INTRODUCTION TO JAVA™ PROGRAMMING

COMPREHENSIVE VERSION

Eighth Edition

Y. Daniel Liang

Armstrong Atlantic State University

Prentice Hall

Boston Columbus Indianapolis New York San Francisco Upper Saddle River
Amsterdam Cape Town Dubai London Madrid Milan Munich Paris Montreal Toronto
Delhi Mexico City Sao Paulo Sydney Hong Kong Seoul Singapore Taipei Tokyo

Vice President and Editorial Director, ECS: Marcia J. Horton
Editor in Chief, Computer Science: Michael Hirsch
Executive Editor: Tracy Dunkelberger
Assistant Editor: Melinda Haggerty
Editorial Assistant: Allison Michael
Vice President, Production: Vince O'Brien
Senior Managing Editor: Scott Disanno
Production Editor: Irwin Zucker
Senior Operations Specialist: Alan Fischer
Marketing Manager: Erin Davis
Marketing Assistant: Mack Patterson
Art Director: Kenny Beck
Cover Image: Male Ruby-throated Hummingbird / Steve Byland / Shutterstock;
Hummingbird, Nazca Lines / Gary Yim / Shutterstock
Art Editor: Greg Dulles
Media Editor: Daniel Sandin

Library of Congress Cataloging-in-Publication Data on file.

Prentice Hall
is an imprint of

PEARSON

www.pearsonhighered.com

10 9 8 7 6 5 4

ISBN-13: 978-0-13-213080-6
ISBN-10: 0-13-213080-7

This book is dedicated to Dr. S. K. Dhall and Dr. S. Lakshmivarahan of the University of Oklahoma, who inspired me in teaching and research. Thank you for being my mentors and advisors.

To Samantha, Michael, and Michelle

PREFACE

This book uses the fundamentals-first approach and teaches programming concepts and techniques in a problem-driven way.

fundamentals-first

The fundamentals-first approach introduces basic programming concepts and techniques before objects and classes. My own experience, confirmed by the experiences of many colleagues, demonstrates that new programmers in order to succeed must learn basic logic and fundamental programming techniques such as loops and stepwise refinement. The fundamental concepts and techniques of loops, methods, and arrays are the foundation for programming. Building the foundation prepares students to learn object-oriented programming, GUI, database, and Web programming.

problem-driven

Problem-driven means focused on problem solving rather than syntax. We make introductory programming interesting by using interesting problems. The central thread of early chapters is on problem solving. Appropriate syntax and library are introduced to support the writing of a program for solving the problems. To support the teaching of programming in a problem-driven way, the book provides a wide variety of problems at various levels of difficulty to motivate students. In order to appeal to students in all majors, the problems cover many application areas in math, science, business, financials, gaming, animation, and multimedia.

Two Versions

comprehensive version

This *comprehensive version* covers fundamentals of programming, object-oriented programming, GUI programming, algorithms and data structures, concurrency, networking, internationalization, advanced GUI, database, and Web programming. It is designed to prepare students to become proficient Java programmers. A *brief version* (Introduction to Java Programming, Brief Version, Eighth Edition) is available for a first course on programming, commonly known as CS1. The brief version contains the first 20 chapters of the comprehensive version.

brief version

What's New in This Edition?

This edition substantially improves *Introduction to Java Programming, Seventh Edition.* The major improvements are as follows:

complete revision

- This edition is completely revised in every detail to enhance clarity, presentation, content, examples, and exercises.

new problems

- In the examples and exercises, which are provided to motivate and stimulate student interest in programming, one-fifth of the problems are new.

early console input

- In the previous edition, console input was covered at the end of Chapter 2. The new edition introduces console input early in Chapter 2 so that students can write interactive programs early.

hand trace box

- The hand trace box is added for many programs to help novice students to read and trace programs.

multidimensional arrays

- Single-dimensional arrays and multidimensional arrays are covered in two chapters to give instructors the flexibility to cover multidimensional arrays later.

Sudoku problem simplified

- The case study for the Sudoku problem has been moved to the Companion Website. A more pedagogically effective simple version of the Sudoku problem is presented instead.

- The design of the API for Java GUI programming is an excellent example of how the object-oriented principle is applied. Students learn better with concrete and visual examples.

So, basic GUI now precedes the introduction of abstract classes and interfaces. The instructor, however, can still choose to cover abstract classes and interfaces before GUI. basic GUI earlier

- Exception handling is covered before abstract classes and interfaces so that students can build robust programs early. The instructor can still choose to cover exception handling later. exception handling earlier
- Chapter 12, "Object-Oriented Design and Patterns," in the previous edition has been replaced by spreading the design guidelines and patterns into several chapters so that these topics can be covered in appropriate context. design guidelines
- The chapter on sorting now follows right after the chapter on algorithm efficiency, so that students can immediately apply algorithm efficiency to sorting algorithms. sorting
- A brand-new bonus Chapter 44 covers Java 2D. Java 2D
- The coverage on data structures is expanded with new bonus chapters on AVL trees, splay trees, 2-4 trees, B-trees, and red-black trees, and hashing. So the book can be used for a full data structures course. new data structures chapters

Learning Strategies

A programming course is quite different from other courses. In a programming course, you learn from examples, from practice, and *from mistakes*. You need to devote a lot of time to writing programs, testing them, and fixing errors. learn from mistakes

For first-time programmers, learning Java is like learning any high-level programming language. The fundamental point is to develop the critical skills of formulating programmatic solutions for real problems and translating them into programs using selection statements, loops, methods, and arrays. programmatic solution

Once you acquire the basic skills of writing programs using loops, methods, and arrays, you can begin to learn how to develop large programs and GUI programs using the object-oriented approach. object-oriented programming

When you know how to program and you understand the concept of object-oriented programming, learning Java becomes a matter of learning the Java API. The Java API establishes a framework for programmers to develop applications using Java. You have to use the classes and interfaces in the API and follow their conventions and rules to create applications. The best way to learn the Java API is to imitate examples and do exercises. Java API

Pedagogical Features

The book uses the following elements to get the most from the material:

- **Objectives** list what students should have learned from the chapter. This will help them determine whether they have met the objectives after completing the chapter.
- **Introduction** opens the discussion with representative problems to give the reader an overview of what to expect from the chapter.
- **Problems** carefully chosen and presented in an easy-to-follow style, teach problem solving and programming concepts. The book uses many small, simple, and stimulating examples to demonstrate important ideas.
- **Chapter Summary** reviews the important subjects that students should understand and remember. It helps them reinforce the key concepts they have learned in the chapter.
- **Review Questions** are grouped by sections to help students track their progress and evaluate their learning.
- **Programming Exercises** are grouped by sections to provide students with opportunities to apply on their own the new skills they have learned. The level of difficulty is rated as easy (no

asterisk), moderate (*), hard (**), or challenging (***). The trick of learning programming is practice, practice, and practice. To that end, the book provides a great many exercises.

- **LiveLab** is a course assessment and management system. Students can submit programs online. The system automatically grades the programs/multiple-choice quizzes and gives students instant feedback. Instructors can create custom programming exercises and quizzes as well as use the system prebuilt exercises and quizzes.
- **Notes**, **Tips**, and **Cautions** are inserted throughout the text to offer valuable advice and insight on important aspects of program development.

Note
Provides additional information on the subject and reinforces important concepts.

Tip
Teaches good programming style and practice.

Caution
Helps students steer away from the pitfalls of programming errors.

Design Guide
Provides the guidelines for designing programs.

Flexible Chapter Orderings

The book is designed to provide flexible chapter orderings to enable GUI, exception handling, recursion, generics, and the Java Collections Framework to be covered earlier or later. The diagram on the next page shows the chapter dependencies.

Organization of the Book

The chapters can be grouped into five parts that, taken together, form a comprehensive introduction to Java programming, data structures and algorithms, and database and Web programming. Because knowledge is cumulative, the early chapters provide the conceptual basis for understanding programming and guide students through simple examples and exercises; subsequent chapters progressively present Java programming in detail, culminating with the development of comprehensive Java applications.

Part I: Fundamentals of Programming (Chapters 1–7)

The first part of the book is a stepping stone, preparing you to embark on the journey of learning Java. You will begin to know Java (Chapter 1) and will learn fundamental programming techniques with primitive data types, variables, constants, assignments, expressions, and operators (Chapter 2), control statements (Chapters 3–4), methods (Chapter 5), and arrays (Chapters 6–7). After Chapter 6, you may jump to Chapter 20 to learn how to write recursive methods for solving inherently recursive problems.

Part II: Object-Oriented Programming (Chapters 8–11, 13–14, 19)

This part introduces object-oriented programming. Java is an object-oriented programming language that uses abstraction, encapsulation, inheritance, and polymorphism to provide great flexibility, modularity, and reusability in developing software. You will learn programming with objects and classes (Chapters 8–10), class inheritance (Chapter 11), polymorphism (Chapter 11), exception handling (Chapter 13), abstract classes (Chapter 14), and interfaces (Chapter 14). Processing strings will be introduced in Chapter 9 along with text I/O. Binary I/O is introduced in Chapter 19.

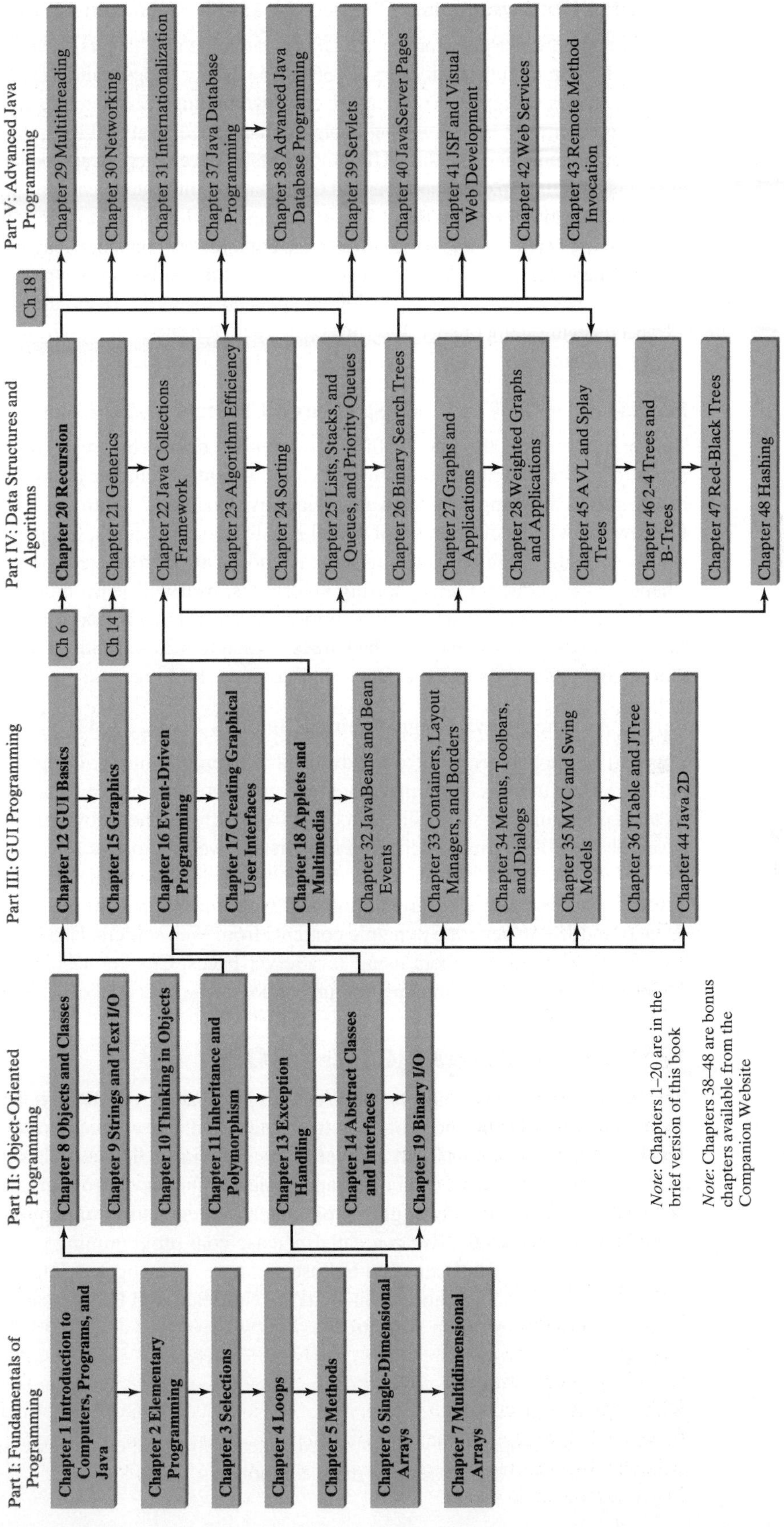

Part I: Fundamentals of Programming
Chapter 1 Introduction to Computers, Programs, and Java
Chapter 2 Elementary Programming
Chapter 3 Selections
Chapter 4 Loops
Chapter 5 Methods
Chapter 6 Single-Dimensional Arrays
Chapter 7 Multidimensional Arrays
Part II: Object-Oriented Programming
Chapter 8 Objects and Classes
Chapter 9 Strings and Text I/O
Chapter 10 Thinking in Objects
Chapter 11 Inheritance and Polymorphism
Chapter 13 Exception Handling
Chapter 14 Abstract Classes and Interfaces
Chapter 19 Binary I/O
Part III: GUI Programming
Chapter 12 GUI Basics
Chapter 15 Graphics
Chapter 16 Event-Driven Programming
Chapter 17 Creating Graphical User Interfaces
Chapter 18 Applets and Multimedia
Chapter 32 JavaBeans and Bean Events
Chapter 33 Containers, Layout Managers, and Borders
Chapter 34 Menus, Toolbars, and Dialogs
Chapter 35 MVC and Swing Models
Chapter 36 JTable and JTree
Chapter 44 Java 2D
Ch 6
Ch 14
Part IV: Data Structures and Algorithms
Chapter 20 Recursion
Chapter 21 Generics
Chapter 22 Java Collections Framework
Chapter 23 Algorithm Efficiency
Chapter 24 Sorting
Chapter 25 Lists, Stacks, and Queues, and Priority Queues
Chapter 26 Binary Search Trees
Chapter 27 Graphs and Applications
Chapter 28 Weighted Graphs and Applications
Chapter 45 AVL and Splay Trees
Chapter 46 2-4 Trees and B-Trees
Chapter 47 Red-Black Trees
Chapter 48 Hashing
Ch 18
Part V: Advanced Java Programming
Chapter 29 Multithreading
Chapter 30 Networking
Chapter 31 Internationalization
Chapter 37 Java Database Programming
Chapter 38 Advanced Java Database Programming
Chapter 39 Servlets
Chapter 40 JavaServer Pages
Chapter 41 JSF and Visual Web Development
Chapter 42 Web Services
Chapter 43 Remote Method Invocation
Note: Chapters 1–20 are in the brief version of this book
Note: Chapters 38–48 are bonus chapters available from the Companion Website

Part III: GUI Programming (Chapters 12, 15–18, 32–36, and 44)

This part introduces elementary Java GUI programming in Chapters 12 and 15–18 and advanced Java GUI programming in Chapters 32–36 and 44. Major topics include GUI basics (Chapter 12), drawing shapes (Chapter 15), event-driven programming (Chapter 16), creating graphical user interfaces (Chapter 17), and writing applets (Chapter 18). You will learn the architecture of Java GUI programming and use the GUI components to develop applications and applets from these elementary GUI chapters. The advanced GUI chapters introduce Java GUI programming in more depth and breadth. You will delve into JavaBeans and learn how to develop custom events and source components in Chapter 32, review and explore new containers, layout managers, and borders in Chapter 33, learn how to create GUI with menus, popup menus, toolbars, dialogs, and internal frames in Chapter 34, develop components using the MVC approach and explore the advanced Swing components `JSpinner`, `JList`, `JComboBox`, `JSpinner`, and `JTable`, and `JTree` in Chapters 35 and 36. Bonus Chapter 44 introduces Java 2D.

Part IV: Algorithms and Data Structures (Chapters 20–28, 45–48)

This part introduces the main subjects in a typical data structures course. Chapter 20 introduces recursion to write methods for solving inherently recursive problems. Chapter 21 introduces generics to improve software reliability. Chapter 22 introduces the Java Collection Framework, which defines a set of useful API for data structures. Chapter 23 introduces measurement of algorithm efficiency in order to choose an appropriate algorithm for applications. Chapter 24 introduces classic sorting algorithms. You will learn how to implement several classic data structures lists, queues, priority queues, binary search trees, AVL trees, splay trees, 2-4 trees, B-trees, and red-black trees in Chapters 25–26 and 45–47. Chapters 27 and 28 introduce graph applications. Chapter 48 introduces hashing.

Part V: Advanced Java Programming (Chapters 29–31, 37–43)

This part of the book is devoted to advanced Java programming. Chapter 29 treats the use of multithreading to make programs more responsive and interactive. Chapter 30 introduces how to write programs that talk with each other from different hosts over the Internet. Chapter 31 covers the use of internationalization support to develop projects for international audiences. Chapter 37 introduces the use of Java to develop database projects, Chapter 38 introduces advanced Java database programming, and Chapters 39 and 40 introduce how to use Java servlets and JSP to generate dynamic contents from Web servers. Chapter 41 introduces rapid Web application development using JavaServer Faces. Chapter 42 introduces Web services. Chapter 43 introduces remote method invocation.

Java Development Tools

IDE tutorials

You can use a text editor, such as the Windows Notepad or WordPad, to create Java programs and to compile and run the programs from the command window. You can also use a Java development tool, such as TextPad, NetBeans, or Eclipse. These tools support an integrated development environment (IDE) for rapidly developing Java programs. Editing, compiling, building, executing, and debugging programs are integrated in one graphical user interface. Using these tools effectively can greatly increase your programming productivity. TextPad is a primitive IDE tool. NetBeans and Eclipse are more sophisticated, but they are easy to use if you follow the tutorials. Tutorials on TextPad, NetBeans and Eclipse can be found in the supplements on the Companion Website.

LiveLab

This book is accompanied by an improved faster Web-based course assessment and management system. The system has three main components:

- **Automatic Grading System:** It can automatically grade programs from the text or created by instructors.
- **Quiz Creation/Submission/Grading System:** It enables instructors to create/modify quizzes that students can take and be graded upon automatically.
- **Tracking grades, attendance, etc:** The system enables the students to track grades and instructors, to view the grades of all students, and to track attendance.

The main features of the Automatic Grading System are as follows:

- Allows students to compile, run and submit exercises. (The system checks whether their program runs correctly—students can continue to run and resubmit the program before the due date.)
- Allows instructors to review submissions; run programs with instructor test cases; correct them; and provide feedback to students.
- Allows instructors to create/modify custom exercises, create public and secret test cases, assign exercises, and set due dates for the whole class or for individuals.
- All the exercises in the text can be assigned to students. Additionally, LiveLab provides extra exercises that are not printed in the text.
- Allows instructors to sort and filter all exercises and check grades (by time frame, student, and/or exercise).
- Allows instructors to delete students from the system.
- Allows students and instructors to track grades on exercises.

The main features of the Quiz System are as follows:

- Allows instructors to create/modify quizzes from test bank or a text file or to create complete new tests online.
- Allows instructors to assign the quizzes to students and set a due date and test time limit for the whole class or for individuals.
- Allows students and instructors to review submitted quizzes.
- Allows students and instructors to track grades on quizzes.

Video Notes are Pearson's new visual tool designed for teaching students key programming concepts and techniques. These short step-by-step videos demonstrate how to solve problems from design through coding. Video Notes allows for self-paced instruction with easy navigation including the ability to select, play, rewind, fast-forward, and stop within each Video Note exercise.

Video Note margin icons in your textbook let you know what a Video Notes video is available for a particular concept or homework problem.

Video Notes are free with the purchase of a new textbook. To purchase access to Video Notes, please go to www.pearsonhighered.com/liang.

Student Resource Materials

The student resources can be accessed through the Publisher's Web site (www.pearsonhighered.com/liang) and the Companion Web site (www.cs.armstrong.edu/liang/intro8e). The resources include:

- Answers to review questions
- Solutions to even-numbered programming exercises

- Source code for book examples
- Interactive self-test (organized by chapter sections)
- LiveLab
- Resource links
- Errata
- Video Notes
- Web Chapters

To access the Video Notes and Web Chapters, students must log onto www.pearsonhighered.com/liang and use the access card located in the front of the book to register and access the material. If there is no access card in the front of this textbook, students can purchase access by visiting www.pearsonhighered.com/liang and selecting *purchase access to premium content.*

Additional Supplements

The text covers the essential subjects. The supplements extend the text to introduce additional topics that might be of interest to readers. The supplements listed in this table are available from the Companion Web site.

Supplements on the Companion Web site

Part I General Supplements
- A Glossary
- B Installing and Configuring JDK
- C Compiling and Running Java from the Command Window
- D Java Coding Style Guidelines
- E Creating Desktop Shortcuts for Java Applications on Windows
- F Using Packages to Organize the Classes in the Text

Part II IDE Supplements
- A TextPad Tutorial
- B NetBeans Tutorial | One Page Startup Instruction
- C Learning Java Effectively with NetBeans
- D Eclipse Tutorial | One Page Startup Instruction
- E Learning Java Effectively with Eclipse

Part III Java Supplements
- A Java Characteristics
- B Discussion on Operator and Operand Evaluations
- C The & and | Operators
- D Bitwise Operations
- E Statement Labels with break and continue
- F Enumerated Types
- G Packages
- H Regular Expressions
- I Formatted Strings
- J The Methods in the Object Class
- K Hiding Data Fields and Static Methods
- L Initialization Blocks
- M Extended Discussions on Overriding Methods
- N Design Patterns
- O Text I/O Prior to JDK 1.5 (Reader and Writer Classes)
- P Assertions
- Q Packaging and Deploying Java Projects
- R Java Web Start
- S GridBagLayout | OverlayLayout | SpringLayout
- T Networking Using Datagram Protocol
- U Creating Internal Frames
- V Pluggable Look and Feel
- W UML Graphical Notations
- X Testing Classes Using JUnit
- Y JNI
- Z The StringTokenizer Class

Part IV Database Supplements
- A SQL Statements for Creating and Initializing Tables Used in the Book

B MySQL Tutorial C Oracle Tutorial D Microsoft Access Tutorial E Introduction to Database Systems F Relational Database Concept G Database Design H SQL Basics I Advanced SQL	Part V Web Programming Supplements A HTML and XHTML Tutorial B CSS Tutorial C XML D Java and XML E Tomcat Tutorial F More Examples on JSF and Visual Web Development

Instructor Resource Materials

The instructor resources can be accessed through the Publisher's Web site (www.pearsonhighered.com/liang) and the Companion Web site (www.cs.armstrong.edu/liang/intro8e). For username and password information to the Liang 8e site, please contact your Pearson Representative.

The resources include:

- PowerPoint lecture slides with source code and run program capacity
- Instructor solutions manual
- Computerized test generator
- Sample exams using multiple choice and short answer questions, write and trace programs, and correcting programming errors.
- LiveLab
- Errata
- Video Notes
- Web Chapters

To access the Video Notes and Web Chapters, instructors must log onto www.pearsonhighered.com/liang and register.

Acknowledgments

I would like to thank Armstrong Atlantic State University for enabling me to teach what I write and for supporting me in writing what I teach. Teaching is the source of inspiration for continuing to improve the book. I am grateful to the instructors and students who have offered comments, suggestions, bug reports, and praise.

This book has been greatly enhanced thanks to outstanding reviews for this and previous editions. The reviewers are: Elizabeth Adams (James Madison University), Syed Ahmed (North Georgia College and State University), Omar Aldawud (Illinois Institute of Technology), Yang Ang (University of Wollongong, Australia), Kevin Bierre (Rochester Institute of Technology), David Champion (DeVry Institute), James Chegwidden (Tarrant County College), Anup Dargar (University of North Dakota), Charles Dierbach (Towson University), Frank Ducrest (University of Louisiana at Lafayette), Erica Eddy (University of Wisconsin at Parkside), Deena Engel (New York University), Henry A Etlinger (Rochester Institute of Technology), James Ten Eyck (Marist College), Olac Fuentes (University of Texas at El Paso), Harold Grossman (Clemson University), Barbara Guillot (Louisiana State University), Ron Hofman (Red River College, Canada), Stephen Hughes (Roanoke College), Vladan Jovanovic (Georgia Southern University), Edwin Kay (Lehigh University), Larry King (University of Texas at Dallas), Nana Kofi (Langara College, Canada), George Koutsogiannakis (Illinois

Institute of Technology), Roger Kraft (Purdue University at Calumet), Hong Lin (DeVry Institute), Dan Lipsa (Armstrong Atlantic State University), James Madison (Rensselaer Polytechnic Institute), Frank Malinowski (Darton College), Tim Margush (University of Akron), Debbie Masada (Sun Microsystems), Blayne Mayfield (Oklahoma State University), John McGrath (J.P. McGrath Consulting), Shyamal Mitra (University of Texas at Austin), Michel Mitri (James Madison University), Kenrick Mock (University of Alaska Anchorage), Jun Ni (University of Iowa), Benjamin Nystuen (University of Colorado at Colorado Springs), Maureen Opkins (CA State University, Long Beach), Gavin Osborne (University of Saskatchewan), Kevin Parker (Idaho State University), Dale Parson (Kutztown University), Mark Pendergast (Florida Gulf Coast University), Richard Povinelli (Marquette University), Roger Priebe (University of Texas at Austin), Mary Ann Pumphrey (De Anza Junior College), Pat Roth (Southern Polytechnic State University), Ronald F. Taylor (Wright State University), Carolyn Schauble (Colorado State University), David Scuse (University of Manitoba), Ashraf Shirani (San Jose State University), Daniel Spiegel (Kutztown University), Amr Sabry (Indiana University), Lixin Tao (Pace University), Russ Tront (Simon Fraser University), Deborah Trytten (University of Oklahoma), Kent Vidrine (George Washington University), and Bahram Zartoshty (California State University at Northridge).

It is a great pleasure, honor, and privilege to work with Pearson. I would like to thank Tracy Dunkelberger and her colleagues Marcia Horton, Margaret Waples, Erin Davis, Michael Hirsh, Matt Goldstein, Jake Warde, Melinda Haggerty, Allison Michael, Scott Disanno, Irwin Zucker, and their colleagues for organizing, producing, and promoting this project, and Robert Lentz for copy editing.

As always, I am indebted to my wife, Samantha, for her love, support, and encouragement.

Y. Daniel Liang
y.daniel.liang@gmail.com
www.cs.armstrong.edu/liang
www.pearsonhighered.com/liang

BRIEF CONTENTS

Chapters are available from the companion Web site at www.pearsonhighered.com/liang:

APPENDIXES

CONTENTS

Video Notes

Locations of **Video Notes**

http://www.pearsonhighered.com/liang

CHAPTER 1

INTRODUCTION TO COMPUTERS, PROGRAMS, AND JAVA

Objectives

- To review computer basics, programs, and operating systems (§§1.2–1.4).
- To explore the relationship between Java and the World Wide Web (§1.5).
- To distinguish the terms API, IDE, and JDK (§1.6).
- To write a simple Java program (§1.7).
- To display output on the console (§1.7).
- To explain the basic syntax of a Java program (§1.7).
- To create, compile, and run Java programs (§1.8).
- (GUI) To display output using the `JOptionPane` output dialog boxes (§1.9).

1.1 Introduction

why Java?

You use word processors to write documents, Web browsers to explore the Internet, and email programs to send email. These are all examples of software that runs on computers. Software is developed using programming languages. There are many programming languages—so *why Java*? The answer is that Java enables users to develop and deploy applications on the Internet for servers, desktop computers, and small hand-held devices. The future of computing is being profoundly influenced by the Internet, and Java promises to remain a big part of that future. Java is *the* Internet programming language.

You are about to begin an exciting journey, learning a powerful programming language. At the outset, it is helpful to review computer basics, programs, and operating systems and to become familiar with number systems. If you are already familiar with such terms as CPU, memory, disks, operating systems, and programming languages, you may skip the review in §§1.2–1.4.

1.2 What Is a Computer?

hardware
software

A computer is an electronic device that stores and processes data. It includes both *hardware* and *software*. In general, hardware comprises the visible, physical elements of the computer, and software provides the invisible instructions that control the hardware and make it perform specific tasks. Writing instructions for computers to perform is called computer programming. Knowing computer hardware isn't essential to your learning a programming language, but it does help you understand better the effect of the program instructions. This section introduces computer hardware components and their functions.

A computer consists of the following major hardware components (Figure 1.1):

- Central processing unit (CPU)
- Memory (main memory)
- Storage devices (e.g., disks, CDs, tapes)
- Input and output devices (e.g., monitors, keyboards, mice, printers)
- Communication devices (e.g., modems and network interface cards (NICs))

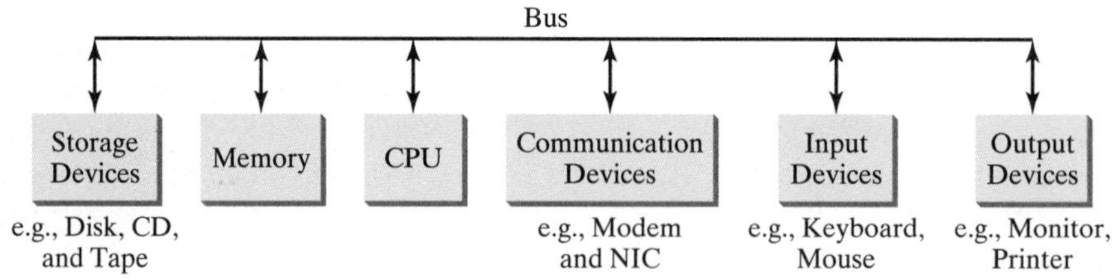
Bus
Storage Devices
Memory
CPU
Communication Devices
Input Devices
Output Devices
e.g., Disk, CD, and Tape
e.g., Modem and NIC
e.g., Keyboard, Mouse
e.g., Monitor, Printer

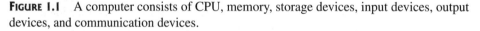

FIGURE 1.1 A computer consists of CPU, memory, storage devices, input devices, output devices, and communication devices.

bus

The components are connected through a subsystem called a *bus* that transfers data or power between them.

1.2.1 Central Processing Unit

CPU

The *central processing unit* (CPU) is the computer's brain. It retrieves instructions from memory and executes them. The CPU usually has two components: a *control unit* and an *arithmetic/logic unit*. The control unit controls and coordinates the actions of the other components. The arithmetic/logic unit performs numeric operations (addition, subtraction, multiplication, division) and logical operations (comparisons).

Today's CPU is built on a small silicon semiconductor chip having millions of transistors. Every computer has an internal clock, which emits electronic pulses at a constant rate. These pulses are used to control and synchronize the pace of operations. The higher the clock speed, the more instructions are executed in a given period of time. The unit of measurement of clock speed is the *hertz (Hz)*, with 1 hertz equaling 1 pulse per second. The clock speed of a computer is usually stated in megahertz (MHz) (1 MHz is 1 million Hz). CPU speed has been improved continuously. Intel's Pentium 3 Processor runs at about 500 megahertz and Pentium 4 Processor at about 3 gigahertz (GHz) (1 GHz is 1000 MHz).

speed
hertz
megahertz
gigahertz

1.2.2 Memory

To store and process information, computers use *off* and *on* electrical states, referred to by convention as *0* and *1*. These 0s and 1s are interpreted as digits in the binary number system and called *bits* (*b*inary dig*its*). Data of various kinds, such as numbers, characters, and strings, are encoded as series of bits. Data and program instructions for the CPU to execute are stored as groups of bits, or bytes, each byte composed of eight bits, in a computer's *memory*. A memory unit is an ordered sequence of *bytes*, as shown in Figure 1.2.

bit
byte

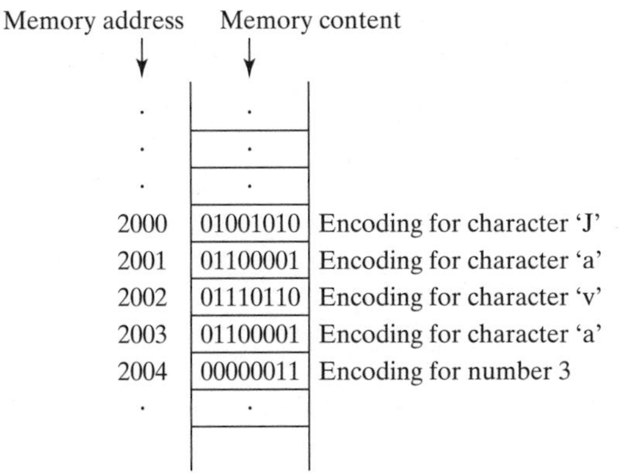
Memory address
Memory content
2000
01001010
Encoding for character 'J'
2001
01100001
Encoding for character 'a'
2002
01110110
Encoding for character 'v'
2003
01100001
Encoding for character 'a'
2004
00000011
Encoding for number 3

FIGURE 1.2 Memory stores data and program instructions.

The programmer need not be concerned about the encoding and decoding of data, which the system performs automatically, based on the encoding scheme. In the popular ASCII encoding scheme, for example, character `'J'` is represented by `01001010` in one byte.

A byte is the minimum storage unit. A small number such as `3` can be stored in a single byte. To store a number that cannot fit into a single byte, the computer uses several adjacent bytes. No two data items can share or split the same byte.

A memory byte is never empty, but its initial content may be meaningless to your program. The current content of a memory byte is lost whenever new information is placed in it.

A program and its data must be brought to memory before they can be executed.

Every byte has a unique address. The address is used to locate the byte for storing and retrieving data. Since bytes can be accessed in any order, the memory is also referred to as *random-access memory* (*RAM*). Today's personal computers usually have at least 1 gigabyte of RAM. Computer storage size is measured in bytes, kilobytes (KB), megabytes (MB), gigabytes (GB), and terabytes (TB). A *kilobyte* is $2^{10} = 1024$, about 1000 bytes, a *megabyte* is $2^{20} = 1048576$, about 1 million bytes, a *gigabyte* is about 1 billion bytes, and a terabyte is about 1000 gigabytes. Like the CPU, memory is built on silicon semiconductor chips having thousands of transistors embedded on their surface. Compared to CPU chips, memory chips are less complicated, slower, and less expensive.

RAM
megabyte

1.2.3 Storage Devices

Memory is volatile, because information is lost when the power is turned off. Programs and data are permanently stored on storage devices and are moved, when the computer actually uses them, to memory, which is much faster than storage devices.

There are four main types of storage devices:

- Disk drives
- CD drives (CD-R, CD-RW, and DVD)
- Tape drives
- USB flash drives

drive

Drives are devices for operating a medium, such as disks, CDs, and tapes.

Disks

hard disk

Each computer has at least one hard drive. *Hard disks* are for permanently storing data and programs. The hard disks of the latest PCs store from 80 to 250 gigabytes. Often disk drives are encased inside the computer. Removable hard disks are also available.

CDs and DVDs

CD-R

CD-RW

CD stands for compact disk. There are two types of CD drives: CD-R and CD-RW. A *CD-R* is for read-only permanent storage; the user cannot modify its contents once they are recorded. A *CD-RW* can be used like a hard disk and can be both read and rewritten. A single CD can hold up to 700 MB. Most software is distributed through CD-ROMs. Most new PCs are equipped with a CD-RW drive that can work with both CD-R and CD-RW.

DVD stands for digital versatile disc or digital video disk. DVDs and CDs look alike, and you can use either to store data. A DVD can hold more information than a CD. A standard DVD's storage capacity is 4.7 GB.

Tapes

Tapes are mainly used for backup of data and programs. Unlike disks and CDs, tapes store information sequentially. The computer must retrieve information in the order it was stored. Tapes are very slow. It would take one to two hours to back up a 1-gigabyte hard disk. The new trend is to back up data using flash drives or external hard disks.

USB Flash Drives

USB flash drives are devices for storing and transporting data. A flash drive is small—about the size of a pack of gum. It acts like a portable hard drive that can be plugged into your computer's USB port. USB flash drives are currently available with up to 32 GB storage capacity.

1.2.4 Input and Output Devices

Input and output devices let the user communicate with the computer. The common input devices are *keyboards* and *mice*. The common output devices are *monitors* and *printers*.

The Keyboard

A computer *keyboard* resembles a typewriter keyboard with extra keys added for certain special functions.

function key

Function keys are located at the top of the keyboard and are numbered with prefix F. Their use depends on the software.

modifier key

A *modifier key* is a special key (e.g., *Shift*, *Alt*, *Ctrl*) that modifies the normal action of another key when the two are pressed in combination.

The *numeric keypad,* located on the right-hand corner of the keyboard, is a separate set of keys for quick input of numbers.

numeric keypad

Arrow keys, located between the main keypad and the numeric keypad, are used to move the cursor up, down, left, and right.

The *Insert, Delete, Page Up, and Page Down keys*, located above the arrow keys, are used in word processing for performing insert, delete, page up, and page down.

The Mouse

A *mouse* is a pointing device. It is used to move an electronic pointer called a cursor around the screen or to click on an object on the screen to trigger it to respond.

The Monitor

The *monitor* displays information (text and graphics). The screen resolution and dot pitch determine the quality of the display.

The *screen resolution* specifies the number of pixels per square inch. Pixels (short for "picture elements") are tiny dots that form an image on the screen. A common resolution for a 17-inch screen, for example, is 1024 pixels wide and 768 pixels high. The resolution can be set manually. The higher the resolution, the sharper and clearer the image is.

screen resolution

The *dot pitch* is the amount of space between pixels in millimeters. The smaller the dot pitch, the better the display.

dot pitch

1.2.5 Communication Devices

Computers can be networked through communication devices, such as the dialup modem (*mo*dulator/*dem*odulator), DSL, cable modem, network interface card, and wireless. A dialup modem uses a phone line and can transfer data at a speed up to 56,000 bps (bits per second). A *DSL* (digital subscriber line) also uses a phone line and can transfer data twenty times faster. A cable modem uses the TV cable line maintained by the cable company and is as fast as a DSL. A network interface card (NIC) is a device that connects a computer to a local area network (LAN). The *LAN* is commonly used in universities and business and government organizations. A typical *NIC* called *10BaseT* can transfer data at 10 *mbps* (million bits per second). Wireless is becoming popular. Every laptop sold today is equipped with a wireless adapter that enables the computer to connect with the Internet.

modem

DSL

NIC

LAN

mbps

1.3 Programs

Computer *programs*, known as *software*, are instructions to the computer, telling it what to do. Computers do not understand human languages, so you need to use computer languages in computer programs. *Programming* is the creation of a program that is executable by a computer and performs the required tasks.

software

programming

A computer's native language, which differs among different types of computers, is its *machine language*—a set of built-in primitive instructions. These instructions are in the form of binary code, so in telling the machine what to do, you have to enter binary code. Programming in machine language is a tedious process. Moreover, the programs are highly difficult to read and modify. For example, to add two numbers, you might have to write an instruction in binary like this:

machine language

```
1101101010011010
```

Assembly language is a low-level programming language in which a mnemonic is used to represent each of the machine-language instructions. For example, to add two numbers, you might write an instruction in assembly code like this:

assembly language

```
ADDF3 R1, R2, R3
```

assembler

Assembly languages were developed to make programming easy. However, since the computer cannot understand assembly language, a program called an *assembler* is used to convert assembly-language programs into machine code, as shown in Figure 1.3.

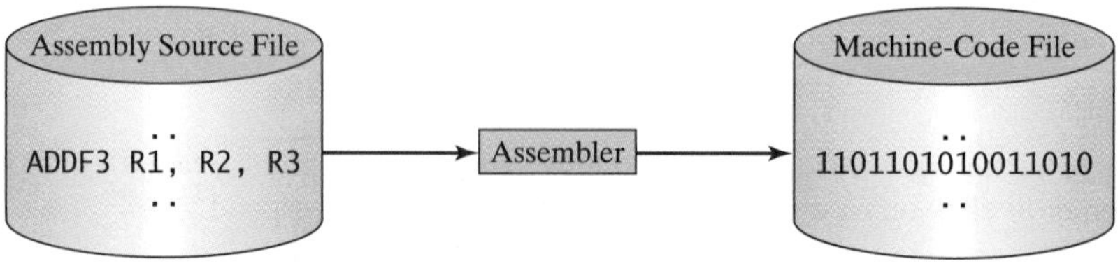
Assembly Source File
..
ADDF3 R1, R2, R3
..
Assembler
Machine-Code File
..
1101101010011010
..

FIGURE 1.3 Assembler translates assembly-language instructions to machine code.

Assembly programs are written in terms of machine instructions with easy-to-remember mnemonic names. Since assembly language is machine dependent, an assembly program can be executed only on a particular kind of machine. The high-level languages were developed in order to transcend platform specificity and make programming easier.

high-level language

The *high-level languages* are English-like and easy to learn and program. Here, for example, is a high-level language statement that computes the area of a circle with radius 5:

```
area = 5 * 5 * 3.1415;
```

Among the more than one hundred high-level languages, the following are well known:

- COBOL (COmmon Business Oriented Language)
- FORTRAN (FORmula TRANslation)
- BASIC (Beginner's All-purpose Symbolic Instruction Code)
- Pascal (named for Blaise Pascal)
- Ada (named for Ada Lovelace)
- C (developed by the designer of B)
- Visual Basic (Basic-like visual language developed by Microsoft)
- Delphi (Pascal-like visual language developed by Borland)
- C++ (an object-oriented language, based on C)
- C# (a Java-like language developed by Microsoft)
- Java

Each of these languages was designed for a specific purpose. COBOL was designed for business applications and is used primarily for business data processing. FORTRAN was designed for mathematical computations and is used mainly for numeric computations. BASIC was designed to be learned and used easily. Ada was developed for the Department of Defense and is used mainly in defense projects. C combines the power of an assembly language with the ease of use and portability of a high-level language. Visual Basic and Delphi are used in developing graphical user interfaces and in rapid application development. C++ is popular for system software projects such as writing compilers and operating systems. The Microsoft Windows operating system was coded using C++. C# (pronounced C sharp) is a new language developed by Microsoft for developing applications based on the Microsoft .NET platform. Java, developed by Sun Microsystems, is widely used for developing platform-independent Internet applications.

A program written in a high-level language is called a *source program* or *source code*. Since a computer cannot understand a source program, a program called a *compiler* is used to translate it into a machine-language program. The machine-language program is then linked with other supporting library code to form an executable file, which can be run on the machine, as shown in Figure 1.4. On Windows, executable files have extension .exe.

source program

compiler

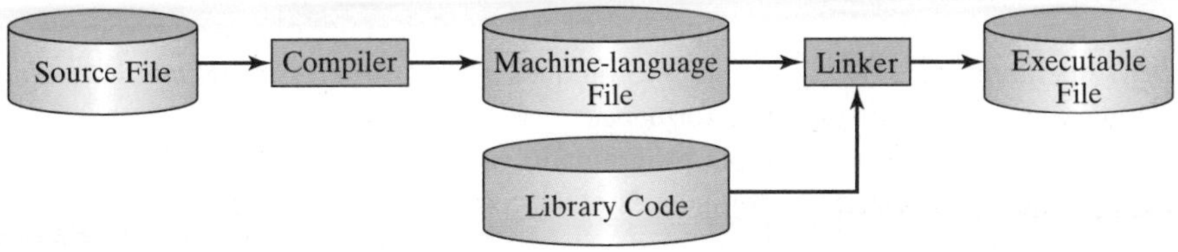
Source File
Compiler
Machine-language File
Linker
Executable File
Library Code

FIGURE 1.4 A source program is compiled into a machine-language file, which is then linked with the system library to form an executable file.

1.4 Operating Systems

The *operating system* (*OS*) is the most important program that runs on a computer, which manages and controls a computer's activities. The popular operating systems are Microsoft Windows, Mac OS, and Linux. Application programs, such as a Web browser or a word processor, cannot run without an operating system. The interrelationship of hardware, operating system, application software, and the user is shown in Figure 1.5.

OS

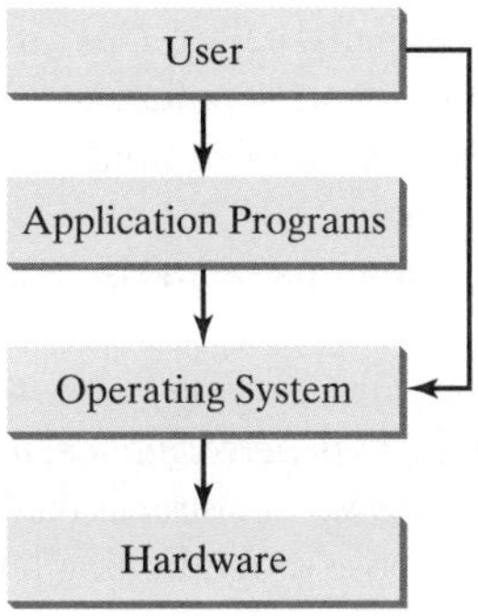
User
Application Programs
Operating System
Hardware

FIGURE 1.5 The operating system is the software that controls and manages the system.

The major tasks of an operating system are:

- Controlling and monitoring system activities
- Allocating and assigning system resources
- Scheduling operations

1.4.1 Controlling and Monitoring System Activities

Operating systems perform basic tasks, such as recognizing input from the keyboard, sending output to the monitor, keeping track of files and directories on the disk, and controlling peripheral devices, such as disk drives and printers. They also make sure that different programs and users running at the same time do not interfere with each other, and they are responsible for security, ensuring that unauthorized users do not access the system.

1.4.2 Allocating and Assigning System Resources

The operating system is responsible for determining what computer resources a program needs (e.g., CPU, memory, disks, input and output devices) and for allocating and assigning them to run the program.

1.4.3 Scheduling Operations

The OS is responsible for scheduling programs to make efficient use of system resources. Many of today's operating systems support such techniques as *multiprogramming*, *multithreading*, or *multiprocessing* to increase system performance.

multiprogramming

Multiprogramming allows multiple programs to run simultaneously by sharing the CPU. The CPU is much faster than the computer's other components. As a result, it is idle most of the time—for example, while waiting for data to be transferred from the disk or from other sources. A multiprogramming OS takes advantage of this situation by allowing multiple programs to use the CPU when it would otherwise be idle. For example, you may use a word processor to edit a file at the same time as the Web browser is downloading a file.

multithreading

Multithreading allows concurrency within a program, so that its subtasks can run at the same time. For example, a word-processing program allows users to simultaneously edit text and save it to a file. In this example, editing and saving are two tasks within the same application. These two tasks may run on separate threads concurrently.

multiprocessing

Multiprocessing, or parallel processing, uses two or more processors together to perform a task. It is like a surgical operation where several doctors work together on one patient.

1.5 Java, World Wide Web, and Beyond

This book introduces Java programming. Java was developed by a team led by James Gosling at Sun Microsystems. Originally called *Oak*, it was designed in 1991 for use in embedded chips in consumer electronic appliances. In 1995, renamed *Java*, it was redesigned for developing Internet applications. For the history of Java, see java.sun.com/features/1998/05/birthday.html.

Java has become enormously popular. Its rapid rise and wide acceptance can be traced to its design characteristics, particularly its promise that you can write a program once and run it anywhere. As stated by Sun, Java is *simple*, *object oriented*, *distributed*, *interpreted*, *robust*, *secure*, *architecture neutral*, *portable*, *high performance*, *multithreaded*, and *dynamic*. For the anatomy of Java characteristics, see www.cs.armstrong.edu/liang/JavaCharacteristics.pdf.

Java is a full-featured, general-purpose programming language that can be used to develop robust mission-critical applications. Today, it is employed not only for Web programming, but also for developing standalone applications across platforms on servers, desktops, and mobile devices. It was used to develop the code to communicate with and control the robotic rover on Mars. Many companies that once considered Java to be more hype than substance are now using it to create distributed applications accessed by customers and partners across the Internet. For every new project being developed today, companies are asking how they can use Java to make their work easier.

The World Wide Web is an electronic information repository that can be accessed on the Internet from anywhere in the world. The Internet, the Web's infrastructure, has been around for more than thirty years. The colorful World Wide Web and sophisticated Web browsers are the major reason for the Internet's popularity.

The primary authoring language for the Web is the Hypertext Markup Language (HTML). HTML is a simple language for laying out documents, linking documents on the Internet, and bringing images, sound, and video alive on the Web. However, it cannot interact with the user except through simple forms. Web pages in HTML are essentially static and flat.

applet

Java initially became attractive because Java programs can be run from a Web browser. Such programs are called *applets*. Applets employ a modern graphical interface with buttons, text fields, text areas, radio buttons, and so on, to interact with users on the Web and process their requests. Applets make the Web responsive, interactive, and fun to use. Figure 1.6 shows an applet running from a Web browser for playing a Tic Tac Toe game.

Enter this URL from a Web browser

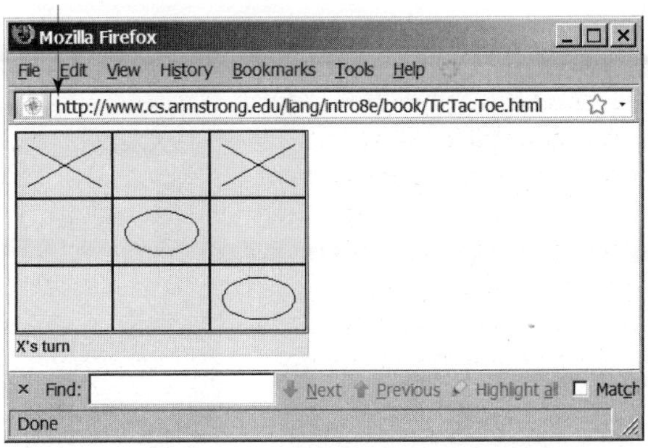
Mozilla Firefox
File Edit View History Bookmarks Tools Help
http://www.cs.armstrong.edu/liang/intro8e/book/TicTacToe.html
X's turn
Find:
Next
Previous
Highlight all
Match
Done

FIGURE 1.6 A Java applet for playing TicTacToe is embedded in an HTML page.

Tip

For a demonstration of Java applets, visit java.sun.com/applets. This site provides a rich Java resource as well as links to other cool applet demo sites. java.sun.com is the official Sun Java Website.

Java can also be used to develop applications on the server side. These applications can be run from a Web server to generate dynamic Web pages. The automatic grading system for this book, as shown in Figure 1.7, was developed using Java.

Enter this URL from a Web browser

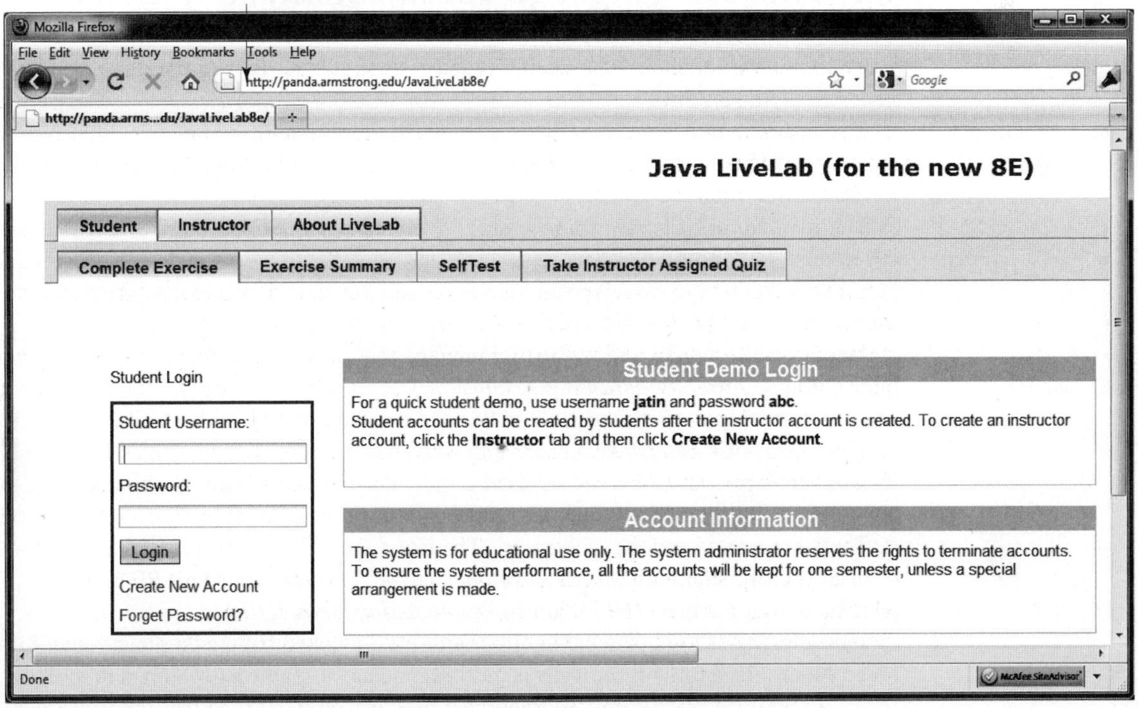
Mozilla Firefox
File Edit View History Bookmarks Tools Help
http://panda.armstrong.edu/JavaLiveLab8e/
Google
http://panda.arms...du/JavaLiveLab8e/
Java LiveLab (for the new 8E)
Student
Instructor
About LiveLab
Complete Exercise
Exercise Summary
SelfTest
Take Instructor Assigned Quiz
Student Login
Student Username:
Password:
Login
Create New Account
Forget Password?
Student Demo Login
For a quick student demo, use username jatin and password abc.
Student accounts can be created by students after the instructor account is created. To create an instructor account, click the Instructor tab and then click Create New Account.
Account Information
The system is for educational use only. The system administrator reserves the rights to terminate accounts. To ensure the system performance, all the accounts will be kept for one semester, unless a special arrangement is made.
Done
McAfee SiteAdvisor

FIGURE 1.7 Java was used to develop an automatic grading system to accompany this book.

Java is a versatile programming language. You can use it to develop applications on your desktop and on the server. You can also use it to develop applications for small hand-held devices. Figure 1.8 shows a Java-programmed calendar displayed on a BlackBerry© and on a cell phone.

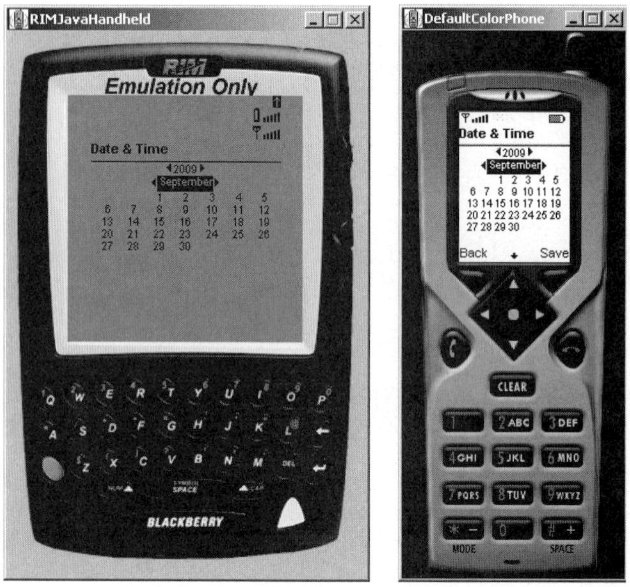
RIMJavaHandheld
Emulation Only
Date & Time
2009
September
BLACKBERRY
DefaultColorPhone
Date & Time
2009
September
Back
Save
CLEAR
MODE
SPACE

FIGURE 1.8 Java can be used to develop applications for hand-held and wireless devices, such as a BlackBerry© (left) and a cell phone (right).

1.6 The Java Language Specification, API, JDK, and IDE

Computer languages have strict rules of usage. If you do not follow the rules when writing a program, the computer will be unable to understand it. The Java language specification and Java API define the Java standard.

Java language specification

The *Java language specification* is a technical definition of the language that includes the syntax and semantics of the Java programming language. The complete Java language specification can be found at java.sun.com/docs/books/jls.

API

The *application program interface (API)* contains predefined classes and interfaces for developing Java programs. The Java language specification is stable, but the API is still expanding. At the Sun Java Website (java.sun.com), you can view and download the latest version of the Java API.

Java SE, EE, and ME

Java is a full-fledged and powerful language that can be used in many ways. It comes in three editions: *Java Standard Edition (Java SE)*, *Java Enterprise Edition (Java EE)*, and *Java Micro Edition (Java ME)*. Java SE can be used to develop client-side standalone applications or applets. Java EE can be used to develop server-side applications, such as Java servlets and JavaServer Pages. Java ME can be used to develop applications for mobile devices, such as cell phones. This book uses Java SE to introduce Java programming.

JDK 1.6 = JDK 6

There are many versions of Java SE. The latest, Java SE 6, will be used in this book. Sun releases each version with a *Java Development Toolkit (JDK)*. For Java SE 6, the Java Development Toolkit is called *JDK 1.6* (also known as *Java 6 or JDK 6*).

Java IDE

JDK consists of a set of separate programs, each invoked from a command line, for developing and testing Java programs. Besides JDK, you can use a Java development tool (e.g., NetBeans, Eclipse, and TextPad)—software that provides an *integrated development environment (IDE)* for rapidly developing Java programs. Editing, compiling, building, debugging, and online help are integrated in one graphical user interface. Just enter source code in one window or open an existing file in a window, then click a button, menu item, or function key to compile and run the program.

1.7 A Simple Java Program

Let us begin with a simple Java program that displays the message "Welcome to Java!" on the console. *Console* refers to text entry and display device of a computer. The program is shown in Listing 1.1.

console

Video Note
First Java program

LISTING 1.1 Welcome.java

class
main method
display message

```
1 public class Welcome {
2   public static void main(String[] args) {
3     // Display message Welcome to Java! to the console
4     System.out.println("Welcome to Java!");
5   }
6 }
```

```
Welcome to Java!
```

line numbers

The *line numbers* are displayed for reference purposes but are not part of the program. So, don't type line numbers in your program.

class name

Line 1 defines a class. Every Java program must have at least one class. Each class has a name. By convention, class names start with an uppercase letter. In this example, the *class name* is `Welcome`.

main method

Line 2 defines the *main method*. In order to run a class, the class must contain a method named `main`. The program is executed from the `main` method.

A method is a construct that contains statements. The `main` method in this program contains the `System.out.println` statement. This statement prints a message `"Welcome to Java!"` to the console (line 4). Every statement in Java ends with a semicolon (`;`), known as the *statement terminator*.

statement terminator

reserved word

Reserved words, or *keywords,* have a specific meaning to the compiler and cannot be used for other purposes in the program. For example, when the compiler sees the word `class`, it understands that the word after `class` is the name for the class. Other reserved words in this program are `public`, `static`, and `void`.

comment

Line 3 is a *comment* that documents what the program is and how it is constructed. Comments help programmers to communicate and understand the program. They are not programming statements and thus are ignored by the compiler. In Java, comments are preceded by two slashes (`//`) on a line, called a *line comment*, or enclosed between `/*` and `*/` on one or several lines, called a *block comment*. When the compiler sees `//`, it ignores all text after `//` on the same line. When it sees `/*`, it scans for the next `*/` and ignores any text between `/*` and `*/`. Here are examples of comments:

```
// This application program prints Welcome to Java!
/* This application program prints Welcome to Java! */
/* This application program
   prints Welcome to Java! */
```

block

A pair of braces in a program forms a *block* that groups the program's components. In Java, each block begins with an opening brace (`{`) and ends with a closing brace (`}`). Every class has a *class block* that groups the data and methods of the class. Every method has a *method block* that groups the statements in the method. Blocks can be *nested*, meaning that one block can be placed within another, as shown in the following code.

```
public class Welcome {
  public static void main(String[] args) {
    System.out.println("Welcome to Java!");
  }
}
```

Class block

Method block

matching braces

Tip

An opening brace must be matched by a closing brace. Whenever you type an opening brace, immediately type a closing brace to prevent the missing-brace error. Most Java IDEs automatically insert the closing brace for each opening brace.

Note

You are probably wondering why the `main` method is declared this way and why `System.out.println(...)` is used to display a message to the console. For the time being, simply accept that this is how things are done. Your questions will be fully answered in subsequent chapters.

case sensitive

Caution

Java source programs are case sensitive. It would be wrong, for example, to replace `main` in the program with `Main`.

syntax rules

Note

Like any programming language, Java has its own syntax, and you need to write code that obeys the *syntax rules*. If your program violates the rules—for example if the semicolon is missing, a brace is missing, a quotation mark is missing, or `String` is misspelled—the Java compiler will report syntax errors. Try to compile the program with these errors and see what the compiler reports.

The program in Listing 1.1 displays one message. Once you understand the program, it is easy to extend it to display more messages. For example, you can rewrite the program to display three messages, as shown in Listing 1.2.

LISTING 1.2 Welcome1.java

class
main method
display message

```java
public class Welcome1 {
  public static void main(String[] args) {
    System.out.println("Programming is fun!");
    System.out.println("Fundamentals First");
    System.out.println("Problem Driven");
  }
}
```

```
Programming is fun!
Fundamentals First
Problem Driven
```

Further, you can perform mathematical computations and display the result to the console. Listing 1.3 gives an example of evaluating $\frac{10.5 + 2 \times 3}{45 - 3.5}$.

LISTING 1.3 ComputeExpression.java

```
public class ComputeExpression {
  public static void main(String[] args) {
    System.out.println((10.5 + 2 * 3) / (45 - 3.5));
  }
}
```

class
main method
compute expression

```
0.39759036144578314
```

The multiplication operator in Java is *. As you see, it is a straightforward process to translate an arithmetic expression to a Java expression. We will discuss Java expressions further in Chapter 2.

1.8 Creating, Compiling, and Executing a Java Program

You have to create your program and compile it before it can be executed. This process is repetitive, as shown in Figure 1.9. If your program has compilation errors, you have to modify the program to fix them, then recompile it. If your program has runtime errors or does not produce the correct result, you have to modify the program, recompile it, and execute it again.

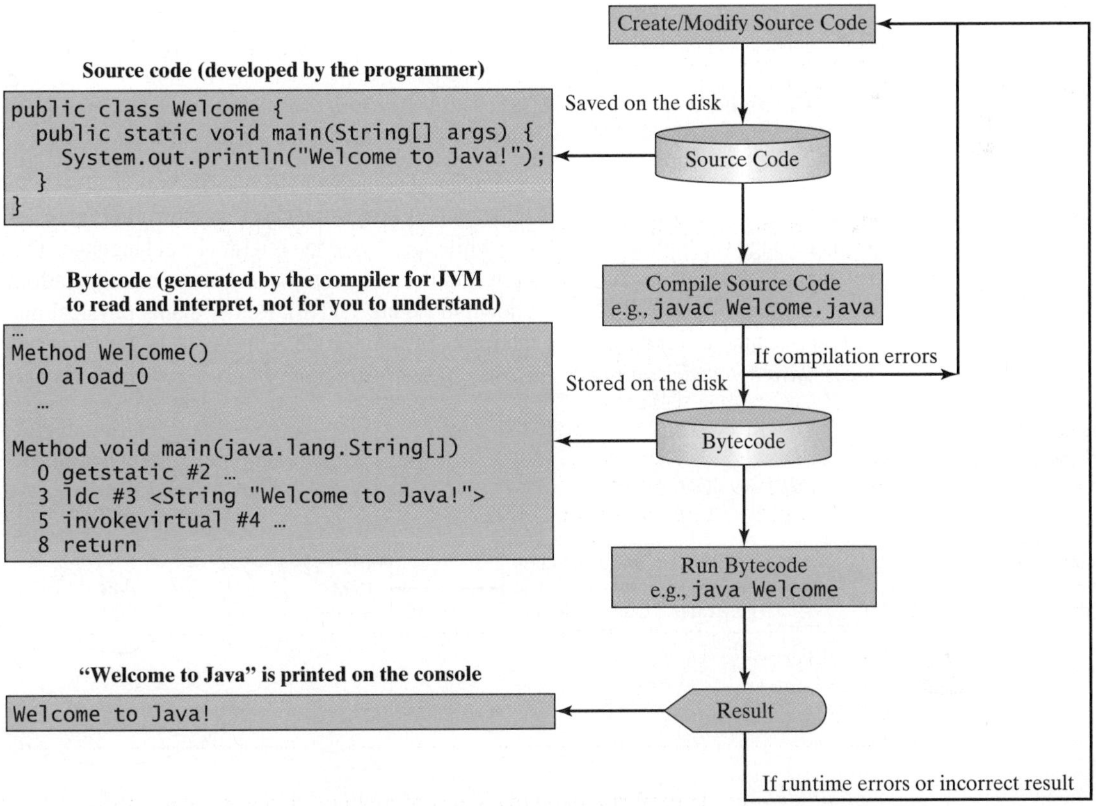
Create/Modify Source Code
Source code (developed by the programmer)
public class Welcome {
  public static void main(String[] args) {
    System.out.println("Welcome to Java!");
  }
}
Saved on the disk
Source Code
Bytecode (generated by the compiler for JVM to read and interpret, not for you to understand)
...
Method Welcome()
  0 aload_0
  ...
Method void main(java.lang.String[])
  0 getstatic #2 ...
  3 ldc #3 <String "Welcome to Java!">
  5 invokevirtual #4 ...
  8 return
Compile Source Code
e.g., javac Welcome.java
If compilation errors
Stored on the disk
Bytecode
Run Bytecode
e.g., java Welcome
"Welcome to Java" is printed on the console
Welcome to Java!
Result
If runtime errors or incorrect result

FIGURE 1.9 The Java program-development process consists of repeatedly creating/modifying source code, compiling, and executing programs.

editor

You can use any text *editor* or IDE to create and edit a Java source-code file. This section demonstrates how to create, compile, and run Java programs from a command window. If you wish to use an IDE such as Eclipse, NetBeans, or TextPad, please refer to Supplement II for tutorials. From the command window, you can use the NotePad to create the Java source code file, as shown in Figure 1.10.

Video Note
Brief Eclipse Tutorial

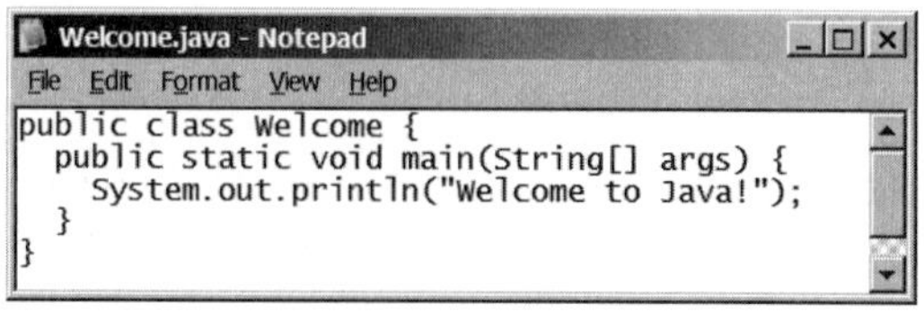
Welcome.java - Notepad
File Edit Format View Help
public class Welcome {
  public static void main(String[] args) {
    System.out.println("Welcome to Java!");
  }
}

FIGURE 1.10 You can create the Java source file using Windows NotePad.

file name

Note

The source file must end with the extension .java and must have exactly the same name as the public class name. For example, the file for the source code in Listing 1.1 should be named Welcome.java, since the public class name is **`Welcome`**.

A Java compiler translates a Java source file into a Java bytecode file. The following command compiles Welcome.java:

compile

```
javac Welcome.java
```

Supplement I.B

Supplement I.C

Note

You must first install and configure JDK before compiling and running programs. See Supplement I.B, "Installing and Configuring JDK 6," on how to install JDK and set up the environment to compile and run Java programs. If you have trouble compiling and running programs, please see Supplement I.C, "Compiling and Running Java from the Command Window." This supplement also explains how to use basic DOS commands and how to use Windows NotePad and WordPad to create and edit files. All the supplements are accessible from the Companion Website.

.class bytecode file

If there are no syntax errors, the *compiler* generates a bytecode file with a .class extension. So the preceding command generates a file named **Welcome. class**, as shown in Figure 1.11(a). The Java language is a high-level language while Java bytecode is a low-level language. The bytecode is similar to machine instructions but is architecture neutral and can run on any platform that has a Java Virtual Machine (JVM), as shown in Figure 1.11(b). Rather than a physical machine, the virtual machine is a program that interprets Java bytecode. This is one of Java's primary advantages: *Java bytecode can run on a variety of hardware platforms and operating systems.*

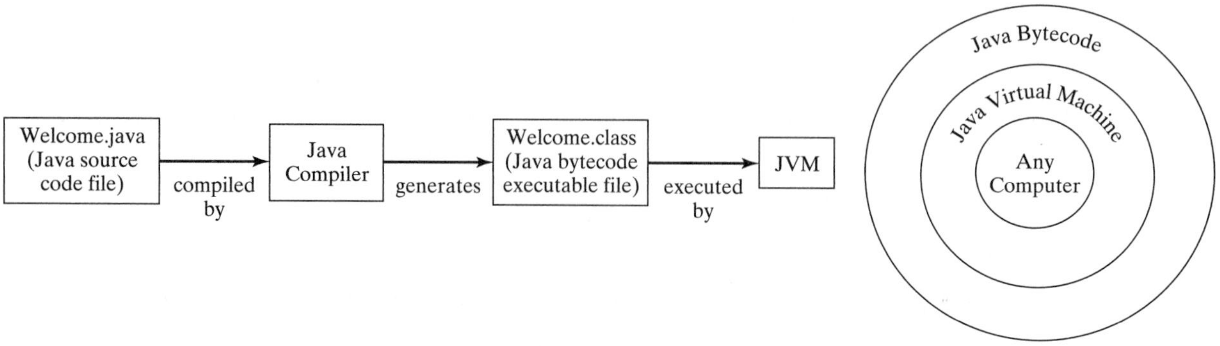
Welcome.java (Java source code file)
compiled by
Java Compiler
generates
Welcome.class (Java bytecode executable file)
executed by
JVM
Java Bytecode
Java Virtual Machine
Any Computer

(a) (b)

FIGURE 1.11 (a) Java source code is translated into bytecode. (b) Java bytecode can be executed on any computer with a Java Virtual Machine.

To execute a Java program is to run the program's bytecode. You can execute the bytecode on any platform with a JVM. Java bytecode is interpreted. Interpreting translates the individual steps in the bytecode into the target machine-language code one at a time rather than translating the whole program as a single unit. Each step is executed immediately after it is translated.

interpreting bytecode

The following command runs the bytecode:

```
java Welcome
```

run

Figure 1.12 shows the **javac** command for compiling Welcome.java. The compiler generated the Welcome.class file. This file is executed using the **java** command.

Video Note
Compile and run a Java program

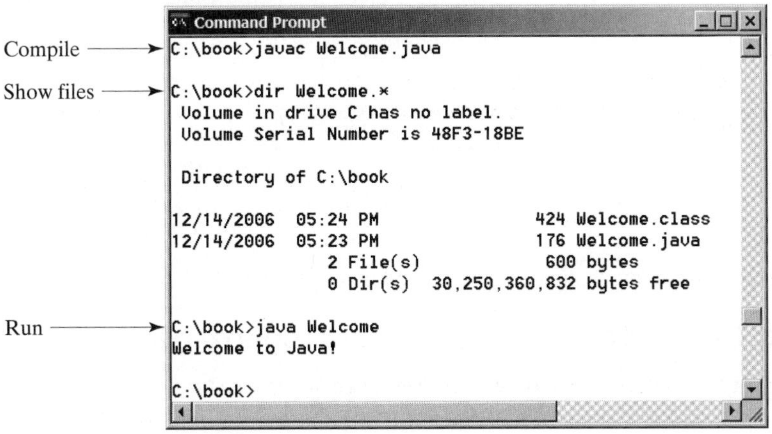
Command Prompt
Compile
C:\book>javac Welcome.java
Show files
C:\book>dir Welcome.*
Volume in drive C has no label.
Volume Serial Number is 48F3-18BE
Directory of C:\book
12/14/2006 05:24 PM 424 Welcome.class
12/14/2006 05:23 PM 176 Welcome.java
2 File(s) 600 bytes
0 Dir(s) 30,250,360,832 bytes free
Run
C:\book>java Welcome
Welcome to Java!
C:\book>

FIGURE 1.12 The output of Listing 1.1 displays the message "Welcome to Java!"

Note

For simplicity and consistency, all source code and class files are placed under **c:\book** unless specified otherwise.

c:\book

Caution

Do not use the extension .class in the command line when executing the program. Use **java ClassName** to run the program. If you use **java ClassName.class** in the command line, the system will attempt to fetch **ClassName.class.class**.

java ClassName

Tip

If you execute a class file that does not exist, a `NoClassDefFoundError` will occur. If you execute a class file that does not have a `main` method or you mistype the `main` method (e.g., by typing `Main` instead of `main`), a `NoSuchMethodError` will occur.

`NoClassDefFoundError`

`NoSuchMethodError`

Note

When executing a Java program, the JVM first loads the bytecode of the class to memory using a program called the *class loader*. If your program uses other classes, the class loader dynamically loads them just before they are needed. After a class is loaded, the JVM uses a program called *bytecode verifier* to check the validity of the bytecode and ensure that the bytecode does not violate Java's security restrictions. Java enforces strict security to make sure that Java programs arriving from the network do not harm your computer.

class loader

bytecode verifier

Pedagogical Note

Instructors may require students to use packages for organizing programs. For example, you may place all programs in this chapter in a package named *chapter1*. For instructions on how to use packages, please see Supplement I.F, "Using Packages to Organize the Classes in the Text."

using package

1.9 (GUI) Displaying Text in a Message Dialog Box

JOptionPane

showMessageDialog

The program in Listing 1.1 displays the text on the console, as shown in Figure 1.12. You can rewrite the program to display the text in a message dialog box. To do so, you need to use the `showMessageDialog` method in the `JOptionPane` class. `JOptionPane` is one of the many predefined classes in the Java system that you can reuse rather than "reinventing the wheel." You can use the `showMessageDialog` method to display any text in a message dialog box, as shown in Figure 1.13. The new program is given in Listing 1.4.

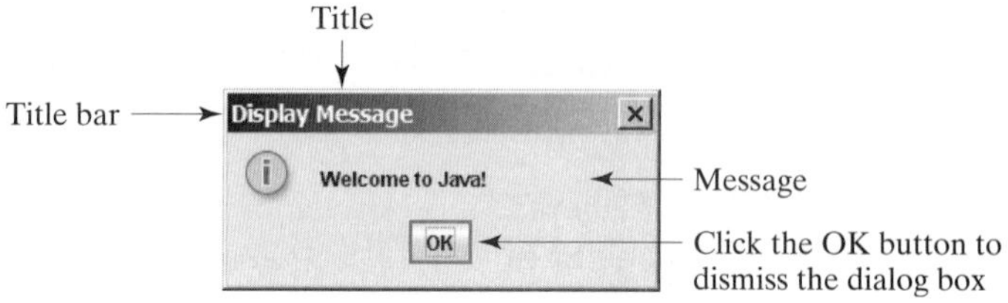
Title
Title bar
Display Message
Welcome to Java!
OK
Message
Click the OK button to dismiss the dialog box

FIGURE 1.13 "Welcome to Java!" is displayed in a message box.

LISTING 1.4 `WelcomeInMessageDialogBox.java`

block comment

import

main method

display message

```
 1 /*  This application program displays Welcome to Java!
 2  *  in a message dialog box.
 3  */
 4 import javax.swing.JOptionPane;
 5
 6 public class WelcomeInMessageDialogBox {
 7   public static void main(String[] args) {
 8     // Display Welcome to Java! in a message dialog box
 9     JOptionPane.showMessageDialog(null, "Welcome to Java!");
10   }
11 }
```

package

This program uses a Java class `JOptionPane` (line 9). Java's predefined classes are grouped into packages. `JOptionPane` is in the `javax.swing` package. `JOptionPane` is imported to the program using the `import` statement in line 4 so that the compiler can locate the class without the full name `javax.swing.JOptionPane`.

Note

If you replace `JOptionPane` on line 9 with `javax.swing.JOptionPane`, you don't need to import it in line 4. `javax.swing.JOptionPane` is the full name for the `JOptionPane` class.

The `showMessageDialog` method is a *static* method. Such a method should be invoked by using the class name followed by a dot operator (`.`) and the method name with arguments. Methods will be introduced in Chapter 5, "Methods." The `showMessageDialog` method can be invoked with two arguments, as shown below.

Message
Welcome to Java!
OK
JOptionPane.showMessageDialog(null,
"Welcome to Java!");

The first argument can always be **null**. **null** is a Java keyword that will be fully introduced in Chapter 8, "Objects and Classes." The second argument is a string for text to be displayed.

two versions of **showMessageDialog**

There are several ways to use the **showMessageDialog** method. For the time being, you need to know only two ways. One is to use a statement, as shown in the example:

```
JOptionPane.showMessageDialog(null, x);
```

where x is a string for the text to be displayed.

The other is to use a statement like this one:

```
JOptionPane.showMessageDialog(null, x,
  y, JOptionPane.INFORMATION_MESSAGE);
```

where x is a string for the text to be displayed, and y is a string for the title of the message box. The fourth argument can be **JOptionPane.INFORMATION_MESSAGE**, which causes the icon ( ) to be displayed in the message box, as shown in the following example.

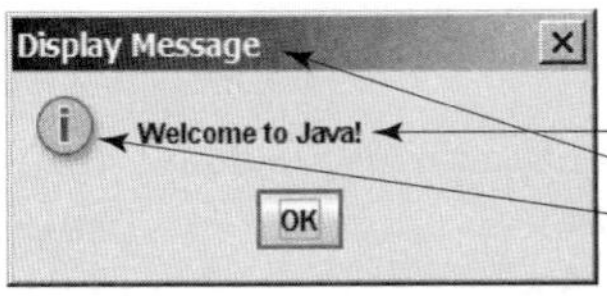
Display Message
Welcome to Java!
OK

```
JOptionPane.showMessageDialog(null,
  "Welcome to Java!",
  "Display Message",
  JOptionPane.INFORMATION_MESSAGE);
```

Note

There are two types of **import** statements: *specific import* and *wildcard import*. The *specific import* specifies a single class in the import statement. For example, the following statement imports **JOptionPane** from package **javax.swing**.

specific import

```
import javax.swing.JOptionPane;
```

The *wildcard import* imports all the classes in a package. For example, the following statement imports all classes from package **javax.swing**.

wildcard import

```
import javax.swing.*;
```

The information for the classes in an imported package is not read in at compile time or runtime unless the class is used in the program. The import statement simply tells the compiler where to locate the classes. There is no performance difference between a specific import and a wildcard import declaration.

no performance difference

Note

Recall that you have used the **System** class in the statement ***System.out.println("Welcome to Java");*** in Listing 1.1. The **System** class is not imported because it is in the **java.lang** package. All the classes in the **java.lang** package are *implicitly* imported in every Java program.

java.lang implicitly imported

Key Terms

compiler 7
console 11
dot pitch 5
DSL (digital subscriber line) 5
hardware 2
high-level language 6
Integrated Development Environment (IDE) 10
java command 15
javac command 15
Java Development Toolkit (JDK) 10
Java Virtual Machine (JVM) 14
keyword (or reserved word) 11
line comment 11
machine language 5
main method 11
memory 3
modem 5
network interface card (NIC) 5
operating system (OS) 7
pixel 5
program 5
programming 5
resolution 5
software 5
source code 7
source file 14
specific import 17
storage devices 4
statement 11
wildcard import 17

Supplement I.A

Note

The above terms are defined in the present chapter. Supplement I.A, "Glossary," lists all the key terms and descriptions in the book, organized by chapters.

Chapter Summary

1. A computer is an electronic device that stores and processes data.
2. A computer includes both *hardware* and *software*.
3. Hardware is the physical aspect of the computer that can be seen.
4. Computer *programs*, known as *software*, are the invisible instructions that control the hardware and make it perform tasks.
5. Computer programming is the writing of instructions (i.e., code) for computers to perform.
6. The central processing unit (CPU) is a computer's brain. It retrieves instructions from memory and executes them.
7. Computers use zeros and ones because digital devices have two stable states, referred to by convention as zero and one.
8. A bit is a binary digit 0 or 1.
9. A byte is a sequence of 8 bits.
10. A kilobyte is about 1000 bytes, a megabyte about 1 million bytes, a gigabyte about 1 billion bytes, and a terabyte about 1000 gigabytes.
11. Memory stores data and program instructions for the CPU to execute.
12. A memory unit is an ordered sequence of bytes.
13. Memory is volatile, because information is lost when the power is turned off.

14. Programs and data are permanently stored on storage devices and are moved to memory when the computer actually uses them.

15. The machine language is a set of primitive instructions built into every computer.

16. Assembly language is a low-level programming language in which a mnemonic is used to represent each machine-language instruction.

17. High-level languages are English-like and easy to learn and program.

18. A program written in a high-level language is called a source program.

19. A compiler is a software program that translates the source program into a machine-language program.

20. The operating system (OS) is a program that manages and controls a computer's activities.

21. Java is platform independent, meaning that you can write a program once and run it anywhere.

22. Java programs can be embedded in HTML pages and downloaded by Web browsers to bring live animation and interaction to Web clients.

23. Java source files end with the .java extension.

24. Every class is compiled into a separate bytecode file that has the same name as the class and ends with the .class extension.

25. To compile a Java source-code file from the command line, use the **javac** command.

26. To run a Java class from the command line, use the **java** command.

27. Every Java program is a set of class definitions. The keyword `class` introduces a class definition. The contents of the class are included in a block.

28. A block begins with an opening brace ({) and ends with a closing brace (}). Methods are contained in a class.

29. A Java program must have a `main` method. The `main` method is the entry point where the program starts when it is executed.

30. Every statement in Java ends with a semicolon (`;`), known as the *statement terminator.*

31. *Reserved words,* or *keywords,* have a specific meaning to the compiler and cannot be used for other purposes in the program.

32. In Java, comments are preceded by two slashes (`//`) on a line, called a *line comment*, or enclosed between `/*` and `*/` on one or several lines, called a block comment.

33. Java source programs are case sensitive.

34. There are two types of `import` statements: *specific import* and *wildcard import*. The *specific import* specifies a single class in the import statement. The *wildcard import* imports all the classes in a package.

Review Questions

Note

Answers to review questions are on the Companion Website.

Sections 1.2–1.4

1.1 Define hardware and software.

1.2 List the main components of the computer.

1.3 Define machine language, assembly language, and high-level programming language.

1.4 What is a source program? What is a compiler?

1.5 What is the JVM?

1.6 What is an operating system?

Sections 1.5–1.6

1.7 Describe the history of Java. Can Java run on any machine? What is needed to run Java on a computer?

1.8 What are the input and output of a Java compiler?

1.9 List some Java development tools. Are tools like NetBeans and Eclipse different languages from Java, or are they dialects or extensions of Java?

1.10 What is the relationship between Java and HTML?

Sections 1.7–1.9

1.11 Explain the Java keywords. List some Java keywords you learned in this chapter.

1.12 Is Java case sensitive? What is the case for Java keywords?

1.13 What is the Java source filename extension, and what is the Java bytecode filename extension?

1.14 What is a comment? Is the comment ignored by the compiler? How do you denote a comment line and a comment paragraph?

1.15 What is the statement to display a string on the console? What is the statement to display the message "Hello world" in a message dialog box?

1.16 The following program is wrong. Reorder the lines so that the program displays `morning` followed by `afternoon`.

```
  public static void main(String[] args) {
  }

public class Welcome {
    System.out.println("afternoon");
    System.out.println("morning");
}
```

1.17 Identify and fix the errors in the following code:

```
public class Welcome {
  public void Main(String[] args) {
    System.out.println('Welcome to Java!);
  }
)
```

1.18 What is the command to compile a Java program? What is the command to run a Java program?

1.19 If a `NoClassDefFoundError` occurs when you run a program, what is the cause of the error?

1.20 If a `NoSuchMethodError` occurs when you run a program, what is the cause of the error?

1.21 Why does the `System` class not need to be imported?

1.22 Are there any performance differences between the following two `import` statements?

```
import javax.swing.JOptionPane;

import javax.swing.*;
```

1.23 Show the output of the following code:

```
public class Test {
  public static void main(String[] args) {
    System.out.println("3.5 * 4 / 2 - 2.5 is ");
    System.out.println(3.5 * 4 / 2 - 2.5);
  }
}
```

Programming Exercises

Note

Solutions to even-numbered exercises are on the Companion Website. Solutions to all exercises are on the Instructor Resource Website. The level of difficulty is rated easy (no star), moderate (*), hard (**), or challenging (***).

level of difficulty

1.1 (*Displaying three messages*) Write a program that displays `Welcome to Java`, `Welcome to Computer Science`, and `Programming is fun`.

1.2 (*Displaying five messages*) Write a program that displays `Welcome to Java` five times.

1.3* (*Displaying a pattern*) Write a program that displays the following pattern:

```
    J     A     V     V     A
    J    A A     V   V     A A
J   J   AAAAA     V V     AAAAA
 J J   A     A     V     A     A
```

1.4 (*Printing a table*) Write a program that displays the following table:

```
a     a^2    a^3
1     1      1
2     4      8
3     9      27
4     16     64
```

1.5 (*Computing expressions*) Write a program that displays the result of

$$\frac{9.5 \times 4.5 - 2.5 \times 3}{45.5 - 3.5}.$$

1.6 (*Summation of a series*) Write a program that displays the result of $1 + 2 + 3 + 4 + 5 + 6 + 7 + 8 + 9$.

1.7 (*Approximating π*) π can be computed using the following formula:

$$\pi = 4 \times \left(1 - \frac{1}{3} + \frac{1}{5} - \frac{1}{7} + \frac{1}{9} - \frac{1}{11} + \frac{1}{13} + \cdots\right)$$

Write a program that displays the result of $4 \times \left(1 - \frac{1}{3} + \frac{1}{5} - \frac{1}{7} + \frac{1}{9} - \frac{1}{11} + \frac{1}{13}\right)$. Use `1.0` instead of `1` in your program.

CHAPTER 2

ELEMENTARY PROGRAMMING

Objectives

- To write Java programs to perform simple calculations (§2.2).
- To obtain input from the console using the `Scanner` class (§2.3).
- To use identifiers to name variables, constants, methods, and classes (§2.4).
- To use variables to store data (§§2.5–2.6).
- To program with assignment statements and assignment expressions (§2.6).
- To use constants to store permanent data (§2.7).
- To declare Java primitive data types: `byte`, `short`, `int`, `long`, `float`, `double`, and `char` (§2.8.1).
- To use Java operators to write numeric expressions (§§2.8.2–2.8.3).
- To display the current time (§2.9).
- To use shorthand operators (§2.10).
- To cast the value of one type to another type (§2.11).
- To compute loan payments (§2.12).
- To represent characters using the `char` type (§2.13).
- To compute monetary changes (§2.14).
- To represent a string using the `String` type (§2.15).
- To become familiar with Java documentation, programming style, and naming conventions (§2.16).
- To distinguish syntax errors, runtime errors, and logic errors and debug errors (§2.17).
- (GUI) To obtain input using the `JOptionPane` input dialog boxes (§2.18).

2.1 Introduction

In Chapter 1 you learned how to create, compile, and run a Java program. Now you will learn how to solve practical problems programmatically. Through these problems, you will learn elementary programming using primitive data types, variables, constants, operators, expressions, and input and output.

2.2 Writing Simple Programs

problem

To begin, let's look at a simple problem for computing the area of a circle. How do we write a program for solving this problem?

algorithm

pseudocode

Writing a program involves designing algorithms and translating algorithms into code. An *algorithm* describes how a problem is solved in terms of the actions to be executed and the order of their execution. Algorithms can help the programmer plan a program before writing it in a programming language. Algorithms can be described in natural languages or in *pseudocode* (i.e., natural language mixed with programming code). The algorithm for this program can be described as follows:

1. Read in the radius.
2. Compute the area using the following formula:

$$area = radius \times radius \times \pi$$

3. Display the area.

Many of the problems you will encounter when taking an introductory course in programming can be described with simple, straightforward algorithms.

When you *code*, you translate an algorithm into a program. You already know that every Java program begins with a class declaration in which the keyword `class` is followed by the class name. Assume that you have chosen `ComputeArea` as the class name. The outline of the program would look like this:

```
public class ComputeArea {
  // Details to be given later
}
```

As you know, every Java program must have a `main` method where program execution begins. So the program is expanded as follows:

```
public class ComputeArea {
  public static void main(String[] args) {
    // Step 1: Read in radius

    // Step 2: Compute area

    // Step 3: Display the area
  }
}
```

The program needs to read the radius entered by the user from the keyboard. This raises two important issues:

- Reading the radius.
- Storing the radius in the program.

variable

Let's address the second issue first. In order to store the radius, the program needs to declare a symbol called a *variable*. A variable designates a location in memory for storing data and computational results in the program. A variable has a name that can be used to access the memory location.

Rather than using `x` and `y` as variable names, choose descriptive names: in this case, `radius` for radius, and `area` for area. To let the compiler know what `radius` and `area` are, specify their data types. Java provides simple data types for representing integers, floating-point numbers (i.e., numbers with a decimal point), characters, and Boolean types. These types are known as *primitive data types* or *fundamental types.*

descriptive names

floating-point number

primitive data types

Declare `radius` and `area` as double-precision floating-point numbers. The program can be expanded as follows:

```
public class ComputeArea {
  public static void main(String[] args) {
    double radius;
    double area;

    // Step 1: Read in radius

    // Step 2: Compute area

    // Step 3: Display the area
  }
}
```

The program declares `radius` and `area` as variables. The reserved word `double` indicates that `radius` and `area` are double-precision floating-point values stored in the computer.

The first step is to read in `radius`. Reading a number from the keyboard is not a simple matter. For the time being, let us assign a fixed value to `radius` in the program.

The second step is to compute `area` by assigning the result of the expression `radius * radius * 3.14159` to `area`.

In the final step, display `area` on the console by using the `System.out.println` method.

The complete program is shown in Listing 2.1. A sample run of the program is shown in Figure 2.1.

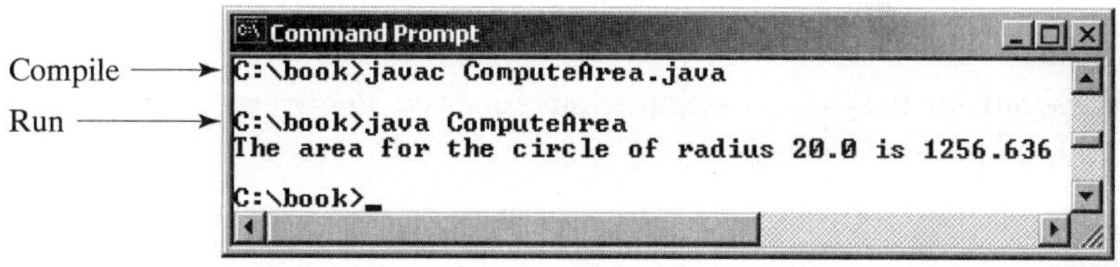
Compile
Run
Command Prompt
C:\book>javac ComputeArea.java
C:\book>java ComputeArea
The area for the circle of radius 20.0 is 1256.636
C:\book>_

FIGURE 2.1 The program displays the area of a circle.

LISTING 2.1 ComputeArea.java

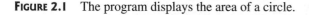

```
public class ComputeArea {
  public static void main(String[] args) {
    double radius; // Declare radius
    double area; // Declare area

    // Assign a radius
    radius = 20; // New value is radius

    // Compute area
    area = radius * radius * 3.14159;

    // Display results
```

```
13     System.out.println("The area for the circle of radius " +
14       radius + " is " + area);
15   }
16 }
```

declaring variable

assign value

Variables such as radius and area correspond to memory locations. Every variable has a name, a type, a size, and a value. Line 3 declares that radius can store a double value. The value is not defined until you assign a value. Line 7 assigns 20 into radius. Similarly, line 4 declares variable area, and line 10 assigns a value into area. The following table shows the value in the memory for area and radius as the program is executed. Each row in the table shows the values of variables after the statement in the corresponding line in the program is executed. Hand trace is helpful to understand how a program works, and it is also a useful tool for finding errors in the program.

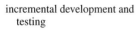

line#	radius	area
3	no value	
4		no value
7	20	
10		1256.636

concatenating strings

concatenating strings with numbers

The plus sign (+) has two meanings: one for addition and the other for concatenating strings. The plus sign (+) in lines 13–14 is called a *string concatenation operator*. It combines two strings if two operands are strings. If one of the operands is a nonstring (e.g., a number), the nonstring value is converted into a string and concatenated with the other string. So the plus signs (+) in lines 13–14 concatenate strings into a longer string, which is then displayed in the output. Strings and string concatenation will be discussed further in §2.15, "The String Type."

breaking a long string

Caution

A string constant cannot cross lines in the source code. Thus the following statement would result in a compile error:

```
System.out.println("Introduction to Java Programming,
  by Y. Daniel Liang");
```

To fix the error, break the string into separate substrings, and use the concatenation operator (+) to combine them:

```
System.out.println("Introduction to Java Programming, " +
  "by Y. Daniel Liang");
```

incremental development and testing

Tip

This example consists of three steps. It is a good approach to develop and test these steps incrementally by adding them one at a time.

2.3 Reading Input from the Console

Video Note
Obtain input

In Listing 2.1, the radius is fixed in the source code. To use a different radius, you have to modify the source code and recompile it. Obviously, this is not convenient. You can use the Scanner class for console input.

Java uses System.out to refer to the standard output device and System.in to the standard input device. By default the output device is the display monitor, and the input device is the keyboard. To perform console output, you simply use the `println` method to display a primitive value or a string to the console. Console input is not directly supported in Java, but you can use the `Scanner` class to create an object to read input from `System.in`, as follows:

```
Scanner input = new Scanner(System.in);
```

The syntax `new Scanner(System.in)` creates an object of the `Scanner` type. The syntax `Scanner input` declares that `input` is a variable whose type is `Scanner`. The whole line `Scanner input = new Scanner(System.in)` creates a `Scanner` object and assigns its reference to the variable `input`. An object may invoke its methods. To invoke a method on an object is to ask the object to perform a task. You can invoke the methods in Table 2.1 to read various types of input.

TABLE 2.1 Methods for `Scanner` Objects

Method	*Description*
`nextByte()`	reads an integer of the `byte` type.
`nextShort()`	reads an integer of the `short` type.
`nextInt()`	reads an integer of the `int` type.
`nextLong()`	reads an integer of the `long` type.
`nextFloat()`	reads a number of the `float` type.
`nextDouble()`	reads a number of the `double` type.
`next()`	reads a string that ends before a whitespace character.
`nextLine()`	reads a line of text (i.e., a string ending with the *Enter* key pressed).

For now, we will see how to read a number that includes a decimal point by invoking the `nextDouble()` method. Other methods will be covered when they are used. Listing 2.2 rewrites Listing 2.1 to prompt the user to enter a radius.

LISTING 2.2 ComputeAreaWithConsoleInput.java

```java
import java.util.Scanner; // Scanner is in the java.util package

public class ComputeAreaWithConsoleInput {
  public static void main(String[] args) {
    // Create a Scanner object
    Scanner input = new Scanner(System.in);

    // Prompt the user to enter a radius
    System.out.print("Enter a number for radius: ");
    double radius = input.nextDouble() ;

    // Compute area
    double area = radius * radius * 3.14159;

    // Display result
    System.out.println("The area for the circle of radius " +
      radius + " is " + area);
  }
}
```

import class

create a **Scanner**

read a **double**

```
Enter a number for radius: 2.5 ↵Enter
The area for the circle of radius 2.5 is 19.6349375
```

```
Enter a number for radius: 23 ↵Enter
The area for the circle of radius 23.0 is 1661.90111
```

The `Scanner` class is in the `java.util` package. It is imported in line 1. Line 6 creates a `Scanner` object.

The statement in line 9 displays a message to prompt the user for input.

```
System.out.print ("Enter a number for radius: ");
```

`print` vs. `println`

The `print` method is identical to the `println` method except that `println` moves the cursor to the next line after displaying the string, but `print` does not advance the cursor to the next line when completed.

The statement in line 10 reads an input from the keyboard.

```
double radius = input.nextDouble();
```

After the user enters a number and presses the *Enter* key, the number is read and assigned to `radius`.

More details on objects will be introduced in Chapter 8, "Objects and Classes." For the time being, simply accept that this is how to obtain input from the console.

Listing 2.3 gives another example of reading input from the keyboard. The example reads three numbers and displays their average.

Listing 2.3 ComputeAverage.java

import class · create a **`Scanner`** · read a **`double`**

```
import java.util.Scanner; // Scanner is in the java.util package

public class ComputeAverage {
  public static void main(String[] args) {
    // Create a Scanner object
    Scanner input = new Scanner(System.in);

    // Prompt the user to enter three numbers
    System.out.print("Enter three numbers: ");
    double number1 = input.nextDouble() ;
    double number2 = input.nextDouble() ;
    double number3 = input.nextDouble() ;

    // Compute average
    double average = (number1 + number2 + number3) / 3;

    // Display result
    System.out.println("The average of " + number1 + " " + number2
      + " " + number3 + " is " + average);
  }
}
```

enter input in one line

```
Enter three numbers: 1 2 3 ↵Enter
The average of 1.0 2.0 3.0 is 2.0
```

enter input in multiple lines

```
Enter three numbers: 10.5 ↵Enter
11 ↵Enter
11.5 ↵Enter
The average of 10.5 11.0 11.5 is 11.0
```

The code for importing the `Scanner` class (line 1) and creating a `Scanner` object (line 6) are the same as in the preceding example as well as in all new programs you will write.

Line 9 prompts the user to enter three numbers. The numbers are read in lines 10–12. You may enter three numbers separated by spaces, then press the *Enter* key, or enter each number followed by a press of the *Enter* key, as shown in the sample runs of this program.

2.4 Identifiers

As you see in Listing 2.3, `ComputeAverage`, `main`, `input`, `number1`, `number2`, `number3`, and so on are the names of things that appear in the program. Such names are called *identifiers*. All identifiers must obey the following rules:

identifier naming rules

- An identifier is a sequence of characters that consists of letters, digits, underscores (_), and dollar signs ($).
- An identifier must start with a letter, an underscore (_), or a dollar sign ($). It cannot start with a digit.
- An identifier cannot be a reserved word. (See Appendix A, "Java Keywords," for a list of reserved words.)
- An identifier cannot be `true`, `false`, or `null`.
- An identifier can be of any length.

For example, `$2`, `ComputeArea`, `area`, `radius`, and `showMessageDialog` are legal identifiers, whereas `2A` and `d+4` are not because they do not follow the rules. The Java compiler detects illegal identifiers and reports syntax errors.

Note

Since Java is case sensitive, `area`, `Area`, and `AREA` are all different identifiers.

case sensitive

Tip

Identifiers are for naming variables, constants, methods, classes, and packages. Descriptive identifiers make programs easy to read.

descriptive names

Tip

Do not name identifiers with the $ character. By convention, the $ character should be used only in mechanically generated source code.

the $ character

2.5 Variables

why called variables?

As you see from the programs in the preceding sections, variables are used to store values to be used later in a program. They are called variables because their values can be changed. In the program in Listing 2.2, `radius` and `area` are variables of double-precision, floating-point type. You can assign any numerical value to `radius` and `area`, and the values of `radius` and `area` can be reassigned. For example, you can write the code shown below to compute the area for different radii:

```
// Compute the first area
radius = 1.0;
area = radius * radius * 3.14159;
System.out.println("The area is " + area + " for radius " + radius);

// Compute the second area
radius = 2.0;
area = radius * radius * 3.14159;
System.out.println("The area is " + area + " for radius " + radius);
```

Variables are for representing data of a certain type. To use a variable, you declare it by telling the compiler its name as well as what type of data it can store. The *variable declaration* tells the compiler to allocate appropriate memory space for the variable based on its data type. The syntax for declaring a variable is

```
datatype variableName;
```

declaring variables

Here are some examples of variable declarations:

```
int count;            // Declare count to be an integer variable;
double radius;        // Declare radius to be a double variable;
double interestRate; // Declare interestRate to be a double variable;
```

The examples use the data types `int`, `double`, and `char`. Later you will be introduced to additional data types, such as `byte`, `short`, `long`, `float`, `char`, and `boolean`.

If variables are of the same type, they can be declared together, as follows:

```
datatype variable1, variable2, ..., variablen;
```

The variables are separated by commas. For example,

```
int i, j, k; // Declare i, j, and k as int variables
```

Note

naming variables

By convention, variable names are in lowercase. If a name consists of several words, concatenate all of them and capitalize the first letter of each word except the first. Examples of variables are `radius` and `interestRate`.

initializing variables

Variables often have initial values. You can declare a variable and initialize it in one step. Consider, for instance, the following code:

```
int count = 1;
```

This is equivalent to the next two statements:

```
int count;
x = 1;
```

You can also use a shorthand form to declare and initialize variables of the same type together. For example,

```
int i = 1, j = 2;
```

Tip

A variable must be declared before it can be assigned a value. A variable declared in a method must be assigned a value before it can be used.

Whenever possible, declare a variable and assign its initial value in one step. This will make the program easy to read and avoid programming errors.

2.6 Assignment Statements and Assignment Expressions

assignment statement
assignment operator

After a variable is declared, you can assign a value to it by using an *assignment statement*. In Java, the equal sign (=) is used as the *assignment operator*. The syntax for assignment statements is as follows:

```
variable = expression;
```

An *expression* represents a computation involving values, variables, and operators that, taking them together, evaluates to a value. For example, consider the following code: expression

```
int x = 1;                    // Assign 1 to variable x
double radius = 1.0;          // Assign 1.0 to variable radius
x = 5 * (3 / 2) + 3 * 2;  // Assign the value of the expression to x
x = y + 1;                    // Assign the addition of y and 1 to x
area = radius * radius * 3.14159; // Compute area
```

A variable can also be used in an expression. For example,

```
x = x + 1;
```

In this assignment statement, the result of x + 1 is assigned to x. If x is 1 before the statement is executed, then it becomes 2 after the statement is executed.

To assign a value to a variable, the variable name must be on the left of the assignment operator. Thus, 1 = x would be wrong.

Note

In mathematics, x = 2 * x + 1 denotes an equation. However, in Java, x = 2 * x + 1 is an assignment statement that evaluates the expression 2 * x + 1 and assigns the result to x.

In Java, an assignment statement is essentially an expression that evaluates to the value to be assigned to the variable on the left-hand side of the assignment operator. For this reason, an assignment statement is also known as an *assignment expression*. For example, the following statement is correct: assignment expression

```
System.out.println(x = 1);
```

which is equivalent to

```
x = 1;
System.out.println(x);
```

The following statement is also correct:

```
i = j = k = 1;
```

which is equivalent to

```
k = 1;
j = k;
i = j;
```

Note

In an assignment statement, the data type of the variable on the left must be compatible with the data type of the value on the right. For example, int x = 1.0 would be illegal, because the data type of x is int. You cannot assign a double value (1.0) to an int variable without using type casting. Type casting is introduced in §2.11 "Numeric Type Conversions."

2.7 Named Constants

The value of a variable may change during the execution of a program, but a *named constant* or simply *constant* represents permanent data that never changes. In our ComputeArea program, π is a constant. If you use it frequently, you don't want to keep typing 3.14159; instead, you can declare a constant for π. Here is the syntax for declaring a constant: constant

```
final datatype CONSTANTNAME = VALUE;
```

A constant must be declared and initialized in the same statement. The word final is a Java keyword for declaring a constant. For example, you can declare π as a constant and rewrite Listing 2.1 as follows:

```
// ComputeArea.java: Compute the area of a circle
public class ComputeArea {
  public static void main(String[] args) {
    final double PI = 3.14159; // Declare a constant

    // Assign a radius
    double radius = 20;

    // Compute area
    double area = radius * radius * PI;

    // Display results
    System.out.println("The area for the circle of radius " +
      radius + " is " + area);
  }
}
```

naming constants

Caution

By convention, constants are named in uppercase: PI, not pi or Pi.

benefits of constants

Note

There are three benefits of using constants: (1) you don't have to repeatedly type the same value; (2) if you have to change the constant value (e.g., from 3.14 to 3.14159 for PI), you need to change it only in a single location in the source code; (3) a descriptive name for a constant makes the program easy to read.

2.8 Numeric Data Types and Operations

Every data type has a range of values. The compiler allocates memory space for each variable or constant according to its data type. Java provides eight primitive data types for numeric values, characters, and Boolean values. This section introduces numeric data types.

Table 2.2 lists the six numeric data types, their ranges, and their storage sizes.

TABLE 2.2 Numeric Data Types

Name	*Range*	*Storage Size*
byte	-2^7 (−128) to 2^7-1 (127)	8-bit signed
short	-2^{15} (−32768) to $2^{15}-1$ (32767)	16-bit signed
int	-2^{31} (−2147483648) to $2^{31}-1$ (2147483647)	32-bit signed
long	-2^{63} to $2^{63}-1$ (i.e., −9223372036854775808 to 9223372036854775807)	64-bit signed
float	Negative range: −3.4028235E + 38 to −1.4E−45 Positive range: 1.4E–45 to 3.4028235E + 38	32-bit IEEE 754
double	Negative range: −1.7976931348623157E + 308 to −4.9E−324 Positive range: 4.9E − 324 to 1.7976931348623157E + 308	64-bit IEEE 754

Note

IEEE 754 is a standard approved by the Institute of Electrical and Electronics Engineers for representing floating-point numbers on computers. The standard has been widely adopted. Java has adopted the 32-bit **IEEE 754** for the `float` type and the 64-bit **IEEE 754** for the `double` type. The **IEEE 754** standard also defines special values as given in Appendix E, "Special Floating-Point Values."

Java uses four types for integers: `byte`, `short`, `int`, and `long`. Choose the type that is most appropriate for your variable. For example, if you know an integer stored in a variable is within a range of byte, declare the variable as a `byte`. For simplicity and consistency, we will use `int` for integers most of the time in this book. integer types

Java uses two types for floating-point numbers: `float` and `double`. The `double` type is twice as big as `float`. So, the `double` is known as *double precision*, `float` as *single precision*. Normally you should use the `double` type, because it is more accurate than the `float` type. floating point

Caution

When a variable is assigned a value that is too large (*in size*) to be stored, it causes *overflow*. For example, executing the following statement causes *overflow*, because the largest value that can be stored in a variable of the `int` type is `2147483647`. `2147483648` is too large. what is overflow?

```
int value = 2147483647 + 1; // value will actually be -2147483648
```

Likewise, executing the following statement causes *overflow*, because the smallest value that can be stored in a variable of the `int` type is `-2147483648`. `-2147483649` is too large in size to be stored in an `int` variable.

```
int value = -2147483648 - 1; // value will actually be 2147483647
```

Java does not report warnings or errors on overflow. So be careful when working with numbers close to the maximum or minimum range of a given type.

When a floating-point number is too small (i.e., too close to zero) to be stored, it causes *underflow*. Java approximates it to zero. So normally you should not be concerned with underflow. what is underflow?

2.8.1 Numeric Operators

The operators for numeric data types include the standard arithmetic operators: addition (+), subtraction (–), multiplication (*), division (/), and remainder (%), as shown in Table 2.3. operators +, -, *, /, %

When both operands of a division are integers, the result of the division is an integer. The fractional part is truncated. For example, `5 / 2` yields `2`, not `2.5`, and `-5 / 2` yields `-2`, not `-2.5`. To perform regular mathematical division, one of the operands must be a floating-point number. For example, `5.0 / 2` yields `2.5`. integer division

The `%` operator yields the remainder after division. The left-hand operand is the dividend and the right-hand operand the divisor. Therefore, `7 % 3` yields `1`, `12 % 4` yields `0`, `26 % 8` yields `2`, and `20 % 13` yields `7`.

TABLE 2.3 Numeric Operators

Name	*Meaning*	*Example*	*Result*
+	Addition	34 + 1	35
-	Subtraction	34.0 – 0.1	33.9
*	Multiplication	300 * 30	9000
/	Division	1.0 / 2.0	0.5
%	Remainder	20 % 3	2

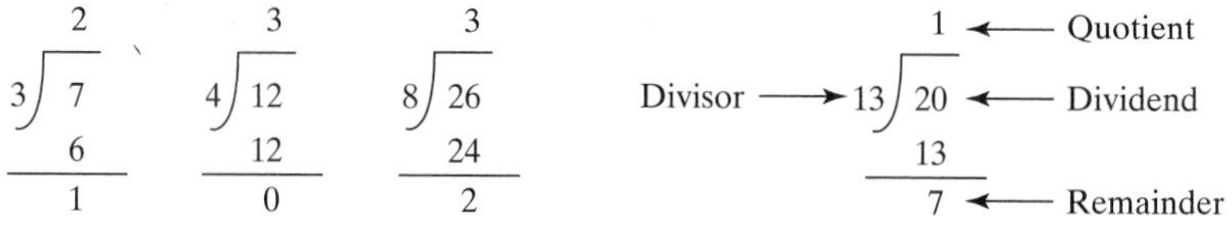
Quotient
Divisor
Dividend
Remainder

The % operator is often used for positive integers but can be used also with negative integers and floating-point values. The remainder is negative only if the dividend is negative. For example, -7 % 3 yields -1, -12 % 4 yields 0, -26 % -8 yields -2, and 20 % -13 yields 7.

Remainder is very useful in programming. For example, an even number % 2 is always 0 and an odd number % 2 is always 1. So you can use this property to determine whether a number is even or odd. If today is Saturday, it will be Saturday again in 7 days. Suppose you and your friends are going to meet in 10 days. What day is in 10 days? You can find that the day is Tuesday using the following expression:

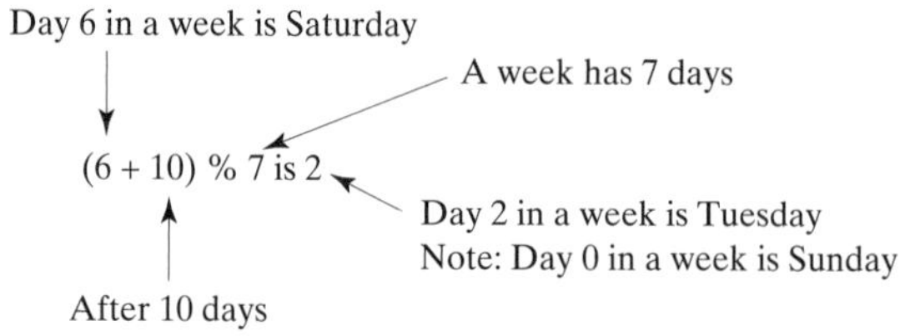
Day 6 in a week is Saturday
A week has 7 days
(6 + 10) % 7 is 2
Day 2 in a week is Tuesday
Note: Day 0 in a week is Sunday
After 10 days

Listing 2.4 gives a program that obtains minutes and remaining seconds from an amount of time in seconds. For example, 500 seconds contains 8 minutes and 20 seconds.

LISTING 2.4 DisplayTime.java

import **Scanner**
create a **Scanner**
read an integer
divide
remainder

```
1 import java.util.Scanner;
2
3 public class DisplayTime {
4   public static void main(String[] args) {
5     Scanner input = new Scanner(System.in);
6     // Prompt the user for input
7     System.out.print("Enter an integer for seconds: ");
8     int seconds = input.nextInt() ;
9
10    int minutes = seconds / 60 ; // Find minutes in seconds
11    int remainingSeconds = seconds % 60 ; // Seconds remaining
12    System.out.println(seconds + " seconds is " + minutes +
13      " minutes and " + remainingSeconds + " seconds");
14  }
15 }
```

```
Enter an integer for seconds: 500 ↵Enter
500 seconds is 8 minutes and 20 seconds
```

line#	seconds	minutes	remainingSeconds
8	500		
10		8	
11			20

The nextInt() method (line 8) reads an integer for seconds. Line 4 obtains the minutes using seconds / 60. Line 5 (seconds % 60) obtains the remaining seconds after taking away the minutes.

The + and - operators can be both unary and binary. A *unary* operator has only one operand; a *binary* operator has two. For example, the - operator in -5 is a unary operator to negate number 5, whereas the - operator in 4 - 5 is a binary operator for subtracting 5 from 4.

unary operator
binary operator

Note

Calculations involving floating-point numbers are approximated because these numbers are not stored with complete accuracy. For example,

floating-point approximation

```
System.out.println(1.0 - 0.1 - 0.1 - 0.1 - 0.1 - 0.1);
```

displays 0.5000000000000001, not 0.5, and

```
System.out.println(1.0 - 0.9);
```

displays 0.09999999999999998, not 0.1. Integers are stored precisely. Therefore, calculations with integers yield a precise integer result.

2.8.2 Numeric Literals

A *literal* is a constant value that appears directly in a program. For example, 34 and 0.305 are literals in the following statements:

literal

```
int numberOfYears = 34;
double weight = 0.305;
```

Integer Literals

An integer literal can be assigned to an integer variable as long as it can fit into the variable. A compile error will occur if the literal is too large for the variable to hold. The statement byte b = 128, for example, will cause a compile error, because 128 cannot be stored in a variable of the byte type. (Note that the range for a byte value is from −128 to 127.)

An integer literal is assumed to be of the int type, whose value is between -2^{31} (−2147483648) and $2^{31} - 1$ (2147483647). To denote an integer literal of the long type, append the letter L or l to it (e.g., 2147483648L). L is preferred because l (lowercase L) can easily be confused with 1 (the digit one). To write integer 2147483648 in a Java program, you have to write it as 2147483648L, because 2147483648 exceeds the range for the int value.

long literal

Note

By default, an integer literal is a decimal integer number. To denote an octal integer literal, use a leading *0* (zero), and to denote a hexadecimal integer literal, use a leading *0x* or *0X* (zero x). For example, the following code displays the decimal value 65535 for hexadecimal number FFFF.

octal and hex literals

```
System.out.println(0xFFFF);
```

Hexadecimal numbers, binary numbers, and octal numbers are introduced in Appendix F, "Number Systems."

Floating-Point Literals

Floating-point literals are written with a decimal point. By default, a floating-point literal is treated as a double type value. For example, 5.0 is considered a double value, not a float value. You can make a number a float by appending the letter f or F, and you can make a number a double by appending the letter d or D. For example, you can use 100.2f or 100.2F for a float number, and 100.2d or 100.2D for a double number.

suffix d or D
suffix f or F

Note

The double type values are more accurate than the float type values. For example,

double vs. float

```
System.out.println("1.0 / 3.0 is " + 1.0 / 3.0);
```

displays `1.0 / 3.0 is 0.3333333333333333`.

```
System.out.println("1.0F / 3.0F is " + 1.0F / 3.0F);
```

displays `1.0F / 3.0F is 0.33333334`.

Scientific Notation

Floating-point literals can also be specified in scientific notation; for example, `1.23456e+2`, the same as `1.23456e2`, is equivalent to $1.23456 \times 10^2 = 123.456$, and `1.23456e-2` is equivalent to $1.23456 \times 10^{-2} = 0.0123456$. `E` (or `e`) represents an exponent and can be in either lowercase or uppercase.

why called floating-point?

Note

The `float` and `double` types are used to represent numbers with a decimal point. Why are they called *floating-point numbers*? These numbers are stored in scientific notation. When a number such as `50.534` is converted into scientific notation, such as `5.0534e+1`, its decimal point is moved (i.e., floated) to a new position.

2.8.3 Evaluating Java Expressions

Writing a numeric expression in Java involves a straightforward translation of an arithmetic expression using Java operators. For example, the arithmetic expression

$$\frac{3 + 4x}{5} - \frac{10(y - 5)(a + b + c)}{x} + 9\left(\frac{4}{x} + \frac{9 + x}{y}\right)$$

can be translated into a Java expression as:

```
(3 + 4 * x) / 5 - 10 * (y - 5) * (a + b + c) / x +
9 * (4 / x + (9 + x) / y)
```

evaluating an expression

Though Java has its own way to evaluate an expression behind the scene, the result of a Java expression and its corresponding arithmetic expression are the same. Therefore, you can safely apply the arithmetic rule for evaluating a Java expression. Operators contained within pairs of parentheses are evaluated first. Parentheses can be nested, in which case the expression in the inner parentheses is evaluated first. Multiplication, division, and remainder operators are applied next. If an expression contains several multiplication, division, and remainder operators, they are applied from left to right. Addition and subtraction operators are applied last. If an expression contains several addition and subtraction operators, they are applied from left to right. Here is an example of how an expression is evaluated:

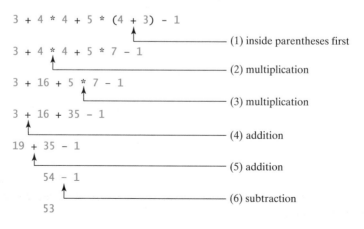

```
3 + 4 * 4 + 5 * (4 + 3) - 1
                   ↑
                   └──────────── (1) inside parentheses first
3 + 4 * 4 + 5 * 7 - 1
      ↑
      └──────────────────────── (2) multiplication
3 + 16 + 5 * 7 - 1
           ↑
           └─────────────────── (3) multiplication
3 + 16 + 35 - 1
  ↑
  └──────────────────────────── (4) addition
19 + 35 - 1
   ↑
   └─────────────────────────── (5) addition
     54 - 1
        ↑
        └────────────────────── (6) subtraction
     53
```

Listing 2.5 gives a program that converts a Fahrenheit degree to Celsius using the formula $celsius = \left(\frac{5}{9}\right)(fahrenheit - 32)$.

LISTING 2.5 FahrenheitToCelsius.java

```
1  import java.util.Scanner;
2
3  public class FahrenheitToCelsius {
4    public static void main(String[] args) {
5      Scanner input = new Scanner(System.in);
6
7      System.out.print("Enter a degree in Fahrenheit: ");
8      double fahrenheit = input.nextDouble();
9
10     // Convert Fahrenheit to Celsius
11     double celsius = (5.0 / 9) * (fahrenheit - 32);
12     System.out.println("Fahrenheit " + fahrenheit + " is " +
13       celsius + " in Celsius");
14   }
15 }
```

divide

```
Enter a degree in Fahrenheit: 100 ↵Enter
Fahrenheit 100.0 is 37.77777777777778 in Celsius
```

line#	fahrenheit	celsius
8	100	
11		37.77777777777778

Be careful when applying division. Division of two integers yields an integer in Java. $\frac{5}{9}$ is translated to `5.0 / 9` instead of `5 / 9` in line 11, because `5 / 9` yields `0` in Java.

integer vs. decimal division

2.9 Problem: Displaying the Current Time

Video Note
Use operators / and %

The problem is to develop a program that displays the current time in GMT (Greenwich Mean Time) in the format hour:minute:second, such as 13:19:8.

The `currentTimeMillis` method in the `System` class returns the current time in milliseconds elapsed since the time `00:00:00` on January 1, 1970 GMT, as shown in Figure 2.2. This time is known as the *Unix epoch,* because `1970` was the year when the Unix operating system was formally introduced.

currentTimeMillis

Unix epoch

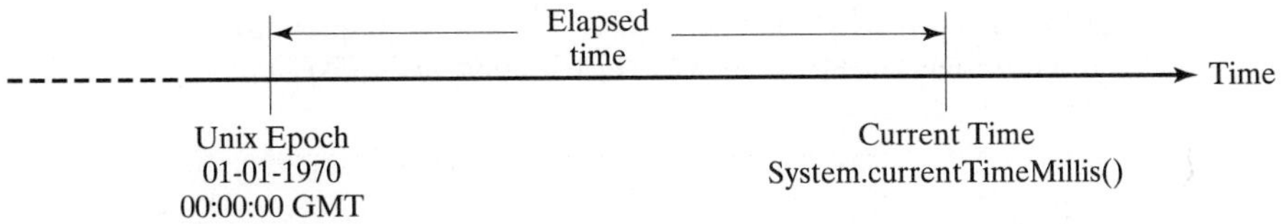
Elapsed time
Time
Unix Epoch
01-01-1970
00:00:00 GMT
Current Time
System.currentTimeMillis()

FIGURE 2.2 The `System.currentTimeMillis()` returns the number of milliseconds since the Unix epoch.

You can use this method to obtain the current time, and then compute the current second, minute, and hour as follows.

1. Obtain the total milliseconds since midnight, Jan 1, 1970, in `totalMilliseconds` by invoking `System.currentTimeMillis()` (e.g., `1203183086328` milliseconds).
2. Obtain the total seconds `totalSeconds` by dividing `totalMilliseconds` by `1000` (e.g., `1203183086328` milliseconds / `1000` = `1203183086` seconds).
3. Compute the current second from `totalSeconds % 60` (e.g., `1203183086` seconds % `60` = `26`, which is the current second).
4. Obtain the total minutes `totalMinutes` by dividing `totalSeconds` by `60` (e.g., `1203183086` seconds / `60` = `20053051` minutes).
5. Compute the current minute from `totalMinutes % 60` (e.g., `20053051` minutes % `60` = `31`, which is the current minute).
6. Obtain the total hours `totalHours` by dividing `totalMinutes` by `60` (e.g., `20053051` minutes / `60` = `334217` hours).
7. Compute the current hour from `totalHours % 24` (e.g., `334217` hours % `24` = `17`, which is the current hour).

Listing 2.6 gives the complete program.

LISTING 2.6 ShowCurrentTime.java

totalMilliseconds **totalSeconds** **currentSecond** **totalMinutes** **currentMinute** **totalHours** **currentHour**

```
public class ShowCurrentTime {
  public static void main(String[] args) {
    // Obtain the total milliseconds since midnight, Jan 1, 1970
    long totalMilliseconds = System.currentTimeMillis();

    // Obtain the total seconds since midnight, Jan 1, 1970
    long totalSeconds = totalMilliseconds / 1000;

    // Compute the current second in the minute in the hour
    long currentSecond = (int)(totalSeconds % 60);

    // Obtain the total minutes
    long totalMinutes = totalSeconds / 60;

    // Compute the current minute in the hour
    long currentMinute = totalMinutes % 60;

    // Obtain the total hours
    long totalHours = totalMinutes / 60;

    // Compute the current hour
    long currentHour = totalHours % 24;

    // Display results
    System.out.println("Current time is " + currentHour + ":"
      + currentMinute + ":" + currentSecond + " GMT");
  }
}
```

```
Current time is 17:31:26 GMT
```

line# / variables	4	7	10	13	16	19	22
totalMilliseconds	1203183086328						
totalSeconds		1203183086					
currentSecond			26				
totalMinutes				20053051			
currentMinute					31		
totalHours						334217	
currentHour							17

When `System.currentTimeMillis()` (line 4) is invoked, it returns the difference, measured in milliseconds, between the current GMT and midnight, January 1, 1970 GMT. This method returns the milliseconds as a `long` value. So, all the variables are declared as the `long` type in this program.

2.10 Shorthand Operators

Very often the current value of a variable is used, modified, and then reassigned back to the same variable. For example, the following statement adds the current value of `i` with `8` and assigns the result back to `i`:

```
i = i + 8;
```

Java allows you to combine assignment and addition operators using a shorthand operator. For example, the preceding statement can be written as:

```
i += 8;
```

The += is called the *addition assignment operator*. Other shorthand operators are shown in Table 2.4.

addition assignment operator

TABLE 2.4 Shorthand Operators

Operator	*Name*	*Example*	*Equivalent*
+=	Addition assignment	`i += 8`	`i = i + 8`
-=	Subtraction assignment	`i -= 8`	`i = i - 8`
*=	Multiplication assignment	`i *= 8`	`i = i * 8`
/=	Division assignment	`i /= 8`	`i = i / 8`
%=	Remainder assignment	`i %= 8`	`i = i % 8`

Caution

There are no spaces in the shorthand operators. For example, + = should be +=.

Note

Like the assignment operator (=), the operators (+=, -=, *=, /=, %=) can be used to form an assignment statement as well as an expression. For example, in the following code, x += 2 is a statement in the first line and an expression in the second line.

```
x += 2; // Statement
System.out.println(x += 2); // Expression
```

There are two more shorthand operators for incrementing and decrementing a variable by 1. These are handy, because that's often how much the value needs to be changed. The two operators are ++ and --. For example, the following code increments i by 1 and decrements j by 1.

```
int i = 3, j = 3;
i++; // i becomes 4
j--; // j becomes 2
```

The ++ and -- operators can be used in prefix or suffix mode, as shown in Table 2.5.

TABLE 2.5 Increment and Decrement Operators

Operator	*Name*	*Description*	*Example (assume i = 1)*
++var	preincrement	Increment var by 1 and use the new var value	int j = ++i; // j is 2, // i is 2
var++	postincrement	Increment var by 1, but use the original var value	int j = i++; // j is 1, // i is 2
--var	predecrement	Decrement var by 1 and use the new var value	int j = --i; // j is 0, // i is 0
var--	postdecrement	Decrement var by 1 and use the original var value	int j = ++i; // j is 1, // i is 0

If the operator is *before* (prefixed to) the variable, the variable is incremented or decremented by 1, then the *new* value of the variable is returned. If the operator is *after* (suffixed to) the variable, then the variable is incremented or decremented by 1, but the original *old* value of the variable is returned. Therefore, the prefixes ++x and --x are referred to, respectively, as the *preincrement operator* and the *predecrement operator*; and the suffixes x++ and x-- are referred to, respectively, as the *postincrement operator* and the *postdecrement operator*. The prefix form of ++ (or --) and the suffix form of ++ (or --) are the same if they are used in isolation, but they cause different effects when used in an expression. The following code illustrates this:

preincrement, predecrement
postincrement, postdecrement

```
int i = 10;
int newNum = 10 * i++;      Same effect as →   int newNum = 10 * i;
                                               i = i + 1;
```

In this case, i is incremented by 1, then the *old* value of i is returned and used in the multiplication. So newNum becomes 100. If i++ is replaced by ++i as follows,

```
int i = 10;
int newNum = 10 * (++i);    Same effect as →   i = i + 1;
                                               int newNum = 10 * i;
```

i is incremented by 1, and the new value of i is returned and used in the multiplication. Thus newNum becomes 110.

Here is another example:

```
double x = 1.0;
double y = 5.0;
double z = x-- + (++y);
```

After all three lines are executed, y becomes 6.0, z becomes 7.0, and x becomes 0.0.

The increment operator ++ and the decrement operator -- can be applied to all integer and floating-point types. These operators are often used in loop statements. A *loop statement* is a construct that controls how many times an operation or a sequence of operations is performed in succession. This construct, and the topic of loop statements, are introduced in Chapter 4, "Loops."

Tip

Using increment and decrement operators makes expressions short, but it also makes them complex and difficult to read. Avoid using these operators in expressions that modify multiple variables or the same variable multiple times, such as this one: `int k = ++i + i`.

2.11 Numeric Type Conversions

Can you perform binary operations with two operands of different types? Yes. If an integer and a floating-point number are involved in a binary operation, Java automatically converts the integer to a floating-point value. So, 3 * 4.5 is same as 3.0 * 4.5.

You can always assign a value to a numeric variable whose type supports a larger range of values; thus, for instance, you can assign a long value to a float variable. You cannot, however, assign a value to a variable of a type with smaller range unless you use *type casting*. Casting is an operation that converts a value of one data type into a value of another data type. Casting a variable of a type with a small range to a variable of a type with a larger range is known as *widening a type*. Casting a variable of a type with a large range to a variable of a type with a smaller range is known as *narrowing a type*. Widening a type can be performed automatically without explicit casting. Narrowing a type must be performed explicitly.

widening a type

narrowing a type

The syntax is the target type in parentheses, followed by the variable's name or the value to be cast. For example, the following statement

type casting

```
System.out.println((int)1.7);
```

displays 1. When a double value is cast into an int value, the fractional part is truncated.

The following statement

```
System.out.println((double)1 / 2);
```

displays 0.5, because 1 is cast to 1.0 first, then 1.0 is divided by 2. However, the statement

```
System.out.println(1 / 2);
```

displays 0, because 1 and 2 are both integers and the resulting value should also be an integer.

Caution

Casting is necessary if you are assigning a value to a variable of a smaller type range, such as assigning a double value to an int variable. A compile error will occur if casting is not used in situations of this kind. Be careful when using casting. Loss of information might lead to inaccurate results.

possible loss of precision

Note

Casting does not change the variable being cast. For example, **d** is not changed after casting in the following code:

```
double d = 4.5;
int i = (int)d;  // i becomes 4, but d is not changed, still 4.5
```

Note

To assign a variable of the **int** type to a variable of the **short** or **byte** type, explicit casting must be used. For example, the following statements have a compile error:

```
int i = 1;
byte b = i; // Error because explicit casting is required
```

However, so long as the integer literal is within the permissible range of the target variable, explicit casting is not needed to assign an integer literal to a variable of the **short** or **byte** type. Please refer to §2.8.2, "Numeric Literals."

Listing 2.7 gives a program that displays the sales tax with two digits after the decimal point.

LISTING 2.7 SalesTax.java

casting

```
1 import java.util.Scanner;
2
3 public class SalesTax {
4   public static void main(String[] args) {
5     Scanner input = new Scanner(System.in);
6
7     System.out.print("Enter purchase amount: ");
8     double purchaseAmount = input.nextDouble();
9
10    double tax = purchaseAmount * 0.06;
11    System.out.println("Sales tax is " + (int)(tax * 100) / 100.0);
12  }
13 }
```

```
Enter purchase amount: 197.55 ↵Enter
Sales tax is 11.85
```

line#	purchaseAmount	tax	output
8	197.55		
10		11.853	
11			11.85

formatting numbers

Variable **purchaseAmount** is **197.55** (line 8). The sales tax is **6%** of the purchase, so the **tax** is evaluated as **11.853** (line 10). Note that

```
tax * 100 is 1185.3
(int)(tax * 100) is 1185
(int)(tax * 100) / 100.0 is 11.85
```

So, the statement in line 11 displays the tax **11.85** with two digits after the decimal point.

2.12 Problem: Computing Loan Payments

Video Note
Program computations

The problem is to write a program that computes loan payments. The loan can be a car loan, a student loan, or a home mortgage loan. The program lets the user enter the interest rate, number of years, and loan amount, and displays the monthly and total payments.

The formula to compute the monthly payment is as follows:

$$monthlyPayment = \frac{loanAmount \times monthlyInterestRate}{1 - \dfrac{1}{(1 + monthlyInterestRate)^{numberOfYears \times 12}}}$$

You don't have to know how this formula is derived. Nonetheless, given the monthly interest rate, number of years, and loan amount, you can use it to compute the monthly payment.

In the formula, you have to compute $(1 + monthlyInterestRate)^{numberOfYears \times 12}$. The `pow(a, b)` method in the `Math` class can be used to compute a^b. The `Math` class, which comes with the Java API, is available to all Java programs. For example,

pow(a, b) method

```
System.out.println(Math.pow(2, 3)); // Display 8
System.out.println(Math.pow(4, 0.5)); // Display 4
```

$(1 + monthlyInterestRate)^{numberOfYears \times 12}$ can be computed using `Math.pow(1 + monthlyInterestRate, numberOfYears * 12)`.

Here are the steps in developing the program:

1. Prompt the user to enter the annual interest rate, number of years, and loan amount.
2. Obtain the monthly interest rate from the annual interest rate.
3. Compute the monthly payment using the preceding formula.
4. Compute the total payment, which is the monthly payment multiplied by 12 and multiplied by the number of years.
5. Display the monthly payment and total payment.

Listing 2.8 gives the complete program.

LISTING 2.8 ComputeLoan.java

```
import java.util.Scanner;

public class ComputeLoan {
  public static void main(String[] args) {
    // Create a Scanner
    Scanner input = new Scanner(System.in);

    // Enter yearly interest rate
    System.out.print("Enter yearly interest rate, for example 8.25: ");
    double annualInterestRate = input.nextDouble();

    // Obtain monthly interest rate
    double monthlyInterestRate = annualInterestRate / 1200;

    // Enter number of years
    System.out.print(
      "Enter number of years as an integer, for example 5: ");
    int numberOfYears = input.nextInt();

    // Enter loan amount
    System.out.print("Enter loan amount, for example 120000.95: ");
```

import class

create a Scanner

enter interest rate

enter years

enter loan amount

monthlyPayment

totalPayment

casting

casting

```
22      double loanAmount = input.nextDouble();
23
24      // Calculate payment
25      double monthlyPayment = loanAmount * monthlyInterestRate / (1
26        - 1 / Math.pow(1 + monthlyInterestRate, numberOfYears * 12));
27      double totalPayment = monthlyPayment * numberOfYears * 12;
28
29      // Display results
30     System.out.println("The monthly payment is " +
31       (int)(monthlyPayment * 100) / 100.0);
32     System.out.println("The total payment is " +
33       (int)(totalPayment * 100) / 100.0);
34   }
35 }
```

```
Enter yearly interest rate, for example 8.25: 5.75 ↵Enter
Enter number of years as an integer, for example 5: 15 ↵Enter
Enter loan amount, for example 120000.95: 250000 ↵Enter
The monthly payment is 2076.02
The total payment is 373684.53
```

variables \ line#	10	13	18	22	25	27
annualInterestRate	5.75					
monthlyInterestRate		0.0047916666666				
numberOfYears			15			
loanAmount				250000		
monthlyPayment					2076.0252175	
totalPayment						373684.539

Line 10 reads the yearly interest rate, which is converted into monthly interest rate in line 13. If you entered an input other than a numeric value, a runtime error would occur.

Choose the most appropriate data type for the variable. For example, `numberOfYears` is best declared as an `int` (line 18), although it could be declared as a `long`, `float`, or `double`. Note that `byte` might be the most appropriate for `numberOfYears`. For simplicity, however, the examples in this book will use `int` for integer and `double` for floating-point values.

The formula for computing the monthly payment is translated into Java code in lines 25–27.

Casting is used in lines 31 and 33 to obtain a new `monthlyPayment` and `totalPayment` with two digits after the decimal point.

java.lang package

The program uses the `Scanner` class, imported in line 1. The program also uses the `Math` class; why isn't it imported? The `Math` class is in the `java.lang` package. All classes in the `java.lang` package are implicitly imported. So, there is no need to explicitly import the `Math` class.

2.13 Character Data Type and Operations

char type

The character data type, `char`, is used to represent a single character. A character literal is enclosed in single quotation marks. Consider the following code:

```
char letter = 'A';
char numChar = '4';
```

The first statement assigns character A to the char variable letter. The second statement assigns digit character 4 to the char variable numChar.

Caution

A string literal must be enclosed in quotation marks. A character literal is a single character enclosed in single quotation marks. So "A" is a string, and 'A' is a character.

char literal

2.13.1 Unicode and ASCII code

character encoding

Computers use binary numbers internally. A character is stored in a computer as a sequence of 0s and 1s. Mapping a character to its binary representation is called *encoding*. There are different ways to encode a character. How characters are encoded is defined by an *encoding scheme*.

Unicode

original Unicode

supplementary Unicode

Java supports *Unicode*, an encoding scheme established by the Unicode Consortium to support the interchange, processing, and display of written texts in the world's diverse languages. Unicode was originally designed as a 16-bit character encoding. The primitive data type char was intended to take advantage of this design by providing a simple data type that could hold any character. However, it turned out that the 65,536 characters possible in a 16-bit encoding are not sufficient to represent all the characters in the world. The Unicode standard therefore has been extended to allow up to 1,112,064 characters. Those characters that go beyond the original 16-bit limit are called *supplementary characters*. Java supports supplementary characters. The processing and representing of supplementary characters are beyond the scope of this book. For simplicity, this book considers only the original 16-bit Unicode characters. These characters can be stored in a char type variable.

A 16-bit Unicode takes two bytes, preceded by \u, expressed in four hexadecimal digits that run from '\u0000' to '\uFFFF'. For example, the word "welcome" is translated into Chinese using two characters, 欢迎. The Unicodes of these two characters are "\u6B22\u8FCE".

Listing 2.9 gives a program that displays two Chinese characters and three Greek letters.

LISTING 2.9 DisplayUnicode.java

```
import javax.swing.JOptionPane;

public class DisplayUnicode {
  public static void main(String[] args) {
    JOptionPane.showMessageDialog(null,
      "\u6B22\u8FCE \u03b1 \u03b2 \u03b3",
      "\u6B22\u8FCE Welcome",
      JOptionPane.INFORMATION_MESSAGE);
  }
}
```

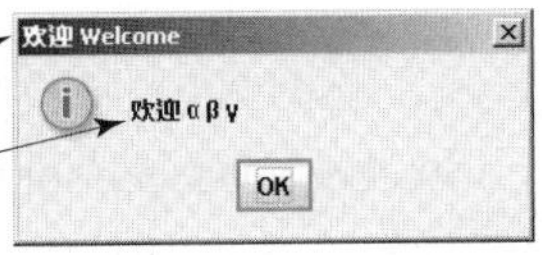
欢迎 Welcome
欢迎 α β γ
OK

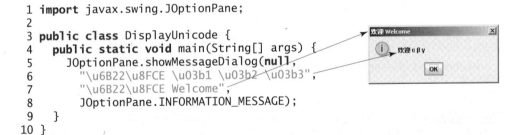

If no Chinese font is installed on your system, you will not be able to see the Chinese characters. The Unicodes for the Greek letters α β γ are \u03b1 \u03b2 \u03b3.

ASCII

Most computers use *ASCII* (*American Standard Code for Information Interchange*), a 7-bit encoding scheme for representing all uppercase and lowercase letters, digits, punctuation marks, and control characters. Unicode includes ASCII code, with '\u0000' to '\u007F' corresponding to the 128 ASCII characters. (See Appendix B, "The ASCII Character Set," for a list of ASCII characters and their decimal and hexadecimal codes.) You can use ASCII characters such as 'X', '1', and '$' in a Java program as well as Unicodes. Thus, for example, the following statements are equivalent:

```
char letter = 'A';
char letter = '\u0041'; // Character A's Unicode is 0041
```

Both statements assign character A to char variable letter.

char increment and decrement

Note

The increment and decrement operators can also be used on **char** variables to get the next or preceding Unicode character. For example, the following statements display character **b**.

```
char ch = 'a';
System.out.println(++ch);
```

2.13.2 Escape Sequences for Special Characters

Suppose you want to print a message with quotation marks in the output. Can you write a statement like this?

```
System.out.println("He said "Java is fun"");
```

No, this statement has a syntax error. The compiler thinks the second quotation character is the end of the string and does not know what to do with the rest of characters.

backslash

To overcome this problem, Java defines escape sequences to represent special characters, as shown in Table 2.6. An escape sequence begins with the backslash character (\) followed by a character that has a special meaning to the compiler.

TABLE 2.6 Java Escape Sequences

Character Escape Sequence	*Name*	*Unicode Code*
\b	Backspace	\u0008
\t	Tab	\u0009
\n	Linefeed	\u000A
\f	Formfeed	\u000C
\r	Carriage Return	\u000D
\\	Backslash	\u005C
\'	Single Quote	\u0027
\"	Double Quote	\u0022

So, now you can print the quoted message using the following statement:

```
System.out.println("He said \"Java is fun\"");
```

The output is

```
He said "Java is fun"
```

2.13.3 Casting between char and Numeric Types

A **char** can be cast into any numeric type, and vice versa. When an integer is cast into a **char**, only its lower 16 bits of data are used; the other part is ignored. For example:

```
char ch = (char)0XAB0041; // the lower 16 bits hex code 0041 is
                          // assigned to ch
System.out.println(ch);   // ch is character A
```

When a floating-point value is cast into a **char**, the floating-point value is first cast into an **int**, which is then cast into a **char**.

```
char ch = (char)65.25;    // decimal 65 is assigned to ch
System.out.println(ch);   // ch is character A
```

When a **char** is cast into a numeric type, the character's Unicode is cast into the specified numeric type.

```
int i = (int)'A'; // the Unicode of character A is assigned to i
System.out.println(i);   // i is 65
```

Implicit casting can be used if the result of a casting fits into the target variable. Otherwise, explicit casting must be used. For example, since the Unicode of 'a' is 97, which is within the range of a byte, these implicit castings are fine:

```
byte b = 'a';
int i = 'a';
```

But the following casting is incorrect, because the Unicode \uFFF4 cannot fit into a byte:

```
byte b = '\uFFF4';
```

To force assignment, use explicit casting, as follows:

```
byte b = (byte)'\uFFF4';
```

Any positive integer between 0 and FFFF in hexadecimal can be cast into a character implicitly. Any number not in this range must be cast into a char explicitly.

Note

numeric operators on characters

All numeric operators can be applied to char operands. A char operand is automatically cast into a number if the other operand is a number or a character. If the other operand is a string, the character is concatenated with the string. For example, the following statements

```
int i = '2' + '3'; // (int)'2' is 50 and (int)'3' is 51
System.out.println("i is " + i); // i is 101

int j = 2 + 'a'; // (int)'a' is 97
System.out.println("j is " + j); // j is 99
System.out.println(j + " is the Unicode for character "
  + (char)j);

System.out.println("Chapter " + '2');
```

display

```
i is 101
j is 99
99 is the Unicode for character c
Chapter 2
```

Note

The Unicodes for lowercase letters are consecutive integers starting from the Unicode for 'a', then for 'b', 'c', ..., and 'z'. The same is true for the uppercase letters. Furthermore, the Unicode for 'a' is greater than the Unicode for 'A'. So 'a' - 'A' is the same as 'b' - 'B'. For a lowercase letter *ch*, its corresponding uppercase letter is (char)('A' + (ch - 'a')).

2.14 Problem: Counting Monetary Units

Suppose you want to develop a program that classifies a given amount of money into smaller monetary units. The program lets the user enter an amount as a double value representing a total in dollars and cents, and outputs a report listing the monetary equivalent in dollars, quarters, dimes, nickels, and pennies, as shown in the sample run.

Your program should report the maximum number of dollars, then the maximum number of quarters, and so on, in this order.

Here are the steps in developing the program:

1. Prompt the user to enter the amount as a decimal number, such as 11.56.
2. Convert the amount (e.g., 11.56) into cents (1156).
3. Divide the cents by 100 to find the number of dollars. Obtain the remaining cents using the cents remainder 100.
4. Divide the remaining cents by 25 to find the number of quarters. Obtain the remaining cents using the remaining cents remainder 25.
5. Divide the remaining cents by 10 to find the number of dimes. Obtain the remaining cents using the remaining cents remainder 10.
6. Divide the remaining cents by 5 to find the number of nickels. Obtain the remaining cents using the remaining cents remainder 5.
7. The remaining cents are the pennies.
8. Display the result.

The complete program is given in Listing 2.10.

Listing 2.10 ComputeChange.java

import class
enter input
dollars
quarters
dimes
nickels
pennies
prepare output

```
import java.util.Scanner;

public class ComputeChange {
  public static void main(String[] args) {
    // Create a Scanner
    Scanner input = new Scanner(System.in);

    // Receive the amount
    System.out.print(
      "Enter an amount in double, for example 11.56: ");
    double amount = input.nextDouble();

    int remainingAmount = (int)(amount * 100);

    // Find the number of one dollars
    int numberOfOneDollars = remainingAmount / 100;
    remainingAmount = remainingAmount % 100;

    // Find the number of quarters in the remaining amount
    int numberOfQuarters = remainingAmount / 25;
    remainingAmount = remainingAmount % 25;

    // Find the number of dimes in the remaining amount
    int numberOfDimes = remainingAmount / 10;
    remainingAmount = remainingAmount % 10;

    // Find the number of nickels in the remaining amount
    int numberOfNickels = remainingAmount / 5;
    remainingAmount = remainingAmount % 5;

    // Find the number of pennies in the remaining amount
    int numberOfPennies = remainingAmount;

    // Display results
    System.out.println("Your amount " + amount + " consists of \n" +
```

```
36          "\t" + numberOfOneDollars + " dollars\n" +
37          "\t" + numberOfQuarters + " quarters\n" +
38          "\t" + numberOfDimes + " dimes\n" +
39          "\t" + numberOfNickels + " nickels\n" +
40          "\t" + numberOfPennies + " pennies");
41    }
42 }
```

```
Enter an amount in double, for example 11.56: 11.56 ↵Enter
Your amount 11.56 consists of
       11 dollars
       2 quarters
       0 dimes
       1 nickels
       1 pennies
```

variables \ line#	11	13	16	17	20	21	24	25	28	29	32
Amount	11.56										
remainingAmount		1156		56		6		6		1	
numberOfOneDollars			11								
numberOfQuarters					2						
numberOfDimes							0				
numberOfNickles									1		
numberOfPennies											1

The variable `amount` stores the amount entered from the console (line 11). This variable is not changed, because the amount has to be used at the end of the program to display the results. The program introduces the variable `remainingAmount` (line 13) to store the changing `remainingAmount`.

The variable `amount` is a `double` decimal representing dollars and cents. It is converted to an `int` variable `remainingAmount`, which represents all the cents. For instance, if `amount` is `11.56`, then the initial `remainingAmount` is `1156`. The division operator yields the integer part of the division. So `1156 / 100` is `11`. The remainder operator obtains the remainder of the division. So `1156 % 100` is `56`.

The program extracts the maximum number of singles from the total amount and obtains the remaining amount in the variable `remainingAmount` (lines 16–17). It then extracts the maximum number of quarters from `remainingAmount` and obtains a new `remainingAmount` (lines 20–21). Continuing the same process, the program finds the maximum number of dimes, nickels, and pennies in the remaining amount.

loss of precision

One serious problem with this example is the possible loss of precision when casting a `double` amount to an `int remainingAmount`. This could lead to an inaccurate result. If you try to enter the amount `10.03`, `10.03 * 100` becomes `1002.9999999999999`. You will find that the program displays `10` dollars and `2` pennies. To fix the problem, enter the amount as an integer value representing cents (see Exercise 2.9).

As shown in the sample run, 0 dimes, 1 nickels, and 1 pennies are displayed in the result. It would be better not to display 0 dimes, and to display 1 nickel and 1 penny using the singular forms of the words. You will learn how to use selection statements to modify this program in the next chapter (see Exercise 3.7).

2.15 The String Type

The char type represents only one character. To represent a string of characters, use the data type called String. For example, the following code declares the message to be a string with value "Welcome to Java".

```
String message = "Welcome to Java";
```

String is actually a predefined class in the Java library just like the classes System, JOptionPane, and Scanner. The String type is not a primitive type. It is known as a *reference type*. Any Java class can be used as a reference type for a variable. Reference data types will be thoroughly discussed in Chapter 8, "Objects and Classes." For the time being, you need to know only how to declare a String variable, how to assign a string to the variable, and how to concatenate strings.

concatenating strings and numbers

As first shown in Listing 2.1, two strings can be concatenated. The plus sign (+) is the concatenation operator if one of the operands is a string. If one of the operands is a nonstring (e.g., a number), the nonstring value is converted into a string and concatenated with the other string. Here are some examples:

```
// Three strings are concatenated
String message = "Welcome " + "to " + "Java";

// String Chapter is concatenated with number 2
String s = "Chapter" + 2; // s becomes Chapter2

// String Supplement is concatenated with character B
String s1 = "Supplement" + 'B'; // s1 becomes SupplementB
```

If neither of the operands is a string, the plus sign (+) is the addition operator that adds two numbers.

The shorthand += operator can also be used for string concatenation. For example, the following code appends the string "and Java is fun" with the string "Welcome to Java" in message.

```
message += " and Java is fun";
```

So the new message is "Welcome to Java and Java is fun".

Suppose that i = 1 and j = 2, what is the output of the following statement?

```
System.out.println("i + j is " + i + j);
```

The output is "i + j is 12" because "i + j is " is concatenated with the value of i first. To force i + j to be executed first, enclose i + j in the parentheses, as follows:

```
System.out.println("i + j is " + (i + j));
```

reading strings

To read a string from the console, invoke the next() method on a Scanner object. For example, the following code reads three strings from the keyboard:

```
Scanner input = new Scanner(System.in);
System.out.println("Enter three strings: ");
String s1 = input.next();
```

```
String s2 = input.next();
String s3 = input.next();
System.out.println("s1 is " + s1);
System.out.println("s2 is " + s2);
System.out.println("s3 is " + s3);
```

```
Enter a string: Welcome to Java ↵Enter
s1 is Welcome
s2 is to
s3 is Java
```

The **next()** method reads a string that ends with a whitespace character (i.e., **' '**, **'\t'**, **'\f'**, **'\r'**, or **'\n'**).

You can use the **nextLine()** method to read an entire line of text. The **nextLine()** method reads a string that ends with the *Enter* key pressed. For example, the following statements read a line of text.

```
Scanner input = new Scanner(System.in);
System.out.println("Enter a string: ");
String s = input.nextLine();
System.out.println("The string entered is " + s);
```

```
Enter a string: Welcome to Java ↵Enter
The string entered is "Welcome to Java"
```

Important Caution

To *avoid input errors*, do not use **nextLine()** after **nextByte()**, **nextShort()**, **nextInt()**, **nextLong()**, **nextFloat()**, **nextDouble()**, and **next()**. The reasons will be explained in §9.7.3, "How Does **Scanner** Work?"

avoiding input errors

2.16 Programming Style and Documentation

programming style

documentation

Programming style deals with what programs look like. A program can compile and run properly even if written on only one line, but writing it all on one line would be bad programming style because it would be hard to read. *Documentation* is the body of explanatory remarks and comments pertaining to a program. Programming style and documentation are as important as coding. Good programming style and appropriate documentation reduce the chance of errors and make programs easy to read. So far you have learned some good programming styles. This section summarizes them and gives several guidelines. More detailed guidelines can be found in Supplement I.D, "Java Coding Style Guidelines," on the Companion Website.

2.16.1 Appropriate Comments and Comment Styles

Include a summary at the beginning of the program to explain what the program does, its key features, and any unique techniques it uses. In a long program, you should also include comments that introduce each major step and explain anything that is difficult to read. It is important to make comments concise so that they do not crowd the program or make it difficult to read.

javadoc comment

In addition to line comment **//** and block comment **/***, Java supports comments of a special type, referred to as *javadoc comments*. javadoc comments begin with **/**** and end with ***/**. They can be extracted into an HTML file using JDK's **javadoc** command. For more information, see java.sun.com/j2se/javadoc.

Use javadoc comments (/** ... */) for commenting on an entire class or an entire method. These comments must precede the class or the method header in order to be extracted in a javadoc HTML file. For commenting on steps inside a method, use line comments (//).

2.16.2 Naming Conventions

Make sure that you choose descriptive names with straightforward meanings for the variables, constants, classes, and methods in your program. Names are case sensitive. Listed below are the conventions for naming variables, methods, and classes.

naming variables and methods

- Use lowercase for variables and methods. If a name consists of several words, concatenate them into one, making the first word lowercase and capitalizing the first letter of each subsequent word—for example, the variables `radius` and `area` and the method `showInputDialog`.

naming classes

- Capitalize the first letter of each word in a class name—for example, the class names `ComputeArea`, `Math`, and `JOptionPane`.

naming constants

- Capitalize every letter in a constant, and use underscores between words—for example, the constants `PI` and `MAX_VALUE`.

It is important to follow the naming conventions to make programs easy to read.

naming classes

Caution

Do not choose class names that are already used in the Java library. For example, since the `Math` class is defined in Java, you should not name your class `Math`.

using full descriptive names

Tip

Avoid using abbreviations for identifiers. Using complete words is more descriptive. For example, `numberOfStudents` is better than `numStuds`, `numOfStuds`, or `numOfStudents`.

2.16.3 Proper Indentation and Spacing

indent code

A consistent indentation style makes programs clear and easy to read, debug, and maintain. *Indentation* is used to illustrate the structural relationships between a program's components or statements. Java can read the program even if all of the statements are in a straight line, but humans find it easier to read and maintain code that is aligned properly. Indent each subcomponent or statement at least *two* spaces more than the construct within which it is nested.

A single space should be added on both sides of a binary operator, as shown in the following statement:

```
int i= 3+4 * 4;        ← Bad style

int i = 3 + 4 * 4;     ← Good style
```

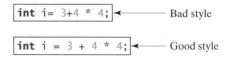

A single space line should be used to separate segments of the code to make the program easier to read.

2.16.4 Block Styles

A block is a group of statements surrounded by braces. There are two popular styles, *next-line* style and *end-of-line* style, as shown below.

```
public class Test
{
  public static void main(String[] args)
  {
    System.out.println("Block Styles");
  }
}
```

Next-line style

```
public class Test {
  public static void main(String[] args) {
    System.out.println("Block Styles");
  }
}
```

End-of-line style

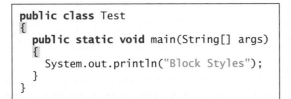

The next-line style aligns braces vertically and makes programs easy to read, whereas the end-of-line style saves space and may help avoid some subtle programming errors. Both are acceptable block styles. The choice depends on personal or organizational preference. You should use a block style consistently. Mixing styles is not recommended. This book uses the *end-of-line* style to be consistent with the Java API source code.

2.17 Programming Errors

Programming errors are unavoidable, even for experienced programmers. Errors can be categorized into three types: syntax errors, runtime errors, and logic errors.

2.17.1 Syntax Errors

syntax errors

Errors that occur during compilation are called *syntax errors* or *compile errors*. Syntax errors result from errors in code construction, such as mistyping a keyword, omitting some necessary punctuation, or using an opening brace without a corresponding closing brace. These errors are usually easy to detect, because the compiler tells you where they are and what caused them. For example, the following program has a syntax error, as shown in Figure 2.3.

Compile

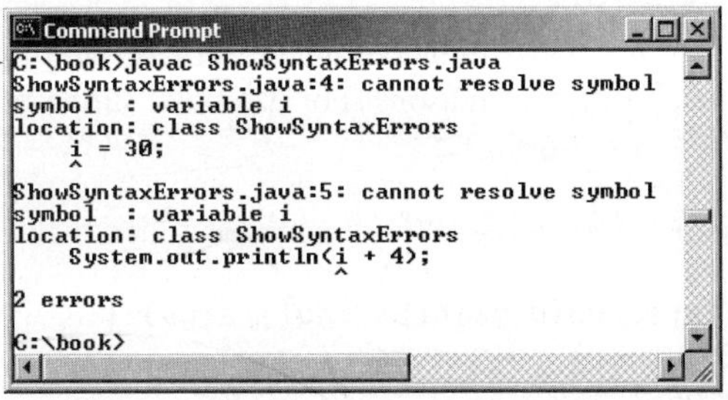
Command Prompt
C:\book>javac ShowSyntaxErrors.java
ShowSyntaxErrors.java:4: cannot resolve symbol
symbol : variable i
location: class ShowSyntaxErrors
    i = 30;
    ^
ShowSyntaxErrors.java:5: cannot resolve symbol
symbol : variable i
location: class ShowSyntaxErrors
    System.out.println(i + 4);
                       ^
2 errors
C:\book>

FIGURE 2.3 The compiler reports syntax errors.

```
// ShowSyntaxErrors.java: The program contains syntax errors
public class ShowSyntaxErrors {
  public static void main(String[] args) {
    i = 30;
    System.out.println(i + 4);
  }
}
```

syntax error

Two errors are detected. Both are the result of not declaring variable `i`. Since a single error will often display many lines of compile errors, it is a good practice to start debugging from the top line and work downward. Fixing errors that occur earlier in the program may also fix additional errors that occur later.

2.17.2 Runtime Errors

runtime errors

Runtime errors are errors that cause a program to terminate abnormally. They occur while a program is running if the environment detects an operation that is impossible to carry out. Input errors typically cause runtime errors.

An *input error* occurs when the user enters an unexpected input value that the program cannot handle. For instance, if the program expects to read in a number, but instead the user enters a string, this causes data-type errors to occur in the program. To prevent input errors, the program should prompt the user to enter values of the correct type. It may display a message such as "Please enter an integer" before reading an integer from the keyboard.

Another common source of runtime errors is division by zero. This happens when the divisor is zero for integer divisions. For instance, the following program would cause a runtime error, as shown in Figure 2.4.

Run

Command Prompt
C:\book>java ShowRuntimeErrors
Exception in thread "main" java.lang.ArithmeticException: / by zero
at ShowRuntimeErrors.main(ShowRuntimeErrors.java:4)
C:\book>

FIGURE 2.4 The runtime error causes the program to terminate abnormally.

runtime error

```
// ShowRuntimeErrors.java: Program contains runtime errors
public class ShowRuntimeErrors {
  public static void main(String[] args) {
    int i = 1 / 0 ;
  }
}
```

2.17.3 Logic Errors

Logic errors occur when a program does not perform the way it was intended to. Errors of this kind occur for many different reasons. For example, suppose you wrote the following program to add `number1` to `number2`.

```
// ShowLogicErrors.java: The program contains a logic error
public class ShowLogicErrors {
  public static void main(String[] args) {
    // Add number1 to number2
    int number1 = 3;
    int number2 = 3;
    number2 += number1 + number2;
    System.out.println("number2 is " + number2);
  }
}
```

The program does not have syntax errors or runtime errors, but it does not print the correct result for `number2`. See if you can find the error.

2.17.4 Debugging

In general, syntax errors are easy to find and easy to correct, because the compiler gives indications as to where the errors came from and why they are wrong. Runtime errors are not difficult to find, either, since the reasons and locations of the errors are displayed on the console when the program aborts. Finding logic errors, on the other hand, can be very challenging.

Logic errors are called *bugs*. The process of finding and correcting errors is called *debugging*. A common approach is to use a combination of methods to narrow down to the part of the program where the bug is located. You can *hand-trace* the program (i.e., catch errors by reading the program), or you can insert print statements in order to show the values of the variables or the execution flow of the program. This approach might work for a short, simple program. But for a large, complex program, the most effective approach is to use a debugger utility.

bugs
debugging
hand traces

Pedagogical NOTE

An IDE not only helps debug errors but also is an effective pedagogical tool. Supplement II shows you how to use a debugger to trace programs and how debugging can help you to learn Java effectively.

learning tool

2.18 (GUI) Getting Input from Input Dialogs

You can obtain input from the console. Alternatively, you may obtain input from an input dialog box by invoking the `JOptionPane.showInputDialog` method, as shown in Figure 2.5.

`JOptionPane` class

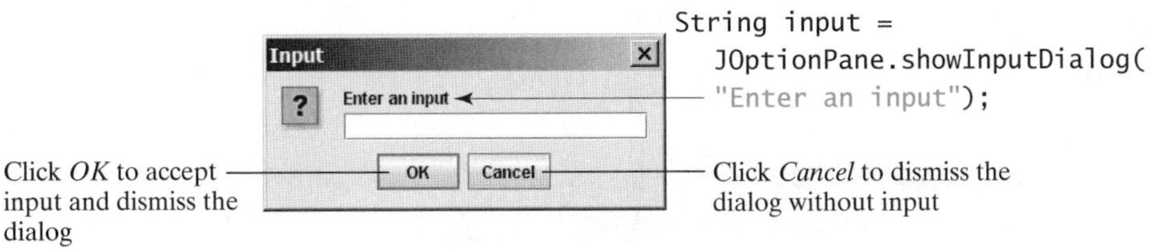
Input
Enter an input
OK
Cancel
String input =
JOptionPane.showInputDialog(
"Enter an input");
Click *OK* to accept input and dismiss the dialog
Click *Cancel* to dismiss the dialog without input

FIGURE 2.5 The input dialog box enables the user to enter a string.

When this method is executed, a dialog is displayed to enable you to enter an input value. After entering a string, click *OK* to accept the input and dismiss the dialog box. The input is returned from the method as a string.

There are several ways to use the `showInputDialog` method. For the time being, you need to know only two ways to invoke it.

`showInputDialog` method

One is to use a statement like this one:

```
JOptionPane.showInputDialog(x);
```

where `x` is a string for the prompting message.

The other is to use a statement such as the following:

```
String string = JOptionPane.showInputDialog(null, x,
  y, JOptionPane.QUESTION_MESSAGE);
```

where `x` is a string for the prompting message and `y` is a string for the title of the input dialog box, as shown in the example below.

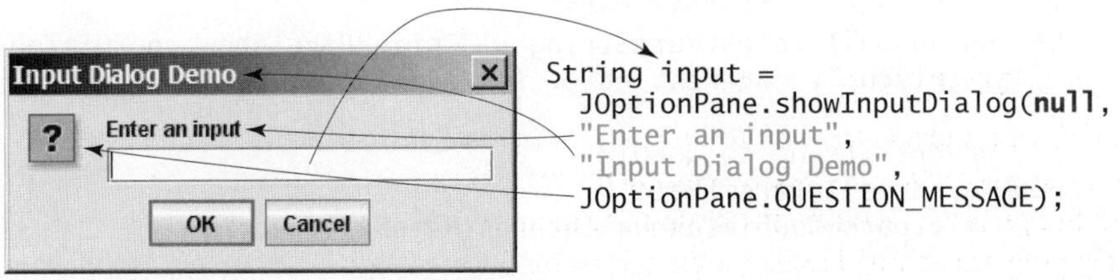
Input Dialog Demo
Enter an input
OK
Cancel
String input =
JOptionPane.showInputDialog(null,
"Enter an input",
"Input Dialog Demo",
JOptionPane.QUESTION_MESSAGE);

2.18.1 Converting Strings to Numbers

The input returned from the input dialog box is a string. If you enter a numeric value such as `123`, it returns `"123"`. You have to convert a string into a number to obtain the input as a number.

`Integer.parseInt` method

To convert a string into an `int` value, use the `parseInt` method in the `Integer` class, as follows:

```
int intValue = Integer.parseInt(intString);
```

where `intString` is a numeric string such as `"123"`.

`Double.parseDouble` method

To convert a string into a `double` value, use the `parseDouble` method in the `Double` class, as follows:

```
double doubleValue = Double.parseDouble(doubleString);
```

where `doubleString` is a numeric string such as `"123.45"`.

The `Integer` and `Double` classes are both included in the `java.lang` package, and thus they are automatically imported.

2.18.2 Using Input Dialog Boxes

Listing 2.8, ComputeLoan.java, reads input from the console. Alternatively, you can use input dialog boxes.

Listing 2.11 gives the complete program. Figure 2.6 shows a sample run of the program.

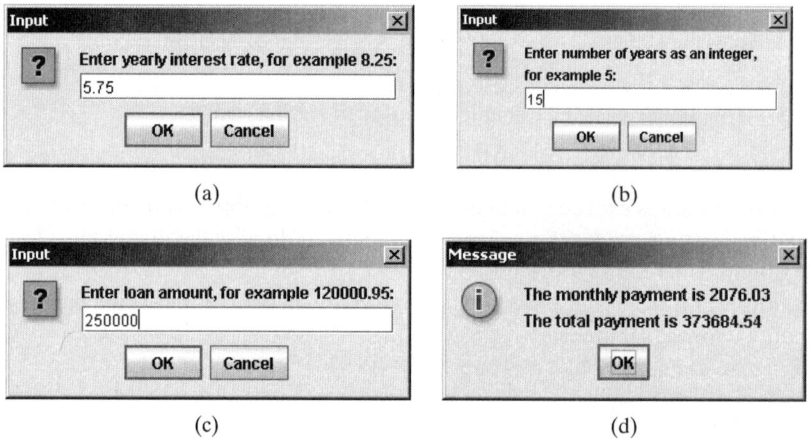
Input
Enter yearly interest rate, for example 8.25:
5.75
OK
Cancel
(a)
Input
Enter number of years as an integer,
for example 5:
15
OK
Cancel
(b)
Input
Enter loan amount, for example 120000.95:
250000
OK
Cancel
(c)
Message
The monthly payment is 2076.03
The total payment is 373684.54
OK
(d)

FIGURE 2.6 The program accepts the annual interest rate (a), number of years (b), and loan amount (c), then displays the monthly payment and total payment (d).

LISTING 2.11 `ComputeLoanUsingInputDialog.java`

enter interest rate

convert string to double

```
import javax.swing.JOptionPane;

public class ComputeLoanUsingInputDialog {
  public static void main(String[] args) {
    // Enter yearly interest rate
    String annualInterestRateString = JOptionPane.showInputDialog(
      "Enter yearly interest rate, for example 8.25:");

    // Convert string to double
    double annualInterestRate =
      Double.parseDouble(annualInterestRateString);

```

```
13      // Obtain monthly interest rate
14      double monthlyInterestRate = annualInterestRate / 1200;
15
16      // Enter number of years
17      String numberOfYearsString = JOptionPane.showInputDialog(
18        "Enter number of years as an integer, \nfor example 5:");
19
20      // Convert string to int
21      int numberOfYears = Integer.parseInt(numberOfYearsString);
22
23      // Enter loan amount
24      String loanString = JOptionPane.showInputDialog(
25        "Enter loan amount, for example 120000.95:");
26
27      // Convert string to double
28      double loanAmount = Double.parseDouble(loanString);
29
30      // Calculate payment
31      double monthlyPayment = loanAmount * monthlyInterestRate / (1
32        - 1 / Math.pow(1 + monthlyInterestRate, numberOfYears * 12));
33      double totalPayment = monthlyPayment * numberOfYears * 12;
34
35      // Format to keep two digits after the decimal point
36      monthlyPayment = (int)(monthlyPayment * 100) / 100.0;
37      totalPayment = (int)(totalPayment * 100) / 100.0;
38
39      // Display results
40      String output = "The monthly payment is " + monthlyPayment +
41        "\nThe total payment is " + totalPayment;
42      JOptionPane.showMessageDialog(null, output);
43    }
44  }
```

monthlyPayment

totalPayment

preparing output

The showInputDialog method in lines 6–7 displays an input dialog. Enter the interest rate as a double value and click *OK* to accept the input. The value is returned as a string that is assigned to the String variable annualInterestRateString. The Double.parseDouble(annualInterestRateString) (line 11) is used to convert the string into a double value. If you entered an input other than a numeric value or clicked *Cancel* in the input dialog box, a runtime error would occur. In Chapter 13, "Exception Handling," you will learn how to handle the exception so that the program can continue to run.

Pedagogical Note

For obtaining input you can use JOptionPane or Scanner, whichever is convenient. For consistency most examples in this book use Scanner for getting input. You can easily revise the examples using JOptionPane for getting input.

JOptionPane or Scanner?

Key Terms

algorithm 24
assignment operator (=) 30
assignment statement 30
backslash (\) 46
byte type 27
casting 41
char type 44
constant 31
data type 25
debugger 55
debugging 55
declaration 30
decrement operator (--) 41
double type 33
encoding 45
final 31

Chapter Summary

1. Identifiers are names for things in a program.
2. An identifier is a sequence of characters that consists of letters, digits, underscores (_), and dollar signs ($).
3. An identifier must start with a letter or an underscore. It cannot start with a digit.
4. An identifier cannot be a reserved word.
5. An identifier can be of any length.
6. Choosing descriptive identifiers can make programs easy to read.
7. Variables are used to store data in a program
8. To declare a variable is to tell the compiler what type of data a variable can hold.
9. By convention, variable names are in lowercase.
10. In Java, the equal sign (=) is used as the *assignment operator*.
11. A variable declared in a method must be assigned a value before it can be used.
12. A *named constant* (or simply a *constant*) represents permanent data that never changes.
13. A named constant is declared by using the keyword `final`.
14. By convention, constants are named in uppercase.
15. Java provides four integer types (`byte`, `short`, `int`, `long`) that represent integers of four different sizes.

16. Java provides two floating-point types (`float`, `double`) that represent floating-point numbers of two different precisions.

17. Java provides operators that perform numeric operations: + (addition), – (subtraction), * (multiplication), / (division), and % (remainder).

18. Integer arithmetic (/) yields an integer result.

19. The numeric operators in a Java expression are applied the same way as in an arithmetic expression.

20. Java provides shorthand operators += (addition assignment), –= (subtraction assignment), *= (multiplication assignment), /= (division assignment), and %= (remainder assignment).

21. The increment operator (++) and the decrement operator (––) increment or decrement a variable by `1`.

22. When evaluating an expression with values of mixed types, Java automatically converts the operands to appropriate types.

23. You can explicitly convert a value from one type to another using the `(type)exp` notation.

24. Casting a variable of a type with a small range to a variable of a type with a larger range is known as *widening a type*.

25. Casting a variable of a type with a large range to a variable of a type with a smaller range is known as *narrowing a type*.

26. Widening a type can be performed automatically without explicit casting. Narrowing a type must be performed explicitly.

27. Character type (`char`) represents a single character.

28. The character \ is called the escape character.

29. Java allows you to use escape sequences to represent special characters such as `'\t'` and `'\n'`.

30. The characters `' '`, `'\t'`, `'\f'`, `'\r'`, and `'\n'` are known as the whitespace characters.

31. In computer science, midnight of January 1, 1970, is known as the *Unix epoch*.

32. Programming errors can be categorized into three types: syntax errors, runtime errors, and logic errors.

33. Errors that occur during compilation are called *syntax errors* or *compile errors*.

34. *Runtime errors* are errors that cause a program to terminate abnormally.

35. *Logic errors* occur when a program does not perform the way it was intended to.

Review Questions

Sections 2.2–2.7

2.1 Which of the following identifiers are valid? Which are Java keywords?

```
applet, Applet, a++, --a, 4#R, $4, #44, apps
class, public, int, x, y, radius
```

2.2 Translate the following algorithm into Java code:

- Step 1: Declare a `double` variable named `miles` with initial value `100`;
- Step 2: Declare a `double` constant named `MILES_PER_KILOMETER` with value `1.609`;
- Step 3: Declare a `double` variable named `kilometers`, multiply miles and `MILES_PER_KILOMETER`, and assign the result to `kilometers`.
- Step 4: Display `kilometers` to the console.

What is `kilometers` after Step 4?

2.3 What are the benefits of using constants? Declare an `int` constant `SIZE` with value `20`.

Sections 2.8–2.10

2.4 Assume that `int a = 1` and `double d = 1.0`, and that each expression is independent. What are the results of the following expressions?

```
a = 46 / 9;
a = 46 % 9 + 4 * 4 - 2;
a = 45 + 43 % 5 * (23 * 3 % 2);
a %= 3 / a + 3;
d = 4 + d * d + 4;
d += 1.5 * 3 + (++a);
d -= 1.5 * 3 + a++;
```

2.5 Show the result of the following remainders.

```
56 % 6
78 % -4
-34 % 5
-34 % -5
5 % 1
1 % 5
```

2.6 If today is Tuesday, what will be the day in 100 days?

2.7 Find the largest and smallest `byte`, `short`, `int`, `long`, `float`, and `double`. Which of these data types requires the least amount of memory?

2.8 What is the result of `25 / 4`? How would you rewrite the expression if you wished the result to be a floating-point number?

2.9 Are the following statements correct? If so, show the output.

```
System.out.println("25 / 4 is " + 25 / 4);
System.out.println("25 / 4.0 is " + 25 / 4.0);
System.out.println("3 * 2 / 4 is " + 3 * 2 / 4);
System.out.println("3.0 * 2 / 4 is " + 3.0 * 2 / 4);
```

2.10 How would you write the following arithmetic expression in Java?

$$\frac{4}{3(r + 34)} - 9(a + bc) + \frac{3 + d(2 + a)}{a + bd}$$

2.11 Suppose m and r are integers. Write a Java expression for mr^2 to obtain a floating-point result.

2.12 Which of these statements are true?

(a) Any expression can be used as a statement.
(b) The expression x++ can be used as a statement.
(c) The statement x = x + 5 is also an expression.
(d) The statement x = y = x = 0 is illegal.

2.13 Which of the following are correct literals for floating-point numbers?

```
12.3, 12.3e+2, 23.4e-2, -334.4, 20, 39F, 40D
```

2.14 Identify and fix the errors in the following code:

```
public class Test {
  public void main(string[] args) {
    int i;
    int k = 100.0;
    int j = i + 1;

    System.out.println("j is " + j + " and
      k is " + k);
  }
}
```

2.15 How do you obtain the current minute using the `System.currentTimeMillis()` method?

Section 2.11

2.16 Can different types of numeric values be used together in a computation?

2.17 What does an explicit conversion from a `double` to an `int` do with the fractional part of the *double* value? Does casting change the variable being cast?

2.18 Show the following output.

```
float f = 12.5F;
int i = (int)f;
System.out.println("f is " + f);
System.out.println("i is " + i);
```

Section 2.13

2.19 Use print statements to find out the ASCII code for '1', 'A', 'B', 'a', 'b'. Use print statements to find out the character for the decimal code 40, 59, 79, 85, 90. Use print statements to find out the character for the hexadecimal code 40, 5A, 71, 72, 7A.

2.20 Which of the following are correct literals for characters?

```
'1', '\u345dE', '\u3fFa', '\b', \t
```

2.21 How do you display characters \ and "?

2.22 Evaluate the following:

```
int i = '1';
int j = '1' + '2';
int k = 'a';
char c = 90;
```

2.23 Can the following conversions involving casting be allowed? If so, find the converted result.

```
char c = 'A';
i = (int)c;
float f = 1000.34f;
int i = (int)f;

double d = 1000.34;
int i = (int)d;

int i = 97;
char c = (char)i;
```

2.24 Show the output of the following program:

```
public class Test {
  public static void main(String[] args) {
    char x = 'a';
    char y = 'c';

    System.out.println(++x);
    System.out.println(y++);
    System.out.println(x - y);
  }
}
```

Section 2.15

2.25 Show the output of the following statements (write a program to verify your result):

```
System.out.println("1" + 1);
System.out.println('1' + 1);
System.out.println("1" + 1 + 1);
System.out.println("1" + (1 + 1));
System.out.println('1' + 1 + 1);
```

2.26 Evaluate the following expressions (write a program to verify your result):

```
1 + "Welcome " + 1 + 1
1 + "Welcome " + (1 + 1)
1 + "Welcome " + ('\u0001' + 1)
1 + "Welcome " + 'a' + 1
```

Sections 2.16–2.17

2.27 What are the naming conventions for class names, method names, constants, and variables? Which of the following items can be a constant, a method, a variable, or a class according to the Java naming conventions?

```
MAX_VALUE, Test, read, readInt
```

2.28 Reformat the following program according to the programming style and documentation guidelines. Use the next-line brace style.

```
public class Test
{
  // Main method
  public static void main(String[] args) {
```

```
    /** Print a line */
    System.out.println("2 % 3 = "+2%3);
    }
  }
```

2.29 Describe syntax errors, runtime errors, and logic errors.

Section 2.18

2.30 Why do you have to import `JOptionPane` but not the `Math` class?

2.31 How do you prompt the user to enter an input using a dialog box?

2.32 How do you convert a string to an integer? How do you convert a string to a double?

PROGRAMMING EXERCISES

Note

sample runs

Students can run all exercises by downloading **`exercise8e.zip`** from **`www.cs.armstrong.edu/liang/intro8e/exercise8e.zip`** and use the command **`java -cp exercise8e.zip Exercisei_j`** to run Exercise*i_j*. For example, to run Exercise2_1, use

```
java -cp exercise8e.zip Exercise2_1
```

This will give you an idea how the program runs.

Debugging TIP

learn from examples

The compiler usually gives a reason for a syntax error. If you don't know how to correct it, compare your program closely, character by character, with similar examples in the text.

Sections 2.2–2.9

2.1 (*Converting Celsius to Fahrenheit*) Write a program that reads a Celsius degree in double from the console, then converts it to Fahrenheit and displays the result. The formula for the conversion is as follows:

```
fahrenheit = (9 / 5) * celsius + 32
```

Hint: In Java, `9 / 5` is `1`, but `9.0 / 5` is `1.8`.

Here is a sample run:

```
Enter a degree in Celsius: 43 ↵Enter
43 Celsius is 109.4 Fahrenheit
```

2.2 (*Computing the volume of a cylinder*) Write a program that reads in the radius and length of a cylinder and computes volume using the following formulas:

```
area = radius * radius * π
volume = area * length
```

Here is a sample run:

```
Enter the radius and length of a cylinder: 5.5 12 ↵Enter
The area is 95.0331
The volume is 1140.4
```

2.3 (*Converting feet into meters*) Write a program that reads a number in feet, converts it to meters, and displays the result. One foot is 0.305 meter. Here is a sample run:

```
Enter a value for feet: 16 ↵Enter
16 feet is 4.88 meters
```

2.4 (*Converting pounds into kilograms*) Write a program that converts pounds into kilograms. The program prompts the user to enter a number in pounds, converts it to kilograms, and displays the result. One pound is 0.454 kilograms. Here is a sample run:

```
Enter a number in pounds: 55.5 ↵Enter
55.5 pounds is 25.197 kilograms
```

2.5* (*Financial application: calculating tips*) Write a program that reads the subtotal and the gratuity rate, then computes the gratuity and total. For example, if the user enters 10 for subtotal and 15% for gratuity rate, the program displays $1.5 as gratuity and $11.5 as total. Here is a sample run:

```
Enter the subtotal and a gratuity rate: 15.69 15 ↵Enter
The gratuity is 2.35 and total is 18.04
```

2.6** (*Summing the digits in an integer*) Write a program that reads an integer between 0 and 1000 and adds all the digits in the integer. For example, if an integer is 932, the sum of all its digits is 14.

Hint: Use the % operator to extract digits, and use the / operator to remove the extracted digit. For instance, 932 % 10 = 2 and 932 / 10 = 93.

Here is a sample run:

```
Enter a number between 0 and 1000: 999 ↵Enter
The sum of the digits is 27
```

2.7* (*Finding the number of years*) Write a program that prompts the user to enter the minutes (e.g., 1 billion) and displays the number of years and days for the minutes. For simplicity, assume a year has 365 days. Here is a sample run:

```
Enter the number of minutes: 1000000000 ↵Enter
1000000000 minutes is approximately 1902 years and 214 days.
```

Section 2.13

2.8* (*Finding the character of an ASCII code*) Write a program that receives an ASCII code (an integer between `0` and `128`) and displays its character. For example, if the user enters `97`, the program displays character `a`. Here is a sample run:

```
Enter an ASCII code: 69 ↵ Enter
The character for ASCII code 69 is E
```

2.9* (*Financial application: monetary units*) Rewrite Listing 2.10, ComputeChange.java, to fix the possible loss of accuracy when converting a `double` value to an `int` value. Enter the input as an integer whose last two digits represent the cents. For example, the input `1156` represents `11` dollars and `56` cents.

Section 2.18

2.10* (*Using the GUI input*) Rewrite Listing 2.10, ComputeChange.java, using the GUI input and output.

Comprehensive

2.11* (*Financial application: payroll*) Write a program that reads the following information and prints a payroll statement:

Employee's name (e.g., Smith)

Number of hours worked in a week (e.g., 10)

Hourly pay rate (e.g., 6.75)

Federal tax withholding rate (e.g., 20%)

State tax withholding rate (e.g., 9%)

Write this program in two versions: (a) Use dialog boxes to obtain input and display output; (b) Use console input and output. A sample run of the console input and output is shown below:

```
Enter employee's name: Smith ↵ Enter
Enter number of hours worked in a week: 10 ↵ Enter
Enter hourly pay rate: 6.75 ↵ Enter
Enter federal tax withholding rate: 0.20 ↵ Enter
Enter state tax withholding rate: 0.09 ↵ Enter
Employee Name: Smith
Hours Worked:  10.0
Pay Rate:  $6.75
Gross Pay:  $67.5
Deductions:
  Federal Withholding (20.0%):  $13.5
  State Withholding (9.0%):  $6.07
  Total Deduction:  $19.57
Net Pay:  $47.92
```

2.12* (*Financial application: calculating interest*) If you know the balance and the annual percentage interest rate, you can compute the interest on the next monthly payment using the following formula:

$$\text{interest} = \text{balance} \times (\text{annualInterestRate} / 1200)$$

Write a program that reads the balance and the annual percentage interest rate and displays the interest for the next month in two versions: (a) Use dialog boxes to obtain input and display output; (b) Use console input and output. Here is a sample run:

```
Enter balance and interest rate (e.g., 3 for 3%): 1000 3.5 ↵Enter
The interest is 2.91667
```

2.13* (*Financial application: calculating the future investment value*) Write a program that reads in investment amount, annual interest rate, and number of years, and displays the future investment value using the following formula:

```
futureInvestmentValue =
  investmentAmount x (1 + monthlyInterestRate)^(numberOfYears*12)
```

For example, if you enter amount `1000`, annual interest rate `3.25%`, and number of years `1`, the future investment value is `1032.98`.

Hint: Use the `Math.pow(a, b)` method to compute `a` raised to the power of `b`.

Here is a sample run:

```
Enter investment amount: 1000 ↵Enter
Enter monthly interest rate: 4.25 ↵Enter
Enter number of years: 1 ↵Enter
Accumulated value is 1043.34
```

Video Note
Compute BMI

2.14* (*Health application: computing BMI*) Body Mass Index (BMI) is a measure of health on weight. It can be calculated by taking your weight in kilograms and dividing by the square of your height in meters. Write a program that prompts the user to enter a weight in pounds and height in inches and display the BMI. Note that one pound is `0.45359237` kilograms and one inch is `0.0254` meters. Here is a sample run:

```
Enter weight in pounds: 95.5 ↵Enter
Enter height in inches: 50 ↵Enter
BMI is 26.8573
```

2.15** (*Financial application: compound value*) Suppose you save `$100` *each* month into a savings account with the annual interest rate 5%. So, the monthly interest rate is 0.05 / 12 = 0.00417. After the first month, the value in the account becomes

```
100 * (1 + 0.00417) = 100.417
```

After the second month, the value in the account becomes

```
(100 + 100.417) * (1 + 0.00417) = 201.252
```

After the third month, the value in the account becomes

```
(100 + 201.252) * (1 + 0.00417) = 302.507
```

and so on.

Write a program to display the account value after the sixth month. (In Exercise 4.30, you will use a loop to simplify the code and display the account value for any month.)

2.16 (*Science: calculating energy*) Write a program that calculates the energy needed to heat water from an initial temperature to a final temperature. Your program should prompt the user to enter the amount of water in kilograms and the initial and final temperatures of the water. The formula to compute the energy is

```
Q = M * (final temperature – initial temperature) * 4184
```

where `M` is the weight of water in kilograms, temperatures are in degrees Celsius, and energy `Q` is measured in joules. Here is a sample run:

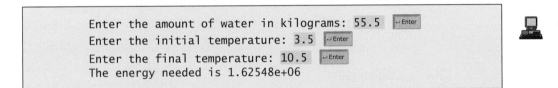

```
Enter the amount of water in kilograms: 55.5 [Enter]
Enter the initial temperature: 3.5 [Enter]
Enter the final temperature: 10.5 [Enter]
The energy needed is 1.62548e+06
```

2.17* (*Science: wind-chill temperature*) How cold is it outside? The temperature alone is not enough to provide the answer. Other factors including wind speed, relative humidity, and sunshine play important roles in determining coldness outside. In 2001, the National Weather Service (NWS) implemented the new wind-chill temperature to measure the coldness using temperature and wind speed. The formula is given as follows:

$$t_{wc} = 35.74 + 0.6215t_a - 35.75v^{0.16} + 0.4275t_a v^{0.16}$$

where t_a is the outside temperature measured in degrees Fahrenheit and v is the speed measured in miles per hour. t_{wc} is the wind-chill temperature. The formula cannot be used for wind speeds below 2 mph or temperatures below −58°F or above 41°F.

Write a program that prompts the user to enter a temperature between −58°F and 41°F and a wind speed greater than or equal to `2` and displays the wind-chill temperature. Use `Math.pow(a, b)` to compute $v^{0.16}$. Here is a sample run:

```
Enter the temperature in Fahrenheit: 5.3 [Enter]
Enter the wind speed miles per hour: 6 [Enter]
The wind chill index is -5.56707
```

2.18 (*Printing a table*) Write a program that displays the following table:

```
a     b     pow(a, b)
1     2     1
2     3     8
3     4     81
4     5     1024
5     6     15625
```

2.19 (*Random character*) Write a program that displays a random uppercase letter using the `System.CurrentTimeMillis()` method.

2.20 (*Geometry: distance of two points)* Write a program that prompts the user to enter two points `(x1, y1)` and `(x2, y2)` and displays their distances. The formula for computing the distance is $\sqrt{(x_2 - x_1)^2 + (y_2 - y_1)^2}$. Note you can use the `Math.pow(a, 0.5)` to compute $\sqrt{a}$. Here is a sample run:

```
Enter x1 and y1: 1.5 -3.4 Enter
Enter x2 and y2: 4 5 Enter
The distance of the two points is 8.764131445842194
```

2.21* (*Geometry: area of a triangle*) Write a program that prompts the user to enter three points `(x1, y1)`, `(x2, y2)`, `(x3, y3)` of a triangle and displays its area. The formula for computing the area of a triangle is

$$s = (side1 + side2 + side3)/2;$$

$$area = \sqrt{s(s - side1)(s - side2)(s - side3)}$$

Here is a sample run.

```
Enter three points for a triangle: 1.5 -3.4 4.6 5 9.5 -3.4 Enter
The area of the triangle is 33.6
```

2.22 (*Geometry: area of a hexagon*) Write a program that prompts the user to enter the side of a hexagon and displays its area. The formula for computing the area of a hexagon is

$$Area = \frac{3\sqrt{3}}{2}s^2,$$

where s is the length of a side. Here is a sample run:

```
Enter the side: 5.5 Enter
The area of the hexagon is 78.5895
```

2.23 (*Physics: acceleration*) Average acceleration is defined as the change of velocity divided by the time taken to make the change, as shown in the following formula:

$$a = \frac{v_1 - v_0}{t}$$

Write a program that prompts the user to enter the starting velocity v_0 in meters/second, the ending velocity v_1 in meters/second, and the time span t in seconds, and displays the average acceleration. Here is a sample run:

```
Enter v0, v1, and t: 5.5 50.9 4.5 ↵Enter
The average acceleration is 10.0889
```

2.24 (*Physics: finding runway length*) Given an airplane's acceleration a and take-off speed v, you can compute the minimum runway length needed for an airplane to take off using the following formula:

$$length = \frac{v^2}{2a}$$

Write a program that prompts the user to enter v in meters/second (m/s) and the acceleration a in meters/second squared (m/s^2), and displays the minimum runway length. Here is a sample run:

```
Enter v and a: 60 3.5 ↵Enter
The minimum runway length for this airplane is 514.286
```

2.25* (*Current time*) Listing 2.6, ShowCurrentTime.java, gives a program that displays the current time in GMT. Revise the program so that it prompts the user to enter the time zone offset to GMT and displays the time in the specified time zone. Here is a sample run:

```
Enter the time zone offset to GMT: -5 ↵Enter
The current time is 4:50:34
```

CHAPTER 3

SELECTIONS

Objectives

- To declare `boolean` type and write Boolean expressions using comparison operators (§3.2).
- To program `AdditionQuiz` using Boolean expressions (§3.3).
- To implement selection control using one-way `if` statements (§3.4)
- To program the `GuessBirthday` game using one-way `if` statements (§3.5).
- To implement selection control using two-way `if` statements (§3.6).
- To implement selection control using nested `if` statements (§3.7).
- To avoid common errors in `if` statements (§3.8).
- To program using selection statements for a variety of examples(`SubtractionQuiz`, `BMI`, `ComputeTax`) (§3.9–3.11).
- To generate random numbers using the `Math.random()` method (§3.9).
- To combine conditions using logical operators (`&&`, `||`, and `!`) (§3.12).
- To program using selection statements with combined conditions (`LeapYear`, `Lottery`) (§§3.13–3.14).
- To implement selection control using `switch` statements (§3.15).
- To write expressions using the conditional operator (§3.16).
- To format output using the `System.out.printf` method and to format strings using the `String.format` method (§3.17).
- To examine the rules governing operator precedence and associativity (§3.18).
- (GUI) To get user confirmation using confirmation dialogs (§3.19).

3.1 Introduction

problem

If you enter a negative value for **radius** in Listing 2.2, ComputeAreaWithConsoleInput.java, the program prints an invalid result. If the radius is negative, you don't want the program to compute the area. How can you deal with this situation?

Like all high-level programming languages, Java provides selection statements that let you choose actions with two or more alternative courses. You can use the following selection statement to replace lines 12–17 in Listing 2.2:

```
if (radius < 0)
  System.out.println("Incorrect input");
else {
  area = radius * radius * 3.14159;
  System.out.println("Area is " + area);
}
```

Selection statements use conditions. Conditions are Boolean expressions. This chapter first introduces Boolean types, values, comparison operators, and expressions.

3.2 boolean Data Type

comparison operators

How do you compare two values, such as whether a radius is greater than **0**, equal to **0**, or less than **0**? Java provides six *comparison operators* (also known as *relational operators*), shown in Table 3.1, which can be used to compare two values (assume radius is **5** in the table).

TABLE 3.1 Comparison Operators

Operator	*Name*	*Example*	*Result*
<	less than	radius < 0	false
<=	less than or equal to	radius <= 0	false
>	greater than	radius > 0	true
>=	greater than or equal to	radius >= 0	true
==	equal to	radius == 0	false
!=	not equal to	radius != 0	true

compare characters

Note

You can also compare characters. Comparing characters is the same as comparing their Unicodes. For example, **'a'** is larger than **'A'** because the Unicode of **'a'** is larger than the Unicode of **'A'**. See Appendix B, "The ASCII Character Sets," to find the order of characters.

== vs. =

Caution

The equality comparison operator is two equal signs (==), not a single equal sign (=). The latter symbol is for assignment.

The result of the comparison is a Boolean value: **true** or **false**. For example, the following statement displays **true**:

```
double radius = 1;
System.out.println(radius > 0);
```

Boolean variable

A variable that holds a Boolean value is known as a *Boolean variable*. The **boolean** data type is used to declare Boolean variables. A **boolean** variable can hold one of the two values:

`true` and `false`. For example, the following statement assigns `true` to the variable `lightsOn`:

```
boolean lightsOn = true;
```

`true` and `false` are literals, just like a number such as `10`. They are reserved words and cannot be used as identifiers in your program.

Boolean literals

3.3 Problem: A Simple Math Learning Tool

Video Note
Program addition quiz

Suppose you want to develop a program to let a first-grader practice addition. The program randomly generates two single-digit integers, `number1` and `number2`, and displays to the student a question such as "What is 7 + 9?", as shown in the sample run. After the student types the answer, the program displays a message to indicate whether it is true or false.

There are several ways to generate random numbers. For now, generate the first integer using `System.currentTimeMillis() % 10` and the second using `System.currentTimeMillis() * 7 % 10`. Listing 3.1 gives the program. Lines 5–6 generate two numbers, `number1` and `number2`. Line 14 obtains an answer from the user. The answer is graded in line 18 using a Boolean expression `number1 + number2 == answer`.

LISTING 3.1 AdditionQuiz.java

```
 1 import java.util.Scanner;
 2
 3 public class AdditionQuiz {
 4   public static void main(String[] args) {
 5     int number1 = (int)(System.currentTimeMillis() % 10);
 6     int number2 = (int)(System.currentTimeMillis() * 7 % 10);
 7
 8     // Create a Scanner
 9     Scanner input = new Scanner(System.in);
10
11     System.out.print(
12       "What is " + number1 + " + " + number2 + "? ");
13
14     int answer = input.nextInt();
15
16     System.out.println(
17       number1 + " + " + number2 + " = " + answer + " is " +
18       (number1 + number2 == answer));
19   }
20 }
```

generate number1
generate number2
show question
display result

```
What is 1 + 7? 8 ↵Enter
1 + 7 = 8 is true
```

```
What is 4 + 8? 9 ↵Enter
4 + 8 = 9 is false
```

line#	number1	number2	answer	output
5	4			
6		8		
14			9	
16				4 + 8 = 9 is false

3.4 if Statements

why **if** statement?

The preceding program displays a message such as "6 + 2 = 7 is false." If you wish the message to be "6 + 2 = 7 is incorrect," you have to use a selection statement to carry out this minor change.

This section introduces selection statements. Java has several types of selection statements: one-way if statements, two-way if statements, nested if statements, switch statements, and conditional expressions.

3.4.1 One-Way if Statements

A one-way if statement executes an action if and only if the condition is true. The syntax for a one-way if statement is shown below:

if statement

```
if (boolean-expression) {
  statement(s);
}
```

The execution flow chart is shown in Figure 3.1(a).

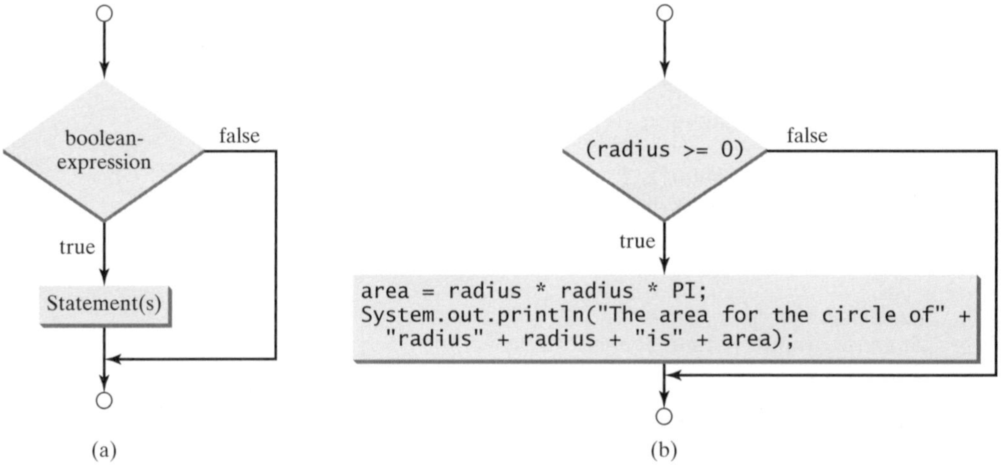
boolean-
expression
false
true
Statement(s)
(a)
(radius >= 0)
false
true
area = radius * radius * PI;
System.out.println("The area for the circle of" +
  "radius" + radius + "is" + area);
(b)

FIGURE 3.1 An if statement executes statements if the boolean-expression evaluates to true.

If the boolean-expression evaluates to true, the statements in the block are executed. As an example, see the following code:

```
if (radius >= 0) {
  area = radius * radius * PI;
  System.out.println("The area for the circle of radius " +
    radius + " is " + area);
}
```

The flow chart of the preceding statement is shown in Figure 3.1(b). If the value of radius is greater than or equal to 0, then the area is computed and the result is displayed; otherwise, the two statements in the block will not be executed.

The boolean-expression is enclosed in parentheses. For example, the code in (a) below is wrong. It should be corrected, as shown in (b).

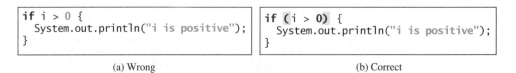

```
if i > 0 {
  System.out.println("i is positive");
}
```

(a) Wrong

```
if (i > 0) {
  System.out.println("i is positive");
}
```

(b) Correct

The block braces can be omitted if they enclose a single statement. For example, the following statements are equivalent.

```
if (i > 0) {
  System.out.println("i is positive");
}
```

(a)

Equivalent

```
if (i > 0)
  System.out.println("i is positive");
```

(b)

Listing 3.2 gives a program that prompts the user to enter an integer. If the number is a multiple of 5, print HiFive. If the number is divisible by 2, print HiEven.

LISTING 3.2 SimpleIfDemo.java

```
1 import java.util.Scanner;
2
3 public class SimpleIfDemo {
4   public static void main(String[] args) {
5     Scanner input = new Scanner(System.in);
6     System.out.println("Enter an integer: ");
7     int number = input.nextInt();
8
9     if (number % 5 == 0)
10      System.out.println("HiFive");
11
12    if (number % 2 == 0)
13      System.out.println("HiEven");
14  }
15 }
```

enter input

check 5

check even

```
Enter an integer: 4 ↵Enter
HiEven
```

```
Enter an integer: 30 ↵Enter
HiFive
HiEven
```

The program prompts the user to enter an integer (line 7) and displays HiFive if it is divisible by 5 (lines 9–10) and HiEven if it is divisible by 2 (lines 12–13).

3.5 Problem: Guessing Birthdays

You can find out the date of the month when your friend was born by asking five questions. Each question asks whether the day is in one of the five sets of numbers.

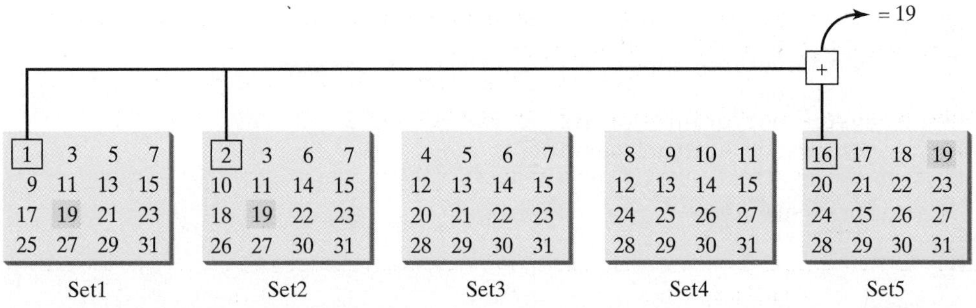
= 19
+
1 3 5 7
9 11 13 15
17 19 21 23
25 27 29 31
2 3 6 7
10 11 14 15
18 19 22 23
26 27 30 31
4 5 6 7
12 13 14 15
20 21 22 23
28 29 30 31
8 9 10 11
12 13 14 15
24 25 26 27
28 29 30 31
16 17 18 19
20 21 22 23
24 25 26 27
28 29 30 31
Set1
Set2
Set3
Set4
Set5

The birthday is the sum of the first numbers in the sets where the day appears. For example, if the birthday is **19**, it appears in Set1, Set2, and Set5. The first numbers in these three sets are **1**, **2**, and **16**. Their sum is **19**.

Listing 3.3 gives a program that prompts the user to answer whether the day is in Set1 (lines 41–47), in Set2 (lines 50–56), in Set3 (lines 59–65), in Set4 (lines 68–74), and in Set5 (lines 77–83). If the number is in the set, the program adds the first number in the set to **day** (lines 47, 56, 65, 74, 83).

LISTING 3.3 GuessBirthday.java

```
1 import java.util.Scanner;
2
3 public class GuessBirthday {
4   public static void main(String[] args) {
5     String set1 =
6       " 1  3  5  7\n" +
7       " 9 11 13 15\n" +
8       "17 19 21 23\n" +
9       "25 27 29 31";
10
11    String set2 =
12      " 2  3  6  7\n" +
13      "10 11 14 15\n" +
14      "18 19 22 23\n" +
15      "26 27 30 31";
16
17    String set3 =
18      " 4  5  6  7\n" +
19      "12 13 14 15\n" +
20      "20 21 22 23\n" +
21      "28 29 30 31";
22
23    String set4 =
24      " 8  9 10 11\n" +
25      "12 13 14 15\n" +
26      "24 25 26 27\n" +
27      "28 29 30 31";
28
29    String set5 =
30      "16 17 18 19\n" +
31      "20 21 22 23\n" +
32      "24 25 26 27\n" +
33      "28 29 30 31";
34
```

day to be determined

```
35    int day = 0;
36
37    // Create a Scanner
38    Scanner input = new Scanner(System.in);
39
40    // Prompt the user to answer questions
41    System.out.print("Is your birthday in Set1?\n");
42    System.out.print(set1);
43    System.out.print("\nEnter 0 for No and 1 for Yes: ");
44    int answer = input.nextInt();
45
```

in Set1?

```
46    if (answer == 1)
47      day += 1;
48
```

```
    // Prompt the user to answer questions
    System.out.print("\nIs your birthday in Set2?\n" );
    System.out.print(set2);
    System.out.print("\nEnter 0 for No and 1 for Yes: ");
    answer = input.nextInt();

    if (answer == 1)
      day += 2;

    // Prompt the user to answer questions
    System.out.print("Is your birthday in Set3?\n");
    System.out.print(set3);
    System.out.print("\nEnter 0 for No and 1 for Yes: ");
    answer = input.nextInt();

    if (answer == 1)
      day += 4;

    // Prompt the user to answer questions
    System.out.print("\nIs your birthday in Set4?\n");
    System.out.print(set4);
    System.out.print("\nEnter 0 for No and 1 for Yes: ");
    answer = input.nextInt();

    if (answer == 1)
      day += 8;

    // Prompt the user to answer questions
    System.out.print("\nIs your birthday in Set5?\n");
    System.out.print(set5);
    System.out.print("\nEnter 0 for No and 1 for Yes: ");
    answer = input.nextInt();

    if (answer == 1)
      day += 16;

    System.out.println("\nYour birthday is " + day + "!");
  }
}
```

in Set2?

in Set3?

in Set4?

in Set5?

```
Is your birthday in Set1?
 1  3  5  7
 9 11 13 15
17 19 21 23
25 27 29 31
Enter 0 for No and 1 for Yes: 1 ↵Enter
Is your birthday in Set2?
 2  3  6  7
10 11 14 15
18 19 22 23
26 27 30 31
Enter 0 for No and 1 for Yes: 1 ↵Enter
Is your birthday in Set3?
 4  5  6  7
12 13 14 15
20 21 22 23
28 29 30 31
Enter 0 for No and 1 for Yes: 0 ↵Enter
```

```
Is your birthday in Set4?
 8  9 10 11
12 13 14 15
24 25 26 27
28 29 30 31
Enter 0 for No and 1 for Yes: 0 ↵Enter

Is your birthday in Set5?
16 17 18 19
20 21 22 23
24 25 26 27
28 29 30 31
Enter 0 for No and 1 for Yes: 1 ↵Enter
Your birthday is 19
```

line#	day	answer	output
35	0		
44		1	
47	1		
53		1	
56	3		
62		0	
71		0	
80		1	
83	19		
			Your birthday is 19

mathematics behind the game

The game is easy to program. You may wonder how the game was created. The mathematics behind the game is actually quite simple. The numbers are not grouped together by accident. The way they are placed in the five sets is deliberate. The starting numbers in the five sets are **1**, **2**, **4**, **8**, and **16**, which correspond to **1**, **10**, **100**, **1000**, and **10000** in binary. A binary number for decimal integers between **1** and **31** has at most five digits, as shown in Figure 3.2(a). Let it be $b_5b_4b_3b_2b_1$. So, $b_5b_4b_3b_2b_1 = b_5\,0000 + b_4\,000 + b_3\,00 + b_2\,0 + b_1$, as shown in Figure 3.2(b). If a day's binary number has a digit **1** in b_k, the number should appear in Set*k*. For example, number **19** is binary **10011**, so it appears in Set1, Set2, and Set5. It is binary **1 + 10 + 10000 = 10011** or decimal **1 + 2 + 16 = 19**. Number **31** is binary **11111**, so it appears in Set1, Set2, Set3, Set4, and Set5. It is binary **1 + 10 + 100 + 1000 + 10000 = 11111** or decimal **1 + 2 + 4 + 8 + 16 = 31**.

Decimal	Binary
1	00001
2	00010
3	00011
...	
19	10011
...	
31	11111

(a)

```
  b5 0 0 0 0                      10000
     b4 0 0 0                      1000
        b3 0 0         10000        100
           b2 0           10         10
+             b1     +     1     +    1
  ----------------   --------    -------
  b5 b4 b3 b2 b1       10011      11111
                          19         31
```

(b)

FIGURE 3.2 (a) A number between **1** and **31** can be represented using a 5-digit binary number. (b) A 5-digit binary number can be obtained by adding binary numbers **1**, **10**, **100**, **1000**, or **10000**.

3.6 Two-Way if Statements

A one-way `if` statement takes an action if the specified condition is `true`. If the condition is `false`, nothing is done. But what if you want to take alternative actions when the condition is `false`? You can use a two-way `if` statement. The actions that a two-way `if` statement specifies differ based on whether the condition is `true` or `false`.

Here is the syntax for a two-way `if` statement:

```
if (boolean-expression) {
  statement(s)-for-the-true-case;
}
else {
  statement(s)-for-the-false-case;
}
```

The flow chart of the statement is shown in Figure 3.3.

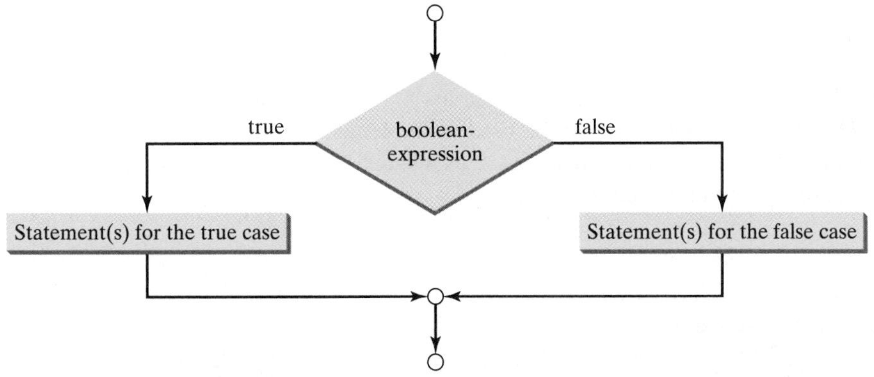
true
boolean-
expression
false
Statement(s) for the true case
Statement(s) for the false case

FIGURE 3.3 An `if ... else` statement executes statements for the true case if the `boolean-expression` evaluates to `true`; otherwise, statements for the false case are executed.

If the `boolean-expression` evaluates to `true`, the statement(s) for the true case are executed; otherwise, the statement(s) for the false case are executed. For example, consider the following code:

two-way **if** statement

```
if (radius >= 0) {
  area = radius * radius * PI;
  System.out.println("The area for the circle of radius " +
    radius + " is " + area);
}
else {
  System.out.println("Negative input");
}
```

If `radius >= 0` is `true`, `area` is computed and displayed; if it is `false`, the message `"Negative input"` is printed.

As usual, the braces can be omitted if there is only one statement within them. The braces enclosing the `System.out.println("Negative input")` statement can therefore be omitted in the preceding example.

Here is another example of using the `if ... else` statement. The example checks whether a number is even or odd, as follows:

```
if (number % 2 == 0)
  System.out.println(number + " is even.");
else
  System.out.println(number + " is odd.");
```

3.7 Nested `if` Statements

The statement in an `if` or `if ... else` statement can be any legal Java statement, including another `if` or `if ... else` statement. The inner `if` statement is said to be *nested* inside the outer `if` statement. The inner `if` statement can contain another `if` statement; in fact, there is no limit to the depth of the nesting. For example, the following is a nested `if` statement:

nested `if` statement

```
if (i > k) {
  if (j > k)
    System.out.println("i and j are greater than k");
}
else
  System.out.println("i is less than or equal to k");
```

The `if (j > k)` statement is nested inside the `if (i > k)` statement.

The nested `if` statement can be used to implement multiple alternatives. The statement given in Figure 3.4(a), for instance, assigns a letter grade to the variable `grade` according to the score, with multiple alternatives.

```
if (score >= 90.0)
  grade = 'A';
else
  if (score >= 80.0)
    grade = 'B';
  else
    if (score >= 70.0)
      grade = 'C';
    else
      if (score >= 60.0)
        grade = 'D';
      else
        grade = 'F';
```

(a)

Equivalent

This is better

```
if (score >= 90.0)
  grade = 'A';
else if (score >= 80.0)
  grade = 'B';
else if (score >= 70.0)
  grade = 'C';
else if (score >= 60.0)
  grade = 'D';
else
  grade = 'F';
```

(b)

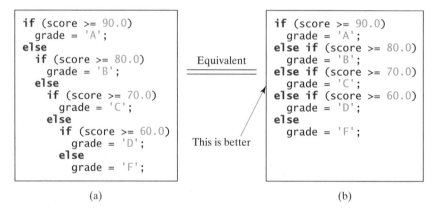

FIGURE 3.4 A preferred format for multiple alternative `if` statements is shown in (b).

The execution of this `if` statement proceeds as follows. The first condition `(score >= 90.0)` is tested. If it is `true`, the grade becomes `'A'`. If it is `false`, the second condition `(score >= 80.0)` is tested. If the second condition is `true`, the grade becomes `'B'`. If that condition is `false`, the third condition and the rest of the conditions (if necessary) continue to be tested until a condition is met or all of the conditions prove to be `false`. If all of the conditions are `false`, the grade becomes `'F'`. Note that a condition is tested only when all of the conditions that come before it are `false`.

The `if` statement in Figure 3.4(a) is equivalent to the `if` statement in Figure 3.4(b). In fact, Figure 3.4(b) is the preferred writing style for multiple alternative `if` statements. This style avoids deep indentation and makes the program easy to read.

Tip

Often, to assign a test condition to a **boolean** variable, new programmers write code as in (a) below:

assign **boolean** variable

```
if (number % 2 == 0)
  even = true;
else
  even = false;
```

(a)

Equivalent

This is shorter

```
boolean even
  = number % 2 == 0;
```

(b)

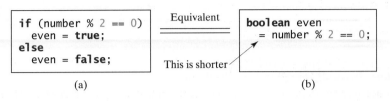

The code can be simplified by assigning the test value directly to the variable, as shown in (b).

3.8 Common Errors in Selection Statements

The following errors are common among new programmers.

Common Error 1: Forgetting Necessary Braces

The braces can be omitted if the block contains a single statement. However, forgetting the braces when they are needed for grouping multiple statements is a common programming error. If you modify the code by adding new statements in an `if` statement without braces, you will have to insert the braces. For example, the code in (a) below is wrong. It should be written with braces to group multiple statements, as shown in (b).

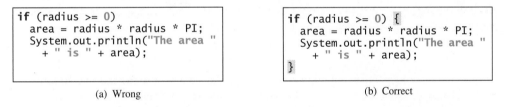

```
if (radius >= 0)
  area = radius * radius * PI;
  System.out.println("The area "
    + " is " + area);
```

(a) Wrong

```
if (radius >= 0) {
  area = radius * radius * PI;
  System.out.println("The area "
    + " is " + area);
}
```

(b) Correct

Common Error 2: Wrong Semicolon at the `if` Line

Adding a semicolon at the `if` line, as shown in (a) below, is a common mistake.

Logic Error

```
if (radius >= 0);
{
  area = radius * radius * PI;
  System.out.println("The area "
    + " is " + area);
}
```

(a)

Equivalent

Empty Block

```
if (radius >= 0) { };
{
  area = radius * radius * PI;
  System.out.println("The area "
    + " is " + area);
}
```

(b)

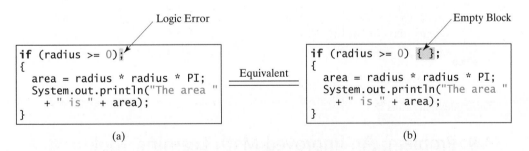

This mistake is hard to find, because it is neither a compilation error nor a runtime error; it is a logic error. The code in (a) is equivalent to that in (b) with an empty block.

This error often occurs when you use the next-line block style. Using the end-of-line block style can help prevent the error.

Common Error 3: Redundant Testing of Boolean Values

To test whether a `boolean` variable is `true` or `false` in a test condition, it is redundant to use the equality comparison operator like the code in (a):

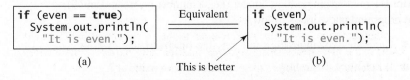

```
if (even == true)
  System.out.println(
    "It is even.");
```

(a)

Equivalent

This is better

```
if (even)
  System.out.println(
    "It is even.");
```

(b)

Instead, it is better to test the `boolean` variable directly, as shown in (b). Another good reason for doing this is to avoid errors that are difficult to detect. Using the = operator instead of the == operator to compare equality of two items in a test condition is a common error. It could lead to the following erroneous statement:

```
if (even = true)
  System.out.println("It is even.");
```

This statement does not have syntax errors. It assigns `true` to `even`, so that `even` is always `true`.

Common Error 4: Dangling `else` Ambiguity

The code in (a) below has two `if` clauses and one `else` clause. Which `if` clause is matched by the `else` clause? The indentation indicates that the `else` clause matches the first `if` clause. However, the `else` clause actually matches the second `if` clause. This situation is known as the *dangling-else ambiguity*. The `else` clause always matches the most recent unmatched `if` clause in the same block. So, the statement in (a) is equivalent to the code in (b).

```
int i = 1;
int j = 2;
int k = 3;

if (i > j)
  if (i > k)
     System.out.println("A");
else
     System.out.println("B");
```

(a)

Equivalent

This is better with correct indentation

```
int i = 1;
int j = 2;
int k = 3;

if (i > j)
  if (i > k)
    System.out.println("A");
  else
    System.out.println("B");
```

(b)

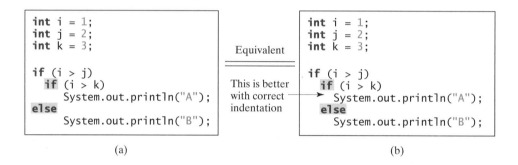

Since `(i > j)` is false, nothing is printed from the statement in (a) and (b). To force the `else` clause to match the first `if` clause, you must add a pair of braces:

```
int i = 1, j = 2, k = 3;

if (i > j) {
  if (i > k)
    System.out.println("A");
}
else
  System.out.println("B");
```

This statement prints `B`.

3.9 Problem: An Improved Math Learning Tool

Video Note
Program subtraction quiz

Suppose you want to develop a program for a first-grader to practice subtraction. The program randomly generates two single-digit integers, `number1` and `number2`, with `number1 > = number2` and displays to the student a question such as "What is 9 – 2?" After the student enters the answer, the program displays a message indicating whether it is correct.

`random()` method

The previous programs generate random numbers using `System.currentTimeMillis()`. A better approach is to use the `random()` method in the `Math` class. Invoking this method returns a random double value `d` such that $0.0 \le d < 1.0$. So, `(int)(Math.random() * 10)` returns a random single-digit integer (i.e., a number between 0 and 9).

The program may work as follows:

- Generate two single-digit integers into `number1` and `number2`.
- If `number1 < number2`, swap `number1` with `number2`.

- Prompt the student to answer "What is number1 – number2?"
- Check the student's answer and display whether the answer is correct.

The complete program is shown in Listing 3.4.

LISTING 3.4 SubtractionQuiz.java

```java
 1 import java.util.Scanner;
 2
 3 public class SubtractionQuiz {
 4   public static void main(String[] args) {
 5     // 1. Generate two random single-digit integers
 6     int number1 = (int)(Math.random() * 10);
 7     int number2 = (int)(Math.random() * 10);
 8
 9     // 2. If number1 < number2, swap number1 with number2
10     if (number1 < number2) {
11       int temp = number1;
12       number1 = number2;
13       number2 = temp;
14     }
15
16     // 3. Prompt the student to answer "What is number1 - number2?"
17     System.out.print
18       ("What is " + number1 + " - " + number2 + "? ");
19     Scanner input = new Scanner(System.in);
20     int answer = input.nextInt();
21
22     // 4. Grade the answer and display the result
23     if (number1 - number2 == answer)
24       System.out.println("You are correct!");
25     else
26       System.out.println("Your answer is wrong\n" + number1 + " - "
27         + number2 + " should be " + (number1 - number2));
28   }
29 }
```

random numbers

get answer

check the answer

```
What is 6 - 6? 0 ↵Enter
You are correct!
```

```
What is 9 - 2? 5 ↵Enter
Your answer is wrong
9 - 2 should be 7
```

line#	number1	number2	temp	answer	output
6	2				
7		9			
11			2		
12	9				
13		2			
20				5	
26					Your answer is wrong 9 – 2 should be 7

To swap two variables **number1** and **number2**, a temporary variable **temp** (line 11) is used to first hold the value in **number1**. The value in **number2** is assigned to **number1** (line 12), and the value in **temp** is assigned to **number2** (line 13).

3.10 Problem: Computing Body Mass Index

Body Mass Index (BMI) is a measure of health on weight. It can be calculated by taking your weight in kilograms and dividing by the square of your height in meters. The interpretation of BMI for people 16 years or older is as follows:

BMI	Interpretation
below 16	seriously underweight
16–18	underweight
18–24	normal weight
24–29	overweight
29–35	seriously overweight
above 35	gravely overweight

Write a program that prompts the user to enter a weight in pounds and height in inches and display the BMI. Note that one pound is **0.45359237** kilograms and one inch is **0.0254** meters. Listing 3.5 gives the program.

LISTING 3.5 ComputeBMI.java

input weight

input height

compute **bmi**

display output

```
import java.util.Scanner;

public class ComputeAndInterpretBMI {
  public static void main(String[] args) {
    Scanner input = new Scanner(System.in);

    // Prompt the user to enter weight in pounds
    System.out.print("Enter weight in pounds: ");
    double weight = input.nextDouble();

    // Prompt the user to enter height in inches
    System.out.print("Enter height in inches: ");
    double height = input.nextDouble();

    final double KILOGRAMS_PER_POUND = 0.45359237; // Constant
    final double METERS_PER_INCH = 0.0254; // Constant

    // Compute BMI
    double weightInKilograms = weight * KILOGRAMS_PER_POUND;
    double heightInMeters = height * METERS_PER_INCH;
    double bmi = weightInKilograms /
      (heightInMeters * heightInMeters);

    // Display result
    System.out.printf("Your BMI is %5.2f\n", bmi);
    if (bmi < 16)
      System.out.println("You are seriously underweight");
    else if (bmi < 18)
      System.out.println("You are underweight");
    else if (bmi < 24)
      System.out.println("You are normal weight");
```

```
32      else if (bmi < 29)
33        System.out.println("You are overweight");
34      else if (bmi < 35)
35        System.out.println("You are seriously overweight");
36      else
37        System.out.println("You are gravely overweight");
38    }
39 }
```

```
Enter weight in pounds: 146 ↵Enter
Enter height in inches: 70 ↵Enter
Your BMI is 20.948603801493316
You are normal weight
```

line#	weight	height	WeightInKilograms	heightInMeters	bmi	output
9	146					
13		70				
19			66.22448602			
20				1.778		
21					20.9486	
25						Your BMI is 20.95
31						You are normal weight

Two constants **KILOGRAMS_PER_POUND** and **METERS_PER_INCH** are defined in lines 15–16. Using constants here makes programs easy to read.

3.11 Problem: Computing Taxes

The United States federal personal income tax is calculated based on filing status and taxable income. There are four filing statuses: single filers, married filing jointly, married filing separately, and head of household. The tax rates vary every year. Table 3.2 shows the rates for 2009. If you are, say, single with a taxable income of $10,000, the first $8,350 is taxed at 10% and the other $1,650 is taxed at 15%. So, your tax is $1,082.5

Video Note
Use multiple alternative if statements

TABLE 3.2 2009 U.S. Federal Personal Tax Rates

Marginal Tax Rate	*Single*	*Married Filing Jointly or Qualified Widow(er)*	*Married Filing Separately*	*Head of Household*
10%	$0 – $8,350	$0 – $16,700	$0 – $8,350	$0 – $11,950
15%	$8,351 – $33,950	$16,701 – $67,900	$8,351 – $33,950	$11,951 – $45,500
25%	$33,951 – $82,250	$67,901 – $137,050	$33,951 – $68,525	$45,501 – $117,450
28%	$82,251 – $171,550	$137,051 – $208,850	$68,525 – $104,425	$117,451 – $190,200
33%	$171,551 – $372,950	$208,851 – $372,950	$104,426 – $186,475	$190,201 – $372,950
35%	$372,951+	$372,951+	$186,476+	$372,951+

You are to write a program to compute personal income tax. Your program should prompt the user to enter the filing status and taxable income and compute the tax. Enter 0 for single filers, 1 for married filing jointly, 2 for married filing separately, and 3 for head of household.

Your program computes the tax for the taxable income based on the filing status. The filing status can be determined using `if` statements outlined as follows:

```
if (status == 0) {
  // Compute tax for single filers
}
else if (status == 1) {
  // Compute tax for married filing jointly
}
else if (status == 2) {
  // Compute tax for married filing separately
}
else if (status == 3) {
  // Compute tax for head of household
}
else {
  // Display wrong status
}
```

For each filing status there are six tax rates. Each rate is applied to a certain amount of taxable income. For example, of a taxable income of $400,000 for single filers, $8,350 is taxed at 10%, (33,950 – 8,350) at 15%, (82,250 – 33,950) at 25%, (171,550 – 82,250) at 28%, (372,950 – 171,550) at 33%, and (400,000 – 372,950) at 35%.

Listing 3.6 gives the solution to compute taxes for single filers. The complete solution is left as an exercise.

LISTING 3.6 ComputeTax.java

input status
input income
compute tax

```
import java.util.Scanner;

public class ComputeTax {
  public static void main(String[] args) {
    // Create a Scanner
    Scanner input = new Scanner(System.in);

    // Prompt the user to enter filing status
    System.out.print(
      "(0-single filer, 1-married jointly,\n" +
      "2-married separately, 3-head of household)\n" +
      "Enter the filing status: ");
    int status = input.nextInt();

    // Prompt the user to enter taxable income
    System.out.print("Enter the taxable income: ");
    double income = input.nextDouble();

    // Compute tax
    double tax = 0;

    if (status == 0) { // Compute tax for single filers
      if (income <= 8350)
        tax = income * 0.10;
      else if (income <= 33950)
        tax = 8350 * 0.10 + (income - 8350) * 0.15;
      else if (income <= 82250)
        tax = 8350 * 0.10 + (33950 - 8350) * 0.15 +
```

```
29          (income - 33950) * 0.25;
30        else if (income <= 171550)
31          tax = 8350 * 0.10 + (33950 - 8350) * 0.15 +
32            (82250 - 33950) * 0.25 + (income - 82250) * 0.28;
33        else if (income <= 372950)
34          tax = 8350 * 0.10 + (33950 - 8350) * 0.15 +
35            (82250 - 33950) * 0.25 + (171550 - 82250) * 0.28 +
36            (income - 171550) * 0.35;
37        else
38          tax = 8350 * 0.10 + (33950 - 8350) * 0.15 +
39            (82250 - 33950) * 0.25 + (171550 - 82250) * 0.28 +
40            (372950 - 171550) * 0.33 + (income - 372950) * 0.35;
41      }
42      else if (status == 1) { // Compute tax for married file jointly
43        // Left as exercise
44      }
45      else if (status == 2) { // Compute tax for married separately
46        // Left as exercise
47      }
48      else if (status == 3) { // Compute tax for head of household
49        // Left as exercise
50      }
51      else {
52        System.out.println("Error: invalid status");
53        System.exit(0);
54      }
55
56      // Display the result
57      System.out.println("Tax is " + (int)(tax * 100) / 100.0);
58    }
59  }
```

exit program

display output

```
(0-single filer, 1-married jointly,
2-married separately, 3-head of household)
Enter the filing status: 0 ↵Enter
Enter the taxable income: 400000 ↵Enter
Tax is 117683.5
```

line#	status	income	tax	output
13	0			
17		400000		
20			0	
38			117683.5	
57				Tax is 117683.5

The program receives the filing status and taxable income. The multiple alternative `if` statements (lines 22, 42, 45, 48, 51) check the filing status and compute the tax based on the filing status.

`System.exit(0)` (line 53) is defined in the `System` class. Invoking this method terminates the program. The argument `0` indicates that the program is terminated normally.

System.exit(0)

An initial value of `0` is assigned to `tax` (line 20). A syntax error would occur if it had no initial value, because all of the other statements that assign values to `tax` are within the `if` statement. The compiler thinks that these statements may not be executed and therefore reports a syntax error.

test all cases

To test a program, you should provide the input that covers all cases. For this program, your input should cover all statuses (0, 1, 2, 3). For each status, test the tax for each of the six brackets. So, there are a total of 24 cases.

Tip

incremental development and testing

For all programs, you should write a small amount of code and test it before moving on to add more code. This is called *incremental development and testing*. This approach makes debugging easier, because the errors are likely in the new code you just added.

3.12 Logical Operators

Sometimes, whether a statement is executed is determined by a combination of several conditions. You can use logical operators to combine these conditions. *Logical operators*, also known as *Boolean operators*, operate on Boolean values to create a new Boolean value. Table 3.3 gives a list of Boolean operators. Table 3.4 defines the not (!) operator. The not (!) operator negates true to false and false to true. Table 3.5 defines the and (&&) operator. The and (&&) of two Boolean operands is true if and only if both operands are true. Table 3.6 defines the or (||) operator. The or (||) of two Boolean operands is true if at least one of the operands is true. Table 3.7 defines the exclusive or (^) operator. The exclusive or (^) of two Boolean operands is true if and only if the two operands have different Boolean values.

TABLE 3.3 Boolean Operators

Operator	*Name*	*Description*
!	not	logical negation
&&	and	logical conjunction
||	or	logical disjunction
^	exclusive or	logical exclusion

TABLE 3.4 Truth Table for Operator !

p	*!p*	*Example (assume age = 24, gender = 'F')*
true	false	!(age > 18) is false, because (age > 18) is true.
false	true	!(gender == 'M') is true, because (gender == 'M') is false.

TABLE 3.5 Truth Table for Operator &&

p1	*p2*	*p1 && p2*	*Example (assume* age = 24, gender = 'F'*)*
false	false	false	(age > 18) && (gender == 'F') is true, because (age > 18) and (gender == 'F') are both true.
false	true	false	
true	false	false	(age > 18) && (gender != 'F') is false, because (gender != 'F') is false.
true	true	true	

TABLE 3.6 Truth Table for Operator ||

p1	*p2*	*p1* || *p2*	*Example (assume* age = 24, gender = 'F'*)*
false	false	false	(age > 34) || (gender == 'F') is true, because (gender == 'F') is true.
false	true	true	
true	false	true	(age > 34) || (gender == 'M') is false, because (age > 34) and (gender == 'M') are both false.
true	true	true	

TABLE 3.7 Truth Table for Operator ^

p1	*p2*	*p1* ^ *p2*	*Example (assume* age = 24, gender = 'F'*)*
false	false	false	(age > 34) ^ (gender == 'F') is true, because (age > 34) is false but (gender == 'F') is true.
false	true	true	
true	false	true	(age > 34) || (gender == 'M') is false, because (age > 34) and (gender == 'M') are both false.
true	true	false	

Listing 3.7 gives a program that checks whether a number is divisible by 2 and 3, by 2 or 3, and by 2 or 3 but not both:

LISTING 3.7 TestBooleanOperators.java

```
import java.util.Scanner;                                   // import class

public class TestBooleanOperators {
  public static void main(String[] args) {
    // Create a Scanner
    Scanner input = new Scanner(System.in);

    // Receive an input
    System.out.print("Enter an integer: ");
    int number = input.nextInt();                           // input

    System.out.println("Is " + number +
      "\n\tdivisible by 2 and 3? " +
      (number % 2 == 0 && number % 3 == 0 )                 // and
      + "\n\tdivisible by 2 or 3? " +
      (number % 2 == 0 || number % 3 == 0 ) +               // or
      "\n\tdivisible by 2 or 3, but not both? "
      + (number % 2 == 0 ^ number % 3 == 0 ));              // exclusive or
  }
}
```

```
Enter an integer: 18 [Enter]
Is 18
  divisible by 2 and 3? true
  divisible by 2 or 3? true
  divisible by 2 or 3, but not both? false
```

A long string is formed by concatenating the substrings in lines 12–18. The three `\n` characters display the string in four lines. `(number % 2 == 0 && number % 3 == 0)` (line 14) checks whether the number is divisible by `2` and `3`. `(number % 2 == 0 || number % 3 == 0)` (line 16) checks whether the number is divisible by `2` or `3`. `(number % 2 == 0 ^ number % 3 == 0)` (line 20) checks whether the number is divisible by `2` or `3`, but not both.

Caution

In mathematics, the expression

```
1 <= numberOfDaysInAMonth <= 31
```

incompatible operands

is correct. However, it is incorrect in Java, because `1 <= numberOfDaysInAMonth` is evaluated to a `boolean` value, which cannot be compared with `31`. Here, two operands (a `boolean` value and a numeric value) are *incompatible*. The correct expression in Java is

```
(1 <= numberOfDaysInAMonth) && (numberOfDaysInAMonth <= 31)
```

Note

cannot cast **boolean**

As shown in the preceding chapter, a `char` value can be cast into an `int` value, and vice versa. A `boolean` value, however, cannot be cast into a value of another type, nor can a value of another type be cast into a `boolean` value.

Note

De Morgan's law

De Morgan's law, named after Indian-born British mathematician and logician Augustus De Morgan (1806–1871), can be used to simplify Boolean expressions. The law states

```
!(condition1 && condition2) is same as !condition1 || !condition2
!(condition1 || condition2) is same as !condition1 && !condition2
```

For example,

```
!(n == 2 || n == 3) is same as n != 2 && n != 3
!(n % 2 == 0 && n % 3 == 0) is same as n % 2 != 0 || n % 3 != 0
```

conditional operator

short-circuit operator

If one of the operands of an `&&` operator is `false`, the expression is `false`; if one of the operands of an `||` operator is `true`, the expression is `true`. Java uses these properties to improve the performance of these operators. When evaluating `p1 && p2`, Java first evaluates `p1` and then, if `p1` is `true`, evaluates `p2`; if `p1` is `false`, it does not evaluate `p2`. When evaluating `p1 || p2`, Java first evaluates `p1` and then, if `p1` is `false`, evaluates `p2`; if `p1` is `true`, it does not evaluate `p2`. Therefore, `&&` is referred to as the *conditional* or *short-circuit AND* operator, and || is referred to as the *conditional* or *short-circuit OR* operator.

3.13 Problem: Determining Leap Year

leap year

A year is a *leap year* if it is divisible by `4` but not by `100` or if it is divisible by `400`. So you can use the following Boolean expressions to check whether a year is a leap year:

```
// A leap year is divisible by 4
boolean isLeapYear = (year % 4 == 0);

// A leap year is divisible by 4 but not by 100
isLeapYear = isLeapYear && (year % 100 != 0);

// A leap year is divisible by 4 but not by 100 or divisible by 400
isLeapYear = isLeapYear || (year % 400 == 0);
```

or you can combine all these expressions into one like this:

```
isLeapYear = (year % 4 == 0 && year % 100 != 0) || (year % 400 == 0);
```

Listing 3.8 gives the program that lets the user enter a year and checks whether it is a leap year.

LISTING 3.8 LeapYear.java

```java
import java.util.Scanner;

public class LeapYear {
  public static void main(String[] args) {
    // Create a Scanner
    Scanner input = new Scanner(System.in);
    System.out.print("Enter a year: ");
    int year = input.nextInt();

    // Check if the year is a leap year
    boolean isLeapYear =
      (year % 4 == 0 && year % 100 != 0) || (year % 400 == 0);

    // Display the result
    System.out.println(year + " is a leap year? " + isLeapYear);
  }
}
```

input

leap year?

display result

```
Enter a year: 2008 ↵Enter
2008 is a leap year? true

Enter a year: 2002 ↵Enter
2002 is a leap year? false
```

3.14 Problem: Lottery

Suppose you want to develop a program to play lottery. The program randomly generates a lottery of a two-digit number, prompts the user to enter a two-digit number, and determines whether the user wins according to the following rule:

1. If the user input matches the lottery in exact order, the award is $10,000.
2. If all the digits in the user input match all the digits in the lottery, the award is $3,000.
3. If one digit in the user input matches a digit in the lottery, the award is $1,000.

The complete program is shown in Listing 3.9.

LISTING 3.9 Lottery.java

```java
import java.util.Scanner;

public class Lottery {
  public static void main(String[] args) {
    // Generate a lottery
    int lottery = (int)(Math.random() * 100);

    // Prompt the user to enter a guess
    Scanner input = new Scanner(System.in);
    System.out.print("Enter your lottery pick (two digits): ");
    int guess = input.nextInt();

    //  Get digits from lottery
    int  lotteryDigit1 = lottery / 10;
```

generate a lottery

enter a guess

exact match?

match all digits?

match one digit?

```
15     int lotteryDigit2 = lottery % 10;
16
17     // Get digits from guess
18     int guessDigit1 = guess / 10;
19     int guessDigit2 = guess % 10;
20
21     System.out.println("The lottery number is " + lottery);
22
23     // Check the guess
24     if (guess == lottery)
25       System.out.println("Exact match: you win $10,000");
26     else if (guessDigit2 == lotteryDigit1
27           && guessDigit1 == lotteryDigit2)
28       System.out.println("Match all digits: you win $3,000");
29     else if (guessDigit1 == lotteryDigit1
30           || guessDigit1 == lotteryDigit2
31           || guessDigit2 == lotteryDigit1
32           || guessDigit2 == lotteryDigit2)
33       System.out.println("Match one digit: you win $1,000");
34     else
35       System.out.println("Sorry, no match");
36   }
37 }
```

```
Enter your lottery pick (two digits): 45 [Enter]
The lottery number is 12
Sorry, no match
```

```
Enter your lottery pick: 23 [Enter]
The lottery number is 34
Match one digit: you win $1,000
```

line# / variable	6	11	14	15	18	19	33
lottery	34						
guess		23					
lotteryDigit1			3				
lotteryDigit2				4			
guessDigit1					2		
guessDigit2						3	
output							Match one digit: you win $1,000

The program generates a lottery using the `random()` method (line 6) and prompts the user to enter a guess (line 11). Note that `guess % 10` obtains the last digit from `guess` and `guess / 10` obtains the first digit from `guess`, since `guess` is a two-digit number (lines 18–19).

The program checks the guess against the lottery number in this order:

1. First check whether the guess matches the lottery exactly (line 24).
2. If not, check whether the reversal of the guess matches the lottery (lines 26–27).

3. If not, check whether one digit is in the lottery (lines 29–32).
4. If not, nothing matches.

3.15 switch Statements

The `if` statement in Listing 3.6, ComputeTax.java, makes selections based on a single `true` or `false` condition. There are four cases for computing taxes, which depend on the value of `status`. To fully account for all the cases, nested `if` statements were used. Overuse of nested `if` statements makes a program difficult to read. Java provides a `switch` statement to handle multiple conditions efficiently. You could write the following `switch` statement to replace the nested `if` statement in Listing 3.6:

```
switch (status) {
  case 0:  compute taxes for single filers;
           break;
  case 1:  compute taxes for married filing jointly;
           break;
  case 2:  compute taxes for married filing separately;
           break;
  case 3:  compute taxes for head of household;
           break;
  default: System.out.println("Errors: invalid status");
           System.exit(0);
}
```

The flow chart of the preceding `switch` statement is shown in Figure 3.5.

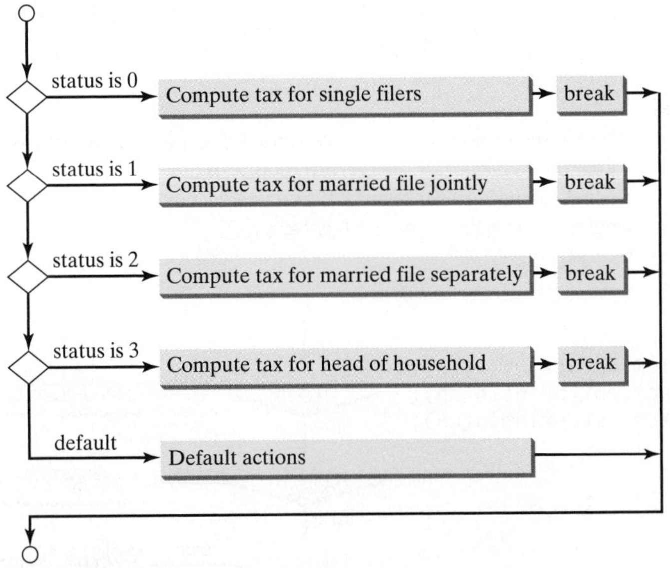
status is 0
Compute tax for single filers
break
status is 1
Compute tax for married file jointly
break
status is 2
Compute tax for married file separately
break
status is 3
Compute tax for head of household
break
default
Default actions

FIGURE 3.5 The `switch` statement checks all cases and executes the statements in the matched case.

This statement checks to see whether the status matches the value `0`, `1`, `2`, or `3`, in that order. If matched, the corresponding tax is computed; if not matched, a message is displayed. Here is the full syntax for the `switch` statement:

`switch` statement

```
switch (switch-expression) {
  case value1: statement(s)1;
               break;
```

```
    case value2: statement(s)2;
                 break;
    ...
    case valueN: statement(s)N;
                 break;
    default:     statement(s)-for-default;
}
```

The **switch** statement observes the following rules:

- The **switch-expression** must yield a value of **char**, **byte**, **short**, or **int** type and must always be enclosed in parentheses.
- The **value1**, ..., and **valueN** must have the same data type as the value of the **switch-expression**. Note that **value1**, ..., and **valueN** are constant expressions, meaning that they cannot contain variables, such as **1 + x**.
- When the value in a **case** statement matches the value of the **switch-expression**, the statements *starting from this case* are executed until either a **break** statement or the end of the switch statement is reached.
- The keyword **break** is optional. The **break** statement immediately ends the **switch** statement.
- The **default** case, which is optional, can be used to perform actions when none of the specified cases matches the **switch-expression**.
- The **case** statements are checked in sequential order, but the order of the cases (including the default case) does not matter. However, it is good programming style to follow the logical sequence of the cases and place the default case at the end.

Caution

without **break**

fall-through behavior

Do not forget to use a **break** statement when one is needed. Once a case is matched, the statements starting from the matched case are executed until a **break** statement or the end of the **switch** statement is reached. This is referred to as *fall-through* behavior. For example, the following code prints character **a** three times if **ch** is **'a'**:

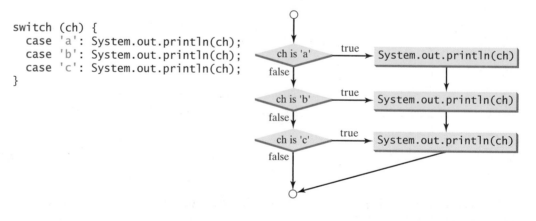

```
switch (ch) {
  case 'a': System.out.println(ch);
  case 'b': System.out.println(ch);
  case 'c': System.out.println(ch);
}
```

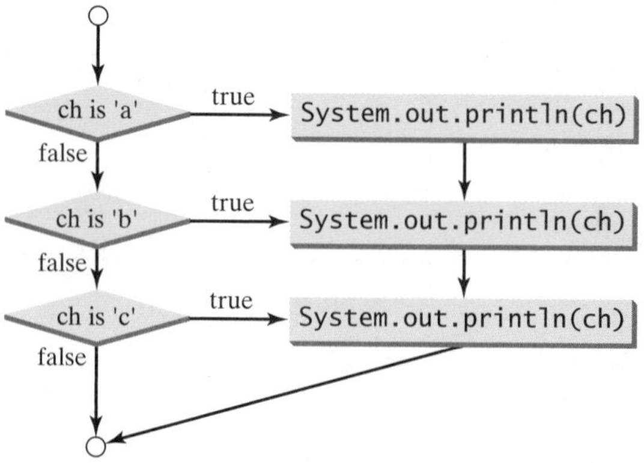
ch is 'a'
true
System.out.println(ch)
false
ch is 'b'
true
System.out.println(ch)
false
ch is 'c'
true
System.out.println(ch)
false

Tip

To avoid programming errors and improve code maintainability, it is a good idea to put a comment in a case clause if **break** is purposely omitted.

3.16 Conditional Expressions

You might want to assign a value to a variable that is restricted by certain conditions. For example, the following statement assigns `1` to `y` if `x` is greater than `0`, and `-1` to `y` if `x` is less than or equal to `0`.

```
if (x > 0)
  y = 1;
else
  y = -1;
```

Alternatively, as in this example, you can use a conditional expression to achieve the same result.

```
y = (x > 0) ? 1 : -1;
```

Conditional expressions are in a completely different style, with no explicit `if` in the statement. The syntax is shown below:

```
boolean-expression ? expression1 : expression2;
```

conditional expression

The result of this conditional expression is `expression1` if `boolean-expression` is true; otherwise the result is `expression2`.

Suppose you want to assign the larger number between variable `num1` and `num2` to `max`. You can simply write a statement using the conditional expression:

```
max = (num1 > num2) ? num1 : num2;
```

For another example, the following statement displays the message "num is even" if `num` is even, and otherwise displays "num is odd."

```
System.out.println((num % 2 == 0) ? "num is even" : "num is odd");
```

Note

The symbols `?` and `:` appear together in a conditional expression. They form a conditional operator. It is called a *ternary operator* because it uses three operands. It is the only ternary operator in Java.

3.17 Formatting Console Output

If you wish to display only two digits after the decimal point in a floating-point value, you may write the code like this:

```
double x = 2.0 / 3;
System.out.println("x is " + (int)(x * 100) / 100.0);
```

```
x is 0.66
```

printf

However, a better way to accomplish this task is to format the output using the `printf` method. The syntax to invoke this method is

```
System.out.printf(format, item1, item2, ..., itemk)
```

where `format` is a string that may consist of substrings and format specifiers.

specifier

A format specifier specifies how an item should be displayed. An item may be a numeric value, a character, a Boolean value, or a string. A simple specifier consists of a percent sign (%) followed by a conversion code. Table 3.8 lists some frequently used simple specifiers:

TABLE 3.8 Frequently Used Specifiers

Specifier	*Output*	*Example*
`%b`	a Boolean value	true or false
`%c`	a character	'a'
`%d`	a decimal integer	200
`%f`	a floating-point number	45.460000
`%e`	a number in standard scientific notation	4.556000e+01
`%s`	a string	"Java is cool"

Here is an example:

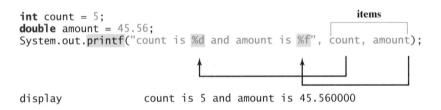

```
int count = 5;                                                  items
double amount = 45.56;
System.out.printf("count is %d and amount is %f", count, amount);

display             count is 5 and amount is 45.560000
```

Items must match the specifiers in order, in number, and in exact type. For example, the specifier for `count` is `%d` and for `amount` is `%f`. By default, a floating-point value is displayed with six digits after the decimal point. You can specify the width and precision in a specifier, as shown in the examples in Table 3.9.

TABLE 3.9 Examples of Specifying Width and Precision

Example	*Output*
`%5c`	Output the character and add four spaces before the character item.
`%6b`	Output the Boolean value and add one space before the false value and two spaces before the true value.
`%5d`	Output the integer item with width at least 5. If the number of digits in the item is $<$ 5, add spaces before the number. If the number of digits in the item is $>$ 5, the width is automatically increased.
`%10.2f`	Output the floating-point item with width at least 10 including a decimal point and two digits after the point. Thus there are 7 digits allocated before the decimal point. If the number of digits before the decimal point in the item is $<$ 7, add spaces before the number. If the number of digits before the decimal point in the item is $>$ 7, the width is automatically increased.
`%10.2e`	Output the floating-point item with width at least 10 including a decimal point, two digits after the point and the exponent part. If the displayed number in scientific notation has width less than 10, add spaces before the number.
`%12s`	Output the string with width at least 12 characters. If the string item has less than 12 characters, add spaces before the string. If the string item has more than 12 characters, the width is automatically increased.

The code presented in the beginning of this section for displaying only two digits after the decimal point in a floating-point value can be revised using the **printf** method as follows:

```
double x = 2.0 / 3;
System.out.printf("x is %4.2f", x);
display          x is 0.67
```

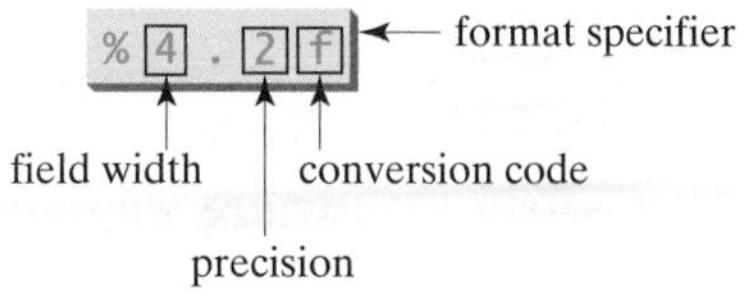

% 4 . 2 f
format specifier
field width
conversion code
precision

By default, the output is right justified. You can put the minus sign (-) in the specifier to specify that the item is left justified in the output within the specified field. For example, the following statements left justify

```
System.out.printf("%8d%8s%8.1f\n", 1234, "Java", 5.6);
System.out.printf("%-8d%-8s%-8.1f \n", 1234, "Java", 5.6);
```

display

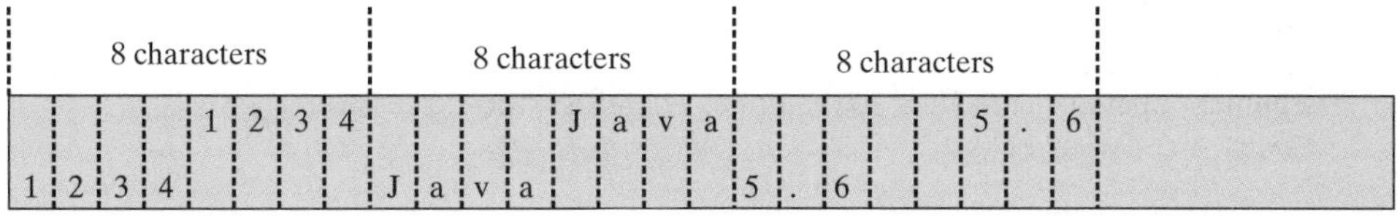

8 characters
8 characters
8 characters
1 2 3 4
J a v a
5 . 6
1 2 3 4
J a v a
5 . 6

Caution

The items must match the specifiers in exact type. The item for the specifier **%f** or **%e** must be a floating-point type value such as 40.0, not 40. Thus an **int** variable cannot match **%f** or **%e**.

Tip

The **%** sign denotes a specifier. To output a literal **%** in the format string, use **%%**.

3.18 Operator Precedence and Associativity

Operator precedence and associativity determine the order in which operators are evaluated. Suppose that you have this expression:

```
3 + 4 * 4 > 5 * (4 + 3) - 1
```

What is its value? What is the execution order of the operators?

Arithmetically, the expression in the parentheses is evaluated first. (Parentheses can be nested, in which case the expression in the inner parentheses is executed first.) When evaluating an expression without parentheses, the operators are applied according to the precedence rule and the associativity rule.

The precedence rule defines precedence for operators, as shown in Table 3.10, which contains the operators you have learned so far. Operators are listed in decreasing order of precedence from top to bottom. Operators with the same precedence appear in the same group. (See Appendix C, "Operator Precedence Chart," for a complete list of Java operators and their precedence.) precedence

If operators with the same precedence are next to each other, their *associativity* determines the order of evaluation. All binary operators except assignment operators are *left associative*. For example, since + and – are of the same precedence and are left associative, the expression associativity

```
a - b + c - d   ==equivalent==   ((a - b) + c) - d
```

TABLE 3.10 Operator Precedence Chart

Precedence	*Operator*
↓	var++ and var-- (Postfix)
	+, - (Unary plus and minus), ++var and --var (Prefix)
	(type) (Casting)
	! (Not)
	*, /, % (Multiplication, division, and remainder)
	+, - (Binary addition and subtraction)
	<, <=, >, >= (Comparison)
	==, != (Equality)
	^ (Exclusive OR)
	&& (AND)
	|| (OR)
	=, +=, -=, *=, /=, %= (Assignment operator)

Assignment operators are *right associative*. Therefore, the expression

```
a = b += c = 5    equivalent    a = (b += (c = 5))
```

Suppose a, b, and c are 1 before the assignment; after the whole expression is evaluated, a becomes 6, b becomes 6, and c becomes 5. Note that left associativity for the assignment operator would not make sense.

Note

behind the scenes

Java has its own way to evaluate an expression internally. The result of a Java evaluation is the same as that of its corresponding arithmetic evaluation. Interested readers may refer to Supplement III.B for more discussions on how an expression is evaluated in Java *behind the scenes*.

3.19 (GUI) Confirmation Dialogs

You have used **showMessageDialog** to display a message dialog box and **showInputDialog** to display an input dialog box. Occasionally it is useful to answer a question with a confirmation dialog box. A confirmation dialog can be created using the following statement:

```
int option =
  JOptionPane.showConfirmDialog
    (null, "Continue");
```

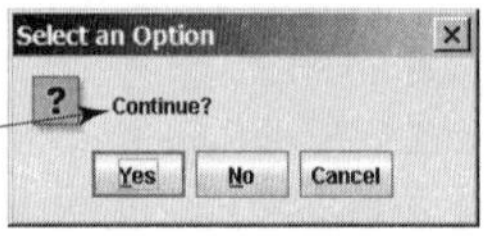
Select an Option
Continue?
Yes
No
Cancel

When a button is clicked, the method returns an option value. The value is **JOptionPane.YES_OPTION** (0) for the *Yes* button, **JOptionPane.NO_OPTION** (1) for the *No* button, and **JOptionPane.CANCEL_OPTION** (2) for the *Cancel* button.

You may rewrite the guess-birthday program in Listing 3.3 using confirmation dialog boxes, as shown in Listing 3.10. Figure 3.6 shows a sample run of the program for the day **19**.

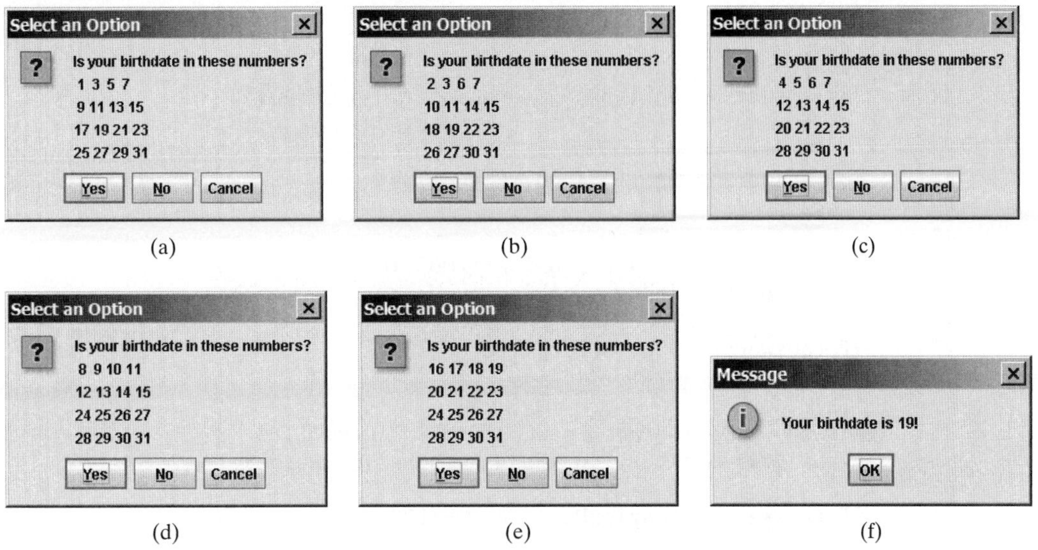
Select an Option
Is your birthdate in these numbers?
1 3 5 7
9 11 13 15
17 19 21 23
25 27 29 31
Yes No Cancel
(a)
Select an Option
Is your birthdate in these numbers?
2 3 6 7
10 11 14 15
18 19 22 23
26 27 30 31
Yes No Cancel
(b)
Select an Option
Is your birthdate in these numbers?
4 5 6 7
12 13 14 15
20 21 22 23
28 29 30 31
Yes No Cancel
(c)
Select an Option
Is your birthdate in these numbers?
8 9 10 11
12 13 14 15
24 25 26 27
28 29 30 31
Yes No Cancel
(d)
Select an Option
Is your birthdate in these numbers?
16 17 18 19
20 21 22 23
24 25 26 27
28 29 30 31
Yes No Cancel
(e)
Message
Your birthdate is 19!
OK
(f)

FIGURE 3.6 Click Yes in (a), Yes in (b), No in (c), No in (d), and Yes in (e).

LISTING 3.10 GuessBirthdayUsingConfirmationDialog.java

import class

```
import javax.swing.JOptionPane;

public class GuessBirthdayUsingConfirmationDialog {
  public static void main(String[] args) {
    String set1 =
      " 1  3  5  7\n" +
      " 9 11 13 15\n" +
      "17 19 21 23\n" +
      "25 27 29 31";

    String set2 =
      " 2  3  6  7\n" +
      "10 11 14 15\n" +
      "18 19 22 23\n" +
      "26 27 30 31";

    String set3 =
      " 4  5  6  7\n" +
      "12 13 14 15\n" +
      "20 21 22 23\n" +
      "28 29 30 31";

    String set4 =
      " 8  9 10 11\n" +
      "12 13 14 15\n" +
      "24 25 26 27\n" +
      "28 29 30 31";

    String set5 =
      "16 17 18 19\n" +
      "20 21 22 23\n" +
      "24 25 26 27\n" +
      "28 29 30 31";

```

set1

set2

set3

set4

set5

confirmation dialog

in set1?

in set2?

in set3?

in set4?

in set5?

```java
35      int day = 0;
36
37      // Prompt the user to answer questions
38      int answer = JOptionPane.showConfirmDialog(null,
39        "Is your birthday in these numbers?\n" + set1);
40
41      if (answer == JOptionPane.YES_OPTION)
42        day += 1;
43
44      answer = JOptionPane.showConfirmDialog(null,
45        "Is your birthday in these numbers?\n" + set2);
46
47      if (answer == JOptionPane.YES_OPTION)
48        day += 2;
49
50      answer = JOptionPane.showConfirmDialog(null,
51        "Is your birthday in these numbers?\n" + set3);
52
53      if (answer == JOptionPane.YES_OPTION)
54        day += 4;
55
56      answer = JOptionPane.showConfirmDialog(null,
57        "Is your birthday in these numbers?\n" + set4);
58
59      if (answer == JOptionPane.YES_OPTION)
60        day += 8;
61
62      answer = JOptionPane.showConfirmDialog(null,
63        "Is your birthday in these numbers?\n" + set5);
64
65      if (answer == JOptionPane.YES_OPTION)
66        day += 16;
67
68      JOptionPane.showMessageDialog(null, "Your birthday is " +
69        day + "!");
70    }
71  }
```

The program displays confirmation dialog boxes to prompt the user to answer whether a number is in Set1 (line 38), Set2 (line 44), Set3 (line 50), Set4 (line 56), and Set5 (line 62). If the answer is Yes, the first number in the set is added to `day` (lines 42, 48, 54, 60, and 66).

Key Terms

Chapter Summary

1. A `boolean` variable stores a `true` or `false` value.

2. The relational operators (<, <=, ==, !=, >, >=) work with numbers and characters, and yield a Boolean value.

3. The Boolean operators &&, ||, !, and ^ operate with Boolean values and variables.

4. When evaluating p1 && p2, Java first evaluates p1 and then evaluates p2 if p1 is true; if p1 is false, it does not evaluate p2. When evaluating p1 || p2, Java first evaluates p1 and then evaluates p2 if p1 is false; if p1 is true, it does not evaluate p2. Therefore, && is referred to as the conditional or short-circuit AND operator, and || is referred to as the conditional or short-circuit OR operator.

5. Selection statements are used for programming with alternative courses. There are several types of selection statements: if statements, if ... else statements, nested if statements, switch statements, and conditional expressions.

6. The various if statements all make control decisions based on a Boolean expression. Based on the true or false evaluation of the expression, these statements take one of two possible courses.

7. The switch statement makes control decisions based on a switch expression of type char, byte, short, or int.

8. The keyword break is optional in a switch statement, but it is normally used at the end of each case in order to terminate the remainder of the switch statement. If the break statement is not present, the next case statement will be executed.

Review Questions

Section 3.2

3.1 List six comparison operators.

3.2 Can the following conversions involving casting be allowed? If so, find the converted result.

```
boolean b = true;
i = (int)b;

int i = 1;
boolean b = (boolean)i;
```

Sections 3.3–3.11

3.3 What is the printout of the code in (a) and (b) if number is 30 and 35, respectively?

```
if (number % 2 == 0)
  System.out.println(number + " is even.");

  System.out.println(number + " is odd.");
```

(a)

```
if (number % 2 == 0)
  System.out.println(number + " is even.");
else
  System.out.println(number + " is odd.");
```

(b)

3.4 Suppose x = 3 and y = 2; show the output, if any, of the following code. What is the output if x = 3 and y = 4? What is the output if x = 2 and y = 2? Draw a flow chart of the code:

```
if (x > 2) {
  if (y > 2) {
```

```
      z = x + y;
      System.out.println("z is " + z);
    }
  }
  else
    System.out.println("x is " + x);
```

3.5 Which of the following statements are equivalent? Which ones are correctly indented?

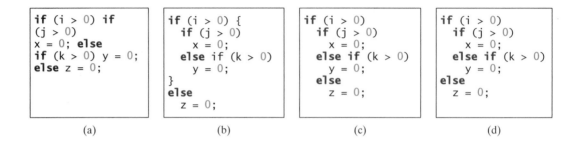

```
if (i > 0) if
(j > 0)
x = 0; else
if (k > 0) y = 0;
else z = 0;
```

(a)

```
if (i > 0) {
  if (j > 0)
    x = 0;
  else if (k > 0)
    y = 0;
}
else
  z = 0;
```

(b)

```
if (i > 0)
  if (j > 0)
    x = 0;
  else if (k > 0)
    y = 0;
  else
    z = 0;
```

(c)

```
if (i > 0)
  if (j > 0)
    x = 0;
  else if (k > 0)
    y = 0;
else
  z = 0;
```

(d)

3.6 Suppose x = 2 and y = 3. Show the output, if any, of the following code. What is the output if x = 3 and y = 2? What is the output if x = 3 and y = 3?

(*Hint*: Indent the statement correctly first.)

```
if (x > 2)
  if (y > 2) {
    int z = x + y;
    System.out.println("z is " + z);
  }
else
  System.out.println("x is " + x);
```

3.7 Are the following two statements equivalent?

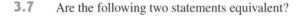

```
if (income <= 10000)
  tax = income * 0.1;
else if (income <= 20000)
  tax = 1000 +
    (income - 10000) * 0.15;
```

```
if (income <= 10000)
  tax = income * 0.1;
else if (income > 10000 &&
         income <= 20000)
  tax = 1000 +
    (income - 10000) * 0.15;
```

3.8 Which of the following is a possible output from invoking `Math.random()`?

`323.4, 0.5, 34, 1.0, 0.0, 0.234`

3.9 How do you generate a random integer `i` such that $0 \leq i < 20$? How do you generate a random integer `i` such that $10 \leq i < 20$? How do you generate a random integer `i` such that $10 \leq i \leq 50$?

3.10 Write an `if` statement that assigns `1` to `x` if `y` is greater than `0`.

3.11 (a) Write an `if` statement that increases `pay` by 3% if `score` is greater than `90`. (b) Write an `if` statement that increases `pay` by 3% if `score` is greater than `90`, otherwise increases `pay` by 1%.

3.12 What is wrong in the following code?

```
if (score >= 60.0)
  grade = 'D';
else if (score >= 70.0)
  grade = 'C';
else if (score >= 80.0)
  grade = 'B';
else if (score >= 90.0)
  grade = 'A';
else
  grade = 'F';
```

3.13 Rewrite the following statement using a Boolean expression:

```
if (count % 10 == 0)
  newLine = true;
else
  newLine = false;
```

Sections 3.12–3.14

3.14 Assuming that x is 1, show the result of the following Boolean expressions.

```
(true) && (3 > 4)
!(x > 0) && (x > 0)
(x > 0) || (x < 0)
(x != 0) || (x == 0)
(x >= 0) || (x < 0)
(x != 1) == !(x == 1)
```

3.15 Write a Boolean expression that evaluates to `true` if a number stored in variable `num` is between 1 and 100.

3.16 Write a Boolean expression that evaluates to `true` if a number stored in variable `num` is between 1 and 100 or the number is negative.

3.17 Assume that x and y are `int` type. Which of the following are legal Java expressions?

```
x > y > 0
x = y && y
x /= y
x or y
x and y
(x != 0) || (x = 0)
```

3.18 Suppose that x is 1. What is x after the evaluation of the following expression?

```
(x >= 1) && (x++ > 1)
(x > 1) && (x++ > 1)
```

3.19 What is the value of the expression `ch >= 'A' && ch <= 'Z'` if `ch` is `'A'`, `'p'`, `'E'`, or `'5'`?

3.20 Suppose, when you run the program, you enter input 2 3 6 from the console. What is the output?

```
public class Test {
  public static void main(String[] args) {
    java.util.Scanner input = new java.util.Scanner(System.in);
    double x = input.nextDouble();
```

```
        double y = input.nextDouble();
        double z = input.nextDouble();

        System.out.println("(x < y && y < z) is " + (x < y && y < z));
        System.out.println("(x < y || y < z) is " + (x < y || y < z));
        System.out.println("!(x < y) is " + !(x < y));
        System.out.println("(x + y < z) is " + (x + y < z));
        System.out.println("(x + y < z) is " + (x + y < z));
    }
}
```

3.21 Write a Boolean expression that evaluates `true` if `age` is greater than `13` and less than `18`.

3.22 Write a Boolean expression that evaluates `true` if `weight` is greater than `50` or height is greater than `160`.

3.23 Write a Boolean expression that evaluates `true` if `weight` is greater than `50` and height is greater than `160`.

3.24 Write a Boolean expression that evaluates `true` if either `weight` is greater than `50` or height is greater than `160`, but not both.

Section 3.15

3.25 What data types are required for a `switch` variable? If the keyword `break` is not used after a case is processed, what is the next statement to be executed? Can you convert a `switch` statement to an equivalent `if` statement, or vice versa? What are the advantages of using a `switch` statement?

3.26 What is `y` after the following `switch` statement is executed?

```
x = 3; y = 3;
switch (x + 3) {
  case 6:  y = 1;
  default: y += 1;
}
```

3.27 Use a `switch` statement to rewrite the following `if` statement and draw the flow chart for the `switch` statement:

```
if (a == 1)
  x += 5;
else if (a == 2)
  x += 10;
else if (a == 3)
  x += 16;
else if (a == 4)
  x += 34;
```

3.28 Write a `switch` statement that assigns a `String` variable `dayName` with Sunday, Monday, Tuesday, Wednesday, Thursday, Friday, Saturday, if `day` is `0`, `1`, `2`, `3`, `4`, `5`, `6`, accordingly.

Section 3.16

3.29 Rewrite the following `if` statement using the conditional operator:

```
if (count % 10 == 0)
  System.out.print(count + "\n");
else
  System.out.print(count + " ");
```

3.30 Rewrite the following statement using a conditional expression:

```
if (temperature > 90)
  pay = pay * 1.5;
else
  pay = pay * 1.1;
```

Section 3.17

3.31 What are the specifiers for outputting a Boolean value, a character, a decimal integer, a floating-point number, and a string?

3.32 What is wrong in the following statements?

```
(a) System.out.printf("%5d %d", 1, 2, 3);
(b) System.out.printf("%5d %f", 1);
(c) System.out.printf("%5d %f", 1, 2);
```

3.33 Show the output of the following statements.

```
(a) System.out.printf("amount is %f %e\n", 32.32, 32.32);
(b) System.out.printf("amount is %5.4f %5.4e\n", 32.32, 32.32);
(c) System.out.printf("%6b\n", (1 > 2));
(d) System.out.printf("%6s\n", "Java");
(e) System.out.printf("%-6b%s\n", (1 > 2), "Java");
(f) System.out.printf("%6b%-s\n", (1 > 2), "Java");
```

3.34 How do you create a formatted string?

Section 3.18

3.35 List the precedence order of the Boolean operators. Evaluate the following expressions:

```
true || true && false
true && true || false
```

3.36 True or false? All the binary operators except = are left associative.

3.37 Evaluate the following expressions:

```
2 * 2 - 3 > 2 && 4 - 2 > 5
2 * 2 - 3 > 2 || 4 - 2 > 5
```

3.38 Is `(x > 0 && x < 10)` the same as `((x > 0) && (x < 10))`? Is `(x > 0 || x < 10)` the same as `((x > 0) || (x < 10))`? Is `(x > 0 || x < 10 && y < 0)` the same as `(x > 0 || (x < 10 && y < 0))`?

Section 3.19

3.39 How do you display a confirmation dialog? What value is returned when invoking `JOptionPane.showConfirmDialog`?

Programming Exercises

Pedagogical Note

For each exercise, students should carefully analyze the problem requirements and design strategies for solving the problem before coding. think before coding document analysis and design

Pedagogical Note

Instructors may ask students to document analysis and design for selected exercises. Students should use their own words to analyze the problem, including the input, output, and what needs to be computed, and describe how to solve the problem in pseudocode.

learn from mistakes

Debugging Tip

Before you ask for help, read and explain the program to yourself, and trace it using several representative inputs by hand or using an IDE debugger. You learn how to program by debugging your own mistakes.

Section 3.2

3.1* (*Algebra: solving quadratic equations*) The two roots of a quadratic equation $ax^2 + bx + c = 0$ can be obtained using the following formula:

$$r_1 = \frac{-b + \sqrt{b^2 - 4ac}}{2a} \text{ and } r_2 = \frac{-b - \sqrt{b^2 - 4ac}}{2a}$$

$b^2 - 4ac$ is called the discriminant of the quadratic equation. If it is positive, the equation has two real roots. If it is zero, the equation has one root. If it is negative, the equation has no real roots.

Write a program that prompts the user to enter values for *a*, *b*, and *c* and displays the result based on the discriminant. If the discriminant is positive, display two roots. If the discriminant is `0`, display one root. Otherwise, display "The equation has no real roots".

Note you can use `Math.pow(x, 0.5)` to compute $\sqrt{x}$. Here are some sample runs.

```
Enter a, b, c: 1.0 3 1 [Enter]
The roots are -0.381966 and -2.61803
```

```
Enter a, b, c: 1 2.0 1 [Enter]
The root is -1
```

```
Enter a, b, c: 1 2 3 [Enter]
The equation has no real roots
```

3.2 (*Checking whether a number is even*) Write a program that reads an integer and checks whether it is even. Here are the sample runs of this program:

```
Enter an integer: 25 [Enter]
Is 25 an even number? false
```

```
Enter an integer: 2000 [Enter]
Is 2000 an even number? true
```

Sections 3.3–3.8

3.3* (*Algebra: solving* 2 × 2 *linear equations*) You can use Cramer's rule to solve the following 2 × 2 system of linear equation:

$$ax + by = e \qquad x = \frac{ed - bf}{ad - bc} \qquad y = \frac{af - ec}{ad - bc}$$
$$cx + dy = f$$

Write a program that prompts the user to enter a, b, c, d, e, and f and display the result. If $ad - bc$ is 0, report that "The equation has no solution".

```
Enter a, b, c, d, e, f: 9.0 4.0 3.0 -5.0 -6.0 -21.0 ↵Enter
x is -2.0 and y is 3.0
```

```
Enter a, b, c, d, e, f: 1.0 2.0 2.0 4.0 4.0 5.0 ↵Enter
The equation has no solution
```

3.4** (*Game: learning addition*) Write a program that generates two integers under 100 and prompts the user to enter the sum of these two integers. The program then reports true if the answer is correct, false otherwise. The program is similar to Listing 3.1.

3.5** (*Game: addition for three numbers*) The program in Listing 3.1 generates two integers and prompts the user to enter the sum of these two integers. Revise the program to generate three single-digit integers and prompt the user to enter the sum of these three integers.

3.6* (*Health application: BMI*) Revise Listing 3.5, ComputeBMI.java, to let the user enter weight, feet, and inches. For example, if a person is 5 feet and 10 inches, you will enter 5 for feet and 10 for inches.

3.7 (*Financial application: monetary units*) Modify Listing 2.10, ComputeChange.java, to display the nonzero denominations only, using singular words for single units such as 1 dollar and 1 penny, and plural words for more than one unit such as 2 dollars and 3 pennies. (Use input 23.67 to test your program.)

Video Note
Sort three integers

3.8* (*Sorting three integers*) Write a program that sorts three integers. The integers are entered from the input dialogs and stored in variables num1, num2, and num3, respectively. The program sorts the numbers so that $num1 \le num2 \le num3$.

3.9 (*Business: checking ISBN*) An **ISBN** (International Standard Book Number) consists of 10 digits $d_1d_2d_3d_4d_5d_6d_7d_8d_9d_{10}$. The last digit d_{10} is a checksum, which is calculated from the other nine digits using the following formula:

$$(d_1 \times 1 + d_2 \times 2 + d_3 \times 3 + d_4 \times 4 + d_5 \times 5 +$$
$$d_6 \times 6 + d_7 \times 7 + d_8 \times 8 + d_9 \times 9)\ \%\ 11$$

If the checksum is 10, the last digit is denoted X according to the ISBN convention. Write a program that prompts the user to enter the first 9 digits and displays the 10-digit ISBN (including leading zeros). Your program should read the input as an integer. For example, if you enter 013601267, the program should display 0136012671.

3.10* (*Game: addition quiz*) Listing 3.4, SubtractionQuiz.java, randomly generates a subtraction question. Revise the program to randomly generate an addition question with two integers less than 100.

Sections 3.9–3.19

3.11* (*Finding the number of days in a month*) Write a program that prompts the user to enter the month and year and displays the number of days in the month. For example, if the user entered month `2` and year `2000`, the program should display that February 2000 has 29 days. If the user entered month `3` and year `2005`, the program should display that March 2005 has 31 days.

3.12 (*Checking a number*) Write a program that prompts the user to enter an integer and checks whether the number is divisible by both `5` and `6`, or neither of them, or just one of them. Here are some sample runs for inputs `10`, `30`, and `23`.

```
10 is divisible by 5 or 6, but not both
30 is divisible by both 5 and 6
23 is not divisible by either 5 or 6
```

3.13 (*Financial application: computing taxes*) Listing 3.6, ComputeTax.java, gives the source code to compute taxes for single filers. Complete Listing 3.6 to give the complete source code.

3.14 (*Game: head or tail*) Write a program that lets the user guess the head or tail of a coin. The program randomly generates an integer `0` or `1`, which represents head or tail. The program prompts the user to enter a guess and reports whether the guess is correct or incorrect.

3.15* (*Game: lottery*) Revise Listing 3.9, Lottery.java, to generate a lottery of a three-digit number. The program prompts the user to enter a three-digit number and determines whether the user wins according to the following rule:

1. If the user input matches the lottery in exact order, the award is $10,000.
2. If all the digits in the user input match all the digits in the lottery, the award is $3,000.
3. If one digit in the user input matches a digit in the lottery, the award is $1,000.

3.16 (*Random character*) Write a program that displays a random uppercase letter using the `Math.random()` method.

3.17* (*Game: scissor, rock, paper*) Write a program that plays the popular scissor-rock-paper game. (A scissor can cut a paper, a rock can knock a scissor, and a paper can wrap a rock.) The program randomly generates a number `0`, `1`, or `2` representing scissor, rock, and paper. The program prompts the user to enter a number `0`, `1`, or `2` and displays a message indicating whether the user or the computer wins, loses, or draws. Here are sample runs:

```
scissor (0), rock (1), paper (2): 1 Enter
The computer is scissor. You are rock. You won
```

```
scissor (0), rock (1), paper (2): 2 Enter
The computer is paper. You are paper too. It is a draw
```

3.18* (*Using the input dialog box*) Rewrite Listing 3.8, LeapYear.java, using the input dialog box.

3.19 (*Validating triangles*) Write a program that reads three edges for a triangle and determines whether the input is valid. The input is valid if the sum of any two edges is greater than the third edge. Here are the sample runs of this program:

```
Enter three edges: 1 2.5 1 Enter
Can edges 1, 2.5, and 1 form a triangle? false
```

```
Enter three edges: 2.5 2 1 Enter
Can edges 2.5, 2, and 1 form a triangle? true
```

3.20* (*Science: wind-chill temperature*) Exercise 2.17 gives a formula to compute the wind-chill temperature. The formula is valid for temperature in the range between −58°F and 41°F and wind speed greater than or equal to 2. Write a program that prompts the user to enter a temperature and a wind speed. The program displays the wind-chill temperature if the input is valid, otherwise displays a message indicating whether the temperature and/or wind speed is invalid.

Comprehensives

3.21** (*Science: day of the week*) Zeller's congruence is an algorithm developed by Christian Zeller to calculate the day of the week. The formula is

$$h = \left(q + \left\lfloor \frac{26(m+1)}{10} \right\rfloor + k + \left\lfloor \frac{k}{4} \right\rfloor + \left\lfloor \frac{j}{4} \right\rfloor + 5j\right) \% 7$$

where

- h is the day of the week (0: Saturday, 1: Sunday, 2: Monday, 3: Tuesday, 4: Wednesday, 5: Thursday, 6: Friday).
- q is the day of the month.
- m is the month (3: March, 4: April, . . . , 12: December). January and February are counted as months 13 and 14 of the previous year.
- j is the century (i.e., $\left\lfloor \frac{year}{100} \right\rfloor$).
- k is the year of the century (i.e., *year* % 7).

Write a program that prompts the user to enter a year, month, and day of the month, and displays the name of the day of the week. Here are some sample runs:

```
Enter year: (e.g., 2008): 2002 Enter
Enter month: 1-12: 3 Enter
Enter the day of the month: 1-31: 26 Enter
Day of the week is Tuesday
```

```
Enter year: (e.g., 2008): 2011 Enter
Enter month: 1-12: 5 Enter
Enter the day of the month: 1-31: 2 Enter
Day of the week is Thursday
```

(*Hint*: $\lfloor n \rfloor$ = (int)n for a positive n. January and February are counted as 13 and 14 in the formula. So you need to convert the user input 1 to 13 and 2 to 14 for the month and change the year to the previous year.)

3.22** (*Geometry: point in a circle?*) Write a program that prompts the user to enter a point (x, y) and checks whether the point is within the circle centered at (0, 0) with radius 10. For example, (4, 5) is inside the circle and (9, 9) is outside the circle, as shown in Figure 3.7(a).

(*Hint*: A point is in the circle if its distance to (0, 0) is less than or equal to 10. The formula for computing the distance is $\sqrt{(x_2 - x_1)^2 + (y_2 - y_1)^2}$.) Two sample runs are shown below.)

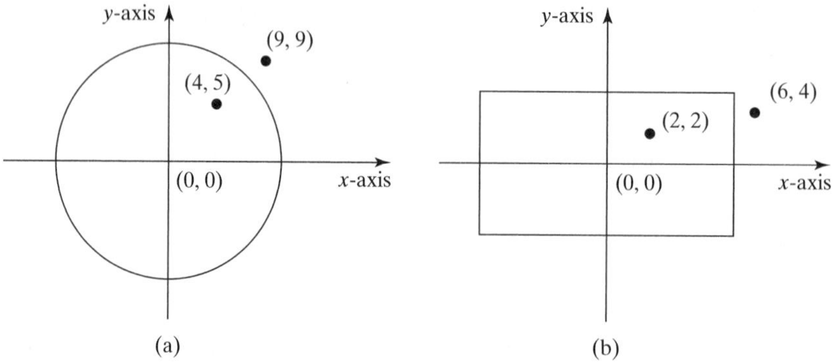
y-axis
(9, 9)
(4, 5)
(0, 0)
x-axis
(a)
y-axis
(6, 4)
(2, 2)
(0, 0)
x-axis
(b)

FIGURE 3.7 (a) Points inside and outside of the circle; (b) Points inside and outside of the rectangle.

```
Enter a point with two coordinates: 4 5 ↵Enter
Point (4.0, 5.0) is in the circle
```

```
Enter a point with two coordinates: 9 9 ↵Enter
Point (9.0, 9.0) is not in the circle
```

3.23** (*Geometry: point in a rectangle?*) Write a program that prompts the user to enter a point (x, y) and checks whether the point is within the rectangle centered at (0, 0) with width 10 and height 5. For example, (2, 2) is inside the rectangle and (6, 4) is outside the circle, as shown in Figure 3.7(b).

(*Hint*: A point is in the rectangle if its horizontal distance to (0, 0) is less than or equal to 10 / 2 and its vertical distance to (0, 0) is less than or equal to 5 / 2.] Here are two sample runs. Two sample runs are shown below.)

```
Enter a point with two coordinates: 2 2 ↵Enter
Point (2.0, 2.0) is in the rectangle
```

```
Enter a point with two coordinates: 6 4 ↵Enter
Point (6.0, 4.0) is not in the rectangle
```

3.24** (*Game: picking a card*) Write a program that simulates picking a card from a deck of 52 cards. Your program should display the rank (Ace, 2, 3, 4, 5, 6, 7, 8, 9, 10, Jack, Queen, King) and suit (Clubs, Diamonds, Hearts, Spades) of the card. Here is a sample run of the program:

```
The card you picked is Jack of Hearts
```

3.25** (*Computing the perimeter of a triangle*) Write a program that reads three edges for a triangle and computes the perimeter if the input is valid. Otherwise, display that the input is invalid. The input is valid if the sum of any two edges is greater than the third edge.

3.26 (*Using the &&, || and ^ operators*) Write a program that prompts the user to enter an integer and determines whether it is divisible by 5 and 6, whether it is divisible by 5 or 6, and whether it is divisible by 5 or 6, but not both. Here is a sample run of this program:

```
Enter an integer: 10 ↵Enter
Is 10 divisible by 5 and 6? false
Is 10 divisible by 5 or 6? true
Is 10 divisible by 5 or 6, but not both? true
```

3.27** (*Geometry: points in triangle?*) Suppose a right triangle is placed in a plane as shown below. The right-angle point is placed at (0, 0), and the other two points are placed at (200, 0), and (0, 100). Write a program that prompts the user to enter a point with x- and y-coordinates and determines whether the point is inside the triangle. Here are the sample runs:

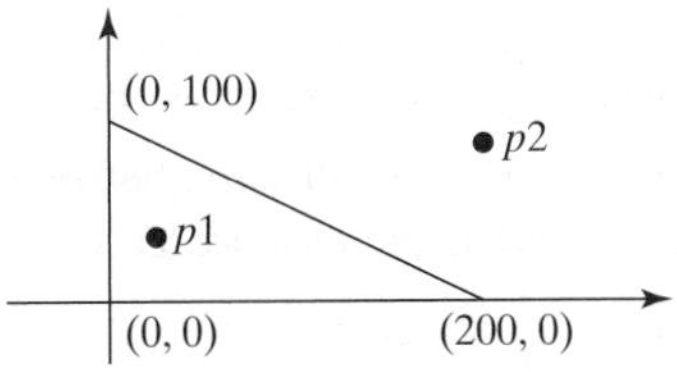
(0, 100)
p2
p1
(0, 0)
(200, 0)

```
Enter a point's x- and y-coordinates: 100.5 25.5 ↵Enter
The point is in the triangle
```

```
Enter a point's x- and y-coordinates: 100.5 50.5 ↵Enter
The point is not in the triangle
```

3.28** (*Geometry: two rectangles*) Write a program that prompts the user to enter the center *x*-, *y*-coordinates, width, and height of two rectangles and determines whether the second rectangle is inside the first or overlaps with the first, as shown in Figure 3.8.

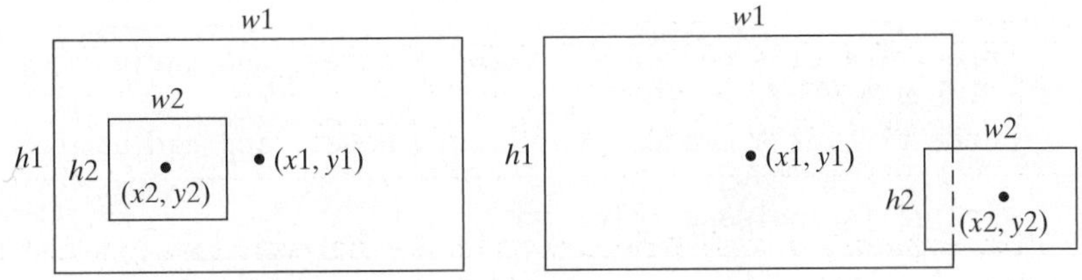
w1
w2
h1
h2
(x2, y2)
(x1, y1)
(a)
w1
h1
(x1, y1)
w2
h2
(x2, y2)
(b)

FIGURE 3.8 (a) A rectangle is inside another one. (b) A rectangle overlaps another one.

Here are the sample runs:

```
Enter r1's center x-, y-coordinates, width, and height:
  2.5 4 2.5 43 ↵Enter
Enter r2's center x-, y-coordinates, width, and height:
  1.5 5 0.5 3 ↵Enter
r2 is inside r1
```

```
Enter r1's center x-, y-coordinates, width, and height:
  1 2 3 5.5 ↵Enter
Enter r2's center x-, y-coordinates, width, and height:
  3 4 4.5 5 ↵Enter
r2 overlaps r1
```

```
Enter r1's center x-, y-coordinates, width, and height:
  1 2 3 3 ↵Enter
Enter r2's center x-, y-coordinates, width, and height:
  40 45 3 2 ↵Enter
r2 does not overlap r1
```

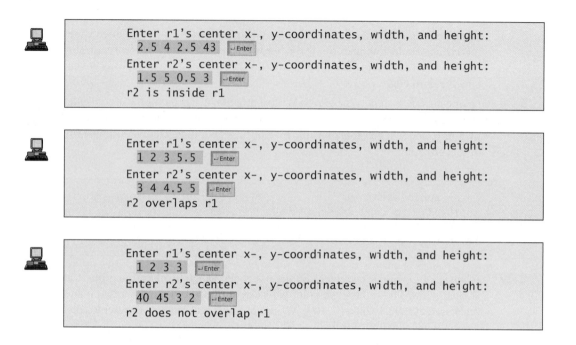

3.29** (*Geometry: two circles*) Write a program that prompts the user to enter the center coordinates and radii of two circles and determines whether the second circle is inside the first or overlaps with the first, as shown in Figure 3.9.

(*Hint*: circle2 is inside circle1 if the distance between the two centers <= `|r1 - r2|` and circle2 overlaps circle1 if the distance between the two centers <= `r1 + r2`.)

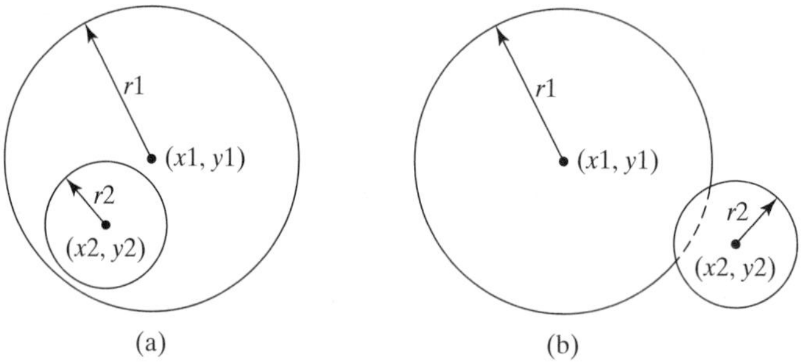
r1
(x1, y1)
r2
(x2, y2)
(a)
r1
(x1, y1)
r2
(x2, y2)
(b)

FIGURE 3.9 (a) A circle is inside another circle. (b) A circle overlaps another circle.

Here are the sample runs:

```
Enter circle1's center x-, y-coordinates, and radius:
  0.5 5.1 13 ↵Enter
Enter circle2's center x-, y-coordinates, and radius:
  1 1.7 4.5 ↵Enter
circle2 is inside circle1
```

```
Enter circle1's center x-, y-coordinates, and radius:
  3.4 5.7 5.5 ↵Enter
Enter circle2's center x-, y-coordinates, and radius:
  6.7 3.5 3 ↵Enter
circle2 overlaps circle1
```

```
Enter circle1's center x-, y-coordinates, and radius:
  3.4 5.5 1 ↵Enter
Enter circle2's center x-, y-coordinates, and radius:
  5.5 7.2 1 ↵Enter
circle2 does not overlap circle1
```

CHAPTER 4

LOOPS

Objectives

- To write programs for executing statements repeatedly using a `while` loop (§4.2).
- To develop a program for `GuessNumber` (§4.2.1).
- To follow the loop design strategy to develop loops (§4.2.2).
- To develop a program for `SubtractionQuizLoop` (§4.2.3).
- To control a loop with a sentinel value (§4.2.4).
- To obtain large input from a file using input redirection rather than typing from the keyboard (§4.2.4).
- To write loops using `do-while` statements (§4.3).
- To write loops using `for` statements (§4.4).
- To discover the similarities and differences of three types of loop statements (§4.5).
- To write nested loops (§4.6).
- To learn the techniques for minimizing numerical errors (§4.7).
- To learn loops from a variety of examples (`GCD`, `FutureTuition`, `MonteCarloSimulation`) (§4.8).
- To implement program control with `break` and `continue` (§4.9).
- (GUI) To control a loop with a confirmation dialog (§4.10).

4.1 Introduction

Suppose that you need to print a string (e.g., "Welcome to Java!") a hundred times. It would be tedious to have to write the following statement a hundred times:

```
          System.out.println("Welcome to Java!");
100 times System.out.println("Welcome to Java!");
          ...
          System.out.println("Welcome to Java!");
```

problem

why loop?

So, how do you solve this problem?

Java provides a powerful construct called a *loop* that controls how many times an operation or a sequence of operations is performed in succession. Using a loop statement, you simply tell the computer to print a string a hundred times without having to code the print statement a hundred times, as follows:

```
int count = 0;
while (count < 100) {
  System.out.println("Welcome to Java!");
  count++;
}
```

The variable count is initially 0. The loop checks whether (count < 100) is true. If so, it executes the loop body to print the message "Welcome to Java!" and increments count by 1. It repeatedly executes the loop body until (count < 100) becomes false. When (count < 100) is false (i.e., when count reaches 100), the loop terminates and the next statement after the loop statement is executed.

Loops are constructs that control repeated executions of a block of statements. The concept of looping is fundamental to programming. Java provides three types of loop statements: while loops, do-while loops, and for loops.

4.2 The while Loop

The syntax for the while loop is as follows:

while loop

```
while (loop-continuation-condition) {
  // Loop body
  Statement(s);
}
```

loop body

iteration

Figure 4.1(a) shows the while-loop flow chart. The part of the loop that contains the statements to be repeated is called the *loop body*. A one-time execution of a loop body is referred to as an *iteration of the loop*. Each loop contains a loop-continuation-condition, a Boolean expression that controls the execution of the body. It is evaluated each time to determine if the loop body is executed. If its evaluation is true, the loop body is executed; if its evaluation is false, the entire loop terminates and the program control turns to the statement that follows the while loop.

The loop for printing Welcome to Java! a hundred times introduced in the preceding section is an example of a while loop. Its flow chart is shown in Figure 4.1(b). The loop-continuation-condition is (count < 100) and loop body contains two statements as shown below:

loop-continuation-condition

```
int count = 0;
while (count < 100) {
  System.out.println("Welcome to Java!");   } loop body
  count++;
}
```

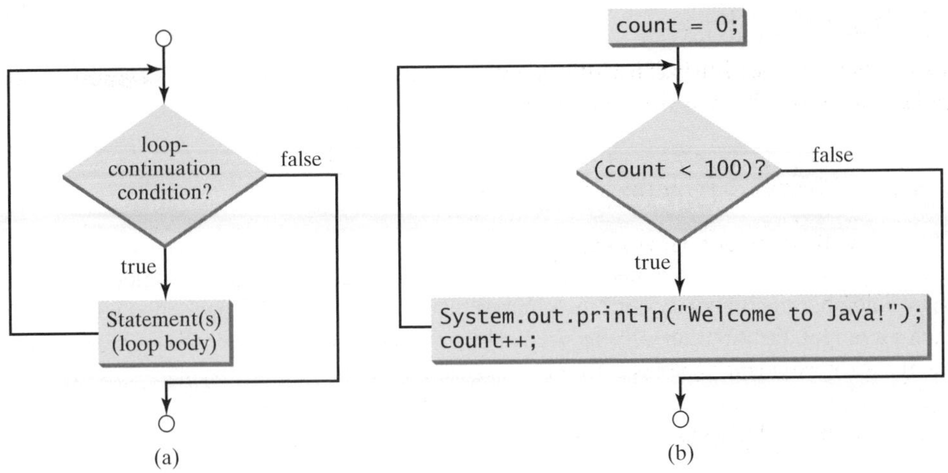
loop-
continuation
condition?
false
true
Statement(s)
(loop body)
(a)
count = 0;
(count < 100)?
false
true
System.out.println("Welcome to Java!");
count++;
(b)

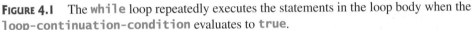

FIGURE 4.1 The `while` loop repeatedly executes the statements in the loop body when the `loop-continuation-condition` evaluates to `true`.

In this example, you know exactly how many times the loop body needs to be executed. So a control variable `count` is used to count the number of executions. This type of loop is known as a *counter-controlled loop*.

counter-controlled loop

Note

The `loop-continuation-condition` must always appear inside the parentheses. The braces enclosing the loop body can be omitted only if the loop body contains one or no statement.

Here is another example to help understand how a loop works.

```
int sum = 0, i = 1;
while (i < 10) {
  sum = sum + i;
  i++;
}
System.out.println("sum is " + sum); // sum is 45
```

If `i < 10` is `true`, the program adds `i` to `sum`. Variable `i` is initially set to `1`, then incremented to `2`, `3`, and up to `10`. When `i` is `10`, `i < 10` is `false`, the loop exits. So, the sum is `1 + 2 + 3 + ... + 9 = 45`.

What happens if the loop is mistakenly written as follows:

```
int sum = 0, i = 1;
while (i < 10) {
  sum = sum + i;
}
```

This loop is infinite, because `i` is always `1` and `i < 10` will always be `true`.

Caution

Make sure that the `loop-continuation-condition` eventually becomes `false` so that the program will terminate. A common programming error involves infinite loops. That is, the program cannot terminate because of a mistake in the `loop-continuation-condition`.

infinite loop

Programmers often make mistakes to execute a loop one more or less time. This is commonly known as the *off-by-one error*. For example, the following loop displays `Welcome to Java` 101 times rather than 100 times. The error lies in the condition, which should be `count < 100` rather than `count <= 100`.

off-by-one error

```
int count = 0;
while (count <= 100) {
  System.out.println("Welcome to Java!");
  count++;
}
```

4.2.1 Problem: Guessing Numbers

Video Note
Guess a number

The problem is to guess what a number a computer has in mind. You will write a program that randomly generates an integer between 0 and 100, inclusive. The program prompts the user to enter a number continuously until the number matches the randomly generated number. For each user input, the program tells the user whether the input is too low or too high, so the user can make the next guess intelligently. Here is a sample run:

```
Guess a magic number between 0 and 100

Enter your guess: 50 ↵Enter
Your guess is too high

Enter your guess: 25 ↵Enter
Your guess is too high

Enter your guess: 12 ↵Enter
Your guess is too high

Enter your guess: 6 ↵Enter
Your guess is too low

Enter your guess: 9 ↵Enter
Yes, the number is 9
```

intelligent guess

The magic number is between 0 and 100. To minimize the number of guesses, enter 50 first. If your guess is too high, the magic number is between 0 and 49. If your guess is too low, the magic number is between 51 and 100. So, you can eliminate half of the numbers from further consideration after one guess.

think before coding

How do you write this program? Do you immediately begin coding? No. It is important to *think before coding*. Think how you would solve the problem without writing a program. You need first to generate a random number between 0 and 100, inclusive, then to prompt the user to enter a guess, and then to compare the guess with the random number.

code incrementally

It is a good practice to *code incrementally* one step at a time. For programs involving loops, if you don't know how to write a loop right away, you may first write the code for executing the loop one time, and then figure out how to repeatedly execute the code in a loop. For this program, you may create an initial draft, as shown in Listing 4.1:

LISTING 4.1 GuessNumberOneTime.java

```
import java.util.Scanner;

public class GuessNumberOneTime {
  public static void main(String[] args) {
    // Generate a random number to be guessed
    int number = (int)(Math.random() * 101);          // generate a number

    Scanner input = new Scanner(System.in);
    System.out.println("Guess a magic number between 0 and 100");

    // Prompt the user to guess the number
    System.out.print("\nEnter your guess: ");
    int guess = input.nextInt();                      // enter a guess
```

```
14
15      if (guess == number)
16        System.out.println("Yes, the number is " + number);
17      else if (guess > number)
18        System.out.println("Your guess is too high");
19      else
20        System.out.println("Your guess is too low");
21    }
22 }
```

correct guess?

too high?

too low?

When you run this program, it prompts the user to enter a guess only once. To let the user enter a guess repeatedly, you may put the code in lines 11–20 in a loop as follows:

```
while (true) {
  // Prompt the user to guess the number
  System.out.print("\nEnter your guess: ");
  guess = input.nextInt();

  if (guess == number)
    System.out.println("Yes, the number is " + number);
  else if (guess > number)
    System.out.println("Your guess is too high");
  else
    System.out.println("Your guess is too low");
} // End of loop
```

This loop repeatedly prompts the user to enter a guess. However, this loop is not correct, because it never terminates. When **guess** matches **number**, the loop should end. So, the loop can be revised as follows:

```
while (guess != number) {
  // Prompt the user to guess the number
  System.out.print("\nEnter your guess: ");
  guess = input.nextInt();

  if (guess == number)
    System.out.println("Yes, the number is " + number);
  else if (guess > number)
    System.out.println("Your guess is too high");
  else
    System.out.println("Your guess is too low");
} // End of loop
```

The complete code is given in Listing 4.2.

LISTING 4.2 GuessNumber.java

```
import java.util.Scanner;

public class GuessNumber {
  public static void main(String[] args) {
    // Generate a random number to be guessed
    int number = (int)(Math.random() * 101);

    Scanner input = new Scanner(System.in);
    System.out.println("Guess a magic number between 0 and 100");

    int guess = -1;
    while (guess != number) {
```

generate a number

enter a guess

too high?

too low?

```
13       // Prompt the user to guess the number
14       System.out.print("\nEnter your guess: ");
15       guess = input.nextInt();
16
17       if (guess == number)
18         System.out.println("Yes, the number is " + number);
19       else if (guess > number)
20         System.out.println("Your guess is too high");
21       else
22         System.out.println("Your guess is too low");
23     } // End of loop
24   }
25 }
```

	line#	number	guess	output
	6	8		
	11		-1	
iteration 1	15		50	
	20			Your guess is too high
iteration 2	15		25	
	20			Your guess is too high
iteration 3	15		12	
	20			Your guess is too high
iteration 4	15		6	
	22			Your guess is too low
iteration 5	15		9	
	20			Yes, the number is 9

The program generates the magic number in line 6 and prompts the user to enter a guess continuously in a loop (lines 12–23). For each guess, the program checks whether the guess is correct, too high, or too low (lines 17–22). When the guess is correct, the program exits the loop (line 12). Note that `guess` is initialized to `-1`. Initializing it to a value between `0` and `100` would be wrong, because that could be the number to be guessed.

4.2.2 Loop Design Strategies

Writing a correct loop is not an easy task for novice programmers. Consider three steps when writing a loop.

Step 1: Identify the statements that need to be repeated.

Step 2: Wrap these statements in a loop like this:

```
while (true) {
  Statements;
}
```

Step 3: Code the loop-continuation-condition and add appropriate statements for controlling the loop.

```
while (loop-continuation-condition) {
  Statements;
  Additional statements for controlling the loop;
}
```

4.2.3 Problem: An Advanced Math Learning Tool

Video Note
Multiple subtraction quiz

The Math subtraction learning tool program in Listing 3.4, SubtractionQuiz.java, generates just one question for each run. You can use a loop to generate questions repeatedly. How do you write the code to generate five questions? Follow the loop design strategy. First identify the statements that need to be repeated. These are the statements for obtaining two random numbers, prompting the user with a subtraction question, and grading the question. Second, wrap the statements in a loop. Third, add a loop control variable and the loop-continuation-condition to execute the loop five times.

Listing 4.3 gives a program that generates five questions and, after a student answers all five, reports the number of correct answers. The program also displays the time spent on the test and lists all the questions.

LISTING 4.3 SubtractionQuizLoop.java

```
import java.util.Scanner;

public class SubtractionQuizLoop {
  public static void main(String[] args) {
    final int NUMBER_OF_QUESTIONS = 5; // Number of questions
    int correctCount = 0; // Count the number of correct answers
    int count = 0; // Count the number of questions
    long startTime = System.currentTimeMillis();
    String output = ""; // output string is initially empty
    Scanner input = new Scanner(System.in);

    while (count < NUMBER_OF_QUESTIONS) {
      // 1. Generate two random single-digit integers
      int number1 = (int)(Math.random() * 10);
      int number2 = (int)(Math.random() * 10);

      // 2. If number1 < number2, swap number1 with number2
      if (number1 < number2) {
        int temp = number1;
        number1 = number2;
        number2 = temp;
      }

      // 3. Prompt the student to answer "What is number1 - number2?"
      System.out.print(
        "What is " + number1 + " - " + number2 + "? ");
      int answer = input.nextInt();

      // 4. Grade the answer and display the result
      if (number1 - number2 == answer) {
        System.out.println("You are correct!");
        correctCount++;
      }
      else
        System.out.println("Your answer is wrong.\n" + number1
          + " - " + number2 + " should be " + (number1 - number2));

```

get start time

loop

display a question

grade an answer

increase correct count

increase control variable
prepare output
end loop
get end time
test time
display result

```
38       // Increase the count
39       count++;
40
41       output += "\n" + number1 + "-" + number2 + "=" + answer +
42         ((number1 - number2 == answer) ? " correct" : " wrong");
43     }
44
45     long endTime = System.currentTimeMillis();
46     long testTime = endTime - startTime;
47
48     System.out.println("Correct count is " + correctCount +
49       "\nTest time is " + testTime / 1000 + " seconds\n" + output);
50   }
51 }
```

```
What is 9 - 2? 7 ↵Enter
You are correct!

What is 3 - 0? 3 ↵Enter
You are correct!

What is 3 - 2? 1 ↵Enter
You are correct!

What is 7 - 4? 4 ↵Enter
Your answer is wrong.
7 - 4 should be 3

What is 7 - 5? 4 ↵Enter
Your answer is wrong.
7 - 5 should be 2

Correct count is 3
Test time is 1021 seconds

9-2=7 correct
3-0=3 correct
3-2=1 correct
7-4=4 wrong
7-5=4 wrong
```

The program uses the control variable **count** to control the execution of the loop. **count** is initially **0** (line 7) and is increased by **1** in each iteration (line 39). A subtraction question is displayed and processed in each iteration. The program obtains the time before the test starts in line 8 and the time after the test ends in line 45, and computes the test time in line 46. The test time is in milliseconds and is converted to seconds in line 49.

4.2.4 Controlling a Loop with a Sentinel Value

sentinel value

Another common technique for controlling a loop is to designate a special value when reading and processing a set of values. This special input value, known as a *sentinel value*, signifies the end of the loop. A loop that uses a sentinel value to control its execution is called a *sentinel-controlled loop*.

Listing 4.4 writes a program that reads and calculates the sum of an unspecified number of integers. The input **0** signifies the end of the input. Do you need to declare a new variable for each input value? No. Just use one variable named **data** (line 12) to store the input value and use a variable named **sum** (line 15) to store the total. Whenever a value is read, assign it to **data** and, if it is not zero, add it to **sum** (line 17).

LISTING 4.4 SentinelValue.java

```
1 import java.util.Scanner;
2
3 public class SentinelValue {
4   /** Main method */
5   public static void main(String[] args) {
6     // Create a Scanner
7     Scanner input = new Scanner(System.in);
8
9     // Read an initial data
10    System.out.print(
11      "Enter an int value (the program exits if the input is 0): ");
12    int data = input.nextInt();
13
14    // Keep reading data until the input is 0
15    int sum = 0;
16    while (data != 0) {
17      sum += data;
18
19      // Read the next data
20      System.out.print(
21        "Enter an int value (the program exits if the input is 0): ");
22      data = input.nextInt();
23    }
24
25    System.out.println("The sum is " + sum);
26  }
27 }
```

input

loop

end of loop

display result

```
Enter an int value (the program exits if the input is 0): 2 ↵Enter
Enter an int value (the program exits if the input is 0): 3 ↵Enter
Enter an int value (the program exits if the input is 0): 4 ↵Enter
Enter an int value (the program exits if the input is 0): 0 ↵Enter
The sum is 9
```

	line#	data	sum	output
	12	2		
	15		0	
iteration 1	17		2	
	22	3		
iteration 2	17		5	
	22	4		
iteration 3	17		9	
	22	0		
	25			The sum is 9

If **data** is not **0**, it is added to **sum** (line 17) and the next item of input data is read (lines 20–22). If **data** is **0**, the loop body is no longer executed and the **while** loop terminates. The input value **0** is the sentinel value for this loop. Note that if the first input read is **0**, the loop body never executes, and the resulting sum is **0**.

Caution

numeric error

Don't use floating-point values for equality checking in a loop control. Since floating-point values are approximations for some values, using them could result in imprecise counter values and inaccurate results.

Consider the following code for computing `1 + 0.9 + 0.8 + ... + 0.1`:

```
double item = 1; double sum = 0;
while (item != 0) { // No guarantee item will be 0
  sum += item;
  item -= 0.1;
}
System.out.println(sum);
```

Variable `item` starts with `1` and is reduced by `0.1` every time the loop body is executed. The loop should terminate when `item` becomes `0`. However, there is no guarantee that item will be exactly `0`, because the floating-point arithmetic is approximated. This loop seems OK on the surface, but it is actually an infinite loop.

4.2.5 Input and Output Redirections

In the preceding example, if you have a large number of data to enter, it would be cumbersome to type from the keyboard. You may store the data separated by whitespaces in a text file, say input.txt, and run the program using the following command:

```
java SentinelValue < input.txt
```

input redirection

This command is called *input redirection*. The program takes the input from the file input.txt rather than having the user to type the data from the keyboard at runtime. Suppose the contents of the file are

```
2 3 4 5 6 7 8 9 12 23 32
23 45 67 89 92 12 34 35 3 1 2 4 0
```

The program should get `sum` to be `518`.

output redirection

Similarly, there is *output redirection*, which sends the output to a file rather than displaying it on the console. The command for output redirection is:

```
java ClassName > output.txt
```

Input and output redirection can be used in the same command. For example, the following command gets input from input.txt and sends output to output.txt:

```
java SentinelValue < input.txt > output.txt
```

Please run the program and see what contents are in output.txt.

4.3 The do-while Loop

The `do-while` loop is a variation of the `while` loop. Its syntax is given below:

do-while loop

```
do {
  // Loop body;
  Statement(s);
} while (loop-continuation-condition);
```

Its execution flow chart is shown in Figure 4.2.

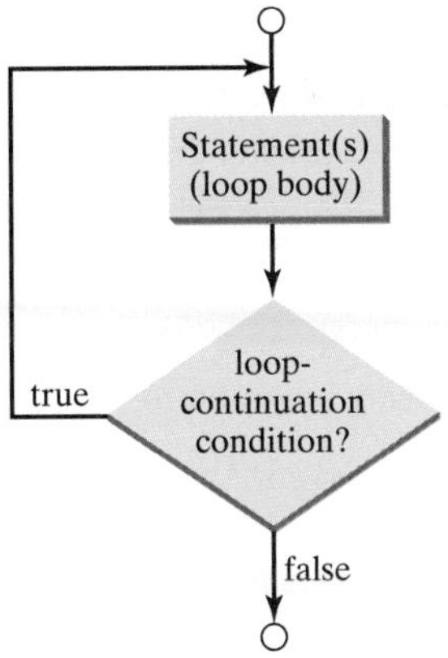
Statement(s)
(loop body)
loop-
continuation
condition?
true
false

FIGURE 4.2 The `do-while` loop executes the loop body first, then checks the `loop-continuation-condition` to determine whether to continue or terminate the loop.

The loop body is executed first. Then the `loop-continuation-condition` is evaluated. If the evaluation is `true`, the loop body is executed again; if it is `false`, the `do-while` loop terminates. The difference between a `while` loop and a `do-while` loop is the order in which the `loop-continuation-condition` is evaluated and the loop body executed. The `while` loop and the `do-while` loop have equal expressive power. Sometimes one is a more convenient choice than the other. For example, you can rewrite the `while` loop in Listing 4.4 using a `do-while` loop, as shown in Listing 4.5:

LISTING 4.5 TestDoWhile.java

```
import java.util.Scanner;

public class TestDoWhile {
  /** Main method */
  public static void main(String[] args) {
    int data;
    int sum = 0;

    // Create a Scanner
    Scanner input = new Scanner(System.in);

    // Keep reading data until the input is 0
    do {                                                    loop
      // Read the next data
      System.out.print(
        "Enter an int value (the program exits if the input is 0): ");
      data = input.nextInt();

      sum += data;
    } while (data != 0);                                    end loop

    System.out.println("The sum is " + sum);
  }
}
```

```
Enter an int value (the program exits if the input is 0): 3 Enter
Enter an int value (the program exits if the input is 0): 5 Enter
Enter an int value (the program exits if the input is 0): 6 Enter
Enter an int value (the program exits if the input is 0): 0 Enter
The sum is 14
```

Tip

Use the do-while loop if you have statements inside the loop that must be executed *at least once*, as in the case of the do-while loop in the preceding TestDoWhile program. These statements must appear before the loop as well as inside it if you use a while loop.

4.4 The **for** Loop

Often you write a loop in the following common form:

```
i = initialValue;  // Initialize loop control variable
while (i < endValue) {
  // Loop body
  ...
  i++; // Adjust loop control variable
}
```

A for loop can be used to simplify the proceding loop:

```
for (i = initialValue; i < endValue; i++) {
  // Loop body
  ...
}
```

In general, the syntax of a for loop is as shown below:

for loop

```
for (initial-action; loop-continuation-condition;
     action-after-each-iteration) {
  // Loop body;
  Statement(s);
}
```

The flow chart of the for loop is shown in Figure 4.3(a).

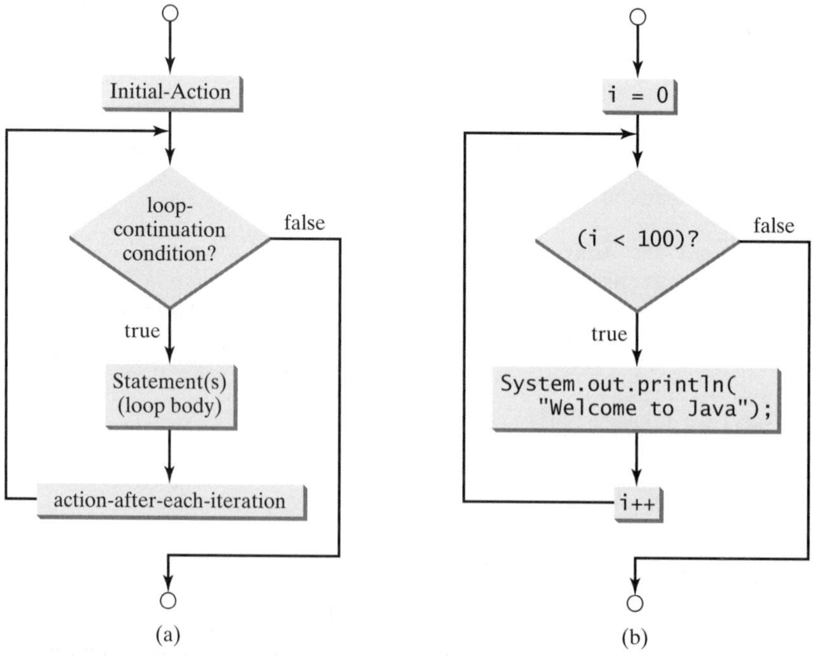
Initial-Action
loop-continuation condition?
false
true
Statement(s) (loop body)
action-after-each-iteration
(a)
i = 0
(i < 100)?
false
true
System.out.println(
"Welcome to Java");
i++
(b)

FIGURE 4.3 A for loop performs an initial action once, then repeatedly executes the statements in the loop body, and performs an action after an iteration when the loop-continuation-condition evaluates to true.

The `for` loop statement starts with the keyword `for`, followed by a pair of parentheses enclosing the control structure of the loop. This structure consists of `initial-action`, `loop-continuation-condition`, and `action-after-each-iteration`. The control structure is followed by the loop body enclosed inside braces. The `initial-action`, `loop-continuation-condition`, and `action-after-each-iteration` are separated by semicolons.

A `for` loop generally uses a variable to control how many times the loop body is executed and when the loop terminates. This variable is referred to as a *control variable*. The `initial-action` often initializes a control variable, the `action-after-each-iteration` usually increments or decrements the control variable, and the `loop-continuation-condition` tests whether the control variable has reached a termination value. For example, the following `for` loop prints `Welcome to Java!` a hundred times: control variable

```
int i;
for (i = 0; i < 100; i++) {
  System.out.println("Welcome to Java!");
}
```

The flow chart of the statement is shown in Figure 4.3(b). The `for` loop initializes `i` to `0`, then repeatedly executes the `println` statement and evaluates `i++` while `i` is less than `100`.

The `initial-action`, `i = 0`, initializes the control variable, `i`. The `loop-continuation-condition`, `i < 100`, is a Boolean expression. The expression is evaluated right after the initialization and at the beginning of each iteration. If this condition is `true`, the loop body is executed. If it is `false`, the loop terminates and the program control turns to the line following the loop. **`initial-action`**

The `action-after-each-iteration`, `i++`, is a statement that adjusts the control variable. This statement is executed after each iteration. It increments the control variable. Eventually, the value of the control variable should force the `loop-continuation-condition` to become `false`. Otherwise the loop is infinite. **`action-after-each-iteration`**

The loop control variable can be declared and initialized in the for loop. Here is an example:

```
for (int i = 0; i < 100; i++) {
  System.out.println("Welcome to Java!");
}
```

If there is only one statement in the loop body, as in this example, the braces can be omitted. omitting braces

Tip

The control variable must be declared inside the control structure of the loop or before the loop. If the loop control variable is used only in the loop, and not elsewhere, it is good programming practice to declare it in the `initial-action` of the `for` loop. If the variable is declared inside the loop control structure, it cannot be referenced outside the loop. In the preceding code, for example, you cannot reference `i` outside the `for` loop, because it is declared inside the `for` loop. declare control variable

Note

The `initial-action` in a `for` loop can be a list of zero or more comma-separated variable declaration statements or assignment expressions. For example, for loop variations

```
for (int i = 0, j = 0; (i + j < 10); i++, j++) {
  // Do something
}
```

The `action-after-each-iteration` in a `for` loop can be a list of zero or more comma-separated statements. For example,

```
for (int i = 1; i < 100; System.out.println(i), i++ );
```

This example is correct, but it is a bad example, because it makes the code difficult to read. Normally, you declare and initialize a control variable as an initial action and increment or decrement the control variable as an action after each iteration.

Note

If the `loop-continuation-condition` in a `for` loop is omitted, it is implicitly `true`. Thus the statement given below in (a), which is an infinite loop, is the same as in (b). To avoid confusion, though, it is better to use the equivalent loop in (c):

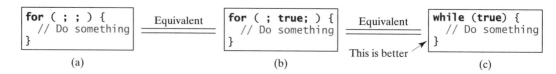

(a)
```
for ( ; ; ) {
  // Do something
}
```
Equivalent

(b)
```
for ( ; true; ) {
  // Do something
}
```
Equivalent — This is better

(c)
```
while (true) {
  // Do something
}
```

4.5 Which Loop to Use?

pretest loop
posttest loop

The `while` loop and `for` loop are called *pretest loops* because the continuation condition is checked before the loop body is executed. The `do-while` loop is called a *posttest loop* because the condition is checked after the loop body is executed. The three forms of loop statements, `while`, `do-while`, and `for`, are expressively equivalent; that is, you can write a loop in any of these three forms. For example, a `while` loop in (a) in the following figure can always be converted into the `for` loop in (b):

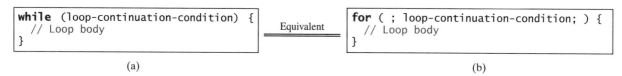

(a)
```
while (loop-continuation-condition) {
  // Loop body
}
```
Equivalent

(b)
```
for ( ; loop-continuation-condition; ) {
  // Loop body
}
```

A `for` loop in (a) in the next figure can generally be converted into the `while` loop in (b) except in certain special cases (see Review Question 4.17 for such a case):

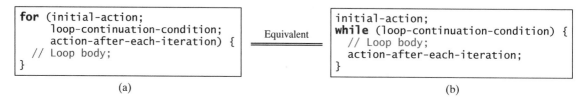

(a)
```
for (initial-action;
     loop-continuation-condition;
     action-after-each-iteration) {
  // Loop body;
}
```
Equivalent

(b)
```
initial-action;
while (loop-continuation-condition) {
  // Loop body;
  action-after-each-iteration;
}
```

Use the loop statement that is most intuitive and comfortable for you. In general, a `for` loop may be used if the number of repetitions is known in advance, as, for example, when you need to print a message a hundred times. A `while` loop may be used if the number of repetitions is not fixed, as in the case of reading the numbers until the input is `0`. A `do-while` loop can be used to replace a `while` loop if the loop body has to be executed before the continuation condition is tested.

Caution

Adding a semicolon at the end of the `for` clause before the loop body is a common mistake, as shown below in (a). In (a), the semicolon signifies the end of the loop prematurely. The loop body is actually empty, as shown in (b). (a) and (b) are equivalent.

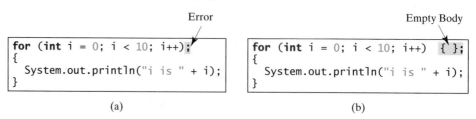

(a) Error
```
for (int i = 0; i < 10; i++);
{
  System.out.println("i is " + i);
}
```

(b) Empty Body
```
for (int i = 0; i < 10; i++) { };
{
  System.out.println("i is " + i);
}
```

Similarly, the loop in (c) is also wrong. (c) is equivalent to (d).

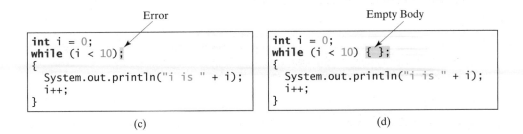

Error

```
int i = 0;
while (i < 10);
{
  System.out.println("i is " + i);
  i++;
}
```

(c)

Empty Body

```
int i = 0;
while (i < 10) { };
{
  System.out.println("i is " + i);
  i++;
}
```

(d)

These errors often occur when you use the next-line block style. Using the end-of-line block style can avoid errors of this type.

In the case of the `do-while` loop, the semicolon is needed to end the loop.

```
int i = 0;
do {
  System.out.println("i is " + i);
  i++;
} while (i < 10);
```

Correct

4.6 Nested Loops

Nested loops consist of an outer loop and one or more inner loops. Each time the outer loop is repeated, the inner loops are reentered, and started anew.

Listing 4.6 presents a program that uses nested `for` loops to print a multiplication table.

LISTING 4.6 `MultiplicationTable.java`

```
public class MultiplicationTable {
  /** Main method */
  public static void main(String[] args) {
    // Display the table heading
    System.out.println("           Multiplication Table");

    // Display the number title
    System.out.print("    ");
    for (int j = 1; j <= 9; j++)
      System.out.print("   " + j);

    System.out.println("\n-----------------------------------------");

    // Print table body
    for (int i = 1; i <= 9; i++) {
      System.out.print(i + " | ");
      for (int j = 1; j <= 9; j++) {
        // Display the product and align properly
        System.out.printf("%4d", i * j);
      }
      System.out.println()
    }
  }
}
```

table title

outer loop

inner loop

```
           Multiplication Table
        1   2   3   4   5   6   7   8   9
-----------------------------------------
1 |     1   2   3   4   5   6   7   8   9
2 |     2   4   6   8  10  12  14  16  18
3 |     3   6   9  12  15  18  21  24  27
4 |     4   8  12  16  20  24  28  32  36
5 |     5  10  15  20  25  30  35  40  45
6 |     6  12  18  24  30  36  42  48  54
7 |     7  14  21  28  35  42  49  56  63
8 |     8  16  24  32  40  48  56  64  72
9 |     9  18  27  36  45  54  63  72  81
```

The program displays a title (line 5) on the first line in the output. The first `for` loop (lines 9–10) displays the numbers `1` through `9` on the second line. A dash (`-`) line is displayed on the third line (line 12).

The next loop (lines 15–22) is a nested `for` loop with the control variable `i` in the outer loop and `j` in the inner loop. For each `i`, the product `i * j` is displayed on a line in the inner loop, with `j` being `1`, `2`, `3`, . . . , `9`.

4.7 Minimizing Numeric Errors

Video Note
Minimize numeric errors

Numeric errors involving floating-point numbers are inevitable. This section discusses how to minimize such errors through an example.

Listing 4.7 presents an example summing a series that starts with `0.01` and ends with `1.0`. The numbers in the series will increment by `0.01`, as follows: `0.01 + 0.02 + 0.03` and so on.

LISTING 4.7 TestSum.java

loop

```
1 public class TestSum {
2   public static void main(String[] args) {
3     // Initialize sum
4     float sum = 0;
5
6     // Add 0.01, 0.02, ..., 0.99, 1 to sum
7     for (float i = 0.01f; i <= 1.0f; i = i + 0.01f)
8       sum += i;
9
10    // Display result
11    System.out.println("The sum is " + sum);
12  }
13 }
```

```
The sum is 50.499985
```

The `for` loop (lines 7–8) repeatedly adds the control variable `i` to `sum`. This variable, which begins with `0.01`, is incremented by `0.01` after each iteration. The loop terminates when `i` exceeds `1.0`.

The `for` loop initial action can be any statement, but it is often used to initialize a control variable. From this example, you can see that a control variable can be a `float` type. In fact, it can be any data type.

The exact sum should be 50.50, but the answer is 50.499985. The result is imprecise because computers use a fixed number of bits to represent floating-point numbers, and thus they cannot represent some floating-point numbers exactly. If you change float in the program to double, as follows, you should see a slight improvement in precision, because a double variable takes 64 bits, whereas a float variable takes 32.

double precision

```
// Initialize sum
double sum = 0;

// Add 0.01, 0.02, ..., 0.99, 1 to sum
for (double i = 0.01; i <= 1.0; i = i + 0.01)
  sum += i;
```

However, you will be stunned to see that the result is actually 49.50000000000003. What went wrong? If you print out i for each iteration in the loop, you will see that the last i is slightly larger than 1 (not exactly 1). This causes the last i not to be added into sum. The fundamental problem is that the floating-point numbers are represented by approximation. To fix the problem, use an integer count to ensure that all the numbers are added to sum. Here is the new loop:

numeric error

```
double currentValue = 0.01;

for (int count = 0; count < 100; count++) {
  sum += currentValue;
  currentValue += 0.01;
}
```

After this loop, sum is 50.50000000000003. This loop adds the numbers from small to big. What happens if you add numbers from big to small (i.e., 1.0, 0.99, 0.98, ..., 0.02, 0.01 in this order) as follows:

```
double currentValue = 1.0;

for (int count = 0; count < 100; count++) {
  sum += currentValue;
  currentValue -= 0.01;
}
```

After this loop, sum is 50.49999999999995. Adding from big to small is less accurate than adding from small to big. This phenomenon is an artifact of the finite-precision arithmetic. Adding a very small number to a very big number can have no effect if the result requires more precision than the variable can store. For example, the inaccurate result of 100000000.0 + 0.000000001 is 100000000.0. To obtain more accurate results, carefully select the order of computation. Adding the smaller numbers before the big numbers is one way to minimize error.

avoiding numeric error

4.8 Case Studies

Loops are fundamental in programming. The ability to write loops is essential in learning Java programming. *If you can write programs using loops, you know how to program!* For this reason, this section presents three additional examples of solving problems using loops.

4.8.1 Problem: Finding the Greatest Common Divisor

The greatest common divisor of two integers 4 and 2 is 2. The greatest common divisor of two integers 16 and 24 is 8. How do you find the greatest common divisor? Let the two input integers be n1 and n2. You know that number 1 is a common divisor, but it may not be the gcd

greatest common divisor. So, you can check whether k (for k = 2, 3, 4, and so on) is a common divisor for n1 and n2, until k is greater than n1 or n2. Store the common divisor in a variable named gcd. Initially, gcd is 1. Whenever a new common divisor is found, it becomes the new gcd. When you have checked all the possible common divisors from 2 up to n1 or n2, the value in variable gcd is the greatest common divisor. The idea can be translated into the following loop:

```
int gcd = 1; // Initial gcd is 1
int k = 2; // Possible gcd

while (k <= n1 && k <= n2) {
  if (n1 % k == 0 && n2 % k == 0)
    gcd = k; // Update gcd
  k++; // Next possible gcd
}

// After the loop, gcd is the greatest common divisor for n1 and n2
```

Listing 4.8 presents the program that prompts the user to enter two positive integers and finds their greatest common divisor.

LISTING 4.8 GreatestCommonDivisor.java

input
input
gcd
check divisor
output

```
import java.util.Scanner;

public class GreatestCommonDivisor {
  /** Main method */
  public static void main(String[] args) {
    // Create a Scanner
    Scanner input = new Scanner(System.in);

    // Prompt the user to enter two integers
    System.out.print("Enter first integer: ");
    int n1 = input.nextInt();
    System.out.print("Enter second integer: ");
    int n2 = input.nextInt();

    int gcd = 1; // Initial gcd is 1
    int k = 2; // Possible gcd
    while (k <= n1 && k <= n2) {
      if (n1 % k == 0 && n2 % k == 0)
        gcd = k; // Update gcd
      k++;
    }

    System.out.println("The greatest common divisor for " + n1 +
      " and " + n2 + " is " + gcd);
  }
}
```

```
Enter first integer: 125 ↵Enter
Enter second integer: 2525 ↵Enter
The greatest common divisor for 125 and 2525 is 25
```

think before you type

How did you write this program? Did you immediately begin to write the code? No. It is important to *think before you type*. Thinking enables you to generate a logical solution for the problem without concern about how to write the code. Once you have a logical solution, type the code to translate the solution into a Java program. The translation is not unique. For example, you could use a for loop to rewrite the code as follows:

```
for (int k = 2; k <= n1 && k <= n2; k++) {
  if (n1 % k == 0 && n2 % k == 0)
    gcd = k;
}
```

multiple solutions

A problem often has multiple solutions. The gcd problem can be solved in many ways. Exercise 4.15 suggests another solution. A more efficient solution is to use the classic Euclidean algorithm. See http://www.cut-the-knot.org/blue/Euclid.shtml for more information.

erroneous solutions

You might think that a divisor for a number n1 cannot be greater than n1 / 2. So you would attempt to improve the program using the following loop:

```
for (int k = 2; k <= n1 / 2 && k <= n2 / 2 ; k++) {
  if (n1 % k == 0 && n2 % k == 0)
    gcd = k;
}
```

This revision is wrong. Can you find the reason? See Review Question 4.14 for the answer.

4.8.2 Problem: Predicating the Future Tuition

Suppose that the tuition for a university is $10,000 this year and tuition increases 7% every year. In how many years will the tuition be doubled?

Before you can write a program to solve this problem, first consider how to solve it by hand. The tuition for the second year is the tuition for the first year * 1.07. The tuition for a future year is the tuition of its preceding year * 1.07. So, the tuition for each year can be computed as follows:

```
double tuition = 10000;   int year = 1  // Year 1
tuition = tuition * 1.07; year++;       // Year 2
tuition = tuition * 1.07; year++;       // Year 3
tuition = tuition * 1.07; year++;       // Year 4
...
```

Keep computing tuition for a new year until it is at least 20000. By then you will know how many years it will take for the tuition to be doubled. You can now translate the logic into the following loop:

```
double tuition = 10000;   // Year 1
int year = 1;
while (tuition < 20000) {
  tuition = tuition * 1.07;
  year++;
}
```

The complete program is shown in Listing 4.9.

LISTING 4.9 FutureTuition.java

```
public class FutureTuition {
  public static void main(String[] args) {
    double tuition = 10000;   // Year 1
    int year = 1;
    while (tuition < 20000) {
```

loop

next year's tuition

```
6         tuition = tuition * 1.07;
7         year++;
8       }
9
10      System.out.println("Tuition will be doubled in "
11        + year + " years");
12    }
13 }
```

```
Tuition will be doubled in 12 years
```

The `while` loop (lines 5–8) is used to repeatedly compute the tuition for a new year. The loop terminates when tuition is greater than or equal to 20000.

4.8.3 Problem: Problem: Monte Carlo Simulation

Monte Carlo simulation uses random numbers and probability to solve problems. This method has a wide range of applications in computational mathematics, physics, chemistry, and finance. This section gives an example of using Monte Carlo simulation for estimating π.

To estimate π using the Monte Carlo method, draw a circle with its bounding square as shown below.

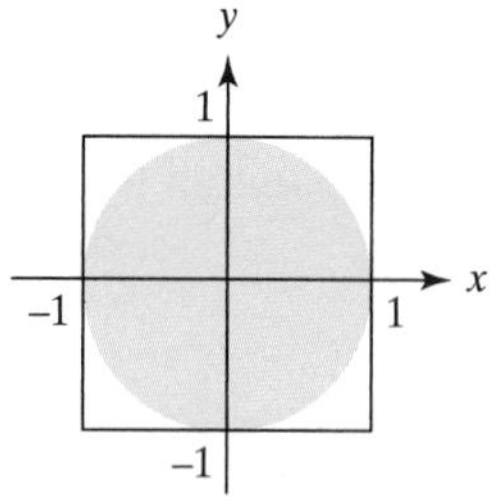

y
1
x
–1
1
–1

Assume the radius of the circle is 1. So, the circle area is π and the square area is 4. Randomly generate a point in the square. The probability for the point to fall in the circle is `circleArea / squareArea = π / 4`.

Write a program that randomly generates `1000000` points in the square and let `numberOfHits` denote the number of points that fall in the circle. So, `numberOfHits` is approximately `1000000 * (π / 4)`. π can be approximated as `4 * numberOfHits / 1000000`. The complete program is shown in Listing 4.10.

LISTING 4.10 MonteCarloSimulation.java

generate random points

check inside circle

estimate pi

```
public class MonteCarloSimulation {
  public static void main(String[] args) {
    final int NUMBER_OF_TRIALS = 10000000;
    int numberOfHits = 0;

    for (int i = 0; i < NUMBER_OF_TRIALS; i++) {
      double x = Math.random() * 2.0 - 1;
      double y = Math.random() * 2.0 - 1;
      if (x * x + y * y <= 1)
        numberOfHits++;
    }

    double pi = 4.0 * numberOfHits / NUMBER_OF_TRIALS;
```

```
14     System.out.println("PI is " + pi);
15   }
16 }
```

```
PI is 3.14124
```

The program repeatedly generates a random point (x, y) in the square in lines 7–8:

```
double x = Math.random() * 2.0 - 1;
double y = Math.random() * 2.0 - 1;
```

If $x^2 + y^2 \leq 1$, the point is inside the circle and `numberOfHits` is incremented by `1`. π is approximately `4 * numberOfHits / NUMBER_OF_TRIALS` (line 13).

4.9 Keywords *break* and *continue*

Pedagogical Note

Two keywords, `break` and `continue`, can be used in loop statements to provide additional controls. Using `break` and `continue` can simplify programming in some cases. Overusing or improperly using them, however, can make programs difficult to read and debug. (*Note to instructors*: You may skip this section without affecting the rest of the book.)

You have used the keyword `break` in a `switch` statement. You can also use `break` in a loop to immediately terminate the loop. Listing 4.11 presents a program to demonstrate the effect of using `break` in a loop. **break**

LISTING 4.11 TestBreak.java

```
1 public class TestBreak {
2   public static void main(String[] args) {
3     int sum = 0;
4     int number = 0;
5
6     while (number < 20) {
7       number++;
8       sum += number;
9       if (sum >= 100)
10        break;
11    }
12
13    System.out.println("The number is " + number);
14    System.out.println("The sum is " + sum);
15  }
16 }
```

break

```
The number is 14
The sum is 105
```

The program in Listing 4.11 adds integers from `1` to `20` in this order to `sum` until `sum` is greater than or equal to `100`. Without the `if` statement (line 9), the program calculates the sum of the numbers from `1` to `20`. But with the `if` statement, the loop terminates when `sum` becomes greater than or equal to `100`. Without the `if` statement, the output would be:

```
The number is 20
The sum is 210
```

continue

You can also use the continue keyword in a loop. When it is encountered, it ends the current iteration. Program control goes to the end of the loop body. In other words, continue breaks out of an iteration while the break keyword breaks out of a loop. Listing 4.12 presents a program to demonstrate the effect of using continue in a loop.

LISTING 4.12 TestContinue.java

continue

```
 1 public class TestContinue {
 2   public static void main(String[] args) {
 3     int sum = 0;
 4     int number = 0;
 5
 6     while (number < 20) {
 7       number++;
 8       if (number == 10 || number == 11)
 9         continue;
10       sum += number;
11     }
12
13     System.out.println("The sum is " + sum);
14   }
15 }
```

```
The sum is 189
```

The program in Listing 4.12 adds integers from 1 to 20 except 10 and 11 to sum. With the if statement in the program (line 8), the continue statement is executed when number becomes 10 or 11. The continue statement ends the current iteration so that the rest of the statement in the loop body is not executed; therefore, number is not added to sum when it is 10 or 11. Without the if statement in the program, the output would be as follows:

```
The sum is 210
```

In this case, all of the numbers are added to sum, even when number is 10 or 11. Therefore, the result is 210, which is 21 more than it was with the if statement.

Note

The continue statement is always inside a loop. In the while and do-while loops, the loop-continuation-condition is evaluated immediately after the continue statement. In the for loop, the action-after-each-iteration is performed, then the loop-continuation-condition is evaluated, immediately after the continue statement.

You can always write a program without using break or continue in a loop. See Review Question 4.18. In general, using break and continue is appropriate only if it simplifies coding and makes programs easier to read.

Listing 4.2 gives a program for guessing a number. You can rewrite it using a break statement, as shown in Listing 4.13.

LISTING 4.13 GuessNumberUsingBreak.java

generate a number

loop continuously

enter a guess

break

```java
import java.util.Scanner;

public class GuessNumberUsingBreak {
  public static void main(String[] args) {
    // Generate a random number to be guessed
    int number = (int)(Math.random() * 101);

    Scanner input = new Scanner(System.in);
    System.out.println("Guess a magic number between 0 and 100");

    while (true) {
      // Prompt the user to guess the number
      System.out.print("\nEnter your guess: ");
      int guess = input.nextInt();

      if (guess == number) {
        System.out.println("Yes, the number is " + number);
        break;
      }
      else if (guess > number)
        System.out.println("Your guess is too high");
      else
        System.out.println("Your guess is too low");
    } // End of loop
  }
}
```

Using the `break` statement makes this program simpler and easier to read. However, you should use `break` and `continue` with caution. Too many `break` and `continue` statements will produce a loop with many exit points and make the program difficult to read.

Note

goto

Some programming languages have a `goto` statement. The `goto` statement indiscriminately transfers control to any statement in the program and executes it. This makes your program vulnerable to errors. The `break` and `continue` statements in Java are different from `goto` statements. They operate only in a loop or a `switch` statement. The `break` statement breaks out of the loop, and the `continue` statement breaks out of the current iteration in the loop.

4.9.1 Problem: Displaying Prime Numbers

An integer greater than `1` is *prime* if its only positive divisor is `1` or itself. For example, `2`, `3`, `5`, and `7` are prime numbers, but `4`, `6`, `8`, and `9` are not.

The problem is to display the first 50 prime numbers in five lines, each of which contains ten numbers. The problem can be broken into the following tasks:

- Determine whether a given number is prime.
- For `number` = `2`, `3`, `4`, `5`, `6`, . . . , test whether it is prime.
- Count the prime numbers.
- Print each prime number, and print ten numbers per line.

Obviously, you need to write a loop and repeatedly test whether a new `number` is prime. If the `number` is prime, increase the count by `1`. The `count` is `0` initially. When it reaches `50`, the loop terminates.

Here is the algorithm for the problem:

```
Set the number of prime numbers to be printed as
  a constant NUMBER_OF_PRIMES;
Use count to track the number of prime numbers and
  set an initial count to 0;
Set an initial number to 2;

while (count < NUMBER_OF_PRIMES) {
  Test whether number is prime;

  if number is prime {
    Print the prime number and increase the count;
  }

  Increment number by 1;
}
```

To test whether a number is prime, check whether it is divisible by 2, 3, 4, up to `number/2`. If a divisor is found, the number is not a prime. The algorithm can be described as follows:

```
Use a boolean variable isPrime to denote whether
  the number is prime; Set isPrime to true initially;

for (int divisor = 2; divisor <= number / 2; divisor++) {
  if (number % divisor == 0) {
    Set isPrime to false
    Exit the loop;
  }
}
```

The complete program is given in Listing 4.14.

Listing 4.14 PrimeNumber.java

```java
public class PrimeNumber {
  public static void main(String[] args) {
    final int NUMBER_OF_PRIMES = 50; // Number of primes to display
    final int NUMBER_OF_PRIMES_PER_LINE = 10; // Display 10 per line
    int count = 0; // Count the number of prime numbers
    int number = 2; // A number to be tested for primeness

    System.out.println("The first 50 prime numbers are \n");

    // Repeatedly find prime numbers
    while (count < NUMBER_OF_PRIMES) {
      // Assume the number is prime
      boolean isPrime = true; // Is the current number prime?

      // Test whether number is prime
      for (int divisor = 2; divisor <= number / 2; divisor++) {
        if (number % divisor == 0) { // If true, number is not prime
          isPrime = false; // Set isPrime to false
          break; // Exit the for loop
        }
      }

      // Print the prime number and increase the count
      if (isPrime) {
        count++; // Increase the count
```

count prime numbers

check primeness

exit loop

print if prime

```
26
27         if (count % NUMBER_OF_PRIMES_PER_LINE == 0) {
28           // Print the number and advance to the new line
29           System.out.println(number);
30         }
31         else
32           System.out.print(number + " ");
33       }
34
35       // Check if the next number is prime
36       number++;
37     }
38   }
39 }
```

```
The first 50 prime numbers are

2 3 5 7 11 13 17 19 23 29
31 37 41 43 47 53 59 61 67 71
73 79 83 89 97 101 103 107 109 113
127 131 137 139 149 151 157 163 167 173
179 181 191 193 197 199 211 223 227 229
```

subproblem

This is a complex program for novice programmers. The key to developing a programmatic solution to this problem, and to many other problems, is to break it into subproblems and develop solutions for each of them in turn. Do not attempt to develop a complete solution in the first trial. Instead, begin by writing the code to determine whether a given number is prime, then expand the program to test whether other numbers are prime in a loop.

To determine whether a number is prime, check whether it is divisible by a number between 2 and number/2 inclusive (line 16). If so, it is not a prime number (line 18); otherwise, it is a prime number. For a prime number, display it. If the count is divisible by 10 (lines 27–30), advance to a new line. The program ends when the count reaches 50.

The program uses the break statement in line 19 to exit the for loop as soon as the number is found to be a nonprime. You can rewrite the loop (lines 16–21) without using the break statement, as follows:

```
for (int divisor = 2; divisor <= number / 2 && isPrime;
     divisor++) {
  // If true, the number is not prime
  if (number % divisor == 0) {
    // Set isPrime to false, if the number is not prime
    isPrime = false;
  }
}
```

However, using the break statement makes the program simpler and easier to read in this case.

4.10 (GUI) Controlling a Loop with a Confirmation Dialog

confirmation dialog

A sentinel-controlled loop can be implemented using a confirmation dialog. The answers *Yes* or *No* continue or terminate the loop. The template of the loop may look as follows:

```
int option = JOptionPane.YES_OPTION;
while (option == JOptionPane.YES_OPTION) {
  System.out.println("continue loop");
  option = JOptionPane.showConfirmDialog(null, "Continue?");
}
```

Listing 4.15 rewrites Listing 4.4, SentinelValue.java, using a confirmation dialog box. A sample run is shown in Figure 4.4.

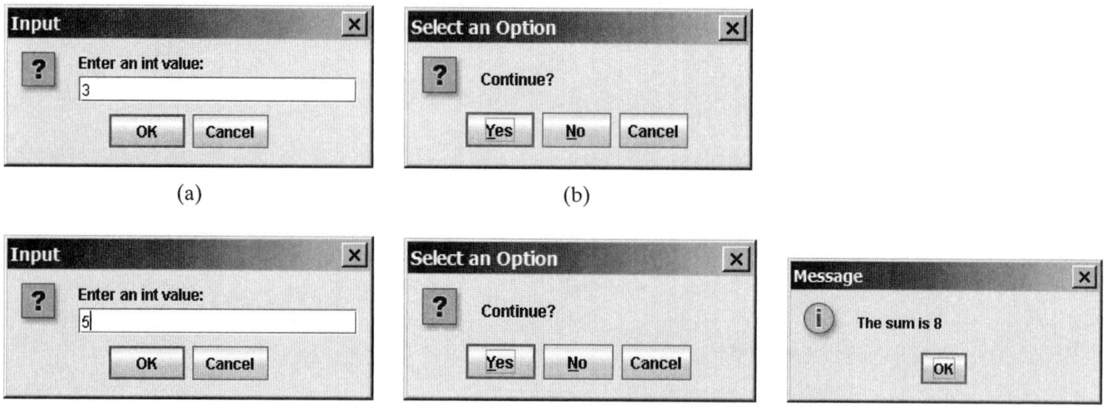
Input
Enter an int value:
3
OK
Cancel
Select an Option
Continue?
Yes
No
Cancel
Input
Enter an int value:
5
OK
Cancel
Select an Option
Continue?
Yes
No
Cancel
Message
The sum is 8
OK

(a) (b) (c) (d) (e)

FIGURE 4.4 The user enters 3 in (a), clicks Yes in (b), enters 5 in (c), clicks No in (d), and the result is shown in (e).

LISTING 4.15 SentinelValueUsingConfirmationDialog.java

confirmation option (line 8); check option (line 9); input dialog (line 11); confirmation dialog (line 17); message dialog (line 20)

```
1 import javax.swing.JOptionPane;
2
3 public class SentinelValueUsingConfirmationDialog {
4   public static void main(String[] args) {
5     int sum = 0;
6
7     // Keep reading data until the user answers No
8     int option = JOptionPane.YES_OPTION;
9     while (option == JOptionPane.YES_OPTION) {
10      // Read the next data
11      String dataString = JOptionPane.showInputDialog(
12        "Enter an int value: ");
13      int data = Integer.parseInt(dataString);
14
15      sum += data;
16
17      option = JOptionPane.showConfirmDialog(null, "Continue?");
18    }
19
20    JOptionPane.showMessageDialog(null, "The sum is " + sum);
21  }
22 }
```

A program displays an input dialog to prompt the user to enter an integer (line 11) and adds it to `sum` (line 15). Line 17 displays a confirmation dialog to let the user decide whether to continue the input. If the user clicks *Yes*, the loop continues; otherwise the loop exits. Finally the program displays the result in a message dialog box (line 20).

KEY TERMS

`break` statement 136
`continue` statement 136
`do-while` loop 124
`for` loop 126
loop control structure 127
infinite loop 117

Chapter Summary

1. There are three types of repetition statements: the `while` loop, the `do-while` loop, and the `for` loop.

2. The part of the loop that contains the statements to be repeated is called the *loop body*.

3. A one-time execution of a loop body is referred to as an *iteration of the loop*.

4. An infinite loop is a loop statement that executes infinitely.

5. In designing loops, you need to consider both the loop control structure and the loop body.

6. The `while` loop checks the `loop-continuation-condition` first. If the condition is `true`, the loop body is executed; if it is `false`, the loop terminates.

7. The `do-while` loop is similar to the `while` loop, except that the `do-while` loop executes the loop body first and then checks the `loop-continuation-condition` to decide whether to continue or to terminate.

8. Since the `while` loop and the `do-while` loop contain the `loop-continuation-condition`, which is dependent on the loop body, the number of repetitions is determined by the loop body. The `while` loop and the `do-while` loop often are used when the number of repetitions is unspecified.

9. A *sentinel value* is a special value that signifies the end of the loop.

10. The `for` loop generally is used to execute a loop body a predictable number of times; this number is not determined by the loop body.

11. The `for` loop control has three parts. The first part is an initial action that often initializes a control variable. The second part, the loop-continuation-condition, determines whether the loop body is to be executed. The third part is executed after each iteration and is often used to adjust the control variable. Usually, the loop control variables are initialized and changed in the control structure.

12. The `while` loop and `for` loop are called *pretest loops* because the continuation condition is checked before the loop body is executed.

13. The `do-while` loop is called *posttest loop* because the condition is checked after the loop body is executed.

14. Two keywords, `break` and `continue`, can be used in a loop.

15. The break keyword immediately ends the innermost loop, which contains the break.

16. The continue keyword only ends the current iteration.

Review Questions

Sections 4.2–4.4

4.1 Analyze the following code. Is count < 100 always true, always false, or sometimes true or sometimes false at Point A, Point B, and Point C?

```
int count = 0;
while (count < 100) {
  // Point A
  System.out.println("Welcome to Java!\n");
  count++;
  // Point B
}
  // Point C
```

4.2 What is wrong if guess is initialized to 0 in line 11 in Listing 4.2?

4.3 How many times is the following loop body repeated? What is the printout of the loop?

```
int i = 1;
while (i < 10)
  if (i % 2 == 0)
    System.out.println(i);
```

(a)

```
int i = 1;
while (i < 10)
  if (i % 2 == 0)
    System.out.println(i++);
```

(b)

```
int i = 1;
while (i < 10)
  if ((i++) % 2 == 0)
    System.out.println(i);
```

(c)

4.4 What are the differences between a while loop and a do-while loop? Convert the following while loop into a do-while loop.

```
int sum = 0;
int number = input.nextInt();
while (number != 0) {
  sum += number;
  number = input.nextInt();
}
```

4.5 Do the following two loops result in the same value in sum?

```
for (int i = 0; i < 10; ++i) {
  sum += i;
}
```

(a)

```
for (int i = 0; i < 10; i++) {
  sum += i;
}
```

(b)

4.6 What are the three parts of a for loop control? Write a for loop that prints the numbers from 1 to 100.

4.7 Suppose the input is 2 3 4 5 0. What is the output of the following code?

```
import java.util.Scanner;

public class Test {
```

```
  public static void main(String[] args) {
    Scanner input = new Scanner(System.in);

    int number, max;
    number = input.nextInt();
    max = number;

    while (number != 0) {
      number = input.nextInt();
      if (number > max)
        max = number;
    }

    System.out.println("max is " + max);
    System.out.println("number " + number);
  }
}
```

4.8 Suppose the input is 2 3 4 5 0. What is the output of the following code?

```
import java.util.Scanner;

public class Test {
  public static void main(String[] args) {
    Scanner input = new Scanner(System.in);

    int number, sum = 0, count;

    for (count = 0; count < 5; count++) {
      number = input.nextInt();
      sum += number;
    }

    System.out.println("sum is " + sum);
    System.out.println("count is " + count);
  }
}
```

4.9 Suppose the input is 2 3 4 5 0. What is the output of the following code?

```
import java.util.Scanner;

public class Test {
  public static void main(String[] args) {
    Scanner input = new Scanner(System.in);

    int number, max;
    number = input.nextInt();
    max = number;

    do {
      number = input.nextInt();
      if (number > max)
        max = number;
    } while (number != 0);

    System.out.println("max is " + max);
    System.out.println("number " + number);
  }
}
```

4.10 What does the following statement do?

```
for ( ; ; ) {
  do something;
}
```

4.11 If a variable is declared in the `for` loop control, can it be used after the loop exits?

4.12 Can you convert a `for` loop to a `while` loop? List the advantages of using `for` loops.

4.13 Convert the following `for` loop statement to a `while` loop and to a `do-while` loop:

```
long sum = 0;
for (int i = 0; i <= 1000; i++)
  sum = sum + i;
```

4.14 Will the program work if `n1` and `n2` are replaced by `n1 / 2` and `n2 / 2` in line 17 in Listing 4.8?

Section 4.9

4.15 What is the keyword `break` for? What is the keyword `continue` for? Will the following program terminate? If so, give the output.

```
int balance = 1000;
while (true) {
  if (balance < 9)
    break;
  balance = balance - 9;
}

System.out.println("Balance is "
  + balance);
```

(a)

```
int balance = 1000;
while (true) {
  if (balance < 9)
    continue;
  balance = balance - 9;
}

System.out.println("Balance is "
  + balance);
```

(b)

4.16 Can you always convert a `while` loop into a `for` loop? Convert the following `while` loop into a `for` loop.

```
int i = 1;
int sum = 0;
while (sum < 10000) {
  sum = sum + i;
  i++;
}
```

4.17 The `for` loop on the left is converted into the `while` loop on the right. What is wrong? Correct it.

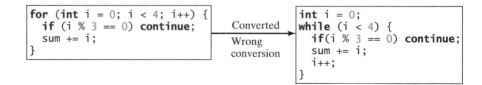

```
for (int i = 0; i < 4; i++) {
  if (i % 3 == 0) continue;
  sum += i;
}
```

Converted → Wrong conversion

```
int i = 0;
while (i < 4) {
  if(i % 3 == 0) continue;
  sum += i;
  i++;
}
```

4.18 Rewrite the programs `TestBreak` and `TestContinue` in Listings 4.11 and 4.12 without using `break` and `continue`.

4.19 After the `break` statement is executed in the following loop, which statement is executed? Show the output.

```
for (int i = 1; i < 4; i++) {
  for (int j = 1; j < 4; j++) {
    if (i * j > 2)
      break;

    System.out.println(i * j);
  }

  System.out.println(i);
}
```

4.20 After the `continue` statement is executed in the following loop, which statement is executed? Show the output.

```
for (int i = 1; i < 4; i++) {
  for (int j = 1; j < 4; j++) {
    if (i * j > 2)
      continue;

    System.out.println(i * j);
  }

  System.out.println(i);
}
```

Comprehensive

4.21 Identify and fix the errors in the following code:

```
public class Test {
  public void main(String[] args) {
    for (int i = 0; i < 10; i++);
      sum += i;

    if (i < j);
      System.out.println(i)
    else
      System.out.println(j);

    while (j < 10);
    {
      j++;
    };

    do {
      j++;
    } while (j < 10)
  }
}
```

4.22 What is wrong with the following programs?

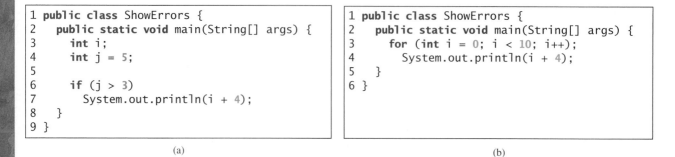

```
public class ShowErrors {
  public static void main(String[] args) {
    int i;
    int j = 5;

    if (j > 3)
      System.out.println(i + 4);
  }
}
```

(a)

```
public class ShowErrors {
  public static void main(String[] args) {
    for (int i = 0; i < 10; i++);
      System.out.println(i + 4);
  }
}
```

(b)

4.23 Show the output of the following programs. (*Tip*: Draw a table and list the variables in the columns to trace these programs.)

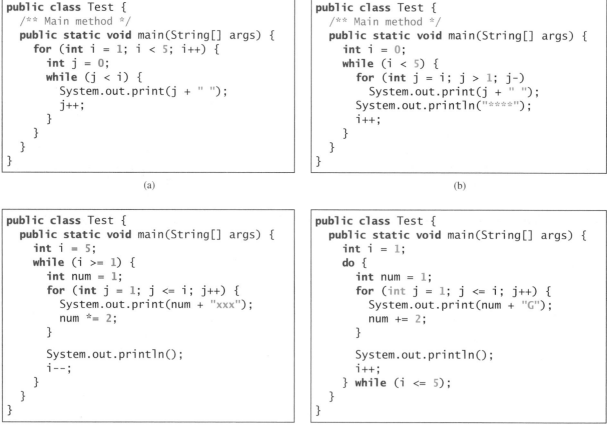

```
public class Test {
  /** Main method */
  public static void main(String[] args) {
    for (int i = 1; i < 5; i++) {
      int j = 0;
      while (j < i) {
        System.out.print(j + " ");
        j++;
      }
    }
  }
}
```

(a)

```
public class Test {
  /** Main method */
  public static void main(String[] args) {
    int i = 0;
    while (i < 5) {
      for (int j = i; j > 1; j-)
        System.out.print(j + " ");
      System.out.println("****");
      i++;
    }
  }
}
```

(b)

```
public class Test {
  public static void main(String[] args) {
    int i = 5;
    while (i >= 1) {
      int num = 1;
      for (int j = 1; j <= i; j++) {
        System.out.print(num + "xxx");
        num *= 2;
      }

      System.out.println();
      i--;
    }
  }
}
```

(c)

```
public class Test {
  public static void main(String[] args) {
    int i = 1;
    do {
      int num = 1;
      for (int j = 1; j <= i; j++) {
        System.out.print(num + "G");
        num += 2;
      }

      System.out.println();
      i++;
    } while (i <= 5);
  }
}
```

(d)

4.24 What is the output of the following program? Explain the reason.

```
int x = 80000000;

while (x > 0)
  x++;

System.out.println("x is " + x);
```

4.25 Count the number of iterations in the following loops.

```
int count = 0;
while (count < n) {
  count++;
}
```

(a)

```
for (int count = 0;
    count <= n; count++) {
}
```

(b)

```
int count = 5;
while (count < n) {
  count++;
}
```

(c)

```
int count = 5;
while (count < n) {
  count = count + 3;
}
```

(d)

Programming Exercises

Pedagogical Note

For each problem, read it several times until you understand the problem. Think how to solve the problem before coding. Translate your logic into a program.

read and think before coding

A problem often can be solved in many different ways. Students are encouraged to explore various solutions.

explore solutions

Sections 4.2–4.7

4.1* (*Counting positive and negative numbers and computing the average of numbers*) Write a program that reads an unspecified number of integers, determines how many positive and negative values have been read, and computes the total and average of the input values (not counting zeros). Your program ends with the input 0. Display the average as a floating-point number. Here is a sample run:

```
Enter an int value, the program exits if the input is 0:
  1 2 -1 3 0 ↵Enter
The number of positives is 3
The number of negatives is 1
The total is 5
The average is 1.25
```

4.2 (*Repeating additions*) Listing 4.3, SubtractionQuizLoop.java, generates five random subtraction questions. Revise the program to generate ten random addition questions for two integers between 1 and 15. Display the correct count and test time.

4.3 (*Conversion from kilograms to pounds*) Write a program that displays the following table (note that 1 kilogram is 2.2 pounds):

```
Kilograms      Pounds
1                2.2
3                6.6
...
197            433.4
199            437.8
```

4.4 (*Conversion from miles to kilometers*) Write a program that displays the following table (note that 1 mile is 1.609 kilometers):

```
Miles     Kilometers
1         1.609
2         3.218
...
9         14.481
10        16.090
```

4.5 (*Conversion from kilograms to pounds*) Write a program that displays the following two tables side by side (note that 1 kilogram is 2.2 pounds):

```
Kilograms     Pounds          Pounds          Kilograms
1             2.2             20              9.09
3             6.6             25              11.36
...
197           433.4           510             231.82
199           437.8           515             234.09
```

4.6 (*Conversion from miles to kilometers*) Write a program that displays the following two tables side by side (note that 1 mile is 1.609 kilometers):

```
Miles     Kilometers     Kilometers      Miles
1         1.609          20              12.430
2         3.218          25              15.538
...
9         14.481         60              37.290
10        16.090         65              40.398
```

4.7** (*Financial application: computing future tuition*) Suppose that the tuition for a university is $10,000 this year and increases 5% every year. Write a program that computes the tuition in ten years and the total cost of four years' worth of tuition starting ten years from now.

4.8 (*Finding the highest score*) Write a program that prompts the user to enter the number of students and each student's name and score, and finally displays the name of the student with the highest score.

4.9* (*Finding the two highest scores*) Write a program that prompts the user to enter the number of students and each student's name and score, and finally displays the student with the highest score and the student with the second-highest score.

4.10 (*Finding numbers divisible by* 5 and 6) Write a program that displays all the numbers from 100 to 1000, ten per line, that are divisible by 5 and 6.

4.11 (*Finding numbers divisible by* 5 or 6, *but not both*) Write a program that displays all the numbers from 100 to 200, ten per line, that are divisible by 5 or 6, but not both.

4.12 (*Finding the smallest* n such that $n^2 > 12,000$) Use a `while` loop to find the smallest integer n such that n^2 is greater than 12,000.

4.13 (*Finding the largest* n such that $n^3 < 12,000$) *Use a* `while` loop to find the largest integer n such that n^3 is less than 12,000.

4.14* (*Displaying the ACSII character table*) Write a program that prints the characters in the ASCII character table from '!' to '~'. Print ten characters per line. The ASCII table is shown in Appendix B.

Section 4.8

4.15* (*Computing the greatest common divisor*) Another solution for Listing 4.8 to find the greatest common divisor of two integers `n1` and `n2` is as follows: First find `d` to be the minimum of `n1` and `n2`, then check whether `d`, `d-1`, `d-2`, . . . , `2`, or `1` is a divisor for both `n1` and `n2` in this order. The first such common divisor is the greatest common divisor for `n1` and `n2`. Write a program that prompts the user to enter two positive integers and displays the gcd.

4.16** (*Finding the factors of an integer*) Write a program that reads an integer and displays all its smallest factors in increasing order. For example, if the input integer is `120`, the output should be as follows: `2`, `2`, `2`, `3`, `5`.

4.17** (*Displaying pyramid*) Write a program that prompts the user to enter an integer from `1` to `15` and displays a pyramid, as shown in the following sample run:

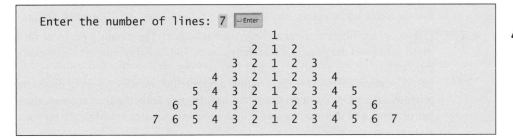

```
Enter the number of lines: 7 ↵Enter
                        1
                     2  1  2
                  3  2  1  2  3
               4  3  2  1  2  3  4
            5  4  3  2  1  2  3  4  5
         6  5  4  3  2  1  2  3  4  5  6
      7  6  5  4  3  2  1  2  3  4  5  6  7
```

4.18* (*Printing four patterns using loops*) Use nested loops that print the following patterns in four separate programs:

```
Pattern I       Pattern II      Pattern III     Pattern IV
1               1 2 3 4 5 6               1     1 2 3 4 5 6
1 2             1 2 3 4 5               2 1       1 2 3 4 5
1 2 3           1 2 3 4               3 2 1         1 2 3 4
1 2 3 4         1 2 3               4 3 2 1           1 2 3
1 2 3 4 5       1 2               5 4 3 2 1             1 2
1 2 3 4 5 6     1               6 5 4 3 2 1               1
```

4.19** (*Printing numbers in a pyramid pattern*) Write a nested `for` loop that prints the following output:

```
                              1
                          1   2   1
                      1   2   4   2   1
                  1   2   4   8   4   2   1
              1   2   4   8  16   8   4   2   1
          1   2   4   8  16  32  16   8   4   2   1
      1   2   4   8  16  32  64  32  16   8   4   2   1
  1   2   4   8  16  32  64 128  64  32  16   8   4   2   1
```

4.20* (*Printing prime numbers between 2 and 1000*) Modify Listing 4.14 to print all the prime numbers between 2 and 1000, inclusive. Display eight prime numbers per line.

Comprehensive

4.21** (*Financial application: comparing loans with various interest rates*) Write a program that lets the user enter the loan amount and loan period in number of years and displays the monthly and total payments for each interest rate starting from 5% to 8%, with an increment of 1/8. Here is a sample run:

```
Loan Amount: 10000 ↵Enter
Number of Years: 5 ↵Enter
Interest Rate            Monthly Payment    Total Payment

5%                       188.71             11322.74
5.125%                   189.28             11357.13
5.25%                    189.85             11391.59
...
7.875%                   202.17             12129.97
8.0%                     202.76             12165.83
```

For the formula to compute monthly payment, see Listing 2.8, ComputeLoan.java.

Video Note
Display loan schedule

4.22** (*Financial application: loan amortization schedule*) The monthly payment for a given loan pays the principal and the interest. The monthly interest is computed by multiplying the monthly interest rate and the balance (the remaining principal). The principal paid for the month is therefore the monthly payment minus the monthly interest. Write a program that lets the user enter the loan amount, number of years, and interest rate and displays the amortization schedule for the loan. Here is a sample run:

```
Loan Amount: 10000
Number of Years: 1
Annual Interest Rate: 7%

Monthly Payment: 865.26
Total Payment: 10383.21

Payment#          Interest          Principal          Balance

1                 58.33             806.93             9193.07
2                 53.62             811.64             8381.43
...
11                10.0              855.26             860.27
12                5.01              860.25             0.01
```

Note

The balance after the last payment may not be zero. If so, the last payment should be the normal monthly payment plus the final balance.

Hint: Write a loop to print the table. Since the monthly payment is the same for each month, it should be computed before the loop. The balance is initially the loan amount. For each iteration in the loop, compute the interest and principal, and update the balance. The loop may look like this:

```
for (i = 1; i <= numberOfYears * 12; i++) {
  interest = monthlyInterestRate * balance;
  principal = monthlyPayment - interest;
  balance = balance - principal;
  System.out.println(i + "\t\t" + interest
    + "\t\t" + principal + "\t\t" + balance);
}
```

4.23* (*Obtaining more accurate results*) In computing the following series, you will obtain more accurate results by computing from right to left rather than from left to right:

$$1 + \frac{1}{2} + \frac{1}{3} + \ldots + \frac{1}{n}$$

Write a program that compares the results of the summation of the preceding series, computing from left to right and from right to left with `n = 50000`.

4.24* (*Summing a series*) Write a program to sum the following series:

$$\frac{1}{3} + \frac{3}{5} + \frac{5}{7} + \frac{7}{9} + \frac{9}{11} + \frac{11}{13} + \ldots + \frac{95}{97} + \frac{97}{99}$$

4.25** (*Computing π*) You can approximate π by using the following series:

$$\pi = 4\left(1 - \frac{1}{3} + \frac{1}{5} - \frac{1}{7} + \frac{1}{9} - \frac{1}{11} + \ldots + \frac{1}{2i-1} - \frac{1}{2i+1}\right)$$

Write a program that displays the π value for `i = 10000, 20000, ...,` and `100000`.

4.26** (*Computing e*) You can approximate `e` using the following series:

$$e = 1 + \frac{1}{1!} + \frac{1}{2!} + \frac{1}{3!} + \frac{1}{4!} + \ldots + \frac{1}{i!}$$

Write a program that displays the `e` value for `i = 10000, 20000, ...,` and `100000`.

(*Hint*: Since $i! = i \times (i - 1) \times \ldots \times 2 \times 1$, then $\frac{1}{i!}$ is $\frac{1}{i(i-1)!}$

Initialize `e` and `item` to be `1` and keep adding a new `item` to `e`. The new item is the previous item divided by `i` for i = `2, 3, 4, ....`)

4.27** (*Displaying leap years*) Write a program that displays all the leap years, ten per line, in the twenty-first century (from 2001 to 2100).

4.28** (*Displaying the first days of each month*) Write a program that prompts the user to enter the year and first day of the year, and displays the first day of each month in the year on the console. For example, if the user entered the year `2005`, and `6` for Saturday, January 1, 2005, your program should display the following output (note that Sunday is `0`):

```
January 1, 2005 is Saturday
...
December 1, 2005 is Thursday
```

4.29** (*Displaying calendars*) Write a program that prompts the user to enter the year and first day of the year and displays the calendar table for the year on the console. For example, if the user entered the year `2005`, and `6` for Saturday, January 1, 2005, your program should display the calendar for each month in the year, as follows:

January 2005

Sun	Mon	Tue	Wed	Thu	Fri	Sat
						1
2	3	4	5	6	7	8
9	10	11	12	13	14	15
16	17	18	19	20	21	22
23	24	25	26	27	28	29
30	31					

...

December 2005

Sun	Mon	Tue	Wed	Thu	Fri	Sat
				1	2	3
4	5	6	7	8	9	10
11	12	13	14	15	16	17
18	19	20	21	22	23	24
25	26	27	28	29	30	31

4.30* (*Financial application: compound value*) Suppose you save $100 *each* month into a savings account with the annual interest rate 5%. So, the monthly interest rate is `0.05 / 12 = 0.00417`. After the first month, the value in the account becomes

```
100 * (1 + 0.00417) = 100.417
```

After the second month, the value in the account becomes

```
(100 + 100.417) * (1 + 0.00417) = 201.252
```

After the third month, the value in the account becomes

```
(100 + 201.252) * (1 + 0.00417) = 302.507
```

and so on.

Write a program that prompts the user to enter an amount (e.g., 100), the annual interest rate (e.g., 5), and the number of months (e.g., 6) and displays the amount in the savings account after the given month.

4.31* (*Financial application: computing CD value*) Suppose you put $10,000 into a CD with an annual percentage yield of 5.75%. After one month, the CD is worth

```
10000 + 10000 * 5.75 / 1200 = 10047.91
```

After two months, the CD is worth

```
10047.91 + 10047.91 * 5.75 / 1200 = 10096.06
```

After three months, the CD is worth

```
10096.06 + 10096.06 * 5.75 / 1200 = 10144.43
```

and so on.

Write a program that prompts the user to enter an amount (e.g., 10000), the annual percentage yield (e.g., `5.75`), and the number of months (e.g., 18) and displays a table as shown in the sample run.

```
Enter the initial deposit amount: 10000 ↵Enter
Enter annual percentage yield: 5.75 ↵Enter
Enter maturity period (number of months): 18 ↵Enter

Month                 CD Value
1                     10047.91
2                     10096.06
...
17                    10846.56
18                    10898.54
```

4.32** (*Game: lottery*) Revise Listing 3.9, Lottery.java, to generate a lottery of a two-digit number. The two digits in the number are distinct.

(*Hint*: Generate the first digit. Use a loop to continuously generate the second digit until it is different from the first digit.)

4.33** (*Perfect number*) A positive integer is called a *perfect number* if it is equal to the sum of all of its positive divisors, excluding itself. For example, 6 is the first perfect number because 6 = 3 + 2 + 1. The next is 28 = 14 + 7 + 4 + 2 + 1. There are four perfect numbers less than 10000. Write a program to find all these four numbers.

4.34*** (*Game: scissor, rock, paper*) Exercise 3.17 gives a program that plays the scissor-rock-paper game. Revise the program to let the user continuously play until either the user or the computer wins more than two times.

4.35* (*Summation*) Write a program that computes the following summation.

$$\frac{1}{1+\sqrt{2}} + \frac{1}{\sqrt{2}+\sqrt{3}} + \frac{1}{\sqrt{3}+\sqrt{4}} + \ldots + \frac{1}{\sqrt{624}+\sqrt{625}}$$

4.36** (*Business application: checking ISBN*) Use loops to simplify Exercise 3.19.

4.37** (*Decimal to binary*) Write a program that prompts the user to enter a decimal integer and displays its corresponding binary value. Don't use Java's `Integer.toBinaryString(int)` in this program.

4.38** (*Decimal to hex*) Write a program that prompts the user to enter a decimal integer and displays its corresponding hexadecimal value. Don't use Java's `Integer.toHexString(int)` in this program.

4.39* (*Financial application: finding the sales amount*) You have just started a sales job in a department store. Your pay consists of a base salary and a commission. The base salary is $5,000. The scheme shown below is used to determine the commission rate.

Sales Amount	Commission Rate
$0.01–$5,000	8 percent
$5,000.01–$10,000	10 percent
$10,000.01 and above	12 percent

Your goal is to earn $30,000 a year. Write a program that finds out the minimum amount of sales you have to generate in order to make $30,000.

4.40 (*Simulation: head or tail*) Write a program that simulates flipping a coin one million times and displays the number of heads and tails.

4.41** (*Occurrence of max numbers*) Write a program that reads integers, finds the largest of them, and counts its occurrences. Assume that the input ends with number 0. Suppose that you entered 3 5 2 5 5 5 0; the program finds that the largest is 5 and the occurrence count for 5 is 4.

(*Hint*: Maintain two variables, `max` and `count`. `max` stores the current max number, and `count` stores its occurrences. Initially, assign the first number to `max` and 1 to `count`. Compare each subsequent number with `max`. If the number is greater than `max`, assign it to `max` and reset `count` to 1. If the number is equal to `max`, increment `count` by 1.)

```
Enter numbers: 3 5 2 5 5 5 0 ↵Enter
The largest number is 5
The occurrence count of the largest number is 4
```

4.42* (*Financial application: finding the sales amount*) Rewrite Exercise 4.39 as follows:

- Use a `for` loop instead of a `do-while` loop.
- Let the user enter `COMMISSION_SOUGHT` instead of fixing it as a constant.

4.43* (*Simulation: clock countdown*) Write a program that prompts the user to enter the number of seconds, displays a message at every second, and terminates when the time expires. Here is a sample run:

```
Enter the number of second: 3 ↵Enter
2 seconds remaining
1 second remaining
Stopped
```

4.44** (*Monte Carlo simulation*) A square is divided into four smaller regions as shown below in (a). If you throw a dart into the square 1000000 times, what is the probability for a dart to fall into an odd-numbered region? Write a program to simulate the process and display the result.

(*Hint*: Place the center of the square in the center of a coordinate system, as shown in (b). Randomly generate a point in the square and count the number of times a point falls into an odd-numbered region.)

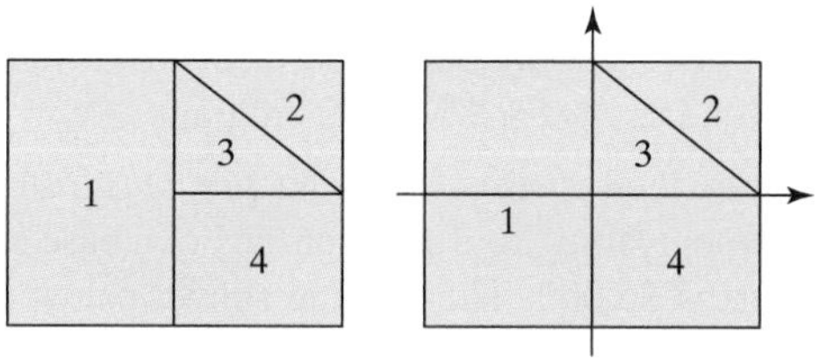
1
2
3
4
1
2
3
4

(a) (b)

4.45* (*Math: combinations*) Write a program that displays all possible combinations for picking two numbers from integers `1` to `7`. Also display the total number of all combinations.

```
1 2
1 3
...
...
```

4.46* (*Computer architecture: bit-level operations*) A `short` value is stored in `16` bits. Write a program that prompts the user to enter a short integer and displays the `16` bits for the integer. Here are sample runs:

```
Enter an integer: 5 ↵Enter
The bits are 0000000000000101
```

```
Enter an integer: -5 ↵Enter
The bits are 1111111111111011
```

(*Hint*: You need to use the bitwise right shift operator (`>>`) and the bitwise AND operator (`&`), which are covered in Supplement III.D on the Companion Website.)

CHAPTER 5

METHODS

Objectives

- To define methods (§5.2).
- To invoke methods with a return value (§5.3).
- To invoke methods without a return value (§5.4).
- To pass arguments by value (§5.5).
- To develop reusable code that is modular, easy to read, easy to debug, and easy to maintain (§5.6).
- To write a method that converts decimals to hexadecimals (§5.7).
- To use method overloading and understand ambiguous overloading (§5.8).
- To determine the scope of variables (§5.9).
- To solve mathematics problems using the methods in the `Math` class (§§5.10–5.11).
- To apply the concept of method abstraction in software development (§5.12).
- To design and implement methods using stepwise refinement (§5.12).

5.1 Introduction

problem

Suppose that you need to find the sum of integers from 1 to 10, from 20 to 30, and from 35 to 45, respectively. You may write the code as follows:

```
int sum = 0;
for (int i = 1; i <= 10; i++)
  sum += i;
System.out.println("Sum from 1 to 10 is " + sum);

sum = 0;
for (int i = 20; i <= 30; i++)
  sum += i;
System.out.println("Sum from 20 to 30 is " + sum);

sum = 0;
for (int i = 35; i <= 45; i++)
  sum += i;
System.out.println("Sum from 35 to 45 is " + sum);
```

why methods?

You may have observed that computing sum from 1 to 10, from 20 to 30, and from 35 to 45 are very similar except that the starting and ending integers are different. Wouldn't it be nice if we could write the common code once and reuse it without rewriting it? We can do so by defining a method. The method is for creating reusable code.

The preceding code can be simplified as follows:

define **sum** method

main method

invoke **sum**

```
 1 public static int sum(int i1, int i2) {
 2   int sum = 0;
 3   for (int i = i1; i <= i2; i++)
 4     sum += i;
 5
 6   return sum;
 7 }
 8
 9  public static void main(String[] args) {
10   System.out.println("Sum from 1 to 10 is " + sum(1, 10));
11   System.out.println("Sum from 20 to 30 is " + sum(20, 30));
12   System.out.println("Sum from 35 to 45 is " + sum(35, 45));
13 }
```

Lines 1–7 define the method named **sum** with two parameters **i** and **j**. The statements in the **main** method invoke **sum(1, 10)** to compute the sum from 1 to 10, **sum(20, 30)** to compute the sum from 20 to 30, and **sum(35, 45)** to compute the sum from 35 to 45.

A method is a collection of statements grouped together to perform an operation. In earlier chapters you have used predefined methods such as **System.out.println**, **JOptionPane.showMessageDialog**, **JOptionPane.showInputDialog**, **Integer.parseInt**, **Double.parseDouble**, **System.exit**, **Math.pow**, and **Math.random**. These methods are defined in the Java library. In this chapter, you will learn how to define your own methods and apply method abstraction to solve complex problems.

5.2 Defining a Method

The syntax for defining a method is as follows:

```
modifier returnValueType methodName(list of parameters) {
  // Method body;
}
```

Let's look at a method created to find which of two integers is bigger. This method, named `max`, has two `int` parameters, `num1` and `num2`, the larger of which is returned by the method. Figure 5.1 illustrates the components of this method.

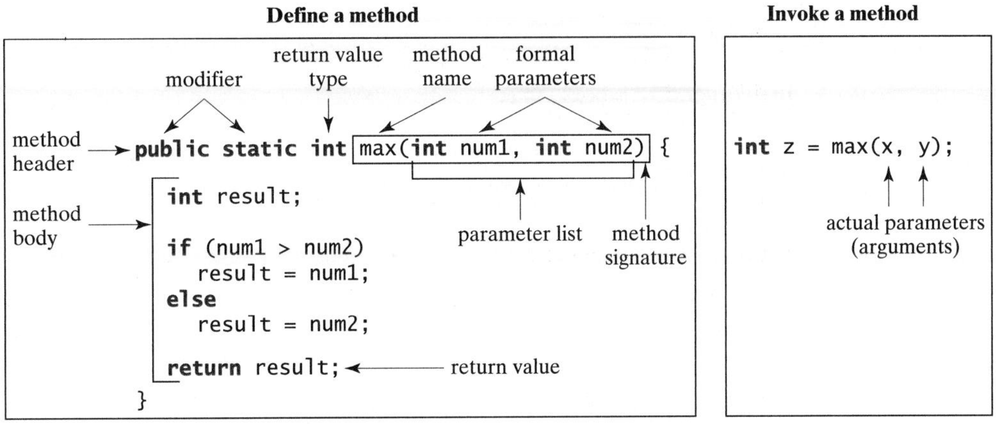
Define a method
Invoke a method
modifier
return value type
method name
formal parameters
method header
public static int max(int num1, int num2) {
method body
int result;
if (num1 > num2)
result = num1;
else
result = num2;
return result;
}
parameter list
method signature
return value
int z = max(x, y);
actual parameters (arguments)

FIGURE 5.1 A method definition consists of a method header and a method body.

method header

The *method header* specifies the *modifiers*, *return value type*, *method name*, and *parameters* of the method. The static modifier is used for all the methods in this chapter. The reason for using it will be discussed in Chapter 8, "Objects and Classes."

A method may return a value. The `returnValueType` is the data type of the value the method returns. Some methods perform desired operations without returning a value. In this case, the `returnValueType` is the keyword `void`. For example, the `returnValueType` is `void` in the `main` method, as well as in `System.exit`, `System.out.println`, and `JOptionPane.showMessageDialog`. If a method returns a value, it is called a *value-returning method*, otherwise it is a *void method*.

value-returning method
void method

The variables defined in the method header are known as *formal parameters* or simply *parameters*. A parameter is like a placeholder. When a method is invoked, you pass a value to the parameter. This value is referred to as an *actual parameter or argument*. The *parameter list* refers to the type, order, and number of the parameters of a method. The method name and the parameter list together constitute the *method signature*. Parameters are optional; that is, a method may contain no parameters. For example, the `Math.random()` method has no parameters.

parameter
argument
parameter list
method signature

The method body contains a collection of statements that define what the method does. The method body of the `max` method uses an `if` statement to determine which number is larger and return the value of that number. In order for a value-returning method to return a result, a return statement using the keyword `return` is *required*. The method terminates when a return statement is executed.

Note

In certain other languages, methods are referred to as *procedures* and *functions*. A value-returning method is called a *function*; a void method is called a *procedure*.

Caution

In the method header, you need to declare a separate data type for each parameter. For instance, `max(int num1, int num2)` is correct, but `max(int num1, num2)` is wrong.

Note

define vs. declare

We say "*define* a method" and "*declare* a variable." We are making a subtle distinction here. A definition defines what the defined item is, but a declaration usually involves allocating memory to store data for the declared item.

5.3 Calling a Method

In creating a method, you define what the method is to do. To use a method, you have to *call* or *invoke* it. There are two ways to call a method, depending on whether the method returns a value or not.

If the method returns a value, a call to the method is usually treated as a value. For example,

```
int larger = max(3, 4);
```

calls `max(3, 4)` and assigns the result of the method to the variable `larger`. Another example of a call that is treated as a value is

```
System.out.println(max(3, 4));
```

which prints the return value of the method call `max(3, 4)`.

If the method returns `void`, a call to the method must be a statement. For example, the method `println` returns `void`. The following call is a statement:

```
System.out.println("Welcome to Java!");
```

Note

A value-returning method can also be invoked as a statement in Java. In this case, the caller simply ignores the return value. This is not often done but is permissible if the caller is not interested in the return value.

When a program calls a method, program control is transferred to the called method. A called method returns control to the caller when its return statement is executed or when its method-ending closing brace is reached.

Listing 5.1 shows a complete program that is used to test the `max` method.

Video Note
Define/invoke max method

LISTING 5.1 TestMax.java

main method

invoke max

define method

```
public class TestMax {
  /** Main method */
  public static void main(String[] args) {
    int i = 5;
    int j = 2;
    int k = max(i, j);
    System.out.println("The maximum between " + i +
      " and " + j + " is " + k);
  }

  /** Return the max between two numbers */
  public static int max(int num1, int num2) {
    int result;

    if (num1 > num2)
      result = num1;
    else
      result = num2;

    return result;
  }
}
```

```
The maximum between 5 and 2 is 5
```

	line#	i	j	k	num1	num2	result
	4	5					
	5		2				
Invoking max	12				5	2	
Invoking max	13						undefined
Invoking max	16						5
	6			5			

This program contains the `main` method and the `max` method. The `main` method is just like any other method except that it is invoked by the JVM. main method

The `main` method's header is always the same. Like the one in this example, it includes the modifiers `public` and `static`, return value type `void`, method name `main`, and a parameter of the `String[]` type. `String[]` indicates that the parameter is an array of `String`, a subject addressed in Chapter 6.

The statements in `main` may invoke other methods that are defined in the class that contains the `main` method or in other classes. In this example, the `main` method invokes `max(i, j)`, which is defined in the same class with the `main` method.

When the `max` method is invoked (line 6), variable `i`'s value `5` is passed to `num1`, and variable `j`'s value `2` is passed to `num2` in the `max` method. The flow of control transfers to the `max` method. The `max` method is executed. When the `return` statement in the `max` method is executed, the `max` method returns the control to its caller (in this case the caller is the `main` method). This process is illustrated in Figure 5.2. max method

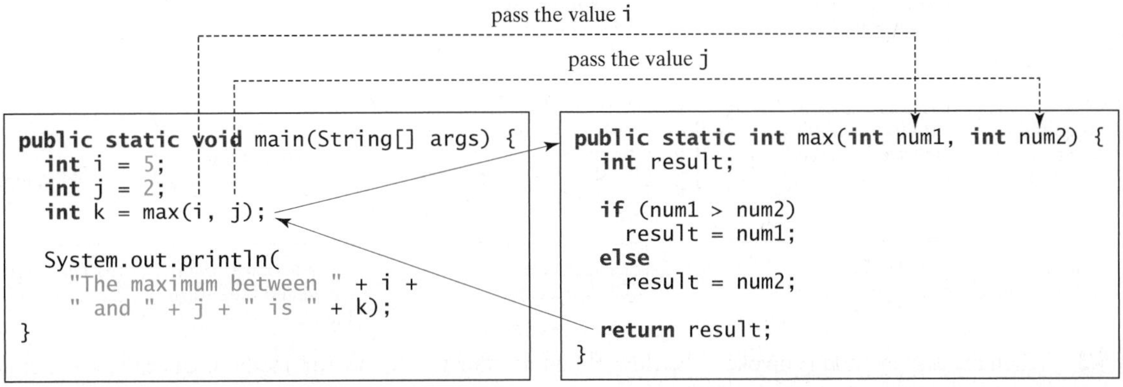
pass the value i
pass the value j
public static void main(String[] args) {
int i = 5;
int j = 2;
int k = max(i, j);
System.out.println(
"The maximum between " + i +
" and " + j + " is " + k);
}
public static int max(int num1, int num2) {
int result;
if (num1 > num2)
result = num1;
else
result = num2;
return result;
}

FIGURE 5.2 When the `max` method is invoked, the flow of control transfers to it. Once the `max` method is finished, it returns control back to the caller.

Caution

A `return` statement is required for a value-returning method. The method shown below in (a) is logically correct, but it has a compile error because the Java compiler thinks it possible that this method returns no value.

To fix this problem, delete *if (n < 0)* in (a), so that the compiler will see a `return` statement to be reached regardless of how the `if` statement is evaluated.

```
public static int sign(int n) {
  if (n > 0)
    return 1;
  else if (n == 0)
    return 0;
  else if (n < 0)
    return -1;
}
```

(a)

Should be

```
public static int sign(int n) {
  if (n > 0)
    return 1;
  else if (n == 0)
    return 0;
  else
    return -1;
}
```

(b)

reusing method

Note

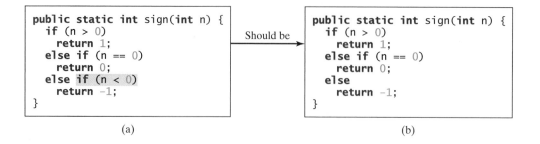

Methods enable code sharing and reuse. The `max` method can be invoked from any class besides `TestMax`. If you create a new class, you can invoke the `max` method using `ClassName.methodName` (i.e., `TestMax.max`).

5.3.1 Call Stacks

stack

Each time a method is invoked, the system stores parameters and variables in an area of memory known as a *stack*, which stores elements in last-in, first-out fashion. When a method calls another method, the caller's stack space is kept intact, and new space is created to handle the new method call. When a method finishes its work and returns to its caller, its associated space is released.

Understanding call stacks helps you to comprehend how methods are invoked. The variables defined in the `main` method are `i`, `j`, and `k`. The variables defined in the `max` method are `num1`, `num2`, and `result`. The variables `num1` and `num2` are defined in the method signature and are parameters of the method. Their values are passed through method invocation. Figure 5.3 illustrates the variables in the stack.

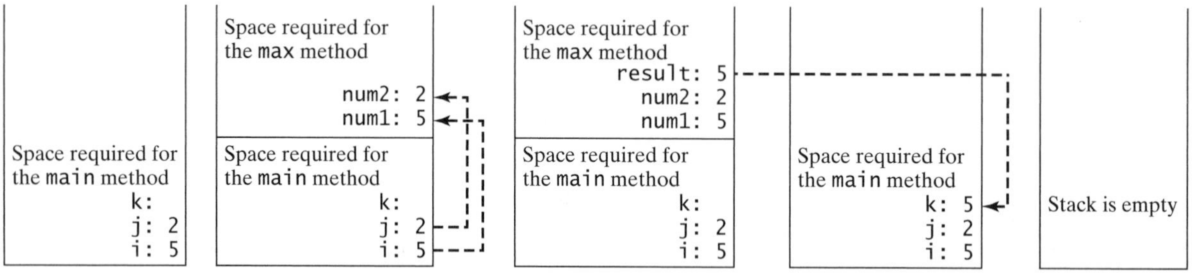
Space required for the main method
k:
j: 2
i: 5
Space required for the max method
num2: 2
num1: 5
Space required for the main method
k:
j: 2
i: 5
Space required for the max method
result: 5
num2: 2
num1: 5
Space required for the main method
k:
j: 2
i: 5
Space required for the main method
k: 5
j: 2
i: 5
Stack is empty

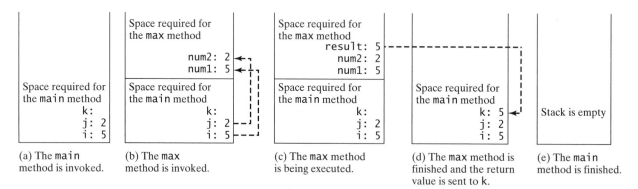

(a) The `main` method is invoked. (b) The `max` method is invoked. (c) The `max` method is being executed. (d) The `max` method is finished and the return value is sent to `k`. (e) The `main` method is finished.

FIGURE 5.3 When the `max` method is invoked, the flow of control transfers to the `max` method. Once the `max` method is finished, it returns control back to the caller.

5.4 `void` Method Example

Video Note
Use void method

The preceding section gives an example of a value-returning method. This section shows how to define and invoke a `void` method. Listing 5.2 gives a program that defines a method named `printGrade` and invokes it to print the grade for a given score.

LISTING 5.2 TestVoidMethod.java

main method

```
public class TestVoidMethod {
  public static void main(String[] args) {
    System.out.print("The grade is ");
```

```
4      printGrade(78.5);
5
6      System.out.print("The grade is ");
7      printGrade(59.5);
8    }
9
10   public static void printGrade(double score) {
11     if (score >= 90.0) {
12       System.out.println('A');
13     }
14     else if (score >= 80.0) {
15       System.out.println('B');
16     }
17     else if (score >= 70.0) {
18       System.out.println('C');
19     }
20     else if (score >= 60.0) {
21       System.out.println('D');
22     }
23     else {
24       System.out.println('F');
25     }
26   }
27 }
```

invoke **printGrade**

printGrade method

```
The grade is C
The grade is F
```

The **printGrade** method is a **void** method. It does not return any value. A call to a **void** method must be a statement. So, it is invoked as a statement in line 4 in the **main** method. Like any Java statement, it is terminated with a semicolon.

invoke void method

To see the differences between a void and a value-returning method, let us redesign the **printGrade** method to return a value. The new method, which we call **getGrade**, returns the grade as shown in Listing 5.3.

void vs. value-returned

LISTING 5.3 TestReturnGradeMethod.java

```
public class TestReturnGradeMethod {
  public static void main(String[] args) {
    System.out.print("The grade is " + getGrade(78.5));
    System.out.print("\nThe grade is " + getGrade(59.5));
  }

  public static char getGrade(double score) {
    if (score >= 90.0)
      return 'A';
    else if (score >= 80.0)
      return 'B';
    else if (score >= 70.0)
      return 'C';
    else if (score >= 60.0)
      return 'D';
    else
      return 'F';
  }
}
```

main method

invoke **printGrade**

printGrade method

```
The grade is C
The grade is F
```

The **getGrade** method defined in lines 7–18 returns a character grade based on the numeric score value. The caller invokes this method in lines 3–4.

The **getGrade** method can be invoked by a caller wherever a character may appear. The **printGrade** method does not return any value. It must be also invoked as a statement.

Note

return in void method

A **return** statement is not needed for a **void** method, but it can be used for terminating the method and returning to the method's caller. The syntax is simply

```
return;
```

This is not often done, but sometimes it is useful for circumventing the normal flow of control in a **void** method. For example, the following code has a return statement to terminate the method when the score is invalid.

```
public static void printGrade(double score) {
  if (score < 0 || score > 100) {
    System.out.println("Invalid score");
    return;
  }

  if (score >= 90.0) {
    System.out.println('A');
  }
  else if (score >= 80.0) {
    System.out.println('B');
  }
  else if (score >= 70.0) {
    System.out.println('C');
  }
  else if (score >= 60.0) {
    System.out.println('D');
  }
  else {
    System.out.println('F');
  }
}
```

5.5 Passing Parameters by Values

parameter order association

The power of a method is its ability to work with parameters. You can use **println** to print any string and **max** to find the maximum between any two **int** values. When calling a method, you need to provide arguments, which must be given in the same order as their respective parameters in the method signature. This is known as *parameter order association*. For example, the following method prints a message **n** times:

```
public static void nPrintln(String message, int n) {
  for (int i = 0; i < n; i++)
    System.out.println(message);
}
```

You can use **nPrintln("Hello", 3)** to print **"Hello"** three times. The **nPrintln("Hello", 3)** statement passes the actual string parameter **"Hello"** to the parameter **message**; passes **3** to **n**;

and prints "Hello" three times. However, the statement `nPrintln(3, "Hello")` would be wrong. The data type of `3` does not match the data type for the first parameter, `message`, nor does the second parameter, `"Hello"`, match the second parameter, `n`.

Caution

The arguments must match the parameters in *order*, *number*, and *compatible type*, as defined in the method signature. Compatible type means that you can pass an argument to a parameter without explicit casting, such as passing an `int` value argument to a `double` value parameter.

When you invoke a method with a parameter, the value of the argument is passed to the parameter. This is referred to as *pass-by-value*. If the argument is a variable rather than a literal value, the value of the variable is passed to the parameter. The variable is not affected, regardless of the changes made to the parameter inside the method. As shown in Listing 5.4, the value of `x` (`1`) is passed to the parameter `n` to invoke the `increment` method (line 5). `n` is incremented by `1` in the method (line 10), but `x` is not changed no matter what the method does.

pass-by-value

LISTING 5.4 Increment.java

```
1 public class Increment {
2   public static void main(String[] args) {
3     int x = 1;
4     System.out.println("Before the call, x is " + x);
5     increment(x);
6     System.out.println("after the call, x is " + x);
7   }
8
9   public static void increment(int n) {
10    n++;
11    System.out.println("n inside the method is " + n);
12  }
13 }
```

invoke increment

increment **n**

```
Before the call, x is 1
n inside the method is 2
after the call, x is 1
```

Listing 5.5 gives another program that demonstrates the effect of passing by value. The program creates a method for swapping two variables. The `swap` method is invoked by passing two arguments. Interestingly, the values of the arguments are not changed after the method is invoked.

LISTING 5.5 TestPassByValue.java

```
public class TestPassByValue {
  /** Main method */
  public static void main(String[] args) {
    // Declare and initialize variables
    int num1 = 1;
    int num2 = 2;

    System.out.println("Before invoking the swap method, num1 is " +
      num1 + " and num2 is " + num2);

    // Invoke the swap method to attempt to swap two variables
    swap(num1, num2);
```

false swap

```
13
14     System.out.println("After invoking the swap method, num1 is " +
15       num1 + " and num2 is " + num2);
16   }
17
18   /** Swap two variables */
19   public static void swap(int n1, int n2) {
20     System.out.println("\tInside the swap method");
21     System.out.println("\t\tBefore swapping n1 is " + n1
22       + " n2 is " + n2);
23
24     // Swap n1 with n2
25     int temp = n1;
26     n1 = n2;
27     n2 = temp;
28
29     System.out.println("\t\tAfter swapping n1 is " + n1
30       + " n2 is " + n2);
31   }
32 }
```

```
Before invoking the swap method, num1 is 1 and num2 is 2
  Inside the swap method
    Before swapping n1 is 1 n2 is 2
    After swapping n1 is 2 n2 is 1
After invoking the swap method, num1 is 1 and num2 is 2
```

Before the swap method is invoked (line 12), num1 is 1 and num2 is 2. After the swap method is invoked, num1 is still 1 and num2 is still 2. Their values have not been swapped. As shown in Figure 5.4, the values of the arguments num1 and num2 are passed to n1 and n2, but n1 and n2 have their own memory locations independent of num1 and num2. Therefore, changes in n1 and n2 do not affect the contents of num1 and num2.

Another twist is to change the parameter name n1 in swap to num1. What effect does this have? No change occurs, because it makes no difference whether the parameter and the argument have the same name. The parameter is a variable in the method with its own memory space. The variable is allocated when the method is invoked, and it disappears when the method is returned to its caller.

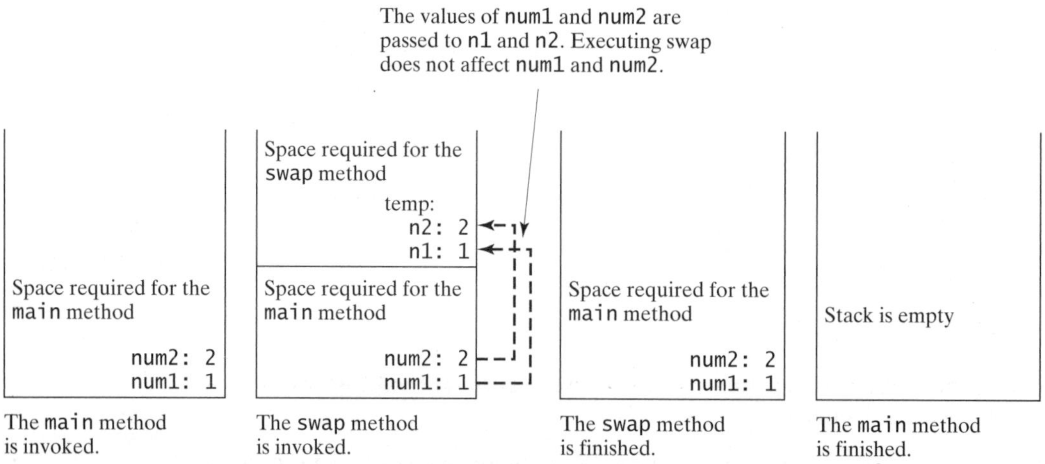
The values of num1 and num2 are passed to n1 and n2. Executing swap does not affect num1 and num2.
Space required for the main method
num2: 2
num1: 1
The main method is invoked.
Space required for the swap method
temp:
n2: 2
n1: 1
Space required for the main method
num2: 2
num1: 1
The swap method is invoked.
Space required for the main method
num2: 2
num1: 1
The swap method is finished.
Stack is empty
The main method is finished.

FIGURE 5.4 The values of the variables are passed to the parameters of the method.

Note

For simplicity, Java programmers often say *passing an argument* x *to a parameter* y, which actually means *passing the value of* x *to* y.

5.6 Modularizing Code

Methods can be used to reduce redundant code and enable code reuse. Methods can also be used to modularize code and improve the quality of the program.

Video Note
Modularize code

Listing 4.8 gives a program that prompts the user to enter two integers and displays their greatest common divisor. You can rewrite the program using a method, as shown in Listing 5.6.

LISTING 5.6 GreatestCommonDivisorMethod.java

```
import java.util.Scanner;

public class GreatestCommonDivisorMethod {
  /** Main method */
  public static void main(String[] args) {
    // Create a Scanner
    Scanner input = new Scanner(System.in);

    // Prompt the user to enter two integers
    System.out.print("Enter first integer: ");
    int n1 = input.nextInt();
    System.out.print("Enter second integer: ");
    int n2 = input.nextInt();

    System.out.println("The greatest common divisor for " + n1 +
      " and " + n2 + " is " + gcd(n1, n2));
  }

  /** Return the gcd of two integers */
  public static int gcd(int n1, int n2) {
    int gcd = 1; // Initial gcd is 1
    int k = 2;   // Possible gcd

    while (k <= n1 && k <= n2) {
      if (n1 % k == 0 && n2 % k == 0)
        gcd = k; // Update gcd
      k++;
    }

    return gcd; // Return gcd
  }
}
```

invoke **gcd**

compute gcd

return gcd

```
Enter first integer: 45 [Enter]
Enter second integer: 75 [Enter]
The greatest common divisor for 45 and 75 is 15
```

By encapsulating the code for obtaining the gcd in a method, this program has several advantages:

1. It isolates the problem for computing the gcd from the rest of the code in the main method. Thus, the logic becomes clear and the program is easier to read.

2. The errors on computing gcd are confined in the **gcd** method, which narrows the scope of debugging.

3. The **gcd** method now can be reused by other programs.

Listing 5.7 applies the concept of code modularization to improve Listing 4.14, PrimeNumber.java.

LISTING 5.7 PrimeNumberMethod.java

invoke **printPrimeNumbers**

printPrimeNumbers method

invoke **isPrime**

isPrime method

```
public class PrimeNumberMethod {
  public static void main(String[] args) {
    System.out.println("The first 50 prime numbers are \n");
    printPrimeNumbers(50);
  }

  public static void printPrimeNumbers(int numberOfPrimes) {
    final int NUMBER_OF_PRIMES_PER_LINE = 10; // Display 10 per line
    int count = 0; // Count the number of prime numbers
    int number = 2; // A number to be tested for primeness

    // Repeatedly find prime numbers
    while (count < numberOfPrimes) {
      // Print the prime number and increase the count
      if (isPrime(number) ) {
        count++; // Increase the count

        if (count % NUMBER_OF_PRIMES_PER_LINE == 0) {
          // Print the number and advance to the new line
          System.out.printf("%-5s\n", number);
        }
        else
          System.out.printf("%-5s", number);
      }

      // Check whether the next number is prime
      number++;
    }
  }

  /** Check whether number is prime */
  public static boolean isPrime(int number) {
    for (int divisor = 2; divisor <= number / 2; divisor++) {
      if (number % divisor == 0) { // If true, number is not prime
        return false; // number is not a prime
      }
    }

    return true; // number is prime
  }
}
```

```
The first 50 prime numbers are

2    3    5    7    11   13   17   19   23   29
31   37   41   43   47   53   59   61   67   71
73   79   83   89   97   101  103  107  109  113
127  131  137  139  149  151  157  163  167  173
179  181  191  193  197  199  211  223  227  229
```

We divided a large problem into two subproblems. As a result, the new program is easier to read and easier to debug. Moreover, the methods `printPrimeNumbers` and `isPrime` can be reused by other programs.

5.7 Problem: Converting Decimals to Hexadecimals

Hexadecimals are often used in computer systems programming. Appendix F introduces number systems. This section presents a program that converts a decimal to a hexadecimal.

To convert a decimal number d to a hexadecimal number is to find the hexadecimal digits $h_n, h_{n-1}, h_{n-2}, \ldots, h_2, h_1$, and h_0 such that

$$d = h_n \times 16^n + h_{n-1} \times 16^{n-1} + h_{n-2} \times 16^{n-2} + \ldots + h_2 \times 16^2 + h_1 \times 16^1 + h_0 \times 16^0$$

These numbers can be found by successively dividing d by 16 until the quotient is 0. The remainders are $h_0, h_1, h_2, \ldots, h_{n-2}, h_{n-1}$, and h_n.

For example, the decimal number `123` is `7B` in hexadecimal. The conversion is done as follows:

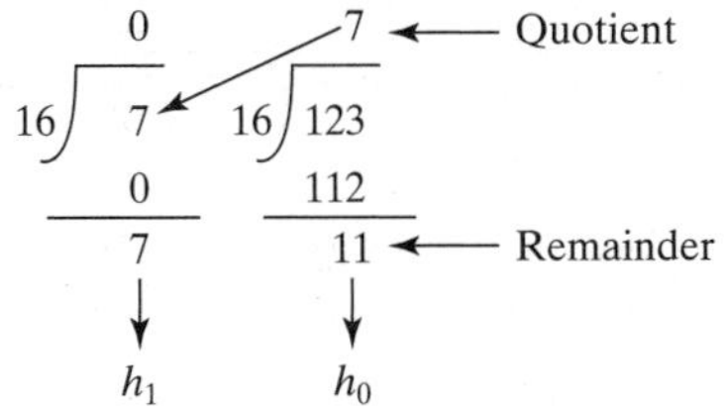
Quotient
Remainder

Listing 5.8 gives a program that prompts the user to enter a decimal number and converts it into a hex number as a string.

LISTING 5.8 `Decimal2HexConversion.java`

```
import java.util.Scanner;

public class Decimal2HexConversion {
  /** Main method */
  public static void main(String[] args) {
    // Create a Scanner
    Scanner input = new Scanner(System.in);

    // Prompt the user to enter a decimal integer
    System.out.print("Enter a decimal number: ");
    int decimal = input.nextInt();

    System.out.println("The hex number for decimal " +
      decimal + " is " + decimalToHex(decimal));
  }

  /** Convert a decimal to a hex as a string */
  public static String decimalToHex(int decimal) {
    String hex = "";

    while (decimal != 0) {
      int hexValue = decimal % 16;
      hex = toHexChar(hexValue) + hex;
      decimal = decimal / 16;
```

input string

hex to decimal

hex char to decimal

to uppercase

```
25      }
26
27      return hex;
28    }
29
30    /** Convert an integer to a single hex digit in a character */
31    public static char toHexChar(int hexValue) {
32      if (hexValue <= 9 && hexValue >= 0)
33        return (char)(hexValue + '0');
34      else  // hexValue <= 15 && hexValue >= 10
35        return (char)(hexValue - 10 + 'A');
36    }
37  }
```

```
Enter a decimal number: 1234 ↵Enter
The hex number for decimal 1234 is 4D2
```

	line#	decimal	hex	hexValue	toHexChar(hexValue)
	19	1234	“ ”		
iteration 1	22			2	
	23		“2”		2
	24	77			
iteration 2	22			13	
	23		“D2”		D
	24	4			
iteration 3	22			4	
	23		“4D2”		4
	24	0			

The program uses the `decimalToHex` method (lines 18–28) to convert a decimal integer to a hex number as a string. The method gets the remainder of the division of the decimal integer by `16` (line 22). The remainder is converted into a character by invoking the `toHexChar` method (line 23). The character is then appended to the hex string (line 23). The hex string is initially empty (line 19). Divide the decimal number by `16` to remove a hex digit from the number (line 24). The method repeatedly performs these operations in a loop until quotient becomes `0` (lines 21–25).

The `toHexChar` method (lines 31–36) converts a `hexValue` between `0` and `15` into a hex character. If `hexValue` is between `0` and `9`, it is converted to `(char)(hexValue + '0')` (line 33). Recall when adding a character with an integer, the character's Unicode is used in the evaluation. For example, if `hexValue` is `5`, `(char)(hexValue + '0')` returns `'5'`. Similarly, if `hexValue` is between `10` and `15`, it is converted to `(char)(hexValue + 'A')` (line 35). For example, if `hexValue` is `11`, `(char)(hexValue + 'A')` returns `'B'`.

5.8 Overloading Methods

The `max` method that was used earlier works only with the `int` data type. But what if you need to determine which of two floating-point numbers has the maximum value? The solution is to create another method with the same name but different parameters, as shown in the following code:

```
public static double max(double num1, double num2) {
  if (num1 > num2)
    return num1;
  else
    return num2;
}
```

If you call `max` with `int` parameters, the `max` method that expects `int` parameters will be invoked; if you call `max` with `double` parameters, the `max` method that expects `double` parameters will be invoked. This is referred to as *method overloading*; that is, two methods have the same name but different parameter lists within one class. The Java compiler determines which method is used based on the method signature.

method overloading

Listing 5.9 is a program that creates three methods. The first finds the maximum integer, the second finds the maximum double, and the third finds the maximum among three double values. All three methods are named `max`.

LISTING 5.9 TestMethodOverloading.java

```
public class TestMethodOverloading {
  /** Main method */
  public static void main(String[] args) {
    // Invoke the max method with int parameters
    System.out.println("The maximum between 3 and 4 is "
      + max(3, 4));

    // Invoke the max method with the double parameters
    System.out.println("The maximum between 3.0 and 5.4 is "
      + max(3.0, 5.4));

    // Invoke the max method with three double parameters
    System.out.println("The maximum between 3.0, 5.4, and 10.14 is "
      + max(3.0, 5.4, 10.14));
  }

  /** Return the max between two int values */
  public static int max(int num1, int num2) {
    if (num1 > num2)
      return num1;
    else
      return num2;
  }

  /** Find the max between two double values */
  public static double max(double num1, double num2) {
    if (num1 > num2)
      return num1;
    else
      return num2;
  }

  /** Return the max among three double values */
  public static double max(double num1, double num2, double num3) {
    return max(max(num1, num2), num3);
  }
}
```

overloaded **max**

overloaded **max**

overloaded **max**

```
The maximum between 3 and 4 is 4
The maximum between 3.0 and 5.4 is 5.4
The maximum between 3.0, 5.4, and 10.14 is 10.14
```

When calling `max(3, 4)` (line 6), the `max` method for finding the maximum of two integers is invoked. When calling `max(3.0, 5.4)` (line 10), the `max` method for finding the maximum of two doubles is invoked. When calling `max(3.0, 5.4, 10.14)` (line 14), the `max` method for finding the maximum of three double values is invoked.

Can you invoke the `max` method with an `int` value and a `double` value, such as `max(2, 2.5)`? If so, which of the `max` methods is invoked? The answer to the first question is yes. The answer to the second is that the `max` method for finding the maximum of two `double` values is invoked. The argument value 2 is automatically converted into a `double` value and passed to this method.

You may be wondering why the method `max(double, double)` is not invoked for the call `max(3, 4)`. Both `max(double, double)` and `max(int, int)` are possible matches for `max(3, 4)`. The Java compiler finds the most specific method for a method invocation. Since the method `max(int, int)` is more specific than `max(double, double)`, `max(int, int)` is used to invoke `max(3, 4)`.

Note

Overloaded methods must have different parameter lists. You cannot overload methods based on different modifiers or return types.

Note

ambiguous invocation

Sometimes there are two or more possible matches for an invocation of a method, but the compiler cannot determine the most specific match. This is referred to as *ambiguous invocation*. Ambiguous invocation causes a compile error. Consider the following code:

```
public class AmbiguousOverloading {
  public static void main(String[] args) {
    System.out.println(max(1, 2) );
  }

  public static double max(int num1, double num2) {
    if (num1 > num2)
      return num1;
    else
      return num2;
  }

  public static double max(double num1, int num2) {
    if (num1 > num2)
      return num1;
    else
      return num2;
  }
}
```

Both `max(int, double)` and `max(double, int)` are possible candidates to match `max(1, 2)`. Since neither is more specific than the other, the invocation is ambiguous, resulting in a compile error.

5.9 The Scope of Variables

The *scope of a variable* is the part of the program where the variable can be referenced. A variable defined inside a method is referred to as a *local variable.*

local variable

The scope of a local variable starts from its declaration and continues to the end of the block that contains the variable. A local variable must be declared and assigned a value before it can be used.

A parameter is actually a local variable. The scope of a method parameter covers the entire method.

A variable declared in the initial-action part of a `for`-loop header has its scope in the entire loop. But a variable declared inside a `for`-loop body has its scope limited in the loop body from its declaration to the end of the block that contains the variable, as shown in Figure 5.5.

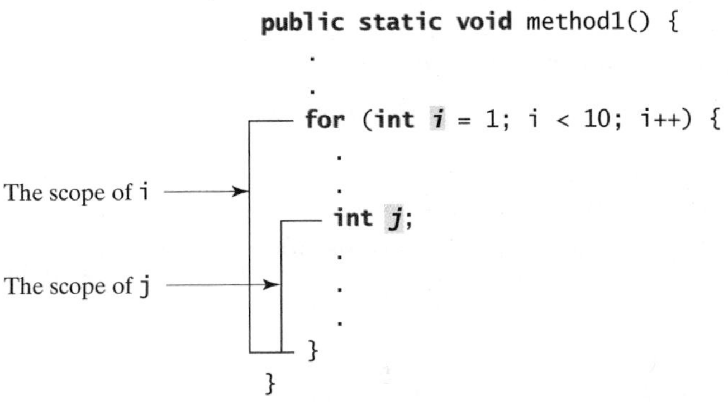

public static void method1() {
for (int i = 1; i < 10; i++) {
The scope of i
int j;
The scope of j
}
}

FIGURE 5.5 A variable declared in the initial action part of a `for`-loop header has its scope in the entire loop.

You can declare a local variable with the same name in different blocks in a method, but you cannot declare a local variable twice in the same block or in nested blocks, as shown in Figure 5.6.

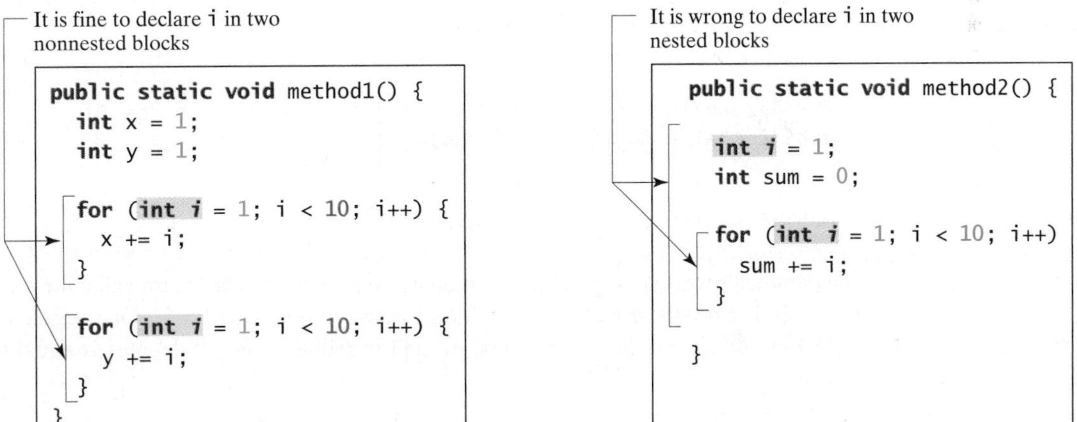

It is fine to declare i in two nonnested blocks
public static void method1() {
int x = 1;
int y = 1;
for (int i = 1; i < 10; i++) {
x += i;
}
for (int i = 1; i < 10; i++) {
y += i;
}
}
It is wrong to declare i in two nested blocks
public static void method2() {
int i = 1;
int sum = 0;
for (int i = 1; i < 10; i++)
sum += i;
}
}

FIGURE 5.6 A variable can be declared multiple times in nonnested blocks but only once in nested blocks.

Caution

Do not declare a variable inside a block and then attempt to use it outside the block. Here is an example of a common mistake:

```
for (int i = 0; i < 10; i++) {
}
System.out.println(i);
```

The last statement would cause a syntax error, because variable i is not defined outside of the for loop.

5.10 The Math Class

The Math class contains the methods needed to perform basic mathematical functions. You have already used the pow(a, b) method to compute a^b in Listing 2.8, ComputeLoan.java, and the Math.random() method in Listing 3.4, SubtractionQuiz.java. This section introduces other useful methods in the Math class. They can be categorized as *trigonometric methods*, *exponent methods*, and *service methods*. Besides methods, the Math class provides two useful double constants, PI and E (the base of natural logarithms). You can use these constants as Math.PI and Math.E in any program.

5.10.1 Trigonometric Methods

The Math class contains the following trigonometric methods:

```
/** Return the trigonometric sine of an angle in radians */
public static double sin(double radians)

/** Return the trigonometric cosine of an angle in radians */
public static double cos(double radians)

/** Return the trigonometric tangent of an angle in radians */
public static double tan(double radians)

/** Convert the angle in degrees to an angle in radians */
public static double toRadians(double degree)

/** Convert the angle in radians to an angle in degrees */
public static double toDegrees(double radians)

/** Return the angle in radians for the inverse of sin */
public static double asin(double a)

/** Return the angle in radians for the inverse of cos */
public static double acos(double a)

/** Return the angle in radians for the inverse of tan */
public static double atan(double a)
```

The parameter for sin, cos, and tan is an angle in radians. The return value for asin, acos, and atan is a degree in radians in the range between $-\pi/2$ and $\pi/2$. One degree is equal to $\pi/180$ in radians, 90 degrees is equal to $\pi/2$ in radians, and 30 degrees is equal to $\pi/6$ in radians.

For example,

```
Math.toDegrees(Math.PI / 2) returns 90.0
Math.toRadians(30) returns π/6
Math.sin(0) returns 0.0
Math.sin(Math.toRadians(270)) returns -1.0
Math.sin(Math.PI / 6) returns 0.5
Math.sin(Math.PI / 2) returns 1.0
Math.cos(0) returns 1.0
Math.cos(Math.PI / 6) returns 0.866
Math.cos(Math.PI / 2) returns 0
Math.asin(0.5) returns π/6
```

5.10.2 Exponent Methods

There are five methods related to exponents in the Math class:

```
/** Return e raised to the power of x (e^x) */
public static double exp(double x)

/** Return the natural logarithm of x (ln(x) = log_e(x)) */
public static double log(double x)

/** Return the base 10 logarithm of x (log_10(x)) */
public static double log10(double x)

/** Return a raised to the power of b (a^b) */
public static double pow(double a, double b)

/** Return the square root of x (√x) for x >= 0 */
public static double sqrt(double x)
```

For example,

```
Math.exp(1) returns 2.71828
Math.log(Math.E) returns 1.0
Math.log10(10) returns 1.0
Math.pow(2, 3) returns 8.0
Math.pow(3, 2) returns 9.0
Math.pow(3.5, 2.5) returns 22.91765
Math.sqrt(4) returns 2.0
Math.sqrt(10.5) returns 3.24
```

5.10.3 The Rounding Methods

The Math class contains five rounding methods:

```
/** x is rounded up to its nearest integer. This integer is
  * returned as a double value. */
public static double ceil(double x)

/** x is rounded down to its nearest integer. This integer is
  * returned as a double value. */
public static double floor(double x)

/** x is rounded to its nearest integer. If x is equally close
  * to two integers, the even one is returned as a double. */
public static double rint(double x)

/** Return (int)Math.floor(x + 0.5). */
public static int round(float x)

/** Return (long)Math.floor(x + 0.5). */
public static long round(double x)
```

For example,

```
Math.ceil(2.1) returns 3.0
Math.ceil(2.0) returns 2.0
Math.ceil(-2.0) returns -2.0
Math.ceil(-2.1) returns -2.0
Math.floor(2.1) returns 2.0
Math.floor(2.0) returns 2.0
```

```
Math.floor(-2.0) returns -2.0
Math.floor(-2.1) returns -3.0
Math.rint(2.1) returns 2.0
Math.rint(-2.0) returns -2.0
Math.rint(-2.1) returns -2.0
Math.rint(2.5) returns 2.0
Math.rint(3.5) returns 4.0
Math.rint(-2.5) returns -2.0
Math.round(2.6f) returns 3 // Returns int
Math.round(2.0) returns 2  // Returns long
Math.round(-2.0f) returns -2
Math.round(-2.6) returns -3
```

5.10.4 The min, max, and abs Methods

The min and max methods are overloaded to return the minimum and maximum numbers between two numbers (int, long, float, or double). For example, max(3.4, 5.0) returns 5.0, and min(3, 2) returns 2.

The abs method is overloaded to return the absolute value of the number (int, long, float, and double). For example,

```
Math.max(2, 3) returns 3
Math.max(2.5, 3) returns 3.0
Math.min(2.5, 3.6) returns 2.5
Math.abs(-2) returns 2
Math.abs(-2.1) returns 2.1
```

5.10.5 The random Method

You have used the random() method to generate a random double value greater than or equal to 0.0 and less than 1.0 (0 <= Math.random() < 1.0). This method is very useful. You can use it to write a simple expression to generate random numbers in any range. For example,

(int) (Math.random( ) * 10) ⟶ Returns a random integer between 0 and 9

50 + (int) (Math.random( ) * 50) ⟶ Returns a random integer between 50 and 99

In general,

a + Math.random( ) * b ⟶ Returns a random number between a and a + b excluding a + b

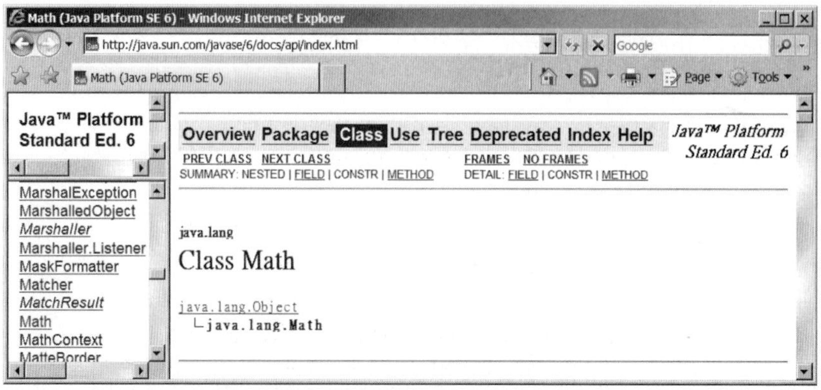
Math (Java Platform SE 6) - Windows Internet Explorer
http://java.sun.com/javase/6/docs/api/index.html
Math (Java Platform SE 6)
Java™ Platform Standard Ed. 6
Overview Package Class Use Tree Deprecated Index Help
Java™ Platform Standard Ed. 6
PREV CLASS NEXT CLASS
FRAMES NO FRAMES
SUMMARY: NESTED | FIELD | CONSTR | METHOD
DETAIL: FIELD | CONSTR | METHOD
MarshalException
MarshalledObject
Marshaller
Marshaller.Listener
MaskFormatter
Matcher
MatchResult
Math
MathContext
java.lang
Class Math
java.lang.Object
java.lang.Math

FIGURE 5.7 You can view the documentation for Java API online.

Tip

You can view the complete documentation for the `Math` class online at http://java.sun.com/javase/6/docs/api/index.html, as shown in Figure 5.7.

Note

Not all classes need a `main` method. The `Math` class and `JOptionPane` class do not have `main` methods. These classes contain methods for other classes to use.

5.11 Case Study: Generating Random Characters

Computer programs process numerical data and characters. You have seen many examples that involve numerical data. It is also important to understand characters and how to process them. This section presents an example for generating random characters.

As introduced in §2.13, every character has a unique Unicode between 0 and FFFF in hexadecimal (65535 in decimal). To generate a random character is to generate a random integer between 0 and 65535 using the following expression (note that since `0 <= Math.random() < 1.0`, you have to add 1 to 65535):

```
(int)(Math.random() * (65535 + 1))
```

Now let us consider how to generate a random lowercase letter. The Unicodes for lowercase letters are consecutive integers starting from the Unicode for `'a'`, then that for `'b'`, `'c'`, . . . , and `'z'`. The Unicode for `'a'` is

```
(int)'a'
```

So a random integer between `(int)'a'` and `(int)'z'` is

```
(int)((int)'a' + Math.random() * ((int)'z' - (int)'a' + 1)
```

As discussed in §2.13.3, all numeric operators can be applied to the `char` operands. The `char` operand is cast into a number if the other operand is a number or a character. Thus the preceding expression can be simplified as follows:

```
'a' + Math.random() * ('z' - 'a' + 1)
```

and a random lowercase letter is

```
(char)('a' + Math.random() * ('z' - 'a' + 1))
```

To generalize the foregoing discussion, a random character between any two characters `ch1` and `ch2` with `ch1 < ch2` can be generated as follows:

```
(char)(ch1 + Math.random() * (ch2 - ch1 + 1))
```

This is a simple but useful discovery. Let us create a class named `RandomCharacter` in Listing 5.10 with five overloaded methods to get a certain type of character randomly. You can use these methods in your future projects.

LISTING 5.10 RandomCharacter.java

```
public class RandomCharacter {
  /** Generate a random character between ch1 and ch2 */
  public static char getRandomCharacter(char ch1, char ch2) {
    return (char)(ch1 + Math.random() * (ch2 - ch1 + 1));
  }
```

getRandomCharacter

getRandomLowerCaseLetter()

getRandomUpperCaseLetter()

getRandomDigitCharacter()

getRandomCharacter()

```

  /** Generate a random lowercase letter */
  public static char getRandomLowerCaseLetter() {
    return getRandomCharacter('a', 'z');
  }

  /** Generate a random uppercase letter */
  public static char getRandomUpperCaseLetter() {
    return getRandomCharacter('A', 'Z');
  }

  /** Generate a random digit character */
  public static char getRandomDigitCharacter() {
    return getRandomCharacter('0', '9');
  }

  /** Generate a random character */
  public static char getRandomCharacter() {
    return getRandomCharacter('\u0000', '\uFFFF');
  }
}
```

Listing 5.11 gives a test program that displays 175 random lowercase letters.

LISTING 5.11 TestRandomCharacter.java

constants

lower-case letter

```
 1 public class TestRandomCharacter {
 2   /** Main method */
 3   public static void main(String[] args) {
 4     final int NUMBER_OF_CHARS = 175;
 5     final int CHARS_PER_LINE = 25;
 6
 7     // Print random characters between 'a' and 'z', 25 chars per line
 8     for (int i = 0; i < NUMBER_OF_CHARS; i++) {
 9       char ch = RandomCharacter.getRandomLowerCaseLetter();
10       if ((i + 1) % CHARS_PER_LINE == 0)
11         System.out.println(ch);
12       else
13         System.out.print(ch);
14     }
15   }
16 }
```

```
gmjsohezfkgtazqgmswfclrao
pnrunulnwmaztlfjedmpchcif
lalqdgivxkxpbzulrmqmbhikr
lbnrjlsopfxahssqhwuuljvbe
xbhdotzhpehbqmuwsfktwsoli
cbuwkzgxpmtzihgatdslvbwbz
bfesoklwbhnooygiigzdxuqni
```

Line 9 invokes **getRandomLowerCaseLetter()** defined in the **RandomCharacter** class. Note that **getRandomLowerCaseLetter()** does not have any parameters, but you still have to use the parentheses when defining and invoking the method.

parentheses required

5.12 Method Abstraction and Stepwise Refinement

method abstraction

The key to developing software is to apply the concept of abstraction. You will learn many levels of abstraction from this book. *Method abstraction* is achieved by separating the use of a method from its implementation. The client can use a method without knowing how it is implemented. The details of the implementation are encapsulated in the method and hidden from the client who invokes the method. This is known as *information hiding* or *encapsulation*. If you decide to change the implementation, the client program will not be affected, provided that you do not change the method signature. The implementation of the method is hidden from the client in a "black box," as shown in Figure 5.8.

information hiding

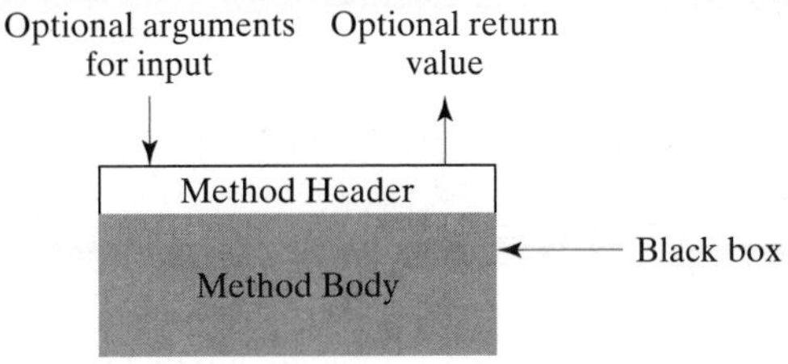
Optional arguments for input
Optional return value
Method Header
Method Body
Black box

FIGURE 5.8 The method body can be thought of as a black box that contains the detailed implementation for the method.

You have already used the `System.out.print` method to display a string, the `JOptionPane.showInputDialog` method to read a string from a dialog box, and the `max` method to find the maximum number. You know how to write the code to invoke these methods in your program, but as a user of these methods, you are not required to know how they are implemented.

The concept of method abstraction can be applied to the process of developing programs. When writing a large program, you can use the *divide-and-conquer* strategy, also known as *stepwise refinement*, to decompose it into subproblems. The subproblems can be further decomposed into smaller, more manageable problems.

divide and conquer
stepwise refinement

Suppose you write a program that displays the calendar for a given month of the year. The program prompts the user to enter the year and the month, then displays the entire calendar for the month, as shown in the following sample run:

```
Enter full year (e.g., 2001): 2006 ↵Enter
Enter month in number between 1 and 12: 6 ↵Enter
          June 2006
-----------------------------------
 Sun  Mon  Tue  Wed  Thu  Fri  Sat
                       1    2    3
   4    5    6    7    8    9   10
  11   12   13   14   15   16   17
  18   19   20   21   22   23   24
  25   26   27   28   29   30
```

Let us use this example to demonstrate the divide-and-conquer approach.

5.12.1 Top-Down Design

How would you get started on such a program? Would you immediately start coding? Beginning programmers often start by trying to work out the solution to every detail. Although details are important in the final program, concern for detail in the early stages may block the problem-solving process. To make problem solving flow as smoothly as possible, this example begins by using method abstraction to isolate details from design and only later implements the details.

For this example, the problem is first broken into two subproblems: get input from the user, and print the calendar for the month. At this stage, you should be concerned with what the subproblems will achieve, not with how to get input and print the calendar for the month. You can draw a structure chart to help visualize the decomposition of the problem (see Figure 5.9(a)).

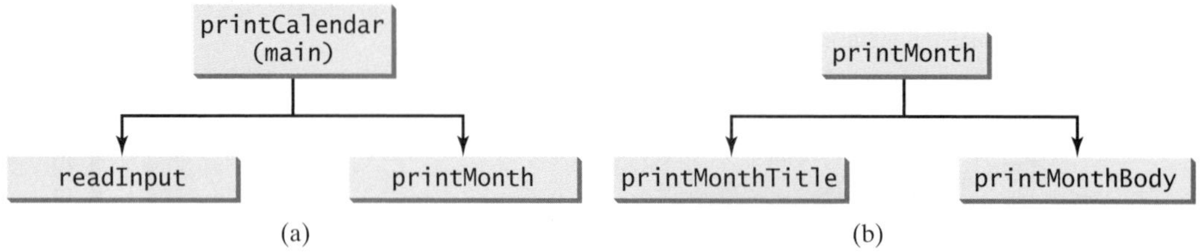
printCalendar
(main)
readInput
printMonth
(a)
printMonth
printMonthTitle
printMonthBody
(b)

FIGURE 5.9 The structure chart shows that the `printCalendar` problem is divided into two subproblems, `readInput` and `printMonth`, and that `printMonth` is divided into two smaller subproblems, `printMonthTitle` and `printMonthBody`.

The problem of printing the calendar for a given month can be broken into two subproblems: print the month title, and print the month body, as shown in Figure 5.9(b). The month title consists of three lines: month and year, a dash line, and the names of the seven days of the week. You need to get the month name (e.g., January) from the numeric month (e.g., 1). This is accomplished in `getMonthName` (see Figure 5.10(a)).

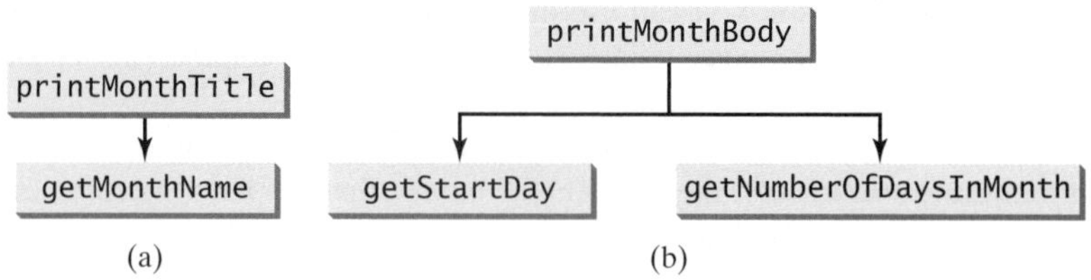
printMonthTitle
getMonthName
(a)
printMonthBody
getStartDay
getNumberOfDaysInMonth
(b)

FIGURE 5.10 (a) To `printMonthTitle`, you need `getMonthName`. (b) The `printMonthBody` problem is refined into several smaller problems.

In order to print the month body, you need to know which day of the week is the first day of the month (`getStartDay`) and how many days the month has (`getNumberOfDaysInMonth`), as shown in Figure 5.10(b). For example, December 2005 has 31 days, and December 1, 2005, is Thursday.

How would you get the start day for the first date in a month? There are several ways to do so. For now, we'll use the following approach. Assume you know that the start day (`startDay1800 = 3`) for Jan 1, 1800, was Wednesday. You could compute the total number of

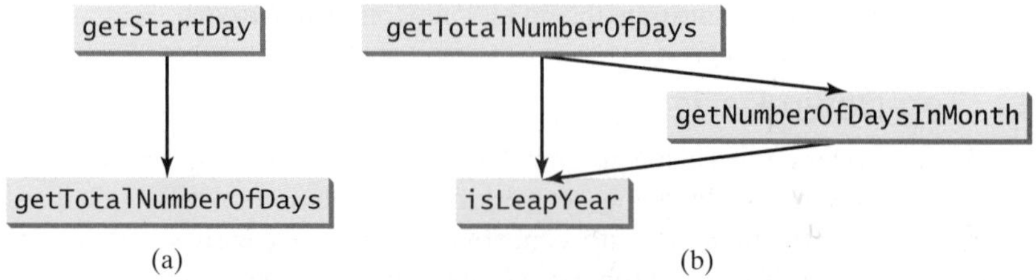
getStartDay
getTotalNumberOfDays
(a)
getTotalNumberOfDays
getNumberOfDaysInMonth
isLeapYear
(b)

FIGURE 5.11 (a) To `getStartDay`, you need `getTotalNumberOfDays`. (b) The `getTotalNumberOfDays` problem is refined into two smaller problems.

days (totalNumberOfDays) between Jan 1, 1800, and the first date of the calendar month. The start day for the calendar month is (totalNumberOfDays + startDay1800) % 7, since every week has seven days. So the getStartDay problem can be further refined as getTotalNumberOfDays, as shown in Figure 5.11(a).

To get the total number of days, you need to know whether the year is a leap year and the number of days in each month. So getTotalNumberOfDays is further refined into two subproblems: isLeapYear and getNumberOfDaysInMonth, as shown in Figure 5.11(b). The complete structure chart is shown in Figure 5.12.

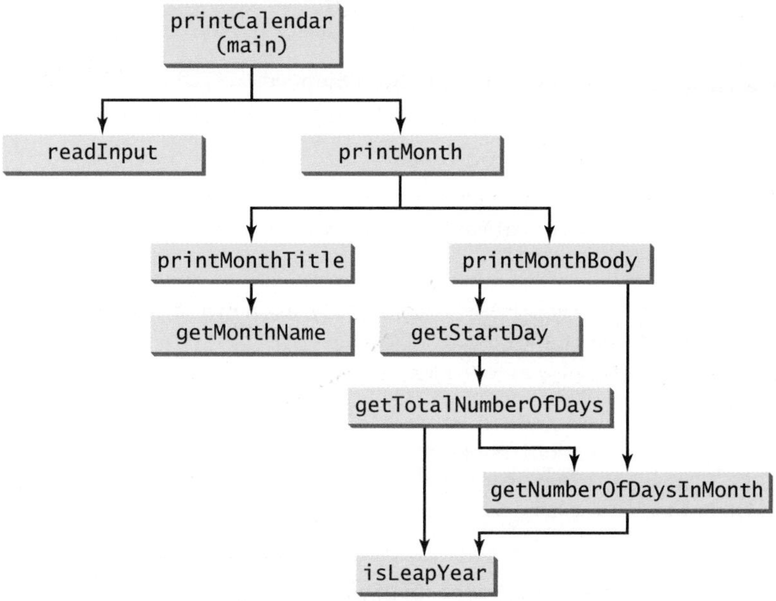
printCalendar (main)
readInput
printMonth
printMonthTitle
printMonthBody
getMonthName
getStartDay
getTotalNumberOfDays
getNumberOfDaysInMonth
isLeapYear

FIGURE 5.12 The structure chart shows the hierarchical relationship of the subproblems in the program.

5.12.2 Top-Down or Bottom-Up Implementation

Now we turn our attention to implementation. In general, a subproblem corresponds to a method in the implementation, although some are so simple that this is unnecessary. You would need to decide which modules to implement as methods and which to combine in other methods. Decisions of this kind should be based on whether the overall program will be easier to read as a result of your choice. In this example, the subproblem readInput can be simply implemented in the main method.

You can use either a "top-down" or a "bottom-up" approach. The top-down approach implements one method in the structure chart at a time from the top to the bottom. Stubs can be used for the methods waiting to be implemented. A *stub* is a simple but incomplete version of a method. The use of stubs enables you to quickly build the framework of the program. Implement the main method first, then use a stub for the printMonth method. For example, let printMonth display the year and the month in the stub. Thus, your program may begin like this:

top-down approach

stub

```
public class PrintCalendar {
  /** Main method */
  public static void main(String[] args) {
    Scanner input = new Scanner(System.in);

    // Prompt the user to enter year
    System.out.print("Enter full year (e.g., 2001): ");
    int year = input.nextInt();
```

```
    // Prompt the user to enter month
    System.out.print("Enter month as number between 1 and 12: ");
    int month = input.nextInt();

    // Print calendar for the month of the year
    printMonth(year, month);
  }

  /** A stub for printMonth may look like this */
  public static void printMonth(int year, int month) {
    System.out.print(month + " " + year);
  }

  /** A stub for printMonthTitle may look like this */
  public static void printMonthTitle(int year, int month) {
  }

  /** A stub for getMonthBody may look like this */
  public static void printMonthBody(int year, int month) {
  }

  /** A stub for getMonthName may look like this */
  public static String getMonthName(int month) {
    return "January"; // A dummy value
  }

  /** A stub for getMonthName may look like this */
  public static int getStartDay(int year, int month) {
    return 1; // A dummy value
  }

  /** A stub for getTotalNumberOfDays may look like this */
  public static int getTotalNumberOfDays(int year, int month) {
    return 10000; // A dummy value
  }

  /** A stub for getNumberOfDaysInMonth may look like this */
  public static int getNumberOfDaysInMonth(int year, int month) {
    return 31; // A dummy value
  }

  /** A stub for getTotalNumberOfDays may look like this */
  public static boolean isLeapYear(int year) {
    return true; // A dummy value
  }
}
```

Compile and test the program, and fix any errors. You can now implement the `printMonth` method. For methods invoked from the `printMonth` method, you can again use stubs.

bottom-up approach

The bottom-up approach implements one method in the structure chart at a time from the bottom to the top. For each method implemented, write a test program to test it. The top-down and bottom-up approaches are both fine. Both approaches implement methods incrementally, help to isolate programming errors, and make debugging easy. Sometimes they can be used together.

5.12.3 Implementation Details

The `isLeapYear(int year)` method can be implemented using the following code:

```
return (year % 400 == 0 || (year % 4 == 0 && year % 100 != 0));
```

Use the following facts to implement `getTotalNumberOfDaysInMonth(int year, int month)`:

- January, March, May, July, August, October, and December have 31 days.
- April, June, September, and November have 30 days.
- February has 28 days during a regular year and 29 days during a leap year. A regular year, therefore, has 365 days, a leap year 366 days.

To implement `getTotalNumberOfDays(int year, int month)`, you need to compute the total number of days (`totalNumberOfDays`) between January 1, 1800, and the first day of the calendar month. You could find the total number of days between the year 1800 and the calendar year and then figure out the total number of days prior to the calendar month in the calendar year. The sum of these two totals is `totalNumberOfDays`.

To print a body, first pad some space before the start day and then print the lines for every week.

The complete program is given in Listing 5.12.

Listing 5.12 PrintCalendar.java

```
import java.util.Scanner;

public class PrintCalendar {
  /** Main method */
  public static void main(String[] args) {
    Scanner input = new Scanner(System.in);

    // Prompt the user to enter year
    System.out.print("Enter full year (e.g., 2001): ");
    int year = input.nextInt();

    // Prompt the user to enter month
    System.out.print("Enter month in number between 1 and 12: ");
    int month = input.nextInt();

    // Print calendar for the month of the year
    printMonth(year, month);
  }

  /** Print the calendar for a month in a year */
  public static void printMonth(int year, int month) {
    // Print the headings of the calendar
    printMonthTitle(year, month);

    // Print the body of the calendar
    printMonthBody(year, month);
  }

  /** Print the month title, e.g., May, 1999 */
  public static void printMonthTitle(int year, int month) {
    System.out.println("         " + getMonthName(month)
      + " " + year);
    System.out.println("-----------------------------");
    System.out.println(" Sun Mon Tue Wed Thu Fri Sat");
  }

  /** Get the English name for the month */
  public static String getMonthName(int month) {
    String monthName = " ";
```

printMonth

printMonthTitle

getMonthName

```
    switch (month) {
      case 1: monthName = "January"; break;
      case 2: monthName = "February"; break;
      case 3: monthName = "March"; break;
      case 4: monthName = "April"; break;
      case 5: monthName = "May"; break;
      case 6: monthName = "June"; break;
      case 7: monthName = "July"; break;
      case 8: monthName = "August"; break;
      case 9: monthName = "September"; break;
      case 10: monthName = "October"; break;
      case 11: monthName = "November"; break;
      case 12: monthName = "December";
    }

    return monthName;
  }

  /** Print month body */
```

getMonthBody

```
  public static void printMonthBody(int year, int month) {
    // Get start day of the week for the first date in the month
    int startDay = getStartDay(year, month);

    // Get number of days in the month
    int numberOfDaysInMonth = getNumberOfDaysInMonth(year, month);

    // Pad space before the first day of the month
    int i = 0;
    for (i = 0; i < startDay; i++)
      System.out.print("    ");

    for (i = 1; i <= numberOfDaysInMonth; i++) {
      System.out.printf("%4d", i);

      if ((i + startDay) % 7 == 0)
        System.out.println();
    }

   System.out.println();
 }

  /** Get the start day of month/1/year */
```

getStartDay

```
  public static int getStartDay(int year, int month) {
    final int START_DAY_FOR_JAN_1_1800 = 3;
    // Get total number of days from 1/1/1800 to month/1/year
    int totalNumberOfDays = getTotalNumberOfDays(year, month);

    // Return the start day for month/1/year
    return (totalNumberOfDays + START_DAY_FOR_JAN_1_1800) % 7;
  }

  /** Get the total number of days since January 1, 1800 */
```

getTotalNumberOfDays

```
  public static int getTotalNumberOfDays(int year, int month) {
    int total = 0;

    // Get the total days from 1800 to 1/1/year
    for (int i = 1800; i < year; i++)
      if (isLeapYear(i))
```

```
        total = total + 366;
      else
        total = total + 365;

    // Add days from Jan to the month prior to the calendar month
    for (int i = 1; i < month; i++)
      total = total + getNumberOfDaysInMonth(year, i);

    return total;
  }

  /** Get the number of days in a month */
  public static int getNumberOfDaysInMonth(int year, int month) {
    if (month == 1 || month == 3 || month == 5 || month == 7 ||
     month == 8 || month == 10 || month == 12)
     return 31;

    if (month == 4 || month == 6 || month == 9 || month == 11)
      return 30;

    if (month == 2) return isLeapYear(year) ? 29 : 28;

    return 0; // If month is incorrect
  }

  /** Determine if it is a leap year */
  public static boolean isLeapYear(int year) {
    return year % 400 == 0 || (year % 4 == 0 && year % 100 != 0);
  }
}
```

getNumberOfDaysInMonth

isLeapYear

The program does not validate user input. For instance, if the user enters either a month not in the range between 1 and 12 or a year before 1800, the program displays an erroneous calendar. To avoid this error, add an `if` statement to check the input before printing the calendar.

This program prints calendars for a month but could easily be modified to print calendars for a whole year. Although it can print months only after January 1800, it could be modified to trace the day of a month before 1800.

Note

Method abstraction modularizes programs in a neat, hierarchical manner. Programs written as collections of concise methods are easier to write, debug, maintain, and modify. This writing style also promotes method reusability.

incremental development and testing

Tip

When implementing a large program, use the top-down or bottom-up approach. Do not write the entire program at once. Using these approaches seems to take more development time (because you repeatedly compile and run the program), but it actually saves time and makes debugging easier.

Key Terms

actual parameter 157
argument 157
ambiguous invocation 170
divide and conquer 177
formal parameter (i.e., parameter) 157
information hiding 177
method 156
method abstraction 176

Chapter Summary

1. Making programs modular and reusable is one of the central goals in software engineering. Java provides many powerful constructs that help to achieve this goal. Methods are one such construct.

2. The method header specifies the *modifiers*, *return value type*, *method name*, and *parameters* of the method. The static modifier is used for all the methods in this chapter.

3. A method may return a value. The `returnValueType` is the data type of the value the method returns. If the method does not return a value, the `returnValueType` is the keyword `void`.

4. The *parameter list* refers to the type, order, and number of the parameters of a method. The method name and the parameter list together constitute the *method signature*. Parameters are optional; that is, a method may contain no parameters.

5. A return statement can also be used in a `void` method for terminating the method and returning to the method's caller. This is useful occasionally for circumventing the normal flow of control in a method.

6. The arguments that are passed to a method should have the same number, type, and order as the parameters in the method signature.

7. When a program calls a method, program control is transferred to the called method. A called method returns control to the caller when its return statement is executed or when its method-ending closing brace is reached.

8. A value-returning method can also be invoked as a statement in Java. In this case, the caller simply ignores the return value.

9. Each time a method is invoked, the system stores parameters and local variables in a space known as a *stack*. When a method calls another method, the caller's stack space is kept intact, and new space is created to handle the new method call. When a method finishes its work and returns to its caller, its associated space is released.

10. A method can be overloaded. This means that two methods can have the same name, as long as their method parameter lists differ.

11. A variable declared in a method is called a local variable. The scope of a local variable starts from its declaration and continues to the end of the block that contains the variable. A local variable must be declared and initialized before it is used.

12. *Method abstraction* is achieved by separating the use of a method from its implementation. The client can use a method without knowing how it is implemented. The details of the implementation are encapsulated in the method and hidden from the client who invokes the method. This is known as *information hiding* or *encapsulation*.

13. Method abstraction modularizes programs in a neat, hierarchical manner. Programs written as collections of concise methods are easier to write, debug, maintain, and modify than would otherwise be the case. This writing style also promotes method reusability.

14. When implementing a large program, use the top-down or bottom-up coding approach. Do not write the entire program at once. This approach seems to take more time for coding (because you are repeatedly compiling and running the program), but it actually saves time and makes debugging easier.

Review Questions

Sections 5.2–5.4

5.1 What are the benefits of using a method? How do you define a method? How do you invoke a method?

5.2 What is the `return` type of a `main` method?

5.3 Can you simplify the `max` method in Listing 5.1 using the conditional operator?

5.4 True or false? A call to a method with a `void` return type is always a statement itself, but a call to a value-returning method is always a component of an expression.

5.5 What would be wrong with not writing a `return` statement in a value-returning method? Can you have a `return` statement in a `void` method? Does the `return` statement in the following method cause syntax errors?

```
public static void xMethod(double x, double y) {
  System.out.println(x + y);
  return x + y;
}
```

5.6 Define the terms parameter, argument, and method signature.

5.7 Write method headers for the following methods:

- Computing a sales commission, given the sales amount and the commission rate.
- Printing the calendar for a month, given the month and year.
- Computing a square root.
- Testing whether a number is even, and returning `true` if it is.
- Printing a message a specified number of times.
- Computing the monthly payment, given the loan amount, number of years, and annual interest rate.
- Finding the corresponding uppercase letter, given a lowercase letter.

5.8 Identify and correct the errors in the following program:

```
public class Test {
  public static method1(int n, m) {
    n += m;
    method2(3.4);
  }

  public static int method2(int n) {
    if (n > 0) return 1;
    else if (n == 0) return 0;
    else if (n < 0) return -1;
  }
}
```

5.9 Reformat the following program according to the programming st yle and documentation guidelines proposed in §2.16, "Programming Style and Documentation." Use the next-line brace style.

```
public class Test {
  public static double method1(double i,double j)
  {
  while (i<j) {
    j--;
  }

  return j;
  }
}
```

Sections 5.5–5.7

5.10 How is an argument passed to a method? Can the argument have the same name as its parameter?

5.11 What is pass-by-value? Show the result of the following programs:

```
public class Test {
  public static void main(String[] args) {
    int max = 0;
    max(1, 2, max);
    System.out.println(max);
  }

  public static void max(
      int value1, int value2, int max) {
    if (value1 > value2)
      max = value1;
    else
      max = value2;
  }
}
```

(a)

```
public class Test {
  public static void main(String[] args) {
    int i = 1;
    while (i <= 6) {
      method1(i, 2);
      i++;
    }
  }

  public static void method1(
      int i, int num) {
    for (int j = 1; j <= i; j++) {
      System.out.print(num + " ");
      num *= 2;
    }

    System.out.println();
  }
}
```

(b)

```
public class Test {
  public static void main(String[] args) {
    // Initialize times
    int times = 3;
    System.out.println("Before the call,"
      + " variable times is " + times);

    // Invoke nPrintln and display times
    nPrintln("Welcome to Java!", times);
    System.out.println("After the call,"
      + " variable times is " + times);
  }

  // Print the message n times
  public static void nPrintln(
      String message, int n) {
    while (n > 0) {
      System.out.println("n = " + n);
      System.out.println(message);
      n--;
    }
  }
}
```

(c)

```
public class Test {
  public static void main(String[] args) {
    int i = 0;
    while (i <= 4) {
      method1(i);
      i++;
    }

    System.out.println("i is " + i);
  }

  public static void method1(int i) {
    do {
      if (i % 3 != 0)
        System.out.print(i + " ");
      i--;
    }
    while (i >= 1);

    System.out.println();
  }
}
```

(d)

5.12 For (a) in the preceding question, show the contents of the stack just before the method `max` is invoked, just as `max` is entered, just before `max` is returned, and right after `max` is returned.

Section 5.8

5.13 What is method overloading? Is it permissible to define two methods that have the same name but different parameter types? Is it permissible to define two methods in a class that have identical method names and parameter lists but different return value types or different modifiers?

5.14 What is wrong in the following program?

```
public class Test {
  public static void method(int x) {
  }

  public static int method(int y) {
    return y;
  }
}
```

Section 5.9

5.15 Identify and correct the errors in the following program:

```
public class Test {
  public static void main(String[] args) {
    nPrintln("Welcome to Java!", 5);
  }

  public static void nPrintln(String message, int n) {
    int n = 1;
```

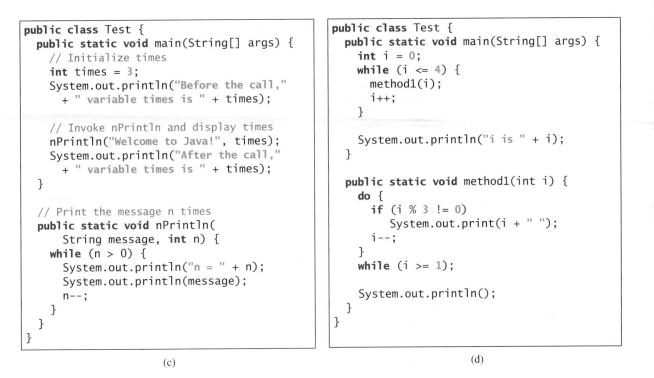

```
    for (int i = 0; i < n; i++)
      System.out.println(message);
  }
}
```

Section 5.10

5.16 True or false? The argument for trigonometric methods represents an angle in radians.

5.17 Write an expression that returns a random integer between `34` and `55`. Write an expression that returns a random integer between `0` and `999`. Write an expression that returns a random number between `5.5` and `55.5`. Write an expression that returns a random lowercase letter.

5.18 Evaluate the following method calls:

(a) Math.sqrt(4)
(b) Math.sin(2 * Math.PI)
(c) Math.cos(2 * Math.PI)
(d) Math.pow(2, 2)
(e) Math.log(Math.E)
(f) Math.exp(1)
(g) Math.max(2, Math.min(3, 4))
(h) Math.rint(−2.5)
(i) Math.ceil(−2.5)
(j) Math.floor(−2.5)
(k) Math.round(−2.5F)
(l) Math.round(−2.5)
(m) Math.rint(2.5)
(n) Math.ceil(2.5)
(o) Math.floor(2.5)
(p) Math.round(2.5F)
(q) Math.round(2.5)
(r) Math.round(Math.abs(−2.5))

Programming Exercises

Sections 5.2–5.9

5.1 (*Math: pentagonal numbers*) A pentagonal number is defined as $n(3n-1)/2$ for $n = 1, 2, \ldots$, and so on. So, the first few numbers are 1, 5, 12, 22, ... Write the following method that returns a pentagonal number:

```
public static int getPentagonalNumber(int n)
```

Write a test program that displays the first 100 pentagonal numbers with 10 numbers on each line.

5.2* (*Summing the digits in an integer*) Write a method that computes the sum of the digits in an integer. Use the following method header:

```
public static int sumDigits(long n)
```

For example, `sumDigits(234)` returns `9` $(2 + 3 + 4)$.

(*Hint*: Use the `%` operator to extract digits, and the `/` operator to remove the extracted digit. For instance, to extract `4` from `234`, use `234 % 10` (= 4). To remove `4` from `234`, use `234 / 10` (= 23). Use a loop to repeatedly extract and remove the digit until all the digits are extracted. Write a test program that prompts the user to enter an integer and displays the sum of all its digits.)

5.3** (*Palindrome integer*) Write the following two methods

```
// Return the reversal of an integer, i.e. reverse(456) returns 654
public static int reverse(int number)

// Return true if number is palindrome
public static boolean isPalindrome(int number)
```

Use the `reverse` method to implement `isPalindrome`. A number is a palindrome if its reversal is the same as itself. Write a test program that prompts the user to enter an integer and reports whether the integer is a palindrome.

5.4* (*Displaying an integer reversed*) Write the following method to display an integer in reverse order:

```
public static void reverse(int number)
```

For example, `reverse(3456)` displays `6543`. Write a test program that prompts the user to enter an integer and displays its reversal.

5.5* (*Sorting three numbers*) Write the following method to display three numbers in increasing order:

```
public static void displaySortedNumbers(
  double num1, double num2, double num3)
```

5.6* (*Displaying patterns*) Write a method to display a pattern as follows:

```
              1
            2 1
          3 2 1
...
n n-1 ... 3 2 1
```

The method header is

```
public static void displayPattern(int n)
```

5.7* (*Financial application: computing the future investment value*) Write a method that computes future investment value at a given interest rate for a specified number of years. The future investment is determined using the formula in Exercise 2.13.

Use the following method header:

```
public static double futureInvestmentValue(
  double investmentAmount, double monthlyInterestRate, int years)
```

For example, `futureInvestmentValue(10000, 0.05/12, 5)` returns `12833.59`.

Write a test program that prompts the user to enter the investment amount (e.g., 1000) and the interest rate (e.g., 9%) and prints a table that displays future value for the years from 1 to 30, as shown below:

```
The amount invested: 1000
Annual interest rate: 9%
Years        Future Value
1               1093.80
2               1196.41
...
29             13467.25
30             14730.57
```

5.8 (*Conversions between Celsius and Fahrenheit*) Write a class that contains the following two methods:

```
/** Converts from Celsius to Fahrenheit */
public static double celsiusToFahrenheit(double celsius)

/** Converts from Fahrenheit to Celsius */
public static double fahrenheitToCelsius(double fahrenheit)
```

The formula for the conversion is:

```
fahrenheit = (9.0 / 5) * celsius + 32
```

Write a test program that invokes these methods to display the following tables:

```
Celsius        Fahrenheit        Fahrenheit        Celsius

40.0           104.0             120.0             48.89
39.0           102.2             110.0             43.33
...
32.0           89.6              40.0              4.44
31.0           87.8              30.0              -1.11
```

5.9 (*Conversions between feet and meters*) Write a class that contains the following two methods:

```
/** Converts from feet to meters */
public static double footToMeter(double foot)

/** Converts from meters to feet */
public static double meterToFoot(double meter)
```

The formula for the conversion is:

```
meter = 0.305 * foot
```

Write a test program that invokes these methods to display the following tables:

```
Feet       Meters       Meters       Feet

1.0        0.305        20.0         65.574
2.0        0.61         25.0         81.967
...
9.0        2.745        60.0         196.721
10.0       3.05         65.0         213.115
```

5.10 (*Using the `isPrime` Method*) Listing 5.7, PrimeNumberMethod.java, provides the `isPrime(int number)` method for testing whether a number is prime. Use this method to find the number of prime numbers less than `10000`.

5.11 (*Financial application: computing commissions*) Write a method that computes the commission, using the scheme in Exercise 4.39. The header of the method is as follows:

```
public static double computeCommission(double salesAmount)
```

Write a test program that displays the following table:

Sales Amount	Commission
10000	900.0
15000	1500.0
...	
95000	11100.0
100000	11700.0

5.12 (*Displaying characters*) Write a method that prints characters using the following header:

```
public static void printChars(char ch1, char ch2, int
  numberPerLine)
```

This method prints the characters between `ch1` and `ch2` with the specified numbers per line. Write a test program that prints ten characters per line from `'1'` to `'Z'`.

5.13* (*Summing series*) Write a method to compute the following series:

$$m(i) = \frac{1}{2} + \frac{2}{3} + \ldots + \frac{i}{i+1}$$

Write a test program that displays the following table:

i	m(i)
1	0.5000
2	1.1667
...	
19	16.4023
20	17.3546

5.14* (*Computing series*) Write a method to compute the following series:

Video Note
Compute π

$$m(i) = 4\left(1 - \frac{1}{3} + \frac{1}{5} - \frac{1}{7} + \frac{1}{9} - \frac{1}{11} + \ldots + \frac{1}{2i-1} - \frac{1}{2i+1}\right)$$

Write a test program that displays the following table:

i	m(i)
10	3.04184
20	3.09162
...	
90	3.13048
100	3.13159

5.15* (*Financial application: printing a tax table*) Listing 3.6 gives a program to compute tax. Write a method for computing tax using the following header:

```
public static double computetax(int status, double taxableIncome)
```

Use this method to write a program that prints a tax table for taxable income from \$50,000 to \$60,000 with intervals of \$50 for all four statuses, as follows:

Taxable Income	Single	Married Joint	Married Separate	Head of a House
50000	8688	6665	8688	7353
50050	8700	6673	8700	7365
...				
59950	11175	8158	11175	9840
60000	11188	8165	11188	9853

5.16* (*Number of days in a year*) Write a method that returns the number of days in a year using the following header:

```
public static int numberOfDaysInAYear(int year)
```

Write a test program that displays the number of days in year from 2000 to 2010.

Sections 5.10–5.11

5.17* (*Displaying matrix of 0s and 1s*) Write a method that displays an n-by-n matrix using the following header:

```
public static void printMatrix(int n)
```

Each element is 0 or 1, which is generated randomly. Write a test program that prints a 3-by-3 matrix that may look like this:

```
0 1 0
0 0 0
1 1 1
```

5.18 (*Using the* Math.sqrt *method*) Write a program that prints the following table using the sqrt method in the Math class.

```
Number        SquareRoot
0                 0.0000
2                 1.4142
...
18                4.2426
20                4.4721
```

5.19* (*The* MyTriangle *class*) Create a class named MyTriangle that contains the following two methods:

```
/** Returns true if the sum of any two sides is
 *  greater than the third side. */
public static boolean isValid(
  double side1, double side2, double side3)

/** Returns the area of the triangle. */
public static double area(
  double side1, double side2, double side3)
```

Write a test program that reads three sides for a triangle and computes the area if the input is valid. Otherwise, it displays that the input is invalid. The formula for computing the area of a triangle is given in Exercise 2.21.

5.20 (*Using trigonometric methods*) Print the following table to display the sin value and cos value of degrees from 0 to 360 with increments of 10 degrees. Round the value to keep four digits after the decimal point.

```
Degree       Sin          Cos
0            0.0000       1.0000
10           0.1736       0.9848
...
350          -0.1736      0.9848
360          0.0000       1.0000
```

5.21** (*Statistics: computing mean and standard deviation*) In business applications, you are often asked to compute the mean and standard deviation of data. The mean is simply the average of the numbers. The standard deviation is a statistic that tells you how tightly all the various data are clustered around the mean in a set of data. For example, what is the average age of the students in a class? How close are the ages? If all the students are the same age, the deviation is 0. Write a program that prompts the user to enter ten numbers, and displays the mean and standard deviations of these numbers using the following formula:

$$mean = \frac{\sum_{i=1}^{n} x_i}{n} = \frac{x_1 + x_2 + \ldots + x_n}{n} \qquad deviation = \sqrt{\frac{\sum_{i=1}^{n} x_i^2 - \frac{\left(\sum_{i=1}^{n} x_i\right)^2}{n}}{n-1}}$$

Here is a sample run:

```
Enter ten numbers: 1 2 3 4.5 5.6 6 7 8 9 10 ↵Enter
The mean is 5.61
The standard deviation is 2.99794
```

5.22** (*Math: approximating the square root*) Implement the `sqrt` method. The square root of a number, `num`, can be approximated by repeatedly performing a calculation using the following formula:

```
nextGuess = (lastGuess + (num / lastGuess)) / 2
```

When `nextGuess` and `lastGuess` are almost identical, `nextGuess` is the approximated square root.

The initial guess can be any positive value (e.g., `1`). This value will be the starting value for `lastGuess`. If the difference between `nextGuess` and `lastGuess` is less than a very small number, such as `0.0001`, you can claim that `nextGuess` is the approximated square root of `num`. If not, `nextGuess` becomes `lastGuess` and the approximation process continues.

Sections 5.10–5.11

5.23* (*Generating random characters*) Use the methods in `RandomCharacter` in Listing 5.10 to print 100 uppercase letters and then 100 single digits, printing ten per line.

5.24** (*Displaying current date and time*) Listing 2.9, ShowCurrentTime.java, displays the current time. Improve this example to display the current date and time. The calendar example in Listing 5.12, PrintCalendar.java, should give you some ideas on how to find year, month, and day.

5.25** (*Converting milliseconds to hours, minutes, and seconds*) Write a method that converts milliseconds to hours, minutes, and seconds using the following header:

```
public static String convertMillis(long millis)
```

The method returns a string as hours:minutes:seconds. For example, `convertMillis(5500)` returns a string 0:0:5, `convertMillis(100000)` returns a string 0:1:40, and `convertMillis(555550000)` returns a string 154:19:10.

Comprehensive

5.26** (*Palindromic prime*) A *palindromic prime* is a prime number and also palindromic. For example, 131 is a prime and also a palindromic prime. So are 313 and 757. Write a program that displays the first 100 palindromic prime numbers. Display 10 numbers per line and align the numbers properly, as follows:

```
   2     3     5     7    11   101   131   151   181   191
 313   353   373   383   727   757   787   797   919   929
...
```

5.27** (*Emirp*) An *emirp* (prime spelled backward) is a nonpalindromic prime number whose reversal is also a prime. For example, 17 is a prime and 71 is a prime. So, 17 and 71 are emirps. Write a program that displays the first 100 emirps. Display 10 numbers per line and align the numbers properly, as follows:

```
  13   17   31   37   71   73   79   97  107  113
 149  157  167  179  199  311  337  347  359  389
 ...
```

5.28** (*Mersenne prime*) A prime number is called a *Mersenne prime* if it can be written in the form $2^p - 1$ for some positive integer p. Write a program that finds all Mersenne primes with $p \leq 31$ and displays the output as follows:

```
p        2^p - 1
2           3
3           7
5          31
...
```

5.29** (*Game: craps*) Craps is a popular dice game played in casinos. Write a program to play a variation of the game, as follows:

Roll two dice. Each die has six faces representing values 1, 2, . . . , and 6, respectively. Check the sum of the two dice. If the sum is 2, 3, or 12 (called *craps*), you lose; if the sum is 7 or 11 (called *natural*), you win; if the sum is another value (i.e., 4, 5, 6, 8, 9, or 10), a *point* is established. Continue to roll the dice until either a 7 or the same point value is rolled. If 7 is rolled, you lose. Otherwise, you win.

Your program acts as a single player. Here are some sample runs.

```
You rolled 5 + 6 = 11
You win
```

```
You rolled 1 + 2 = 3
You lose
```

```
You rolled 4 + 4 = 8
point is 8
You rolled 6 + 2 = 8
You win
```

```
You rolled 3 + 2 = 5
point is 5
You rolled 2 + 5 = 7
You lose
```

5.30** (*Twin primes*) Twin primes are a pair of prime numbers that differ by 2. For example, 3 and 5 are twin primes, 5 and 7 are twin primes, and 11 and 13 are twin primes. Write a program to find all twin primes less than 1000. Display the output as follows:

```
(3, 5)
(5, 7)
...
```

5.31** (*Financial: credit card number validation*) Credit card numbers follow certain patterns. A credit card number must have between 13 and 16 digits. It must start with:

- 4 for Visa cards
- 5 for Master cards
- 37 for American Express cards
- 6 for Discover cards

In 1954, Hans Luhn of IBM proposed an algorithm for validating credit card numbers. The algorithm is useful to determine whether a card number is entered correctly or whether a credit card is scanned correctly by a scanner. All credit card numbers are generated following this validity check, commonly known as the *Luhn check* or the *Mod 10 check*, which can be described as follows (for illustration, consider the card number 4388576018402626):

1. Double every second digit from right to left. If doubling of a digit results in a two-digit number, add up the two digits to get a single-digit number.

   2 * 2 = 4
   2 * 2 = 4
   4 * 2 = 8
   1 * 2 = 2
   6 * 2 = 12 (1 + 2 = 3)
   5 * 2 = 10 (1 + 0 = 1)
   8 * 2 = 16 (1 + 6 = 7)
   4 * 2 = 8

2. Now add all single-digit numbers from Step 1.

   4 + 4 + 8 + 2 + 3 + 1 + 7 + 8 = 37

3. Add all digits in the odd places from right to left in the card number.

   6 + 6 + 0 + 8 + 0 + 7 + 8 + 3 = 38

4. Sum the results from Step 2 and Step 3.

   37 + 38 = 75

5. If the result from Step 4 is divisible by 10, the card number is valid; otherwise, it is invalid. For example, the number 4388576018402626 is invalid, but the number 4388576018410707 is valid.

Write a program that prompts the user to enter a credit card number as a `long` integer. Display whether the number is valid or invalid. Design your program to use the following methods:

```
/** Return true if the card number is valid */
public static boolean isValid(long number)

/** Get the result from Step 2 */
public static int sumOfDoubleEvenPlace(long number)
```

```
/** Return this number if it is a single digit, otherwise, return
 * the sum of the two digits */
public static int getDigit(int number)

/** Return sum of odd place digits in number */
public static int sumOfOddPlace(long number)

/** Return true if the digit d is a prefix for number */
public static boolean prefixMatched(long number, int d)

/** Return the number of digits in d */
public static int getSize(long d)

/** Return the first k number of digits from number. If the
 * number of digits in number is less than k, return number. */
public static long getPrefix(long number, int k)
```

5.32** (*Game: chance of winning at craps*) Revise Exercise 5.29 to run it `10000` times and display the number of winning games.

5.33*** (*Current date and time*) Invoking `System.currentTimeMillis()` returns the elapse time in milliseconds since midnight of January 1, 1970. Write a program that displays the date and time. Here is a sample run:

```
Current date and time is May 16, 2009 10:34:23
```

5.34** (*Printing calendar*) Exercise 3.21 uses Zeller's congruence to calculate the day of the week. Simplify Listing 5.12, PrintCalendar.java, using Zeller's algorithm to get the start day of the month.

5.35 (*Geometry: area of a pentagon*) The area of a pentagon can be computed using the following formula:

$$Area = \frac{5 \times s^2}{4 \times \tan\left(\frac{\pi}{5}\right)}$$

Write a program that prompts the user to enter the side of a pentagon and displays its area.

5.36* (*Geometry: area of a regular polygon*) A regular polygon is an n-sided polygon in which all sides are of the same length and all angles have the same degree (i.e., the polygon is both equilateral and equiangular). The formula for computing the area of a regular polygon is

$$Area = \frac{n \times s^2}{4 \times \tan\left(\frac{\pi}{n}\right)}.$$

Write a method that returns the area of a regular polygon using the following header:

```
public static double area(int n, double side)
```

Write a main method that prompts the user to enter the number of sides and the side of a regular polygon and displays its area.

Chapter 6

Single-Dimensional Arrays

Objectives

- To describe why arrays are necessary in programming (§6.1).
- To declare array reference variables and create arrays (§§6.2.1–6.2.2).
- To initialize the values in an array (§6.2.3).
- To access array elements using indexed variables (§6.2.4).
- To declare, create, and initialize an array using an array initializer (§6.2.5).
- To program common array operations (displaying arrays, summing all elements, finding min and max elements, random shuffling, shifting elements) (§6.2.6).
- To simplify programming using the for-each loops (§6.2.7).
- To apply arrays in the `LottoNumbers` and `DeckOfCards` problems (§§6.3–6.4).
- To copy contents from one array to another (§6.5).
- To develop and invoke methods with array arguments and return value (§6.6–6.7).
- To define a method with variable-length argument list (§6.8).
- To search elements using the linear (§6.9.1) or binary (§6.9.2) search algorithm.
- To sort an array using the selection sort (§6.10.1)
- To sort an array using the insertion sort (§6.10.2).
- To use the methods in the `Arrays` class (§6.11).

6.1 Introduction

problem

Often you will have to store a large number of values during the execution of a program. Suppose, for instance, that you need to read 100 numbers, compute their average, and find out how many numbers are above the average. Your program first reads the numbers and computes their average, then compares each number with the average to determine whether it is above the average. In order to accomplish this task, the numbers must all be stored in variables. You have to declare 100 variables and repeatedly write almost identical code 100 times.

why array?

Writing a program this way would be impractical. So, how do you solve this problem?

what is array?

An efficient, organized approach is needed. Java and most other high-level languages provide a data structure, the *array*, which stores a fixed-size sequential collection of elements of the same type. In the present case, you can store all 100 numbers into an array and access them through a single array variable. The solution may look like this:

declare array (line 4); store number in array (line 10); get average (line 14); above average? (line 18)

```
 1 public class AnalyzeNumbers {
 2   public static void main(String[] args) {
 3     final int NUMBER_OF_ELEMENTS = 100;
 4     double[] numbers = new double[NUMBER_OF_ELEMENTS];
 5     double sum = 0;
 6 
 7     java.util.Scanner input = new java.util.Scanner(System.in);
 8     for (int i = 0; i < NUMBER_OF_ELEMENTS; i++) {
 9       System.out.print("Enter a new number: ");
10       numbers[i] = input.nextDouble();
11       sum += numbers[i];
12     }
13 
14     double average = sum / NUMBER_OF_ELEMENTS;
15 
16     int count = 0; // The number of elements above average
17     for (int i = 0; i < NUMBER_OF_ELEMENTS; i++)
18       if (numbers[i] > average)
19         count++;
20 
21     System.out.println("Average is " + average);
22     System.out.println("Number of elements above the average "
23       + count);
24   }
25 }
```

The program creates an array of 100 elements in line 4, stores numbers into the array in line 10, adds each number to sum in line 11, and obtains the average in line 14. It then compares each number in the array with the average to count the number of values above the average (lines 16–19).

This chapter introduces single-dimensional arrays. The next chapter will introduce two-dimensional and multidimensional arrays.

6.2 Array Basics

An array is used to store a collection of data, but often we find it more useful to think of an array as a collection of variables of the same type. Instead of declaring individual variables, such as number0, number1, . . . , and number99, you declare one array variable such as numbers and use numbers[0], numbers[1], . . . , and numbers[99] to represent individual variables. This section introduces how to declare array variables, create arrays, and process arrays using indexed variables.

6.2.1 Declaring Array Variables

To use an array in a program, you must declare a variable to reference the array and specify the array's *element type*. Here is the syntax for declaring an array variable:

element type

```
elementType[] arrayRefVar;
```

The `elementType` can be any data type, and all elements in the array will have the same data type. For example, the following code declares a variable `myList` that references an array of double elements.

```
double[] myList;
```

Note

You can also use `elementType arrayRefVar[]` to declare an array variable. This style comes from the C language and was adopted in Java to accommodate C programmers. The style `elementType[] arrayRefVar` is preferred.

preferred syntax

6.2.2 Creating Arrays

Unlike declarations for primitive data type variables, the declaration of an array variable does not allocate any space in memory for the array. It creates only a storage location for the reference to an array. If a variable does not contain a reference to an array, the value of the variable is `null`. You cannot assign elements to an array unless it has already been created. After an array variable is declared, you can create an array by using the `new` operator with the following syntax:

```
arrayRefVar = new elementType[arraySize];
```

new operator

This statement does two things: (1) it creates an array using `new elementType[arraySize]`; (2) it assigns the reference of the newly created array to the variable `arrayRefVar`.

Declaring an array variable, creating an array, and assigning the reference of the array to the variable can be combined in one statement, as shown below:

```
elementType arrayRefVar = new elementType[arraySize];
```

or

```
elementType arrayRefVar[] = new elementType[arraySize];
```

Here is an example of such a statement:

```
double[] myList = new double[10];
```

This statement declares an array variable, `myList`, creates an array of ten elements of `double` type, and assigns its reference to `myList`. To assign values to the elements, use the syntax:

```
arrayRefVar[index] = value;
```

For example, the following code initializes the array.

```
myList[0] = 5.6;
myList[1] = 4.5;
myList[2] = 3.3;
myList[3] = 13.2;
```

```
myList[4] = 4.0;
myList[5] = 34.33;
myList[6] = 34.0;
myList[7] = 45.45;
myList[8] = 99.993;
myList[9] = 11123;
```

The array is pictured in Figure 6.1.

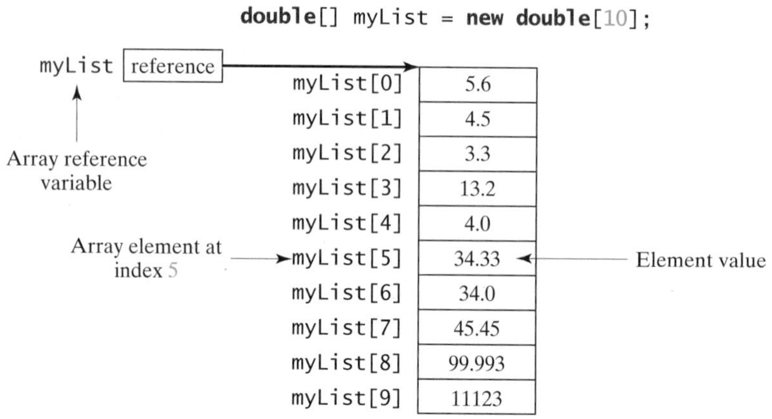
double[] myList = new double[10];
myList
reference
Array reference variable
Array element at index 5
myList[0]
myList[1]
myList[2]
myList[3]
myList[4]
myList[5]
myList[6]
myList[7]
myList[8]
myList[9]
5.6
4.5
3.3
13.2
4.0
34.33
34.0
45.45
99.993
11123
Element value

FIGURE 6.1 The array `myList` has ten elements of `double` type and `int` indices from `0` to `9`.

array vs. array variable

> **Note**
> An array variable that appears to hold an array actually contains a reference to that array. Strictly speaking, an array variable and an array are different, but most of the time the distinction can be ignored. Thus it is all right to say, for simplicity, that `myList` is an array, instead of stating, at greater length, that `myList` is a variable that contains a reference to an array of ten double elements.

6.2.3 Array Size and Default Values

array length

When space for an array is allocated, the array size must be given, specifying the number of elements that can be stored in it. The size of an array cannot be changed after the array is created. Size can be obtained using `arrayRefVar.length`. For example, `myList.length` is `10`.

default values

When an array is created, its elements are assigned the default value of `0` for the numeric primitive data types, `'\u0000'` for `char` types, and `false` for `boolean` types.

6.2.4 Array Indexed Variables

0 based

The array elements are accessed through the index. Array indices are `0` based; that is, they range from `0` to `arrayRefVar.length-1`. In the example in Figure 6.1, `myList` holds ten `double` values, and the indices are from `0` to `9`.

indexed variables

Each element in the array is represented using the following syntax, known as an *indexed variable*:

```
arrayRefVar[index];
```

For example, `myList[9]` represents the last element in the array `myList`.

> **Caution**
> Some languages use parentheses to reference an array element, as in `myList(9)`. But Java uses brackets, as in `myList[9]`.

After an array is created, an indexed variable can be used in the same way as a regular variable. For example, the following code adds the values in `myList[0]` and `myList[1]` to `myList[2]`.

```
myList[2] = myList[0] + myList[1];
```

The following loop assigns `0` to `myList[0]`, `1` to `myList[1]`, . . . , and `9` to `myList[9]`:

```
for (int i = 0; i < myList.length; i++) {
  myList[i] = i;
}
```

6.2.5 Array Initializers

Java has a shorthand notation, known as the *array initializer*, which combines in one statement declaring an array, creating an array, and initializing, using the following syntax:

```
elementType[] arrayRefVar = {value0, value1, ..., valuek};
```

For example,

```
double[] myList = {1.9, 2.9, 3.4, 3.5};
```

This statement declares, creates, and initializes the array `myList` with four elements, which is equivalent to the statements shown below:

```
double[] myList = new double[4];
myList[0] = 1.9;
myList[1] = 2.9;
myList[2] = 3.4;
myList[3] = 3.5;
```

Caution

The `new` operator is not used in the array-initializer syntax. Using an array initializer, you have to declare, create, and initialize the array all in one statement. Splitting it would cause a syntax error. Thus the next statement is wrong:

```
double[] myList;
myList = {1.9, 2.9, 3.4, 3.5};
```

6.2.6 Processing Arrays

When processing array elements, you will often use a `for` loop—for two reasons:

- All of the elements in an array are of the same type. They are evenly processed in the same fashion repeatedly using a loop.
- Since the size of the array is known, it is natural to use a `for` loop.

Assume the array is created as follows:

```
double[] myList = new double[10];
```

Here are some examples of processing arrays:

1. (*Initializing arrays with input values*) The following loop initializes the array `myList` with user input values.

```
java.util.Scanner input = new java.util.Scanner(System.in);
System.out.print("Enter " + myList.length + " values: ");
for (int i = 0; i < myList.length; i++)
  myList[i] = input.nextDouble();
```

2. (*Initializing arrays with random values*) The following loop initializes the array **myList** with random values between **0.0** and **100.0**, but less than **100.0**.

```
for (int i = 0; i < myList.length; i++) {
  myList[i] = Math.random() * 100;
}
```

3. (*Displaying arrays*) To print an array, you have to print each element in the array using a loop like the following:

```
for (int i = 0; i < myList.length; i++) {
  System.out.print(myList[i] + " ");
}
```

print character array

Tip

For an array of the **char[]** type, it can be printed using one print statement. For example, the following code displays **Dallas**:

```
char[] city = {'D', 'a', 'l', 'l', 'a', 's'};
System.out.println(city);
```

4. (*Summing all elements*) Use a variable named **total** to store the sum. Initially **total** is **0**. Add each element in the array to **total** using a loop like this:

```
double total = 0;
for (int i = 0; i < myList.length; i++) {
  total += myList[i];
}
```

5. (*Finding the largest element*) Use a variable named **max** to store the largest element. Initially **max** is **myList[0]**. To find the largest element in the array **myList**, compare each element with **max**, and update **max** if the element is greater than **max**.

```
double max = myList[0];
for (int i = 1; i < myList.length; i++) {
  if (myList[i] > max) max = myList[i];
}
```

6. (*Finding the smallest index of the largest element*) Often you need to locate the largest element in an array. If an array has more than one largest element, find the smallest index of such an element. Suppose the array **myList** is {**1**, **5**, **3**, **4**, **5**, **5**}. The largest element is **5** and the smallest index for **5** is **1**. Use a variable named **max** to store the largest element and a variable named **indexOfMax** to denote the index of the largest element. Initially **max** is **myList[0]**, and **indexOfMax** is **0**. Compare each element in **myList** with **max**, and update **max** and **indexOfMax** if the element is greater than **max**.

```
double max = myList[0];
int indexOfMax = 0;
for (int i = 1; i < myList.length; i++) {
  if (myList[i] > max) {
    max = myList[i];
    indexOfMax = i;
  }
}
```

What is the consequence if **(myList[i] > max)** is replaced by **(myList[i] >= max)**?

Video Note
Random shuffling

7. (*Random shuffling*) In many applications, you need to randomly reorder the elements in an array. This is called a *shuffling*. To accomplish this, for each element **myList[i]**, randomly generate an index **j** and swap **myList[i]** with **myList[j]**, as follows:

```
for (int i = 0; i < myList.length; i++) {
  // Generate an index j randomly
  int index = (int) (Math.random()
    * mylist.length);

  // Swap myList[i] with myList[j]
  double temp = myList[i];
  myList[i] = myList[index]
  myList[index] = temp;
}
```

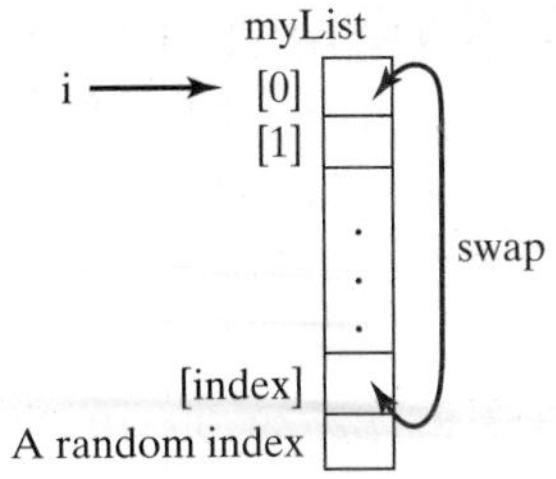
myList
i
[0]
[1]
swap
[index]
A random index

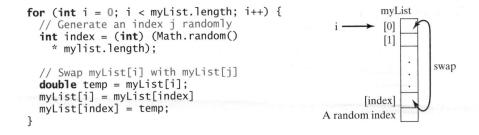

8. (*Shifting elements*) Sometimes you need to shift the elements left or right. Here is an example to shift the elements one position to the left and fill the last element with the first element:

```
double temp = myList[0]; // Retain the first element

// Shift elements left
for (int i = 1; i < myList.length; i++) {
  myList[i - 1] = myList[i];
}

// Move the first element to fill in the last position
myList[myList.length - 1] = temp;
```

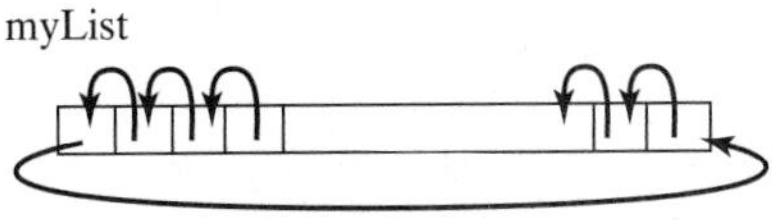
myList

6.2.7 For-each Loops

Java supports a convenient `for` loop, known as a *for-each loop* or *enhanced for loop*, which enables you to traverse the array sequentially without using an index variable. For example, the following code displays all the elements in the array `myList`:

```
for (double u: myList) {
  System.out.println(u);
}
```

You can read the code as "for each element `u` in `myList` do the following." Note that the variable, `u`, must be declared the same type as the elements in `myList`.

In general, the syntax for a `for-each` loop is

```
for (elementType element: arrayRefVar) {
  // Process the element
}
```

You still have to use an index variable if you wish to traverse the array in a different order or change the elements in the array.

Caution

Accessing an array out of bounds is a common programming error that throws a runtime `ArrayIndexOutOfBoundsException`. To avoid it, make sure that you do not use an index beyond `arrayRefVar.length - 1`.

`ArrayIndexOutOfBounds-Exception`

Programmers often mistakenly reference the first element in an array with index `1`, but it should be `0`. This is called the *off-by-one error*. It is a common error in a loop to use `<=` where `<` should be used. For example, the following loop is wrong,

off-by-one error

```
for (int i = 0; i <= list.length; i++)
  System.out.print(list[i] + " ");
```

The `<=` should be replaced by `<`.

Video Note
Lotto numbers

6.3 Problem: Lotto Numbers

Each ticket for the Pick-10 lotto has `10` unique numbers ranging from `1` to `99`. Suppose you buys a lot of tickets and like to have them cover all numbers from `1` to `99`. Write a program that reads the ticket numbers from a file and checks whether all numbers are covered. Assume the last number in the file is `0`. Suppose the file contains the numbers

```
80 3 87 62 30 90 10 21 46 27
12 40 83 9 39 88 95 59 20 37
80 40 87 67 31 90 11 24 56 77
11 48 51 42 8 74 1 41 36 53
52 82 16 72 19 70 44 56 29 33
54 64 99 14 23 22 94 79 55 2
60 86 34 4 31 63 84 89 7 78
43 93 97 45 25 38 28 26 85 49
47 65 57 67 73 69 32 71 24 66
92 98 96 77 6 75 17 61 58 13
35 81 18 15 5 68 91 50 76
0
```

Your program should display

```
The tickets cover all numbers
```

Suppose the file contains the numbers

```
11 48 51 42 8 74 1 41 36 53
52 82 16 72 19 70 44 56 29 33
0
```

Your program should display

```
The tickets don't cover all numbers
```

How do you mark a number as covered? You can create an array with `99` `boolean` elements. Each element in the array can be used to mark whether a number is covered. Let the array be `isCovered`. Initially, each element is `false`, as shown in Figure 6.2(a). Whenever a number is read, its corresponding element is set to `true`. Suppose the numbers entered are `1`, `2`, `3`, `99`, `0`. When number `1` is read, `isCovered[0]` is set to `true` (see Figure 6.2(b)). When number `2` is read, `isCovered[2 - 1]` is set to `true` (see Figure 6.2(c)). When number `3` is read,

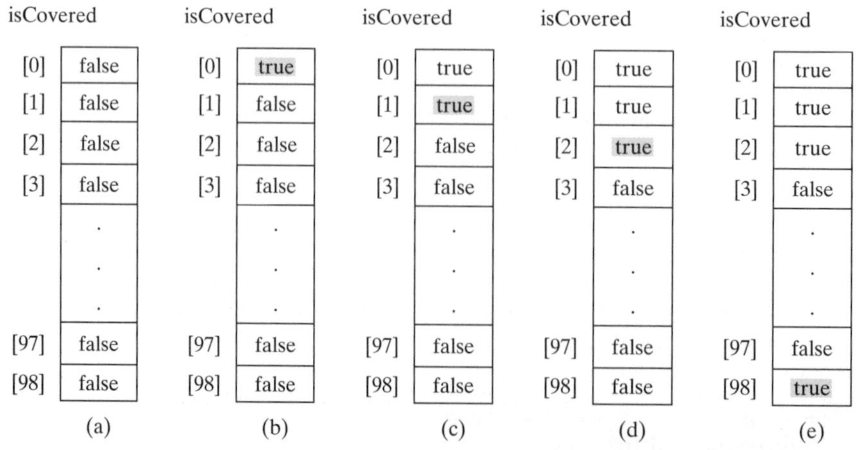

isCovered
[0] [1] [2] [3] [97] [98]
false
true
(a)
(b)
(c)
(d)
(e)

Figure 6.2 If number `i` appears in a Lotto ticket, `isCovered[i-1]` is set to true.

isCovered[3 - 1] is set to true (see Figure 6.2(d)). When number 99 is read, set isCovered[98] to true (see Figure 6.2(e)).

The algorithm for the program can be described as follows:

```
for each number k read from the file,
  mark number k as covered by setting isCovered[k - 1] true;

if every isCovered[i] is true
  The tickets cover all numbers
else
  The tickets don't cover all numbers
```

The complete program is given in Listing 6.1.

LISTING 6.1 LottoNumbers.java

```
 1 import java.util.Scanner;
 2
 3 public class LottoNumbers {
 4   public static void main(String args[]) {
 5     Scanner input = new Scanner(System.in);
 6     boolean[] isCovered = new boolean[99]; // Default is false
 7
 8     // Read each number and mark its corresponding element covered
 9     int number = input.nextInt();
10     while (number != 0) {
11       isCovered[number - 1] = true;
12       number = input.nextInt();
13     }
14
15     // Check whether all covered
16     boolean allCovered = true; // Assume all covered initially
17     for (int i = 0; i < 99; i++)
18       if (!isCovered[i]) {
19         allCovered = false; // Find one number not covered
20         break;
21       }
22
23     // Display result
24     if (allCovered)
25       System.out.println("The tickets cover all numbers");
26     else
27       System.out.println("The tickets don't cover all numbers");
28   }
29 }
```

create and initialize array

read number

mark number covered

read number

check **allCovered**?

Suppose you have created a text file named LottoNumbers.txt that contains the input data 2 5 6 5 4 3 23 43 2 0. You can run the program using the following command:

```
java LottoNumbers < LottoNumbers.txt
```

The program can be traced as follows:

The program creates an array of 99 boolean elements and initializes each element to false (line 6). It reads the first number from the file (line 9). The program then repeats the following operations in a loop:

- If the number is not zero, set its corresponding value in array isCovered to true (line 11);
- Read the next number (line 12).

line	Representative elements in array isCovered							number	allCovered
	[1]	[2]	[3]	[4]	[5]	[22]	[42]		
6	false	false	false	false	false	false	false		
9								2	
11	true								
12								5	
11				true					
12								6	
11					true				
12								5	
11				true					
12								4	
11			true						
12								3	
11		true							
12								23	
11						true			
12								43	
11							true		
12								2	
11	true								
12								0	
16									true
18(i=0)									false

When the input is 0, the input ends. The program checks whether all numbers are covered in lines 16–21 and displays the result in lines 24–27.

6.4 Problem: Deck of Cards

The problem is to write a program that picks four cards randomly from a deck of 52 cards. All the cards can be represented using an array named deck, filled with initial values 0 to 51, as follows:

```
int[] deck = new int[52];

// Initialize cards
for (int i = 0; i < deck.length; i++)
  deck[i] = i;
```

Card numbers 0 to 12, 13 to 25, 26 to 38, 39 to 51 represent 13 Spades, 13 Hearts, 13 Diamonds, and 13 Clubs, respectively, as shown in Figure 6.3. After shuffling the array deck, pick the first four cards from deck. cardNumber / 13 determines the suit of the card and cardNumber % 13 determines the rank of the card.

Listing 6.2 gives the solution to the problem.

LISTING 6.2 DeckOfCards.java

```
public class DeckOfCards {
  public static void main(String[] args) {
    int[] deck = new int[52];
    String[] suits = {"Spades", "Hearts", "Diamonds", "Clubs"};
    String[] ranks = {"Ace", "2", "3", "4", "5", "6", "7", "8", "9",
      "10", "Jack", "Queen", "King"};

    // Initialize cards
    for (int i = 0; i < deck.length; i++)
      deck[i] = i;

    // Shuffle the cards
    for (int i = 0; i < deck.length; i++) {
      // Generate an index randomly
      int index = (int)(Math.random() * deck.length);
      int temp = deck[i];
      deck[i] = deck[index];
      deck[index] = temp;
    }

    // Display the first four cards
    for (int i = 0; i < 4; i++) {
      String suit = suits[deck[i] / 13];
      String rank = ranks[deck[i] % 13];
      System.out.println("Card number " + deck[i] + ": "
        + rank + " of " + suit);
    }
  }
}
```

create array **deck**
array of strings
array of strings
initialize deck
shuffle deck
suit of a card
rank of a card

```
Card number 6: 7 of Spades
Card number 48: 10 of Clubs
Card number 11: Queen of Spades
Card number 24: Queen of Hearts
```

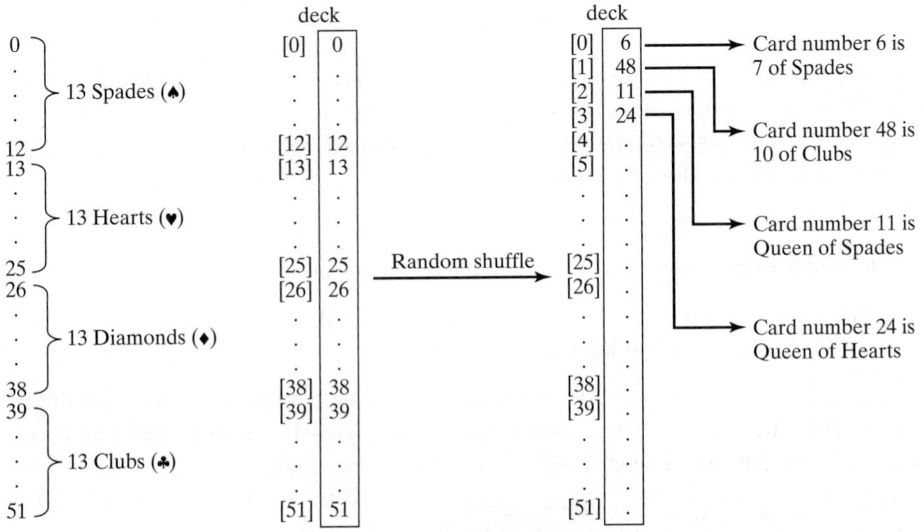
13 Spades (♠)
13 Hearts (♥)
13 Diamonds (♦)
13 Clubs (♣)
deck
Random shuffle
deck
Card number 6 is 7 of Spades
Card number 48 is 10 of Clubs
Card number 11 is Queen of Spades
Card number 24 is Queen of Hearts

FIGURE 6.3 52 cards are stored in an array named **deck**.

The program defines an array `suits` for four suits (line 4) and an array `ranks` for 13 cards in a suits (lines 5–6). Each element in these arrays is a string.

The `deck` is initialized with values `0` to `51` in lines 9–10. A deck value `0` represents card Ace of Spades, `1` represents card 2 of Spades, `13` represents card Ace of Hearts, `14` represents card 2 of Hearts.

Lines 13–19 randomly shuffle the deck. After a deck is shuffled, `deck[i]` contains an arbitrary value. `deck[i] / 13` is `0`, `1`, `2`, or `3`, which determines a suit (line 23). `deck[i] % 13` is a value between `0` and `12`, which determines a rank (line 24).

6.5 Copying Arrays

Often, in a program, you need to duplicate an array or a part of an array. In such cases you could attempt to use the assignment statement (=), as follows:

copy reference

```
list2 = list1;
```

garbage collection

This statement does not copy the contents of the array referenced by `list1` to `list2`, but merely copies the reference value from `list1` to `list2`. After this statement, `list1` and `list2` reference to the same array, as shown in Figure 6.4. The array previously referenced by `list2` is no longer referenced; it becomes garbage, which will be automatically collected by the Java Virtual Machine.

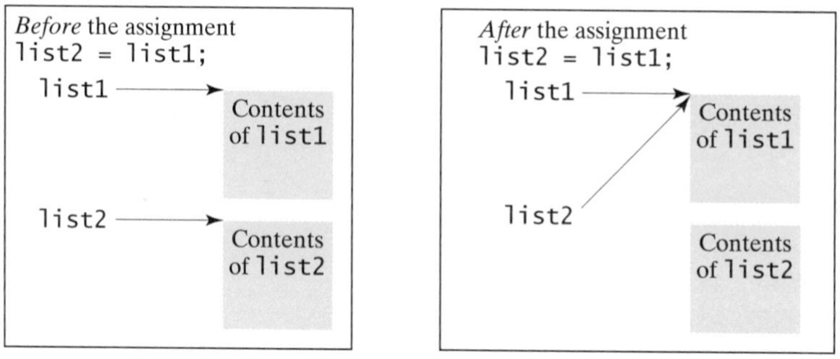

Before the assignment
list2 = list1;
list1
Contents of list1
list2
Contents of list2
After the assignment
list2 = list1;
list1
Contents of list1
list2
Contents of list2

FIGURE 6.4 Before the assignment statement, `list1` and `list2` point to separate memory locations. After the assignment, the reference of the `list1` array is passed to `list2`.

In Java, you can use assignment statements to copy primitive data type variables, but not arrays. Assigning one array variable to another array variable actually copies one reference to another and makes both variables point to the same memory location.

There are three ways to copy arrays:

- Use a loop to copy individual elements one by one.
- Use the static `arraycopy` method in the `System` class.
- Use the `clone` method to copy arrays; this will be introduced in Chapter 14, "Abstract Classes and Interfaces."

You can write a loop to copy every element from the source array to the corresponding element in the target array. The following code, for instance, copies `sourceArray` to `targetArray` using a `for` loop.

```
int[] sourceArray = {2, 3, 1, 5, 10};
int[] targetArray = new int[sourceArray.length];
```

```
for (int i = 0; i < sourceArray.length; i++) {
  targetArray[i] = sourceArray[i];
}
```

Another approach is to use the arraycopy method in the java.lang.System class to copy arrays instead of using a loop. The syntax for arraycopy is shown below:

```
arraycopy(sourceArray, src_pos, targetArray, tar_pos, length);
```

arraycopy method

The parameters src_pos and tar_pos indicate the starting positions in sourceArray and targetArray, respectively. The number of elements copied from sourceArray to targetArray is indicated by length. For example, you can rewrite the loop using the following statement:

```
System.arraycopy(sourceArray, 0, targetArray, 0, sourceArray.length);
```

The arraycopy method does not allocate memory space for the target array. The target array must have already been created with its memory space allocated. After the copying takes place, targetArray and sourceArray have the same content but independent memory locations.

Note

The arraycopy method violates the Java naming convention. By convention, this method should be named arrayCopy (i.e., with an uppercase C).

6.6 Passing Arrays to Methods

Just as you can pass primitive type values to methods, you can also pass arrays to methods. For example, the following method displays the elements in an int array:

```
public static void printArray(int[] array) {
  for (int i = 0; i < array.length; i++) {
    System.out.print(array[i] + " ");
  }
}
```

You can invoke it by passing an array. For example, the following statement invokes the printArray method to display 3, 1, 2, 6, 4, and 2.

```
printArray(new int[]{3, 1, 2, 6, 4, 2});
```

Note

The preceding statement creates an array using the following syntax:

```
new elementType[]{value0, value1, ..., valuek};
```

There is no explicit reference variable for the array. Such array is called an *anonymous array*.

anonymous arrays

Java uses *pass-by-value* to pass arguments to a method. There are important differences between passing the values of variables of primitive data types and passing arrays.

pass-by-value

- For an argument of a primitive type, the argument's value is passed.
- For an argument of an array type, the value of the argument is a reference to an array; this reference value is passed to the method. Semantically, it can be best described as *pass-by-sharing*, i.e., the array in the method is the same as the array being passed. So if you change the array in the method, you will see the change outside the method.

pass-by-sharing

Take the following code, for example:

```
public class Test {
  public static void main(String[] args) {
    int x = 1; // x represents an int value
    int[] y = new int[10]; // y represents an array of int values

    m(x, y); // Invoke m with arguments x and y

    System.out.println("x is " + x);
    System.out.println("y[0] is " + y[0]);
  }

  public static void m(int number, int[] numbers) {
    number = 1001; // Assign a new value to number
    numbers[0] = 5555; // Assign a new value to numbers[0]
  }
}
```

```
x is 1
y[0] is 5555
```

You will see that after m is invoked, x remains 1, but y[0] is 5555. This is because y and numbers, although they are independent variables, reference to the same array, as illustrated in Figure 6.5. When m(x, y) is invoked, the values of x and y are passed to number and numbers. Since y contains the reference value to the array, numbers now contains the same reference value to the same array.

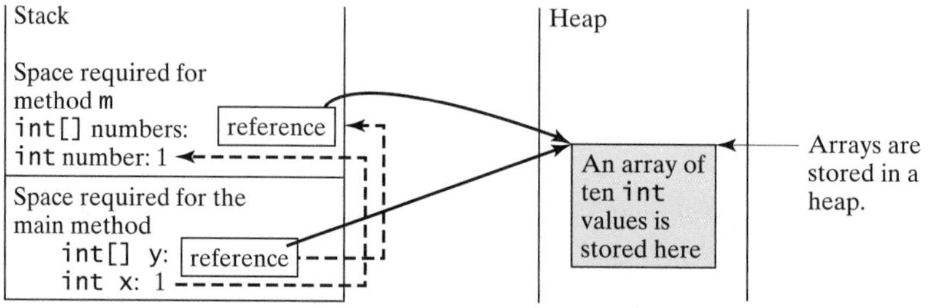
Stack
Space required for method m
int[] numbers: reference
int number: 1
Space required for the main method
int[] y: reference
int x: 1
Heap
An array of ten int values is stored here
Arrays are stored in a heap.

Figure 6.5 The primitive type value in x is passed to number, and the reference value in y is passed to numbers.

heap

Note

The JVM stores the array in an area of memory called the *heap*, which is used for dynamic memory allocation where blocks of memory are allocated and freed in an arbitrary order.

6.6.1 Passing Array Arguments

Listing 6.3 gives another program that shows the difference between passing a primitive data type value and an array reference variable to a method.

The program contains two methods for swapping elements in an array. The first method, named swap, fails to swap two int arguments. The second method, named swapFirstTwoInArray, successfully swaps the first two elements in the array argument.

LISTING 6.3 TestPassArray.java

```
public class TestPassArray {
  /** Main method */
  public static void main(String[] args) {
    int[] a = {1, 2};

    // Swap elements using the swap method
    System.out.println("Before invoking swap");
    System.out.println("array is {" + a[0] + ", " + a[1] + "}");
    swap(a[0], a[1]);
    System.out.println("After invoking swap");
    System.out.println("array is {" + a[0] + ", " + a[1] + "}");

    // Swap elements using the swapFirstTwoInArray method
    System.out.println("Before invoking swapFirstTwoInArray");
    System.out.println("array is {" + a[0] + ", " + a[1] + "}");
    swapFirstTwoInArray(a);
    System.out.println("After invoking swapFirstTwoInArray");
    System.out.println("array is {" + a[0] + ", " + a[1] + "}");
  }

  /** Swap two variables */
  public static void swap(int n1, int n2) {
    int temp = n1;
    n1 = n2;
    n2 = temp;
  }

  /** Swap the first two elements in the array */
  public static void swapFirstTwoInArray(int[] array) {
    int temp = array[0];
    array[0] = array[1];
    array[1] = temp;
  }
}
```

false swap

swap array elements

```
Before invoking swap
array is {1, 2}
After invoking swap
array is {1, 2}
Before invoking swapFirstTwoInArray
array is {1, 2}
After invoking swapFirstTwoInArray
array is {2, 1}
```

As shown in Figure 6.6, the two elements are not swapped using the `swap` method. However, they are swapped using the `swapFirstTwoInArray` method. Since the parameters in the `swap` method are primitive type, the values of `a[0]` and `a[1]` are passed to `n1` and `n2` inside the method when invoking `swap(a[0], a[1])`. The memory locations for `n1` and `n2` are independent of the ones for `a[0]` and `a[1]`. The contents of the array are not affected by this call.

The parameter in the `swapFirstTwoInArray` method is an array. As shown in Figure 6.6, the reference of the array is passed to the method. Thus the variables `a` (outside the method) and `array` (inside the method) both refer to the same array in the same memory location. Therefore, swapping `array[0]` with `array[1]` inside the method `swapFirstTwoInArray` is the same as swapping `a[0]` with `a[1]` outside of the method.

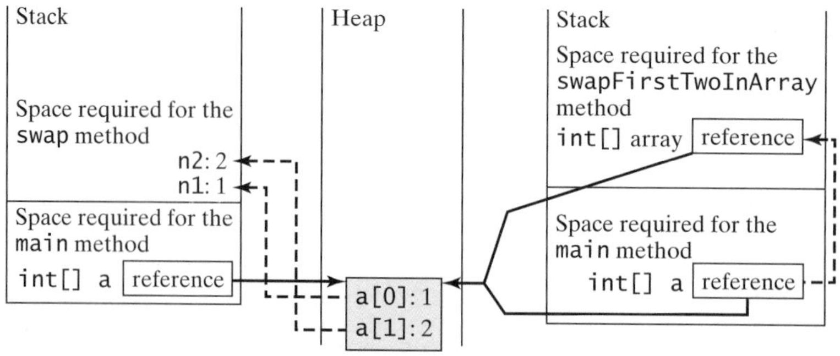

Stack
Space required for the swap method
n2: 2
n1: 1
Space required for the main method
int[] a reference
Heap
a[0]: 1
a[1]: 2
Stack
Space required for the swapFirstTwoInArray method
int[] array reference
Space required for the main method
int[] a reference

Invoke swap(int n1, int n2). The primitive type values in a[0] and a[1] are passed to the swap method.

The arrays are stored in a heap.

Invoke swapFirstTwoInArray(int[] array). The reference value in a is passed to the swapFirstTwoInArray method.

FIGURE 6.6 When passing an array to a method, the reference of the array is passed to the method.

6.7 Returning an Array from a Method

You can pass arrays when invoking a method. A method may also return an array. For example, the method shown below returns an array that is the reversal of another array:

create array

return array

```
 1 public static int[] reverse(int[] list) {
 2   int[] result = new int[list.length];
 3
 4   for (int i = 0, j = result.length - 1;
 5        i < list.length; i++, j--) {
 6     result[j] = list[i];
 7   }
 8
 9   return result;
10 }
```

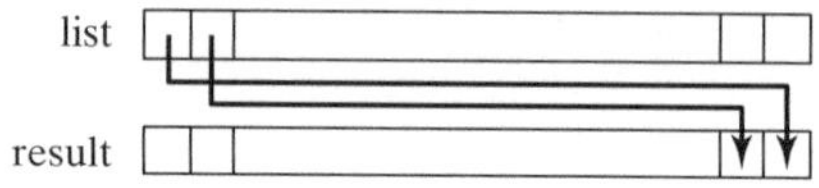

list
result

Line 2 creates a new array result. Lines 4–7 copy elements from array list to array result. Line 9 returns the array. For example, the following statement returns a new array list2 with elements 6, 5, 4, 3, 2, 1.

```
int[] list1 = {1, 2, 3, 4, 5, 6};
int[] list2 = reverse(list1);
```

6.7.1 Case Study: Counting the Occurrences of Each Letter

Listing 6.4 presents a program to count the occurrences of each letter in an array of characters. The program does the following:

1. Generate 100 lowercase letters randomly and assign them to an array of characters, as shown in Figure 6.7(a). You can obtain a random letter by using the getRandomLowerCaseLetter() method in the RandomCharacter class in Listing 5.10

2. Count the occurrences of each letter in the array. To do so, create an array, say counts, of 26 int values, each of which counts the occurrences of a letter, as shown in Figure 6.7(b). That is, counts[0] counts the number of a's, counts[1] counts the number of b's, and so on.

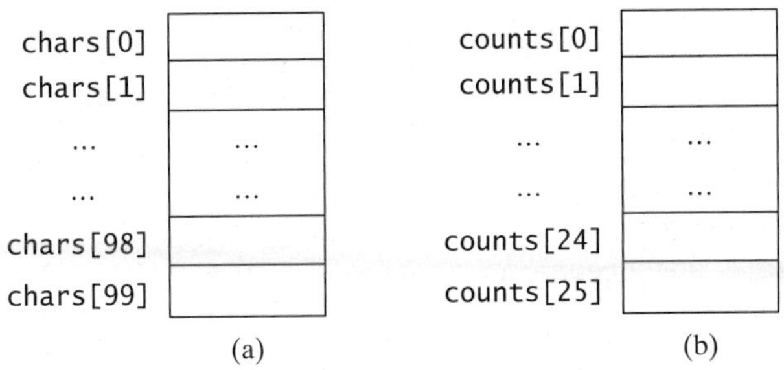
chars[0]
chars[1]
...
...
chars[98]
chars[99]
(a)
counts[0]
counts[1]
...
...
counts[24]
counts[25]
(b)

FIGURE 6.7 The chars array stores 100 characters, and the counts array stores 26 counts, each of which counts the occurrences of a letter.

LISTING 6.4 CountLettersInArray.java

```
public class CountLettersInArray {
  /** Main method */
  public static void main(String[] args) {
    // Declare and create an array
    char[] chars = createArray();

    // Display the array
    System.out.println("The lowercase letters are:");
    displayArray(chars);

    // Count the occurrences of each letter
    int[] counts = countLetters(chars);

    // Display counts
    System.out.println();
    System.out.println("The occurrences of each letter are:");
    displayCounts(counts);
  }

  /** Create an array of characters */
  public static char[] createArray() {
    // Declare an array of characters and create it
    char[] chars = new char[100];

    // Create lowercase letters randomly and assign
    // them to the array
    for (int i = 0; i < chars.length; i++)
      chars[i] = RandomCharacter.getRandomLowerCaseLetter();

    // Return the array
    return chars;
  }

  /** Display the array of characters */
  public static void displayArray(char[] chars) {
    // Display the characters in the array 20 on each line
    for (int i = 0; i < chars.length; i++) {
      if ((i + 1) % 20 == 0)
        System.out.println(chars[i]);
```

create array

pass array

return array

pass array

```
40       else
41         System.out.print(chars[i] + " ");
42     }
43   }
44
45   /** Count the occurrences of each letter */
46   public static int[] countLetters(char[] chars) {
47     // Declare and create an array of 26 int
48     int[] counts = new int[26];
49
50     // For each lowercase letter in the array, count it
51     for (int i = 0; i < chars.length; i++)
52       counts[chars[i] - 'a']++;
53
54     return counts;
55   }
56
57   /** Display counts */
58   public static void displayCounts(int[] counts) {
59     for (int i = 0; i < counts.length; i++) {
60       if ((i + 1) % 10 == 0)
61         System.out.println(counts[i] + " " + (char)(i + 'a'));
62       else
63         System.out.print(counts[i] + " " + (char)(i + 'a') + " ");
64     }
65   }
66 }
```

count

```
The lowercase letters are:
e y l s r i b k j v j h a b z n w b t v
s c c k r d w a m p w v u n q a m p l o
a z g d e g f i n d x m z o u l o z j v
h w i w n t g x w c d o t x h y v z y z
q e a m f w p g u q t r e n n w f c r f

The occurrences of each letter are:
5 a 3 b 4 c 4 d 4 e 4 f 4 g 3 h 3 i 3 j
2 k 3 l 4 m 6 n 4 o 3 p 3 q 4 r 2 s 4 t
3 u 5 v 8 w 3 x 3 y 6 z
```

The `createArray` method (lines 21–32) generates an array of `100` random lowercase letters. Line 5 invokes the method and assigns the array to `chars`. What would be wrong if you rewrote the code as follows?

```
char[] chars = new char[100];
chars = createArray();
```

You would be creating two arrays. The first line would create an array by using `new char[100]`. The second line would create an array by invoking `createArray()` and assign the reference of the array to `chars`. The array created in the first line would be garbage because it is no longer referenced. Java automatically collects garbage behind the scenes. Your program would compile and run correctly, but it would create an array unnecessarily.

Invoking `getRandomLowerCaseLetter()` (line 28) returns a random lowercase letter. This method is defined in the `RandomCharacter` class in Listing 5.10.

The `countLetters` method (lines 46–55) returns an array of `26 int` values, each of which stores the number of occurrences of a letter. The method processes each letter in the array and increases its count by one. A brute-force approach to count the occurrences of each letter might be as follows:

```
for (int i = 0; i < chars.length; i++)
  if (chars[i] == 'a')
    counts[0]++;
  else if (chars[i] == 'b')
    counts[1]++;
  ...
```

But a better solution is given in lines 51–52.

```
  for (int i = 0; i < chars.length; i++)
    counts[chars[i] - 'a']++;
```

If the letter (**chars[i]**) is **'a'**, the corresponding count is **counts['a' - 'a']** (i.e., **counts[0]**). If the letter is **'b'**, the corresponding count is **counts['b' - 'a']** (i.e., **counts[1]**), since the Unicode of **'b'** is one more than that of **'a'**. If the letter is **'z'**, the corresponding count is **counts['z' - 'a']** (i.e., **counts[25]**), since the Unicode of **'z'** is **25** more than that of **'a'**.

Figure 6.8 shows the call stack and heap *during* and *after* executing **createArray**. See Review Question 6.14 to show the call stack and heap for other methods in the program.

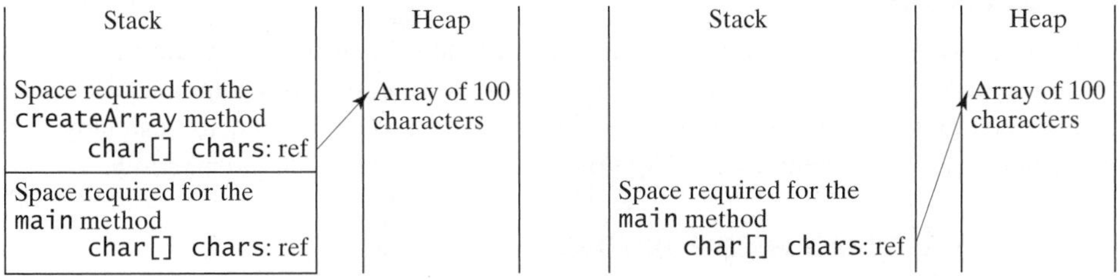
Stack
Heap
Space required for the createArray method
char[] chars: ref
Array of 100 characters
Space required for the main method
char[] chars: ref
Stack
Heap
Array of 100 characters
Space required for the main method
char[] chars: ref

(a) Executing createArray in line 5 (b) After exiting createArray in line 5

FIGURE 6.8 (a) An array of 100 characters is created when executing **createArray**. (b) This array is returned and assigned to the variable **chars** in the **main** method.

6.8 Variable-Length Argument Lists

You can pass a variable number of arguments of the same type to a method. The parameter in the method is declared as follows:

```
typeName... parameterName
```

In the method declaration, you specify the type followed by an ellipsis (...). Only one variable-length parameter may be specified in a method, and this parameter must be the last parameter. Any regular parameters must precede it.

Java treats a variable-length parameter as an array. You can pass an array or a variable number of arguments to a variable-length parameter. When invoking a method with a variable number of arguments, Java creates an array and passes the arguments to it. Listing 6.5 contains a method that prints the maximum value in a list of an unspecified number of values.

LISTING 6.5 VarArgsDemo.java

```
public class VarArgsDemo {
  public static void main(String[] args) {
    printMax(34, 3, 3, 2, 56.5);
```

pass variable-length arg list

pass an array arg

a variable-length arg parameter

```
4      printMax(new double[]{1, 2, 3});
5    }
6
7    public static void printMax(double... numbers) {
8      if (numbers.length == 0) {
9        System.out.println("No argument passed");
10       return;
11     }
12
13     double result = numbers[0];
14
15     for (int i = 1; i < numbers.length; i++)
16       if (numbers[i] > result)
17         result = numbers[i];
18
19     System.out.println("The max value is " + result);
20   }
21 }
```

Line 3 invokes the `printMax` method with a variable-length argument list passed to the array `numbers`. If no arguments are passed, the length of the array is `0` (line 8).

Line 4 invokes the `printMax` method with an array.

6.9 Searching Arrays

linear search

binary search

Searching is the process of looking for a specific element in an array—for example, discovering whether a certain score is included in a list of scores. Searching is a common task in computer programming. Many algorithms and data structures are devoted to searching. This section discusses two commonly used approaches, *linear search* and *binary search*.

6.9.1 The Linear Search Approach

The linear search approach compares the key element `key` sequentially with each element in the array. It continues to do so until the key matches an element in the array or the array is exhausted without a match being found. If a match is made, the linear search returns the index of the element in the array that matches the key. If no match is found, the search returns `-1`. The `linearSearch` method in Listing 6.6 gives the solution:

LISTING 6.6 `LinearSearch.java`

```
public class LinearSearch {
  /** The method for finding a key in the list */
  public static int linearSearch(int[] list, int key) {
    for (int i = 0; i < list.length; i++) {
      if (key == list[i])
        return i;
    }
    return -1;
  }
}
```

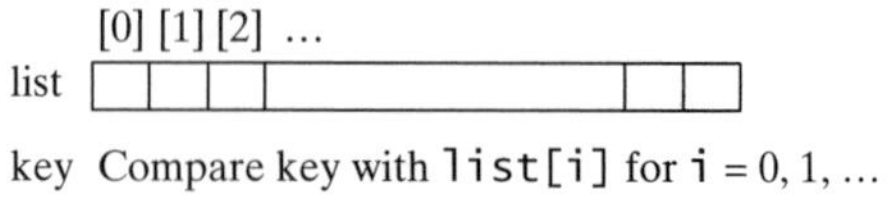
[0] [1] [2] ...
list
key Compare key with list[i] for i = 0, 1, ...

To better understand this method, trace it with the following statements:

```
int[] list = {1, 4, 4, 2, 5, -3, 6, 2};
int i = linearSearch(list, 4);  // Returns 1
int j = linearSearch(list, -4); // Returns -1
int k = linearSearch(list, -3); // Returns 5
```

The linear search method compares the key with each element in the array. The elements can be in any order. On average, the algorithm will have to compare half of the elements in an array before finding the key, if it exists. Since the execution time of a linear search increases linearly as the number of array elements increases, linear search is inefficient for a large array.

6.9.2 The Binary Search Approach

Binary search is the other common search approach for a list of values. For binary search to work, the elements in the array must already be ordered. Assume that the array is in ascending order. The binary search first compares the key with the element in the middle of the array. Consider the following three cases:

- If the key is less than the middle element, you need to continue to search for the key only in the first half of the array.
- If the key is equal to the middle element, the search ends with a match.
- If the key is greater than the middle element, you need to continue to search for the key only in the second half of the array.

Clearly, the binary search method eliminates half of the array after each comparison. Sometimes you eliminate half of the elements, and sometimes you eliminate half plus one. Suppose that the array has n elements. For convenience, let `n` be a power of `2`. After the first comparison, `n/2` elements are left for further search; after the second comparison, `(n/2)/2` elements are left. After the `k`th comparison, $n/2^k$ elements are left for further search. When $k = \log_2 n$, only one element is left in the array, and you need only one more comparison. Therefore, in the worst case when using the binary search approach, you need $\log_2 n+1$ comparisons to find an element in the sorted array. In the worst case for a list of `1024` (2^{10}) elements, binary search requires only `11` comparisons, whereas a linear search requires `1023` comparisons in the worst case.

The portion of the array being searched shrinks by half after each comparison. Let `low` and `high` denote, respectively, the first index and last index of the array that is currently being searched. Initially, `low` is `0` and `high` is `list.length–1`. Let `mid` denote the index of the middle element. So `mid` is `(low + high)/2`. Figure 6.9 shows how to find key `11` in the list {`2, 4, 7, 10, 11, 45, 50, 59, 60, 66, 69, 70, 79`} using binary search.

You now know how the binary search works. The next task is to implement it in Java. Don't rush to give a complete implementation. Implement it incrementally, one step at a time. You may start with the first iteration of the search, as shown in Figure 6.10(a). It compares the key with the middle element in the list whose `low` index is `0` and `high` index is `list.length - 1`.

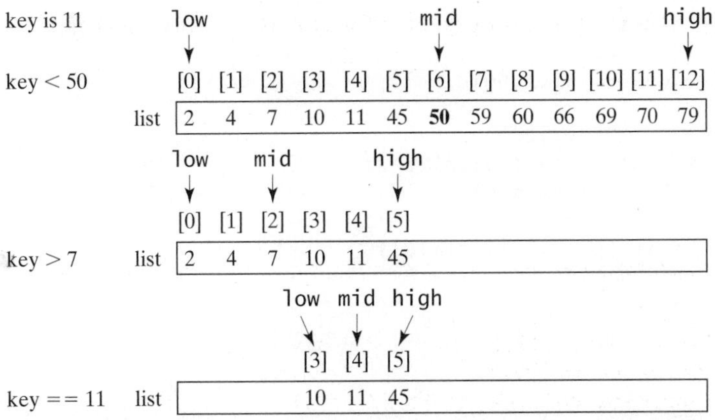
key is 11
low
mid
high
key < 50
[0] [1] [2] [3] [4] [5] [6] [7] [8] [9] [10] [11] [12]
list 2 4 7 10 11 45 50 59 60 66 69 70 79
low mid high
[0] [1] [2] [3] [4] [5]
key > 7
list 2 4 7 10 11 45
low mid high
[3] [4] [5]
key == 11
list 10 11 45

FIGURE 6.9 Binary search eliminates half of the list from further consideration after each comparison.

If `key < list[mid]`, set the `high` index to `mid - 1`; if `key == list[mid]`, a match is found and return `mid`; if `key > list[mid]`, set the `low` index to `mid + 1`.

```
public static int binarySearch(
    int[] list, int key) {
  int low = 0;
  int high = list.length - 1;


    int mid = (low + high) / 2;
    if (key < list[mid])
      high = mid - 1;
    else if (key == list[mid])
      return mid;
    else
      low = mid + 1;



}
```

(a) Version 1

```
public static int binarySearch(
    int[] list, int key) {
  int low = 0;
  int high = list.length - 1;

  while (high >= low) {
    int mid = (low + high) / 2;
    if (key < list[mid])
      high = mid - 1;
    else if (key == list[mid])
      return mid;
    else
      low = mid + 1;
  }

  return -1; // Not found
}
```

(b) Version 2

FIGURE 6.10 Binary search is implemented incrementally.

Next consider implementing the method to perform search repeatedly by adding a loop, as shown in Figure 6.10(b). The search ends if the key is found, or if the key is not found when `low > high`.

why not -1?

When the key is not found, `low` is the insertion point where a key would be inserted to maintain the order of the list. It is more useful to return the insertion point than `-1`. The method must return a negative value to indicate that the key is not in the list. Can it simply return `-low`? No. If key is less than `list[0]`, `low` would be `0`. `-0` is `0`. This would indicate that key matches `list[0]`. A good choice is to let the method return `-low - 1` if the key is not in the list. Returning `-low - 1` indicates not only that the key is not in the list, but also where the key would be inserted.

The complete program is given in Listing 6.7.

LISTING 6.7 BinarySearch.java

```
public class BinarySearch {
  /** Use binary search to find the key in the list */
  public static int binarySearch(int[] list, int key) {
    int low = 0;
    int high = list.length - 1;

    while (high >= low) {
      int mid = (low + high) / 2;
      if (key < list[mid])
        high = mid - 1;
      else if (key == list[mid])
        return mid;
      else
        low = mid + 1;
    }

    return -low - 1; // Now high < low, key not found
  }
}
```

first half

second half

The binary search returns the index of the search key if it is contained in the list (line 12). Otherwise, it returns `-low - 1` (line 17).

What would happens if we replaced `(high >= low)` in line 7 with `(high > low)`? The search would miss a possible matching element. Consider a list with just one element. The search would miss the element.

Does the method still work if there are duplicate elements in the list? Yes, as long as the elements are sorted in increasing order. The method returns the index of one of the matching elements if the element is in the list.

To better understand this method, trace it with the following statements and identify `low` and `high` when the method returns.

```
int[] list = {2, 4, 7, 10, 11, 45, 50, 59, 60, 66, 69, 70, 79};
int i = BinarySearch.binarySearch(list, 2); // Returns 0
int j = BinarySearch.binarySearch(list, 11); // Returns 4
int k = BinarySearch.binarySearch(list, 12); // Returns -6
int l = BinarySearch.binarySearch(list, 1); // Returns -1
int m = BinarySearch.binarySearch(list, 3); // Returns -2
```

Here is the table that lists the `low` and `high` values when the method exits and the value returned from invoking the method.

Method	Low	High	Value Returned
binarySearch(list, 2)	0	1	0
binarySearch(list, 11)	3	5	4
binarySearch(list, 12)	5	4	−6
binarySearch(list, 1)	0	−1	−1
binarySearch(list, 3)	1	0	−2

Note

Linear search is useful for finding an element in a small array or an unsorted array, but it is inefficient for large arrays. Binary search is more efficient, but it requires that the array be presorted.

binary search benefits

6.10 Sorting Arrays

Sorting, like searching, is a common task in computer programming. Many different algorithms have been developed for sorting. This section introduces two simple, intuitive sorting algorithms: *selection sort* and *insertion sort.*

6.10.1 Selection Sort

Video Note
Selection sort

Suppose that you want to sort a list in ascending order. Selection sort finds the smallest number in the list and places it first. It then finds the smallest number remaining and places it next to first, and so on, until only a single number remains. Figure 6.11 shows how to sort a list {`2`, `9`, `5`, `4`, `8`, `1`, `6`} using selection sort.

You know how the selection-sort approach works. The task now is to implement it in Java. Beginners find it difficult to develop a complete solution on the first attempt. Start by writing the code for the first iteration to find the largest element in the list and swap it with the last element, and then observe what would be different for the second iteration, the third, and so on. The insight this gives will enable you to write a loop that generalizes all the iterations.

The solution can be described as follows:

```
for (int i = 0; i < list.length - 1; i++) {
  select the smallest element in list[i..list.length-1];
  swap the smallest with list[i], if necessary;
    // list[i] is in its correct position.
    // The next iteration apply on list[i+1..list.length-1]
}
```

Listing 6.8 implements the solution.

LISTING 6.8 SelectionSort.java

select

swap

```
1 public class SelectionSort {
2   /** The method for sorting the numbers */
3   public static void selectionSort(double[] list) {
4     for (int i = 0; i < list.length - 1; i++) {
5       // Find the minimum in the list[i..list.length-1]
6       double currentMin = list[i];
7       int currentMinIndex = i;
8
9       for (int j = i + 1; j < list.length; j++) {
10        if (currentMin > list[j]) {
11          currentMin = list[j];
12          currentMinIndex = j;
13        }
14      }
15
16      // Swap list[i] with list[currentMinIndex] if necessary;
17      if (currentMinIndex != i) {
18        list[currentMinIndex] = list[i];
19        list[i] = currentMin;
20      }
21    }
22  }
23 }
```

The `selectionSort(double[] list)` method sorts any array of `double` elements. The method is implemented with a nested `for` loop. The outer loop (with the loop control variable `i`) (line 4) is iterated in order to find the smallest element in the list, which ranges from `list[i]` to `list[list.length-1]`, and exchange it with `list[i]`.

The variable `i` is initially `0`. After each iteration of the outer loop, `list[i]` is in the right place. Eventually, all the elements are put in the right place; therefore, the whole list is sorted.

To understand this method better, trace it with the following statements:

```
double[] list = {1, 9, 4.5, 6.6, 5.7, -4.5};
SelectionSort.selectionSort(list);
```

6.10.2 Insertion Sort

Suppose that you want to sort a list in ascending order. The insertion-sort algorithm sorts a list of values by repeatedly inserting a new element into a sorted sublist until the whole list is sorted. Figure 6.12 shows how to sort the list {2, 9, 5, 4, 8, 1, 6} using insertion sort.

The algorithm can be described as follows:

```
for (int i = 1; i < list.length; i++) {
  insert list[i] into a sorted sublist list[0..i-1] so that
  list[0..i] is sorted.
}
```

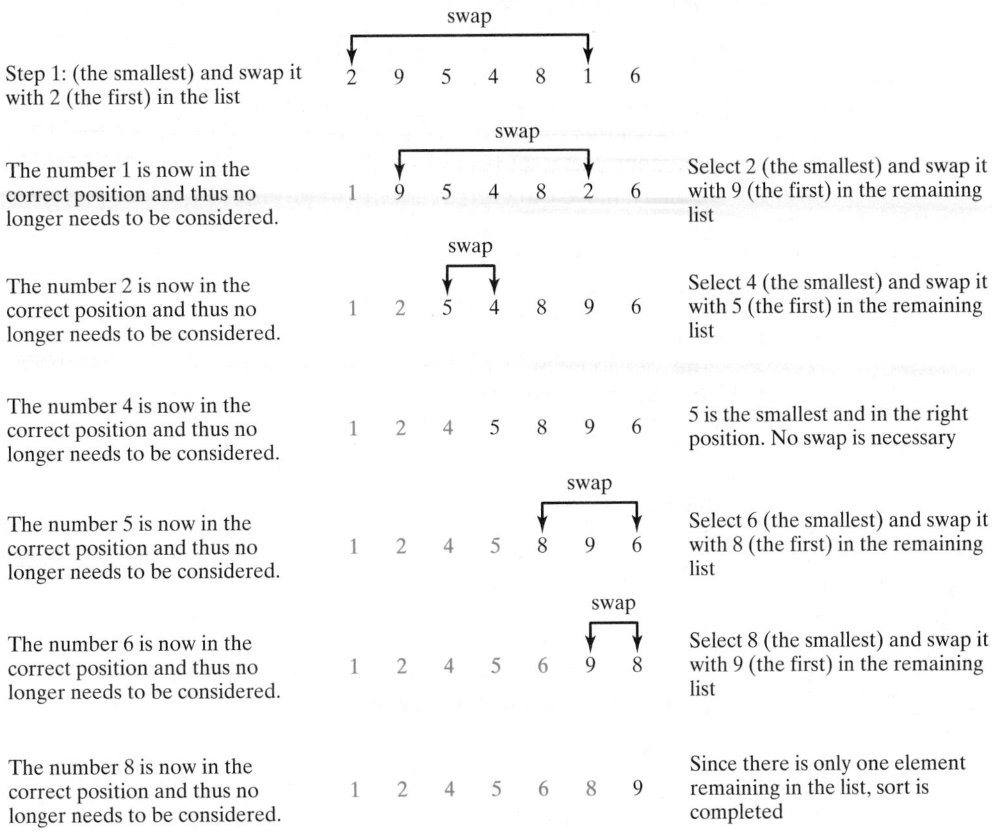
swap
Step 1: (the smallest) and swap it with 2 (the first) in the list
2 9 5 4 8 1 6
swap
The number 1 is now in the correct position and thus no longer needs to be considered.
1 9 5 4 8 2 6
Select 2 (the smallest) and swap it with 9 (the first) in the remaining list
swap
The number 2 is now in the correct position and thus no longer needs to be considered.
1 2 5 4 8 9 6
Select 4 (the smallest) and swap it with 5 (the first) in the remaining list
The number 4 is now in the correct position and thus no longer needs to be considered.
1 2 4 5 8 9 6
5 is the smallest and in the right position. No swap is necessary
swap
The number 5 is now in the correct position and thus no longer needs to be considered.
1 2 4 5 8 9 6
Select 6 (the smallest) and swap it with 8 (the first) in the remaining list
swap
The number 6 is now in the correct position and thus no longer needs to be considered.
1 2 4 5 6 9 8
Select 8 (the smallest) and swap it with 9 (the first) in the remaining list
The number 8 is now in the correct position and thus no longer needs to be considered.
1 2 4 5 6 8 9
Since there is only one element remaining in the list, sort is completed

FIGURE 6.11 Selection sort repeatedly selects the smallest number and swaps it with the first number in the list.

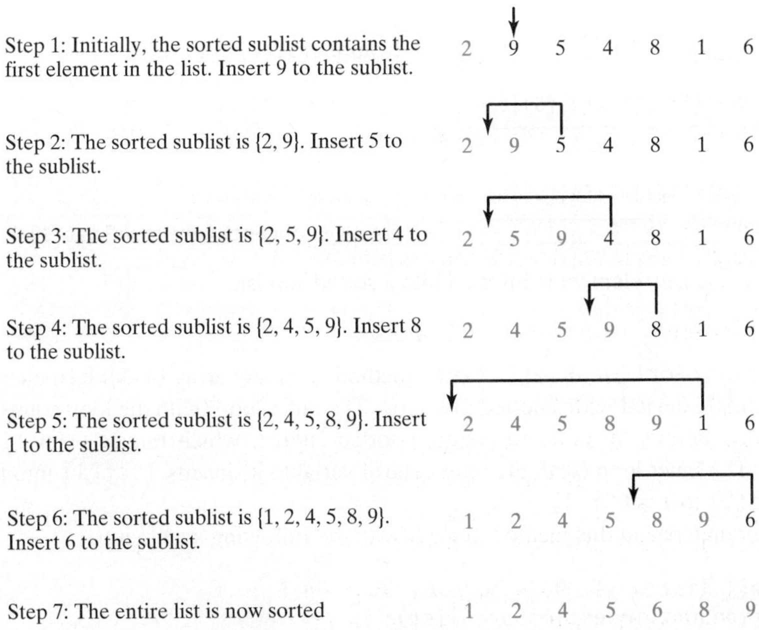
Step 1: Initially, the sorted sublist contains the first element in the list. Insert 9 to the sublist.
2 9 5 4 8 1 6
Step 2: The sorted sublist is {2, 9}. Insert 5 to the sublist.
2 9 5 4 8 1 6
Step 3: The sorted sublist is {2, 5, 9}. Insert 4 to the sublist.
2 5 9 4 8 1 6
Step 4: The sorted sublist is {2, 4, 5, 9}. Insert 8 to the sublist.
2 4 5 9 8 1 6
Step 5: The sorted sublist is {2, 4, 5, 8, 9}. Insert 1 to the sublist.
2 4 5 8 9 1 6
Step 6: The sorted sublist is {1, 2, 4, 5, 8, 9}. Insert 6 to the sublist.
1 2 4 5 8 9 6
Step 7: The entire list is now sorted
1 2 4 5 6 8 9

FIGURE 6.12 Insertion sort repeatedly inserts a new element into a sorted sublist.

To insert `list[i]` into `list[0..i-1]`, save `list[i]` into a temporary variable, say `currentElement`. Move `list[i-1]` to `list[i]` if `list[i-1] > currentElement`, move `list[i-2]` to `list[i-1]` if `list[i-2] > currentElement`, and so on, until `list[i-k] <= currentElement` or `k > i` (we pass the first element of the sorted list). Assign `currentElement` to `list[i-k+1]`. For example, to insert 4 into {2, 5, 9} in Step 3 in Figure 6.13, move `list[2]` (9) to `list[3]` since 9 > 4, move `list[1]` (5) to `list[2]` since 5 > 4. Finally, move `currentElement` (4) to `list[1]`.

The algorithm can be expanded and implemented as in Listing 6.9.

LISTING 6.9 InsertionSort.java

shift (line 9)
insert (line 14)

```
 1 public class InsertionSort {
 2   /** The method for sorting the numbers */
 3   public static void insertionSort(double[] list) {
 4     for (int i = 1; i < list.length; i++) {
 5       /** insert list[i] into a sorted sublist list[0..i-1] so that
 6            list[0..i] is sorted. */
 7       double currentElement = list[i];
 8       int k;
 9       for (k = i - 1; k >= 0 && list[k] > currentElement; k--) {
10         list[k + 1] = list[k];
11       }
12
13       // Insert the current element into list[k + 1]
14       list[k + 1] = currentElement;
15     }
16   }
17 }
```

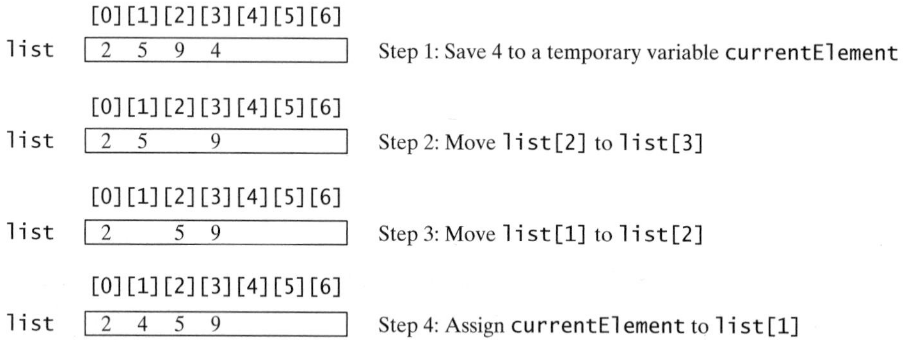
[0][1][2][3][4][5][6]
list
2 5 9 4
Step 1: Save 4 to a temporary variable currentElement
[0][1][2][3][4][5][6]
list
2 5 9
Step 2: Move list[2] to list[3]
[0][1][2][3][4][5][6]
list
2 5 9
Step 3: Move list[1] to list[2]
[0][1][2][3][4][5][6]
list
2 4 5 9
Step 4: Assign currentElement to list[1]

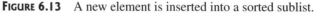

FIGURE 6.13 A new element is inserted into a sorted sublist.

The `insertionSort(double[] list)` method sorts any array of `double` elements. The method is implemented with a nested `for` loop. The outer loop (with the loop control variable `i`) (line 4) is iterated in order to obtain a sorted sublist, which ranges from `list[0]` to `list[i]`. The inner loop (with the loop control variable `k`) inserts `list[i]` into the sublist from `list[0]` to `list[i-1]`.

To better understand this method, trace it with the following statements:

```
double[] list = {1, 9, 4.5, 6.6, 5.7, -4.5};
InsertionSort.insertionSort(list);
```

6.11 The Arrays Class

The `java.util.Arrays` class contains various static methods for sorting and searching arrays, comparing arrays, and filling array elements. These methods are overloaded for all primitive types.

You can use the `sort` method to sort a whole array or a partial array. For example, the following code sorts an array of numbers and an array of characters. sort

```
double[] numbers = {6.0, 4.4, 1.9, 2.9, 3.4, 3.5};
java.util.Arrays.sort(numbers); // Sort the whole array

char[] chars = {'a', 'A', '4', 'F', 'D', 'P'};
java.util.Arrays.sort(chars, 1, 3); // Sort part of the array
```

Invoking `sort(numbers)` sorts the whole array `numbers`. Invoking `sort(chars, 1, 3)` sorts a partial array from `chars[1]` to `chars[3-1]`.

You can use the `binarySearch` method to search for a key in an array. The array must be presorted in increasing order. If the key is not in the array, the method returns `-(insertion index + 1)`. For example, the following code searches the keys in an array of integers and an array of characters. binarySearch

```
int[] list = {2, 4, 7, 10, 11, 45, 50, 59, 60, 66, 69, 70, 79};
System.out.println("(1) Index is " +
  java.util.Arrays.binarySearch(list, 11));
System.out.println("(2) Index is " +
  java.util.Arrays.binarySearch(list, 12));

char[] chars = {'a', 'c', 'g', 'x', 'y', 'z'};
System.out.println("(3) Index is " +
  java.util.Arrays.binarySearch(chars, 'a'));
System.out.println("(4) Index is " +
  java.util.Arrays.binarySearch(chars, 't'));
```

The output of the preceding code is

(1) Index is 4
(2) Index is -6
(3) Index is 0
(4) Index is -4

You can use the `equals` method to check whether two arrays are equal. Two arrays are equal if they have the same contents. In the following code, `list1` and `list2` are equal, but `list2` and `list3` are not. equals

```
int[] list1 = {2, 4, 7, 10};
int[] list2 = {2, 4, 7, 10};
int[] list3 = {4, 2, 7, 10};
System.out.println(java.util.Arrays.equals(list1, list2)); // true
System.out.println(java.util.Arrays.equals(list2, list3)); // false
```

You can use the `fill` method to fill in all or part of the array. For example, the following code fills `list1` with `5` and fills `8` into elements `list2[1]` and `list2[3-1]`. fill

```
int[] list1 = {2, 4, 7, 10};
int[] list2 = {2, 4, 7, 10};
java.util.Arrays.fill(list1, 5); // Fill 5 to the whole array
java.util.Arrays.fill(list2, 1, 3, 8); // Fill 8 to a partial array
```

Key Terms

Chapter Summary

1. A variable is declared as an array type using the syntax `elementType[] arrayRefVar` or `elementType arrayRefVar[]`. The style `elementType[] arrayRefVar` is preferred, although `elementType arrayRefVar[]` is legal.

2. Unlike declarations for primitive data type variables, the declaration of an array variable does not allocate any space in memory for the array. An array variable is not a primitive data type variable. An array variable contains a reference to an array.

3. You cannot assign elements to an array unless it has already been created. You can create an array by using the `new` operator with the following syntax: `new elementType[arraySize]`.

4. Each element in the array is represented using the syntax `arrayRefVar[index]`. An index must be an integer or an integer expression.

5. After an array is created, its size becomes permanent and can be obtained using `arrayRefVar.length`. Since the index of an array always begins with `0`, the last index is always `arrayRefVar.length - 1`. An out-of-bounds error will occur if you attempt to reference elements beyond the bounds of an array.

6. Programmers often mistakenly reference the first element in an array with index `1`, but it should be `0`. This is called the *index off-by-one error.*

7. When an array is created, its elements are assigned the default value of `0` for the numeric primitive data types, `'\u0000'` for char types, and `false` for `boolean` types.

8. Java has a shorthand notation, known as the *array initializer*, which combines in one statement declaring an array, creating an array, and initializing, using the syntax: `elementType[] arrayRefVar = {value0, value1, ..., valuek}`.

9. When you pass an array argument to a method, you are actually passing the reference of the array; that is, the called method can modify the elements in the caller's original array.

Review Questions

Section 6.2

6.1 How do you declare and create an array?

6.2 How do you access elements of an array?

6.3 Is memory allocated for an array when it is declared? When is the memory allocated for an array? What is the printout of the following code?

```
int x = 30;
int[] numbers = new int[x];
x = 60;
System.out.println("x is " + x);
System.out.println("The size of numbers is " + numbers.length);
```

6.4 Indicate true or false for the following statements:

- Every element in an array has the same type.
- The array size is fixed after it is declared.
- The array size is fixed after it is created.
- The elements in an array must be of primitive data type.

6.5 Which of the following statements are valid array declarations?

```
int i = new int(30);
double d[] = new double[30];
char[] r = new char(1..30);
int i[] = (3, 4, 3, 2);
float f[] = {2.3, 4.5, 6.6};
char[] c = new char();
```

6.6 What is the array index type? What is the lowest index? What is the representation of the third element in an array named `a`?

6.7 Write statements to do the following:

a. Create an array to hold `10` double values.
b. Assign value `5.5` to the last element in the array.
c. Display the sum of the first two elements.
d. Write a loop that computes the sum of all elements in the array.
e. Write a loop that finds the minimum element in the array.
f. Randomly generate an index and display the element of this index in the array.
g. Use an array initializer to create another array with initial values `3.5`, `5.5`, `4.52`, and `5.6`.

6.8 What happens when your program attempts to access an array element with an invalid index?

6.9 Identify and fix the errors in the following code:

```
public class Test {
  public static void main(String[] args) {
    double[100] r;

    for (int i = 0; i < r.length(); i++);
      r(i) = Math.random * 100;
  }
}
```

Section 6.3

6.10 Use the `arraycopy()` method to copy the following array to a target array `t`:

```
int[] source = {3, 4, 5};
```

6.11 Once an array is created, its size cannot be changed. Does the following code resize the array?

```
int[] myList;
myList = new int[10];
// Some time later you want to assign a new array to myList
myList = new int[20];
```

Sections 6.4–6.7

6.12 When an array is passed to a method, a new array is created and passed to the method. Is this true?

6.13 Show the output of the following two programs:

```
public class Test {
  public static void main(String[] args) {
    int number = 0;
    int[] numbers = new int[1];

    m(number, numbers);

    System.out.println("number is " + number
      + " and numbers[0] is " + numbers[0]);
  }

  public static void m(int x, int[] y) {
    x = 3;
    y[0] = 3;
  }
}
```

a

```
public class Test {
  public static void main(String[] args) {
    int[] list = {1, 2, 3, 4, 5};
    reverse(list);
    for (int i = 0; i < list.length; i++)
      System.out.print(list[i] + " ");
  }

  public static void  reverse(int[] list) {
    int[] newList = new int[list.length];

    for (int i = 0; i < list.length; i++)
      newList[i] = list[list.length - 1 - i];

    list = newList;
  }
}
```

b

6.14 Where are the arrays stored during execution? Show the contents of the stack and heap during and after executing `createArray`, `displayArray`, `countLetters`, `displayCounts` in Listing 6.4.

Section 6.8

6.15 What is wrong in the following method declaration?

```
public static void print(String... strings, double... numbers)
public static void print(double... numbers, String name)
public static double... print(double d1, double d2)
```

6.16 Can you invoke the `printMax` method in Listing 6.5 using the following statements?

```
printMax(1, 2, 2, 1, 4);
printMax(new double[]{1, 2, 3});
printMax(new int[]{1, 2, 3});
```

Sections 6.9–6.10

6.17 Use Figure 6.9 as an example to show how to apply the binary search approach to a search for key 10 and key 12 in list {2, 4, 7, 10, 11, 45, 50, 59, 60, 66, 69, 70, 79}.

6.18 Use Figure 6.11 as an example to show how to apply the selection-sort approach to sort {`3.4`, `5`, `3`, `3.5`, `2.2`, `1.9`, `2`}.

6.19 Use Figure 6.12 as an example to show how to apply the insertion-sort approach to sort {`3.4`, `5`, `3`, `3.5`, `2.2`, `1.9`, `2`}.

6.20 How do you modify the `selectionSort` method in Listing 6.8 to sort numbers in decreasing order?

6.21 How do you modify the `insertionSort` method in Listing 6.9 to sort numbers in decreasing order?

Section 6.11

6.22 What types of array can be sorted using the `java.util.Arrays.sort` method? Does this `sort` method create a new array?

6.23 To apply `java.util.Arrays.binarySearch(array, key)`, should the array be sorted in increasing order, in decreasing order, or neither?

6.24 Show the contents of the array after the execution of each line.

```
int[] list = {2, 4, 7, 10};
java.util.Arrays.fill(list, 7);
java.util.Arrays.fill(list, 1, 3, 8);
System.out.print(java.util.Arrays.equals(list, list));
```

Programming Exercises

Section 6.2

6.1* (*Assigning grades*) Write a program that reads student scores, gets the best score, and then assigns grades based on the following scheme:

Grade is A if score is >= best − 10;

Grade is B if score is >= best − 20;

Grade is C if score is >= best − 30;

Grade is D if score is >= best − 40;

Grade is F otherwise.

The program prompts the user to enter the total number of students, then prompts the user to enter all of the scores, and concludes by displaying the grades. Here is a sample run:

```
Enter the number of students: 4 ↵Enter
Enter 4 scores: 40 55 70 58 ↵Enter
Student 0 score is 40 and grade is C
Student 1 score is 55 and grade is B
Student 2 score is 70 and grade is A
Student 3 score is 58 and grade is B
```

6.2 (*Reversing the numbers entered*) Write a program that reads ten integers and displays them in the reverse of the order in which they were read.

6.3** (*Counting occurrence of numbers*) Write a program that reads the integers between `1` and `100` and counts the occurrences of each. Assume the input ends with `0`. Here is a sample run of the program:

```
Enter the integers between 1 and 100: 2 5 6 5 4 3 23
  43 2 0 ↵Enter
2 occurs 2 times
3 occurs 1 time
4 occurs 1 time
5 occurs 2 times
6 occurs 1 time
23 occurs 1 time
43 occurs 1 time
```

Note that if a number occurs more than one time, the plural word "times" is used in the output.

6.4 (*Analyzing scores*) Write a program that reads an unspecified number of scores and determines how many scores are above or equal to the average and how many scores are below the average. Enter a negative number to signify the end of the input. Assume that the maximum number of scores is `10`.

6.5** (*Printing distinct numbers*) Write a program that reads in ten numbers and displays distinct numbers (i.e., if a number appears multiple times, it is displayed only once). *Hint*: Read a number and store it to an array if it is new. If the number is already in the array, ignore it. After the input, the array contains the distinct numbers. Here is the sample run of the program:

```
Enter ten numbers: 1 2 3 2 1 6 3 4 5 2 ↵Enter
The distinct numbers are: 1 2 3 6 4 5
```

6.6* (*Revising Listing 4.14, PrimeNumber.java*) Listing 4.14 determines whether a number `n` is prime by checking whether `2`, `3`, `4`, `5`, `6`, ..., `n/2` is a divisor. If a divisor is found, `n` is not prime. A more efficient approach is to check whether any of the prime numbers less than or equal to $\sqrt{n}$ can divide `n` evenly. If not, `n` is prime. Rewrite Listing 4.11 to display the first 50 prime numbers using this approach. You need to use an array to store the prime numbers and later use them to check whether they are possible divisors for `n`.

6.7* (*Counting single digits*) Write a program that generates `100` random integers between `0` and `9` and displays the count for each number. (*Hint*: Use `(int)(Math.random() * 10)` to generate a random integer between 0 and 9. Use an array of ten integers, say `counts`, to store the counts for the number of 0s, 1s, ..., 9s.)

Sections 6.4–6.7

6.8 (*Averaging an array*) Write two overloaded methods that return the average of an array with the following headers:

```
public static int average(int[] array)
public static double average(double[] array)
```

Write a test program that prompts the user to enter ten double values, invokes this method, and displays the average value.

6.9 (*Finding the smallest element*) Write a method that finds the smallest element in an array of integers using the following header:

```
public static double min(double[] array)
```

Write a test program that prompts the user to enter ten numbers, invokes this method to return the minimum value, and displays the minimum value. Here is a sample run of the program:

```
Enter ten numbers: 1.9 2.5 3.7 2 1.5 6 3 4 5 2 ↵Enter
The minimum number is: 1.5
```

6.10 (*Finding the index of the smallest element*) Write a method that returns the index of the smallest element in an array of integers. If the number of such elements is greater than 1, return the smallest index. Use the following header:

```
public static int indexOfSmallestElement(double[] array)
```

Write a test program that prompts the user to enter ten numbers, invokes this method to return the index of the smallest element, and displays the index.

6.11* (*Statistics: computing deviation*) Exercise 5.21 computes the standard deviation of numbers. This exercise uses a different but equivalent formula to compute the standard deviation of **n** numbers.

$$mean = \frac{\sum_{i=1}^{n} x_i}{n} = \frac{x_1 + x_2 + \ldots + x_n}{n} \qquad deviation = \sqrt{\frac{\sum_{i=1}^{n}(x_i - mean)^2}{n - 1}}$$

To compute deviation with this formula, you have to store the individual numbers using an array, so that they can be used after the mean is obtained.

Your program should contain the following methods:

```
/** Compute the deviation of double values*/
public static double deviation(double[] x)

/** Compute the mean of an array of double values*/
public static double mean(double[] x)
```

Write a test program that prompts the user to enter ten numbers and displays the mean and deviation, as shown in the following sample run:

```
Enter ten numbers: 1.9 2.5 3.7 2 1 6 3 4 5 2 ↵Enter
The mean is 3.11
The standard deviation is 1.55738
```

6.12* (*Reversing an array*) The **reverse** method in §6.7 reverses an array by copying it to a new array. Rewrite the method that reverses the array passed in the argument and returns this array. Write a test program that prompts the user to enter ten numbers, invokes the method to reverse the numbers, and displays the numbers.

Section 6.8

6.13* (*Random number chooser*) Write a method that returns a random number between **1** and **54**, excluding the numbers passed in the argument. The method header is specified as follows:

```
public static int getRandom(int... numbers)
```

6.14 (*Computing gcd*) Write a method that returns the gcd of an unspecified number of integers. The method header is specified as follows:

```
public static int gcd(int... numbers)
```

Write a test program that prompts the user to enter five numbers, invokes the method to find the gcd of these numbers, and displays the gcd.

Sections 6.9–6.10

6.15 (*Eliminating duplicates*) Write a method to eliminate the duplicate values in the array using following method header:

```
public static int[] eliminateDuplicates(int[] numbers)
```

Write a test program that reads in ten integers, invokes the method, and displays the result. Here is the sample run of the program:

```
Enter ten numbers: 1 2 3 2 1 6 3 4 5 2 ↵Enter
The distinct numbers are: 1 2 3 6 4 5
```

6.16 (*Execution time*) Write a program that randomly generates an array of `100000` integers and a key. Estimate the execution time of invoking the `linearSearch` method in Listing 6.6. Sort the array and estimate the execution time of invoking the `binarySearch` method in Listing 6.7. You can use the following code template to obtain the execution time:

```
long startTime = System.currentTimeMillis();
perform the task;
long endTime = System.currentTimeMillis();
long executionTime = endTime - startTime;
```

6.17* (*Revising selection sort*) In §6.10.1, you used selection sort to sort an array. The selection-sort method repeatedly finds the smallest number in the current array and swaps it with the first number in the array. Rewrite this program by finding the largest number and swapping it with the last number in the array. Write a test program that reads in ten double numbers, invokes the method, and displays the sorted numbers.

6.18** (*Bubble sort*) Write a sort method that uses the bubble-sort algorithm. The bubble-sort algorithm makes several passes through the array. On each pass, successive neighboring pairs are compared. If a pair is in decreasing order, its values are swapped; otherwise, the values remain unchanged. The technique is called a *bubble sort* or *sinking sort* because the smaller values gradually "bubble" their way to the top and the larger values "sink" to the bottom. Use {`6.0`, `4.4`, `1.9`, `2.9`, `3.4`, `2.9`, `3.5`} to test the method. Write a test program that reads in ten double numbers, invokes the method, and displays the sorted numbers.

6.19** (*Sorting students*) Write a program that prompts the user to enter the number of students, the students' names, and their scores, and prints student names in decreasing order of their scores.

6.20*** (*Game: Eight Queens*) The classic Eight Queens puzzle is to place eight queens on a chessboard such that no two queens can attack each other (i.e., no two queens are on the same row, same column, or same diagonal). There are many possible solutions. Write a program that displays one such solution. A sample output is shown below:

```
|Q| | | | | | | |
| | | | |Q| | | |
| | | | | | | |Q|
| | | | | |Q| | |
| | |Q| | | | | |
| | | | | | |Q| |
| |Q| | | | | | |
| | | |Q| | | | |
```

6.21*** (*Game: bean machine*) The bean machine, also known as a quincunx or the Galton box, is a device for statistic experiments named after English scientist Sir Francis Galton. It consists of an upright board with evenly spaced nails (or pegs) in a triangular form, as shown in Figure 6.14.

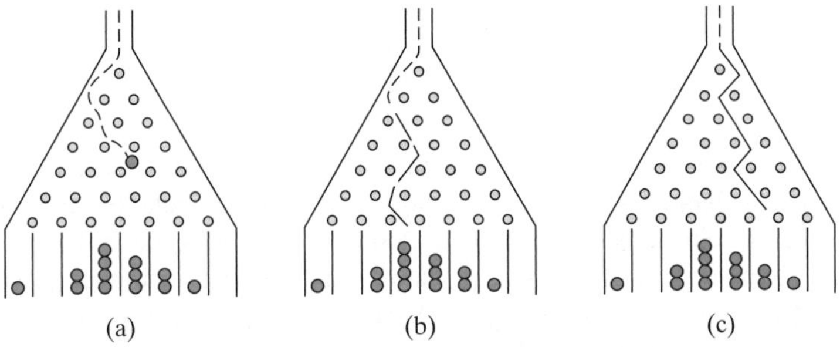

FIGURE 6.14 Each ball takes a random path and falls into a slot.

Balls are dropped from the opening of the board. Every time a ball hits a nail, it has a 50% chance of falling to the left or to the right. The piles of balls are accumulated in the slots at the bottom of the board.

Write a program that simulates the bean machine. Your program should prompt the user to enter the number of the balls and the number of the slots in the machine. Simulate the falling of each ball by printing its path. For example, the path for the ball in Figure 6.14(b) is LLRRLLR and the path for the ball in Figure 6.14(c) is RLRRLRR. Display the final buildup of the balls in the slots in a histogram. Here is a sample run of the program:

```
Enter the number of balls to drop: 5 [Enter]
Enter the number of slots in the bean machine: 7 [Enter]

LRLRLRR
RRLLLRR
LLRLLRR
RRLLLLL
LRLRRLR

  0
  0
000
```

(*Hint*: Create an array named `slots`. Each element in `slots` stores the number of balls in a slot. Each ball falls into a slot via a path. The number of R's in a path is the position of the slot where the ball falls. For example, for the path

LRLRLRR, the ball falls into `slots[4]`, and for the path is RRLLLLL, the ball falls into `slots[2]`.)

6.22*** (*Game: multiple Eight Queens solutions*) Exercise 6.20 finds one solution for the Eight Queens problem. Write a program to count all possible solutions for the eight queens problem and display all solutions.

6.23** (*Game: locker puzzle*) A school has 100 lockers and 100 students. All lockers are closed on the first day of school. As the students enter, the first student, denoted S1, opens every locker. Then the second student, S2, begins with the second locker, denoted L2, and closes every other locker. Student S3 begins with the third locker and changes every third locker (closes it if it was open, and opens it if it was closed). Student S4 begins with locker L4 and changes every fourth locker. Student S5 starts with L5 and changes every fifth locker, and so on, until student S100 changes L100.

After all the students have passed through the building and changed the lockers, which lockers are open? Write a program to find your answer.

(*Hint*: Use an array of `100 boolean` elements, each of which indicates whether a locker is open (`true`) or closed (`false`). Initially, all lockers are closed.)

Video Note
Coupon collector's problem

6.24** (*Simulation: coupon collector's problem*) Coupon collector is a classic statistic problem with many practical applications. The problem is to pick objects from a set of objects repeatedly and find out how many picks are needed for all the objects to be picked at least once. A variation of the problem is to pick cards from a shuffled deck of `52` cards repeatedly and find out how many picks are needed before you see one of each suit. Assume a picked card is placed back in the deck before picking another. Write a program to simulate the number of picks needed to get four cards from each suit and display the four cards picked (it is possible a card may be picked twice). Here is a sample run of the program:

```
Queen of Spades
5 of Clubs
Queen of Hearts
4 of Diamonds
Number of picks: 12
```

6.25 (*Algebra: solving quadratic equations*) Write a method for solving a quadratic equation using the following header:

```
public static int solveQuadratic(double[] eqn, double[] roots)
```

The coefficients of a quadratic equation $ax^2 + bx + c = 0$ are passed to the array `eqn` and the noncomplex roots are stored in roots. The method returns the number of roots. See Programming Exercise 3.1 on how to solve a quadratic equation.

Write a program that prompts the user to enter values for a, b, and c and displays the number of roots and all noncomplex roots.

6.26 (*Strictly identical arrays*) Two arrays `list1` and `list2` are *strictly identical* if they have the same length and `list1[i]` is equal to `list2[i]` for each `i`. Write a method that returns `true` if `list1` and `list2` are strictly identical, using the following header:

```
public static boolean equal(int[] list1, int[] list2)
```

Write a test program that prompts the user to enter two lists of integers and displays whether the two are strictly identical. Here are the sample runs. Note that the first number in the input indicates the number of the elements in the list.

```
Enter list1: 5 2 5 6 1 6
Enter list2: 5 2 5 6 1 6
Two lists are strictly identical
```

```
Enter list1: 5 2 5 6 6 1
Enter list2: 5 2 5 6 1 6
Two lists are not strictly identical
```

6.27 (*Identical arrays*) Two arrays `list1` and `list2` are *identical* if they have the same contents. Write a method that returns `true` if `list1` and `list2` are identical, using the following header:

```
public static boolean equal(int[] list1, int[] list2)
```

Write a test program that prompts the user to enter two lists of integers and displays whether the two are identical. Here are the sample runs. Note that the first number in the input indicates the number of the elements in the list.

```
Enter list1: 5 2 5 6 6 1
Enter list2: 5 5 2 6 1 6
Two lists are identical
```

```
Enter list1: 5 5 5 6 6 1
Enter list2: 5 2 5 6 1 6
Two lists are not identical
```

6.28 (*Math: combinations*) Write a program that prompts the user to enter 10 integers and displays all combinations of picking two numbers from the 10.

6.29 (*Game: picking four cards*) Write a program that picks four cards from a deck of 52 cards and computes their sum. An Ace, King, Queen, and Jack represent 1, 13, 12, and 11, respectively. Your program should display the number of picks that yields the sum of 24.

6.30 (*Pattern recognition: consecutive four equal numbers*) Write the following method that tests whether the array has four consecutive numbers with the same value.

```
public static boolean isConsecutiveFour(int[] values)
```

Write a test program that prompts the user to enter a series of integers and displays true if the series contains four consecutive numbers with the same value. Otherwise, display false. Your program should first prompt the user to enter the input size—i.e., the number of values in the series.

CHAPTER 7

MULTIDIMENSIONAL ARRAYS

Objectives

- To give examples of representing data using two-dimensional arrays (§7.1).
- To declare variables for two-dimensional arrays, create arrays, and access array elements in a two-dimensional array using row and column indexes (§7.2).
- To program common operations for two-dimensional arrays (displaying arrays, summing all elements, finding min and max elements, and random shuffling) (§7.3).
- To pass two-dimensional arrays to methods (§7.4).
- To write a program for grading multiple-choice questions using two-dimensional arrays (§7.5).
- To solve the closest-pair problem using two-dimensional arrays (§7.6).
- To check a Sudoku solution using two-dimensional arrays (§7.7).
- To use multidimensional arrays (§7.8).

7.1 Introduction

problem

The preceding chapter introduced how to use one-dimensional arrays to store linear collections of elements. You can use a two-dimensional array to store a matrix or a table. For example, the following table that describes the distances between the cities can be stored using a two-dimensional array.

Distance Table (in miles)

	Chicago	Boston	New York	Atlanta	Miami	Dallas	Houston
Chicago	0	983	787	714	1375	967	1087
Boston	983	0	214	1102	1763	1723	1842
New York	787	214	0	888	1549	1548	1627
Atlanta	714	1102	888	0	661	781	810
Miami	1375	1763	1549	661	0	1426	1187
Dallas	967	1723	1548	781	1426	0	239
Houston	1087	1842	1627	810	1187	239	0

7.2 Two-Dimensional Array Basics

How do you declare a variable for two-dimensional arrays? How do you create a two-dimensional array? How do you access elements in a two-dimensional array? This section addresses these issues.

7.2.1 Declaring Variables of Two-Dimensional Arrays and Creating Two-Dimensional Arrays

Here is the syntax for declaring a two-dimensional array:

```
elementType[][] arrayRefVar;
```

or

```
elementType arrayRefVar[][]; // Allowed, but not preferred
```

As an example, here is how you would declare a two-dimensional array variable `matrix` of `int` values:

```
int[][] matrix;
```

or

```
int matrix[][]; // This style is allowed, but not preferred
```

You can create a two-dimensional array of `5`-by-`5` `int` values and assign it to `matrix` using this syntax:

```
matrix = new int[5][5];
```

Two subscripts are used in a two-dimensional array, one for the row and the other for the column. As in a one-dimensional array, the index for each subscript is of the `int` type and starts from `0`, as shown in Figure 7.1(a).

To assign the value `7` to a specific element at row `2` and column `1`, as shown in Figure 7.1(b), you can use the following:

```
matrix[2][1] = 7;
```

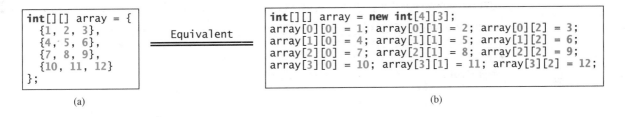

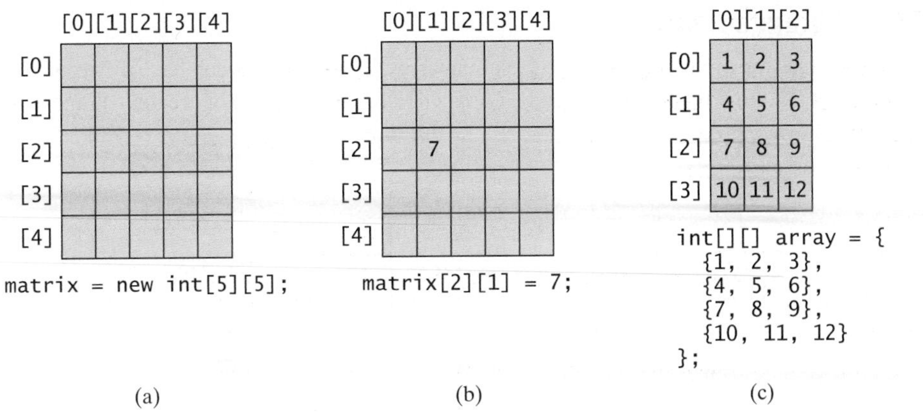
[0][1][2][3][4]
[0]
[1]
[2]
[3]
[4]
matrix = new int[5][5];
[0][1][2][3][4]
[0]
[1]
[2]
[3]
[4]
7
matrix[2][1] = 7;
[0][1][2]
[0]
[1]
[2]
[3]
1 2 3
4 5 6
7 8 9
10 11 12
int[][] array = {
{1, 2, 3},
{4, 5, 6},
{7, 8, 9},
{10, 11, 12}
};
(a)
(b)
(c)

FIGURE 7.1 The index of each subscript of a two-dimensional array is an `int` value, starting from `0`.

Caution

It is a common mistake to use `matrix[2, 1]` to access the element at row `2` and column `1`. In Java, each subscript must be enclosed in a pair of square brackets.

You can also use an array initializer to declare, create, and initialize a two-dimensional array. For example, the following code in (a) creates an array with the specified initial values, as shown in Figure 7.1(c). This is equivalent to the code in (b).

```
int[][] array = {
  {1, 2, 3},
  {4, 5, 6},
  {7, 8, 9},
  {10, 11, 12}
};
```

(a)

Equivalent

```
int[][] array = new int[4][3];
array[0][0] = 1; array[0][1] = 2; array[0][2] = 3;
array[1][0] = 4; array[1][1] = 5; array[1][2] = 6;
array[2][0] = 7; array[2][1] = 8; array[2][2] = 9;
array[3][0] = 10; array[3][1] = 11; array[3][2] = 12;
```

(b)

7.2.2 Obtaining the Lengths of Two-Dimensional Arrays

A two-dimensional array is actually an array in which each element is a one-dimensional array. The length of an array `x` is the number of elements in the array, which can be obtained using `x.length`. `x[0]`, `x[1]`, . . . , and `x[x.length-1]` are arrays. Their lengths can be obtained using `x[0].length`, `x[1].length`, . . . , and `x[x.length-1].length`.

For example, suppose `x = new int[3][4]`, `x[0]`, `x[1]`, and `x[2]` are one-dimensional arrays and each contains four elements, as shown in Figure 7.2. `x.length` is `3`, and `x[0].length`, `x[1].length`, and `x[2].length` are `4`.

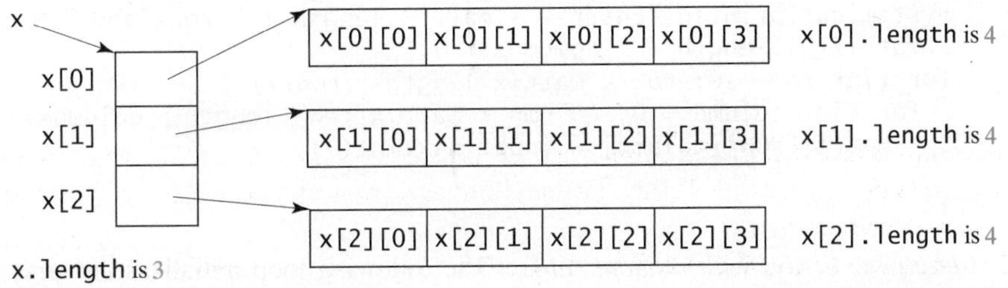
x
x[0]
x[1]
x[2]
x[0][0] x[0][1] x[0][2] x[0][3]
x[1][0] x[1][1] x[1][2] x[1][3]
x[2][0] x[2][1] x[2][2] x[2][3]
x[0].length is 4
x[1].length is 4
x[2].length is 4
x.length is 3

FIGURE 7.2 A two-dimensional array is a one-dimensional array in which each element is another one-dimensional array.

7.2.3 Ragged Arrays

Each row in a two-dimensional array is itself an array. Thus the rows can have different lengths. An array of this kind is known as a *ragged array*. Here is an example of creating a ragged array:

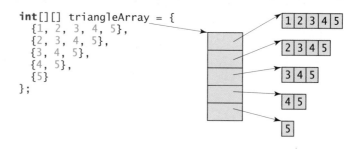

```
int[][] triangleArray = {
  {1, 2, 3, 4, 5},
  {2, 3, 4, 5},
  {3, 4, 5},
  {4, 5},
  {5}
};
```

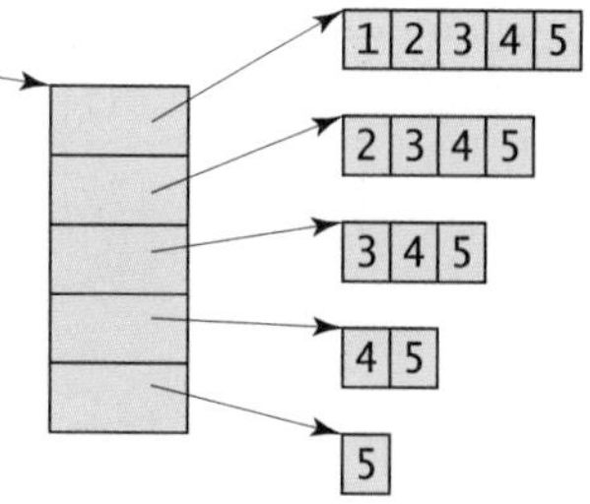

1 2 3 4 5
2 3 4 5
3 4 5
4 5
5

As can be seen, `triangleArray[0].length` is 5, `triangleArray[1].length` is 4, `triangleArray[2].length` is 3, `triangleArray[3].length` is 2, and `triangleArray[4].length` is 1.

If you don't know the values in a ragged array in advance, but know the sizes, say the same as before, you can create a ragged array using the syntax that follows:

```
int[][] triangleArray = new int[5][] ;
triangleArray[0] = new int[5];
triangleArray[1] = new int[4];
triangleArray[2] = new int[3];
triangleArray[3] = new int[2];
triangleArray[4] = new int[1];
```

You can now assign values to the array. For example,

```
triangleArray[0][3] = 50;
triangleArray[4][0] = 45;
```

Note

The syntax `new int[5][]` for creating an array requires the first index to be specified. The syntax `new int[][]` would be wrong.

7.3 Processing Two-Dimensional Arrays

Suppose an array `matrix` is created as follows:

```
int[][] matrix = new int[10][10];
```

Here are some examples of processing two-dimensional arrays:

1. (*Initializing arrays with input values*) The following loop initializes the array with user input values:

```
java.util.Scanner input = new Scanner(System.in);
System.out.println("Enter " + matrix.length + " rows and " +
  matrix[0].length + " columns: ");
for (int row = 0; row < matrix.length ; row++) {
  for (int column = 0; column < matrix[row].length ; column++) {
    matrix[row][column] = input.nextInt();
  }
}
```

2. (*Initializing arrays with random values*) The following loop initializes the array with random values between 0 and 99:

```
for (int row = 0; row < matrix.length ; row++) {
  for (int column = 0; column < matrix[row].length ; column++) {
```

```
      matrix[row][column] = (int)(Math.random() * 100);
    }
  }
```

3. (*Printing arrays*) To print a two-dimensional array, you have to print each element in the array using a loop like the following:

```
for (int row = 0; row < matrix.length ; row++) {
  for (int column = 0; column < matrix[row].length ; column++) {
    System.out.print(matrix[row][column] + " ");
  }

  System.out.println();
}
```

4. (*Summing all elements*) Use a variable named `total` to store the sum. Initially `total` is `0`. Add each element in the array to `total` using a loop like this:

```
int total = 0;
for (int row = 0; row < matrix.length; row++) {
  for (int column = 0; column < matrix[row].length; column++) {
    total += matrix[row][column];
  }
}
```

5. (*Summing elements by column*) For each column, use a variable named `total` to store its sum. Add each element in the column to `total` using a loop like this:

```
for (int column = 0; column < matrix[0].length; column++) {
  int total = 0;
  for (int row = 0; row < matrix.length; row++)
    total += matrix[row][column];
  System.out.println("Sum for column " + column + " is " +
    total);
}
```

6. (*Which row has the largest sum?*) Use variables `maxRow` and `indexOfMaxRow` to track the largest sum and index of the row. For each row, compute its sum and update `maxRow` and `indexOfMaxRow` if the new sum is greater.

Video Note
find the row with the largest sum

```
int maxRow = 0;
int indexOfMaxRow = 0;

// Get sum of the first row in maxRow
for (int column = 0; column < matrix[0].length; column++) {
  maxRow += matrix[0][column];
}

for (int row = 1; row < matrix.length; row++) {
  int totalOfThisRow = 0;
  for (int column = 0; column < matrix[row].length; column++)
    totalOfThisRow += matrix[row][column];

  if (totalOfThisRow > maxRow) {
    maxRow = totalOfThisRow;
    indexOfMaxRow = row;
  }
}

System.out.println("Row " + indexOfMaxRow
  + " has the maximum sum of " + maxRow);
```

7. (*Random shuffling*) Shuffling the elements in a one-dimensional array was introduced in §6.2.6. How do you shuffle all the elements in a two-dimensional array? To accomplish this, for each element `matrix[i][j]`, randomly generate indices `i1` and `j1` and swap `matrix[i][j]` with `matrix[i1][j1]`, as follows:

```
for (int i = 0; i < matrix.length; i++) {
  for (int j = 0; j < matrix[i].length; j++) {
    int i1 = (int)(Math.random() * matrix.length);
    int j1 = (int)(Math.random() * matrix[i].length);

    // Swap matrix[i][j] with matrix[i1][j1]
    int temp = matrix[i][j];
    matrix[i][j] = matrix[i1][j1];
    matrix[i1][j1] = temp;
  }
}
```

7.4 Passing Two-Dimensional Arrays to Methods

You can pass a two-dimensional array to a method just as you pass a one-dimensional array. Listing 7.1 gives an example with a method that returns the sum of all the elements in a matrix.

LISTING 7.1 PassTwoDimensionalArray.java

```
import java.util.Scanner;

public class PassTwoDimensionalArray {
  public static void main(String[] args) {
    // Create a Scanner
    Scanner input = new Scanner(System.in);

    // Enter array values
    int[][] m = new int[3][4];
    System.out.println("Enter " + m.length + " rows and "
      + m[0].length + " columns: ");
    for (int i = 0; i < m.length; i++)
      for (int j = 0; j < m[i].length; j++)
        m[i][j] = input.nextInt();

    // Display result
    System.out.println("\nSum of all elements is " + sum(m));
  }

  public static int sum(int[][] m) {
    int total = 0;
    for (int row = 0; row < m.length; row++) {
      for (int column = 0; column < m[row].length; column++) {
        total += m[row][column];
      }
    }

    return total;
  }
}
```

pass array

```
Enter 3 rows and 4 columns:
1 2 3 4 ↵Enter
5 6 7 8 ↵Enter
9 10 11 12 ↵Enter
Sum of all elements is 78
```

The method `sum` (line 20) has a two-dimensional array argument. You can obtain the number of rows using `m.length` (line 22) and the number of columns in a specified row using `m[row].column` (line 23).

7.5 Problem: Grading a Multiple-Choice Test

The problem is to write a program that grades multiple-choice tests. Suppose there are eight students and ten questions, and the answers are stored in a two-dimensional array. Each row records a student's answers to the questions, as shown in the following array.

Video Note
Grade multiple-choice test

Students' Answers to the Questions:

	0	1	2	3	4	5	6	7	8	9
Student 0	A	B	A	C	C	D	E	E	A	D
Student 1	D	B	A	B	C	A	E	E	A	D
Student 2	E	D	D	A	C	B	E	E	A	D
Student 3	C	B	A	E	D	C	E	E	A	D
Student 4	A	B	D	C	C	D	E	E	A	D
Student 5	B	B	E	C	C	D	E	E	A	D
Student 6	B	B	A	C	C	D	E	E	A	D
Student 7	E	B	E	C	C	D	E	E	A	D

The key is stored in a one-dimensional array:

Key to the Questions:

	0	1	2	3	4	5	6	7	8	9
Key	D	B	D	C	C	D	A	E	A	D

Your program grades the test and displays the result. It compares each student's answers with the key, counts the number of correct answers, and displays it. Listing 7.2 gives the program.

LISTING 7.2 `GradeExam.java`

```
public class GradeExam {
  /** Main method */
  public static void main(String[] args) {
    // Students' answers to the questions
    char[][] answers = {
      {'A', 'B', 'A', 'C', 'C', 'D', 'E', 'E', 'A', 'D'},
      {'D', 'B', 'A', 'B', 'C', 'A', 'E', 'E', 'A', 'D'},
      {'E', 'D', 'D', 'A', 'C', 'B', 'E', 'E', 'A', 'D'},
      {'C', 'B', 'A', 'E', 'D', 'C', 'E', 'E', 'A', 'D'},
      {'A', 'B', 'D', 'C', 'C', 'D', 'E', 'E', 'A', 'D'},
      {'B', 'B', 'E', 'C', 'C', 'D', 'E', 'E', 'A', 'D'},
      {'B', 'B', 'A', 'C', 'C', 'D', 'E', 'E', 'A', 'D'},
      {'E', 'B', 'E', 'C', 'C', 'D', 'E', 'E', 'A', 'D'}};
```

2-D array

1-D array

compare with key

```
14
15     // Key to the questions
16     char[] keys = {'D', 'B', 'D', 'C', 'C', 'D', 'A', 'E', 'A', 'D'};
17
18     // Grade all answers
19     for (int i = 0; i < answers.length ; i++) {
20       // Grade one student
21       int correctCount = 0;
22       for (int j = 0; j < answers[i].length ; j++) {
23         if (answers[i][j] == keys[j] )
24           correctCount++;
25       }
26
27       System.out.println("Student " + i + "'s correct count is " +
28         correctCount);
29     }
30   }
31 }
```

```
Student 0's correct count is 7
Student 1's correct count is 6
Student 2's correct count is 5
Student 3's correct count is 4
Student 4's correct count is 8
Student 5's correct count is 7
Student 6's correct count is 7
Student 7's correct count is 7
```

The statement in lines 5–13 declares, creates, and initializes a two-dimensional array of characters and assigns the reference to `answers` of the `char[][]` type.

The statement in line 16 declares, creates, and initializes an array of `char` values and assigns the reference to `keys` of the `char[]` type.

Each row in the array `answers` stores a student's answer, which is graded by comparing it with the key in the array `keys`. The result is displayed immediately after a student's answer is graded.

7.6 Problem: Finding a Closest Pair

The GPS navigation system is becoming increasingly popular. The system uses the graph and geometric algorithms to calculate distances and map a route. This section presents a geometric problem for finding a closest pair of points.

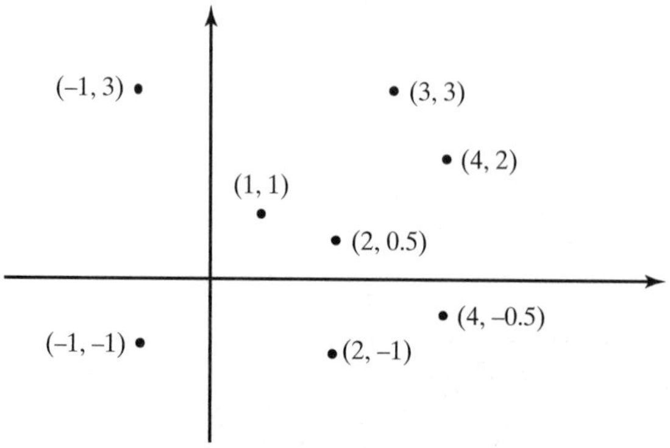

(–1, 3)
(3, 3)
(4, 2)
(1, 1)
(2, 0.5)
(4, –0.5)
(–1, –1)
(2, –1)

	x	y
0	–1	3
1	–1	–1
2	1	1
3	2	0.5
4	2	–1
5	3	3
6	4	2
7	4	–0.5

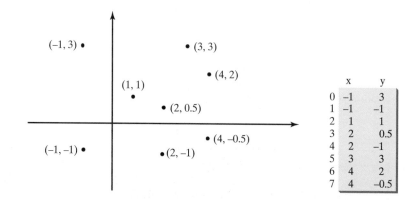

FIGURE 7.3 Points can be represented in a two-dimensional array.

Given a set of points, the closest-pair problem is to find the two points that are nearest to each other. In Figure 7.3, for example, points (1, 1) and (2, 0.5) are closest to each other. There are several ways to solve this problem. An intuitive approach is to compute the distances between all pairs of points and find the one with the minimum distance, as implemented in Listing 7.3.

LISTING 7.3 FindNearestPoints.java

```
import java.util.Scanner;

public class FindNearestPoints {
  public static void main(String[] args) {
    Scanner input = new Scanner(System.in);
    System.out.print("Enter the number of points: ");
    int numberOfPoints = input.nextInt();

    // Create an array to store points
    double[][] points = new double[numberOfPoints][2];
    System.out.print("Enter " + numberOfPoints + " points: ");
    for (int i = 0; i < points.length; i++) {
      points[i][0] = input.nextDouble();
      points[i][1] = input.nextDouble();
    }

    // p1 and p2 are the indices in the points array
    int p1 = 0, p2 = 1; // Initial two points
    double shortestDistance = distance(points[p1][0], points[p1][1],
      points[p2][0], points[p2][1]); // Initialize shortestDistance

    // Compute distance for every two points
    for (int i = 0; i < points.length; i++) {
      for (int j = i + 1; j < points.length; j++) {
        double distance = distance(points[i][0], points[i][1],
          points[j][0], points[j][1]); // Find distance

        if (shortestDistance > distance) {
          p1 = i; // Update p1
          p2 = j; // Update p2
          shortestDistance = distance; // Update shortestDistance
        }
      }
    }

    // Display result
    System.out.println("The closest two points are " +
      "(" + points[p1][0] + ", " + points[p1][1] + ") and (" +
      points[p2][0] + ", " + points[p2][1] + ")");
  }

  /** Compute the distance between two points (x1, y1) and (x2, y2)*/
  public static double distance(
      double x1, double y1, double x2, double y2) {
    return Math.sqrt((x2 - x1) * (x2 - x1) + (y2 - y1) * (y2 - y1));
  }
}
```

number of points

2-D array

read points

track two points

track **shortestDistance**

for each point **i**

for each point **j**

distance between **i** and **j**

distance between two points

update **shortestDistance**

```
Enter the number of points: 8 ↵Enter
Enter 8 points: -1 3  -1 -1  1 1  2 0.5  2 -1  3 3  4 2 4 -0.5 ↵Enter
The closest two points are (1, 1) and (2, 0.5)
```

The program prompts the user to enter the number of points (lines 6–7). The points are read from the console and stored in a two-dimensional array named `points` (lines 12–15). The program uses variable `shortestDistance` (line 19) to store the distance between two nearest points, and the indices of these two points in the `points` array are stored in `p1` and `p2` (line 18).

For each point at index `i`, the program computes the distance between `points[i]` and `points[j]` for all `j > i` (lines 23–34). Whenever a shorter distance is found, the variable `shortestDistance` and `p1` and `p2` are updated (lines 28–32).

The distance between two points `(x1, y1)` and `(x2, y2)` can be computed using the formula $\sqrt{(x_2 - x_1)^2 + (y_2 - y_1)^2}$ (lines 43–46).

The program assumes that the plane has at least two points. You can easily modify the program to handle the case if the plane has zero or one point.

multiple closest pairs

Note that there might be more than one closest pair of points with the same minimum distance. The program finds one such pair. You may modify the program to find all closest pairs in Programming Exercise 7.8.

Tip

input file

It is cumbersome to enter all points from the keyboard. You may store the input in a file, say FindNearestPoints.txt, and compile and run the program using the following command:

```
java FindNearestPoints < FindNearestPoints.txt
```

7.7 Problem: Sudoku

Video Note
Sudoku

This book teaches how to program using a wide variety of problems with various levels of difficulty. We use simple, short, and stimulating examples to introduce programming and problem-solving techniques and use interesting and challenging examples to motivate students. This section presents an interesting problem of a sort that appears in the newspaper every day. It is a number-placement puzzle, commonly known as *Sudoku*. This is a very challenging problem. To make it accessible to the novice, this section presents a solution to a simplified version of the Sudoku problem, which is to verify whether a solution is correct. The complete solution for solving the Sudoku problem is presented in Supplement VII.A.

fixed cells

free cells

Sudoku is a 9 × 9 grid divided into smaller 3 × 3 boxes (also called regions or blocks), as shown in Figure 7.4(a). Some cells, called *fixed cells*, are populated with numbers from `1` to `9`. The objective is to fill the empty cells, also called *free cells*, with numbers `1` to `9` so that every row, every column, and every 3 × 3 box contains the numbers `1` to `9`, as shown in Figure 7.4(b).

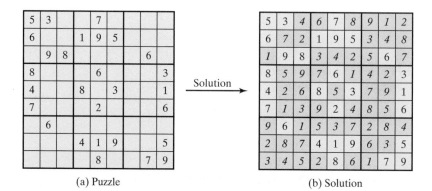

5	3			7				
6			1	9	5			
	9	8					6	
8				6				3
4			8		3			1
7				2				6
	6							
			4	1	9			5
				8			7	9

(a) Puzzle

Solution →

5	3	4	6	7	8	9	1	2
6	7	2	1	9	5	3	4	8
1	9	8	3	4	2	5	6	7
8	5	9	7	6	1	4	2	3
4	2	6	8	5	3	7	9	1
7	1	3	9	2	4	8	5	6
9	6	1	5	3	7	2	8	4
2	8	7	4	1	9	6	3	5
3	4	5	2	8	6	1	7	9

(b) Solution

FIGURE 7.4 The Sudoku puzzle in (a) is solved in (b).

For convenience, we use value 0 to indicate a free cell, as shown in Figure 7.5(a). The grid can be naturally represented using a two-dimensional array, as shown in Figure 7.5(a).

representing a grid

5	3	0	0	7	0	0	0	0
6	0	0	1	9	5	0	0	0
0	9	8	0	0	0	0	6	0
8	0	0	0	6	0	0	0	3
4	0	0	8	0	3	0	0	1
7	0	0	0	2	0	0	0	6
0	6	0	0	0	0	0	0	0
0	0	0	4	1	9	0	0	5
0	0	0	0	8	0	0	7	9

(a)

```
int[][] grid =
  {{5, 3, 0, 0, 7, 0, 0, 0, 0},
   {6, 0, 0, 1, 9, 5, 0, 0, 0},
   {0, 9, 8, 0, 0, 0, 0, 6, 0},
   {8, 0, 0, 0, 6, 0, 0, 0, 3},
   {4, 0, 0, 8, 0, 3, 0, 0, 1},
   {7, 0, 0, 0, 2, 0, 0, 0, 6},
   {0, 6, 0, 0, 0, 0, 2, 8, 0},
   {0, 0, 0, 4, 1, 9, 0, 0, 5},
   {0, 0, 0, 0, 8, 0, 0, 7, 9}
  };
```

(b)

FIGURE 7.5 A grid can be represented using a two-dimensional array.

To find a solution for the puzzle we must replace each 0 in the grid with an appropriate number from 1 to 9. For the solution in Figure 7.4(b), the grid should be as shown in Figure 7.6.

```
A solution grid is
  {{5, 3, 4, 6, 7, 8, 9, 1, 2},
   {6, 7, 2, 1, 9, 5, 3, 4, 8},
   {1, 9, 8, 3, 4, 2, 5, 6, 7},
   {8, 5, 9, 7, 6, 1, 4, 2, 3},
   {4, 2, 6, 8, 5, 3, 7, 9, 1},
   {7, 1, 3, 9, 2, 4, 8, 5, 6},
   {9, 6, 1, 5, 3, 7, 2, 8, 4},
   {2, 8, 7, 4, 1, 9, 6, 3, 5},
   {3, 4, 5, 2, 8, 6, 1, 7, 9}
  };
```

FIGURE 7.6 A solution is stored in `grid`.

A simplified version of the Sudoku problem is to check the validity of a solution. The program in Listing 7.4 prompts the user to enter a solution and reports whether it is valid.

LISTING 7.4 CheckSudokuSolution.java

```
import java.util.Scanner;

public class CheckSudokuSolution {
  public static void main(String[] args) {
    // Read a Sudoku solution
    int[][] grid = readASolution();

    System.out.println(isValid(grid) ? "Valid solution" :
      "Invalid solution");
  }

  /** Read a Sudoku solution from the console */
  public static int[][] readASolution() {
    // Create a Scanner
    Scanner input = new Scanner(System.in);
```

read input

solution valid?

read solution

check solution

check rows

check columns

check small boxes

all valid

contains 1 to 9 ?

copy of array

sort array

check 1 to 9

```

    System.out.println("Enter a Sudoku puzzle solution:");
    int[][] grid = new int[9][9];
    for (int i = 0; i < 9; i++)
      for (int j = 0; j < 9; j++)
        grid[i][j] = input.nextInt();

    return grid;
  }

  /** Check whether a solution is valid */
  public static boolean isValid(int[][] grid) {
    // Check whether each row has numbers 1 to 9
    for (int i = 0; i < 9; i++)
      if (!is1To9(grid[i]) ) // If grid[i] does not contain 1 to 9
        return false;

    // Check whether each column has numbers 1 to 9
    for (int j = 0; j < 9; j++) {
      // Obtain a column in the one-dimensional array
      int[] column = new int[9];
      for (int i = 0; i < 9; i++) {
        column[i] = grid[i][j];
      }

      if (!is1To9(column) ) // If column does not contain 1 to 9
        return false;
    }

    // Check whether each 3-by-3 box has numbers 1 to 9
    for (int i = 0; i < 3; i++) {
      for (int j = 0; j < 3; j++) {
        // The starting element in a small 3-by-3 box
        int k = 0;
        int[] list = new int[9]; // Get all numbers in the box to list
        for (int row = i * 3; row < i * 3 + 3; row ++)
          for (int column = j * 3; column < j * 3 + 3; column++)
            list[k++] = grid[row][column];

        if (!is1To9(list) ) // If list does not contain 1 to 9
          return false;
      }
    }

    return true; // The fixed cells are valid
  }

  /** Check whether the one-dimensional array contains 1 to 9 */
  public static boolean is1To9(int[] list) {
    // Make a copy of the array
    int[] temp = new int[list.length];
    System.arraycopy(list, 0, temp, 0, list.length);

    // Sort the array
    java.util.Arrays.sort(temp);

    // Check whether the list contains 1, 2, 3, ..., 9
    for (int i = 0; i < 9; i++)
```

```
74          if (temp[i] != i + 1)
75            return false;
76
77        return true; // The list contains exactly 1 to 9
78      }
79    }
```

```
Enter a Sudoku puzzle solution:
9 6 3 1 7 4 2 5 8 ↵Enter
1 7 8 3 2 5 6 4 9 ↵Enter
2 5 4 6 8 9 7 3 1 ↵Enter
8 2 1 4 3 7 5 9 6 ↵Enter
4 9 6 8 5 2 3 1 7 ↵Enter
7 3 5 9 6 1 8 2 4 ↵Enter
5 8 9 7 1 3 4 6 2 ↵Enter
3 1 7 2 4 6 9 8 5 ↵Enter
6 4 2 5 9 8 1 7 3 ↵Enter
Valid solution
```

The program invokes the `readASolution()` method (line 6) to read a Sudoku solution and return a two-dimensional array representing a Sudoku grid.

`isValid` method

check rows

The `isValid(grid)` method (lines 27–61) checks whether every row contains numbers `1` to `9` (lines 29–31). `grid` is a two-dimensional array. `grid[i]` is a one-dimensional array for the *i*th row. Invoking `is1To9(grid[i])` returns `true` if the row `grid[i]` contains exactly numbers from `1` to `9` (line 30).

check columns

To check whether each column in `grid` has numbers `1` to `9`, get a column into a one-dimensional array (lines 36–39) and invoke the `is1To9` method to check whether it has `1` to `9` (line 41).

check small boxes

To check whether each small 3 × 3 box in `grid` has numbers `1` to `9`, get a box into a one-dimensional array (lines 49–53) and invoke the `is1To9` method to check whether it has `1` to `9` (line 55).

How do you locate all the cells in the same box? First, locate the starting cells of the 3 × 3 boxes. They are at `(3i, 3j)` for `i = 0, 1, 2` and `j = 0, 1, 2`, as illustrated in Figure 7.7.

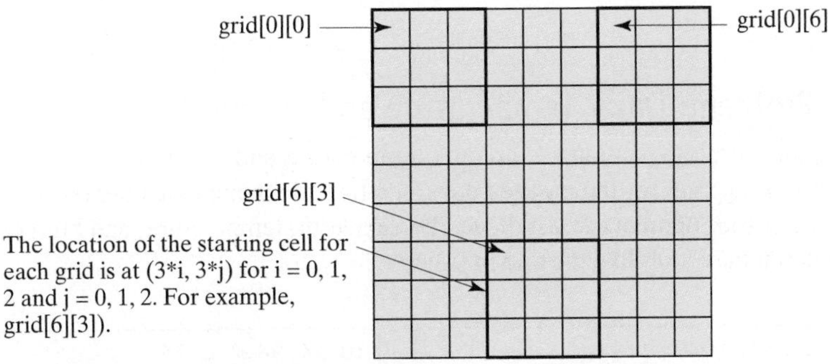
grid[0][0]
grid[0][6]
grid[6][3]
The location of the starting cell for each grid is at (3*i, 3*j) for i = 0, 1, 2 and j = 0, 1, 2. For example, grid[6][3]).

FIGURE 7.7 The location of the first cell in a 3 × 3 box determines the locations of other cells in the box.

With this observation, you can easily identify all the cells in the box. Suppose grid[r][c] is the starting cell of a 3 × 3 box. The cells in the box can be traversed in a nested loop as follows:

```
// Get all cells in a 3-by-3 box starting at grid[r][c]
for (int row = r; row < r + 3; row++)
  for (int column = c; column < c + 3; column++)
    // grid[row][column] is in the box
```

All the numbers in a small box are collected into a one-dimensional array list (line 53), and invoking is1To9(list) checks whether list contains numbers 1 to 9 (line 55).

is1To9 method

The is1To9(list) method (lines 64–78) checks whether array list contains exactly numbers 1 to 9. It first copies list to a new array temp, then sorts temp. Note that if you sort list, the contents of grid will be changed. After temp is sorted, the numbers in temp should be 1, 2, ..., 9, if temp contains exactly 1 to 9. The loop in lines 73–75 checks whether this is the case.

input file

It is cumbersome to enter 81 numbers from the console. When you test the program, you may store the input in a file, say CheckSudokuSolution.txt, and run the program using the following command:

```
java CheckSudokuSoluton < CheckSudokuSoluton.txt
```

7.8 Multidimensional Arrays

In the preceding section, you used a two-dimensional array to represent a matrix or a table. Occasionally, you will need to represent n-dimensional data structures. In Java, you can create n-dimensional arrays for any integer n.

The way to declare two-dimensional array variables and create two-dimensional arrays can be generalized to declare n-dimensional array variables and create n-dimensional arrays for $n >= 3$. For example, the following syntax declares a three-dimensional array variable scores, creates an array, and assigns its reference to scores.

```
double[][][] data = new double[10][24][2];
```

A multidimensional array is actually an array in which each element is another array. A three-dimensional array consists of an array of two-dimensional arrays, each of which is an array of one-dimensional arrays. For example, suppose x = new int[2][2][5], x[0] and x[1] are two-dimensional arrays. X[0][0], x[0][1], x[1][0], and x[1][1] are one-dimensional arrays and each contains five elements. x.length is 2, x[0].length and x[1].length are 2, and X[0][0].length, x[0][1].length, x[1][0].length, and x[1][1].length are 5.

7.8.1 Problem: Daily Temperature and Humidity

Suppose a meteorology station records the temperature and humidity at each hour of every day and stores the data for the past ten days in a text file named weather.txt. Each line of the file consists of four numbers that indicate the day, hour, temperature, and humidity. The contents of the file may look like the one in (a):

```
1 1 76.4 0.92
1 2 77.7 0.93
...
10 23 97.7 0.71
10 24 98.7 0.74
```

(a)

```
10 24 98.7 0.74
1 2 77.7 0.93
...
10 23 97.7 0.71
1 1 76.4 0.92
```

(b)

Note that the lines in the file are not necessary in order. For example, the file may appear as shown in (b).

Your task is to write a program that calculates the average daily temperature and humidity for the 10 days. You can use the input redirection to read the file and store the data in a three-dimensional array, named data. The first index of data ranges from 0 to 9 and represents 10 days, the second index ranges from 0 to 23 and represents 24 hours, and the third index ranges from 0 to 1 and represents temperature and humidity, respectively. Note that the days are numbered from 1 to 10 and hours from 1 to 24 in the file. Since the array index starts from 0, data[0][0][0] stores the temperature in day 1 at hour 1 and data[9][23][1] stores the humidity in day 10 at hour 24.

The program is given in Listing 7.5.

LISTING 7.5 Weather.java

```
import java.util.Scanner;

public class Weather {
  public static void main(String[] args) {
    final int NUMBER_OF_DAYS = 10;
    final int NUMBER_OF_HOURS = 24;
    double[][][] data
      = new double[NUMBER_OF_DAYS][NUMBER_OF_HOURS][2];

    Scanner input = new Scanner(System.in);
    // Read input using input redirection from a file
    for (int k = 0; k < NUMBER_OF_DAYS * NUMBER_OF_HOURS; k++) {
      int day = input.nextInt();
      int hour = input.nextInt();
      double temperature = input.nextDouble();
      double humidity = input.nextDouble();
      data[day - 1][hour - 1][0] = temperature;
      data[day - 1][hour - 1][1] = humidity;
    }

    // Find the average daily temperature and humidity
    for (int i = 0; i < NUMBER_OF_DAYS; i++) {
      double dailyTemperatureTotal = 0, dailyHumidityTotal = 0;
      for (int j = 0; j < NUMBER_OF_HOURS; j++) {
        dailyTemperatureTotal += data[i][j][0];
        dailyHumidityTotal += data[i][j][1];
      }

      // Display result
      System.out.println("Day " + i + "'s average temperature is "
        + dailyTemperatureTotal / NUMBER_OF_HOURS);
      System.out.println("Day " + i + "'s average humidity is "
        + dailyHumidityTotal / NUMBER_OF_HOURS);
    }
  }
}
```

three-dimensional array

```
Day 0's average temperature is 77.7708
Day 0's average humidity is 0.929583
Day 1's average temperature is 77.3125
Day 1's average humidity is 0.929583
...
Day 9's average temperature is 79.3542
Day 9's average humidity is 0.9125
```

You can use the following command to run the program:

```
java Weather < Weather.txt
```

A three-dimensional array for storing temperature and humidity is created in line 8. The loop in lines 12–19 reads the input to the array. You can enter the input from the keyboard, but doing so will be awkward. For convenience, we store the data in a file and use the input redirection to read the data from the file. The loop in lines 24–27 adds all temperatures for each hour in a day to `dailyTemperatureTotal` and all humidity for each hour to `dailyHumidityTotal`. The average daily temperature and humidity are displayed in lines 30–33.

7.8.2 Problem: Guessing Birthdays

Listing 3.3, GuessBirthday.java, gives a program that guesses a birthday. The program can be simplified by storing the numbers in five sets in a three-dimensional array, and it prompts the user for the answers using a loop, as shown in Listing 7.6. The sample run of the program can be the same as shown in Listing 3.3.

LISTING 7.6 GuessBirthdayUsingArray.java

three-dimensional array

Set i

```
import java.util.Scanner;

public class GuessBirthdayUsingArray {
  public static void main(String[] args) {
    int day = 0; // Day to be determined
    int answer;

    int[][][] dates = {
      {{ 1,  3,  5,  7},
       { 9, 11, 13, 15},
       {17, 19, 21, 23},
       {25, 27, 29, 31}},
      {{ 2,  3,  6,  7},
       {10, 11, 14, 15},
       {18, 19, 22, 23},
       {26, 27, 30, 31}},
      {{ 4,  5,  6,  7},
       {12, 13, 14, 15},
       {20, 21, 22, 23},
       {28, 29, 30, 31}},
      {{ 8,  9, 10, 11},
       {12, 13, 14, 15},
       {24, 25, 26, 27},
       {28, 29, 30, 31}},
      {{16, 17, 18, 19},
       {20, 21, 22, 23},
       {24, 25, 26, 27},
       {28, 29, 30, 31}}};

    // Create a Scanner
    Scanner input = new Scanner(System.in);

    for (int i = 0; i < 5; i++) {
      System.out.println("Is your birthday in Set" + (i + 1) + "?");
      for (int j = 0; j < 4; j++) {
        for (int k = 0; k < 4; k++)
          System.out.printf("%4d", dates[i][j][k]);
        System.out.println();
      }
```

```
40
41         System.out.print("\nEnter 0 for No and 1 for Yes: ");
42         answer = input.nextInt();
43
44         if (answer == 1)
45           day += dates[i][0][0];
46       }
47
48       System.out.println("Your birth day is " + day);
49     }
50 }
```

add to Set i

A three-dimensional array dates is created in Lines 8–28. This array stores five sets of numbers. Each set is a 4-by-4 two-dimensional array.

The loop starting from line 33 displays the numbers in each set and prompts the user to answer whether the birthday is in the set (lines 41–42). If the day is in the set, the first number (dates[i][0][0]) in the set is added to variable day (line 45).

Chapter Summary

1. A two-dimensional array can be used to store a table.
2. A variable for two-dimensional arrays can be declared using the syntax: elementType[][] arrayVar.
3. A two-dimensional array can be created using the syntax: new elementType[ROW_SIZE][COLUMN_SIZE].
4. Each element in a two-dimensional array is represented using the syntax: arrayVar[rowIndex][columnIndex].
5. You can create and initialize a two-dimensional array using an array initializer with the syntax: elementType[][] arrayVar = {{row values}, ..., {row values}}.
6. You can use arrays of arrays to form multidimensional arrays. For example, a variable for three-dimensional arrays can be declared as elementType[][][] arrayVar and a three-dimensional array can be created using new elementType[size1][size2][size3].

Review Questions

7.1 Declare and create a 4-by-5 int matrix.

7.2 Can the rows in a two-dimensional array have different lengths?

7.3 What is the output of the following code?

```
int[][] array = new int[5][6];
int[] x = {1, 2};
array[0] = x;
System.out.println("array[0][1] is " + array[0][1]);
```

7.4 Which of the following statements are valid array declarations?

```
int[][] r = new int[2];

int[] x = new int[];

int[][] y = new int[3][];
```

7.5 Why does the `is1To9` method need to copy `list` to `temp`? What happens if you replace the code in lines 66–70 in Listing 7.4 with the following code:

```
java.util.Arrays.sort(list);
```

7.6 Declare and create a `4` × `6` × `5` `int` array.

PROGRAMMING EXERCISES

7.1* (*Summing all the numbers in a matrix*) Write a method that sums all the integers in a matrix of integers using the following header:

```
public static double sumMatrix(int[][] m)
```

Write a test program that reads a 4-by-4 matrix and displays the sum of all its elements. Here is a sample run:

```
Enter a 4-by-4 matrix row by row:
1 2 3 4 ↵Enter
5 6 7 8 ↵Enter
9 10 11 12 ↵Enter
13 14 15 16 ↵Enter
Sum of the matrix is 136
```

7.2* (*Summing the major diagonal in a matrix*) Write a method that sums all the integers in the major diagonal in an $n \times n$ matrix of integers using the following header:

```
public static int sumMajorDiagonal(int[][] m)
```

Write a test program that reads a 4-by-4 matrix and displays the sum of all its elements on the major diagonal. Here is a sample run:

```
Enter a 4-by-4 matrix row by row:
1 2 3 4 ↵Enter
5 6 7 8 ↵Enter
9 10 11 12 ↵Enter
13 14 15 16 ↵Enter
Sum of the elements in the major diagonal is 34
```

7.3* (*Sorting students on grades*) Rewrite Listing 7.2, GradeExam.java, to display the students in increasing order of the number of correct answers.

7.4** (*Computing the weekly hours for each employee*) Suppose the weekly hours for all employees are stored in a two-dimensional array. Each row records an employee's seven-day work hours with seven columns. For example, the array shown below stores the work hours for eight employees. Write a program that displays employees and their total hours in decreasing order of the total hours.

	Su	M	T	W	H	F	Sa
Employee 0	2	4	3	4	5	8	8
Employee 1	7	3	4	3	3	4	4
Employee 2	3	3	4	3	3	2	2
Employee 3	9	3	4	7	3	4	1
Employee 4	3	5	4	3	6	3	8
Employee 5	3	4	4	6	3	4	4
Employee 6	3	7	4	8	3	8	4
Employee 7	6	3	5	9	2	7	9

7.5 (*Algebra: adding two matrices*) Write a method to add two matrices. The header of the method is as follows:

```
public static double[][] addMatrix(double[][] a, double[][] b)
```

In order to be added, the two matrices must have the same dimensions and the same or compatible types of elements. Let **c** be the resulting matrix. Each element c_{ij} is $a_{ij} + b_{ij}$. For example, for two 3 × 3 matrices **a** and **b**, **c** is

$$\begin{pmatrix} a_{11}\ a_{12}\ a_{13} \\ a_{21}\ a_{22}\ a_{23} \\ a_{31}\ a_{32}\ a_{33} \end{pmatrix} + \begin{pmatrix} b_{11}\ b_{12}\ b_{13} \\ b_{21}\ b_{22}\ b_{23} \\ b_{31}\ b_{32}\ b_{33} \end{pmatrix} = \begin{pmatrix} a_{11} + b_{11} & a_{12} + b_{12} & a_{13} + b_{13} \\ a_{21} + b_{21} & a_{22} + b_{22} & a_{23} + b_{23} \\ a_{31} + b_{31} & a_{32} + b_{32} & a_{33} + b_{33} \end{pmatrix}$$

Write a test program that prompts the user to enter two 3 × 3 matrices and displays their sum. Here is a sample run:

```
Enter matrix1: 1 2 3 4 5 6 7 8 9 ↵Enter
Enter matrix2: 0 2 4 1 4.5 2.2 1.1 4.3 5.2 ↵Enter
The matrices are added as follows
 1.0 2.0 3.0      0.0 2.0 4.0       1.0 4.0 7.0
 4.0 5.0 6.0  +   1.0 4.5 2.2   =   5.0 9.5 8.2
 7.0 8.0 9.0      1.1 4.3 5.2       8.1 12.3 14.2
```

7.6** (*Algebra: multiplying two matrices*) Write a method to multiply two matrices. The header of the method is as follows:

Video Note
Multiply two matrices

```
public static double[][] multiplyMatrix(double[][] a, double[][] b)
```

To multiply matrix **a** by matrix **b**, the number of columns in **a** must be the same as the number of rows in **b**, and the two matrices must have elements of the same or compatible types. Let **c** be the result of the multiplication. Assume the column size of matrix a is **n**. Each element c_{ij} is $a_{i1} \times b_{1j} + a_{i2} \times b_{2j} + \ldots + a_{in} \times b_{nj}$. For example, for two 3 × 3 matrices **a** and **b**, **c** is

$$\begin{pmatrix} a_{11}\ a_{12}\ a_{13} \\ a_{21}\ a_{22}\ a_{23} \\ a_{31}\ a_{32}\ a_{33} \end{pmatrix} \times \begin{pmatrix} b_{11}\ b_{12}\ b_{13} \\ b_{21}\ b_{22}\ b_{23} \\ b_{31}\ b_{32}\ b_{33} \end{pmatrix} = \begin{pmatrix} c_{11}\ c_{12}\ c_{13} \\ c_{21}\ c_{22}\ c_{23} \\ c_{31}\ c_{32}\ c_{33} \end{pmatrix}$$

where $c_{ij} = a_{i1} \times b_{1j} + a_{i2} \times b_{2j} + a_{i3} \times b_{3j}$.

Write a test program that prompts the user to enter two 3 × 3 matrices and displays their product. Here is a sample run:

```
Enter matrix1: 1 2 3 4 5 6 7 8 9 ↵Enter
Enter matrix2: 0 2 4 1 4.5 2.2 1.1 4.3 5.2 ↵Enter
The matrices are multiplied as follows:
 1 2 3       0 2.0 4.0       5.3 23.9 24
 4 5 6   *   1 4.5 2.2   =   11.6 56.3 58.2
 7 8 9       1.1 4.3 5.2     17.9 88.7 92.4
```

7.7* (*Points nearest to each other*) Listing 7.3 gives a program that finds two points in a two-dimensional space nearest to each other. Revise the program so that it finds two points in a three-dimensional space nearest to each other. Use a two-dimensional array to represent the points. Test the program using the following points:

```
double[][] points = {{-1, 0, 3}, {-1, -1, -1}, {4, 1, 1},
  {2, 0.5, 9}, {3.5, 2, -1}, {3, 1.5, 3}, {-1.5, 4, 2},
  {5.5, 4, -0.5}};
```

The formula for computing the distance between two points `(x1, y1, z1)` and `(x2, y2, z2)` is $\sqrt{(x_2 - x_1)^2 + (y_2 - y_1)^2 + (z_2 - z_1)^2}$.

7.8** (*All closest pairs of points*) Revise Listing 7.3, FindNearestPoints.java, to find all closest pairs of points with same minimum distance.

7.9*** (*Game: playing a TicTacToe game*) In a game of TicTacToe, two players take turns marking an available cell in a `3` × `3` grid with their respective tokens (either X or O). When one player has placed three tokens in a horizontal, vertical, or diagonal row on the grid, the game is over and that player has won. A draw (no winner) occurs when all the cells on the grid have been filled with tokens and neither player has achieved a win. Create a program for playing TicTacToe.

The program prompts two players to enter X token and O token alternately. Whenever a token is entered, the program redisplays the board on the console and determines the status of the game (win, draw, or continue). Here is a sample run:

```
-------------
|   |   |   |
-------------
|   |   |   |
-------------
|   |   |   |
-------------
Enter a row (1, 2, or 3) for player X: 1 ↵Enter
Enter a column (1, 2, or 3) for player X: 1 ↵Enter
-------------
|   |   |   |
-------------
|   | X |   |
-------------
|   |   |   |
-------------
Enter a row (1, 2, or 3) for player O: 1 ↵Enter
Enter a column (1, 2, or 3) for player O: 2 ↵Enter
-------------
|   |   |   |
-------------
|   | X | O |
-------------
|   |   |   |
-------------
```

```
Enter a row (1, 2, or 3) for player X:
...
-------------
| X |   |   |
-------------
| O | X | O |
-------------
|   |   | X |
-------------
X player won
```

7.10* (*Game: TicTacToe board*) Write a program that randomly fills in 0s and 1s into a TicTacToe board, prints the board, and finds the rows, columns, or diagonals with all 0s or 1s. Use a two-dimensional array to represent a TicTacToe board. Here is a sample run of the program:

```
001
001
111
All 1s on row 2
All 1s on column 2
```

7.11** (*Game: nine heads and tails*) Nine coins are placed in a 3-by-3 matrix with some face up and some face down. You can represent the state of the coins using a 3-by-3 matrix with values 0 (head) and 1 (tail). Here are some examples:

```
0 0 0    1 0 1    1 1 0    1 0 1    1 0 0
0 1 0    0 0 1    1 0 0    1 1 0    1 1 1
0 0 0    1 0 0    0 0 1    1 0 0    1 1 0
```

Each state can also be represented using a binary number. For example, the preceding matrices correspond to the numbers

```
000010000 101001100 110100001 101110100 100111110
```

There are a total of 512 possibilities. So, you can use decimal numbers 0, 1, 2, 3, . . . , and 511 to represent all states of the matrix. Write a program that prompts the user to enter a number between 0 and 511 and displays the corresponding matrix with characters H and T. Here is a sample run:

```
Enter a number between 0 and 511: 7 ↵Enter
H H H
H H H
T T T
```

The user entered 7, which corresponds to 000000111. Since 0 stands for H and 1 for T, the output is correct.

7.12** (*Financial application: computing tax*) Rewrite Listing 3.6, ComputeTax.java, using arrays. For each filing status, there are six tax rates. Each rate is applied to a certain amount of taxable income. For example, from the taxable income of \$400,000 for a single filer, \$8,350 is taxed at 10%, (33,950 – 8,350) at 15%, (82,250 – 33,950) at 25%, (171,550 – 82,550) at 28%, (372,550 – 82,250) at 33%, and (400,000 – 372,950) at 36%. The six rates are the same for all filing statuses, which can be represented in the following array:

```
double[] rates = {0.10, 0.15, 0.25, 0.28, 0.33, 0.35};
```

The brackets for each rate for all the filing statuses can be represented in a two-dimensional array as follows:

```
int[][] brackets = {
  {8350, 33950, 82250, 171550, 372950},    // Single filer
  {16700, 67900, 137050, 20885, 372950}, // Married jointly
  {8350, 33950, 68525, 104425, 186475}, // Married separately
  {11950, 45500, 117450, 190200, 372950} // Head of household
};
```

Suppose the taxable income is $400,000 for single filers. The tax can be computed as follows:

```
tax = brackets[0][0] * rates[0] +
  (brackets[0][1] - brackets[0][0]) * rates[1] +
  (brackets[0][2] - brackets[0][1]) * rates[2] +
  (brackets[0][3] - brackets[0][2]) * rates[3] +
  (brackets[0][4] - brackets[0][3]) * rates[4] +
  (400000 - brackets[0][4]) * rates[5]
```

7.13* (*Locating the largest element*) Write the following method that returns the location of the largest element in a two-dimensional array.

```
public static int[] locateLargest(double[][] a)
```

The return value is a one-dimensional array that contains two elements. These two elements indicate the row and column indices of the largest element in the two-dimensional array. Write a test program that prompts the user to enter a two-dimensional array and displays the location of the largest element in the array. Here is a sample run:

```
Enter the number of rows and columns of the array: 3 4 Enter
Enter the array:
23.5 35 2 10 Enter
4.5 3 45 3.5 Enter
35 44 5.5 9.6 Enter
The location of the largest element is at (1, 2)
```

7.14** (*Exploring matrix*) Write a program that prompts the user to enter the length of a square matrix, randomly fills in 0s and 1s into the matrix, prints the matrix, and finds the rows, columns, and diagonals with all 0s or 1s. Here is a sample run of the program:

```
Enter the size for the matrix: 4 Enter
0111
0000
0100
1111
All 0s on row 1
All 1s on row 3
No same numbers on a column
No same numbers on the major diagonal
No same numbers on the sub-diagonal
```

7.15* (*Geometry: same line?*) Suppose a set of points are given. Write a program to check whether all the points are on the same line. Use the following sets to test your program:

```
double[][] set1 = {{1, 1}, {2, 2}, {3, 3}, {4, 4}};
double[][] set2 = {{0, 1}, {1, 2}, {4, 5}, {5, 6}};
double[][] set3 = {{0, 1}, {1, 2}, {4, 5}, {4.5, 4}};
```

7.16* (*Sorting two-dimensional array*) Write a method to sort a two-dimensional array using following header:

```
public static void sort(int m[][])
```

The method performs a primary sort on rows and a secondary sort on columns. For example, the array `{{4, 2}, {1, 7}, {4, 5}, {1, 2}, {1, 1}, {4, 1}}` will be sorted to `{{1, 1}, {1, 2}, {1, 7}, {4, 1}, {4, 2}, {4, 5}}`.

7.17*** (*Financial tsunami*) Banks lend money to each other. In tough economic times, if a bank goes bankrupt, it may not be able to pay back the loan. A bank's total assets are its current balance plus its loans to other banks. Figure 7.8 is a diagram that shows five banks. The banks' current balances are `25`, `125`, `175`, `75`, and `181` million dollars, respectively. The directed edge from node 1 to node 2 indicates that bank 1 lends `40` million dollars to bank 2.

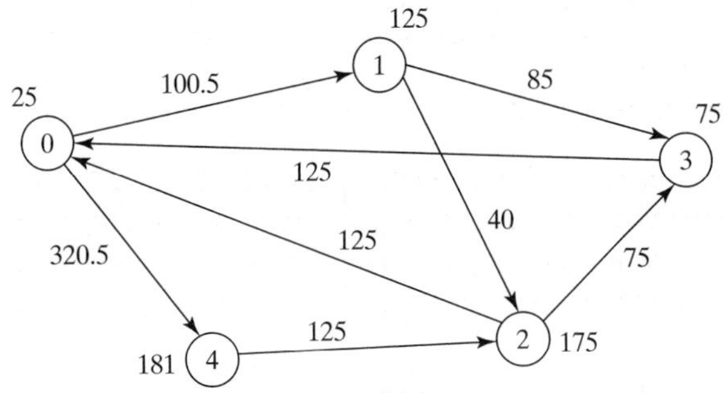
125
1
100.5
85
25
75
0
3
125
40
125
320.5
75
125
2
175
181
4

FIGURE 7.8 Banks lend money to each other.

If a bank's total assets are under a certain limit, the bank is unsafe. The money it borrowed cannot be returned to the lender, and the lender cannot count the loan in its total assets. Consequently, the lender may also be unsafe, if its total assets are under the limit. Write a program to find all unsafe banks. Your program reads the input as follows. It first reads two integers `n` and `limit`, where `n` indicates the number of banks and `limit` is the minimum total assets for keeping a bank safe. It then reads `n` lines that describe the information for `n` banks with id from `0` to `n-1`. The first number in the line is the bank's balance, the second number indicates the number of banks that borrowed money from the bank, and the rest are pairs of two numbers. Each pair describes a borrower. The first number in the pair is the borrower's id and the second is the amount borrowed. For example, the input for the five banks in Figure 7.8 is as follows (note that the limit is `201`):

```
5 201
25 2 1 100.5 4 320.5
125 2 2 40 3 85
175 2 0 125 3 75
75 1 0 125
181 1 2 125
```

The total assets of bank 3 are (`75 + 125`), which is under `201`. So bank 3 is unsafe. After bank 3 becomes unsafe, the total assets of bank 1 fall below (`125 + 40`). So, bank 1 is also unsafe. The output of the program should be

Unsafe banks are 3 1

(*Hint*: Use a two-dimensional array `borrowers` to represent loans. `borrowers[i][j]` indicates the loan that bank i loans to bank j. Once bank j becomes unsafe, `borrowers[i][j]` should be set to `0`.)

7.18* (*Shuffling rows*) Write a method that shuffles the rows in a two-dimensional `int` array using the following header:

```
public static void shuffle(int[][] m)
```

Write a test program that shuffles the following matrix:

```
int[][] m = {{1, 2}, {3, 4}, {5, 6}, {7, 8}, {9, 10}};
```

7.19** (*Pattern recognition: consecutive four equal numbers*) Write the following method that tests whether a two-dimensional array has four consecutive numbers of the same value, either horizontally, vertically, or diagonally.

```
public static boolean isConsecutiveFour(int[][] values)
```

Write a test program that prompts the user to enter the number of rows and columns of a two-dimensional array and then the values in the array and displays true if the array contains four consecutive numbers with the same value. Otherwise, display false. Here are some examples of the true cases:

0	1	0	3	1	6	1
0	1	6	8	6	0	1
5	6	2	1	8	2	9
6	5	6	1	1	9	1
1	3	6	1	4	0	7
3	3	3	3	4	0	7

0	1	0	3	1	6	1
0	1	6	8	6	0	1
5	5	2	1	8	2	9
6	5	6	1	1	9	1
1	5	6	1	4	0	7
3	5	3	3	4	0	7

0	1	0	3	1	6	1
0	1	6	8	6	0	1
5	6	2	1	6	2	9
6	5	6	6	1	9	1
1	3	6	1	4	0	7
3	6	3	3	4	0	7

0	1	0	3	1	6	1
0	1	6	8	6	0	1
9	6	2	1	8	2	9
6	9	6	1	1	9	1
1	3	9	1	4	0	7
3	3	3	9	4	0	7

7.20*** (*Game: connect four*) Connect four is a two-player board game in which the players alternately drop colored disks into a seven-column, six-row vertically-suspended grid, as shown below.

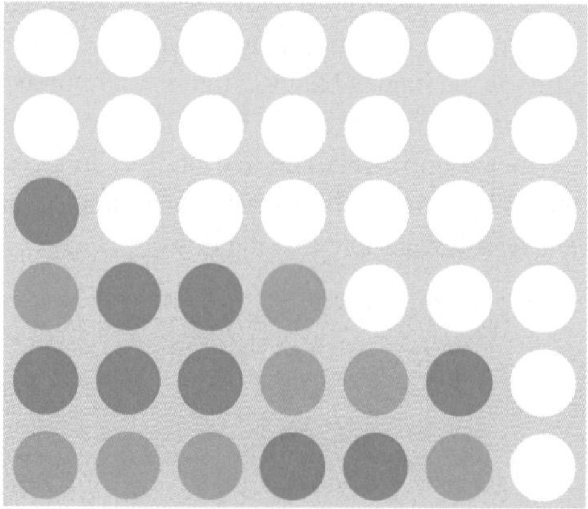

The objective of the game is to connect four same-colored disks in a row, a column, or a diagonal before your opponent can do likewise. The program prompts two players to drop a RED or YELLOW disk alternately. Whenever a disk is dropped, the program redisplays the board on the console and determines the status of the game (win, draw, or continue). Here is a sample run:

```
| | | | | | | |
| | | | | | | |
| | | | | | | |
| | | | | | | |
| | | | | | | |
| | | | | | | |
———————————————
Drop a red disk at column (0–6): 0 ↵Enter
| | | | | | | |
| | | | | | | |
| | | | | | | |
| | | | | | | |
| | | | | | | |
|R| | | | | | |
———————————————
Drop a yellow disk at column (0–6): 3 ↵Enter
| | | | | | | |
| | | | | | | |
| | | | | | | |
| | | | | | | |
| | | | | | | |
|R| | |Y| | | |
...
...
...
Drop a yellow disk at column (0–6): 6 ↵Enter
| | | | | | | |
| | | | | | | |
| | | |R| | | |
| | | |Y|R|Y| |
| | |R|Y|Y|Y|Y|
|R|Y|R|Y|R|R|R|
———————————————
The yellow player won
```

7.21*** (*Game: multiple Sudoku solutions*) The complete solution for the Sudoku problem is given in Supplement VII.A. A Sudoku problem may have multiple solutions. Modify Sudoku.java in Supplement VII.A to display the total number of the solutions. Display two solutions if multiple solutions exist.

7.22* (*Algebra:* 2 × 2 *matrix inverse*) The inverse of a square matrix **A** is denoted A^{-1}, such that $A \times A^{-1} = I$, where **I** is the identity matrix with all **1**'s on the diagonal and **0** on all other cells. For example, the inverse of matrix $\begin{bmatrix} 1 & 2 \\ 3 & 4 \end{bmatrix}$ is $\begin{bmatrix} -0.5 & 1 \\ 1.5 & 0 \end{bmatrix}$, i.e.,

$$\begin{bmatrix} 1 & 2 \\ 3 & 4 \end{bmatrix} \times \begin{bmatrix} -0.5 & 1 \\ 1.5 & 0 \end{bmatrix} = \begin{bmatrix} 1 & 0 \\ 0 & 1 \end{bmatrix}$$

The inverse of a 2×2 matrix A can be obtained using the following formula:

$$A = \begin{bmatrix} a & b \\ c & d \end{bmatrix} \qquad A^{-1} = \frac{1}{ad - bc}\begin{bmatrix} d & -b \\ -c & a \end{bmatrix}$$

Implement the following method to obtain an inverse of the matrix:

```
public static double[][] inverse(double[][] A)
```

The method returns `null` if `ad – bc` is `0`.

Write a test program that prompts the user to enter `a`, `b`, `c`, `d` for a matrix and displays its inverse matrix. Here is a sample run:

```
Enter a, b, c, d: 1 2 3 4 [Enter]
-2.0 1.0
1.5 -0.5
```

```
Enter a, b, c, d: 0.5 2 1.5 4.5 [Enter]
-6.0 2.6666666666666665
2.0 -0.6666666666666666
```

7.23* (*Algebra: 3 × 3 matrix inverse*) The inverse of a square matrix `A` is denoted `A`$^{-1}$, such that `A×A`$^{-1}$ = `I`, where `I` is the identity matrix with all `1`'s on the diagonal and `0` on all other cells. The inverse of matrix $\begin{bmatrix} 1 & 2 & 1 \\ 2 & 3 & 1 \\ 4 & 5 & 3 \end{bmatrix}$, for example, is

$$\begin{bmatrix} -2 & 0.5 & 0.5 \\ 1 & 0.5 & -0.5 \\ 1 & -1.5 & 0.5 \end{bmatrix}$$

—that is,

$$\begin{bmatrix} 1 & 2 & 1 \\ 2 & 3 & 1 \\ 4 & 5 & 3 \end{bmatrix} \times \begin{bmatrix} -2 & 0.5 & 0.5 \\ 1 & 0.5 & -0.5 \\ 1 & -1.5 & 0.5 \end{bmatrix} = \begin{bmatrix} 1 & 0 & 0 \\ 0 & 1 & 0 \\ 0 & 0 & 1 \end{bmatrix}$$

The inverse of a 3×3 matrix

$$A = \begin{bmatrix} a_{11} & a_{12} & a_{13} \\ a_{21} & a_{22} & a_{23} \\ a_{31} & a_{32} & a_{33} \end{bmatrix}$$

can be obtained using the following formula if $|A| \neq 0$:

$$A^{-1} = \frac{1}{|A|}\begin{bmatrix} a_{22}a_{33} - a_{23}a_{32} & a_{13}a_{32} - a_{12}a_{33} & a_{12}a_{23} - a_{13}a_{22} \\ a_{23}a_{31} - a_{21}a_{33} & a_{11}a_{33} - a_{13}a_{31} & a_{13}a_{21} - a_{11}a_{23} \\ a_{21}a_{32} - a_{22}a_{31} & a_{12}a_{31} - a_{11}a_{32} & a_{11}a_{22} - a_{12}a_{21} \end{bmatrix}$$

$$|A| = \begin{vmatrix} a_{11} & a_{12} & a_{13} \\ a_{21} & a_{22} & a_{23} \\ a_{31} & a_{32} & a_{33} \end{vmatrix} = a_{11}a_{22}a_{33} + a_{31}a_{12}a_{23} + a_{13}a_{21}a_{32}$$

$$- a_{13}a_{22}a_{31} - a_{11}a_{23}a_{32} - a_{33}a_{21}a_{12}.$$

Implement the following function to obtain an inverse of the matrix:

```
public static double[][] inverse(double[][] A)
```

The method returns `null` if `|A|` is `0`.

Write a test program that prompts the user to enter $a_{11}, a_{12}, a_{13}, a_{21}, a_{22}, a_{23}, a_{31}, a_{32}, a_{33}$ for a matrix and displays its inverse matrix. Here is a sample run:

```
Enter a11, a12, a13, a21, a22, a23, a31, a32, a33:
 1 2 1 2 3 1 4 5 3 [Enter]
-2 0.5 0.5
1 0.5 -0.5
1 -1.5 0.5
```

```
Enter a11, a12, a13, a21, a22, a23, a31, a32, a33:
 1 4 2 2 5 8 2 1 8 [Enter]
2.0 -1.875 1.375
0.0 0.25 -0.25
-0.5 0.4375 -0.1875
```

CHAPTER 8

OBJECTS AND CLASSES

Objectives

- To describe objects and classes, and use classes to model objects (§8.2).
- To use UML graphical notations to describe classes and objects (§8.2).
- To demonstrate defining classes and creating objects (§8.3).
- To create objects using constructors (§8.4).
- To access objects via object reference variables (§8.5).
- To define a reference variable using a reference type (§8.5.1).
- To access an object's data and methods using the object member access operator (`.`) (§8.5.2).
- To define data fields of reference types and assign default values for an object's data fields (§8.5.3).
- To distinguish between object reference variables and primitive data type variables (§8.5.4).
- To use classes `Date`, `Random`, and `JFrame` in the Java library (§8.6).
- To distinguish between instance and static variables and methods (§8.7).
- To define private data fields with appropriate `get` and `set` methods (§8.8).
- To encapsulate data fields to make classes easy to maintain (§8.9).
- To develop methods with object arguments and differentiate between primitive-type arguments and object-type arguments (§8.10).
- To store and process objects in arrays (§8.11).

8.1 Introduction

why OOP?

Having learned the material in earlier chapters, you are able to solve many programming problems using selections, loops, methods, and arrays. However, these Java features are not sufficient for developing graphical user interfaces and large-scale software systems. Suppose you want to develop a GUI (graphical user interface, pronounced *goo-ee*) as shown in Figure 8.1. How do you program it?

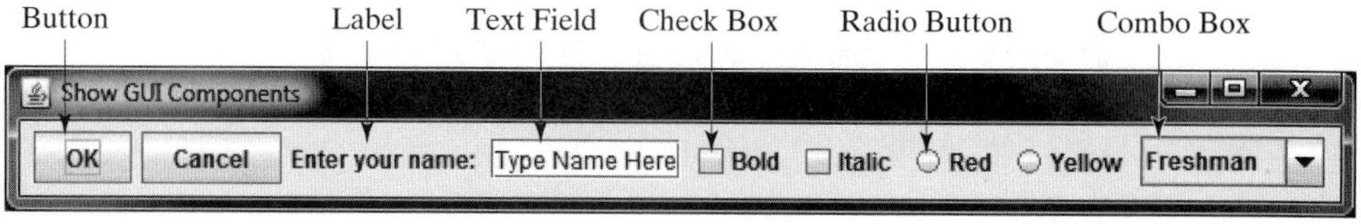
Button
Label
Text Field
Check Box
Radio Button
Combo Box
Show GUI Components
OK
Cancel
Enter your name:
Type Name Here
Bold
Italic
Red
Yellow
Freshman

FIGURE 8.1 The GUI objects are created from classes.

This chapter begins the introduction of object-oriented programming, which will enable you to develop GUI and large-scale software systems effectively.

8.2 Defining Classes for Objects

object

Object-oriented programming (OOP) involves programming using objects. An *object* represents an entity in the real world that can be distinctly identified. For example, a student, a desk, a circle, a button, and even a loan can all be viewed as objects. An object has a unique identity, state, and behavior.

state

- The *state* of an object (also known as its *properties* or *attributes*) is represented by *data fields* with their current values. A circle object, for example, has a data field `radius`, which is the property that characterizes a circle. A rectangle object has data fields `width` and `height`, which are the properties that characterize a rectangle.

behavior

- The *behavior* of an object (also known as its *actions*) is defined by methods. To invoke a method on an object is to ask the object to perform an action. For example, you may define a method named `getArea()` for circle objects. A circle object may invoke `getArea()` to return its area.

contract
instantiation
object
instance

Objects of the same type are defined using a common class. A class is a template, blueprint, or *contract* that defines what an object's data fields and methods will be. An object is an instance of a class. You can create many instances of a class. Creating an instance is referred to as *instantiation*. The terms *object* and *instance* are often interchangeable. The relationship between classes and objects is analogous to that between an apple-pie recipe and apple pies. You can make as many apple pies as you want from a single recipe. Figure 8.2 shows a class named `Circle` and its three objects.

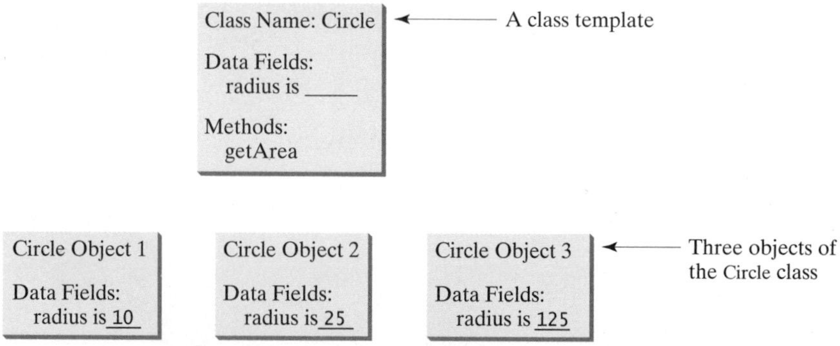
Class Name: Circle
A class template
Data Fields:
radius is _____
Methods:
getArea
Circle Object 1
Data Fields:
radius is 10
Circle Object 2
Data Fields:
radius is 25
Circle Object 3
Data Fields:
radius is 125
Three objects of the Circle class

FIGURE 8.2 A class is a template for creating objects.

A Java class uses variables to define data fields and methods to define actions. Additionally, a class provides methods of a special type, known as *constructors*, which are invoked to create a new object. A constructor can perform any action, but constructors are designed to perform initializing actions, such as initializing the data fields of objects. Figure 8.3 shows an example of defining the class for circle objects.

class
data field
method
constructor

```
class Circle {
  /** The radius of this circle */
  double radius = 1.0;                          ← Data field

  /** Construct a circle object */
  Circle() {
  }
                                                ← Constructors
  /** Construct a circle object */
  Circle(double newRadius) {
    radius = newRadius;
  }

  /** Return the area of this circle */
  double getArea() {                            ← Method
    return radius * radius * Math.PI;
  }
}
```

FIGURE 8.3 A class is a construct that defines objects of the same type.

The `Circle` class is different from all of the other classes you have seen thus far. It does not have a `main` method and therefore cannot be run; it is merely a definition for circle objects. The class that contains the `main` method will be referred to in this book, for convenience, as the *main class*.

main class

The illustration of class templates and objects in Figure 8.2 can be standardized using UML (Unified Modeling Language) notations. This notation, as shown in Figure 8.4, is called a *UML class diagram*, or simply a *class diagram*. In the class diagram, the data field is denoted as

class diagram

```
dataFieldName: dataFieldType
```

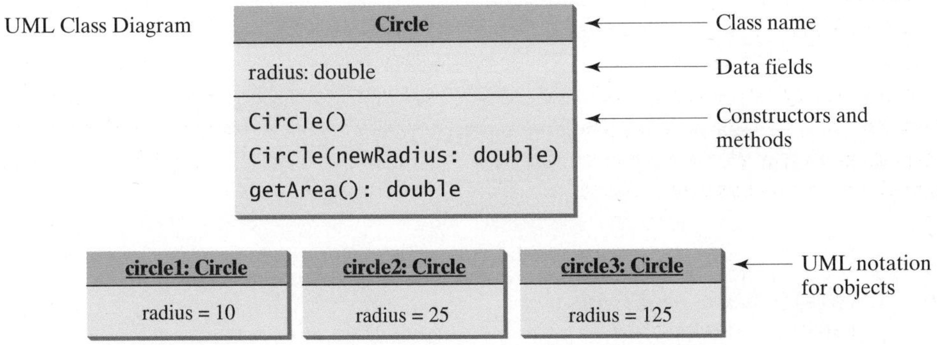
UML Class Diagram
Circle
radius: double
Circle()
Circle(newRadius: double)
getArea(): double
Class name
Data fields
Constructors and methods
circle1: Circle
radius = 10
circle2: Circle
radius = 25
circle3: Circle
radius = 125
UML notation for objects

FIGURE 8.4 Classes and objects can be represented using UML notations.

The constructor is denoted as

```
ClassName(parameterName: parameterType)
```

The method is denoted as

```
methodName(parameterName: parameterType): returnType
```

8.3 Example: Defining Classes and Creating Objects

This section gives two examples of defining classes and uses the classes to create objects. Listing 8.1 is a program that defines the `Circle` class and uses it to create objects. To avoid a naming conflict with several improved versions of the `Circle` class introduced later in this book, the `Circle` class in this example is named `Circle1`.

The program constructs three circle objects with radius `1.0`, `25`, and `125` and displays the radius and area of each of the three circles. Change the radius of the second object to `100` and display its new radius and area.

LISTING 8.1 `TestCircle1.java`

main class
main method
create object
create object
create object
class **Circle1**
data field
no-arg constructor
second constructor
method

```java
public class TestCircle1 {
  /** Main method */
  public static void main(String[] args) {
    // Create a circle with radius 1.0
    Circle1 circle1 = new Circle1();
    System.out.println("The area of the circle of radius "
      + circle1.radius + " is " + circle1.getArea() );

    // Create a circle with radius 25
    Circle1 circle2 = new Circle1(25);
    System.out.println("The area of the circle of radius "
      + circle2.radius + " is " + circle2.getArea());

    // Create a circle with radius 125
    Circle1 circle3 = new Circle1(125);
    System.out.println("The area of the circle of radius "
      + circle3.radius + " is " + circle3.getArea());

    // Modify circle radius
    circle2.radius = 100;
    System.out.println("The area of the circle of radius "
      + circle2.radius + " is " + circle2.getArea() );
  }
}

// Define the circle class with two constructors
class Circle1 {
  double radius ;

  /** Construct a circle with radius 1 */
  Circle1() {
    radius = 1.0;
  }

  /** Construct a circle with a specified radius */
  Circle1(double newRadius) {
    radius = newRadius;
  }

  /** Return the area of this circle */
  double getArea() {
    return radius * radius * Math.PI;
  }
}
```

```
The area of the circle of radius 1.0 is 3.141592653589793
The area of the circle of radius 25.0 is 1963.4954084936207
The area of the circle of radius 125.0 is 49087.385212340516
The area of the circle of radius 100.0 is 31415.926535897932
```

The program contains two classes. The first of these, `TestCircle1`, is the main class. Its sole purpose is to test the second class, `Circle1`. Such a program that uses the class is often referred to as a *client* of the class. When you run the program, the Java runtime system invokes the `main` method in the main class.

client

You can put the two classes into one file, but only one class in the file can be a public class. Furthermore, the public class must have the same name as the file name. Therefore, the file name is TestCircle1.java, since `TestCircle1` is public.

public class

The main class contains the `main` method (line 3) that creates three objects. As in creating an array, the `new` operator is used to create an object from the constructor. `new Circle1()` creates an object with radius `1.0` (line 5), `new Circle1(25)` creates an object with radius `25` (line 10), and `new Circle1(125)` creates an object with radius `125` (line 15).

These three objects (referenced by `circle1`, `circle2`, and `circle3`) have different data but the same methods. Therefore, you can compute their respective areas by using the `getArea()` method. The data fields can be accessed via the reference of the object using `circle1.radius`, `circle2.radius`, and `circle3.radius`, respectively. The object can invoke its method via the reference of the object using `circle1.getArea()`, `circle2.getArea()`, and `circle3.getArea()`, respectively.

These three objects are independent. The radius of `circle2` is changed to `100` in line 20. The object's new radius and area is displayed in lines 21–22.

There are many ways to write Java programs. For instance, you can combine the two classes in the example into one, as shown in Listing 8.2.

LISTING 8.2 Circle1.java

main method

```
1 public class Circle1 {
2   /** Main method */
3   public static void main(String[] args) {
4     // Create a circle with radius 1.0
5     Circle1 circle1 = new Circle1();
6     System.out.println("The area of the circle of radius "
7       + circle1.radius + " is " + circle1.getArea() );
8
9     // Create a circle with radius 25
10    Circle1 circle2 = new Circle1(25);
11    System.out.println("The area of the circle of radius "
12      + circle2.radius + " is " + circle2.getArea());
13
14    // Create a circle with radius 125
15    Circle1 circle3 = new Circle1(125);
16    System.out.println("The area of the circle of radius "
17      + circle3.radius + " is " + circle3.getArea());
18
19    // Modify circle radius
20    circle2.radius = 100;
21    System.out.println("The area of the circle of radius "
22      + circle2.radius + " is " + circle2.getArea());
23  }
24
```

data field
no-arg constructor
second constructor
method

```
  double radius;

  /** Construct a circle with radius 1 */
  Circle1() {
    radius = 1.0;
  }

  /** Construct a circle with a specified radius */
  Circle1(double newRadius) {
    radius = newRadius;
  }

  /** Return the area of this circle */
  double getArea() {
    return radius * radius * Math.PI;
  }
}
```

Since the combined class has a `main` method, it can be executed by the Java interpreter. The `main` method is the same as in Listing 1.1. This demonstrates that you can test a class by simply adding a `main` method in the same class.

As another example, consider TV sets. Each TV is an object with states (current channel, current volume level, power on or off) and behaviors (change channels, adjust volume, turn on/off). You can use a class to model TV sets. The UML diagram for the class is shown in Figure 8.5.

Listing 8.3 gives a program that defines the `TV` class.

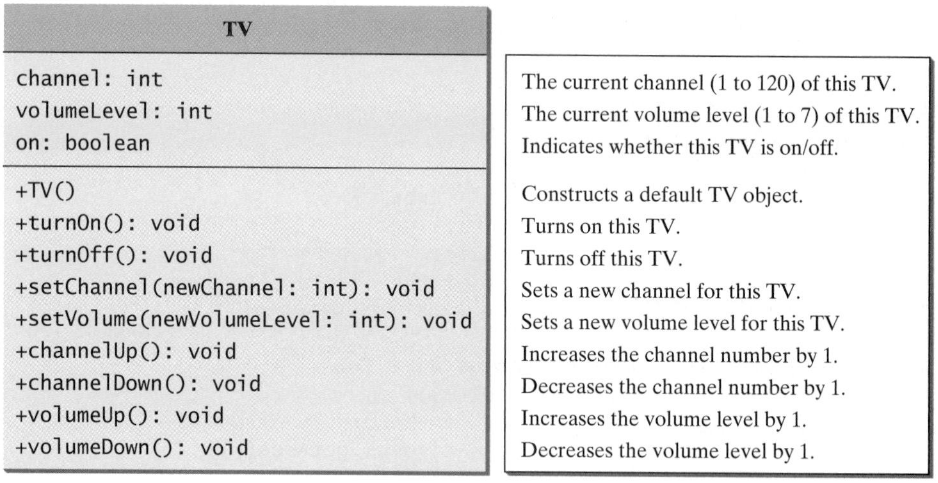
TV
channel: int
volumeLevel: int
on: boolean
+TV()
+turnOn(): void
+turnOff(): void
+setChannel(newChannel: int): void
+setVolume(newVolumeLevel: int): void
+channelUp(): void
+channelDown(): void
+volumeUp(): void
+volumeDown(): void
The current channel (1 to 120) of this TV.
The current volume level (1 to 7) of this TV.
Indicates whether this TV is on/off.
Constructs a default TV object.
Turns on this TV.
Turns off this TV.
Sets a new channel for this TV.
Sets a new volume level for this TV.
Increases the channel number by 1.
Decreases the channel number by 1.
Increases the volume level by 1.
Decreases the volume level by 1.

FIGURE 8.5 The TV class models TV sets.

LISTING 8.3 TV.java

data fields
constructor

```
public class TV {
  int channel = 1; // Default channel is 1
  int volumeLevel = 1; // Default volume level is 1
  boolean on = false; // By default TV is off

  public TV() {
  }

```

```java
  public void turnOn() {
    on = true;
  }

  public void turnOff() {
    on = false;
  }

  public void setChannel(int newChannel) {
    if (on && newChannel >= 1 && newChannel <= 120)
      channel = newChannel;
  }

  public void setVolume(int newVolumeLevel) {
    if (on && newVolumeLevel >= 1 && newVolumeLevel <= 7)
      volumeLevel = newVolumeLevel;
  }

  public void channelUp() {
    if (on && channel < 120)
      channel++;
  }

  public void channelDown() {
    if (on && channel > 1)
      channel--;
  }

  public void volumeUp() {
    if (on && volumeLevel < 7)
      volumeLevel++;
  }

  public void volumeDown() {
    if (on && volumeLevel > 1)
      volumeLevel--;
  }
}
```

turn on TV
turn off TV
set a new channel
set a new volume
increase channel
decrease channel
increase volume
decrease volume

Note that the channel and volume level are not changed if the TV is not on. Before either of these is changed, its current value is checked to ensure that it is within the correct range.

Listing 8.4 gives a program that uses the TV class to create two objects.

Listing 8.4 TestTV.java

```java
public class TestTV {
  public static void main(String[] args) {
    TV tv1 = new TV();
    tv1.turnOn();
    tv1.setChannel(30);
    tv1.setVolume(3);

    TV tv2 = new TV();
    tv2.turnOn();
    tv2.channelUp();
    tv2.channelUp();
    tv2.volumeUp();

    System.out.println("tv1's channel is " + tv1.channel
      + " and volume level is " + tv1.volumeLevel );
```

main method
create a TV
turn on
set a new channel
set a new volume
create a TV
turn on
increase channel
increase volume
display state

```
16     System.out.println("tv2's channel is " + tv2.channel
17       + " and volume level is " + tv2.volumeLevel);
18   }
19 }
```

```
tv1's channel is 30 and volume level is 3
tv2's channel is 3 and volume level is 2
```

The program creates two objects in lines 3 and 8 and invokes the methods on the objects to perform actions for setting channels and volume levels and for increasing channels and volumes. The program displays the state of the objects in lines 14–17. The methods are invoked using a syntax such as `tv1.turnOn()` (line 4). The data fields are accessed using a syntax such as `tv1.channel` (line 14).

These examples have given you a glimpse of classes and objects. You may have many questions regarding constructors, objects, reference variables, and accessing data fields, and invoking object's methods. The sections that follow discuss these issues in detail.

8.4 Constructing Objects Using Constructors

Constructors are a special kind of method. They have three peculiarities:

constructor's name

- A constructor must have the same name as the class itself.

no return type

- Constructors do not have a return type—not even `void`.

new operator

- Constructors are invoked using the `new` operator when an object is created. Constructors play the role of initializing objects.

overloaded constructors

The constructor has exactly the same name as the defining class. Like regular methods, constructors can be overloaded (i.e., multiple constructors can have the same name but different signatures), making it easy to construct objects with different initial data values.

no **void**

It is a common mistake to put the `void` keyword in front of a constructor. For example,

```
public void Circle() {
}
```

In this case, `Circle()` is a method, not a constructor.

constructing objects

Constructors are used to construct objects. To construct an object from a class, invoke a constructor of the class using the `new` operator, as follows:

```
new ClassName(arguments);
```

For example, `new Circle()` creates an object of the `Circle` class using the first constructor defined in the `Circle` class, and `new Circle(25)` creates an object using the second constructor defined in the `Circle` class.

no-arg constructor

A class normally provides a constructor without arguments (e.g., `Circle()`). Such a constructor is referred to as a *no-arg* or *no-argument constructor*.

default constructor

A class may be defined without constructors. In this case, a no-arg constructor with an empty body is implicitly defined in the class. This constructor, called *a default constructor,* is provided automatically *only if no constructors are explicitly defined in the class.*

8.5 Accessing Objects via Reference Variables

Newly created objects are allocated in the memory. They can be accessed via reference variables.

8.5.1 Reference Variables and Reference Types

reference variable

Objects are accessed via object *reference variables*, which contain references to the objects. Such variables are declared using the following syntax:

```
ClassName objectRefVar;
```

reference type

A class is essentially a programmer-defined type. A class is a *reference type*, which means that a variable of the class type can reference an instance of the class. The following statement declares the variable `myCircle` to be of the `Circle` type:

```
Circle myCircle;
```

The variable `myCircle` can reference a `Circle` object. The next statement creates an object and assigns its reference to `myCircle`:

```
myCircle = new Circle();
```

Using the syntax shown below, you can write a single statement that combines the declaration of an object reference variable, the creation of an object, and the assigning of an object reference to the variable.

```
ClassName objectRefVar = new ClassName();
```

Here is an example:

```
Circle myCircle = new Circle();
```

The variable `myCircle` holds a reference to a `Circle` object.

object vs. object reference variable

Note

An object reference variable that appears to hold an object actually contains a reference to that object. Strictly speaking, an object reference variable and an object are different, but most of the time the distinction can be ignored. So it is fine, for simplicity, to say that `myCircle` is a `Circle` object rather than use the longer-winded description that `myCircle` is a variable that contains a reference to a `Circle` object.

array object

Note

Arrays are treated as objects in Java. Arrays are created using the `new` operator. An array variable is actually a variable that contains a reference to an array.

8.5.2 Accessing an Object's Data and Methods

dot operator

After an object is created, its data can be accessed and its methods invoked using the dot operator (`.`), also known as the *object member access operator*:

- `objectRefVar.dataField` references a data field in the object.
- `objectRefVar.method(arguments)` invokes a method on the object.

For example, `myCircle.radius` references the radius in `myCircle`, and `myCircle.getArea()` invokes the `getArea` method on `myCircle`. Methods are invoked as operations on objects.

instance variable

instance method

calling object

The data field `radius` is referred to as an *instance variable*, because it is dependent on a specific instance. For the same reason, the method `getArea` is referred to as an *instance method*, because you can invoke it only on a specific instance. The object on which an instance method is invoked is called a *calling object*.

Caution

invoking methods

Recall that you use **Math.methodName(arguments)** (e.g., **Math.pow(3, 2.5)**) to invoke a method in the **Math** class. Can you invoke **getArea()** using **Circle.getArea()**? The answer is no. All the methods in the **Math** class are static methods, which are defined using the **static** keyword. However, **getArea()** is an instance method, and thus nonstatic. It must be invoked from an object using **objectRefVar.methodName(arguments)** (e.g., **myCircle.getArea()**). Further explanation is given in §8.7, "Static Variables, Constants, and Methods."

Note

Usually you create an object and assign it to a variable. Later you can use the variable to reference the object. Occasionally an object does not need to be referenced later. In this case, you can create an object without explicitly assigning it to a variable, as shown below:

```
new Circle();
```

or

```
System.out.println("Area is " + new Circle(5).getArea());
```

anonymous object

The former statement creates a **Circle** object. The latter creates a **Circle** object and invokes its **getArea** method to return its area. An object created in this way is known as an *anonymous object*.

8.5.3 Reference Data Fields and the null Value

reference data fields

The data fields can be of reference types. For example, the following **Student** class contains a data field **name** of the **String** type. **String** is a predefined Java class.

```
class Student {
  String name; // name has default value null
  int age; // age has default value 0
  boolean isScienceMajor; // isScienceMajor has default value false
  char gender; // c has default value '\u0000'
}
```

null value

If a data field of a reference type does not reference any object, the data field holds a special Java value, **null**. **null** is a literal just like **true** and **false**. While **true** and **false** are Boolean literals, **null** is a literal for a reference type.

default field values

The default value of a data field is **null** for a reference type, **0** for a numeric type, **false** for a **boolean** type, and **'\u0000'** for a **char** type. However, Java assigns no default value to a local variable inside a method. The following code displays the default values of data fields **name**, **age**, **isScienceMajor**, and **gender** for a **Student** object:

```
class Test {
  public static void main(String[] args) {
    Student student = new Student();
    System.out.println("name? " + student.name);
    System.out.println("age? " + student.age);
    System.out.println("isScienceMajor? " + student.isScienceMajor);
    System.out.println("gender? " + student.gender);
  }
}
```

The code below has a compile error, because local variables **x** and **y** are not initialized:

```
class Test {
  public static void main(String[] args) {
```

```
    int x; // x has no default value
    String y; // y has no default value
    System.out.println("x is " + x);
    System.out.println("y is " + y);
  }
}
```

Caution

NullPointerException

NullPointerException is a common runtime error. It occurs when you invoke a method on a reference variable with null value. Make sure you assign an object reference to the variable before invoking the method through the reference variable.

8.5.4 Differences Between Variables of Primitive Types and Reference Types

Every variable represents a memory location that holds a value. When you declare a variable, you are telling the compiler what type of value the variable can hold. For a variable of a primitive type, the value is of the primitive type. For a variable of a reference type, the value is a reference to where an object is located. For example, as shown in Figure 8.6, the value of int variable i is int value 1, and the value of Circle object c holds a reference to where the contents of the Circle object are stored in the memory.

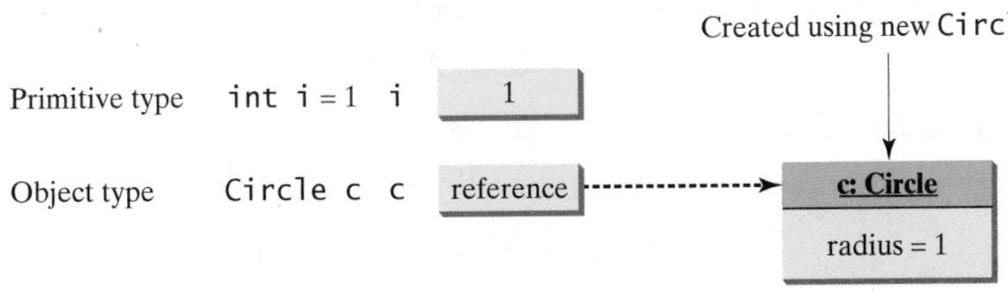
Created using new Circle()
Primitive type
int i = 1
i
1
Object type
Circle c
c
reference
c: Circle
radius = 1

FIGURE 8.6 A variable of a primitive type holds a value of the primitive type, and a variable of a reference type holds a reference to where an object is stored in memory.

When you assign one variable to another, the other variable is set to the same value. For a variable of a primitive type, the real value of one variable is assigned to the other variable. For a variable of a reference type, the reference of one variable is assigned to the other variable. As shown in Figure 8.7, the assignment statement i = j copies the contents of j into i for primitive variables. As shown in Figure 8.8, the assignment statement c1 = c2 copies the reference of c2 into c1 for reference variables. After the assignment, variables c1 and c2 refer to the same object.

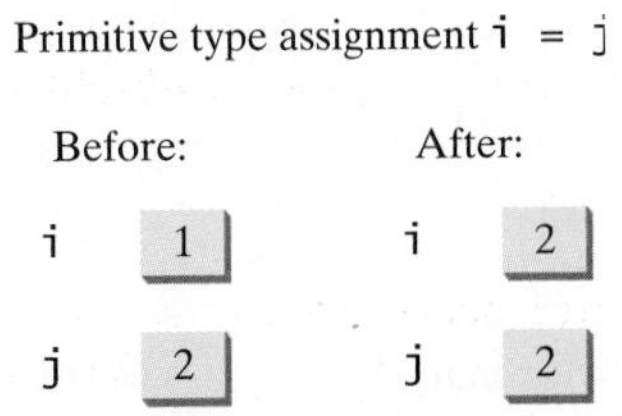
Primitive type assignment i = j
Before:
After:
i
1
i
2
j
2
j
2

FIGURE 8.7 Primitive variable j is copied to variable i.

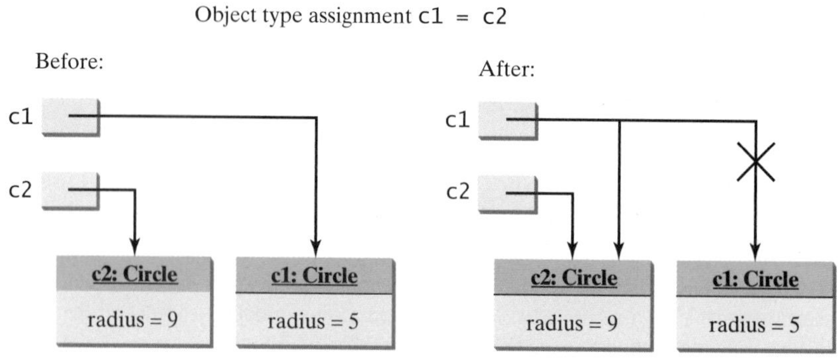
Object type assignment c1 = c2
Before:
After:
c1
c2
c1
c2
c2: Circle
radius = 9
c1: Circle
radius = 5
c2: Circle
radius = 9
c1: Circle
radius = 5

FIGURE 8.8 Reference variable `c2` is copied to variable `c1`.

Note

As shown in Figure 8.8, after the assignment statement `c1 = c2`, `c1` points to the same object referenced by `c2`. The object previously referenced by `c1` is no longer useful and therefore is now known as *garbage*. Garbage occupies memory space. The Java runtime system detects garbage and automatically reclaims the space it occupies. This process is called *garbage collection*.

garbage
garbage collection

Tip

If you know that an object is no longer needed, you can explicitly assign `null` to a reference variable for the object. The JVM will automatically collect the space if the object is not referenced by any reference variable.

8.6 Using Classes from the Java Library

Listing 8.1 defined the `Circle1` class and created objects from the class. You will frequently use the classes in the Java library to develop programs. This section gives some examples of the classes in the Java library.

8.6.1 The `Date` Class

In Listing 2.8, ShowCurrentTime.java, you learned how to obtain the current time using `System.currentTimeMillis()`. You used the division and remainder operators to extract current second, minute, and hour. Java provides a system-independent encapsulation of date and time in the `java.util.Date` class, as shown in Figure 8.9.

java.util.Date class

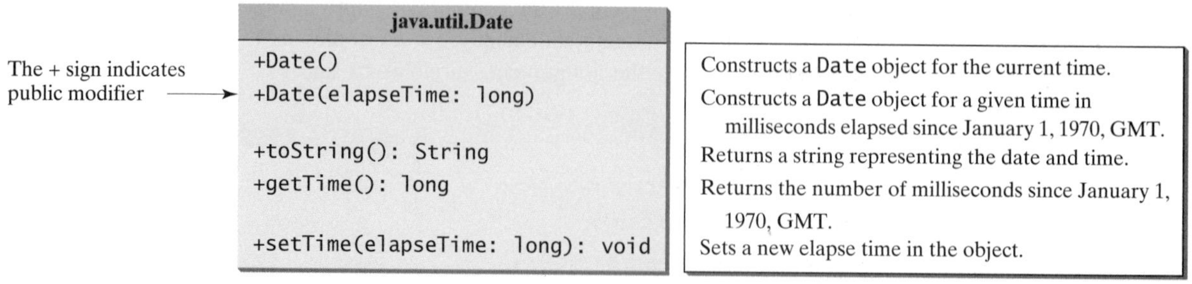
The + sign indicates public modifier
java.util.Date
+Date()
+Date(elapseTime: long)
+toString(): String
+getTime(): long
+setTime(elapseTime: long): void
Constructs a Date object for the current time.
Constructs a Date object for a given time in milliseconds elapsed since January 1, 1970, GMT.
Returns a string representing the date and time.
Returns the number of milliseconds since January 1, 1970, GMT.
Sets a new elapse time in the object.

FIGURE 8.9 A `Date` object represents a specific date and time.

You can use the no-arg constructor in the `Date` class to create an instance for the current date and time, its `getTime()` method to return the elapsed time since January 1, 1970, GMT, and its `toString` method to return the date and time as a string. For example, the following code

```
java.util.Date date = new java.util.Date() ;
System.out.println("The elapsed time since Jan 1, 1970 is " +
  date.getTime() + " milliseconds");
System.out.println(date.toString() );
```

create object

get elapsed time
invoke **toString**

displays the output like this:

```
The elapsed time since Jan 1, 1970 is 1100547210284 milliseconds
Mon Nov 15 14:33:30 EST 2004
```

The **Date** class has another constructor, **Date(long elapseTime)**, which can be used to construct a **Date** object for a given time in milliseconds elapsed since January 1, 1970, GMT.

8.6.2 The Random Class

You have used **Math.random()** to obtain a random **double** value between **0.0** and **1.0** (excluding **1.0**). Another way to generate random numbers is to use the **java.util.Random** class, as shown in Figure 8.10, which can generate a random **int**, **long**, **double**, **float**, and **boolean** value.

java.util.Random	
+Random()	Constructs a Random object with the current time as its seed.
+Random(seed: long)	Constructs a Random object with a specified seed.
+nextInt(): int	Returns a random int value.
+nextInt(n: int): int	Returns a random int value between 0 and n (exclusive).
+nextLong(): long	Returns a random long value.
+nextDouble(): double	Returns a random double value between 0.0 and 1.0 (exclusive).
+nextFloat(): float	Returns a random float value between 0.0F and 1.0F (exclusive).
+nextBoolean(): boolean	Returns a random boolean value.

FIGURE 8.10 A **Random** object can be used to generate random values.

When you create a **Random** object, you have to specify a seed or use the default seed. The no-arg constructor creates a **Random** object using the current elapsed time as its seed. If two **Random** objects have the same seed, they will generate identical sequences of numbers. For example, the following code creates two **Random** objects with the same seed, **3**.

```
Random random1 = new Random(3);
System.out.print("From random1: ");
for (int i = 0; i < 10; i++)
  System.out.print(random1.nextInt(1000) + " ");

Random random2 = new Random(3);
System.out.print("\nFrom random2: ");
for (int i = 0; i < 10; i++)
  System.out.print(random2.nextInt(1000) + " ");
```

The code generates the same sequence of random **int** values:

```
From random1: 734 660 210 581 128 202 549 564 459 961
From random2: 734 660 210 581 128 202 549 564 459 961
```

Note

The ability to generate the same sequence of random values is useful in software testing and many other applications. In software testing, you can test your program using a fixed sequence of numbers before using different sequences of random numbers.

same sequence

8.6.3 Displaying GUI Components

Pedagogical Note

Graphical user interface (GUI) components are good examples for teaching OOP. Simple GUI examples are introduced for this purpose. The full introduction to GUI programming begins with Chapter 12, "GUI Basics."

When you develop programs to create graphical user interfaces, you will use Java classes such as `JFrame`, `JButton`, `JRadioButton`, `JComboBox`, and `JList` to create frames, buttons, radio buttons, combo boxes, lists, and so on. Listing 8.5 is an example that creates two windows using the `JFrame` class. The output of the program is shown in Figure 8.11.

Window 1
Window 2

FIGURE 8.11 The program creates two windows using the `JFrame` class.

LISTING 8.5 TestFrame.java

create an object (line 5)
invoke a method (line 6)
create an object (line 12)
invoke a method (line 13)

```
 1 import javax.swing.JFrame;
 2
 3 public class TestFrame {
 4   public static void main(String[] args) {
 5     JFrame frame1 = new JFrame();
 6     frame1.setTitle("Window 1");
 7     frame1.setSize(200, 150);
 8     frame1.setLocation(200, 100);
 9     frame1.setDefaultCloseOperation(JFrame.EXIT_ON_CLOSE);
10     frame1.setVisible(true);
11
12     JFrame frame2 = new JFrame();
13     frame2.setTitle("Window 2");
14     frame2.setSize(200, 150);
15     frame2.setLocation(410, 100);
16     frame2.setDefaultCloseOperation(JFrame.EXIT_ON_CLOSE);
17     frame2.setVisible(true);
18   }
19 }
```

This program creates two objects of the `JFrame` class (lines 5, 12) and then uses the methods `setTitle`, `setSize`, `setLocation`, `setDefaultCloseOperation`, and `setVisible` to set the properties of the objects. The `setTitle` method sets a title for the window (lines 6, 13). The `setSize` method sets the window's width and height (lines 7, 14). The `setLocation` method specifies the location of the window's upper-left corner (lines 8, 15). The `setDefaultCloseOperation` method terminates the program when the frame is closed (lines 9, 16). The `setVisible` method displays the window.

You can add graphical user interface components, such as buttons, labels, text fields, check boxes, and combo boxes to the window. The components are defined using classes. Listing 8.6 gives an example of creating a graphical user interface, as shown in Figure 8.1.

Video Note
Use classes

LISTING 8.6 GUIComponents.java

```
 1 import javax.swing.*;
 2
 3 public class GUIComponents {
 4   public static void main(String[] args) {
 5     // Create a button with text OK
 6     JButton jbtOK = new JButton("OK");
 7
 8     // Create a button with text Cancel
 9     JButton jbtCancel = new JButton("Cancel");
10
11     // Create a label with text "Enter your name: "
12     JLabel jlblName = new JLabel("Enter your name: ");
13
14     // Create a text field with text "Type Name Here"
15     JTextField jtfName = new JTextField("Type Name Here");
16
17     // Create a check box with text bold
18     JCheckBox jchkBold = new JCheckBox("Bold");
19
20     // Create a check box with text italic
21     JCheckBox jchkItalic = new JCheckBox("Italic");
22
23     // Create a radio button with text red
24     JRadioButton jrbRed = new JRadioButton("Red");
25
26     // Create a radio button with text yellow
27     JRadioButton jrbYellow = new JRadioButton("Yellow");
28
29     // Create a combo box with several choices
30     JComboBox jcboColor = new JComboBox(new String[]{"Freshman",
31       "Sophomore", "Junior", "Senior"});
32
33     // Create a panel to group components
34     JPanel panel = new JPanel();
35     panel.add(jbtOK); // Add the OK button to the panel
36     panel.add(jbtCancel); // Add the Cancel button to the panel
37     panel.add(jlblName); // Add the label to the panel
38     panel.add(jtfName); // Add the text field to the panel
39     panel.add(jchkBold); // Add the check box to the panel
40     panel.add(jchkItalic); // Add the check box to the panel
41     panel.add(jrbRed); // Add the radio button to the panel
42     panel.add(jrbYellow); // Add the radio button to the panel
43     panel.add(jcboColor); // Add the combo box to the panel
44
45     JFrame frame = new JFrame(); // Create a frame
46     frame.add(panel); // Add the panel to the frame
47     frame.setTitle("Show GUI Components");
48     frame.setSize(450, 100);
49     frame.setLocation(200, 100);
50     frame.setDefaultCloseOperation(JFrame.EXIT_ON_CLOSE);
51     frame.setVisible(true);
52   }
53 }
```

create a button
create a button
create a label
create a text field
create a check box
create a check box
create a radio button
create a radio button
create a combo box
create a panel
add to panel
create a frame
add panel to frame
display frame

This program creates GUI objects using the classes `JButton`, `JLabel`, `JTextField`, `JCheckBox`, `JRadioButton`, and `JComboBox` (lines 6–31). Then, using the `JPanel` class (line 34), it then creates a panel object and adds to it the button, label, text field, check box, radio button, and combo box (lines 35–43). The program then creates a frame and adds the panel to the frame (line 45). The frame is displayed in line 51.

8.7 Static Variables, Constants, and Methods

instance variable

Video Note
static vs. instance

The data field `radius` in the circle class in Listing 8.1 is known as an *instance variable*. An instance variable is tied to a specific instance of the class; it is not shared among objects of the same class. For example, suppose that you create the following objects:

```
Circle circle1 = new Circle();
Circle circle2 = new Circle(5);
```

The `radius` in `circle1` is independent of the `radius` in `circle2` and is stored in a different memory location. Changes made to `circle1`'s `radius` do not affect `circle2`'s `radius`, and vice versa.

static variable

If you want all the instances of a class to share data, use *static variables*, also known as *class variables*. Static variables store values for the variables in a common memory location. Because of this common location, if one object changes the value of a static variable, all objects of the same class are affected. Java supports static methods as well as static variables. *Static methods* can be called without creating an instance of the class.

static method

Let us modify the `Circle` class by adding a static variable `numberOfObjects` to count the number of circle objects created. When the first object of this class is created, `numberOfObjects` is `1`. When the second object is created, `numberOfObjects` becomes `2`. The UML of the new circle class is shown in Figure 8.12. The `Circle` class defines the instance variable `radius` and the static variable `numberOfObjects`, the instance methods `getRadius`, `setRadius`, and `getArea`, and the static method `getNumberOfObjects`. (Note that static variables and methods are underlined in the UML class diagram.)

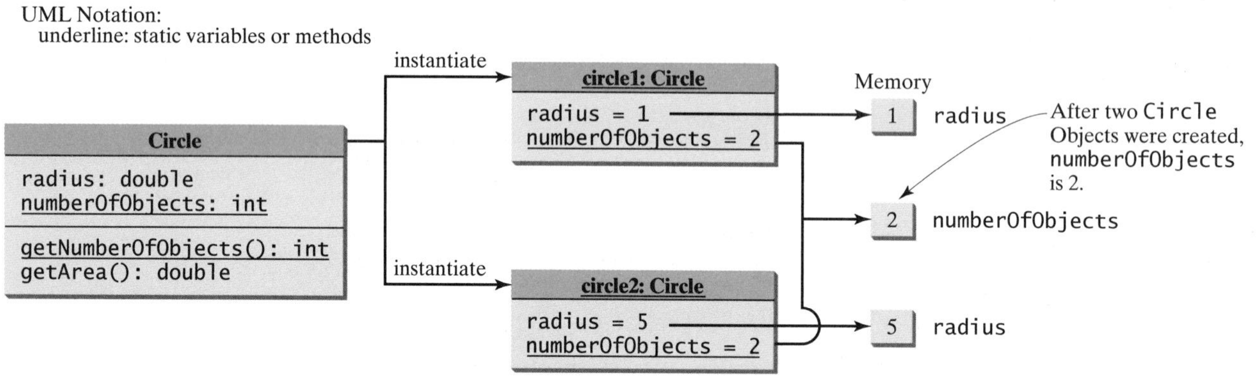
UML Notation:
underline: static variables or methods
Circle
radius: double
numberOfObjects: int
getNumberOfObjects(): int
getArea(): double
instantiate
circle1: Circle
radius = 1
numberOfObjects = 2
instantiate
circle2: Circle
radius = 5
numberOfObjects = 2
Memory
1 radius
2 numberOfObjects
5 radius
After two Circle Objects were created, numberOfObjects is 2.

FIGURE 8.12 Instance variables belong to the instances and have memory storage independent of one another. Static variables are shared by all the instances of the same class.

To declare a static variable or define a static method, put the modifier `static` in the variable or method declaration. The static variable `numberOfObjects` and the static method `getNumberOfObjects()` can be declared as follows:

declare static variable

```
static int numberOfObjects;
```

define static method

```
static int getNumberObjects() {
  return numberOfObjects;
}
```

Constants in a class are shared by all objects of the class. Thus, constants should be declared `final static`. For example, the constant `PI` in the `Math` class is defined as:

declare constant

```
final static double PI = 3.14159265358979323846;
```

The new circle class, named Circle2, is declared in Listing 8.7:

LISTING 8.7 Circle2.java

```
public class Circle2 {
  /** The radius of the circle */
  double radius;

  /** The number of objects created */
  static int numberOfObjects = 0;

  /** Construct a circle with radius 1 */
  Circle2() {
    radius = 1.0;
    numberOfObjects++;
  }

  /** Construct a circle with a specified radius */
  Circle2(double newRadius) {
    radius = newRadius;
    numberOfObjects++;
  }

  /** Return numberOfObjects */
  static int getNumberOfObjects() {
    return numberOfObjects;
  }

  /** Return the area of this circle */
  double getArea() {
    return radius * radius * Math.PI;
  }
}
```

static variable

increase by 1

increase by 1

static method

Method getNumberOfObjects() in Circle2 is a static method. Other examples of static methods are showMessageDialog and showInputDialog in the JOptionPane class and all the methods in the Math class. The main method is static, too.

Instance methods (e.g., getArea()) and instance data (e.g., radius) belong to instances and can be used only after the instances are created. They are accessed via a reference variable. Static methods (e.g., getNumberOfObjects()) and static data (e.g., numberOfObjects) can be accessed from a reference variable or from their class name.

The program in Listing 8.8 demonstrates how to use instance and static variables and methods and illustrates the effects of using them.

LISTING 8.8 TestCircle2.java

```
public class TestCircle2 {
  /** Main method */
  public static void main(String[] args) {
    System.out.println("Before creating objects");
    System.out.println("The number of Circle objects is " +
      Circle2.numberOfObjects);

     // Create c1
     Circle2 c1 = new Circle2();

    // Display c1 BEFORE c2 is created
    System.out.println("\nAfter creating c1");
    System.out.println("c1: radius (" + c1.radius +
      ") and number of Circle objects (" +
```

static variable

instance variable

static variable

instance variable

static variable

static variable

```
15        c1.numberOfObjects + ")");
16
17      // Create c2
18      Circle2 c2 = new Circle2(5);
19
20      // Modify c1
21      c1.radius = 9;
22
23      // Display c1 and c2 AFTER c2 was created
24      System.out.println("\nAfter creating c2 and modifying c1");
25      System.out.println("c1: radius (" + c1.radius +
26        ") and number of Circle objects (" +
27        c1.numberOfObjects + ")");
28      System.out.println("c2: radius (" + c2.radius +
29        ") and number of Circle objects (" +
30        c2.numberOfObjects + ")");
31    }
32  }
```

```
Before creating objects
The number of Circle objects is 0

After creating c1
c1: radius (1.0) and number of Circle objects (1)

After creating c2 and modifying c1
c1: radius (9.0) and number of Circle objects (2)
c2: radius (5.0) and number of Circle objects (2)
```

When you compile `TestCircle2.java`, the Java compiler automatically compiles `Circle2.java` if it has not been compiled since the last change.

Static variables and methods can be accessed without creating objects. Line 6 displays the number of objects, which is `0`, since no objects have been created.

The `main` method creates two circles, `c1` and `c2` (lines 9, 18). The instance variable `radius` in `c1` is modified to become `9` (line 21). This change does not affect the instance variable `radius` in `c2`, since these two instance variables are independent. The static variable `numberOfObjects` becomes `1` after `c1` is created (line 9), and it becomes `2` after `c2` is created (line 18).

Note that `PI` is a constant defined in `Math`, and `Math.PI` references the constant. `c.numberOfObjects` could be replaced by `Circle2.numberOfObjects`. This improves readability, because the reader can easily recognize the static variable. You can also replace `Circle2.numberOfObjects` by `Circle2.getNumberOfObjects()`.

use class name

Tip

Use `ClassName.methodName(arguments)` to invoke a static method and `ClassName.staticVariable` to access a static variable. This improves readability, because the user can easily recognize the static method and data in the class.

Static variables and methods can be used from instance or static methods in the class. However, instance variables and methods can be used only from instance methods, not from static methods, since static variables and methods don't belong to a particular object. Thus the code given below is wrong.

```
public class Foo {
  int i = 5;
  static int k = 2;

  public static void main(String[] args) {
    int j = i; // Wrong because i is an instance variable
    m1(); // Wrong because m1() is an instance method
```

```
8     }
9
10    public void m1() {
11      // Correct since instance and static variables and methods
12      // can be used in an instance method
13      i = i + k + m2(i, k);
14    }
15
16    public static int m2(int i, int j) {
17      return (int)(Math.pow(i, j));
18    }
19  }
```

Note that if you replace the code in lines 5–8 with the following new code, the program is fine, because the instance data field `i` and method `m1` are now accessed from an object `foo` (lines 6–7):

```
1  public class Foo {
2    int i = 5;
3    static int k = 2;
4
5    public static void main(String[] args) {
6      Foo foo = new Foo();
7      int j = foo.i; // OK, foo.i accesses the object's instance variable
8      foo.m1();     // OK. Foo.m1() invokes object's instance method
9    }
10
11   public void m1() {
12     i = i + k + m2(i, k);
13   }
14
15   public static int m2(int i, int j) {
16     return (int)(Math.pow(i, j));
17   }
18 }
```

Design Guide

instance or static?

How do you decide whether a variable or method should be an instance one or a static one? A variable or method that is dependent on a specific instance of the class should be an instance variable or method. A variable or method that is not dependent on a specific instance of the class should be a static variable or method. For example, every circle has its own radius. Radius is dependent on a specific circle. Therefore, **radius** is an instance variable of the **Circle** class. Since the **getArea** method is dependent on a specific circle, it is an instance method. None of the methods in the **Math** class, such as **random**, **pow**, **sin**, and **cos**, is dependent on a specific instance. Therefore, these methods are static methods. The **main** method is static and can be invoked directly from a class.

Caution

common design error

It is a common design error to define an instance method that should have been defined static. For example, the method **factorial(int n)** should be defined static, as shown below, because it is independent of any specific instance.

```
public class Test {
  public int factorial(int n) {
    int result = 1;
    for (int i = 1; i <= n; i++)
      result *= i;

    return result;
  }
}
```

(a) Wrong design

```
public class Test {
  public static int factorial(int n)
    int result = 1;
    for (int i = 1; i <= n; i++)
      result *= i;

    return result;
  }
}
```

(b) Correct design

8.8 Visibility Modifiers

You can use the public visibility modifier for classes, methods, and data fields to denote that they can be accessed from any other classes. If no visibility modifier is used, then by default the classes, methods, and data fields are accessible by any class in the same package. This is known as *package-private* or *package-access*.

using packages

Note

Packages can be used to organize classes. To do so, you need to add the following line as the first noncomment and nonblank statement in the program:

```
package packageName;
```

If a class is defined without the package statement, it is said to be placed in the *default package*.

Java recommends that you place classes into packages rather using a default package. For simplicity, however, this book uses default packages. For more information on packages, see Supplement III.G, "Packages."

In addition to the public and default visibility modifiers, Java provides the private and protected modifiers for class members. This section introduces the private modifier. The protected modifier will be introduced in §11.13, "The protected Data and Methods."

The private modifier makes methods and data fields accessible only from within its own class. Figure 8.13 illustrates how a public, default, and private data field or method in class C1 can be accessed from a class C2 in the same package and from a class C3 in a different package.

```
package p1;

public class C1 {
  public int x;
  int y;
  private int z;

  public void m1() {
  }
  void m2() {
  }
  private void m3() {
  }
}
```

```
package p1;

public class C2 {
  void aMethod()  {
    C1 o = new C1();
    can access o.x;
    can access o.y;
    cannot access o.z;

    can invoke o.m1();
    can invoke o.m2();
    cannot invoke o.m3();
  }
}
```

```
package p2;

public class C3 {
  void aMethod()  {
    C1 o = new C1();
    can access o.x;
    cannot access o.y;
    cannot access o.z;

    can invoke o.m1();
    cannot invoke o.m2();
    cannot invoke o.m3();
  }
}
```

FIGURE 8.13 The private modifier restricts access to its defining class, the default modifier restricts access to a package, and the public modifier enables unrestricted access.

If a class is not defined public, it can be accessed only within the same package. As shown in Figure 8.14, C1 can be accessed from C2 but not from C3.

```
package p1;

class C1 {
  ...
}
```

```
package p1;

public class C2 {
  can access C1
}
```

```
package p2;

public class C3 {
  cannot access C1;
  can access C2;
}
```

FIGURE 8.14 A nonpublic class has package-access.

A visibility modifier specifies how data fields and methods in a class can be accessed from outside the class. There is no restriction on accessing data fields and methods from inside the class. As shown in Figure 8.15(b), an object foo of the Foo class cannot access its private members, because foo is in the Test class. As shown in Figure 8.15(a), an object foo of the Foo class can access its private members, because foo is defined inside its own class.

inside access

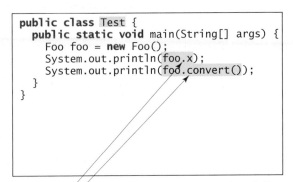

```
public class Foo {
  private boolean x;

  public static void main(String[] args) {
    Foo foo = new Foo();
    System.out.println(foo.x);
    System.out.println(foo.convert());
  }

  private int convert() {
    return x ? 1 :  1;
  }
}
```

(a) This is OK because object foo is used inside the Foo class

```
public class Test {
  public static void main(String[] args) {
    Foo foo = new Foo();
    System.out.println(foo.x);
    System.out.println(foo.convert());
  }
}
```

(b) This is wrong because x and convert are private in Foo.

FIGURE 8.15 An object can access its private members if it is defined in its own class.

Caution

The private modifier applies only to the members of a class. The public modifier can apply to a class or members of a class. Using modifiers public and private on local variables would cause a compile error.

Note

In most cases, the constructor should be public. However, if you want to prohibit the user from creating an instance of a class, use a private constructor. For example, there is no reason to create an instance from the Math class, because all of its data fields and methods are static. To prevent the user from creating objects from the Math class, the constructor in java.lang.Math is defined as follows:

private constructor

```
private Math() {
}
```

8.9 Data Field Encapsulation

The data fields radius and numberOfObjects in the Circle2 class in Listing 8.7 can be modified directly (e.g., myCircle.radius = 5 or Circle2.numberOfObjects = 10). This is not a good practice—for two reasons:

Video Note
Data field encapsulation

- First, data may be tampered with. For example, numberOfObjects is to count the number of objects created, but it may be mistakenly set to an arbitrary value (e.g., Circle2.numberOfObjects = 10).
- Second, the class becomes difficult to maintain and vulnerable to bugs. Suppose you want to modify the Circle2 class to ensure that the radius is nonnegative after other programs have already used the class. You have to change not only the Circle2 class but also the programs that use it, because the clients may have modified the radius directly (e.g., myCircle.radius = -5).

To prevent direct modifications of data fields, you should declare the data fields private, using the private modifier. This is known as *data field encapsulation.*

data field encapsulation

A private data field cannot be accessed by an object from outside the class that defines the private field. But often a client needs to retrieve and modify a data field. To make a private data field accessible, provide a *get* method to return its value. To enable a private data field to be updated, provide a *set* method to set a new value.

accessor
mutator

Note

Colloquially, a **get** method is referred to as a *getter* (or *accessor*), and a **set** method is referred to as a *setter* (or *mutator*).

A `get` method has the following signature:

```
public returnType getPropertyName()
```

boolean accessor

If the `returnType` is `boolean`, the `get` method should be defined as follows by convention:

```
public boolean isPropertyName()
```

A `set` method has the following signature:

```
public void setPropertyName(dataType propertyValue)
```

Let us create a new circle class with a private data-field radius and its associated accessor and mutator methods. The class diagram is shown in Figure 8.16. The new circle class, named `Circle3`, is defined in Listing 8.9:

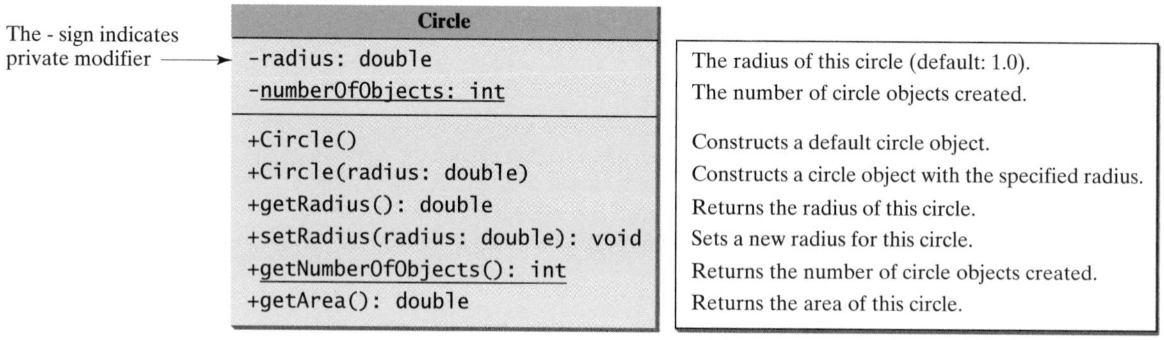
The - sign indicates private modifier
Circle
-radius: double
-numberOfObjects: int
+Circle()
+Circle(radius: double)
+getRadius(): double
+setRadius(radius: double): void
+getNumberOfObjects(): int
+getArea(): double
The radius of this circle (default: 1.0).
The number of circle objects created.
Constructs a default circle object.
Constructs a circle object with the specified radius.
Returns the radius of this circle.
Sets a new radius for this circle.
Returns the number of circle objects created.
Returns the area of this circle.

FIGURE 8.16 The `Circle` class encapsulates circle properties and provides get/set and other methods.

LISTING 8.9 Circle3.java

encapsulate **radius**

encapsulate **numberOfObjects**

```
public class Circle3 {
  /** The radius of the circle */
  private double radius = 1;

  /** The number of the objects created */
  private static int numberOfObjects = 0;

  /** Construct a circle with radius 1 */
  public Circle3() {
    numberOfObjects++;
  }

  /** Construct a circle with a specified radius */
  public Circle3(double newRadius) {
    radius = newRadius;
    numberOfObjects++;
  }

```

```
19   /** Return radius */
20   public double getRadius() {
21     return radius;
22   }
23
24   /** Set a new radius */
25   public void setRadius(double newRadius) {
26     radius = (newRadius >= 0) ? newRadius : 0;
27   }
28
29   /** Return numberOfObjects */
30   public static int getNumberOfObjects() {
31     return numberOfObjects;
32   }
33
34   /** Return the area of this circle */
35   public double getArea() {
36     return radius * radius * Math.PI;
37   }
38 }
```

access method

mutator method

access method

The getRadius() method (lines 20–22) returns the radius, and the setRadius(newRadius) method (line 25–27) sets a new radius into the object. If the new radius is negative, 0 is set to the radius in the object. Since these methods are the only ways to read and modify radius, you have total control over how the radius property is accessed. If you have to change the implementation of these methods, you need not change the client programs. This makes the class easy to maintain.

Listing 8.10 gives a client program that uses the Circle class to create a Circle object and modifies the radius using the setRadius method.

LISTING 8.10 TestCircle3.java

```
public class TestCircle3 {
  /** Main method */
  public static void main(String[] args) {
    // Create a Circle with radius 5.0
    Circle3 myCircle = new Circle3(5.0);
    System.out.println("The area of the circle of radius "
      + myCircle.getRadius() + " is " + myCircle.getArea() );

    // Increase myCircle's radius by 10%
    myCircle.setRadius(myCircle.getRadius() * 1.1);
    System.out.println("The area of the circle of radius "
      + myCircle.getRadius() + " is " + myCircle.getArea() );

    System.out.println("The number of objects created is "
      + Circle3.getNumberOfObjects() );
  }
}
```

invoke public method

invoke public method

invoke public method

The data field radius is declared private. Private data can be accessed only within their defining class. You cannot use myCircle.radius in the client program. A compile error would occur if you attempted to access private data from a client.

Since numberOfObjects is private, it cannot be modified. This prevents tampering. For example, the user cannot set numberOfObjects to 100. The only way to make it 100 is to create 100 objects of the Circle class.

Suppose you combined TestCircle and Circle into one class by moving the main method in TestCircle into Circle. Could you use myCircle.radius in the main method? See Review Question 8.15 for the answer.

Design Guide

To prevent data from being tampered with and to make the class easy to maintain, declare data fields private.

8.10 Passing Objects to Methods

You can pass objects to methods. Like passing an array, passing an object is actually passing the reference of the object. The following code passes the `myCircle` object as an argument to the `printCircle` method:

pass an object

```
public class Test {
  public static void main(String[] args) {
    // Circle3 is defined in Listing 8.9
    Circle3 myCircle = new Circle3(5.0);
    printCircle(myCircle);
  }

  public static void printCircle(Circle3 c) {
    System.out.println("The area of the circle of radius "
      + c.getRadius() + " is " + c.getArea());
  }
}
```

pass-by-value

Java uses exactly one mode of passing arguments: pass-by-value. In the preceding code, the value of `myCircle` is passed to the `printCircle` method. This value is a reference to a `Circle` object.

Let us demonstrate the difference between passing a primitive type value and passing a reference value with the program in Listing 8.11:

Listing 8.11 TestPassObject.java

pass object

object parameter

```
public class TestPassObject {
  /** Main method */
  public static void main(String[] args) {
    // Create a Circle object with radius 1
    Circle3 myCircle = new Circle3(1);

    // Print areas for radius 1, 2, 3, 4, and 5.
    int n = 5;
    printAreas(myCircle, n);

    // See myCircle.radius and times
    System.out.println("\n" + "Radius is " + myCircle.getRadius());
    System.out.println("n is " + n);
  }

  /** Print a table of areas for radius */
  public static void printAreas(Circle3 c, int times) {
    System.out.println("Radius \t\tArea");
    while (times >= 1) {
      System.out.println(c.getRadius() + "\t\t" + c.getArea());
      c.setRadius(c.getRadius() + 1);
      times--;
    }
  }
}
```

```
Radius                              Area
 1.0                                 3.141592653589793
 2.0                                12.566370614359172
 3.0                                29.274333882308138
 4.0                                50.26548245743669
 5.0                                79.53981633974483
Radius is 6.0
n is 5
```

The Circle3 class is defined in Listing 8.9. The program passes a Circle3 object myCircle and an integer value from n to invoke printAreas(myCircle, n) (line 9), which prints a table of areas for radii 1, 2, 3, 4, 5, as shown in the sample output.

Figure 8.17 shows the call stack for executing the methods in the program. Note that the objects are stored in a heap.

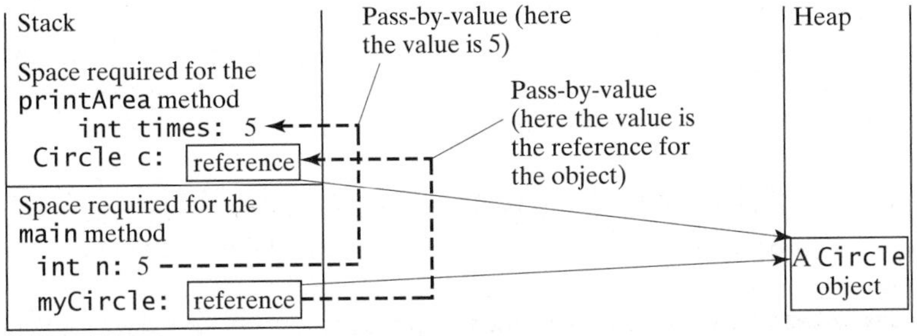

Stack
Space required for the printArea method
int times: 5
Circle c: reference
Space required for the main method
int n: 5
myCircle: reference
Pass-by-value (here the value is 5)
Pass-by-value (here the value is the reference for the object)
Heap
A Circle object

FIGURE 8.17 The value of n is passed to times, and the reference of myCircle is passed to c in the printAreas method.

When passing an argument of a primitive data type, the value of the argument is passed. In this case, the value of n (5) is passed to times. Inside the printAreas method, the content of times is changed; this does not affect the content of n.

When passing an argument of a reference type, the reference of the object is passed. In this case, c contains a reference for the object that is also referenced via myCircle. Therefore, changing the properties of the object through c inside the printAreas method has the same effect as doing so outside the method through the variable myCircle. Pass-by-value on references can be best described semantically as *pass-by-sharing*; i.e., the object referenced in the method is the same as the object being passed.

pass-by-sharing

8.11 Array of Objects

In Chapter 6, "Single-Dimensional Arrays," arrays of primitive type elements were created. You can also create arrays of objects. For example, the following statement declares and creates an array of ten Circle objects:

```
Circle[] circleArray = new Circle[10];
```

To initialize the circleArray, you can use a for loop like this one:

```
for (int i = 0; i < circleArray.length; i++) {
  circleArray[i] = new Circle();
}
```

An array of objects is actually an *array of reference variables*. So, invoking `circleArray[1].getArea()` involves two levels of referencing, as shown in Figure 8.18. `circleArray` references the entire array. `circleArray[1]` references a `Circle` object.

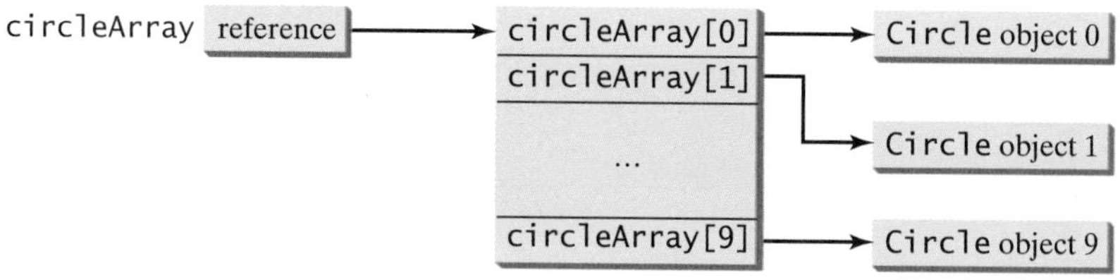
circleArray
reference
circleArray[0]
circleArray[1]
...
circleArray[9]
Circle object 0
Circle object 1
Circle object 9

FIGURE 8.18 In an array of objects, an element of the array contains a reference to an object.

Note

When an array of objects is created using the **new** operator, each element in the array is a reference variable with a default value of `null`.

Listing 8.12 gives an example that demonstrates how to use an array of objects. The program summarizes the areas of an array of circles. The program creates `circleArray`, an array composed of five `Circle` objects; it then initializes circle radii with random values and displays the total area of the circles in the array.

LISTING 8.12 TotalArea.java

array of objects

return array of objects

pass array of objects

```
public class TotalArea {
  /** Main method */
  public static void main(String[] args) {
    // Declare circleArray
    Circle3[] circleArray;

    // Create circleArray
    circleArray = createCircleArray() ;

    // Print circleArray and total areas of the circles
    printCircleArray(circleArray);
  }

  /** Create an array of Circle objects */
  public static Circle3[] createCircleArray() {
    Circle3[] circleArray = new Circle3[5];

    for (int i = 0; i < circleArray.length; i++) {
      circleArray[i] = new Circle3(Math.random() * 100);
    }

    // Return Circle array
    return circleArray;
  }

  /** Print an array of circles and their total area */
  public static void printCircleArray(Circle3[] circleArray) {
    System.out.printf("%-30s%-15s\n", "Radius", "Area");
    for (int i = 0; i < circleArray.length; i++) {
      System.out.printf("%-30f%-15f\n", circleArray[i].getRadius(),
        circleArray[i].getArea());
    }

    System.out.println("----------------------------------------------");
```

```
35
36     // Compute and display the result
37     System.out.printf("%-30s%-15f\n", "The total area of circles is",
38       sum(circleArray));
39   }
40
41   /** Add circle areas */
42   public static double sum(Circle3[] circleArray) {
43     // Initialize sum
44     double sum = 0;
45
46     // Add areas to sum
47     for (int i = 0; i < circleArray.length; i++)
48       sum += circleArray[i].getArea();
49
50     return sum;
51   }
52 }
```

pass array of objects

```
Radius                                  Area
70.577708                          15648.941866
44.152266                           6124.291736
24.867853                           1942.792644
 5.680718                            101.380949
36.734246                           4239.280350
-----------------------------------------------------
The total area of circles is       28056.687544
```

The program invokes `createCircleArray()` (line 8) to create an array of five `Circle` objects. Several `Circle` classes were introduced in this chapter. This example uses the `Circle` class introduced in §8.9, "Data Field Encapsulation."

The circle radii are randomly generated using the `Math.random()` method (line 19). The `createCircleArray` method returns an array of `Circle` objects (line 23). The array is passed to the `printCircleArray` method, which displays the radius and area of each circle and the total area of the circles.

The sum of the circle areas is computed using the `sum` method (line 38), which takes the array of `Circle` objects as the argument and returns a `double` value for the total area.

Key Terms

accessor method (getter) 284
action 264
attribute 264
behavior 264
class 265
client 267
constructor 268
data field 268
data-field encapsulation 283
default constructor 270
dot operator (.) 271
instance 271
instance method 271
instance variable 271
instantiation 264
mutator method (setter) 285
`null` 272
no-arg constructor 266
object-oriented programming (OOP) 264
Unified Modeling Language (UML) 265
package-private (or package-access) 282
private 283
property 264
public 282
reference variable 271
reference type 271
state 264
static method 278
static variable 278

Chapter Summary

1. A class is a template for objects. It defines the properties of objects and provides constructors for creating objects and methods for manipulating them.

2. A class is also a data type. You can use it to declare object reference variables. An object reference variable that appears to hold an object actually contains a reference to that object. Strictly speaking, an object reference variable and an object are different, but most of the time the distinction can be ignored.

3. An object is an instance of a class. You use the `new` operator to create an object, and the dot (`.`) operator to access members of that object through its reference variable.

4. An instance variable or method belongs to an instance of a class. Its use is associated with individual instances. A static variable is a variable shared by all instances of the same class. A static method is a method that can be invoked without using instances.

5. Every instance of a class can access the class's static variables and methods. For clarity, however, it is better to invoke static variables and methods using `ClassName.variable` and `ClassName.method`.

6. Modifiers specify how the class, method, and data are accessed. A `public` class, method, or data is accessible to all clients. A `private` method or data is accessible only inside the class.

7. You can provide a `get` method or a `set` method to enable clients to see or modify the data. Colloquially, a `get` method is referred to as a *getter* (or *accessor*), and a `set` method as a *setter* (or *mutator*).

8. A `get` method has the signature `public returnType getPropertyName()`. If the `returnType` is `boolean`, the `get` method should be defined as `public boolean isPropertyName()`. A `set` method has the signature `public void setPropertyName(dataType propertyValue)`.

9. All parameters are passed to methods using pass-by-value. For a parameter of a primitive type, the actual value is passed; for a parameter of a reference type, the reference for the object is passed.

10. A Java array is an object that can contain primitive type values or object type values. When an array of objects is created, its elements are assigned the default value of `null`.

Review Questions

Sections 8.2–8.5

8.1 Describe the relationship between an object and its defining class. How do you define a class? How do you declare an object reference variable? How do you create an object? How do you declare and create an object in one statement?

8.2 What are the differences between constructors and methods?

8.3 Is an array an object or a primitive type value? Can an array contain elements of an object type as well as a primitive type? Describe the default value for the elements of an array.

8.4 What is wrong with the following program?

```
public class ShowErrors {
  public static void main(String[] args) {
    ShowErrors t = new ShowErrors(5);
  }
}
```

(a)

```
public class ShowErrors {
  public static void main(String[] args) {
    ShowErrors t = new ShowErrors();
    t.x();
  }
}
```

(b)

```
public class ShowErrors {
  public void method1() {
    Circle c;
    System.out.println("What is radius "
      + c.getRadius());
    c = new Circle();
  }
}
```

(c)

```
public class ShowErrors {
  public static void main(String[] args) {
    C c = new C(5.0);
    System.out.println(c.value);
  }
}

class C {
  int value = 2;
}
```

(d)

8.5 What is wrong in the following code?

```
class Test {
  public static void main(String[] args) {
    A a = new A();
    a.print();
  }
}

class A {
  String s;

  A(String s) {
    this.s = s;
  }

  public void print() {
    System.out.print(s);
  }
}
```

8.6 What is the printout of the following code?

```
public class Foo {
  private boolean x;

  public static void main(String[] args) {
    Foo foo = new Foo();
    System.out.println(foo.x);
  }
}
```

Section 8.6

8.7 How do you create a `Date` for the current time? How do you display the current time?

8.8 How do you create a `JFrame`, set a title in a frame, and display a frame?

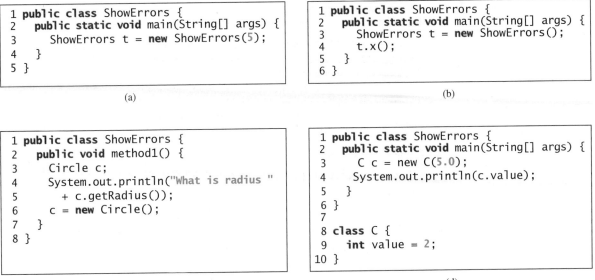

8.9 Which packages contain the classes `Date`, `JFrame`, `JOptionPane`, `System`, and `Math`?

Section 8.7

8.10 Suppose that the class `Foo` is defined in (a). Let `f` be an instance of `Foo`. Which of the statements in (b) are correct?

```
public class Foo {
  int i;
  static String s;

  void imethod() {
  }

  static void smethod() {
  }
}
```

(a)

```
System.out.println(f.i);
System.out.println(f.s);
f.imethod();
f.smethod();
System.out.println(Foo.i);
System.out.println(Foo.s);
Foo.imethod();
Foo.smethod();
```

(b)

8.11 Add the `static` keyword in the place of `?` if appropriate.

```
public class Test {
  private int count;

  public ? void main(String[] args) {
    ...
  }

  public ? int getCount() {
    return count;
  }

  public ? int factorial(int n) {
    int result = 1;
    for (int i = 1; i <= n; i++)
      result *= i;

    return result;
  }
}
```

8.12 Can you invoke an instance method or reference an instance variable from a static method? Can you invoke a static method or reference a static variable from an instance method? What is wrong in the following code?

```
public class Foo {
  public static void main(String[] args) {
    method1();
  }

  public void method1() {
    method2();
  }

  public static void method2() {
    System.out.println("What is radius " + c.getRadius());
  }

  Circle c = new Circle();
}
```

Sections 8.8–8.9

8.13 What is an accessor method? What is a mutator method? What are the naming conventions for accessor methods and mutator methods?

8.14 What are the benefits of data-field encapsulation?

8.15 In the following code, `radius` is private in the `Circle` class, and `myCircle` is an object of the `Circle` class. Does the highlighted code below cause any problems? Explain why.

```
public class Circle {
  private double radius = 1.0;

  /** Find the area of this circle */
  public double getArea() {
    return radius * radius * Math.PI;
  }

  public static void main(String[] args) {
    Circle myCircle = new Circle();
    System.out.println("Radius is " + myCircle.radius);
  }
}
```

Section 8.10

8.16 Describe the difference between passing a parameter of a primitive type and passing a parameter of a reference type. Show the output of the following program:

```
public class Test {
  public static void main(String[] args) {
    Count myCount = new Count();
    int times = 0;

    for (int i = 0; i < 100; i++)
      increment(myCount, times);

    System.out.println("count is " + myCount.count);
    System.out.println("times is " + times);
  }

  public static void increment(Count c, int times) {
    c.count++;
    times++;
  }
}
```

```
public class Count {
  public int count;

  public Count(int c) {
    count = c;
  }

  public Count() {
    count = 1;
  }
}
```

8.17 Show the output of the following program:

```
public class Test {
  public static void main(String[] args) {
    Circle circle1 = new Circle(1);
    Circle circle2 = new Circle(2);

    swap1(circle1, circle2);
    System.out.println("After swap1: circle1 = " +
      circle1.radius + " circle2 = " + circle2.radius);

    swap2(circle1, circle2);
    System.out.println("After swap2: circle1 = " +
      circle1.radius + " circle2 = " + circle2.radius);
  }
```

```
  public static void swap1(Circle x, Circle y) {
    Circle temp = x;
    x = y;
    y = temp;
  }

  public static void swap2(Circle x, Circle y) {
    double temp = x.radius;
    x.radius = y.radius;
    y.radius = temp;
  }
}

class Circle {
  double radius;

  Circle(double newRadius) {
    radius = newRadius;
  }
}
```

8.18 Show the printout of the following code:

```
public class Test {
  public static void main(String[] args) {
    int[] a = {1, 2};
    swap(a[0], a[1]);
    System.out.println("a[0] = " + a[0]
      + " a[1] = " + a[1]);
  }

  public static void swap(int n1, int n2) {
    int temp = n1;
    n1 = n2;
    n2 = temp;
  }
}
```

(a)

```
public class Test {
  public static void main(String[] args) {
    int[] a = {1, 2};
    swap(a);
    System.out.println("a[0] = " + a[0]
      + " a[1] = " + a[1]);
  }

  public static void swap(int[] a) {
    int temp = a[0];
    a[0] = a[1];
    a[1] = temp;
  }
}
```

(b)

```
public class Test {
  public static void main(String[] args) {
    T t = new T();
    swap(t);
    System.out.println("e1 = " + t.e1
      + " e2 = " + t.e2);
  }

  public static void swap(T t) {
    int temp = t.e1;
    t.e1 = t.e2;
    t.e2 = temp;
  }
}

class T {
  int e1 = 1;
  int e2 = 2;
}
```

(c)

```
public class Test {
  public static void main(String[] args) {
    T t1 = new T();
    T t2 = new T();
    System.out.println("t1's i = " +
      t1.i + " and j = " + t1.j);
    System.out.println("t2's i = " +
      t2.i + " and j = " + t2.j);
  }
}

class T {
  static int i = 0;
  int j = 0;

  T() {
    i++;
    j = 1;
  }
}
```

(d)

8.19 What is the output of the following program?

```
import java.util.Date;

public class Test {
  public static void main(String[] args) {
    Date date = null;
    m1(date);
    System.out.println(date);
  }

  public static void m1(Date date) {
    date = new Date();
  }
}
```

(a)

```
import java.util.Date;

public class Test {
  public static void main(String[] args) {
    Date date = new Date(1234567);
    m1(date);
    System.out.println(date.getTime());
  }

  public static void m1(Date date) {
    date = new Date(7654321);
  }
}
```

(b)

```
import java.util.Date;

public class Test {
  public static void main(String[] args) {
    Date date = new Date(1234567);
    m1(date);
    System.out.println(date.getTime());
  }

  public static void m1(Date date) {
    date.setTime(7654321);
  }
}
```

(c)

```
import java.util.Date;

public class Test {
  public static void main(String[] args) {
    Date date = new Date(1234567);
    m1(date);
    System.out.println(date.getTime());
  }

  public static void m1(Date date) {
    date = null;
  }
}
```

(d)

Section 8.11

8.20 What is wrong in the following code?

```
public class Test {
  public static void main(String[] args) {
    java.util.Date[] dates = new java.util.Date[10];
    System.out.println(dates[0]);
    System.out.println(dates[0].toString());
  }
}
```

PROGRAMMING EXERCISES

Pedagogical Note

The exercises in Chapters 8–14 achieve three objectives:

three objectives

- Design classes and draw UML class diagrams;
- Implement classes from the UML;
- Use classes to develop applications.

Solutions for the UML diagrams for the even-numbered exercises can be downloaded from the Student Website and all others can be downloaded from the Instructor Website.

Sections 8.2–8.5

8.1 (*The `Rectangle` class*) Following the example of the `Circle` class in §8.2, design a class named `Rectangle` to represent a rectangle. The class contains:

- Two `double` data fields named `width` and `height` that specify the width and height of the rectangle. The default values are `1` for both `width` and `height`.
- A no-arg constructor that creates a default rectangle.
- A constructor that creates a rectangle with the specified `width` and `height`.
- A method named `getArea()` that returns the area of this rectangle.
- A method named `getPerimeter()` that returns the perimeter.

Draw the UML diagram for the class. Implement the class. Write a test program that creates two `Rectangle` objects—one with width `4` and height `40` and the other with width `3.5` and height `35.9`. Display the width, height, area, and perimeter of each rectangle in this order.

8.2 (*The `Stock` class*) Following the example of the `Circle` class in §8.2, design a class named `Stock` that contains:

- A string data field named `symbol` for the stock's symbol.
- A string data field named `name` for the stock's name.
- A `double` data field named `previousClosingPrice` that stores the stock price for the previous day.
- A `double` data field named `currentPrice` that stores the stock price for the current time.
- A constructor that creates a stock with specified symbol and name.
- A method named `getChangePercent()` that returns the percentage changed from `previousClosingPrice` to `currentPrice`.

Draw the UML diagram for the class. Implement the class. Write a test program that creates a `Stock` object with the stock symbol JAVA, the name Sun Microsystems Inc, and the previous closing price of `4.5`. Set a new current price to `4.35` and display the price-change percentage.

Section 8.6

8.3* (*Using the `Date` class*) Write a program that creates a `Date` object, sets its elapsed time to `10000`, `100000`, `10000000`, `10000000`, `100000000`, `1000000000`, `10000000000`, `100000000000`, and displays the date and time using the `toString()` method, respectively.

8.4* (*Using the `Random` class*) Write a program that creates a `Random` object with seed `1000` and displays the first 50 random integers between `0` and `100` using the `nextInt(100)` method.

8.5* (*Using the `GregorianCalendar` class*) Java API has the `GregorianCalendar` class in the `java.util` package that can be used to obtain the year, month, and day of a date. The no-arg constructor constructs an instance for the current date, and the methods `get(GregorianCalendar.YEAR)`, `get(GregorianCalendar.MONTH)`, and `get(GregorianCalendar.DAY_OF_MONTH)` return the year, month, and day. Write a program to perform two tasks:

- Display the current year, month, and day.
- The `GregorianCalendar` class has the `setTimeInMillis(long)`, which can be used to set a specified elapsed time since January 1, 1970. Set the value to `1234567898765L` and display the year, month, and day.

Sections 8.7–8.9

8.6** (*Displaying calendars*) Rewrite the `PrintCalendar` class in Listing 5.12 to display calendars in a message dialog box. Since the output is generated from several static methods in the class, you may define a static `String` variable `output` for storing the output and display it in a message dialog box.

8.7 (*The* `Account` *class*) Design a class named `Account` that contains:

- A private `int` data field named `id` for the account (default `0`).
- A private `double` data field named `balance` for the account (default `0`).
- A private `double` data field named `annualInterestRate` that stores the current interest rate (default `0`). Assume all accounts have the same interest rate.
- A private `Date` data field named `dateCreated` that stores the date when the account was created.
- A no-arg constructor that creates a default account.
- A constructor that creates an account with the specified id and initial balance.
- The accessor and mutator methods for `id`, `balance`, and `annualInterestRate`.
- The accessor method for `dateCreated`.
- A method named `getMonthlyInterestRate()` that returns the monthly interest rate.
- A method named `withdraw` that withdraws a specified amount from the account.
- A method named `deposit` that deposits a specified amount to the account.

Draw the UML diagram for the class. Implement the class. Write a test program that creates an `Account` object with an account ID of 1122, a balance of $20,000, and an annual interest rate of 4.5%. Use the `withdraw` method to withdraw $2,500, use the `deposit` method to deposit $3,000, and print the balance, the monthly interest, and the date when this account was created.

8.8 (*The* `Fan` *class*) Design a class named `Fan` to represent a fan. The class contains:

Video Note
The Fan class

- Three constants named `SLOW`, `MEDIUM`, and `FAST` with values `1`, `2`, and `3` to denote the fan speed.
- A private `int` data field named `speed` that specifies the speed of the fan (default `SLOW`).
- A private `boolean` data field named `on` that specifies whether the fan is on (default `false`).
- A private `double` data field named `radius` that specifies the radius of the fan (default `5`).
- A string data field named `color` that specifies the color of the fan (default `blue`).
- The accessor and mutator methods for all four data fields.
- A no-arg constructor that creates a default fan.
- A method named `toString()` that returns a string description for the fan. If the fan is on, the method returns the fan speed, color, and radius in one combined string. If the fan is not on, the method returns fan color and radius along with the string "fan is off" in one combined string.

Draw the UML diagram for the class. Implement the class. Write a test program that creates two `Fan` objects. Assign maximum speed, radius `10`, color `yellow`, and turn it on to the first object. Assign medium speed, radius `5`, color `blue`, and turn it off to the second object. Display the objects by invoking their `toString` method.

8.9** (*Geometry: n-sided regular polygon*) In an *n*-sided regular polygon all sides have the same length and all angles have the same degree (i.e., the polygon is both equilateral and equiangular). Design a class named **RegularPolygon** that contains:

- A private **int** data field named **n** that defines the number of sides in the polygon with default value **3**.
- A private **double** data field named **side** that stores the length of the side with default value **1**.
- A private **double** data field named **x** that defines the *x*-coordinate of the center of the polygon with default value **0**.
- A private **double** data field named **y** that defines the *y*-coordinate of the center of the polygon with default value **0**.
- A no-arg constructor that creates a regular polygon with default values.
- A constructor that creates a regular polygon with the specified number of sides and length of side, centered at (**0**, **0**).
- A constructor that creates a regular polygon with the specified number of sides, length of side, and *x*-and *y*-coordinates.
- The accessor and mutator methods for all data fields.
- The method **getPerimeter()** that returns the perimeter of the polygon.
- The method **getArea()** that returns the area of the polygon. The formula for computing the area of a regular polygon is

$$Area = \frac{n \times s^2}{4 \times \tan\left(\frac{p}{n}\right)}.$$

Draw the UML diagram for the class. Implement the class. Write a test program that creates three **RegularPolygon** objects, created using the no-arg constructor, using **RegularPolygon(6, 4)**, and using **RegularPolygon(10, 4, 5.6, 7.8)**. For each object, display its perimeter and area.

8.10* (*Algebra: quadratic equations*) Design a class named **QuadraticEquation** for a quadratic equation $ax^2 + bx + x = 0$. The class contains:

- Private data fields **a**, **b**, and **c** that represents three coefficients.
- A constructor for the arguments for **a**, **b**, and **c**.
- Three **get** methods for **a**, **b**, and **c**.
- A method named **getDiscriminant()** that returns the discriminant, which is $b^2 - 4ac$.
- The methods named **getRoot1()** and **getRoot2()** for returning two roots of the equation

$$r_1 = \frac{-b + \sqrt{b^2 - 4ac}}{2a} \text{ and } r_2 = \frac{-b - \sqrt{b^2 - 4ac}}{2a}$$

These methods are useful only if the discriminant is nonnegative. Let these methods return **0** if the discriminant is negative.

Draw the UML diagram for the class. Implement the class. Write a test program that prompts the user to enter values for *a*, *b*, and *c* and displays the result based on the discriminant. If the discriminant is positive, display the two roots. If the discriminant is **0**, display the one root. Otherwise, display "The equation has no roots." See Exercise 3.1 for sample runs.

8.11* (*Algebra: 2 × 2 linear equations*) Design a class named `LinearEquation` for a 2 × 2 system of linear equations:

$$ax + by = e \qquad x = \frac{ed - bf}{ad - bc} \qquad y = \frac{af - ec}{ad - bc}$$
$$cx + dy = f$$

The class contains:

- Private data fields `a`, `b`, `c`, `d`, `e`, and `f`.
- A constructor with the arguments for `a`, `b`, `c`, `d`, `e`, and `f`.
- Six `get` methods for `a`, `b`, `c`, `d`, `e`, and `f`.
- A method named `isSolvable()` that returns true if $ad - bc$ is not `0`.
- Methods `getX()` and `getY()` that return the solution for the equation.

Draw the UML diagram for the class. Implement the class. Write a test program that prompts the user to enter `a`, `b`, `c`, `d`, `e`, and `f` and displays the result. If $ad - bc$ is `0`, report that "The equation has no solution." See Exercise 3.3 for sample runs.

8.12** (*Geometry: intersection*) Suppose two line segments intersect. The two endpoints for the first line segment are (`x1`, `y1`) and (`x2`, `y2`) and for the second line segment are (`x3`, `y3`) and (`x4`, `y5`). Write a program that prompts the user to enter these four endpoints and displays the intersecting point.

(*Hint*: Use the `LinearEquation` class from the preceding exercise.)

```
Enter the endpoints of the first line segment: 2.0 2.0 0 0 ↵Enter
Enter the endpoints of the second line segment: 0 2.0 2.0 0 ↵Enter
The intersecting point is: (1.0, 1.0)
```

8.13** (*The `Location` class*) Design a class named `Location` for locating a maximal value and its location in a two-dimensional array. The class contains public data fields `row`, `column`, and `maxValue` that store the maximal value and its indices in a two dimensional array with `row` and `column` as `int` type and `maxValue` as `double` type.

Write the following method that returns the location of the largest element in a two-dimensional array.

```
public static Location locateLargest(double[][] a)
```

The return value is an instance of `Location`. Write a test program that prompts the user to enter a two-dimensional array and displays the location of the largest element in the array. Here is a sample run:

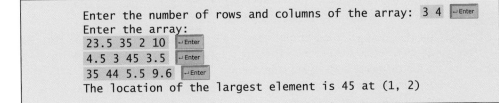

```
Enter the number of rows and columns of the array: 3 4 ↵Enter
Enter the array:
23.5 35 2 10 ↵Enter
4.5 3 45 3.5 ↵Enter
35 44 5.5 9.6 ↵Enter
The location of the largest element is 45 at (1, 2)
```

CHAPTER 9

STRINGS AND TEXT I/O

Objectives

- To use the String class to process fixed strings (§9.2).
- To use the Character class to process a single character (§9.3).
- To use the StringBuilder/StringBuffer class to process flexible strings (§9.4).
- To distinguish among the String, StringBuilder, and StringBuffer classes (§9.2–9.4).
- To learn how to pass arguments to the main method from the command line (§9.5).
- To discover file properties and to delete and rename files using the File class (§9.6).
- To write data to a file using the PrintWriter class (§9.7.1).
- To read data from a file using the Scanner class (§9.7.2).
- (GUI) To open files using a dialog box (§9.8).

9.1 Introduction

problem

Often you encounter problems that involve string processing and file input and output. Suppose you need to write a program that replaces all occurrences of a word in a file with a new word. How do you accomplish this? This chapter introduces strings and text files, which will enable you to solve problems of this type. (Since no new concepts are introduced here, instructors may assign this chapter for students to study on their own.)

9.2 The `String` Class

A *string* is a sequence of characters. In many languages, strings are treated as an array of characters, but in Java a string is an object. The `String` class has 11 constructors and more than 40 methods for manipulating strings. Not only is it very useful in programming, but also it is a good example for learning classes and objects.

9.2.1 Constructing a String

You can create a string object from a string literal or from an array of characters. To create a string from a string literal, use a syntax like this one:

```
String newString = new String(stringLiteral);
```

The argument `stringLiteral` is a sequence of characters enclosed inside double quotes. The following statement creates a `String` object `message` for the string literal `"Welcome to Java"`:

```
String message = new String("Welcome to Java");
```

string literal object

Java treats a string literal as a `String` object. So, the following statement is valid:

```
String message = "Welcome to Java";
```

You can also create a string from an array of characters. For example, the following statements create the string "Good Day":

```
char[] charArray = {'G', 'o', 'o', 'd', ' ', 'D', 'a', 'y'};
String message = new String(charArray);
```

Note

string variable, string object, string value

A `String` variable holds a reference to a `String` object that stores a string value. Strictly speaking, the terms `String` *variable*, `String` *object*, and *string value* are different, but most of the time the distinctions between them can be ignored. For simplicity, the term *string* will often be used to refer to `String` variable, `String` object, and string value.

9.2.2 Immutable Strings and Interned Strings

immutable

A `String` object is immutable; its contents cannot be changed. Does the following code change the contents of the string?

```
String s = "Java";
s = "HTML";
```

The answer is no. The first statement creates a `String` object with the content "Java" and assigns its reference to `s`. The second statement creates a new `String` object with the content "HTML" and assigns its reference to `s`. The first `String` object still exists after the assignment, but it can no longer be accessed, because variable `s` now points to the new object, as shown in Figure 9.1.

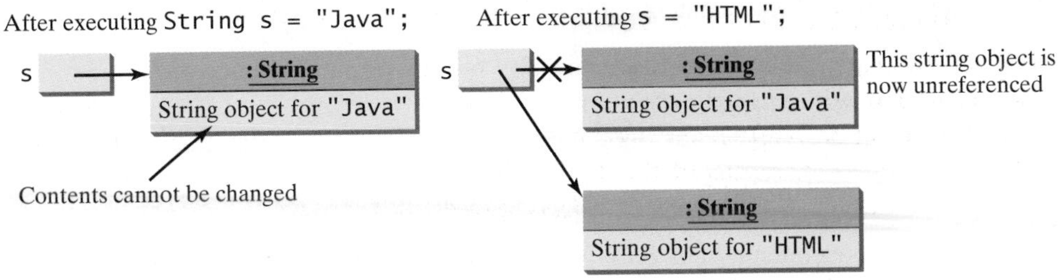
After executing String s = "Java";
s
: String
String object for "Java"
Contents cannot be changed
After executing s = "HTML";
s
: String
String object for "Java"
This string object is now unreferenced
: String
String object for "HTML"

FIGURE 9.1 Strings are immutable; once created, their contents cannot be changed.

Since strings are immutable and are ubiquitous in programming, the JVM uses a unique instance for string literals with the same character sequence in order to improve efficiency and save memory. Such an instance is called *interned*. For example, the following statements: interned string

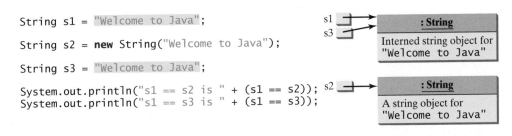

```
String s1 = "Welcome to Java";

String s2 = new String("Welcome to Java");

String s3 = "Welcome to Java";

System.out.println("s1 == s2 is " + (s1 == s2));
System.out.println("s1 == s3 is " + (s1 == s3));
```

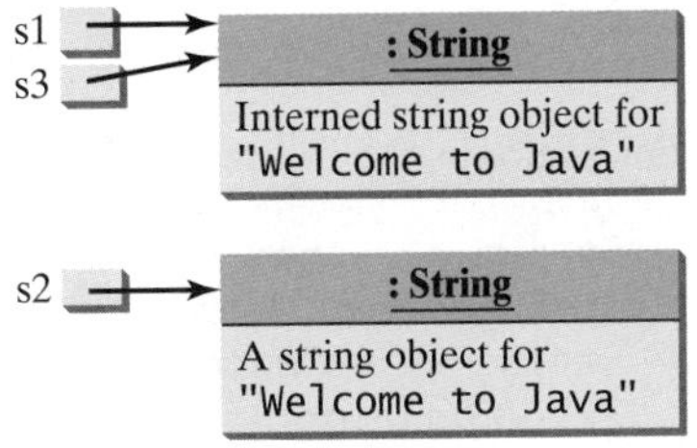
s1
s3
: String
Interned string object for "Welcome to Java"
s2
: String
A string object for "Welcome to Java"

display

```
s1 == s2 is false
s1 == s3 is true
```

In the preceding statements, `s1` and `s3` refer to the same interned string "Welcome to Java", therefore `s1 == s3` is `true`. However, `s1 == s2` is `false`, because `s1` and `s2` are two different string objects, even though they have the same contents.

9.2.3 String Comparisons

The `String` class provides the methods for comparing strings, as shown in Figure 9.2.

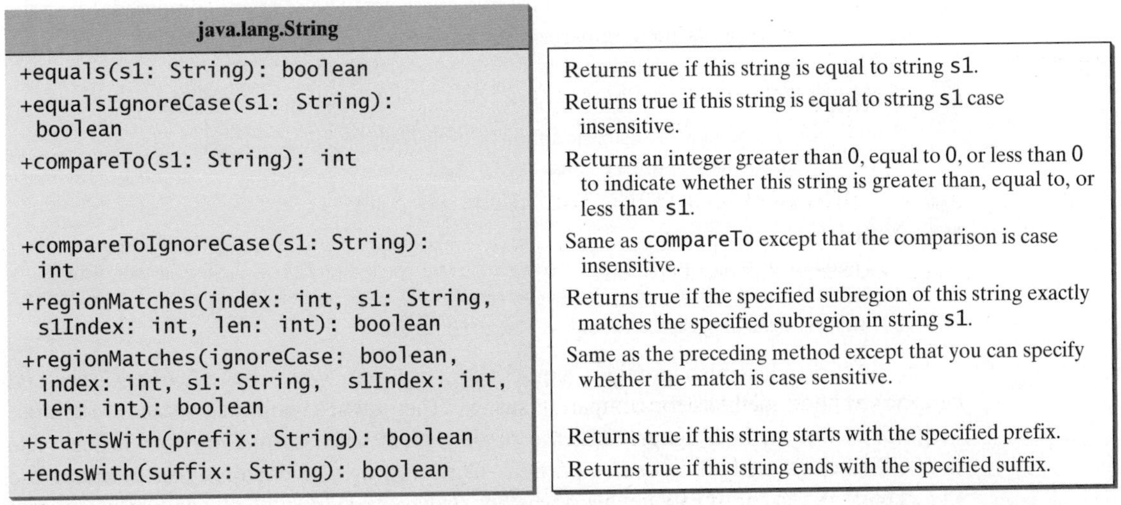
java.lang.String
+equals(s1: String): boolean
+equalsIgnoreCase(s1: String): boolean
+compareTo(s1: String): int
+compareToIgnoreCase(s1: String): int
+regionMatches(index: int, s1: String, s1Index: int, len: int): boolean
+regionMatches(ignoreCase: boolean, index: int, s1: String, s1Index: int, len: int): boolean
+startsWith(prefix: String): boolean
+endsWith(suffix: String): boolean
Returns true if this string is equal to string s1.
Returns true if this string is equal to string s1 case insensitive.
Returns an integer greater than 0, equal to 0, or less than 0 to indicate whether this string is greater than, equal to, or less than s1.
Same as compareTo except that the comparison is case insensitive.
Returns true if the specified subregion of this string exactly matches the specified subregion in string s1.
Same as the preceding method except that you can specify whether the match is case sensitive.
Returns true if this string starts with the specified prefix.
Returns true if this string ends with the specified suffix.

FIGURE 9.2 The `String` class contains the methods for comparing strings.

How do you compare the contents of two strings? You might attempt to use the == operator, as follows:

==

```
if (string1 == string2)
  System.out.println("string1 and string2 are the same object");
else
  System.out.println("string1 and string2 are different objects");
```

However, the == operator checks only whether `string1` and `string2` refer to the same object; it does not tell you whether they have the same contents. Therefore, you cannot use the == operator to find out whether two string variables have the same contents. Instead, you should use the `equals` method. The code given below, for instance, can be used to compare two strings:

`string1.equals(string2)`

```
if (string1.equals(string2))
  System.out.println("string1 and string2 have the same contents");
else
  System.out.println("string1 and string2 are not equal");
```

For example, the following statements display `true` and then `false`.

```
String s1 = new String("Welcome to Java");
String s2 = "Welcome to Java";
String s3 = "Welcome to C++";
System.out.println(s1.equals(s2)); // true
System.out.println(s1.equals(s3)); // false
```

The `compareTo` method can also be used to compare two strings. For example, consider the following code:

`s1.compareTo(s2)`

```
s1.compareTo(s2)
```

The method returns the value `0` if `s1` is equal to `s2`, a value less than `0` if `s1` is lexicographically (i.e., in terms of Unicode ordering) less than `s2`, and a value greater than `0` if `s1` is lexicographically greater than `s2`.

The actual value returned from the `compareTo` method depends on the offset of the first two distinct characters in `s1` and `s2` from left to right. For example, suppose `s1` is `"abc"` and `s2` is `"abg"`, and `s1.compareTo(s2)` returns `-4`. The first two characters (`a` vs. `a`) from `s1` and `s2` are compared. Because they are equal, the second two characters (`b` vs. `b`) are compared. Because they are also equal, the third two characters (`c` vs. `g`) are compared. Since the character `c` is `4` less than `g`, the comparison returns `-4`.

Caution

Syntax errors will occur if you compare strings by using comparison operators, such as >, >=, <, or <=. Instead, you have to use `s1.compareTo(s2)`.

Note

The `equals` method returns `true` if two strings are equal and `false` if they are not. The `compareTo` method returns `0`, a positive integer, or a negative integer, depending on whether one string is equal to, greater than, or less than the other string.

The `String` class also provides `equalsIgnoreCase`, `compareToIgnoreCase`, and `regionMatches` methods for comparing strings. The `equalsIgnoreCase` and `compareToIgnoreCase` methods ignore the case of the letters when comparing two strings. The `regionMatches` method compares portions of two strings for equality. You can also use `str.startsWith(prefix)` to check whether string `str` starts with a specified prefix, and `str.endsWith(suffix)` to check whether string `str` ends with a specified `suffix`.

9.2.4 String Length, Characters, and Combining Strings

The `String` class provides the methods for obtaining length, retrieving individual characters, and concatenating strings, as shown in Figure 9.3.

java.lang.String	
+length(): int	Returns the number of characters in this string.
+charAt(index: int): char	Returns the character at the specified index from this string.
+concat(s1: String): String	Returns a new string that concatenates this string with string s1.

FIGURE 9.3 The `String` class contains the methods for getting string length, individual characters, and combining strings.

You can get the length of a string by invoking its `length()` method. For example, `message.length()` returns the length of the string `message`. **length()**

Caution

`length` is a method in the `String` class but is a property of an array object. So you have to use `s.length()` to get the number of characters in string `s`, and `a.length` to get the number of elements in array `a`. **length()**

The `s.charAt(index)` method can be used to retrieve a specific character in a string `s`, where the index is between `0` and `s.length()-1`. For example, `message.charAt(0)` returns the character `W`, as shown in Figure 9.4. **charAt(index)**

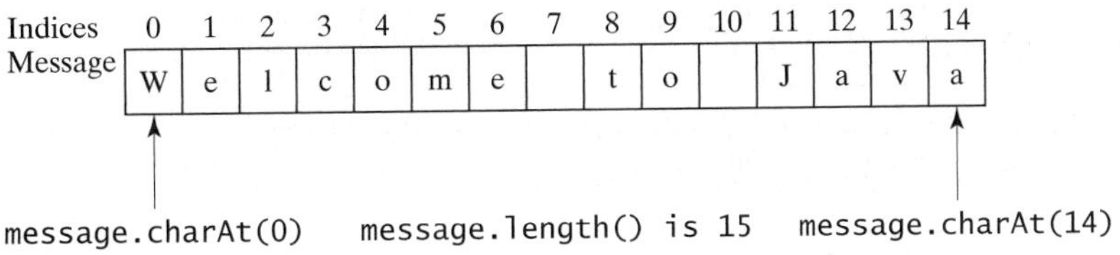
Indices 0 1 2 3 4 5 6 7 8 9 10 11 12 13 14
Message
W e l c o m e t o J a v a
message.charAt(0)
message.length() is 15
message.charAt(14)

FIGURE 9.4 A `String` object is represented using an array internally.

Note

When you use a string, you often know its literal value. For convenience, Java allows you to use the string literal to refer directly to strings without creating new variables. Thus, `"Welcome to Java".charAt(0)` is correct and returns `W`. string literal

Note

A string value is represented using a private array variable internally. The array cannot be accessed outside of the `String` class. The `String` class provides many public methods, such as `length()` and `charAt(index)`, to retrieve the array information. This is a good example of encapsulation: the data field of the class is hidden from the user through the private modifier, and thus the user cannot directly manipulate it. If the array were not private, the user would be able to change the string content by modifying the array. This would violate the tenet that the `String` class is immutable. encapsulating string

Caution

Attempting to access characters in a string `s` out of bounds is a common programming error. To avoid it, make sure that you do not use an index beyond `s.length() - 1`. For example, `s.charAt(s.length())` would cause a `StringIndexOutOfBoundsException`. string index range

You can use the **concat** method to concatenate two strings. The statement shown below, for example, concatenates strings **s1** and **s2** into **s3**:

s1.concat(s2)

```
String s3 = s1.concat(s2);
```

Since string concatenation is heavily used in programming, Java provides a convenient way to accomplish it. You can use the plus (+) sign to concatenate two or more strings. So the above statement is equivalent to

s1 + s2

```
String s3 = s1 + s2;
```

The following code combines the strings **message**, **" and "**, and **"HTML"** into one string:

```
String myString = message + " and " + "HTML";
```

Recall that the + sign can also concatenate a number with a string. In this case, the number is converted into a string and then concatenated. Note that at least one of the operands must be a string in order for concatenation to take place.

9.2.5 Obtaining Substrings

You can obtain a single character from a string using the **charAt** method, as shown in Figure 9.3. You can also obtain a substring from a string using the **substring** method in the **String** class, as shown in Figure 9.5.

java.lang.String	
+substring(beginIndex: int): String	Returns this string's substring that begins with the character at the specified beginIndex and extends to the end of the string, as shown in Figure 9.6.
+substring(beginIndex: int, endIndex: int): String	Returns this string's substring that begins at the specified beginIndex and extends to the character at index endIndex – 1, as shown in Figure 9.6. Note that the character at endIndex is not part of the substring.

Figure 9.5 The **String** class contains the methods for obtaining substrings.

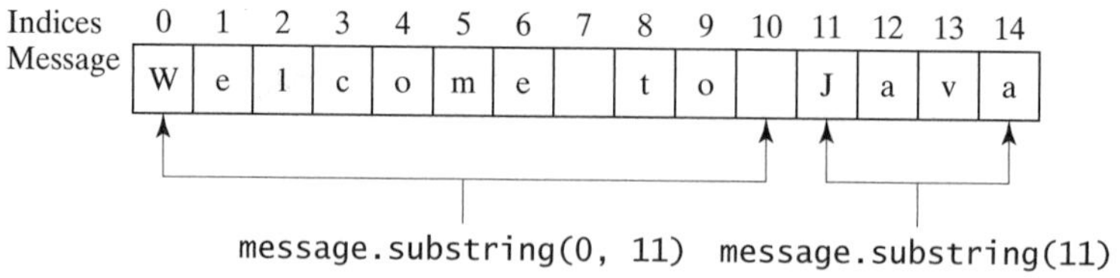
Indices
Message
0 1 2 3 4 5 6 7 8 9 10 11 12 13 14
W e l c o m e t o J a v a
message.substring(0, 11)
message.substring(11)

Figure 9.6 The **substring** method obtains a substring from a string.

For example,

```
String message = "Welcome to Java".substring(0, 11) + "HTML";
```

The string **message** now becomes **"Welcome to HTML"**.

beginIndex <= endIndex

Note

If **beginIndex** is **endIndex**, **substring(beginIndex, endIndex)** returns an empty string with length **0**. If **beginIndex** > **endIndex**, it would be a runtime error.

9.2.6 Converting, Replacing, and Splitting Strings

The `String` class provides the methods for converting, replacing, and splitting strings, as shown in Figure 9.7.

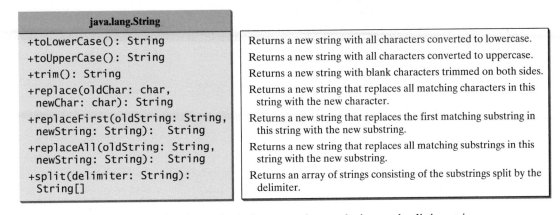

java.lang.String	
+toLowerCase(): String	Returns a new string with all characters converted to lowercase.
+toUpperCase(): String	Returns a new string with all characters converted to uppercase.
+trim(): String	Returns a new string with blank characters trimmed on both sides.
+replace(oldChar: char, newChar: char): String	Returns a new string that replaces all matching characters in this string with the new character.
+replaceFirst(oldString: String, newString: String): String	Returns a new string that replaces the first matching substring in this string with the new substring.
+replaceAll(oldString: String, newString: String): String	Returns a new string that replaces all matching substrings in this string with the new substring.
+split(delimiter: String): String[]	Returns an array of strings consisting of the substrings split by the delimiter.

FIGURE 9.7 The `String` class contains the methods for converting, replacing, and splitting strings.

Once a string is created, its contents cannot be changed. The methods `toLowerCase`, `toUpperCase`, `trim`, `replace`, `replaceFirst`, and `replaceAll` return a new string derived from the original string (without changing the original string!). The `toLowerCase` and `toUpperCase` methods return a new string by converting all the characters in the string to lowercase or uppercase. The `trim` method returns a new string by eliminating blank characters from both ends of the string. Several versions of the `replace` methods are provided to replace a character or a substring in the string with a new character or a new substring.

For example,

```
"Welcome".toLowerCase() returns a new string, welcome.
"Welcome".toUpperCase() returns a new string, WELCOME.
"  Welcome  ".trim() returns a new string, Welcome.
"Welcome".replace('e', 'A') returns a new string, WAlcomA.
"Welcome".replaceFirst("e", "AB") returns a new string, WABlcome.
"Welcome".replace("e", "AB") returns a new string, WABlcomAB.
"Welcome".replace("el", "AB") returns a new string, WABcome.
```

toLowerCase()
toUpperCase()
trim()
replace
replaceFirst
replace
replace

The `split` method can be used to extract tokens from a string with the specified delimiters. For example, the following code split

```
String[] tokens = "Java#HTML#Perl".split("#", 0);
for (int i = 0; i < tokens.length; i++)
  System.out.print(tokens[i] + " ");
```

displays

Java HTML Perl

9.2.7 Matching, Replacing and Splitting by Patterns

You can match, replace, or split a string by specifying a pattern. This is an extremely useful and powerful feature, commonly known as *regular expression*. Regular expressions seem complex to beginning students. For this reason, two simple patterns are used in this section. Please refer to Supplement III.H, "Regular Expressions," for further studies. regular expression

matches(regex)

Let us begin with the matches method in the String class. At first glance, the matches method is very similar to the equals method. For example, the following two statements both evaluate to true.

```
"Java".matches("Java");
"Java".equals("Java");
```

However, the matches method is more powerful. It can match not only a fixed string, but also a set of strings that follow a pattern. For example, the following statements all evaluate to true:

```
"Java is fun".matches("Java.*")
"Java is cool".matches("Java.*")
"Java is powerful".matches("Java.*")
```

"Java.*" in the preceding statements is a regular expression. It describes a string pattern that begins with Java followed by *any* zero or more characters. Here, the substring .* matches any zero or more characters.

The replaceAll, replaceFirst, and split methods can be used with a regular expression. For example, the following statement returns a new string that replaces $, +, or # in "a+b$#c" with the string NNN.

replaceAll(regex)

```
String s = "a+b$#c".replaceAll("[$+#]", "NNN");
System.out.println(s);
```

Here the regular expression [$+#] specifies a pattern that matches $, +, or #. So, the output is aNNNbNNNNNNc.

The following statement splits the string into an array of strings delimited by punctuation marks.

split(regex)

```
String[] tokens = "Java,C?C#,C++".split("[.,:;?]");

for (int i = 0; i < tokens.length; i++)
  System.out.println(tokens[i]);
```

Here the regular expression [.,:;?] specifies a pattern that matches ., ,, :, ;, or ?. Each of these characters is a delimiter for splitting the string. So, the string is split into Java, C, C#, and C++, which are stored into array tokens.

9.2.8 Finding a Character or a Substring in a String

The String class provides several overloaded indexOf and lastIndexOf methods to find a character or a substring in a string, as shown in Figure 9.8.

For example,

indexOf

```
"Welcome to Java".indexOf('W') returns 0.
"Welcome to Java".indexOf('o') returns 4.
"Welcome to Java".indexOf('o', 5) returns 9.
"Welcome to Java".indexOf("come") returns 3.
"Welcome to Java".indexOf("Java", 5) returns 11.
"Welcome to Java".indexOf("java", 5) returns -1.
```

lastIndexOf

```
"Welcome to Java".lastIndexOf('W') returns 0.
"Welcome to Java".lastIndexOf('o') returns 9.
"Welcome to Java".lastIndexOf('o', 5) returns 4.
"Welcome to Java".lastIndexOf("come") returns 3.
"Welcome to Java".lastIndexOf("Java", 5) returns -1.
"Welcome to Java".lastIndexOf("Java") returns 11.
```

java.lang.String	
+indexOf(ch: char): int	Returns the index of the first occurrence of ch in the string. Returns -1 if not matched.
+indexOf(ch: char, fromIndex: int): int	Returns the index of the first occurrence of ch after fromIndex in the string. Returns -1 if not matched.
+indexOf(s: String): int	Returns the index of the first occurrence of string s in this string. Returns -1 if not matched.
+indexOf(s: String, fromIndex: int): int	Returns the index of the first occurrence of string s in this string after fromIndex. Returns -1 if not matched.
+lastIndexOf(ch: int): int	Returns the index of the last occurrence of ch in the string. Returns -1 if not matched.
+lastIndexOf(ch: int, fromIndex: int): int	Returns the index of the last occurrence of ch before fromIndex in this string. Returns -1 if not matched.
+lastIndexOf(s: String): int	Returns the index of the last occurrence of string s. Returns -1 if not matched.
+lastIndexOf(s: String, fromIndex: int): int	Returns the index of the last occurrence of string s before fromIndex. Returns -1 if not matched.

FIGURE 9.8 The `String` class contains the methods for matching substrings.

9.2.9 Conversion between Strings and Arrays

Strings are not arrays, but a string can be converted into an array, and vice versa. To convert a string to an array of characters, use the `toCharArray` method. For example, the following statement converts the string `"Java"` to an array.

toCharArray

```
char[] chars = "Java".toCharArray();
```

So `chars[0]` is `'J'`, `chars[1]` is `'a'`, `chars[2]` is `'v'`, and `chars[3]` is `'a'`.

You can also use the `getChars(int srcBegin, int srcEnd, char[] dst, int dstBegin)` method to copy a substring of the string from index `srcBegin` to index `srcEnd-1` into a character array `dst` starting from index `dstBegin`. For example, the following code copies a substring "3720" in "CS3720" from index `2` to index `6-1` into the character array `dst` starting from index `4`.

getChars

```
char[]  dst = {'J', 'A', 'V', 'A', '1', '3', '0', '1'};
"CS3720".getChars(2, 6, dst, 4);
```

Thus `dst` becomes `{'J', 'A', 'V', 'A', '3', '7', '2', '0'}`.

To convert an array of characters into a string, use the `String(char[])` constructor or the `valueOf(char[])` method. For example, the following statement constructs a string from an array using the `String` constructor.

```
String str = new String(new char[]{'J', 'a', 'v', 'a'});
```

The next statement constructs a string from an array using the `valueOf` method.

valueOf

```
String str = String.valueOf(new char[]{'J', 'a', 'v', 'a'});
```

9.2.10 Converting Characters and Numeric Values to Strings

overloaded `valueOf`

The static `valueOf` method can be used to convert an array of characters into a string. There are several overloaded versions of the `valueOf` method that can be used to convert a character and numeric values to strings with different parameter types, `char`, `double`, `long`, `int`, and `float`, as shown in Figure 9.9.

java.lang.String	
+valueOf(c: char): String	Returns a string consisting of the character c.
+valueOf(data: char[]): String	Returns a string consisting of the characters in the array.
+valueOf(d: double): String	Returns a string representing the double value.
+valueOf(f: float): String	Returns a string representing the float value.
+valueOf(i: int): String	Returns a string representing the int value.
+valueOf(l: long): String	Returns a string representing the long value.
+valueOf(b: boolean): String	Returns a string representing the boolean value.

FIGURE 9.9 The `String` class contains the static methods for creating strings from primitive type values.

For example, to convert a `double` value `5.44` to a string, use `String.valueOf(5.44)`. The return value is a string consisting of the characters `'5'`, `'.'`, `'4'`, and `'4'`.

Note

Use `Double.parseDouble(str)` or `Integer.parseInt(str)` to convert a string to a `double` value or an `int` value.

9.2.11 Formatting Strings

The `String` class contains the static `format` method in the `String` class to create a formatted string. The syntax to invoke this method is

```
String.format(format, item1, item2, ..., itemk)
```

This method is similar to the `printf` method except that the `format` method returns a formatted string, whereas the `printf` method displays a formatted string. For example,

```
String s = String.format("%5.2f", 45.556);
```

creates a formatted string `"45.56"`.

9.2.12 Problem: Checking Palindromes

Video Note
Check palindrome

A string is a palindrome if it reads the same forward and backward. The words "mom," "dad," and "noon," for instance, are all palindromes.

The problem is to write a program that prompts the user to enter a string and reports whether the string is a palindrome. One solution is to check whether the first character in the string is the same as the last character. If so, check whether the second character is the same as the second-to-last character. This process continues until a mismatch is found or all the characters in the string are checked, except for the middle character if the string has an odd number of characters.

To implement this idea, use two variables, say `low` and `high`, to denote the position of two characters at the beginning and the end in a string `s`, as shown in Listing 9.1 (lines 22, 25). Initially, `low` is `0` and `high` is `s.length() – 1`. If the two characters at these positions match, increment `low` by `1` and decrement `high` by `1` (lines 31–32). This process continues until (`low >= high`) or a mismatch is found.

LISTING 9.1 CheckPalindrome.java

```
1 import java.util.Scanner;
2
3 public class CheckPalindrome {
4   /** Main method */
```

```
5    public static void main(String[] args) {
6      // Create a Scanner
7      Scanner input = new Scanner(System.in);
8
9      // Prompt the user to enter a string
10     System.out.print("Enter a string: ");
11     String s = input.nextLine();
12
13     if (isPalindrome(s))
14       System.out.println(s + " is a palindrome");
15     else
16       System.out.println(s + " is not a palindrome");
17   }
18
19   /** Check if a string is a palindrome */
20   public static boolean isPalindrome(String s) {
21     // The index of the first character in the string
22     int low = 0;
23
24     // The index of the last character in the string
25     int high = s.length() - 1;
26
27     while (low < high) {
28       if (s.charAt(low) != s.charAt(high))
29         return false; // Not a palindrome
30
31       low++;
32       high--;
33     }
34
35     return true; // The string is a palindrome
36   }
37 }
```

input string

low index

high index

update indices

```
Enter a string: noon ↵Enter
noon is a palindrome

Enter a string: moon ↵Enter
moon is not a palindrome
```

The `nextLine()` method in the `Scanner` class (line 11) reads a line into `s`. `isPalindrome(s)` checks whether `s` is a palindrome (line 13).

9.2.13 Problem: Converting Hexadecimals to Decimals

Section 5.7 gives a program that converts a decimal to a hexadecimal. This section presents a program that converts a hex number into a decimal.

Given a hexadecimal number $h_n h_{n-1} h_{n-2} \ldots h_2 h_1 h_0$, the equivalent decimal value is

$$h_n \times 16^n + h_{n-1} \times 16^{n-1} + h_{n-2} \times 16^{n-2} + \ldots + h_2 \times 16^2 + h_1 \times 16^1 + h_0 \times 16^0$$

For example, the hex number **AB8C** is

$$10 \times 16^3 + 11 \times 16^2 + 8 \times 16^1 + 12 \times 16^0 = 43916$$

Our program will prompt the user to enter a hex number as a string and convert it into a decimal using the following method:

```
public static int hexToDecimal(String hex)
```

A brute-force approach is to convert each hex character into a decimal number, multiply it by 16^i for a hex digit at the `i`'s position, and add all the items together to obtain the equivalent decimal value for the hex number.

Note that

$$h_n \times 16^n + h_{n-1} \times 16^{n-1} + h_{n-2} \times 16^{n-2} + \ldots + h_1 \times 16^1 + h_0 \times 16^0$$
$$= (\ldots((h_n \times 16 + h_{n-1}) \times 16 + h_{n-2}) \times 16 + \ldots + h_1) \times 16 + h_0$$

This observation leads to the following efficient algorithm for converting a hex string to a decimal number:

```
int decimalValue = 0;
for (int i = 0; i < hex.length(); i++) {
  char hexChar = hex.charAt(i);
  decimalValue = decimalValue * 16 + hexCharToDecimal(hexChar);
}
```

Here is a trace of the algorithm for hex number `AB8C`:

	i	hexChar	hexCharToDecimal(hexChar)	decimalValue
before the loop				0
after the 1st iteration	0	A	10	10
after the 2nd iteration	1	B	11	10 * 16 + 11
after the 3rd iteration	2	8	8	(10 * 16 + 11) * 16 + 8
after the 4th iteration	3	C	12	((10 * 16 + 11) * 16 + 8) * 16 + 12

Listing 9.2 gives the complete program.

LISTING 9.2 `HexToDecimalConversion.java`

input string

hex to decimal

```
import java.util.Scanner;

public class HexToDecimalConversion {
  /** Main method */
  public static void main(String[] args) {
    // Create a Scanner
    Scanner input = new Scanner(System.in);

    // Prompt the user to enter a string
    System.out.print("Enter a hex number: ");
    String hex = input.nextLine();

    System.out.println("The decimal value for hex number "
      + hex + " is " + hexToDecimal(hex.toUpperCase()));
  }

  public static int hexToDecimal(String hex) {
    int decimalValue = 0;
    for (int i = 0; i < hex.length(); i++) {
      char hexChar = hex.charAt(i);
      decimalValue = decimalValue * 16 + hexCharToDecimal(hexChar);
    }

```

```
24     return decimalValue;
25   }
26
27   public static int hexCharToDecimal(char ch) {
28     if (ch >= 'A' && ch <= 'F')
29       return 10 + ch - 'A';
30     else // ch is '0', '1', ..., or '9'
31       return ch - '0';
32   }
33 }
```

hex char to decimal

```
Enter a hex number: AB8C ↵Enter
The decimal value for hex number AB8C is 43916
```

```
Enter a hex number: af71 ↵Enter
The decimal value for hex number af71 is 44913
```

The program reads a string from the console (line 11), and invokes the `hexToDecimal` method to convert a hex string to decimal number (line 14). The characters can be in either lowercase or uppercase. They are converted to uppercase before invoking the `hexToDecimal` method (line 14).

The `hexToDecimal` method is defined in lines 17–25 to return an integer. The length of the string is determined by invoking `hex.length()` in line 19.

The `hexCharToDecimal` method is defined in lines 27–32 to return a decimal value for a hex character. The character can be in either lowercase or uppercase. Recall that to subtract two characters is to subtract their Unicodes. For example, `'5' - '0'` is `5`.

9.3 The **Character** Class

Java provides a wrapper class for every primitive data type. These classes are `Character`, `Boolean`, `Byte`, `Short`, `Integer`, `Long`, `Float`, and `Double` for `char`, `boolean`, `byte`, `short`, `int`, `long`, `float`, and `double`. All these classes are in the `java.lang` package. They enable the primitive data values to be treated as objects. They also contain useful methods for processing primitive values. This section introduces the `Character` class. The other wrapper classes will be introduced in Chapter 14, "Abstract Classes and Interfaces."

The `Character` class has a constructor and several methods for determining a character's category (uppercase, lowercase, digit, and so on) and for converting characters from uppercase to lowercase, and vice versa, as shown in Figure 9.10.

You can create a `Character` object from a `char` value. For example, the following statement creates a `Character` object for the character `'a'`.

```
Character character = new Character('a');
```

The `charValue` method returns the character value wrapped in the `Character` object. The `compareTo` method compares this character with another character and returns an integer that is the difference between the Unicodes of this character and the other character. The `equals` method returns `true` if and only if the two characters are the same. For example, suppose `charObject` is `new Character('b')`:

```
charObject.compareTo(new Character('a')) returns 1
charObject.compareTo(new Character('b')) returns 0
charObject.compareTo(new Character('c')) returns -1
charObject.compareTo(new Character('d')) returns -2
```

java.lang.Character	
+Character(value: char)	Constructs a character object with char value.
+charValue(): char	Returns the char value from this object.
+compareTo(anotherCharacter: Character): int	Compares this character with another.
+equals(anotherCharacter: Character): boolean	Returns true if this character is equal to another.
+isDigit(ch: char): boolean	Returns true if the specified character is a digit.
+isLetter(ch: char): boolean	Returns true if the specified character is a letter.
+isLetterOrDigit(ch: char): boolean	Returns true if the character is a letter or a digit.
+isLowerCase(ch: char): boolean	Returns true if the character is a lowercase letter.
+isUpperCase(ch: char): boolean	Returns true if the character is an uppercase letter.
+toLowerCase(ch: char): char	Returns the lowercase of the specified character.
+toUpperCase(ch: char): char	Returns the uppercase of the specified character.

FIGURE 9.10 The `Character` class provides the methods for manipulating a character.

```
charObject.equals(new Character('b')) returns true
charObject.equals(new Character('d')) returns false
```

Most of the methods in the `Character` class are static methods. The `isDigit(char ch)` method returns `true` if the character is a digit. The `isLetter(char ch)` method returns `true` if the character is a letter. The `isLetterOrDigit(char ch)` method returns `true` if the character is a letter or a digit. The `isLowerCase(char ch)` method returns `true` if the character is a lowercase letter. The `isUpperCase(char ch)` method returns `true` if the character is an uppercase letter. The `toLowerCase(char ch)` method returns the lowercase letter for the character, and the `toUpperCase(char ch)` method returns the uppercase letter for the character.

9.3.1 Problem: Counting Each Letter in a String

The problem is to write a program that prompts the user to enter a string and counts the number of occurrences of each letter in the string regardless of case.

Here are the steps to solve this problem:

1. Convert all the uppercase letters in the string to lowercase using the `toLowerCase` method in the `String` class.

2. Create an array, say `counts` of `26 int` values, each of which counts the occurrences of a letter. That is, `counts[0]` counts the number of `a`'s, `counts[1]` counts the number of `b`'s, and so on.

3. For each character in the string, check whether it is a (lowercase) letter. If so, increment the corresponding count in the array.

Listing 9.3 gives the complete program:

LISTING 9.3 CountEachLetter.java

```java
import java.util.Scanner;

public class CountEachLetter {
  /** Main method */
  public static void main(String[] args) {
    // Create a Scanner
    Scanner input = new Scanner(System.in);
```

```
 8
 9     // Prompt the user to enter a string
10     System.out.print("Enter a string: ");
11     String s = input.nextLine();
12
13     // Invoke the countLetters method to count each letter
14     int[] counts = countLetters(s.toLowerCase()) ;
15
16     // Display results
17     for (int i = 0; i < counts.length; i++) {
18       if (counts[i] != 0)
19         System.out.println((char)('a' + i) + " appears  " +
20           counts[i] + ((counts[i] == 1) ? " time" : " times"));
21     }
22   }
23
24   /** Count each letter in the string */
25   public static int[] countLetters(String s ) {
26     int[] counts = new int[26];
27
28     for (int i = 0; i < s.length() ; i++) {
29       if (Character.isLetter(s.charAt(i)) )
30         counts[s.charAt(i) - 'a']++;
31     }
32
33     return counts;
34   }
35 }
```

input string

count letters

count a letter

```
Enter a string: abababx ↵Enter
a appears  3 times
b appears  3 times
x appears  1 time
```

The main method reads a line (line 11) and counts the number of occurrences of each letter in the string by invoking the `countLetters` method (line 14). Since the case of the letters is ignored, the program uses the `toLowerCase` method to convert the string into all lowercase and pass the new string to the `countLetters` method.

The `countLetters` method (lines 25–34) returns an array of `26` elements. Each element counts the number of occurrences of a letter in the string `s`. The method processes each character in the string. If the character is a letter, its corresponding count is increased by `1`. For example, if the character (`s.charAr(i)`) is `'a'`, the corresponding count is `counts['a' - 'a']` (i.e., `counts[0]`). If the character is `'b'`, the corresponding count is `counts['b' - 'a']` (i.e., `counts[1]`), since the Unicode of `'b'` is `1` more than that of `'a'`. If the character is `'z'`, the corresponding count is `counts['z' - 'a']` (i.e., `counts[25]`), since the Unicode of `'z'` is `25` more than that of `'a'`.

9.4 The **StringBuilder/StringBuffer** Class

The `StringBuilder/StringBuffer` class is an alternative to the `String` class. In general, a `StringBuilder/StringBuffer` can be used wherever a string is used. `StringBuilder/StringBuffer` is more flexible than `String`. You can add, insert, or append new contents into a `StringBuilder` or a `StringBuffer`, whereas the value of a `String` object is fixed, once the string is created.

StringBuilder

The StringBuilder class is similar to StringBuffer except that the methods for modifying buffer in StringBuffer are synchronized. Use StringBuffer if it may be accessed by multiple tasks concurrently. Using StringBuilder is more efficient if it is accessed by a single task. The constructors and methods in StringBuffer and StringBuilder are almost the same. This section covers StringBuilder. You may replace StringBuilder by StringBuffer. The program can compile and run without any other changes.

StringBuilder constructors

The StringBuilder class has three constructors and more than 30 methods for managing the builder and modifying strings in the builder. You can create an empty string builder or a string builder from a string using the constructors, as shown in Figure 9.11.

java.lang.StringBuilder	
+StringBuilder()	Constructs an empty string builder with capacity 16.
+StringBuilder(capacity: int)	Constructs a string builder with the specified capacity.
+StringBuilder(s: String)	Constructs a string builder with the specified string.

FIGURE 9.11 The StringBuilder class contains the constructors for creating instances of StringBuilder.

9.4.1 Modifying Strings in the StringBuilder

You can append new contents at the end of a string builder, insert new contents at a specified position in a string builder, and delete or replace characters in a string builder, using the methods listed in Figure 9.12:

java.lang.StringBuilder	
+append(data: char[]): StringBuilder	Appends a char array into this string builder.
+append(data: char[], offset: int, len: int): StringBuilder	Appends a subarray in data into this string builder.
+append(v: *aPrimitiveType*): StringBuilder	Appends a primitive type value as a string to this builder.
+append(s: String): StringBuilder	Appends a string to this string builder.
+delete(startIndex: int, endIndex: int): StringBuilder	Deletes characters from startIndex to endIndex-1.
+deleteCharAt(index: int): StringBuilder	Deletes a character at the specified index.
+insert(index: int, data: char[], offset: int, len: int): StringBuilder	Inserts a subarray of the data in the array to the builder at the specified index.
+insert(offset: int, data: char[]): StringBuilder	Inserts data into this builder at the position offset.
+insert(offset: int, b: *aPrimitiveType*): StringBuilder	Inserts a value converted to a string into this builder.
+insert(offset: int, s: String): StringBuilder	Inserts a string into this builder at the position offset.
+replace(startIndex: int, endIndex: int, s: String): StringBuilder	Replaces the characters in this builder from startIndex to endIndex-1 with the specified string.
+reverse(): StringBuilder	Reverses the characters in the builder.
+setCharAt(index: int, ch: char): void	Sets a new character at the specified index in this builder.

FIGURE 9.12 The StringBuilder class contains the methods for modifying string builders.

The StringBuilder class provides several overloaded methods to append boolean, char, char array, double, float, int, long, and String into a string builder. For example, the following code appends strings and characters into stringBuilder to form a new string, "Welcome to Java".

```
StringBuilder stringBuilder = new StringBuilder();
```

```
stringBuilder.append("Welcome");
stringBuilder.append(' ');
stringBuilder.append("to");
stringBuilder.append(' ');
stringBuilder.append("Java");
```

append

The `StringBuilder` class also contains overloaded methods to insert `boolean`, `char`, `char array`, `double`, `float`, `int`, `long`, and `String` into a string builder. Consider the following code:

```
stringBuilder.insert(11, "HTML and ");
```

insert

Suppose `stringBuilder` contains `"Welcome to Java"` before the `insert` method is applied. This code inserts `"HTML and "` at position 11 in `stringBuilder` (just before `J`). The new `stringBuilder` is `"Welcome to HTML and Java"`.

You can also delete characters from a string in the builder using the two `delete` methods, reverse the string using the `reverse` method, replace characters using the `replace` method, or set a new character in a string using the `setCharAt` method.

For example, suppose `stringBuilder` contains `"Welcome to Java"` before each of the following methods is applied.

`stringBuilder.delete(8, 11)` changes the builder to `Welcome Java`. **delete**
`stringBuilder.deleteCharAt(8)` changes the builder to `Welcome o Java`. **deleteCharAt**
`stringBuilder.reverse()` changes the builder to `avaJ ot emocleW`. **reverse**
`stringBuilder.replace(11, 15, "HTML")` changes the builder to `Welcome to HTML`. **replace**
`stringBuilder.setCharAt(0, 'w')` sets the builder to `welcome to Java`. **setCharAt**

All these modification methods except `setCharAt` do two things:

1. Change the contents of the string builder
2. Return the reference of the string builder

For example, the following statement

```
StringBuilder stringBuilder1 = stringBuilder.reverse();
```

reverses the string in the builder and assigns the reference of the builder to `stringBuilder1`. Thus, `stringBuilder` and `stringBuilder1` both point to the same `StringBuilder` object. Recall that a value-returning method may be invoked as a statement, if you are not interested in the return value of the method. In this case, the return value is simply ignored. For example, in the following statement

ignore return value

```
stringBuilder.reverse();
```

the return value is ignored.

Tip

If a string does not require any change, use `String` rather than `StringBuilder`. Java can perform some optimizations for `String`, such as sharing interned strings.

`String` or `StringBuilder`?

9.4.2 The `toString`, `capacity`, `length`, `setLength`, and `charAt` Methods

The `StringBuilder` class provides the additional methods for manipulating a string builder and obtaining its properties, as shown in Figure 9.13.

java.lang.StringBuilder	
+toString(): String	Returns a string object from the string builder.
+capacity(): int	Returns the capacity of this string builder.
+charAt(index: int): char	Returns the character at the specified index.
+length(): int	Returns the number of characters in this builder.
+setLength(newLength: int): void	Sets a new length in this builder.
+substring(startIndex: int): String	Returns a substring starting at startIndex.
+substring(startIndex: int, endIndex: int): String	Returns a substring from startIndex to endIndex-1.
+trimToSize(): void	Reduces the storage size used for the string builder.

FIGURE 9.13 The `StringBuilder` class contains the methods for modifying string builders.

`capacity()`

The `capacity()` method returns the current capacity of the string builder. The capacity is the number of characters it is able to store without having to increase its size.

`length()`
`setLength(int)`

The `length()` method returns the number of characters actually stored in the string builder. The `setLength(newLength)` method sets the length of the string builder. If the `newLength` argument is less than the current length of the string builder, the string builder is truncated to contain exactly the number of characters given by the `newLength` argument. If the `newLength` argument is greater than or equal to the current length, sufficient null characters (`'\u0000'`) are appended to the string builder so that `length` becomes the `newLength` argument. The `newLength` argument must be greater than or equal to `0`.

`charAt(int)`

The `charAt(index)` method returns the character at a specific `index` in the string builder. The index is `0` based. The first character of a string builder is at index `0`, the next at index `1`, and so on. The `index` argument must be greater than or equal to `0`, and less than the length of the string builder.

length and capacity

Note

The length of the string is always less than or equal to the capacity of the builder. The length is the actual size of the string stored in the builder, and the capacity is the current size of the builder. The builder's capacity is automatically increased if more characters are added to exceed its capacity. Internally, a string builder is an array of characters, so the builder's capacity is the size of the array. If the builder's capacity is exceeded, the array is replaced by a new array. The new array size is `2 * (the previous array size + 1)`.

initial capacity

trimToSize()

Tip

You can use `new StringBuilder(initialCapacity)` to create a `StringBuilder` with a specified initial capacity. By carefully choosing the initial capacity, you can make your program more efficient. If the capacity is always larger than the actual length of the builder, the JVM will never need to reallocate memory for the builder. On the other hand, if the capacity is too large, you will waste memory space. You can use the `trimToSize()` method to reduce the capacity to the actual size.

9.4.3 Problem: Ignoring Nonalphanumeric Characters When Checking Palindromes

Listing 9.1, CheckPalindrome.java, considered all the characters in a string to check whether it was a palindrome. Write a new program that ignores nonalphanumeric characters in checking whether a string is a palindrome.

Here are the steps to solve the problem:

1. Filter the string by removing the nonalphanumeric characters. This can be done by creating an empty string builder, adding each alphanumeric character in the string to a string builder, and returning the string from the string builder. You can use the

isLetterOrDigit(ch) method in the Character class to check whether character ch is a letter or a digit.

2. Obtain a new string that is the reversal of the filtered string. Compare the reversed string with the filtered string using the equals method.

The complete program is shown in Listing 9.4.

LISTING 9.4 PalindromeIgnoreNonAlphanumeric.java

```
import java.util.Scanner;

public class PalindromeIgnoreNonAlphanumeric {
  /** Main method */
  public static void main(String[] args) {
    // Create a Scanner
    Scanner input = new Scanner(System.in);

    // Prompt the user to enter a string
    System.out.print("Enter a string: ");
    String s = input.nextLine();

    // Display result
    System.out.println("Ignoring nonalphanumeric characters, \nis "
      + s + " a palindrome? " + isPalindrome(s));
  }

  /** Return true if a string is a palindrome */
  public static boolean isPalindrome(String s) {
    // Create a new string by eliminating nonalphanumeric chars
    String s1 = filter(s);

    // Create a new string that is the reversal of s1
    String s2 = reverse(s1);

    // Compare if the reversal is the same as the original string
    return s2.equals(s1);
  }

  /** Create a new string by eliminating nonalphanumeric chars */
  public static String filter(String s) {
    // Create a string builder
    StringBuilder stringBuilder = new StringBuilder();

    // Examine each char in the string to skip alphanumeric char
    for (int i = 0; i < s.length(); i++) {
      if (Character.isLetterOrDigit(s.charAt(i))) {
        stringBuilder.append(s.charAt(i));
      }
    }

    // Return a new filtered string
    return stringBuilder.toString();
  }

  /** Create a new string by reversing a specified string */
  public static String reverse(String s) {
    StringBuilder stringBuilder = new StringBuilder(s);
    stringBuilder.reverse(); // Invoke reverse in StringBuilder
    return stringBuilder.toString();
  }
}
```

check palindrome

add letter or digit

```
Enter a string: ab<c>cb?a ↵Enter
Ignoring nonalphanumeric characters,
is ab<c>cb?a a palindrome? true

Enter a string: abcc><?cab ↵Enter
Ignoring nonalphanumeric characters,
is abcc><?cab a palindrome? false
```

The `filter(String s)` method (lines 31–44) examines each character in string `s` and copies it to a string builder if the character is a letter or a numeric character. The `filter` method returns the string in the builder. The `reverse(String s)` method (lines 47–52) creates a new string that reverses the specified string `s`. The `filter` and `reverse` methods both return a new string. The original string is not changed.

The program in Listing 9.1 checks whether a string is a palindrome by comparing pairs of characters from both ends of the string. Listing 9.4 uses the `reverse` method in the `StringBuilder` class to reverse the string, then compares whether the two strings are equal to determine whether the original string is a palindrome.

9.5 Command-Line Arguments

Perhaps you have already noticed the unusual declarations for the `main` method, which has parameter `args` of `String[]` type. It is clear that `args` is an array of strings. The `main` method is just like a regular method with a parameter. You can call a regular method by passing actual parameters. Can you pass arguments to `main`? Yes, of course you can. For example, the `main` method in class `TestMain` is invoked by a method in `A`, as shown below:

```
public class A {
  public static void main(String[] args) {
    String[] strings = {"New York",
      "Boston", "Atlanta"};
    TestMain.main(strings);
  }
}
```

```
public class TestMain {
  public static void main(String[] args) {
    for (int i = 0; i < args.length; i++)
      System.out.println(args[i]);
  }
}
```

A main method is just a regular method. Furthermore, you can pass arguments from the command line.

9.5.1 Passing Strings to the `main` Method

You can pass strings to a `main` method from the command line when you run the program. The following command line, for example, starts the program `TestMain` with three strings: `arg0`, `arg1`, and `arg2`:

```
java TestMain arg0 arg1 arg2
```

`arg0`, `arg1`, and `arg2` are strings, but they don't have to appear in double quotes on the command line. The strings are separated by a space. A string that contains a space must be enclosed in double quotes. Consider the following command line:

```
java TestMain "First num" alpha 53
```

It starts the program with three strings: `"First num"`, `alpha`, and `53`, a numeric string. Since `"First num"` is a string, it is enclosed in double quotes. Note that `53` is actually treated as a string. You can use `"53"` instead of `53` in the command line.

When the `main` method is invoked, the Java interpreter creates an array to hold the command-line arguments and pass the array reference to `args`. For example, if you invoke a program with `n` arguments, the Java interpreter creates an array like this one:

```
args = new String[n];
```

The Java interpreter then passes `args` to invoke the `main` method.

Note

If you run the program with no strings passed, the array is created with `new String[0]`. In this case, the array is empty with length `0`. `args` references to this empty array. Therefore, `args` is not `null`, but `args.length` is `0`.

9.5.2 Problem: Calculator

Video Note
Command-line argument

Suppose you are to develop a program that performs arithmetic operations on integers. The program receives three arguments: an integer followed by an operator and another integer. For example, to add two integers, use this command:

```
java Calculator 2 + 3
```

The program will display the following output:

```
2 + 3 = 5
```

Figure 9.14 shows sample runs of the program.

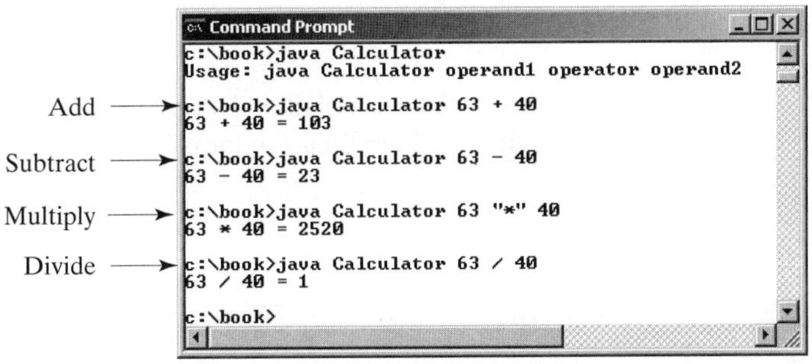
Command Prompt
c:\book>java Calculator
Usage: java Calculator operand1 operator operand2
Add
c:\book>java Calculator 63 + 40
63 + 40 = 103
Subtract
c:\book>java Calculator 63 - 40
63 - 40 = 23
Multiply
c:\book>java Calculator 63 "*" 40
63 * 40 = 2520
Divide
c:\book>java Calculator 63 / 40
63 / 40 = 1
c:\book>

FIGURE 9.14 The program takes three arguments (operand1 operator operand2) from the command line and displays the expression and the result of the arithmetic operation.

The strings passed to the main program are stored in `args`, which is an array of strings. The first string is stored in `args[0]`, and `args.length` is the number of strings passed.

Here are the steps in the program:

- Use `args.length` to determine whether three arguments have been provided in the command line. If not, terminate the program using `System.exit(0)`.
- Perform a binary arithmetic operation on the operands `args[0]` and `args[2]` using the operator specified in `args[1]`.

The program is shown in Listing 9.5.

LISTING 9.5 Calculator.java

```
public class Calculator {
  /** Main method */
  public static void main(String[] args) {
```

check operator

```
4     // Check number of strings passed
5     if (args.length != 3) {
6       System.out.println(
7         "Usage: java Calculator operand1 operator operand2");
8       System.exit(0);
9     }
10
11    // The result of the operation
12    int result = 0;
13
14    // Determine the operator
15    switch (args[1].charAt(0)) {
16      case '+': result = Integer.parseInt(args[0]) +
17                         Integer.parseInt(args[2]);
18                break;
19      case '-': result = Integer.parseInt(args[0]) -
20                         Integer.parseInt(args[2]);
21                break;
22      case '*': result = Integer.parseInt(args[0]) *
23                         Integer.parseInt(args[2]);
24                break;
25      case '/': result = Integer.parseInt(args[0]) /
26                         Integer.parseInt(args[2]);
27    }
28
29    // Display result
30    System.out.println(args[0] + ' ' + args[1] + ' ' + args[2]
31      + " = " + result);
32  }
33 }
```

`Integer.parseInt(args[0])` (line 16) converts a digital string into an integer. The string must consist of digits. If not, the program will terminate abnormally.

special * character

Note

In the sample run, "*" had to be used instead of * for the command

```
java Calculator 63 "*" 40
```

The * symbol refers to all the files in the current directory when it is used on a command line. Therefore, in order to specify the multiplication operator, the * must be enclosed in quote marks in the command line. The following program displays all the files in the current directory when issuing the command `java Test *`:

```
public class Test {
  public static void main(String[] args) {
    for (int i = 0; i < args.length; i++)
      System.out.println(args[i]);
  }
}
```

9.6 The File Class

why file?

Data stored in variables, arrays, and objects are temporary; they are lost when the program terminates. To permanently store the data created in a program, you need to save them in a file on a disk or a CD. The file can be transported and can be read later by other programs. Since data are stored in files, this section introduces how to use the `File` class to obtain file properties and to delete and rename files. The next section introduces how to read/write data from/to text files.

Every file is placed in a directory in the file system. An *absolute file name* contains a file name with its complete path and drive letter. For example, **c:\book\Welcome.java** is the absolute file name for the file **Welcome.java** on the Windows operating system. Here **c:\book** is referred to as the *directory path* for the file. Absolute file names are machine dependent. On the Unix platform, the absolute file name may be **/home/liang/book/Welcome.java**, where **/home/liang/book** is the directory path for the file **Welcome.java**.

absolute file name

directory path

The `File` class is intended to provide an abstraction that deals with most of the machine-dependent complexities of files and path names in a machine-independent fashion. The `File` class contains the methods for obtaining file properties and for renaming and deleting files, as shown in Figure 9.15. However, *the* `File` *class does not contain the methods for reading and writing file contents.*

java.io.File	
`+File(pathname: String)`	Creates a `File` object for the specified path name. The path name may be a directory or a file.
`+File(parent: String, child: String)`	Creates a `File` object for the child under the directory parent. The child may be a file name or a subdirectory.
`+File(parent: File, child: String)`	Creates a `File` object for the child under the directory parent. The parent is a `File` object. In the preceding constructor, the parent is a string.
`+exists(): boolean`	Returns true if the file or the directory represented by the `File` object exists.
`+canRead(): boolean`	Returns true if the file represented by the `File` object exists and can be read.
`+canWrite(): boolean`	Returns true if the file represented by the `File` object exists and can be written.
`+isDirectory(): boolean`	Returns true if the `File` object represents a directory.
`+isFile(): boolean`	Returns true if the `File` object represents a file.
`+isAbsolute(): boolean`	Returns true if the `File` object is created using an absolute path name.
`+isHidden(): boolean`	Returns true if the file represented in the `File` object is hidden. The exact definition of *hidden* is system dependent. On Windows, you can mark a file hidden in the File Properties dialog box. On Unix systems, a file is hidden if its name begins with a period character '.'.
`+getAbsolutePath(): String`	Returns the complete absolute file or directory name represented by the `File` object.
`+getCanonicalPath(): String`	Returns the same as `getAbsolutePath()` except that it removes redundant names, such as "." and "..", from the path name, resolves symbolic links (on Unix platforms), and converts drive letters to standard uppercase (on Win32 platforms).
`+getName(): String`	Returns the last name of the complete directory and file name represented by the `File` object. For example, new `File("c:\\book\\test.dat").getName()` returns `test.dat`.
`+getPath(): String`	Returns the complete directory and file name represented by the `File` object. For example, new `File("c:\\book\\test.dat").getPath()` returns `c:\book\test.dat`.
`+getParent(): String`	Returns the complete parent directory of the current directory or the file represented by the `File` object. For example, new `File("c:\\book\\test.dat").getParent()` returns `c:\book`.
`+lastModified(): long`	Returns the time that the file was last modified.
`+length(): long`	Returns the size of the file, or 0 if it does not exist or if it is a directory.
`+listFile(): File[]`	Returns the files under the directory for a directory `File` object.
`+delete(): boolean`	Deletes this file. The method returns true if the deletion succeeds.
`+renameTo(dest: File): boolean`	Renames this file. The method returns true if the operation succeeds.

FIGURE 9.15 The `File` class can be used to obtain file and directory properties and to delete and rename files.

The file name is a string. The `File` class is a wrapper class for the file name and its directory path. For example, `new File("c:\\book")` creates a `File` object for the directory **c:\book**, and `new File("c:\\book\\test.dat")` creates a `File` object for the file **c:\\book\\test.dat**, both on Windows. You can use the `File` class's `isDirectory()` method to check whether the object represents a directory, and the `isFile()` method to check whether the object represents a file.

Caution

The directory separator for Windows is a backslash (\). The backslash is a special character in Java and should be written as \\ in a string literal (see Table 2.6).

\ in file names

Note

Constructing a `File` instance does not create a file on the machine. You can create a `File` instance for any file name regardless whether it exists or not. You can invoke the `exists()` method on a `File` instance to check whether the file exists.

relative file name

Java directory separator (/)

Do not use absolute file names in your program. If you use a file name such as `"c:\\book\\Welcome.java"`, it will work on Windows but not on other platforms. You should use a file name relative to the current directory. For example, you may create a `File` object using `new File("Welcome.java")` for the file **Welcome.java** in the current directory. You may create a `File` object using `new File("image/us.gif")` for the file **us.gif** under the **image** directory in the current directory. The forward slash (/) is the Java directory separator, which is the same as on Unix. The statement `new File("image/us.gif")` works on Windows, Unix, and any other platform.

Listing 9.6 demonstrates how to create a `File` object and use the methods in the `File` class to obtain its properties. The program creates a `File` object for the file **us.gif**. This file is stored under the **image** directory in the current directory.

Listing 9.6 TestFileClass.java

create a `File`, `exists()`, `length()`, `canRead()`, `canWrite()`, `isDirectory()`, `isFile()`, `isAbsolute()`, `isHidden()`, `getAbsolutePath()`, `lastModified()`

```
1 public class TestFileClass {
2   public static void main(String[] args) {
3     java.io.File file = new java.io.File("image/us.gif");
4     System.out.println("Does it exist? " + file.exists());
5     System.out.println("The file has " + file.length() + " bytes");
6     System.out.println("Can it be read? " + file.canRead());
7     System.out.println("Can it be written? " + file.canWrite());
8     System.out.println("Is it a directory? " + file.isDirectory());
9     System.out.println("Is it a file? " + file.isFile());
10    System.out.println("Is it absolute? " + file.isAbsolute());
11    System.out.println("Is it hidden? " + file.isHidden());
12    System.out.println("Absolute path is " +
13      file.getAbsolutePath());
14    System.out.println("Last modified on " +
15      new java.util.Date(file.lastModified()));
16  }
17 }
```

The `lastModified()` method returns the date and time when the file was last modified, measured in milliseconds since the beginning of Unix time (00:00:00 GMT, January 1, 1970). The `Date` class is used to display it in a readable format in lines 14–15.

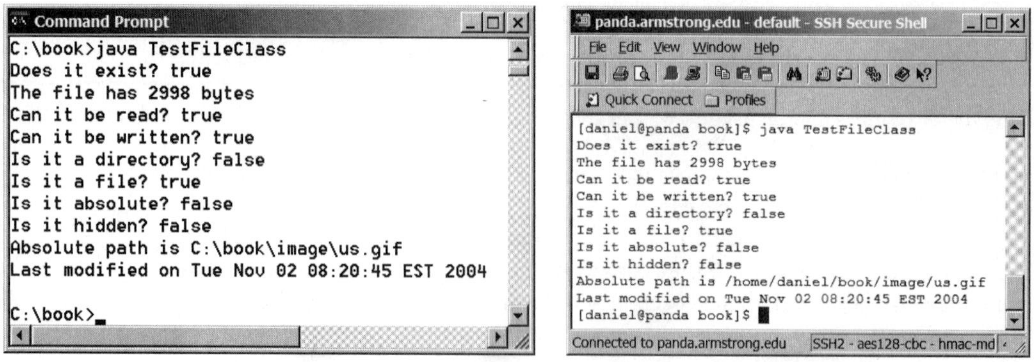
Command Prompt
C:\book>java TestFileClass
Does it exist? true
The file has 2998 bytes
Can it be read? true
Can it be written? true
Is it a directory? false
Is it a file? true
Is it absolute? false
Is it hidden? false
Absolute path is C:\book\image\us.gif
Last modified on Tue Nov 02 08:20:45 EST 2004
C:\book>
panda.armstrong.edu - default - SSH Secure Shell
File Edit View Window Help
Quick Connect Profiles
[daniel@panda book]$ java TestFileClass
Does it exist? true
The file has 2998 bytes
Can it be read? true
Can it be written? true
Is it a directory? false
Is it a file? true
Is it absolute? false
Is it hidden? false
Absolute path is /home/daniel/book/image/us.gif
Last modified on Tue Nov 02 08:20:45 EST 2004
[daniel@panda book]$
Connected to panda.armstrong.edu
SSH2 - aes128-cbc - hmac-md

(a) On Windows (b) On Unix

Figure 9.16 The program creates a `File` object and displays file properties.

Figure 9.16(a) shows a sample run of the program on Windows, and Figure 9.16(b), a sample run on Unix. As shown in the figures, the path-naming conventions on Windows are different from those on Unix.

9.7 File Input and Output

A `File` object encapsulates the properties of a file or a path but does not contain the methods for creating a file or for reading/writing data from/to a file. In order to perform I/O, you need to create objects using appropriate Java I/O classes. The objects contain the methods for reading/writing data from/to a file. This section introduces how to read/write strings and numeric values from/to a text file using the `Scanner` and `PrintWriter` classes.

9.7.1 Writing Data Using `PrintWriter`

The `java.io.PrintWriter` class can be used to create a file and write data to a text file. First, you have to create a `PrintWriter` object for a text file as follows:

```
PrintWriter output = new PrintWriter(filename);
```

Then, you can invoke the `print`, `println`, and `printf` methods on the `PrintWriter` object to write data to a file. Figure 9.17 summarizes frequently used methods in `PrintWriter`.

java.io.PrintWriter	
`+PrintWriter(file: File)`	Creates a `PrintWriter` object for the specified file object.
`+PrintWriter(filename: String)`	Creates a `PrintWriter` object for the specified file-name string.
`+print(s: String): void`	Writes a string to the file.
`+print(c: char): void`	Writes a character to the file.
`+print(cArray: char[]): void`	Writes an array of characters to the file.
`+print(i: int): void`	Writes an `int` value to the file.
`+print(l: long): void`	Writes a `long` value to the file.
`+print(f: float): void`	Writes a `float` value to the file.
`+print(d: double): void`	Writes a `double` value to the file.
`+print(b: boolean): void`	Writes a `boolean` value to the file.
Also contains the overloaded `println` methods.	A `println` method acts like a `print` method; additionally it prints a line separator. The line-separator string is defined by the system. It is `\r\n` on Windows and `\n` on Unix.
Also contains the overloaded `printf` methods.	The `printf` method was introduced in §3.17, "Formatting Console Output."

FIGURE 9.17 The `PrintWriter` class contains the methods for writing data to a text file.

Listing 9.7 gives an example that creates an instance of `PrintWriter` and writes two lines to the file "scores.txt". Each line consists of first name (a string), middle-name initial (a character), last name (a string), and score (an integer).

LISTING 9.7 `WriteData.java`

```
public class WriteData {
  public static void main(String[] args) throws Exception {
    java.io.File file = new java.io.File("scores.txt");
    if (file.exists()) {
      System.out.println("File already exists");
      System.exit(0);
    }

    // Create a file
    java.io.PrintWriter output = new java.io.PrintWriter(file);
```

throws an exception

create **File** object

file exist?

create **PrintWriter**

print data
close file

```
11
12       // Write formatted output to the file
13       output.print("John T Smith ");
14       output.println(90);
15       output.print("Eric K Jones ");
16       output.println(85);
17
18       // Close the file
19       output.close();
20     }
21 }
```

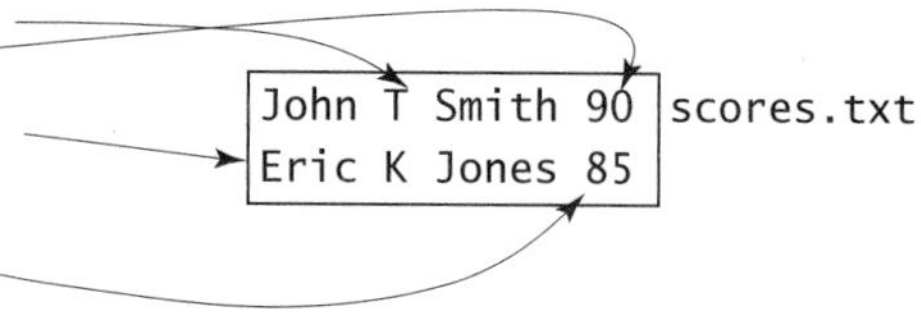
John T Smith 90
Eric K Jones 85
scores.txt

Lines 3–7 check whether the file scores.txt exists. If so, exit the program (line 6).

create a file

Invoking the constructor of **PrintWriter** will create a new file if the file does not exist. If the file already exists, the current content in the file will be discarded.

throws Exception

Invoking the constructor of **PrintWriter** may throw an I/O exception. Java forces you to write the code to deal with this type of exception. You will learn how to handle it in Chapter 13, "Exception Handling." For now, simply declare ***throws Exception*** in the method header (line 2).

print method

You have used the **System.out.print** and **System.out.println** methods to write text to the console. **System.out** is a standard Java object for the console. You can create objects for writing text to any file using **print**, **println**, and **printf** (lines 13–16).

close file

The **close()** method must be used to close the file. If this method is not invoked, the data may not be saved properly in the file.

9.7.2 Reading Data Using Scanner

The **java.util.Scanner** class was used to read strings and primitive values from the console in §2.3, "Reading Input from the Console." A **Scanner** breaks its input into tokens delimited by whitespace characters. To read from the keyboard, you create a **Scanner** for **System.in**, as follows:

```
Scanner input = new Scanner(System.in);
```

To read from a file, create a **Scanner** for a file, as follows:

```
Scanner input = new Scanner(new File(filename));
```

Figure 9.18 summarizes frequently used methods in **Scanner**.

java.util.Scanner	
+Scanner(source: File)	Creates a scanner that produces values scanned from the specified file.
+Scanner(source: String)	Creates a scanner that produces values scanned from the specified string.
+close()	Closes this scanner.
+hasNext(): boolean	Returns true if this scanner has more data to be read.
+next(): String	Returns next token as a string from this scanner.
+nextLine(): String	Returns a line ending with the line separator from this scanner.
+nextByte(): byte	Returns next token as a byte from this scanner.
+nextShort(): short	Returns next token as a short from this scanner.
+nextInt(): int	Returns next token as an int from this scanner.
+nextLong(): long	Returns next token as a long from this scanner.
+nextFloat(): float	Returns next token as a float from this scanner.
+nextDouble(): double	Returns next token as a double from this scanner.
+useDelimiter(pattern: String): Scanner	Sets this scanner's delimiting pattern and returns this scanner.

FIGURE 9.18 The **Scanner** class contains the methods for scanning data.

Listing 9.8 gives an example that creates an instance of Scanner and reads data from the file "scores.txt".

LISTING 9.8 ReadData.java

```
1 import java.util.Scanner;
2
3 public class ReadData {
4   public static void main(String[] args) throws Exception {
5     // Create a File instance
6     java.io.File file = new java.io.File("scores.txt");
7
8     // Create a Scanner for the file
9     Scanner input = new Scanner(file);
10
11    // Read data from a file
12    while (input.hasNext()) {
13      String firstName = input.next();
14      String mi = input.next();
15      String lastName = input.next();
16      int score = input.nextInt();
17      System.out.println(
18        firstName + " " + mi + " " + lastName + " " + score);
19    }
20
21    // Close the file
22    input.close();
23  }
24 }
```

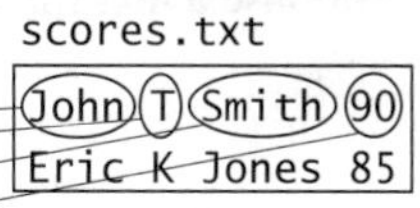
scores.txt
John T Smith 90
Eric K Jones 85

create a File

create a Scanner

has next?
read items

close file

Note that new Scanner(String) creates a Scanner for a given string. To create a Scanner to read data from a file, you have to use the java.io.File class to create an instance of the File using the constructor new File(filename) (line 6), and use new Scanner(File) to create a Scanner for the file (line 9).

File class

Invoking the constructor new Scanner(File) may throw an I/O exception. So the main method declares throws Exception in line 4.

throws Exception

Each iteration in the while loop reads first name, mi, last name, and score from the text file (lines 12–19). The file is closed in line 22.

It is not necessary to close the input file (line 22), but it is a good practice to do so to release the resources occupied by the file.

close file

9.7.3 How Does Scanner Work?

The nextByte(), nextShort(), nextInt(), nextLong(), nextFloat(), nextDouble(), and next() methods are known as *token-reading methods*, because they read tokens separated by delimiters. By default, the delimiters are whitespace. You can use the useDelimiter-(String regex) method to set a new pattern for delimiters.

token-reading method

change delimiter

How does an input method work? A token-reading method first skips any delimiters (whitespace by default), then reads a token ending at a delimiter. The token is then automatically converted into a value of the byte, short, int, long, float, or double type for nextByte(), nextShort(), nextInt(), nextLong(), nextFloat(), and nextDouble(), respectively. For the next() method, no conversion is performed. If the token does not match the expected type, a runtime exception java.util.InputMismatchException will be thrown.

InputMismatchException

Both methods next() and nextLine() read a string. The next() method reads a string delimited by delimiters, but nextLine() reads a line ending with a line separator.

next() vs. nextLine()

line separator

Note

The line-separator string is defined by the system. It is `\r\n` on Windows and `\n` on Unix. To get the line separator on a particular platform, use

```
String lineSeparator = System.getProperty("line.separator");
```

If you enter input from a keyboard, a line ends with the *Enter* key, which corresponds to the `\n` character.

behavior of **nextLine()**

The token-reading method does not read the delimiter after the token. If the `nextLine()` is invoked after a token-reading method, the method reads characters that start from this delimiter and end with the line separator. The line separator is read, but it is not part of the string returned by `nextLine()`.

input from file

Suppose a text file named test.txt contains a line

```
34 567
```

After the following code is executed,

```
Scanner input = new Scanner(new File("test.txt"));
int intValue = input.nextInt();
String line = input.nextLine();
```

`intValue` contains `34` and `line` contains characters `' '`, `'5'`, `'6'`, `'7'`.

input from keyboard

What happens if the input is *entered from the keyboard*? Suppose you enter `34`, the *Enter* key, `567`, and the *Enter* key for the following code:

```
Scanner input = new Scanner(System.in);
int intValue = input.nextInt();
String line = input.nextLine();
```

You will get `34` in `intValue` and an empty string in `line`. Why? Here is the reason. The token-reading method `nextInt()` reads in `34` and stops at the delimiter, which in this case is a line separator (the *Enter* key). The `nextLine()` method ends after reading the line separator and returns the string read before the line separator. Since there are no characters before the line separator, `line` is empty.

9.7.4 Problem: Replacing Text

Suppose you are to write a program named `ReplaceText` that replaces all occurrences of a string in a text file with a new string. The file name and strings are passed as command-line arguments as follows:

```
java ReplaceText sourceFile targetFile oldString newString
```

For example, invoking

```
java ReplaceText FormatString.java t.txt StringBuilder StringBuffer
```

replaces all the occurrences of `StringBuilder` by `StringBuffer` in FormatString.java and saves the new file in t.txt.

Listing 9.9 gives the solution to the problem. The program checks the number of arguments passed to the `main` method (lines 7–11), checks whether the source and target files exist (lines 14–25), creates a `Scanner` for the source file (line 28), creates a `PrintWriter` for the target file, and repeatedly reads a line from the source file (line 32), replaces the text (line 33), and writes a new line to the target file (line 34). You must close the output file (line 38) to ensure that data are saved to the file properly.

LISTING 9.9 ReplaceText.java

```
import java.io.*;
import java.util.*;

public class ReplaceText {
  public static void main(String[] args) throws Exception {
    // Check command-line parameter usage
    if (args.length != 4) {
      System.out.println(
        "Usage: java ReplaceText sourceFile targetFile oldStr newStr");
      System.exit(0);
    }

    // Check if source file exists
    File sourceFile = new File(args[0]);
    if (!sourceFile.exists()) {
       System.out.println("Source file " + args[0] + " does not exist");
       System.exit(0);
    }

    // Check if target file exists
    File targetFile = new File(args[1]);
    if (targetFile.exists()) {
      System.out.println("Target file " + args[1] + " already exists");
      System.exit(0);
    }

    // Create a Scanner for input and a PrintWriter for output
    Scanner input = new Scanner(sourceFile);
    PrintWriter output = new PrintWriter(targetFile);

    while (input.hasNext()) {
      String s1 = input.nextLine();
      String s2 = s1.replaceAll(args[2], args[3]);
      output.println(s2);
    }

    input.close();
    output.close();
  }
}
```

check command usage
source file exists?
target file exists?
create a **Scanner**
create a **PrintWriter**
has next?
read a line
close file

9.8 (GUI) File Dialogs

Java provides the **javax.swing.JFileChooser** class for displaying a file dialog, as shown in Figure 9.19. From this dialog box, the user can choose a file.

Listing 9.10 gives a program that prompts the user to choose a file and displays its contents on the console.

LISTING 9.10 ReadFileUsingJFileChooser.java

```
import java.util.Scanner;
import javax.swing.JFileChooser;

public class ReadFileUsingJFileChooser {
  public static void main(String[] args) throws Exception {
    JFileChooser fileChooser = new JFileChooser();
    if (fileChooser.showOpenDialog(null)
```

create a **JFileChooser**
display file chooser

check status

getSelectedFile

```
8            == JFileChooser.APPROVE_OPTION) {
9          // Get the selected file
10         java.io.File file = fileChooser.getSelectedFile();
11
12         // Create a Scanner for the file
13         Scanner input = new Scanner(file);
14
15         // Read text from the file
16         while (input.hasNext()) {
17           System.out.println(input.nextLine());
18         }
19
20         // Close the file
21         input.close();
22       }
23       else {
24         System.out.println("No file selected");
25       }
26     }
27   }
```

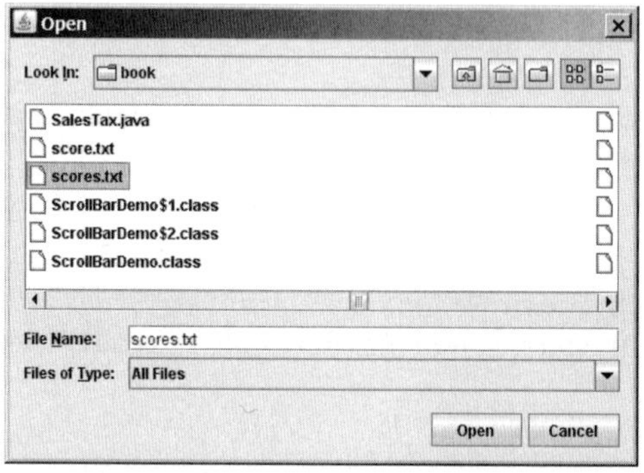
Open
Look In: book
SalesTax.java
score.txt
scores.txt
ScrollBarDemo$1.class
ScrollBarDemo$2.class
ScrollBarDemo.class
File Name: scores.txt
Files of Type: All Files
Open
Cancel

FIGURE 9.19 `JFileChooser` can be used to display a file dialog for opening a file.

showOpenDialog

APPROVE_OPTION

getSelectedFile

The program creates a `JFileChooser` in line 6. The `showOpenDialog(null)` method displays a dialog box, as shown in Figure 9.19. The method returns an `int` value, either `APPROVE_OPTION` or `CANCEL_OPTION`, which indicates whether the *Open* button or the *Cancel* button was clicked.

The `getSelectedFile()` method (line 10) returns the selected file from the file dialog box. Line 13 creates a scanner for the file. The program continuously reads the lines from the file and displays them to the console (lines 16–18).

CHAPTER SUMMARY

1. Strings are objects encapsulated in the `String` class. A string can be constructed using one of the 11 constructors or using a string literal shorthand initializer.

2. A `String` object is immutable; its contents cannot be changed. To improve efficiency and save memory, the JVM stores two literal strings that have the same character sequence in a unique object. This unique object is called an interned string object.

3. You can get the length of a string by invoking its `length()` method, retrieve a character at the specified `index` in the string using the `charAt(index)` method, and use the `indexOf` and `lastIndexOf` methods to find a character or a substring in a string.

4. You can use the concat method to concatenate two strings, or the plus (+) sign to concatenate two or more strings.

5. You can use the substring method to obtain a substring from the string.

6. You can use the equals and compareTo methods to compare strings. The equals method returns true if two strings are equal, and false if they are not equal. The compareTo method returns 0, a positive integer, or a negative integer, depending on whether one string is equal to, greater than, or less than the other string.

7. The Character class is a wrapper class for a single character. The Character class provides useful static methods to determine whether a character is a letter (isLetter(char)), a digit (isDigit(char)), uppercase (isUpperCase(char)), or lowercase (isLowerCase(char)).

8. The StringBuilder/StringBuffer class can be used to replace the String class. The String object is immutable, but you can add, insert, or append new contents into a StringBuilder/StringBuffer object. Use String if the string contents do not require any change, and use StringBuilder/StringBuffer if they change.

9. You can pass strings to the main method from the command line. Strings passed to the main program are stored in args, which is an array of strings. The first string is represented by args[0], and args.length is the number of strings passed.

10. The File class is used to obtain file properties and manipulate files. It does not contain the methods for creating a file or for reading/writing data from/to a file.

11. You can use Scanner to read string and primitive data values from a text file and use PrintWriter to create a file and write data to a text file.

12. The JFileChooser class can be used to display files graphically.

Review Questions

Section 9.2

9.1 Suppose that s1, s2, s3, and s4 are four strings, given as follows:

```
String s1 = "Welcome to Java";
String s2 = s1;
String s3 = new String("Welcome to Java");
String s4 = "Welcome to Java";
```

What are the results of the following expressions?

```
(1) s1 == s2                 (9) s1.indexOf('j')
(2) s2 == s3                 (10) s1.indexOf("to")
(3) s1.equals(s2)            (11) s1.lastIndexOf('a')
(4) s2.equals(s3)            (12) s1.lastIndexOf("o", 15)
(5) s1.compareTo(s2)         (13) s1.length()
(6) s2.compareTo(s3)         (14) s1.substring(5)
(7) s1 == s4                 (15) s1.substring(5, 11)
(8) s1.charAt(0)             (16) s1.startsWith("Wel")
```

```
(17) s1.endsWith("Java")        (21) s1.replace('o', 'T')
(18) s1.toLowerCase()           (22) s1.replaceAll("o", "T")
(19) s1.toUpperCase()           (23) s1.replaceFirst("o", "T")
(20) "  Welcome ".trim()        (24) s1.toCharArray()
```

To create a string "Welcome to Java", you may use a statement like this:

```
String s = "Welcome to Java";
```

or

```
String s = new String("Welcome to Java);
```

Which one is better? Why?

9.2 Suppose that `s1` and `s2` are two strings. Which of the following statements or expressions are incorrect?

```
String s = new String("new string");
String s3 = s1 + s2;
String s3 = s1 - s2;
s1 == s2;
s1 >= s2;
s1.compareTo(s2);
int i = s1.length();
char c = s1(0);
char c = s1.charAt(s1.length());
```

9.3 What is the printout of the following code?

```
String s1 = "Welcome to Java";
String s2 = s1.replace("o", "abc");
System.out.println(s1);
System.out.println(s2);
```

9.4 Let `s1` be `" Welcome "` and `s2` be `" welcome "`. Write the code for the following statements:

- Check whether `s1` is equal to `s2` and assign the result to a Boolean variable `isEqual`.
- Check whether `s1` is equal to `s2`, ignoring case, and assign the result to a Boolean variable `isEqual`.
- Compare `s1` with `s2` and assign the result to an `int` variable `x`.
- Compare `s1` with `s2`, ignoring case, and assign the result to an `int` variable `x`.
- Check whether `s1` has prefix `"AAA"` and assign the result to a Boolean variable `b`.
- Check whether `s1` has suffix `"AAA"` and assign the result to a Boolean variable `b`.
- Assign the length of `s1` to an `int` variable `x`.
- Assign the first character of `s1` to a `char` variable `x`.
- Create a new string `s3` that combines `s1` with `s2`.
- Create a substring of `s1` starting from index `1`.
- Create a substring of `s1` from index `1` to index `4`.
- Create a new string `s3` that converts `s1` to lowercase.
- Create a new string `s3` that converts `s1` to uppercase.
- Create a new string `s3` that trims blank spaces on both ends of `s1`.
- Replace all occurrences of character `e` with `E` in `s1` and assign the new string to `s3`.
- Split `"Welcome to Java and HTML"` into an array `tokens` delimited by a space.
- Assign the index of the first occurrence of character `e` in `s1` to an `int` variable `x`.
- Assign the index of the last occurrence of string `abc` in `s1` to an `int` variable `x`.

9.5 Does any method in the `String` class change the contents of the string?

9.6 Suppose string `s` is created using `new String()`; what is `s.length()`?

9.7 How do you convert a `char`, an array of characters, or a number to a string?

9.8 Why does the following code cause a `NullPointerException`?

```
public class Test {
  private String text;

  public Test(String s) {
    String text = s;
  }

  public static void main(String[] args) {
    Test test = new Test("ABC");
    System.out.println(test.text.toLowerCase());
  }
}
```

9.9 What is wrong in the following program?

```
public class Test {
  String text;

  public void Test(String s) {
    this.text = s;
  }

  public static void main(String[] args) {
    Test test = new Test("ABC");
    System.out.println(test);
  }
}
```

Section 9.3

9.10 How do you determine whether a character is in lowercase or uppercase?

9.11 How do you determine whether a character is alphanumeric?

Section 9.4

9.12 What is the difference between `StringBuilder` and `StringBuffer`?

9.13 How do you create a string builder for a string? How do you get the string from a string builder?

9.14 Write three statements to reverse a string `s` using the `reverse` method in the `StringBuilder` class.

9.15 Write a statement to delete a substring from a string `s` of `20` characters, starting at index `4` and ending with index `10`. Use the `delete` method in the `StringBuilder` class.

9.16 What is the internal structure of a string and a string builder?

9.17 Suppose that `s1` and `s2` are given as follows:

```
StringBuilder s1 = new StringBuilder("Java");
StringBuilder s2 = new StringBuilder("HTML");
```

Show the value of `s1` after each of the following statements. Assume that the statements are independent.

```
(1) s1.append(" is fun");        (7) s1.deleteCharAt(3);
(2) s1.append(s2);               (8) s1.delete(1, 3);
(3) s1.insert(2, "is fun");      (9) s1.reverse();
(4) s1.insert(1, s2);            (10) s1.replace(1, 3, "Computer");
(5) s1.charAt(2);                (11) s1.substring(1, 3);
(6) s1.length();                 (12) s1.substring(2);
```

9.18 Show the output of the following program:

```
public class Test {
  public static void main(String[] args) {
    String s = "Java";
    StringBuilder builder = new StringBuilder(s);
    change(s, builder);

    System.out.println(s);
    System.out.println(builder);
  }

  private static void change(String s, StringBuilder builder) {
    s = s + " and HTML";
    builder.append(" and HTML");
  }
}
```

Section 9.5

9.19 This book declares the `main` method as

```
public static void main(String[] args)
```

Can it be replaced by one of the following lines?

```
public static void main(String args[])

public static void main(String[] x)

public static void main(String x[])

static void main(String x[])
```

9.20 Show the output of the following program when invoked using

1. **java Test I have a dream**
2. **java Test "1 2 3"**
3. **java Test**
4. **java Test** "*"
5. **java Test** *

```
public class Test {
  public static void main(String[] args) {
    System.out.println("Number of strings is " + args.length);
    for (int i = 0; i < args.length; i++)
      System.out.println(args[i]);
  }
}
```

Section 9.6

9.21 What is wrong about creating a `File` object using the following statement?

```
new File("c:\book\test.dat");
```

9.22 How do you check whether a file already exists? How do you delete a file? How do you rename a file? Can you find the file size (the number of bytes) using the `File` class?

9.23 Can you use the `File` class for I/O? Does creating a `File` object create a file on the disk?

Section 9.7

9.24 How do you create a `PrintWriter` to write data to a file? What is the reason to declare `throws Exception` in the main method in Listing 9.7, WriteData.java? What would happen if the `close()` method were not invoked in Listing 9.7?

9.25 Show the contents of the file temp.txt after the following program is executed.

```
public class Test {
  public static void main(String[] args) throws Exception {
    java.io.PrintWriter output = new
      java.io.PrintWriter("temp.txt");
    output.printf("amount is %f %e\r\n", 32.32, 32.32);
    output.printf("amount is %5.4f %5.4e\r\n", 32.32, 32.32);
    output.printf("%6b\r\n", (1 > 2));
    output.printf("%6s\r\n", "Java");
    output.close();
  }
}
```

9.26 How do you create a `Scanner` to read data from a file? What is the reason to define `throws Exception` in the main method in Listing 9.8, ReadData.java? What would happen if the `close()` method were not invoked in Listing 9.8?

9.27 What will happen if you attempt to create a `Scanner` for a nonexistent file? What will happen if you attempt to create a `PrintWriter` for an existing file?

9.28 Is the line separator the same on all platforms? What is the line separator on Windows?

9.29 Suppose you enter `45 57.8 789`, then press the *Enter* key. Show the contents of the variables after the following code is executed.

```
Scanner input = new Scanner(System.in);
int intValue = input.nextInt();
double doubleValue = input.nextDouble();
String line = input.nextLine();
```

9.30 Suppose you enter `45`, the *Enter* key, `57.8`, the *Enter* key, `789`, the *Enter* key. Show the contents of the variables after the following code is executed.

```
Scanner input = new Scanner(System.in);
int intValue = input.nextInt();
double doubleValue = input.nextDouble();
String line = input.nextLine();
```

PROGRAMMING EXERCISES

Sections 9.2–9.3

9.1* (*Checking SSN*) Write a program that prompts the user to enter a social security number in the format DDD-DD-DDDD, where D is a digit. The program displays `"Valid SSN"` for a correct social security number and `"Invalid SSN"` otherwise.

9.2** (*Checking substrings*) You can check whether a string is a substring of another string by using the `indexOf` method in the `String` class. Write your own method for this function. Write a program that prompts the user to enter two strings, and check whether the first string is a substring of the second.

9.3** (*Checking password*) Some Websites impose certain rules for passwords. Write a method that checks whether a string is a valid password. Suppose the password rule is as follows:

- A password must have at least eight characters.
- A password consists of only letters and digits.
- A password must contain at least two digits.

Write a program that prompts the user to enter a password and displays `"Valid Password"` if the rule is followed or `"Invalid Password"` otherwise.

9.4 (*Occurrences of a specified character*) Write a method that finds the number of occurrences of a specified character in the string using the following header:

```
public static int count(String str, char a)
```

For example, `count("Welcome", 'e')` returns `2`. Write a test program that prompts the user to enter a string followed by a character and displays the number of occurrences of the character in the string.

9.5** (*Occurrences of each digit in a string*) Write a method that counts the occurrences of each digit in a string using the following header:

```
public static int[] count(String s)
```

The method counts how many times a digit appears in the string. The return value is an array of ten elements, each of which holds the count for a digit. For example, after executing `int[] counts = count("12203AB3")`, `counts[0]` is `1`, `counts[1]` is `1`, `counts[2]` is `2`, `counts[3]` is `2`.

Write a test program that prompts the user to enter a string and displays the number of occurrences of each digit in the string.

9.6* (*Counting the letters in a string*) Write a method that counts the number of letters in a string using the following header:

```
public static int countLetters(String s)
```

Write a test program that prompts the user to enter a string and displays the number of letters in the string.

9.7* (*Phone keypads*) The international standard letter/number mapping found on the telephone is shown below:

1	2	3
	ABC	DEF
4	5	6
GHI	JKL	MNO
7	8	9
PQRS	TUV	WXYZ
	0	

Write a method that returns a number, given an uppercase letter, as follows:

```
public static int getNumber(char uppercaseLetter)
```

Write a test program that prompts the user to enter a phone number as a string. The input number may contain letters. The program translates a letter (upper- or lowercase) to a digit and leaves all other characters intact. Here is a sample run of the program:

```
Enter a string: 1-800-Flowers
1-800-3569377
```

```
Enter a string: 1800flowers
18003569377
```

9.8* (*Binary to decimal*) Write a method that parses a binary number as a string into a decimal integer. The method header is as follows:

```
public static int binaryToDecimal(String binaryString)
```

For example, binary string 10001 is 17 ($1 \times 2^4 + 0 \times 2^3 + 0 \times 2^2 + 0 \times 2 + 1 = 17$). So, `binaryToDecimal("10001")` returns `17`. Note that `Integer.parseInt("10001", 2)` parses a binary string to a decimal value. Do not use this method in this exercise.

Write a test program that prompts the user to enter a binary string and displays the corresponding decimal integer value.

Section 9.4

9.9** (*Binary to hex*) Write a method that parses a binary number into a hex number. The method header is as follows:

```
public static String binaryToHex(String binaryValue)
```

Write a test program that prompts the user to enter a binary number and displays the corresponding hexadecimal value.

9.10** (*Decimal to binary*) Write a method that parses a decimal number into a binary number as a string. The method header is as follows:

Video Note
Number conversion

```
public static String decimalToBinary(int value)
```

Write a test program that prompts the user to enter a decimal integer value and displays the corresponding binary value.

9.11** (*Sorting characters in a string*) Write a method that returns a sorted string using the following header:

```
public static String sort(String s)
```

For example, `sort("acb")` returns `abc`.

Write a test program that prompts the user to enter a string and displays the sorted string.

9.12** (*Anagrams*) Write a method that checks whether two words are anagrams. Two words are anagrams if they contain the same letters in any order. For example, `"silent"` and `"listen"` are anagrams. The header of the method is as follows:

```
public static boolean isAnagram(String s1, String s2)
```

Write a test program that prompts the user to enter two strings and, if they are anagrams, displays "anagram", otherwise displays "not anagram".

Section 9.5

9.13* (*Passing a string to check palindromes*) Rewrite Listing 9.1 by passing the string as a command-line argument.

9.14* (*Summing integers*) Write two programs. The first program passes an unspecified number of integers as separate strings to the main method and displays their total. The second program passes an unspecified number of integers delimited by one space in a string to the main method and displays their total. Name the two programs Exercise9_14a and Exercise9_14b, as shown in Figure 9.20.

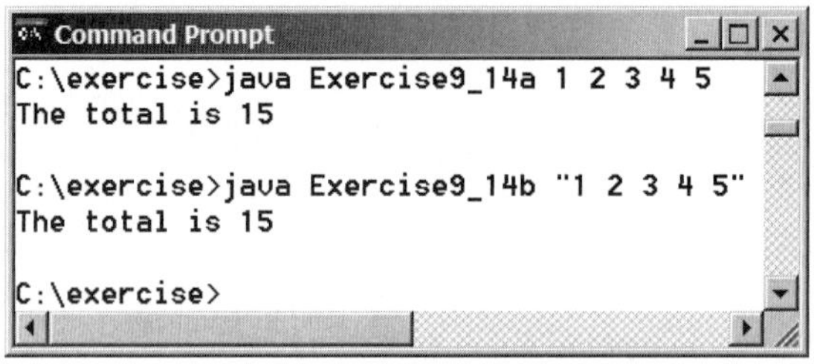
Command Prompt
C:\exercise>java Exercise9_14a 1 2 3 4 5
The total is 15
C:\exercise>java Exercise9_14b "1 2 3 4 5"
The total is 15
C:\exercise>

FIGURE 9.20 The program adds all the numbers passed from the command line.

9.15* (*Finding the number of uppercase letters in a string*) Write a program that passes a string to the main method and displays the number of uppercase letters in a string.

Sections 9.7–9.8

9.16** (*Reformatting Java source code*) Write a program that converts the Java source code from the next-line brace style to the end-of-line brace style. For example, the Java source in (a) below uses the next-line brace style. Your program converts it to the end-of-line brace style in (b).

```
public class Test
{
  public static void main(String[] args)
  {
    // Some statements
  }
}
```

(a) Next-line brace style

```
public class Test {
  public static void main(String[] args) {
    // Some statements
  }
}
```

(b) End-of-line brace style

Your program can be invoked from the command line with the Java source-code file as the argument. It converts the Java source code to a new format. For example, the following command converts the Java source-code file **Test.java** to the end-of-line brace style.

```
java Exercise9_16 Test.java
```

9.17* (*Counting characters, words, and lines in a file*) Write a program that will count the number of characters (excluding control characters '\r' and '\n'), words, and lines, in a file. Words are separated by spaces, tabs, carriage return, or line-feed characters. The file name should be passed as a command-line argument, as shown in Figure 9.21.

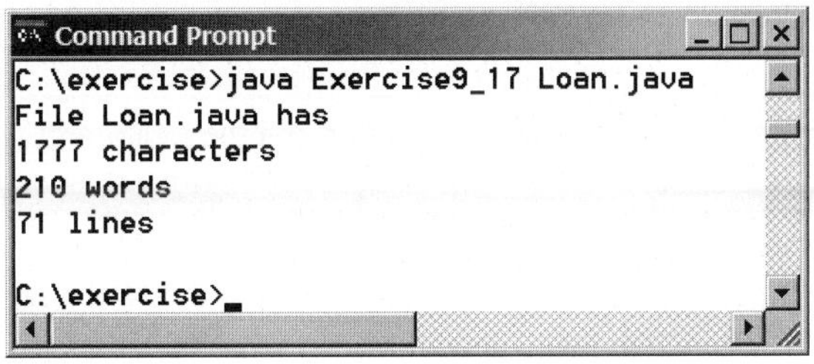
Command Prompt
C:\exercise>java Exercise9_17 Loan.java
File Loan.java has
1777 characters
210 words
71 lines
C:\exercise>_

FIGURE 9.21 The program displays the number of characters, words, and lines in the given file.

9.18* (*Processing scores in a text file*) Suppose that a text file **Exercise9_18.txt** contains an unspecified number of scores. Write a program that reads the scores from the file and displays their total and average. Scores are separated by blanks.

9.19* (*Writing/Reading data*) Write a program to create a file named **Exercise9_19.txt** if it does not exist. Write `100` integers created randomly into the file using text I/O. Integers are separated by spaces in the file. Read the data back from the file and display the sorted data.

9.20** (*Replacing text*) Listing 9.9, ReplaceText.java, gives a program that replaces text in a source file and saves the change into a new file. Revise the program to save the change into the original file. For example, invoking

```
java Exercise9_20 file oldString newString
```

replaces `oldString` in the source file with `newString`.

9.21** (*Removing text*) Write a program that removes all the occurrences of a specified string from a text file. For example, invoking

```
java Exercise9_21 John filename
```

removes string `John` from the specified file.

Comprehensive

9.22** (*Guessing the capitals*) Write a program that repeatedly prompts the user to enter a capital for a state, as shown in Figure 9.22(a). Upon receiving the user input, the program reports whether the answer is correct, as shown in Figure 9.22(b). Assume that `50` states and their capitals are stored in a two-dimensional array, as shown in Figure 9.23. The program prompts the user to answer all ten states' capitals and displays the total correct count.

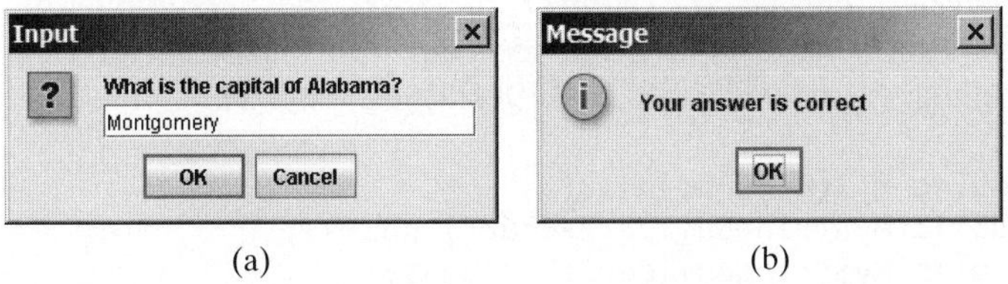
Input
What is the capital of Alabama?
Montgomery
OK
Cancel
(a)
Message
Your answer is correct
OK
(b)

FIGURE 9.22 The program prompts the user to enter the capital in (a) and reports the correctness of the answer.

```
Alabama          Montgomery
Alaska           Juneau
Arizona          Phoenix
...              ...
...              ...
```

FIGURE 9.23 A two-dimensional array stores states and their capitals.

9.23** (*Implementing the* **String** *class*) The **String** class is provided in the Java library. Provide your own implementation for the following methods (name the new class **MyString1**):

```
public MyString1(char[] chars);
public char charAt(int index);
public int length();
public MyString1 substring(int begin, int end);
public MyString1 toLowerCase();
public boolean equals(MyString1 s);
public static MyString1 valueOf(int i);
```

9.24** (*Implementing the* **String** *class*) The **String** class is provided in the Java library. Provide your own implementation for the following methods (name the new class **MyString2**):

```
public MyString2(String s);
public int compare(String s);
public MyString2 substring(int begin);
public MyString2 toUpperCase();
public char[] toChars();
public static MyString2 valueOf(boolean b);
```

9.25 (*Implementing the* **Character** *class*) The **Character** class is provided in the Java library. Provide your own implementation for this class. Name the new class **MyCharacter**.

9.26** (*Implementing the* **StringBuilder** *class*) The **StringBuilder** class is provided in the Java library. Provide your own implementation for the following methods (name the new class **MyStringBuilder1**):

```
public MyStringBuilder1(String s);
public MyStringBuilder1 append(MyStringBuilder1 s);
public MyStringBuilder1 append(int i);
public int length();
public char charAt(int index);
public MyStringBuilder1 toLowerCase();
public MyStringBuilder1 substring(int begin, int end);
public String toString();
```

9.27** (*Implementing the* **StringBuilder** *class*) The **StringBuilder** class is provided in the Java library. Provide your own implementation for the following methods (name the new class **MyStringBuilder2**):

```
public MyStringBuilder2();
public MyStringBuilder2(char[] chars);
public MyStringBuilder2(String s);
public MyStringBuilder2 insert(int offset, MyStringBuilder2 s);
```

```
public MyStringBuilder2 reverse();
public MyStringBuilder2 substring(int begin);
public MyStringBuilder2 toUpperCase();
```

9.28* (*Common prefix*) Write a method that returns the common prefix of two strings. For example, the common prefix of "distance" and "disinfection" is "dis". The header of the method is as follows:

```
public static String prefix(String s1, String s2)
```

If the two strings have no common prefix, the method returns an empty string.

Write a main method that prompts the user to enter two strings and display their common prefix.

9.29** (*New string split method*) The split method in the String class returns an array of strings consisting of the substrings split by the delimiters. However, the delimiters are not returned. Implement the following new method that returns an array of strings consisting of the substrings split by the matches, including the matches.

```
public static String[] split(String s, String regex)
```

For example, split("ab#12#453", "#") returns ab, #, 12, #, 453 in an array of String, and split("a?b?gf#e", "[?#]") returns a, b, ?, b, gf, #, and e in an array of String.

9.30** (*Financial: credit card number validation*) Rewrite Exercise 5.31 using a string input for credit card number. Redesign the program using the following method:

```
/** Return true if the card number is valid */
public static boolean isValid(String cardNumber)

/** Get the result from Step 2 */
public static int sumOfDoubleEvenPlace(String cardNumber)

/** Return this number if it is a single digit; otherwise,
  * return the sum of the two digits */
public static int getDigit(int number)

/** Return sum of odd place digits in number */
public static int sumOfOddPlace(String cardNumber)
```

9.31*** (*Game: hangman*) Write a hangman game that randomly generates a word and prompts the user to guess one letter at a time, as shown in the sample run. Each letter in the word is displayed as an asterisk. When the user makes a correct guess, the actual letter is then displayed. When the user finishes a word, display the number of misses and ask the user whether to continue for another word. Declare an array to store words, as follows:

```
// Use any words you wish
String[] words = {"write", "that", ...};
```

```
(Guess) Enter a letter in word ******* > p
(Guess) Enter a letter in word p****** > r
(Guess) Enter a letter in word pr**r** > p
     p is already in the word
(Guess) Enter a letter in word pr**r** > o
(Guess) Enter a letter in word pro*r** > g
(Guess) Enter a letter in word progr** > n
     n is not in the word
(Guess) Enter a letter in word progr** > m
(Guess) Enter a letter in word progr*m > a
The word is program. You missed 1 time

Do you want to guess for another word? Enter y or n>
```

9.32** (*Checking ISBN*) Use string operations to simplify Exercise 3.9. Enter the first 9 digits of an ISBN number as a string.

9.33*** (*Game: hangman*) Rewrite Exercise 9.31. The program reads the words stored in a text file named **Exercise9_33.txt**. Words are delimited by spaces.

9.34** (*Replacing text*) Revise Exercise9_20 to replace a string in a file with a new string for all files in the specified directory using the following command:

java Exercise9_34 dir oldString newString

9.35* (*Bioinformatics: finding genes*) Biologists use a sequence of letters **A**, **C**, **T**, and **G** to model a genome. A gene is a substring of a genome that starts after a triplet **ATG** and ends before a triplet **TAG**, **TAA**, or **TGA**. Furthermore, the length of a gene string is a multiple of 3 and the gene does not contain any of the triplets **ATG**, **TAG**, **TAA**, and **TGA**. Write a program that prompts the user to enter a genome and displays all genes in the genome. If no gene is found in the input sequence, displays no gene. Here are the sample runs:

```
Enter a genome string: TTATGTTTTAAGGATGGGGCGTTAGTT [Enter]
TTT
GGGCGT
```

```
Enter a genome string: TGTGTGTATAT [Enter]
no gene is found
```

CHAPTER 10

THINKING IN OBJECTS

Objectives

- To create immutable objects from immutable classes to protect the contents of objects (§10.2).
- To determine the scope of variables in the context of a class (§10.3).
- To use the keyword `this` to refer to the calling object itself (§10.4).
- To apply class abstraction to develop software (§10.5).
- To explore the differences between the procedural paradigm and object-oriented paradigm (§10.6).
- To develop classes for modeling composition relationships (§10.7).
- To design programs using the object-oriented paradigm (§§10.8–10.10).
- To design classes that follow the class-design guidelines (§10.11).

10.1 Introduction

The preceding two chapters introduced objects and classes. You learned how to define classes, create objects, and use objects from several classes in the Java API (e.g., `Date`, `Random`, `String`, `StringBuilder`, `File`, `Scanner`, `PrintWriter`). This book's approach is to teach problem solving and fundamental programming techniques before object-oriented programming. This chapter will show how procedural and object-oriented programming differ. You will see the benefits of object-oriented programming and learn to use it effectively.

Our focus here is on class design. We will use several examples to illustrate the advantages of the object-oriented approach. The examples involve designing new classes and using them in applications. We first introduce some language features supporting these examples.

10.2 Immutable Objects and Classes

immutable object

immutable class

Normally, you create an object and allow its contents to be changed later. Occasionally it is desirable to create an object whose contents cannot be changed, once the object is created. We call such an object an *immutable object* and its class an *immutable class*. The `String` class, for example, is immutable. If you deleted the `set` method in the `Circle` class in Listing 8.9, the class would be immutable, because radius is private and cannot be changed without a `set` method.

If a class is immutable, then all its data fields must be private and it cannot contain public `set` methods for any data fields. A class with all private data fields and no mutators is not necessarily immutable. For example, the following `Student` class has all private data fields and no `set` methods, but it is not an immutable class.

`Student` class

```
public class Student {
  private int id;
  private String name;
  private java.util.Date dateCreated;

  public Student(int ssn, String newName) {
    id = ssn;
    name = newName;
    dateCreated = new java.util.Date();
  }

  public int getId() {
    return id;
  }

  public String getName() {
    return name;
  }

  public java.util.Date getDateCreated() {
    return dateCreated;
  }
}
```

As shown in the code below, the data field `dateCreated` is returned using the `getDateCreated()` method. This is a reference to a `Date` object. Through this reference, the content for `dateCreated` can be changed.

```
public class Test {
  public static void main(String[] args) {
    Student student = new Student(111223333, "John");
    java.util.Date dateCreated = student.getDateCreated();
```

```
        dateCreated.setTime(200000); // Now dateCreated field is changed!
    }
}
```

For a class to be immutable, it must meet the following requirements:

- all data fields private;
- no mutator methods;
- no accessor method that returns a reference to a data field that is mutable.

10.3 The Scope of Variables

Chapter 5, "Methods," discussed local variables and their scope rules. Local variables are declared and used inside a method locally. This section discusses the scope rules of all the variables in the context of a class.

Instance and static variables in a class are referred to as the *class's variables* or *data fields*. A variable defined inside a method is referred to as a local variable. The scope of a class's variables is the entire class, regardless of where the variables are declared. A class's variables and methods can appear in any order in the class, as shown in Figure 10.1(a). The exception is when a data field is initialized based on a reference to another data field. In such cases, the other data field must be declared first, as shown in Figure 10.1(b). For consistency, this book declares data fields at the beginning of the class.

```
public class Circle {
  public double findArea() {
    return radius * radius * Math.PI;
  }

  private double radius = 1;
}
```

(a) variable `radius` and method `findArea()` can be declared in any order

```
public class Foo {
  private int i;
  private int j = i + 1;
}
```

(b) `i` has to be declared before `j` because `j`'s initial value is dependent on `i`.

FIGURE 10.1 Members of a class can be declared in any order, with one exception.

You can declare a class's variable only once, but you can declare the same variable name in a method many times in different nonnesting blocks.

If a local variable has the same name as a class's variable, the local variable takes precedence and the class's variable with the same name is *hidden*. For example, in the following program, `x` is defined as an instance variable and as a local variable in the method.

```
public class Foo {
  private int x = 0; // Instance variable
  private int y = 0;

  public Foo() {
  }

  public void p() {
    int x = 1; // Local variable
    System.out.println("x = " + x);
    System.out.println("y = " + y);
  }
}
```

What is the printout for `f.p()`, where `f` is an instance of `Foo`? The printout for `f.p()` is `1` for `x` and `0` for `y`. Here is why:

- x is declared as a data field with the initial value of 0 in the class, but is also declared in the method p() with an initial value of 1. The latter x is referenced in the System.out.println statement.
- y is declared outside the method p(), but is accessible inside it.

Tip

To avoid confusion and mistakes, do not use the names of instance or static variables as local variable names, except for method parameters.

10.4 The this Reference

hidden data fields

The this keyword is the name of a reference that refers to a calling object itself. One of its common uses is to reference a class's *hidden data fields*. For example, a data-field name is often used as the parameter name in a set method for the data field. In this case, the data field is hidden in the set method. You need to reference the hidden data-field name in the method in order to set a new value to it. A hidden static variable can be accessed simply by using the ClassName.StaticVariable reference. A hidden instance variable can be accessed by using the keyword this, as shown in Figure 10.2(a).

```
public class Foo {
  int i = 5;
  static double k = 0;

  void setI(int i) {
    this.i = i;
  }

  static void setK(double k) {
    Foo.k = k;
  }
}
```

(a)

```
Suppose that f1 and f2 are two objects of Foo.

Invoking f1.setI(10) is to execute
   this.i = 10, where this refers f1

Invoking f2.setI(45) is to execute
   this.i = 45, where this refers f2
```

(b)

FIGURE 10.2 The keyword this refers to the calling object that invokes the method.

The this keyword gives us a way to refer to the object that invokes an instance method within the code of the instance method. The line this.i = i means "assign the value of parameter i to the data field i of the calling object." The keyword this refers to the object that invokes the instance method setI, as shown in Figure 10.2(b). The line Foo.k = k means that the value in parameter k is assigned to the static data field k of the class, which is shared by all the objects of the class.

call another constructor

Another common use of the this keyword is to enable a constructor to invoke another constructor of the same class. For example, you can rewrite the Circle class as follows:

```
public class Circle {
  private double radius;

  public Circle(double radius) {
    this.radius = radius;
  }

  public Circle() {
    this(1.0);
  }

  public double getArea() {
    return this.radius * this.radius * Math.PI;
  }
}
```

this must be explicitly used to reference the data field radius of the object being constructed

this is used to invoke another constructor

Every instance variable belongs to an instance represented by this, which is normally omitted

The line `this(1.0)` in the second constructor invokes the first constructor with a `double` value argument.

Tip

If a class has multiple constructors, it is better to implement them using `this(arg-list)` as much as possible. In general, a constructor with no or fewer arguments can invoke the constructor with more arguments using `this(arg-list)`. This often simplifies coding and makes the class easier to read and to maintain.

Note

Java requires that the `this(arg-list)` statement appear first in the constructor before any other statements.

10.5 Class Abstraction and Encapsulation

In Chapter 5, "Methods," you learned about method abstraction and used it in program development. Java provides many levels of abstraction. *Class abstraction* is the separation of class implementation from the use of a class. The creator of a class describes it and lets the user know how it can be used. The collection of methods and fields that are accessible from outside the class, together with the description of how these members are expected to behave, serves as the *class's contract*. As shown in Figure 10.3, the user of the class does not need to know how the class is implemented. The details of implementation are encapsulated and hidden from the user. This is known as *class encapsulation*. For example, you can create a `Circle` object and find the area of the circle without knowing how the area is computed.

class abstraction

class encapsulation

Class implementation is like a black box hidden from the clients
Class
Class Contract (signatures of public methods and public constants)
Clients use the class through the contract of the class

FIGURE 10.3 Class abstraction separates class implementation from the use of the class.

Class abstraction and encapsulation are two sides of the same coin. Many real-life examples illustrate the concept of class abstraction. Consider, for instance, building a computer system. Your personal computer has many components—a CPU, memory, disk, motherboard, fan, and so on. Each component can be viewed as an object that has properties and methods. To get the components to work together, you need know only how each component is used and how it interacts with the others. You don't need to know how the components work internally. The internal implementation is encapsulated and hidden from you. You can build a computer without knowing how a component is implemented.

The computer-system analogy precisely mirrors the object-oriented approach. Each component can be viewed as an object of the class for the component. For example, you might have a class that models all kinds of fans for use in a computer, with properties such as fan size and speed and methods such as start and stop. A specific fan is an instance of this class with specific property values.

As another example, consider getting a loan. A specific loan can be viewed as an object of a `Loan` class. Interest rate, loan amount, and loan period are its data properties, and computing monthly payment and total payment are its methods. When you buy a car, a loan object is created by instantiating the class with your loan interest rate, loan amount, and loan period. You can then use the methods to find the monthly payment and total payment of your loan. As a user of the `Loan` class, you don't need to know how these methods are implemented.

Listing 2.8, ComputeLoan.java, presented a program for computing loan payments. The program cannot be reused in other programs. One way to fix this problem is to define static methods for computing monthly payment and total payment. However, this solution has limitations. Suppose you wish to associate a date with the loan. The ideal way is to create an

Video Note
The **Loan** class

Loan	
-annualInterestRate: double	The annual interest rate of the loan (default: 2.5).
-numberOfYears: int	The number of years for the loan (default: 1).
-loanAmount: double	The loan amount (default: 1000).
-loanDate: java.util.Date	The date this loan was created.
+Loan()	Constructs a default Loan object.
+Loan(annualInterestRate: double, numberOfYears: int,loanAmount: double)	Constructs a loan with specified interest rate, years, and loan amount.
+getAnnualInterestRate(): double	Returns the annual interest rate of this loan.
+getNumberOfYears(): int	Returns the number of the years of this loan.
+getLoanAmount(): double	Returns the amount of this loan.
+getLoanDate(): java.util.Date	Returns the date of the creation of this loan.
+setAnnualInterestRate(annualInterestRate: double): void	Sets a new annual interest rate to this loan.
+setNumberOfYears(numberOfYears: int): void	Sets a new number of years to this loan.
+setLoanAmount(loanAmount: double): void	Sets a new amount for this loan.
+getMonthlyPayment(): double	Returns the monthly payment of this loan.
+getTotalPayment(): double	Returns the total payment of this loan.

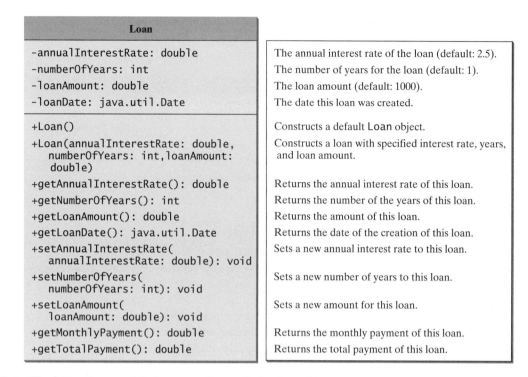

FIGURE 10.4 The Loan class models the properties and behaviors of loans.

object that ties the properties for loan information and date together. Figure 10.4 shows the UML class diagram for the Loan class.

The UML diagram in Figure 10.4 serves as the contract for the Loan class. Throughout this book, you will play the roles of both class user and class developer. The user can use the class without knowing how the class is implemented. Assume that the Loan class is available. We begin by writing a test program that uses the Loan class (Listing 10.1).

LISTING 10.1 TestLoanClass.java

```
import java.util.Scanner;

public class TestLoanClass {
  /** Main method */
  public static void main(String[] args) {
    // Create a Scanner
    Scanner input = new Scanner(System.in);

    // Enter yearly interest rate
    System.out.print(
      "Enter yearly interest rate, for example, 8.25: ");
    double annualInterestRate = input.nextDouble();

    // Enter number of years
    System.out.print("Enter number of years as an integer: ");
    int numberOfYears = input.nextInt();

    // Enter loan amount
    System.out.print("Enter loan amount, for example, 120000.95: ");
```

```
20     double loanAmount =  input.nextDouble();
21
22     // Create a Loan object
23     Loan loan =
24       new Loan(annualInterestRate, numberOfYears, loanAmount);
25
26     // Display loan date, monthly payment, and total payment
27     System.out.printf("The loan was created on %s\n" +
28       "The monthly payment is %.2f\nThe total payment is %.2f\n",
29       loan.getLoanDate().toString(), loan.getMonthlyPayment(),
30       loan.getTotalPayment());
31   }
32 }
```

create Loan object

invoke instance method

invoke instance method

```
Enter yearly interest rate, for example, 8.25: 2.5 ↵Enter
Enter number of years as an integer: 5 ↵Enter
Enter loan amount, for example, 120000.95: 1000 ↵Enter
The loan was created on Sat Jun 10 21:12:50 EDT 2006
The monthly payment is 17.74
The total payment is 1064.84
```

The **main** method reads interest rate, payment period (in years), and loan amount; creates a **Loan** object; and then obtains the monthly payment (line 29) and total payment (line 30) using the instance methods in the **Loan** class.

The **Loan** class can be implemented as in Listing 10.2.

Listing 10.2 Loan.java

```
public class Loan {
  private double annualInterestRate;
  private int numberOfYears;
  private double loanAmount;
  private java.util.Date loanDate;

  /** Default constructor */
  public Loan() {
    this(2.5, 1, 1000);
  }

  /** Construct a loan with specified annual interest rate,
      number of years, and loan amount
    */
  public Loan(double annualInterestRate, int numberOfYears,
      double loanAmount) {
    this.annualInterestRate = annualInterestRate;
    this.numberOfYears = numberOfYears;
    this.loanAmount = loanAmount;
    loanDate = new java.util.Date();
  }

  /** Return annualInterestRate */
  public double getAnnualInterestRate() {
    return annualInterestRate;
  }
```

no-arg constructor

constructor

```

  /** Set a new annualInterestRate */
  public void setAnnualInterestRate(double annualInterestRate) {
    this.annualInterestRate = annualInterestRate;
  }

  /** Return numberOfYears */
  public int getNumberOfYears() {
    return numberOfYears;
  }

  /** Set a new numberOfYears */
  public void setNumberOfYears(int numberOfYears) {
    this.numberOfYears = numberOfYears;
  }

  /** Return loanAmount */
  public double getLoanAmount() {
    return loanAmount;
  }

  /** Set a newloanAmount */
  public void setLoanAmount(double loanAmount) {
    this.loanAmount = loanAmount;
  }

  /** Find monthly payment */
  public double getMonthlyPayment() {
    double monthlyInterestRate = annualInterestRate / 1200;
    double monthlyPayment = loanAmount * monthlyInterestRate / (1 -
      (Math.pow(1 / (1 + monthlyInterestRate), numberOfYears * 12)));
    return monthlyPayment;
  }

  /** Find total payment */
  public double getTotalPayment() {
    double totalPayment = getMonthlyPayment() * numberOfYears * 12;
    return totalPayment;
  }

  /** Return loan date */
  public java.util.Date getLoanDate() {
    return loanDate;
  }
}
```

From a class developer's perspective, a class is designed for use by many different customers. In order to be useful in a wide range of applications, a class should provide a variety of ways for customization through constructors, properties, and methods.

The `Loan` class contains two constructors, four `get` methods, three `set` methods, and the methods for finding monthly payment and total payment. You can construct a `Loan` object by using the no-arg constructor or the one with three parameters: annual interest rate, number of years, and loan amount. When a loan object is created, its date is stored in the `loanDate` field. The `getLoanDate` method returns the date. The three `get` methods, `getAnnualInterest`, `getNumberOfYears`, and `getLoanAmount`, return annual interest rate, payment years, and loan amount, respectively. All the data properties and methods in this class are tied to a specific instance of the `Loan` class. Therefore, they are instance variables or methods.

Important Pedagogical Tip

The UML diagram for the **Loan** class is shown in Figure 10.4. Students should begin by writing a test program that uses the **Loan** class even though they don't know how the **Loan** class is implemented. This has three benefits:

- It demonstrates that developing a class and using a class are two separate tasks.
- It enables you to skip the complex implementation of certain classes without interrupting the sequence of the book.
- It is easier to learn how to implement a class if you are familiar with the class through using it.

For all the examples from now on, you may first create an object from the class and try to use its methods and then turn your attention to its implementation.

10.6 Object-Oriented Thinking

Chapters 1–7 introduced fundamental programming techniques for problem solving using loops, methods, and arrays. The study of these techniques lays a solid foundation for object-oriented programming. Classes provide more flexibility and modularity for building reusable software. This section improves the solution for a problem introduced in Chapter 3 using the object-oriented approach. From the improvements, you will gain insight on the differences between procedural and object-oriented programming and see the benefits of developing reusable code using objects and classes.

Listing 3.5, ComputeBMI.java, presented a program for computing body mass index. The code cannot be reused in other programs. To make it reusable, define a static method to compute body mass index as follows:

```
public static double getBMI(double weight, double height)
```

This method is useful for computing body mass index for a specified weight and height. However, it has limitations. Suppose you need to associate the weight and height with a person's name and birth date. You may declare separate variables to store these values. But these values are not tightly coupled. The ideal way to couple them is to create an object that contains them. Since these values are tied to individual objects, they should be stored in instance data fields. You can define a class named `BMI`, as shown in Figure 10.5.

Video Note
The BMI class

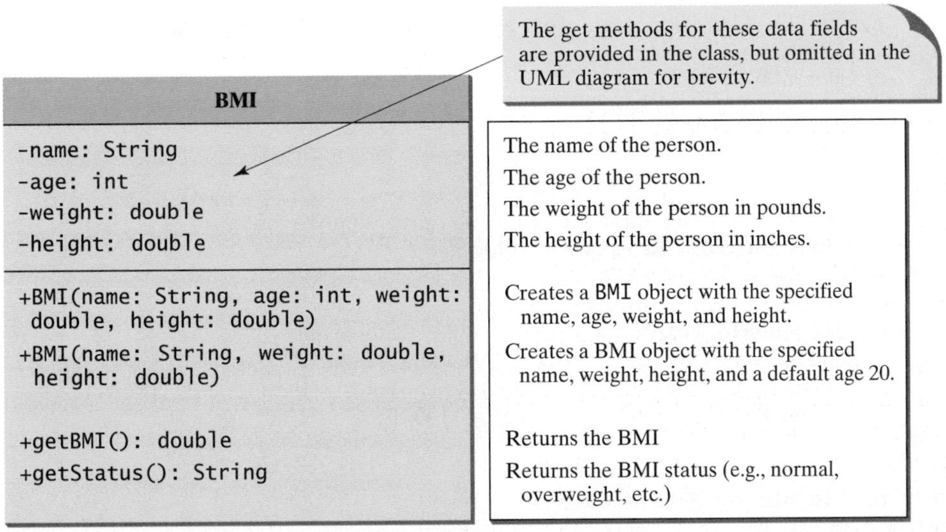
The get methods for these data fields are provided in the class, but omitted in the UML diagram for brevity.
BMI
-name: String
-age: int
-weight: double
-height: double
+BMI(name: String, age: int, weight: double, height: double)
+BMI(name: String, weight: double, height: double)
+getBMI(): double
+getStatus(): String
The name of the person.
The age of the person.
The weight of the person in pounds.
The height of the person in inches.
Creates a BMI object with the specified name, age, weight, and height.
Creates a BMI object with the specified name, weight, height, and a default age 20.
Returns the BMI
Returns the BMI status (e.g., normal, overweight, etc.)

FIGURE 10.5 The `BMI` class encapsulates BMI information.

Assume that the BMI class is available. Listing 10.3 gives a test program that uses this class.

LISTING 10.3 UseBMIClass.java

create an object / invoke instance method

```
 1 public class UseBMIClass {
 2   public static void main(String[] args) {
 3     BMI bmi1 = new BMI("John Doe", 18, 145, 70);
 4     System.out.println("The BMI for " + bmi1.getName() + " is "
 5       + bmi1.getBMI() + " " + bmi1.getStatus());
 6
 7     BMI bmi2 = new BMI("Peter King", 215, 70);
 8     System.out.println("The BMI for " + bmi2.getName() + " is "
 9       + bmi2.getBMI() + " " + bmi2.getStatus());
10   }
11 }
```

```
The BMI for John Doe is 20.81 normal weight
The BMI for Peter King is 30.85 seriously overweight
```

Line 3 creates an object bmi1 for John Doe and line 7 creates an object bmi2 for Peter King. You can use the instance methods getName(), getBMI(), and getStatus() to return the BMI information in a BMI object.

The BMI class can be implemented as in Listing 10.4.

LISTING 10.4 BMI.java

constructor / constructor / getBMI / getStatus

```
public class BMI {
  private String name;
  private int age;
  private double weight; // in pounds
  private double height; // in inches
  public static final double KILOGRAMS_PER_POUND = 0.45359237;
  public static final double METERS_PER_INCH = 0.0254;

  public BMI(String name, int age, double weight, double height) {
    this.name = name;
    this.age = age;
    this.weight = weight;
    this.height = height;
  }

  public BMI(String name, double weight, double height) {
    this(name, 20, weight, height);
  }

  public double getBMI() {
    double bmi = weight * KILOGRAMS_PER_POUND /
      ((height * METERS_PER_INCH) * (height * METERS_PER_INCH));
    return Math.round(bmi * 100) / 100.0;
  }

  public String getStatus() {
    double bmi = getBMI();
    if (bmi < 16)
      return "seriously underweight";
    else if (bmi < 18)
```

```
      return "underweight";
    else if (bmi < 24)
      return "normal weight";
    else if (bmi < 29)
      return "overweight";
    else if (bmi < 35)
      return "seriously overweight";
    else
      return "gravely overweight";
  }

  public String getName() {
    return name;
  }

  public int getAge() {
    return age;
  }

  public double getWeight() {
    return weight;
  }

  public double getHeight() {
    return height;
  }
}
```

The mathematic formula for computing the BMI using weight and height is given in §3.10. The instance method `getBMI()` returns the BMI. Since the weight and height are instance data fields in the object, the `getBMI()` method can use these properties to compute the BMI for the object.

The instance method `getStatus()` returns a string that interprets the BMI. The interpretation is also given in §3.10.

Procedural vs. Object-Oriented Paradigms

This example demonstrates the advantages of the object-oriented paradigm over the procedural paradigm. The procedural paradigm focuses on designing methods. The object-oriented paradigm couples data and methods together into objects. Software design using the object-oriented paradigm focuses on objects and operations on objects. The object-oriented approach combines the power of the procedural paradigm with an added dimension that integrates data with operations into objects.

In procedural programming, data and operations on the data are separate, and this methodology requires sending data to methods. Object-oriented programming places data and the operations that pertain to them in an object. This approach solves many of the problems inherent in procedural programming. The object-oriented programming approach organizes programs in a way that mirrors the real world, in which all objects are associated with both attributes and activities. Using objects improves software reusability and makes programs easier to develop and easier to maintain. Programming in Java involves thinking in terms of objects; a Java program can be viewed as a collection of cooperating objects.

10.7 Object Composition

An object can contain another object. The relationship between the two is called *composition*. In Listing 10.4, you defined the `BMI` class to contain a `String` data field. The relationship between `BMI` and `String` is composition.

Composition is actually a special case of the aggregation relationship. Aggregation models *has-a* relationships and represents an ownership relationship between two objects. The owner object is called an *aggregating object* and its class an *aggregating class*. The subject object is called an *aggregated object* and its class an *aggregated class*.

composition

An object may be owned by several other aggregating objects. If an object is exclusively owned by an aggregating object, the relationship between them is referred to as *composition*. For example, "a student has a name" is a composition relationship between the **Student** class and the **Name** class, whereas "a student has an address" is an aggregation relationship between the **Student** class and the **Address** class, since an address may be shared by several students. In UML, a filled diamond is attached to an aggregating class (e.g., **Student**) to denote the composition relationship with an aggregated class (e.g., **Name**), and an empty diamond is attached to an aggregating class (e.g., **Student**) to denote the aggregation relationship with an aggregated class (e.g., **Address**), as shown in Figure 10.6.

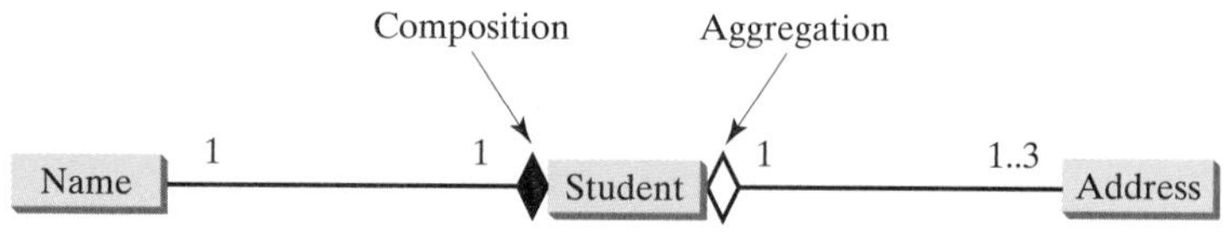
Composition
Aggregation
Name
1
1
Student
1
1..3
Address

FIGURE 10.6 A student has a name and an address.

multiplicity

Each class involved in a relationship may specify a *multiplicity*. A multiplicity could be a number or an interval that specifies how many objects of the class are involved in the relationship. The character * means an unlimited number of objects, and the interval **m..n** means that the number of objects should be between **m** and **n**, inclusive. In Figure 10.6, each student has only one address, and each address may be shared by up to **3** students. Each student has one name, and a name is unique for each student.

An aggregation relationship is usually represented as a data field in the aggregating class. For example, the relationship in Figure 10.6 can be represented as follows:

```
public class Name {
  ...
}
```

Aggregated class

```
public class Student {
  private Name name;
  private Address address;

  ...
}
```

Aggregating class

```
public class Address {
  ...
}
```

Aggregated class

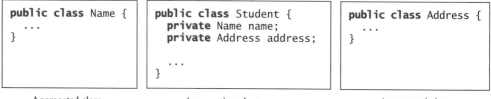

Aggregation may exist between objects of the same class. For example, a person may have a supervisor. This is illustrated in Figure 10.7.

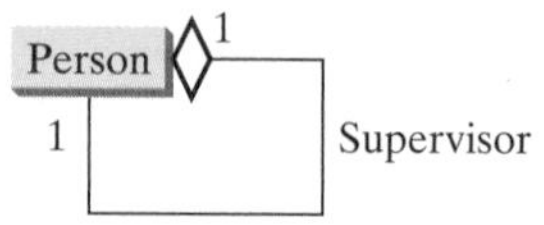
Person
1
1
Supervisor

FIGURE 10.7 A person may have a supervisor.

In the relationship "a person has a supervisor," as shown in Figure 10.7, a supervisor can be represented as a data field in the **Person** class, as follows:

```
public class Person {
  // The type for the data is the class itself
```

```java
    private Person supervisor;

    ...
}
```

If a person may have several supervisors, as shown in Figure 10.8(a), you may use an array to store supervisors, as shown in Figure 10.8(b).

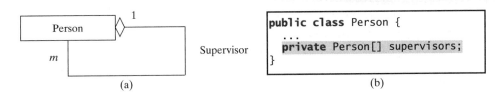

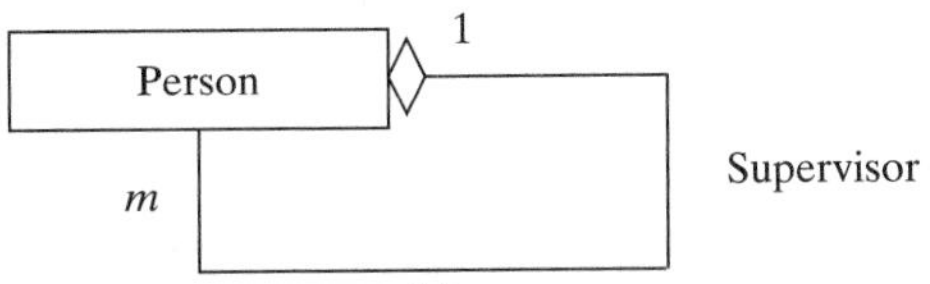
Person
1
m
Supervisor

(a)

```java
public class Person {
  ...
  private Person[] supervisors;
}
```

(b)

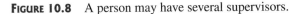

FIGURE 10.8 A person may have several supervisors.

Note

Since aggregation and composition relationships are represented using classes in similar ways, many texts don't differentiate them and call both compositions.

aggregation or composition

10.8 Designing the **Course** Class

This book's philosophy is *teaching by example and learning by doing*. The book provides a wide variety of examples to demonstrate object-oriented programming. The next three sections offer additional examples on designing classes.

Suppose you need to process course information. Each course has a name and has students enrolled. You should be able to add/drop a student to/from the course. You can use a class to model the courses, as shown in Figure 10.9.

Course	
`-courseName: String`	The name of the course.
`-students: String[]`	An array to store the students for the course.
`-numberOfStudents: int`	The number of students (default: 0).
`+Course(courseName: String)`	Creates a course with the specified name.
`+getCourseName(): String`	Returns the course name.
`+addStudent(student: String): void`	Adds a new student to the course.
`+dropStudent(student: String): void`	Drops a student from the course.
`+getStudents(): String[]`	Returns the students for the course.
`+getNumberOfStudents(): int`	Returns the number of students for the course.

FIGURE 10.9 The `Course` class models the courses.

A `Course` object can be created using the constructor `Course(String name)` by passing a course name. You can add students to the course using the `addStudent(String student)` method, drop a student from the course using the `dropStudent(String student)` method, and return all the students for the course using the `getStudents()` method. Suppose the class is available; Listing 10.5 gives a test class that creates two courses and adds students to them.

LISTING 10.5 TestCourse.java

create a course
add a student
number of students
return students

```
public class TestCourse {
  public static void main(String[] args) {
    Course course1 = new Course("Data Structures");
    Course course2 = new Course("Database Systems");

    course1.addStudent("Peter Jones");
    course1.addStudent("Brian Smith");
    course1.addStudent("Anne Kennedy");

    course2.addStudent("Peter Jones");
    course2.addStudent("Steve Smith");

    System.out.println("Number of students in course1: "
      + course1.getNumberOfStudents());
    String[] students = course1.getStudents();
    for (int i = 0; i < course1.getNumberOfStudents(); i++)
      System.out.print(students[i] + ", ");

    System.out.println();
    System.out.print("Number of students in course2: "
      + course2.getNumberOfStudents());
  }
}
```

```
Number of students in course1: 3
Peter Jones, Brian Smith, Anne Kennedy,
Number of students in course2: 2
```

The Course class is implemented in Listing 10.6. It uses an array to store the students for the course. For simplicity, assume that the maximum course enrollment is 100. The array is created using new String[100] in line 3. The addStudent method (line 10) adds a student to the array. Whenever a new student is added to the course, numberOfStudents is increased (line 12). The getStudents method returns the array. The dropStudent method (line 27) is left as an exercise.

LISTING 10.6 Course.java

create students
add a course
return students

```
1 public class Course {
2   private String courseName;
3   private String[] students = new String[100];
4   private int numberOfStudents;
5
6   public Course(String courseName) {
7     this.courseName = courseName;
8   }
9
10  public void addStudent(String student) {
11    students[numberOfStudents] = student;
12    numberOfStudents++;
13  }
14
15  public String[] getStudents() {
16    return students;
17  }
18
```

```
19   public int getNumberOfStudents() {
20     return numberOfStudents;
21   }
22
23   public String getCourseName() {
24     return courseName;
25   }
26
27   public void dropStudent(String student) {
28     // Left as an exercise in Exercise 10.9
29   }
30 }
```

number of students

The array size is fixed to be 100 (line 3) in Listing 10.6. You can improve it to automatically increase the array size in Exercise 10.9.

When you create a Course object, an array object is created. A Course object contains a reference to the array. For simplicity, you can say that the Course object contains the array.

The user can create a Course and manipulate it through the public methods addStudent, dropStudent, getNumberOfStudents, and getStudents. However, the user doesn't need to know how these methods are implemented. The Course class encapsulates the internal implementation. This example uses an array to store students. You may use a different data structure to store students. The program that uses Course does not need to change as long as the contract of the public methods remains unchanged.

10.9 Designing a Class for Stacks

Recall that a stack is a data structure that holds data in a last-in, first-out fashion, as shown in Figure 10.10.

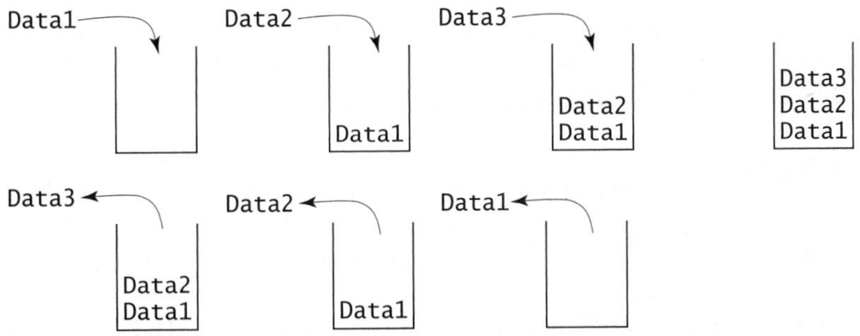
Data1
Data2
Data3
Data1
Data2
Data1
Data3
Data2
Data1
Data3
Data2
Data1
Data2
Data1
Data1

FIGURE 10.10 A stack holds data in a last-in, first-out fashion.

stack

Stacks have many applications. For example, the compiler uses a stack to process method invocations. When a method is invoked, its parameters and local variables are pushed into a stack. When a method calls another method, the new method's parameters and local variables are pushed into the stack. When a method finishes its work and returns to its caller, its associated space is released from the stack.

You can define a class to model stacks. For simplicity, assume the stack holds the int values. So, name the stack class StackOfIntegers. The UML diagram for the class is shown in Figure 10.11.

Video Note
The **StackOfInteger** class

Suppose that the class is available. Let us write a test program in Listing 10.7 that uses the class to create a stack (line 3), stores ten integers 0, 1, 2, . . . , and 9 (line 6), and displays them in reverse order (line 9).

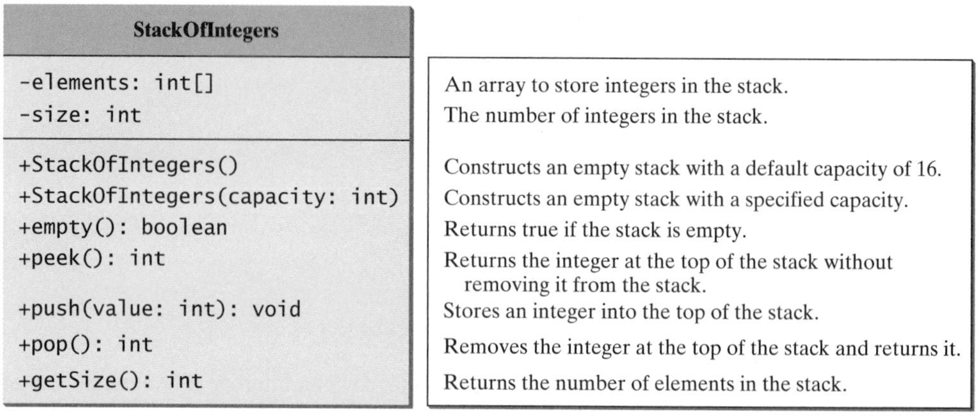
StackOfIntegers
-elements: int[]
-size: int
+StackOfIntegers()
+StackOfIntegers(capacity: int)
+empty(): boolean
+peek(): int
+push(value: int): void
+pop(): int
+getSize(): int
An array to store integers in the stack.
The number of integers in the stack.
Constructs an empty stack with a default capacity of 16.
Constructs an empty stack with a specified capacity.
Returns true if the stack is empty.
Returns the integer at the top of the stack without removing it from the stack.
Stores an integer into the top of the stack.
Removes the integer at the top of the stack and returns it.
Returns the number of elements in the stack.

FIGURE 10.11 The `StackOfIntegers` class encapsulates the stack storage and provides the operations for manipulating the stack.

LISTING 10.7 TestStackOfIntegers.java

create a stack

push to stack

pop from stack

```
public class TestStackOfIntegers {
  public static void main(String[] args) {
    StackOfIntegers stack = new StackOfIntegers();

    for (int i = 0; i < 10; i++)
      stack.push(i);

    while (!stack.empty())
      System.out.print(stack.pop() + " ");
  }
}
```

```
9 8 7 6 5 4 3 2 1 0
```

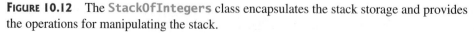

How do you implement the `StackOfIntegers` class? The elements in the stack are stored in an array named `elements`. When you create a stack, the array is also created. The no-arg constructor creates an array with the default capacity of `16`. The variable `size` counts the number of elements in the stack, and `size – 1` is the index of the element at the top of the stack, as shown in Figure 10.12. For an empty stack, `size` is `0`.

The `StackOfIntegers` class is implemented in Listing 10.8. The methods `empty()`, `peek()`, `pop()`, and `getSize()` are easy to implement. To implement `push(int value)`, assign `value` to `elements[size]` if `size < capacity` (line 24). If the stack is full (i.e.,

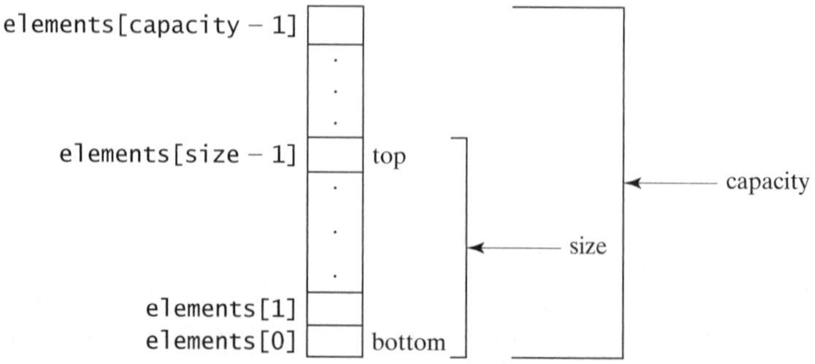
elements[capacity – 1]
elements[size – 1]
top
capacity
size
elements[1]
elements[0]
bottom

FIGURE 10.12 The `StackOfIntegers` class encapsulates the stack storage and provides the operations for manipulating the stack.

`size >= capacity`), create a new array of twice the current capacity (line 19), copy the contents of the current array to the new array (line 20), and assign the reference of the new array to the current array in the stack (line 21). Now you can add the new value to the array (line 24).

LISTING 10.8 StackOfIntegers.java

```
1 public class StackOfIntegers {
2   private int[] elements;
3   private int size;
4   public static final int DEFAULT_CAPACITY = 16;
5
6   /** Construct a stack with the default capacity 16 */
7   public StackOfIntegers() {
8     this(DEFAULT_CAPACITY);
9   }
10
11  /** Construct a stack with the specified maximum capacity */
12  public StackOfIntegers(int capacity) {
13    elements = new int[capacity];
14  }
15
16  /** Push a new integer into the top of the stack */
17  public void push(int value) {
18    if (size >= elements.length) {
19      int[] temp = new int[elements.length * 2];
20      System.arraycopy(elements, 0, temp, 0, elements.length);
21      elements = temp;
22    }
23
24    elements[size++] = value;
25  }
26
27  /** Return and remove the top element from the stack */
28  public int pop() {
29    return elements[--size];
30  }
31
32  /** Return the top element from the stack */
33  public int peek() {
34    return elements[size - 1];
35  }
36
37  /** Test whether the stack is empty */
38  public boolean empty() {
39    return size == 0;
40  }
41
42  /** Return the number of elements in the stack */
43  public int getSize() {
44    return size;
45  }
46 }
```

max capacity 16

double the capacity

add to stack

10.10 Designing the **GuessDate** Class

Listing 3.3, GuessBirthday.java, and Listing 7.6, GuessBirthdayUsingArray.java, presented two programs for guessing birthdays. Both programs use the same data developed with the procedural paradigm. The majority of code in these two programs is to define the five sets of data. You cannot reuse the code in these two programs. To make the code reusable, design a class to encapsulate the data, as defined in Figure 10.13.

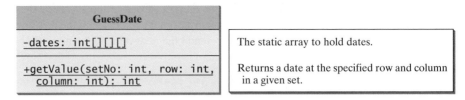

GuessDate	
-dates: int[][][]	The static array to hold dates.
+getValue(setNo: int, row: int, column: int): int	Returns a date at the specified row and column in a given set.

FIGURE 10.13 The GuessDate class defines data for guessing birthdays.

Note that getValue is defined as a static method because it is not dependent on a specific object of the GuessDate class. The GuessDate class encapsulates dates as a private member. The user of this class need not know how dates is implemented or even that the dates field exists in the class. All the user needs to know is how to use this method to access dates. Suppose this class is available. As shown in §3.5, there are five sets of dates. Invoking getValue(setNo, row, column) returns the date at the specified row and column in the given set. For example, getValue(1, 0, 0) returns 2.

Assume that the GuessDate class is available. Listing 10.9 is a test program that uses this class.

LISTING 10.9 UseGuessDateClass.java

```
import java.util.Scanner;

public class UseGuessDateClass {
  public static void main(String[] args) {
    int date = 0; // Date to be determined
    int answer;

    // Create a Scanner
    Scanner input = new Scanner(System.in);

    for (int i = 0; i < 5; i++) {
      System.out.println("Is your birthday in Set" + (i + 1) + "?");
      for (int j = 0; j < 4; j++) {
        for (int k = 0; k < 4; k++)
          System.out.print(GuessDate.getValue(i, j, k) + "  ");
        System.out.println();
      }

      System.out.print("\nEnter 0 for No and 1 for Yes: ");
      answer = input.nextInt();

      if (answer == 1)
        date += GuessDate.getValue(i, 0, 0);
    }

    System.out.println("Your birthday is " + date);
  }
}
```

invoke static method (line 15)

invoke static method (line 23)

```
Is your birthday in Set1?
1  3  5  7
9  11  13  15
17  19  21  23
25  27  29  31
Enter 0 for No and 1 for Yes: 0 ↵Enter
```

```
Is your birthday in Set2?
2  3  6  7
10  11  14  15
18  19  22  23
26  27  30  31
Enter 0 for No and 1 for Yes: 1 ↵Enter

Is your birthday in Set3?
4  5  6  7
12  13  14  15
20  21  22  23
28  29  30  31
Enter 0 for No and 1 for Yes: 0 ↵Enter

Is your birthday in Set4?
8  9  10  11
12  13  14  15
24  25  26  27
28  29  30  31
Enter 0 for No and 1 for Yes: 1 ↵Enter

Is your birthday in Set5?
16  17  18  19
20  21  22  23
24  25  26  27
28  29  30  31
Enter 0 for No and 1 for Yes: 1 ↵Enter

Your birthday is 26
```

Since `getValue` is a static method, you don't need to create an object in order to invoke it. `GuessDate.getValue(i, j, k)` (line 15) returns the date at row `i` and column `k` in Set `i`.

The `GuessDate` class can be implemented in Listing 10.10.

LISTING 10.10 GuessDate.java

static field

```
public class GuessDate {
  private final static int[][][] dates = {
    {{ 1,  3,  5,  7},
     { 9, 11, 13, 15},
     {17, 19, 21, 23},
     {25, 27, 29, 31}},
    {{ 2,  3,  6,  7},
     {10, 11, 14, 15},
     {18, 19, 22, 23},
     {26, 27, 30, 31}},
    {{ 4,  5,  6,  7},
     {12, 13, 14, 15},
     {20, 21, 22, 23},
     {28, 29, 30, 31}},
    {{ 8,  9, 10, 11},
     {12, 13, 14, 15},
     {24, 25, 26, 27},
     {28, 29, 30, 31}},
    {{16, 17, 18, 19},
     {20, 21, 22, 23},
     {24, 25, 26, 27},
     {28, 29, 30, 31}}};
```

private constructor

static method

```
23
24   /** Prevent the user from creating objects from GuessDate */
25   private GuessDate() {
26   }
27
28   /** Return a date at the specified row and column in a given set */
29   public static int getValue(int setNo, int k, int j) {
30     return dates[setNo][k][j];
31   }
32 }
```

This class uses a three-dimensional array to store dates (lines 2–22). You may use a different data structure (i.e., five two-dimensional arrays for representing five sets of numbers). The implementation of the `getValue` method will change, but the program that uses `GuessDate` does not need to change as long as the contract of the public method `getValue` remains unchanged. This shows the benefit of data encapsulation.

benefit of data encapsulation

private constructor

The class defines a private no-arg constructor (line 25) to prevent the user from creating objects for this class. Since all methods are static in this class, there is no need to create objects from this class.

10.11 Class Design Guidelines

You have learned how to design classes from the preceding two examples and from many other examples in the preceding chapters. Here are some guidelines.

10.11.1 Cohesion

coherent purpose

A class should describe a single entity, and all the class operations should logically fit together to support a coherent purpose. You can use a class for students, for example, but you should not combine students and staff in the same class, because students and staff are different entities.

separating responsibilities

A single entity with too many responsibilities can be broken into several classes to separate responsibilities. The classes `String`, `StringBuilder`, and `StringBuffer` all deal with strings, for example, but have different responsibilities. The `String` class deals with immutable strings, the `StringBuilder` class is for creating mutable strings, and the `StringBuffer` class is similar to `StringBuilder` except that `StringBuffer` contains synchronized methods for updating strings.

10.11.2 Consistency

naming conventions

Follow standard Java programming style and naming conventions. Choose informative names for classes, data fields, and methods. A popular style is to place the data declaration before the constructor and place constructors before methods.

naming consistency

Choose names consistently. It is not a good practice to choose different names for similar operations. For example, the `length()` method returns the size of a `String`, a `StringBuilder`, and a `StringBuffer`. It would be inconsistent if different names were used for this method in these classes.

no-arg constructor

In general, you should consistently provide a public no-arg constructor for constructing a default instance. If a class does not support a no-arg constructor, document the reason. If no constructors are defined explicitly, a public default no-arg constructor with an empty body is assumed.

If you want to prevent users from creating an object for a class, you may declare a private constructor in the class, as is the case for the `Math` class and the `GuessDate` class.

10.11.3 Encapsulation

A class should use the `private` modifier to hide its data from direct access by clients. This makes the class easy to maintain.

encapsulating data fields

Provide a `get` method only if you want the field to be readable, and provide a `set` method only if you want the field to be updateable. For example, the `Course` class provides a `get` method for `courseName`, but no `set` method, because the user is not allowed to change the course name, once it is created.

10.11.4 Clarity

Cohesion, consistency, and encapsulation are good guidelines for achieving design clarity. Additionally, a class should have a clear contract that is easy to explain and easy to understand.

easy to explain

Users can incorporate classes in many different combinations, orders, and environments. Therefore, you should design a class that imposes no restrictions on what or when the user can do with it, design the properties in a way that lets the user set them in any order and with any combination of values, and design methods that function independently of their order of occurrence. For example, the `Loan` class contains the properties `loanAmount`, `numberOfYears`, and `annualInterestRate`. The values of these properties can be set in any order.

independent methods

Methods should be defined intuitively without generating confusion. For example, the `substring(int beginIndex, int endIndex)` method in the `String` class is somehow confusing. The method returns a substring from `beginIndex` to `endIndex - 1`, rather than `endIndex`.

intuitive meaning

You should not declare a data field that can be derived from other data fields. For example, the following `Person` class has two data fields: `birthDate` and `age`. Since `age` can be derived from `birthDate`, age should not be declared as a data field.

independent properties

```
public class Person {
  private java.util.Date birthDate;
  private int age;

  ...
}
```

10.11.5 Completeness

Classes are designed for use by many different customers. In order to be useful in a wide range of applications, a class should provide a variety of ways for customization through properties and methods. For example, the `String` class contains more than 40 methods that are useful for a variety of applications.

10.11.6 Instance vs. Static

A variable or method that is dependent on a specific instance of the class should be an instance variable or method. A variable that is shared by all the instances of a class should be declared static. For example, the variable `numberOfObjects` in `Circle3` in Listing 8.9, is shared by all the objects of the `SimpleCircle1` class and therefore is declared static. A method that is not dependent on a specific instance should be declared as a static method. For instance, the `getNumberOfObjects` method in `Circle3` is not tied to any specific instance and therefore is declared as a static method.

Always reference static variables and methods from a class name (rather than a reference variable) to improve readability and avoid errors.

Do not pass a parameter from a constructor to initialize a static data field. It is better to use a `set` method to change the static data field. The class in (a) below is better replaced by (b).

```java
public class SomeThing {
  private int t1;
  private static int t2;

  public SomeThing(int t1, int t2) {
    ...
  }
}
```

(a)

```java
public class SomeThing {
  private int t1;
  private static int t2;

  public SomeThing(int t1) {
    ...
  }

  public static void setT2(int t2) {
    SomeThing.t2 = t2;
  }
}
```

(b)

Instance and static are integral parts of object-oriented programming. A data field or method is either instance or static. Do not mistakenly overlook static data fields or methods. It is a common design error to define an instance method that should have been static. For example, the `factorial(int n)` method for computing the factorial of `n` should be defined static, because it is independent of any specific instance.

common design error

A constructor is always instance, because it is used to create a specific instance. A static variable or method can be invoked from an instance method, but an instance variable or method cannot be invoked from a static method.

Key Terms

class abstraction 347
class encapsulation 347
class's contract 347
class's variable 345
immutable class 344
immutable object 344
stack 357
`this` keyword 346

Chapter Summary

1. Once it is created, an immutable object cannot be modified. To prevent users from modifying an object, you may define immutable classes.

2. The scope of instance and static variables is the entire class, regardless of where the variables are declared. Instance and static variables can be declared anywhere in the class. For consistency, they are declared at the beginning of the class.

3. The keyword `this` can be used to refer to the calling object. It can also be used inside a constructor to invoke another constructor of the same class.

4. The procedural paradigm focuses on designing methods. The object-oriented paradigm couples data and methods together into objects. Software design using the object-oriented paradigm focuses on objects and operations on objects. The object-oriented approach combines the power of the procedural paradigm with an added dimension that integrates data with operations into objects.

Review Questions

Section 10.2

10.1 If a class contains only private data fields and no set methods, is the class immutable?

10.2 If all the data fields in a class are private and primitive type, and the class contains no `set` methods, is the class immutable?

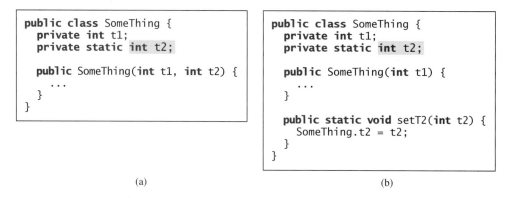

10.3 Is the following class immutable?

```
public class A {
  private int[] values;

  public int[] getValues() {
    return values;
  }
}
```

10.4 If you redefine the **Loan** class in Listing 10.2 without **set** methods, is the class immutable?

Section 10.3

10.5 What is the output of the following program?

```
public class Foo {
  private static int i = 0;
  private static int j = 0;

  public static void main(String[] args) {
    int i = 2;
    int k = 3;

    {
      int j = 3;
      System.out.println("i + j is " + i + j);
    }

    k = i + j;
    System.out.println("k is " + k);
    System.out.println("j is " + j);
  }
}
```

Section 10.4

10.6 Describe the role of the **this** keyword. What is wrong in the following code?

```
public class C {
  private int p;

  public C() {
    System.out.println("C's no-arg constructor invoked");
    this(0);
  }

  public C(int p) {
    p = p;
  }

  public void setP(int p) {
    p = p;
  }
}
```

Programming Exercises

10.1* (*The* `Time` *class*) Design a class named `Time`. The class contains:

- Data fields `hour`, `minute`, and `second` that represent a time.
- A no-arg constructor that creates a `Time` object for the current time. (The values of the data fields will represent the current time.)
- A constructor that constructs a `Time` object with a specified elapsed time since midnight, Jan 1, 1970, in milliseconds. (The values of the data fields will represent this time.)
- A constructor that constructs a `Time` object with the specified hour, minute, and second.
- Three `get` methods for the data fields `hour`, `minute`, and `second`, respectively.
- A method named `setTime(long elapseTime)` that sets a new time for the object using the elapsed time.

Draw the UML diagram for the class. Implement the class. Write a test program that creates two `Time` objects (using `new Time()` and `new Time(555550000)`) and display their hour, minute, and second.

(*Hint:* The first two constructors will extract hour, minute, and second from the elapsed time. For example, if the elapsed time is `555550` seconds, the hour is `10`, the minute is `19`, and the second is `9`. For the no-arg constructor, the current time can be obtained using `System.currentTimeMills()`, as shown in Listing 2.6, ShowCurrentTime.java.)

10.2 (*The* `BMI` *class*) Add the following new constructor in the `BMI` class:

```
/** Construct a BMI with the specified name, age, weight,
 * feet and inches
 */
public BMI(String name, int age, double weight, double feet,
double inches)
```

10.3 (*The* `MyInteger` *class*) Design a class named `MyInteger`. The class contains:

- An `int` data field named `value` that stores the `int` value represented by this object.
- A constructor that creates a `MyInteger` object for the specified `int` value.
- A `get` method that returns the `int` value.
- Methods `isEven()`, `isOdd()`, and `isPrime()` that return `true` if the value is even, odd, or prime, respectively.
- Static methods `isEven(int)`, `isOdd(int)`, and `isPrime(int)` that return `true` if the specified value is even, odd, or prime, respectively.
- Static methods `isEven(MyInteger)`, `isOdd(MyInteger)`, and `isPrime(MyInteger)` that return `true` if the specified value is even, odd, or prime, respectively.
- Methods `equals(int)` and `equals(MyInteger)` that return `true` if the value in the object is equal to the specified value.
- A static method `parseInt(char[])` that converts an array of numeric characters to an `int` value.
- A static method `parseInt(String)` that converts a string into an `int` value.

Draw the UML diagram for the class. Implement the class. Write a client program that tests all methods in the class.

10.4 (*The `MyPoint` class*) Design a class named `MyPoint` to represent a point with x- and y-coordinates. The class contains:

Video Note
The **MyPoint** class

- Two data fields x and y that represent the coordinates with get methods.
- A no-arg constructor that creates a point (0, 0).
- A constructor that constructs a point with specified coordinates.
- Two get methods for data fields x and y, respectively.
- A method named `distance` that returns the distance from this point to another point of the `MyPoint` type.
- A method named `distance` that returns the distance from this point to another point with specified x- and y-coordinates.

Draw the UML diagram for the class. Implement the class. Write a test program that creates two points (0, 0) and (10, 30.5) and displays the distance between them.

10.5* (*Displaying the prime factors*) Write a program that prompts the user to enter a positive integer and displays all its smallest factors in decreasing order. For example, if the integer is 120, the smallest factors are displayed as 5, 3, 2, 2, 2. Use the `StackOfIntegers` class to store the factors (e.g., 2, 2, 2, 3, 5) and retrieve and display them in reverse order.

10.6* (*Displaying the prime numbers*) Write a program that displays all the prime numbers less than 120 in decreasing order. Use the `StackOfIntegers` class to store the prime numbers (e.g., 2, 3, 5, ...) and retrieve and display them in reverse order.

10.7** (*Game: ATM machine*) Use the `Account` class created in Exercise 8.7 to simulate an ATM machine. Create ten accounts in an array with id 0, 1, ..., 9, and initial balance $100. The system prompts the user to enter an id. If the id is entered incorrectly, ask the user to enter a correct id. Once an id is accepted, the main menu is displayed as shown in the sample run. You can enter a choice 1 for viewing the current balance, 2 for withdrawing money, 3 for depositing money, and 4 for exiting the main menu. Once you exit, the system will prompt for an id again. So, once the system starts, it will not stop.

```
Enter an id: 4 [Enter]

Main menu
1: check balance
2: withdraw
3: deposit
4: exit
Enter a choice: 1 [Enter]
The balance is 100.0

Main menu
1: check balance
2: withdraw
3: deposit
4: exit
Enter a choice: 2 [Enter]
Enter an amount to withdraw: 3 [Enter]
```

```
Main menu
1: check balance
2: withdraw
3: deposit
4: exit
Enter a choice: 1 ↵Enter
The balance is 97.0

Main menu
1: check balance
2: withdraw
3: deposit
4: exit
Enter a choice: 3 ↵Enter
Enter an amount to deposit: 10 ↵Enter

Main menu
1: check balance
2: withdraw
3: deposit
4: exit
Enter a choice: 1 ↵Enter
The balance is 107.0

Main menu
1: check balance
2: withdraw
3: deposit
4: exit
Enter a choice: 4 ↵Enter

Enter an id:
```

10.8** (*Financial: the* `Tax` *class*) Exercise 7.12 writes a program for computing taxes using arrays. Design a class named `Tax` to contain the following instance data fields:

- `int filingStatus`: One of the four tax-filing statuses: `0`—single filer, `1`—married filing jointly, `2`—married filing separately, and `3`—head of household. Use the public static constants `SINGLE_FILER` (`0`), `MARRIED_JOINTLY` (`1`), `MARRIED_SEPARATELY` (`2`), `HEAD_OF_HOUSEHOLD` (`3`) to represent the status.
- `int[][] brackets`: Stores the tax brackets for each filing status.
- `double[] rates`: Stores the tax rates for each bracket.
- `double taxableIncome`: Stores the taxable income.

Provide the `get` and `set` methods for each data field and the `getTax()` method that returns the tax. Also provide a no-arg constructor and the constructor `Tax(filingStatus, brackets, rates, taxableIncome)`.

Draw the UML diagram for the class. Implement the class. Write a test program that uses the `Tax` class to print the 2001 and 2009 tax tables for taxable income from $50,000 to $60,000 with intervals of $1,000 for all four statuses. The tax rates for the year 2009 were given in Table 3.2. The tax rates for 2001 are shown in Table 10.1.

TABLE 10.1 2001 United States Federal Personal Tax Rates

Tax rate	*Single filers*	*Married filing jointly or qualifying widow(er)*	*Married filing separately*	*Head of household*
15%	Up to $27,050	Up to $45,200	UP to $22,600	UP to $36,250
27.5%	$27,051–$65,550	$45,201–$109,250	$22,601–$54,625	$36,251–$93,650
30.5%	$65,551–$136,750	$109,251–$166,500	$54,626–$83,250	$93,651–$151,650
35.5%	$136,751–$297,350	$166,501–$297,350	$83,251–148,675	$151,651–$297,350
39.1%	$297,351 or more	$297,351 or more	$148,676 or more	$297,351 or more

10.9** (*The* `Course` *class*) Revise the `Course` class as follows:

- The array size is fixed in Listing 10.6. Improve it to automatically increase the array size by creating a new larger array and copying the contents of the current array to it.
- Implement the `dropStudent` method.
- Add a new method named `clear()` that removes all students from the course.

Write a test program that creates a course, adds three students, removes one, and displays the students in the course.

10.10* (*Game: The* `GuessDate` *class*) Modify the `GuessDate` class in Listing 10.10. Instead of representing dates in a three-dimensional array, use five two-dimensional arrays to represent the five sets of numbers. So you need to declare:

```
private static int[][] set1 = {{1,  3,  5,  7}, ... };
private static int[][] set2 = {{2,  3,  6,  7}, ... };
private static int[][] set3 = {{4,  5,  6,  7}, ... };
private static int[][] set4 = {{8,  9, 10, 11}, ... };
private static int[][] set5 = {{16, 17, 18, 19}, ... };
```

10.11* (*Geometry: The* `Circle2D` *class*) Define the `Circle2D` class that contains:

- Two `double` data fields named `x` and `y` that specify the center of the circle with `get` methods.
- A data field `radius` with a `get` method.
- A no-arg constructor that creates a default circle with (`0`, `0`) for (`x`, `y`) and `1` for `radius`.
- A constructor that creates a circle with the specified `x`, `y`, and `radius`.
- A method `getArea()` that returns the area of the circle.
- A method `getPerimeter()` that returns the perimeter of the circle.
- A method `contains(double x, double y)` that returns `true` if the specified point (`x`, `y`) is inside this circle. See Figure 10.14(a).
- A method `contains(Circle2D circle)` that returns `true` if the specified circle is inside this circle. See Figure 10.14(b).
- A method `overlaps(Circle2D circle)` that returns `true` if the specified circle overlaps with this circle. See Figure 10.14(c).

Draw the UML diagram for the class. Implement the class. Write a test program that creates a `Circle2D` object `c1` (`new Circle2D(2, 2, 5.5)`), displays its area and perimeter, and displays the result of `c1.contains(3, 3)`, `c1.contains(new Circle2D(4, 5, 10.5))`, and `c1.overlaps(new Circle2D(3, 5, 2.3))`.

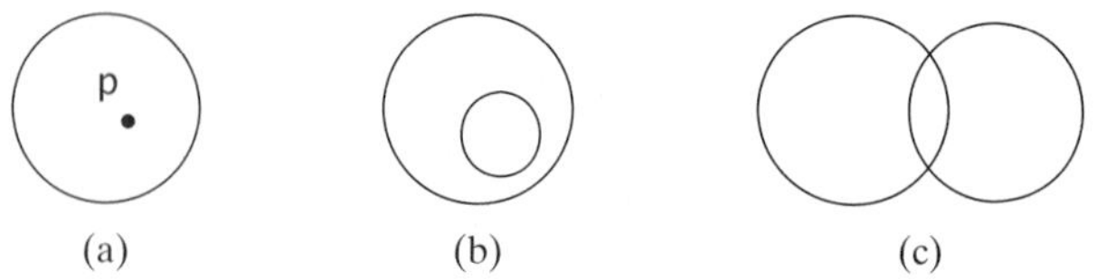
p
(a)
(b)
(c)

FIGURE 10.14 (a) A point is inside the circle. (b) A circle is inside another circle. (c) A circle overlaps another circle.

10.12* (*Geometry: The* `MyRectangle2D` *class*) Define the `MyRectangle2D` class that contains:

- Two `double` data fields named `x` and `y` that specify the center of the rectangle with `get` and `set` methods. (Assume that the rectangle sides are parallel to `x-` or `y-` axes.)
- The data fields `width` and `height` with `get` and `set` methods.
- A no-arg constructor that creates a default rectangle with (`0`, `0`) for (`x`, `y`) and `1` for both `width` and `height`.
- A constructor that creates a rectangle with the specified `x`, `y`, `width`, and `height`.
- A method `getArea()` that returns the area of the rectangle.
- A method `getPerimeter()` that returns the perimeter of the rectangle.
- A method `contains(double x, double y)` that returns `true` if the specified point (`x`, `y`) is inside this rectangle. See Figure 10.15(a).
- A method `contains(MyRectangle2D r)` that returns `true` if the specified rectangle is inside this rectangle. See Figure 10.15(b).
- A method `overlaps(MyRectangle2D r)` that returns `true` if the specified rectangle overlaps with this rectangle. See Figure 10.15(c).

Draw the UML diagram for the class. Implement the class. Write a test program that creates a `MyRectangle2D` object `r1` (`new MyRectangle2D(2, 2, 5.5, 4.9)`), displays its area and perimeter, and displays the result of `r1.contains(3, 3)`, `r1.contains(new MyRectangle2D(4, 5, 10.5, 3.2))`, and `r1.overlaps(new MyRectangle2D(3, 5, 2.3, 5.4))`.

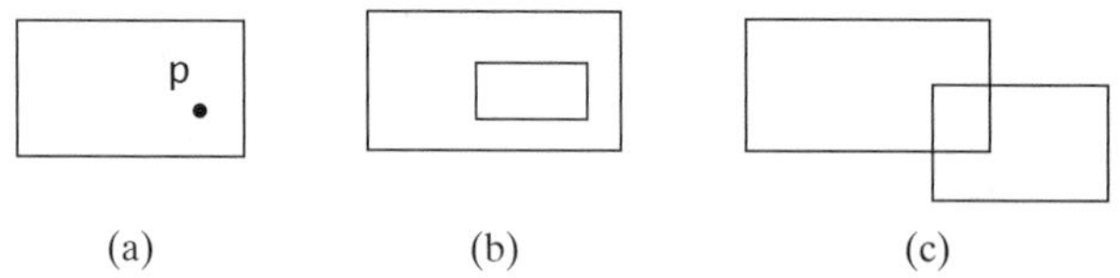
p
(a)
(b)
(c)

FIGURE 10.15 (a) A point is inside the rectangle. (b) A rectangle is inside another rectangle. (c) A rectangle overlaps another rectangle.

10.13*** (*Geometry: The* `Triangle2D` *class*) Define the `Triangle2D` class that contains:

- Three points named `p1`, `p2`, and `p3` with the type `MyPoint` with `get` and `set` methods. `MyPoint` is defined in Exercise 10.4.
- A no-arg constructor that creates a default triangle with points (`0`, `0`), (`1`, `1`), and (`2`, `5`).
- A constructor that creates a triangle with the specified points.
- A method `getArea()` that returns the area of the triangle.
- A method `getPerimeter()` that returns the perimeter of the triangle.

- A method `contains(MyPoint p)` that returns `true` if the specified point `p` is inside this triangle. See Figure 10.16(a).
- A method `contains(Triangle2D t)` that returns `true` if the specified triangle is inside this triangle. See Figure 10.16(b).
- A method `overlaps(Triangle2D t)` that returns `true` if the specified triangle overlaps with this triangle. See Figure 10.16(c).

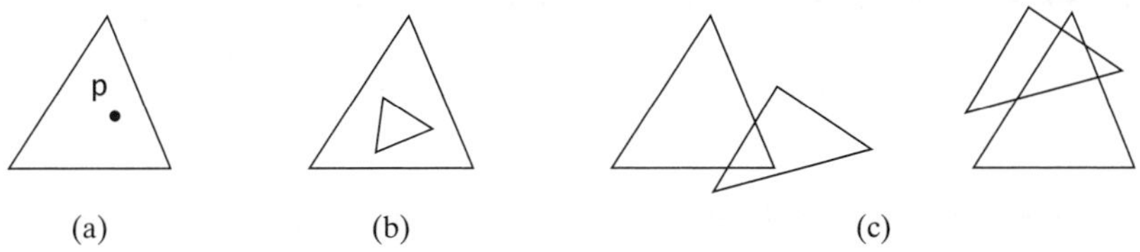
p
(a)
(b)
(c)

FIGURE 10.16 (a) A point is inside the triangle. (b) A triangle is inside another triangle. (c) A triangle overlaps another triangle.

Draw the UML diagram for the class. Implement the class. Write a test program that creates a `Triangle2D` objects `t1` (`new Triangle2D(new MyPoint(2.5, 2), new MyPoint(4.2, 3), MyPoint(5, 3.5))`), displays its area and perimeter, and displays the result of `t1.contains(3, 3)`, `r1.contains(new Triangle2D(new MyPoint(2.9, 2), new MyPoint(4, 1), MyPoint(1, 3.4)))`, and `t1.overlaps(new Triangle2D(new MyPoint(2, 5.5), new MyPoint(4, -3), MyPoint(2, 6.5)))`.

(*Hint*: For the formula to compute the area of a triangle, see Exercise 5.19. Use the `java.awt.geo.Line2D` class in the Java API to implement the `contains` and `overlaps` methods. The `Line2D` class contains the methods for checking whether two line segments intersect and whether a line contains a point, etc. Please see the Java API for more information on `Line2D`. To detect whether a point is inside a triangle, draw three dashed lines, as shown in Figure 10.17. If the point is inside a triangle, each dashed line should intersect a side only once. If a dashed line intersects a side twice, then the point must be outside the triangle.)

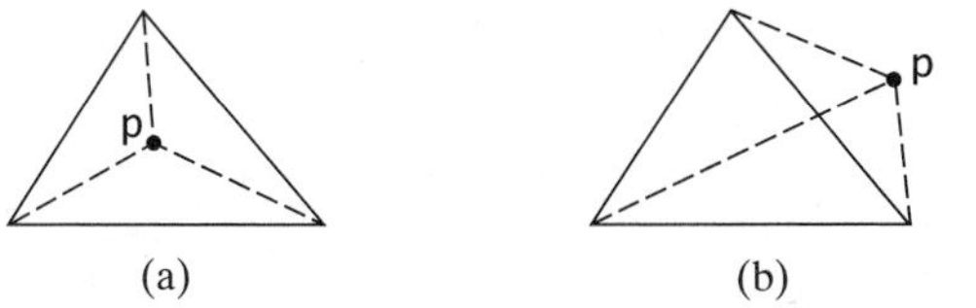
p
p
(a)
(b)

FIGURE 10.17 (a) A point is inside the triangle. (b) A point is outside the triangle.

10.14* (*The `MyDate` class*) Design a class named `MyDate`. The class contains:

- Data fields `year`, `month`, and `day` that represent a date.
- A no-arg constructor that creates a `MyDate` object for the current date.
- A constructor that constructs a `MyDate` object with a specified elapsed time since midnight, Jan 1, 1970, in milliseconds.
- A constructor that constructs a `MyDate` object with the specified year, month, and day.
- Three `get` methods for the data fields `year`, `month`, and `day`, respectively.
- A method named `setDate(long elapsedTime)` that sets a new date for the object using the elapsed time.

Draw the UML diagram for the class. Implement the class. Write a test program that creates two `Date` objects (using `new Date()` and `new Date(34355555133101L)`) and display their hour, minute, and second.

(*Hint*: The first two constructors will extract year, month, and day from the elapsed time. For example, if the elapsed time is `561555550000` milliseconds, the year is `1987`, the month is `10`, and the day is `17`. For the no-arg constructor, the current time can be obtained using `System.currentTimeMills()`, as shown in Listing 2.6, ShowCurrentTime.java.)

CHAPTER 11

INHERITANCE AND POLYMORPHISM

Objectives

- To develop a subclass from a superclass through inheritance (§11.2).
- To invoke the superclass's constructors and methods using the `super` keyword (§11.3).
- To override instance methods in the subclass (§11.4).
- To distinguish differences between overriding and overloading (§11.5).
- To explore the `toString()` method in the `Object` class (§11.6).
- To discover polymorphism and dynamic binding (§§11.7–11.8).
- To describe casting and explain why explicit downcasting is necessary (§11.9).
- To explore the `equals` method in the `Object` class (§11.10).
- To store, retrieve, and manipulate objects in an `ArrayList` (§11.11).
- To implement a `Stack` class using `ArrayList` (§11.12).
- To enable data and methods in a superclass accessible in subclasses using the `protected` visibility modifier (§11.13).
- To prevent class extending and method overriding using the `final` modifier (§11.14).

11.1 Introduction

why inheritance?

Object-oriented programming allows you to derive new classes from existing classes. This is called *inheritance*. Inheritance is an important and powerful feature in Java for reusing software. Suppose you are to define classes to model circles, rectangles, and triangles. These classes have many common features. What is the best way to design these classes so to avoid redundancy and make the system easy to comprehend and easy to maintain? The answer is to use inheritance.

11.2 Superclasses and Subclasses

Video Note
Geometric class hierarchy

You use a class to model objects of the same type. Different classes may have some common properties and behaviors, which can be generalized in a class that can be shared by other classes. Inheritance enables you to define a general class and later extend it to more specialized classes. The specialized classes inherit the properties and methods from the general class.

Consider geometric objects. Suppose you want to design the classes to model geometric objects such as circles and rectangles. Geometric objects have many common properties and behaviors. They can be drawn in a certain color, filled or unfilled. Thus a general class

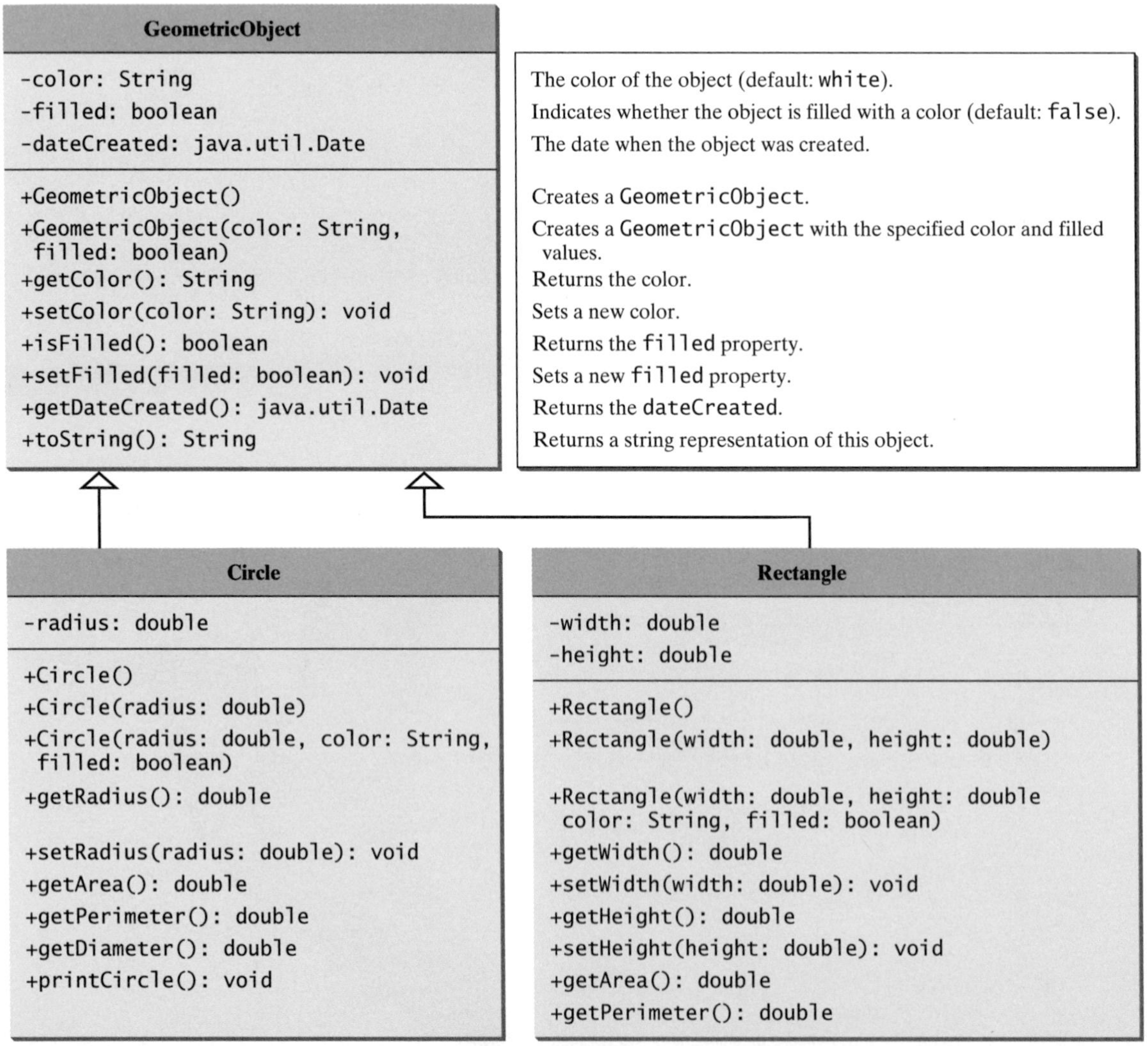
GeometricObject
-color: String
-filled: boolean
-dateCreated: java.util.Date
+GeometricObject()
+GeometricObject(color: String, filled: boolean)
+getColor(): String
+setColor(color: String): void
+isFilled(): boolean
+setFilled(filled: boolean): void
+getDateCreated(): java.util.Date
+toString(): String
The color of the object (default: white).
Indicates whether the object is filled with a color (default: false).
The date when the object was created.
Creates a GeometricObject.
Creates a GeometricObject with the specified color and filled values.
Returns the color.
Sets a new color.
Returns the filled property.
Sets a new filled property.
Returns the dateCreated.
Returns a string representation of this object.
Circle
-radius: double
+Circle()
+Circle(radius: double)
+Circle(radius: double, color: String, filled: boolean)
+getRadius(): double
+setRadius(radius: double): void
+getArea(): double
+getPerimeter(): double
+getDiameter(): double
+printCircle(): void
Rectangle
-width: double
-height: double
+Rectangle()
+Rectangle(width: double, height: double)
+Rectangle(width: double, height: double color: String, filled: boolean)
+getWidth(): double
+setWidth(width: double): void
+getHeight(): double
+setHeight(height: double): void
+getArea(): double
+getPerimeter(): double

FIGURE 11.1 The `GeometricObject` class is the superclass for `Circle` and `Rectangle`.

GeometricObject can be used to model all geometric objects. This class contains the properties color and filled and their appropriate get and set methods. Assume that this class also contains the dateCreated property and the getDateCreated() and toString() methods. The toString() method returns a string representation for the object. Since a circle is a special type of geometric object, it shares common properties and methods with other geometric objects. Thus it makes sense to define the Circle class that extends the GeometricObject class. Likewise, Rectangle can also be declared as a subclass of GeometricObject. Figure 11.1 shows the relationship among these classes. An arrow pointing to the superclass is used to denote the inheritance relationship between the two classes involved.

subclass
superclass

In Java terminology, a class C1 extended from another class C2 is called a *subclass*, and C2 is called a *superclass*. A superclass is also referred to as a *parent class,* or a *base class*, and a subclass as a *child class*, an *extended class*, or a *derived class*. A subclass inherits accessible data fields and methods from its superclass and may also add new data fields and methods.

The Circle class inherits all accessible data fields and methods from the GeometricObject class. In addition, it has a new data field, radius, and its associated get and set methods. It also contains the getArea(), getPerimeter(), and getDiameter() methods for returning the area, perimeter, and diameter of the circle.

The Rectangle class inherits all accessible data fields and methods from the GeometricObject class. In addition, it has the data fields width and height and the associated get and set methods. It also contains the getArea() and getPerimeter() methods for returning the area and perimeter of the rectangle.

The GeometricObject, Circle, and Rectangle classes are shown in Listings 11.1, 11.2, and 11.3.

Note

avoid naming conflict

To avoid naming conflict with the improved GeometricObject, Circle, and Rectangle classes introduced in the next chapter, name these classes GeometricObject1, Circle4, and Rectangle1 in this chapter. For convenience, we will still refer to them in the text as GeometricObject, Circle, and Rectangle classes. The best way to avoid naming conflict would be to place these classes in a different package. However, for simplicity and consistency, all classes in this book are placed in the default package.

Listing 11.1 GeometricObject1.java

data fields · *constructor* · *date constructed*

```
public class GeometricObject1 {
  private String color = "white";
  private boolean filled;
  private java.util.Date dateCreated;

  /** Construct a default geometric object */
  public GeometricObject1() {
    dateCreated = new java.util.Date();
  }

  /** Construct a geometric object with the specified color
    * and filled value */
  public GeometricObject1(String Color, boolean filled) {
    dateCreated = new java.util.Date();
    this.color = color;
    this.filled = filled;
  }

  /** Return color */
  public String getColor() {
    return color;
  }
```

```java

  /** Set a new color */
  public void setColor(String color) {
    this.color = color;
  }

  /** Return filled. Since filled is boolean,
     its get method is named isFilled */
  public boolean isFilled() {
    return filled;
  }

  /** Set a new filled */
  public void setFilled(boolean filled) {
    this.filled = filled;
  }

  /** Get dateCreated */
  public java.util.Date getDateCreated() {
    return dateCreated;
  }

  /** Return a string representation of this object */
  public String toString() {
    return "created on " + dateCreated + "\ncolor: " + color +
      " and filled: " + filled;
  }
}
```

LISTING 11.2 Circle4.java

data fields

constructor

methods

```java
public class Circle4 extends GeometricObject1 {
  private double radius;

  public Circle4() {
  }

  public Circle4(double radius) {
    this.radius = radius;
  }

  public Circle4(double radius, String color, boolean filled) {
    this.radius = radius;
    setColor(color);
    setFilled(filled);
  }

  /** Return radius */
  public double getRadius() {
    return radius;
  }

  /** Set a new radius */
  public void setRadius(double radius) {
    this.radius = radius;
  }

  /** Return area */
  public double getArea() {
    return radius * radius * Math.PI;
  }
```

```
31
32    /** Return diameter */
33    public double getDiameter() {
34      return 2 * radius;
35    }
36
37    /** Return perimeter */
38    public double getPerimeter() {
39      return 2 * radius * Math.PI;
40    }
41
42    /* Print the circle info */
43    public void printCircle() {
44      System.out.println("The circle is created " + getDateCreated() +
45        " and the radius is " + radius);
46    }
47  }
```

The Circle class extends the GeometricObject class (Listing 11.2) using the following syntax:

```
    Subclass                    Superclass

  public class Circle extends GeometricObject
```

The keyword extends (line 1) tells the compiler that the Circle class extends the GeometricObject class, thus inheriting the methods getColor, setColor, isFilled, setFilled, and toString.

The overloaded constructor Circle(double radius, string color, boolean filled) is implemented by invoking the setColor and setFilled methods to set the color and filled properties (lines 11–15). These two public methods are defined in the base class GeometricObject and are inherited in Circle. So, they can be used in the derived class.

private member in base class

You might attempt to use the data fields color and filled directly in the constructor as follows:

```
public Circle4(double radius, String color, boolean filled) {
  this.radius = radius;
  this.color = color; // Illegal
  this.filled = filled; // Illegal
}
```

This is wrong, because the private data fields color and filled in the GeometricObject class cannot be accessed in any class other than in the GeometricObject class itself. The only way to read and modify color and filled is through their get and set methods.

The Rectangle class (Listing 11.3) extends the GeometricObject class (Listing 11.2) using the following syntax:

```
    Subclass                         Superclass

  public class Rectangle extends GeometricObject
```

The keyword `extends` (line 1) tells the compiler that the `Rectangle` class extends the `GeometricObject` class, thus inheriting the methods `getColor`, `setColor`, `isFilled`, `setFilled`, and `toString`.

Listing 11.3 Rectangle1.java

data fields

constructor

methods

```
1 public class Rectangle1 extends GeometricObject1 {
2   private double width;
3   private double height;
4
5   public Rectangle1() {
6   }
7
8   public Rectangle1(double width, double height) {
9     this.width = width;
10    this.height = height;
11  }
12
13  public Rectangle1(double width, double height, String color,
14      boolean filled) {
15    this.width = width;
16    this.height = height;
17    setColor(color);
18    setFilled(filled);
19  }
20
21  /** Return width */
22  public double getWidth() {
23    return width;
24  }
25
26  /** Set a new width */
27  public void setWidth(double width) {
28    this.width = width;
29  }
30
31  /** Return height */
32  public double getHeight() {
33    return height;
34  }
35
36  /** Set a new height */
37  public void setHeight(double height) {
38    this.height = height;
39  }
40
41  /** Return area */
42  public double getArea() {
43    return width * height;
44  }
45
46  /** Return perimeter */
47  public double getPerimeter() {
48    return 2 * (width + height);
49  }
50 }
```

The code in Listing 11.4 creates objects of `Circle` and `Rectangle` and invokes the methods on these objects. The `toString()` method is inherited from the `GeometricObject` class and is invoked from a `Circle` object (line 4) and a `Rectangle` object (line 10).

LISTING 11.4 TestCircleRectangle.java

```
public class TestCircleRectangle {
  public static void main(String[] args) {
    Circle4 circle = new Circle4(1);
    System.out.println("A circle " + circle.toString());
    System.out.println("The radius is " + circle.getRadius());
    System.out.println("The area is " + circle.getArea());
    System.out.println("The diameter is " + circle.getDiameter());

    Rectangle1 rectangle = new Rectangle1(2, 4);
    System.out.println("\nA rectangle " + rectangle.toString());
    System.out.println("The area is " + rectangle.getArea());
    System.out.println("The perimeter is " +
      rectangle.getPerimeter());
  }
}
```

Circle object
invoke **toString**

Rectangle object
invoke **toString**

```
A circle created on Thu Sep 24 20:31:02 EDT 2009
color: white and filled: false
The radius is 1.0
The area is 3.141592653589793
The diameter is 2.0

A rectangle created on Thu Sep 24 20:31:02 EDT 2009
color: white and filled: false
The area is 8.0
The perimeter is 12.0
```

The following points regarding inheritance are worthwhile to note:

- Contrary to the conventional interpretation, a subclass is not a subset of its superclass. In fact, a subclass usually contains more information and methods than its superclass. *(more in subclass)*

- Private data fields in a superclass are not accessible outside the class. Therefore, they cannot be used directly in a subclass. They can, however, be accessed/mutated through public accessor/mutator if defined in the superclass. *(private data fields)*

- Not all *is-a* relationships should be modeled using inheritance. For example, a square is a rectangle, but you should not define a **Square** class to extend a **Rectangle** class, because there is nothing to extend (or supplement) from a rectangle to a square. Rather you should define a **Square** class to extend the **GeometricObject** class. For class **A** to extend class **B**, **A** should contain more detailed information than **B**. *(nonextensible is-a)*

- Inheritance is used to model the *is-a* relationship. Do not blindly extend a class just for the sake of reusing methods. For example, it makes no sense for a **Tree** class to extend a **Person** class, even though they share common properties such as height and weight. A subclass and its superclass must have the *is-a* relationship. *(no blind extension)*

- Some programming languages allow you to derive a subclass from several classes. This capability is known as *multiple inheritance*. Java, however, does not allow multiple inheritance. A Java class may inherit directly from only one superclass. This restriction is known as *single inheritance*. If you use the **extends** keyword to define a subclass, it allows only one parent class. Nevertheless, multiple inheritance can be achieved through interfaces, which will be introduced in §14.4, "Interfaces." *(multiple inheritance)* *(single inheritance)*

11.3 Using the **super** Keyword

A subclass inherits accessible data fields and methods from its superclass. Does it inherit constructors? Can superclass constructors be invoked from subclasses? This section addresses these questions and their ramification.

§10.4, "The `this` Reference," introduced the use of the keyword `this` to reference the calling object. The keyword `super` refers to the superclass of the class in which `super` appears. It can be used in two ways:

- To call a superclass constructor.
- To call a superclass method.

11.3.1 Calling Superclass Constructors

The syntax to call a superclass constructor is:

```
super(), or super(parameters);
```

The statement `super()` invokes the no-arg constructor of its superclass, and the statement `super(arguments)` invokes the superclass constructor that matches the `arguments`. The statement `super()` or `super(arguments)` must appear in the first line of the subclass constructor; this is the only way to explicitly invoke a superclass constructor. For example, the constructor in lines 11–15 in Listing 11.2 can be replaced by the following code:

```
public Circle4(double radius, String color, boolean filled) {
  super(color, filled);
  this.radius = radius;
}
```

Caution

You must use the keyword `super` to call the superclass constructor, and the call must be the first statement in the constructor. Invoking a superclass constructor's name in a subclass causes a syntax error.

Note

A constructor is used to construct an instance of a class. Unlike properties and methods, the constructors of a superclass are not inherited in the subclass. They can only be invoked from the constructors of the subclasses, using the keyword `super`.

11.3.2 Constructor Chaining

A constructor may invoke an overloaded constructor or its superclass constructor. If neither is invoked explicitly, the compiler automatically puts `super()` as the first statement in the constructor. For example,

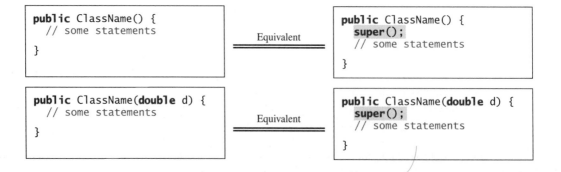

```
public ClassName() {
  // some statements
}
```

Equivalent

```
public ClassName() {
  super();
  // some statements
}
```

```
public ClassName(double d) {
  // some statements
}
```

Equivalent

```
public ClassName(double d) {
  super();
  // some statements
}
```

In any case, constructing an instance of a class invokes the constructors of all the superclasses along the inheritance chain. When constructing an object of a subclass, the subclass constructor first invokes its superclass constructor before performing its own tasks. If the superclass is derived from another class, the superclass constructor invokes its parent-class constructor before performing its own tasks. This process continues until the last constructor along the inheritance hierarchy is called. This is *constructor chaining*.

constructor chaining

Consider the following code:

```
1 public class Faculty extends Employee {
2   public static void main(String[] args) {
3     new Faculty();
4   }
5
6   public Faculty() {
7     System.out.println("(4) Performs Faculty's tasks");
8   }
9 }
10
11 class Employee extends Person {
12   public Employee() {
13     this("(2) Invoke Employee's overloaded constructor");
14     System.out.println("(3) Performs Employee's tasks ");
15   }
16
17   public Employee(String s) {
18     System.out.println(s);
19   }
20 }
21
22 class Person {
23   public Person() {
24     System.out.println("(1) Performs Person's tasks");
25   }
26 }
```

invoke overloaded constructor

```
(1) Performs Person's tasks
(2) Invoke Employee's overloaded constructor
(3) Performs Employee's tasks
(4) Performs Faculty's tasks
```

The program produces the preceding output. Why? Let us discuss the reason. In line 3, **new Faculty()** invokes **Faculty**'s no-arg constructor. Since **Faculty** is a subclass of **Employee**, **Employee**'s no-arg constructor is invoked before any statements in **Faculty**'s constructor are executed. **Employee**'s no-arg constructor invokes **Employee**'s second constructor (line 12). Since **Employee** is a subclass of **Person**, **Person**'s no-arg constructor is invoked before any statements in **Employee**'s second constructor are executed. This process is pictured in the figure below.

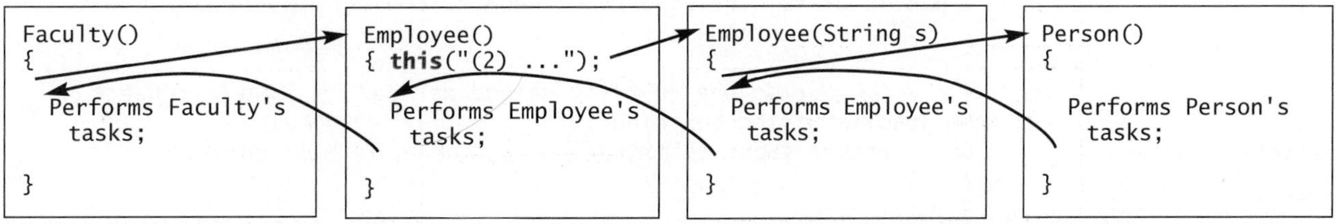
Faculty()
{
Performs Faculty's tasks;
}
Employee()
{ this("(2) ...");
Performs Employee's tasks;
}
Employee(String s)
{
Performs Employee's tasks;
}
Person()
{
Performs Person's tasks;
}

no-arg constructor

Caution

If a class is designed to be extended, it is better to provide a no-arg constructor to avoid programming errors. Consider the following code:

```
public class Apple extends Fruit {
}

class Fruit {
  public Fruit(String name) {
    System.out.println("Fruit's constructor is invoked");
  }
}
```

Since no constructor is explicitly defined in `Apple`, `Apple`'s default no-arg constructor is defined implicitly. Since `Apple` is a subclass of `Fruit`, `Apple`'s default constructor automatically invokes `Fruit`'s no-arg constructor. However, `Fruit` does not have a no-arg constructor, because `Fruit` has an explicit constructor defined. Therefore, the program cannot be compiled.

no-arg constructor

Design Guide

It is better to provide a no-arg constructor (if desirable) for every class to make the class easy to extend and to avoid errors.

11.3.3 Calling Superclass Methods

The keyword `super` can also be used to reference a method other than the constructor in the superclass. The syntax is like this:

```
super.method(parameters);
```

You could rewrite the `printCircle()` method in the `Circle` class as follows:

```
public void printCircle() {
  System.out.println("The circle is created " +
    super.getDateCreated() + " and the radius is " + radius);
}
```

It is not necessary to put `super` before `getDateCreated()` in this case, however, because `getDateCreated` is a method in the `GeometricObject` class and is inherited by the `Circle` class. Nevertheless, in some cases, as shown in the next section, the keyword `super` is needed.

11.4 Overriding Methods

A subclass inherits methods from a superclass. Sometimes it is necessary for the subclass to modify the implementation of a method defined in the superclass. This is referred to as *method overriding*.

method overriding

The `toString` method in the `GeometricObject` class returns the string representation for a geometric object. This method can be overridden to return the string representation for a circle. To *override* it, add the following new method in Listing 11.2, Circle4.java:

toString in superclass

```
public class Circle4 extends GeometricObject1 {
  // Other methods are omitted

  /** Override the toString method defined in GeometricObject */
  public String toString() {
    return super.toString() + "\nradius is " + radius;
  }
}
```

The toString() method is defined in the GeometricObject class and modified in the Circle class. Both methods can be used in the Circle class. To invoke the toString method defined in the GeometricObject class from the Circle class, use super.toString() (line 6).

Can a subclass of Circle access the toString method defined in the GeometricObject class using a syntax such as super.super.toString()? No. This is a syntax error.

no super.super.methodName()

Several points are worth noting:

- An instance method can be overridden only if it is accessible. Thus a private method cannot be overridden, because it is not accessible outside its own class. If a method defined in a subclass is private in its superclass, the two methods are completely unrelated.

override accessible instance method

- Like an instance method, a static method can be inherited. However, a static method cannot be overridden. If a static method defined in the superclass is redefined in a subclass, the method defined in the superclass is hidden. The hidden static methods can be invoked using the syntax SuperClassName.staticMethodName.

cannot override static method

11.5 Overriding vs. Overloading

You have learned about overloading methods in §5.8. Overloading means to define multiple methods with the same name but different signatures. Overriding means to provide a new implementation for a method in the subclass. The method is already defined in the superclass.

To override a method, the method must be defined in the subclass using the same signature and the same return type.

Let us use an example to show the differences between overriding and overloading. In (a) below, the method p(double i) in class A overrides the same method defined in class B. In (b), however, the class B has two overloaded methods p(double i) and p(int i). The method p(double i) is inherited from B.

```
public class Test {
  public static void main(String[] args) {
    A a = new A();
    a.p(10);
    a.p(10.0);
  }
}

class B {
  public void p(double i) {
    System.out.println(i * 2);
  }
}

class A extends B {
  // This method overrides the method in B
  public void p(double i) {
    System.out.println(i);
  }
}
```

(a)

```
public class Test {
  public static void main(String[] args) {
    A a = new A();
    a.p(10);
    a.p(10.0);
  }
}

class B {
  public void p(double i) {
    System.out.println(i * 2);
  }
}

class A extends B {
  // This method overloads the method in B
  public void p(int i) {
    System.out.println(i);
  }
}
```

(b)

When you run the Test class in (a), both a.p(10) and a.p(10.0) invoke the p(double i) method defined in class A to display 10.0. When you run the Test class in (b), a.p(10) invokes the p(int i) method defined in class B to display 20, and a.p(10.0) invokes the p(double i) method defined in class A to display 10.0.

11.6 The Object Class and Its toString() Method

Every class in Java is descended from the **java.lang.Object** class. If no inheritance is specified when a class is defined, the superclass of the class is **Object** by default. For example, the following two class definitions are the same:

```
public class ClassName {
  ...
}
```

Equivalent

```
public class ClassName extends Object {
  ...
}
```

Classes such as **String**, **StringBuilder**, **Loan**, and **GeometricObject** are implicitly subclasses of **Object** (as are all the main classes you have seen in this book so far). It is important to be familiar with the methods provided by the **Object** class so that you can use them in your classes. We will introduce the **toString** method in the **Object** class in this section.

toString()

The signature of the **toString()** method is

```
public String toString()
```

string representation

Invoking **toString()** on an object returns a string that describes the object. By default, it returns a string consisting of a class name of which the object is an instance, an at sign (@), and the object's memory address in hexadecimal. For example, consider the following code for the **Loan** class defined in Listing 10.2:

```
Loan loan = new Loan();
System.out.println(loan.toString());
```

The code displays something like **Loan@15037e5**. This message is not very helpful or informative. Usually you should override the **toString** method so that it returns a descriptive string representation of the object. For example, the **toString** method in the **Object** class was overridden in the **GeometricObject** class in lines 46-49 in Listing 11.1 as follows:

```
public String toString() {
  return "created on " + dateCreated + "\ncolor: " + color +
    " and filled: " + filled;
}
```

Note

print object

You can also pass an object to invoke **System.out.println(object)** or **System.out.print(object)**. This is equivalent to invoking **System.out.println(object.toString())** or **System.out.print(object.toString())**. So you could replace **System.out.println(loan.toString())** with **System.out.println(loan)**.

11.7 Polymorphism

The three pillars of object-oriented programming are encapsulation, inheritance, and polymorphism. You have already learned the first two. This section introduces polymorphism.

subtype

supertype

First let us define two useful terms: subtype and supertype. A class defines a type. A type defined by a subclass is called a *subtype* and a type defined by its superclass is called a *supertype*. So, you can say that **Circle** is a subtype of **GeometricObject** and **GeometricObject** is a supertype for **Circle**.

The inheritance relationship enables a subclass to inherit features from its superclass with additional new features. A subclass is a specialization of its superclass; every instance of a subclass is also an instance of its superclass, but not vice versa. For example, every circle is a geometric object, but not every geometric object is a circle. Therefore, you can always pass an instance of a subclass to a parameter of its superclass type. Consider the code in Listing 11.5.

LISTING 11.5 `PolymorphismDemo.java`

```
1 public class PolymorphismDemo {
2   /** Main method */
3   public static void main(String[] args) {
4     // Display circle and rectangle properties
5     displayObject(new Circle4(1, "red", false));
6     displayObject(new Rectangle1(1, 1, "black", true));
7   }
8
9   /** Display geometric object properties */
10  public static void displayObject(GeometricObject1 object) {
11    System.out.println("Created on " + object.getDateCreated() +
12      ". Color is " + object.getColor());
13  }
14 }
```

polymorphic call

polymorphic call

```
Created on Mon Mar 09 19:25:20 EDT 2009. Color is white
Created on Mon Mar 09 19:25:20 EDT 2009. Color is black
```

Method `displayObject` (line 10) takes a parameter of the `GeometricObject` type. You can invoke `displayObject` by passing any instance of `GeometricObject` (e.g., `new Circle4(1, "red", false)` and `new Rectangle1(1, 1, "black", false)` in lines 5–6). An object of a subclass can be used wherever its superclass object is used. This is commonly known as *polymorphism* (from a Greek word meaning "many forms"). In simple terms, polymorphism means that a variable of a supertype can refer to a subtype object.

what is polymorphism?

11.8 Dynamic Binding

A method may be defined in a superclass and overridden in its subclass. For example, the `toString()` method is defined in the `Object` class and overridden in `GeometricObject1`. Consider the following code:

```
Object o = new GeometricObject();
System.out.println(o.toString());
```

Which `toString()` method is invoked by `o`? To answer this question, we first introduce two terms: declared type and actual type. A variable must be declared a type. The type of a variable is called its *declared type*. Here `o`'s declared type is `Object`. A variable of a reference type can hold a `null` value or a reference to an instance of the declared type. The instance may be created using the constructor of the declared type or its subtype. The *actual type* of the variable is the actual class for the object referenced by the variable. Here `o`'s actual type is `GeometricObject`, since `o` references to an object created using `new GeometricObject()`. Which `toString()` method is invoked by `o` is determined by `o`'s actual type. This is known as *dynamic binding*.

declared type

actual type

Dynamic binding works as follows: Suppose an object `o` is an instance of classes C_1, C_2, ..., C_{n-1}, and C_n, where C_1 is a subclass of C_2, C_2 is a subclass of C_3, ..., and C_{n-1} is a subclass of C_n, as shown in Figure 11.2. That is, C_n is the most general class, and C_1 is the most specific

dynamic binding

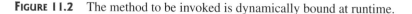

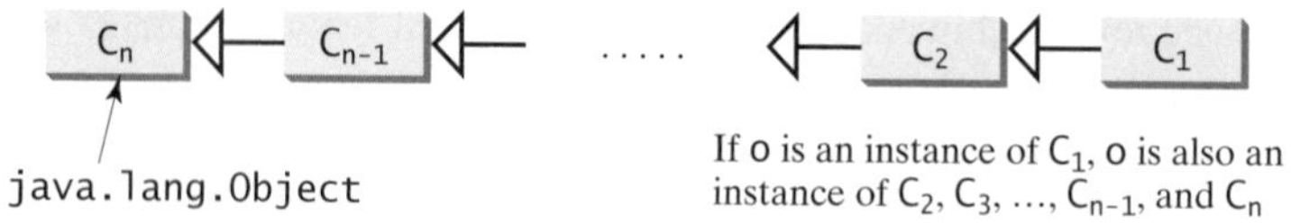
C_n
C_{n-1}
.....
C_2
C_1
java.lang.Object
If o is an instance of C_1, o is also an instance of C_2, C_3, ..., C_{n-1}, and C_n

FIGURE 11.2 The method to be invoked is dynamically bound at runtime.

class. In Java, C_n is the `Object` class. If `o` invokes a method `p`, the JVM searches the implementation for the method `p` in C_1, C_2, . . . , C_{n-1}, and C_n, in this order, until it is found. Once an implementation is found, the search stops and the first-found implementation is invoked.

Listing 11.6 gives an example to demonstrate dynamic binding.

Video Note
polymorphism and dynamic binding demo

LISTING 11.6 DynamicBindingDemo.java

polymorphic call (line 3) · dynamic binding (line 10) · override `toString()` (line 18) · override `toString()` (line 24)

```
 1 public class DynamicBindingDemo {
 2   public static void main(String[] args) {
 3     m(new GraduateStudent());
 4     m(new Student());
 5     m(new Person());
 6     m(new Object());
 7   }
 8
 9   public static void m(Object x) {
10     System.out.println(x.toString());
11   }
12 }
13
14 class GraduateStudent extends Student {
15 }
16
17 class Student extends Person {
18   public String toString() {
19     return "Student";
20   }
21 }
22
23 class Person extends Object {
24   public String toString() {
25     return "Person";
26   }
27 }
```

```
Student
Student
Person
java.lang.Object@130c19b
```

Method `m` (line 9) takes a parameter of the `Object` type. You can invoke `m` with any object (e.g., `new GraduateStudent()`, `new Student()`, `new Person()`, and `new Object()`) in lines 3–6).

When the method `m(Object x)` is executed, the argument `x`'s `toString` method is invoked. `x` may be an instance of `GraduateStudent`, `Student`, `Person`, or `Object`. Classes `GraduateStudent`, `Student`, `Person`, and `Object` have their own implementations of the `toString` method. Which implementation is used will be determined by `x`'s actual type at runtime. Invoking `m(new GraduateStudent())` (line 3) causes the `toString` method defined in the `Student` class to be invoked.

Invoking `m(new Student())` (line 4) causes the `toString` method defined in the `Student` class to be invoked.

Invoking `m(new Person())` (line 5) causes the `toString` method defined in the `Person` class to be invoked. Invoking `m(new Object())` (line 6) causes the `toString` method defined in the `Object` class to be invoked.

Matching a method signature and binding a method implementation are two separate issues. The *declared type* of the reference variable decides which method to match at compile time. The compiler finds a matching method according to parameter type, number of parameters, and order of the parameters at compile time. A method may be implemented in several subclasses. The JVM dynamically binds the implementation of the method at runtime, decided by the actual type of the variable. matching vs. binding

11.9 Casting Objects and the `instanceof` Operator

You have already used the casting operator to convert variables of one primitive type to another. Casting can also be used to convert an object of one class type to another within an inheritance hierarchy. In the preceding section, the statement

```
m(new Student());
```

assigns the object `new Student()` to a parameter of the `Object` type. This statement is equivalent to

```
Object o = new Student(); // Implicit casting
m(o);
```

The statement `Object o = new Student()`, known as *implicit casting*, is legal because an instance of `Student` is automatically an instance of `Object`. implicit casting

Suppose you want to assign the object reference `o` to a variable of the `Student` type using the following statement:

```
Student b = o;
```

In this case a compile error would occur. Why does the statement `Object o = new Student()` work but `Student b = o` doesn't? The reason is that a `Student` object is always an instance of `Object`, but an `Object` is not necessarily an instance of `Student`. Even though you can see that `o` is really a `Student` object, the compiler is not clever enough to know it. To tell the compiler that `o` is a `Student` object, use an *explicit casting*. The syntax is similar to the one used for casting among primitive data types. Enclose the target object type in parentheses and place it before the object to be cast, as follows: explicit casting

```
Student b = (Student)o; // Explicit casting
```

It is always possible to cast an instance of a subclass to a variable of a superclass (known as *upcasting*), because an instance of a subclass is *always* an instance of its superclass. When casting an instance of a superclass to a variable of its subclass (known as *downcasting*), explicit casting must be used to confirm your intention to the compiler with the (`SubclassName`) cast notation. For the casting to be successful, you must make sure that the object to be cast is an instance of the subclass. If the superclass object is not an instance of the subclass, a runtime *`ClassCastException`* occurs. For example, if an object is not an instance of `Student`, it cannot be cast into a variable of `Student`. It is a good practice, therefore, to ensure that the object is an instance of another object before attempting a casting. This can be accomplished by using the *instanceof* operator. Consider the following code: upcasting downcasting ClassCastException instanceof

```
Object myObject = new Circle();
... // Some lines of code
```

```
/** Perform casting if myObject is an instance of Circle */
if (myObject instanceof Circle) {
  System.out.println("The circle diameter is " +
    ((Circle)myObject).getDiameter());
  ...
}
```

You may be wondering why casting is necessary. Variable `myObject` is declared `Object`. The *declared type* decides which method to match at compile time. Using `myObject.getDiameter()` would cause a compile error, because the `Object` class does not have the `getDiameter` method. The compiler cannot find a match for `myObject.getDiameter()`. It is necessary to cast `myObject` into the `Circle` type to tell the compiler that `myObject` is also an instance of `Circle`.

Why not define `myObject` as a `Circle` type in the first place? To enable generic programming, it is a good practice to define a variable with a supertype, which can accept a value of any subtype.

lowercase keywords

Note

`instanceof` is a Java keyword. Every letter in a Java keyword is in lowercase.

casting analogy

Tip

To help understand casting, you may also consider the analogy of fruit, apple, and orange with the `Fruit` class as the superclass for `Apple` and `Orange`. An apple is a fruit, so you can always safely assign an instance of `Apple` to a variable for `Fruit`. However, a fruit is not necessarily an apple, so you have to use explicit casting to assign an instance of `Fruit` to a variable of `Apple`.

Listing 11.7 demonstrates polymorphism and casting. The program creates two objects (lines 5–6), a circle and a rectangle, and invokes the `displayObject` method to display them (lines 9–10). The `displayObject` method displays the area and diameter if the object is a circle (line 15), and the area if the object is a rectangle (line 21).

Listing 11.7 CastingDemo.java

polymorphic call (line 17)

polymorphic call (line 23)

```
 1 public class CastingDemo {
 2   /** Main method */
 3   public static void main(String[] args) {
 4     // Create and initialize two objects
 5     Object object1 = new Circle4(1);
 6     Object object2 = new Rectangle1(1, 1);
 7
 8     // Display circle and rectangle
 9     displayObject(object1);
10     displayObject(object2);
11   }
12
13   /** A method for displaying an object */
14   public static void displayObject(Object object) {
15     if (object instanceof Circle4) {
16       System.out.println("The circle area is " +
17         ((Circle4)object).getArea());
18       System.out.println("The circle diameter is " +
19         ((Circle4)object).getDiameter());
20     }
21     else if (object instanceof Rectangle1) {
22       System.out.println("The rectangle area is " +
23         ((Rectangle1)object).getArea());
24     }
25   }
26 }
```

```
The circle area is 3.141592653589793
The circle diameter is 2.0
The rectangle area is 1.0
```

The `displayObject(Object object)` method is an example of generic programming. It can be invoked by passing any instance of `Object`.

The program uses implicit casting to assign a `Circle` object to `object1` and a `Rectangle` object to `object2` (lines 5–6), then invokes the `displayObject` method to display the information on these objects (lines 9–10).

In the `displayObject` method (lines 14–25), explicit casting is used to cast the object to `Circle` if the object is an instance of `Circle`, and the methods `getArea` and `getDiameter` are used to display the area and diameter of the circle.

Casting can be done only when the source object is an instance of the target class. The program uses the `instanceof` operator to ensure that the source object is an instance of the target class before performing a casting (line 15).

Explicit casting to `Circle` (lines 17, 19) and to `Rectangle` (line 23) is necessary because the `getArea` and `getDiameter` methods are not available in the `Object` class.

Caution

. precedes casting

The object member access operator (`.`) precedes the casting operator. Use parentheses to ensure that casting is done before the `.` operator, as in

```
((Circle)object).getArea());
```

11.10 The **Object**'s **equals** Method

`equals(Object)`

Another method defined in the `Object` class that is often used is the `equals` method. Its signature is

```
public boolean equals(Object o)
```

This method tests whether two objects are equal. The syntax for invoking it is:

```
object1.equals(object2);
```

The default implementation of the `equals` method in the `Object` class is:

```
public boolean equals(Object obj) {
  return (this == obj);
}
```

This implementation checks whether two reference variables point to the same object using the == operator. You should override this method in your custom class to test whether two distinct objects have the same content.

You have already used the `equals` method to compare two strings in §9.2, "The `String` Class." The `equals` method in the `String` class is inherited from the `Object` class and is overridden in the `String` class to test whether two strings are identical in content. You can override the `equals` method in the `Circle` class to compare whether two circles are equal based on their radius as follows:

```
public boolean equals(Object o) {
  if (o instanceof Circle) {
    return radius == ((Circle)o).radius;
  }
```

```
      else
        return false;
    }
```

== vs. equals

Note

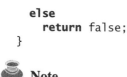

The == comparison operator is used for comparing two primitive data type values or for determining whether two objects have the same references. The **equals** method is intended to test whether two objects have the same contents, provided that the method is overridden in the defining class of the objects. The == operator is stronger than the **equals** method, in that the == operator checks whether the two reference variables refer to the same object.

equals(Object)

Caution

Using the signature **equals(SomeClassName obj)** (e.g., **equals(Circle c)**) to override the **equals** method in a subclass is a common mistake. You should use **equals(Object obj)**. See Review Question 11.15.

11.11 The ArrayList Class

Video Note
the **ArrayList** class

Now we are ready to introduce a very useful class for storing objects. You can create an array to store objects. But, once the array is created, its size is fixed. Java provides the **ArrayList** class that can be used to store an unlimited number of objects. Figure 11.3 shows some methods in **ArrayList**.

java.util.ArrayList	
+ArrayList()	Creates an empty list.
+add(o: Object): void	Appends a new element o at the end of this list.
+add(index: int, o: Object): void	Adds a new element o at the specified index in this list.
+clear(): void	Removes all the elements from this list.
+contains(o: Object): boolean	Returns true if this list contains the element o.
+get(index: int): Object	Returns the element from this list at the specified index.
+indexOf(o: Object): int	Returns the index of the first matching element in this list.
+isEmpty(): boolean	Returns true if this list contains no elements.
+lastIndexOf(o: Object): int	Returns the index of the last matching element in this list.
+remove(o: Object): boolean	Removes the element o from this list.
+size(): int	Returns the number of elements in this list.
+remove(index: int): boolean	Removes the element at the specified index.
+set(index: int, o: Object): Object	Sets the element at the specified index.

FIGURE 11.3 An **ArrayList** stores an unlimited number of objects.

Listing 11.8 gives an example of using **ArrayList** to store objects.

LISTING 11.8 TestArrayList.java

create **ArrayList**

add element

```
public class TestArrayList {
  public static void main(String[] args) {
    // Create a list to store cities
    java.util.ArrayList cityList = new java.util.ArrayList();

    // Add some cities in the list
    cityList.add("London");
```

```java
    // cityList now contains [London]
    cityList.add("Denver");
    // cityList now contains [London, Denver]
    cityList.add("Paris");
    // cityList now contains [London, Denver, Paris]
    cityList.add("Miami");
    // cityList now contains [London, Denver, Paris, Miami]
    cityList.add("Seoul");
    // contains [London, Denver, Paris, Miami, Seoul]
    cityList.add("Tokyo");
    // contains [London, Denver, Paris, Miami, Seoul, Tokyo]

    System.out.println("List size? " + cityList.size() );
    System.out.println("Is Miami in the list? " +
      cityList.contains("Miami") );
    System.out.println("The location of Denver in the list? "
      + cityList.indexOf("Denver"));
    System.out.println("Is the list empty? " +
      cityList.isEmpty() ); // Print false

    // Insert a new city at index 2
    cityList.add(2, "Xian");
    // contains [London, Denver, Xian, Paris, Miami, Seoul, Tokyo]

    // Remove a city from the list
    cityList.remove("Miami");
    // contains [London, Denver, Xian, Paris, Seoul, Tokyo]

    // Remove a city at index 1
    cityList.remove(1);
    // contains [London, Xian, Paris, Seoul, Tokyo]

    // Display the contents in the list
    System.out.println(cityList.toString());

    // Display the contents in the list in reverse order
    for (int i = cityList.size() - 1; i >= 0; i--)
      System.out.print(cityList.get(i) + " ");
    System.out.println();

    // Create a list to store two circles
    java.util.ArrayList list = new java.util.ArrayList();

    // Add two circles
    list.add(new Circle4(2));
    list.add(new Circle4(3));

    // Display the area of the first circle in the list
    System.out.println("The area of the circle? " +
      ((Circle4)list.get(0)).getArea());
  }
}
```

list size

contains element?

element index

is empty?

remove element

remove element

toString()

get element

create **ArrayList**

```
List size? 6
Is Miami in the list? true
The location of Denver in the list? 1
Is the list empty? false
[London, Xian, Paris, Seoul, Tokyo]
Tokyo Seoul Paris Xian London
The area of the circle? 12.566370614359172
```

The program creates an `ArrayList` using its no-arg constructor (line 4). The `add` method adds any instance of `Object` into the list. Since `String` is a subclass of `Object`, strings can be added to the list. The `add` method (lines 7–17) adds an object to the end of list. So, after `cityList.add("London")` (line 7), the list contains

```
[London]
```

add(Object)

After `cityList. add("Denver")` (line 9), the list contains

```
[London, Denver]
```

After adding Paris, Miami, Seoul, and Tokyo (lines 11–17), the list would contain

```
[London, Denver, Paris, Miami, Seoul, Tokyo]
```

size()

Invoking `size()` (line 20) returns the size of the list, which is currently `6`. Invoking `contains("Miami")` (line 22) checks whether the object is in the list. In this case, it returns `true`, since `Miami` is in the list. Invoking `indexOf("Denver")` (line 24) returns the index of the object in the list, which is `1`. If the object is not in the list, it returns `-1`. The `isEmpty()` method (line 26) checks whether the list is empty. It returns `false`, since the list is not empty.

add(index, Object)

The statement `cityList.add(2, "Xian")` (line 29) inserts an object to the list at the specified index. After this statement, the list becomes

```
[London, Denver, Xian, Paris, Miami, Seoul, Tokyo]
```

remove(Object)

The statement `cityList. remove("Miami")` (line 33) removes the object from the list. After this statement, the list becomes

```
[London, Denver, Xian, Paris, Seoul, Tokyo]
```

remove(index)

The statement `cityList. remove(1)` (line 37) removes the object at the specified index from the list. After this statement, the list becomes

```
[London, Xian, Paris, Seoul, Tokyo]
```

The statement in line 41 is same as

```
System.out.println(cityList);
```

toString()

The `toString()` method returns a string representation for the list in the form of `[e0.toString(), e1.toString(), ..., ek.toString()]`, where `e0`, `e1`, . . . , and `ek` are the elements in the list.

getIndex()

The `get(index)` method (line 45) returns the object at the specified index.

compiler warning

Note

You will get the following warning when compiling this program from the command prompt:

```
Note: TestArrayList.java uses unchecked or unsafe operations.
Note: Recompile with -Xlint:unchecked for details.
```

This warning can be eliminated using generic types discussed in Chapter 21, "Generics". For now, ignore it. Despite the warning, the program will be compiled just fine to produce a .class file.

array vs. **ArrayList**

`ArrayList` objects can be used like arrays, but there are many differences. Table 11.1 lists their similarities and differences.

Once an array is created, its size is fixed. You can access an array element using the square-bracket notation (e.g., `a[index]`). When an `ArrayList` is created, its size is `0`. You cannot use the `get` and `set` methods if the element is not in the list. It is easy to add, insert,

TABLE 11.1 Differences and Similarities between Arrays and `ArrayList`

Operation	*Array*	*ArrayList*
Creating an array/ArrayList	`Object[] a = new Object[10]`	`ArrayList list = new ArrayList();`
Accessing an element	`a[index]`	`list.get(index);`
Updating an element	`a[index] = "London";`	`list.set(index, "London");`
Returning size	`a.length`	`list.size();`
Adding a new element		`list.add("London");`
Inserting a new element		`list.add(index, "London");`
Removing an element		`list.remove(index);`
Removing an element		`list.remove(Object);`
Removing all elements		`list.clear();`

and remove elements in a list, but it is rather complex to add, insert, and remove elements in an array. You have to write code to manipulate the array in order to perform these operations.

Note

`java.util.Vector` is also a class for storing objects, which is very similar to the `ArrayList` class. All the methods in `ArrayList` are also available in `Vector`. The `Vector` class was introduced in JDK 1.1. The `ArrayList` class introduced in JDK 1.2 was intended to replace the `Vector` class.

`Vector` class

11.12 A Custom Stack Class

Video Note
the `MyStack` class

"Designing a Class for Stacks" in §10.8 presented a stack class for storing `int` values. This section introduces a stack class to store objects. You can use an `ArrayList` to implement `Stack`, as shown in Listing 11.9. The UML diagram for the class is shown in Figure 11.4.

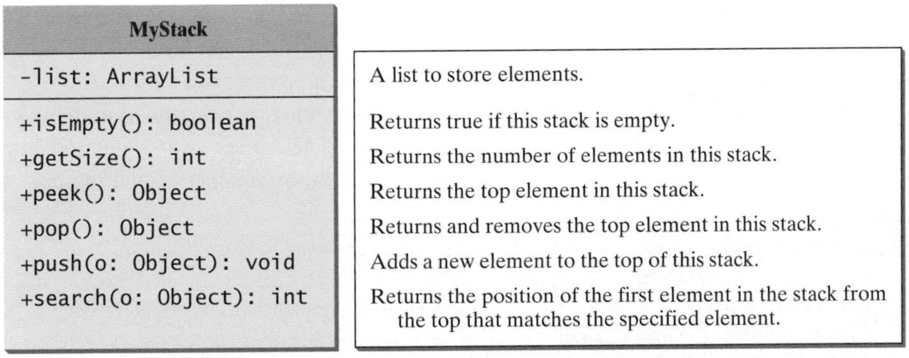
MyStack
-list: ArrayList
+isEmpty(): boolean
+getSize(): int
+peek(): Object
+pop(): Object
+push(o: Object): void
+search(o: Object): int
A list to store elements.
Returns true if this stack is empty.
Returns the number of elements in this stack.
Returns the top element in this stack.
Returns and removes the top element in this stack.
Adds a new element to the top of this stack.
Returns the position of the first element in the stack from the top that matches the specified element.

FIGURE 11.4 The `MyStack` class encapsulates the stack storage and provides the operations for manipulating the stack.

LISTING 11.9 MyStack.java

```
public class MyStack {
  private java.util.ArrayList list = new java.util.ArrayList();

  public boolean isEmpty() {
    return list.isEmpty();
  }
```

array list

stack empty?

get stack size
peek stack
remove
push
search

```
 7
 8   public int getSize() {
 9     return list.size();
10   }
11
12   public Object peek() {
13     return list.get(getSize() - 1);
14   }
15
16   public Object pop() {
17     Object o = list.get(getSize() - 1);
18     list.remove(getSize() - 1);
19     return o;
20   }
21
22   public void push(Object o) {
23     list.add(o);
24   }
25
26   public int search(Object o) {
27     return list.lastIndexOf(o);
28   }
29
30   /** Override the toString in the Object class */
31   public String toString() {
32     return "stack: " + list.toString();
33   }
34 }
```

An array list is created to store the elements in the stack (line 2). The `isEmpty()` method (lines 4–6) returns `list.isEmpty()`. The `getSize()` method (lines 8–10) returns `list.size()`. The `peek()` method (lines 12–14) retrieves the element at the top of the stack without removing it. The end of the list is the top of the stack. The `pop()` method (lines 16–20) removes the top element from the stack and returns it. The `push(Object element)` method (lines 22–24) adds the specified element to the stack. The `search(Object element)` method checks whether the specified element is in the stack, and it returns the index of first-matching element in the stack from the top by invoking `list.lastIndexOf(o)`. The `toString()` method (lines 31–33) defined in the `Object` class is overridden to display the contents of the stack by invoking `list.toString()`. The `toString()` method implemented in `ArrayList` returns a string representation of all the elements in an array list.

composition
has-a
is-a

Design Guide

In Listing 11.9, `MyStack` contains `ArrayList`. The relationship between `MyStack` and `ArrayList` is *composition*. While inheritance models an is-a relationship, composition models a has-a relationship. You may also implement `MyStack` as a subclass of `ArrayList` (see Exercise 11.4). Using composition is better, however, because it enables you to define a completely new stack class without inheriting the unnecessary and inappropriate methods from `ArrayList`.

11.13 The **protected** Data and Methods

So far you have used the `private` and `public` keywords to specify whether data fields and methods can be accessed from the outside of the class. Private members can be accessed only from the inside of the class, and public members can be accessed from any other classes.

why **protected**?

Often it is desirable to allow subclasses to access data fields or methods defined in the superclass, but not allow nonsubclasses to access these data fields and methods. To do so, you can use the `protected` keyword. A protected data field or method in a superclass can be accessed in its subclasses.

The modifiers `private`, `protected`, and `public` are known as *visibility* or *accessibility modifiers* because they specify how class and class members are accessed. The visibility of these modifiers increases in this order:

Visibility increases →

private, none (if no modifier is used), protected, public

Table 11.2 summarizes the accessibility of the members in a class. Figure 11.5 illustrates how a public, protected, default, and private datum or method in class C1 can be accessed from a class C2 in the same package, from a subclass C3 in the same package, from a subclass C4 in a different package, and from a class C5 in a different package.

TABLE 11.2 Data and Methods Visibility

Modifier on members in a class	*Accessed from the same class*	*Accessed from the same package*	*Accessed from a subclass*	*Accessed from a different package*
public	✓	✓	✓	✓
protected	✓	✓	✓	–
(default)	✓	✓	–	–
private	✓	–	–	–

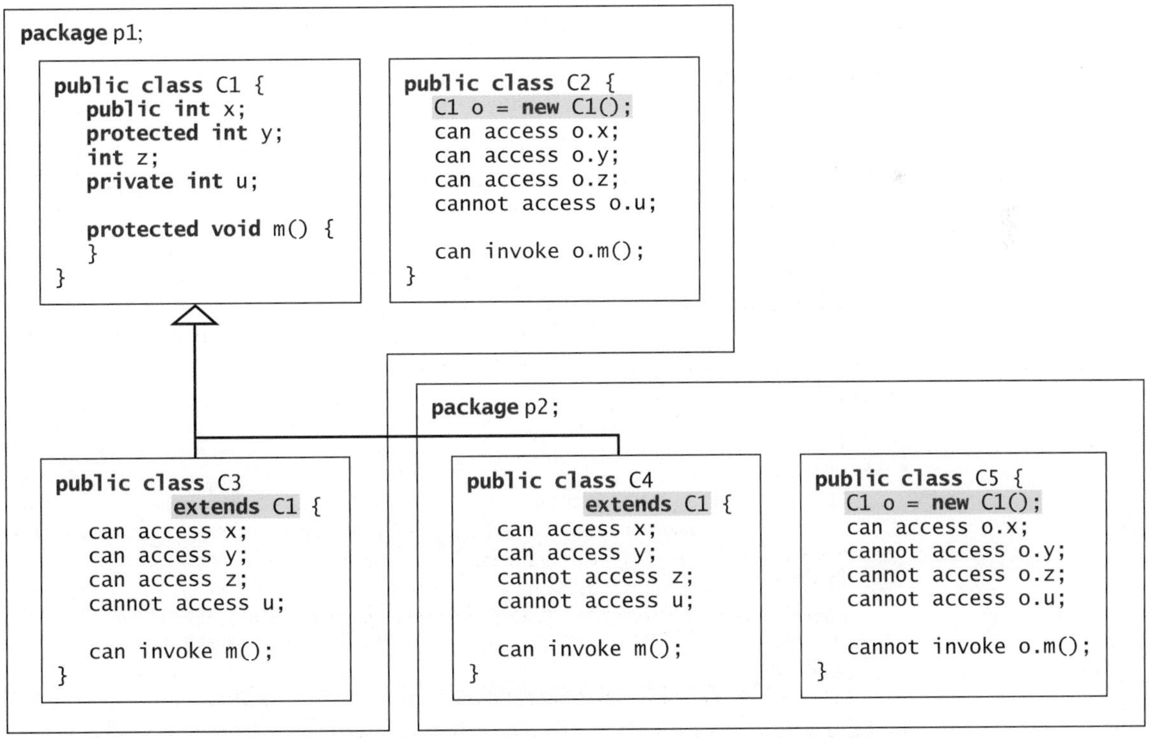
package p1;
public class C1 {
public int x;
protected int y;
int z;
private int u;
protected void m() {
}
}
public class C2 {
C1 o = new C1();
can access o.x;
can access o.y;
can access o.z;
cannot access o.u;
can invoke o.m();
}
public class C3
extends C1 {
can access x;
can access y;
can access z;
cannot access u;
can invoke m();
}
package p2;
public class C4
extends C1 {
can access x;
can access y;
cannot access z;
cannot access u;
can invoke m();
}
public class C5 {
C1 o = new C1();
can access o.x;
cannot access o.y;
cannot access o.z;
cannot access o.u;
cannot invoke o.m();
}

FIGURE 11.5 Visibility modifiers are used to control how data and methods are accessed.

Use the `private` modifier to hide the members of the class completely so that they cannot be accessed directly from outside the class. Use no modifiers in order to allow the members of the class to be accessed directly from any class within the same package but not from other packages. Use the **protected** modifier to enable the members of the class to be accessed by the subclasses in any package or classes in the same package. Use the **public** modifier to enable the members of the class to be accessed by any class.

Your class can be used in two ways: for creating instances of the class, and for defining subclasses by extending the class. Make the members **private** if they are not intended for use from outside the class. Make the members **public** if they are intended for the users of the class. Make the fields or methods **protected** if they are intended for the extenders of the class but not the users of the class.

The **private** and **protected** modifiers can be used only for members of the class. The **public** modifier and the default modifier (i.e., no modifier) can be used on members of the class as well on the class. A class with no modifier (i.e., not a public class) is not accessible by classes from other packages.

change visibility

Note

A subclass may override a protected method in its superclass and change its visibility to public. However, a subclass cannot weaken the accessibility of a method defined in the superclass. For example, if a method is defined as public in the superclass, it must be defined as public in the subclass.

11.14 Preventing Extending and Overriding

You may occasionally want to prevent classes from being extended. In such cases, use the **final** modifier to indicate that a class is final and cannot be a parent class. The **Math** class is a final class. The **String**, **StringBuilder**, and **StringBuffer** classes are also final classes. For example, the following class is final and cannot be extended:

```
public final class C {
  // Data fields, constructors, and methods omitted
}
```

You also can define a method to be final; a final method cannot be overridden by its subclasses.

For example, the following method is final and cannot be overridden:

```
public class Test {
  // Data fields, constructors, and methods omitted

  public final void m() {
    // Do something
  }
}
```

Note

The modifiers are used on classes and class members (data and methods), except that the **final** modifier can also be used on local variables in a method. A final local variable is a constant inside a method.

Key Terms

actual type 385
array list 393
casting objects 387
composition 394
constructor chaining 381
declared type 385
dynamic binding 385
final 396

Chapter Summary

1. You can derive a new class from an existing class. This is known as class inheritance. The new class is called a subclass, child class or extended class. The existing class is called a *superclass, parent class*, or *base class*.

2. A constructor is used to construct an instance of a class. Unlike properties and methods, the constructors of a superclass are not inherited in the subclass. They can be invoked only from the constructors of the subclasses, using the keyword `super`.

3. A constructor may invoke an overloaded constructor or its superclass's constructor. The call must be the first statement in the constructor. If none of them is invoked explicitly, the compiler puts `super()` as the first statement in the constructor, which invokes the superclass's no-arg constructor.

4. To override a method, the method must be defined in the subclass using the same signature as in its superclass.

5. An instance method can be overridden only if it is accessible. Thus a private method cannot be overridden, because it is not accessible outside its own class. If a method defined in a subclass is private in its superclass, the two methods are completely unrelated.

6. Like an instance method, a static method can be inherited. However, a static method cannot be overridden. If a static method defined in the superclass is redefined in a subclass, the method defined in the superclass is hidden.

7. Every class in Java is descended from the `java.lang.Object` class. If no inheritance is specified when a class is defined, its superclass is `Object`.

8. If a method's parameter type is a superclass (e.g., `Object`), you may pass an object to this method of any of the parameter's subclasses (e.g., `Circle` or `String`). When an object (e.g., a `Circle` object or a `String` object) is used in the method, the particular implementation of the method of the object that is invoked (e.g., `toString`) is determined dynamically.

9. It is always possible to cast an instance of a subclass to a variable of a superclass, because an instance of a subclass is *always* an instance of its superclass. When casting an instance of a superclass to a variable of its subclass, explicit casting must be used to confirm your intention to the compiler with the (`SubclassName`) cast notation.

10. A class defines a type. A type defined by a subclass is called a *subtype* and a type defined by its superclass is called a *supertype*.

11. When invoking an instance method from a reference variable, the *actual type of* the variable decides which implementation of the method is used *at runtime*. When

accessing a field or a static method, the *declared type* of the reference variable decides which method is used *at compile time*.

12. You can use `obj instanceof AClass` to test whether an object is an instance of a class.

13. You can use the `protected` modifier to prevent the data and methods from being accessed by nonsubclasses from a different package.

14. You can use the `final` modifier to indicate that a class is final and cannot be a parent class and to indicate that a method is final and cannot be overridden.

Review Questions

Sections 11.2–11.5

11.1 What is the printout of running the class `C` in (a)? What problem arises in compiling the program in (b)?

```
class A {
  public A() {
    System.out.println(
      "A's no-arg constructor is invoked");
  }
}

class B extends A {
}

public class C {
  public static void main(String[] args) {
    B b = new B();
  }
}
```

(a)

```
class A {
  public A(int x) {
  }
}

class B extends A {
  public B() {
  }
}

public class C {
  public static void main(String[] args) {
    B b = new B();
  }
}
```

(b)

11.2 True or false?

1. A subclass is a subset of a superclass.
2. When invoking a constructor from a subclass, its superclass's no-arg constructor is always invoked.
3. You can override a private method defined in a superclass.
4. You can override a static method defined in a superclass.

11.3 Identify the problems in the following classes:

```
public class Circle {
  private double radius;

  public Circle(double radius) {
    radius = radius;
  }

  public double getRadius() {
    return radius;
  }

  public double getArea() {
    return radius * radius * Math.PI;
  }
```

```
}

class B extends Circle {
  private double length;

  B(double radius, double length) {
    Circle(radius);
    length = length;
  }

  /** Override getArea() */
  public double getArea() {
    return getArea() * length;
  }
}
```

11.4 How do you explicitly invoke a superclass's constructor from a subclass?

11.5 How do you invoke an overridden superclass method from a subclass?

11.6 Explain the difference between method overloading and method overriding.

11.7 If a method in a subclass has the same signature as a method in its superclass with the same return type, is the method overridden or overloaded?

11.8 If a method in a subclass has the same signature as a method in its superclass with a different return type, will this be a problem?

11.9 If a method in a subclass has the same name as a method in its superclass with different parameter types, is the method overridden or overloaded?

Sections 11.6–11.9

11.10 Does every class have a `toString` method and an `equals` method? Where do they come from? How are they used? Is it appropriate to override these methods?

11.11 Show the output of following program:

```
public class Test {
  public static void main(String[] args) {
    A a = new A(3);
  }
}

class A extends B {
  public A(int t) {
    System.out.println("A's constructor is invoked");
  }
}

class B {
  public B() {
    System.out.println("B's constructor is invoked");
  }
}
```

Is the no-arg constructor of `Object` invoked when `new A(3)` is invoked?

11.12 For the `GeometricObject` and `Circle` classes in Listings 11.1 and 11.2, answer the following questions:

(a) Are the following Boolean expressions true or false?

```
Circle circle = new Circle(1);
GeometricObject object1 = new GeometricObject();
```

```
(circle instanceof GeometricObject)
(object1 instanceof GeometricObject)
(circle instanceof Circle)
(object1 instanceof Circle)
```

(b) Can the following statements be compiled?

```
Circle circle = new Circle(5);
GeometricObject object = circle;
```

(c) Can the following statements be compiled?

```
GeometricObject object = new GeometricObject();
Circle circle = (Circle)object;
```

11.13 Suppose that Fruit, Apple, Orange, GoldenDelicious, and Macintosh are declared, as shown in Figure 11.6.

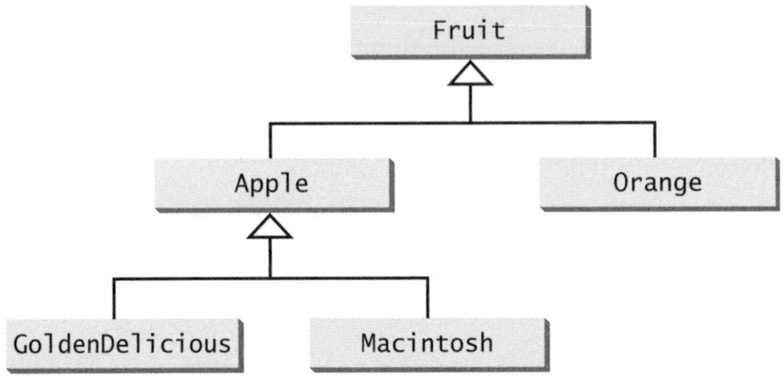
Fruit
Apple
Orange
GoldenDelicious
Macintosh

FIGURE 11.6 GoldenDelicious and Macintosh are subclasses of Apple; Apple and Orange are subclasses of Fruit.

Assume that the following declaration is given:

```
Fruit fruit = new GoldenDelicious();
Orange orange = new Orange();
```

Answer the following questions:

(1) Is fruit instanceof Fruit?
(2) Is fruit instanceof Orange?
(3) Is fruit instanceof Apple?
(4) Is fruit instanceof GoldenDelicious?
(5) Is fruit instanceof Macintosh?
(6) Is orange instanceof Orange?
(7) Is orange instanceof Fruit?
(8) Is orange instanceof Apple?
(9) Suppose the method makeAppleCider is defined in the Apple class. Can fruit invoke this method? Can orange invoke this method?
(10) Suppose the method makeOrangeJuice is defined in the Orange class. Can orange invoke this method? Can fruit invoke this method?
(11) Is the statement Orange p = new Apple() legal?
(12) Is the statement Macintosh p = new Apple() legal?
(13) Is the statement Apple p = new Macintosh() legal?

11.14 What is wrong in the following code?

```
public class Test {
  public static void main(String[] args) {
    Object fruit = new Fruit();
    Object apple = (Apple)fruit;
  }
}

class Apple extends Fruit {
}

class Fruit {
}
```

Section 11.10

11.15 When overriding the `equals` method, a common mistake is mistyping its signature in the subclass. For example, the `equals` method is incorrectly written as `equals(Circle circle)`, as shown in (a) in the code below; instead, it should be `equals(Object circle)`, as shown in (b). Show the output of running class `Test` with the `Circle` class in (a) and in (b), respectively.

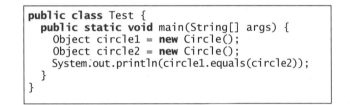

```
public class Test {
  public static void main(String[] args) {
    Object circle1 = new Circle();
    Object circle2 = new Circle();
    System.out.println(circle1.equals(circle2));
  }
}
```

```
class Circle {
  double radius;

  public boolean equals(Circle circle) {
    return this.radius == circle.radius;
  }
}
```

(a)

```
class Circle {
  double radius;

  public boolean equals(Object circle ) {
    return this.radius ==
      ((Circle)circle).radius;
  }
}
```

(b)

Sections 11.11–11.12

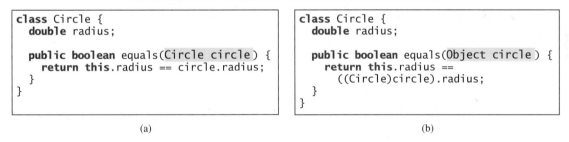

11.16 How do you create an `ArrayList`? How do you append an object to a list? How do you insert an object at the beginning of a list? How do you find the number of objects in a list? How do you remove a given object from a list? How do you remove the last object from the list? How do you check whether a given object is in a list? How do you retrieve an object at a specified index from a list?

11.17 There are three errors in the code below. Identify them.

```
ArrayList list = new ArrayList();
list.add("Denver");
list.add("Austin");
list.add(new java.util.Date());
String city = list.get(0);
list.set(3, "Dallas");
System.out.println(list.get(3));
```

Sections 11.13–11.14

11.18 What modifier should you use on a class so that a class in the same package can access it, but a class in a different package cannot access it?

11.19 What modifier should you use so that a class in a different package cannot access the class, but its subclasses in any package can access it?

11.20 In the code below, classes A and B are in the same package. If the question marks are replaced by blanks, can class B be compiled? If the question marks are replaced by `private`, can class B be compiled? If the question marks are replaced by `protected`, can class B be compiled?

```
package p1;

public class A {
   ?    int i;

   ?    void m() {
     ...
  }
}
```

(a)

```
package p1;

public class B extends A {
  public void m1(String[] args) {
    System.out.println(i);
    m();
  }
}
```

(b)

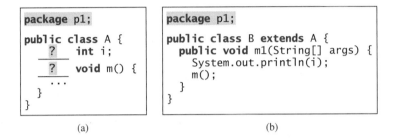

11.21 In the code below, classes A and B are in different packages. If the question marks are replaced by blanks, can class B be compiled? If the question marks are replaced by `private`, can class B be compiled? If the question marks are replaced by `protected`, can class B be compiled?

```
package p1;

public class A {
   ?    int i;

   ?    void m() {
     ...
  }
}
```

(a)

```
package p2;

public class B extends A {
  public void m1(String[] args) {
    System.out.println(i);
    m();
  }
}
```

(b)

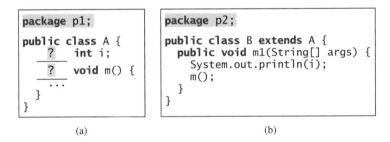

11.22 How do you prevent a class from being extended? How do you prevent a method from being overridden?

Comprehensive

11.23 Define the following terms: inheritance, superclass, subclass, the keywords `super` and `this`, casting objects, the modifiers `protected` and `final`.

11.24 Indicate true or false for the following statements:

- A protected datum or method can be accessed by any class in the same package.
- A protected datum or method can be accessed by any class in different packages.
- A protected datum or method can be accessed by its subclasses in any package.
- A final class can have instances.
- A final class can be extended.
- A final method can be overridden.
- You can always successfully cast an instance of a subclass to a superclass.
- You can always successfully cast an instance of a superclass to a subclass.

11.25 Describe the difference between method matching and method binding.

11.26 What is polymorphism? What is dynamic binding?

PROGRAMMING EXERCISES

Sections 11.2–11.4

11.1 (*The* `Triangle` *class*) Design a class named `Triangle` that extends `GeometricObject`. The class contains:

- Three `double` data fields named `side1`, `side2`, and `side3` with default values `1.0` to denote three sides of the triangle.
- A no-arg constructor that creates a default triangle.
- A constructor that creates a triangle with the specified `side1`, `side2`, and `side3`.
- The accessor methods for all three data fields.
- A method named `getArea()` that returns the area of this triangle.
- A method named `getPerimeter()` that returns the perimeter of this triangle.
- A method named `toString()` that returns a string description for the triangle.

For the formula to compute the area of a triangle, see Exercise 2.21. The `toString()` method is implemented as follows:

```
return "Triangle: side1 = " + side1 + " side2 = " + side2 +
  " side3 = " + side3;
```

Draw the UML diagram for the classes `Triangle` and `GeometricObject`. Implement the class. Write a test program that creates a `Triangle` object with sides `1`, `1.5`, `1`, color `yellow` and `filled true`, and displays the area, perimeter, color, and whether filled or not.

Sections 11.5–11.11

11.2 (*The* `Person`, `Student`, `Employee`, `Faculty`, *and* `Staff` *classes*) Design a class named `Person` and its two subclasses named `Student` and `Employee`. Make `Faculty` and `Staff` subclasses of `Employee`. A person has a name, address, phone number, and email address. A student has a class status (freshman, sophomore, junior, or senior). Define the status as a constant. An employee has an office, salary, and date hired. Define a class named `MyDate` that contains the fields `year`, `month`, and `day`. A faculty member has office hours and a rank. A staff member has a title. Override the `toString` method in each class to display the class name and the person's name.

Draw the UML diagram for the classes. Implement the classes. Write a test program that creates a `Person`, `Student`, `Employee`, `Faculty`, and `Staff`, and invokes their `toString()` methods.

11.3 (*Subclasses of* `Account`) In Exercise 8.7, the `Account` class was defined to model a bank account. An account has the properties account number, balance, annual interest rate, and date created, and methods to deposit and withdraw funds. Create two subclasses for checking and saving accounts. A checking account has an overdraft limit, but a savings account cannot be overdrawn.

Draw the UML diagram for the classes. Implement the classes. Write a test program that creates objects of `Account`, `SavingsAccount`, and `CheckingAccount` and invokes their `toString()` methods.

11.4 (*Implementing `MyStack` using inheritance*) In Listing 11.9, `MyStack` is implemented using composition. Create a new stack class that extends `ArrayList`.
Draw the UML diagram for the classes. Implement `MyStack`. Write a test program that prompts the user to enter five strings and displays them in reverse order.

11.5 (*The `Course` class*) Rewrite the `Course` class in Listing 10.6. Use an `ArrayList` to replace an array to store students. You should not change the original contract of the `Course` class (i.e., the definition of the constructors and methods should not be changed).

11.6 (*Using `ArrayList`*) Write a program that creates an `ArrayList` and adds a `Loan` object, a `Date` object, a string, a `JFrame` object, and a `Circle` object to the list, and use a loop to display all the elements in the list by invoking the object's `toString()` method.

11.7*** (*Implementing `ArrayList`*) `ArrayList` is implemented in the Java API. Implement `ArrayList` and the methods defined in Figure 11.3. (*Hint*: Use an array to store the elements in `ArrayList`. If the size of the `ArrayList` exceeds the capacity of the current array, create a new array that doubles the size of the current array and copy the contents of the current to the new array.)

11.8** (*New `Account` class*) An `Account` class was specified in Exercise 8.7. Design a new `Account` class as follows:

- Add a new data field `name` of the `String` type to store the name of the customer.
- Add a new constructor that constructs an account with the specified name, id, and balance.
- Add a new data field named `transactions` whose type is `ArrayList` that stores the transaction for the accounts. Each transaction is an instance of the `Transaction` class. The `Transaction` class is defined as shown in Figure 11.7.
- Modify the `withdraw` and `deposit` methods to add a transaction to the `transactions` array list.
- All other properties and methods are same as in Exercise 8.7.

Write a test program that creates an `Account` with annual interest rate `1.5%`, balance `1000`, id `1122`, and name `George`. Deposit $30, $40, $50 to the account and withdraw $5, $4, $2 from the account. Print an account summary that shows account holder name, interest rate, balance, and all transactions.

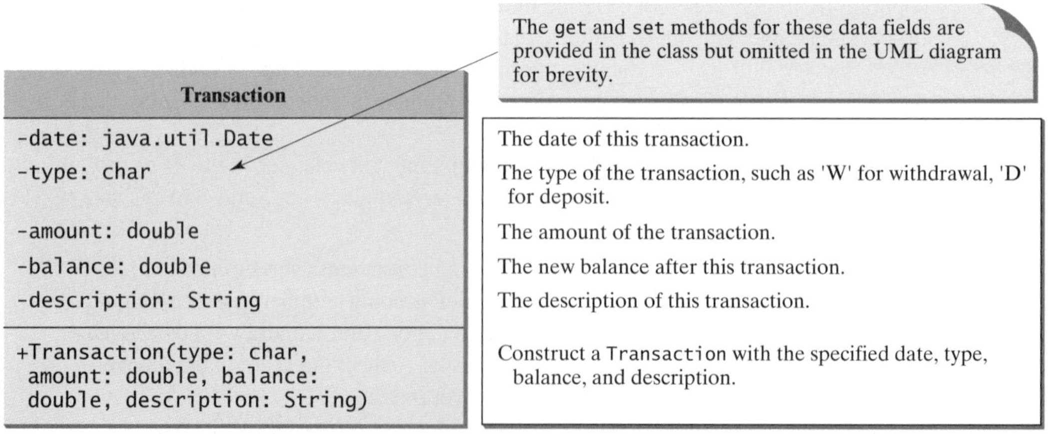
The get and set methods for these data fields are provided in the class but omitted in the UML diagram for brevity.
Transaction
-date: java.util.Date
-type: char
-amount: double
-balance: double
-description: String
+Transaction(type: char, amount: double, balance: double, description: String)
The date of this transaction.
The type of the transaction, such as 'W' for withdrawal, 'D' for deposit.
The amount of the transaction.
The new balance after this transaction.
The description of this transaction.
Construct a Transaction with the specified date, type, balance, and description.

FIGURE 11.7 The `Transaction` class describes a transaction for a bank account.

Chapter 12

GUI Basics

Objectives

- To distinguish between Swing and AWT (§12.2).
- To describe the Java GUI API hierarchy (§12.3).
- To create user interfaces using frames, panels, and simple GUI components (§12.4).
- To understand the role of layout managers (§12.5).
- To use the `FlowLayout`, `GridLayout`, and `BorderLayout` managers to lay out components in a container (§12.5).
- To use `JPanel` to make panels as subcontainers (§12.6).
- To specify colors and fonts using the `Color` and `Font` classes (§§12.7–12.8).
- To apply common features such as borders, tool tips, fonts, and colors on Swing components (§12.9).
- To use borders to visually group user-interface components (§12.9).
- To create image icons using the `ImageIcon` class (§12.10).

12.1 Introduction

The design of the API for Java GUI programming is an excellent example of how the object-oriented principle is applied. This chapter serves two purposes. First, it introduces the basics of Java GUI programming. Second, it uses GUI to demonstrate OOP. Specifically, this chapter will introduce the framework of Java GUI API and discuss GUI components and their relationships, containers and layout managers, colors, fonts, borders, image icons, and tool tips.

12.2 Swing vs. AWT

We used simple GUI examples to demonstrate OOP in §8.6.3, "Displaying GUI Components." We used the GUI components such as `JButton`, `JLabel`, `JTextField`, `JRadioButton`, and `JComboBox`. Why do the GUI component classes have the prefix *J*? Instead of `JButton`, why not name it simply `Button`? In fact, there is a class already named `Button` in the `java.awt` package.

When Java was introduced, the GUI classes were bundled in a library known as the Abstract Windows Toolkit (AWT). AWT is fine for developing simple graphical user interfaces, but not for developing comprehensive GUI projects. Besides, AWT is prone to platform-specific bugs. The AWT user-interface components were replaced by a more robust, versatile, and flexible library known as *Swing components*. Swing components are painted directly on canvases using Java code, except for components that are subclasses of `java.awt.Window` or `java.awt.Panel`, which must be drawn using native GUI on a specific platform. Swing components depend less on the target platform and use less of the native GUI resource. For this reason, Swing components that don't rely on native GUI are referred to as *lightweight components*, and AWT components are referred to as *heavyweight components*.

Swing components

lightweight

heavyweight

To distinguish new Swing component classes from their AWT counterparts, the Swing GUI component classes are named with a prefixed *J*. Although AWT components are still supported in Java, it is better to learn to how program using Swing components, because the AWT user-interface components will eventually fade away. This book uses Swing GUI components exclusively.

why prefix J?

12.3 The Java GUI API

The GUI API contains classes that can be classified into three groups: *component classes, container classes*, and *helper classes*. Their hierarchical relationships are shown in Figure 12.1.

The component classes, such as `JButton`, `JLabel`, and `JTextField`, are for creating the user interface. The container classes, such as `JFrame`, `JPanel`, and `JApplet`, are used to contain other components. The helper classes, such as `Graphics`, `Color`, `Font`, `FontMetrics`, and `Dimension`, are used to support GUI components.

Note

The `JFrame`, `JApplet`, `JDialog`, and `JComponent` classes and their subclasses are grouped in the `javax.swing` package. All the other classes in Figure 12.1 are grouped in the `java.awt` package.

12.3.1 Component Classes

An instance of `Component` can be displayed on the screen. `Component` is the root class of all the user-interface classes including container classes, and `JComponent` is the root class of all the lightweight Swing components. Both `Component` and `JComponent` are abstract classes. Abstract classes will be introduced in Chapter 14, "Abstract Classes and Interfaces." For now, all you need to know is that abstract classes are same as classes except that you cannot create instances using the `new` operator. For example, you cannot use `new JComponent()` to create an

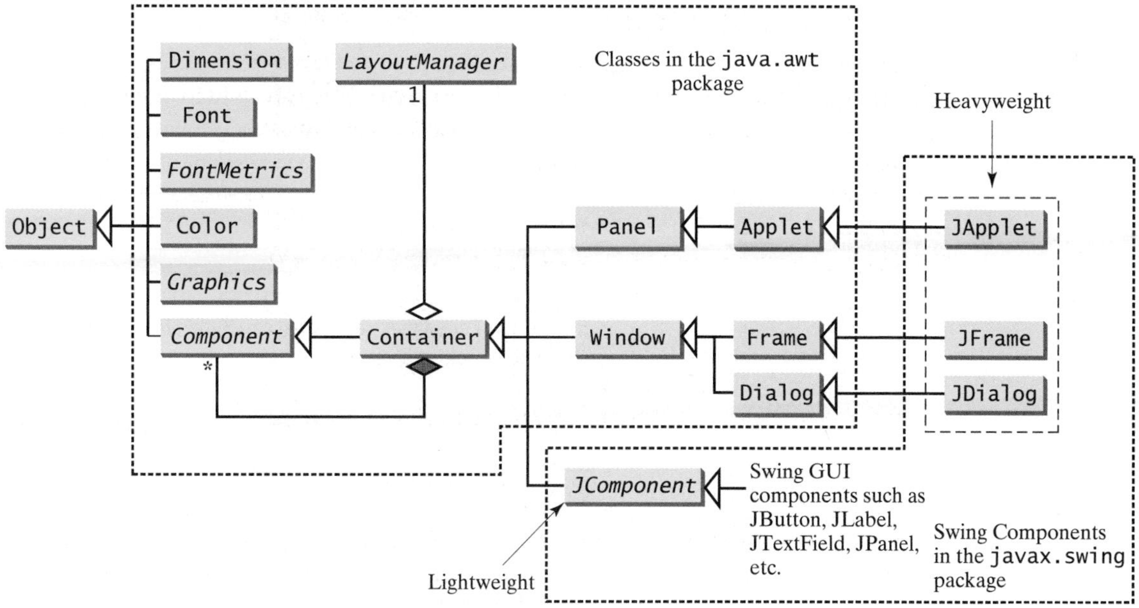
Dimension
LayoutManager
1
Classes in the java.awt package
Heavyweight
Font
FontMetrics
Object
Color
Panel
Applet
JApplet
Graphics
Component
Container
Window
Frame
JFrame
*
Dialog
JDialog
JComponent
Swing GUI components such as JButton, JLabel, JTextField, JPanel, etc.
Swing Components in the javax.swing package
Lightweight

FIGURE 12.1 Java GUI programming utilizes the classes shown in this hierarchical diagram.

instance of `JComponent`. However, you can use the constructors of concrete subclasses of `JComponent` to create `JComponent` instances. It is important to become familiar with the class inheritance hierarchy. For example, the following statements all display true:

```
JButton jbtOK = new JButton("OK");
System.out.println(jbtOK instanceof JButton);
System.out.println(jbtOK instanceof JComponent);
System.out.println(jbtOK instanceof Container);
System.out.println(jbtOK instanceof Component);
System.out.println(jbtOK instanceof Object);
```

12.3.2 Container Classes

An instance of `Container` can hold instances of `Component`. Container classes are GUI components that are used to contain other GUI components. `Window`, `Panel`, `Applet`, `Frame`, and `Dialog` are the container classes for AWT components. To work with Swing components, use `Container`, `JFrame`, `JDialog`, `JApplet`, and `JPanel`, as described in Table 12.1.

TABLE 12.1 GUI Container Classes

Container Class	*Description*
`java.awt.Container`	is used to group components. Frames, panels, and applets are its subclasses.
`javax.swing.JFrame`	is a window not contained inside another window. It is used to hold other Swing user-interface components in Java GUI applications.
`javax.swing.JPanel`	is an invisible container that holds user-interface components. Panels can be nested. You can place panels inside a container that includes a panel. `JPanel` is also often used as a canvas to draw graphics.
`javax.swing.JApplet`	is a subclass of `Applet`. You must extend `JApplet` to create a Swing-based Java applet.
`javax.swing.JDialog`	is a popup window or message box generally used as a temporary window to receive additional information from the user or to provide notification that an event has occurred.

12.3.3 GUI Helper Classes

The helper classes, such as `Graphics`, `Color`, `Font`, `FontMetrics`, `Dimension`, and `LayoutManager`, are not subclasses of `Component`. They are used to describe the properties of GUI components, such as graphics context, colors, fonts, and dimension, as described in Table 12.2.

TABLE 12.2 GUI Helper Classes

Helper Class	*Description*
`java.awt.Graphics`	is an abstract class that provides the methods for drawing strings, lines, and simple shapes.
`java.awt.Color`	deals with the colors of GUI components. For example, you can specify background or foreground colors in components like `JFrame` and `JPanel`, or you can specify colors of lines, shapes, and strings in drawings.
`java.awt.Font`	specifies fonts for the text and drawings on GUI components. For example, you can specify the font type (e.g., SansSerif), style (e.g., bold), and size (e.g., 24 points) for the text on a button.
`java.awt.FontMetrics`	is an abstract class used to get the properties of the fonts.
`java.awt.Dimension`	encapsulates the width and height of a component (in integer precision) in a single object.
`java.awt.LayoutManager`	specifies how components are arranged in a container.

Note

The helper classes are in the `java.awt` package. The Swing components do not replace all the classes in AWT, only the AWT GUI component classes (e.g., `Button`, `TextField`, `TextArea`). The AWT helper classes are still useful in GUI programming.

12.4 Frames

To create a user interface, you need to create either a frame or an applet to hold the user-interface components. Creating Java applets will be introduced in Chapter 18, "Applets and Multimedia." This section introduces frames.

12.4.1 Creating a Frame

To create a frame, use the `JFrame` class, as shown in Figure 12.2.

The program in Listing 12.1 creates a frame:

LISTING 12.1 `MyFrame.java`

import package
create frame
set size
center frame
close upon exit
display the frame

```
import javax.swing.JFrame;

public class MyFrame {
  public static void main(String[] args) {
    JFrame frame = new JFrame("MyFrame"); // Create a frame
    frame.setSize(400, 300); // Set the frame size
    frame.setLocationRelativeTo(null); // Center a frame
    frame.setDefaultCloseOperation(JFrame.EXIT_ON_CLOSE);
    frame.setVisible(true); // Display the frame
  }
}
```

javax.swing.JFrame	
`+JFrame()`	Creates a default frame with no title.
`+JFrame(title: String)`	Creates a frame with the specified title.
`+setSize(width: int, height: int): void`	Sets the size of the frame.
`+setLocation(x: int, y: int): void`	Sets the upper-left-corner location of the frame.
`+setVisible(visible: boolean): void`	Sets true to display the frame.
`+setDefaultCloseOperation(mode: int): void`	Specifies the operation when the frame is closed.
`+setLocationRelativeTo(c: Component): void`	Sets the location of the frame relative to the specified component. If the component is null, the frame is centered on the screen.
`+pack(): void`	Automatically sets the frame size to hold the components in the frame.

FIGURE 12.2 `JFrame` is a top-level container to hold GUI components.

The frame is not displayed until the `frame.setVisible(true)` method is invoked. `frame.setSize(400, 300)` specifies that the frame is `400` pixels wide and `300` pixels high. If the `setSize` method is not used, the frame will be sized to display just the title bar. Since the `setSize` and `setVisible` methods are both defined in the `Component` class, they are inherited by the `JFrame` class. Later you will see that these methods are also useful in many other subclasses of `Component`.

When you run the `MyFrame` program, a window will be displayed on the screen (see Figure 12.3(a)).

Title bar
Content pane
MyFrame
(a)
MyFrameWithComponents
OK
Title bar
Content pane
(b)

FIGURE 12.3 (a) The program creates and displays a frame with the title `MyFrame`. (b) An OK button is added to the frame.

Invoking `setLocationRelativeTo(null)` (line 7) centers the frame on the screen. Invoking `setDefaultCloseOperation(JFrame.EXIT_ON_CLOSE)` (line 8) tells the program to terminate when the frame is closed. If this statement is not used, the program does not terminate when the frame is closed. In that case, you have to stop the program by pressing *Ctrl+C* at the DOS prompt window in Windows or stop the process by using the kill command in Unix. If you run the program from an IDE such as Eclipse or NetBeans, you need to click the red Terminate button in the Console pane to stop the program.

Note

Recall that a pixel is the smallest unit of space available for drawing on the screen. You can think of a pixel as a small rectangle and think of the screen as paved with pixels. The *resolution* specifies the number of pixels per square inch. The more pixels the screen has, the higher the screen's resolution. The higher the resolution, the finer the detail you can see.

pixel and resolution

Note

You should invoke the `setSize(w, h)` method before invoking `setLocationRelativeTo(null)` to center the frame.

`setSize` before centering

12.4.2 Adding Components to a Frame

The frame shown in Figure 12.3(a) is empty. Using the add method, you can add components into the frame, as in Listing 12.2.

LISTING 12.2 MyFrameWithComponents.java

create a button
add to frame
set size
exit upon closing window
center the frame
set visible

```
 1 import javax.swing.*;
 2
 3 public class MyFrameWithComponents {
 4   public static void main(String[] args) {
 5     JFrame frame = new JFrame("MyFrameWithComponents");
 6
 7     // Add a button into the frame
 8     JButton jbtOK = new JButton("OK");
 9     frame.add(jbtOK);
10
11     frame.setSize(400, 300);
12     frame.setDefaultCloseOperation(JFrame.EXIT_ON_CLOSE);
13     frame.setLocationRelativeTo(null); // Center the frame
14     frame.setVisible(true);
15   }
16 }
```

Each JFrame contains a content pane. A content pane is an instance of java.awt.Container. The GUI components such as buttons are placed in the content pane in a frame. In earlier version of Java, you had to use the getContentPane method in the JFrame class to return the content pane of the frame, then invoke the content pane's add method to place a component into the content pane, as follows:

```
java.awt.Container container = frame.getContentPane();
container.add(jbtOK);
```

This was cumbersome. The new version of Java since Java 5 allows you to place components into the content pane by invoking a frame's add method, as follows:

```
frame.add(jbtOK);
```

content-pane delegation

This new feature is called *content-pane delegation*. Strictly speaking, a component is added into the content pane of a frame. For simplicity we say that a component is added to a frame.

An object of JButton was created using new JButton("OK"), and this object was added to the content pane of the frame (line 9).

The add(Component comp) method defined in the Container class adds an instance of Component to the container. Since JButton is a subclass of Component, an instance of JButton is also an instance of Component. To remove a component from a container, use the remove method. The following statement removes the button from the container:

```
container.remove(jbtOK);
```

When you run the program MyFrameWithComponents, the window will be displayed as in Figure 12.3(b). The button is always centered in the frame and occupies the entire frame no matter how you resize it. This is because components are put in the frame by the content pane's layout manager, and the default layout manager for the content pane places the button in the center. In the next section, you will use several different layout managers to place components in the desired locations.

12.5 Layout Managers

In many other window systems, the user-interface components are arranged by using hard-coded pixel measurements. For example, put a button at location (10, 10) in the window. Using hard-coded pixel measurements, the user interface might look fine on one system but be unusable on another. Java's layout managers provide a level of abstraction that automatically maps your user interface on all window systems.

The Java GUI components are placed in containers, where they are arranged by the container's layout manager. In the preceding program, you did not specify where to place the OK button in the frame, but Java knows where to place it, because the layout manager works behind the scenes to place components in the correct locations. A layout manager is created using a layout manager class.

Layout managers are set in containers using the `setLayout(aLayoutManager)` method. For example, you can use the following statements to create an instance of `XLayout` and set it in a container:

```
LayoutManager layoutManager = new XLayout();
container.setLayout(layoutManager);
```

This section introduces three basic layout managers: `FlowLayout`, `GridLayout`, and `BorderLayout`.

12.5.1 FlowLayout

Video Note
Use `FlowLayout`

`FlowLayout` is the simplest layout manager. The components are arranged in the container from left to right in the order in which they were added. When one row is filled, a new row is started. You can specify the way the components are aligned by using one of three constants: `FlowLayout.RIGHT`, `FlowLayout.CENTER`, or `FlowLayout.LEFT`. You can also specify the gap between components in pixels. The class diagram for `FlowLayout` is shown in Figure 12.4.

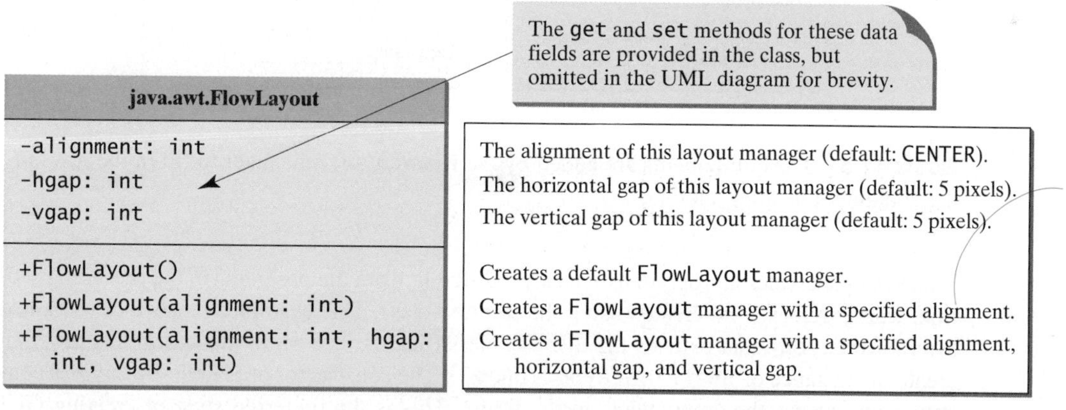
The get and set methods for these data fields are provided in the class, but omitted in the UML diagram for brevity.
java.awt.FlowLayout
-alignment: int
-hgap: int
-vgap: int
+FlowLayout()
+FlowLayout(alignment: int)
+FlowLayout(alignment: int, hgap: int, vgap: int)
The alignment of this layout manager (default: CENTER).
The horizontal gap of this layout manager (default: 5 pixels).
The vertical gap of this layout manager (default: 5 pixels).
Creates a default FlowLayout manager.
Creates a FlowLayout manager with a specified alignment.
Creates a FlowLayout manager with a specified alignment, horizontal gap, and vertical gap.

FIGURE 12.4 `FlowLayout` lays out components row by row.

Listing 12.3 gives a program that demonstrates flow layout. The program adds three labels and text fields into the frame with a `FlowLayout` manager, as shown in Figure 12.5.

LISTING 12.3 ShowFlowLayout.java

```
import javax.swing.JLabel;
import javax.swing.JTextField;
import javax.swing.JFrame;
```

extends **JFrame**
set layout
add label
add text field
create frame
set visible

```
 4 import java.awt.FlowLayout;
 5
 6 public class ShowFlowLayout extends JFrame {
 7   public ShowFlowLayout() {
 8     // Set FlowLayout, aligned left with horizontal gap 10
 9     // and vertical gap 20 between components
10     setLayout(new FlowLayout(FlowLayout.LEFT, 10, 20));
11
12     // Add labels and text fields to the frame
13     add(new JLabel("First Name"));
14     add(new JTextField(8));
15     add(new JLabel("MI"));
16     add(new JTextField(1));
17     add(new JLabel("Last Name"));
18     add(new JTextField(8));
19   }
20
21   /** Main method */
22   public static void main(String[] args) {
23     ShowFlowLayout frame = new ShowFlowLayout();
24     frame.setTitle("ShowFlowLayout");
25     frame.setSize(200, 200);
26     frame.setLocationRelativeTo(null); // Center the frame
27     frame.setDefaultCloseOperation(JFrame.EXIT_ON_CLOSE);
28     frame.setVisible(true);
29   }
30 }
```

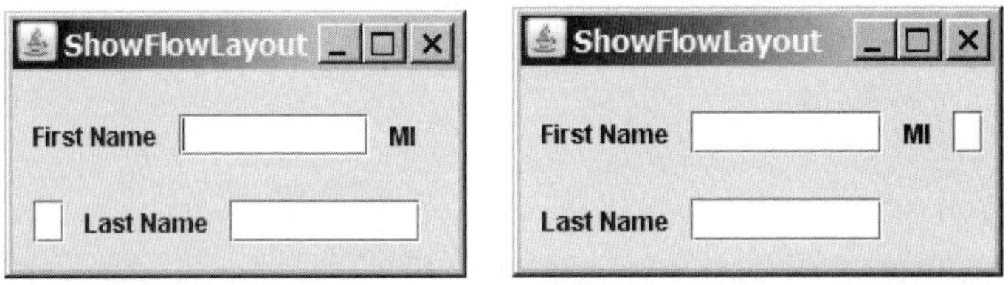
ShowFlowLayout
First Name
MI
Last Name
ShowFlowLayout
First Name
MI
Last Name

(a) (b)

FIGURE 12.5 The components are added by the `FlowLayout` manager to fill in the rows in the container one after another.

This example creates a program using a style different from the programs in the preceding section, where frames were created using the `JFrame` class. This example creates a class named `ShowFlowLayout` that extends the `JFrame` class (line 6). The `main` method in this program creates an instance of `ShowFlowLayout` (line 23). The constructor of `ShowFlowLayout` constructs and places the components in the frame. This is the preferred style of creating GUI applications—for three reasons:

- Creating a GUI application means creating a frame, so it is natural to define a frame to extend `JFrame`.
- The frame may be further extended to add new components or functions.
- The class can be easily reused. For example, you can create multiple frames by creating multiple instances of the class.

Using one style consistently makes programs easy to read. From now on, most of the GUI main classes will extend the `JFrame` class. The constructor of the main class constructs the user interface. The `main` method creates an instance of the main class and then displays the frame.

In this example, the `FlowLayout` manager is used to place components in a frame. If you resize the frame, the components are automatically rearranged to fit. In Figure 12.5(a), the first row has three components, but in Figure 12.5(a), the first row has four components, because the width has been increased.

If you replace the `setLayout` statement (line 10) with `setLayout(new FlowLayout-(FlowLayout.RIGHT, 0, 0))`, all the rows of buttons will be right aligned with no gaps.

An anonymous `FlowLayout` object was created in the statement (line 10):

```
setLayout(new FlowLayout(FlowLayout.LEFT, 10, 20));
```

which is equivalent to:

```
FlowLayout layout = new FlowLayout(FlowLayout.LEFT, 10, 20);
setLayout(layout);
```

This code creates an explicit reference to the object `layout` of the `FlowLayout` class. The explicit reference is not necessary, because the object is not directly referenced in the `ShowFlowLayout` class.

Suppose you add the same button into the frame ten times; will ten buttons appear in the frame? No, a GUI component such as a button can be added into only one container and only once in a container. Adding a button into a container multiple times is the same as adding it once.

Caution

Do not forget to put the `new` operator before a layout manager class when setting a layout style—for example, `setLayout(new FlowLayout())`.

Note

The constructor `ShowFlowLayout()` does not explicitly invoke the constructor `JFrame()`, but the constructor `JFrame()` is invoked implicitly. See §11.3.2, "Constructor Chaining."

12.5.2 `GridLayout`

The `GridLayout` manager arranges components in a grid (matrix) formation. The components are placed in the grid from left to right, starting with the first row, then the second, and so on, in the order in which they are added. The class diagram for `GridLayout` is shown in Figure 12.6.

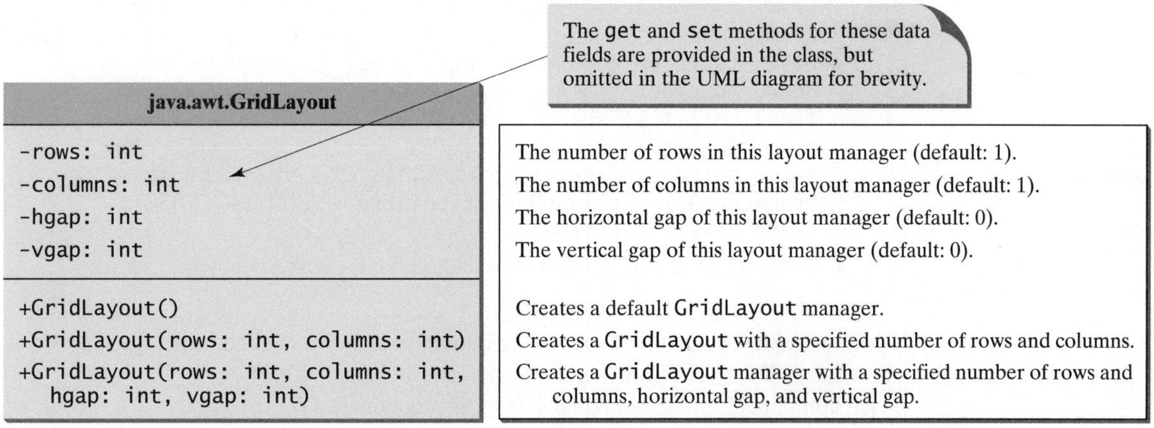
The get and set methods for these data fields are provided in the class, but omitted in the UML diagram for brevity.
java.awt.GridLayout
-rows: int
-columns: int
-hgap: int
-vgap: int
+GridLayout()
+GridLayout(rows: int, columns: int)
+GridLayout(rows: int, columns: int, hgap: int, vgap: int)
The number of rows in this layout manager (default: 1).
The number of columns in this layout manager (default: 1).
The horizontal gap of this layout manager (default: 0).
The vertical gap of this layout manager (default: 0).
Creates a default GridLayout manager.
Creates a GridLayout with a specified number of rows and columns.
Creates a GridLayout manager with a specified number of rows and columns, horizontal gap, and vertical gap.

FIGURE 12.6 `GridLayout` lays out components in equal-sized cells on a grid.

You can specify the number of rows and columns in the grid. The basic rule is as follows:

- The number of rows or the number of columns can be zero, but not both. If one is zero and the other is nonzero, the nonzero dimension is fixed, while the zero dimension is determined dynamically by the layout manager. For example, if you specify zero rows and three columns for a grid that has ten components, `GridLayout` creates three fixed columns of four rows, with the last row containing one component. If you specify three rows and zero columns for a grid that has ten components, `GridLayout` creates three fixed rows of four columns, with the last row containing two components.

- If both the number of rows and the number of columns are nonzero, the number of rows is the dominating parameter; that is, the number of rows is fixed, and the layout manager dynamically calculates the number of columns. For example, if you specify three rows and three columns for a grid that has ten components, `GridLayout` creates three fixed rows of four columns, with the last row containing two components.

Listing 12.4 gives a program that demonstrates grid layout. The program is similar to the one in Listing 12.3. It adds three labels and three text fields to the frame of `GridLayout` instead of `FlowLayout`, as shown in Figure 12.7.

LISTING 12.4 ShowGridLayout.java

set layout
add label
add text field
create a frame
set visible

```
import javax.swing.JLabel;
import javax.swing.JTextField;
import javax.swing.JFrame;
import java.awt.GridLayout;

public class ShowGridLayout extends JFrame {
  public ShowGridLayout() {
    // Set GridLayout, 3 rows, 2 columns, and gaps 5 between
    // components horizontally and vertically
    setLayout(new GridLayout(3, 2, 5, 5));

    // Add labels and text fields to the frame
    add(new JLabel("First Name"));
    add(new JTextField(8));
    add(new JLabel("MI"));
    add(new JTextField(1));
    add(new JLabel("Last Name"));
    add(new JTextField(8));
  }

  /** Main method */
  public static void main(String[] args) {
    ShowGridLayout frame = new ShowGridLayout();
    frame.setTitle("ShowGridLayout");
    frame.setSize(200, 125);
    frame.setLocationRelativeTo(null); // Center the frame
    frame.setDefaultCloseOperation(JFrame.EXIT_ON_CLOSE);
    frame.setVisible(true);
  }
}
```

If you resize the frame, the layout of the buttons remains unchanged (i.e., the number of rows and columns does not change, and the gaps don't change either).

All components are given equal size in the container of `GridLayout`.

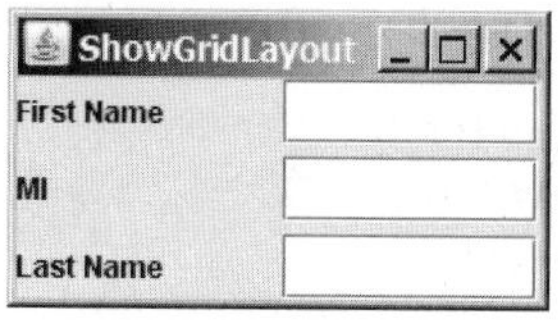
ShowGridLayout
First Name
MI
Last Name

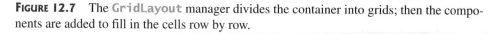

FIGURE 12.7 The `GridLayout` manager divides the container into grids; then the components are added to fill in the cells row by row.

Replacing the `setLayout` statement (line 10) with `setLayout(new GridLayout(3, 10))` would still yield three rows and *two* columns. The `columns` parameter is ignored because the `rows` parameter is nonzero. The actual number of columns is calculated by the layout manager.

What would happen if the `setLayout` statement (line 10) were replaced with `setLayout(new GridLayout(4, 2))` or with `setLayout(new GridLayout(2, 2))`? Please try it yourself.

Note

In `FlowLayout` and `GridLayout`, the order in which the components are added to the container is important. It determines the location of the components in the container.

12.5.3 `BorderLayout`

The `BorderLayout` manager divides a container into five areas: East, South, West, North, and Center. Components are added to a `BorderLayout` by using `add(Component, index)`, where `index` is a constant `BorderLayout.EAST`, `BorderLayout.SOUTH`, `BorderLayout.WEST`, `BorderLayout.NORTH`, or `BorderLayout.CENTER`. The class diagram for `BorderLayout` is shown in Figure 12.8.

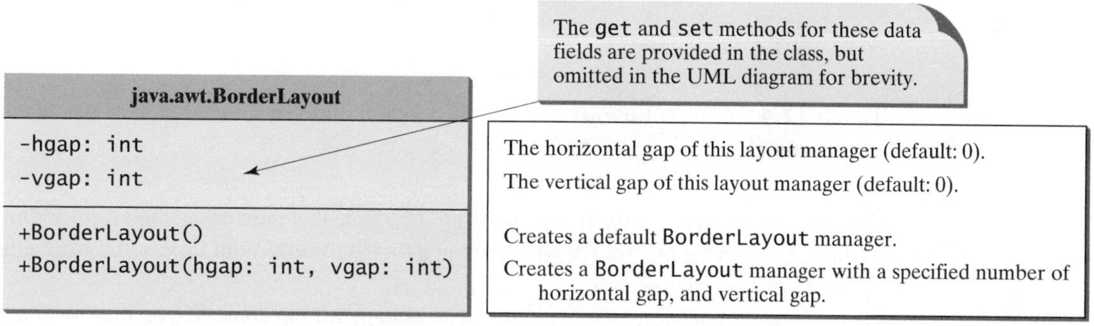
The get and set methods for these data fields are provided in the class, but omitted in the UML diagram for brevity.
java.awt.BorderLayout
-hgap: int
-vgap: int
+BorderLayout()
+BorderLayout(hgap: int, vgap: int)
The horizontal gap of this layout manager (default: 0).
The vertical gap of this layout manager (default: 0).
Creates a default BorderLayout manager.
Creates a BorderLayout manager with a specified number of horizontal gap, and vertical gap.

FIGURE 12.8 `BorderLayout` lays out components in five areas.

The components are laid out according to their preferred sizes and their placement in the container. The North and South components can stretch horizontally; the East and West components can stretch vertically; the Center component can stretch both horizontally and vertically to fill any empty space.

Listing 12.5 gives a program that demonstrates border layout. The program adds five buttons labeled `East`, `South`, `West`, `North`, and `Center` into the frame with a `BorderLayout` manager, as shown in Figure 12.9.

LISTING 12.5 ShowBorderLayout.java

set layout

add buttons

create a frame

set visible

```
1 import javax.swing.JButton;
2 import javax.swing.JFrame;
3 import java.awt.BorderLayout;
4
5 public class ShowBorderLayout extends JFrame {
6   public ShowBorderLayout() {
7     // Set BorderLayout with horizontal gap 5 and vertical gap 10
8     setLayout(new BorderLayout(5, 10));
9
10    // Add buttons to the frame
11    add(new JButton("East"), BorderLayout.EAST);
12    add(new JButton("South"), BorderLayout.SOUTH);
13    add(new JButton("West"), BorderLayout.WEST);
14    add(new JButton("North"), BorderLayout.NORTH);
15    add(new JButton("Center"), BorderLayout.CENTER);
16  }
17
18  /** Main method */
19  public static void main(String[] args) {
20    ShowBorderLayout frame = new ShowBorderLayout();
21    frame.setTitle("ShowBorderLayout");
22    frame.setSize(300, 200);
23    frame.setLocationRelativeTo(null); // Center the frame
24    frame.setDefaultCloseOperation(JFrame.EXIT_ON_CLOSE);
25    frame.setVisible(true);
26  }
27 }
```

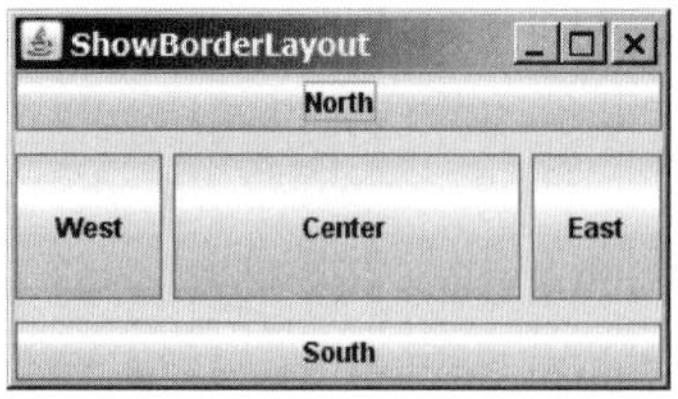
ShowBorderLayout
North
West
Center
East
South

FIGURE 12.9 BorderLayout divides the container into five areas, each of which can hold a component.

The buttons are added to the frame (lines 11–15). Note that the add method for BorderLayout is different from the one for FlowLayout and GridLayout. With BorderLayout you specify where to put the components.

It is unnecessary to place components to occupy all the areas. If you remove the East button from the program and rerun it, you will see that the center stretches rightward to occupy the East area.

Note

BorderLayout interprets the absence of an index specification as BorderLayout.CENTER. For example, add(component) is the same as add(Component, BorderLayout.CENTER). If you add two components into a container of BorderLayout, as follows,

```
container.add(component1);
container.add(component2);
```

only the last component is displayed.

12.5.4 Properties of Layout Managers

Layout managers have properties that can be changed dynamically. FlowLayout has alignment, hgap, and vgap properties. You can use the setAlignment, setHgap, and setVgap methods to specify the alignment and the horizontal and vertical gaps. GridLayout has the rows, columns, hgap, and vgap properties. You can use the setRows, setColumns, setHgap, and setVgap methods to specify the number of rows, the number of columns, and the horizontal and vertical gaps. BorderLayout has the hgap and vgap properties. You can use the setHgap and setVgap methods to specify the horizontal and vertical gaps.

In the preceding sections an anonymous layout manager is used because the properties of a layout manager do not change, once it is created. If you have to change the properties of a layout manager dynamically, the layout manager must be explicitly referenced by a variable. You can then change the properties of the layout manager through the variable. For example, the following code creates a layout manager and sets its properties:

```
// Create a layout manager
FlowLayout flowLayout = new FlowLayout();

// Set layout properties
flowLayout.setAlignment(FlowLayout.RIGHT);
flowLayout.setHgap(10);
flowLayout.setVgap(20);
```

12.6 Using Panels as Subcontainers

Video Note
Use panels as subcontainers

Suppose that you want to place ten buttons and a text field in a frame. The buttons are placed in grid formation, but the text field is placed on a separate row. It is difficult to achieve the desired look by placing all the components in a single container. With Java GUI programming, you can divide a window into panels. Panels act as subcontainers to group user-interface components. You add the buttons in one panel, then add the panel into the frame.

The Swing version of panel is JPanel. You can use new JPanel() to create a panel with a default FlowLayout manager or new JPanel(LayoutManager) to create a panel with the specified layout manager. Use the add(Component) method to add a component to the panel. For example, the following code creates a panel and adds a button to it:

```
JPanel p = new JPanel();
p.add(new JButton("OK"));
```

Panels can be placed inside a frame or inside another panel. The following statement places panel p into frame f:

```
f.add(p);
```

Listing 12.6 gives an example that demonstrates using panels as subcontainers. The program creates a user interface for a microwave oven, as shown in Figure 12.10.

LISTING 12.6 TestPanels.java

```
import java.awt.*;
import javax.swing.*;

public class TestPanels extends JFrame {
  public TestPanels() {
    // Create panel p1 for the buttons and set GridLayout
    JPanel p1 = new JPanel();
    p1.setLayout(new GridLayout(4, 3));

```

panel p1

panel p2

add p2 to frame

```
10      // Add buttons to the panel
11      for (int i = 1; i <= 9; i++) {
12        p1.add(new JButton("" + i));
13      }
14
15      p1.add(new JButton("" + 0));
16      p1.add(new JButton("Start"));
17      p1.add(new JButton("Stop"));
18
19      // Create panel p2 to hold a text field and p1
20      JPanel p2 = new JPanel(new BorderLayout());
21      p2.add(new JTextField("Time to be displayed here"),
22        BorderLayout.NORTH);
23      p2.add(p1, BorderLayout.CENTER);
24
25      // add contents into the frame
26      add(p2, BorderLayout.EAST);
27      add(new JButton("Food to be placed here"),
28        BorderLayout.CENTER);
29    }
30
31    /** Main method */
32    public static void main(String[] args) {
33      TestPanels frame = new TestPanels();
34      frame.setTitle("The Front View of a Microwave Oven");
35      frame.setSize(400, 250);
36      frame.setLocationRelativeTo(null); // Center the frame
37      frame.setDefaultCloseOperation(JFrame.EXIT_ON_CLOSE);
38      frame.setVisible(true);
39    }
40  }
```

The Front View of a Microwave Oven
Frame
Content panel
Button
Time to be displayed here
Panel p2
Food to be placed here
1
2
3
4
5
6
7
8
9
0
Start
Stop
Panel p1

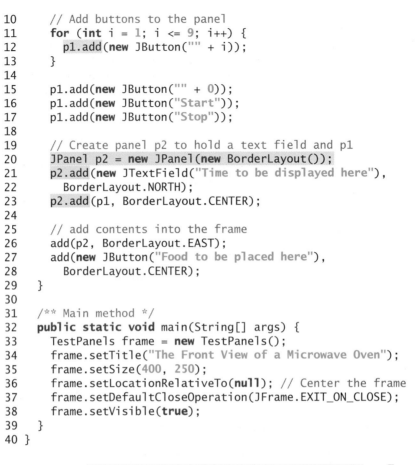

FIGURE 12.10 The program uses panels to organize components.

The `setLayout` method is defined in `java.awt.Container`. Since `JPanel` is a subclass of `Container`, you can use `setLayout` to set a new layout manager in the panel (line 8). Lines 7–8 can be replaced by `JPanel p1 = new JPanel(new GridLayout(4, 3))`.

To achieve the desired layout, the program uses panel `p1` of `GridLayout` to group the number buttons, the *Stop* button, and the *Start* button, and panel `p2` of `BorderLayout` to hold a text field in the north and `p1` in the center. The button representing the food is placed in the center of the frame, and `p2` is placed in the east of the frame.

The statement (lines 21–22)

```
p2.add(new JTextField("Time to be displayed here"),
  BorderLayout.NORTH);
```

creates an instance of `JTextField` and adds it to `p2`. `JTextField` is a GUI component that can be used for user input as well as to display values.

> **Note**
> It is worthwhile to note that the **Container** class is the superclass for GUI component classes, such as **JButton**. Every GUI component is a container. In theory, you could use the **setLayout** method to set the layout in a button and add components into a button, because all the public methods in the **Container** class are inherited into **JButton**, but for practical reasons you should not use buttons as containers.

superclass **Container**

12.7 The **Color** Class

You can set colors for GUI components by using the **java.awt.Color** class. Colors are made of red, green, and blue components, each represented by an **int** value that describes its intensity, ranging from **0** (darkest shade) to **255** (lightest shade). This is known as the *RGB model*.

You can create a color using the following constructor:

```
public Color(int r, int g, int b);
```

in which **r**, **g**, and **b** specify a color by its red, green, and blue components. For example,

```
Color color = new Color(128, 100, 100);
```

> **Note**
> The arguments **r**, **g**, **b** are between **0** and **255**. If a value beyond this range is passed to the argument, an **IllegalArgumentException** will occur.

IllegalArgumentException

You can use the **setBackground(Color c)** and **setForeground(Color c)** methods defined in the **java.awt.Component** class to set a component's background and foreground colors. Here is an example of setting the background and foreground of a button:

```
JButton jbtOK = new JButton("OK");
jbtOK.setBackground(color);
jbtOK.setForeground(new Color(100, 1, 1));
```

Alternatively, you can use one of the 13 standard colors (**BLACK**, **BLUE**, **CYAN**, **DARK_GRAY**, **GRAY**, **GREEN**, **LIGHT_GRAY**, **MAGENTA**, **ORANGE**, **PINK**, **RED**, **WHITE**, and **YELLOW**) defined as constants in **java.awt.Color**. The following code, for instance, sets the foreground color of a button to red:

```
jbtOK.setForeground(Color.RED);
```

12.8 The **Font** Class

You can create a font using the **java.awt.Font** class and set fonts for the components using the **setFont** method in the **Component** class.

The constructor for **Font** is:

```
public Font(String name, int style, int size);
```

You can choose a font name from **SansSerif**, **Serif**, **Monospaced**, **Dialog**, or **DialogInput**, choose a style from **Font.PLAIN** (**0**), **Font.BOLD** (**1**), **Font.ITALIC** (**2**), and **Font.BOLD** + **Font.ITALIC** (**3**), and specify a font size of any positive integer. For example, the following statements create two fonts and set one font to a button.

```
Font font1 = new Font("SansSerif", Font.BOLD, 16);
Font font2 = new Font("Serif", Font.BOLD + Font.ITALIC, 12);

JButton jbtOK = new JButton("OK");
jbtOK.setFont(font1);
```

Tip

find available fonts

If your system supports other fonts, such as "Times New Roman," you can use it to create a `Font` object. To find the fonts available on your system, you need to obtain an instance of `java.awt.GraphicsEnvironment` using its static method `getLocalGraphicsEnvironment()`. `GraphicsEnvironment` is an abstract class that describes the graphics environment on a particular system. You can use its `getAllFonts()` method to obtain all the available fonts on the system and its `getAvailableFontFamilyNames()` method to obtain the names of all the available fonts. For example, the following statements print all the available font names in the system:

```
GraphicsEnvironment e =
  GraphicsEnvironment.getLocalGraphicsEnvironment();
String[] fontnames = e.getAvailableFontFamilyNames();

for (int i = 0; i < fontnames.length; i++)
  System.out.println(fontnames[i]);
```

12.9 Common Features of Swing GUI Components

Component

Video Note
Use Swing common properties

In this chapter you have used several GUI components (e.g., `JFrame`, `Container`, `JPanel`, `JButton`, `JLabel`, `JTextField`). Many more GUI components will be introduced in this book. It is important to understand the common features of Swing GUI components. The

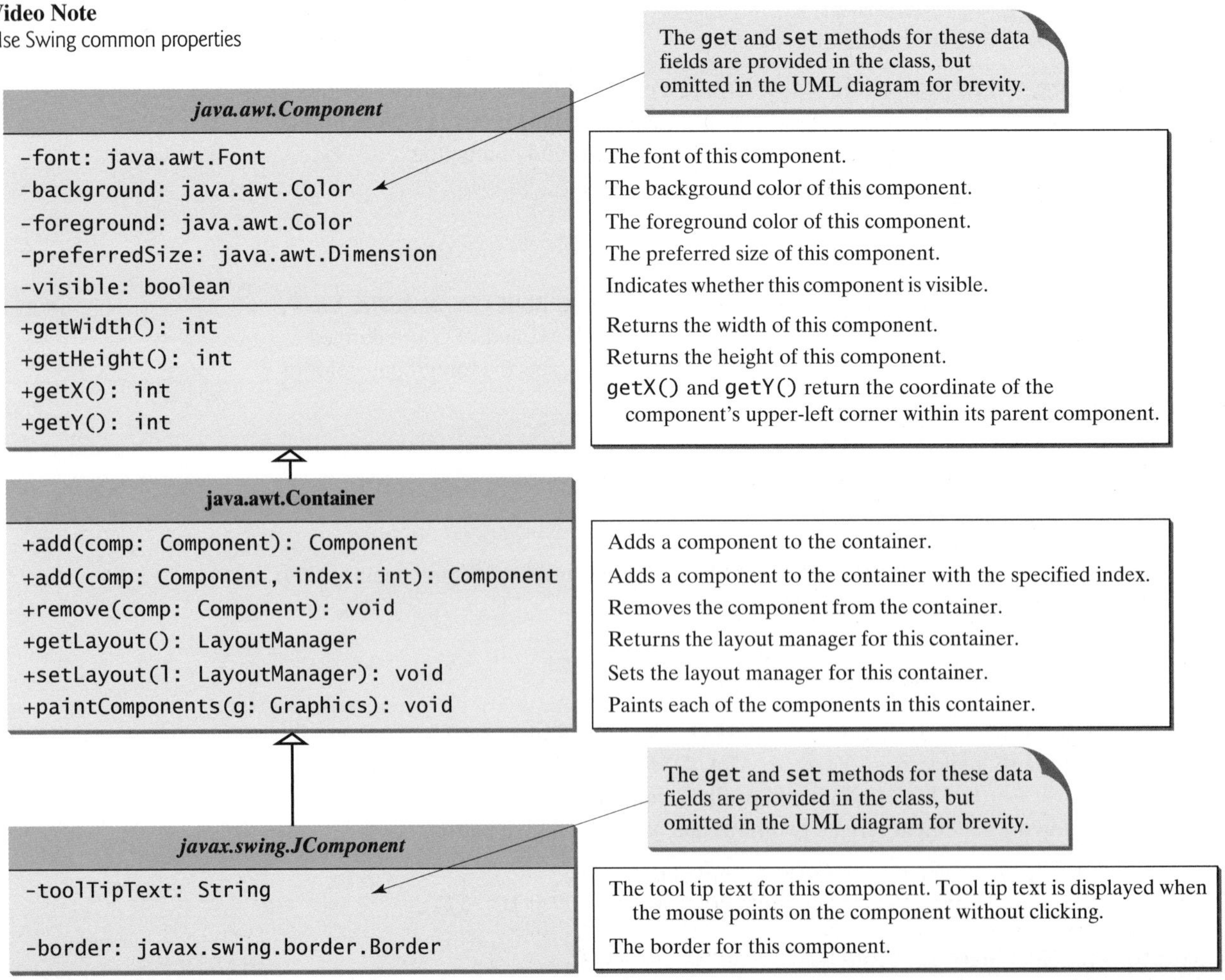
The get and set methods for these data fields are provided in the class, but omitted in the UML diagram for brevity.
java.awt.Component
-font: java.awt.Font
-background: java.awt.Color
-foreground: java.awt.Color
-preferredSize: java.awt.Dimension
-visible: boolean
+getWidth(): int
+getHeight(): int
+getX(): int
+getY(): int
The font of this component.
The background color of this component.
The foreground color of this component.
The preferred size of this component.
Indicates whether this component is visible.
Returns the width of this component.
Returns the height of this component.
getX() and getY() return the coordinate of the component's upper-left corner within its parent component.
java.awt.Container
+add(comp: Component): Component
+add(comp: Component, index: int): Component
+remove(comp: Component): void
+getLayout(): LayoutManager
+setLayout(l: LayoutManager): void
+paintComponents(g: Graphics): void
Adds a component to the container.
Adds a component to the container with the specified index.
Removes the component from the container.
Returns the layout manager for this container.
Sets the layout manager for this container.
Paints each of the components in this container.
The get and set methods for these data fields are provided in the class, but omitted in the UML diagram for brevity.
javax.swing.JComponent
-toolTipText: String
-border: javax.swing.border.Border
The tool tip text for this component. Tool tip text is displayed when the mouse points on the component without clicking.
The border for this component.

FIGURE 12.11 All the Swing GUI components inherit the public methods from `Component`, `Container`, and `JComponent`.

Container

JComponent

`Component` class is the root for all GUI components and containers. All Swing GUI components (except `JFrame`, `JApplet`, and `JDialog`) are subclasses of `JComponent`, as shown in Figure 12.1. Figure 12.11 lists some frequently used methods in `Component`, `Container`, and `JComponent` for manipulating properties such as font, color, size, tool tip text, and border.

A *tool tip* is text displayed on a component when you move the mouse on the component. It is often used to describe the function of a component.

You can set a border on any object of the `JComponent` class. Swing has several types of borders. To create a titled border, use `new TitledBorder(String title)`. To create a line border, use `new LineBorder(Color color, int width)`, where `width` specifies the thickness of the line.

Listing 12.7 is an example to demonstrate Swing common features. The example creates a panel `p1` to hold three buttons (line 8) and a panel `p2` to hold two labels (line 25), as shown in Figure 12.12. The background of the button `jbtLeft` is set to white (line 12) and the foreground of the button `jbtCenter` is set to green (line 13). The tool tip of the button `jbtRight` is set in line 14. Titled borders are set on panels `p1` and `p2` (lines 18, 36) and line borders are set on the labels (lines 32–33).

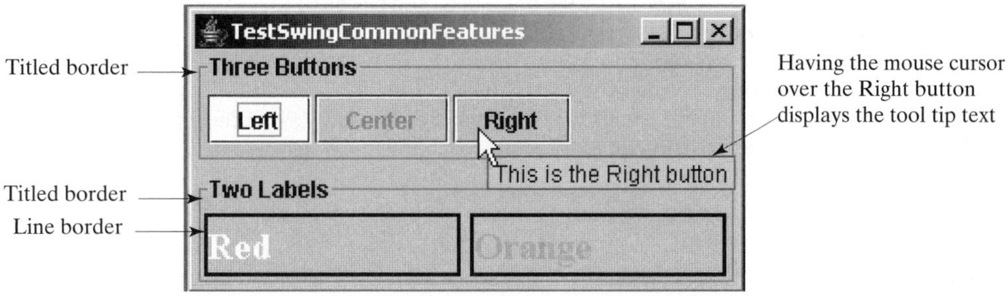
Titled border
Titled border
Line border
TestSwingCommonFeatures
Three Buttons
Left
Center
Right
This is the Right button
Two Labels
Red
Orange
Having the mouse cursor over the Right button displays the tool tip text

FIGURE 12.12 The font, color, border, and tool tip text are set in the message panel.

LISTING 12.7 TestSwingCommonFeatures.java

```
 1 import java.awt.*;
 2 import javax.swing.*;
 3 import javax.swing.border.*;
 4
 5 public class TestSwingCommonFeatures extends JFrame {
 6   public TestSwingCommonFeatures() {
 7     // Create a panel to group three buttons
 8     JPanel p1 = new JPanel(new FlowLayout(FlowLayout.LEFT, 2, 2));
 9     JButton jbtLeft = new JButton("Left");
10     JButton jbtCenter = new JButton("Center");
11     JButton jbtRight = new JButton("Right");
12     jbtLeft.setBackground(Color.WHITE);
13     jbtCenter.setForeground(Color.GREEN);
14     jbtRight.setToolTipText("This is the Right button");
15     p1.add(jbtLeft);
16     p1.add(jbtCenter);
17     p1.add(jbtRight);
18     p1.setBorder(new TitledBorder("Three Buttons"));
19
20     // Create a font and a line border
21     Font largeFont = new Font("TimesRoman", Font.BOLD, 20);
22     Border lineBorder = new LineBorder(Color.BLACK, 2);
23
24     // Create a panel to group two labels
```

set background (line 12)
set foreground (line 13)
set tool tip text (line 14)
set titled border (line 18)
create a font (line 21)
create a border (line 22)

```
25     JPanel p2 = new JPanel(new GridLayout(1, 2, 5, 5));
26     JLabel jlblRed = new JLabel("Red");
27     JLabel jlblOrange = new JLabel("Orange");
28     jlblRed.setForeground(Color.RED);
29     jlblOrange.setForeground(Color.ORANGE);
30     jlblRed.setFont(largeFont);
31     jlblOrange.setFont(largeFont);
32     jlblRed.setBorder(lineBorder);
33     jlblOrange.setBorder(lineBorder);
34     p2.add(jlblRed);
35     p2.add(jlblOrange);
36     p2.setBorder(new TitledBorder("Two Labels"));
37
38     // Add two panels to the frame
39     setLayout(new GridLayout(2, 1, 5, 5));
40     add(p1);
41     add(p2);
42   }
43
44   public static void main(String[] args) {
45     // Create a frame and set its properties
46     JFrame frame = new TestSwingCommonFeatures();
47     frame.setTitle("TestSwingCommonFeatures");
48     frame.setSize(300, 150);
49     frame.setLocationRelativeTo(null); // Center the frame
50     frame.setDefaultCloseOperation(JFrame.EXIT_ON_CLOSE);
51     frame.setVisible(true);
52   }
53 }
```

set foreground (line 28)
set font (line 30)
set line border (line 32)
set titled border (line 36)

property default values

Note

The same property may have different default values in different components. For example, the `visible` property in `JFrame` is `false` by default, but it is `true` in every instance of `JComponent` (e.g., `JButton` and `JLabel`) by default. To display a `JFrame`, you have to invoke `setVisible(true)` to set the `visible` property `true`, but you don't have to set this property for a `JButton` or a `JLabel`, because it is already `true`. To make a `JButton` or a `JLabel` invisible, you may invoke `setVisible(false)`. Please run the program and see the effect after inserting the following two statements in line 37:

```
jbtLeft.setVisible(false);
jlblRed.setVisible(false);
```

12.10 Image Icons

image-file format

An icon is a fixed-size picture; typically it is small and used to decorate components. Images are normally stored in image files. Java currently supports three image formats: GIF (Graphics Interchange Format), JPEG (Joint Photographic Experts Group), and PNG (Portable Network Graphics). The image file names for these types end with .gif, .jpg, and .png, respectively. If you have a bitmap file or image files in other formats, you can use image-processing utilities to convert them into GIF, JPEG, or PNG format for use in Java.

To display an image icon, first create an `ImageIcon` object using `new javax.swing.ImageIcon(filename)`. For example, the following statement creates an icon from an image file `us.gif` in the `image` directory under the current class path:

create **ImageIcon**

```
ImageIcon icon = new ImageIcon("image/us.gif");
```

file path character

"`image/us.gif`" is located in "`c:\book\image\us.gif`." The back slash (\) is the Windows file path notation. In Unix, the forward slash (/) should be used. In Java, the forward slash (/) is used to denote a relative file path under the Java classpath (e.g., `image/us.gif`, as in this example).

Tip

File names are not case sensitive in Windows but are case sensitive in Unix. To enable your programs to run on all platforms, name all the image files consistently, using lowercase.

naming files consistently

An image icon can be displayed in a label or a button using `new JLabel(imageIcon)` or `new JButton(imageIcon)`. Listing 12.8 demonstrates displaying icons in labels and buttons. The example creates two labels and two buttons with icons, as shown in Figure 12.13.

LISTING 12.8 TestImageIcon.java

```
import javax.swing.*;
import java.awt.*;

public class TestImageIcon extends JFrame {
  private ImageIcon usIcon = new ImageIcon("image/us.gif");
  private ImageIcon myIcon = new ImageIcon("image/my.jpg");
  private ImageIcon frIcon = new ImageIcon("image/fr.gif");
  private ImageIcon ukIcon = new ImageIcon("image/uk.gif");

  public TestImageIcon() {
    setLayout(new GridLayout(1, 4, 5, 5));
    add(new JLabel(usIcon));
    add(new JLabel(myIcon));
    add(new JButton(frIcon));
    add(new JButton(ukIcon));
  }

  /** Main method */
  public static void main(String[] args) {
    TestImageIcon frame = new TestImageIcon();
    frame.setTitle("TestImageIcon");
    frame.setSize(200, 200);
    frame.setLocationRelativeTo(null); // Center the frame
    frame.setDefaultCloseOperation(JFrame.EXIT_ON_CLOSE);
    frame.setVisible(true);
  }
}
```

create image icons

a label with image

a button with image

TestImageIcon

FIGURE 12.13 The image icons are displayed in labels and buttons.

Note

GUI components cannot be shared by containers, because one GUI component can appear in only one container at a time. Therefore, the relationship between a component and a container is the composition denoted by a solid diamond, as shown in Figure 12.1.

sharing borders and icons

Note

Borders and icons can be shared. Thus you can create a border or icon and use it to set the `border` or `icon` property for any GUI component. For example, the following statements set a border `b` for two panels `p1` and `p2`:

```
p1.setBorder(b);
p2.setBorder(b);
```

The following statements set an icon in two buttons `jbt1` and `jbt2`:

```
jbt1.setIcon(icon);
jbt2.setIcon(icon);
```

splash screen

Tip

A *splash screen* is an image that is displayed while the application is starting up. If your program takes a long time to load, you may display a splash screen to alert the user. For example, the following command:

```
java -splash:image/us.gif TestImageIcon
```

displays an image while the program `TestImageIcon` is being loaded.

Key Terms

AWT 406
heavyweight component 406
lightweight component 406
layout manager 411
Swing 406
splash screen 424

Chapter Summary

1. Every container has a layout manager that is used to position and place components in the container in the desired locations. Three simple and frequently used layout managers are `FlowLayout`, `GridLayout`, and `BorderLayout`.
2. You can use a `JPanel` as a subcontainer to group components to achieve a desired layout.
3. Use the `add` method to place components to a `JFrame` or a `JPanel`. By default, the frame's layout is `BorderLayout`, and the `JPanel`'s layout is `FlowLayout`.
4. You can set colors for GUI components by using the `java.awt.Color` class. Colors are made of red, green, and blue components, each represented by an unsigned byte value that describes its intensity, ranging from `0` (darkest shade) to `255` (lightest shade). This is known as the *RGB model.*
5. To create a `Color` object, use `new Color(r, g, b)`, in which `r`, `g`, and `b` specify a color by its red, green, and blue components. Alternatively, you can use one of the 13 standard colors (`BLACK`, `BLUE`, `CYAN`, `DARK_GRAY`, `GRAY`, `GREEN`, `LIGHT_GRAY`, `MAGENTA`, `ORANGE`, `PINK`, `RED`, `WHITE`, `YELLOW`) defined as constants in `java.awt.Color`.
6. Every Swing GUI component is a subclass of `javax.swing.JComponent`, and `JComponent` is a subclass of `java.awt.Component`. The properties `font`, `background`, `foreground`, `height`, `width`, and `preferredSize` in `Component` are inherited in these subclasses, as are `toolTipText` and `border` in `JComponent`.
7. You can use borders on any Swing components. You can create an image icon using the `ImageIcon` class and display it in a label and a button. Icons and borders can be shared.

Review Questions

Sections 12.3–12.4

12.1 Which class is the root of the Java GUI component classes? Is a container class a subclass of `Component`? Which class is the root of the Swing GUI component classes?

12.2 Explain the difference between AWT GUI components, such as `java.awt.Button`, and Swing components, such as `javax.swing.JButton`.

12.3 How do you create a frame? How do you set the size for a frame? How do you get the size of a frame? How do you add components to a frame? What would happen if the statements `frame.setSize(400, 300)` and `frame.setVisible(true)` were swapped in Listing 12.2 `MyFrameWithComponents`?

12.4 Determine whether the following statements are true or false:

- You can add a button to a frame.
- You can add a frame to a panel.
- You can add a panel to a frame.
- You can add any number of components to a panel or a frame.
- You can derive a class from `JButton`, `JPanel`, or `JFrame`.

12.5 The following program is supposed to display a button in a frame, but nothing is displayed. What is the problem?

```
public class Test extends javax.swing.JFrame {
  public Test() {
    add(new javax.swing.JButton("OK"));
  }

  public static void main(String[] args) {
    javax.swing.JFrame frame = new javax.swing.JFrame();
    frame.setSize(100, 200);
    frame.setVisible(true);
  }
}
```

12.6 Which of the following statements have syntax errors?

```
Component c1 = new Component();
JComponent c2 = new JComponent();
Component c3 = new JButton();
JComponent c4 = new JButton();
Container c5 = new JButton();
c5.add(c4);
Object c6 = new JButton();
c5.add(c6);
```

Sections 12.5

12.7 Why do you need to use layout managers? What is the default layout manager for a frame? How do you add a component to a frame?

12.8 Describe `FlowLayout`. How do you create a `FlowLayout` manager? How do you add a component to a `FlowLayout` container? Is there a limit to the number of components that can be added to a `FlowLayout` container?

12.9 Describe `GridLayout`. How do you create a `GridLayout` manager? How do you add a component to a `GridLayout` container? Is there a limit to the number of components that can be added to a `GridLayout` container?

12.10 Describe `BorderLayout`. How do you create a `BorderLayout` manager? How do you add a component to a `BorderLayout` container?

Section 12.6

12.11 How do you create a panel with a specified layout manager?

12.12 What is the default layout manager for a `JPanel`? How do you add a component to a `JPanel`?

12.13 Can you use the `setTitle` method in a panel? What is the purpose of using a panel?

12.14 Since a GUI component class such as `JButton` is a subclass of `Container`, can you add components into a button?

Sections 12.7–12.8

12.15 How do you create a color? What is wrong about creating a `Color` using `new Color(400, 200, 300)`? Which of two colors is darker, `new Color(10, 0, 0)` or `new Color(200, 0, 0)`?

12.16 How do you create a font? How do you find all available fonts on your system?

Sections 12.9–12.10

12.17 How do you set background color, foreground color, font, and tool tip text on a Swing GUI component? Why is the tool tip text not displayed in the following code?

```
import javax.swing.*;

public class Test extends JFrame {
  private JButton jbtOK = new JButton("OK");

  public static void main(String[] args) {
    // Create a frame and set its properties
    JFrame frame = new Test();
    frame.setTitle("Logic Error");
    frame.setSize(200, 100);
    frame.setDefaultCloseOperation(JFrame.EXIT_ON_CLOSE);
    frame.setVisible(true);
  }

  public Test() {
    jbtOK.setToolTipText("This is a button");
    add(new JButton("OK"));
  }
}
```

12.18 Show the output of the following code:

```
import javax.swing.*;

public class Test {
  public static void main(String[] args) {
    JButton jbtOK = new JButton("OK");
    System.out.println(jbtOK.isVisible());

    JFrame frame = new JFrame();
    System.out.println(frame.isVisible());
  }
}
```

12.19 How do you create an `ImageIcon` from the file **image/us.gif** in the class directory?

12.20 What happens if you add a button to a container several times, as shown below? Does it cause syntax errors? Does it cause runtime errors?

```
JButton jbt = new JButton();
JPanel panel = new JPanel();
panel.add(jbt);
panel.add(jbt);
panel.add(jbt);
```

12.21 Will the following code display three buttons? Will the buttons display the same icon?

```
import javax.swing.*;
import java.awt.*;

public class Test extends JFrame  {
  public static void main(String[] args) {
    // Create a frame and set its properties
    JFrame frame = new Test();
    frame.setTitle("ButtonIcons");
    frame.setSize(200, 100);
    frame.setDefaultCloseOperation(JFrame.EXIT_ON_CLOSE);
    frame.setVisible(true);
  }

  public Test() {
    ImageIcon usIcon = new ImageIcon("image/us.gif");
    JButton jbt1 = new JButton(usIcon);
    JButton jbt2 = new JButton(usIcon);

    JPanel p1 = new JPanel();
    p1.add(jbt1);

    JPanel p2 = new JPanel();
    p2.add(jbt2);

    JPanel p3 = new JPanel();
    p2.add(jbt1);

    add(p1, BorderLayout.NORTH);
    add(p2, BorderLayout.SOUTH);
    add(p3, BorderLayout.CENTER);
  }
}
```

12.22 Can a border or an icon be shared by GUI components?

Programming Exercises

Sections 12.5–12.6

12.1 (*Using the* `FlowLayout` *manager*) Write a program that meets the following requirements (see Figure 12.14):

- Create a frame and set its layout to `FlowLayout`.
- Create two panels and add them to the frame.
- Each panel contains three buttons. The panel uses `FlowLayout`.

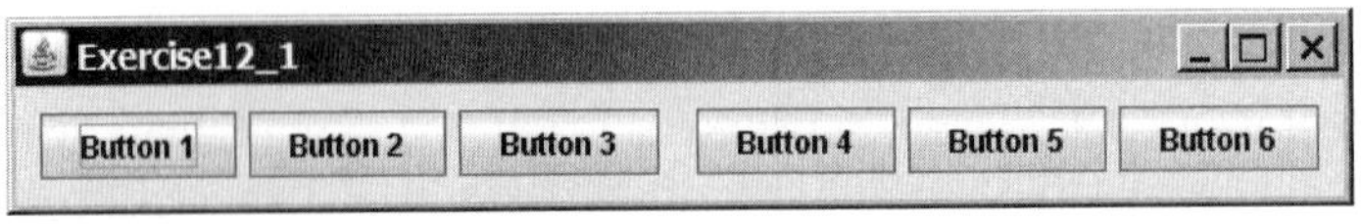
Exercise12_1
Button 1
Button 2
Button 3
Button 4
Button 5
Button 6

FIGURE 12.14 Exercise 12.1 places the first three buttons in one panel and the other three buttons in another panel.

12.2 (*Using the `BorderLayout` manager*) Rewrite the preceding program to create the same user interface, but instead of using `FlowLayout` for the frame, use `BorderLayout`. Place one panel in the south of the frame and the other in the center.

12.3 (*Using the `GridLayout` manager*) Rewrite the preceding program to create the same user interface. Instead of using `FlowLayout` for the panels, use a `GridLayout` of two rows and three columns.

12.4 (*Using `JPanel` to group buttons*) Rewrite the preceding program to create the same user interface. Instead of creating buttons and panels separately, define a class that extends the `JPanel` class. Place three buttons in your panel class, and create two panels from the user-defined panel class.

12.5 (*Displaying labels*) Write a program that displays four lines of text in four labels, as shown in Figure 12.15(a). Add a line border on each label.

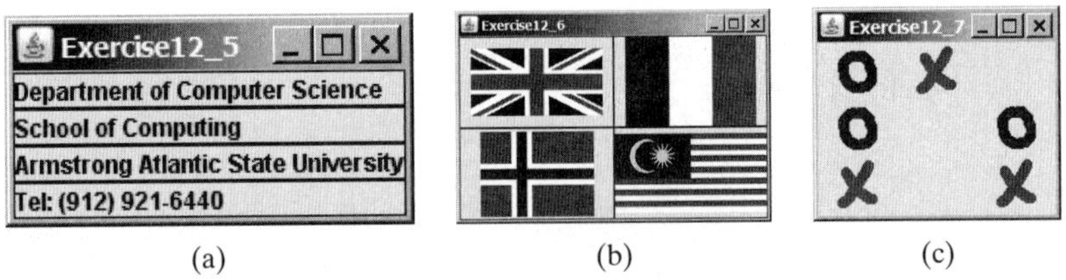
Exercise12_5
Department of Computer Science
School of Computing
Armstrong Atlantic State University
Tel: (912) 921-6440
Exercise12_6
Exercise12_7
(a)
(b)
(c)

FIGURE 12.15 (a) Exercise 12.5 displays four labels. (b) Exercise 12.6 displays four icons. (c) Exercise 12.7 displays a TicTacToe board with image icons in labels.

Sections 12.7–12.10

12.6 (*Displaying icons*) Write a program that displays four icons in four labels, as shown in Figure 12.15(b). Add a line border on each label. (Use any images of your choice or those in the book, which can be obtained along with the book's source code.)

12.7** (*Game: displaying a TicTacToe board*) Display a frame that contains nine labels. A label may display an image icon for X, an image icon for O, or nothing, as shown in Figure 12.15(c). What to display is randomly decided. Use the `Math.random()` method to generate an integer `0`, `1`, or `2`, which corresponds to displaying a cross image icon, a not image icon, or nothing. The cross and not images are in the files `x.gif` and `o.gif`, which are under the image directory in www.cs.armstrong.edu/liang/intro8e/book.zip).

12.8* (*Swing common features*) Display a frame that contains six labels. Set the background of the labels to white. Set the foreground of the labels to black, blue, cyan, green, magenta, and orange, respectively, as shown in Figure 12.16(a). Set the border of each label to a line border with the yellow color. Set the font of each label to TimesRoman, bold, and 20 pixels. Set the text and tool tip text of each label to the name of its foreground color.

Exercise12_8
black
blue
cyan
green
magenta
orange
Exercise12_9
Exercise12_10

(a) (b) (c)

FIGURE 12.16 (a) Six labels are placed in the frame. (b) Three cards are randomly selected. (c) A checkerboard is displayed using buttons.

12.9* (*Game: displaying three cards*) Display a frame that contains three labels. Each label displays a card, as shown in Figure 12.16(b). The card image files are named 1.png, 2.png, . . . , 54.png and stored in the `image/card` directory. All three cards are distinct and selected randomly. The image files can be obtained from www.cs.armstrong.edu/liang/intro8e/book.zip.

12.10* (*Game: displaying a checkerboard*) Write a program that displays a checkerboard in which each white and black cell is a `JButton` with a background black or white, as shown in Figure 12.16(c).

Video Note
Display a checker board

CHAPTER 13

EXCEPTION HANDLING

Objectives

- To get an overview of exceptions and exception handling (§13.2).
- To explore the advantages of using exception handling (§13.3).
- To distinguish exception types: `Error` (fatal) vs. `Exception` (nonfatal) and checked vs. unchecked (§13.4).
- To declare exceptions in a method header (§13.5.1).
- To throw exceptions in a method (§13.5.2).
- To write a `try-catch` block to handle exceptions (§13.5.3).
- To explain how an exception is propagated (§13.5.3).
- To use the `finally` clause in a `try-catch` block (§13.6).
- To use exceptions only for unexpected errors (§13.7).
- To rethrow exceptions in a `catch` block (§13.8).
- To create chained exceptions (§13.9).
- To define custom exception classes (§13.10).

13.1 Introduction

Runtime errors occur while a program is running if the environment detects an operation that is impossible to carry out. For example, if you access an array using an index out of bounds, your program will get a runtime error with an `ArrayIndexOutOfBoundsException`. To read data from a file, you need to create a `Scanner` object using `new Scanner(new File(filename))` (see Listing 9.6). If the file does not exist, your program will get a runtime error with a `FileNotFoundException`.

In Java, runtime errors are caused by exceptions. An exception is an object that represents an error or a condition that prevents execution from proceeding normally. If the exception is not handled, the program will terminate abnormally. How can you handle the exception so that the program can continue to run or else terminate gracefully? This is the subject we introduce in this chapter.

13.2 Exception-Handling Overview

Video Note
Exception-handling advantages

To demonstrate exception handling, including how an exception object is created and thrown, we begin with an example (Listing 13.1) that reads in two integers and displays their quotient.

LISTING 13.1 Quotient.java

reads two integers

integer division

```
import java.util.Scanner;

public class Quotient {
  public static void main(String[] args) {
    Scanner input = new Scanner(System.in);

    // Prompt the user to enter two integers
    System.out.print("Enter two integers: ");
    int number1 = input.nextInt();
    int number2 = input.nextInt();

    System.out.println(number1 + " / " + number2 + " is " +
      (number1 / number2));
  }
}
```

```
Enter two integers: 5 2 [Enter]
5 / 2 is 2
```

```
Enter two integers: 3 0 [Enter]
Exception in thread "main" java.lang.ArithmeticException: / by zero
                at Quotient.main(Quotient.java:11)
```

If you entered `0` for the second number, a runtime error would occur, because you cannot divide an integer by `0`. (*Recall that a floating-point number divided by* `0` *does not raise an exception.*) A simple way to fix the error is to add an `if` statement to test the second number, as shown in Listing 13.2.

LISTING 13.2 QuotientWithIf.java

```
import java.util.Scanner;

public class QuotientWithIf {
```

```
  public static void main(String[] args) {
    Scanner input = new Scanner(System.in);

    // Prompt the user to enter two integers
    System.out.print("Enter two integers: ");
    int number1 = input.nextInt();
    int number2 = input.nextInt();

    if (number2 != 0)
      System.out.println(number1 + " / " + number2
        + " is " + (number1 / number2));
    else
      System.out.println("Divisor cannot be zero ");
  }
}
```

reads two integers

test number2

```
Enter two integers: 5 0 ↵Enter
Divisor cannot be zero
```

In order to demonstrate the concept of exception handling, including how to create, throw, catch, and handle an exception, we rewrite Listing 13.2 as shown in Listing 13.3.

Listing 13.3 QuotientWithException.java

```
import java.util.Scanner;

public class QuotientWithException {
  public static void main(String[] args) {
    Scanner input = new Scanner(System.in);

    // Prompt the user to enter two integers
    System.out.print("Enter two integers: ");
    int number1 = input.nextInt();
    int number2 = input.nextInt();

    try {
      if (number2 == 0)
        throw new ArithmeticException("Divisor cannot be zero");

      System.out.println(number1 + " / " + number2 + " is " +
        (number1 / number2));
    }
    catch (ArithmeticException ex) {
      System.out.println("Exception: an integer " +
        "cannot be divided by zero ");
    }

    System.out.println("Execution continues ...");
  }
}
```

reads two integers

`try` block

`catch` block

```
Enter two integers: 5 3 ↵Enter
5 / 3 is 1
Execution continues ...
```

```
Enter two integers: 5 0 ↵Enter
Exception: an integer cannot be divided by zero
Execution continues ...
```

The program contains a `try` block and a `catch` block. The `try` block (lines 12–18) contains the code that is executed in normal circumstances. The `catch` block (lines 19–22) contains the code that is executed when `number2` is `0`. In this event the program throws an exception by executing

throw statement

```
throw new ArithmeticException("Divisor cannot be zero");
```

exception

throwing exception

The value thrown, in this case `new ArithmeticException("Divisor cannot be zero")`, is called an *exception*. The execution of a `throw` statement is called *throwing an exception*. The exception is an object created from an exception class. In this case, the exception class is `java.lang.ArithmeticException`.

handle exception

When an exception is thrown, the normal execution flow is interrupted. As the name suggests, to "throw an exception" is to pass the exception from one place to another. The exception is caught by the `catch` block. The code in the `catch` block is executed to *handle the exception*. Afterward, the statement (line 24) after the `catch` block is executed.

The `throw` statement is analogous to a method call, but instead of calling a method, it calls a `catch` block. In this sense, a `catch` block is like a method definition with a parameter that matches the type of the value being thrown. Unlike a method, after the `catch` block is executed, however, the program control does not return to the `throw` statement; instead, it executes the next statement after the `catch` block.

The identifier `ex` in the `catch`–block header

```
catch (ArithmeticException ex)
```

catch–block parameter

acts very much like a parameter in a method. So this parameter is referred to as a `catch`–block parameter. The type (e.g., `ArithmeticException`) preceding `ex` specifies what kind of exception the `catch` block can catch. Once the exception is caught, you can access the thrown value from this parameter in the body of a catch block.

In summary, a template for a `try-throw-catch` block may look like this:

```
try {
  Code to try;
  Throw an exception with a throw statement or
    from method if necessary;
  More code to try;
}
catch (type ex) {
  Code to process the exception;
}
```

An exception may be thrown directly by using a `throw` statement in a `try` block, or by invoking a method that may throw an exception.

13.3 Exception-Handling Advantages

You have seen from Listing 13.3 how an exception is created, thrown, caught, and handled. You may wonder what the benefits are. To see these benefits, we rewrite Listing 13.3 to compute a quotient using a method, as shown in Listing 13.4.

LISTING 13.4 QuotientWithMethod.java

```
 1 import java.util.Scanner;
 2
 3 public class QuotientWithMethod {
 4   public static int quotient(int number1, int number2) {
 5     if (number2 == 0)
 6       throw new ArithmeticException("Divisor cannot be zero");
 7
 8     return number1 / number2;
 9   }
10
11   public static void main(String[] args) {
12     Scanner input = new Scanner(System.in);
13
14     // Prompt the user to enter two integers
15     System.out.print("Enter two integers: ");
16     int number1 = input.nextInt();
17     int number2 = input.nextInt();
18
19     try {
20       int result = quotient(number1, number2);
21       System.out.println(number1 + " / " + number2 + " is "
22         + result);
23     }
24     catch (ArithmeticException ex) {
25       System.out.println("Exception: an integer " +
26         "cannot be divided by zero ");
27     }
28
29     System.out.println("Execution continues ...");
30   }
31 }
```

If an ArithmeticException occurs (line 20 → line 25)

quotient method

throw exception

reads two integers

try block

invoke method

catch block

```
Enter two integers: 5 3 ↵Enter
5 / 3 is 1
Execution continues ...
```

```
Enter two integers: 5 0 ↵Enter
Exception: an integer cannot be divided by zero
Execution continues ...
```

Method **quotient** (lines 4–9) returns the quotient of two integers. If **number2** is **0**, it cannot return a value. So, an exception is thrown in line 6.

The main method invokes **quotient** (line 20). If the quotient method executes normally, it returns a value to the caller. If the **quotient** method encounters an exception, it throws the exception back to its caller. The caller's **catch** block handles the exception.

advantage

Now you see the *advantages* of using exception handling. It enables a method to throw an exception to its caller. The caller can handle this exception. Without this capability, the called method itself must handle the exception or terminate the program. Often the called method does not know what to do in case of error. This is typically the case for the library methods. The library method can detect the error, but only the caller knows what needs to be done when an error occurs. The essential benefit of exception handling is to separate the detection of an error (done in a called method) from the handling of an error (done in the calling method).

Many library methods *throw exceptions*. Listing 13.5 gives an example that handles `FileNotFoundException` for invoking the `Scanner(File file)` constructor.

Listing 13.5 FileNotFoundExceptionDemo.java

try block
create a Scanner
catch block

If a FileNotFoundException occurs

```
1 import java.util.Scanner;
2 import java.io.*;
3
4 public class FileNotFoundExceptionDemo {
5   public static void main(String[] args) {
6     Scanner inputFromConsole = new Scanner(System.in);
7     // Prompt the user to enter a file name
8     System.out.print("Enter a file name: ");
9     String filename = inputFromConsole.nextLine();
10
11     try {
12       Scanner inputFromFile = new Scanner(new File(filename));
13       System.out.println("File " + filename + " exists ");
14       // Processing file ...
15     }
16     catch (FileNotFoundException ex) {
17       System.out.println("Exception: " +  filename + " not found");
18     }
19   }
20 }
```

```
Enter a file name: c:\book\Welcome.java [Enter]
File c:\book\Welcome.java exists
```

```
Enter a file name: c:\book\Test10.java [Enter]
Exception: c:\book\Test10.java not found
```

The program creates a `Scanner` for a file (line 12). If the file does not exist, the constructor throws a `FileNotFoundException`, which is caught in the `catch` block.

Listing 13.6 gives an example that handles an `InputMismatchException` exception.

Listing 13.6 InputMismatchExceptionDemo.java

try block
create a Scanner

If an InputMismatchException occurs

```
import java.util.*;

public class InputMismatchExceptionDemo {
  public static void main(String[] args) {
    Scanner input = new Scanner(System.in);
    boolean continueInput = true;

    do {
      try {
        System.out.print("Enter an integer: ");
        int number = input.nextInt();

        // Display the result
        System.out.println(
```

```
15          "The number entered is " + number);
16
17        continueInput = false;
18      }
19      catch (InputMismatchException ex) {
20        System.out.println("Try again. (" +
21          "Incorrect input: an integer is required)");
22        input.nextLine(); // Discard input
23      }
24    } while (continueInput);
25  }
26 }
```

catch block

```
Enter an integer: 3.5 [Enter]
Try again. (Incorrect input: an integer is required)
Enter an integer: 4 [Enter]
The number entered is 4
```

When executing `input.nextInt()` (line 11), an `InputMismatchException` occurs if the input entered is not an integer. Suppose `3.5` is entered. An `InputMismatchException` occurs and the control is transferred to the `catch` block. The statements in the `catch` block are now executed. The statement `input.nextLine()` in line 22 discards the current input line so that the user can enter a new line of input. The variable `continueInput` controls the loop. Its initial value is `true` (line 6), and it is changed to `false` (line 17) when a valid input is received.

13.4 Exception Types

The preceding sections used `ArithmeticException`, `FileNotFoundException`, and `InputMismatchException`. Are there any other types of exceptions you can use? Yes. There are many predefined exception classes in the Java API. Figure 13.1 shows some of them.

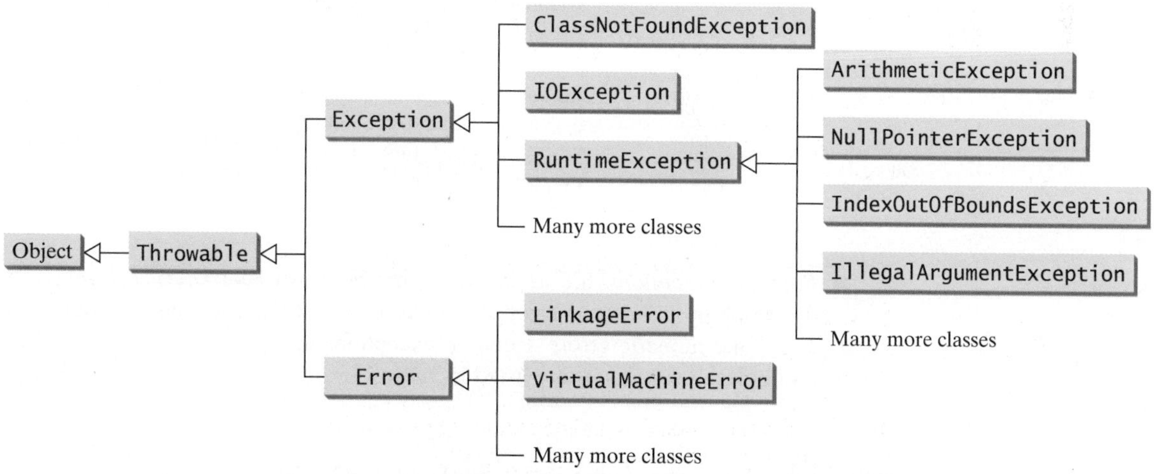

Object
Throwable
Exception
Error
ClassNotFoundException
IOException
RuntimeException
Many more classes
ArithmeticException
NullPointerException
IndexOutOfBoundsException
IllegalArgumentException
Many more classes
LinkageError
VirtualMachineError
Many more classes

FIGURE 13.1 Exceptions thrown are instances of the classes shown in this diagram, or of subclasses of one of these classes.

Note

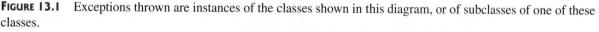

The class names `Error`, `Exception`, and `RuntimeException` are somewhat confusing. All three of these classes are exceptions, and all of the errors discussed here occur at runtime.

The `Throwable` class is the root of exception classes. All Java exception classes inherit directly or indirectly from `Throwable`. You can create your own exception classes by extending `Exception` or a subclass of `Exception`.

The exception classes can be classified into three major types: system errors, exceptions, and runtime exceptions.

system error

- *System errors* are thrown by the JVM and represented in the `Error` class. The `Error` class describes internal system errors. Such errors rarely occur. If one does, there is little you can do beyond notifying the user and trying to terminate the program gracefully. Examples of subclasses of `Error` are listed in Table 13.1.

TABLE 13.1 Examples of Subclasses of `Error`

Class	*Possible Reason for Exception*
`LinkageError`	A class has some dependency on another class, but the latter class has changed incompatibly after the compilation of the former class.
`VirtualMachineError`	The JVM is broken or has run out of the resources it needs in order to continue operating.

exception

- *Exceptions* are represented in the `Exception` class, which describes errors caused by your program and by external circumstances. These errors can be caught and handled by your program. Examples of subclasses of `Exception` are listed in Table 13.2.

TABLE 13.2 Examples of Subclasses of `Exception`

Class	*Possible Reason for Exception*
`ClassNotFoundException`	Attempt to use a class that does not exist. This exception would occur, for example, if you tried to run a nonexistent class using the **java** command, or if your program were composed of, say, three class files, only two of which could be found.
`IOException`	Related to input/output operations, such as invalid input, reading past the end of a file, and opening a nonexistent file. Examples of subclasses of `IOException` are `InterruptedIOException`, `EOFException` (EOF is short for End Of File), and `FileNotFoundException`.

runtime exception

- *Runtime exceptions* are represented in the `RuntimeException` class, which describes programming errors, such as bad casting, accessing an out-of-bounds array, and numeric errors. Runtime exceptions are generally thrown by the JVM. Examples of subclasses are listed in Table 13.3.

TABLE 13.3 Examples of Subclasses of `RuntimeException`

Class	*Possible Reason for Exception*
`ArithmeticException`	Dividing an integer by zero. Note that floating-point arithmetic does not throw exceptions. See Appendix E, "Special Floating-Point Values."
`NullPointerException`	Attempt to access an object through a `null` reference variable.
`IndexOutOfBoundsException`	Index to an array is out of range.
`IllegalArgumentException`	A method is passed an argument that is illegal or inappropriate.

RuntimeException, **Error**, and their subclasses are known as *unchecked exceptions*. All other exceptions are known as *checked exceptions*, meaning that the compiler forces the programmer to check and deal with them.

unchecked exception
checked exception

In most cases, unchecked exceptions reflect programming logic errors that are unrecoverable. For example, a **NullPointerException** is thrown if you access an object through a reference variable before an object is assigned to it; an **IndexOutOfBoundsException** is thrown if you access an element in an array outside the bounds of the array. These are logic errors that should be corrected in the program. Unchecked exceptions can occur anywhere in a program. To avoid cumbersome overuse of **try-catch** blocks, Java does not mandate that you write code to catch or declare unchecked exceptions.

Caution

At present, Java does not throw integer overflow or underflow exceptions. The following statement adds **1** to the maximum integer.

integer overflow/underflow

```
int number = Integer.MAX_VALUE + 1;
System.out.println(number);
```

It displays **-2147483648**, which is logically incorrect. The cause of this problem is overflow; that is, the result exceeds the maximum for an **int** value.

A future version of Java may fix this problem by throwing an overflow exception.

13.5 More on Exception Handling

The preceding sections gave you an overview of exception handling and introduced several predefined exception types. This section provides an in-depth discussion of exception handling.

Java's exception-handling model is based on three operations: *declaring an exception*, *throwing an exception*, and *catching an exception*, as shown in Figure 13.2.

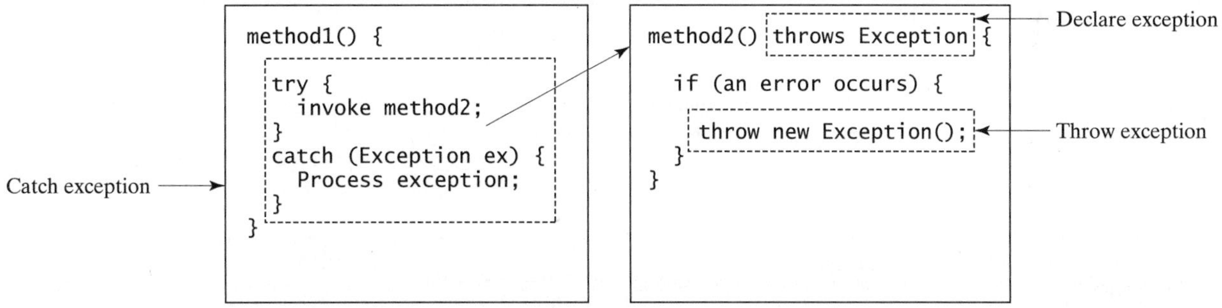
method1() {
try {
invoke method2;
}
catch (Exception ex) {
Process exception;
}
}
Catch exception
method2() throws Exception {
if (an error occurs) {
throw new Exception();
}
}
Declare exception
Throw exception

FIGURE 13.2 Exception handling in Java consists of declaring exceptions, throwing exceptions, and catching and processing exceptions.

13.5.1 Declaring Exceptions

In Java, the statement currently being executed belongs to a method. The Java interpreter invokes the **main** method to start executing a program. Every method must state the types of checked exceptions it might throw. This is known as *declaring exceptions*. Because system errors and runtime errors can happen to any code, Java does not require that you declare **Error** and **RuntimeException** (unchecked exceptions) explicitly in the method. However, all other exceptions thrown by the method must be explicitly declared in the method header so that the caller of the method is informed of the exception.

declare exception

To declare an exception in a method, use the `throws` keyword in the method header, as in this example:

```
public void myMethod() throws IOException
```

The `throws` keyword indicates that `myMethod` might throw an `IOException`. If the method might throw multiple exceptions, add a list of the exceptions, separated by commas, after `throws`:

```
public void myMethod()
  throws Exception1, Exception2, ..., ExceptionN
```

Note

If a method does not declare exceptions in the superclass, you cannot override it to declare exceptions in the subclass.

13.5.2 Throwing Exceptions

throw exception

A program that detects an error can create an instance of an appropriate exception type and throw it. This is known as *throwing an exception*. Here is an example: Suppose the program detects that an argument passed to the method violates the method contract (e.g., the argument must be nonnegative, but a negative argument is passed); the program can create an instance of `IllegalArgumentException` and throw it, as follows:

```
IllegalArgumentException ex =
  new IllegalArgumentException("Wrong Argument");
throw ex;
```

Or, if you prefer, you can use the following:

```
throw new IllegalArgumentException("Wrong Argument");
```

Note

exception message

`IllegalArgumentException` is an exception class in the Java API. In general, each exception class in the Java API has at least two constructors: a no-arg constructor, and a constructor with a `String` argument that describes the exception. This argument is called the *exception message*, which can be obtained using `getMessage()`.

Tip

`throws` and **`throw`**

The keyword to declare an exception is `throws`, and the keyword to throw an exception is `throw`.

13.5.3 Catching Exceptions

catch exception

You now know how to declare an exception and how to throw an exception. When an exception is thrown, it can be caught and handled in a try-catch block, as follows:

```
try {
  statements;  // Statements that may throw exceptions
}
catch (Exception1 exVar1) {
  handler for exception1;
}
catch (Exception2 exVar2) {
  handler for exception2;
}
...
```

```
catch (ExceptionN exVar3) {
  handler for exceptionN;
}
```

If no exceptions arise during the execution of the try block, the catch blocks are skipped.

If one of the statements inside the try block throws an exception, Java skips the remaining statements in the try block and starts the process of finding the code to handle the exception. The code that handles the exception is called the *exception handler*; it is found by propagating the exception backward through a chain of method calls, starting from the current method. Each catch block is examined in turn, from first to last, to see whether the type of the exception object is an instance of the exception class in the catch block. If so, the exception object is assigned to the variable declared, and the code in the catch block is executed. If no handler is found, Java exits this method, passes the exception to the method that invoked the method, and continues the same process to find a handler. If no handler is found in the chain of methods being invoked, the program terminates and prints an error message on the console. The process of finding a handler is called *catching an exception*.

exception handler

Suppose the main method invokes method1, method1 invokes method2, method2 invokes method3, and method3 throws an exception, as shown in Figure 13.3. Consider the following scenario:

- If the exception type is Exception3, it is caught by the catch block for handling exception ex3 in method2. statement5 is skipped, and statement6 is executed.
- If the exception type is Exception2, method2 is aborted, the control is returned to method1, and the exception is caught by the catch block for handling exception ex2 in method1. statement3 is skipped, and statement4 is executed.
- If the exception type is Exception1, method1 is aborted, the control is returned to the main method, and the exception is caught by the catch block for handling exception ex1 in the main method. statement1 is skipped, and statement2 is executed.
- If the exception type is not caught in method2, method1, and main, the program terminates. statement1 and statement2 are not executed.

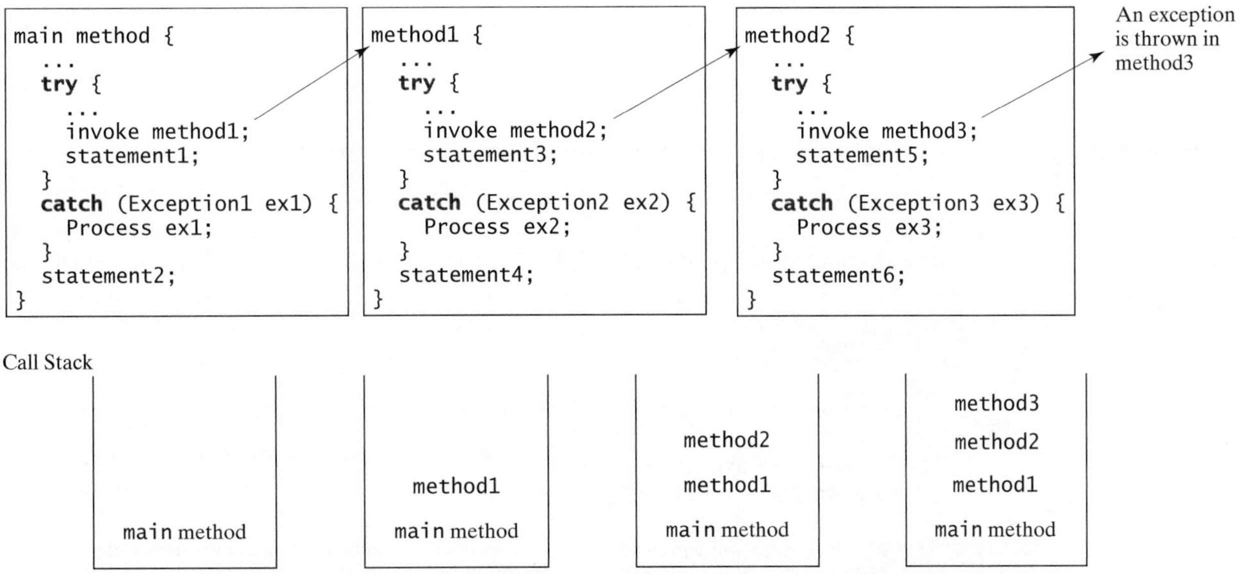
main method {
...
try {
...
invoke method1;
statement1;
}
catch (Exception1 ex1) {
Process ex1;
}
statement2;
}
method1 {
...
try {
...
invoke method2;
statement3;
}
catch (Exception2 ex2) {
Process ex2;
}
statement4;
}
method2 {
...
try {
...
invoke method3;
statement5;
}
catch (Exception3 ex3) {
Process ex3;
}
statement6;
}
An exception is thrown in method3
Call Stack
main method
method1
main method
method2
method1
main method
method3
method2
method1
main method

FIGURE 13.3 If an exception is not caught in the current method, it is passed to its caller. The process is repeated until the exception is caught or passed to the main method.

catch block

Note

Various exception classes can be derived from a common superclass. If a **catch** block catches exception objects of a superclass, it can catch all the exception objects of the subclasses of that superclass.

order of exception handlers

Note

The order in which exceptions are specified in **catch** blocks is important. A compile error will result if a catch block for a superclass type appears before a catch block for a subclass type. For example, the ordering in (a) below is erroneous, because **RuntimeException** is a subclass of **Exception**. The correct ordering should be as shown in (b).

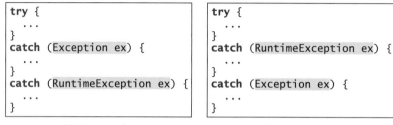

```
try {
  ...
}
catch (Exception ex) {
  ...
}
catch (RuntimeException ex) {
  ...
}
```

(a) Wrong order

```
try {
  ...
}
catch (RuntimeException ex) {
  ...
}
catch (Exception ex) {
  ...
}
```

(b) Correct order

catch or declare checked exceptions

Note

Java forces you to deal with checked exceptions. If a method declares a checked exception (i.e., an exception other than **Error** or **RuntimeException**), you must invoke it in a **try-catch** block or declare to throw the exception in the calling method. For example, suppose that method **p1** invokes method **p2**, and **p2** may throw a checked exception (e.g., **IOException**); you have to write the code as shown in (a) or (b) below.

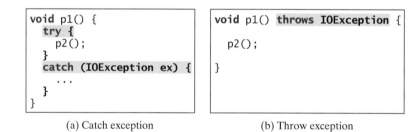

```
void p1() {
  try {
    p2();
  }
  catch (IOException ex) {
    ...
  }
}
```

(a) Catch exception

```
void p1() throws IOException {

  p2();

}
```

(b) Throw exception

13.5.4 Getting Information from Exceptions

methods in **Throwable**

An exception object contains valuable information about the exception. You may use the following instance methods in the **java.lang.Throwable** class to get information regarding the exception, as shown in Figure 13.4. The **printStackTrace()** method prints stack trace

java.lang.Throwable	
+getMessage(): String	Returns the message of this object.
+toString(): String	Returns the concatenation of three strings: (1) the full name of the exception class; (2) ": " (a colon and a space); (3) the getMessage() method.
+printStackTrace(): void	Prints the Throwable object and its call stack trace information on the console.
+getStackTrace(): StackTraceElement[]	Returns an array of stack trace elements representing the stack trace pertaining to this throwable.

FIGURE 13.4 Throwable is the root class for all exception objects.

information on the console. The `getStackTrace()` method provides programmatic access to the stack trace information printed by `printStackTrace()`.

Listing 13.7 gives an example that uses the methods in `Throwable` to display exception information. Line 4 invokes the `sum` method to return the sum of all the elements in the array. There is an error in line 23 that causes the `ArrayIndexOutOfBoundsException`, a subclass of `IndexOutOfBoundsException`. This exception is caught in the try-catch block. Lines 7, 8, 9 display the stack trace, exception message, and exception object and message using the `printStackTrace()`, `getMessage()`, and `toString()` methods, as shown in Figure 13.5. Line 10 brings stack trace elements into an array. Each element represents a method call. You can obtain the method (line 12), class name (line 13), and exception line number (line 14) for each element.

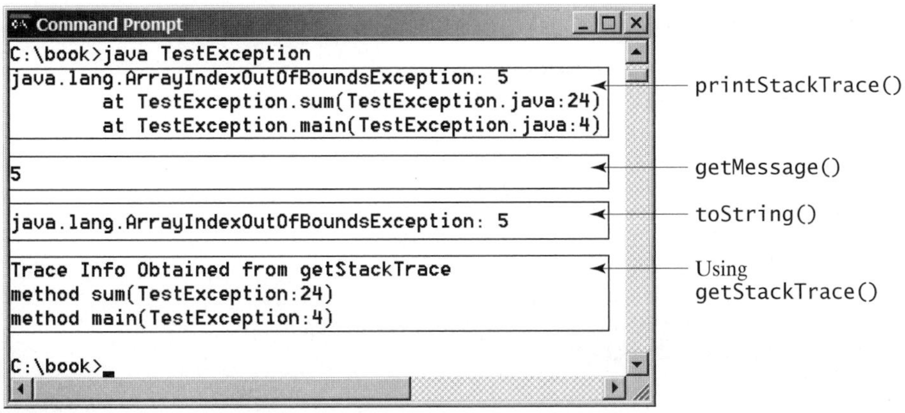
Command Prompt
C:\book>java TestException
java.lang.ArrayIndexOutOfBoundsException: 5
at TestException.sum(TestException.java:24)
at TestException.main(TestException.java:4)
5
java.lang.ArrayIndexOutOfBoundsException: 5
Trace Info Obtained from getStackTrace
method sum(TestException:24)
method main(TestException:4)
C:\book>
printStackTrace()
getMessage()
toString()
Using getStackTrace()

FIGURE 13.5 You can use the `printStackTrace()`, `getMessage()`, `toString()`, and `getStackTrace()` methods to obtain information from exception objects.

LISTING 13.7 TestException.java

```
 1 public class TestException  {
 2   public static void main(String[] args) {
 3     try {
 4       System.out.println(sum(new int[] {1, 2, 3, 4, 5}));
 5     }
 6     catch (Exception ex) {
 7       ex.printStackTrace();
 8       System.out.println("\n" + ex.getMessage());
 9       System.out.println("\n" + ex.toString());
10
11       System.out.println("\nTrace Info Obtained from getStackTrace");
12       StackTraceElement[] traceElements = ex.getStackTrace();
13       for (int i = 0; i < traceElements.length; i++) {
14         System.out.print("method " + traceElements[i].getMethodName());
15         System.out.print("(" + traceElements[i].getClassName() + ":");
16         System.out.println(traceElements[i].getLineNumber() + ")");
17       }
18     }
19   }
20
21   private static int sum(int[] list) {
22     int result = 0;
23     for (int i = 0; i <= list.length; i++)
24       result += list[i];
25     return result;
26   }
27 }
```

invoke sum

printStackTrace()
getMessage()
toString()

13.5.5 Example: Declaring, Throwing, and Catching Exceptions

This example demonstrates declaring, throwing, and catching exceptions by modifying the **setRadius** method in the **Circle** class in Listing 8.9, Circle3.java. The new **setRadius** method throws an exception if the radius is negative.

Rename the circle class given in Listing 13.8 as **CircleWithException**, which is the same as **Circle3** except that the **setRadius(double newRadius)** method throws an **IllegalArgumentException** if the argument **newRadius** is negative.

LISTING 13.8 CircleWithException.java

declare exception

throw exception

```
public class CircleWithException {
  /** The radius of the circle */
  private double radius;

  /** The number of the objects created */
  private static int numberOfObjects = 0;

  /** Construct a circle with radius 1 */
  public CircleWithException() {
    this(1.0);
  }

  /** Construct a circle with a specified radius */
  public CircleWithException(double newRadius) {
    setRadius(newRadius);
    numberOfObjects++;
  }

  /** Return radius */
  public double getRadius() {
    return radius;
  }

  /** Set a new radius */
  public void setRadius(double newRadius)
      throws IllegalArgumentException {
    if (newRadius >= 0)
      radius =  newRadius;
    else
      throw new IllegalArgumentException(
        "Radius cannot be negative");
  }

  /** Return numberOfObjects */
  public static int getNumberOfObjects() {
    return numberOfObjects;
  }

  /** Return the area of this circle */
  public double findArea() {
    return radius * radius * 3.14159;
  }
}
```

A test program that uses the new **Circle** class is given in Listing 13.9.

LISTING 13.9 TestCircleWithException.java

```
public class TestCircleWithException {
  public static void main(String[] args) {
```

```
3      try {
4        CircleWithException c1 = new CircleWithException(5);
5        CircleWithException c2 = new CircleWithException(-5);
6        CircleWithException c3 = new CircleWithException(0);
7      }
8      catch (IllegalArgumentException ex) {
9        System.out.println(ex);
10     }
11
12     System.out.println("Number of objects created: " +
13       CircleWithException.getNumberOfObjects());
14   }
15 }
```

try

catch

```
java.lang.IllegalArgumentException: Radius cannot be negative
Number of objects created: 1
```

The original `Circle` class remains intact except that the class name is changed to `CircleWithException`, a new constructor `CircleWithException(newRadius)` is added, and the `setRadius` method now declares an exception and throws it if the radius is negative.

The `setRadius` method declares to throw `IllegalArgumentException` in the method header (lines 25–32 in `CircleWithException.java`). The `CircleWithException` class would still compile if the `throws IllegalArgumentException` clause were removed from the method declaration, since it is a subclass of `RuntimeException` and every method can throw `RuntimeException` (unchecked exception) regardless of whether it is declared in the method header.

The test program creates three `CircleWithException` objects, `c1`, `c2`, and `c3`, to test how to handle exceptions. Invoking `new CircleWithException(-5)` (line 5 in Listing 13.9) causes the `setRadius` method to be invoked, which throws an `IllegalArgumentException`, because the radius is negative. In the `catch` block, the type of the object `ex` is `IllegalArgumentException`, which matches the exception object thrown by the `setRadius` method. So, this exception is caught by the `catch` block.

The exception handler prints a short message, `ex.toString()` (line 9), about the exception, using `System.out.println(ex)`.

Note that the execution continues in the event of the exception. If the handlers had not caught the exception, the program would have abruptly terminated.

The test program would still compile if the `try` statement were not used, because the method throws an instance of `IllegalArgumentException`, a subclass of `RuntimeException` (unchecked exception). If a method throws an exception other than `RuntimeException` and `Error`, the method must be invoked within a `try-catch` block.

13.6 The **finally** Clause

Occasionally, you may want some code to be executed regardless of whether an exception occurs or is caught. Java has a `finally` clause that can be used to accomplish this objective. The syntax for the `finally` clause might look like this:

```
try {
  statements;
}
catch (TheException ex) {
  handling ex;
}
```

```
finally {
  finalStatements;
}
```

The code in the `finally` block is executed under all circumstances, regardless of whether an exception occurs in the `try` block or is caught. Consider three possible cases:

- If no exception arises in the `try` block, `finalStatements` is executed, and the next statement after the `try` statement is executed.
- If a statement causes an exception in the `try` block that is caught in a `catch` block, the rest of statements in the `try` block are skipped, the `catch` block is executed, and the `finally` clause is executed. The next statement after the `try` statement is executed.
- If one of the statements causes an exception that is not caught in any `catch` block, the other statements in the `try` block are skipped, the `finally` clause is executed, and the exception is passed to the caller of this method.

The `finally` block executes even if there is a `return` statement prior to reaching the `finally` block.

omitting catch block

Note

The `catch` block may be omitted when the `finally` clause is used.

A common use of the `finally` clause is in I/O programming. To ensure that a file is closed under all circumstances, you may place a file closing statement in the `finally` block, as shown in Listing 13.10.

Listing 13.10 FinallyDemo.java

try

catch

finally

```
 1 public class FinallyDemo {
 2   public static void main(String[] args) {
 3     java.io.PrintWriter output = null;
 4 
 5     try {
 6       // Create a file
 7       output = new java.io.PrintWriter("text.txt");
 8 
 9       // Write formatted output to the file
10       output.println("Welcome to Java");
11     }
12     catch (java.io.IOException ex) {
13       ex.printStackTrace();
14     }
15     finally {
16       // Close the file
17       if (output != null) output.close();
18     }
19 
20     System.out.println("End of program");
21   }
22 }
```

The statements in lines 7 and 10 may throw an `IOException`, so they are placed inside a `try` block. The statement `output.close()` closes the `PrintWriter` object output in the `finally` block. This statement is executed regardless of whether an exception occurs in the `try` block or is caught.

13.7 When to Use Exceptions

The `try` block contains the code that is executed in normal circumstances. The `catch` block contains the code that is executed in exceptional circumstances. Exception handling separates error-handling code from normal programming tasks, thus making programs easier to read and to modify. Be aware, however, that exception handling usually requires more time and resources, because it requires instantiating a new exception object, rolling back the call stack, and propagating the exception through the chain of methods invoked to search for the handler.

An exception occurs in a method. If you want the exception to be processed by its caller, you should create an exception object and throw it. If you can handle the exception in the method where it occurs, there is no need to throw or use exceptions.

In general, common exceptions that may occur in multiple classes in a project are candidates for exception classes. Simple errors that may occur in individual methods are best handled locally without throwing exceptions.

When should you use a try-catch block in the code? Use it when you have to deal with unexpected error conditions. Do not use a try-catch block to deal with simple, expected situations. For example, the following code

```
try {
  System.out.println(refVar.toString());
}
catch (NullPointerException ex) {
  System.out.println("refVar is null");
}
```

is better replaced by

```
if (refVar != null)
  System.out.println(refVar.toString());
else
  System.out.println("refVar is null");
```

Which situations are exceptional and which are expected is sometimes difficult to decide. The point is not to abuse exception handling as a way to deal with a simple logic test.

13.8 Rethrowing Exceptions

Java allows an exception handler to rethrow the exception if the handler cannot process the exception or simply wants to let its caller be notified of the exception. The syntax may look like this:

```
try {
  statements;
}
catch (TheException ex) {
  perform operations before exits;
  throw ex;
}
```

The statement `throw ex` rethrows the exception to the caller so that other handlers in the caller get a chance to process the exception `ex`.

13.9 Chained Exceptions

In the preceding section, the catch block rethrows the original exception. Sometimes, you may need to throw a new exception (with additional information) along with the original exception.

This is called *chained exceptions*. Listing 13.11 illustrates how to create and throw chained exceptions.

LISTING 13.11 ChainedExceptionDemo.java

stack trace

chained exception

throw exception

```
 1 public class ChainedExceptionDemo {
 2   public static void main(String[] args) {
 3     try {
 4       method1();
 5     }
 6     catch (Exception ex) {
 7       ex.printStackTrace();
 8     }
 9   }
10
11   public static void method1() throws Exception {
12     try {
13       method2();
14     }
15     catch (Exception ex) {
16       throw new Exception("New info from method1", ex);
17     }
18   }
19
20   public static void method2() throws Exception {
21     throw new Exception("New info from method2");
22   }
23 }
```

```
java.lang.Exception: New info from method1
       at ChainedExceptionDemo.method1(ChainedExceptionDemo.java:16)
       at ChainedExceptionDemo.main(ChainedExceptionDemo.java:4)
Caused by: java.lang.Exception: New info from method2
       at ChainedExceptionDemo.method2(ChainedExceptionDemo.java:21)
       at ChainedExceptionDemo.method1(ChainedExceptionDemo.java:13)
       ... 1 more
```

The `main` method invokes `method1` (line 4), `method1` invokes `method2` (line 13), and `method2` throws an exception (line 21). This exception is caught in the `catch` block in `method1` and is wrapped in a new exception in line 16. The new exception is thrown and caught in the `catch` block in the `main` method in line 4. The sample output shows the output from the `printStackTrace()` method in line 7. The new exception thrown from `method1` is displayed first, followed by the original exception thrown from `method2`.

13.10 Creating Custom Exception Classes

Video Note
Create custom exception classes

Java provides quite a few exception classes. Use them whenever possible instead of creating your own exception classes. However, if you run into a problem that cannot be adequately described by the predefined exception classes, you can create your own exception class, derived from `Exception` or from a subclass of `Exception`, such as `IOException`.

In Listing 13.8, CircleWithException.java, the `setRadius` method throws an exception if the radius is negative. Suppose you wish to pass the radius to the handler. In that case, you may create a custom exception class, as shown in Listing 13.12.

LISTING 13.12 InvalidRadiusException.java

```
1 public class InvalidRadiusException extends Exception {
2   private double radius;
3
4   /** Construct an exception */
5   public InvalidRadiusException(double radius) {
6     super("Invalid radius " + radius);
7     this.radius = radius;
8   }
9
10  /** Return the radius */
11  public double getRadius() {
12    return radius;
13  }
14 }
```

extends Exception

This custom exception class extends `java.lang.Exception` (line 1). The `Exception` class extends `java.lang.Throwable`. All the methods (e.g., `getMessage()`, `toString()`, and `printStackTrace()`) in `Exception` are inherited from `Throwable`. The `Exception` class contains four constructors. Among them, the following two constructors are often used:

java.lang.Exception	
+Exception()	Constructs an exception with no message.
+Exception(message: String)	Constructs an exception with the specified message.

Line 6 invokes the superclass's constructor with a message. This message will be set in the exception object and can be obtained by invoking `getMessage()` on the object.

Tip

Most exception classes in the Java API contain two constructors: a no-arg constructor and a constructor with a message parameter.

To create an `InvalidRadiusException`, you have to pass a radius. So, the `setRadius` method in Listing 13.8 can be modified as follows:

```
/** Set a new radius */
public void setRadius(double newRadius)
    throws InvalidRadiusException {
  if (newRadius >= 0)
    radius =  newRadius;
  else
    throw new InvalidRadiusException(newRadius);
}
```

The following code creates a circle object and sets its radius to -5.

```
try {
  CircleWithException1 c = new CircleWithException1(4);
  c.setRadius(-5);
}
catch (InvalidRadiusException ex ) {
  System.out.println("The invalid radius is " + ex.getRadius());
}
```

Invoking `setRadius(-5)` throws an `InvalidRadiusException`, which is caught by the handler. The handler displays the radius in the exception object `ex`.

checked custom exception

Tip

Can you define a custom exception class by extending `RuntimeException`? Yes, but it is not a good way to go, because it makes your custom exception unchecked. It is better to make a custom exception checked, so that the complier can force these exceptions to be caught in your program.

Key Terms

chained exception 448
checked exception 438
declare exception 439
exception 438
exception propagation 441
throw exception 436
unchecked exception 438

Chapter Summary

1. Exception handling enables a method to throw an exception to its caller.
2. A Java exception is an instance of a class derived from `java.lang.Throwable`. Java provides a number of predefined exception classes, such as `Error`, `Exception`, `RuntimeException`, `ClassNotFoundException`, `NullPointerException`, and `ArithmeticException`. You can also define your own exception class by extending `Exception`.
3. Exceptions occur during the execution of a method. `RuntimeException` and `Error` are unchecked exceptions; all other exceptions are checked.
4. When declaring a method, you have to declare a checked exception if the method might throw it, thus telling the compiler what can go wrong.
5. The keyword for declaring an exception is `throws`, and the keyword for throwing an exception is `throw`.
6. To invoke the method that declares checked exceptions, you must enclose the method call in a `try` statement. When an exception occurs during the execution of the method, the `catch` block catches and handles the exception.
7. If an exception is not caught in the current method, it is passed to its caller. The process is repeated until the exception is caught or passed to the `main` method.
8. Various exception classes can be derived from a common superclass. If a `catch` block catches the exception objects of a superclass, it can also catch all the exception objects of the subclasses of that superclass.
9. The order in which exceptions are specified in a `catch` block is important. A compile error will result if you do not specify an exception object of a class before an exception object of the superclass of that class.
10. When an exception occurs in a method, the method exits immediately if it does not catch the exception. If the method is required to perform some task before exiting, you can catch the exception in the method and then rethrow it to the real handler.
11. The code in the `finally` block is executed under all circumstances, regardless of whether an exception occurs in the `try` block or is caught.

12. Exception handling separates error-handling code from normal programming tasks, thus making programs easier to read and to modify.

13. Exception handling should not be used to replace simple tests. You should test simple exceptions whenever possible, and reserve exception handling for dealing with situations that cannot be handled with `if` statements.

Review Questions

Sections 13.1–13.3

13.1 Describe the Java `Throwable` class, its subclasses, and the types of exceptions. What `RuntimeException` will the following programs throw, if any?

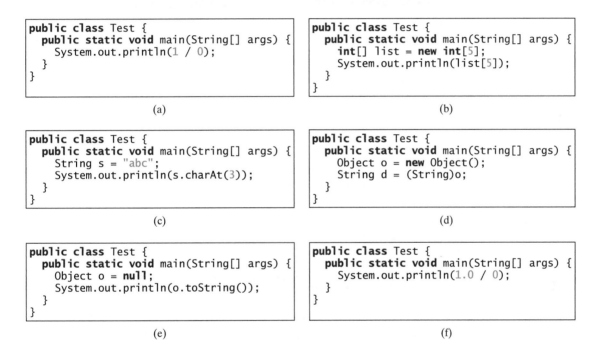

```
public class Test {
  public static void main(String[] args) {
    System.out.println(1 / 0);
  }
}
```

(a)

```
public class Test {
  public static void main(String[] args) {
    int[] list = new int[5];
    System.out.println(list[5]);
  }
}
```

(b)

```
public class Test {
  public static void main(String[] args) {
    String s = "abc";
    System.out.println(s.charAt(3));
  }
}
```

(c)

```
public class Test {
  public static void main(String[] args) {
    Object o = new Object();
    String d = (String)o;
  }
}
```

(d)

```
public class Test {
  public static void main(String[] args) {
    Object o = null;
    System.out.println(o.toString());
  }
}
```

(e)

```
public class Test {
  public static void main(String[] args) {
    System.out.println(1.0 / 0);
  }
}
```

(f)

13.2 Show the output of the following code.

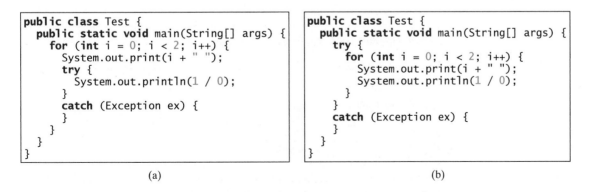

```
public class Test {
  public static void main(String[] args) {
    for (int i = 0; i < 2; i++) {
      System.out.print(i + " ");
      try {
        System.out.println(1 / 0);
      }
      catch (Exception ex) {
      }
    }
  }
}
```

(a)

```
public class Test {
  public static void main(String[] args) {
    try {
      for (int i = 0; i < 2; i++) {
        System.out.print(i + " ");
        System.out.println(1 / 0);
      }
    }
    catch (Exception ex) {
    }
  }
}
```

(b)

13.3 Point out the problem in the following code. Does the code throw any exceptions?

```
long value = Long.MAX_VALUE + 1;
System.out.println(value);
```

13.4 What is the purpose of declaring exceptions? How do you declare an exception, and where? Can you declare multiple exceptions in a method header?

13.5 What is a checked exception, and what is an unchecked exception?

13.6 How do you throw an exception? Can you throw multiple exceptions in one `throw` statement?

13.7 What is the keyword `throw` used for? What is the keyword `throws` used for?

13.8 What does the JVM do when an exception occurs? How do you catch an exception?

13.9 What is the printout of the following code?

```
public class Test {
  public static void main(String[] args) {
    try {
      int value = 30;
      if (value < 40)
        throw new Exception("value is too small");
    }
    catch (Exception ex) {
      System.out.println(ex.getMessage());
    }
    System.out.println("Continue after the catch block");
  }
}
```

What would be the printout if the line

```
int value = 30;
```

were changed to

```
int value = 50;
```

13.10 Suppose that `statement2` causes an exception in the following `try-catch` block:

```
try {
  statement1;
  statement2;
  statement3;
}
catch (Exception1 ex1) {
}
catch (Exception2 ex2) {
}

statement4;
```

Answer the following questions:

- Will `statement3` be executed?
- If the exception is not caught, will `statement4` be executed?
- If the exception is caught in the `catch` block, will `statement4` be executed?
- If the exception is passed to the caller, will `statement4` be executed?

13.11 What is displayed when the following program is run?

```
public class Test {
  public static void main(String[] args) {
```

```
    try {
      int[] list = new int[10];
      System.out.println("list[10] is " + list[10]);
    }
    catch (ArithmeticException ex) {
      System.out.println("ArithmeticException");
    }
    catch (RuntimeException ex) {
      System.out.println("RuntimeException");
    }
    catch (Exception ex) {
      System.out.println("Exception");
    }
  }
}
```

13.12 What is displayed when the following program is run?

```
public class Test {
  public static void main(String[] args) {
    try {
      method();
      System.out.println("After the method call");
    }
    catch (ArithmeticException ex) {
      System.out.println("ArithmeticException");
    }
    catch (RuntimeException ex) {
      System.out.println("RuntimeException");
    }
    catch (Exception e) {
      System.out.println("Exception");
    }
  }

  static void method() throws Exception {
    System.out.println(1 / 0);
  }
}
```

13.13 What is displayed when the following program is run?

```
public class Test {
  public static void main(String[] args) {
    try {
      method();
      System.out.println("After the method call");
    }
    catch (RuntimeException ex) {
      System.out.println("RuntimeException in main");
    }
    catch (Exception ex) {
      System.out.println("Exception in main");
    }
  }

  static void method() throws Exception {
    try {
      String s ="abc";
      System.out.println(s.charAt(3));
    }
```

```
      catch (RuntimeException ex) {
        System.out.println("RuntimeException in method()");
      }
      catch (Exception ex) {
        System.out.println("Exception in method()");
      }
    }
  }
```

13.14 What does the method `getMessage()` do?

13.15 What does the method `printStackTrace` do?

13.16 Does the presence of a `try-catch` block impose overhead when no exception occurs?

13.17 Correct a compile error in the following code:

```
public void m(int value) {
  if (value < 40)
    throw new Exception("value is too small");
}
```

Sections 13.4–13.10

13.18 Suppose that `statement2` causes an exception in the following statement:

```
try {
  statement1;
  statement2;
  statement3;
}
catch (Exception1 ex1) {
}
catch (Exception2 ex2) {
}
catch (Exception3 ex3) {
  throw ex3;
}
finally {
  statement4;
};
statement5;
```

Answer the following questions:

- Will `statement5` be executed if the exception is not caught?
- If the exception is of type `Exception3`, will `statement4` be executed, and will `statement5` be executed?

13.19 Suppose the `setRadius` method throws the `RadiusException` defined in §13.7. What is displayed when the following program is run?

```
public class Test {
  public static void main(String[] args) {
    try {
      method();
      System.out.println("After the method call");
    }
    catch (RuntimeException ex) {
      System.out.println("RuntimeException in main");
    }
```

```
    catch (Exception ex) {
      System.out.println("Exception in main");
    }
  }

  static void method() throws Exception {
    try {
      Circle c1 = new Circle(1);
      c1.setRadius(-1);
      System.out.println(c1.getRadius());
    }
    catch (RuntimeException ex) {
      System.out.println("RuntimeException in method()");
    }
    catch (Exception ex) {
      System.out.println("Exception in method()");
      throw ex;
    }
  }
}
```

13.20 The following method checks whether a string is a numeric string:

```
public static boolean isNumeric(String token) {
  try {
    Double.parseDouble(token);
    return true;
  }
  catch (java.lang.NumberFormatException ex) {
    return false;
  }
}
```

Is it correct? Rewrite it without using exceptions.

Programming Exercises

Sections 13.2–13.10

13.1* (*NumberFormatException*) Listing 9.5, Calculator.java, is a simple command-line calculator. Note that the program terminates if any operand is nonnumeric. Write a program with an exception handler that deals with nonnumeric operands; then write another program without using an exception handler to achieve the same objective. Your program should display a message that informs the user of the wrong operand type before exiting (see Figure 13.6).

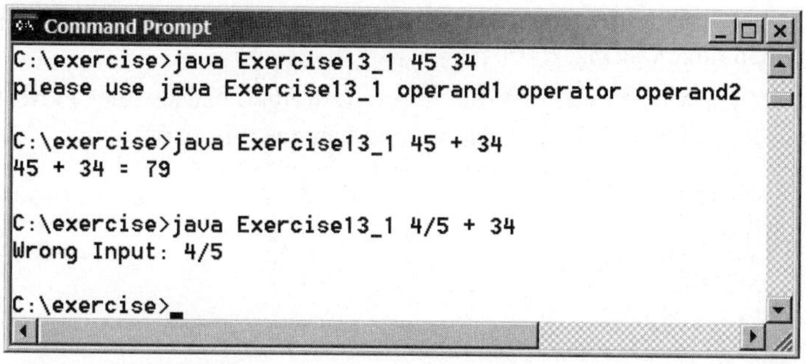
Command Prompt
C:\exercise>java Exercise13_1 45 34
please use java Exercise13_1 operand1 operator operand2
C:\exercise>java Exercise13_1 45 + 34
45 + 34 = 79
C:\exercise>java Exercise13_1 4/5 + 34
Wrong Input: 4/5
C:\exercise>

FIGURE 13.6 The program performs arithmetic operations and detects input errors.

13.2* (*NumberFormatException*) Write a program that prompts the user to read two integers and displays their sum. Your program should prompt the user to read the number again if the input is incorrect.

13.3* (*ArrayIndexOutBoundsException*) Write a program that meets the following requirements:

- Create an array with `100` randomly chosen integers.
- Prompt the user to enter the index of the array, then display the corresponding element value. If the specified index is out of bounds, display the message **Out of Bounds**.

13.4* (*IllegalArgumentException*) Modify the `Loan` class in Listing 10.2 to throw `IllegalArgumentException` if the loan amount, interest rate, or number of years is less than or equal to zero.

13.5* (*IllegalTriangleException*) Exercise 11.1 defined the `Triangle` class with three sides. In a triangle, the sum of any two sides is greater than the other side. The `Triangle` class must adhere to this rule. Create the `IllegalTriangleException` class, and modify the constructor of the `Triangle` class to throw an `IllegalTriangleException` object if a triangle is created with sides that violate the rule, as follows:

```
/** Construct a triangle with the specified sides */
public Triangle(double side1, double side2, double side3)
  throws IllegalTriangleException {
  // Implement it
}
```

13.6* (*NumberFormatException*) Listing 9.2 implements the `hexToDecimal(String hexString)` method, which converts a hex string into a decimal number. Implement the `hexToDecimal` method to throw a `NumberFormatException` if the string is not a hex string.

13.7* (*NumberFormatException*) Exercise 9.8 specifies the `binaryToDecimal(String binaryString)` method, which converts a binary string into a decimal number. Implement the `binaryToDecimal` method to throw a `NumberFormatException` if the string is not a binary string.

Video Note
`HexFormatException`

13.8* (*HexFormatException*) Exercise 13.6 implements the `hexToDecimal` method to throw a `NumberFormatException` if the string is not a hex string. Define a custom exception called `HexFormatException`. Implement the `hexToDecimal` method to throw a `HexFormatException` if the string is not a hex string.

13.9* (*BinaryFormatException*) Exercise 13.7 implements the `binaryToDecimal` method to throw a `BinaryFormatException` if the string is not a binary string. Define a custom exception called `BinaryFormatException`. Implement the `binaryToDecimal` method to throw a `BinaryFormatException` if the string is not a binary string.

13.10* (*OutOfMemoryError*) Write a program that causes the JVM to throw an `OutOfMemoryError` and catches and handles this error.

CHAPTER 14

ABSTRACT CLASSES AND INTERFACES

Objectives

- To design and use abstract classes (§14.2).
- To process a calendar using the `Calendar` and `GregorianCalendar` classes (§14.3).
- To specify common behavior for objects using interfaces (§14.4).
- To define interfaces and define classes that implement interfaces (§14.4).
- To define a natural order using the `Comparable` interface (§14.5).
- To enable objects to listen for action events using the `ActionListener` interface (§14.6).
- To make objects cloneable using the `Cloneable` interface (§14.7).
- To explore the similarities and differences between an abstract class and an interface (§14.8).
- To create objects for primitive values using the wrapper classes (`Byte`, `Short`, `Integer`, `Long`, `Float`, `Double`, `Character`, and `Boolean`) (§14.9).
- To create a generic sort method (§14.10).
- To simplify programming using automatic conversion between primitive types and wrapper class types (§14.11).
- To use the `BigInteger` and `BigDecimal` classes for computing very large numbers with arbitrary precisions (§14.12).
- To design the `Rational` class for defining the `Rational` type (§14.13).

14.1 Introduction

problem

You have learned how to write simple programs to create and display GUI components. Can you write the code to respond to user actions, such as clicking a button? As shown in Figure 14.1, when a button is clicked, a message is displayed on the console.

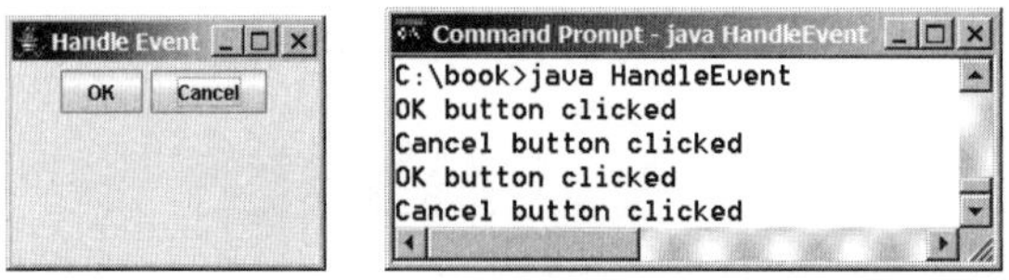
Handle Event
OK
Cancel
Command Prompt - java HandleEvent
C:\book>java HandleEvent
OK button clicked
Cancel button clicked
OK button clicked
Cancel button clicked

FIGURE 14.1 The program responds to button-clicking action events.

In order to write such code, you have to know interfaces. An interface is for defining common behavior for classes (especially unrelated classes). Before discussing interfaces, we introduce a closely related subject: abstract classes.

14.2 Abstract Classes

Video Note
Abstract **GeometricObject Class**

abstract class

In the inheritance hierarchy, classes become more specific and concrete *with each new subclass*. If you move from a subclass back up to a superclass, the classes become more general and less specific. Class design should ensure that a superclass contains common features of its subclasses. Sometimes a superclass is so abstract that it cannot have any specific instances. Such a class is referred to as an *abstract class*.

abstract method
abstract modifier

In Chapter 11, `GeometricObject` was defined as the superclass for `Circle` and `Rectangle`. `GeometricObject` models common features of geometric objects. Both `Circle` and `Rectangle` contain the `getArea()` and `getPerimeter()` methods for computing the area and perimeter of a circle and a rectangle. Since you can compute areas and perimeters for all geometric objects, it is better to define the `getArea()` and `getPerimeter()` methods in the `GeometricObject` class. However, these methods cannot be implemented in the `GeometricObject` class, because their implementation depends on the specific type of geometric object. Such methods are referred to as *abstract methods* and are denoted using the `abstract` modifier in the method header. After you define the methods in `GeometricObject`, it becomes an abstract class. Abstract classes are denoted using the `abstract` modifier in the class header. In UML graphic notation, the names of abstract classes and their abstract methods are italicized, as shown in Figure 14.2. Listing 14.1 gives the source code for the new `GeometricObject` class.

LISTING 14.1 GeometricObject.java

abstract class

```
public abstract class GeometricObject {
  private String color = "white";
  private boolean filled;
  private java.util.Date dateCreated;

  /** Construct a default geometric object */
  protected GeometricObject() {
    dateCreated = new java.util.Date();
  }

  /** Construct a geometric object with color and filled value */
  protected GeometricObject(String color, boolean filled) {
    dateCreated = new java.util.Date();
```

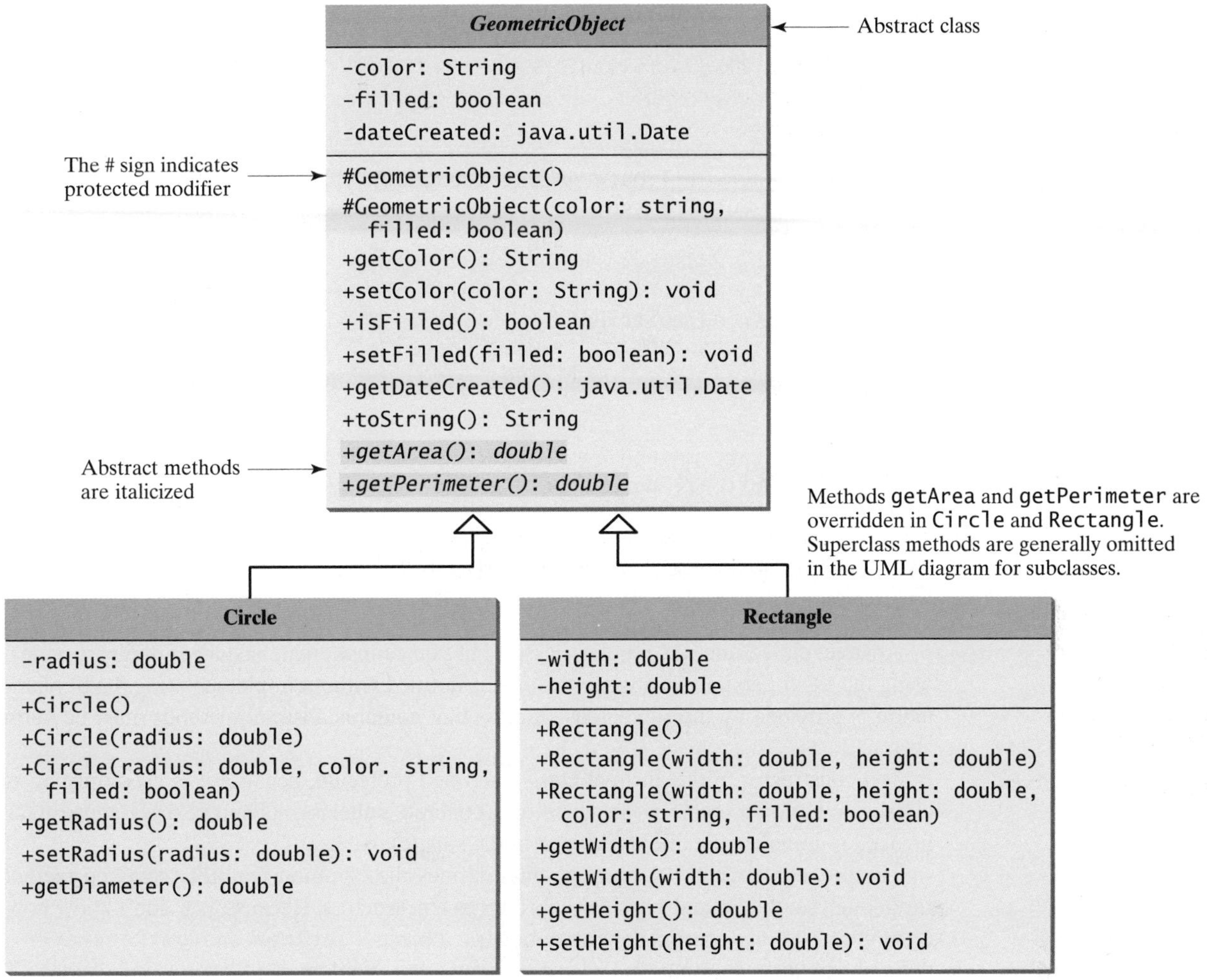
GeometricObject
-color: String
-filled: boolean
-dateCreated: java.util.Date
#GeometricObject()
#GeometricObject(color: string, filled: boolean)
+getColor(): String
+setColor(color: String): void
+isFilled(): boolean
+setFilled(filled: boolean): void
+getDateCreated(): java.util.Date
+toString(): String
+getArea(): double
+getPerimeter(): double
Abstract class
The # sign indicates protected modifier
Abstract methods are italicized
Methods getArea and getPerimeter are overridden in Circle and Rectangle. Superclass methods are generally omitted in the UML diagram for subclasses.
Circle
-radius: double
+Circle()
+Circle(radius: double)
+Circle(radius: double, color. string, filled: boolean)
+getRadius(): double
+setRadius(radius: double): void
+getDiameter(): double
Rectangle
-width: double
-height: double
+Rectangle()
+Rectangle(width: double, height: double)
+Rectangle(width: double, height: double, color: string, filled: boolean)
+getWidth(): double
+setWidth(width: double): void
+getHeight(): double
+setHeight(height: double): void

FIGURE 14.2 The new `GeometricObject` class contains abstract methods.

```
    this.color = color;
    this.filled = filled;
  }

  /** Return color */
  public String getColor() {
    return color;
  }

  /** Set a new color */
  public void setColor(String color) {
    this.color = color;
  }

  /** Return filled. Since filled is boolean,
   *  the get method is named isFilled */
  public boolean isFilled() {
    return filled;
  }

```

abstract method

abstract method

```
  /** Set a new filled */
  public void setFilled(boolean filled) {
    this.filled = filled;
  }

  /** Get dateCreated */
  public java.util.Date getDateCreated() {
    return dateCreated;
  }

  /** Return a string representation of this object */
  public String toString() {
    return "created on " + dateCreated + "\ncolor: " + color +
      " and filled: " + filled;
  }

  /** Abstract method getArea */
  public abstract double getArea();

  /** Abstract method getPerimeter */
  public abstract double getPerimeter();
}
```

Abstract classes are like regular classes, but you cannot create instances of abstract classes using the **new** operator. An abstract method is defined without implementation. Its implementation is provided by the subclasses. A class that contains abstract methods must be defined abstract.

why protected constructor?

The constructor in the abstract class is defined protected, because it is used only by subclasses. When you create an instance of a concrete subclass, its superclass's constructor is invoked to initialize data fields defined in the superclass.

implementing **Circle**
implementing **Rectangle**

The **GeometricObject** abstract class defines the common features (data and methods) for geometric objects and provides appropriate constructors. Because you don't know how to compute areas and perimeters of geometric objects, **getArea** and **getPerimeter** are defined as abstract methods. These methods are implemented in the subclasses. The implementation of **Circle** and **Rectangle** is the same as in Listings 14.2 and 14.3, except that they extend the **GeometricObject** class defined in this chapter, as follows:

LISTING 14.2 Circle.java

extends abstract **GeometricObject**

```
public class Circle extends GeometricObject {
  // Same as lines 2-46 in Listing 11.2, so omitted
}
```

LISTING 14.3 Rectangle.java

extends abstract **GeometricObject**

```
public class Rectangle extends GeometricObject {
  // Same as lines 2-49 in Listing 11.3, so omitted
}
```

14.2.1 Why Abstract Methods?

You may be wondering what advantage is gained by defining the methods **getArea** and **getPerimeter** as abstract in the **GeometricObject** class instead of defining them only in each subclass. The following example shows the benefits of defining them in the **GeometricObject** class.

The example in Listing 14.4 creates two geometric objects, a circle and a rectangle, invokes the **equalArea** method to check whether they have equal areas and invokes the **displayGeometricObject** method to display them.

LISTING 14.4 TestGeometricObject.java

```
1 public class TestGeometricObject {
2   /** Main method */
3   public static void main(String[] args) {
4     // Create two geometric objects
5     GeometricObject geoObject1 = new Circle(5);
6     GeometricObject geoObject2 = new Rectangle(5, 3);
7
8     System.out.println("The two objects have the same area? " +
9       equalArea(geoObject1, geoObject2) );
10
11    // Display circle
12    displayGeometricObject(geoObject1);
13
14    // Display rectangle
15    displayGeometricObject(geoObject2);
16  }
17
18  /** A method for comparing the areas of two geometric objects */
19  public static boolean equalArea(GeometricObject object1,
20      GeometricObject object2) {
21    return object1.getArea() == object2.getArea();
22  }
23
24  /** A method for displaying a geometric object */
25  public static void displayGeometricObject(GeometricObject object) {
26    System.out.println();
27    System.out.println("The area is " + object.getArea());
28    System.out.println("The perimeter is " + object.getPerimeter());
29  }
30 }
```

create a circle
create a rectangle
equalArea
displayGeometricObject

```
The two objects have the same area? false

The area is 78.53981633974483
The perimeter is 31.41592653589793

The area is 14.0
The perimeter is 16.0
```

The methods getArea() and getPerimeter() defined in the GeometricObject class are overridden in the Circle class and the Rectangle class. The statements (lines 5–6)

```
GeometricObject geoObject1 = new Circle(5);
GeometricObject geoObject2 = new Rectangle(5, 3);
```

create a new circle and rectangle and assign them to the variables geoObject1 and geoObject2. These two variables are of the GeometricObject type.

When invoking equalArea(geoObject1, geoObject2) (line 9), the getArea() method defined in the Circle class is used for object1.getArea(), since geoObject1 is a circle, and the getArea() method defined in the Rectangle class is used for object2.getArea(), since geoObject2 is a rectangle.

Similarly, when invoking displayGeometricObject(geoObject1) (line 12), the methods getArea and getPerimeter defined in the Circle class are used, and when invoking displayGeometricObject(geoObject2) (line 15), the methods getArea and getPerimeter defined in the Rectangle class are used. The JVM dynamically determines which of these methods to invoke at runtime, depending on the type of object.

Note that you could not define the equalArea method for comparing whether two geometric objects have the same area if the getArea method were not defined in GeometricObject. So, you see the benefits of defining the abstract methods in GeometricObject.

why abstract methods?

14.2.2 Interesting Points on Abstract Classes

The following points on abstract classes are worth noting:

abstract method in abstract class

- An abstract method cannot be contained in a nonabstract class. If a subclass of an abstract superclass does not implement all the abstract methods, the subclass must be defined abstract. In other words, in a nonabstract subclass extended from an abstract class, all the abstract methods must be implemented. Also note that abstract methods are nonstatic.

object cannot be created from abstract class

- An abstract class cannot be instantiated using the new operator, but you can still define its constructors, which are invoked in the constructors of its subclasses. For instance, the constructors of GeometricObject are invoked in the Circle class and the Rectangle class.

abstract class without abstract method

- A class that contains abstract methods must be abstract. However, it is possible to define an abstract class that contains no abstract methods. In this case, you cannot create instances of the class using the new operator. This class is used as a base class for defining a new subclass.

superclass of abstract class may be concrete

- A subclass can be abstract even if its superclass is concrete. For example, the Object class is concrete, but its subclasses, such as GeometricObject, may be abstract.

concrete method overridden to be abstract

- A subclass can override a method from its superclass to define it abstract. This is *very unusual* but is useful when the implementation of the method in the superclass becomes invalid in the subclass. In this case, the subclass must be defined abstract.

abstract class as type

- You cannot create an instance from an abstract class using the new operator, but an abstract class can be used as a data type. Therefore, the following statement, which creates an array whose elements are of the GeometricObject type, is correct.

```
GeometricObject[] objects = new GeometricObject[10];
```

  You can then create an instance of GeometricObject and assign its reference to the array like this:

```
objects[0] = new Circle();
```

14.3 Example: **Calendar** and **GregorianCalendar**

Video Note
Calendar and **Gregorian-Calendar** Classes

An instance of java.util.Date represents a specific instant in time with millisecond precision. java.util.Calendar is an abstract base class for extracting detailed calendar information, such as year, month, date, hour, minute, and second. Subclasses of Calendar can implement specific calendar systems, such as the Gregorian calendar, the lunar calendar, and the Jewish calendar. Currently, java.util.GregorianCalendar for the Gregorian calendar is supported in Java, as shown in Figure 14.3. The add method is abstract in the Calendar class, because its implementation is dependent on a concrete calendar system.

abstract **add** method

You can use new GregorianCalendar() to construct a default GregorianCalendar with the current time and new GregorianCalendar(year, month, date) to construct a GregorianCalendar with the specified year, month, and date. The month parameter is 0 based—that is, 0 is for January.

constructing calendar

get(field)

The get(int field) method defined in the Calendar class is useful for extracting the date and time information from a Calendar object. The fields are defined as constants, as shown in Table 14.1.

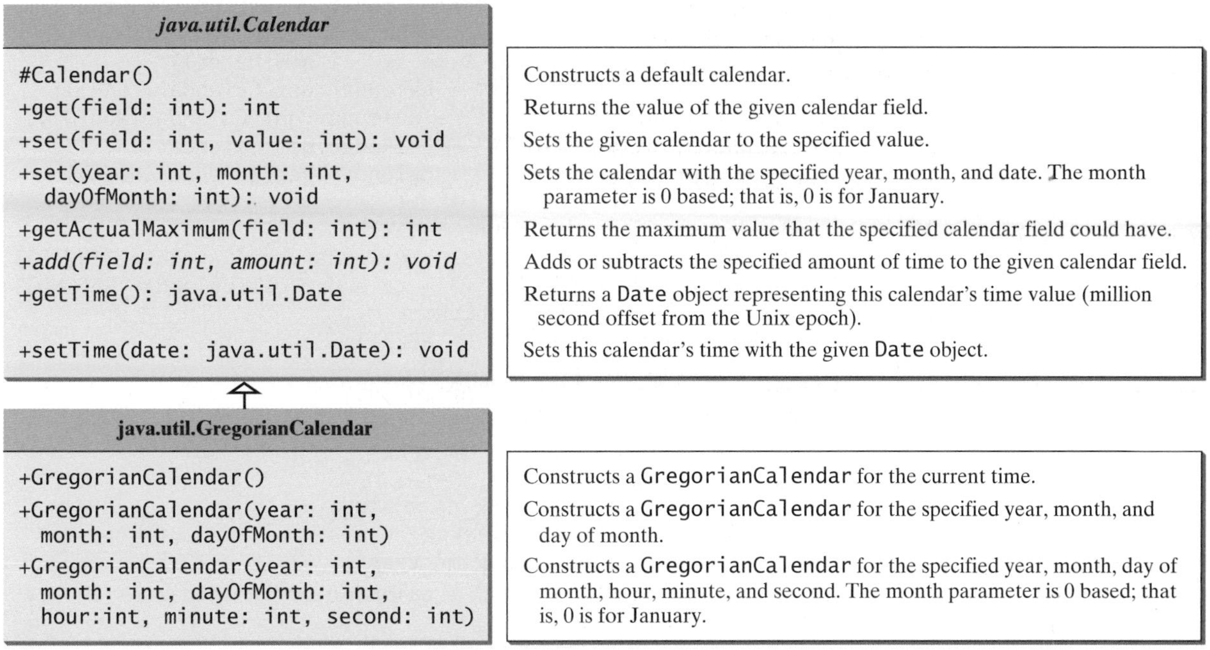
java.util.Calendar
#Calendar()
+get(field: int): int
+set(field: int, value: int): void
+set(year: int, month: int, dayOfMonth: int): void
+getActualMaximum(field: int): int
+add(field: int, amount: int): void
+getTime(): java.util.Date
+setTime(date: java.util.Date): void
Constructs a default calendar.
Returns the value of the given calendar field.
Sets the given calendar to the specified value.
Sets the calendar with the specified year, month, and date. The month parameter is 0 based; that is, 0 is for January.
Returns the maximum value that the specified calendar field could have.
Adds or subtracts the specified amount of time to the given calendar field.
Returns a Date object representing this calendar's time value (million second offset from the Unix epoch).
Sets this calendar's time with the given Date object.
java.util.GregorianCalendar
+GregorianCalendar()
+GregorianCalendar(year: int, month: int, dayOfMonth: int)
+GregorianCalendar(year: int, month: int, dayOfMonth: int, hour:int, minute: int, second: int)
Constructs a GregorianCalendar for the current time.
Constructs a GregorianCalendar for the specified year, month, and day of month.
Constructs a GregorianCalendar for the specified year, month, day of month, hour, minute, and second. The month parameter is 0 based; that is, 0 is for January.

FIGURE 14.3 The abstract `Calendar` class defines common features of various calendars.

TABLE 14.1 Field constants in the `Calendar` class

Constant	*Description*
YEAR	The year of the calendar.
MONTH	The month of the calendar with 0 for January.
DATE	The day of the calendar.
HOUR	The hour of the calendar (12-hour notation).
HOUR_OF_DAY	The hour of the calendar (24-hour notation).
MINUTE	The minute of the calendar.
SECOND	The second of the calendar.
DAY_OF_WEEK	The day number within the week with 1 for Sunday.
DAY_OF_MONTH	Same as DATE.
DAY_OF_YEAR	The day number in the year with 1 for the first day of the year.
WEEK_OF_MONTH	The week number within the month with 1 for the first week.
WEEK_OF_YEAR	The week number within the year with 1 for the first week.
AM_PM	Indicator for AM or PM (0 for AM and 1 for PM).

Listing 14.5 gives an example that displays the date and time information for the current time.

LISTING 14.5 TestCalendar.java

```
import java.util.*;

public class TestCalendar {
  public static void main(String[] args) {
```

calendar for current time

extract fields in calendar

create a calendar

```java
    // Construct a Gregorian calendar for the current date and time
    Calendar calendar = new GregorianCalendar();
    System.out.println("Current time is " + new Date());
    System.out.println("YEAR:\t" + calendar.get(Calendar.YEAR));
    System.out.println("MONTH:\t" + calendar.get(Calendar.MONTH));
    System.out.println("DATE:\t" + calendar.get(Calendar.DATE));
    System.out.println("HOUR:\t" + calendar.get(Calendar.HOUR));
    System.out.println("HOUR_OF_DAY:\t" +
      calendar.get(Calendar.HOUR_OF_DAY));
    System.out.println("MINUTE:\t" + calendar.get(Calendar.MINUTE));
    System.out.println("SECOND:\t" + calendar.get(Calendar.SECOND));
    System.out.println("DAY_OF_WEEK:\t" +
      calendar.get(Calendar.DAY_OF_WEEK));
    System.out.println("DAY_OF_MONTH:\t" +
      calendar.get(Calendar.DAY_OF_MONTH));
    System.out.println("DAY_OF_YEAR: " +
      calendar.get(Calendar.DAY_OF_YEAR));
    System.out.println("WEEK_OF_MONTH: " +
      calendar.get(Calendar.WEEK_OF_MONTH));
    System.out.println("WEEK_OF_YEAR: " +
      calendar.get(Calendar.WEEK_OF_YEAR));
    System.out.println("AM_PM: " + calendar.get(Calendar.AM_PM));

    // Construct a calendar for September 11, 2001
    Calendar calendar1 = new GregorianCalendar(2001, 8, 11);
    System.out.println("September 11, 2001 is a " +
      dayNameOfWeek(calendar1.get(Calendar.DAY_OF_WEEK)));
  }

  public static String dayNameOfWeek(int dayOfWeek) {
    switch (dayOfWeek) {
      case 1: return "Sunday";
      case 2: return "Monday";
      case 3: return "Tuesday";
      case 4: return "Wednesday";
      case 5: return "Thursday";
      case 6: return "Friday";
      case 7: return "Saturday";
      default: return null;
    }
  }
}
```

```
Current time is Sun Sep 09 21:23:59 EDT 2007
YEAR:          2007
MONTH:         8
DATE:          9
HOUR:          9
HOUR_OF_DAY:   21
MINUTE:        23
SECOND:        59
DAY_OF_WEEK:   1
DAY_OF_MONTH:  9
DAY_OF_YEAR:   252
WEEK_OF_MONTH: 3
WEEK_OF_YEAR:  37
AM_PM:         1
September 11, 2001 is a Tuesday
```

The `set(int field, value)` method defined in the `Calendar` class can be used to set a field. For example, you can use `calendar.set(Calendar.DAY_OF_MONTH, 1)` to set the `calendar` to the first day of the month.

set(field, value)

The `add(field, value)` method adds the specified amount to a given field. For example, `add(Calendar.DAY_OF_MONTH, 5)` adds five days to the current time of the calendar. `add(Calendar.DAY_OF_MONTH, -5)` subtracts five days from the current time of the calendar.

add(field, amount)

To obtain the number of days in a month, use `calendar.getActualMaximum(Calendar.DAY_OF_MONTH)`. For example, if the `calendar` were for March, this method would return `31`.

getActualMaximum(field)

You can set a time represented in a `Date` object for the `calendar` by invoking `calendar. setTime(date)` and retrieve the time by invoking `calendar. getTime()`.

setTime(Date)
getTime()

14.4 Interfaces

Video Note
The concept of interface

An interface is a classlike construct that contains only constants and abstract methods. In many ways an interface is similar to an abstract class, but its intent is to specify common behavior for objects. For example, using appropriate interfaces, you can specify that the objects are comparable, edible, and/or cloneable.

To distinguish an interface from a class, Java uses the following syntax to define an interface:

```
modifier interface InterfaceName {
  /** Constant declarations */
  /** Method signatures */
}
```

Here is an example of an interface:

```
public interface Edible {
  /** Describe how to eat */
  public abstract String howToEat();
}
```

An interface is treated like a special class in Java. Each interface is compiled into a separate bytecode file, just like a regular class. As with an abstract class, you cannot create an instance from an interface using the `new` operator, but in most cases you can use an interface more or less the same way you use an abstract class. For example, you can use an interface as a data type for a reference variable, as the result of casting, and so on.

You can now use the `Edible` interface to specify whether an object is edible. This is accomplished by letting the class for the object implement this interface using the `implements` keyword. For example, the classes `Chicken` and `Fruit` in Listing 14.6 (lines 14, 23) implement the `Edible` interface. The relationship between the class and the interface is known as *interface inheritance*. Since interface inheritance and class inheritance are essentially the same, we will simply refer to both as inheritance.

interface inheritance

Listing 14.6 TestEdible.java

```
1 public class TestEdible {
2   public static void main(String[] args) {
3     Object[] objects = {new Tiger(), new Chicken(), new Apple()};
4     for (int i = 0; i < objects.length; i++)
5       if (objects[i] instanceof Edible)
6         System.out.println(((Edible)objects[i]).howToEat());
7   }
8 }
9
10 class Animal {
```

Animal class

implements Edible
howToEat()
Tiger class
implements Edible
Apple class
Orange class

```java
11   // Data fields, constructors, and methods omitted here
12 }
13
14 class Chicken extends Animal implements Edible {
15   public String howToEat() {
16     return "Chicken: Fry it";
17   }
18 }
19
20 class Tiger extends Animal {
21 }
22
23 abstract class Fruit implements Edible {
24   // Data fields, constructors, and methods omitted here
25 }
26
27 class Apple extends Fruit {
28   public String howToEat() {
29     return "Apple: Make apple cider";
30   }
31 }
32
33 class Orange extends Fruit {
34   public String howToEat() {
35     return "Orange: Make orange juice";
36   }
37 }
```

```
Chicken: Fry it
Apple: Make apple cider
```

The **Chicken** class extends **Animal** and implements **Edible** to specify that chickens are edible. When a class implements an interface, it implements all the methods defined in the interface with the exact signature and return type. The **Chicken** class implements the **howToEat** method (lines 15–17).

The **Fruit** class implements **Edible**. Since it does not implement the **howToEat** method, **Fruit** must be denoted **abstract** (line 23). The concrete subclasses of **Fruit** must implement the **howToEat** method. The **Apple** and **Orange** classes implements the **howToEat** method (lines 28, 34).

The **main** method creates an array with three objects for **Tiger**, **Chicken**, and **Apple** (line 3) and invokes the **howToEat** method if the element is edible (line 6).

Note

omitting modifiers

Since all data fields are ***public final static*** and all methods are ***public abstract*** in an interface, Java allows these modifiers to be omitted. Therefore the following interface definitions are equivalent:

```java
public interface T {
  public static final int K = 1;

  public abstract void p();
}
```

Equivalent

```java
public interface T {
  int K = 1;

  void p();
}
```

Tip

A constant defined in an interface can be accessed using the syntax **InterfaceName.CONSTANT_NAME** (e.g., **T.K**).

accessing constants

14.5 Example: The Comparable Interface

Suppose you want to design a generic method to find the larger of two objects of the same type, such as two students, two dates, two circles, two rectangles, or two squares. In order to accomplish this, the two objects must be comparable. So, the common behavior for the objects is comparable. Java provides the **Comparable** interface for this purpose. The interface is defined as follows:

java.lang.Comparable

```
// Interface for comparing objects, defined in java.lang
package java.lang;

public interface Comparable {
  public int compareTo(Object o);
}
```

The **compareTo** method determines the order of this object with the specified object **o** and returns a negative integer, zero, or a positive integer if this object is less than, equal to, or greater than **o**.

Many classes in the Java library (e.g., **String** and **Date**) implement **Comparable** to define a natural order for the objects. If you examine the source code of these classes, you will see the keyword **implements** used in the classes, as shown below:

```
public class String extends Object
    implements Comparable {
  // class body omitted
}
```

```
public class Date extends Object
    implements Comparable {
  // class body omitted
}
```

Thus, strings are comparable, and so are dates. Let **s** be a **String** object and **d** be a **Date** object. All the following expressions are **true**.

```
s instanceof String
s instanceof Object
s instanceof Comparable
```

```
d instanceof java.util.Date
d instanceof Object
d instanceof Comparable
```

A generic **max** method for finding the larger of two objects can be defined, as shown in (a) or (b) below:

```
// Max.java: Find a maximum object
public class Max {
  /** Return the maximum of two objects */
  public static Comparable max
      (Comparable o1, Comparable o2) {
    if (o1.compareTo(o2) > 0)
      return o1;
    else
      return o2;
  }
}
```

(a)

```
// Max.java: Find a maximum object
public class Max {
  /** Return the maximum of two objects */
  public static Object max
      (Object o1, Object o2) {
    if (((Comparable)o1).compareTo(o2) > 0)
      return o1;
    else
      return o2;
  }
}
```

(b)

(a) is simpler

The max method in (a) is simpler than the one in (b). In the Max class in (b), o1 is declared as Object, and (Comparable)o1 tells the compiler to cast o1 into Comparable so that the compareTo method can be invoked from o1. However, no casting is needed in the Max class in (a), since o1 is declared as Comparable.

(a) is more robust

The max method in (a) is more robust than the one in (b). You must invoke the max method with two comparable objects. Suppose you invoke max with two noncomparable objects:

```
Max.max(anyObject1, anyObject2);
```

The compiler will detect the error using the max method in (a), because anyObject1 is not an instance of Comparable. Using the max method in (b), this line of code will compile fine but will have a runtime ClassCastException, because anyObject1 is not an instance of Comparable and cannot be cast into Comparable.

From now on, assume that the max method in (a) is in the text. Since strings are comparable and dates are comparable, you can use the max method to find the larger of two instances of String or Date. Here is an example:

```
String s1 = "abcdef";
String s2 = "abcdee";
String s3 = (String)Max.max(s1, s2);
```

```
Date d1 = new Date();
Date d2 = new Date();
Date d3 = (Date)Max.max(d1, d2);
```

The return value from the max method is of the Comparable type. So you need to cast it to String or Date explicitly.

You cannot use the max method to find the larger of two instances of Rectangle, because Rectangle does not implement Comparable. However, you can define a new rectangle class that implements Comparable. The instances of this new class are comparable. Let this new class be named ComparableRectangle, as shown in Listing 14.7.

LISTING 14.7 ComparableRectangle.java

implements **Comparable**

implement **compareTo**

```
public class ComparableRectangle extends Rectangle
    implements Comparable {
  /** Construct a ComparableRectangle with specified properties */
  public ComparableRectangle(double width, double height) {
    super(width, height);
  }

  /** Implement the compareTo method defined in Comparable */
  public int compareTo(Object o) {
    if (getArea() > ((ComparableRectangle)o).getArea())
      return 1;
    else if (getArea() < ((ComparableRectangle)o).getArea())
      return -1;
    else
      return 0;
  }
}
```

ComparableRectangle extends Rectangle and implements Comparable, as shown in Figure 14.4. The keyword implements indicates that ComparableRectangle inherits all the constants from the Comparable interface and implements the methods in the interface. The compareTo method compares the areas of two rectangles. An instance of ComparableRectangle is also an instance of Rectangle, GeometricObject, Object, and Comparable.

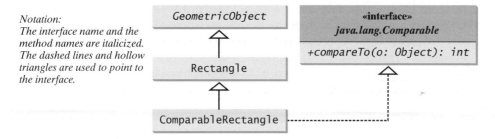

Notation:
The interface name and the method names are italicized. The dashed lines and hollow triangles are used to point to the interface.

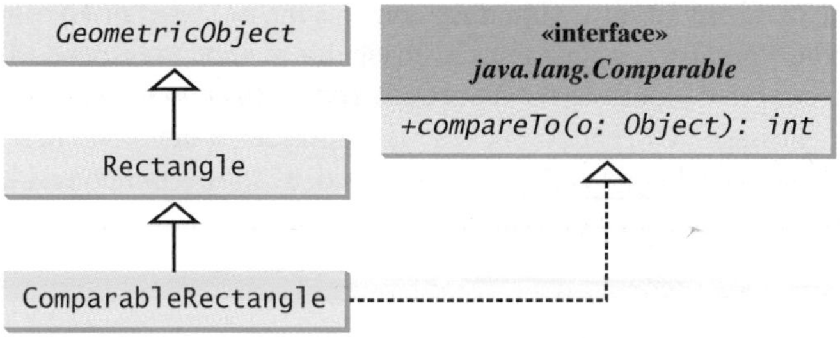
GeometricObject
«interface»
java.lang.Comparable
+compareTo(o: Object): int
Rectangle
ComparableRectangle

FIGURE 14.4 ComparableRectangle extends Rectangle and implements Comparable.

You can now use the max method to find the larger of two objects of ComparableRectangle. Here is an example:

```
ComparableRectangle rectangle1 = new ComparableRectangle(4, 5);
ComparableRectangle rectangle2 = new ComparableRectangle(3, 6);
System.out.println(Max.max(rectangle1, rectangle2));
```

benefits of interface

An interface provides another form of generic programming. It would be difficult to use a generic max method to find the maximum of the objects without using an interface in this example, because multiple inheritance would be necessary to inherit Comparable and another class, such as Rectangle, at the same time.

The Object class contains the equals method, which is intended for the subclasses of the Object class to override in order to compare whether the contents of the objects are the same. Suppose that the Object class contains the compareTo method, as defined in the Comparable interface; the new max method can be used to compare a list of *any* objects. Whether a compareTo method should be included in the Object class is debatable. Since the compareTo method is not defined in the Object class, the Comparable interface is defined in Java to enable objects to be compared if they are instances of the Comparable interface. It is strongly recommended (though not required) that compareTo should be consistent with equals. That is, for two objects o1 and o2, o1.compareTo(o2) == 0 if and only if o1.equals(o2) is true.

14.6 Example: The ActionListener Interface

Now you are ready to write a short program to address the problem proposed in the introduction of this chapter. The program displays two buttons in the frame, as shown in Figure 14.1. To respond to a button click, you need to write the code to process the button-clicking action. The button is a *source object* where the action originates. You need to create an object capable of handling the action event on a button. This object is called a *listener*, as shown in Figure 14.5.

Not all objects can be listeners for an action event. To be a listener, two requirements must be met:

ActionListener interface

1. The object must be an instance of the ActionListener interface. This interface defines the common behavior for all action listeners.

addActionListener (listener)

2. The ActionListener object listener must be registered with the source using the method source. addActionListener(listener).

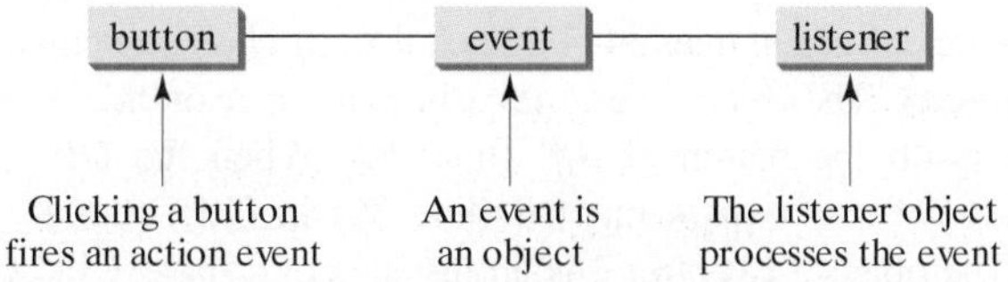
button
event
listener
Clicking a button
fires an action event
An event is
an object
The listener object
processes the event

FIGURE 14.5 A listener object processes the event fired from the source object.

The `ActionListener` interface contains the `actionPerformed` method for processing the event. Your listener class must override this method to respond to the event. Listing 14.8 gives the code that processes the `ActionEvent` on the two buttons. When you click the *OK* button, the message "OK button clicked" is displayed. When you click the *Cancel* button, the message "Cancel button clicked" is displayed, as shown in Figure 14.1.

LISTING 14.8 HandleEvent.java

create listener

register listener

listener class

process event

listener class

process event

```
 1 import javax.swing.*;
 2 import java.awt.event.*;
 3
 4 public class HandleEvent extends JFrame {
 5   public HandleEvent() {
 6     // Create two buttons
 7     JButton jbtOK = new JButton("OK");
 8     JButton jbtCancel = new JButton("Cancel");
 9
10     // Create a panel to hold buttons
11     JPanel panel = new JPanel();
12     panel.add(jbtOK);
13     panel.add(jbtCancel);
14
15     add(panel); // Add panel to the frame
16
17     // Register listeners
18     OKListenerClass listener1 = new OKListenerClass();
19     CancelListenerClass listener2 = new CancelListenerClass();
20     jbtOK.addActionListener(listener1);
21     jbtCancel.addActionListener(listener2);
22   }
23
24   public static void main(String[] args) {
25     JFrame frame = new HandleEvent();
26     frame.setTitle("Handle Event");
27     frame.setSize(200, 150);
28     frame.setLocation(200, 100);
29     frame.setDefaultCloseOperation(JFrame.EXIT_ON_CLOSE);
30     frame.setVisible(true);
31   }
32 }
33
34 class OKListenerClass implements ActionListener {
35   public void actionPerformed(ActionEvent e) {
36     System.out.println("OK button clicked");
37   }
38 }
39
40 class CancelListenerClass implements ActionListener {
41   public void actionPerformed(ActionEvent e) {
42     System.out.println("Cancel button clicked");
43   }
44 }
```

Two listener classes are defined in lines 34–44. Each listener class implements `ActionListener` to process `ActionEvent`. The object `listener1` is an instance of `OKListenerClass` (line 18), which is registered with the button `jbtOK` (line 20). When the *OK* button is clicked, the `actionPerformed(ActionEvent)` method (line 36) in `OKListenerClass` is invoked to process the event. The object `listener2` is an instance of `CancelListenerClass` (line 19), which is registered with the button `jbtCancel` in line 21. When the *OK* button is clicked, the `actionPerformed(ActionEvent)` method (line 42) in `CancelListenerClass` is invoked to process the event. Ways to process events will be discussed further in Chapter 16, "Event-Driven Programming."

14.7 Example: The **Cloneable** Interface

Often it is desirable to create a copy of an object. You need to use the `clone` method and understand the `Cloneable` interface, which is the subject of this section.

An interface contains constants and abstract methods, but the `Cloneable` interface is a special case. The `Cloneable` interface in the `java.lang` package is defined as follows:

java.lang.Cloneable

```
package java.lang;

public interface Cloneable {
}
```

marker interface

This interface is empty. An interface with an empty body is referred to as a *marker interface*. A marker interface does not contain constants or methods. It is used to denote that a class possesses certain desirable properties. A class that implements the `Cloneable` interface is marked cloneable, and its objects can be cloned using the `clone()` method defined in the `Object` class.

Many classes in the Java library (e.g., `Date`, `Calendar`, and `ArrayList`) implement `Cloneable`. Thus, the instances of these classes can be cloned. For example, the following code

```
1 Calendar calendar = new GregorianCalendar(2003, 2, 1);
2 Calendar calendar1 = calendar;
3 Calendar calendar2 = (Calendar)calendar.clone();
4 System.out.println("calendar == calendar1 is " +
5   (calendar == calendar1));
6 System.out.println("calendar == calendar2 is " +
7   (calendar == calendar2));
8 System.out.println("calendar.equals(calendar2) is " +
9   calendar.equals(calendar2));
```

displays

```
calendar == calendar1 is true
calendar == calendar2 is false
calendar.equals(calendar2) is true
```

In the preceding code, line 2 copies the reference of `calendar` to `calendar1`, so `calendar` and `calendar1` point to the same `Calendar` object. Line 3 creates a new object that is the clone of `calendar` and assigns the new object's reference to `calendar2`. `calendar2` and `calendar` are different objects with the same contents.

clone arrays

You can clone an array using the `clone` method. For example, the following code

```
int[] list1 = {1, 2};
int[] list2 = list1.clone();
list1[0] = 7; list1[1] = 8;

System.out.println("list1 is " + list1[0] + ", " + list1[1]);
System.out.println("list2 is " + list2[0] + ", " + list2[1]);
```

displays

```
list1 is 7, 8
list2 is 1, 2
```

how to implement **Cloneable**

To define a custom class that implements the **Cloneable** interface, the class must override the **clone()** method in the **Object** class. Listing 14.9 defines a class named **House** that implements **Cloneable** and **Comparable**.

LISTING 14.9 House.java

```
1 public class House implements Cloneable, Comparable {
2   private int id;
3   private double area;
4   private java.util.Date whenBuilt;
5
6   public House(int id, double area) {
7     this.id = id;
8     this.area = area;
9     whenBuilt = new java.util.Date();
10  }
11
12  public int getId() {
13    return id;
14  }
15
16  public double getArea() {
17    return area;
18  }
19
20  public java.util.Date getWhenBuilt() {
21    return whenBuilt;
22  }
23
24  /** Override the protected clone method defined in the Object
25    class, and strengthen its accessibility */
26  public Object clone() throws CloneNotSupportedException {
27    return super.clone();
28  }
29
30  /** Implement the compareTo method defined in Comparable */
31  public int compareTo(Object o) {
32    if (area > ((House)o).area)
33      return 1;
34    else if (area < ((House)o).area)
35      return -1;
36    else
37      return 0;
38  }
39 }
```

This exception is thrown if **House** does not implement **Cloneable**

The **House** class implements the **clone** method (lines 26–28) defined in the **Object** class. The header is:

```
protected native Object clone() throws CloneNotSupportedException;
```

The keyword **native** indicates that this method is not written in Java but is implemented in the JVM for the native platform. The keyword **protected** restricts the method to be accessed in the same package or in a subclass. For this reason, the **House** class must override the method and change the visibility modifier to **public** so that the method can be used in any package. Since the **clone** method implemented for the native platform in the **Object** class performs the task of cloning objects, the **clone** method in the **House** class simply invokes **super.clone()**. The **clone** method defined in the **Object** class may throw **CloneNotSupportedException**.

CloneNotSupported-Exception

The House class implements the compareTo method (lines 31–38) defined in the Comparable interface. The method compares the areas of two houses.

You can now create an object of the House class and create an identical copy from it, as follows:

```
House house1 = new House(1, 1750.50);
House house2 = (House)house1.clone();
```

house1 and house2 are two different objects with identical contents. The clone method in the Object class copies each field from the original object to the target object. If the field is of a primitive type, its value is copied. For example, the value of area (double type) is copied from house1 to house2. If the field is of an object, the reference of the field is copied. For example, the field whenBuilt is of the Date class, so its reference is copied into house2, as shown in Figure 14.6. Therefore, house1.whenBuilt == house2.whenBuilt is true, although house1 == house2 is false. This is referred to as a *shallow copy* rather than a *deep copy*, meaning that if the field is of an object type, the object's reference is copied rather than its contents.

shallow copy
deep copy

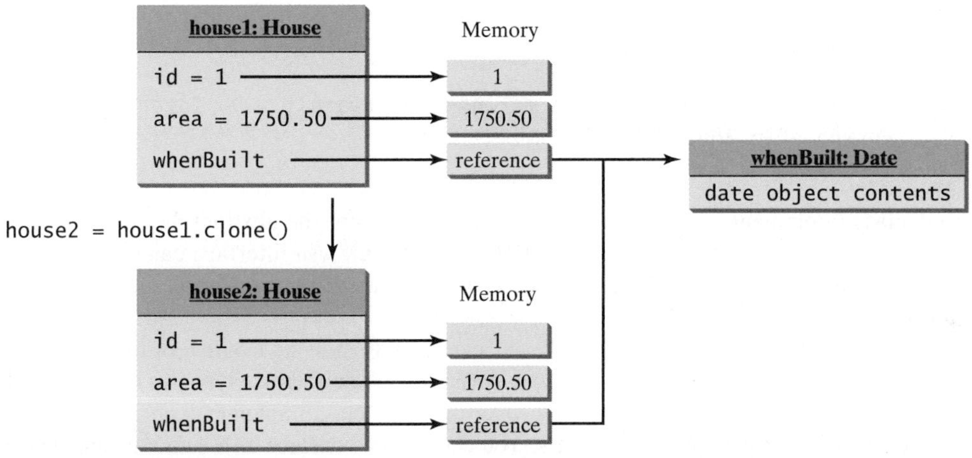

house1: House
id = 1
area = 1750.50
whenBuilt
Memory
1
1750.50
reference
whenBuilt: Date
date object contents
house2 = house1.clone()
house2: House
id = 1
area = 1750.50
whenBuilt
Memory
1
1750.50
reference

FIGURE 14.6 The clone method copies the values of primitive type fields and the references of object type fields.

If you want to perform a deep copy, you can override the clone method with custom cloning operations after invoking super.clone(). See Exercise 14.4.

Caution

If the House class does not override the clone() method, the program will receive a syntax error, because clone() is protected in java.lang.Object. If House does not implement java.lang.Cloneable, invoking super.clone() (line 27) in House.java will cause a CloneNotSupportedException. Thus, to enable cloning an object, the class for the object must override the clone() method and implement Cloneable.

14.8 Interfaces vs. Abstract Classes

An interface can be used more or less the same way as an abstract class, but defining an interface is different from defining an abstract class. Table 14.2 summarizes the differences.

Java allows only single inheritance for class extension but allows multiple extensions for interfaces. For example,

TABLE 14.2 Interfaces vs. Abstract Classes

	Variables	*Constructors*	*Methods*
Abstract class	No restrictions.	Constructors are invoked by subclasses through constructor chaining. An abstract class cannot be instantiated using the new operator.	No restrictions.
Interface	All variables must be `public static final`.	No constructors. An interface cannot be instantiated using the new operator.	All methods must be public abstract instance methods.

```
public class NewClass extends BaseClass
    implements Interface1, ..., InterfaceN {
  ...
}
```

subinterface

An interface can inherit other interfaces using the `extends` keyword. Such an interface is called a *subinterface*. For example, `NewInterface` in the following code is a subinterface of `Interface1`, ..., and `InterfaceN`.

```
public interface NewInterface extends Interface1, ..., InterfaceN {
  // constants and abstract methods
}
```

A class implementing `NewInterface` must implement the abstract methods defined in `NewInterface`, `Interface1`, ..., and `InterfaceN`. An interface can extend other interfaces but not classes. A class can extend its superclass and implement multiple interfaces.

All classes share a single root, the `Object` class, but there is no single root for interfaces. Like a class, an interface also defines a type. A variable of an interface type can reference any instance of the class that implements the interface. If a class implements an interface, the interface is like a superclass for the class. You can use an interface as a data type and cast a variable of an interface type to its subclass, and vice versa. For example, suppose that `c` is an instance of `Class2` in Figure 14.7. `c` is also an instance of `Object`, `Class1`, `Interface1`, `Interface1_1`, `Interface1_2`, `Interface2_1`, and `Interface2_2`.

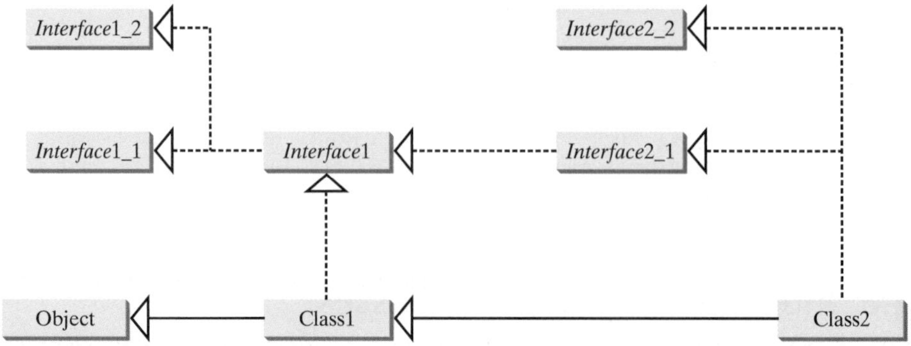
Interface1_2
Interface2_2
Interface1_1
Interface1
Interface2_1
Object
Class1
Class2

FIGURE 14.7 `Class1` implements `Interface1`; `Interface1` extends `Interface1_1` and `Interface1_2`. `Class2` extends `Class1` and implements `Interface2_1` and `Interface2_2`.

Note

Class names are nouns. Interface names may be adjectives or nouns. For example, both **java.lang.Comparable** and **java.awt.event.ActionListener** are interfaces. **Comparable** is an adjective, and **ActionListener** is a noun.

naming convention

Design Guide

Abstract classes and interfaces can both be used to specify common behavior of objects. How do you decide whether to use an interface or a class? In general, a *strong is-a relationship* that clearly describes a parent-child relationship should be modeled using classes. For example, Gregorian calendar is a calendar, so the relationship between the class **java.util.GregorianCalendar** and **java.util.Calendar** is modeled using class inheritance. A *weak is-a relationship*, also known as an *is-kind-of relationship*, indicates that an object possesses a certain property. A weak is-a relationship can be modeled using interfaces. For example, all strings are comparable, so the **String** class implements the **Comparable** interface.

is-a relationship
is-kind-of relationship

In general, interfaces are preferred over abstract classes because an interface can define a common supertype for unrelated classes. Interfaces are more flexible than classes. Consider the **Animal** class. Suppose the **howToEat** method is defined in the **Animal** class, as follows:

interface preferred

```
abstract class Animal {
  public abstract String howToEat();
}
```

Animal class

Two subclasses of **Animal** are defined as follows:

```
class Chicken extends Animal {
  public String howToEat() {
    return "Fry it";
  }
}
```

Chicken class

```
class Duck extends Animal {
  public String howToEat() {
    return "Roast it";
  }
}
```

Duck class

Given this inheritance hierarchy, polymorphism enables you to hold a reference to a **Chicken** object or a **Duck** object in a variable of type **Animal**, as in the following code:

```
public static void main(String[] args) {
  Animal animal = new Chicken();
  eat(animal);

  animal = new Duck();
  eat(animal);
}

public static void eat(Animal animal) {
  animal.howToEat();
}
```

The JVM dynamically decides which **howToEat** method to invoke based on the actual object that invokes the method.

You can define a subclass of **Animal**. However, there is a restriction. The subclass must be for another animal (e.g., **Turkey**).

Interfaces don't have this restriction. Interfaces give you more flexibility than classes, because you don't have make everything fit into one type of class. You may define the howToEat() method in an interface and let it serve as a common supertype for other classes. For example,

```
public static void main(String[] args) {
  Edible stuff = new Chicken();
  eat(stuff);

  stuff = new Duck();
  eat(stuff);

  stuff = new Broccoli();
  eat(stuff);
}

public static void eat(Edible stuff) {
  stuff.howToEat();
}
```

Edible interface

```
interface Edible {
  public String howToEat();
}
```

Chicken class

```
class Chicken implements Edible {
  public String howToEat() {
    return "Fry it";
  }
}
```

Duck class

```
class Duck implements Edible {
  public String howToEat() {
    return "Roast it";
  }
}
```

Broccoli class

```
class Broccoli implements Edible {
  public String howToEat() {
    return "Stir-fry it";
  }
}
```

To define a class that represents edible objects, simply let the class implement the Edible interface. The class is now a subtype of the Edible type. Any Edible object can be passed to invoke the eat method.

14.9 Processing Primitive Data Type Values as Objects

Owing to performance considerations, primitive data types are not used as objects in Java. Because of the overhead of processing objects, the language's performance would be adversely affected if primitive data types were treated as objects. However, many Java methods require the use of objects as arguments. For example, the add(object) method in the ArrayList class adds an object to an ArrayList. Java offers a convenient way to incorporate, or wrap, a primitive data type into an object (e.g., wrapping int into the Integer class, and wrapping double into the Double class). The corresponding class is called a *wrapper class*. By using a wrapper object instead of a primitive data type variable, you can take advantage of generic programming.

why wrapper class?

Java provides Boolean, Character, Double, Float, Byte, Short, Integer, and Long wrapper classes for primitive data types. These classes are grouped in the java.lang package. Their inheritance hierarchy is shown in Figure 14.8.

why wrapper class?

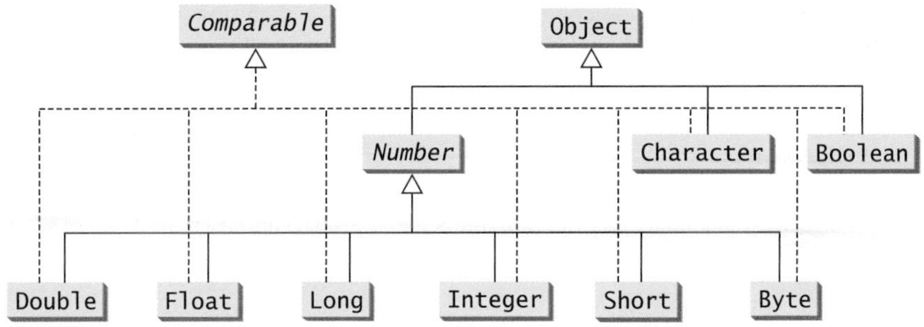
Comparable
Object
Number
Character
Boolean
Double
Float
Long
Integer
Short
Byte

FIGURE 14.8 The `Number` class is an abstract superclass for `Double`, `Float`, `Long`, `Integer`, `Short`, and `Byte`.

Note

naming convention

Most wrapper class names for a primitive type are the same as the primitive data type name with the first letter capitalized. The exceptions are `Integer` and `Character`.

Each numeric wrapper class extends the abstract `Number` class, which contains the methods `doubleValue()`, `floatValue()`, `intValue()`, `longValue()`, `shortValue()`, and `byteValue()`. These methods "convert" objects into primitive type values. Each wrapper class overrides the `toString` and `equals` methods defined in the `Object` class. Since all the wrapper classes implement the `Comparable` interface, the `compareTo` method is implemented in these classes.

Wrapper classes are very similar to each other. The `Character` class was introduced in Chapter 9, "Strings and Text I/O." The `Boolean` class wraps a Boolean value `true` or `false`. This section uses `Integer` and `Double` as examples to introduce the numeric wrapper classes. The key features of `Integer` and `Double` are shown in Figure 14.9.

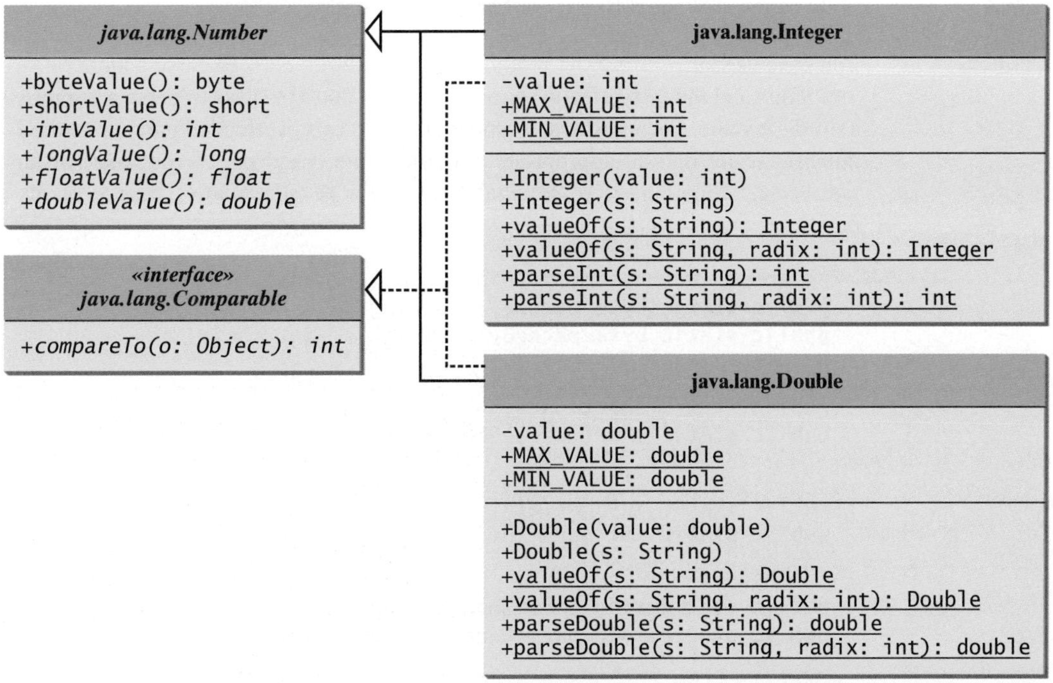
java.lang.Number
+byteValue(): byte
+shortValue(): short
+intValue(): int
+longValue(): long
+floatValue(): float
+doubleValue(): double
«interface»
java.lang.Comparable
+compareTo(o: Object): int
java.lang.Integer
-value: int
+MAX_VALUE: int
+MIN_VALUE: int
+Integer(value: int)
+Integer(s: String)
+valueOf(s: String): Integer
+valueOf(s: String, radix: int): Integer
+parseInt(s: String): int
+parseInt(s: String, radix: int): int
java.lang.Double
-value: double
+MAX_VALUE: double
+MIN_VALUE: double
+Double(value: double)
+Double(s: String)
+valueOf(s: String): Double
+valueOf(s: String, radix: int): Double
+parseDouble(s: String): double
+parseDouble(s: String, radix: int): double

FIGURE 14.9 The wrapper classes provide constructors, constants, and conversion methods for manipulating various data types.

constructors

You can construct a wrapper object either from a primitive data type value or from a string representing the numeric value—for example, `new Double(5.0)`, `new Double("5.0")`, `new Integer(5)`, and `new Integer("5")`.

no no-arg constructor
immutable

The wrapper classes do not have no-arg constructors. The instances of all wrapper classes are immutable; this means that, once the objects are created, their internal values cannot be changed.

constants

Each numeric wrapper class has the constants `MAX_VALUE` and `MIN_VALUE`. `MAX_VALUE` represents the maximum value of the corresponding primitive data type. For `Byte`, `Short`, `Integer`, and `Long`, `MIN_VALUE` represents the minimum `byte`, `short`, `int`, and `long` values. For `Float` and `Double`, `MIN_VALUE` represents the minimum *positive* `float` and `double` values. The following statements display the maximum integer (2,147,483,647), the minimum positive float (1.4E −45), and the maximum double floating-point number (1.79769313486231570e+308d).

```
System.out.println("The maximum integer is " + Integer.MAX_VALUE);
System.out.println("The minimum positive float is " +
  Float.MIN_VALUE);
System.out.println(
  "The maximum double-precision floating-point number is " +
  Double.MAX_VALUE);
```

conversion methods

Each numeric wrapper class implements the abstract methods `doubleValue()`, `floatValue()`, `intValue()`, `longValue()`, and `shortValue()`, which are defined in the `Number` class. These methods return a `double`, `float`, `int`, `long`, or `short` value for the wrapper object.

static **valueOf** methods

The numeric wrapper classes have a useful static method, `valueOf(String s)`. This method creates a new object initialized to the value represented by the specified string. For example,

```
Double doubleObject = Double.valueOf("12.4");
Integer integerObject = Integer.valueOf("12");
```

static parsing methods

You have used the `parseInt` method in the `Integer` class to parse a numeric string into an `int` value and the `parseDouble` method in the `Double` class to parse a numeric string into a `double` value. Each numeric wrapper class has two overloaded parsing methods to parse a numeric string into an appropriate numeric value based on `10` (decimal) or any specified radix (e.g., `2` for binary, `8` for octal, and `16` for hexadecimal). These methods are shown below:

```
// These two methods are in the Byte class
public static byte parseByte(String s)
public static byte parseByte(String s, int radix)

// These two methods are in the Short class
public static short parseShort(String s)
public static short parseShort(String s, int radix)

// These two methods are in the Integer class
public static int parseInt(String s)
public static int parseInt(String s, int radix)

// These two methods are in the Long class
public static long parseLong(String s)
public static long parseLong(String s, int radix)

// These two methods are in the Float class
public static float parseFloat(String s)
public static float parseFloat(String s, int radix)
```

```
// These two methods are in the Double class
public static double parseDouble(String s)
public static double parseDouble(String s, int radix)
```

For example,

```
Integer.parseInt("11", 2) returns 3;
Integer.parseInt("12", 8) returns 10;
Integer.parseInt("13", 10) returns 13;
Integer.parseInt("1A", 16) returns 26;
```

`Integer.parseInt("12", 2)` would raise a runtime exception because `12` is not a binary number.

14.10 Sorting an Array of Objects

This example presents a static generic method for sorting an array of comparable objects. The objects are instances of the `Comparable` interface, and they are compared using the `compareTo` method. The method can be used to sort an array of any objects as long as their classes implement the `Comparable` interface.

To test the method, the program sorts an array of integers, an array of double numbers, an array of characters, and an array of strings. The program is shown in Listing 14.10.

LISTING 14.10 GenericSort.java

```
public class GenericSort {
  public static void main(String[] args) {
    // Create an Integer array
    Integer[] intArray = {new Integer(2), new Integer(4),
      new Integer(3)};

    // Create a Double array
    Double[] doubleArray = {new Double(3.4), new Double(1.3),
      new Double(-22.1)};

    // Create a Character array
    Character[] charArray = {new Character('a'),
      new Character('J'), new Character('r')};

    // Create a String array
    String[] stringArray = {"Tom", "John", "Fred"};

    // Sort the arrays
    sort(intArray);
    sort(doubleArray);
    sort(charArray);
    sort(stringArray);

    // Display the sorted arrays
    System.out.print("Sorted Integer objects: ");
    printList(intArray);
    System.out.print("Sorted Double objects: ");
    printList(doubleArray);
    System.out.print("Sorted Character objects: ");
    printList(charArray);
    System.out.print("Sorted String objects: ");
    printList(stringArray);
  }

```

sort **Integer** objects
sort **Double** objects
sort **Character** objects
sort **String** objects

generic sort method

compareTo

```
  /** Sort an array of comparable objects */
  public static void sort(Comparable[] list) {
    Comparable currentMin;
    int currentMinIndex;

    for (int i = 0; i < list.length - 1; i++) {
      // Find the maximum in the list[0..i]
      currentMin = list[i];
      currentMinIndex = i;

      for (int j = i + 1; j < list.length; j++) {
        if (currentMin.compareTo(list[j]) > 0) {
          currentMin = list[j];
          currentMinIndex = j;
        }
      }

      // Swap list[i] with list[currentMinIndex] if necessary;
      if (currentMinIndex != i) {
        list[currentMinIndex] = list[i];
        list[i] = currentMin;
      }
    }
  }

  /** Print an array of objects */
  public static void printList(Object[] list) {
    for (int i = 0; i < list.length; i++)
      System.out.print(list[i] + " ");
    System.out.println();
  }
}
```

```
Sorted Integer objects: 2 3 4
Sorted Double objects: -22.1 1.3 3.4
Sorted Character objects: J a r
Sorted String objects: Fred John Tom
```

The algorithm for the **sort** method is the same as in §6.10.1, "Selection Sort." The **sort** method in §6.10.1 sorts an array of **double** values. The **sort** method in this example can sort an array of any object type, provided that the objects are also instances of the **Comparable** interface. This is another example of *generic programming*. Generic programming enables a method to operate on arguments of generic types, making it reusable with multiple types.

Integer, **Double**, **Character**, and **String** implement **Comparable**, so the objects of these classes can be compared using the **compareTo** method. The **sort** method uses the **compareTo** method to determine the order of the objects in the array.

Arrays.sort method

Tip

Java provides a static **sort** method for sorting an array of any object type in the **java.util.Arrays** class, provided that the elements in the array are comparable. Thus you can use the following code to sort arrays in this example:

```
java.util.Arrays.sort(intArray);
java.util.Arrays.sort(doubleArray);
java.util.Arrays.sort(charArray);
java.util.Arrays.sort(stringArray);
```

Note

Arrays are objects. An array is an instance of the `Object` class. Furthermore, if `A` is a subtype of `B`, every instance of `A[]` is an instance of `B[]`. Therefore, the following statements are all true:

```
new int[10] instanceof Object
new Integer[10] instanceof Object
new Integer[10] instanceof Comparable[]
new Integer[10] instanceof Number[]
new Number[10] instanceof Object[]
```

Caution

Although an `int` value can be assigned to a `double` type variable, `int[]` and `double[]` are two incompatible types. Therefore, you cannot assign an `int[]` array to a variable of `double[]` or `Object[]` type.

14.11 Automatic Conversion between Primitive Types and Wrapper Class Types

Java allows primitive types and wrapper classes to be converted automatically. For example, the following statement in (a) can be simplified as in (b) due to autoboxing:

(a)		(b)
`Integer intObject = new Integer(2);`	Equivalent	`Integer intObject = 2;` (autoboxing)

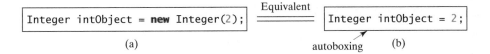

Converting a primitive value to a wrapper object is called *boxing*. The reverse conversion is called *unboxing*. The compiler will automatically box a primitive value that appears in a context requiring an object, and will unbox an object that appears in a context requiring a primitive value. Consider the following example: boxing unboxing

```
1 Integer[] intArray = {1, 2, 3};
2 System.out.println(intArray[0] + intArray[1] + intArray[2]);
```

In line 1, primitive values `1`, `2`, and `3` are automatically boxed into objects `new Integer(1)`, `new Integer(2)`, and `new Integer(3)`. In line 2, objects `intArray[0]`, `intArray[1]`, and `intArray[2]` are automatically converted into `int` values that are added together.

14.12 The BigInteger and BigDecimal Classes

If you need to compute with very large integers or high-precision floating-point values, you can use the `BigInteger` and `BigDecimal` classes in the `java.math` package. Both are *immutable*. Both extend the `Number` class and implement the `Comparable` interface. The largest integer of the `long` type is `Long.MAX_VALUE` (i.e., `9223372036854775807`). An instance of `BigInteger` can represent an integer of any size. You can use `new BigInteger(String)` and `new BigDecimal(String)` to create an instance of `BigInteger` and `BigDecimal`, use the `add`, `subtract`, `multiple`, `divide`, and `remainder` methods to perform arithmetic operations, and use the `compareTo` method to compare two big numbers. For example, the following code creates two `BigInteger` objects and multiplies them. immutable

```
BigInteger a = new BigInteger("9223372036854775807");
BigInteger b = new BigInteger("2");
BigInteger c = a.multiply(b); // 9223372036854775807 * 2
System.out.println(c);
```

The output is 18446744073709551614.

There is no limit to the precision of a BigDecimal object. The divide method may throw an ArithmeticException if the result cannot be terminated. However, you can use the overloaded divide(BigDecimal d, int scale, int roundingMode) method to specify a scale and a rounding mode to avoid this exception, where scale is the minimum number of digits after the decimal point. For example, the following code creates two BigDecimal objects and performs division with scale 20 and rounding mode BigDecimal.ROUND_UP.

```
BigDecimal a = new BigDecimal(1.0);
BigDecimal b = new BigDecimal(3);
BigDecimal c = a.divide(b, 20, BigDecimal.ROUND_UP);
System.out.println(c);
```

The output is 0.33333333333333333334.

Note that the factorial of an integer can be very large. Listing 14.11 gives a method that can return the factorial of any integer.

LISTING 14.11 LargeFactorial.java

```
 1 import java.math.*;
 2
 3 public class LargeFactorial {
 4   public static void main(String[] args) {
 5     System.out.println("50! is \n" + factorial(50));
 6   }
 7
 8   public static BigInteger factorial(long n) {
 9     BigInteger result = BigInteger.ONE;                        // constant
10     for (int i = 1; i <= n; i++)
11       result = result.multiply(new BigInteger(i + ""));        // multiply
12
13     return result;
14   }
15 }
```

```
50! is
30414093201713378043612608166064768844377641568960512000000000000
```

BigInteger.ONE (line 9) is a constant defined in the BigInteger class. BigInteger.ONE is same as new BigInteger("1").

A new result is obtained by invoking the multiply method (line 11).

14.13 Case Study: The **Rational** Class

A rational number has a numerator and a denominator in the form a/b, where a is the numerator and b the denominator. For example, 1/3, 3/4, and 10/4 are rational numbers.

A rational number cannot have a denominator of 0, but a numerator of 0 is fine. Every integer i is equivalent to a rational number i/1. Rational numbers are used in exact computations involving fractions—for example, 1/3 = 0.33333 .... This number cannot be precisely represented in floating-point format using data type double or float. To obtain the exact result, we must use rational numbers.

Java provides data types for integers and floating-point numbers, but not for rational numbers. This section shows how to design a class to represent rational numbers.

Since rational numbers share many common features with integers and floating-point numbers, and `Number` is the root class for numeric wrapper classes, it is appropriate to define `Rational` as a subclass of `Number`. Since rational numbers are comparable, the `Rational` class should also implement the `Comparable` interface. Figure 14.10 illustrates the `Rational` class and its relationship to the `Number` class and the `Comparable` interface.

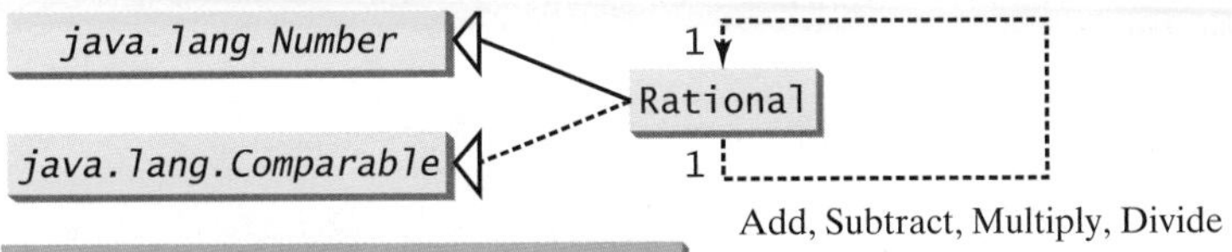
java.lang.Number
java.lang.Comparable
Rational
1
1
Add, Subtract, Multiply, Divide

Rational	
-numerator: long	The numerator of this rational number.
-denominator: long	The denominator of this rational number.
+Rational()	Creates a rational number with numerator 0 and denominator 1.
+Rational(numerator: long, denominator: long)	Creates a rational number with specified numerator and denominator.
+getNumerator(): long	Returns the numerator of this rational number.
+getDenominator(): long	Returns the denominator of this rational number.
+add(secondRational: Rational): Rational	Returns the addition of this rational with another.
+subtract(secondRational: Rational): Rational	Returns the subtraction of this rational with another.
+multiply(secondRational: Rational): Rational	Returns the multiplication of this rational with another.
+divide(secondRational: Rational): Rational	Returns the division of this rational with another.
+toString(): String	Returns a string in the form "numerator / denominator." Returns numerator if denominator is 1.
-gcd(n: long, d: long): long	Returns the greatest common divisor between n and d.

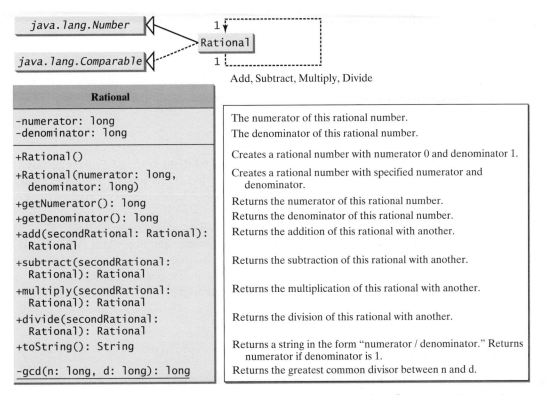

FIGURE 14.10 The properties, constructors, and methods of the `Rational` class are illustrated in UML.

A rational number consists of a numerator and a denominator. There are many equivalent rational numbers—for example, `1/3 = 2/6 = 3/9 = 4/12`. The numerator and the denominator of `1/3` have no common divisor except `1`, so `1/3` is said to be in lowest terms.

To reduce a rational number to its lowest terms, you need to find the greatest common divisor (GCD) of the absolute values of its numerator and denominator, then divide both numerator and denominator by this value. You can use the method for computing the GCD of two integers `n` and `d`, as suggested in Listing 4.8, GreatestCommonDivisor.java. The numerator and denominator in a `Rational` object are reduced to their lowest terms.

As usual, let us first write a test program to create two `Rational` objects and test its methods. Listing 14.12 is a test program.

LISTING 14.12 TestRationalClass.java

```
public class TestRationalClass {
  /** Main method */
  public static void main(String[] args) {
    // Create and initialize two rational numbers r1 and r2.
    Rational r1 = new Rational(4, 2);
    Rational r2 = new Rational(2, 3);

```

create a **Rational**
create a **Rational**

add

```
8     // Display results
9     System.out.println(r1 + " + " + r2 + " = " + r1.add(r2));
10    System.out.println(r1 + " - " + r2 + " = " + r1.subtract(r2));
11    System.out.println(r1 + " * " + r2 + " = " + r1.multiply(r2));
12    System.out.println(r1 + " / " + r2 + " = " + r1.divide(r2));
13    System.out.println(r2 + " is " + r2.doubleValue());
14  }
15 }
```

```
2 + 2/3 = 8/3
2 - 2/3 = 4/3
2 * 2/3 = 4/3
2 / 2/3 = 3
2/3 is 0.6666666666666666
```

The `main` method creates two rational numbers, `r1` and `r2` (lines 5–6), and displays the results of `r1 + r2`, `r1 - r2`, `r1 x r2`, and `r1 / r2` (lines 9–12). To perform `r1 + r2`, invoke `r1.add(r2)` to return a new `Rational` object. Similarly, `r1.subtract(r2)` is for `r1 - r2`, `r1.multiply(r2)` for `r1 x r2`, and `r1.divide(r2)` for `r1 / r2`.

The `doubleValue()` method displays the double value of `r2` (line 13). The `doubleValue()` method is defined in `java.lang.Number` and overridden in `Rational`.

Note that when a string is concatenated with an object using the plus sign (+), the object's string representation from the `toString()` method is used to concatenate with the string. So `r1 + " + " + r2 + " = " + r1.add(r2)` is equivalent to `r1.toString() + " + " + r2.toString() + " = " + r1.add(r2).toString()`.

The `Rational` class is implemented in Listing 14.13.

Listing 14.13 Rational.java

```
public class Rational extends Number implements Comparable {
  // Data fields for numerator and denominator
  private long numerator = 0;
  private long denominator = 1;

  /** Construct a rational with default properties */
  public Rational() {
    this(0, 1);
  }

  /** Construct a rational with specified numerator and denominator */
  public Rational(long numerator, long denominator) {
    long gcd = gcd(numerator, denominator);
    this.numerator = ((denominator > 0) ? 1 : -1) * numerator / gcd;
    this.denominator = Math.abs(denominator) / gcd;
  }

  /** Find GCD of two numbers */
  private static long gcd(long n, long d) {
    long n1 = Math.abs(n);
    long n2 = Math.abs(d);
    int gcd = 1;

    for (int k = 1; k <= n1 && k <= n2; k++) {
      if (n1 % k == 0 && n2 % k == 0)
        gcd = k;
    }
```

```java

    return gcd;
  }

  /** Return numerator */
  public long getNumerator() {
    return numerator;
  }

  /** Return denominator */
  public long getDenominator() {
    return denominator;
  }

  /** Add a rational number to this rational */
  public Rational add(Rational secondRational) {
    long n = numerator * secondRational.getDenominator() +
      denominator * secondRational.getNumerator();
    long d = denominator * secondRational.getDenominator();
    return new Rational(n, d);
  }
```

$\frac{a}{b} + \frac{c}{d} = \frac{ad + bc}{bd}$

```java

  /** Subtract a rational number from this rational */
  public Rational subtract(Rational secondRational) {
    long n = numerator * secondRational.getDenominator()
      - denominator * secondRational.getNumerator();
    long d = denominator * secondRational.getDenominator();
    return new Rational(n, d);
  }
```

$\frac{a}{b} - \frac{c}{d} = \frac{ad - bc}{bd}$

```java

  /** Multiply a rational number to this rational */
  public Rational multiply(Rational secondRational) {
    long n = numerator * secondRational.getNumerator();
    long d = denominator * secondRational.getDenominator();
    return new Rational(n, d);
  }
```

$\frac{a}{b} \times \frac{c}{d} = \frac{ac}{bd}$

```java

  /** Divide a rational number from this rational */
  public Rational divide(Rational secondRational) {
    long n = numerator * secondRational.getDenominator();
    long d = denominator * secondRational.numerator;
    return new Rational(n, d);
  }
```

$\frac{a}{b} \div \frac{c}{d} = \frac{ad}{bc}$

```java

  /** Override the toString() method */
  public String toString() {
    if (denominator == 1)
      return numerator + "";
    else
      return numerator + "/" + denominator;
  }

  /** Override the equals method in the Object class */
  public boolean equals(Object parm1) {
    if ((this.subtract((Rational)(parm1))).getNumerator() == 0)
      return true;
    else
      return false;
  }

```

```
88    /** Implement the abstract intValue method in java.lang.Number */
89    public int intValue() {
90      return (int)doubleValue();
91    }
92
93    /** Implement the abstract floatValue method in java.lang.Number */
94    public float floatValue() {
95      return (float)doubleValue();
96    }
97
98    /** Implement the doubleValue method in java.lang.Number */
99    public double doubleValue() {
100     return numerator * 1.0 / denominator;
101   }
102
103   /** Implement the abstract longValue method in java.lang.Number */
104   public long longValue() {
105     return (long)doubleValue();
106   }
107
108   /** Implement the compareTo method in java.lang.Comparable */
109   public int compareTo(Object o) {
110     if ((this.subtract((Rational)o)).getNumerator() > 0)
111       return 1;
112     else if ((this.subtract((Rational)o)).getNumerator() < 0)
113       return -1;
114     else
115       return 0;
116   }
117 }
```

The rational number is encapsulated in a **Rational** object. Internally, a rational number is represented in its lowest terms (line 13), and the numerator determines its sign (line 14). The denominator is always positive (line 15).

The **gcd()** method (lines 19–30 in the **Rational** class) is private; it is not intended for use by clients. The **gcd()** method is only for internal use by the **Rational** class. The **gcd()** method is also static, since it is not dependent on any particular **Rational** object.

The **abs(x)** method (lines 20–21 in the **Rational** class) is defined in the **Math** class that returns the absolute value of **x**.

Two **Rational** objects can interact with each other to perform add, subtract, multiply, and divide operations. These methods return a new **Rational** object (lines 43–70).

The methods **toString** and **equals** in the **Object** class are overridden in the **Rational** class (lines 73–91). The **toString()** method returns a string representation of a **Rational** object in the form **numerator/denominator**, or simply **numerator** if **denominator** is **1**. The **equals(Object other)** method returns true if this rational number is equal to the other rational number.

The abstract methods **intValue**, **longValue**, **floatValue**, and **doubleValue** in the **Number** class are implemented in the **Rational** class (lines 88–106). These methods return **int**, **long**, **float**, and **double** value for this rational number.

The **compareTo(Object other)** method in the **Comparable** interface is implemented in the **Rational** class (lines 109–116) to compare this rational number to the other rational number.

Tip

The **get** methods for the properties **numerator** and **denominator** are provided in the **Rational** class, but the **set** methods are not provided, so, once a **Rational** object is created, its contents cannot be changed. The **Rational** class is immutable. The **String** class and the wrapper classes for primitive type values are also immutable.

immutable

Tip

The numerator and denominator are represented using two variables. It is possible to use an array of two integers to represent the numerator and denominator. See Exercise 14.18. The signatures of the public methods in the **Rational** class are not changed, although the internal representation of a rational number is changed. This is a good example to illustrate the idea that the data fields of a class should be kept private so as to encapsulate the implementation of the class from the use of the class.

encapsulation

The **Rational** class has serious limitations. It can easily overflow. For example, the following code will display an incorrect result, because the denominator is too large.

overflow

```
public class Test {
  public static void main(String[] args) {
    Rational r1 = new Rational(1, 123456789);
    Rational r2 = new Rational(1, 123456789);
    Rational r3 = new Rational(1, 123456789);
    System.out.println("r1 * r2 * r3 is " +
      r1.multiply(r2.multiply(r3)));
  }
}
```

```
r1 * r2 * r3 is -1/2204193661661244627
```

To fix it, you may implement the **Rational** class using the **BigInteger** for numerator and denominator (see Exercise 14.19).

Key Terms

Chapter Summary

1. Abstract classes are like regular classes with data and methods, but you cannot create instances of abstract classes using the **new** operator.

2. An abstract method cannot be contained in a nonabstract class. If a subclass of an abstract superclass does not implement all the inherited abstract methods of the superclass, the subclass must be defined abstract.

3. A class that contains abstract methods must be abstract. However, it is possible to define an abstract class that contains no abstract methods.

4. A subclass can be abstract even if its superclass is concrete.

5. An interface is a classlike construct that contains only constants and abstract methods. In many ways, an interface is similar to an abstract class, but an abstract class can contain constants and abstract methods as well as variables and concrete methods.

6. An interface is treated like a special class in Java. Each interface is compiled into a separate bytecode file, just like a regular class.

7. The `java.lang.Comparable` interface defines the `compareTo` method. Many classes in the Java library implement `Comparable`.

8. The `java.lang.Cloneable` interface is a marker interface. An object of the class that implements the `Cloneable` interface is cloneable.

9. A class can extend only one superclass but can implement one or more interfaces.

10. An interface can extend one or more interfaces.

11. Many Java methods require the use of objects as arguments. Java offers a convenient way to incorporate, or wrap, a primitive data type into an object (e.g., wrapping `int` into the `Integer` class, and wrapping `double` into the `Double` class). The corresponding class is called a *wrapper class*. By using a wrapper object instead of a primitive data type variable, you can take advantage of generic programming.

12. Java can automatically convert a primitive type value to its corresponding wrapper object in the context and vice versa.

13. The `BigInteger` class is useful to compute and process integers of any size. The `BigDecimal` class can be used to compute and process floating-point numbers with any arbitrary precision.

Review Questions

Section 14.2

14.1 Which of the following classes definitions defines a legal abstract class?

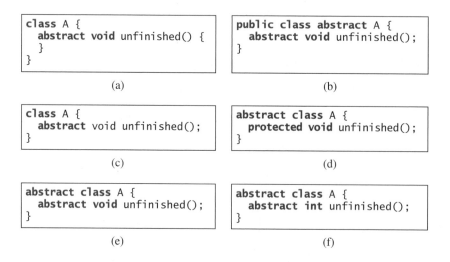

```
class A {
  abstract void unfinished() {
  }
}
```

(a)

```
public class abstract A {
  abstract void unfinished();
}
```

(b)

```
class A {
  abstract void unfinished();
}
```

(c)

```
abstract class A {
  protected void unfinished();
}
```

(d)

```
abstract class A {
  abstract void unfinished();
}
```

(e)

```
abstract class A {
  abstract int unfinished();
}
```

(f)

14.2 The `getArea` and `getPerimeter` methods may be removed from the `GeometricObject` class. What are the benefits of defining `getArea` and `getPerimeter` as abstract methods in the `GeometricObject` class?

14.3 True or false? An abstract class can be used just like a nonabstract class except that you cannot use the `new` operator to create an instance from the abstract class.

Sections 14.4–14.6

14.4 Which of the following is a correct interface?

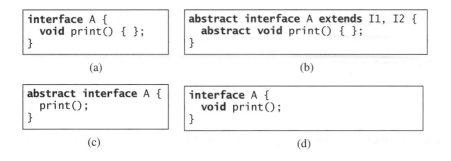

```
interface A {
  void print() { };
}
```
(a)

```
abstract interface A extends I1, I2 {
  abstract void print() { };
}
```
(b)

```
abstract interface A {
  print();
}
```
(c)

```
interface A {
  void print();
}
```
(d)

14.5 True or false? If a class implements `Comparable`, the object of the class can invoke the `compareTo` method.

14.6 Two `max` methods are defined in §14.5. Explain why the `max` with the signature `max(Comparable, Comparable)` is better than the one with the signature `max(Object, Object)`.

14.7 You can define the `compareTo` method in a class without implementing the `Comparable` interface. What are the benefits of implementing the `Comparable` interface?

14.8 True or false? If a class implements `java.awt.event.ActionListener`, the object of the class can invoke the `actionPerformed` method.

Sections 14.7–14.8

14.9 Can you invoke the `clone()` method to clone an object if the class for the object does not implement the `java.lang.Cloneable`? Does the `Date` class implement `Cloneable`?

14.10 What would happen if the `House` class (defined in Listing 14.9) did not override the `clone()` method or if `House` did not implement `java.lang.Cloneable`?

14.11 Show the printout of the following code:

```
java.util.Date date = new java.util.Date();
java.util.Date date1 = date;
java.util.Date date2 = (java.util.Date)(date.clone());
System.out.println(date == date1);
System.out.println(date == date2);
System.out.println(date.equals(date2));
```

14.12 Show the printout of the following code:

```
java.util.ArrayList list = new java.util.ArrayList();
list.add("New York");
java.util.ArrayList list1 = list;
java.util.ArrayList list2 = (java.util.ArrayList)(list.clone());
list.add("Atlanta");
System.out.println(list == list1);
System.out.println(list == list2);
System.out.println("list is " + list);
System.out.println("list1 is " + list1);
System.out.println("list2.get(0) is " + list2.get(0));
System.out.println("list2.size() is " + list2.size());
```

14.13 What is wrong in the following code?

```
public class Test {
  public static void main(String[] args) {
    GeometricObject x = new Circle(3);
    GeometricObject y = x.clone();
    System.out.println(x == y);
  }
}
```

14.14 Give an example to show why interfaces are preferred over abstract classes.

Section 14.9

14.15 Describe primitive-type wrapper classes. Why do you need these wrapper classes?

14.16 Can each of the following statements be compiled?

```
Integer i = new Integer("23");
Integer i = new Integer(23);
Integer i = Integer.valueOf("23");
Integer i = Integer.parseInt("23", 8);
Double d = new Double();
Double d = Double.valueOf("23.45");
int i = (Integer.valueOf("23")).intValue();
double d = (Double.valueOf("23.4")).doubleValue();
int i = (Double.valueOf("23.4")).intValue();
String s = (Double.valueOf("23.4")).toString();
```

14.17 How do you convert an integer into a string? How do you convert a numeric string into an integer? How do you convert a double number into a string? How do you convert a numeric string into a double value?

14.18 Why do the following two lines of code compile but cause a runtime error?

```
Number numberRef = new Integer(0);
Double doubleRef = (Double)numberRef;
```

14.19 Why do the following two lines of code compile but cause a runtime error?

```
Number[] numberArray = new Integer[2];
numberArray[0] = new Double(1.5);
```

14.20 What is wrong in the following code?

```
public class Test {
  public static void main(String[] args) {
    Number x = new Integer(3);
    System.out.println(x.intValue());
    System.out.println(x.compareTo(new Integer(4)));
  }
}
```

14.21 What is wrong in the following code?

```
public class Test {
  public static void main(String[] args) {
    Number x = new Integer(3);
    System.out.println(x.intValue());
    System.out.println((Integer)x.compareTo(new Integer(4)));
  }
}
```

14.22 What is the output of the following code?

```
public class Test {
  public static void main(String[] args) {
    System.out.println(Integer.parseInt("10"));
    System.out.println(Integer.parseInt("10", 10));
    System.out.println(Integer.parseInt("10", 16));
    System.out.println(Integer.parseInt("11"));
    System.out.println(Integer.parseInt("11", 10));
    System.out.println(Integer.parseInt("11", 16));
  }
}
```

Sections 14.10–14.12

14.23 What are autoboxing and autounboxing? Are the following statements correct?

```
Number x = 3;
Integer x = 3;
Double x = 3;
Double x = 3.0;
int x = new Integer(3);
int x = new Integer(3) + new Integer(4);
double y = 3.4;
y.intValue();

JOptionPane.showMessageDialog(null, 45.5);
```

14.24 Can you assign `new int[10]`, `new String[100]`, `new Object[50]`, or `new Calendar[20]` into a variable of `Object[]` type?

14.25 What is the output of the following code?

```
public class Test {
  public static void main(String[] args) {
    java.math.BigInteger x = new java.math.BigInteger("3");
    java.math.BigInteger y = new java.math.BigInteger("7");
    x.add(y);
    System.out.println(x);
  }
}
```

Comprehensive

14.26 Define the following terms: abstract classes, interfaces. What are the similarities and differences between abstract classes and interfaces?

14.27 Indicate true or false for the following statements:

- An abstract class can have instances created using the constructor of the abstract class.
- An abstract class can be extended.
- An interface is compiled into a separate bytecode file.
- A subclass of a nonabstract superclass cannot be abstract.
- A subclass cannot override a concrete method in a superclass to define it abstract.
- An abstract method must be nonstatic
- An interface can have static methods.
- An interface can extend one or more interfaces.

- An interface can extend an abstract class.
- An abstract class can extend an interface.

Programming Exercises

Sections 14.1–14.7

14.1* (*Enabling GeometricObject comparable*) Modify the GeometricObject class to implement the Comparable interface, and define a static max method in the GeometricObject class for finding the larger of two GeometricObject objects. Draw the UML diagram and implement the new GeometricObject class. Write a test program that uses the max method to find the larger of two circles and the larger of two rectangles.

14.2* (*The ComparableCircle class*) Create a class named ComparableCircle that extends Circle and implements Comparable. Draw the UML diagram and implement the compareTo method to compare the circles on the basis of area. Write a test class to find the larger of two instances of ComparableCircle objects.

14.3* (*The Colorable interface*) Design an interface named Colorable with a void method named howToColor(). Every class of a colorable object must implement the Colorable interface. Design a class named Square that extends GeometricObject and implements Colorable. Implement howToColor to display a message "Color all four sides".

Draw a UML diagram that involves Colorable, Square, and GeometricObject. Write a test program that creates an array of five GeometricObjects. For each object in the array, invoke its howToColor method if it is colorable.

14.4* (*Revising the House class*) Rewrite the House class in Listing 14.9 to perform a deep copy on the whenBuilt field.

14.5* (*Enabling Circle comparable*) Rewrite the Circle class in Listing 14.2 to extend GeometricObject and implement the Comparable interface. Override the equals method in the Object class. Two Circle objects are equal if their radii are the same. Draw the UML diagram that involves Circle, GeometricObject, and Comparable.

Video Note
Redesign the **Rectangle** class

14.6* (*Enabling Rectangle comparable*) Rewrite the Rectangle class in Listing 14.3 to extend GeometricObject and implement the Comparable interface. Override the equals method in the Object class. Two Rectangle objects are equal if their areas are the same. Draw the UML diagram that involves Rectangle, GeometricObject, and Comparable.

14.7* (*The Octagon class*) Write a class named Octagon that extends GeometricObject and implements the Comparable and Cloneable interfaces. Assume that all eight sides of the octagon are of equal size. The area can be computed using the following formula:

$$area = \left(2 + 4/\sqrt{2}\right)*side*side$$

Draw the UML diagram that involves Octagon, GeometricObject, Comparable, and Cloneable. Write a test program that creates an Octagon object with side value 5 and displays its area and perimeter. Create a new object using the clone method and compare the two objects using the compareTo method.

14.8* (*Summing the areas of geometric objects*) Write a method that sums the areas of all the geometric objects in an array. The method signature is:

```
public static double sumArea(GeometricObject[] a)
```

Write a test program that creates an array of four objects (two circles and two rectangles) and computes their total area using the `sumArea` method.

14.9* (*Finding the largest object*) Write a method that returns the largest object in an array of objects. The method signature is:

```
public static Object max(Comparable[] a)
```

All the objects are instances of the `Comparable` interface. The order of the objects in the array is determined using the `compareTo` method.

Write a test program that creates an array of ten strings, an array of ten integers, and an array of ten dates, and finds the largest string, integer, and date in the arrays.

14.10** (*Displaying calendars*) Rewrite the `PrintCalendar` class in Listing 5.12 to display a calendar for a specified month using the `Calendar` and `GregorianCalendar` classes. Your program receives the month and year from the command line. For example:

```
java Exercise14_10 1 2010
```

This displays the calendar shown in Figure 14.11.

You also can run the program without the year. In this case, the year is the current year. If you run the program without specifying a month and a year, the month is the current month.

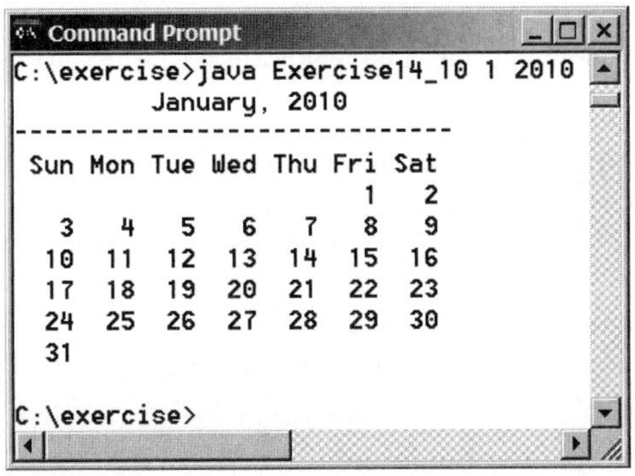
Command Prompt
C:\exercise>java Exercise14_10 1 2010
January, 2010

Sun Mon Tue Wed Thu Fri Sat
1 2
3 4 5 6 7 8 9
10 11 12 13 14 15 16
17 18 19 20 21 22 23
24 25 26 27 28 29 30
31
C:\exercise>

FIGURE 14.11 The program displays a calendar for January 2010.

Section 14.12

14.11** (*Divisible by 5 or 6*) Find the first ten numbers (greater than `Long.MAX_VALUE`) that are divisible by 5 or 6.

14.12** (*Divisible by 2 or 3*) Find the first ten numbers with 50 decimal digits that are divisible by 2 or 3.

14.13** (*Square numbers*) Find the first ten square numbers that are greater than `Long.MAX_VALUE`. A square number is a number in the form of n^2.

14.14** (*Large prime numbers*) Write a program that finds five prime numbers larger than `Long.MAX_VALUE`.

14.15** (*Mersenne prime*) A prime number is called a *Mersenne prime* if it can be written in the form $2^p - 1$ for some positive integer p. Write a program that finds all Mersenne primes with $p \le 100$ and displays the output as shown below. (You have to use `BigInteger` to store the number, because it is too big to be stored in `long`. Your program may take several hours to complete.)

```
p          2^p - 1

2          3
3          7
5          31
...
```

Section 14.13

14.16** (*Approximating e*) Exercise 4.26 approximates e using the following series:

$$e = 1 + \frac{1}{1!} + \frac{1}{2!} + \frac{1}{3!} + \frac{1}{4!} + \ldots + \frac{1}{i!}$$

In order to get better precision, use `BigDecimal` with `25` digits of precision in the computation. Write a program that displays the `e` value for `i` = `100`, `200`, . . . , and `1000`.

14.17 (*Using the* `Rational` *class*) Write a program that will compute the following summation series using the `Rational` class:

$$\frac{1}{2} + \frac{2}{3} + \frac{3}{4} + \ldots + \frac{98}{99} + \frac{99}{100}$$

You will discover that output is incorrect because of integer overflow (too large). To fix this problem, see Exercise 14.19.

14.18* (*Demonstrating the benefits of encapsulation*) Rewrite the `Rational` class in §14.13 using a new internal representation for numerator and denominator. Create an array of two integers as follows:

```
private long[] r = new long[2];
```

Use `r[0]` to represent the numerator and `r[1]` to represent the denominator. The signatures of the methods in the `Rational` class are not changed, so a client application that uses the previous `Rational` class can continue to use this new `Rational` class without being recompiled.

14.19** (*Using* `BigInteger` *for the* `Rational` *class*) Redesign and implement the `Rational` class in §14.13 using `BigInteger` for numerator and denominator.

14.20* (*Creating a rational-number calculator*) Write a program similar to Listing 9.5, Calculator.java. Instead of using integers, use rationals, as shown in Figure 14.12.

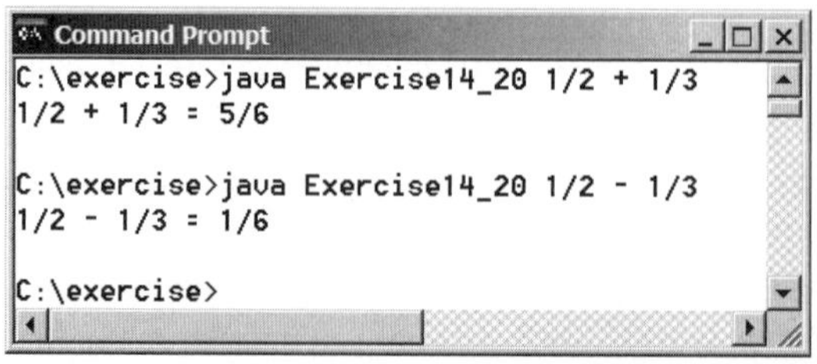
Command Prompt
C:\exercise>java Exercise14_20 1/2 + 1/3
1/2 + 1/3 = 5/6
C:\exercise>java Exercise14_20 1/2 - 1/3
1/2 - 1/3 = 1/6
C:\exercise>

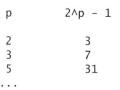

FIGURE 14.12 The program takes three arguments (operand1, operator, and operand2) from the command line and displays the expression and the result of the arithmetic operation.

You will need to use the `split` method in the `String` class, introduced in §9.2.6, "Converting, Replacing, and Splitting Strings," to retrieve the numerator string and denominator string, and convert strings into integers using the `Integer.parseInt` method.

14.21* (*Math: The `Complex` class*) A complex number is a number of the form $a + bi$, where a and b are real numbers and i is $\sqrt{-1}$. The numbers `a` and `b` are known as the real part and imaginary part of the complex number, respectively. You can perform addition, subtraction, multiplication, and division for complex numbers using the following formula:

$$a + bi + c + di = (a + c) + (b + d)i$$

$$a + bi - (c + di) = (a - c) + (b - d)i$$

$$(a + bi)*(c + di) = (ac - bd) + (bc + ad)i$$

$$(a + bi)/(c + di) = (ac + bd)/(c^2 + d^2) + (bc - ad)i/(c^2 + d^2)$$

You can also obtain the absolute value for a complex number using the following formula:

$$|a + bi| = \sqrt{a^2 + b^2}$$

Design a class named `Complex` for representing complex numbers and the methods `add`, `subtract`, `multiply`, `divide`, and `abs` for performing complex-number operations, and override the `toString` method for returning a string representation for a complex number. The `toString` method returns `a + bi` as a string. If `b` is `0`, it simply returns `a`.

Provide three constructors `Complex(a, b)`, `Complex(a)`, and `Complex()`. `Complex()` creates a `Complex` object for number `0` and `Complex(a)` creates a `Complex` object with `0` for `b`. Also provide the `getRealPart()` and `getImaginaryPart()` methods for returning the real and imaginary part of the complex number, respectively.

Write a test program that prompts the user to enter two complex numbers and display the result of their addition, subtraction, multiplication, and division. Here is a sample run:

```
Enter the first complex number: 3.5 5.5 [Enter]
Enter the second complex number: -3.5 1 [Enter]
3.5 + 5.5i + -3.5 + 1.0i = 0.0 + 6.5i
3.5 + 5.5i - -3.5 + 1.0i = 7.0 + 4.5i
3.5 + 5.5i * -3.5 + 1.0i = -17.75 + -15.75i
3.5 + 5.5i / -3.5 + 1.0i = -0.5094 + -1.7i
|3.5 + 5.5i| = 6.519202405202649
```

Chapter 15

Graphics

Objectives

- To describe Java coordinate systems in a GUI component (§15.2).
- To draw things using the methods in the `Graphics` class (§15.3).
- To override the `paintComponent` method to draw things on a GUI component (§15.3).
- To use a panel as a canvas to draw things (§15.3).
- To draw strings, lines, rectangles, ovals, arcs, and polygons (§§15.4, 15.6–15.7).
- To obtain font properties using `FontMetrics` and know how to center a message (§15.8).
- To display an image in a GUI component (§15.11).
- To develop reusable GUI components `FigurePanel`, `MessagePanel`, `StillClock`, and `ImageViewer` (§§15.5, 15.9, 15.10, 15.12).

15.1 Introduction

Problem

Suppose you wish to draw shapes such as a bar chart, a clock, or a stop sign, as shown in Figure 15.1. How do you do so?

This chapter describes how to use the methods in the **Graphics** class to draw strings, lines, rectangles, ovals, arcs, polygons, and images, and how to develop reusable GUI components.

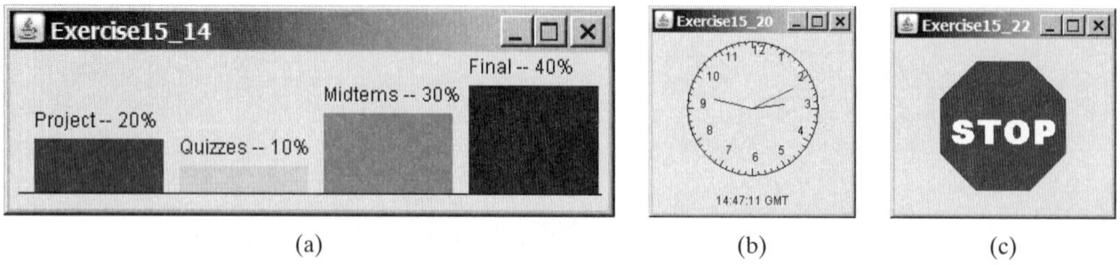

Exercise15_14
Final -- 40%
Midtems -- 30%
Project -- 20%
Quizzes -- 10%
Exercise15_20
14:47:11 GMT
Exercise15_22
STOP
(a)
(b)
(c)

FIGURE 15.1 You can draw shapes using the drawing methods in the **Graphics** class.

15.2 Graphical Coordinate Systems

To paint, you need to specify where to paint. Each component has its own coordinate system with the origin (**0**, **0**) at the upper-left corner. The *x*-coordinate increases to the right, and the *y*-coordinate increases downward. Note that the Java coordinate system differs from the conventional coordinate system, as shown in Figure 15.2.

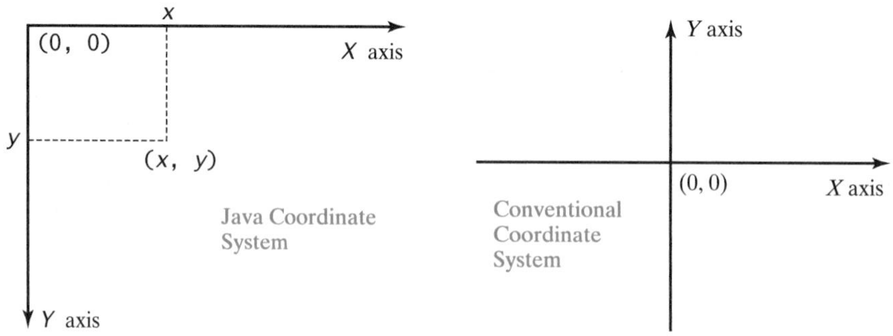

x
(0, 0)
X axis
y
(x, y)
Java Coordinate System
Y axis
Y axis
(0, 0)
X axis
Conventional Coordinate System

FIGURE 15.2 The Java coordinate system is measured in pixels, with **(0, 0)** at its upper-left corner.

The location of the upper-left corner of a component **c1** (e.g., a button) inside its parent component **c2** (e.g., a panel) can be located using **c1.getX()** and **c1.getY()**. As shown in Figure 15.3, **(x1, y1) = (c1.getX(), c1.getY())**, **(x2, y2) = (c2.getX(), c2.getY())**, and **(x3, y3) = (c3.getX(), c3.getY())**.

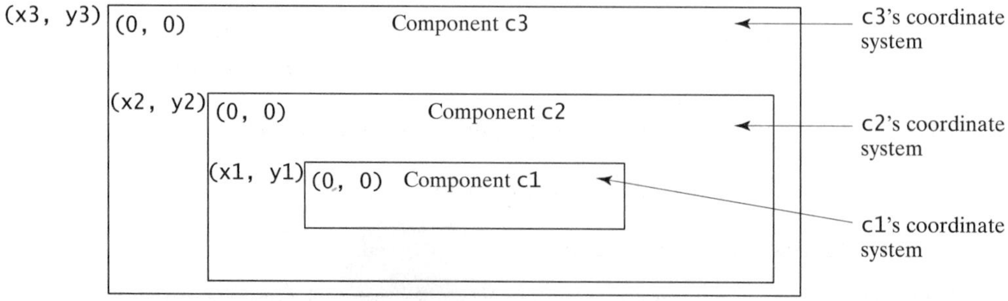

(x3, y3)
(0, 0)
Component c3
c3's coordinate system
(x2, y2)
(0, 0)
Component c2
c2's coordinate system
(x1, y1)
(0, 0)
Component c1
c1's coordinate system

FIGURE 15.3 Each GUI component has its own coordinate system.

15.3 The Graphics Class

The Graphics class provides the methods for drawing strings, lines, rectangles, ovals, arcs, polygons, and polylines, as shown in Figure 15.4.

Think of a GUI component as a piece of paper and the Graphics object as a pencil or paintbrush. You can apply the methods in the Graphics class to draw things on a GUI component.

java.awt.Graphics	
+setColor(color: Color): void	Sets a new color for subsequent drawings.
+setFont(font: Font): void	Sets a new font for subsequent drawings.
+drawString(s: String, x: int, y: int): void	Draws a string starting at point (x, y).
+drawLine(x1: int, y1: int, x2: int, y2: int): void	Draws a line from (x1, y1) to (x2, y2).
+drawRect(x: int, y: int, w: int, h: int): void	Draws a rectangle with specified upper-left corner point at (x,y) and width w and height h.
+fillRect(x: int, y: int, w: int, h: int): void	Draws a filled rectangle with specified upper-left corner point at (x, y) and width w and height h.
+drawRoundRect(x: int, y: int, w: int, h: int, aw: int, ah: int): void	Draws a round-cornered rectangle with specified arc width aw and arc height ah.
+fillRoundRect(x: int, y: int, w: int, h: int, aw: int, ah: int): void	Draws a filled round-cornered rectangle with specified arc width aw and arc height ah.
+draw3DRect(x: int, y: int, w: int, h: int, raised: boolean): void	Draws a 3-D rectangle raised above the surface or sunk into the surface.
+fill3DRect(x: int, y: int, w: int, h: int, raised: boolean): void	Draws a filled 3-D rectangle raised above the surface or sunk into the surface.
+drawOval(x: int, y: int, w: int, h: int): void	Draws an oval bounded by the rectangle specified by the parameters x, y, w, and h.
+fillOval(x: int, y: int, w: int, h: int): void	Draws a filled oval bounded by the rectangle specified by the parameters x, y, w, and h.
+drawArc(x: int, y: int, w: int, h: int, startAngle: int, arcAngle: int): void	Draws an arc conceived as part of an oval bounded by the rectangle specified by the parameters x, y, w, and h.
+fillArc(x: int, y: int, w: int, h: int, startAngle: int, arcAngle: int): void	Draws a filled arc conceived as part of an oval bounded by the rectangle specified by the parameters x, y, w, and h.
+drawPolygon(xPoints: int[], yPoints: int[], nPoints: int): void	Draws a closed polygon defined by arrays of x- and y-coordinates. Each pair of (x[i], y[i])-coordinates is a point.
+fillPolygon(xPoints: int[], yPoints: int[], nPoints: int): void	Draws a filled polygon defined by arrays of x- and y-coordinates. Each pair of (x[i], y[i])-coordinates is a point.
+drawPolygon(g: Polygon): void	Draws a closed polygon defined by a Polygon object.
+fillPolygon(g: Polygon): void	Draws a filled polygon defined by a Polygon object.
+drawPolyline(xPoints: int[], yPoints: int[], nPoints: int): void	Draws a polyline defined by arrays of x- and y-coordinates. Each pair of (x[i], y[i])-coordinates is a point.

FIGURE 15.4 The Graphics class contains the methods for drawing strings and shapes.

The Graphics class–an abstract class—provides a device-independent graphics interface for displaying figures and images on the screen on different platforms. Whenever a component (e.g., a button, a label, a panel) is displayed, the JVM automatically creates a Graphics object for the component on the native platform and passes this object to invoke the paintComponent method to display the drawings.

The signature of the paintComponent method is as follows:

```
protected void paintComponent(Graphics g)
```

This method, defined in the JComponent class, is invoked whenever a component is first displayed or redisplayed.

In order to draw things on a component, you need to define a class that extends `JPanel` and overrides its `paintComponent` method to specify what to draw. Listing 15.1 gives an example that draws a line and a string on a panel, as shown in Figure 15.5.

LISTING 15.1 TestPaintComponent.java

create a panel (line 6)
new panel class (line 19)
override **paintComponent** (line 20)
draw things in the superclass (line 21)
draw line (line 22)
draw string (line 23)

```
 1 import javax.swing.*;
 2 import java.awt.Graphics;
 3
 4 public class TestPaintComponent extends JFrame {
 5   public TestPaintComponent() {
 6     add(new NewPanel());
 7   }
 8
 9   public static void main(String[] args) {
10     TestPaintComponent frame = new TestPaintComponent();
11     frame.setTitle("TestPaintComponent");
12     frame.setSize(200, 100);
13     frame.setLocationRelativeTo(null); // Center the frame
14     frame.setDefaultCloseOperation(JFrame.EXIT_ON_CLOSE);
15     frame.setVisible(true);
16   }
17 }
18
19 class NewPanel extends JPanel {
20   protected void paintComponent(Graphics g) {
21     super.paintComponent(g);
22     g.drawLine(0, 0, 50, 50);
23     g.drawString("Banner", 0, 40);
24   }
25 }
```

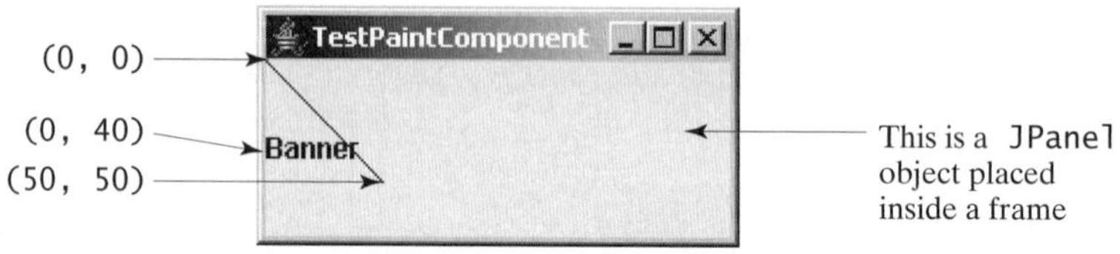

TestPaintComponent
(0, 0)
(0, 40)
(50, 50)
Banner
This is a JPanel object placed inside a frame

FIGURE 15.5 A line and a string are drawn on a panel.

The `paintComponent` method is automatically invoked to paint graphics when the component is first displayed or whenever the component needs to be redisplayed. Invoking `super.paintComponent(g)` (line 21) invokes the `paintComponent` method defined in the superclass. This is necessary to ensure that the viewing area is cleared before a new drawing is displayed. Line 22 invokes the `drawLine` method to draw a line from (0, 0) to (50, 50). Line 23 invokes the `drawString` method to draw a string.

All the drawing methods have parameters that specify the locations of the subjects to be drawn. All measurements in Java are made in pixels. The string "Banner" is drawn at location (0, 40).

The JVM invokes `paintComponent` to draw things on a component. The user should never invoke `paintComponent` directly. For this reason, the protected visibility is sufficient for `paintComponent`.

Panels are invisible and are used as small containers that group components to achieve a desired layout. Another important use of `JPanel` is for drawing. You can draw things on any Swing GUI component, but normally you should use a `JPanel` as a canvas upon which to draw things. What happens if you replace `JPanel` with `JLabel` in line 19 as follows?

```
class NewPanel extends JLabel {
```

The program will work, but it is not preferred, because JLabel is designed for creating a label, not for drawing. For consistency, this book will define a canvas class by subclassing JPanel.

extends JPanel?

Tip

Some textbooks define a canvas class by subclassing JComponent. The problem is that, if you wish to set a background in the canvas, you have to write the code to paint the background color. A simple setBackground(Color color) method will not set a background color in a JComponent.

extends JComponent?

15.4 Drawing Strings, Lines, Rectangles, and Ovals

The drawString(String s, int x, int y) method draws a string starting at the point (x, y), as shown in Figure 15.6(a).

drawString

The drawLine(int x1, int y1, int x2, int y2) method draws a straight line from point (x1, y1) to point (x2, y2), as shown in Figure 15.6(b).

drawLine

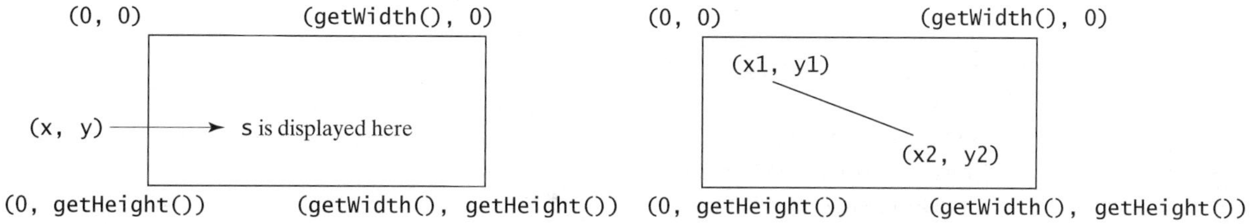
(0, 0)
(getWidth(), 0)
(x, y)
s is displayed here
(0, getHeight())
(getWidth(), getHeight())
(0, 0)
(getWidth(), 0)
(x1, y1)
(x2, y2)
(0, getHeight())
(getWidth(), getHeight())

(a) **drawString** (b) **drawLine**

Figure 15.6 (a) The drawString(s, x, y) method draws a string starting at (x, y). (b) The drawLine(x1, y1, x2, y2) method draws a line between two specified points.

Java provides six methods for drawing rectangles in outline or filled with color. You can draw or fill plain rectangles, round-cornered rectangles, or three-dimensional rectangles.

The drawRect(int x, int y, int w, int h) method draws a plain rectangle, and the fillRect(int x, int y, int w, int h) method draws a filled rectangle. The parameters x and y represent the upper-left corner of the rectangle, and w and h are its width and height (see Figure 15.7).

drawRect
fillRect

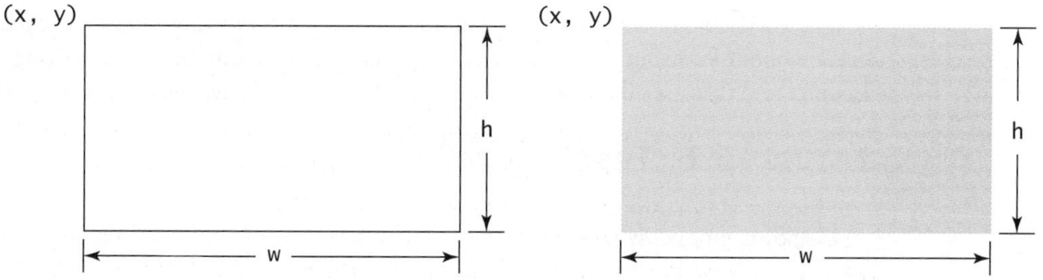
(x, y)
h
w
(x, y)
h
w

(a) Plain rectangle (b) Filled rectangle

Figure 15.7 (a) The drawRect(x, y, w, h) method draws a rectangle. (b) The fillRect(x, y, w, h) method draws a filled rectangle.

The drawRoundRect(int x, int y, int w, int h, int aw, int ah) method draws a round-cornered rectangle, and the fillRoundRect(int x, int y, int w, int h, int aw, int ah) method draws a filled round-cornered rectangle. Parameters x, y, w, and h are the same as in the drawRect method, parameter aw is the horizontal diameter of the arcs at the

drawRoundRect
fillRoundRect

corner, and `ah` is the vertical diameter of the arcs at the corner (see Figure 15.8(a)). In other words, `aw` and `ah` are the width and the height of the oval that produces a quarter-circle at each corner.

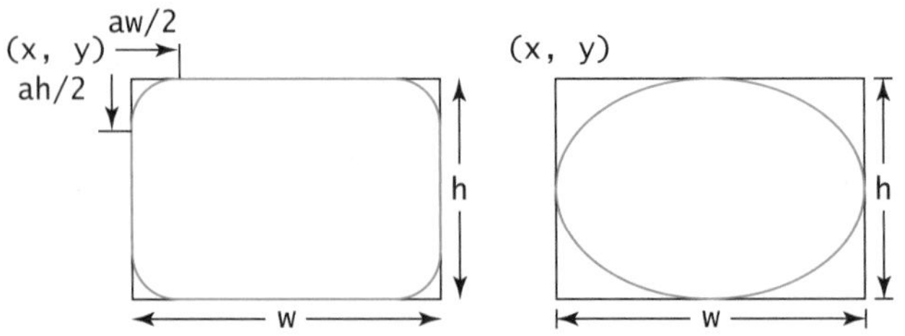
aw/2
(x, y)
ah/2
h
w
(x, y)
h
w

(a) **drawRoundRect** (b) **drawOval**

FIGURE 15.8 (a) The `drawRoundRect(x, y, w, h, aw, ah)` method draws a round-cornered rectangle. (b) The `drawOval(x, y, w, h)` method draws an oval based on its bounding rectangle.

draw3DRect
fill3DRect

The `draw3DRect(int x, int y, int w, int h, boolean raised)` method draws a 3D rectangle and the `fill3DRect(int x, int y, int w, int h, boolean raised)` method draws a filled 3D rectangle. The parameters `x`, `y`, `w`, and `h` are the same as in the `drawRect` method. The last parameter, a Boolean value, indicates whether the rectangle is raised above the surface or sunk into the surface.

drawOval
fillOval

Depending on whether you wish to draw an oval in outline or filled solid, you can use either the `drawOval(int x, int y, int w, int h)` method or the `fillOval(int x, int y, int w, int h)` method. An oval is drawn based on its bounding rectangle. Parameters `x` and `y` indicate the top-left corner of the bounding rectangle, and `w` and `h` indicate the width and height, respectively, of the bounding rectangle, as shown in Figure 15.8(b).

15.5 Case Study: The `FigurePanel` Class

Video Note
The **FigurePanel** class

This example develops a useful class for displaying various figures. The class enables the user to set the figure type and specify whether the figure is filled, and it displays the figure on a panel. The UML diagram for the class is shown in Figure 15.9. The panel can display lines, rectangles, round-cornered rectangles, and ovals. Which figure to display is decided by the `type` property. If the `filled` property is `true`, the rectangle, round-cornered rectangle, and oval are filled in the panel.

The UML diagram serves as the contract for the `FigurePanel` class. The user can use the class without knowing how the class is implemented. Let us begin by writing a program in Listing 15.2 that uses the class to display six figure panels, as shown in Figure 15.10.

LISTING 15.2 `TestFigurePanel.java`

create figures

```
import java.awt.*;
import javax.swing.*;

public class TestFigurePanel extends JFrame {
  public TestFigurePanel() {
    setLayout(new GridLayout(2, 3, 5, 5));
    add(new FigurePanel(FigurePanel.LINE));
    add(new FigurePanel(FigurePanel.RECTANGLE));
    add(new FigurePanel(FigurePanel.ROUND_RECTANGLE));
    add(new FigurePanel(FigurePanel.OVAL));
    add(new FigurePanel(FigurePanel.RECTANGLE, true));
```

```
    add(new FigurePanel(FigurePanel.ROUND_RECTANGLE, true));
  }

  public static void main(String[] args) {
    TestFigurePanel frame = new TestFigurePanel();
    frame.setSize(400, 200);
    frame.setTitle("TestFigurePanel");
    frame.setLocationRelativeTo(null); // Center the frame
    frame.setDefaultCloseOperation(JFrame.EXIT_ON_CLOSE);
    frame.setVisible(true);
  }
}
```

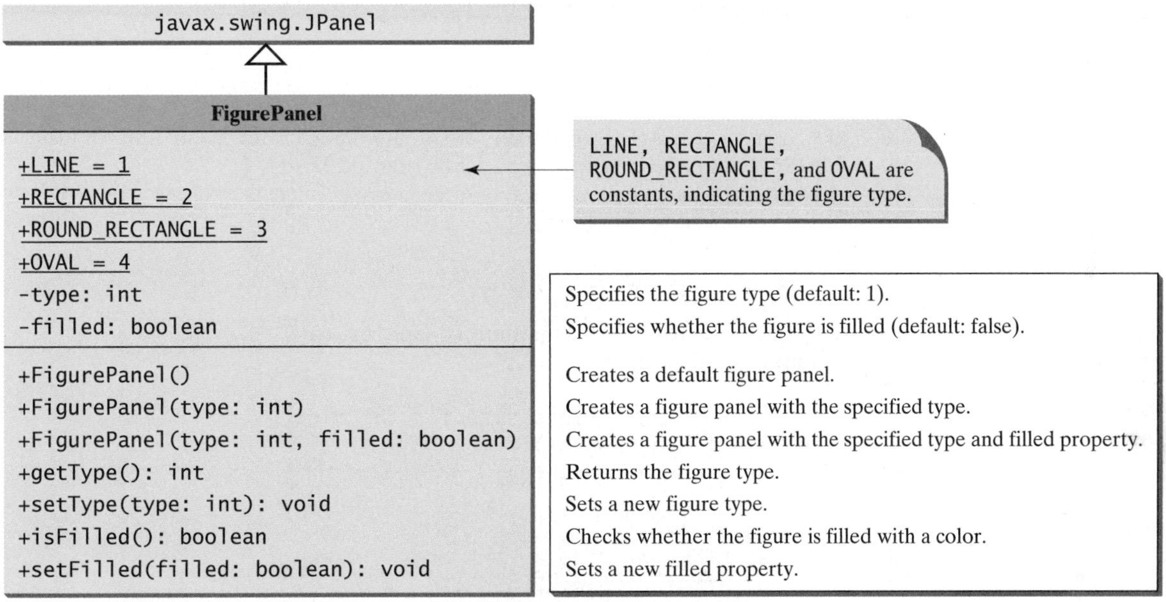

javax.swing.JPanel
FigurePanel
+LINE = 1
+RECTANGLE = 2
+ROUND_RECTANGLE = 3
+OVAL = 4
-type: int
-filled: boolean
+FigurePanel()
+FigurePanel(type: int)
+FigurePanel(type: int, filled: boolean)
+getType(): int
+setType(type: int): void
+isFilled(): boolean
+setFilled(filled: boolean): void
LINE, RECTANGLE, ROUND_RECTANGLE, and OVAL are constants, indicating the figure type.
Specifies the figure type (default: 1).
Specifies whether the figure is filled (default: false).
Creates a default figure panel.
Creates a figure panel with the specified type.
Creates a figure panel with the specified type and filled property.
Returns the figure type.
Sets a new figure type.
Checks whether the figure is filled with a color.
Sets a new filled property.

FIGURE 15.9 FigurePanel displays various types of figures on the panel.

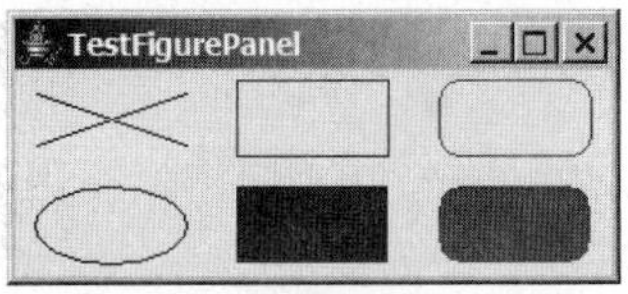

TestFigurePanel

FIGURE 15.10 Six FigurePanel objects are created to display six figures.

The FigurePanel class is implemented in Listing 15.3. Four constants—LINE, RECTANGLE, ROUND_RECTANGLE, and OVAL—are declared in lines 6–9. Four types of figures are drawn according to the type property (line 37). The setColor method (lines 39, 44, 53, 62) sets a new color for the drawing.

LISTING 15.3 FigurePanel.java

```
1 import java.awt.*;
2 import javax.swing.JPanel;
3
4 public class FigurePanel extends JPanel {
```

constants
override **paintComponent(g)**
check type
draw lines
fill a rectangle
draw a rectangle
fill round-cornered rect
draw round-cornered rect
fill an oval

```java
  // Define constants
  public static final int LINE = 1;
  public static final int RECTANGLE = 2;
  public static final int ROUND_RECTANGLE = 3;
  public static final int OVAL = 4;

  private int type = 1;
  private boolean filled = false;

  /** Construct a default FigurePanel */
  public FigurePanel() {
  }

  /** Construct a FigurePanel with the specified type */
  public FigurePanel(int type) {
    this.type = type;
  }

  /** Construct a FigurePanel with the specified type and filled */
  public FigurePanel(int type, boolean filled) {
    this.type = type;
    this.filled = filled;
  }

  /** Draw a figure on the panel */
  protected void paintComponent(Graphics g) {
    super.paintComponent(g);

    // Get the appropriate size for the figure
    int width = getWidth();
    int height = getHeight();

    switch (type) {
      case LINE: // Display two cross lines
        g.setColor(Color.BLACK);
        g.drawLine(10, 10, width - 10, height - 10);
        g.drawLine(width - 10, 10, 10, height - 10);
        break;
      case RECTANGLE: // Display a rectangle
        g.setColor(Color.BLUE);
        if (filled)
          g.fillRect((int)(0.1 * width), (int)(0.1 * height),
            (int)(0.8 * width), (int)(0.8 * height));
        else
          g.drawRect((int)(0.1 * width), (int)(0.1 * height),
            (int)(0.8 * width), (int)(0.8 * height));
        break;
      case ROUND_RECTANGLE: // Display a round-cornered rectangle
        g.setColor(Color.RED);
        if (filled)
          g.fillRoundRect((int)(0.1 * width), (int)(0.1 * height),
            (int)(0.8 * width), (int)(0.8 * height), 20, 20);
        else
          g.drawRoundRect((int)(0.1 * width), (int)(0.1 * height),
            (int)(0.8 * width), (int)(0.8 * height), 20, 20);
        break;
      case OVAL: // Display an oval
        g.setColor(Color.BLACK);
        if (filled)
          g.fillOval((int)(0.1 * width), (int)(0.1 * height),
```

```
65            (int)(0.8 * width), (int)(0.8 * height));
66        else
67          g.drawOval((int)(0.1 * width), (int)(0.1 * height),
68            (int)(0.8 * width), (int)(0.8 * height));
69      }
70    }
71
72    /** Set a new figure type */
73    public void setType(int type) {
74      this.type = type;
75      repaint();
76    }
77
78    /** Return figure type */
79    public int getType() {
80      return type;
81    }
82
83    /** Set a new filled property */
84    public void setFilled(boolean filled) {
85      this.filled = filled;
86      repaint();
87    }
88
89    /** Check if the figure is filled */
90    public boolean isFilled() {
91      return filled;
92    }
93
94    /** Specify preferred size */
95    public Dimension getPreferredSize() {
96      return new Dimension(80, 80);
97    }
98  }
```

draw an oval

repaint panel

repaint panel

override `getPreferredSize()`

The `repaint` method (lines 75, 86) is defined in the `Component` class. Invoking `repaint` causes the `paintComponent` method to be called. The `repaint` method is invoked to refresh the viewing area. Typically, you call it if you have new things to display.

Caution

The `paintComponent` method should never be invoked directly. It is invoked either by the JVM whenever the viewing area changes or by the `repaint` method. You should override the `paintComponent` method to tell the system how to paint the viewing area, but never override the `repaint` method.

don't invoke `paintComponent`

Note

The `repaint` method lodges a request to update the viewing area and returns immediately. Its effect is asynchronous, meaning that it is up to the JVM to execute the `paintComponent` method on a separate thread.

request repaint using `repaint()`

`getPreferedSize()`

The `getPreferredSize()` method (lines 95–97), defined in `Component`, is overridden in `FigurePanel` to specify the preferred size for the layout manager to consider when laying out a `FigurePanel` object. This property may or may not be considered by the layout manager, depending on its rules. For example, a component uses its preferred size in a container with a `FlowLayout` manager, but its preferred size may be ignored if it is placed in a container with a `GridLayout` manager. It is a good practice to override `getPreferredSize()` in a subclass of `JPanel` to specify a preferred size, because the default preferred size for a `JPanel` is `0` by `0`.

15.6 Drawing Arcs

An arc is conceived as part of an oval bounded by a rectangle. The methods to draw or fill an arc are as follows:

```
drawArc(int x, int y, int w, int h, int startAngle, int arcAngle);
fillArc(int x, int y, int w, int h, int startAngle, int arcAngle);
```

Parameters `x`, `y`, `w`, and `h` are the same as in the `drawOval` method; parameter `startAngle` is the starting angle; `arcAngle` is the spanning angle (i.e., the angle covered by the arc). Angles are measured in degrees and follow the usual mathematical conventions (i.e., `0` degrees is in the easterly direction, and positive angles indicate counterclockwise rotation from the easterly direction); see Figure 15.11.

Listing 15.4 is an example of how to draw arcs; the output is shown in Figure 15.12.

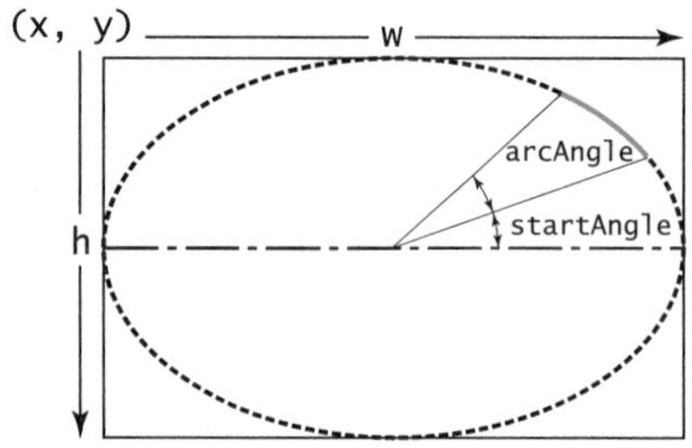
(x, y)
w
h
arcAngle
startAngle

FIGURE 15.11 The `drawArc` method draws an arc based on an oval with specified angles.

LISTING 15.4 DrawArcs.java

add a panel

override **paintComponent**

```
import javax.swing.JFrame;
import javax.swing.JPanel;
import java.awt.Graphics;

public class DrawArcs extends JFrame {
  public DrawArcs() {
    setTitle("DrawArcs");
    add(new ArcsPanel());
  }

  /** Main method */
  public static void main(String[] args) {
    DrawArcs frame = new DrawArcs();
    frame.setSize(250, 300);
    frame.setLocationRelativeTo(null); // Center the frame
    frame.setDefaultCloseOperation(JFrame.EXIT_ON_CLOSE);
    frame.setVisible(true);
  }
}

// The class for drawing arcs on a panel
class ArcsPanel extends JPanel {
  // Draw four blades of a fan
  protected void paintComponent(Graphics g) {
    super.paintComponent(g);

    int xCenter = getWidth() / 2;
    int yCenter = getHeight() / 2;
    int radius = (int)(Math.min(getWidth(), getHeight()) * 0.4);

```

```
    int x = xCenter - radius;
    int y = yCenter - radius;

    g.fillArc(x, y, 2 * radius, 2 * radius, 0, 30);
    g.fillArc(x, y, 2 * radius, 2 * radius, 90, 30);
    g.fillArc(x, y, 2 * radius, 2 * radius, 180, 30);
    g.fillArc(x, y, 2 * radius, 2 * radius, 270, 30);
  }
}
```

30° arc from 0°
30° arc from 90°
30° arc from 180°
30° arc from 270°

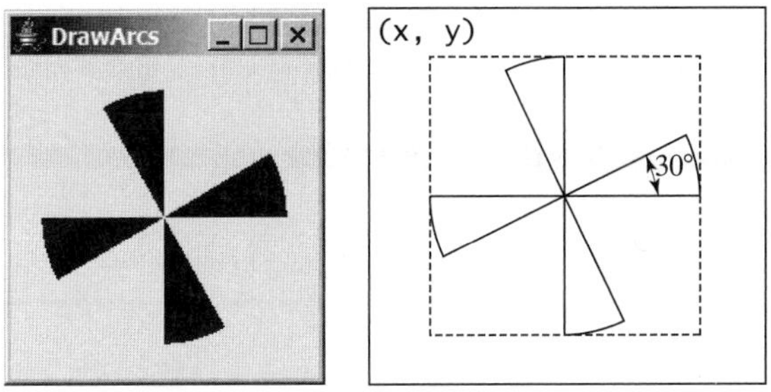
DrawArcs
(x, y)
30°

FIGURE 15.12 The program draws four filled arcs.

negative degrees

Angles may be negative. A negative starting angle sweeps clockwise from the easterly direction, as shown in Figure 15.13. A negative spanning angle sweeps clockwise from the starting angle. The following two statements draw the same arc:

```
g.fillArc(x, y, 2 * radius, 2 * radius, -30, -20);
g.fillArc(x, y, 2 * radius, 2 * radius, -50, 20);
```

The first statement uses negative starting angle `-30` and negative spanning angle `-20`, as shown in Figure 15.13(a). The second statement uses negative starting angle `-50` and positive spanning angle `20`, as shown in Figure 15.13(b).

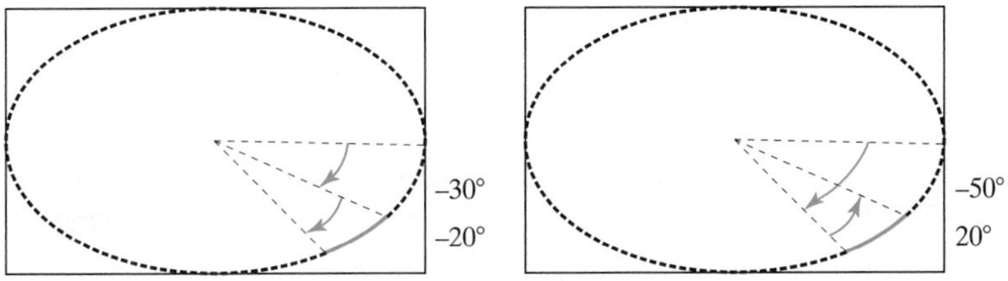
–30°
–20°
–50°
20°

(a) Negative starting angle –30° and negative spanning angle –20°

(b) Negative starting angle –50° and positive spanning angle 20°

FIGURE 15.13 Angles may be negative.

15.7 Drawing Polygons and Polylines

To draw a polygon, first create a `Polygon` object using the `Polygon` class, as shown in Figure 15.14.

A polygon is a closed two-dimensional region. This region is bounded by an arbitrary number of line segments, each being one side (or edge) of the polygon. A polygon comprises a list of `(x, y)`-coordinate pairs in which each pair defines a vertex of the polygon, and two successive pairs are the endpoints of a line that is a side of the polygon. The first and final points are joined by a line segment that closes the polygon.

Here is an example of creating a polygon and adding points into it:

```
Polygon polygon = new Polygon();
polygon.addPoint(40, 20);
```

```
polygon.addPoint(70, 40);
polygon.addPoint(60, 80);
polygon.addPoint(45, 45);
polygon.addPoint(20, 60);
```

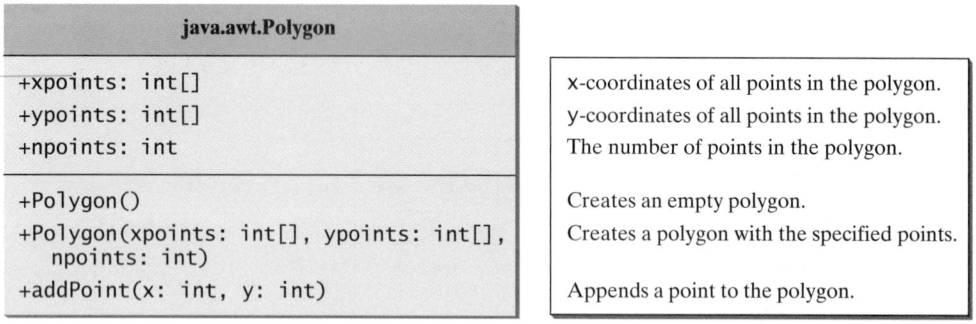
java.awt.Polygon
+xpoints: int[]
+ypoints: int[]
+npoints: int
+Polygon()
+Polygon(xpoints: int[], ypoints: int[], npoints: int)
+addPoint(x: int, y: int)
x-coordinates of all points in the polygon.
y-coordinates of all points in the polygon.
The number of points in the polygon.
Creates an empty polygon.
Creates a polygon with the specified points.
Appends a point to the polygon.

FIGURE 15.14 The `Polygon` class models a polygon.

After these points are added, `xpoints` is {40, 70, 60, 45, 20}, `ypoints` is {20, 40, 80, 45, 60}, and `npoints` is 5. `xpoints`, `ypoints`, and `npoints` are public data fields in `Polygon`, which is a bad design. In principle, all data fields should be kept private.

To draw or fill a polygon, use one of the following methods in the `Graphics` class:

```
drawPolygon(Polygon polygon);

fillPolygon(Polygon polygon);

drawPolygon(int[] xpoints, int[] ypoints, int npoints);

fillPolygon(int[] xpoints, int[] ypoints, int npoints);
```

For example:

```
int x[] = {40, 70, 60, 45, 20};
int y[] = {20, 40, 80, 45, 60};
g.drawPolygon(x, y, x.length);
```

The drawing method opens the polygon by drawing lines between point `(x[i], y[i])` and point `(x[i+1], y[i+1])` for `i = 0, ... , x.length-1`; it closes the polygon by drawing a line between the first and last points (see Figure 15.15(a)).

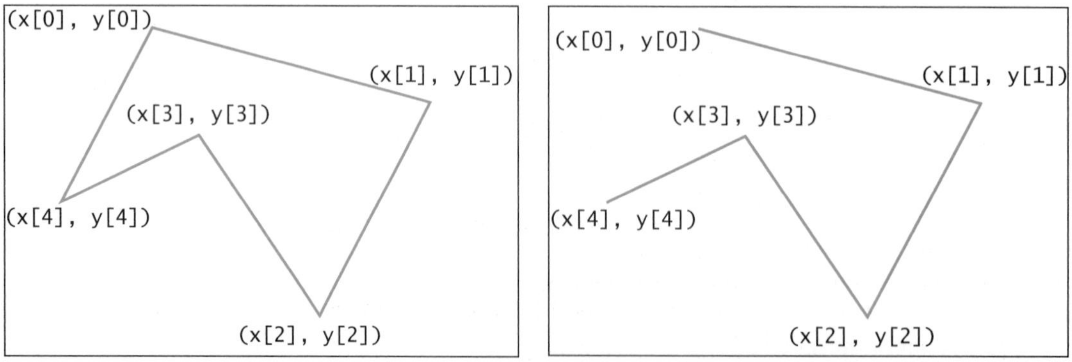
(x[0], y[0])
(x[1], y[1])
(x[3], y[3])
(x[4], y[4])
(x[2], y[2])
(x[0], y[0])
(x[1], y[1])
(x[3], y[3])
(x[4], y[4])
(x[2], y[2])

(a) Polygon (b) Polyline

FIGURE 15.15 The `drawPolygon` method draws a polygon, and the `polyLine` method draws a polyline.

To draw a polyline, use the `drawPolyline(int[] x, int[] y, int nPoints)` method, which draws a sequence of connected lines defined by arrays of `x`- and `y`-coordinates. For example, the following code draws the polyline, as shown in Figure 15.15(b).

```
int x[] = {40, 70, 60, 45, 20};
int y[] = {20, 40, 80, 45, 60};
g.drawPolyline(x, y, x.length);
```

Listing 15.5 is an example of how to draw a hexagon, with the output shown in Figure 15.16.

LISTING 15.5 DrawPolygon.java

```
import javax.swing.JFrame;
import javax.swing.JPanel;
import java.awt.Graphics;
import java.awt.Polygon;

public class DrawPolygon extends JFrame {
  public DrawPolygon() {
    setTitle("DrawPolygon");
    add(new PolygonsPanel());
  }

  /** Main method */
  public static void main(String[] args) {
    DrawPolygon frame = new DrawPolygon();
    frame.setSize(200, 250);
    frame.setLocationRelativeTo(null); // Center the frame
    frame.setDefaultCloseOperation(JFrame.EXIT_ON_CLOSE);
    frame.setVisible(true);
  }
}

// Draw a polygon in the panel
class PolygonsPanel extends JPanel {
  protected void paintComponent(Graphics g) {
    super.paintComponent(g);

    int xCenter = getWidth() / 2;
    int yCenter = getHeight() / 2;
    int radius = (int)(Math.min(getWidth(), getHeight()) * 0.4);

    // Create a Polygon object
    Polygon polygon = new Polygon();

    // Add points to the polygon in this order
    polygon.addPoint(xCenter + radius, yCenter);
    polygon.addPoint((int)(xCenter + radius *
      Math.cos(2 * Math.PI / 6)), (int)(yCenter - radius *
      Math.sin(2 * Math.PI / 6)));
    polygon.addPoint((int)(xCenter + radius *
      Math.cos(2 * 2 * Math.PI / 6)), (int)(yCenter - radius *
      Math.sin(2 * 2 * Math.PI / 6)));
    polygon.addPoint((int)(xCenter + radius *
      Math.cos(3 * 2 * Math.PI / 6)), (int)(yCenter - radius *
      Math.sin(3 * 2 * Math.PI / 6)));
    polygon.addPoint((int)(xCenter + radius *
      Math.cos(4 * 2 * Math.PI / 6)), (int)(yCenter - radius *
      Math.sin(4 * 2 * Math.PI / 6)));
    polygon.addPoint((int)(xCenter + radius *
```

add a panel

`paintComponent`

add a point

```
        Math.cos(5 * 2 * Math.PI / 6)), (int)(yCenter - radius *
        Math.sin(5 * 2 * Math.PI / 6)));

      // Draw the polygon
      g.drawPolygon(polygon);
    }
  }
```

draw polygon

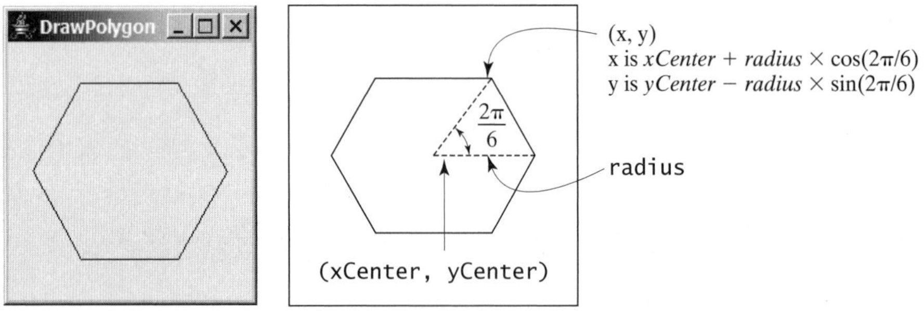
DrawPolygon
(x, y)
x is *xCenter* + *radius* × cos(2π/6)
y is *yCenter* − *radius* × sin(2π/6)
2π
6
radius
(xCenter, yCenter)

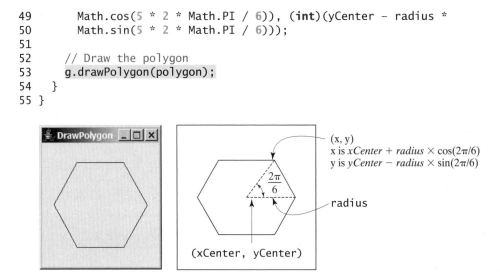

FIGURE 15.16 The program uses the `drawPolygon` method to draw a polygon.

15.8 Centering a String Using the FontMetrics Class

You can display a string at any location in a panel. Can you display it centered? To do so, you need to use the `FontMetrics` class to measure the exact width and height of the string for a particular font. `FontMetrics` can measure the following attributes for a given font (see Figure 15.17):

- **Leading,** pronounced *ledding*, is the amount of space between lines of text.
- **Ascent** is the distance from the baseline to the ascent line. The top of most characters in the font will be under the ascent line, but some may extend above the ascent line.
- **Descent** is the distance from the baseline to the descent line. The bottom of most descending characters (e.g., *j*, *y*, and *g*) in the font will be above the descent line, but some may extend below the descent line.
- **Height** is the sum of leading, ascent, and descent.

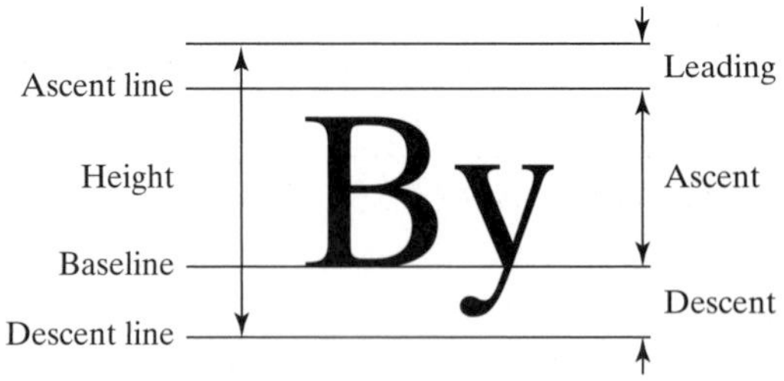
Ascent line
Height
Baseline
Descent line
By
Leading
Ascent
Descent

FIGURE 15.17 The `FontMetrics` class can be used to determine the font properties of characters for a given font.

`FontMetrics` is an abstract class. To get a `FontMetrics` object for a specific font, use the following `getFontMetrics` methods defined in the `Graphics` class:

- **`public FontMetrics getFontMetrics(Font font)`**
  Returns the font metrics of the specified font.
- **`public FontMetrics getFontMetrics()`**
  Returns the font metrics of the current font.

You can use the following instance methods in the FontMetrics class to obtain the attributes of a font and the width of a string when it is drawn using the font:

```
public int getAscent() // Return the ascent
public int getDescent() // Return the descent
public int getLeading() // Return the leading
public int getHeight() // Return the height
public int stringWidth(String str) // Return the width of the string
```

Listing 15.6 gives an example that displays a message in the center of the panel, as shown in Figure 15.18.

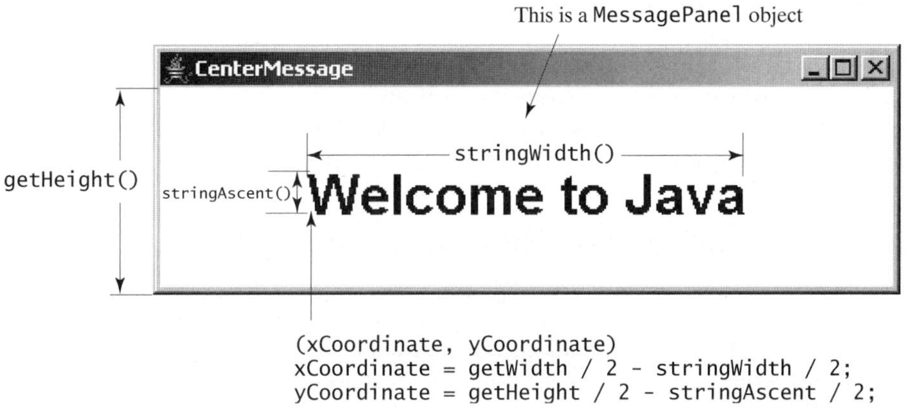
This is a MessagePanel object
CenterMessage
stringWidth()
getHeight()
stringAscent()
Welcome to Java
(xCoordinate, yCoordinate)
xCoordinate = getWidth / 2 - stringWidth / 2;
yCoordinate = getHeight / 2 - stringAscent / 2;

FIGURE 15.18 The program uses the FontMetrics class to measure the string width and height and displays it at the center of the panel.

LISTING 15.6 TestCenterMessage.java

```
import javax.swing.*;
import java.awt.*;

public class TestCenterMessage extends JFrame{
  public TestCenterMessage() {
    CenterMessage messagePanel = new CenterMessage();
    add(messagePanel);
    messagePanel.setBackground(Color.WHITE);
    messagePanel.setFont(new Font("Californian FB", Font.BOLD, 30));
  }

  /** Main method */
  public static void main(String[] args) {
    TestCenterMessage frame = new TestCenterMessage();
    frame.setSize(300, 150);
    frame.setLocationRelativeTo(null); // Center the frame
    frame.setDefaultCloseOperation(JFrame.EXIT_ON_CLOSE);
    frame.setVisible(true);
  }
}

class CenterMessage extends JPanel {
  /** Paint the message */
  protected void paintComponent(Graphics g) {
    super.paintComponent(g);
```

create a message panel
add a message panel
set background
set font
override **paintComponent**

get **FontMetrics**

```
26
27      // Get font metrics for the current font
28      FontMetrics fm = g.getFontMetrics();
29
30      // Find the center location to display
31      int stringWidth = fm.stringWidth("Welcome to Java");
32      int stringAscent = fm.getAscent();
33
34      // Get the position of the leftmost character in the baseline
35      int xCoordinate = getWidth() / 2 - stringWidth / 2;
36      int yCoordinate = getHeight() / 2 + stringAscent / 2;
37
38      g.drawString("Welcome to Java", xCoordinate, yCoordinate);
39    }
40  }
```

The methods `getWidth()` and `getHeight()` (lines 35–36) defined in the `Component` class return the component's width and height, respectively.

Since the message is `centered`, the first character of the string should be positioned at (`xCoordinate`, `yCoordinate`), as shown in Figure 15.18.

15.9 Case Study: The `MessagePanel` Class

Video Note
The **MessagePanel** class

This case study develops a useful class that displays a message in a panel. The class enables the user to set the location of the message, center the message, and move the message with the specified interval. The contract of the class is shown in Figure 15.19.

Let us first write a test program in Listing 15.7 that uses the `MessagePanel` class to display four message panels, as shown in Figure 15.20.

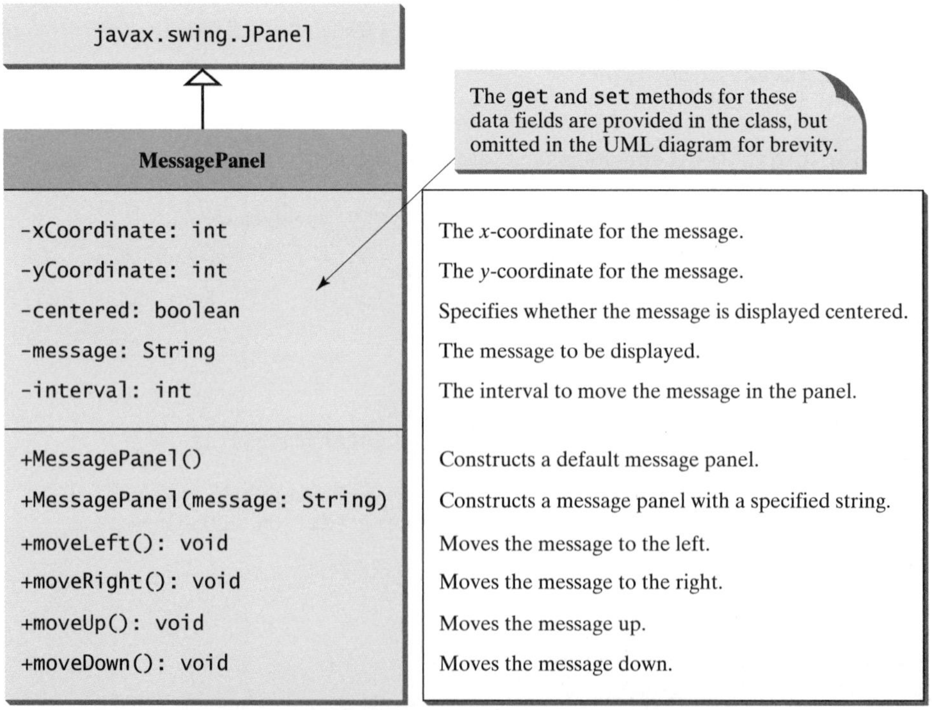
javax.swing.JPanel
MessagePanel
The get and set methods for these data fields are provided in the class, but omitted in the UML diagram for brevity.
-xCoordinate: int
-yCoordinate: int
-centered: boolean
-message: String
-interval: int
+MessagePanel()
+MessagePanel(message: String)
+moveLeft(): void
+moveRight(): void
+moveUp(): void
+moveDown(): void
The x-coordinate for the message.
The y-coordinate for the message.
Specifies whether the message is displayed centered.
The message to be displayed.
The interval to move the message in the panel.
Constructs a default message panel.
Constructs a message panel with a specified string.
Moves the message to the left.
Moves the message to the right.
Moves the message up.
Moves the message down.

FIGURE 15.19 `MessagePanel` displays a message on the panel.

TestMessagePanel
Wecome to Java
Java is fun
Java is cool
I love Java

FIGURE 15.20 `TestMessagePanel` uses `MessagePanel` to display four message panels.

LISTING 15.7 TestMessagePanel.java

```java
import java.awt.*;
import javax.swing.*;

public class TestMessagePanel extends JFrame {
  public TestMessagePanel() {
    MessagePanel messagePanel1 = new MessagePanel("Wecome to Java");
    MessagePanel messagePanel2 = new MessagePanel("Java is fun");
    MessagePanel messagePanel3 = new MessagePanel("Java is cool");
    MessagePanel messagePanel4 = new MessagePanel("I love Java");
    messagePanel1.setFont(new Font("SansSerif", Font.ITALIC, 20));
    messagePanel2.setFont(new Font("Courier", Font.BOLD, 20));
    messagePanel3.setFont(new Font("Times", Font.ITALIC, 20));
    messagePanel4.setFont(new Font("Californian FB", Font.PLAIN, 20));
    messagePanel1.setBackground(Color.RED);
    messagePanel2.setBackground(Color.CYAN);
    messagePanel3.setBackground(Color.GREEN);
    messagePanel4.setBackground(Color.WHITE);
    messagePanel1.setCentered(true);

    setLayout(new GridLayout(2, 2));
    add(messagePanel1);
    add(messagePanel2);
    add(messagePanel3);
    add(messagePanel4);
  }

  public static void main(String[] args) {
    TestMessagePanel frame = new TestMessagePanel();
    frame.setSize(300, 200);
    frame.setTitle("TestMessagePanel");
    frame.setLocationRelativeTo(null); // Center the frame
    frame.setDefaultCloseOperation(JFrame.EXIT_ON_CLOSE);
    frame.setVisible(true);
  }
}
```

create message panel
set font
set background
add message panel

The rest of this section explains how to implement the `MessagePanel` class. Since you can use the class without knowing how it is implemented, you may skip the implementation if you wish.

skip implementation?

The `MessagePanel` class is implemented in Listing 15.8. The program seems long but is actually simple, because most of the methods are `get` and `set` methods, and each method is relatively short and easy to read.

LISTING 15.8 MessagePanel.java

```java
import java.awt.FontMetrics;
import java.awt.Dimension;
import java.awt.Graphics;
```

```java
import javax.swing.JPanel;

public class MessagePanel extends JPanel {
  /** The message to be displayed */
  private String message = "Welcome to Java";

  /** The x-coordinate where the message is displayed */
  private int xCoordinate = 20;

  /** The y-coordinate where the message is displayed */
  private int yCoordinate = 20;

  /** Indicate whether the message is displayed in the center */
  private boolean centered;

  /** The interval for moving the message horizontally and
    vertically */
  private int interval = 10;

  /** Construct with default properties */
  public MessagePanel() {
  }

  /** Construct a message panel with a specified message */
  public MessagePanel(String message) {
    this.message = message;
  }

  /** Return message */
  public String getMessage() {
    return message;
  }

  /** Set a new message */
  public void setMessage(String message) {
    this.message = message;
    repaint();
  }

  /** Return xCoordinator */
  public int getXCoordinate() {
    return xCoordinate;
  }

  /** Set a new xCoordinator */
  public void setXCoordinate(int x) {
    this.xCoordinate = x;
    repaint();
  }

  /** Return yCoordinator */
  public int getYCoordinate() {
    return yCoordinate;
  }

  /** Set a new yCoordinator */
  public void setYCoordinate(int y) {
    this.yCoordinate = y;
```

repaint panel

repaint panel

```
    repaint();
  }

  /** Return centered */
  public boolean isCentered() {
    return centered;
  }

  /** Set a new centered */
  public void setCentered(boolean centered) {
    this.centered = centered;
    repaint();
  }

  /** Return interval */
  public int getInterval() {
    return interval;
  }

  /** Set a new interval */
  public void setInterval(int interval) {
    this.interval = interval;
    repaint();
  }

  /** Paint the message */
  protected void paintComponent(Graphics g) {
    super.paintComponent(g);

    if (centered) {
      // Get font metrics for the current font
      FontMetrics fm = g.getFontMetrics();

      // Find the center location to display
      int stringWidth = fm.stringWidth(message);
      int stringAscent = fm.getAscent();
      // Get the position of the leftmost character in the baseline
      xCoordinate = getWidth() / 2 - stringWidth / 2;
      yCoordinate = getHeight() / 2 + stringAscent / 2;
    }

    g.drawString(message, xCoordinate, yCoordinate);
  }

  /** Move the message left */
  public void moveLeft() {
    xCoordinate -= interval;
    repaint();
  }

  /** Move the message right */
  public void moveRight() {
    xCoordinate += interval;
    repaint();
  }

  /** Move the message up */
  public void moveUp() {
    yCoordinate -= interval;
```

repaint panel

repaint panel

repaint panel

override **paintComponent**

check centered

override getPreferredSize

```
121       repaint();
122     }
123
124     /** Move the message down */
125     public void moveDown() {
126       yCoordinate += interval;
127       repaint();
128     }
129
130     /** Override get method for preferredSize */
131     public Dimension getPreferredSize() {
132       return new Dimension(200, 30);
133     }
134   }
```

The `paintComponent` method displays the message centered, if the `centered` property is `true` (line 91). `message` is initialized to "Welcome to Java" in line 8. If it were not initialized, a `NullPointerException` runtime error would occur when you created a `MessagePanel` using the no-arg constructor, because `message` would be `null` in line 103.

Caution

The `MessagePanel` class uses the properties `xCoordinate` and `yCoordinate` to specify the position of the message displayed on the panel. Do not use the property names `x` and `y`, because they are already defined in the `Component` class to return the position of the component in the parent's coordinate system using `getX()` and `getY()`.

Note

The `Component` class has the `setBackground`, `setForeground`, and `setFont` methods. These methods are for setting colors and fonts for the entire component. Suppose you want to draw several messages in a panel with different colors and fonts; you have to use the `setColor` and `setFont` methods in the `Graphics` class to set the color and font for the current drawing.

design classes for reuse

Note

A key feature of Java programming is the reuse of classes. Throughout this book, reusable classes are developed and later reused. `MessagePanel` is an example, as are `Loan` in Listing 10.2 and `FigurePanel` in Listing 15.3. `MessagePanel` can be reused whenever you need to display a message on a panel. To make your class reusable in a wide range of applications, you should provide a variety of ways to use it. `MessagePanel` provides many properties and methods that will be used in several examples in the book. The next section presents a useful and reusable class for displaying a clock on a panel graphically.

15.10 Case Study: The `StillClock` Class

Video Note
The **StillClock** class

This case study develops a class that displays a clock on a panel. The contract of the class is shown in Figure 15.21.

Let us first write a test program in Listing 15.9 that uses the `StillClock` class to display an analog clock and uses the `MessagePanel` class to display the hour, minute, and second in a panel, as shown in Figure 15.22(a).

LISTING 15.9 DisplayClock.java

```
import java.awt.*;
import javax.swing.*;

public class DisplayClock extends JFrame {
  public DisplayClock() {
```

```
    // Create an analog clock for the current time
    StillClock clock = new StillClock();

    // Display hour, minute, and second in the message panel
    MessagePanel messagePanel = new MessagePanel(clock.getHour() +
      ":" + clock.getMinute() + ":" + clock.getSecond());
    messagePanel.setCentered(true);
    messagePanel.setForeground(Color.blue);
    messagePanel.setFont(new Font("Courier", Font.BOLD, 16));

    // Add the clock and message panel to the frame
    add(clock);
    add(messagePanel, BorderLayout.SOUTH);
  }

  public static void main(String[] args) {
    DisplayClock frame = new DisplayClock();
    frame.setTitle("DisplayClock");
    frame.setSize(300, 350);
    frame.setLocationRelativeTo(null); // Center the frame
    frame.setDefaultCloseOperation(JFrame.EXIT_ON_CLOSE);
    frame.setVisible(true);
  }
}
```

create a clock

create a message panel

add a clock

add a message panel

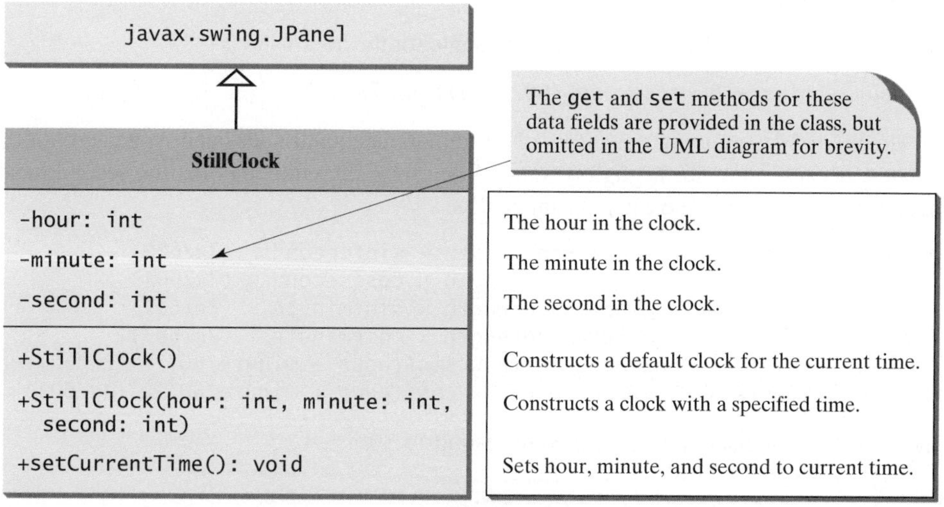
javax.swing.JPanel
StillClock
-hour: int
-minute: int
-second: int
+StillClock()
+StillClock(hour: int, minute: int, second: int)
+setCurrentTime(): void
The get and set methods for these data fields are provided in the class, but omitted in the UML diagram for brevity.
The hour in the clock.
The minute in the clock.
The second in the clock.
Constructs a default clock for the current time.
Constructs a clock with a specified time.
Sets hour, minute, and second to current time.

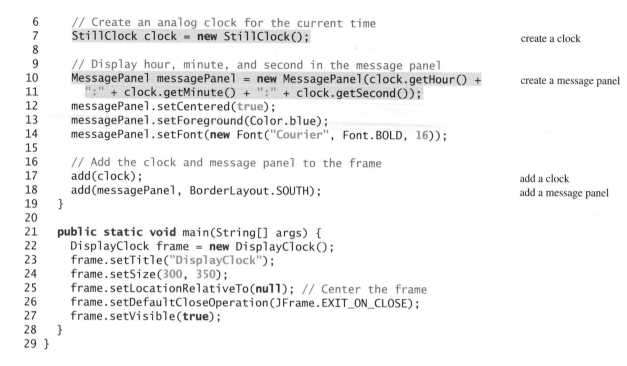

FIGURE 15.21 `StillClock` displays an analog clock.

The rest of this section explains how to implement the `StillClock` class. Since you can use the class without knowing how it is implemented, you may skip the implementation if you wish.

skip implementation?

implementation

To draw a clock, you need to draw a circle and three hands for second, minute, and hour. To draw a hand, you need to specify the two ends of the line. As shown in Figure 15.22(b), one end is the center of the clock at `(xCenter, yCenter)`; the other end, at `(xEnd, yEnd)`, is determined by the following formula:

```
xEnd = xCenter + handLength × sin(θ)
yEnd = yCenter - handLength × cos(θ)
```

Since there are 60 seconds in one minute, the angle for the second hand is

```
second × (2π/60)
```

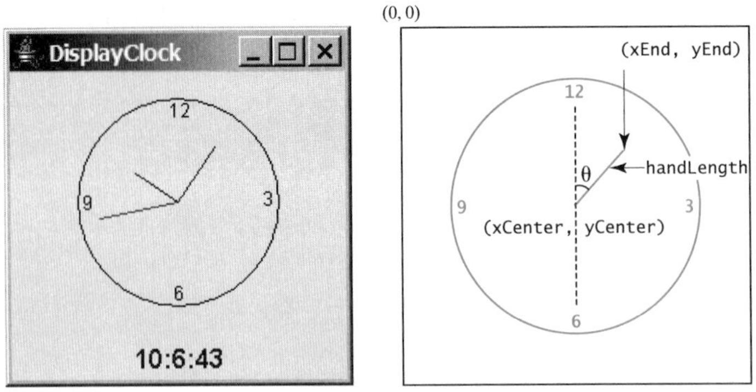
DisplayClock
12
9
3
6
10:6:43
(0, 0)
(xEnd, yEnd)
12
θ
handLength
9
3
(xCenter, yCenter)
6

(a) (b)

FIGURE 15.22 (a) The DisplayClock program displays a clock that shows the current time. (b) The endpoint of a clock hand can be determined, given the spanning angle, the hand length, and the center point.

The position of the minute hand is determined by the minute and second. The exact minute value combined with seconds is `minute + second/60`. For example, if the time is 3 minutes and 30 seconds, the total minutes are 3.5. Since there are 60 minutes in one hour, the angle for the minute hand is

```
(minute + second/60) × (2π/60)
```

Since one circle is divided into 12 hours, the angle for the hour hand is

```
(hour + minute/60 + second/(60 × 60)) × (2π/12)
```

For simplicity in computing the angles of the minute hand and hour hand, you can omit the seconds, because they are negligibly small. Therefore, the endpoints for the second hand, minute hand, and hour hand can be computed as:

```
xSecond = xCenter + secondHandLength × sin(second × (2π/60))
ySecond = yCenter - secondHandLength × cos(second × (2π/60))
xMinute = xCenter + minuteHandLength × sin(minute × (2π/60))
yMinute = yCenter - minuteHandLength × cos(minute × (2π/60))
xHour = xCenter + hourHandLength × sin((hour + minute/60) × (2π/60))
yHour = yCenter - hourHandLength × cos((hour + minute/60) × (2π/60))
```

The `StillClock` class is implemented in Listing 15.10.

LISTING 15.10 StillClock.java

```
import java.awt.*;
import javax.swing.*;
import java.util.*;

public class StillClock extends JPanel {
  private int hour;
  private int minute;
  private int second;

  /** Construct a default clock with the current time*/
  public StillClock() {
    setCurrentTime();
  }

  /** Construct a clock with specified hour, minute, and second */
```

```
  public StillClock(int hour, int minute, int second) {
    this.hour = hour;
    this.minute = minute;
    this.second = second;
  }

  /** Return hour */
  public int getHour() {
    return hour;
  }

  /** Set a new hour */
  public void setHour(int hour) {
    this.hour = hour;
    repaint();
  }

  /** Return minute */
  public int getMinute() {
    return minute;
  }

  /** Set a new minute */
  public void setMinute(int minute) {
    this.minute = minute;
    repaint();
  }

  /** Return second */
  public int getSecond() {
    return second;
  }

  /** Set a new second */
  public void setSecond(int second) {
    this.second = second;
    repaint();
  }

  /** Draw the clock */
  protected void paintComponent(Graphics g) {
    super.paintComponent(g);

    // Initialize clock parameters
    int clockRadius =
      (int)(Math.min(getWidth(), getHeight()) * 0.8 * 0.5);
    int xCenter = getWidth() / 2;
    int yCenter = getHeight() / 2;

    // Draw circle
    g.setColor(Color.BLACK);
    g.drawOval(xCenter - clockRadius, yCenter - clockRadius,
      2 * clockRadius, 2 * clockRadius);
    g.drawString("12", xCenter - 5, yCenter - clockRadius + 12);
    g.drawString("9", xCenter - clockRadius + 3, yCenter + 5);
    g.drawString("3", xCenter + clockRadius - 10, yCenter + 3);
    g.drawString("6", xCenter - 3, yCenter + clockRadius - 3);

    // Draw second hand
    int sLength = (int)(clockRadius * 0.8);
```

repaint panel

repaint panel

repaint panel

override **paintComponent**

```
76      int xSecond = (int)(xCenter + sLength *
77        Math.sin(second * (2 * Math.PI / 60)));
78      int ySecond = (int)(yCenter - sLength *
79        Math.cos(second * (2 * Math.PI / 60)));
80      g.setColor(Color.red);
81      g.drawLine(xCenter, yCenter, xSecond, ySecond);
82
83      // Draw minute hand
84      int mLength = (int)(clockRadius * 0.65);
85      int xMinute = (int)(xCenter + mLength *
86        Math.sin(minute * (2 * Math.PI / 60)));
87      int yMinute = (int)(yCenter - mLength *
88        Math.cos(minute * (2 * Math.PI / 60)));
89      g.setColor(Color.blue);
90      g.drawLine(xCenter, yCenter, xMinute, yMinute);
91
92      // Draw hour hand
93      int hLength = (int)(clockRadius * 0.5);
94      int xHour = (int)(xCenter + hLength *
95        Math.sin((hour % 12 + minute / 60.0) * (2 * Math.PI / 12)));
96      int yHour = (int)(yCenter - hLength *
97        Math.cos((hour % 12 + minute / 60.0) * (2 * Math.PI / 12)));
98      g.setColor(Color.green);
99      g.drawLine(xCenter, yCenter, xHour, yHour);
100   }
101
102   public void setCurrentTime() {
103     // Construct a calendar for the current date and time
104     Calendar calendar = new GregorianCalendar();
105
106     // Set current hour, minute and second
107     this.hour = calendar.get(Calendar.HOUR_OF_DAY);
108     this.minute = calendar.get(Calendar.MINUTE);
109     this.second = calendar.get(Calendar.SECOND);
110   }
111
112   public Dimension getPreferredSize() {
113     return new Dimension(200, 200);
114   }
115 }
```

get current time

override **getPreferredSize**

The program enables the clock size to adjust as the frame resizes. Every time you resize the frame, the `paintComponent` method is automatically invoked to paint the new frame. The `paintComponent` method displays the clock in proportion to the panel width (`getWidth()`) and height (`getHeight()`) (lines 60–63 in `StillClock`).

15.11 Displaying Images

You learned how to create image icons and display them in labels and buttons in §12.10, "Image Icons." For example, the following statements create an image icon and display it in a label:

```
ImageIcon icon = new ImageIcon("image/us.gif");
JLabel jlblImage = new JLabel(imageIcon);
```

An image icon displays a fixed-size image. To display an image in a flexible size, you need to use the `java.awt.Image` class. An image can be created from an image icon using the `getImage()` method as follows:

```
Image image = imageIcon.getImage();
```

Using a label as an area for displaying images is simple and convenient, but you don't have much control over how the image is displayed. A more flexible way to display images is to use the **drawImage** method of the **Graphics** class on a panel. Four versions of the **drawImage** method are shown in Figure 15.23.

java.awt.Graphics	
+drawImage(image: Image, x: int, y: int, bgcolor: Color, observer: ImageObserver): void	Draws the image in a specified location. The image's top-left corner is at (*x*, *y*) in the graphics context's coordinate space. Transparent pixels in the image are drawn in the specified color bgcolor. The observer is the object on which the image is displayed. The image is cut off if it is larger than the area it is being drawn on.
+drawImage(image: Image, x: int, y: int, observer: ImageObserver): void	Same as the preceding method except that it does not specify a background color.
+drawImage(image: Image, x: int, y: int, width: int, height: int, observer: ImageObserver): void	Draws a scaled version of the image that can fill all of the available space in the specified rectangle.
+drawImage(image: Image, x: int, y: int, width: int, height: int, bgcolor: Color, observer: ImageObserver): void	Same as the preceding method except that it provides a solid background color behind the image being drawn.

FIGURE 15.23 You can apply the **drawImage** method on a **Graphics** object to display an image in a GUI component.

ImageObserver specifies a GUI component for receiving notifications of image information as the image is constructed. To draw images using the **drawImage** method in a Swing component, such as **JPanel**, override the **paintComponent** method to tell the component how to display the image in the panel.

Listing 15.11 gives the code that displays an image from **image/us.gif**. The file **image/us.gif** (line 20) is under the class directory. An **Image** object is obtained in line 21. The **drawImage** method displays the image to fill in the whole panel, as shown in Figure 15.24.

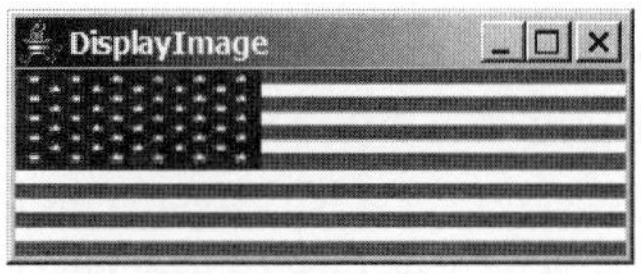
DisplayImage

FIGURE 15.24 An image is displayed in a panel.

LISTING 15.11 DisplayImage.java

```
1 import java.awt.*;
2 import javax.swing.*;
3
4 public class DisplayImage extends JFrame {
5   public DisplayImage() {
6     add(new ImagePanel());
7   }
8
9   public static void main(String[] args) {
10    JFrame frame = new DisplayImage();
11    frame.setTitle("DisplayImage");
12    frame.setSize(300, 300);
13    frame.setLocationRelativeTo(null); // Center the frame
14    frame.setDefaultCloseOperation(JFrame.EXIT_ON_CLOSE);
```

add panel

panel class
create image icon
get image
override **paintComponent**
draw image

```
    frame.setVisible(true);
  }
}

class ImagePanel extends JPanel {
  private ImageIcon imageIcon = new ImageIcon("image/us.gif");
  private Image image = imageIcon.getImage();

  /** Draw image on the panel */
  protected void paintComponent(Graphics g) {
    super.paintComponent(g);

    if (image != null)
      g.drawImage(image, 0, 0, getWidth(), getHeight(), this);
  }
}
```

15.12 Case Study: The `ImageViewer` Class

Displaying an image is a common task in Java programming. This case study develops a reusable component named `ImageViewer` that displays an image on a panel. The class contains the properties `image`, `stretched`, `xCoordinate`, and `yCoordinate`, with associated accessor and mutator methods, as shown in Figure 15.25.

stretchable image

You can use images in Swing components such as `JLabel` and `JButton`, but these images are not stretchable. The image in an `ImageViewer` can be stretched.

Let us write a test program in Listing 15.12 that displays six images using the `ImageViewer` class. Figure 15.26 shows a sample run of the program.

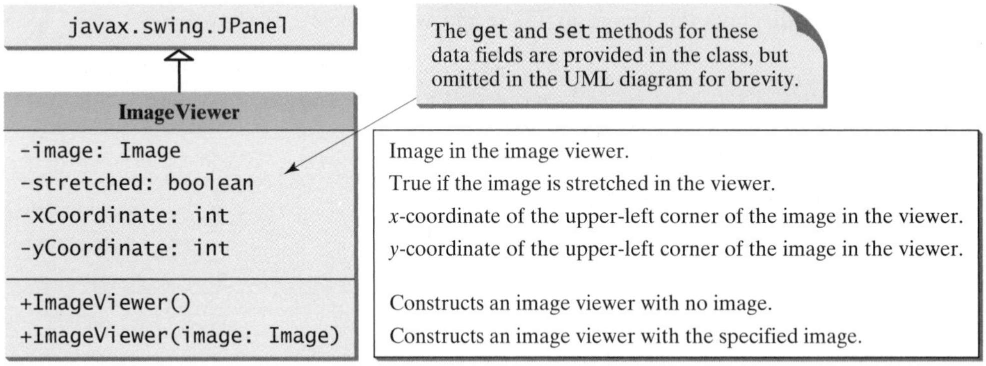
javax.swing.JPanel
The get and set methods for these data fields are provided in the class, but omitted in the UML diagram for brevity.
ImageViewer
-image: Image
-stretched: boolean
-xCoordinate: int
-yCoordinate: int
+ImageViewer()
+ImageViewer(image: Image)
Image in the image viewer.
True if the image is stretched in the viewer.
x-coordinate of the upper-left corner of the image in the viewer.
y-coordinate of the upper-left corner of the image in the viewer.
Constructs an image viewer with no image.
Constructs an image viewer with the specified image.

FIGURE 15.25 The `ImageViewer` class displays an image on a panel.

SixFlags

FIGURE 15.26 Six images are displayed in six `ImageViewer` components.

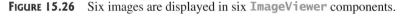

Listing 15.12 SixFlags.java

```
import javax.swing.*;
import java.awt.*;

public class SixFlags extends JFrame {
  public SixFlags() {
    Image image1 = new ImageIcon("image/us.gif").getImage();
    Image image2 = new ImageIcon("image/ca.gif").getImage();
    Image image3 = new ImageIcon("image/india.gif").getImage();
    Image image4 = new ImageIcon("image/uk.gif").getImage();
    Image image5 = new ImageIcon("image/china.gif").getImage();
    Image image6 = new ImageIcon("image/norway.gif").getImage();

    setLayout(new GridLayout(2, 0, 5, 5));
    add(new ImageViewer(image1));
    add(new ImageViewer(image2));
    add(new ImageViewer(image3));
    add(new ImageViewer(image4));
    add(new ImageViewer(image5));
    add(new ImageViewer(image6));
  }

  public static void main(String[] args) {
    SixFlags frame = new SixFlags();
    frame.setTitle("SixFlags");
    frame.setSize(400, 320);
    frame.setLocationRelativeTo(null); // Center the frame
    frame.setDefaultCloseOperation(JFrame.EXIT_ON_CLOSE);
    frame.setVisible(true);
  }
}
```

create image

create image viewer

The `ImageViewer` class is implemented in Listing 15.13. (*Note: You may skip the implementation.*) The accessor and mutator methods for the properties `image`, `stretched`, `xCoordinate`, and `yCoordinate` are easy to implement. The `paintComponent` method (lines 26–35) displays the image on the panel. Line 29 ensures that the image is not `null` before displaying it. Line 30 checks whether the image is stretched or not.

implementation

skip implementation?

Listing 15.13 ImageViewer.java

```
 1 import java.awt.*;
 2 import javax.swing.*;
 3
 4 public class ImageViewer extends JPanel {
 5   /** Hold value of property image. */
 6   private java.awt.Image image;
 7
 8   /** Hold value of property stretched. */
 9   private boolean stretched = true;
10
11   /** Hold value of property xCoordinate. */
12   private int xCoordinate;
13
14   /** Hold value of property yCoordinate. */
15   private int yCoordinate;
16
```

properties

constructor

```
  /** Construct an empty image viewer */
  public ImageViewer() {
  }

  /** Construct an image viewer for a specified Image object */
```

constructor

```
  public ImageViewer(Image image) {
    this.image = image;
  }

  protected void paintComponent(Graphics g) {
    super.paintComponent(g);

```

image null?

```
    if (image != null)
      if (isStretched())
```

stretched

```
        g.drawImage(image, xCoordinate, yCoordinate,
          getWidth(), getHeight(), this);
      else
```

nonstretched

```
        g.drawImage(image, xCoordinate, yCoordinate, this);
  }

  /** Return value of property image */
  public java.awt.Image getImage() {
    return image;
  }

  /** Set a new value for property image */
  public void setImage(java.awt.Image image) {
    this.image = image;
    repaint();
  }

  /** Return value of property stretched */
  public boolean isStretched() {
    return stretched;
  }

  /** Set a new value for property stretched */
  public void setStretched(boolean stretched) {
    this.stretched = stretched;
    repaint();
  }

  /** Return value of property xCoordinate */
  public int getXCoordinate() {
    return xCoordinate;
  }

  /** Set a new value for property xCoordinate */
  public void setXCoordinate(int xCoordinate) {
    this.xCoordinate = xCoordinate;
    repaint();
  }

  /** Return value of property yCoordinate */
  public int getYCoordinate() {
    return yCoordinate;
  }

  /** Set a new value for property yCoordinate */
```

```
  public void setYCoordinate(int yCoordinate) {
    this.yCoordinate = yCoordinate;
    repaint();
  }
}
```

Chapter Summary

1. Each component has its own coordinate system with the origin (0, 0) at the upper-left corner of the window. The *x*-coordinate increases to the right, and the *y*-coordinate increases downward.

2. The Graphics class is an abstract class for displaying figures and images on the screen on different platforms. The Graphics class is implemented on the native platform in the JVM. When you use the paintComponent(g) method to paint on a GUI component, this g is an instance of a concrete subclass of the abstract Graphics class for the specific platform. The Graphics class encapsulates the platform details and enables you to draw things uniformly without concern for the specific platform.

3. Invoking super.paintComponent(g) is necessary to ensure that the viewing area is cleared before a new drawing is displayed. The user can request the component to be redisplayed by invoking the repaint() method defined in the Component class. Invoking repaint() causes paintComponent to be invoked by the JVM. The user should never invoke paintComponent directly. For this reason, the protected visibility is sufficient for paintComponent.

4. Normally you use JPanel as a canvas. To draw on a JPanel, you create a new class that extends JPanel and overrides the paintComponent method to tell the panel how to draw things.

5. You can set fonts for the components or subjects you draw, and use font metrics to measure font size. Fonts and font metrics are encapsulated in the classes Font and FontMetrics. FontMetrics can be used to compute the exact length and width of a string, which is helpful for measuring the size of a string in order to display it in the right position.

6. The Component class has the setBackground, setForeground, and setFont methods. These methods are used to set colors and fonts for the entire component. Suppose you want to draw several messages in a panel with different colors and fonts; you have to use the setColor and setFont methods in the Graphics class to set the color and font for the current drawing.

7. To display an image, first create an image icon. You can then use ImageIcon's getImage() method to get an Image object for the image and draw the image using the drawImage method in the java.awt.Graphics class.

Review Questions

Sections 15.2–15.3

15.1 Suppose that you want to draw a new message below an existing message. Should the x-coordinate, y-coordinate, or both increase or decrease?

15.2 Why is the Graphics class abstract? How is a Graphics object created?

15.3 Describe the paintComponent method. Where is it defined? How is it invoked? Can it be directly invoked? How can a program cause this method to be invoked?

15.4 Why is the `paintComponent` method `protected`? What happens if you change it to `public` or `private` in a subclass? Why is `super.paintComponent(g)` invoked in line 21 in Listing 15.1 and in line 31 in Listing 15.3?

15.5 Can you draw things on any Swing GUI component? Why should you use a panel as a canvas for drawings rather than a label or a button?

Sections 15.4-15.7

15.6 Describe the methods for drawing strings, lines, rectangles, round-cornered rectangles, 3D rectangles, ovals, arcs, polygons, and polylines.

15.7 Describe the methods for filling rectangles, round-cornered rectangle, ovals, arcs, and polygons.

15.8 How do you `get` and `set` colors and fonts in a `Graphics` object?

15.9 Write a statement to draw the following shapes:

- Draw a thick line from (10, 10) to (70, 30). You can draw several lines next to each other to create the effect of one thick line.
- Draw/fill a rectangle of width 100 and height 50 with the upper-left corner at (10, 10).
- Draw/fill a round-cornered rectangle with width 100, height 200, corner horizontal diameter 40, and corner vertical diameter 20.
- Draw/fill a circle with radius 30.
- Draw/fill an oval with width 50 and height 100.
- Draw the upper half of a circle with radius 50.
- Draw/fill a polygon connecting the following points: (20, 40), (30, 50), (40, 90), (90, 10), (10, 30).

Sections 15.8–15.10

15.10 How do you find the leading, ascent, descent, and height of a font? How do you find the exact length in pixels of a string in a `Graphics` object?

15.11 If `message` is not initialized in line 8 in Listing 15.8, MessagePanel.java, what will happen when you create a `MessagePanel` using its no-arg constructor?

15.12 The following program is supposed to display a message on a panel, but nothing is displayed. There are problems in lines 2 and 14. Correct them.

```
1 public class TestDrawMessage extends javax.swing.JFrame {
2   public void TestDrawMessage() {
3     add(new DrawMessage());
4   }
5
6   public static void main(String[] args) {
7     javax.swing.JFrame frame = new TestDrawMessage();
8     frame.setSize(100, 200);
9     frame.setVisible(true);
10  }
11 }
12
13 class DrawMessage extends javax.swing.JPanel {
14   protected void PaintComponent(java.awt.Graphics g) {
15     super.paintComponent(g);
16     g.drawString("Welcome to Java", 20, 20);
17   }
18 }
```

Sections 15.11–15.12

15.13 How do you create an `Image` object from the `ImageIcon` object?

15.14 How do you create an `ImageIcon` object from an `Image` object?

15.15 Describe the `drawImage` method in the `Graphics` class.

15.16 Explain the differences between displaying images in a `JLabel` and in a `JPanel`.

15.17 Which package contains `ImageIcon`, and which contains `Image`?

Programming Exercises

Sections 15.2–15.7

15.1* (*Displaying a 3 × 3 grid*) Write a program that displays a 3 × 3 grid, as shown in Figure 15.27(a). Use red color for vertical lines and blue for horizontals.

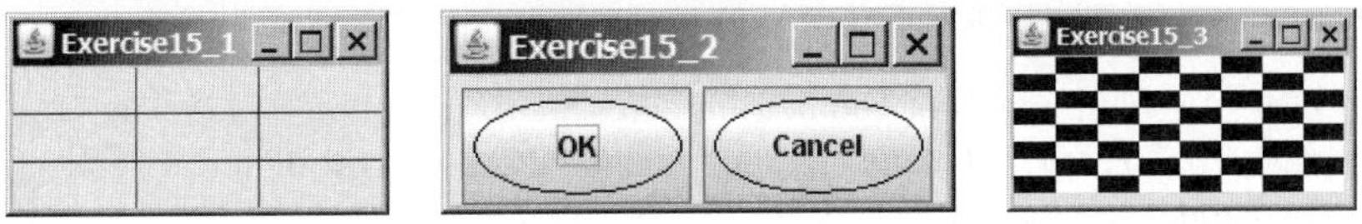
Exercise15_1
Exercise15_2
OK
Cancel
Exercise15_3

(a) (b) (c)

Figure 15.27 (a) Exercise 15.1 displays a grid. (b) Exercise 15.2 displays two objects of `OvalButton`. (c) Exercise 15.3 displays a checkerboard.

15.2** (*Creating a custom button class*) Develop a custom button class named `OvalButton` that extends `JButton` and displays the button text inside an oval. Figure 15.27(b) shows two buttons created using the `OvalButton` class.

15.3* (*Displaying a checkerboard*) Exercise 12.10 displays a checkerboard in which each white and black cell is a `JButton`. Rewrite a program that draws a checkerboard on a `JPanel` using the drawing methods in the `Graphics` class, as shown in Figure 15.27(c).

15.4* (*Displaying a multiplication table*) Write a program that displays a multiplication table in a panel using the drawing methods, as shown in Figure 15.28(a).

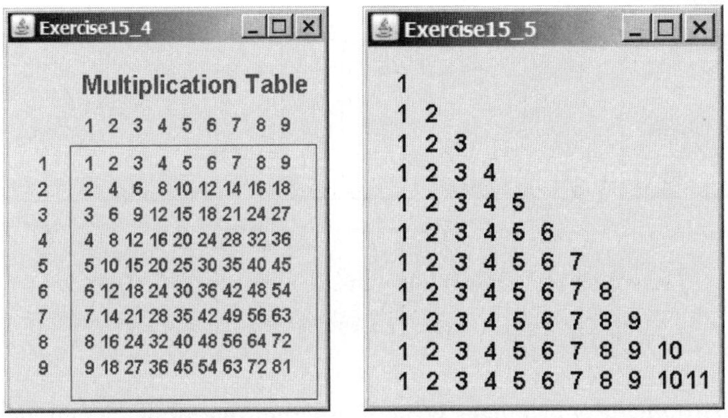
Exercise15_4
Multiplication Table
1 2 3 4 5 6 7 8 9
1 1 2 3 4 5 6 7 8 9
2 2 4 6 8 10 12 14 16 18
3 3 6 9 12 15 18 21 24 27
4 4 8 12 16 20 24 28 32 36
5 5 10 15 20 25 30 35 40 45
6 6 12 18 24 30 36 42 48 54
7 7 14 21 28 35 42 49 56 63
8 8 16 24 32 40 48 56 64 72
9 9 18 27 36 45 54 63 72 81
Exercise15_5
1
1 2
1 2 3
1 2 3 4
1 2 3 4 5
1 2 3 4 5 6
1 2 3 4 5 6 7
1 2 3 4 5 6 7 8
1 2 3 4 5 6 7 8 9
1 2 3 4 5 6 7 8 9 10
1 2 3 4 5 6 7 8 9 1011

(a) (b)

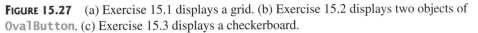

Figure 15.28 (a) Exercise 15.4 displays a multiplication table. (b) Exercise 15.5 displays numbers in a triangle formation.

15.5** (*Displaying numbers in a triangular pattern*) Write a program that displays numbers in a triangular pattern, as shown in Figure 15.28(b). The number of lines in the display changes to fit the window as the window resizes.

15.6** (*Improving `FigurePanel`*) The `FigurePanel` class in Listing 15.3 can display lines, rectangles, round-cornered rectangles, and ovals. Add appropriate new code in the class to display arcs and polygons. Write a test program to display the shapes as shown in Figure 15.29(a) using the new `FigurePanel` class.

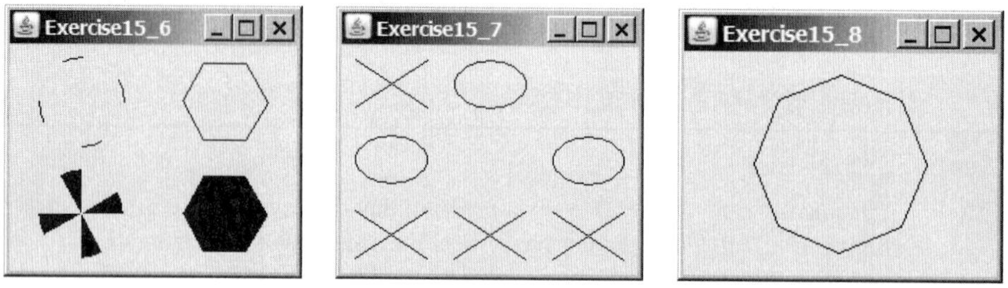
Exercise15_6
Exercise15_7
Exercise15_8

(a) (b) (c)

FIGURE 15.29 (a) Four panels of geometric figures are displayed in a frame of `GridLayout`. (b) `TicTacToe` cells randomly display X, O, or nothing. (c) Exercise 15.8 draws an octagon.

15.7** (*Displaying a TicTacToe board*) Create a custom panel that displays `X`, `O`, or nothing. What to display is randomly decided whenever a panel is repainted. Use the `Math.random()` method to generate an integer `0`, `1`, or `2`, which corresponds to displaying `X`, `O`, or nothing. Create a frame that contains nine custom panels, as shown in Figure 15.29(b).

15.8** (*Drawing an octagon*) Write a program that draws an octagon, as shown in Figure 15.29(c).

15.9* (*Creating four fans*) Write a program that places four fans in a frame of `GridLayout` with two rows and two columns, as shown in Figure 15.30(a).

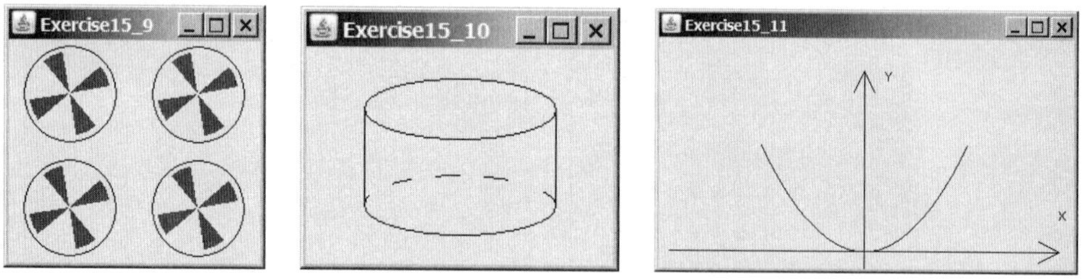
Exercise15_9
Exercise15_10
Exercise15_11
Y
X

(a) (b) (c)

FIGURE 15.30 (a) Exercise 15.9 draws four fans. (b) Exercise 15.10 draws a cylinder. (c) Exercise 15.11 draws a diagram for function $f(x) = x^2$.

15.10* (*Displaying a cylinder*) Write a program that draws a cylinder, as shown in Figure 15.30(b).

15.11** (*Plotting the square function*) Write a program that draws a diagram for the function $f(x) = x^2$ (see Figure 15.30(c)).

Hint: Add points to a polygon `p` using the following loop:

```
double scaleFactor = 0.1;

for (int x = -100; x <= 100; x++) {
  p.addPoint(x + 200, 200 - (int)(scaleFactor * x * x));
}
```

Connect the points using **g.drawPolyline(p.xpoints, p.ypoints, p.npoints)** for a **Graphics** object **g**. **p.xpoints** returns an array of **x**-coordinates, **p.ypoints** an array of **y**-coordinates, and **p.npoints** the number of points in **Polygon** object **p**.

15.12** (*Plotting the sine function*) Write a program that draws a diagram for the sine function, as shown in Figure 15.31(a).

Video Note
Plot a sine function

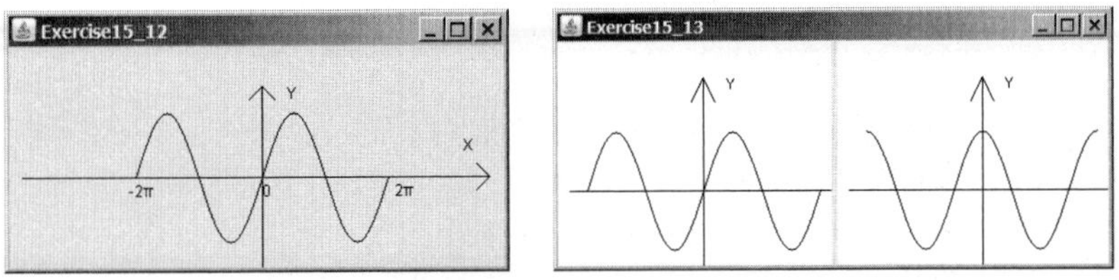

Exercise15_12
Y
X
-2π
0
2π
Exercise15_13
Y
Y

(a) (b)

FIGURE 15.31 (a) Exercise 15.12 draws a diagram for function $f(x) = sin(x)$. (b) Exercise 15.13 draws the sine and cosine functions.

Hint: The Unicode for π is **\u03c0**. To display -2π, use **g.drawString("-2\u03c0", x, y)**. For a trigonometric function like **sin(x)**, **x** is in radians. Use the following loop to add the points to a polygon **p**:

```
for (int x = -100; x <= 100; x++) {
  p.addPoint(x + 200,
    100 - (int)(50 * Math.sin((x / 100.0) * 2 * Math.PI)));
}
```

-2π is at (**100**, **100**), the center of the axis is at (**200**, **100**), and 2π is at (**300**, **100**). Use the **drawPolyline** method in the **Graphics** class to connect the points.

15.13** (*Plotting functions using abstract methods*) Write an abstract class that draws the diagram for a function. The class is defined as follows:

```
public abstract class AbstractDrawFunction extends JPanel {
  /** Polygon to hold the points */
  private Polygon p = new Polygon();

  protected AbstractDrawFunction () {
    drawFunction();
  }

  /** Return the y-coordinate */
  abstract double f(double x);

  /** Obtain points for x-coordinates 100, 101, ..., 300 */
  public void drawFunction() {
    for (int x = -100; x <= 100; x++) {
      p.addPoint(x + 200, 200 - (int)f(x));
    }
  }

  /** Implement paintComponent to draw axes, labels, and
   *  connecting points
   */
  protected void paintComponent(Graphics g) {
    // To be completed by you
  }
}
```

Test the class with the following functions:

```
f(x) = x²;
f(x) = sin(x);
f(x) = cos(x);
f(x) = tan(x);
f(x) = cos(x) + 5sin(x);
f(x) = 5cos(x) + sin(x);
f(x) = log(x) + x²;
```

For each function, create a class that extends the `AbstractDrawFunction` class and implements the `f` method. Figure 15.31(b) displays the drawings for the sine function and the cosine function.

15.14** (*Displaying a bar chart*) Write a program that uses a bar chart to display the percentages of the overall grade represented by projects, quizzes, midterm exams, and the final exam, as shown in Figure 15.1(a). Suppose that projects take `20` percent and are displayed in red, quizzes take `10` percent and are displayed in blue, midterm exams take `30` percent and are displayed in green, and the final exam takes `40` percent and is displayed in orange.

15.15** (*Displaying a pie chart*) Write a program that uses a pie chart to display the percentages of the overall grade represented by projects, quizzes, midterm exam, and the final exam, as shown in Figure 15.32(a). Suppose that projects take `20` percent and are displayed in red, quizzes take `10` percent and are displayed in blue, midterm exam takes `30` percent and are displayed in green, and the final exam takes `40` percent and is displayed in orange.

15.16 (*Obtaining font information*) Write a program that displays the message "Java is fun" in a panel. Set the panel's font to `TimesRoman`, `bold`, and `20` pixel. Display the font's leading, ascent, descent, height, and the string width as a tool tip text for the panel, as shown in Figure 15.32(b).

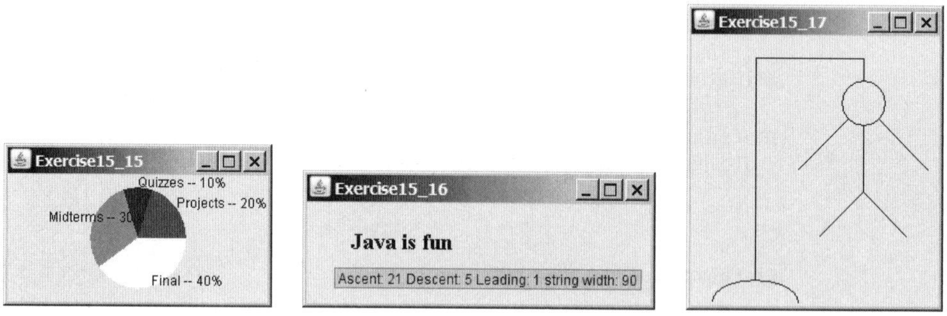
Exercise15_15
Quizzes -- 10%
Projects -- 20%
Midterms -- 30%
Final -- 40%
Exercise15_16
Java is fun
Ascent: 21 Descent: 5 Leading: 1 string width: 90
Exercise15_17

(a) (b) (c)

FIGURE 15.32 (a) Exercise 15.15 uses a pie chart to show the percentages of projects, quizzes, midterm exam, and final exam in the overall grade. (b) Exercise 15.16 displays font properties in a tool tip text. (c) Exercise 15.17 draws a sketch for the hangman game.

15.17 (*Game: hangman*) Write a program that displays a drawing for the popular hangman game, as shown in Figure 15.32(c).

15.18 (*Using the `StillClock` class*) Write a program that displays two clocks. The hour, minute, and second values are `4`, `20`, `45` for the first clock and `22`, `46`, `15` for the second clock, as shown in Figure 15.33(a).

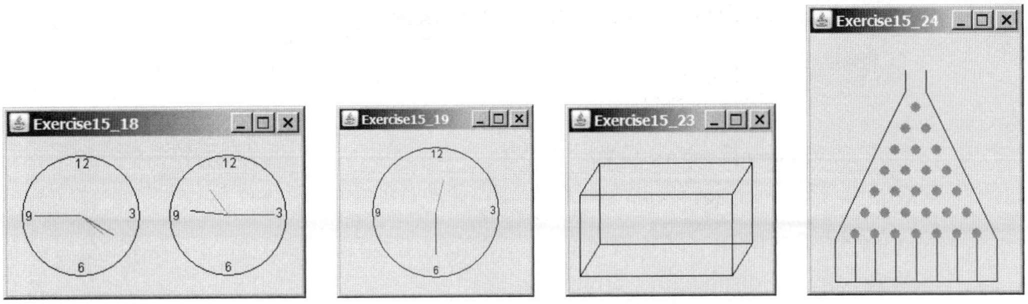
Exercise15_18
12
9
3
6
12
9
3
6
Exercise15_19
12
9
3
6
Exercise15_23
Exercise15_24

(a) (b) (c) (d)

FIGURE 15.33 (a) Exercise 15.18 displays two clocks. (b) Exercise 15.19 displays a clock with random hour and minute values. (c) Exercise 15.23 displays a rectanguloid. (d) Exercise 15.24 simulates a bean machine.

15.19* (*Random time*) Modify the `StillClock` class with three new Boolean properties—`hourHandVisible`, `minuteHandVisible`, and `secondHandVisible`—and their associated accessor and mutator methods. You can use the `set` methods to make a hand visible or invisible. Write a test program that displays only the hour and minute hands. The hour and minute values are randomly generated. The hour is between `0` and `11`, and the minute is either `0` or `30`, as shown in Figure 15.33(b).

15.20** (*Drawing a detailed clock*) Modify the `StillClock` class in §15.12, "Case Study: The `StillClock` Class," to draw the clock with more details on the hours and minutes, as shown in Figure 15.1(b).

15.21** (*Displaying a TicTacToe board with images*) Rewrite Exercise 12.7 to display an image in a `JPanel` instead of displaying an image icon in a `JLabel`.

15.22** (*Displaying a STOP sign*) Write a program that displays a STOP sign, as shown in Figure 15.1(c). The hexagon is in red and the sign is in white.

(*Hint*: See Listing 15.5, DrawPolygon.java, and Listing 15.6, TestCenterMessage.java.)

15.23 (*Displaying a rectanguloid*) Write a program that displays a rectanguloid, as shown in Figure 15.33(c). The cube should grow and shrink as the frame grows or shrinks.

15.24** (*Game: bean machine*) Write a program that displays a bean machine introduced in Exercise 6.21. The bean machine should be centered in a resizable panel, as shown in Figure 15.33(d).

15.25** (*Geometry: displaying an n-sided regular polygon*) Create a subclass of `JPanel`, named `RegularPolygonPanel`, to paint an *n*-sided regular polygon. The class contains a property named `numberOfSides`, which specifies the number of sides in the polygon. The polygon is centered at the center of the panel. The size of the polygon is proportional to the size of the panel. Create a pentagon, hexagon, heptagon, and octagon, nonagon, and decagon from `RegularPolygonPanel` and display them in a frame, as shown in Figure 15.34(a).

15.26 (*Using the `MessagePanel` class*) Write a program that displays four messages, as shown in Figure 15.34(b).

15.27** (*Displaying a graph*) A graph consists of vertices and edges that connect vertices. Write a program that reads a graph from a file and displays it on a panel. The first line in the file contains a number that indicates the number of vertices (`n`). The vertices are labeled as `0`, `1`, ..., `n-1`. Each subsequent line, with the

Exercise15_25
(a)
Exercise15_26
HTML
Java
Tomcat
PHP
(b)

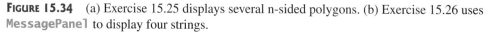

FIGURE 15.34 (a) Exercise 15.25 displays several n-sided polygons. (b) Exercise 15.26 uses `MessagePanel` to display four strings.

format `u x y v1, v2, ...`, describes that the vertex `u` is located at position (`x`, `y`) with edges (`u`, `v1`), (`u`, `v2`), etc. Figure 15.35(a) gives an example of the file for a graph. Your program prompts the user to enter the name of the file, reads data from the file, and displays the graph on a panel, as shown in Figure 15.35(b).

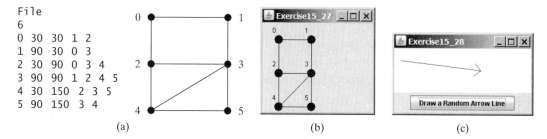

```
File
6
0 30  30  1 2
1 90  30  0 3
2 30  90  0 3 4
3 90  90  1 2 4 5
4 30  150  2 3 5
5 90  150  3 4
```

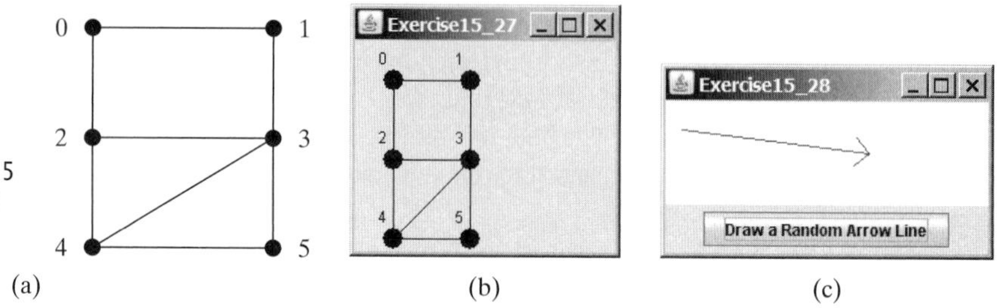
0
1
2
3
4
5
(a)
Exercise15_27
0
1
2
3
4
5
(b)
Exercise15_28
Draw a Random Arrow Line
(c)

FIGURE 15.35 (a)-(b) The program reads the information about the graph and displays it visually. (c) The program displays an arrow line.

15.28** (*Drawing an arrow line*) Write a static method that draws an arrow line from a starting point to an ending point using the following method header:

```
public static void drawArrowLine(int x1, int y1,
  int x2, int y2, Graphics g)
```

Write a test program that randomly draws an arrow line when the *Draw Random Arrow Line* button is clicked, as shown in Figure 15.35(c).

CHAPTER 16

EVENT-DRIVEN PROGRAMMING

Objectives

- To describe events, event sources, and event classes (§16.2).
- To define listener classes, register listener objects with the source object, and write the code to handle events (§16.3).
- To define listener classes using inner classes (§16.4).
- To define listener classes using anonymous inner classes (§16.5).
- To explore various coding styles for creating and registering listeners (§16.6).
- To get input from text field upon clicking a button (§16.7).
- To write programs to deal with `WindowEvent` (§16.8).
- To simplify coding for listener classes using listener interface adapters (§16.9).
- To write programs to deal with `MouseEvent` (§16.10).
- To write programs to deal with `KeyEvent` (§16.11).
- To use the `javax.swing.Timer` class to control animations (§16.12).

16.1 Introduction

problem

Suppose you wish to write a GUI program that lets the user enter the loan amount, annual interest rate, and number of years and click the *Compute Loan* button to obtain the monthly payment and total payment, as shown in Figure 16.1(a). How do you accomplish the task? You have to use event-driven programming to write the code to respond to the button-clicking event.

LoanCalculator
Enter loan amount, interest rate, and year
Annual Interest Rate 4.5
Number of Years 4
Loan Amount 5000
Monthly Payment 114.02
Total Payment 5472.84
Compute Payment
Exercise16_14
Exercise16_14
Exercise16_14
(a)
(b)
(c)
(d)

FIGURE 16.1 (a) The program computes loan payments. (b)–(d) A flag is rising upward.

problem

Suppose you wish to write a program that animates a rising flag, as shown in Figure 16.1(b)–(d). How do you accomplish the task? There are several ways to solve this problem. An effective one is to use a timer in event-driven programming, which is the subject of this chapter.

In event-driven programming, code is executed when an event occurs (e.g., a button click, a mouse movement, or a timer). §14.6, "Example: The `ActionListener` Interface," gave you a taste of event-driven programming. You probably have many questions, such as why a listener class is defined to implement the `ActionListener` interface. This chapter will give you all the answers.

16.2 Event and Event Source

event

When you run a Java GUI program, the program interacts with the user, and the events drive its execution. An *event* can be defined as a signal to the program that something has happened. Events are triggered either by external user actions, such as mouse movements, button clicks, and keystrokes, or by internal program activities, such as a timer. The program can choose to respond to or ignore an event.

fire event
source object

The component that creates an event and fires it is called the *source object* or *source component*. For example, a button is the source object for a button-clicking action event. An event is an instance of an event class. The root class of the event classes is `java.util.EventObject`. The hierarchical relationships of some event classes are shown in Figure 16.2.

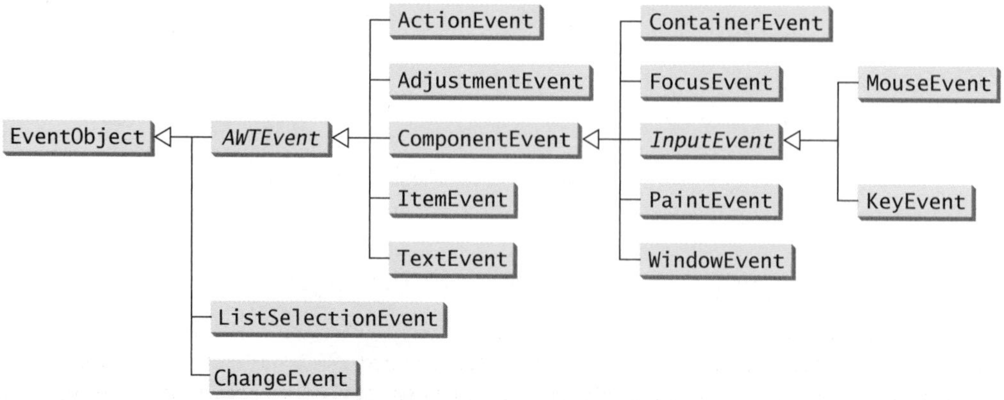
EventObject
AWTEvent
ActionEvent
AdjustmentEvent
ComponentEvent
ItemEvent
TextEvent
ListSelectionEvent
ChangeEvent
ContainerEvent
FocusEvent
InputEvent
PaintEvent
WindowEvent
MouseEvent
KeyEvent

FIGURE 16.2 An event is an object of the `EventObject` class.

An event object contains whatever properties are pertinent to the event. You can identify the source object of an event using the **getSource()** instance method in the **EventObject** class. The subclasses of **EventObject** deal with special types of events, such as action events, window events, component events, mouse events, and key events. Table 16.1 lists external user actions, source objects, and event types fired.

getSource()

TABLE 16.1 User Action, Source Object, and Event Type

User Action	*Source Object*	*Event Type Fired*
Click a button	**JButton**	**ActionEvent**
Press return on a text field	**JTextField**	**ActionEvent**
Select a new item	**JComboBox**	**ItemEvent, ActionEvent**
Select item(s)	**JList**	**ListSelectionEvent**
Click a check box	**JCheckBox**	**ItemEvent, ActionEvent**
Click a radio button	**JRadioButton**	**ItemEvent, ActionEvent**
Select a menu item	**JMenuItem**	**ActionEvent**
Move the scroll bar	**JScrollBar**	**AdjustmentEvent**
Move the scroll bar	**JSlider**	**ChangeEvent**
Window opened, closed, iconified, deiconified, or closing	**Window**	**WindowEvent**
Mouse pressed, released, clicked, entered, or exited	**Component**	**MouseEvent**
Mouse moved or dragged	**Component**	**MouseEvent**
Key released or pressed	**Component**	**KeyEvent**
Component added or removed from the container	**Container**	**ContainerEvent**
Component moved, resized, hidden, or shown	**Component**	**ComponentEvent**
Component gained or lost focus	**Component**	**FocusEvent**

Note

If a component can fire an event, any subclass of the component can fire the same type of event. For example, every GUI component can fire **MouseEvent**, **KeyEvent**, **FocusEvent**, and **ComponentEvent**, since **Component** is the superclass of all GUI components.

Note

All the event classes in Figure 16.2 are included in the **java.awt.event** package except **ListSelectionEvent** and **ChangeEvent**, which are in the **javax.swing.event** package. AWT events were originally designed for AWT components, but many Swing components fire them.

16.3 Listeners, Registrations, and Handling Events

Java uses a delegation-based model for event handling: a source object fires an event, and an object interested in the event handles it. The latter object is called a *listener*. For an object to be a listener for an event on a source object, two things are needed, as shown in Figure 16.3.

listener

ActionEvent/ActionListener

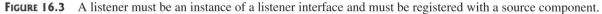

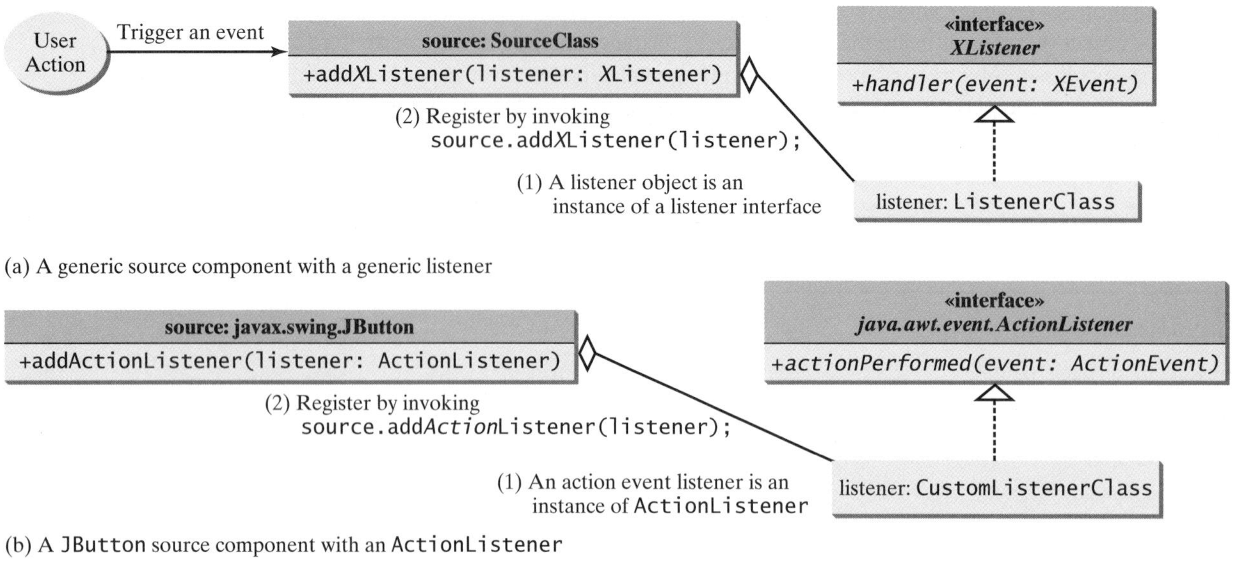
User Action
Trigger an event
source: SourceClass
+addXListener(listener: XListener)
«interface»
XListener
+handler(event: XEvent)
(2) Register by invoking
source.addXListener(listener);
(1) A listener object is an
instance of a listener interface
listener: ListenerClass
(a) A generic source component with a generic listener
source: javax.swing.JButton
+addActionListener(listener: ActionListener)
«interface»
java.awt.event.ActionListener
+actionPerformed(event: ActionEvent)
(2) Register by invoking
source.addActionListener(listener);
(1) An action event listener is an
instance of ActionListener
listener: CustomListenerClass
(b) A JButton source component with an ActionListener

FIGURE 16.3 A listener must be an instance of a listener interface and must be registered with a source component.

listener interface
*X*Listener/*X*Event
handler

1. The listener object must be an instance of the corresponding event-listener interface to ensure that the listener has the correct method for processing the event. Java provides a listener interface for every type of event. The listener interface is usually named `XListener` for `XEvent`, with the exception of `MouseMotionListener`. For example, the corresponding listener interface for `ActionEvent` is `ActionListener`; each listener for `ActionEvent` should implement the `ActionListener` interface. Table 16.2 lists event types, the corresponding listener interfaces, and the methods defined in the listener interfaces. The listener interface contains the method(s), known as the *handler(s)*, for processing the event.

register listener

2. The listener object must be registered by the source object. Registration methods depend on the event type. For `ActionEvent`, the method is `addActionListener`. In general, the method is named `addXListener` for `XEvent`. A source object may fire several types of events. It maintains, for each event, a list of registered listeners and notifies them by invoking the *handler* of the listener object to respond to the event, as shown in Figure 16.4. (Figure 16.4 shows the internal implementation of a source class. You don't have to know how a source class such as `JButton` is implemented in order to use it. Nevertheless, this knowledge will help you to understand the Java event-driven programming framework).

Let's revisit Listing 14.8, HandleEvent.java. Since a `JButton` object fires `ActionEvent`, a listener object for `ActionEvent` must be an instance of `ActionListener`, so the listener class implements `ActionListener` in line 34. The source object invokes `addActionListener(listener)` to register a listener, as follows:

create source object
create listener object
register listener

```
JButton jbtOK = new JButton("OK"); // Line 7 in Listing 14.8
ActionListener listener1
  = new OKListenerClass(); // Line 18 in Listing 14.8
jbtOK.addActionListener(listener1); // Line 20 in Listing 14.8
```

When you click the button, the `JButton` object fires an `ActionEvent` and passes it to invoke the listener's `actionPerformed` method to handle the event.

TABLE 16.2 Events, Event Listeners, and Listener Methods

Event Class (Handlers)	*Listener Interface*	*Listener Methods*
`ActionEvent`	`ActionListener`	`actionPerformed(ActionEvent)`
`ItemEvent`	`ItemListener`	`itemStateChanged(ItemEvent)`
`MouseEvent`	`MouseListener`	`mousePressed(MouseEvent)`
		`mouseReleased(MouseEvent)`
		`mouseEntered(MouseEvent)`
		`mouseExited(MouseEvent)`
		`mouseClicked(MouseEvent)`
	`MouseMotionListener`	`mouseDragged(MouseEvent)`
		`mouseMoved(MouseEvent)`
`KeyEvent`	`KeyListener`	`keyPressed(KeyEvent)`
		`keyReleased(KeyEvent)`
		`keyTyped(KeyEvent)`
`WindowEvent`	`WindowListener`	`windowClosing(WindowEvent)`
		`windowOpened(WindowEvent)`
		`windowIconified(WindowEvent)`
		`windowDeiconified(WindowEvent)`
		`windowClosed(WindowEvent)`
		`windowActivated(WindowEvent)`
		`windowDeactivated(WindowEvent)`
`ContainerEvent`	`ContainerListener`	`componentAdded(ContainerEvent)`
		`componentRemoved(ContainerEvent)`
`ComponentEvent`	`ComponentListener`	`componentMoved(ComponentEvent)`
		`componentHidden(ComponentEvent)`
		`componentResized(ComponentEvent)`
		`componentShown(ComponentEvent)`
`FocusEvent`	`FocusListener`	`focusGained(FocusEvent)`
		`focusLost(FocusEvent)`
`AdjustmentEvent`	`AdjustmentListener`	`adjustmentValueChanged(AdjustmentEvent)`
`ChangeEvent`	`ChangeListener`	`stateChanged(ChangeEvent)`
`ListSelectionEvent`	`ListSelectionListener`	`valueChanged(ListSelectionEvent)`

The event object contains information pertinent to the event, which can be obtained using the methods, as shown in Figure 16.5. For example, you can use `e.getSource()` to obtain the source object in order to determine whether it is a button, a check box, or a radio button. For an action event, you can use `e.getWhen()` to obtain the time when the event occurs.

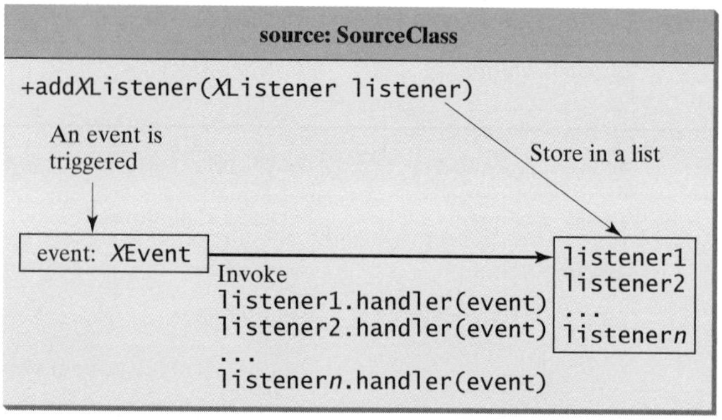

source: SourceClass
+addXListener(XListener listener)
An event is triggered
Store in a list
event: XEvent
Invoke
listener1.handler(event)
listener2.handler(event)
...
listenern.handler(event)
listener1
listener2
...
listenern

(a) Internal function of a generic source object

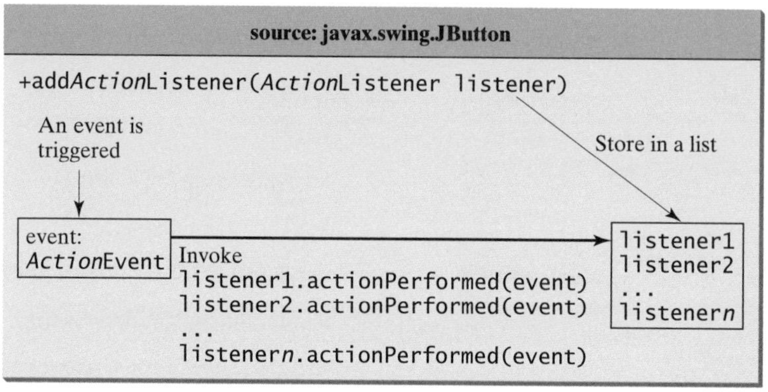

source: javax.swing.JButton
+addActionListener(ActionListener listener)
An event is triggered
Store in a list
event: ActionEvent
Invoke
listener1.actionPerformed(event)
listener2.actionPerformed(event)
...
listenern.actionPerformed(event)
listener1
listener2
...
listenern

(b) Internal function of a `JButton` object

FIGURE 16.4 The source object notifies the listeners of the event by invoking the handler of the listener object.

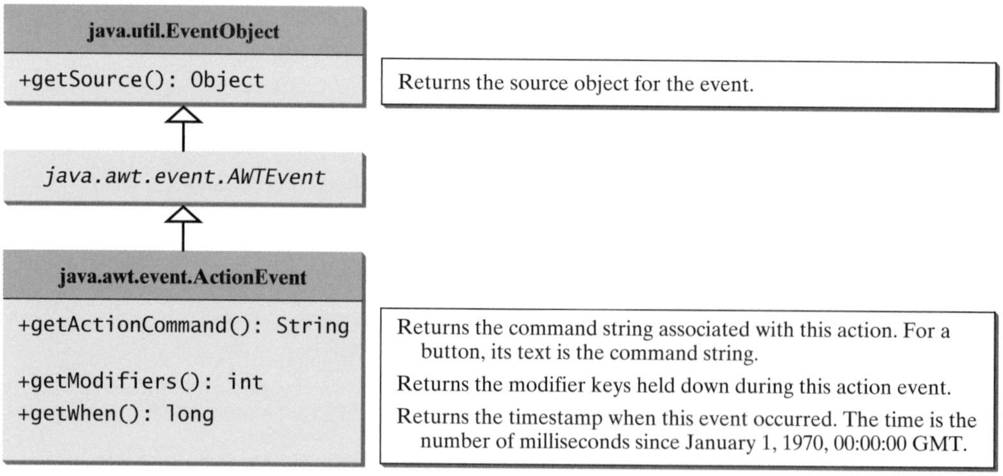

java.util.EventObject
+getSource(): Object
Returns the source object for the event.
java.awt.event.AWTEvent
java.awt.event.ActionEvent
+getActionCommand(): String
+getModifiers(): int
+getWhen(): long
Returns the command string associated with this action. For a button, its text is the command string.
Returns the modifier keys held down during this action event.
Returns the timestamp when this event occurred. The time is the number of milliseconds since January 1, 1970, 00:00:00 GMT.

FIGURE 16.5 You can obtain useful information from an event object.

We now write a program that uses two buttons to control the size of a circle, as shown in Figure 16.6.

first version

We will develop this program incrementally. First we write a program in Listing 16.1 that displays the user interface with a circle in the center (line 14) and two buttons in the bottom (line 15).

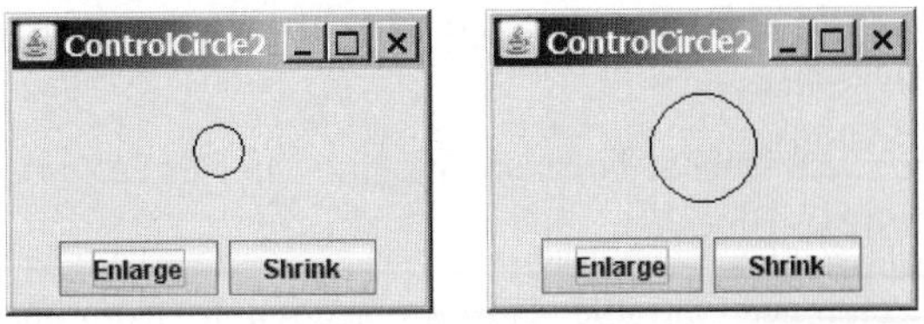
ControlCircle2
Enlarge
Shrink
ControlCircle2
Enlarge
Shrink

Figure 16.6 The user clicks the *Enlarge* and *Shrink* buttons to enlarge and shrink the size of the circle.

Listing 16.1 ControlCircle1.java

buttons

circle canvas

CirclePanel class

paint the circle

```java
import javax.swing.*;
import java.awt.*;

public class ControlCircle1 extends JFrame {
  private JButton jbtEnlarge = new JButton("Enlarge");
  private JButton jbtShrink = new JButton("Shrink");
  private CirclePanel canvas = new CirclePanel();

  public ControlCircle1() {
    JPanel panel = new JPanel(); // Use the panel to group buttons
    panel.add(jbtEnlarge);
    panel.add(jbtShrink);

    this.add(canvas, BorderLayout.CENTER); // Add canvas to center
    this.add(panel, BorderLayout.SOUTH); // Add buttons to the frame
  }

  /** Main method */
  public static void main(String[] args) {
    JFrame frame = new ControlCircle1();
    frame.setTitle("ControlCircle1");
    frame.setLocationRelativeTo(null); // Center the frame
    frame.setDefaultCloseOperation(JFrame.EXIT_ON_CLOSE);
    frame.setSize(200, 200);
    frame.setVisible(true);
  }
}

class CirclePanel extends JPanel {
  private int radius = 5; // Default circle radius

  /** Repaint the circle */
  protected void paintComponent(Graphics g) {
    super.paintComponent(g);
    g.drawOval(getWidth() / 2 - radius, getHeight() / 2 - radius,
      2 * radius, 2 * radius);
  }
}
```

second version

How do you use the buttons to enlarge or shrink the circle? When the *Enlarge* button is clicked, you want the circle to be repainted with a larger radius. How can you accomplish this? You can expand the program in Listing 16.1 into Listing 16.2 with the following features:

1. Define a listener class named `EnlargeListener` that implements `ActionListener` (lines 31–35).
2. Create a listener and register it with `jbtEnlarge` (line 18).

3. Add a method named `enlarge()` in `CirclePanel` to increase the radius, then repaint the panel (lines 41–44).

4. Implement the `actionPerformed` method in `EnlargeListener` to invoke `canvas.enlarge()` (line 33).

5. To make the reference variable `canvas` accessible from the `actionPerformed` method, define `EnlargeListener` as an inner class of the `ControlCircle2` class (lines 31–35). Inner classes are defined inside another class. We will introduce inner classes in the next section.

6. To avoid compile errors, the `CirclePanel` class (lines 37–52) now is also defined as an inner class in `ControlCircle2`,since an old `CirclePanel` class is already defined in Listing 16.1.

Video Note
Listener and its registration

LISTING 16.2 ControlCircle2.java

```
1 import javax.swing.*;
2 import java.awt.*;
3 import java.awt.event.*;
4
5 public class ControlCircle2 extends JFrame {
6   private JButton jbtEnlarge = new JButton("Enlarge");
7   private JButton jbtShrink = new JButton("Shrink");
8   private CirclePanel canvas = new CirclePanel();
9
10  public ControlCircle2() {
11    JPanel panel = new JPanel(); // Use the panel to group buttons
12    panel.add(jbtEnlarge);
13    panel.add(jbtShrink);
14
15    this.add(canvas, BorderLayout.CENTER); // Add canvas to center
16    this.add(panel, BorderLayout.SOUTH); // Add buttons to the frame
17
18    jbtEnlarge.addActionListener(new EnlargeListener());
19  }
20
21  /** Main method */
22  public static void main(String[] args) {
23    JFrame frame = new ControlCircle2();
24    frame.setTitle("ControlCircle2");
25    frame.setLocationRelativeTo(null); // Center the frame
26    frame.setDefaultCloseOperation(JFrame.EXIT_ON_CLOSE);
27    frame.setSize(200, 200);
28    frame.setVisible(true);
29  }
30
31  class EnlargeListener implements ActionListener { // Inner class
32    public void actionPerformed(ActionEvent e) {
33      canvas.enlarge();
34    }
35  }
36
37  class CirclePanel extends JPanel { // Inner class
38    private int radius = 5; // Default circle radius
39
40    /** Enlarge the circle */
41    public void enlarge() {
42      radius++;
```

create/register listener

listener class

`CirclePanel` class

`enlarge` method

```
        repaint();
      }

      /** Repaint the circle */
      protected void paintComponent(Graphics g) {
        super.paintComponent(g);
        g.drawOval(getWidth() / 2 - radius, getHeight() / 2 - radius,
          2 * radius, 2 * radius);
      }
    }
}
```

the Shrink button

Similarly you can add the code for the *Shrink* button to display a smaller circle when the *Shrink* button is clicked.

16.4 Inner Classes

An *inner class*, or *nested class,* is a class defined within the scope of another class. The code in Figure 16.7(a) defines two separate classes, **Test** and **A**. The code in Figure 16.7(b) defines **A** as an inner class in **Test**.

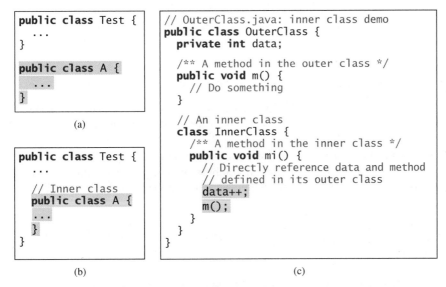

```
public class Test {
  ...
}

public class A {
  ...
}
```

(a)

```
public class Test {
  ...

  // Inner class
  public class A {
    ...
  }
}
```

(b)

```
// OuterClass.java: inner class demo
public class OuterClass {
  private int data;

  /** A method in the outer class */
  public void m() {
    // Do something
  }

  // An inner class
  class InnerClass {
    /** A method in the inner class */
    public void mi() {
      // Directly reference data and method
      // defined in its outer class
      data++;
      m();
    }
  }
}
```

(c)

FIGURE 16.7 Inner classes combine dependent classes into the primary class.

The class **InnerClass** defined inside **OuterClass** in Figure 16.7(c) is another example of an inner class. An inner class may be used just like a regular class. Normally, you define a class an inner class if it is used only by its outer class. An inner class has the following features:

- An inner class is compiled into a class named ***OuterClassName$InnerClassName*.class**. For example, the inner class **A** in **Test** is compiled into ***Test$A*.class** in Figure 16.7(b).
- An inner class can reference the data and methods defined in the outer class in which it nests, so you need not pass the reference of an object of the outer class to the constructor of the inner class. For this reason, inner classes can make programs simple and concise.
- An inner class can be defined with a visibility modifier subject to the same visibility rules applied to a member of the class.

- An inner class can be defined `static`. A `static` inner class can be accessed using the outer class name. A `static` inner class cannot access nonstatic members of the outer class.
- Objects of an inner class are often created in the outer class. But you can also create an object of an inner class from another class. If the inner class is nonstatic, you must first create an instance of the outer class, then use the following syntax to create an object for the inner class:

```
OuterClass.InnerClass innerObject = outerObject.new InnerClass();
```

- If the inner class is static, use the following syntax to create an object for it:

```
OuterClass.InnerClass innerObject = new OuterClass.InnerClass();
```

A simple use of inner classes is to combine dependent classes into a primary class. This reduces the number of source files. It also makes class files easy to organize, since they are all named with the primary class as the prefix. For example, rather than creating two source files, **Test.java** and **A.java**, in Figure 16.7(a), you can combine class `A` into class `Test` and create just one source file **Test.java** in Figure 16.7(b). The resulting class files are **Test.class** and **Test$A.class**.

Another practical use of inner classes is to avoid class-naming conflict. Two versions of `CirclePanel` are defined in Listings 16.1 and 16.2. You can define them as inner classes to avoid conflict.

16.5 Anonymous Class Listeners

A listener class is designed specifically to create a listener object for a GUI component (e.g., a button). The listener class will not be shared by other applications and therefore is appropriate to be defined inside the frame class as an inner class.

anonymous inner class

Inner-class listeners can be shortened using anonymous inner classes. An *anonymous inner class* is an inner class without a name. It combines defining an inner class and creating an instance of the class in one step. The inner class in Listing 16.2 can be replaced by an anonymous inner class as shown below.

```
public ControlCircle2() {
  // Omitted

  jbtEnlarge.addActionListener(
    new EnlargeListener());
}

class EnlargeListener
    implements ActionListener {
  public void actionPerformed(ActionEvent e) {
    canvas.enlarge();
  }
}
```

(a) Inner class EnlargeListener

```
public ControlCircle2() {
  // Omitted

  jbtEnlarge.addActionListener(
    new class EnlargeListener
        implements ActionListener() {
      public void
          actionPerformed(ActionEvent e) {
        canvas.enlarge();
      }
    });
}
```

(b) Anonymous inner class

The syntax for an anonymous inner class is as follows:

```
new SuperClassName/InterfaceName() {
  // Implement or override methods in superclass or interface

  // Other methods if necessary
}
```

Since an anonymous inner class is a special kind of inner class, it is treated like an inner class with the following features:

- An anonymous inner class must always extend a superclass or implement an interface, but it cannot have an explicit `extends` or `implements` clause.
- An anonymous inner class must implement all the abstract methods in the superclass or in the interface.
- An anonymous inner class always uses the no-arg constructor from its superclass to create an instance. If an anonymous inner class implements an interface, the constructor is `Object()`.
- An anonymous inner class is compiled into a class named `OuterClassName$n.class`. For example, if the outer class `Test` has two anonymous inner classes, they are compiled into `Test$1.class` and `Test$2.class`.

Listing 16.3 gives an example that handles the events from four buttons, as shown in Figure 16.8.

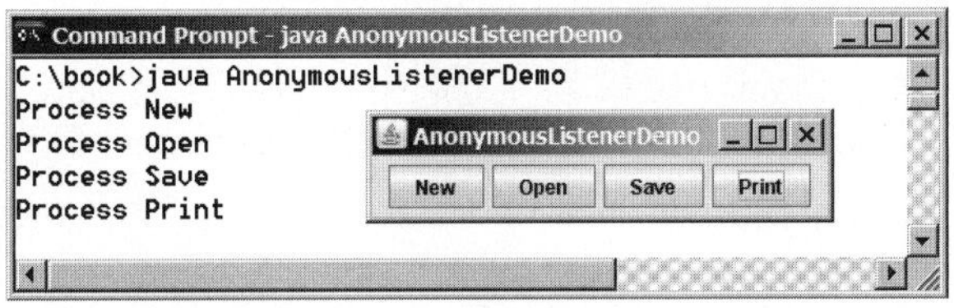
Command Prompt - java AnonymousListenerDemo
C:\book>java AnonymousListenerDemo
Process New
Process Open
Process Save
Process Print
AnonymousListenerDemo
New
Open
Save
Print

FIGURE 16.8 The program handles the events from four buttons.

LISTING 16.3 AnonymousListenerDemo.java

Video Note
Anonymous listener

```
import javax.swing.*;
import java.awt.event.*;

public class AnonymousListenerDemo extends JFrame {
  public AnonymousListenerDemo() {
    // Create four buttons
    JButton jbtNew = new JButton("New");
    JButton jbtOpen = new JButton("Open");
    JButton jbtSave = new JButton("Save");
    JButton jbtPrint = new JButton("Print");

    // Create a panel to hold buttons
    JPanel panel = new JPanel();
    panel.add(jbtNew);
    panel.add(jbtOpen);
    panel.add(jbtSave);
    panel.add(jbtPrint);

    add(panel);

    // Create and register anonymous inner-class listener
    jbtNew.addActionListener(
      new ActionListener() {
        public void actionPerformed(ActionEvent e) {
          System.out.println("Process New");
        }
      }
    );
```

anonymous listener
handle event

```
29
30     jbtOpen.addActionListener(
31       new ActionListener() {
32         public void actionPerformed(ActionEvent e) {
33           System.out.println("Process Open");
34         }
35       }
36     );
37
38     jbtSave.addActionListener(
39       new ActionListener() {
40         public void actionPerformed(ActionEvent e) {
41           System.out.println("Process Save");
42         }
43       }
44     );
45
46     jbtPrint.addActionListener(
47       new ActionListener() {
48         public void actionPerformed(ActionEvent e) {
49           System.out.println("Process Print");
50         }
51       }
52     );
53   }
54
55   /** Main method */
56   public static void main(String[] args) {
57     JFrame frame = new AnonymousListenerDemo();
58     frame.setTitle("AnonymousListenerDemo");
59     frame.setLocationRelativeTo(null); // Center the frame
60     frame.setDefaultCloseOperation(JFrame.EXIT_ON_CLOSE);
61     frame.pack();
62     frame.setVisible(true);
63   }
64 }
```

The program creates four listeners using anonymous inner classes (lines 22–52). Without using anonymous inner classes, you would have to create four separate classes. An anonymous listener works the same way as an inner class listener. The program is condensed using an anonymous inner class.

Anonymous inner classes are compiled into `OuterClassName$#.class`, where `#` starts at `1` and is incremented for each anonymous class the compiler encounters. In this example, the anonymous inner class is compiled into `AnonymousListenerDemo$1.class`, `AnonymousListenerDemo$2.class`, `AnonymousListenerDemo$3.class`,and `AnonymousListenerDemo$4.class`.

pack()

Instead of using the `setSize` method to set the size for the frame, the program uses the `pack()` method (line 61), which automatically sizes the frame according to the size of the components placed in it.

16.6 Alternative Ways of Defining Listener Classes

There are many other ways to define the listener classes. For example, you may rewrite Listing 16.3 by creating just one listener, register the listener with the buttons, and let the listener detect the event source—i.e., which button fires the event—as shown in Listing 16.4.

LISTING 16.4 DetectSourceDemo.java

```java
import javax.swing.*;
import java.awt.event.*;

public class DetectSourceDemo extends JFrame {
  // Create four buttons
  private JButton jbtNew = new JButton("New");
  private JButton jbtOpen = new JButton("Open");
  private JButton jbtSave = new JButton("Save");
  private JButton jbtPrint = new JButton("Print");

  public DetectSourceDemo() {
    // Create a panel to hold buttons
    JPanel panel = new JPanel();
    panel.add(jbtNew);
    panel.add(jbtOpen);
    panel.add(jbtSave);
    panel.add(jbtPrint);

    add(panel);

    // Create a listener
    ButtonListener listener = new ButtonListener();

    // Register listener with buttons
    jbtNew.addActionListener(listener);
    jbtOpen.addActionListener(listener);
    jbtSave.addActionListener(listener);
    jbtPrint.addActionListener(listener);
  }

  class ButtonListener implements ActionListener {
    public void actionPerformed(ActionEvent e) {
      if (e.getSource() == jbtNew)
        System.out.println("Process New");
      else if (e.getSource() == jbtOpen)
        System.out.println("Process Open");
      else if (e.getSource() == jbtSave)
        System.out.println("Process Save");
      else if (e.getSource() == jbtPrint)
        System.out.println("Process Print");
    }
  }

  /** Main method */
  public static void main(String[] args) {
    JFrame frame = new DetectSourceDemo();
    frame.setTitle("DetectSourceDemo");
    frame.setLocationRelativeTo(null); // Center the frame
    frame.setDefaultCloseOperation(JFrame.EXIT_ON_CLOSE);
    frame.pack();
    frame.setVisible(true);
  }
}
```

create listener

register listener

listener class

handle event

This program defines just one inner listener class (lines 31–42), creates a listener from the class (line 22), and registers it to four buttons (lines 25–28). When a button is clicked, the button fires an **ActionEvent** and invokes the listener's **actionPerformed** method. The **actionPerformed** method checks the source of the event using the **getSource()** method for the event (lines 33, 35, 37, 39) and determines which button fired the event.

You may also rewrite Listing 16.3 by defining the custom frame class that implements **ActionListener**, as shown in Listing 16.5.

Listing 16.5 FrameAsListenerDemo.java

implement **ActionListener**

register listeners

handle event

```
import javax.swing.*;
import java.awt.event.*;

public class FrameAsListenerDemo extends JFrame
    implements ActionListener {
  // Create four buttons
  private JButton jbtNew = new JButton("New");
  private JButton jbtOpen = new JButton("Open");
  private JButton jbtSave = new JButton("Save");
  private JButton jbtPrint = new JButton("Print");

  public FrameAsListenerDemo() {
    // Create a panel to hold buttons
    JPanel panel = new JPanel();
    panel.add(jbtNew);
    panel.add(jbtOpen);
    panel.add(jbtSave);
    panel.add(jbtPrint);

    add(panel);

    // Register listener with buttons
    jbtNew.addActionListener(this);
    jbtOpen.addActionListener(this);
    jbtSave.addActionListener(this);
    jbtPrint.addActionListener(this);
  }

  /** Implement actionPerformed */
  public void actionPerformed(ActionEvent e) {
    if (e.getSource() == jbtNew)
      System.out.println("Process New");
    else if (e.getSource() == jbtOpen)
      System.out.println("Process Open");
    else if (e.getSource() == jbtSave)
      System.out.println("Process Save");
    else if (e.getSource() == jbtPrint)
      System.out.println("Process Print");
  }

  /** Main method */
  public static void main(String[] args) {
    JFrame frame = new FrameAsListenerDemo();
    frame.setTitle("FrameAsListenerDemo");
    frame.setLocationRelativeTo(null); // Center the frame
    frame.setDefaultCloseOperation(JFrame.EXIT_ON_CLOSE);
    frame.pack();
    frame.setVisible(true);
  }
}
```

The frame class extends `JFrame` and implements `ActionListener` (line 5). So the class is a listener class for action events. The listener is registered to four buttons (lines 23–26). When a button is clicked, the button fires an `ActionEvent` and invokes the listener's `actionPerformed` method. The `actionPerformed` method checks the source of the event using the `getSource()` method for the event (lines 31, 33, 35, 37) and determines which button fired the event.

This design is not desirable because it places too many responsibilities into one class. It is better to design a listener class that is solely responsible for handling events. This design makes the code easy to read and easy to maintain.

You can define listener classes in many ways. Which way is preferred? Defining listener classes using inner class or anonymous inner class has become a standard for event-handling programming because it generally provides clear, clean, and concise code. So, we will consistently use it in this book.

16.7 Problem: Loan Calculator

Now you can write the program for the loan-calculator problem presented in the introduction of this chapter. Here are the major steps in the program:

1. Create the user interface, as shown in Figure 16.9.

   a. Create a panel of a `GridLayout` with `5` rows and `2` columns. Add labels and text fields into the panel. Set a title "Enter loan amount, interest rate, and years" for the panel.

   b. Create another panel with a `FlowLayout(FlowLayout.RIGHT)` and add a button into the panel.

   c. Add the first panel to the center of the frame and the second panel to the south side of the frame.

2. Process the event.

   Create and register the listener for processing the button-clicking action event. The handler obtains the user input on loan, interest rate, and number of years, computes the monthly and total payments, and displays the values in the text fields.

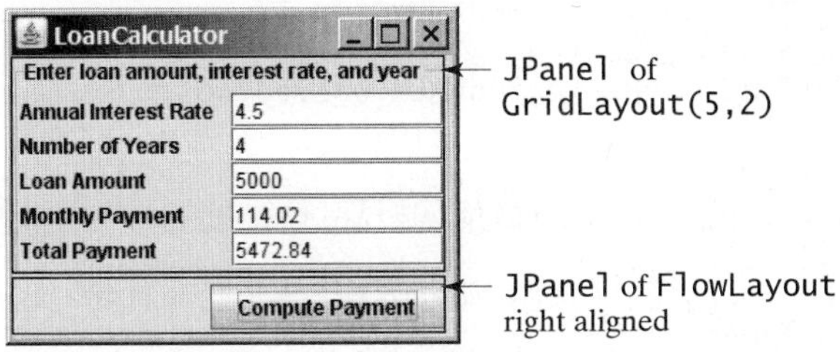
LoanCalculator
Enter loan amount, interest rate, and year
Annual Interest Rate
4.5
Number of Years
4
Loan Amount
5000
Monthly Payment
114.02
Total Payment
5472.84
Compute Payment
JPanel of GridLayout(5,2)
JPanel of FlowLayout right aligned

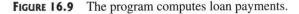

FIGURE 16.9 The program computes loan payments.

The complete program is given in Listing 16.6.

LISTING 16.6 LoanCalculator.java

```
import java.awt.*;
import java.awt.event.*;
import javax.swing.*;
import javax.swing.border.TitledBorder;

public class LoanCalculator extends JFrame {
  // Create text fields for interest rate,
```

text fields · button · create UI · add to frame · register listener · get input · create loan · set result

```java
  // year, loan amount, monthly payment, and total payment
  private JTextField jtfAnnualInterestRate = new JTextField();
  private JTextField jtfNumberOfYears = new JTextField();
  private JTextField jtfLoanAmount = new JTextField();
  private JTextField jtfMonthlyPayment = new JTextField();
  private JTextField jtfTotalPayment = new JTextField();

  // Create a Compute Payment button
  private JButton jbtComputeLoan = new JButton("Compute Payment");

  public LoanCalculator() {
    // Panel p1 to hold labels and text fields
    JPanel p1 = new JPanel(new GridLayout(5, 2));
    p1.add(new JLabel("Annual Interest Rate"));
    p1.add(jtfAnnualInterestRate);
    p1.add(new JLabel("Number of Years"));
    p1.add(jtfNumberOfYears);
    p1.add(new JLabel("Loan Amount"));
    p1.add(jtfLoanAmount);
    p1.add(new JLabel("Monthly Payment"));
    p1.add(jtfMonthlyPayment);
    p1.add(new JLabel("Total Payment"));
    p1.add(jtfTotalPayment);
    p1.setBorder(new
      TitledBorder("Enter loan amount, interest rate, and year"));

    // Panel p2 to hold the button
    JPanel p2 = new JPanel(new FlowLayout(FlowLayout.RIGHT));
    p2.add(jbtComputeLoan);

    // Add the panels to the frame
    add(p1, BorderLayout.CENTER);
    add(p2, BorderLayout.SOUTH);

    // Register listener
    jbtComputeLoan.addActionListener(new ButtonListener());
  }

  /** Handle the Compute Payment button */
  private class ButtonListener implements ActionListener {
    public void actionPerformed(ActionEvent e) {
      // Get values from text fields
      double interest =
        Double.parseDouble(jtfAnnualInterestRate.getText());
      int year =
        Integer.parseInt(jtfNumberOfYears.getText());
      double loanAmount =
        Double.parseDouble(jtfLoanAmount.getText());

      // Create a loan object
      Loan loan = new Loan(interest, year, loanAmount);

      // Display monthly payment and total payment
      jtfMonthlyPayment.setText(String.format("%.2f",
        loan.getMonthlyPayment()));
      jtfTotalPayment.setText(String.format("%.2f",
        loan.getTotalPayment()));
    }
  }

```

```java
68   public static void main(String[] args) {
69     LoanCalculator frame = new LoanCalculator();
70     frame.pack();
71     frame.setTitle("LoanCalculator");
72     frame.setLocationRelativeTo(null); // Center the frame
73     frame.setDefaultCloseOperation(JFrame.EXIT_ON_CLOSE);
74     frame.setVisible(true);
75   }
76 }
```

The user interface is created in the constructor (lines 18–44). The button is the source of the event. A listener is created and registered with the button (line 43).

The listener class (lines 47–66) implements the `actionPerformed` method. When the button is clicked, the `actionPerformed` method is invoked to get the interest rate (line 51), number of years (line 53), and loan amount (line 55). Invoking `jtfAnnualInterestRate.getText()` returns the string text in the `jtfAnnualInterestRate` text field. The loan is used for computing the loan payments. This class was introduced in Listing 10.2, Loan.java. Invoking `loan.getMonthlyPayment()` returns the monthly payment for the loan. The `String.format` method uses the `printf` like syntax to format a number into a desirable format. Invoking the `setText` method on a text field sets a string value in the text field (line 61).

16.8 Window Events

The preceding sections used action events. Other events can be processed similarly. This section gives an example of handling `WindowEvent`. Any subclass of the `Window` class can fire the following window events: window opened, closing, closed, activated, deactivated, iconified, and deiconified. The program in Listing 16.7 creates a frame, listens to the window events, and displays a message to indicate the occurring event. Figure 16.10 shows a sample run of the program.

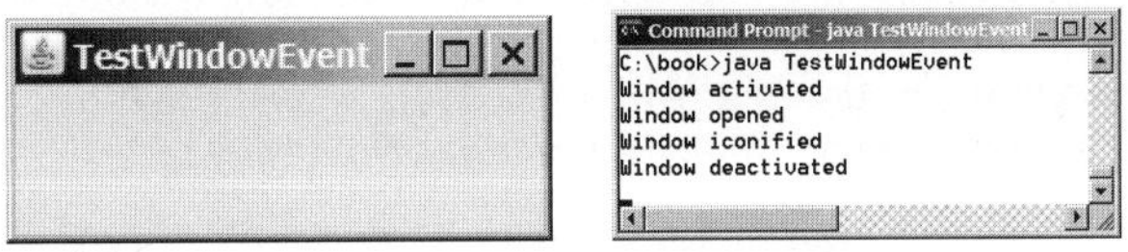
TestWindowEvent
Command Prompt - java TestWindowEvent
C:\book>java TestWindowEvent
Window activated
Window opened
Window iconified
Window deactivated

FIGURE 16.10 The window events are displayed on the console when you run the program from the command prompt.

LISTING 16.7 TestWindowEvent.java

```java
import java.awt.event.*;
import javax.swing.JFrame;

public class TestWindowEvent extends JFrame {
  public static void main(String[] args) {
    TestWindowEvent frame = new TestWindowEvent();
    frame.setSize(220, 80);
    frame.setLocationRelativeTo(null); // Center the frame
    frame.setDefaultCloseOperation(JFrame.EXIT_ON_CLOSE);
    frame.setTitle("TestWindowEvent");
    frame.setVisible(true);
  }

  public TestWindowEvent() {
    addWindowListener(new WindowListener() {
      /**
       * Handler for window-deiconified event
```

```
   * Invoked when a window is changed from a minimized
   * to a normal state.
   */
```

implement handler

```
  public void windowDeiconified(WindowEvent event) {
    System.out.println("Window deiconified");
  }

  /**
   * Handler for window-iconified event
   * Invoked when a window is changed from a normal to a
   * minimized state. For many platforms, a minimized window
   * is displayed as the icon specified in the window's
   * iconImage property.
   */
```

implement handler

```
  public void windowIconified(WindowEvent event) {
    System.out.println("Window iconified");
  }

  /**
   * Handler for window-activated event
   * Invoked when the window is set to be the user's
   * active window, which means the window (or one of its
   * subcomponents) will receive keyboard events.
   */
```

implement handler

```
  public void windowActivated(WindowEvent event) {
    System.out.println("Window activated");
  }

  /**
   * Handler for window-deactivated event
   * Invoked when a window is no longer the user's active
   * window, which means that keyboard events will no longer
   * be delivered to the window or its subcomponents.
   */
```

implement handler

```
  public void windowDeactivated(WindowEvent event) {
    System.out.println("Window deactivated");
  }

  /**
   * Handler for window-opened event
   * Invoked the first time a window is made visible.
   */
  public void windowOpened(WindowEvent event) {
    System.out.println("Window opened");
  }

  /**
   * Handler for window-closing event
   * Invoked when the user attempts to close the window
   * from the window's system menu.  If the program does not
   * explicitly hide or dispose the window while processing
   * this event, the window-closing operation will be cancelled.
   */
```

implement handler

```
  public void windowClosing(WindowEvent event) {
    System.out.println("Window closing");
  }

  /**
   * Handler for window-closed event
   * Invoked when a window has been closed as the result
```

```
       * of calling dispose on the window.
       */
      public void windowClosed(WindowEvent event) {
        System.out.println("Window closed");
      }
    });
  }
}
```

implement handler

The WindowEvent can be fired by the Window class or by any subclass of Window. Since JFrame is a subclass of Window, it can fire WindowEvent.

TestWindowEvent extends JFrame and implements WindowListener. The WindowListener interface defines several abstract methods (windowActivated, windowClosed, windowClosing, windowDeactivated, windowDeiconified, windowIconified, windowOpened) for handling window events when the window is activated, closed, closing, deactivated, deiconified, iconified, or opened.

When a window event, such as activation, occurs, the windowActivated method is invoked. Implement the windowActivated method with a concrete response if you want the event to be processed.

16.9 Listener Interface Adapters

Because the methods in the WindowListener interface are abstract, you must implement all of them even if your program does not care about some of the events. For convenience, Java provides support classes, called *convenience adapters*, which provide default implementations for all the methods in the listener interface. The default implementation is simply an empty body. Java provides convenience listener adapters for every AWT listener interface with multiple handlers. A convenience listener adapter is named *X*Adapter for *X*Listener. For example, WindowAdapter is a convenience listener adapter for WindowListener. Table 16.3 lists the convenience adapters.

convenience adapter

TABLE 16.3 Convenience Adapters

Adapter	*Interface*
WindowAdapter	WindowListener
MouseAdapter	MouseListener
MouseMotionAdapter	MouseMotionListener
KeyAdapter	KeyListener
ContainerAdapter	ContainerListener
ComponentAdapter	ComponentListener
FocusAdapter	FocusListener

Using WindowAdapter, the preceding example can be simplified as shown in Listing 16.8, if you are interested only in the window-activated event. The WindowAdapter class is used to create an anonymous listener instead of WindowListener (line 15). The windowActivated handler is implemented in line 16.

LISTING 16.8 AdapterDemo.java

```
1 import java.awt.event.*;
2 import javax.swing.JFrame;
3
4 public class AdapterDemo extends JFrame {
```

```
  public static void main(String[] args) {
    AdapterDemo frame = new AdapterDemo();
    frame.setSize(220, 80);
    frame.setLocationRelativeTo(null); // Center the frame
    frame.setDefaultCloseOperation(JFrame.EXIT_ON_CLOSE);
    frame.setTitle("AdapterDemo");
    frame.setVisible(true);
  }

  public AdapterDemo() {
    addWindowListener(new WindowAdapter() {
      public void windowActivated(WindowEvent event) {
        System.out.println("Window activated");
      }
    });
  }
}
```

register listener

implement handler

16.10 Mouse Events

A mouse event is fired whenever a mouse is pressed, released, clicked, moved, or dragged on a component. The `MouseEvent` object captures the event, such as the number of clicks associated with it or the location (`x`- and `y`-coordinates) of the mouse, as shown in Figure 16.11.

Since the `MouseEvent` class inherits `InputEvent`, you can use the methods defined in the `InputEvent` class on a `MouseEvent` object.

`Point` class

The `java.awt.Point` class represents a point on a component. The class contains two public variables, `x` and `y`, for coordinates. To create a `Point`, use the following constructor:

```
Point(int x, int y)
```

This constructs a `Point` object with the specified `x`- and `y`-coordinates. Normally, the data fields in a class should be private, but this class has two public data fields.

Java provides two listener interfaces, `MouseListener` and `MouseMotionListener`, to handle mouse events, as shown in Figure 16.12. Implement the `MouseListener` interface to

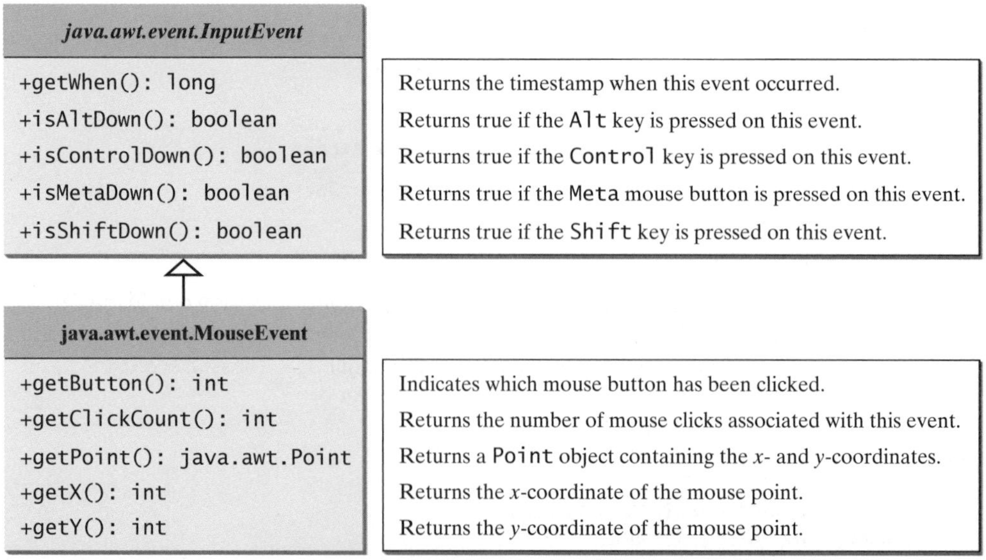
java.awt.event.InputEvent
+getWhen(): long
+isAltDown(): boolean
+isControlDown(): boolean
+isMetaDown(): boolean
+isShiftDown(): boolean
Returns the timestamp when this event occurred.
Returns true if the Alt key is pressed on this event.
Returns true if the Control key is pressed on this event.
Returns true if the Meta mouse button is pressed on this event.
Returns true if the Shift key is pressed on this event.
java.awt.event.MouseEvent
+getButton(): int
+getClickCount(): int
+getPoint(): java.awt.Point
+getX(): int
+getY(): int
Indicates which mouse button has been clicked.
Returns the number of mouse clicks associated with this event.
Returns a Point object containing the x- and y-coordinates.
Returns the x-coordinate of the mouse point.
Returns the y-coordinate of the mouse point.

FIGURE 16.11 The `MouseEvent` class encapsulates information for mouse events.

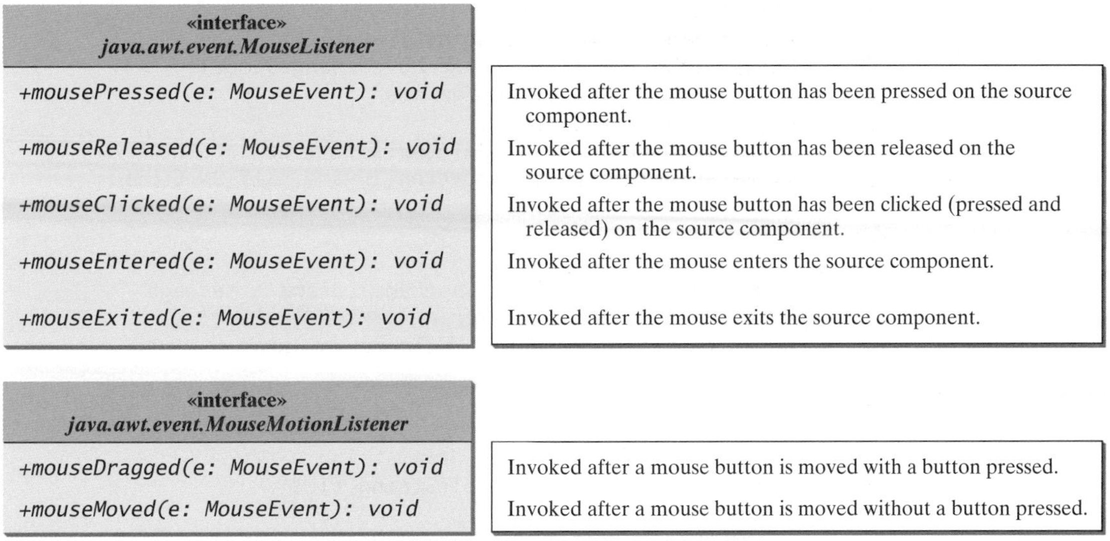
«interface»
java.awt.event.MouseListener
+mousePressed(e: MouseEvent): void
+mouseReleased(e: MouseEvent): void
+mouseClicked(e: MouseEvent): void
+mouseEntered(e: MouseEvent): void
+mouseExited(e: MouseEvent): void
Invoked after the mouse button has been pressed on the source component.
Invoked after the mouse button has been released on the source component.
Invoked after the mouse button has been clicked (pressed and released) on the source component.
Invoked after the mouse enters the source component.
Invoked after the mouse exits the source component.
«interface»
java.awt.event.MouseMotionListener
+mouseDragged(e: MouseEvent): void
+mouseMoved(e: MouseEvent): void
Invoked after a mouse button is moved with a button pressed.
Invoked after a mouse button is moved without a button pressed.

FIGURE 16.12 The `MouseListener` interface handles mouse pressed, released, clicked, entered, and exited events. The `MouseMotionListener` interface handles mouse dragged and moved events.

listen for such actions as pressing, releasing, entering, exiting, or clicking the mouse, and implement the `MouseMotionListener` interface to listen for such actions as dragging or moving the mouse.

16.10.1 Example: Moving a Message on a Panel Using a Mouse

This example writes a program that displays a message in a panel, as shown in Listing 16.9. You can use the mouse to move the message. The message moves as the mouse drags and is always displayed at the mouse point. A sample run of the program is shown in Figure 16.13.

MoveMessageDemo
Welcome to Java

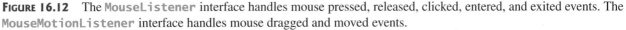

FIGURE 16.13 You can move the message by dragging the mouse.

LISTING 16.9 MoveMessageDemo.java

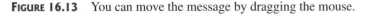

Video Note
Move message using the mouse

```
import java.awt.*;
import java.awt.event.*;
import javax.swing.*;

public class MoveMessageDemo extends JFrame {
  public MoveMessageDemo() {
    // Create a MovableMessagePanel instance for moving a message
    MovableMessagePanel p = new MovableMessagePanel
      ("Welcome to Java");

    // Place the message panel in the frame
    setLayout(new BorderLayout());
    add(p);
  }

```

create a panel

inner class
set a new message
anonymous listener
override handler
new location
repaint
paint message

```java
16   /** Main method */
17   public static void main(String[] args) {
18     MoveMessageDemo frame = new MoveMessageDemo();
19     frame.setTitle("MoveMessageDemo");
20     frame.setSize(200, 100);
21     frame.setLocationRelativeTo(null); // Center the frame
22     frame.setDefaultCloseOperation(JFrame.EXIT_ON_CLOSE);
23     frame.setVisible(true);
24   }
25
26   // Inner class: MovableMessagePanel draws a message
27   static class MovableMessagePanel extends JPanel {
28     private String message = "Welcome to Java";
29     private int x = 20;
30     private int y = 20;
31
32     /** Construct a panel to draw string s */
33     public MovableMessagePanel(String s) {
34       message = s;
35       addMouseMotionListener(new MouseMotionAdapter() {
36         /** Handle mouse-dragged event */
37         public void mouseDragged(MouseEvent e) {
38           // Get the new location and repaint the screen
39           x = e.getX();
40           y = e.getY();
41           repaint();
42         }
43       });
44     }
45
46     /** Paint the component */
47     protected void paintComponent(Graphics g) {
48       super.paintComponent(g);
49       g.drawString(message, x, y);
50     }
51   }
52 }
```

The `MovableMessagePanel` class extends `JPanel` to draw a message (line 27). Additionally, it handles redisplaying the message when the mouse is dragged. This class is defined as an inner class inside the main class because it is used only in this class. Furthermore, the inner class is defined static because it does not reference any instance members of the main class.

The `MouseMotionListener` interface contains two handlers, `mouseMoved` and `mouseDragged`, for handling mouse-motion events. When you move the mouse with the button pressed, the `mouseDragged` method is invoked to repaint the viewing area and display the message at the mouse point. When you move the mouse without pressing the button, the `mouseMoved` method is invoked.

Because the listener is interested only in the mouse-dragged event, the anonymous inner-class listener extends `MouseMotionAdapter` to override the `mouseDragged` method. If the inner class implemented the `MouseMotionListener` interface, you would have to implement all of the handlers, even if your listener did not care about some of the events.

The `mouseDragged` method is invoked when you move the mouse with a button pressed. This method obtains the mouse location using `getX` and `getY` methods (lines 39–40) in the `MouseEvent` class. This becomes the new location for the message. Invoking the `repaint()` method (line 41) causes `paintComponent` to be invoked (line 47), which displays the message in a new location.

16.11 Key Events

Key events enable the use of the keys to control and perform actions or get input from the keyboard. A key event is fired whenever a key is pressed, released, or typed on a component. The KeyEvent object describes the nature of the event (namely, that a key has been pressed, released, or typed) and the value of the key, as shown in Figure 16.14. Java provides the KeyListener interface to handle key events, as shown in Figure 16.15.

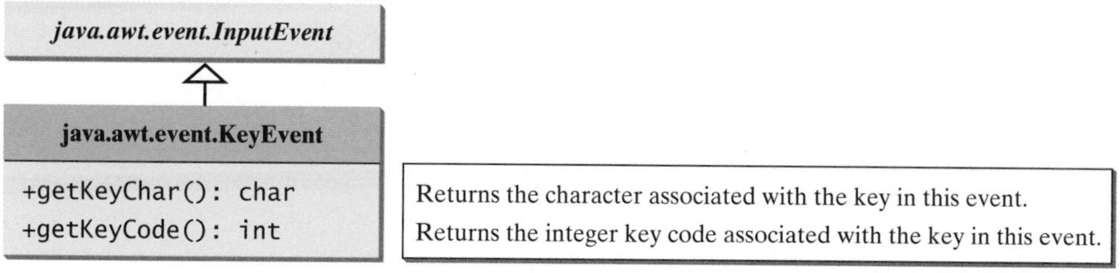
java.awt.event.InputEvent
java.awt.event.KeyEvent
+getKeyChar(): char
+getKeyCode(): int
Returns the character associated with the key in this event.
Returns the integer key code associated with the key in this event.

FIGURE 16.14 The KeyEvent class encapsulates information about key events.

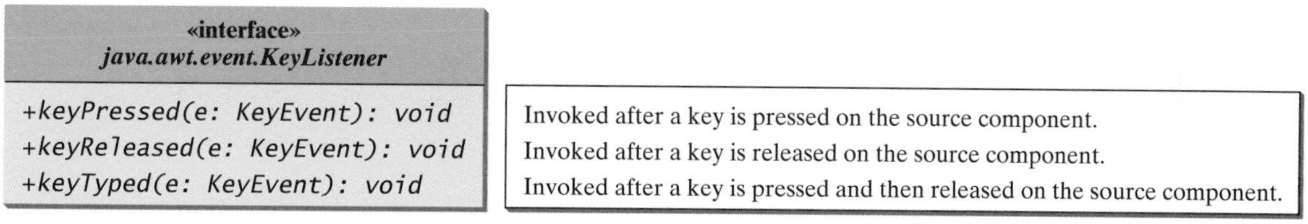
«interface»
java.awt.event.KeyListener
+keyPressed(e: KeyEvent): void
+keyReleased(e: KeyEvent): void
+keyTyped(e: KeyEvent): void
Invoked after a key is pressed on the source component.
Invoked after a key is released on the source component.
Invoked after a key is pressed and then released on the source component.

FIGURE 16.15 The KeyListener interface handles key pressed, released, and typed events.

The keyPressed handler is invoked when a key is pressed, the keyReleased handler is invoked when a key is released, and the keyTyped handler is invoked when a Unicode character is entered. If a key does not have a Unicode (e.g., function keys, modifier keys, action keys, and control keys), the keyTyped handler will be not be invoked.

Every key event has an associated key character or key code that is returned by the getKeyChar() or getKeyCode() method in KeyEvent. The key codes are constants defined in Table 16.4. For a key of the Unicode character, the key code is the same as the Unicode value.

TABLE 16.4 Key Constants

Constant	*Description*	*Constant*	*Description*
VK_HOME	The Home key	VK_SHIFT	The Shift key
VK_END	The End key	VK_BACK_SPACE	The Backspace key
VK_PGUP	The Page Up key	VK_CAPS_LOCK	The Caps Lock key
VK_PGDN	The Page Down key	VK_NUM_LOCK	The Num Lock key
VK_UP	The up-arrow key	VK_ENTER	The Enter key
VK_DOWN	The down-arrow key	VK_UNDEFINED	The keyCode unknown
VK_LEFT	The left-arrow key	VK_F1 to VK_F12	The function keys from F1 to F12
VK_RIGHT	The right-arrow key		
VK_ESCAPE	The Esc key	VK_0 to VK_9	The number keys from 0 to 9
VK_TAB	The Tab key	VK_A to VK_Z	The letter keys from A to Z
VK_CONTROL	The Control key		

For the key-pressed and key-released events, `getKeyCode()` returns the value as defined in the table. For the key-typed event, `getKeyCode()` returns `VK_UNDEFINED`, while `getKeyChar()` returns the character entered.

The program in Listing 16.10 displays a user-input character. The user can move the character up, down, left, and right, using the arrow keys `VK_UP`, `VK_DOWN`, `VK_LEFT`, and `VK_RIGHT`. Figure 16.16 contains a sample run of the program.

KeyEventDemo
J

FIGURE 16.16 The program responds to key events by displaying a character and moving it up, down, left, or right.

LISTING 16.10 KeyEventDemo.java

create a panel
focusable
inner class
register listener
override handler
get the key pressed

```
import java.awt.*;
import java.awt.event.*;
import javax.swing.*;

public class KeyEventDemo extends JFrame {
  private KeyboardPanel keyboardPanel = new KeyboardPanel();

  /** Initialize UI */
  public KeyEventDemo() {
    // Add the keyboard panel to accept and display user input
    add(keyboardPanel);

    // Set focus
    keyboardPanel.setFocusable(true);
  }

  /** Main method */
  public static void main(String[] args) {
    KeyEventDemo frame = new KeyEventDemo();
    frame.setTitle("KeyEventDemo");
    frame.setSize(300, 300);
    frame.setLocationRelativeTo(null); // Center the frame
    frame.setDefaultCloseOperation(JFrame.EXIT_ON_CLOSE);
    frame.setVisible(true);
  }

  // Inner class: KeyboardPanel for receiving key input
  static class KeyboardPanel extends JPanel {
    private int x = 100;
    private int y = 100;
    private char keyChar = 'A'; // Default key

    public KeyboardPanel() {
      addKeyListener(new KeyAdapter() {
        public void keyPressed(KeyEvent e) {
          switch (e.getKeyCode()) {
            case KeyEvent.VK_DOWN: y += 10; break;
            case KeyEvent.VK_UP: y -= 10; break;
            case KeyEvent.VK_LEFT: x -= 10; break;
            case KeyEvent.VK_RIGHT: x += 10; break;
            default: keyChar = e.getKeyChar();
          }
```

```
43
44             repaint();
45           }
46         });
47       }
48
49       /** Draw the character */
50       protected void paintComponent(Graphics g) {
51         super.paintComponent(g);
52
53         g.setFont(new Font("TimesRoman", Font.PLAIN, 24));
54         g.drawString(String.valueOf(keyChar), x, y);
55       }
56     }
57 }
```

repaint

redraw character

The `KeyboardPanel` class extends `JPanel` to display a character (line 28). This class is defined as an inner class inside the main class, because it is used only in this class. Furthermore, the inner class is defined static, because it does not reference any instance members of the main class.

Because the program gets input from the keyboard, it listens for `KeyEvent` and extends `KeyAdapter` to handle key input (line 34).

When a key is pressed, the `keyPressed` handler is invoked. The program uses `e.getKeyCode()` to obtain the key code and `e.getKeyChar()` to get the character for the key. When a nonarrow key is pressed, the character is displayed (line 41). When an arrow key is pressed, the character moves in the direction indicated by the arrow key (lines 37–40).

focusable

Only a focused component can receive `KeyEvent`. To make a component focusable, set its `isFocusable` property to `true` (line 14).

efficient?

Every time the component is repainted, a new font is created for the `Graphics` object in line 53. This is not efficient. It is better to create the font once as a data field.

16.12 Animation Using the `Timer` Class

Not all source objects are GUI components. The `javax.swing.Timer` class is a source component that fires an `ActionEvent` at a predefined rate. Figure 16.17 lists some of the methods in the class.

javax.swing.Timer	
`+Timer(delay: int, listener: ActionListener)`	Creates a `Timer` object with a specified delay in milliseconds and an `ActionListener`.
`+addActionListener(listener: ActionListener): void`	Adds an `ActionListener` to the timer.
`+start(): void`	Starts this timer.
`+stop(): void`	Stops this timer.
`+setDelay(delay: int): void`	Sets a new delay value for this timer.

FIGURE 16.17 A `Timer` object fires an `ActionEvent` at a fixed rate.

A `Timer` object serves as the source of an `ActionEvent`. The listeners must be instances of `ActionListener` and registered with a `Timer` object. You create a `Timer` object using its sole constructor with a delay and a listener, where `delay` specifies the number of milliseconds between two action events. You can add additional listeners using the `addActionListener` method and adjust the `delay` using the `setDelay` method. To start the timer, invoke the `start()` method. To stop the timer, invoke the `stop()` method.

The `Timer` class can be used to control animations. For example, you can use it to display a moving message, as shown in Figure 16.18, with the code in Listing 16.11.

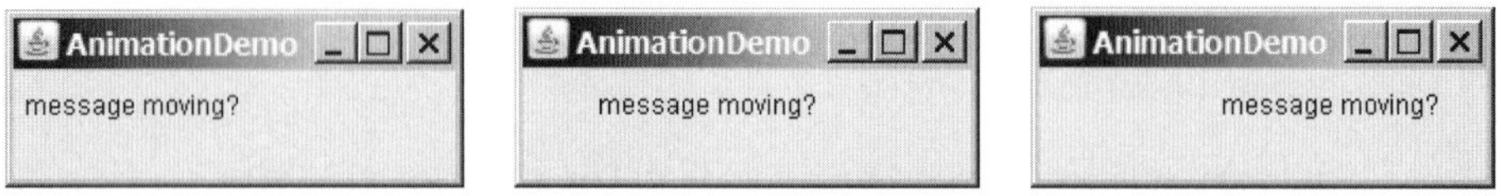
AnimationDemo
message moving?
AnimationDemo
message moving?
AnimationDemo
message moving?

FIGURE 16.18 A message moves in the panel.

LISTING 16.11 AnimationDemo.java

create panel
set message
create timer
start timer
reset x-coordinate
move message

```java
import java.awt.*;
import java.awt.event.*;
import javax.swing.*;

public class AnimationDemo extends JFrame {
  public AnimationDemo() {
    // Create a MovingMessagePanel for displaying a moving message
    add(new MovingMessagePanel("message moving?"));
  }

  /** Main method */
  public static void main(String[] args) {
    AnimationDemo frame = new AnimationDemo();
    frame.setTitle("AnimationDemo");
    frame.setSize(280, 100);
    frame.setLocationRelativeTo(null); // Center the frame
    frame.setDefaultCloseOperation(JFrame.EXIT_ON_CLOSE);
    frame.setVisible(true);
  }

  // Inner class: Displaying a moving message
  static class MovingMessagePanel extends JPanel {
    private String message = "Welcome to Java";
    private int xCoordinate = 0;
    private int yCoordinate = 20;

    public MovingMessagePanel(String message) {
      this.message = message;

      // Create a timer
      Timer timer = new Timer(1000, new TimerListener());
      timer.start();
    }

    /** Paint message */
    protected void paintComponent(Graphics g) {
      super.paintComponent(g);

      if (xCoordinate > getWidth()) {
        xCoordinate = -20;
      }
      xCoordinate += 5;
      g.drawString(message, xCoordinate, yCoordinate);
    }
```

```
45
46     class TimerListener implements ActionListener {
47       /** Handle ActionEvent */
48       public void actionPerformed(ActionEvent e) {
49         repaint();
50       }
51     }
52   }
53 }
```

listener class

event handler

repaint

The `MovingMessagePanel` class extends `JPanel` to display a message (line 22). This class is defined as an inner class inside the main class, because it is used only in this class. Furthermore, the inner class is defined static, because it does not reference any instance members of the main class.

An inner class listener is defined in line 46 to listen for `ActionEvent`. Line 31 creates a `Timer` for the listener. The timer is started in line 32. The timer fires an `ActionEvent` every second, and the listener responds in line 49 to repaint the panel. When a panel is painted, its `x`-coordinate is increased (line 42), so the message is displayed to the right. When the `x`-coordinate exceeds the bound of the panel, it is reset to `-20` (line 40), so the message continues moving from left to right.

In §15.12, "Case Study: The `StillClock` Class," you drew a `StillClock` to show the current time. The clock does not tick after it is displayed. What can you do to make the clock display a new current time every second? The key to making the clock tick is to repaint it every second with a new current time. You can use a timer to control the repainting of the clock with the code in Listing 16.12.

Listing 16.12 ClockAnimation.java

Video Note
Animate a clock

```
import java.awt.event.*;
import javax.swing.*;

public class ClockAnimation extends JFrame {
  private StillClock clock = new StillClock();

  public ClockAnimation() {
    add(clock);

    // Create a timer with delay 1000 ms
    Timer timer = new Timer(1000, new TimerListener());
    timer.start();
  }

  private class TimerListener implements ActionListener {
    /** Handle the action event */
    public void actionPerformed(ActionEvent e) {
      // Set new time and repaint the clock to display current time
      clock.setCurrentTime();
      clock.repaint();
    }
  }

  /** Main method */
  public static void main(String[] args) {
    JFrame frame = new ClockAnimation();
    frame.setTitle("ClockAnimation");
    frame.setSize(200, 200);
    frame.setLocationRelativeTo(null); // Center the frame
    frame.setDefaultCloseOperation(JFrame.EXIT_ON_CLOSE);
```

create a clock

create a timer

start timer

listener class

implement handler

set new time

repaint

```
31     frame.setVisible(true);
32   }
33 }
```

The program displays a running clock, as shown in Figure 16.19. `ClockAnimation` creates a `StillClock` (line 5). Line 11 creates a `Timer` for a `ClockAnimation`. The timer is started in line 12. The timer fires an `ActionEvent` every second, and the listener responds to set a new time (line 19) and repaint the clock (line 20). The `setCurrentTime()` method defined in `StillClock` sets the current time in the clock.

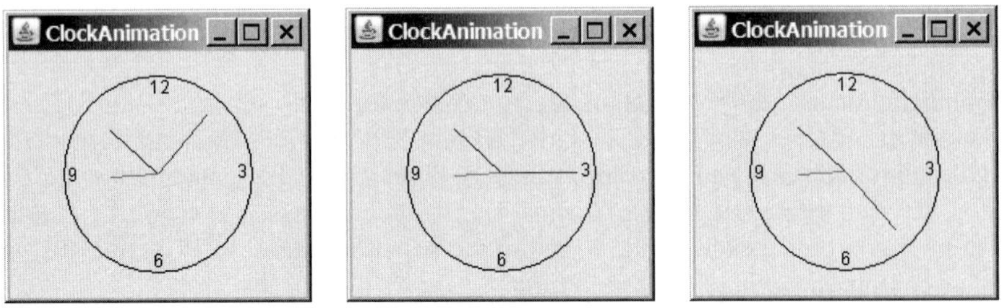
ClockAnimation
12
9
3
6
ClockAnimation
12
9
3
6
ClockAnimation
12
9
3
6

FIGURE 16.19 A live clock is displayed in the panel.

Key Terms

- anonymous inner class 542
- convenience listener adapter 551
- event 534
- event delegation 535
- event handler 559
- event listener 535
- event-listener interface 536
- event object 535
- event registration 535
- event source (source object) 535
- event-driven programming 534
- inner class 554

Chapter Summary

1. The root class of the event classes is `java.util.EventObject`. The subclasses of `EventObject` deal with special types of events, such as action events, window events, component events, mouse events, and key events. You can identify the source object of an event using the `getSource()` instance method in the `EventObject` class. If a component can fire an event, any subclass of the component can fire the same type of event.

2. The listener object's class must implement the corresponding event-listener interface. Java provides a listener interface for every event class. The listener interface is usually named `XListener` for `XEvent`, with the exception of `MouseMotionListener`. For example, the corresponding listener interface for `ActionEvent` is `ActionListener`; each listener for `ActionEvent` should implement the `ActionListener` interface. The listener interface contains the method(s), known as the *handler(s)*, which process the events.

3. The listener object must be registered by the source object. Registration methods depend on the event type. For `ActionEvent`, the method is `addActionListener`. In general, the method is named `addXListener` for `XEvent`.

4. An *inner class*, or *nested class,* is defined within the scope of another class. An inner class can reference the data and methods defined in the outer class in which it nests, so you need not pass the reference of the outer class to the constructor of the inner class.

5. Convenience adapters are support classes that provide default implementations for all the methods in the listener interface. Java provides convenience listener adapters for every AWT listener interface with multiple handlers. A convenience listener adapter is named *X*Adapter for *X*Listener.

6. A source object may fire several types of events. For each event, the source object maintains a list of registered listeners and notifies them by invoking the *handler* on the listener object to process the event.

7. A mouse event is fired whenever a mouse is clicked, released, moved, or dragged on a component. The mouse-event object captures the event, such as the number of clicks associated with it or the location (`x`- and `y`-coordinates) of the mouse point.

8. Java provides two listener interfaces, `MouseListener` and `MouseMotionListener`, to handle mouse events, implement the `MouseListener` interface to listen for such actions as mouse pressed, released, clicked, entered, or exited, and implement the `MouseMotionListener` interface to listen for such actions as mouse dragged or moved.

9. A `KeyEvent` object describes the nature of the event (namely, that a key has been pressed, released, or typed) and the value of the key.

10. The `keyPressed` handler is invoked when a key is pressed, the `keyReleased` handler is invoked when a key is released, and the `keyTyped` handler is invoked when a Unicode character key is entered. If a key does not have a Unicode (e.g., function keys, modifier keys, action keys, and control keys), the `keyTyped` handler will be not be invoked.

11. You can use the `Timer` class to control Java animations. A timer fires an `ActionEvent` at a fixed rate. The listener updates the painting to simulate an animation.

Review Questions

Sections 16.2–16.3

16.1 Can a button fire a `WindowEvent`? Can a button fire a `MouseEvent`? Can a button fire an `ActionEvent`?

16.2 Why must a listener be an instance of an appropriate listener interface? Explain how to register a listener object and how to implement a listener interface.

16.3 Can a source have multiple listeners? Can a listener listen on multiple sources? Can a source be a listener for itself?

16.4 How do you implement a method defined in the listener interface? Do you need to implement all the methods defined in the listener interface?

Sections 16.4–16.9

16.5 Can an inner class be used in a class other than the class in which it nests?

16.6 Can the modifiers `public`, `private`, and `static` be used on inner classes?

16.7 If class `A` is an inner class in class `B`, what is the .class file for `A`? If class B contains two anonymous inner classes, what are the .class file names for these two classes?

16.8 What is wrong in the following code?

```java
import java.swing.*;
import java.awt.*;

public class Test extends JFrame {
  public Test() {
    JButton jbtOK = new JButton("OK");
    add(jbtOK);
  }

  private class Listener
      implements ActionListener {
    public void actionPerform
        (ActionEvent e) {
      System.out.println
        (jbtOK.getActionCommand());
    }
  }

  /** Main method omitted */
}
```

(a)

```java
import java.awt.event.*;
import javax.swing.*;

public class Test extends JFrame {
  public Test() {
    JButton jbtOK = new JButton("OK");
    add(jbtOK);
    jbtOK.addActionListener(
      new ActionListener() {
        public void actionPerformed
            (ActionEvent e) {
          System.out.println
            (jbtOK.getActionCommand());
        }
    } // Something missing here
  }

  /** Main method omitted */
}
```

(b)

16.9 What is the difference between the `setSize(width, height)` method and the `pack()` method in `JFrame`?

Sections 16.10–16.11

16.10 What method do you use to get the source of an event? What method do you use to get the timestamp for an action event, a mouse event, or a key event? What method do you use to get the mouse-point position for a mouse event? What method do you use to get the key character for a key event?

16.11 What is the listener interface for mouse pressed, released, clicked, entered, and exited? What is the listener interface for mouse moved and dragged?

16.12 Does every key in the keyboard have a Unicode? Is a key code in the `KeyEvent` class equivalent to a Unicode?

16.13 Is the `keyPressed` handler invoked after a key is pressed? Is the `keyReleased` handler invoked after a key is released? Is the `keyTyped` handler invoked after *any* key is typed?

Section 16.12

16.14 How do you create a timer? How do you start a timer? How do you stop a timer?

16.15 Does the `Timer` class have a no-arg constructor? Can you add multiple listeners to a timer?

Programming Exercises

Sections 16.2–16.9

16.1 (*Finding which button has been clicked on the console*) Add the code to Exercise 12.1 that will display a message on the console indicating which button has been clicked.

16.2 (*Using `ComponentEvent`*) Any GUI component can fire a `ComponentEvent`. The `ComponentListener` defines the `componentMoved`, `componentResized`, `componentShown`, and `componentHidden` methods for processing component events. Write a test program to demonstrate `ComponentEvent`.

16.3* (*Moving the ball*) Write a program that moves the ball in a panel. You should define a panel class for displaying the ball and provide the methods for moving the button left, right, up, and down, as shown in Figure 16.20(a).

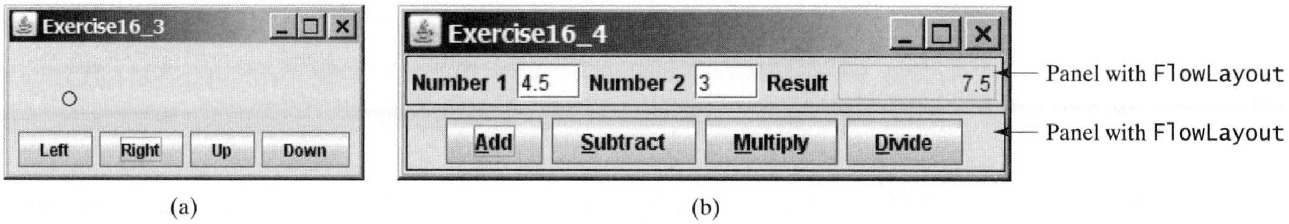
Exercise16_3
Left
Right
Up
Down
Exercise16_4
Number 1
4.5
Number 2
3
Result
7.5
Add
Subtract
Multiply
Divide
Panel with FlowLayout
Panel with FlowLayout
(a)
(b)

FIGURE 16.20 (a) Exercise 16.3 displays which button is clicked on a message panel. (b) The program performs addition, subtraction, multiplication, and division on double numbers.

16.4* (*Creating a simple calculator*) Write a program to perform add, subtract, multiply, and divide operations (see Figure 16.20(b)).

16.5* (*Creating an investment-value calculator*) Write a program that calculates the future value of an investment at a given interest rate for a specified number of years. The formula for the calculation is as follows:

```
futureValue = investmentAmount * (1 + monthlyInterestRate)^(years*12)
```

Use text fields for interest rate, investment amount, and years. Display the future amount in a text field when the user clicks the *Calculate* button, as shown in Figure 16.21(a).

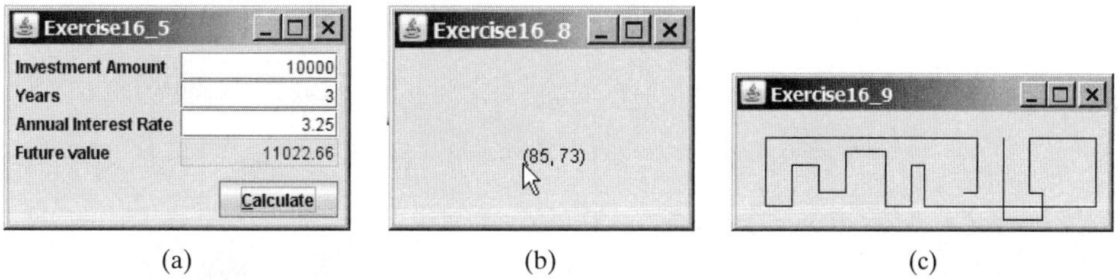
Exercise16_5
Investment Amount
10000
Years
3
Annual Interest Rate
3.25
Future value
11022.66
Calculate
Exercise16_8
(85, 73)
Exercise16_9
(a)
(b)
(c)

FIGURE 16.21 (a) The user enters the investment amount, years, and interest rate to compute future value. (b) Exercise 16.8 displays the mouse position. (c) Exercise 16.9 uses the arrow keys to draw the lines.

Section 16.10

16.6** (*Alternating two messages*) Write a program to rotate with a mouse click two messages displayed on a panel, "Java is fun" and "Java is powerful".

16.7* (*Setting background color using a mouse*) Write a program that displays the background color of a panel as black when the mouse is pressed and as white when the mouse is released.

16.8* (*Displaying the mouse position*) Write two programs, such that one displays the mouse position when the mouse is clicked (see Figure 16.21(b)) and the other displays the mouse position when the mouse is pressed and ceases to display it when the mouse is released.

Section 16.11

16.9* (*Drawing lines using the arrow keys*) Write a program that draws line segments using the arrow keys. The line starts from the center of the frame and draws toward east, north, west, or south when the right-arrow key, up-arrow key, left-arrow key, or down-arrow key is clicked, as shown in Figure 16.21(c).

16.10** (*Entering and displaying a string*) Write a program that receives a string from the keyboard and displays it on a panel. The *Enter* key signals the end of a string. Whenever a new string is entered, it is displayed on the panel.

16.11* (*Displaying a character*) Write a program to get a character input from the keyboard and display the character where the mouse points.

Section 16.12

16.12** (*Displaying a running fan*) Listing 15.4, DrawArcs.java, displays a motionless fan. Write a program that displays a running fan.

16.13** (*Slide show*) Twenty-five slides are stored as image files (slide0.jpg, slide1.jpg, . . . , slide24.jpg) in the image directory downloadable along with the source code in the book. The size of each image is 800 $\times$ 600. Write a Java application that automatically displays the slides repeatedly. Each slide is shown for a second. The slides are displayed in order. When the last slide finishes, the first slide is redisplayed, and so on.

(*Hint*: Place a label in the frame and set a slide as an image icon in the label.)

Video Note
Animate a rising flag

16.14** (*Raising flag*) Write a Java program that animates raising a flag, as shown in Figure 16.1. (See §15.11, "Displaying Images," on how to display images.)

16.15** (*Racing car*) Write a Java program that simulates car racing, as shown in Figure 16.22(a). The car moves from left to right. When it hits the right end, it restarts from the left and continues the same process. You can use a timer to control animation. Redraw the car with a new base coordinates (x, y), as shown in Figure 16.22(b).

Exercise16_15
Exercise16_15
x
x+20
x+40
y-30
y-20
y-10
y
(x,y)

(a) (b)

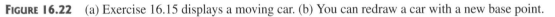

FIGURE 16.22 (a) Exercise 16.15 displays a moving car. (b) You can redraw a car with a new base point.

16.16* (*Displaying a flashing label*) Write a program that displays a flashing label.

(*Hint*: To make the label flash, you need to repaint the panel alternately with the label and without it (blank screen) at a fixed rate. Use a `boolean` variable to control the alternation.)

16.17* (*Controlling a moving label*) Modify Listing 16.11, AnimationDemo.java, to control a moving label using the mouse. The label freezes when the mouse is pressed, and moves again when the button is released.

Comprehensive

16.18* (*Moving a circle using keys*) Write a program that moves a circle up, down, left, or right using the arrow keys.

16.19** (*Geometry: inside a circle?*) Write a program that draws a fixed circle centered at (`100`, `60`) with radius `50`. Whenever a mouse is moved, display the message indicating whether the mouse point is inside the circle, as shown in Figure 16.23(a).

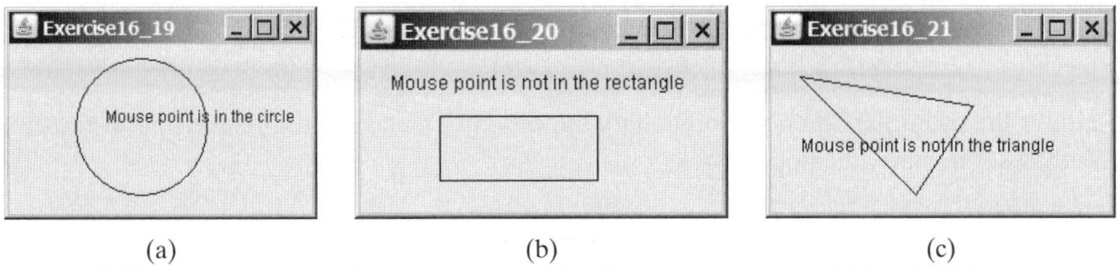
Exercise16_19
Mouse point is in the circle
Exercise16_20
Mouse point is not in the rectangle
Exercise16_21
Mouse point is not in the triangle
(a)
(b)
(c)

FIGURE 16.23 Detect whether a point is inside a circle, a rectangle, or a triangle.

16.20** (*Geometry: inside a rectangle?*) Write a program that draws a fixed rectangle centered at (`100`, `60`) with width `100` and height `40`. Whenever a mouse is moved, display the message indicating whether the mouse point is inside the rectangle, as shown in Figure 16.23(b). To detect whether a point is inside a rectangle, use the `MyRectangle2D` class defined in Exercise 10.12.

16.21** (*Geometry: inside a triangle?*) Write a program that draws a fixed triangle with three vertices at (`20`, `20`), (`100`, `100`), and (`140`, `40`). Whenever a mouse is moved, display the message indicating whether the mouse point is inside the triangle, as shown in Figure 16.23(c). To detect whether a point is inside a triangle, use the `Triangle2D` class defined in Exercise 10.13.

16.22*** (*Game: bean-machine animation*) Write a program that animates a bean machine introduced in Exercise 15.24. The animation terminates after ten balls are dropped, as shown in Figure 16.24.

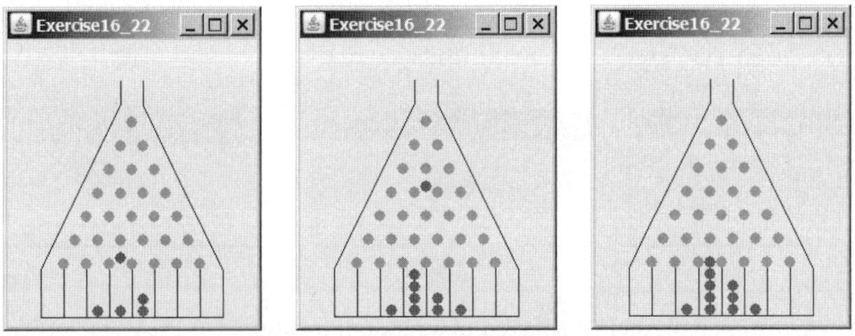
Exercise16_22
Exercise16_22
Exercise16_22

FIGURE 16.24 The balls are dropped to the bean machine.

16.23*** (*Geometry: closest pair of points*) Write a program that lets the user click on the panel to dynamically create points. Initially, the panel is empty. When a panel has two or more points, highlight the pair of closest points. Whenever a new point is created, a new pair of closest points is highlighted. Display the points using small circles and highlight the points using filled circles, as shown in Figure 16.25(a)–(c).

(*Hint*: store the points in an `ArrayList`.)

16.24* (*Controlling a clock*) Modify Listing 16.12 ClockAnimation.java to add two methods `start()` and `stop()` to start and stop the clock. Write a program

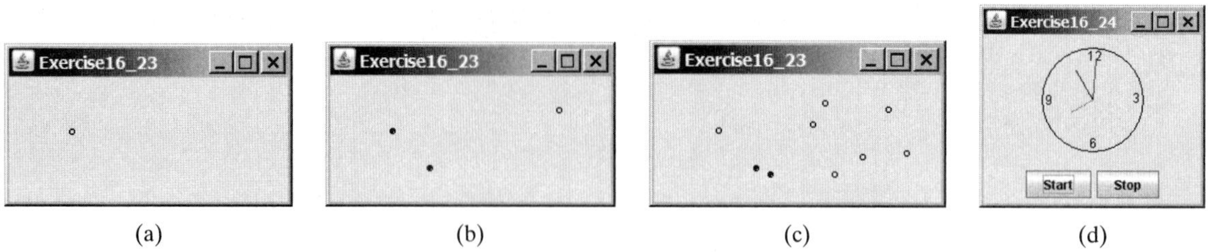
Exercise16_23
Exercise16_23
Exercise16_23
Exercise16_24
12
9
3
6
Start
Stop
(a)
(b)
(c)
(d)

FIGURE 16.25 Exercise 16.23 allows the user to create new points with a mouse click and highlights the pair of the closest points. Exercise 16.24 allows the user to start and stop a clock.

that lets the user control the clock with the *Start* and *Stop* buttons, as shown in Figure 16.25(d).

16.25*** (*Game: hitting balloons*) Write a program that displays a balloon in a random position in a panel (Figure 16.26(a)). Use the left- and right-arrow keys to point the gun left or right to aim at the balloon (Figure 16.26(b)). Press the up-arrow key to fire a small ball from the gun (Figure 16.26(c)). Once the ball hits the balloon, the debris is displayed (Figure 16.26(e)) and a new balloon is displayed in a random location (Figure 16.26(f)). If the ball misses the balloon, the ball disappears once it hits the boundary of the panel. You can then press the up-arrow key to fire another ball. Whenever you press the left- or the right-arrow key, the gun turns 5 degrees left or right. (Instructors may modify the game as follows: 1. display the number of the balloons destroyed; 2. display a countdown timer (e.g., 60 seconds) and terminate the game once the time expires; 3. allow the balloon to rise dynamically.)

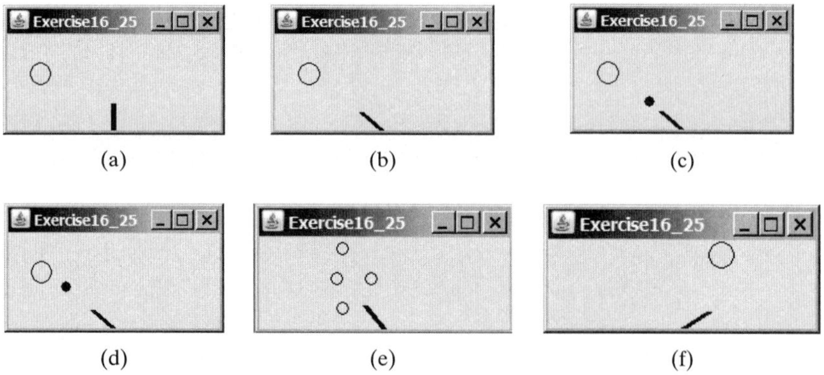
Exercise16_25
Exercise16_25
Exercise16_25
Exercise16_25
Exercise16_25
Exercise16_25
(a)
(b)
(c)
(d)
(e)
(f)

FIGURE 16.26 (a) A balloon is displayed in a random location. (b) Press the left-/right-arrow keys to aim the balloon. (c) Press the up-arrow key to fire a ball. (d) The ball moves straight toward the balloon. (e) The ball hits the balloon. (f) A new balloon is displayed in a random position.

16.26** (*Moving a circle using mouse*) Write a program that displays a circle with radius `10` pixels. You can point the mouse inside the circle and drag (i.e., move with mouse pressed) the circle wherever the mouse goes, as shown in Figure 16.27(a)–(b).

16.27*** (*Game: eye-hand coordination*) Write a program that displays a circle of radius `10` pixels filled with a random color at a random location on a panel, as shown in Figure 16.27(c). When you click the circle, it is gone and a new random-color circle is displayed at another random location. After twenty circles are clicked, display the time spent in the panel, as shown in Figure 16.27(d).

Exercise16_26
Exercise16_26
Exercise16_27
Exercise16_27
Time spent: 51515 milliseconds
(a)
(b)
(c)
(d)

FIGURE 16.27 (a)–(b) You can point, drag, and move the circle. (c) When you click a circle, a new circle is displayed at a random location. (d) After 20 circles are clicked, the time spent in the panel is displayed.

16.28*** (*Simulation: self-avoiding random walk*) A self-avoiding walk in a lattice is a path from one point to another which does not visit the same point twice. Self-avoiding walks have applications in physics, chemistry, and mathematics. They can be used to model chainlike entities such as solvents and polymers. Write a program that displays a random path that starts from the center and ends at a point on the boundary, as shown in Figure 16.28(a), or ends at a dead-end point (i.e., surrounded by four points that are already visited), as shown in Figure 16.28(b). Assume the size of the lattice is **16** by **16**.

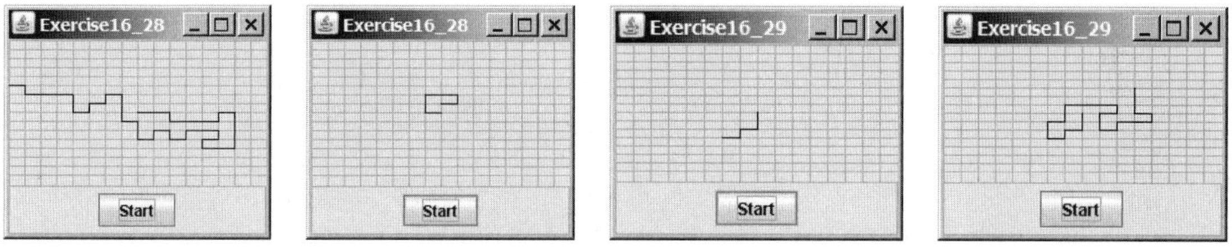
Exercise16_28
Start
Exercise16_28
Start
Exercise16_29
Start
Exercise16_29
Start
(a)
(b)
(c)
(d)

FIGURE 16.28 (a) A path ends at a boundary point. (b) A path ends at dead-end point. (c)–(d) Animation shows the progress of a path step by step.

16.29*** (*Animation: self-avoiding random walk*) Revise the preceding exercise to display the walk step by step in an animation, as shown in Figure 16.28(c)–(d).

16.30** (*Simulation: self-avoiding random walk*) Write a simulation program to show that the chance of getting dead-end paths increases as the grid size increases. Your program simulates lattices with size from 10 to 80. For each lattice size, simulate a self-avoiding random walk 10000 times and display the probability of the dead-end paths, as shown in the following sample output:

```
For a lattice of size 10, the probability of dead-end paths is 10.6%
For a lattice of size 11, the probability of dead-end paths is 14.0%
...
For a lattice of size 80, the probability of dead-end paths is 99.5%
```

16.31* (*Geometry: displaying an n-sided regular polygon*) Exercise 15.25 created the `RegularPolygonPanel` for displaying an n-sided regular polygon. Write a program that displays a regular polygon and uses two buttons named *+1* and *−1* to increase or decrease the size of the polygon, as shown in Figure 16.29(a)–(b).

16.32** (*Geometry: adding and removing points*) Write a program that lets the user click on the panel to dynamically create and remove points. When the user right-click the mouse, a point is created and displayed at the mouse point, and

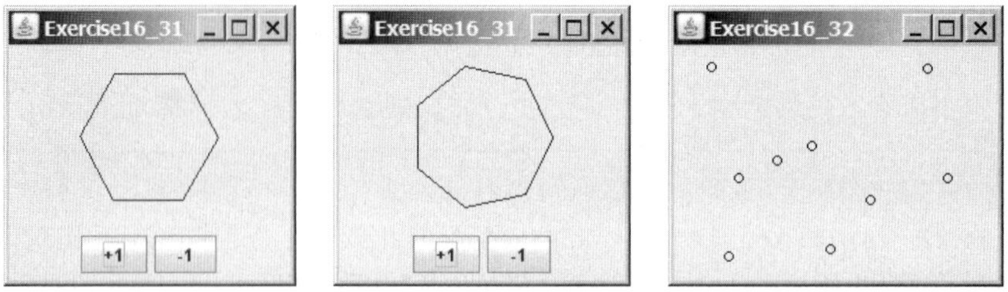
Exercise16_31
+1
-1
Exercise16_31
+1
-1
Exercise16_32

FIGURE 16.29 Clicking the *+1* or *−1* button increases or decreases the number of sides of a regular polygon in Exercise 16.31. Exercise 16.32 allows the user to create/remove points dynamically.

the user can remove a point by pointing to it and left-clicking the mouse, as shown in Figure 16.29(c).

16.33** (*Geometry: palindrome*) Write a program that animates a palindrome swing, as shown in Figure 16.30. Press the up-arrow key to increase the speed and the down-arrow key to decrease it. Press the *S* key to stop animation and the *R* key to resume.

Exercise16_33
Exercise16_33
Exercise16_33

FIGURE 16.30 Exercise 16.33 animates a palindrome swing.

16.34** (*Game: hangman*) Write a program that animates a hangman game swing, as shown in Figure 16.31. Press the up-arrow key to increase the speed and the down-arrow key to decrease it. Press the *S* key to stop animation and the *R* key to resume.

Exercise16_34
Exercise16_34
Exercise16_34

FIGURE 16.31 Exercise 16.34 animates a hangman game.

16.35*** (*Game: hangman*) Exercise 9.31 presents a console version of the popular hangman game. Write a GUI program that lets a user play the game. The user guesses a word by entering one letter at a time, as shown in Figure 16.32(a). If the user misses seven times, a hanging man swings, as shown in Figure 16.32(b)–(c). Once a word is finished, the user can press the *Enter* key to continue to guess another word.

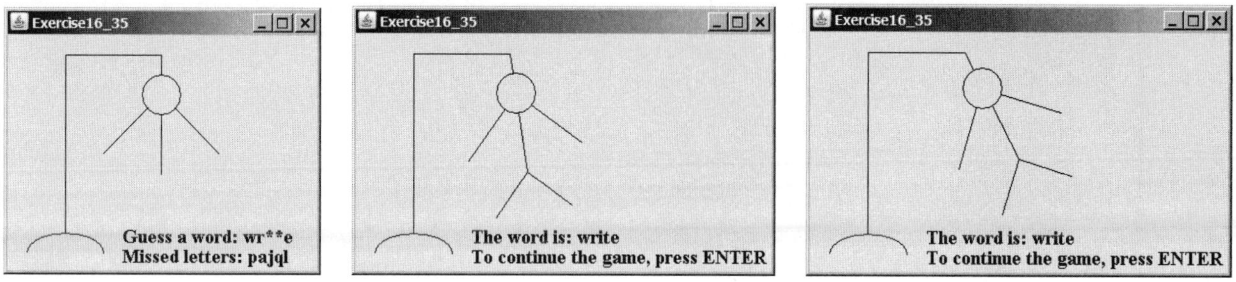
Exercise16_35
Guess a word: wr**e
Missed letters: pajql
Exercise16_35
The word is: write
To continue the game, press ENTER
Exercise16_35
The word is: write
To continue the game, press ENTER

(a) (b) (c)

FIGURE 16.32 Exercise 16.35 develops a complete hangman game.

16.36* (*Flipping coins*) Write a program that displays head (`H`) or tail (`T`) for each of nine coins, as shown in Figure 16.33. When a cell is clicked, the coin is flipped. A cell is a `JLable`. Write a custom cell class that extends `JLable` with the mouse listener for handling the clicks. When the program starts, all cells initially display `H`.

Exercise16_36
H H H
H H H
H H H
Exercise16_36
H H H
T T T
H H H

FIGURE 16.33 Exercise 16.36 enables the user to click a cell to flip a coin.

CHAPTER 17

CREATING GRAPHICAL USER INTERFACES

Objectives

- To create graphical user interfaces with various user-interface components: `JButton`, `JCheckBox`, `JRadioButton`, `JLabel`, `JTextField`, `JTextArea`, `JComboBox`, `JList`, `JScrollBar`, and `JSlider` (§§17.2–17.11).
- To create listeners for various types of events (§§17.2–17.11).
- To explore `JButton` (§17.2)
- To explore `JCheckBox` (§17.3)
- To explore `JRadioButton` (§17.4)
- To explore `JLabel` (§17.5)
- To explore `JTextField` (§17.6)
- To explore `JTextArea` (§17.7)
- To explore `JComboBox` (§17.8)
- To explore `JList` (§17.9)
- To explore `JScrollBar` (§17.10)
- To explore `JSlider` (§17.11)
- To display multiple windows in an application (§17.12).

17.1 Introduction

GUI

A graphical user interface (GUI) makes a system user friendly and easy to use. Creating a GUI requires creativity and knowledge of how GUI components work. Since the GUI components in Java are very flexible and versatile, you can create a wide assortment of useful user interfaces.

Many Java IDEs provide tools for visually designing and developing GUI interfaces. This enables you to rapidly assemble the elements of a user interface (UI) for a Java application or applet with minimum coding. Tools, however, cannot do everything. You have to modify the programs they produce. Consequently, before you begin to use the visual tools, you must understand the basic concepts of Java GUI programming.

Previous chapters briefly introduced several GUI components. This chapter introduces the frequently used GUI components in detail (see Figure 17.1). (Since this chapter introduces no new concepts, instructors may assign it for students to study on their own.)

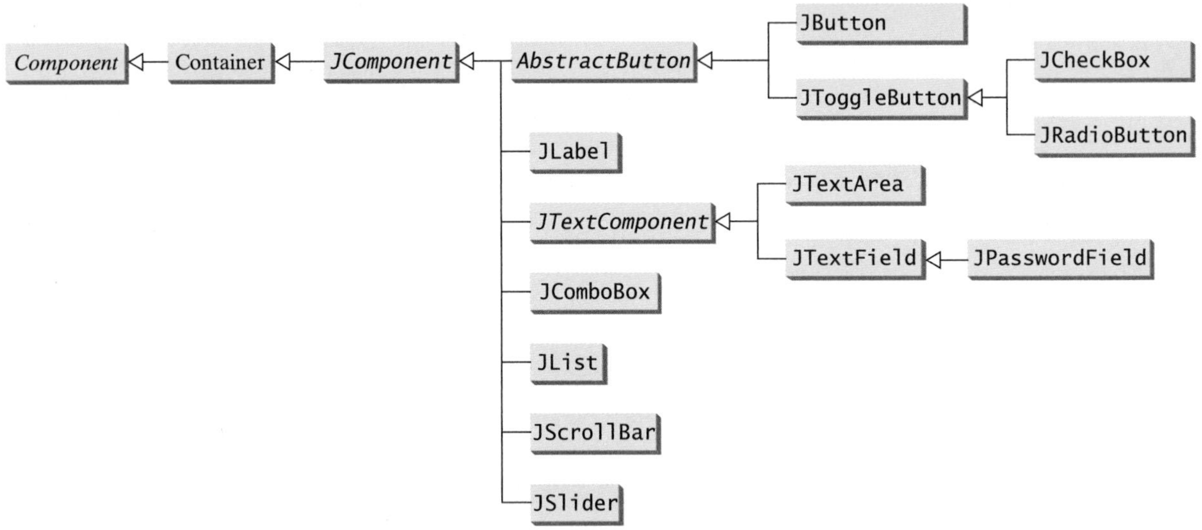
Component
Container
JComponent
AbstractButton
JButton
JToggleButton
JCheckBox
JRadioButton
JLabel
JTextComponent
JTextArea
JTextField
JPasswordField
JComboBox
JList
JScrollBar
JSlider

FIGURE 17.1 These Swing GUI components are frequently used to create user interfaces.

naming convention for components

Note

Throughout this book, the prefixes `jbt`, `jchk`, `jrb`, `jlbl`, `jtf`, `jpf`, `jta`, `jcbo`, `jlst`, `jscb`, and `jsld` are used to name reference variables for `JButton`, `JCheckBox`, `JRadioButton`, `JLabel`, `JTextField`, `JPasswordField`, `JTextArea`, `JComboBox`, `JList`, `JScrollBar`, and `JSlider`.

17.2 Buttons

AbstractButton
JButton

A *button* is a component that triggers an action event when clicked. Swing provides regular buttons, toggle buttons, check box buttons, and radio buttons. The common features of these buttons are defined in `javax.swing. AbstractButton`, as shown in Figure 17.2.

This section introduces the regular buttons defined in the `JButton` class. `JButton` inherits `AbstractButton` and provides several constructors to create buttons, as shown in Figure 17.3.

17.2.1 Icons, Pressed Icons, and Rollover Icons

A regular button has a default icon, a pressed icon, and a rollover icon. Normally you use the default icon. The other icons are for special effects. A pressed icon is displayed when a button is pressed, and a rollover icon is displayed when the mouse is over the button but not pressed.

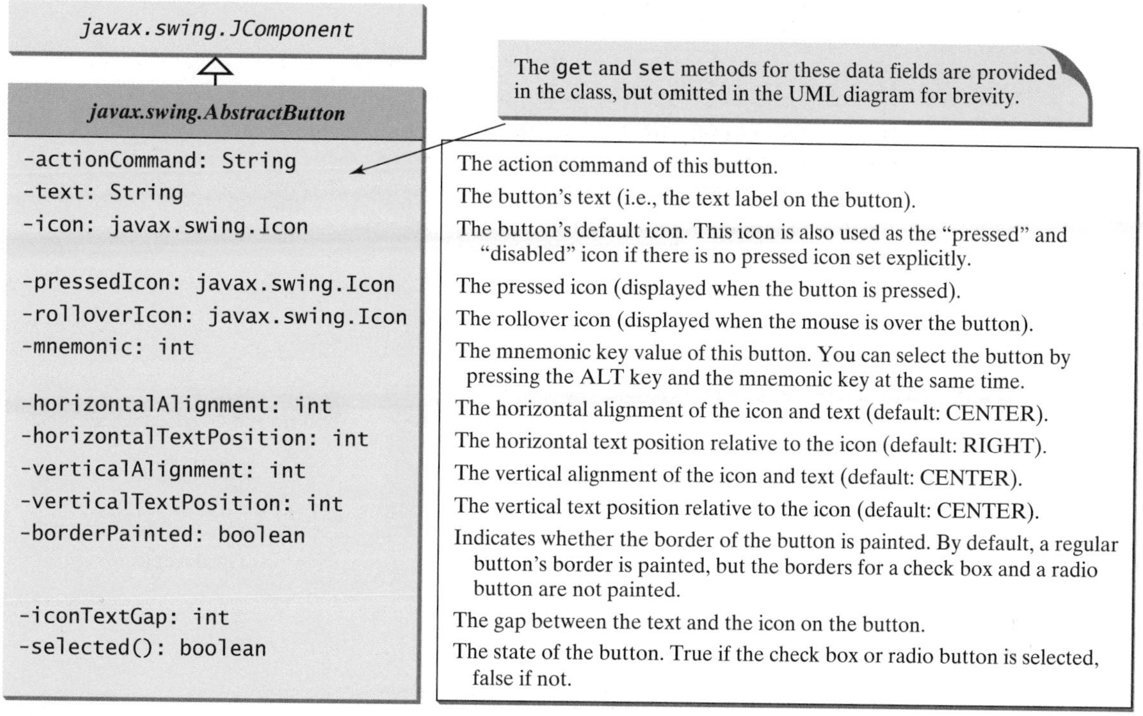
javax.swing.JComponent
javax.swing.AbstractButton
-actionCommand: String
-text: String
-icon: javax.swing.Icon
-pressedIcon: javax.swing.Icon
-rolloverIcon: javax.swing.Icon
-mnemonic: int
-horizontalAlignment: int
-horizontalTextPosition: int
-verticalAlignment: int
-verticalTextPosition: int
-borderPainted: boolean
-iconTextGap: int
-selected(): boolean
The get and set methods for these data fields are provided in the class, but omitted in the UML diagram for brevity.
The action command of this button.
The button's text (i.e., the text label on the button).
The button's default icon. This icon is also used as the "pressed" and "disabled" icon if there is no pressed icon set explicitly.
The pressed icon (displayed when the button is pressed).
The rollover icon (displayed when the mouse is over the button).
The mnemonic key value of this button. You can select the button by pressing the ALT key and the mnemonic key at the same time.
The horizontal alignment of the icon and text (default: CENTER).
The horizontal text position relative to the icon (default: RIGHT).
The vertical alignment of the icon and text (default: CENTER).
The vertical text position relative to the icon (default: CENTER).
Indicates whether the border of the button is painted. By default, a regular button's border is painted, but the borders for a check box and a radio button are not painted.
The gap between the text and the icon on the button.
The state of the button. True if the check box or radio button is selected, false if not.

FIGURE 17.2 `AbstractButton` defines common features of different types of buttons.

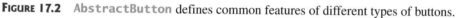

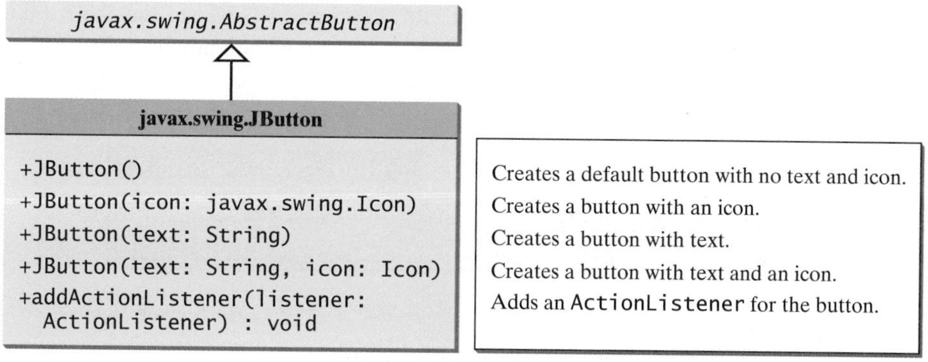
javax.swing.AbstractButton
javax.swing.JButton
+JButton()
+JButton(icon: javax.swing.Icon)
+JButton(text: String)
+JButton(text: String, icon: Icon)
+addActionListener(listener: ActionListener) : void
Creates a default button with no text and icon.
Creates a button with an icon.
Creates a button with text.
Creates a button with text and an icon.
Adds an ActionListener for the button.

FIGURE 17.3 `JButton` defines a regular push button.

For example, Listing 17.1 displays the American flag as a regular icon, the Canadian flag as a pressed icon, and the British flag as a rollover icon, as shown in Figure 17.4.

LISTING 17.1 TestButtonIcons.java

```
import javax.swing.*;

public class TestButtonIcons extends JFrame  {
  public static void main(String[] args) {
    // Create a frame and set its properties
    JFrame frame = new TestButtonIcons();
    frame.setTitle("ButtonIcons");
    frame.setSize(200, 100);
    frame.setLocationRelativeTo(null); // Center the frame
    frame.setDefaultCloseOperation(JFrame.EXIT_ON_CLOSE);
```

create icons
regular icon
pressed icon
rollover icon
add a button

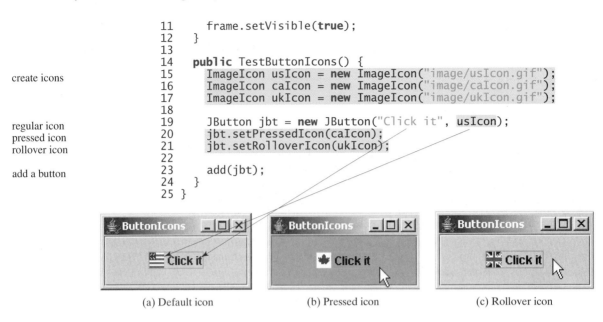

```
    frame.setVisible(true);
  }

  public TestButtonIcons() {
    ImageIcon usIcon = new ImageIcon("image/usIcon.gif");
    ImageIcon caIcon = new ImageIcon("image/caIcon.gif");
    ImageIcon ukIcon = new ImageIcon("image/ukIcon.gif");

    JButton jbt = new JButton("Click it", usIcon);
    jbt.setPressedIcon(caIcon);
    jbt.setRolloverIcon(ukIcon);

    add(jbt);
  }
}
```

ButtonIcons
Click it
ButtonIcons
Click it
ButtonIcons
Click it

(a) Default icon (b) Pressed icon (c) Rollover icon

FIGURE 17.4 A button can have several types of icons.

17.2.2 Alignments

horizontal alignment

Horizontal alignment specifies how the icon and text are placed horizontally on a button. You can set the horizontal alignment using `setHorizontalAlignment(int)` with one of the five constants `LEADING`, `LEFT`, `CENTER`, `RIGHT`, `TRAILING`, as shown in Figure 17.5. At present, `LEADING` and `LEFT` are the same, and `TRAILING` and `RIGHT` are the same. Future implementation may distinguish them. The default horizontal alignment is `SwingConstants.CENTER`.

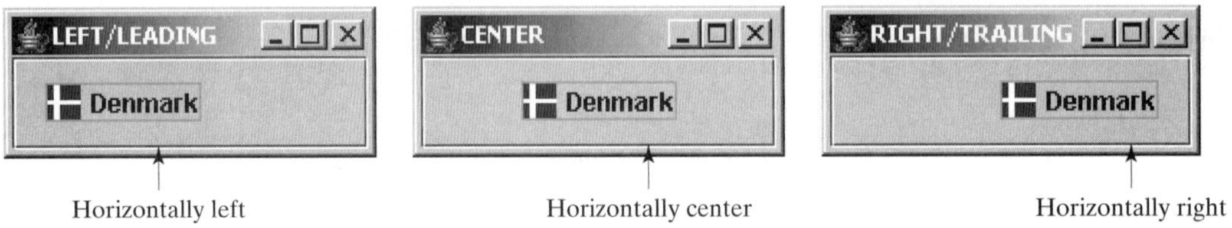
LEFT/LEADING
Denmark
CENTER
Denmark
RIGHT/TRAILING
Denmark
Horizontally left
Horizontally center
Horizontally right

FIGURE 17.5 You can specify how the icon and text are placed on a button horizontally.

vertical alignment

Vertical alignment specifies how the icon and text are placed vertically on a button. You can set the vertical alignment using `setVerticalAlignment(int)` with one of the three constants `TOP`, `CENTER`, `BOTTOM`, as shown in Figure 17.6. The default vertical alignment is `SwingConstants.CENTER`.

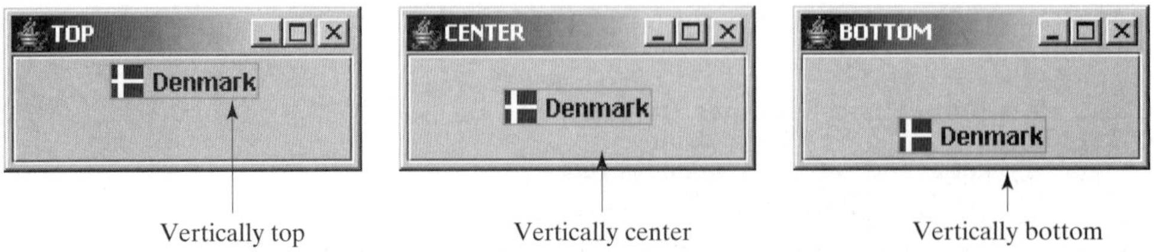
TOP
Denmark
CENTER
Denmark
BOTTOM
Denmark
Vertically top
Vertically center
Vertically bottom

FIGURE 17.6 You can specify how the icon and text are placed on a button vertically.

17.2.3 Text Positions

horizontal text position

Horizontal text position specifies the horizontal position of the text relative to the icon. You can set the horizontal text position using `setHorizontalTextPosition(int)` with one of the five constants `LEADING`, `LEFT`, `CENTER`, `RIGHT`, `TRAILING`, as shown in Figure 17.7. At present, `LEADING` and `LEFT` are the same, and `TRAILING` and `RIGHT` are the same. Future implementation may distinguish them. The default horizontal text position is `SwingConstants.RIGHT`.

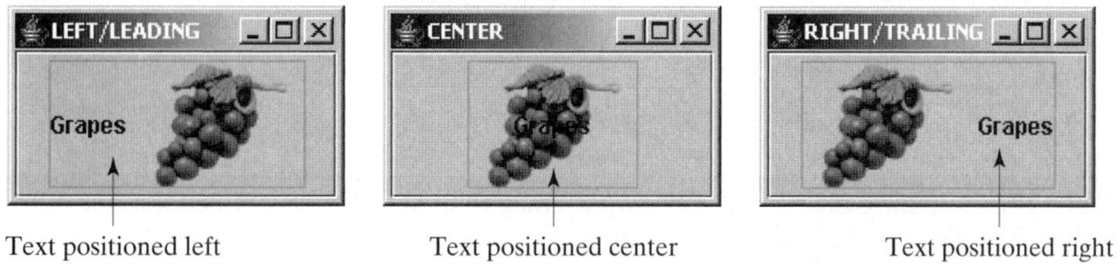
LEFT/LEADING
Grapes
CENTER
Grapes
RIGHT/TRAILING
Grapes
Text positioned left
Text positioned center
Text positioned right

FIGURE 17.7 You can specify the horizontal position of the text relative to the icon.

vertical text position

Vertical text position specifies the vertical position of the text relative to the icon. You can set the vertical text position using `setVerticalTextPosition(int)` with one of the three constants `TOP`, `CENTER`, `BOTTOM`, as shown in Figure 17.8. The default vertical text position is `SwingConstants.CENTER`.

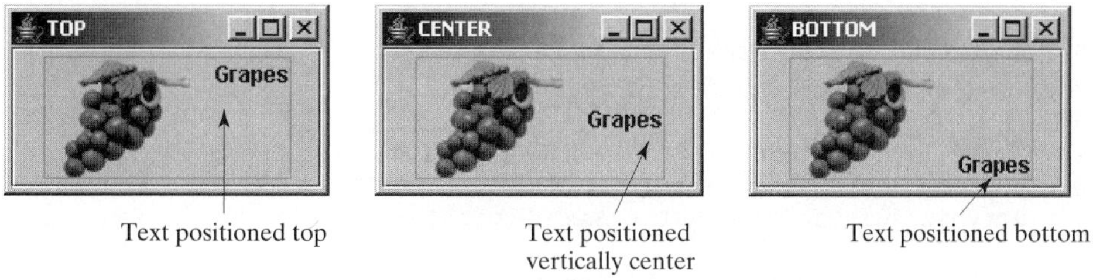
TOP
Grapes
CENTER
Grapes
BOTTOM
Grapes
Text positioned top
Text positioned vertically center
Text positioned bottom

FIGURE 17.8 You can specify the vertical position of the text relative to the icon.

Note

The constants `LEFT`, `CENTER`, `RIGHT`, `LEADING`, `TRAILING`, `TOP`, and `BOTTOM` used in `AbstractButton` are also used in many other Swing components. These constants are centrally defined in the `javax.swing.SwingConstants` interface. Since all Swing GUI components implement `SwingConstants`, you can reference the constants through `SwingConstants` or a GUI component. For example, `SwingConstants.CENTER` is the same as `JButton.CENTER`.

SwingConstants

`JButton` can fire many types of events, but often you need to add listeners to respond to an `ActionEvent`. When a button is pressed, it fires an `ActionEvent`.

17.2.4 Using Buttons

Video Note
Use buttons

This section presents a program, shown in Listing 17.2, that displays a message on a panel and uses two buttons, <= and =>, to move the message on the panel to the left or right. The layout of the UI is shown in Figure 17.9.

Here are the major steps in the program:

1. Create the user interface.
   Create a `MessagePanel` object to display the message. The `MessagePanel` class was created in Listing 15.8, MessagePanel.java. Place it in the center of the frame. Create two buttons, <= and =>, on a panel. Place the panel in the south of the frame.

2. Process the event.
   Create and register listeners for processing the action event to move the message left or right according to whether the left or right button was clicked.

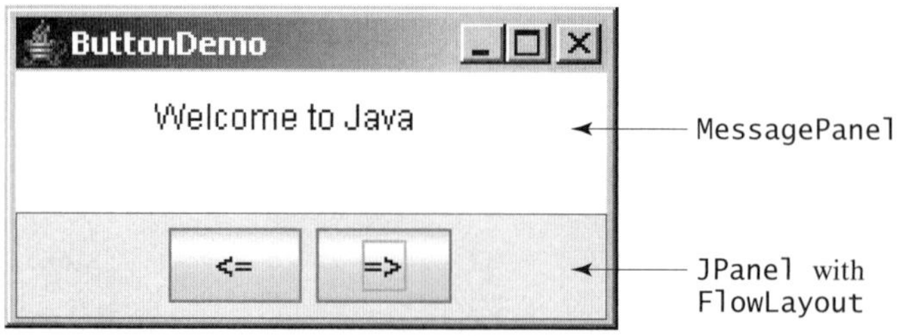
ButtonDemo
Welcome to Java
<=
=>
MessagePanel
JPanel with
FlowLayout

FIGURE 17.9 Clicking the <= and => buttons causes the message on the panel to move to the left and right, respectively.

LISTING 17.2 ButtonDemo.java

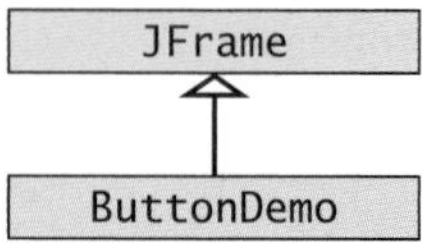
JFrame
ButtonDemo

create frame

create UI

mnemonic

```
import java.awt.*;
import java.awt.event.ActionListener;
import java.awt.event.ActionEvent;
import javax.swing.*;

public class ButtonDemo extends JFrame {
  // Create a panel for displaying message
  protected MessagePanel messagePanel
    = new MessagePanel("Welcome to Java");

  // Declare two buttons to move the message left and right
  private JButton jbtLeft = new JButton("<=");
  private JButton jbtRight = new JButton("=>");

  public static void main(String[] args) {
    ButtonDemo frame = new ButtonDemo();
    frame.setTitle("ButtonDemo");
    frame.setSize(250, 100);
    frame.setLocationRelativeTo(null); // Center the frame
    frame.setDefaultCloseOperation(JFrame.EXIT_ON_CLOSE);
    frame.setVisible(true);
  }

  public ButtonDemo() {
    // Set the background color of messagePanel
    messagePanel.setBackground(Color.white);

    // Create Panel jpButtons to hold two Buttons "<=" and "right =>"
    JPanel jpButtons = new JPanel();
    jpButtons.add(jbtLeft);
    jpButtons.add(jbtRight);

    // Set keyboard mnemonics
    jbtLeft.setMnemonic('L');
    jbtRight.setMnemonic('R');

    // Set icons and remove text
//    jbtLeft.setIcon(new ImageIcon("image/left.gif"));
//    jbtRight.setIcon(new ImageIcon("image/right.gif"));
//    jbtLeft.setText(null);
```

```
41 //     jbtRight.setText(null);
42
43     // Set tool tip text on the buttons
44     jbtLeft.setToolTipText("Move message to left");
45     jbtRight.setToolTipText("Move message to right");
46
47     // Place panels in the frame
48     setLayout(new BorderLayout());
49     add(messagePanel, BorderLayout.CENTER);
50     add(jpButtons, BorderLayout.SOUTH);
51
52     // Register listeners with the buttons
53     jbtLeft.addActionListener(new ActionListener() {
54       public void actionPerformed(ActionEvent e) {
55         messagePanel.moveLeft();
56       }
57     });
58     jbtRight.addActionListener(new ActionListener() {
59       public void actionPerformed(ActionEvent e) {
60         messagePanel.moveRight();
61       }
62     });
63   }
64 }
```

tool tip

register listener

register listener

messagePanel (line 8) is deliberately declared protected so that it can be referenced by a subclass in future examples.

You can set an icon image on the button by using the setIcon method. If you uncomment the following code in lines 38–41:

```
// jbtLeft.setIcon(new ImageIcon("image/left.gif"));
// jbtRight.setIcon(new ImageIcon("image/right.gif"));
// jbtLeft.setText(null);
// jbtRight.setText(null);
```

the texts are replaced by the icons, as shown in Figure 17.10(a). "image/left.gif" is located in "c:\book\image\left.gif". Note that the backslash is the Windows file-path notation. In Java, the forward slash should be used.

ButtonDemo
Welcome to Java
ButtonDemo
Welcome to Java
Left
Right
ButtonDemo
Welcome to Java
Move message to right Alt-R

(a) (b) (c)

Figure 17.10 You can set an icon on a JButton and access a button using its mnemonic key.

You can set text and an icon on a button at the same time, if you wish, as shown in Figure 17.10(b). By default, the text and icon are centered horizontally and vertically.

The button can also be accessed by using the keyboard mnemonics. Pressing *Alt+L* is equivalent to clicking the <= button, since you set the mnemonic property to 'L' in the left button (line 34). If you change the left button text to "Left" and the right button text to "Right", the L and R in the captions of these buttons will be underlined, as shown in Figure 17.10(b).

Each button has a tool tip text (lines 44–45), which appears when the mouse is set on the button without being clicked, as shown in Figure 17.10(c).

locating **MessagePanel**

Note

Since `MessagePanel` is not in the Java API, you should place MessagePanel.java in the same directory with ButtonDemo.java.

17.3 Check Boxes

toggle button

A *toggle button* is a two-state button like a light switch. `JToggleButton` inherits `AbstractButton` and implements a toggle button. Often `JToggleButton`'s subclasses `JCheckBox` and `JRadioButton` are used to enable the user to toggle a choice on or off. This section introduces `JCheckBox`. `JRadioButton` will be introduced in the next section.

Video Note
Use check boxes

`JCheckBox` inherits all the properties from `AbstractButton`, such as `text`, `icon`, `mnemonic`, `verticalAlignment`, `horizontalAlignment`, `horizontalTextPosition`, `verticalTextPosition`, and `selected`, and provides several constructors to create check boxes, as shown in Figure 17.11.

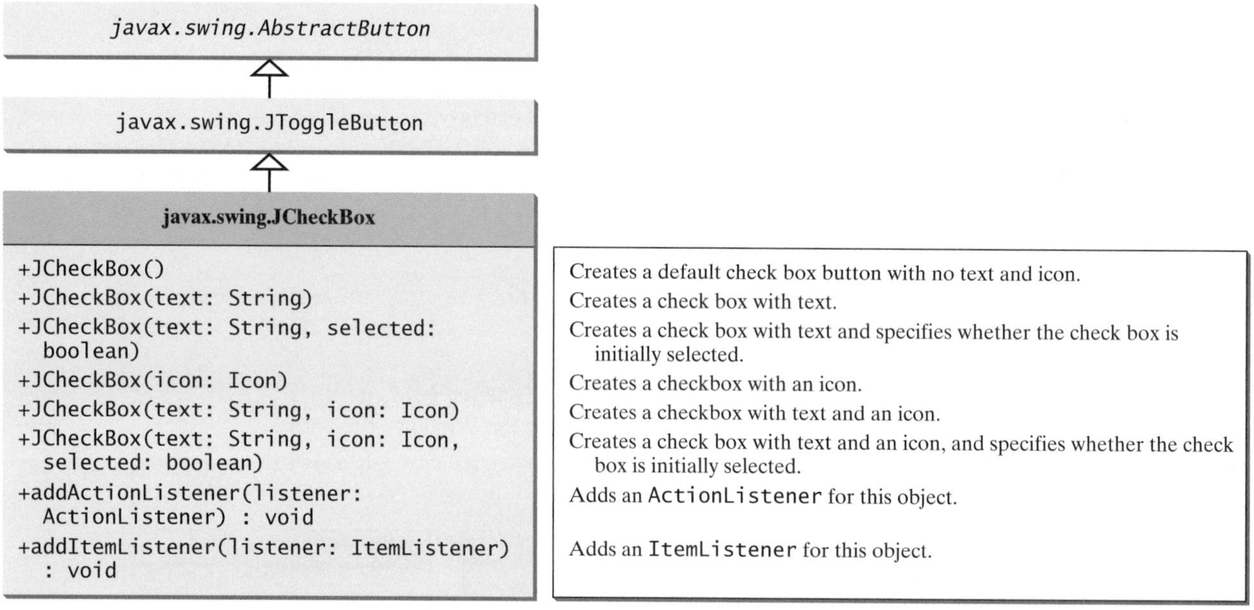
javax.swing.AbstractButton
javax.swing.JToggleButton
javax.swing.JCheckBox
+JCheckBox()
+JCheckBox(text: String)
+JCheckBox(text: String, selected: boolean)
+JCheckBox(icon: Icon)
+JCheckBox(text: String, icon: Icon)
+JCheckBox(text: String, icon: Icon, selected: boolean)
+addActionListener(listener: ActionListener) : void
+addItemListener(listener: ItemListener) : void
Creates a default check box button with no text and icon.
Creates a check box with text.
Creates a check box with text and specifies whether the check box is initially selected.
Creates a checkbox with an icon.
Creates a checkbox with text and an icon.
Creates a check box with text and an icon, and specifies whether the check box is initially selected.
Adds an ActionListener for this object.
Adds an ItemListener for this object.

FIGURE 17.11 `JCheckBox` defines a check box button.

Here is an example of a check box with text Student, foreground `red`, background `white`, mnemonic key `'S'`, and initially selected.

```
JCheckBox jchk = new JCheckBox("Student", true);
jchk.setForeground(Color.RED);
jchk.setBackground(Color.WHITE);
jchk.setMnemonic('S');
```

Student

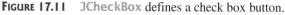

When a check box is clicked (checked or unchecked), it fires an `ItemEvent` and then an `ActionEvent`. To see if a check box is selected, use the `isSelected()` method.

Listing 17.3 gives a program that adds three check boxes named *Centered*, *Bold*, and *Italic* to the preceding example to let the user specify whether the message is centered, bold, or italic, as shown in Figure 17.12.

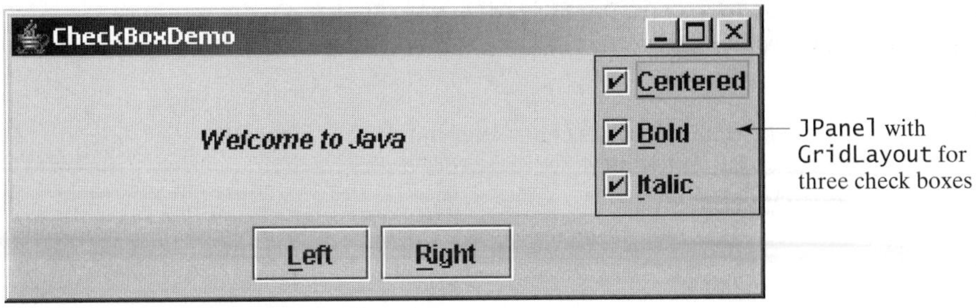
CheckBoxDemo
Centered
Bold
Italic
Welcome to Java
Left
Right
JPanel with GridLayout for three check boxes

FIGURE 17.12 Three check boxes are added to specify how the message is displayed.

There are at least two approaches to writing this program. The first is to revise the preceding ButtonDemo class to insert the code for adding the check boxes and processing their events. The second is to create a subclass that extends ButtonDemo. Please implement the first approach as an exercise. Listing 17.3 gives the code to implement the second approach.

LISTING 17.3 CheckBoxDemo.java

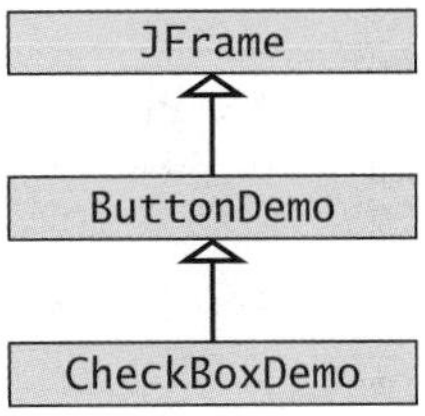
JFrame
ButtonDemo
CheckBoxDemo

```
import java.awt.*;
import java.awt.event.*;
import javax.swing.*;

public class CheckBoxDemo extends ButtonDemo {
  // Create three check boxes to control the display of message
  private JCheckBox jchkCentered = new JCheckBox("Centered");
  private JCheckBox jchkBold = new JCheckBox("Bold");
  private JCheckBox jchkItalic = new JCheckBox("Italic");

  public static void main(String[] args) {
    CheckBoxDemo frame = new CheckBoxDemo();
    frame.setTitle("CheckBoxDemo");
    frame.setSize(500, 200);
    frame.setLocationRelativeTo(null); // Center the frame
    frame.setDefaultCloseOperation(JFrame.EXIT_ON_CLOSE);
    frame.setVisible(true);
  }

  public CheckBoxDemo() {
    // Set mnemonic keys
    jchkCentered.setMnemonic('C');
    jchkBold.setMnemonic('B');
    jchkItalic.setMnemonic('I');

    // Create a new panel to hold check boxes
    JPanel jpCheckBoxes = new JPanel();
    jpCheckBoxes.setLayout(new GridLayout(3, 1));
    jpCheckBoxes.add(jchkCentered);
    jpCheckBoxes.add(jchkBold);
    jpCheckBoxes.add(jchkItalic);
    add(jpCheckBoxes, BorderLayout.EAST);

    // Register listeners with the check boxes
    jchkCentered.addActionListener(new ActionListener() {
      public void actionPerformed(ActionEvent e) {
        messagePanel.setCentered(jchkCentered.isSelected());
      }
    });
    jchkBold.addActionListener(new ActionListener() {
```

create frame

create UI

register listener

register listener

set a new font

```
41       public void actionPerformed(ActionEvent e) {
42         setNewFont();
43       }
44     });
45     jchkItalic.addActionListener(new ActionListener() {
46       public void actionPerformed(ActionEvent e) {
47         setNewFont();
48       }
49     });
50   }
51
52   private void setNewFont() {
53     // Determine a font style
54     int fontStyle = Font.PLAIN;
55     fontStyle += (jchkBold.isSelected() ? Font.BOLD : Font.PLAIN);
56     fontStyle += (jchkItalic.isSelected() ? Font.ITALIC : Font.PLAIN);
57
58     // Set font for the message
59     Font font = messagePanel.getFont();
60     messagePanel.setFont(
61       new Font(font.getName(), fontStyle, font.getSize()));
62   }
63 }
```

`CheckBoxDemo` extends `ButtonDemo` and adds three check boxes to control how the message is displayed. When a `CheckBoxDemo` is constructed (line 12), its superclass's no-arg constructor is invoked, so you don't have to rewrite the code that is already in the constructor of `ButtonDemo`.

When a check box is checked or unchecked, the listener's `actionPerformed` method is invoked to process the event. When the *Centered* check box is checked or unchecked, the `centered` property of the `MessagePanel` class is set to `true` or `false`.

The current font name and size used in `MessagePanel` are obtained from `messagePanel.getFont()` using the `getName()` and `getSize()` methods. The font styles (`Font.BOLD` and `Font.ITALIC`) are specified in the check boxes. If no font style is selected, the font style is `Font.PLAIN`. Font styles are combined by adding together the selected integers representing the fonts.

The keyboard mnemonics *C*, *B*, and *I* are set on the check boxes *Centered*, *Bold*, and *Italic*, respectively (lines 22–24). You can use a mouse click or a shortcut key to select a check box.

The `setFont` method (line 60) defined in the `Component` class is inherited in the `MessagePanel` class. This method automatically invokes the `repaint` method. Invoking `setFont` in `messagePanel` automatically repaints the message.

A check box fires an `ActionEvent` and an `ItemEvent` when it is clicked. You could process either the `ActionEvent` or the `ItemEvent` to redisplay the message. The example processes the `ActionEvent`. If you wish to process the `ItemEvent`, create a listener for `ItemEvent` and register it with a check box. The listener must implement the `itemStateChanged` handler to process an `ItemEvent`. For example, the following code registers an `ItemListener` with `jchkCentered`:

```
// To listen for ItemEvent
jchkCentered.addItemListener(new ItemListener() {
  /** Handle ItemEvent */
  public void itemStateChanged(ItemEvent e) {
    messagePanel.setCentered(jchkCentered.isSelected());
  }
});
```

17.4 Radio Buttons

Video Note
Use radio buttons

Radio buttons, also known as *option buttons*, enable you to choose a single item from a group of choices. In appearance radio buttons resemble check boxes, but check boxes display a square that is either checked or blank, whereas radio buttons display a circle that is either filled (if selected) or blank (if not selected).

JRadioButton inherits AbstractButton and provides several constructors to create radio buttons, as shown in Figure 17.13. These constructors are similar to the constructors for JCheckBox.

javax.swing.AbstractButton

↑

javax.swing.JToggleButton

↑

javax.swing.JRadioButton	
+JRadioButton()	Creates a default radio button with no text and icon.
+JRadioButton(text: String)	Creates a radio button with text.
+JRadioButton(text: String, selected: boolean)	Creates a radio button with text and specifies whether the radio button is initially selected.
+JRadioButton(icon: Icon)	Creates a radio button with an icon.
+JRadioButton(text: String, icon: Icon)	Creates a radio button with text and an icon.
+JRadioButton(text: String, icon: Icon, selected: boolean)	Creates a radio button with text and an icon, and specifies whether the radio button is initially selected.
+addActionEvent(listener: ActionListener): void	Adds an ActionListener for this object.
+addItemListener(listener: ItemListener) : void	Adds an ItemListener for this object.

FIGURE 17.13 JRadioButton defines a radio button.

Here is an example of a radio button with text Student, red foreground, white background, mnemonic key S, and initially selected.

```
JRadioButton jrb = new JRadioButton("Student", true);
jrb.setForeground(Color.RED);
jrb.setBackground(Color.WHITE);
jrb.setMnemonic('S');
```

Student

To group radio buttons, you need to create an instance of java.swing.ButtonGroup and use the add method to add them to it, as follows:

```
ButtonGroup group = new ButtonGroup();
group.add(jrb1);
group.add(jrb2);
```

This code creates a radio-button group for radio buttons jrb1 and jrb2 so that they are selected mutually exclusively. Without grouping, jrb1 and jrb2 would be independent.

GUI helper class

Note

ButtonGroup is not a subclass of java.awt.Component, so a ButtonGroup object cannot be added to a container.

When a radio button is changed (selected or deselected), it fires an ItemEvent and then an ActionEvent. To see if a radio button is selected, use the isSelected() method.

Listing 17.4 gives a program that adds three radio buttons named *Red*, *Green*, and *Blue* to the preceding example to let the user choose the color of the message, as shown in Figure 17.14.

JPanel with GridLayout for three radio buttons
RadioButtonDemo
Red
Green
Blue
Welcome to Java
Centered
Bold
Italic
Left
Right

FIGURE 17.14 Three radio buttons are added to specify the color of the message.

Again there are at least two approaches to writing this program. The first is to revise the preceding CheckBoxDemo class to insert the code for adding the radio buttons and processing their events. The second is to create a subclass that extends CheckBoxDemo. Listing 17.4 gives the code to implement the second approach.

LISTING 17.4 RadioButtonDemo.java

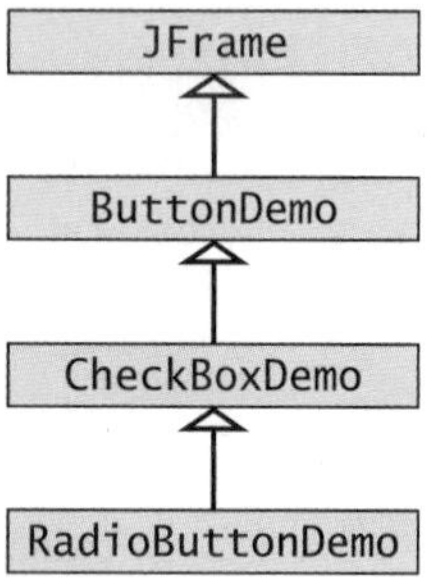
JFrame
ButtonDemo
CheckBoxDemo
RadioButtonDemo

create frame

create UI

```
import java.awt.*;
import java.awt.event.*;
import javax.swing.*;

public class RadioButtonDemo extends CheckBoxDemo {
  // Declare radio buttons
  private JRadioButton jrbRed, jrbGreen, jrbBlue;

  public static void main(String[] args) {
    RadioButtonDemo frame = new RadioButtonDemo();
    frame.setSize(500, 200);
    frame.setLocationRelativeTo(null); // Center the frame
    frame.setDefaultCloseOperation(JFrame.EXIT_ON_CLOSE);
    frame.setTitle("RadioButtonDemo");
    frame.setVisible(true);
  }

  public RadioButtonDemo() {
    // Create a new panel to hold check boxes
    JPanel jpRadioButtons = new JPanel();
    jpRadioButtons.setLayout(new GridLayout(3, 1));
    jpRadioButtons.add(jrbRed = new JRadioButton("Red"));
    jpRadioButtons.add(jrbGreen = new JRadioButton("Green"));
    jpRadioButtons.add(jrbBlue = new JRadioButton("Blue"));
```

```
25     add(jpRadioButtons, BorderLayout.WEST);
26
27     // Create a radio-button group to group three buttons
28     ButtonGroup group = new ButtonGroup();
29     group.add(jrbRed);
30     group.add(jrbGreen);
31     group.add(jrbBlue);
32
33     // Set keyboard mnemonics
34     jrbRed.setMnemonic('E');
35     jrbGreen.setMnemonic('G');
36     jrbBlue.setMnemonic('U');
37
38     // Register listeners for radio buttons
39     jrbRed.addActionListener(new ActionListener() {
40       public void actionPerformed(ActionEvent e) {
41         messagePanel.setForeground(Color.red);
42       }
43     });
44     jrbGreen.addActionListener(new ActionListener() {
45       public void actionPerformed(ActionEvent e) {
46         messagePanel.setForeground(Color.green);
47       }
48     });
49     jrbBlue.addActionListener(new ActionListener() {
50       public void actionPerformed(ActionEvent e) {
51         messagePanel.setForeground(Color.blue);
52       }
53     });
54
55     // Set initial message color to blue
56     jrbBlue.setSelected(true);
57     messagePanel.setForeground(Color.blue);
58   }
59 }
```

group buttons (line 28)

register listener (line 39)

register listener (line 44)

register listener (line 49)

`RadioButtonDemo` extends `CheckBoxDemo` and adds three radio buttons to specify the message color. When a radio button is clicked, its action event listener sets the corresponding foreground color in `messagePanel`.

The keyboard mnemonics `'R'` and `'B'` are already set for the *Right* button and *Bold* check box. To avoid conflict, the keyboard mnemonics `'E'`, `'G'`, and `'U'` are set on the radio buttons *Red*, *Green*, and *Blue*, respectively (lines 34–36).

The program creates a `ButtonGroup` and puts three `JRadioButton` instances (`jrbRed`, `jrbGreen`, and `jrbBlue`) in the group (lines 28–31).

A radio button fires an `ActionEvent` and an `ItemEvent` when it is selected or deselected. You could process either the `ActionEvent` or the `ItemEvent` to choose a color. The example processes the `ActionEvent`. Please rewrite the code using the `ItemEvent` as an exercise.

17.5 Labels

A *label* is a display area for a short text, an image, or both. It is often used to label other components (usually text fields). Figure 17.15 lists the constructors and methods in `JLabel`.

`JLabel` inherits all the properties from `JComponent` and has many properties similar to the ones in `JButton`, such as `text`, `icon`, `horizontalAlignment`, `verticalAlignment`, `horizontalTextPosition`, `verticalTextPosition`, and `iconTextGap`. For example, the following code displays a label with text and an icon:

```
// Create an image icon from an image file
ImageIcon icon = new ImageIcon("image/grapes.gif");

// Create a label with a text, an icon,
// with centered horizontal alignment
JLabel jlbl = new JLabel("Grapes", icon, SwingConstants.CENTER);

//Set label's text alignment and gap between text and icon
jlbl.setHorizontalTextPosition(SwingConstants.CENTER);
jlbl.setVerticalTextPosition(SwingConstants.BOTTOM);
jlbl.setIconTextGap(5);
```

Text and Icon Label
Grapes

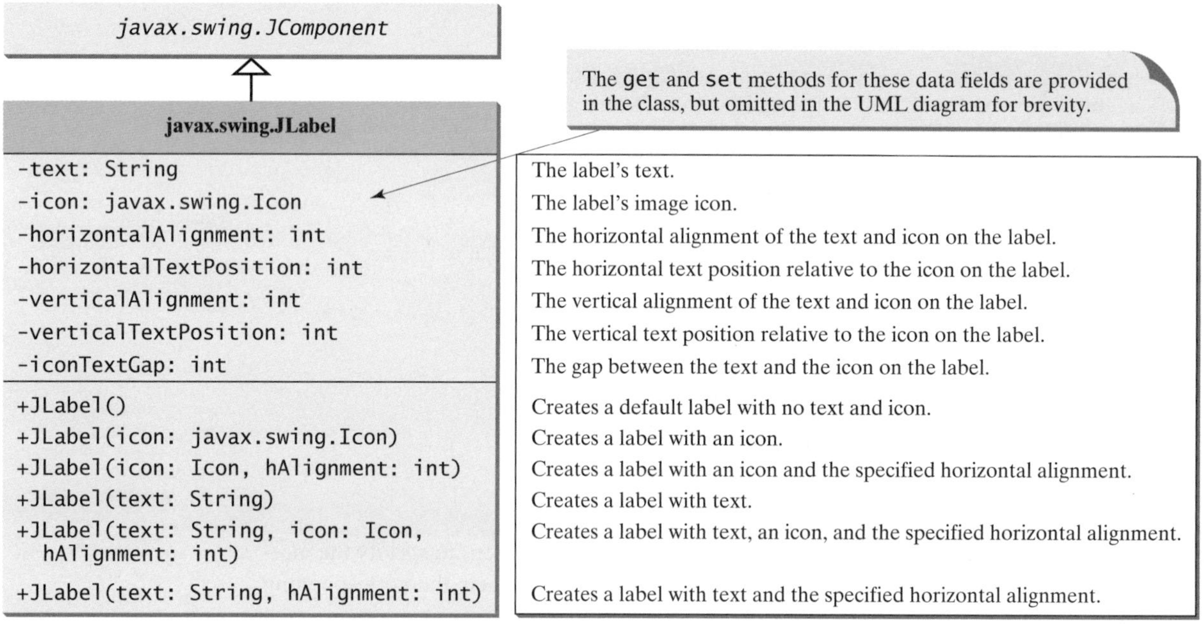
javax.swing.JComponent
The get and set methods for these data fields are provided in the class, but omitted in the UML diagram for brevity.
javax.swing.JLabel
-text: String
-icon: javax.swing.Icon
-horizontalAlignment: int
-horizontalTextPosition: int
-verticalAlignment: int
-verticalTextPosition: int
-iconTextGap: int
+JLabel()
+JLabel(icon: javax.swing.Icon)
+JLabel(icon: Icon, hAlignment: int)
+JLabel(text: String)
+JLabel(text: String, icon: Icon, hAlignment: int)
+JLabel(text: String, hAlignment: int)
The label's text.
The label's image icon.
The horizontal alignment of the text and icon on the label.
The horizontal text position relative to the icon on the label.
The vertical alignment of the text and icon on the label.
The vertical text position relative to the icon on the label.
The gap between the text and the icon on the label.
Creates a default label with no text and icon.
Creates a label with an icon.
Creates a label with an icon and the specified horizontal alignment.
Creates a label with text.
Creates a label with text, an icon, and the specified horizontal alignment.
Creates a label with text and the specified horizontal alignment.

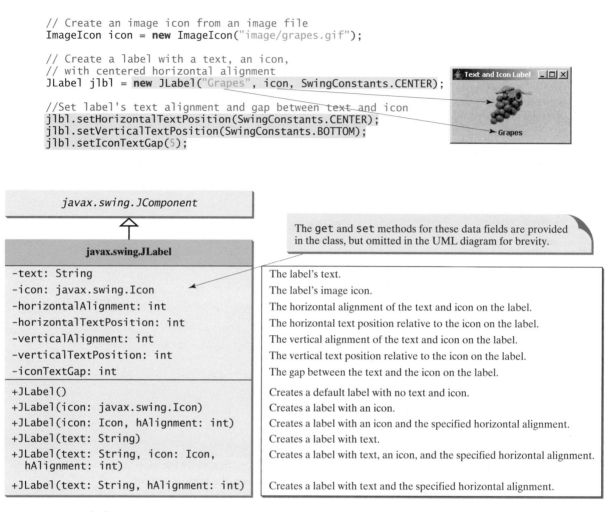

FIGURE 17.15 `JLabel` displays text or an icon, or both.

17.6 Text Fields

Video Note
Use labels and text fields

A *text field* can be used to enter or display a string. `JTextField` is a subclass of `JTextComponent`. Figure 17.16 lists the constructors and methods in `JTextField`.

`JTextField` inherits `JTextComponent`, which inherits `JComponent`. Here is an example of creating a text field with red foreground color and right horizontal alignment:

```
JTextField jtfMessage = new JTextField("T-Strom");
jtfMessage.setForeground(Color.RED);
jtfMessage.setHorizontalAlignment(SwingConstants.RIGHT);
```

When you move the cursor in the text field and press the *Enter* key, it fires an `ActionEvent`.

Listing 17.5 gives a program that adds a text field to the preceding example to let the user set a new message, as shown in Figure 17.17.

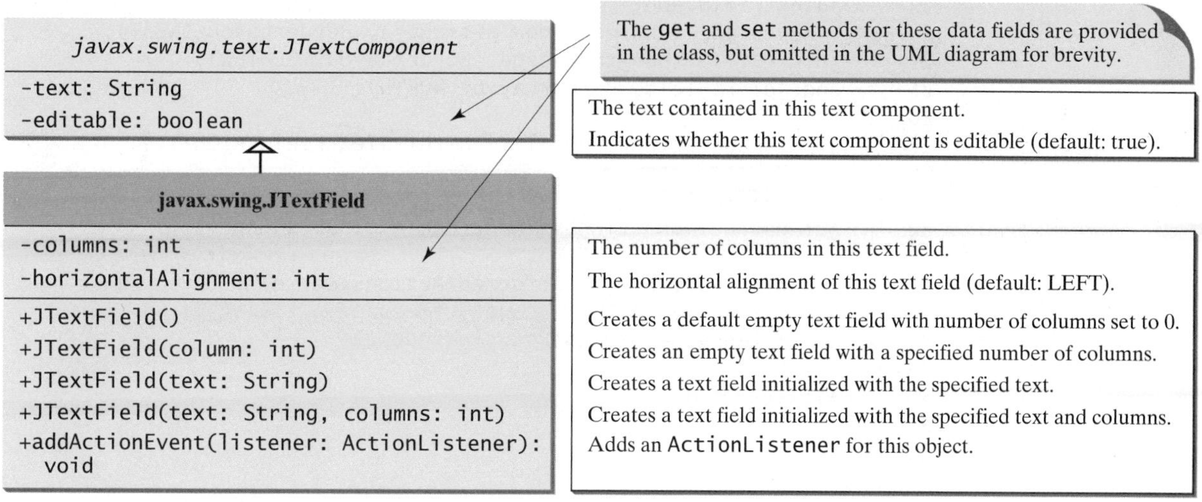
javax.swing.text.JTextComponent
-text: String
-editable: boolean
The get and set methods for these data fields are provided in the class, but omitted in the UML diagram for brevity.
The text contained in this text component.
Indicates whether this text component is editable (default: true).
javax.swing.JTextField
-columns: int
-horizontalAlignment: int
+JTextField()
+JTextField(column: int)
+JTextField(text: String)
+JTextField(text: String, columns: int)
+addActionEvent(listener: ActionListener): void
The number of columns in this text field.
The horizontal alignment of this text field (default: LEFT).
Creates a default empty text field with number of columns set to 0.
Creates an empty text field with a specified number of columns.
Creates a text field initialized with the specified text.
Creates a text field initialized with the specified text and columns.
Adds an ActionListener for this object.

FIGURE 17.16 `JTextField` enables you to enter or display a string.

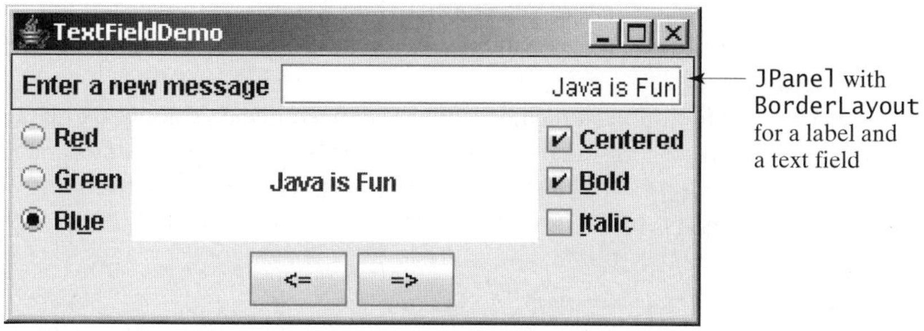
TextFieldDemo
Enter a new message
Java is Fun
Red
Green
Blue
Java is Fun
Centered
Bold
Italic
<=
=>
JPanel with BorderLayout for a label and a text field

FIGURE 17.17 A label and a text field are added to set a new message.

LISTING 17.5 TextFieldDemo.java

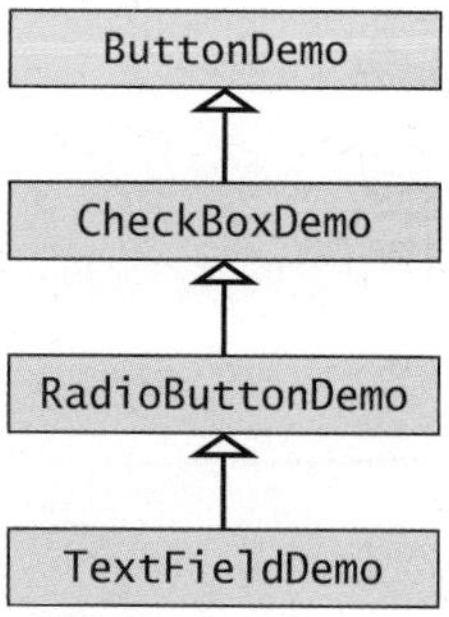
ButtonDemo
CheckBoxDemo
RadioButtonDemo
TextFieldDemo

```java
import java.awt.*;
import java.awt.event.*;
import javax.swing.*;

public class TextFieldDemo extends RadioButtonDemo {
  private JTextField jtfMessage = new JTextField(10);

  /** Main method */
  public static void main(String[] args) {
    TextFieldDemo frame = new TextFieldDemo();
    frame.pack();
    frame.setTitle("TextFieldDemo");
    frame.setLocationRelativeTo(null); // Center the frame
    frame.setDefaultCloseOperation(JFrame.EXIT_ON_CLOSE);
    frame.setVisible(true);
  }

  public TextFieldDemo() {
    // Create a new panel to hold label and text field
    JPanel jpTextField = new JPanel();
    jpTextField.setLayout(new BorderLayout(5, 0));
```

create frame
pack frame
create UI

```
22      jpTextField.add(
23        new JLabel("Enter a new message"), BorderLayout.WEST);
24      jpTextField.add(jtfMessage, BorderLayout.CENTER);
25      add(jpTextField, BorderLayout.NORTH);
26
27      jtfMessage.setHorizontalAlignment(JTextField.RIGHT);
28
29      // Register listener
30      jtfMessage.addActionListener(new ActionListener() {
31        /** Handle ActionEvent */
32        public void actionPerformed(ActionEvent e) {
33          messagePanel.setMessage(jtfMessage.getText());
34          jtfMessage.requestFocusInWindow();
35        }
36      });
37    }
38  }
```

listener

TextFieldDemo extends RadioButtonDemo and adds a label and a text field to let the user enter a new message. After you set a new message in the text field and press the *Enter* key, a new message is displayed. Pressing the *Enter* key on the text field triggers an action event. The listener sets a new message in messagePanel (line 33).

pack()

The pack() method (line 11) automatically sizes the frame according to the size of the components placed in it.

requestFocusInWindow()

The requestFocusInWindow() method (line 34) defined in the Component class requests the component to receive input focus. Thus, jtfMessage.requestFocusInWindow() requests the input focus on jtfMessage. You will see the cursor on jtfMessage after the actionPerformed method is invoked.

JPasswordField

Note

If a text field is used for entering a password, use JPasswordField to replace JTextField. JPasswordField extends JTextField and hides the input text with echo characters (e.g., ******). By default, the echo character is *. You can specify a new echo character using the setEchoChar(char) method.

17.7 Text Areas

If you want to let the user enter multiple lines of text, you have to create several instances of JTextField. A better alternative is to use JTextArea, which enables the user to enter multiple lines of text. Figure 17.18 lists the constructors and methods in JTextArea.

Like JTextField, JTextArea inherits JTextComponent, which contains the methods getText, setText, isEditable, and setEditable. Here is an example of creating a text area with 5 rows and 20 columns, line-wrapped on words, red foreground color, and Courier font, bold, 20 pixels.

wrap line
wrap word

```
JTextArea jtaNote = new JTextArea("This is a text area", 5, 20);
jtaNote.setLineWrap(true);
jtaNote.setWrapStyleWord(true);
jtaNote.setForeground(Color.red);
jtaNote.setFont(new Font("Courier", Font.BOLD, 20));
```

JTextArea does not handle scrolling, but you can create a JScrollPane object to hold an instance of JTextArea and let JScrollPane handle scrolling for JTextArea, as follows:

```
// Create a scroll pane to hold text area
JScrollPane scrollPane = new JScrollPane(jta = new JTextArea());
add(scrollPane, BorderLayout.CENTER);
```

Listing 17.7 gives a program that displays an image and a text in a label, and a text in a text area, as shown in Figure 17.19.

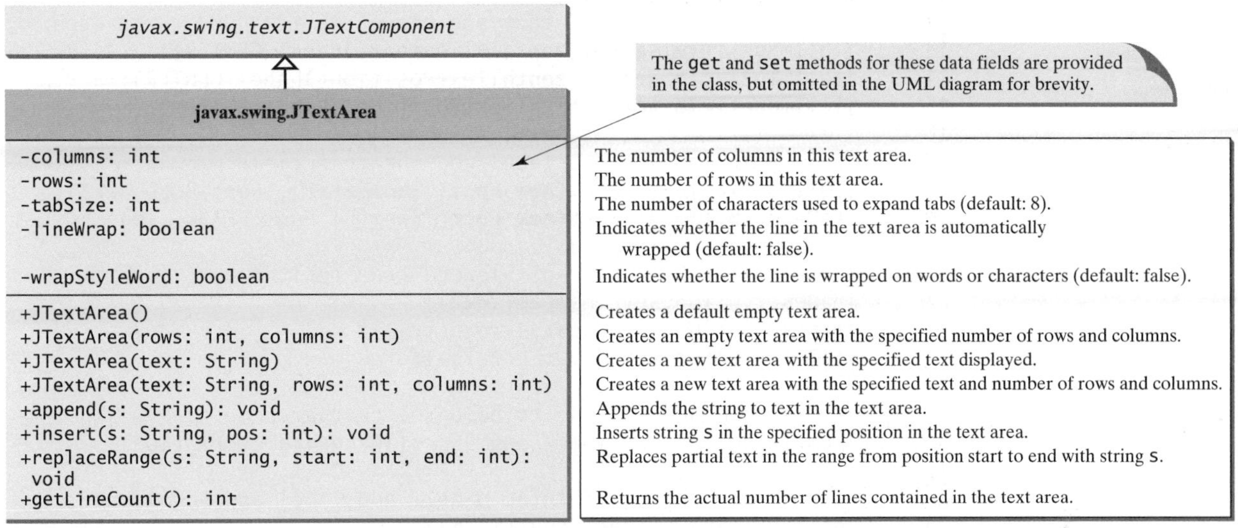
javax.swing.text.JTextComponent
javax.swing.JTextArea
-columns: int
-rows: int
-tabSize: int
-lineWrap: boolean
-wrapStyleWord: boolean
+JTextArea()
+JTextArea(rows: int, columns: int)
+JTextArea(text: String)
+JTextArea(text: String, rows: int, columns: int)
+append(s: String): void
+insert(s: String, pos: int): void
+replaceRange(s: String, start: int, end: int): void
+getLineCount(): int
The get and set methods for these data fields are provided in the class, but omitted in the UML diagram for brevity.
The number of columns in this text area.
The number of rows in this text area.
The number of characters used to expand tabs (default: 8).
Indicates whether the line in the text area is automatically wrapped (default: false).
Indicates whether the line is wrapped on words or characters (default: false).
Creates a default empty text area.
Creates an empty text area with the specified number of rows and columns.
Creates a new text area with the specified text displayed.
Creates a new text area with the specified text and number of rows and columns.
Appends the string to text in the text area.
Inserts string s in the specified position in the text area.
Replaces partial text in the range from position start to end with string s.
Returns the actual number of lines contained in the text area.

FIGURE 17.18 `JTextArea` enables you to enter or display multiple lines of characters.

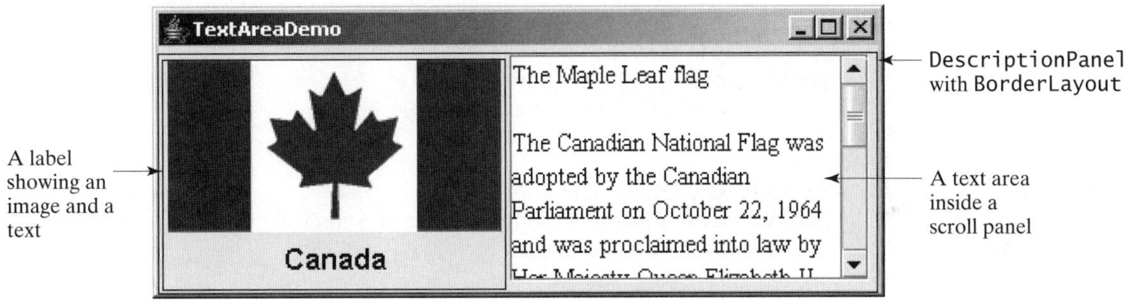
TextAreaDemo
The Maple Leaf flag
The Canadian National Flag was
adopted by the Canadian
Parliament on October 22, 1964
and was proclaimed into law by
Canada
DescriptionPanel with BorderLayout
A label showing an image and a text
A text area inside a scroll panel

FIGURE 17.19 The program displays an image in a label, a title in a label, and a text in the text area.

Here are the major steps in the program:

1. Create a class named `DescriptionPanel` that extends `JPanel`, as shown in Listing 17.6. This class contains a text area inside a scroll pane, and a label for displaying an image icon and a title. This class is used in the present example and will be reused in later examples.

2. Create a class named `TextAreaDemo` that extends `JFrame`, as shown in Listing 17.7. Create an instance of `DescriptionPanel` and add it to the center of the frame. The relationship between `DescriptionPanel` and `TextAreaDemo` is shown in Figure 17.20.

LISTING 17.6 DescriptionPanel.java

```
import javax.swing.*;
import java.awt.*;

public class DescriptionPanel extends JPanel {
  /** Label for displaying an image icon and a text */
  private JLabel jlblImageTitle = new JLabel();

```

label

text area · label properties · wrap line · wrap word · read only · scroll pane

```
  /** Text area for displaying text */
  private JTextArea jtaDescription = new JTextArea();

  public DescriptionPanel() {
    // Center the icon and text and place the text under the icon
    jlblImageTitle.setHorizontalAlignment(JLabel.CENTER);
    jlblImageTitle.setHorizontalTextPosition(JLabel.CENTER);
    jlblImageTitle.setVerticalTextPosition(JLabel.BOTTOM);

    // Set the font in the label and the text field
    jlblImageTitle.setFont(new Font("SansSerif", Font.BOLD, 16));
    jtaDescription.setFont(new Font("Serif", Font.PLAIN, 14));

    // Set lineWrap and wrapStyleWord true for the text area
    jtaDescription.setLineWrap(true);
    jtaDescription.setWrapStyleWord(true);
    jtaDescription.setEditable(false);

    // Create a scroll pane to hold the text area
    JScrollPane scrollPane = new JScrollPane(jtaDescription);

    // Set BorderLayout for the panel, add label and scrollpane
    setLayout(new BorderLayout(5, 5));
    add(scrollPane, BorderLayout.CENTER);
    add(jlblImageTitle, BorderLayout.WEST);
  }

  /** Set the title */
  public void setTitle(String title) {
    jlblImageTitle.setText(title);
  }

  /** Set the image icon */
  public void setImageIcon(ImageIcon icon) {
    jlblImageTitle.setIcon(icon);
  }

  /** Set the text description */
  public void setDescription(String text) {
    jtaDescription.setText(text);
  }
}
```

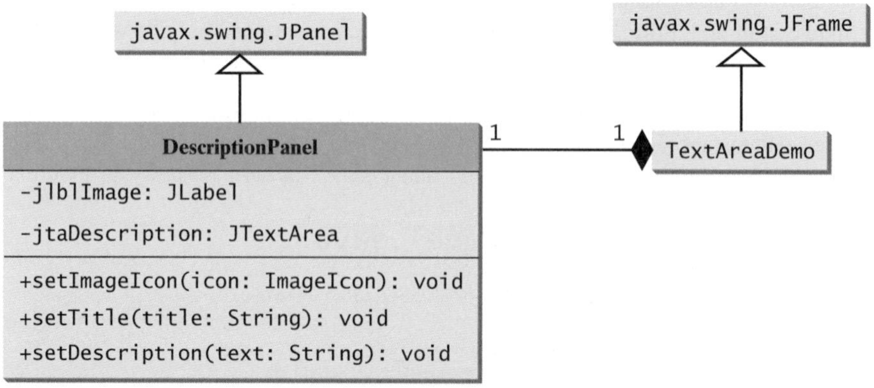
javax.swing.JPanel
javax.swing.JFrame
DescriptionPanel
-jlblImage: JLabel
-jtaDescription: JTextArea
+setImageIcon(icon: ImageIcon): void
+setTitle(title: String): void
+setDescription(text: String): void
1
1
TextAreaDemo

FIGURE 17.20 TextAreaDemo uses DescriptionPanel to display an image, title, and text description of a national flag.

The text area is inside a `JScrollPane` (line 27), which provides scrolling functions for the text area. Scroll bars automatically appear if there is more text than the physical size of the text area, and disappear if the text is deleted and the remaining text does not exceed the text area size.

The `lineWrap` property is set to `true` (line 22) so that the line is automatically wrapped when the text cannot fit in one line. The `wrapStyleWord` property is set to `true` (line 23) so that the line is wrapped on words rather than characters. The text area is set noneditable (line 24), so you cannot edit the description in the text area.

It is not necessary to create a separate class for `DescriptionPanel` in this example. Nevertheless, this class was created for reuse in the next section, where you will use it to display a description panel for various images.

LISTING 17.7 TextAreaDemo.java

```
 1 import java.awt.*;
 2 import javax.swing.*;
 3
 4 public class TextAreaDemo extends JFrame {
 5   // Declare and create a description panel
 6   private DescriptionPanel descriptionPanel = new DescriptionPanel();
 7
 8   public static void main(String[] args) {
 9     TextAreaDemo frame = new TextAreaDemo();
10     frame.pack();
11     frame.setLocationRelativeTo(null); // Center the frame
12     frame.setDefaultCloseOperation(JFrame.EXIT_ON_CLOSE);
13     frame.setTitle("TextAreaDemo");
14     frame.setVisible(true);
15   }
16
17   public TextAreaDemo() {
18     // Set title, text and image in the description panel
19     descriptionPanel.setTitle("Canada");
20     String description = "The Maple Leaf flag \n\n" +
21       "The Canadian National Flag was adopted by the Canadian " +
22       "Parliament on October 22, 1964 and was proclaimed into law " +
23       "by Her Majesty Queen Elizabeth II (the Queen of Canada) on " +
24       "February 15, 1965. The Canadian Flag (colloquially known " +
25       "as The Maple Leaf Flag) is a red flag of the proportions " +
26       "two by length and one by width, containing in its center a " +
27       "white square, with a single red stylized eleven-point " +
28       "maple leaf centered in the white square.";
29     descriptionPanel.setDescription(description);
30     descriptionPanel.setImageIcon(new ImageIcon("image/ca.gif"));
31
32     // Add the description panel to the frame
33     setLayout(new BorderLayout());
34     add(descriptionPanel, BorderLayout.CENTER);
35   }
36 }
```

create **decriptionPanel**

create frame

create UI

add **decriptionPanel**

`TextAreaDemo` simply creates an instance of `DescriptionPanel` (line 6) and sets the title (line 19), image (line 30), and text in the description panel (line 29). `DescriptionPanel` is a subclass of `JPanel`. `DescriptionPanel` contains a label for displaying an image icon and a text title, and a text area for displaying a description of the image.

17.8 Combo Boxes

A *combo box*, also known as a *choice list* or *drop-down list*, contains a list of items from which the user can choose. It is useful in limiting a user's range of choices and avoids the cumbersome validation of data input. Figure 17.21 lists several frequently used constructors and methods in JComboBox.

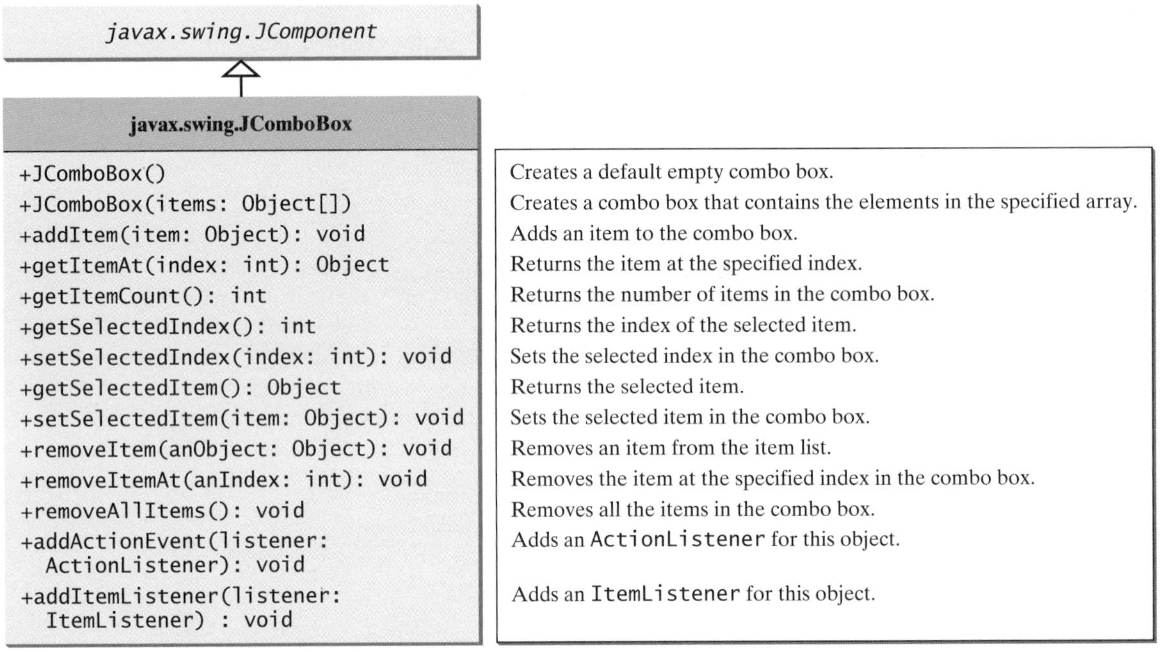
javax.swing.JComponent
javax.swing.JComboBox
+JComboBox()
+JComboBox(items: Object[])
+addItem(item: Object): void
+getItemAt(index: int): Object
+getItemCount(): int
+getSelectedIndex(): int
+setSelectedIndex(index: int): void
+getSelectedItem(): Object
+setSelectedItem(item: Object): void
+removeItem(anObject: Object): void
+removeItemAt(anIndex: int): void
+removeAllItems(): void
+addActionEvent(listener: ActionListener): void
+addItemListener(listener: ItemListener) : void
Creates a default empty combo box.
Creates a combo box that contains the elements in the specified array.
Adds an item to the combo box.
Returns the item at the specified index.
Returns the number of items in the combo box.
Returns the index of the selected item.
Sets the selected index in the combo box.
Returns the selected item.
Sets the selected item in the combo box.
Removes an item from the item list.
Removes the item at the specified index in the combo box.
Removes all the items in the combo box.
Adds an ActionListener for this object.
Adds an ItemListener for this object.

FIGURE 17.21 JComboBox enables you to select an item from a set of items.

The following statements create a combo box with four items, red foreground, white background, and the second item selected.

```
JComboBox jcb = new JComboBox(new Object[]
  {"Item 1", "Item 2", "Item 3", "Item 4"});
jcb.setForeground(Color.red);
jcb.setBackground(Color.white);
jcb.setSelectedItem("Item 2");
```

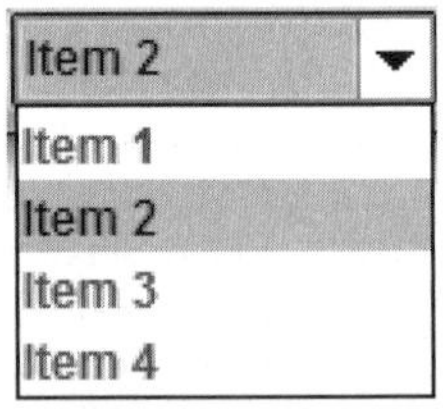
Item 2
Item 1
Item 2
Item 3
Item 4

JComboBox can fire ActionEvent and ItemEvent, among many other events. Whenever an item is selected, an ActionEvent is fired. Whenever a new item is selected, JComboBox fires ItemEvent twice, once for deselecting the previously selected item, and the other for selecting the currently selected item. Note that no ItemEvent is fired if the current item is reselected. To respond to an ItemEvent, you need to implement the itemStateChanged(ItemEvent e) handler for processing a choice. To get data from a JComboBox menu, you can use getSelectedItem() to return the currently selected item, or e.getItem() method to get the item from the itemStateChanged(ItemEvent e) handler.

Listing 17.8 gives a program that lets users view an image and a description of a country's flag by selecting the country from a combo box, as shown in Figure 17.22.

Here are the major steps in the program:

1. Create the user interface.
   Create a combo box with country names as its selection values. Create a DescriptionPanel object. The DescriptionPanel class was introduced in the preceding

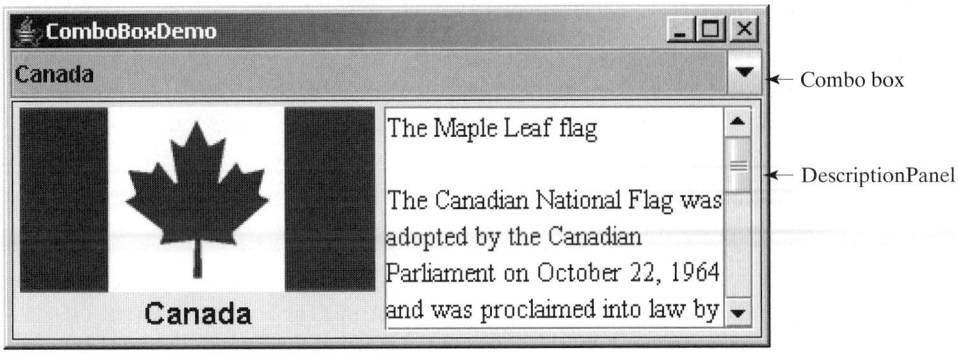
ComboBoxDemo
Canada
Combo box
The Maple Leaf flag
The Canadian National Flag was adopted by the Canadian Parliament on October 22, 1964 and was proclaimed into law by
DescriptionPanel
Canada

FIGURE 17.22 A country's info, including a flag image and a description of the flag, is displayed when the country is selected in the combo box.

example. Place the combo box in the north of the frame and the description panel in the center of the frame.

2. Process the event.
   Create a listener to implement the `itemStateChanged` handler to set the flag title, image, and text in the description panel for the selected country name.

LISTING 17.8 ComboBoxDemo.java

```
import java.awt.*;
import java.awt.event.*;
import javax.swing.*;

public class ComboBoxDemo extends JFrame {
  // Declare an array of Strings for flag titles
  private String[] flagTitles = {"Canada", "China", "Denmark",
    "France", "Germany", "India", "Norway", "United Kingdom",
    "United States of America"};

  // Declare an ImageIcon array for the national flags of 9 countries
  private ImageIcon[] flagImage = {
    new ImageIcon("image/ca.gif"),
    new ImageIcon("image/china.gif"),
    new ImageIcon("image/denmark.gif"),
    new ImageIcon("image/fr.gif"),
    new ImageIcon("image/germany.gif"),
    new ImageIcon("image/india.gif"),
    new ImageIcon("image/norway.gif"),
    new ImageIcon("image/uk.gif"),
    new ImageIcon("image/us.gif")
  };

  // Declare an array of strings for flag descriptions
  private String[] flagDescription = new String[9];

  // Declare and create a description panel
  private DescriptionPanel descriptionPanel = new DescriptionPanel();

  // Create a combo box for selecting countries
  private JComboBox jcbo = new JComboBox(flagTitles);

  public static void main(String[] args) {
    ComboBoxDemo frame = new ComboBoxDemo();
```

country

image icon

description

combo box

```
35     frame.pack();
36     frame.setTitle("ComboBoxDemo");
37     frame.setLocationRelativeTo(null); // Center the frame
38     frame.setDefaultCloseOperation(JFrame.EXIT_ON_CLOSE);
39     frame.setVisible(true);
40   }
41
42   public ComboBoxDemo() {
43     // Set text description
44     flagDescription[0] = "The Maple Leaf flag \n\n" +
45       "The Canadian National Flag was adopted by the Canadian " +
46       "Parliament on October 22, 1964 and was proclaimed into law " +
47       "by Her Majesty Queen Elizabeth II (the Queen of Canada) on " +
48       "February 15, 1965. The Canadian Flag (colloquially known " +
49       "as The Maple Leaf Flag) is a red flag of the proportions " +
50       "two by length and one by width, containing in its center a " +
51       "white square, with a single red stylized eleven-point " +
52       "maple leaf centered in the white square.";
53     flagDescription[1] = "Description for China ... ";
54     flagDescription[2] = "Description for Denmark ... ";
55     flagDescription[3] = "Description for France ... ";
56     flagDescription[4] = "Description for Germany ... ";
57     flagDescription[5] = "Description for India ... ";
58     flagDescription[6] = "Description for Norway ... ";
59     flagDescription[7] = "Description for UK ... ";
60     flagDescription[8] = "Description for US ... ";
61
62     // Set the first country (Canada) for display
63     setDisplay(0);
64
65     // Add combo box and description panel to the list
66     add(jcbo, BorderLayout.NORTH);
67     add(descriptionPanel, BorderLayout.CENTER);
68
69     // Register listener
70     jcbo.addItemListener(new ItemListener() {
71       /** Handle item selection */
72       public void itemStateChanged(ItemEvent e) {
73         setDisplay(jcbo.getSelectedIndex());
74       }
75     });
76   }
77
78   /** Set display information on the description panel */
79   public void setDisplay(int index) {
80     descriptionPanel.setTitle(flagTitles[index]);
81     descriptionPanel.setImageIcon(flagImage[index]);
82     descriptionPanel.setDescription(flagDescription[index]);
83   }
84 }
```

create UI

listener

The listener listens to **ItemEvent** from the combo box and implements **ItemListener** (lines 70–75). Instead of using **ItemEvent**, you may rewrite the program to use **ActionEvent** for handling combo-box item selection.

The program stores the flag information in three arrays: **flagTitles**, **flagImage**, and **flagDescription** (lines 7–25). The array **flagTitles** contains the names of nine countries, the array **flagImage** contains images of the nine countries' flags, and the array **flagDescription** contains descriptions of the flags.

The program creates an instance of `DescriptionPanel` (line 28), which was presented in Listing 17.6, DescriptionPanel.java. The program creates a combo box with initial values from `flagTitles` (line 31). When the user selects an item in the combo box, the `itemStateChanged` handler is executed, finds the selected index, and sets its corresponding flag title, flag image, and flag description on the panel.

17.9 Lists

A *list* is a component that basically performs the same function as a combo box but enables the user to choose a single value or multiple values. The Swing `JList` is very versatile. Figure 17.23 lists several frequently used constructors and methods in `JList`.

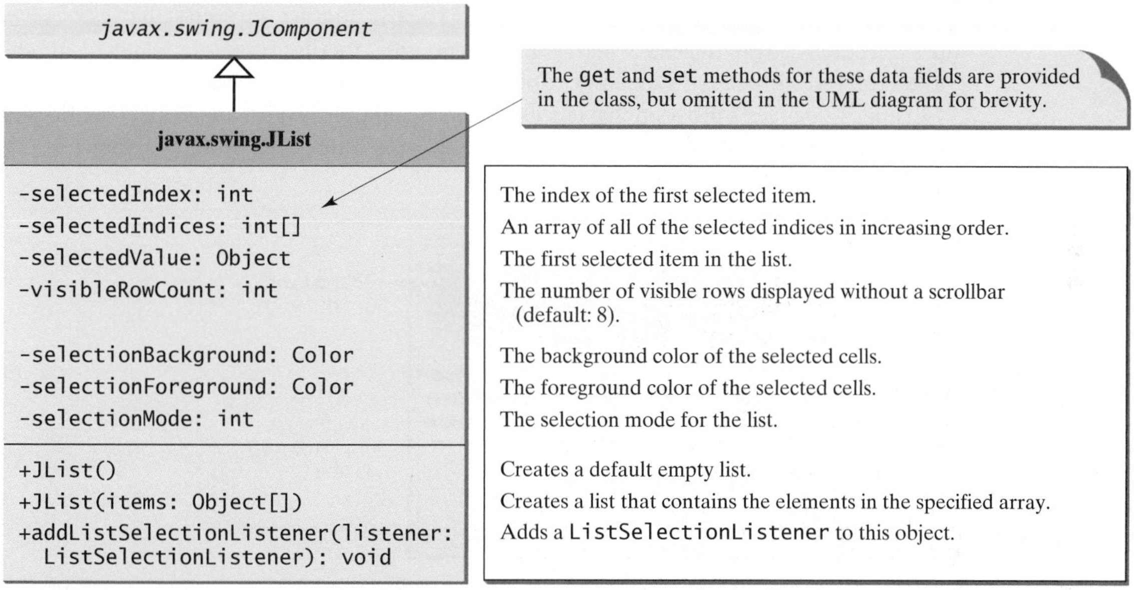
javax.swing.JComponent
The get and set methods for these data fields are provided in the class, but omitted in the UML diagram for brevity.
javax.swing.JList
-selectedIndex: int
-selectedIndices: int[]
-selectedValue: Object
-visibleRowCount: int
-selectionBackground: Color
-selectionForeground: Color
-selectionMode: int
+JList()
+JList(items: Object[])
+addListSelectionListener(listener: ListSelectionListener): void
The index of the first selected item.
An array of all of the selected indices in increasing order.
The first selected item in the list.
The number of visible rows displayed without a scrollbar (default: 8).
The background color of the selected cells.
The foreground color of the selected cells.
The selection mode for the list.
Creates a default empty list.
Creates a list that contains the elements in the specified array.
Adds a ListSelectionListener to this object.

FIGURE 17.23 `JList` enables you to select multiple items from a set of items.

`selectionMode` is one of the three values (`SINGLE_SELECTION`, `SINGLE_INTERVAL_SELECTION`, `MULTIPLE_INTERVAL_SELECTION`) defined in `javax.swing.ListSelectionModel` that indicate whether a single item, single-interval item, or multiple-interval item can be selected. Single selection allows only one item to be selected. Single-interval selection allows multiple selections, but the selected items must be contiguous. Multiple-interval selection allows selections of multiple contiguous items without restrictions, as shown in Figure 17.24. The default value is `MULTIPLE_INTERVAL_SELECTION`.

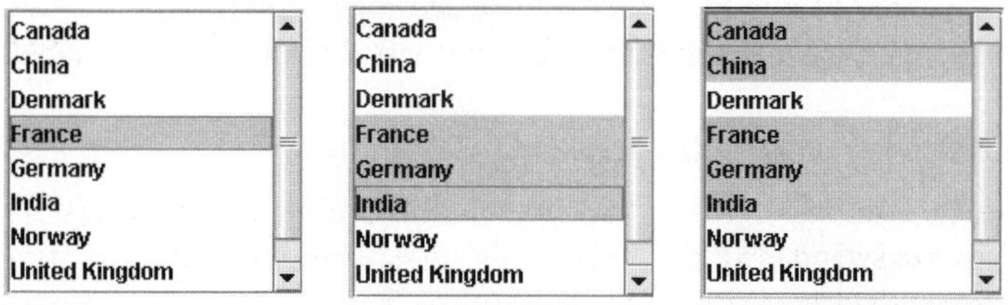
Canada
China
Denmark
France
Germany
India
Norway
United Kingdom

(a) Single selection (b) Single-interval selection (c) Multiple-interval selection

FIGURE 17.24 `JList` has three selection modes: single selection, single-interval selection, and multiple-interval selection.

The following statements create a list with six items, `red` foreground, `white` background, `pink` selection foreground, `black` selection background, and visible row count `4`.

```
JList jlst = new JList(new Object[]
  {"Item 1", "Item 2", "Item 3", "Item 4", "Item 5", "Item 6"});
jlst.setForeground(Color.RED);
jlst.setBackground(Color.WHITE);
jlst.setSelectionForeground(Color.PINK);
jlst.setSelectionBackground(Color.BLACK);
jlst.setVisibleRowCount(4);
```

Lists do not scroll automatically. To make a list scrollable, create a scroll pane and add the list to it.

`JList` fires `javax.swing.event.ListSelectionEvent` to notify the listeners of the selections. The listener must implement the `valueChanged` handler in the `javax.swing.event.ListSelectionListener` interface to process the event.

Listing 17.9 gives a program that lets users select countries in a list and display the flags of the selected countries in the labels. Figure 17.25 shows a sample run of the program.

ListDemo
Canada
China
Denmark
France
Germany
India
Norway
United Kingdom
United States of America
JList inside a scroll pane
JPanel with GridLayout
An image is displayed on a Jlabel

FIGURE 17.25 When the countries in the list are selected, corresponding images of their flags are displayed in the labels.

Here are the major steps in the program:

1. Create the user interface.
   Create a list with nine country names as selection values, and place the list inside a scroll pane. Place the scroll pane in the west of the frame. Create nine labels to be used to display the countries' flag images. Place the labels in the panel, and place the panel in the center of the frame.

2. Process the event.
   Create a listener to implement the `valueChanged` method in the `ListSelectionListener` interface to set the selected countries' flag images in the labels.

LISTING 17.9 ListDemo.java

```
import java.awt.*;
import javax.swing.*;
import javax.swing.event.*;

public class ListDemo extends JFrame {
  final int NUMBER_OF_FLAGS = 9;

  // Declare an array of Strings for flag titles
  private String[] flagTitles = {"Canada", "China", "Denmark",
```

```
    "France", "Germany", "India", "Norway", "United Kingdom",
    "United States of America"};

  // The list for selecting countries
  private JList jlst = new JList(flagTitles);

  // Declare an ImageIcon array for the national flags of 9 countries
  private ImageIcon[] imageIcons = {
    new ImageIcon("image/ca.gif"),
    new ImageIcon("image/china.gif"),
    new ImageIcon("image/denmark.gif"),
    new ImageIcon("image/fr.gif"),
    new ImageIcon("image/germany.gif"),
    new ImageIcon("image/india.gif"),
    new ImageIcon("image/norway.gif"),
    new ImageIcon("image/uk.gif"),
    new ImageIcon("image/us.gif")
  };

  // Arrays of labels for displaying images
  private JLabel[] jlblImageViewer = new JLabel[NUMBER_OF_FLAGS];

  public static void main(String[] args) {
    ListDemo frame = new ListDemo();
    frame.setSize(650, 500);
    frame.setTitle("ListDemo");
    frame.setLocationRelativeTo(null); // Center the frame
    frame.setDefaultCloseOperation(JFrame.EXIT_ON_CLOSE);
    frame.setVisible(true);
  }

  public ListDemo() {
    // Create a panel to hold nine labels
    JPanel p = new JPanel(new GridLayout(3, 3, 5, 5));

    for (int i = 0; i < NUMBER_OF_FLAGS; i++) {
      p.add(jlblImageViewer[i] = new JLabel());
      jlblImageViewer[i].setHorizontalAlignment
        (SwingConstants.CENTER);
    }

    // Add p and the list to the frame
    add(p, BorderLayout.CENTER);
    add(new JScrollPane(jlst), BorderLayout.WEST);

    // Register listeners
    jlst.addListSelectionListener(new ListSelectionListener() {
      /** Handle list selection */
      public void valueChanged(ListSelectionEvent e) {
        // Get selected indices
        int[] indices = jlst.getSelectedIndices();

        int i;
        // Set icons in the labels
        for (i = 0; i < indices.length; i++) {
          jlblImageViewer[i].setIcon(imageIcons[indices[i]]);
        }

        // Remove icons from the rest of the labels
        for (; i < NUMBER_OF_FLAGS; i++) {
```

create frame

create UI

event handler

```
70             jlblImageViewer[i].setIcon(null);
71           }
72         }
73       });
74     }
75   }
```

The anonymous inner-class listener listens to `ListSelectionEvent` for handling the selection of country names in the list (lines 56–73). `ListSelectionEvent` and `ListSelectionListener` are defined in the `javax.swing.event` package, so this package is imported in the program (line 3).

The program creates an array of nine labels for displaying flag images for nine countries. The program loads the images of the nine countries into an image array (lines 17–27) and creates a list of the nine countries in the same order as in the image array (lines 9–11). Thus the index `0` of the image array corresponds to the first country in the list.

The list is placed in a scroll pane (line 53) so that it can be scrolled when the number of items in the list extends beyond the viewing area.

By default, the selection mode of the list is multiple-interval, which allows the user to select multiple items from different blocks in the list. When the user selects countries in the list, the `valueChanged` handler (lines 58–73) is executed, which gets the indices of the selected item and sets their corresponding image icons in the label to display the flags.

17.10 Scroll Bars

`JScrollBar` is a component that enables the user to select from a range of values, as shown in Figure 17.26.

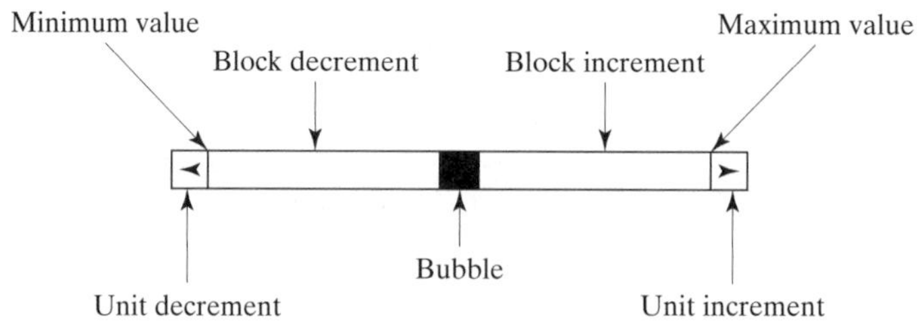
Minimum value
Block decrement
Block increment
Maximum value
Bubble
Unit decrement
Unit increment

FIGURE 17.26 A scroll bar represents a range of values graphically.

Normally, the user changes the value of the scroll bar by making a gesture with the mouse. For example, the user can drag the scroll bar's bubble up and down, or click in the scroll bar's unit-increment or block-increment areas. Keyboard gestures can also be mapped to the scroll bar. By convention, the Page Up and Page Down keys are equivalent to clicking in the scroll bar's block-increment and block-decrement areas.

Note

The width of the scroll bar's track corresponds to `maximum + visibleAmount`. When a scroll bar is set to its maximum value, the left side of the bubble is at `maximum`, and the right side is at `maximum + visibleAmount`.

`JScrollBar` has the following properties, as shown in Figure 17.27.

When the user changes the value of the scroll bar, the scroll bar fires an instance of `AdjustmentEvent`, which is passed to every registered listener. An object that wishes to be notified of changes to the scroll bar's value must implement the `adjustmentValueChanged` method in the `java.awt.event.AdjustmentListener` interface.

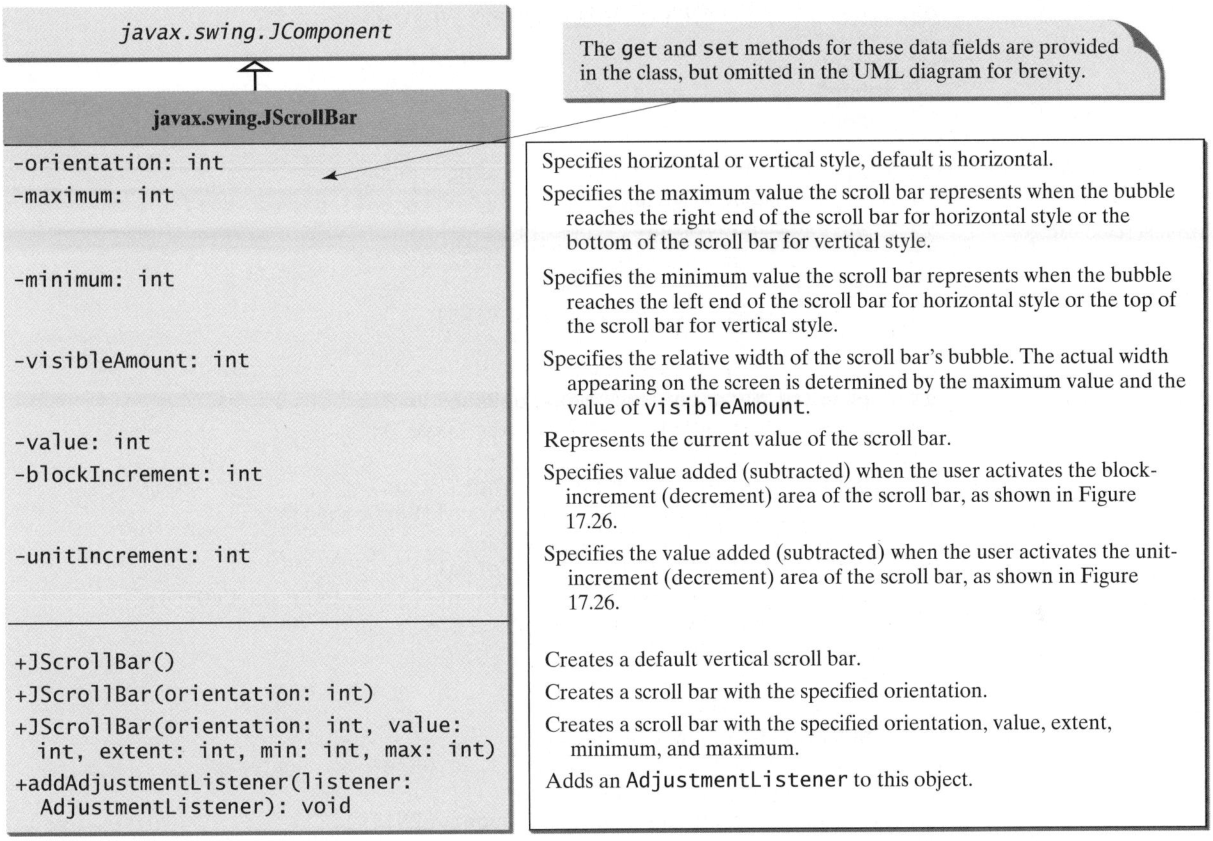
javax.swing.JComponent
The get and set methods for these data fields are provided in the class, but omitted in the UML diagram for brevity.
javax.swing.JScrollBar
-orientation: int
-maximum: int
-minimum: int
-visibleAmount: int
-value: int
-blockIncrement: int
-unitIncrement: int
+JScrollBar()
+JScrollBar(orientation: int)
+JScrollBar(orientation: int, value: int, extent: int, min: int, max: int)
+addAdjustmentListener(listener: AdjustmentListener): void
Specifies horizontal or vertical style, default is horizontal.
Specifies the maximum value the scroll bar represents when the bubble reaches the right end of the scroll bar for horizontal style or the bottom of the scroll bar for vertical style.
Specifies the minimum value the scroll bar represents when the bubble reaches the left end of the scroll bar for horizontal style or the top of the scroll bar for vertical style.
Specifies the relative width of the scroll bar's bubble. The actual width appearing on the screen is determined by the maximum value and the value of visibleAmount.
Represents the current value of the scroll bar.
Specifies value added (subtracted) when the user activates the block-increment (decrement) area of the scroll bar, as shown in Figure 17.26.
Specifies the value added (subtracted) when the user activates the unit-increment (decrement) area of the scroll bar, as shown in Figure 17.26.
Creates a default vertical scroll bar.
Creates a scroll bar with the specified orientation.
Creates a scroll bar with the specified orientation, value, extent, minimum, and maximum.
Adds an AdjustmentListener to this object.

FIGURE 17.27 `JScrollBar` enables you to select from a range of values.

Listing 17.10 gives a program that uses horizontal and vertical scroll bars to control a message displayed on a panel. The horizontal scroll bar is used to move the message to the left or the right, and the vertical scroll bar to move it up and down. A sample run of the program is shown in Figure 17.28.

ScrollBarDemo
Message panel
Welcome to Java
Vertical scroll bar
Horizontal scroll bar

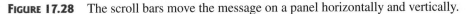

FIGURE 17.28 The scroll bars move the message on a panel horizontally and vertically.

Here are the major steps in the program:

1. Create the user interface.
   Create a `MessagePanel` object and place it in the center of the frame. Create a vertical scroll bar and place it in the east of the frame. Create a horizontal scroll bar and place it in the south of the frame.

2. Process the event.
   Create listeners to implement the `adjustmentValueChanged` handler to move the message according to the bar movement in the scroll bars.

LISTING 17.10 ScrollBarDemo.java

horizontal scroll bar

vertical scroll bar

create frame

create UI

add scroll bar

adjustment listener

adjustment listener

```
import java.awt.*;
import java.awt.event.*;
import javax.swing.*;

public class ScrollBarDemo extends JFrame {
  // Create horizontal and vertical scroll bars
  private JScrollBar jscbHort =
    new JScrollBar(JScrollBar.HORIZONTAL);
  private JScrollBar jscbVert =
    new JScrollBar(JScrollBar.VERTICAL);

  // Create a MessagePanel
  private MessagePanel messagePanel =
    new MessagePanel("Welcome to Java");

  public static void main(String[] args) {
    ScrollBarDemo frame = new ScrollBarDemo();
    frame.setTitle("ScrollBarDemo");
    frame.setLocationRelativeTo(null); // Center the frame
    frame.setDefaultCloseOperation(JFrame.EXIT_ON_CLOSE);
    frame.pack();
    frame.setVisible(true);
  }

  public ScrollBarDemo() {
    // Add scroll bars and message panel to the frame
    setLayout(new BorderLayout());
    add(messagePanel, BorderLayout.CENTER);
    add(jscbVert, BorderLayout.EAST);
    add(jscbHort, BorderLayout.SOUTH);

    // Register listener for the scroll bars
    jscbHort.addAdjustmentListener(new AdjustmentListener() {
      public void adjustmentValueChanged(AdjustmentEvent e) {
        // getValue() and getMaximumValue() return int, but for better
        // precision, use double
        double value = jscbHort.getValue();
        double maximumValue = jscbHort.getMaximum();
        double newX = (value * messagePanel.getWidth() /
          maximumValue);
        messagePanel.setXCoordinate((int)newX);
      }
    });
    jscbVert.addAdjustmentListener(new AdjustmentListener() {
      public void adjustmentValueChanged(AdjustmentEvent e) {
        // getValue() and getMaximumValue() return int, but for better
        // precision, use double
        double value = jscbVert.getValue();
        double maximumValue = jscbVert.getMaximum();
        double newY = (value * messagePanel.getHeight() /
          maximumValue);
        messagePanel.setYCoordinate((int)newY);
      }
    });
  }
}
```

The program creates two scroll bars (`jscbVert` and `jscbHort`) (lines 7–10) and an instance of `MessagePanel` (`messagePanel`) (lines 13–14). `messagePanel` is placed in the center of the frame; `jscbVert` and `jscbHort` are placed in the east and south sections of the frame (lines 29–30), respectively.

You can specify the orientation of the scroll bar in the constructor or use the `setOrientation` method. By default, the property value is `100` for `maximum`, `0` for `minimum`, `10` for `blockIncrement`, and `10` for `visibleAmount`.

When the user drags the bubble, or clicks the increment or decrement unit, the value of the scroll bar changes. An instance of `AdjustmentEvent` is fired and passed to the listener by invoking the `adjustmentValueChanged` handler. The listener for the vertical scroll bar moves the message up and down (lines 33–43), and the listener for the horizontal bar moves the message to right and left (lines 44–54).

The maximum value of the vertical scroll bar corresponds to the height of the panel, and the maximum value of the horizontal scroll bar corresponds to the width of the panel. The ratio between the current and maximum values of the horizontal scroll bar is the same as the ratio between the `x` value and the width of the message panel. Similarly, the ratio between the current and maximum values of the vertical scroll bar is the same as the ratio between the `y` value and the height of the message panel. The `x`-coordinate and `y`-coordinate are set in response to the scroll bar adjustments (lines 39, 50).

17.11 Sliders

`JSlider` is similar to `JScrollBar`, but `JSlider` has more properties and can appear in many forms. Figure 17.29 shows two sliders.

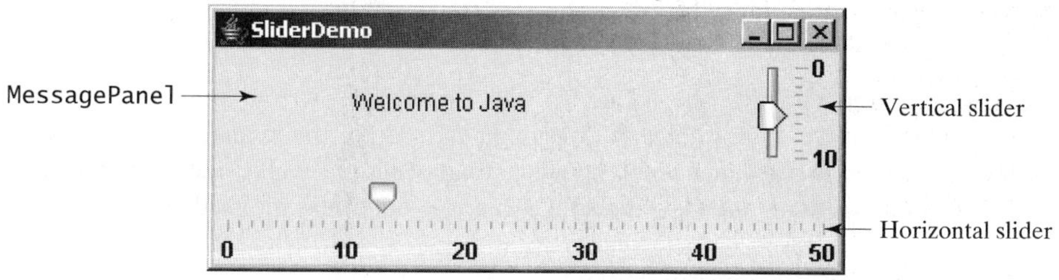
SliderDemo
MessagePanel
Welcome to Java
0
10
Vertical slider
Horizontal slider
0 10 20 30 40 50

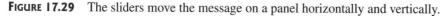

FIGURE 17.29 The sliders move the message on a panel horizontally and vertically.

`JSlider` lets the user graphically select a value by sliding a knob within a bounded interval. The slider can show both major tick marks and minor tick marks between them. The number of pixels between the tick marks is controlled by the `majorTickSpacing` and `minorTickSpacing` properties. Sliders can be displayed horizontally or vertically, with or without ticks, and with or without labels. The frequently used constructors and properties in `JSlider` are shown in Figure 17.30.

Note

The values of a vertical scroll bar increase from top to bottom, but the values of a vertical slider decrease from top to bottom by default.

Note

All the properties listed in Figure 17.30 have the associated `get` and `set` methods, which are omitted for brevity. By convention, the `get` method for a Boolean property is named *`is<PropertyName>()`*. In the `JSlider` class, the `get` methods for `paintLabels`, `paintTicks`, `paintTrack`, and `inverted` are `getPaintLabels()`, `getPaintTicks()`, `getPaintTrack()`, and `getInverted()`, which violate the naming convention.

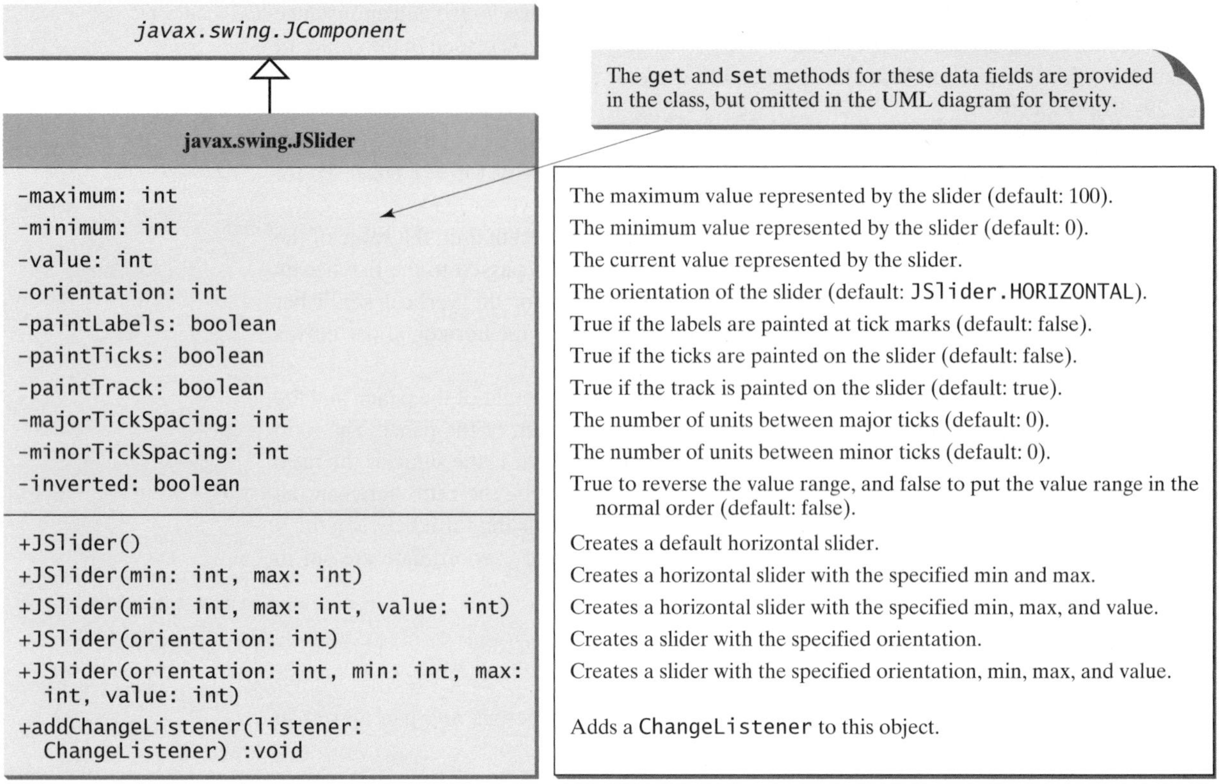
javax.swing.JComponent
The get and set methods for these data fields are provided in the class, but omitted in the UML diagram for brevity.
javax.swing.JSlider
-maximum: int
-minimum: int
-value: int
-orientation: int
-paintLabels: boolean
-paintTicks: boolean
-paintTrack: boolean
-majorTickSpacing: int
-minorTickSpacing: int
-inverted: boolean
+JSlider()
+JSlider(min: int, max: int)
+JSlider(min: int, max: int, value: int)
+JSlider(orientation: int)
+JSlider(orientation: int, min: int, max: int, value: int)
+addChangeListener(listener: ChangeListener) :void
The maximum value represented by the slider (default: 100).
The minimum value represented by the slider (default: 0).
The current value represented by the slider.
The orientation of the slider (default: JSlider.HORIZONTAL).
True if the labels are painted at tick marks (default: false).
True if the ticks are painted on the slider (default: false).
True if the track is painted on the slider (default: true).
The number of units between major ticks (default: 0).
The number of units between minor ticks (default: 0).
True to reverse the value range, and false to put the value range in the normal order (default: false).
Creates a default horizontal slider.
Creates a horizontal slider with the specified min and max.
Creates a horizontal slider with the specified min, max, and value.
Creates a slider with the specified orientation.
Creates a slider with the specified orientation, min, max, and value.
Adds a ChangeListener to this object.

FIGURE 17.30 `JSlider` enables you to select from a range of values.

When the user changes the value of the slider, the slider fires an instance of `javax.swing.event.ChangeEvent`, which is passed to any registered listeners. Any object that wishes to be notified of changes to the slider's value must implement the `stateChanged` method in the `ChangeListener` interface defined in the package `javax.swing.event`.

Listing 17.11 writes a program that uses the sliders to control a message displayed on a panel, as shown in Figure 17.29. Here are the major steps in the program:

1. Create the user interface.
   Create a `MessagePanel` object and place it in the center of the frame. Create a vertical slider and place it in the east of the frame. Create a horizontal slider and place it in the south of the frame.

2. Process the event.
   Create listeners to implement the `stateChanged` handler in the `ChangeListener` interface to move the message according to the knot movement in the slider.

LISTING 17.11 SliderDemo.java

horizontal slider
vertical slider

```
import java.awt.*;
import javax.swing.*;
import javax.swing.event.*;

public class SliderDemo extends JFrame {
  // Create horizontal and vertical sliders
  private JSlider jsldHort = new JSlider(JSlider.HORIZONTAL);
  private JSlider jsldVert = new JSlider(JSlider.VERTICAL);

```

```java
  // Create a MessagePanel
  private MessagePanel messagePanel =
    new MessagePanel("Welcome to Java");

  public static void main(String[] args) {
    SliderDemo frame = new SliderDemo();
    frame.setTitle("SliderDemo");
    frame.setLocationRelativeTo(null); // Center the frame
    frame.setDefaultCloseOperation(JFrame.EXIT_ON_CLOSE);
    frame.pack();
    frame.setVisible(true);
  }

  public SliderDemo() {
    // Add sliders and message panel to the frame
    setLayout(new BorderLayout(5, 5));
    add(messagePanel, BorderLayout.CENTER);
    add(jsldVert, BorderLayout.EAST);
    add(jsldHort, BorderLayout.SOUTH);

    // Set properties for sliders
    jsldHort.setMaximum(50);
    jsldHort.setPaintLabels(true);
    jsldHort.setPaintTicks(true);
    jsldHort.setMajorTickSpacing(10);
    jsldHort.setMinorTickSpacing(1);
    jsldHort.setPaintTrack(false);
    jsldVert.setInverted(true);
    jsldVert.setMaximum(10);
    jsldVert.setPaintLabels(true);
    jsldVert.setPaintTicks(true);
    jsldVert.setMajorTickSpacing(10);
    jsldVert.setMinorTickSpacing(1);

    // Register listener for the sliders
    jsldHort.addChangeListener(new ChangeListener() {
      /** Handle scroll-bar adjustment actions */
      public void stateChanged(ChangeEvent e) {
        // getValue() and getMaximumValue() return int, but for better
        // precision, use double
        double value = jsldHort.getValue();
        double maximumValue = jsldHort.getMaximum();
        double newX = (value * messagePanel.getWidth() /
          maximumValue);
        messagePanel.setXCoordinate((int)newX);
      }
    });
    jsldVert.addChangeListener(new ChangeListener() {
      /** Handle scroll-bar adjustment actions */
      public void stateChanged(ChangeEvent e) {
        // getValue() and getMaximumValue() return int, but for better
        // precision, use double
        double value = jsldVert.getValue();
        double maximumValue = jsldVert.getMaximum();
        double newY = (value * messagePanel.getHeight() /
          maximumValue);
        messagePanel.setYCoordinate((int) newY);
      }
    });
  }
}
```

create frame

create UI

slider properties

listener

listener

`JSlider` is similar to `JScrollBar` but has more features. As shown in this example, you can specify maximum, labels, major ticks, and minor ticks on a `JSlider` (lines 31–35). You can also choose to hide the track (line 36). Since the values of a vertical slider decrease from top to bottom, the `setInverted` method reverses the order (line 37).

`JSlider` fires `ChangeEvent` when the slider is changed. The listener needs to implement the `stateChanged` handler in `ChangeListener` (lines 45–68). Note that `JScrollBar` fires `AdjustmentEvent` when the scroll bar is adjusted.

17.12 Creating Multiple Windows

Occasionally, you may want to create multiple windows in an application. The application opens a new window to perform a specified task. The new windows are called *subwindows,* and the main frame is called the *main window*.

To create a subwindow from an application, you need to define a subclass of `JFrame` that specifies the task and tells the new window what to do. You can then create an instance of this subclass in the application and launch the new window by setting the frame instance to be visible.

Listing 17.12 gives a program that creates a main window with a text area in the scroll pane and a button named *Show Histogram*. When the user clicks the button, a new window appears that displays a histogram to show the occurrences of the letters in the text area. Figure 17.31 contains a sample run of the program.

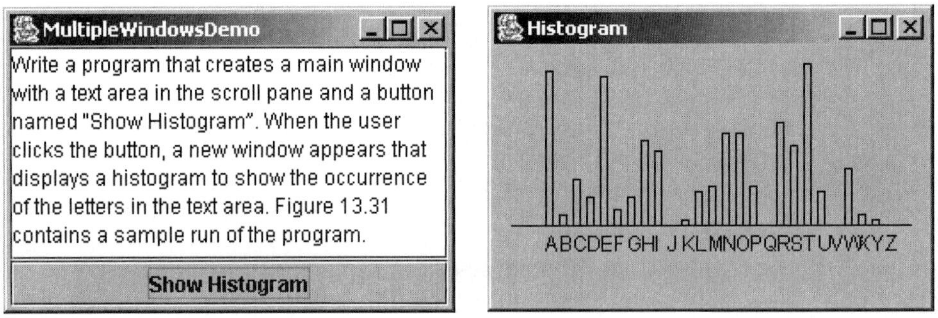
MultipleWindowsDemo
Write a program that creates a main window with a text area in the scroll pane and a button named "Show Histogram". When the user clicks the button, a new window appears that displays a histogram to show the occurrence of the letters in the text area. Figure 13.31 contains a sample run of the program.
Show Histogram
Histogram
ABCDEFGHIJKLMNOPQRSTUVWXYZ

FIGURE 17.31 The histogram is displayed in a separate frame.

Here are the major steps in the program:

1. Create a main class for the frame named `MultipleWindowsDemo` in Listing 17.12. Add a text area inside a scroll pane, and place the scroll pane in the center of the frame. Create a button *Show Histogram* and place it in the south of the frame.

2. Create a subclass of `JPanel` named `Histogram` in Listing 17.13. The class contains a data field named `count` of the `int[]` type, which counts the occurrences of `26` letters. The values in `count` are displayed in the histogram.

3. Implement the `actionPerformed` handler in `MultipleWindowsDemo`, as follows:

   a. Create an instance of `Histogram`. Count the letters in the text area and pass the count to the `Histogram` object.

   b. Create a new frame and place the `Histogram` object in the center of frame. Display the frame.

LISTING 17.12 MultipleWindowsDemo.java

```
import java.awt.*;
import java.awt.event.*;
import javax.swing.*;

public class MultipleWindowsDemo extends JFrame {
  private JTextArea jta;
  private JButton jbtShowHistogram = new JButton("Show Histogram");
  private Histogram histogram = new Histogram();

  // Create a new frame to hold the histogram panel
  private JFrame histogramFrame = new JFrame();

  public MultipleWindowsDemo() {
    // Store text area in a scroll pane
    JScrollPane scrollPane = new JScrollPane(jta = new JTextArea());
    scrollPane.setPreferredSize(new Dimension(300, 200));
    jta.setWrapStyleWord(true);
    jta.setLineWrap(true);

    // Place scroll pane and button in the frame
    add(scrollPane, BorderLayout.CENTER);
    add(jbtShowHistogram, BorderLayout.SOUTH);

    // Register listener
    jbtShowHistogram.addActionListener(new ActionListener() {
      /** Handle the button action */
      public void actionPerformed(ActionEvent e) {
        // Count the letters in the text area
        int[] count = countLetters();

        // Set the letter count to histogram for display
        histogram.showHistogram(count);

        // Show the frame
        histogramFrame.setVisible(true);
      }
    });

    // Create a new frame to hold the histogram panel
    histogramFrame.add(histogram);
    histogramFrame.pack();
    histogramFrame.setTitle("Histogram");
  }

  /** Count the letters in the text area */
  private int[] countLetters() {
    // Count for 26 letters
    int[] count = new int[26];

    // Get contents from the text area
    String text = jta.getText();

    // Count occurrences of each letter (case insensitive)
    for (int i = 0; i < text.length(); i++) {
      char character = text.charAt(i);
```

create subframe

create UI

display subframe

```java
      if ((character >= 'A') && (character <= 'Z')) {
        count[character - 'A']++;
      }
      else if ((character >= 'a') && (character <= 'z')) {
        count[character - 'a']++;
      }
    }

    return count; // Return the count array
  }

  public static void main(String[] args) {
    MultipleWindowsDemo frame = new MultipleWindowsDemo();
    frame.setLocationRelativeTo(null); // Center the frame
    frame.setDefaultCloseOperation(JFrame.EXIT_ON_CLOSE);
    frame.setTitle("MultipleWindowsDemo");
    frame.pack();
    frame.setVisible(true);
  }
}
```

create main frame

LISTING 17.13 Histogram.java

```java
import javax.swing.*;
import java.awt.*;

public class Histogram extends JPanel {
  // Count the occurrences of 26 letters
  private int[] count;

  /** Set the count and display histogram */
  public void showHistogram(int[] count) {
    this.count = count;
    repaint();
  }

  /** Paint the histogram */
  protected void paintComponent(Graphics g) {
    if (count == null) return; // No display if count is null

    super.paintComponent(g);

    // Find the panel size and bar width and interval dynamically
    int width = getWidth();
    int height = getHeight();
    int interval = (width - 40) / count.length;
    int individualWidth = (int)(((width - 40) / 24) * 0.60);

    // Find the maximum count. The maximum count has the highest bar
    int maxCount = 0;
    for (int i = 0; i < count.length; i++) {
      if (maxCount < count[i])
        maxCount = count[i];
    }

    // x is the start position for the first bar in the histogram
    int x = 30;

    // Draw a horizontal base line
```

paint histogram

```
    g.drawLine(10, height - 45, width - 10, height - 45);
    for (int i = 0; i < count.length; i++) {
      // Find the bar height
      int barHeight =
        (int)(((double)count[i] / (double)maxCount) * (height - 55));

      // Display a bar (i.e. rectangle)
      g.drawRect(x, height - 45 - barHeight, individualWidth,
        barHeight);

      // Display a letter under the base line
      g.drawString((char)(65 + i) + "", x, height - 30);

      // Move x for displaying the next character
      x += interval;
    }
  }

  /** Override getPreferredSize */
  public Dimension getPreferredSize() {
    return new Dimension(300, 300);
  }
}
```

preferredSize

The program contains two classes: `MultipleWindowsDemo` and `Histogram`. Their relationship is shown in Figure 17.32.

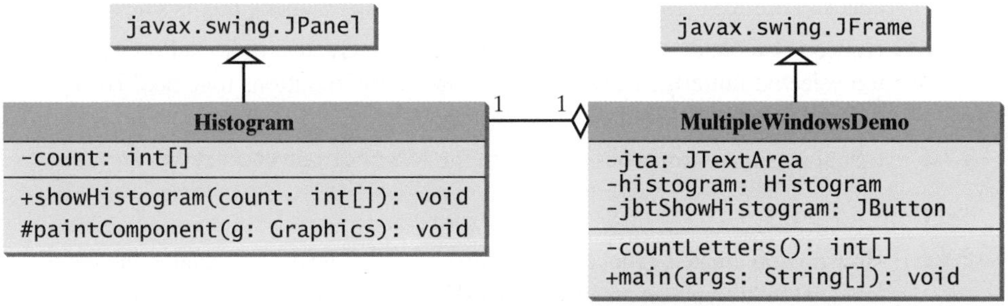

javax.swing.JPanel
javax.swing.JFrame
Histogram
-count: int[]
+showHistogram(count: int[]): void
#paintComponent(g: Graphics): void
1
1
MultipleWindowsDemo
-jta: JTextArea
-histogram: Histogram
-jbtShowHistogram: JButton
-countLetters(): int[]
+main(args: String[]): void

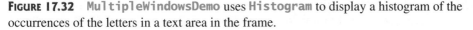

FIGURE 17.32 `MultipleWindowsDemo` uses `Histogram` to display a histogram of the occurrences of the letters in a text area in the frame.

`MultipleWindowsDemo` is a frame that holds a text area in a scroll pane and a button. `Histogram` is a subclass of `JPanel` that displays a histogram for the occurrences of letters in the text area.

When the user clicks the *Show Histogram* button, the handler counts the occurrences of letters in the text area. Letters are counted regardless of their case. Nonletter characters are not counted. The count is stored in an `int` array of `26` elements. The first element in the array stores the count for letter `'a'` or `'A'`, and the last element stores the count for letter `'z'` or `'Z'`. The `count` array is passed to the histogram for display.

The `MultipleWindowsDemo` class contains a `main` method. The `main` method creates an instance of `MultipleWindowsDemo` and displays the frame. The `MultipleWindowsDemo` class also contains an instance of `JFrame`, named `histogramFrame`, which holds an instance of `Histogram`. When the user clicks the *Show Histogram* button, `histogramFrame` is set visible to display the histogram.

The height and width of the bars in the histogram are determined dynamically according to the window size of the histogram.

You cannot add an instance of `JFrame` to a container. For example, adding `histogramFrame` to the main frame would cause a runtime exception. However, you can create a frame instance and set it visible to launch a new window.

Chapter Summary

1. You learned how to create graphical user interfaces using Swing GUI components `JButton`, `JCheckBox`, `JRadioButton`, `JLabel`, `JTextField`, `JTextArea`, `JComboBox`, `JList`, `JScrollBar`, and `JSlider`. You also learned how to handle events on these components.
2. You can display a text and icon on buttons (`JButton`, `JCheckBox`, `JRadioButton`) and labels (`JLabel`).

Review Questions

Sections 17.2–17.4

17.1 How do you create a button labeled OK? How do you change text on a button? How do you set an icon, a pressed icon, and a rollover icon in a button?

17.2 Given a `JButton` object `jbtOK`, write statements to set the button's foreground to `red`, background to `yellow`, mnemonic to `'K'`, tool tip text to `"Click OK to proceed"`, horizontal alignment to `RIGHT`, vertical alignment to `BOTTOM`, horizontal text position to `LEFT`, vertical text position to `TOP`, and icon text gap to `5`.

17.3 How do you create a check box? How do you create a check box with the box checked initially? How do you determine whether a check box is selected?

17.4 How do you create a radio button? How do you create a radio button with the button selected initially? How do you group the radio buttons together? How do you determine whether a radio button is selected?

17.5 List at least five properties defined in the `AbstractButton` class.

Sections 17.5–17.9

17.6 How do you create a label named `"Address"`? How do you change the name on a label? How do you set an icon in a label?

17.7 Given a `JLabel` object `jlblMap`, write statements to set the label's foreground to `red`, background to `yellow`, mnemonic to `'K'`, tool tip text to `"Map image"`, horizontal alignment to `RIGHT`, vertical alignment to `BOTTOM`, horizontal text position to `LEFT`, vertical text position to `TOP`, and icon text gap to `5`.

17.8 How do you create a text field with `10` columns and the default text `"Welcome to Java"`? How do you write the code to check whether a text field is empty?

17.9 How do you create a text area with ten rows and 20 columns? How do you insert three lines into the text area? How do you create a scrollable text area?

17.10 How do you create a combo box, add three items to it, and retrieve a selected item?

17.11 How do you create a list with an array of strings?

Sections 17.10–17.12

17.12 How do you create a horizontal scroll bar? What event can a scroll bar fire?

17.13 How do you create a vertical slider? What event can a slider fire?

17.14 Explain how to create and show multiple frames in an application.

Programming Exercises

Pedagogical Note

Instructors may assign the exercises from the next chapter as exercises for this chapter. Instead of writing Java applets, ask students to write Java applications.

additional exercises

Sections 17.2–17.5

17.1* (*Revising Listing 17.2, ButtonDemo.java*) Rewrite Listing 17.2 to add a group of radio buttons to select background colors. The available colors are red, yellow, white, gray, and green (see Figure 17.33).

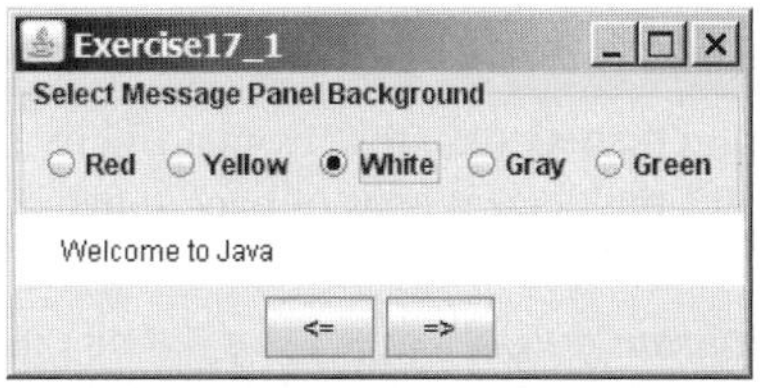
Exercise17_1
Select Message Panel Background
Red
Yellow
White
Gray
Green
Welcome to Java
<=
=>

Figure 17.33 The <= and => buttons move the message on the panel, and you can also set the background color for the message.

17.2* (*Selecting geometric figures*) Write a program that draws various figures, as shown in Figure 17.34. The user selects a figure from a radio button and specifies whether it is filled in a check box. (*Hint*: Use the `FigurePanel` class introduced in Listing 15.3 to display a figure.)

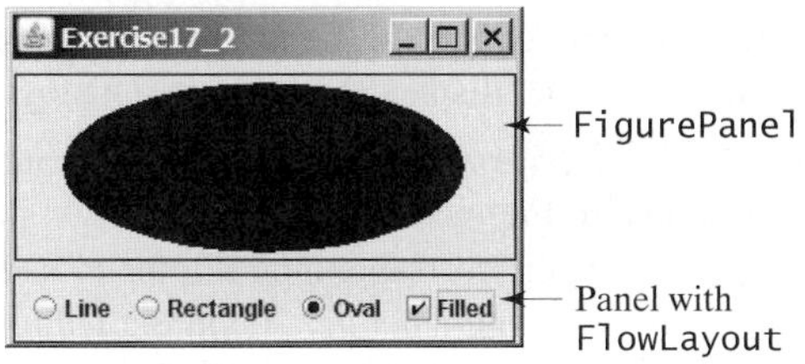
Exercise17_2
FigurePanel
Line
Rectangle
Oval
Filled
Panel with FlowLayout

Figure 17.34 The program displays lines, rectangles, and ovals when you select a shape type.

17.3** (*Traffic lights*) Write a program that simulates a traffic light. The program lets the user select one of three lights: red, yellow, or green. When a radio button is selected, the light is turned on, and only one light can be on at a time (see Figure 17.35). No light is on when the program starts.

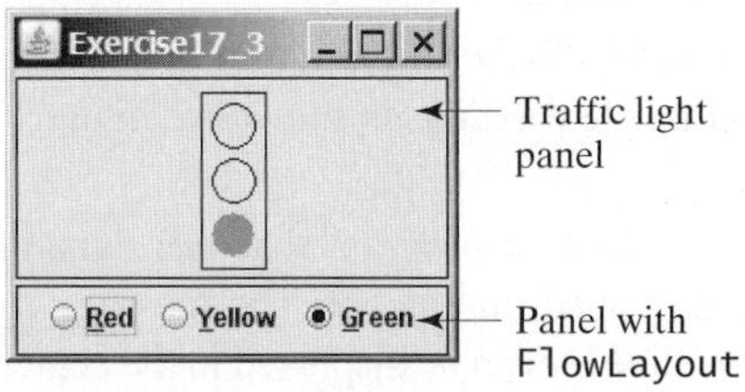
Exercise17_3
Traffic light panel
Red
Yellow
Green
Panel with FlowLayout

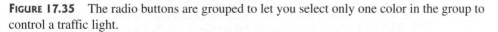

Figure 17.35 The radio buttons are grouped to let you select only one color in the group to control a traffic light.

Sections 17.6–17.10

17.4** (*Text Viewer*) Write a program that displays a text file in a text area, as shown in Figure 17.36. The user enters a file name in a text field and clicks the *View* button; the file is then displayed in a text area.

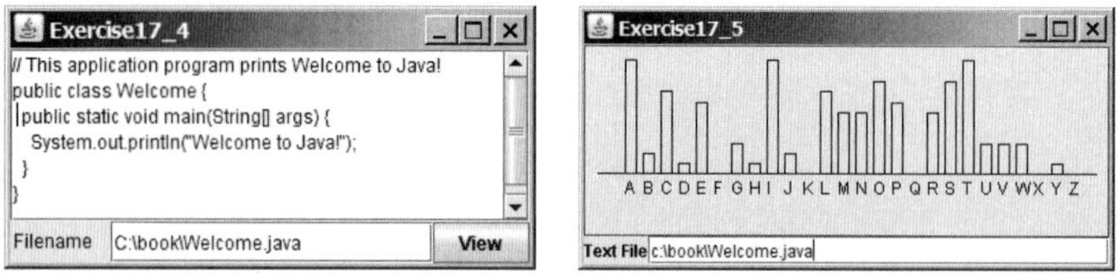
Exercise17_4
// This application program prints Welcome to Java!
public class Welcome {
public static void main(String[] args) {
System.out.println("Welcome to Java!");
}
}
Filename
C:\book\Welcome.java
View
Exercise17_5
A B C D E F G H I J K L M N O P Q R S T U V W X Y Z
Text File
c:\book\Welcome.java

(a) (b)

FIGURE 17.36 (a) The program displays the text from a file to a text area. (b) The program displays a histogram that shows the occurrences of each letter in the file.

17.5** (*Creating a histogram for occurrences of letters*) In Listing 17.12, MultipleWindowsDemo.java, you developed a program that displays a histogram to show the occurrences of each letter in a text area. Reuse the `Histogram` class created in Listing 17.12 to write a program that will display a histogram on a panel. The histogram should show the occurrences of each letter in a text file, as shown in Figure 17.36(b). Assume that the letters are not case sensitive.

- Place a panel that will display the histogram in the center of the frame.
- Place a label and a text field in a panel, and put the panel in the south side of the frame. The text file will be entered from this text field.
- Pressing the *Enter* key on the text field causes the program to count the occurrences of each letter and display the count in a histogram.

17.6* (*Creating a miles/kilometers converter*) Write a program that converts miles and kilometers, as shown in Figure 17.37. If you enter a value in the Mile text field and press the *Enter* key, the corresponding kilometer is displayed in the Kilometer text field. Likewise, if you enter a value in the Kilometer text field and press the *Enter* key, the corresponding mile is displayed in the Mile text field.

Exercise17_6
Mile
1
Kilometer
1.602307322544464
Panel with GridLayout for two labels
Panel with BorderLayout
Panel with GridLayout for two text fields

FIGURE 17.37 The program converts miles to kilometers, and vice versa.

17.7* (*Setting clock time*) Write a program that displays a clock time and sets it with the input from three text fields, as shown in Figure 17.38. Use the `StillClock` in Listing 15.10.

17.8** (*Selecting a font*) Write a program that can dynamically change the font of a message to be displayed on a panel. The message can be displayed in bold and italic at the same time, or can be displayed in the center of the panel. You can select the font name or font size from combo boxes, as shown in Figure 17.39. The available font names can be obtained using `getAvailableFontFamilyNames()` in `GraphicsEnvironment` (§12.8, "The `Font` Class"). The combo box for font size is initialized with numbers from `1` to `100`.

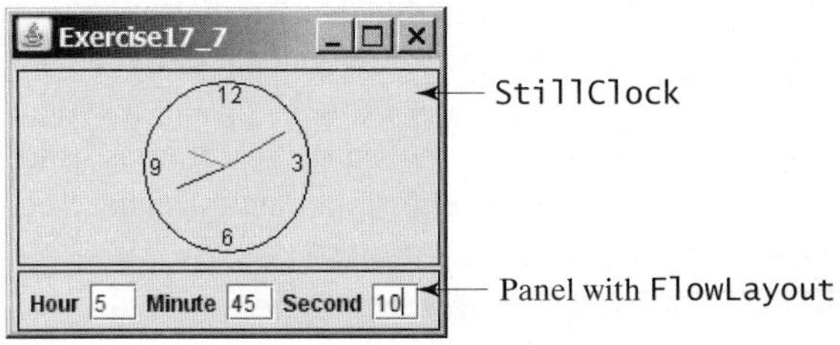
Exercise17_7
12
9
3
6
StillClock
Hour 5 Minute 45 Second 10
Panel with FlowLayout

FIGURE 17.38 The program displays the time specified in the text fields.

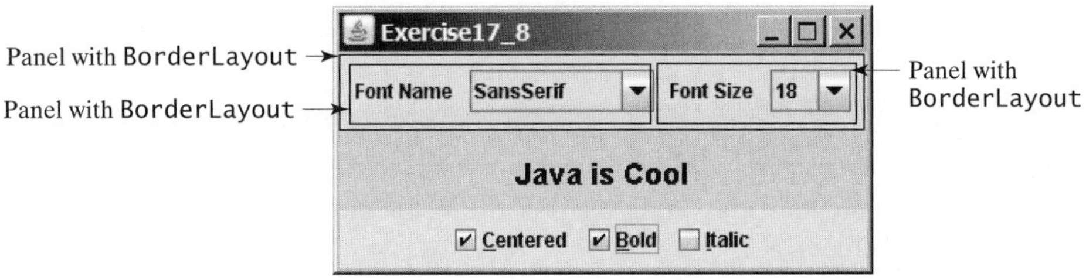
Exercise17_8
Panel with BorderLayout
Panel with BorderLayout
Font Name SansSerif
Font Size 18
Panel with BorderLayout
Java is Cool
Centered Bold Italic

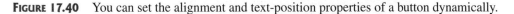

FIGURE 17.39 You can dynamically set the font for the message.

17.9** (*Demonstrating `JLabel` properties*) Write a program to let the user dynamically set the properties `horizontalAlignment`, `verticalAlignment`, `horizontalTextAlignment`, and `verticalTextAlignment`, as shown in Figure 17.40.

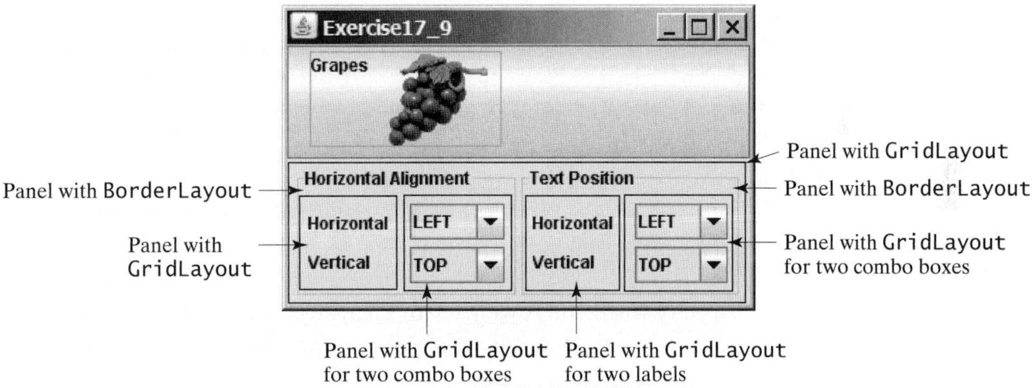
Exercise17_9
Grapes
Panel with GridLayout
Horizontal Alignment
Text Position
Panel with BorderLayout
Panel with BorderLayout
Horizontal
LEFT
Vertical
TOP
Horizontal
LEFT
Vertical
TOP
Panel with GridLayout
Panel with GridLayout for two combo boxes
Panel with GridLayout for two combo boxes
Panel with GridLayout for two labels

FIGURE 17.40 You can set the alignment and text-position properties of a button dynamically.

17.10* (*Adding new features into Listing 17.2, ButtonDemo.java, incrementally*) Improve Listing 17.2 incrementally, as follows (see Figure 17.41):

1. Add a text field labeled `"Enter a new message"` in the same panel with the buttons. When you type a new message in the text field and press the *Enter* key, the new message is displayed in the message panel.
2. Add a combo box labeled `"Select an interval"` in the same panel with the buttons. The combo box enables the user to select a new interval for moving the message. The selection values range from `5` to `100` with interval `5`. The user can also type a new interval in the combo box.
3. Add three radio buttons that enable the user to select the foreground color for the message as `Red`, `Green`, and `Blue`. The radio buttons are grouped in a panel, and the panel is placed in the north of the frame's content pane.

4. Add three check boxes that enable the user to center the message and display it in italic or bold. Place the check boxes in the same panel with the radio buttons.
5. Add a border titled `"Message Panel"` on the message panel, add a border titled `"South Panel"` on the panel for buttons, and add a border titled `"North Panel"` on the panel for radio buttons and check boxes.

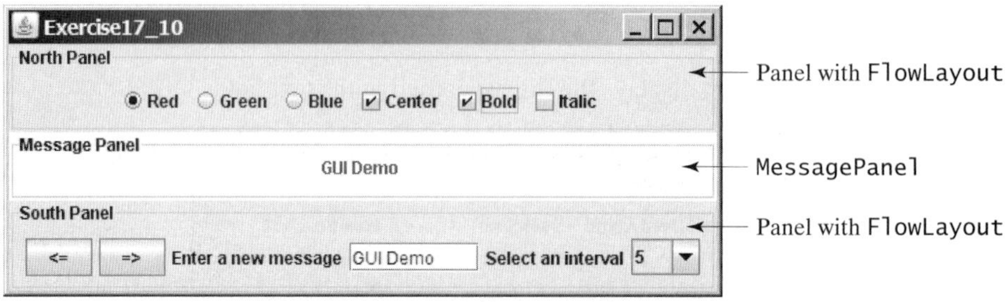
Exercise17_10
North Panel
Red
Green
Blue
Center
Bold
Italic
Message Panel
GUI Demo
South Panel
<=
=>
Enter a new message
GUI Demo
Select an interval
5
Panel with FlowLayout
MessagePanel
Panel with FlowLayout

FIGURE 17.41 The program uses buttons, labels, text fields, combo boxes, radio buttons, check boxes, and borders.

17.11* (*Demonstrating `JTextField` properties*) Write a program that sets the horizontal-alignment and column-size properties of a text field dynamically, as shown in Figure 17.42.

Exercise17_11
Text field
Type any thing
Horizontal Alignment
Left
Center
Right
Column Size
30

FIGURE 17.42 You can set the horizontal-alignment and column-size properties of a text field dynamically.

17.12* (*Demonstrating `JTextArea` properties*) Write a program that demonstrates the wrapping styles of the text area. The program uses a check box to indicate whether the text area is wrapped. In the case where the text area is wrapped, you need to specify whether it is wrapped by characters or by words, as shown in Figure 17.43.

Video Note
Use text areas

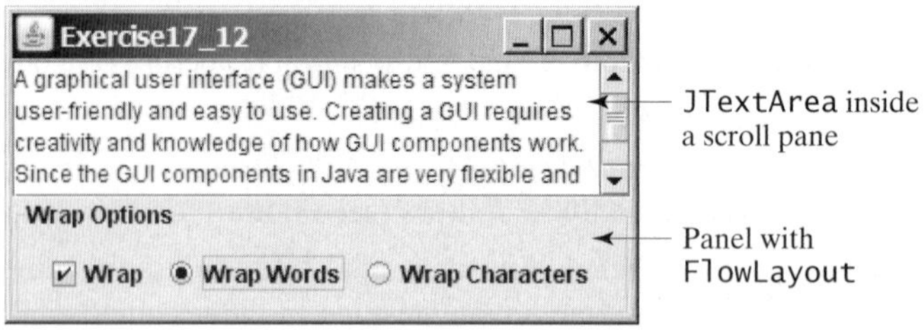
Exercise17_12
A graphical user interface (GUI) makes a system
user-friendly and easy to use. Creating a GUI requires
creativity and knowledge of how GUI components work.
Since the GUI components in Java are very flexible and
Wrap Options
Wrap
Wrap Words
Wrap Characters
JTextArea inside a scroll pane
Panel with FlowLayout

FIGURE 17.43 You can set the options to wrap a text area by characters or by words dynamically.

17.13* (*Comparing loans with various interest rates*) Rewrite Exercise 4.21 to create a user interface, as shown in Figure 17.44. Your program should let the user enter the loan amount and loan period in number of years from a text field, and should display the monthly and total payments for each interest rate starting from `5` percent to `8` percent, with increments of one-eighth, in a text area.

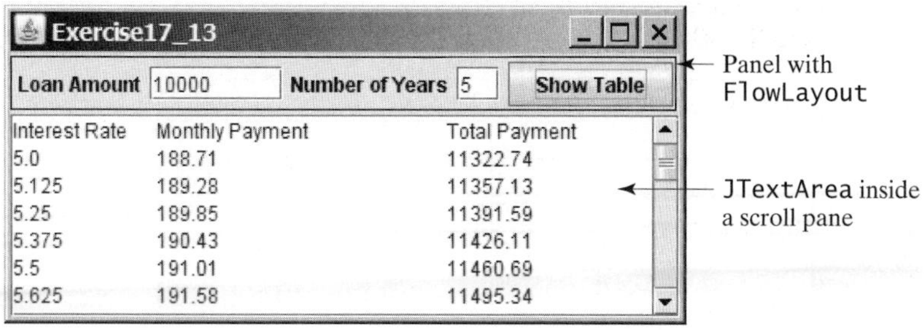
Exercise17_13
Loan Amount 10000 Number of Years 5 Show Table
Interest Rate Monthly Payment Total Payment
5.0 188.71 11322.74
5.125 189.28 11357.13
5.25 189.85 11391.59
5.375 190.43 11426.11
5.5 191.01 11460.69
5.625 191.58 11495.34
Panel with FlowLayout
JTextArea inside a scroll pane

FIGURE 17.44 The program displays a table for monthly payments and total payments on a given loan based on various interest rates.

17.14* (*Using `JComboBox` and `JList`*) Write a program that demonstrates selecting items in a list. The program uses a combo box to specify a selection mode, as shown in Figure 17.45. When you select items, they are displayed in a label below the list.

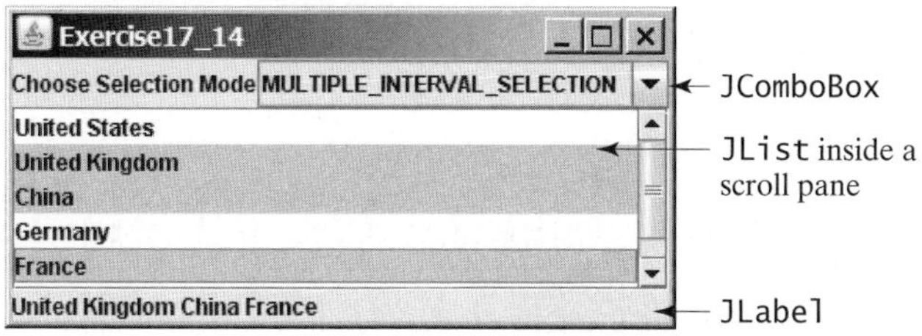
Exercise17_14
Choose Selection Mode MULTIPLE_INTERVAL_SELECTION
United States
United Kingdom
China
Germany
France
United Kingdom China France
JComboBox
JList inside a scroll pane
JLabel

FIGURE 17.45 You can choose single selection, single-interval selection, or multiple-interval selection in a list.

Sections 17.11–17.13

17.15** (*Using `JScrollBar`*) Write a program that uses scroll bars to select the foreground color for a label, as shown in Figure 17.46. Three horizontal scroll bars are used for selecting the red, green, and blue components of the color. Use a title border on the panel that holds the scroll bars.

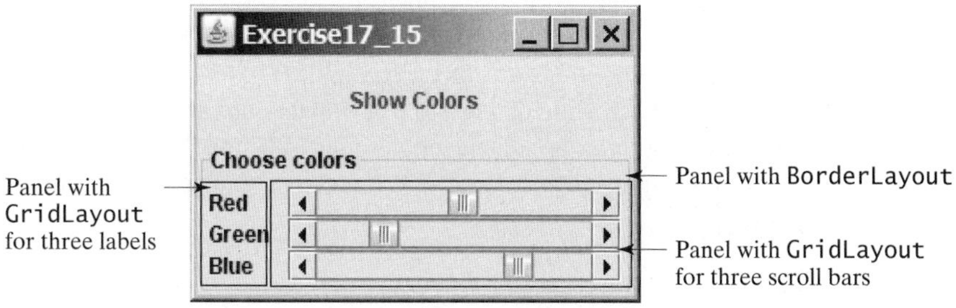
Exercise17_15
Show Colors
Choose colors
Red
Green
Blue
Panel with GridLayout for three labels
Panel with BorderLayout
Panel with GridLayout for three scroll bars

FIGURE 17.46 The foreground color changes in the label as you adjust the scroll bars.

17.16** (*Using `JSlider`*) Revise the preceding exercise using sliders.

17.17*** (*Displaying a calendar*) Write a program that displays the calendar for the current month, as shown in Figure 17.47. Use labels, and set texts on the labels to display the calendar. Use the `GregorianCalendar` class in §14.3, "Example: `Calendar` and `GregorianCalendar`," to obtain the information about month, year, first day of the month, and number of days in the month.

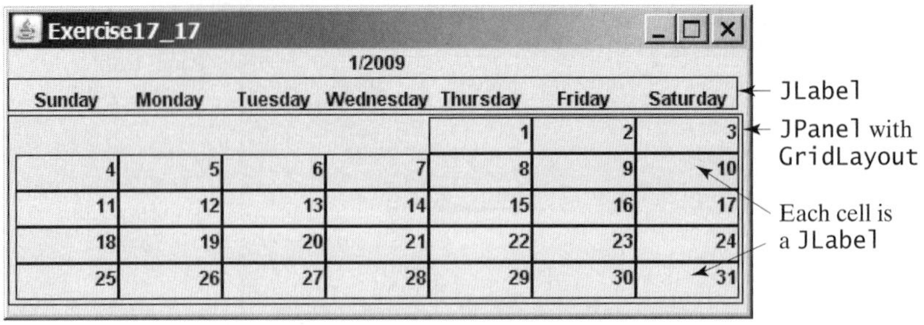
Exercise17_17
1/2009
Sunday Monday Tuesday Wednesday Thursday Friday Saturday
1 2 3
4 5 6 7 8 9 10
11 12 13 14 15 16 17
18 19 20 21 22 23 24
25 26 27 28 29 30 31
JLabel
JPanel with GridLayout
Each cell is a JLabel

FIGURE 17.47 The program displays the calendar for the current month.

17.18* (*Revising Listing 17.12, MultipleWindowsDemo.java*) Instead of displaying the occurrences of the letters using the `Histogram` component in Listing 17.12, use a bar chart, so that the display is as shown in Figure 17.48.

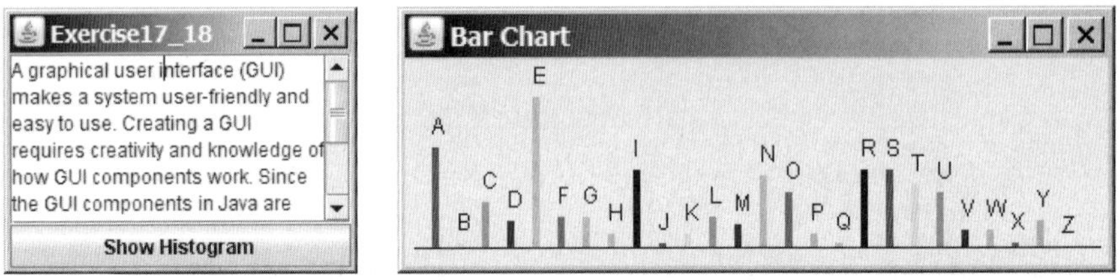
Exercise17_18
A graphical user interface (GUI) makes a system user-friendly and easy to use. Creating a GUI requires creativity and knowledge of how GUI components work. Since the GUI components in Java are
Show Histogram
Bar Chart
A B C D E F G H I J K L M N O P Q R S T U V W X Y Z

FIGURE 17.48 The number of occurrences of each letter is displayed in a bar chart.

17.19** (*Displaying country flag and flag description*) Listing 17.8, ComboBoxDemo.java, gives a program that lets users view a country's flag image and description by selecting the country from a combo box. The description is a string coded in the program. Rewrite the program to read the text description from a file. Suppose that the descriptions are stored in the file **description0.txt**, . . . , and **description8.txt** under the `text` directory for the nine countries Canada, China, Denmark, France, Germany, India, Norway, the United Kingdom, and the United States, in this order.

17.20** (*Slide show*) Exercise 16.13 developed a slide show using images. Rewrite Exercise 16.13 to develop a slide show using text files. Suppose ten text files named `slide0.txt`, `slide1.txt`, . . . , and `slide9.txt` are stored in the `text` directory. Each slide displays the text from one file. Each slide is shown for a second. The slides are displayed in order. When the last slide finishes, the first slide is redisplayed, and so on. Use a text area to display the slide.

CHAPTER 18

APPLETS AND MULTIMEDIA

Objectives

- To convert GUI applications to applets (§18.2).
- To embed applets in Web pages (§18.3).
- To run applets from Web browsers and from the appletviewer (§§18.3.1–18.3.2).
- To understand the applet security sandbox model (§18.4).
- To write a Java program that can run both as an application and as an applet (§18.5).
- To override the applet life-cycle methods `init`, `start`, `stop`, and `destroy` (§18.6).
- To pass string values to applets from HTML (§18.7).
- To develop an animation for a bouncing ball (§18.8).
- To develop an applet for the TicTacToe game (§18.9).
- To locate resources (images and audio) using the `URL` class (§18.10).
- To play audio in any Java program (§18.11).

18.1 Introduction

When browsing the Web, often the graphical user interface and animation you see are developed by the use of Java. The programs used are called Java applets. Suppose you want to develop a Java applet for the Sudoku game, as shown in Figure 18.1. How do you write this program?

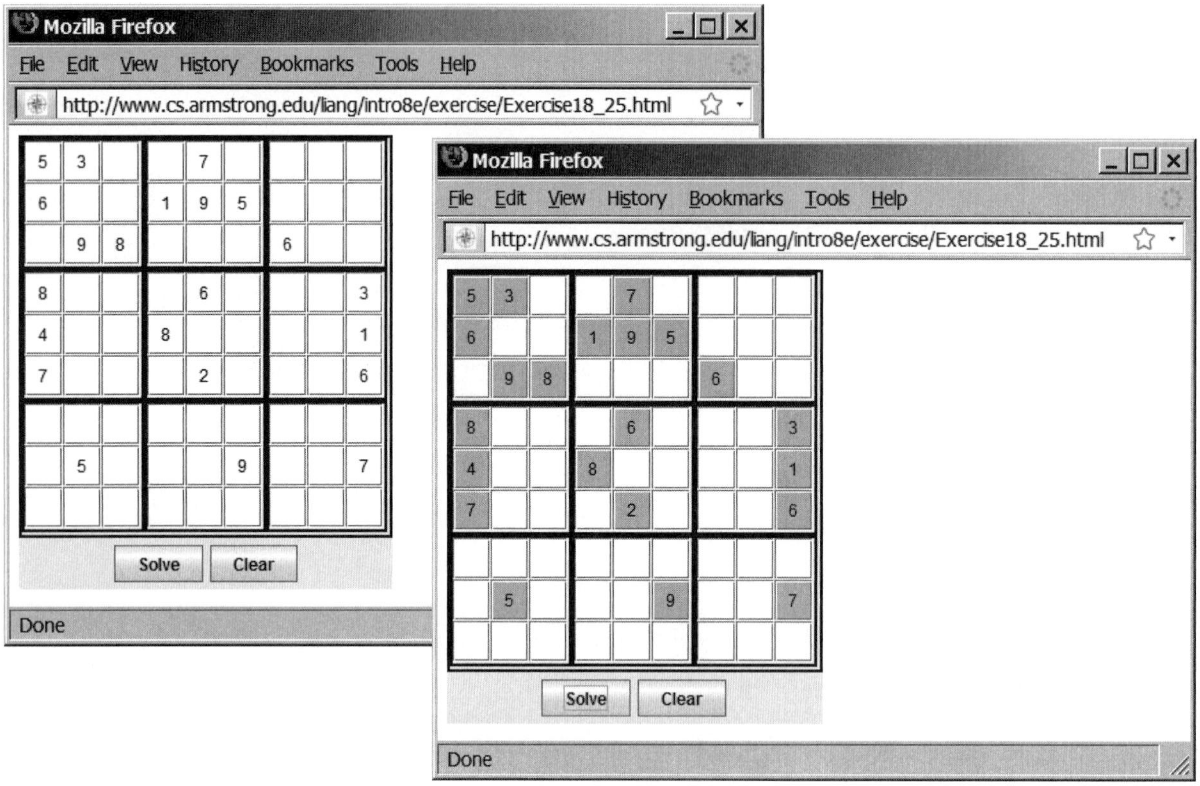
Mozilla Firefox
File Edit View History Bookmarks Tools Help
http://www.cs.armstrong.edu/liang/intro8e/exercise/Exercise18_25.html
Solve
Clear
Done
Mozilla Firefox
File Edit View History Bookmarks Tools Help
http://www.cs.armstrong.edu/liang/intro8e/exercise/Exercise18_25.html
Solve
Clear
Done

FIGURE 18.1 The Sudoku game is displayed in a Web browser.

In this chapter, you will learn how to write Java applets, explore the relationship between applets and the Web browser, and discover the similarities and differences between applications and applets. You will also learn how to create multimedia Java applications and applets with images and audio.

18.2 Developing Applets

Video Note
First applet

So far, you have used only Java applications. Everything you have learned about writing applications, however, applies also to writing applets. Applications and applets share many common programming features, although they differ slightly in some aspects. For example, every application must have a `main` method, which is invoked by the Java interpreter. Java applets, on the other hand, do not need a `main` method. They run in the Web browser environment. Because applets are invoked from a Web page, Java provides special features that enable applets to run from a Web browser.

The `Applet` class provides the essential framework that enables applets to be run from a Web browser. While every Java application has a `main` method that is executed when the application starts, applets do not have a `main` method. Instead they depend on the browser to run. Every applet is a subclass of `java.applet.Applet`. The `Applet` class is an AWT class and is not designed to work with Swing components. To use Swing components in Java applets, you need to create a Java applet that extends `javax.swing.JApplet`, which is a subclass of `java.applet.Applet`.

Every Java GUI program you have developed can be converted into an applet by replacing `JFrame` with `JApplet` and deleting the `main` method. Figure 18.2(a) shows a Java GUI application program, which can be converted into a Java applet as shown in Figure 18.2(b).

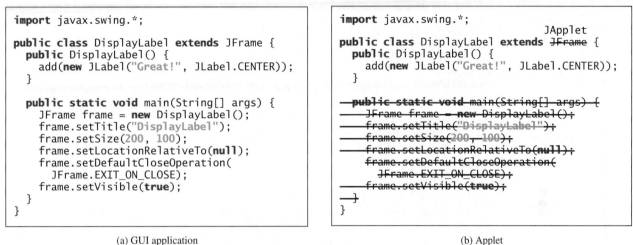

```
import javax.swing.*;

public class DisplayLabel extends JFrame {
  public DisplayLabel() {
    add(new JLabel("Great!", JLabel.CENTER));
  }

  public static void main(String[] args) {
    JFrame frame = new DisplayLabel();
    frame.setTitle("DisplayLabel");
    frame.setSize(200, 100);
    frame.setLocationRelativeTo(null);
    frame.setDefaultCloseOperation(
      JFrame.EXIT_ON_CLOSE);
    frame.setVisible(true);
  }
}
```

(a) GUI application

```
import javax.swing.*;
                                            JApplet
public class DisplayLabel extends ~~JFrame~~ {
  public DisplayLabel() {
    add(new JLabel("Great!", JLabel.CENTER));
  }

  ~~public static void main(String[] args) {~~
    ~~JFrame frame = new DisplayLabel();~~
    ~~frame.setTitle("DisplayLabel");~~
    ~~frame.setSize(200, 100);~~
    ~~frame.setLocationRelativeTo(null);~~
    ~~frame.setDefaultCloseOperation(~~
      ~~JFrame.EXIT_ON_CLOSE);~~
    ~~frame.setVisible(true);~~
  ~~}~~
}
```

(b) Applet

FIGURE 18.2 You can convert a GUI application into an applet.

Listing 18.1 gives the complete code for the applet.

LISTING 18.1 DisplayLabel.java

```
import javax.swing.*;

public class DisplayLabel extends JApplet {
  public DisplayLabel() {
    add(new JLabel("Great!", JLabel.CENTER));
  }
}
```

extend **JApplet**

Like `JFrame`, `JApplet` is a container that can contain other GUI components (see the GUI class diagrams in Figure 14.1).

18.3 The HTML File and the <applet> Tag

To run an applet from a browser, you need to create an HTML file with the `<applet>` tag.

HTML is a markup language that presents static documents on the Web. It uses tags to instruct the Web browser how to render a Web page and contains a tag called `<applet>` that incorporates applets into a Web page.

The HTML file in Listing 18.2 invokes the **DisplayLabel.class**:

LISTING 18.2 DisplayLabel.html

```
<html>
  <head>
    <title>Java Applet Demo</title>
  </head>
  <body>
```

applet class

```
    <applet
      code = "DisplayLabel.class"
      width = 250
      height = 50>
    </applet>
  </body>
</html>
```

A *tag* is an instruction to the Web browser. The browser interprets the tag and decides how to display or otherwise treat the subsequent contents of the HTML document. Tags are enclosed inside brackets. The first word in a tag, called the *tag name*, describes tag functions. A tag can have additional attributes, sometimes with values after an equals sign, which further define the tag's action. For example, in the preceding HTML file, <applet> is the tag name, and code, width, and height are attributes. The width and height attributes specify the rectangular viewing area of the applet.

Most tags have a *start tag* and a corresponding *end tag*. The tag has a specific effect on the region between the start tag and the end tag. For example, <applet...>...</applet> tells the browser to display an applet. An end tag is always the start tag's name preceded by a slash.

HTML tag

An HTML document begins with the <html> tag, which declares that the document is written in HTML. Each document has two parts, a *head* and a *body*, defined by <head> and <body> tags, respectively. The head part contains the document title, including the <title> tag and other information the browser can use when rendering the document, and the body part holds the actual contents of the document. The header is optional. For more information, refer to Supplement V.A, "HTML and XHTML Tutorial."

<applet> tag

The complete syntax of the <applet> tag is as follows:

```
<applet
  [codebase = applet_url]
  code = classfilename.class
  width = applet_viewing_width_in_pixels
  height = applet_viewing_height_in_pixels
  [archive = archivefile]
  [vspace = vertical_margin]
  [hspace = horizontal_margin]
  [align = applet_alignment]
  [alt = alternative_text]
>
<param name = param_name1 value = param_value1>
<param name = param_name2 value = param_value2>
...
<param name = param_name3 value = param_value3>
</applet>
```

<param> tag

The code, width, and height attributes are required; all the others are optional. The <param> tag will be introduced in §18.7, "Passing Strings to Applets." The other attributes are explained below.

codebase attribute

- **codebase** specifies a base where your classes are loaded. If this attribute is not used, the Web browser loads the applet from the directory in which the HTML page is located. If your applet is located in a different directory from the HTML page, you must specify the applet_url for the browser to load the applet. This attribute enables you to load the class from anywhere on the Internet. The classes used by the applet are dynamically loaded when needed.

archive attribute

- **archive** instructs the browser to load an archive file that contains all the class files needed to run the applet. Archiving allows the Web browser to load all the classes from a single compressed file at one time, thus reducing loading time and improving performance. To create archives, see Supplement III.Q, "Packaging and Deploying Java Projects."

- **vspace** and **hspace** specify the size, in pixels, of the blank margin to pad around the applet vertically and horizontally.
- **align** specifies how the applet will be aligned in the browser. One of nine values is used: **left**, **right**, **top**, **texttop**, **middle**, **absmiddle**, **baseline**, **bottom**, or **absbottom**.
- **alt** specifies the text to be displayed in case the browser cannot run Java.

18.3.1 Viewing Applets from a Web Browser

To display an applet from a Web browser, open the applet's HTML file (e.g., DisplayLabel.html). Its output is shown in Figure 18.3(a).

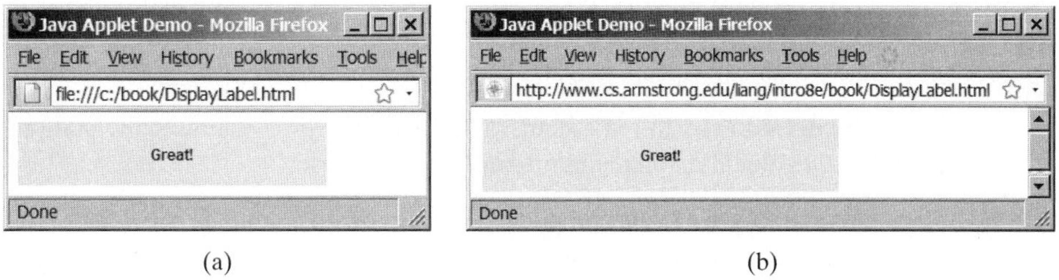
Java Applet Demo - Mozilla Firefox
File Edit View History Bookmarks Tools Help
file:///c:/book/DisplayLabel.html
Great!
Done
(a)
Java Applet Demo - Mozilla Firefox
File Edit View History Bookmarks Tools Help
http://www.cs.armstrong.edu/liang/intro8e/book/DisplayLabel.html
Great!
Done
(b)

FIGURE 18.3 The DisplayLabel program is loaded from a local host in (a) and from a Web server in (b).

To make your applet accessible on the Web, you need to store the DisplayLabel.class and DisplayLabel.html on a Web server, as shown in Figure 18.4. You can view the applet from an appropriate URL. For example, I have uploaded these two files on Web server www.cs.armstrong.edu/. As shown in Figure 18.3(b), you can access the applet from www.cs.armstrong.edu/liang/intro8e/book/DisplayLabel.html.

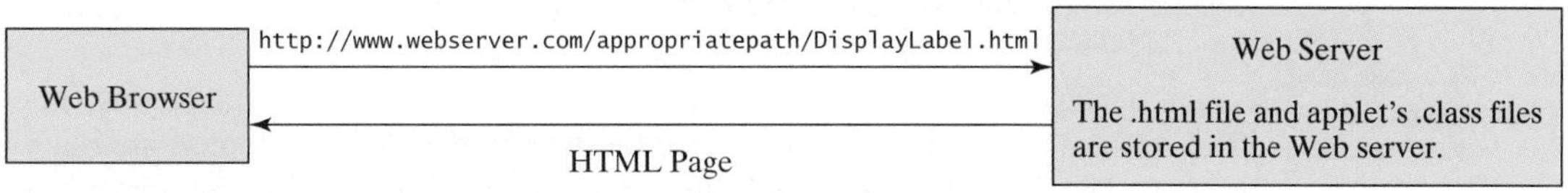
Web Browser
http://www.webserver.com/appropriatepath/DisplayLabel.html
HTML Page
Web Server
The .html file and applet's .class files are stored in the Web server.

FIGURE 18.4 A Web browser requests an HTML page from a Web server.

18.3.2 Viewing Applets Using the Applet Viewer Utility

You can test the applet using the applet viewer utility, which can be invoked from the DOS prompt using the **appletviewer** command from **c:\book**, as shown in Figure 18.5(a). Its output is shown in Figure 18.5(b). appletviewer

The applet viewer functions as a browser. It is convenient for testing applets during development without launching a Web browser.

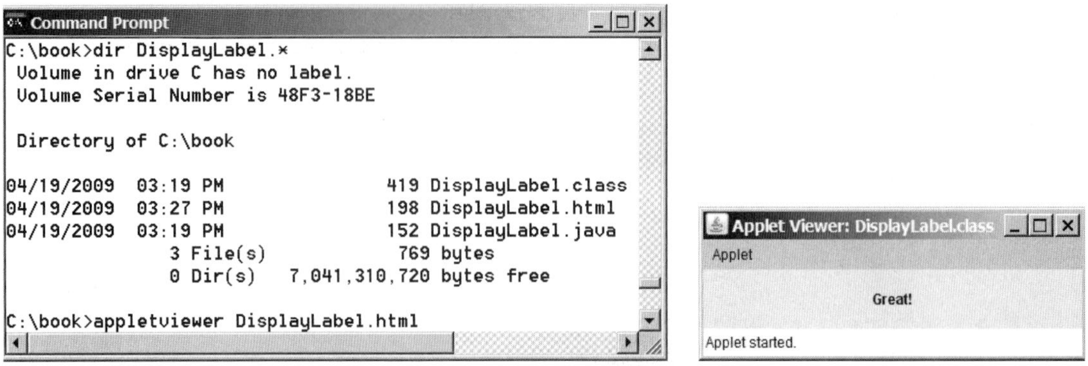
Command Prompt
C:\book>dir DisplayLabel.*
Volume in drive C has no label.
Volume Serial Number is 48F3-18BE
Directory of C:\book
04/19/2009 03:19 PM 419 DisplayLabel.class
04/19/2009 03:27 PM 198 DisplayLabel.html
04/19/2009 03:19 PM 152 DisplayLabel.java
3 File(s) 769 bytes
0 Dir(s) 7,041,310,720 bytes free
C:\book>appletviewer DisplayLabel.html
Applet Viewer: DisplayLabel.class
Applet
Great!
Applet started.

(a) (b)

FIGURE 18.5 The appletviewer command runs a Java applet in the applet viewer utility.

18.4 Applet Security Restrictions

Java uses the so-called "sandbox security model" for executing applets to prevent destructive programs from damaging the system on which the browser is running. Applets are not allowed to use resources outside the "sandbox." Specifically, the sandbox restricts the following activities:

- Applets are not allowed to read from, or write to, the file system of the computer. Otherwise, they could damage the files and spread viruses.
- Applets are not allowed to run programs on the browser's computer. Otherwise, they might call destructive local programs and damage the local system on the user's computer.
- Applets are not allowed to establish connections between the user's computer and any other computer, except for the server where the applets are stored. This restriction prevents the applet from connecting the user's computer to another computer without the user's knowledge.

signed applet

Note

You can create *signed applets* to circumvent the security restrictions. See java.sun.com/developer/onlineTraining/Programming/JDCBook/signed.html for detailed instructions on how to create signed applets.

18.5 Enabling Applets to Run as Applications

Video Note
Run applets standalone

Despite some differences, the `JFrame` class and the `JApplet` class have a lot in common. Since they both are subclasses of the `Container` class, all their user-interface components, layout managers, and event-handling features are the same. Applications, however, are invoked from the static `main` method by the Java interpreter, and applets are run by the Web browser. The Web browser creates an instance of the applet using the applet's no-arg constructor and controls and executes the applet.

In general, an applet can be converted to an application without loss of functionality. An application can be converted to an applet as long as it does not violate the security restrictions imposed on applets. You can implement a `main` method in an applet to enable the applet to run as an application. This feature has both theoretical and practical implications. Theoretically, it blurs the difference between applets and applications. You can write a class that is both an applet and an application. From the standpoint of practicality, it is convenient to be able to run a program in two ways.

How do you write such program? Suppose you have an applet named `MyApplet`. To enable it to run as an application, you need only add a `main` method in the applet with the implementation, as follows:

```
public static void main(String[] args) {
  // Create a frame
  JFrame frame = new JFrame("Applet is in the frame");

  // Create an instance of the applet
  MyApplet applet = new MyApplet();

  // Add the applet to the frame
  frame.add(applet, BorderLayout.CENTER);

  // Display the frame
  frame.setSize(300, 300);
  frame.setLocationRelativeTo(null); // Center the frame
  frame.setDefaultCloseOperation(JFrame.EXIT_ON_CLOSE);
  frame.setVisible(true);
}
```

create frame

create applet

add applet

show frame

You can revise the `DisplayLabel` class in Listing 18.1 to enable it to run standalone by adding a `main` method in Listing 18.3.

Listing 18.3 New DisplayLabel.java with a main Method

```
1 import javax.swing.*;
2
3 public class DisplayLabel extends JApplet {
4   public DisplayLabel() {
5     add(new JLabel("Great!", JLabel.CENTER));
6   }
7
8   public static void main(String[] args) {
9     // Create a frame
10    JFrame frame = new JFrame("Applet is in the frame");
11
12    // Create an instance of the applet
13    DisplayLabel applet = new DisplayLabel();
14
15    // Add the applet to the frame
16    frame.add(applet);
17
18    // Display the frame
19    frame.setSize(300, 100);
20    frame.setLocationRelativeTo(null); // Center the frame
21    frame.setDefaultCloseOperation(JFrame.EXIT_ON_CLOSE);
22    frame.setVisible(true);
23  }
24 }
```

new main method

When the applet is run from a Web browser, the browser creates an instance of the applet and displays it. When the applet is run standalone, the main method is invoked to create a frame (line 10) to hold the applet. The applet is created (line 13) and added to the frame (line 16). The frame is displayed in line 22.

18.6 Applet Life-Cycle Methods

applet container

Applets are actually run from the *applet container*, which is a plug-in of a Web browser. The `Applet` class contains the `init()`, `start()`, `stop()`, and `destroy()` methods, known as the *life-cycle methods*. These methods are called by the applet container to control the execution of an applet. They are implemented with an empty body in the `Applet` class. So, they do nothing by default. You may override them in a subclass of `Applet` to perform desired operations. Figure 18.6 shows how the applet container calls these methods.

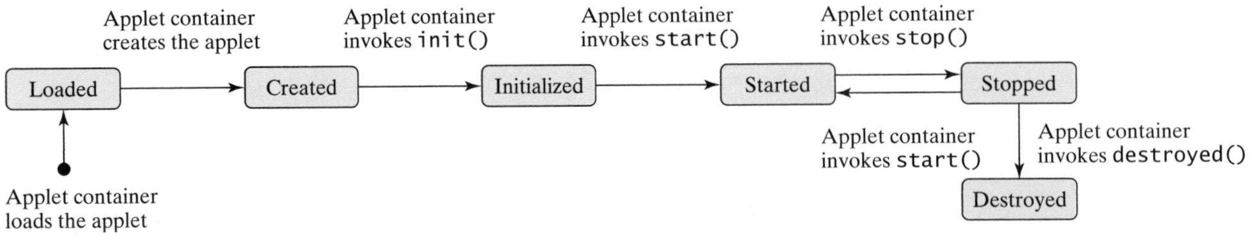

Applet container creates the applet
Applet container invokes init()
Applet container invokes start()
Applet container invokes stop()
Loaded
Created
Initialized
Started
Stopped
Applet container invokes start()
Applet container invokes destroyed()
Applet container loads the applet
Destroyed

FIGURE 18.6 The applet container uses the `init`, `start`, `stop`, and `destroy` methods to control the applet.

18.6.1 The `init` Method

`init()`

The `init` method is invoked after the applet is created. If a subclass of `Applet` has an initialization to perform, it should override this method. The functions usually implemented in this method include getting string parameter values from the `<applet>` tag in the HTML page.

18.6.2 The `start` Method

`start()`

The `start` method is invoked after the `init` method. It is also called when the user returns to the Web page containing the applet after surfing other pages.

A subclass of `Applet` overrides this method if it has any operation that needs to be performed whenever the Web page containing the applet is visited. An applet with animation, for example, might start the timer to resume animation.

18.6.3 The `stop` Method

`stop()`

The `stop` method is the opposite of the `start` method. The `start` method is called when the user moves back to the page that contains the applet. The `stop` method is invoked when the user leaves the page.

A subclass of `Applet` overrides this method if it has any operation to be performed each time the Web page containing the applet is no longer visible. An applet with animation, for example, might stop the timer to pause animation.

18.6.4 The `destroy` Method

`destroy()`

The `destroy` method is invoked when the browser exits normally to inform the applet that it is no longer needed and should release any resources it has allocated. The `stop` method is always called before the `destroy` method.

A subclass of `Applet` overrides this method if it has any operation to be performed before it is destroyed. Usually, you won't need to override this method unless you wish to release specific resources that the applet created.

18.7 Passing Strings to Applets

In §9.5, "Command-Line Arguments," you learned how to pass strings to Java applications from a command line. Strings are passed to the `main` method as an array of strings. When the application starts, the main method can use these strings. There is no main method in an applet, however, and applets are not run from the command line by the Java interpreter.

How, then, can applets accept arguments? In this section, you will learn how to pass strings to Java applets. To be passed to an applet, a parameter must be declared in the HTML file and must be read by the applet when it is initialized. Parameters are declared using the <param> tag. The <param> tag must be embedded in the <applet> tag and has no end tag. Its syntax is given below:

```
<param name = parametername value = stringvalue />
```

This tag specifies a parameter and its corresponding string value.

Note

No comma separates the parameter name from the parameter value in the HTML code. The HTML parameter names are not case sensitive.

Suppose you want to write an applet to display a message. The message is passed as a parameter. In addition, you want the message to be displayed at a specific location with x-coordinate and y-coordinate, which are passed as two parameters. The parameters and their values are listed in Table 18.1.

TABLE 18.1 Parameter Names and Values for the DisplayMessage Applet

Parameter Name	*Parameter Value*
MESSAGE	"Welcome to Java"
X	20
Y	30

The HTML source file is given in Listing 18.4.

LISTING 18.4 DisplayMessage.html

```
<html>
  <head>
    <title>Passing Strings to Java Applets</title>
  </head>
  <body>
    <p>This applet gets a message from the HTML
       page and displays it.</p>
    <applet
      code = "DisplayMessage.class"
      width = 200
      height = 50
      alt = "You must have a Java 2-enabled browser to view the applet"
    >
      <param name = MESSAGE value = "Welcome to Java" />
      <param name = X value = 20 />
      <param name = Y value = 30 />
    </applet>
  </body>
</html>
```

To read the parameter from the applet, use the following method defined in the Applet class:

```
public String getParameter(String parametername);
```

This returns the value of the specified parameter.

The applet is given in Listing 18.5. A sample run of the applet is shown in Figure 18.7.

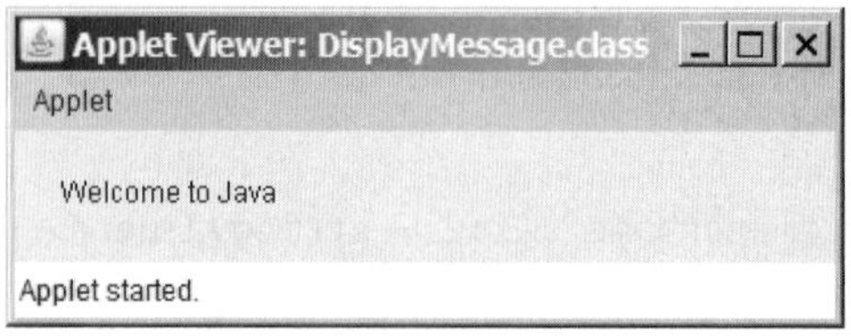
Applet Viewer: DisplayMessage.class
Applet
Welcome to Java
Applet started.

FIGURE 18.7 The applet displays the message `Welcome to Java` passed from the HTML page.

LISTING 18.5 DisplayMessage.java

getParameter

add to applet

```
 1 import javax.swing.*;
 2
 3 public class DisplayMessage extends JApplet {
 4   /** Initialize the applet */
 5   public void init() {
 6     // Get parameter values from the HTML file
 7     String message = getParameter("MESSAGE");
 8     int x = Integer.parseInt(getParameter("X"));
 9     int y = Integer.parseInt(getParameter("Y"));
10
11     // Create a message panel
12     MessagePanel messagePanel = new MessagePanel(message);
13     messagePanel.setXCoordinate(x);
14     messagePanel.setYCoordinate(y);
15
16     // Add the message panel to the applet
17     add(messagePanel);
18   }
19 }
```

The program gets the parameter values from the HTML in the `init` method. The values are strings obtained using the `getParameter` method (lines 7–9). Because `x` and `y` are `int`, the program uses `Integer.parseInt(string)` to parse a digital string into an `int` value.

If you change *`Welcome to Java`* in the HTML file to *`Welcome to HTML`*, and reload the HTML file in the Web browser, you should see *`Welcome to HTML`* displayed. Similarly, the `x` and `y` values can be changed to display the message in a desired location.

Caution

The `Applet`'s `getParameter` method can be invoked only after an instance of the applet is created. Therefore, this method cannot be invoked in the constructor of the applet class. You should invoke it from the `init` method.

You can add a main method to enable this applet to run standalone. The applet takes the parameters from the HTML file when it runs as an applet and takes the parameters from the command line when it runs standalone. The program, as shown in Listing 18.6, is identical to `DisplayMessage` except for the addition of a new `main` method and of a variable named `isStandalone` to indicate whether it is running as an applet or as an application.

LISTING 18.6 DisplayMessageApp.java

```
import javax.swing.*;
import java.awt.Font;
import java.awt.BorderLayout;

public class DisplayMessageApp extends JApplet {
  private String message = "A default message"; // Message to display
  private int x = 20; // Default x-coordinate
  private int y = 20; // Default y-coordinate

  /** Determine whether it is an application */
  private boolean isStandalone = false;

  /** Initialize the applet */
  public void init() {
    if (!isStandalone) {
      // Get parameter values from the HTML file
      message = getParameter("MESSAGE");
      x = Integer.parseInt(getParameter("X"));
      y = Integer.parseInt(getParameter("Y"));
    }

    // Create a message panel
    MessagePanel messagePanel = new MessagePanel(message);
    messagePanel.setFont(new Font("SansSerif", Font.BOLD, 20));
    messagePanel.setXCoordinate(x);
    messagePanel.setYCoordinate(y);

    // Add the message panel to the applet
    add(messagePanel);
  }

  /** Main method to display a message
     @param args[0] x-coordinate
     @param args[1] y-coordinate
     @param args[2] message
    */
  public static void main(String[] args) {
    // Create a frame
    JFrame frame = new JFrame("DisplayMessageApp");

    // Create an instance of the applet
    DisplayMessageApp applet = new DisplayMessageApp();

    // It runs as an application
    applet.isStandalone = true;

    // Get parameters from the command line
    applet.getCommandLineParameters(args);

    // Add the applet instance to the frame
    frame.add(applet, BorderLayout.CENTER);

    // Invoke applet's init method
    applet.init();
    applet.start();

    // Display the frame
    frame.setSize(300, 300);
```

isStandalone

applet params

standalone

command params

```
59      frame.setLocationRelativeTo(null); // Center the frame
60      frame.setDefaultCloseOperation(JFrame.EXIT_ON_CLOSE);
61      frame.setVisible(true);
62    }
63
64    /** Get command-line parameters */
65    private void getCommandLineParameters(String[] args) {
66      // Check usage and get x, y and message
67      if (args.length != 3) {
68        System.out.println(
69          "Usage: java DisplayMessageApp x y message");
70        System.exit(0);
71      }
72      else {
73        x = Integer.parseInt(args[0]);
74        y = Integer.parseInt(args[1]);
75        message = args[2];
76      }
77    }
78  }
```

When you run the program as an applet, the **main** method is ignored. When you run it as an application, the **main** method is invoked. Sample runs of the program as an application and as an applet are shown in Figure 18.8.

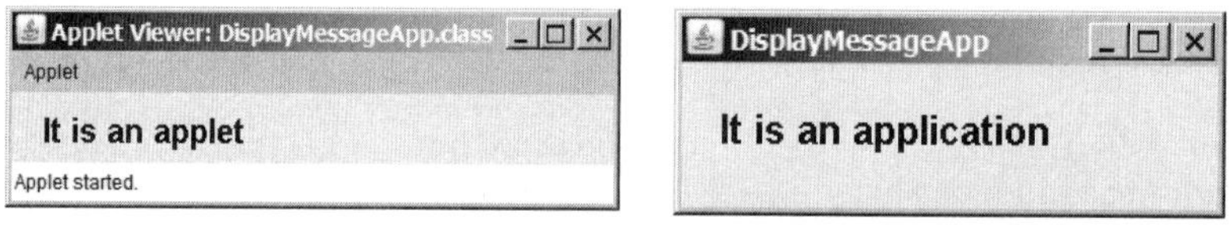
Applet Viewer: DisplayMessageApp.class
Applet
It is an applet
Applet started.
DisplayMessageApp
It is an application

FIGURE 18.8 The **DisplayMessageApp** class can run as an application and as an applet.

The **main** method creates a **JFrame** object **frame** and creates a **JApplet** object **applet**, then places the applet **applet** into the frame **frame** and invokes its **init** method. The application runs just like an applet.

The **main** method sets **isStandalone true** (line 45) so that it does not attempt to retrieve HTML parameters when the **init** method is invoked.

The **setVisible(true)** method (line 61) is invoked *after* the components are added to the applet, and the applet is added to the frame to ensure that the components will be visible. Otherwise, the components are not shown when the frame starts.

omitting **main** method

Important Pedagogical Note

From now on, all the GUI examples will be created as applets with a **main** method. Thus you will be able to run the program either as an applet or as an application. For brevity, the **main** method is not listed in the text.

18.8 Case Study: Bouncing Ball

This section presents an applet that displays a ball bouncing in a panel. Use two buttons to suspend and resume the movement, and use a scroll bar to control the bouncing speed, as shown in Figure 18.9.

Here are the major steps to complete this example:

1. Create a subclass of **JPanel** named **Ball** to display a ball bouncing, as shown in Listing 18.7.

BounceBallApp
Suspend
Resume
BounceBallApp
Suspend
Resume
BounceBallApp
Suspend
Resume

FIGURE 18.9 The ball's movement is controlled by the Suspend and Resume buttons and the scroll bar.

2. Create a subclass of `JPanel` named `BallControl` to contain the ball with a scroll bar and two control buttons *Suspend* and *Resume*, as shown in Listing 18.8.
3. Create an applet named `BounceBallApp` to contain an instance of `BallControl` and enable the applet to run standalone, as shown in Listing 18.9.

The relationship among these classes is shown in Figure 18.10.

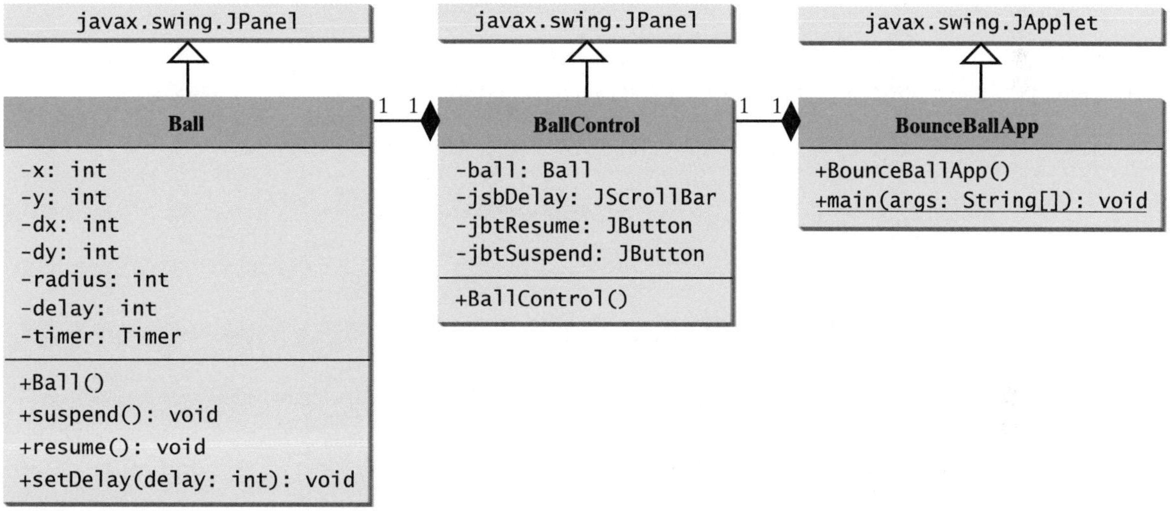
javax.swing.JPanel
javax.swing.JPanel
javax.swing.JApplet
Ball
-x: int
-y: int
-dx: int
-dy: int
-radius: int
-delay: int
-timer: Timer
+Ball()
+suspend(): void
+resume(): void
+setDelay(delay: int): void
1 1
BallControl
-ball: Ball
-jsbDelay: JScrollBar
-jbtResume: JButton
-jbtSuspend: JButton
+BallControl()
1 1
BounceBallApp
+BounceBallApp()
+main(args: String[]): void

FIGURE 18.10 `BounceBallApp` contains `BallControl`, and `BallControl` contains `Ball`.

LISTING 18.7 Ball.java

```
import javax.swing.Timer;
import java.awt.*;
import javax.swing.*;
import java.awt.event.*;

public class Ball extends JPanel {
  private int delay = 10;

  // Create a timer with delay 1000 ms
  private Timer timer = new Timer(delay, new TimerListener());

  private int x = 0; private int y = 0; // Current ball position
  private int radius = 5; // Ball radius
  private int dx = 2; // Increment on ball's x-coordinate
  private int dy = 2; // Increment on ball's y-coordinate

```

timer delay

create timer

start timer
timer listener
repaint ball
paint ball

```
17   public Ball() {
18     timer.start();
19   }
20
21   private class TimerListener implements ActionListener {
22     /** Handle the action event */
23     public void actionPerformed(ActionEvent e) {
24       repaint();
25     }
26   }
27
28   protected void paintComponent(Graphics g) {
29     super.paintComponent(g);
30
31     g.setColor(Color.red);
32
33     // Check boundaries
34     if (x < radius) dx = Math.abs(dx);
35     if (x > getWidth() - radius) dx = -Math.abs(dx);
36     if (y < radius) dy = Math.abs(dy);
37     if (y > getHeight() - radius) dy = -Math.abs(dy);
38
39     // Adjust ball position
40     x += dx;
41     y += dy;
42     g.fillOval(x - radius, y - radius, radius * 2, radius * 2);
43   }
44
45   public void suspend() {
46     timer.stop(); // Suspend timer
47   }
48
49   public void resume() {
50     timer.start(); // Resume timer
51   }
52
53   public void setDelay(int delay) {
54     this.delay = delay;
55     timer.setDelay(delay);
56   }
57 }
```

The use of `Timer` to control animation was introduced in §16.12, "Animation Using the `Timer` Class." `Ball` extends `JPanel` to display a moving ball. The timer listener implements `ActionListener` to listen for `ActionEvent` (line 21). Line 10 creates a `Timer` for a `Ball`. The timer is started in line 18 when a `Ball` is constructed. The timer fires an `ActionEvent` at a fixed rate. The listener responds in line 24 to repaint the ball to animate ball movement. The center of the ball is at (`x`, `y`), which changes to (`x + dx`, `y + dy`) on the next display (lines 40–41). The `suspend` and `resume` methods (lines 45–51) can be used to stop and start the timer. The `setDelay(int)` method (lines 53–56) sets a new delay.

Listing 18.8 BallControl.java

button

```
import javax.swing.*;
import java.awt.event.*;
import java.awt.*;

public class BallControl extends JPanel {
  private Ball ball = new Ball();
```

```
7   private JButton jbtSuspend = new JButton("Suspend");
8   private JButton jbtResume = new JButton("Resume");
9   private JScrollBar jsbDelay = new JScrollBar();
10
11  public BallControl() {
12    // Group buttons in a panel
13    JPanel panel = new JPanel();
14    panel.add(jbtSuspend);
15    panel.add(jbtResume);
16
17    // Add ball and buttons to the panel
18    ball.setBorder(new javax.swing.border.LineBorder(Color.red));
19    jsbDelay.setOrientation(JScrollBar.HORIZONTAL);
20    ball.setDelay(jsbDelay.getMaximum());
21    setLayout(new BorderLayout());
22    add(jsbDelay, BorderLayout.NORTH);
23    add(ball, BorderLayout.CENTER);
24    add(panel, BorderLayout.SOUTH);
25
26    // Register listeners
27    jbtSuspend.addActionListener(new ActionListener() {
28      public void actionPerformed(ActionEvent e) {
29        ball.suspend();
30      }
31    });
32    jbtResume.addActionListener(new ActionListener() {
33      public void actionPerformed(ActionEvent e) {
34        ball.resume();
35      }
36    });
37    jsbDelay.addAdjustmentListener(new AdjustmentListener() {
38      public void adjustmentValueChanged(AdjustmentEvent e) {
39        ball.setDelay(jsbDelay.getMaximum() - e.getValue());
40      }
41    });
42  }
43 }
```

scroll bar

create UI

register listener

suspend

register listener

resume

register listener

new delay

The **BallControl** class extends **JPanel** to display the ball with a scroll bar and two control buttons. When the *Suspend* button is clicked, the ball's **suspend()** method is invoked to suspend the ball movement (line 29). When the *Resume* button is clicked, the ball's **resume()** method is invoked to resume the ball movement (line 34). The bouncing speed can be changed using the scroll bar.

LISTING 18.9 BounceBallApp.java

```
import java.awt.*;
import javax.swing.*;

public class BounceBallApp extends JApplet {
  public BounceBallApp() {
    add(new BallControl());
  }
}
```

add **BallControl**

main method omitted

The **BounceBallApp** class simply places an instance of **BallControl** in the applet. The **main** method is provided in the applet (not displayed in the listing for brevity) so that you can also run it standalone.

18.9 Case Study: TicTacToe

Video Note
TicTacToe

From the many examples in this and earlier chapters you have learned about objects, classes, arrays, class inheritance, GUI, event-driven programming, and applets. Now it is time to put what you have learned to work in developing comprehensive projects. In this section, you will develop a Java applet with which to play the popular game of TicTacToe.

Two players take turns marking an available cell in a 3×3 grid with their respective tokens (either X or O). When one player has placed three tokens in a horizontal, vertical, or diagonal row on the grid, the game is over and that player has won. A draw (no winner) occurs when all the cells on the grid have been filled with tokens and neither player has achieved a win. Figure 18.11 shows the representative sample runs of the example.

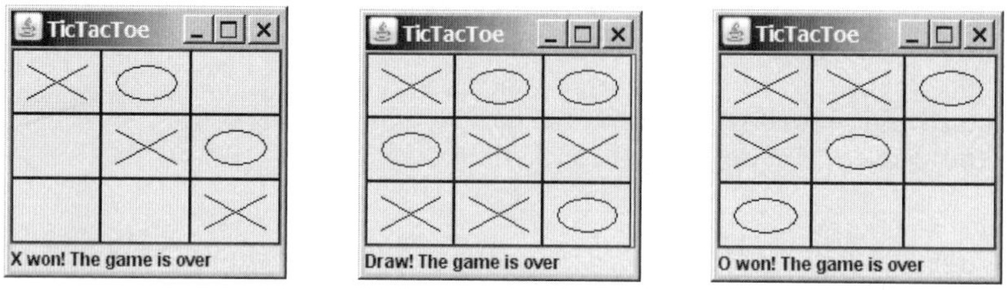
TicTacToe
X won! The game is over
TicTacToe
Draw! The game is over
TicTacToe
O won! The game is over

(a) The X player won the game (b) Draw-no winners (c) The O player won the game

FIGURE 18.11 Two players play a TicTacToe game.

All the examples you have seen so far show simple behaviors that are easy to model with classes. The behavior of the TicTacToe game is somewhat more complex. To create classes that model the behavior, you need to study and understand the game.

Assume that all the cells are initially empty, and that the first player takes the X token, the second player the O token. To mark a cell, the player points the mouse to the cell and clicks it. If the cell is empty, the token (X or O) is displayed. If the cell is already filled, the player's action is ignored.

From the preceding description, it is obvious that a cell is a GUI object that handles the mouse-click event and displays tokens. Such an object could be either a button or a panel. Drawing on panels is more flexible than drawing on buttons, because on a panel the token (X or O) can be drawn in any size, but on a button it can be displayed only as a text label. Therefore, a panel should be used to model a cell. How do you know the state of the cell (empty, X, or O)? You use a property named `token` of `char` type in the `Cell` class. The `Cell` class is responsible for drawing the token when an empty cell is clicked. So you need to write the code for listening to the `MouseEvent` and for painting the shapes for tokens X and O. The `Cell` class can be defined as shown in Figure 18.12.

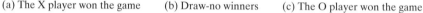

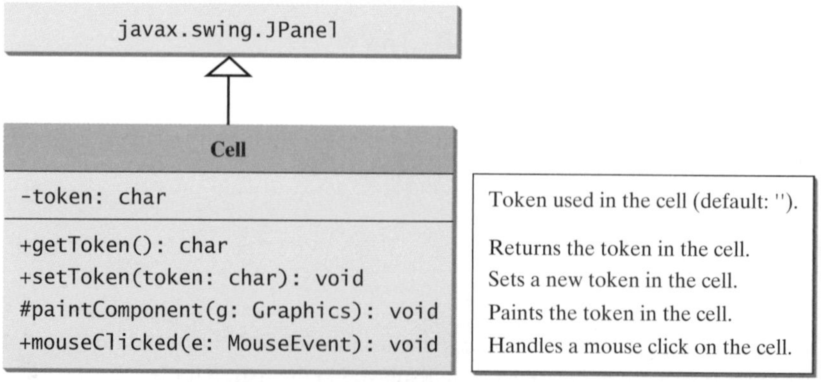
javax.swing.JPanel
Cell
-token: char
+getToken(): char
+setToken(token: char): void
#paintComponent(g: Graphics): void
+mouseClicked(e: MouseEvent): void
Token used in the cell (default: '').
Returns the token in the cell.
Sets a new token in the cell.
Paints the token in the cell.
Handles a mouse click on the cell.

FIGURE 18.12 The `Cell` class paints the token on a cell.

The TicTacToe board consists of nine cells, created using `new Cell[3][3]`. To determine which player's turn it is, you can introduce a variable named `whoseTurn` of `char` type. `whoseTurn` is initially X, then changes to O, and subsequently changes between X and O whenever a new cell is occupied. When the game is over, set `whoseTurn` to `' '`.

How do you know whether the game is over, whether there is a winner, and who the winner, if any, is? You can create a method named `isWon(char token)` to check whether a specified token has won and a method named `isFull()` to check whether all the cells are occupied.

Clearly, two classes emerge from the foregoing analysis. One is the `Cell` class, which handles operations for a single cell; the other is the `TicTacToe` class, which plays the whole game and deals with all the cells. The relationship between these two classes is shown in Figure 18.13.

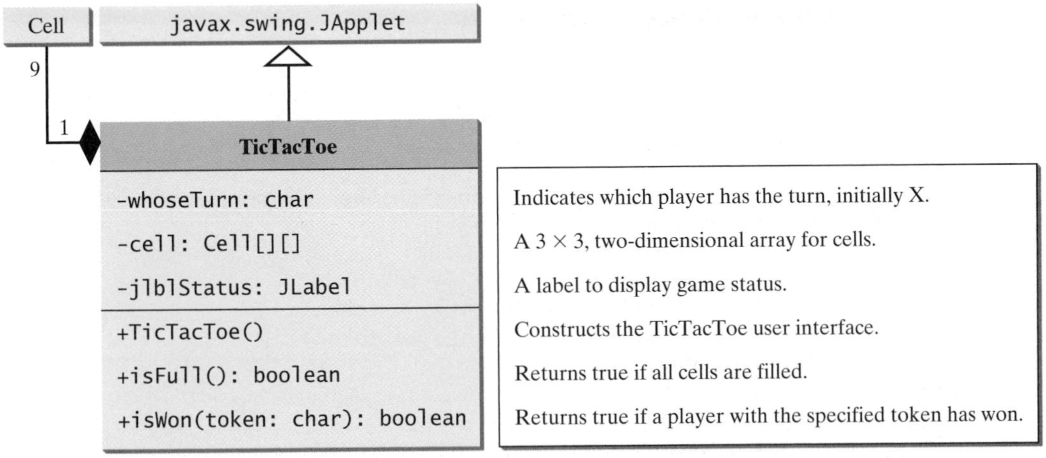
Cell
javax.swing.JApplet
9
1
TicTacToe
-whoseTurn: char
-cell: Cell[][]
-jlblStatus: JLabel
+TicTacToe()
+isFull(): boolean
+isWon(token: char): boolean
Indicates which player has the turn, initially X.
A 3 × 3, two-dimensional array for cells.
A label to display game status.
Constructs the TicTacToe user interface.
Returns true if all cells are filled.
Returns true if a player with the specified token has won.

FIGURE 18.13 The `TicTacToe` class contains nine cells.

Since the `Cell` class is only to support the `TicTacToe` class, it can be defined as an inner class in `TicTacToe`. The complete program is given in Listing 18.10:

LISTING 18.10 TicTacToe.java

main class **TicTacToe**

```
import java.awt.*;
import java.awt.event.*;
import javax.swing.*;
import javax.swing.border.LineBorder;

public class TicTacToe extends JApplet {
  // Indicate which player has a turn; initially it is the X player
  private char whoseTurn = 'X';

  // Create and initialize cells
  private Cell[][] cells =  new Cell[3][3];

  // Create and initialize a status label
  private JLabel jlblStatus = new JLabel("X's turn to play");

  /** Initialize UI */
  public TicTacToe() {
    // Panel p to hold cells
    JPanel p = new JPanel(new GridLayout(3, 3, 0, 0));
    for (int i = 0; i < 3; i++)
      for (int j = 0; j < 3; j++)
        p.add(cells[i][j] = new Cell());
```

```java

    // Set line borders on the cells panel and the status label
    p.setBorder(new LineBorder(Color.red, 1));
    jlblStatus.setBorder(new LineBorder(Color.yellow, 1));

    // Place the panel and the label to the applet
    add(p, BorderLayout.CENTER);
    add(jlblStatus, BorderLayout.SOUTH);
  }

  /** Determine whether the cells are all occupied */
```

check **isFull**

```java
  public boolean isFull() {
    for (int i = 0; i < 3; i++)
      for (int j = 0; j < 3; j++)
        if (cells[i][j].getToken() == ' ')
          return false;

    return true;
  }

  /** Determine whether the player with the specified token wins */
  public boolean isWon(char token) {
```

check rows

```java
    for (int i = 0; i < 3; i++)
      if ((cells[i][0].getToken() == token)
          && (cells[i][1].getToken() == token)
          && (cells[i][2].getToken() == token)) {
        return true;
      }

```

check columns

```java
    for (int j = 0; j < 3; j++)
      if ((cells[0][j].getToken() ==  token)
          && (cells[1][j].getToken() == token)
          && (cells[2][j].getToken() == token)) {
        return true;
      }

```

check major diagonal

```java
    if ((cells[0][0].getToken() == token)
        && (cells[1][1].getToken() == token)
        && (cells[2][2].getToken() == token)) {
      return true;
    }

```

check subdiagonal

```java
    if ((cells[0][2].getToken() == token)
        && (cells[1][1].getToken() == token)
        && (cells[2][0].getToken() == token)) {
      return true;
    }

    return false;
  }

  // An inner class for a cell
```

inner class **Cell**

```java
  public class Cell extends JPanel {
    // Token used for this cell
    private char token = ' ';

    public Cell() {
      setBorder(new LineBorder(Color.black, 1)); // Set cell's border
```

register listener

```java
      addMouseListener(new MyMouseListener());  // Register listener
    }
```

```
 83
 84     /** Return token */
 85     public char getToken() {
 86       return token;
 87     }
 88
 89     /** Set a new token */
 90     public void setToken(char c) {
 91       token = c;
 92       repaint();
 93     }
 94
 95     /** Paint the cell */
 96     protected void paintComponent(Graphics g) {
 97       super.paintComponent(g);
 98
 99       if (token == 'X') {
100         g.drawLine(10, 10, getWidth() - 10, getHeight() - 10);
101         g.drawLine(getWidth() - 10, 10, 10, getHeight() - 10);
102       }
103       else if (token == 'O') {
104         g.drawOval(10, 10, getWidth() - 20, getHeight() - 20);
105       }
106     }
107
108     private class MyMouseListener extends MouseAdapter {
109       /** Handle mouse click on a cell */
110       public void mouseClicked(MouseEvent e) {
111         // If cell is empty and game is not over
112         if (token == ' ' && whoseTurn != ' ') {
113           setToken(whoseTurn); // Set token in the cell
114
115           // Check game status
116           if (isWon(whoseTurn)) {
117             jlblStatus.setText(whoseTurn + " won! The game is over");
118             whoseTurn = ' '; // Game is over
119           }
120           else if (isFull()) {
121             jlblStatus.setText("Draw! The game is over");
122             whoseTurn = ' '; // Game is over
123           }
124           else {
125             // Change the turn
126             whoseTurn = (whoseTurn == 'X') ? 'O': 'X';
127             // Display whose turn
128             jlblStatus.setText(whoseTurn + "'s turn");
129           }
130         }
131       }
132     }
133   }
134 }
```

paint cell

listener class

`main` method omitted

The `TicTacToe` class initializes the user interface with nine cells placed in a panel of `GridLayout` (lines 19–22). A label named `jlblStatus` is used to show the status of the game (line 14). The variable `whoseTurn` (line 8) is used to track the next type of token to be placed in a cell. The methods `isFull` (lines 34-41) and `isWon` (lines 44–72) are for checking the status of the game.

Since `Cell` is an inner class in `TicTacToe`, the variable (`whoseTurn`) and methods (`isFull` and `isWon`) defined in `TicTacToe` can be referenced from the `Cell` class. The inner class makes programs simple and concise. If `Cell` were not declared as an inner class of `TicTacToe`, you would have to pass an object of `TicTacToe` to `Cell` in order for the variables and methods in `TicTacToe` to be used in `Cell`. You will rewrite the program without using an inner class in Exercise 18.6.

The listener for `MouseEvent` is registered for the cell (line 81). If an empty cell is clicked and the game is not over, a token is set in the cell (line 113). If the game is over, `whoseTurn` is set to `' '` (lines 118, 122). Otherwise, `whoseTurn` is alternated to a new turn (line 126).

incremental development and testing

Tip

Use an incremental approach in developing and testing a Java project of this kind. The foregoing program can be divided into five steps:

1. Lay out the user interface and display a fixed token X on a cell.
2. Enable the cell to display a fixed token X upon a mouse click.
3. Coordinate between the two players so as to display tokens X and O alternately.
4. Check whether a player wins, or whether all the cells are occupied without a winner.
5. Implement displaying a message on the label upon each move by a player.

18.10 Locating Resources Using the URL Class

You have used the `ImageIcon` class to create an icon from an image file and used the `setIcon` method or the constructor to place the icon in a GUI component, such as a button or a label. For example, the following statements create an `ImageIcon` and set it on a `JLabel` object `jlbl`:

```
ImageIcon imageIcon = new ImageIcon("c:\\book\\image\\us.gif");
jlbl.setIcon(imageIcon);
```

This approach presents a problem. The file location is fixed, because it uses the absolute file path on the Windows platform. As a result, the program cannot run on other platforms and cannot run as an applet. Assume that `image/us.gif` is under the class directory. You can circumvent this problem by using a relative path as follows:

```
ImageIcon imageIcon = new ImageIcon("image/us.gif");
```

This works fine with Java applications on all platforms but not with Java applets, because applets cannot load local files. To enable it to work with both applications and applets, you need to locate the file's URL.

why URL class?

The `java.net.URL` class can be used to identify files (image, audio, text, and so on) on the Internet. In general, a URL (Uniform Resource Locator) is a pointer to a "resource" on a local machine or a remote host. A resource can be something as simple as a file or a directory.

A URL for a file can also be accessed from a class in a way that is independent of the location of the file, as long as the file is located in the class directory. Recall that the class directory is where the class is stored. To obtain the URL of a resource file, use the following statements in an applet or application:

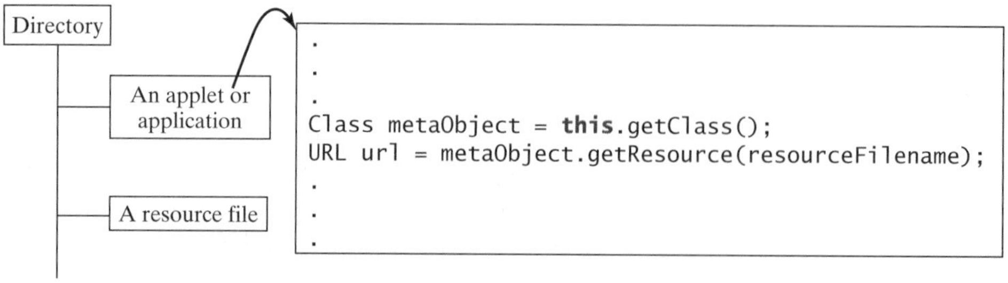
Directory
An applet or application
A resource file
.
.
.
Class metaObject = this.getClass();
URL url = metaObject.getResource(resourceFilename);
.
.
.

The `getClass()` method returns an instance of the `java.lang.Class` class. This instance is automatically created by the JVM for every class loaded into the memory. This instance, also known as a *meta object*, contains the information about the class file such as class name,

meta object

constructors, and methods. You can obtain the URL of a file in the class path by invoking the `getResource(filename)` method on the meta object. For example, if the class file is in `c:\book`, the following statements obtain a URL for `c:\book\image\us.gif`.

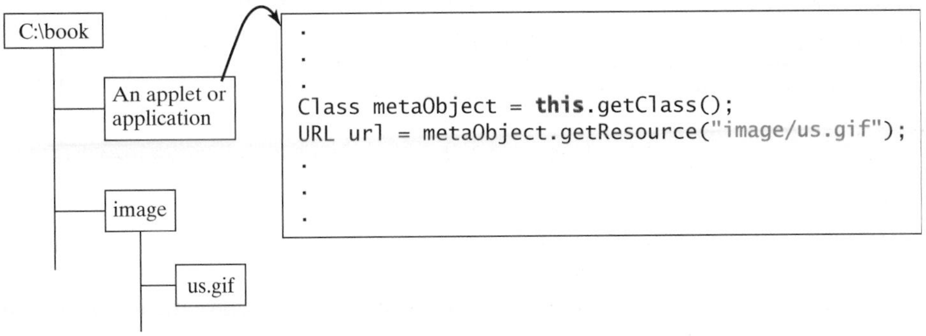
C:\book
An applet or application
image
us.gif
.
.
.
Class metaObject = this.getClass();
URL url = metaObject.getResource("image/us.gif");
.
.
.

You can now create an `ImageIcon` using

```
ImageIcon imageIcon = new ImageIcon(url);
```

Listing 18.11 gives the code that displays an image from `image/us.gif` in the class directory. The file `image/us.gif` is under the class directory, and its URL is obtained using the `getResource` method (line 5). A label with an image icon is created in line 6. The image icon is obtained from the URL.

LISTING 18.11 DisplayImageWithURL.java

```
1 import javax.swing.*;
2
3 public class DisplayImageWithURL extends JApplet {
4   public DisplayImageWithURL() {
5     java.net.URL url = this.getClass().getResource("image/us.gif");
6     add(new JLabel(new ImageIcon(url)));
7   }
8 }
```

get image URL (line 5)
create a label (line 6)
`main` method omitted

If you replace the code in lines 5–6 with the following code,

```
add(new JLabel(new ImageIcon("image/us.gif")));
```

you can still run the program standalone, but not from a browser.

18.11 Playing Audio in Any Java Program

There are several formats for audio files. Java programs can play audio files in the WAV, AIFF, MIDI, AU, and RMF formats.

To play an audio file in Java (application or applet), first create an *audio clip object* for the file. The audio clip is created once and can be played repeatedly without reloading the file. To create an audio clip, use the static method `newAudioClip()` in the `java.applet.Applet` class:

```
AudioClip audioClip = Applet.newAudioClip(url);
```

Audio originally could be played only from Java applets. For this reason, the `AudioClip` interface is in the `java.applet` package. Since JDK 1.2, audio can be played in any Java program.

The following statements, for example, create an `AudioClip` for the `beep.au` audio file in the class directory:

```
Class metaObject = this.getClass();
URL url = metaObject.getResource("beep.au");
AudioClip audioClip = Applet.newAudioClip(url);
```

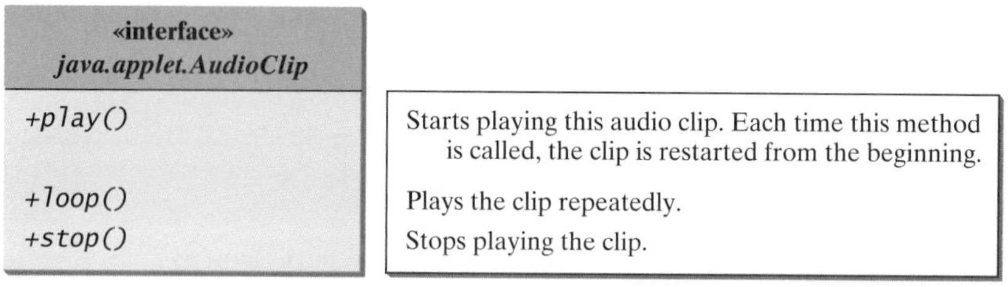
«interface»
java.applet.AudioClip
+play()
+loop()
+stop()
Starts playing this audio clip. Each time this method is called, the clip is restarted from the beginning.
Plays the clip repeatedly.
Stops playing the clip.

FIGURE 18.14 The `AudioClip` interface provides the methods for playing sound.

To manipulate a sound for an audio clip, use the `play()`, `loop()`, and `stop()` methods in `java.applet.AudioClip`, as shown in Figure 18.14.

Listing 18.12 gives the code that displays the Danish flag and plays the Danish national anthem repeatedly. The image file `image/denmark.gif` and audio file `audio/denmark.mid` are stored under the class directory. Line 12 obtains the audio file URL. Line 13 creates an audio clip for the file. Line 14 repeatedly plays the audio.

LISTING 18.12 DisplayImagePlayAudio.java

```
 1 import javax.swing.*;
 2 import java.net.URL;
 3 import java.applet.*;
 4
 5 public class DisplayImagePlayAudio extends JApplet {
 6   private AudioClip audioClip;
 7
 8   public DisplayImagePlayAudio() {
 9     URL urlForImage = getClass().getResource("image/denmark.gif");
10     add(new JLabel(new ImageIcon(urlForImage)));
11
12     URL urlForAudio = getClass().getResource("audio/denmark.mid");
13     audioClip = Applet.newAudioClip(urlForAudio);
14     audioClip.loop();
15   }
16
17   public void start() {
18     if (audioClip != null) audioClip.loop();
19   }
20
21   public void stop() {
22     if (audioClip != null) audioClip.stop();
23   }
24 }
```

get image URL (line 9)
create a label (line 10)
get audio URL (line 12)
create an audio clip (line 13)
play audio repeatedly (line 14)
start audio (line 18)
stop audio (line 22)
main method omitted (line 24)

The `stop` method (lines 21–23) stops the audio when the applet is not displayed, and the `start` method (lines 17–19) restarts the audio when the applet is redisplayed. Try to run this applet from a browser and observe the effect without the `stop` and `start` methods.

Run this program standalone from the main method and from a Web browser to test it. Recall that, for brevity, the `main` method in all applets is not printed in the listing.

18.12 Case Study: Multimedia Animations

This case study presents a multimedia animation with images and audio. The images are for seven national flags, named `flag0.gif`, `flag1.gif`, . . . , `flag6.gif` for Denmark, Germany, China, India, Norway, U.K., and U.S. They are stored under the `image` directory in the class path. The audio consists of national anthems for these seven nations, named

anthem0.mid, **anthem1.mid**, ..., and **anthem6.mid**. They are stored under the **audio** directory in the class path.

The program presents the nations, starting from the first one. For each nation, it displays its flag and plays its anthem. When the audio for a nation finishes, the next nation is presented, and so on. After the last nation is presented, the program starts to present all the nations again. You may suspend animation by clicking the *Suspend* button and resume it by clicking the *Resume* button, as shown in Figure 18.15. You can also directly select a nation from a combo box.

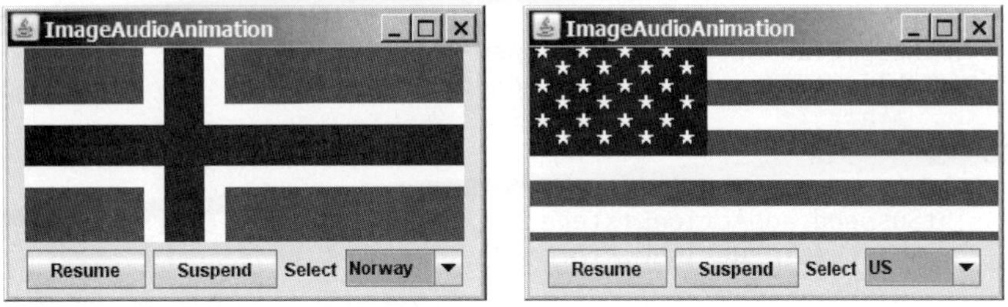
ImageAudioAnimation
Resume
Suspend
Select
Norway
ImageAudioAnimation
Resume
Suspend
Select
US

FIGURE 18.15 The applet displays a sequence of images and plays audio.

The program is given in Listing 18.13. A timer is created to control the animation (line 15). The timer delay for each presentation is the play time for the anthem. You can find the play time for an audio file using RealPlayer or Windows Media. The delay times are stored in an array named **delays** (lines 13–14). The delay time for the first audio file (the Danish anthem) is 48 seconds.

LISTING 18.13 ImageAudioAnimation.java

Video Note
Audio and image

```
 1 import java.awt.*;
 2 import java.awt.event.*;
 3 import javax.swing.*;
 4 import java.applet.*;
 5
 6 public class ImageAudioAnimation extends JApplet {
 7   private final static int NUMBER_OF_NATIONS = 7;
 8   private int current = 0;
 9   private ImageIcon[] icons = new ImageIcon[NUMBER_OF_NATIONS];
10   private AudioClip[] audioClips = new AudioClip[NUMBER_OF_NATIONS];
11   private AudioClip currentAudioClip;
12
13   private int[] delays =
14     {48000, 54000, 59000, 54000, 59000, 31000, 68000};
15   private Timer timer = new Timer(delays[0], new TimerListener());
16
17   private JLabel jlblImageLabel = new JLabel();
18   private JButton jbtResume = new JButton("Resume");
19   private JButton jbtSuspend = new JButton("Suspend");
20   private JComboBox jcboNations = new JComboBox(new Object[]
21     {"Denmark", "Germany", "China", "India", "Norway", "UK", "US"});
22
23   public ImageAudioAnimation() {
24     // Load image icons and audio clips
25     for (int i = 0; i < NUMBER_OF_NATIONS; i++) {
26       icons[i] = new ImageIcon(getClass().getResource(
27         "image/flag" + i + ".gif"));
28       audioClips[i] = Applet.newAudioClip(
```

image icons
audio clips
current audio clip
audio play time
timer
GUI components
create icons
create audio clips

create UI

register listener

start animation

register listener

stop animation

register listener

select a nation

present a nation

set a new delay

```
        getClass().getResource("audio/anthem" + i + ".mid"));
    }

    JPanel panel = new JPanel();
    panel.add(jbtResume);
    panel.add(jbtSuspend);
    panel.add(new JLabel("Select"));
    panel.add(jcboNations);
    add(jlblImageLabel, BorderLayout.CENTER);
    add(panel, BorderLayout.SOUTH);

    jbtResume.addActionListener(new ActionListener() {
      public void actionPerformed(ActionEvent e) {
        start();
      }
    });
    jbtSuspend.addActionListener(new ActionListener() {
      public void actionPerformed(ActionEvent e) {
        stop();
      }
    });
    jcboNations.addActionListener(new ActionListener() {
      public void actionPerformed(ActionEvent e) {
        stop();
        current = jcboNations.getSelectedIndex();
        presentNation(current);
        timer.start();
      }
    });

    timer.start();
    jlblImageLabel.setIcon(icons[0]);
    jlblImageLabel.setHorizontalAlignment(JLabel.CENTER);
    currentAudioClip = audioClips[0];
    currentAudioClip.play();
  }

  private class TimerListener implements ActionListener {
    public void actionPerformed(ActionEvent e) {
      current = (current + 1) % NUMBER_OF_NATIONS;
      presentNation(current);
    }
  }

  private void presentNation(int index) {
    jlblImageLabel.setIcon(icons[index]);
    jcboNations.setSelectedIndex(index);
    currentAudioClip = audioClips[index];
    currentAudioClip.play();
    timer.setDelay(delays[index]);
  }

  public void start() {
    timer.start();
    currentAudioClip.play();
  }
```

```
85
86   public void stop() {
87     timer.stop();
88     currentAudioClip.stop();
89   }
90 }
```

stop audio clip

main method omitted

A label is created in line 17 to display a flag image. An array of flag images for seven nations is created in lines 26–27. An array of audio clips is created in lines 28–29. Each audio clip is created for an audio file through the URL of the current class. The audio files are stored in the same directory with the applet class file.

The combo box for country names is created in lines 20–21. When a new country name in the combo box is selected, the current presentation is stopped and a new selected nation is presented (lines 52–55).

The `presentNation(index)` method (lines 73–79) presents a nation with the specified index. It sets a new image in the label (line 74), synchronizes with the combo box by setting the selected index (line 75), plays the new audio, and sets a new delay time (line 78).

The applet's `start` and `stop` methods are overridden to resume and suspend the animation (lines 81–89).

Key Terms

applet 616
applet container 620
archive 616
HTML 616
tag 616
signed applet 618

Chapter Summary

1. `JApplet` is a subclass of `Applet`. It is used for developing Java applets with Swing components.
2. The applet bytecode must be specified, using the `<applet>` tag in an HTML file to tell the Web browser where to find the applet. The applet can accept string parameters from HTML using the `<param>` tag.
3. The applet container controls and executes applets through the `init`, `start`, `stop`, and `destroy` methods in the `Applet` class.
4. When an applet is loaded, the applet container creates an instance of it by invoking its no-arg constructor. The `init` method is invoked after the applet is created. The `start` method is invoked after the `init` method. It is also called whenever the applet becomes active again after the page containing the applet is revisited. The `stop` method is invoked when the applet becomes inactive.
5. The `destroy` method is invoked when the browser exits normally to inform the applet that it is no longer needed and should release any resources it has allocated. The `stop` method is always called before the `destroy` method.

6. The procedures for writing applications and writing applets are very similar. An applet can easily be converted into an application, and vice versa. Moreover, an applet can be written with a main method to run standalone.

7. You can pass arguments to an applet using the `param` attribute in the applet's tag in HTML. To retrieve the value of the parameter, invoke the `getParameter(paramName)` method.

8. The `Applet`'s `getParameter` method can be invoked only after an instance of the applet is created. Therefore, this method cannot be invoked in the constructor of the applet class. You should invoke this method from the `init` method.

9. You learned how to incorporate images and audio in Java applications and applets. To load audio and images for Java applications and applets, you have to create a URL for the audio and image. You can create a `URL` from a file under the class directory.

10. To play an audio, create an audio clip from the `URL` for the audio source. You can use the `AudioClip`'s `play()` method to play it once, the `loop()` method to play it repeatedly, and the `stop()` method to stop it.

Review Questions

Sections 18.2–18.6

18.1 Is every applet an instance of `java.applet.Applet`? Is every applet an instance of `javax.swing.JApplet`?

18.2 Describe the `init()`, `start()`, `stop()`, and `destroy()` methods in the `Applet` class.

18.3 How do you add components to a `JApplet`? What is the default layout manager of the content pane of `JApplet`?

18.4 Why does the applet in (a) below display nothing? Why does the applet in (b) have a runtime `NullPointerException` on the highlighted line?

```java
import javax.swing.*;

public class WelcomeApplet extends JApplet {
  public void WelcomeApplet() {
    JLabel jlblMessage =
      new JLabel("It is Java");
  }
}
```

(a)

```java
import javax.swing.*;

public class WelcomeApplet extends JApplet {
  private JLabel jlblMessage;

  public WelcomeApplet() {
    JLabel jlblMessage =
      new JLabel("It is Java");
  }

  public void init() {
    add(jlblMessage);
  }
}
```

(b)

18.5 Describe the `<applet>` HTML tag. How do you pass parameters to an applet?

18.6 Where is the `getParameter` method defined?

18.7 What is wrong if the `DisplayMessage` applet is revised as follows?

```java
public class DisplayMessage extends JApplet {
  /** Initialize the applet */
  public DisplayMessage() {
    // Get parameter values from the HTML file
    String message = getParameter("MESSAGE");
    int x =
      Integer.parseInt(getParameter("X"));
    int y =
      Integer.parseInt(getParameter("Y"));

    // Create a message panel
    MessagePanel messagePanel =
      new MessagePanel(message);
    messagePanel.setXCoordinate(x);
    messagePanel.setYCoordinate(y);

    // Add the message panel to the applet
    add(messagePanel);
  }
}
```

(a) Revision 1

```java
public class DisplayMessage extends JApplet {
  private String message;
  private int x;
  private int y;

  /** Initialize the applet */
  public void init() {
    // Get parameter values from the HTML file
    message = getParameter("MESSAGE");
    x = Integer.parseInt(getParameter("X"));
    y = Integer.parseInt(getParameter("Y"));
  }

  public DisplayMessage() {
    // Create a message panel
    MessagePanel messagePanel =
      new  MessagePanel(message);
    messagePanel.setXCoordinate(x);
    messagePanel.setYCoordinate(y);

    // Add the message panel to the applet
    add(messagePanel);
  }
}
```

(b) Revision 2

18.8 What are the differences between applications and applets? How do you run an application, and how do you run an applet? Is the compilation process different for applications and applets? List some security restrictions on applets.

18.9 Can you place a frame in an applet?

18.10 Can you place an applet in a frame?

18.11 Delete `super.paintComponent(g)` on line 97 in TicTacToe.java in Listing 18.5 and run the program to see what happens.

Sections 18.9–18.10

18.12 How do you create a `URL` object for the file image/us.gif in the class directory?

18.13 How do you create an `ImageIcon` from the file image/us.gif in the class directory?

Section 18.11

18.14 What types of audio files are used in Java?

18.15 How do you create an audio clip from a file anthem/us.mid in the class directory?

18.16 How do you play, repeatedly play, and stop an audio clip?

Programming Exercises

Pedagogical Note

For every applet in the exercise, add a main method to enable it to run standalone.

run standalone

Sections 18.2–18.6

18.1 (*Converting applications to applets*) Convert Listing 17.2, ButtonDemo.java, into an applet.

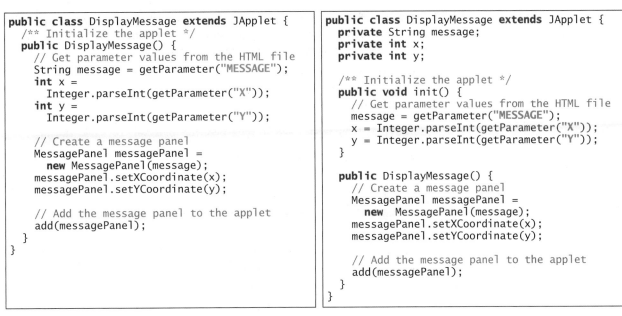

18.2* (*Passing strings to applets*) Rewrite Listing 18.5, DisplayMessage.java to display a message with a standard color, font, and size. The `message`, `x`, `y`, `color`, `fontname`, and `fontsize` are parameters in the `<applet>` tag, as shown below:

```
<applet
  code = "Exercise18_2.class"
  width = 200
  height = 50
  alt = "You must have a Java-enabled browser to view the applet"
>
  <param name = MESSAGE value = "Welcome to Java" />
  <param name = X value = 40 />
  <param name = Y value = 50 />
  <param name = COLOR value = "red" />
  <param name = FONTNAME value = "Monospaced" />
  <param name = FONTSIZE value = 20 />
</applet>
```

18.3 (*Loan calculator*) Write an applet for calculating loan payment, as shown in Figure 18.16. The user can enter the interest rate, the number of years, and the loan amount and click the *Compute Payment* button to display the monthly payment and total payment.

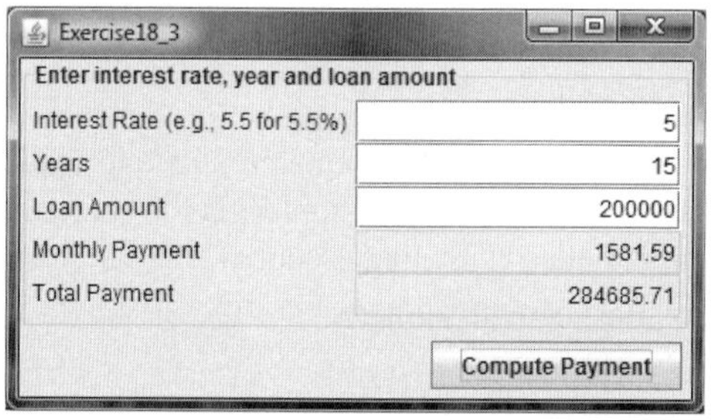

Exercise18_3
Enter interest rate, year and loan amount
Interest Rate (e.g., 5.5 for 5.5%)
5
Years
15
Loan Amount
200000
Monthly Payment
1581.59
Total Payment
284685.71
Compute Payment

FIGURE 18.16 The applet computes the loan payment.

18.4* (*Converting applications to applets*) Rewrite ClockAnimation in Listing 16.12 as an applet and enable it to run standalone.

18.5** (*Game: a clock learning tool*) Develop a clock applet to show a first-grade student how to read a clock. Modify Exercise 15.19 to display a detailed clock with an hour hand and a minute hand in an applet, as shown in Figure 18.17(a). The hour and minute values are randomly generated. The hour is between `0` and `11`, and the minute is `0`, `15`, `30`, or `45`. Upon a mouse click, a new random time is displayed on the clock.

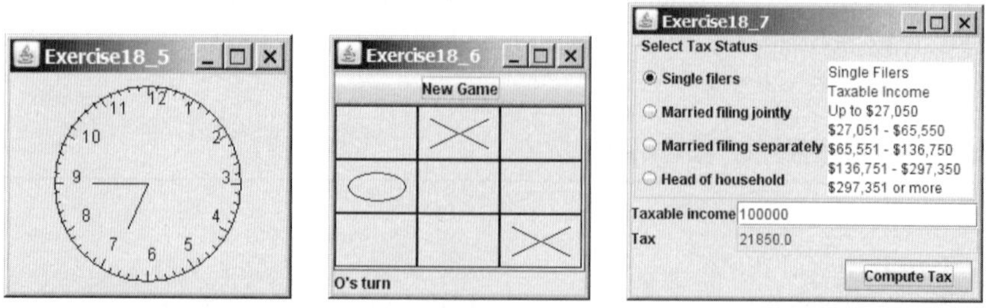

Exercise18_5
12
1
2
3
4
5
6
7
8
9
10
11
Exercise18_6
New Game
O's turn
Exercise18_7
Select Tax Status
Single filers
Married filing jointly
Married filing separately
Head of household
Single Filers
Taxable Income
Up to $27,050
$27,051 - $65,550
$65,551 - $136,750
$136,751 - $297,350
$297,351 or more
Taxable income
100000
Tax
21850.0
Compute Tax

(a) (b) (c)

FIGURE 18.17 (a) Upon a mouse click on the clock, the clock time is randomly displayed. (b) The *New Game* button starts a new game. (c) The tax calculator computes the tax for the specified taxable income and tax status.

18.6** (*Game: TicTacToe*) Rewrite the program in §18.9, "Case Study: TicTacToe," with the following modifications:

- Declare `Cell` as a separate class rather than an inner class.
- Add a button named *New Game*, as shown in Figure 18.17(b). The *New Game* button starts a new game.

18.7** (*Financial application: tax calculator*) Create an applet to compute tax, as shown in Figure 18.17(c). The applet lets the user select the tax status and enter the taxable income to compute the tax based on the 2001 federal tax rates, as shown in Exercise 10.8.

18.8*** (*Creating a calculator*) Use various panels of `FlowLayout`, `GridLayout`, and `BorderLayout` to lay out the following calculator and to implement addition (+), subtraction (-), division (/), square root (`sqrt`), and modulus (`%`) functions (see Figure 18.18(a)).

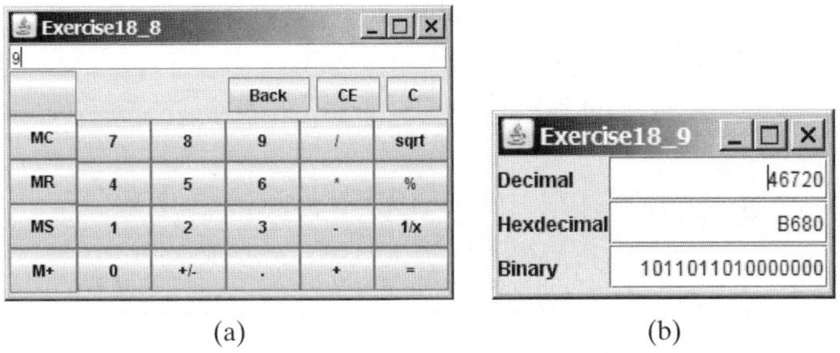

Exercise18_8
9
Back
CE
C
MC
7
8
9
/
sqrt
MR
4
5
6
*
%
MS
1
2
3
-
1/x
M+
0
+/-
.
+
=
(a)
Exercise18_9
Decimal
46720
Hexdecimal
B680
Binary
1011011010000000
(b)

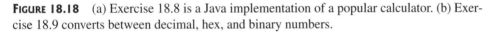

FIGURE 18.18 (a) Exercise 18.8 is a Java implementation of a popular calculator. (b) Exercise 18.9 converts between decimal, hex, and binary numbers.

18.9* (*Converting numbers*) Write an applet that converts between decimal, hex, and binary numbers, as shown in Figure 18.18(b). When you enter a decimal value on the decimal-value text field and press the *Enter* key, its corresponding hex and binary numbers are displayed in the other two text fields. Likewise, you can enter values in the other fields and convert them accordingly.

18.10** (*Repainting a partial area*) When you repaint the entire viewing area of a panel, sometimes only a tiny portion of the viewing area is changed. You can improve the performance by repainting only the affected area, but do not invoke `super.paintComponent(g)` when repainting the panel, because this will cause the entire viewing area to be cleared. Use this approach to write an applet to display the temperatures of each hour during the last 24 hours in a histogram. Suppose that temperatures between 50 and 90 degrees Fahrenheit are obtained randomly and are updated every hour. The temperature of the current hour needs to be redisplayed, while the others remain unchanged. Use a unique color to highlight the temperature for the current hour (see Figure 18.19(a)).

18.11** (*Simulation: a running fan*) Write a Java applet that simulates a running fan, as shown in Figure 18.19(b). The buttons *Start*, *Stop*, and *Reverse* control the fan. The scrollbar controls the fan's speed. Create a class named `Fan`, a subclass of `JPanel`, to display the fan. This class also contains the methods to suspend and resume the fan, set its speed, and reverse its direction. Create a class named `FanControl` that contains a fan, and three buttons and a scroll bar to control the fan. Create a Java applet that contains an instance of `FanControl`.

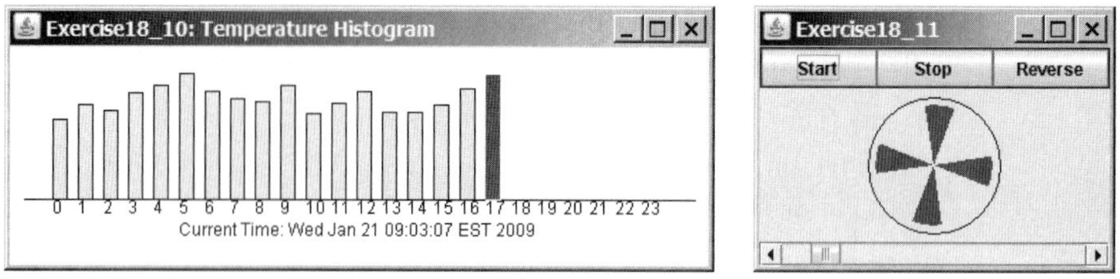
Exercise18_10: Temperature Histogram
0 1 2 3 4 5 6 7 8 9 10 11 12 13 14 15 16 17 18 19 20 21 22 23
Current Time: Wed Jan 21 09:03:07 EST 2009
Exercise18_11
Start
Stop
Reverse

(a) (b)

FIGURE 18.19 (a) The histogram displays the average temperature of every hour in the last 24 hours. (b) The program simulates a running fan.

18.12** (*Controlling a group of fans*) Write a Java applet that displays three fans in a group, with control buttons to start and stop all of them, as shown in Figure 18.20.

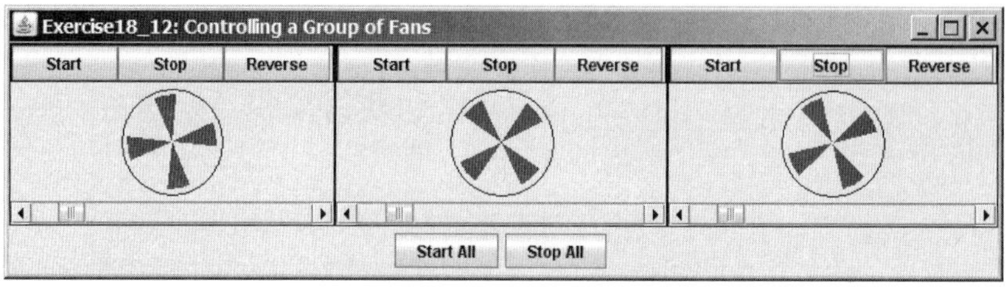
Exercise18_12: Controlling a Group of Fans
Start
Stop
Reverse
Start
Stop
Reverse
Start
Stop
Reverse
Start All
Stop All

FIGURE 18.20 The program runs and controls a group of fans.

18.13*** (*Creating an elevator simulator*) Write an applet that simulates an elevator going up and down (see Figure 18.21). The buttons on the left indicate the floor where the passenger is now located. The passenger must click a button on the left to request that the elevator come to his or her floor. On entering the elevator, the passenger clicks a button on the right to request that it go to the specified floor.

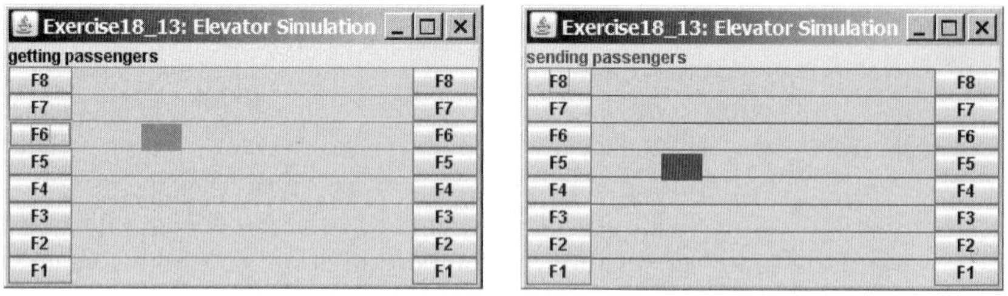
Exercise18_13: Elevator Simulation
getting passengers
F8
F7
F6
F5
F4
F3
F2
F1
Exercise18_13: Elevator Simulation
sending passengers
F8
F7
F6
F5
F4
F3
F2
F1

FIGURE 18.21 The program simulates elevator operations.

18.14* (*Controlling a group of clocks*) Write a Java applet that displays three clocks in a group, with control buttons to start and stop all of them, as shown in Figure 18.22.

Video Note
Control a group of clocks

Sections 18.10–18.12

18.15* (*Enlarging and shrinking an image*) Write an applet that will display a sequence of images from a single image file in different sizes. Initially, the viewing area for this image has a width of 300 and a height of 300. Your program should continuously shrink the viewing area by 1 in width and 1 in height until it reaches a width of 50 and a height of 50. At that point, the viewing area

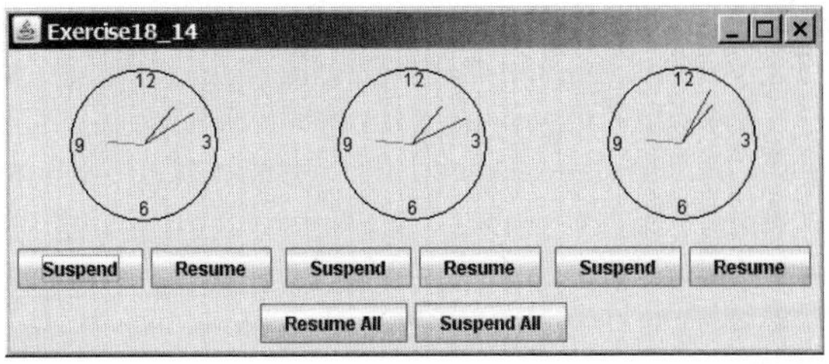
Exercise18_14
Suspend
Resume
Suspend
Resume
Suspend
Resume
Resume All
Suspend All

FIGURE 18.22 Three clocks run independently with individual control and group control.

should continuously enlarge by 1 in width and 1 in height until it reaches a width of 300 and a height of 300. The viewing area should shrink and enlarge (alternately) to create animation for the single image.

18.16*** (*Simulating a stock ticker*) Write a Java applet that displays a stock-index ticker (see Figure 18.23). The stock-index information is passed from the `<param>` tag in the HTML file. Each index has four parameters: Index Name (e.g., S&P 500), Current Time (e.g., 15:54), the index from the previous day (e.g., 919.01), and Change (e.g., 4.54). Use at least five indexes, such as Dow Jones, S&P 500, NASDAQ, NIKKEI, and Gold & Silver Index. Display positive changes in green and negative changes in red. The indexes move from right to left in the applet's viewing area. The applet freezes the ticker when the mouse button is pressed; it moves again when the mouse button is released.

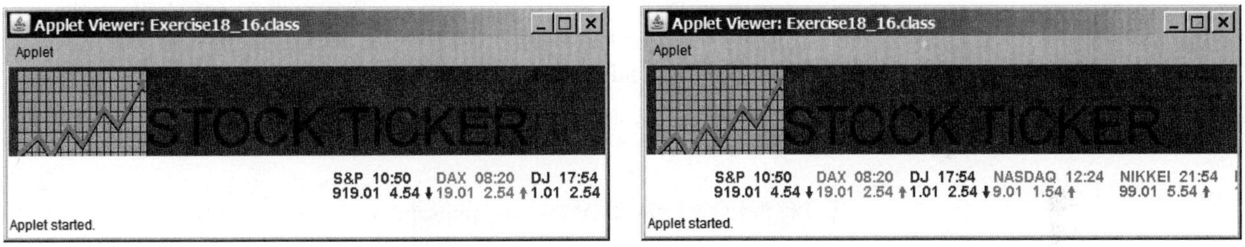
Applet Viewer: Exercise18_16.class
Applet
STOCK TICKER
S&P 10:50 DAX 08:20 DJ 17:54
919.01 4.54 19.01 2.54 1.01 2.54
Applet started.
Applet Viewer: Exercise18_16.class
Applet
STOCK TICKER
S&P 10:50 DAX 08:20 DJ 17:54 NASDAQ 12:24 NIKKEI 21:54
919.01 4.54 19.01 2.54 1.01 2.54 9.01 1.54 99.01 5.54
Applet started.

FIGURE 18.23 The program displays a stock-index ticker.

18.17** (*Racing cars*) Write an applet that simulates four cars racing, as shown in Figure 18.24(a). You can set the speed for each car, with 1 being the highest.

Exercise18_17
Car 1: 10
Car 2: 20
Car 3: 30
Car 4: 40
Applet Viewer: Exercise18_18.class
Applet
Canada
The Maple Leaf flag The Canadian National Flag was adopted by the Canadian Parliament on October 22, 1964 and was proclaimed into law by Her Majesty Queen Elizabeth II (the Queen of Canada) on February 15, 1965. The Canadian Flag (colloquially known as The
Applet started.

(a) (b)

FIGURE 18.24 (a) You can set the speed for each car. (b) This applet shows each country's flag, name, and description, one after another, and reads the description that is currently shown.

18.18** (*Showing national flags*) Write an applet that introduces national flags, one after the other, by presenting each one's photo, name, and description (see Figure 18.24(b)) along with audio that reads the description.

Suppose your applet displays the flags of eight countries. Assume that the photo image files, named **flag0.gif**, **flag1.gif**, and so on, up to **flag7.gif**, are stored in a subdirectory named **image** in the applet's directory. The length of each audio is less than 10 seconds. Assume that the name and description of each country's flag are passed from the HTML using the parameters `name0`, `name1`, ..., `name7`, and `description0`, `description1`, ..., and `description7`. Pass the number of countries as an HTML parameter using `numberOfCountries`. Here is an example:

```
<param name = "numberOfCountries" value = 8>
<param name = "name0" value = "Canada">
<param name = "description0" value = "The Maple Leaf flag
The Canadian National Flag was adopted by the Canadian
Parliament on October 22, 1964 and was proclaimed into law
by Her Majesty Queen Elizabeth II (the Queen of Canada) on
February 15, 1965. The Canadian Flag (colloquially known
as The Maple Leaf Flag) is a red flag of the proportions
two by length and one by width, containing in its center a
white square, with a single red stylized eleven-point
maple leaf centered in the white square.">
```

Hint: Use the `DescriptionPanel` class to display the image, name, and the text. The `DescriptionPanel` class was introduced in Listing 17.6.

18.19*** (*Bouncing balls*) The example in §18.8 simulates a bouncing ball. Extend the example to allow multiple balls, as shown in Figure 18.25(a). You may use the *+1* or *−1* button to increase or decrease the number of the balls, and use the *Suspend* and *Resume* buttons to freeze the balls or resume bouncing. For each ball, assign a random color.

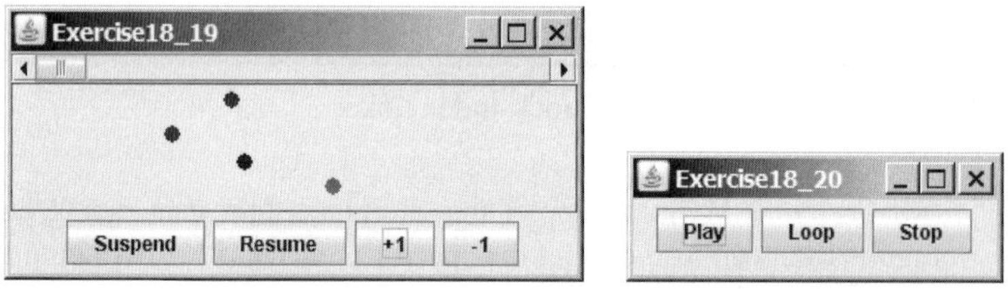
Exercise18_19
Suspend
Resume
+1
-1
Exercise18_20
Play
Loop
Stop

(a) (b)

FIGURE 18.25 (a) The applet allows you to add or remove bouncing balls. (b) Click *Play* to play an audio clip once, click *Loop* to play an audio repeatedly, and click *Stop* to terminate playing.

18.20* (*Playing, looping, and stopping a sound clip*) Write an applet that meets the following requirements:

- Get an audio file. The file is in the class directory.
- Place three buttons labeled *Play*, *Loop*, and *Stop*, as shown in Figure 18.25(b).
- If you click the *Play* button, the audio file is played once. If you click the *Loop* button, the audio file keeps playing repeatedly. If you click the *Stop* button, the playing stops.
- The applet can run as an application.

18.21** (*Creating an alarm clock*) Write an applet that will display a digital clock with a large display panel that shows hour, minute, and second. This clock should allow the user to set an alarm. Figure 18.26(a) shows an example of such a clock. To turn on the alarm, check the *Alarm* check box. To specify the alarm time, click the *Set alarm* button to display a new frame, as shown in Figure 18.26(b). You can set the alarm time in the frame.

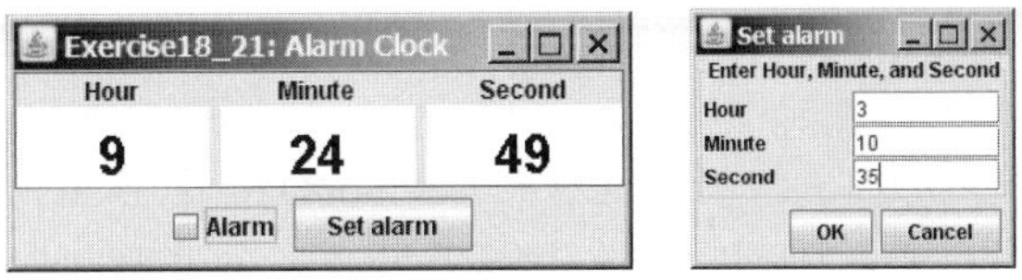
Exercise18_21: Alarm Clock
Hour
Minute
Second
9
24
49
Alarm
Set alarm
Set alarm
Enter Hour, Minute, and Second
Hour
3
Minute
10
Second
35
OK
Cancel

(a) (b)

FIGURE 18.26 The program displays current hour, minute, and second and enables you to set an alarm.

18.22** (*Creating an image animator with audio*) Create animation using the applet (see Figure 18.27) to meet the following requirements:

- Allow the user to specify the animation speed. The user can enter the speed in a text field.
- Get the number of frames and the image file-name prefix from the user. For example, if the user enters **n** for the number of frames and **L** for the image prefix, then the files are **L1**, **L2**, and so on, to **L*n***. Assume that the images are stored in the **image** directory, a subdirectory of the applet's directory.
- Allow the user to specify an audio file name. The audio file is stored in the same directory as the applet. The sound is played while the animation runs.

Exercise18_22
Start Animation
Learning Java
Enter information for animation
Animation speed in millisecon...
1000
Image file prefix
L
Number of images
24
Audio file
ticker.au

FIGURE 18.27 This applet lets the user select image files, audio file, and animation speed.

18.23** (*Simulation: raising flag and playing anthem*) Create an applet that displays a flag rising up, as shown in Figure 15.1. As the national flag rises, play the national anthem. (You may use a flag image and anthem audio file from Listing 18.13.)

Comprehensive

18.24** (*Game: guessing birthdays*) Listing 3.3, GuessBirthday.java, gives a program for guessing a birthday. Create an applet for guessing birthdays as shown in Figure 18.28. The applet prompts the user to check whether the date is in any of the five sets. The date is displayed in the text field upon clicking the *Guess Birthday* button.

18.25*** (*Game: Sudoku*) §7.7 introduced the Sudoku problem. Write a program that lets the user enter the input from the text fields in an applet, as shown in Figure 18.1. Clicking the *Solve* button displays the result.

Exercise18_24
Check the boxes if your birthday is in these sets
1 3 5 7
9 11 13 15
17 19 21 23
25 27 29 31
2 3 6 7
10 11 14 15
18 19 22 23
26 27 30 31
4 5 6 7
12 13 14 15
20 21 22 23
28 29 30 31
8 9 10 11
12 13 14 15
24 25 26 27
28 29 30 31
16 17 18 19
20 21 22 23
24 25 26 27
28 29 30 31
Guess Birthday
19

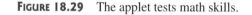

FIGURE 18.28 This applet guesses the birthdays.

18.26*** (*Game: math quiz*) Listing 3.1, AdditionQuiz.java, and Listing 3.4, SubtractionQuiz.java, generate and grade Math quizzes. Write an applet that allows the user to select a question type and difficulty level, as shown in Figure 18.29(a). When the user clicks the *Start* button, the program begins to generate a question. After the user enters an answer with the *Enter* key, a new question is displayed. When the user clicks the *Start* button, the elapse time is displayed. The time is updated every second until the *Stop* button is clicked. The correct count is updated whenever a correct answer is made.

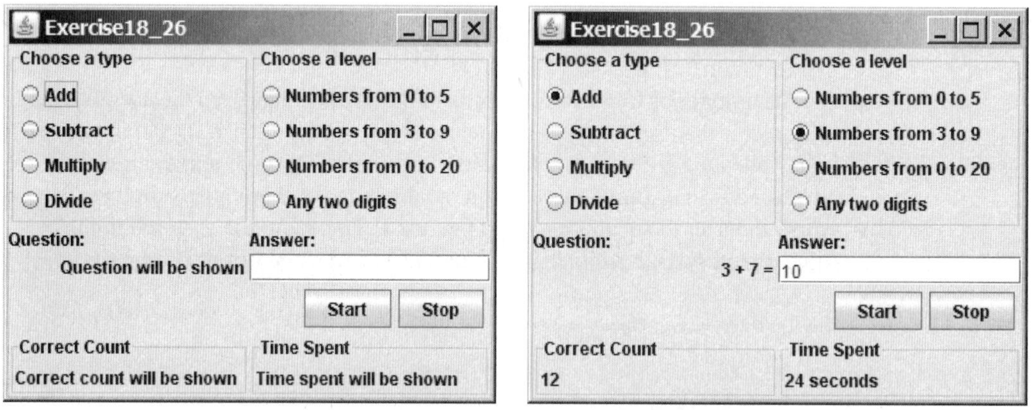
Exercise18_26
Choose a type
Add
Subtract
Multiply
Divide
Choose a level
Numbers from 0 to 5
Numbers from 3 to 9
Numbers from 0 to 20
Any two digits
Question:
Question will be shown
Answer:
Start
Stop
Correct Count
Correct count will be shown
Time Spent
Time spent will be shown
Exercise18_26
Choose a type
Add
Subtract
Multiply
Divide
Choose a level
Numbers from 0 to 5
Numbers from 3 to 9
Numbers from 0 to 20
Any two digits
Question:
3 + 7 =
Answer:
10
Start
Stop
Correct Count
12
Time Spent
24 seconds

(a) Before a session starts

(b) After a session is started

FIGURE 18.29 The applet tests math skills.

18.27*** (*Simulation: traffic control*) Exercise 17.3 uses the radio buttons to change the traffic lights. Revise the program that simulates traffic control at an intersection, as shown in Figure 18.30. When the light turns red, the traffic flows

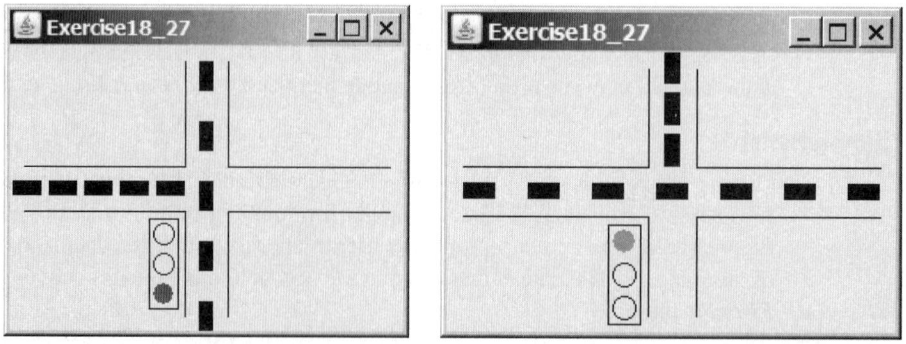
Exercise18_27
Exercise18_27

(a) The traffic flows vertically

(b) The traffic flows horizontally

FIGURE 18.30 The applet simulates traffic control.

vertically; when the light turns green, the traffic flows horizontally. The light changes automatically every one minute. Before the light changes to red from green, it first changes to yellow for a brief five seconds.

18.28** (*Geometry: two circles intersect?*) The `Circle2D` class was defined in Exercise 10.11. Write an applet that enables the user to specify the location and size of the circles and displays whether the two circles intersect, as shown in Figure 18.31(a).

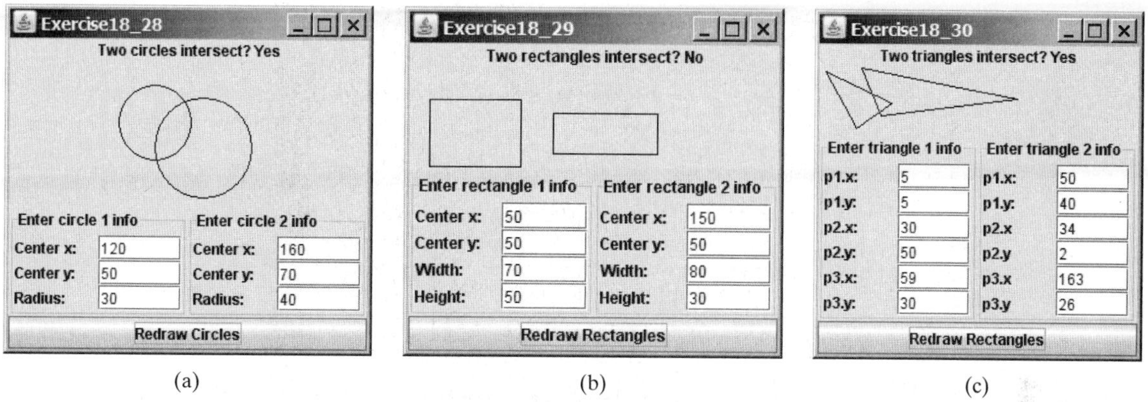

Exercise18_28
Two circles intersect? Yes
Enter circle 1 info
Enter circle 2 info
Center x: 120
Center y: 50
Radius: 30
Center x: 160
Center y: 70
Radius: 40
Redraw Circles
(a)
Exercise18_29
Two rectangles intersect? No
Enter rectangle 1 info
Enter rectangle 2 info
Center x: 50
Center y: 50
Width: 70
Height: 50
Center x: 150
Center y: 50
Width: 80
Height: 30
Redraw Rectangles
(b)
Exercise18_30
Two triangles intersect? Yes
Enter triangle 1 info
Enter triangle 2 info
p1.x: 5
p1.y: 5
p2.x: 30
p2.y: 50
p3.x: 59
p3.y: 30
p1.x: 50
p1.y: 40
p2.x 34
p2.y 2
p3.x 163
p3.y 26
Redraw Rectangles
(c)

FIGURE 18.31 Check whether two circles, two rectangles, and two triangles are overlapping.

18.29** (*Geometry: two rectangles intersect?*) The `MyRectangle2D` class was defined in Exercise 10.12. Write an applet that enables the user to specify the location and size of the rectangles and displays whether the two rectangles intersect, as shown in Figure 18.31(b).

18.30** (*Geometry: two triangles intersect?*) The `Triangle2D` class was defined in Exercise 10.13. Write an applet that enables the user to specify the location of the two triangles and displays whether the two triangles intersect, as shown in Figure 18.31(c).

18.31*** (*Game: bean-machine animation*) Write an applet that animates a bean machine introduced in Exercise 16.22. The applet lets you set the number of slots, as shown in Figure 18.32. Click *Start* to start or restart the animation and click *Stop* to stop.

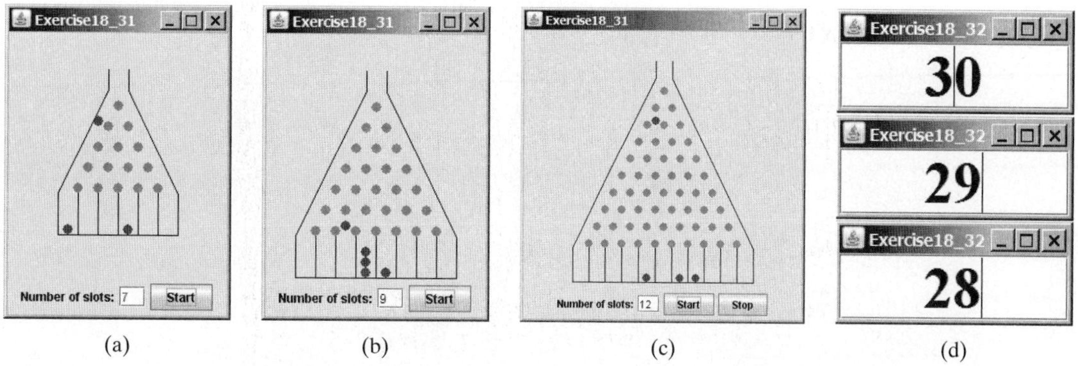

Exercise18_31
Number of slots: 7
Start
(a)
Exercise18_31
Number of slots: 9
Start
(b)
Exercise18_31
Number of slots: 12
Start
Stop
(c)
Exercise18_32
30
Exercise18_32
29
Exercise18_32
28
(d)

FIGURE 18.32 (a)–(c) The applet controls a bean-machine animation. (d) The applet counts down the time.

18.32* (*Count-down alarm*) Write an applet that allows the user to enter time in minutes in the text field and press the *Enter* key to count down the minutes, as shown in Figure 18.32(d). The remaining minutes are redisplayed every one minute. When the minutes are expired, the program starts to play music continuously.

18.33** (*Pattern recognition: consecutive four equal numbers*) Write an applet for Exercise 7.19, as shown in Figure 18.33 (a–b). Let the user enter the numbers in the text fields in a grid of 6 rows and 7 columns. The user can click the *Solve* button to highlight a sequence of four equal numbers, if it exists.

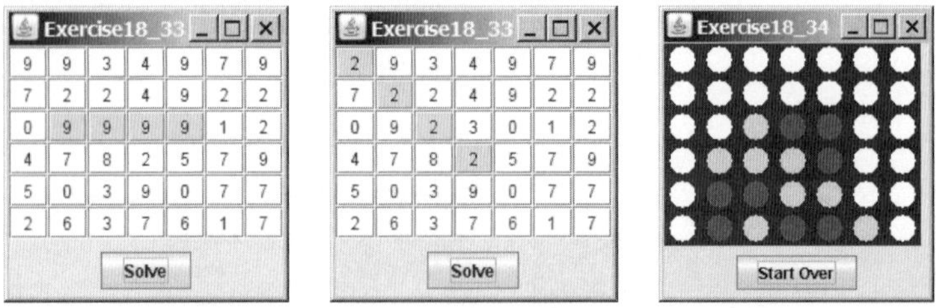
Exercise18_33
9 9 3 4 9 7 9
7 2 2 4 9 2 2
0 9 9 9 9 1 2
4 7 8 2 5 7 9
5 0 3 9 0 7 7
2 6 3 7 6 1 7
Solve
Exercise18_33
2 9 3 4 9 7 9
7 2 2 4 9 2 2
0 9 2 3 0 1 2
4 7 8 2 5 7 9
5 0 3 9 0 7 7
2 6 3 7 6 1 7
Solve
Exercise18_34
Start Over

(a) (b) (c)

FIGURE 18.33 (a)–(b) Clicking the *Solve* button to highlight the four consecutive numbers in a row, a column, or a diagonal. (c) The applet enables two players to play the connect-four game.

18.34*** (*Game: connect four*) Exercise 7.20 enables two players to play the connect-four game on the console. Rewrite the program using an applet, as shown in Figure 18.33(c). The applet enables two players to place red and yellow discs in turn. To place a disk, the player needs to click on an available cell. An *available cell* is unoccupied and whose downward neighbor is occupied. The applet flashes the four winning cells if a player wins and reports no winners if all cells are occupied with no winners.

CHAPTER 19

BINARY I/O

Objectives

- To discover how I/O is processed in Java (§19.2).
- To distinguish between text I/O and binary I/O (§19.3).
- To read and write bytes using `FileInputStream` and `FileOutputStream` (§19.4.1).
- To filter data using base classes `FilterInputStream`/`FilterOutputStream` (§19.4.2).
- To read and write primitive values and strings using `DataInputStream`/`DataOutputStream` (§19.4.3).
- To store and restore objects using `ObjectOutputStream` and `ObjectInputStream`, and to understand how objects are serialized and what kind of objects can be serialized (§19.6).
- To implement the `Serializable` interface to make objects serializable (§19.6.1).
- To serialize arrays (§19.6.2).
- To read and write files using the `RandomAccessFile` class (§19.7).

19.1 Introduction

text file
binary file
why binary I/O?

Data stored in a text file are represented in human-readable form. Data stored in a binary file are represented in binary form. You cannot read binary files. They are designed to be read by programs. For example, Java source programs are stored in text files and can be read by a text editor, but Java classes are stored in binary files and are read by the JVM. The advantage of binary files is that they are more efficient to process than text files.

Although it is not technically precise and correct, you can envision a text file as consisting of a sequence of characters and a binary file as consisting of a sequence of bits. For example, the decimal integer `199` is stored as the sequence of three characters, `'1'`, `'9'`, `'9'`, in a text file, and the same integer is stored as a `byte`-type value `C7` in a binary file, because decimal `199` equals hex `C7`($199 = 12 \times 16^1 + 7$).

text I/O
binary I/O

Java offers many classes for performing file input and output. These can be categorized as *text I/O classes* and *binary I/O classes.* In §9.7, "File Input and Output," you learned how to read/write strings and numeric values from/to a text file using `Scanner` and `PrintWriter`. This section introduces the classes for performing binary I/O.

19.2 How is I/O Handled in Java?

Recall that a `File` object encapsulates the properties of a file or a path but does not contain the methods for reading/writing data from/to a file. In order to perform I/O, you need to create objects using appropriate Java I/O classes. The objects contain the methods for reading/writing data from/to a file. For example, to write text to a file named **temp.txt**, you may create an object using the `PrintWriter` class as follows:

```
PrintWriter output = new PrintWriter("temp.txt");
```

You can now invoke the `print` method from the object to write a string into the file. For example, the following statement writes `"Java 101"` to the file.

```
output.print("Java 101");
```

The next statement closes the file.

```
output.close();
```

There are many I/O classes for various purposes. In general, these can be classified as input classes and output classes. An input class contains the methods to read data, and an output class contains the methods to write data. `PrintWriter` is an example of an output class, and `Scanner` is an example of an input class. The following code creates an input object for the file **temp.txt** and reads data from the file.

```
Scanner input = new Scanner(new File("temp.txt"));
System.out.println(input.nextLine());
```

If **temp.txt** contains `"Java 101"`, `input.nextLine()` returns string `"Java 101"`.

input stream
output stream

Figure 19.1 illustrates Java I/O programming. An input object reads a stream of data from a file, and an output object writes a stream of data to a file. An input object is also called an *input stream* and an output object an *output stream.*

19.3 Text I/O vs. Binary I/O

Computers do not differentiate binary files and text files. All files are stored in binary format, and thus all files are essentially binary files. Text I/O is built upon binary I/O to provide a level of abstraction for character encoding and decoding, as shown in Figure 19.2(a). Encoding and decoding are automatically performed for text I/O. The JVM converts a Unicode to a file-specific

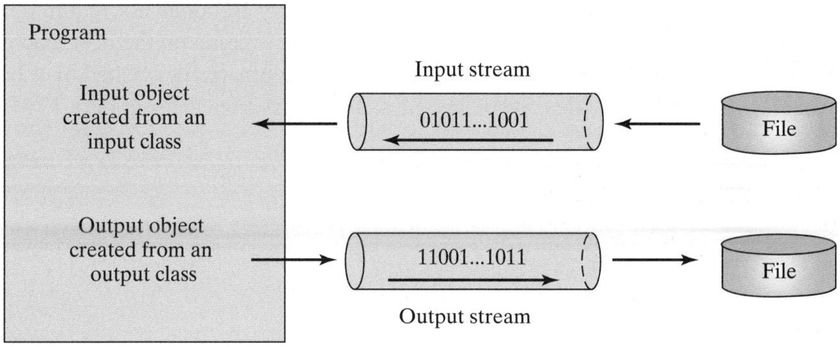
Program
Input object created from an input class
Output object created from an output class
Input stream
01011...1001
Output stream
11001...1011
File
File

FIGURE 19.1 The program receives data through an input object and sends data through an output object.

encoding when writing a character and converts a file-specific encoding to a Unicode when reading a character. For example, suppose you write string "199" using text I/O to a file. Each character is written to the file. Since the Unicode for character '1' is 0x0031, the Unicode 0x0031 is converted to a code that depends on the encoding scheme for the file. (Note that the prefix 0x denotes a hex number.) In the United States, the default encoding for text files on Windows is ASCII. The ASCII code for character '1' is 49 (0x31 in hex) and for character '9' is 57 (0x39 in hex). So to write the characters "199", three bytes—0x31, 0x39, and 0x39—are sent to the output, as shown in Figure 19.2(a).

Note

The new version of Java supports supplementary Unicode. For simplicity, however, this book considers only the original Unicode from 0 to FFFF.

supplementary Unicode

Binary I/O does not require conversions. If you write a numeric value to a file using binary I/O, the exact value in the memory is copied into the file. For example, a byte-type value 199 is represented as 0xC7 ($199 = 12 \times 16^1 + 7$) in the memory and appears exactly as 0xC7 in the file, as shown in Figure 19.2(b). When you read a byte using binary I/O, one byte value is read from the input.

In general, you should use text input to read a file created by a text editor or a text output program, and use binary input to read a file created by a Java binary output program.

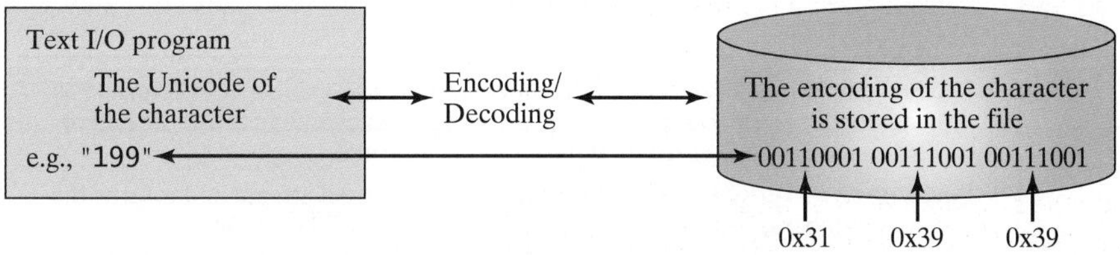
Text I/O program
The Unicode of the character
e.g., "199"
Encoding/ Decoding
The encoding of the character is stored in the file
00110001 00111001 00111001
0x31
0x39
0x39

(a)

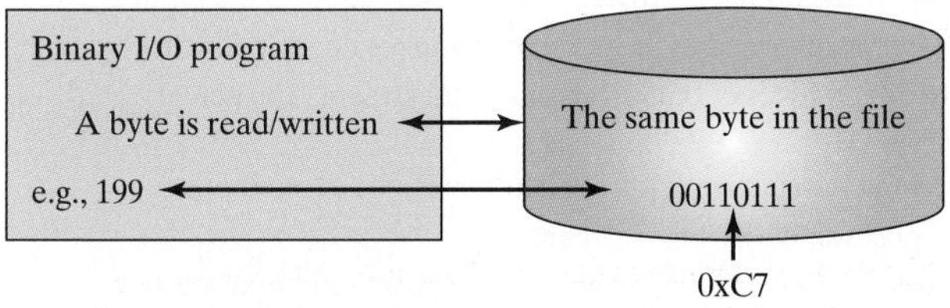
Binary I/O program
A byte is read/written
e.g., 199
The same byte in the file
00110111
0xC7

(b)

FIGURE 19.2 Text I/O requires encoding and decoding, whereas binary I/O does not.

Binary I/O is more efficient than text I/O, because binary I/O does not require encoding and decoding. Binary files are independent of the encoding scheme on the host machine and thus are portable. Java programs on any machine can read a binary file created by a Java program. This is why Java class files are binary files. Java class files can run on a JVM on any machine.

.txt and .dat

Note

For consistency, this book uses the extension `.txt` to name text files and `.dat` to name binary files.

19.4 Binary I/O Classes

The design of the Java I/O classes is a good example of applying inheritance, where common operations are generalized in superclasses, and subclasses provide specialized operations. Figure 19.3 lists some of the classes for performing binary I/O. `InputStream` is the root for binary input classes, and `OutputStream` is the root for binary output classes. Figures 19.4 and 19.5 list all the methods in `InputStream` and `OutputStream`.

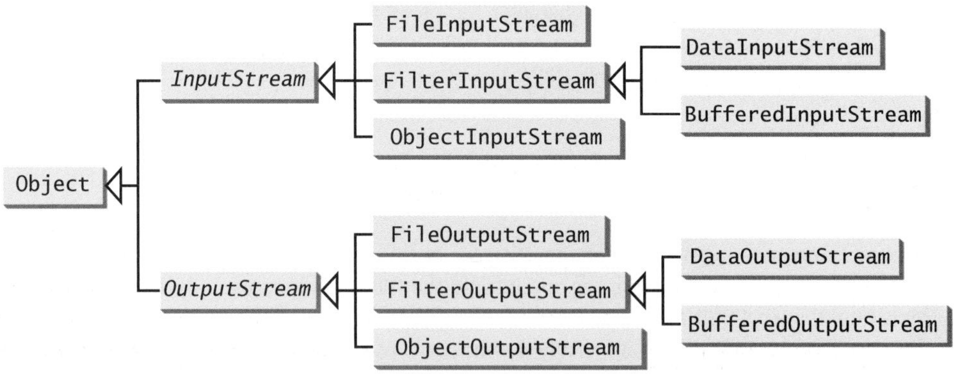
Object
InputStream
FileInputStream
FilterInputStream
ObjectInputStream
DataInputStream
BufferedInputStream
OutputStream
FileOutputStream
FilterOutputStream
ObjectOutputStream
DataOutputStream
BufferedOutputStream

FIGURE 19.3 `InputStream`, `OutputStream`, and their subclasses are for binary I/O.

java.io.InputStream	
`+read(): int`	Reads the next byte of data from the input stream. The value byte is returned as an `int` value in the range `0` to `255`. If no byte is available because the end of the stream has been reached, the value –1 is returned.
`+read(b: byte[]): int`	Reads up to `b.length` bytes into array `b` from the input stream and returns the actual number of bytes read. Returns –1 at the end of the stream.
`+read(b: byte[], off: int, len: int): int`	Reads bytes from the input stream and stores them in `b[off]`, `b[off+1]`, . . ., `b[off+len-1]`. The actual number of bytes read is returned. Returns –1 at the end of the stream.
`+available(): int`	Returns an estimate of the number of bytes that can be read from the input stream.
`+close(): void`	Closes this input stream and releases any system resources occupied by it.
`+skip(n: long): long`	Skips over and discards `n` bytes of data from this input stream. The actual number of bytes skipped is returned.
`+markSupported(): boolean`	Tests whether this input stream supports the `mark` and `reset` methods.
`+mark(readlimit: int): void`	Marks the current position in this input stream.
`+reset(): void`	Repositions this stream to the position at the time the `mark` method was last called on this input stream.

FIGURE 19.4 The abstract `InputStream` class defines the methods for the input stream of bytes.

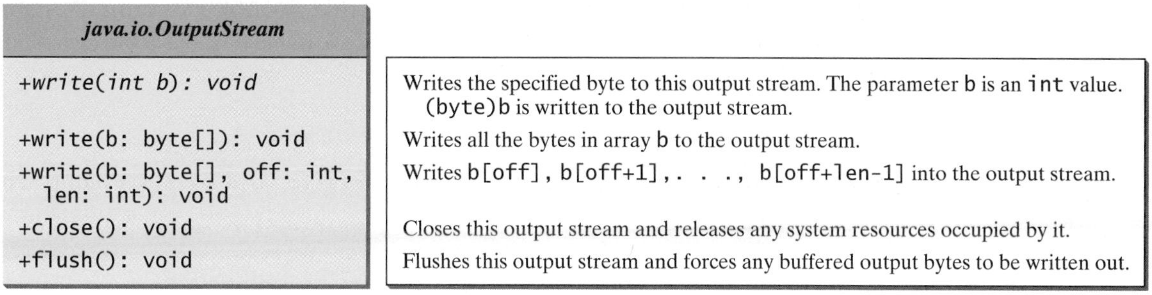
java.io.OutputStream
+write(int b): void
+write(b: byte[]): void
+write(b: byte[], off: int, len: int): void
+close(): void
+flush(): void
Writes the specified byte to this output stream. The parameter b is an int value. (byte)b is written to the output stream.
Writes all the bytes in array b to the output stream.
Writes b[off], b[off+1], . . ., b[off+len-1] into the output stream.
Closes this output stream and releases any system resources occupied by it.
Flushes this output stream and forces any buffered output bytes to be written out.

FIGURE 19.5 The abstract `OutputStream` class defines the methods for the output stream of bytes.

Note

All the methods in the binary I/O classes are declared to throw `java.io.IOException` or a subclass of `java.io.IOException`.

throws IOException

19.4.1 `FileInputStream`/`FileOutputStream`

`FileInputStream/FileOutputStream` is for reading/writing bytes from/to files. All the methods in these classes are inherited from `InputStream` and `OutputStream`. `FileInputStream/FileOutputStream` does not introduce new methods. To construct a `FileInputStream`, use the following constructors, as shown in Figure 19.6:

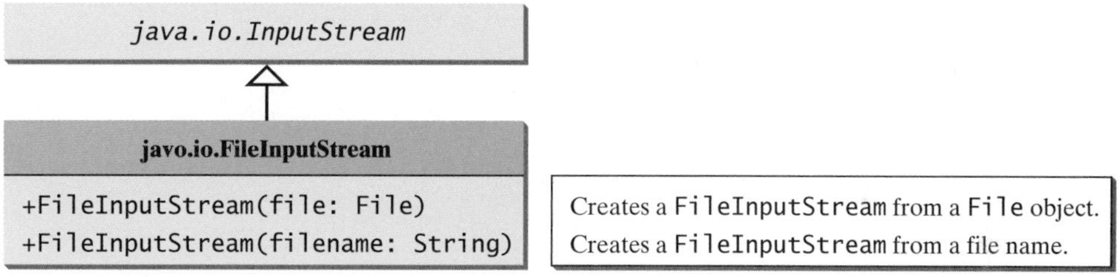
java.io.InputStream
javo.io.FileInputStream
+FileInputStream(file: File)
+FileInputStream(filename: String)
Creates a FileInputStream from a File object.
Creates a FileInputStream from a file name.

FIGURE 19.6 `FileInputStream` inputs a stream of bytes from a file.

A `java.io.FileNotFoundException` will occur if you attempt to create a `FileInputStream` with a nonexistent file.

FileNotFoundException

To construct a `FileOutputStream`, use the constructors shown in Figure 19.7.

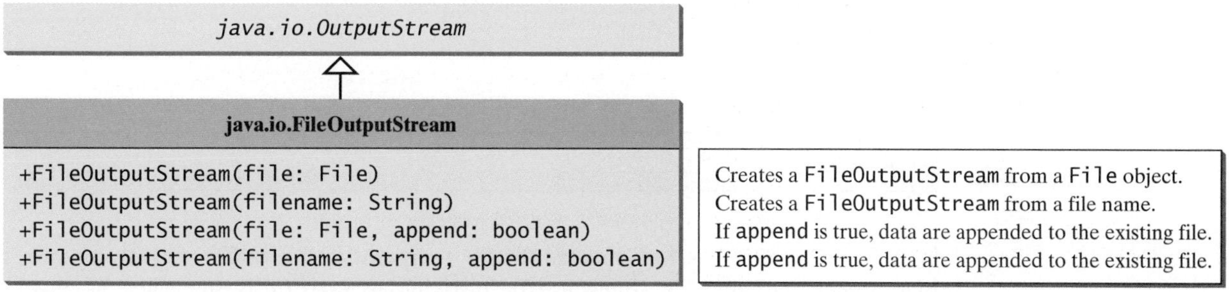
java.io.OutputStream
java.io.FileOutputStream
+FileOutputStream(file: File)
+FileOutputStream(filename: String)
+FileOutputStream(file: File, append: boolean)
+FileOutputStream(filename: String, append: boolean)
Creates a FileOutputStream from a File object.
Creates a FileOutputStream from a file name.
If append is true, data are appended to the existing file.
If append is true, data are appended to the existing file.

FIGURE 19.7 `FileOutputStream` outputs a stream of bytes to a file.

If the file does not exist, a new file will be created. If the file already exists, the first two constructors will delete the current content of the file. To retain the current content and append new data into the file, use the last two constructors by passing `true` to the `append` parameter.

IOException

Almost all the methods in the I/O classes throw `java.io.IOException`. Therefore you have to declare `java.io.IOException` to throw in the method or place the code in a `try-catch` block, as shown below:

Declaring exception in the method

```
public static void main(String[] args)
    throws IOException {
  // Perform I/O operations
}
```

Using try-catch block

```
public static void main(String[] args) {
  try {
    // Perform I/O operations
  }
  catch (IOException ex) {
    ex.printStackTrace();
  }
}
```

Listing 19.1 uses binary I/O to write ten byte values from `1` to `10` to a file named **temp.dat** and reads them back from the file.

LISTING 19.1 TestFileStream.java

import · output stream · output · input stream · input

```
1 import java.io.*;
2
3 public class TestFileStream {
4   public static void main(String[] args) throws IOException {
5     // Create an output stream to the file
6     FileOutputStream output = new FileOutputStream("temp.dat");
7
8     // Output values to the file
9     for (int i = 1; i <= 10; i++)
10      output.write(i);
11
12    // Close the output stream
13    output.close();
14
15    // Create an input stream for the file
16    FileInputStream input = new FileInputStream("temp.dat");
17
18    // Read values from the file
19    int value;
20    while ((value = input.read()) != -1)
21      System.out.print(value + " ");
22
23    // Close the output stream
24    input.close();
25  }
26 }
```

```
1 2 3 4 5 6 7 8 9 10
```

A `FileOutputStream` is created for file **temp.dat** in line 6. The `for` loop writes ten byte values into the file (lines 9–10). Invoking `write(i)` is the same as invoking `write((byte)i)`. Line 13 closes the output stream. Line 16 creates a `FileInputStream` for file **temp.dat**. Values are read from the file and displayed on the console in lines 19–21. The expression `((value = input.read()) != -1)` (line 20) reads a byte from `input.read()`, assigns it to `value`, and checks whether it is `-1`. The input value of `-1` signifies the end of a file.

end of a file

The file **temp.dat** created in this example is a binary file. It can be read from a Java program but not from a text editor, as shown in Figure 19.8.

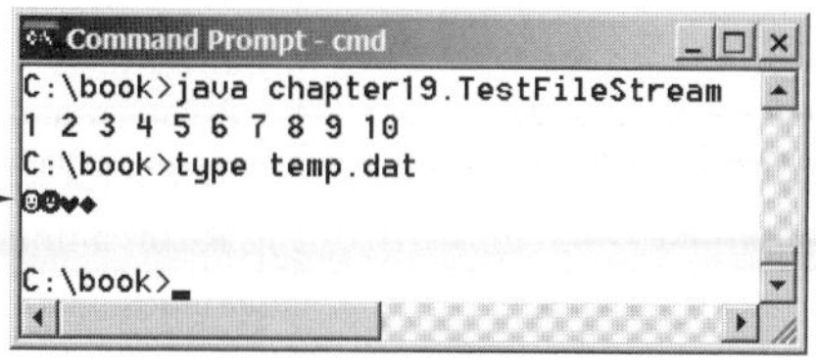
Binary data
Command Prompt - cmd
C:\book>java chapter19.TestFileStream
1 2 3 4 5 6 7 8 9 10
C:\book>type temp.dat
C:\book>_

FIGURE 19.8 A binary file cannot be displayed in text mode.

Tip

When a stream is no longer needed, always close it using the `close()` method. Not closing streams may cause data corruption in the output file, or other programming errors.

close stream

Note

The root directory for the file is the classpath directory. For the example in this book, the root directory is **c:\book**. So the file **temp.dat** is located at **c:\book**. If you wish to place **temp.dat** in a specific directory, replace line 8 by

where is the file?

```
FileOutputStream output =
  new FileOutputStream("directory/temp.dat");
```

Note

An instance of `FileInputStream` can be used as an argument to construct a `Scanner`, and an instance of `FileOutputStream` can be used as an argument to construct a `PrintWriter`. You can create a `PrintWriter` to append text into a file using

appending to text file

```
new PrintWriter(new FileOutputStream("temp.txt", true));
```

If **temp.txt** does not exist, it is created. If **temp.txt** already exists, new data are appended to the file.

19.4.2 FilterInputStream/FilterOutputStream

Filter streams are streams that filter bytes for some purpose. The basic byte input stream provides a `read` method that can be used only for reading bytes. If you want to read integers, doubles, or strings, you need a filter class to wrap the byte input stream. Using a filter class enables you to read integers, doubles, and strings instead of bytes and characters. `FilterInputStream` and `FilterOutputStream` are the base classes for filtering data. When you need to process primitive numeric types, use `DataInputStream` and `DataOutputStream` to filter bytes.

19.4.3 DataInputStream/DataOutputStream

`DataInputStream` reads bytes from the stream and converts them into appropriate primitive type values or strings. `DataOutputStream` converts primitive type values or strings into bytes and outputs the bytes to the stream.

`DataInputStream` extends `FilterInputStream` and implements the `DataInput` interface, as shown in Figure 19.9. `DataOutputStream` extends `FilterOutputStream` and implements the `DataOutput` interface, as shown in Figure 19.10.

`DataInputStream` implements the methods defined in the `DataInput` interface to read primitive data type values and strings. `DataOutputStream` implements the methods defined in the `DataOutput` interface to write primitive data type values and strings. Primitive values

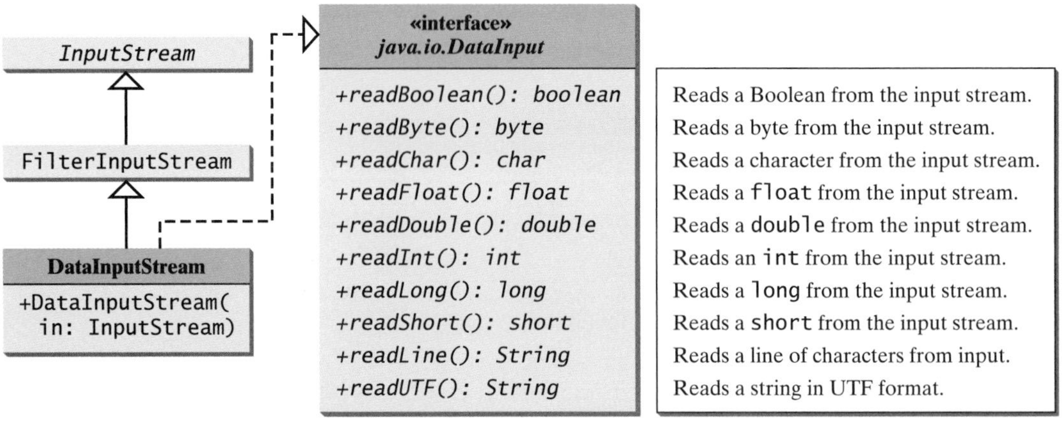
InputStream
FilterInputStream
DataInputStream
+DataInputStream(
in: InputStream)
«interface»
java.io.DataInput
+readBoolean(): boolean
+readByte(): byte
+readChar(): char
+readFloat(): float
+readDouble(): double
+readInt(): int
+readLong(): long
+readShort(): short
+readLine(): String
+readUTF(): String
Reads a Boolean from the input stream.
Reads a byte from the input stream.
Reads a character from the input stream.
Reads a float from the input stream.
Reads a double from the input stream.
Reads an int from the input stream.
Reads a long from the input stream.
Reads a short from the input stream.
Reads a line of characters from input.
Reads a string in UTF format.

FIGURE 19.9 `DataInputStream` filters an input stream of bytes into primitive data type values and strings.

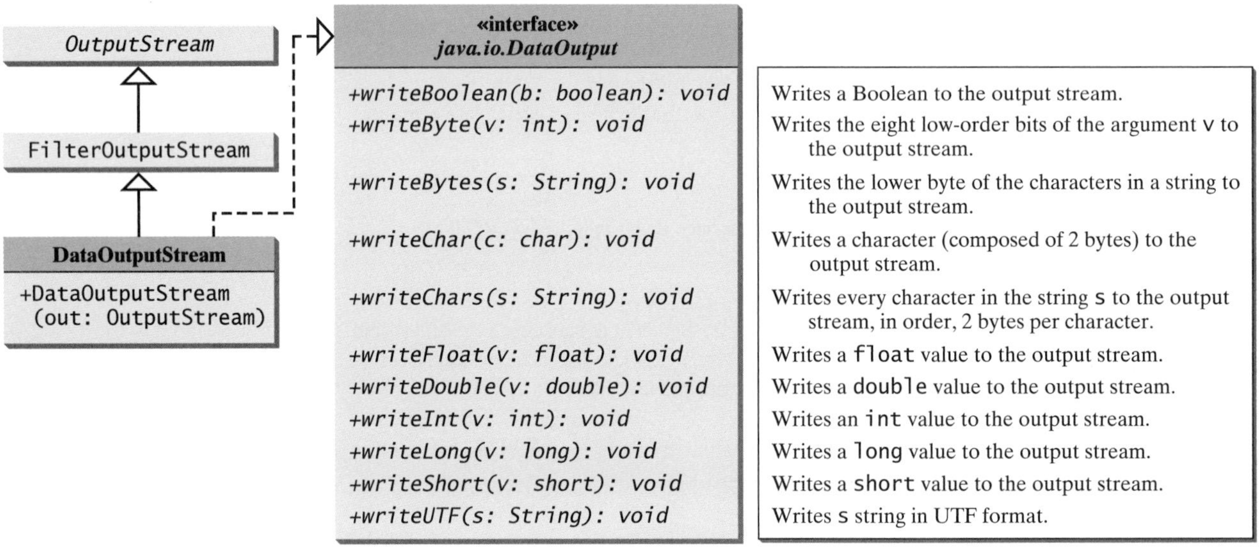
OutputStream
FilterOutputStream
DataOutputStream
+DataOutputStream
(out: OutputStream)
«interface»
java.io.DataOutput
+writeBoolean(b: boolean): void
+writeByte(v: int): void
+writeBytes(s: String): void
+writeChar(c: char): void
+writeChars(s: String): void
+writeFloat(v: float): void
+writeDouble(v: double): void
+writeInt(v: int): void
+writeLong(v: long): void
+writeShort(v: short): void
+writeUTF(s: String): void
Writes a Boolean to the output stream.
Writes the eight low-order bits of the argument v to the output stream.
Writes the lower byte of the characters in a string to the output stream.
Writes a character (composed of 2 bytes) to the output stream.
Writes every character in the string s to the output stream, in order, 2 bytes per character.
Writes a float value to the output stream.
Writes a double value to the output stream.
Writes an int value to the output stream.
Writes a long value to the output stream.
Writes a short value to the output stream.
Writes s string in UTF format.

FIGURE 19.10 `DataOutputStream` enables you to write primitive data type values and strings into an output stream.

are copied from memory to the output without any conversions. Characters in a string may be written in several ways, as discussed in the next section.

Characters and Strings in Binary I/O

A Unicode consists of two bytes. The `writeChar(char c)` method writes the Unicode of character `c` to the output. The `writeChars(String s)` method writes the Unicode for each character in the string `s` to the output. The `writeBytes(String s)` method writes the lower byte of the Unicode for each character in the string `s` to the output. The high byte of the Unicode is discarded. The `writeBytes` method is suitable for strings that consist of ASCII characters, since an ASCII code is stored only in the lower byte of a Unicode. If a string consists of non-ASCII characters, you have to use the `writeChars` method to write the string.

The `writeUTF(String s)` method writes two bytes of length information to the output stream, followed by the modified UTF-8 representation of every character in the string `s`. UTF-8 is a coding scheme that allows systems to operate with both ASCII and Unicode. Most operating systems use ASCII. Java uses Unicode. The ASCII character set is a subset of the Unicode character set. Since most applications need only the ASCII character set, it is a waste to represent an 8-bit ASCII character as a 16-bit Unicode character. The modified UTF-8 scheme stores a character using one, two, or three bytes. Characters are coded in one byte if their code is less than or equal to 0x7F, in two bytes if their code is greater than 0x7F and less than or equal to 0x7FF, or in three bytes if their code is greater than 0x7FF.

UTF-8 scheme

The initial bits of a UTF-8 character indicate whether a character is stored in one byte, two bytes, or three bytes. If the first bit is 0, it is a one-byte character. If the first bits are 110, it is the first byte of a two-byte sequence. If the first bits are 1110, it is the first byte of a three-byte sequence. The information that indicates the number of characters in a string is stored in the first two bytes preceding the UTF-8 characters. For example, writeUTF("ABCDEF") actually writes eight bytes (i.e., 00 06 41 42 43 44 45 46) to the file, because the first two bytes store the number of characters in the string.

The writeUTF(String s) method converts a string into a series of bytes in the UTF-8 format and writes them into a binary stream. The readUTF() method reads a string that has been written using the writeUTF method.

The UTF-8 format has the advantage of saving a byte for each ASCII character, because a Unicode character takes up two bytes and an ASCII character in UTF-8 only one byte. If most of the characters in a long string are regular ASCII characters, using UTF-8 is efficient.

Using DataInputStream/DataOutputStream

Data streams are used as wrappers on existing input, and output streams to filter data in the original stream. They are created using the following constructors (see Figures 19.9 and 19.10):

```
public DataInputStream(InputStream instream)
public DataOutputStream(OutputStream outstream)
```

The statements given below create data streams. The first statement creates an input stream for file **in.dat**; the second statement creates an output stream for file **out.dat**.

```
DataInputStream input =
  new DataInputStream(new FileInputStream("in.dat"));
DataOutputStream output =
  new DataOutputStream(new FileOutputStream("out.dat"));
```

Listing 19.2 writes student names and scores to a file named **temp.dat** and reads the data back from the file.

LISTING 19.2 TestDataStream.java

```
import java.io.*;

public class TestDataStream {
  public static void main(String[] args) throws IOException {
    // Create an output stream for file temp.dat
    DataOutputStream output =
      new DataOutputStream(new FileOutputStream("temp.dat"));

    // Write student test scores to the file
    output.writeUTF("John");
    output.writeDouble(85.5);
    output.writeUTF("Jim");
    output.writeDouble(185.5);
    output.writeUTF("George");
    output.writeDouble(105.25);

    // Close output stream
    output.close();

    // Create an input stream for file temp.dat
    DataInputStream input =
      new DataInputStream(new FileInputStream("temp.dat"));

```

output stream

output

close stream

input stream

input

```
24      // Read student test scores from the file
25      System.out.println(input.readUTF() + " " + input.readDouble());
26      System.out.println(input.readUTF() + " " + input.readDouble());
27      System.out.println(input.readUTF() + " " + input.readDouble());
28    }
29  }
```

```
John 85.5
Jim 185.5
George 105.25
```

A `DataOutputStream` is created for file **temp.dat** in lines 6–7. Student names and scores are written to the file in lines 10–15. Line 18 closes the output stream. A `DataInputStream` is created for the same file in lines 21–22. Student names and scores are read back from the file and displayed on the console in lines 25–27.

`DataInputStream` and `DataOutputStream` read and write Java primitive type values and strings in a machine-independent fashion, thereby enabling you to write a data file on one machine and read it on another machine that has a different operating system or file structure. An application uses a data output stream to write data that can later be read by a program using a data input stream.

Caution

You have to read data in the same order and format in which they are stored. For example, since names are written in UTF-8 using `writeUTF`, you must read names using `readUTF`.

Detecting End of File

EOFException

If you keep reading data at the end of an `InputStream`, an `EOFException` will occur. This exception may be used to detect the end of file, as shown in Listing 19.3.

Listing 19.3 DetectEndOfFile.java

output stream / output / close stream / input stream / input / EOFException

```
import java.io.*;

public class DetectEndOfFile {
  public static void main(String[] args) {
    try {
      DataOutputStream output = new DataOutputStream
        (new FileOutputStream("test.dat"));
      output.writeDouble(4.5);
      output.writeDouble(43.25);
      output.writeDouble(3.2);
      output.close();

      DataInputStream input = new DataInputStream
        (new FileInputStream("test.dat"));
      while (true) {
        System.out.println(input.readDouble());
      }
    }
    catch (EOFException ex) {
      System.out.println("All data read");
    }
    catch (IOException ex) {
      ex.printStackTrace();
    }
  }
}
```

```
4.5
43.25
3.2
All data read
```

The program writes three double values to the file using DataOutputStream (lines 6–10), and reads the data using DataInputStream (lines 13–17). When reading past the end of file, an EOFException is thrown. The exception is caught in line 19.

19.4.4 BufferedInputStream/BufferedOutputStream

BufferedInputStream/BufferedOutputStream can be used to speed up input and output by reducing the number of reads and writes. BufferedInputStream/BufferedOutputStream does not contain new methods. All the methods in BufferedInputStream/BufferedOutputStream are inherited from the InputStream/OutputStream classes. BufferedInputStream/BufferedOutputStream adds a buffer in the stream for storing bytes for efficient processing.

You may wrap a BufferedInputStream/BufferedOutputStream on any InputStream/OutputStream using the constructors shown in Figures 19.11 and 19.12.

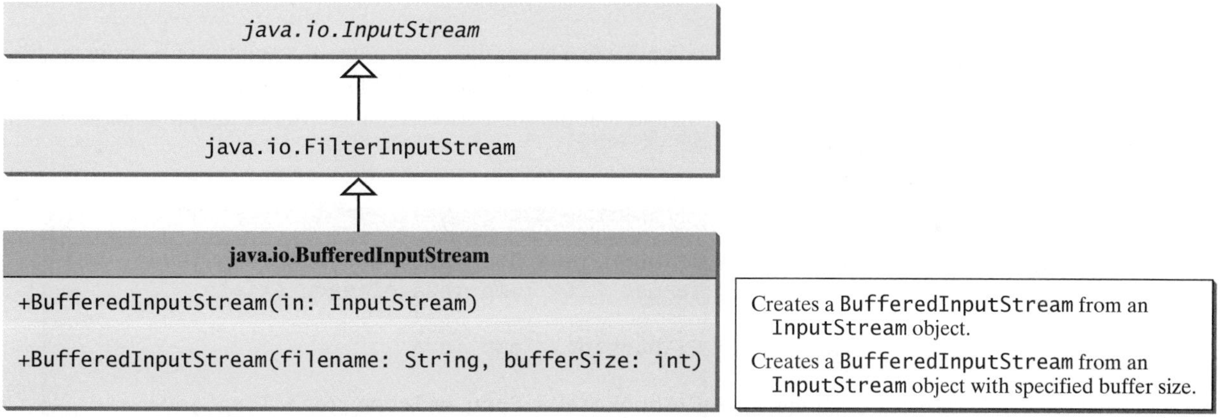
java.io.InputStream
java.io.FilterInputStream
java.io.BufferedInputStream
+BufferedInputStream(in: InputStream)
+BufferedInputStream(filename: String, bufferSize: int)
Creates a BufferedInputStream from an InputStream object.
Creates a BufferedInputStream from an InputStream object with specified buffer size.

FIGURE 19.11 BufferedInputStream buffers input stream.

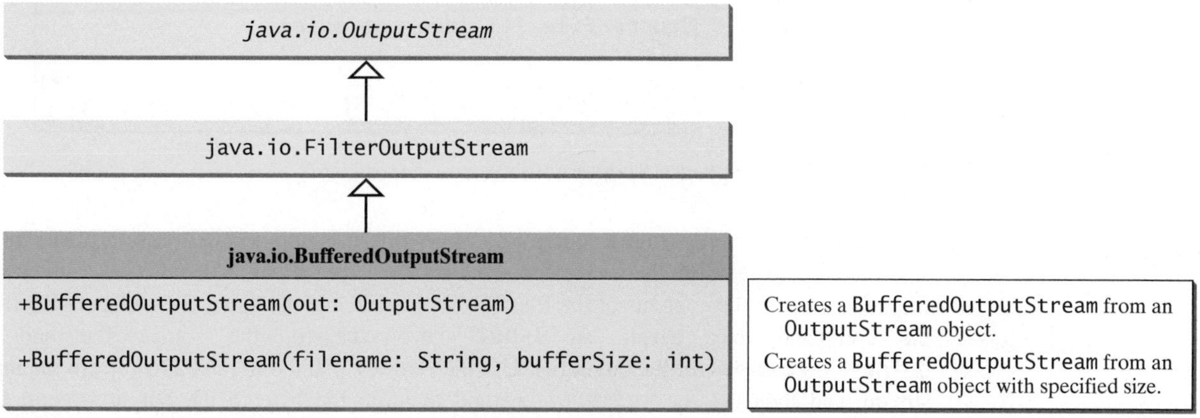
java.io.OutputStream
java.io.FilterOutputStream
java.io.BufferedOutputStream
+BufferedOutputStream(out: OutputStream)
+BufferedOutputStream(filename: String, bufferSize: int)
Creates a BufferedOutputStream from an OutputStream object.
Creates a BufferedOutputStream from an OutputStream object with specified size.

FIGURE 19.12 BufferedOutputStream buffers output stream.

If no buffer size is specified, the default size is `512` bytes. A buffered input stream reads as many data as possible into its buffer in a single read call. By contrast, a buffered output stream calls the write method only when its buffer fills up or when the `flush()` method is called.

You can improve the performance of the `TestDataStream` program in the preceding example by adding buffers in the stream in lines 6–7 and 13–14 as follows:

```
DataOutputStream output = new DataOutputStream(
  new BufferedOutputStream (new FileOutputStream("temp.dat")));

DataInputStream input = new DataInputStream(
  new BufferedInputStream (new FileInputStream("temp.dat")));
```

Tip

You should always use buffered IO to speed up input and output. For small files, you may not notice performance improvements. However, for large files—over 100 MB—you will see substantial improvements using buffered IO.

19.5 Problem: Copying Files

Video Note
Copy file

This section develops a program that copies files. The user needs to provide a source file and a target file as command-line arguments using the following command:

```
java Copy source target
```

The program copies a source file to a target file and displays the number of bytes in the file. If the source does not exist, the user is told that the file has not been found. If the target file already exists, the user is told that the file exists. A sample run of the program is shown in Figure 19.13.

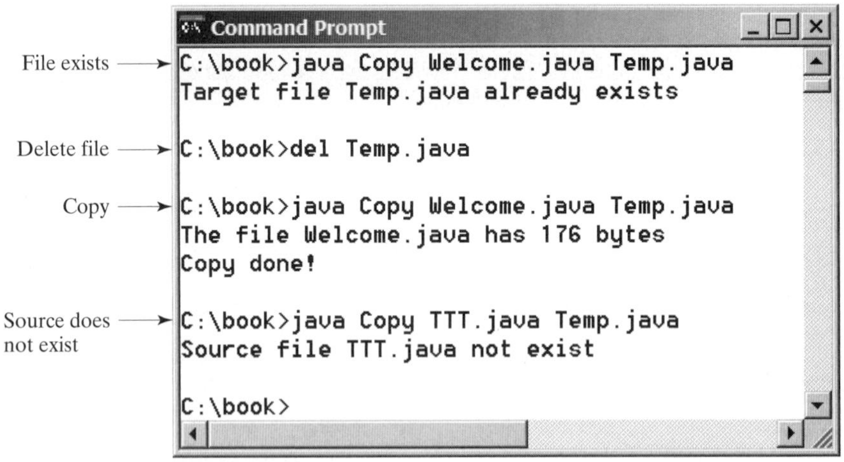
Command Prompt
File exists
C:\book>java Copy Welcome.java Temp.java
Target file Temp.java already exists
Delete file
C:\book>del Temp.java
Copy
C:\book>java Copy Welcome.java Temp.java
The file Welcome.java has 176 bytes
Copy done!
Source does not exist
C:\book>java Copy TTT.java Temp.java
Source file TTT.java not exist
C:\book>

FIGURE 19.13 The program copies a file.

To copy the contents from a source to a target file, it is appropriate to use a binary input stream to read bytes from the source file and a binary output stream to send bytes to the target file, regardless of the contents of the file. The source file and the target file are specified from the command line. Create an `InputFileStream` for the source file and an `OutputFileStream` for the target file. Use the `read()` method to read a byte from the input stream, and then use the `write(b)` method to write the byte to the output stream. Use `BufferedInputStream` and `BufferedOutputStream` to improve the performance. Listing 19.4 gives the solution to the problem.

LISTING 19.4 Copy.java

```
1 import java.io.*;
2
3 public class Copy {
4   /** Main method
5      @param args[0] for sourcefile
6      @param args[1] for target file
7    */
8   public static void main(String[] args) throws IOException {
9     // Check command-line parameter usage
10    if (args.length != 2) {
11      System.out.println(
12        "Usage: java Copy sourceFile targetfile");
13      System.exit(0);
14    }
15
16    // Check whether source file exists
17    File sourceFile = new File(args[0]);
18    if (!sourceFile.exists()) {
19       System.out.println("Source file " + args[0] + " not exist");
20       System.exit(0);
21    }
22
23    // Check whether target file exists
24    File targetFile = new File(args[1]);
25    if (targetFile.exists()) {
26      System.out.println("Target file " + args[1] + " already
27        exists");
28      System.exit(0);
29    }
30
31    // Create an input stream
32    BufferedInputStream input =
33      new BufferedInputStream(new FileInputStream(sourceFile));
34
35    // Create an output stream
36    BufferedOutputStream output =
37      new BufferedOutputStream(new FileOutputStream(targetFile));
38
39    // Continuously read a byte from input and write it to output
40    int r; int numberOfBytesCopied = 0;
41    while ((r = input.read()) != -1) {
42      output.write((byte)r);
43      numberOfBytesCopied++;
44    }
45
46    // Close streams
47    input.close();
48    output.close();
49
50    // Display the file size
51    System.out.println(numberOfBytesCopied + " bytes copied");
52  }
53 }
```

check usage
source file
target file
input stream
output stream
read
write
close stream

The program first checks whether the user has passed two required arguments from the command line in lines 10–14.

The program uses the `File` class to check whether the source file and target file exist. If the source file does not exist (lines 18–21) or if the target file already exists, exit the program.

An input stream is created using BufferedInputStream wrapped on FileInputStream in lines 32–33, and an output stream is created using BufferedOutputStream wrapped on FileOutputStream in lines 36–37.

The expression ((r = input.read()) != -1) (line 41) reads a byte from input.read(), assigns it to r, and checks whether it is -1. The input value of -1 signifies the end of a file. The program continuously reads bytes from the input stream and sends them to the output stream until all of the bytes have been read.

19.6 Object I/O

Video Note
Object I/O

DataInputStream/DataOutputStream enables you to perform I/O for primitive type values and strings. ObjectInputStream/ObjectOutputStream enables you to perform I/O for objects in addition to primitive type values and strings. Since ObjectInputStream/ObjectOutputStream contains all the functions of DataInputStream/DataOutputStream, you can replace DataInputStream/DataOutputStream completely with ObjectInputStream/ObjectOutputStream.

ObjectInputStream extends InputStream and implements ObjectInput and ObjectStreamConstants, as shown in Figure 19.14. ObjectInput is a subinterface of DataInput. DataInput is shown in Figure 19.9. ObjectStreamConstants contains the constants to support ObjectInputStream/ObjectOutputStream.

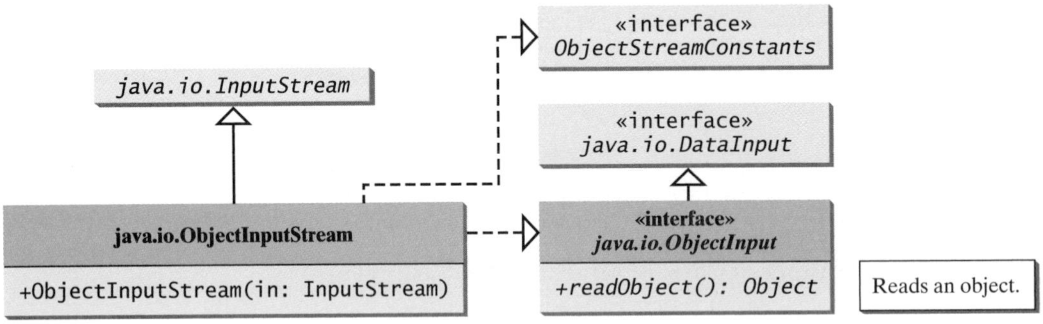
«interface»
ObjectStreamConstants
java.io.InputStream
«interface»
java.io.DataInput
java.io.ObjectInputStream
«interface»
java.io.ObjectInput
+ObjectInputStream(in: InputStream)
+readObject(): Object
Reads an object.

FIGURE 19.14 ObjectInputStream can read objects, primitive type values, and strings.

ObjectOutputStream extends OutputStream and implements ObjectOutput and ObjectStreamConstants, as shown in Figure 19.15. ObjectOutput is a subinterface of DataOutput. DataOutput is shown in Figure 19.10.

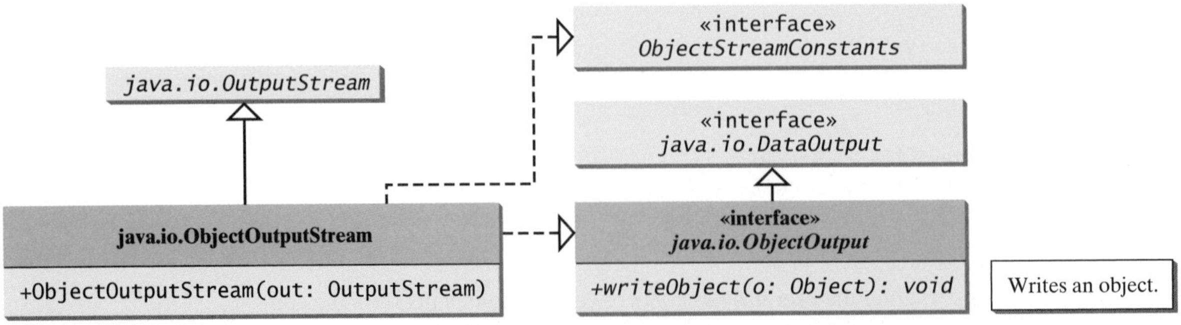
«interface»
ObjectStreamConstants
java.io.OutputStream
«interface»
java.io.DataOutput
java.io.ObjectOutputStream
«interface»
java.io.ObjectOutput
+ObjectOutputStream(out: OutputStream)
+writeObject(o: Object): void
Writes an object.

FIGURE 19.15 ObjectOutputStream can write objects, primitive type values, and strings.

You may wrap an ObjectInputStream/ObjectOutputStream on any InputStream/OutputStream using the following constructors:

```
// Create an ObjectInputStream
public ObjectInputStream(InputStream in)

// Create an ObjectOutputStream
public ObjectOutputStream(OutputStream out)
```

Listing 19.5 writes student names, scores, and current date to a file named **object.dat**.

Listing 19.5 TestObjectOutputStream.java

```
1 import java.io.*;
2
3 public class TestObjectOutputStream {
4   public static void main(String[] args) throws IOException {
5     // Create an output stream for file object.dat
6     ObjectOutputStream output =
7       new ObjectOutputStream(new FileOutputStream("object.dat"));
8
9     // Write a string, double value, and object to the file
10    output.writeUTF("John");
11    output.writeDouble(85.5);
12    output.writeObject(new java.util.Date());
13
14    // Close output stream
15    output.close();
16  }
17 }
```

output stream

output

An ObjectOutputStream is created to write data into file **object.dat** in lines 6–7. A string, a double value, and an object are written to the file in lines 10–12. To improve performance, you may add a buffer in the stream using the following statement to replace lines 6–7:

```
ObjectOutputStream output = new ObjectOutputStream(
  new BufferedOutputStream(new FileOutputStream("object.dat")));
```

Multiple objects or primitives can be written to the stream. The objects must be read back from the corresponding ObjectInputStream with the same types and in the same order as they were written. Java's safe casting should be used to get the desired type. Listing 19.6 reads data back from **object.dat**.

Listing 19.6 TestObjectInputStream.java

```
import java.io.*;

public class TestObjectInputStream {
  public static void main(String[] args)
    throws ClassNotFoundException, IOException {
    // Create an input stream for file object.dat
    ObjectInputStream input =
      new ObjectInputStream(new FileInputStream("object.dat"));

    // Write a string, double value, and object to the file
    String name = input.readUTF();
    double score = input.readDouble();
    java.util.Date date = (java.util.Date)(input.readObject());
    System.out.println(name + " " + score + " " + date);

```

input stream

input

```
16      // Close output stream
17      input.close();
18    }
19  }
```

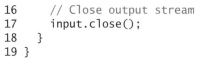

```
John 85.5 Mon Jun 26 17:17:29 EDT 2006
```

ClassNotFoundException

The `readObject()` method may throw `java.lang.ClassNotFoundException`. The reason is that when the JVM restores an object, it first loads the class for the object if the class has not been loaded. Since `ClassNotFoundException` is a checked exception, the `main` method declares to throw it in line 5. An `ObjectInputStream` is created to read input from **object.dat** in lines 7–8. You have to read the data from the file in the same order and format as they were written to the file. A string, a double value, and an object are read in lines 11–13. Since `readObject()` returns an `Object`, it is cast into `Date` and assigned to a `Date` variable in line 13.

19.6.1 The `Serializable` Interface

serializable

Not every object can be written to an output stream. Objects that can be so written are said to be *serializable*. A serializable object is an instance of the `java.io.Serializable` interface, so the object's class must implement `Serializable`.

The `Serializable` interface is a marker interface. Since it has no methods, you don't need to add additional code in your class that implements `Serializable`. Implementing this interface enables the Java serialization mechanism to automate the process of storing objects and arrays.

serialization

deserialization

To appreciate this automation feature, consider what you otherwise need to do in order to store an object. Suppose you want to store a `JButton` object. To do this you need to store all the current values of the properties (e.g., color, font, text, alignment) in the object. Since `JButton` is a subclass of `AbstractButton`, the property values of `AbstractButton` have to be stored as well as the properties of all the superclasses of `AbstractButton`. If a property is of an object type (e.g., `background` of the `Color` type), storing it requires storing all the property values inside this object. As you can see, this is a very tedious process. Fortunately, you don't have to go through it manually. Java provides a built-in mechanism to automate the process of writing objects. This process is referred to as *object serialization*, which is implemented in `ObjectOutputStream`. In contrast, the process of reading objects is referred to as *object deserialization*, which is implemented in `ObjectInputStream`.

NotSerializable-Exception

Many classes in the Java API implement `Serializable`. The utility classes, such as `java.util.Date`, and all the Swing GUI component classes implement `Serializable`. Attempting to store an object that does not support the `Serializable` interface would cause a `NotSerializableException`.

When a serializable object is stored, the class of the object is encoded; this includes the class name and the signature of the class, the values of the object's instance variables, and the closure of any other objects referenced from the initial object. The values of the object's static variables are not stored.

Note

nonserializable fields

transient

If an object is an instance of `Serializable` but contains nonserializable instance data fields, can it be serialized? The answer is no. To enable the object to be serialized, mark these data fields with the `transient` keyword to tell the JVM to ignore them when writing the object to an object stream. Consider the following class:

```
public class Foo implements java.io.Serializable {
  private int v1;
  private static double v2;
  private transient A v3 = new A();
}

class A { } // A is not serializable
```

When an object of the Foo class is serialized, only variable v1 is serialized. Variable v2 is not serialized because it is a static variable, and variable v3 is not serialized because it is marked transient. If v3 were not marked transient, a java.io.NotSerializable-Exception would occur.

Note

duplicate objects

If an object is written to an object stream more than once, will it be stored in multiple copies? No, it will not. When an object is written for the first time, a serial number is created for it. The JVM writes the complete content of the object along with the serial number into the object stream. After the first time, only the serial number is stored if the same object is written again. When the objects are read back, their references are the same, since only one object is actually created in the memory.

19.6.2 Serializing Arrays

An array is serializable if all its elements are serializable. An entire array can be saved using writeObject into a file and later can be restored using readObject. Listing 19.7 stores an array of five int values and an array of three strings and reads them back to display on the console.

LISTING 19.7 TestObjectStreamForArray.java

```java
import java.io.*;

public class TestObjectStreamForArray {
  public static void main(String[] args)
      throws ClassNotFoundException, IOException {
    int[] numbers = {1, 2, 3, 4, 5};
    String[] strings = {"John", "Jim", "Jake"};

    // Create an output stream for file array.dat
    ObjectOutputStream output =
      new ObjectOutputStream(new FileOutputStream
        ("array.dat", true));

    // Write arrays to the object output stream
    output.writeObject(numbers);
    output.writeObject(strings);

    // Close the stream
    output.close();

    // Create an input stream for file array.dat
    ObjectInputStream input =
      new ObjectInputStream(new FileInputStream("array.dat"));

    int[] newNumbers = (int[])(input.readObject());
    String[] newStrings = (String[])(input.readObject());

    // Display arrays
    for (int i = 0; i < newNumbers.length; i++)
      System.out.print(newNumbers[i] + " ");
    System.out.println();

    for (int i = 0; i < newStrings.length; i++)
      System.out.print(newStrings[i] + " ");
  }
}
```

output stream

store array

input stream

restore array

```
1 2 3 4 5
John Jim Jake
```

Lines 15–16 write two arrays into file **array.dat**. Lines 25–26 read three arrays back in the same order they were written. Since `readObject()` returns `Object`, casting is used to cast the objects into `int[]` and `String[]`.

19.7 Random-Access Files

read-only

write-only

sequential

All of the streams you have used so far are known as *read-only* or *write-only* streams. The external files of these streams are *sequential* files that cannot be updated without creating a new file. It is often necessary to modify files or to insert new records into files. Java provides the `RandomAccessFile` class to allow a file to be read from and written to at random locations.

The `RandomAccessFile` class implements the `DataInput` and `DataOutput` interfaces, as shown in Figure 19.16. The `DataInput` interface shown in Figure 19.9 defines the methods (e.g., `readInt`, `readDouble`, `readChar`, `readBoolean`, `readUTF`) for reading primitive type values and strings, and the `DataOutput` interface shown in Figure 19.10 defines the methods (e.g., `writeInt`, `writeDouble`, `writeChar`, `writeBoolean`, `writeUTF`) for writing primitive type values and strings.

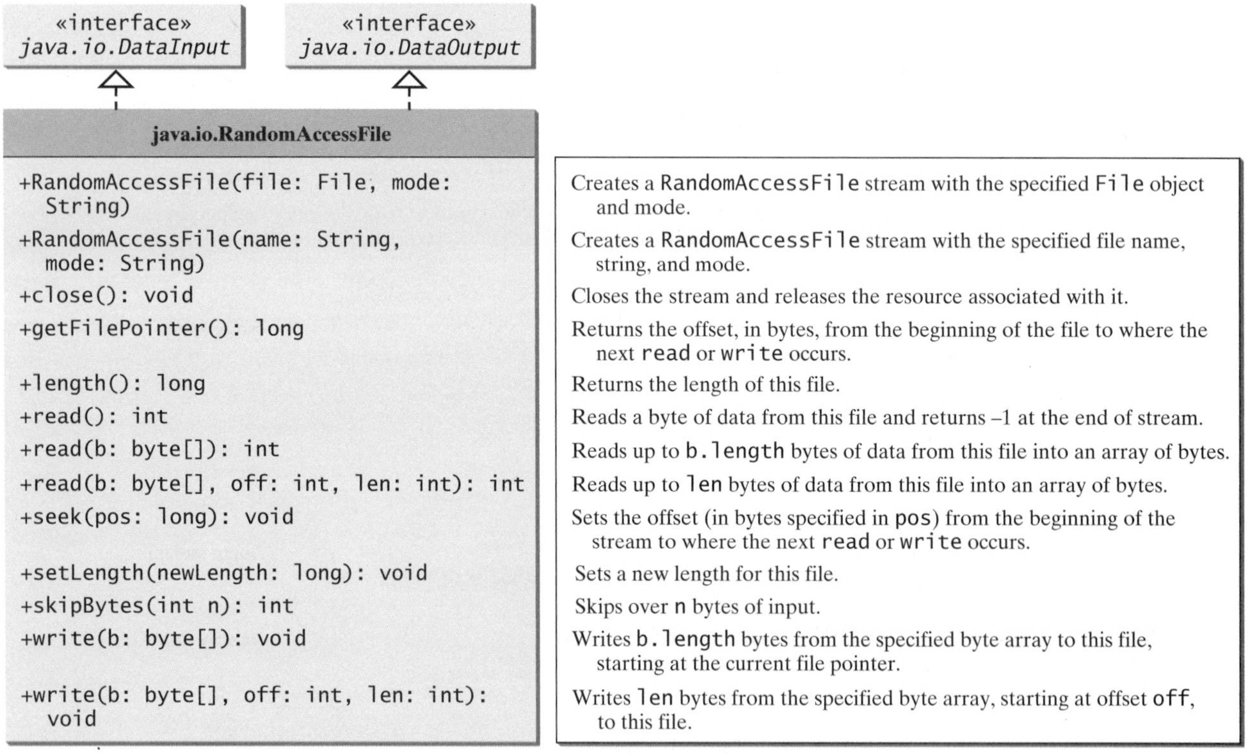
«interface»
java.io.DataInput
«interface»
java.io.DataOutput
java.io.RandomAccessFile
+RandomAccessFile(file: File, mode: String)
+RandomAccessFile(name: String, mode: String)
+close(): void
+getFilePointer(): long
+length(): long
+read(): int
+read(b: byte[]): int
+read(b: byte[], off: int, len: int): int
+seek(pos: long): void
+setLength(newLength: long): void
+skipBytes(int n): int
+write(b: byte[]): void
+write(b: byte[], off: int, len: int): void
Creates a RandomAccessFile stream with the specified File object and mode.
Creates a RandomAccessFile stream with the specified file name, string, and mode.
Closes the stream and releases the resource associated with it.
Returns the offset, in bytes, from the beginning of the file to where the next read or write occurs.
Returns the length of this file.
Reads a byte of data from this file and returns –1 at the end of stream.
Reads up to b.length bytes of data from this file into an array of bytes.
Reads up to len bytes of data from this file into an array of bytes.
Sets the offset (in bytes specified in pos) from the beginning of the stream to where the next read or write occurs.
Sets a new length for this file.
Skips over n bytes of input.
Writes b.length bytes from the specified byte array to this file, starting at the current file pointer.
Writes len bytes from the specified byte array, starting at offset off, to this file.

FIGURE 19.16 `RandomAccessFile` implements the `DataInput` and `DataOutput` interfaces with additional methods to support random access.

When creating a `RandomAccessFile`, you can specify one of two modes ("`r`" or "`rw`"). Mode "`r`" means that the stream is read-only, and mode "`rw`" indicates that the stream allows both read and write. For example, the following statement creates a new stream, `raf`, that allows the program to read from and write to the file **test.dat**:

```
RandomAccessFile raf = new RandomAccessFile("test.dat", "rw");
```

If **test.dat** already exists, `raf` is created to access it; if **test.dat** does not exist, a new file named **test.dat** is created, and `raf` is created to access the new file. The method `raf.length()` returns the number of bytes in **test.dat** at any given time. If you append new data into the file, `raf.length()` increases.

Tip

If the file is not intended to be modified, open it with the `"r"` mode. This prevents unintentional modification of the file.

file pointer

A random-access file consists of a sequence of bytes. A special marker called a *file pointer* is positioned at one of these bytes. A read or write operation takes place at the location of the file pointer. When a file is opened, the file pointer is set at the beginning of the file. When you read or write data to the file, the file pointer moves forward to the next data item. For example, if you read an `int` value using `readInt()`, the JVM reads `4` bytes from the file pointer, and now the file pointer is `4` bytes ahead of the previous location, as shown in Figure 19.17.

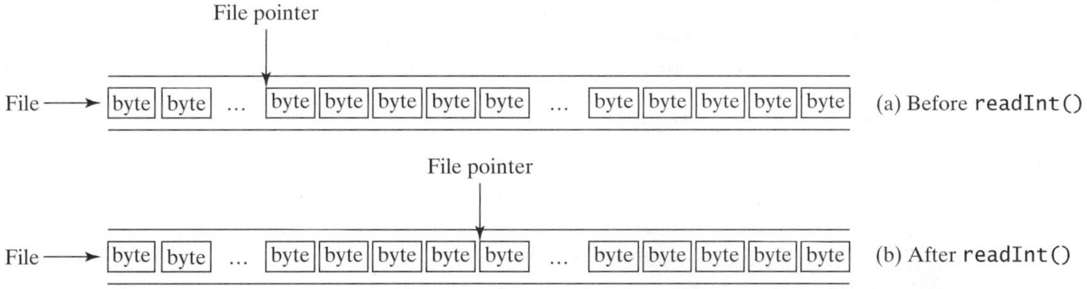
File pointer
File
byte byte ... byte byte byte byte byte ... byte byte byte byte byte
(a) Before readInt()
File pointer
File
byte byte ... byte byte byte byte byte ... byte byte byte byte byte
(b) After readInt()

FIGURE 19.17 After an `int` value is read, the file pointer is moved 4 bytes ahead.

For a `RandomAccessFile raf`, you can use the `raf.seek(position)` method to move the file pointer to a specified position. `raf.seek(0)` moves it to the beginning of the file, and `raf.seek(raf.length())` moves it to the end of the file. Listing 19.8 demonstrates `RandomAccessFile`. A large case study of using `RandomAccessFile` to organize an address book is given in Supplement VII.B.

LISTING 19.8 TestRandomAccessFile.java

```
import java.io.*;

public class TestRandomAccessFile {
  public static void main(String[] args) throws IOException {
    // Create a random-access file
    RandomAccessFile inout = new RandomAccessFile("inout.dat", "rw");

    // Clear the file to destroy the old contents, if any
    inout.setLength(0);

    // Write new integers to the file
    for (int i = 0; i < 200; i++)
      inout.writeInt(i);

    // Display the current length of the file
    System.out.println("Current file length is " + inout.length());

```

RandomAccessFile

empty file

write

move pointer
read

```
18     // Retrieve the first number
19     inout.seek(0); // Move the file pointer to the beginning
20     System.out.println("The first number is " + inout.readInt());
21
22     // Retrieve the second number
23     inout.seek(1 * 4); // Move the file pointer to the second number
24     System.out.println("The second number is " + inout.readInt());
25
26     // Retrieve the tenth number
27     inout.seek(9 * 4); // Move the file pointer to the tenth number
28     System.out.println("The tenth number is " + inout.readInt());
29
30     // Modify the eleventh number
31     inout.writeInt(555);
32
33     // Append a new number
34     inout.seek(inout.length()); // Move the file pointer to the end
35     inout.writeInt(999);
36
37     // Display the new length
38     System.out.println("The new length is " + inout.length());
39
40     // Retrieve the new eleventh number
41     inout.seek(10 * 4); // Move the file pointer to the next number
42     System.out.println("The eleventh number is " + inout.readInt());
43
44     inout.close();
45   }
46 }
```

close file

```
Current file length is 800
The first number is 0
The second number is 1
The tenth number is 9
The new length is 804
The eleventh number is 555
```

A `RandomAccessFile` is created for the file named **inout.dat** with mode "`rw`" to allow both read and write operations in line 6.

`inout.setLength(0)` sets the length to `0` in line 9. This, in effect, destroys the old contents of the file.

The `for` loop writes `200` `int` values from `0` to `199` into the file in lines 12–13. Since each `int` value takes `4` bytes, the total length of the file returned from `inout.length()` is now `800` (line 16), as shown in sample output.

Invoking `inout.seek(0)` in line 19 sets the file pointer to the beginning of the file. `inout.readInt()` reads the first value in line 20 and moves the file pointer to the next number. The second number is read in line 23.

`inout.seek(9 * 4)` (line 27) moves the file pointer to the tenth number. `inout.readInt()` reads the tenth number and moves the file pointer to the eleventh number in line 28. `inout.write(555)` writes a new eleventh number at the current position (line 31). The previous eleventh number is destroyed.

`inout.seek(inout.length())` moves the file pointer to the end of the file (line 34). `inout.writeInt(999)` writes a `999` to the file. Now the length of the file is increased by `4`, so `inout.length()` returns `804` (line 38).

`inout.seek(10 * 4)` moves the file pointer to the eleventh number in line 41. The new eleventh number, `555`, is displayed in line 42.

Key Terms

binary I/O 650
deserialization 664
file pointer 667
random-access file 667
sequential-access file 666
serialization 664
stream 650
text I/O 650

Chapter Summary

1. I/O can be classified into text I/O and binary I/O. Text I/O interprets data in sequences of characters. Binary I/O interprets data as raw binary values. How text is stored in a file depends on the encoding scheme for the file. Java automatically performs encoding and decoding for text I/O.

2. The `InputStream` and `OutputStream` classes are the roots of all binary I/O classes. `FileInputStream/FileOutputStream` associates a file for binary input/output. `BufferedInputStream/BufferedOutputStream` can be used to wrap on any binary I/O stream to improve performance. `DataInputStream/DataOutputStream` can be used to read/write primitive values and strings.

3. `ObjectInputStream/ObjectOutputStream` can be used to read/write objects in addition to primitive values and strings. To enable object serialization, the object's defining class must implement the `java.io.Serializable` marker interface.

4. The `RandomAccessFile` class enables you to read and write data to a file. You can open a file with the "`r`" mode to indicate that it is read-only, or with the "`rw`" mode to indicate that it is updateable. Since the `RandomAccessFile` class implements `DataInput` and `DataOutput` interfaces, many methods in `RandomAccessFile` are the same as those in `DataInputStream` and `DataOutputStream`.

Review Questions

Sections 19.1–19.2

19.1 What is a text file, and what is a binary file? Can you view a text file or a binary file using a text editor?

19.2 How do you read or write data in Java? What is a stream?

Section 19.3

19.3 What are the differences between text I/O and binary I/O?

19.4 How is a Java character represented in the memory, and how is a character represented in a text file?

19.5 If you write string "`ABC`" to an ASCII text file, what values are stored in the file?

19.6 If you write string "`100`" to an ASCII text file, what values are stored in the file? If you write a numeric byte-type value `100` using binary I/O, what values are stored in the file?

19.7 What is the encoding scheme for representing a character in a Java program? By default, what is the encoding scheme for a text file on Windows?

Section 19.4

19.8 Why do you have to declare to throw `IOException` in the method or use a try-catch block to handle `IOException` for Java IO programs?

19.9 Why should you always close streams?

19.10 InputStream reads bytes. Why does the read() method return an int instead of a byte? Find the abstract methods in InputStream and OutputStream.

19.11 Does FileInputStream/FileOutputStream introduce any new methods? How do you create a FileInputStream/FileOutputStream?

19.12 What will happen if you attempt to create an input stream on a nonexistent file? What will happen if you attempt to create an output stream on an existing file? Can you append data to an existing file?

19.13 How do you append data to an existing text file using java.io.PrintWriter?

19.14 Suppose a file contains an unspecified number of double values. Theses values were written to the file using the writeDouble method using a DataOutputStream. How do you write a program to read all these values? How do you detect the end of file?

19.15 What is written to a file using writeByte(91) on a FileOutputStream?

19.16 How do you check the end of a file in a binary input stream (FileInputStream, DataInputStream)?

19.17 What is wrong in the following code?

```
import java.io.*;

public class Test {
  public static void main(String[] args) {
    try {
      FileInputStream fis = new FileInputStream("test.dat");
    }
    catch (IOException ex) {
      ex.printStackTrace();
    }
    catch (FileNotFoundException ex) {
      ex.printStackTrace();
    }
  }
}
```

19.18 Suppose you run the program on Windows using the default ASCII encoding. After the program is finished, how many bytes are in the file **t.txt**? Show the contents of each byte.

```
public class Test {
  public static void main(String[] args)
      throws java.io.IOException {
    java.io.PrintWriter output =
      new java.io.PrintWriter("t.txt");
    output.printf("%s", "1234");
    output.printf("%s", "5678");
    output.close();
  }
}
```

19.19 After the program is finished, how many bytes are in the file **t.dat**? Show the contents of each byte.

```
import java.io.*;

public class Test {
  public static void main(String[] args) throws IOException {
    DataOutputStream output = new DataOutputStream(
```

```
      new FileOutputStream("t.dat"));
    output.writeInt(1234);
    output.writeInt(5678);
    output.close();
  }
}
```

19.20 For each of the following statements on a DataOutputStream out, how many bytes are sent to the output?

```
output.writeChar('A');
output.writeChars("BC");
output.writeUTF("DEF");
```

19.21 What are the advantages of using buffered streams? Are the following statements correct?

```
BufferedInputStream input1 =
  new BufferedInputStream(new FileInputStream("t.dat"));

DataInputStream input2 = new DataInputStream(
  new BufferedInputStream(new FileInputStream("t.dat")));

ObjectInputStream input3 = new ObjectInputStream(
  new BufferedInputStream(new FileInputStream("t.dat")));
```

Section 19.6

19.22 What types of objects can be stored using the ObjectOutputStream? What is the method for writing an object? What is the method for reading an object? What is the return type of the method that reads an object from ObjectInputStream?

19.23 If you serialize two objects of the same type, will they take the same amount of space? If not, give an example.

19.24 Is it true that any instance of java.io.Serializable can be successfully serialized? Are the static variables in an object serialized? How do you mark an instance variable not to be serialized?

19.25 Can you write an array to an ObjectOutputStream?

19.26 Is it true that DataInputStream/DataOutputStream can always be replaced by ObjectInputStream/ObjectOutputStream?

19.27 What will happen when you attempt to run the following code?

```
import java.io.*;

public class Test {
  public static void main(String[] args) throws IOException {
    ObjectOutputStream output =
      new ObjectOutputStream(new FileOutputStream("object.dat"));

    output.writeObject(new A());
  }
}

class A implements Serializable {
  B b = new B();
}

class B {
}
```

Section 19.7

19.28 Can `RandomAccessFile` streams read and write a data file created by `DataOutputStream`? Can `RandomAccessFile` streams read and write objects?

19.29 Create a `RandomAccessFile` stream for the file **address.dat** to allow the updating of student information in the file. Create a `DataOutputStream` for the file **address.dat**. Explain the differences between these two statements.

19.30 What happens if the file **test.dat** does not exist when you attempt to compile and run the following code?

```
import java.io.*;

public class Test {
  public static void main(String[] args) {
    try {
      RandomAccessFile raf =
        new RandomAccessFile("test.dat", "r");
      int i = raf.readInt();
    }
    catch (IOException ex) {
      System.out.println("IO exception");
    }
  }
}
```

Programming Exercises

Section 19.3

19.1* (*Creating a text file*) Write a program to create a file named **Exercise19_1.txt** if it does not exist. Append new data to it. Write 100 integers created randomly into the file using text I/O. Integers are separated by a space.

Section 19.4

19.2* (*Creating a binary data file*) Write a program to create a file named **Exercise19_2.dat** if it does not exist. Append new data to it. Write 100 integers created randomly into the file using binary I/O.

19.3* (*Summing all the integers in a binary data file*) Suppose a binary data file named **Exercise19_3.dat** has been created using `writeInt(int)` in `DataOutputStream`. The file contains an unspecified number of integers. Write a program to find the sum of integers.

19.4* (*Converting a text file into UTF*) Write a program that reads lines of characters from a text and writes each line as a UTF-8 string into a binary file. Display the sizes of the text file and the binary file. Use the following command to run the program:

```
java Exercise19_4 Welcome.java Welcome.utf
```

Section 19.6

19.5* (*Storing objects and arrays into a file*) Write a program that stores an array of five `int` values `1`, `2`, `3`, `4` and `5`, a `Date` object for current time, and a `double` value `5.5` into the file named **Exercise19_5.dat**.

19.6* (*Storing* `Loan` *objects*) The `Loan` class, in Listing 10.2, does not implement `Serializable`. Rewrite the `Loan` class to implement `Serializable`. Write a program that creates five `Loan` objects and stores them in a file named **Exercise19_6.dat**.

19.7* (*Restoring objects from a file*) Suppose a file named **Exercise19_7.dat** has been created using the `ObjectOutputStream`. The file contains `Loan` objects. The `Loan` class, in Listing 10.2, does not implement `Serializable`. Rewrite the `Loan` class to implement `Serializable`. Write a program that reads the `Loan` objects from the file and computes the total loan amount. Suppose you don't know how many `Loan` objects are in the file. Use `EOFException` to end the loop.

Section 19.7

19.8* (*Updating count*) Suppose you want to track how many times a program has been executed. You may store an `int` to count the file. Increase the count by `1` each time this program is executed. Let the program be **Exercise19_8** and store the count in **Exercise19_8.dat**.

19.9*** (*Address book*) Supplement VII.B gives a case study of using random-access files for creating and manipulating an address book. Modify the case study by adding an *Update* button, as shown in Figure 19.18, to enable the user to modify the address that is being displayed.

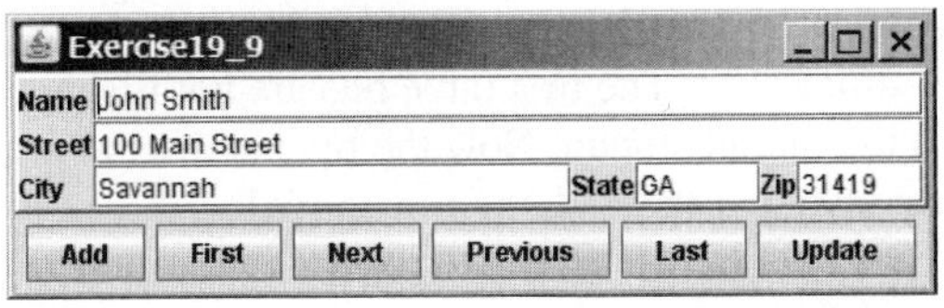
Exercise19_9
Name John Smith
Street 100 Main Street
City Savannah
State GA
Zip 31419
Add
First
Next
Previous
Last
Update

FIGURE 19.18 The application can store, retrieve, and update addresses from a file.

Comprehensive

19.10* (*Splitting files*) Suppose you wish to back up a huge file (e.g., a 10-GB AVI file) to a CD-R. You can achieve it by splitting the file into smaller pieces and backing up these pieces separately. Write a utility program that splits a large file into smaller ones using the following command:

Video Note
Split a large file

```
java Exercise19_10 SourceFile numberOfPieces
```

The command creates files SourceFile.1, SourceFile.2, . . . , SourceFile.n, where `n` is `numberOfPieces` and the output files are about the same size.

19.11** (*Splitting files GUI*) Rewrite Exercise 19.10 with a GUI, as shown in Figure 19.19(a).

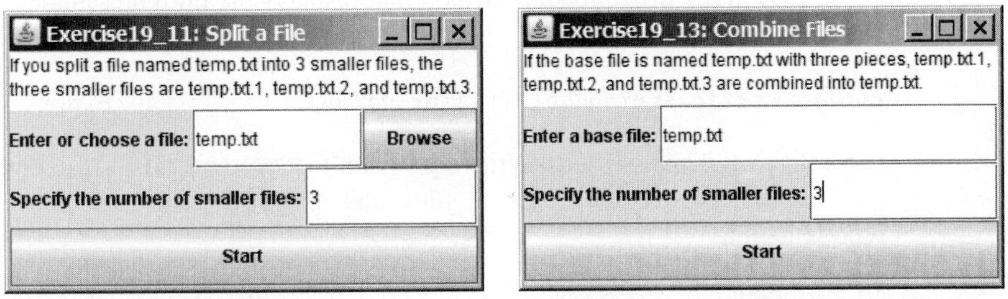
Exercise19_11: Split a File
If you split a file named temp.txt into 3 smaller files, the three smaller files are temp.txt.1, temp.txt.2, and temp.txt.3.
Enter or choose a file: temp.txt
Browse
Specify the number of smaller files: 3
Start
Exercise19_13: Combine Files
If the base file is named temp.txt with three pieces, temp.txt.1, temp.txt.2, and temp.txt.3 are combined into temp.txt.
Enter a base file: temp.txt
Specify the number of smaller files: 3
Start

(a) (b)

FIGURE 19.19 (a) The program splits a file. (b) The program combines files into a new file.

19.12* (*Combining files*) Write a utility program that combines the files together into a new file using the following command:

java Exercise19_12 SourceFile1 . . . SoureFilen TargetFile

The command combines SourceFile1, . . . , and SourceFilen into TargetFile.

19.13* (*Combining files GUI*) Rewrite Exercise 19.12 with a GUI, as shown in Figure 19.19(b).

19.14 (*Encrypting files*) Encode the file by adding `5` to every byte in the file. Write a program that prompts the user to enter an input file name and an output file name and saves the encrypted version of the input file to the output file.

19.15 (*Decrypting files*) Suppose a file is encrypted using the scheme in Exercise 19.14. Write a program to decode an encrypted file. Your program should prompt the user to enter an input file name and an output file name and should save the unencrypted version of the input file to the output file.

19.16 (*Frequency of characters*) Write a program that prompts the user to enter the name of an ASCII text file and display the frequency of the characters in the file.

19.17** (*`BitOutputStream`*) Implement a class named `BitOutputStream`, as shown in Figure 19.20, for writing bits to an output stream. The `writeBit(char bit)` method stores the bit in a byte variable. When you create a `BitOutputStream`, the byte is empty. After invoking `writeBit('1')`, the byte becomes `00000001`. After invoking `writeBit("0101")`, the byte becomes `00010101`. The first three bits are not filled yet. When a byte is full, it is sent to the output stream. Now the byte is reset to empty. You must close the stream by invoking the `close()` method. If the byte is not empty and not full, the `close()` method first fills the zeros to make a full `8` bits in the byte, and then output the byte and close the stream. For a hint, see Exercise 4.46. Write a test program that sends the bits `010000100100001001101` to the file named **Exercise19_17.dat**.

BitOutputStream	
+BitOutputStream(file: File)	Creates a `BitOutputStream` to write bit to the file.
+writeBit(char bit): void	Write a bit '0' or '1' to the output stream.
+writeBit(String bit): void	Write a string of bits to the output stream.
+close(): void	This method must be invoked to close the stream.

FIGURE 19.20 `BitOutputStream` outputs a stream of bits to a file.

19.18* (*View bits*) Write the following method that displays the bit representation for the last byte in an integer:

```
public static String getBits(int value)
```

For a hint, see Exercise 4.46. Write a program that prompts the user to enter a file name, reads bytes from a file, and displays each byte's binary representation.

19.19* (*View hex*) Write a program that prompts the user to enter a file name, reads bytes from a file, and displays each byte's hex representation. (*Hint*: You may first convert the byte value into an 8-bit string, then convert the bit string into a two-digit hex string.)

19.20** (*Binary Editor*) Write a GUI application that lets the user enter a file name in the text field and press the *Enter* key to display its binary representation in a text area. The user can also modify the binary code and save it back to the file, as shown in Figure 19.21(a).

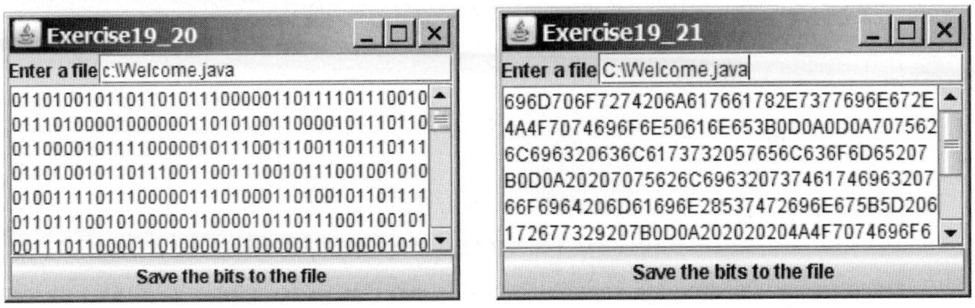
Exercise19_20
Enter a file
c:\Welcome.java
Save the bits to the file
Exercise19_21
Enter a file
C:\Welcome.java
Save the bits to the file

(a) (b)

FIGURE 19.21 The exercises enable the user to manipulate the contents of the file in binary and hex.

19.21** (*Hex Editor*) Write a GUI application that lets the user enter a file name in the text field and press the *Enter* key to display its hex representation in a text area. The user can also modify the hex code and save it back to the file, as shown in Figure 19.21(b).

CHAPTER 20

RECURSION

Objectives

- To describe what a recursive method is and the benefits of using recursion (§20.1).
- To develop recursive methods for recursive mathematical functions (§§20.2–20.3).
- To explain how recursive method calls are handled in a call stack (§§20.2–20.3).
- To use an overloaded helper method to derive a recursive method (§20.5).
- To solve selection sort using recursion (§20.5.1).
- To solve binary search using recursion (§20.5.2).
- To get the directory size using recursion (§20.6).
- To solve the Towers of Hanoi problem using recursion (§20.7).
- To draw fractals using recursion (§20.8).
- To solve the Eight Queens problem using recursion (§20.9).
- To discover the relationship and difference between recursion and iteration (§20.10).
- To know tail-recursive methods and why they are desirable (§20.11).

20.1 Introduction

search word problem

Suppose you want to find all the files under a directory that contain a particular word. How do you solve this problem? There are several ways to do so. An intuitive and effective solution is to use recursion by searching the files in the subdirectories recursively.

Eight Queens problem

The classic Eight Queens puzzle is to place eight queens on a chessboard such that no two can attack each other (i.e., no two queens are on the same row, same column, or same diagonal), as shown in Figure 20.1. How do you write a program to solve this problem? A good approach is to use recursion.

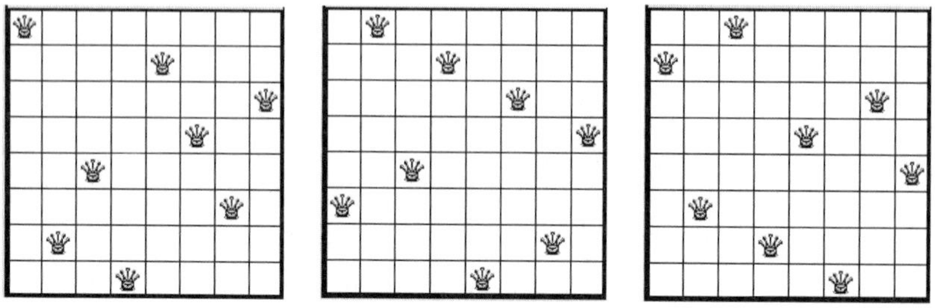

FIGURE 20.1 The Eight Queens problem can be solved using recursion.

recursive method

To use recursion is to program using *recursive methods*—methods that directly or indirectly invoke themselves. Recursion is a useful programming technique. In some cases, it enables you to develop a natural, straightforward, simple solution to an otherwise difficult problem. This chapter introduces the concepts and techniques of recursive programming and illustrates by examples how to "think recursively."

20.2 Problem: Computing Factorials

Many mathematical functions are defined using recursion. We begin with a simple example. The factorial of a number `n` can be recursively defined as follows:

```
0! = 1;
n! = n × (n - 1) × ... × 2 × 1 = n × (n - 1)!; n > 0
```

How do you find `n!` for a given `n`? To find `1!` is easy, because you know that `0!` is `1`, and `1!` is `1` × `0!`. Assuming that you know `(n - 1)!`, you can obtain `n!` immediately using `n` × `(n - 1)!`. Thus, the problem of computing `n!` is reduced to computing `(n - 1)!`. When computing `(n - 1)!`, you can apply the same idea recursively until `n` is reduced to `0`.

Let `factorial(n)` be the method for computing `n!`. If you call the method with `n = 0`, it immediately returns the result. The method knows how to solve the simplest case, which is referred to as the *base case* or the *stopping condition*. If you call the method with `n > 0`, it reduces the problem into a subproblem for computing the factorial of `n - 1`. The subproblem is essentially the same as the original problem, but is simpler or smaller. Because the subproblem has the same property as the original, you can call the method with a different argument, which is referred to as a *recursive call*.

base case or stopping condition

recursive call

The recursive algorithm for computing `factorial(n)` can be simply described as follows:

```
if (n == 0)
  return 1;
else
  return n * factorial(n - 1);
```

A recursive call can result in many more recursive calls, because the method keeps on dividing a subproblem into new subproblems. For a recursive method to terminate, the problem must eventually be reduced to a stopping case, at which point the method returns a result to its caller. The caller then performs a computation and returns the result to its own caller. This process continues until the result is passed back to the original caller. The original problem can now be solved by multiplying `n` by the result of `factorial(n - 1)`.

Listing 20.1 gives a complete program that prompts the user to enter a nonnegative integer and displays the factorial for the number.

LISTING 20.1 ComputeFactorial.java

```
1 import java.util.Scanner;
2
3 public class ComputeFactorial {
4   /** Main method */
5   public static void main(String[] args) {
6     // Create a Scanner
7     Scanner input = new Scanner(System.in);
8     System.out.print("Enter a nonnegative integer: ");
9     int n = input.nextInt();
10
11     // Display factorial
12     System.out.println("Factorial of " + n + " is " + factorial(n));
13   }
14
15   /** Return the factorial for a specified number */
16   public static long factorial(int n) {
17     if (n == 0) // Base case
18       return 1;
19     else
20       return n * factorial(n - 1); // Recursive call
21   }
22 }
```

base case

recursion

```
Enter a nonnegative integer: 4 ↵Enter
Factorial of 4 is 24
```

```
Enter a nonnegative integer: 10 ↵Enter
Factorial of 10 is 3628800
```

The `factorial` method (lines 16–21) is essentially a direct translation of the recursive mathematical definition for the factorial into Java code. The call to `factorial` is recursive because it calls itself. The parameter passed to `factorial` is decremented until it reaches the base case of `0`.

Figure 20.2 illustrates the execution of the recursive calls, starting with `n = 4`. The use of stack space for recursive calls is shown in Figure 20.3.

Caution

If recursion does not reduce the problem in a manner that allows it to eventually converge into the base case, infinite recursion can occur. For example, suppose you mistakenly write the `factorial` method as follows:

infinite recursion

```
public static long factorial(int n) {
  return n * factorial(n - 1);
}
```

The method runs infinitely and causes a `StackOverflowError`.

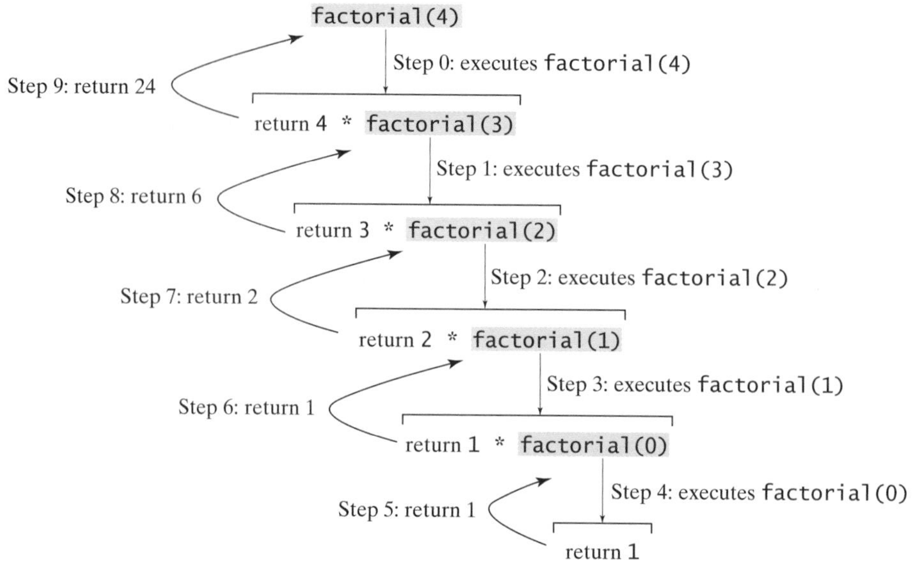
factorial(4)
Step 0: executes factorial(4)
Step 9: return 24
return 4 * factorial(3)
Step 1: executes factorial(3)
Step 8: return 6
return 3 * factorial(2)
Step 2: executes factorial(2)
Step 7: return 2
return 2 * factorial(1)
Step 3: executes factorial(1)
Step 6: return 1
return 1 * factorial(0)
Step 4: executes factorial(0)
Step 5: return 1
return 1

FIGURE 20.2 Invoking `factorial(4)` spawns recursive calls to `factorial`.

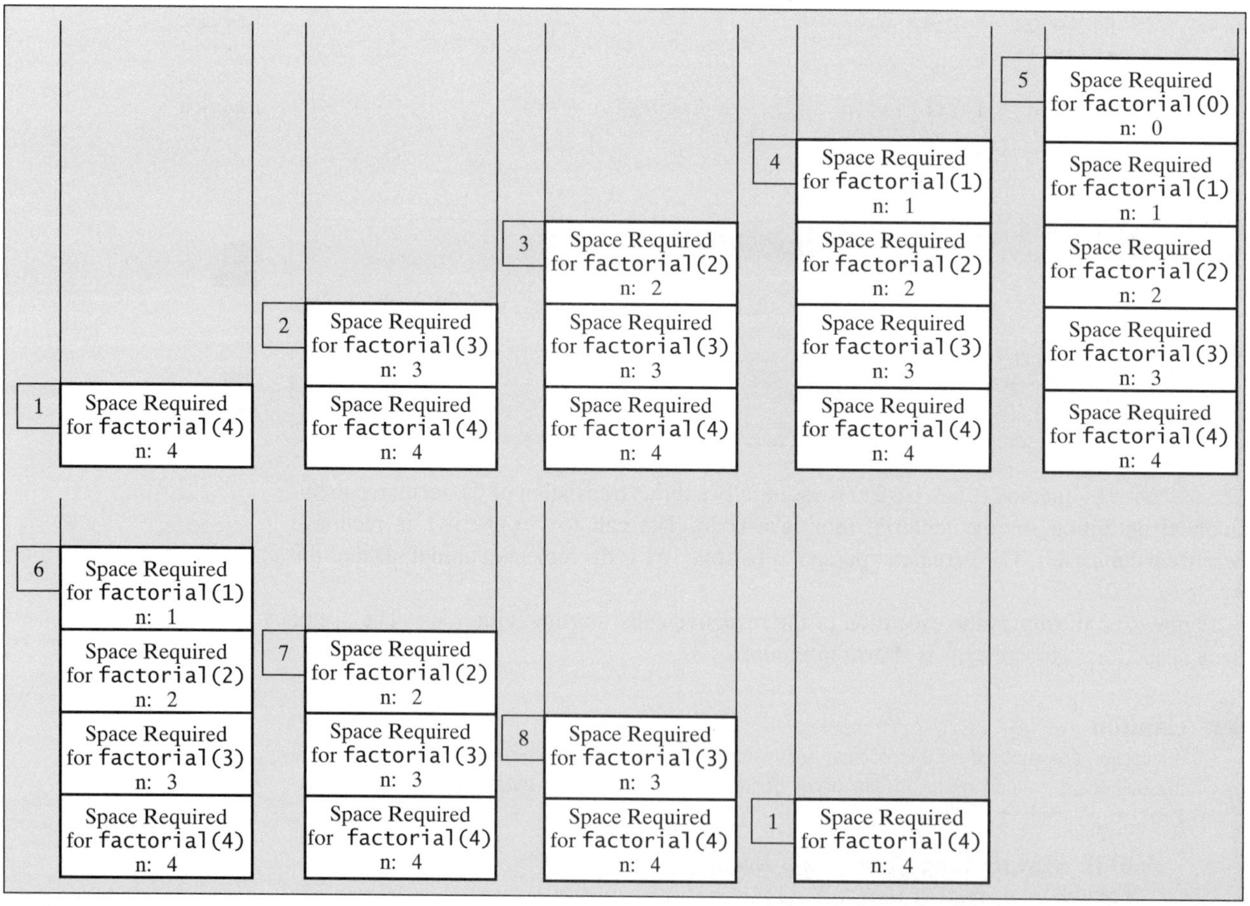
1
Space Required for factorial(4) n: 4
2
Space Required for factorial(3) n: 3
Space Required for factorial(4) n: 4
3
Space Required for factorial(2) n: 2
Space Required for factorial(3) n: 3
Space Required for factorial(4) n: 4
4
Space Required for factorial(1) n: 1
Space Required for factorial(2) n: 2
Space Required for factorial(3) n: 3
Space Required for factorial(4) n: 4
5
Space Required for factorial(0) n: 0
Space Required for factorial(1) n: 1
Space Required for factorial(2) n: 2
Space Required for factorial(3) n: 3
Space Required for factorial(4) n: 4
6
Space Required for factorial(1) n: 1
Space Required for factorial(2) n: 2
Space Required for factorial(3) n: 3
Space Required for factorial(4) n: 4
7
Space Required for factorial(2) n: 2
Space Required for factorial(3) n: 3
Space Required for factorial(4) n: 4
8
Space Required for factorial(3) n: 3
Space Required for factorial(4) n: 4
1
Space Required for factorial(4) n: 4

FIGURE 20.3 When `factorial(4)` is being executed, the `factorial` method is called recursively, causing stack space to dynamically change.

Pedagogical Note

It is simpler and more efficient to implement the `factorial` method using a loop. However, we use the recursive `factorial` method here to demonstrate the concept of recursion. Later in this chapter, we will present some problems that are inherently recursive and are difficult to solve without using recursion.

20.3 Problem: Computing Fibonacci Numbers

The `factorial` method in the preceding section could easily be rewritten without using recursion. In some cases, however, using recursion enables you to give a natural, straightforward, simple solution to a program that would otherwise be difficult to solve. Consider the well-known Fibonacci-series problem:

The series:	0	1	1	2	3	5	8	13	21	34	55	89	...
indices:	0	1	2	3	4	5	6	7	8	9	10	11	

The Fibonacci series begins with `0` and `1`, and each subsequent number is the sum of the preceding two. The series can be recursively defined as follows:

```
fib(0) = 0;
fib(1) = 1;
fib(index) = fib(index - 2) + fib(index - 1); index >= 2
```

The Fibonacci series was named for Leonardo Fibonacci, a medieval mathematician, who originated it to model the growth of the rabbit population. It can be applied in numeric optimization and in various other areas.

How do you find `fib(index)` for a given `index`? It is easy to find `fib(2)`, because you know `fib(0)` and `fib(1)`. Assuming that you know `fib(index - 2)` and `fib(index - 1)`, you can obtain `fib(index)` immediately. Thus, the problem of computing `fib(index)` is reduced to computing `fib(index - 2)` and `fib(index - 1)`. When doing so, you apply the idea recursively until `index` is reduced to `0` or `1`.

The base case is `index = 0` or `index = 1`. If you call the method with `index = 0` or `index = 1`, it immediately returns the result. If you call the method with `index >= 2`, it divides the problem into two subproblems for computing `fib(index - 1)` and `fib(index - 2)` using recursive calls. The recursive algorithm for computing `fib(index)` can be simply described as follows:

```
if (index == 0)
  return 0;
else if (index == 1)
  return 1;
else
  return fib(index - 1) + fib(index - 2);
```

Listing 20.2 gives a complete program that prompts the user to enter an index and computes the Fibonacci number for the index.

LISTING 20.2 ComputeFibonacci.java

```
import java.util.Scanner;

public class ComputeFibonacci {
  /** Main method */
  public static void main(String args[]) {
    // Create a Scanner
    Scanner input = new Scanner(System.in);
    System.out.print("Enter an index for the Fibonacci number: ");
```

```
    int index = input.nextInt();

    // Find and display the Fibonacci number
    System.out.println(
      "Fibonacci number at index " + index + " is " + fib(index));
  }

  /** The method for finding the Fibonacci number */
  public static long fib(long index) {
    if (index == 0) // Base case
      return 0;
    else if (index == 1) // Base case
      return 1;
    else  // Reduction and recursive calls
      return fib(index - 1) + fib(index - 2);
  }
}
```

base case

base case

recursion

```
Enter an index for the Fibonacci number: 1
Fibonacci number at index 1 is 1
```

```
Enter an index for the Fibonacci number: 6 ↵Enter
Fibonacci number at index 6 is 8
```

```
Enter an index for the Fibonacci number: 7 ↵Enter
Fibonacci number at index 7 is 13
```

The program does not show the considerable amount of work done behind the scenes by the computer. Figure 20.4, however, shows successive recursive calls for evaluating `fib(4)`. The original method, `fib(4)`, makes two recursive calls, `fib(3)` and `fib(2)`, and then returns `fib(3) + fib(2)`. But in what order are these methods called? In Java, operands are evaluated from left to right. `fib(2)` is called after `fib(3)` is completely evaluated. The labels in Figure 20.4 show the order in which methods are called.

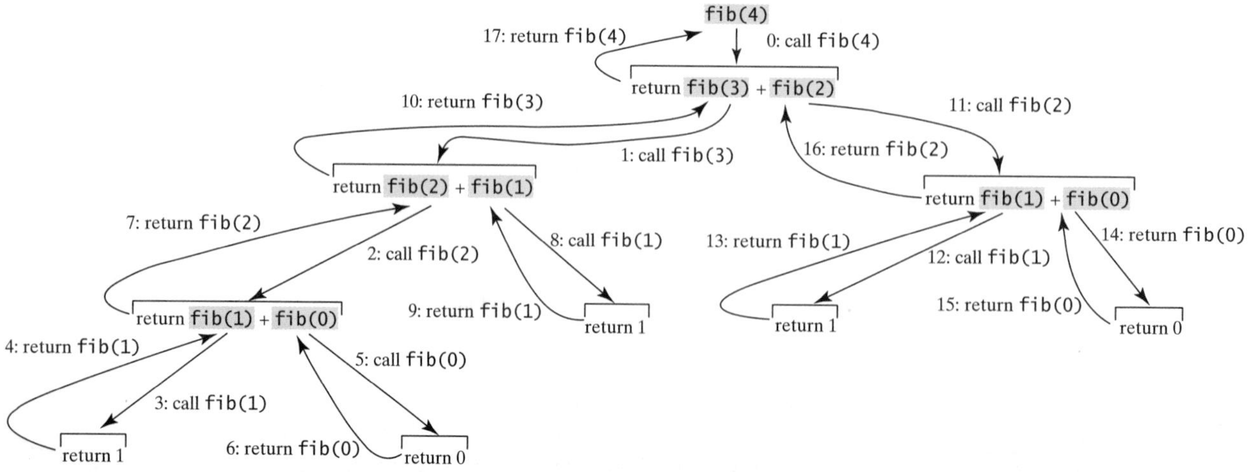

fib(4)
0: call fib(4)
17: return fib(4)
return fib(3) + fib(2)
10: return fib(3)
1: call fib(3)
11: call fib(2)
16: return fib(2)
return fib(2) + fib(1)
return fib(1) + fib(0)
7: return fib(2)
2: call fib(2)
8: call fib(1)
9: return fib(1)
return 1
13: return fib(1)
12: call fib(1)
14: return fib(0)
15: return fib(0)
return 1
return 0
return fib(1) + fib(0)
4: return fib(1)
3: call fib(1)
5: call fib(0)
6: return fib(0)
return 1
return 0

FIGURE 20.4 Invoking `fib(4)` spawns recursive calls to `fib`.

As shown in Figure 20.4, there are many duplicated recursive calls. For instance, `fib(2)` is called twice, `fib(1)` three times, and `fib(0)` twice. In general, computing `fib(index)` requires roughly twice as many recursive calls as does computing `fib(index - 1)`. As you try larger index values, the number of calls substantially increases.

Besides the large number of recursive calls, the computer requires more time and space to run recursive methods.

Pedagogical Note

The recursive implementation of the `fib` method is very simple and straightforward, but not efficient. See Exercise 20.2 for an efficient solution using loops. Though it is not practical, the recursive `fib` method is a good example of how to write recursive methods.

20.4 Problem Solving Using Recursion

recursion characteristics

The preceding sections presented two classic recursion examples. All recursive methods have the following characteristics:

if-else

- The method is implemented using an `if-else` or a `switch` statement that leads to different cases.

base cases

- One or more base cases (the simplest case) are used to stop recursion.

reduction

- Every recursive call reduces the original problem, bringing it increasingly closer to a base case until it becomes that case.

In general, to solve a problem using recursion, you break it into subproblems. Each subproblem is almost the same as the original problem but smaller in size. You can apply the same approach to each subproblem to solve it recursively.

Let us consider the simple problem of printing a message `n` times. You can break the problem into two subproblems: one is to print the message one time and the other is to print it `n - 1` times. The second problem is the same as the original problem but smaller in size. The base case for the problem is `n == 0`. You can solve this problem using recursion as follows:

recursive call

```
public static void nPrintln(String message, int times) {
  if (times >= 1) {
    System.out.println(message);
    nPrintln(message, times - 1);
  } // The base case is times == 0
}
```

Note that the `fib` method in the preceding example returns a value to its caller, but the `nPrintln` method is `void` and does not.

think recursively

If you *think recursively*, you can use recursion to solve many of the problems presented in earlier chapters of this book. Consider the palindrome problem in Listing 9.1. Recall that a string is a palindrome if it reads the same from the left and from the right. For example, mom and dad are palindromes, but uncle and aunt are not. The problem of checking whether a string is a palindrome can be divided into two subproblems:

- Check whether the first character and the last character of the string are equal.
- Ignore the two end characters and check whether the rest of the substring is a palindrome.

The second subproblem is the same as the original problem but smaller in size. There are two base cases: (1) the two end characters are not same; (2) the string size is `0` or `1`. In case 1, the string is not a palindrome; and in case 2, the string is a palindrome. The recursive method for this problem can be implemented as shown in Listing 20.3.

LISTING 20.3 RecursivePalindromeUsingSubstring.java

method header
base case
base case
recursive call

```
1 public class RecursivePalindromeUsingSubstring {
2   public static boolean isPalindrome(String s) {
3     if (s.length() <= 1) // Base case
4       return true;
5     else if (s.charAt(0) != s.charAt(s.length() - 1)) // Base case
6       return false;
7     else
8       return isPalindrome(s.substring(1, s.length() - 1));
9   }
10
11   public static void main(String[] args) {
12     System.out.println("Is moon a palindrome? "
13       + isPalindrome("moon"));
14     System.out.println("Is noon a palindrome? "
15       + isPalindrome("noon"));
16     System.out.println("Is a a palindrome? " + isPalindrome("a"));
17     System.out.println("Is aba a palindrome? " +
18       isPalindrome("aba"));
19     System.out.println("Is ab a palindrome? " + isPalindrome("ab"));
20   }
21 }
```

```
Is moon a palindrome? false
Is noon a palindrome? true
Is a a palindrome? true
Is aba a palindrome? true
Is ab a palindrome? false
```

The `substring` method in line 8 creates a new string that is the same as the original string except without the first and last characters. Checking whether a string is a palindrome is equivalent to checking whether the substring is a palindrome if the two end characters in the original string are the same.

20.5 Recursive Helper Methods

The preceding recursive `isPalindrome` method is not efficient, because it creates a new string for every recursive call. To avoid creating new strings, you can use the low and high indices to indicate the range of the substring. These two indices must be passed to the recursive method. Since the original method is `isPalindrome(String s)`, you have to create a new method `isPalindrome(String s, int low, int high)` to accept additional information on the string, as shown in Listing 20.4.

LISTING 20.4 RecursivePalindrome.java

helper method
base case
base case

```
public class RecursivePalindrome {
  public static boolean isPalindrome(String s) {
    return isPalindrome(s, 0, s.length() - 1);
  }

  public static boolean isPalindrome(String s, int low, int high) {
    if (high <= low) // Base case
      return true;
    else if (s.charAt(low) != s.charAt(high)) // Base case
      return false;
```

```
    else
      return isPalindrome(s, low + 1, high - 1);
  }

  public static void main(String[] args) {
    System.out.println("Is moon a palindrome? "
      + isPalindrome("moon"));
    System.out.println("Is noon a palindrome? "
      + isPalindrome("noon"));
    System.out.println("Is a a palindrome? " + isPalindrome("a"));
    System.out.println("Is aba a palindrome? " + isPalindrome("aba"));
    System.out.println("Is ab a palindrome? " + isPalindrome("ab"));
  }
}
```

Two overloaded `isPalindrome` methods are defined. The first, `isPalindrome(String s)`, checks whether a string is a palindrome, and the second, `isPalindrome(String s, int low, int high)`, checks whether a substring `s(low..high)` is a palindrome. The first method passes the string `s` with `low = 0` and `high = s.length() - 1` to the second method. The second method can be invoked recursively to check a palindrome in an ever-shrinking substring. It is a common design technique in recursive programming to define a second method that receives additional parameters. Such a method is known as a *recursive helper method*.

recursive helper method

Helper methods are very useful in designing recursive solutions for problems involving strings and arrays. The sections that follow give two more examples.

20.5.1 Selection Sort

Selection sort was introduced in §6.10.1, "Selection Sort." Recall that it finds the smallest number in the list and places it first. It then finds the smallest number remaining and places it after the first, and so on until the remaining list contains only a single number. The problem can be divided into two subproblems:

- Find the smallest number in the list and swap it with the first number.
- Ignore the first number and sort the remaining smaller list recursively.

The base case is that the list contains only one number. Listing 20.5 gives the recursive sort method.

LISTING 20.5 RecursiveSelectionSort.java

```
public class RecursiveSelectionSort {
  public static void sort(double[] list) {
    sort(list, 0, list.length - 1); // Sort the entire list
  }

  public static void sort(double[] list, int low, int high) {
    if (low < high) {
      // Find the smallest number and its index in list(low .. high)
      int indexOfMin = low;
      double min = list[low];
      for (int i = low + 1; i <= high; i++) {
        if (list[i] < min) {
          min = list[i];
          indexOfMin = i;
        }
      }

      // Swap the smallest in list(low .. high) with list(low)
```

helper method

base case

recursive call

```
      list[indexOfMin] = list[low];
      list[low] = min;

      // Sort the remaining list(low+1 .. high)
      sort(list, low + 1, high);
    }
  }
}
```

Two overloaded `sort` methods are defined. The first method, `sort(double[] list)`, sorts an array in `list[0..list.length - 1]` and the second method `sort(double[] list, int low, int high)` sorts an array in `list[low..high]`. The second method can be invoked recursively to sort an ever-shrinking subarray.

20.5.2 Binary Search

Video Note
Binary search

Binary search was introduced in §6.9.2. For binary search to work, the elements in the array must already be ordered. The binary search first compares the key with the element in the middle of the array. Consider the following three cases:

- Case 1: If the key is less than the middle element, recursively search the key in the first half of the array.
- Case 2: If the key is equal to the middle element, the search ends with a match.
- Case 3: If the key is greater than the middle element, recursively search the key in the second half of the array.

Case 1 and Case 3 reduce the search to a smaller list. Case 2 is a base case when there is a match. Another base case is that the search is exhausted without a match. Listing 20.6 gives a clear, simple solution for the binary search problem using recursion.

LISTING 20.6 Recursive Binary Search Method

helper method

base case

recursive call

base case

recursive call

```
public class RecursiveBinarySearch {
  public static int recursiveBinarySearch(int[] list, int key) {
    int low = 0;
    int high = list.length - 1;
    return recursiveBinarySearch(list, key, low, high);
  }

  public static int recursiveBinarySearch(int[] list, int key,
      int low, int high) {
    if (low > high)  // The list has been exhausted without a match
      return -low - 1;

    int mid = (low + high) / 2;
    if (key < list[mid])
      return recursiveBinarySearch(list, key, low, mid - 1);
    else if (key == list[mid])
      return mid;
    else
      return recursiveBinarySearch(list, key, mid + 1, high);
  }
}
```

The first method finds a key in the whole list. The second method finds a key in the list with index from `low` to `high`.

The first `binarySearch` method passes the initial array with `low = 0` and `high = list.length - 1` to the second `binarySearch` method. The second method is invoked recursively to find the key in an ever-shrinking subarray.

20.6 Problem: Finding the Directory Size

Video Note
Directory size

The preceding examples can easily be solved without using recursion. This section presents a problem that is difficult to solve without using recursion. The problem is to find the size of a directory. The size of a directory is the sum of the sizes of all files in the directory. A directory d may contain subdirectories. Suppose a directory contains files $f_1, f_2, \ldots, f_m$ and subdirectories $d_1, d_2, \ldots, d_n$, as shown in Figure 20.5.

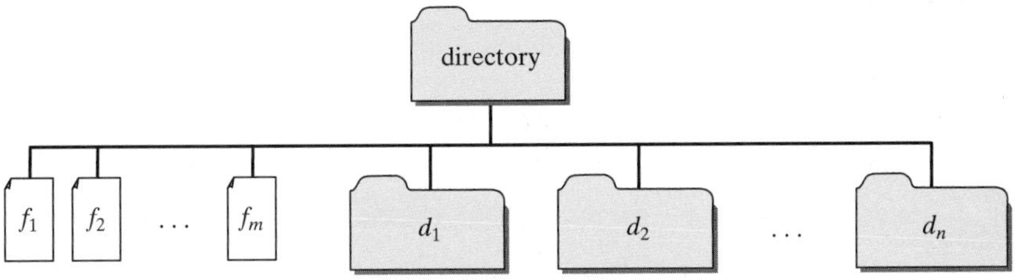
directory
f1
f2
...
fm
d1
d2
...
dn

FIGURE 20.5 A directory contains files and subdirectories.

The size of the directory can be defined recursively as follows:

$$size(d) = size(f_1) + size(f_2) + \ldots + size(f_m) + size(d_1) + size(d_2) + \ldots + size(d_n)$$

The `File` class, introduced in §9.6, can be used to represent a file or a directory and obtain the properties for files and directories. Two methods in the `File` class are useful for this problem:

- The `length()` method returns the size of a file.
- The `listFiles()` method returns an array of `File` objects under a directory.

Listing 20.7 gives a program that prompts the user to enter a directory or a file and displays its size.

LISTING 20.7 `DirectorySize.java`

```
import java.io.File;
import java.util.Scanner;

public class DirectorySize {
  public static void main(String[] args) {
    // Prompt the user to enter a directory or a file
    System.out.print("Enter a directory or a file: ");
    Scanner input = new Scanner(System.in);
    String directory = input.nextLine();

    // Display the size
    System.out.println(getSize(new File(directory)) + " bytes");
  }

  public static long getSize(File file) {
    long size = 0; // Store the total size of all files

    if (file.isDirectory()) {
```

invoke method

`getSize` method

is directory?

all subitems

recursive call

base case

```
19      File[] files = file.listFiles(); // All files and subdirectories
20      for (int i = 0; i < files.length; i++) {
21        size += getSize(files[i]); // Recursive call
22      }
23    }
24    else { // Base case
25      size += file.length();
26    }
27
28    return size;
29  }
30 }
```

```
Enter a directory or a file: c:\book ↵Enter
48619631 bytes
```

```
Enter a directory or a file: c:\book\Welcome.java ↵Enter
172 bytes
```

```
Enter a directory or a file: c:\book\NonExistentFile ↵Enter
0 bytes
```

If the `file` object represents a directory (line 18), each subitem (file or subdirectory) in the directory is recursively invoked to obtain its size (line 21). If the `file` object represents a file (line 24), the file size is obtained (line 25).

What happens if an incorrect or a nonexistent directory is entered? The program will detect that it is not a directory and invoke `file.length()` (line 25), which returns `0`. So, in this case, the `getSize` method will return `0`.

testing base cases

Tip

To avoid mistakes, it is a good practice to test base cases. For example, you should test the program for an input of file, an empty directory, a nonexistent directory, and a nonexistent file.

20.7 Problem: Towers of Hanoi

The Towers of Hanoi problem is a classic problem that can be solved easily using recursion but is difficult to solve otherwise.

The problem involves moving a specified number of disks of distinct sizes from one tower to another while observing the following rules:

- There are n disks labeled 1, 2, 3, . . . , n and three towers labeled A, B, and C.
- No disk can be on top of a smaller disk at any time.
- All the disks are initially placed on tower A.
- Only one disk can be moved at a time, and it must be the top disk on a tower.

The objective of the problem is to move all the disks from A to B with the assistance of C. For example, if you have three disks, the steps to move all of the disks from A to B are shown in Figure 20.6.

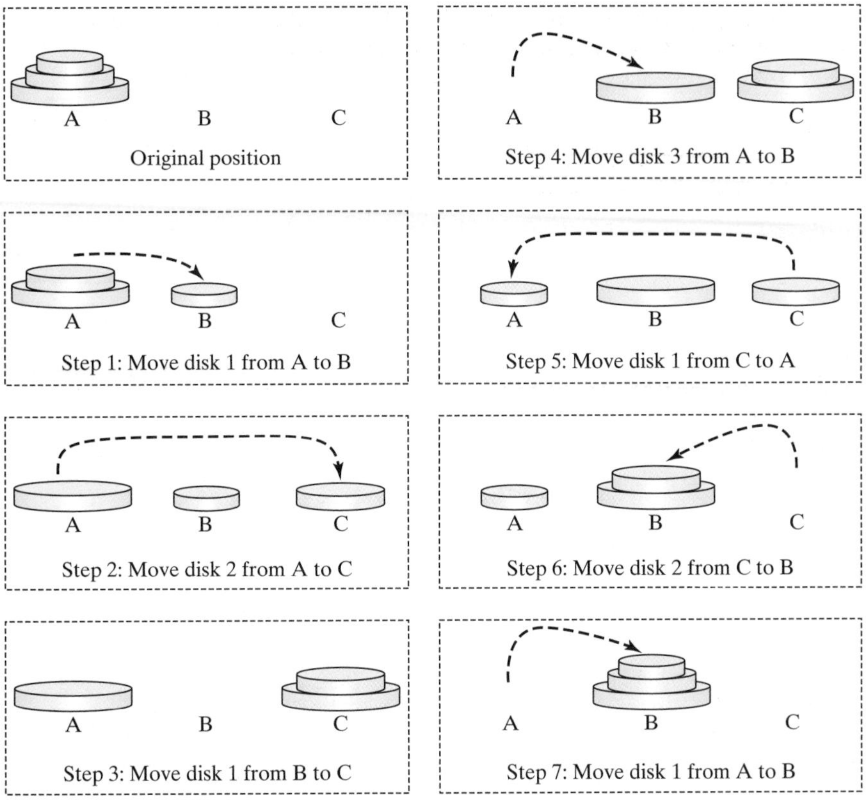
A
B
C
Original position
Step 1: Move disk 1 from A to B
Step 2: Move disk 2 from A to C
Step 3: Move disk 1 from B to C
Step 4: Move disk 3 from A to B
Step 5: Move disk 1 from C to A
Step 6: Move disk 2 from C to B
Step 7: Move disk 1 from A to B

FIGURE 20.6 The goal of the Towers of Hanoi problem is to move disks from tower A to tower B without breaking the rules.

Note

The Towers of Hanoi is a classic computer-science problem, to which many Websites are devoted. One of them worth looking at is www.cut-the-knot.com/recurrence/hanoi.html.

In the case of three disks, you can find the solution manually. For a larger number of disks, however—even for four—the problem is quite complex. Fortunately, the problem has an inherently recursive nature, which leads to a straightforward recursive solution.

The base case for the problem is `n = 1`. If `n == 1`, you could simply move the disk from A to B. When `n > 1`, you could split the original problem into three subproblems and solve them sequentially.

1. Move the first `n - 1` disks from A to C with the assistance of tower B, as shown in Step 1 in Figure 20.7.
2. Move disk `n` from A to B, as shown in Step 2 in Figure 20.7.
3. Move `n - 1` disks from C to B with the assistance of tower A, as shown in Step 3 in Figure 20.7.

The following method moves *n* disks from the `fromTower` to the `toTower` with the assistance of the `auxTower`:

```
void moveDisks(int n, char fromTower, char toTower, char auxTower)
```

The algorithm for the method can be described as follows:

```
if (n == 1) // Stopping condition
  Move disk 1 from the fromTower to the toTower;
else {
```

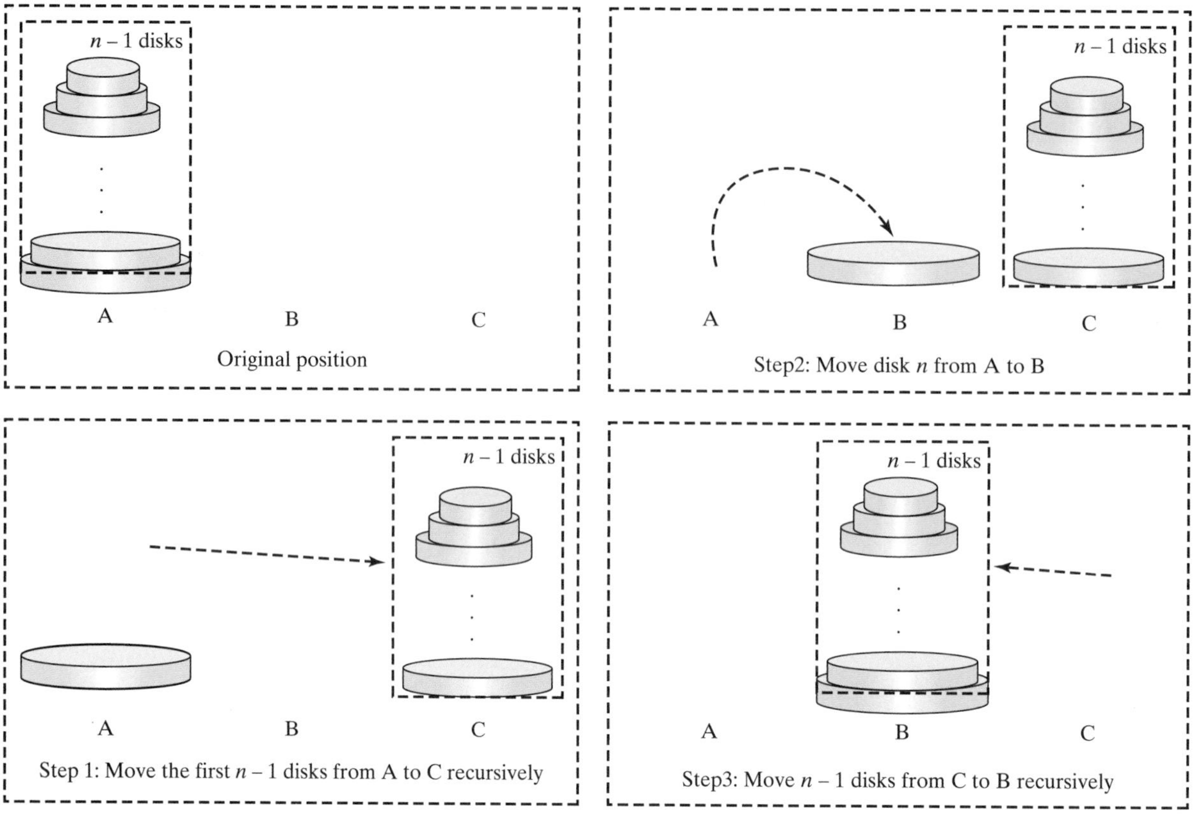
n – 1 disks
A
B
C
Original position
n – 1 disks
A
B
C
Step2: Move disk n from A to B
n – 1 disks
A
B
C
Step 1: Move the first n – 1 disks from A to C recursively
n – 1 disks
A
B
C
Step3: Move n – 1 disks from C to B recursively

FIGURE 20.7 The Towers of Hanoi problem can be decomposed into three subproblems.

```
    moveDisks(n - 1, fromTower, auxTower, toTower);
    Move disk n from the fromTower to the toTower;
    moveDisks(n - 1, auxTower, toTower, fromTower);
  }
```

Listing 20.8 gives a program that prompts the user to enter the number of disks and invokes the recursive method `moveDisks` to display the solution for moving the disks.

LISTING 20.8 TowersOfHanoi.java

```java
import java.util.Scanner;

public class TowersOfHanoi {
  /** Main method */
  public static void main(String[] args) {
    // Create a Scanner
    Scanner input = new Scanner(System.in);
    System.out.print("Enter number of disks: ");
    int n = input.nextInt();

    // Find the solution recursively
    System.out.println("The moves are:");
    moveDisks(n, 'A', 'B', 'C');
  }

  /** The method for finding the solution to move n disks
      from fromTower to toTower with auxTower */
```

```java
  public static void moveDisks(int n, char fromTower,
      char toTower, char auxTower) {
    if (n == 1) // Stopping condition
      System.out.println("Move disk " + n + " from " +
        fromTower + " to " + toTower);
    else {
      moveDisks(n - 1, fromTower, auxTower, toTower);
      System.out.println("Move disk " + n + " from " +
        fromTower + " to " + toTower);
      moveDisks(n - 1, auxTower, toTower, fromTower);
    }
  }
}
```

base case

recursion

recursion

```
Enter number of disks: 4 ↵Enter
The moves are:
Move disk 1 from A to C
Move disk 2 from A to B
Move disk 1 from C to B
Move disk 3 from A to C
Move disk 1 from B to A
Move disk 2 from B to C
Move disk 1 from A to C
Move disk 4 from A to B
Move disk 1 from C to B
Move disk 2 from C to A
Move disk 1 from B to A
Move disk 3 from C to B
Move disk 1 from A to C
Move disk 2 from A to B
Move disk 1 from C to B
```

This problem is inherently recursive. Using recursion makes it possible to find a natural, simple solution. It would be difficult to solve the problem without using recursion.

Consider tracing the program for `n = 3`. The successive recursive calls are shown in Figure 20.8. As you can see, writing the program is easier than tracing the recursive calls. The system uses stacks to trace the calls behind the scenes. To some extent, recursion provides a level of abstraction that hides iterations and other details from the user.

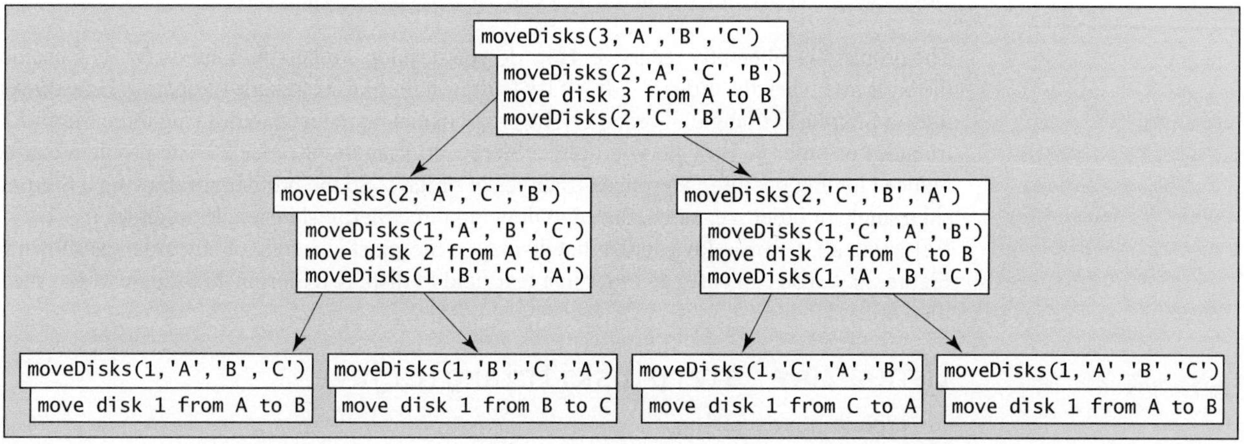
moveDisks(3,'A','B','C')
moveDisks(2,'A','C','B')
move disk 3 from A to B
moveDisks(2,'C','B','A')
moveDisks(2,'A','C','B')
moveDisks(1,'A','B','C')
move disk 2 from A to C
moveDisks(1,'B','C','A')
moveDisks(2,'C','B','A')
moveDisks(1,'C','A','B')
move disk 2 from C to B
moveDisks(1,'A','B','C')
moveDisks(1,'A','B','C')
move disk 1 from A to B
moveDisks(1,'B','C','A')
move disk 1 from B to C
moveDisks(1,'C','A','B')
move disk 1 from C to A
moveDisks(1,'A','B','C')
move disk 1 from A to B

FIGURE 20.8 Invoking `moveDisks(3, 'A', 'B', 'C')` spawns calls to `moveDisks` recursively.

20.8 Problem: Fractals

Video Note
Fractal (Sierpinski triangle)

A *fractal* is a geometrical figure, but unlike triangles, circles, and rectangles, fractals can be divided into parts, each a reduced-size copy of the whole. There are many interesting examples of fractals. This section introduces a simple fractal, the *Sierpinski triangle*, named after a famous Polish mathematician.

A Sierpinski triangle is created as follows:

1. Begin with an equilateral triangle, which is considered to be a Sierpinski fractal of order (or level) 0, as shown in Figure 20.9(a).
2. Connect the midpoints of the sides of the triangle of order 0 to create a Sierpinski triangle of order 1 (Figure 20.9(b)).
3. Leave the center triangle intact. Connect the midpoints of the sides of the three other triangles to create a Sierpinski triangle of order 2 (Figure 20.9(c)).
4. You can repeat the same process recursively to create a Sierpinski triangle of order 3, 4, . . . , and so on (Figure 20.9(d)).

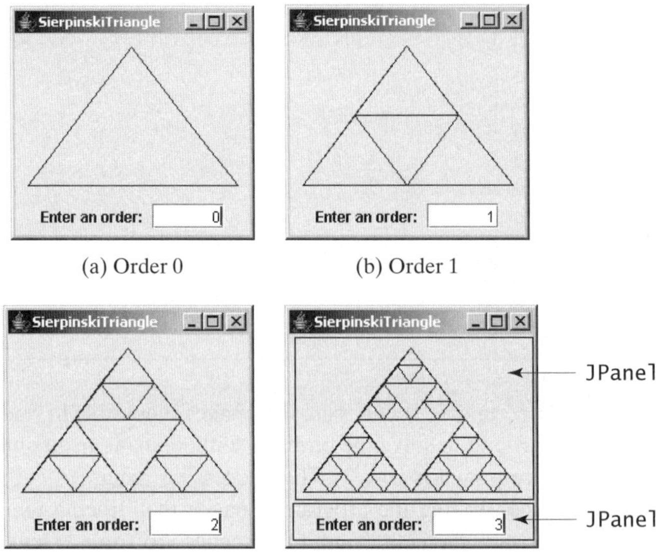
SierpinskiTriangle
Enter an order:
0
SierpinskiTriangle
Enter an order:
1
SierpinskiTriangle
Enter an order:
2
SierpinskiTriangle
JPanel
Enter an order:
3
JPanel

(a) Order 0 (b) Order 1

(c) Order 2 (d) Order 3

FIGURE 20.9 A Sierpinski triangle is a pattern of recursive triangles.

The problem is inherently recursive. How do you develop a recursive solution for it? Consider the base case when the order is 0. It is easy to draw a Sierpinski triangle of order 0. How do you draw a Sierpinski triangle of order 1? The problem can be reduced to drawing three Sierpinski triangles of order 0. How do you draw a Sierpinski triangle of order 2? The problem can be reduced to drawing three Sierpinski triangles of order 1. So the problem of drawing a Sierpinski triangle of order n can be reduced to drawing three Sierpinski triangles of order n - 1.

Listing 20.9 gives a Java applet that displays a Sierpinski triangle of any order, as shown in Figure 20.9. You can enter an order in a text field to display a Sierpinski triangle of the specified order.

LISTING 20.9 SierpinskiTriangle.java

```
import javax.swing.*;
import java.awt.*;
import java.awt.event.*;
```

```
public class SierpinskiTriangle extends JApplet {
  private JTextField jtfOrder = new JTextField("0", 5); // Order
  private SierpinskiTrianglePanel trianglePanel =
    new SierpinskiTrianglePanel(); // To display the pattern

  public SierpinskiTriangle() {
    // Panel to hold label, text field, and a button
    JPanel panel = new JPanel();
    panel.add(new JLabel("Enter an order: "));
    panel.add(jtfOrder);
    jtfOrder.setHorizontalAlignment(SwingConstants.RIGHT);

    // Add a Sierpinski triangle panel to the applet
    add(trianglePanel);
    add(panel, BorderLayout.SOUTH);

    // Register a listener
    jtfOrder.addActionListener(new ActionListener() {
      public void actionPerformed(ActionEvent e) {
        trianglePanel.setOrder(Integer.parseInt(jtfOrder.getText()));
      }
    });
  }

  static class SierpinskiTrianglePanel extends JPanel {
    private int order = 0;

    /** Set a new order */
    public void setOrder(int order) {
      this.order = order;
      repaint();
    }

    protected void paintComponent(Graphics g) {
      super.paintComponent(g);

      // Select three points in proportion to the panel size
      Point p1 = new Point(getWidth() / 2, 10);
      Point p2 = new Point(10, getHeight() - 10);
      Point p3 = new Point(getWidth() - 10, getHeight() - 10);

      displayTriangles(g, order, p1, p2, p3);
    }

    private static void displayTriangles(Graphics g, int order,
        Point p1, Point p2, Point p3) {
      if (order >= 0) {
        // Draw a triangle to connect three points
        g.drawLine(p1.x, p1.y, p2.x, p2.y);
        g.drawLine(p1.x, p1.y, p3.x, p3.y);
        g.drawLine(p2.x, p2.y, p3.x, p3.y);

        // Get the midpoint on each edge in the triangle
        Point p12 = midpoint(p1, p2);
        Point p23 = midpoint(p2, p3);
        Point p31 = midpoint(p3, p1);

        // Recursively display three triangles
        displayTriangles(g, order - 1, p1, p12, p31);
```

listener
set a new order
three initial points
draw a triangle
top subtriangle

left subtriangle
right subtriangle

```
64        displayTriangles(g, order - 1, p12, p2, p23);
65        displayTriangles(g, order - 1, p31, p23, p3);
66      }
67    }
68
69    private static Point midpoint(Point p1, Point p2) {
70      return new Point((p1.x + p2.x) / 2, (p1.y + p2.y) / 2);
71    }
72  }
73 }
```

main method omitted

The initial triangle has three points set in proportion to the panel size (lines 42–44). The `displayTriangles(g, order, p1, p2, p3)` method (lines 49–67) performs the following tasks if `order >= 0`:

1. Display a triangle to connect three points `p1`, `p2`, and `p3` in lines 53–55 , as shown in Figure 20.10(a).
2. Obtain a midpoint between `p1` and `p2` (line 58), a midpoint between `p2` and `p3` (line 59), and a midpoint between `p3` and `p1` (line 60), as shown in Figure 20.10(b).
3. Recursively invoke `displayTriangles` with a reduced order to display three smaller Sierpinski triangles (lines 63–66). Note each small Sierpinski triangle is structurally identical to the original big Sierpinski triangle except that the order of a small triangle is one less, as shown in Figure 20.10(b).

A Sierpinski triangle is displayed in a `SierpinskiTrianglePanel`. The `order` property in the inner class `SierpinskiTrianglePanel` specifies the order for the Sierpinski triangle. The `Point` class, introduced in §16.10, "Mouse Events," represents a point on a component. The `midpoint(Point p1, Point p2)` method returns the midpoint between `p1` and `p2` (lines 72–74).

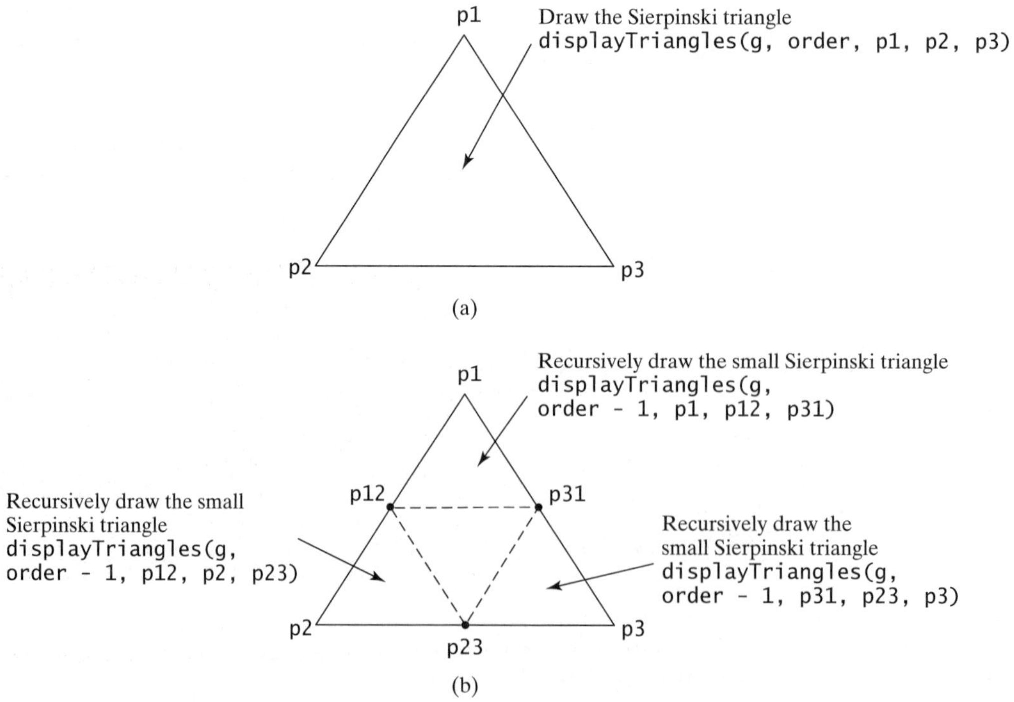
p1
Draw the Sierpinski triangle
displayTriangles(g, order, p1, p2, p3)
p2
p3
(a)
p1
Recursively draw the small Sierpinski triangle
displayTriangles(g,
order - 1, p1, p12, p31)
p12
p31
Recursively draw the small
Sierpinski triangle
displayTriangles(g,
order - 1, p12, p2, p23)
Recursively draw the
small Sierpinski triangle
displayTriangles(g,
order - 1, p31, p23, p3)
p2
p23
p3
(b)

FIGURE 20.10 Drawing a Sierpinski triangle spawns calls to draw three small Sierpinski triangles recursively.

20.9 Problem: Eight Queens

This section gives a recursive solution to the Eight Queens problem presented at the beginning of the chapter. The task is to find a solution to place a queen in each row on a chessboard such that no two queens can attack each other. You may use a two-dimensional array to represent a chessboard. However, since each row can have only one queen, it is sufficient to use a one-dimensional array to denote the position of the queen in the row. So, you may define array queens as follows:

```
int[] queens = new int[8];
```

Assign j to queens[i] to denote that a queen is placed in row i and column j. Figure 20.11(a) shows the contents of array queens for the chessboard in Figure 20.11(b).

queens[0]	0
queens[1]	4
queens[2]	7
queens[3]	5
queens[4]	2
queens[5]	6
queens[6]	1
queens[7]	3

(a)

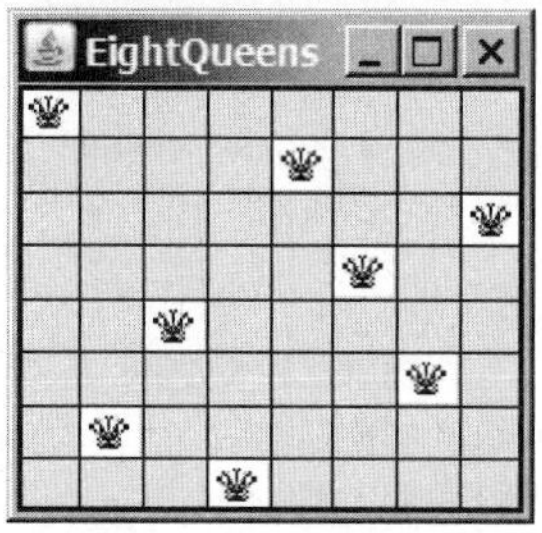
EightQueens

(b)

FIGURE 20.11 queens[i] denotes the position of the queen in row i.

Listing 20.10 gives the program that displays a solution for the Eight Queens problem.

LISTING 20.10 EightQueens.java

```
import java.awt.*;
import javax.swing.*;

public class EightQueens extends JApplet {
  public static final int SIZE = 8; // The size of the chessboard
  private int[] queens = new int[SIZE]; // Queen positions

  public EightQueens() {
    search(0); // Search for a solution from row 0
    add(new ChessBoard(), BorderLayout.CENTER); // Display solution
  }

  /** Check if a queen can be placed at row i and column j */
  private boolean isValid(int row, int column) {
    for (int i = 1; i <= row; i++)
      if (queens[row - i] == column // Check column
        || queens[row - i] == column - i // Check upleft diagonal
        || queens[row - i] == column + i) // Check upright diagonal
        return false; // There is a conflict
    return true; // No conflict
  }

  /** Search for a solution starting from a specified row */
  private boolean search(int row) {
    if (row == SIZE) // Stopping condition
      return true; // A solution found to place 8 queens in 8 rows

    for (int column = 0; column < SIZE; column++) {
```

search for solution

check whether valid

search this row

search columns

search next row

found

main method omitted

```
29        queens[row] = column; // Place a queen at (row, column)
30        if (isValid(row, column) && search(row + 1))
31          return true; // Found, thus return true to exit for loop
32      }
33
34      // No solution for a queen placed at any column of this row
35      return false;
36    }
37
38    class ChessBoard extends JPanel {
39      private Image queenImage =
40        new ImageIcon("image/queen.jpg").getImage();
41
42      ChessBoard() {
43        this.setBorder(BorderFactory.createLineBorder(Color.BLACK, 2));
44      }
45
46      protected void paintComponent(Graphics g) {
47        super.paintComponent(g);
48
49        // Paint the queens
50        for (int i = 0; i < SIZE; i++) {
51          int j = queens[i]; // The position of the queen in row i
52          g.drawImage(queenImage, j * getWidth() / SIZE,
53            i * getHeight() / SIZE, getWidth() / SIZE,
54            getHeight() / SIZE, this);
55        }
56
57        // Draw the horizontal and vertical lines
58        for (int i = 1; i < SIZE; i++) {
59          g.drawLine(0, i * getHeight() / SIZE,
60            getWidth(), i * getHeight() / SIZE);
61          g.drawLine(i * getWidth() / SIZE, 0,
62            i * getWidth() / SIZE, getHeight());
63        }
64      }
65    }
66  }
```

The program invokes search(0) (line 9) to start a search for a solution at row 0, which recursively invokes search(1), search(2), . . . , and search(7) (line 30).

The recursive search(row) method returns true if all row are filled (lines 25–26). The method checks whether a queen can be placed in column 0, 1, 2, . . . , and 7 in a for loop (line 28). Place a queen in the column (line 29). If the placement is valid, recursively search for the next row by invoking search(row + 1) (line 30). If search is successful, return true (line 31) to exit the for loop. In this case, there is no need to look for the next column in the row. If there is no solution for a queen to be placed on any column of this row, the method returns false (line 35).

Suppose you invoke search(row) for row 3, as shown in Figure 20.12(a). The method tries to fill in a queen in column 0, 1, 2, and so on in this order. For each trial, the isValid(row, column) method (line 30) is called to check whether placing a queen at the specified position causes a conflict with the queens placed earlier. It ensures that no queen is placed in the same column (line 16), no queen is placed in the upper left diagonal (line 17), and no queen is placed in the upper right diagonal (line 18), as shown in Figure 20.12(a). If isValid(row, column) returns false, check the next column, as shown Figure 20.12(b). If isValid(row, column) returns true, recursively invoke search(row + 1), as shown in Figure 20.12(d). If search(row + 1) returns false, check the next column on the preceding row, as shown Figure 20.12(c).

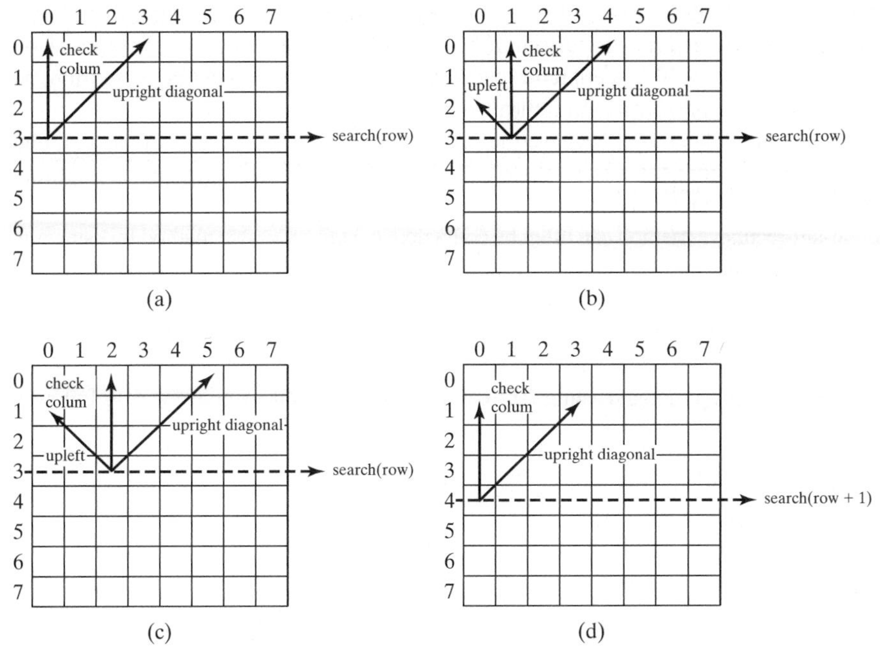

check colum
upright diagonal
search(row)
(a)
upleft
check colum
upright diagonal
search(row)
(b)
check colum
upleft
upright diagonal
search(row)
(c)
check colum
upright diagonal
search(row + 1)
(d)

FIGURE 20.12 Invoking `search(row)` fills in a queen in a column on the row.

20.10 Recursion vs. Iteration

Recursion is an alternative form of program control. It is essentially repetition without a loop. When you use loops, you specify a loop body. The repetition of the loop body is controlled by the loop control structure. In recursion, the method itself is called repeatedly. A selection statement must be used to control whether to call the method recursively or not.

Recursion bears substantial overhead. Each time the program calls a method, the system must assign space for all of the method's local variables and parameters. This can consume considerable memory and requires extra time to manage the additional space. recursion overhead

Any problem that can be solved recursively can be solved nonrecursively with iterations. Recursion has some negative aspects: it uses up too much time and too much memory. Why, then, should you use it? In some cases, using recursion enables you to specify for an inherently recursive problem a clear, simple solution that would otherwise be difficult to obtain. Examples are the directory-size problem, the Towers of Hanoi problem, and the fractal problem, which are rather difficult to solve without using recursion. recursion advantages

The decision whether to use recursion or iteration should be based on the nature of, and your understanding of, the problem you are trying to solve. The rule of thumb is to use whichever approach can best develop an intuitive solution that naturally mirrors the problem. If an iterative solution is obvious, use it. It will generally be more efficient than the recursive option. recursion or iteration?

Note

Your recursive program could run out of memory, causing a `StackOverflowError`. `StackOverflowError`

Tip

If you are concerned about your program's performance, avoid using recursion, because it takes more time and consumes more memory than iteration. performance concern

20.11 Tail Recursion

A recursive method is said to be *tail recursive* if there are no pending operations to be performed on return from a recursive call. For example, the recursive `isPalindrome` method (lines 6–13) in Listing 20.4 is tail recursive because there are no pending operations after recursively invoking `isPalindrome` in line 12. However, the recursive `factorial` method (lines 16-21) in Listing 20.1 is not tail recursive, because there is a pending operation, namely multiplication, to be performed on return from each recursive call.

Tail recursion is desirable, because the method ends when the last recursive call ends. So there is no need to store the intermediate calls in the stack. Some compilers can optimize tail recursion to reduce stack space.

A non-tail-recursive method can often be converted to a tail-recursive method by using auxiliary parameters. These parameters are used to contain the result. The idea is to incorporate the pending operations into the auxiliary parameters in such a way that the recursive call no longer has a pending operation. You may define a new auxiliary recursive method with the auxiliary parameters. This method may overload the original method with the same name but a different signature. For example, the `factorial` method in Listing 20.1 can be written in a tail-recursive way as follows:

original method
invoke auxiliary method
auxiliary method
recursive call

```
 1 /** Return the factorial for a specified number */
 2 public static long factorial(int n) {
 3   return factorial(n, 1); // Call auxiliary method
 4 }
 5
 6 /** Auxiliary tail-recursive method for factorial */
 7 private static long factorial(int n, int result) {
 8   if (n == 1)
 9     return result;
10   else
11     return factorial(n - 1, n * result); // Recursive call
12 }
```

The first `factorial` method simply invokes the second auxiliary method (line 3). The second method contains an auxiliary parameter `result` that stores the result for factorial of `n`. This method is invoked recursively in line 11. There is no pending operation after a call is returned. The final result is returned in line 9, which is also the return value from invoking `factorial(n, 1)` in line 3.

Key Terms

base case 678	recursive helper method 685
infinite recursion 679	stopping condition 678
recursive method 678	tail recursion 697

Chapter Summary

1. A recursive method is one that directly or indirectly invokes itself. For a recursive method to terminate, there must be one or more base cases.
2. Recursion is an alternative form of program control. It is essentially repetition without a loop control. It can be used to specify simple, clear solutions for inherently recursive problems that would otherwise be difficult to solve.
3. Sometimes the original method needs to be modified to receive additional parameters in order to be invoked recursively. A recursive helper method can be defined for this purpose.
4. Recursion bears substantial overhead. Each time the program calls a method, the system must assign space for all of the method's local variables and parameters. This can consume considerable memory and requires extra time to manage the additional space.
5. A recursive method is said to be *tail recursive* if there are no pending operations to be performed on return from a recursive call. Some compilers can optimize tail recursion to reduce stack space.

Review Questions

Sections 20.1–20.3

20.1 What is a recursive method? Describe the characteristics of recursive methods. What is an infinite recursion?

20.2 Write a recursive mathematical definition for computing 2^n for a positive integer n.

20.3 Write a recursive mathematical definition for computing x^n for a positive integer n and a real number x.

20.4 Write a recursive mathematical definition for computing $1 + 2 + 3 + \cdots + n$ for a positive integer.

20.5 How many times is the `factorial` method in Listing 20.1 invoked for `factorial(6)`?

20.6 How many times is the `fib` method in Listing 20.2 invoked for `fib(6)`?

Sections 20.4–20.6

20.7 Show the call stack for `isPalindrome("abcba")` using the methods defined in Listing 20.3 and Listing 20.4, respectively.

20.8 Show the call stack for `selectionSort(new double[]{2, 3, 5, 1})` using the method defined in Listing 20.5.

20.9 What is a recursive helper method?

Section 20.7

20.10 How many times is the `moveDisks` method in Listing 20.8 invoked for `moveDisks(5, 'A', 'B', 'C')`?

Section 20.9

20.11 Which of the following statements are true?

- Any recursive method can be converted into a nonrecursive method.
- Recursive methods take more time and memory to execute than nonrecursive methods.
- Recursive methods are *always* simpler than nonrecursive methods.
- There is always a selection statement in a recursive method to check whether a base case is reached.

20.12 What is the cause for the stack-overflow exception?

Comprehensive

20.13 Show the output of the following program:

```
public class Test {
  public static void main(String[] args) {
    System.out.println(
      "Sum is " + xMethod(5));
  }

  public static int xMethod(int n) {
    if (n == 1)
      return 1;
    else
      return n + xMethod(n - 1);
  }
}
```

```
public class Test {
  public static void main(String[] args) {
    xMethod(1234567);
  }

  public static void xMethod(int n) {
    if (n > 0) {
      System.out.print(n % 10);
      xMethod(n / 10);
    }
  }
}
```

20.14 Show the output of the following two programs:

```
public class Test {
  public static void main(String[] args) {
    xMethod(5);
  }

  public static void xMethod(int n) {
    if (n > 0) {
      System.out.print(n + " ");
      xMethod(n - 1);
    }
  }
}
```

```
public class Test {
  public static void main(String[] args) {
    xMethod(5);
  }

  public static void xMethod(int n) {
    if (n > 0) {
      xMethod(n - 1);
      System.out.print(n + " ");
    }
  }
}
```

20.15 What is wrong in the following method?

```
public class Test {
  public static void main(String[] args) {
    xMethod(1234567);
  }

  public static void xMethod(double n) {
    if (n != 0) {
      System.out.print(n);
      xMethod(n / 10);
    }
  }
}
```

```
public class Test {
  public static void main(String[] args) {
    Test test = new Test();
    System.out.println(test.toString());
  }

  public Test() {
    Test test = new Test();
  }
}
```

20.16 Identify tail-recursive methods in this chapter.

20.17 Rewrite the `fib` method in Listing 20.2 using tail recursion.

Programming Exercises

Sections 20.2–20.3

20.1* (*Factorial*) Using the `BigInteger` class introduced in §14.12, you can find the factorial for a large number (e.g., `100!`). Write a program that prompts the user to enter an integer and displays its factorial. Implement the method using recursion.

20.2* (*Fibonacci numbers*) Rewrite the `fib` method in Listing 20.2 using iterations.

Hint: To compute `fib(n)` without recursion, you need to obtain `fib(n - 2)` and `fib(n - 1)` first. Let `f0` and `f1` denote the two previous Fibonacci numbers. The current Fibonacci number would then be `f0 + f1`. The algorithm can be described as follows:

```
f0 = 0; // For fib(0)
f1 = 1; // For fib(1)

for (int i = 1; i <= n; i++) {
  currentFib = f0 + f1;
  f0 = f1;
  f1 = currentFib;
}

// After the loop, currentFib is fib(n)
```

20.3* (*Computing greatest common divisor using recursion*) The `gcd(m, n)` can also be defined recursively as follows:

- If `m % n` is `0`, `gcd (m, n)` is `n`.
- Otherwise, `gcd(m, n)` is `gcd(n, m % n)`.

Write a recursive method to find the GCD. Write a test program that computes `gcd(24, 16)` and `gcd(255, 25)`.

20.4 (*Summing series*) Write a recursive method to compute the following series:

$$m(i) = 1 + \frac{1}{2} + \frac{1}{3} + \cdots + \frac{1}{i}$$

20.5 (*Summing series*) Write a recursive method to compute the following series:

$$m(i) = \frac{1}{3} + \frac{2}{5} + \frac{3}{7} + \frac{4}{9} + \frac{5}{11} + \frac{6}{13} + \cdots + \frac{i}{2i + 1}$$

20.6* (*Summing series*) Write a recursive method to compute the following series:

$$m(i) = \frac{1}{2} + \frac{2}{3} + \cdots + \frac{i}{i + 1}$$

20.7* (*Fibonacci series*) Modify Listing 20.2, ComputeFibonacci.java, so that the program finds the number of times the `fib` method is called.

(*Hint*: Use a static variable and increment it every time the method is called.)

Section 20.4

20.8* (*Printing the digits in an integer reversely*) Write a recursive method that displays an `int` value reversely on the console using the following header:

```
public static void reverseDisplay(int value)
```

For example, `reverseDisplay(12345)` displays `54321`.

20.9* (*Printing the characters in a string reversely*) Write a recursive method that displays a string reversely on the console using the following header:

```
public static void reverseDisplay(String value)
```

For example, `reverseDisplay("abcd")` displays `dcba`.

20.10* (*Occurrences of a specified character in a string*) Write a recursive method that finds the number of occurrences of a specified letter in a string using the following method header.

```
public static int count(String str, char a)
```

For example, `count("Welcome", 'e')` returns `2`.

20.11* (*Summing the digits in an integer using recursion*) Write a recursive method that computes the sum of the digits in an integer. Use the following method header:

```
public static int sumDigits(long n)
```

For example, `sumDigits(234)` returns $2 + 3 + 4 = 9$.

Section 20.5

20.12** (*Printing the characters in a string reversely*) Rewrite Exercise 20.9 using a helper method to pass the substring high index to the method. The helper method header is:

```
public static void reverseDisplay(String value, int high)
```

20.13* (*Finding the largest number in an array*) Write a recursive method that returns the largest integer in an array.

20.14* (*Finding the number of uppercase letters in a string*) Write a recursive method to return the number of uppercase letters in a string.

20.15* (*Occurrences of a specified character in a string*) Rewrite Exercise 20.10 using a helper method to pass the substring high index to the method. The helper method header is:

```
public static int count(String str, char a, int high)
```

20.16* (*Finding the number of uppercase letters in an array*) Write a recursive method to return the number of uppercase letters in an array of characters. You need to define the following two methods. The second one is a recursive helper method.

```
public static int count(char[] chars)
public static int count(char[] chars, int high)
```

20.17* (*Occurrences of a specified character in an array*) Write a recursive method that finds the number of occurrences of a specified character in an array. You need to define the following two methods. The second one is a recursive helper method.

```
public static int count(char[] chars, char ch)
public static int count(char[] chars, char ch, int high)
```

Sections 20.6

20.18* (*Towers of Hanoi*) Modify Listing 20.8, TowersOfHanoi.java, so that the program finds the number of moves needed to move *n* disks from tower A to tower B.

(*Hint*: Use a static variable and increment it every time the method is called.)

20.19* (*Sierpinski triangle*) Revise Listing 20.9 to develop an applet that lets the user use the *Increase* and *Decrease* buttons to increase or decrease the current order by 1, as shown in Figure 20.13(a). The initial order is 0. If the current order is 0, the *Decrease* button is ignored.

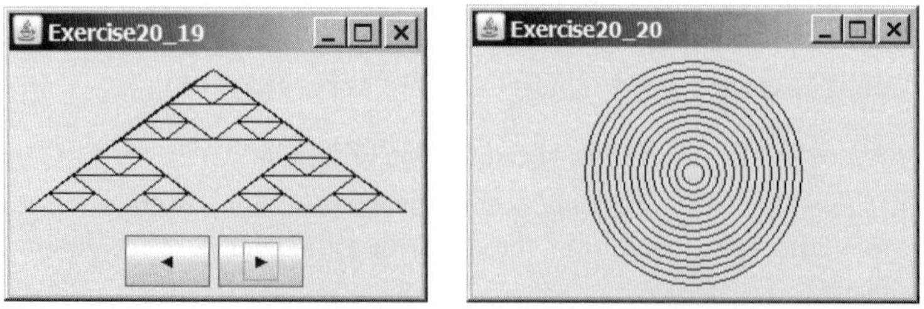

Exercise20_19
Exercise20_20

(a) (b)

FIGURE 20.13 (a) Exercise 20.19 uses the *Increase* and *Decrease* buttons to increase or decrease the current order by 1. (b) Exercise 20.20 draws ovals using a recursive method.

20.20* (*Displaying circles*) Write a Java applet that displays ovals, as shown in Figure 20.13(b). The ovals are centered in the panel. The gap between two adjacent ovals is 10 pixels, and the gap between the panel and the largest oval is also 10.

Comprehensive

20.21* (*Decimal to binary*) Write a recursive method that converts a decimal number into a binary number as a string. The method header is as follows:

```
public static String decimalToBinary(int value)
```

20.22* (*Decimal to hex*) Write a recursive method that converts a decimal number into a hex number as a string. The method header is as follows:

```
public static String decimalToHex(int value)
```

20.23* (*Binary to decimal*) Write a recursive method that parses a binary number as a string into a decimal integer. The method header is as follows:

```
public static int binaryToDecimal(String binaryString)
```

20.24* (*Hex to decimal*) Write a recursive method that parses a hex number as a string into a decimal integer. The method header is as follows:

```
public static int hexToDecimal(String hexString)
```

20.25** (*String permutation*) Write a recursive method to print all the permutations of a string. For example, for a string abc, the printout is

```
abc
acb
bac
bca
cab
cba
```

(*Hint*: Define the following two methods. The second is a helper method.)

```
public static void displayPermuation(String s)
public static void displayPermuation(String s1, String s2)
```

The first method simply invokes `displayPermuation("", s)`. The second method uses a loop to move a character from s2 to s1 and recursively invoke it with a new s1 and s2. The base case is that s2 is empty and prints s1 to the console.

20.26** (*Creating a maze*) Write an applet that will find a path in a maze, as shown in Figure 20.14(a). The maze is represented by an 8×8 board. The path must meet the following conditions:

- The path is between the upper-left corner cell and the lower-right corner cell in the maze.
- The applet enables the user to place or remove a mark on a cell. A path consists of adjacent unmarked cells. Two cells are said to be adjacent if they are horizontal or vertical neighbors, but not if they are diagonal neighbors.
- The path does not contain cells that form a square. The path in Figure 20.14(b), for example, does not meet this condition. (The condition makes a path easy to identify on the board.)

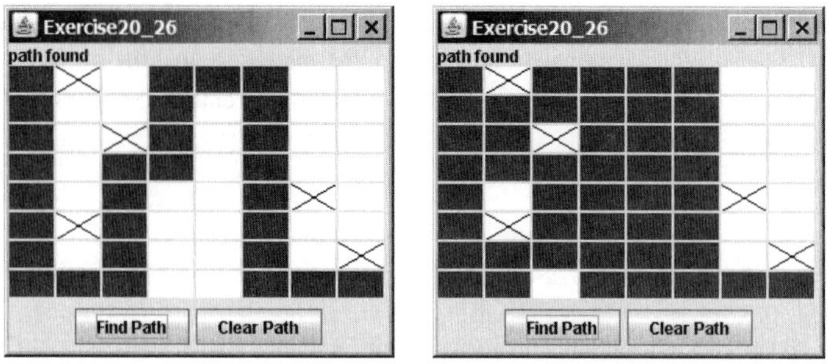

Exercise20_26
path found
Find Path
Clear Path
Exercise20_26
path found
Find Path
Clear Path

(a) Correct path (b) Illegal path

FIGURE 20.14 The program finds a path from the upper-left corner to the bottom-right corner.

20.27** (*Koch snowflake fractal*) The text presented the Sierpinski triangle fractal. In this exercise, you will write an applet to display another fractal, called the *Koch snowflake*, named after a famous Swedish mathematician. A Koch snowflake is created as follows:

1. Begin with an equilateral triangle, which is considered to be the Koch fractal of order (or level) 0, as shown in Figure 20.15(a).
2. Divide each line in the shape into three equal line segments and draw an outward equilateral triangle with the middle line segment as the base to create a Koch fractal of order 1, as shown in Figure 20.15(b).
3. Repeat step 2 to create a Koch fractal of order 2, 3, . . . , and so on, as shown in Figure 20.15(c–d).

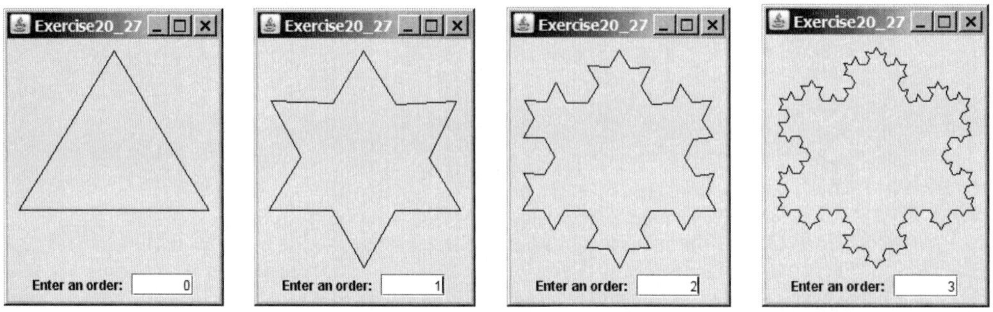

Exercise20_27
Enter an order: 0
Exercise20_27
Enter an order: 1
Exercise20_27
Enter an order: 2
Exercise20_27
Enter an order: 3

(a) (b) (c) (d)

FIGURE 20.15 A Koch snowflake is a fractal starting with a triangle.

20.28** (*Nonrecursive directory size*) Rewrite Listing 20.7, DirectorySize.java, without using recursion.

20.29* (*Number of files in a directory*) Write a program that prompts the user to enter a directory and displays the number of the files in the directory.

20.30** (*Finding words*) Write a program that finds all occurrences of a word in all the files under a directory, recursively. Pass the parameters from the command line as follows:

```
java Exercise20_30 dirName word
```

Video Note
Search a string in a directory

20.31** (*Replacing words*) Write a program that replaces all occurrences of a word with a new word in all the files under a directory, recursively. Pass the parameters from the command line as follows:

```
java Exercise20_31 dirName oldWord newWord
```

20.32*** (*Game: Knight's Tour*) The Knight's Tour is an ancient puzzle. The objective is to move a knight, starting from any square on a chessboard, to every other square once, as shown in Figure 20.16(a). Note that the knight makes only L-shape moves (two spaces in one direction and one space in a perpendicular direction). As shown in Figure 20.16(b), the knight can move to eight squares. Write a program that displays the moves for the knight in an applet, as shown in Figure 20.16(c).

(*Hint*: A brute-force approach for this problem is to move the knight from one square to another available square arbitrarily. Using such an approach, your program will take a long time to finish. A better approach is to employ some heuristics. A knight has two, three, four, six, or eight possible moves, depending on its location. Intuitively, you should attempt to move the knight to the least accessible squares first and leave those more accessible squares open, so there will be a better chance of success at the end of the search.)

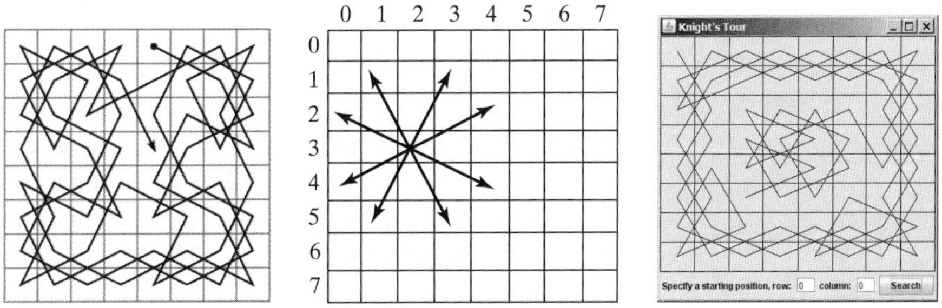
0 1 2 3 4 5 6 7
0
1
2
3
4
5
6
7
Knight's Tour
Specify a starting position, row: 0 column: 0
Search

(a) (b) (c)

FIGURE 20.16 (a) A knight traverses all squares once. (b) A knight makes an L-shape move. (c) An applet displays a knight tour path.

20.33*** (*Game: Knight's Tour animation*) Write an applet for the Knight's Tour problem. Your applet should let the user move a knight to any starting square and click the *Solve* button to animate a knight moving along the path, as shown in Figure 20.17.

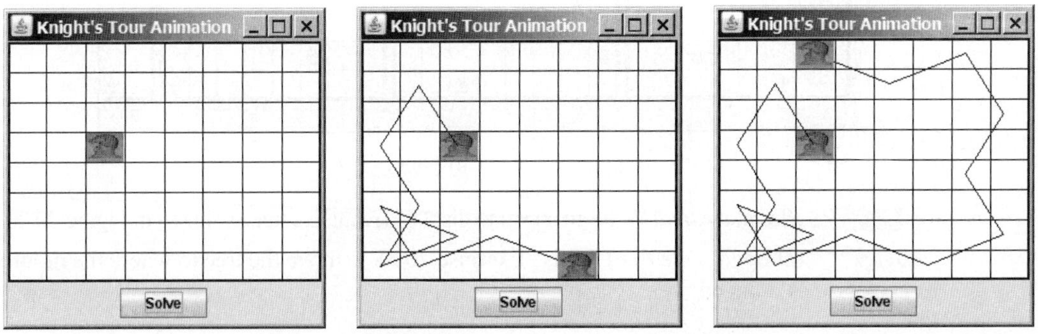
Knight's Tour Animation
Solve
Knight's Tour Animation
Solve
Knight's Tour Animation
Solve

FIGURE 20.17 A knight traverses along the path.

20.34** (*Game: Sudoku*) Write a program to solve the Sudoku problem using recursion.

20.35** (*H-tree fractal*) An H-tree is a fractal defined as follows:

1. Begin with a letter H. The three lines of the H are of the same length, as shown in Figure 20.18(a).
2. The letter H (in its sans-serif form, H) has four endpoints. Draw an H centered at each of the four endpoints to an H-tree of order 1, as shown in Figure 20.18(b). These H's are half the size of the H that contains the four endpoints.
3. Repeat step 2 to create a H-tree of order 2, 3, . . . , and so on, as shown in Figure 20.18(c–d).

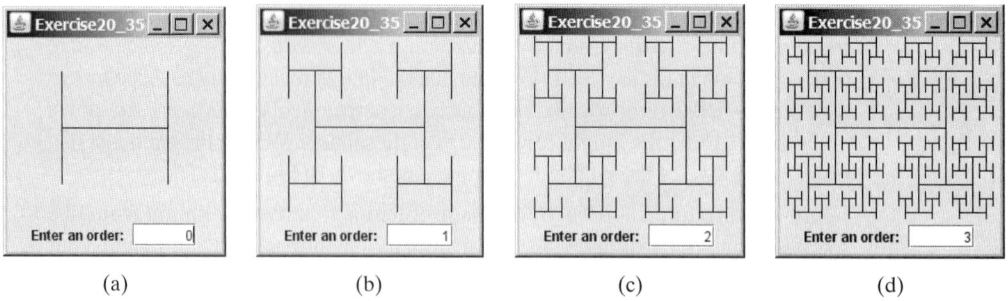
Exercise20_35
Enter an order: 0
(a)
Exercise20_35
Enter an order: 1
(b)
Exercise20_35
Enter an order: 2
(c)
Exercise20_35
Enter an order: 3
(d)

FIGURE 20.18 An H-tree is a fractal starting with three lines of equal length in an H-shape.

The H-tree is used in VLSI design as a clock distribution network for routing timing signals to all parts of a chip with equal propagation delays. Write an applet that draws an H-tree, as shown in Figure 20.18.

20.36*** (*Game: all Sudoku solutions*) Rewrite Exercise 20.34 to find all possible solutions to a Sudoku problem.

20.37*** (*Game: multiple Eight Queens solution*) Write an applet to display all possible solutions for the Eight Queens puzzle in a scroll pane, as shown in Figure 20.19. For each solution, put a label to denote the solution number.

Hint: Place all solution panels into one panel and place this one panel into a `JScrollPane`. The solution panel class should override the `getPreferredSize()` method to ensure that a solution panel is displayed properly. See Listing 15.3, FigurePanel.java, on how to override `getPreferredSize()`.

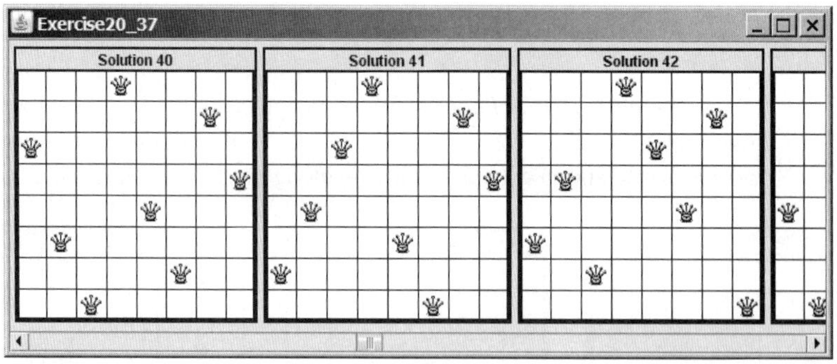
Exercise20_37
Solution 40
Solution 41
Solution 42

FIGURE 20.19 All solutions are placed in a scroll pane.

20.38** (*Recursive tree*) Write an applet to display a recursive tree as shown in Figure 20.20.

20.39** (*Dragging the tree*) Revise Exercise 20.38 to move the tree to where the mouse is dragged.

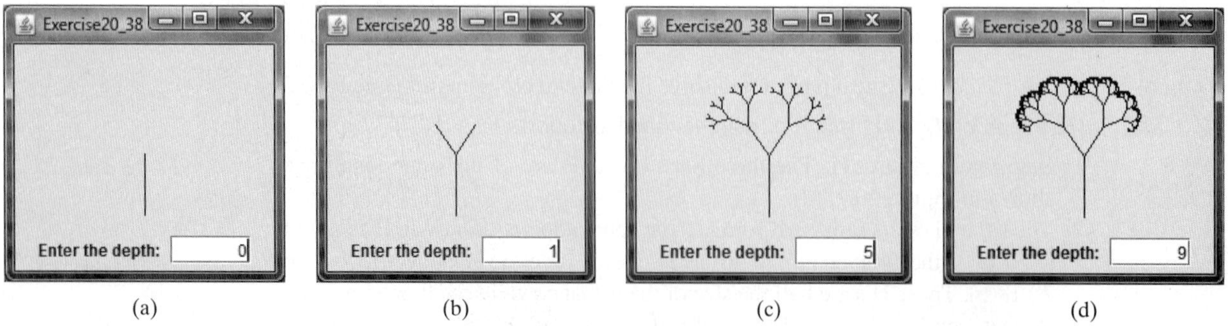
Exercise20_38
Enter the depth: 0
(a)
Exercise20_38
Enter the depth: 1
(b)
Exercise20_38
Enter the depth: 5
(c)
Exercise20_38
Enter the depth: 9
(d)

FIGURE 20.20 A recursive tree with the specified depth.

CHAPTER 21

GENERICS

Objectives

- To describe the benefits of generics (§21.1).
- To use generic classes and interfaces (§21.2).
- To define generic classes and interfaces (§21.3).
- To explain why generic types can improve reliability and readability (§21.3).
- To define and use generic methods and bounded generic types (§21.4).
- To use raw types for backward compatibility (§21.5).
- To explain why wildcard generic types are necessary (§21.6).
- To describe generic type erasure and list certain restrictions and limitations on generic types caused by type erasure (§21.7).
- To design and implement generic matrix classes (§21.8).

21.1 Introduction

what is generics?

Generics is the capability to parameterize types. With this capability, you can define a class or a method with generic types that the compiler can replace with concrete types. For example, you may define a generic stack class that stores the elements of a generic type. From this generic class, you may create a stack object for holding strings and a stack object for holding numbers. Here, strings and numbers are concrete types that replace the generic type.

why generics?

The key benefit of generics is to enable errors to be detected at compile time rather than at runtime. A generic class or method permits you to specify allowable types of objects that the class or method may work with. If you attempt to use an incompatible object, the compiler can detect the errors.

This chapter explains how to define and use generic classes, interfaces, and methods and demonstrates how generics can be used to improve software reliability and readability. It can be intertwined with Chapter 14, "Abstract Classes and Interfaces."

21.2 Motivations and Benefits

Since JDK 1.5, Java allows you to define generic classes, interfaces, and methods. Several interfaces and classes in the Java API are modified using generics. For example, prior to JDK 1.5 the `java.lang.Comparable` interface was defined as shown in Figure 21.1(a), but since JDK 1.5 it is modified as shown in Figure 21.1(b).

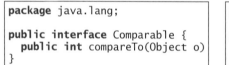

```
package java.lang;

public interface Comparable {
  public int compareTo(Object o)
}
```

(a) Prior to JDK 1.5

```
package java.lang;

public interface Comparable<T> {
  public int compareTo(T o)
}
```

(b) JDK 1.5

FIGURE 21.1 The `java.lang.Comparable` interface is redefined since JDK 1.5 with a generic type.

formal generic type
actual concrete type
generic instantiation

Here, <T> represents a *formal generic type*, which can be replaced later with an *actual concrete type*. Replacing a generic type is called a *generic instantiation*. By convention, a single capital letter such as `E` or `T` is used to denote a formal generic type.

To see the benefits of using generics, let us examine the code in Figures 21.2. The statement in Figure 21.2(a) declares that `c` is a reference variable whose type is `Comparable` and invokes the `compareTo` method to compare a `Date` object with a string. The code compiles fine, but it has a runtime error because a string cannot be compared with a date.

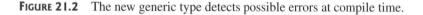

```
Comparable c = new Date();
System.out.println(c.compareTo("red"));
```

(a) Prior to JDK 1.5

```
Comparable<Date> c = new Date();
System.out.println(c.compareTo("red"));
```

(b) JDK 1.5

FIGURE 21.2 The new generic type detects possible errors at compile time.

The statement in Figure 21.2(b) declares that `c` is a reference variable whose type is `Comparable<Date>` and invokes the `compareTo` method to compare a `Date` object with a string. The code has a compile error, because the argument passed to the `compareTo` method must be of the `Date` type. Since the errors can be detected at compile time rather than at runtime, the generic type makes the program more reliable.

reliable

ArrayList was introduced in §11.11, "The ArrayList Class." This class is a generic class since JDK 1.5. Figure 21.3 shows the class diagram for ArrayList before and since JDK 1.5, respectively.

```
java.util.ArrayList
-------------------------------------
+ArrayList()
+add(o: Object): void
+add(index: int, o: Object): void
+clear(): void
+contains(o: Object): boolean
+get(index:int): Object
+indexOf(o: Object): int
+isEmpty(): boolean
+lastIndexOf(o: Object): int
+remove(o: Object): boolean
+size(): int
+remove(index: int): boolean
+set(index: int, o: Object): Object
```

(a) ArrayList before JDK 1.5

```
java.util.ArrayList<E>
-------------------------------------
+ArrayList()
+add(o: E): void
+add(index: int, o: E): void
+clear(): void
+contains(o: Object): boolean
+get(index:int): E
+indexOf(o: Object): int
+isEmpty(): boolean
+lastIndexOf(o: Object): int
+remove(o: Object): boolean
+size(): int
+remove(index: int): boolean
+set(index: int, o: E): E
```

(b) ArrayList in JDK 1.5

FIGURE 21.3 ArrayList is a generic class since JDK 1.5.

For example, the following statement creates a list for strings:

```
ArrayList<String> list = new ArrayList<String>();
```

You can now add *only strings* into the list. For example, only string allowed

```
list.add("Red");
```

If you attempt to add a nonstring, a compile error will occur. For example, the following statement is now illegal, because list can contain only strings.

```
list.add(new Integer(1));
```

Generic types must be reference types. You cannot replace a generic type with a primitive type such as int, double, or char. For example, the following statement is wrong: generic reference type

```
ArrayList<int> intList = new ArrayList<int>();
```

To create an ArrayList object for int values, you have to use:

```
ArrayList<Integer> intList = new ArrayList<Integer>();
```

You can add an int value to intList. For example,

```
intList.add(5);
```

Java automatically wraps 5 into new Integer(5). This is called *autoboxing*, as introduced in §14.11, "Automatic Conversion between Primitive Types and Wrapper Class Types." autoboxing

Casting is not needed to retrieve a value from a list with a specified element type, because the compiler already knows the element type. For example, the following statements create a list that contains strings, add strings to the list, and retrieve strings from the list. no casting needed

```
ArrayList<String> list = new ArrayList<String>();
list.add("Red");
list.add("White");
String s = list.get(0); // No casting is needed
```

Prior to JDK 1.5, without using generics, you would have had to cast the return value to `String` as follows:

```
String s = (String)(list.get(0)); // Casting needed prior to JDK 1.5
```

autounboxing

If the elements are of wrapper types, such as `Integer`, `Double`, and `Character`, you can directly assign an element to a primitive type variable. This is called *autounboxing*, as introduced in §14.11. For example, see the following code:

```
1 ArrayList<Double> list = new ArrayList<Double>();
2 list.add(5.5); // 5.5 is automatically converted to new Double(5.5)
3 list.add(3.0); // 3.0 is automatically converted to new Double(3.0)
4 Double doubleObject = list.get(0); // No casting is needed
5 double d = list.get(1); // Automatically converted to double
```

In lines 2 and 3, `5.5` and `3.0` are automatically converted into `Double` objects and added to `list`. In line 4, the first element in `list` is assigned to a `Double` variable. No casting is necessary, because `list` is declared for `Double` objects. In line 5, the second element in `list` is assigned to a `double` variable. The object in `list.get(1)` is automatically converted into a primitive type value.

21.3 Defining Generic Classes and Interfaces

Let us revise the stack class in §11.12, "A Custom Stack Class," to generalize the element type with a generic type. The new stack class, named `GenericStack`, is shown in Figure 21.4 and is implemented in Listing 21.1.

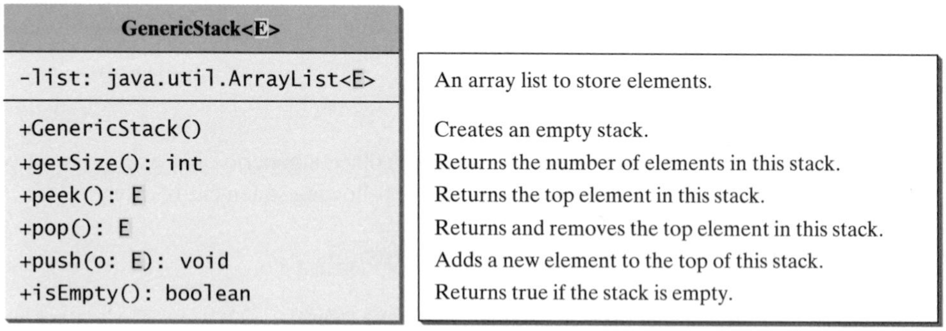
GenericStack<E>
-list: java.util.ArrayList<E>
+GenericStack()
+getSize(): int
+peek(): E
+pop(): E
+push(o: E): void
+isEmpty(): boolean
An array list to store elements.
Creates an empty stack.
Returns the number of elements in this stack.
Returns the top element in this stack.
Returns and removes the top element in this stack.
Adds a new element to the top of this stack.
Returns true if the stack is empty.

FIGURE 21.4 The `GenericStack` class encapsulates the stack storage and provides the operations for manipulating the stack.

LISTING 21.1 GenericStack.java

generic type **E** declared
generic array list
getSize

```
public class GenericStack<E> {
  private java.util.ArrayList<E> list = new java.util.ArrayList<E>();

  public int getSize() {
    return list.size();
  }

```

peek push pop isEmpty

```
  public E peek() {
    return list.get(getSize() - 1);
  }

  public void push(E o) {
    list.add(o);
  }

  public E pop() {
    E o = list.get(getSize() - 1);
    list.remove(getSize() - 1);
    return o;
  }

  public boolean isEmpty() {
    return list.isEmpty();
  }
}
```

Here is an example that creates a stack to hold strings and adds three strings to the stack:

```
GenericStack<String> stack1 = new GenericStack<String>();
stack1.push("London");
stack1.push("Paris");
stack1.push("Berlin");
```

Here is another example that creates a stack to hold integers and adds three integers to the stack:

```
GenericStack<Integer> stack2 = new GenericStack<Integer>();
stack2.push(1); // auto boxing 1 to new Integer(1)
stack2.push(2);
stack2.push(3);
```

benefits of using generic types

Instead of using a generic type, you could simply make the type element **Object**, which can accommodate any object type. However, using generic types can improve software reliability and readability, because certain errors can be detected at compile time rather than at runtime. For example, since **stack1** is declared **GenericStack<String>**, only strings can be added to the stack. It would be a compile error if you attempted to add an integer to **stack1**.

Caution

generic class constructor

To create a stack of strings, you use **new GenericStack<String>()**. This could mislead you into thinking that the constructor of **GenericStack** should be defined as

```
public GenericStack<E>()
```

This is wrong. It should be defined

```
public GenericStack()
```

Note

multiple generic parameters

Occasionally, a generic class may have more than one parameter. In this case, place the parameters together inside the brackets, separated by commas—for example, **<E1, E2, E3>**.

inheritance with generics

Note

You can define a class or an interface as a subtype of a generic class or interface. For example, the **java.lang.String** class is defined to implement the **Comparable** interface in the Java API as follows:

```
public class String implements Comparable<String>
```

21.4 Generic Methods

generic method

You can define generic interfaces (e.g., the **Comparable** interface in Figure 21.1(b)) and classes (e.g., the **GenericStack** class in Listing 21.1). You can also use generic types to define generic methods. For example, Listing 21.2 defines a generic method **print** (lines 10–14) to print an array of objects. Line 6 passes an array of integer objects to invoke the generic **print** method. Line 7 invokes **print** with an array of strings.

LISTING 21.2 GenericMethodDemo.java

generic method

```
1 public class GenericMethodDemo {
2   public static void main(String[] args ) {
3     Integer[] integers = {1, 2, 3, 4, 5};
4     String[] strings = {"London", "Paris", "New York", "Austin"};
5
6     GenericMethodDemo.<Integer>print(integers);
7     GenericMethodDemo.<String>print(strings);
8   }
9
10   public static <E> void print(E[] list) {
11     for (int i = 0; i < list.length; i++)
12       System.out.print(list[i] + " ");
13     System.out.println();
14   }
15 }
```

invoke generic method

To invoke a generic method, prefix the method name with the actual type in angle brackets. For example,

```
GenericMethodDemo.<Integer>print(integers);
GenericMethodDemo.<String>print(strings);
```

bounded generic type

A generic type can be specified as a subtype of another type. Such a generic type is called *bounded*. For example, Listing 21.3 revises the **equalArea** method in Listing 11.4, TestGeometricObject.java, to test whether two geometric objects have the same area. The bounded generic type **<E extends GeometricObject>** (line 7) specifies that **E** is a generic subtype of **GeometricObject**. You must invoke **equalArea** by passing two instances of **GeometricObject**.

LISTING 21.3 BoundedTypeDemo.java

Rectangle in Listing 14.3
Circle in Listing 14.2
bounded generic type

```
1 public class BoundedTypeDemo {
2   public static void main(String[] args ) {
3     Rectangle rectangle = new Rectangle(2, 2);
4     Circle circle = new Circle(2);
5
6     System.out.println("Same area? " +
7       BoundedTypeDemo.<GeometricObject>equalArea(rectangle, circle));
8   }
9
10   public static <E extends GeometricObject> boolean equalArea(
11       E object1, E object2) {
```

```
    return object1.getArea() == object2.getArea();
  }
}
```

Note

An unbounded generic type <E> is the same as <E extends Object>.

Note

generic class parameter vs. generic method parameter

To define a generic type for a class, place it after the class name, such as GenericStack<E>. To define a generic type for a method, place the generic type before the method return type, such as <E> void max(E o1, E o2).

21.5 Raw Type and Backward Compatibility

You may use a generic class without specifying a concrete type like this:

```
GenericStack stack = new GenericStack(); // raw type
```

This is roughly equivalent to

```
GenericStack<Object> stack = new GenericStack<Object>();
```

raw type

backward compatibility

A generic class such as GenericStack and ArrayList used without a type parameter is called a *raw type*. Use of raw type is allowed for backward compatibility with the earlier versions of Java. For example, generic type is used in java.lang.Comparable since JDK 1.5, but a lot of code still uses the raw type Comparable, as shown in Listing 21.4 (also see the Max class in §14.5, "Example: The Comparable Interface"):

LISTING 21.4 Max.java

raw type

```
1 public class Max {
2   /** Return the maximum between two objects */
3   public static Comparable max(Comparable o1, Comparable o2) {
4     if (o1.compareTo(o2) > 0)
5       return o1;
6     else
7       return o2;
8   }
9 }
```

Comparable o1 and Comparable o2 are raw type declarations. *Raw type is unsafe*. For example, you might invoke the max method using

```
Max.max("Welcome", 23); // 23 is autoboxed into new Integer(23)
```

Xlint:unchecked

This would cause a runtime error, because you cannot compare a string with an integer object. The Java compiler displays a warning on line 3 when compiled with the option *-Xlint:unchecked*, as shown in Figure 21.5.

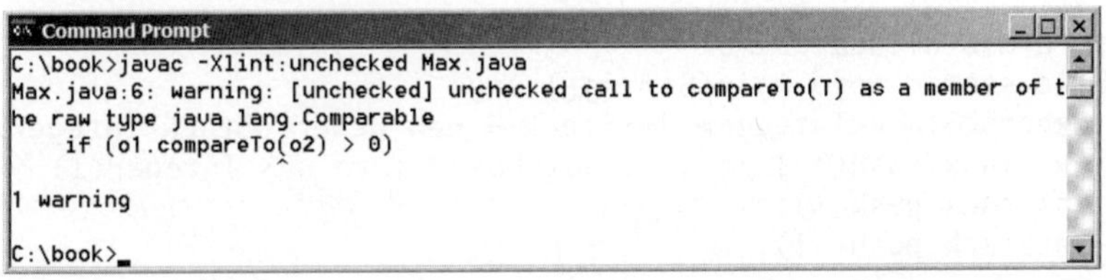
Command Prompt
C:\book>javac -Xlint:unchecked Max.java
Max.java:6: warning: [unchecked] unchecked call to compareTo(T) as a member of the raw type java.lang.Comparable
if (o1.compareTo(o2) > 0)
1 warning
C:\book>

FIGURE 21.5 The unchecked warnings are displayed using the compiler option -Xlint:unchecked.

A better way to write the max method is to use a generic type, as shown in Listing 21.5.

Listing 21.5 Max1.java

bounded type

```
public class Max1 {
  /** Return the maximum between two objects */
  public static <E extends Comparable<E>> E max(E o1, E o2) {
    if (o1.compareTo(o2) > 0)
      return o1;
    else
      return o2;
  }
}
```

If you invoke the max method using

```
Max1.max("Welcome", 23); // 23 is autoboxed into new Integer(23)
```

a compile error will be displayed, because two arguments of the max method in Max1 must have the same type (e.g., two strings or two integer objects). Furthermore, the type E must be a subtype of Comparable<E>.

As another example, in the following code you may declare a raw type stack in line 1, assign new GenericStack<String> to it in line 2, and push a string and an integer object to the stack in lines 3 and 4.

```
1 GenericStack stack;
2 stack = new GenericStack<String>();
3 stack.push("Welcome to Java");
4 stack.push(new Integer(2));
```

Line 4 is unsafe because the stack is intended to store strings, but an Integer object is added into the stack. Line 3 should be OK, but the compiler will show warnings on both line 3 and line 4, because it cannot follow the semantic meaning of the program. All the compiler knows is that stack is a raw type, and performing certain operations is unsafe. Therefore, warnings are displayed to alert potential problems.

Tip

Since raw types are unsafe, this book will not use them from here on.

21.6 Wildcard Generic Types

What are wildcard generic types and why are needed? Listing 21.6 gives an example to demonstrate the needs. The example defines a generic max method for finding the maximum in a stack of numbers (lines 12–22). The main method creates a stack of integer objects, adds three integers to the stack, and invokes the max method to find the maximum number in the stack.

Listing 21.6 WildCardDemo1.java

GenericStack<Integer> type

```
1 public class WildCardDemo1 {
2   public static void main(String[] args ) {
3     GenericStack<Integer> intStack = new GenericStack<Integer>();
4     intStack.push(1); // 1 is autoboxed into new Integer(1)
5     intStack.push(2);
6     intStack.push(-2);
7
8     System.out.print("The max number is " + max(intStack));
9   }
```

```
10
11   /** Find the maximum in a stack of numbers */
12   public static double max(GenericStack<Number> stack) {
13     double max = stack.pop().doubleValue(); // Initialize max
14
15     while (!stack.isEmpty()) {
16       double value = stack.pop().doubleValue();
17       if (value > max)
18         max = value;
19     }
20
21     return max;
22   }
23 }
```

GenericStack<Number> type

The program in Listing 21.6 has a compile error in line 8 because intStack is not an instance of GenericStack<Number>. So you cannot invoke max(intStack).

The fact is that Integer is a subtype of Number, but GenericStack<Integer> is not a subtype of GenericStack<Number>. To circumvent this problem, use wildcard generic types. A wildcard generic type has three forms—?, ? extends T, or ? super T, where T is a generic type.

unbounded wildcard

bounded wildcard

lower bound wildcard

The first form, ?, called an *unbounded wildcard*, is the same as ? extends Object. The second form, ? extends T, called a *bounded wildcard*, represents T or an unknown subtype of T. The third form, ? super T, called a *lower-bound wildcard*, denotes T or an unknown supertype of T.

You can fix the error by replacing line 12 in Listing 21.6 as follows:

```
public static double max(GenericStack<? extends Number> stack) {
```

<? extends Number> is a wildcard type that represents Number or a subtype of Number. So it is legal to invoke max(new GenericStack<Integer>()) or max(new GenericStack<Double>()).

Listing 21.7 shows an example of using the ? wildcard in the print method that prints objects in a stack and empties the stack. <?> is a wildcard that represents any object type. It is equivalent to <? Extends Object>. What happens if you replace GenericStack<?> by GenericStack<Object>? It would be wrong to invoke print(intStack), because instack is not an instance of GenericStack<Object>. Please note that GenericStack<Integer> is not a subtype of GenericStack<Object>, although Integer is a subtype of Object.

LISTING 21.7 WildCardDemo2.java

```
public class WildCardDemo2 {
  public static void main(String[] args ) {
    GenericStack<Integer> intStack = new GenericStack<Integer>();
    intStack.push(1); // 1 is autoboxed into new Integer(1)
    intStack.push(2);
    intStack.push(-2);

    print(intStack);
  }

  /** Prints objects and empties the stack */
  public static void print(GenericStack<?> stack) {
    while (!stack.isEmpty()) {
      System.out.print(stack.pop() + " ");
    }
  }
}
```

GenericStack<Integer> type

wildcard type

why <? Super T>

When is the wildcard <? super T> needed? Consider the example in Listing 21.8. The example creates a stack of strings in stack1 (line 3) and a stack of objects in stack2 (line 4) and invokes add(stack1, stack2) (line 8) to add the strings in stack1 into stack2. GenericStack<? super T> is used to declare stack2 in line 13. If <? super T> is replaced by <T>, a compile error will occur on add(stack1, stack2) in line 8, because stack1's type is GenericStack<String> and stack2's type is GenericStack<Object>. <? super T> represents type T or a supertype of T. Object is a supertype of String.

LISTING 21.8 WildCardDemo3.java

GenericStack<Integer> type

<? Super T> type

```
1 public class WildCardDemo3 {
2   public static void main(String[] args) {
3     GenericStack<String> stack1 = new GenericStack<String>();
4     GenericStack<Object> stack2 = new GenericStack<Object>();
5     stack2.push("Java");
6     stack2.push(2);
7     stack1.push("Sun");
8     add(stack1, stack2);
9     WildCardDemo2.print(stack2);
10  }
11
12  public static <T> void add(GenericStack<T> stack1,
13      GenericStack<? super T> stack2) {
14    while (!stack1.isEmpty())
15      stack2.push(stack1.pop());
15  }
16 }
```

The inheritance relationship involving generic types and wildcard types is summarized in Figure 21.6. In this figure, A and B represent classes or interfaces, and E is a generic type parameter.

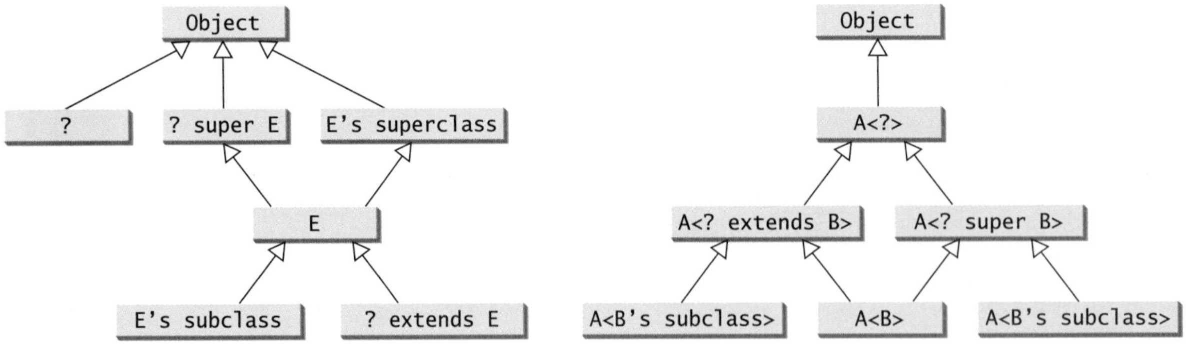
Object
?
? super E
E's superclass
E
E's subclass
? extends E
Object
A<?>
A<? extends B>
A<? super B>
A<B's subclass>
A<B>
A<B's subclass>

FIGURE 21.6 The relationship between generic types and wildcard types.

21.7 Erasure and Restrictions on Generics

type erasure

Generics are implemented using an approach called *type erasure*. The compiler uses the generic type information to compile the code, but erases it afterward. So the generic information is not available at runtime. This approach enables the generic code to be backward compatible with the legacy code that uses raw types.

erase generics

The generics are present at compile time. Once the compiler confirms that a generic type is used safely, it converts it to a raw type. For example, the compiler checks whether generics is used correctly for the following code in (a) and translates it into the equivalent code in (b) for runtime use. The code in (b) uses the raw type.

```
ArrayList<String> list = new ArrayList<String> ();
list.add("Oklahoma");
String state = list.get(0);
```

(a)

```
ArrayList list = new ArrayList();
list.add("Oklahoma");
String state = (String)(list.get(0));
```

(b)

When generic classes, interfaces, and methods are compiled, the compiler replaces the generic type with the `Object` type. For example, the compiler would convert the following method in (a) into (b).

replace generic type

```
public static <E> void print(E[] list) {
  for (int i = 0; i < list.length; i++)
    System.out.print(list[i] + " ");
  System.out.println();
}
```

(a)

```
public static Object void print(Object[] list) {
  for (int i = 0; i < list.length; i++)
    System.out.print(list[i] + " ");
  System.out.println();
}
```

(b)

If a generic type is bounded, the compiler replaces it with the bounded type. For example, the compiler would convert the following method in (a) into (b).

replace bounded type

```
public static <E extends GeometricObject>
    boolean equalArea(
      E object1,
      E object2) {
  return object1.getArea() ==
    object2.getArea();
}
```

(a)

```
public static GeometricObject
    boolean equalArea(
      GeometricObject object1,
      GeometricObject object2) {
  return object1.getArea() ==
    object2.getArea();
}
```

(b)

It is important to note that a generic class is shared by all its instances regardless of its actual concrete type. Suppose `list1` and `list2` are created as follows:

important fact

```
ArrayList<String> list1 = new ArrayList<String>();
ArrayList<Integer> list2 = new ArrayList<Integer>();
```

Although `ArrayList<String>` and `ArrayList<Integer>` are two types at compile time, only one `ArrayList` class is loaded into the JVM at runtime. `list1` and `list2` are both instances of `ArrayList`. So the following statements display `true`:

```
System.out.println(list1 instanceof ArrayList);
System.out.println(list2 instanceof ArrayList);
```

But the expression `list1 instanceof ArrayList<String>` is wrong. Since `ArrayList<String>` is not stored as a separate class in the JVM, using it at runtime makes no sense.

Because generic types are erased at runtime, there are certain restrictions on how generic types can be used. Here are some of the restrictions:

Restriction 1: Cannot Use *new E()*

You cannot create an instance using a generic type parameter. For example, the following statement is wrong:

```
E object = new E();
```

no **new E()**

The reason is that `new E()` is executed at runtime, but the generic type `E` is not available at runtime.

Restriction 2: Cannot Use *new E[]*

You cannot create an array using a generic type parameter. For example, the following statement is wrong:

no **new** E[capacity]

```
E[] elements = new E[capacity];
```

You can circumvent this limitation by creating an array of the `Object` type and then casting it to `E[]`, as follows:

```
E[] elements = (E[])new Object[capacity];
```

unavoidable compile warning

However, casting to `(E[])` causes an unchecked compile warning. The warning occurs because the compiler is not certain that casting will succeed at runtime. For example, if `E` is `String` and `new Object[]` is an array of `Integer` objects, `(String[])(new Object[])` will cause a `ClassCastException`. This type of compile warning is the limitation of Java generics and is unavoidable.

Generic array creation using a generic class is not allowed, either. For example, the following code is wrong:

```
ArrayList<String>[] list = new ArrayList<String>[10];
```

You can use the following code to circumvent this restriction:

```
ArrayList<String>[] list = (ArrayList<String>[])new
  ArrayList[10];
```

You will get a compile warning.

Restriction 3: A Generic Type Parameter of a Class Is Not Allowed in a Static Context

Since all instances of a generic class have the same runtime class, the static variables and methods of a generic class are shared by all its instances. Therefore, it is illegal to refer to a generic type parameter for a class in a static method, field, or initializer. For example, the following code is illegal:

```
public class Test<E> {
  public static void m(E o1) { // Illegal
  }

  public static E o1; // Illegal

  static {
    E o2; // Illegal
  }
}
```

Restriction 4: Exception Classes Cannot be Generic

A generic class may not extend `java.lang.Throwable`, so the following class declaration would be illegal:

```
public class MyException<T> extends Exception {
}
```

Why? If it were allowed, you would have a catch clause for MyException<T> as follows:

```
try {
  ...
}
catch (MyException<T> ex) {
  ...
}
```

The JVM has to check the exception thrown from the try clause to see if it matches the type specified in a catch clause. This is impossible, because the type information is not present at runtime.

21.8 Case Study: Generic Matrix Class

This section presents a case study on designing classes for matrix operations using generic types. The addition and multiplication operations for all matrices are similar except that their element types differ. Therefore, you can design a superclass that describes the common operations shared by matrices of all types regardless of their element types, and you can create subclasses tailored to specific types of matrices. This case study gives implementations for two types: int and Rational. For the int type, the wrapper class Integer should be used to wrap an int value into an object, so that the object is passed in the methods for operations.

The class diagram is shown in Figure 21.7. The methods addMatrix and multiplyMatrix add and multiply two matrices of a generic type E[][]. The static method printResult displays the matrices, the operations, and their result. The methods add, multiply, and zero are abstract, because their implementations depend on the specific type of the array elements. For example, the zero() method returns 0 for the Integer type and 0/1 for the Rational type. These methods will be implemented in the subclasses in which the matrix element type is specified.

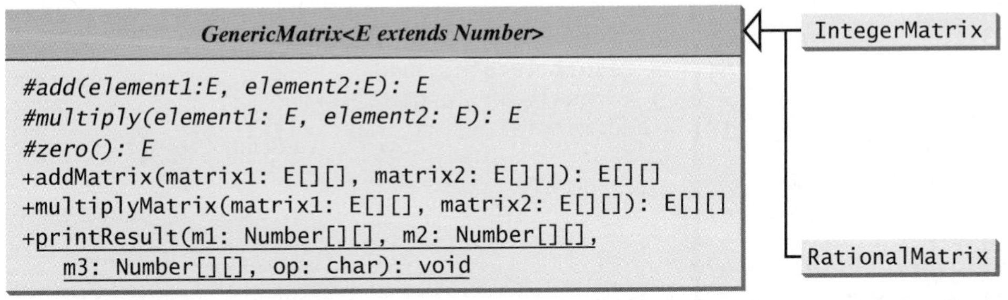
GenericMatrix<E extends Number>
#add(element1:E, element2:E): E
#multiply(element1: E, element2: E): E
#zero(): E
+addMatrix(matrix1: E[][], matrix2: E[][]): E[][]
+multiplyMatrix(matrix1: E[][], matrix2: E[][]): E[][]
+printResult(m1: Number[][], m2: Number[][],
m3: Number[][], op: char): void
IntegerMatrix
RationalMatrix

FIGURE 21.7 The GenericMatrix class is an abstract superclass for IntegerMatrix and RationalMatrix.

IntegerMatrix and RationalMatrix are concrete subclasses of GenericMatrix. These two classes implement the add, multiply, and zero methods defined in the GenericMatrix class.

Listing 21.9 implements the GenericMatrix class. <E extends Number> in line 3 specifies that the generic type is a subtype of Number. Three abstract methods add, multiply, and zero are defined in lines 3, 6, and 9. These methods are abstract because we cannot implement them without knowing the exact type of the elements. The addMaxtrix (lines 12–30) and multiplyMatrix (lines 33–57) methods implement the methods for adding and multiplying two matrices. All these methods must be nonstatic, because they use generic type E for the class. The printResult method (lines 59–84) is static because it is not tied to specific instances.

The matrix element type is generic. This enables you to use an object of any class as long as you can implement the abstract `add`, `multiply`, and `zero` methods in subclasses.

The `addMatrix` and `multiplyMatrix` methods (lines 12–57) are concrete methods. They are ready to use as long as the `add`, `multiply`, and `zero` methods are implemented in the subclasses.

The `addMatrix` and `multiplyMatrix` methods check the bounds of the matrices before performing operations. If the two matrices have incompatible bounds, the program throws an exception (lines 16, 36).

LISTING 21.9 GenericMatrix.java

bounded generic type (line 1); abstract method (line 3); abstract method (line 6); abstract method (line 9); add two matrices (line 12); multiply two matrices (line 33)

```
1 public abstract class GenericMatrix<E extends Number> {
2   /** Abstract method for adding two elements of the matrices */
3   protected abstract E add(E o1, E o2);
4
5   /** Abstract method for multiplying two elements of the matrices */
6   protected abstract E multiply(E o1, E o2);
7
8   /** Abstract method for defining zero for the matrix element */
9   protected abstract E zero();
10
11  /** Add two matrices */
12  public E[][] addMatrix(E[][] matrix1, E[][] matrix2) {
13    // Check bounds of the two matrices
14    if ((matrix1.length != matrix2.length) ||
15        (matrix1[0].length != matrix2.length)) {
16      throw new RuntimeException(
17        "The matrices do not have the same size");
18    }
19
20    E[][] result =
21      (E[][])new Number[matrix1.length][matrix1[0].length];
22
23    // Perform addition
24    for (int i = 0; i < result.length; i++)
25      for (int j = 0; j < result[i].length; j++) {
26        result[i][j] = add(matrix1[i][j], matrix2[i][j]);
27      }
28
29    return result;
30  }
31
32  /** Multiply two matrices */
33  public E[][] multiplyMatrix(E[][] matrix1, E[][] matrix2) {
34    // Check bounds
35    if (matrix1[0].length != matrix2.length) {
36      throw new RuntimeException(
37        "The matrices do not have compatible size");
38    }
39
40    // Create result matrix
41    E[][] result =
42      (E[][])new Number[matrix1.length][matrix2[0].length];
43
44    // Perform multiplication of two matrices
45    for (int i = 0; i < result.length; i++) {
46      for (int j = 0; j < result[0].length; j++) {
47        result[i][j] = zero();
48
```

```
        for (int k = 0; k < matrix1[0].length; k++) {
          result[i][j] = add(result[i][j],
            multiply(matrix1[i][k], matrix2[k][j]));
        }
      }
    }

    return result;
  }

  /** Print matrices, the operator, and their operation result */
  public static void printResult(
      Number[][] m1, Number[][] m2, Number[][] m3, char op) {
    for (int i = 0; i < m1.length; i++) {
      for (int j = 0; j < m1[0].length; j++)
        System.out.print(" " + m1[i][j]);

      if (i == m1.length / 2)
        System.out.print( "  " + op + "  " );
      else
        System.out.print( "     " );

      for (int j = 0; j < m2.length; j++)
        System.out.print(" " + m2[i][j]);

      if (i == m1.length / 2)
        System.out.print( "  =  " );
      else
        System.out.print( "     " );

      for (int j = 0; j < m3.length; j++)
        System.out.print(m3[i][j] + " ");

      System.out.println();
    }
  }
}
```

display result

Listing 21.10 implements the IntegerMatrix class. The class extends GenericMatrix<Integer> in line 1. After the generic instantiation, the add method in GenericMatrix<Integer> is now Integer add(Integer o1, Integer o2). The add, multiply and zero methods are implemented for Integer objects. These methods are still protected, because they are invoked only by the addMatrix and multiplyMatrix methods.

Listing 21.10 IntegerMatrix.java

```
1 public class IntegerMatrix extends GenericMatrix<Integer> {
2   /** Implement the add method for adding two matrix elements */
3   protected Integer add(Integer o1, Integer o2) {
4     return o1 + o2;
5   }
6
7   /** Implement the multiply method for multiplying two
8      matrix elements */
9   protected Integer multiply(Integer o1, Integer o2) {
10    return o1 * o2;
11  }
12
```

extends generic type

implement add

implement multiply

implement zero

```
  /** Implement the zero method to specify zero for Integer */
  protected Integer zero() {
    return 0;
  }
}
```

Listing 21.11 implements the `RationalMatrix` class. The `Rational` class was introduced in §14.13, "Case Study: The `Rational` Class." `Rational` is a subtype of `Number`. The `RationalMatrix` class extends `GenericMatrix<Rational>` in line 1. After the generic instantiation, the `add` method in `GenericMatrix<Rational>` is now `Rational add(Rational o1, Rational o2)`. The `add`, `multiply`, and `zero` methods are implemented for `Rational` objects. These methods are still protected, because they are invoked only by the `addMatrix` and `multiplyMatrix` methods.

Listing 21.11 RationalMatrix.java

extends generic type

implement add

implement multiply

implement zero

```
 1 public class RationalMatrix extends GenericMatrix<Rational> {
 2   /** Implement the add method for adding two rational elements */
 3   protected Rational add(Rational r1, Rational r2) {
 4     return r1.add(r2);
 5   }
 6
 7   /** Implement the multiply method for multiplying
 8      two rational elements */
 9   protected Rational multiply(Rational r1, Rational r2) {
10     return r1.multiply(r2);
11   }
12
13   /** Implement the zero method to specify zero for Rational */
14   protected Rational zero() {
15     return new Rational(0,1);
16   }
17 }
```

Listing 21.12 gives a program that creates two `Integer` matrices (lines 4–5) and an `IntegerMatrix` object (line 8), and adds and multiplies two matrices in lines 12 and 16.

Listing 21.12 TestIntegerMatrix.java

create matrices

create **IntegerMatrix**

add two matrices

multiply two matrices

```
 1 public class TestIntegerMatrix {
 2   public static void main(String[] args) {
 3     // Create Integer arrays m1, m2
 4     Integer[][] m1 = new Integer[][]{{1, 2, 3}, {4, 5, 6}, {1, 1, 1}};
 5     Integer[][] m2 = new Integer[][]{{1, 1, 1}, {2, 2, 2}, {0, 0, 0}};
 6
 7     // Create an instance of IntegerMatrix
 8     IntegerMatrix integerMatrix = new IntegerMatrix();
 9
10     System.out.println("\nm1 + m2 is ");
11     GenericMatrix.printResult(
12       m1, m2, integerMatrix.addMatrix(m1, m2), '+');
13
14     System.out.println("\nm1 * m2 is ");
15     GenericMatrix.printResult(
16       m1, m2, integerMatrix.multiplyMatrix(m1, m2), '*');
17   }
18 }
```

```
m1 + m2 is
 1 2 3     1 1 1     2 3 4
 4 5 6  +  2 2 2  =  6 7 8
 1 1 1     0 0 0     1 1 1

m1 * m2 is
 1 2 3     1 1 1     5  5  5
 4 5 6  *  2 2 2  =  14 14 14
 1 1 1     0 0 0     3  3  3
```

Listing 21.13 gives a program that creates two `Rational` matrices (lines 4–10) and a `RationalMatrix` object (line 13) and adds and multiplies two matrices in lines 17 and 21.

LISTING 21.13 TestRationalMatrix.java

```
1 public class TestRationalMatrix {
2   public static void main(String[] args) {
3     // Create two Rational arrays m1 and m2
4     Rational[][] m1 = new Rational[3][3];
5     Rational[][] m2 = new Rational[3][3];
6     for (int i = 0; i < m1.length; i++)
7       for (int j = 0; j < m1[0].length; j++) {
8         m1[i][j] = new Rational(i + 1, j + 5);
9         m2[i][j] = new Rational(i + 1, j + 6);
10      }
11
12    // Create an instance of RationalMatrix
13    RationalMatrix rationalMatrix = new RationalMatrix();
14
15    System.out.println("\nm1 + m2 is ");
16    GenericMatrix.printResult(
17      m1, m2, rationalMatrix.addMatrix(m1, m2), '+');
18
19    System.out.println("\nm1 * m2 is ");
20    GenericMatrix.printResult(
21      m1, m2, rationalMatrix.multiplyMatrix(m1, m2), '*');
22  }
23 }
```

create matrices

create **RationalMatrix**

add two matrices

multiply two matrices

```
m1 + m2 is
 1/5 1/6 1/7     1/6 1/7 1/8     11/30 13/42 15/56
 2/5 1/3 2/7  +  1/3 2/7 1/4  =  11/15 13/21 15/28
 3/5 1/2 3/7     1/2 3/7 3/8     11/10 13/14 45/56

m1 * m2 is
 1/5 1/6 1/7     1/6 1/7 1/8     101/630 101/735 101/840
 2/5 1/3 2/7  *  1/3 2/7 1/4  =  101/315 202/735 101/420
 3/5 1/2 3/7     1/2 3/7 3/8     101/210 101/245 101/280
```

KEY TERMS

actual concrete type 708
bounded generic type 712
formal generic type 708
generic instantiation 708
raw type 713
unbounded wildcard (<?>) 715
bounded wildcard (<? extends E>) 715
lower bound wildcard (<? super E>) 715

Chapter Summary

1. Generics is the capability to parameterize types. With it you can define a class or a method with generic types that can be replaced with concrete types by the compiler.
2. The key benefit of generics is to enable errors to be detected at compile time rather than at runtime.
3. A generic class or method permits you to specify allowable types of objects that the class or method may work with. If you attempt to use the class or method with an incompatible object, the compiler can detect the errors.
4. A generic type defined in a class, interface, or a static method is called a *formal generic type*, which can be replaced later with an *actual concrete type*. Replacing a generic type is called a *generic instantiation*.
5. A generic class such as `ArrayList` used without a type parameter is called a *raw type*. Use of raw type is allowed for backward compatibility with the earlier versions of Java.
6. A wildcard generic type has three forms: `?`, `? extends T`, or `? super T`, where `T` is a generic type. The first form, `?`, called an *unbounded wildcard*, is the same as `? extends Object`. The second form, `? extends T`, called a *bounded wildcard*, represents `T` or an unknown subtype of `T`. The third form, `? super T`, called a *lower bound wildcard*, denotes `T` or an unknown supertype of `T`.
7. Generics are implemented using an approach called *type erasure*. The compiler uses the generic type information to compile the code but erases it afterward. So the generic information is not available at runtime. This approach enables the generic code to be backward compatible with the legacy code that uses raw types.
8. You cannot create an instance using a generic type parameter.
9. You cannot create an array using a generic type parameter.
10. You cannot use a generic type parameter of a class in a static context.
11. Generic type parameters cannot be used in exception classes.

Review Questions

Sections 21.2–21.4

21.1 Are there any compile errors in (a) and (b)?

```
ArrayList dates = new ArrayList();
dates.add(new Date());
dates.add(new String());
```

(a)

```
ArrayList<Date> dates =
  new ArrayList<Date>();
dates.add(new Date());
dates.add(new String());
```

(b)

21.2 What is wrong in (a)? Is the code in (b) correct?

```
ArrayList dates = new ArrayList();
dates.add(new Date());
Date date = dates.get(0);
```

(a)

```
ArrayList<Date> dates =
  new ArrayList<Date>();
dates.add(new Date());
Date date = dates.get(0);
```

(b)

CHAPTER 22

JAVA COLLECTIONS FRAMEWORK

Objectives

- To describe the Java Collections Framework hierarchy (§§22.1–22.2).
- To use the common methods defined in the Collection interface for operating sets and lists (§22.3).
- To use the Iterator interface to traverse a collection (§22.4).
- To use the for-each loop to simplify traversing a collection (§22.4).
- To explore how and when to use HashSet (§22.4.1), LinkedHashSet (§22.4.2), or TreeSet (§22.4.3) to store elements.
- To compare elements using the Comparable interface and the Comparator interface (§22.5).
- To explore how and when to use ArrayList or LinkedList to store elements (§22.6).
- To use the static utility methods in the Collections class for sorting, searching, shuffling lists, and finding the largest and smallest element in collections (§22.7).
- To compare performance of sets and lists (§22.8).
- To distinguish between Vector and ArrayList and to use the Stack class for creating stacks (§22.9).
- To explore the relationships among Collection,Queue, LinkedList, and PriorityQueue and to create priority queues using the PriorityQueue class (§22.10).
- To tell the differences between Collection and Map and describe when and how to use HashMap, LinkedHashMap,and TreeMap to store values associated with keys (§22.11).
- To obtain singleton sets, lists, and maps, and unmodifiable sets, lists, and maps, using the static methods in the Collections class (§22.12).

22.1 Introduction

data structure

A *data structure* is a collection of data organized in some fashion. The structure not only stores data but also supports operations for accessing and manipulating the data. You have learned `ArrayList`, which is a data structure to store elements in a list. Java provides several more data structures that can be used to organize and manipulate data efficiently. These data structures are commonly known as *Java Collections Framework*.

container

In object-oriented thinking, a data structure, also known as a *container*, is an object that stores other objects, referred to as data or elements. Some people refer to data structures as *container objects*. To define a data structure is essentially to define a class. The class for a data structure should use data fields to store data and provide methods to support such operations as search, insertion, and deletion. To create a data structure is therefore to create an instance from the class. You can then apply the methods on the instance to manipulate the data structure, such as inserting an element into or deleting an element from the data structure.

The Java Collections Framework supports two types of containers:

collection

- One for storing a collection of elements, simply called a *collection*.

map

- The other for storing key/value pairs, called a *map*.

Maps are efficient data structures for fast searching an element using a key. We will introduce maps later in this chapter. Now we turn our attention to collections.

22.2 Collections

set
list
queue

The Java Collections Framework supports three major types of collections: `Set`, `List`, and `Queue`. An instance of `Set` stores a group of nonduplicate elements. An instance of `List` stores an ordered collection of elements. An instance of `Queue` stores objects that are processed in first-in, first-out fashion. The common features of these collections are defined in the interfaces, and implementations are provided in concrete classes, as shown in Figure 22.1.

Note

All the interfaces and classes defined in the Java Collections Framework are grouped in the `java.util` package.

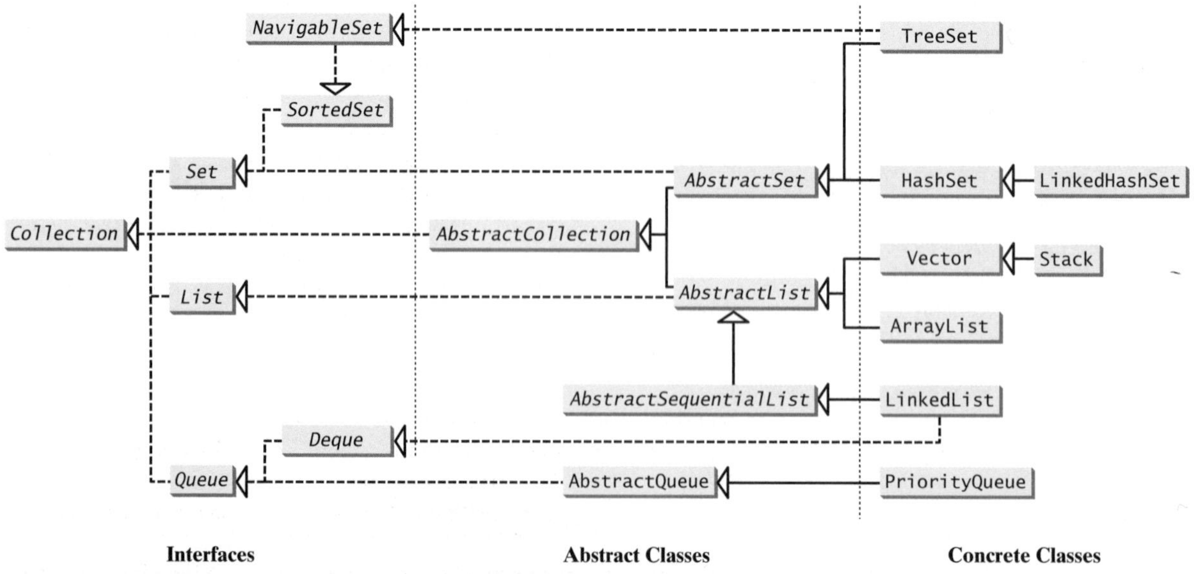
NavigableSet
TreeSet
SortedSet
Set
AbstractSet
HashSet
LinkedHashSet
Collection
AbstractCollection
Vector
Stack
List
AbstractList
ArrayList
AbstractSequentialList
LinkedList
Deque
Queue
AbstractQueue
PriorityQueue
Interfaces
Abstract Classes
Concrete Classes

FIGURE 22.1 A collection is a container that stores objects.

Design Guide

The design of the Java Collections Framework is an excellent example of using interfaces, abstract classes, and concrete classes. The interfaces define the framework. The abstract classes provide partial implementation for convenience. The concrete classes implement the interfaces with concrete data structures.

Note

All the concrete classes in the Java Collections Framework implement the `java.lang.Cloneable` and `java.io.Serializable` interfaces. Thus their instances can be cloned and serialized.

Cloneable
Serializable

22.3 The `Collection` Interface and the `AbstractCollection` Class

The `Collection` interface is the root interface for manipulating a collection of objects. Its public methods are listed in Figure 22.2. The `AbstractCollection` class is a convenience class that provides partial implementation for the `Collection` interface. It implements all the methods in `Collection` except the `size` and `iterator` methods. These are implemented in appropriate subclasses.

basic operations

The `Collection` interface provides the basic operations for adding and removing elements in a collection. The `add` method adds an element to the collection. The `addAll` method adds all the elements in the specified collection to this collection. The `remove` method removes an element from the collection. The `removeAll` method removes the elements from this collection that are present in the specified collection. The `retainAll` method retains the elements in

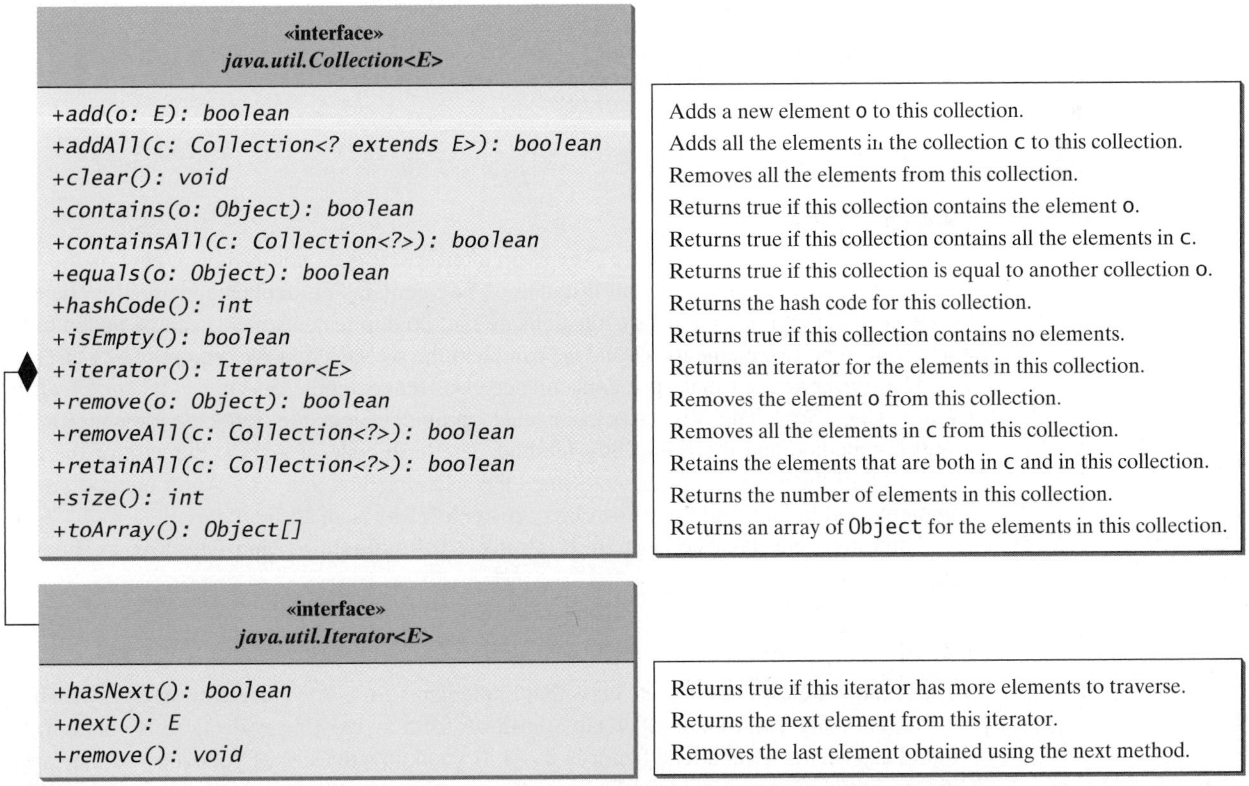
«interface»
java.util.Collection<E>
+add(o: E): boolean
+addAll(c: Collection<? extends E>): boolean
+clear(): void
+contains(o: Object): boolean
+containsAll(c: Collection<?>): boolean
+equals(o: Object): boolean
+hashCode(): int
+isEmpty(): boolean
+iterator(): Iterator<E>
+remove(o: Object): boolean
+removeAll(c: Collection<?>): boolean
+retainAll(c: Collection<?>): boolean
+size(): int
+toArray(): Object[]
Adds a new element o to this collection.
Adds all the elements in the collection c to this collection.
Removes all the elements from this collection.
Returns true if this collection contains the element o.
Returns true if this collection contains all the elements in c.
Returns true if this collection is equal to another collection o.
Returns the hash code for this collection.
Returns true if this collection contains no elements.
Returns an iterator for the elements in this collection.
Removes the element o from this collection.
Removes all the elements in c from this collection.
Retains the elements that are both in c and in this collection.
Returns the number of elements in this collection.
Returns an array of Object for the elements in this collection.
«interface»
java.util.Iterator<E>
+hasNext(): boolean
+next(): E
+remove(): void
Returns true if this iterator has more elements to traverse.
Returns the next element from this iterator.
Removes the last element obtained using the next method.

FIGURE 22.2 The `Collection` interface contains the methods for manipulating the elements in a collection, and you can obtain an iterator object for traversing elements in the collection.

this collection that are also present in the specified collection. All these methods return `boolean`. The return value is `true` if the collection is changed as a result of the method execution. The `clear()` method simply removes all the elements from the collection.

set operations

Note

The methods `addAll`, `removeAll`, and `retainAll` are similar to the set union, difference, and intersection operations.

query operations

The `Collection` interface provides various query operations. The `size` method returns the number of elements in the collection. The `contains` method checks whether the collection contains the specified element. The `containsAll` method checks whether the collection contains all the elements in the specified collection. The `isEmpty` method returns `true` if the collection is empty.

The `Collection` interface provides the `toArray()` method that returns an array representation for the collection.

iterator

A collection may be a set or a list. The `Iterator` interface provides a uniform way for traversing elements in various types of collections. The `iterator` method in the `Collection` interface returns an instance of the `Iterator` interface, as shown in Figure 22.2, which provides sequential access to the elements in the collection using the `next()` method. You can also use the `hasNext()` method to check whether there are more elements in the iterator, and the `remove()` method to remove the last element returned by the iterator.

Design Note

Unsupported Operations

Some of the methods in the `Collection` interface cannot be implemented in the concrete subclass. In this case, the method would throw `java.lang.UnsupportedOperationException`, a subclass of `RuntimeException`. This is a good design that you can use in your project. If a method has no meaning in the subclass, you can implement it as follows:

```
public void someMethod() {
  throw new UnsupportedOperationException
    ("Method not supported");
}
```

22.4 Sets

no duplicates

The `Set` interface extends the `Collection` interface. It does not introduce new methods or constants, but it stipulates that an instance of `Set` contains no duplicate elements. The concrete classes that implement `Set` must ensure that no duplicate elements can be added to the set. That is, no two elements `e1` and `e2` can be in the set such that `e1.equals(e2)` is `true`.

The `AbstractSet` class is a convenience class that extends `AbstractCollection` and implements `Set`. The `AbstractSet` class provides concrete implementations for the `equals` method and the `hashCode` method. The hash code of a set is the sum of the hash codes of all the elements in the set. Since the `size` method and `iterator` method are not implemented in the `AbstractSet` class, `AbstractSet` is an abstract class.

Three concrete classes of `Set` are `HashSet`, `LinkedHashSet`, and `TreeSet`, as shown in Figure 22.3.

22.4.1 HashSet

The `HashSet` class is a concrete class that implements `Set`. You can create an empty hash set using its no-arg constructor or create a hash set from an existing collection. By default, the initial capacity is `16` and load factor is `0.75`. If you know the size of your set, you may specify the initial capacity and load factor in the constructor. Otherwise, use the default setting. Load factor is a value between `0.0` and `1.0`.

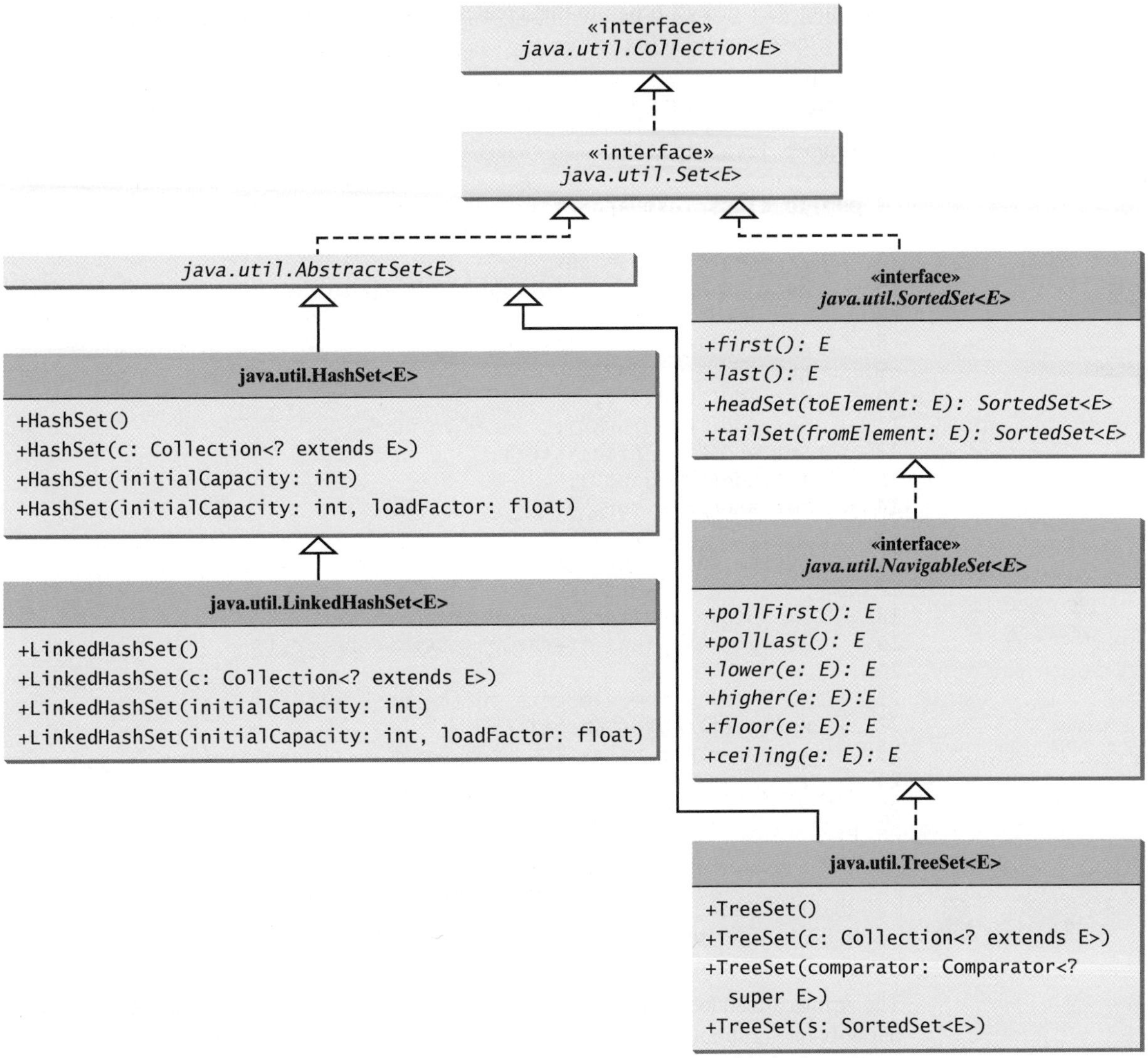

«interface»
java.util.Collection<E>
«interface»
java.util.Set<E>
java.util.AbstractSet<E>
«interface»
java.util.SortedSet<E>
+first(): E
+last(): E
+headSet(toElement: E): SortedSet<E>
+tailSet(fromElement: E): SortedSet<E>
java.util.HashSet<E>
+HashSet()
+HashSet(c: Collection<? extends E>)
+HashSet(initialCapacity: int)
+HashSet(initialCapacity: int, loadFactor: float)
«interface»
java.util.NavigableSet<E>
+pollFirst(): E
+pollLast(): E
+lower(e: E): E
+higher(e: E):E
+floor(e: E): E
+ceiling(e: E): E
java.util.LinkedHashSet<E>
+LinkedHashSet()
+LinkedHashSet(c: Collection<? extends E>)
+LinkedHashSet(initialCapacity: int)
+LinkedHashSet(initialCapacity: int, loadFactor: float)
java.util.TreeSet<E>
+TreeSet()
+TreeSet(c: Collection<? extends E>)
+TreeSet(comparator: Comparator<? super E>)
+TreeSet(s: SortedSet<E>)

FIGURE 22.3 The Java Collections Framework provides three concrete set classes.

Load factor measures how full the set is allowed to be before its capacity is increased. When the number of elements exceeds the product of the capacity and load factor, the capacity is automatically doubled. For example, if the capacity is 16 and load factor is 0.75, the capacity will be doubled to 32 when the size reaches 12 (16 * 0.75 = 12). Higher load factor decreases the space costs but increases the search time. Generally, the default load factor 0.75 is a good trade-off between time and space costs. load factor

A HashSet can be used to store *duplicate-free* elements. For efficiency, objects added to a hash set need to implement the hashCode method in a manner that properly disperses the hash code. Recall that hashCode is defined in the Object class. The hash codes of two objects must be the same if the two objects are equal. Two unequal objects may have the same hash code, but you should implement the hashCode method to avoid too many such cases. Most of the classes in the Java API implement the hashCode method. For example, the hashCode in the Integer class returns its int value. The hashCode in the Character class returns the Unicode of the character. The hashCode in the String class returns $s_0 * 31^{(n-1)} + s_1 * 31^{(n-2)} + \ldots + s_{n-1}$, where s_i is s.charAt(i). **hashCode()**

Listing 22.1 gives a program that creates a hash set to store strings and uses an iterator to traverse the elements in the set.

LISTING 22.1 TestHashSet.java

create set
add element
get iterator
traverse iterator

```
1 import java.util.*;
2 
3 public class TestHashSet {
4   public static void main(String[] args) {
5     // Create a hash set
6     Set<String> set = new HashSet<String>();
7 
8     // Add strings to the set
9     set.add("London");
10    set.add("Paris");
11    set.add("New York");
12    set.add("San Francisco");
13    set.add("Beijing");
14    set.add("New York");
15 
16    System.out.println(set);
17 
18    // Obtain an iterator for the hash set
19    Iterator<String> iterator = set.iterator();
20 
21    // Display the elements in the hash set
22    while (iterator.hasNext()) {
23      System.out.print(iterator.next().toUpperCase() + " ");
24    }
25  }
26 }
```

```
[San Francisco, New York, Paris, Beijing, London]
SAN FRANCISCO NEW YORK PARIS BEIJING LONDON
```

The strings are added to the set (lines 9–14). "New York" is added to the set more than once, but only one is stored, because a set does not allow duplicates.

As shown in the output, the strings are not stored in the order in which they are inserted into the set. There is no particular order for the elements in a hash set. To impose an order on them, you need to use the LinkedHashSet class, which is introduced in the next section.

for-each loop

Tip

You can simplify the code in lines 18–24 using a for-each loop without using an iterator, as follows:

```
for (Object element: set)
  System.out.print(element);
```

This loop is read as "for each element in the set, do the following." The for-each loop can be used for arrays (see §6.2.7) as well as any instance of Collection.

Since a set is an instance of Collection, all methods defined in Collection can be used for sets. Listing 22.2 gives an example that explores the methods in the Collection interface.

LISTING 22.2 TestMethodsInCollection.java

create a set

```
public class TestMethodsInCollection {
  public static void main(String[] args) {
    // Create set1
    java.util.Set<String> set1 = new java.util.HashSet<String>();
```

```java

    // Add strings to set1
    set1.add("London");
    set1.add("Paris");
    set1.add("New York");
    set1.add("San Francisco");
    set1.add("Beijing");

    System.out.println("set1 is " + set1);
    System.out.println(set1.size() + " elements in set1");

    // Delete a string from set1
    set1.remove("London");
    System.out.println("\nset1 is " + set1);
    System.out.println(set1.size() + " elements in set1");

    // Create set2
    java.util.Set<String> set2 = new java.util.HashSet<String>();

    // Add strings to set2
    set2.add("London");
    set2.add("Shanghai");
    set2.add("Paris");
    System.out.println("\nset2 is " + set2);
    System.out.println(set2.size() + " elements in set2");

    System.out.println("\nIs Taipei in set2? "
      + set2.contains("Taipei"));

    set1.addAll(set2);
    System.out.println("\nAfter adding set2 to set1, set1 is "
      + set1);

    set1.removeAll(set2);
    System.out.println("After removing set2 from set1, set1 is "
      + set1);

    set1.retainAll(set2);
    System.out.println("After removing common elements in set2 "
      + "from set1, set1 is " + set1);
  }
}
```

add element

get size

remove element

create a set

add element

contains element?

addAll

removeAll

retainAll

```
set1 is [San Francisco, New York, Paris, Beijing, London]
5 elements in set1

set1 is [San Francisco, New York, Paris, Beijing]
4 elements in set1

set2 is [Shanghai, Paris, London]
3 elements in set2

Is Taipei in set2? false

After adding set2 to set1, set1 is
  [San Francisco, New York, Shanghai, Paris, Beijing, London]

After removing set2 from set1, set1 is
  [San Francisco, New York, Beijing]

After removing common elements in set2 from set1, set1 is []
```

The program creates two sets (lines 4, 22). The `size()` method returns the number of the elements in a set (line 14). Line 17

```
set1.remove("London");
```

removes `"New York"` from `set1`.

The `contains` method (line 32) checks whether an element is in the set.

Line 34

```
set1.addAll(set2);
```

adds `set2` to `set1`. So, `set1` becomes `[San Francisco, New York, Shanghai, Paris, Beijing, London]`.

Line 38

```
set1.removeAll(set2);
```

removes `set2` from `set1`. So, `set1` becomes `[San Francisco, New York, Beijing]`.

Line 42

```
set1.retainAll(set2);
```

retains the common elements in `set1`. Since `set1` and `set2` have no common elements, `set1` becomes empty.

22.4.2 `LinkedHashSet`

`LinkedHashSet` extends `HashSet` with a linked-list implementation that supports an ordering of the elements in the set. The elements in a `HashSet` are not ordered, but the elements in a `LinkedHashSet` can be retrieved in the order in which they were inserted into the set. A `LinkedHashSet` can be created by using one of its four constructors, as shown in Figure 22.3. These constructors are similar to the constructors for `HashSet`.

Listing 22.3 gives a test program for `LinkedHashSet`. The program simply replaces `HashSet` by `LinkedHashSet` in Listing 22.1.

LISTING 22.3 `TestLinkedHashSet.java`

create linked hash set · add element · display elements

```
import java.util.*;

public class TestLinkedHashSet {
  public static void main(String[] args) {
    // Create a hash set
    Set<String> set = new LinkedHashSet<String>();

    // Add strings to the set
    set.add("London");
    set.add("Paris");
    set.add("New York");
    set.add("San Francisco");
    set.add("Beijing");
    set.add("New York");

    System.out.println(set);

    // Display the elements in the hash set
    for (Object element: set)
      System.out.print(element.toString().toLowerCase() + " ");
  }
}
```

```
[London, Paris, New York, San Francisco, Beijing]
london paris new york san francisco beijing
```

A LinkedHashSet is created in line 6. As shown in the output, the strings are stored in the order in which they are inserted. Since LinkedHashSet is a set, it does not store duplicate elements.

The LinkedHashSet maintains the order in which the elements are inserted. To impose a different order (e.g., increasing or decreasing order), you can use the TreeSet class introduced in the next section.

Tip

If you don't need to maintain the order in which the elements are inserted, use HashSet, which is more efficient than LinkedHashSet.

22.4.3 TreeSet

SortedSet is a subinterface of Set, which guarantees that the elements in the set are sorted. Additionally, it provides the methods first() and last() for returning the first and last elements in the set, and headSet(toElement) and tailSet(fromElement) for returning a portion of the set whose elements are less than toElement and greater than or equal to fromElement.

NavigableSet extends SortedSet to provide navigation methods lower(e), floor(e), ceiling(e), and higher(e) that return elements respectively less than, less than or equal, greater than or equal, and greater than a given element and return null if there is no such element. The pollFirst() and pollLast() methods remove and return the first and last element in the tree set, respectively.

TreeSet implements the SortedSet interface. To create a TreeSet, use a constructor, as shown in Figure 22.3. You can add objects into a tree set as long as they can be compared with each other. There are two ways to compare objects.

- Use the Comparable interface. Since the objects added to the set are instances of Comparable, they can be compared using the compareTo method. The Comparable interface was introduced in §14.5. Several classes in the Java API, such as String, Date, Calendar, and all the wrapper classes for the primitive types, implement the Comparable interface. This approach is referred to as *natural order*.

  Comparable
  natural order

- If the class for the elements does not implement the Comparable interface, or if you don't want to use the compareTo method in the class that implements the Comparable interface, specify a comparator for the elements in the set. This approach is referred to as *order by comparator*. It will be introduced in §22.5, "The Comparator Interface."

  Comparator
  order by comparator

Listing 22.4 gives an example of ordering elements using the Comparable interface. The preceding example in Listing 22.3 displays all the strings in their insertion order. This example rewrites the preceding example to display the strings in alphabetical order using the TreeSet class.

LISTING 22.4 TestTreeSet.java

```
import java.util.*;

public class TestTreeSet {
  public static void main(String[] args) {
    // Create a hash set
    Set<String> set = new HashSet<String>();
```

create hash set

create tree set

display elements

```
 7
 8      // Add strings to the set
 9      set.add("London");
10      set.add("Paris");
11      set.add("New York");
12      set.add("San Francisco");
13      set.add("Beijing");
14      set.add("New York");
15
16      TreeSet<String> treeSet = new TreeSet<String>(set);
17      System.out.println("Sorted tree set: " + treeSet);
18
19      // Use the methods in SortedSet interface
20      System.out.println("first(): " + treeSet.first());
21      System.out.println("last(): " + treeSet.last());
22      System.out.println("headSet(): " + treeSet.headSet("New York"));
23      System.out.println("tailSet(): " + treeSet.tailSet("New York"));
24
25      // Use the methods in NavigableSet interface
26      System.out.println("lower(\"P\"): " + treeSet.lower("P"));
27      System.out.println("higher(\"P\"): " + treeSet.higher("P"));
28      System.out.println("floor(\"P\"): " + treeSet.floor("P"));
29      System.out.println("ceiling(\"P\"): " + treeSet.ceiling("P"));
30      System.out.println("pollFirst(): " + treeSet.pollFirst());
31      System.out.println("pollLast(): " + treeSet.pollLast());
32      System.out.println("New tree set: " + treeSet);
33    }
34  }
```

```
Sorted tree set: [Beijing, London, New York, Paris, San Francisco]
first(): Beijing
last(): San Francisco
headSet(): [Beijing, London]
tailSet(): [New York, Paris, San Francisco]
lower("P"): New York
higher("P"): Paris
floor("P"): New York
ceiling("P"): Paris
pollFirst(): Beijing
pollLast(): San Francisco
New tree set: [London, New York, Paris]
```

The example creates a hash set filled with strings, then creates a tree set for the same strings. The strings are sorted in the tree set using the `compareTo` method in the `Comparable` interface.

The elements in the set are sorted once you create a `TreeSet` object from a `HashSet` object using `new TreeSet(hashSet)` (line 16). You may rewrite the program to create an instance of `TreeSet` using its no-arg constructor, and add the strings into the `TreeSet` object. Then, every time a string is added to the `TreeSet` object, the elements in it will be reordered. The approach used in the example is generally more efficient because it requires only a one-time sorting.

`treeSet.first()` returns the first element in `treeSet` (line 20). `treeSet.last()` returns the last element in `treeSet` (line 21). `treeSet.headSet("New York")` returns the elements in `treeSet` before New York (line 22). `treeSet.tailSet("New York")` returns the elements in `treeSet` after New York, including New York (line 23).

`treeSet.lower("P")` returns the largest element less than `"P"` in `treeSet` (line 26). `treeSet.higher("P")` returns the smallest element greater than `"P"` in `treeSet` (line 27).

`treeSet.floor("P")` returns the largest element less than or equal to `"P"` in `treeSet` (line 28). `treeSet.ceiling("P")` returns the smallest element greater than or equal to `"P"` in `treeSet` (line 29). `treeSet.pollFirst()` removes the first element in `treeSet` and returns the removed element (line 30). `treeSet.pollLast()` removes the last element in `treeSet` and returns the removed element (line 31).

Note

All the concrete classes in Java Collections Framework (see Figure 22.1) have at least two constructors. One is the no-arg constructor that constructs an empty collection. The other constructs instances from a collection. Thus the `TreeSet` class has the constructor `TreeSet(Collection c)` for constructing a `TreeSet` from a collection `c`. In this example, `new TreeSet(hashSet)` creates an instance of `TreeSet` from the collection `hashSet`.

Tip

If you don't need to maintain a sorted set when updating a set, you should use a hash set, because it takes less time to insert and remove elements in a hash set. When you need a set to be sorted, you can create a tree set from the hash set.

22.5 The Comparator Interface

Sometimes you want to insert elements into a tree set. The elements may not be instances of `java.lang.Comparable`. You can define a comparator to compare these elements. To do so, create a class that implements the `java.util.Comparator` interface. The `Comparator` interface has two methods, `compare` and `equals`.

- **public int** `compare(Object element1, Object element2)`
  Returns a negative value if `element1` is less than `element2`, a positive value if `element1` is greater than `element2`, and zero if they are equal.
- **public boolean** `equals(Object element)`
  Returns true if the specified object is also a comparator and imposes the same ordering as this comparator.

The `equals` method is also defined in the `Object` class. Therefore, you will not get a compile error even if you don't implement the `equals` method in your custom comparator class. However, in some cases implementing this method may improve performance by allowing programs to determine quickly whether two distinct comparators impose the same order.

Listing 22.5 defines a `Comparator` for geometric objects. The `GeometricObject` class was introduced in §14.2, "Abstract Classes." Line 4 implements `Comparator<GeometricObject>`. Line 5 overrides the `compare` method to compare two geometric objects. The comparator class also implements `Serializable`. It is generally a good idea for comparators to implement `Serializable`, as they may be used as ordering methods in serializable data structures such as `TreeSet`. In order for the data structure to serialize successfully, the comparator (if provided) must implement `Serializable`.

LISTING 22.5 GeometricObjectComparator.java

```
1 import java.util.Comparator;
2
3 public class GeometricObjectComparator
4     implements Comparator<GeometricObject>, java.io.Serializable {
5   public int compare(GeometricObject o1, GeometricObject o2) {
6     double area1 = o1.getArea();
7     double area2 = o2.getArea();
8
9     if (area1 < area2)
```

implements **Comparator**
implements **compare**

```
      return -1;
    else if (area1 == area2)
      return 0;
    else
      return 1;
  }
}
```

If you create a `TreeSet` using its no-arg constructor, the `compareTo` method is used to compare the elements in the set, assuming that the class of the elements implements the `Comparable` interface. To use a comparator, you have to use the constructor `TreeSet(Comparator comparator)` to create a sorted set that uses the `compare` method in the comparator to order the elements in the set.

Listing 22.6 gives a program that demonstrates how to sort elements in a tree set using the `Comparator` interface. The example creates a tree set of geometric objects in lines 6–11. The geometric objects are sorted using the `compare` method in the `Comparator` interface.

Listing 22.6 TestTreeSetWithComparator.java

tree set

display elements

```
1 import java.util.*;
2
3 public class TestTreeSetWithComparator {
4   public static void main(String[] args) {
5     // Create a tree set for geometric objects using a comparator
6     Set<GeometricObject> set =
7       new TreeSet<GeometricObject>(new GeometricObjectComparator());
8     set.add(new Rectangle(4, 5));
9     set.add(new Circle(40));
10    set.add(new Circle(40));
11    set.add(new Rectangle(4, 1));
12
13    // Display geometric objects in the tree set
14    System.out.println("A sorted set of geometric objects");
15    for (GeometricObject element: set)
16      System.out.println("area = " + element.getArea());
17  }
18 }
```

```
A sorted set of geometric objects
area = 4.0
area = 20.0
area = 5022.548245743669
```

The `Circle` and `Rectangle` classes were defined in §14.2, "Abstract Classes." They are all subclasses of `GeometricObject`.

Two circles of the same radius are added to the set in the tree set (lines 9–10), but only one is stored, because the two circles are equal and the set does not allow duplicates.

Comparable vs. **Comparator**

Note

`Comparable` is used to compare the objects of the class that implement `Comparable`. `Comparator` can be used to compare the objects of the class that doesn't implement `Comparable`.

22.6 Lists

A set stores nonduplicate elements. To allow duplicate elements to be stored in a collection, you need to use a list. A list can not only store duplicate elements but also allow the user to specify where they are stored. The user can access elements by an index. The `List` interface extends `Collection` to define an ordered collection with duplicates allowed. The `List` interface adds position-oriented operations, as well as a new list iterator that enables the user to traverse the list bidirectionally. The new methods in the `List` interface are shown in Figure 22.4.

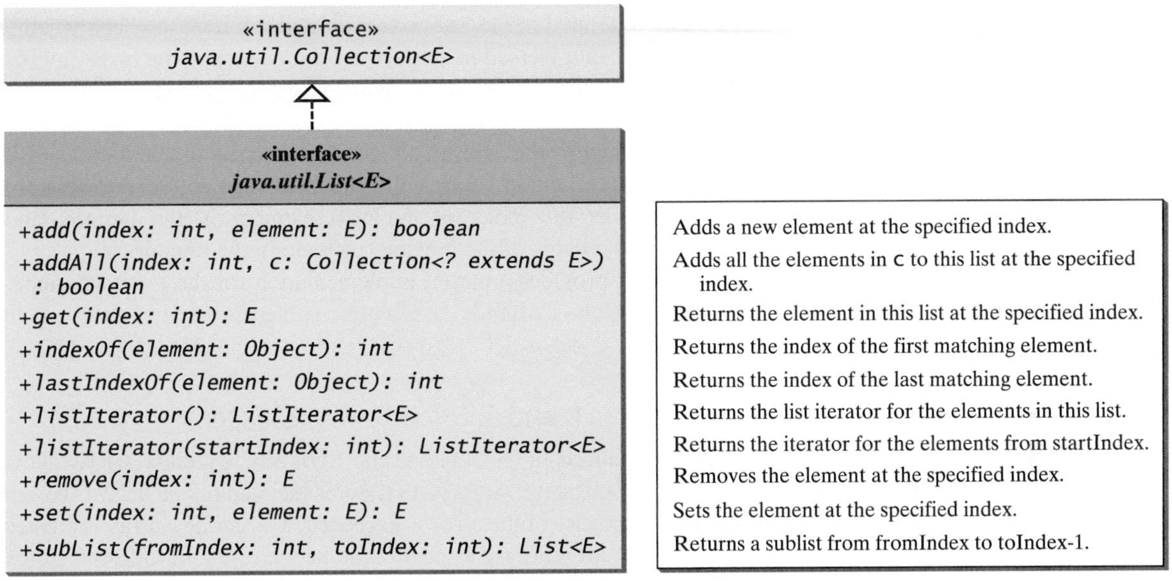
«interface»
java.util.Collection<E>
«interface»
java.util.List<E>
+add(index: int, element: E): boolean
+addAll(index: int, c: Collection<? extends E>) : boolean
+get(index: int): E
+indexOf(element: Object): int
+lastIndexOf(element: Object): int
+listIterator(): ListIterator<E>
+listIterator(startIndex: int): ListIterator<E>
+remove(index: int): E
+set(index: int, element: E): E
+subList(fromIndex: int, toIndex: int): List<E>
Adds a new element at the specified index.
Adds all the elements in c to this list at the specified index.
Returns the element in this list at the specified index.
Returns the index of the first matching element.
Returns the index of the last matching element.
Returns the list iterator for the elements in this list.
Returns the iterator for the elements from startIndex.
Removes the element at the specified index.
Sets the element at the specified index.
Returns a sublist from fromIndex to toIndex-1.

FIGURE 22.4 The `List` interface stores elements in sequence, permitting duplicates.

The `add(index, element)` method is used to insert an element at a specified index, and the `addAll(index, collection)` method to insert a collection at a specified index. The `remove(index)` method is used to remove an element at the specified index from the list. A new element can be set at the specified index using the `set(index, element)` method.

The `indexOf(element)` method is used to obtain the index of the specified element's first occurrence in the list, and the `lastIndexOf(element)` method to obtain the index of its last occurrence. A sublist can be obtained by using the `subList(fromIndex, toIndex)` method.

The `listIterator()` or `listIterator(startIndex)` method returns an instance of `ListIterator`. The `ListIterator` interface extends the `Iterator` interface to add bidirectional traversal of the list. The methods in `ListIterator` are listed in Figure 22.5.

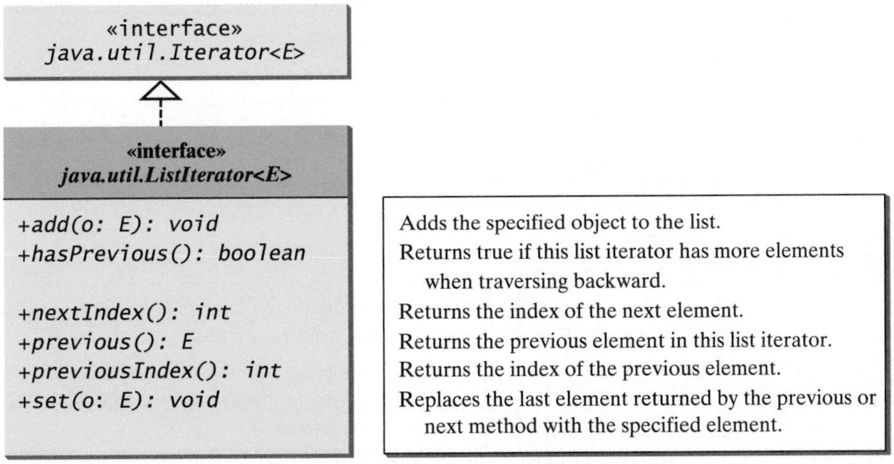
«interface»
java.util.Iterator<E>
«interface»
java.util.ListIterator<E>
+add(o: E): void
+hasPrevious(): boolean
+nextIndex(): int
+previous(): E
+previousIndex(): int
+set(o: E): void
Adds the specified object to the list.
Returns true if this list iterator has more elements when traversing backward.
Returns the index of the next element.
Returns the previous element in this list iterator.
Returns the index of the previous element.
Replaces the last element returned by the previous or next method with the specified element.

FIGURE 22.5 `ListIterator` enables traversal of a list bidirectionally.

The add(element) method inserts the specified element into the list. The element is inserted immediately before the next element that would be returned by the next() method defined in the Iterator interface, if any, and after the element that would be returned by the previous() method, if any. If the list contains no elements, the new element becomes the sole element on the list. The set(element) method can be used to replace the last element returned by the next method or the previous method with the specified element.

The hasNext() method defined in the Iterator interface is used to check whether the iterator has more elements when traversed in the forward direction, and the hasPrevious() method to check whether the iterator has more elements when traversed in the backward direction.

The next() method defined in the Iterator interface returns the next element in the iterator, and the previous() method returns the previous element in the iterator. The nextIndex() method returns the index of the next element in the iterator, and the previousIndex() returns the index of the previous element in the iterator.

The AbstractList class provides a partial implementation for the List interface. The AbstractSequentialList class extends AbstractList to provide support for linked lists.

22.6.1 The ArrayList and LinkedList Classes

The ArrayList class (introduced in §11.11) and the LinkedList class are two concrete implementations of the List interface. ArrayList stores elements in an array. The array is dynamically created. If the capacity of the array is exceeded, a larger new array is created and all the elements from the current array are copied to the new array. LinkedList stores elements in a linked list. Which of the two classes you use depends on your specific needs. If you need to support random access through an index without inserting or removing elements except at the end, ArrayList offers the most efficient collection. If, however, your application requires the insertion or deletion of elements anywhere in the list, you should choose LinkedList. A list can grow or shrink dynamically. Once it is created, an array is fixed. If your application does not require the insertion or deletion of elements, an array is the most efficient data structure.

ArrayList is a resizable-array implementation of the List interface. It also provides methods for manipulating the size of the array used internally to store the list, as shown in Figure 22.6. Each ArrayList instance has a capacity, which is the size of the array used to store the elements in the list. It is always at least as large as the list size. As elements are added to an ArrayList, its capacity grows automatically. An ArrayList does not automatically shrink.

trimToSize()

You can use the trimToSize() method to reduce the array capacity to the size of the list. An ArrayList can be constructed using its no-arg constructor, ArrayList(Collection), or ArrayList(initialCapacity).

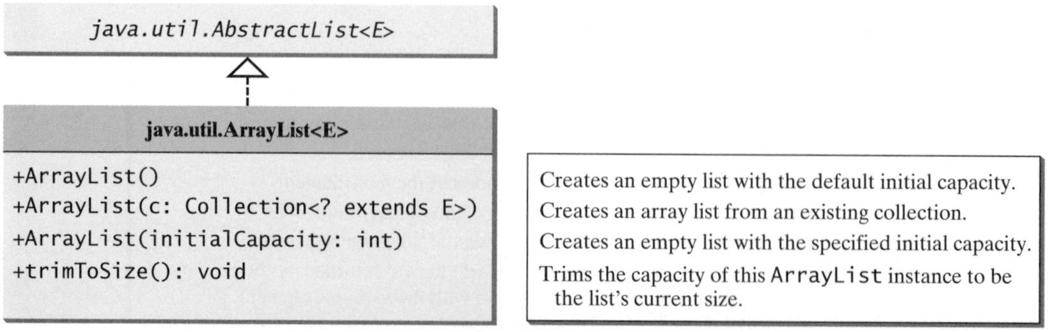
java.util.AbstractList<E>
java.util.ArrayList<E>
+ArrayList()
+ArrayList(c: Collection<? extends E>)
+ArrayList(initialCapacity: int)
+trimToSize(): void
Creates an empty list with the default initial capacity.
Creates an array list from an existing collection.
Creates an empty list with the specified initial capacity.
Trims the capacity of this ArrayList instance to be the list's current size.

FIGURE 22.6 ArrayList implements List using an array.

LinkedList is a linked list implementation of the List interface. In addition to implementing the List interface, this class provides the methods for retrieving, inserting, and removing elements from both ends of the list, as shown in Figure 22.7. A LinkedList can be constructed using its no-arg constructor or LinkedList(Collection).

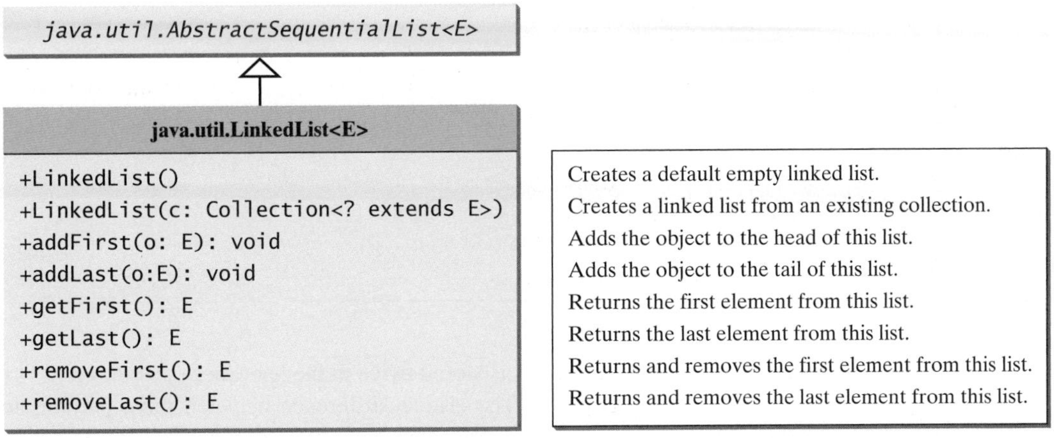
java.util.AbstractSequentialList<E>
java.util.LinkedList<E>
+LinkedList()
+LinkedList(c: Collection<? extends E>)
+addFirst(o: E): void
+addLast(o:E): void
+getFirst(): E
+getLast(): E
+removeFirst(): E
+removeLast(): E
Creates a default empty linked list.
Creates a linked list from an existing collection.
Adds the object to the head of this list.
Adds the object to the tail of this list.
Returns the first element from this list.
Returns the last element from this list.
Returns and removes the first element from this list.
Returns and removes the last element from this list.

FIGURE 22.7 LinkedList provides methods for adding and inserting elements at both ends of the list.

Listing 22.7 gives a program that creates an array list filled with numbers and inserts new elements into specified locations in the list. The example also creates a linked list from the array list and inserts and removes elements from the list. Finally, the example traverses the list forward and backward.

LISTING 22.7 TestArrayAndLinkedList.java

```
import java.util.*;

public class TestArrayAndLinkedList {
  public static void main(String[] args) {
    List<Integer> arrayList = new ArrayList<Integer>();
    arrayList.add(1); // 1 is autoboxed to new Integer(1)
    arrayList.add(2);
    arrayList.add(3);
    arrayList.add(1);
    arrayList.add(4);
    arrayList.add(0, 10);
    arrayList.add(3, 30);

    System.out.println("A list of integers in the array list:");
    System.out.println(arrayList);

    LinkedList<Object> linkedList = new LinkedList<Object>(arrayList);
    linkedList.add(1, "red");
    linkedList.removeLast();
    linkedList.addFirst("green");

    System.out.println("Display the linked list forward:");
    ListIterator<Object> listIterator = linkedList.listIterator();
    while (listIterator.hasNext()) {
      System.out.print(listIterator.next() + " ");
    }
    System.out.println();
```

array list

linked list

list iterator

list iterator

```
28
29      System.out.println("Display the linked list backward:");
30      listIterator = linkedList.listIterator(linkedList.size());
31      while (listIterator.hasPrevious()) {
32        System.out.print(listIterator.previous() + " ");
33      }
34    }
35 }
```

```
A list of integers in the array list:
[10, 1, 2, 30, 3, 1, 4]
Display the linked list forward:
green 10 red 1 2 30 3 1
Display the linked list backward:
1 3 30 2 1 red 10 green
```

A list can hold identical elements. Integer `1` is stored twice in the list (lines 6, 9). `ArrayList` and `LinkedList` are operated similarly. The critical difference between them pertains to internal implementation, which affects their performance. `ArrayList` is efficient for retrieving elements and for inserting and removing elements from the end of the list. `LinkedList` is efficient for inserting and removing elements anywhere in the list.

`Arrays.asList(T... a)` method

Tip

Java provides the static `asList` method for creating a list from a variable-length argument list of a generic type. Thus you can use the following code to create a list of strings and a list of integers:

```
List<String> list1 = Arrays.asList("red", "green", "blue");
List<Integer> list2 = Arrays.asList(10, 20, 30, 40, 50);
```

22.7 Static Methods for Lists and Collections

You can use `TreeSet` to store sorted elements in a set. But there is no sorted list. However, the Java Collections Framework provides static methods in the `Collections` class that can be used to sort a list. The `Collections` class also contains the `binarySearch`, `reverse`, `shuffle`, `copy`, and `fill` methods on lists, and `max`, `min`, `disjoint`, and `frequency` methods on collections, as shown in Figure 22.8.

You can sort the comparable elements in a list in its natural order through the `compareTo` method in the `Comparable` interface. You may also specify a comparator to sort elements. For example, the following code sorts strings in a list.

sort list

```
List<String> list = Arrays.asList("red", "green", "blue");
Collections.sort(list);
System.out.println(list);
```

The output is `[blue, green, red]`.

ascending order

descending order

The preceding code sorts a list in ascending order. To sort it in descending order, you may simply use the `Collections.reverseOrder()` method to return a `Comparator` object that orders the elements in reverse order. For example, the following code sorts a list of strings in descending order.

```
List<String> list = Arrays.asList("yellow", "red", "green", "blue");
Collections.sort(list, Collections.reverseOrder());
System.out.println(list);
```

The output is `[yellow, red, green, blue]`.

	java.util.Collections	
List	+sort(list: List): void	Sorts the specified list.
	+sort(list: List, c: Comparator): void	Sorts the specified list with the comparator.
	+binarySearch(list: List, key: Object): int	Searches the key in the sorted list using binary searc
	+binarySearch(list: List, key: Object, c: Comparator): int	Searches the key in the sorted list using binary search with the comparator.
	+reverse(list: List): void	Reverses the specified list.
	+reverseOrder(): Comparator	Returns a comparator with the reverse ordering.
	+shuffle(list: List): void	Shuffles the specified list randomly.
	+shuffle(list: List, rmd: Random): void	Shuffles the specified list with a random object.
	+copy(des: List, src: List): void	Copies from the source list to the destination list.
	+nCopies(n: int, o: Object): List	Returns a list consisting of *n* copies of the object.
	+fill(list: List, o: Object): void	Fills the list with the object.
Collection	+max(c: Collection): Object	Returns the `max` object in the collection.
	+max(c: Collection, c: Comparator): Object	Returns the `max` object using the comparator.
	+min(c: Collection): Object	Returns the `min` object in the collection.
	+min(c: Collection, c: Comparator): Object	Returns the `min` object using the comparator.
	+disjoint(c1: Collection, c2: Collection): boolean	Returns true if `c1` and `c2` have no elements in common.
	+frequency(c: Collection, o: Object): int	Returns the number of occurrences of the specified element in the collection.

FIGURE 22.8 The `Collections` class contains static methods for manipulating lists and collections.

binarySearch

You can use the `binarySearch` method to search for a key in a list. The list must be presorted in increasing order. If the key is not in the list, the method returns $-(insertion\ point + 1)$. Recall that the insertion point is where the item would fall in the list if it were present. For example, the following code searches the keys in a list of integers and a list of strings.

```
List<Integer> list1 =
  Arrays.asList(2, 4, 7, 10, 11, 45, 50, 59, 60, 66);
System.out.println("(1) Index: " + Collections.binarySearch(list1, 7));
System.out.println("(2) Index: " + Collections.binarySearch(list1, 9));

List<String> list2 = Arrays.asList("blue", "green", "red");
System.out.println("(3) Index: " +
  Collections.binarySearch(list2, "red"));
System.out.println("(4) Index: " +
  Collections.binarySearch(list2, "cyan"));
```

The output of the preceding code is

```
(1) Index: 2
(2) Index: -4
(3) Index: 2
(4) Index: -2
```

reverse

You can use the `reverse` method to reverse the elements in a list. For example, the following code displays `[blue, green, red, yellow]`.

```
List<String> list = Arrays.asList("yellow", "red", "green", "blue");
Collections.reverse(list);
System.out.println(list);
```

shuffle

You can use the `shuffle(List)` method to randomly reorder the elements in a list. For example, the following code shuffles the elements in `list`.

```
List<String> list = Arrays.asList("yellow", "red", "green", "blue");
Collections.shuffle(list);
System.out.println(list);
```

You can also use the `shuffle(List, Random)` method to randomly reorder the elements in a list with a specified `Random` object. Using a specified `Random` object is useful to generate a list with identical sequences of elements for the same original list. For example, the following code shuffles the elements in `list`.

```
List<String> list1 = Arrays.asList("yellow", "red", "green", "blue");
List<String> list2 = Arrays.asList("yellow", "red", "green", "blue");
Collections.shuffle(list1, new Random(20));
Collections.shuffle(list2, new Random(20));
System.out.println(list1);
System.out.println(list2);
```

You will see that `list1` and `list2` have the same sequence of elements before and after the shuffling.

copy

You can use the `copy(det, src)` method to copy all the elements from a source list to a destination list on the same index. The destination must be as long as the source list. If it is longer, the remaining elements in the source list are not affected. For example, the following code copies `list2` to `list1`.

```
List<String> list1 = Arrays.asList("yellow", "red", "green", "blue");
List<String> list2 = Arrays.asList("white", "black");
Collections.copy(list1, list2);
System.out.println(list1);
```

The output for `list1` is `[white, black, green, blue]`. The `copy` method performs a shallow copy. Only the references of the elements from the source list are copied.

nCopies

You can use the `nCopies(int n, Object o)` method to create an immutable list that consists of `n` copies of the specified object. For example, the following code creates a list with five `Calendar` objects.

```
List<GregorianCalendar> list1 = Collections.nCopies
  (5, new GregorianCalendar(2005, 0, 1));
```

The list created from the `nCopies` method is immutable, so you cannot add, remove, or update elements in the list. All the elements have the same references.

fill

You can use the `fill(List list, Object o)` method to replace all the elements in the list with the specified element. For example, the following code displays `[black, black, black]`.

```
List<String> list = Arrays.asList("red", "green", "blue");
Collections.fill(list, "black");
System.out.println(list);
```

max and min methods

You can use the `max` and `min` methods for finding the maximum and minimum elements in a collection. The elements must be comparable using the `Comparable` interface or the `Comparator` interface. For example, the following code displays the largest and smallest strings in a collection.

```
Collection<String> collection = Arrays.asList("red", "green", "blue");
System.out.println(Collections.max(collection));
System.out.println(Collections.min(collection));
```

`disjoint` method

The `disjoint(collection1, collection2)` method returns `true` if the two collections have no elements in common. For example, in the following code, `disjoint(collection1, collection2)` returns `false`, but `disjoint(collection1, collection3)` returns `true`.

```
Collection<String> collection1 = Arrays.asList("red", "cyan");
Collection<String> collection2 = Arrays.asList("red", "blue");
Collection<String> collection3 = Arrays.asList("pink", "tan");
System.out.println(Collections.disjoint(collection1, collection2));
System.out.println(Collections.disjoint(collection1, collection3));
```

`frequency` method

The `frequency(collection, element)` method finds the number of occurrences of the element in the collection. For example, `frequency(collection, "red")` returns `2` in the following code.

```
Collection<String> collection = Arrays.asList("red", "cyan", "red");
System.out.println(Collections.frequency(collection, "red"));
```

22.8 Performance of Sets and Lists

We now conduct an interesting experiment to test the performance of sets and lists. Listing 22.8 gives a program that shows the execution time of adding and removing elements in a hash set, linked hash set, tree set, array list, and linked list.

Listing 22.8 SetListPerformanceTest.java

```
import java.util.*;

public class SetListPerformanceTest {
  public static void main(String[] args) {
    // Create a hash set, and test its performance
    Collection<Integer> set1 = new HashSet<Integer>();
    System.out.println("Time for hash set is " +
      getTestTime(set1, 500000) + " milliseconds");

    // Create a linked hash set, and test its performance
    Collection<Integer> set2 = new LinkedHashSet<Integer>();
    System.out.println("Time for linked hash set is " +
      getTestTime(set2, 500000) + " milliseconds");

    // Create a tree set, and test its performance
    Collection<Integer> set3 = new TreeSet<Integer>();
    System.out.println("Time for tree set is " +
      getTestTime(set3, 500000) + " milliseconds");

    // Create an array list, and test its performance
    Collection<Integer> list1 = new ArrayList<Integer>();
    System.out.println("Time for array list is " +
      getTestTime(list1, 60000) + " milliseconds");

    // Create a linked list, and test its performance
    Collection<Integer> list2 = new LinkedList<Integer>();
    System.out.println("Time for linked list is " +
      getTestTime(list2, 60000) + " milliseconds");
  }

  public static long getTestTime(Collection<Integer> c, int size) {
    long startTime = System.currentTimeMillis();

```

a hash set

a linked hash set

a tree set

an array list

a linked list

start time

shuffle
add to container
shuffle
remove from container
end time
return elapsed time

```
34     // Add numbers 0, 1, 2, ..., size - 1 to the array list
35     List<Integer> list = new ArrayList<Integer>();
36     for (int i = 0; i < size; i++)
37       list.add(i);
38
39     Collections.shuffle(list); // Shuffle the array list
40
41     // Add the elements to the container
42     for (int element: list)
43       c.add(element);
44
45     Collections.shuffle(list); // Shuffle the array list
46
47     // Remove the element from the container
48     for (int element: list)
49       c.remove(element);
50
51     long endTime = System.currentTimeMillis();
52     return endTime - startTime; // Return the execution time
53   }
54 }
```

```
Time for hash set is 1437 milliseconds
Time for linked hash set is 1891 milliseconds
Time for tree set is 2891 milliseconds
Time for array list is 13797 milliseconds
Time for linked list is 15344 milliseconds
```

The `getTestTime` method creates a list of distinct integers from `0` to `size - 1` (lines 35–37), shuffles the list (line 39), adds the elements from the list to a container `c` (lines 42–43), shuffles the list again (line 45), removes the elements from the container (lines 48–49), and finally returns the execution time (line 52).

The program creates a hash set (line 6), a linked hash set (line 11), a tree set (line 16), an array list (line 21), and a linked list (line 26). The program obtains the execution time for adding and removing `500000` elements in the three sets and adding and removing `60000` elements in the two lists.

sets are better

As you see, sets are much more efficient than lists. If sets are sufficient for your application, use sets. Furthermore, if no particular order is needed for your application, choose hash sets.

The program tested general remove operations for array lists and linked lists. Their complexity is about the same. Please note that linked lists are more efficient than array lists for insertion and deletion anywhere in the list except at the end.

22.9 The **Vector** and **Stack** Classes

The Java Collections Framework was introduced with Java 2. Several data structures were supported earlier, among them the `Vector` and `Stack` classes. These classes were redesigned to fit into the Java Collections Framework, but all their old-style methods are retained for compatibility.

`Vector` is the same as `ArrayList`, except that it contains synchronized methods for accessing and modifying the vector. Synchronized methods can prevent data corruption when a vector is accessed and modified by two or more threads concurrently. For the many applications that do not require synchronization, using `ArrayList` is more efficient than using `Vector`.

The `Vector` class implements the `List` interface. It also has the methods contained in the original `Vector` class defined prior to Java 2, as shown in Figure 22.9.

«interface»
java.util.List<E>

java.util.Vector<E>

java.util.Vector<E>	
+Vector()	Creates a default empty vector with initial capacity 10.
+Vector(c: Collection<? extends E>)	Creates a vector from an existing collection.
+Vector(initialCapacity: int)	Creates a vector with the specified initial capacity.
+Vector(initCapacity: int, capacityIncr: int)	Creates a vector with the specified initial capacity and increment.
+addElement(o: E): void	Appends the element to the end of this vector.
+capacity(): int	Returns the current capacity of this vector.
+copyInto(anArray: Object[]): void	Copies the elements in this vector to the array.
+elementAt(index: int): E	Returns the object at the specified index.
+elements(): Enumeration<E>	Returns an enumeration of this vector.
+ensureCapacity(): void	Increases the capacity of this vector.
+firstElement(): E	Returns the first element in this vector.
+insertElementAt(o: E, index: int): void	Inserts o to this vector at the specified index.
+lastElement(): E	Returns the last element in this vector.
+removeAllElements(): void	Removes all the elements in this vector.
+removeElement(o: Object): boolean	Removes the first matching element in this vector.
+removeElementAt(index: int): void	Removes the element at the specified index.
+setElementAt(o: E, index: int): void	Sets a new element at the specified index.
+setSize(newSize: int): void	Sets a new size in this vector.
+trimToSize(): void	Trims the capacity of this vector to its size.

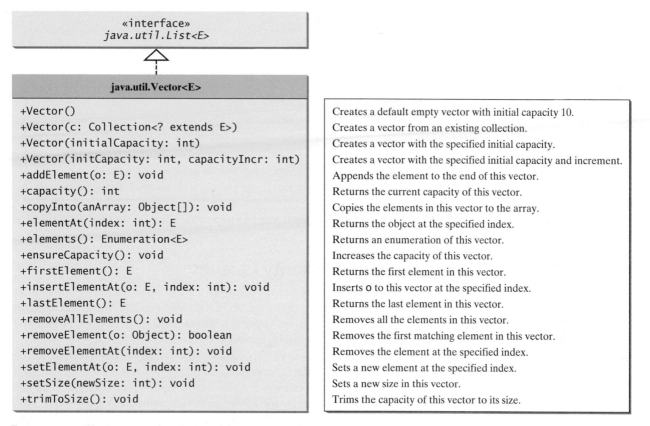

FIGURE 22.9 The `Vector` class in Java 2 implements `List` and also retains all the methods in the original `Vector` class.

Most of the additional methods in the `Vector` class listed in the UML diagram in Figure 22.9 are similar to the methods in the `List` interface. These methods were introduced before the Java Collections Framework. For example, `addElement(Object element)` is the same as the `add(Object element)` method, except that the `addElement` method is synchronized. Use the `ArrayList` class if you don't need synchronization. It works much faster than `Vector`.

Note

The `elements()` method returns an `Enumeration`. The `Enumeration` interface was introduced prior to Java 2 and was superseded by the `Iterator` interface.

Note

`Vector` is widely used in Java programming because it was the Java resizable array implementation before Java 2. Many of the Swing data models use vectors.

In the Java Collections Framework, `Stack` is implemented as an extension of `Vector`, as illustrated in Figure 22.10.

The `Stack` class was introduced prior to Java 2. The methods shown in Figure 22.10 were used before Java 2. The `empty()` method is the same as `isEmpty()`. The `peek()` method looks at the element at the top of the stack without removing it. The `pop()` method removes the top element from the stack and returns it. The `push(Object element)` method adds the specified element to the stack. The `search(Object element)` method checks whether the specified element is in the stack.

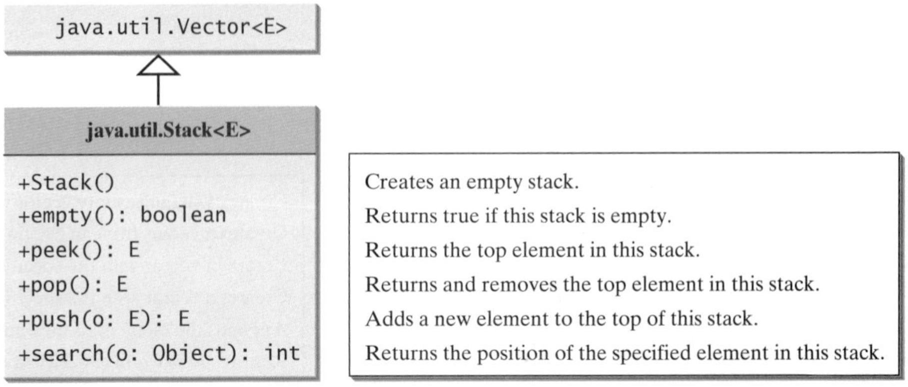
java.util.Vector<E>
java.util.Stack<E>
+Stack()
+empty(): boolean
+peek(): E
+pop(): E
+push(o: E): E
+search(o: Object): int
Creates an empty stack.
Returns true if this stack is empty.
Returns the top element in this stack.
Returns and removes the top element in this stack.
Adds a new element to the top of this stack.
Returns the position of the specified element in this stack.

FIGURE 22.10 The `Stack` class extends `Vector` to provide a last-in, first-out data structure.

22.10 Queues and Priority Queues

A queue is a first-in, first-out data structure. Elements are appended to the end of the queue and are removed from the beginning of the queue. In a priority queue, elements are assigned priorities. When accessing elements, the element with the highest priority is removed first. This section introduces queues and priority queues in the Java API.

Queue interface

The `Queue` interface extends `java.util.Collection` with additional insertion, extraction, and inspection operations, as shown in Figure 22.11.

queue operations

The `offer` method is used to add an element to the queue. This method is similar to the `add` method in the `Collection` interface, but the `offer` method is preferred for queues. The `poll` and `remove` methods are similar, except that `poll()` returns `null` if the queue is empty, whereas `remove()` throws an exception. The `peek` and `element` methods are similar, except that `peek()` returns `null` if the queue is empty, whereas `element()` throws an exception.

22.10.1 `Deque` and `LinkedList`

The `LinkedList` class implements the `Deque` interface, which extends the `Queue` interface, as shown in Figure 22.12. So you can use `LinkedList` to create a queue.

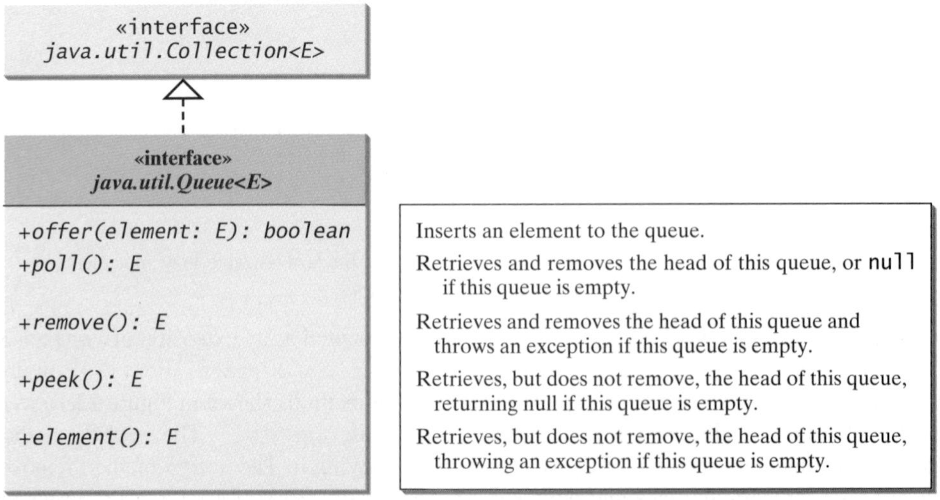
«interface»
java.util.Collection<E>
«interface»
java.util.Queue<E>
+offer(element: E): boolean
+poll(): E
+remove(): E
+peek(): E
+element(): E
Inserts an element to the queue.
Retrieves and removes the head of this queue, or null if this queue is empty.
Retrieves and removes the head of this queue and throws an exception if this queue is empty.
Retrieves, but does not remove, the head of this queue, returning null if this queue is empty.
Retrieves, but does not remove, the head of this queue, throwing an exception if this queue is empty.

FIGURE 22.11 The `Queue` interface extends `Collection` to provide additional insertion, extraction, and inspection operations.

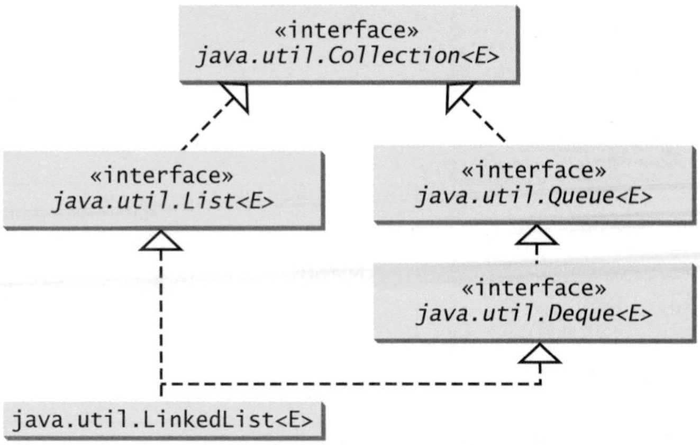
«interface»
java.util.Collection<E>
«interface»
java.util.List<E>
«interface»
java.util.Queue<E>
«interface»
java.util.Deque<E>
java.util.LinkedList<E>

FIGURE 22.12 `LinkedList` implements `List` and `Deque`.

`Deque` supports element insertion and removal at both ends. The name *deque* is short for "double-ended queue" and is usually pronounced "deck". The `Deque` interface extends `Queue` with additional methods for inserting and removing elements from the both ends of the queue. The methods `addFirst(e)`, `removeFirst()`, `addLast(e)`, `removeLast()`, `getFirst()`, and `getLast()` are defined in the `Deque` interface.

Listing 22.9 shows an example of using a queue to store strings. Line 4 creates a queue using `LinkedList`. Four strings are added to the queue in lines 5–8. The `size()` method defined in the `Collection` interface returns the number of elements in the queue (line 10). The `remove()` method retrieves and removes the element at the head of the queue (line 11).

LISTING 22.9 TestQueue.java

```
 1 public class TestQueue {
 2   public static void main(String[] args) {
 3     java.util.Queue<String> queue =
 4       new java.util.LinkedList<String>();
 5     queue.offer("Oklahoma");
 6     queue.offer("Indiana");
 7     queue.offer("Georgia");
 8     queue.offer("Texas");
 9
10     while (queue.size() > 0)
11       System.out.print(queue.remove() + " ");
12   }
13 }
```

creates a queue
inserts an element
queue size
remove element

```
Oklahoma Indiana Georgia Texas
```

PriorityQueue class

The `PriorityQueue` class implements a priority queue, as shown in Figure 22.13. By default, the priority queue orders its elements according to their natural ordering using `Comparable`. The element with the least value is assigned the highest priority and thus is removed from the queue first. If there are several elements with the same highest priority, the tie is broken arbitrarily. You can also specify an ordering using `Comparator` in the constructor `PriorityQueue(initialCapacity, comparator)`.

Listing 22.10 shows an example of using a priority queue to store strings. Line 5 creates a priority queue for strings using its no-arg constructor. This priority queue orders the strings using their natural order, so the strings are removed from the queue in increasing order. Lines 16–17

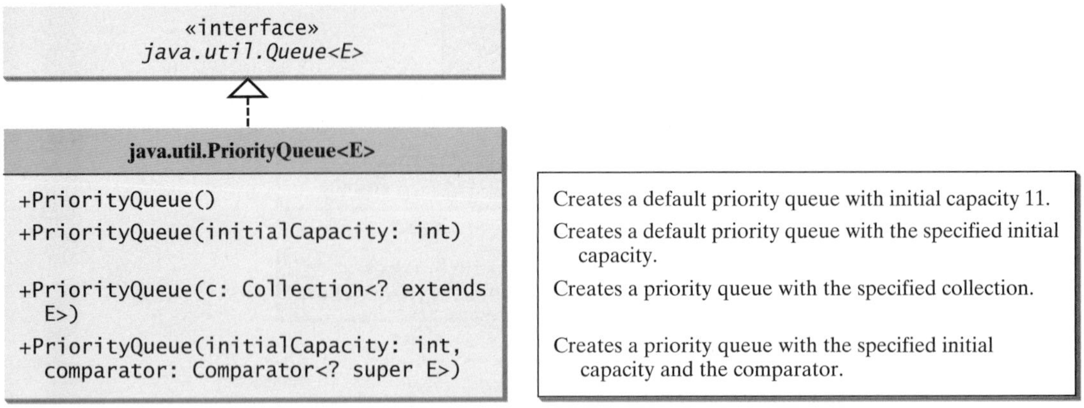
«interface»
java.util.Queue<E>
java.util.PriorityQueue<E>
+PriorityQueue()
+PriorityQueue(initialCapacity: int)
+PriorityQueue(c: Collection<? extends E>)
+PriorityQueue(initialCapacity: int, comparator: Comparator<? super E>)
Creates a default priority queue with initial capacity 11.
Creates a default priority queue with the specified initial capacity.
Creates a priority queue with the specified collection.
Creates a priority queue with the specified initial capacity and the comparator.

FIGURE 22.13 The `PriorityQueue` class implements a priority queue.

create a priority queue using the comparator obtained from `Collections.reverseOrder()`, which orders the elements in reverse order, so the strings are removed from the queue in decreasing order.

LISTING 22.10 PriorityQueueDemo.java

```java
import java.util.*;

public class PriorityQueueDemo {
  public static void main(String[] args) {
    PriorityQueue<String> queue1 = new PriorityQueue<String>();
    queue1.offer("Oklahoma");
    queue1.offer("Indiana");
    queue1.offer("Georgia");
    queue1.offer("Texas");

    System.out.println("Priority queue using Comparable:");
    while (queue1.size() > 0) {
      System.out.print(queue1.remove() + " ");
    }

    PriorityQueue<String> queue2 = new PriorityQueue<String>(
      4, Collections.reverseOrder());
    queue2.offer("Oklahoma");
    queue2.offer("Indiana");
    queue2.offer("Georgia");
    queue2.offer("Texas");

    System.out.println("\nPriority queue using Comparator:");
    while (queue2.size() > 0) {
      System.out.print(queue2.remove() + " ");
    }
  }
}
```

a default queue
inserts an element
a queue with comparator
comparator

```
Priority queue using Comparable:
Georgia Indiana Oklahoma Texas
Priority queue using Comparator:
Texas Oklahoma Indiana Georgia
```

22.11 Maps

Suppose your program stores a million students and frequently searches for a student using the social security number. An efficient data structure for this task is the *map*. A map is a container that stores the elements along with the keys. The keys are like indexes. In `List`, the indexes are integers. In `Map`, the keys can be any objects. A map cannot contain duplicate keys. Each key maps to one value. A key and its corresponding value form an entry, which is actually stored in a map, as shown in Figure 22.14.

why map?

There are three types of maps: `HashMap`, `LinkedHashMap`, and `TreeMap`. The common features of these maps are defined in the `Map` interface. Their relationship is shown in Figure 22.15.

The `Map` interface provides the methods for querying, updating, and obtaining a collection of values and a set of keys, as shown in Figure 22.16.

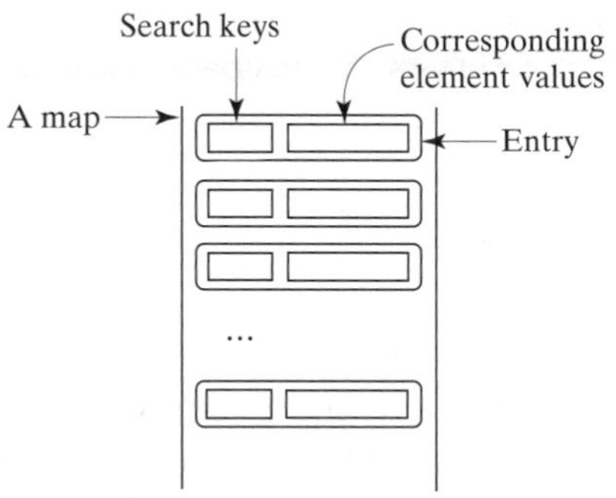
Search keys
Corresponding element values
A map
Entry
...

FIGURE 22.14 The entries consisting of key/value pairs are stored in a map.

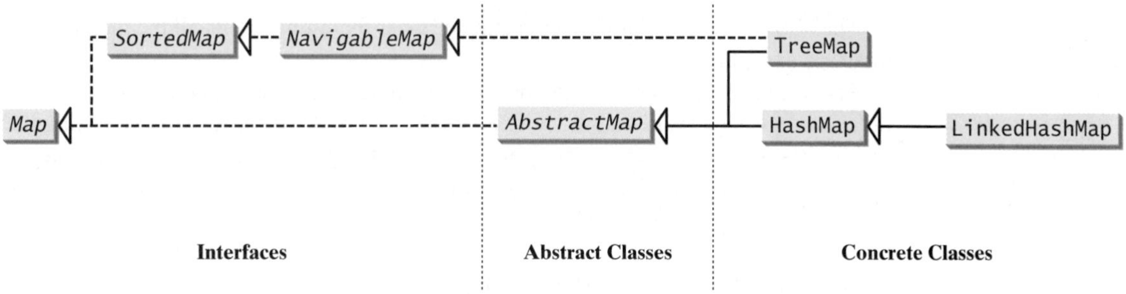
SortedMap
NavigableMap
TreeMap
Map
AbstractMap
HashMap
LinkedHashMap
Interfaces
Abstract Classes
Concrete Classes

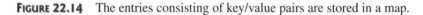

FIGURE 22.15 A map stores key/value pairs.

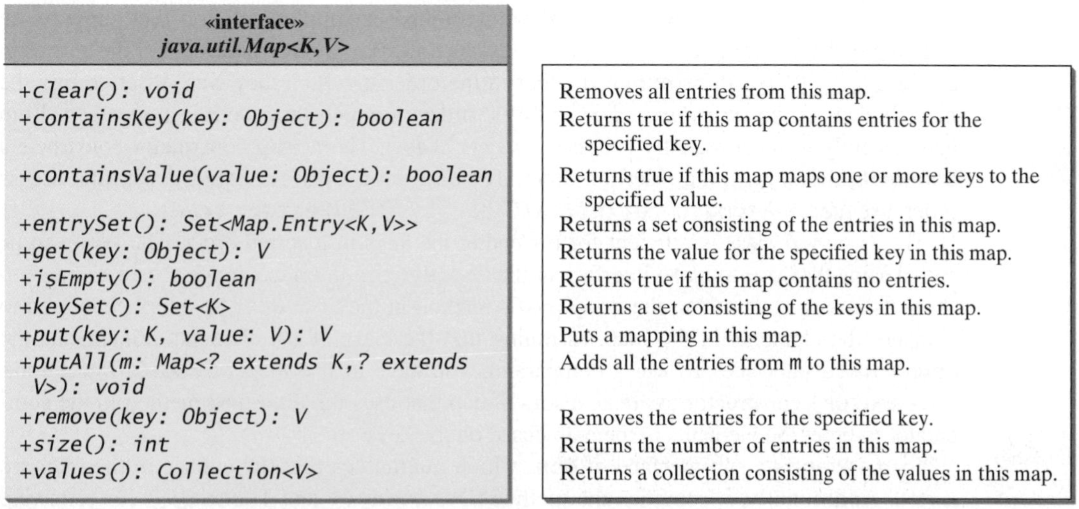
«interface»
java.util.Map<K,V>
+clear(): void
+containsKey(key: Object): boolean
+containsValue(value: Object): boolean
+entrySet(): Set<Map.Entry<K,V>>
+get(key: Object): V
+isEmpty(): boolean
+keySet(): Set<K>
+put(key: K, value: V): V
+putAll(m: Map<? extends K,? extends V>): void
+remove(key: Object): V
+size(): int
+values(): Collection<V>
Removes all entries from this map.
Returns true if this map contains entries for the specified key.
Returns true if this map maps one or more keys to the specified value.
Returns a set consisting of the entries in this map.
Returns the value for the specified key in this map.
Returns true if this map contains no entries.
Returns a set consisting of the keys in this map.
Puts a mapping in this map.
Adds all the entries from m to this map.
Removes the entries for the specified key.
Returns the number of entries in this map.
Returns a collection consisting of the values in this map.

FIGURE 22.16 The `Map` interface maps keys to values.

update methods

The *update methods* include `clear`, `put`, `putAll`, and `remove`. The `clear()` method removes all entries from the map. The `put(K key, V value)` method associates a value with a key in the map. If the map formerly contained a mapping for this key, the old value associated with the key is returned. The `putAll(Map m)` method adds the specified map to this map. The `remove(Object key)` method removes the map elements for the specified key from the map.

query methods

The *query methods* include `containsKey`, `containsValue`, `isEmpty`, and `size`. The `containsKey(Object key)` method checks whether the map contains a mapping for the specified key. The `containsValue(Object value)` method checks whether the map contains a mapping for this value. The `isEmpty()` method checks whether the map contains any mappings. The `size()` method returns the number of mappings in the map.

`keySet()`
`values()`
`entrySet()`

You can obtain a set of the keys in the map using the `keySet()` method, and a collection of the values in the map using the `values()` method. The `entrySet()` method returns a set of objects that implement the `Map.Entry<K, V>` interface, where `Entry` is an inner interface for the `Map` interface, as shown in Figure 22.17. Each object in the set is a specific key/value pair in the underlying map.

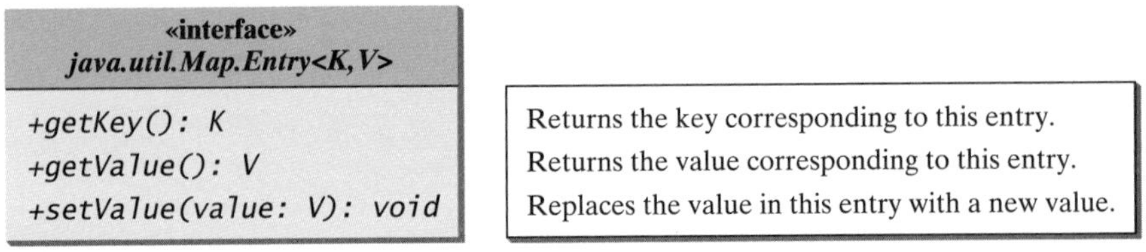
«interface»
java.util.Map.Entry<K, V>
+getKey(): K
+getValue(): V
+setValue(value: V): void
Returns the key corresponding to this entry.
Returns the value corresponding to this entry.
Replaces the value in this entry with a new value.

FIGURE 22.17 The `Map.Entry` interface operates on an entry in the map.

`AbstractMap`

The `AbstractMap` class is a convenience class that implements all the methods in the `Map` interface except the `entrySet()` method.

The `SortedMap` interface extends the `Map` interface to maintain the mapping in ascending order of keys with additional methods `firstKey()` and `lastKey()` for returning the lowest and highest key, `headMap(toKey)` for returning the portion of the map whose keys are less than `toKey`, and `tailMap(fromKey)` for returning the portion of the map whose keys are greater than or equal to `fromKey`.

concrete implementation

The `HashMap`, `LinkedHashMap`, and `TreeMap` classes are three *concrete implementations* of the `Map` interface, as shown in Figure 22.18.

`HashMap`

The `HashMap` class is efficient for locating a value, inserting a mapping, and deleting a mapping.

`LinkedHashMap`

`LinkedHashMap` extends `HashMap` with a linked-list implementation that supports an ordering of the entries in the map. The entries in a `HashMap` are not ordered, but the entries in a `LinkedHashMap` can be retrieved either in the order in which they were inserted into the map (known as the *insertion order*) or in the order in which they were last accessed, from least recently to most recently accessed (*access order*). The no-arg constructor constructs a `LinkedHashMap` with the insertion order. To construct a `LinkedHashMap` with the access order, use the `LinkedHashMap(initialCapacity, loadFactor, true)`.

insertion order
access order

`TreeMap`

The `TreeMap` class is efficient for traversing the keys in a sorted order. The keys can be sorted using the `Comparable` interface or the `Comparator` interface. If you create a `TreeMap` using its no-arg constructor, the `compareTo` method in the `Comparable` interface is used to compare the elements in the map, assuming that the class of the elements implements the `Comparable` interface. To use a comparator, you have to use the `TreeMap(Comparator comparator)` constructor to create a sorted map that uses the `compare` method in the comparator to order the elements in the map based on the keys.

`SortedMap`

`SortedMap` is a subinterface of `Map`, which guarantees that the entries in the map are sorted. Additionally, it provides the methods `firstKey()` and `lastKey()` for returning the first and last keys in the map, and `headMap(toKey)` and `tailMap(fromKey)` for

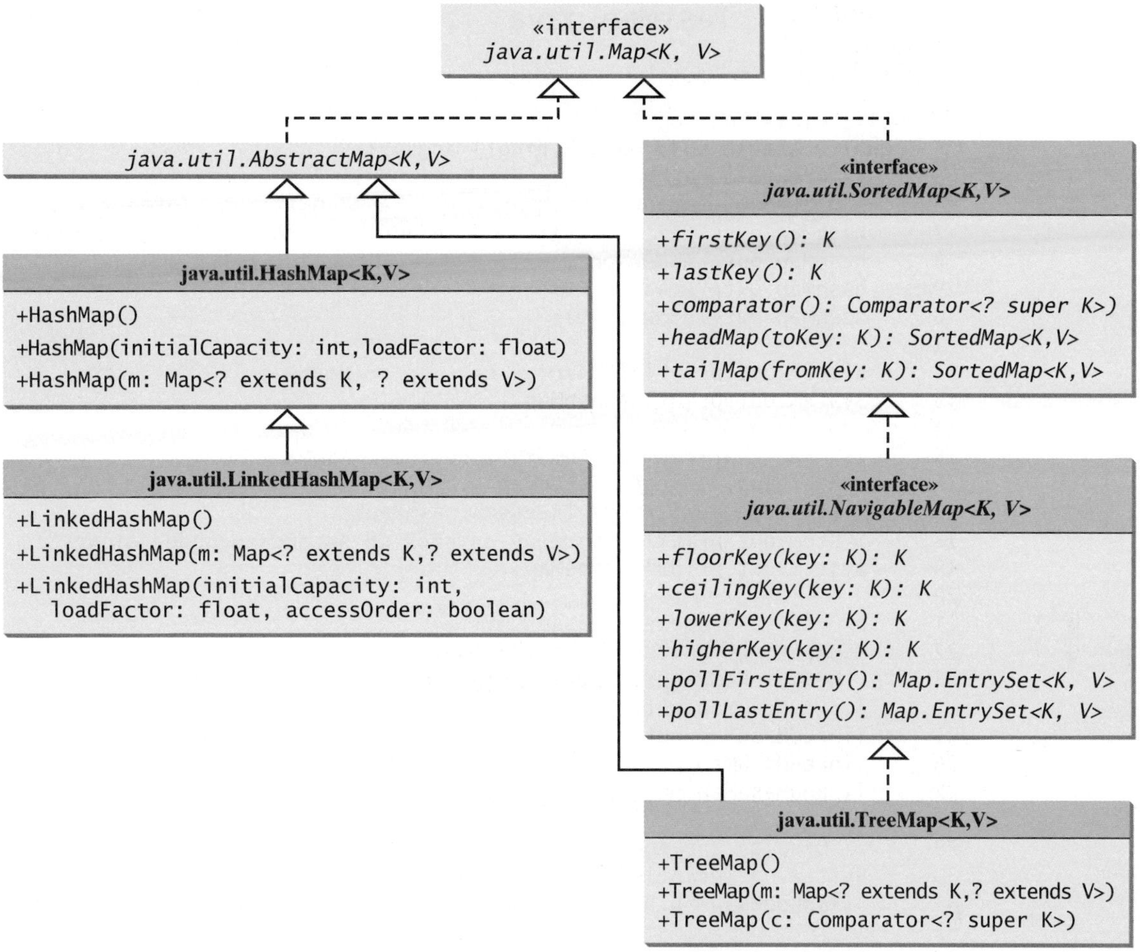
«interface»
java.util.Map<K, V>
java.util.AbstractMap<K, V>
«interface»
java.util.SortedMap<K, V>
+firstKey(): K
+lastKey(): K
+comparator(): Comparator<? super K>)
+headMap(toKey: K): SortedMap<K, V>
+tailMap(fromKey: K): SortedMap<K, V>
java.util.HashMap<K,V>
+HashMap()
+HashMap(initialCapacity: int, loadFactor: float)
+HashMap(m: Map<? extends K, ? extends V>)
java.util.LinkedHashMap<K,V>
+LinkedHashMap()
+LinkedHashMap(m: Map<? extends K,? extends V>)
+LinkedHashMap(initialCapacity: int, loadFactor: float, accessOrder: boolean)
«interface»
java.util.NavigableMap<K, V>
+floorKey(key: K): K
+ceilingKey(key: K): K
+lowerKey(key: K): K
+higherKey(key: K): K
+pollFirstEntry(): Map.EntrySet<K, V>
+pollLastEntry(): Map.EntrySet<K, V>
java.util.TreeMap<K,V>
+TreeMap()
+TreeMap(m: Map<? extends K,? extends V>)
+TreeMap(c: Comparator<? super K>)

FIGURE 22.18 The Java Collections Framework provides three concrete map classes.

returning a portion of the map whose keys are less than `toKey` and greater than or equal to `fromKey`.

`NavigableMap` extends `SortedMap` to provide navigation methods `lowerKey(key)`, `floorKey(key)`, `ceilingKey(key)`, and `higherKey(key)` that return keys respectively less than, less than or equal, greater than or equal, and greater than a given key and return `null` if there is no such key. The `pollFirstEntry()` and `pollLastEntry()` methods remove and return the first and last entry in the tree map, respectively. **NavigableMap**

Note

Prior to Java 2, `java.util.Hashtable` was used for mapping keys with elements. `Hashtable` was redesigned to fit into the Java Collections Framework with all its methods retained for compatibility. `Hashtable` implements the `Map` interface and is used in the same way as `HashMap`, except that `Hashtable` is synchronized. **Hashtable**

Listing 22.11 gives an example that creates a hash map, a linked hash map, and a tree map that map students to ages. The program first creates a hash map with the student's name as its key and the age as its value. The program then creates a tree map from the hash map and displays the mappings in ascending order of the keys. Finally, the program creates a linked hash map, adds the same entries to the map, and displays the entries.

LISTING 22.11 TestMap.java

create map
add entry
tree map
linked hash map

```
1 import java.util.*;
2
3 public class TestMap {
4   public static void main(String[] args) {
5     // Create a HashMap
6     Map<String, Integer> hashMap = new HashMap<String, Integer>();
7     hashMap.put("Smith", 30);
8     hashMap.put("Anderson", 31);
9     hashMap.put("Lewis", 29);
10    hashMap.put("Cook", 29);
11
12    System.out.println("Display entries in HashMap");
13    System.out.println(hashMap + "\n");
14
15    // Create a TreeMap from the previous HashMap
16    Map<String, Integer> treeMap =
17      new TreeMap<String, Integer>(hashMap);
18    System.out.println("Display entries in ascending order of key");
19    System.out.println(treeMap);
20
21    // Create a LinkedHashMap
22    Map<String, Integer> linkedHashMap =
23      new LinkedHashMap<String, Integer>(16, 0.75f, true);
24    linkedHashMap.put("Smith", 30);
25    linkedHashMap.put("Anderson", 31);
26    linkedHashMap.put("Lewis", 29);
27    linkedHashMap.put("Cook", 29);
28
29    // Display the age for Lewis
30    System.out.println("The age for " + "Lewis is " +
31      linkedHashMap.get("Lewis").intValue());
32
33    System.out.println("\nDisplay entries in LinkedHashMap");
34    System.out.println(linkedHashMap);
35  }
36 }
```

```
Display entries in HashMap
{Cook=29, Smith=30, Lewis=29, Anderson=31}

Display entries in ascending order of key
{Anderson=31, Cook=29, Lewis=29, Smith=30}
The age for Lewis is 29

Display entries in LinkedHashMap
{Smith=30, Anderson=31, Cook=29, Lewis=29}
```

As shown in the output, the entries in the `HashMap` are in random order. The entries in the `TreeMap` are in increasing order of the keys. The entries in the `LinkedHashMap` are in the order of their access, from least recently accessed to most recently.

All the concrete classes that implement the `Map` interface have at least two constructors. One is the no-arg constructor that constructs an empty map, and the other constructs a map from an instance of `Map`. Thus `new TreeMap<String, Integer>(hashMap)` (lines 16–17) constructs a tree map from a hash map.

You can create an insertion-ordered or access-ordered linked hash map. An access-ordered linked hash map is created in lines 22–23. The most recently accessed entry is placed at the end of the map. The entry with the key Lewis is last accessed in line 31, so it is displayed last in line 34.

Tip

If you don't need to maintain an order in a map when updating it, use a **HashMap**. When you need to maintain the insertion order or access order in the map, use a **LinkedHashMap**. When you need the map to be sorted on keys, use a **TreeMap**.

22.11.1 Case Study: Occurrences of Words

This case study writes a program that counts the occurrences of words in a text and displays the words and their occurrences in alphabetical order of words. The program uses a **TreeMap** to store an entry consisting of a word and its count. For each word, check whether it is already a key in the map. If not, add to the map an entry with the word as the key and value **1**. Otherwise, increase the value for the word (key) by **1** in the map. Assume the words are case insensitive; e.g., **Good** is treated the same as **good**.

Listing 22.12 gives the solution to the problem.

LISTING 22.12 CountOccurrenceOfWords.java

```java
import java.util.*;

public class CountOccurrenceOfWords {
  public static void main(String[] args) {
    // Set text in a string
    String text = "Good morning. Have a good class. " +
      "Have a good visit. Have fun!";

    // Create a TreeMap to hold words as key and count as value
    TreeMap<String, Integer> map = new TreeMap<String, Integer>();

    String[] words = text.split("[ \n\t\r.,;:!?(){");
    for (int i = 0; i < words.length; i++) {
      String key = words[i].toLowerCase();

      if (key.length() > 0) {
        if (map.get(key) == null) {
          map.put(key, 1);
        }
        else {
          int value = map.get(key).intValue();
          value++;
          map.put(key, value);
        }
      }
    }

    // Get all entries into a set
    Set<Map.Entry<String, Integer>> entrySet = map.entrySet();

    // Get key and value from each entry
    for (Map.Entry<String, Integer> entry: entrySet)
      System.out.println(entry.getValue() + "\t" + entry.getKey());
  }
}
```

tree map
split string
add entry
add entry
tree map
entry set
display entry

```
2       a
1       class
1       fun
3       good
3       have
1       morning
1       visit
```

The program creates a `TreeMap` (line 10) to store pairs of words and their occurrence counts. The words serve as the keys. Since all elements in the map must be stored as objects, the count is wrapped in an `Integer` object.

The program extracts a word from a text using the `split` method (line 12) in the `String` class (see §9.2.7). For each word extracted, the program checks whether it is already stored as a key in the map (line 17). If not, a new pair consisting of the word and its initial count (`1`) is stored to the map (line 18). Otherwise, the count for the word is incremented by `1` (lines 21–23).

The program obtains the entries of the map in a set (line 29), and traverses the set to display the count and the key in each entry (lines 32–33).

Since the map is a tree map, the entries are displayed in increasing order of words. To display them in ascending order of the occurrence counts, see Exercise 22.8.

Now sit back and think how you would write this program without using `map`. Your new program will be longer and more complex. You will find that `map` is a very efficient and powerful data structure for solving problems such as this.

22.12 Singleton and Unmodifiable Collections and Maps

The `Collections` class contains the static methods for lists and collections. It also contains the methods for creating singleton sets, lists, and maps, and for creating unmodifiable sets, lists, and maps, as shown in Figure 22.19.

The `Collections` class defines three constants: one for an empty set, one for an empty list, and one for an empty map (`EMPTY_SET`, `EMPTY_LIST`, and `EMPTY_MAP`). The class also provides the `singleton(Object o)` method for creating an immutable set containing only a single item, the `singletonList(Object o)` method for creating an immutable list containing

java.util.Collections	
+singleton(o: Object): Set	Returns a singleton set containing the specified object.
+singletonList(o: Object): List	Returns a singleton list containing the specified object.
+singletonMap(key: Object, value: Object): Map	Returns a singleton map with the key and value pair.
+unmodifiedCollection(c: Collection): Collection	Returns an unmodified collection.
+unmodifiableList(list: List): List	Returns an unmodified list.
+unmodifiableMap(m: Map): Map	Returns an unmodified map.
+unmodifiableSet(s: Set): Set	Returns an unmodified set.
+unmodifiableSortedMap(s: SortedMap): SortedMap	Returns an unmodified sorted map.
+unmodifiableSortedSet(s: SortedSet): SortedSet	Returns an unmodified sorted set.

FIGURE 22.19 The `Collections` class contains the static methods for creating singleton and unmodifiable sets, lists, and maps.

only a single item, and the `singletonMap(Object key, Object value)` method for creating an immutable map containing only a single mapping.

The `Collections` class also provides six static methods for creating read-only collections: `unmodifiableCollection(Collection c)`, `unmodifiableList(List list)`, `unmodifiableMap(Map m)`, `unmodifiableSet(Set set)`, `unmodifiableSortedMap(SortedMap m)`, and `unmodifiableSortedSet(SortedSet s)`. The read-only collections prevent the data in the collections from being modified, and they offer better performance for read-only operations.

KEY TERMS

collection 728
comparator 735
data structure 728
hash map 752
hash set 730
linked hash map 752
linked hash set 734
linked list 741
list 738
map 751
priority queue 749
queue 748
set 728
tree map 752
tree set 735

CHAPTER SUMMARY

1. The Java Collections Framework supports *sets*, *lists*, *queue*, and *maps*. They are defined in the interfaces `Set`, `List`, `Queue`, and `Map`.

2. A *set* stores a group of nonduplicate elements.

3. A *list* stores an ordered collection of elements.

4. A *map* stores key/value pairs.

5. All the concrete classes in the Java Collections Framework implement the `Cloneable` and `Serializable` interfaces. Thus their instances can be cloned and serialized.

6. A set stores nonduplicate elements. To allow duplicate elements to be stored in a collection, you need to use a list. A list not only can store duplicate elements but also allows the user to specify where they are stored. The user can access elements by an index.

7. Three types of sets are supported: `HashSet`, `LinkedHashSet`, and `TreeSet`. `HashSet` stores elements in an unpredictable order. `LinkedHashSet` stores elements in the order they were inserted. `TreeSet` stores elements sorted. All the methods in `HashSet`, `LinkedHashSet`, and `TreeSet` are inherited from the `Collection` interface.

8. Two types of lists are supported: `ArrayList` and `LinkedList`. `ArrayList` is a resizable-array implementation of the `List` interface. All the methods in `ArrayList` are defined in `List`. `LinkedList` is a linked-list implementation of the `List` interface. In addition to implementing the `List` interface, this class provides the methods for retrieving, inserting, and removing elements from both ends of the list.

9. The `Vector` class implements the `List` interface. In Java 2, `Vector` is the same as `ArrayList`, except that the methods for accessing and modifying the vector are synchronized. The `Stack` class extends the `Vector` class and provides several methods for manipulating the stack.

10. The `Queue` interface represents a queue. The `PriorityQueue` class implements `Queue` for a priority queue.

11. The `Collection` interface represents a collection of elements stored in a set or a list. The `Map` interface maps keys to the elements. The keys are like indexes. In `List`, the indexes are integers. In `Map`, the keys can be any objects. A map cannot contain duplicate keys. Each key can map to at most one value. The `Map` interface provides the methods for querying, updating, and obtaining a collection of values and a set of keys.

12. Three types of maps are supported: `HashMap`, `LinkedHashMap`, and `TreeMap`. `HashMap` is efficient for locating a value, inserting a mapping, and deleting a mapping. `LinkedHashMap` supports ordering of the entries in the map. The entries in a `HashMap` are not ordered, but the entries in a `LinkedHashMap` can be retrieved either in the order in which they were inserted into the map (known as the *insertion order*) or in the order in which they were last accessed, from least recently accessed to most recently (*access order*). `TreeMap` is efficient for traversing the keys in a sorted order. The keys can be sorted using the `Comparable` interface or the `Comparator` interface.

Review Questions

Sections 22.1–22.3

22.1 Describe the Java Collections Framework. List the interfaces, convenience abstract classes, and concrete classes.

22.2 Can a collection object be cloned and serialized?

22.3 What method do you use to add all the elements from one collection to this collection?

22.4 When should a method throw an `UnsupportedOperationException`?

Section 22.4

22.5 How do you create an instance of `Set`? How do you insert a new element in a set? How do you remove an element from a set? How do you find the size of a set?

22.6 What are the differences between `HashSet`, `LinkedHashSet`, and `TreeSet`?

22.7 How do you traverse the elements in a set? Can you traverse the elements in a set in an arbitrary order?

22.8 How do you sort the elements in a set using the `compareTo` method in the `Comparable` interface? How do you sort the elements in a set using the `Comparator` interface? What would happen if you added an element that could not be compared with the existing elements in a tree set?

22.9 Suppose that `set1` is a set that contains the strings `"red"`,`"yellow"`, `"green"`, and that `set2` is another set that contains the strings `"red"`, `"yellow"`, `"blue"`. Answer the following questions:

- What are `set1` and `set2` after executing `set1.addAll(set2)`?
- What are `set1` and `set2` after executing `set1.add(set2)`?
- What are `set1` and `set2` after executing `set1.removeAll(set2)`?
- What are `set1` and `set2` after executing `set1.remove(set2)`?
- What are `set1` and `set2` after executing `set1.retainAll(set2)`?
- What is `set1` after executing `set1.clear()`?

22.10 Show the output of the following code:

```
import java.util.*;

public class Test {
```

```
    public static void main(String[] args) {
      LinkedHashSet<String> set1 = new LinkedHashSet<String>();
      set1.add("New York");
      LinkedHashSet<String> set2 = set1;
      LinkedHashSet<String> set3 =
        (LinkedHashSet<String>)(set1.clone());
      set1.add("Atlanta");
      System.out.println("set1 is " + set1);
      System.out.println("set2 is " + set2);
      System.out.println("set3 is " + set3);
    }
  }
```

22.11 Show the output of the following code:

```
  import java.util.*;
  import java.io.*;

  public class Test {
    public static void main(String[] args) throws Exception {
      ObjectOutputStream output = new ObjectOutputStream(
        new FileOutputStream("c:\\test.dat"));
      LinkedHashSet<String> set1 = new LinkedHashSet<String>();
      set1.add("New York");
      LinkedHashSet<String> set2 =
        (LinkedHashSet<String>)set1.clone();
      set1.add("Atlanta");
      output.writeObject(set1);
      output.writeObject(set2);
      output.close();

      ObjectInputStream input = new ObjectInputStream(
        new FileInputStream("c:\\test.dat"));
      set1 = (LinkedHashSet)input.readObject();
      set2 = (LinkedHashSet)input.readObject();
      System.out.println(set1);
      System.out.println(set2);
      output.close();
    }
  }
```

Section 22.5

22.12 What are the differences between the `Comparable` interface and the `Comparator` interface? In which package is `Comparable`, and in which package is `Comparator`?

22.13 The `Comparator` interface contains the `equals` method. Why is the method not implemented in the `GeometricObjectComparator` class in this section?

Section 22.6

22.14 How do you add and remove elements from a list? How do you traverse a list in both directions?

22.15 Suppose that `list1` is a list that contains the strings `"red"`, `"yellow"`, `"green"`, and that `list2` is another list that contains the strings `"red"`, `"yellow"`, `"blue"`. Answer the following questions:

- What are `list1` and `list2` after executing `list1.addAll(list2)`?
- What are `list1` and `list2` after executing `list1.add(list2)`?
- What are `list1` and `list2` after executing `list1.removeAll(list2)`?
- What are `list1` and `list2` after executing `list1.remove(list2)`?

- What are list1 and list2 after executing list1.retainAll(list2)?
- What is list1 after executing list1.clear()?

22.16 What are the differences between ArrayList and LinkedList? Are all the methods in ArrayList also in LinkedList? What methods are in LinkedList but not in ArrayList?

22.17 How do you create a set or a list from an array of objects?

Section 22.7

22.18 Are all the methods in the Collections class static?

22.19 Which of the following static methods in the Collections class are for lists, and which are for collections?

```
sort, binarySearch, reverse, shuffle, max, min, disjoint,
  frequency
```

22.20 Show the printout of the following code:

```
import java.util.*;

public class Test {
  public static void main(String[] args) {
    List<String> list =
      Arrays.asList("yellow", "red", "green", "blue");
    Collections.reverse(list);
    System.out.println(list);

    List<String> list1 =
      Arrays.asList("yellow", "red", "green", "blue");
    List<String> list2 = Arrays.asList("white", "black");
    Collections.copy(list1, list2);
    System.out.println(list1);

    Collection<String> c1 = Arrays.asList("red", "cyan");
    Collection<String> c2 = Arrays.asList("red", "blue");
    Collection<String> c3 = Arrays.asList("pink", "tan");
    System.out.println(Collections.disjoint(c1, c2));
    System.out.println(Collections.disjoint(c1, c3));

    Collection<String> collection =
      Arrays.asList("red", "cyan", "red");
    System.out.println(Collections.frequency(collection, "red"));
  }
}
```

22.21 Which method can you use to sort the elements in an ArrayList or a LinkedList? Which method can you use to sort an array of strings?

22.22 Which method can you use to perform binary search for elements in an ArrayList or a LinkedList? Which method can you use to perform binary search for an array of strings?

22.23 Write a statement to find the largest element in an array of comparable objects.

Section 22.9

22.24 How do you create an instance of Vector? How do you add or insert a new element into a vector? How do you remove an element from a vector? How do you find the size of a vector?

22.25 How do you create an instance of Stack? How do you add a new element into a stack? How do you remove an element from a stack? How do you find the size of a stack?

22.26 Does Listing 22.1, TestHashSet.java, compile and run if line 7 (`Set set = new HashSet()`) is replaced by one of the following statements?

```
Collection set = new LinkedHashSet();
Collection set = new TreeSet();
Collection set = new ArrayList();
Collection set = new LinkedList();
Collection set = new Vector();
Collection set = new Stack();
```

Section 22.10

22.27 Is `java.util.Queue` a subinterface of `java.util.Collection`, `java.util.Set`, or `java.util.List`? Does `LinkedList` implement `Queue`?

22.28 How do you create a priority queue for integers? By default, how are elements ordered in a priority queue? Is the element with the least value assigned the highest priority in a priority queue?

22.29 How do you create a priority queue that reverses the natural order of the elements?

Section 22.11

22.30 How do you create an instance of `Map`? How do you add into a map an entry consisting of a key and a value? How do you remove an entry from a map? How do you find the size of a map? How do you traverse entries in a map?

22.31 Describe and compare `HashMap`, `LinkedHashMap`, and `TreeMap`.

22.32 Show the printout of the following code:

```
public class Test {
  public static void main(String[] args) {
    Map map = new LinkedHashMap();
    map.put("123", "John Smith");
    map.put("111", "George Smith");
    map.put("123", "Steve Yao");
    map.put("222", "Steve Yao");
    System.out.println("(1) " + map);
    System.out.println("(2) " + new TreeMap(map));
  }
}
```

PROGRAMMING EXERCISES

Section 22.4

22.1 (*Performing set operations on hash sets*) Create two hash sets {`"George"`, `"Jim"`, `"John"`, `"Blake"`, `"Kevin"`, `"Michael"`} and {`"George"`, `"Katie"`, `"Kevin"`, `"Michelle"`, `"Ryan"`} and find their union, difference, and intersection. (You may clone the sets to preserve the original sets from being changed by these set methods.)

22.2 (*Displaying nonduplicate words in ascending order*) Write a program that reads words from a text file and displays all the nonduplicate words in ascending order. The text file is passed as a command-line argument.

22.3** (*Counting the keywords in Java source code*) Write a program that reads a Java source-code file and reports the number of keywords (including `null`, `true`, and `false`) in the file. Pass the Java file name from the command line.

(*Hint*: Create a set to store all the Java keywords.)

Section 22.5

22.4 (*Performing set operations on array lists*) Create two array lists {"George", "Jim", "John", "Blake", "Kevin", "Michael"} and {"George", "Katie", "Kevin", "Michelle", "Ryan"} and find their union, difference, and intersection. (You may clone the lists to preserve the original lists from being changed by these methods.)

22.5* (*Displaying words in ascending alphabetical order*) Write a program that reads words from a text file and displays all the words (duplicates allowed) in ascending alphabetical order. The text file is passed as a command-line argument.

Section 22.7

22.6* (*Storing numbers in a linked list*) Write a program that lets the user enter numbers from a graphical user interface and display them in a text area, as shown in Figure 22.20. Use a linked list to store the numbers. Do not store duplicate numbers. Add the buttons *Sort*, *Shuffle*, and *Reverse* to sort, shuffle, and reverse the list.

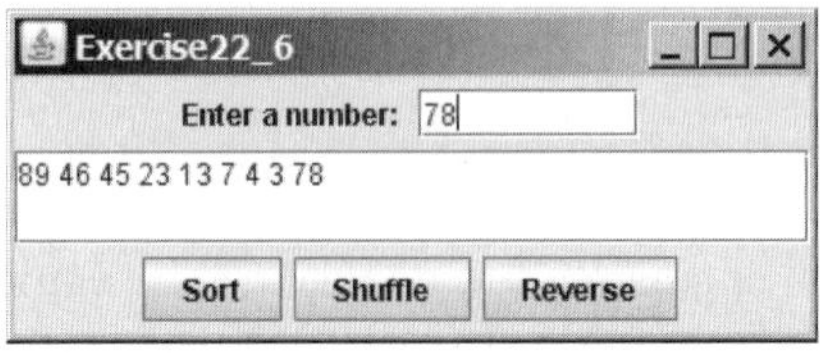
Exercise22_6
Enter a number: 78
89 46 45 23 13 7 4 3 78
Sort
Shuffle
Reverse

FIGURE 22.20 The numbers are stored in a list and displayed in the text area.

Section 22.11

22.7* (*Counting the occurrences of numbers entered*) Write a program that reads an unspecified number of integers and finds the one that has the most occurrences. Your input ends when the input is 0. For example, if you entered 2 3 40 3 5 4 -3 3 3 2 0, the number 3 occurred most often. Please enter one number at a time. If not one but several numbers have the most occurrences, all of them should be reported. For example, since 9 and 3 appear twice in the list 9 30 3 9 3 2 4, both occurrences should be reported.

22.8** (*Revising Listing 22.12, CountOccurrenceOfWords.java*) Rewrite Listing 22.12 to display the words in ascending order of occurrence counts.

Hint: Create a class named `WordOccurrence` that implements the `Comparable` interface. The class contains two fields, `word` and `count`. The `compareTo` method compares the counts. For each pair in the hash set in Listing 22.12, create an instance of `WordOccurrence` and store it in an array list. Sort the array list using the `Collections.sort` method. What would be wrong if you stored the instances of `WordOccurrence` in a tree set?

22.9** (*Counting the occurrences of words in a text file*) Rewrite Listing 22.12 to read the text from a text file. The text file is passed as a command-line argument. Words are delimited by whitespace, punctuation marks (,;.:?), quotation marks ('"), and parentheses. Count words in case-insensitive fashion (e.g., consider `Good` and `good` to be the same word). Don't count the word if the first character is not a letter. Display the output in alphabetical order of words with each word preceded by its occurrence count.

22.10*** (*Syntax highlighting*) Write a program that converts a Java file into an HTML file. In the HTML file, the keywords, comments, and literals are displayed in bold navy, green, and blue, respectively. Use the command line to pass a Java file and an HTML file. For example, the following command

```
java Exercise22_10 Welcome.java Welcome.HTML
```

converts ComputeArea.java into ComputeArea.HTML. Figure 22.21(a) shows a Java file. The corresponding HTML file is shown in Figure 22.21(b).

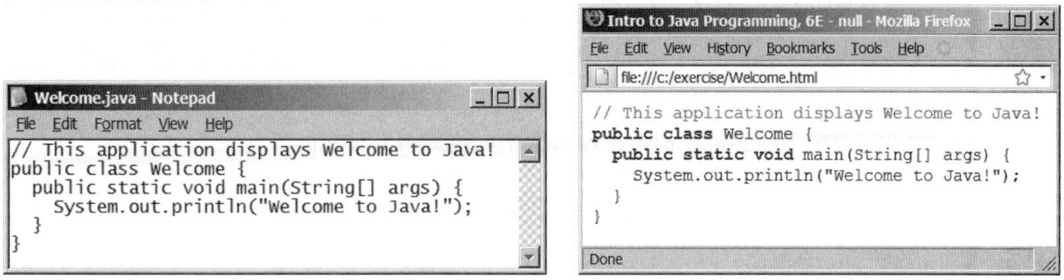
Welcome.java - Notepad
File Edit Format View Help
// This application displays Welcome to Java!
public class Welcome {
public static void main(String[] args) {
System.out.println("Welcome to Java!");
}
}
Intro to Java Programming, 6E - null - Mozilla Firefox
File Edit View History Bookmarks Tools Help
file:///c:/exercise/Welcome.html
// This application displays Welcome to Java!
public class Welcome {
public static void main(String[] args) {
System.out.println("Welcome to Java!");
}
}
Done

(a) (b)

FIGURE 22.21 The Java code in plain text in (a) is displayed in HTML with syntax highlighted in (b).

22.11* (*Guessing the capitals*) Rewrite Exercise 9.22 so that the questions are randomly displayed.

22.12* (*Sort points in a plane*) Write a program that meets the following requirements:

- Define a class named `Point` with two data fields `x` and `y` to represent a point's *x* and *y* coordinates. Implement the `Comparable` interface for comparing the points on *x*-coordinates and on *y*-coordinates if *x*-coordinates are identical.
- Define a class named `CompareY` that implements `Comparator<Point>`. Implement the `compare` method to compare two points on their *y*-coordinates and on their *x*-coordinates if *y*-coordinates are identical.
- Randomly create `100` points and apply the `Arrays.sort` method to display the points in increasing order of their *x*-coordinates and in increasing order of their *y*-coordinates, respectively.

22.13** (*Game: lottery*) Revise Exercise 3.15 to add an additional $2,000 award if two digits from the user input are in the lottery number.

(*Hint*: Sort the three digits for lottery and for user input in two lists and use the `Collection`'s `containsAll` method to check whether the two digits in the user input are in the lottery.)

22.14** (*Guessing the capitals using maps*) Rewrite Exercise 9.22 to store pairs of state and its capital in a map. Your program should prompt the user to enter a state and should display the capital for the state.

22.15*** (*Game: Sudoku*) Revise Exercise 18.25 to display all solutions of the Sudoku game, as shown in Figure 22.22(a). When you click the *Solve* button, the program stores all solutions in an `ArrayList`. Each element in the list is a two-dimensional 9-by-9 grid. If the program has multiple solutions, the *Next* button appears as shown in Figure 22.22(b). You can click the *Next* button to display the next solution, as shown in Figure 22.22(c). When the *Clear* button is clicked, the cells are cleared and the *Next* button is hidden.

Exercise22_15
Solve
Clear
Exercise22_15
Solve
Clear
Next
Exercise22_15
Solve
Clear
Next

(a) (b) (c)

FIGURE 22.22 The program can display multiple Sudoku solutions.

CHAPTER 23

ALGORITHM EFFICIENCY

Objectives

- To estimate algorithm efficiency using the Big *O* notation (§23.2).
- To explain growth rates and why constants and nondominating terms can be ignored in the estimation (§23.2).
- To determine the complexity of various types of algorithms (§23.3).
- To analyze the binary search algorithm (§23.4.1).
- To analyze the selection sort algorithm (§23.4.2).
- To analyze the insertion sort algorithm (§23.4.3).
- To analyze the Towers of Hanoi algorithm (§23.4.4).
- To describe common growth functions (constant, logarithmic, log-linear, quadratic, cubic, exponential) (§23.4.5).
- To design efficient algorithms for finding Fibonacci numbers (§23.5).
- To design efficient algorithms for finding gcd (§23.6).
- To design efficient algorithms for finding prime numbers (§23.7).
- To design efficient algorithms for finding a closest pair of points (§23.8).

23.1 Introduction

what is algorithm efficiency?

Suppose two algorithms perform the same task, such as search (linear search vs. binary search) or sort (selection sort vs. insertion sort). Which one is better? To answer this question, we might implement these algorithms in Java and run the programs to get execution time. But there are two problems with this approach:

1. First, many tasks run concurrently on a computer. The execution time of a particular program depends on the system load.
2. Second, the execution time depends on specific input. Consider, for example, linear search and binary search. If an element to be searched happens to be the first in the list, linear search will find the element quicker than binary search.

growth rate

It is very difficult to compare algorithms by measuring their execution time. To overcome these problems, a theoretical approach was developed to analyze algorithms independent of computers and specific input. This approach approximates the effect of a change on the size of the input. In this way, you can see how fast an algorithm's execution time increases as the input size increases, so you can compare two algorithms by examining their *growth rates*.

Pedagogical Note

If you are not taking a data structures course, you may skip this chapter.

23.2 Big O Notation

Big O notation

Consider linear search. The linear search algorithm compares the key with the elements in the array sequentially until the key is found or the array is exhausted. If the key is not in the array, it requires n comparisons for an array of size n. If the key is in the array, it requires $n/2$ comparisons on average. The algorithm's execution time is proportional to the size of the array. If you double the size of the array, you will expect the number of comparisons to double. The algorithm grows at a linear rate. The growth rate has an order of magnitude of n. Computer scientists use the Big O notation to represent "order of magnitude." Using this notation, the complexity of the linear search algorithm is $O(n)$, pronounced as "*order of n*."

best-case

worst-case

average-case

For the same input size, an algorithm's execution time may vary, depending on the input. An input that results in the shortest execution time is called the *best-case* input, and an input that results in the longest execution time is the *worst-case* input. Best case and worst case are not representative, but worst-case analysis is very useful. You can be assured that the algorithm will never be slower than the worst case. An average-case analysis attempts to determine the average amount of time among all possible inputs of the same size. Average-case analysis is ideal, but difficult to perform, because for many problems it is hard to determine the relative probabilities and distributions of various input instances. Worst-case analysis is easier to perform, so the analysis is generally conducted for the worst case.

ignoring multiplicative constants

The linear search algorithm requires n comparisons in the worst case and $n/2$ comparisons in the average case if you are nearly always looking for something known to be in the list. Using the Big O notation, both cases require $O(n)$ time. The multiplicative constant (1/2) can be omitted. Algorithm analysis is focused on growth rate. The multiplicative constants have no impact on growth rates. The growth rate for $n/2$ or $100n$ is the same as for n, as illustrated in Table 23.1. Therefore, $O(n) = O(n/2) = O(100n)$.

large input size

ignoring nondominating terms

Consider the algorithm for finding the maximum number in an array of n elements. To find the maximum number if n is 2, it takes one comparison; if n is 3, two comparisons. In general, it takes $n - 1$ comparisons to find the maximum number in a list of n elements. Algorithm analysis is for large input size. If the input size is small, there is no significance in estimating an algorithm's efficiency. As n grows larger, the n part in the expression $n - 1$ dominates the complexity. The Big O notation allows you to ignore the nondominating part (e.g., -1 in the

TABLE 23.1 Growth Rates

n \ $f(n)$	n	$n/2$	$100n$	
100	100	50	10000	
200	200	100	20000	
	2	2	2	$f(200) / f(100)$

expression $n - 1$) and highlight the important part (e.g., n in the expression $n - 1$). So, the complexity of this algorithm is $O(n)$.

The Big O notation estimates the execution time of an algorithm in relation to the input size. If the time is not related to the input size, the algorithm is said to take *constant time* with the notation $O(1)$. For example, a method that retrieves an element at a given index in an array takes constant time, because the time does not grow as the size of the array increases. constant time

The following mathematical summations are often useful in algorithm analysis: useful summations

$$1 + 2 + 3 + \cdots + (n-1) + n = \frac{n(n+1)}{2}$$

$$a^0 + a^1 + a^2 + a^3 + \cdots + a^{(n-1)} + a^n = \frac{a^{n+1} - 1}{a - 1}$$

$$2^0 + 2^1 + 2^2 + 2^3 + \cdots + 2^{(n-1)} + 2^n = \frac{2^{n+1} - 1}{2 - 1} = 2^{n+1} - 1$$

23.3 Examples: Determining Big O

This section gives several examples of determining Big O for repetition, sequence, and selection statements.

Example 1

Consider the time complexity for the following loop:

```
for (i = 1; i <= n; i++) {
  k = k + 5;
}
```

It is a constant time, c, for executing

```
k = k + 5;
```

Since the loop is executed n times, the time complexity for the loop is

$$T(n) = (\text{a constant } c) * n = O(n).$$

Example 2

What is the time complexity for the following loop?

```
for (i = 1; i <= n; i++) {
  for (j = 1; j <= n; j++) {
    k = k + i + j;
  }
}
```

It is a constant time, c, for executing

```
k = k + i + j;
```

The outer loop executes n times. For each iteration in the outer loop, the inner loop is executed n times. So, the time complexity for the loop is

$$T(n) = (\text{a constant } c) * n * n = O(n^2)$$

quadratic time

An algorithm with the $O(n^2)$ time complexity is called a *quadratic algorithm*. The quadratic algorithm grows quickly as the problem size increases. If you double the input size, the time for the algorithm is quadrupled. Algorithms with a nested loop are often quadratic.

Example 3

Consider the following loop:

```
for (i = 1; i <= n; i++) {
  for (j = 1; j <= i; j++) {
    k = k + i + j;
  }
}
```

The outer loop executes n times. For $i = 1, 2, \ldots,$ the inner loop is executed one time, two times, and n times. So, the time complexity for the loop is

$$\begin{aligned} T(n) &= c + 2c + 3c + 4c + \cdots + nc \\ &= cn(n + 1)/2 \\ &= (c/2)n^2 + (c/2)n \\ &= O(n^2) \end{aligned}$$

Example 4

Consider the following loop:

```
for (i = 1; i <= n; i++) {
  for (j = 1; j <= 20; j++) {
    k = k + i + j;
  }
}
```

The inner loop executes 20 times, and the outer loop n times. So, the time complexity for the loop is

$$T(n) = 20 * c * n = O(n)$$

Example 5

Consider the following sequences:

```
for (j = 1; j <= 10; j++) {
  k = k + 4;
}

for (i = 1; i <= n; i++) {
  for (j = 1; j <= 20; j++) {
    k = k + i + j;
  }
}
```

The first loop executes 10 times, and the second loop 20 * n times. So, the time complexity for the loop is

$$T(n) = 10 * c + 20 * c * n = O(n)$$

Example 6

Consider the following selection statement:

```
if (list.contains(e)) {
  System.out.println(e);
}
else
  for (Object t: list) {
    System.out.println(t);
  }
```

Suppose the list contains n elements. The execution time for `list.contains(e)` is $O(n)$. The loop in the `else` clause takes $O(n)$ time. So, the time complexity for the entire statement is

$$\begin{aligned} T(n) &= \text{if test time} + \text{worst-case time (if clause, else clause)} \\ &= O(n) + O(n) = O(n) \end{aligned}$$

Example 7

Consider the computation of a^n for an integer n. A simple algorithm would multiply a n times, as follows:

```
result = 1;
for (int i = 1; i <= n; i++)
  result *= a;
```

The algorithm takes $O(n)$ time. Without loss of generality, assume $n = 2^k$. You can improve the algorithm using the following scheme:

```
result = a;
for (int i = 1; i <= k; i++)
  result = result * result;
```

The algorithm takes $O(\log n)$ time. For an arbitrary n, you can revise the algorithm and prove that the complexity is still $O(\log n)$. (See Review Question 23.7.)

Note

For simplicity, since $O(\log n) = O(\log_2 n) = O(\log_a n)$, the constant base is omitted. omitting base

23.4 Analyzing Algorithm Time Complexity

You have used many algorithms in this book. This section will analyze the complexity of several well-known algorithms: binary search, selection sort, insertion sort, and Tower of Hanoi.

23.4.1 Analyzing Binary Search

The binary search algorithm presented in Listing 6.7, BinarySearch.java, searches a key in a sorted array. Each iteration in the algorithm contains a fixed number of operations, denoted by *c.* Let $T(n)$ denote the time complexity for a binary search on a list of n elements. Without loss of generality, assume n is a power of 2 and $k = \log n$. Since binary search eliminates half of the input after two comparisons,

$$\begin{aligned} T(n) &= T\left(\frac{n}{2}\right) + c = T\left(\frac{n}{2^2}\right) + c + c = T\left(\frac{n}{2^k}\right) + kc \\ &= T(1) + c \log n = 1 + (\log n)c \\ &= O(\log n) \end{aligned}$$

logarithmic time

Ignoring constants and nondominating terms, the complexity of the binary search algorithm is $O(\log n)$. An algorithm with the $O(\log n)$ time complexity is called a *logarithmic algorithm*. The base of the log is 2, but the base does not affect a logarithmic growth rate, so it can be omitted. The logarithmic algorithm grows slowly as the problem size increases. If you square the input size, you only double the time for the algorithm.

23.4.2 Analyzing Selection Sort

The selection sort algorithm presented in Listing 6.8, SelectionSort.java, finds the smallest number in the list and places it first. It then finds the smallest number remaining and places it after the first, and so on until the list contains only a single number. The number of comparisons is $n - 1$ for the first iteration, $n - 2$ for the second iteration, and so on. Let $T(n)$ denote the complexity for selection sort and c denote the total number of other operations such as assignments and additional comparisons in each iteration. So,

$$\begin{aligned} T(n) &= (n - 1) + c + (n - 2) + c + \cdots + 2 + c + 1 + c \\ &= \frac{(n - 1)(n - 1 + 1)}{2} + c(n - 1) = \frac{n^2}{2} - \frac{n}{2} + cn - c \\ &= O(n^2) \end{aligned}$$

Therefore, the complexity of the selection sort algorithm is $O(n^2)$.

23.4.3 Analyzing Insertion Sort

The insertion sort algorithm presented in Listing 6.9, InsertionSort.java, sorts a list of values by repeatedly inserting a new element into a sorted partial array until the whole array is sorted. At the kth iteration, to insert an element into an array of size k, it may take k comparisons to find the insertion position, and k moves to insert the element. Let $T(n)$ denote the complexity for insertion sort and c denote the total number of other operations such as assignments and additional comparisons in each iteration. So,

$$\begin{aligned} T(n) &= (2 + c) + (2 \times 2 + c) + \cdots + (2 \times (n - 1) + c) \\ &= 2(1 + 2 + \cdots + n - 1) + c(n - 1) \\ &= 2\frac{(n - 1)n}{2} + cn - c = n^2 - n + cn - c \\ &= O(n^2) \end{aligned}$$

Therefore, the complexity of the insertion sort algorithm is $O(n^2)$. So, the selection sort and insertion sort are of the same time complexity.

23.4.4 Analyzing the Towers of Hanoi Problem

The Towers of Hanoi problem presented in Listing 20.8, TowersOfHanoi.java, recursively moves n disks from tower A to tower B with the assistance of tower C as follows:

1. Move the first $n - 1$ disks from A to C with the assistance of tower B.
2. Move disk n from A to B.
3. Move $n - 1$ disks from C to B with the assistance of tower A.

Let $T(n)$ denote the complexity for the algorithm that moves n disks and c denote the constant time to move one disk; i.e., $T(1)$ is c. So,

$$\begin{aligned} T(n) &= T(n-1) + c + T(n-1) \\ &= 2T(n-1) + c \\ &= 2(2T(n-2) + c) + c \\ &= 2(2(2T(n-3) + c) + c) + c \\ &= 2^{n-1}T(1) + 2^{n-2}c + \cdots + 2c + c \\ &= 2^{n-1}c + 2^{n-2}c + \cdots + 2c + c = (2^n - 1)c = O(2^n) \end{aligned}$$

An algorithm with $O(2^n)$ time complexity is called an *exponential algorithm*. As the input size increases, the time for the exponential algorithm grows exponentially. Exponential algorithms are not practical for large input size.

$O(2^n)$
exponential time

23.4.5 Comparing Common Growth Functions

The preceding sections analyzed the complexity of several algorithms. Table 23.2 lists some common growth functions and shows how growth rates change as the input size doubles from $n = 25$ to $n = 50$.

These functions are ordered as follows, as illustrated in Figure 23.1.

$$O(1) < O(\log n) < O(n) < O(n \log n) < O(n^2) < O(n^3) < O(2^n)$$

TABLE 23.2 Change of Growth Rates

Function	*Name*	$n = 25$	$n = 50$	*f*(50)/*f*(25)
$O(1)$	Constant time	1	1	1
$O(\log n)$	Logarithmic time	4.64	5.64	1.21
$O(n)$	Linear time	25	50	2
$O(n\log n)$	Log-linear time	116	282	2.43
$O(n^2)$	Quadratic time	625	2500	4
$O(n^3)$	Cubic time	15625	125000	8
$O(2^n)$	Exponential time	3.36×10^7	1.27×10^{15}	3.35×10^7

23.5 Case Studies: Finding Fibonacci Numbers

Section 20.3, "Problem: Computing Fibonacci Numbers," gave a recursive method for finding the Fibonacci number, as follows:

```
/** The method for finding the Fibonacci number */
public static long fib(long index) {
```

```
    if (index == 0) // Base case
      return 0;
    else if (index == 1) // Base case
      return 1;
    else  // Reduction and recursive calls
      return fib(index - 1) + fib(index - 2);
}
```

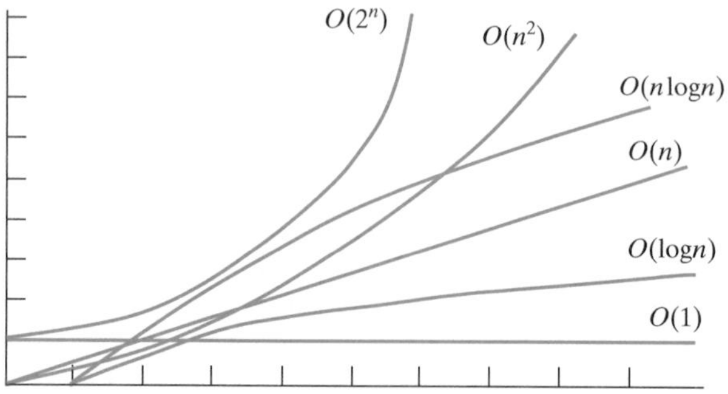

$O(2^n)$
$O(n^2)$
$O(n\log n)$
$O(n)$
$O(\log n)$
$O(1)$

FIGURE 23.1 As the size n increases, the function grows.

We can now prove that the complexity of this algorithm is $O(2^n)$. For convenience, let the index be n. Let $T(n)$ denote the complexity for the algorithm that finds fib(n) and c denote the constant time for comparing index with `0` and `1;` i.e., $T(1)$ is c. So,

$$\begin{aligned} T(n) &= T(n-1) + T(n-2) + c \\ &\le 2T(n-1) + c \\ &\le 2(2T(n-2) + c) + c \\ &= 2^2T(n-2) + 2c + c \end{aligned}$$

Similar to the analysis of the Towers of Hanoi problem, we can show that $T(n)$ is $O(2^n)$.

This algorithm is not efficient. Is there an efficient algorithm for finding a Fibonacci number? The trouble in the recursive `fib` method is that the method is invoked redundantly with the same arguments. For example, to compute `fib(4)`, `fib(3)` and `fib(2)` are invoked. To compute `fib(3)`, `fib(2)` and `fib(1)` are invoked. Note that `fib(2)` is redundantly invoked. We can improve it by avoiding repeated calling of the `fib` method with the same argument. Note that a new Fibonacci number is obtained by adding the preceding two numbers in the

```
                   f0 f1 f2
Fibonacci series: 0  1  1  2  3  5  8  13  21  34  55  89 ...
         indices: 0  1  2  3  4  5  6  7   8   9   10  11

                      f0 f1 f2
Fibonacci series: 0  1  1  2  3  5  8  13  21  34  55  89 ...
         indices: 0  1  2  3  4  5  6  7   8   9   10  11

                                               f0  f1  f2
Fibonacci series: 0  1  1  2  3  5  8  13  21  34  55  89 ...
         indices: 0  1  2  3  4  5  6  7   8   9   10  11
```

FIGURE 23.2 Variables `f0`, `f1`, and `f2` store three consecutive Fibonacci numbers in the series.

sequence. If you use two variables `f0` and `f1` to store the two preceding numbers, the new number `f2` can be immediately obtained by adding `f0` with `f1`. Now you should update `f0` and `f1` by assigning `f1` to `f0` and assigning `f2` to `f1`, as shown in Figure 23.2.

The new method is implemented in Listing 23.1.

LISTING 23.1 ImprovedFibonacci.java

```
import java.util.Scanner;

public class ImprovedFibonacci {
  /** Main method */
  public static void main(String args[]) {
    // Create a Scanner
    Scanner input = new Scanner(System.in);
    System.out.print("Enter an index for the Fibonacci number: ");
    int index = input.nextInt();

    // Find and display the Fibonacci number
    System.out.println(
      "Fibonacci number at index " + index + " is " + fib(index));
  }

  /** The method for finding the Fibonacci number */
  public static long fib(long n) {
    long f0 = 0; // For fib(0)
    long f1 = 1; // For fib(1)
    long f2 = 1; // For fib(2)

    if (n == 0)
      return f0;
    else if (n == 1)
      return f1;
    else if (n == 2)
      return f2;

    for (int i = 3; i <= n; i++) {
      f0 = f1;
      f1 = f2;
      f2 = f0 + f1;
    }

    return f2;
  }
}
```

input

invoke fib

f0

f1

f2

update f0, f1, f2

```
Enter an index for the Fibonacci number: 6 ↵Enter
Fibonacci number at index 6 is 8
```

```
Enter an index for the Fibonacci number: 7 ↵Enter
Fibonacci number at index 7 is 13
```

Obviously, the complexity of this new algorithm is $O(n)$. This is a tremendous improvement over the recursive $O(2^n)$ algorithm.

$O(n)$

23.6 Case Studies: Finding Greatest Common Divisors

This section presents several algorithms in the search for an efficient algorithm for finding the greatest common divisor between two integers.

gcd

The greatest common divisor of two integers is the largest number that can evenly divide both integers. Listing 4.8, GreatestCommonDivisor.java, presented a brute-force algorithm for finding the greatest common divisor (GCD) of two integers `m` and `n`. The algorithm checks whether `k` (for `k` = `2`, `3`, `4`, and so on) is a common divisor for `n1` and `n2`, until `k` is greater than `n1` or `n2`. The algorithm can be described as follows:

```
public static int gcd(int m, int n) {
  int gcd = 1;

  for (int k = 2; k <= m && k <= n; k++) {
    if (m % k == 0 && n % k == 0)
      gcd = k;
  }

  return gcd;
}
```

assume $m \geq n$

$O(n)$

Assuming $m \geq n$, the complexity of this algorithm is obviously $O(n)$.

improved solutions

Is there any better algorithm for finding the gcd? Rather than searching a possible divisor from `1` up, it is more efficient to search from `n` down. Once a divisor is found, the divisor is the gcd. So you can improve the algorithm using the following loop:

```
for (int k = n; k >= 1; k--) {
  if (m % k == 0 && n % k == 0) {
    gcd = k;
    break;
  }
}
```

This algorithm is better than the preceding one, but its worst-case time complexity is still $O(n)$.

A divisor for a number `n` cannot be greater than `n / 2`. So you can further improve the algorithm using the following loop:

```
for (int k = m / 2; k >= 1; k--) {
  if (m % k == 0 && n % k == 0) {
    gcd = k;
    break;
  }
}
```

However, this algorithm is incorrect, because `n` can be a divisor for `m`. This case must be considered. The correct algorithm is shown in Listing 23.2.

Listing 23.2 GCD1.java

check divisor

```
import java.util.Scanner;

public class GCD1 {
  /** Find gcd for integers m and n */
  public static int gcd(int m, int n) {
    int gcd = 1;

    if (m % n == 0) return n;

```

```
    for (int k = n / 2; k >= 1; k--) {
      if (m % k == 0 && n % k == 0) {
        gcd = k;
        break;
      }
    }

    return gcd;
  }

  /** Main method */
  public static void main(String[] args) {
    // Create a Scanner
    Scanner input = new Scanner(System.in);

    // Prompt the user to enter two integers
    System.out.print("Enter first integer: ");
    int m = input.nextInt();
    System.out.print("Enter second integer: ");
    int n = input.nextInt();

    System.out.println("The greatest common divisor for " + m +
      " and " + n + " is " + gcd(m, n));
  }
}
```

gcd found

input

input

```
Enter first integer: 2525 [Enter]
Enter second integer: 125 [Enter]
The greatest common divisor for 2525 and 125 is 25
```

```
Enter first integer: 3 [Enter]
Enter second integer: 3 [Enter]
The greatest common divisor for 3 and 3 is 3
```

Assuming $m \geq n$, the `for` loop is executed at most n / 2 times, which cuts the time by half from the previous algorithm. The time complexity of this algorithm is still $O(n)$, but practically, it is much faster than the algorithm in Listing 4.8.

O(n)

Note

The Big *O* notation provides a good theoretical estimate of algorithm efficiency. However, two algorithms of the same time complexity are not necessarily equally efficient. As shown in the preceding example, both algorithms in Listings 4.8 and 23.2 have the same complexity, but in practice the one in Listing 23.2 is obviously better.

practical consideration

A more efficient algorithm for finding gcd was discovered by Euclid around 300 B.C. This is one of the oldest known algorithms. It can be defined recursively as follows:

improved solutions

Let `gcd(m, n)` denote the gcd for integers `m` and `n`:

- If `m % n` is `0`, `gcd (m, n)` is `n`.
- Otherwise, `gcd(m, n)` is `gcd(n, m % n)`.

It is not difficult to prove the correctness of the algorithm. Suppose `m % n = r`. So, `m = qn + r`, where `q` is the quotient of `m / n`. Any number that is divisible by `m` and `n` must also be divisible by `r`. Therefore, `gcd(m, n)` is the same as `gcd(n, r)`, where `r = m % n`. The algorithm can be implemented as in Listing 23.3.

LISTING 23.3 GCD2.java

base case; reduction; input; input

```
import java.util.Scanner;

public class GCD2 {
  /** Find gcd for integers m and n */
  public static int gcd(int m, int n) {
    if (m % n == 0)
      return n;
    else
      return gcd(n, m % n);
  }

  /** Main method */
  public static void main(String[] args) {
    // Create a Scanner
    Scanner input = new Scanner(System.in);

    // Prompt the user to enter two integers
    System.out.print("Enter first integer: ");
    int m = input.nextInt();
    System.out.print("Enter second integer: ");
    int n = input.nextInt();

    System.out.println("The greatest common divisor for " + m +
      " and " + n + " is " + gcd(m, n));
  }
}
```

```
Enter first integer: 2525 ↵Enter
Enter second integer: 125 ↵Enter
The greatest common divisor for 2525 and 125 is 25
```

```
Enter first integer: 3 ↵Enter
Enter second integer: 3 ↵Enter
The greatest common divisor for 3 and 3 is 3
```

best case; average case; worst case

In the best case when `m % n` is `0`, the algorithm takes just one step to find the gcd. It is difficult to analyze the average case. However, we can prove that the worst-case time complexity is $O(\log n)$.

Assuming $m \geq n$, we can show that `m % n < m / 2`, as follows:

- If `n <= m / 2`, `m % n < m / 2`, since the remainder of m divided by n is always less than n.
- If `n > m / 2`, `m % n = m – n < m / 2`. Therefore, `m % n < m / 2`.

Euclid's algorithm recursively invokes the `gcd` method. It first calls `gcd(m, n)`, then calls `gcd(n, m % n)`, and `gcd(m % n, n % (m % n))`, and so on, as follows:

```
  gcd(m, n)
= gcd(n, m % n)
= gcd(m % n, n % (m % n))
= ...
```

Since `m % n < m / 2` and `n % (m % n) < n / 2`, the argument passed to the gcd method is reduced by half after every two iterations. After invoking gcd two times, the second parameter is less than $n/2$. After invoking gcd four times, the second parameter is less than $n/4$. After invoking gcd six times, the second parameter is less than $\frac{n}{2^3}$. Let k be the number of times the gcd method is invoked. After invoking gcd k times, the second parameter is less than $\frac{n}{2^{(k/2)}}$, which is greater than or equal to 1. That is,

$$\frac{n}{2^{(k/2)}} \geq 1 \quad => \quad n \geq 2^{(k/2)} \quad => \quad \log n \geq k/2 \quad => \quad k \leq 2 \log n$$

Therefore, $k \leq 2 \log n$. So, the time complexity of the gcd method is $O(\log n)$.

The worst case occurs when the two numbers result in most divisions. It turns out that two successive Fibonacci numbers will result in most divisions. Recall that the Fibonacci series begins with 0 and 1, and each subsequent number is the sum of the preceding two numbers in the series, such as:

0 1 1 2 3 5 8 13 21 34 55 89 ...

The series can be recursively defined as

```
fib(0) = 0;
fib(1) = 1;
fib(index) = fib(index - 2) + fib(index - 1); index >= 2
```

For two successive Fibonacci numbers `fib(index)` and `fib(index -1)`,

```
gcd(fib(index), fib(index - 1))
= gcd(fib(index - 1), fib(index - 2))
= gcd(fib(index - 2), fib(index - 3))
= gcd(fib(index - 3), fib(index - 4))
= ...
= gcd(fib(2), fib(1))
= 1
```

For example,

```
gcd(21, 13)
= gcd(13, 8)
= gcd(8, 5)
= gcd(5, 3)
= gcd(3, 2)
= gcd(2, 1)
= 1
```

So, the number of times the gcd method is invoked is the same as the index. We can prove that $index \leq 1.44 \log n$, where $n = \text{fib}(\text{index} - 1)$. This is a tighter bound than $index \leq 2 \log n$.

Table 23.3 summarizes the complexity of three algorithms for finding the gcd.

TABLE 23.3 Comparisons of GCD Algorithms

	Listing 4.8	*Listing 23.2*	*Listing 23.3*
Complexity	$O(n)$	$O(n)$	$O(\log n)$

23.7 Case Studies: Finding Prime Numbers

A $100,000 award awaits the first individual or group who discovers a prime number with at least 10,000,000 decimal digits (www.eff.org/awards/coop.php). This section presents several algorithms in the search for an efficient algorithm for finding the prime numbers.

what is prime?

An integer greater than 1 is *prime* if its only positive divisor is 1 or itself. For example, 2, 3, 5, and 7 are prime numbers, but 4, 6, 8, and 9 are not.

How do you determine whether a number n is prime? Listing 4.14 presented a brute-force algorithm for finding prime numbers. The algorithm checks whether 2, 3, 4, 5, ..., or n - 1 is divisible by n. If not, n is prime. This algorithm takes $O(n)$ time to check whether n is prime. Note that you need to check only whether 2, 3, 4, 5, ..., and n/2 is divisible by n. If not, n is prime. The algorithm is slightly improved, but it is still of $O(n)$.

In fact, we can prove that if n is not a prime, n must have a factor that is greater than 1 and less than or equal to $\sqrt{n}$. Here is the proof. Since n is not a prime, there exist two numbers p and q such that n = pq with $1 < p \le q$. Note that $n = \sqrt{n}\sqrt{n}$. p must be less than or equal to $\sqrt{n}$. Hence, you need to check only whether 2, 3, 4, 5, ..., or $\sqrt{n}$ is divisible by n. If not, n is prime. This significantly reduces the time complexity of the algorithm to $O(\sqrt{n})$.

Now consider the algorithm for finding all the prime numbers up to n. A straightforward implementation is to check whether i is prime for i = 2, 3, 4, ..., n. The program is given in Listing 23.4.

LISTING 23.4 PrimeNumbers.java

check prime

increase count

```
import java.util.Scanner;

public class PrimeNumbers {
  public static void main(String[] args) {
    Scanner input = new Scanner(System.in);
    System.out.print("Find all prime numbers <= n, enter n: ");
    int n = input.nextInt();

    final int NUMBER_PER_LINE = 10; // Display 10 per line
    int count = 0; // Count the number of prime numbers
    int number = 2; // A number to be tested for primeness

    System.out.println("The prime numbers are:");

    // Repeatedly find prime numbers
    while (number <= n) {
      // Assume the number is prime
      boolean isPrime = true; // Is the current number prime?

      // Test if number is prime
      for (int divisor = 2; divisor <= (int)(Math.sqrt(number));
          divisor++) {
        if (number % divisor == 0) { // If true, number is not prime
          isPrime = false; // Set isPrime to false
          break; // Exit the for loop
        }
      }

      // Print the prime number and increase the count
      if (isPrime) {
        count++; // Increase the count

        if (count % NUMBER_PER_LINE == 0) {
          // Print the number and advance to the new line
```

```
35         System.out.printf("%7d\n", number);
36       }
37       else
38         System.out.printf("%7d", number);
39     }
40
41     // Check if the next number is prime
42     number++;
43   }
44
45   System.out.println("\n" + count +
46     " prime(s) less than or equal to " + n);
47   }
48 }
```

check next number

```
Find all prime numbers <= n, enter n: 1000 ↵Enter
The prime numbers are:
      2      3      5      7     11     13     17     19     23     29
     31     37     41     43     47     53     59     61     67     71
...
...
168 prime(s) less than or equal to 1000
```

The program is not efficient if you have to compute `Math.sqrt(number)` for every iteration of the for loop (line 21). A good compiler should evaluate `Math.sqrt(number)` only once for the entire for loop. To ensure this happens, you may explicitly replace line 21 by the following two lines:

```
int squareRoot = (int)(Math.sqrt(number));
for (int divisor = 2; divisor <= squareRoot; divisor++) {
```

In fact, there is no need to actually compute `Math.sqrt(number)` for every `number`. You need look only for the perfect squares such as `4`, `9`, `16`, `25`, `36`, `49`, and so on. Note that for all the numbers between `36` and `48`, inclusively, their `(int)(Math.sqrt(number))` is `6`. With this insight, you can replace the code in lines 16–26 with the following:

```
...
int squareRoot = 1;

// Repeatedly find prime numbers
while (number <= n) {
  // Assume the number is prime
  boolean isPrime = true; // Is the current number prime?

  if (squareRoot * squareRoot < number) squareRoot++;

  // Test if number is prime
  for (int divisor = 2; divisor <= squareRoot; divisor++) {
    if (number % divisor == 0) { // If true, number is not prime
      isPrime = false; // Set isPrime to false
      break; // Exit the for loop
    }
  }
...
```

Now we turn our attention to analyzing the complexity of this program. Since it takes $\sqrt{i}$ steps in the for loop (lines 21–27) to check whether number i is prime, the algorithm takes

$\sqrt{2} + \sqrt{3} + \sqrt{4} + \cdots + \sqrt{n}$ steps to find all the prime numbers less than or equal to n. Observe that

$$\sqrt{2} + \sqrt{3} + \sqrt{4} + \cdots + \sqrt{n} \leq n\sqrt{n}$$

Therefore, the time complexity for this algorithm is $O(n\sqrt{n})$.

To determine whether i is prime, the algorithm checks whether 2, 3, 4, 5, ..., and $\sqrt{i}$ are divisible by i. This algorithm can be further improved. In fact, you need to check only whether the prime numbers from 2 to $\sqrt{i}$ are possible divisors for i.

We can prove that if i is not prime, there must exist a prime number p such that $i = pq$ and $p \leq q$. Here is the proof. Assume that i is not prime; let p be the smallest factor of i. p must be prime, otherwise, p has a factor k with $2 \leq k < p$. k is also a factor of i, which contradicts that p be the smallest factor of i. Therefore, if i is not prime, you can find a prime number from 2 to $\sqrt{i}$ that is divisible by i. This leads to a more efficient algorithm for finding all prime numbers up to n, as shown in Listing 23.5.

LISTING 23.5 EfficientPrimeNumbers.java

```
import java.util.Scanner;

public class EfficientPrimeNumbers {
  public static void main(String[] args) {
    Scanner input = new Scanner(System.in);
    System.out.print("Find all prime numbers <= n, enter n: ");
    int n = input.nextInt();

    // A list to hold prime numbers
    java.util.List<Integer> list =
      new java.util.ArrayList<Integer>();

    final int NUMBER_PER_LINE = 10; // Display 10 per line
    int count = 0; // Count the number of prime numbers
    int number = 2; // A number to be tested for primeness
    int squareRoot = 1; // Check whether number <= squareRoot

    System.out.println("The prime numbers are \n");

    // Repeatedly find prime numbers
    while (number <= n) {
      // Assume the number is prime
      boolean isPrime = true; // Is the current number prime?

      if (squareRoot * squareRoot < number) squareRoot++;

      // Test whether number is prime
      for (int k = 0; k < list.size()
                        && list.get(k) <= squareRoot; k++) {
        if (number % list.get(k) == 0) { // If true, not prime
          isPrime = false; // Set isPrime to false
          break; // Exit the for loop
        }
      }

      // Print the prime number and increase the count
      if (isPrime) {
        count++; // Increase the count
        list.add(number); // Add a new prime to the list
        if (count % NUMBER_PER_LINE == 0) {
```

check prime

increase count

```
            // Print the number and advance to the new line
            System.out.println(number);
          }
          else
            System.out.print(number + " ");
        }

        // Check whether the next number is prime
        number++;
      }

      System.out.println("\n" + count +
        " prime(s) less than or equal to " + n);
    }
}
```

check next number

```
Find all prime numbers <= n, enter n: 1000 ↵Enter
The prime numbers are:
    2    3    5    7   11   13   17   19   23   29
   31   37   41   43   47   53   59   61   67   71
...
...
168 prime(s) less than or equal to 1000
```

Let $\pi(i)$ denote the number of prime numbers less than or equal to i. The primes under 20 are 2, 3, 5, 7, 11, 13, 17, and 19. So, $\pi(2)$ is 1, $\pi(3)$ is 2, $\pi(6)$ is 3, and $\pi(20)$ is 8. It has been proved that $\pi(i)$ is approximately $\frac{i}{\log i}$ (see primes.utm.edu/howmany.shtml).

For each number i, the algorithm checks whether a prime number less than or equal to $\sqrt{i}$ is divisible by i. The number of the prime numbers less than or equal to $\sqrt{i}$ is $\frac{\sqrt{i}}{\log \sqrt{i}} = \frac{2\sqrt{i}}{\log i}$. Thus, the complexity for finding all prime numbers up to n is

$$\frac{2\sqrt{2}}{\log 2} + \frac{2\sqrt{3}}{\log 3} + \frac{2\sqrt{4}}{\log 4} + \frac{2\sqrt{5}}{\log 5} + \frac{2\sqrt{6}}{\log 6} + \frac{2\sqrt{7}}{\log 7} + \frac{2\sqrt{8}}{\log 8} + \cdots + \frac{2\sqrt{n}}{\log n}$$

Since $\frac{\sqrt{i}}{\log i} < \frac{\sqrt{n}}{\log n}$ for $i < n$ and $n \geq 16$,

$$\frac{2\sqrt{2}}{\log 2} + \frac{2\sqrt{3}}{\log 3} + \frac{2\sqrt{4}}{\log 4} + \frac{2\sqrt{5}}{\log 5} + \frac{2\sqrt{6}}{\log 6} + \frac{2\sqrt{7}}{\log 7} + \frac{2\sqrt{8}}{\log 8} + \cdots + \frac{2\sqrt{n}}{\log n} < \frac{2n\sqrt{n}}{\log n}$$

Therefore, the complexity of this algorithm is $O\left(\frac{n\sqrt{n}}{\log n}\right)$.

Is there any algorithm better than $O\left(\frac{n\sqrt{n}}{\log n}\right)$? Let us examine the well-known Eratosthenes algorithm for finding prime numbers. Eratosthenes (276–194 B.C.) was a Greek mathematician who devised a clever algorithm, known as the *Sieve of Eratosthenes*, for finding all prime numbers $\leq n$. His algorithm is to use an array named primes of n Boolean values. Initially, all elements in primes are set true. Since the multiples of 2 are not prime, set primes[2 * i] to false for all $2 \leq i \leq n/2$, as shown in Figure 23.3. Since we don't care about primes[0] and primes[1], these values are marked × in the figure.

Sieve of Eratosthenes

primes array

index	0	1	2	3	4	5	6	7	8	9	10	11	12	13	14	15	16	17	18	19	20	21	22	23	24	25	26	27
initial	×	×	T	T	T	T	T	T	T	T	T	T	T	T	T	T	T	T	T	T	T	T	T	T	T	T	T	T
$k = 2$	×	×	T	T	F	T	F	T	F	T	F	T	F	T	F	T	F	T	F	T	F	T	F	T	F	T	F	T
$k = 3$	×	×	T	T	F	T	F	T	F	F	F	T	F	T	F	F	F	T	F	T	F	F	F	T	F	T	F	F
$k = 5$	×	×	(T)	(T)	F	(T)	F	(T)	F	F	F	(T)	F	(T)	F	F	F	(T)	F	(T)	F	F	F	(T)	F	F	F	F

FIGURE 23.3 The values in `primes` are changed with each prime number `k`.

Since the multiples of 3 are not prime, set `primes[3 * i]` to `false` for all $3 \leq i \leq n/3$. Since the multiples of 5 are not prime, set `primes[5 * i]` to `false` for all $5 \leq i \leq n/5$. Note that you don't need to consider the multiples of 4, because the multiples of 4 are also the multiples of 2, which have already been considered. Similarly, multiples of 6, 8, 9 need not be considered. You only need to consider the multiples of a prime number k = 2, 3, 5, 7, 11, ..., and set the corresponding element in `primes` to `false`. Afterward, if `primes[i]` is still true, then i is a prime number. As shown in Figure 23.3, 2, 3, 5, 7, 11, 13, 17, 19, 23 are prime numbers. Listing 23.6 gives the program for finding the prime numbers using the *Sieve of Eratosthenes* algorithm.

LISTING 23.6 SieveOfEratosthenes.java

sieve

initialize sieve

nonprime

```
import java.util.Scanner;

public class SieveOfEratosthenes {
  public static void main(String[] args) {
    Scanner input = new Scanner(System.in);
    System.out.print("Find all prime numbers <= n, enter n: ");
    int n = input.nextInt();

    boolean[] primes = new boolean[n + 1]; // Prime number sieve

    // Initialize primes[i] to true
    for (int i = 0; i < primes.length; i++) {
      primes[i] = true;
    }

    for (int k = 2; k <= n / k; k++) {
      if (primes[k]) {
        for (int i = k; i <= n / k; i++) {
          primes[k * i] = false; // k * i is not prime
        }
      }
    }

    int count = 0; // Count the number of prime numbers found so far
    // Print prime numbers
    for (int i = 2; i < primes.length; i++) {
      if (primes[i]) {
        count++;
        if (count % 10 == 0)
          System.out.printf("%7d\n", i);
        else
          System.out.printf("%7d", i);
      }
    }

    System.out.println("\n" + count +
```

```
37        " prime(s) less than or equal to " + n);
38    }
39 }
```

```
Find all prime numbers <= n, enter n: 1000 ↵Enter
The prime numbers are:
     2      3      5      7     11     13     17     19     23     29
    31     37     41     43     47     53     59     61     67     71
...
...
168 prime(s) less than or equal to 1000
```

Note that `k <= n / k` (line 16). Otherwise, `k * i` would be greater than `n` (line 19). What is the time complexity of this algorithm?

For each prime number `k` (line 17), the algorithm sets `primes[k * i]` to `false` (line 19). This is performed `n / k - k + 1` times in the for loop (line 18). Thus, the complexity for finding all prime numbers up to `n` is

$$\frac{n}{2} - 2 + 1 + \frac{n}{3} - 3 + 1 + \frac{n}{5} - 5 + 1 + \frac{n}{7} - 7 + 1 + \frac{n}{11} - 11 + 1 \ldots$$

$$= O\left(\frac{n}{2} + \frac{n}{3} + \frac{n}{5} + \frac{n}{7} + \frac{n}{11} + \cdots\right) < O(n\pi(n))$$

$$= O\left(n\frac{\sqrt{n}}{\log n}\right)$$

This upper bound $O\left(\frac{n\sqrt{n}}{\log n}\right)$ is very loose. The actual time complexity is much better than $O\left(\frac{n\sqrt{n}}{\log n}\right)$. The Sieve of Eratosthenes algorithm is good for a small `n` such that the array `primes` can fit in the memory.

Table 23.4 summarizes the complexity of three algorithms for finding all prime numbers up to *n*.

TABLE 23.4 Comparisons of Prime-Number Algorithms

	Listing 4.14	*Listing 23.4*	*Listing 23.5*	*Listing 23.6*
Complexity	$O(n^2)$	$O\left(n\sqrt{n}\right)$	$O\left(\frac{n\sqrt{n}}{\log n}\right)$	$O\left(\frac{n\sqrt{n}}{\log n}\right)$

23.8 Case Studies: Closest Pair of Points

Given a set of points, the closest-pair problem is to find the two points that are nearest to each other. Section 7.3, "Problem: Finding a Closest Pair," presented an intuitive algorithm for finding a closest pair of points. The algorithm computes the distances between all pairs of points and finds the one with the minimum distance. Clearly, the algorithm takes $O(n^2)$ time. Can you beat this algorithm?

One approach you can use is to divide and conquer, as described in Listing 23.7:

LISTING 23.7 Algorithm for Finding a Closest Pair

```
Step 1: Sort the points in increasing order of x-coordinates. For the
points with the same x-coordinates, sort on y-coordinates. This results
in a sorted list S of points.
```

```
Step 2: Divide S into two subsets S1 and S2 of the equal size using the
midpoint in the sorted list. Let the midpoint be in S1. Recursively find
the closest pair in S1 and S2. Let d1 and d2 denote the distance of the
closest pairs in the two subsets, respectively.

Step 3: Find the closest pair between a point in S1 and a point in S2 and
denote their distance to be d3. The closest pair is the one with the
distance min(d1, d2, d3).
```

Selection sort and insertion sort take $O(n^2)$ time. In Chapter 24 we will introduce merge sort and heap sort. These sorting algorithms take $O(n\log n)$ time. So, Step 1 can be done in $O(n\log n)$ time.

Step 3: can be done in $O(n)$ time. Let $d = \min(d_1, d_2)$. We already know that the closest-pair distance cannot be larger than d. For a point in S_1 and a point in S_2 to form a closest pair in S, the left point must be in **stripL** and the right point in **stripR**, as pictured in Figure 23.4(a).

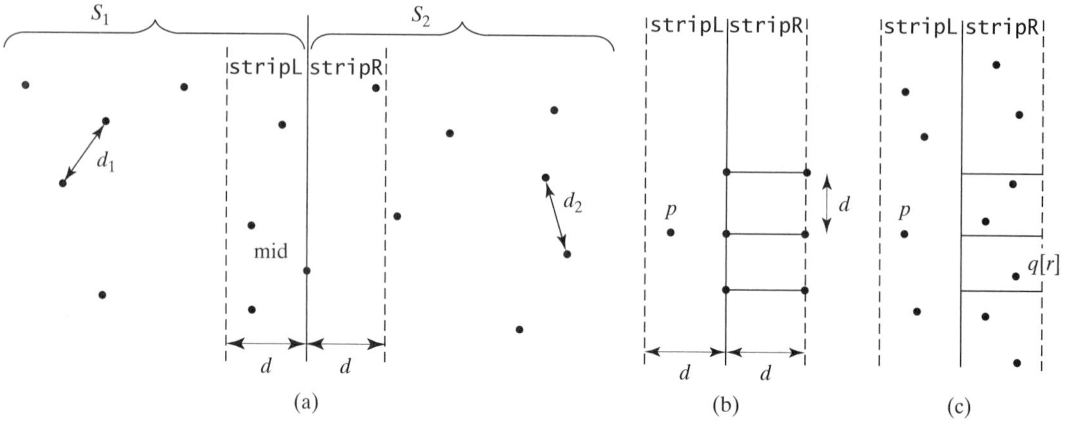

S1
S2
stripL
stripR
d1
d2
mid
d
p
q[r]
(a)
(b)
(c)

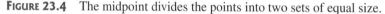

FIGURE 23.4 The midpoint divides the points into two sets of equal size.

Further, for a point p in **stripL**, you need only consider a right point within the $d \times 2d$ rectangle, as shown in 23.2(b). Any right point outside the rectangle cannot form a closest pair with p. Since the closest-pair distance in S_2 is greater than or equal to d, there can be at most six points in the rectangle. So, for each point in **stripL**, at most six points in **stripR** need to be considered.

For each point p in **stripL**, how do you locate the points in the corresponding $d \times 2d$ rectangle area in **stripR**? This can be done efficiently if the points in **stripL** and **stripR** are sorted in increasing order of their y-coordinates. Let **pointsOrderedOnY** be the list of the points sorted in increasing order of y-coordinates. **pointsOrderedOnY** can be obtained beforehand in the algorithm. **stripL** and **stripR** can be obtained from **pointsOrderedOnY** in Step 3 as shown in Listing 23.8

LISTING 23.8 Algorithm for obtaining **stripL** and **stripR**

```
for each point p in pointsOrderedOnY
  if (p is in S1 and mid.x - p.x <= d)
    append p to stripL;                      // stripL
  else if (p is in S2 and p.x - mid.x <= d)
    append p to stripR;                      // stripR
```

Let the points in **stripL** and **stripR** be $\{p_0, p_1, \ldots, p_k\}$ and $\{q_0, q_1, \ldots, q_t\}$. A closest pair between a point in **stripL** and a point in **stripR** can be found using the algorithm described in Listing 23.9.

LISTING 23.9 Algorithm for Finding a Closest Pair in Step 3

```
d = min(d1, d2);
r = 0; // r is the index in stripR
```

```
3 for (each point p in stripL) {
4   // Skip the points below the rectangle area
5   while (r < stripR.length && q[r].y <= p.y - d)
6     r++;
7
8   let r1 = r;
9   while (r1 < stripR.length && |q[r1].y - p.y| <= d) {
10    // Check if (p, q[r1]) is a possible closest pair
11    if (distance(p, q[r1]) < d) {
12      d = distance(p, q[r1]);
13      (p, q[r1]) is now the current closed pair;
14    }
15
16    r1 = r1 + 1;
17  }
18 }
```

update closest pair

The points in `stripL` are considered from $p_0, p_1, \ldots, p_k$ in this order. For a point `p` in `stripL`, skip the points in `stripR` that are below `p.y – d` (lines 5–6). Once a point is skipped, it will no longer be considered. The `while` loop (lines 9–17) checks whether `(p, q[r1])` is a possible closest pair. There are at most six such `q[r1]`'s. So, the complexity for finding a closest pair in Step 3 is $O(n)$.

Let $T(n)$ denote the time complexity for the algorithm. So,

$$T(n) = 2T(n/2) + O(n) = O(n \log n)$$

Therefore, a closest pair of points can be found in O($n$log n) time. The complete implementation of this algorithm is left as an exercise (see Exercise 23.9).

23.9 Preview of Other Algorithms

The examples in this chapter have demonstrated how to analyze and design efficient algorithms for several well-known problems. Chapter 24 will introduce efficient algorithms for internal and external sorting. Chapter 25 will introduce efficient algorithms for implementing lists, stacks, and queues. Chapter 26 will introduce efficient algorithms for implementing trees, heaps, and priority queues. Chapters 27-28 will introduce efficient algorithms and data structures for graph problems. Chapters 45–47 will introduce AVL trees, splay trees, 2-3 trees, B-trees, and red-black trees. Chapter 48 will introduce hashing. For the algorithms in these chapters, we will also analyze their complexities. Recurrence relations are a useful tool for analyzing algorithm complexity. Table 23.5 summarizes the common recurrence relations.

TABLE 23.5 Common Recurrence Functions

Recurrence Relation	*Result*	*Example*
$T(n) = T(n/2) + O(1)$	$T(n) = O(\log n)$	Binary search, Euclid's GCD
$T(n) = T(n-1) + O(1)$	$T(n) = O(n)$	Linear search
$T(n) = 2T(n/2) + O(1)$	$T(n) = O(n)$	
$T(n) = 2T(n/2) + O(n)$	$T(n) = O(n \log n)$	Merge sort (Chapter 26)
$T(n) = 2T(n/2) + O(n \log n)$	$T(n) = O(n \log^2 n)$	
$T(n) = T(n-1) + O(n)$	$T(n) = O(n^2)$	Selection sort, insertion sort
$T(n) = 2T(n-1) + O(1)$	$T(n) = O(2^n)$	Towers of Hanoi
$T(n) = T(n-1) + T(n-2) + O(1)$	$T(n) = O(2^n)$	Recursive Fibonacci algorithm

Key Terms

average-case analysis 766
best-case analysis 766
Big *O* notation 766
constant time 767
exponential time 771
growth rate 766
logarithmic time 770
quadratic time 768
worst-case analysis 766

Chapter Summary

1. The Big *O* notation is a theoretical approach for analyzing the performance of an algorithm. It estimates how fast an algorithm's execution time increases as the input size increases. So you can compare two algorithms by examining their *growth rates*.
2. An input that results in the shortest execution time is called the *best-case* input and one that results in the longest execution time is called the *worst-case* input. Best case and worst case are not representative, but worst-case analysis is very useful. You can be assured that the algorithm will never be slower than the worst case.
3. An average-case analysis attempts to determine the average amount of time among all possible input of the same size. Average-case analysis is ideal, but difficult to perform, because for many problems it is hard to determine the relative probabilities and distributions of various input instances.
4. If the time is not related to the input size, the algorithm is said to take *constant time* with the notation $O(1)$.
5. Linear search takes $O(n)$ time. An algorithm with the $O(n)$ time complexity is called a *linear algorithm*. Binary search takes $O(\log n)$ time. An algorithm with the $O(\log n)$ time complexity is called a *logarithmic algorithm*.
6. The worst-time complexity for selection sort and insertion sort is $O(n^2)$. An algorithm with the $O(n^2)$ time complexity is called a *quadratic algorithm*.
7. The time complexity for the Towers of Hanoi problem is $O(2^n)$. An algorithm with the $O(2^n)$ time complexity is called an *exponential algorithm*.
8. A Fibonacci number at a given index can be found in $O(n)$ time.
9. Euclid's gcd algorithm takes $O(\log n)$ time.
10. All prime numbers less than or equal to n can be found in $O\left(\frac{n\sqrt{n}}{\log n}\right)$ time.

Review Questions

Sections 23.2

23.1 Put the following growth functions in order:

$$\frac{5n^3}{4032}, 44 \log n, 10n \log n, 500, 2n^2, \frac{2^n}{45}, 3n$$

23.2 Count the number of iterations in the following loops.

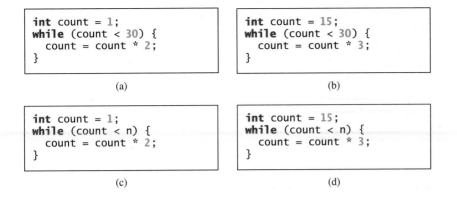

```
int count = 1;
while (count < 30) {
  count = count * 2;
}
```

(a)

```
int count = 15;
while (count < 30) {
  count = count * 3;
}
```

(b)

```
int count = 1;
while (count < n) {
  count = count * 2;
}
```

(c)

```
int count = 15;
while (count < n) {
  count = count * 3;
}
```

(d)

23.3 How many stars are displayed in the following code if n is 10? How many if n is 20? Use the Big *O* notation to estimate the time complexity.

```
for (int i = 0; i < n; i++) {
  System.out.print('*');
}
```

```
for (int i = 0; i < n; i++) {
  for (int j = 0; j < n; j++) {
    System.out.print('*');
  }
}
```

```
for (int k = 0; k < n; k++) {
  for (int i = 0; i < n; i++) {
    for (int j = 0; j < n; j++) {
      System.out.print('*');
    }
  }
}
```

```
for (int k = 0; k < 10; k++) {
  for (int i = 0; i < n; i++) {
    for (int j = 0; j < n; j++) {
      System.out.print('*');
    }
  }
}
```

23.4 Use the Big *O* notation to estimate the time complexity of the following methods:

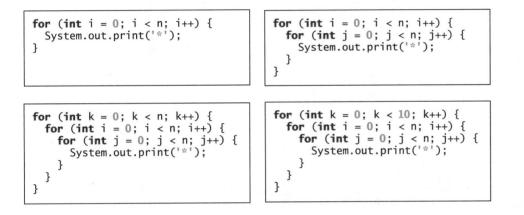

```
public static void mA(int n) {
  for (int i = 0; i < n; i++) {
    System.out.print(Math.random());
  }
}
```

```
public static void mB(int n) {
  for (int i = 0; i < n; i++) {
    for (int j = 0; j < i; j++)
      System.out.print(Math.random());
  }
}
```

```
public static void mC(int[] m) {
  for (int i = 0; i < m.length; i++) {
    System.out.print(m[i]);
  }

  for (int i = m.length - 1; i >= 0; )
  {
    System.out.print(m[i]);
    i--;
  }
}
```

```
public static void mD(int[] m) {
  for (int i = 0; i < m.length; i++) {
    for (int j = 0; j < i; j++)
      System.out.print(m[i] * m[j]);
  }
}
```

23.5 Estimate the time complexity for adding two $n \times m$ matrices, and for multiplying an $n \times m$ matrix by an $m \times k$ matrix.

23.6 Analyze the following sorting algorithm:

```
for (int i = 0; i < list.length -1; i++) {
  if (list[i] > list[i + 1]) {
    swap list[i] with list[i + 1];
    i = -1;
  }
}
```

23.7 Example 7 in §23.3 assumes $n = 2^k$. Revise the algorithm for an arbitrary n and prove that the complexity is still $O(\log n)$.

Programming Exercises

23.1* (*Maximum consecutive increasingly ordered substring*) Write a program that prompts the user to enter a string and displays the maximum consecutive increasingly ordered substring. Analyze the time complexity of your program. Here is a sample run:

```
Enter a string: Welcome ↵Enter
Wel
```

23.2** (*Maximum increasingly ordered subsequence*) Write a program that prompts the user to enter a string and displays the maximum increasingly ordered substring. Analyze the time complexity of your program. Here is a sample run:

```
Enter a string: Welcome ↵Enter
Welo
```

23.3* (*Pattern matching*) Write a program that prompts the user to enter two strings and tests whether the second string is a substring in the first string. *Suppose the neighboring characters in the string are distinct.* (Don't use the `indexOf` method in the `String` class.) Analyze the time complexity of your algorithm. Your algorithm needs to be at least `O(n)` time. Here is a sample run of the program:

```
Enter a string s1: Welcome to Java ↵Enter
Enter a string s2: come ↵Enter
matched at index 3
```

23.4* (*Pattern matching*) Write a program that prompts the user to enter two strings and tests whether the second string is a substring in the first string. (Don't use the `indexOf` method in the `String` class.) Analyze the time complexity of your algorithm. Here is a sample run of the program:

```
Enter a string s1: Mississippi ↵Enter
Enter a string s2: sip ↵Enter
matched at index 6
```

23.5* (*Same-number subsequence*) Write an $O(n)$ program that prompts the user to enter a sequence of integers ending with `0` and finds longest subsequence with the same number. Here is a sample run of the program:

```
Enter a series of numbers ending with 0:
  2 4 4 8 8 8 8 2 4 4 0 [Enter]
The longest same number sequence starts at index
  3 with 4 values of 8
```

23.6* (*Execution time for GCD*) Write a program that obtains the execution time for finding the GCD of every two consecutive Fibonacci numbers from the index 40 to index 45 using the algorithms in Listings 23.2 and 23.3. Your program should print a table like this:

	40	41	42	43	44	45
Listing 23.2 GCD1						
Listing 23.3 GCD2						

(*Hint*: You can use the code template below to obtain the execution time.)

```
long startTime = System.currentTimeMillis();
perform the task;
long endTime = System.currentTimeMillis();
long executionTime = endTime - startTime;
```

23.7** (*Execution time for prime numbers*) Write a program that obtains the execution time for finding all the prime numbers less than 8,000,000, 10,000,000, 12,000,000, 14,000,000, 16,000,000, and 18,000,000 using the algorithms in Listings 23.4–23.6. Your program should print a table like this:

	8000000	10000000	12000000	14000000	16000000	18000000
Listing 23.4						
Listing 23.5						
Listing 23.6						

23.8** (*All prime numbers up to* `10,000,000,000`) Write a program that finds all prime numbers up to `10,000,000,000`. There are approximately `455,052,511` such prime numbers. Your program should meet the following requirements:

- Your program should store the prime numbers in a binary data file, named **Exercise23_8.dat.** When a new prime number is found, the number is appended to the file.
- To find whether a new number is prime, your program should load the prime numbers from the file to an array of the `long` type of size `10000`. If no number in the array is a divisor for the new number, continue to read the next `10000` prime numbers from the data file, until a divisor is found or all numbers in the file are read. If no divisor is found, the new number is prime.

- Since this program takes a long time to finish, you should run it as a batch job from a Unix machine. If the machine is shut down and rebooted, your program should resume by using the prime numbers stored in the binary data file rather than start over from the scratch.

23.9 (*Last 100 prime numbers*) Exercise 23.8 stores the prime numbers in a file named **Exercise23_8.dat**. Write an efficient program that reads the last `100` numbers in the file.

(*Hint*: Don't read all numbers from the file. Skip all numbers before the last 100 numbers in the file.)

23.10 (*Number of prime numbers*) Exercise 23.8 stores the prime numbers in a file named **Exercise23_8.dat**. Write a program that finds the number of the prime numbers less than or equal to `10`, `100`, `1,000`, `10,000`, `100,000`, `1,000,000`, `10,000,000`, `100,000,000`, `1,000,000,000`, and `10,000,000,000`. Your program should read the data from Exercise23_8.dat. Note that the data file may continue to grow as more prime numbers are stored to the file.

23.11*** (*Closest pair of points*) Section 23.8 introduced an algorithm for finding a closest pair of points using a divide-and-conquer approach. Implement the algorithm to meet the following requirements:

- Define the classes `Point` and `CompareY` in the same way as in Exercise 22.12.
- Define a class named `Pair` with data fields `p1` and `p2` to represent two points, and a method named `getDistance()` that returns the distance of the two points.
- Implement the following methods:

```
/** Return the distance of the closest pair of points */
public static Pair getClosestPair(double[][] points)

/** Return the distance of the closest pair of points */
public static Pair getClosestPair(Point[] points)

/** Return the distance of the closest pair of points
  * in pointsOrderedOnX[low..high]. This is a recursive
  * method. pointsOrderedOnX and pointsOrderedOnY are
  * not changed in the subsequent recursive calls.
  */
public static Pair distance(Point[] pointsOrderedOnX,
    int low, int high, Point[] pointsOrderedOnY)

/** Compute the distance between two points p1 and p2 */
public static double distance(Point p1, Point p2)

/** Compute the distance between points (x1, y1)
  and (x2, y2) */
public static double distance(double x1, double y1,
    double x2, double y2)
```

CHAPTER 24

SORTING

Objectives

- To study and analyze time efficiency of various sorting algorithms (§§24.2–24.7).
- To design, implement, and analyze bubble sort (§24.2).
- To design, implement, and analyze merge sort (§24.3).
- To design, implement, and analyze quick sort (§24.4).
- To design and implement a heap (§24.5).
- To design, implement, and analyze heap sort (§24.5).
- To design, implement, and analyze bucket sort and radix sort (§24.6).
- To design, implement, and analyze external sort for large amounts of data in a file (§24.7).

24.1 Introduction

why study sorting?

Sorting is a classic subject in computer science. There are three reasons to study sorting algorithms. First, sorting algorithms illustrate many creative approaches to problem solving, and these approaches can be applied to solve other problems. Second, sorting algorithms are good for practicing fundamental programming techniques using selection statements, loops, methods, and arrays. Third, sorting algorithms are excellent examples to demonstrate algorithm performance.

what data to sort?

The data to be sorted might be integers, doubles, characters, or objects. Section 6.10, "Sorting Arrays," presented selection sort and insertion sort for numeric values. The selection sort algorithm was extended to sort an array of objects in §14.10, "Sorting an Array of Objects." The Java API contains several overloaded sort methods for sorting primitive type values and objects in the `java.util.Arrays` and `java.util.Collections` class. For simplicity, this section assumes:

1. data to be sorted are integers,
2. data are stored in an array, and
3. data are sorted in ascending order.

The programs can be easily modified to sort other types of data, to sort in descending order, or to sort data in an `ArrayList` or a `LinkedList`.

There are many algorithms for sorting. You have already learned selection sort and insertion sort. This chapter introduces bubble sort, merge sort, quick sort, bucket sort, radix sort, and external sort.

Note

The whole chapter is optional. No chapter in the book depends on this chapter.

24.2 Bubble Sort

The bubble sort algorithm makes several passes through the array. On each pass, successive neighboring pairs are compared. If a pair is in decreasing order, its values are swapped; otherwise, the values remain unchanged. The technique is called a *bubble sort* or *sinking sort*, because the smaller values gradually "bubble" their way to the top and the larger values sink to the bottom. After first pass, the last element becomes the largest in the array. After the second pass, the second-to-last element becomes the second largest in the array. This process is continued until all elements are sorted.

bubble sort illustration

Figure 24.1(a) shows the first pass of a bubble sort of an array of six elements (2 9 5 4 8 1). Compare the elements in the first pair (2 and 9), and no swap is needed because they are already in order. Compare the elements in the second pair (9 and 5), and swap 9 with 5 because 9 is greater than 5. Compare the elements in the third pair (9 and 4), and swap 9 with

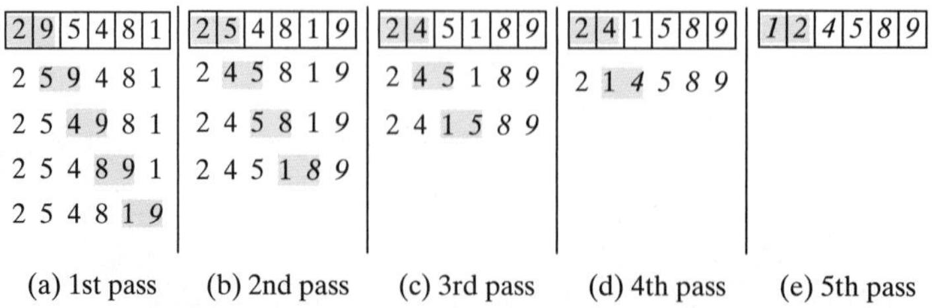
2 9 5 4 8 1
2 5 9 4 8 1
2 5 4 9 8 1
2 5 4 8 9 1
2 5 4 8 1 9
2 5 4 8 1 9
2 4 5 8 1 9
2 4 5 8 1 9
2 4 5 1 8 9
2 4 5 1 8 9
2 4 5 1 8 9
2 4 1 5 8 9
2 4 1 5 8 9
2 1 4 5 8 9
1 2 4 5 8 9
(a) 1st pass
(b) 2nd pass
(c) 3rd pass
(d) 4th pass
(e) 5th pass

FIGURE 24.1 Each pass compares and orders the pairs of elements sequentially.

4. Compare the elements in the fourth pair (9 and 8), and swap 9 with 8. Compare the elements in the fifth pair (9 and 1), and swap 9 with 1. The pairs being compared are highlighted and the numbers already sorted are italicized.

The first pass places the largest number (9) as the last in the array. In the second pass, as shown in Figure 24.1(b), you compare and order pairs of elements sequentially. There is no need to consider the last pair, because the last element in the array is already the largest. In the third pass, as shown in Figure 24.1(c), you compare and order pairs of elements sequentially except the last two elements, because they are already ordered. So in the *k*th pass, you don't need to consider the last $k - 1$ elements, because they are already ordered.

The algorithm for bubble sort can be described in Listing 24.1:

algorithm

LISTING 24.1 Bubble Sort Algorithm

```
for (int k = 1; k < list.length; k++) {
  // Perform the kth pass
  for (int i = 0; i < list.length - k; i++) {
    if (list[i] > list[i + 1])
      swap list[i] with list[i + 1];
  }
}
```

Note that if no swap takes place in a pass, there is no need to perform the next pass, because all the elements are already sorted. You may use this property to improve the preceding algorithm as in Listing 24.2.

LISTING 24.2 Improved Bubble Sort Algorithm

```
boolean needNextPass = true;
for (int k = 1; k < list.length && needNextPass; k++) {
  // Array may be sorted and next pass not needed
  needNextPass = false;
  // Perform the kth pass
  for (int i = 0; i < list.length - k; i++) {
    if (list[i] > list[i + 1]) {
      swap list[i] with list[i + 1];
      needNextPass = true; // Next pass still needed
    }
  }
}
```

The algorithm can be implemented as in Listing 24.3:

LISTING 24.3 BubbleSort.java

perform one pass

```
public class BubbleSort {
  /** Bubble sort method */
  public static void bubbleSort(int[] list) {
    boolean needNextPass = true;

    for (int k = 1; k < list.length && needNextPass; k++) {
      // Array may be sorted and next pass not needed
      needNextPass = false;
      for (int i = 0; i < list.length - k; i++) {
        if (list[i] > list[i + 1]) {
          // Swap list[i] with list[i + 1]
          int temp = list[i];
          list[i] = list[i + 1];
          list[i + 1] = temp;

```

```
            needNextPass = true; // Next pass still needed
          }
        }
      }
    }

    /** A test method */
    public static void main(String[] args) {
      int[] list = {2, 3, 2, 5, 6, 1, -2, 3, 14, 12};
      bubbleSort(list);
      for (int i = 0; i < list.length; i++)
        System.out.print(list[i] + " ");
    }
  }
```

```
-2 1 2 2 3 3 5 6 12 14
```

24.2.1 Bubble Sort Time

In the best-case, the bubble sort algorithm needs just the first pass to find that the array is already sorted. No next pass is needed. Since the number of comparisons is $n - 1$ in the first pass, the best-case time for bubble sort is $O(n)$.

In the worst case, the bubble sort algorithm requires $n - 1$ passes. The first pass takes $n - 1$ comparisons; the second pass takes $n - 2$ comparisons; and so on; the last pass takes 1 comparison. So, the total number of comparisons is:

$$(n-1) + (n-2) + \cdots + 2 + 1$$

$$= \frac{(n-1)n}{2} = \frac{n^2}{2} - \frac{n}{2} = O(n^2)$$

Therefore, the worst-case time for bubble sort is $O(n^2)$.

24.3 Merge Sort

The merge sort algorithm can be described recursively as follows: The algorithm divides the array into two halves and applies merge sort on each half recursively. After the two halves are sorted, merge them. The algorithm is given in Listing 24.4.

LISTING 24.4 Merge Sort Algorithm

base condition
sort first half
sort second half
merge two halves

```
public static void mergeSort(int[] list) {
  if (list.length > 1) {
    mergeSort(list[0 ... list.length / 2]);
    mergeSort(list[list.length / 2 + 1 ... list.length]);
    merge list[0 ... list.length / 2] with
      list[list.length / 2 + 1 ... list.length];
  }
}
```

merge sort illustration

Figure 24.2 illustrates a merge sort of an array of eight elements (2 9 5 4 8 1 6 7). The original array is split into (2 9 5 4) and (8 1 6 7). Apply merge sort on these two subarrays recursively to split (1 9 5 4) into (1 9) and (5 4) and (8 1 6 7) into (8 1) and (6 7). This process continues until the subarray contains only one element. For example, array (2 9) is split into subarrays (2) and (9). Since array (2) contains a single element, it cannot be further split. Now merge (2) with (9) into a new sorted array (2 9); merge (5) with (4) into a new sorted array (4 5). Merge

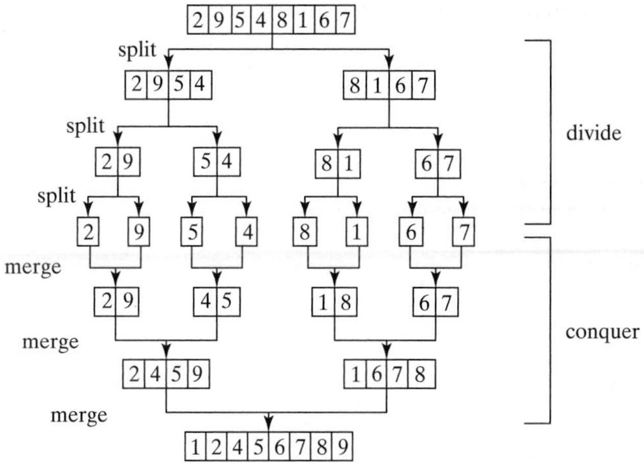
2 9 5 4 8 1 6 7
split
2 9 5 4
8 1 6 7
split
2 9
5 4
8 1
6 7
split
2
9
5
4
8
1
6
7
merge
2 9
4 5
1 8
6 7
merge
2 4 5 9
1 6 7 8
merge
1 2 4 5 6 7 8 9
divide
conquer

FIGURE 24.2 Merge sort employs a divide-and-conquer approach to sort the array.

(2 9) with (4 5) into a new sorted array (2 4 5 9), and finally merge (2 4 5 9) with (1 6 7 8) into a new sorted array (1 2 4 5 6 7 8 9).

The recursive call continues dividing the array into subarrays until each subarray contains only one element. The algorithm then merges these small subarrays into larger sorted subarrays until one sorted array results.

The merge sort algorithm is implemented in Listing 24.5.

LISTING 24.5 MergeSort.java

```java
public class MergeSort {
  /** The method for sorting the numbers */
  public static void mergeSort(int[] list) {
    if (list.length > 1) {
      // Merge sort the first half
      int[] firstHalf = new int[list.length / 2];
      System.arraycopy(list, 0, firstHalf, 0, list.length / 2);
      mergeSort(firstHalf);

      // Merge sort the second half
      int secondHalfLength = list.length - list.length / 2;
      int[] secondHalf = new int[secondHalfLength];
      System.arraycopy(list, list.length / 2,
        secondHalf, 0, secondHalfLength);
      mergeSort(secondHalf);

      // Merge firstHalf with secondHalf
      int[] temp = merge(firstHalf, secondHalf);
      System.arraycopy(temp, 0, list, 0, temp.length);
    }
  }

  /** Merge two sorted lists */
  private static int[] merge(int[] list1, int[] list2) {
    int[] temp = new int[list1.length + list2.length];

    int current1 = 0; // Current index in list1
    int current2 = 0; // Current index in list2
    int current3 = 0; // Current index in temp

```

base case

sort first half

sort second half

merge two halves

copy to original array

list1 to temp

list2 to temp

rest of list1 to temp

rest of list2 to temp

```
31     while (current1 < list1.length && current2 < list2.length) {
32       if (list1[current1] < list2[current2])
33         temp[current3++] = list1[current1++];
34       else
35         temp[current3++] = list2[current2++];
36     }
37 
38     while (current1 < list1.length)
39       temp[current3++] = list1[current1++];
40 
41     while (current2 < list2.length)
42       temp[current3++] = list2[current2++];
43 
44     return temp;
45   }
46 
47   /** A test method */
48   public static void main(String[] args) {
49     int[] list = {2, 3, 2, 5, 6, 1, -2, 3, 14, 12};
50     mergeSort(list);
51     for (int i = 0; i < list.length; i++)
52       System.out.print(list[i] + " ");
53   }
54 }
```

The `mergeSort` method (lines 3–21) creates a new array `firstHalf`, which is a copy of the first half of `list` (line 7). The algorithm invokes `mergeSort` recursively on `firstHalf` (line 8). The length of the `firstHalf` is `list.length / 2` and the length of the `secondHalf` is `list.length - list.length / 2`. The new array `secondHalf` was created to contain the second part of the original array `list`. The algorithm invokes `mergeSort` recursively on `secondHalf` (line 15). After `firstHalf` and `secondHalf` are sorted, they are merged to become a new sorted array in `temp` (line 18). Finally, temp is assigned to the original array `list` (line 19). So, array `list` is now sorted.

The `merge` method (lines 24–45) merges two sorted arrays. This method merges arrays `list1` and `list2` into a temporary array `temp`. So, `temp.length` is `list1.length + list2.length` (line 25). `current1` and `current2` point to the current element to be considered in `list1` and `list2` (lines 27–28). The method repeatedly compares the current elements from `list1` and `list2` and moves the smaller one to `temp`. `current1` is increased by `1` (line 33) if the smaller one is in `list1` and `current2` is increased by `1` (line 35) if the smaller one is in `list2`. Finally, all the elements in one of the lists are moved to `temp`. If there are still unmoved elements in `list1`, copy them to `temp` (lines 38–39). If there are still unmoved elements in `list2`, copy them to `temp` (lines 41–42). The method returns `temp` as the new sorted array in line 44.

Figure 24.3 illustrates how to merge two arrays `list1` (2 4 5 9) and `list2` (1 6 7 8). Initially the current elements to be considered in the arrays are 2 and 1. Compare them and move the smaller element 1 to `temp`, as shown in Figure 24.3(a). `current2` and `current3` are increased by 1. Continue to compare the current elements in the two arrays and move the smaller one to `temp` until one of the arrays is completely moved. As shown in Figure 24.3(b), all the elements in `list2` are moved to `temp` and `current1` points to element 9 in `list1`. Copy 9 to `temp`, as shown in Figure 24.3(c).

24.3.1 Merge Sort Time

time analysis

Let $T(n)$ denote the time required for sorting an array of n elements using merge sort. Without loss of generality, assume n is a power of 2. The merge sort algorithm splits the array into two

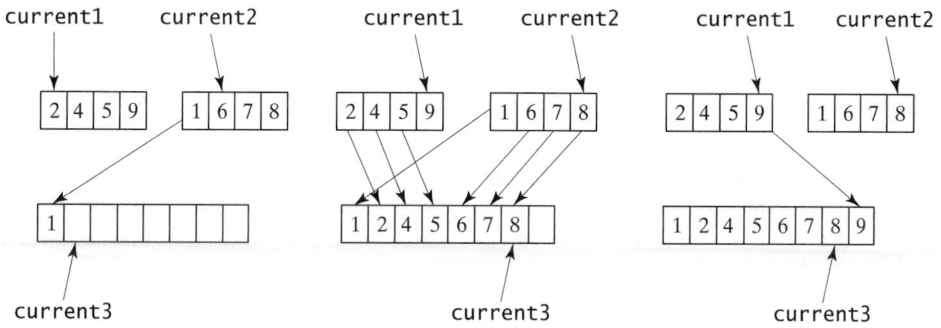
current1
current2
2 4 5 9
1 6 7 8
1
current3
current1
current2
2 4 5 9
1 6 7 8
1 2 4 5 6 7 8
current3
current1
current2
2 4 5 9
1 6 7 8
1 2 4 5 6 7 8 9
current3

(a) After moving 1 to `temp` (b) After moving all the elements in `list2` to `temp` (c) After moving 9 to `temp`

FIGURE 24.3 Two sorted arrays are merged into one sorted array.

subarrays, sorts the subarrays using the same algorithm recursively, and then merges the subarrays. So,

$$T(n) = T\left(\frac{n}{2}\right) + T\left(\frac{n}{2}\right) + mergetime$$

The first $T\left(\frac{n}{2}\right)$ is the time for sorting the first half of the array and the second $T\left(\frac{n}{2}\right)$ is the time for sorting the second half. To merge two subarrays, it takes at most $n - 1$ comparisons to compare the elements from the two subarrays and n moves to move elements to the temporary array. So, the total time is $2n - 1$. Therefore,

$$T(n) = T\left(\frac{n}{2}\right) + T\left(\frac{n}{2}\right) + 2n - 1 = O(n \log n)$$

The complexity of merge sort is $O(n \log n)$. This algorithm is better than selection sort, insertion sort, and bubble sort. The `sort` method in the `java.util.Arrays` class is implemented using a variation of the merge sort algorithm.

$O(n \log n)$ merge sort

24.4 Quick Sort

Quick sort, developed by C. A. R. Hoare (1962), works as follows: The algorithm selects an element, called the *pivot*, in the array. Divide the array into two parts such that all the elements in the first part are less than or equal to the pivot and all the elements in the second part are greater than the pivot. Recursively apply the quick sort algorithm to the first part and then the second part. The algorithm is described in Listing 24.6.

LISTING 24.6 Quick Sort Algorithm

```
public static void quickSort(int[] list) {
  if (list.length > 1) {
    select a pivot;
    partition list into list1 and list2 such that
      all elements in list1 <= pivot and
      all elements in list2 >
    quickSort(list1);
    quickSort(list2);
  }
}
```

base condition
select the pivot
partition the list
sort first part
sort second part

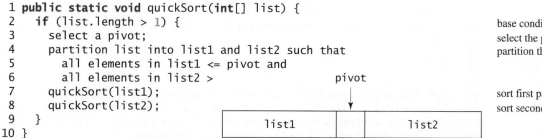

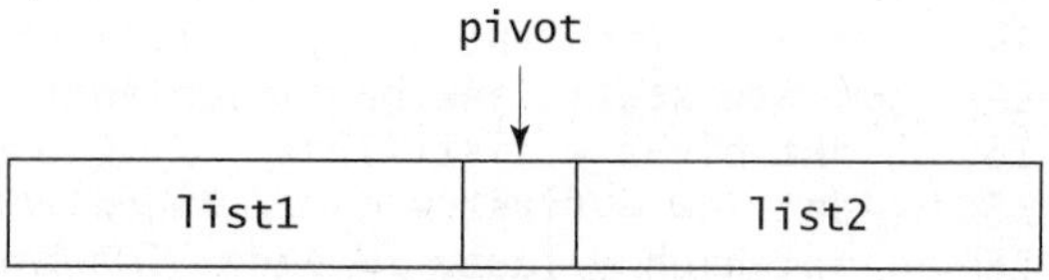
pivot
list1
list2

how to partition

Each partition places the pivot in the right place. The selection of the pivot affects the performance of the algorithm. Ideally, you should choose the pivot that divides the two parts evenly. For simplicity, assume the first element in the array is chosen as the pivot. Exercise 24.4 proposes an alternative strategy for selecting the pivot.

quick sort illustration

Figure 24.4 illustrates how to sort an array (5 2 9 3 8 4 0 1 6 7) using quick sort. Choose the first element 5 as the pivot. The array is partitioned into two parts, as shown in Figure 24.4(b). The highlighted pivot is placed in the right place in the array. Apply quick sort on two partial arrays (4 2 1 3 0) and then (8 9 6 7). The pivot 4 partitions (4 2 1 3 0) into just one partial array (0 2 1 3), as shown in Figure 24.4(c). Apply quick sort on (0 2 1 3). The pivot 0 partitions it to just one partial array (2 1 3), as shown in Figure 24.4(d). Apply quick sort on (2 1 3). The pivot 2 partitions it to (1) and (3), as shown in Figure 24.4(e). Apply quick sort on (1). Since the array contains just one element, no further partition is needed.

The quick sort algorithm is implemented in Listing 24.7. There are two overloaded `quickSort` methods in the class. The first method (line 2) is used to sort an array. The second is a helper method (line 6) that sorts a partial array with a specified range.

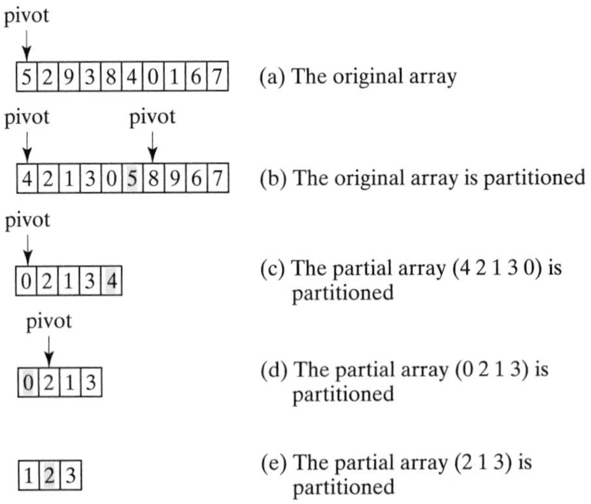
pivot
5 2 9 3 8 4 0 1 6 7
(a) The original array
pivot pivot
4 2 1 3 0 5 8 9 6 7
(b) The original array is partitioned
pivot
0 2 1 3 4
(c) The partial array (4 2 1 3 0) is partitioned
pivot
0 2 1 3
(d) The partial array (0 2 1 3) is partitioned
1 2 3
(e) The partial array (2 1 3) is partitioned

FIGURE 24.4 The quick sort algorithm is recursively applied to partial arrays.

LISTING 24.7 QuickSort.java

sort method · helper method · recursive call

```
1 public class QuickSort {
2   public static void quickSort(int[] list) {
3     quickSort(list, 0, list.length - 1);
4   }
5
6   private static void quickSort(int[] list, int first, int last) {
7     if (last > first) {
8       int pivotIndex = partition(list, first, last);
9       quickSort(list, first, pivotIndex - 1);
10      quickSort(list, pivotIndex + 1, last);
11    }
12  }
13
14  /** Partition the array list[first..last] */
15  private static int partition(int[] list, int first, int last) {
16    int pivot = list[first]; // Choose the first element as the pivot
17    int low = first + 1; // Index for forward search
18    int high = last; // Index for backward search
19
```

```
20     while (high > low) {
21       // Search forward from left
22       while (low <= high && list[low] <= pivot)
23         low++;
24
25       // Search backward from right
26       while (low <= high && list[high] > pivot)
27         high--;
28
29       // Swap two elements in the list
30       if (high > low) {
31         int temp = list[high];
32         list[high] = list[low];
33         list[low] = temp;
34       }
35     }
36
37     while (high > first && list[high] >= pivot)
38       high--;
39
40     // Swap pivot with list[high]
41     if (pivot > list[high]) {
42       list[first] = list[high];
43       list[high] = pivot;
44       return high;
45     }
46     else {
47       return first;
48     }
49   }
50
51   /** A test method */
52   public static void main(String[] args) {
53     int[] list = {2, 3, 2, 5, 6, 1, -2, 3, 14, 12};
54     quickSort(list);
55     for (int i = 0; i < list.length; i++)
56       System.out.print(list[i] + " ");
57   }
58 }
```

forward

backward

swap

place pivot

pivot's new index

pivot's original index

```
-2 1 2 2 3 3 5 6 12 14
```

The `partition` method (lines 15–49) partitions array `list[first..last]` using the pivot. The first element in the partial array is chosen as the pivot (line 16). Initially `low` points to the second element in the partial array (line 17) and `high` points to the last element in the partial array (line 18).

The method search for the first element from left forward in the array that is greater than the pivot (lines 22–23), then search for the first element from right backward in the array that is less than or equal to the pivot (lines 26–27). Swap these two elements. Repeat the same search and swap operations until all the elements are searched in a while loop (lines 20–35).

The method returns the new index for the pivot that divides the partial array into two parts if the pivot has been moved (line 44). Otherwise, return the original index for the pivot (line 47).

partition illustration

Figure 24.5 illustrates how to partition an array (5 2 9 3 8 4 0 1 6 7). Choose the first element 5 as the pivot. Initially `low` is the index that points to element 2 and `high` points to element 7, as shown in Figure 24.5(a). Advance index `low` forward to search for the first element (9) that is greater than the pivot and move index `high` backward to search for the first element (1) that is less than or equal to the pivot, as shown in Figure 24.5(b). Swap 9 with 1, as shown in Figure 24.5(c). Continue the search and move `low` to point to element 8 and `high` to point

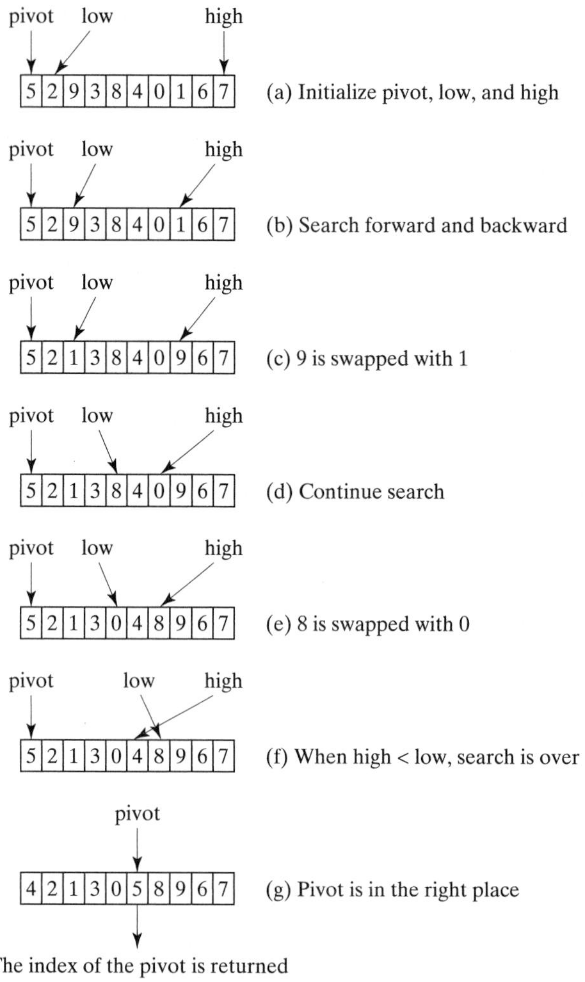
pivot
low
high
5 2 9 3 8 4 0 1 6 7
(a) Initialize pivot, low, and high
5 2 9 3 8 4 0 1 6 7
(b) Search forward and backward
5 2 1 3 8 4 0 9 6 7
(c) 9 is swapped with 1
5 2 1 3 8 4 0 9 6 7
(d) Continue search
5 2 1 3 0 4 8 9 6 7
(e) 8 is swapped with 0
5 2 1 3 0 4 8 9 6 7
(f) When high < low, search is over
4 2 1 3 0 5 8 9 6 7
(g) Pivot is in the right place
The index of the pivot is returned

FIGURE 24.5 The partition method returns the index of the pivot after it is put in the right place.

to element 0, as shown in Figure 24.5(d). Swap element 8 with 0, as shown in Figure 24.5(e). Continue to move `low` until it passes `high`, as shown in Figure 24.5(f). Now all the elements are examined. Swap the pivot with element 4 at index `high`. The final partition is shown in Figure 24.5(g). The index of the pivot is returned when the method is finished.

24.4.1 Quick Sort Time

$O(n)$ partition time

To partition an array of n elements, it takes n comparisons and n moves in the worst case. So, the time required for partition is $O(n)$.

$O(n^2)$ worst-case time

In the worst case, the pivot divides the array each time into one big subarray with the other empty. The size of the big subarray is one less than the one before divided. The algorithm requires $(n-1)+(n-2)+\cdots+2+1=O(n^2)$ time.

$O(n \log n)$ best-case time

In the best case, the pivot divides the array each time into two parts of about the same size. Let $T(n)$ denote the time required for sorting an array of n elements using quick sort. So,

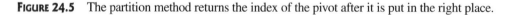

`recursive quick sort on two subarrays` → $T\left(\frac{n}{2}\right) + T\left(\frac{n}{2}\right)$; `partition time` → n

$$T(n) = T\left(\frac{n}{2}\right) + T\left(\frac{n}{2}\right) + n.$$

Similar to the merge sort analysis, $T(n) = O(n \log n)$.

On the average, each time the pivot will not divide the array into two parts of the same size or one empty part. Statistically, the sizes of the two parts are very close. So the average time is $O(n\log n)$. The exact average-case analysis is beyond the scope of this book.

O(nlogn) average-case time

quick sort vs. merge sort

Both merge sort and quick sort employ the divide-and-conquer approach. For merge sort, the bulk of work is to merge two sublists, which takes place *after* the sublists are sorted. For quick sort, the bulk of work is to partition the list into two sublists, which takes place *before* the sublists are sorted. Merge sort is more efficient than quick sort in the worst case, but the two are equally efficient in the average case. Merge sort requires a temporary array for merging two subarrays. Quick sort does not need additional array space. So, quick sort is more space efficient than merge sort.

24.5 Heap Sort

root

left subtree

right subtree

length

depth

Heap sort uses a binary heap, which is a complete binary tree. A binary tree is a hierarchical structure. It either is empty or consists of an element, called the *root*, and two distinct binary trees, called the *left subtree* and *right subtree*. The *length* of a path is the number of the edges in the path. The *depth* of a node is the length of the path from the root to the node.

A *heap* is a binary tree with the following properties:

- It is a complete binary tree.
- Each node is greater than or equal to any of its children.

complete binary tree

A binary tree is *complete* if each of its levels is full, except that the last level may not be full and all the leaves on the last level are placed leftmost. For example, in Figure 24.6, the binary trees in (a) and (b) are complete, but the binary trees in (c) and (d) are not complete. Further, the binary tree in (a) is a heap, but the binary tree in (b) is not a heap, because the root (39) is less than its right child (42).

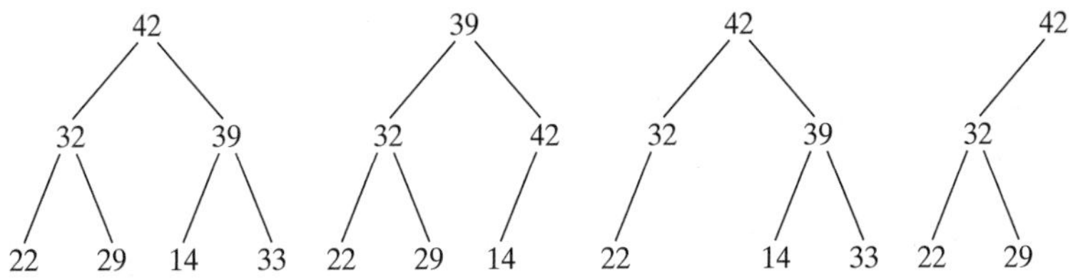
42
32
39
22
29
14
33
39
32
42
22
29
14
42
32
39
22
14
33
42
32
22
29

(a) A heap (b) (c) (d)

FIGURE 24.6 A heap is a special complete binary tree.

heap animation

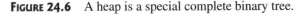

Pedagogical Note

A heap can be implemented efficiently for inserting keys and for deleting the root. Follow the link www.cs.armstrong.edu/liang/animation/HeapAnimation.html to see how a heap works, as shown in Figure 24.7.

24.5.1 Storing a Heap

A heap can be stored in an `ArrayList` or an array if the heap size is known in advance. The heap in Figure 24.8(a) can be stored using the array in Figure 24.8(b). The root is at position 0, and its two children are at positions 1 and 2. For a node at position i, its left child is at position $2i + 1$, its right child is at position $2i + 2$, and its parent is $(i - 1)/2$. For example, the node for element 39 is at position 4, so its left child (element 14) is at 9 $(2 \times 4 + 1)$, its right child (element 33) is at 10 $(2 \times 4 + 2)$, and its parent (element 42) is at 1 $((4 - 1)/2)$.

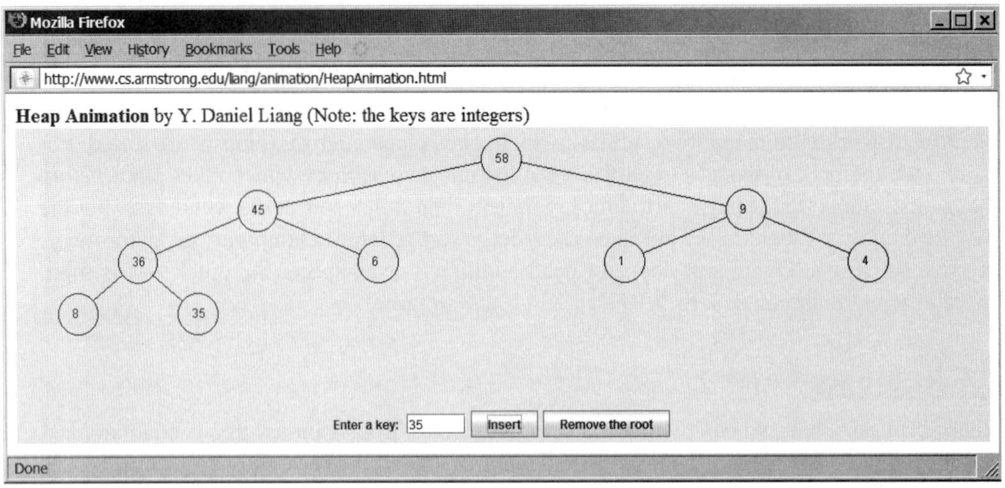
Mozilla Firefox
File Edit View History Bookmarks Tools Help
http://www.cs.armstrong.edu/liang/animation/HeapAnimation.html
Heap Animation by Y. Daniel Liang (Note: the keys are integers)
58
45
9
36
6
1
4
8
35
Enter a key: 35
Insert
Remove the root
Done

FIGURE 24.7 The animation tool enables you to insert a key and delete the root visually.

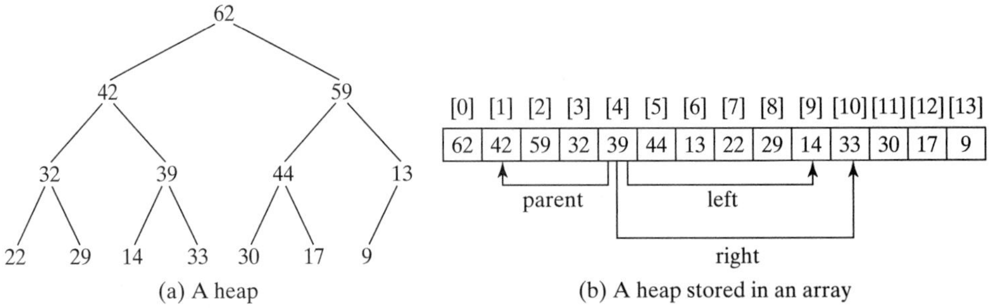
62
42
59
32
39
44
13
22
29
14
33
30
17
9
(a) A heap
[0] [1] [2] [3] [4] [5] [6] [7] [8] [9] [10] [11] [12] [13]
62 42 59 32 39 44 13 22 29 14 33 30 17 9
parent
left
right
(b) A heap stored in an array

FIGURE 24.8 A binary heap can be implemented using an array.

24.5.2 Adding a New Node

To add a new node to the heap, first add it to the end of the heap and then rebuild the tree as follows:

```
Let the last node be the current node;
while (the current node is greater than its parent) {
  Swap the current node with its parent;
  Now the current node is one level up;
}
```

Suppose the heap is initially empty. The heap is shown in Figure 24.9, after adding numbers 3, 5, 1, 19, 11, and 22 in this order.

Now consider adding 88 into the heap. Place the new node 88 at the end of the tree, as shown in Figure 24.10(a). Swap 88 with 19, as shown in Figure 25.17(b). Swap 88 with 22, as shown in Figure 24.10(c).

24.5.3 Removing the Root

Often you need to remove the max element, which is the root in a heap. After the root is removed, the tree must be rebuilt to maintain the heap property. The algorithm for rebuilding the tree can be described as follows:

```
Move the last node to replace the root;
Let the root be the current node;
```

```
while (the current node has children and the current node is
       smaller than one of its children) {
  Swap the current node with the larger of its children;
  Now the current node is one level down;
}
```

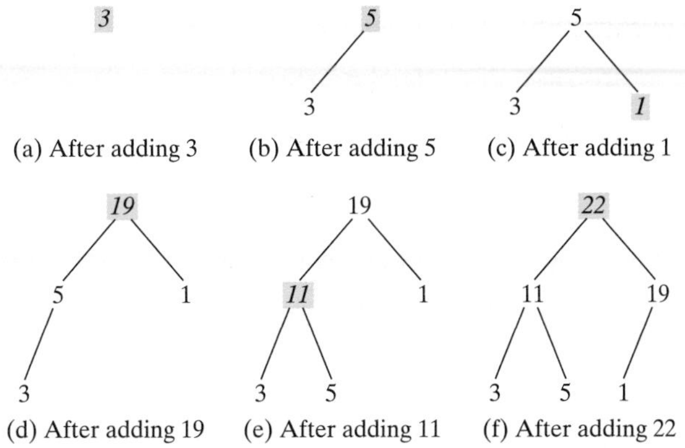
(a) After adding 3
(b) After adding 5
(c) After adding 1
(d) After adding 19
(e) After adding 11
(f) After adding 22

FIGURE 24.9 Elements 3, 5, 1, 19, 11, and 22 are inserted into the heap.

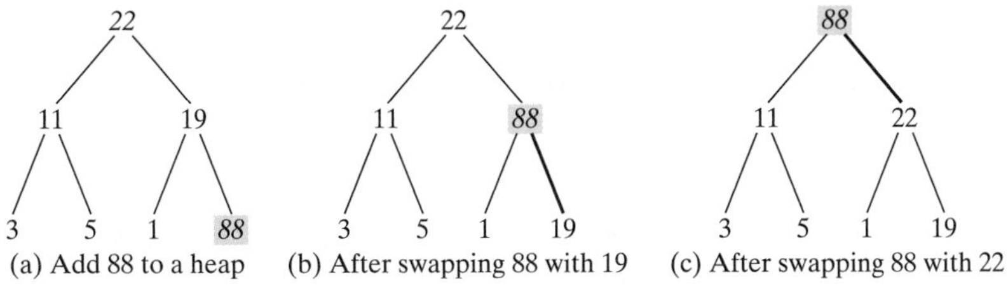
(a) Add 88 to a heap
(b) After swapping 88 with 19
(c) After swapping 88 with 22

FIGURE 24.10 Rebuild the heap after adding a new node.

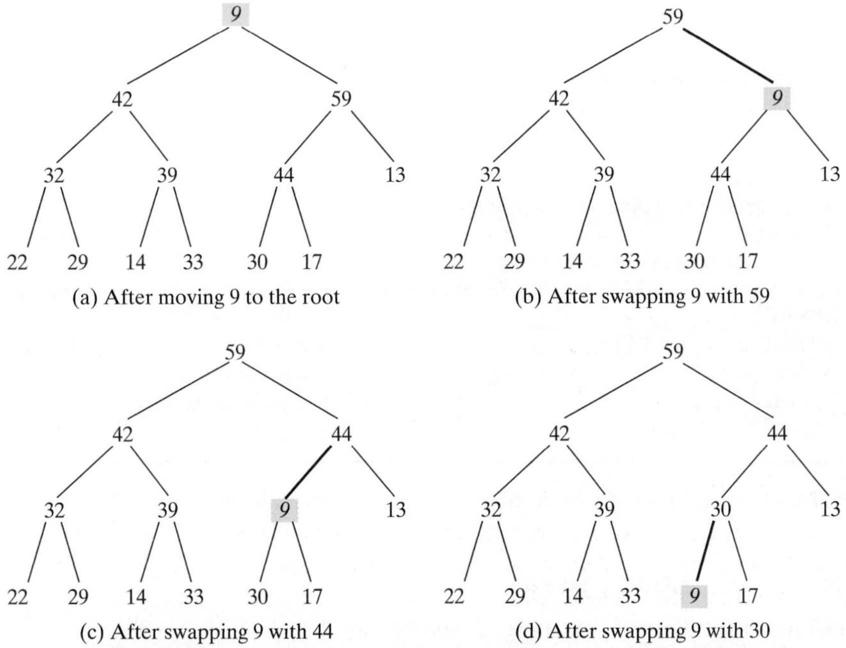
(a) After moving 9 to the root
(b) After swapping 9 with 59
(c) After swapping 9 with 44
(d) After swapping 9 with 30

FIGURE 24.11 Rebuild the heap after the root 62 is removed.

Figure 24.11 shows the process of rebuilding a heap after the root 62 is removed from Figure 24.8(a). Move the last node 9 to the root as shown in Figure 24.11(a). Swap 9 with 59 as shown in Figure 24.11(b). Swap 9 with 44 as shown in Figure 24.11(c). Swap 9 with 30 as shown in Figure 24.11(d).

Figure 24.12 shows the process of rebuilding a heap after the root 59 is removed from Figure 24.11(d). Move the last node 17 to the root, as shown in Figure 24.12(a). Swap 17 with 44 as shown in Figure 24.12(b). Swap 17 with 30 as shown in Figure 24.12(c).

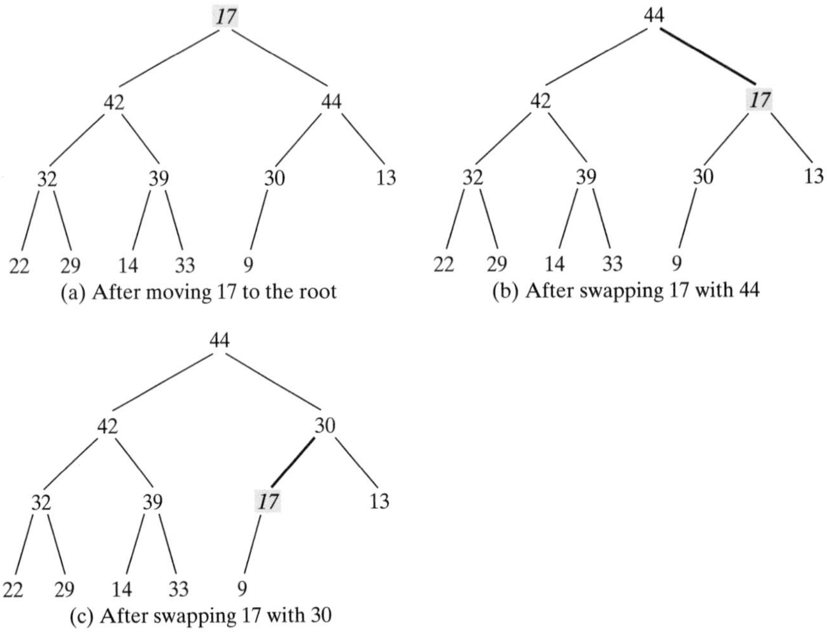
17
42 44
32 39 30 13
22 29 14 33 9
(a) After moving 17 to the root
44
42 17
32 39 30 13
22 29 14 33 9
(b) After swapping 17 with 44
44
42 30
32 39 17 13
22 29 14 33 9
(c) After swapping 17 with 30

FIGURE 24.12 Rebuild the heap after the root 59 is removed.

24.5.4 The Heap Class

Now you are ready to design and implement the Heap class. The class diagram is shown in Figure 24.13. Its implementation is given in Listing 24.8.

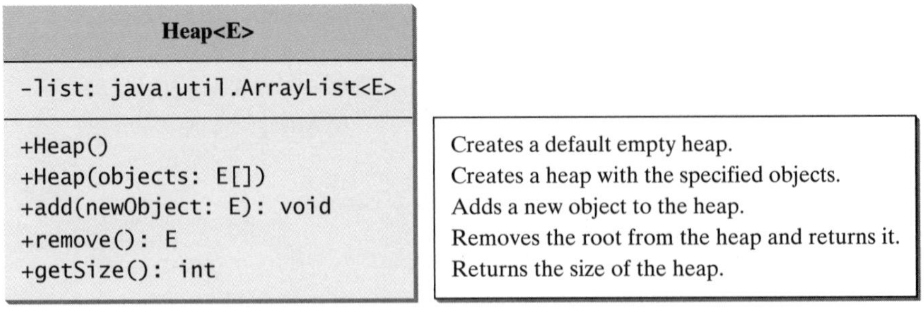
Heap<E>
-list: java.util.ArrayList<E>
+Heap()
+Heap(objects: E[])
+add(newObject: E): void
+remove(): E
+getSize(): int
Creates a default empty heap.
Creates a heap with the specified objects.
Adds a new object to the heap.
Removes the root from the heap and returns it.
Returns the size of the heap.

FIGURE 24.13 Heap provides operations for manipulating a heap.

LISTING 24.8 Heap.java

internal heap representation

```
public class Heap<E extends Comparable> {
  private java.util.ArrayList<E> list = new java.util.ArrayList<E>();

```

```java
  /** Create a default heap */
  public Heap() {
  }

  /** Create a heap from an array of objects */
  public Heap(E[] objects) {
    for (int i = 0; i < objects.length; i++)
      add(objects[i]);
  }

  /** Add a new object into the heap */
  public void add(E newObject) {
    list.add(newObject); // Append to the heap
    int currentIndex = list.size() - 1; // The index of the last node

    while (currentIndex > 0) {
      int parentIndex = (currentIndex - 1) / 2;
      // Swap if the current object is greater than its parent
      if (list.get(currentIndex).compareTo(
          list.get(parentIndex)) > 0) {
        E temp = list.get(currentIndex);
        list.set(currentIndex, list.get(parentIndex));
        list.set(parentIndex, temp);
      }
      else
        break; // The tree is a heap now

      currentIndex = parentIndex;
    }
  }

  /** Remove the root from the heap */
  public E remove() {
    if (list.size() == 0) return null;

    E removedObject = list.get(0);
    list.set(0, list.get(list.size() - 1));
    list.remove(list.size() - 1);

    int currentIndex = 0;
    while (currentIndex < list.size()) {
      int leftChildIndex = 2 * currentIndex + 1;
      int rightChildIndex = 2 * currentIndex + 2;

      // Find the maximum between two children
      if (leftChildIndex >= list.size()) break; // The tree is a heap
      int maxIndex = leftChildIndex;
      if (rightChildIndex < list.size()) {
        if (list.get(maxIndex).compareTo(
            list.get(rightChildIndex)) < 0) {
          maxIndex = rightChildIndex;
        }
      }

      // Swap if the current node is less than the maximum
      if (list.get(currentIndex).compareTo(
          list.get(maxIndex)) < 0) {
        E temp = list.get(maxIndex);
        list.set(maxIndex, list.get(currentIndex));
        list.set(currentIndex, temp);
```

no-arg constructor

constructor

add a new object

append the object

swap with parent

heap now

remove the root

empty heap

root

new root

remove the last

adjust the tree

compare two children

swap with the larger child

```
64          currentIndex = maxIndex;
65        }
66        else
67          break; // The tree is a heap
68      }
69
70      return removedObject;
71    }
72
73    /** Get the number of nodes in the tree */
74    public int getSize() {
75      return list.size();
76    }
77  }
```

A heap is represented using an array list internally (line 2). You may change it to other data structures, but the Heap class contract will remain unchanged.

The add(E newObject) method (lines 15–33) appends the object to the tree and then swaps it with its parent if it is greater than its parent. This process continues until the new object becomes the root or is not greater than its parent.

The remove() method (lines 36–71) removes and returns the root. To maintain the heap property, the method moves the last object to the root position and swaps it with its larger child if it is less than the larger child. This process continues until the last object becomes a leaf or is not less than its children.

24.5.5 Sorting Using the Heap Class

To sort an array using a heap, first create an object using the Heap class, add all the elements to the heap using the add method, and remove all the elements from the heap using the remove method. The elements are removed in descending order. Listing 24.9 gives an algorithm for sorting an array using a heap.

Listing 24.9 HeapSort.java

```
public class HeapSort {
  /** Heap sort method */
  public static <E extends Comparable> void heapSort(E[] list) {
    // Create a Heap of integers
    Heap<E> heap = new Heap<E>();

    // Add elements to the heap
    for (int i = 0; i < list.length; i++)
      heap.add(list[i]);

    // Remove elements from the heap
    for (int i = list.length - 1; i >= 0; i--)
      list[i] = heap.remove();
  }

  /** A test method */
  public static void main(String[] args) {
    Integer[] list = {2, 3, 2, 5, 6, 1, -2, 3, 14, 12};
    heapSort(list);
    for (int i = 0; i < list.length; i++)
      System.out.print(list[i] + " ");
  }
}
```

create a **Heap**

add element

remove element

invoke sort method

```
-2 1 2 2 3 3 5 6 12 14
```

24.5.6 Heap Sort Time Complexity

height of a heap

Let us turn our attention to analyzing the time complexity for the heap sort. Let h denote the height for a heap of n elements. Since a heap is a complete binary tree, the first level has 1 node, the second level has 2 nodes, the kth level has 2^{k-1} nodes, the $(h - 1)$th level has 2^{h-2} nodes, and the hth level has at least 1 and at most 2^{h-1} nodes. Therefore,

$$1 + 2 + \cdots + 2^{h-2} < n \leq 1 + 2 + \cdots + 2^{h-2} + 2^{h-1}$$

i.e.,

$$2^{h-1} - 1 < n \leq 2^h - 1$$
$$2^{h-1} < n + 1 \leq 2^h$$
$$h - 1 < \log(n + 1) \leq h$$

Thus, $h < \log(n + 1) + 1$ and $\log(n + 1) \leq h$. Therefore, $\log(n + 1) \leq h < \log(n + 1) + 1$. Hence, the height of the heap is $O(\log n)$.

$O(n \log n)$ worst-case time

Since the `add` method traces a path from a leaf to a root, it takes at most h steps to add a new element to the heap. So, the total time for constructing an initial heap is $O(n \log n)$ for an array of n elements. Since the `remove` method traces a path from a root to a leaf, it takes at most h steps to rebuild a heap after removing the root from the heap. Since the `remove` method is invoked n times, the total time for producing a sorted array from a heap is $O(n \log n)$.

heap sort vs. merge sort

Both merge sort and heap sort requires $O(n \log n)$ time. Merge sort requires a temporary array for merging two subarrays. Heap sort does not need additional array space. So, heap sort is more space efficient than merge sort.

24.6 Bucket Sort and Radix Sort

All sort algorithms discussed so far are general sorting algorithms that work for any types of keys (e.g., integers, strings, and any comparable objects). These algorithms sort the elements by comparing their keys. The lower bound for general sorting algorithms is $O(n \log n)$. So, no sorting algorithms based on comparisons can perform better than $O(n \log n)$. However, if the keys are small integers, you can use bucket sort without having to compare the keys.

The bucket sort algorithm works as follows. Assume the keys are in the range from `0` to `N-1`. We need `N` buckets labeled `0`, `1`, . . . , and `N-1`. If an element's key is `i`, the element is put into the bucket `i`. Each bucket holds the elements with the same key value. You can use an `ArrayList` to implement a bucket.

The bucket sort algorithm for sorting a list of elements can be described as follows:

```
void bucketSort(E[] list) {
  E[] buckets = (E[])new java.util.ArrayList[N];

  // Distribute the elements from list to buckets
  for (int i = 0; i < list.length; i++) {
    int key = list[i].getKey();

    if (buckets[key] == null)
      buckets[key] = new java.util.ArrayList();

    buckets[key].add(list[i]);
  }
```

```
      // Now move the elements from the buckets back to list
      int k = 0; // k is an index for list
      for (int i = 0; i < buckets.length; i++) {
        if (buckets[i] != null) {
          for (int j = 0; j < buckets[i].size(); j++)
            list[k++] = buckets[i].get(j);
        }
      }
    }
```

Clearly, it takes $O(n + N)$ time to sort the list and uses $O(n + N)$ space, where n is the list size.

Note that if N is too large, bucket sort is not desirable. You can use radix sort. Radix sort is based on bucket sort, but it uses only ten buckets.

stable

It is worthwhile to note that bucket sort is *stable*, meaning that if two elements in the original list have the same key value, their order is not changed in the sorted list. That is, if element e_1 and element e_2 have the same key and e_1 precedes e_2 in the original list, e_1 still precedes e_2 in the sorted list.

Again assume that the keys are positive integers. The idea for the radix sort is to divide the keys into subgroups based on their radix positions. It applies bucket sort repeatedly for the key values on radix positions, starting from the least-significant position.

Consider sorting the elements with the keys:

```
331, 454, 230, 34, 343, 45, 59, 453, 345, 231, 9
```

queue

Apply the bucket sort on the last radix position. The elements are put into the buckets as follows:

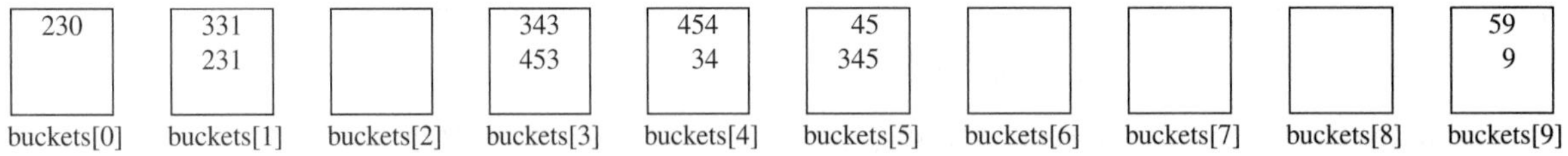
230
331
231
343
453
454
34
45
345
59
9
buckets[0]
buckets[1]
buckets[2]
buckets[3]
buckets[4]
buckets[5]
buckets[6]
buckets[7]
buckets[8]
buckets[9]

After being removed from the buckets, the elements are in the following order:

```
230, 331, 231, 343, 453, 454, 34, 45, 345, 59, 9
```

queue

Apply the bucket sort on the second-to-last radix position. The elements are put into the buckets as follows:

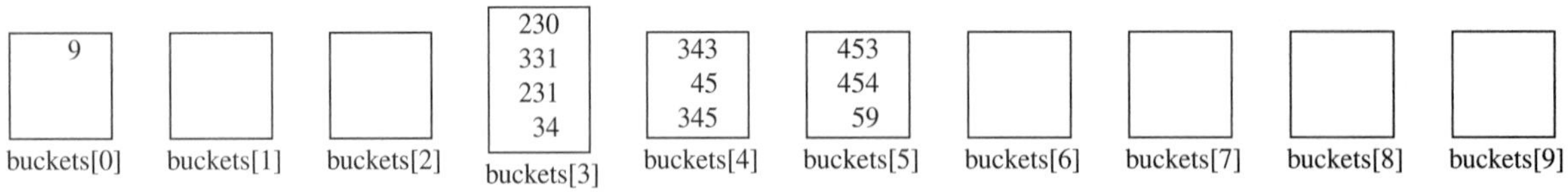
9
230
331
231
34
343
45
345
453
454
59
buckets[0]
buckets[1]
buckets[2]
buckets[3]
buckets[4]
buckets[5]
buckets[6]
buckets[7]
buckets[8]
buckets[9]

After being removed from the buckets, the elements are in the following order:

```
9, 230, 331, 231, 34, 343, 45, 345, 453, 454, 59
```

(Note that 9 is 009.)

queue

Apply the bucket sort on the third-to-last radix position. The elements are put into the buckets as follows:

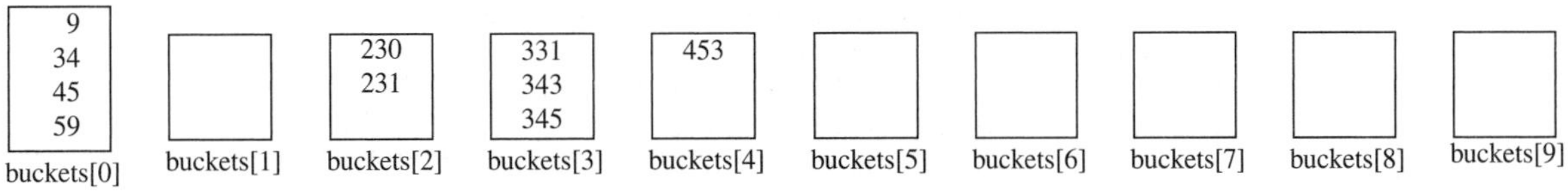
9
34
45
59
230
231
331
343
345
453
buckets[0]
buckets[1]
buckets[2]
buckets[3]
buckets[4]
buckets[5]
buckets[6]
buckets[7]
buckets[8]
buckets[9]

After being removed from the buckets, the elements are in the following order:

```
9, 34, 45, 59, 230, 231, 331, 343, 345, 453
```

The elements are now sorted.

In general, radix sort takes $O(dn)$ time to sort n elements with integer keys, where d is the maximum number of the radix positions among all keys.

24.7 External Sort

All the sort algorithms discussed in the preceding sections assume that all data to be sorted are available at one time in internal memory such as an array. To sort data stored in an external file, you may first bring data to the memory, then sort them internally. However, if the file is too large, all data in the file cannot be brought to memory at one time. This section discusses how to sort data in a large external file.

For simplicity, assume that two million `int` values are stored in a binary file named **largedata.dat**. This file was created using the program in Listing 24.10:

LISTING 24.10 CreateLargeFile.java

```
import java.io.*;

public class CreateLargeFile {
  public static void main(String[] args) throws Exception {
    DataOutputStream output = new DataOutputStream(
      new BufferedOutputStream(
      new FileOutputStream("largedata.dat")));

    for (int i = 0; i < 800004; i++)
      output.writeInt((int)(Math.random() * 1000000));

    output.close();

    // Display first 100 numbers
    DataInputStream input =
      new DataInputStream(new FileInputStream("largedata.dat"));
    for (int i = 0; i < 100; i++)
      System.out.print(input.readInt() + " ");

    input.close();
  }
}
```

a binary output stream

output an **int** value

close output file

read an **int** value

close input file

```
569193 131317 608695 776266 767910 624915 458599 5010 ... (omitted)
```

A variation of merge sort can be used to sort this file in two phases:

Phase I: Repeatedly bring data from the file to an array, sort the array using an internal sorting algorithm, and output the data from the array to a temporary file. This process is shown in Figure 24.14. Ideally, you want to create a large array, but its maximum size depends on how

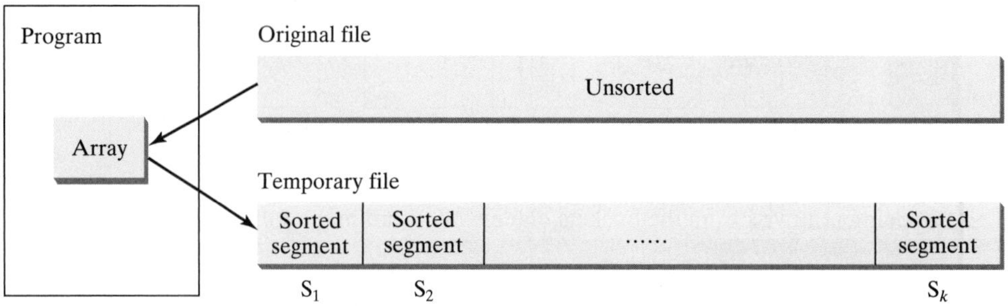
Program
Array
Original file
Unsorted
Temporary file
Sorted segment
Sorted segment
......
Sorted segment
S1
S2
Sk

FIGURE 24.14 The original file is sorted in segments.

much memory is allocated to the JVM by the operating system. Assume that the maximum array size is 100000 `int` values. In the temporary file, every 100000 `int` values are sorted. They are denoted as $S_1, S_2, \ldots,$ and S_k, where the last segment, S_k, may contain less than 100000 values.

Phase II: Merge a pair of sorted segments (e.g., S_1 with S_2, S_3 with $S_4, \ldots,$ and so on) into a larger sorted segment and save the new segment into a new temporary file. Continue the same process until one sorted segment results. Figure 24.15 shows how to merge eight segments.

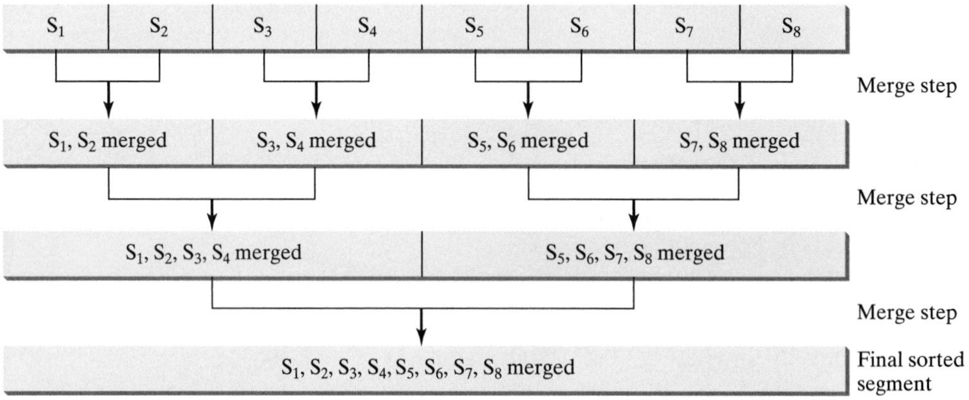
S1
S2
S3
S4
S5
S6
S7
S8
Merge step
S1, S2 merged
S3, S4 merged
S5, S6 merged
S7, S8 merged
Merge step
S1, S2, S3, S4 merged
S5, S6, S7, S8 merged
Merge step
S1, S2, S3, S4, S5, S6, S7, S8 merged
Final sorted segment

FIGURE 24.15 Sorted segments are merged iteratively.

Note

It is not necessary to merge two successive segments. For example, you may merge S_1 with S_5, S_2 with S_6, S_3 with S_7, and S_4 with S_8, in the first merge step. This observation is useful in implementing Phase II efficiently.

24.7.1 Implementing Phase I

Listing 24.11 gives the method that reads each segment of data from a file, sorts the segment, and stores the sorted segments into a new file. The method returns the number of segments.

LISTING 24.11 Creating Initial Sorted Segments

```
1 /** Sort original file into sorted segments */
2 private static int initializeSegments
3     (int segmentSize, String originalFile, String f1)
4     throws Exception {
5   int[] list = new int[segmentSize];
6   DataInputStream input = new DataInputStream(
7     new BufferedInputStream(new FileInputStream(originalFile)));
8   DataOutputStream output = new DataOutputStream(
9     new BufferedOutputStream(new FileOutputStream(f1)));
10
11   int numberOfSegments = 0;
12   while (input.available() > 0) {
13     numberOfSegments++;
14     int i = 0;
15     for ( ; input.available() > 0 && i < segmentSize; i++) {
16       list[i] = input.readInt();
17     }
18
19     // Sort an array list[0..i-1]
20     java.util.Arrays.sort(list, 0, i);
21
22     // Write the array to f1.dat
23     for (int j = 0; j < i; j++) {
24       output.writeInt(list[j]);
25     }
26   }
27
28   input.close();
29   output.close();
30
31   return numberOfSegments;
32 }
```

original file (line 7)
file with sorted segments (line 9)
sort a segment (line 20)
output to file (line 24)
close file (line 28)
return # of segments (line 31)

The method creates an array with the max size in line 5, a data input stream for the original file in line 6, and a data output stream for a temporary file in line 8. Buffered streams are used to improve performance.

Lines 14–17 read a segment of data from the file into the array. Line 20 sorts the array. Lines 23–25 write the data in the array to the temporary file.

The number of segments is returned in line 31. Note that every segment has `MAX_ARRAY_SIZE` number of elements except the last segment, which may have fewer elements.

24.7.2 Implementing Phase II

In each merge step, two sorted segments are merged to form a new segment. The size of the new segment is doubled. The number of segments is reduced by half after each merge step. A segment is too large to be brought to an array in memory. To implement a merge step, copy half the number of segments from file **f1.dat** to a temporary file **f2.dat**. Then merge the first remaining segment in **f1.dat** with the first segment in **f2.dat** into a temporary file named **f3.dat**, as shown in Figure 24.16.

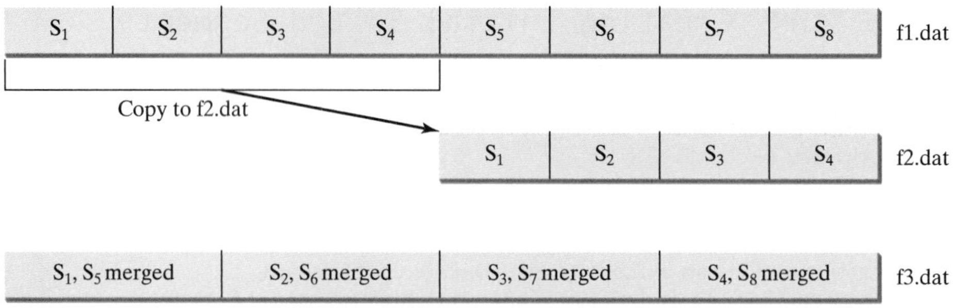
S1
S2
S3
S4
S5
S6
S7
S8
f1.dat
Copy to f2.dat
S1
S2
S3
S4
f2.dat
S1, S5 merged
S2, S6 merged
S3, S7 merged
S4, S8 merged
f3.dat

FIGURE 24.16 Sorted segments are merged iteratively.

> **Note**
> **f1.dat** may have one segment more than **f2.dat**. If so, move the last segment into **f3.dat** after the merge.

Listing 24.12 gives a method that copies the first half of the segments in **f1.dat** to **f2.dat**. Listing 24.13 gives a method that merges a pair of segments in **f1.dat** and **f2.dat**. Listing 24.14 gives a method that merges two segments.

LISTING 24.12 Copying First Half Segments

input stream **f1**
output stream **f2**
segments copied

```
private static void copyHalfToF2(int numberOfSegments,
    int segmentSize, DataInputStream f1, DataOutputStream f2)
    throws Exception {
  for (int i = 0; i < (numberOfSegments / 2) * segmentSize; i++) {
    f2.writeInt(f1.readInt());
  }
}
```

LISTING 24.13 Merging All Segments

input stream **f1** and **f2**
output stream **f3**
merge two segments
extra segment in **f1**

```
private static void mergeSegments(int numberOfSegments,
    int segmentSize, DataInputStream f1, DataInputStream f2,
    DataOutputStream f3) throws Exception {
  for (int i = 0; i < numberOfSegments; i++) {
    mergeTwoSegments(segmentSize, f1, f2, f3);
  }

  // f1 may have one extra segment, copy it to f3
  while (f1.available() > 0) {
    f3.writeInt(f1.readInt());
  }
}
```

LISTING 24.14 Merging Two Segments

input stream **f1** and **f2**
output stream **f3**
read from **f1**
read from **f2**

```
private static void mergeTwoSegments(int segmentSize,
    DataInputStream f1, DataInputStream f2,
    DataOutputStream f3) throws Exception {
  int intFromF1 = f1.readInt();
  int intFromF2 = f2.readInt();
  int f1Count = 1;
  int f2Count = 1;
```

```
  while (true) {
    if (intFromF1 < intFromF2) {
      f3.writeInt(intFromF1);
      if (f1.available() == 0 || f1Count++ >= segmentSize) {
        f3.writeInt(intFromF2);
        break;
      }
      else {
        intFromF1 = f1.readInt();
      }
    }
    else {
      f3.writeInt(intFromF2);
      if (f2.available() == 0 || f2Count++ >= segmentSize) {
        f3.writeInt(intFromF1);
        break;
      }
      else {
        intFromF2 = f2.readInt();
      }
    }
  }

  while (f1.available() > 0 && f1Count++ < segmentSize) {
    f3.writeInt(f1.readInt());
  }

  while (f2.available() > 0 && f2Count++ < segmentSize) {
    f3.writeInt(f2.readInt());
  }
}
```

write to f3

segment in **f1** finished

write to **f3**

segment in **f2** finished

remaining **f1** segment

remaining **f2** segment

24.7.3 Combining Two Phases

Listing 24.15 gives the complete program for sorting `int` values in **largedata.dat** and storing the sorted data in **sortedlargedata.dat**.

LISTING 24.15 SortLargeFile.java

```
import java.io.*;

public class SortLargeFile {
  public static final int MAX_ARRAY_SIZE = 100000;
  public static final int BUFFER_SIZE = 100000;

  public static void main(String[] args) throws Exception {
    // Sort largedata.dat to sortedfile.dat
    sort("largedata.dat", "sortedfile.dat");

    // Display the first 100 numbers in the sorted file
    displayFile("sortedfile.dat");
  }

  /** Sort data in source file and into target file */
  public static void sort(String sourcefile, String targetfile)
      throws Exception {
```

max array size

IO stream buffer size

create initial segments
merge recursively
merge one step
merge recursively
final sorted file
input stream **f1Input**
output stream **f2Output**
copy half segments to **f2**
close **f2Output**
input stream **f2Input**
output stream **f3Output**
merge two segments
close streams

```java
    // Implement Phase 1: Create initial segments
    int numberOfSegments =
      initializeSegments(MAX_ARRAY_SIZE, sourcefile, "f1.dat");

    // Implement Phase 2: Merge segments recursively
    merge(numberOfSegments, MAX_ARRAY_SIZE,
      "f1.dat", "f2.dat", "f3.dat", targetfile);
  }

  /** Sort original file into sorted segments */
  private static int initializeSegments
      (int segmentSize, String originalFile, String f1)
      throws Exception {
    // Same as Listing 24.11, so omitted
  }

  private static void merge(int numberOfSegments, int segmentSize,
      String f1, String f2, String f3, String targetfile)
      throws Exception {
    if (numberOfSegments > 1) {
      mergeOneStep(numberOfSegments, segmentSize, f1, f2, f3);
      merge((numberOfSegments + 1) / 2, segmentSize * 2,
        f3, f1, f2, targetfile);
    }
    else { // Rename f1 as the final sorted file
      File sortedFile = new File(targetfile);
      if (sortedFile.exists()) sortedFile.delete();
      new File(f1).renameTo(sortedFile);
    }
  }

  private static void mergeOneStep(int numberOfSegments,
      int segmentSize, String f1, String f2, String f3)
      throws Exception {
    DataInputStream f1Input = new DataInputStream(
      new BufferedInputStream(new FileInputStream(f1), BUFFER_SIZE));
    DataOutputStream f2Output = new DataOutputStream(
      new BufferedOutputStream(new FileOutputStream(f2), BUFFER_SIZE));

    // Copy half number of segments from f1.dat to f2.dat
    copyHalfToF2(numberOfSegments, segmentSize, f1Input, f2Output);
    f2Output.close();

    // Merge remaining segments in f1 with segments in f2 into f3
    DataInputStream f2Input = new DataInputStream(
      new BufferedInputStream(new FileInputStream(f2), BUFFER_SIZE));
    DataOutputStream f3Output = new DataOutputStream(
      new BufferedOutputStream(new FileOutputStream(f3), BUFFER_SIZE));

    mergeSegments(numberOfSegments / 2,
      segmentSize, f1Input, f2Input, f3Output);

    f1Input.close();
    f2Input.close();
    f3Output.close();
  }

  /** Copy first half number of segments from f1.dat to f2.dat */
  private static void copyHalfToF2(int numberOfSegments,
      int segmentSize, DataInputStream f1, DataOutputStream f2)
```

```
80        throws Exception {
81      // Same as Listing 24.12, so omitted
82    }
83
84    /** Merge all segments */
85    private static void mergeSegments(int numberOfSegments,
86        int segmentSize, DataInputStream f1, DataInputStream f2,
87        DataOutputStream f3) throws Exception {
88      // Same as Listing 24.13, so omitted
89    }
90
91    /** Merges two segments */
92    private static void mergeTwoSegments(int segmentSize,
93      DataInputStream f1, DataInputStream f2,
94      DataOutputStream f3) throws Exception {
95      // Same as Listing 24.14, so omitted
96    }
97
98    /** Display the first 100 numbers in the specified file */
99    public static void displayFile(String filename) {
100     try {
101       DataInputStream input =
102         new DataInputStream(new FileInputStream(filename));
103       for (int i = 0; i < 100; i++)
104         System.out.print(input.readInt() + " ");
105       input.close();
106     }
107     catch (IOException ex) {
108       ex.printStackTrace();
109     }
110   }
111 }
112
```

display file

```
0 1 1 1 2 2 2 3 3 4 5 6 8 8 9 9 9 10 10 11 ... (omitted)
```

Before you run this program, first run Listing 24.10, CreateLargeFile.java, to create **largedata.dat**. Invoking `sort("largedata.dat", "sortedfile.dat")` (line 9) reads data from `largedata.dat` and writes sorted data `sortedfile.dat`. Invoking `displayFile("sortedfile.dat")` (line 12) displays the first `100` numbers in the specified file. Note that the files are created using binary I/O. You cannot view them using a text editor such as Notepad.

The `sort` method first creates initial segments from the original array and stores the sorted segments in a new file **f1.dat** (lines 19–20), then produces a sorted file in `targetfile` (lines 23–24).

The `merge` method

```
merge(int numberOfSegments, int segmentSize,
  String f1, String f2, String f3, String targetfile)
```

merges the segments in `f1` into `f3` using `f2` to assist the merge. The `merge` method is invoked recursively with many merge steps. Each merge step reduces the `numberOfSegments` by half and doubles the sorted segment size. After completion of one merge step, the next merge step merges the new segments in `f3` to `f2` using `f1` to assist the merge. So the statement to invoke the new merge method is

```
merge((numberOfSegments + 1) / 2, segmentSize * 2,
  f3, f1, f2, targetfile);
```

The `numberOfSegments` for the next merge step is `(numberOfSegments + 1) / 2`. For example, if `numberOfSegments` is `5`, `numberOfSegments` is `3` for the next merge step, because every two segments are merged but one is left unmerged.

The recursive `merge` method ends when `numberOfSegments` is `1`. In this case, `f1` contains sorted data. File `f1` is renamed to `targetfile` (line 47).

24.7.4 External Sort Analysis

In the external sort, the dominating cost is that of I/O. Assume n is the number of elements to be sorted in the file. In Phase I, n number of elements are read from the original file and output to a temporary file. So, the I/O for Phase I is $O(n)$.

In Phase II, before the first merge step, the number of sorted segments is $\frac{n}{c}$, where c is `MAX_ARRAY_SIZE`. Each merge step reduces the number of segments by half. So, after the first merge step, the number of segments is $\frac{n}{2c}$. After the second merge step,the number of segments is $\frac{n}{2^2c}$. After the third merge step, the number of segments is $\frac{n}{2^3c}$. After $\log\left(\frac{n}{c}\right)$ merge steps, the number of segments has been reduced to 1. Therefore, the total number of merge steps is $\log\left(\frac{n}{c}\right)$.

In each merge step, half the number of segments are read from file `f1` and then written into a temporary file `f2`. The remaining segments in `f1` are merged with the segments in `f2`. The number of I/Os in each merge step is $O(n)$. Since the total number of merge steps is $\log\left(\frac{n}{c}\right)$, the total number of I/Os is

$$O(n) \times \log\left(\frac{n}{c}\right) = O(n \log n)$$

Therefore, the complexity of the external sort is $O(n \log n)$.

Key Terms

bubble sort 792
bucket sort 792
external sort 809
heap 801
heap sort 806
merge sort 794
quick sort 797
radix sort 807

Chapter Summary

1. The worst-case complexity for selection sort, insertion sort, bubble sort, and quick sort is $O(n^2)$.
2. The average-case and worst-case complexity for merge sort is $O(n \log n)$. The average time for quick sort is also $O(n \log n)$.
3. Heaps are a useful data structure for designing efficient algorithms such as sorting. You learned how to define and implement a heap class, and how to insert and delete elements to/from a heap.
4. The time complexity for heap sort is $O(n \log n)$.

5. Bucket sort and radix sort are specialized sorting algorithms for integer keys. These algorithms sort keys using buckets rather than comparing keys. They are more efficient than general sorting algorithms.

6. A variation of merge sort can be applied to sort large amounts of data from external files.

Review Questions

Sections 24.2–24.4

24.1 Use Figure 24.1 as an example to show how to apply bubble sort on {45, 11, 50, 59, 60, 2, 4, 7, 10}.

24.2 Use Figure 24.2 as an example to show how to apply merge sort on {45, 11, 50, 59, 60, 2, 4, 7, 10}.

24.3 Use Figure 24.4 as an example to show how to apply quick sort on {45, 11, 50, 59, 60, 2, 4, 7, 10}.

Section 24.5

24.4 What is a complete binary tree? What is a heap? Describe how to remove the root from a heap and how to add a new object to a heap.

24.5 What is the return value from invoking the `remove` method if the heap is empty?

24.6 Add the elements `4`, `5`, `1`, `2`, `9`, `3` into a heap in this order. Draw the diagrams to show the heap after each element is added.

24.7 Show the heap after the root in the heap in Figure 24.12(c) is removed.

24.8 What is the time complexity of inserting a new element into a heap and what is the time complexity of deleting an element from a heap?

24.9 Show the steps of creating a heap using {45, 11, 50, 59, 60, 2, 4, 7, 10}.

24.10 Given the following heap, show the steps of removing all nodes from the heap.

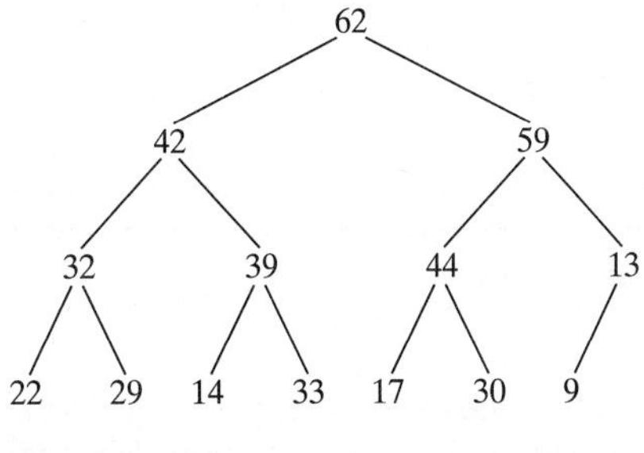
62
42
59
32
39
44
13
22
29
14
33
17
30
9

Section 24.7

24.11 Ten numbers {2, 3, 4, 0, 5, 6, 7, 9, 8, 1} are stored in the external file **largedata.dat**. Trace the SortLargeFile program by hand with `MAX_ARRAY_SIZE` 2.

Programming Exercises

Sections 24.2–24.4

24.1 (*Generic bubble sort*) Write the following two generic methods using bubble sort. The first method sorts the elements using the `Comparable` interface and the second uses the `Comparator` interface.

```
public static <E extends Comparable<E>> void bubbleSort(E[] list)
public static <E> void bubbleSort(E[] list,
  Comparator<? super E> comparator)
```

24.2 (*Generic merge sort*) Write the following two generic methods using merge sort. The first method sorts the elements using the Comparable interface and the second uses the Comparator interface.

```
public static <E extends Comparable<E>> void mergeSort(E[] list)
public static <E> void mergeSort(E[] list,
  Comparator<? super E> comparator)
```

24.3 (*Generic quick sort*) Write the following two generic methods using quick sort. The first method sorts the elements using the Comparable interface and the second uses the Comparator interface.

```
public static <E extends Comparable<E>> void quickSort(E[] list)
public static <E> void quickSort(E[] list,
  Comparator<? super E> comparator)
```

24.4 (*Improving quick sort*) The quick sort algorithm presented in the book selects the first element in the list as the pivot. Revise it by selecting the median among the first, middle, and last elements in the list.

24.5* (*Generic heap sort*) Write the following two generic methods using heap sort. The first method sorts the elements using the Comparable interface and the second uses the Comparator interface.

```
public static <E extends Comparable<E>> void heapSort(E[] list)
public static <E> void heapSort(E[] list,
  Comparator<? super E> comparator)
```

24.6 (*Checking order*) Write the following overloaded methods that check whether an array is ordered in ascending order or descending order. By default, the method checks ascending order. To check descending order, pass false to the ascending argument in the method.

```
public static boolean ordered(int[] list)
public static boolean ordered(int[] list, boolean ascending)
public static boolean ordered(double[] list)
public static boolean ordered(double[] list, boolean descending)
public static <E extends Comparable<E>> boolean ordered(E[] list)
public static <E extends Comparable<E>> boolean ordered
  (E[] list, boolean ascending)
public static <E> boolean ordered(E[] list,
  Comparator<? super E> comparator)
public static <E> boolean ordered(E[] list,
  Comparator<? super E> comparator, boolean ascending)
```

Section 24.5

24.7 (*Min-heap*) The heap presented in the text is also known as a *max-heap*, in which each node is greater than or equal to any of its children. A *min-heap* is a heap in which each node is less than or equal to any of its children. Revise the Heap class in Listing 24.8 to implement a min-heap.

24.8* (*Sorting using a heap*) Implement the following sort method using a heap.

```
public static <E extends Comparable<E>> void sort(E[] list)
```

24.9* (*Generic Heap using `Comparator`*) Revise `Heap` in Listing 24.8, using a generic parameter and a `Comparator` for comparing objects. Define a new constructor with a `Comparator` as its argument as follows:

```
Heap(Comparator<? super E> comparator)
```

24.10** (*Heap visualization*) Write a Java applet that displays a heap graphically, as shown in Figure 24.7. The applet lets you insert and delete an element from the heap.

24.11 (*Heap `clone` and `equals`*) Implement the `clone` and `equals` method in the `Heap` class.

Section 24.6

24.12* (*Radix sort*) Write a program that randomly generates 1000000 integers and sorts them using radix sort.

24.13* (*Execution time for sorting*) Write a program that obtains the execution time of selection sort, radix sort, bubble sort, merge sort, quick sort, and heap sort for input size 50000, 100,000, 150,000, 200,000, 250,000, and 300,000. Your program should create data randomly and print a table like this:

Array size	Selection Sort	Radix Sort	Bubble Sort	Merge Sort	Quick Sort	Heap Sort
50000						
100000						
150000						
200000						
250000						
300000						

(*Hint*: You can use the code template below to obtain the execution time.)

```
long startTime = System.currentTimeMillis();
perform the task;
long endTime = System.currentTimeMillis();
long executionTime = endTime - startTime;
```

The text gives a recursive quick sort. Write a nonrecursive version in this exercise.

Section 24.7

24.14* (*Execution time for external sorting*) Write a program that obtains the execution time of external sort for integers of size 5,000,000, 10,000,000, 15,000,000, 20,000,000, 25,000,000, and 30,000,000. Your program should print a table like this:

File size	5000000	10000000	15000000	20000000	25000000	30000000
Time						

CHAPTER 25

LISTS, STACKS, QUEUES, AND PRIORITY QUEUES

Objectives

- To design common features of lists in an interface and provide skeleton implementation in an abstract class (§25.2).
- To design and implement a dynamic list using an array (§25.3).
- To design and implement a dynamic list using a linked structure (§25.4).
- To explore variations of linked lists (§25.5).
- To design and implement a queue using a linked list (§25.6).
- To design and implement a priority queue using a heap (§25.7).
- To evaluate expressions using stacks (§25.8).

25.1 Introduction

Lists, stacks, queues, and priority queues are classic data structures typically covered in a data structures course. They are supported in the Java API, and their uses were presented in Chapter 22, "Java Collections Framework." This chapter will examine how these data structures are implemented under the hood and give an interesting application on evaluating expressions using stacks. Implementation of sets and maps is covered in Chapters 45–48.

25.2 Common Features for Lists

A list is a popular data structure for storing data in sequential order—for example, a list of students, a list of available rooms, a list of cities, a list of books. The operations listed below are typical of most lists:

- Retrieve an element from a list.
- Insert a new element to a list.
- Delete an element from a list.
- Find how many elements are in a list.
- Find whether an element is in a list.
- Find whether a list is empty.

There are two ways to implement a list. One is to use an *array* to store the elements. Arrays are dynamically created. If the capacity of the array is exceeded, create a new, larger array and copy all the elements from the current array to the new array. The other approach is to use a *linked structure*. A linked structure consists of nodes. Each node is dynamically created to hold an element. All the nodes are linked together to form a list. Thus you can define two classes for lists. For convenience, let's name these two classes `MyArrayList` and `MyLinkedList`. These two classes have common operations but different implementations.

abstract class for interface

Design Guide

The common operations can be generalized in an interface or an abstract class. A good strategy is to combine the virtues of interfaces and abstract classes by providing both an interface and an abstract class in the design so that the user can use either of them, whichever is convenient. The abstract class provides a skeletal implementation of the interface, which minimizes the effort required to implement the interface.

list animation

Pedagogical Note

Follow the link www.cs.armstrong.edu/liang/animation/ArrayListAnimation.html and www.cs.armstrong.edu/liang/animation/LinkedListAnimation.html to see how array lists and linked lists work, as shown in Figure 25.1.

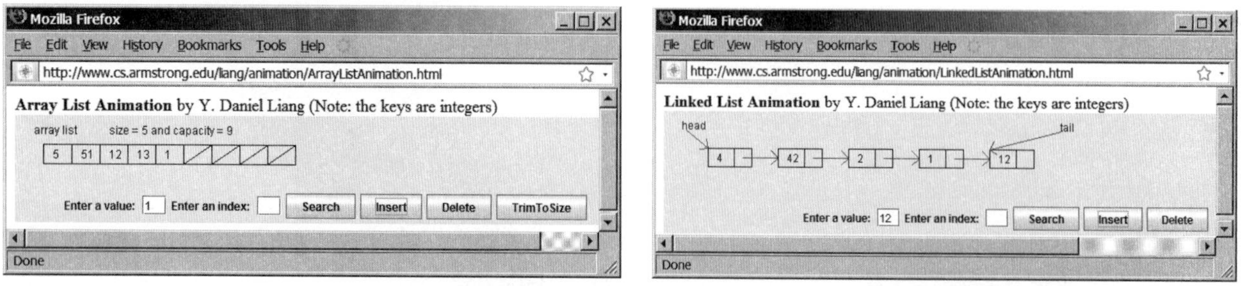
Mozilla Firefox
http://www.cs.armstrong.edu/liang/animation/ArrayListAnimation.html
Array List Animation by Y. Daniel Liang (Note: the keys are integers)
array list size = 5 and capacity = 9
5 51 12 13 1
Enter a value: 1 Enter an index:
Search Insert Delete TrimToSize
Done
Mozilla Firefox
http://www.cs.armstrong.edu/liang/animation/LinkedListAnimation.html
Linked List Animation by Y. Daniel Liang (Note: the keys are integers)
head
tail
4 42 2 1 12
Enter a value: 12 Enter an index:
Search Insert Delete
Done

(a) Array list animation

(b) Linked list animation

FIGURE 25.1 The animation tool enables you to see how array lists and linked lists work visually.

Let us name the interface `MyList` and the convenience class `MyAbstractList`. Figure 25.2 shows the relationship of `MyList`, `MyAbstractList`, `MyArrayList`, and `MyLinkedList`. The methods in `MyList` and the methods implemented in `MyAbstractList` are shown in Figure 25.3. Listing 25.1 gives the source code for `MyList`.

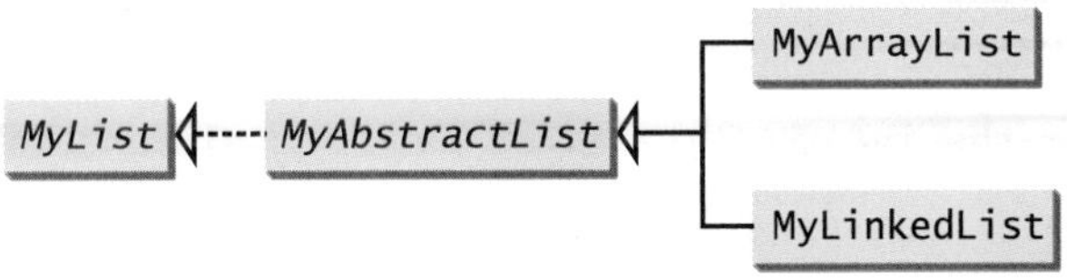
MyArrayList
MyList
MyAbstractList
MyLinkedList

FIGURE 25.2 `MyList` defines a common interface for `MyAbstractList`, `MyArrayList`, and `MyLinkedList`.

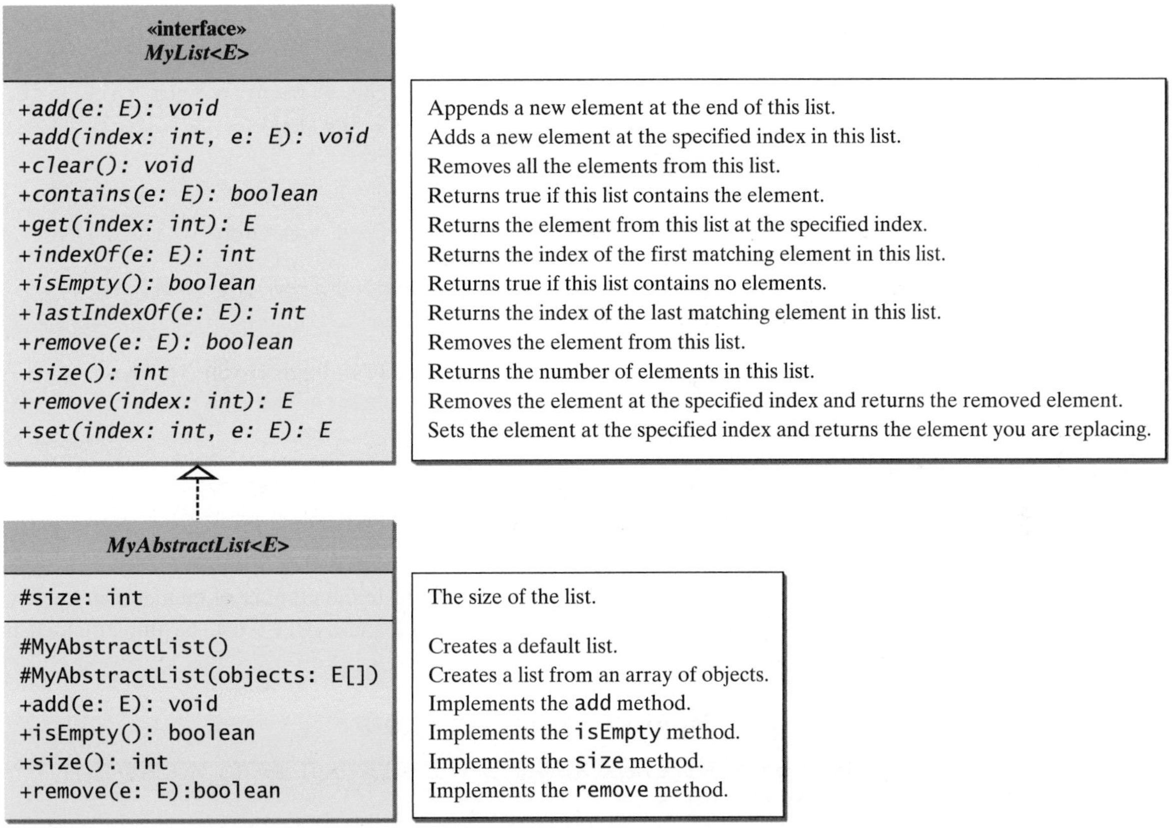
«interface»
MyList<E>
+add(e: E): void
+add(index: int, e: E): void
+clear(): void
+contains(e: E): boolean
+get(index: int): E
+indexOf(e: E): int
+isEmpty(): boolean
+lastIndexOf(e: E): int
+remove(e: E): boolean
+size(): int
+remove(index: int): E
+set(index: int, e: E): E
Appends a new element at the end of this list.
Adds a new element at the specified index in this list.
Removes all the elements from this list.
Returns true if this list contains the element.
Returns the element from this list at the specified index.
Returns the index of the first matching element in this list.
Returns true if this list contains no elements.
Returns the index of the last matching element in this list.
Removes the element from this list.
Returns the number of elements in this list.
Removes the element at the specified index and returns the removed element.
Sets the element at the specified index and returns the element you are replacing.
MyAbstractList<E>
#size: int
#MyAbstractList()
#MyAbstractList(objects: E[])
+add(e: E): void
+isEmpty(): boolean
+size(): int
+remove(e: E):boolean
The size of the list.
Creates a default list.
Creates a list from an array of objects.
Implements the add method.
Implements the isEmpty method.
Implements the size method.
Implements the remove method.

FIGURE 25.3 `List` supports many methods for manipulating a list. `MyAbstractList` provides a partial implementation of the `List` interface.

LISTING 25.1 MyList.java

```
public interface MyList<E> {
  /** Add a new element at the end of this list */
  public void add(E e);

  /** Add a new element at the specified index in this list */
  public void add(int index, E e);

```

add(e)

add(index, e)

clear() contains(e) get(index) indexOf(e) isEmpty(e) lastIndexOf(e) remove(e) remove(index) set(index, e) size(e)

```
  /** Clear the list */
  public void clear();

  /** Return true if this list contains the element */
  public boolean contains(E e);

  /** Return the element from this list at the specified index */
  public E get(int index);

  /** Return the index of the first matching element in this list.
   *  Return -1 if no match. */
  public int indexOf(E e);

  /** Return true if this list contains no elements */
  public boolean isEmpty();

  /** Return the index of the last matching element in this list
   *  Return -1 if no match. */
  public int lastIndexOf(E e);

  /** Remove the first occurrence of the element o from this list.
   *  Shift any subsequent elements to the left.
   *  Return true if the element is removed. */
  public boolean remove(E e);

  /** Remove the element at the specified position in this list
   *  Shift any subsequent elements to the left.
   *  Return the element that was removed from the list. */
  public E remove(int index);

  /** Replace the element at the specified position in this list
   *  with the specified element and return the new set. */
  public Object set(int index, E e);

  /** Return the number of elements in this list */
  public int size();
}
```

MyAbstractList declares variable size to indicate the number of elements in the list. The methods isEmpty(), and size(), add(E), and remove(E) can be implemented in the class in Listing 25.2.

Listing 25.2 MyAbstractList.java

size, no-arg constructor, constructor, implement **add**

```
public abstract class MyAbstractList<E> implements MyList<E> {
  protected int size = 0; // The size of the list

  /** Create a default list */
  protected MyAbstractList() {
  }

  /** Create a list from an array of objects */
  protected MyAbstractList(E[] objects) {
    for (int i = 0; i < objects.length; i++)
      add(objects[i]);
  }

  /** Add a new element at the end of this list */
  public void add(E e) {
```

```java
    add(size, e);
  }

  /** Return true if this list contains no elements */
  public boolean isEmpty() {
    return size == 0;
  }

  /** Return the number of elements in this list */
  public int size() {
    return size;
  }

  /** Remove the first occurrence of the element o from this list.
   *  Shift any subsequent elements to the left.
   *  Return true if the element is removed. */
  public boolean remove(E e) {
    if (indexOf(e) >= 0) {
      remove(indexOf(e));
      return true;
    }
    else
      return false;
  }
}
```

implement **isEmpty()**

implement **size()**

implement **remove(E e)**

The following sections give the implementation for `MyArrayList` and `MyLinkedList`, respectively.

Design Guide

Protected data fields are rarely used. However, making `size` a protected data field in the `MyAbstractList` class is a good choice. The subclass of `MyAbstractList` can access `size`, but nonsubclasses of `MyAbstractList` in different packages cannot access it. As a general rule, you may declare protected data fields in abstract classes.

protected data field

25.3 Array Lists

Array is a fixed-size data structure. Once an array is created, its size cannot be changed. Nevertheless, you can still use arrays to implement dynamic data structures. The trick is to create a larger new array to replace the current array, if the current array cannot hold new elements in the list.

Initially, an array, say `data` of `E[]` type, is created with a default size. When inserting a new element into the array, first make sure that there is enough room in the array. If not, create a new array twice as large as the current one. Copy the elements from the current array to the new array. The new array now becomes the current array. Before inserting a new element at a specified index, shift all the elements after the index to the right and increase the list size by `1`, as shown in Figure 25.4.

Note

The data array is of type `E[]`. Each cell in the array actually stores the reference of an object.

To remove an element at a specified index, shift all the elements after the index to the left by one position and decrease the list size by `1`, as shown in Figure 25.5.

`MyArrayList` uses an array to implement `MyAbstractList`, as shown in Figure 25.6. Its implementation is given in Listing 25.3.

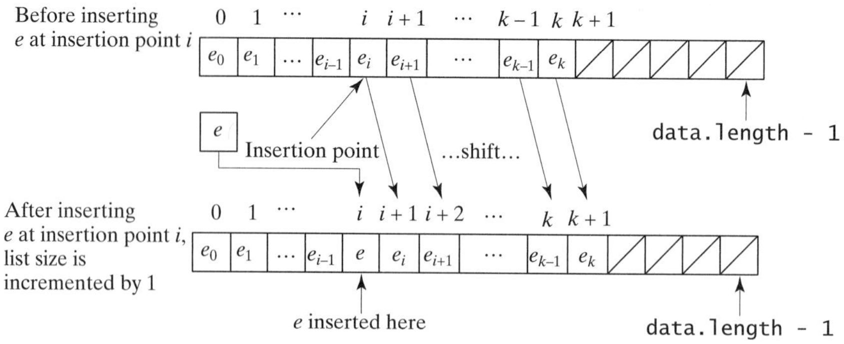
Before inserting
e at insertion point i
Insertion point
...shift...
data.length - 1
After inserting
e at insertion point i,
list size is
incremented by 1
e inserted here
data.length - 1

FIGURE 25.4 Inserting a new element into the array requires that all the elements after the insertion point be shifted one position to the right, so that the new element can be inserted at the insertion point.

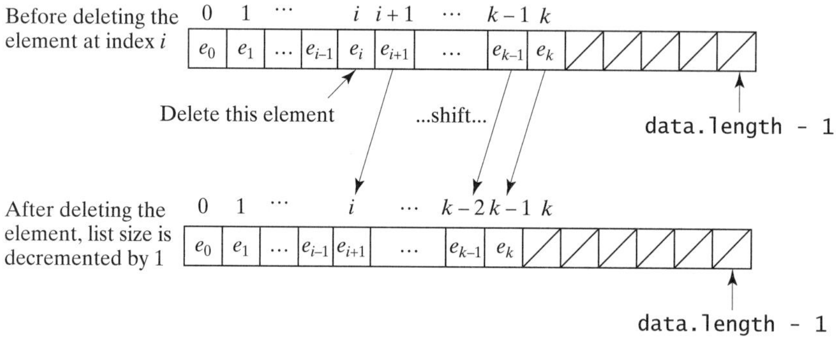
Before deleting the
element at index i
Delete this element
...shift...
data.length - 1
After deleting the
element, list size is
decremented by 1
data.length - 1

FIGURE 25.5 Deleting an element from the array requires that all the elements after the deletion point be shifted one position to the left.

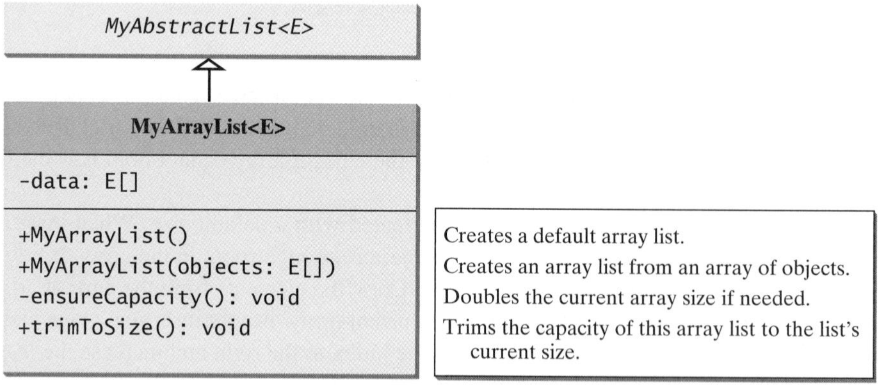
MyAbstractList<E>
MyArrayList<E>
-data: E[]
+MyArrayList()
+MyArrayList(objects: E[])
-ensureCapacity(): void
+trimToSize(): void
Creates a default array list.
Creates an array list from an array of objects.
Doubles the current array size if needed.
Trims the capacity of this array list to the list's current size.

FIGURE 25.6 `MyArrayList` implements a list using an array.

LISTING 25.3 MyArrayList.java

initial capacity
array

```
public class MyArrayList<E> extends MyAbstractList<E> {
  public static final int INITIAL_CAPACITY = 16;
  private E[] data = (E[])new Object[INITIAL_CAPACITY];

  /** Create a default list */
```

no-arg constructor

```
  public MyArrayList() {
  }

  /** Create a list from an array of objects */
```

constructor

```
  public MyArrayList(E[] objects) {
    for (int i = 0; i < objects.length; i++)
      add(objects[i]); // Warning: don't use super(objects)!
  }

  /** Add a new element at the specified index in this list */
```

add

```
  public void add(int index, E e) {
    ensureCapacity();

    // Move the elements to the right after the specified index
    for (int i = size - 1; i >= index; i--)
      data[i + 1] = data[i];

    // Insert new element to data[index]
    data[index] = e;

    // Increase size by 1
    size++;
  }

  /** Create a new larger array, double the current size + 1 */
```

ensureCapacity

double capacity + 1

```
  private void ensureCapacity() {
    if (size >= data.length) {
      E[] newData = (E[])(new Object[size * 2 + 1]);
      System.arraycopy(data, 0, newData, 0, size);
      data = newData;
    }
  }

  /** Clear the list */
```

clear

```
  public void clear() {
    data = (E[])new Object[INITIAL_CAPACITY];
    size = 0;
  }

  /** Return true if this list contains the element */
```

contains

```
  public boolean contains(E e) {
    for (int i = 0; i < size; i++)
      if (e.equals(data[i])) return true;

    return false;
  }

  /** Return the element from this list at the specified index */
```

get

```
  public E get(int index) {
    return data[index];
  }

  /** Return the index of the first matching element in this list.
   *  Return -1 if no match. */
```

indexOf

```
  public int indexOf(E e) {
    for (int i = 0; i < size; i++)
      if (e.equals(data[i])) return i;

```

```
    return -1;
  }

  /** Return the index of the last matching element in this list
   *  Return -1 if no match. */
```

lastIndexOf

```
  public int lastIndexOf(E e) {
    for (int i = size - 1; i >= 0; i--)
      if (e.equals(data[i])) return i;

    return -1;
  }

  /** Remove the element at the specified position in this list
   *  Shift any subsequent elements to the left.
   *  Return the element that was removed from the list. */
```

remove

```
  public E remove(int index) {
    E e = data[index];

    // Shift data to the left
    for (int j = index; j < size - 1; j++)
      data[j] = data[j + 1];

    data[size - 1] = null; // This element is now null

    // Decrement size
    size--;

    return e;
  }

  /** Replace the element at the specified position in this list
   *  with the specified element. */
```

set

```
  public E set(int index, E e) {
    E old = data[index];
    data[index] = e;
    return old;
  }

  /** Override toString() to return elements in the list */
```

toString

```
  public String toString() {
    StringBuilder result = new StringBuilder("[");

    for (int i = 0; i < size; i++) {
      result.append(data[i]);
      if (i < size - 1) result.append(", ");
    }

    return result.toString() + "]";
  }

  /** Trims the capacity to current size */
  public void trimToSize() {
    if (size != data.length) {
      // If size == capacity, no need to trim
      E[] newData = (E[])(new Object[size]);
      System.arraycopy(data, 0, newData, 0, size);
      data = newData;
    }
  }
}
```

A node can be defined as a class, as follows:

```
class Node<E> {
  E element;
  Node<E> next;

  public Node(E e) {
    element = e;
  }
}
```

The variable head refers to the first node in the list, and the variable tail to the last node. If the list is empty, both head and tail are null. Here is an example that creates a linked list to hold three nodes. Each node stores a string element.

Step 1: Declare head and tail:

```
Node<E> head = null;
Node<E> tail = null;
```

The list is empty now

head and tail are both null. The list is empty.

Step 2: Create the first node and append it to the list:

After the first node is inserted in the list, head and tail point to this node, as shown in Figure 25.8.

```
head = new Node<E>("Chicago");
last = head;
```

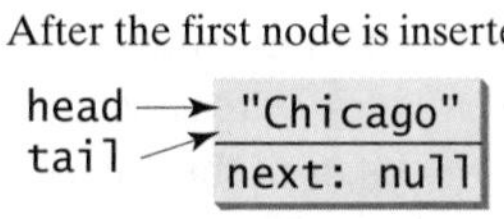
After the first node is inserted
head
tail
"Chicago"
next: null

FIGURE 25.8 Append the first node to the list.

Step 3: Create the second node and append it into the list:

To append the second node to the list, link the first node with the new node, as shown in Figure 25.9(a). The new node is now the tail node. So you should move tail to point to this new node, as shown in Figure 25.9(b).

Step 4: Create the third node and append it to the list:

```
tail.next = new Node<E>("Denver");
```

```
tail = tail.next;
```

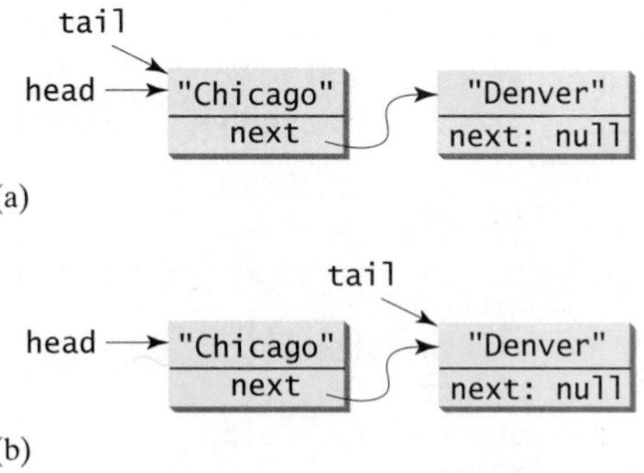
tail
head
"Chicago"
next
"Denver"
next: null
(a)
tail
head
"Chicago"
next
"Denver"
next: null
(b)

FIGURE 25.9 Append the second node to the list.

To append the new node to the list, link the last node in the list with the new node, as shown in Figure 25.10(a). The new node is now the tail node. So you should move tail to point to this new node, as shown in Figure 25.10(b).

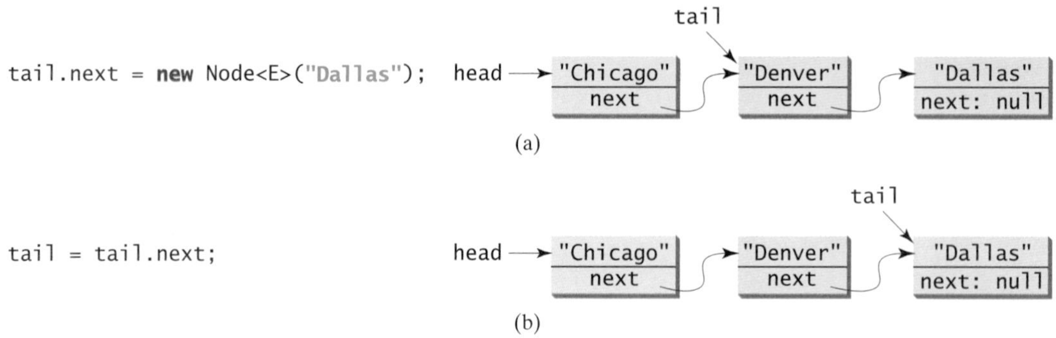
tail.next = new Node<E>("Dallas");
head
"Chicago"
next
tail
"Denver"
next
"Dallas"
next: null
(a)
tail = tail.next;
head
"Chicago"
next
"Denver"
next
tail
"Dallas"
next: null
(b)

FIGURE 25.10 Append the third node to the list.

Each node contains the element and a data field named *next* that points to the next element. If the node is the last in the list, its pointer data field `next` contains the value `null`. You can use this property to detect the last node. For example, you may write the following loop to traverse all the nodes in the list.

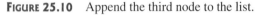

current pointer
check last node
next node

```
1 Node current = head;
2 while (current != null) {
3   System.out.println(current.element);
4   current = current.next;
5 }
```

The variable `current` points initially to the first node in the list (line 1). In the loop, the element of the current node is retrieved (line 3), and then `current` points to the next node (line 4). The loop continues until the current node is `null`.

25.4.2 The `LinkedList` Class

`MyLinkedList` uses a linked structure to implement a dynamic list. It extends `MyAbstractList`. In addition, it provides the methods `addFirst`, `addLast`, `removeFirst`, `removeLast`, `getFirst`, and `getLast`, as shown in Figure 25.11.

Assuming that the class has been implemented, Listing 25.5 gives a test program that uses the class.

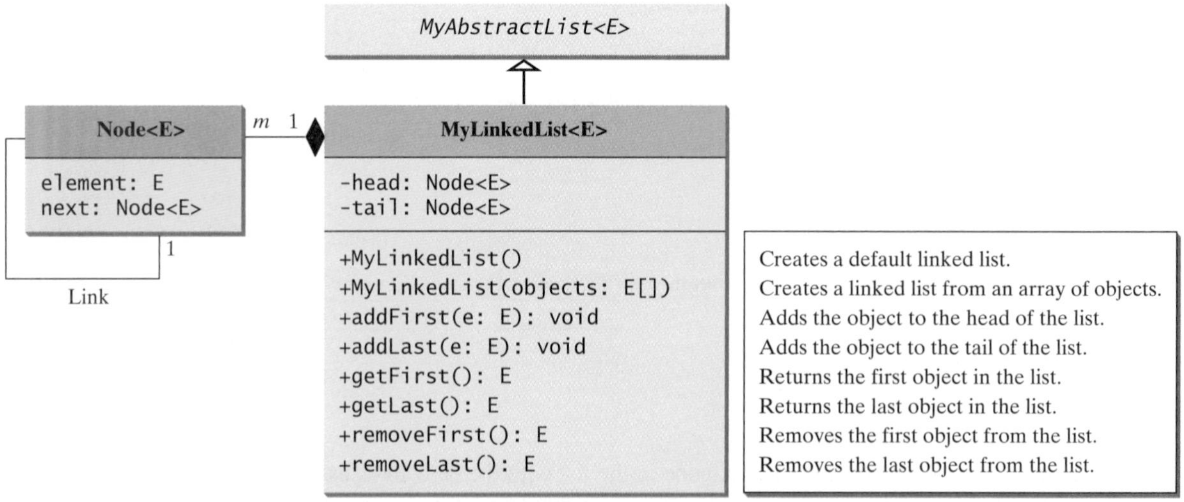
MyAbstractList<E>
Node<E>
element: E
next: Node<E>
Link
m
1
1
MyLinkedList<E>
-head: Node<E>
-tail: Node<E>
+MyLinkedList()
+MyLinkedList(objects: E[])
+addFirst(e: E): void
+addLast(e: E): void
+getFirst(): E
+getLast(): E
+removeFirst(): E
+removeLast(): E
Creates a default linked list.
Creates a linked list from an array of objects.
Adds the object to the head of the list.
Adds the object to the tail of the list.
Returns the first object in the list.
Returns the last object in the list.
Removes the first object from the list.
Removes the last object from the list.

FIGURE 25.11 `MyLinkedList` implements a list using a linked list of nodes.

LISTING 25.5 TestLinkedList.java

```
public class TestLinkedList {
  /** Main method */
  public static void main(String[] args) {
    // Create a list for strings
    MyLinkedList<String> list = new MyLinkedList<String>();

    // Add elements to the list
    list.add("America"); // Add it to the list
    System.out.println("(1) " + list);

    list.add(0, "Canada"); // Add it to the beginning of the list
    System.out.println("(2) " + list);

    list.add("Russia"); // Add it to the end of the list
    System.out.println("(3) " + list);

    list.addLast("France"); // Add it to the end of the list
    System.out.println("(4) " + list);

    list.add(2, "Germany"); // Add it to the list at index 2
    System.out.println("(5) " + list);

    list.add(5, "Norway"); // Add it to the list at index 5
    System.out.println("(6) " + list);

    list.add(0, "Poland"); // Same as list.addFirst("Poland")
    System.out.println("(7) " + list);

    // Remove elements from the list
    list.remove(0); // Same as list.remove("Australia") in this case
    System.out.println("(8) " + list);

    list.remove(2); // Remove the element at index
    System.out.println("(9) " + list);

    list.remove(list.size() - 1); // Remove the last element
    System.out.println("(10) " + list);
  }
}
```

create list
append element
print list
insert element
append element
append element
insert element
insert element
insert element
remove element
remove element
remove element

```
(1) [America]
(2) [Canada, America]
(3) [Canada, America, Russia]
(4) [Canada, America, Russia, France]
(5) [Canada, America, Germany, Russia, France]
(6) [Canada, America, Germany, Russia, France, Norway]
(7) [Poland, Canada, America, Germany, Russia, France, Norway]
(8) [Canada, America, Germany, Russia, France, Norway]
(9) [Canada, America, Russia, France, Norway]
(10) [Canada, America, Russia, France]
```

25.4.3 Implementing `MyLinkedList`

Now let us turn our attention to implementing the `MyLinkedList` class. We will discuss how to implement methods `addFirst`, `addLast`, `add(index, e)`, `removeFirst`, `removeLast`, and `remove(index)` and leave other methods in the `MyLinkedList` class as exercises.

25.4.3.1 Implementing **addFirst(e)**

The `addFirst(e)` method creates a new node for holding element `e`. The new node becomes the first node in the list. It can be implemented as follows:

create a node
link with head
head to new node
increase size
was empty?

```
1 public void addFirst(E e) {
2   Node<E> newNode = new Node<E>(e); // Create a new node
3   newNode.next = head; // link the new node with the head
4   head = newNode; // head points to the new node
5   size++; // Increase list size
6
7   if (tail == null) // the new node is the only node in list
8     tail = head;
9 }
```

The `addFirst(e)` method creates a new node to store the element (line 2) and insert the node to the beginning of the list (line 3), as shown in Figure 25.12(a). After the insertion, `head` should point to this new element node (line 4), as shown in Figure 25.12(b).

If the list is empty (line 7), both `head` and `tail` will point to this new node (line 8). After the node is created, `size` should be increased by `1` (line 5).

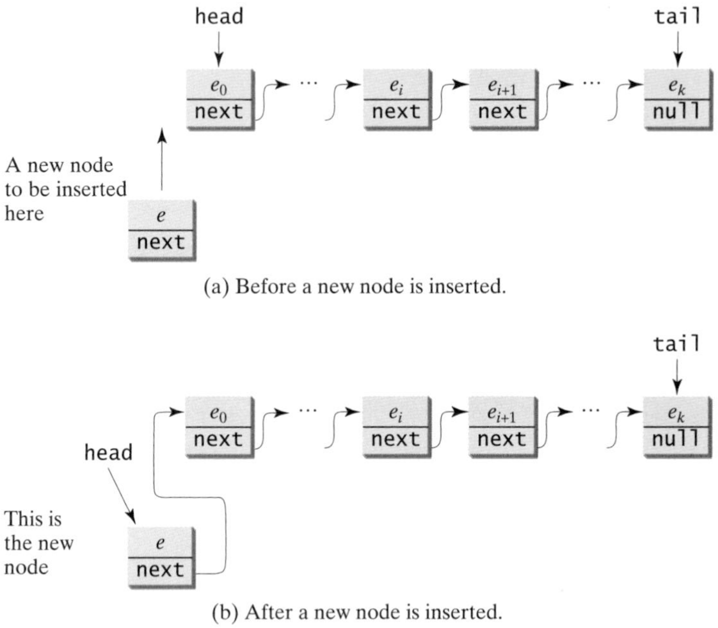
head
tail
e0
next
ei
next
ei+1
next
ek
null
A new node to be inserted here
e
next
(a) Before a new node is inserted.
tail
e0
next
ei
next
ei+1
next
ek
null
head
This is the new node
e
next
(b) After a new node is inserted.

FIGURE 25.12 A new element is added to the beginning of the list.

25.4.3.2 Implementing **addLast(e)**

The `addLast(e)` method creates a node to hold the element and appends the node at the end of the list. It can be implemented as follows:

create a node

```
public void addLast(E e) {
  Node<E> newNode = new Node<E>(e); // Create a new node for e

  if (tail == null) {
    head = tail = newNode; // The only node in list
  }
```

```
7  else {
8    tail.next = newNode; // Link the new with the last node
9    tail = tail.next; // tail now points to the last node
10 }
11
12   size++; // Increase size
13 }
```

increase size

The addLast(e) method creates a new node to store the element (line 2) and appends it to the end of the list (line 8). Consider two cases:

1. If the list is empty (line 4), both head and tail will point to this new node (line 5);
2. Otherwise, link the node with the last node in the list (line 8). tail should now point to this new node (line 9), as shown in Figure 25.13(b).

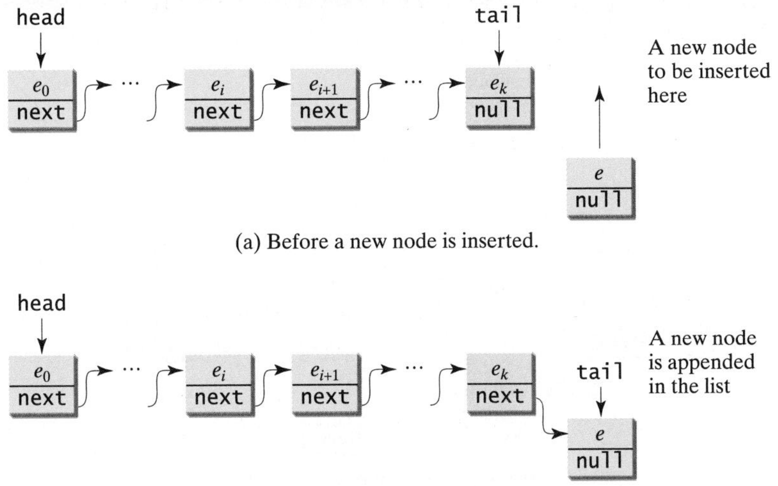
head
tail
A new node
to be inserted
here
e_0
next
e_i
next
e_{i+1}
next
e_k
null
e
null
head
tail
A new node
is appended
in the list
e_0
next
e_i
next
e_{i+1}
next
e_k
next
e
null

(a) Before a new node is inserted.

(b) After a new node is inserted.

FIGURE 25.13 A new element is added at the end of the list.

In any case, after the node is created, the size should be increased by 1 (line 12).

25.4.3.3 Implementing add(index, e)

The add(index, e) method inserts an element into the list at the specified index. It can be implemented as follows:

```
public void add(int index, E e) {
  if (index == 0) addFirst(e); // Insert first
  else if (index >= size) addLast(e); // Insert last
  else { // Insert in the middle
    Node<E> current = head;
    for (int i = 1; i < index; i++)
      current = current.next;
    Node<E> temp = current.next;
    current.next = new Node<E>(e);
    (current.next).next = temp;
    size++;
  }
}
```

insert first
insert last
create a node
increase size

There are three cases when inserting an element into the list:

1. If `index` is `0`, invoke `addFirst(e)` (line 2) to insert the element at the beginning of the list;

2. If `index` is greater than or equal to `size`, invoke `addLast(e)` (line 3) to insert the element at the end of the list;

3. Otherwise, create a new node to store the new element and locate where to insert it. As shown in Figure 25.14(b), the new node is to be inserted between the nodes `current` and `temp`, as shown in Figure 25.14(a). The method assigns the new node to `current.next` and assigns `temp` to the new node's `next`, as shown in Figure 25.14(b). The size is now increased by `1` (line 11).

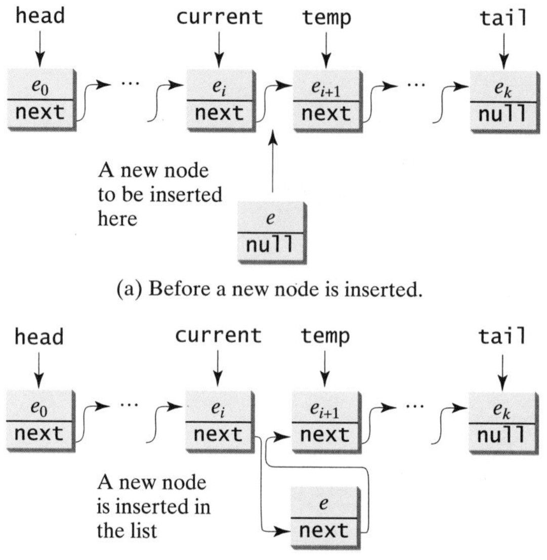
head
current
temp
tail
e_0
next
e_i
next
e_{i+1}
next
e_k
null
A new node to be inserted here
e
null
head
current
temp
tail
e_0
next
e_i
next
e_{i+1}
next
e_k
null
A new node is inserted in the list
e
next

(a) Before a new node is inserted.

(b) After a new node is inserted.

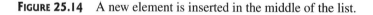

FIGURE 25.14 A new element is inserted in the middle of the list.

25.4.3.4 Implementing **removeFirst()**

The `removeFirst()` method is to remove the first element from the list. It can be implemented as follows:

nothing to remove
keep old head
new head
decrease **size**
destroy the node

```
1 public E removeFirst() {
2   if (size == 0) return null; // Nothing to delete
3   else {
4     Node<E> temp = head; // Keep the first node temporarily
5     head = head.next; // Move head to point to the next node
6     size--; // Reduce size by 1
7     if (head == null) tail = null; // List becomes empty
8     return temp.element; // Return the deleted element
9   }
10 }
```

Consider two cases:

1. If the list is empty, there is nothing to delete, so return `null` (line 2);

2. Otherwise, remove the first node from the list by pointing `head` to the second node, as shown in Figure 25.15. The size is reduced by `1` after the deletion (line 6). If there is one element, after removing the element, `tail` should be set to `null` (line 7).

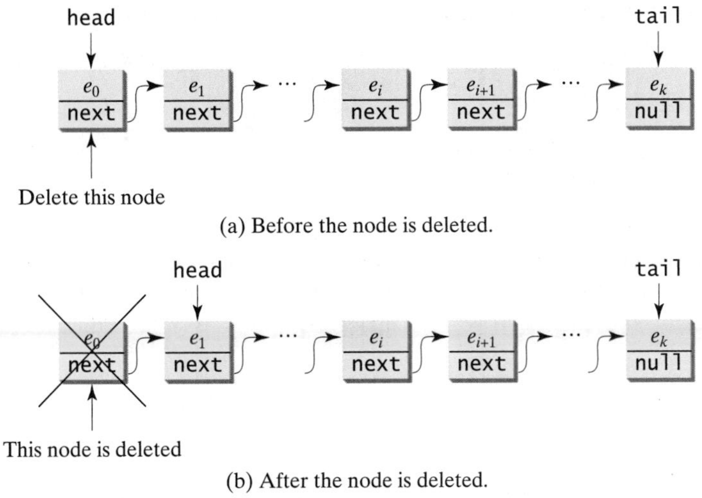
head
tail
next
null
Delete this node
(a) Before the node is deleted.
This node is deleted
(b) After the node is deleted.

FIGURE 25.15 The first node is deleted from the list.

25.4.3.5 Implementing **removeLast()**

The `removeLast()` method removes the last element from the list. It can be implemented as follows:

```
1 public E removeLast() {
2   if (size == 0) return null; // Nothing to remove
3   else if (size == 1) // Only one element in the list
4   {
5     Node<E> temp = head;
6     head = tail = null;  // list becomes empty
7     size = 0;
8     return temp.element;
9   }
10  else
11  {
12    Node<E> current = head;
13
14    for (int i = 0; i < size - 2; i++)
15      current = current.next;
16
17    Node<E> temp = tail;
18    tail = current;
19    tail.next = null;
20    size--;
21    return temp.element;
22  }
23 }
```

empty?
size 1?
head and tail null
size is 0
return element
size > 1?
move tail
reduce size
return element

Consider three cases:

1. If the list is empty, return `null` (line 2);
2. If the list contains only one node, this node is destroyed; `head` and `tail` both become `null` (line 6);
3. Otherwise, the last node is destroyed (line 18) and the `tail` is repositioned to point to the second-to-last node, as shown in Figure 25.16(a). For the last two cases, the size is reduced by `1` after the deletion (lines 7, 20) and the element value of the deleted node is returned (lines 8, 21).

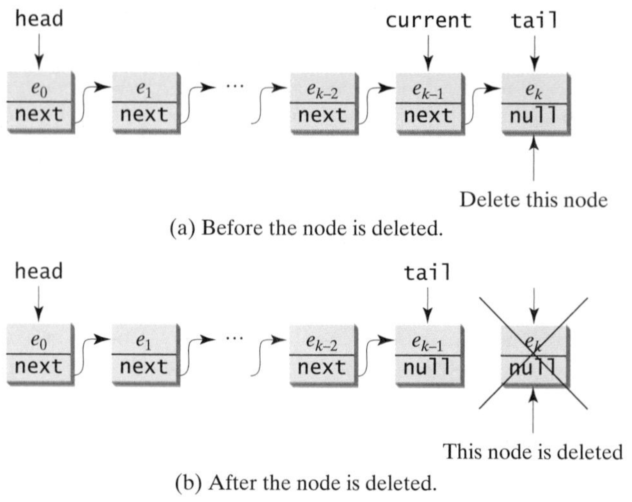
head
current
tail
e0
next
e1
next
ek–2
next
ek–1
next
ek
null
Delete this node
(a) Before the node is deleted.
head
tail
e0
next
e1
next
ek–2
next
ek–1
null
This node is deleted
(b) After the node is deleted.

FIGURE 25.16 The last node is deleted from the list.

25.4.3.6 Implementing **remove(index)**

The `remove(index)` method finds the node at the specified index and then removes it. It can be implemented as follows:

```
1 public E remove(int index) {
2   if (index < 0 || index >= size) return null; // Out of range
3   else if (index == 0) return removeFirst(); // Remove first
4   else if (index == size - 1) return removeLast(); // Remove last
5   else {
6     Node<E> previous = head;
7
8     for (int i = 1; i < index; i++) {
9       previous = previous.next;
10    }
11
12    Node<E> current = previous.next;
13    previous.next = current.next;
14    size--;
15    return current.element;
16  }
17 }
```

out of range (line 2); remove first (line 3); remove last (line 4); locate previous (line 8); locate current (line 12); remove from list (line 13); reduce size (line 14); return element (line 15)

Consider four cases:

1. If `index` is beyond the range of the list (i.e., `index < 0 || index >= size`), return `null` (line 2);
2. If `index` is `0`, invoke `removeFirst()` to remove the first node (line 3);
3. If `index` is `size - 1`, invoke `removeLast()` to remove the last node (line 4);
4. Otherwise, locate the node at the specified `index`. Let `current` denote this node and `previous` denote the node before this node, as shown in Figure 25.17(a). Assign `current.next` to `previous.next` to eliminate the current node, as shown in Figure 25.17(b).

Listing 25.6 gives the implementation of `MyLinkedList`. The implementation of `get(index)`, `indexOf(e)`, `lastIndexOf(e)`, `contains(e)`, and `set(index, e)` is omitted and left as an exercise.

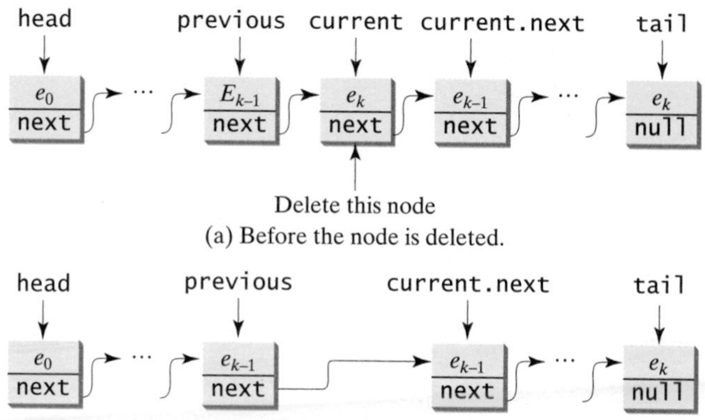
head
previous
current
current.next
tail
e_0
next
E_{k-1}
next
e_k
next
e_{k-1}
next
e_k
null
Delete this node
head
previous
current.next
tail
e_0
next
e_{k-1}
next
e_{k-1}
next
e_k
null

(a) Before the node is deleted.

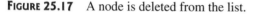

(b) After the node is deleted.

FIGURE 25.17 A node is deleted from the list.

LISTING 25.6 MyLinkedList.java

```
public class MyLinkedList<E> extends MyAbstractList<E> {
  private Node<E> head, tail;

  /** Create a default list */
  public MyLinkedList() {
  }

  /** Create a list from an array of objects */
  public MyLinkedList(E[] objects) {
    super(objects);
  }

  /** Return the head element in the list */
  public E getFirst() {
    if (size == 0) {
      return null;
    }
    else {
      return head.element;
    }
  }

  /** Return the last element in the list */
  public E getLast() {
    if (size == 0) {
      return null;
    }
    else {
      return tail.element;
    }
  }

  /** Add an element to the beginning of the list */
  public void addFirst(E e) {
    // Implemented in §25.4.3.1, so omitted here
  }

  /** Add an element to the end of the list */
  public void addLast(E e) {
```

head, tail

no-arg constructor

constructor

`getFirst`

`getLast`

`addFirst`

`addLast`

```java
    // Implemented in §25.4.3.2, so omitted here
  }

  /** Add a new element at the specified index in this list
   * The index of the head element is 0 */
```

add

```java
  public void add(int index, E e) {
    // Implemented in §25.4.3.3, so omitted here
  }

  /** Remove the head node and
   *  return the object that is contained in the removed node. */
```

removeFirst

```java
  public E removeFirst() {
    // Implemented in §25.4.3.4, so omitted here
  }

  /** Remove the last node and
   * return the object that is contained in the removed node. */
```

removeLast

```java
  public E removeLast() {
    // Implemented in §25.4.3.5, so omitted here
  }

  /** Remove the element at the specified position in this list.
   *  Return the element that was removed from the list. */
```

remove

```java
  public E remove( int index) {
    // Implemented in §25.4.3.6, so omitted here
  }

  /** Override toString() to return elements in the list */
```

toString

```java
  public String toString() {
    StringBuilder result = new StringBuilder("[");

    Node<E> current = head;
    for (int i = 0; i < size; i++) {
      result.append(current.element);
      current = current.next;
      if (current != null) {
        result.append(", "); // Separate two elements with a comma
      }
      else {
        result.append("]"); // Insert the closing ] in the string
      }
    }

    return result.toString();
  }

  /** Clear the list */
```

clear

```java
  public void clear() {
    head = tail = null;
  }

  /** Return true if this list contains the element o */
```

contains

```java
  public boolean contains(E e) {
    System.out.println("Implementation left as an exercise");
    return true;
  }

  /** Return the element from this list at the specified index */
```

get

```java
  public E get(int index) {
    System.out.println("Implementation left as an exercise");
```

```java
    return null;
  }

  /** Return the index of the head matching element in this list.
   *  Return -1 if no match. */
  public int indexOf(E e) {
    System.out.println("Implementation left as an exercise");
    return 0;
  }

  /** Return the index of the last matching element in this list
   *  Return -1 if no match. */
  public int lastIndexOf(E e) {
    System.out.println("Implementation left as an exercise");
    return 0;
  }

  /** Replace the element at the specified position in this list
   *  with the specified element. */
  public E set(int index, E e) {
    System.out.println("Implementation left as an exercise");
    return null;
  }

  private static class Node<E> {
    E element;
    Node<E> next;

    public Node(E element) {
      this.element = element;
    }
  }
}
```

indexOf

lastIndexOf

set

Node inner class

25.4.4 MyArrayList vs. MyLinkedList

Both `MyArrayList` and `MyLinkedList` can be used to store a list. `MyArrayList` is implemented using an array and `MyLinkedList` is implemented using a linked list. The overhead of `MyArrayList` is smaller than that of `MyLinkedList`. However, `MyLinkedList` is more efficient if you need to insert and delete the elements from anywhere in the list. Table 25.1 summarizes the complexity of the methods in `MyArrayList`, and `MyLinkedList`. Note that `MyArrayList` is the same as `java.util.ArrayList` and `MyLinkedList` is the same as `java.util.LinkedList`.

TABLE 25.1 Time Complexities for Methods in `MyArrayList` and `MyLinkedList`

Methods	*MyArrayList/ArrayList*	*MyLinkedList/LinkedList*
add(e: E)	$O(1)$	$O(1)$
add(index: int, e: E)	$O(n)$	$O(n)$
clear()	$O(1)$	$O(1)$
contains(e: E)	$O(n)$	$O(n)$
get(index: int)	$O(1)$	$O(n)$
indexOf(e: E)	$O(n)$	$O(n)$

isEmpty()	$O(1)$	$O(1)$
lastIndexOf(e: E)	$O(n)$	$O(n)$
remove(e: E)	$O(n)$	$O(n)$
size()	$O(1)$	$O(1)$
remove(index: int)	$O(n)$	$O(n)$
set(index: int, e: E)	$O(n)$	$O(n)$
addFirst(e: E)	$O(n)$	$O(1)$
removeFirst()	$O(n)$	$O(1)$

25.5 Variations of Linked Lists

The linked list introduced in the preceding section is known as a *singly linked list*. It contains a pointer to the list's first node, and each node contains a pointer to the next node sequentially. Several variations of the linked list are useful in certain applications.

A *circular, singly linked list* is like a singly linked list, except that the pointer of the last node points back to the first node, as shown in Figure 25.18(a). Note that `tail` is not needed for circular linked lists. A good application of a circular linked list is in the operating system that serves multiple users in a timesharing fashion. The system picks a user from a circular list and grants a small amount of CPU time, then moves on to the next user in the list.

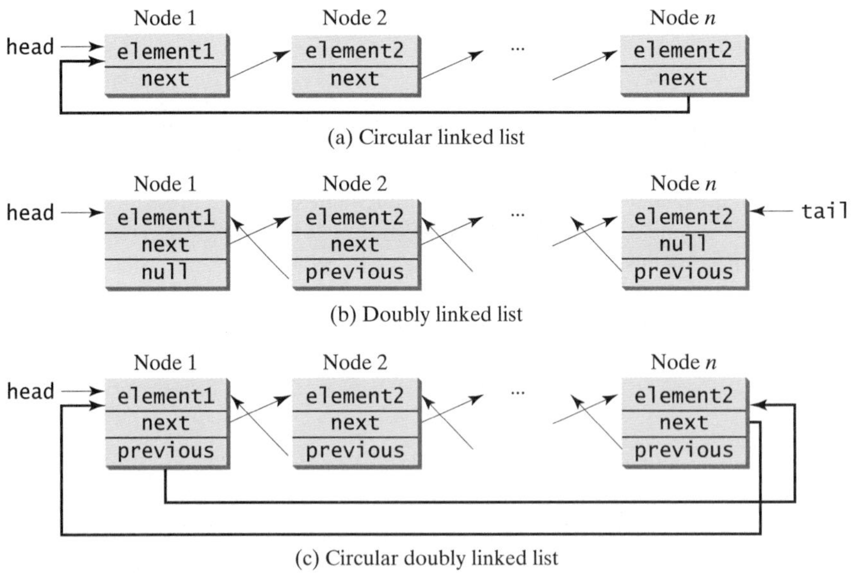
Node 1
Node 2
Node n
head
element1
next
element2
next
...
element2
next
(a) Circular linked list
Node 1
Node 2
Node n
head
element1
next
null
element2
next
previous
element2
null
previous
tail
(b) Doubly linked list
Node 1
Node 2
Node n
head
element1
next
previous
element2
next
previous
element2
next
previous
(c) Circular doubly linked list

FIGURE 25.18 Linked lists may appear in various forms.

A *doubly linked list* contains the nodes with two pointers. One points to the next node and the other to the previous node, as shown in Figure 25.18(b). These two pointers are conveniently called *a forward pointer* and *a backward pointer*. So, a doubly linked list can be traversed forward and backward.

A *circular, doubly linked list* is a doubly linked list, except that the forward pointer of the last node points to the first node and the backward pointer of the first pointer points to the last node, as shown in Figure 25.18(c).

The implementations of these linked lists are left as exercises.

25.6 Stacks and Queues

A stack can be viewed as a special type of list whose elements are accessed, inserted, and deleted only from the end (top), as shown in Figure 10.10. A queue represents a waiting list. It can be viewed as a special type of list whose elements are inserted into the end (tail) of the queue, and are accessed and deleted from the beginning (head), as shown in Figure 25.19.

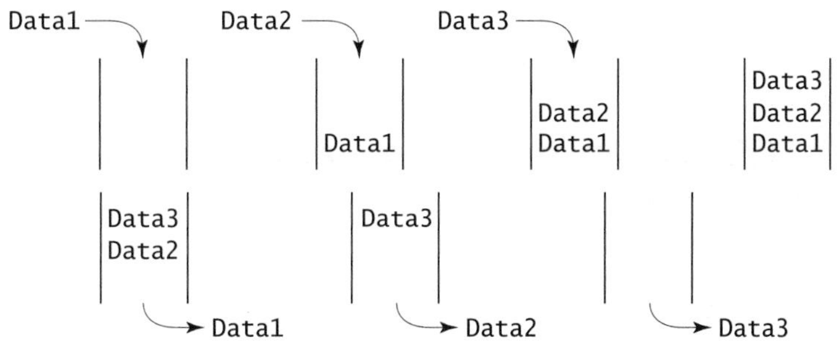
Data1
Data2
Data3
Data1
Data2
Data1
Data3
Data2
Data1
Data3
Data2
Data3
Data1
Data2
Data3

FIGURE 25.19 A queue holds objects in a first-in, first-out fashion.

Pedagogical Note

Follow the links www.cs.armstrong.edu/liang/animation/StackAnimation.html and www.cs.armstrong.edu/liang/animation/QueueAnimation.html to see how stacks and queues work, as shown in Figure 25.20.

stack and queue animation

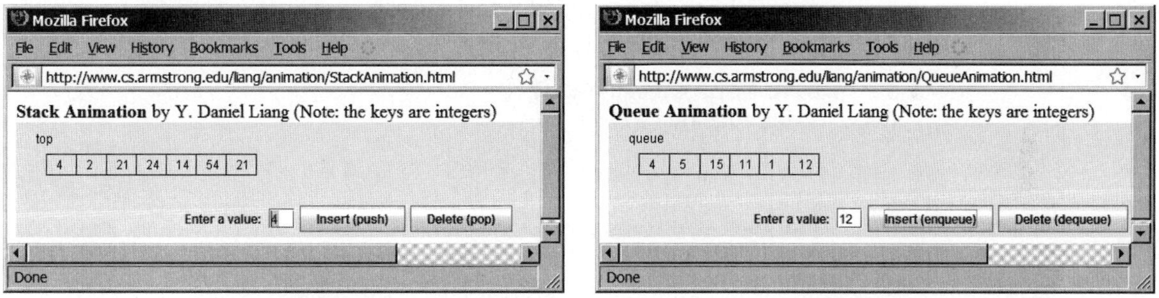
Mozilla Firefox
http://www.cs.armstrong.edu/liang/animation/StackAnimation.html
Stack Animation by Y. Daniel Liang (Note: the keys are integers)
top
4 2 21 24 14 54 21
Enter a value: 4
Insert (push)
Delete (pop)
Done
Mozilla Firefox
http://www.cs.armstrong.edu/liang/animation/QueueAnimation.html
Queue Animation by Y. Daniel Liang (Note: the keys are integers)
queue
4 5 15 11 1 12
Enter a value: 12
Insert (enqueue)
Delete (dequeue)
Done

(a) Stack animation

(b) Queue animation

FIGURE 25.20 The animation tool enables you to see how stacks and queues work visually.

Since the insertion and deletion operations on a stack are made only at the end of the stack, it is more efficient to implement a stack with an array list than with a linked list. Since deletions are made at the beginning of the list, it is more efficient to implement a queue using a linked list than an array list. This section implements a stack class using an array list and a queue using a linked list.

There are two ways to design the stack and queue classes:

- Using inheritance: You can define a stack class by extending `ArrayList`, and a queue class by extending `LinkedList`, as shown in Figure 25.21(a). inheritance
- Using composition: You can define an array list as a data field in the stack class, and a linked list as a data field in the queue class, as shown in Figure 25.21(b). composition

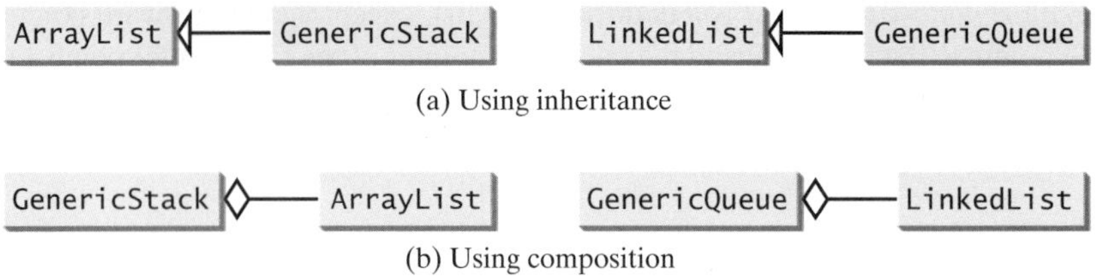
ArrayList
GenericStack
LinkedList
GenericQueue
(a) Using inheritance
GenericStack
ArrayList
GenericQueue
LinkedList
(b) Using composition

FIGURE 25.21 GenericStack and GenericQueue may be implemented using inheritance or composition.

Both designs are fine, but using composition is better because it enables you to define a completely new stack class and queue class without inheriting the unnecessary and inappropriate methods from the array list and linked list. The implementation of the stack class using the composition approach was given in Listing 21.1, GenericStack.java. Listing 25.7 implements the queue class using the composition approach. Figure 25.22 shows the UML of the class.

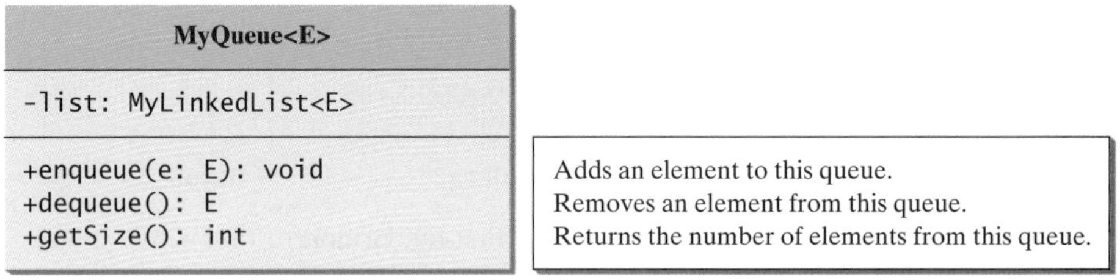
MyQueue<E>
-list: MyLinkedList<E>
+enqueue(e: E): void
+dequeue(): E
+getSize(): int
Adds an element to this queue.
Removes an element from this queue.
Returns the number of elements from this queue.

FIGURE 25.22 GenericQueue uses a linked list to provide a first-in, first-out data structure.

LISTING 25.7 GenericQueue.java

linked list · enqueue · dequeue · getSize · toString

```
 1 public class GenericQueue<E> {
 2   private java.util.LinkedList<E> list
 3     = new java.util.LinkedList<E>();
 4
 5   public void enqueue(E e) {
 6     list.addLast(e);
 7   }
 8
 9   public E dequeue() {
10     return list.removeFirst();
11   }
12
13   public int getSize() {
14     return list.size();
15   }
16
17   public String toString() {
18     return "Queue: " + list.toString();
19   }
20 }
```

A linked list is created to store the elements in a queue (lines 2–3). The enqueue(e) method (lines 5–7) adds element e into the tail of the queue. The dequeue() method (lines 9–11) removes an element from the head of the queue and returns the removed element. The getSize() method (lines 13–15) returns the number of elements in the queue.

Listing 25.8 gives an example that creates a stack using GenericStack and a queue using GenericQueue. It uses the push (enqueue) method to add strings to the stack (queue) and the pop (dequeue) method to remove strings from the stack (queue).

LISTING 25.8 TestStackQueue.java

```java
public class TestStackQueue {
  public static void main(String[] args) {
    // Create a stack
    GenericStack<String> stack =
      new GenericStack<String>();

    // Add elements to the stack
    stack.push("Tom"); // Push it to the stack
    System.out.println("(1) " + stack);

    stack.push("John"); // Push it to the the stack
    System.out.println("(2) " + stack);

    stack.push("George"); // Push it to the stack
    stack.push("Michael"); // Push it to the stack
    System.out.println("(3) " + stack);

    // Remove elements from the stack
    System.out.println("(4) " + stack.pop());
    System.out.println("(5) " + stack.pop());
    System.out.println("(6) " + stack);

    // Create a queue
    GenericQueue<String> queue = new GenericQueue<String>();

    // Add elements to the queue
    queue.enqueue("Tom"); // Add it to the queue
    System.out.println("(7) " + queue);

    queue.enqueue("John"); // Add it to the queue
    System.out.println("(8) " + queue);

    queue.enqueue("George"); // Add it to the queue
    queue.enqueue("Michael"); // Add it to the queue
    System.out.println("(9) " + queue);

    // Remove elements from the queue
    System.out.println("(10) " + queue.dequeue());
    System.out.println("(11) " + queue.dequeue());
    System.out.println("(12) " + queue);
  }
}
```

```
(1) stack: [Tom]
(2) stack: [Tom, John]
(3) stack: [Tom, John, George, Michael]
(4) Michael
(5) George
(6) stack: [Tom, John]
(7) Queue: [Tom]
(8) Queue: [Tom, John]
(9) Queue: [Tom, John, George, Michael]
(10) Tom
(11) John
(12) Queue: [George, Michael]
```

Stack time complexity

Queue time complexity

For a stack, the `push(e)` method adds an element to the top of the stack, and the `pop()` method removes the top element from the stack and returns the removed element. It is easy to see that the time complexity for the `push` and `pop` methods is $O(1)$.

For a queue, the `enqueue(o)` method adds an element to the tail of the queue, and the `dequeue()` method removes the element from the head of the queue. It is easy to see that the time complexity for the `enqueue` and `dequeue` methods is $O(1)$.

25.7 Priority Queues

An ordinary queue is a first-in, first-out data structure. Elements are appended to the end of the queue and removed from the beginning. In a priority queue, elements are assigned with priorities. When accessing elements, the element with the highest priority is removed first. A priority queue has a largest-in, first-out behavior. For example, the emergency room in a hospital assigns priority numbers to patients; the patient with the highest priority is treated first.

A priority queue can be implemented using a heap, where the root is the object with the highest priority in the queue. Heap was introduced in §24.5, "Heap Sort." The class diagram for the priority queue is shown in Figure 25.23. Its implementation is given in Listing 25.9.

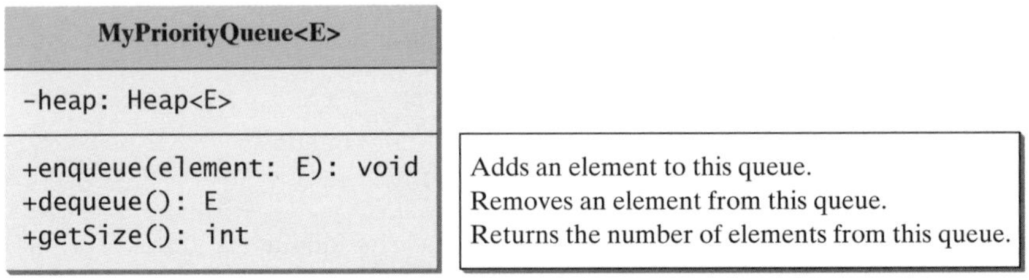
MyPriorityQueue<E>
-heap: Heap<E>
+enqueue(element: E): void
+dequeue(): E
+getSize(): int
Adds an element to this queue.
Removes an element from this queue.
Returns the number of elements from this queue.

FIGURE 25.23 `MyPriorityQueue` uses a heap to provide a largest-in, first-out data structure.

LISTING 25.9 MyPriorityQueue.java

heap for priority queue

enqueue

dequeue

getsize

```
public class MyPriorityQueue<E extends Comparable> {
  private Heap<E> heap = new Heap<E>();

  public void enqueue(E newObject) {
    heap.add(newObject);
  }

  public E dequeue() {
    return heap.remove();
  }

  public int getSize() {
    return heap.getSize();
  }
}
```

Listing 25.10 gives an example of using a priority queue for patients. The `Patient` class is defined in lines 18–34. Four patients are created with associated priority values in lines 3–6. Line 8 creates a priority queue. The patients are enqueued in lines 9–12. Line 15 dequeues a patient from the queue.

LISTING 25.10 TestPriorityQueue.java

```java
public class TestPriorityQueue {
  public static void main(String[] args) {
    Patient patient1 = new Patient("John", 2);
    Patient patient2 = new Patient("Jim", 1);
    Patient patient3 = new Patient("Tim", 5);
    Patient patient4 = new Patient("Cindy", 7);

    MyPriorityQueue priorityQueue = new MyPriorityQueue();
    priorityQueue.enqueue(patient1);
    priorityQueue.enqueue(patient2);
    priorityQueue.enqueue(patient3);
    priorityQueue.enqueue(patient4);

    while (priorityQueue.getSize() > 0)
      System.out.print(priorityQueue.dequeue() + " ");
  }

  static class Patient implements Comparable {
    private String name;
    private int priority;

    public Patient(String name, int priority) {
      this.name = name;
      this.priority = priority;
    }

    public String toString() {
      return name + "(priority:" + priority + ")";
    }

    public int compareTo(Object o) {
      return this.priority - ((Patient)o).priority;
    }
  }
}
```

create a patient

create a priority queue

add to queue

remove from queue

inner class **Patient**

compareTo

```
Cindy(priority:7) Tim(priority:5) John(priority:2) Jim(priority:1)
```

25.8 Case Study: Evaluating Expressions

Stacks and queues have many applications. This section gives an application of using stacks. You can enter an arithmetic expression from Google to evaluate the expression as shown in Figure 25.24.

How does Google evaluate an expression? This section presents a program that evaluates a *compound expression* with multiple operators and parentheses (e.g., `(15 + 2) * 34 - 2`). For simplicity, assume that the operands are integers and the operators are of four types: `+`, `-`, `*`, and `/`.

compound expression

The problem can be solved using two stacks, named `operandStack` and `operatorStack`, for storing operands and operators, respectively. Operands and operators are pushed into the stacks before they are processed. When an *operator is processed*, it is popped from `operatorStack` and applied on the first two operands from `operandStack` (the two operands are popped from `operandStack`). The resultant value is pushed back to `operandStack`.

process an operator

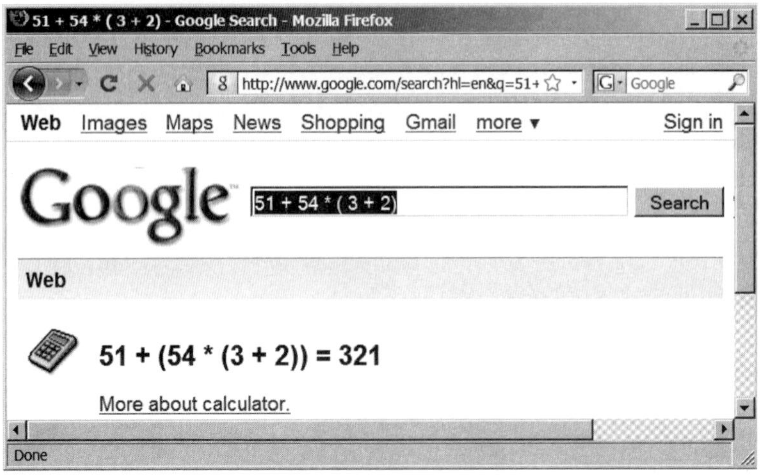
51 + 54 * (3 + 2) - Google Search - Mozilla Firefox
File Edit View History Bookmarks Tools Help
http://www.google.com/search?hl=en&q=51+
Google
Web Images Maps News Shopping Gmail more ▾
Sign in
Google
51 + 54 * (3 + 2)
Search
Web
51 + (54 * (3 + 2)) = 321
More about calculator.
Done

FIGURE 25.24 You can evaluate an arithmetic expression from Google.

The algorithm proceeds in two phases:

Phase 1: Scanning expression
The program scans the expression from left to right to extract operands, operators, and the parentheses.

1.1 If the extracted item is an operand, push it to `operandStack`.

1.2 If the extracted item is a `+` or `-` operator, process all the operators at the top of `operatorStack`, push the extracted operator to `operatorStack`.

1.3 If the extracted item is a `*` or `/` operator, process all the operators `*` and `/` at the top of `operatorStack`, push the extracted operator to `operatorStack`.

1.4 If the extracted item is a `(` symbol, push it to `operatorStack`.

1.5 If the extracted item is a `)` symbol, repeatedly process the operators from the top of `operatorStack` until seeing the `(` symbol on the stack.

Phase 2: Clearing stack
Repeatedly process the operators from the top of `operatorStack` until `operatorStack` is empty.

Table 25.2 shows how the algorithm is applied to evaluate the expression `(1 + 2) * 4 - 3`.
Listing 25.11 gives the program. Figure 25.25 gives some sample output.

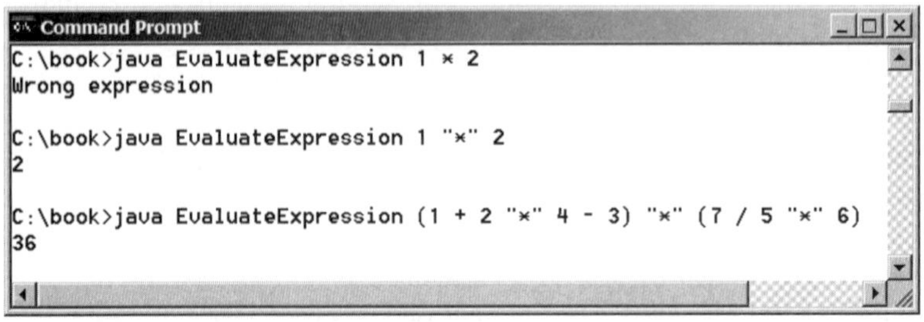
Command Prompt
C:\book>java EvaluateExpression 1 * 2
Wrong expression
C:\book>java EvaluateExpression 1 "*" 2
2
C:\book>java EvaluateExpression (1 + 2 "*" 4 - 3) "*" (7 / 5 "*" 6)
36

FIGURE 25.25 The program takes an expression as command-line arguments.

TABLE 25.2 Evaluating an expression

Expression	*Scan*	*Action*	OperandStack	OperatorStack
(1 + 2) * 4 − 3	(	Phase 1.4		(
(1 + 2) * 4 − 3	1	Phase 1.1	1	(
(1 + 2) * 4 − 3	+	Phase 1.2	1	+ (
(1 + 2) * 4 − 3	2	Phase 1.1	2 1	+ (
(1 + 2) * 4 − 3	)	Phase 1.5	3	
(1 + 2) * 4 − 3	*	Phase 1.3	3	*
(1 + 2) * 4 − 3	4	Phase 1.1	4 3	*
(1 + 2) * 4 − 3	−	Phase 1.2	12	−
(1 + 2) * 4 − 3	3	Phase 1.1	3 12	−
(1 + 2) * 4 − 3	none	Phase 2	9	

LISTING 25.11 EvaluateExpression.java

```
public class EvaluateExpression {
  public static void main(String[] args) {
    // Check number of arguments passed
    if (args.length < 1) {
      System.out.println(
        "Usage: java EvaluateExpression expression");
      System.exit(0);
    }

    String expression = "";
    for (int i = 0; i < args.length; i++)
      expression += args[i];

    try {
      System.out.println(evaluateExpression(expression));
    }
    catch (Exception ex) {
      System.out.println("Wrong expression");
    }
  }

  /** Evaluate an expression */
  public static int evaluateExpression(String expression) {
    // Create operandStack to store operands
```

check usage

concatenate arguments

evaluate expression

exception

operandStack

operatorStack

extract tokens

more tokens?

+ or - scanned

* or / scanned

(scanned

) scanned

an operand scanned

```
    GenericStack<Integer> operandStack
      = new GenericStack<Integer>();

    // Create operatorStack to store operators
    GenericStack<Character> operatorStack
      = new GenericStack<Character>();

    // Extract operands and operators
    java.util.StringTokenizer tokens =
      new java.util.StringTokenizer(expression, "()+-/*", true);

    // Phase 1: Scan tokens
    while (tokens.hasMoreTokens()) {
      String token = tokens.nextToken().trim(); // Extract a token
      if (token.length() == 0) // Blank space
        continue; // Back to the while loop to extract the next token
      else if (token.charAt(0) == '+' || token.charAt(0) == '-') {
        // Process all +, -, *, / in the top of the operator stack
        while (!operatorStack.isEmpty() &&
          (operatorStack.peek() == '+' ||
           operatorStack.peek() == '-' ||
           operatorStack.peek() == '*' ||
           operatorStack.peek() == '/')) {
          processAnOperator(operandStack, operatorStack);
        }

        // Push the + or - operator into the operator stack
        operatorStack.push(token.charAt(0));
      }
      else if (token.charAt(0) == '*' || token.charAt(0) == '/') {
        // Process all *, / in the top of the operator stack
        while (!operatorStack.isEmpty() &&
          (operatorStack.peek() == '*' ||
          operatorStack.peek() == '/')) {
          processAnOperator(operandStack, operatorStack);
        }

        // Push the * or / operator into the operator stack
        operatorStack.push(token.charAt(0));
      }
      else if (token.trim().charAt(0) == '(') {
        operatorStack.push('('); // Push '(' to stack
      }
      else if (token.trim().charAt(0) == ')') {
        // Process all the operators in the stack until seeing '('
        while (operatorStack.peek() != '(') {
          processAnOperator(operandStack, operatorStack);
        }

        operatorStack.pop(); // Pop the '(' symbol from the stack
      }
      else { // An operand scanned
        // Push an operand to the stack
        operandStack.push(new Integer(token));
      }
    }

```

```
82     // Phase 2: process all the remaining operators in the stack
83     while (!operatorStack.isEmpty()) {
84       processAnOperator(operandStack, operatorStack);
85     }
86
87     // Return the result
88     return operandStack.pop();
89   }
90
91   /** Process one operator: Take an operator from operatorStack and
92    *  apply it on the operands in the operandStack */
93   public static void processAnOperator(
94       GenericStack<Integer> operandStack,
95       GenericStack<Character> operatorStack) {
96     char op = operatorStack.pop();
97     int op1 = operandStack.pop();
98     int op2 = operandStack.pop();
99     if (op == '+')
100      operandStack.push(op2 + op1);
101    else if (op == '-')
102      operandStack.push(op2 - op1);
103    else if (op == '*')
104      operandStack.push(op2 * op1);
105    else if (op == '/')
106      operandStack.push(op2 / op1);
107    }
108 }
```

clear **operatorStack**

return result

process +

process -

process *

process /

The program takes an expression as command-line arguments and concatenates all arguments into a string (lines 11–12). The `evaluateExpression` method creates two stacks `operandStack` and `operatorStack` (lines 25, 29) and uses `StringTokenizer` to extract tokens with operators and parentheses as delimiters (lines 33–34). The `StringTokenizer` class is introduced in Supplement III.Z, "The `StringTokenizer` Class." Normally, you use the `split` method in the `String` class to separate and extract tokens, ignoring delimiters from a string, but `StringTokenizer` is useful to extract tokens including delimiters.

The program scans each token in the `while` loop (lines 37–80). If a token is empty, skip it (line 39). If a token is an operand, push it to `operandStack` (line 78). If a token is a `+` or `-` operator (line 41), process all the operators from the top of `operatorStack` if any (lines 43–49) and push the newly scanned operator to the stack (line 52). If a token is a `*` or `/` operator (line 54), process all the `*` and `/` operators from the top of `operatorStack` if any (lines 56–60) and push the newly scanned operator to the stack (line 63). If a token is a `(` symbol (line 65), push it to `operatorStack`. If a token is a `)` symbol (line 68), process all the operators from the top of `operatorStack` until seeing the `)` symbol (lines 70–72) and pop the `)` symbol from the stack.

After all tokens are considered, the program processes the remaining operators in `operatorStack` (lines 83–85).

The `processAnOperator` method (lines 93–107) processes an operator. The method pops the operator from `operatorStack` (line 96) and pops two operands from `operandStack` (lines 97–98). Depending on the operator, the method performs an operation and pushes the result of the operation back to `operandStack` (lines 100, 102, 104, 106).

special * character

Recall that the `*` character has special meaning when passed as a command-line argument (see the Note after Listing 9.5 Calculator.java). You have to use `"*"` to replace `*`, as shown in Figure 25.25.

Chapter Summary

1. You learned how to implement lists, stacks, and queues.
2. To define a data structure is essentially to define a class. The class for a data structure should use data fields to store data and provide methods to support such operations as insertion and deletion.
3. To create a data structure is to create an instance from the class. You can then apply the methods on the instance to manipulate the data structure, such as inserting an element into the data structure or deleting an element from the data structure.
4. You learned how to implement a priority queue using a heap.
5. Stacks can be applied to evaluate expressions.

Review Questions

Sections 25.1–25.2

25.1 What is a data structure? What is an object-oriented data structure?

25.2 What are the limitations of the array data type?

25.3 `MyArrayList` is implemented using an array, and an array is a fixed-size data structure. Why is `MyArrayList` considered a dynamic data structure?

25.4 What are the benefits of defining both the `MyList` interface and the `MyAbstractList` class? What is a convenience class?

25.5 What is wrong in the following code?

```
MyArrayList<String> list = new MyArrayList<String>();
list.add(100);
```

25.6 What is wrong if lines 11–12 in MyArrayList.java

```
for (int i = 0; i < objects.length; i++)
  add(objects[i]);
```

are replaced by

```
super(objects);
```

or

```
data = objects;
size = objects.length;
```

25.7 If you change the code in line 33 in Listing 25.3 MyArrayList.java from

```
E[] newData = (E[])(new Object[size * 2] + 1);
```

to

```
E[] newData = (E[])(new Object[size * 2]);
```

The program is incorrect. Can you find the reason?

25.8 If the number of elements in the program is fixed, what data structure should you use? If the number of elements in the program changes, what data structure should you use?

25.9 If you have to add or delete the elements anywhere in a list, should you use `ArrayList` or `LinkedList`?

Section 25.3

25.10 You can use inheritance or composition to design the data structures for stacks and queues. Discuss the pros and cons of these two approaches.

25.11 Which lines of the following code are wrong?

```
MyList list = new MyArrayList();
list.add("Tom");
list = new MyLinkedList();
list.add("Tom");
list = new GenericStack();
list.add("Tom");
```

Section 25.7

25.12 What is a priority queue?

Programming Exercises

Section 25.2

25.1 (*Adding set operations in `MyList`*) Add and implement the following methods in `MyList` and implement them in `MyAbstractList`:

```
/** Adds the elements in otherList to this list.
  * Returns true if this list changed as a result of the call */
public boolean addAll(MyList<E> otherList)

/** Removes all the elements in otherList from this list
  * Returns true if this list changed as a result of the call */
public boolean removeAll(MyList<E> otherList)

/** Retains the elements in this list that are also in otherList
  * Returns true if this list changed as a result of the call */
public boolean retainAll(MyList<E> otherList)
```

Write a test program that creates two `MyArrayList`s, `list1` and `list2`, with the initial values `{"Tom", "George", "Peter", "Jean", "Jane"}` and `{"Tom", "George", "Michael", "Michelle", "Daniel"}`, then invokes `list1.addAll(list2)`, `list1.removeAll(list2)`, and `list1.retainAll(list2)` and displays the resulting new `list1`.

25.2* (*Completing the implementation of `MyLinkedList`*) The implementations of methods `clear()`, `contains(Object o)`, `get(int index)`, `indexOf(Object o)`, `lastIndexOf(Object o)`, and `set(int index, Object o)` are omitted in the text. Implement these methods.

25.3* (*Creating a two-way linked list*) The `MyLinkedList` class used in Listing 25.6 is a one-way directional linked list that enables one-way traversal of the list. Modify the `Node` class to add the new field name `previous` to refer to the previous node in the list, as follows:

```
public class Node {
  Object element;
  Node next;
  Node previous;
```

```
    public Node(Object o) {
      element = o;
    }
  }
```

Simplify the implementation of the `add(Object element, int index)` and `remove(int index)` methods to take advantage of the bidirectional linked list.

Section 25.6

25.4 (*Using the* `Stack` *class*) Write a program that displays the first 50 prime numbers in descending order. Use a stack to store prime numbers.

25.5 (*Implementing* `GenericQueue` *using inheritance*) In §25.6, "Stacks and Queues," `GenericQueue` is implemented using composition. Define a new queue class that extends `MyLinkedList`.

25.6* (*Matching grouping symbols*) A Java program contains various pairs of grouping symbols, such as:

- Parentheses: `(` and `)`.
- Braces: `{` and `}`.
- Brackets: `[` and `]`.

Note that the grouping symbols cannot overlap. For example, `(a{b)}` is illegal. Write a program to check whether a Java source-code file has correct pairs of grouping symbols. Pass the source-code file name as a command-line argument.

25.7** (*Game: the 24-point card game*) The 24-point game is to pick any four cards from 52 cards, as shown in Figure 25.26. Note that two Jokers are excluded. Each card represents a number. An Ace, King, Queen, and Jack represent `1`, `13`, `12`, and `11`, respectively. Enter an expression that uses the four numbers from the four selected cards. Each number must be used once and only once. You can use the operators (addition, subtraction, multiplication, and division) and parentheses in the expression. The expression must evaluate to `24`. After entering the expression, click the *Verify* button to check whether the numbers in the expression are currently selected and whether the result of the expression is correct. Display the verification in a dialog box. Note that such an expression might not exist. In this case, click the *Refresh* button to get another set of four cards. Assume that images are stored in files named **1.png**, **2.png**, . . . , **52.png**, in the order of spades, hearts, diamonds, and clubs. So, the first 13 images are for spades 1, 2, 3, . . . , and 13.

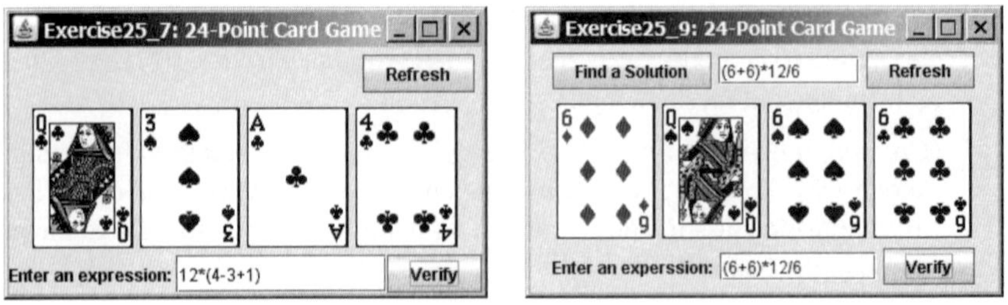
Exercise25_7: 24-Point Card Game
Refresh
Enter an expression: 12*(4-3+1)
Verify
Exercise25_9: 24-Point Card Game
Find a Solution
(6+6)*12/6
Refresh
Enter an experssion: (6+6)*12/6
Verify

(a) (b)

FIGURE 25.26 (a) The user enters an expression consisting of the numbers in the cards. (b) The program can automatically find a solution if one exists.

25.8** (*Postfix notation*) Postfix notation is a way of writing expressions without using parentheses. For example, the expression `(1 + 2) * 3` would be written as `1 2 + 3 *`. A postfix expression is evaluated using a stack. Scan a postfix expression from left to right. A variable or constant is pushed to the stack. When an operator is encountered, apply the operator with the top two operands in the stack and replace the two operands with the result. The following diagram shows how to evaluate `1 2 + 3 *`.

Write a program to evaluate postfix expressions. Pass the expression as command-line arguments.

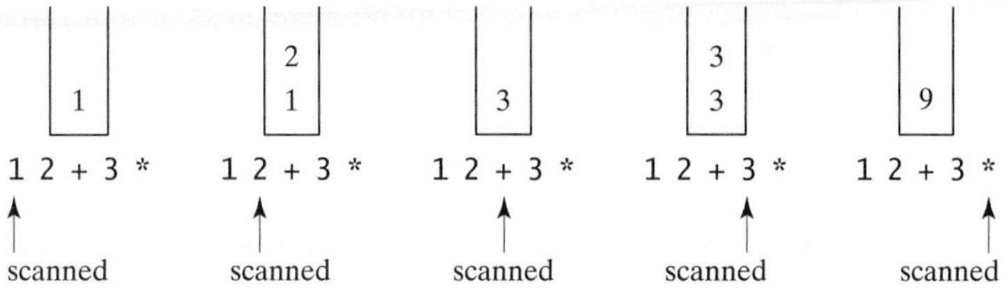

1
2
1
3
3
3
9
1 2 + 3 *
1 2 + 3 *
1 2 + 3 *
1 2 + 3 *
1 2 + 3 *
scanned
scanned
scanned
scanned
scanned

25.9*** (*Game: the 24-point card game*) Improve Exercise 25.7 to enable the computer to display the expression if one exists, as shown in Figure 25.26(b). Otherwise, report that the expression does not exist.

25.10** (*Converting infix to postfix*) Write a method that converts an infix expression into a postfix expression using the following header:

```
public static String infixToPostfix(String expression)
```

For example, the method should convert the infix expression `(1 + 2) * 3` to `1 2 + 3 *` and `2 * (1 + 3)` to `2 1 3 + *`.

25.11*** (*Game: the 24-point card game*) This exercise is a variation of the 24-point card game described in Exercise 25.7. Write an applet to check whether there is a 24-point solution for the four specified numbers. The applet lets the user enter four values, each between `1` and `13`, as shown in Figure 25.27. The user can then click the *Solve* button to display the solution or display no solutions if none exist.

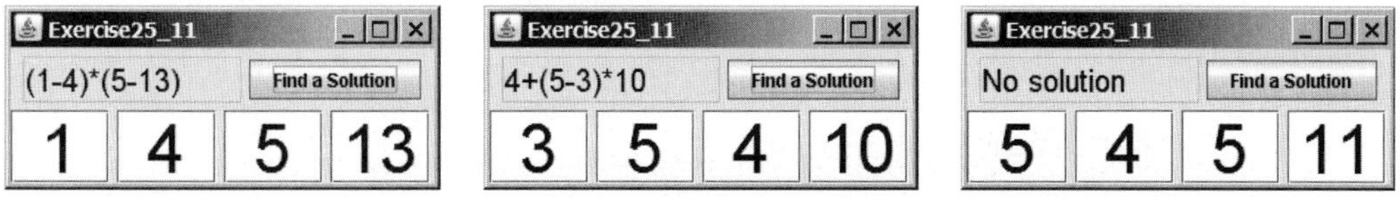

Exercise25_11
(1-4)*(5-13)
Find a Solution
1
4
5
13
Exercise25_11
4+(5-3)*10
Find a Solution
3
5
4
10
Exercise25_11
No solution
Find a Solution
5
4
5
11

FIGURE 25.27 The user enters four numbers and the program finds a solution.

25.12** (*Implementing `MyArrayList`*) Implement `MyArrayList` by extending `java.util.AbstractList`. Please study the Java API to learn the details of `java.util.AbstractList`.

25.13** (*Implementing `MyLinkedList`*) Implement `MyLinkedList` by extending `java.util.AbstractSequentialList`. Please study the Java API to learn the details of `java.util.AbstractSequentialList`.

25.14* (*Generic* `PriorityQueue` using `Comparator`) Revise `MyPriorityQueue` in Listing 25.9, using a generic parameter for comparing objects. Define a new constructor with a `Comparator` as its argument as follows:

```
PriorityQueue(Comparator<? super E> comparator)
```

25.15*** (*Game: solution ratio for 24-point game*) When you pick four cards from a deck of 52 cards for the 24-point game introduced in Exercise 25.7, the four cards may not have a 24-point solution. What is the number of all possible picks of four cards from 52 cards? Among all possible picks, how many of them have 24-point solutions? What is the success ratio [i.e., (number of picks with solutions)/(number of all possible picks of four cards)]? Write a program to find these answers.

25.16* (*Animation: array list*) Write an applet to animate search, insertion, and deletion in an array list, as shown in Figure 25.1(a). The *Search* button searches whether the specified value is in the list. The *Delete* button deletes the specified value from the list. The *Insert* button inserts the value into the specified index in the list.

25.17** (*Animation: linked list*) Write an applet to animate search, insertion, and deletion in a linked list, as shown in Figure 25.1(b). The *Search* button searches whether the specified value is in the list. The *Delete* button deletes the specified value from the list. The *Insert* button inserts the value into the specified index in the list.

25.18* (*Animation: stack*) Write an applet to animate push and pop of a stack, as shown in Figure 25.20(a).

25.19* (*Animation: queue*) Write an applet to animate the enqueue and dequeue operations on a queue, as shown in Figure 25.20(b).

CHAPTER 26

BINARY SEARCH TREES

Objectives

- To design and implement a binary search tree (§26.2).
- To represent binary trees using linked data structures (§26.2.1).
- To search an element in a binary search tree (§26.2.2).
- To insert an element into a binary search tree (§26.2.3).
- To traverse elements in a binary tree (§26.2.4).
- To delete elements from a binary search tree (§26.3).
- To display a binary tree graphically (§26.4).
- To create iterators for traversing a binary tree (§26.5).
- To implement Huffman coding for compressing data using a binary tree (§26.6).

26.1 Introduction

A tree is a classic data structure with many important applications. A tree provides a hierarchical organization in which data are stored in the nodes. This chapter introduces binary search trees. You have used iterators in the Java collections framework. This chapter will also demonstrate how to implement iterators for traversing elements in a binary tree.

26.2 Binary Search Trees

root
left subtree
right subtree

Recall that a list, stack, or queue is a linear structure that consists of a sequence of elements. A binary tree is a hierarchical structure. It either is empty or consists of an element, called the *root*, and two distinct binary trees, called the *left subtree* and *right subtree*, either or both of which may be empty. Examples of binary trees are shown in Figure 26.1.

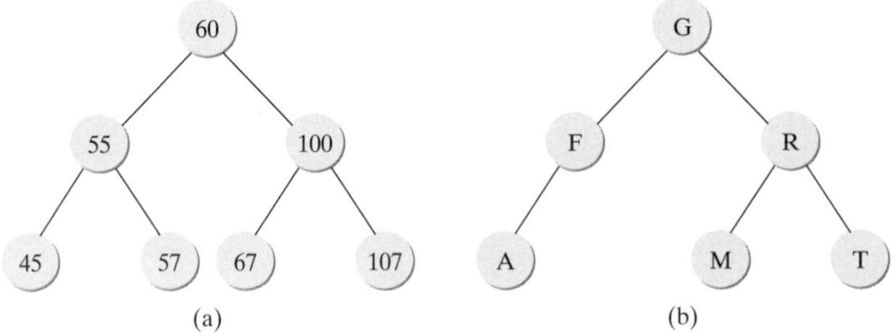
60
55
100
45
57
67
107
(a)
G
F
R
A
M
T
(b)

FIGURE 26.1 Each node in a binary tree has zero, one, or two subtrees.

length
depth
level
sibling
leaf
height

The *length* of a path is the number of the edges in the path. The *depth* of a node is the length of the path from the root to the node. The set of all nodes at a given depth is sometimes called a *level* of the tree. *Siblings* are nodes that share the same parent node. The root of a left (right) subtree of a node is called a *left (right) child* of the node. A node without children is called a *leaf*. The *height* of an empty tree is 0. The height of a nonempty tree is the length of the path from the root node to its furthest leaf + 1. Consider the tree in Figure 26.1(a). The length of the path from node 60 to 45 is 2. The depth of node 60 is 0, the depth of node 55 is 1, and the depth of node 45 is 2. The height of the tree is 3. Nodes 45 and 57 are siblings. Nodes 45, 57, 67, and 107 are in the same level.

binary search tree

A special type of binary tree called a *binary search tree* (BST) is often useful. A BST (with no duplicate elements) has the property that for every node in the tree, the value of any node in its left subtree is less than the value of the node, and the value of any node in its right subtree is greater than the value of the node. The binary trees in Figure 26.1 are all BSTs. This section is concerned with BSTs.

BST animation

Pedagogical Note

Follow the link www.cs.armstrong.edu/liang/animation/BSTAnimation.html to see how a BST works, as shown in Figure 26.2.

26.2.1 Representing Binary Search Trees

A binary tree can be represented using a set of linked nodes. Each node contains a value and two links named *left* and *right* that reference the left child and right child, respectively, as shown in Figure 26.3.

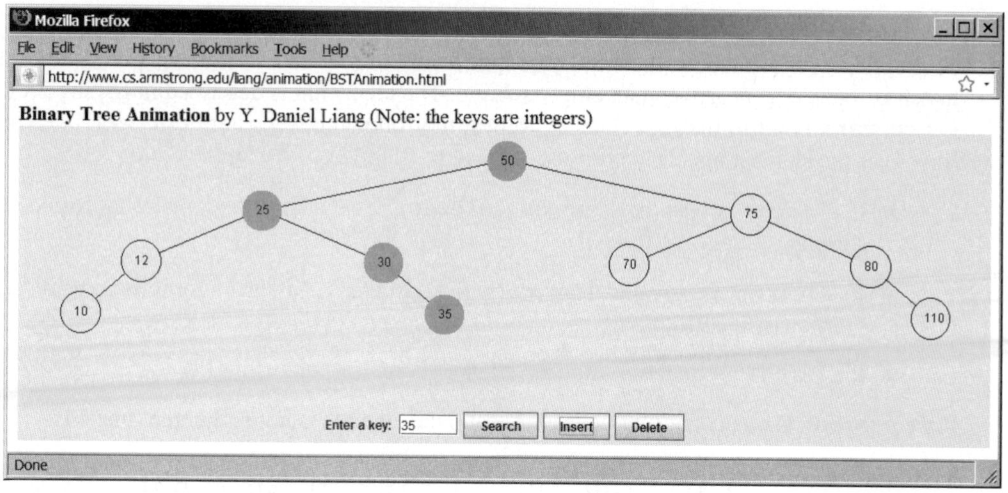
Mozilla Firefox
File Edit View History Bookmarks Tools Help
http://www.cs.armstrong.edu/liang/animation/BSTAnimation.html
Binary Tree Animation by Y. Daniel Liang (Note: the keys are integers)
50
25
75
12
30
70
80
10
35
110
Enter a key: 35
Search
Insert
Delete
Done

FIGURE 26.2 The animation tool enables you to insert, delete, and search elements visually.

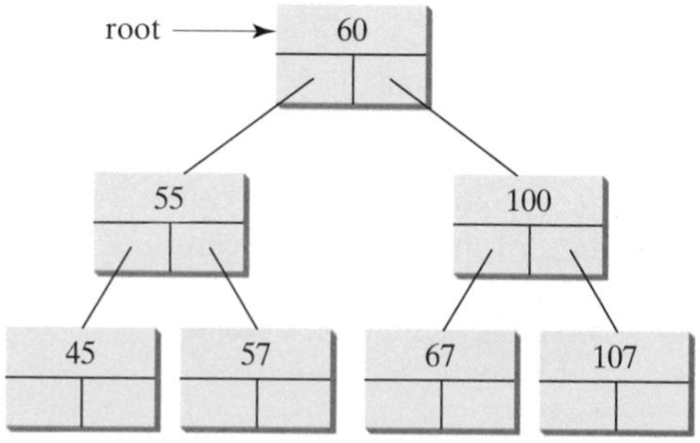
root
60
55
100
45
57
67
107

FIGURE 26.3 A binary tree can be represented using a set of linked nodes.

A node can be defined as a class, as follows:

```
class TreeNode<E> {
  E element;
  TreeNode<E> left;
  TreeNode<E> right;

  public TreeNode(E e) {
    element = e;
  }
}
```

The variable `root` refers to the root node of the tree. If the tree is empty, `root` is `null`. The following code creates the first three nodes of the tree in Figure 26.3.

```
// Create the root node
TreeNode<Integer> root = new TreeNode<Integer>(new Integer(60));

// Create the left child node
root.left = new TreeNode<Integer>(new Integer(55));

// Create the right child node
root.right = new TreeNode<Integer>(new Integer(100));
```

26.2.2 Searching for an Element

To search for an element in the BST, you start from the root and scan down from it until a match is found or you arrive at an empty subtree. The algorithm is described in Listing 26.1. Let `current` point to the root (line 2). Repeat the following steps until `current` is `null` (line 4) or the element matches `current.element` (line 12).

- If `element` is less than `current.element`, assign `current.left` to `current` (line 6).
- If `element` is greater than `current.element`, assign `current.right` to `current` (line 9).
- If `element` is equal to `current.element`, return `true` (line 12).

If the `current` is `null`, the subtree is empty and the element is not in the tree (line 14).

LISTING 26.1 Searching for an Element in a BST

start from root
left subtree
right subtree
found
not found

```
 1 public boolean search(E element) {
 2   TreeNode<E> current = root; // Start from the root
 3
 4   while (current != null)
 5     if (element < current.element) {
 6       current = current.left; // Go left
 7     }
 8     else if (element > current.element) {
 9       current = current.right; // Go right
10     }
11     else // Element matches current.element
12       return true; // Element is found
13
14   return false; // Element is not in the tree
15 }
```

26.2.3 Inserting an Element into a BST

To insert an element into a BST, you need to locate where to insert it in the tree. The key idea is to locate the parent for the new node. Listing 26.2 gives the algorithm.

LISTING 26.2 Inserting an Element into a BST

create a new node
locate parent
left child
right child

```
boolean insert(E e) {
  if (tree is empty)
    // Create the node for e as the root;
  else {
    // Locate the parent node
    parent = current = root;
    while (current != null)
      if (e < the value in current.element) {
        parent = current;  // Keep the parent
        current = current.left; // Go left
      }
      else if (e > the value in current.element) {
        parent = current; // Keep the parent
        current = current.right; // Go right
      }
      else
        return false; // Duplicate node not inserted

```

```
19       // Create a new node for e and attach it to parent
20
21       return true; // Element inserted
22     }
23 }
```

If the tree is empty, create a root node with the new element (lines 2–3). Otherwise, locate the parent node for the new element node (lines 6–17). Create a new node for the element and link this node to its parent node. If the new element is less than the parent element, the node for the new element will be the left child of the parent. If the new element is greater than the parent element, the node for the new element will be the right child of the parent.

For example, to insert **101** into the tree in Figure 26.3, after the **while** loop finishes in the algorithm, **parent** points to the node for **107**, as shown in Figure 26.4(a). The new node for **101** becomes the left child of the parent. To insert **59** into the tree, after the **while** finishes in the algorithm, the parent points to the node for **57**, as shown in Figure 26.4(b). The new node for **59** becomes the right child of the parent.

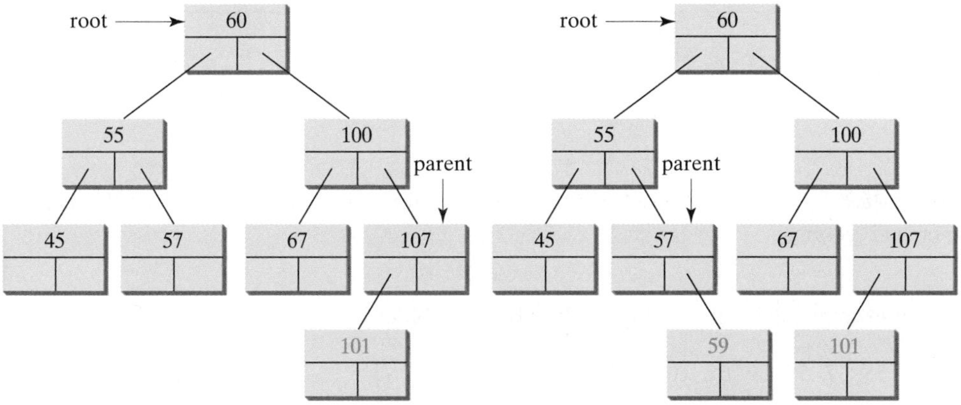
root
60
55
100
parent
45
57
67
107
101
root
60
55
parent
100
45
57
67
107
59
101

(a) Inserting 101 (b) Inserting 59

FIGURE 26.4 Two new elements are inserted into the tree.

26.2.4 Tree Traversal

Tree traversal is the process of visiting each node in the tree exactly once. There are several ways to traverse a tree. This section presents *inorder, preorder, postorder, depth-first, and breadth-first* traversals.

inorder

With inorder traversal, the left subtree of the current node is visited recursively first, then the current node, and finally the right subtree of the current node recursively. The inorder traversal displays all the nodes in a BST in increasing order.

postorder

With postorder traversal, the left subtree of the current node is visited recursively first, then the recursively right subtree of the current node, and finally the current node itself. An application of postorder is to find the size of the directory in a file system. As shown in Figure 26.5, each directory is an internal node and a file is a leaf node. You can apply postorder to get the size of each file and subdirectory before finding the size of the root directory.

preorder
depth-first

With preorder traversal, the current node is visited first, then recursively the left subtree of the current node, and finally recursively the right subtree of the current node. Depth-first traversal is the same as preorder traversal. An application of preorder is to print a structure document. As shown in Figure 26.6, you can print the table of contents in a book using the preorder.

breadth-first

With breadth-first traversal, the nodes are visited level by level. First the root is visited, then all the children of the root from left to right, then the grandchildren of the root from left to right, and so on.

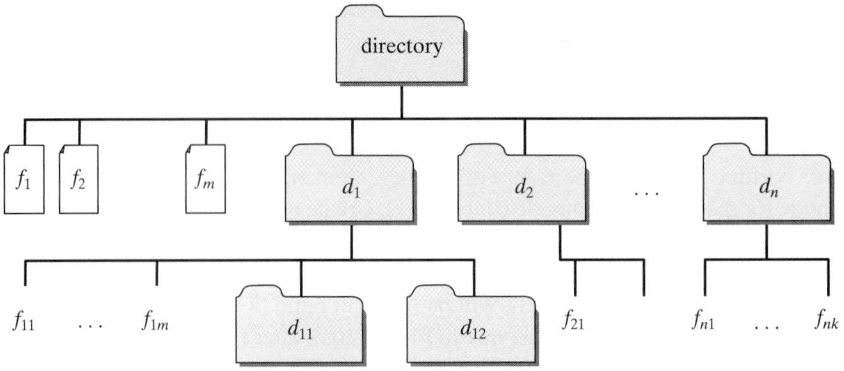
directory
f_1
f_2
f_m
d_1
d_2
...
d_n
f_{11} ... f_{1m}
d_{11}
d_{12}
f_{21}
f_{n1} ... f_{nk}

FIGURE 26.5 A directory contains files and subdirectories.

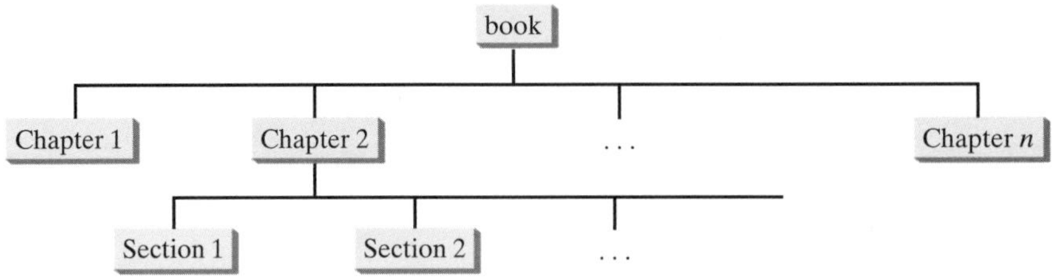
book
Chapter 1
Chapter 2
...
Chapter *n*
Section 1
Section 2
...

FIGURE 26.6 A tree can be used to represent a structured document such as a book, chapters, and sections.

For example, in the tree in Figure 26.4(b), the inorder is

```
45 55 57 59 60 67 100 101 107
```

The postorder is

```
45 59 57 55 67 101 107 100 60
```

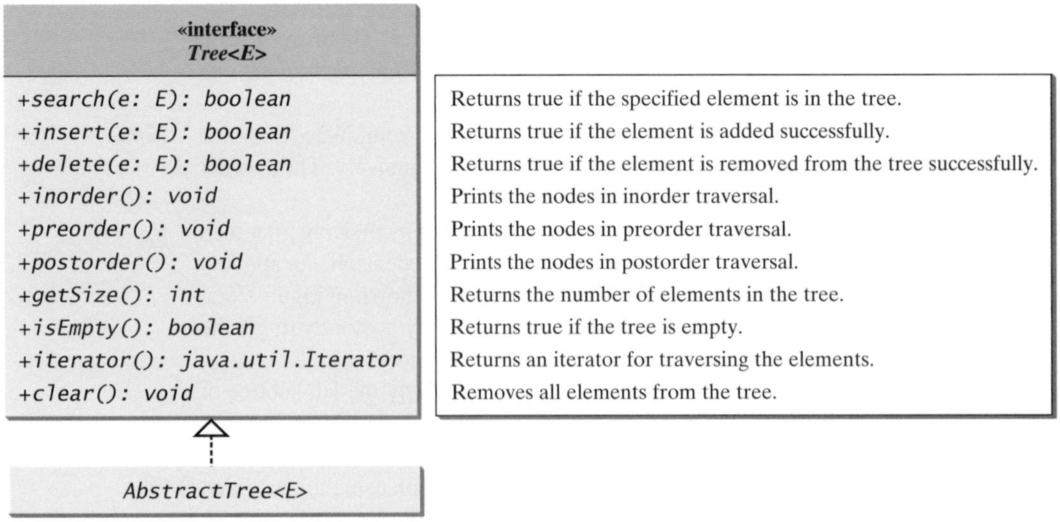
«interface»
Tree<E>
+search(e: E): boolean
+insert(e: E): boolean
+delete(e: E): boolean
+inorder(): void
+preorder(): void
+postorder(): void
+getSize(): int
+isEmpty(): boolean
+iterator(): java.util.Iterator
+clear(): void
Returns true if the specified element is in the tree.
Returns true if the element is added successfully.
Returns true if the element is removed from the tree successfully.
Prints the nodes in inorder traversal.
Prints the nodes in preorder traversal.
Prints the nodes in postorder traversal.
Returns the number of elements in the tree.
Returns true if the tree is empty.
Returns an iterator for traversing the elements.
Removes all elements from the tree.
AbstractTree<E>

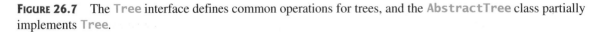

FIGURE 26.7 The `Tree` interface defines common operations for trees, and the `AbstractTree` class partially implements `Tree`.

The preorder is

```
60 55 45 57 59 100 67 107 101
```

The breadth-first traversal is

```
60 55 100 45 57 67 107 59 101
```

26.2.5 The BinaryTree Class

Following the design pattern for the Java collections framework API, we use an interface named `Tree` to define all common operations for trees and provide an abstract class named `AbstractTree` that partially implements `Tree`, as shown in Figure 26.7. A concrete `BinaryTree` class can be defined to extend `AbstractTree`, as shown in Figure 26.8.

Listings 26.3, 26.4, and 26.5 give the implementation for `Tree`, `AbstractTree`, and `BinaryTree`.

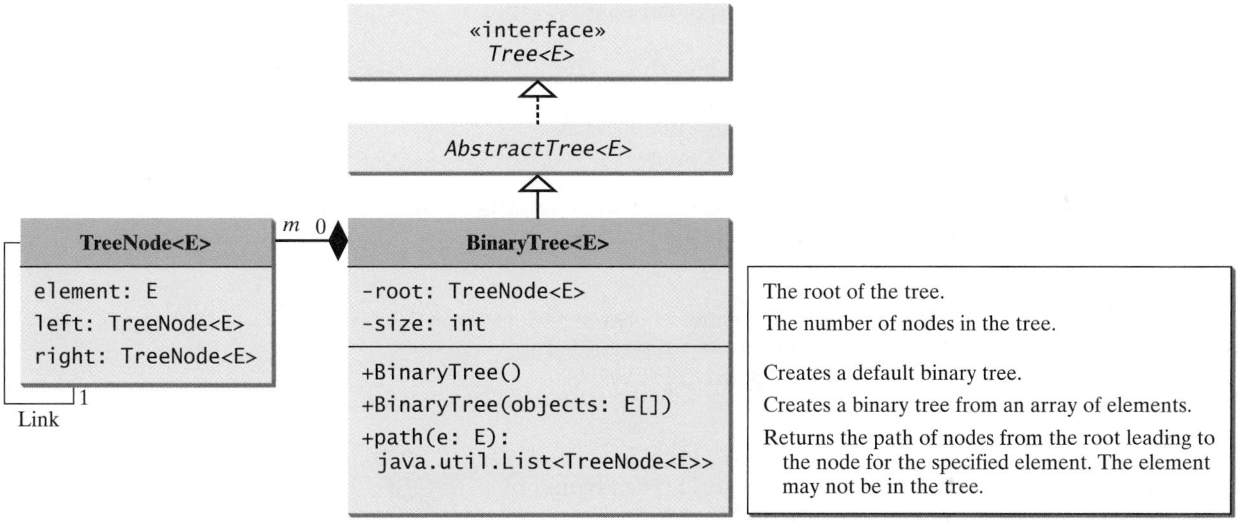
«interface»
Tree<E>
AbstractTree<E>
TreeNode<E>
element: E
left: TreeNode<E>
right: TreeNode<E>
Link
1
m
0
BinaryTree<E>
-root: TreeNode<E>
-size: int
+BinaryTree()
+BinaryTree(objects: E[])
+path(e: E): java.util.List<TreeNode<E>>
The root of the tree.
The number of nodes in the tree.
Creates a default binary tree.
Creates a binary tree from an array of elements.
Returns the path of nodes from the root leading to the node for the specified element. The element may not be in the tree.

FIGURE 26.8 The `BinaryTree` class defines a concrete BST.

LISTING 26.3 Tree.java

```
public interface Tree<E extends Comparable<E>> {
  /** Return true if the element is in the tree */
  public boolean search(E e);

  /** Insert element e into the binary search tree
   * Return true if the element is inserted successfully */
  public boolean insert(E e);

  /** Delete the specified element from the tree
   * Return true if the element is deleted successfully */
  public boolean delete(E e);

  /** Inorder traversal from the root*/
  public void inorder();

  /** Postorder traversal from the root */
  public void postorder();
```

interface · **search** · **insert** · **delete** · **inorder** · **postorder**

```java

  /** Preorder traversal from the root */
  public void preorder();

  /** Get the number of nodes in the tree */
  public int getSize();

  /** Return true if the tree is empty */
  public boolean isEmpty();

  /** Return an iterator to traverse elements in the tree */
  public java.util.Iterator iterator();
}
```

preorder
getSize
isEmpty
iterator

LISTING 26.4 AbstractTree.java

```java
public abstract class AbstractTree<E extends Comparable<E>>
    implements Tree<E> {
  /** Inorder traversal from the root*/
  public void inorder() {
  }

  /** Postorder traversal from the root */
  public void postorder() {
  }

  /** Preorder traversal from the root */
  public void preorder() {
  }

  /** Return true if the tree is empty */
  public boolean isEmpty() {
    return getSize() == 0;
  }

  /** Return an iterator to traverse elements in the tree */
  public java.util.Iterator iterator() {
    return null;
  }
}
```

abstract class
default **inorder** implementation
default **postorder** implementation
default **preorder** implementation
isEmpty implementation
default **iterator** implementation

LISTING 26.5 BinaryTree.java

```java
public class BinaryTree<E extends Comparable<E>>
    extends AbstractTree<E> {
  protected TreeNode<E> root;
  protected int size = 0;

  /** Create a default binary search tree */
  public BinaryTree() {
  }

  /** Create a binary search tree from an array of objects */
  public BinaryTree(E[] objects) {
    for (int i = 0; i < objects.length; i++)
      insert(objects[i]);
  }

  /** Return true if the element is in the tree */
  public boolean search(E e) {
```

BinaryTree class
root
size
no-arg constructor
constructor
search

```java
    TreeNode<E> current = root; // Start from the root

    while (current != null) {
      if (e.compareTo(current.element) < 0) {
        current = current.left;
      }
      else if (e.compareTo(current.element) > 0) {
        current = current.right;
      }
      else // element matches current.element
        return true; // Element is found
    }

    return false;
  }

  /** Insert element e into the binary search tree
   * Return true if the element is inserted successfully */
  public boolean insert(E e) {
    if (root == null)
      root = createNewNode(e); // Create a new root
    else {
      // Locate the parent node
      TreeNode<E> parent = null;
      TreeNode<E> current = root;
      while (current != null)
        if (e.compareTo(current.element) < 0) {
          parent = current;
          current = current.left;
        }
        else if (e.compareTo(current.element) > 0) {
          parent = current;
          current = current.right;
        }
        else
          return false; // Duplicate node not inserted

      // Create the new node and attach it to the parent node
      if (e.compareTo(parent.element) < 0)
        parent.left = createNewNode(e);
      else
        parent.right = createNewNode(e);
    }

    size++;
    return true; // Element inserted
  }

  protected TreeNode<E> createNewNode(E e) {
    return new TreeNode<E>(e);
  }

  /** Inorder traversal from the root*/
  public void inorder() {
    inorder(root);
  }

  /** Inorder traversal from a subtree */
  protected void inorder(TreeNode<E> root) {
    if (root == null) return;
```

compare objects

insert

new root

compare objects

link to parent

increase size

create new node

inorder

recursive helper method

```
    inorder(root.left);
    System.out.print(root.element + " ");
    inorder(root.right);
  }

  /** Postorder traversal from the root */
  public void postorder() {
    postorder(root);
  }

  /** Postorder traversal from a subtree */
  protected void postorder(TreeNode<E> root) {
    if (root == null) return;
    postorder(root.left);
    postorder(root.right);
    System.out.print(root.element + " ");
  }

  /** Preorder traversal from the root */
  public void preorder() {
    preorder(root);
  }

  /** Preorder traversal from a subtree */
  protected void preorder(TreeNode<E> root) {
    if (root == null) return;
    System.out.print(root.element + " ");
    preorder(root.left);
    preorder(root.right);
  }

  /** Inner class tree node */
  public static class TreeNode<E extends Comparable<E>> {
    E element;
    TreeNode<E> left;
    TreeNode<E> right;

    public TreeNode(E e) {
      element = e;
    }
  }

  /** Get the number of nodes in the tree */
  public int getSize() {
    return size;
  }

  /** Returns the root of the tree */
  public TreeNode getRoot() {
    return root;
  }

  /** Returns a path from the root leading to the specified element */
  public java.util.ArrayList<TreeNode<E>> path(E e) {
    java.util.ArrayList<TreeNode<E>> list =
      new java.util.ArrayList<TreeNode<E>>();
    TreeNode<E> current = root; // Start from the root

    while (current != null) {
      list.add(current); // Add the node to the list
```

postorder (line 84); recursive helper method (line 89); preorder (line 97); recursive helper method (line 102); inner class (line 110); **getSize** (line 121); **getRoot** (line 126); **path** (line 131)

```
      if (e.compareTo(current.element) < 0) {
        current = current.left;
      }
      else if (e.compareTo(current.element) > 0) {
        current = current.right;
      }
      else
        break;
    }

    return list; // Return an array of nodes
  }

  /** Delete an element from the binary search tree.
   * Return true if the element is deleted successfully
   * Return false if the element is not in the tree */
  public boolean delete(E e) {
    // Locate the node to be deleted and also locate its parent node
    TreeNode<E> parent = null;
    TreeNode<E> current = root;
    while (current != null) {
      if (e.compareTo(current.element) < 0) {
        parent = current;
        current = current.left;
      }
      else if (e.compareTo(current.element) > 0) {
        parent = current;
        current = current.right;
      }
      else
        break; // Element is in the tree pointed by current
    }

    if (current == null)
      return false; // Element is not in the tree

    // Case 1: current has no left children
    if (current.left == null) {
      // Connect the parent with the right child of the current node
      if (parent == null) {
        root = current.right;
      }
      else {
        if (e.compareTo(parent.element) < 0)
          parent.left = current.right;
        else
          parent.right = current.right;
      }
    }
    else {
      // Case 2: The current node has a left child
      // Locate the rightmost node in the left subtree of
      // the current node and also its parent
      TreeNode<E> parentOfRightMost = current;
      TreeNode<E> rightMost = current.left;

      while (rightMost.right != null) {
        parentOfRightMost = rightMost;
        rightMost = rightMost.right; // Keep going to the right
      }
```

delete

locate **parent**

locate **current**

current found

not found

Case 1

reconnect parent

reconnect parent

Case 2

locate **parentOfRightMost**

locate **rightMost**

replace current
reconnect **parentOfRightMost**
reduce size
successful deletion
default iterator
inorder iterator
inner class
internal list
current position
obtain inorder list
hasNext in iterator?
get next element

```

      // Replace the element in current by the element in rightMost
      current.element = rightMost.element;

      // Eliminate rightmost node
      if (parentOfRightMost.right == rightMost)
        parentOfRightMost.right = rightMost.left;
      else
        // Special case: parentOfRightMost == current
        parentOfRightMost.left = rightMost.left;
    }

    size--;
    return true; // Element inserted
  }

  /** Obtain an iterator. Use inorder. */
  public java.util.Iterator iterator() {
    return inorderIterator();
  }

  /** Obtain an inorder iterator */
  public java.util.Iterator inorderIterator() {
    return new InorderIterator();
  }

  // Inner class InorderIterator
  class InorderIterator implements java.util.Iterator {
    // Store the elements in a list
    private java.util.ArrayList<E> list =
      new java.util.ArrayList<E>();
    private int current = 0; // Point to the current element in list

    public InorderIterator() {
      inorder(); // Traverse binary tree and store elements in list
    }

    /** Inorder traversal from the root*/
    private void inorder() {
      inorder(root);
    }

    /** Inorder traversal from a subtree */
    private void inorder(TreeNode<E> root) {
      if (root == null)return;
      inorder(root.left);
      list.add(root.element);
      inorder(root.right);
    }

    /** Next element for traversing? */
    public boolean hasNext() {
      if (current < list.size())
        return true;

      return false;
    }

    /** Get the current element and move cursor to the next */
    public Object next() {
```

```
258        return list.get(current++);
259      }
260
261      /** Remove the current element and refresh the list */
262      public void remove() {
263        delete(list.get(current)); // Delete the current element
264        list.clear(); // Clear the list
265        inorder(); // Rebuild the list
266      }
267    }
268
269    /** Remove all elements from the tree */
270    public void clear() {
271      root = null;
272      size = 0;
273    }
274  }
```

remove the current

refresh list

The `insert(E e)` method (lines 36–64) creates a node for element `e` and inserts it into the tree. If the tree is empty, the node becomes the root. Otherwise, the method finds an appropriate parent for the node to maintain the order of the tree. If the element is already in the tree, the method returns `false`; otherwise it returns `true`.

The `inorder()` method (lines 71–81) invokes `inorder(root)` to traverse the entire tree. The method `inorder(TreeNode root)` traverses the tree with the specified root. This is a recursive method. It recursively traverses the left subtree, then the root, and finally the right subtree. The traversal ends when the tree is empty.

The `postorder()` method (lines 84–94) and the `preorder()` method (lines 97–107) are implemented similarly using recursion.

The `path(E e)` method (lines 131–149) returns a path of the nodes as an array list. The path starts from the root leading to the element. The element may not be in the tree. For example, in Figure 26.4(a), `path(45)` contains the nodes for elements `60`, `55`, and `45`, and `path(58)` contains the nodes for elements `60`, `55`, and `57`.

The implementation of `delete()` and `iterator()` (lines 151–267) will be discussed in §§26.3 and 26.4.

Listing 26.6 gives an example that creates a binary search tree using `BinaryTree` (line 4). The program adds strings into the tree (lines 5–11), traverses the tree in inorder, postorder, and preorder (lines 14–20), searches an element (line 24), and obtains a path from the node containing `Peter` to the root (lines 28–31).

LISTING 26.6 TestBinaryTree.java

```
 1 public class TestBinaryTree {
 2   public static void main(String[] args) {
 3     // Create a BinaryTree
 4     BinaryTree<String> tree = new BinaryTree<String>();
 5     tree.insert("George");
 6     tree.insert("Michael");
 7     tree.insert("Tom");
 8     tree.insert("Adam");
 9     tree.insert("Jones");
10     tree.insert("Peter");
11     tree.insert("Daniel");
12
13     // Traverse tree
14     System.out.print("Inorder (sorted): ");
15     tree.inorder();
16     System.out.print("\nPostorder: ");
```

create tree

`insert`

inorder

postorder

preorder

getSize

search

```
17      tree.postorder();
18      System.out.print("\nPreorder: ");
19      tree.preorder();
20      System.out.print("\nThe number of nodes is " + tree.getSize());
21
22      // Search for an element
23      System.out.print("\nIs Peter in the tree? " +
24        tree.search("Peter"));
25
26      // Get a path from the root to Peter
27      System.out.print("\nA path from the root to Peter is: ");
28      java.util.ArrayList<BinaryTree.TreeNode<String>>  path
29        = tree.path("Peter");
30      for (int i = 0; path != null && i < path.size(); i++)
31        System.out.print(path.get(i).element + " ");
32
33      Integer[] numbers = {2, 4, 3, 1, 8, 5, 6, 7};
34      BinaryTree<Integer> intTree = new BinaryTree<Integer>(numbers);
35      System.out.print("\nInorder (sorted): ");
36      intTree.inorder();
37    }
38 }
```

```
Inorder (sorted): Adam Daniel George Jones Michael Peter Tom
Postorder: Daniel Adam Jones Peter Tom Michael George
Preorder: George Adam Daniel Michael Jones Tom Peter
The number of nodes is 7
Is Peter in the tree? true
A path from the root to Peter is: George Michael Tom Peter
Inorder (sorted): 1 2 3 4 5 6 7 8
```

The program checks `path != null` in line 30 to ensure that the path is not `null` before invoking `path.get(i)`. This is an example of defensive programming to avoid potential runtime errors.

The program creates another tree for storing `int` values (line 34). After all the elements are inserted into the trees, the trees should appear as shown in Figure 26.9.

If the elements are inserted in a different order (e.g., Daniel, Adam, Jones, Peter, Tom, Michael, George), the tree will look different. However, the inorder traversal prints elements in the same order as long as the set of elements is the same. The inorder traversal displays a sorted list.

26.3 Deleting Elements in a BST

The `insert(element)` method was presented in §26.2.3. Often you need to delete an element from a binary search tree. Doing so is far more complex than adding an element into a binary search tree.

locating element

To delete an element from a binary search tree, you need to first locate the node that contains the element and also its parent node. Let `current` point to the node that contains the element in the binary search tree and `parent` point to the parent of the `current` node. The `current` node may be a left child or a right child of the `parent` node. There are two cases to consider:

Case 1: The current node does not have a left child, as shown in Figure 26.10(a). Simply connect the parent with the right child of the current node, as shown in Figure 26.10(b).

For example, to delete node `10` in Figure 26.11(a). Connect the parent of node `10` with the right child of node `10`, as shown in Figure 26.11(b).

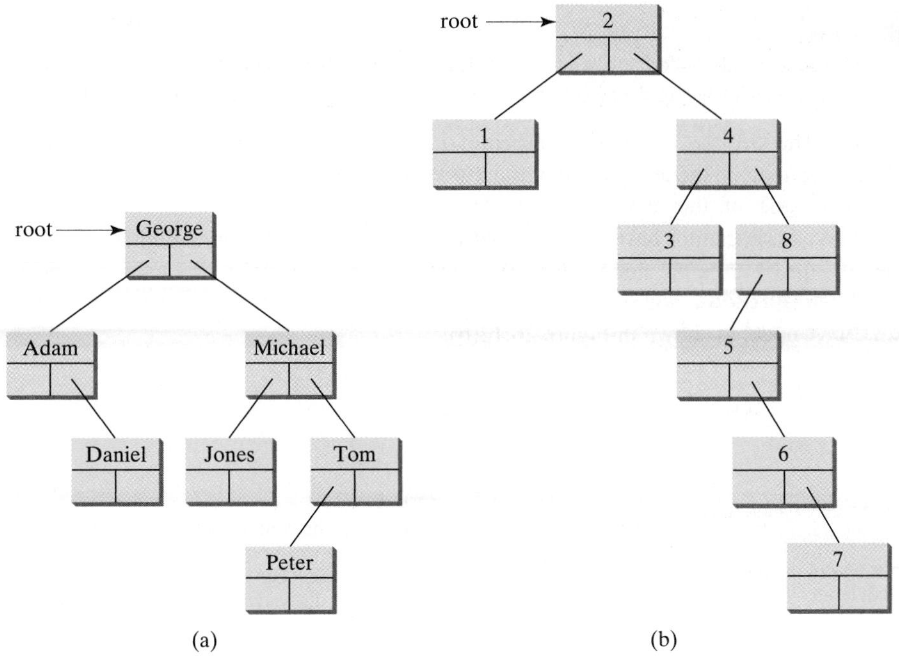
root
George
Adam
Michael
Daniel
Jones
Tom
Peter
(a)
root
2
1
4
3
8
5
6
7
(b)

FIGURE 26.9 The BSTs are pictured here after they are created.

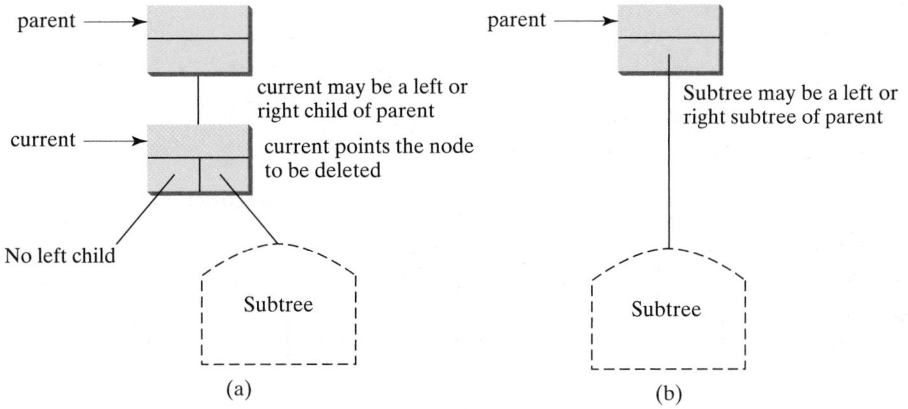
parent
current may be a left or
right child of parent
current
current points the node
to be deleted
No left child
Subtree
(a)
parent
Subtree may be a left or
right subtree of parent
Subtree
(b)

FIGURE 26.10 Case 1: the current node has no left child.

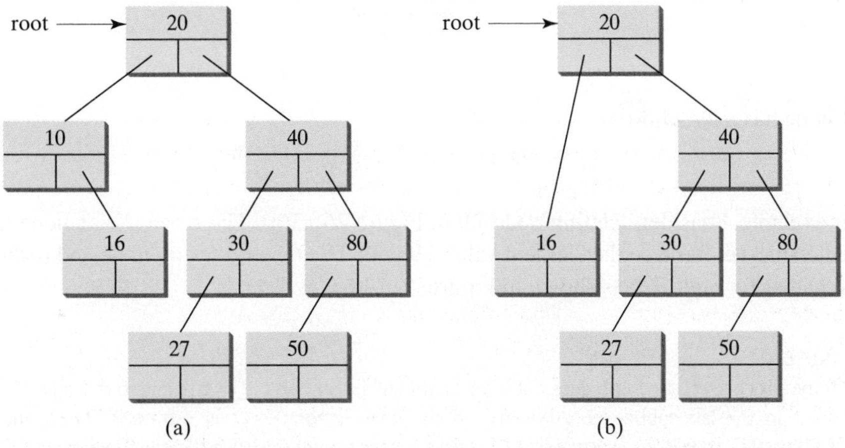
root
20
10
40
16
30
80
27
50
(a)
root
20
40
16
30
80
27
50
(b)

FIGURE 26.11 Case 1: deleting node 10 from (a) results in (b).

delete a leaf

Note

If the current node is a leaf, it falls into Case 1. For example, to delete element 16 in Figure 26.11(a), connect its right child to the parent of node 16. In this case, the right child of node 16 is null.

Case 2: The current node has a left child. Let rightMost point to the node that contains the largest element in the left subtree of the current node and parentOfRightMost point to the parent node of the rightMost node, as shown in Figure 26.12(a). Note that the rightMost node cannot have a right child but may have a left child. Replace the element value in the current node with the one in the rightMost node, connect the parentOfRightMost node with the left child of the rightMost node, and delete the rightMost node, as shown in Figure 26.12(b).

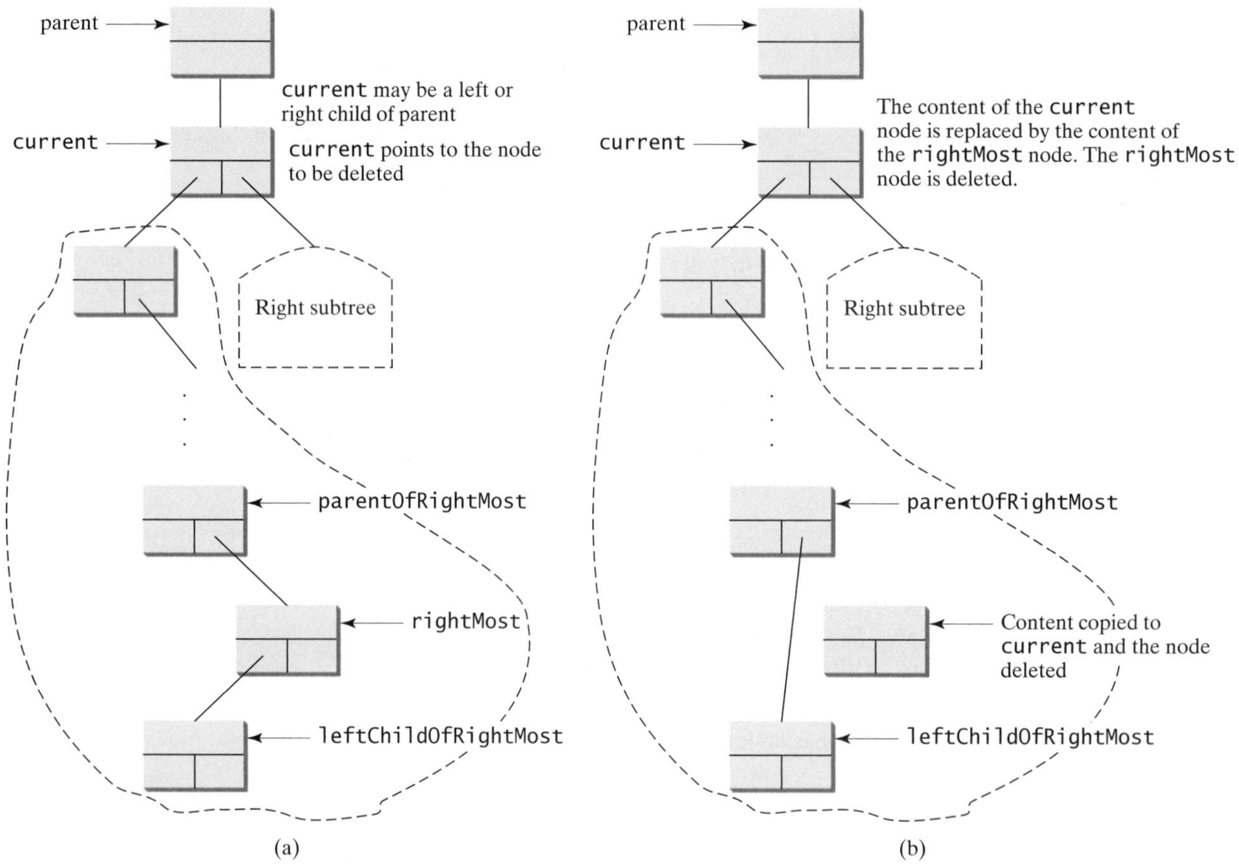
parent
current
current may be a left or right child of parent
current points to the node to be deleted
Right subtree
parentOfRightMost
rightMost
leftChildOfRightMost
(a)
parent
current
The content of the current node is replaced by the content of the rightMost node. The rightMost node is deleted.
Right subtree
parentOfRightMost
Content copied to current and the node deleted
leftChildOfRightMost
(b)

FIGURE 26.12 Case 2: the current node has a left child.

For example, consider deleting node 20 in Figure 26.13(a). The rightMost node has the element value 16. Replace the element value 20 with 16 in the current node and make node 10 the parent for node 14, as shown in Figure 26.13(b).

Note

special case

If the left child of current does not have a right child, current.left points to the large element in the left subtree of current. In this case, rightMost is current.left and parentOfRightMost is current. You have to take care of this special case to reconnect the right child of rightMost with parentOfRightMost.

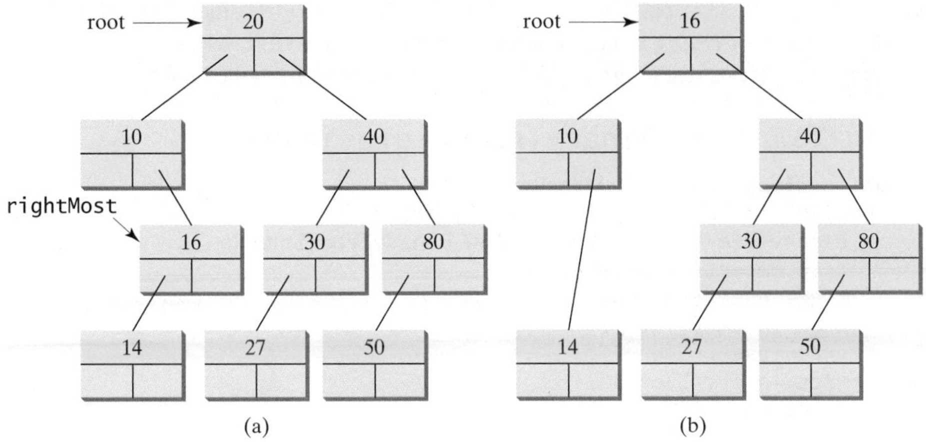
root
20
10
40
rightMost
16
30
80
14
27
50
(a)
root
16
10
40
30
80
14
27
50
(b)

FIGURE 26.13 Case 2: deleting node 20 from (a) results in (b).

The algorithm for deleting an element from a binary search tree can be described in Listing 26.7.

`delete` method

LISTING 26.7 Deleting an Element from a BST

```
boolean delete(E e) {
  Locate element e in the tree;
  if element e is not found
    return true;

  Let current be the node that contains e and parent be
    the parent of current;

  if (current has no left child) // Case 1
    Connect the right child of
      current with parent; now current is not referenced, so
    it is eliminated;
  else // Case 2
    Locate the rightmost node in the left subtree of current.
    Copy the element value in the rightmost node to current.
    Connect the parent of the rightmost to the left child
      of rightmost;

  return true; // Element deleted
}
```

not in the tree

locate parent

case 1

case 2

The complete implementation of the `delete` method is given in lines 154–212 in Listing 26.5. The method locates the node (named `current`) to be deleted and also locates its parent (named `parent`) in lines 158–169. If `current` is `null`, the element is not in tree. So, the method returns `false` (line 172). Please note that if `current` is `root`, `parent` is `null`. If the tree is empty, both `current` and `parent` are `null`.

Case 1 of the algorithm is covered in lines 175–186. In this case, the `current` node has no left child (i.e., `current.left == null`). If `parent` is `null`, assign `current.right` to `root` (lines 177–179). Otherwise, assign `current.right` to `parent.left` or `parent.right`, depending on whether `current` is a left or right child of `parent` (181–184).

Case 2 of the algorithm is covered in lines 187–208. In this case, the `current` has a left child. The algorithm locates the rightmost node (named `rightMost`) in the left subtree of the current node and also its parent (named `parentOfRightMost`) (lines 194–197). Replace the element in `current` by the element in `rightMost` (line 200); assign `rightMost.left` to `parentOfRightMost.right` or `parentOfRightMost.right` (lines 203–207), depending on whether `rightMost` is a right or left child of `parentOfRightMost`.

Listing 26.8 gives a test program that deletes the elements from the binary search tree.

LISTING 26.8 TestBinaryTreeDelete.java

delete an element

delete an element

delete an element

```java
public class TestBinaryTreeDelete {
  public static void main(String[] args) {
    BinaryTree<String> tree = new BinaryTree<String>();
    tree.insert("George");
    tree.insert("Michael");
    tree.insert("Tom");
    tree.insert("Adam");
    tree.insert("Jones");
    tree.insert("Peter");
    tree.insert("Daniel");
    printTree(tree);

    System.out.println("\nAfter delete George:");
    tree.delete("George");
    printTree(tree);

    System.out.println("\nAfter delete Adam:");
    tree.delete("Adam");
    printTree(tree);

    System.out.println("\nAfter delete Michael:");
    tree.delete("Michael");
    printTree(tree);
  }

  public static void printTree(BinaryTree tree) {
    // Traverse tree
    System.out.print("Inorder (sorted): ");
    tree.inorder();
    System.out.print("\nPostorder: ");
    tree.postorder();
    System.out.print("\nPreorder: ");
    tree.preorder();
    System.out.print("\nThe number of nodes is " + tree.getSize());
    System.out.println();
  }
}
```

```
Inorder (sorted): Adam Daniel George Jones Michael Peter Tom
Postorder: Daniel Adam Jones Peter Tom Michael George
Preorder: George Adam Daniel Michael Jones Tom Peter
The number of nodes is 7

After delete George:
Inorder (sorted): Adam Daniel Jones Michael Peter Tom
Postorder: Adam Jones Peter Tom Michael Daniel
Preorder: Daniel Adam Michael Jones Tom Peter
The number of nodes is 6

After delete Adam:
Inorder (sorted): Daniel Jones Michael Peter Tom
Postorder: Jones Peter Tom Michael Daniel
```

```
Preorder: Daniel Michael Jones Tom Peter
The number of nodes is 5

After delete Michael:
Inorder (sorted): Daniel Jones Peter Tom
Postorder: Peter Tom Jones Daniel
Preorder: Daniel Jones Tom Peter
The number of nodes is 4
```

Figures 26.14–26.16 show how the tree evolves as the elements are deleted from it.

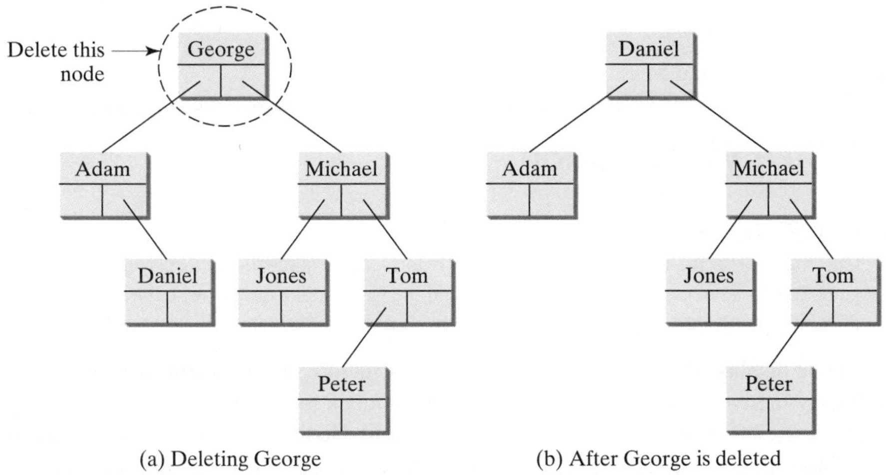
Delete this node
George
Adam
Michael
Daniel
Jones
Tom
Peter
(a) Deleting George
Daniel
Adam
Michael
Jones
Tom
Peter
(b) After George is deleted

FIGURE 26.14 Deleting George falls in Case 2.

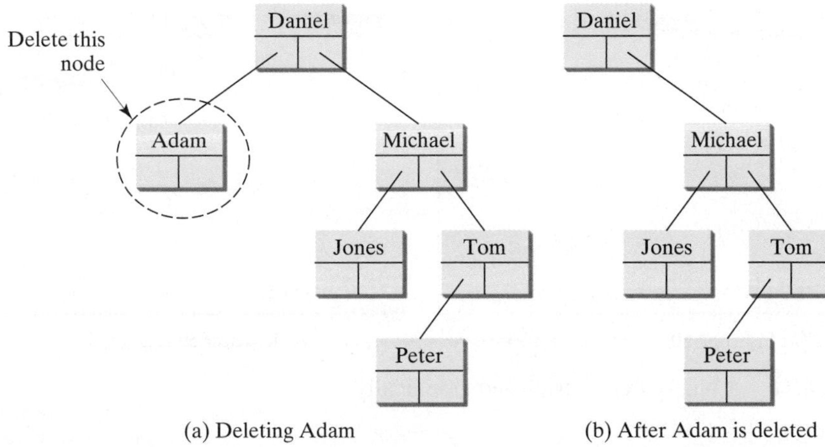
Delete this node
Daniel
Adam
Michael
Jones
Tom
Peter
(a) Deleting Adam
Daniel
Michael
Jones
Tom
Peter
(b) After Adam is deleted

FIGURE 26.15 Deleting Adam falls in Case 1.

Note

It is obvious that the time complexity for the inorder, preorder, and postorder is $O(n)$, since each node is traversed only once. The time complexity for search, insertion, and deletion is the height of the tree. In the worst case, the height of the tree is $O(n)$.

BST time complexity

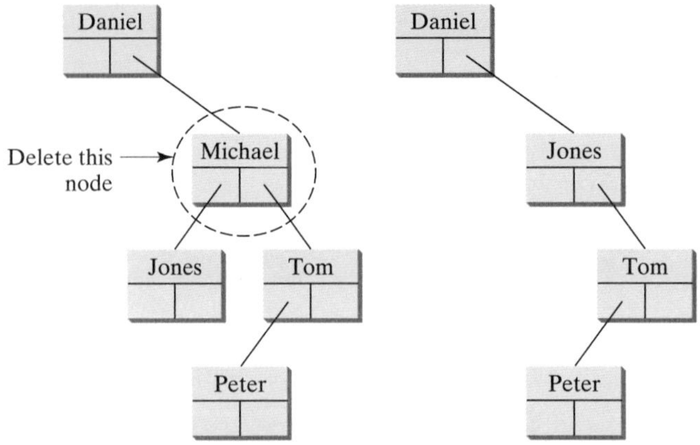
Daniel
Delete this node
Michael
Jones
Tom
Peter
Daniel
Jones
Tom
Peter

(a) Deleting Michael (b) After Michael is deleted

FIGURE 26.16 Deleting Michael falls in Case 2.

26.4 Tree Visualization

Pedagogical Note

One challenge facing the data-structure course is to motivate students. To display a binary tree graphically will not only help students understand the working of a binary tree but also stimulate their interest in programming. Students can apply visualization techniques in other projects.

How do you display a binary tree? It is a recursive structure. You can simply display the root, then display the two subtrees recursively. The techniques for displaying the Sierpinski triangle (Listing 20.9 SierpinskiTriangle.java) can be applied to display a binary tree. You can display a binary tree using recursion. For simplicity, we assume the keys are positive integers less than 100. Listings 26.9 and 26.10 give the program, and Figure 26.17 shows some sample runs of the program.

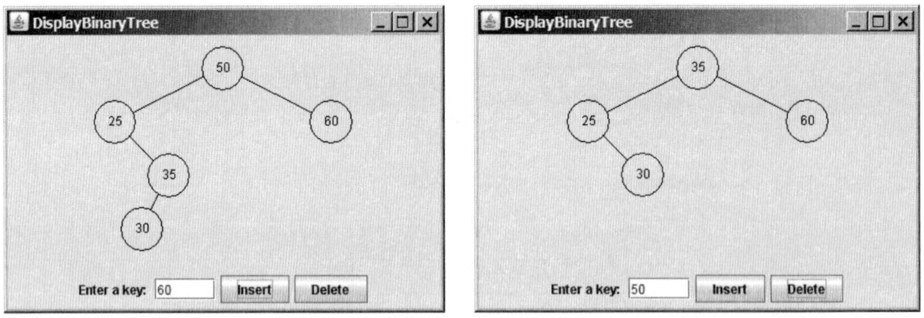
DisplayBinaryTree
50
25
60
35
30
Enter a key: 60
Insert
Delete
DisplayBinaryTree
35
25
60
30
Enter a key: 50
Insert
Delete

(a) Inserting 50, 25, 35, 30, and 60 (b) After 50 is deleted

FIGURE 26.17 A binary tree is displayed graphically.

LISTING 26.9 DisplayBinaryTree.java

create a view

main method omitted

```
import javax.swing.*;

public class DisplayBinaryTree extends JApplet {
  public DisplayBinaryTree() {
    add(new TreeControl(new BinaryTree<Integer>()));
  }
}
```

LISTING 26.10 TreeControl.java

```java
import java.awt.*;
import java.awt.event.*;
import javax.swing.*;

public class TreeControl extends JPanel {
  private BinaryTree<Integer> tree; // A binary tree to be displayed
  private JTextField jtfKey = new JTextField(5);
  private TreeView TreeView = new TreeView();
  private JButton jbtInsert = new JButton("Insert");
  private JButton jbtDelete = new JButton("Delete");

  /** Construct a view for a binary tree */
  public TreeControl(BinaryTree<Integer> tree) {
    this.tree = tree; // Set a binary tree to be displayed
    setUI();
  }

  /** Initialize UI for binary tree */
  private void setUI() {
    this.setLayout(new BorderLayout());
    add(view, BorderLayout.CENTER);
    JPanel panel = new JPanel();
    panel.add(new JLabel("Enter a key: "));
    panel.add(jtfKey);
    panel.add(jbtInsert);
    panel.add(jbtDelete);
    add(panel, BorderLayout.SOUTH);

    // Listener for the Insert button
    jbtInsert.addActionListener(new ActionListener() {
      public void actionPerformed(ActionEvent e) {
        int key = Integer.parseInt(jtfKey.getText());
        if (tree.search(key)) { // key is in the tree already
          JOptionPane.showMessageDialog(null,
            key + " is already in the tree");
        }
        else {
          tree.insert(key); // Insert a new key
          view.repaint(); // Redisplay the tree
        }
      }
    });

    // Listener for the Delete button
    jbtDelete.addActionListener(new ActionListener() {
      public void actionPerformed(ActionEvent e) {
        int key = Integer.parseInt(jtfKey.getText());
        if (!tree.search(key)) { // key is not in the tree
          JOptionPane.showMessageDialog(null,
            key + " is not in the tree");
        }
        else {
          tree.delete(key); // Delete a key
          view.repaint(); // Redisplay the tree
        }
      }
    });
  }
```

binary tree

paint tree

create UI

insert button listener

insert key

repaint the tree

delete button listener

delete key

repaint the tree

TreeView class
display tree
paint a node
connect two nodes
draw left subtree
connect two nodes
draw right subtree

```java

  // Inner class TreeView for displaying a tree on a panel
  class TreeView extends JPanel {
    private int radius = 20; // Tree node radius
    private int vGap = 50; // Gap between two levels in a tree

    protected void paintComponent(Graphics g) {
      super.paintComponent(g);

      if (tree.getRoot() != null) {
        // Display tree recursively
        displayTree(g, tree.getRoot(), getWidth() / 2,  30,
          getWidth() / 4);
      }
    }

    /** Display a subtree rooted at position (x, y) */
    private void displayTree(Graphics g, BinaryTree.TreeNode root,
        int x, int y, int hGap) {
      // Display the root
      g.drawOval(x - radius, y - radius, 2 * radius, 2 * radius);
      g.drawString(root.element + "", x - 6, y + 4);

      if (root.left != null) {
        // Draw a line to the left node
        connectLeftChild(g, x - hGap, y + vGap, x, y);
        // Draw the left subtree recursively
        displayTree(g, root.left, x - hGap, y + vGap,  hGap / 2);
      }

      if (root.right != null) {
        // Draw a line to the right node
        connectRightChild(g, x + hGap, y + vGap, x, y);
        // Draw the right subtree recursively
        displayTree(g, root.right, x + hGap, y + vGap, hGap / 2);
      }
    }

    /** Connect a parent at (x2, y2) with
     * its left child at (x1, y1) */
    private void connectLeftChild(Graphics g,
        int x1, int y1, int x2, int y2) {
      double d = Math.sqrt(vGap * vGap + (x2 - x1) * (x2 - x1));
      int x11 = (int)(x1 + radius * (x2 - x1) / d);
      int y11 = (int)(y1 - radius * vGap / d);
      int x21 = (int)(x2 - radius * (x2 - x1) / d);
      int y21 = (int)(y2 + radius * vGap / d);
      g.drawLine(x11, y11, x21, y21);
    }

    /** Connect a parent at (x2, y2) with
     * its right child at (x1, y1) */
    private void connectRightChild(Graphics g,
        int x1, int y1, int x2, int y2) {
      double d = Math.sqrt(vGap * vGap + (x2 - x1) * (x2 - x1));
      int x11 = (int)(x1 - radius * (x1 - x2) / d);
      int y11 = (int)(y1 - radius * vGap / d);
      int x21 = (int)(x2 + radius * (x1 - x2) / d);
      int y21 = (int)(y2 + radius * vGap / d);
      g.drawLine(x11, y11, x21, y21);
```

```
119       }
120     }
121 }
```

After a new key is inserted into the tree (line 38), the tree is repainted (line 39) to reflect the change. After a key is deleted (line 53), the tree is repainted (line 54) to reflect the change.

The node is displayed as a circle with `radius 20` (line 62). The distance between two levels in the tree is defined in `vGap 50` (line 63). `hGap` (line 77) defines the distance between two nodes horizontally. This value is reduced by half (`hGap / 2`) in the next level when the `displayTree` method is called recursively (lines 86, 93). Note that `vGap` is not changed in the tree.

Invoking `connectLeftChild` connects a parent with its left child. You need to find the two endpoints (`x11`, `y11`) and (`x21`, `y21`) in order to connect the two nodes, as shown in Figure 26.18. The mathematical calculation for finding the two ends is illustrated in Figure 26.18. Note that

$$d = \sqrt{vGap^2 + (x_2 - x_1)^2}$$

$$\frac{x_{11} - x_1}{radius} = \frac{x_2 - x_1}{d}, \quad \text{so} \quad x_{11} = x_1 + radius \times \frac{x_2 - x_1}{d},$$

$$\frac{y_{11} - y_1}{radius} = \frac{y_2 - y_1}{d}, \quad \text{so} \quad y_{11} = y_1 + radius \times \frac{y_2 - y_1}{d}$$

Invoking `connectRightChild` connects a parent with its right child. The mathematical calculation for the two ends of the line is similar to the case for connecting a parent with its left child.

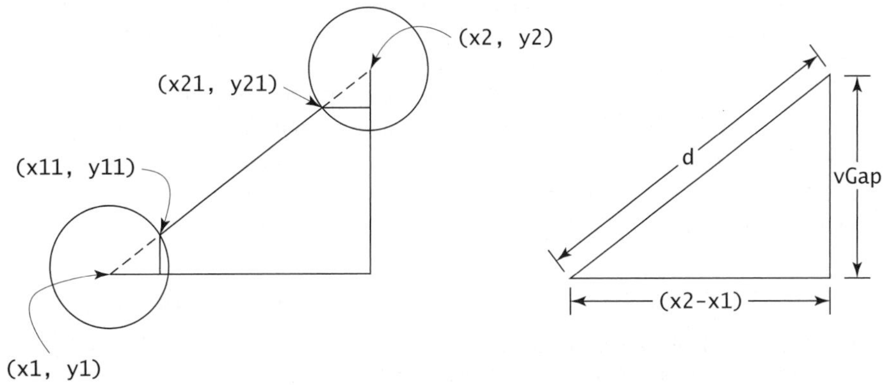
(x2, y2)
(x21, y21)
(x11, y11)
(x1, y1)
d
vGap
(x2-x1)

FIGURE 26.18 You need to find the position of the endpoints to connect two nodes.

The program assumes that the keys are integers. You can easily modify the program with a generic type to display keys of characters or short strings.

26.5 Iterators

The methods `inorder()`, `preorder()`, and `postorder()` display the elements in `inorder`, `preorder`, and `postorder` in a binary tree. These methods are limited to displaying the elements in a tree. If you wish to process the elements in a binary tree rather than displaying them, these methods cannot be used. A more useful approach is to provide an iterator. An *iterator* is an object that provides a uniform way of traversing the elements in a container, such as a set, list, or binary tree. iterator

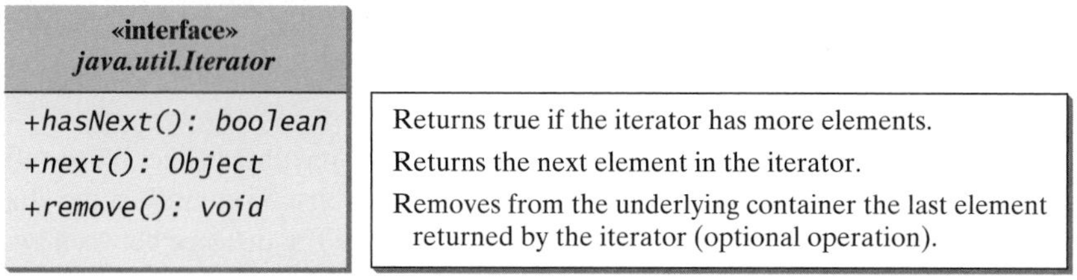
«interface»
java.util.Iterator
+hasNext(): boolean
+next(): Object
+remove(): void
Returns true if the iterator has more elements.
Returns the next element in the iterator.
Removes from the underlying container the last element returned by the iterator (optional operation).

FIGURE 26.19 The `Iterator` interface defines a uniform way of traversing the elements in a container.

Java provides the `java.util.Iterator` interface (see Figure 26.19), which defines the common features of iterators. All the containers (set, list, and map) in the collections framework support iterators.

how to create an iterator

To enable the iterator to be used in a wide range of applications, you should define your iterator class as a subtype of `java.util.Iterator`. You can traverse a binary tree in inorder, preorder, or postorder. So, you may define three iterator classes, named `InorderIterator`, `PreorderIterator`, and `PostorderIterator`. Since these classes are dependent on the `BinaryTree` class, it is appropriate to define them as inner classes in `BinaryTree`. Also it is convenient to add three methods named `inorderIterator()`, `preorderIterator()`, and `postorderIterator()` to return the iterator objects.

The implementation of `inorderIterator()` is shown in lines in Listing 26.5. The implementation of `preorderIterator()` and `postorderIterator()` is left as an exercise.

The `InorderIterator` constructor invokes the `inorder` method. The `inorder(root)` method (lines 241–246) stores all the elements from the tree in `list`. The elements are traversed in `inorder`.

Once an `Iterator` object is created, its `current` value is initialized to `0` (line 229), which points to the first element in the list. Invoking the `next()` method returns the current element and moves current to point to the next element in the list (line 258).

The `hasNext()` method checks whether current is still in the range of `list` (line 250).

The `remove()` method removes the current element from the tree (line 263). Afterward, a new list is created (lines 264–265). Note that `current` does not need to be changed.

Listing 26.11 gives a test program that stores the strings in a BST and displays all strings in uppercase.

LISTING 26.11 TestBinaryTreeWithIterator.java

get an iterator
hasNext?
get current element

```
public class TestBinaryTreeWithIterator {
  public static void main(String[] args) {
    BinaryTree<String> tree = new BinaryTree<String>();
    tree.insert("George");
    tree.insert("Michael");
    tree.insert("Tom");
    tree.insert("Adam");
    tree.insert("Jones");
    tree.insert("Peter");
    tree.insert("Daniel");

    java.util.Iterator iterator = tree.inorderIterator();
    while (iterator.hasNext()) {
      System.out.println(((String)(iterator.next())).toUpperCase());
    }
  }
}
```

```
ADAM
DANIEL
GEORGE
JONES
MICHAEL
PETER
TOM
```

The program constructs an iterator (line 12), which enables you to process all elements in the tree (lines 13–14).

Design Guide

iterator pattern
advantages of iterators

Iterator is an important software design pattern. It provides a uniform way of traversing the elements in a container, while hiding the container's structural details. By implementing the same interface `java.util.Iterator`, you can write a program that traverses the elements of all containers in the same way.

Note

variations of iterators

`java.util.Iterator` defines a forward iterator, which traverses the element in the iterator in a forward direction, and each element can be traversed only once. Java API also provides the `java.util.ListIterator`, which supports traversing in both forward and backward directions. If your data structure warrants flexible traversing, you may define iterator classes as a subtype of `java.util.ListIterator`.

26.6 Case Study: Data Compression

You have used the utilities such as WinZip to compress files. There are many algorithms for compressing data. This section introduces Huffman coding, invented by David Huffman in 1952.

In ASCII, every character is encoded in 8 bits. Huffman coding compresses data by using fewer bits to encode characters that occur more frequently. The codes for characters are constructed based on the occurrence of characters in the text using a binary tree, called the *Huffman coding tree*. Suppose the text is `Mississippi`. Its Huffman tree can be shown as in Figure 26.20(a). The left and right edges of a node are assigned a value `0` and `1`, respectively. Each character is a leaf in the tree. The code for the character consists of the edge values in the path from the root to the leaf, as shown in Figure 26.20(b). Since `i` and `s` appear more than `M` and `p` in the text, they are assigned shorter codes.

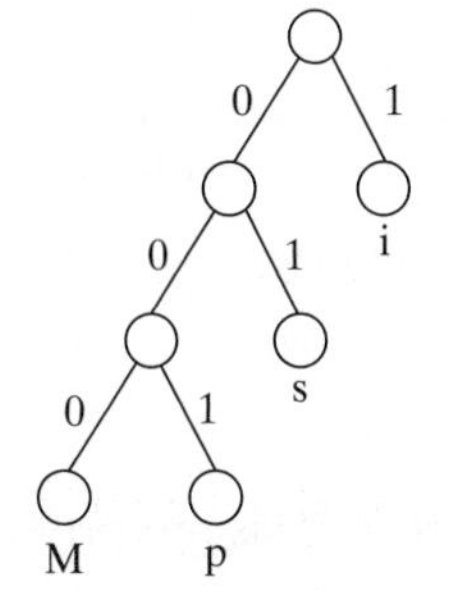
0
1
i
0
1
s
0
1
M
p

(a) Huffman coding tree

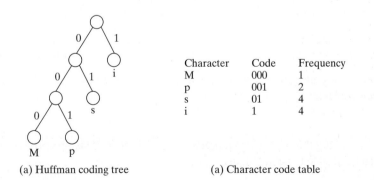

Character	Code	Frequency
M	000	1
p	001	2
s	01	4
i	1	4

(a) Character code table

FIGURE 26.20 The codes for characters are constructed based on the occurrence of characters in the text using a coding tree.

decoding

The coding tree is also used for decoding a sequence of bits into a text. To do so, start with the first bit in the sequence and determine whether to go to the left or right branch of the root in the tree based on the bit value. Consider the next bit and continue go down to the left or right branch based on the bit value. When you reach a leaf, you have found a character. The next bit in the stream is the first bit of the next character. For example, the stream `011001` is decoded to `sip` with `01` matching `s`, `1` matching `i`, and `001` matching `p`.

constructing coding tree

To construct a *Huffman coding tree*, use a greedy algorithm as follows:

1. Begin with a forest of trees. Each tree contains a node for a character. The weight of the node is the frequency of the character in the text.

2. Repeat this step until there is only one tree:
   Choose two trees with the smallest weight and create a new node as their parent. The weight of the new tree is the sum of the weight of the subtrees.

For each interior node, assign its left edge a value `0` and right edge a value `1`. All leaf nodes represent characters in the text.

Here is an example of building a coding tree for the text `Mississippi`. The frequency table for the characters is shown in Figure 26.20(b). Initially the forest contains single-node trees, as shown in Figure 26.21(a). The trees are repeatedly combined to form large trees until only one tree is left, as shown in Figures 26.21(b), (c), and (d).

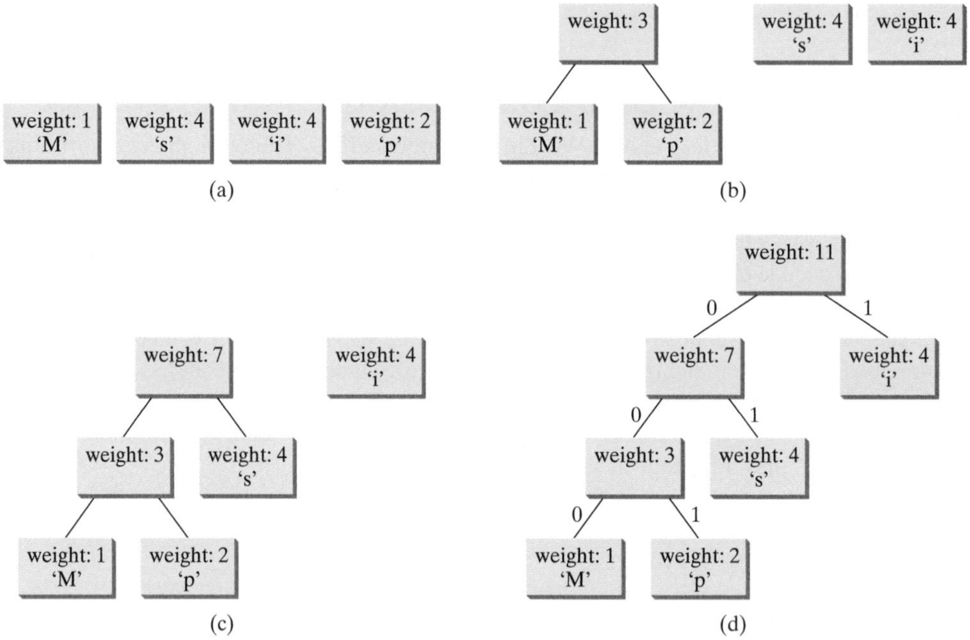

weight: 1 'M'
weight: 4 's'
weight: 4 'i'
weight: 2 'p'
(a)
weight: 3
weight: 4 's'
weight: 4 'i'
weight: 1 'M'
weight: 2 'p'
(b)
weight: 7
weight: 4 'i'
weight: 3
weight: 4 's'
weight: 1 'M'
weight: 2 'p'
(c)
weight: 11
0
1
weight: 7
weight: 4 'i'
0
1
weight: 3
weight: 4 's'
0
1
weight: 1 'M'
weight: 2 'p'
(d)

FIGURE 26.21 The coding tree is built using a greedy algorithm by repeatedly combining two smallest-weighted trees.

prefix property

It is worth noting that no code is a prefix of another code. This property ensures that the streams can be decoded unambiguously.

Pedagogical Note

Huffman coding animation

Follow the link www.cs.armstrong.edu/liang/animation/HuffmanCodingAnimation.html to see how Huffman coding works, as shown in Figure 26.22.

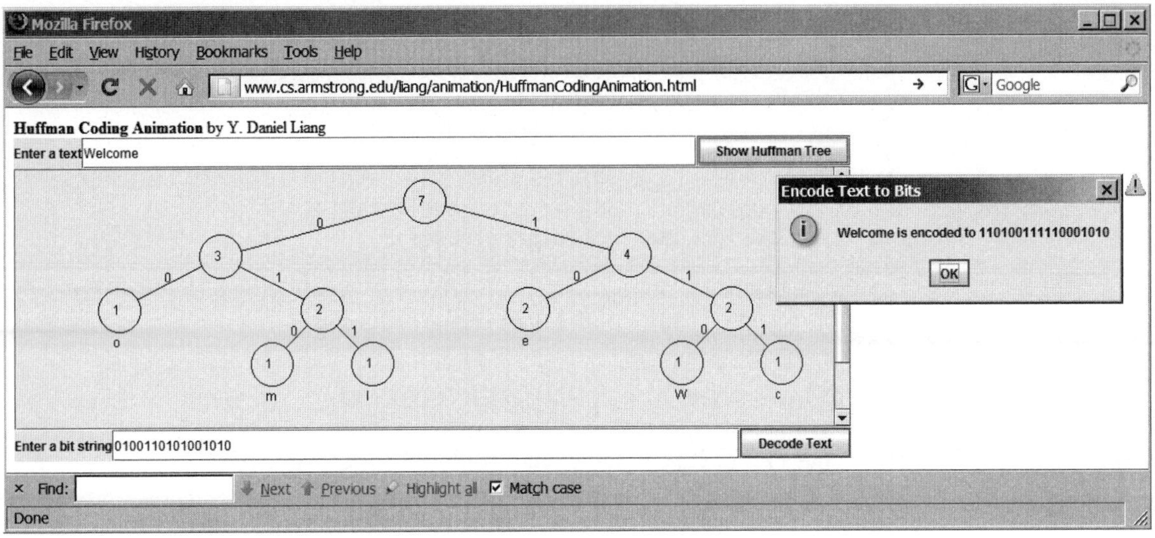

Mozilla Firefox
File Edit View History Bookmarks Tools Help
www.cs.armstrong.edu/liang/animation/HuffmanCodingAnimation.html
Google
Huffman Coding Animation by Y. Daniel Liang
Enter a text Welcome
Show Huffman Tree
Encode Text to Bits
Welcome is encoded to 110100111110001010
OK
Enter a bit string 0100110101001010
Decode Text
Find: Next Previous Highlight all Match case
Done

FIGURE 26.22 The animation tool enables you to create and view a Huffman tree, and it performs encoding and decoding using the tree.

Listing 26.12 gives a program that prompts the user to enter a string, displays the frequency table of the characters in the string, and displays the Huffman code for each character.

LISTING 26.12 HuffmanCode.java

```
import java.util.Scanner;

public class HuffmanCode {
  public static void main(String[] args) {
    Scanner input = new Scanner(System.in);
    System.out.print("Enter a text: ");
    String text = input.nextLine();

    int[] counts = getCharacterFrequency(text); // Count frequency

    System.out.printf("%-15s%-15s%-15s%-15s\n",
      "ASCII Code", "Character", "Frequency", "Code");

    Tree tree = getHuffmanTree(counts); // Create a Huffman tree
    String[] codes = getCode(tree.root); // Get codes

    for (int i = 0; i < codes.length; i++)
      if (counts[i] != 0) // (char)i is not in text if counts[i] is 0
        System.out.printf("%-15d%-15s%-15d%-15s\n",
          i, (char)i + "", counts[i], codes[i]);
  }

  /** Get Huffman codes for the characters
   * This method is called once after a Huffman tree is  built
   */
  public static String[] getCode(Tree.Node root) {
    if (root == null) return null;
    String[] codes = new String[2 * 128];
    assignCode(root, codes);
    return codes;
  }
```

count frequency

get Huffman tree

code for each character

getCode

```java

  /* Recursively get codes to the leaf node */
```

assignCode

```java
  private static void assignCode(Tree.Node root, String[] codes) {
    if (root.left != null) {
      root.left.code = root.code + "0";
      assignCode(root.left, codes);

      root.right.code = root.code + "1";
      assignCode(root.right, codes);
    }
    else {
      codes[(int)root.element] = root.code;
    }
  }

  /** Get a Huffman tree from the codes */
```

getHuffmanTree

```java
  public static Tree getHuffmanTree(int[] counts) {
    // Create a heap to hold trees
    Heap<Tree> heap = new Heap<Tree>(); // Defined in Listing 24.10
    for (int i = 0; i < counts.length; i++) {
      if (counts[i] > 0)
        heap.add(new Tree(counts[i], (char)i)); // A leaf node tree
    }

    while (heap.getSize() > 1) {
      Tree t1 = heap.remove(); // Remove the smallest-weight tree
      Tree t2 = heap.remove(); // Remove the next smallest
      heap.add(new Tree(t1, t2)); // Combine two trees
    }

    return heap.remove(); // The final tree
  }

  /** Get the frequency of the characters */
```

getCharacterFrequency

```java
  public static int[] getCharacterFrequency(String text) {
    int[] counts = new int[256]; // 256 ASCII characters

    for (int i = 0; i < text.length(); i++)
      counts[(int)text.charAt(i)]++; // Count the characters in text

    return counts;
  }

  /** Define a Huffman coding tree */
```

Huffman tree

```java
  public static class Tree implements Comparable<Tree>  {
    Node root; // The root of the tree

    /** Create a tree with two subtrees */
    public Tree(Tree t1, Tree t2) {
      root = new Node();
      root.left = t1.root;
      root.right = t2.root;
      root.weight = t1.root.weight + t2.root.weight;
    }

    /** Create a tree containing a leaf node */
    public Tree(int weight, char element) {
      root = new Node(weight, element);
    }

```

```
92       /** Compare trees based on their weights */
93       public int compareTo(Tree o) {
94         if (root.weight < o.root.weight) // Purposely reverse the order
95           return 1;
96         else if (root.weight == o.root.weight)
97           return 0;
98         else
99           return -1;
100      }
101
102      public class Node {
103        char element; // Stores the character for a leaf node
104        int weight; // weight of the subtree rooted at this node
105        Node left; // Reference to the left subtree
106        Node right; // Reference to the right subtree
107        String code = ""; // The code of this node from the root
108
109        /** Create an empty node */
110        public Node() {
111        }
112
113        /** Create a node with the specified weight and character */
114        public Node(int weight, char element) {
115          this.weight = weight;
116          this.element = element;
117        }
118      }
119    }
120  }
```

tree node

```
Enter text: Welcome [Enter]
ASCII Code     Character     Frequency     Code
87             W             1             110
99             c             1             111
101            e             2             10
108            l             1             011
109            m             1             010
111            o             1             00
```

getCharacterFrequency

The program prompts the user to enter a text string (lines 5–7) and counts the frequency of the characters in the text (line 9). The `getCharacterFrequency` method (lines 66–73) creates an array `counts` to count the occurrences of each of the 256 ASCII characters in the text. If a character appears in the text, its corresponding count is increased by `1` (line 70).

`Node` class

`Tree` class

The program obtains a Huffman coding tree based on `counts` (line 14). The tree consists of linked nodes. The `Node` class is defined in lines 102–118. Each node consists of the properties `element` (storing character), `weight` (storing weight of the subtree under this node), `left` (linking to the left subtree), `right` (linking to the right subtree), and `code` (storing the Huffman code for the character). The `Tree` class (lines 76–119) contains the root property. From the root, you can access all the nodes in the tree. The `Tree` class implements `Comparable`. The trees are comparable based on their weights. The compare order is purposely reversed (lines 93–100) so that the smallest-weight tree is removed first from the heap of trees.

getHuffmanTree

The `getHuffmanTree` method returns a Huffman coding tree. Initially, the single-node trees are created and added to the heap (lines 50–54). In each iteration of the `while` loop (lines 56–60), two smallest-weight trees are removed from the heap and are combined to form a big tree, and then the new tree is added to the heap. This process continues until the heap contains just one tree, which is our final Huffman tree for the text.

assignCode
getCodes

The `assignCode` method assigns the code for each node in the tree (lines 34–45). The `getCodes` method gets the code for each character in the leaf node (lines 26–31). The element `codes[i]` contains the code for character `(char)i`, where `i` is from `0` to `255`. Note that `codes[i]` is `null` if `(char)i` is not in the text.

Key Terms

Chapter Summary

1. A BST is a hierarchical data structure. You learned how to define and implement a BST class. You learned how to insert and delete elements to/from a BST. You learned how to traverse a BST using inorder, postorder, preorder, depth-first, and breadth-first search.
2. An iterator is an object that provides a uniform way of traversing the elements in a container, such as a set, a list, or a binary tree. You learned how to define and implement iterator classes for traversing the elements in a binary tree.
3. Huffman coding is a scheme for compressing data by using fewer bits to encode characters that occur more frequently. The codes for characters are constructed based on the occurrence of characters in the text using a binary tree, called the *Huffman coding tree*.

Review Questions

Section 26.2

26.1 Show the result of inserting `44` into Figure 26.4(b).

26.2 Show the inorder, preorder, and postorder of traversing the elements in the binary tree, as shown in Figure 26.1(b).

26.3 If a set of the same elements is inserted into a BST in two different orders, will the two corresponding BSTs look the same? Will the inorder traversal be the same? Will the postorder traversal be the same? Will the preorder traversal be the same?

26.4 What is the time complexity of inserting an element into a BST?

Section 26.3

26.5 Show the result of deleting `55` from the tree in Figure 26.4(b).

26.6 Show the result of deleting `60` from the tree in Figure 26.4(b).

26.7 What is the time complexity of deleting an element from a BST?

26.8 Is the algorithm correct if lines 202–207 in Case 2 of the `delete()` method are replaced by the following code?

```
parentOfRightMost.right = rightMost.left;
```

Section 26.4

26.9 What is an iterator?

26.10 Why should you define an interator class to be a subtype of `java.util.Iterator`?

PROGRAMMING EXERCISES

Section 26.2

26.1* (*Adding new methods in* `BinaryTree`) Add the following new methods in `BinaryTree`.

```
/** Displays the nodes in breadth-first traversal */
public void breadthFirstTraversal()

/** Returns the height of this binary tree, i.e., the
  * number of the nodes in the longest path of the root to a
    leaf */
public int height()
```

26.2* (*Testing full binary tree*) A full binary tree is a binary tree with the leaves on the same level. Add a method in the `BinaryTree` class to return true if the tree is full.

(*Hint*: The number of nodes in a full binary tree is $2^{\text{depth}} - 1$.)

```
/** Returns true if the tree is a full binary tree */
boolean isFullBinaryTree()
```

26.3** (*Implementing inorder without using recursion*) Implement the `inorder` method in `BinaryTree` using a stack instead of recursion.

26.4** (*Implementing preorder without using recursion*) Implement the `preorder` method in `BinaryTree` using a stack instead of recursion.

26.5** (*Implementing postorder without using recursion*) Implement the `postorder` method in `BinaryTree` using a stack instead of recursion.

26.6** (*Finding the leaves*) Add a method in the `BinaryTree` class to return the number of the leaves as follows:

```
/** Returns the number of leaf nodes */
public int getNumberOfLeaves()
```

26.7** (*Finding the nonleaves*) Add a method in the `BinaryTree` class to return the number of the nonleaves as follows:

```
/** Returns the number of nonleaf nodes */
public int getNumberofNonLeaves()
```

Section 26.5

26.8** (*Implementing iterator on* `MyArrayList`) Define an inner class named `MyArrayListIterator` in `MyArrayList` for traversing the elements on `MyArrayList`. `MyArrayListIterator` should implement `java.util.Iterator`. Add a method `iterator()` that returns an instance of `MyArrayListIterator` in the `MyArrayList` class.

26.9** (*Implementing iterator on* `MyLinkedList`) Define an inner class named `MyLinkedListIterator` in `MyLinkedList` for traversing the elements on `MyLinkedList`. `MyLinkedListIterator` should implement `java.util.Iterator`. Add a method `iterator()` that returns an instance of `MyLinkedListIterator` in the `MyLinkedList` class.

26.10*** (*Implementing bidirectional iterator*) The `java.util.Iterator` interface defines a forward iterator. The Java API also provides the `java.util.ListIterator` interface that defines a bidirectional iterator. Study `ListIterator` and define a bidirectional iterator for the `BinaryTree` class.

26.11** (*Tree* `clone` *and* `equals`) Implement the `clone` and `equals` method in the `BinaryTree` class.

Comprehensive

26.12** (*BST search visualization*) Write a Java applet that displays a search path, as shown in Figure 26.23(a). The applet allows the user to enter a key. If the key is not in the tree, a message dialog box is displayed. Otherwise, the nodes in the path from the root leading to the key are displayed in green.

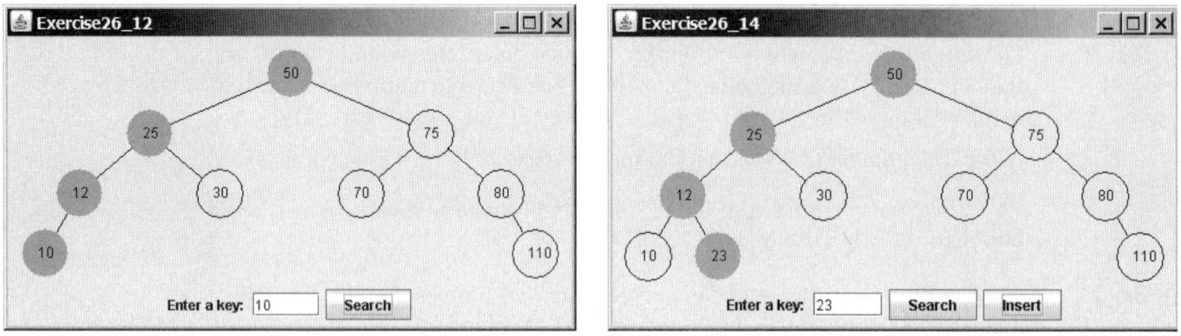
Exercise26_12
50
25
75
12
30
70
80
10
110
Enter a key: 10
Search
Exercise26_14
50
25
75
12
30
70
80
10
23
110
Enter a key: 23
Search
Insert

(a) (b)

FIGURE 26.23 (a) The search path is highlighted in green. (b) The applet animates how an insertion is performed.

26.13** (*BST animation*) The preceding exercise simply highlights a search path. Write a Java applet that animates how a search is performed. First you see that the root is searched, and then a subtree is searched recursively. When a node is searched, the node is highlighted in green. The search stops when a key is found in the tree, or displays that a key is not in the tree.

26.14** (*BST insert animation*) Add an *Insert* button to the preceding exercise to animate how insertion is performed, as shown in Figure 26.23(b). When the *Insert* button is clicked, the applet first animates a search. If the key is already in the tree, display a dialog box. Otherwise, insert the key and repaint the tree.

26.15** (*BST animation*) Write a Java applet that animates the binary search tree `insert`, `delete`, and `search` methods, as shown in Figure 26.2.

26.16* (*Generic* `BinaryTree` *using* `Comparator`) Revise `BinaryTree` in Listing 26.5, using a generic parameter and a `Comparator` for comparing objects. Define a new constructor with a `Comparator` as its argument as follows:

```
BinaryTree(Comparator<? super E> comparator)
```

26.17* (*Parent reference for* `BinaryTree`) Redefine `TreeNode` by adding a reference to a node's parent, as shown below:

BinaryTree.TreeNode<E>
#element: E #left: TreeNode<E> #right: TreeNode<E> #parent: TreeNode<E>

Add the following two new methods in `BinaryTree`:

```
/** Returns the parent for the specified node. */
public TreeNode<E> getParent(TreeNode<E> node)

/** Returns the path from the specified node to the root
  * in an array list. */
public ArrayList<TreeNode<E>> getPath(TreeNode<E> node)
```

Write a test program that adds numbers `1`, `2`, ..., `100` to the tree and displays the paths for all leaf nodes.

26.18** (*Add new buttons in* `TreeControl`) Modify Listing 26.10, TreeControl.java, to add three new buttons *Show Inorder, Show Preorder,* and *Show Postorder* to display the result in a message dialog box, as shown in Figure 26.24. You need also to modify BinaryTree.java to implement the `inorder()`, `preorder()`, and `postorder()` methods so that each of these methods returns a `List` of node elements in inorder, preorder, and postorder, as follows:

```
public java.util.List<E> inorderList();
public java.util.List<E> preorderList();
public java.util.List<E> postorderList();
```

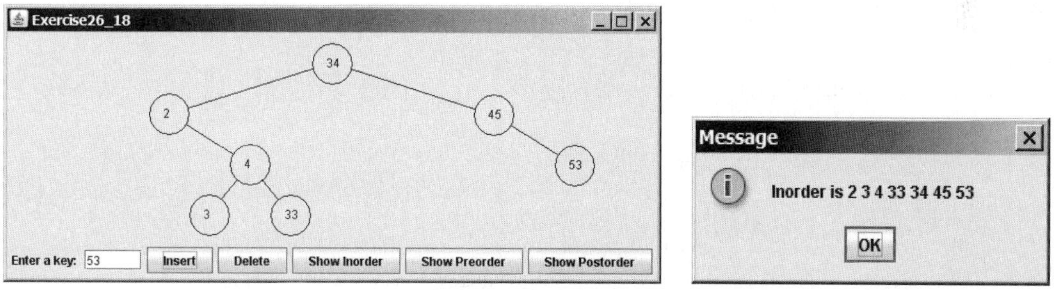

Exercise26_18
34
2
45
4
53
3
33
Enter a key: 53
Insert
Delete
Show Inorder
Show Preorder
Show Postorder
Message
Inorder is 2 3 4 33 34 45 53
OK

FIGURE 26.24 When you click the *Show Inorder* button in (a), the tree nodes are displayed in an inorder in a message dialog box in (b).

26.19** (*Animation: heap*) Write an applet to display a heap visually as shown in Figure 24.7.

26.20*** (*Data compression: Huffman coding*) Write a program that prompts the user to enter a file name, displays the frequency table of the characters in the file, and displays the Huffman code for each character.

26.21*** (*Data compression: Huffman coding animation*) Write an applet that enables the user to enter a text and displays the Huffman coding tree based on the text, as shown in Figure 26.25(a). Display the weight of the subtree inside a subtree's root circle. Display each leaf node's character. Display the encoded bits for the text in a dialog box, as shown in Figure 26.25(b). When the user clicks the *Decode Text* button, a bit string is decoded into a text, as shown in Figure 26.25(c).

26.22*** (*Compressing a file*) Write a program that prompts the user to enter a file name, obtains the Huffman codes for the characters in the file, and encode the text into a new file. Assume the original file is named `abc`. The encoded file should be named as `abc.new`. Also store the array of the codes for `256` ASCII characters using `ObjectOutputStream` to a file name `abc.huf`.

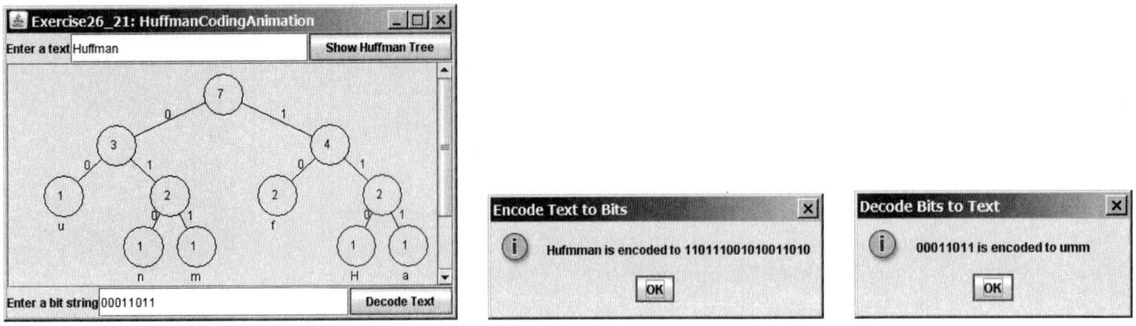
Exercise26_21: HuffmanCodingAnimation
Enter a text Huffman
Show Huffman Tree
Enter a bit string 00011011
Decode Text
Encode Text to Bits
Hufmman is encoded to 110111001010011010
OK
Decode Bits to Text
00011011 is encoded to umm
OK

(a) (b) (c)

FIGURE 26.25 The animation shows the coding tree for a given text in (a), encoded bits in (b), and the text for the given bit sequence in (c).

26.23*** (*Decompressing a file*) The preceding exercise compresses a file to generate two files `filename.huf` and `filename.new`. Write a program that decompresses the file. The program prompts the user to enter the file name and decompresses it into a file named `filename`.

CHAPTER 27

GRAPHS AND APPLICATIONS

Objectives

- To model real-world problems using graphs and explain the Seven Bridges of Königsberg problem (§27.1).
- To describe the graph terminologies: vertices, edges, simple graphs, weighted/unweighted graphs, and directed/undirected graphs (§27.2).
- To represent vertices and edges using lists, adjacent matrices, and adjacent lists (§27.3).
- To model graphs using the `Graph` interface, the `AbstractGraph` class, and the `UnweightedGraph` class (§27.4).
- To display graphs visually (§27.5).
- To represent the traversal of a graph using the `AbstractGraph.Tree` class (§27.6).
- To design and implement depth-first search (§27.7).
- To design and implement breadth-first search (§27.8).
- To solve the nine-tail problem using breadth-first search (§27.9).
- To solve the Knight's Tour problem by reducing it to a Hamiltonian path problem (§27.10).

27.1 Introduction

Shortest distance

Graphs play an important role in modeling real-world problems. For example, the problem to find the shortest distance between two cities can be modeled using a graph, where the vertices represent cities and the edges represent the roads and distances between two adjacent cities, as shown in Figure 27.1. The problem of finding the shortest distance between two cities is reduced to finding a shortest path between two vertices in a graph.

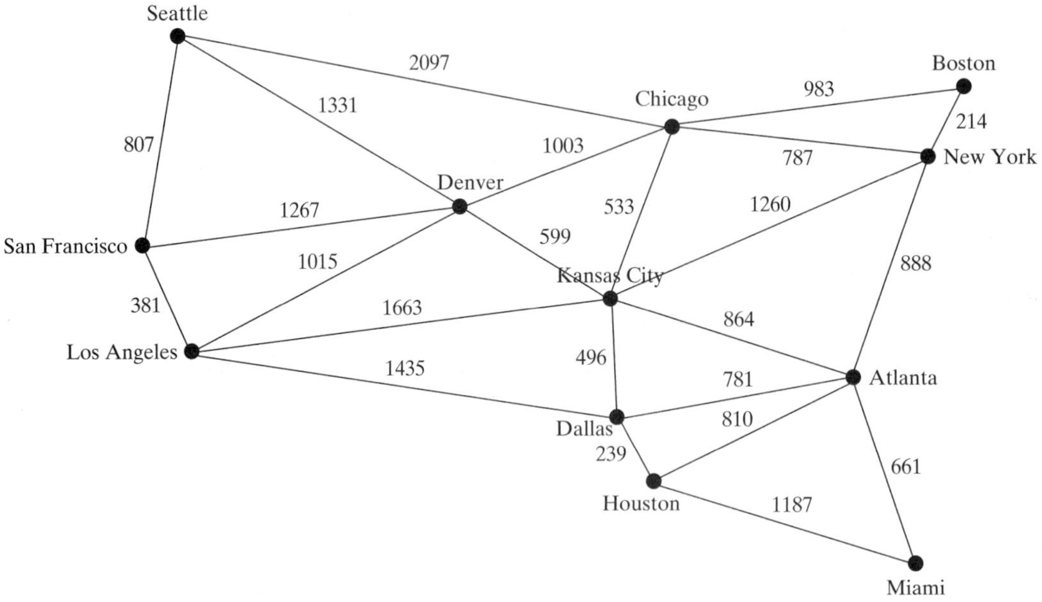
Seattle
2097
1331
807
Chicago
983
Boston
214
1003
787
New York
Denver
1267
533
1260
San Francisco
599
1015
Kansas City
888
381
1663
864
Los Angeles
1435
496
781
Atlanta
810
Dallas
239
661
Houston
1187
Miami

FIGURE 27.1 A graph can be used to model the distance between the cities.

graph theory

Seven Bridges of Königsberg

The study of graph problems is known as *graph theory*. Graph theory was founded by Leonard Euler in 1736, when he introduced graph terminology to solve the famous *Seven Bridges of Königsberg* problem. The city of Königsberg, Prussia (now Kaliningrad, Russia) was divided by the Pregel River. There were two islands on the river. The city and islands were connected by seven bridges, as shown in Figure 27.2(a). The question is, can one take a walk, cross each bridge exactly once, and return to the starting point? Euler proved that it is not possible.

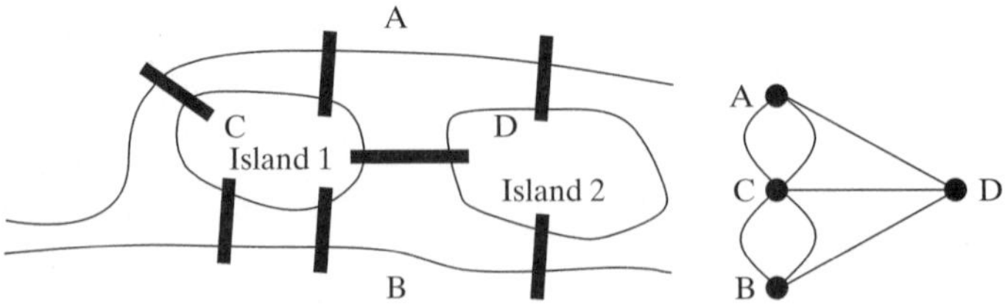
A
C
Island 1
D
Island 2
B
A
C
D
B

(a) Seven bridges sketch (b) Graph model

FIGURE 27.2 Seven bridges connected islands and land.

To establish a proof, Euler first abstracted the Königsberg city map by eliminating all streets, producing the sketch shown in Figure 27.2(a). Second, he replaced each land mass with a dot, called a vertex or a node, and each bridge with a line, called an edge, as shown in Figure 27.2(b). This structure with vertices and edges is called a graph.

Looking at the graph, we ask whether there is a path starting from any vertex, traversing all edges exactly once, and returning to the starting vertex. Euler proved that for such path to exist, each vertex must have an even number of edges. Therefore, the *Seven Bridges of Königsberg* problem has no solution.

Graph problems are often solved using algorithms. Graph algorithms have many applications in various areas, such as in computer science, mathematics, biology, engineering, economics, genetics, and social sciences. This chapter presents the algorithms for depth-first search and breadth-first search, and their applications. The next chapter presents the algorithms for finding a minimum spanning tree and shortest paths in weighted graphs, and their applications.

27.2 Basic Graph Terminologies

This chapter does not assume that the reader has prior knowledge of graph theory or discrete mathematics. We use plain and simple terms to define graphs.

What is a graph? A *graph* is a mathematical structure that represents relationships among entities in the real world. For example, the graph in Figure 27.1 represents the roads and their distances among cities, and the graph in Figure 27.2(b) represents the bridges among land masses. what is a graph?

A graph consists of a nonempty set of vertices, nodes, or points, and a set of edges that connect the vertices. For convenience, we define a graph as G = (V, E), where V represents a set of vertices and E represents a set of edges. For example, V and E for the graph in Figure 27.1 are as follows: define a graph

```
V = {"Seattle", "San Francisco", "Los Angeles",
  "Denver", "Kansas City", "Chicago", "Boston", "New York",
  "Atlanta", "Miami", "Dallas", "Houston"};

E = {{"Seattle", "San Francisco"},{"Seattle", "Chicago"},
     {"Seattle", "Denver"}, {"San Francisco", "Denver"},
       ...
    };
```

A graph may be directed or undirected. In a directed graph, each edge has a direction, which indicates that you can move from one vertex to the other through the edge. You may model parent/child relationships using a directed graph, where an edge from vertex A to B indicates that A is a parent of B. directed vs. undirected

Figure 27.3(a) shows a directed graph. In an undirected graph, you can move in both directions between vertices. The graph in Figure 27.1 is undirected.

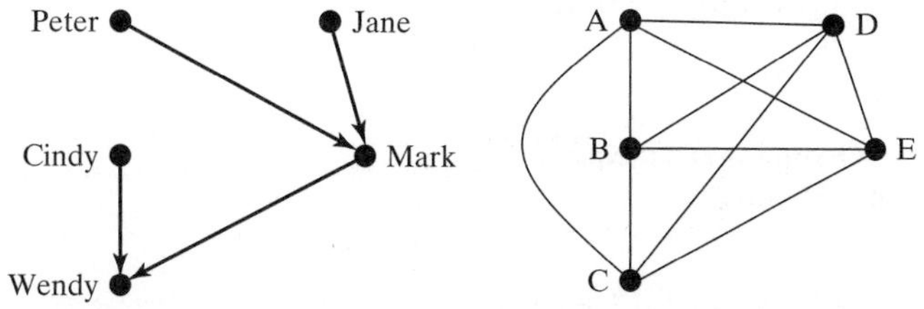
Peter
Jane
Cindy
Mark
Wendy
A
D
B
E
C

(a) A directed graph (b) A complete graph

FIGURE 27.3 Graphs may appear in many forms.

Edges may be weighted or unweighted. For example, each edge in the graph in Figure 27.1 has a weight that represents the distance between two cities. weighted vs. unweighted

Two vertices in a graph are said to be *adjacent* if they are connected by the same edge. Similarly two edges are said to be *adjacent* if they are connected to the same vertex. An edge adjacent

incident
degree

in a graph that joins two vertices is said to be *incident* to both vertices. The *degree* of a vertex is the number of edges incident to it.

neighbor

Two vertices are called *neighbors* if they are adjacent. Similarly two edges are called *neighbors* if they are adjacent.

loop
parallel edge
simple graph
complete graph

A *loop* is an edge that links a vertex to itself. If two vertices are connected by two or more edges, these edges are called *parallel edges*. A *simple graph* is one that has no loops and parallel edges. A *complete graph* is the one in which every two pairs of vertices are connected, as shown in Figure 27.3(b).

spanning tree

Assume that the graph is connected and undirected. A *spanning tree* of a graph is a subgraph that is a tree and connects all vertices in the graph.

27.3 Representing Graphs

To write a program that processes and manipulates graphs, you have to store or represent graphs in the computer.

27.3.1 Representing Vertices

The vertices can be stored in an array. For example, you can store all the city names in the graph in Figure 27.1 using the following array:

```
String[] vertices = {"Seattle", "San Francisco", "Los Angeles",
  "Denver", "Kansas City", "Chicago", "Boston", "New York",
  "Atlanta", "Miami", "Dallas", "Houston"};
```

vertex type

Note

The vertices can be objects of any type. For example, you may consider cities as objects that contain the information such as name, population, and mayor. So, you may define vertices as follows:

```
City city0 = new City("Seattle", 563374, "Greg Nickels");
...
City city11 = new City("Houston", 1000203, "Bill White");
Object[] vertices = {city0, city1, ..., city11};

public class City {
  private String cityName;
  private int population;
  private String mayor;

  public City(String cityName, int population, String mayor) {
    this.cityName = cityName;
    this.population = population;
    this.mayor = mayor;
  }

  public String getCityName() {
    return cityName;
  }

  public int getPopulation() {
    return population;
  }

  public String getMayor() {
    return mayor;
  }
```

```
    public void setMayor(String mayor) {
      this.mayor = mayor;
    }

    public void setPopulation(int population) {
      this.population = population;
    }
  }
```

The vertices can be conveniently labeled using natural numbers $0, 1, 2, \ldots, n - 1$, for a graphs for n vertices. So, `vertices[0]` represents `"Seattle"`, `vertices[1]` represents `"San Francisco"`, and so on, as shown in Figure 27.4.

`vertices[0]`	Seattle
`vertices[1]`	San Francisco
`vertices[2]`	Los Angeles
`vertices[3]`	Denver
`vertices[4]`	Kansas City
`vertices[5]`	Chicago
`vertices[6]`	Boston
`vertices[7]`	New York
`vertices[8]`	Atlanta
`vertices[9]`	Miami
`vertices[10]`	Dallas
`vertices[11]`	Houston

FIGURE 27.4 An array stores the vertex names.

Note

You can reference a vertex by its name or its index, whichever is convenient. Obviously, it is easy to access a vertex via its index in a program.

reference vertex

27.3.2 Representing Edges: Edge Array

The edges can be represented using a two-dimensional array. For example, you can store all the edges in the graph in Figure 27.1 using the following array:

```
int[][] edges = {
  {0, 1}, {0, 3}, {0, 5},
  {1, 0}, {1, 2}, {1, 3},
  {2, 1}, {2, 3}, {2, 4}, {2, 10},
  {3, 0}, {3, 1}, {3, 2}, {3, 4}, {3, 5},
  {4, 2}, {4, 3}, {4, 5}, {4, 7}, {4, 8}, {4, 10},
  {5, 0}, {5, 3}, {5, 4}, {5, 6}, {5, 7},
  {6, 5}, {6, 7},
  {7, 4}, {7, 5}, {7, 6}, {7, 8},
  {8, 4}, {8, 7}, {8, 9}, {8, 10}, {8, 11},
```

```
  {9, 8}, {9, 11},
  {10, 2}, {10, 4}, {10, 8}, {10, 11},
  {11, 8}, {11, 9}, {11, 10}
};
```

array edge

This is known as the *edge representation using arrays*.

27.3.3 Representing Edges: Edge Objects

Another way to represent the edges is to define edges as objects and store the edges in a **java.util.ArrayList**. The **Edge** class can be defined as follows:

```
public class Edge {
  int u;
  int v;

  public Edge(int u, int v) {
    this.u = u;
    this.v = v;
  }
}
```

For example, you can store all the edges in the graph in Figure 27.1 using the following list:

```
java.util.ArrayList<Edge> list = new java.util.ArrayList<Edge>();
list.add(new Edge(0, 1));
list.add(new Edge(0, 3));
list.add(new Edge(0, 5));
...
```

Storing **Edge** objects in an **ArrayList** is useful if you don't know the edges in advance.

Representing edges using edge array or **Edge** objects in §27.3.2 and §27.3.3 is intuitive for input, but not efficient for internal processing. The next two sections introduce the representation of graphs using adjacency matrices and adjacency lists. These two data structures are efficient for processing graphs.

27.3.4 Representing Edges: Adjacency Matrices

Assume that the graph has n vertices. You can use a two-dimensional $n \times n$ matrix, say **adjacencyMatrix**, to represent edges. Each element in the array is **0** or **1**. **adjacencyMatrix[i][j]** is **1** if there is an edge from vertex i to vertex j; otherwise, **adjacencyMatrix[i][j]** is **0**. If the graph is undirected, the matrix is symmetric, because **adjacencyMatrix[i][j]** is the same as **adjacencyMatrix[j][i]**. For example, the edges in the graph in Figure 27.1 can be represented using an adjacency matrix as follows:

```
int[][] adjacencyMatrix = {
  {0, 1, 0, 1, 0, 1, 0, 0, 0, 0, 0, 0}, // Seattle
  {1, 0, 1, 1, 0, 0, 0, 0, 0, 0, 0, 0}, // San Francisco
  {0, 1, 0, 1, 1, 1, 0, 0, 0, 0, 0, 0}, // Los Angeles
  {1, 1, 1, 0, 1, 1, 0, 0, 0, 0, 0, 0}, // Denver
  {0, 0, 1, 1, 0, 1, 0, 1, 1, 0, 1, 0}, // Kansas City
  {1, 0, 0, 1, 1, 0, 1, 1, 0, 0, 0, 0}, // Chicago
  {0, 0, 0, 0, 0, 1, 0, 1, 0, 0, 0, 0}, // Boston
  {0, 0, 0, 0, 1, 1, 1, 0, 1, 0, 0, 0}, // New York
  {0, 0, 0, 1, 1, 0, 0, 1, 0, 1, 1, 1}, // Atlanta
  {0, 0, 0, 0, 0, 0, 0, 0, 1, 0, 0, 1}, // Miami
  {0, 0, 1, 0, 1, 0, 0, 0, 1, 0, 0, 1}, // Dallas
  {0, 0, 0, 0, 0, 0, 0, 0, 1, 1, 1, 0}  // Houston
};
```

Note

Since the matrix is symmetric for an undirected graph, to save storage you may use a ragged array.

ragged array

The adjacency matrix for the directed graph in Figure 27.3(a) can be represented as follows:

```
int[][] a = {{0, 0, 1, 0, 0}, // Peter
             {0, 0, 1, 0, 0}, // Jane
             {0, 0, 0, 0, 1}, // Mark
             {0, 0, 0, 0, 1}, // Cindy
             {0, 0, 0, 0, 0}  // Wendy
            };
```

27.3.5 Representing Edges: Adjacency Lists

To represent edges using adjacency lists, define an array of lists. The array has *n* entries. Each entry is a linked list. The linked list for vertex *i* contains all the vertices *j* such that there is an edge from vertex *i* to vertex *j*. For example, to represent the edges in the graph in Figure 27.1, you may create an array of linked lists as follows:

```
java.util.LinkedList[] neighbors = new java.util.LinkedList[12];
```

`lists[0]` contains all vertices adjacent to vertex `0` (i.e., Seattle), `lists[1]` contains all vertices adjacent to vertex `1` (i.e., San Francisco), and so on, as shown in Figure 27.5.

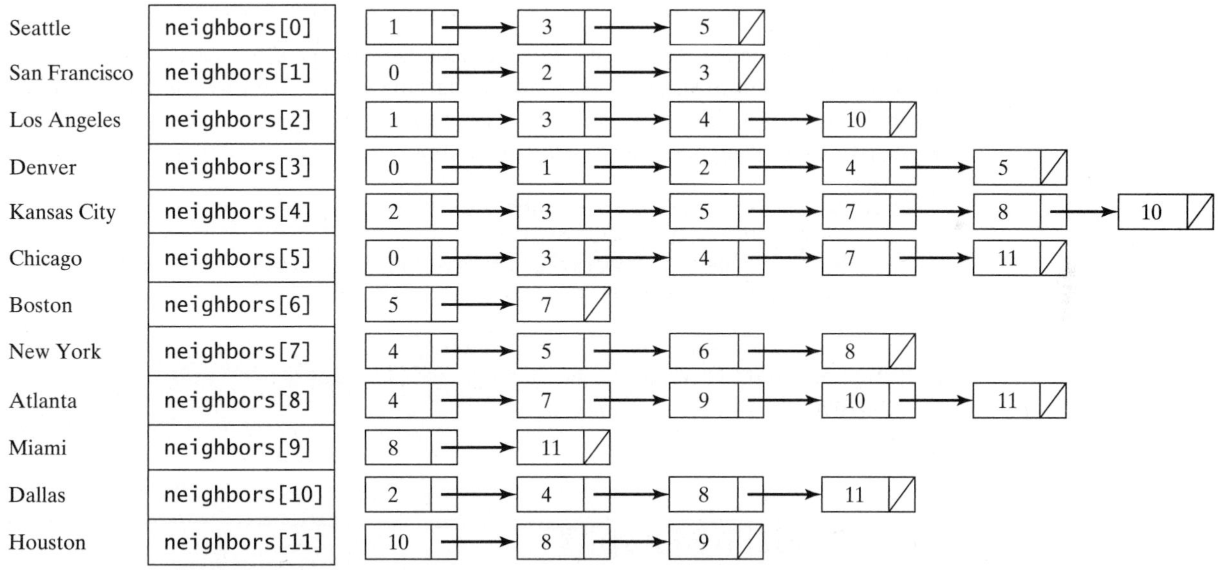

Seattle neighbors[0] 1 3 5
San Francisco neighbors[1] 0 2 3
Los Angeles neighbors[2] 1 3 4 10
Denver neighbors[3] 0 1 2 4 5
Kansas City neighbors[4] 2 3 5 7 8 10
Chicago neighbors[5] 0 3 4 7 11
Boston neighbors[6] 5 7
New York neighbors[7] 4 5 6 8
Atlanta neighbors[8] 4 7 9 10 11
Miami neighbors[9] 8 11
Dallas neighbors[10] 2 4 8 11
Houston neighbors[11] 10 8 9

FIGURE 27.5 Edges in the graph in Figure 27.1 are represented using linked lists.

To represent the edges in the graph in Figure 27.3(a), you may create an array of linked lists as follows:

```
java.util.LinkedList[] neighbors = new java.util.LinkedList[5];
```

`lists[0]` contains all vertices pointed from vertex `0` via directed edges, `lists[1]` contains all vertices pointed from vertex `1` via directed edges, and so on, as shown in Figure 27.6.

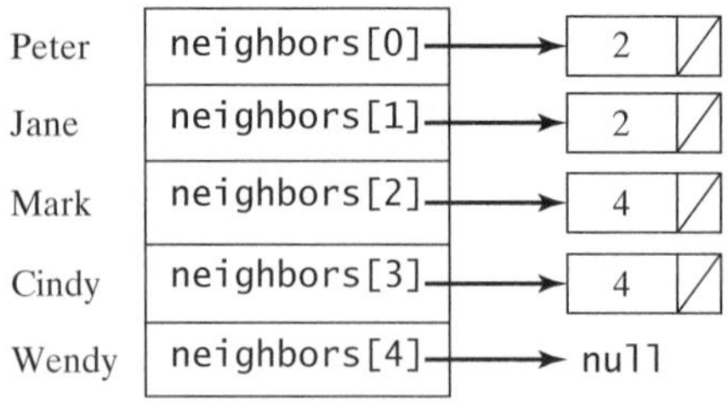
Peter
Jane
Mark
Cindy
Wendy
neighbors[0]
neighbors[1]
neighbors[2]
neighbors[3]
neighbors[4]
2
2
4
4
null

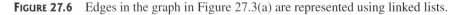

FIGURE 27.6 Edges in the graph in Figure 27.3(a) are represented using linked lists.

adjacency matrices vs. adjacency lists

Note

You can represent a graph using an adjacency matrix or adjacency lists. Which one is better? If the graph is dense (i.e., there are a lot of edges), using an adjacency matrix is preferred. If the graph is very sparse (i.e., very few edges), using adjacency lists is better, because using an adjacency matrix would waste a lot of space.

Both adjacency matrices and adjacency lists may be used in a program to make algorithms more efficient. For example, it takes $O(1)$ constant time to check whether two vertices are connected using an adjacency matrix and it takes linear time $O(m)$ to print all edges in a graph using adjacency lists, where m is the number of edges.

Note

Adjacency matrices and adjacency lists are two common representations for graphs, but they are not the only ways to represent graphs. For example, you may define a vertex as an object with a method `getNeighbors()` that returns all its neighbors. For simplicity, the text will use adjacency lists to represent graphs. Other representations will be explored in the exercises.

other representations

using **ArrayList**

For flexibility and simplicity, we will use array lists to represent arrays. Also we will use array lists instead of linked lists, because our algorithms only require searching for adjacent vertices in the list. Using array lists is more efficient for our algorithms. Using array lists, the adjacency list in Figure 27.5 can be built as follows:

```
List<ArrayList<Integer>> neighbors
  = new ArrayList<List<Integer>>();
neighbors.add(new ArrayList<Integer>());
neighbors.get(0).add(1); neighbors.get(0).add(3);
  neighbors.get(0).add(5);
neighbors.add(new ArrayList<Integer>());
neighbors.get(1).add(0); neighbors.get(1).add(2);
  neighbors.get(1).add(3);
...
...
```

27.4 Modeling Graphs

The Java Collections Framework serves as a good example for designing complex data structures. The common features of data structures are defined in the interfaces (e.g., `Collection`, `Set`, `List`), as shown in Figure 22.1. Abstract classes (e.g., `AbstractCollection`, `AbstractSet`, `AbstractList`) partially implement the interfaces. Concrete classes (e.g., `HashSet`, `LinkedHashSet`, `TreeSet`, `ArrayList`, `LinkedList`, `PriorityQueue`) provide concrete implementations. This design pattern is useful to model graphs. We will define an interface named `Graph` that contains all common operations of graphs and an abstract class named `AbstractGraph` that partially implements the `Graph` interface. Many concrete graphs may be added to the design. For example, we will define such graphs named `UnweightedGraph` and `WeightedGraph`. The relationships of these interfaces and classes are illustrated in Figure 27.7.

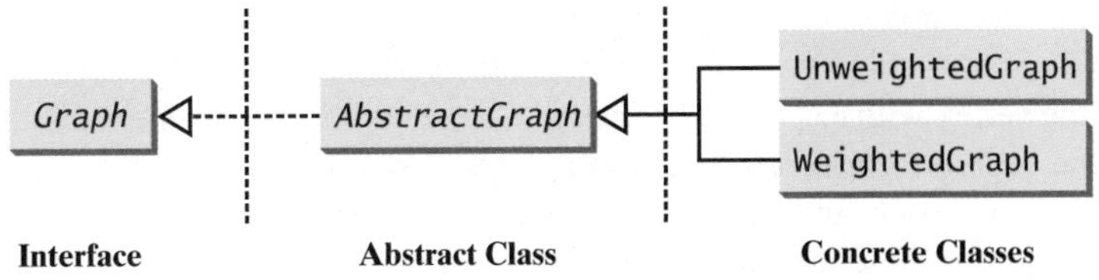
Graph
AbstractGraph
UnweightedGraph
WeightedGraph
Interface
Abstract Class
Concrete Classes

FIGURE 27.7 Graphs can be modeled using interfaces, abstract classes, and concrete classes.

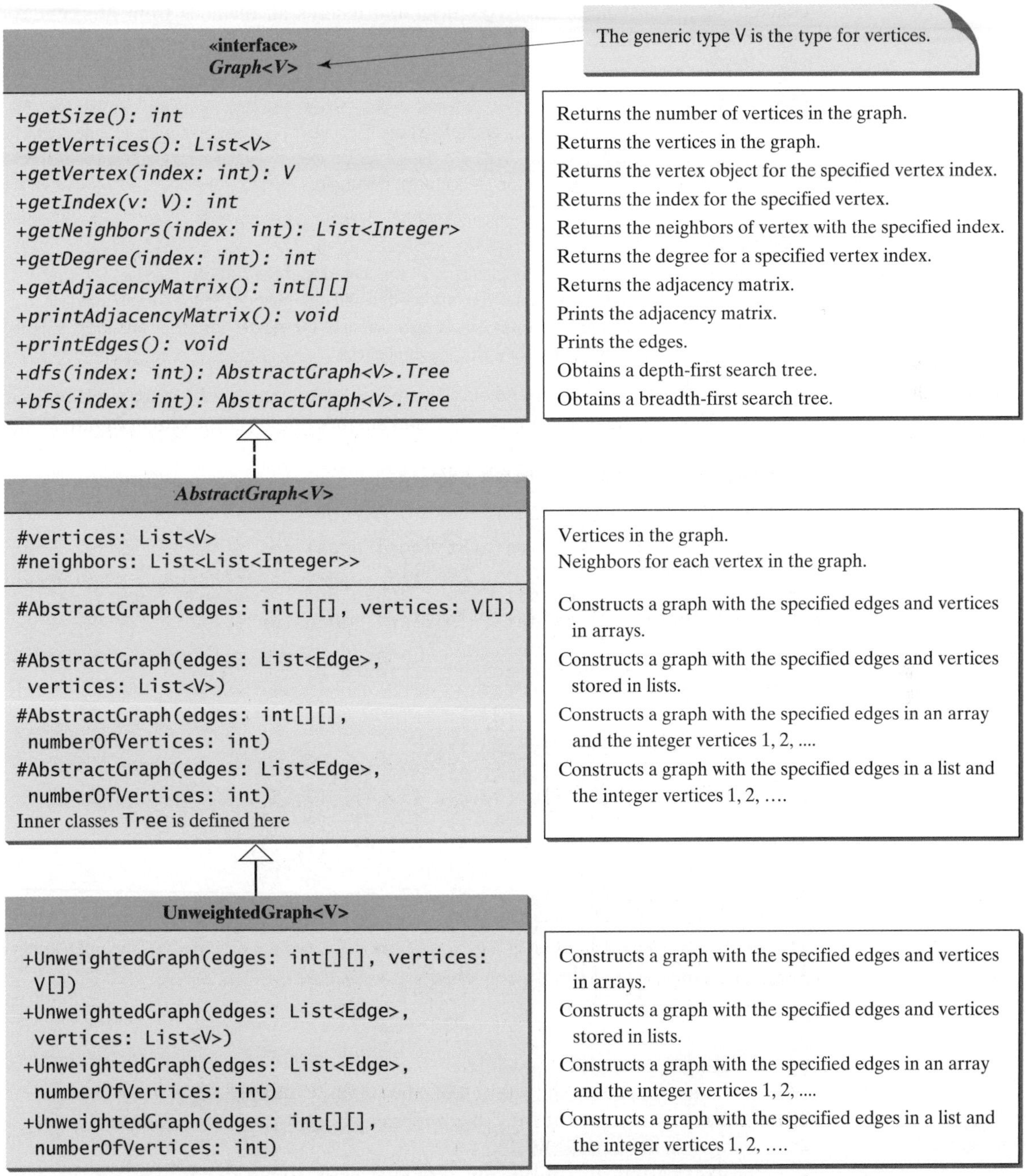
«interface»
Graph<V>
The generic type V is the type for vertices.
+getSize(): int
+getVertices(): List<V>
+getVertex(index: int): V
+getIndex(v: V): int
+getNeighbors(index: int): List<Integer>
+getDegree(index: int): int
+getAdjacencyMatrix(): int[][]
+printAdjacencyMatrix(): void
+printEdges(): void
+dfs(index: int): AbstractGraph<V>.Tree
+bfs(index: int): AbstractGraph<V>.Tree
Returns the number of vertices in the graph.
Returns the vertices in the graph.
Returns the vertex object for the specified vertex index.
Returns the index for the specified vertex.
Returns the neighbors of vertex with the specified index.
Returns the degree for a specified vertex index.
Returns the adjacency matrix.
Prints the adjacency matrix.
Prints the edges.
Obtains a depth-first search tree.
Obtains a breadth-first search tree.
AbstractGraph<V>
#vertices: List<V>
#neighbors: List<List<Integer>>
#AbstractGraph(edges: int[][], vertices: V[])
#AbstractGraph(edges: List<Edge>, vertices: List<V>)
#AbstractGraph(edges: int[][], numberOfVertices: int)
#AbstractGraph(edges: List<Edge>, numberOfVertices: int)
Inner classes Tree is defined here
Vertices in the graph.
Neighbors for each vertex in the graph.
Constructs a graph with the specified edges and vertices in arrays.
Constructs a graph with the specified edges and vertices stored in lists.
Constructs a graph with the specified edges in an array and the integer vertices 1, 2, ...
Constructs a graph with the specified edges in a list and the integer vertices 1, 2, ...
UnweightedGraph<V>
+UnweightedGraph(edges: int[][], vertices: V[])
+UnweightedGraph(edges: List<Edge>, vertices: List<V>)
+UnweightedGraph(edges: List<Edge>, numberOfVertices: int)
+UnweightedGraph(edges: int[][], numberOfVertices: int)
Constructs a graph with the specified edges and vertices in arrays.
Constructs a graph with the specified edges and vertices stored in lists.
Constructs a graph with the specified edges in an array and the integer vertices 1, 2, ...
Constructs a graph with the specified edges in a list and the integer vertices 1, 2, ...

FIGURE 27.8 The Graph interface defines the common operations for all types of graphs.

What are the common operations for a graph? In general, you need to get the number of vertices in a graph, get all vertices in a graph, get the vertex object with a specified index, get the index of the vertex with a specified name, get the neighbors for a vertex, get the adjacency matrix, get the degree for a vertex, perform a depth-first search, and perform a breadth-first search. Depth-first search and breadth-first search will be introduced in the next section. Figure 27.8 illustrates these methods in the UML diagram.

AbstractGraph does not introduce any new methods. A list of vertices and a list of adjacency lists for the vertices are defined in the **AbstractGraph** class. With these data fields, it is sufficient to implement all the methods defined in the **Graph** interface.

UnweightedGraph simply extends **AbstractGraph** with four constructors for creating the concrete **Graph** instances. **UnweightedGraph** inherits all methods from **AbstractGraph**, and it does not introduce any new methods.

vertices and their indices

Note

You can create a graph with any type of vertices. Each vertex is associated with an index, which is the same as the index of the vertex in the list for vertices. If you create a graph without specifying the vertices, the vertices are the same as their indices.

why **AbstractGraph**?

Note

The **AbstractGraph** class implements all the methods in the **Graph** interface. So, why is it defined as abstract? In the future, you may need to add new methods to the **Graph** interface that cannot be implemented in **AbstractGraph**. To make the classes easy to maintain, it is desirable to define the **AbstractGraph** class as abstract.

Assume all these interfaces and classes are available. Listing 27.1 gives a test program that creates a graph for the one in Figure 27.1 and another graph for the one in Figure 27.3(a).

LISTING 27.1 TestGraph.java

vertices · edges · create a graph · number of vertices · get vertex

```
public class TestGraph {
  public static void main(String[] args) {
    String[] vertices = {"Seattle", "San Francisco", "Los Angeles",
      "Denver", "Kansas City", "Chicago", "Boston", "New York",
      "Atlanta", "Miami", "Dallas", "Houston"};

    // Edge array for graph in Figure 27.1
    int[][] edges = {
      {0, 1}, {0, 3}, {0, 5},
      {1, 0}, {1, 2}, {1, 3},
      {2, 1}, {2, 3}, {2, 4}, {2, 10},
      {3, 0}, {3, 1}, {3, 2}, {3, 4}, {3, 5},
      {4, 2}, {4, 3}, {4, 5}, {4, 7}, {4, 8}, {4, 10},
      {5, 0}, {5, 3}, {5, 4}, {5, 6}, {5, 7},
      {6, 5}, {6, 7},
      {7, 4}, {7, 5}, {7, 6}, {7, 8},
      {8, 4}, {8, 7}, {8, 9}, {8, 10}, {8, 11},
      {9, 8}, {9, 11},
      {10, 2}, {10, 4}, {10, 8}, {10, 11},
      {11, 8}, {11, 9}, {11, 10}
    };

    Graph<String> graph1 =
      new UnweightedGraph<String>(edges, vertices);
    System.out.println("The number of vertices in graph1: "
      + graph1.getSize());
    System.out.println("The vertex with index 1 is "
      + graph1.getVertex(1));
```

```java
    System.out.println("The index for Miami is " +
      graph1.getIndex("Miami"));
    System.out.println("The edges for graph1:");
    graph1.printEdges();
    System.out.println("Adjacency matrix for graph1:");
    graph1.printAdjacencyMatrix();

    // List of Edge objects for graph in Figure 27.3(a)
    String[] names = {"Peter", "Jane", "Mark", "Cindy", "Wendy"};
    java.util.ArrayList<AbstractGraph.Edge> edgeList
      = new java.util.ArrayList<AbstractGraph.Edge>();
    edgeList.add(new AbstractGraph.Edge(0, 2));
    edgeList.add(new AbstractGraph.Edge(1, 2));
    edgeList.add(new AbstractGraph.Edge(2, 4));
    edgeList.add(new AbstractGraph.Edge(3, 4));
    // Create a graph with 5 vertices
    Graph<String> graph2 = new UnweightedGraph<String>
      (edgeList, java.util.Arrays.asList(names));
    System.out.println("The number of vertices in graph2: "
      + graph2.getSize());
    System.out.println("The edges for graph2:");
    graph2.printEdges();
    System.out.println("\nAdjacency matrix for graph2:");
    graph2.printAdjacencyMatrix();

    for (int i = 0; i < 5; i++)
      System.out.println("vertex " + i + ": " + graph2.getVertex(i));
  }
}
```

get index

print edges

print adjacency matrix

list of **Edge** objects

create a graph

print edges

print adjacency matrix

```
The number of vertices in graph1: 12
The vertex with index 1 is San Francisco
The index for Miami is 9
The edges for graph1:
Vertex 0: (0, 1) (0, 3) (0, 5)
Vertex 1: (1, 0) (1, 2) (1, 3)
Vertex 2: (2, 1) (2, 3) (2, 4) (2, 10)
Vertex 3: (3, 0) (3, 1) (3, 2) (3, 4) (3, 5)
Vertex 4: (4, 2) (4, 3) (4, 5) (4, 7) (4, 8) (4, 10)
Vertex 5: (5, 0) (5, 3) (5, 4) (5, 6) (5, 7)
Vertex 6: (6, 5) (6, 7)
Vertex 7: (7, 4) (7, 5) (7, 6) (7, 8)
Vertex 8: (8, 4) (8, 7) (8, 9) (8, 10) (8, 11)
Vertex 9: (9, 8) (9, 11)
Vertex 10: (10, 2) (10, 4) (10, 8) (10, 11)
Vertex 11: (11, 8) (11, 9) (11, 10)
Adjacency matrix for graph1:
0 1 0 1 0 1 0 0 0 0 0 0
1 0 1 1 0 0 0 0 0 0 0 0
0 1 0 1 1 0 0 0 0 0 1 0
1 1 1 0 1 1 0 0 0 0 0 0
0 0 1 1 0 1 0 1 1 0 1 0
1 0 0 1 1 0 1 1 0 0 0 0
0 0 0 0 0 1 0 1 0 0 0 0
0 0 0 0 1 1 1 0 1 0 0 0
0 0 0 0 1 0 0 1 0 1 1 1
0 0 0 0 0 0 0 0 1 0 0 1
0 0 1 0 1 0 0 0 1 0 0 1
0 0 0 0 0 0 0 0 1 1 1 0
```

```
The number of vertices in graph2: 5
The edges for graph2:
Vertex 0: (0, 2)
Vertex 1: (1, 2)
Vertex 2: (2, 4)
Vertex 3: (3, 4)
Vertex 4:

Adjacency matrix for graph2:
0 0 1 0 0
0 0 1 0 0
0 0 0 0 1
0 0 0 0 1
0 0 0 0 0
vertex 0: Peter
vertex 1: Jane
vertex 2: Mark
vertex 3: Cindy
vertex 4: Wendy
```

The program creates **graph1** for the graph in Figure 27.1 in lines 3–24. The vertices for **graph1** are defined in lines 3–5. The edges for **graph1** are defined in 8–21. The edges are represented using a two-dimensional array. For each row **i** in the array, **edges[i][0]** and **edges[i][1]** indicate that there is an edge from vertex **edges[i][0]** to vertex **edges[i][1]**. For example, the first row {**0**, **1**} represents the edge from vertex **0** (**edges[0][0]**) to vertex **1** (**edges[0][1]**). The row {**0**, **5**} represents the edge from vertex **0** (**edges[2][0]**) to vertex **5** (**edges[2][1]**). The graph is created in line 24. Line 32 invokes the **printEdges()** method on **graph1** to display all edges in **graph1**. Line 34 invokes the **printAdjacencyMatrix()** method on **graph1** to display the adjacency matrix for **graph1**.

The program creates **graph2** for the graph in Figure 27.3(a) in lines 37–46. The edges for **graph2** are defined in lines 40–43. **graph2** is created using a list of **Edge** objects in line 46. Line 50 invokes the **printEdges()** method on **graph2** to display all edges in **graph2**. Line 52 invokes the **printAdjacencyMatrix()** method on **graph2** to display the adjacency matrix for **graph1**.

Note that both graphs contain the vertices of strings. The vertices are associated with indices **0**, **1**, . . . , **n-1**. The index is the location of the vertex in **vertices**. For example, the index of vertex **Miami** is **9**.

Now we turn our attention to implementing the interface and classes. Listings 27.2, 27.3, and 27.4 give the **Graph** interface, the **AbstractGraph** class, and the **UnweightedGraph** class, respectively.

Listing 27.2 Graph.java

getSize

getVertices

getVertex

```
public interface Graph<V> {
  /** Return the number of vertices in the graph */
  public int getSize();

  /** Return the vertices in the graph */
  public java.util.List<V> getVertices();

  /** Return the object for the specified vertex index */
  public V getVertex(int index);

```

```java
  /** Return the index for the specified vertex object */
  public int getIndex(V v);

  /** Return the neighbors of vertex with the specified index */
  public java.util.List<Integer> getNeighbors(int index);

  /** Return the degree for a specified vertex */
  public int getDegree(int v);

  /** Return the adjacency matrix */
  public int[][] getAdjacencyMatrix();

  /** Print the adjacency matrix */
  public void printAdjacencyMatrix();

  /** Print the edges */
  public void printEdges();

  /** Obtain a depth-first search tree */
  public AbstractGraph<V>.Tree dfs(int v);

  /** Obtain a breadth-first search tree */
  public AbstractGraph<V>.Tree bfs(int v);
}
```

`getIndex` `getNeighbors` `getDegree` `getAdjacencyMatrix` `printAdjacencyMatrix` `printEdges` `dfs` `bfs`

LISTING 27.3 AbstractGraph.java

```java
import java.util.*;

public abstract class AbstractGraph<V> implements Graph<V> {
  protected List<V> vertices; // Store vertices
  protected List<List<Integer>> neighbors; // Adjacency lists

  /** Construct a graph from edges and vertices stored in arrays */
  protected AbstractGraph(int[][] edges, V[] vertices) {
    this.vertices = new ArrayList<V>();
    for (int i = 0; i < vertices.length; i++)
      this.vertices.add(vertices[i]);

    createAdjacencyLists(edges, vertices.length);
  }

  /** Construct a graph from edges and vertices stored in List */
  protected AbstractGraph(List<Edge> edges, List<V> vertices) {
    this.vertices = vertices;
    createAdjacencyLists(edges, vertices.size());
  }

  /** Construct a graph for integer vertices 0, 1, 2 and edge list */
  protected AbstractGraph(List<Edge> edges, int numberOfVertices) {
    vertices = new ArrayList<V>(); // Create vertices
    for (int i = 0; i < numberOfVertices; i++) {
      vertices.add((V)(new Integer(i))); // vertices is {0, 1, ...}
    }
    createAdjacencyLists(edges, numberOfVertices);
  }

```

constructor

constructor

constructor

constructor

```
  /** Construct a graph from integer vertices 0, 1, and edge array */
  protected AbstractGraph(int[][] edges, int numberOfVertices) {
    vertices = new ArrayList<V>(); // Create vertices
    for (int i = 0; i < numberOfVertices; i++) {
      vertices.add((V)(new Integer(i))); // vertices is {0, 1, ...}
    }
    createAdjacencyLists(edges, numberOfVertices);
  }

  /** Create adjacency lists for each vertex */
  private void createAdjacencyLists(
      int[][] edges, int numberOfVertices) {
    // Create a linked list
    neighbors = new ArrayList<List<Integer>>();
    for (int i = 0; i < numberOfVertices; i++) {
      neighbors.add(new ArrayList<Integer>());
    }

    for (int i = 0; i < edges.length; i++) {
      int u = edges[i][0];
      int v = edges[i][1];
      neighbors.get(u).add(v);
    }
  }

  /** Create adjacency lists for each vertex */
  private void createAdjacencyLists(
      List<Edge> edges, int numberOfVertices) {
    // Create a linked list
    neighbors = new ArrayList<List<Integer>>();
    for (int i = 0; i < numberOfVertices; i++) {
      neighbors.add(new ArrayList<Integer>());
    }

    for (Edge edge: edges) {
      neighbors.get(edge.u).add(edge.v);
    }
  }

  /** Return the number of vertices in the graph */
```

getSize

```
  public int getSize() {
    return vertices.size();
  }

  /** Return the vertices in the graph */
```

getVertices

```
  public List<V> getVertices() {
    return vertices;
  }

  /** Return the object for the specified vertex */
```

getVertex

```
  public V getVertex(int index) {
    return vertices.get(index);
  }

  /** Return the index for the specified vertex object */
```

getIndex

```
  public int getIndex(V v) {
    return vertices.indexOf(v);
  }

```

getNeighbors

```
  /** Return the neighbors of vertex with the specified index */
  public List<Integer> getNeighbors(int index) {
    return neighbors.get(index);
  }

```

getDegrees

```
  /** Return the degree for a specified vertex */
  public int getDegree(int v) {
    return neighbors.get(v).size();
  }

```

getAdjacencyMatrix

```
  /** Return the adjacency matrix */
  public int[][] getAdjacencyMatrix() {
    int[][] adjacencyMatrix = new int[getSize()][getSize()];

    for (int i = 0; i < neighbors.size(); i++) {
      for (int j = 0; j < neighbors.get(i).size(); j++) {
        int v = neighbors.get(i).get(j);
        adjacencyMatrix[i][v] = 1;
      }
    }

    return adjacencyMatrix;
  }

```

printAdjacencyMatrix

```
  /** Print the adjacency matrix */
  public void printAdjacencyMatrix() {
    int[][] adjacencyMatrix = getAdjacencyMatrix();
    for (int i = 0; i < adjacencyMatrix.length; i++) {
      for (int j = 0; j < adjacencyMatrix[0].length; j++) {
        System.out.print(adjacencyMatrix[i][j] + " ");
      }

      System.out.println();
    }
  }

```

printEdges

```
  /** Print the edges */
  public void printEdges() {
    for (int u = 0; u < neighbors.size(); u++) {
      System.out.print("Vertex " + u + ": ");
      for (int j = 0; j < neighbors.get(u).size(); j++) {
        System.out.print("(" + u + ", " +
          neighbors.get(u).get(j) + ") ");
      }
      System.out.println();
    }
  }

```

Edge inner class

```
  /** Edge inner class inside the AbstractGraph class */
  public static class Edge {
    public int u; // Starting vertex of the edge
    public int v; // Ending vertex of the edge

    /** Construct an edge for (u, v) */
    public Edge(int u, int v) {
      this.u = u;
      this.v = v;
    }
  }

```

dfs method

bfs method

```
  /** Obtain a DFS tree starting from vertex v */
  /** To be discussed in Section 27.6 */
  public Tree dfs(int v) {
    List<Integer> searchOrders = new ArrayList<Integer>();
    int[] parent = new int[vertices.size()];
    for (int i = 0; i < parent.length; i++)
      parent[i] = -1; // Initialize parent[i] to -1

    // Mark visited vertices
    boolean[] isVisited = new boolean[vertices.size()];

    // Recursively search
    dfs(v, parent, searchOrders, isVisited);

    // Return a search tree
    return new Tree(v, parent, searchOrders);
  }

  /** Recursive method for DFS search */
  private void dfs(int v, int[] parent, List<Integer> searchOrders,
      boolean[] isVisited) {
    // Store the visited vertex
    searchOrders.add(v);
    isVisited[v] = true; // Vertex v visited

    for (int i : neighbors.get(v)) {
      if (!isVisited[i]) {
        parent[i] = v; // The parent of vertex i is v
        dfs(i, parent, searchOrders, isVisited); // Recursive search
      }
    }
  }

  /** Starting bfs search from vertex v */
  /** To be discussed in Section 27.7 */
  public Tree bfs(int v) {
    List<Integer> searchOrders = new ArrayList<Integer>();
    int[] parent = new int[vertices.size()];
    for (int i = 0; i < parent.length; i++)
      parent[i] = -1; // Initialize parent[i] to -1

    java.util.LinkedList<Integer> queue =
      new java.util.LinkedList<Integer>(); // list used as a queue
    boolean[] isVisited = new boolean[vertices.size()];
    queue.offer(v); // Enqueue v
    isVisited[v] = true; // Mark it visited

    while (!queue.isEmpty()) {
      int u = queue.poll(); // Dequeue to u
      searchOrders.add(u); // u searched
      for (int w : neighbors.get(u)) {
        if (!isVisited[w]) {
          queue.offer(w); // Enqueue w
          parent[w] = u; // The parent of w is u
          isVisited[w] = true; // Mark it visited
        }
      }
    }

```

```
    return new Tree(v, parent, searchOrders);
  }

  /** Tree inner class inside the AbstractGraph class */
  /** To be discussed in Section 27.5 */
  public class Tree {
    private int root; // The root of the tree
    private int[] parent; // Store the parent of each vertex
    private List<Integer> searchOrders; // Store the search order

    /** Construct a tree with root, parent, and searchOrder */
    public Tree(int root, int[] parent, List<Integer> searchOrders) {
      this.root = root;
      this.parent = parent;
      this.searchOrders = searchOrders;
    }

    /** Construct a tree with root and parent without a
     *  particular order */
    public Tree(int root, int[] parent) {
      this.root = root;
      this.parent = parent;
    }

    /** Return the root of the tree */
    public int getRoot() {
      return root;
    }

    /** Return the parent of vertex v */
    public int getParent(int v) {
      return parent[v];
    }

    /** Return an array representing search order */
    public List<Integer> getSearchOrders() {
      return searchOrders;
    }

    /** Return number of vertices found */
    public int getNumberOfVerticesFound() {
      return searchOrders.size();
    }

    /** Return the path of vertices from a vertex index to the root */
    public List<V> getPath(int index) {
      ArrayList<V> path = new ArrayList<V>();

      do {
        path.add(vertices.get(index));
        index = parent[index];
      }
      while (index != -1);

      return path;
    }

    /** Print a path from the root to vertex v */
    public void printPath(int index) {
      List<V> path = getPath(index);
```

Tree inner class

```
269       System.out.print("A path from " + vertices.get(root) + " to " +
270         vertices.get(index) + ": ");
271       for (int i = path.size() - 1; i >= 0; i--)
272         System.out.print(path.get(i) + " ");
273     }
274
275     /** Print the whole tree */
276     public void printTree() {
277       System.out.println("Root is: " + vertices.get(root));
278       System.out.print("Edges: ");
279       for (int i = 0; i < parent.length; i++) {
280         if (parent[i] != -1) {
281           // Display an edge
282           System.out.print("(" + vertices.get(parent[i]) + ", " +
283             vertices.get(i) + ") ");
284         }
285       }
286       System.out.println();
287     }
288   }
289 }
```

LISTING 27.4 UnweightedGraph.java

```
import java.util.*;

public class UnweightedGraph<V> extends AbstractGraph<V> {
  /** Construct a graph from edges and vertices stored in arrays */
```

constructor

```
  public UnweightedGraph(int[][] edges, V[] vertices) {
    super(edges, vertices);
  }

  /** Construct a graph from edges and vertices stored in List */
```

constructor

```
  public UnweightedGraph(List<Edge> edges, List<V> vertices) {
    super(edges, vertices);
  }

  /** Construct a graph for integer vertices 0, 1, 2 and edge list */
```

constructor

```
  public UnweightedGraph(List<Edge> edges, int numberOfVertices) {
    super(edges, numberOfVertices);
  }

  /** Construct a graph from integer vertices 0, 1, and edge array */
```

constructor

```
  public UnweightedGraph(int[][] edges, int numberOfVertices) {
    super(edges, numberOfVertices);
  }
}
```

The code in the `Graph` interface in Listing 27.2 and the `UnweightedGraph` class are straightforward. Let us digest the code in the `AbstractGraph` class in Listing 27.3.

The `AbstractGraph` class defines the data field `vertices` (line 4) to store vertices and `neighbors` (line 5) to store edges in adjacency lists. `neighbors.get(i)` stores all vertices adjacent to vertex `i`. Four overloaded constructors are defined in lines 8–38 to create graphs from arrays or lists of edges and vertices. The `createAdjacencyLists(int[][] edges, int numberOfVertice)` method creates adjacency lists from edges in an array (lines 41–54). The `createAdjacencyLists(List<Edge> edges, int numberOfVertice)` method creates adjacency lists from edges in a list (lines 57–68).

The `getAdjacencyMatrix()` method (lines 101–112) returns a two-dimensional array for representing an adjacency matrix of the edges. The `printAdjacencyMatrix()` method (lines 115–124) displays the adjacency matrix. The `printEdges()` method (lines 127–136) displays all vertices and edges adjacent to each vertex.

The code in lines 150–288 gives the methods for finding a depth-first search tree and a breadth-first search tree, which will be introduced in §§27.7–27.8.

27.5 Graph Visualization

The preceding section introduced how to model a graph using the `Graph` interface, `AbstractGraph` class, and `UnweightedGraph` class. This section introduces how to display graphs graphically. In order to display a graph, you need to know where each vertex is displayed and the name of each vertex. To ensure a graph can be displayed, we define an interface named `Displayable` in Listing 27.5 and make vertices instances of `Displayable`.

Listing 27.5 Displayable.java

`Displayable` interface

```java
public interface Displayable {
  public int getX(); // Get x-coordinate of the vertex
  public int getY(); // Get y-coordinate of the vertex
  public String getName(); // Get display name of the vertex
}
```

A graph with `Displayable` vertices can now be displayed on a panel named `GraphView` as shown in Listing 27.6.

Listing 27.6 GraphView.java

`Displayable` interface

```java
public class GraphView extends javax.swing.JPanel {
  private Graph<? extends Displayable> graph;

  public GraphView(Graph<? extends Displayable> graph) {
    this.graph = graph;
  }

  protected void paintComponent(java.awt.Graphics g) {
    super.paintComponent(g);

    // Draw vertices
    java.util.List<? extends Displayable> vertices
      = graph.getVertices();
    for (int i = 0; i < graph.getSize(); i++) {
      int x = vertices.get(i).getX();
      int y = vertices.get(i).getY();
      String name = vertices.get(i).getName();

      g.fillOval(x - 8, y - 8, 16, 16); // Display a vertex
      g.drawString(name, x - 12, y - 12); // Display the name
    }

    // Draw edges for pair of vertices
    for (int i = 0; i < graph.getSize(); i++) {
      java.util.List<Integer> neighbors = graph.getNeighbors(i);
      for (int j = 0; j < neighbors.size(); j++) {
        int v = neighbors.get(j);
        int x1 = graph.getVertex(i).getX();
        int y1 = graph.getVertex(i).getY();
        int x2 = graph.getVertex(v).getX();
```

```
31         int y2 = graph.getVertex(v).getY();
32
33         g.drawLine(x1, y1, x2, y2); // Draw an edge for (i, v)
34       }
35     }
36   }
37 }
```

To display a graph on a panel, simply create an instance of **GraphView** by passing the graph as an argument in the constructor (line 4). The class for the vertex of the graph must implement the **Displayable** interface in order to display the vertices (lines 12–21). For each vertex index **i**, invoking **graph.getNeighbors(i)** returns its adjacency list (line 25). From this list, you can find all vertices that are adjacent to **i** and draw a line to connect **i** with its adjacent vertex (lines 27–33).

Listing 27.7 gives an example of displaying the graph in Figure 27.1, as shown in Figure 27.9.

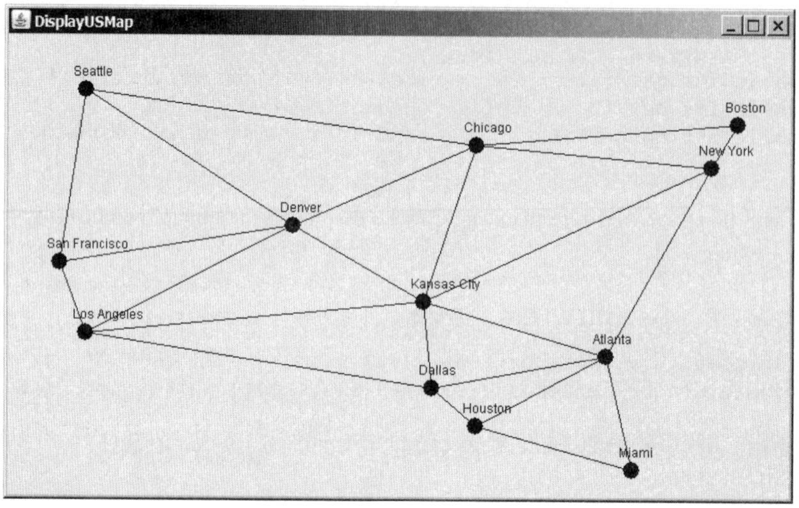
DisplayUSMap
Seattle
Boston
Chicago
New York
Denver
San Francisco
Kansas City
Los Angeles
Atlanta
Dallas
Houston
Miami

FIGURE 27.9 The graph is displayed on the panel.

LISTING 27.7 DisplayUSMap.java

```
import javax.swing.*;

public class DisplayUSMap extends JApplet {
  private City[] vertices = {new City("Seattle", 75, 50),
    new City("San Francisco", 50, 210),
    new City("Los Angeles", 75, 275), new City("Denver", 275, 175),
    new City("Kansas City", 400, 245),
    new City("Chicago", 450, 100), new City("Boston", 700, 80),
    new City("New York", 675, 120), new City("Atlanta", 575, 295),
    new City("Miami", 600, 400), new City("Dallas", 408, 325),
    new City("Houston", 450, 360) };

  // Edge array for graph in Figure 27.1
  private int[][] edges = {
    {0, 1}, {0, 3}, {0, 5}, {1, 0}, {1, 2}, {1, 3},
    {2, 1}, {2, 3}, {2, 4}, {2, 10},
    {3, 0}, {3, 1}, {3, 2}, {3, 4}, {3, 5},
    {4, 2}, {4, 3}, {4, 5}, {4, 7}, {4, 8}, {4, 10},
    {5, 0}, {5, 3}, {5, 4}, {5, 6}, {5, 7},
    {6, 5}, {6, 7}, {7, 4}, {7, 5}, {7, 6}, {7, 8},
```

```
21      {8, 4}, {8, 7}, {8, 9}, {8, 10}, {8, 11},
22      {9, 8}, {9, 11}, {10, 2}, {10, 4}, {10, 8}, {10, 11},
23      {11, 8}, {11, 9}, {11, 10}
24    };
25
26    private Graph<City> graph
27      = new UnweightedGraph<City>(edges, vertices);
28
29    public DisplayUSMap() {
30      add(new GraphView(graph));
31    }
32
33    static class City implements Displayable {
34      private int x, y;
35      private String name;
36
37      City(String name, int x, int y) {
38        this.name = name;
39        this.x = x;
40        this.y = y;
41      }
42
43      public int getX() {
44        return x;
45      }
46
47      public int getY() {
48        return y;
49      }
50
51      public String getName() {
52        return name;
53      }
54    }
55  }
```

create a graph

create a **GraphView**

City class

main method omitted

The class **City** is defined to model the vertices with the coordinates and name (lines 33–54). The program creates a graph with the vertices of the **City** type (line 27). Since **City** implements **Displayable**, a **GraphView** object can be created for the graph to be displayed in the panel (line 30).

27.6 Graph Traversals

depth-first

breadth-first

Graph traversal is the process of visiting each vertex in the graph exactly once. There are two popular ways to traverse a graph: *depth-first traversal* (or *depth-first search*) and *breadth-first traversal* (or *breadth-first search*). Both traversals result in a spanning tree, which can be modeled using a class, as shown in Figure 27.10. Note that **Tree** is an inner class defined in the **AbstractGraph** class. **AbstractGraph<V>.Tree** is different from the **Tree** interface defined in §26.2.5. **AbstractGraph.Tree** is a specialized class designed for describing the parent-child relationship of the nodes, whereas the **Tree** interface defines common operations such as search, insert, and delete in a tree. Since there is no need to perform these operations for a spanning tree, **AbstractGraph<V>.Tree** is not defined as a subtype of **Tree**.

The **Tree** class is defined as an inner class in the **AbstractGraph** class in lines 214–288 in Listing 27.3.

The **Tree** class has two constructors. The first constructs a tree with a search order and the second without a search order. The second constructor will be used in the next chapter for finding the minimum spanning tree and shortest path where search order is not important.

AbstractGraph<V>.Tree	
-root: int	The root of the tree.
-parent: int[]	The parents of the vertices.
-searchOrders: List<Integer>	The orders for traversing the vertices.
+Tree(root: int, parent: int[], searchOrders: List<Integer>)	Constructs a tree with the specified root, parent, and searchOrders.
+Tree(root: int, parent: int[])	Constructs a tree with the specified root and parent.
+getRoot(): int	Returns the root of the tree.
+getSearchOrders(): List<Integer>	Returns the order of vertices searched.
+getParent(index: int): int	Returns the parent for the specified vertex index.
+getNumberOfVerticesFound(): int	Returns the number of vertices searched.
+getPath(index: int): List<V>	Returns a list of vertices from the specified vertex index to the root.
+printPath(index: int): void	Displays a path from the root to the specified vertex.
+printTree(): void	Displays tree with the root and all edges.

FIGURE 27.10 The Tree class describes the nodes with parent-child relationship.

The Tree class defines seven methods. The getRoot() method returns the root of the tree. You can get the order of the vertices searched by invoking the getSearchOrders() method. You can invoke getParent(v) to find the parent of vertex v in the search. Invoking getNumberOfVerticesFound() returns the number of vertices searched. Invoking getPath(index) returns a list of vertices from the specified vertex index to the root. Invoking printPath(v) displays a path from the root to v. You can display all edges in the tree using the printTree() method.

Sections 27.7 and 27.8 will introduce depth-first search and breadth-first search, respectively. Both searches will result in an instance of the Tree class.

27.7 Depth-First Search (DFS)

The depth-first search of a graph is like the depth-first search of a tree discussed in §26.2.4, "Tree Traversal." In the case of a tree, the search starts from the root. In a graph, the search may start from any vertex.

A depth-first search of a tree first visits the root, then recursively visits the subtrees of the root. Similarly, the depth-first search of a graph first visits a vertex, then recursively visits all vertices adjacent to that vertex. The difference is that the graph may contain cycles, which may lead to an infinite recursion. To avoid this problem, you need to track the vertices that have already been visited.

The search is called depth-first, because it searches "deeper" in the graph as much as possible. The search starts from some vertex *v*. After visiting *v*, it next visits the first unvisited neighbor of *v*. If *v* has no unvisited neighbor, backtrack to the vertex from which we reached *v*.

27.7.1 Depth-First Search Algorithm

The algorithm for the depth-first search can be described in Listing 27.8.

LISTING 27.8 Depth-First Search Algorithm

visit v

```
dfs(vertex v) {
  visit v;
```

```
  for each neighbor w of v
    if (w has not been visited) {
      dfs(w);
    }
}
```

check a neighbor
recursive search

You may use an array named `isVisited` to denote whether a vertex has been visited. Initially, `isVisited[i]` is `false` for each vertex *i*. Once a vertex, say *v*, is visited, `isVisited[v]` is set to `true`.

Consider the graph in Figure 27.11(a). Suppose you start the depth-first search from vertex 0. First visit 0, then any of its neighbors, say 1. Now 1 is visited, as shown in Figure 27.11(b). Vertex 1 has three neighbors—0, 2, and 4. Since 0 has already been visited, you will visit either 2 or 4. Let us pick 2. Now 2 is visited, as shown in Figure 27.11(c). 2 has three neighbors 0, 1, and 3. Since 0 and 1 have already been visited, pick 3. 3 is now visited, as shown in Figure 27.11(d). At this point, the vertices have been visited in this order:

0, 1, 2, 3

Since all the neighbors of 3 have been visited, backtrack to 2. Since all the vertices of 2 have been visited, backtrack to 1. 4 is adjacent to 1, but 4 has not been visited. So, visit 4, as shown in Figure 27.11(e). Since all the neighbors of 4 have been visited, backtrack to 1. Since all the neighbors of 1 have been visited, backtrack to 0. Since all the neighbors of 0 have been visited, the search ends.

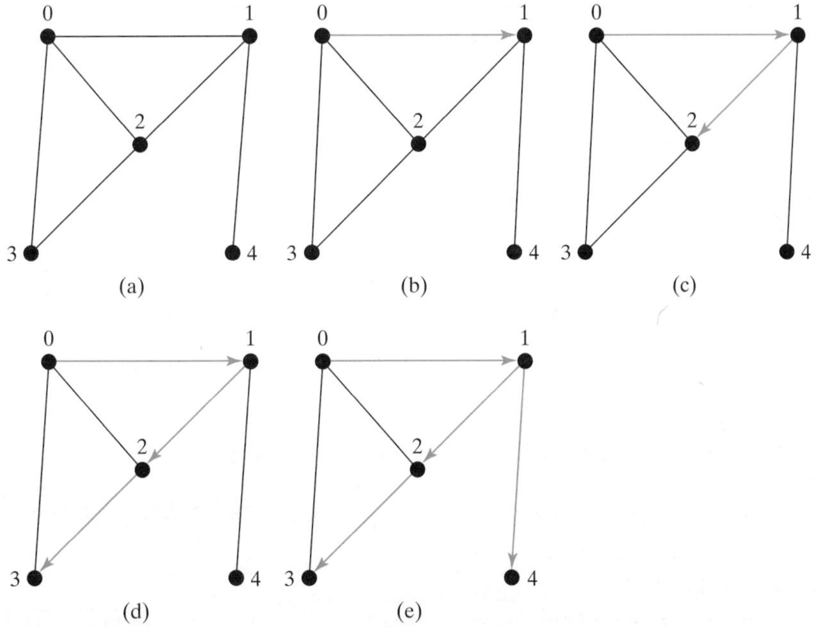
(a)
(b)
(c)
(d)
(e)

FIGURE 27.11 Depth-first search visits a node and its neighbors recursively.

DFS time complexity

Since each edge and each vertex is visited only once, the time complexity of the `dfs` method is `O(|E| + |V|)`, where `|E|` denotes the number of edges and `|V|` the number of vertices.

27.7.2 Implementation of Depth-First Search

The algorithm is described in Listing 27.8 using recursion. It is natural to use recursion to implement it. Alternatively, you can use a stack (see Exercise 27.3).

The `dfs(int v)` method is implemented in lines 152–181 in Listing 27.3. It returns an instance of the `Tree` class with vertex `v` as the root. The method stores the vertices searched in a list `searchOrders` (line 153), the parent of each vertex in an array `parent` (line 154), and uses the `isVisited` array to indicate whether a vertex has been visited (line 159). It invokes the helper method `dfs(v, parent, searchOrders, isVisited)` to perform a depth-first search (line 162).

In the recursive helper method, the search starts from vertex `v`. `v` is added to `searchOrders` in line 172 and is marked visited (line 173). For each unvisited neighbor of `v`, the method is recursively invoked to perform a depth-first search. When a vertex `i` is visited, the parent of `i` is stored in `parent[i]` (line 177). The method returns when all vertices are visited for a connected graph, or in a connected component.

Listing 27.9 gives a test program that displays a DFS for the graph in Figure 27.1 starting from Chicago. The graphical illustration of the DFS starting from Chicago is shown in Figure 27.12. For an interactive GUI program, see Exercise 27.19.

Listing 27.9 TestDFS.java

vertices
edges
create a graph
get DFS
get search order

```java
public class TestDFS {
  public static void main(String[] args) {
    String[] vertices = {"Seattle", "San Francisco", "Los Angeles",
      "Denver", "Kansas City", "Chicago", "Boston", "New York",
      "Atlanta", "Miami", "Dallas", "Houston"};

    int[][] edges = {
      {0, 1}, {0, 3}, {0, 5},
      {1, 0}, {1, 2}, {1, 3},
      {2, 1}, {2, 3}, {2, 4}, {2, 10},
      {3, 0}, {3, 1}, {3, 2}, {3, 4}, {3, 5},
      {4, 2}, {4, 3}, {4, 5}, {4, 7}, {4, 8}, {4, 10},
      {5, 0}, {5, 3}, {5, 4}, {5, 6}, {5, 7},
      {6, 5}, {6, 7},
      {7, 4}, {7, 5}, {7, 6}, {7, 8},
      {8, 4}, {8, 7}, {8, 9}, {8, 10}, {8, 11},
      {9, 8}, {9, 11},
      {10, 2}, {10, 4}, {10, 8}, {10, 11},
      {11, 8}, {11, 9}, {11, 10}
    };

    Graph<String> graph =
      new UnweightedGraph<String>(edges, vertices);
    AbstractGraph<String>.Tree dfs = graph.dfs(5); // 5 is Chicago

    java.util.List<Integer> searchOrders = dfs.getSearchOrders();
    System.out.println(dfs.getNumberOfVerticesFound() +
      " vertices are searched in this DFS order:");
    for (int i = 0; i < searchOrders.size(); i++)
      System.out.print(graph.getVertex(searchOrders.get(i)) + " ");
    System.out.println();

    for (int i = 0; i < searchOrders.size(); i++)
      if (dfs.getParent(i) != -1)
       System.out.println("parent of " + graph.getVertex(i) +
         " is " + graph.getVertex(dfs.getParent(i)));
  }
}
```

```
12 vertices are searched in this DFS order:
  Chicago Seattle San Francisco Los Angeles Denver
  Kansas City New York Boston Atlanta Miami Houston Dallas
parent of Seattle is Chicago
parent of San Francisco is Seattle
parent of Los Angeles is San Francisco
parent of Denver is Los Angeles
parent of Kansas City is Denver
parent of Boston is New York
parent of New York is Kansas City
parent of Atlanta is New York
parent of Miami is Atlanta
parent of Dallas is Houston
parent of Houston is Miami
```

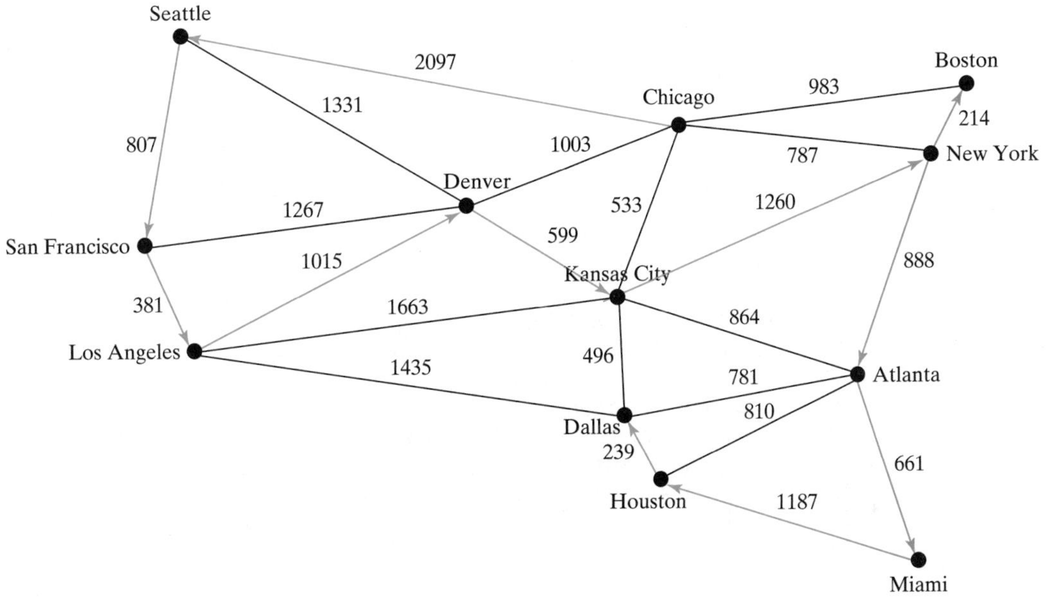
Seattle
2097
1331
807
Chicago
983
Boston
214
1003
787
New York
Denver
533
1260
1267
599
San Francisco
1015
Kansas City
888
381
1663
864
Los Angeles
1435
496
781
Atlanta
810
Dallas
239
661
Houston
1187
Miami

FIGURE 27.12 DFS search starts from Chicago.

27.7.3 Applications of the DFS

The depth-first search can be used to solve many problems, such as the following:

- Detecting whether a graph is connected. Search the graph starting from any vertex. If the number of vertices searched is the same as the number of vertices in the graph, the graph is connected. Otherwise, the graph is not connected. (See Exercise 27.1.)
- Detecting whether there is a path between two vertices. (See Exercise 27.5.)
- Finding a path between two vertices. (See Exercise 27.5.)
- Finding all connected components. A connected component is a maximal connected subgraph in which every pair of vertices are connected by a path. (See Exercise 27.4.)

- Detecting whether there is a cycle in the graph. (See Exercise 27.6.)
- Finding a cycle in the graph. (See Exercise 27.7.)

The first four problems can be easily solved using the `dfs` method in Listing 27.3. To detect or find a cycle in the graph, you have to slightly modify the `dfs` method.

27.8 Breadth-First Search (BFS)

The breadth-first traversal of a graph is like the breadth-first traversal of a tree discussed in §26.2.4, "Tree Traversal." With breadth-first traversal of a tree, the nodes are visited level by level. First the root is visited, then all the children of the root, then the grandchildren of the root, and so on. Similarly, the breadth-first search of a graph first visits a vertex, then all its adjacent vertices, then all the vertices adjacent to those vertices, and so on. To ensure that each vertex is visited only once, skip a vertex if it has already been visited.

27.8.1 Breadth-First Search Algorithm

The algorithm for the breadth-first search starting from vertex *v* in a graph can be described in Listing 27.10.

LISTING 27.10 Breadth-First Search Algorithm

create a queue
enqueue v
dequeue into u
u traversed
check a neighbor w
is w visited?
enqueue w

```
bfs(vertex v) {
  create an empty queue for storing vertices to be visited;
  add v into the queue;
  mark v visited;

  while the queue is not empty {
    dequeue a vertex, say u, from the queue
    add u into a list of traversed vertices;
    for each neighbor w of u
      if w has not been visited {
        add w into the queue;
        mark w visited;
      }
  }
}
```

Consider the graph in Figure 27.13(a). Suppose you start the breadth-first search from vertex 0. First visit 0, then all its visited neighbors, 1, 2, and 3, as shown in 27.13(b). Vertex 1 has three neighbors, 0, 2, and 4. Since 0 and 2 have already been visited, you will now visit just 4, as shown in Figure 27.13(c). Vertex 2 has three neighbors, 0, 1, and 3, which are all visited. Vertex 3 has three neighbors, 0, 2, and 4, which are all visited. Vertex 4 has two neighbors, 1 and 3, which are all visited. So, the search ends.

BFS time complexity

Since each edge and each vertex is visited only once, the time complexity of the `bfs` method is `O(|E| + |V|)`, where `|E|` denotes the number of edges and `|V|` the number of vertices.

27.8.2 Implementation of Breadth-First Search

The `bfs(int v)` method is defined in the `Graph` interface and implemented in the `AbstractGraph` class (lines 185–210). It returns an instance of the `Tree` class with vertex `v` as the root. The method stores the vertices searched in a list `searchOrders` (line 186), the parent of each vertex in an array `parent` (line 187), uses a linked list for a queue (lines 191–192), and uses the `isVisited` array to indicate whether a vertex has been visited (line 193). The search starts from vertex `v`. `v` is added to the queue in line 194 and is marked visited (line 195). The method now examines each vertex `u` in the queue (line 198) and adds it to

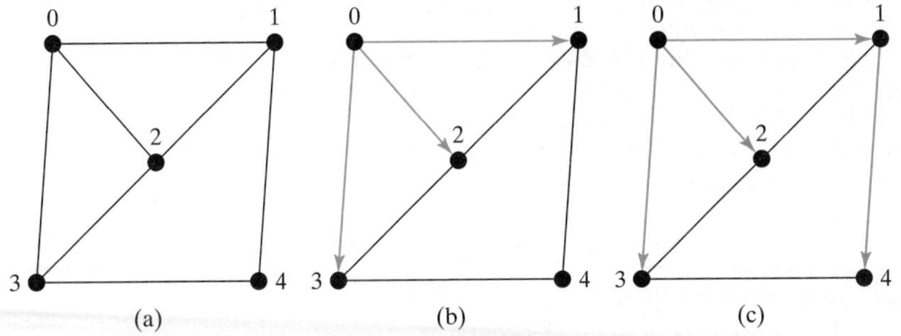
0
1
2
3
4
(a)
(b)
(c)

FIGURE 27.13 Breadth-first search visits a node, then its neighbors, then its neighbors' neighbors, and so on.

searchOrders (line 199). The method adds each unvisited neighbor w of u to the queue (line 202), set its parent to u (line 203), and mark it visited (line 204).

Listing 27.11 gives a test program that displays a BFS for the graph in Figure 27.1 starting from Chicago. The graphical illustration of the BFS starting from Chicago is shown in Figure 27.14. For an interactive GUI program, see Exercise 27.19.

LISTING 27.11 TestBFS.java

```java
public class TestBFS {
  public static void main(String[] args) {
    String[] vertices = {"Seattle", "San Francisco", "Los Angeles",
      "Denver", "Kansas City", "Chicago", "Boston", "New York",
      "Atlanta", "Miami", "Dallas", "Houston"};

    int[][] edges = {
      {0, 1}, {0, 3}, {0, 5},
      {1, 0}, {1, 2}, {1, 3},
      {2, 1}, {2, 3}, {2, 4}, {2, 10},
      {3, 0}, {3, 1}, {3, 2}, {3, 4}, {3, 5},
      {4, 2}, {4, 3}, {4, 5}, {4, 7}, {4, 8}, {4, 10},
      {5, 0}, {5, 3}, {5, 4}, {5, 6}, {5, 7},
      {6, 5}, {6, 7},
      {7, 4}, {7, 5}, {7, 6}, {7, 8},
      {8, 4}, {8, 7}, {8, 9}, {8, 10}, {8, 11},
      {9, 8}, {9, 11},
      {10, 2}, {10, 4}, {10, 8}, {10, 11},
      {11, 8}, {11, 9}, {11, 10}
    };

    Graph<String> graph =
      new UnweightedGraph<String>(edges, vertices);
    AbstractGraph<String>.Tree bfs = graph.bfs(5); // 5 is Chicago

    java.util.List<Integer> searchOrders = bfs.getSearchOrders();
    System.out.println(bfs.getNumberOfVerticesFound() +
      " vertices are searched in this order:");
    for (int i = 0; i < searchOrders.size(); i++)
      System.out.println(graph.getVertex(searchOrders.get(i)));

    for (int i = 0; i < searchOrders.size(); i++)
      if (bfs.getParent(i) != -1)
        System.out.println("parent of " + graph.getVertex(i) +
          " is " + graph.getVertex(bfs.getParent(i)));
  }
}
```

vertices

edges

create a graph

create a bfs tree

get search order

```
12 vertices are searched in this order:
  Chicago Seattle Denver Kansas City Boston New York
  San Francisco Los Angeles Atlanta Dallas Miami Houston
parent of Seattle is Chicago
parent of San Francisco is Seattle
parent of Los Angeles is Denver
parent of Denver is Chicago
parent of Kansas City is Chicago
parent of Boston is Chicago
parent of New York is Chicago
parent of Atlanta is Kansas City
parent of Miami is Atlanta
parent of Dallas is Kansas City
parent of Houston is Atlanta
```

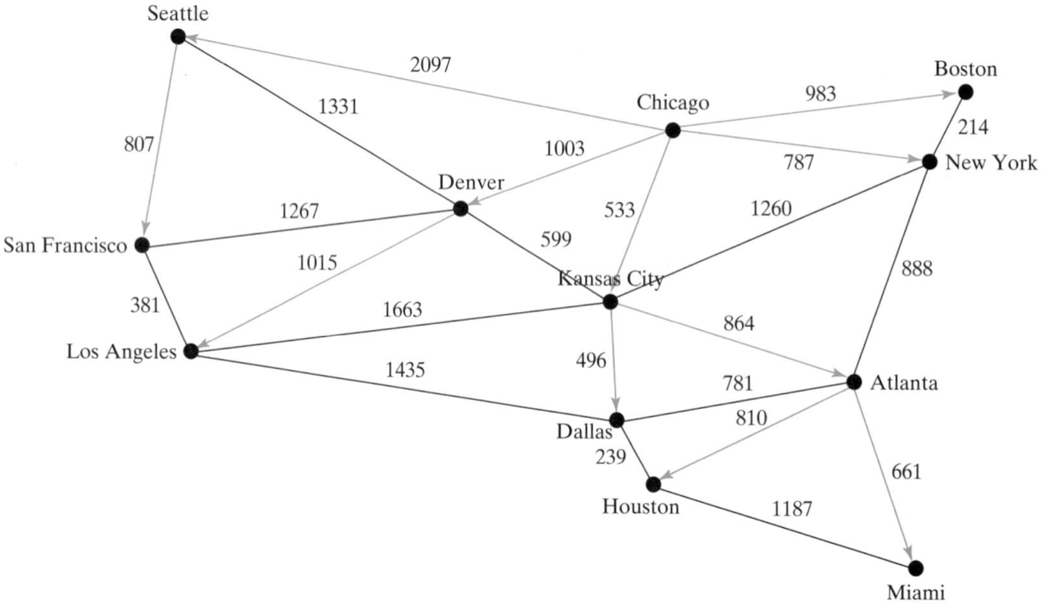
Seattle
2097
Boston
1331
Chicago
983
807
214
1003
787
New York
Denver
1267
533
1260
San Francisco
599
1015
Kansas City
888
381
1663
864
Los Angeles
1435
496
781
Atlanta
810
Dallas
239
661
Houston
1187
Miami

FIGURE 27.14 BFS search starts from Chicago.

The graphical illustration of the BFS starting from Chicago is shown in Figure 27.14.

27.8.3 Applications of the BFS

Many of the problems solved by the DFS can also be solved using the BFS. Specifically, the BFS can be used to solve the following problems:

- Detecting whether a graph is connected. A graph is connected if there is a path between any two vertices in the graph.
- Detecting whether there is a path between two vertices.
- Finding a shortest path between two vertices. You can prove that the path between the root and any node in the BFS tree is the shortest path between the root and the node. (See Review Question 27.10.)
- Finding all connected components. A connected component is a maximal connected subgraph in which every pair of vertices are connected by a path.

- Detecting whether there is a cycle in the graph. (See Exercise 27.6.)
- Finding a cycle in the graph. (See Exercise 27.7.)
- Testing whether a graph is bipartite. A graph is bipartite if the vertices of the graph can be divided into two disjoint sets such that no edges exist between vertices in the same set. (See Exercise 27.8.)

27.9 Case Study: The Nine Tail Problem

The DFS and BFS algorithms have many applications. This section applies the BFS to solve the nine tail problem.

The problem is stated as follows. Nine coins are placed in a three-by-three matrix with some face up and some face down. A legal move is to take any coin that is face up and reverse it, together with the coins adjacent to it (this does not include coins that are diagonally adjacent). Your task is to find the minimum number of moves that lead to all coins face down. For example, you start with the nine coins as shown in Figure 27.15(a). After you flip the second coin in the last row, the nine coins are now as shown in Figure 27.15(b). After you flip the second coin in the first row, the nine coins are all face down, as shown in Figure 27.15(c).

H	H	H
T	T	T
H	H	H

(a)

H	H	H
T	H	T
T	T	T

(b)

T	T	T
T	T	T
T	T	T

(c)

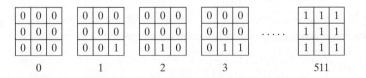

FIGURE 27.15 The problem is solved when all coins are face down.

We will write a program that prompts the user to enter an initial state of the nine coins and displays the solution, as shown in the following sample run.

```
Enter an initial nine coin H's and T's: HHHTTTHHH [Enter]

The steps to flip the coins are
HHH
TTT
HHH

HHH
THT
TTT

TTT
TTT
TTT
```

Each state of the nine coins represents a node in the graph. For example, the three states in Figure 27.15 correspond to three nodes in the graph. For convenience, we use a 3×3 matrix to represent all nodes and use 0 for head and 1 for tail. Since there are nine cells and each cell is either 0 or 1, there are a total of 2^9(512) nodes, labeled 0, 1, . . . , and 511, as shown in Figure 27.16.

0	0	0
0	0	0
0	0	0

0

0	0	0
0	0	0
0	0	1

1

0	0	0
0	0	0
0	1	0

2

0	0	0
0	0	0
0	1	1

3

.....

1	1	1
1	1	1
1	1	1

511

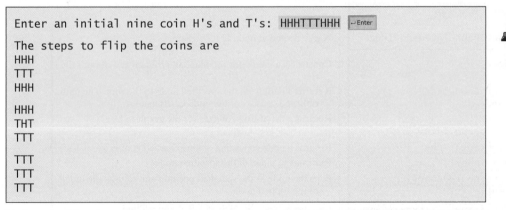

FIGURE 27.16 There are total of 512 nodes, labeled in this order as 0, 1, 2, . . . , 511.

We assign an edge from node u to v if there is a legal move from v to u. Figure 27.17 shows the directed edges to node 56.

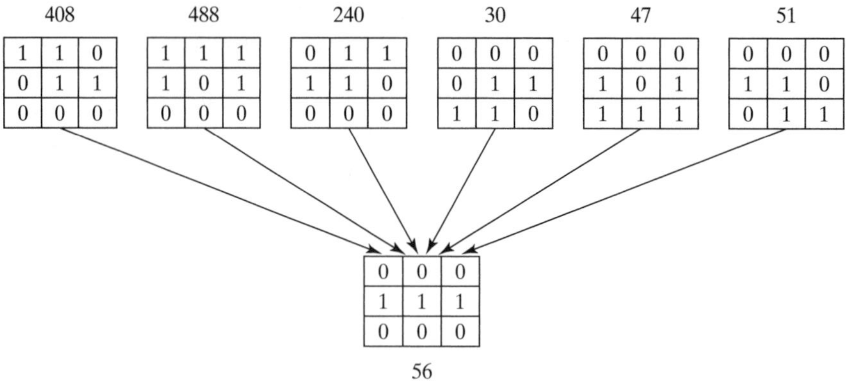
408
488
240
30
47
51
56

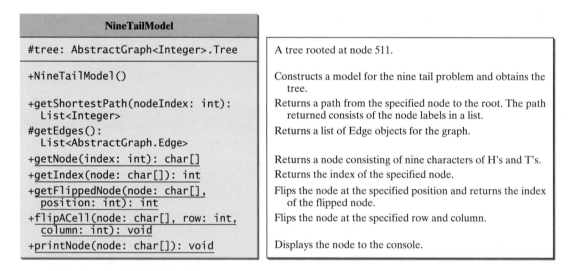

FIGURE 27.17 If node v becomes node u after cells are flipped, assign an edge from u to v.

The last node in Figure 27.16 represents the state of nine face-down coins. For convenience, we call this last node the *target node*. So, the target node is labeled 511. Suppose the initial state of the nine tail problem corresponds to the node s. The problem is reduced to finding a shortest path from node s to the target node, which is equivalent to finding a path from node s to the target node in a BFS tree rooted at the target node.

Now the task is to build a graph that consists of 512 nodes labeled 0, 1, 2, . . . , 511, and edges among the nodes. Once the graph is created, obtain a BFS tree rooted at node 511. From the BFS tree, you can find the shortest path from the root to any vertex. We will create a class named NineTailModel, which contains the method to get the shortest path from the target node to any other node. The class UML diagram is shown in Figure 27.18.

NineTailModel	
#tree: AbstractGraph<Integer>.Tree	A tree rooted at node 511.
+NineTailModel()	Constructs a model for the nine tail problem and obtains the tree.
+getShortestPath(nodeIndex: int): List<Integer>	Returns a path from the specified node to the root. The path returned consists of the node labels in a list.
#getEdges(): List<AbstractGraph.Edge>	Returns a list of Edge objects for the graph.
+getNode(index: int): char[]	Returns a node consisting of nine characters of H's and T's.
+getIndex(node: char[]): int	Returns the index of the specified node.
+getFlippedNode(node: char[], position: int): int	Flips the node at the specified position and returns the index of the flipped node.
+flipACell(node: char[], row: int, column: int): void	Flips the node at the specified row and column.
+printNode(node: char[]): void	Displays the node to the console.

FIGURE 27.18 The NineTailModel class models the nine tail problem using a graph.

Visually, a node is represented in a 3×3 matrix with letters H and T. In our program, we use a single-dimensional array of nine characters to represent a node. For example, the node for vertex 1 in Figure 27.16 is represented as {'H', 'H', 'H', 'H', 'H', 'H', 'H', 'H', 'T'} in the array.

The getEdges() method returns a list of Edge objects.

The getNode(index) method returns the node for the specified index. For example, getNode(0) returns the node that contains nine H's. getNode(511) returns the node that contains nine T's. The getIndex(node) method returns the index of the node.

Note that the data field `tree` and methods `getEdges()`, `getFlippedNode(node, position)`, and `flipACell(node, row, column)` are defined protected so that they can be accessed from subclasses in the next chapter.

The `getFlippedNode(char[] node, int position)` method flips the node at the specified position and its adjacent positions. This method returns the index of the new node. For example, for node 56 in Figure 27.17, flip it at position 0, and you will get node 51. If you flip node 56 at position 1, you will get node 47.

The `flipACell(char[] node, int row, int column)` method flips a node at the specified row and column. For example, if you flip node 56 at row 0 and column 0, the new node is 408. If you flip node 56 at row 2 and column 0, the new node is 30.

Listing 27.12 shows the source code for NineTailModel.java.

LISTING 27.12 NineTailModel.java

```
import java.util.*;

public class NineTailModel {
  public final static int NUMBER_OF_NODES = 512;
  protected AbstractGraph<Integer>.Tree tree; // Define a tree

  /** Construct a model */
  public NineTailModel() {
    // Create edges
    List<AbstractGraph.Edge> edges = getEdges();

    // Create a graph
    UnweightedGraph<Integer> graph = new UnweightedGraph<Integer>(
      edges, NUMBER_OF_NODES);

    // Obtain a BSF tree rooted at the target node
    tree = graph.bfs(511);
  }

  /** Create all edges for the graph */
  private List<AbstractGraph.Edge> getEdges() {
    List<AbstractGraph.Edge> edges =
      new ArrayList<AbstractGraph.Edge>(); // Store edges

    for (int u = 0; u < NUMBER_OF_NODES; u++) {
      for (int k = 0; k < 9; k++) {
        char[] node = getNode(u); // Get the node for vertex u
        if (node[k] == 'H') {
          int v = getFlippedNode(node, k);
          // Add edge (v, u) for a legal move from node u to node v
          edges.add(new AbstractGraph.Edge(v, u));
        }
      }
    }

    return edges;
  }

  public static int getFlippedNode(char[] node, int position) {
    int row = position / 3;
    int column = position % 3;

    flipACell(node, row, column);
    flipACell(node, row - 1, column);
```

declare a tree

create edges

create graph

create tree

get edges

add an edge

flip cells

```
    flipACell(node, row + 1, column);
    flipACell(node, row, column - 1);
    flipACell(node, row, column + 1);

    return getIndex(node);
  }

  public static void flipACell(char[] node, int row, int column) {
    if (row >= 0 && row <= 2 && column >= 0 && column <= 2) {
      // Within the boundary
      if (node[row * 3 + column] == 'H')
        node[row * 3 + column] = 'T'; // Flip from H to T
      else
        node[row * 3 + column] = 'H'; // Flip from T to H
    }
  }

  public static int getIndex(char[] node) {
    int result = 0;

    for (int i = 0; i < 9; i++)
      if (node[i] == 'T')
        result = result * 2 + 1;
      else
        result = result * 2 + 0;

    return result;
  }

  public static char[] getNode(int index) {
    char[] result = new char[9];

    for (int i = 0; i < 9; i++) {
      int digit = index % 2;
      if (digit == 0)
        result[8 - i] = 'H';
      else
        result[8 - i] = 'T';
      index = index / 2;
    }

    return result;
  }

  public List<Integer> getShortestPath(int nodeIndex) {
    return tree.getPath(nodeIndex);
  }

  public static void printNode(char[] node) {
    for (int i = 0; i < 9; i++)
      if (i % 3 != 2)
        System.out.print(node[i]);
      else
        System.out.println(node[i]);

    System.out.println();
  }
}
```

Margin notes: flip a cell; get index for a node; get node for an index; shortest path; display a node

For example:
index: 3
node: HHHHHHHTT

H	H	H
H	H	H
H	T	T

For example:
node: THHHHHHTT
index: 259

T	H	H
H	H	H
H	T	T

The constructor (lines 8–18) creates a graph with `512` nodes, and each edge corresponds to the move from one node to the other (line 10). From the graph, a BFS tree rooted at the target node `511` is obtained (line 17).

To create edges, the `getEdges` method (lines 21–37) checks each node `u` to see if it can be flipped to another node `v`. If so, add `(v, u)` to the `Edge` vector (line 31). The `getFlippedNode(node, position)` method finds a flipped node by flipping an `H` cell and its neighbors in a node (lines 43–47). The `flipACell(node, row, column)` method actually flips an `H` cell and its neighbors in a node (lines 52–60).

The `getIndex(node)` method is implemented in the same way as converting a binary number to a decimal (lines 62–72). The `getNode(index)` method returns a node consisting of letters `H` and `T`'s (lines 74–87).

The `getShortestpath(nodeIndex)` method invokes the `getPath(nodeIndex)` method to get the vertices in the shortest path from the specified node to the target node (lines 89–91).

The `printNode(node)` method displays a node to the console (lines 93–101).

Listing 27.13 gives a program that prompts the user to enter an initial node and displays the steps to reach the target node.

LISTING 27.13 `NineTail.java`

```
 1 import java.util.Scanner;
 2
 3 public class NineTail {
 4   public static void main(String[] args) {
 5     // Prompt the user to enter nine coins H's and T's
 6     System.out.print("Enter an initial nine coin H's and T's: ");
 7     Scanner input = new Scanner(System.in);
 8     String s = input.nextLine();
 9     char[] initialNode = s.toCharArray();
10
11     NineTailModel model = new NineTailModel();
12     java.util.List<Integer> path =
13       model.getShortestPath(NineTailModel.getIndex(initialNode));
14
15     System.out.println("The steps to flip the coins are ");
16     for (int i = 0; i < path.size(); i++)
17       NineTailModel.printNode(
18         NineTailModel.getNode(path.get(i).intValue()));
19   }
20 }
```

initial node

create model

get shortest path

The program prompts the user to enter an initial node with nine letters, `H`'s and `T`'s, as a string in line 8, obtains an array of characters from the string (line 9), creates a model to create a graph and get the BFS tree (line 11), obtains a shortest path from the initial node to the target node (lines 12–13), and displays the nodes in the path (lines 16–18).

27.10 Case Study: The Knight's Tour Problem

Graph algorithms are used in everyday life. Delivery companies such as UPS and FedEx use graph algorithms to determine the best delivery routes for their drivers. Google uses graph algorithms to map the best travel routes. The key to solving a real-world problem using graph algorithms is to model the problem into a graph problem. In the preceding section, we model the nine tail problem into the problem of finding a shortest path between two vertices in a graph. This section introduces a solution of the Knight's Tour problem using graph algorithms.

The Knight's Tour is a well-known classic problem. The objective is to move a knight, starting from any square on a chessboard, to every other square once. Note that the knight makes only L-shaped moves (two spaces in one direction and one space in a perpendicular direction). As shown in Figure 27.19(a), the knight can move to eight squares.

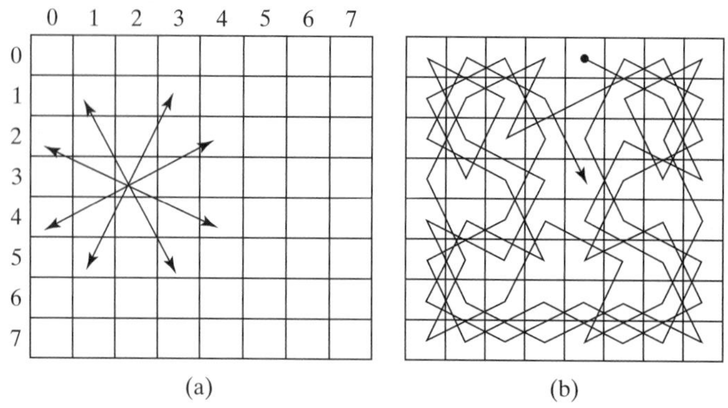
0 1 2 3 4 5 6 7
0
1
2
3
4
5
6
7
(a)
(b)

FIGURE 27.19 (a) A knight makes an L-shaped move. (b) A solution for a knight to traverse all squares once.

Hamiltonian path
Hamiltonian cycle

There are several approaches to solving this problem. One approach is to reduce it to a problem for finding a *Hamiltonian path* in a graph—that is, a path that visits each vertex in the graph exactly once. A *Hamiltonian cycle* visits each vertex in the graph exactly once and returns to the starting vertex. To solve the Knight's Tour problem, create a graph with `64` vertices representing all the squares in the chessboard. Two vertices are connected if a knight can move between them.

We will write an applet that lets the user specify a starting square and displays a tour, as shown in Figure 27.20.

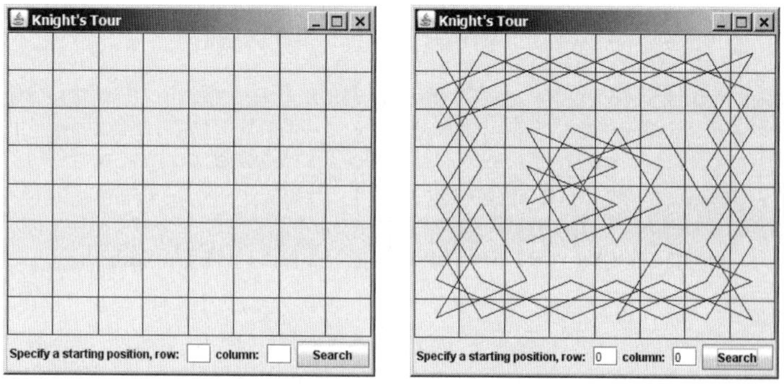
Knight's Tour
Specify a starting position, row:
column:
Search
Knight's Tour
Specify a starting position, row: 0
column: 0
Search

FIGURE 27.20 The applet displays a knight's tour.

A graph model was built for the nine tail problem in the preceding section. In the same spirit, we will build a graph model for the Knight's Tour problem. We will create two classes: `KnightTourApp` and `KnightTourModel`. The `KnightTourApp` class is responsible for user interaction and for displaying the solution, and the `KnightTourModel` class creates a graph for modeling this problem, as shown in Figure 27.21.

The `KnightTourModel` class is given in Listing 27.14 to create the vertices and the edges. For convenience, the vertices are labeled `0`, `1`, `2`, . . . , `63`. A square in the chessboard at row `i` and column `j` corresponds to the vertex (`i * 8 + j`). The `getEdges()` method (lines 20–70) creates all edges and adds them to the `edges` list. For each node `u` at square (`i`, `j`), check eight possible edges from `u` (lines 28–66), as shown in Figure 27.22. The model builds a graph from the edges and nodes (line 11). The method `getHamiltonianPath(int v)` returns a Hamiltonian path from the specified starting vertex `v` by applying the `getHamiltonianPath` method on the graph.

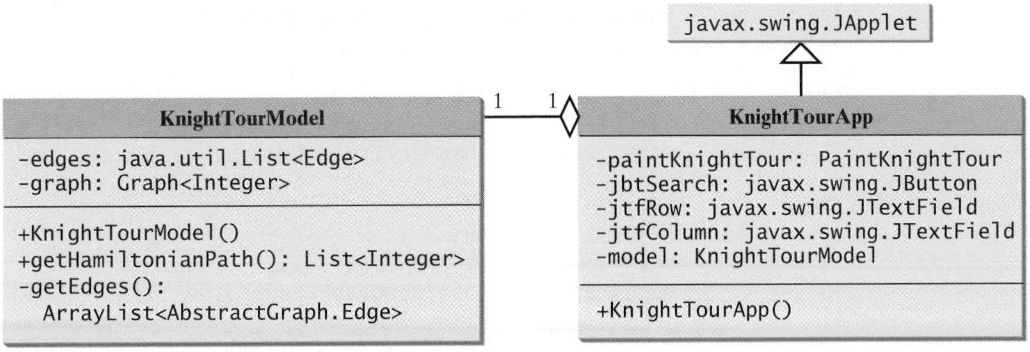
javax.swing.JApplet
KnightTourModel
-edges: java.util.List<Edge>
-graph: Graph<Integer>
+KnightTourModel()
+getHamiltonianPath(): List<Integer>
-getEdges():
ArrayList<AbstractGraph.Edge>
1
1
KnightTourApp
-paintKnightTour: PaintKnightTour
-jbtSearch: javax.swing.JButton
-jtfRow: javax.swing.JTextField
-jtfColumn: javax.swing.JTextField
-model: KnightTourModel
+KnightTourApp()

Figure 27.21 `KnightTourModel` creates a graph for modeling the problem and `KnightTourApp` presents a view for the solution.

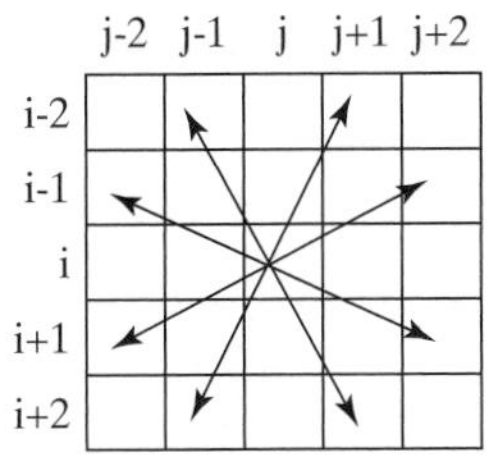
j-2 j-1 j j+1 j+2
i-2
i-1
i
i+1
i+2

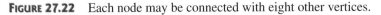

Figure 27.22 Each node may be connected with eight other vertices.

Listing 27.14 KnightTourModel.java

```
import java.util.*;

public class KnightTourModel {
  private UnweightedGraph<Integer> graph; // Define a graph

  public KnightTourModel() {
    // (u, v) is an edge if a knight can move from u and v
    ArrayList<AbstractGraph.Edge> edges = getEdges();

    // Create a graph with 64 vertices labeled 0 to 63
    graph = new UnweightedGraph<Integer>(edges, 64);
  }

  /** Get a Hamiltonian path starting from vertex v */
  public List<Integer> getHamiltonianPath(int v) {
    return graph.getHamiltonianPath(v);
  }

  /** Create edges for the graph */
  public static ArrayList<AbstractGraph.Edge> getEdges() {
    ArrayList<AbstractGraph.Edge> edges
      = new ArrayList<AbstractGraph.Edge>(); // Store edges
    for (int i = 0; i < 8; i++)
      for (int j = 0; j < 8; j++) {
        int u = i * 8 + j; // The vertex label

        // Check eight possible edges from u
        if (i - 1 >= 0 && j - 2 >= 0) {
          int v1 = (i - 1) * 8 + (j - 2);
```

edges
declare a graph
create edges
Hamiltonian path
create edges
vertex label
find an edge

```
          edges.add(new AbstractGraph.Edge(u, v1));
        }

        if (i - 2 >= 0 && j - 1 >= 0) {
          int v2 = (i - 2) * 8 + (j - 1);
          edges.add(new AbstractGraph.Edge(u, v2));
        }

        if (i - 2 >= 0 && j + 1 <= 7) {
          int v3 = (i - 2) * 8 + (j + 1);
          edges.add(new AbstractGraph.Edge(u, v3));
        }

        if (i - 1 >= 0 && j + 2 <= 7) {
          int v4 = (i - 1) * 8 + (j + 2);
          edges.add(new AbstractGraph.Edge(u, v4));
        }

        if (i + 1 <= 7 && j + 2 <= 7) {
          int v5 = (i + 1) * 8 + (j + 2);
          edges.add(new AbstractGraph.Edge(u, v5));
        }

        if (i + 2 <= 7 && j + 1 <= 7) {
          int v6 = (i + 2) * 8 + (j + 1);
          edges.add(new AbstractGraph.Edge(u, v6));
        }

        if (i + 2 <= 7 && j - 1 >= 0) {
          int v7 = (i + 2) * 8 + (j - 1);
          edges.add(new AbstractGraph.Edge(u, v7));
        }

        if (i + 1 <= 7 && j - 2 >= 0) {
          int v8 = (i + 1) * 8 + (j - 2);
          edges.add(new AbstractGraph.Edge(u, v8));
        }
      }

    return edges;
  }
}
```

Now the question is: how can you find a Hamiltonian path in a graph? You can apply the DFS approach to search for a subpath that contains unvisited vertices as deep as possible. In the DFS, after a vertex is visited, it will never be revisited. In the process of finding a Hamiltonian path, you may have to backtrack to revisit the same vertex in order to search for a new path. The algorithm can be described in Listing 27.15.

LISTING 27.15 Hamiltonian Path Algorithm

visit v

all visited?

check a neighbor

```
/** hamiltonianPath(v) is to find a Hamiltonian path for
 *  all unvisited vertices. */
boolean hamiltonianPath(vertex v) {
  isVisited[v] = true;

  if (all vertices are marked visited)
    return true;

  for each neighbor u of v
```

recursive search

```
10     if (u is not visited && hamiltonianPath(u)) {
11       next[v] = u; // u is the next vertex in the path from v
12       return true;
13     }
14
15   isVisited[v] = false; // Backtrack
16   return false; // No path starting from v
17 }
```

To find a Hamiltonian path starting from v, the algorithm first visits v and then recursively finds a Hamiltonian path for the remaining unvisited vertices starting from a neighbor of v (line 10). If so, a Hamiltonian path is found; otherwise, a Hamiltonian path from v does not exist (line 16).

time complexity

Let $T(n)$ denote the time for finding a Hamiltonian path in a graph of n vertices and d be the largest degree among all vertices. Clearly,

$$T(n) = O(d \times T(n-1)) = O(d \times d \times T(n-2)) = O(d^n)$$

NP-complete

This is an exponential-time algorithm. Can you develop an algorithm in polynomial time? No. It has been proven that the Hamiltonian path problem is *NP-complete*, meaning that no polynomial-time algorithm for such problems can be found. However, you can apply some heuristic to speed up the search. Intuitively, you should attempt to search the vertices with small degrees and leave those vertices with large degrees open, so there will be a better chance of success at the end of the search.

Add the following two methods in the Graph interface.

```
/** Return a Hamiltonian path from the specified vertex object
  * Return null if the graph does not contain a Hamiltonian path */
 public java.util.List<Integer> getHamiltonianPath(V vertex);

 /** Return a Hamiltonian path from the specified vertex label
  * Return null if the graph does not contain a Hamiltonian path */
 public java.util.List<Integer> getHamiltonianPath(int index);
```

Implement these methods in the AbstractGraph class as follows:

```
/** Return a Hamiltonian path from the specified vertex object
  * Return null if the graph does not contain a Hamiltonian path */
public List<Integer> getHamiltonianPath(V vertex) {
  return getHamiltonianPath(getIndex(vertex));
}

/** Return a Hamiltonian path from the specified vertex label
  * Return null if the graph does not contain a Hamiltonian path */
public List<Integer> getHamiltonianPath(int v) {
  // A path starts from v. (i, next[i]) represents an edge in
  // the path. isVisited[i] tracks whether i is currently in the
  // path.
  int[] next = new int[getSize()];
  for (int i = 0; i < next.length; i++)
    next[i] = -1; // Indicate no subpath from i is found yet

  boolean[] isVisited = new boolean[getSize()];

  // The vertices in the Hamiltonian path are stored in result
  List<Integer> result = null;

  // To speed up search, reorder the adjacency list for each
  // vertex so that the vertices in the list are in increasing
```

reorder adjacency list

recursive search

```
    // order of their degrees
    for (int i = 0; i < getSize(); i++)
      reorderNeigborsBasedOnDegree(neighbors.get(i));

    if (getHamiltonianPath(v, next, isVisited)) {
      result = new ArrayList<Integer>(); // Create a list for path
      int vertex = v; // Starting from v
      while (vertex != -1) {
        result.add(vertex); // Add vertex to the result list
        vertex = next[vertex]; // Get the next vertex in the path
      }
    }

    return result; // return null if no Hamiltonian path is found
  }

  /** Reorder the adjacency list in increasing order of degrees */
  private void reorderNeigborsBasedOnDegree(List<Integer> list) {
    for (int i = list.size() - 1; i >= 1; i--) {
      // Find the maximum in the list[0..i]
      int currentMaxDegree = getDegree(list.get(0));
      int currentMaxIndex = 0;

      for (int j = 1; j <= i; j++) {
        if (currentMaxDegree < getDegree(list.get(j))) {
          currentMaxDegree = getDegree(list.get(j));
          currentMaxIndex = j;
        }
      }

      // Swap list[i] with list[currentMaxIndex] if necessary;
      if (currentMaxIndex != i) {
        int temp = list.get(currentMaxIndex);
        list.set(currentMaxIndex, list.get(i));
        list.set(i, temp);
      }
    }
  }

  /** Return true if all elements in array isVisited are true */
  private boolean allVisited(boolean[] isVisited) {
    boolean result = true;

    for (int i = 0; i < getSize(); i++)
      result = result && isVisited[i];

    return result;
   }

  /** Search for a Hamiltonian path from v */
  private boolean getHamiltonianPath(int v, int[] next,
       boolean[] isVisited) {
    isVisited[v] = true; // Mark vertex v visited

    if (allVisited(isVisited))
      return true; // The path now includes all vertices, thus found

    for (int i = 0; i < neighbors.get(v).size(); i++) {
      int u = neighbors.get(v).get(i);
      if (!isVisited[u] &&
```

```
87          getHamiltonianPath(u, next, isVisited)) {
88        next[v] = u; // Edge (v, u) is in the path
89        return true;
90      }
91    }
92
93    isVisited[v] = false; // Backtrack, v is marked unvisited now
94    return false; // No Hamiltonian path exists from vertex v
95  }
```

The `getHamiltonianPath(V vertex)` finds a Hamiltonian path for the specified vertex object, and the `getHamiltonianPath(int index)` finds a Hamiltonian path for the specified vertex index. `getIndex(vertex)` returns the label for the vertex object (line 4).

To implement the `getHamiltonianPath(int v)` method, first create an array `next`, which keeps track of the `next` vertex in the path (line 13). `next[v]` denotes the next vertex in the path after `v`. Initially, `next[i]` is set to `-1` for all vertices `i` (line 15). The `isVisited` array keeps track of the vertices that are currently in the path (line 17). Initially, all elements in `isVisited` are `false`.

heuristics

To speed up search, the adjacency list for every vertex is reordered in increasing order of their degrees (line 26). So, the vertices with small degrees will be visited earlier.

The recursive `getHamiltonianPath(v, next, isVisited)` method is invoked to find a Hamiltonian path starting from `v`. When a vertex `v` is visited, `isVisited[v]` is set to `true` (line 79). If all the vertices are visited, the search returns `true` (line 82). For each neighbor of `v`, recursively search a Hamiltonian subpath starting from a neighbor of `v` (line 85). If a subpath is found, set `u` to `next[v]` and return `true` (line 89). After all neighbors of `v` are searched without success, backtrack by setting `v` unvisited (line 93) and return `false` to indicate a path or a subpath is not found (line 94).

The `KnightTourApp` class is given in Listing 27.16 to create the GUI. An instance of the `KnightTourModel` class is created in line 7. The path of the knight's tour is displayed in an instance of `PaintKnightTour` panel (line 8). The user specifies the row and column of the starting square and clicks the *Search* button to display the path (line 24).

LISTING 27.16 KnightTourApp.java

```
 1 import java.util.List;
 2 import javax.swing.*;
 3 import java.awt.*;
 4 import java.awt.event.*;
 5
 6 public class KnightTourApp extends JApplet {
 7   private KnightTourModel model = new KnightTourModel();               // model
 8   private PaintKnightTour paintKnightTour = new PaintKnightTour();     // paint panel
 9   private JTextField jtfRow = new JTextField(2);
10   private JTextField jtfColumn = new JTextField(2);
11   private JButton jbtSearch = new JButton("Search");
12
13   public KnightTourApp() {
14     JPanel panel = new JPanel();
15     panel.add(new JLabel("Specify a starting position, row: "));
16     panel.add(jtfRow);
17     panel.add(new JLabel("column: "));
18     panel.add(jtfColumn);
19     panel.add(jbtSearch);
20     add(paintKnightTour, BorderLayout.CENTER);
21     add(panel, BorderLayout.SOUTH);
22
23     jbtSearch.addActionListener(new ActionListener() {                 // button listener
```

display path
find path

```
      public void actionPerformed(ActionEvent e) {
        int position = Integer.parseInt(jtfRow.getText()) * 8 +
          Integer.parseInt(jtfColumn.getText());
        paintKnightTour.displayPath(
          model.getHamiltonianPath(position));
      }
    });
  }

  /** A panel to paint the chessboard and the knight's tour */
  private static class PaintKnightTour extends JPanel {
    private List<Integer> path; // A knight's tour path

    public PaintKnightTour() {
      setBorder(BorderFactory.createLineBorder(Color.black, 1));
    }

    public void displayPath(List<Integer> path) {
      this.path = path;
      repaint();
    }

    protected void paintComponent(Graphics g) {
      super.paintComponent(g);

      // Display horizontal lines
      for (int i = 0; i < 8; i++)
        g.drawLine(0, i * getHeight() / 8,
          getWidth(), i * getHeight() / 8);

      // Display vertical lines
      for (int i = 0; i < 8; i++)
        g.drawLine(i * getWidth() / 8, 0,
          (int)i * getWidth() / 8, getHeight());

      if (path == null) return; // No path to be displayed yet

      for (int i = 0; i < path.size() - 1; i++) {
        int u = path.get(i);
        int v = path.get(i + 1);

        // Knight moves from u and v. Draw a line to connect u and v
        g.drawLine((u % 8) * getWidth() / 8 + getWidth() / 16,
          (u / 8) * getHeight() / 8 + getHeight() / 16,
          (v % 8) * getWidth() / 8 + getWidth() / 16,
          (v / 8) * getHeight() / 8 + getHeight() / 16);
      }
    }
  }
}
```

display path

main method omitted

KEY TERMS

adjacency list 897
adjacent vertices 893
adjacency matrix 896
breadth-first search 916
complete graph 894
degree 894
depth-first search 912
directed graph 893

graph 892
incident edges 894
parallel edge 894
Seven Bridges of Königsberg 892
simple graph 894
spanning tree 894
weighted graph 893
undirected graph 893
unweighted graph 893

Chapter Summary

1. A graph is a useful mathematical structure that represents relationships among entities in the real world. You learned how to model graphs using classes and interfaces, how to represent vertices and edges using arrays and linked lists, and how to implement operations for vertices and edges.

2. Graph traversal is the process of visiting each vertex in the graph exactly once. You learned two popular ways for traversing a graph: depth-first search (DFS) and breadth-first search (BFS).

3. DFS and BFS can be used to solve many problems such as detecting whether a graph is connected, detecting whether there is a cycle in the graph, and finding a shortest path between two vertices.

Review Questions

Sections 27.1–27.3

27.1 What is the famous *Seven Bridges of Königsberg* problem?

27.2 What is a graph? Explain the following terms: undirected graph, directed graph, weighted graph, degree of a vertex, parallel edge, simple graph, and complete graph.

27.3 How do you represent vertices in a graph? How do you represent edges using an edge array? How do you represent an edge using an edge object? How do you represent edges using an adjacency matrix? How do you represent edges using adjacency lists?

27.4 Represent the following graph using an edge array, a list of edge objects, an adjacent matrix, and an adjacent list, respectively.

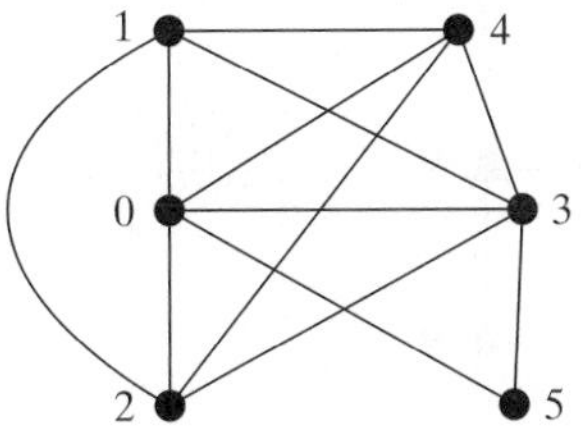
1
4
0
3
2
5

Sections 27.4–27.7

27.5 Describe the relationships among `Graph`, `AbstractGraph`, and `UnweightedGraph`.

27.6 What is the return type from invoking `dfs(v)` and `bfs(v)`?

27.7 What are depth-first search and breadth-first search?

27.8 Show the DFS and BFS for the graph in Figure 27.1 starting from vertex Atlanta.

27.9 The depth-first search algorithm described in Listing 27.8 uses recursion. Alternatively you may use a stack to implement it, as shown below. Point out the error in this algorithm and give a correct algorithm.

```
// Wrong version
dfs(vertex v) {
  push v into the stack;
  mark v visited;

  while (the stack is not empty) {
    pop a vertex, say u, from the stack
    visit u;
    for each neighbor w of u
      if (w has not been visited)
        push w into the stack;
  }
}
```

27.10 Prove that the path between the root and any node in the BFS tree is the shortest path between the root and the node.

Section 27.8

27.11 What is returned after invoking `getIndex("HTHTTTHHH".toCharArray())` in Listing 27.12? What is returned after invoking `getNode(46)` in Listing 27.12?

Programming Exercises

Sections 27.6–27.7

27.1* (*Testing whether a graph is connected*) Write a program that reads a graph from a file and determines whether the graph is connected. The first line in the file contains a number that indicates the number of vertices (`n`). The vertices are labeled as `0, 1, ..., n-1`. Each subsequent line, with the format `u v1 v2 ...`, describes edges (`u, v1`), (`u, v2`), and so on. Figure 27.23 gives the examples of two files for their corresponding graphs.

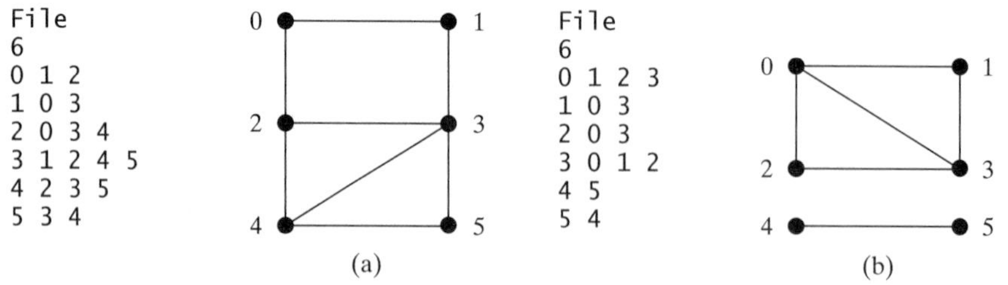
File
6
0 1 2
1 0 3
2 0 3 4
3 1 2 4 5
4 2 3 5
5 3 4
0
1
2
3
4
5
(a)
File
6
0 1 2 3
1 0 3
2 0 3
3 0 1 2
4 5
5 4
0
1
2
3
4
5
(b)

Figure 27.23 The vertices and edges of a graph can be stored in a file.

Your program should prompt the user to enter the name of the file, should read data from a file, create an instance `g` of `UnweightedGraph`, invoke `g.printEdges()` to display all edges, and invokes `dfs()` to obtain an instance `tree` of `AbstractGraph.Tree`. If `tree.getNumberOfVerticeFound()` is the same as the number of vertices in the graph, the graph is connected. Here is a sample run of the program:

```
Enter a file name: c:\exercise\Exercise27_1a.txt ↵Enter
The number of vertices is 6
Vertex 0: (0, 1) (0, 2)
Vertex 1: (1, 0) (1, 3)
Vertex 2: (2, 0) (2, 3) (2, 4)
Vertex 3: (3, 1) (3, 2) (3, 4) (3, 5)
Vertex 4: (4, 2) (4, 3) (4, 5)
Vertex 5: (5, 3) (5, 4)
The graph is connected
```

(*Hint*: Use `new UnweightedGraph(list, numberOfVertices)` to create a graph, where `list` contains a list of `AbstractGraph.Edge` objects. Use `new AbstractGraph.Edge(u, v)` to create an edge. Read the first line to get the number of vertices. Read each subsequent line into a string `s` and use `s.split("[\\s+]")` to extract the vertices from the string and create edges from the vertices.)

27.2* (*Creating a file for a graph*) Modify Listing 27.1, TestGraph.java, to create a file for representing `graph1`. The file format is described in Exercise 27.1. Create the file from the array defined in lines 8–21 in Listing 27.1. The number of vertices for the graph is `12`, which will be stored in the first line of the file. The contents of the file should be as follows:

```
12
0 1 3 5
1 0 2 3
2 1 3 4 10
3 0 1 2 4 5
4 2 3 5 7 8 10
5 0 3 4 6 7
6 5 7
7 4 5 6 8
8 4 7 9 10 11
9 8 11
10 2 4 8 11
11 8 9 10
```

27.3* (*Implementing DFS using a stack*) The depth-first search algorithm described in Listing 27.8 uses recursion. Implement it without using recursion.

27.4* (*Finding connected components*) Add a new method in `AbstractGraph` to find all connected components in a graph with the following header:

```java
public List<Integer> getConnectedComponents();
```

The method returns a `List<Integer>`. Each element in the list is another list that contains all the vertices in a connected component. For example, if the graph has three connected components, the method returns a list with three elements, each containing the vertices in a connected component.

27.5* (*Finding paths*) Add a new method in `AbstractGraph` to find a path between two vertices with the following header:

```java
public List<Integer> getPath(int u, int v);
```

The method returns a `List<Integer>` that contains all the vertices in a path from `u` to `v` in this order. Using the BFS approach, you can obtain a shortest path from `u` to `v`. If there is no path from `u` to `v`, the method returns `null`.

27.6* (*Detecting cycles*) Add a new method in `AbstractGraph` to determine whether there is a cycle in the graph with the following header:

```
public boolean isCyclic();
```

27.7* (*Finding a cycle*) Add a new method in `AbstractGraph` to find a cycle in the graph with the following header:

```
public List<Integer> getACycle();
```

The method returns a `List` that contains all the vertices in a cycle from `u` to `v` in this order. If the graph has no cycles, the method returns `null`.

27.8** (*Testing bipartite*) Recall that a graph is bipartite if its vertices can be divided into two disjoint sets such that no edges exist between vertices in the same set. Add a new method in `AbstractGraph` to detect whether the graph is bipartite:

```
public boolean isBipartite();
```

27.9** (*Getting bipartite sets*) Add a new method in `AbstractGraph` to return two bipartite sets if the graph is bipartite:

```
public List<List<Integer>> getBipartite();
```

The method returns a `List` that contains two sublists, each of which contains a set of vertices. If the graph is not bipartite, the method returns `null`.

27.10* (*Finding a shortest path*) Write a program that reads a connected graph from a file. The graph is stored in a file using the same format specified in Exercise 27.1. Your program should prompt the user to enter the name of the file, then two vertices, and should display the shortest path between the two vertices. For example, for the graph in Figure 27.23(a), a shortest path between `0` and `5` may be displayed as `0 1 3 5`.

Here is a sample run of the program:

```
Enter a file name: c:\exercise\Exercise27_1a.txt [Enter]
Enter two vertices (integer indexes): 0 5 [Enter]
The number of vertices is 6
Vertex 0: (0, 1) (0, 2)
Vertex 1: (1, 0) (1, 3)
Vertex 2: (2, 0) (2, 3) (2, 4)
Vertex 3: (3, 1) (3, 2) (3, 4) (3, 5)
Vertex 4: (4, 2) (4, 3) (4, 5)
Vertex 5: (5, 3) (5, 4)
The path is 0 1 3 5
```

27.11** (*Revising Listing 27.12, NineTail.java*) The program in Listing 27.12 lets the user enter an input for the nine tail program from the console and displays the result on the console. Write an applet that lets the user set an initial state of the nine coins (see Figure 27.24(a)) and click the *Solve* button to display the solution, as shown in Figure 27.24(b). Initially, the user can click the mouse button to flip a coin.

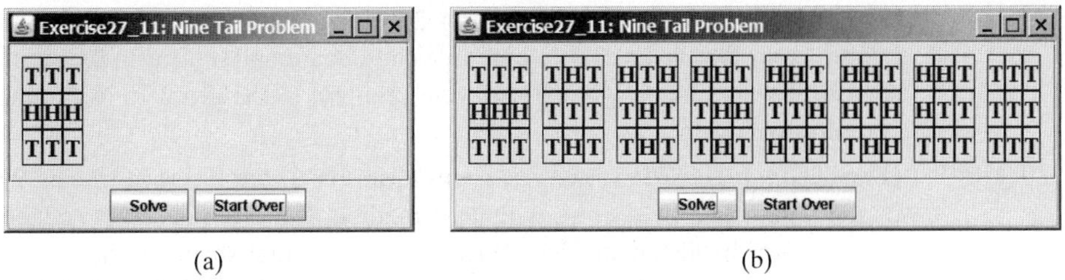
Exercise27_11: Nine Tail Problem
Solve
Start Over
(a)
Exercise27_11: Nine Tail Problem
Solve
Start Over
(b)

FIGURE 27.24 The applet solves the nine tail problem.

27.12** (*Variation of the nine tail problem*) In the nine tail problem, when you flip a head, the horizontal and vertical neighboring cells are also flipped. Rewrite the program, assuming that all neighboring cells including the diagonal neighbors are also flipped.

27.13** (*4 × 4 16 tail model*) The nine tail problem in the text uses a 3 × 3 matrix. Assume that you have 16 coins placed in a 4 × 4 matrix. Create a new model class named `TailModel16`. Create an instance of the model and save the object into a file named **Exercise27_13.dat**.

27.14** (*4 × 4 16 tail view*) Listing 27.13, NineTail.java, presents a view for the nine tail problem. Revise this program for the 4 × 4 16 tail problem. Your program should read the model object created from the preceding exercise.

27.15** (*Dynamic graphs*) Add the following methods in the `Graph` interface to dynamically add and remove vertices and edges:

```
// Add a vertex to the graph and return true if succeeded
public boolean add(Object vertex)

// Remove a vertex from the graph and return true if succeeded
public boolean remove(Object vertex)

// Add an edge to the graph and return true if succeeded
public boolean add(Edge edge)

// Remove an edge from the graph and return true if succeeded
public boolean remove(Edge edge)
```

For simplicity, assume the vertices are labeled with integers `1`, `2`, . . . , and so on.

27.16** (*Induced subgraph*) Given an undirected graph G = (V, E) and an integer *k*, find an induced subgraph H of G of maximum size such that all vertices of H have degree >= *k*, or conclude that no such induced subgraph exists. Implement the method with the following header:

```
public static Graph maxInducedSubgraph(Graph edge, int k)
```

The method returns `null` if such subgraph does not exist.

(*Hint*: An intuitive approach is to remove vertices whose degree is less than k. As vertices are removed with their adjacent edges, the degrees of other vertices may be reduced. Continue the process until no vertices can be removed, or all the vertices are removed.)

27.17*** (*Hamiltonian cycle*) Add the following method in the `Graph` interface and implement it in the `AbstractGraph` class:

```
/** Return a Hamiltonian cycle
  * Return null if the graph contains no Hamiltonian cycle */
public List<Integer> getHamiltonianCycle()
```

27.18*** (*Knight's Tour cycle*) Rewrite Listing 27.16, KnightTourApp.java, to find a knight's tour that visits each square in a chessboard and returns to the starting square. Reduce the Knight's Tour cycle problem to the problem of finding a Hamiltonian cycle.

27.19** (*Displaying a DFS/BFS tree in a graph*) Modify `GraphView` in Listing 27.6 to add a new data field `tree` with a set method. If a `tree` is set, the edges in the tree are displayed in blue. Write a program that displays the graph in Figure 27.1 and the DFS/BFS tree starting from a specified city, as shown in Figure 27.25(a). If a city not in the map is entered, the program displays a dialog box to alert the user, as shown in Figure 27.25(b).

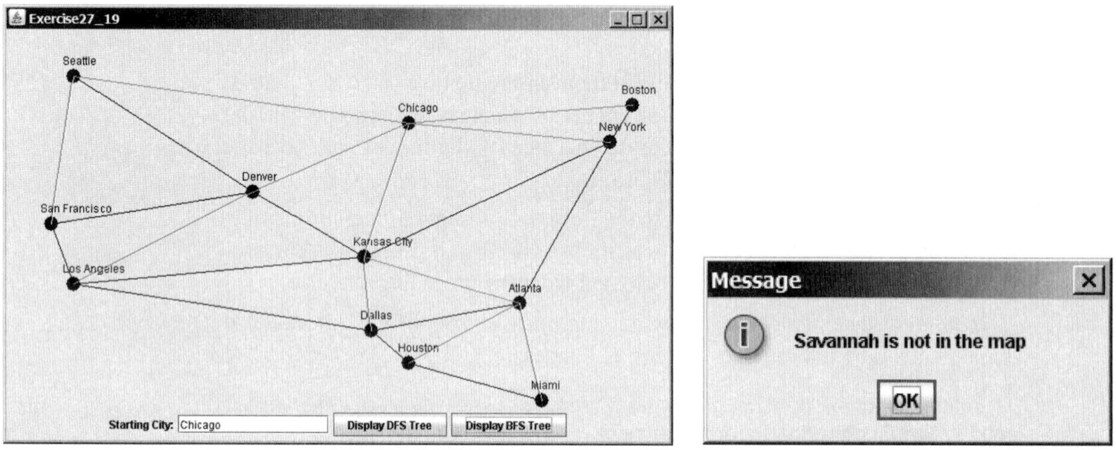
Exercise27_19
Seattle
Boston
Chicago
New York
Denver
San Francisco
Kansas City
Los Angeles
Atlanta
Dallas
Houston
Miami
Starting City:
Chicago
Display DFS Tree
Display BFS Tree
Message
Savannah is not in the map
OK

(a) (b)

FIGURE 27.25 The program displays a DFS/BFS tree in the graph.

27.20* (*Displaying a graph*) Write a program that reads a graph from a file and displays it. The first line in the file contains a number that indicates the number of vertices (`n`). The vertices are labeled `0`, `1`, ..., `n-1`. Each subsequent line, with the format `u x y v1 v2 ...`, describes the position of `u` at (`x`, `y`) and edges (`u`, `v1`), (`u`, `v2`), and so on. Figure 27.26(a) gives an example of the file for their corresponding graph. Your program prompts the user to enter the name of the file, reads data from a file, and displays the graph on a panel using `GraphView`, as shown in Figure 27.26(b).

```
File
7
0 30 30 1 2
1 90 30 0 3 6
2 30 90 0 3 4
3 90 90 1 2 4 5
4 30 150 2 3 5
5 90 150 3 4 6
6 130 90 1 5
```

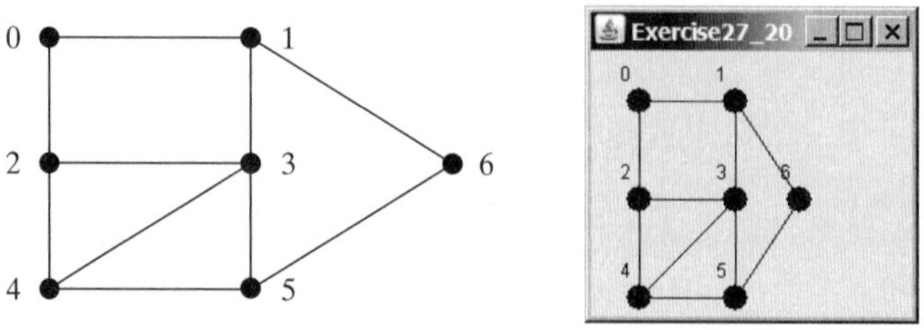
0
1
2
3
6
4
5
Exercise27_20

(a) (b)

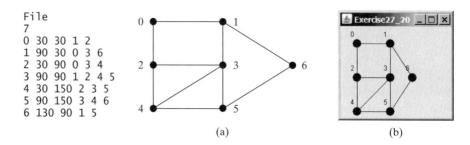

FIGURE 27.26 The program reads the information about the graph and displays it visually.

27.21*** (*Dynamic graphs*) Write a program that lets the user create a graph dynamically. The user can create a vertex by entering its index and location, as shown in Figure 27.27. The user can also create an edge to connect two vertices. To make this program work, add the following two methods in the `AbstractGraph` class.

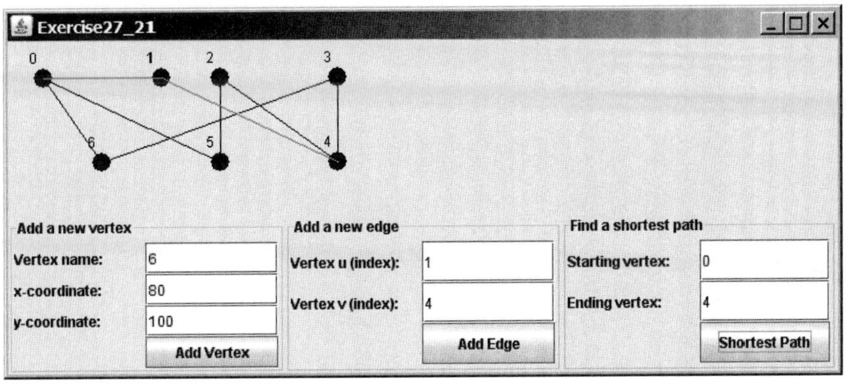

Exercise27_21
0
1
2
3
6
5
4
Add a new vertex
Vertex name:
6
x-coordinate:
80
y-coordinate:
100
Add Vertex
Add a new edge
Vertex u (index):
1
Vertex v (index):
4
Add Edge
Find a shortest path
Starting vertex:
0
Ending vertex:
4
Shortest Path

FIGURE 27.27 The program can add vertices and edges and display a shortest path between two specified vertices.

```
public void addVertex(V vertex)

public void addEdge(int u, int v)
```

To simplify the program, assume that vertex names are the same as vertex indices. You have to add the vertex indices `0`, `1`, . . . , `n`, in this order. The user may specify two vertices and let the program display their shortest path in blue.

CHAPTER 28

WEIGHTED GRAPHS AND APPLICATIONS

Objectives

- To represent weighted edges using adjacency matrices and priority queues (§28.2).
- To model weighted graphs using the `WeightedGraph` class that extends the `AbstractGraph` class (§28.3).
- To design and implement the algorithm for finding a minimum spanning tree (§28.4).
- To define the `MST` class that extends the `Tree` class (§28.4).
- To design and implement the algorithm for finding single-source shortest paths (§28.5).
- To define the `ShortestPathTree` class that extends the `Tree` class (§28.5).
- To solve the weighted nine tail problem using the shortest-path algorithm (§28.6).

28.1 Introduction

The preceding chapter introduced the concept of graphs. You learned how to represent edges using edge arrays, edge lists, adjacency matrices, and adjacency lists, and how to model a graph using the **Graph** interface, the **AbstractGraph** class, and the **UnweightedGraph** class. The preceding chapter also introduced two important techniques for traversing graphs: depth-first search and breadth-first search, and applied traversal to solve practical problems. This chapter will introduce weighted graphs. You will learn the algorithm for finding a minimum spanning tree in §28.4 and the algorithm for finding shortest paths in §28.5.

28.2 Representing Weighted Graphs

There are two types of weighted graphs: vertex weighted and edge weighted. In a vertex-weighted graph, each vertex is assigned a weight. In an edge-weighted graph, each edge is assigned a weight. Of the two types, edge-weighted graphs have more applications. This chapter considers edge-weighted graphs.

Weighted graphs can be represented in the same way as unweighted graphs, except that you have to represent the weights on the edges. As with unweighted graphs, the vertices in weighted graphs can be stored in an array. This section introduces three representations for the edges in weighted graphs.

28.2.1 Representing Weighted Edges: Edge Array

Weighted edges can be represented using a two-dimensional array. For example, you can store all the edges in the graph in Figure 28.1 using the following array:

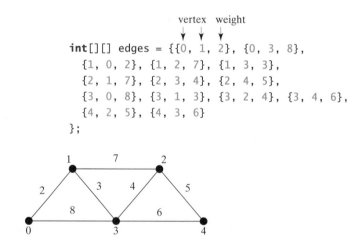

```
                         vertex  weight
int[][] edges = {{0, 1, 2}, {0, 3, 8},
  {1, 0, 2}, {1, 2, 7}, {1, 3, 3},
  {2, 1, 7}, {2, 3, 4}, {2, 4, 5},
  {3, 0, 8}, {3, 1, 3}, {3, 2, 4}, {3, 4, 6},
  {4, 2, 5}, {4, 3, 6}
};
```

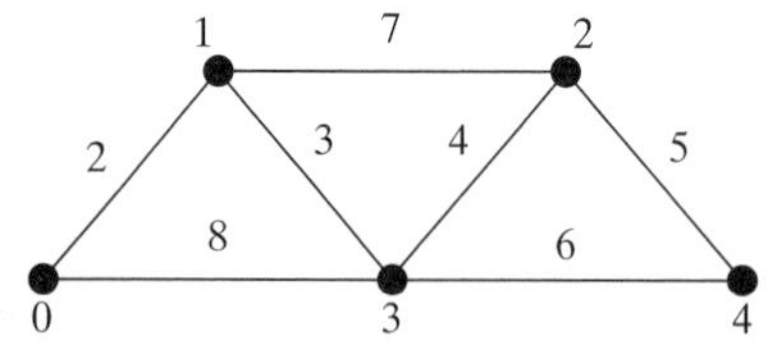
1
7
2
2
3
4
5
8
6
0
3
4

FIGURE 28.1 Each edge is assigned a weight on an edge-weighted graph.

integer weights

Note

For simplicity, we assume that the *weights are integers*. Weights can be of any type. In that case, you may use a two-dimensional array of the **Object** type as follows:

```
Object[][] edges = {
  {new Integer(0), new Integer(1), new SomeTypeForWeight(2)},
  {new Integer(0), new Integer(3), new SomeTypeForWeight(8)},
  ...
};
```

28.2.2 Weighted Adjacency Matrices

Assume that the graph has n vertices. You can use a two-dimensional $n \times n$ matrix, say `weights`, to represent the weights on edges. `weights[i][j]` represents the weight on edge (`i`, `j`). If vertices `i` and `j` are not connected, `weights[i][j]` is `null`. For example, the weights in the graph in Figure 28.1 can be represented using an adjacency matrix as follows:

```
Integer[][] adjacencyMatrix = {
  {null, 2, null, 8, null },
  {2, null, 7, 3, null },
  {null, 7, null, 4, 5},
  {8, 3, 4, null, 6},
  {null, null, 5, 6, null}
```

	0	1	2	3	4
0	null	2	null	8	null
1	2	null	7	3	null
2	null	7	null	4	5
3	8	3	4	null	6
4	null	null	5	6	null

28.2.3 Priority Adjacency Lists

Another way to represent the edges is to define edges as objects. The `AbstractGraph.Edge` class was defined to represent edges in unweighted graphs. For weighted edges, we define the `WeightedEdge` class as shown in Listing 28.1.

LISTING 28.1 `WeightedEdge.java`

```
public class WeightedEdge extends AbstractGraph.Edge
    implements Comparable<WeightedEdge> {
  public int weight; // The weight on edge (u, v)

  /** Create a weighted edge on (u, v) */
  public WeightedEdge(int u, int v, int weight) {
    super(u, v);
    this.weight = weight;
  }

  /** Compare two edges on weights */
  public int compareTo(WeightedEdge edge) {
    if (weight > edge.weight)
      return 1;
    else if (weight == edge.weight)
      return 0;
    else
      return -1;
  }
}
```

edge weight

constructor

compare edges

`AbstractGraph.Edge` is an inner class defined in the `AbstractGraph` class. It represents an edge from vertex `u` to `v`. `WeightedEdge` extends `AbstractGraph.Edge` with a new property `weight`.

To create a `WeightedEdge` object, use `new WeightedEdge(i, j, w)`, where `w` is the weight on edge (`i`, `j`). Often it is desirable to store a vertex's adjacent edges in a priority queue so that you can remove the edges in increasing order of their weights. For this reason, the `Edge` class implements the `Comparable` interface.

For unweighted graphs, we use adjacency lists to represent edges. For weighted graphs, we still use adjacency lists, but the lists are priority queues. For example, the adjacency lists for the vertices in the graph in Figure 28.1 can be represented as follows:

```
java.util.PriorityQueue<WeightedEdge>[] queues =
  new java.util.PriorityQueue<WeightedEdge>[5];
```

queues[0]	WeightedEdge(0, 1, 2)	WeightedEdge(0, 3, 8)		
queues[1]	WeightedEdge(1, 0, 2)	WeightedEdge(1, 3, 3)	WeightedEdge(1, 2, 7)	
queues[2]	WeightedEdge(2, 3, 4)	WeightedEdge(2, 4, 5)	WeightedEdge(2, 1, 7)	
queues[3]	WeightedEdge(3, 1, 3)	WeightedEdge(3, 2, 4)	WeightedEdge(3, 4, 6)	WeightedEdge(3, 0, 8)
queues[4]	WeightedEdge(4, 2, 5)	WeightedEdge(4, 3, 6)		

`queues[i]` stores all edges adjacent to vertex `i`.

For flexibility, we will use an array list rather than a fixed-sized array to represent `queues`.

28.3 The `WeightedGraph` Class

The preceding chapter designed the `Graph` interface, the `AbstractGraph` class, and the `UnweightedGraph` class for modeling graphs. Following this pattern, we design `WeightedGraph` as a subclass of `AbstractGraph`, as shown in Figure 28.2.

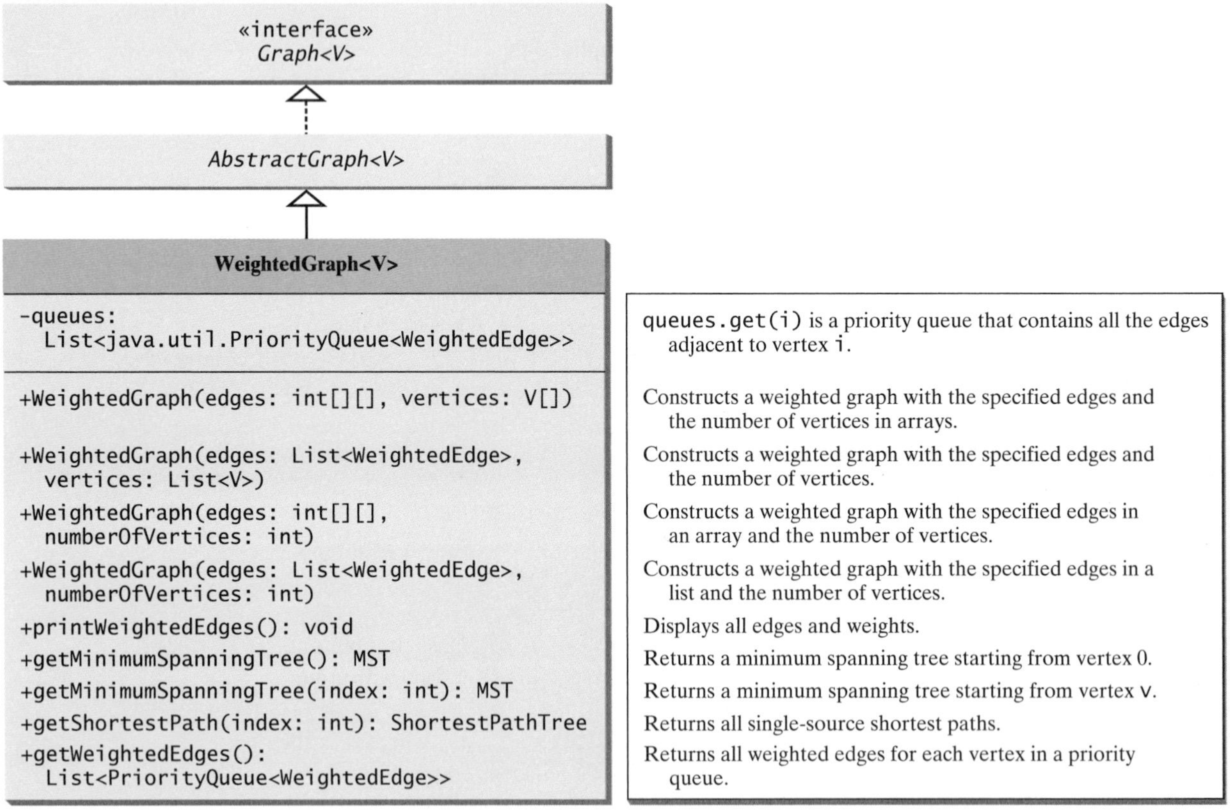
«interface»
Graph<V>
AbstractGraph<V>
WeightedGraph<V>
-queues:
List<java.util.PriorityQueue<WeightedEdge>>
+WeightedGraph(edges: int[][], vertices: V[])
+WeightedGraph(edges: List<WeightedEdge>, vertices: List<V>)
+WeightedGraph(edges: int[][], numberOfVertices: int)
+WeightedGraph(edges: List<WeightedEdge>, numberOfVertices: int)
+printWeightedEdges(): void
+getMinimumSpanningTree(): MST
+getMinimumSpanningTree(index: int): MST
+getShortestPath(index: int): ShortestPathTree
+getWeightedEdges(): List<PriorityQueue<WeightedEdge>>
queues.get(i) is a priority queue that contains all the edges adjacent to vertex i.
Constructs a weighted graph with the specified edges and the number of vertices in arrays.
Constructs a weighted graph with the specified edges and the number of vertices.
Constructs a weighted graph with the specified edges in an array and the number of vertices.
Constructs a weighted graph with the specified edges in a list and the number of vertices.
Displays all edges and weights.
Returns a minimum spanning tree starting from vertex 0.
Returns a minimum spanning tree starting from vertex v.
Returns all single-source shortest paths.
Returns all weighted edges for each vertex in a priority queue.

FIGURE 28.2 `WeightedGraph` extends `AbstractGraph`.

`WeightedGraph` simply extends `AbstractGraph` with four constructors for creating concrete `WeightedGraph` instances. `WeightedGraph` inherits all methods from `AbstractGraph` and also introduces the new methods for obtaining minimum spanning trees and for finding single-source all shortest paths. Minimum spanning trees and shortest paths will be introduced in §28.4 and §28.5, respectively.

Listing 28.2 implements `WeightedGraph`. Priority adjacency lists (line 5) are used internally to store adjacent edges for a vertex. When a `WeightedGraph` is constructed, its priority adjacency lists are created (lines 10, 16, 22, and 29). The methods `getMinimumSpanningTree()` (lines 74–158) and `getShortestPaths()` (lines 161–241) will be introduced in the upcoming sections.

LISTING 28.2 WeightedGraph.java

```
1 import java.util.*;
2
3 public class WeightedGraph<V> extends AbstractGraph<V> {
4   // Priority adjacency lists
5   private List<PriorityQueue<WeightedEdge>> queues;
6
7   /** Construct a WeightedGraph from edges and vertices in arrays */
8   public WeightedGraph(int[][] edges, V[] vertices) {
9     super(edges, vertices);
10    createQueues(edges, vertices.length);
11  }
12
13  /** Construct a WeightedGraph from edges and vertices in List */
14  public WeightedGraph(int[][] edges, int numberOfVertices) {
15    super(edges, numberOfVertices);
16    createQueues(edges, numberOfVertices);
17  }
18
19  /** Construct a WeightedGraph from vertices 0, 1, 2 and edge list */
20  public WeightedGraph(List<WeightedEdge> edges, List<V> vertices) {
21    super((List)edges, vertices);
22    createQueues(edges, vertices.size());
23  }
24
25  /** Construct a WeightedGraph from vertices 0, 1, and edge array */
26  public WeightedGraph(List<WeightedEdge> edges,
27      int numberOfVertices) {
28    super((List)edges, numberOfVertices);
29    createQueues(edges, numberOfVertices);
30  }
31
32  /** Create priority adjacency lists from edge arrays */
33  private void createQueues(int[][] edges, int numberOfVertices) {
34    queues = new ArrayList<PriorityQueue<WeightedEdge>>();
35    for (int i = 0; i < numberOfVertices; i++) {
36      queues.add(new PriorityQueue<WeightedEdge>()); // Create a queue
37    }
38
39    for (int i = 0; i < edges.length; i++) {
40      int u = edges[i][0];
41      int v = edges[i][1];
42      int weight = edges[i][2];
43      // Insert an edge into the queue
44      queues.get(u).offer(new WeightedEdge(u, v, weight));
45    }
46  }
47
48  /** Create priority adjacency lists from edge lists */
49  private void createQueues(List<WeightedEdge> edges,
50      int numberOfVertices) {
51    queues = new ArrayList<PriorityQueue<WeightedEdge>>();
```

priority queue (line 5)
constructor (line 8)
superclass constructor (line 9)
create priority queues (line 10)
constructor (line 14)
constructor (line 20)
constructor (line 26)
create priority queues (line 33)
create queues (line 36)
fill queues (line 44)
create priority queues (line 51)

create queues

fill queues

print edges

minimum spanning tree
start from vertex 0

minimum spanning tree
vertices in tree
add to tree
number of vertices
parent array
initialize parent
total weight
a copy of queues
more vertices?
every **u** in tree
remove visited vertex
queues.get(u) is empty

```
    for (int i = 0; i < numberOfVertices; i++) {
      queues.add(new PriorityQueue<WeightedEdge>()); // Create a queue
    }

    for (WeightedEdge edge: edges) {
      queues.get(edge.u).offer(edge); // Insert an edge into the queue
    }
  }

  /** Display edges with weights */
  public void printWeightedEdges() {
    for (int i = 0; i < queues.size(); i++) {
      System.out.print("Vertex " + i + ": ");
      for (WeightedEdge edge : queues.get(i)) {
        System.out.print("(" + edge.u +
          ", " + edge.v + ", " + edge.weight + ") ");
      }
      System.out.println();
    }
  }

  /** Get a minimum spanning tree rooted at vertex 0 */
  public MST getMinimumSpanningTree() {
    return getMinimumSpanningTree(0);
  }

  /** Get a minimum spanning tree rooted at a specified vertex */
  public MST getMinimumSpanningTree(int startingIndex) {
    List<Integer> T = new ArrayList<Integer>();
    // T initially contains the startingVertex;
    T.add(startingIndex);

    int numberOfVertices = vertices.size(); // Number of vertices
    int[] parent = new int[numberOfVertices]; // Parent of a vertex
    // Initially set the parent of all vertices to -1
    for (int i = 0; i < parent.length; i++)
      parent[i] = -1;
    int totalWeight = 0; // Total weight of the tree thus far

    // Clone the queue, so as to keep the original queue intact
    List<PriorityQueue<WeightedEdge>> queues = deepClone(this.queues);

    // All vertices are found?
    while (T.size() < numberOfVertices) {
      // Search for the vertex with the smallest edge adjacent to
      // a vertex in T
      int v = -1;
      double smallestWeight = Double.MAX_VALUE;
      for (int u : T) {
        while (!queues.get(u).isEmpty() &&
          T.contains(queues.get(u).peek().v)) {
          // Remove the edge from queues.get(u) if the adjacent
          // vertex of u is already in T
          queues.get(u).remove();
        }

        if (queues.get(u).isEmpty()) {
          continue; // Consider the next vertex in T
        }

```

```
        // Current smallest weight on an edge adjacent to u
        WeightedEdge edge = queues.get(u).peek();
        if (edge.weight < smallestWeight) {
          v = edge.v;
          smallestWeight = edge.weight;
          // If v is added to the tree, u will be its parent
          parent[v] = u;
        }
      } // End of for

      T.add(v); // Add a new vertex to the tree
      totalWeight += smallestWeight;
    } // End of while

    return new MST(startingIndex, parent, T, totalWeight);
  }

  /** Clone an array of queues */
  private List<PriorityQueue<WeightedEdge>> deepClone(
    List<PriorityQueue<WeightedEdge>> queues) {
    List<PriorityQueue<WeightedEdge>> copiedQueues =
      new ArrayList<PriorityQueue<WeightedEdge>>();

    for (int i = 0; i < queues.size(); i++) {
      copiedQueues.add(new PriorityQueue<WeightedEdge>());
      for (WeightedEdge e : queues.get(i)) {
        copiedQueues.get(i).add(e);
      }
    }

    return copiedQueues;
  }

  /** MST is an inner class in WeightedGraph */
  public class MST extends Tree {
    private int totalWeight; // Total weight of all edges in the tree

    public MST(int root, int[] parent, List<Integer> searchOrder,
        int totalWeight) {
      super(root, parent, searchOrder);
      this.totalWeight = totalWeight;
    }

    public int getTotalWeight() {
      return totalWeight;
    }
  }

  /** Find single-source shortest paths */
  public ShortestPathTree getShortestPath(int sourceIndex) {
    // T stores the vertices whose path found so far
    List<Integer> T = new ArrayList<Integer>();
    // T initially contains the sourceVertex;
    T.add(sourceIndex);

    // vertices is defined in AbstractGraph
    int numberOfVertices = vertices.size();

    // parent[v] stores the previous vertex of v in the path
    int[] parent = new int[numberOfVertices];
```

smallest edge to **u**
update **smallestWeight**
add to tree
update **totalWeight**
clone queue
clone every element
MST inner class
total weight in tree
vertices found
add source
number of vertices
parent array

parent of root
costs array
source cost
a copy of queues
more vertices left?
determine one
remove visited vertex
queues.get(u) is empty
smallest edge to **u**
update **smallestCost**
v now found
add to **T**
create a path
costs
constructor
get cost

```
    parent[sourceIndex] = -1; // The parent of source is set to -1

    // costs[v] stores the cost of the path from v to the source
    int[] costs = new int[numberOfVertices];
    for (int i = 0; i < costs.length; i++) {
      costs[i] = Integer.MAX_VALUE; // Initial cost set to infinity
    }
    costs[sourceIndex] = 0; // Cost of source is 0

    // Get a copy of queues
    List<PriorityQueue<WeightedEdge>> queues = deepClone(this.queues);

    // Expand verticesFound
    while (T.size() < numberOfVertices) {
      int v = -1; // Vertex to be determined
      int smallestCost = Integer.MAX_VALUE; // Set to infinity
      for (int u : T) {
        while (!queues.get(u).isEmpty() &&
          T.contains(queues.get(u).peek().v)) {
         queues.get(u).remove(); // Remove the vertex in verticesFound
        }

        if (queues.get(u).isEmpty()) {
          // All vertices adjacent to u are in verticesFound
          continue;
        }

        WeightedEdge e = queues.get(u).peek();
        if (costs[u] + e.weight < smallestCost) {
          v = e.v;
          smallestCost = costs[u] + e.weight;
          // If v is added to the tree, u will be its parent
          parent[v] = u;
        }
      } // End of for

      T.add(v); // Add a new vertex to T
      costs[v] = smallestCost;
    } // End of while

    // Create a ShortestPathTree
    return new ShortestPathTree(sourceIndex, parent, T, costs);
  }

  /** ShortestPathTree is an inner class in WeightedGraph */
  public class ShortestPathTree extends Tree {
    private int[] costs; // costs[v] is the cost from v to source

    /** Construct a path */
    public ShortestPathTree(int source, int[] parent,
        List<Integer> searchOrder, int[] costs) {
      super(source, parent, searchOrder);
      this.costs = costs;
    }

    /** Return the cost for a path from the root to vertex v */
    public int getCost(int v) {
      return costs[v];
    }
```

```
232     /** Print paths from all vertices to the source */
233     public void printAllPaths() {
234       System.out.println("All shortest paths from " +
235         vertices.get(getRoot()) + " are:");
236       for (int i = 0; i < costs.length; i++) {
237         printPath(i); // Print a path from i to the source
238         System.out.println("(cost: " + costs[i] + ")"); // Path cost
239       }
240     }
241   }
242
243   public List<PriorityQueue<WeightedEdge>> getWeightedEdges() {
244     return queues;
245   }
246 }
```

print all paths

return edges

When you construct a `WeightedGraph`, its superclass's constructor is invoked (lines 9, 15, 21, 28) to initialize the properties `vertices` and `neighbors` in `AbstractGraph`. Additionally, priority queues are created for instances of `WeightedGraph`.

Listing 28.3 gives a test program that creates a graph for the one in Figure 27.1 and another graph for the one in Figure 28.1.

LISTING 28.3 TestWeightedGraph.java

```
public class TestWeightedGraph {
  public static void main(String[] args) {
    String[] vertices = {"Seattle", "San Francisco", "Los Angeles",
      "Denver", "Kansas City", "Chicago", "Boston", "New York",
      "Atlanta", "Miami", "Dallas", "Houston"};

    int[][] edges = {
      {0, 1, 807}, {0, 3, 1331}, {0, 5, 2097},
      {1, 0, 807}, {1, 2, 381}, {1, 3, 1267},
      {2, 1, 381}, {2, 3, 1015}, {2, 4, 1663}, {2, 10, 1435},
      {3, 0, 1331}, {3, 1, 1267}, {3, 2, 1015}, {3, 4, 599},
        {3, 5, 1003},
      {4, 2, 1663}, {4, 3, 599}, {4, 5, 533}, {4, 7, 1260},
        {4, 8, 864}, {4, 10, 496},
      {5, 0, 2097}, {5, 3, 1003}, {5, 4, 533},
        {5, 6, 983}, {5, 7, 787},
      {6, 5, 983}, {6, 7, 214},
      {7, 4, 1260}, {7, 5, 787}, {7, 6, 214}, {7, 8, 888},
      {8, 4, 864}, {8, 7, 888}, {8, 9, 661},
        {8, 10, 781}, {8, 11, 810},
      {9, 8, 661}, {9, 11, 1187},
      {10, 2, 1435}, {10, 4, 496}, {10, 8, 781}, {10, 11, 239},
      {11, 8, 810}, {11, 9, 1187}, {11, 10, 239}
    };

    WeightedGraph<String> graph1 =
      new WeightedGraph<String>(edges, vertices);
    System.out.println("The number of vertices in graph1: "
      + graph1.getSize());
    System.out.println("The vertex with index 1 is "
      + graph1.getVertex(1));
    System.out.println("The index for Miami is " +
      graph1.getIndex("Miami"));
    System.out.println("The edges for graph1:");
    graph1.printWeightedEdges();

```

vertices

edges

create graph

print edges

edges

create graph

print edges

```
37     edges = new int[][]{
38       {0, 1, 2}, {0, 3, 8},
39       {1, 0, 2}, {1, 2, 7}, {1, 3, 3},
40       {2, 1, 7}, {2, 3, 4}, {2, 4, 5},
41       {3, 0, 8}, {3, 1, 3}, {3, 2, 4}, {3, 4, 6},
42       {4, 2, 5}, {4, 3, 6}
43     };
44     WeightedGraph<Integer> graph2 =
45       new WeightedGraph<Integer>(edges, 5);
46     System.out.println("\nThe edges for graph2:");
47     graph2.printWeightedEdges();
48   }
49 }
```

```
The number of vertices in graph1: 12
The vertex with index 1 is San Francisco
The index for Miami is 9
The edges for graph1:
Vertex 0: (0, 1, 807) (0, 3, 1331) (0, 5, 2097)
Vertex 1: (1, 2, 381) (1, 0, 807) (1, 3, 1267)
Vertex 2: (2, 1, 381) (2, 3, 1015) (2, 4, 1663) (2, 10, 1435)
Vertex 3: (3, 4, 599) (3, 5, 1003) (3, 1, 1267)
  (3, 0, 1331) (3, 2, 1015)
Vertex 4: (4, 10, 496) (4, 8, 864) (4, 5, 533) (4, 2, 1663)
  (4, 7, 1260) (4, 3, 599)
Vertex 5: (5, 4, 533) (5, 7, 787) (5, 3, 1003)
  (5, 0, 2097) (5, 6, 983)
Vertex 6: (6, 7, 214) (6, 5, 983)
Vertex 7: (7, 6, 214) (7, 8, 888) (7, 5, 787) (7, 4, 1260)
Vertex 8: (8, 9, 661) (8, 10, 781) (8, 4, 864)
  (8, 7, 888) (8, 11, 810)
Vertex 9: (9, 8, 661) (9, 11, 1187)
Vertex 10: (10, 11, 239) (10, 4, 496) (10, 8, 781) (10, 2, 1435)
Vertex 11: (11, 10, 239) (11, 9, 1187) (11, 8, 810)

The edges for graph2:
Vertex 0: (0, 1, 2) (0, 3, 8)
Vertex 1: (1, 0, 2) (1, 2, 7) (1, 3, 3)
Vertex 2: (2, 3, 4) (2, 1, 7) (2, 4, 5)
Vertex 3: (3, 1, 3) (3, 4, 6) (3, 2, 4) (3, 0, 8)
Vertex 4: (4, 2, 5) (4, 3, 6)
```

The program creates `graph1` for the graph in Figure 27.1 in lines 3–27. The vertices for `graph1` are defined in lines 3–5. The edges for `graph1` are defined in lines 7–24. The edges are represented using a two-dimensional array. For each row `i` in the array, `edges[i][0]` and `edges[i][1]` indicate that there is an edge from vertex `edges[i][0]` to vertex `edges[i][1]` and the weight for the edge is `edges[i][2]`. For example, the first row {`0`, `1`, `807`} represents the edge from vertex `0` (`edges[0][0]`) to vertex `1` (`edges[0][1]`) with weight `807` (`edges[0][2]`). The row {`0`, `5`, `2097`} represents the edge from vertex `0` (`edges[2][0]`) to vertex `5` (`edges[2][1]`) with weight `2097` (`edges[2][2]`). Line 35 invokes the `printWeightedEdges()` method on `graph1` to display all edges in `graph1`.

The program creates the edges for `graph2` for the graph in Figure 28.1 in lines 37–45. Line 47 invokes the `printWeightedEdges()` method on `graph2` to display all edges in `graph2`.

Note

The adjacent edges for each vertex are stored in a priority queue. When you remove an edge from the queue, the one with the smallest weight is always removed. However, if you traverse the edges in the queue, the edges are not necessarily in increasing order of weights.

Traversing priority queue

28.4 Minimum Spanning Trees

A graph may have many spanning trees. Suppose that the edges are weighted. A minimum spanning tree has the minimum total weights. For example, the trees in Figures 28.3(b), 28.3(c), 28.3(d) are spanning trees for the graph in Figure 28.3(a). The trees in Figures 28.3(c) and 28.3(d) are minimum spanning trees.

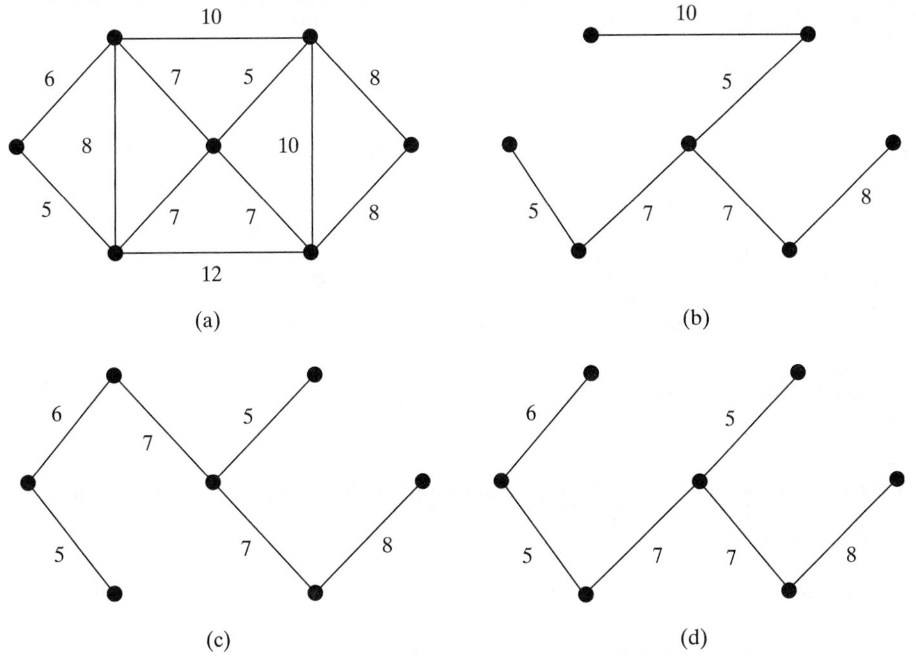
10
6
7
5
8
8
10
5
7
7
8
12
(a)
10
5
5
7
7
8
(b)
6
5
7
5
7
8
(c)
6
5
5
7
7
8
(d)

FIGURE 28.3 The tree in (c) and (d) are minimum spanning trees of the graph in (a).

The problem of finding a minimum spanning tree has many applications. Consider a company with branches in many cities. The company wants to lease telephone lines to connect all branches together. The phone company charges different amounts of money to connect different pairs of cities. There are many ways to connect all branches together. The cheapest way is to find a spanning tree with the minimum total rates.

28.4.1 Minimum Spanning Tree Algorithms

How do you find a minimum spanning tree? There are several well-known algorithms for doing so. This section introduces Prim's algorithm. Prim's algorithm starts with a spanning tree T that contains an arbitrary vertex. The algorithm expands the tree by adding a vertex with the smallest edge incident to a vertex already in the tree. The algorithm is described in Listing 28.4.

Prim's algorithm

LISTING 28.4 Prim's Minimum Spanning Tree Algorithm

add initial vertex
more vertices?
find a vertex
add to tree

```
minimumSpanningTree() {
  Let V denote the set of vertices in the graph;
  Let T be a set for the vertices in the spanning tree;
  Initially, add the starting vertex to T;

  while (size of T < n) {
    find u in T and v in V - T with the smallest weight
      on the edge (u, v), as shown in Figure 28.4;
    add v to T;
  }
}
```

The algorithm starts by adding the starting vertex into T. It then continuously adds a vertex (say v) from V – T into T. v is the vertex that is adjacent to a vertex in T with the smallest weight on the edge. For example, there are five edges connecting vertices in T and V – T, as shown in Figure 28.4, (u, v) is the one with the smallest weight.

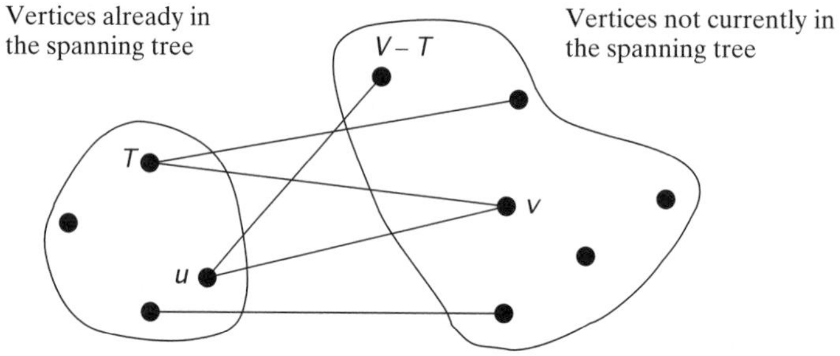
Vertices already in the spanning tree
V – T
Vertices not currently in the spanning tree
T
u
v

FIGURE 28.4 Find a vertex u in T that connects a vertex v in V – T with the smallest weight.

example

Consider the graph in Figure 28.5. The algorithm adds the vertices to T in this order:

1. Add vertex 0 to T.
2. Add vertex 5 to T, since Edge(5, 0, 5) has the smallest weight among all edges incident to a vertex in T, as shown in Figure 28.5(a).
3. Add vertex 1 to T, since Edge(1, 0, 6) has the smallest weight among all edges incident to a vertex T, as shown in Figure 28.5(b).
4. Add vertex 6 to T, since Edge(6, 1, 7) has the smallest weight among all edges incident to a vertex T, as shown in Figure 28.5(c).
5. Add vertex 2 to T, since Edge(2, 6, 5) has the smallest weight among all edges incident to a vertex T, as shown in Figure 28.5(d).
6. Add vertex 4 to T, since Edge(4, 6, 7) has the smallest weight among all edges incident to a vertex T, as shown in Figure 28.5(e).
7. Add vertex 3 to T, since Edge(3, 2, 8) has the smallest weight among all edges incident to a vertex T, as shown in Figure 28.5(f).

unique tree?

Note

A minimum spanning tree is not unique. For example, both (c) and (d) in Figure 28.5 are minimum spanning trees for the graph in Figure 28.5(a). However, if the weights are distinct, the graph has a unique minimum spanning tree.

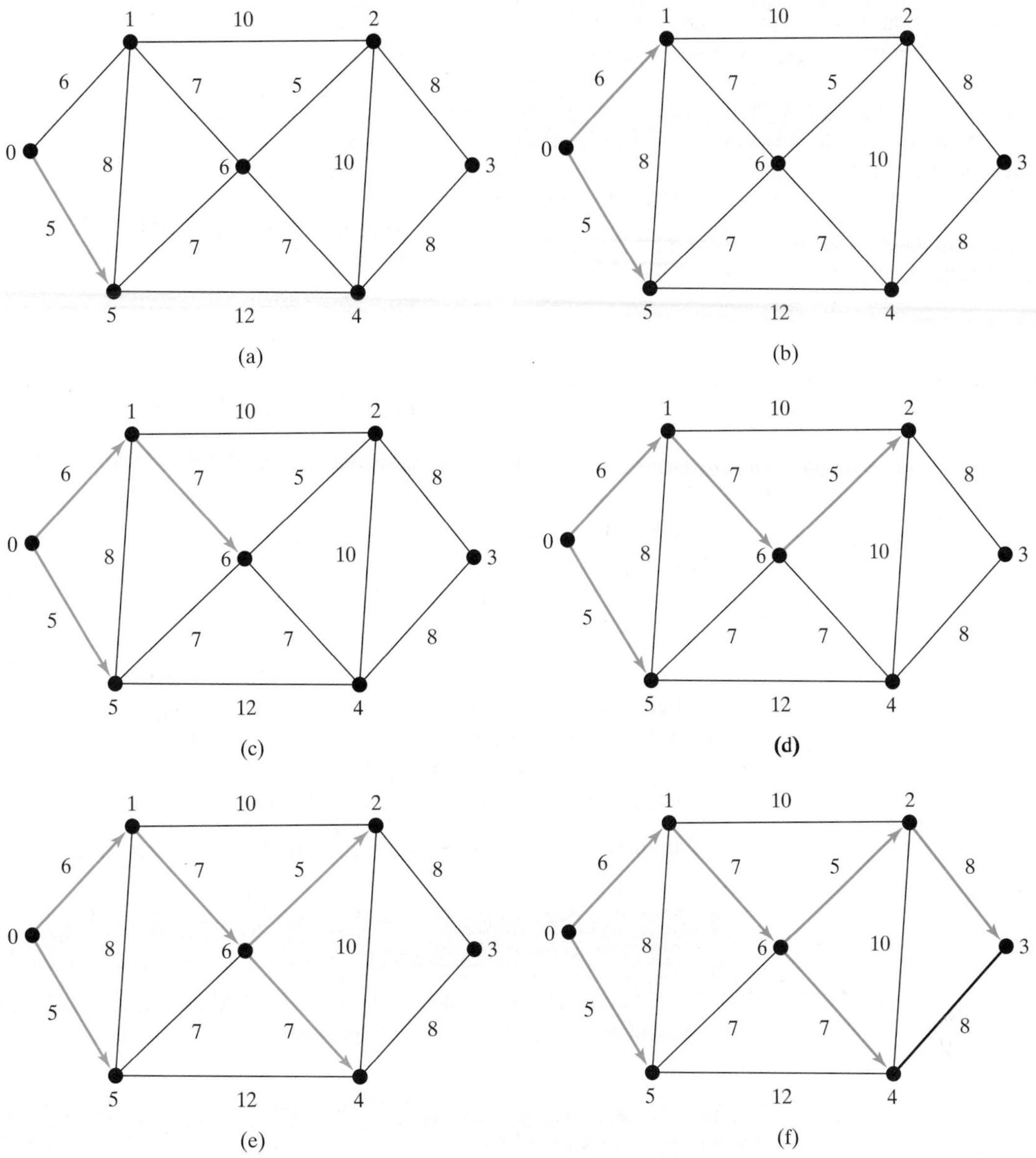
(a)
(b)
(c)
(d)
(e)
(f)

FIGURE 28.5 The adjacent vertices with the smallest weight are added successively to `T`.

Note

Assume that the graph is connected and undirected. If a graph is not connected or directed, the algorithm will not work. You may modify the algorithm to find a spanning forest for any undirected graph.

connected and undirected

28.4.2 Implementation of the MST Algorithm

The `getMinimumSpanningTree(int v)` method is defined in the `WeightedGraph` class. It returns an instance of the `MST` class, as shown in Figure 28.2. The `MST` class is defined as an inner class in the `WeightedGraph` class, which extends the `Tree` class, as shown in Figure 28.6. The `Tree` class was shown in Figure 27.10. The `MST` class was implemented in lines 146–158 in Listing 28.2.

`getMinimumSpanningTree()`

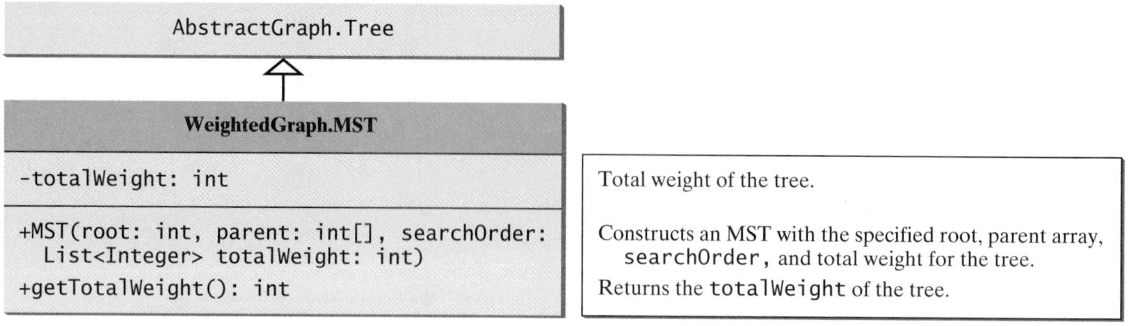
AbstractGraph.Tree
WeightedGraph.MST
-totalWeight: int
+MST(root: int, parent: int[], searchOrder: List<Integer> totalWeight: int)
+getTotalWeight(): int
Total weight of the tree.
Constructs an MST with the specified root, parent array, searchOrder, and total weight for the tree.
Returns the totalWeight of the tree.

FIGURE 28.6 The MST class extends the Tree class.

The `getMinimumSpanningTree` method was implemented in lines 79–127 in Listing 28.2. The `getMinimumSpanningTree(int startingVertex)` method first adds `startingVertex` to `T` (line 82). `T` is a list that stores the vertices added into the spanning tree (line 80). `vertices` is defined as a protected data field in the `AbstractGraph` class, which is an array that stores all vertices in the graph. `vertices.size()` returns the number of the vertices in the graph (line 84).

A vertex is added to `T` if it is adjacent to one of the vertices in `T` with the smallest weight (line 122). Such a vertex is found using the following procedure:

1. For each vertex `u` in `T`, find its neighbor with the smallest weight to `u`. All the neighbors of `u` are stored in `queues.get(u)`. `queues.get(u).peek()` (line 102) returns the adjacent edge with the smallest weight. If a neighbor is already in `T`, remove it (line 105). To keep the original queues intact, a copy is created in line 92. After lines 101–110, `queues.get(u).peek()` (line 113) returns the vertex with the smallest weight to `u`.

2. Compare all these neighbors and find the one with the smallest weight (lines 114–119).

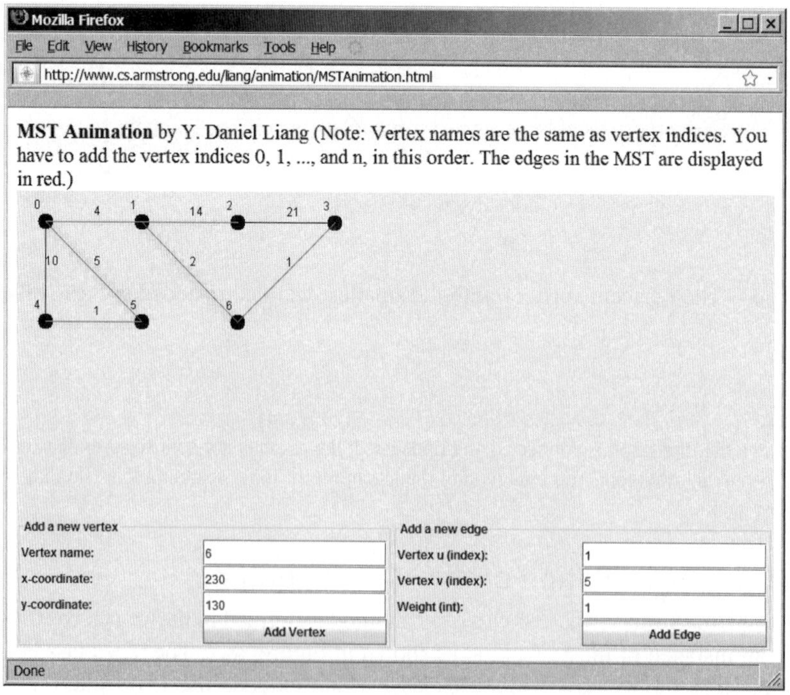
Mozilla Firefox
File Edit View History Bookmarks Tools Help
http://www.cs.armstrong.edu/liang/animation/MSTAnimation.html
MST Animation by Y. Daniel Liang (Note: Vertex names are the same as vertex indices. You have to add the vertex indices 0, 1, ..., and n, in this order. The edges in the MST are displayed in red.)
0
1
2
3
4
5
6
4
14
21
10
5
2
1
1
Add a new vertex
Vertex name:
6
x-coordinate:
230
y-coordinate:
130
Add Vertex
Add a new edge
Vertex u (index):
1
Vertex v (index):
5
Weight (int):
1
Add Edge
Done

FIGURE 28.7 The animation tool enables you to create a graph dynamically and displays its MST.

After a new vertex is added to T (line 122), totalWeight is updated (line 123). Once all vertices are added to T, an instance of MST is created (line 126). Note that the method will not work if the graph is not connected. However, you can modify it to obtain a partial MST.

The MST class extends the Tree class (line 146). To create an instance of MST, pass root, parent, T, and totalWeight (lines 126). The data fields root, parent, and searchOrder are defined in the Tree class, which is an inner class defined in AbstractGraph.

For each vertex, the program constructs a priority queue for its adjacent edges. It takes $O(\log|V|)$ time to insert an edge into a priority queue and the same time to remove an edge from the priority queue. So the overall time complexity for the program is $O(|E|\log|V|)$, where $|E|$ denotes the number of edges and $|V|$ the number of vertices.

time complexity

Pedagogical Note

Follow the link www.cs.armstrong.edu/liang/animation/MSTAnimation.html to see how to create a weighted graph dynamically and display its MST, as shown in Figure 28.7.

MST animation

Listing 28.5 gives a test program that displays minimum spanning trees for the graph in Figure 27.1 and the graph in Figure 28.1, respectively.

LISTING 28.5 TestMinimumSpanningTree.java

```
public class TestMinimumSpanningTree {
  public static void main(String[] args) {
    String[] vertices = {"Seattle", "San Francisco", "Los Angeles",
      "Denver", "Kansas City", "Chicago", "Boston", "New York",
      "Atlanta", "Miami", "Dallas", "Houston"};

    int[][] edges = {
      {0, 1, 807}, {0, 3, 1331}, {0, 5, 2097},
      {1, 0, 807}, {1, 2, 381}, {1, 3, 1267},
      {2, 1, 381}, {2, 3, 1015}, {2, 4, 1663}, {2, 10, 1435},
      {3, 0, 1331}, {3, 1, 1267}, {3, 2, 1015}, {3, 4, 599},
        {3, 5, 1003},
      {4, 2, 1663}, {4, 3, 599}, {4, 5, 533}, {4, 7, 1260},
        {4, 8, 864}, {4, 10, 496},
      {5, 0, 2097}, {5, 3, 1003}, {5, 4, 533},
        {5, 6, 983}, {5, 7, 787},
      {6, 5, 983}, {6, 7, 214},
      {7, 4, 1260}, {7, 5, 787}, {7, 6, 214}, {7, 8, 888},
      {8, 4, 864}, {8, 7, 888}, {8, 9, 661},
        {8, 10, 781}, {8, 11, 810},
      {9, 8, 661}, {9, 11, 1187},
      {10, 2, 1435}, {10, 4, 496}, {10, 8, 781}, {10, 11, 239},
      {11, 8, 810}, {11, 9, 1187}, {11, 10, 239}
    };

    WeightedGraph<String> graph1 =
      new WeightedGraph<String>(edges, vertices);
    WeightedGraph<String>.MST tree1 = graph1.getMinimumSpanningTree();
    System.out.println("Total weight is " + tree1.getTotalWeight());
    tree1.printTree();

    edges = new int[][]{
      {0, 1, 2}, {0, 3, 8},
      {1, 0, 2}, {1, 2, 7}, {1, 3, 3},
      {2, 1, 7}, {2, 3, 4}, {2, 4, 5},
      {3, 0, 8}, {3, 1, 3}, {3, 2, 4}, {3, 4, 6},
      {4, 2, 5}, {4, 3, 6}
    };
```

create vertices
create edges
create **graph1**
MST for **graph1**
total weight
print tree
create edges

create **graph2**

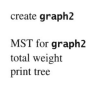

MST for **graph2**

total weight

print tree

```
39
40      WeightedGraph<Integer> graph2 =
41        new WeightedGraph<Integer>(edges, 5);
42      WeightedGraph<Integer>.MST tree2 =
43        graph2.getMinimumSpanningTree(1);
44      System.out.println("Total weight is " + tree2.getTotalWeight());
45      tree2.printTree();
46    }
47  }
```

```
Total weight is 6513
Root is: Seattle
Edges: (Seattle, San Francisco) (San Francisco, Los Angeles)
  (Los Angeles, Denver) (Denver, Kansas City) (Kansas City, Chicago)
  (New York, Boston) (Chicago, New York) (Dallas, Atlanta)
  (Atlanta, Miami) (Kansas City, Dallas) (Dallas, Houston)

Total weight is 14
Root is: 1
Edges: (1, 0) (3, 2) (1, 3) (2, 4)
```

The program creates a weighted graph for Figure 27.1 in line 27. It then invokes `getMinimumSpanningTree()` (line 28) to return an `MST` that represents a minimum spanning tree for the graph. Invoking `printTree()` (line 30) on the `MST` object displays the edges in the tree. Note that `MST` is a subclass of `Tree`. The `printTree()` method is defined in the `Tree` class.

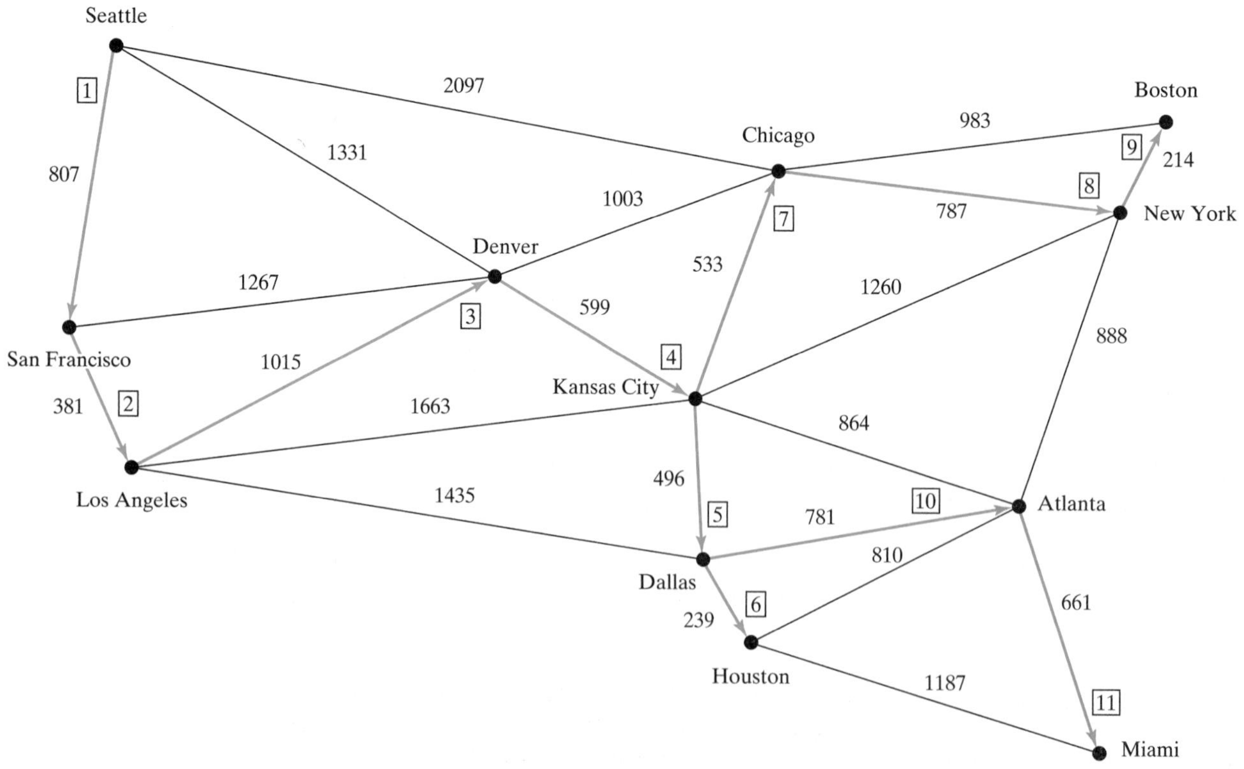
Seattle
Boston
Chicago
New York
Denver
San Francisco
Kansas City
Los Angeles
Atlanta
Dallas
Houston
Miami
2097
983
1331
807
214
1003
787
533
1267
1260
599
888
1015
381
1663
864
496
1435
781
810
239
661
1187
1
2
3
4
5
6
7
8
9
10
11

FIGURE 28.8 The edges in the minimum spanning tree for the cities are highlighted.

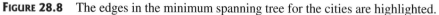

graphical illustration

The graphical illustration of the minimum spanning tree is shown in Figure 28.8. The vertices are added to the tree in this order: Seattle, San Francisco, Los Angeles, Denver, Kansas City, Dallas, Houston, Chicago, New York, Boston, Atlanta, and Miami.

28.5 Finding Shortest Paths

Section 27.1 introduced the problem of finding the shortest distance between two cities for the graph in Figure 27.1. The answer to this problem is to find a shortest path between two vertices in the graph.

28.5.1 Shortest-Path Algorithms

Given a graph with nonnegative weights on the edges, a well-known algorithm for finding a single-source shortest path was discovered by Edsger Dijkstra, a Dutch computer scientist. Dijkstra's algorithm uses `costs[v]` to store the cost of the shortest path from vertex `v` to the source vertex `s`. So `costs[s]` is `0`. Initially assign infinity to `costs[v]` to indicate that no path is found from `v` to `s`. Let `V` denote all vertices in the graph and `T` denote the set of the vertices whose costs have been found so far. Initially, the source vertex `s` is in `T`. The algorithm repeatedly finds a vertex `u` in `T` and a vertex `v` in `V - T` such that `costs[u] + w(u, v)` is the smallest, and moves `v` to `T`. Here `w(u, v)` denotes the weight on edge (`u`, `v`).

The algorithm is described in Listing 28.6.

LISTING 28.6 Dijkstra's Single-Source Shortest-Path Algorithm

```
 1 shortestPath(s) {
 2   Let V denote the set of vertices in the graph;
 3   Let T be a set that contains the vertices whose
 4     paths to s have been found;
 5   Initially T contains source vertex s with costs[s] = 0;
 6
 7   while (size of T < n) {
 8     find v in V - T with the smallest costs[u] + w(u, v) value
 9       among all u in T;
10     add v to T and costs[v] = costs[u] + w(u, v);
11   }
12 }
```

add initial vertex (line 5)
more vertex (line 7)
find next vertex (line 8)
add a vertex (line 10)

This algorithm is very similar to Prim's for finding a minimum spanning tree. Both algorithms divide the vertices into two sets `T` and `V - T`. In the case of Prim's algorithm, set `T` contains the vertices that are already added to the tree. In the case of Dijkstra's, set `T` contains the vertices whose shortest paths to the source have been found. Both algorithms repeatedly find a vertex from `V - T` and add it to `T`. In the case of Prim's algorithm, the vertex is adjacent to some vertex in the set with the minimum weight on the edge. In the case of Dijkstra's, the vertex is adjacent to some vertex in the set with the minimum total cost to the source.

The algorithm starts by adding the source vertex `s` into `T` and sets `costs[s]` to `0` (line 5) It then continuously adds a vertex (say `v`) from `V - T` into `T`. `v` is the vertex that is adjacent to a vertex in `T` with the smallest `costs[u] + w(u, v)`. For example, there are five edges connecting vertices in `T` and `V - T`, as shown in Figure 28.9; `(u, v)` is the one with the smallest `costs[u] + w(u, v)`. After `v` is added to `T`, set `costs[v]` to `costs[u] + w(u, v)` (line 10).

Let us illustrate Dijkstra's algorithm using the graph in Figure 28.10(a). Suppose the source vertex is `1`. So, `costs[1]` is `0` and the costs for all other vertices are initially ∞, as shown in Figure 28.10(b). We use the `parent[i]` to denote the parent of `i` in the path. For convenience, set the parent of the source node to `-1`.

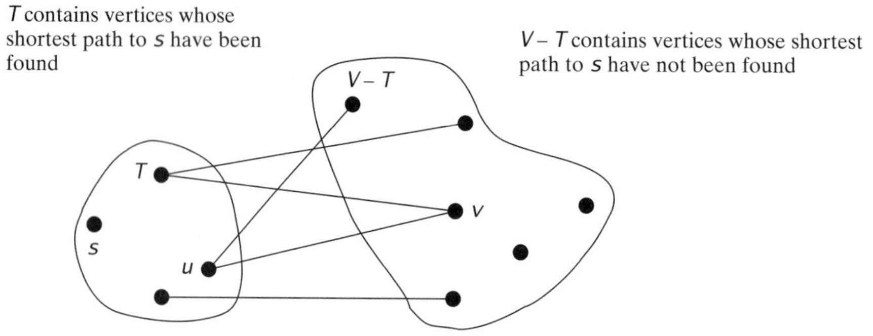
T contains vertices whose shortest path to s have been found
V – T contains vertices whose shortest path to s have not been found
V – T
T
v
s
u

FIGURE 28.9 Find a vertex u in T that connects a vertex v in V – T with the smallest costs[u] + w(u, v).

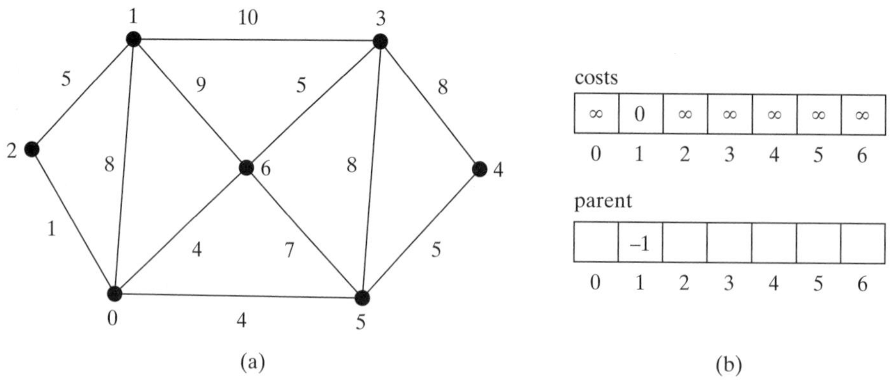
costs
∞ 0 ∞ ∞ ∞ ∞ ∞
0 1 2 3 4 5 6
parent
–1
0 1 2 3 4 5 6
(a)
(b)

FIGURE 28.10 The algorithm will find all shortest paths from source vertex 1.

Initially set T contains the source vertex. Vertices 2, 0, 6, and 3 are adjacent to the vertices in T, and vertex 2 has the path of smallest cost to source vertex 1. So add 2 to T. costs[2] now becomes 5, as shown in Figure 28.11.

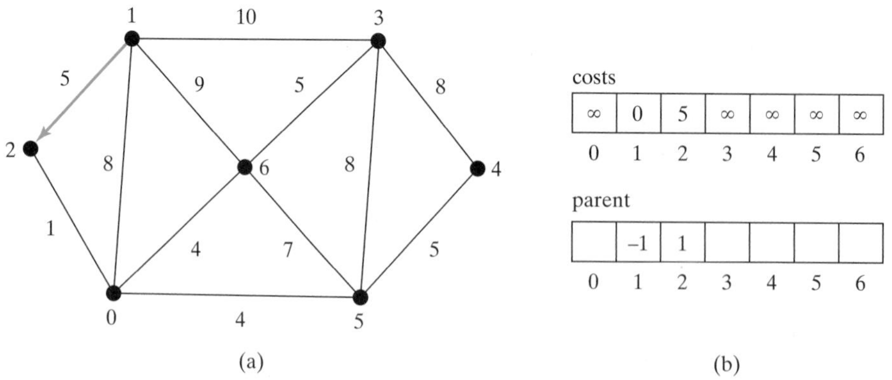
costs
∞ 0 5 ∞ ∞ ∞ ∞
0 1 2 3 4 5 6
parent
–1 1
0 1 2 3 4 5 6
(a)
(b)

FIGURE 28.11 Now vertices 1 and 2 are in the set T.

Now T contains {1, 2}. Vertices 0, 6, and 3 are adjacent to the vertices in T, and vertex 0 has a path of smallest cost to source vertex 1. So add 1 to T. costs[0] now becomes 6, as shown in Figure 28.12.

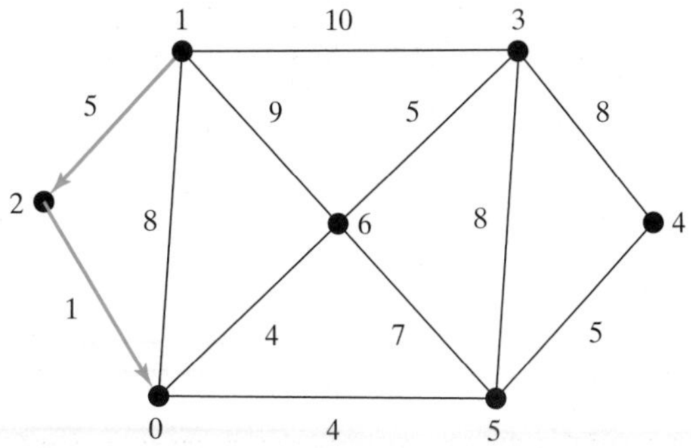
1
10
3
5
9
5
8
2
8
6
8
4
1
4
7
5
0
4
5

(a)

costs

6	0	5	∞	∞	∞	∞
0	1	2	3	4	5	6

parent

2	–1	1				
0	1	2	3	4	5	6

(b)

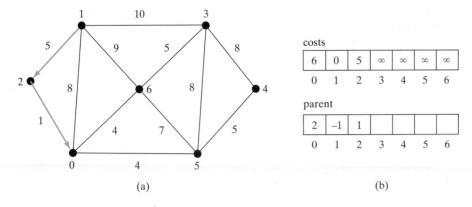

FIGURE 28.12 Now vertices {1, 2, 0} are in the set T.

Now T contains {1, 2, 0}. Vertices 3, 6, and 5 are adjacent to the vertices in T, and vertex 6 has the path of smallest cost to source vertex 1. So add 6 to T. `costs[6]` now becomes 9, as shown in Figure 28.13.

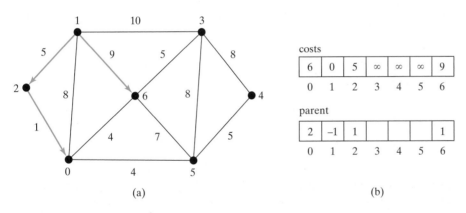

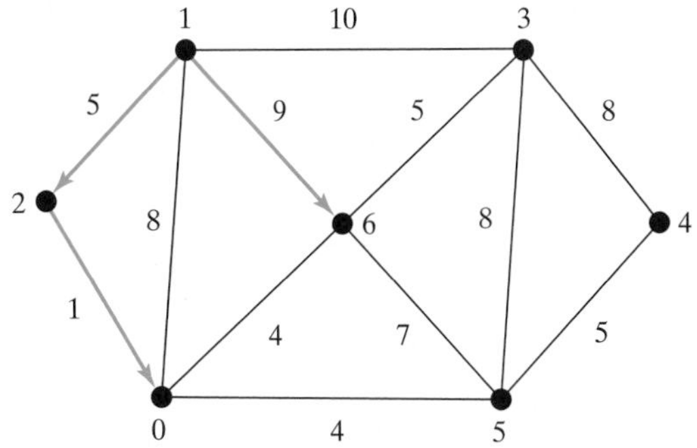
1
10
3
5
9
5
8
2
8
6
8
4
1
4
7
5
0
4
5

(a)

costs

6	0	5	∞	∞	∞	9
0	1	2	3	4	5	6

parent

2	–1	1				1
0	1	2	3	4	5	6

(b)

FIGURE 28.13 Now vertices {1, 2, 0, 6} are in the set T.

Now T contains {1, 2, 0, 6}. Vertices 3 and 5 are adjacent to the vertices in T, and both vertices have a path of the same smallest cost to source vertex 1. You can choose either 3 or 5. Let us add 3 to T. `costs[3]` now becomes 10, as shown in Figure 28.14.

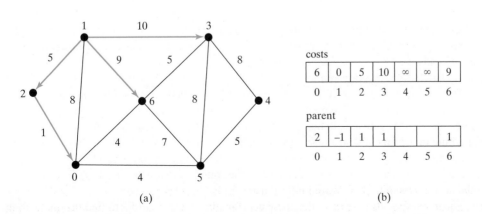

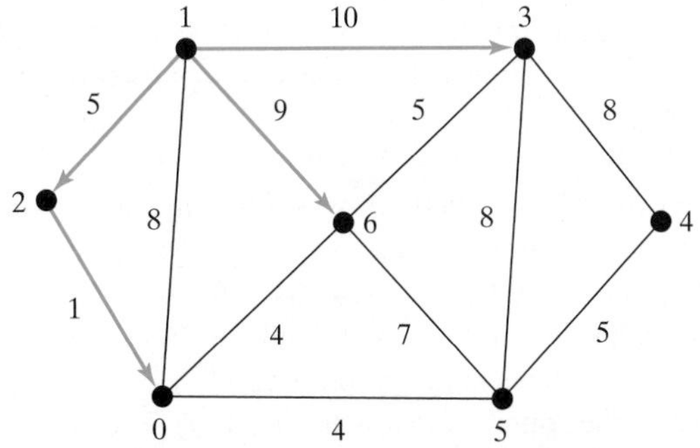
1
10
3
5
9
5
8
2
8
6
8
4
1
4
7
5
0
4
5

(a)

costs

6	0	5	10	∞	∞	9
0	1	2	3	4	5	6

parent

2	–1	1	1			1
0	1	2	3	4	5	6

(b)

FIGURE 28.14 Now vertices {1, 2, 0, 6, 3} are in the set T.

Now T contains {1, 2, 0, 6, 3}. Vertices 4 and 5 are adjacent to the vertices in T, and vertex 5 has the path of smallest cost to source vertex 1. So add 5 to T. `costs[5]` now becomes 10, as shown in Figure 28.15.

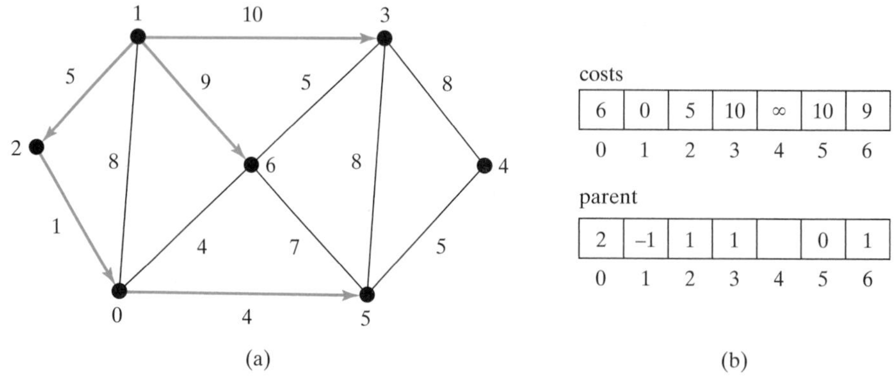
costs
6 0 5 10 ∞ 10 9
0 1 2 3 4 5 6
parent
2 –1 1 1 0 1
0 1 2 3 4 5 6
(a)
(b)

FIGURE 28.15 Now vertices {1, 2, 0, 6, 3, 5} are in the set T.

Now T contains {1, 2, 0, 6, 3, 5}. The smallest cost for a path to connect 4 with 1 is 15, as shown in Figure 28.16.

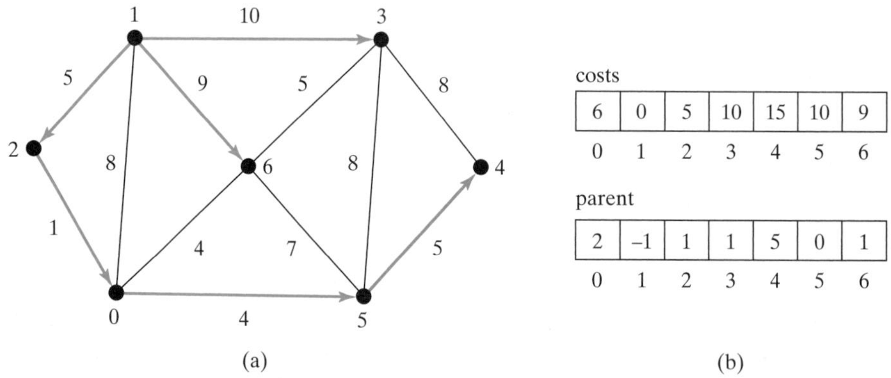
costs
6 0 5 10 15 10 9
0 1 2 3 4 5 6
parent
2 –1 1 1 5 0 1
0 1 2 3 4 5 6
(a)
(b)

FIGURE 28.16 Now vertices {1, 2, 6, 0, 3, 5, 4} are in set T.

28.5.2 Implementation of the Shortest-Paths Algorithm

shortest-path tree

As you see, the algorithm essentially finds all shortest paths from a source vertex, which produces a tree rooted at the source vertex. We call this tree a *single-source all-shortest-path tree* (or simply a *shortest-path tree*). To model this tree, define a class named `ShortestPathTree` that extends the `Tree` class, as shown in Figure 28.17. `ShortestPathTree` is defined as an inner class in `WeightedGraph` in lines 217–241 in Listing 28.2.

The `getShortestPath(int sourceVertex)` method was implemented in lines 161–214 in Listing 28.2. The method first adds `sourceVertex` to `T` (line 165). `T` is a list that stores the vertices whose path has been found (line 163). `vertices` is defined as a protected data field in the `AbstractGraph` class, which is an array that stores all vertices in the graph. `vertices.size()` returns the number of the vertices in the graph (line 168).

Each vertex is assigned a cost. The cost of the source vertex is 0 (line 179). The cost of all other vertices is initially assigned infinity (line 177).

The method needs to remove the elements from the queues in order to find the one with the smallest total cost. To keep the original queues intact, queues are cloned in line 182.

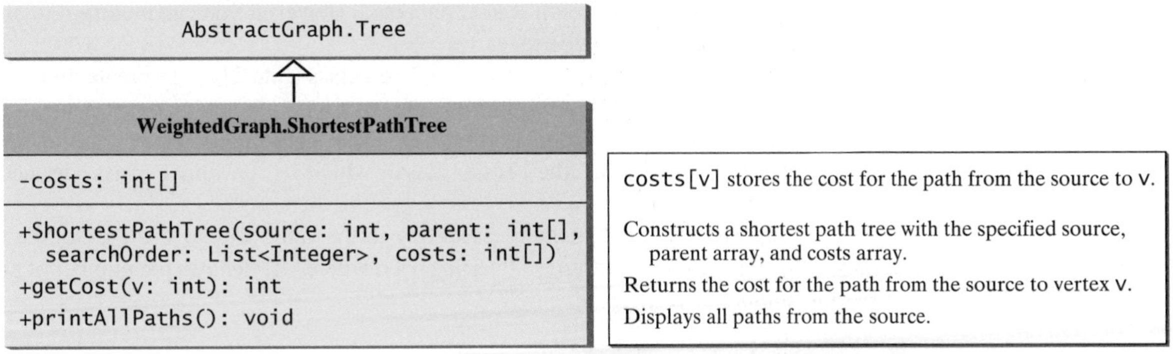
AbstractGraph.Tree
WeightedGraph.ShortestPathTree
-costs: int[]
+ShortestPathTree(source: int, parent: int[], searchOrder: List<Integer>, costs: int[])
+getCost(v: int): int
+printAllPaths(): void
costs[v] stores the cost for the path from the source to v.
Constructs a shortest path tree with the specified source, parent array, and costs array.
Returns the cost for the path from the source to vertex v.
Displays all paths from the source.

FIGURE 28.17 `WeightedGraph.ShortestPathTree` extends `AbstractGraph.Tree`.

A vertex is added to `T` if it is adjacent to one of the vertices in `T` with the smallest cost (line 208). Such a vertex is found using the following procedure:

1. For each vertex `u` in `T`, find its incident edge `e` with the smallest weight to `u`. All the incident edges to `u` are stored in `queues.get(u)`. `queues.get(u).peek()` (line 190) returns the incident edge with the smallest weight. If `e.v` is already in `T`, remove `e` from `queues.get(u)` (line 194). After lines 189–197, `queues.get(u).peek()` returns the edge `e` such that `e` has the smallest weight to `u` and `e.v` is not in `T` (line 199).

2. Compare all these edges and find the one with the smallest value on `costs[u] + e.getWeight()` (line 202).

After a new vertex is added to `T` (line 208), the cost of this vertex is updated (line 209). Once all vertices are added to `T`, an instance of `ShortestPathTree` is created (line 213). Note that

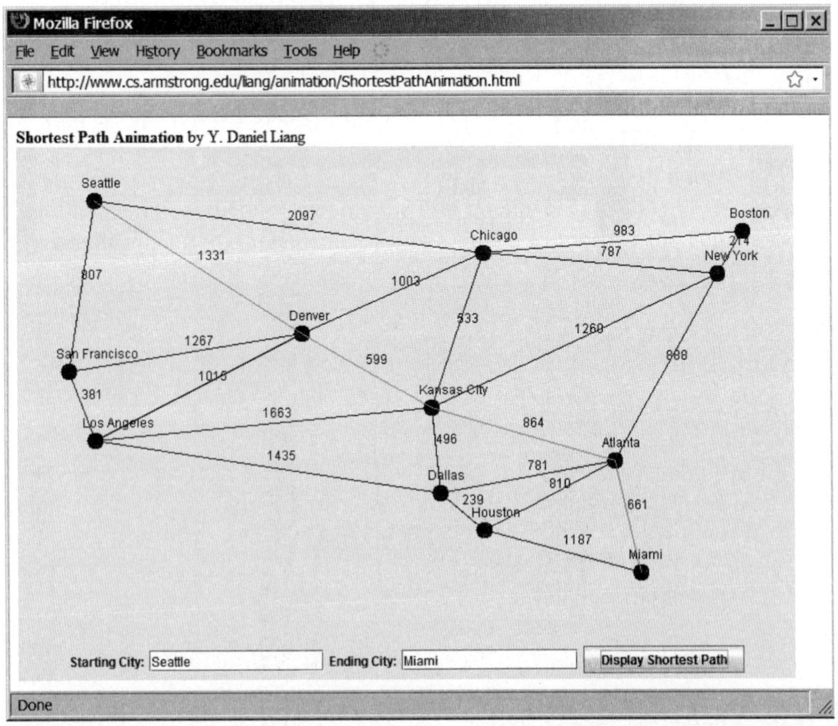
Mozilla Firefox
File Edit View History Bookmarks Tools Help
http://www.cs.armstrong.edu/liang/animation/ShortestPathAnimation.html
Shortest Path Animation by Y. Daniel Liang
Seattle
Boston
Chicago
New York
Denver
San Francisco
Kansas City
Los Angeles
Atlanta
Dallas
Houston
Miami
2097
983
1331
787
807
1003
533
1267
1260
599
888
1015
381
1663
864
496
1435
781
810
239
661
1187
Starting City: Seattle
Ending City: Miami
Display Shortest Path
Done

FIGURE 28.18 The animation tool enables you to create a graph dynamically and displays its MST.

the method will not work if the graph is not connected. However, you can modify it to obtain the shortest paths to all connected vertices.

ShortestPathTree class

The `ShortestPathTree` class extends the `Tree` class (line 217). To create an instance of `ShortestPathTree`, pass `sourceVertex`, `parent`, `T`, and `costs` (lines 213). `sourceVertex` becomes the root in the tree. The data fields `root`, `parent`, and `searchOrder` are defined in the `Tree` class, which is an inner class defined in `AbstractGraph`.

Dijkstra's algorithm time complexity

Dijkstra's algorithm is implemented essentially in the same way as Prim's. So, the time complexity for Dijkstra's algorithm is $O(|E|\log|V|)$, where $|E|$ denotes the number of edges and $|V|$ the number of vertices.

Pedagogical Note

Shortest-path animation

Follow the link www.cs.armstrong.edu/liang/animation/ShortestPathAnimation.html to see how to find a shortest path between any two cities, as shown in Figure 28.18.

Listing 28.7 gives a test program that displays all shortest paths from Chicago to all other cities in Figure 27.1 and all shortest paths from vertex `3` to all vertices for the graph in Figure 28.1, respectively.

LISTING 28.7 TestShortestPath.java

vertices · edges · create **graph1** · shortest path

```
public class TestShortestPath {
  public static void main(String[] args) {
    String[] vertices = {"Seattle", "San Francisco", "Los Angeles",
      "Denver", "Kansas City", "Chicago", "Boston", "New York",
      "Atlanta", "Miami", "Dallas", "Houston"};

    int[][] edges = {
      {0, 1, 807}, {0, 3, 1331}, {0, 5, 2097},
      {1, 0, 807}, {1, 2, 381}, {1, 3, 1267},
      {2, 1, 381}, {2, 3, 1015}, {2, 4, 1663}, {2, 10, 1435},
      {3, 0, 1331}, {3, 1, 1267}, {3, 2, 1015}, {3, 4, 599},
        {3, 5, 1003},
      {4, 2, 1663}, {4, 3, 599}, {4, 5, 533}, {4, 7, 1260},
        {4, 8, 864}, {4, 10, 496},
      {5, 0, 2097}, {5, 3, 1003}, {5, 4, 533},
        {5, 6, 983}, {5, 7, 787},
      {6, 5, 983}, {6, 7, 214},
      {7, 4, 1260}, {7, 5, 787}, {7, 6, 214}, {7, 8, 888},
      {8, 4, 864}, {8, 7, 888}, {8, 9, 661},
        {8, 10, 781}, {8, 11, 810},
      {9, 8, 661}, {9, 11, 1187},
      {10, 2, 1435}, {10, 4, 496}, {10, 8, 781}, {10, 11, 239},
      {11, 8, 810}, {11, 9, 1187}, {11, 10, 239}
    };

    WeightedGraph<String> graph1 =
      new WeightedGraph<String>(edges, vertices);
    WeightedGraph<String>.ShortestPathTree tree1 =
      graph1.getShortestPath(5);
    tree1.printAllPaths();

    // Display shortest paths from Houston to Chicago
    System.out.print("Shortest path from Houston to Chicago: ");
    java.util.List<String> path = tree1.getPath(11);
    for (String s: path) {
      System.out.print(s + " ");
    }
```

```
38
39     edges = new int [][]{
40       {0, 1, 2}, {0, 3, 8},
41       {1, 0, 2}, {1, 2, 7}, {1, 3, 3},
42       {2, 1, 7}, {2, 3, 4}, {2, 4, 5},
43       {3, 0, 8}, {3, 1, 3}, {3, 2, 4}, {3, 4, 6},
44       {4, 2, 5}, {4, 3, 6}
45     };
46     WeightedGraph<Integer> graph2 =
47       new WeightedGraph<Integer>(edges, 5);
48     WeightedGraph<Integer>.ShortestPathTree tree2 =
49       graph2.getShortestPath(3);
50     tree2.printAllPaths();
51   }
52 }
```

create edges

create **graph2**

print paths

```
All shortest paths from Chicago are:
A path from Chicago to Seattle: Chicago Seattle (cost: 2097)
A path from Chicago to San Francisco:
  Chicago Denver San Francisco (cost: 2270)
A path from Chicago to Los Angeles:
  Chicago Denver Los Angeles (cost: 2018)
A path from Chicago to Denver: Chicago Denver (cost: 1003)
A path from Chicago to Kansas City: Chicago Kansas City (cost: 533)
A path from Chicago to Chicago: Chicago (cost: 0)
A path from Chicago to Boston: Chicago Boston (cost: 983)
A path from Chicago to New York: Chicago New York (cost: 787)
A path from Chicago to Atlanta:
  Chicago Kansas City Atlanta (cost: 1397)
A path from Chicago to Miami:
  Chicago Kansas City Atlanta Miami (cost: 2058)
A path from Chicago to Dallas:
  Chicago Kansas City Dallas (cost: 1029)
A path from Chicago to Houston:
  Chicago Kansas City Dallas Houston (cost: 1268)

Shortest path from Chicago to Houston:
  Chicago Kansas City Dallas Houston

All shortest paths from 3 are:
A path from 3 to 0: 3 1 0 (cost: 5)
A path from 3 to 1: 3 1 (cost: 3)
A path from 3 to 2: 3 2 (cost: 4)
A path from 3 to 3: 3 (cost: 0)
A path from 3 to 4: 3 4 (cost: 6)
```

The program creates a weighted graph for Figure 27.1 in line 27. It then invokes the `getShortestPath(5)` method to return a `Path` object that contains all shortest paths from vertex `5` (i.e., Chicago). Invoking `printPath()` on the `ShortestPathTree` object displays all the paths.

The graphical illustration of all shortest paths from `Chicago` is shown in Figure 28.19. The shortest paths from Chicago to the cities are found in this order: `Kansas City`, `New York`, `Boston`, `Denver`, `Dallas`, `Houston`, `Atlanta`, `Los Angeles`, `Miami`, `Seattle`, and `San Francisco`.

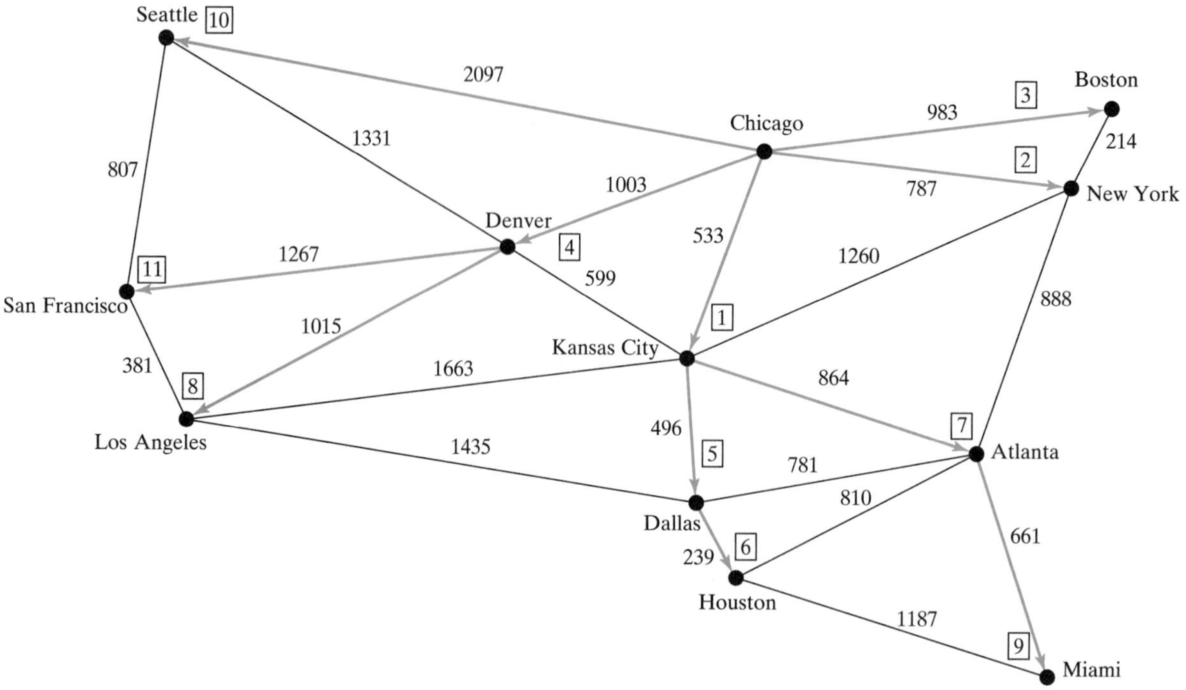
Seattle 10
2097
1331
807
Chicago
983
3
Boston
214
2
1003
787
New York
Denver
4
533
1267
1260
11
599
San Francisco
888
1
1015
Kansas City
381
1663
864
8
Los Angeles
496
7
Atlanta
1435
5
781
810
Dallas
661
239
6
Houston
1187
9
Miami

FIGURE 28.19 The shortest paths from Chicago to all other cities are highlighted.

28.6 Case Study: The Weighted Nine Tail Problem

Section 27.9 presented the nine tail problem and solved it using the BFS algorithm. This section presents a variation of the problem and solves it using the shortest-path algorithm.

The nine tail problem is to find the minimum number of the moves that lead to all coins face down. Each move flips a head coin and its neighbors. The weighted nine tail problem assigns the number of flips as a weight on each move. For example, you can move from the coins in Figure 28.20(a) to those in Figure 28.20(b) by flipping the first coin in the first row and its two neighbors. So the weight for this move is 3.

H	H	H
T	T	T
H	H	H

(a)

T	T	H
H	T	T
H	H	H

(b)

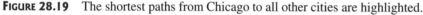

FIGURE 28.20 The weight for each move is the number of flips for the move.

The weighted nine tail problem is to find the minimum number of flips that lead to all coins face down. The problem can be reduced to finding the shortest path from a starting node to the target node in an edge-weighted graph. The graph has 512 nodes. Create an edge from node `v` to `u` if there is a move from node `u` to node `v`. Assign the number of flips to be the weight of the edge.

Recall that in §27.9 we defined a class `NineTailModel` for modeling the nine tail problem. We now define a new class named `WeightedNineTailModel` that extends `NineTailModel`, as shown in Figure 28.21.

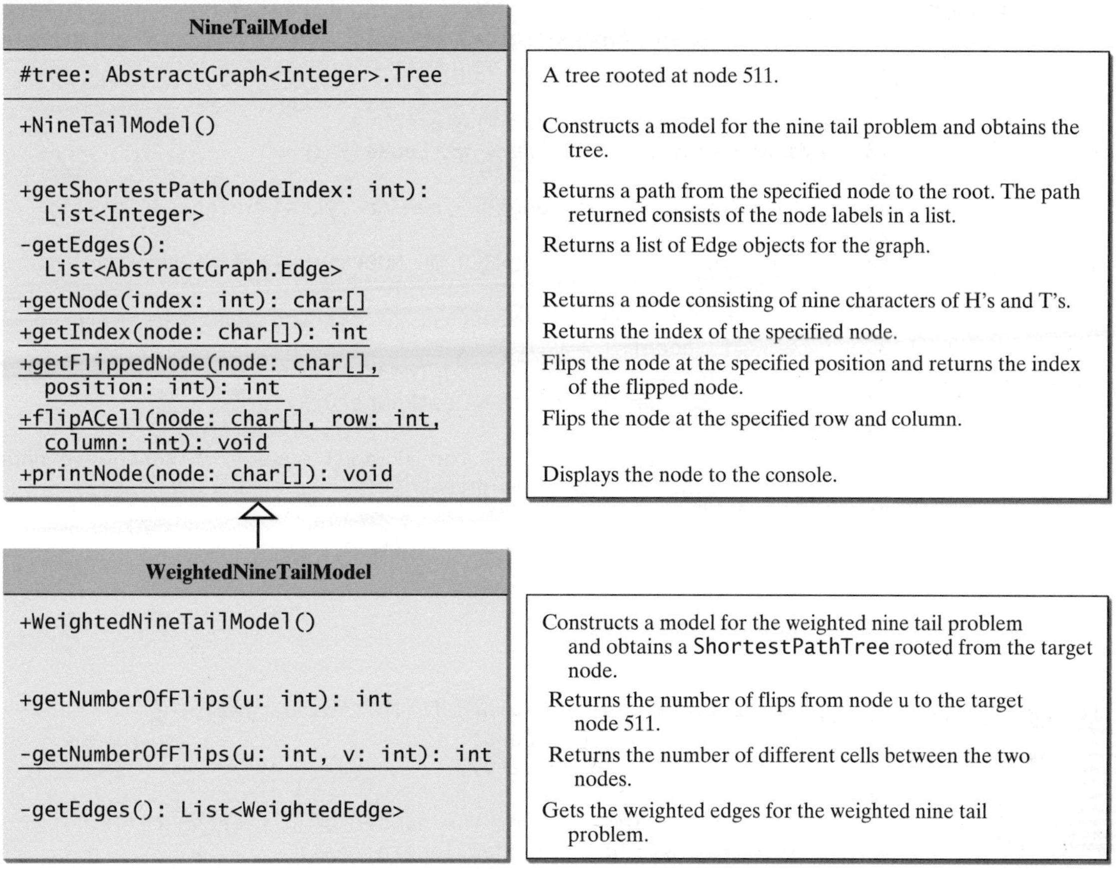
NineTailModel
#tree: AbstractGraph<Integer>.Tree
+NineTailModel()
+getShortestPath(nodeIndex: int): List<Integer>
-getEdges(): List<AbstractGraph.Edge>
+getNode(index: int): char[]
+getIndex(node: char[]): int
+getFlippedNode(node: char[], position: int): int
+flipACell(node: char[], row: int, column: int): void
+printNode(node: char[]): void
A tree rooted at node 511.
Constructs a model for the nine tail problem and obtains the tree.
Returns a path from the specified node to the root. The path returned consists of the node labels in a list.
Returns a list of Edge objects for the graph.
Returns a node consisting of nine characters of H's and T's.
Returns the index of the specified node.
Flips the node at the specified position and returns the index of the flipped node.
Flips the node at the specified row and column.
Displays the node to the console.
WeightedNineTailModel
+WeightedNineTailModel()
+getNumberOfFlips(u: int): int
-getNumberOfFlips(u: int, v: int): int
-getEdges(): List<WeightedEdge>
Constructs a model for the weighted nine tail problem and obtains a ShortestPathTree rooted from the target node.
Returns the number of flips from node u to the target node 511.
Returns the number of different cells between the two nodes.
Gets the weighted edges for the weighted nine tail problem.

FIGURE 28.21 `WeightedNineTailModel` extends `NineTailModel`.

The `NineTailModel` class creates a `Graph` and obtains a `Tree` rooted at the target node `511`. `WeightedNineTailModel` is the same as `NineTailModel` except that it creates a `WeightedGraph` and obtains a `ShortestPathTree` rooted at the target node `511`. `WeightedNineTailModel` extends `NineTailModel`. The method `getEdges()` finds all edges in the graph. The `getNumberOfFlips(int u, int v)` method returns the number of flips from node `u` to node `v`. The `getNumberOfFlips(int u)` method returns the number of flips from node `u` to the target node.

Listing 28.8 implements `WeightedNineTailModel`.

LISTING 28.8 WeightedNineTailModel.java

```
import java.util.*;

public class WeightedNineTailModel extends NineTailModel {
  /** Construct a model */
  public WeightedNineTailModel() {
    // Create edges
    List<WeightedEdge> edges = getEdges();

    // Create a graph
    WeightedGraph<Integer> graph = new WeightedGraph<Integer>(
      edges, NUMBER_OF_NODES);

```

extends **NineTailModel**

constructor

get edges

create a graph

get a tree

get weighted edges

get adjacent node

add an edge

number of flips

total number of flips

```
13     // Obtain a BSF tree rooted at the target node
14     tree = graph.getShortestPath(511);
15   }
16
17   /** Create all edges for the graph */
18   private List<WeightedEdge> getEdges() {
19     // Store edges
20     List<WeightedEdge> edges = new ArrayList<WeightedEdge>();
21
22     for (int u = 0; u < NUMBER_OF_NODES; u++) {
23       for (int k = 0; k < 9; k++) {
24         char[] node = getNode(u); // Get the node for vertex u
25         if (node[k] == 'H') {
26           int v = getFlippedNode(node, k);
27           int numberOfFlips = getNumberOfFlips(u, v);
28
29           // Add edge (v, u) for a legal move from node u to node v
30           edges.add(new WeightedEdge(v, u, numberOfFlips));
31         }
32       }
33     }
34
35     return edges;
36   }
37
38   private static int getNumberOfFlips(int u, int v) {
39     char[] node1 = getNode(u);
40     char[] node2 = getNode(v);
41
42     int count = 0; // Count the number of different cells
43     for (int i = 0; i < node1.length; i++)
44       if (node1[i] != node2[i]) count++;
45
46     return count;
47   }
48
49   public int getNumberOfFlips(int u) {
50     return
51       ((WeightedGraph<Integer>.ShortestPathTree)tree).getCost(u);
52   }
53 }
```

`WeightedNineTailModel` extends `NineTailModel` to build a `WeightedGraph` to model the weighted nine tail problem (lines 10–11). For each node `u`, the `getEdges()` method finds a flipped node `v` and assigns the number of flips as the weight for edge (`u`, `v`) (line 30). The `getNumberOfFlips(int u, int v)` method returns the number of flips from node `u` to node `v` (lines 38–47). The number of flips is the number of the different cells between the two nodes (line 44).

The `WeightedNineTailModel` constructs a `WeightedGraph` (lines 10–11) and obtains a `ShortestPathTree` rooted at the target node `511` (line 14). Note that `tree` is a protected data field defined `NineTailModel` and `ShortestPathTree` is a subclass of `Tree`. The methods defined in `NineTailModel` use the `tree` property.

The `getNumberOfFlips(int u)` method (lines 49–52) returns the number of flips from node `u` to the target node, which is the cost of the path from node `u` to the target node. This cost can be obtained by invoking the `getCost(u)` method defined in the `ShortestPathTree` class (line 51).

Listing 28.9 gives a program that prompts the user to enter an initial node and displays the minimum number of flips to reach the target node.

LISTING 28.9 WeightedNineTail.java

```
1 import java.util.Scanner;
2
3 public class WeightedNineTail {
4   public static void main(String[] args) {
5     // Prompt the user to enter nine coins H's and T's
6     System.out.print("Enter an initial nine coin H's and T's: ");
7     Scanner input = new Scanner(System.in);
8     String s = input.nextLine();
9     char[] initialNode = s.toCharArray();
10
11    WeightedNineTailModel model = new WeightedNineTailModel();
12    java.util.List<Integer> path =
13      model.getShortestPath(NineTailModel.getIndex(initialNode));
14
15    System.out.println("The steps to flip the coins are ");
16    for (int i = 0; i < path.size(); i++)
17      NineTailModel.printNode(
18        NineTailModel.getNode(path.get(i).intValue()));
19
20    System.out.println("The number of flips is " +
21      model.getNumberOfFlips(NineTailModel.getIndex(initialNode)));
22  }
23 }
```

initial node

create model

get shortest path

print node

number of flips

```
Enter an initial nine coin H's and T's: HHHTTTHHH Enter

The steps to flip the coins are
HHH
TTT
HHH

HHH
THT
TTT

TTT
TTT
TTT

The number of flips is 8
```

The program prompts the user to enter an initial node with nine letters, H's and T's, as a string in line 8, obtains an array of characters from the string (line 9), creates a model (line 11), obtains a shortest path from the initial node to the target node (lines 12–13), displays the nodes in the path (lines 16–18), and invokes `getNumberOfFlips` to get the number of flips needed to reach to the target node (line 21).

KEY TERMS

Chapter Summary

1. You can use adjacency matrices or priority queues to represent weighted edges.
2. A spanning tree of a graph is a subgraph that is a tree and connects all vertices in the graph. You learned how to implement Prim's algorithm for finding a minimum spanning tree.
3. You learned how to implement Dijkstra's algorithm for finding shortest paths.

Review Questions

Section 28.4

28.1 Find a minimum spanning tree for the following graph.

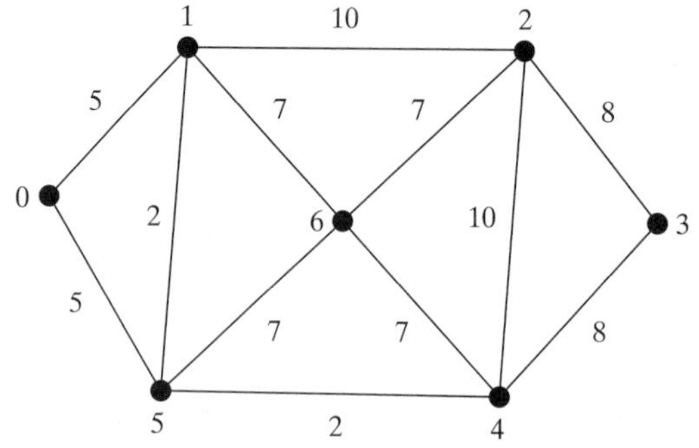
1
10
2
5
7
7
8
0
2
6
10
3
5
7
7
8
5
2
4

28.2 Is the minimum spanning tree unique if all edges have different weights?

28.3 If you use an adjacency matrix to represent weighted edges, what will be the time complexity for Prim's algorithm?

28.4 What happens to the `getMinimumSpanningTree()` method in `WeightedGraph` if the graph is not connected? Verify your answer by writing a test program that creates an unconnected graph and invokes the `getMinimumSpanningTree()` method. How do you fix the problem by obtaining a partial MST?

Section 28.5

28.5 Trace Dijkstra's algorithm for finding the shortest paths from Boston to all other cities in Figure 27.1.

28.6 Is the shortest path between two vertices unique if all edges have different weights?

28.7 If you use an adjacency matrix to represent weighted edges, what would be the time complexity for Dijkstra's algorithm?

28.8 What happens to the `getShortestPath()` method in `WeightedGraph` if the graph is not connected? Verify your answer by writing a test program that creates an unconnected graph and invoke the `getShortestPath()` method.

Programming Exercises

28.1* (*Kruskal's algorithm*) The text introduced Prim's algorithm for finding a minimum spanning tree. Kruskal's algorithm is another well-known algorithm for finding a minimum spanning tree. The algorithm repeatedly finds a minimum-weight edge and adds it to the tree if it does not cause a cycle. The process ends when all vertices are in the tree. Design and implement an algorithm for finding an MST using Kruskal's algorithm.

28.2* (*Implementing Prim's algorithm using adjacency matrix*) The text implements Prim's algorithm using priority queues on adjacent edges. Implement the algorithm using adjacency matrix for weighted graphs.

28.3* (*Implementing Dijkstra's algorithm using adjacency matrix*) The text implements Dijkstra's algorithm using priority queues on adjacent edges. Implement the algorithm using adjacency matrix for weighted graphs.

28.4* (*Modifying weight in the nine tail problem*) In the text, we assign the number of the flips as the weight for each move. Assuming that the weight is three times of the number of flips, revise the program.

28.5* (*Prove or disprove*) The conjecture is that both `NineTailModel` and `WeightedNineTailModel` result in the same shortest path. Write a program to prove or disprove it.

(*Hint*: Add a new method named `depth(int v)` in the `AbstractGraph.Tree` class to return the depth of the `v` in the tree. Let `tree1` and `tree2` denote the trees obtained from `NineTailModel` and `WeightedNineTailModel`, respectively. If the depth of a node `u` is the same in `tree1` and in `tree2`, the length of the path from `u` to the target is the same.)

28.6** (*Weighted 4 × 4 16 tail model*) The weighted nine tail problem in the text uses a 3 × 3 matrix. Assume that you have 16 coins placed in a 4 × 4 matrix. Create a new model class named `WeightedTailModel16`. Create an instance of the model and save the object into a file named **Exercise28_6.dat**.

28.7** (*Weighted 4 × 4 16 tail view*) Listing 27.12, NineTailApp.java, presents a view for the nine tail problem. Revise this program for the weighted 4 × 4 16 tail problem. Your program should read the model object created from the preceding exercise.

28.8** (*Traveling salesman problem*) The traveling salesman problem (TSP) is to find a shortest round-trip route that visits each city exactly once and then returns to the starting city. The problem is equivalent to finding a shortest Hamiltonian cycle. Add the following method in the `WeightedGraph` class:

```
// Return a shortest cycle
// Return null if no such cycle exists
public List<Integer> getShortestHamiltonianCycle()
```

28.9* (*Finding a minimum spanning tree*) Write a program that reads a connected graph from a file and displays its minimum spanning tree. The first line in the file contains a number that indicates the number of vertices (`n`). The vertices are labeled as `0`, `1`, ..., `n-1`. Each subsequent line describes the edges in the form of `u1, v1, w1 | u2, v2, w2 | ...`. Each triplet describes an edge and its weight. Figure 28.22 shows an example of the file for the corresponding graph. Note that we assume the graph is undirected. If the graph has an edge (`u`, `v`), it also has an edge (`v`, `u`). Only one edge is represented in the file. When you construct a graph, both edges need to be considered.

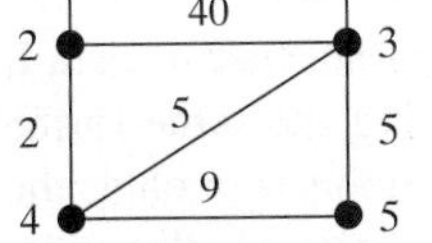

0
1
2
3
4
5
100
3
20
40
5
2
5
9

(a)

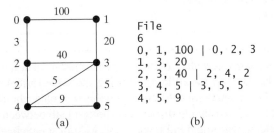

```
File
6
0, 1, 100 | 0, 2, 3
1, 3, 20
2, 3, 40 | 2, 4, 2
3, 4, 5 | 3, 5, 5
4, 5, 9
```

(b)

FIGURE 28.22 The vertices and edges of a weighted graph can be stored in a file.

Your program should prompt the user to enter the name of the file, should read data from a file, create an instance `g` of `WeightedGraph`, invoke `g.printWeightedEdges()` to display all edges, invoke `getMinimumSpanningTree()` to obtain an instance `tree` of `WeightedGraph.MST`, invoke `tree.getTotalWeight()` to display the weight of the minimum spanning tree, and invoke `tree.printTree()` to display the tree. Here is a sample run of the program:

```
Enter a file name: c:\exercise\Exercise28_9.txt [Enter]
The number of vertices is 6
Vertex 0: (0, 2, 3) (0, 1, 100)
Vertex 1: (1, 3, 20) (1, 0, 100)
Vertex 2: (2, 4, 2) (2, 3, 40) (2, 0, 3)
Vertex 3: (3, 4, 5) (3, 5, 5) (3, 1, 20) (3, 2, 40)
Vertex 4: (4, 2, 2) (4, 3, 5) (4, 5, 9)
Vertex 5: (5, 3, 5) (5, 4, 9)
Total weight is 35
Root is: 0
Edges: (3, 1) (0, 2) (4, 3) (2, 4) (3, 5)
```

(*Hint*: Use `new WeightedGraph(list, numberOfVertices)` to create a graph, where `list` contains a list of `WeightedEdge` objects. Use `new WeightedEdge(u, v, w)` to create an edge. Read the first line to get the number of vertices. Read each subsequent line into a string `s` and use `s.split("[\\|]")` to extract the triplets. For each triplet, `triplet.split("[,]")` to extract vertices and weight.)

28.10* (*Creating a file for a graph*) Modify Listing 28.3, TestWeightedGraph.java, to create a file for representing `graph1`. The file format is described in Exercise 28.9. Create the file from the array defined in lines 7–24 in Listing 28.3. The number of vertices for the graph is `12`, which will be stored in the first line of the file. An edge (`u`, `v`) is stored if `u < v`. The contents of the file should be as follows:

```
12
0, 1, 807 | 0, 3, 1331 | 0, 5, 2097
1, 2, 381 | 1, 3, 1267
2, 3, 1015 | 2, 4, 1663 | 2, 10, 1435
3, 4, 599 | 3, 5, 1003
4, 5, 533 | 4, 7, 1260 | 4, 8, 864 | 4, 10, 496
5, 6, 983 | 5, 7, 787
6, 7, 214
7, 8, 888
8, 9, 661 | 8, 10, 781 | 8, 11, 810
9, 11, 1187
10, 11, 239
```

28.11* (*Finding shortest paths*) Write a program that reads a connected graph from a file. The graph is stored in a file using the same format specified in Exercise 28.9. Your program should prompt the user to enter the name of the file, then two vertices, and should display the shortest path between the two vertices. For example, for the graph in Figure 28.21, a shortest path between `0` and `1` may be displayed as `0 2 4 3 1`.

Here is a sample run of the program:

```
Enter a file name: Exercise28_11.txt ↵Enter
Enter two vertices (integer indexes): 0 1 ↵Enter
The number of vertices is 6
Vertex 0: (0, 2, 3) (0, 1, 100)
Vertex 1: (1, 3, 20) (1, 0, 100)
Vertex 2: (2, 4, 2) (2, 3, 40) (2, 0, 3)
Vertex 3: (3, 4, 5) (3, 5, 5) (3, 1, 20) (3, 2, 40)
Vertex 4: (4, 2, 2) (4, 3, 5) (4, 5, 9)
Vertex 5: (5, 3, 5) (5, 4, 9)
A path from 0 to 1: 0 2 4 3 1
```

28.12* (*Displaying weighted graphs*) Revise `GraphView` in Listing 27.6 to display a weighted graph. Write a program that displays the graph in Figure 27.1 as shown in Figure 28.23(a).

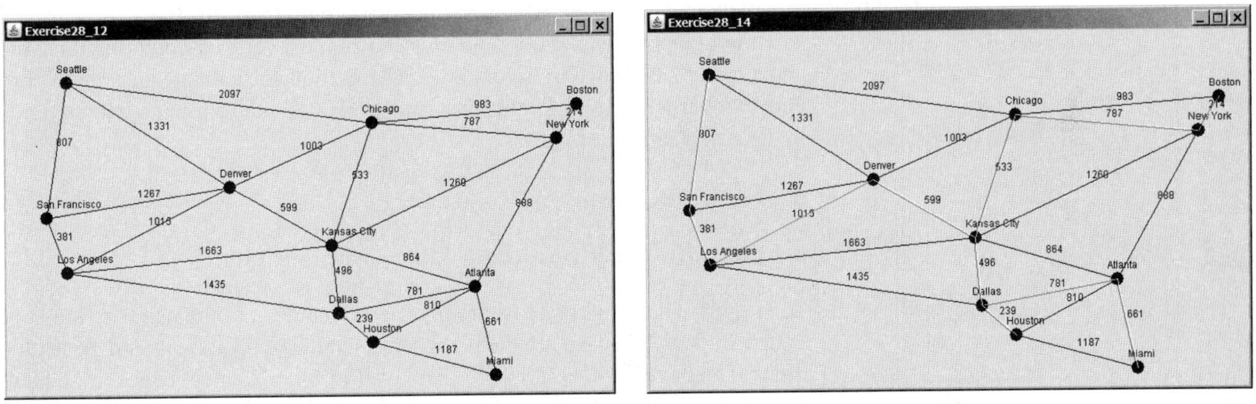
Exercise28_12
Seattle
Boston
New York
Chicago
San Francisco
Denver
Kansas City
Los Angeles
Dallas
Houston
Atlanta
Miami
Exercise28_14

(a) (b)

FIGURE 28.23 (a) Exercise 28.12 displays a weighted graph. (b) Exercise 28.14 displays an MST.

28.13* (*Displaying shortest paths*) Revise `GraphView` in Listing 27.6 to display a weighted graph and a shortest path between the two specified cities, as shown in Figure 28.18. You need to add a data field `path` in `GraphView`. If a `path` is set, the edges in the path are displayed in blue. If a city not in the map is entered, the program displays a dialog box to alert the user.

28.14* (*Displaying a minimum spanning tree*) Revise `GraphView` in Listing 27.6 to display a weighted graph and a minimum spanning tree for the graph in Figure 27.1, as shown in Figure 28.23(b). The edges in the MST are shown in blue.

28.15*** (*Dynamic graphs*) Write a program that lets the users create a weighted graph dynamically. The user can create a vertex by entering its name and location, as shown in Figure 28.24. The user can also create an edge to connect two vertices. To make this program work, add the following two methods in the `WeightedGraph` class.

```
public void addVertex(V vertex)

public void addEdge(int u, int v, int weight)
```

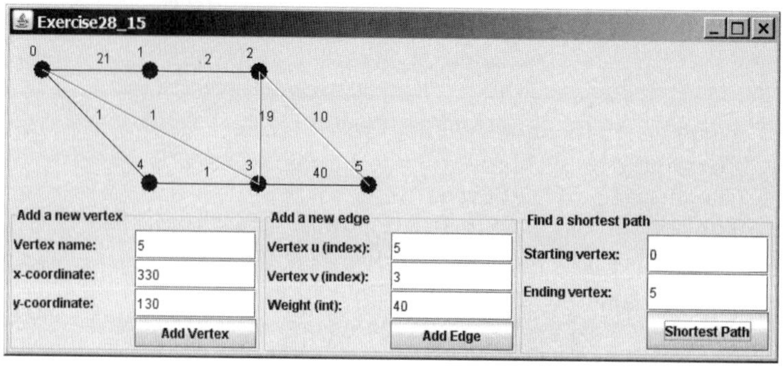
Exercise28_15
0
21
1
2
2
1
1
19
10
4
1
3
40
5
Add a new vertex
Vertex name:
5
x-coordinate:
330
y-coordinate:
130
Add Vertex
Add a new edge
Vertex u (index):
5
Vertex v (index):
3
Weight (int):
40
Add Edge
Find a shortest path
Starting vertex:
0
Ending vertex:
5
Shortest Path

FIGURE 28.24 The program can add vertices and edges and display a shortest path between two specified vertices.

To simplify the program, assume that vertex names are the same as vertex indices. You have to add the vertex indices 0, 1, . . . , and n, in this order. The user may specify two vertices and let the program display their shortest path in blue.

28.16*** (*Displaying a dynamic MST*) Write a program that lets the user create a weighted graph dynamically. The user can create a vertex by entering its name and location, as shown in Figure 28.7. The user can also create an edge to connect two vertices. To make this program work, add the following two methods in the `WeightedGraph` class.

```
public void addVertex(V vertex)

public void addEdge(int u, int v, int weight)
```

To simplify the program, assume that vertex names are the same as those of vertex indices. You have to add the vertex indices 0, 1, . . . , and n, in this order. The edges in the MST are displayed in blue. As new edges are added, the MST is redisplayed.

CHAPTER 29

MULTITHREADING

Objectives

- To get an overview of multithreading (§29.2).
- To develop task classes by implementing the `Runnable` interface (§29.3).
- To create threads to run tasks using the `Thread` class (§29.3).
- To control threads using the methods in the `Thread` class (§29.4).
- To control animations using threads (§§29.5, 29.7).
- To run code in the event dispatch thread (§29.6).
- To execute tasks in a thread pool (§29.8).
- To use synchronized methods or blocks to synchronize threads to avoid race conditions (§29.9).
- To synchronize threads using locks (§29.10).
- To facilitate thread communications using conditions on locks (§§29.11–29.12).
- To use blocking queues to synchronize access to an array queue, linked queue, and priority queue (§29.13).
- To restrict the number of accesses to a shared resource using semaphores (§29.14).
- To use the resource-ordering technique to avoid deadlocks (§29.15).
- To describe the life cycle of a thread (§29.16).
- To create synchronized collections using the static methods in the `Collections` class (§29.17).
- To run time-consuming tasks in a `SwingWorker` rather than in the event dispatch thread (§29.18).
- To display the completion status of a task using `JProgressBar` (§29.19).

29.1 Introduction

multithreading

One of the powerful features of Java is its built-in support for multithreading—the concurrent running of multiple tasks within a program. In many programming languages, you have to invoke system-dependent procedures and functions to implement multithreading. This chapter introduces the concepts of threads and how to develop multithreading programs in Java.

29.2 Thread Concepts

thread
task

A program may consist of many tasks that can run concurrently. A *thread* is the flow of execution, from beginning to end, of a task. It provides the mechanism for running a task. With Java, you can launch multiple threads from a program concurrently. These threads can be executed simultaneously in multiprocessor systems, as shown in Figure 29.1(a).

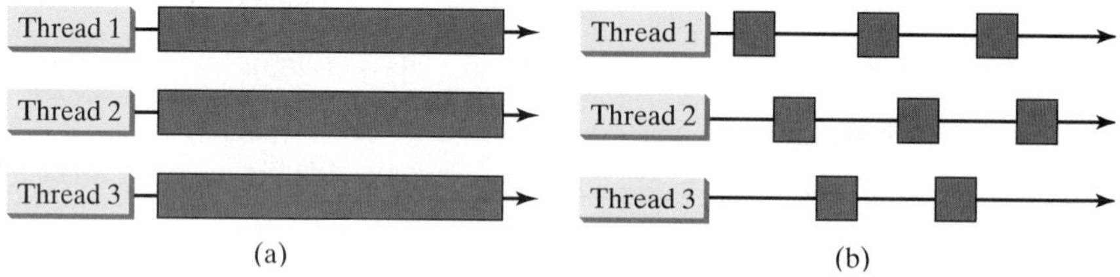
Thread 1
Thread 2
Thread 3
(a)
Thread 1
Thread 2
Thread 3
(b)

FIGURE 29.1 (a) Here multiple threads are running on multiple CPUs. (b) Here multiple threads share a single CPU.

time sharing

In single-processor systems, as shown in Figure 29.1(b), the multiple threads share CPU time known as *time sharing*, and the operating system is responsible for scheduling and allocating resources to them. This arrangement is practical, because most of the time the CPU is idle. It does nothing, for example, while waiting for the user to enter data.

Multithreading can make your program more responsive and interactive, as well as enhance performance. For example, a good word processor lets you print or save a file while you are typing. In some cases, multithreaded programs run faster than single-threaded programs even on single-processor systems. Java provides exceptionally good support for creating and running threads and for locking resources to prevent conflicts.

task
runnable object
thread

When your program executes as an application, the Java interpreter starts a thread for the `main` method. When your program executes as an applet, the Web browser starts a thread to run the applet. You can create additional threads to run concurrent tasks in the program. In Java, each task is an instance of the `Runnable` interface, also called a *runnable object*. A *thread* is essentially an object that facilitates the execution of a task.

29.3 Creating Tasks and Threads

`Thread` class
`Runnable` interface
`run()` method

Tasks are objects. To create tasks, you have to first define a class for tasks. A task class must implement the `Runnable` interface. The `Runnable` interface is rather simple. All it contains is the `run` method. You need to implement this method to tell the system how your thread is going to run. A template for developing a task class is shown in Figure 29.2(a).

Once you have defined a `TaskClass`, you can create a task using its constructor. For example,

creating a task

```
TaskClass task = new TaskClass(...);
```

java.lang.Runnable
TaskClass

```
// Custom task class
public class TaskClass implements Runnable {
  ...
  public TaskClass(...) {
    ...
  }

  // Implement the run method in Runnable
  public void run() {
    // Tell system how to run custom thread
    ...
  }
  ...
}
```

(a)

```
// Client class
public class Client {
  ...
  public void someMethod() {
    ...
    // Create an instance of TaskClass
    TaskClass task = new TaskClass(...);

    // Create a thread
    Thread thread = new Thread(task);

    // Start a thread
    thread.start();
    ...
  }
  ...
}
```

(b)

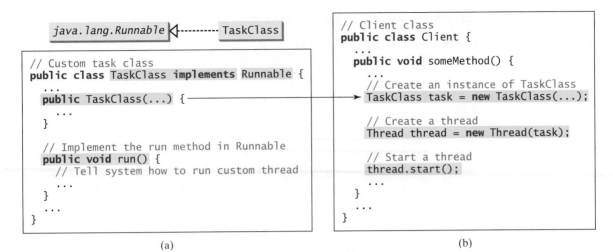

FIGURE 29.2 Define a task class by implementing the `Runnable` interface.

A task must be executed in a thread. The `Thread` class contains the constructors for creating threads and many useful methods for controlling threads. To create a thread for a task, use

creating a thread

```
Thread thread = new Thread(task);
```

You can then invoke the `start()` method to tell the JVM that the thread is ready to run, as follows:

starting a thread

```
thread.start();
```

The JVM will execute the task by invoking the task's `run()` method. Figure 29.2(b) outlines the major steps for creating a task, a thread, and starting the thread.

Listing 29.1 gives a program that creates three tasks and three threads to run them:

- The first task prints the letter *a* 100 times.
- The second task prints the letter *b* 100 times.
- The third task prints the integers 1 through 100.

When you run this program, the three threads will share the CPU and take turns printing letters and numbers on the console. Figure 29.3 shows a sample run of the program.

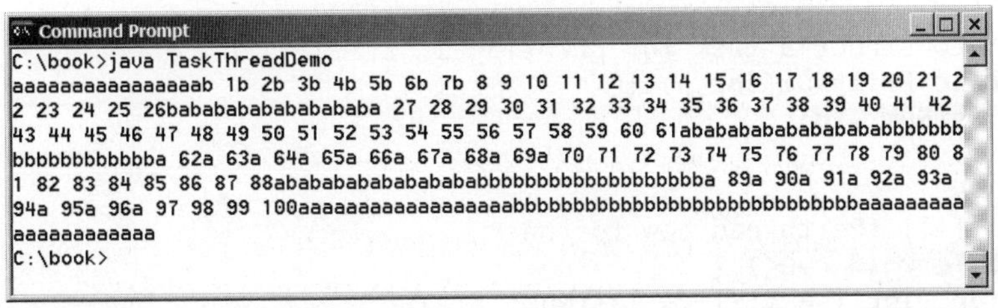
Command Prompt
C:\book>java TaskThreadDemo
aaaaaaaaaaaaaaaab 1b 2b 3b 4b 5b 6b 7b 8 9 10 11 12 13 14 15 16 17 18 19 20 21 2
2 23 24 25 26bababababababababa 27 28 29 30 31 32 33 34 35 36 37 38 39 40 41 42
43 44 45 46 47 48 49 50 51 52 53 54 55 56 57 58 59 60 61abababababababababbbbbb
bbbbbbbbbbbba 62a 63a 64a 65a 66a 67a 68a 69a 70 71 72 73 74 75 76 77 78 79 80 8
1 82 83 84 85 86 87 88abababababababababbbbbbbbbbbbbbbbbba 89a 90a 91a 92a 93a
94a 95a 96a 97 98 99 100aaaaaaaaaaaaaaaaaabbbbbbbbbbbbbbbbbbbbbbbbbbbbbbaaaaaaaaa
aaaaaaaaaaaa
C:\book>

FIGURE 29.3 Tasks `printA`, `printB`, and `print100` are executed simultaneously to display the letter `a` 100 times, the letter `b` 100 times, and the numbers from 1 to 100.

LISTING 29.1 TaskThreadDemo.java

create tasks
create threads
start threads
task class
run
task class
run

```java
public class TaskThreadDemo {
  public static void main(String[] args) {
    // Create tasks
    Runnable printA = new PrintChar('a', 100);
    Runnable printB = new PrintChar('b', 100);
    Runnable print100 = new PrintNum(100);

    // Create threads
    Thread thread1 = new Thread(printA);
    Thread thread2 = new Thread(printB);
    Thread thread3 = new Thread(print100);

    // Start threads
    thread1.start();
    thread2.start();
    thread3.start();
  }
}

// The task for printing a character a specified number of times
class PrintChar implements Runnable {
  private char charToPrint; // The character to print
  private int times; // The number of times to repeat

  /** Construct a task with specified character and number of
   *  times to print the character
   */
  public PrintChar(char c, int t) {
    charToPrint = c;
    times = t;
  }

  /** Override the run() method to tell the system
   *  what task to perform
   */
  public void run() {
    for (int i = 0; i < times; i++) {
      System.out.print(charToPrint);
    }
  }
}

// The task class for printing numbers from 1 to n for a given n
class PrintNum implements Runnable {
  private int lastNum;

  /** Construct a task for printing 1, 2, ... , n */
  public PrintNum(int n) {
    lastNum = n;
  }

  /** Tell the thread how to run */
  public void run() {
    for (int i = 1; i <= lastNum; i++) {
      System.out.print(" " + i);
    }
  }
}
```

The program creates three tasks (lines 4–6). To run them concurrently, three threads are created (lines 9–11). The `start()` method (lines 14–16) is invoked to start a thread that causes the `run()` method in the task to be executed. When the `run()` method completes, the thread terminates.

Because the first two tasks, `printA` and `printB`, have similar functionality, they can be defined in one task class `PrintChar` (lines 21–41). The `PrintChar` class implements `Runnable` and overrides the `run()` method (lines 36–40) with the print-character action. This class provides a framework for printing any single character a given number of times. The runnable objects `printA` and `printB` are instances of the `PrintChar` class.

The `PrintNum` class (lines 44–58) implements `Runnable` and overrides the `run()` method (lines 53–57) with the print-number action. This class provides a framework for printing numbers from *1* to *n*, for any integer *n*. The runnable object `print100` is an instance of the class `printNum` class.

Note

effect of concurrency

If you don't see the effect of these three threads running concurrently, increase the number of characters to be printed. For example, change line 4 to

```
Runnable printA = new PrintChar('a', 10000);
```

Important Note

run() method

The `run()` method in a task specifies how to perform the task. This method is automatically invoked by the JVM. You should not invoke it. Invoking `run()` directly merely executes this method in the same thread; no new thread is started.

29.4 The **Thread** Class

The `Thread` class contains the constructors for creating threads for tasks, and the methods for controlling threads, as shown in Figure 29.4.

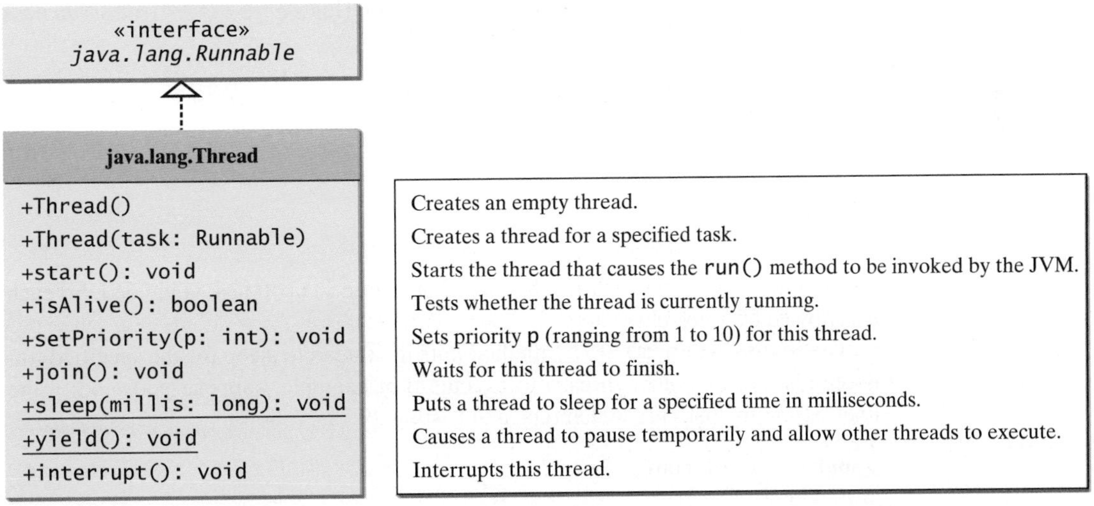
«interface»
java.lang.Runnable
java.lang.Thread
+Thread()
+Thread(task: Runnable)
+start(): void
+isAlive(): boolean
+setPriority(p: int): void
+join(): void
+sleep(millis: long): void
+yield(): void
+interrupt(): void
Creates an empty thread.
Creates a thread for a specified task.
Starts the thread that causes the run() method to be invoked by the JVM.
Tests whether the thread is currently running.
Sets priority p (ranging from 1 to 10) for this thread.
Waits for this thread to finish.
Puts a thread to sleep for a specified time in milliseconds.
Causes a thread to pause temporarily and allow other threads to execute.
Interrupts this thread.

FIGURE 29.4 The `Thread` class contains the methods for controlling threads.

Note

separating task from thread

Since the `Thread` class implements `Runnable`, you could define a class that extends `Thread` and implements the `run` method, as shown in Figure 29.5(a), and then create an object from the class and invoke its `start` method in a client program to start the thread, as shown in Figure 29.5(b).

java.lang.Thread ◁—— CustomThread

```
// Custom thread class
public class CustomThread extends Thread {
  ...
  public CustomThread(...) {
    ...
  }

  // Override the run method in Runnable
  public void run() {
    // Tell system how to perform this task
    ...
  }
  ...
}
```

(a)

```
// Client class
public class Client {
  ...
  public void someMethod() {
    ...
    // Create a thread
    CustomThread thread1 = new CustomThread(...);

    // Start a thread
    thread1.start();
    ...

    // Create another thread
    CustomThread thread2 = new CustomThread(...);

    // Start a thread
    thread2.start();
  }
  ...
}
```

(b)

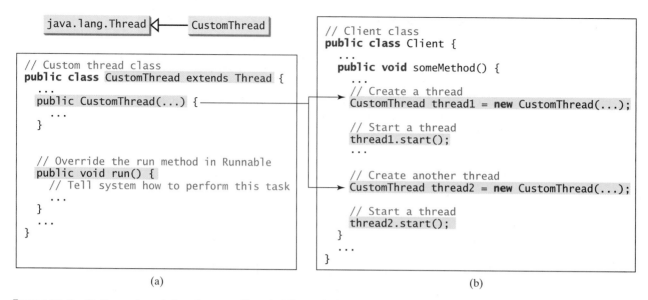

FIGURE 29.5 Define a thread class by extending the Thread class.

This approach is, however, not recommended, because it mixes the task and the mechanism of running the task. Separating the task from the thread is a preferred design.

deprecated method

Note

The Thread class also contains the stop(), suspend(), and resume() methods. As of Java 2, these methods are *deprecated* (or *outdated*) because they are known to be inherently unsafe. Instead of using the stop() method, you should assign null to a Thread variable to indicate that it is stopped.

yield()

You can use the yield() method to temporarily release time for other threads. For example, suppose you modify the code in the run() method (lines 53–57 in PrintNum in TaskThreadDemo.java) in Listing 29.1 as follows:

```
public void run() {
  for (int i = 1; i <= lastNum; i++) {
    System.out.print(" " + i);
    Thread.yield();
  }
}
```

Every time a number is printed, the thread of the print100 task is yielded. So each number is followed by some characters.

sleep(long)

The sleep(long millis) method puts the thread to sleep for the specified time in milliseconds to allow other threads to execute. For example, suppose you modify the code in lines 53–57 in TaskThreadDemo.java in Listing 29.1 as follows:

```
public void run() {
  try {
    for (int i = 1; i <= lastNum; i++) {
      System.out.print(" " + i);
      if (i >= 50) Thread.sleep(1);
    }
  }
  catch (InterruptedException ex) {
  }
}
```

Every time a number (>= 50) is printed, the thread of the print100 task is put to sleep for 1 millisecond.

InterruptedException

The sleep method may throw an InterruptedException, which is a checked exception. Such an exception may occur when a sleeping thread's interrupt() method is called. The interrupt() method is very rarely invoked on a thread, so an InterruptedException is unlikely to occur. But since Java forces you to catch checked exceptions, you have to put it in a try-catch block. If a sleep method is invoked in a loop, you should wrap the loop in a try-catch block, as shown in (a) below. If the loop is outside the try-catch block, as shown in (b), the thread may continue to execute even though it is being interrupted.

```
public void run() {
  try {
    while (...) {
      ...
      Thread.sleep(1000);
    }
  }
  catch (InterruptedException ex) {
    ex.printStackTrace();
  }
}
```

(a) Correct

```
public void run() {
  while (...) {
    try {
      ...
      Thread.sleep(sleepTime);
    }
    catch (InterruptedException ex) {
      ex.printStackTrace();
    }
  }
}
```

(b) Incorrect

join()

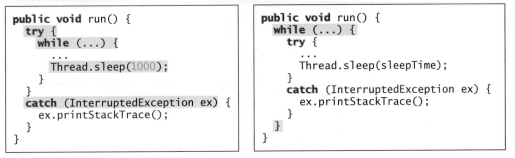

You can use the join() method to force one thread to wait for another thread to finish. For example, suppose you modify the code in lines 53–57 in TaskThreadDemo.java in Listing 29.1 as follows:

```
public void run() {
  Thread thread4 = new Thread(
    new PrintChar('c', 40));
  thread4.start();
  try {
    for (int i = 1; i <= lastNum; i++) {
      System.out.print (" " + i);
      if (i == 50) thread4.join();
    }
  }
  catch (InterruptedException ex) {
  }
}
```

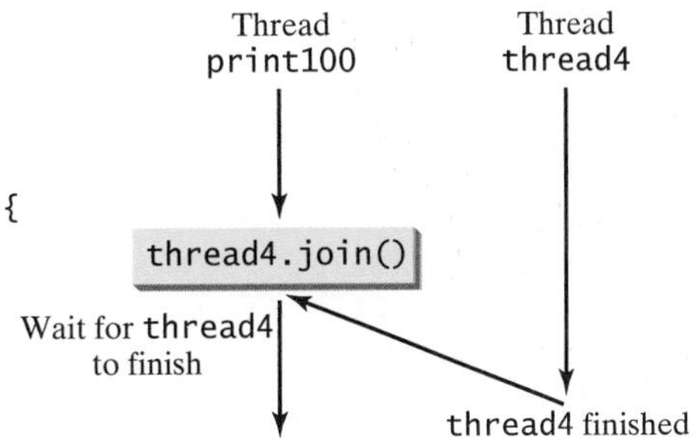
Thread
print100
Thread
thread4
thread4.join()
Wait for thread4
to finish
thread4 finished

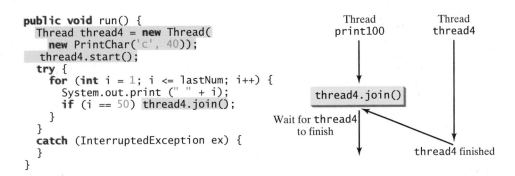

A new thread4 is created. It prints character c 40 times. The numbers from 50 to 100 are printed after thread thread4 is finished.

setPriority(int)

Java assigns every thread a priority. By default, a thread inherits the priority of the thread that spawned it. You can increase or decrease the priority of any thread by using the setPriority method, and you can get the thread's priority by using the getPriority method. Priorities are numbers ranging from 1 to 10. The Thread class has the int constants MIN_PRIORITY, NORM_PRIORITY, and MAX_PRIORITY, representing 1, 5, and 10, respectively. The priority of the main thread is Thread.NORM_PRIORITY.

round-robin scheduling

The JVM always picks the currently runnable thread with the highest priority. A lower-priority thread can run only when no higher-priority threads are running. If all runnable threads have equal priorities, each is assigned an equal portion of the CPU time in a circular queue. This is called the *round-robin scheduling*. For example, suppose you insert the following code in line 16 in TaskThreadDemo.java in Listing 29.1:

```
thread3.setPriority(Thread.MAX_PRIORITY);
```

The thread for the print100 task will be finished first.

Tip

The priority numbers may be changed in a future version of Java. To minimize the impact of any changes, use the constants in the **Thread** class to specify thread priorities.

Tip

contention or starvation

A thread may never get a chance to run if there is always a higher-priority thread running or a same-priority thread that never yields. This situation is known as *contention* or *starvation*. To avoid contention, the thread with high priority must periodically invoke the sleep or yield method to give a thread with a lower or the same priority a chance to run.

29.5 Example: Flashing Text

The use of a `Timer` object to control animations was introduced in §16.12, "Animation Using the `Timer` Class." You can also use a thread to control animation. Listing 29.2 gives an example that displays a flashing text on a label, as shown in Figure 29.6.

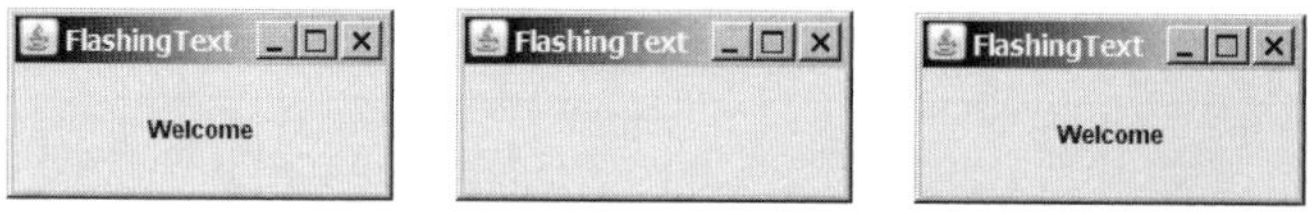
FlashingText
Welcome
FlashingText
FlashingText
Welcome

FIGURE 29.6 The text Welcome blinks.

LISTING 29.2 FlashingText.java

implements Runnable
create a label
add a label
start a thread
how to run
sleep
main method omitted

```
1 import javax.swing.*;
2
3 public class FlashingText extends JApplet implements Runnable {
4   private JLabel jlblText = new JLabel("Welcome", JLabel.CENTER);
5
6   public FlashingText() {
7     add(jlblText);
8     new Thread(this).start();
9   }
10
11   /** Set the text on/off every 200 milliseconds */
12   public void run() {
13     try {
14       while (true) {
15         if (jlblText.getText() == null)
16           jlblText.setText("Welcome");
17         else
18           jlblText.setText(null);
19
20         Thread.sleep(200);
21       }
22     }
23     catch (InterruptedException ex) {
24     }
25   }
26 }
```

`FlashingText` implements `Runnable` (line 3), so it is a task class. Line 8 wraps the task in a thread and starts the thread. The `run` method dictates how to run the thread. It sets a text in the label if the label does not have a text (line 15), and sets its text `null` (line 18) if the label has a text. The text is set and unset to simulate a flashing effect.

thread vs. timer

You can use a timer or a thread to control animation. Which one is better? A timer is a source component that fires an `ActionEvent` at a "fixed rate." When an action event occurs, the timer invokes the listener's `actionPerformed` method to handle the event. The timer and event handling run on the same event dispatch thread. If it takes a long time to handle the event, the actual delay time between two events will be longer than the requested delay time. In this case, you should run event handling on a separate thread. The next section will give an example to illustrate the problem and fix it by running the event handling on a separate thread. In general, threads are more reliable and responsive than timers. If you need a precise delay time or a quick response, it is better to use a thread. Otherwise, using a timer is simpler and more efficient. Timers consume less system resource because they run on the GUI event dispatch thread, so you don't need to spawn new threads for timers.

29.6 GUI Event Dispatch Thread

GUI event handling and painting code executes on a special thread called the *event dispatch thread*. This is necessary because most of Swing methods are not thread-safe. Invoking them from multiple threads may cause conflicts.

invokeLater

invokeAndWait

In certain situations, you need to run the code in the event dispatch thread to avoid possible conflicts. You can use the static methods, `invokeLater` and `invokeAndWait` in the `javax.swing.SwingUtilities` class to run the code in the event dispatch thread. You must put this code in the `run` method of a `Runnable` object and specify the `Runnable` object as the argument to `invokeLater` and `invokeAndWait`. The `invokeLater` method returns immediately, without waiting for the event dispatch thread to execute the code. The `invokeAndWait` method is just like `invokeLater`, except that `invokeAndWait` doesn't return until the event dispatching thread has executed the specified code.

So far, you have launched your GUI application from the main method by creating a frame and making it visible. This works fine for most applications, but if it takes a long time to launch a GUI application, problems may occur. To avoid possible problems in this situation, you should launch GUI creation from the event dispatch thread, as follows:

```
public static void main(String[] args) {
  SwingUtilities.invokeLater(new Runnable() {
    public void run() {
      // The code for creating a frame and setting its properties
    }
  });
}
```

For example, Listing 29.3 gives a simple program that launches the frame from the event dispatch thread.

LISTING 29.3 EventDispatcherThreadDemo.java

```
import javax.swing.*;

public class EventDispatcherThreadDemo extends JApplet {
  public EventDispatcherThreadDemo() {
    add(new JLabel("Hi, it runs from an event dispatch thread"));
  }

  /** Main method */
  public static void main(String[] args) {
    SwingUtilities.invokeLater(new Runnable() {
      public void run() {
        JFrame frame = new JFrame("EventDispatcherThreadDemo");
        frame.add(new EventDispatcherThreadDemo());
```

create frame

```
        frame.setSize(200, 200);
        frame.setDefaultCloseOperation(JFrame.EXIT_ON_CLOSE);
        frame.setLocationRelativeTo(null); // Center the frame
        frame.setVisible(true);
      }
    });
  }
}
```

29.7 Case Study: Clock with Audio

The example creates an applet that displays a running clock and announces the time at one-minute intervals. For example, if the current time is 6:30:00, the applet announces, "six o'-clock thirty minutes A.M." If the current time is 20:20:00, the applet announces, "eight o'clock twenty minutes P.M." Also add a label to display the digital time, as shown in Figure 29.7.

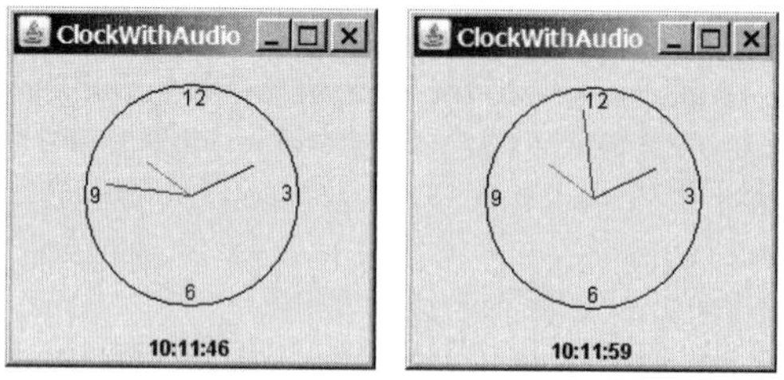
ClockWithAudio
12
9
3
6
10:11:46
ClockWithAudio
12
9
3
6
10:11:59

FIGURE 29.7 The applet displays a clock and announces the time every minute.

audio clips
audio files

To announce the time, the applet plays three audio clips. The first clip announces the hour, the second announces the minute, and the third announces A.M. or P.M. All of the audio files are stored in the directory `audio`, a subdirectory of the applet's class directory. The 12 audio files used to announce the hours are stored in the files **hour0.au**, **hour1.au**, and so on, to **hour11.au**. The 60 audio files used to announce the minutes are stored in the files **minute0.au**, **minute1.au**, and so on, to **minute59.au**. The two audio files used to announce A.M. or P.M. are stored in the file **am.au** and **pm.au**.

You need to play three audio clips on a separate thread to avoid animation delays. To illustrate the problem, let us first write a program without playing the audio on a separate thread.

In §15.10, the `StillClock` class was developed to draw a still clock to show the current time. Create an applet named `ClockWithAudio` (Listing 29.4) that contains an instance of `StillClock` to display an analog clock, and an instance of `JLabel` to display the digit time. Override the `init` method to load the audio files. Use a `Timer` object to set and display the current time continuously at every second. When the second is zero, announce the current time.

LISTING 29.4 `ClockWithAudio.java`

audio clips

```
import java.applet.*;
import javax.swing.*;
import java.awt.event.*;
import java.awt.*;

public class ClockWithAudio extends JApplet {
  protected AudioClip[] hourAudio = new AudioClip[12];
  protected AudioClip[] minuteAudio = new AudioClip[60];

  // Create audio clips for pronouncing am and pm
```

```java
  protected AudioClip amAudio =
    Applet.newAudioClip(this.getClass().getResource("audio/am.au")) ;
  protected AudioClip pmAudio =
    Applet.newAudioClip(this.getClass().getResource("audio/pm.au"));

  // Create a clock
  private StillClock clock = new StillClock();

  // Create a timer
  private Timer timer = new Timer(1000, new TimerListener());

  // Create a label to display time
  private JLabel jlblDigitTime = new JLabel("", JLabel.CENTER);

  /** Initialize the applet */
  public void init() {
    // Create audio clips for pronouncing hours
    for (int i = 0; i < 12; i++)
      hourAudio[i] = Applet.newAudioClip(
        this.getClass().getResource("audio/hour" + i + ".au" ));

    // Create audio clips for pronouncing minutes
    for (int i = 0; i < 60; i++)
      minuteAudio[i] = Applet.newAudioClip(
        this.getClass().getResource("audio/minute" + i + ".au" ));

    // Add clock and time label to the content pane of the applet
    add(clock, BorderLayout.CENTER);
    add(jlblDigitTime, BorderLayout.SOUTH);
  }

  /** Override the applet's start method */
  public void start() {
    timer.start(); // Resume clock
  }

  /** Override the applet's stop method */
  public void stop() {
    timer.stop(); // Suspend clock
  }

  private class TimerListener implements ActionListener {
    public void actionPerformed(ActionEvent e) {
      clock.setCurrentTime();
      clock.repaint();
      jlblDigitTime.setText(clock.getHour() + ":" + clock.getMinute()
        + ":" + clock.getSecond());
      if (clock.getSecond() == 0)
        announceTime(clock.getHour(), clock.getMinute());
    }
  }

  /** Announce the current time at every minute */
  public void announceTime(int hour, int minute) {
    // Announce hour
    hourAudio[hour % 12].play();

    try {
      // Time delay to allow hourAudio play to finish
```

am clip
pm clip
still clock
timer
label
create audio clips
start timer
stop timer
timer listener
set new time
announce time
announce hour

announce minute

announce am

announce pm

main method omitted

```
70         Thread.sleep(1500);
71
72         // Announce minute
73         minuteAudio[minute].play();
74
75         // Time delay to allow minuteAudio play to finish
76         Thread.sleep(1500);
77       }
78       catch(InterruptedException ex) {
79       }
80
81       // Announce am or pm
82       if (hour < 12)
83         amAudio.play();
84       else
85         pmAudio.play();
86     }
87 }
```

The `hourAudio` is an array of twelve audio clips that are used to announce the 12 hours of the day (line 7); the `minuteAudio` is an audio clip that is used to announce the minutes in an hour (line 8). The `amAudio` announces A.M. (line 11); the `pmAudio` announces P.M. (line 13).

The `init()` method creates hour audio clips (lines 29–30) and minute audio clips (lines 34–35), and places a clock and a label in the applet (lines 38–39).

An `ActionEvent` is fired by the timer every second. In the listener's `actionPerformed` method (lines 53–60), the clock is repainted with the new current time, and the digital time is displayed in the label.

In the `announceTime` method (lines 64–86), the `sleep()` method (lines 70, 76) is purposely invoked to ensure that one clip finishes before the next clip starts, so that the clips do not interfere with each other.

The applet's `start()` and `stop()` methods (lines 43–50) are overridden to ensure that the timer starts or stops when the applet is restarted or stopped.

abnormal problem

When you run the preceding program, you will notice that the second hand does not display at the first, second, and third seconds of the minute. This is because `sleep(1500)` is invoked twice in the `announceTime()` method, which takes three seconds to announce the time at the beginning of each minute. Thus, the next action event is delayed for three seconds during the first three seconds of each minute. As a result of this delay, the time is not updated and the clock was not repainted for these three seconds. To fix this problem, you should announce the time on a separate thread. This can be accomplished by modifying the `announceTime` method. Listing 29.5 gives the new program.

Listing 29.5 ClockWithAudioOnSeparateThread.java

omitted

omitted

create a thread

task class

```
// same import statements as in Listing 29.4, so omitted

public class ClockWithAudioOnSeparateThread extends JApplet {
  // same as in lines 7-61 in Listing 29.4, so omitted

  /** Announce the current time at every minute */
  public void announceTime(int h, int m) {
    new Thread(new AnnounceTimeOnSeparateThread(h, m)).start();
  }

  /** Inner class for announcing time */
  class AnnounceTimeOnSeparateThread implements Runnable {
    private int hour, minute;

```

```
15     /** Get Audio clips */
16     public AnnounceTimeOnSeparateThread(int hour, int minute) {
17       this.hour = hour;
18       this.minute = minute;
19     }
20
21     public void run() {
22       // Announce hour
23       hourAudio[hour % 12].play();
24
25       try {
26         // Time delay to allow hourAudio play to finish
27         Thread.sleep(1500);
28
29         // Announce minute
30         minuteAudio[minute].play();
31
32         // Time delay to allow minuteAudio play to finish
33         Thread.sleep(1500);
34       }
35       catch (InterruptedException ex) {
36       }
37
38       // Announce am or pm
39       if (hour < 12)
40         amAudio.play();
41       else
42         pmAudio.play();
43     }
44   }
45 }
```

run thread

main method omitted

The new class ClockWithAudioOnSeparateThread is the same as ClockWithAudio except that the announceTime method is new. The new announceTime method creates a thread (line 8) for the task of announcing time. The task class is defined as an inner class (lines 12–44). The run method (line 21) announces the time on a separate thread.

When running this program, you will discover that the audio does not interfere with the clock animation because an instance of AnnounceTimeOnSeparateThread starts on a separate thread to announce the current time. This thread is independent of the thread on which the actionPerformed method runs.

29.8 Thread Pools

In §29.3, "Creating Tasks and Threads," you learned how to define a task class by implementing java.lang.Runnable, and how to create a thread to run a task like this:

```
Runnable task = new TaskClass(task);
new Thread(task).start();
```

This approach is convenient for a single task execution, but it is not efficient for a large number of tasks, because you have to create a thread for each task. Starting a new thread for each task could limit throughput and cause poor performance. A thread pool is ideal to manage the number of tasks executing concurrently. Java provides the Executor interface for executing tasks in a thread pool and the ExecutorService interface for managing and controlling tasks. ExecutorService is a subinterface of Executor, as shown in Figure 29.8.

To create an Executor object, use the static methods in the Executors class, as shown in Figure 29.9. The newFixedThreadPool(int) method creates a fixed number of threads in

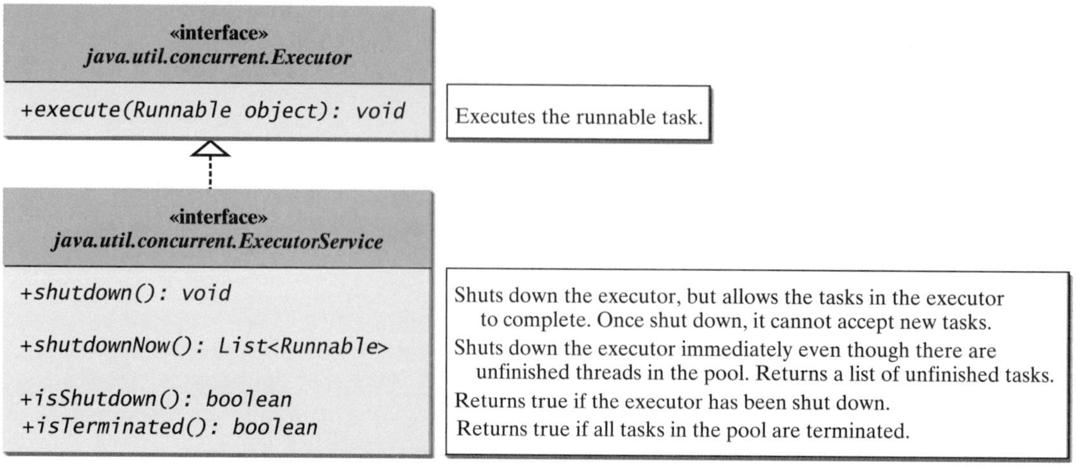
«interface»
java.util.concurrent.Executor
+execute(Runnable object): void
Executes the runnable task.
«interface»
java.util.concurrent.ExecutorService
+shutdown(): void
+shutdownNow(): List<Runnable>
+isShutdown(): boolean
+isTerminated(): boolean
Shuts down the executor, but allows the tasks in the executor to complete. Once shut down, it cannot accept new tasks.
Shuts down the executor immediately even though there are unfinished threads in the pool. Returns a list of unfinished tasks.
Returns true if the executor has been shut down.
Returns true if all tasks in the pool are terminated.

FIGURE 29.8 `Executor` executes threads, and `ExecutorService` manages threads.

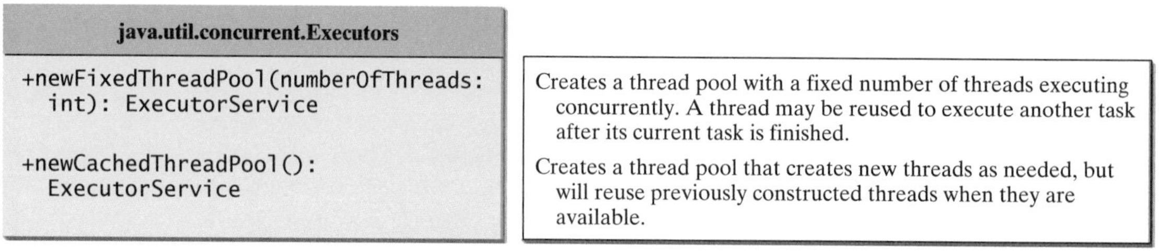
java.util.concurrent.Executors
+newFixedThreadPool(numberOfThreads: int): ExecutorService
+newCachedThreadPool(): ExecutorService
Creates a thread pool with a fixed number of threads executing concurrently. A thread may be reused to execute another task after its current task is finished.
Creates a thread pool that creates new threads as needed, but will reuse previously constructed threads when they are available.

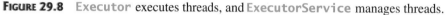

FIGURE 29.9 The `Executors` class provides static methods for creating `Executor` objects.

a pool. If a thread completes executing a task, it can be reused to execute another task. If a thread terminates due to a failure prior to shutdown, a new thread will be created to replace it if all the threads in the pool are not idle and there are tasks waiting for execution. The `newCachedThreadPool()` method creates a new thread if all the threads in the pool are not idle and there are tasks waiting for execution. A thread in a cached pool will be terminated if it has not been used for 60 seconds. A cached pool is efficient for many short tasks.

Listing 29.6 shows how to rewrite Listing 29.1, TaskThreadDemo.java, using a thread pool.

LISTING 29.6 ExecutorDemo.java

create executor

submit task

shut down executor

```java
import java.util.concurrent.*;

public class ExecutorDemo {
  public static void main(String[] args) {
    // Create a fixed thread pool with maximum three threads
    ExecutorService executor = Executors.newFixedThreadPool(3);

    // Submit runnable tasks to the executor
    executor.execute(new PrintChar('a', 100));
    executor.execute(new PrintChar('b', 100));
    executor.execute(new PrintNum(100));

    // Shut down the executor
    executor.shutdown();
  }
}
```

Line 6 creates a thread pool executor with three threads maximum. Classes `PrintChar` and `PrintNum` were defined in TaskThreadDemo.java in Listing 29.1. Line 9 creates a task `new PrintChar('a', 100)` and adds it to the pool. Another two runnable tasks are created and added to the same pool in lines 10–11 similarly. The executor creates three threads to execute three tasks concurrently. Suppose that you replace line 6 by

```
ExecutorService executor = Executors.newFixedThreadPool(1);
```

What will happen? The three runnable tasks will be executed sequentially, because there is only one thread in the pool.

Suppose you replace line 6 by

```
ExecutorService executor = Executors.newCachedThreadPool();
```

What will happen? New threads will be created for each waiting task, so all the tasks will be executed concurrently.

The `shutdown()` method in line 14 tells the executor to shut down. No new tasks can be accepted, but the existing task will continue to finish.

Tip

If you need to create a thread for one task, use the `Thread` class. If you need to create threads for multiple tasks, it is better to use a thread pool.

29.9 Thread Synchronization

A shared resource may be corrupted if it is accessed simultaneously by multiple threads. The following example demonstrates the problem.

Suppose that you create and launch 100 threads, each of which adds a penny to an account. Define a class named `Account` to model the account, a class named `AddAPennyTask` to add a penny to the account, and a main class that creates and launches threads. The relationships of these classes are shown in Figure 29.10. The program is given in Listing 29.7.

Listing 29.7 AccountWithoutSync.java

```
import java.util.concurrent.*;

public class AccountWithoutSync {
  private static Account account = new Account();

  public static void main(String[] args) {
    ExecutorService executor = Executors.newCachedThreadPool();

    // Create and launch 100 threads
    for (int i = 0; i < 100; i++) {
      executor.execute(new AddAPennyTask());
    }

    executor.shutdown();

    // Wait until all tasks are finished
    while (!executor.isTerminated()) {
    }

    System.out.println("What is balance? " + account.getBalance());
  }

```

create executor

submit task

shut down executor

wait for all tasks to terminate

```
23   // A thread for adding a penny to the account
24   private static class AddAPennyTask implements Runnable {
25     public void run() {
26       account.deposit(1);
27     }
28   }
29
30   // An inner class for account
31   private static class Account {
32     private int balance = 0;
33
34     public int getBalance() {
35       return balance;
36     }
37
38     public void deposit(int amount) {
39       int newBalance = balance + amount;
40
41       // This delay is deliberately added to magnify the
42       // data-corruption problem and make it easy to see.
43       try {
44         Thread.sleep(5);
45       }
46       catch (InterruptedException ex) {
47       }
48
49       balance = newBalance;
50     }
51   }
52 }
```

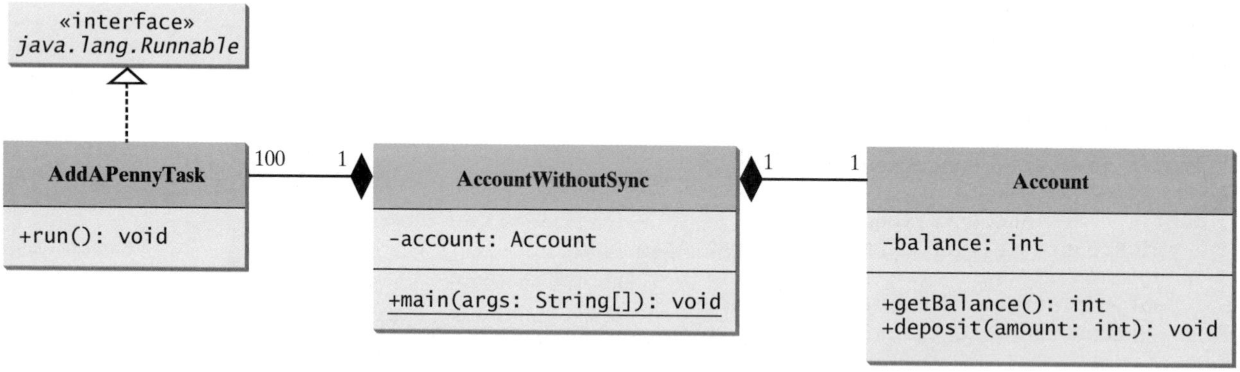
«interface»
java.lang.Runnable
AddAPennyTask
+run(): void
100
1
AccountWithoutSync
-account: Account
+main(args: String[]): void
1
1
Account
-balance: int
+getBalance(): int
+deposit(amount: int): void

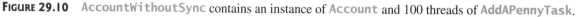

FIGURE 29.10 AccountWithoutSync contains an instance of Account and 100 threads of AddAPennyTask.

The classes AddAPennyTask and Account in lines 24–51 are inner classes. Line 4 creates an Account with initial balance 0. Line 11 creates a task to add a penny to the account and submit the task to the executor. Line 11 is repeated 100 times in lines 10–12. The program repeatedly checks whether all tasks are completed in lines 17–18. The account balance is displayed in line 20 after all tasks are completed.

The program creates 100 threads executed in a thread pool executor (lines 10–12). The isTerminated() method (line 17) is used to test whether the thread is terminated.

The balance of the account is initially 0 (line 32). When all the threads are finished, the balance should be 100, but the output is unpredictable. As can be seen in Figure 29.11, the answers are wrong in the sample run. This demonstrates the data-corruption problem that occurs when all the threads have access to the same data source simultaneously.

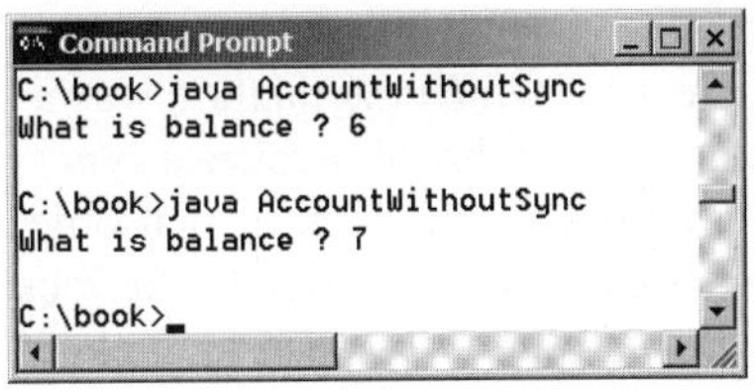
Command Prompt
C:\book>java AccountWithoutSync
What is balance ? 6
C:\book>java AccountWithoutSync
What is balance ? 7
C:\book>_

FIGURE 29.11 The `AccountWithoutSync` program causes data inconsistency.

Lines 39–49 could be replaced by one statement:

```
balance = balance + amount;
```

However, it is highly unlikely, although plausible, that the problem can be replicated using this single statement. The statements in lines 39–49 are deliberately designed to magnify the data-corruption problem and make it easy to see. If you run the program several times but still do not see the problem, increase the sleep time in line 44. This will increase the chances for showing the problem of data inconsistency.

What, then, caused the error in this program? Here is a possible scenario, as shown in Figure 29.12.

Step	Balance	Task 1	Task 2
1	0	`newBalance = balance + 1;`	
2	0		`newBalance = balance + 1;`
3	1	`balance = newBalance;`	
4	1		`balance = newBalance;`

FIGURE 29.12 Task 1 and Task 2 both add 1 to the same balance.

In Step 1, Task 1 gets the balance from the account. In Step 2, Task 2 gets the same balance from the account. In Step 3, Task 1 writes a new balance to the account. In Step 4, Task 2 writes a new balance to the account.

The effect of this scenario is that Task 1 does nothing, because in Step 4 Task 2 overrides Task 1's result. Obviously, the problem is that Task 1 and Task 2 are accessing a common resource in a way that causes conflict. This is a common problem, known as a *race condition*, in multithreaded programs. A class is said to be *thread-safe* if an object of the class does not cause a race condition in the presence of multiple threads. As demonstrated in the preceding example, the `Account` class is not thread-safe.

race condition
thread-safe

29.9.1 The `synchronized` Keyword

To avoid race conditions, it is necessary to prevent more than one thread from simultaneously entering a certain part of the program, known as the *critical region*. The critical region in Listing 29.7 is the entire `deposit` method. You can use the keyword `synchronized` to synchronize the method so that only one thread can access the method at a time. There are several ways to correct the problem in Listing 29.7. One approach is to make `Account` thread-safe by adding the keyword `synchronized` in the `deposit` method in line 38, as follows:

critical region

```
public synchronized void deposit(double amount)
```

A synchronized method acquires a lock before it executes. In the case of an instance method, the lock is on the object for which the method was invoked. In the case of a static method, the lock is on the class. If one thread invokes a synchronized instance method (respectively, static method) on an object, the lock of that object (respectively, class) is acquired first, then the method is executed, and finally the lock is released. Another thread invoking the same method of that object (respectively, class) is blocked until the lock is released.

With the **deposit** method synchronized, the preceding scenario cannot happen. If Task 1 enters the method, Task 2 is blocked until Task 1 finishes the method, as shown in Figure 29.13.

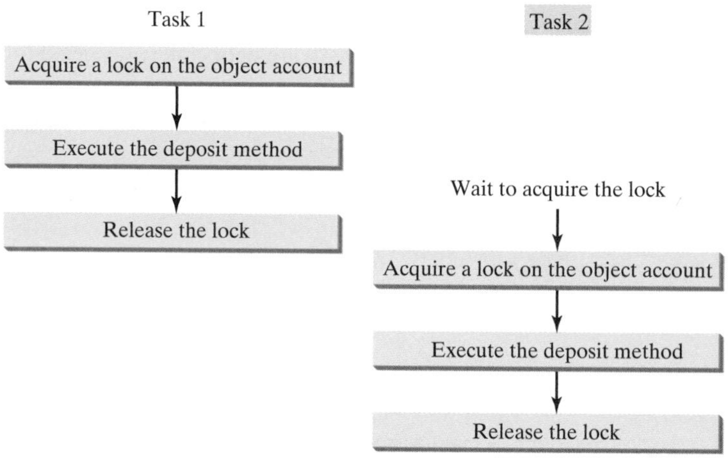
Task 1
Task 2
Acquire a lock on the object account
Execute the deposit method
Release the lock
Wait to acquire the lock
Acquire a lock on the object account
Execute the deposit method
Release the lock

FIGURE 29.13 Task 1 and Task 2 are synchronized.

29.9.2 Synchronizing Statements

synchronized block

Invoking a synchronized instance method of an object acquires a lock on the object, and invoking a synchronized static method of a class acquires a lock on the class. A synchronized statement can be used to acquire a lock on any object, not just *this* object, when executing a block of the code in a method. This block is referred to as a *synchronized block*. The general form of a synchronized statement is as follows:

```
synchronized (expr) {
  statements;
}
```

The expression **expr** must evaluate to an object reference. If the object is already locked by another thread, the thread is blocked until the lock is released. When a lock is obtained on the object, the statements in the synchronized block are executed, and then the lock is released.

Synchronized statements enable you to synchronize part of the code in a method instead of the entire method. This increases concurrency. You can make Listing 29.7 thread-safe by placing the statement in line 26 inside a synchronized block:

```
synchronized (account) {
  account.deposit(1);
}
```

Note

Any synchronized instance method can be converted into a synchronized statement. For example, the following synchronized instance method in (a) is equivalent to (b):

```
public synchronized void xMethod() {
  // method body
}
```

(a)

```
public void xMethod() {
  synchronized (this) {
    // method body
  }
}
```

(b)

29.10 Synchronization Using Locks

In Listing 29.7, 100 tasks deposit a penny to the same account concurrently, which causes conflict. To avoid it, you can simply use the `synchronized` keyword in the `deposit` method, as follows:

```
public synchronized void deposit(double amount)
```

A synchronized instance method implicitly acquires a lock on the instance before it executes the method.

Java enables you to acquire locks explicitly, which gives you more control for coordinating threads. A lock is an instance of the `Lock` interface, which defines the methods for acquiring and releasing locks, as shown in Figure 29.14. A lock may also use the `newCondition()` method to create any number of `Condition` objects, which can be used for thread communications.

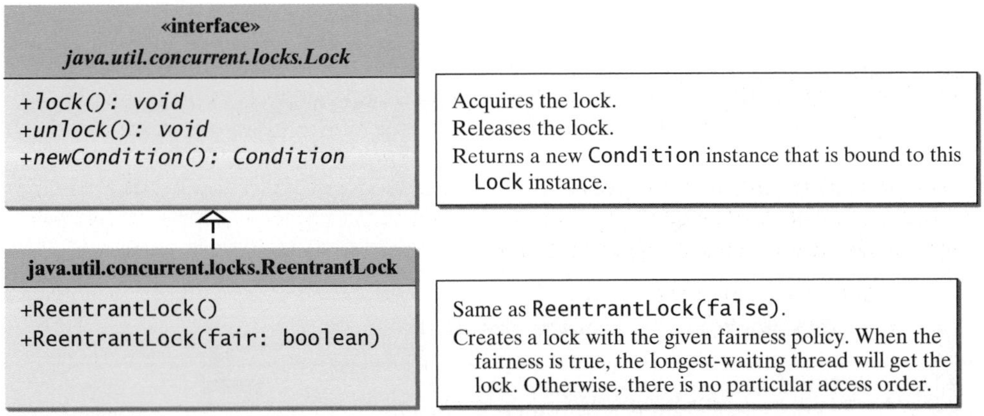
«interface»
java.util.concurrent.locks.Lock
+lock(): void
+unlock(): void
+newCondition(): Condition
Acquires the lock.
Releases the lock.
Returns a new Condition instance that is bound to this Lock instance.
java.util.concurrent.locks.ReentrantLock
+ReentrantLock()
+ReentrantLock(fair: boolean)
Same as ReentrantLock(false).
Creates a lock with the given fairness policy. When the fairness is true, the longest-waiting thread will get the lock. Otherwise, there is no particular access order.

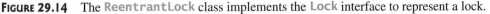

FIGURE 29.14 The `ReentrantLock` class implements the `Lock` interface to represent a lock.

`ReentrantLock` is a concrete implementation of `Lock` for creating mutually exclusive locks. You can create a lock with the specified fairness policy. True fairness policies guarantee that the longest-wait thread will obtain the lock first. False fairness policies grant a lock to a waiting thread arbitrarily. Programs using fair locks accessed by many threads may have poorer overall performance than those using the default setting, but have smaller variances in times to obtain locks and prevent starvation. fairness policy

Listing 29.8 revises AccountWithoutSync.java in Listing 29.7 to synchronize the account modification using explicit locks.

LISTING 29.8 AccountWithSyncUsingLock.java

package for locks

create a lock

acquire the lock

```
import java.util.concurrent.*;
import java.util.concurrent.locks.*;

public class AccountWithSyncUsingLock {
  private static Account account = new Account();

  public static void main(String[] args) {
    ExecutorService executor = Executors.newCachedThreadPool();

    // Create and launch 100 threads
    for (int i = 0; i < 100; i++) {
      executor.execute(new AddAPennyTask());
    }

    executor.shutdown();

    // Wait until all tasks are finished
    while (!executor.isTerminated()) {
    }

    System.out.println("What is balance ? " + account.getBalance());
  }

  // A thread for adding a penny to the account
  public static class AddAPennyTask implements Runnable {
    public void run() {
      account.deposit(1);
    }
  }

  // An inner class for account
  public static class Account {
    private static Lock lock = new ReentrantLock(); // Create a lock
    private int balance = 0;

    public int getBalance() {
      return balance;
    }

    public void deposit(int amount) {
      lock.lock(); // Acquire the lock

      try {
        int newBalance = balance + amount;

        // This delay is deliberately added to magnify the
        // data-corruption problem and make it easy to see.
        Thread.sleep(5);

        balance = newBalance;
      }
      catch (InterruptedException ex) {
      }
      finally {
```

```
55            lock.unlock(); // Release the lock
56          }
57        }
58      }
59    }
```

release the lock

Line 33 creates a lock, line 41 acquires the lock, and line 55 releases the lock.

Tip

It is a good practice to always immediately follow a call to `lock()` with a `try-catch` block and release the lock in the `finally` clause, as shown in lines 41–57, to ensure that the lock is always released.

The example in Listing 29.7 using the synchronized method is simpler than the one in Listing 29.8 using a lock. In general, using `synchronized` methods or statements is simpler than using explicit locks for mutual exclusion. However, using explicit locks is more intuitive and flexible to synchronize threads with conditions, as you will see in the next section.

29.11 Cooperation among Threads

Thread synchronization suffices to avoid race conditions by ensuring the mutual exclusion of multiple threads in the critical region, but sometimes you also need a way for threads to cooperate. Conditions can be used to facilitate communications among threads. A thread can specify what to do under a certain condition. Conditions are objects created by invoking the `newCondition()` method on a `Lock` object. Once a condition is created, you can use its `await()`, `signal()`, and `signalAll()` methods for thread communications, as shown in Figure 29.15. The `await()` method causes the current thread to wait until the condition is signaled. The `signal()` method wakes up one waiting thread, and the `signalAll()` method wakes all waiting threads. condition

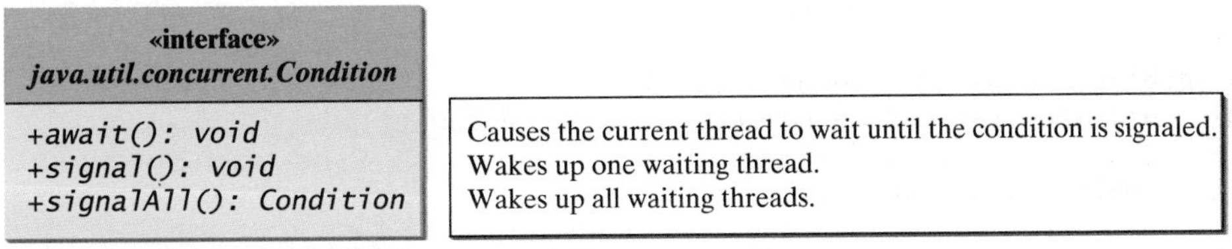
«interface»
java.util.concurrent.Condition
+await(): void
+signal(): void
+signalAll(): Condition
Causes the current thread to wait until the condition is signaled.
Wakes up one waiting thread.
Wakes up all waiting threads.

Figure 29.15 The `Condition` interface defines the methods for performing synchronization.

Let us use an example to demonstrate thread communications. Suppose that you create and launch two tasks, one that deposits to an account, and one that withdraws from the same account. The withdraw task has to wait if the amount to be withdrawn is more than the current balance. Whenever new funds are deposited to the account, the deposit task notifies the withdraw thread to resume. If the amount is still not enough for a withdrawal, the withdraw thread has to continue to wait for a new deposit. thread cooperation example

To synchronize the operations, use a lock with a condition: `newDeposit` (i.e., new deposit added to the account). If the balance is less than the amount to be withdrawn, the withdraw task will wait for the `newDeposit` condition. When the deposit task adds money to the account, the task signals the waiting withdraw task to try again. The interaction between the two tasks is shown in Figure 29.16.

You create a condition from a `Lock` object. To use a condition, you have to first obtain a lock. The `await()` method causes the thread to wait and automatically releases the lock on the condition. Once the condition is right, the thread reacquires the lock and continues executing.

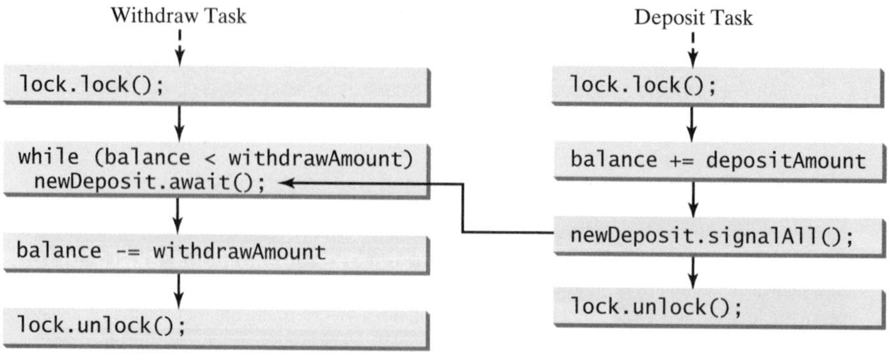
Withdraw Task
lock.lock();
while (balance < withdrawAmount)
  newDeposit.await();
balance -= withdrawAmount
lock.unlock();
Deposit Task
lock.lock();
balance += depositAmount
newDeposit.signalAll();
lock.unlock();

FIGURE 29.16 The condition `newDeposit` is used for communications between the two threads.

Assume that the initial balance is 0 and the amounts to deposit and withdraw are randomly generated. Listing 29.9 gives the program. A sample run of the program is shown in Figure 29.17.

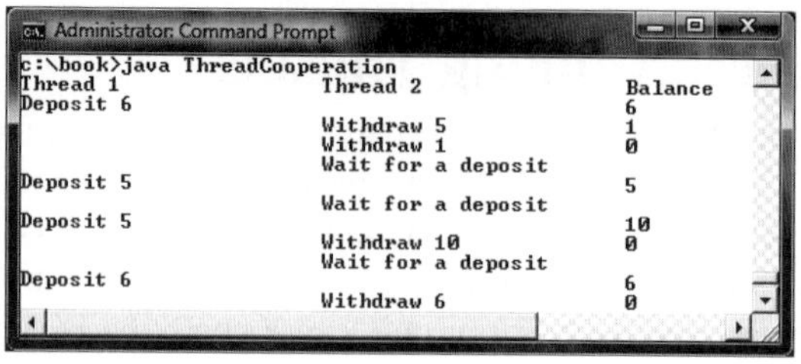
Administrator: Command Prompt
c:\book>java ThreadCooperation
Thread 1 Thread 2 Balance
Deposit 6 6
Withdraw 5 1
Withdraw 1 0
Wait for a deposit
Deposit 5 5
Wait for a deposit
Deposit 5 10
Withdraw 10 0
Wait for a deposit
Deposit 6 6
Withdraw 6 0

FIGURE 29.17 The withdraw task waits if there are not sufficient funds to withdraw.

LISTING 29.9 ThreadCooperation.java

create two threads

```
import java.util.concurrent.*;
import java.util.concurrent.locks.*;

public class ThreadCooperation {
  private static Account account = new Account();

  public static void main(String[] args) {
    // Create a thread pool with two threads
    ExecutorService executor = Executors.newFixedThreadPool(2);
    executor.execute(new DepositTask());
    executor.execute(new WithdrawTask());
    executor.shutdown();

    System.out.println("Thread 1\t\tThread 2\t\tBalance");
  }

  // A task for adding an amount to the account
  public static class DepositTask implements Runnable {
    public void run() {
      try { // Purposely delay it to let the withdraw method proceed
        while (true) {
          account.deposit((int)(Math.random() * 10) + 1);
          Thread.sleep(1000);
        }
      }
      catch (InterruptedException ex) {
        ex.printStackTrace();
      }
    }
```

```
  }

  // A task for subtracting an amount from the account
  public static class WithdrawTask implements Runnable {
    public void run() {
      while (true) {
        account.withdraw((int)(Math.random() * 10) + 1);
      }
    }
  }

  // An inner class for account
  private static class Account {
    // Create a new lock
    private static Lock lock = new ReentrantLock();

    // Create a condition
    private static Condition newDeposit = lock.newCondition();

    private int balance = 0;

    public int getBalance() {
      return balance;
    }

    public void withdraw(int amount) {
      lock.lock(); // Acquire the lock
      try {
        while (balance < amount) {
          System.out.println("\t\t\tWait for a deposit")
          newDeposit.await();
        }

        balance -= amount;
        System.out.println("\t\t\tWithdraw " + amount +
          "\t\t" + getBalance());
      }
      catch (InterruptedException ex) {
        ex.printStackTrace();
      }
      finally {
        lock.unlock(); // Release the lock
      }
    }

    public void deposit(int amount) {
      lock.lock(); // Acquire the lock
      try {
        balance += amount;
        System.out.println("Deposit " + amount +
          "\t\t\t\t\t" + getBalance());

        // Signal thread waiting on the condition
        newDeposit.signalAll();
      }
      finally {
        lock.unlock(); // Release the lock
      }
    }
  }
}
```

create a lock

create a condition

acquire the lock

wait on the condition

release the lock

acquire the lock

signal threads

release the lock

The example creates a new inner class named `Account` to model the account with two methods, `deposit(int)` and `withdraw(int)`, a class named `DepositTask` to add an amount to the balance, a class named `WithdrawTask` to withdraw an amount from the balance, and a main class that creates and launches two threads.

The program creates and submits the deposit task (line 10) and the withdraw task (line 11). The deposit task is purposely put to sleep (line 23) to let the withdraw task run. When there are not enough funds to withdraw, the withdraw task waits (line 59) for notification of the balance change from the deposit task (line 82).

A lock is created in line 44. A condition named `newDeposit` on the lock is created in line 47. A condition is bound to a lock. Before waiting or signaling the condition, a thread must first acquire the lock for the condition. The withdraw task acquires the lock in line 56, waits for the `newDeposit` condition (line 60) when there is not a sufficient amount to withdraw, and releases the lock in line 70. The deposit task acquires the lock in line 75, and signals all waiting threads (line 82) for the `newDeposit` condition after a new deposit is made.

What will happen if you replace the `while` loop in lines 59–60 with the following `if` statement?

```
if (balance < amount) {
  System.out.println("\t\t\tWait for a deposit");
  newDeposit.await();
}
```

The deposit task will notify the withdraw task whenever the balance changes. `(balance < amount)` may still be true when the withdraw task is awakened. Using the `if` statement, the withdraw task may wait forever. Using the loop statement, the withdraw task will have a chance to recheck the condition. Thus you should always test the condition in a loop.

ever-waiting threads

Caution

Once a thread invokes `await()` on a condition, the thread is put to wait for a signal to resume. If you forget to call `signal()` or `signalAll()` on the condition, the thread will wait forever.

`IllegalMonitorState-Exception`

Caution

A condition is created from a `Lock` object. To invoke its method (e.g., `await()`, `signal()`, and `signalAll()`), you must first own the lock. If you invoke these methods without acquiring the lock, an `IllegalMonitorStateException` will be thrown.

29.11.1 Java's Built-in Monitor

Locks and conditions are new in Java 5. Prior to Java 5, thread communications were programmed using the object's built-in monitors. Locks and conditions are more powerful and flexible than the built-in monitor, and in consequence, this section can be completely ignored. However, if you are working with legacy Java code, you may encounter Java's built-in monitor.

A *monitor* is an object with mutual exclusion and synchronization capabilities. Only one thread at a time can execute a method in the monitor. A thread enters the monitor by acquiring a lock on it and exits by releasing the lock. *Any object can be a monitor*. An object becomes a monitor once a thread locks it. Locking is implemented using the `synchronized` keyword on a method or a block. A thread must acquire a lock before executing a synchronized method or block. A thread can wait in a monitor if the condition is not right for it to continue executing in the monitor. You can invoke the `wait()` method on the monitor object to release the lock so that some other thread can get in the monitor and perhaps change the monitor's state. When the condition is right, the other thread can invoke the `notify()` or `notifyAll()` method to signal one or all waiting threads to regain the lock and resume execution. The template for invoking these methods is shown in Figure 29.18.

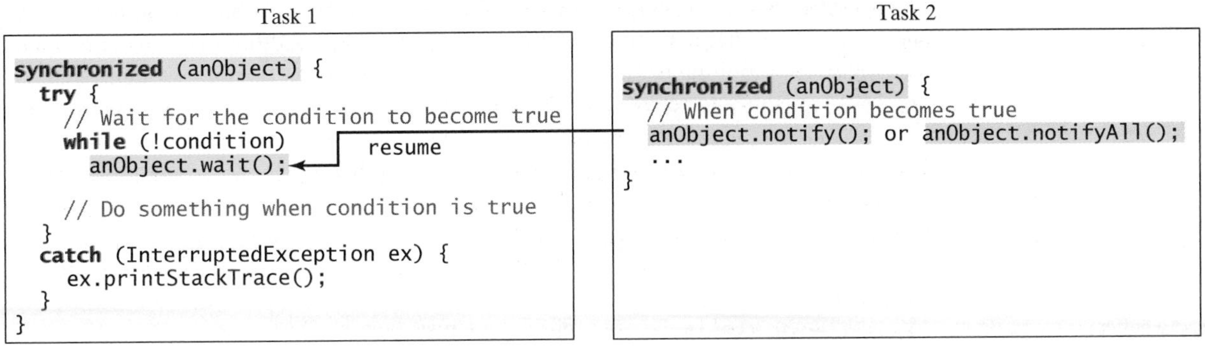
Task 1
synchronized (anObject) {
try {
// Wait for the condition to become true
while (!condition)
anObject.wait();
// Do something when condition is true
}
catch (InterruptedException ex) {
ex.printStackTrace();
}
}
resume
Task 2
synchronized (anObject) {
// When condition becomes true
anObject.notify(); or anObject.notifyAll();
...
}

FIGURE 29.18 The `wait()`, `notify()`, and `notifyAll()` methods coordinate thread communication.

The `wait()`, `notify()`, and `notifyAll()` methods must be called in a synchronized method or a synchronized block on the receiving object of these methods. Otherwise, an `IllegalMonitorStateException` will occur.

When `wait()` is invoked, it pauses the thread and simultaneously releases the lock on the object. When the thread is restarted after being notified, the lock is automatically reacquired.

The `wait()`, `notify()`, and `notifyAll()` methods on an object are analogous to the `await()`, `signal()`, and `signalAll()` methods on a condition.

29.12 Case Study: Producer/Consumer

Consider the classic Consumer/Producer example. Suppose you use a buffer to store integers. The buffer size is limited. The buffer provides the method `write(int)` to add an `int` value to the buffer and the method `read()` to read and delete an `int` value from the buffer. To synchronize the operations, use a lock with two conditions: `notEmpty` (i.e., buffer is not empty) and `notFull` (i.e., buffer is not full). When a task adds an `int` to the buffer, if the buffer is full, the task will wait for the `notFull` condition. When a task deletes an `int` from the buffer, if the buffer is empty, the task will wait for the `notEmpty` condition. The interaction between the two tasks is shown in Figure 29.19.

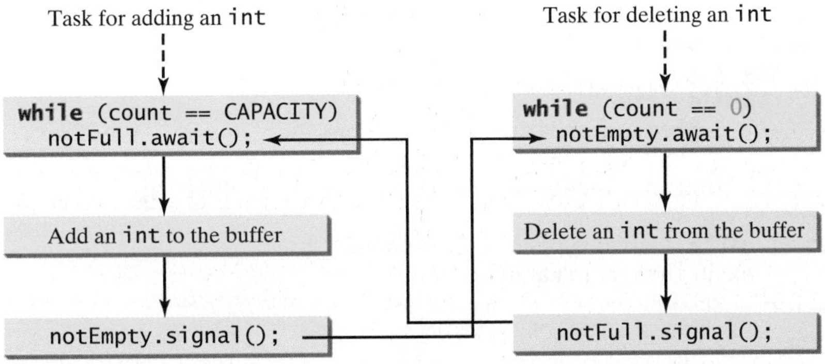
Task for adding an int
while (count == CAPACITY)
notFull.await();
Add an int to the buffer
notEmpty.signal();
Task for deleting an int
while (count == 0)
notEmpty.await();
Delete an int from the buffer
notFull.signal();

FIGURE 29.19 The conditions `notFull` and `notEmpty` are used to coordinate task interactions.

Listing 29.10 presents the complete program. The program contains the `Buffer` class (lines 48–95) and two tasks for repeatedly producing and consuming numbers to and from the buffer (lines 16–45). The `write(int)` method (line 60) adds an integer to the buffer. The `read()` method (line 77) deletes and returns an integer from the buffer.

The buffer is actually a first-in first-out queue (lines 50–51). The conditions `notEmpty` and `notFull` on the lock are created in lines 57–58. The conditions are bound to a lock. A lock must be acquired before a condition can be applied. If you use the `wait()` and `notify()` methods to rewrite this example, you have to designate two objects as monitors.

Listing 29.10 ConsumerProducer.java

create a buffer

create two threads

producer task

consumer task

```
1 import java.util.concurrent.*;
2 import java.util.concurrent.locks.*;
3
4 public class ConsumerProducer {
5   private static Buffer buffer = new Buffer();
6
7   public static void main(String[] args) {
8     // Create a thread pool with two threads
9     ExecutorService executor = Executors.newFixedThreadPool(2);
10    executor.execute(new ProducerTask());
11    executor.execute(new ConsumerTask());
12    executor.shutdown();
13  }
14
15  // A task for adding an int to the buffer
16  private static class ProducerTask implements Runnable {
17    public void run() {
18      try {
19        int i = 1;
20        while (true) {
21          System.out.println("Producer writes " + i);
22          buffer.write(i++); // Add a value to the buffer
23          // Put the thread to sleep
24          Thread.sleep((int)(Math.random() * 10000));
25        }
26      } catch (InterruptedException ex) {
27        ex.printStackTrace();
28      }
29    }
30  }
31
32  // A task for reading and deleting an int from the buffer
33  private static class ConsumerTask implements Runnable {
34    public void run() {
35      try {
36        while (true) {
37          System.out.println("\t\t\tConsumer reads " + buffer.read());
38          // Put the thread into sleep
39          Thread.sleep((int)(Math.random() * 10000));
40        }
41      } catch (InterruptedException ex) {
42        ex.printStackTrace();
43      }
44    }
45  }
46
47  // An inner class for buffer
48  private static class Buffer {
49    private static final int CAPACITY = 1; // buffer size
50    private java.util.LinkedList<Integer> queue =
51      new java.util.LinkedList<Integer>();
52
```

```
    // Create a new lock
    private static Lock lock = new ReentrantLock();

    // Create two conditions
    private static Condition notEmpty = lock.newCondition();
    private static Condition notFull = lock.newCondition();

    public void write(int value) {
      lock.lock(); // Acquire the lock
      try {
        while (queue.size() == CAPACITY) {
          System.out.println("Wait for notFull condition");
          notFull.await();
        }

        queue.offer(value);
        notEmpty.signal(); // Signal notEmpty condition
      } catch (InterruptedException ex) {
        ex.printStackTrace();
      } finally {
        lock.unlock(); // Release the lock
      }
    }

    public int read() {
      int value = 0;
      lock.lock(); // Acquire the lock
      try {
        while (queue.isEmpty()) {
          System.out.println("\t\t\tWait for notEmpty condition");
          notEmpty.await();
        }

        value = queue.remove();
        notFull.signal(); // Signal notFull condition
      } catch (InterruptedException ex) {
        ex.printStackTrace();
      } finally {
        lock.unlock(); // Release the lock
        return value;
      }
    }
  }
}
```

create a lock
create a condition
create a condition
acquire the lock
wait on notFull
signal notEmpty
release the lock
acquire the lock
wait on notEmpty
signal notFull
release the lock

A sample run of the program is shown in Figure 29.20.

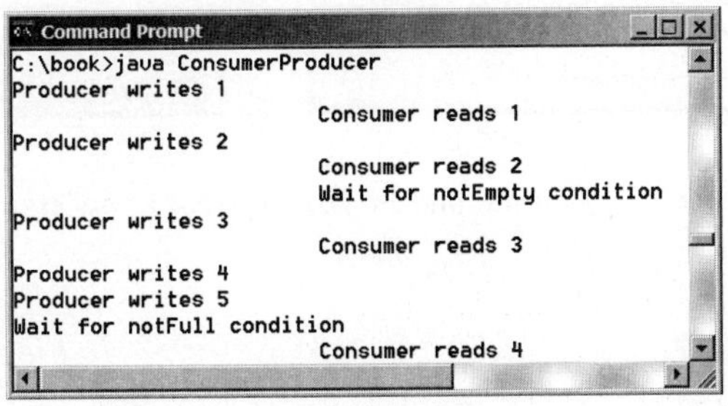
Command Prompt
C:\book>java ConsumerProducer
Producer writes 1
Consumer reads 1
Producer writes 2
Consumer reads 2
Wait for notEmpty condition
Producer writes 3
Consumer reads 3
Producer writes 4
Producer writes 5
Wait for notFull condition
Consumer reads 4

FIGURE 29.20 Locks and conditions are used for communications between the Producer and Consumer threads.

29.13 Blocking Queues

blocking queue

Queues and priority queues were introduced in §22.10. A *blocking queue* causes a thread to block when you try to add an element to a full queue or to remove an element from an empty queue. The `BlockingQueue` interface extends `java.util.Queue` and provides the synchronized `put` and `take` methods for adding an element to the head of the queue and for removing an element from the tail of the queue, as shown in Figure 29.21.

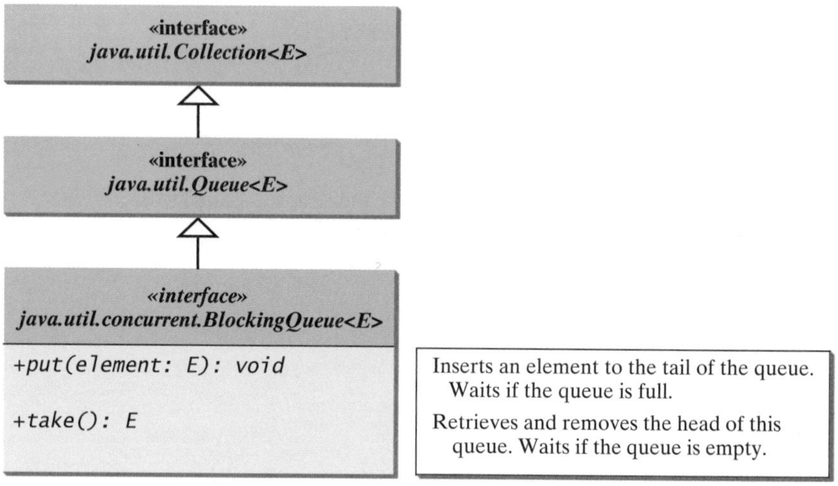
«interface»
java.util.Collection<E>
«interface»
java.util.Queue<E>
«interface»
java.util.concurrent.BlockingQueue<E>
+put(element: E): void
+take(): E
Inserts an element to the tail of the queue. Waits if the queue is full.
Retrieves and removes the head of this queue. Waits if the queue is empty.

FIGURE 29.21 `BlockingQueue` is a subinterface of `Queue`.

Three concrete blocking queues `ArrayBlockingQueue`, `LinkedBlockingQueue`, and `PriorityBlockingQueue` are provided in Java, as shown in Figure 29.22. All are in the `java.util.concurrent` package. `ArrayBlockingQueue` implements a blocking queue using an array. You have to specify a capacity or an optional fairness to construct an `ArrayBlockingQueue`. `LinkedBlockingQueue` implements a blocking queue using a linked list. You may create an unbounded or bounded `LinkedBlockingQueue`. `PriorityBlockingQueue` is a priority queue. You may create an unbounded or bounded priority queue.

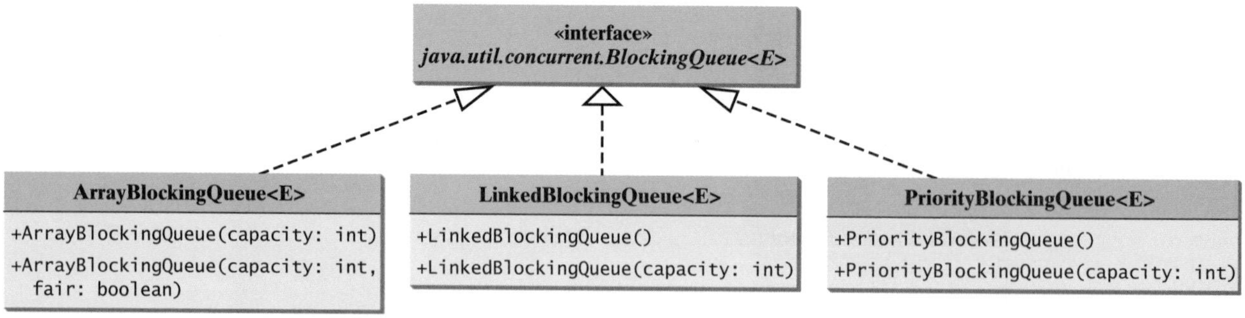
«interface»
java.util.concurrent.BlockingQueue<E>
ArrayBlockingQueue<E>
+ArrayBlockingQueue(capacity: int)
+ArrayBlockingQueue(capacity: int, fair: boolean)
LinkedBlockingQueue<E>
+LinkedBlockingQueue()
+LinkedBlockingQueue(capacity: int)
PriorityBlockingQueue<E>
+PriorityBlockingQueue()
+PriorityBlockingQueue(capacity: int)

FIGURE 29.22 `ArrayBlockingQueue`, `LinkedBlockingQueue`, and `PriorityBlockingQueue` are concrete blocking queues.

Note

unbounded queue

You may create an unbounded `LinkedBlockingQueue` or `PriorityBlockingQueue`. For an unbounded queue, the `put` method will never block.

Listing 29.11 gives an example of using an `ArrayBlockingQueue` to simplify the Consumer/Producer example in Listing 29.10. Line 5 creates an `ArrayBlockingQueue` to store integers. The Producer thread puts an integer to the queue (line 22), and the Consumer thread takes an integer from the queue (line 37).

LISTING 29.11 `ConsumerProducerUsingBlockingQueue.java`

```
1 import java.util.concurrent.*;
2
3 public class ConsumerProducerUsingBlockingQueue {
4   private static ArrayBlockingQueue<Integer> buffer =
5     new ArrayBlockingQueue<Integer>(2);
6
7   public static void main(String[] args) {
8     // Create a thread pool with two threads
9     ExecutorService executor = Executors.newFixedThreadPool(2);
10    executor.execute(new ProducerTask());
11    executor.execute(new ConsumerTask());
12    executor.shutdown();
13  }
14
15  // A task for adding an int to the buffer
16  private static class ProducerTask implements Runnable {
17    public void run() {
18      try {
19        int i = 1;
20        while (true) {
21          System.out.println("Producer writes " + i);
22          buffer.put(i++); // Add any value to the buffer, say, 1
23          // Put the thread to sleep
24          Thread.sleep((int)(Math.random() * 10000));
25        }
26      } catch (InterruptedException ex) {
27        ex.printStackTrace();
28      }
29    }
30  }
31
32  // A task for reading and deleting an int from the buffer
33  private static class ConsumerTask implements Runnable {
34    public void run() {
35      try {
36        while (true) {
37          System.out.println("\t\t\tConsumer reads " + buffer.take());
38          // Put the thread to sleep
39          Thread.sleep((int)(Math.random() * 10000));
40        }
41      } catch (InterruptedException ex) {
42        ex.printStackTrace();
43      }
44    }
45  }
46 }
```

create a buffer

create two threads

producer task

put

consumer task

take

In Listing 29.10, you used locks and conditions to synchronize the Producer and Consumer threads. In this program, hand coding is not necessary, because synchronization is already implemented in `ArrayBlockingQueue`.

29.14 Semaphores

Semaphores can be used to restrict the number of threads that access a shared resource. Before accessing the resource, a thread must acquire a permit from the semaphore. After finishing with the resource, the thread must return the permit back to the semaphore, as shown in Figure 29.23.

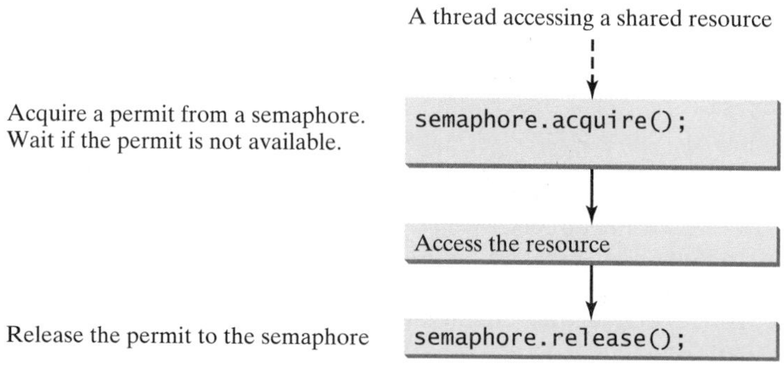
A thread accessing a shared resource
Acquire a permit from a semaphore.
Wait if the permit is not available.
semaphore.acquire();
Access the resource
Release the permit to the semaphore
semaphore.release();

FIGURE 29.23 A limited number of threads can access a shared resource controlled by a semaphore.

To create a semaphore, you have to specify the number of permits with an optional fairness policy, as shown in Figure 29.24. A task acquires a permit by invoking the semaphore's `acquire()` method and releases the permit by invoking the semaphore's `release()` method. Once a permit is acquired, the total number of available permits in a semaphore is reduced by `1`. Once a permit is released, the total number of available permits in a semaphore is increased by `1`.

A semaphore with just one permit can be used to simulate a mutually exclusive lock. Listing 29.12 revises the `Account` inner class in Listing 29.10 using a semaphore to ensure that only one thread at a time can access the `deposit` method.

LISTING 29.12 New Account Inner Class

create a semaphore

acquire a permit

```
// An inner class for account
private static class Account {
  // Create a semaphore
  private static Semaphore semaphore = new Semaphore(1);
  private int balance = 0;

  public int getBalance() {
    return balance;
  }

  public void deposit(int amount) {
    try {
      semaphore.acquire(); // Acquire a permit
      int newBalance = balance + amount;

      // This delay is deliberately added to magnify the
      // data-corruption problem and make it easy to see
      Thread.sleep(5);

      balance = newBalance;
    }
```

```
22       catch (InterruptedException ex) {
23       }
24       finally {
25         semaphore.release(); // Release a permit
26       }
27     }
28 }
```

release a permit

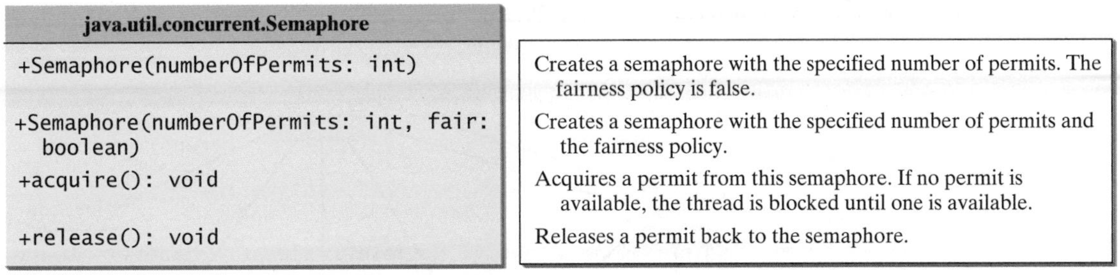

java.util.concurrent.Semaphore
+Semaphore(numberOfPermits: int)
+Semaphore(numberOfPermits: int, fair: boolean)
+acquire(): void
+release(): void
Creates a semaphore with the specified number of permits. The fairness policy is false.
Creates a semaphore with the specified number of permits and the fairness policy.
Acquires a permit from this semaphore. If no permit is available, the thread is blocked until one is available.
Releases a permit back to the semaphore.

FIGURE 29.24 The `Semaphore` class contains the methods for accessing a semaphore.

A semaphore with one permit is created in line 4. A thread first acquires a permit when executing the deposit method in line 13. After the balance is updated, the thread releases the permit in line 25. It is a good practice to always place the `release()` method in the finally clause to ensure that the permit is finally released even in the case of exceptions.

29.15 Avoiding Deadlocks

Sometimes two or more threads need to acquire the locks on several shared objects. This could cause a *deadlock*, in which each thread has the lock on one of the objects and is waiting for the lock on the other object. Consider the scenario with two threads and two objects, as shown in Figure 29.25. Thread 1 has acquired a lock on `object1`, and Thread 2 has acquired a lock on `object2`. Now Thread 1 is waiting for the lock on `object2`, and Thread 2 for the lock on `object1`. Each thread waits for the other to release the lock it needs, and until that happens, neither can continue to run.

deadlock

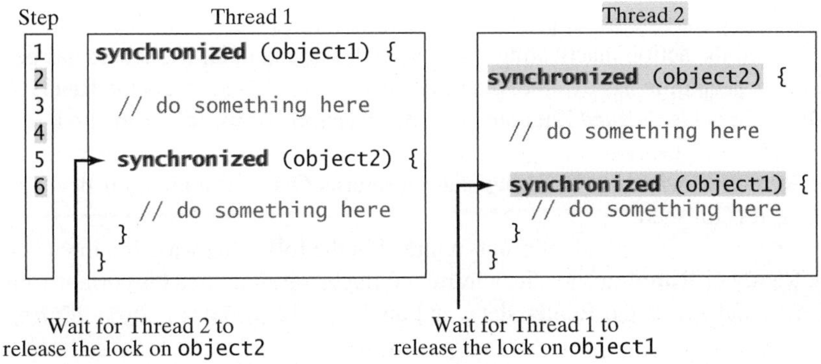

Step
Thread 1
Thread 2
1
2
3
4
5
6
synchronized (object1) {
// do something here
synchronized (object2) {
// do something here
}
}
synchronized (object2) {
// do something here
synchronized (object1) {
// do something here
}
}
Wait for Thread 2 to release the lock on object2
Wait for Thread 1 to release the lock on object1

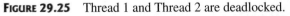

FIGURE 29.25 Thread 1 and Thread 2 are deadlocked.

Deadlock is easily avoided by using a simple technique known as *resource ordering*. With this technique, you assign an order to all the objects whose locks must be acquired and ensure that each thread acquires the locks in that order. For the example in Figure 29.25, suppose that

resource ordering

the objects are ordered as `object1` and `object2`. Using the resource ordering technique, Thread 2 must acquire a lock on `object1` first, then on `object2`. Once Thread 1 acquires a lock on `object1`, Thread 2 has to wait for a lock on `object1`. So Thread 1 will be able to acquire a lock on `object2` and no deadlock will occur.

29.16 Thread States

Tasks are executed in threads. Threads can be in one of five states: New, Ready, Running, Blocked, or Finished (see Figure 29.26).

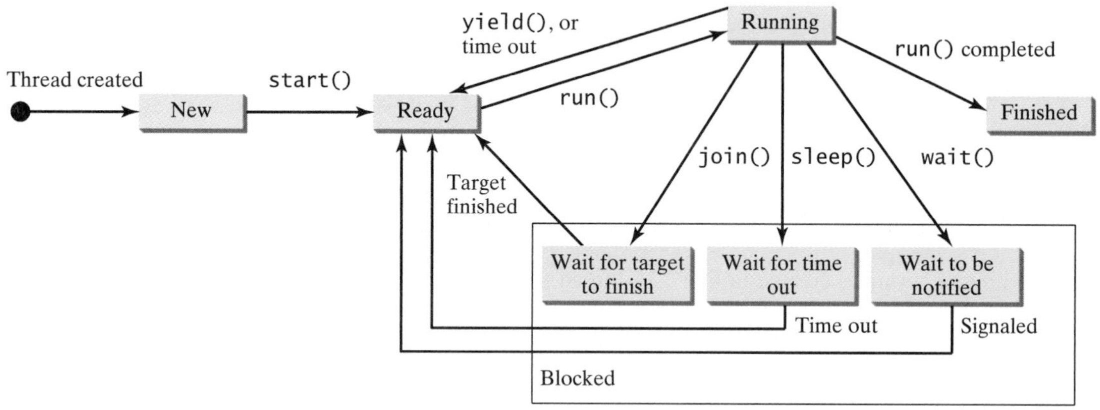

Thread created
New
start()
Ready
yield(), or time out
run()
Running
run() completed
Finished
join()
sleep()
wait()
Target finished
Wait for target to finish
Wait for time out
Wait to be notified
Time out
Signaled
Blocked

FIGURE 29.26 A thread can be in one of five states: New, Ready, Running, Blocked, or Finished.

When a thread is newly created, it enters the ***New** state*. After a thread is started by calling its `start()` method, it enters the ***Ready** state*. A ready thread is runnable but may not be running yet. The operating system has to allocate CPU time to it.

When a ready thread begins executing, it enters the ***Running** state*. A running thread may enter the ***Ready*** state if its given CPU time expires or its `yield()` method is called.

A thread can enter the ***Blocked** state* (i.e., become inactive) for several reasons. It may have invoked the `join()`, `sleep()`, or `wait()` method, or some other thread may have invoked these methods. It may be waiting for an I/O operation to finish. A blocked thread may be reactivated when the action inactivating it is reversed. For example, if a thread has been put to sleep and the sleep time has expired, the thread is reactivated and enters the **Ready** state.

Finally, a thread is *finished* if it completes the execution of its `run()` method.

The `isAlive()` method is used to find out the state of a thread. It returns `true` if a thread is in the **Ready**, **Blocked**, or **Running** state; it returns `false` if a thread is new and has not started or if it is finished.

The `interrupt()` method interrupts a thread in the following way: If a thread is currently in the **Ready** or **Running** state, its interrupted flag is set; if a thread is currently blocked, it is awakened and enters the **Ready** state, and an `java.lang.InterruptedException` is thrown.

29.17 Synchronized Collections

synchronized collection

The classes in the Java Collections Framework are not thread-safe; that is, their contents may be corrupted if they are accessed and updated concurrently by multiple threads. You can protect the data in a collection by locking the collection or by using synchronized collections.

The `Collections` class provides six static methods for wrapping a collection into a synchronized version, as shown in Figure 29.27. The collections created using these methods are called *synchronization wrappers*.

synchronization wrapper

java.util.Collections	
+synchronizedCollection(c: Collection): Collection	Returns a synchronized collection.
+synchronizedList(list: List): List	Returns a synchronized list from the specified list.
+synchronizedMap(m: Map): Map	Returns a synchronized map from the specified map.
+synchronizedSet(s: Set): Set	Returns a synchronized set from the specified set.
+synchronizedSortedMap(s: SortedMap): SortedMap	Returns a synchronized sorted map from the specified sorted map.
+synchronizedSortedSet(s: SortedSet): SortedSet	Returns a synchronized sorted set.

FIGURE 29.27 You can obtain synchronized collections using the methods in the `Collections` class.

Invoking `synchronizedCollection(Collection c)` returns a new `Collection` object, in which all the methods that access and update the original collection `c` are synchronized. These methods are implemented using the `synchronized` keyword. For example, the `add` method is implemented like this:

```
public boolean add(E o) {
  synchronized (this) { return c.add(o); }
}
```

Synchronized collections can be safely accessed and modified by multiple threads concurrently.

Note

The methods in `java.util.Vector`, `java.util.Stack`, and `java.util.Hashtable` are already synchronized. These are old classes introduced in Java. In Java, you should use `java.util.ArrayList` to replace `Vector`, `java.util.LinkedList` to replace `Stack`, and `java.util.Map` to replace `Hashtable`. If synchronization is needed, use a synchronization wrapper.

The synchronization wrapper classes are thread-safe, but the iterator is *fail-fast*. This means that if you are using an iterator to traverse a collection while the underlying collection is being modified by another thread, then the iterator will immediately fail by throwing `java.util.ConcurrentModificationException`, which is a subclass of `RuntimeException`. To avoid this error, you need to create a synchronized collection object and acquire a lock on the object when traversing it. For example, suppose you want to traverse a set; you have to write the code like this:

fail-fast

```
Set hashSet = Collections.synchronizedSet(new HashSet());

synchronized (hashSet) { // Must synchronize it
  Iterator iterator = hashSet.iterator();

  while (iterator.hasNext()) {
    System.out.println(iterator.next());
  }
}
```

Failure to do so may result in nondeterministic behavior, such as `ConcurrentModificationException`.

29.18 SwingWorker

event dispatch thread

As discussed in §29.6, all Swing GUI events are processed in a single *event dispatch thread*. If an event requires a long time to process, the thread cannot attend to other tasks in the queue. To solve this problem, you should run the time-consuming task for processing the event in a separate thread. Java 6 introduced `SwingWorker`. `SwingWorker` is an abstract class that implements `Runnable`. You can define a task class that extends `SwingWorker`, run the time-consuming task and update the GUI using the results produced from the task. Figure 29.28 defines `SwingWorker`.

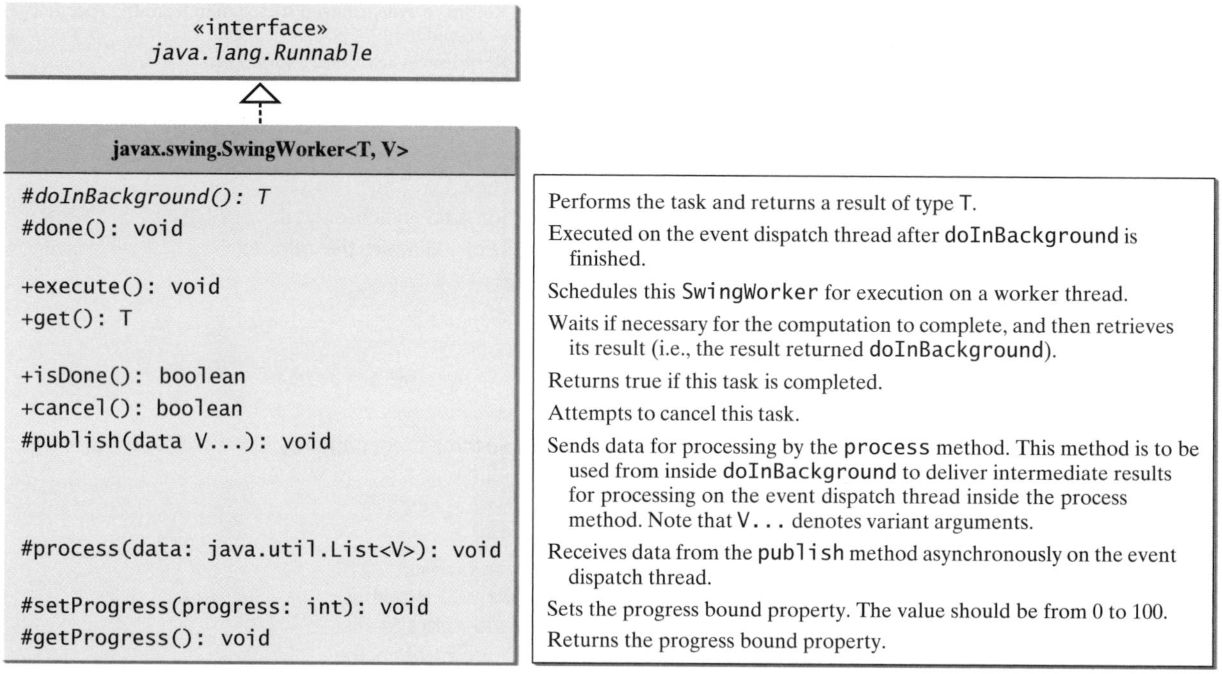
«interface»
java.lang.Runnable
javax.swing.SwingWorker<T, V>
#doInBackground(): T
#done(): void
+execute(): void
+get(): T
+isDone(): boolean
+cancel(): boolean
#publish(data V...): void
#process(data: java.util.List<V>): void
#setProgress(progress: int): void
#getProgress(): void
Performs the task and returns a result of type T.
Executed on the event dispatch thread after doInBackground is finished.
Schedules this SwingWorker for execution on a worker thread.
Waits if necessary for the computation to complete, and then retrieves its result (i.e., the result returned doInBackground).
Returns true if this task is completed.
Attempts to cancel this task.
Sends data for processing by the process method. This method is to be used from inside doInBackground to deliver intermediate results for processing on the event dispatch thread inside the process method. Note that V... denotes variant arguments.
Receives data from the publish method asynchronously on the event dispatch thread.
Sets the progress bound property. The value should be from 0 to 100.
Returns the progress bound property.

FIGURE 29.28 The `SwingWorker` class can be used to process time-consuming tasks.

This section demonstrates basic use of `SwingWorker`. The next section gives an example involving advanced features of `SwingWorker`.

doInBackground()

done()

To use `SwingWorker`, your task class should override `doInBackground()` to perform a time-consuming task and override the `done()` method to update GUI components if necessary. Listing 29.13 gives an example that lets the user specify a number and displays the number of prime numbers less than or equal to the specified number, as shown in Figure 29.29.

SwingWorkerDemo
Using SwingWorker
The number of prime numbers <= 100000 is 9592
Compute
Without Using SwingWorker
The number of prime numbers <= 100000 is 9592
Compute

FIGURE 29.29 You can compare the effect of using versus not using `SwingWorker`.

LISTING 29.13 SwingWorkerDemo.java

```java
import javax.swing.*;
import java.awt.*;
import java.awt.event.*;

public class SwingWorkerDemo extends JApplet {
  private JButton jbtComputeWithSwingWorker = new JButton("Compute");
  private JTextField jtfLimit1 = new JTextField(8);
  private JTextField jtfResult1 = new JTextField(6);
  private JButton jbtCompute = new JButton("Compute");
  private JTextField jtfLimit2 = new JTextField(8);
  private JTextField jtfResult2 = new JTextField(6);

  public SwingWorkerDemo() {
    JPanel panel1 = new JPanel(new GridLayout(2, 1));
    panel1.setBorder(BorderFactory.createTitledBorder(
      "Using SwingWorker"));
    JPanel panel11 = new JPanel();
    panel11.add(new JLabel("The number of prime numbers <= "));
    panel11.add(jtfLimit1);
    panel11.add(new JLabel("is"));
    panel11.add(jtfResult1);
    JPanel panel12 = new JPanel();
    panel12.add(jbtComputeWithSwingWorker);
    panel1.add(panel11);
    panel1.add(panel12);

    JPanel panel2 = new JPanel(new GridLayout(2, 1));
    panel2.setBorder(BorderFactory.createTitledBorder(
      "Without Using SwingWorker"));
    JPanel panel21 = new JPanel();
    panel21.add(new JLabel("The number of prime numbers <= "));
    panel21.add(jtfLimit2);
    panel21.add(new JLabel("is"));
    panel21.add(jtfResult2);
    JPanel panel22 = new JPanel();
    panel22.add(jbtCompute);
    panel2.add(panel21);
    panel2.add(panel22);

    setLayout(new GridLayout(1, 2));
    add(panel1);
    add(panel2);

    jbtComputeWithSwingWorker.addActionListener(new ActionListener() {
       public void actionPerformed(ActionEvent e) {
         new ComputePrime(Integer.parseInt(jtfLimit1.getText()),
           jtfResult1).execute(); // Execute SwingWorker
       }
     });

    jbtCompute.addActionListener(new ActionListener() {
      public void actionPerformed(ActionEvent e) {
        int count = ComputePrime.getNumberOfPrimes(
          Integer.parseInt(jtfLimit2.getText()));
        jtfResult2.setText(count + "");
      }
    });
```

GUI components
create UI
left panel
right panel
add listener
create task
create task
add listener

constructor

override **doInBackground()**

override **done()**

getNumberOfPrimes

main method omitted

```
  }

  /** Task class for SwingWorker */
  static class ComputePrime extends SwingWorker<Integer, Object> {
    private int limit;
    private JTextField result; // Text field in the UI

    /** Construct a runnable Task */
    public ComputePrime(int limit, JTextField result) {
      this.limit = limit;
      this.result = result;
    }

    /** Code run on a background thread */
    protected Integer doInBackground() {
      return getNumberOfPrimes(limit);
    }

    /** Code executed after the background thread finishes */
    protected void done() {
      try {
        result.setText(get().toString()); // Display in text field
      }
      catch (Exception ex) {
        result.setText(ex.getMessage());
      }
    }

    /** Return the number of primes <= limit */
    public static int getNumberOfPrimes(int limit) {
      int count = 0; // Count the number of prime numbers
      int number = 2; // A number to be tested for primeness

      // Repeatedly find prime numbers
      while (number <= limit) {
         // Print the prime number and increase the count
         if (isPrime(number)) {
           count++; // Increase the count
         }

         // Check if the next number is prime
         number++;
       }

       return count;
     }

     /** Check whether number is prime */
     private static boolean isPrime(int number) {
       for (int divisor = 2; divisor <= number / 2; divisor++) {
         if (number % divisor == 0) { // If true, number is not prime
           return false; // number is not a prime
         }
       }

       return true; // number is prime
     }
  }
}
```

The UI consists of two panels. The left panel demonstrates how to compute the number of prime numbers using a `SwingWorker`. The right panel demonstrates how to compute the number of prime numbers without using a `SwingWorker`. You enter a number (e.g., 100000) in the first text field in the panel and click the *Compute* button to display the number of primes in the second text field. When you click the *Compute* button in the left panel, a `SwingWorker` task is created and executed (lines 46–47). Since the task is run on a separate thread, you can continue to use the GUI. However, when you click the *Compute* button in the right panel, the GUI is frozen, because the `getNumberOfPrimes` method is executed on the event dispatch thread (lines 53–54).

using or not using **SwingWorker**

The inner class `ComputePrime` is a `SwingWorker` (line 61). It overrides the `doInBackground` method to run `getNumberOfPrimes` in a background thread (lines 72–74). It also overrides the `done` method to display the result in a text field, once the background thread finishes (lines 77–84).

override **doInBackground**

override **done**

The `ComputePrime` class defines the static `getNumberOfPrimes` method for computing the number of primes (lines 87–103). When you click the *Compute* button in the left panel, this method is executed on a background thread (lines 46–47). When you click the *Compute* button in the right panel, this method is executed in the event dispatch thread (lines 53–54).

static **getNumberOfPrimes**

Tip

Two things to remember when writing Swing GUI programs:

GUI and **SwingWorker**

- Time-consuming tasks should be run in `SwingWorker`.
- Swing components should be accessed from the event dispatch thread only.

29.19 Displaying Progress Using **JProgressBar**

In the preceding example, it may take a long time to finish the computation in the background thread. It is better to inform the user the progress of the computation. You can use the `JProgressBar` to display the progress.

`JProgressBar` is a component that displays a value graphically within a bounded interval. A progress bar is typically used to show the percentage of completion of a lengthy operation; it comprises a rectangular bar that is "filled in" from left to right horizontally or from bottom to top vertically as the operation is performed. It provides the user with feedback on the progress of the operation. For example, when a file is being read, it alerts the user to the progress of the operation, thereby keeping the user attentive.

`JProgressBar` is often implemented using a thread to monitor the completion status of other threads. The progress bar can be displayed horizontally or vertically, as determined by its `orientation` property. The `minimum`, `value`, and `maximum` properties determine the minimum, current, and maximum lengths on the progress bar, as shown in Figure 29.30. Figure 29.31 lists frequently used features of `JProgressBar`.

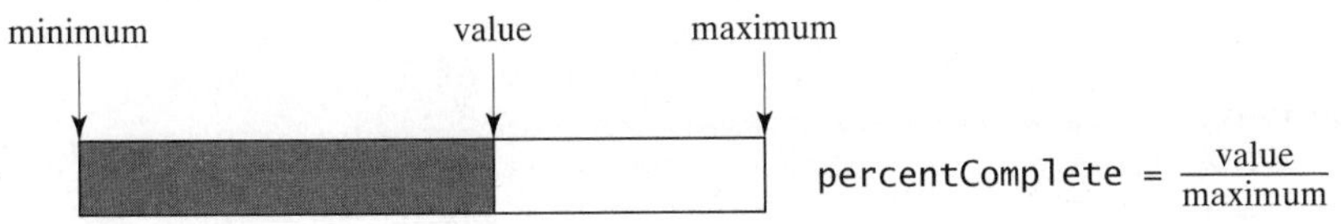
minimum
value
maximum
percentComplete = value / maximum

FIGURE 29.30 `JProgressBar` displays the progress of a task.

Listing 29.14 gives an example that lets the user specify the number of primes, say *n*, and displays the first *n* primes starting from 2, as shown in Figure 29.32. The program displays the primes in the text area and updates the completion status in a progress bar.

javax.swing.JComponent
↑
javax.swing.JProgressBar

`+JProgressBar()`	Creates a horizontal progress bar with min 0 and max 100.
`+JProgressBar(min: int, max: int)`	Creates a horizontal progress bar with specified min and max.
`+JProgressBar(orient: int)`	Creates a progress bar with min 0 and max 100 and a specified orientation.
`+JProgressBar(orient: int, min: int, max: int)`	Creates a progress bar with a specified orientation, min, and max.
`+getMaximum(): int`	Gets the maximum value (default: 100).
`+setMaximum(n: int): void`	Sets a new maximum value.
`+getMinimum(): int`	Gets the minimum value (default: 0).
`+setMinimum(n: int): void`	Sets a new minimum value.
`+getOrientation(): int`	Gets the orientation value (default: `HORIZONTAL`).
`+setOrientation(orient: int): void`	Sets a new minimum value.
`+getPercentComplete(): double`	Returns the percent complete for the progress bar.
`+getValue(): int`	Returns the progress bar's current value.
`+setValue(n: int): void`	Sets the progress bar's current value.
`+getString(): String`	Returns the current value of the progress string.
`+setString(s: String): void`	Sets the value of the progress string.
`+isStringPainted(): boolean`	Returns the value of the `stringPainted` property.
`+setStringPainted(b: boolean): void`	Sets the value of the `stringPainted` property, which determines whether the progress bar should render a progress percentage string (default: false).

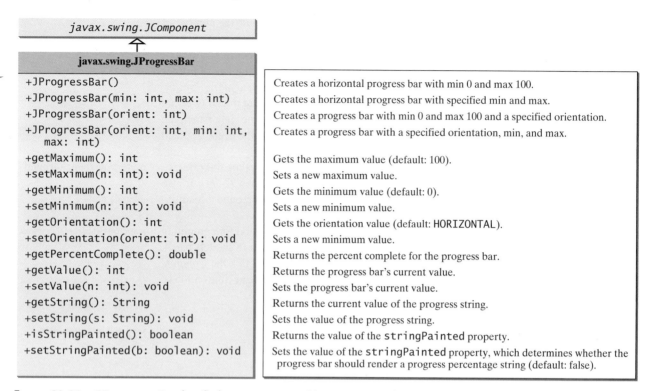

FIGURE 29.31 `JProgressBar` is a Swing component with many properties that enable you to customize a progress bar.

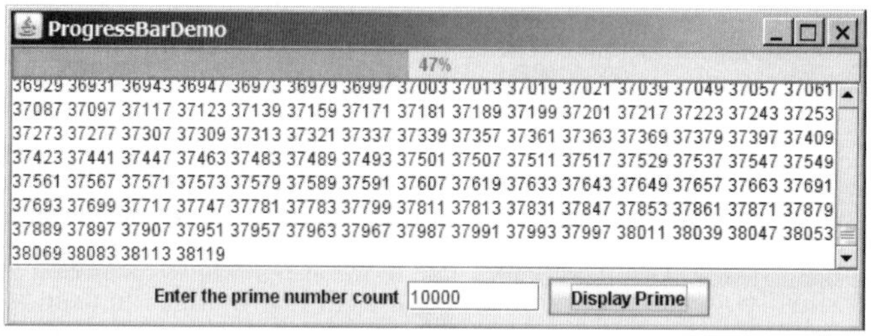
ProgressBarDemo
47%
Enter the prime number count
10000
Display Prime

FIGURE 29.32 The user enters the number of prime numbers and clicks the Display Prime button to display the primes starting from 2 to the text area.

LISTING 29.14 ProgressBarDemo.java

progress bar

JProgressBar properties UI

```
import javax.swing.*;
import java.awt.*;
import java.awt.event.*;
import java.beans.*;

public class ProgressBarDemo extends JApplet {
  private JProgressBar jpb = new JProgressBar();
  private JTextArea jtaResult = new JTextArea();
  private JTextField jtfPrimeCount = new JTextField(8);
  private JButton jbtDisplayPrime = new JButton("Display Prime");

  public ProgressBarDemo() {
    jpb.setStringPainted(true); // Paint the percent in a string
    jpb.setValue(0);
    jpb.setMaximum(100);

```

```
    jtaResult.setWrapStyleWord(true);
    jtaResult.setLineWrap(true);

    JPanel panel = new JPanel();
    panel.add(new JLabel("Enter the prime number count"));
    panel.add(jtfPrimeCount);
    panel.add(jbtDisplayPrime);

    add(jpb, BorderLayout.NORTH);
    add(new JScrollPane(jtaResult), BorderLayout.CENTER);
    add(panel, BorderLayout.SOUTH);

    jbtDisplayPrime.addActionListener(new ActionListener() {
      public void actionPerformed(ActionEvent e) {
        ComputePrime task = new ComputePrime(
          Integer.parseInt(jtfPrimeCount.getText()), jtaResult);

        task.addPropertyChangeListener(new PropertyChangeListener() {
          public void propertyChange(PropertyChangeEvent e) {
            if ("progress".equals(e.getPropertyName())) {
              jpb.setValue((Integer)e.getNewValue());
            }
          }
        });

        task.execute(); // Execute SwingWorker
      }
    });
  }

  /** Task class for SwingWorker */
  static class ComputePrime extends SwingWorker<Integer, Integer> {
    private int count;
    private JTextArea result; // Textarea in the UI

    /** Construct a runnable Task */
    public ComputePrime(int count, JTextArea result) {
      this.count = count;
      this.result = result;
    }

    /** Code run on a background thread */
    protected Integer doInBackground() {
      publishPrimeNumbers(count);

      return 0; // doInBackground must return a value
    }

    /** Override process to display published prime values */
    protected void process(java.util.List<Integer> list) {
      for (int i = 0; i < list.size(); i++)
        result.append(list.get(i) + " ");
    }

    /** Publish the first n prime number */
    private void publishPrimeNumbers(int n) {
      int count = 0; // Count the number of prime numbers
      int number = 2; // A number to be tested for primeness

```

wrap word
wrap line
add button listener
create task
add property listener
get property value
execute task
task class
override **doInBackground**
override **process**
compute primes

set progress property

publish a prime

main method omitted

```
76       // Repeatedly find prime numbers
77       while (count <= n) {
78         // Print the prime number and increase the count
79         if (isPrime(number)) {
80           count++; // Increase the count
81           setProgress(100 * count / n); // Update progress
82           publish(number); // Publish the prime number
83         }
84
85         // Check if the next number is prime
86         number++;
87       }
88     }
89
90     /** Check whether number is prime */
91     private static boolean isPrime(int number) {
92       for (int divisor = 2; divisor <= number / 2; divisor++) {
93         if (number % divisor == 0) { // If true, number is not prime
94           return false; // number is not a prime
95         }
96       }
97
98       return true; // number is prime
99     }
100  }
101 }
```

The **SwingWorker** class generates a **PropertyChangeEvent** whenever the **setProgress** method is invoked. The **setProgress** method (line 81) sets a new progress value between **0** and **100**. This value is wrapped in the **PropertyChangeEvent**. The listener of this event can obtain the progress value using the **getNewValue()** method (line 37). The progress bar is updated using this new progress value (line 37).

The program creates a **JProgressBar** (line 7) and sets its properties (lines 13–15).

override **doInBackground**

The inner class **ComputePrime** is a **SwingWorker** (line 48). It overrides the **doInBackground** method to run **publishPrimeNumbers** in a background thread (line 60). The **publishPrimeNumbers** method finds the specified number of primes starting from **2**. When a prime is found, the **setProgress** method is invoked to set a new progress value (line 81). This causes a **PropertyChangeEvent** to be fired, which is notified to the listener.

override **process**

When a prime is found, the **publish** method is invoked to send the data to the **process** method (line 82). The **process** method is overridden (lines 66–69) to display the primes sent from the **publish** method. The primes are displayed in the text area (line 68).

Key Terms

condition 991
deadlock 1001
event dispatch thread 1004
fail-fast 1003
fairness policy 989
lock 988
monitor 994
multithreading 972
race condition 987
synchronization wrapper 1003
synchronized 988
thread 972
thread-safe 987

Chapter Summary

1. Each task is an instance of the **Runnable** interface. A *thread* is an object that facilitates the execution of a task. You can define a task class by implementing the **Runnable** interface and create a thread by wrapping a task using a **Thread** constructor.

2. After a thread object is created, use the `start()` method to start a thread, and the `sleep(long)` method to put a thread to sleep so that other threads get a chance to run.

3. A thread object never directly invokes the `run` method. The JVM invokes the `run` method when it is time to execute the thread. Your class must override the `run` method to tell the system what the thread will do when it runs.

4. To prevent threads from corrupting a shared resource, use synchronized methods or blocks. A synchronized method acquires a lock before it executes. In the case of an instance method, the lock is on the object for which the method was invoked. In the case of a static (class) method, the lock is on the class.

5. A synchronized statement can be used to acquire a lock on any object, not just *this* object, when executing a block of the code in a method. This block is referred to as a *synchronized block*.

6. You can use explicit locks and conditions to facilitate communications among threads, as well as using the built-in monitor for objects.

7. *Deadlock* occurs when two or more threads acquire locks on multiple objects and each has a lock on one object and is waiting for the lock on the other object. The *resource ordering technique* can be used to avoid deadlock.

8. You can define a task class that extends `SwingWorker`, run the time-consuming task, and update the GUI using the results produced from the task.

9. You can use a `JProgressBar` to track the progress of a thread.

Review Questions

Sections 29.1–29.4

29.1 Why do you need multithreading? How can multiple threads run simultaneously in a single-processor system?

29.2 How do you define a task class? How do you create a thread for a task?

29.3 What would happen if you replaced the `start()` method by the `run()` method in lines 14–16 in Listing 29.1?

```
print100.start();                     print100.run();
printA.start();     Replaced by -->   printA.run();
printB.start();                       printB.run();
```

29.4 What is wrong in the following two programs? Correct the errors.

```
public class Test implements Runnable {
  public static void main(String[] args) {
    new Test();
  }

  public Test() {
    Test task = new Test();
    new Thread(task).start();
  }

  public void run(){
    System.out.println("test");
  }
}
```

(a)

```
public class Test implements Runnable {
  public static void main(String[] args) {
    new Test();
  }

  public Test() {
    Thread t = new Thread(this);
    t.start();
    t.start();

  }
  public void run() {
    System.out.println("test");
  }
}
```

(b)

29.5 Which of the following methods are instance methods in `java.lang.Thread`? Which method may throw an `InterruptedException`? Which of them are deprecated in Java?

```
run, start, stop, suspend, resume, sleep, interrupt, yield, join
```

29.6 If a loop contains a method that throws an `InterruptedException`, why should the loop be placed inside a try-catch block?

29.7 How do you set a priority for a thread? What is the default priority?

Sections 29.5–29.7

29.8 When should you use a timer or a thread to control animation? What are the advantages and disadvantages of using a thread and a timer?

29.9 What is the event dispatch thread? How do you let a task run from the event dispatch thread?

Section 29.8

29.10 What are the benefits of using a thread pool?

29.11 How do you create a thread pool with three fixed threads? How do you submit a task to a thread pool? How do you know that all the tasks are finished?

Sections 29.9–29.12

29.12 Give some examples of possible resource corruption when running multiple threads. How do you synchronize conflicting threads?

29.13 Suppose you place the statement in line 26 of Listing 29.7 AccountWithoutSync.java inside a synchronized block to avoid race conditions, as follows:

```
synchronized (this) {
  account.deposit(1);
}
```

Does it work?

29.14 How do you create a lock object? How do you acquire a lock and release a lock?

29.15 How do you create a condition on a lock? What are the `await()`, `signal()`, and `signalAll()` methods for?

29.16 What would happen if the `while` loop in line 58 of Listing 29.9 ThreadCooperation.java were changed to an `if` statement?

`while (balance < amount)` → Replaced by → `if (balance < amount)`

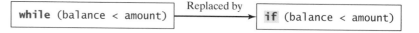

29.17 Why does the following class have a syntax error?

```
import javax.swing.*;

public class Test extends JApplet implements Runnable {
  public void init() throws InterruptedException {
    Thread thread = new Thread(this);
    thread.sleep(1000);
  }

  public synchronized void run() {
  }
}
```

29.18 What is the possible cause for `IllegalMonitorStateException`?

29.19 Can the `wait()`, `notify()`, and `notifyAll()` be invoked from any object? What is the purpose of these methods?

29.20 What is wrong in the following code?

```
synchronized (object1) {
  try {
    while (!condition) object2.wait();
  }
  catch (InterruptedException ex) {
  }
}
```

Section 29.13

29.21 What blocking queues are supported in Java?

29.22 What method do you use to add an element to an `ArrayBlockingQueue`? What happens if the queue is full?

29.23 What method do you use to retrieve an element from an `ArrayBlockingQueue`? What happens if the queue is empty?

Section 29.14

29.24 What are the similarities and differences between a lock and a semaphore?

29.25 How do you create a semaphore that allows three concurrent threads? How do you acquire a semaphore? How do you release a semaphore?

Section 29.15

29.26 What is deadlock? How can you avoid deadlock?

Section 29.17

29.27 What is a synchronized collection? Is `ArrayList` synchronized? How do you make it synchronized?

29.28 Explain why an iterator is fail-fast.

Section 29.19

29.29 For a `JProgressBar`, what is the property that displays the percentage of work completed? How do you set its orientation?

Programming Exercises

Sections 29.1–29.5

29.1* (*Revising Listing 29.1*) Rewrite Listing 29.1 to display the output in a text area, as shown in Figure 29.33.

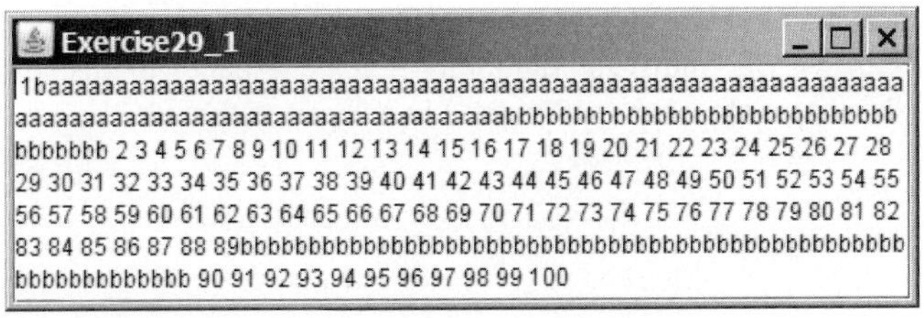
Exercise29_1
bbbbbbb 2 3 4 5 6 7 8 9 10 11 12 13 14 15 16 17 18 19 20 21 22 23 24 25 26 27 28
29 30 31 32 33 34 35 36 37 38 39 40 41 42 43 44 45 46 47 48 49 50 51 52 53 54 55
56 57 58 59 60 61 62 63 64 65 66 67 68 69 70 71 72 73 74 75 76 77 78 79 80 81 82
bbbbbbbbbbbbb 90 91 92 93 94 95 96 97 98 99 100

FIGURE 29.33 The output from three threads is displayed in a text area.

29.2 (*Racing cars*) Rewrite Exercise 18.17 using a thread to control car racing. Compare the program with Exercise 18.17 by setting the delay time to 10 in both programs. Which one runs animation faster?

29.3 (*Raising flags*) Rewrite Exercise 18.23 using a thread to animate flag rising. Compare the program with Exercise 18.23 by setting the delay time to 10 in both programs. Which one runs animation faster?

Sections 29.8–29.12

29.4 (*Synchronizing threads*) Write a program that launches 1000 threads. Each thread adds `1` to a variable `sum` that initially is `0`. You need to pass `sum` by reference to each thread. In order to pass it by reference, define an `Integer` wrapper object to hold `sum`. Run the program with and without synchronization to see its effect.

29.5 (*Running fans*) Rewrite Exercise 18.11 using a thread to control fan animation.

29.6 (*Bouncing balls*) Rewrite Exercise 18.19 using a thread to control car racing.

29.7 (*Controlling a group of clocks*) Rewrite Exercise 18.14 using a thread to control clock animation.

29.8 (*Account synchronization*) Rewrite Listing 29.9, ThreadCooperation.java, using object's `wait()` and `notifyAll()` methods.

29.9 (*Demonstrating `ConcurrentModificationException`*) The iterator is *fail-fast*. Write a program to demonstrate it by creating two threads that concurrently access and modify a set. The first thread creates a hash set filled with numbers, and adds a new number to the set every second. The second thread obtains an iterator for the set and traverses the set back and forth through the iterator every second. You will receive a `ConcurrentModificationException` because the underlying set is being modified in the first thread while the set in the second thread is being traversed.

29.10* (*Using synchronized sets*) Using synchronization, correct the problem in the preceding exercise so that the second thread does not throw `ConcurrentModificationException`.

Section 29.15

29.11* (*Demonstrating deadlock*) Write a program that demonstrates deadlock.

Section 29.18

29.12* (*Using `JProgressBar`*) Create a program that displays an instance of `JProgressBar` and sets its `value` property randomly every 500 milliseconds infinitely.

Comprehensive

29.13*** (*Sorting animation*) Write an animation applet for selection sort, insertion sort, and bubble sort, as shown in Figure 29.34. Create an array of integers `1, 2, ..., 50`. Shuffle it randomly. Create a panel to display the array. You should invoke each sort method in a separate thread.

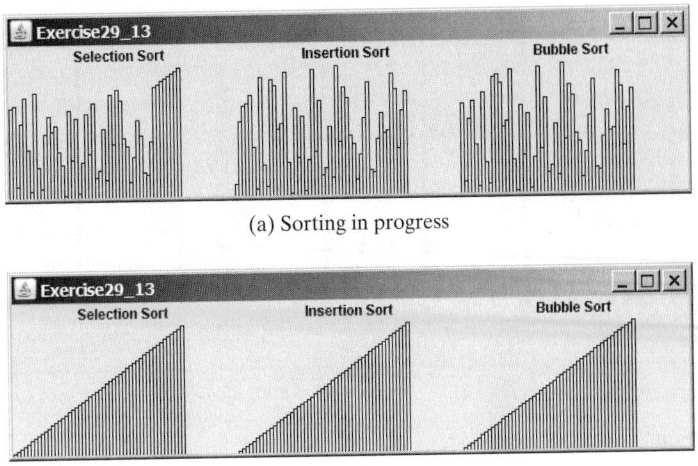
Exercise29_13
Selection Sort
Insertion Sort
Bubble Sort
Exercise29_13
Selection Sort
Insertion Sort
Bubble Sort

(a) Sorting in progress

(b) Sorted

FIGURE 29.34 Three sorting algorithms are illustrated in the animation.

29.14** (*Copying files*) Write a GUI application that copies files. A progress bar is used to display the progress of the copying operation, as shown in Figure 29.35(a).

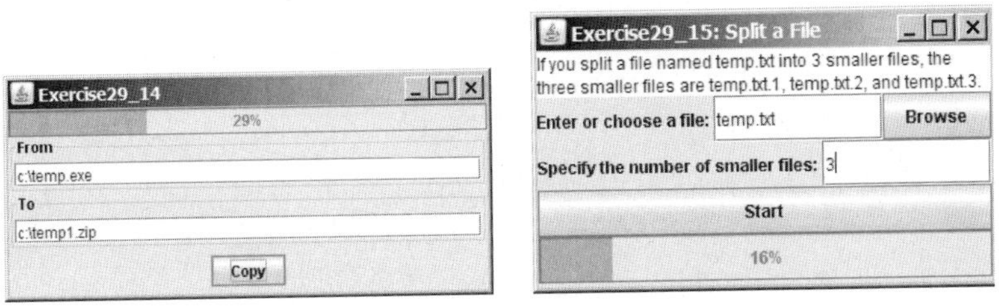
Exercise29_14
29%
From
c:\temp.exe
To
c:\temp1.zip
Copy
Exercise29_15: Split a File
If you split a file named temp.txt into 3 smaller files, the three smaller files are temp.txt.1, temp.txt.2, and temp.txt.3.
Enter or choose a file: temp.txt
Browse
Specify the number of smaller files: 3
Start
16%

(a) (b)

FIGURE 29.35 (a) The user enters the files in the text fields and clicks the *Copy* button to start copying files. (b) The program split a file into several smaller files.

29.15** (*Splitting a file*) Modify Exercise 19.11 to display the percentage of work done in a progress bar, as shown in Figure 29.35(b).

29.16*** (*Sudoku search simulation*) Modify Exercise 18.25 to display the intermediate results of the search. As shown in Figure 29.36(a), number 2 is placed in the first row and last column. This number is invalid, so, the next value 3 is placed in Figure 29.36(b). This number is still invalid, so, the next value 4 is placed in Figure 29.36(c). The simulation displays all the search steps.

Exercise29_16
Solve
Clear

(a) (b) (c)

FIGURE 29.36 The intermediate search steps are displayed in the simulation.

Chapter 30

Networking

Objectives

- To explain terms: TCP, IP, domain name, domain name server, stream-based communication, and packet-based communications (§30.1).
- To create servers using server sockets (§30.2.1) and create clients using client sockets (§30.2.2).
- To implement Java networking programs using stream sockets (§30.2.3).
- To obtain Internet addresses using the `InetAddress` class (§30.3).
- To develop servers for multiple clients (§30.4).
- To develop applets that communicate with the server (§30.5).
- To send and receive objects on a network (§30.6).
- To create applications or applets to retrieve files from a network (§30.7).
- To render HTML files using the `JEditorPane` class (§30.8).
- To develop an interactive `TicTacToe` game played on the Internet (§30.9).

30.1 Introduction

To browse the Web or send email, your computer must be connected to the Internet. The Internet is the global network of millions of computers. Your computer may connect to the Internet through an Internet Service Provider (ISP) using dialup, DSL, or cable modem, or through a local area network (LAN).

When a computer needs to communicate with another computer, it needs to know the other computer's address. An *Internet Protocol* (IP) address uniquely identifies the computer on the Internet. An IP address consists of four dotted decimal numbers between `0` and `255`, such as `130.254.204.36`. Since it is not easy to remember so many numbers, they are often mapped to meaningful names called *domain names*, such as `drake.armstrong.edu`. Special servers called *Domain Name Servers* (DNS) on the Internet translate host names into IP addresses. When a computer contacts `drake.armstrong.edu`, it first asks the DNS to translate this domain name into a numeric IP address and then sends the request using the IP address.

IP address

domain name

domain name server

The Internet Protocol is a low-level protocol for delivering data from one computer to another across the Internet in packets. Two higher-level protocols used in conjunction with the IP are the *Transmission Control Protocol* (TCP) and the *User Datagram Protocol* (UDP). TCP enables two hosts to establish a connection and exchange streams of data. TCP guarantees delivery of data and also guarantees that packets will be delivered in the same order in which they were sent. UDP is a standard, low-overhead, connectionless, host-to-host protocol that is used over the IP. UDP allows an application program on one computer to send a datagram to an application program on another computer.

TCP

Java supports both *stream-based* and *packet-based communications*. *Stream-based communications* use TCP (Transmission Control Protocol) for data transmission, whereas *packet-based communications* use UDP (User Datagram Protocol). Since TCP can detect lost transmissions and resubmit them, transmissions are lossless and reliable. UDP, in contrast, cannot guarantee lossless transmission. Stream-based communications are used in most areas of Java programming and are the focus of this chapter. Packet-based communications are introduced in Supplement III.T, "Networking Using Datagram Protocol."

stream-based

packet-based

30.2 Client/Server Computing

Networking is tightly integrated in Java. Java API provides the classes for creating sockets to facilitate program communications over the Internet. *Sockets* are the endpoints of logical connections between two hosts and can be used to send and receive data. Java treats socket communications much as it treats I/O operations; thus programs can read from or write to sockets as easily as they can read from or write to files.

socket

Network programming usually involves a server and one or more clients. The client sends requests to the server, and the server responds. The client begins by attempting to establish a connection to the server. The server can accept or deny the connection. Once a connection is established, the client and the server communicate through sockets.

The server must be running when a client attempts to connect to the server. The server waits for a connection request from a client. The statements needed to create sockets on a server and a client are shown in Figure 30.1.

30.2.1 Server Sockets

To establish a server, you need to create a *server socket* and attach it to a port, which is where the server listens for connections. The port identifies the TCP service on the socket. Port numbers range from 0 to 65536, but port numbers 0 to 1024 are reserved for privileged services. For instance, the email server runs on port 25, and the Web server usually runs on port 80.

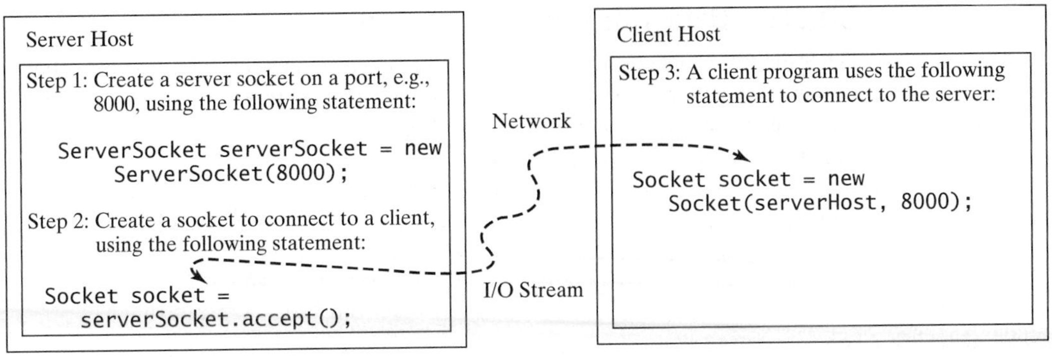
Server Host
Step 1: Create a server socket on a port, e.g., 8000, using the following statement:
ServerSocket serverSocket = new ServerSocket(8000);
Step 2: Create a socket to connect to a client, using the following statement:
Socket socket = serverSocket.accept();
Network
I/O Stream
Client Host
Step 3: A client program uses the following statement to connect to the server:
Socket socket = new Socket(serverHost, 8000);

FIGURE 30.1 The server creates a server socket and, once a connection to a client is established, connects to the client with a client socket.

You can choose any port number that is not currently used by any other process. The following statement creates a server socket `serverSocket`:

```
ServerSocket serverSocket = new ServerSocket(port);
```

server socket

Note

Attempting to create a server socket on a port already in use would cause the `java.net.BindException`.

BindException

30.2.2 Client Sockets

After a server socket is created, the server can use the following statement to listen for connections:

```
Socket socket = serverSocket.accept();
```

This statement waits until a client connects to the server socket. The client issues the following statement to request a connection to a server:

connect to client

```
Socket socket = new Socket(serverName, port);
```

This statement opens a socket so that the client program can communicate with the server. `serverName` is the server's Internet host name or IP address. The following statement creates a socket at port 8000 on the client machine to connect to the host 130.254.204.36:

client socket

```
Socket socket = new Socket("130.254.204.36", 8000)
```

use IP address

Alternatively, you can use the domain name to create a socket, as follows:

```
Socket socket = new Socket("drake.armstrong.edu", 8000);
```

use domain name

When you create a socket with a host name, the JVM asks the DNS to translate the host name into the IP address.

Note

A program can use the host name `localhost` or the IP address `127.0.0.1` to refer to the machine on which a client is running.

localhost

Note

The `Socket` constructor throws a `java.net.UnknownHostException` if the host cannot be found.

UnknownHostException

30.2.3 Data Transmission through Sockets

After the server accepts the connection, communication between server and client is conducted the same as for I/O streams. The statements needed to create the streams and to exchange data between them are shown in Figure 30.2.

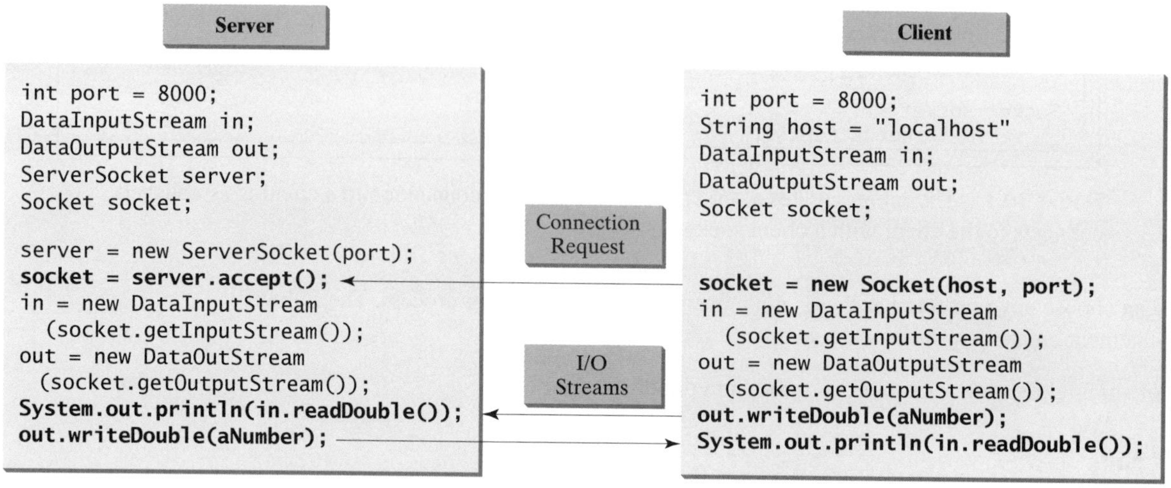
Server
int port = 8000;
DataInputStream in;
DataOutputStream out;
ServerSocket server;
Socket socket;
server = new ServerSocket(port);
socket = server.accept();
in = new DataInputStream
(socket.getInputStream());
out = new DataOutStream
(socket.getOutputStream());
System.out.println(in.readDouble());
out.writeDouble(aNumber);
Connection Request
I/O Streams
Client
int port = 8000;
String host = "localhost"
DataInputStream in;
DataOutputStream out;
Socket socket;
socket = new Socket(host, port);
in = new DataInputStream
(socket.getInputStream());
out = new DataOutputStream
(socket.getOutputStream());
out.writeDouble(aNumber);
System.out.println(in.readDouble());

FIGURE 30.2 The server and client exchange data through I/O streams on top of the socket.

To get an input stream and an output stream, use the `getInputStream()` and `getOutputStream()` methods on a socket object. For example, the following statements create an `InputStream` stream called `input` and an `OutputStream` stream called `output` from a socket:

```
InputStream input = socket.getInputStream();
OutputStream output = socket.getOutputStream();
```

The `InputStream` and `OutputStream` streams are used to read or write bytes. You can use `DataInputStream`, `DataOutputStream`, `BufferedReader`, and `PrintWriter` to wrap on the `InputStream` and `OutputStream` to read or write data, such as `int`, `double`, or `String`. The following statements, for instance, create a `DataInputStream` stream, `input`, and a `DataOutput` stream, `output`, to read and write primitive data values:

```
DataInputStream input = new DataInputStream
  (socket.getInputStream());
DataOutputStream output = new DataOutputStream
  (socket.getOutputStream());
```

The server can use `input.readDouble()` to receive a `double` value from the client, and `output.writeDouble(d)` to send `double` value `d` to the client.

Tip

Recall that binary I/O is more efficient than text I/O because text I/O requires encoding and decoding. Therefore it is better to use binary I/O for transmitting data between a server and a client to improve performance.

30.2.3 A Client/Server Example

This example presents a client program and a server program. The client sends data to a server. The server receives the data, uses it to produce a result, and then sends the result back to the client. The client displays the result on the console. In this example, the data sent from the client comprise the radius of a circle, and the result produced by the server is the area of the circle (see Figure 30.3).

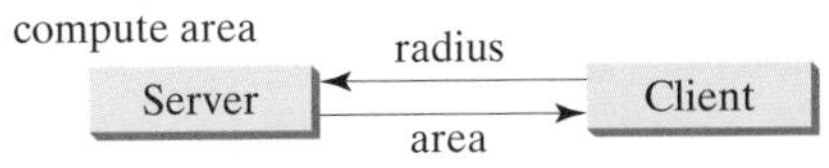
compute area
Server
radius
area
Client

FIGURE 30.3 The client sends the radius to the server; the server computes the area and sends it to the client.

The client sends the radius through a `DataOutputStream` on the output stream socket, and the server receives the radius through the `DataInputStream` on the input stream socket, as shown in Figure 30.4(a). The server computes the area and sends it to the client through a `DataOutputStream` on the output stream socket, and the client receives the area through a `DataInputStream` on the input stream socket, as shown in Figure 30.4(b). The server and client programs are given in Listings 30.1 and 30.2. Figure 30.5 contains a sample run of the server and the client.

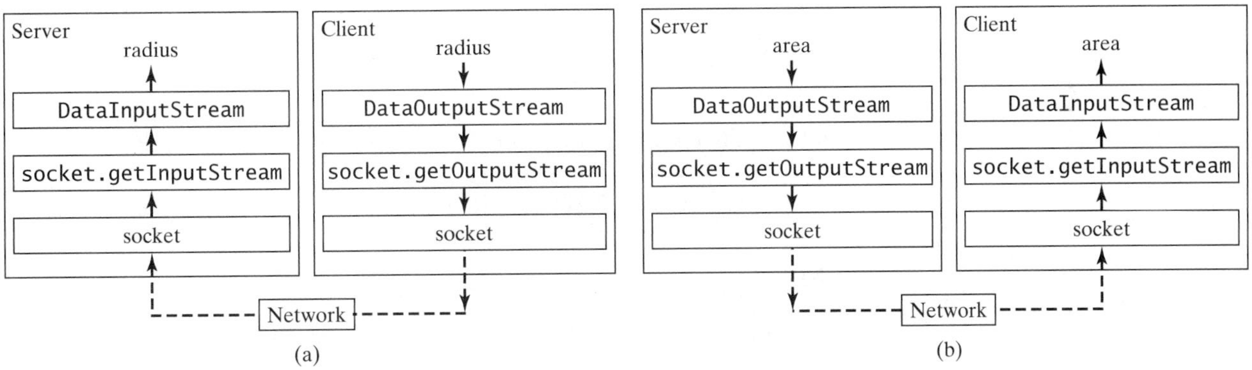
Server
radius
DataInputStream
socket.getInputStream
socket
Client
radius
DataOutputStream
socket.getOutputStream
socket
Network
(a)
Server
area
DataOutputStream
socket.getOutputStream
socket
Client
area
DataInputStream
socket.getInputStream
socket
Network
(b)

FIGURE 30.4 (a) The client sends the radius to the server. (b) The server sends the area to the client.

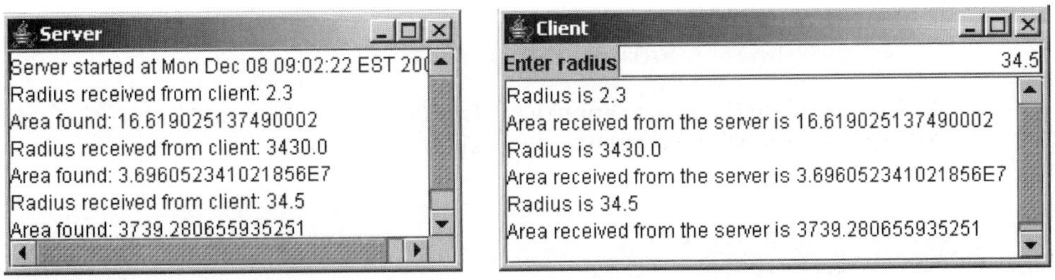
Server
Server started at Mon Dec 08 09:02:22 EST 20
Radius received from client: 2.3
Area found: 16.619025137490002
Radius received from client: 3430.0
Area found: 3.696052341021856E7
Radius received from client: 34.5
Area found: 3739.280655935251
Client
Enter radius
34.5
Radius is 2.3
Area received from the server is 16.619025137490002
Radius is 3430.0
Area received from the server is 3.696052341021856E7
Radius is 34.5
Area received from the server is 3739.280655935251

FIGURE 30.5 The client sends the radius to the server. The server receives it, computes the area, and sends the area to the client.

LISTING 30.1 `Server.java`

```
import java.io.*;
import java.net.*;
import java.util.*;
import java.awt.*;
import javax.swing.*;

```

launch server
server socket
connect client
input from client
output to client
read radius
write area

```java
public class Server extends JFrame {
  // Text area for displaying contents
  private JTextArea jta = new JTextArea();

  public static void main(String[] args) {
    new Server();
  }

  public Server() {
    // Place text area on the frame
    setLayout(new BorderLayout());
    add(new JScrollPane(jta), BorderLayout.CENTER);

    setTitle("Server");
    setSize(500, 300);
    setDefaultCloseOperation(JFrame.EXIT_ON_CLOSE);
    setVisible(true); // It is necessary to show the frame here!

    try {
      // Create a server socket
      ServerSocket serverSocket = new ServerSocket(8000);
      jta.append("Server started at " + new Date() + '\n');

      // Listen for a connection request
      Socket socket = serverSocket.accept();

      // Create data input and output streams
      DataInputStream inputFromClient = new DataInputStream(
        socket.getInputStream());
      DataOutputStream outputToClient = new DataOutputStream(
        socket.getOutputStream());

      while (true) {
        // Receive radius from the client
        double radius = inputFromClient.readDouble();

        // Compute area
        double area = radius * radius * Math.PI;

        // Send area back to the client
        outputToClient.writeDouble(area);

        jta.append("Radius received from client: " + radius + '\n');
        jta.append("Area found: " + area + '\n');
      }
    }
    catch(IOException ex) {
      System.err.println(ex);
    }
  }
}
```

LISTING 30.2 Client.java

```java
import java.io.*;
import java.net.*;
import java.awt.*;
import java.awt.event.*;
import javax.swing.*;
```

```java

public class Client extends JFrame {
  // Text field for receiving radius
  private JTextField jtf = new JTextField();

  // Text area to display contents
  private JTextArea jta = new JTextArea();

  // IO streams
  private DataOutputStream toServer;
  private DataInputStream fromServer;

  public static void main(String[] args) {
    new Client();
  }

  public Client() {
    // Panel p to hold the label and text field
    JPanel p = new JPanel();
    p.setLayout(new BorderLayout());
    p.add(new JLabel("Enter radius"), BorderLayout.WEST);
    p.add(jtf, BorderLayout.CENTER);
    jtf.setHorizontalAlignment(JTextField.RIGHT);

    setLayout(new BorderLayout());
    add(p, BorderLayout.NORTH);
    add(new JScrollPane(jta), BorderLayout.CENTER);

    jtf.addActionListener(new TextFieldListener());

    setTitle("Client");
    setSize(500, 300);
    setDefaultCloseOperation(JFrame.EXIT_ON_CLOSE);
    setVisible(true); // It is necessary to show the frame here!

    try {
      // Create a socket to connect to the server
      Socket socket = new Socket("localhost", 8000);
      // Socket socket = new Socket("130.254.204.36", 8000);
      // Socket socket = new Socket("drake.Armstrong.edu", 8000);

      // Create an input stream to receive data from the server
      fromServer = new DataInputStream(
        socket.getInputStream());

      // Create an output stream to send data to the server
      toServer =
        new DataOutputStream(socket.getOutputStream());
    }
    catch (IOException ex) {
      jta.append(ex.toString() + '\n');
    }
  }

  private class TextFieldListener implements ActionListener {
    public void actionPerformed(ActionEvent e) {
      try {
        // Get the radius from the text field
        double radius = Double.parseDouble(jtf.getText().trim());
```

launch client

register listener

request connection

input from server

output to server

write radius

read radius

```
65
66          // Send the radius to the server
67          toServer.writeDouble(radius);
68          toServer.flush();
69
70          // Get area from the server
71          double area = fromServer.readDouble();
72
73          // Display to the text area
74          jta.append("Radius is " + radius + "\n");
75          jta.append("Area received from the server is "
76            + area + '\n');
77        }
78        catch (IOException ex) {
79          System.err.println(ex);
80        }
81      }
82    }
83 }
```

You start the server program first, then start the client program. In the client program, enter a radius in the text field and press *Enter* to send the radius to the server. The server computes the area and sends it back to the client. This process is repeated until one of the two programs terminates.

The networking classes are in the package `java.net`. This should be imported when writing Java network programs.

The `Server` class creates a `ServerSocket serverSocket` and attaches it to port 8000, using this statement (line 27 in Server.java):

```
ServerSocket serverSocket = new ServerSocket(8000);
```

The server then starts to listen for connection requests, using the following statement (line 31 in Server.java):

```
Socket socket = serverSocket.accept();
```

The server waits until a client requests a connection. After it is connected, the server reads the radius from the client through an input stream, computes the area, and sends the result to the client through an output stream.

The `Client` class uses the following statement to create a socket that will request a connection to the server on the same machine (localhost) at port 8000 (line 43 in Client.java).

```
Socket socket = new Socket("localhost", 8000);
```

If you run the server and the client on different machines, replace `localhost` with the server machine's host name or IP address. In this example, the server and the client are running on the same machine.

If the server is not running, the client program terminates with a `java.net.ConnectException`. After it is connected, the client gets input and output streams—wrapped by data input and output streams—in order to receive and send data to the server.

If you receive a `java.net.BindException` when you start the server, the server port is currently in use. You need to terminate the process that is using the server port and then restart the server.

What happens if the `setVisible(true)` statement in line 23 in Server.java is moved after the `try-catch` block in line 56 in Server.java? The frame will not be displayed, because the `while` loop in the `try-catch` block will not finish until the program terminates.

Note

When you create a server socket, you have to specify a port (e.g., 8000) for the socket. When a client connects to the server (line 43 in Client.java), a socket is created on the client. This socket has its own local port. This port number (e.g., 2047) is automatically chosen by the JVM, as shown in Figure 30.6.

client socket port

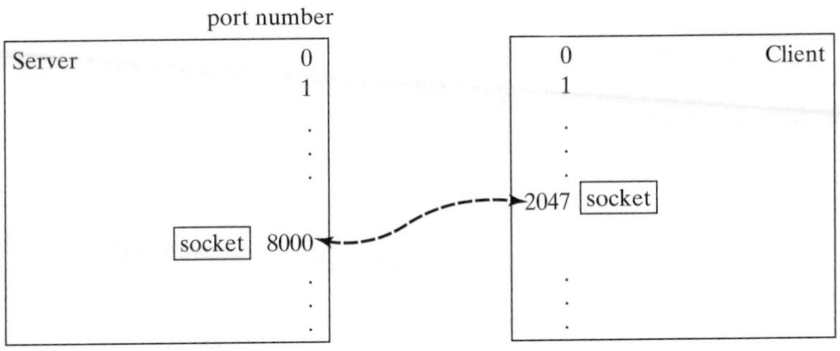
port number
Server
0
1
socket
8000
Client
0
1
2047
socket

FIGURE 30.6 The JVM automatically chooses an available port to create a socket for the client.

To see the local port on the client, insert the following statement in line 46 in Client.java.

```
System.out.println("local port: " + socket.getLocalPort());
```

30.3 The **InetAddress** Class

Occasionally, you would like to know who is connecting to the server. You can use the **InetAddress** class to find the client's host name and IP address. The **InetAddress** class models an IP address. You can use the statement shown below in the server program to get an instance of **InetAddress** on a socket that connects to the client.

```
InetAddress inetAddress = socket.getInetAddress();
```

Next, you can display the client's host name and IP address, as follows:

```
System.out.println("Client's host name is " +
  inetAddress.getHostName());
System.out.println("Client's IP Address is " +
  inetAddress.getHostAddress());
```

You can also create an instance of **InetAddress** from a host name or IP address using the static **getByName** method. For example, the following statement creates an **InetAddress** for the host **liang.armstrong.edu**.

```
InetAddress address = InetAddress.getByName("liang.armstrong.edu");
```

Listing 30.3 gives a program that identifies the host name and IP address of the arguments you pass in from the command line. Line 7 creates an **InetAddress** using the **getByName** method. Lines 8–9 use the **getHostName** and **getHostAddress** methods to get the host name and IP address. Figure 30.7 shows a sample run of the program.

LISTING 30.3 IdentifyHostNameIP.java

```
1 import java.net.*;
2
3 public class IdentifyHostNameIP {
4   public static void main(String[] args) {
```

get an InetAddress
get host name
get host IP

```
    for (int i = 0; i < args.length; i++) {
      try {
        InetAddress address = InetAddress.getByName(args[i]);
        System.out.print("Host name: " + address.getHostName() + " ");
        System.out.println("IP address: " + address.getHostAddress());
      }
      catch (UnknownHostException ex) {
        System.err.println("Unknown host or IP address " + args[i]);
      }
    }
  }
}
```

Administrator: Command Prompt
c:\book>java IdentifyHostNameIP www.whitehouse.gov 130.254.204.34
Host name: www.whitehouse.gov IP address: 96.7.106.135
Host name: panda.Armstrong.EDU IP address: 130.254.204.34
c:\book>

FIGURE 30.7 The program identifies host names and IP addresses.

30.4 Serving Multiple Clients

Multiple clients are quite often connected to a single server at the same time. Typically, a server runs continuously on a server computer, and clients from all over the Internet can connect to it. You can use threads to handle the server's multiple clients simultaneously. Simply create a thread for each connection. Here is how the server handles the establishment of a connection:

```
while (true) {
  Socket socket = serverSocket.accept(); // Connect to a client
  Thread thread = new ThreadClass(socket);
  thread.start();
}
```

The server socket can have many connections. Each iteration of the `while` loop creates a new connection. Whenever a connection is established, a new thread is created to handle communication between the server and the new client; and this allows multiple connections to run at the same time.

Listing 30.4 creates a server class that serves multiple clients simultaneously. For each connection, the server starts a new thread. This thread continuously receives input (the radius of a circle) from clients and sends the results (the area of the circle) back to them (see Figure 30.8). The client program is the same as in Listing 30.2. A sample run of the server with two clients is shown in Figure 30.9.

LISTING 30.4 MultiThreadServer.java

```
import java.io.*;
import java.net.*;
import java.util.*;
import java.awt.*;
import javax.swing.*;

public class MultiThreadServer extends JFrame {
  // Text area for displaying contents
```

```java
  private JTextArea jta = new JTextArea();

  public static void main(String[] args) {
    new MultiThreadServer();
  }

  public MultiThreadServer() {
    // Place text area on the frame
    setLayout(new BorderLayout());
    add(new JScrollPane(jta), BorderLayout.CENTER);

    setTitle("MultiThreadServer");
    setSize(500, 300);
    setDefaultCloseOperation(JFrame.EXIT_ON_CLOSE);
    setVisible(true); // It is necessary to show the frame here!

    try {
      // Create a server socket
      ServerSocket serverSocket = new ServerSocket(8000);
      jta.append("MultiThreadServer started at " + new Date() + '\n');

      // Number a client
      int clientNo = 1;

      while (true) {
        // Listen for a new connection request
        Socket socket = serverSocket.accept();

        // Display the client number
        jta.append("Starting thread for client " + clientNo +
          " at " + new Date() + '\n');

        // Find the client's host name, and IP address
        InetAddress inetAddress = socket.getInetAddress();
        jta.append("Client " + clientNo + "'s host name is "
          + inetAddress.getHostName() + "\n");
        jta.append("Client " + clientNo + "'s IP Address is "
          + inetAddress.getHostAddress() + "\n");

        // Create a new thread for the connection
        HandleAClient task = new HandleAClient(socket);

        // Start the new thread
        new Thread(task).start();

        // Increment clientNo
        clientNo++;
      }
    }
    catch(IOException ex) {
      System.err.println(ex);
    }
  }

  // Inner class
  // Define the thread class for handling new connection
  class HandleAClient implements Runnable {
    private Socket socket; // A connected socket

    /** Construct a thread */
```

server socket

connect client

network information

create task

start thread

task class

I/O

```
69     public HandleAClient(Socket socket) {
70       this.socket = socket;
71     }
72
73     /** Run a thread */
74     public void run() {
75       try {
76         // Create data input and output streams
77         DataInputStream inputFromClient = new DataInputStream(
78           socket.getInputStream());
79         DataOutputStream outputToClient = new DataOutputStream(
80           socket.getOutputStream());
81
82         // Continuously serve the client
83         while (true) {
84           // Receive radius from the client
85           double radius = inputFromClient.readDouble();
86
87           // Compute area
88           double area = radius * radius * Math.PI;
89
90           // Send area back to the client
91           outputToClient.writeDouble(area);
92
93           jta.append("radius received from client: " +
94             radius + '\n');
95           jta.append("Area found: " + area + '\n');
96         }
97       }
98       catch(IOException e) {
99         System.err.println(e);
100      }
101    }
102  }
103 }
```

The server creates a server socket at port 8000 (line 27) and waits for a connection (line 35). When a connection with a client is established, the server creates a new thread to handle the communication (line 49). It then waits for another connection in an infinite `while` loop (lines 33–56).

The threads, which run independently of one another, communicate with designated clients. Each thread creates data input and output streams that receive and send data to a client.

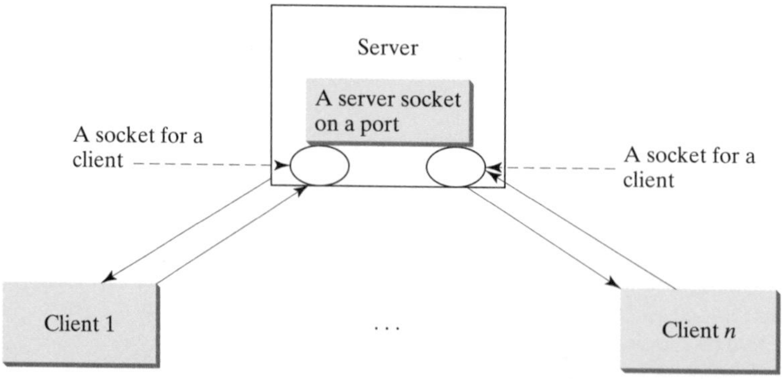
Server
A server socket on a port
A socket for a client
A socket for a client
Client 1
...
Client n

FIGURE 30.8 Multithreading enables a server to handle multiple independent clients.

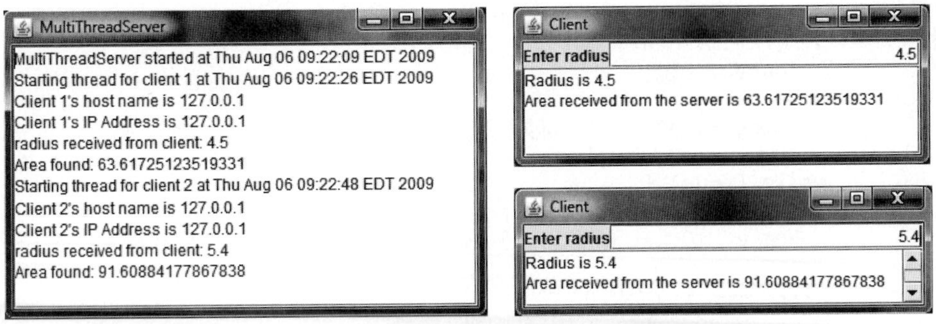
MultiThreadServer
MultiThreadServer started at Thu Aug 06 09:22:09 EDT 2009
Starting thread for client 1 at Thu Aug 06 09:22:26 EDT 2009
Client 1's host name is 127.0.0.1
Client 1's IP Address is 127.0.0.1
radius received from client: 4.5
Area found: 63.61725123519331
Starting thread for client 2 at Thu Aug 06 09:22:48 EDT 2009
Client 2's host name is 127.0.0.1
Client 2's IP Address is 127.0.0.1
radius received from client: 5.4
Area found: 91.60884177867838
Client
Enter radius
4.5
Radius is 4.5
Area received from the server is 63.61725123519331
Client
Enter radius
5.4
Radius is 5.4
Area received from the server is 91.60884177867838

FIGURE 30.9 The server spawns a thread in order to serve a client.

30.5 Applet Clients

Because of security constraints, applets can connect only to the host from which they were loaded. Therefore, the HTML file must be located on the machine on which the server is running. You can obtain the server's host name by invoking `getCodeBase().getHost()` on an applet, so you can write the applet without the host name fixed. Below is an example of how to use an applet to connect to a server.

The applet shows the number of visits made to a Web page. The count should be stored in a file on the server side. Every time the page is visited or reloaded, the applet sends a request to the server, and the server increases the count and sends it to the applet. The applet then displays the new count in a message, such as **You are visitor number 11**, as shown in Figure 30.10. The server and client programs are given in Listings 30.5 and 30.6.

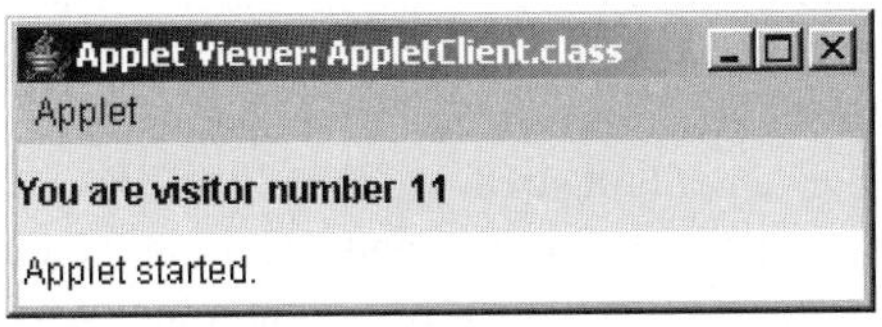
Applet Viewer: AppletClient.class
Applet
You are visitor number 11
Applet started.

FIGURE 30.10 The applet displays the access count on a Web page.

LISTING 30.5 CountServer.java

```
import java.io.*;
import java.net.*;

public class CountServer {
  private RandomAccessFile raf;
  private int count; // Count the access to the server

  public static void main(String[] args) {
    new CountServer();
  }

  public CountServer() {
    try {
      // Create a server socket
      ServerSocket serverSocket = new ServerSocket(8000);
      System.out.println("Server started ");

      // Create or open the count file
      raf = new RandomAccessFile("count.dat", "rw");

```

launch server

server socket

random access file

new file (line 23) · get count (line 25) · connect client (line 29) · send to client (line 32) · update count (line 36)

```
21        // Get the count
22        if (raf.length() == 0)
23          count = 0;
24        else
25          count = raf.readInt();
26
27        while (true) {
28          // Listen for a new connection request
29          Socket socket = serverSocket.accept();
30
31          // Create a DataOutputStream for the socket
32          DataOutputStream outputToClient =
33            new DataOutputStream(socket.getOutputStream());
34
35          // Increase count and send the count to the client
36          count++;
37          outputToClient.writeInt(count);
38
39          // Write new count back to the file
40          raf.seek(0);
41          raf.writeInt(count);
42        }
43      }
44      catch(IOException ex) {
45        ex.printStackTrace();
46      }
47    }
48  }
```

The server creates a `ServerSocket` in line 15 and creates or opens a file using `RandomAccessFile` in line 19. It reads the count from the file in lines 22–31. The server then waits for a connection request from a client (line 29). After a connection with a client is established, the server creates an output stream to the client (lines 32–33), increases the count (line 36), sends the count to the client (line 37), and writes the new count back to the file. This process continues in an infinite `while` loop to handle all clients.

LISTING 30.6 AppletClient.java

```
import java.io.*;
import java.net.*;
import javax.swing.*;

public class AppletClient extends JApplet {
  // Label for displaying the visit count
  private JLabel jlblCount = new JLabel();

  // Indicate if it runs as application
  private boolean isStandAlone = false;

  // Host name or ip
  private String host = "localhost";

  /** Initialize the applet */
  public void init() {
    add(jlblCount);

    try {
      // Create a socket to connect to the server
      Socket socket;
      if (isStandAlone)
```

```
23          socket = new Socket(host, 8000);                               for standalone
24        else
25          socket = new Socket(getCodeBase().getHost(), 8000);            for applet
26
27        // Create an input stream to receive data from the server
28        DataInputStream inputFromServer =
29          new DataInputStream(socket.getInputStream());
30
31        // Receive the count from the server and display it on label
32        int count = inputFromServer.readInt();                           receive count
33        jlblCount.setText("You are visitor number " + count);
34
35        // Close the stream
36        inputFromServer.close();
37      }
38      catch (IOException ex) {
39        ex.printStackTrace();
40      }
41    }
42
43    /** Run the applet as an application */
44    public static void main(String[] args) {
45      // Create a frame
46      JFrame frame = new JFrame("Applet Client");
47
48      // Create an instance of the applet
49      AppletClient applet = new AppletClient();
50      applet.isStandAlone = true;
51
52      // Get host
53      if (args.length == 1) applet.host = args[0];
54
55      // Add the applet instance to the frame
56      frame.getContentPane().add(applet, java.awt.BorderLayout.CENTER);
57
58      // Invoke init() and start()
59      applet.init();
60      applet.start();
61
62      // Display the frame
63      frame.pack();
64      frame.setVisible(true);
65    }
66  }
```

The client is an applet. When it runs as an applet, it uses `getCodeBase().getHost()` (line 25) to return the IP address for the server. When it runs as an application, it passes the URL from the command line (line 53). If the URL is not passed from the command line, by default "localhost" is used for the URL (line 13).

The client creates a socket to connect to the server (lines 21–25), creates an input stream from the socket (lines 28–29), receives the count from the server (line 32), and displays it in the text field (line 33).

30.6 Sending and Receiving Objects

In the preceding examples, you learned how to send and receive data of primitive types. You can also send and receive objects using `ObjectOutputStream` and `ObjectInputStream` on socket streams. To enable passing, the objects must be serializable. The following example demonstrates how to send and receive objects.

The example consists of three classes: StudentAddress.java (Listing 30.7), StudentClient.java (Listing 30.8), and StudentServer.java (Listing 30.9). The client program collects student information from a client and sends it to a server, as shown in Figure 30.11.

The `StudentAddress` class contains the student information: name, street, state, and zip. The `StudentAddress` class implements the `Serializable` interface. Therefore, it can be sent and received using the object output and input streams.

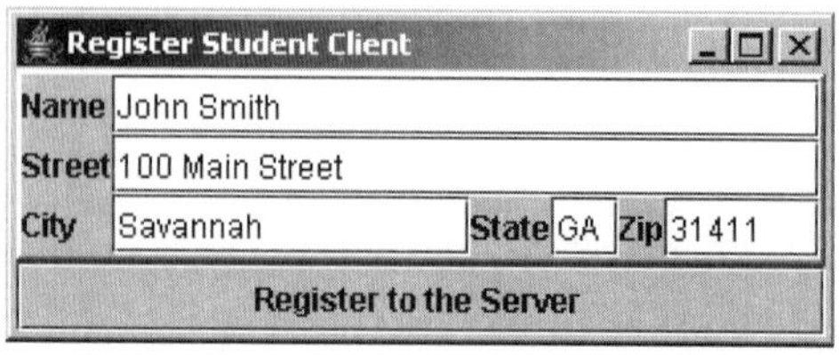
Register Student Client
Name
John Smith
Street
100 Main Street
City
Savannah
State
GA
Zip
31411
Register to the Server

FIGURE 30.11 The client sends the student information in an object to the server.

LISTING 30.7 StudentAddress.java

serialized

```
public class StudentAddress implements java.io.Serializable {
  private String name;
  private String street;
  private String city;
  private String state;
  private String zip;

  public StudentAddress(String name, String street, String city,
    String state, String zip) {
    this.name = name;
    this.street = street;
    this.city = city;
    this.state = state;
    this.zip = zip;
  }

  public String getName() {
    return name;
  }

  public String getStreet() {
    return street;
  }

  public String getCity() {
    return city;
  }

  public String getState() {
    return state;
  }

  public String getZip() {
    return zip;
  }
}
```

The client sends a `StudentAddress` object through an `ObjectOutputStream` on the output stream socket, and the server receives the `Student` object through the `ObjectInputStream` on the input stream socket, as shown in Figure 30.12. The client uses the `writeObject` method in the `ObjectOutputStream` class to send a student to the server, and the server receives the student using the `readObject` method in the `ObjectInputStream` class. The server and client programs are given in Listings 30.8 and 30.9.

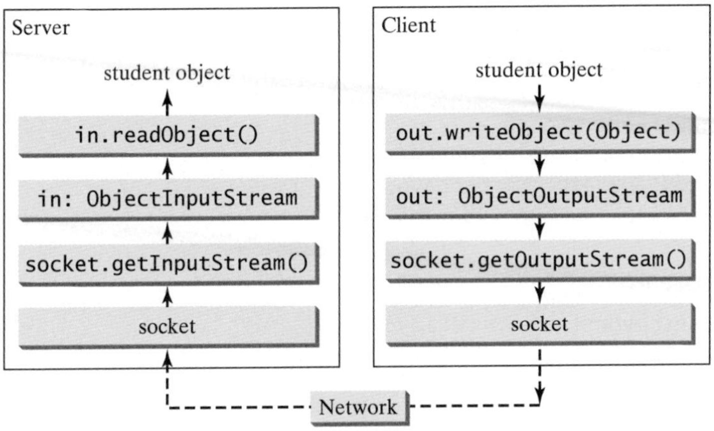
Server
student object
in.readObject()
in: ObjectInputStream
socket.getInputStream()
socket
Client
student object
out.writeObject(Object)
out: ObjectOutputStream
socket.getOutputStream()
socket
Network

FIGURE 30.12 The client sends a `StudentAddress` object to the server.

LISTING 30.8 StudentClient.java

```
import java.io.*;
import java.net.*;
import java.awt.*;
import java.awt.event.*;
import javax.swing.*;
import javax.swing.border.*;

public class StudentClient extends JApplet {
  private JTextField jtfName = new JTextField(32);
  private JTextField jtfStreet = new JTextField(32);
  private JTextField jtfCity = new JTextField(20);
  private JTextField jtfState = new JTextField(2);
  private JTextField jtfZip = new JTextField(5);

  // Button for sending a student to the server
  private JButton jbtRegister = new JButton("Register to the Server");

  // Indicate if it runs as application
  private boolean isStandAlone = false;

  // Host name or ip
  String host = "localhost";

  public void init() {
    // Panel p1 for holding labels Name, Street, and City
    JPanel p1 = new JPanel();                                   create UI
    p1.setLayout(new GridLayout(3, 1));
    p1.add(new JLabel("Name"));
    p1.add(new JLabel("Street"));
    p1.add(new JLabel("City"));

    // Panel jpState for holding state
    JPanel jpState = new JPanel();
```

```java
    jpState.setLayout(new BorderLayout());
    jpState.add(new JLabel("State"), BorderLayout.WEST);
    jpState.add(jtfState, BorderLayout.CENTER);

    // Panel jpZip for holding zip
    JPanel jpZip = new JPanel();
    jpZip.setLayout(new BorderLayout());
    jpZip.add(new JLabel("Zip"), BorderLayout.WEST);
    jpZip.add(jtfZip, BorderLayout.CENTER);

    // Panel p2 for holding jpState and jpZip
    JPanel p2 = new JPanel();
    p2.setLayout(new BorderLayout());
    p2.add(jpState, BorderLayout.WEST);
    p2.add(jpZip, BorderLayout.CENTER);

    // Panel p3 for holding jtfCity and p2
    JPanel p3 = new JPanel();
    p3.setLayout(new BorderLayout());
    p3.add(jtfCity, BorderLayout.CENTER);
    p3.add(p2, BorderLayout.EAST);

    // Panel p4 for holding jtfName, jtfStreet, and p3
    JPanel p4 = new JPanel();
    p4.setLayout(new GridLayout(3, 1));
    p4.add(jtfName);
    p4.add(jtfStreet);
    p4.add(p3);

    // Place p1 and p4 into StudentPanel
    JPanel studentPanel = new JPanel(new BorderLayout());
    studentPanel.setBorder(new BevelBorder(BevelBorder.RAISED));
    studentPanel.add(p1, BorderLayout.WEST);
    studentPanel.add(p4, BorderLayout.CENTER);

    // Add the student panel and button to the applet
    add(studentPanel, BorderLayout.CENTER);
    add(jbtRegister, BorderLayout.SOUTH);

    // Register listener
```

register listener

```java
    jbtRegister.addActionListener(new ButtonListener());

    // Find the IP address of the Web server
    if (!isStandAlone)
```

get server name

```java
      host = getCodeBase().getHost();
  }

  /** Handle button action */
  private class ButtonListener implements ActionListener {
    public void actionPerformed(ActionEvent e) {
      try {
        // Establish connection with the server
```

server socket

```java
        Socket socket = new Socket(host, 8000);

        // Create an output stream to the server
```

output stream

```java
        ObjectOutputStream toServer =
          new ObjectOutputStream(socket.getOutputStream());

        // Get text field
        String name = jtfName.getText().trim();
```

```
        String street = jtfStreet.getText().trim();
        String city = jtfCity.getText().trim();
        String state = jtfState.getText().trim();
        String zip = jtfZip.getText().trim();

        // Create a StudentAddress object and send to the server
        StudentAddress s =
          new StudentAddress(name, street, city, state, zip);
        toServer.writeObject(s);
      }
      catch (IOException ex) {
        System.err.println(ex);
      }
    }
  }

  /** Run the applet as an application */
  public static void main(String[] args) {
    // Create a frame
    JFrame frame = new JFrame("Register Student Client");

    // Create an instance of the applet
    StudentClient applet = new StudentClient();
    applet.isStandAlone = true;

    // Get host
    if (args.length == 1) applet.host = args[0];

    // Add the applet instance to the frame
    frame.add(applet, BorderLayout.CENTER);

    // Invoke init() and start()
    applet.init();
    applet.start();

    // Display the frame
    frame.pack();
    frame.setVisible(true);
  }
}
```

send to server

LISTING 30.9 StudentServer.java

```
import java.io.*;
import java.net.*;

public class StudentServer {
  private ObjectOutputStream outputToFile;
  private ObjectInputStream inputFromClient;

  public static void main(String[] args) {
    new StudentServer();
  }

  public StudentServer() {
    try {
      // Create a server socket
      ServerSocket serverSocket = new ServerSocket(8000);
      System.out.println("Server started ");

```

server socket

output to file
connect to client
input stream
get from client
write to file

```
18        // Create an object ouput stream
19        outputToFile = new ObjectOutputStream(
20          new FileOutputStream("student.dat", true));
21
22        while (true) {
23          // Listen for a new connection request
24          Socket socket = serverSocket.accept();
25
26          // Create an input stream from the socket
27          inputFromClient =
28            new ObjectInputStream(socket.getInputStream());
29
30          // Read from input
31          Object object = inputFromClient.readObject();
32
33          // Write to the file
34          outputToFile.writeObject(object);
35          System.out.println("A new student object is stored");
36        }
37      }
38      catch(ClassNotFoundException ex) {
39        ex.printStackTrace();
40      }
41      catch(IOException ex) {
42        ex.printStackTrace();
43      }
44      finally {
45        try {
46          inputFromClient.close();
47          outputToFile.close();
48        }
49        catch (Exception ex) {
50          ex.printStackTrace();
51        }
52      }
53    }
54  }
```

On the client side, when the user clicks the "Register to the Server" button, the client creates a socket to connect to the host (line 86), creates an **ObjectOutputStream** on the output stream of the socket (lines 89–90), and invokes the **writeObject** method to send the **StudentAddress** object to the server through the object output stream (line 102).

On the server side, when a client connects to the server, the server creates an **ObjectInputStream** on the input stream of the socket (lines 27–28), invokes the **readObject** method to receive the **StudentAddress** object through the object input stream (line 31), and writes the object to a file (line 34).

This program can run either as an applet or as an application. To run it as an application, the host name is passed as a command-line argument.

30.7 Retrieving Files from Web Servers

In previous sections you developed client/server applications. Java allows you to develop clients that retrieve files on a remote host through a Web server. In this case, you don't have to create a custom server program. The Web server can be used to send the files, as shown in Figure 30.13.

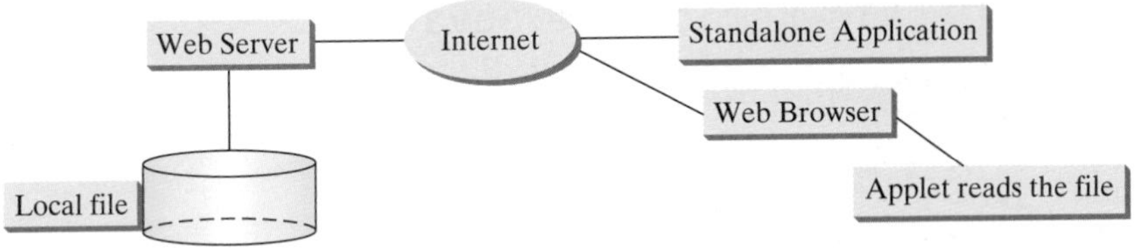
Web Server
Internet
Standalone Application
Web Browser
Local file
Applet reads the file

FIGURE 30.13 The applet client or the application client retrieves files from a Web server.

To retrieve a file, first create a `URL` object for the file. The `java.net.URL` class was introduced in §18.10, "Locating Resource Using the `URL` Class." You can create a URL object using the following constructor:

```
public URL(String spec) throws MalformedURLException
```

For example, the statement given below creates a `URL` object for http://www.cs.armstrong.edu/liang/index.html.

```
try {
  URL url = new URL("http://www.cs.armstrong.edu/liang/index.html");
}
catch (MalformedURLException ex) {
}
```

A `MalformedURLException` is thrown if the URL string has a syntax error. For example, the URL string "http:/www.cs.armstrong.edu/liang/index.html" would cause a `MalformedURLException` runtime error because two slashes (`//`)are required after the colon (`:`).

You can then use the `openStream()` method defined in the `URL` class to open an input stream to the file's URL.

```
InputStream inputStream = url.openStream();
```

Now you can read the data from the input stream. Listing 30.10 gives an example that demonstrates how to retrieve a file from a Web server. The program can run as an application or an applet. The user interface includes a text field in which to enter the URL of the file name, a text area in which to show the file, and a button that can be used to submit an action. A label is added at the bottom of the applet to indicate the status, such as *File loaded successfully* or *Network connection problem*. A sample run of the program is shown in Figure 30.14.

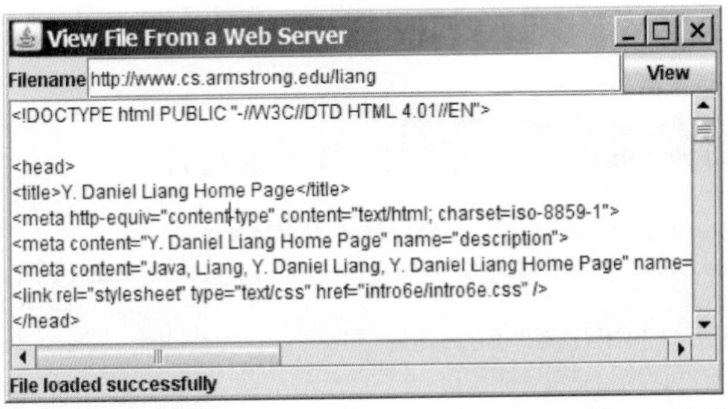
View File From a Web Server
Filename
http://www.cs.armstrong.edu/liang
View
<!DOCTYPE html PUBLIC "-//W3C//DTD HTML 4.01//EN">
<head>
<title>Y. Daniel Liang Home Page</title>
<meta http-equiv="content-type" content="text/html; charset=iso-8859-1">
<meta content="Y. Daniel Liang Home Page" name="description">
<meta content="Java, Liang, Y. Daniel Liang, Y. Daniel Liang Home Page" name=
<link rel="stylesheet" type="text/css" href="intro6e/intro6e.css" />
</head>
File loaded successfully

FIGURE 30.14 The program displays the contents of a specified file on the Web server.

LISTING 30.10 ViewRemoteFile.java

```java
import java.awt.*;
import java.awt.event.*;
import java.io.*;
import java.net.*;
import javax.swing.*;

public class ViewRemoteFile extends JApplet {
  // Button to view the file
  private JButton jbtView = new JButton("View");

  // Text field to receive file name
  private JTextField jtfURL = new JTextField(12);

  // Text area to store file
  private JTextArea jtaFile = new JTextArea();

  // Label to display status
  private JLabel jlblStatus = new JLabel();

  /** Initialize the applet */
  public void init() {
    // Create a panel to hold a label, a text field, and a button
```

create UI

```java
    JPanel p1 = new JPanel();
    p1.setLayout(new BorderLayout());
    p1.add(new JLabel("Filename"), BorderLayout.WEST);
    p1.add(jtfURL, BorderLayout.CENTER);
    p1.add(jbtView, BorderLayout.EAST);

    // Place text area and panel p to the applet
    setLayout(new BorderLayout());
    add(new JScrollPane(jtaFile), BorderLayout.CENTER);
    add(p1, BorderLayout.NORTH);
    add(jlblStatus, BorderLayout.SOUTH);

    // Register listener to handle the "View" button
```

register listener

```java
    jbtView.addActionListener(new ActionListener() {
      public void actionPerformed(ActionEvent e) {
        showFile();
      }
    });
  }

  private void showFile() {
    java.util.Scanner input = null; // Use Scanner for text input
    URL url = null;

    try {
      // Obtain URL from the text field
```

get URL

```java
      url = new URL(jtfURL.getText().trim());

      // Create a Scanner for input stream
```

input stream

```java
      input = new java.util.Scanner(url.openStream());

      // Read a line and append the line to the text area
      while (input.hasNext()) {
```

```
56          jtaFile.append(input.nextLine() + "\n");
57        }
58
59        jlblStatus.setText("File loaded successfully");
60      }
61      catch (MalformedURLException ex) {
62        jlblStatus.setText("URL " + url + " not found.");
63      }
64      catch (IOException e) {
65        jlblStatus.setText(e.getMessage());
66      }
67      finally {
68        if (input != null) input.close();
69      }
70    }
71 }
```

main method omitted

Line 49 `new URL(jtfURL.getText().trim())` creates a `URL` for the file name entered from the text field. Line 52 `url.openStream()` creates an `InputStream` from the URL. After the input stream is established, reading data from the remote file is just like reading data locally. A `Scanner` object is created from the input stream for reading text (line 52). The text from the file is displayed in the text area (line 56).

30.8 JEditorPane

Swing provides a GUI component named `javax.swing.JEditorPane` that can display plain text, HTML, and RTF files automatically. Using it, you don't have to write code to explicitly read data from the files. `JEditorPane` is a subclass of `JTextComponent`. Thus it inherits all the behavior and properties of `JTextComponent`.

To display the content of a file, use the `setPage(URL)` method, as follows:

```
public void setPage(URL url) throws IOException
```

`JEditorPane` generates `javax.swing.event.HyperlinkEvent` when a hyperlink in the editor pane is clicked. Through this event, you can get the URL of the hyperlink and display it using the `setPage(url)` method.

Listing 30.11 gives an example that creates a simple Web browser to render HTML files. The program lets the user enter an HTML file in a text field and press the *Enter* key to display it in an editor pane, as shown in Figure 30.15.

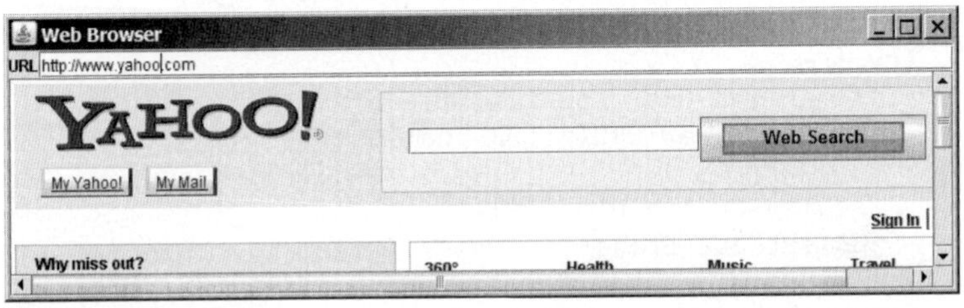
Web Browser
URL http://www.yahoo.com
YAHOO!
Web Search
My Yahoo!
My Mail
Sign In
Why miss out?

FIGURE 30.15 You can specify a URL in the text field and display the HTML file in an editor pane.

LISTING 30.11 WebBrowser.java

create UI
register listener
register listener
get URL
display HTML

```java
import java.awt.*;
import java.awt.event.*;
import javax.swing.*;
import java.net.URL;
import javax.swing.event.*;
import java.io.*;

public class WebBrowser extends JApplet {
  // JEditor pane to view HTML files
  private JEditorPane jep = new JEditorPane();

  // Label for URL
  private JLabel jlblURL = new JLabel("URL");

  // Text field for entering URL
  private JTextField jtfURL = new JTextField();

  /** Initialize the applet */
  public void init() {
    // Create a panel jpURL to hold the label and text field
    JPanel jpURL = new JPanel();
    jpURL.setLayout(new BorderLayout());
    jpURL.add(jlblURL, BorderLayout.WEST);
    jpURL.add(jtfURL, BorderLayout.CENTER);

    // Place jpURL and jspViewer in the applet
    add(new JScrollPane(jspViewer ), BorderLayout.CENTER);
    add(jpURL, BorderLayout.NORTH);

    // Set jep noneditable
    jep.setEditable(false);

    // Register listener
    jep.addHyperlinkListener(new HyperlinkListener() {
      public void hyperlinkUpdate(HyperlinkEvent e) {
        try {
          jep.setPage(e.getURL());
        }
        catch (IOException ex) {
          System.out.println(ex);
        }
      }
    });
    jtfURL.addActionListener(new ActionListener() {
      public void actionPerformed(ActionEvent e) {
        try {
          // Get the URL from text field
          URL url = new URL(jtfURL.getText().trim());

          // Display the HTML file
          jep.setPage(url);
        }
        catch (IOException ex) {
          System.out.println(ex);
        }
      }
```

```
57     });
58   }
59 }
```

main method omitted

In this example, a simple Web browser is created using the `JEditorPane` class (line 10). `JEditorPane` is capable of displaying files in HTML format. To enable scrolling, the editor pane is placed inside a scroll pane (line 27).

The user enters the URL of the HTML file in the text field and presses the *Enter* key to fire an action event to display the URL in the editor pane. To display the URL in the editor pane, simply set the URL in the `page` property of the editor pane (line 51).

The editor pane does not have all the functions of a commercial Web browser, but it is convenient for displaying HTML files, including embedded images.

There are two shortcomings in this program: (1) it cannot view a local HTML file, and (2) to view a remote HTML file, you have to enter a URL beginning with http://. In Exercise 30.11, you will modify the program so that it can also view an HTML file from the local host and accept URLs beginning with either http:// or www.

30.9 Case Studies: Distributed TicTacToe Games

In §18.9, "Case Study: TicTacToe," you developed an applet for the TicTacToe game that enables two players to play on the same machine. In this section, you will learn how to develop a distributed TicTacToe game using multithreads and networking with socket streams. A distributed TicTacToe game enables users to play on different machines from anywhere on the Internet.

You need to develop a server for multiple clients. The server creates a server socket and accepts connections from every two players to form a session. Each session is a thread that communicates with the two players and determines the status of the game. The server can establish any number of sessions, as shown in Figure 30.16.

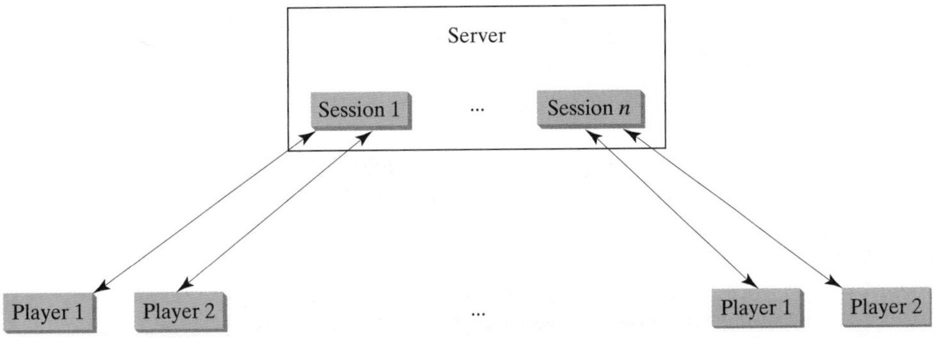

Server
Session 1
...
Session n
Player 1
Player 2
...
Player 1
Player 2

FIGURE 30.16 The server can create many sessions, each of which facilitates a TicTacToe game for two players.

For each session, the first client connecting to the server is identified as player 1 with token `'X'`, and the second client connecting is identified as player 2 with token `'O'`. The server notifies the players of their respective tokens. Once two clients are connected to it, the server starts a thread to facilitate the game between the two players by performing the steps repeatedly, as shown in Figure 30.17.

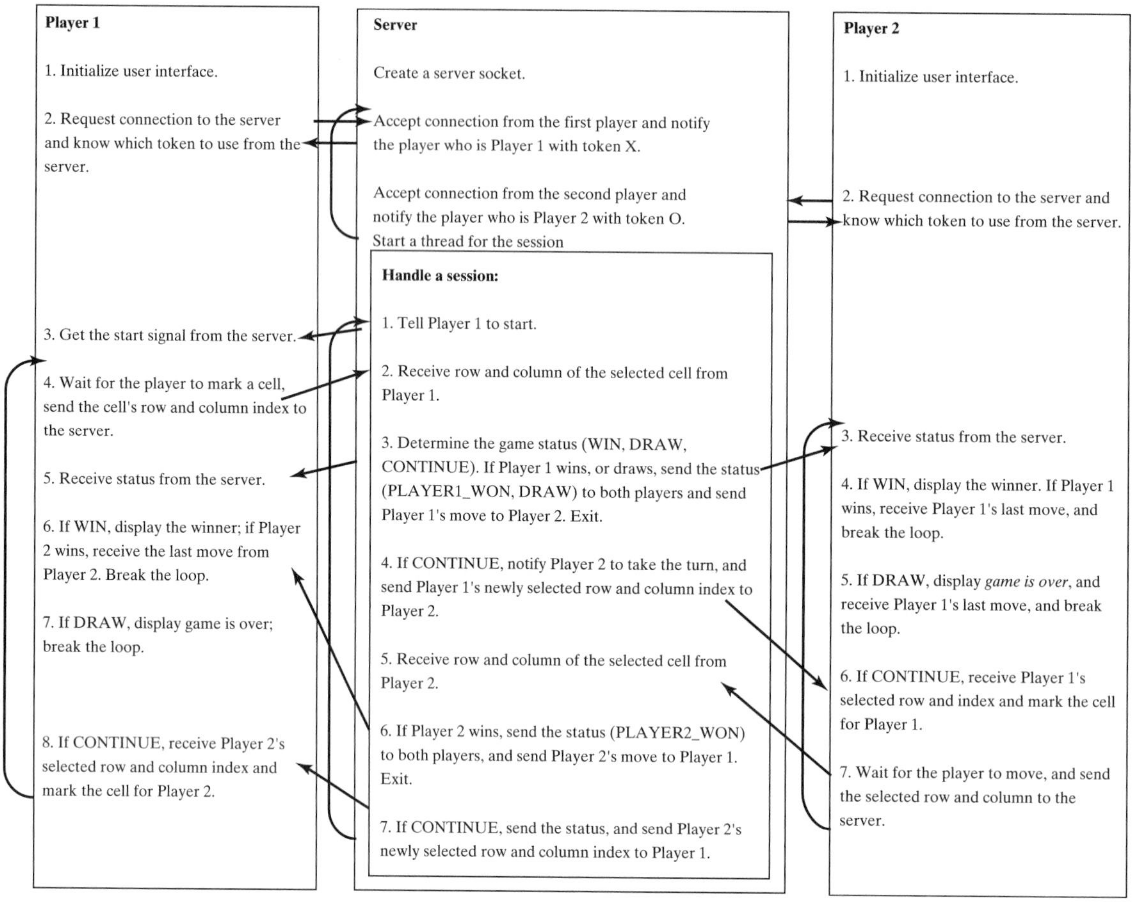

Player 1
1. Initialize user interface.
2. Request connection to the server and know which token to use from the server.
3. Get the start signal from the server.
4. Wait for the player to mark a cell, send the cell's row and column index to the server.
5. Receive status from the server.
6. If WIN, display the winner; if Player 2 wins, receive the last move from Player 2. Break the loop.
7. If DRAW, display game is over; break the loop.
8. If CONTINUE, receive Player 2's selected row and column index and mark the cell for Player 2.
Server
Create a server socket.
Accept connection from the first player and notify the player who is Player 1 with token X.
Accept connection from the second player and notify the player who is Player 2 with token O. Start a thread for the session
Handle a session:
1. Tell Player 1 to start.
2. Receive row and column of the selected cell from Player 1.
3. Determine the game status (WIN, DRAW, CONTINUE). If Player 1 wins, or draws, send the status (PLAYER1_WON, DRAW) to both players and send Player 1's move to Player 2. Exit.
4. If CONTINUE, notify Player 2 to take the turn, and send Player 1's newly selected row and column index to Player 2.
5. Receive row and column of the selected cell from Player 2.
6. If Player 2 wins, send the status (PLAYER2_WON) to both players, and send Player 2's move to Player 1. Exit.
7. If CONTINUE, send the status, and send Player 2's newly selected row and column index to Player 1.
Player 2
1. Initialize user interface.
2. Request connection to the server and know which token to use from the server.
3. Receive status from the server.
4. If WIN, display the winner. If Player 1 wins, receive Player 1's last move, and break the loop.
5. If DRAW, display game is over, and receive Player 1's last move, and break the loop.
6. If CONTINUE, receive Player 1's selected row and index and mark the cell for Player 1.
7. Wait for the player to move, and send the selected row and column to the server.

FIGURE 30.17 The server starts a thread to facilitate communications between the two players.

The server does not have to be a graphical component, but creating it as a frame in which game information can be viewed is user friendly. You can create a scroll pane to hold a text area in the frame and display game information in the text area. The server creates a thread to handle a game session when two players are connected to the server.

The client is responsible for interacting with the players. It creates a user interface with nine cells, and displays the game title and status to the players in the labels. The client class is very similar to the TicTacToe class presented in §18.9, "Case Study: TicTacToe." However, the client in this example does not determine the game status (win or draw), it simply passes the moves to the server and receives the game status from the server.

Based on the foregoing analysis, you can create the following classes:

- **`TicTacToeServer`** serves all the clients in Listing 30.13.
- **`HandleASession`** facilitates the game for two players in Listing 30.13. It is in the same file with TicTacToeServer.java.
- **`TicTacToeClient`** models a player in Listing 30.14.
- **`Cell`** models a cell in the game in Listing 30.14. It is an inner class in `TicTacToeClient`.
- **`TicTacToeConstants`** is an interface that defines the constants shared by all the classes in the example in Listing 30.12.

The relationships of these classes are shown in Figure 30.18.

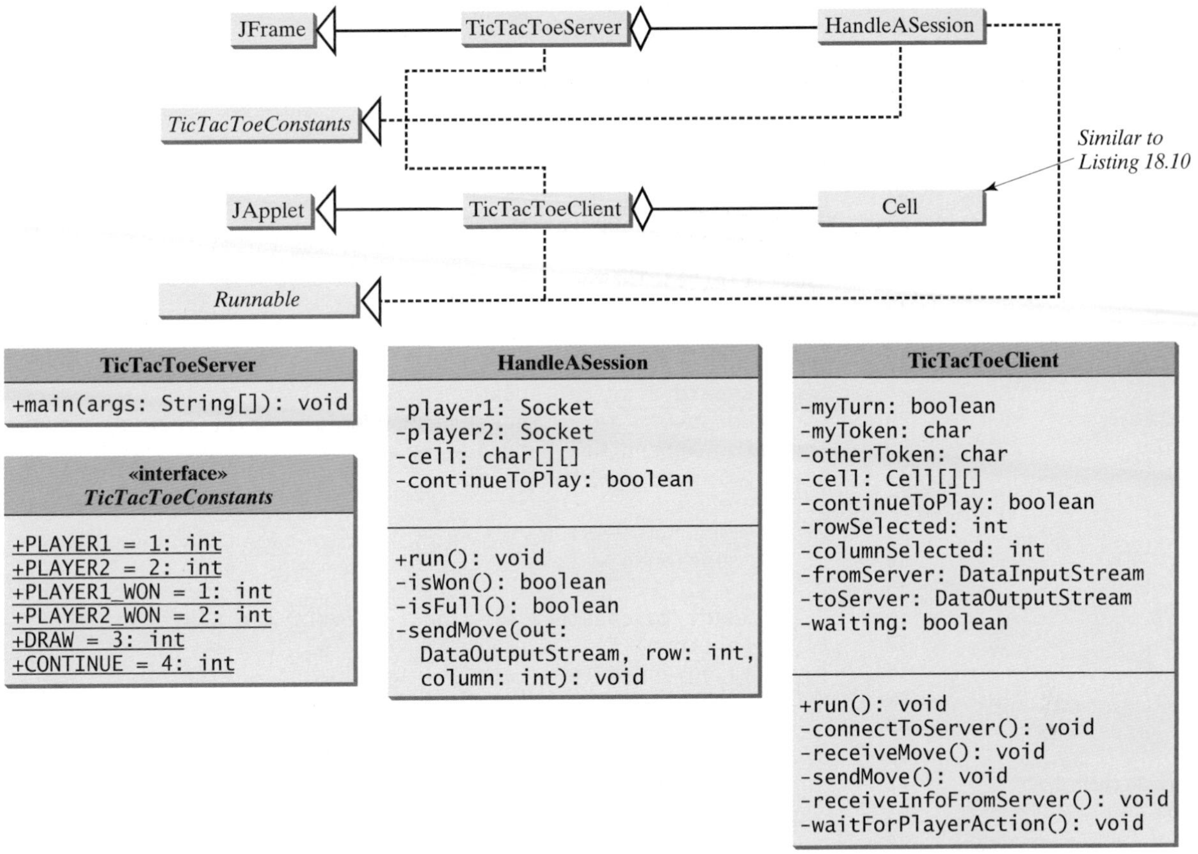
JFrame
TicTacToeServer
HandleASession
TicTacToeConstants
Similar to Listing 18.10
JApplet
TicTacToeClient
Cell
Runnable
TicTacToeServer
+main(args: String[]): void
«interface»
TicTacToeConstants
+PLAYER1 = 1: int
+PLAYER2 = 2: int
+PLAYER1_WON = 1: int
+PLAYER2_WON = 2: int
+DRAW = 3: int
+CONTINUE = 4: int
HandleASession
-player1: Socket
-player2: Socket
-cell: char[][]
-continueToPlay: boolean
+run(): void
-isWon(): boolean
-isFull(): boolean
-sendMove(out: DataOutputStream, row: int, column: int): void
TicTacToeClient
-myTurn: boolean
-myToken: char
-otherToken: char
-cell: Cell[][]
-continueToPlay: boolean
-rowSelected: int
-columnSelected: int
-fromServer: DataInputStream
-toServer: DataOutputStream
-waiting: boolean
+run(): void
-connectToServer(): void
-receiveMove(): void
-sendMove(): void
-receiveInfoFromServer(): void
-waitForPlayerAction(): void

FIGURE 30.18 `TicTacToeServer` creates an instance of `HandleASession` for each session of two players. `TicTacToeClient` creates nine cells in the UI.

LISTING 30.12 TicTacToeConstants.java

```
public interface TicTacToeConstants {
  public static int PLAYER1 = 1; // Indicate player 1
  public static int PLAYER2 = 2; // Indicate player 2
  public static int PLAYER1_WON = 1; // Indicate player 1 won
  public static int PLAYER2_WON = 2; // Indicate player 2 won
  public static int DRAW = 3; // Indicate a draw
  public static int CONTINUE = 4; // Indicate to continue
}
```

LISTING 30.13 TicTacToeServer.java

```
import java.io.*;
import java.net.*;
import javax.swing.*;
import java.awt.*;
import java.util.Date;

public class TicTacToeServer extends JFrame
    implements TicTacToeConstants {
  public static void main(String[] args) {
    TicTacToeServer frame = new TicTacToeServer();
  }

```

run server

create UI
server socket
connect to client
to player1
to player2
a session for two players

```
  public TicTacToeServer() {
    JTextArea jtaLog = new JTextArea();

    // Create a scroll pane to hold text area
    JScrollPane scrollPane = new JScrollPane(jtaLog);

    // Add the scroll pane to the frame
    add(scrollPane, BorderLayout.CENTER);

    setDefaultCloseOperation(JFrame.EXIT_ON_CLOSE);
    setSize(300, 300);
    setTitle("TicTacToeServer");
    setVisible(true);

    try {
      // Create a server socket
      ServerSocket serverSocket = new ServerSocket(8000);
      jtaLog.append(new Date() +
        ": Server started at socket 8000\n");

      // Number a session
      int sessionNo = 1;

      // Ready to create a session for every two players
      while (true) {
        jtaLog.append(new Date() +
          ": Wait for players to join session " + sessionNo + '\n');

        // Connect to player 1
        Socket player1 = serverSocket.accept();

        jtaLog.append(new Date() + ": Player 1 joined session " +
          sessionNo + '\n');
        jtaLog.append("Player 1's IP address" +
          player1.getInetAddress().getHostAddress() + '\n');

        // Notify that the player is Player 1
        new DataOutputStream(
          player1.getOutputStream()).writeInt(PLAYER1);

        // Connect to player 2
        Socket player2 = serverSocket.accept();

        jtaLog.append(new Date() +
          ": Player 2 joined session " + sessionNo + '\n');
        jtaLog.append("Player 2's IP address" +
          player2.getInetAddress().getHostAddress() + '\n');

        // Notify that the player is Player 2
        new DataOutputStream(
          player2.getOutputStream()).writeInt(PLAYER2);

        // Display this session and increment session number
        jtaLog.append(new Date() + ": Start a thread for session " +
          sessionNo++ + '\n');

        // Create a new thread for this session of two players
        HandleASession task = new HandleASession(player1, player2);

        // Start the new thread
```

```
        new Thread(task).start();
      }
    }
    catch(IOException ex) {
      System.err.println(ex);
    }
  }
}

// Define the thread class for handling a new session for two players
class HandleASession implements Runnable, TicTacToeConstants {
  private Socket player1;
  private Socket player2;

  // Create and initialize cells
  private char[][] cell =  new char[3][3];

  private DataInputStream fromPlayer1;
  private DataOutputStream toPlayer1;
  private DataInputStream fromPlayer2;
  private DataOutputStream toPlayer2;

  // Continue to play
  private boolean continueToPlay = true;

  /** Construct a thread */
  public HandleASession(Socket player1, Socket player2) {
    this.player1 = player1;
    this.player2 = player2;

    // Initialize cells
    for (int i = 0; i < 3; i++)
      for (int j = 0; j < 3; j++)
        cell[i][j] = ' ';
  }

  /** Implement the run() method for the thread */
  public void run() {
    try {
      // Create data input and output streams
      DataInputStream fromPlayer1 = new DataInputStream(
        player1.getInputStream());
      DataOutputStream toPlayer1 = new DataOutputStream(
        player1.getOutputStream());
      DataInputStream fromPlayer2 = new DataInputStream(
        player2.getInputStream());
      DataOutputStream toPlayer2 = new DataOutputStream(
        player2.getOutputStream());

      // Write anything to notify player 1 to start
      // This is just to let player 1 know to start
      toPlayer1.writeInt(1);

      // Continuously serve the players and determine and report
      // the game status to the players
      while (true) {
        // Receive a move from player 1
        int row = fromPlayer1.readInt();
        int column = fromPlayer1.readInt();
        cell[row][column] = 'X';
```

```

        // Check if Player 1 wins
        if (isWon('X')) {
          toPlayer1.writeInt(PLAYER1_WON);
          toPlayer2.writeInt(PLAYER1_WON);
          sendMove(toPlayer2, row, column);
          break; // Break the loop
        }
        else if (isFull()) { // Check if all cells are filled
          toPlayer1.writeInt(DRAW);
          toPlayer2.writeInt(DRAW);
          sendMove(toPlayer2, row, column);
          break;
        }
        else {
          // Notify player 2 to take the turn
          toPlayer2.writeInt(CONTINUE);

          // Send player 1's selected row and column to player 2
          sendMove(toPlayer2, row, column);
       }

        // Receive a move from Player 2
        row = fromPlayer2.readInt();
        column = fromPlayer2.readInt();
        cell[row][column] = 'O';

        // Check if Player 2 wins
        if (isWon('O')) {
          toPlayer1.writeInt(PLAYER2_WON);
          toPlayer2.writeInt(PLAYER2_WON);
          sendMove(toPlayer1, row, column);
          break;
        }
        else {
          // Notify player 1 to take the turn
          toPlayer1.writeInt(CONTINUE);

          // Send player 2's selected row and column to player 1
          sendMove(toPlayer1, row, column);
        }
      }
    }
    catch(IOException ex) {
      System.err.println(ex);
    }
  }

  /** Send the move to other player */
  private void sendMove(DataOutputStream out, int row, int column)
      throws IOException {
    out.writeInt(row); // Send row index
    out.writeInt(column); // Send column index
  }

  /** Determine if the cells are all occupied */
  private boolean isFull() {
    for (int i = 0; i < 3; i++)
      for (int j = 0; j < 3; j++)
        if (cell[i][j] == ' ')
```

```
          return false; // At least one cell is not filled

    // All cells are filled
    return true;
  }

  /** Determine if the player with the specified token wins */
  private boolean isWon(char token) {
    // Check all rows
    for (int i = 0; i < 3; i++)
      if ((cell[i][0] == token)
          && (cell[i][1] == token)
          && (cell[i][2] == token)) {
        return true;
      }

    /** Check all columns */
    for (int j = 0; j < 3; j++)
      if ((cell[0][j] == token)
          && (cell[1][j] == token)
          && (cell[2][j] == token)) {
        return true;
      }

    /** Check major diagonal */
    if ((cell[0][0] == token)
        && (cell[1][1] == token)
        && (cell[2][2] == token)) {
      return true;
    }

    /** Check subdiagonal */
    if ((cell[0][2] == token)
        && (cell[1][1] == token)
        && (cell[2][0] == token)) {
      return true;
    }

    /** All checked, but no winner */
    return false;
  }
}
```

LISTING 30.14 TicTacToeClient.java

```
import java.awt.*;
import java.awt.event.*;
import javax.swing.*;
import javax.swing.border.LineBorder;
import java.io.*;
import java.net.*;

public class TicTacToeClient extends JApplet
    implements Runnable, TicTacToeConstants {
  // Indicate whether the player has the turn
  private boolean myTurn = false;

  // Indicate the token for the player
  private char myToken = ' ';

```

```java
  // Indicate the token for the other player
  private char otherToken = ' ';

  // Create and initialize cells
  private Cell [][] cell =  new Cell[3][3];

  // Create and initialize a title label
  private JLabel jlblTitle = new JLabel();

  // Create and initialize a status label
  private JLabel jlblStatus = new JLabel();

  // Indicate selected row and column by the current move
  private int rowSelected;
  private int columnSelected;

  // Input and output streams from/to server
  private DataInputStream fromServer;
  private DataOutputStream toServer;

  // Continue to play?
  private boolean continueToPlay = true;

  // Wait for the player to mark a cell
  private boolean waiting = true;

  // Indicate if it runs as application
  private boolean isStandAlone = false;

  // Host name or ip
  private String host = "localhost";

  /** Initialize UI */
```

create UI

```java
  public void init() {
    // Panel p to hold cells
    JPanel p = new JPanel();
    p.setLayout(new GridLayout(3, 3, 0, 0));
    for (int i = 0; i < 3; i++)
      for (int j = 0; j < 3; j++)
        p.add(cell[i][j] = new Cell(i, j));

    // Set properties for labels and borders for labels and panel
    p.setBorder(new LineBorder(Color.black, 1));
    jlblTitle.setHorizontalAlignment(JLabel.CENTER);
    jlblTitle.setFont(new Font("SansSerif", Font.BOLD, 16));
    jlblTitle.setBorder(new LineBorder(Color.black, 1));
    jlblStatus.setBorder(new LineBorder(Color.black, 1));

    // Place the panel and the labels to the applet
    add(jlblTitle, BorderLayout.NORTH);
    add(p, BorderLayout.CENTER);
    add(jlblStatus, BorderLayout.SOUTH);

    // Connect to the server
```

connect to server

```java
    connectToServer();
  }

  private void connectToServer() {
    try {
      // Create a socket to connect to the server
```

```
      Socket socket;
      if (isStandAlone)
        socket = new Socket(host, 8000);
      else
        socket = new Socket(getCodeBase().getHost(), 8000);

      // Create an input stream to receive data from the server
      fromServer = new DataInputStream(socket.getInputStream());

      // Create an output stream to send data to the server
      toServer = new DataOutputStream(socket.getOutputStream());
    }
    catch (Exception ex) {
      System.err.println(ex);
    }

    // Control the game on a separate thread
    Thread thread = new Thread(this);
    thread.start();
  }

  public void run() {
    try {
      // Get notification from the server
      int player = fromServer.readInt();

      // Am I player 1 or 2?
      if (player == PLAYER1) {
        myToken = 'X';
        otherToken = 'O';
        jlblTitle.setText("Player 1 with token 'X'");
        jlblStatus.setText("Waiting for player 2 to join");

        // Receive startup notification from the server
        fromServer.readInt(); // Whatever read is ignored

        // The other player has joined
        jlblStatus.setText("Player 2 has joined. I start first");

        // It is my turn
        myTurn = true;
      }
      else if (player == PLAYER2) {
        myToken = 'O';
        otherToken = 'X';
        jlblTitle.setText("Player 2 with token 'O'");
        jlblStatus.setText("Waiting for player 1 to move");
      }

      // Continue to play
      while (continueToPlay) {
        if (player == PLAYER1) {
          waitForPlayerAction(); // Wait for player 1 to move
          sendMove(); // Send the move to the server
          receiveInfoFromServer(); // Receive info from the server
        }
        else if (player == PLAYER2) {
          receiveInfoFromServer(); // Receive info from the server
          waitForPlayerAction(); // Wait for player 2 to move
          sendMove(); // Send player 2's move to the server
```

standalone

applet

input from server

output to server

```
        }
      }
    }
    catch (Exception ex) {
    }
  }

  /** Wait for the player to mark a cell */
  private void waitForPlayerAction() throws InterruptedException {
    while (waiting) {
      Thread.sleep(100);
    }

    waiting = true;
  }

  /** Send this player's move to the server */
  private void sendMove() throws IOException {
    toServer.writeInt(rowSelected); // Send the selected row
    toServer.writeInt(columnSelected); // Send the selected column
  }

  /** Receive info from the server */
  private void receiveInfoFromServer() throws IOException {
    // Receive game status
    int status = fromServer.readInt();

    if (status == PLAYER1_WON) {
      // Player 1 won, stop playing
      continueToPlay = false;
      if (myToken == 'X') {
        jlblStatus.setText("I won! (X)");
      }
      else if (myToken == 'O') {
        jlblStatus.setText("Player 1 (X) has won!");
        receiveMove();
      }
    }
    else if (status == PLAYER2_WON) {
      // Player 2 won, stop playing
      continueToPlay = false;
      if (myToken == 'O') {
        jlblStatus.setText("I won! (O)");
      }
      else if (myToken == 'X') {
        jlblStatus.setText("Player 2 (O) has won!");
        receiveMove();
      }
    }
    else if (status == DRAW) {
      // No winner, game is over
      continueToPlay = false;
      jlblStatus.setText("Game is over, no winner!");

      if (myToken == 'O') {
        receiveMove();
      }
    }
    else {
      receiveMove();
```

```
      jlblStatus.setText("My turn");
      myTurn = true; // It is my turn
    }
  }

  private void receiveMove() throws IOException {
    // Get the other player's move
    int row = fromServer.readInt();
    int column = fromServer.readInt();
    cell[row][column].setToken(otherToken);
  }

  // An inner class for a cell
```

model a cell

```
  public class Cell extends JPanel {
    // Indicate the row and column of this cell in the board
    private int row;
    private int column;

    // Token used for this cell
    private char token = ' ';

    public Cell(int row, int column) {
      this.row = row;
      this.column = column;
      setBorder(new LineBorder(Color.black, 1)); // Set cell's border
```

register listener

```
      addMouseListener(new ClickListener());  // Register listener
    }

    /** Return token */
    public char getToken() {
      return token;
    }

    /** Set a new token */
    public void setToken(char c) {
      token = c;
      repaint();
    }

    /** Paint the cell */
    protected void paintComponent(Graphics g) {
      super.paintComponent(g);

      if (token == 'X') {
```

draw X

```
        g.drawLine(10, 10, getWidth() - 10, getHeight() - 10);
        g.drawLine(getWidth() - 10, 10, 10, getHeight() - 10);
      }
      else if (token == 'O') {
```

draw O

```
        g.drawOval(10, 10, getWidth() - 20, getHeight() - 20);
      }
    }

    /** Handle mouse click on a cell */
```

mouse listener

```
    private class ClickListener extends MouseAdapter {
      public void mouseClicked(MouseEvent e) {
        // If cell is not occupied and the player has the turn
        if ((token == ' ') && myTurn) {
          setToken(myToken);  // Set the player's token in the cell
          myTurn = false;
          rowSelected = row;
```

```
          columnSelected = column;
          jlblStatus.setText("Waiting for the other player to move");
          waiting = false; // Just completed a successful move
        }
      }
    }
  }
}
```

main method omitted

The server can serve any number of sessions. Each session takes care of two players. The client can be a Java applet or a Java application. To run a client as a Java applet from a Web browser, the server must run from a Web server. Figures 30.19 and 30.20 show sample runs of the server and the clients.

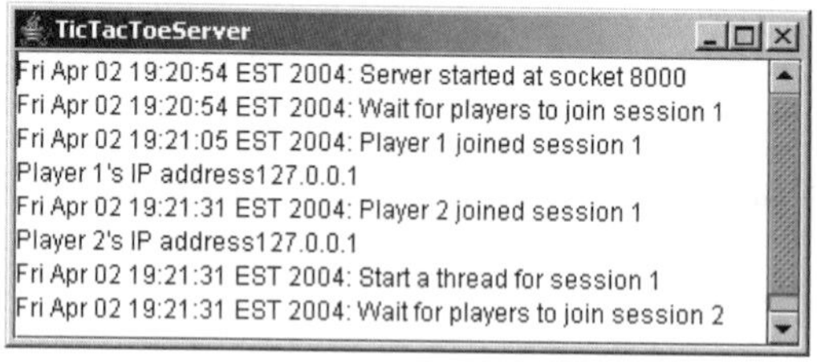
TicTacToeServer
Fri Apr 02 19:20:54 EST 2004: Server started at socket 8000
Fri Apr 02 19:20:54 EST 2004: Wait for players to join session 1
Fri Apr 02 19:21:05 EST 2004: Player 1 joined session 1
Player 1's IP address127.0.0.1
Fri Apr 02 19:21:31 EST 2004: Player 2 joined session 1
Player 2's IP address127.0.0.1
Fri Apr 02 19:21:31 EST 2004: Start a thread for session 1
Fri Apr 02 19:21:31 EST 2004: Wait for players to join session 2

FIGURE 30.19 `TicTacToeServer` accepts connection requests and creates sessions to serve pairs of players.

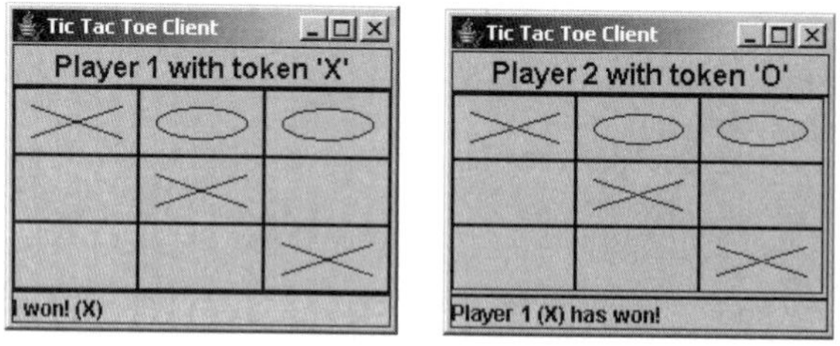
Tic Tac Toe Client
Player 1 with token 'X'
I won! (X)
Tic Tac Toe Client
Player 2 with token 'O'
Player 1 (X) has won!

FIGURE 30.20 `TicTacToeClient` can run as an applet or an application.

The `TicTacToeConstants` interface defines the constants shared by all the classes in the project. Each class that uses the constants needs to implement the interface. Centrally defining constants in an interface is a common practice in Java. For example, all the constants shared by Swing classes are defined in `java.swing.SwingConstants`.

Once a session is established, the server receives moves from the players in alternation. Upon receiving a move from a player, the server determines the status of the game. If the game is not finished, the server sends the status (`CONTINUE`) and the player's move to the other player. If the game is won or drawn, the server sends the status (`PLAYER1_WON`, `PLAYER2_WON`, or `DRAW`) to both players.

The implementation of Java network programs at the socket level is tightly synchronized. An operation to send data from one machine requires an operation to receive data from the other machine. As shown in this example, the server and the client are tightly synchronized to send or receive data.

Chapter Summary

1. Java supports stream sockets and datagram sockets. *Stream sockets* use TCP (Transmission Control Protocol) for data transmission, whereas *datagram sockets* use UDP (User Datagram Protocol). Since TCP can detect lost transmissions and resubmit

them, transmissions are lossless and reliable. UDP, in contrast, cannot guarantee lossless transmission.

2. To create a server, you must first obtain a server socket, using `new ServerSocket(port)`. After a server socket is created, the server can start to listen for connections, using the `accept()` method on the server socket. The client requests a connection to a server by using `new socket(serverName, port)` to create a client socket.

3. Stream socket communication is very much like input/output stream communication after the connection between a server and a client is established. You can obtain an input stream using the `getInputStream()` method and an output stream using the `getOutputStream()` method on the socket.

4. A server must often work with multiple clients at the same time. You can use threads to handle the server's multiple clients simultaneously by creating a thread for each connection.

5. Applets are good for deploying multiple clients. They can run anywhere with a single copy of the program. However, because of security restrictions, an applet client can connect only to the server where the applet is loaded.

6. Java programs can retrieve data from a file on a remote host through a Web server. To do so, first create a URL object using `new URL(urlString)`, then use `openStream()` to get an `InputStream` to read the data from the file.

7. Swing provides a GUI component named `javax.swing.JEditorPane` that can be used to display text, HTML, and RTF files automatically without writing the code to read data from the file explicitly.

Review Questions

Section 30.2

30.1 How do you create a server socket? What port numbers can be used? What happens if a requested port number is already in use? Can a port connect to multiple clients?

30.2 What are the differences between a server socket and a client socket?

30.3 How does a client program initiate a connection?

30.4 How does a server accept a connection?

30.5 How are data transferred between a client and a server?

Sections 30.3–30.4

30.6 How do you find the IP address of a client that connects to a server?

30.7 How do you make a server serve multiple clients?

Sections 30.5–30.6

30.8 Can an applet connect to a server that is different from the machine where the applet is located?

30.9 How do you find the host name of an applet?

30.10 How do you send and receive an object?

Sections 30.7–30.8

30.11 Can an application retrieve a file from a remote host? Can an application update a file on a remote host?

30.12 How do you retrieve a file from a Web server?

30.13 What types of files can be displayed in a `JEditorPane`? How do you display a file in a `JEditorPane`?

PROGRAMMING EXERCISES

Section 30.2

30.1* (*Loan server*) Write a server for a client. The client sends loan information (annual interest rate, number of years, and loan amount) to the server (see Figure 30.21(b)). The server computes monthly payment and total payment and sends them back to the client (see Figure 30.21(a)). Name the client Exercise30_1Client and the server Exercise30_1Server.

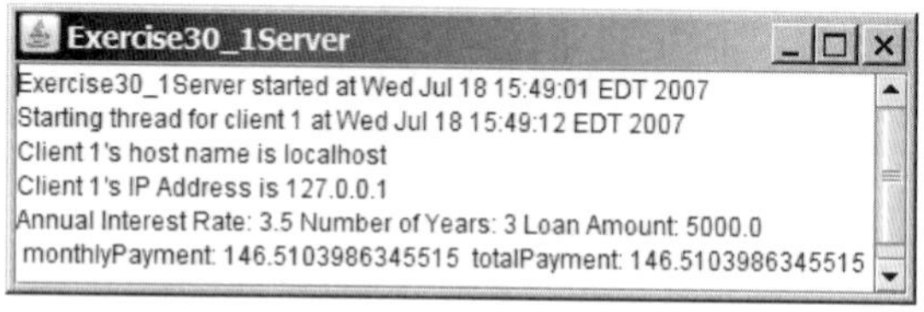
Exercise30_1Server
Exercise30_1Server started at Wed Jul 18 15:49:01 EDT 2007
Starting thread for client 1 at Wed Jul 18 15:49:12 EDT 2007
Client 1's host name is localhost
Client 1's IP Address is 127.0.0.1
Annual Interest Rate: 3.5 Number of Years: 3 Loan Amount: 5000.0
monthlyPayment: 146.5103986345515 totalPayment: 146.5103986345515

(a)

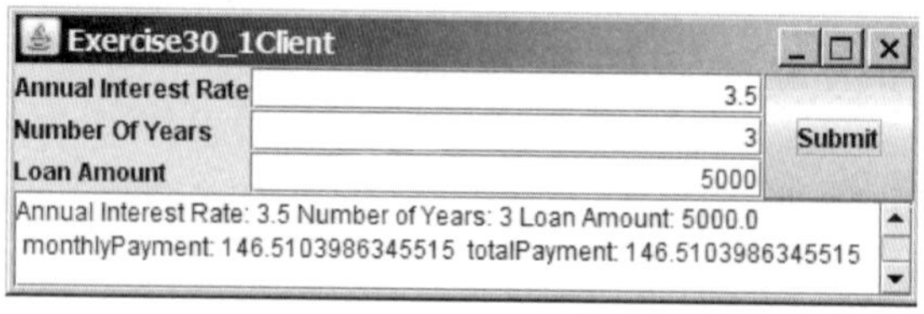
Exercise30_1Client
Annual Interest Rate
3.5
Number Of Years
3
Submit
Loan Amount
5000
Annual Interest Rate: 3.5 Number of Years: 3 Loan Amount: 5000.0
monthlyPayment: 146.5103986345515 totalPayment: 146.5103986345515

(b)

FIGURE 30.21 The client in (b) sends the annual interest rate, number of years, and loan amount to the server and receives the monthly payment and total payment from the server in (a).

30.2 (*Network I/O using* `Scanner` *and* `PrintWriter`) Rewrite the client and server programs in Listings 30.1 and 30.2 using a `Scanner` for input and a `PrintWriter` for output. Name the client Exercise30_2Client and the server Exercise30_2Server.

Sections 30.3–30.4

30.3* (*Loan server for multiple clients*) Revise Exercise 30.1 to write a server for multiple clients.

Section 30.5

30.4 (*Web visit count*) §30.5, "Applet Clients," created an applet that shows the number of visits made to a Web page. The count is stored in a file on the server side. Every time the page is visited or reloaded, the applet sends a request to the server, and the server increases the count and sends it to the applet. The count is stored using a random-access file. When the applet is loaded, the server reads the count from the file, increases it, and saves it back to the file. Rewrite the program to improve its performance. Read the count from the file when the server starts, and save the count to the file when the server stops, using the Stop button, as shown in Figure 30.22. When the server is alive, use a variable to store the count. Name the client Exercise30_4Client and the server Exercise30_4Server. The client program should be the same as in Listing 30.5. Rewrite the server as a GUI application with a *Stop* button that exits the server.

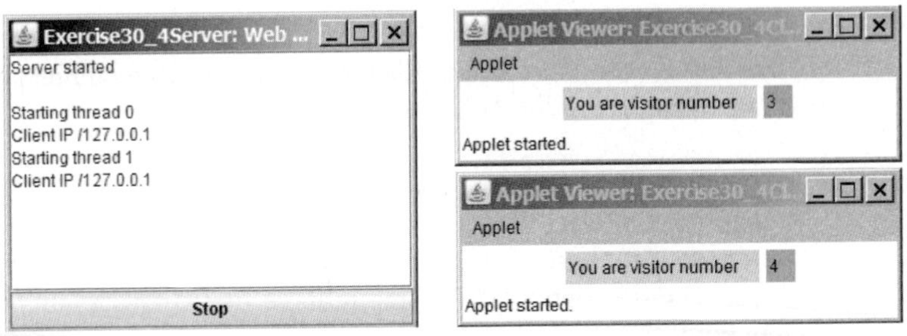
Exercise30_4Server: Web ...
Server started
Starting thread 0
Client IP /127.0.0.1
Starting thread 1
Client IP /127.0.0.1
Stop
Applet Viewer: Exercise30_4Cl...
Applet
You are visitor number
3
Applet started.
Applet Viewer: Exercise30_4Cl...
Applet
You are visitor number
4
Applet started.

FIGURE 30.22 The applet displays how many times this Web page has been accessed. The server stores the count.

30.5 (*Creating a stock ticker in an applet*) Write an applet like the one in Exercise 18.16. Assume that the applet gets the stock index from a file named Exercise30_5.txt stored on the Web server. Enable the applet to run standalone.

Section 30.6

30.6 (*Displaying and adding addresses*) Develop a client/server application to view and add addresses, as shown in Figure 30.23(a).

- Define an `Address` class to hold name, street, city, state, and zip in an object.
- The user can use the buttons *First*, *Next*, *Previous*, and *Last* to view an address, and the *Add* button to add a new address.
- Limit the concurrent connections to two clients.

Name the client Exercise30_6Client and the server Exercise30_6Server.

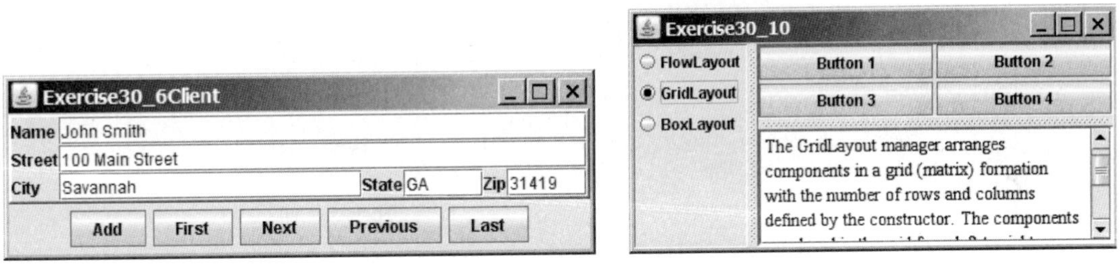
Exercise30_6Client
Name John Smith
Street 100 Main Street
City Savannah
State GA
Zip 31419
Add
First
Next
Previous
Last
Exercise30_10
FlowLayout
GridLayout
BoxLayout
Button 1
Button 2
Button 3
Button 4
The GridLayout manager arranges components in a grid (matrix) formation with the number of rows and columns defined by the constructor. The components

(a) (b)

FIGURE 30.23 (a) You can view and add an address in this applet; (b) The HTML files are displayed in a `JEditorPane`.

30.7* (*Transferring last 100 numbers in an array*) Exercise 23.9 retrieves the last 100 prime numbers from a file Exercise23_8.dat. Write a client program that requests the server to send the last 100 prime numbers in an array. Name the server program Exercise30_7Server and the client program Exercise30_7Client. Assume that the numbers of the `long` type are stored in Exercise23_8.dat in binary format.

30.8* (*Transferring last 100 numbers in an* `ArrayList`) Exercise 23.9 retrieves the last 100 prime numbers from a file Exercise23_8.dat. Write a client program that requests the server to send the last 100 prime numbers in an `ArrayList`. Name the server program Exercise30_8Server and the client program Exercise30_8Client. Assume that the numbers of the `long` type are stored in Exercise23_8.dat in binary format.

Section 30.7

30.9* (*Retrieving remote files*) Revise Listing 30.10, ViewRemoteFile.java, to use `JEditorPane` instead of `JTextArea`.

Section 30.8

30.10* (*Using `JEditorPane`*) Write a program to get descriptions of the layout manager from an HTML file and display it in a `JEditorPane`, as shown in Figure 30.23(b). The descriptions are stored in three files: FlowLayout.html, GridLayout.html, and BoxLayout.html.

30.11* (*Web browser*) Modify Listing 30.11, WebBrowser.java, as follows:

- It accepts an HTML file from a local host. Assume that a local HTML file name begins neither with http:// nor with www.
- It accepts a remote HTML file. A remote HTML file name begins with either http:// or www.

Sections 30.9

30.12** (*Chat*) Write a program that enables two users to chat. Implement one user as the server (Figure 30.24(a)) and the other as the client (Figure 30.24(b)). The server has two text areas: one for entering text and the other (noneditable) for displaying text received from the client. When the user presses the *Enter* key, the current line is sent to the client. The client has two text areas: one for receiving text from the server, and the other for entering text. When the user presses the Enter key, the current line is sent to the server. Name the client Exercise30_12Client and the server Exercise30_12Server.

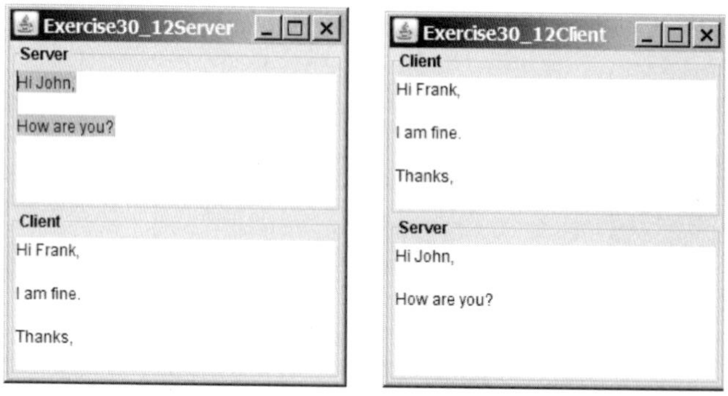
Exercise30_12Server
Server
Hi John,
How are you?
Client
Hi Frank,
I am fine.
Thanks,
Exercise30_12Client
Client
Hi Frank,
I am fine.
Thanks,
Server
Hi John,
How are you?

(a) (b)

FIGURE 30.24 The server and client send and receive text from each other.

30.13*** (*Multiple client chat*) Write a program that enables any number of clients to chat. Implement one server that serves all the clients, as shown in Figure 30.25. Name the client Exercise30_13Client and the server Exercise30_13Server.

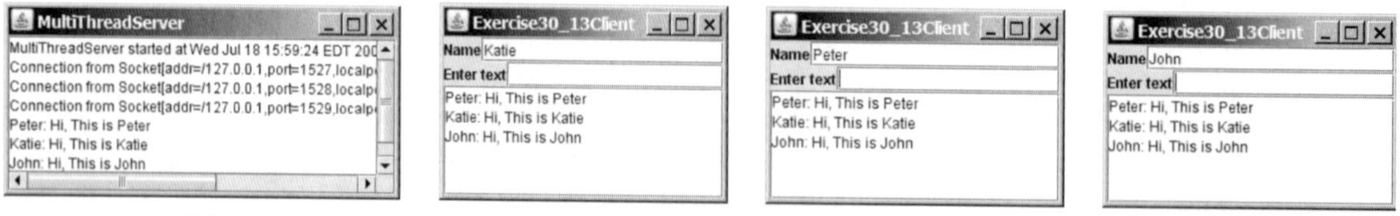
MultiThreadServer
MultiThreadServer started at Wed Jul 18 15:59:24 EDT 200
Connection from Socket[addr=/127.0.0.1,port=1527,localp
Connection from Socket[addr=/127.0.0.1,port=1528,localp
Connection from Socket[addr=/127.0.0.1,port=1529,localp
Peter: Hi, This is Peter
Katie: Hi, This is Katie
John: Hi, This is John
Exercise30_13Client
Name Katie
Enter text
Peter: Hi, This is Peter
Katie: Hi, This is Katie
John: Hi, This is John
Exercise30_13Client
Name Peter
Enter text
Peter: Hi, This is Peter
Katie: Hi, This is Katie
John: Hi, This is John
Exercise30_13Client
Name John
Enter text
Peter: Hi, This is Peter
Katie: Hi, This is Katie
John: Hi, This is John

(a) (b) (c) (d)

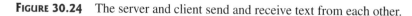

FIGURE 30.25 The server starts in (a) with three clients in (b), (c), and (d).

Chapter 31

Internationalization

Objectives

- To describe Java's internationalization features (§31.1).
- To construct a locale with language, country, and variant (§31.2).
- To display date and time based on locale (§31.3).
- To display numbers, currencies, and percentages based on locale (§31.4).
- To develop applications for international audiences using resource bundles (§31.5).
- To specify encoding schemes for text I/O (§31.6).

31.1 Introduction

Many Web sites maintain several versions of Web pages so that readers can choose one written in a language they understand. Because there are so many languages in the world, it would be highly problematic to create and maintain enough different versions to meet the needs of all clients everywhere. Java comes to the rescue. Java is the first language designed from the ground up to support internationalization. In consequence, it allows your programs to be customized for any number of countries or languages without requiring cumbersome changes in the code.

Here are the major Java features that support internationalization:

Unicode

- Java characters use *Unicode*, a 16-bit encoding scheme established by the Unicode Consortium to support the interchange, processing, and display of written texts in the world's diverse languages. The use of Unicode encoding makes it easy to write Java programs that can manipulate strings in any international language. (To see all the Unicode characters, visit http://mindprod.com/jgloss/reuters.html.)

`Locale` class

- Java provides the `Locale` class to encapsulate information about a specific locale. A `Locale` object determines how locale-sensitive information, such as date, time, and number, is displayed, and how locale-sensitive operations, such as sorting strings, are performed. The classes for formatting date, time, and numbers, and for sorting strings are grouped in the `java.text` package.

`ResourceBundle`

- Java uses the `ResourceBundle` class to separate locale-specific information, such as status messages and GUI component labels, from the program. The information is stored outside the source code and can be accessed and loaded dynamically at runtime from a `ResourceBundle`, rather than hard-coded into the program.

In this chapter, you will learn how to format dates, numbers, currencies, and percentages for different regions, countries, and languages. You will also learn how to use resource bundles to define which images and strings are used by a component, depending on the user's locale and preferences.

31.2 The `Locale` Class

A `Locale` object represents a geographical, political, or cultural region in which a specific language or custom is used. For example, Americans speak English, and the Chinese speak Chinese. The conventions for formatting dates, numbers, currencies, and percentages may differ from one country to another. The Chinese, for instance, use year/month/day to represent the date, while Americans use month/day/year. It is important to realize that locale is not defined only by country. For example, Canadians speak either Canadian English or Canadian French, depending on which region of Canada they reside in.

`locale` property in `Component`

Note

Every Swing user-interface class has a `locale` property inherited from the `Component` class.

To create a `Locale` object, use one of the three constructors with a specified language and optional country and variant, as shown in Figure 31.1.

language

The `language` should be a valid language code—that is, one of the lowercase two-letter codes defined by ISO-639. For example, zh stands for Chinese, da for Danish, en for English, de for German, and ko for Korean. Table 31.1 lists the language codes.

country

The country should be a valid ISO country code—that is, one of the uppercase, two-letter codes defined by ISO-3166. For example, CA stands for Canada, CN for China, DK for Denmark, DE for Germany, and US for the United States. Table 31.2 lists the country codes.

java.util.Locale	
`+Locale(language: String)`	Constructs a locale from a language code.
`+Locale(language: String, country: String)`	Constructs a locale from language and country codes.
`+Locale(language: String, country: String, variant: String)`	Constructs a locale from language, country, and variant codes.
`+getCountry(): String`	Returns the country/region code for this locale.
`+getLanguage(): String`	Returns the language code for this locale.
`+getVariant(): String`	Returns the variant code for this locale.
`+getDefault(): Locale`	Gets the default locale on the machine.
`+getDisplayCountry(): String`	Returns the name of the country as expressed in the current locale.
`+getDisplayLanguage(): String`	Returns the name of the language as expressed in the current locale.
`+getDisplayName(): String`	Returns the name for the locale. For example, the name is `Chinese (China)` for the locale `Locale.CHINA`.
`+getDisplayVariant(): String`	Returns the name for the locale's variant if it exists.
`+getAvailableLocales(): Locale[]`	Returns the available locales in an array.

FIGURE 31.1 The `Locale` class encapsulates a locale.

TABLE 31.1 Common Language Codes

Code	*Language*	*Code*	*Language*
da	Danish	ja	Japanese
de	German	ko	Korean
el	Greek	nl	Dutch
en	English	no	Norwegian
es	Spanish	pt	Portuguese
fi	Finnish	sv	Swedish
fr	French	tr	Turkish
it	Italian	zh	Chinese

TABLE 31.2 Common Country Codes

Code	*Country*	*Code*	*Country*
AT	Austria	IE	Ireland
BE	Belgium	HK	Hong Kong
CA	Canada	IT	Italy
CH	Switzerland	JP	Japan
CN	China	KR	Korea
DE	Germany	NL	Netherlands
DK	Denmark	NO	Norway
ES	Spain	PT	Portugal
FI	Finland	SE	Sweden
FR	France	TR	Turkey
GB	United Kingdom	TW	Taiwan
GR	Greece	US	United States

variant

The argument variant is rarely used and is needed only for exceptional or system-dependent situations to designate information specific to a browser or vendor. For example, the Norwegian language has two sets of spelling rules, a traditional one called *bokmål* and a new one called *nynorsk*. The locale for traditional spelling would be created as follows:

```
new Locale("no", "NO", "B");
```

For convenience, the `Locale` class contains many predefined locale constants. `Locale.CANADA` is for the country Canada and language English; `Locale.CANADA_FRENCH` is for the country Canada and language French. Several other common constants are:

```
Locale.US, Locale.UK, Locale.FRANCE, Locale.GERMANY, Locale.ITALY,
Locale.CHINA, Locale.KOREA, Locale.JAPAN, and Locale.TAIWAN
```

The `Locale` class also provides the following constants based on language:

```
Locale.CHINESE, Locale.ENGLISH, Locale.FRENCH, Locale.GERMAN,
Locale.ITALIAN, Locale.JAPANESE, Locale.KOREAN,
Locale.SIMPLIFIED_CHINESE, and Locale.TRADITIONAL_CHINESE
```

Tip

You can invoke the static method `getAvailableLocales()` in the `Locale` class to obtain all the available locales supported in the system. For example,

```
Locale[] availableLocales = Calendar.getAvailableLocales();
```

returns all the locales in an array.

Tip

Your machine has a default locale. You may override it by supplying the language and region parameters when you run the program, as follows:

```
java -Duser.language=zh -Duser.region=CN MainClass
```

locale sensitive

An operation that requires a `Locale` to perform its task is called *locale sensitive*. Displaying a number such as a date or time, for example, is a locale-sensitive operation; the number should be formatted according to the customs and conventions of the user's locale. The sections that follow introduce locale-sensitive operations.

31.3 Displaying Date and Time

Date

Calendar

Applications often need to obtain date and time. Java provides a system-independent encapsulation of date and time in the `java.util.Date` class; it also provides `java.util.TimeZone` for dealing with time zones, and `java.util.Calendar` for extracting detailed information from `Date`. Different locales have different conventions for displaying date and time. Should the year, month, or day be displayed first? Should slashes, periods, or colons be used to separate fields of the date? What are the names of the months in the language? The `java.text.DateFormat` class can be used to format date and time in a locale-sensitive way for display to the user. The `Date` class was introduced in §8.6.1, "The `Date` Class," and the `Calendar` class and its subclass `GregorianCalendar` were introduced in §14.3, "Example: `Calendar` and `GregorianCalendar`."

31.3.1 The `TimeZone` Class

TimeZone

`TimeZone` represents a time zone offset and also figures out daylight savings. To get a `TimeZone` object for a specified time zone ID, use `TimeZone.getTimeZone(id)`. To set a time zone in a

`Calendar` object, use the `setTimeZone` method with a time zone ID. For example, `cal.setTimeZone(TimeZone.getTimeZone("CST"))` sets the time zone to Central Standard Time. To find all the available time zones supported in Java, use the static method `getAvailableIDs()` in the `TimeZone` class. In general, the international time zone ID is a string in the form of continent/city like Europe/Berlin, Asia/Taipei, and America/Washington. You can also use the static method `getDefault()` in the `TimeZone` class to obtain the default time zone on the host machine.

31.3.2 The DateFormat Class

DateFormat

The `DateFormat` class can be used to format date and time in a number of styles. The `DateFormat` class supports several standard formatting styles. To format date and time, simply create an instance of `DateFormat` using one of the three static methods `getDateInstance`, `getTimeInstance`, and `getDateTimeInstance` and apply the `format(Date)` method on the instance, as shown in Figure 31.2.

java.text.DateFormat	
+format(date: Date): String	Formats a date into a date/time string.
+getDateInstance(): DateFormat	Gets the date formatter with the default formatting style for the default locale.
+getDateInstance(dateStyle: int): DateFormat	Gets the date formatter with the given formatting style for the default locale.
+getDateInstance(dateStyle: int, aLocale: Locale): DateFormat	Gets the date formatter with the given formatting style for the given locale.
+getDateTimeInstance(): DateFormat	Gets the date and time formatter with the default formatting style for the default locale.
+getDateTimeInstance(dateStyle: int, timeStyle: int): DateFormat	Gets the date and time formatter with the given date and time formatting styles for the default locale.
+getDateTimeInstance(dateStyle: int, timeStyle: int, aLocale: Locale): DateFormat	Gets the date and time formatter with the given formatting styles for the given locale.
+getInstance(): DateFormat	Gets a default date and time formatter that uses the SHORT style for both the date and the time.

FIGURE 31.2 The `DateFormat` class formats date and time.

The `dateStyle` and `timeStyle` are one of the following constants: `DateFormat.SHORT`, `DateFormat.MEDIUM`, `DateFormat.LONG`, `DateFormat.FULL`. The exact result depends on the locale, but generally,

- `SHORT` is completely numeric, such as 7/24/98 (for date) and 4:49 PM (for time).
- `MEDIUM` is longer, such as 24-Jul-98 (for date) and 4:52:09 PM (for time).
- `LONG` is even longer, such as July 24, 1998 (for date) and 4:53:16 PM EST (for time).
- `FULL` is completely specified, such as Friday, July 24, 1998 (for date) and 4:54:13 o'clock PM EST (for time).

The statements given below display current time with a specified time zone (CST), formatting style (full date and full time), and locale (US).

```
GregorianCalendar calendar = new GregorianCalendar();
DateFormat formatter = DateFormat.getDateTimeInstance(
  DateFormat.FULL, DateFormat.FULL, Locale.US);
TimeZone timeZone = TimeZone.getTimeZone("CST");
formatter.setTimeZone(timeZone);
System.out.println("The local time is " +
  formatter.format(calendar.getTime()));
```

31.3.3 The SimpleDateFormat Class

SimpleDateFormat

The date and time formatting subclass, SimpleDateFormat, enables you to choose any user-defined pattern for date and time formatting. The constructor shown below can be used to create a SimpleDateFormat object, and the object can be used to convert a Date object into a string with the desired format.

```
public SimpleDateFormat(String pattern)
```

The parameter pattern is a string consisting of characters with special meanings. For example, y means year, M means month, d means day of the month, G is for era designator, h means hour, m means minute of the hour, s means second of the minute, and z means time zone. Therefore, the following code will display a string like "Current time is 1997.11.12 AD at 04:10:18 PST" because the pattern is "yyyy.MM.dd G 'at' hh:mm:ss z".

```
SimpleDateFormat formatter
  = new SimpleDateFormat("yyyy.MM.dd G 'at' hh:mm:ss z");
date currentTime = new Date();
String dateString = formatter.format(currentTime);
System.out.println("Current time is " + dateString);
```

31.3.4 The DateFormatSymbols Class

DateFormatSymbols

The DateFormatSymbols class encapsulates localizable date-time formatting data, such as the names of the months and the names of the days of the week, as shown in Figure 31.3.

For example, the following statement displays the month names and weekday names for the default locale.

```
DateFormatSymbols symbols = new DateFormatSymbols();
String[] monthNames = symbols.getMonths();
for (int i = 0; i < monthNames.length; i++) {
  System.out.println(monthNames[i]); // Display January, ...
}

String[] weekdayNames = symbols.getWeekdays();
for (int i = 0; i < weekdayNames.length; i++) {
  System.out.println(weekdayNames[i]); // Display Sunday, Monday, ...
}
```

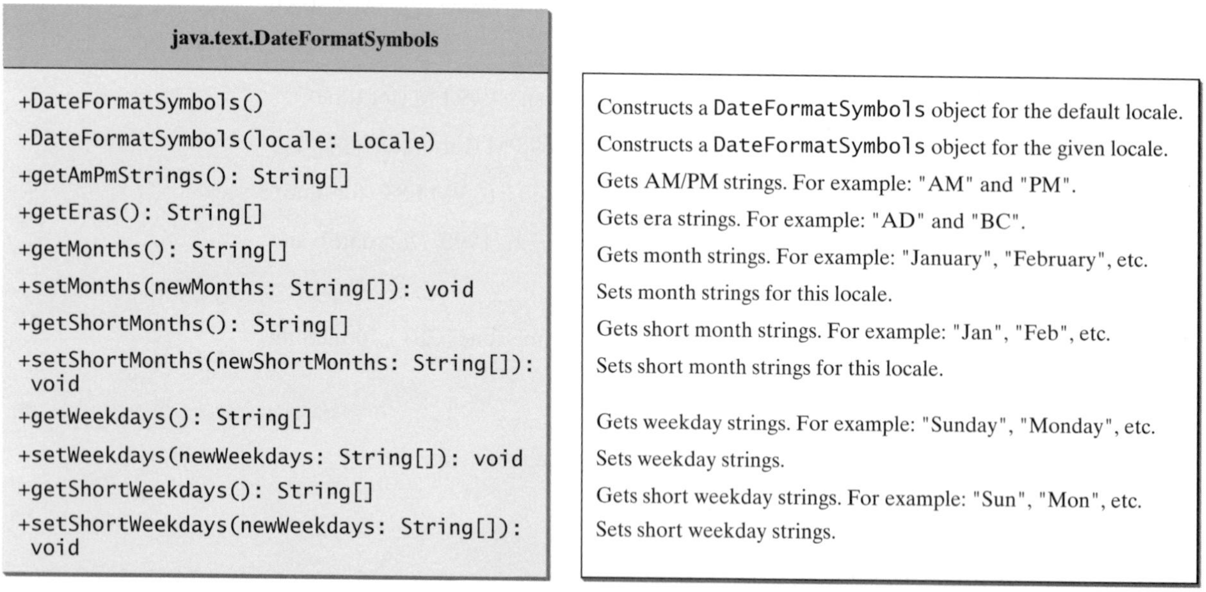
java.text.DateFormatSymbols
+DateFormatSymbols()
+DateFormatSymbols(locale: Locale)
+getAmPmStrings(): String[]
+getEras(): String[]
+getMonths(): String[]
+setMonths(newMonths: String[]): void
+getShortMonths(): String[]
+setShortMonths(newShortMonths: String[]): void
+getWeekdays(): String[]
+setWeekdays(newWeekdays: String[]): void
+getShortWeekdays(): String[]
+setShortWeekdays(newWeekdays: String[]): void
Constructs a DateFormatSymbols object for the default locale.
Constructs a DateFormatSymbols object for the given locale.
Gets AM/PM strings. For example: "AM" and "PM".
Gets era strings. For example: "AD" and "BC".
Gets month strings. For example: "January", "February", etc.
Sets month strings for this locale.
Gets short month strings. For example: "Jan", "Feb", etc.
Sets short month strings for this locale.
Gets weekday strings. For example: "Sunday", "Monday", etc.
Sets weekday strings.
Gets short weekday strings. For example: "Sun", "Mon", etc.
Sets short weekday strings.

FIGURE 31.3 The DateFormatSymbols class encapsulates localizable date-time formatting data.

The following two examples demonstrate how to display date, time, and calendar based on locale. The first example creates a clock and displays date and time in locale-sensitive format. The second example displays several different calendars with the names of the days shown in the appropriate local language.

31.3.5 Example: Displaying an International Clock

Write a program that displays a clock to show the current time based on the specified locale and time zone. The locale and time zone are selected from the combo boxes that contain the available locales and time zones in the system, as shown in Figure 31.4.

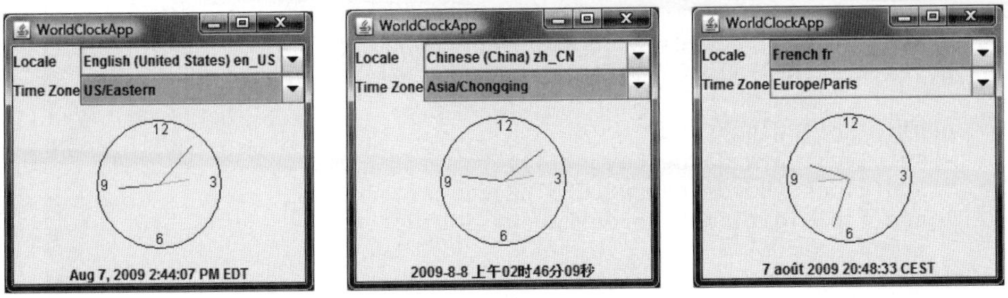
WorldClockApp
Locale
English (United States) en_US
Time Zone
US/Eastern
12
9
3
6
Aug 7, 2009 2:44:07 PM EDT
WorldClockApp
Locale
Chinese (China) zh_CN
Time Zone
Asia/Chongqing
2009-8-8 上午02时46分09秒
WorldClockApp
Locale
French fr
Time Zone
Europe/Paris
7 août 2009 20:48:33 CEST

FIGURE 31.4 The program displays a clock that shows the current time with the specified locale and time zone.

Here are the major steps in the program:

1. Define a subclass of `JPanel` named `WorldClock` (Listing 31.1) to contain an instance of the `StillClock` class (developed in Listing 15.10, StillClock.java), and place it in the center. Create a `JLabel` to display the digit time, and place it in the south. Use the `GregorianCalendar` class to obtain the current time for a specific locale and time zone.
2. Define a subclass of `JPanel` named `WorldClockControl` (Listing 31.2) to contain an instance of `WorldClock` and two instances of `JComboBox` for selecting locales and time zones.
3. Define an applet named `WorldClockApp` (Listing 31.3) to contain an instance of `WorldClockControl` and enable the applet to run standalone.

The relationship among these classes is shown in Figure 31.5.

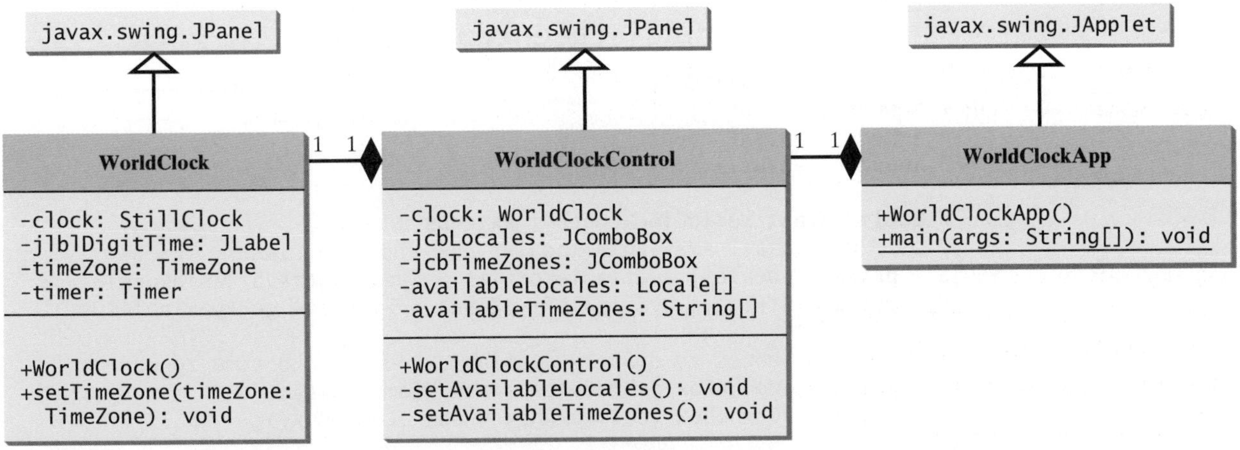
javax.swing.JPanel
javax.swing.JPanel
javax.swing.JApplet
WorldClock
1 1
WorldClockControl
1 1
WorldClockApp
-clock: StillClock
-jlblDigitTime: JLabel
-timeZone: TimeZone
-timer: Timer
+WorldClock()
+setTimeZone(timeZone: TimeZone): void
-clock: WorldClock
-jcbLocales: JComboBox
-jcbTimeZones: JComboBox
-availableLocales: Locale[]
-availableTimeZones: String[]
+WorldClockControl()
-setAvailableLocales(): void
-setAvailableTimeZones(): void
+WorldClockApp()
+main(args: String[]): void

FIGURE 31.5 `WorldClockApp` contains `WorldClockControl`, and `WorldClockControl` contains `WorldClock`.

Listing 31.1 WorldClock.java

create timer · *create clock* · *timer listener class*

```
import javax.swing.*;
import java.awt.*;
import java.awt.event.*;
import java.util.Calendar;
import java.util.TimeZone;
import java.util.GregorianCalendar;
import java.text.*;

public class WorldClock extends JPanel {
  private TimeZone timeZone = TimeZone.getTimeZone("EST");
  private Timer timer = new Timer(1000, new TimerListener());
  private StillClock clock = new StillClock();
  private JLabel jlblDigitTime = new JLabel("", JLabel.CENTER);

  public WorldClock() {
    setLayout(new BorderLayout());
    add(clock, BorderLayout.CENTER);
    add(jlblDigitTime, BorderLayout.SOUTH);
    timer.start();
  }

  public void setTimeZone(TimeZone timeZone) {
    this.timeZone = timeZone;
  }

  private class TimerListener implements ActionListener {
    public void actionPerformed(ActionEvent e) {
      Calendar calendar = new GregorianCalendar(timeZone, getLocale());
      clock.setHour(calendar.get(Calendar.HOUR));
      clock.setMinute(calendar.get(Calendar.MINUTE));
      clock.setSecond(calendar.get(Calendar.SECOND));

      // Display digit time on the label
      DateFormat formatter = DateFormat.getDateTimeInstance
        (DateFormat.MEDIUM, DateFormat.LONG, getLocale());
      formatter.setTimeZone(timeZone);
      jlblDigitTime.setText(formatter.format(calendar.getTime()));
    }
  }
}
```

Listing 31.2 WorldClockControl.java

locales · *time zones* · *combo boxes*

```
import javax.swing.*;
import java.awt.*;
import java.awt.event.*;
import java.util.*;

public class WorldClockControl extends JPanel {
  // Obtain all available locales and time zone ids
  private Locale[] availableLocales = Locale.getAvailableLocales();
  private String[] availableTimeZones = TimeZone.getAvailableIDs();

  // Combo boxes to display available locales and time zones
  private JComboBox jcbLocales = new JComboBox();
  private JComboBox jcbTimeZones = new JComboBox();

```

create clock

```
  // Create a clock
  private WorldClock clock = new WorldClock();

  public WorldClockControl()  {
    // Initialize jcbLocales with all available locales
    setAvailableLocales();

    // Initialize jcbTimeZones with all available time zones
    setAvailableTimeZones();

    // Initialize locale and time zone
    clock.setLocale(
      availableLocales[jcbLocales.getSelectedIndex()]);
    clock.setTimeZone(TimeZone.getTimeZone(
      availableTimeZones[jcbTimeZones.getSelectedIndex()]));

```

create UI

```
    JPanel panel1 = new JPanel();
    panel1.setLayout(new GridLayout(2, 1));
    panel1.add(new JLabel("Locale"));
    panel1.add(new JLabel("Time Zone"));
    JPanel panel2 = new JPanel();

    panel2.setLayout(new GridLayout(2, 1));
    panel2.add(jcbLocales, BorderLayout.CENTER);
    panel2.add(jcbTimeZones, BorderLayout.CENTER);

    JPanel panel3 = new JPanel();
    panel3.setLayout(new BorderLayout());
    panel3.add(panel1, BorderLayout.WEST);
    panel3.add(panel2, BorderLayout.CENTER);

    setLayout(new BorderLayout());
    add(panel3, BorderLayout.NORTH);
    add(clock, BorderLayout.CENTER);

```

new locale

```
    jcbLocales.addActionListener(new ActionListener() {
      public void actionPerformed(ActionEvent e) {
        clock.setLocale(
          availableLocales[jcbLocales.getSelectedIndex()]);
      }
    });
```

new time zone

```
    jcbTimeZones.addActionListener(new ActionListener() {
      public void actionPerformed(ActionEvent e) {
        clock.setTimeZone(TimeZone.getTimeZone(
          availableTimeZones[jcbTimeZones.getSelectedIndex()]));
      }
    });
  }

  private void setAvailableLocales() {
    for (int i = 0; i < availableLocales.length; i++) {
      jcbLocales.addItem(availableLocales[i].getDisplayName() + " "
        + availableLocales[i].toString());
    }
  }

  private void setAvailableTimeZones() {
    // Sort time zones
    Arrays.sort(availableTimeZones);
    for (int i = 0; i < availableTimeZones.length; i++) {
```

```
75        jcbTimeZones.addItem(availableTimeZones[i]);
76      }
77    }
78  }
```

LISTING 31.3 WorldClockApp.java

main method omitted

```
import javax.swing.*;

public class WorldClockApp extends JApplet {
  /** Construct the applet */
  public WorldClockApp() {
    add(new WorldClockControl());
  }
}
```

The WorldClock class uses GregorianCalendar to obtain a Calendar object for the specified locale and time zone (line 28). Since WorldClock extends JPanel, and every GUI component has the locale property, the locale for the calendar is obtained from the WorldClock using getLocale() (line 28).

An instance of StillClock is created (line 12) and placed in the panel (line 17). The clock time is updated every one second using the current Calendar object in lines 28–31.

An instance of DateFormat is created (lines 34–35) and is used to format the date in accordance with the locale (line 37).

The WorldClockControl class contains an instance of WorldClock and two combo boxes. The combo boxes store all the available locales and time zones (lines 64–77). The newly selected locale and time zone are set in the clock (lines 50–61) and used to display a new time based on the current locale and time zone.

31.3.6 Example: Displaying a Calendar

Write a program that displays a calendar based on the specified locale, as shown in Figure 31.6. The user can specify a locale from a combo box that consists of a list of all the available locales supported by the system. When the program starts, the calendar for the current month of the year is displayed. The user can use the *Prior* and *Next* buttons to browse the calendar.

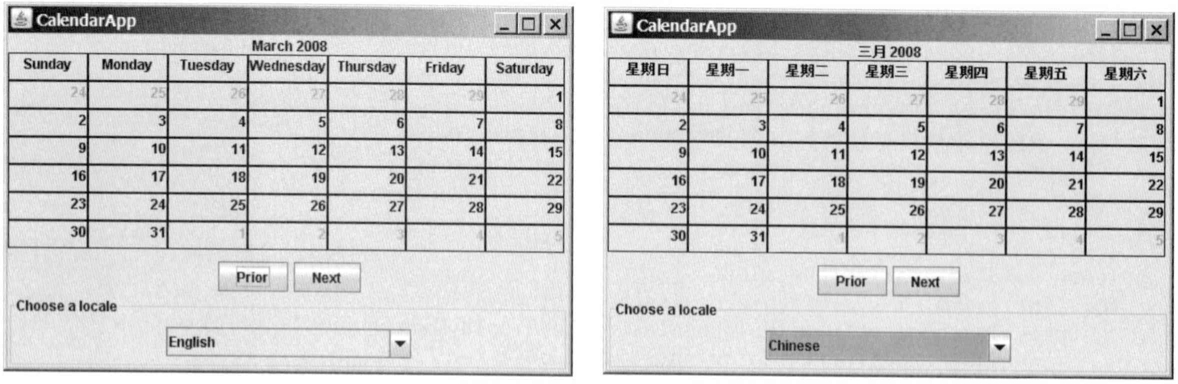
CalendarApp
March 2008
Sunday
Monday
Tuesday
Wednesday
Thursday
Friday
Saturday
Prior
Next
Choose a locale
English
CalendarApp
三月 2008
星期日
星期一
星期二
星期三
星期四
星期五
星期六
Prior
Next
Choose a locale
Chinese

FIGURE 31.6 The calendar applet displays a calendar with a specified locale.

Here are the major steps in the program:

1. Create a subclass of JPanel named CalendarPanel (Listing 31.4) to display the calendar for the given year and month based on the specified locale and time zone.

2. Create an applet named `CalendarApp` (Listing 31.5). Create a panel to hold an instance of `CalendarPanel` and two buttons, *Prior* and *Next*. Place the panel in the center of the applet. Create a combo box and place it in the south of the applet. The relationships among these classes are shown in Figure 31.7.

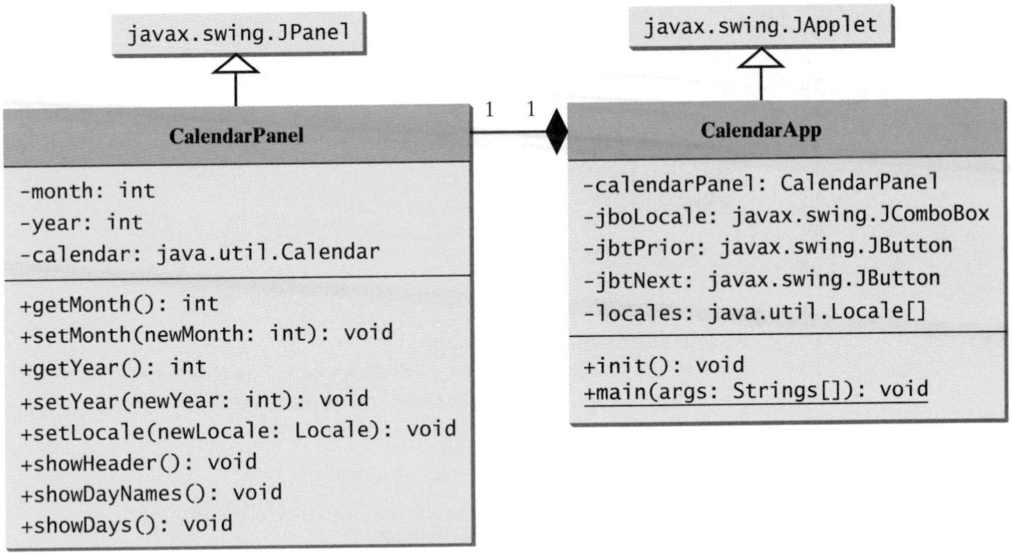
javax.swing.JPanel
javax.swing.JApplet
1
1
CalendarPanel
-month: int
-year: int
-calendar: java.util.Calendar
+getMonth(): int
+setMonth(newMonth: int): void
+getYear(): int
+setYear(newYear: int): void
+setLocale(newLocale: Locale): void
+showHeader(): void
+showDayNames(): void
+showDays(): void
CalendarApp
-calendarPanel: CalendarPanel
-jboLocale: javax.swing.JComboBox
-jbtPrior: javax.swing.JButton
-jbtNext: javax.swing.JButton
-locales: java.util.Locale[]
+init(): void
+main(args: Strings[]): void

FIGURE 31.7 `CalendarApp` contains `CalendarPanel`.

LISTING 31.4 CalendarPanel.java

```java
import java.awt.*;
import javax.swing.*;
import javax.swing.border.LineBorder;
import java.util.*;
import java.text.*;

public class CalendarPanel extends JPanel {
  // The header label
  private JLabel jlblHeader = new JLabel(" ", JLabel.CENTER);

  // Maximum number of labels to display day names and days
  private JLabel[] jlblDay = new JLabel[49];

  private Calendar calendar;
  private int month;  // The specified month
  private int year;  // The specified year

  // Panel jpDays to hold day names and days
  private JPanel jpDays = new JPanel(new GridLayout(0, 7));

  public CalendarPanel() {
    // Create labels for displaying days
    for (int i = 0; i < 49; i++) {
      jlblDay[i] = new JLabel();
      jlblDay[i].setBorder(new LineBorder(Color.black, 1));
      jlblDay[i].setHorizontalAlignment(JLabel.RIGHT);
      jlblDay[i].setVerticalAlignment(JLabel.TOP);
    }

```

label for header
labels for days
calendar
month
year
panel for days
create labels

place header
place day
get current calendar
update calendar
show header
show days
show header
new header
get day names
empty **jpDays** panel
display day names
days before this month

```
    // Place header and calendar body in the panel
    this.setLayout(new BorderLayout());
    this.add(jlblHeader, BorderLayout.NORTH);
    this.add(jpDays, BorderLayout.CENTER);

    // Set current month and year
    calendar = new GregorianCalendar();
    month = calendar.get(Calendar.MONTH);
    year = calendar.get(Calendar.YEAR);
    updateCalendar();

    // Show calendar
    showHeader();
    showDays();
  }

  /** Update the header based on locale */
  private void showHeader() {
    SimpleDateFormat sdf =
      new SimpleDateFormat("MMMM yyyy", getLocale());
    String header = sdf.format(calendar.getTime());
    jlblHeader.setText(header);
  }

  /** Update the day names based on locale */
  private void showDayNames() {
    DateFormatSymbols dfs = new DateFormatSymbols(getLocale());
    String dayNames[] = dfs.getWeekdays();

    // jlblDay[0], jlblDay[1], ..., jlblDay[6] for day names
    for (int i = 0; i < 7; i++) {
      jlblDay[i].setText(dayNames[i + 1]);
      jlblDay[i].setHorizontalAlignment(JLabel.CENTER);
      jpDays.add(jlblDay[i]); // Add to jpDays
    }
  }

  /** Display days */
  public void showDays() {
    jpDays.removeAll(); // Remove all labels from jpDays

    showDayNames(); // Display day names

    // Get the day of the first day in a month
    int startingDayOfMonth = calendar.get(Calendar.DAY_OF_WEEK);

    // Fill the calendar with the days before this month
    Calendar cloneCalendar = (Calendar)calendar.clone();
    cloneCalendar.add(Calendar.DATE, -1); // Becomes preceding month
    int daysInPrecedingMonth = cloneCalendar.getActualMaximum(
          Calendar.DAY_OF_MONTH);

    for (int i = 0; i < startingDayOfMonth - 1; i++) {
      jlblDay[i + 7].setForeground(Color.LIGHT_GRAY);
      jlblDay[i + 7].setText(daysInPrecedingMonth -
        startingDayOfMonth + 2 + i + "");
      jpDays.add(jlblDay[i + 7]); // Add to jpDays
    }

    // Display days of this month
    int daysInCurrentMonth = calendar.getActualMaximum(
```

```java
        Calendar.DAY_OF_MONTH);
    for (int i = 1; i <= daysInCurrentMonth; i++) {
      jlblDay[i - 2 + startingDayOfMonth + 7].
        setForeground(Color.black);
      jlblDay[i - 2 + startingDayOfMonth + 7].setText(i + "");
      jpDays.add(jlblDay[i - 2 + startingDayOfMonth + 7]);
    }

    // Fill the calendar with the days after this month
    int j = 1;
    for (int i = daysInCurrentMonth - 1 + startingDayOfMonth + 7;
        i % 7 != 0; i++) {
      jlblDay[i].setForeground(Color.LIGHT_GRAY);
      jlblDay[i].setText(j++ + "");
      jpDays.add(jlblDay[i]); // Add to jpDays
    }

    jpDays.repaint(); // Repaint the labels in jpDays
  }

  /** Set the calendar to the first day of the
    * specified month and year */
  public void updateCalendar() {
    calendar.set(Calendar.YEAR, year);
    calendar.set(Calendar.MONTH, month);
    calendar.set(Calendar.DATE, 1);
  }

  /** Return month */
  public int getMonth() {
    return month;
  }

  /** Set a new month */
  public void setMonth(int newMonth) {
    month = newMonth;
    updateCalendar();
    showHeader();
    showDays();
  }

  /** Return year */
  public int getYear() {
    return year;
  }

  /** Set a new year */
  public void setYear(int newYear) {
    year = newYear;
    updateCalendar();
    showHeader();
    showDays();
  }

  /** Set a new locale */
  public void changeLocale(Locale newLocale) {
    setLocale(newLocale);
    showHeader();
    showDays();
  }
}
```

days in this month

days after this month

repaint **jpDays**

update calendar

set new month

set new year

set new locale

`CalendarPanel` is created to control and display the calendar. It displays the month and year in the header, and the day names and days in the calendar body. The header and day names are locale sensitive.

showHeader

The `showHeader` method (lines 47–52) displays the calendar title in a form like "MMMM yyyy". The `SimpleDateFormat` class used in the `showHeader` method is a subclass of `DateFormat`. `SimpleDateFormat` allows you to customize the date format to display the date in various nonstandard styles.

showDayNames

The `showDayNames` method (lines 55–65) displays the day names in the calendar. The `DateFormatSymbols` class used in the `showDayNames` method is a class for encapsulating localizable date-time formatting data, such as the names of the months, the names of the days of the week, and the time-zone data. The `getWeekdays` method is used to get an array of day names.

showDays

The `showDays` method (lines 68–109) displays the days for the specified month of the year. As you can see in Figure 31.6, the labels before the current month are filled with the last few days of the preceding month, and the labels after the current month are filled with the first few days of the next month.

To fill the calendar with the days before the current month, a clone of `calendar`, named `cloneCalendar`, is created to obtain the days for the preceding month (line 77). `cloneCalendar` is a copy of `calendar` with separate memory space. Thus you can change the properties of `cloneCalendar` without corrupting the `calendar` object. The `clone()` method is defined in the `Object` class, which was introduced in §14.7, "Example: The `Cloneable` Interface." You can clone any object as long as its defining class implements the `Cloneable` interface. The `Calendar` class implements `Cloneable`.

The `cloneCalendar.getActualMaximum(Calendar.DAY_OF_MONTH)` method (lines 90–91) returns the number of days in the month for the specified calendar.

LISTING 31.5 CalendarApp.java

calendar panel

combo box

locales

create UI

```
import java.awt.*;
import java.awt.event.*;
import javax.swing.*;
import javax.swing.border.*;
import java.util.*;

public class CalendarApp extends JApplet {
  // Create a CalendarPanel for showing calendars
  private CalendarPanel calendarPanel = new CalendarPanel();

  // Combo box for selecting available locales
  private JComboBox jcboLocale = new JComboBox();

  // Declare locales to store available locales
  private Locale[] locales = Calendar.getAvailableLocales();

  // Buttons Prior and Next for displaying prior and next month
  private JButton jbtPrior = new JButton("Prior");
  private JButton jbtNext = new JButton("Next");

  /** Initialize the applet */
  public void init() {
    // Panel jpLocale to hold the combo box for selecting locales
    JPanel jpLocale = new JPanel(new FlowLayout());
    jpLocale.setBorder(new TitledBorder("Choose a locale"));
    jpLocale.add(jcboLocale);

    // Initialize the combo box to add locale names
    for (int i = 0; i < locales.length; i++)
```

```
30        jcboLocale.addItem(locales[i].getDisplayName());
31
32      // Panel jpButtons to hold buttons
33      JPanel jpButtons = new JPanel(new FlowLayout());
34      jpButtons.add(jbtPrior);
35      jpButtons.add(jbtNext);
36
37      // Panel jpCalendar to hold calendarPanel and buttons
38      JPanel jpCalendar = new JPanel(new BorderLayout());
39      jpCalendar.add(calendarPanel, BorderLayout.CENTER);
40      jpCalendar.add(jpButtons, BorderLayout.SOUTH);
41
42      // Place jpCalendar and jpLocale to the applet
43      add(jpCalendar, BorderLayout.CENTER);
44      add(jpLocale, BorderLayout.SOUTH);
45
46      // Register listeners
47      jcboLocale.addActionListener(new ActionListener() {
48        public void actionPerformed(ActionEvent e) {
49          if (e.getSource() == jcboLocale)
50            calendarPanel.changeLocale(
51              locales[jcboLocale.getSelectedIndex()]);
52        }
53      });
54
55      jbtPrior.addActionListener(new ActionListener() {
56        public void actionPerformed(ActionEvent e) {
57          int currentMonth = calendarPanel.getMonth();
58          if (currentMonth == 0) // The previous month is 11 for Dec
59            calendarPanel.setYear(calendarPanel.getYear() - 1);
60            calendarPanel.setMonth((currentMonth - 1) % 12);
61        }});
62
63      jbtNext.addActionListener(new ActionListener() {
64        public void actionPerformed(ActionEvent e) {
65          int currentMonth = calendarPanel.getMonth();
66          if (currentMonth == 11) // The next month is 0 for Jan
67            calendarPanel.setYear(calendarPanel.getYear() + 1);
68
69          calendarPanel.setMonth((currentMonth + 1) % 12);
70        }});
71
72      calendarPanel.changeLocale(
73        locales[jcboLocale.getSelectedIndex()]);
74    }
75  }
```

set a new locale

previous month

next month

main method omitted

`CalendarApp` creates the user interface and handles the button actions and combo box item selections for locales. The `Calendar.getAvailableLocales()` method (line 15) is used to find all the available locales that have calendars. Its `getDisplayName()` method returns the name of each locale and adds the name to the combo box (line 30). When the user selects a locale name in the combo box, a new locale is passed to `calendarPanel`, and a new calendar is displayed based on the new locale (lines 72–73).

31.4 Formatting Numbers

Formatting numbers is highly locale dependent. For example, number 5000.555 is displayed as 5,000.555 in the United States, but as 5 000,555 in France and as 5.000,555 in Germany.

Numbers are formatted using the `java.text.NumberFormat` class, an abstract base class that provides the methods for formatting and parsing numbers, as shown in Figure 31.8.

java.text.NumberFormat	
+getInstance(): NumberFormat	Returns the default number format for the default locale.
+getInstance(locale: Locale): NumberFormat	Returns the default number format for the specified locale.
+getIntegerInstance(): NumberFormat	Returns an integer number format for the default locale.
+getIntegerInstance(locale: Locale): NumberFormat	Returns an integer number format for the specified locale.
+getCurrencyInstance(): NumberFormat	Returns a currency format for the current default locale.
+getNumberInstance(): NumberFormat	Same as `getInstance()`.
+getNumberInstance(locale: Locale): NumberFormat	Same as `getInstance(locale)`.
+getPercentInstance(): NumberFormat	Returns a percentage format for the default locale.
+getPercentInstance(locale: Locale): NumberFormat	Returns a percentage format for the specified locale.
+format(number: double): String	Formats a floating-point number.
+format(number: long): String	Formats an integer.
+getMaximumFractionDigits(): int	Returns the maximum number of allowed fraction digits.
+setMaximumFractionDigits(newValue: int): void	Sets the maximum number of allowed fraction digits.
+getMinimumFractionDigits(): int	Returns the minimum number of allowed fraction digits.
+setMinimumFractionDigits(newValue: int): void	Sets the minimum number of allowed fraction digits.
+getMaximumIntegerDigits(): int	Returns the maximum number of allowed integer digits in a fraction number.
+setMaximumIntegerDigits(newValue: int): void	Sets the maximum number of allowed integer digits in a fraction number.
+getMinimumIntegerDigits(): int	Returns the minimum number of allowed integer digits in a fraction number.
+setMinimumIntegerDigits(newValue: int): void	Sets the minimum number of allowed integer digits in a fraction number.
+isGroupingUsed(): boolean	Returns true if grouping is used in this format. For example, in the English locale, with grouping on, the number 1234567 is formatted as "1,234,567".
+setGroupingUsed(newValue: boolean): void	Sets whether or not grouping will be used in this format.
+parse(source: String): Number	Parses string into a number.
+getAvailableLocales(): Locale[]	Gets the set of locales for which `NumberFormats` are installed.

FIGURE 31.8 The `NumberFormat` class provides the methods for formatting and parsing numbers.

With `NumberFormat`, you can format and parse numbers for any locale. Your code will be completely independent of locale conventions for decimal points, thousands-separators, currency format, and percentage formats.

31.4.1 Plain Number Format

You can get an instance of `NumberFormat` for the current locale using `NumberFormat.getInstance()` or `NumberFormat.getNumberInstance` and for the specified locale using `NumberFormat.getInstance(Locale)` or `NumberFormat.getNumberInstance(Locale)`. You can then invoke `format(number)` on the `NumberFormat` instance to return a formatted number as a string.

For example, to display number 5000.555 in France, use the following code:

```
NumberFormat numberFormat = NumberFormat.getInstance(Locale.FRANCE);
System.out.println(numberFormat.format(5000.555));
```

You can control the display of numbers with such methods as `setMaximumFractionDigits` and `setMinimumFractionDigits`. For example, 5000.555 will be displayed as 5000.6 if you use `numberFormat.setMaximumFractionDigits(1)`.

31.4.2 Currency Format

To format a number as a currency value, use `NumberFormat.getCurrencyInstance()` to get the currency number format for the current locale or `NumberFormat.getCurrencyInstance(Locale)` to get the currency number for the specified locale.

For example, to display number 5000.555 as currency in the United States, use the following code:

```
NumberFormat currencyFormat =
  NumberFormat.getCurrencyInstance(Locale.US);
System.out.println(currencyFormat.format(5000.555));
```

5000.555 is formatted into $5,000,56. If the locale is set to France, the number will be formatted into 5 000,56 €.

31.4.3 Percent Format

To format a number in a percent, use `NumberFormat.getPercentInstance()` or `NumberFormat.getPercentInstance(Locale)` to get the percent number format for the current locale or the specified locale.

For example, to display number 0.555367 as a percent in the United States, use the following code:

```
NumberFormat percentFormat =
  NumberFormat.getPercentInstance(Locale.US);
System.out.println(percentFormat.format(0.555367));
```

0.555367 is formatted into 56%. By default, the format truncates the fraction part in a percent number. If you want to keep three digits after the decimal point, use `percentFormat.setMinimumFractionDigits(3)`. So 0.555367 would be displayed as 55.537%.

31.4.4 Parsing Numbers

You can format a number into a string using the `format(numericalValue)` method. You can also use the `parse(String)` method to convert a formatted plain number, currency value, or percent number with the conventions of a certain locale into an instance of `java.lang.Number`. The `parse` method throws a `java.text.ParseException` if parsing fails. For example, U.S. $5,000.56 can be parsed into a number using the following statements:

```
NumberFormat currencyFormat =
  NumberFormat.getCurrencyInstance(Locale.US);
try {
  Number number = currencyFormat.parse("$5,000.56");
  System.out.println(number.doubleValue());
}
catch (java.text.ParseException ex) {
  System.out.println("Parse failed");
}
```

31.4.5 The DecimalFormat Class

If you want even more control over the format or parsing, cast the NumberFormat you get from the factory methods to a java.text.DecimalFormat, which is a subclass of NumberFormat. You can then use the applyPattern(String pattern) method of the DecimalFormat class to specify the patterns for displaying the number.

A pattern can specify the minimum number of digits before the decimal point and the maximum number of digits after the decimal point. The characters '0' and '#' are used to specify a required digit and an optional digit, respectively. The optional digit is not displayed if it is zero. For example, the pattern "00.0##" indicates minimum two digits before the decimal point and maximum three digits after the decimal point. If there are more actual digits before the decimal point, all of them are displayed. If there are more than three digits after the decimal point, the number of digits is rounded. Applying the pattern "00.0##", number 111.2226 is formatted to 111.223, number 1111.2226 to 1111.223, number 1.22 to 01.22, and number 1 to 01.0. Here is the code:

```
NumberFormat numberFormat = NumberFormat.getInstance(Locale.US);
DecimalFormat decimalFormat = (DecimalFormat)numberFormat;
decimalFormat.applyPattern("00.0##");
System.out.println(decimalFormat.format(111.2226));
System.out.println(decimalFormat.format(1111.2226));
System.out.println(decimalFormat.format(1.22));
System.out.println(decimalFormat.format(1));
```

The character '%' can be put at the end of a pattern to indicate that a number is formatted as a percentage. This causes the number to be multiplied by 100 and appends a percent sign %.

31.4.6 Example: Formatting Numbers

Create a loan calculator for computing loans. The calculator allows the user to choose locales, and displays numbers in accordance with locale-sensitive format. As shown in Figure 31.9, the user enters interest rate, number of years, and loan amount, then clicks the *Compute* button to display the interest rate in percentage format, the number of years in normal number format, and the loan amount, total payment, and monthly payment in currency format. Listing 31.6 gives the solution to the problem.

LISTING 31.6 NumberFormatDemo.java

UI components

```
import java.awt.*;
import java.awt.event.*;
import javax.swing.*;
import javax.swing.border.*;
import java.util.*;
import java.text.NumberFormat;

public class NumberFormatDemo extends JApplet {
  // Combo box for selecting available locales
  private JComboBox jcboLocale = new JComboBox();

  // Text fields for interest rate, year, and loan amount
  private JTextField jtfInterestRate = new JTextField("6.75");
  private JTextField jtfNumberOfYears = new JTextField("15");
  private JTextField jtfLoanAmount = new JTextField("107000");
  private JTextField jtfFormattedInterestRate = new JTextField(10);
  private JTextField jtfFormattedNumberOfYears = new JTextField(10);
  private JTextField jtfFormattedLoanAmount = new JTextField(10);

  // Text fields for monthly payment and total payment
```

```
  private JTextField jtfTotalPayment = new JTextField();
  private JTextField jtfMonthlyPayment = new JTextField();

  // Compute button
  private JButton jbtCompute = new JButton("Compute");

  // Current locale
  private Locale locale = Locale.getDefault();

  // Declare locales to store available locales
  private Locale[] locales = Calendar.getAvailableLocales();

  /** Initialize the combo box */
  public void initializeComboBox() {
    // Add locale names to the combo box
    for (int i = 0; i < locales.length; i++)
      jcboLocale.addItem(locales[i].getDisplayName());
  }

  /** Initialize the applet */
  public void init() {
    // Panel p1 to hold the combo box for selecting locales
    JPanel p1 = new JPanel();
    p1.setLayout(new FlowLayout());
    p1.add(jcboLocale);
    initializeComboBox();
    p1.setBorder(new TitledBorder("Choose a Locale"));

    // Panel p2 to hold the input
    JPanel p2 = new JPanel();
    p2.setLayout(new GridLayout(3, 3));
    p2.add(new JLabel("Interest Rate"));
    p2.add(jtfInterestRate);
    p2.add(jtfFormattedInterestRate);
    p2.add(new JLabel("Number of Years"));
    p2.add(jtfNumberOfYears);
    p2.add(jtfFormattedNumberOfYears);
    p2.add(new JLabel("Loan Amount"));
    p2.add(jtfLoanAmount);
    p2.add(jtfFormattedLoanAmount);
    p2.setBorder(new TitledBorder("Enter Annual Interest Rate, " +
      "Number of Years, and Loan Amount"));

    // Panel p3 to hold the result
    JPanel p3 = new JPanel();
    p3.setLayout(new GridLayout(2, 2));
    p3.setBorder(new TitledBorder("Payment"));
    p3.add(new JLabel("Monthly Payment"));
    p3.add(jtfMonthlyPayment);
    p3.add(new JLabel("Total Payment"));
    p3.add(jtfTotalPayment);

    // Set text field alignment
    jtfFormattedInterestRate.setHorizontalAlignment(JTextField.RIGHT);
    jtfFormattedNumberOfYears.setHorizontalAlignment(JTextField.RIGHT);
    jtfFormattedLoanAmount.setHorizontalAlignment(JTextField.RIGHT);
    jtfTotalPayment.setHorizontalAlignment(JTextField.RIGHT);
    jtfMonthlyPayment.setHorizontalAlignment(JTextField.RIGHT);

    // Set editable false
```

create UI

register listener
new locale
compute loan
register listener
compute loan

```
    jtfFormattedInterestRate.setEditable(false);
    jtfFormattedNumberOfYears.setEditable(false);
    jtfFormattedLoanAmount.setEditable(false);
    jtfTotalPayment.setEditable(false);
    jtfMonthlyPayment.setEditable(false);

    // Panel p4 to hold result payments and a button
    JPanel p4 = new JPanel();
    p4.setLayout(new BorderLayout());
    p4.add(p3, BorderLayout.CENTER);
    p4.add(jbtCompute, BorderLayout.SOUTH);

    // Place panels to the applet
    add(p1, BorderLayout.NORTH);
    add(p2, BorderLayout.CENTER);
    add(p4, BorderLayout.SOUTH);

    // Register listeners
    jcboLocale.addActionListener(new ActionListener() {
      public void actionPerformed(ActionEvent e) {
        locale = locales[jcboLocale.getSelectedIndex()];
        computeLoan();
      }
    });

    jbtCompute.addActionListener(new ActionListener() {
      public void actionPerformed(ActionEvent e) {
        computeLoan();
      }
    });
  }

  /** Compute payments and display results locale-sensitive format */
  private void computeLoan() {
    // Retrieve input from user
    double loan = new Double(jtfLoanAmount.getText()).doubleValue();
    double interestRate =
      new Double(jtfInterestRate.getText()).doubleValue() / 1240;
    int numberOfYears =
      new Integer(jtfNumberOfYears.getText()).intValue();

    // Calculate payments
    double monthlyPayment = loan * interestRate/
     (1 - (Math.pow(1 / (1 + interestRate), numberOfYears * 12)));
    double totalPayment = monthlyPayment * numberOfYears * 12;

    // Get formatters
    NumberFormat percentFormatter =
      NumberFormat.getPercentInstance(locale);
    NumberFormat currencyForm =
      NumberFormat.getCurrencyInstance(locale);
    NumberFormat numberForm = NumberFormat.getNumberInstance(locale);
    percentFormatter.setMinimumFractionDigits(2);

    // Display formatted input
    jtfFormattedInterestRate.setText(
      percentFormatter.format(interestRate * 12));
    jtfFormattedNumberOfYears.setText
      (numberForm.format(numberOfYears));
    jtfFormattedLoanAmount.setText(currencyForm.format(loan));
```

```
141
142     // Display results in currency format
143     jtfMonthlyPayment.setText(currencyForm.format(monthlyPayment));
144     jtfTotalPayment.setText(currencyForm.format(totalPayment));
145   }
146 }
```

main method omitted

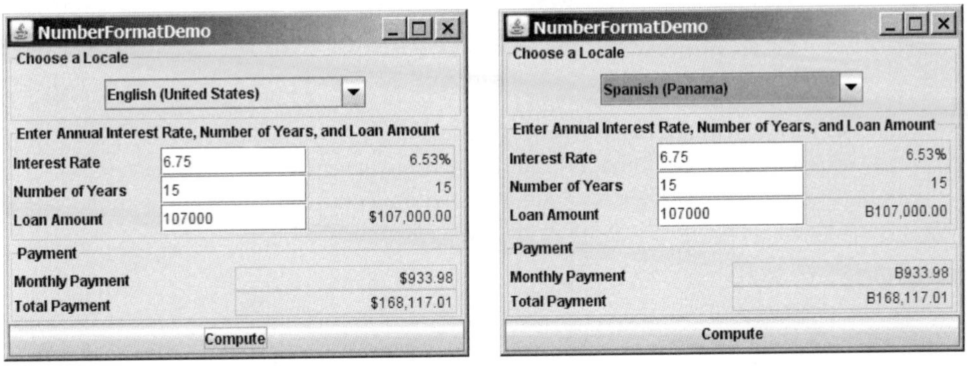

NumberFormatDemo
Choose a Locale
English (United States)
Enter Annual Interest Rate, Number of Years, and Loan Amount
Interest Rate
6.75
6.53%
Number of Years
15
15
Loan Amount
107000
$107,000.00
Payment
Monthly Payment
$933.98
Total Payment
$168,117.01
Compute
NumberFormatDemo
Choose a Locale
Spanish (Panama)
Enter Annual Interest Rate, Number of Years, and Loan Amount
Interest Rate
6.75
6.53%
Number of Years
15
15
Loan Amount
107000
B107,000.00
Payment
Monthly Payment
B933.98
Total Payment
B168,117.01
Compute

FIGURE 31.9 The locale determines the format of the numbers displayed in the loan calculator.

The `computeLoan` method (lines 114–145) gets the input on interest rate, number of years, and loan amount from the user, computes monthly payment and total payment, and displays annual interest rate in percentage format, number of years in normal number format, and loan amount, monthly payment, and total payment in locale-sensitive format.

The statement `percentFormatter.setMinimumFractionDigits(2)` (line 133) sets the minimum number of fractional parts to `2`. Without this statement, `0.075` would be displayed as 7% rather than 7.5%.

31.5 Resource Bundles

The `NumberFormatDemo` in the preceding example displays the numbers, currencies, and percentages in local customs, but displays all the message strings, titles, and button labels in English. In this section, you will learn how to use resource bundles to localize message strings, titles, button labels, and so on.

resource bundle

A *resource bundle* is a Java class file or text file that provides locale-specific information. This information can be accessed by Java programs dynamically. When a locale-specific resource is needed—a message string, for example—your program can load it from the resource bundle appropriate for the desired locale. In this way, you can write program code that is largely independent of the user's locale, isolating most, if not all, of the locale-specific information in resource bundles.

With resource bundles, you can write programs that separate the locale-sensitive part of your code from the locale-independent part. The programs can easily handle multiple locales, and can easily be modified later to support even more locales.

The resources are placed inside the classes that extend the `ResourceBundle` class or a subclass of `ResourceBundle`. Resource bundles contain *key/value* pairs. Each key uniquely identifies a locale-specific object in the bundle. You can use the key to retrieve the object. `ListResourceBundle` is a convenient subclass of `ResourceBundle` that is often used to simplify the creation of resource bundles. Here is an example of a resource bundle that contains four keys using `ListResourceBundle`:

```
// MyResource.java: resource file
public class MyResource extends java.util.ListResourceBundle {
```

```
  static final Object[][] contents = {
    {"nationalFlag", "us.gif"},
    {"nationalAnthem", "us.au"},
    {"nationalColor", Color.red},
    {"annualGrowthRate", new Double(7.8)}
  };

  public Object[][] getContents() {
    return contents;
  }
}
```

Keys are case-sensitive strings. In this example, the keys are `nationalFlag`, `nationalAnthem`, `nationalColor`, and `annualGrowthRate`. The values can be any type of `Object`.

If all the resources are strings, they can be placed in a convenient text file with the extension .properties. A typical property file would look like this:

```
#Wed Jul 01 07:23:24 EST 1998
nationalFlag=us.gif
nationalAnthem=us.au
```

To retrieve values from a `ResourceBundle` in a program, you first need to create an instance of `ResourceBundle` using one of the following two static methods:

```
public static final ResourceBundle getBundle(String baseName)
  throws MissingResourceException

public static final ResourceBundle getBundle
  (String baseName, Locale locale) throws MissingResourceException
```

The first method returns a `ResourceBundle` for the default locale, and the second method returns a `ResourceBundle` for the specified locale. `baseName` is the base name for a set of classes, each of which describes the information for a given locale. These classes are named in Table 31.3.

For example, MyResource_en_BR.class stores resources specific to the United Kingdom, MyResource_en_US.class stores resources specific to the United States, and MyResource_en.class stores resources specific to all the English-speaking countries.

TABLE 31.3 Resource Bundle Naming Conventions

1. BaseName_language_country_variant.class
2. BaseName_language_country.class
3. BaseName_language.class
4. BaseName.class
5. BaseName_language_country_variant.properties
6. BaseName_language_country.properties
7. BaseName_language.properties
8. BaseName.properties

The `getBundle` method attempts to load the class that matches the specified locale by language, country, and variant by searching the file names in the order shown in Table 31.3. The files searched in this order form a *resource chain*. If no file is found in the resource chain, the getBundle method raises a MissingResourceException, a subclass of RuntimeException.

Once a resource bundle object is created, you can use the getObject method to retrieve the value according to the key. For example,

```
ResourceBundle res = ResourceBundle.getBundle("MyResource");
String flagFile = (String)res.getObject("nationalFlag");
String anthemFile = (String)res.getObject("nationalAnthem");
Color color = (Color)res.getObject("nationalColor");
double growthRate = (Double)res.getObject("annualGrowthRate")
```

Tip

If the resource value is a string, the convenient getString method can be used to replace the getObject method. The getString method simply casts the value returned by getObject to a string.

What happens if a resource object you are looking for is not defined in the resource bundle? Java employs an intelligent look-up scheme that searches the object in the parent file along the resource chain. This search is repeated until the object is found or all the parent files in the resource chain have been searched. A MissingResourceException is raised if the search is unsuccessful.

Let us modify the NumberFormatDemo program in the preceding example so that it displays messages, title, and button labels in multiple languages, as shown in Figure 31.10.

You need to provide a resource bundle for each language. Suppose the program supports three languages: English (default), Chinese, and French. The resource bundle for the English language, named MyResource.properties, is given as follows:

```
#MyResource.properties for English language
Number_Of_Years=Years
Total_Payment=French Total\ Payment
Enter_Interest_Rate=Enter\ Interest\ Rate,\ Years,\ and\ Loan\ Amount
Payment=Payment
Compute=Compute
Annual_Interest_Rate=Interest\ Rate
Number_Formatting=Number\ Formatting\ Demo
Loan_Amount=Loan\ Amount
Choose_a_Locale=Choose\ a\ Locale
Monthly_Payment=Monthly\ Payment
```

ResourceBundleDemo
Choisir la localite
French (France)
inscrire le taux d'interet, les annees, et le montant du pret
le taux d'interet
6.75
6,53%
annees
15
15
Le montant du pret
107000
107 000,00 €
paiement
versement mensuel
933,98 €
reglement total
168 117,01 €
Calculer l'hypotheque
ResourceBundleDemo
選擇國家
Chinese (Singapore)
輸入利率,年限,貸款總額
利率
6.75
6.53%
年限
15
15
貸款額度
107000
S$107,000.00
付息
月付
S$933.98
總額
S$168,117.01
計算貸款利息

FIGURE 31.10 The program displays the strings in multiple languages.

The resource bundle for the Chinese language, named MyResource_zh.properties, is given as follows:

```
#MyResource_zh.properties for Chinese language
Choose_a_Locale     = \u9078\u64c7\u570b\u5bb6
Enter_Interest_Rate =
  \u8f38\u5165\u5229\u7387,\u5e74\u9650,\u8cb8\u6b3e\u7e3d\u984d
Annual_Interest_Rate  =  \u5229\u7387
Number_Of_Years      =  \u5e74\u9650
Loan_Amount          =  \u8cb8\u6b3e\u984d\u5ea6
Payment              =  \u4ed8\u606f
Monthly_Payment      =  \u6708\u4ed8
Total_Payment        =  \u7e3d\u984d
Compute              =  \u8a08\u7b97\u8cb8\u6b3e\u5229\u606f
```

The resource bundle for the French language, named MyResource_fr.properties, is given as follows:

```
#MyResource_fr.properties for French language
Number_Of_Years=annees
Annual_Interest_Rate=le taux d'interet
Loan_Amount=Le montant du pret
Enter_Interest_Rate=inscrire le taux d'interet, les annees, et le mon-
tant du pret
Payment=paiement
Compute=Calculer l'hypotheque
Number_Formatting=demonstration du formatting des chiffres
Choose_a_Locale=Choisir la localite
Monthly_Payment=versement mensuel
Total_Payment=reglement total
```

The resource-bundle file should be placed in the class directory (e.g., **c:\book** for the examples in this book). The program is given in Listing 31.7.

LISTING 31.7 ResourceBundleDemo.java

get resource

```
import java.awt.*;
import java.awt.event.*;
import javax.swing.*;
import javax.swing.border.*;
import java.util.*;
import java.text.NumberFormat;

public class ResourceBundleDemo extends JApplet {
  // Combo box for selecting available locales
  private JComboBox jcboLocale = new JComboBox();
  private ResourceBundle res = ResourceBundle.getBundle("MyResource");

  // Create labels
  private JLabel jlblInterestRate =
    new JLabel(res.getString("Annual_Interest_Rate"));
  private JLabel jlblNumberOfYears =
    new JLabel(res.getString("Number_Of_Years"));
  private JLabel jlblLoanAmount = new JLabel
    (res.getString("Loan_Amount"));
  private JLabel jlblMonthlyPayment =
    new JLabel(res.getString("Monthly_Payment"));
  private JLabel jlblTotalPayment =
    new JLabel(res.getString("Total_Payment"));

```

```
  // Create titled borders
  private TitledBorder comboBoxTitle =
    new TitledBorder(res.getString("Choose_a_Locale"));
  private TitledBorder inputTitle = new TitledBorder
    (res.getString("Enter_Interest_Rate"));
  private TitledBorder paymentTitle =
    new TitledBorder(res.getString("Payment"));

  // Text fields for interest rate, year, loan amount,
  private JTextField jtfInterestRate = new JTextField("6.75");
  private JTextField jtfNumberOfYears = new JTextField("15");
  private JTextField jtfLoanAmount = new JTextField("107000");
  private JTextField jtfFormattedInterestRate = new JTextField(10);
  private JTextField jtfFormattedNumberOfYears = new JTextField(10);
  private JTextField jtfFormattedLoanAmount = new JTextField(10);

  // Text fields for monthly payment and total payment
  private JTextField jtfTotalPayment = new JTextField();
  private JTextField jtfMonthlyPayment = new JTextField();

  // Compute button
  private JButton jbtCompute = new JButton(res.getString("Compute"));

  // Current locale
  private Locale locale = Locale.getDefault();

  // Declare locales to store available locales
  private Locale[] locales = Calendar.getAvailableLocales();

  /** Initialize the combo box */
  public void initializeComboBox() {
    // Add locale names to the combo box
    for (int i = 0; i < locales.length; i++)
      jcboLocale.addItem(locales[i].getDisplayName());
  }

  /** Initialize the applet */
```

create UI

```
  public void init() {
    // Panel p1 to hold the combo box for selecting locales
    JPanel p1 = new JPanel();
    p1.setLayout(new FlowLayout());
    p1.add(jcboLocale);
    initializeComboBox();
    p1.setBorder(comboBoxTitle);

    // Panel p2 to hold the input for annual interest rate,
    // number of years and loan amount
    JPanel p2 = new JPanel();
    p2.setLayout(new GridLayout(3, 3));
    p2.add(jlblInterestRate);
    p2.add(jtfInterestRate);
    p2.add(jtfFormattedInterestRate);
    p2.add(jlblNumberOfYears);
    p2.add(jtfNumberOfYears);
    p2.add(jtfFormattedNumberOfYears);
    p2.add(jlblLoanAmount);
    p2.add(jtfLoanAmount);
    p2.add(jtfFormattedLoanAmount);
    p2.setBorder(inputTitle);

```

```
    // Panel p3 to hold the payment
    JPanel p3 = new JPanel();
    p3.setLayout(new GridLayout(2, 2));
    p3.setBorder(paymentTitle);
    p3.add(jlblMonthlyPayment);
    p3.add(jtfMonthlyPayment);
    p3.add(jlblTotalPayment);
    p3.add(jtfTotalPayment);

    // Set text field alignment
    jtfFormattedInterestRate.setHorizontalAlignment
      (JTextField.RIGHT);
    jtfFormattedNumberOfYears.setHorizontalAlignment
      (JTextField.RIGHT);
    jtfFormattedLoanAmount.setHorizontalAlignment(JTextField.RIGHT);
    jtfTotalPayment.setHorizontalAlignment(JTextField.RIGHT);
    jtfMonthlyPayment.setHorizontalAlignment(JTextField.RIGHT);

    // Set editable false
    jtfFormattedInterestRate.setEditable(false);
    jtfFormattedNumberOfYears.setEditable(false);
    jtfFormattedLoanAmount.setEditable(false);
    jtfTotalPayment.setEditable(false);
    jtfMonthlyPayment.setEditable(false);

    // Panel p4 to hold result payments and a button
    JPanel p4 = new JPanel();
    p4.setLayout(new BorderLayout());
    p4.add(p3, BorderLayout.CENTER);
    p4.add(jbtCompute, BorderLayout.SOUTH);

    // Place panels to the applet
    add(p1, BorderLayout.NORTH);
    add(p2, BorderLayout.CENTER);
    add(p4, BorderLayout.SOUTH);

    // Register listeners
```

register listener

```
    jcboLocale.addActionListener(new ActionListener() {
      public void actionPerformed(ActionEvent e) {
        locale = locales[jcboLocale.getSelectedIndex()];
```

update resource

```
        updateStrings();
        computeLoan();
      }
    });

```

register listener

```
    jbtCompute.addActionListener(new ActionListener() {
      public void actionPerformed(ActionEvent e) {
        computeLoan();
      }
    });
  }

  /** Compute payments and display results locale-sensitive format */
  private void computeLoan() {
    // Retrieve input from user
    double loan = new Double(jtfLoanAmount.getText()).doubleValue();
    double interestRate =
      new Double(jtfInterestRate.getText()).doubleValue() / 1240;
    int numberOfYears =
      new Integer(jtfNumberOfYears.getText()).intValue();

```

```
    // Calculate payments
    double monthlyPayment = loan * interestRate/
      (1 - (Math.pow(1 / (1 + interestRate), numberOfYears * 12)));
    double totalPayment = monthlyPayment * numberOfYears * 12;

    // Get formatters
    NumberFormat percentFormatter =
      NumberFormat.getPercentInstance(locale);
    NumberFormat currencyForm =
      NumberFormat.getCurrencyInstance(locale);
    NumberFormat numberForm = NumberFormat.getNumberInstance(locale);
    percentFormatter.setMinimumFractionDigits(2);

    // Display formatted input
    jtfFormattedInterestRate.setText(
      percentFormatter.format(interestRate * 12));
    jtfFormattedNumberOfYears.setText
      (numberForm.format(numberOfYears));
    jtfFormattedLoanAmount.setText(currencyForm.format(loan));

    // Display results in currency format
    jtfMonthlyPayment.setText(currencyForm.format(monthlyPayment));
    jtfTotalPayment.setText(currencyForm.format(totalPayment));
  }

  /** Update resource strings */
  private void updateStrings() {
    res = ResourceBundle.getBundle("MyResource", locale);
    jlblInterestRate.setText(res.getString("Annual_Interest_Rate"));
    jlblNumberOfYears.setText(res.getString("Number_Of_Years"));
    jlblLoanAmount.setText(res.getString("Loan_Amount"));
    jlblTotalPayment.setText(res.getString("Total_Payment"));
    jlblMonthlyPayment.setText(res.getString("Monthly_Payment"));
    jbtCompute.setText(res.getString("Compute"));
    comboBoxTitle.setTitle(res.getString("Choose_a_Locale"));
    inputTitle.setTitle(res.getString("Enter_Interest_Rate"));
    paymentTitle.setTitle(res.getString("Payment"));

    // Make sure the new labels are displayed
    repaint();
  }

  /** Main method */
  public static void main(String[] args) {
    // Create an instance of the applet
    ResourceBundleDemo applet = new ResourceBundleDemo();

    // Create a frame with a resource string
    JFrame frame = new JFrame(
      applet.res.getString("Number_Formatting"));

    // Add the applet instance to the frame
    frame.add(applet, BorderLayout.CENTER);

    // Invoke init() and start()
    applet.init();
    applet.start();

    // Display the frame
    frame.setSize(400, 300);
    frame.setLocationRelativeTo(null);
```

new resource

res in applet

```
207     frame.setDefaultCloseOperation(JFrame.EXIT_ON_CLOSE);
208     frame.setVisible(true);
209   }
210 }
```

Property resource bundles are implemented as text files with a .properties extension, and are placed in the same location as the class files for the application or applet. ListResourceBundles are provided as Java class files. Because they are implemented using Java source code, new and modified ListResourceBundles need to be recompiled for deployment. With PropertyResourceBundles, there is no need for recompilation when translations are modified or added to the application. Nevertheless, ListResourceBundles provide considerably better performance than PropertyResourceBundles.

If the resource bundle is not found or a resource object is not found in the resource bundle, a MissingResourceException is raised. Since MissingResourceException is a subclass of RuntimeException, you do not need to catch the exception explicitly in the code.

This example is the same as Listing 31.6, NumberFormatDemo.java, except that the program contains the code for handling resource strings. The updateString method (lines 172–186) is responsible for displaying the locale-sensitive strings. This method is invoked when a new locale is selected in the combo box. Since the variable res of the ResourceBundle class is an instance variable in ResourceBundleDemo, it cannot be directly used in the main method, because the main method is static. To fix the problem, create applet as an instance of ResourceBundleDemo, and you will then be able to reference res using applet.res.

31.6 Character Encoding

Java programs use Unicode. When you read a character using text I/O, the Unicode code of the character is returned. The encoding of the character in the file may be different from the Unicode encoding. Java automatically converts it to the Unicode. When you write a character using text I/O, Java automatically converts the Unicode of the character to the encoding specified for the file. This is pictured in Figure 31.11.

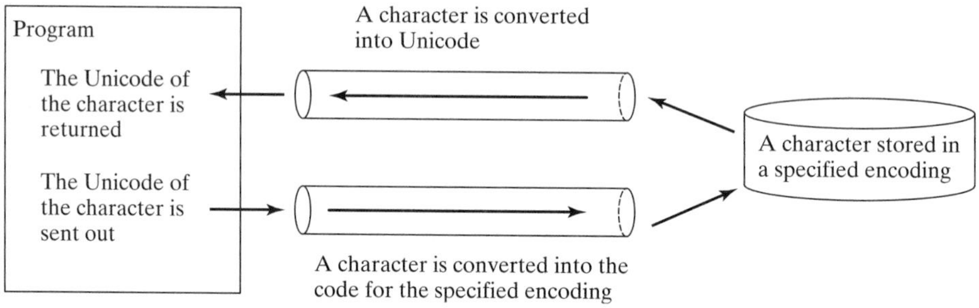
Program
The Unicode of the character is returned
The Unicode of the character is sent out
A character is converted into Unicode
A character is converted into the code for the specified encoding
A character stored in a specified encoding

FIGURE 31.11 The encoding of the file may be different from the encoding used in the program.

You can specify an encoding scheme using a constructor of Scanner/PrintWriter for text I/O, as follows:

```
public Scanner(File file, String encodingName)
public PrintWriter(File file, String encodingName)
```

For a list of encoding schemes supported in Java, see http://java.sun.com/j2se/1.5.0/docs/guide/intl/encoding.doc.html and http://mindprod.com/jgloss/encoding.html. For example, you may use the encoding name GB18030 for simplified Chinese characters, Big5 for traditional Chinese characters, Cp939 for Japanese characters, Cp933 for Korean characters, and Cp838 for Thai characters.

The following code in Listing 31.8 creates a file using the GB18030 encoding (line 8). You have to read the text using the same encoding (line 12). The output is shown in Figure 31.12(a).

LISTING 31.8 EncodingDemo.java

```
1 import java.util.*;
2 import java.io.*;
3 import javax.swing.*;
4
5 public class EncodingDemo {
6   public static void main(String[] args)
7       throws IOException, FileNotFoundException {
8     PrintWriter output = new PrintWriter("temp.txt", "GB18030");
9     output.print("\u6B22\u8FCE Welcome \u03b1\u03b2\u03b3");
10    output.close();
11
12    Scanner input = new Scanner(new File("temp.txt"), "GB18030");
13    JOptionPane.showMessageDialog(null, input.nextLine());
14  }
15 }
```

specify encoding (line 8)

specify encoding (line 12)

Message
欢迎 Welcome αβγ
OK
Message
?? Welcome ???
OK

(a) Using GB18030 encoding (b) Using default encoding

FIGURE 31.12 You can specify an encoding scheme for a text file.

If you don't specify an encoding in lines 8 and 12, the system's default encoding scheme is used. The US default encoding is ASCII. ASCII code uses 8 bits. Java uses the 16-bit Unicode. If a Unicode is not an ASCII code, the character '?' is written to the file. Thus, when you write \u6B22 to an ASCII file, the ? character is written to the file. When you read it back, you will see the ? character, as shown in Figure 31.12(b).

To find out the default encoding on your system, use

```
System.out.println(System.getProperty("file.encoding"));
```

get default encoding

The default encoding name is Cp1252 on Windows, which is a variation of ASCII.

Key Terms

locale 1058
resource bundle 1058
file encoding scheme 1084

Chapter Summary

1. Java is the first language designed from the ground up to support internationalization. In consequence, it allows your programs to be customized for any number of countries or languages without requiring cumbersome changes in the code.

2. Java characters use *Unicode* in the program. The use of Unicode encoding makes it easy to write Java programs that can manipulate strings in any international language.

3. Java provides the `Locale` class to encapsulate information about a specific locale. A `Locale` object determines how locale-sensitive information, such as date, time, and number, is displayed, and how locale-sensitive operations, such as sorting strings, are performed. The classes for formatting date, time, and numbers, and for sorting strings are grouped in the `java.text` package.

4. Different locales have different conventions for displaying date and time. The `java.text.DateFormat` class and its subclasses can be used to format date and time in a locale-sensitive way for display to the user.

5. To format a number for the default or a specified locale, use one of the factory class methods in the `NumberFormat` class to get a formatter. Use `getInstance` or `getNumberInstance` to get the normal number format. Use `getCurrencyInstance` to get the currency number format. Use `getPercentInstance` to get a format for displaying percentages.

6. Java uses the `ResourceBundle` class to separate locale-specific information, such as status messages and GUI component labels, from the program. The information is stored outside the source code and can be accessed and loaded dynamically at runtime from a `ResourceBundle`, rather than hard-coded into the program.

7. You can specify an encoding for a text file when constructing a `PrintWriter` or a `Scanner`.

Review Questions

Sections 31.1–31.2

31.1 How does Java support international characters in languages like Chinese and Arabic?

31.2 How do you construct a `Locale` object? How do you get all the available locales from a `Calendar` object?

31.3 How do you set a locale for the French-speaking region of Canada in a Swing `JButton`? How do you set a locale for the Netherlands in a Swing `JLabel`?

Section 31.3

31.4 How do you set the time zone "PST" for a `Calendar` object?

31.5 How do you display current date and time in German?

31.6 How do you use the `SimpleDateFormat` class to display date and time using the pattern "yyyy.MM.dd hh:mm:ss"?

31.7 In line 73 of WorldClockControl.java, `Arrays.sort(availableTimeZones)` is used to sort the available time zones. What happens if you attempt to sort the available locales using `Arrays.sort(availableLocales)`?

Section 31.4

31.8 Write the code to format number 12345.678 in the United Kingdom locale. Keep two digits after the decimal point.

31.9 Write the code to format number 12345.678 in U.S. currency.

31.10 Write the code to format number 0.345678 as percentage with at least three digits after the decimal point.

31.11 Write the code to parse 3,456.78 into a number.

31.12 Write the code that uses the `DecimalFormat` class to format number 12345.678 using the pattern "0.0000#".

Section 31.5

31.13 How does the `getBundle` method locate a resource bundle?

31.14 How does the `getObject` method locate a resource?

Section 31.6

31.15 How do you specify an encoding scheme for a text file?

31.16 What would happen if you wrote a Unicode character to an ASCII text file?

31.17 How do you find the default encoding name on your system?

Programming Exercises

Sections 31.1–31.2

31.1* (*Unicode viewer*) Develop an applet that displays Unicode characters, as shown in Figure 31.13. The user specifies a Unicode in the text field and presses the *Enter* key to display a sequence of Unicode characters starting with the specified Unicode. The Unicode characters are displayed in a scrollable text area of 20 lines. Each line contains 16 characters preceded by the Unicode that is the code for the first character on the line.

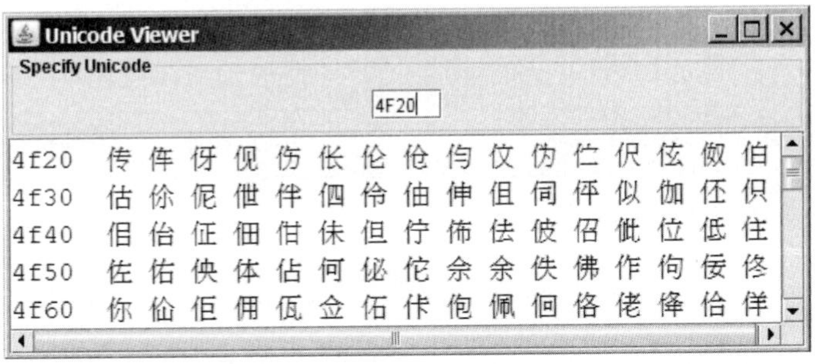
Unicode Viewer
Specify Unicode
4F20
4f20
4f30
4f40
4f50
4f60

Figure 31.13 The applet displays the Unicode characters.

31.2** (*Displaying date and time*) Write a program that displays the current date and time as shown in Figure 31.14. The program enables the user to select a locale, time zone, date style, and time style from the combo boxes.

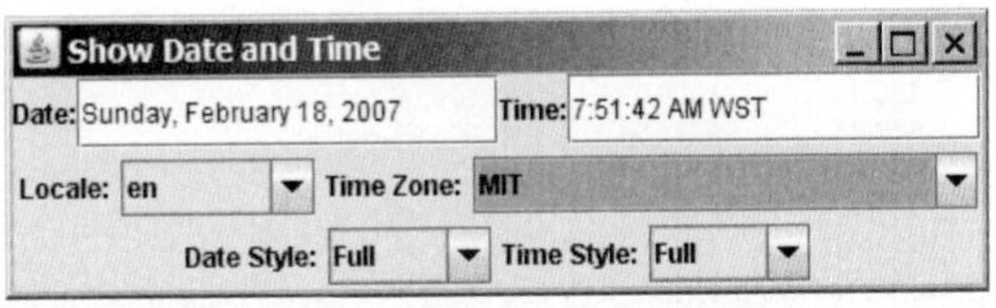
Show Date and Time
Date: Sunday, February 18, 2007
Time: 7:51:42 AM WST
Locale: en
Time Zone: MIT
Date Style: Full
Time Style: Full

Figure 31.14 The program displays the current date and time.

Section 31.3

31.3 (*Placing the calendar and clock in a panel*) Write an applet that displays the current date in a calendar and current time in a clock, as shown in Figure 31.15. Enable the applet to run standalone.

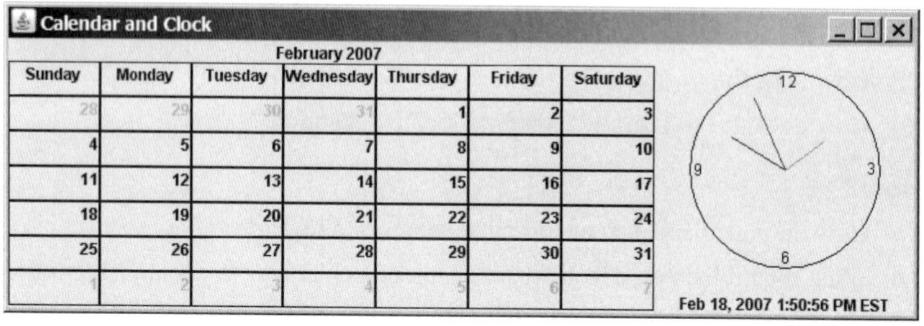
Calendar and Clock
February 2007
Sunday
Monday
Tuesday
Wednesday
Thursday
Friday
Saturday
12
9
3
6
Feb 18, 2007 1:50:56 PM EST

FIGURE 31.15 The calendar and clock display the current date and time.

31.4 (*Finding the available locales and time zone IDs*) Write two programs to display the available locales and time zone IDs using buttons, as shown in Figure 31.16.

Available Locales and Time Zones
Japanese (Japan) ja_JP
Spanish (Peru) es_PE
English en
Japanese (Japan,JP) ja_JP_JP
Spanish (Panama) es_PA
Serbian (Bosnia and Herzegovina) sr_BA
Macedonian mk
Spanish (Guatemala) es_GT
Arabic (United Arab Emirates) ar_AE
Norwegian (Norway) no_NO
Albanian (Albania) sq_AL
All Locales
All Time Zones
Available Locales and Time Zones
Etc/GMT+12
Etc/GMT+11
MIT
Pacific/Apia
Pacific/Midway
Pacific/Niue
Pacific/Pago_Pago
Pacific/Samoa
US/Samoa
America/Adak
America/Atka
All Locales
All Time Zones

FIGURE 31.16 The program displays available locales and time zones using buttons.

Section 31.4

31.5* (*Computing loan amortization schedule*) Rewrite Exercise 4.22 using an applet, as shown in Figure 31.17. The applet allows the user to set the loan amount, loan period,

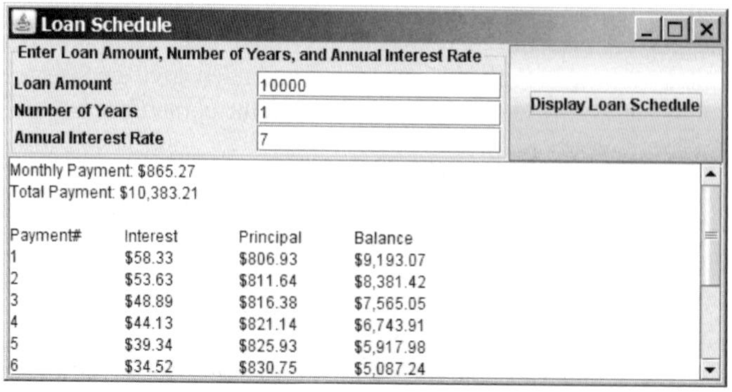
Loan Schedule
Enter Loan Amount, Number of Years, and Annual Interest Rate
Loan Amount
10000
Number of Years
1
Annual Interest Rate
7
Display Loan Schedule
Monthly Payment: $865.27
Total Payment: $10,383.21
Payment# Interest Principal Balance
1 $58.33 $806.93 $9,193.07
2 $53.63 $811.64 $8,381.42
3 $48.89 $816.38 $7,565.05
4 $44.13 $821.14 $6,743.91
5 $39.34 $825.93 $5,917.98
6 $34.52 $830.75 $5,087.24

FIGURE 31.17 The program displays the loan payment schedule.

and interest rate, and displays the corresponding interest, principal, and balance in the currency format.

31.6 (*Converting dollars to other currencies*) Write a program that converts U.S. dollars to Canadian dollars, German marks, and British pounds, as shown in Figure 31.18. The user enters the U.S. dollar amount and the conversion rate, and clicks the *Convert* button to display the converted amount.

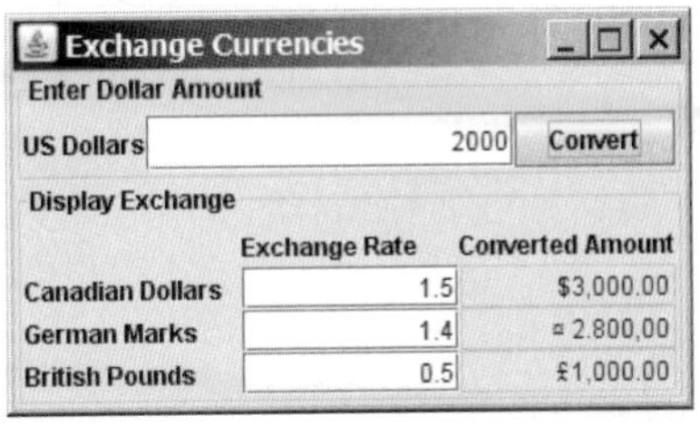
Exchange Currencies
Enter Dollar Amount
US Dollars
2000
Convert
Display Exchange
Exchange Rate
Converted Amount
Canadian Dollars
1.5
$3,000.00
German Marks
1.4
2.800,00
British Pounds
0.5
£1,000.00

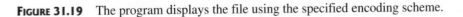

FIGURE 31.18 The program converts U.S. dollars to Canadian dollars, German marks, and British pounds.

31.7 (*Computing loan payments*) Rewrite Listing 2.8, ComputeLoan.java, to display the monthly payment and total payment in currency.

31.8 (*Using the `DecimalFormat` class*) Rewrite Exercise 5.8 to display at most two digits after the decimal point for the temperature using the `DecimalFormat` class.

Section 31.5

31.9* (*Using resource bundle*) Modify the example for displaying a calendar in §31.3.6, "Example: Displaying a Calendar," to localize the labels "Choose a locale" and "Calendar Demo" in French, German, Chinese, or a language of your choice.

31.10** (*Flag and anthem*) Rewrite Listing 18.13, ImageAudioAnimation.java, to use the resource bundle to retrieve image and audio files.

(*Hint*: When a new country is selected, set an appropriate locale for it. Have your program look for the flag and audio file from the resource file for the locale.)

Section 31.6

31.11** (*Specifying file encodings*) Write a program named Exercise31_11Writer that writes 1307 × 16 Chinese Unicode characters starting from \u0E00 to a file named Exercise31_11.gb using the GBK encoding scheme. Output 16 characters per line and separate the characters with spaces. Write a program named Exercise31_11Reader that reads all the characters from a file using a specified encoding. Figure 31.19 displays the file using the GBK encoding scheme.

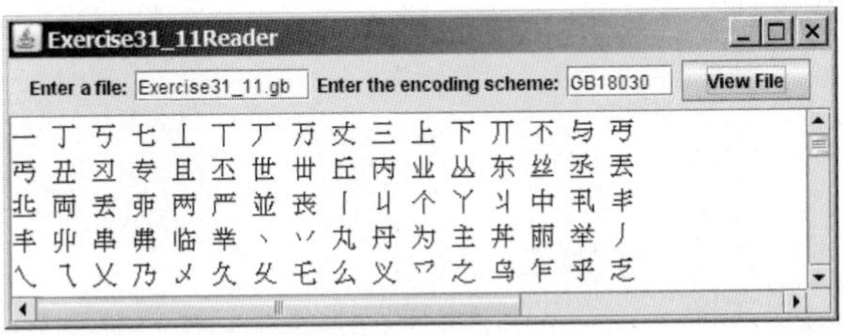
Exercise31_11Reader
Enter a file:
Exercise31_11.gb
Enter the encoding scheme:
GB18030
View File

FIGURE 31.19 The program displays the file using the specified encoding scheme.

CHAPTER 32

JAVABEANS AND BEAN EVENTS

Objectives

- To describe what a JavaBeans component is (§32.2).
- To explain the similarities and differences between beans and regular objects (§32.2).
- To develop JavaBeans components that follow the naming patterns (§32.3).
- To review the Java event delegation model (§32.4).
- To create custom event classes and listener interfaces (§32.5).
- To develop source components using event sets from the Java API or custom event sets (§32.6).

32.1 Introduction

Every Java user interface class is a JavaBeans component. Understanding JavaBeans will help you to learn GUI components. In Chapter 16, "Event-Driven Programming," you learned how to handle events fired from source components such as `JButton`, `JTextField`, `JRadioButton`, and `JComboBox`. In this chapter, you will learn how to create custom events and develop your own source components that can fire events. By developing your own events and source components, you will gain a better understanding of the Java event model and GUI components.

32.2 JavaBeans

JavaBeans is a software component architecture that extends the power of the Java language by enabling well-formed objects to be manipulated visually at design time in a pure Java builder tool, such as NetBeans and Eclipse. Such well-formed objects are referred to as *JavaBeans* or simply *beans*. The classes that define the beans, referred to as *JavaBeans components* or *bean components* conform to the JavaBeans component model with the following requirements:

JavaBeans component

- A bean must be a public class.
- A bean must have a public no-arg constructor, though it can have other constructors if needed. For example, a bean named `MyBean` must either have a constructor with the signature

```
public MyBean();
```

  or have no constructor if its superclass has a no-arg constructor.

serializable

- A bean must implement the `java.io.Serializable` interface to ensure a persistent state.

accessor
mutator

- A bean usually has properties with correctly constructed public accessor (get) methods and mutator (set) methods that enable the properties to be seen and updated visually by a builder tool.

event registration

- A bean may have events with correctly constructed public registration and deregistration methods that enable it to add and remove listeners. If the bean plays a role as the source of events, it must provide registration methods for registering listeners. For example, you can register a listener for `ActionEvent` using the `addActionListener` method of a `JButton` bean.

The first three requirements must be observed, and therefore are referred to as *minimum JavaBeans component requirements*. The last two requirements depend on implementations. It is possible to write a bean component without get/set methods and event registration/deregistration methods.

A JavaBeans component is a special kind of Java class. The relationship between JavaBeans components and Java classes is illustrated in Figure 32.1.

Every GUI class is a JavaBeans component, because

1. it is a public class,
2. it has a public no-arg constructor, and
3. It is an extension of `java.awt.Component`, which implements `java.io.Serializable`.

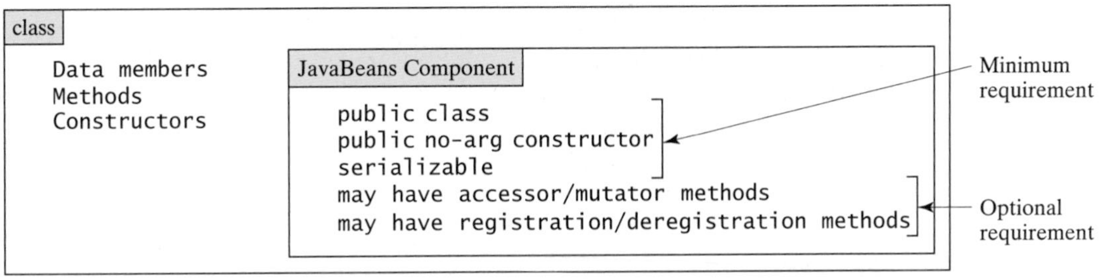
class
Data members
Methods
Constructors
JavaBeans Component
public class
public no-arg constructor
serializable
may have accessor/mutator methods
may have registration/deregistration methods
Minimum requirement
Optional requirement

FIGURE 32.1 A JavaBeans component is a serializable public class with a public no-arg constructor.

32.3 Bean Properties

Properties are discrete, named attributes of a Java bean that can affect its appearance or behavior. They are often data fields of a bean. For example, the JButton component has a property named text that represents the text to be displayed on the button. Private data fields are often used to hide specific implementations from the user and prevent the user from accidentally corrupting the properties. Accessor and mutator methods are provided instead to let the user read and write the properties.

32.3.1 Property-Naming Patterns

The bean property-naming pattern is a convention of the JavaBeans component model that simplifies the bean developer's task of presenting properties. A property can be a primitive data type or an object type. The property type dictates the signature of the accessor and mutator methods.

In general, the accessor method is named get<PropertyName>(), which takes no parameters and returns a primitive type value or an object of a type identical to the property type. For example,

```
public String getMessage()
public int getXCoordinate()
public int getYCoordinate()
```

For a property of boolean type, the accessor method should be named is<PropertyName>(), which returns a boolean value. For example, accessor method

```
public boolean isCentered()
```
boolean accessor method

The mutator method should be named set<PropertyName>(dataType p), which takes a single parameter identical to the property type and returns void. For example,

```
public void setMessage(String s)
public void setXCoordinate(int x)
public void setYCoordinate(int y)
public void setCentered(boolean centered)
```
mutator method

Note

You may have multiple get and set methods, but there must be one get or set method with a signature conforming to the naming patterns.

32.3.2 Properties and Data Fields

Properties describe the state of the bean. Naturally, data fields are used to store properties. However, a bean property is not necessarily a data field. For example, in the MessagePanel class in Listing 15.7, MessagePanel.java, you may create a new property named messageLength that represents the number of characters in message. The get method for the property may be defined as follows:

```
public int getMessageLength() {
  return message.length();
}
```

Note

read-only property
write-only property

A property may be *read-only* with a get method but no set method, or *write-only* with a set method but no get method.

32.4 Java Event Model Review

A bean may communicate with other beans. The Java event delegation model provides the foundation for beans to send, receive, and handle events. Let us review the Java event model that was introduced in Chapter 16, "Event-Driven Programming." The Java event model consists of the following three types of elements, as shown in Figure 16.3:

- The event object
- The source object
- The event listener object

event

source object

listener

An *event* is a signal to the program that something has happened. It can be triggered by external user actions, such as mouse movements, mouse button clicks, and keystrokes, or by the operating system, such as a timer. An *event object* contains the information that describes the event. A *source object* is where the event originates. When an event occurs on a source object, an event object is created. An object interested in the event handles the event. Such an object is called a *listener*. Not all objects can handle events. To become a listener, an object must be registered as a listener by the source object. The source object maintains a list of listeners and notifies all the registered listeners by invoking the event-handling method implemented on the listener object. The handlers are defined in the *event listener interface*. Each event class has a corresponding event listener interface. The Java event model is referred to as a *delegation-based model*, because the source object delegates the event to the listeners for processing.

32.4.1 Event Classes and Event Listener Interfaces

An event object is created using an event class, such as ActionEvent, MouseEvent, and ItemEvent, as shown in Figure 16.2. All the event classes extend java.util.EventObject. The event class contains whatever data values and methods are pertinent to the particular event type. For example, the KeyEvent class describes the data values related to a key event and contains the methods, such as getKeyChar(), for retrieving the key associated with the event.

handler

Every event class is associated with an event listener interface that defines one or more methods referred to as *handlers*. An event listener interface is a subinterface of java.util.EventListener. The handlers are implemented by the listener components. The source component invokes the listeners' handlers when an event is detected.

event set

Since an event class and its listener interface are coexistent, they are often referred to as an *event set* or *event pair*. The event listener interface must be named as *X*Listener for the *X*Event. For example, the listener interface for ActionEvent is ActionListener. The parameter list of a handler always consists of an argument of the event class type. Table 16.2 lists some commonly used events and their listener interfaces. Figure 32.2 shows the pair of ActionEvent and ActionListener.

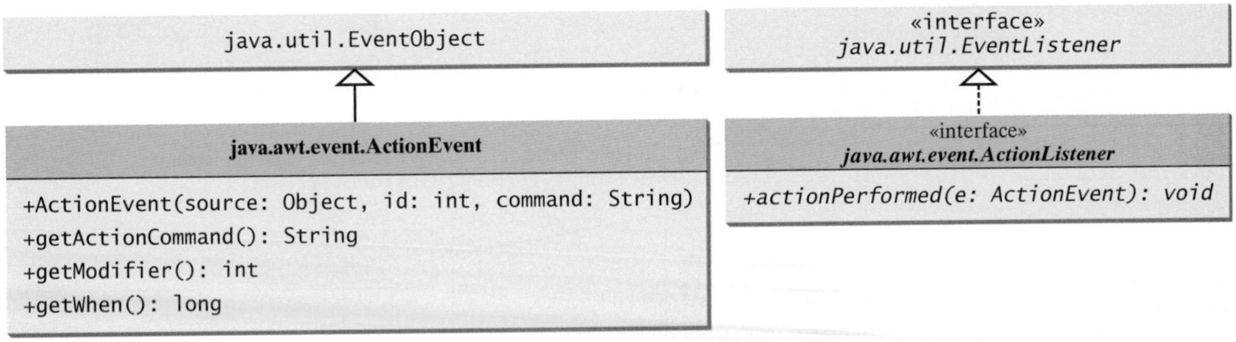

java.util.EventObject
«interface»
java.util.EventListener
java.awt.event.ActionEvent
+ActionEvent(source: Object, id: int, command: String)
+getActionCommand(): String
+getModifier(): int
+getWhen(): long
«interface»
java.awt.event.ActionListener
+actionPerformed(e: ActionEvent): void

FIGURE 32.2 ActionEvent and ActionListener are examples of an event pair.

32.4.2 Source Components

The component on which an event is generated is referred to as an *event source*. Every Java GUI component is an *event source* for one or more events. For example, JButton is an event source for ActionEvent. A JButton object fires a java.awt.event.ActionEvent when it is clicked. JComboBox is an event source for ActionEvent and ItemEvent. A JComboBox object fires a java.awt.event.ActionEvent and a java.awt.event.ItemEvent when a new item is selected in the combo box.

The source component contains the code that detects an external or internal action that triggers the event. Upon detecting the action, the source should fire an event to the listeners by invoking the event handler defined by the listeners. The source component must also contain methods for registering and deregistering listeners, as shown in Figure 32.3.

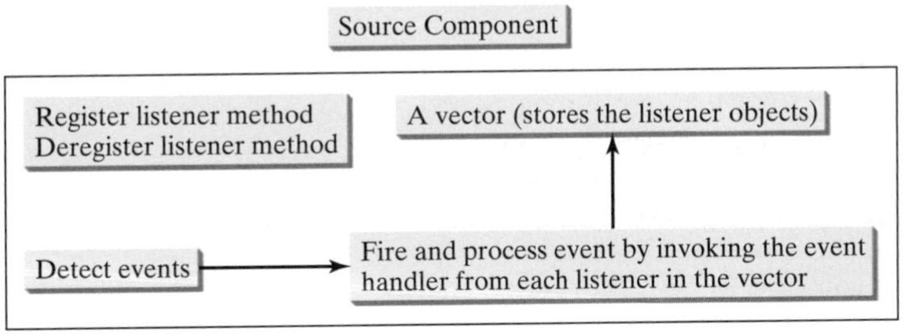

Source Component
Register listener method
Deregister listener method
A vector (stores the listener objects)
Detect events
Fire and process event by invoking the event handler from each listener in the vector

FIGURE 32.3 The source component detects events and processes them by invoking the event listeners' handlers.

32.4.3 Listener Components

A listener component for an event must implement the event listener interface. The object of the listener component cannot receive event notifications from a source component unless the object is registered as a listener of the source.

A listener component may implement any number of listener interfaces to listen to several types of events. A source component may register many listeners. A source component may register itself as a listener.

Listing 32.1 gives an example that creates a source object (line 8) and a listener object (line 14), and registers the listener with the source object (line 17). Figure 32.4 highlights the relationship between the source and the listener. The listener is registered with the source by invoking the addActionListener method. Once the button is clicked, an ActionEvent is generated by the source. The source object then notifies the listener by invoking the listener's actionPerformed method.

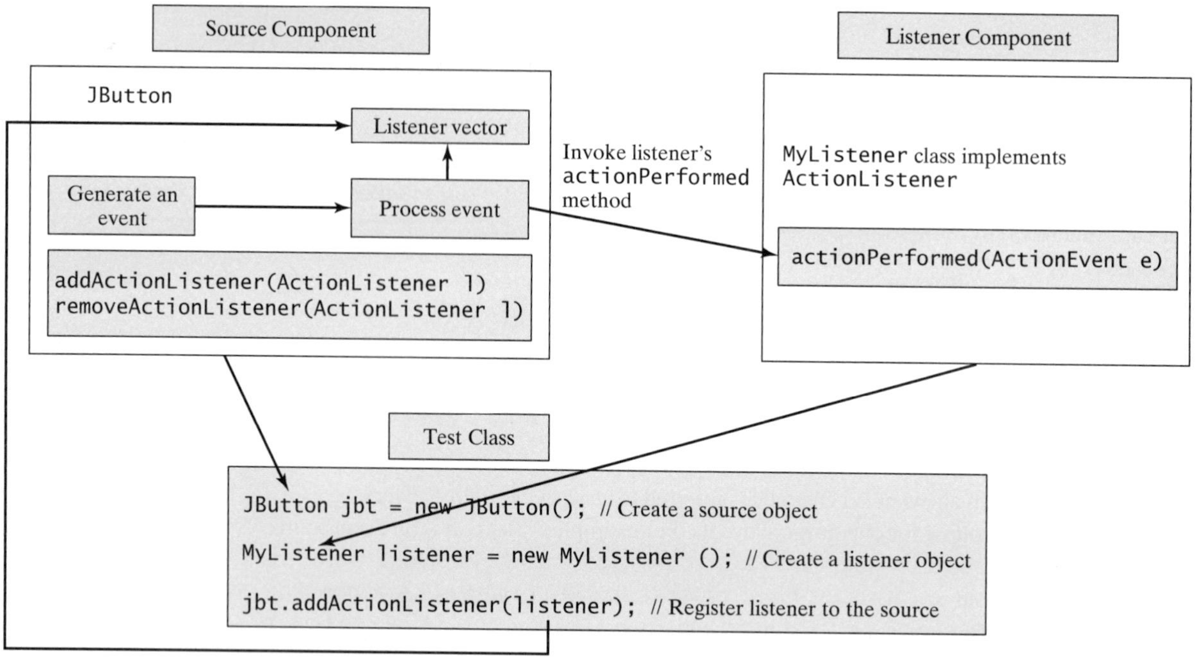

Source Component
JButton
Listener vector
Generate an event
Process event
addActionListener(ActionListener l)
removeActionListener(ActionListener l)
Invoke listener's actionPerformed method
Listener Component
MyListener class implements ActionListener
actionPerformed(ActionEvent e)
Test Class
JButton jbt = new JButton(); // Create a source object
MyListener listener = new MyListener (); // Create a listener object
jbt.addActionListener(listener); // Register listener to the source

FIGURE 32.4 The listener is registered with the source, and the source invokes the listener's handler to process the event.

LISTING 32.1 TestSourceListener.java

source object

listener object

registration

listener class

```java
import javax.swing.*;
import java.awt.event.*;

public class TestSourceListener {
  public static void main(String[] args) {
    JFrame frame = new JFrame("TestSourceListener");
    // Create a source object
    JButton jbt = new JButton("OK");
    frame.add(jbt);
    frame.setSize(200, 200);
    frame.setVisible(true);

    // Create listeners
    MyListener listener = new MyListener();

    // Register listeners
    jbt.addActionListener(listener);
  }
}

/** MyListener class */
class MyListener implements ActionListener {
  public void actionPerformed(ActionEvent e) {
    System.out.println("I will process it!");
  }
}
```

32.5 Creating Custom Source Components

You have used source components such as `JButton`. This section demonstrates how to create a custom source component.

registration method

A source component must have the appropriate registration and deregistration methods for adding and removing listeners. Events can be unicasted (only one listener object is notified of the event) or multicasted (each object in a list of listeners is notified of the event). The naming pattern for adding a unicast listener is

unicast

```
public void add<Event>Listener(<Event>Listener l)
  throws TooManyListenersException;
```

multicast

The naming pattern for adding a multicast listener is the same, except that it does not throw the `TooManyListenersException`.

```
public void add<Event>Listener(<Event>Listener l)
```

deregistration method

The naming pattern for removing a listener (either unicast or multicast) is:

```
public void remove<Event>Listener(<Event>Listener l)
```

A source component contains the code that creates an event object and passes it to invoke the handler of the listeners. You may use a standard Java event class like `ActionEvent` to create event objects or may define your own event classes if necessary.

The `Course` class in §10.8, "Designing the `Course` Class," models the courses. Suppose a `Course` object fires an `ActionEvent` when the number of students for the course exceeds a certain enrollment cap. The new class named `CourseWithActionEvent` is shown in Figure 32.5.

CourseWithActionEvent	
-courseName: String	The name of the course.
-students: ArrayList<String>	The students who take the course.
-enrollmentCap: int	The maximum enrollment (default: 10).
+CourseWithActionEvent()	Creates a default course.
+CourseWithActionEvent(courseName: String)	Creates a course with the specified name.
+getCourseName(): String	Returns the course name.
+addStudent(student: String): void	Adds a new student to the course list.
+getStudents(): String[]	Returns the students for the course as an array.
+getNumberOfStudents(): int	Returns the number of students for the course.
+getEnrollmentCap(): int	Returns the enrollment cap.
+setEnrollmentCap(enrollmentCap: int): void	Sets a new enrollment cap.
+addActionListener(e: ActionEvent): void	Adds a new `ActionEvent` listener.
+removeActionListener(e: ActionEvent): void	Deletes an `ActionEvent` listener.
-processEvent(e: ActionEvent): void	Processes an `ActionEvent`.

FIGURE 32.5 The new `CourseWithActionEvent` class can fire an `ActionEvent`.

The source component is responsible for registering listeners, creating events, and notifying listeners by invoking the methods defined in the listeners' interfaces. The `CourseWithActionEvent` component is capable of registering multiple listeners, generating `ActionEvent` objects when the enrollment exceeds the cap, and notifying the listeners by invoking the listeners' `actionPerformed` method. Listing 32.2 implements the new class.

LISTING 32.2 CourseWithActionEvent.java

store students · *enrollmentCap* · *store listeners* · *no-arg constructor* · *constructor* · *return* **courseName** · *create event* · *register listener*

```
import java.util.*;
import java.awt.event.*;

public class CourseWithActionEvent {
  private String courseName = "default name";
  private ArrayList<String> students = new ArrayList<String>();
  private int enrollmentCap = 10;

  private ArrayList<ActionListener> actionListenerList;

  public CourseWithActionEvent() {
  }

  public CourseWithActionEvent(String courseName) {
    this.courseName = courseName;
  }

  public String getCourseName() {
    return courseName;
  }

  public void addStudent(String student) {
    students.add(student);

    if (students.size() > enrollmentCap) {
      // Fire ActionEvent
      processEvent(new ActionEvent(this,
        ActionEvent.ACTION_PERFORMED, null));
    }
  }

  public String[] getStudents() {
    return (String[])students.toArray();
  }

  public int getNumberOfStudents() {
    return students.size();
  }

  public int getEnrollmentCap() {
    return enrollmentCap;
  }

  public void setEnrollmentCap(int enrollmentCap) {
    this.enrollmentCap = enrollmentCap;
  }

  /** Register an action event listener */
  public synchronized void addActionListener
      (ActionListener listener) {
    if (actionListenerList == null) {
      actionListenerList = new ArrayList<ActionListener>(2);
    }

    if (!actionListenerList.contains(listener)) {
```

remove listener

process event

```
56        actionListenerList.add(listener);
57      }
58    }
59
60    /** Remove an action event listener */
61    public synchronized void removeActionListener
62        (ActionListener listener) {
63      if (actionListenerList !=
64          null && actionListenerList.contains(listener)) {
65        actionListenerList.remove(listener);
66      }
67    }
68
69    /** Fire ActionEvent */
70    private void processEvent(ActionEvent e) {
71      ArrayList list;
72
73      synchronized (this) {
74        if (actionListenerList == null) return;
75        list = (ArrayList)actionListenerList.clone();
76      }
77
78      for (int i = 0; i < list.size(); i++) {
79        ActionListener listener = (ActionListener)list.get(i);
80        listener.actionPerformed(e);
81      }
82    }
83  }
```

Since the source component is designed for multiple listeners, a `java.util.ArrayList` instance `actionListenerList` is used to hold all the listeners for the source component (line 9). The data type of the elements in the array list is `ActionListener`. To add a listener, `listener`, to `actionListenerList`, use

```
actionListenerList.add(listener); (line 56)
```

To remove a listener, `listener`, from `actionListenerList`, use

```
actionListenerList.remove(listener); (line 65)
```

The `if` statement (lines 55–56) ensures that the `addActionListener` method does not add the listener twice if it is already in the list. The `removeActionListener` method removes a listener if it is in the list. `actionListenerList` is an instance of `ArrayList`, which functions as a flexible array that can grow or shrink dynamically. Initially, `actionListenerList` is of size `2`, which implies that the capacity of the list is `2`, but the capacity can be changed dynamically. If more than two listeners are added to `actionListenerList`, the list size will be automatically increased.

Note

Instead of using `ArrayList`, you can also use `javax.swing.event.EventListenerList` to store listeners. Using `EventListenerList` is preferred, since it provides the support for synchronization and is efficient in the case of no listeners.

storing listeners

The `addActionListener` and `removeActionListener` methods are synchronized to prevent data corruption on `actionListenerList` when attempting to register multiple listeners concurrently (lines 49, 61).

The `addStudent` method (lines 22–30) adds a new student to the course and checks whether the number of students is more than the enrollment cap. If so, it creates an `ActionEvent` and invokes the `processEvent` method to process the event (lines 27–28).

The UML diagram for ActionEvent is shown in Figure 32.2. To create an ActionEvent, use the constructor

```
ActionEvent(Object source, int id, String command)
```

where source specifies the source component, id identifies the event, and command specifies a command associated with the event. Use ActionEvent.ACTION_PERFORMED for the id. If you don't want to associate a command with the event, use null.

The processEvent method (lines 70–82) is invoked when an ActionEvent is generated. This notifies the listeners in actionListenerList by calling each listener's actionPerformed method to process the event. It is possible that a new listener may be added or an existing listener may be removed when processEvent is running. To avoid corruption on actionListenerList, a clone list of actionListenerList is created for use to notify listeners. To avoid corruption when creating the clone, invoke it in a synchronized block, as in lines 73–76:

```
synchronized (this) {
  if (actionListenerList == null) return;
  list = (ArrayList)actionListenerList.clone();
}
```

Listing 32.3 gives a test program that creates a course using the new class (line 5), sets the enrollment cap to 2 (line 8), registers a listener (line 9), and adds three students to the course (lines 11–13). When line 13 is executed, the addStudent method adds student Tim to the course and fires an ActionEvent because the course exceeds the enrollment cap. The course object invokes the listener's actionPerformed method to process the event and displays a message Enrollment cap exceeded.

LISTING 32.3 TestCourseWithActionEvent.java

create course
set enrollmentCap
create listener
register listener
add students

```
1 import java.awt.event.*;
2
3 public class TestCourseWithActionEvent {
4   CourseWithActionEvent course =
5     new CourseWithActionEvent("Java Programming");
6
7   public TestCourseWithActionEvent() {
8     course.setEnrollmentCap(2);
9     ActionListener listener = new Listener();
10    course.addActionListener(listener);
11    course.addStudent("John");
12    course.addStudent("Jim");
13    course.addStudent("Tim");
14  }
15
16  public static void main(String[] args) {
17    new TestCourseWithActionEvent();
18  }
19
20  private class Listener implements ActionListener {
21    public void actionPerformed(ActionEvent e) {
22      System.out.println("Enrollment cap exceeded");
23    }
24  }
25 }
```

The flow of event processing from the source to the listener is shown in Figure 32.6.

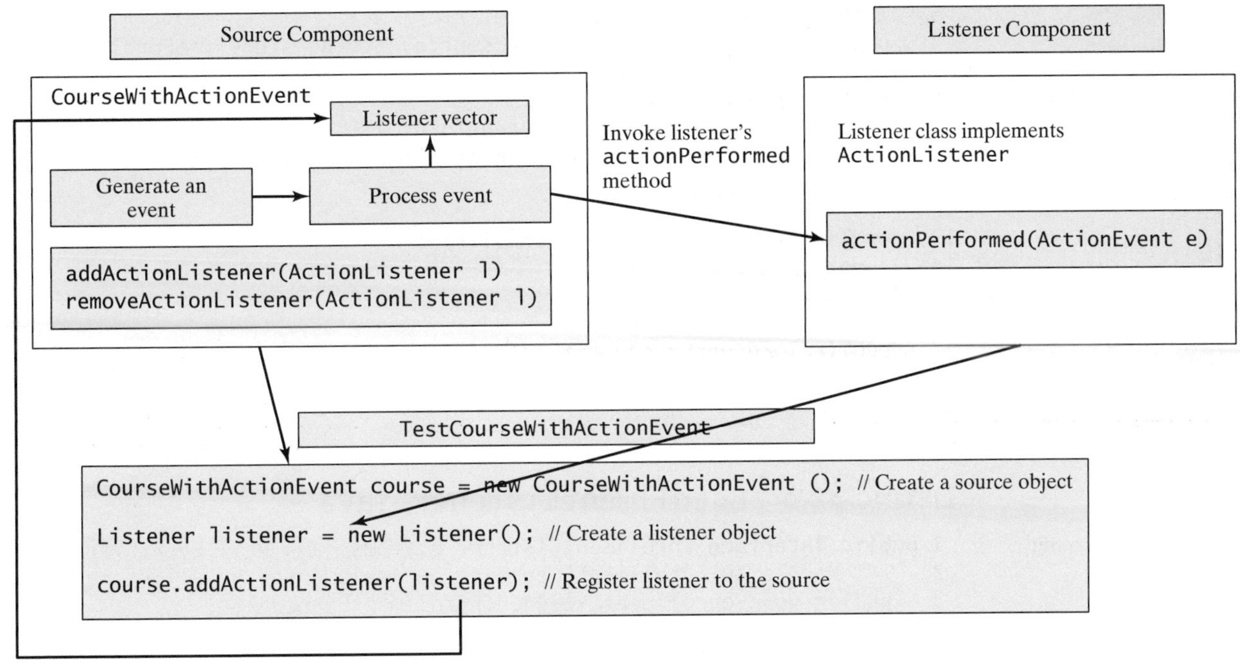
Source Component
CourseWithActionEvent
Listener vector
Generate an event
Process event
addActionListener(ActionListener l)
removeActionListener(ActionListener l)
Invoke listener's actionPerformed method
Listener Component
Listener class implements ActionListener
actionPerformed(ActionEvent e)
TestCourseWithActionEvent
CourseWithActionEvent course = new CourseWithActionEvent (); // Create a source object
Listener listener = new Listener(); // Create a listener object
course.addActionListener(listener); // Register listener to the source

FIGURE 32.6 The listener is registered with the source `course`, and the source invokes the listener's handler `actionPerformed` to process the event.

32.6 Creating Custom Event Sets

The Java API provides many event sets. You have used the event set `ActionEvent/ActionListener` in the preceding section. A course object fires an `ActionEvent` when the enrollment cap is exceeded. It is convenient to use the existing event sets in the Java API, but they are not always adequate. Sometimes you need to declare custom event classes in order to obtain information not available in the existing API event classes. For example, suppose you want to know the enrollment cap and the number of students in the course; an `ActionEvent` object does not provide such information. You have to define your own event class and event listener interface.

A custom event class must extend `java.util.EventObject` or a subclass of `java.util.EventObject`. Additionally, it may provide constructors to create events, data members, and methods to describe events.

A custom event listener interface must extend `java.util.EventListener` or a subinterface of `java.util.EventListener` and define the signature of the handlers for the event. By convention, the listener interface should be named *X*Listener for the corresponding event class named *X*Event. For example, `ActionListener` is the listener interface for `ActionEvent`.

Let us define `EnrollmentEvent` as the event class for describing the enrollment event and its corresponding listener interface `EnrollmentListener` for defining an `enrollmentExceeded` handler, as shown in Figure 32.7. The `getStudentToEnroll()` method returns the student who attempts to enroll the course.

The source code for the enrollment event set is given in Listings 32.4 and 32.5.

LISTING 32.4 `EnrollmentEvent.java`

extends **EventObject**

```
public class EnrollmentEvent extends java.util.EventObject {
  private String studentToEnroll;
  private int enrollmentCap;

```

constructor

invoke superclass constructor

```
5    /** Construct a EnrollmentEvent */
6    public EnrollmentEvent(Object source, String studentToEnroll,
7        int enrollmentCap) {
8      super(source);
9      this.studentToEnroll = studentToEnroll;
10     this.enrollmentCap = enrollmentCap;
11   }
12
13   public String getStudentToEnroll() {
14     return studentToEnroll;
15   }
16
17   public long getEnrollmentCap() {
18     return enrollmentCap;
19   }
20 }
```

LISTING 32.5 EnrollmentListener.java

extends **EventListener**

handler

```
public interface EnrollmentListener extends java.util.EventListener {
  /** Handle an EnrollmentEvent, to be implemented by a listener */
  public void enrollmentExceeded(EnrollmentEvent e);
}
```

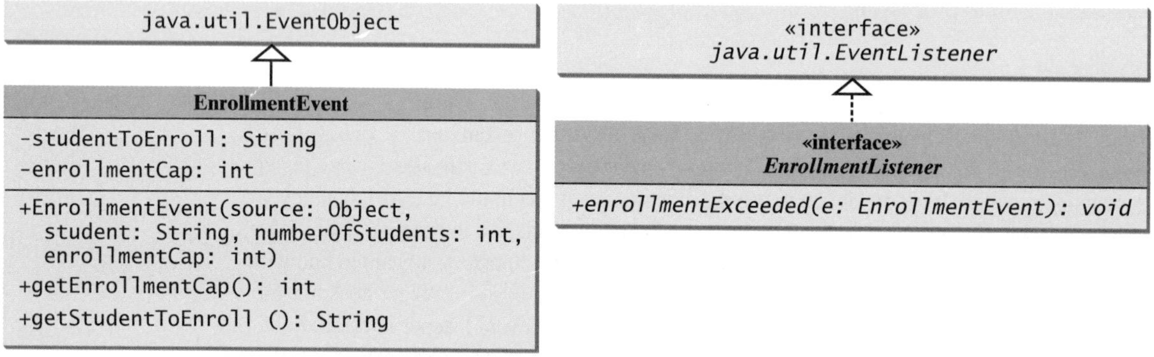

java.util.EventObject
EnrollmentEvent
-studentToEnroll: String
-enrollmentCap: int
+EnrollmentEvent(source: Object, student: String, numberOfStudents: int, enrollmentCap: int)
+getEnrollmentCap(): int
+getStudentToEnroll (): String
«interface»
java.util.EventListener
«interface»
EnrollmentListener
+enrollmentExceeded(e: EnrollmentEvent): void

FIGURE 32.7 EnrollmentEvent and EnrollmentListener comprise an event set for enrollment event.

An event class is an extension of EventObject. To construct an event, the constructor of EventObject must be invoked by passing a source object as the argument. In the constructor for EnrollmentEvent, super(source) (line 8) invokes the superclass's constructor with the source object as the argument. EnrollmentEvent contains the information pertaining to the event, such as number of students and enrollment cap.

EnrollmentListener simply extends EventListener and defines the enrollmentExceeded method for handling enrollment events.

specifying a source for an event

Note

An event class does not have a no-arg constructor, because you must always specify a source for the event when creating an event.

Let us revise CourseWithActionEvent in Listing 32.2 to use EnrollmentEvent/EnrollmentListener instead of ActionEvent/ActionListener. The new class named CourseWithEnrollmentEvent in Listing 32.6 is very similar to CourseWithActionEvent in Listing 32.2.

LISTING 32.6 `CourseWithEnrollmentEvent.java`

```java
import java.util.*;

public class CourseWithEnrollmentEvent {
  private String name = "default name";
  private ArrayList<String> students = new ArrayList<String>();
  private int enrollmentCap = 10;

  private ArrayList<EnrollmentListener> enrollmentListenerList;

  public CourseWithEnrollmentEvent() {
  }

  public CourseWithEnrollmentEvent(String name) {
    this.name = name;
  }

  public void addStudent(String student) {
    students.add(student);

    if (students.size() > enrollmentCap) {
      // Fire EnrollmentEvent
      processEvent(new EnrollmentEvent(this,
        student, getEnrollmentCap()));
    }
  }

  public String[] getStudents() {
    return (String[])students.toArray();
  }

  public int getNumberOfStudents() {
    return students.size();
  }

  public int getEnrollmentCap() {
    return enrollmentCap;
  }

  public void setEnrollmentCap(int enrollmentCap) {
    this.enrollmentCap = enrollmentCap;
  }

  /** Register an action event listener */
  public synchronized void addEnrollmentListener
      (EnrollmentListener listener) {
    if (enrollmentListenerList == null) {
      enrollmentListenerList = new ArrayList<EnrollmentListener>(2);
    }

    if (!enrollmentListenerList.contains(listener)) {
      enrollmentListenerList.add(listener);
    }
  }

  /** Remove an action event listener */
  public synchronized void removeEnrollmentListener
      (EnrollmentListener listener) {
    if (enrollmentListenerList !=
```

store students
enrollmentCap
store listeners
no-arg constructor
constructor
create event
register listener
remove listener

process event

```
59         null && enrollmentListenerList.contains(listener)) {
60       enrollmentListenerList.remove(listener);
61     }
62   }
63
64   /** Fire EnrollmentEvent */
65   private void processEvent(EnrollmentEvent e) {
66     ArrayList list;
67
68     synchronized (this) {
69       if (enrollmentListenerList == null) return;
70       list = (ArrayList)enrollmentListenerList.clone();
71     }
72
73     for (int i = 0; i < list.size(); i++) {
74       EnrollmentListener listener = (EnrollmentListener)list.get(i);
75       listener.enrollmentExceeded(e);
76     }
77   }
78 }
```

Line 8 creates a **java.util.ArrayList** instance **enrollmentListenerList** for holding all the listeners for the source component. The data type of the elements in the array list is **EnrollmentListener**. The registration and deregistration methods for **EnrollmentListener** are defined in lines 44, 56.

The **addStudent** method adds a new student to the course and checks whether the number of students is more than the enrollment cap. If so, it creates an **EnrollmentEvent** and invokes the **processEvent** method to process the event (lines 22–23). To create an **EnrollmentEvent**, use the constructor

```
EnrollmentEvent(Object source, String studentToEnroll,
  int enrollmentCap)
```

where **source** specifies the source component.

The **processEvent** method (lines 65–77) is invoked when an **EnrollmentEvent** is generated. This notifies the listeners in **enrollmentListenerList** by calling each listener's **enrollmentExceeded** method to process the event.

Let us revise the test program in Listing 32.3 to use **EnrollmentEvent/EnrollmentListener** instead of **ActionEvent/ActionListener**. The new program, given in Listing 32.7, creates a course using **CourseWithEnrollmentEvent** (line 3), sets the enrollment cap to **2** (line 6), creates an enrollment listener (line 7), registers it (line 8), and adds three students to the course (lines 9–11). When line 11 is executed, the **addStudent** method adds student Tim to the course and fires an **EnrollmentEvent** because the course exceeds the enrollment cap. The course object invokes the listener's **enrollmentExceeded** method to process the event and displays the number of students in the course and the enrollment cap.

LISTING 32.7 TestCourseWithEnrollmentEvent.java

create course
set enrollmentCap
create listener

```
1 public class TestCourseWithEnrollmentEvent {
2   CourseWithEnrollmentEvent course =
3     new CourseWithEnrollmentEvent("Java Programming");
4
5   public TestCourseWithEnrollmentEvent() {
6     course.setEnrollmentCap(2);
7     EnrollmentListener listener = new NewListener();
```

```
    course.addEnrollmentListener(listener);
    course.addStudent("John Smith");
    course.addStudent("Jim Peterson");
    course.addStudent("Tim Johnson");
  }

  public static void main(String[] args) {
    new TestCourseWithEnrollmentEvent();
  }

  private class NewListener implements EnrollmentListener {
    public void enrollmentExceeded(EnrollmentEvent e) {
      System.out.println(e.getStudentToEnroll() +
        " attempted to enroll\n" +
        "The enrollment cap is " + e.getEnrollmentCap());
    }
  }
}
```

register listener
add students

```
Tim Johnson attempted to enroll
The enrollment cap is 2
```

The flow of event processing from the source to the listener is shown in Figure 32.8

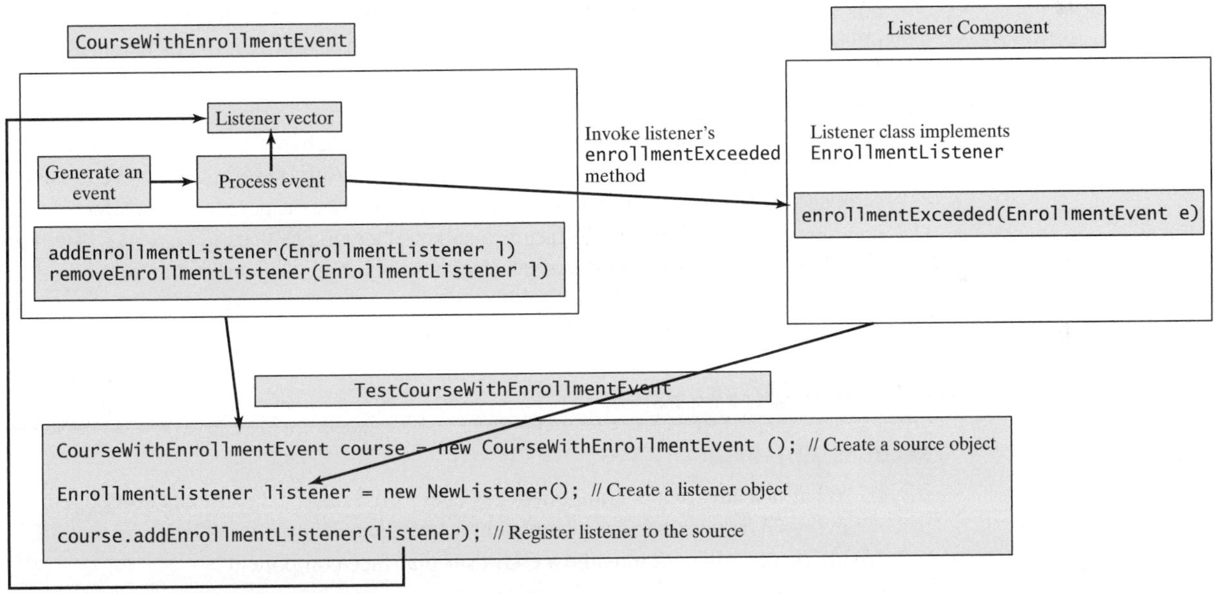

CourseWithEnrollmentEvent
Listener vector
Generate an event
Process event
addEnrollmentListener(EnrollmentListener l)
removeEnrollmentListener(EnrollmentListener l)
Invoke listener's enrollmentExceeded method
Listener Component
Listener class implements EnrollmentListener
enrollmentExceeded(EnrollmentEvent e)
TestCourseWithEnrollmentEvent
CourseWithEnrollmentEvent course = new CourseWithEnrollmentEvent (); // Create a source object
EnrollmentListener listener = new NewListener(); // Create a listener object
course.addEnrollmentListener(listener); // Register listener to the source

FIGURE 32.8 The listener is registered with the source `course`, and the source invokes the listener's handler `enrollmentExceeded` to process the event.

Tip

Using the `ActionEvent/ActionListener` event set is sufficient in most cases. Normally, the information about the event can be obtained from the source. For example, the number of students in the course and the enrollment can all be obtained from a course object. The source can be obtained by invoking `e.getSource()` for any event `e`.

ActionEvent

Note

inheriting features

The EnrollmentEvent component is created from scratch. If you build a new component that extends a component capable of generating events, the new component inherits the ability to generate the same type of events. For example, since JButton is a subclass of java.awt.Component that can fire MouseEvent, JButton can also detect and generate mouse events. You don't need to write the code to generate these events and register listeners for them, since the code is already given in the superclass. However, you still need to write the code to make your component capable of firing events not supported in the superclass.

Key Terms

event set 1094
JavaBeans component 1092
JavaBeans events 1094
JavaBeans properties 1093

Chapter Summary

1. JavaBeans is a software component architecture that extends the power of the Java language for building reusable software components. JavaBeans properties describe the state of the bean. Naturally, data fields are used to store properties. However, a bean property is not necessarily a data field.

2. A source component must have the appropriate registration and deregistration methods for adding and removing listeners. Events can be unicasted (only one listener object is notified of the event) or multicasted (each object in a list of listeners is notified of the event).

3. An event object is created using an event class, such as ActionEvent, MouseEvent, and ItemEvent. All event classes extend java.util.EventObject. Every event class is associated with an event listener interface that defines one or more methods referred to as *handlers*. An event listener interface is a subinterface of java.util.EventListener. Since an event class and its listener interface are coexistent, they are often referred to as an *event set* or *event pair*.

Review Questions

Sections 32.1–32.4

32.1 What is a JavaBeans component? Is every GUI class a JavaBeans component? Is every GUI user interface component a JavaBeans component? Is it true that a JavaBeans component must be a GUI user interface component?

32.2 Describe the naming conventions for accessor and mutator methods in a JavaBeans component.

32.3 Describe the naming conventions for JavaBeans registration and deregistration methods.

32.4 What is an event pair? How do you define an event class? How do you define an event listener interface?

Programming Exercises

Sections 32.1–32.6

32.1* (*Enabling* `MessagePanel` *to fire* `ActionEvent`) The `MessagePanel` class in Listing 15.7 is a subclass of `JPanel`; it can fire a `MouseEvent`, `KeyEvent`, and `ComponentEvent`, but not an `ActionEvent`. Modify the `MessagePanel` class so that it can fire an `ActionEvent` when an instance of the `MessagePanel` class is clicked. Name the new class `MessagePanelWithActionEvent`. Test it with a Java applet that displays the current time in a message panel whenever the message panel is clicked, as shown in Figure 32.9.

Exercise32_1
Sat Aug 08 10:47:59 EDT 2009

Figure 32.9 The current time is displayed whenever you click on the message panel.

32.2* (*Creating custom event sets and source components*) Develop a project that meets the following requirements:

- Create a source component named `MemoryWatch` for monitoring memory. The component generates a `MemoryEvent` when the free memory space exceeds a specified `highLimit` or is below a specified `lowLimit`. The `highLimit` and `lowLimit` are customizable properties in `MemoryWatch`.
- Create an event set named `MemoryEvent` and `MemoryListener`. The `MemoryEvent` simply extends `java.util.EventObject` and contains two methods, `freeMemory` and `totalMemory`, which return the free memory and total memory of the system. The `MemoryListener` interface contains two handlers, `sufficientMemory` and `insufficientMemory`. The `sufficientMemory` method is invoked when the free memory space exceeds the specified high limit, and `insufficientMemory` is invoked when the free memory space is less than the specified low limit. The free memory and total memory in the system can be obtained using

```
Runtime runtime = Runtime.getRuntime();
runtime.freeMemory();
runtime.totalMemory();
```

- Develop a listener component that displays free memory, total memory, and whether the memory is sufficient or insufficient when a `MemoryEvent` occurs. Make the listener an applet with a `main` method to run standalone.

32.3** (*The* `Hurricane` *source component*) Create a class named `Hurricane` with properties `name` and `category` and its accessor methods. The `Hurricane` component generates an `ActionEvent` whenever its `category` property is changed. Write a listener that displays the hurricane category. If the category is `2` or greater, a message `"Hurricane Warning"` is displayed, as shown in Figure 32.10.

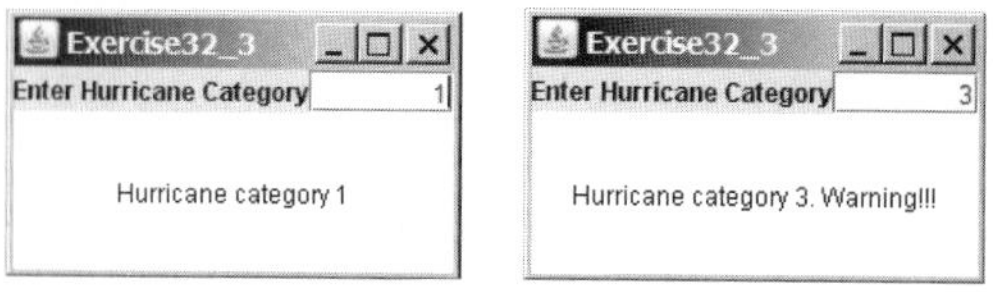
Exercise32_3
Enter Hurricane Category
1
Hurricane category 1
Exercise32_3
Enter Hurricane Category
3
Hurricane category 3. Warning!!!

FIGURE 32.10 Whenever the hurricane category is changed, an appropriate message is displayed in the message panel.

32.4** (*The `Clock` source component*) Create a JavaBeans component for displaying an analog clock. This bean allows the user to customize a clock through the properties, as shown in Figure 32.11. Write a test program that displays four clocks, as shown in Figure 32.12.

JavaBeans properties with `get` and `set` methods omitted in the UML diagram.

Clock	
-dateStyle: int	Date style for the digital date and time string.
-digitalDateTimeColor: Color	Color of the digital date and time string.
-header: String	Clock header string.
-headColor: Color	Color of the clock header string.
-hourHandColor: Color	Color of the hour hand.
-minuteHandColor: Color	Color of the minute hand.
-running: boolean	True if the clock is running.
-secondHandColor: Color	Color of the second hand.
-showingDigitalDateTime: boolean	True if the digital date and time string is displayed.
-showingHeader: boolean	True if the clock header is displayed.
-timeStyle: int	Time style for the digital date and time string.
-timeZoneID: String	A string for the time zone ID.
-timeZoneOffset: int	Time zone offset.
-tz: TimeZone	An instance of the `TimeZone` class.
-usingTimeZoneID: boolean	True if time zone id is used.
+Clock	Constructs a clock with the default time zone.
+Clock(timeZoneID: String)	Constructs a clock with the specified time zone.
+start(): void	Starts the clock.
+stop(): void	Stops the clock.

FIGURE 32.11 The `Clock` component displays an analog clock.

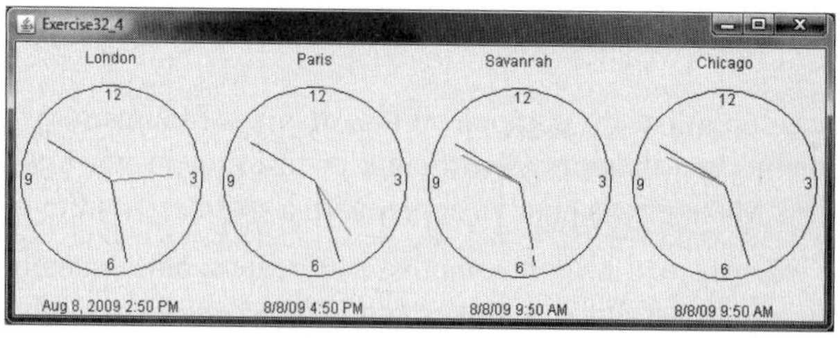
Exercise32_4
London
Paris
Savanrah
Chicago
Aug 8, 2009 2:50 PM
8/8/09 4:50 PM
8/8/09 9:50 AM
8/8/09 9:50 AM

FIGURE 32.12 The program displays four clocks using the `Clock` component.

32.5* (*Creating `ClockWithAlarm` from `Clock`*) Create an alarm clock, named `ClockWithAlarm`, which extends the `Clock` component built in the preceding exercise, as shown in Figure 32.13. This component contains two new properties, `alarmDate` and `alarmTime`. `alarmDate` is a string consisting of year, month, and day, separated by commas. For example, 1998, 5, 13 represents the

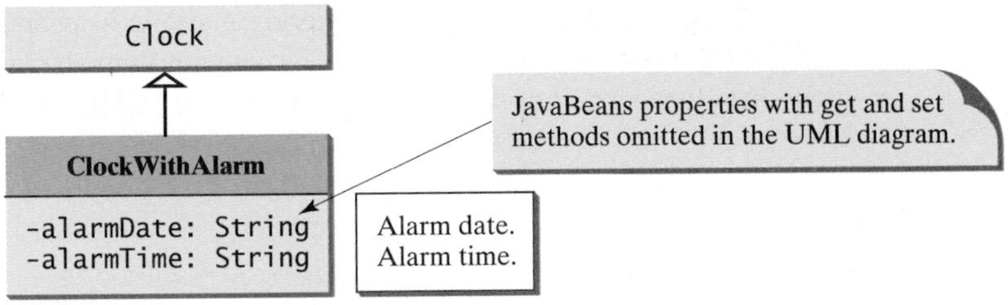
Clock
ClockWithAlarm
-alarmDate: String
-alarmTime: String
JavaBeans properties with get and set methods omitted in the UML diagram.
Alarm date.
Alarm time.

FIGURE 32.13 The `ClockWithAlarm` component extends `Clock` with alarm functions.

year 1998, month 5, and day 13. `alarmTime` is a string consisting of hour, minute, and second, separated by commas. For example, 10,45,2 represents 10 o'clock, 45 minutes, and 2 seconds. When the clock time matches the alarm time, `ClockWithAlarm` fires an `ActionEvent`. Write a test program that displays the alert message "You have an appointment now" on a dialog box at a specified time (e.g., date: 2004,1,1 and time: 10,30,0).

32.6*** (*The `Tick` source component*) Create a custom source component that is capable of generating tick events at variant time intervals, as shown in Figure 32.14. The `Tick` component is similar to `javax.swing.Timer`. The `Timer` class generates a timer at fixed time intervals. This `Tick` component can generate tick events at variant as well as at fixed time intervals.

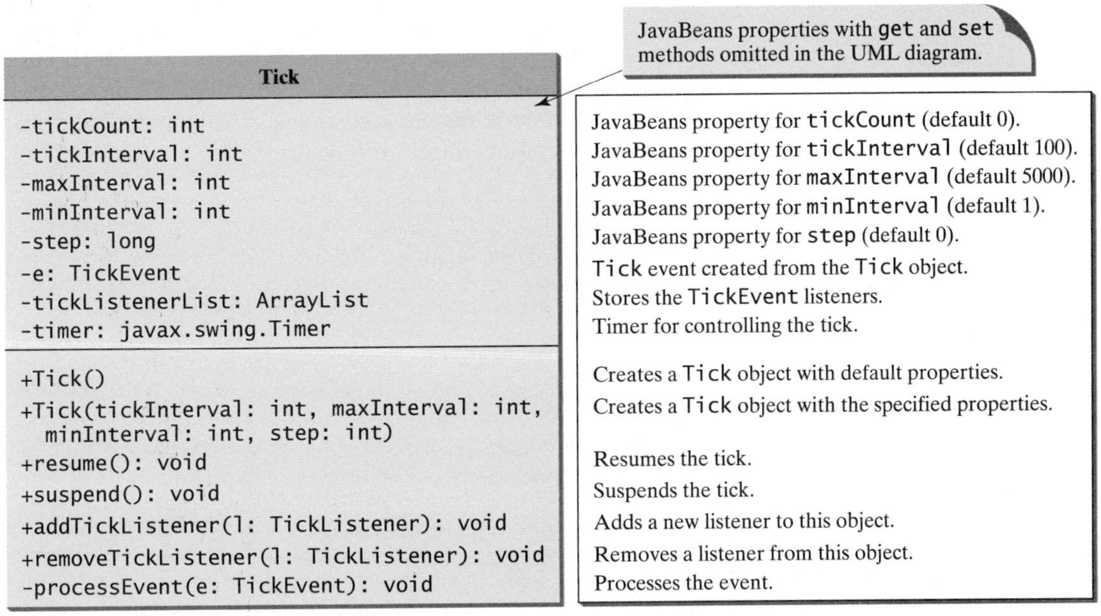
JavaBeans properties with get and set methods omitted in the UML diagram.
Tick
-tickCount: int
-tickInterval: int
-maxInterval: int
-minInterval: int
-step: long
-e: TickEvent
-tickListenerList: ArrayList
-timer: javax.swing.Timer
+Tick()
+Tick(tickInterval: int, maxInterval: int, minInterval: int, step: int)
+resume(): void
+suspend(): void
+addTickListener(l: TickListener): void
+removeTickListener(l: TickListener): void
-processEvent(e: TickEvent): void
JavaBeans property for tickCount (default 0).
JavaBeans property for tickInterval (default 100).
JavaBeans property for maxInterval (default 5000).
JavaBeans property for minInterval (default 1).
JavaBeans property for step (default 0).
Tick event created from the Tick object.
Stores the TickEvent listeners.
Timer for controlling the tick.
Creates a Tick object with default properties.
Creates a Tick object with the specified properties.
Resumes the tick.
Suspends the tick.
Adds a new listener to this object.
Removes a listener from this object.
Processes the event.

FIGURE 32.14 `Tick` is a component that generates `TickEvent`.

The component contains the properties `tickCount`, `tickInterval`, `maxInterval`, `minInterval`, and `step`. The component adjusts the `tickInterval` by adding `step` to it after a tick event occurs. If `step` is 0, `tickInterval` is unchanged. If `step > 0`, `tickInterval` is increased. If `step < 0`, `tickInterval` is decreased. If `tickInterval > maxInterval` or `tickInterval < minInterval`, the component will no longer generate tick events.

The **Tick** component is capable of registering multiple listeners, generating **TickEvent** objects at variant time intervals, and notifying the listeners by invoking the listeners' **handleTick** method. The UML diagram for **TickEvent** and **TickListener** is shown in Figure 32.15.

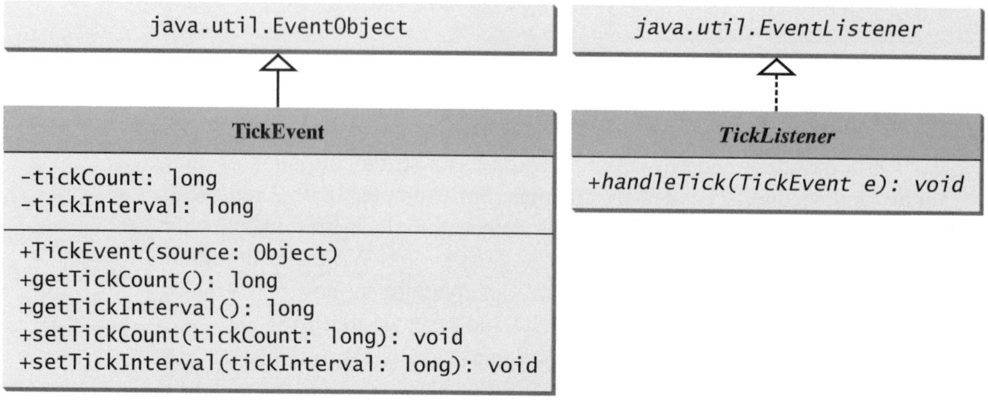
java.util.EventObject
java.util.EventListener
TickEvent
-tickCount: long
-tickInterval: long
+TickEvent(source: Object)
+getTickCount(): long
+getTickInterval(): long
+setTickCount(tickCount: long): void
+setTickInterval(tickInterval: long): void
TickListener
+handleTick(TickEvent e): void

FIGURE 32.15 TickEvent and TickListener comprise an event set for a tick event.

Create an applet named **DisplayMovingMessage**, and create a panel named **MovingMessage** to display the message. Place an instance of the panel in the applet. To enable the message to move rightward, redraw the message with a new incremental *x*-coordinate. Use a **Tick** object to generate a tick event and invoke the **repaint** method to redraw the message when a tick event occurs. To move the message at a decreasing pace, use a positive step (e.g., 10) when constructing a **Tick** object.

CHAPTER 33

CONTAINERS, LAYOUT MANAGERS, AND BORDERS

Objectives

- To explore the internal structures of the Swing container (§33.2).
- To explain how a layout manager works in Java (§33.3).
- To use `CardLayout` and `BoxLayout` (§§33.3.1–33.3.2).
- To use the absolute layout manager to place components in the fixed position (§33.3.3).
- To create custom layout managers (§33.4).
- To use `JScrollPane` to create scroll panes (§33.5).
- To use `JTabbedPane` to create tabbed panes (§33.6).
- To use `JSplitPane` to create split panes (§33.7).
- To use various borders for Swing components (§33.8).

33.1 Introduction

container
layout manager

Chapter 12, "GUI Basics," introduced the concept of containers and the role of layout managers. You learned how to add components into a container and how to use `FlowLayout`, `BorderLayout`, and `GridLayout` to arrange components in a container. A *container* is an object that holds and groups components. A *layout manager* is a special object used to place components in a container. Containers and layout managers play a crucial role in creating user interfaces. This chapter presents a conceptual overview of containers, reviews the layout managers in Java, and introduces several new containers and layout managers. You will also learn how to create custom layout managers and use various borders.

33.2 Swing Container Structures

User interface components like `JButton` cannot be displayed without being placed in a container. A container is a component that holds other components. You do not display a user interface component; you place it in a container, and the container displays the components it contains.

The base class for all containers is `java.awt.Container`, which is a subclass of `java.awt.Component`. The `Container` class has the following essential functions:

- It adds and removes components using various `add` and `remove` methods.
- It maintains a `layout` property for specifying a layout manager that is used to lay out components in the container. Every container has a default layout manager.
- It provides registration methods for the `java.awt.event.ContainerEvent`.

In AWT programming, the `java.awt.Frame` class is used as a top-level container for Java applications, the `java.awt.Applet` class is used for all Java applets, and `java.awt.Dialog` is used for dialog windows. These classes do not work properly with Swing lightweight components. Special versions of `Frame`, `Applet`, and `Dialog` named `JFrame`, `JApplet`, and `JDialog` have been developed to accommodate Swing components. `JFrame` is a subclass of `Frame`, `JApplet` is a subclass of `Applet`, and `JDialog` is a subclass of `Dialog`. `JFrame` and `JApplet` inherit all the functions of their heavyweight counterparts, but they have a more complex internal structure with several layered panes, as shown in Figure 33.1.

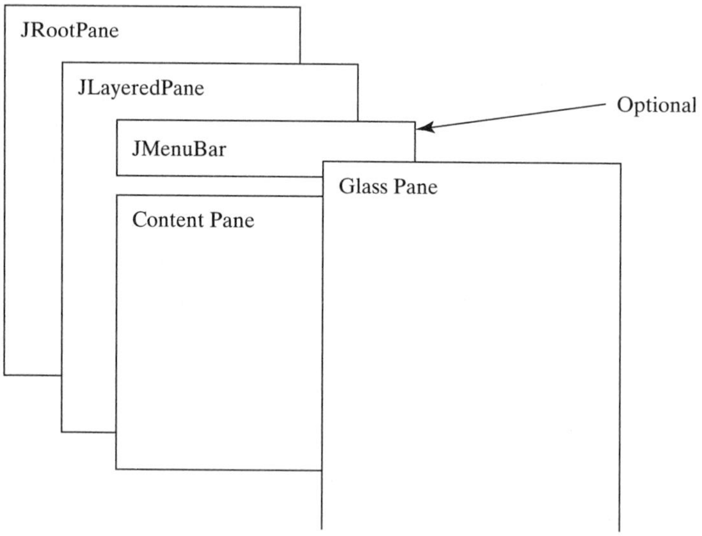
JRootPane
JLayeredPane
JMenuBar
Optional
Glass Pane
Content Pane

FIGURE 33.1 Swing top-level containers use layers of panes to group lightweight components and make them work properly.

javax.swing.JRootPane is a lightweight container used behind the scenes by Swing's top-level containers, such as JFrame, JApplet, and JDialog. javax.swing.JLayeredPane is a container that manages the optional menu bar and the content pane. The content pane is an instance of Container. By default, it is a JPanel with BorderLayout. This is the container where the user interface components are added. To obtain the content pane in a JFrame or in a JApplet, use the getContentPane() method. If you wish to set an instance of Container to be a new content pane, use the setContentPane method. The glass pane floats on top of everything. javax.swing.JGlassPane is a hidden pane by default. If you make the glass pane visible, then it's like a sheet of glass over all the other parts of the root pane. It's completely transparent, unless you implement the glass pane's paint method so that it paints something, and it intercepts input events for the root pane. In general, JRootPane, JLayeredPane, and JGlassPane are not used directly.

Now let us review the three most frequently used Swing containers: JFrame, JApplet, and JPanel.

33.2.1 JFrame

JFrame, a Swing version of Frame, is a top-level container for Java graphics applications. Like Frame, JFrame is displayed as a standalone window with a title bar and a border. The following properties are often useful in JFrame:

- **contentPane** is the content pane of the frame.
- **iconImage** is the image that represents the frame. This image replaces the default Java image on the frame's title bar and is also displayed when the frame is minimized. This property type is Image. You can get an image using the ImageIcon class, as follows:

```
Image image = (new ImageIcon(filename)).getImage();
```

- **jMenuBar** is the optional menu bar for the frame.
- **resizable** is a boolean value indicating whether the frame is resizable. The default value is true.
- **title** specifies the title of the frame.

33.2.2 JApplet

JApplet is a Swing version of Applet. Since it is a subclass of Applet, it has all the functions required by the Web browser. Here are the four essential methods defined in Applet:

```
// Called by the browser when the Web page containing
// this applet is initially loaded
public void init()

// Called by the browser after the init() method and
// every time the Web page is visited.
public void start()

// Called by the browser when the page containing this
// applet becomes inactive.
public void stop()

// Called by the browser when the Web browser exits.
public void destroy()
```

Additionally, JApplet has the contentPane and jMenuBar properties, among others. As with JFrame, you do not place components directly into JApplet; instead you place them into the content pane of the applet. The `Applet` class cannot have a menu bar, but the `JApplet` class allows you to set a menu bar using the `setJMenuBar` method.

Note

When an applet is loaded, the Web browser creates an instance of the applet by invoking the applet's no-arg constructor. So the constructor is invoked before the `init` method.

33.2.3 `JPanel`

Panels act as subcontainers for grouping user interface components. `javax.swing.JPanel` is different from `JFrame` and `JApplet`. First, `JPanel` is not a top-level container; it must be placed inside another container, and it can be placed inside another `JPanel`. Second, since `JPanel` is a subclass of `JComponent`, it is a lightweight component, but `JFrame` and `JApplet` are heavyweight components.

As a subclass of `JComponent`, `JPanel` can take advantage of `JComponent`, such as double buffering and borders. You should draw figures on `JPanel` rather than `JFrame` or `JApplet`, because `JPanel` supports double buffering, which is the technique for eliminating flickers.

33.3 Layout Managers

Every container has a layout manager that is responsible for arranging its components. The container's `setLayout` method can be used to set a layout manager. Certain types of containers have default layout managers. For instance, the content pane of `JFrame` or `JApplet` uses `BorderLayout`, and `JPanel` uses `FlowLayout`.

The layout manager places the components in accordance with its own rules and property settings, and with the constraints associated with each component. Every layout manager has its own specific set of rules. For example, the `FlowLayout` manager places components in rows from left to right and starts a new row when the previous row is filled. The `BorderLayout` manager places components in the north, south, east, west, or center of the container. The `GridLayout` manager places components in a grid of cells in rows and columns from left to right in order.

Some layout managers have properties that can affect the sizing and location of the components in the container. For example, `BorderLayout` has properties called `hgap` (horizontal gap) and `vgap` (vertical gap) that determine the distance between components horizontally and vertically. `FlowLayout` has properties that can be used to specify the alignment (left, center, right) of the components and properties for specifying the horizontal or vertical gap between the components. `GridLayout` has properties that can be used to specify the horizontal or vertical gap between columns and rows and properties for specifying the number of rows and columns. These properties can be retrieved and set using their accessor and mutator methods.

The size of a component in a container is determined by many factors, such as:

- The type of layout manager used by the container.
- The layout constraints associated with each component.
- The size of the container.
- Certain properties common to all components (such as `preferredSize`, `minimumSize`, `maximumSize`, `alignmentX`, and `alignmentY`).

The `preferredSize` property indicates the ideal size at which the component looks best. Depending on the rules of the particular layout manager, this property may or may not be considered. For example, the preferred size of a component is used in a container with a `FlowLayout` manager, but ignored if it is placed in a container with a `GridLayout` manager.

The minimumSize property specifies the minimum size at which the component is useful. For most GUI components, minimumSize is the same as preferredSize. Layout managers generally respect minimumSize more than preferredSize.

The maximumSize property specifies the maximum size needed by a component, so that the layout manager won't wastefully give space to a component that does not need it. For instance, BorderLayout limits the center component's size to its maximum size, and gives the space to edge components.

The alignmentX (alignmentY) property specifies how the component would like to be aligned relative to other components along the x-axis (y-axis). This value should be a number between 0 and 1, where 0 represents alignment along the origin, 1 is aligned the farthest away from the origin, 0.5 is centered, and so on. These two properties are used in the BoxLayout and OverlayLayout.

Java provides a variety of layout managers. You have learned how to use BorderLayout, FlowLayout, and GridLayout. The sections that follow introduce CardLayout, Null layout, and BoxLayout. GridBagLayout, OverlayLayout, and SpringLayout are presented in Supplement III.S.

Tip

If you set a new layout manager in a container, invoke the container's validate() method to force the container to again lay out the components. If you change the properties of a layout manager in a JFrame or JApplet, invoke the doLayout() method to force the container to again lay out the components using the new layout properties. If you change the properties of a layout manager in a JPanel, invoke either doLayout() or revalidate() method to force it to again lay out the components using the new layout properties, but it is better to use revalidate(). Note that validate() is a public method defined in java.awt.Container, revalidate() is a public method defined in javax.swing.JComponent, and doLayout() is a public method defined in java.awt.Container.

33.3.1 CardLayout

CardLayout places components in the container as cards. Only one card is visible at a time, and the container acts as a stack of cards. The ordering of cards is determined by the container's own internal ordering of its component objects. You can specify the size of the horizontal and vertical gaps surrounding a stack of components in a CardLayout manager, as shown in Figure 33.2.

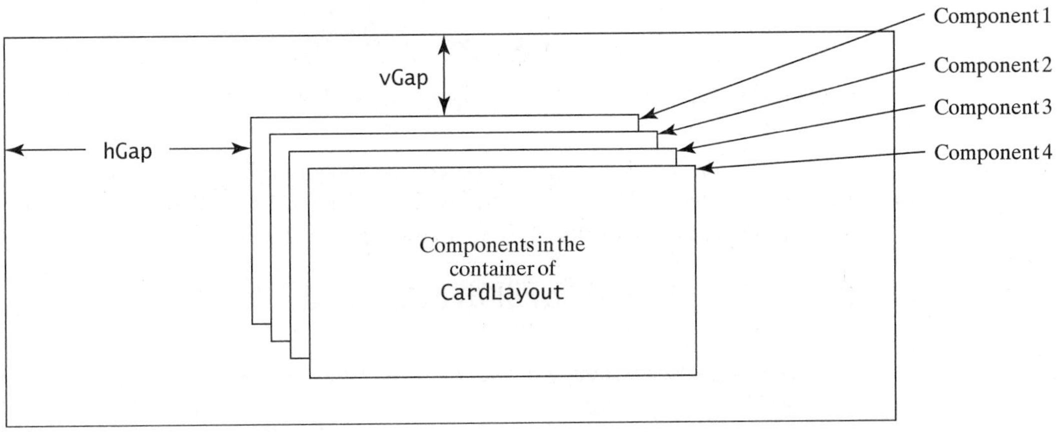
Component 1
Component 2
Component 3
Component 4
vGap
hGap
Components in the container of CardLayout

FIGURE 33.2 The CardLayout places components in the container as a stack of cards.

CardLayout defines a set of methods that allow an application to flip through the cards sequentially or to display a specified card directly, as shown in Figure 33.3.

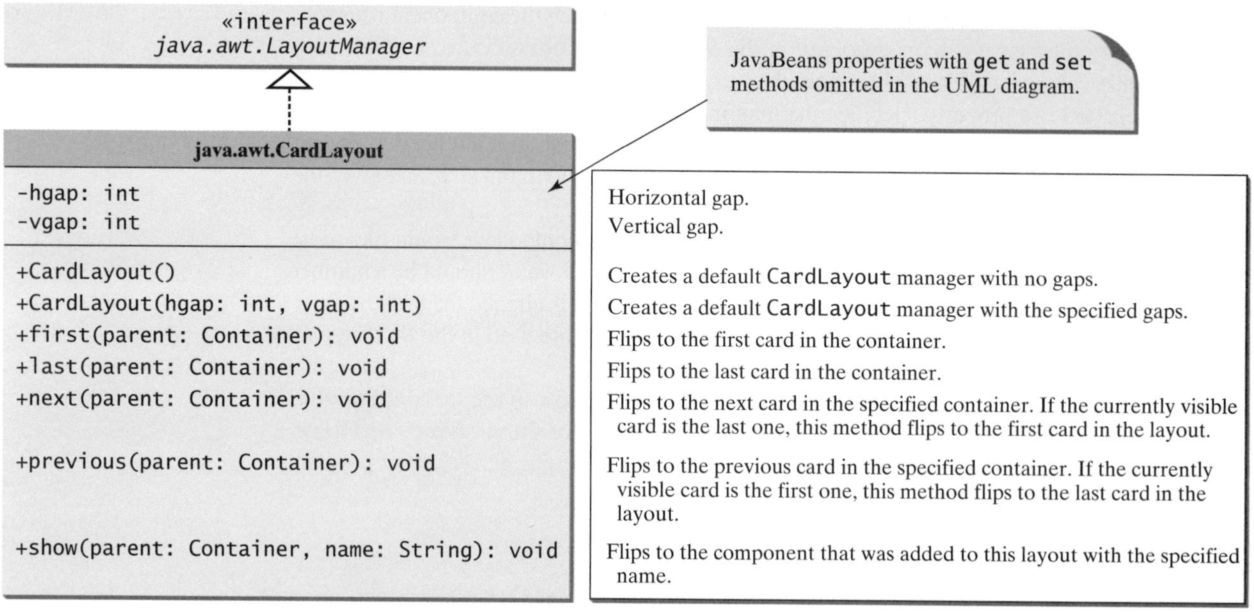
«interface»
java.awt.LayoutManager
java.awt.CardLayout
-hgap: int
-vgap: int
+CardLayout()
+CardLayout(hgap: int, vgap: int)
+first(parent: Container): void
+last(parent: Container): void
+next(parent: Container): void
+previous(parent: Container): void
+show(parent: Container, name: String): void
JavaBeans properties with get and set methods omitted in the UML diagram.
Horizontal gap.
Vertical gap.
Creates a default CardLayout manager with no gaps.
Creates a default CardLayout manager with the specified gaps.
Flips to the first card in the container.
Flips to the last card in the container.
Flips to the next card in the specified container. If the currently visible card is the last one, this method flips to the first card in the layout.
Flips to the previous card in the specified container. If the currently visible card is the first one, this method flips to the last card in the layout.
Flips to the component that was added to this layout with the specified name.

FIGURE 33.3 `CardLayout` contains the methods to flip the card.

To add a component into a container, use the `add(Component c, String name)` method defined in the `LayoutManager` interface. The `String` parameter, `name`, gives an explicit identity to the component in the container.

Listing 33.1 gives a program that creates two panels in a frame. The first panel uses `CardLayout` to hold six labels for displaying images. The second panel uses `FlowLayout` to group four buttons named *First*, *Next*, *Previous*, and *Last*, and a combo box labeled `Image`, as shown in Figure 33.4.

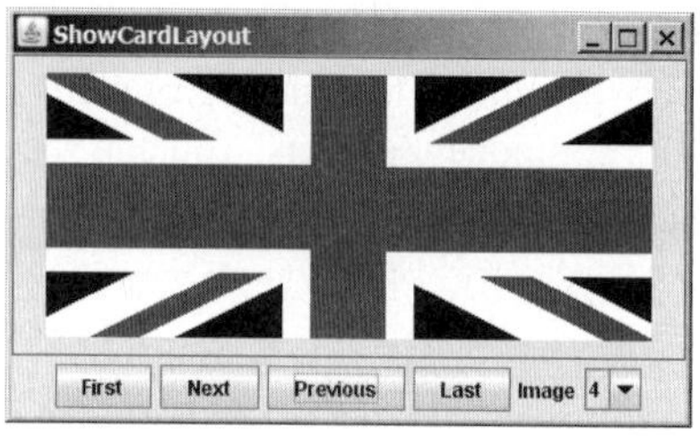
ShowCardLayout
First
Next
Previous
Last
Image
4

FIGURE 33.4 The program shows images in a panel of `CardLayout`.

These buttons control which image will be shown in the `CardLayout` panel. When the user clicks the button named *First*, for example, the first image in the `CardLayout` panel appears. The combo box enables the user to directly select an image.

LISTING 33.1 ShowCardLayout.java

card layout

```
import java.awt.*;
import java.awt.event.*;
import javax.swing.*;

public class ShowCardLayout extends JApplet {
  private CardLayout cardLayout = new CardLayout(20, 10);
  private JPanel cardPanel = new JPanel(cardLayout);
```

```
  private JButton jbtFirst, jbtNext, jbtPrevious, jbtLast;
  private JComboBox jcboImage;
  private final int NUM_OF_FLAGS = 6;

  public ShowCardLayout() {
    cardPanel.setBorder(
      new javax.swing.border.LineBorder(Color.red));

    // Add 9 labels for displaying images into cardPanel
    for (int i = 1; i <= NUM_OF_FLAGS; i++) {
      JLabel label =
        new JLabel(new ImageIcon("image/flag" + i + ".gif"));
      cardPanel.add(label, String.valueOf(i));
    }

    // Panel p to hold buttons and a combo box
    JPanel p = new JPanel();
    p.add(jbtFirst = new JButton("First"));
    p.add(jbtNext = new JButton("Next"));
    p.add(jbtPrevious= new JButton("Previous"));
    p.add(jbtLast = new JButton("Last"));
    p.add(new JLabel("Image"));
    p.add(jcboImage = new JComboBox());

    // Initialize combo box items
    for (int i = 1; i <= NUM_OF_FLAGS; i++)
      jcboImage.addItem(String.valueOf(i));

    // Place panels in the frame
    add(cardPanel, BorderLayout.CENTER);
    add(p, BorderLayout.SOUTH);

    // Register listeners with the source objects
    jbtFirst.addActionListener(new ActionListener() {
      public void actionPerformed(ActionEvent e) {
        // Show the first component in cardPanel
        cardLayout.first(cardPanel);
      }
    });
    jbtNext.addActionListener(new ActionListener() {
      public void actionPerformed(ActionEvent e) {
        // Show the first component in cardPanel
        cardLayout.next(cardPanel);
      }
    });
    jbtPrevious.addActionListener(new ActionListener() {
      public void actionPerformed(ActionEvent e) {
        // Show the first component in cardPanel
        cardLayout.previous(cardPanel);
      }
    });
    jbtLast.addActionListener(new ActionListener() {
      public void actionPerformed(ActionEvent e) {
        // Show the first component in cardPanel
        cardLayout.last(cardPanel);
      }
    });
    jcboImage.addItemListener(new ItemListener() {
      public void itemStateChanged(ItemEvent e) {
```

create UI

register listener

first component

register listener

next component

register listener

previous component

register listener

last component

register listener

```
67        // Show the component at specified index
68        cardLayout.show(cardPanel, (String)e.getItem());
69      }
70    });
71  }
72 }
```

main method omitted

An instance of CardLayout is created in line 6, and a panel of CardLayout is created in line 7. You have already used such statements as setLayout(new FlowLayout()) to create an anonymous layout object and set the layout for a container, instead of creating a separate instance of the layout manager, as in this program. The cardLayout object, however, is useful later in the program to show components in cardPanel. You have to use cardLayout.first(cardPanel) (line 44), for example, to view the first component in cardPanel.

The statement in lines 18–20 adds the image label with the identity String.valueOf(i). Later, when the user selects an image with number i, the identity String.valueOf(i) is used in the cardLayout.show() method (line 68) to view the image with the specified identity.

33.3.2 BoxLayout

javax.swing.BoxLayout is a Swing layout manager that arranges components in a row or a column. To create a BoxLayout, use the following constructor:

```
public BoxlayLayout(Container target, int axis)
```

This constructor is different from other layout constructors. It creates a layout manager that is dedicated to the given target container. The axis parameter is BoxLayout.X_AXIS or BoxLayout.Y_AXIS, which specifies whether the components are laid out horizontally or vertically. For example, the following code creates a horizontal BoxLayout for panel p1:

```
JPanel p1 = new JPanel();
BoxLayout boxLayout = new BoxLayout(p1, BoxLayout.X_AXIS);
p1.setLayout(boxLayout);
```

You still need to invoke the setLayout method on p1 to set the layout manager.

You can use BoxLayout in any container, but it is simpler to use the Box class, which is a container of BoxLayout. To create a Box container, use one of the following two static methods:

```
Box box1 = Box.createHorizontalBox();
Box box2 = Box.createVerticalBox();
```

The former creates a box that contains components horizontally, the latter a box that contains components vertically.

You can add components to a box in the same way that you add them to the containers of FlowLayout or GridLayout using the add method, as follows:

```
box1.add(new JButton("A Button"));
```

You can remove components from a box in the same way that you drop components to a container. The components are laid left to right in a horizontal box, and top to bottom in a vertical box.

BoxLayout is similar to GridLayout but has many unique features.

First, `BoxLayout` respects a component's preferred size, maximum size, and minimum size. If the total preferred size of all the components in the box is less than the box size, then the components are expanded up to their maximum size. If the total preferred size of all the components in the box is greater than the box size, then the components are shrunk down to their minimum size. If the components do not fit at their minimum width, some of them will not be shown. In the `GridLayout`, the container is divided into cells of equal size, and the components are fit in regardless of their preferred maximum or minimum size.

Second, unlike other layout managers, `BoxLayout` considers the component's `alignmentX` or `alignmentY` property. The `alignmentX` property is used to place the component in a vertical box layout, and the `alignmentY` property is used to place it in a horizontal box layout.

Third, `BoxLayout` does not have gaps between the components, but you can use fillers to separate components. A filler is an invisible component. There are three kinds of fillers: struts, rigid areas, and glues.

strut

A *strut* simply adds some space between components. The static method `createHorizontalStrut(int)` in the `Box` class is used to create a horizontal strut, and the static method `createVerticalStrut(int)` to create a vertical strut. For example, the code shown below adds a vertical strut of `8` pixels between two buttons in a vertical box.

```
box2.add(new JButton("Button 1"));
box2.add(Box.createVerticalStrut(8));
box2.add(new JButton("Button 2"));
```

rigid area

A *rigid area* is a two-dimensional space that can be created using the static method `createRigidArea(dimension)` in the `Box` class. For example, the next code adds a rigid area `10` pixels wide and `20` pixels high into a box.

```
box2.add(Box.createRigidArea(new Dimension(10, 20));
```

glue

A *glue* separates components as much as possible. For example, by adding a glue between two components in a horizontal box, you place one component at the left end and the other at the right end. A glue can be created using the `Box.createGlue()` method.

Listing 33.2 shows an example that creates a horizontal box and a vertical box. The horizontal box holds two buttons with print and save icons. The vertical box holds four buttons for selecting flags. When a button in the vertical box is clicked, a corresponding flag icon is displayed in the label centered in the applet, as shown in Figure 33.5.

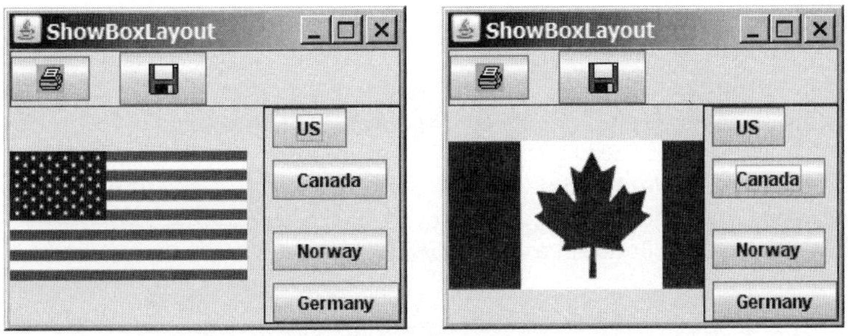
ShowBoxLayout
US
Canada
Norway
Germany
ShowBoxLayout
US
Canada
Norway
Germany

FIGURE 33.5 The components are placed in the containers of `BoxLayout`.

LISTING 33.2 ShowBoxLayout.java

```
import java.awt.*;
import java.awt.event.*;
import javax.swing.*;
```

UI components
BoxLayout container
BoxLayout container
create icons
buttons
create UI
add to box

```

public class ShowBoxLayout extends JApplet {
  // Create two box containers
  private Box box1 = Box.createHorizontalBox();
  private Box box2 = Box.createVerticalBox();

  // Create a label to display flags
  private JLabel jlblFlag = new JLabel();

  // Create image icons for flags
  private ImageIcon imageIconUS =
    new ImageIcon(getClass().getResource("image/us.gif"));
  private ImageIcon imageIconCanada =
    new ImageIcon(getClass().getResource("image/ca.gif"));
  private ImageIcon imageIconNorway =
    new ImageIcon(getClass().getResource("image/norway.gif"));
  private ImageIcon imageIconGermany =
    new ImageIcon(getClass().getResource("image/germany.gif"));
  private ImageIcon imageIconPrint =
    new ImageIcon(getClass().getResource("image/print.gif"));
  private ImageIcon imageIconSave =
    new ImageIcon(getClass().getResource("image/save.gif"));

  // Create buttons to select images
  private JButton jbtUS = new JButton("US");
  private JButton jbtCanada = new JButton("Canada");
  private JButton jbtNorway = new JButton("Norway");
  private JButton jbtGermany = new JButton("Germany");

  public ShowBoxLayout() {
    box1.add(new JButton(imageIconPrint));
    box1.add(Box.createHorizontalStrut(20));
    box1.add(new JButton(imageIconSave));

    box2.add(jbtUS);
    box2.add(Box.createVerticalStrut(8));
    box2.add(jbtCanada);
    box2.add(Box.createGlue());
    box2.add(jbtNorway);
    box2.add(Box.createRigidArea(new Dimension(10, 8)));
    box2.add(jbtGermany);

    box1.setBorder(new javax.swing.border.LineBorder(Color.red));
    box2.setBorder(new javax.swing.border.LineBorder(Color.black));

    add(box1, BorderLayout.NORTH);
    add(box2, BorderLayout.EAST);
    add(jlblFlag, BorderLayout.CENTER);

    // Register listeners
    jbtUS.addActionListener(new ActionListener() {
      public void actionPerformed(ActionEvent e) {
        jlblFlag.setIcon(imageIconUS);
      }
    });
    jbtCanada.addActionListener(new ActionListener() {
      public void actionPerformed(ActionEvent e) {
        jlblFlag.setIcon(imageIconCanada);
      }
```

```
63     });
64     jbtNorway.addActionListener(new ActionListener() {
65       public void actionPerformed(ActionEvent e) {
66         jlblFlag.setIcon(imageIconNorway);
67       }
68     });
69     jbtGermany.addActionListener(new ActionListener() {
70       public void actionPerformed(ActionEvent e) {
71         jlblFlag.setIcon(imageIconGermany);
72       }
73     });
74   }
75 }
```

main method omitted

Two containers of the Box class are created in lines 7–8 using the convenient static methods createHorizontalBox() and createVerticalBox(). The box containers always use the BoxLayout manager. You cannot reset the layout manager for the box containers.

The image icons are created from image files (lines 14–25) through resource URL, introduced in §18.10, "Locating Resource Using the URL Class."

Two buttons with print and save icons are added into the horizontal box (lines 34–36). A horizontal strut with size 20 is added between these two buttons (line 35).

Four buttons with texts US, Canada, Norway, and Germany are added into the vertical box (lines 38–44). A horizontal strut with size 8 is added to separate the US button and the Canada button (line 39). A rigid area is inserted between the Norway button and the Germany button (line 43). A glue is inserted to separate the Canada button and the Norway button as far as possible in the vertical box.

The strut, rigid area, and glue are instances of Component, so they can be added to the box container. In theory, you can add them to a container other than the box container. But they may be ignored and have no effect in other containers.

33.3.3 Using Null Layout Manager

If you have used a Windows-based visual form design tool like Visual Basic, you know that it is easier to create user interfaces with Visual Basic than in Java. This is mainly because in Visual Basic the components are placed in absolute positions and sizes, whereas in Java they are placed in containers using a variety of layout managers. Absolute positions and sizes are fine if the application is developed and deployed on the same platform, but what looks fine on a development system may not look right on a deployment system. To solve this problem, Java provides a set of layout managers that place components in containers in a way that is independent of fonts, screen resolutions, and platform differences.

For convenience, Java also supports an absolute layout, called *null layout*, which enables you to place components at fixed locations. In this case, the component must be placed using the component's instance method setBounds() (defined in java.awt.Component), as follows: null layout

```
public void setBounds(int x, int y, int width, int height);
```

This sets the location and size for the component, as in the next example:

```
JButton jbt = new JButton("Help");
jbt.setBounds(10, 10, 40, 20);
```

The upper-left corner of the *Help* button is placed at (10, 10); the button width is 40, and the height is 20.

Here are the steps of adding a button to a container with a null layout manager:

1. Specify a null layout manager as follows:

set null layout

```
container.setLayout(null);
```

2. Add the component to the container:

```
JButton jbt = new JButton("Help");
container.add(jbt);
```

3. Specify the location where the component is to be placed, using the **setBounds** method:

setBounds

```
jbt.setBounds(10, 10, 40, 20);
```

Listing 33.3 gives a program that places three buttons, as shown in Figure 33.6(a).

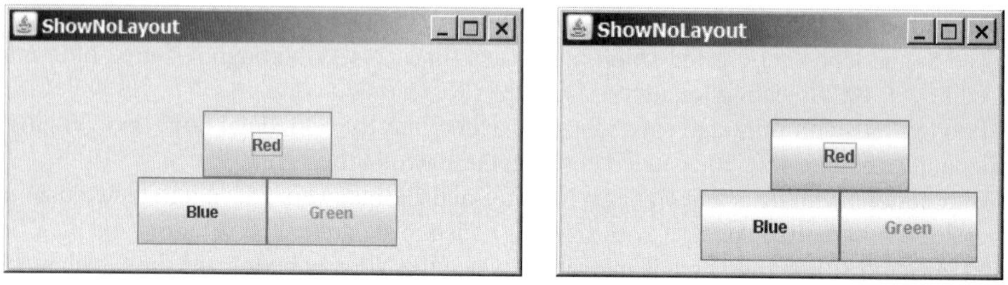
ShowNoLayout
Red
Blue
Green
ShowNoLayout
Red
Blue
Green

(a) (b)

FIGURE 33.6 (a) The components are placed in the frame using a null layout manager. (b) With a null layout manager, the size and positions of the components are fixed.

LISTING 33.3 ShowNoLayout.java

UI components

main method omitted

```
import java.awt.*;
import javax.swing.*;

public class ShowNoLayout extends JApplet {
  private JButton jbtRed = new JButton("Red" );
  private JButton jbtBlue = new JButton("Blue" );
  private JButton jbtGreen = new JButton("Green" );

  public ShowNoLayout() {
    // Set foreground color for the buttons
    jbtRed.setForeground(Color.RED);
    jbtBlue.setForeground(Color.BLUE);
    jbtGreen.setForeground(Color.GREEN);

    // Specify a null layout manager
    setLayout(null);

    // Add components to container
    add(jbtRed);
    add(jbtBlue);
    add(jbtGreen);

    // Put components in the right place
    jbtRed.setBounds(150, 50, 100, 50);
    jbtBlue.setBounds(100, 100, 100, 50);
    jbtGreen.setBounds(200, 100, 100, 50);
  }
}
```

If you run this program on Windows with 1024 × 768 resolution, the layout size is just right. When the program is run on Windows with a higher resolution, the components appear very small and clump together. When it is run on Windows with a lower resolution, they cannot be shown in their entirety.

If you resize the window, you will see that the location and the size of the components are not changed, as shown in Figure 33.6(b).

Tip

Do not use the null-layout-manager to develop platform-independent applications.

33.4 Creating Custom Layout Managers

In addition to the layout managers provided in Java, you can create your own. To do so, you need to understand how a layout manager lays out components. A container's `setLayout` method specifies a layout manager for the container. The layout manager is responsible for laying out the components and displaying them in a desired location with an appropriate size. Every layout manager must directly or indirectly implement the `LayoutManager` interface. For instance, `FlowLayout` directly implements `LayoutManager`, and `BorderLayout` implements `LayoutManager2`, a subclass of `LayoutManager`. The `LayoutManager` interface provides the following methods for laying out components in a container:

- `public void addLayoutComponent(String name, Component comp)`

  Adds the specified component with the specified name to the container.

- `public void layoutContainer(Container parent)`

  Lays out the components in the specified container. In this method, you should provide concrete instructions that specify where the components are to be placed.

- `public Dimension minimumLayoutSize(Container parent)`

  Calculates the minimum size dimensions for the specified panel, given the components in the specified parent container.

- `public Dimension preferredLayoutSize(Container parent)`

  Calculates the preferred size dimensions for the specified panel, given the components in the specified parent container.

- `public void removeLayoutComponent(Component comp)`

  Removes the specified component from the layout.

These methods in `LayoutManager` are invoked by the methods in the `java.awt.Container` class through the layout manager in the container. `Container` contains a property named `layout` (an instance of `LayoutManager`) and the methods for adding and removing components from the container. There are five overloading `add` methods defined in `Container` for adding components with various options. The `remove` method removes a component from the container. The `add` method invokes `addImpl`, which then invokes the `addLayoutComponent` method defined in the `LayoutManager` interface. The `layoutContainer` method in the `LayoutManager` interface is indirectly invoked by the `validate()` method through several calls. The `remove` method invokes `removeLayoutComponent` in `LayoutManager`. The `validate` method is invoked to refresh the container after the components it contains have been added to or modified. The relationship of `Container` and `LayoutManager` is shown in Figure 33.7.

Let us define a custom layout manager named `DiagonalLayout` that places the components in a diagonal. To test `DiagonalLayout`, the example creates an applet with radio

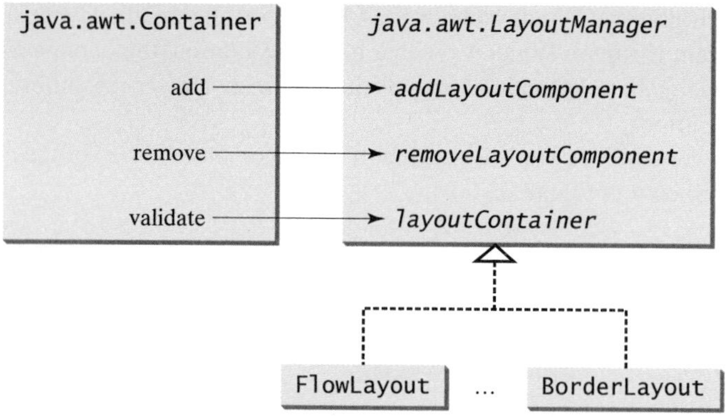
java.awt.Container
add
remove
validate
java.awt.LayoutManager
addLayoutComponent
removeLayoutComponent
layoutContainer
FlowLayout
...
BorderLayout

FIGURE 33.7 The `add`, `remove`, and `validate` methods in `Container` invoke the methods defined in the `LayoutManager` interface.

buttons named "FlowLayout," "GridLayout," and "DiagonalLayout," as shown in Figure 33.8. You can dynamically select one of these three layouts in the panel.

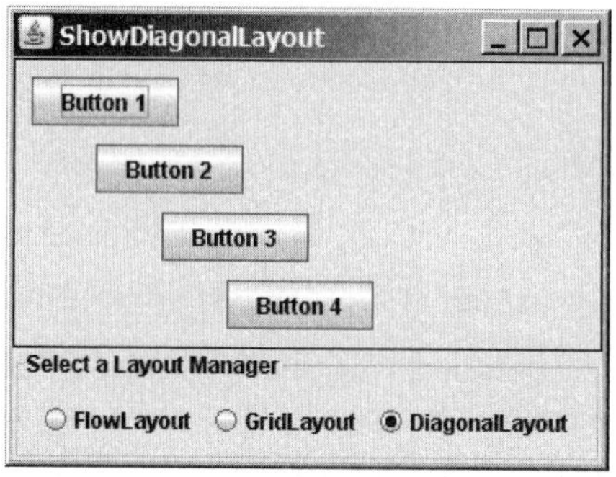
ShowDiagonalLayout
Button 1
Button 2
Button 3
Button 4
Select a Layout Manager
FlowLayout
GridLayout
DiagonalLayout

FIGURE 33.8 The `DiagonalLayout` manager places the components in a diagonal in the container.

`DiagonalLayout` is similar to `FlowLayout`. `DiagonalLayout` arranges components along a diagonal using each component's natural `preferredSize`. It contains three constraints, `gap`, `lastFill`, and `majorDiagonal`, as shown in Figure 33.9. The source code for `DiagonalLayout` is given in Listing 33.4.

LISTING 33.4 DiagonalLayout.java

properties

```
import java.awt.*;

public class DiagonalLayout implements LayoutManager,
    java.io.Serializable {
  /** Vertical gap between the components */
  private int gap = 10;

  /** True if components are placed along the major diagonal */
  private boolean majorDiagonal = true;

  /*True if the last component is stretched to fill the space */
  private boolean lastFill = false;

  /** Constructor */
```

```java
public DiagonalLayout() {
}

public void addLayoutComponent(String name, Component comp) {
  //TODO: implement this java.awt.LayoutManager method;
}

public void removeLayoutComponent(Component comp) {
  //TODO: implement this java.awt.LayoutManager method;
}

public Dimension preferredLayoutSize(Container parent) {
  //TODO: implement this java.awt.LayoutManager method;
  return minimumLayoutSize(parent);
}

public Dimension minimumLayoutSize(Container parent) {
  //TODO: implement this java.awt.LayoutManager method;
  return new Dimension(0, 0);
}

public void layoutContainer(Container parent) {
  //TODO: implement this java.awt.LayoutManager method;
  int numberOfComponents = parent.getComponentCount();

  Insets insets = parent.getInsets();
  int w = parent.getSize().width - insets.left - insets.right;
  int h = parent.getSize().height - insets.bottom - insets.top;

  if (majorDiagonal) {
    int x = 10, y = 10;

    for (int j = 0; j < numberOfComponents; j++) {
      Component c = parent.getComponent(j);
      Dimension d = c.getPreferredSize();

      if (c.isVisible())
        if (lastFill && (j == numberOfComponents - 1))
          c.setBounds(x, y, w - x, h - y);
        else
          c.setBounds(x, y, d.width, d.height);
      x += d.height + gap;
      y += d.height + gap;
    }
  }
  else { // It is subdiagonal
    int x = w - 10, y = 10;

    for (int j = 0; j < numberOfComponents; j++) {
      Component c = parent.getComponent(j);
      Dimension d = c.getPreferredSize();

      if (c.isVisible())
        if (lastFill & (j == numberOfComponents - 1))
          c.setBounds(0, y, x, h - y);
        else
          c.setBounds(x, d.width, y, d.height);

      x -= (d.height + gap);
```

layout container

```
 74         y += d.height + gap;
 75       }
 76     }
 77   }
 78
 79   public int getGap() {
 80     return gap;
 81   }
 82
 83   public void setGap(int gap) {
 84     this.gap = gap;
 85   }
 86
 87   public void setMajorDiagonal(boolean newMajorDiagonal) {
 88     majorDiagonal = newMajorDiagonal;
 89   }
 90
 91   public boolean isMajorDiagonal() {
 92     return majorDiagonal;
 93   }
 94
 95   public void setLastFill(boolean newLastFill) {
 96     lastFill = newLastFill;
 97   }
 98
 99   public boolean isLastFill() {
100     return lastFill;
101   }
102 }
```

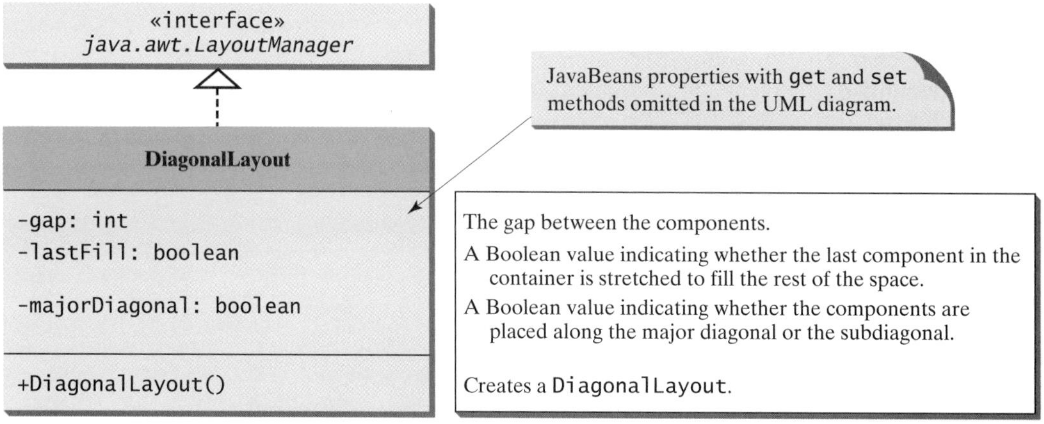
«interface»
java.awt.LayoutManager
JavaBeans properties with get and set methods omitted in the UML diagram.
DiagonalLayout
-gap: int
-lastFill: boolean
-majorDiagonal: boolean
+DiagonalLayout()
The gap between the components.
A Boolean value indicating whether the last component in the container is stretched to fill the rest of the space.
A Boolean value indicating whether the components are placed along the major diagonal or the subdiagonal.
Creates a DiagonalLayout.

FIGURE 33.9 The `DiagonalLayout` manager has three properties with the supporting accessor and mutator methods.

The `DiagonalLayout` class implements the `LayoutManager` and `Serializable` interfaces (lines 3–4). The reason to implement `Serializable` is to make it a JavaBeans component.

The `Insets` class describes the size of the borders of a container. It contains the variables `left`, `right`, `bottom`, and `top`, which correspond to the measurements for the *left border*, *right border*, *top border*, and *bottom border* (lines 40–42).

The `Dimension` class used in `DiagonalLayout` encapsulates the width and height of a component in a single object. The class is associated with certain properties of components. Several methods defined by the `Component` class and the `LayoutManager` interface return a `Dimension` object.

Listing 33.5 gives a test program that uses `DiagonalLayout`.

LISTING 33.5 ShowDiagonalLayout.java

```java
import javax.swing.*;
import javax.swing.border.*;
import java.awt.*;
import java.awt.event.*;

public class ShowDiagonalLayout extends JApplet {
  private FlowLayout flowLayout = new FlowLayout();
  private GridLayout gridLayout = new GridLayout(2, 2);
  private DiagonalLayout diagonalLayout = new DiagonalLayout();

  private JButton jbt1 = new JButton("Button 1");
  private JButton jbt2 = new JButton("Button 2");
  private JButton jbt3 = new JButton("Button 3");
  private JButton jbt4 = new JButton("Button 4");

  private JRadioButton jrbFlowLayout =
    new JRadioButton("FlowLayout");
  private JRadioButton jrbGridLayout =
    new JRadioButton("GridLayout");
  private JRadioButton jrbDiagonalLayout =
    new JRadioButton("DiagonalLayout", true);

  private JPanel jPanel2 = new JPanel();

  public ShowDiagonalLayout() {
    // Set default layout in jPanel2
    jPanel2.setLayout(diagonalLayout);
    jPanel2.add(jbt1);
    jPanel2.add(jbt2);
    jPanel2.add(jbt3);
    jPanel2.add(jbt4);
    jPanel2.setBorder(new LineBorder(Color.black));

    JPanel jPanel1 = new JPanel();
    jPanel1.setBorder(new TitledBorder("Select a Layout Manager"));
    jPanel1.add(jrbFlowLayout);
    jPanel1.add(jrbGridLayout);
    jPanel1.add(jrbDiagonalLayout);

    ButtonGroup buttonGroup1 = new ButtonGroup();
    buttonGroup1.add(jrbFlowLayout);
    buttonGroup1.add(jrbGridLayout);
    buttonGroup1.add(jrbDiagonalLayout);

    add(jPanel1, BorderLayout.SOUTH);
    add(jPanel2, BorderLayout.CENTER);

    jrbFlowLayout.addActionListener(new ActionListener() {
      public void actionPerformed(ActionEvent e) {
        jPanel2.setLayout(flowLayout);
        jPanel2.revalidate();
      }
    });
    jrbGridLayout.addActionListener(new ActionListener() {
      public void actionPerformed(ActionEvent e) {
        jPanel2.setLayout(gridLayout);
        jPanel2.revalidate();
      }
```

diagonal layout

create UI

register listener

register listener

register listener

main method omitted

```
59      });
60      jrbDiagonalLayout.addActionListener(new ActionListener() {
61        public void actionPerformed(ActionEvent e) {
62          jPanel2.setLayout(diagonalLayout);
63          jPanel2.revalidate();
64        }
65      });
66    }
67 }
```

The `TestDiagonalLayout` class enables you to dynamically set the layout in `jPanel2`. When you select a new layout, the layout manager is set in `jPanel2`, and the `revalidate()` method is invoked (lines 51, 57, 63), which in turn invokes the `layoutContainer` method in the `LayoutManager` interface to display the components in the container.

33.5 JScrollPane

Often you need to use a scroll bar to scroll the contents of an object that does not fit completely into the viewing area. `JScrollBar` and `JSlider` can be used for this purpose, but you have to *manually* write the code to implement scrolling with them. `JScrollPane` is a component that supports *automatic* scrolling without coding. It was used to scroll the text area in Listing 17.7, TextAreaDemo.java, and to scroll a list in Listing 17.9, ListDemo.java. In fact, it can be used to scroll any subclass of `JComponent`.

A `JScrollPane` can be viewed as a specialized container with a view port for displaying the contained component. In addition to horizontal and vertical scroll bars, a `JScrollPane` can have a column header, a row header, and corners, as shown in Figure 33.10.

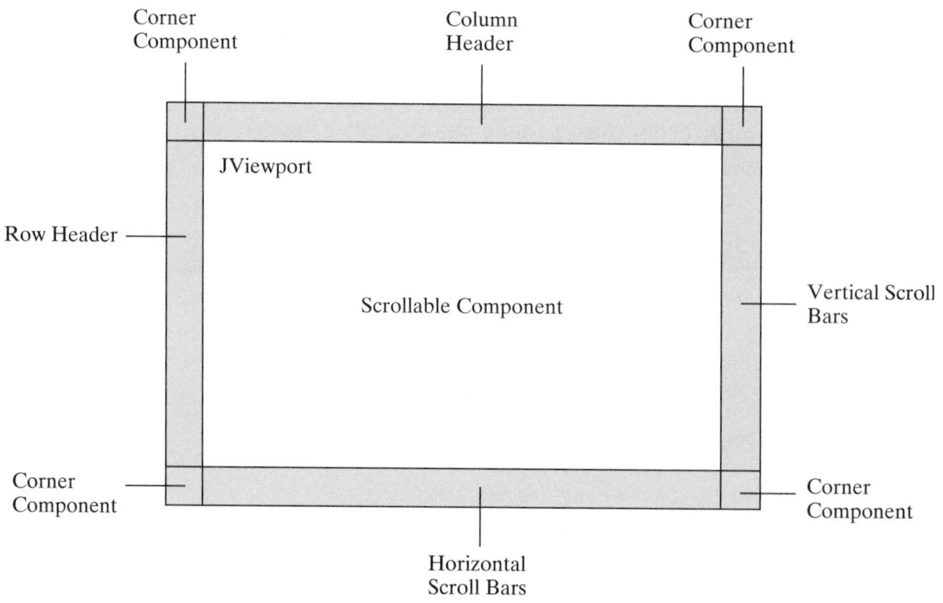
Corner Component
Column Header
Corner Component
JViewport
Row Header
Scrollable Component
Vertical Scroll Bars
Corner Component
Corner Component
Horizontal Scroll Bars

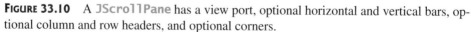

FIGURE 33.10 A `JScrollPane` has a view port, optional horizontal and vertical bars, optional column and row headers, and optional corners.

view port

The *view port* is an instance of `JViewport` through which a scrollable component is displayed. When you add a component to a scroll pane, you are actually placing it in the scroll pane's view port. Figure 33.11 shows the frequently used properties, constructors, and methods in `JScrollPane`.

javax.swing.JComponent ↑ javax.swing.JScrollPane	JavaBeans properties with get and set methods omitted in the UML diagram.
#columnHeader: JViewport	The column header (default: null).
#rowHeader: JViewport	The row header (default: null).
#horizontalScrollBarPolicy: int	The display policy for the horizontal scroll bar (default: JScrollPane.HORIZONTAL_SCROLLBAR_AS_NEEDED).
#verticalScrollBarPolicy: int	The display policy for the horizontal scroll bar (default: JScrollPane.VERTICAL_SCROLLBAR_AS_NEEDED).
#viewport: JViewport	The scroll pane's view port.
#horizontalScrollBar: JScrollBar	The scroll pane's horizontal scroll bar.
#verticalScrollBar: JScrollBar	The scroll pane's vertical scroll bar.
-viewportBorder: Border	The border around the view port.
+JScrollPane()	Creates an empty JScrollPane where both horizontal and vertical scroll bars appear when needed.
+JScrollPane(view: Component)	Creates a JScrollPane that displays the contents of the specified component, where both horizontal and vertical scroll bars appear whenever the component's contents are larger than the view.
+JScrollPane(view: Component, vsbPolicy: int, hsbPolicy: int)	Creates a JScrollPane that displays the contents of the specified component with the specified horizontal and vertical scroll bar policies.
+JScrollPane(vsbPolicy: int, hsbPolicy: int)	Creates an empty JScrollPane with the specified horizontal and vertical scroll bar policies.
+setCorner(key: String, corner: Component): void	Adds a component in one of the scroll pane's corners.
+setViewportView(view: Component): void	Adds a view component to the view port.

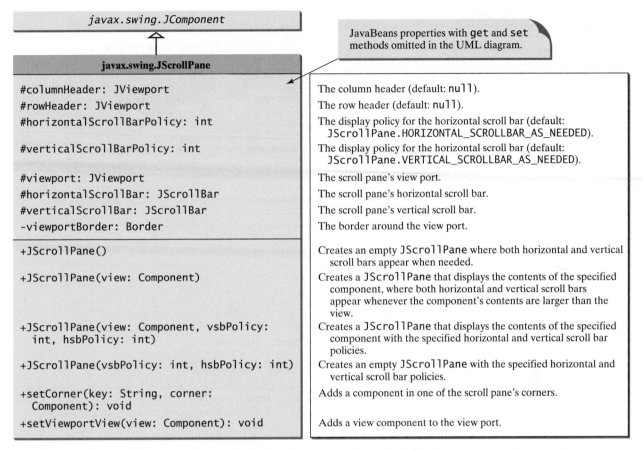

FIGURE 33.11 JScrollPane provides methods for displaying and manipulating the components in a scroll pane.

The constructor always creates a view port regardless of whether the viewing component is specified. Normally, you have the component and you want to place it in a scroll pane. A convenient way to create a scroll pane for a component is to use the `JScrollPane(component)` constructor.

The `vsbPolicy` parameter can be one of the following three values:

```
JScrollPane.VERTICAL_SCROLLBAR_AS_NEEDED
JScrollPane.VERTICAL_SCROLLBAR_NEVER
JScrollPane.VERTICAL_SCROLLBAR_ALWAYS
```

The `hsbPolicy` parameter can be one of the following three values:

```
JScrollPane.HORIZONTAL_SCROLLBAR_AS_NEEDED
JScrollPane.HORIZONTAL_SCROLLBAR_NEVER
JScrollPane.HORIZONTAL_SCROLLBAR_ALWAYS
```

To set a corner component, you can use the `setCorner(String key, Component corner)` method. The legal values for the key are:

```
JScrollPane.LOWER_LEFT_CORNER
JScrollPane.LOWER_RIGHT_CORNER
JScrollPane.UPPER_LEFT_CORNER
JScrollPane.UPPER_RIGHT_CORNER
```

Listing 33.6 shows an example that displays a map in a label and places the label in a scroll pane so that a large map can be scrolled. The program lets you choose a map from a combo box and display it in the scroll pane, as shown in Figure 33.12.

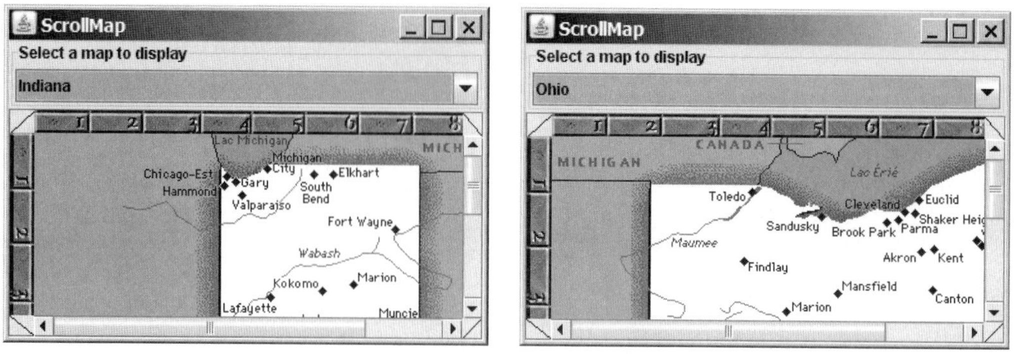
ScrollMap
Select a map to display
Indiana
Chicago-Est
Hammond
Gary
Valparaiso
Michigan City
Elkhart
South Bend
Fort Wayne
Wabash
Kokomo
Marion
Lafayette
Muncie
ScrollMap
Select a map to display
Ohio
CANADA
MICHIGAN
Lac Érié
Toledo
Sandusky
Cleveland
Euclid
Shaker Hei
Brook Park
Parma
Maumee
Findlay
Akron
Kent
Mansfield
Canton
Marion

FIGURE 33.12 The scroll pane can be used to scroll contents automatically.

LISTING 33.6 ScrollMap.java

labels

create UI

scroll pane

```
import java.awt.*;
import java.awt.event.*;
import javax.swing.*;
import javax.swing.border.*;

public class ScrollMap extends JApplet {
  // Create images in labels
  private JLabel lblIndianaMap = new JLabel(
    new ImageIcon(getClass().getResource("image/indianaMap.gif")));
  private JLabel lblOhioMap = new JLabel(
    new ImageIcon(getClass().getResource("image/ohioMap.gif")));

  // Create a scroll pane to scroll map in the labels
  private JScrollPane jspMap = new JScrollPane(lblIndianaMap);

  public ScrollMap() {
    // Create a combo box for selecting maps
    JComboBox jcboMap = new JComboBox(new String[]{"Indiana",
      "Ohio"});

    // Panel p to hold combo box
    JPanel p = new JPanel();
    p.setLayout(new BorderLayout());
    p.add(jcboMap);
    p.setBorder(new TitledBorder("Select a map to display"));

    // Set row header, column header and corner header
    jspMap.setColumnHeaderView(new JLabel(new ImageIcon(getClass().
      getResource("image/horizontalRuler.gif"))));
    jspMap.setRowHeaderView(new JLabel(new ImageIcon(getClass().
      getResource("image/verticalRuler.gif"))));
    jspMap.setCorner(JScrollPane.UPPER_LEFT_CORNER,
      new CornerPanel(JScrollPane.UPPER_LEFT_CORNER));
    jspMap.setCorner(ScrollPaneConstants.UPPER_RIGHT_CORNER,
      new CornerPanel(JScrollPane.UPPER_RIGHT_CORNER));
    jspMap.setCorner(JScrollPane.LOWER_RIGHT_CORNER,
      new CornerPanel(JScrollPane.LOWER_RIGHT_CORNER));
    jspMap.setCorner(JScrollPane.LOWER_LEFT_CORNER,
      new CornerPanel(JScrollPane.LOWER_LEFT_CORNER));

    // Add the scroll pane and combo box panel to the frame
```

```
42       add(jspMap, BorderLayout.CENTER);
43       add(p, BorderLayout.NORTH);
44
45       // Register listener
46       jcboMap.addItemListener(new ItemListener() {
47         /** Show the selected map */
48         public void itemStateChanged(ItemEvent e) {
49           String selectedItem = (String)e.getItem();
50           if (selectedItem.equals("Indiana")) {
51             // Set a new view in the view port
52             jspMap.setViewportView(lblIndianaMap);
53           }
54           else if (selectedItem.equals("Ohio")) {
55             // Set a new view in the view port
56             jspMap.setViewportView(lblOhioMap);
57           }
58
59           // Revalidate the scroll pane
60           jspMap.revalidate();
61         }
62       });
63     }
64   }
65
66   // A panel displaying a line used for scroll pane corner
67   class CornerPanel extends JPanel {
68     // Line location
69     private String location;
70
71     public CornerPanel(String location) {
72       this.location = location;
73     }
74
75     /** Draw a line depending on the location */
76     protected void paintComponent(Graphics g) {
77       super.paintComponents(g);
78
79       if (location == "UPPER_LEFT_CORNER")
80         g.drawLine(0, getHeight(), getWidth(), 0);
81       else if (location == "UPPER_RIGHT_CORNER")
82         g.drawLine(0, 0, getWidth(), getHeight());
83       else if (location == "LOWER_RIGHT_CORNER")
84         g.drawLine(0, getHeight(), getWidth(), 0);
85       else if (location == "LOWER_LEFT_CORNER")
86         g.drawLine(0, 0, getWidth(), getHeight());
87     }
88   }
```

register listener

main method omitted

The program creates a scroll pane to view image maps. The images are created from image files and displayed in labels (lines 8–11). To view an image, the label that contains the image is placed in the scroll pane's view port (line 14).

The scroll pane has a main view, a header view, a column view, and four corner views. Each view is a subclass of `Component`. Since `ImageIcon` is not a subclass of `Component`, it cannot be directly used as a view in the scroll pane. Instead the program places an `ImageIcon` to a label and uses the label as a view.

The `CornerPanel` (lines 67–88) is a subclass of `JPanel` that is used to display a line. How the line is drawn depends on the `location` of the corner. The `location` is a string passed in as a parameter in the `CornerPanel`'s constructor.

Whenever a new map is selected, the label for displaying the map image is set to the scroll pane's view port. The `revalidate()` method (line 60) must be invoked to cause the new image to be displayed. The `revalidate()` method causes a container to lay out its subcomponents again after the components it contains have been added to or modified.

33.6 JTabbedPane

`JTabbedPane` is a useful Swing container that provides a set of mutually exclusive tabs for accessing multiple components, as shown in Figure 33.13.

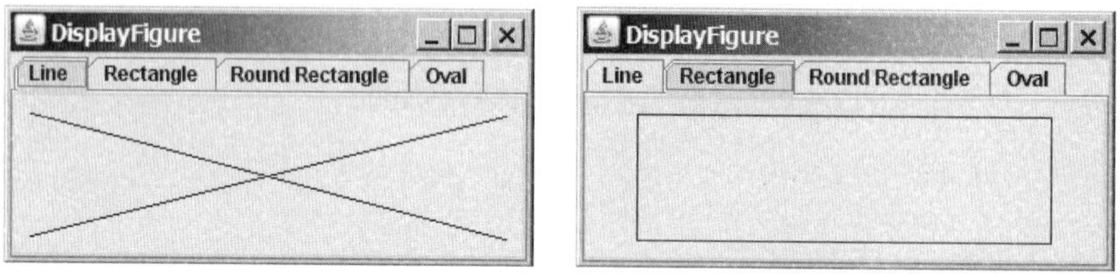
DisplayFigure
Line
Rectangle
Round Rectangle
Oval
DisplayFigure
Line
Rectangle
Round Rectangle
Oval

FIGURE 33.13 `JTabbedPane` displays components through the tabs.

Usually you place the panels inside a `JTabbedPane` and associate a tab with each panel. `JTabbedPane` is easy to use, because the selection of the panel is handled automatically by clicking the corresponding tab. You can switch between a group of panels by clicking on a tab with a given title and/or icon. Figure 33.14 shows the frequently used properties, constructors, and methods in `JTabbedPane`.

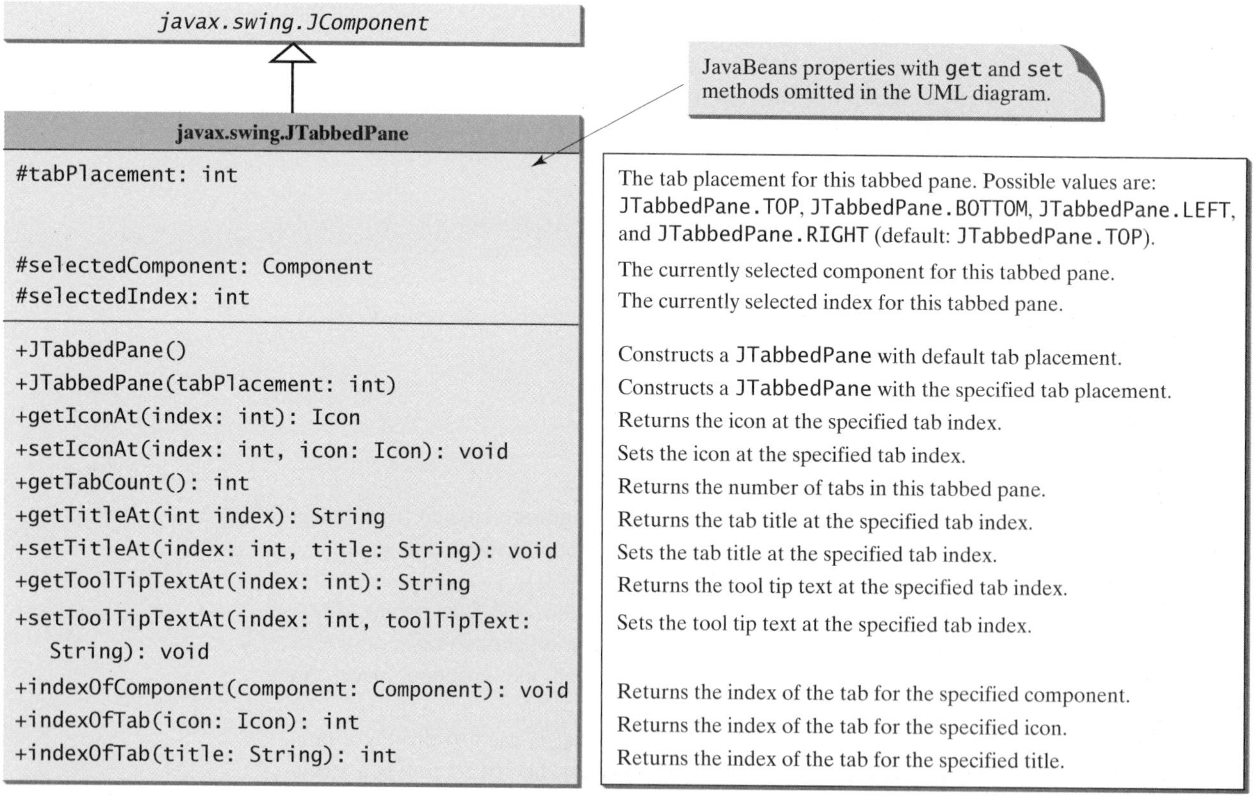
javax.swing.JComponent
JavaBeans properties with get and set methods omitted in the UML diagram.
javax.swing.JTabbedPane
#tabPlacement: int
#selectedComponent: Component
#selectedIndex: int
+JTabbedPane()
+JTabbedPane(tabPlacement: int)
+getIconAt(index: int): Icon
+setIconAt(index: int, icon: Icon): void
+getTabCount(): int
+getTitleAt(int index): String
+setTitleAt(index: int, title: String): void
+getToolTipTextAt(index: int): String
+setToolTipTextAt(index: int, toolTipText: String): void
+indexOfComponent(component: Component): void
+indexOfTab(icon: Icon): int
+indexOfTab(title: String): int
The tab placement for this tabbed pane. Possible values are: JTabbedPane.TOP, JTabbedPane.BOTTOM, JTabbedPane.LEFT, and JTabbedPane.RIGHT (default: JTabbedPane.TOP).
The currently selected component for this tabbed pane.
The currently selected index for this tabbed pane.
Constructs a JTabbedPane with default tab placement.
Constructs a JTabbedPane with the specified tab placement.
Returns the icon at the specified tab index.
Sets the icon at the specified tab index.
Returns the number of tabs in this tabbed pane.
Returns the tab title at the specified tab index.
Sets the tab title at the specified tab index.
Returns the tool tip text at the specified tab index.
Sets the tool tip text at the specified tab index.
Returns the index of the tab for the specified component.
Returns the index of the tab for the specified icon.
Returns the index of the tab for the specified title.

FIGURE 33.14 `JTabbedPane` provides methods for displaying and manipulating the components in the tabbed pane.

Listing 33.7 gives an example that uses a tabbed pane with four tabs to display four types of figures: line, rectangle, rounded rectangle, and oval. You can select a figure to display by clicking the corresponding tab, as shown in Figure 33.13. The `FigurePanel` class for displaying a figure was presented in Listing 15.3 FigurePanel.java. You can use the `type` property to specify a figure type.

LISTING 33.7 DisplayFigure.java

```
import java.awt.*;
import javax.swing.*;

public class DisplayFigure extends JApplet {
  private JTabbedPane jtpFigures = new JTabbedPane();
  private FigurePanel squarePanel = new FigurePanel();
  private FigurePanel rectanglePanel = new FigurePanel();
  private FigurePanel circlePanel = new FigurePanel();
  private FigurePanel ovalPanel = new FigurePanel();

  public DisplayFigure() {
    squarePanel.setType(FigurePanel.LINE);
    rectanglePanel.setType(FigurePanel.RECTANGLE);
    circlePanel.setType(FigurePanel.ROUND_RECTANGLE);
    ovalPanel.setType(FigurePanel.OVAL);

    add(jtpFigures, BorderLayout.CENTER);
    jtpFigures.add(squarePanel, "Line");
    jtpFigures.add(rectanglePanel, "Rectangle");
    jtpFigures.add(circlePanel, "Round Rectangle");
    jtpFigures.add(ovalPanel, "Oval");

    jtpFigures.setToolTipTextAt(0, "Square");
    jtpFigures.setToolTipTextAt(1, "Rectangle");
    jtpFigures.setToolTipTextAt(2, "Circle");
    jtpFigures.setToolTipTextAt(3, "Oval");
  }
}
```

tabbed pane

set type

add tabs

set tool tips

main method omitted

The program creates a tabbed pane to hold four panels, each of which displays a figure. A panel is associated with a tab. The tabs are titled Line, Rectangle, Rounded Rectangle, and Oval.

By default, the tabs are placed at the top of the tabbed pane. You can select a different placement using the `tabPlacement` property.

33.7 JSplitPane

`JSplitPane` is a convenient Swing container that contains two components with a separate bar known as a *divider*, as shown in Figure 33.15.

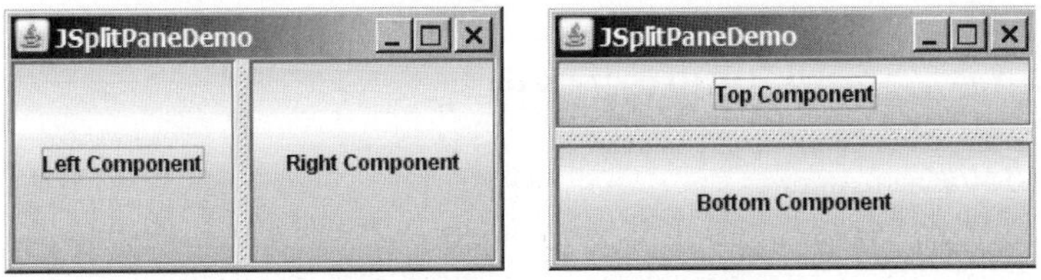
JSplitPaneDemo
Left Component
Right Component
JSplitPaneDemo
Top Component
Bottom Component

(a) Vertical divider (b) Horizontal divider

FIGURE 33.15 `JSplitPane` divides a container into two parts.

The bar can divide the container horizontally or vertically and can be dragged to change the amount of space occupied by each component. Figure 33.16 shows the frequently used properties, constructors, and methods in `JSplitPane`.

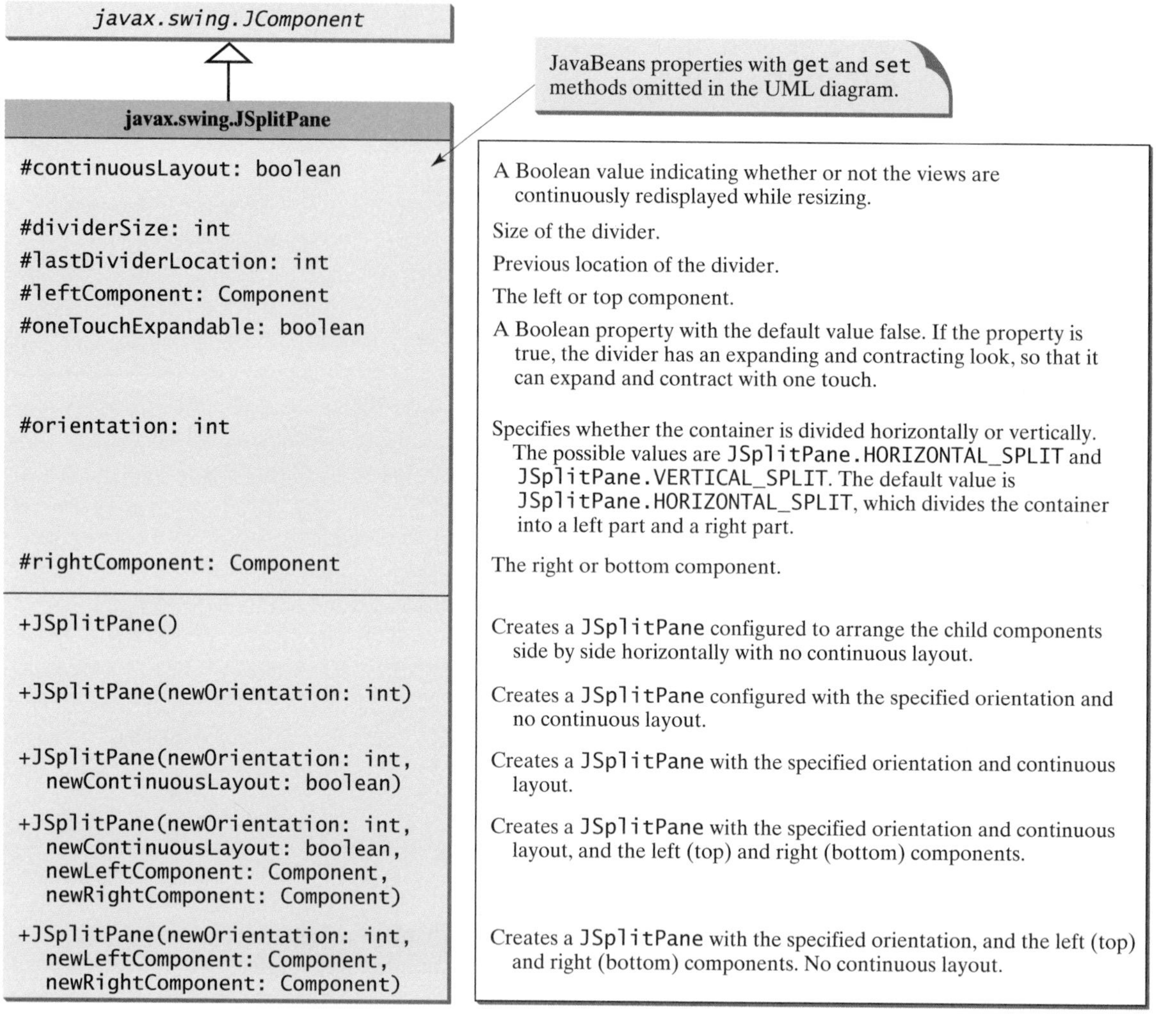
javax.swing.JComponent
JavaBeans properties with get and set methods omitted in the UML diagram.
javax.swing.JSplitPane
#continuousLayout: boolean
A Boolean value indicating whether or not the views are continuously redisplayed while resizing.
#dividerSize: int
Size of the divider.
#lastDividerLocation: int
Previous location of the divider.
#leftComponent: Component
The left or top component.
#oneTouchExpandable: boolean
A Boolean property with the default value false. If the property is true, the divider has an expanding and contracting look, so that it can expand and contract with one touch.
#orientation: int
Specifies whether the container is divided horizontally or vertically. The possible values are JSplitPane.HORIZONTAL_SPLIT and JSplitPane.VERTICAL_SPLIT. The default value is JSplitPane.HORIZONTAL_SPLIT, which divides the container into a left part and a right part.
#rightComponent: Component
The right or bottom component.
+JSplitPane()
Creates a JSplitPane configured to arrange the child components side by side horizontally with no continuous layout.
+JSplitPane(newOrientation: int)
Creates a JSplitPane configured with the specified orientation and no continuous layout.
+JSplitPane(newOrientation: int, newContinuousLayout: boolean)
Creates a JSplitPane with the specified orientation and continuous layout.
+JSplitPane(newOrientation: int, newContinuousLayout: boolean, newLeftComponent: Component, newRightComponent: Component)
Creates a JSplitPane with the specified orientation and continuous layout, and the left (top) and right (bottom) components.
+JSplitPane(newOrientation: int, newLeftComponent: Component, newRightComponent: Component)
Creates a JSplitPane with the specified orientation, and the left (top) and right (bottom) components. No continuous layout.

FIGURE 33.16 `JSplitPane` provides methods to specify the properties of a split pane and for manipulating the components in a split pane.

Listing 33.8 gives an example that uses radio buttons to let the user select a `FlowLayout`, `GridLayout`, or `BoxLayout` manager dynamically for a panel. The panel contains four buttons, as shown in Figure 33.17. The description of the currently selected layout manager is displayed in a text area. The radio buttons, buttons, and text area are placed in two split panes.

LISTING 33.8 ShowLayout.java

```
import java.awt.*;
import java.awt.event.*;
import javax.swing.*;

public class ShowLayout extends JApplet {
  // Get the url for HTML files
```

descriptions

```
  private String flowLayoutDesc = "FlowLayout arranges components " +
    "according to their preferredSize in " +
    "a left-to-right flow, much like lines of text in a paragraph.";
  private String gridLayoutDesc = "GridLayout arranges ...";
  private String boxLayoutDesc = "BoxLayout arranges ...";
```

radio buttons

```
  private JRadioButton jrbFlowLayout =
    new JRadioButton("FlowLayout");
  private JRadioButton jrbGridLayout =
    new JRadioButton("GridLayout", true);
  private JRadioButton jrbBoxLayout =
    new JRadioButton("BoxLayout");

  private JPanel jpComponents = new JPanel();
  private JTextArea jtfDescription = new JTextArea();

  // Create layout managers
```

layout managers

```
  private FlowLayout flowLayout = new FlowLayout();
  private GridLayout gridLayout = new GridLayout(2, 2, 3, 3);
  private BoxLayout boxLayout =
    new BoxLayout(jpComponents, BoxLayout.X_AXIS);

  public ShowLayout() {
    // Create a box to hold radio buttons
    Box jpChooseLayout = Box.createVerticalBox();
    jpChooseLayout.add(jrbFlowLayout);
    jpChooseLayout.add(jrbGridLayout);
    jpChooseLayout.add(jrbBoxLayout);

    // Group radio buttons
    ButtonGroup btg = new ButtonGroup();
    btg.add(jrbFlowLayout);
    btg.add(jrbGridLayout);
    btg.add(jrbBoxLayout);

    // Wrap lines and words
    jtfDescription.setLineWrap(true);
    jtfDescription.setWrapStyleWord(true);

    // Add four buttons to jpComponents
    jpComponents.add(new JButton("Button 1"));
    jpComponents.add(new JButton("Button 2"));
    jpComponents.add(new JButton("Button 3"));
    jpComponents.add(new JButton("Button 4"));

    // Create two split panes to hold jpChooseLayout, jpComponents,
    // and jtfDescription
```

split pane

```
    JSplitPane jSplitPane2 = new JSplitPane(
      JSplitPane.VERTICAL_SPLIT, jpComponents,
      new JScrollPane(jtfDescription));
```

split pane

```
    JSplitPane jSplitPane1 = new JSplitPane(
      JSplitPane.HORIZONTAL_SPLIT, jpChooseLayout, jSplitPane2);

    // Set FlowLayout as default
    jpComponents.setLayout(flowLayout);
    jpComponents.revalidate();
    jtfDescription.setText(flowLayoutDesc);

    add(jSplitPane1, BorderLayout.CENTER);
```

```
66
67      // Register listeners
68      jrbFlowLayout.addActionListener(new ActionListener() {
69        public void actionPerformed(ActionEvent e) {
70          jpComponents.setLayout(flowLayout);
71          jtfDescription.setText(flowLayoutDesc);
72          jpComponents.revalidate();
73        }
74      });
75      jrbGridLayout.addActionListener(new ActionListener() {
76        public void actionPerformed(ActionEvent e) {
77          jpComponents.setLayout(gridLayout);
78          jtfDescription.setText(gridLayoutDesc);
79          jpComponents.revalidate();
80        }
81      });
82      jrbBoxLayout.addActionListener(new ActionListener() {
83        public void actionPerformed(ActionEvent e) {
84          jpComponents.setLayout(boxLayout);
85          jtfDescription.setText(boxLayoutDesc);
86          jpComponents.revalidate();
87        }
88      });
89    }
90  }
```

register listener (line 75)
validate (line 79)
register listener (line 82)
validate (line 86)
main method omitted (line 90)

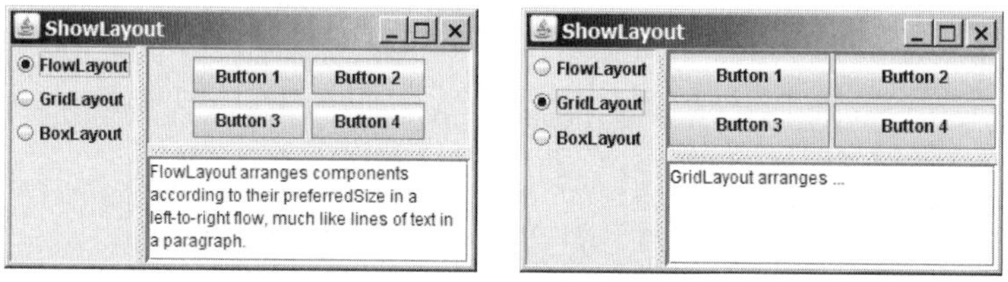
ShowLayout
FlowLayout
GridLayout
BoxLayout
Button 1
Button 2
Button 3
Button 4
FlowLayout arranges components according to their preferredSize in a left-to-right flow, much like lines of text in a paragraph.
ShowLayout
FlowLayout
GridLayout
BoxLayout
Button 1
Button 2
Button 3
Button 4
GridLayout arranges ...

FIGURE 33.17 You can adjust the component size in the split panes.

Split panes can be embedded. Adding a split pane to an existing split pane results in three split panes. The program creates two split panes (lines 54–58) to hold a panel for radio buttons, a panel for buttons, and a scroll pane.

The radio buttons are used to select layout managers. A selected layout manager is used in the panel for laying out the buttons (lines 68–88). The scroll pane contains a `JTextArea` for displaying the text that describes the selected layout manager (line 56).

33.8 Swing Borders

Swing provides a variety of borders that you can use to decorate components. You learned how to create titled borders and line borders in §12.9, "Common Features of Swing GUI Components." This section introduces borders in more detail.

A Swing border is defined in the `Border` interface. Every instance of `JComponent` can set a border through the `border` property defined in `JComponent`. If a border is present, it replaces the inset. The `AbstractBorder` class implements an empty border with no size. This provides a convenient base class from which other border classes can easily be defined. There are eight concrete border classes, `BevelBorder`, `SoftBevelBorder`, `CompoundBorder`, `EmptyBorder`, `EtchedBorder`, `LineBorder`, `MatteBorder`, and `TitledBorder`, as shown in Figure 33.18.

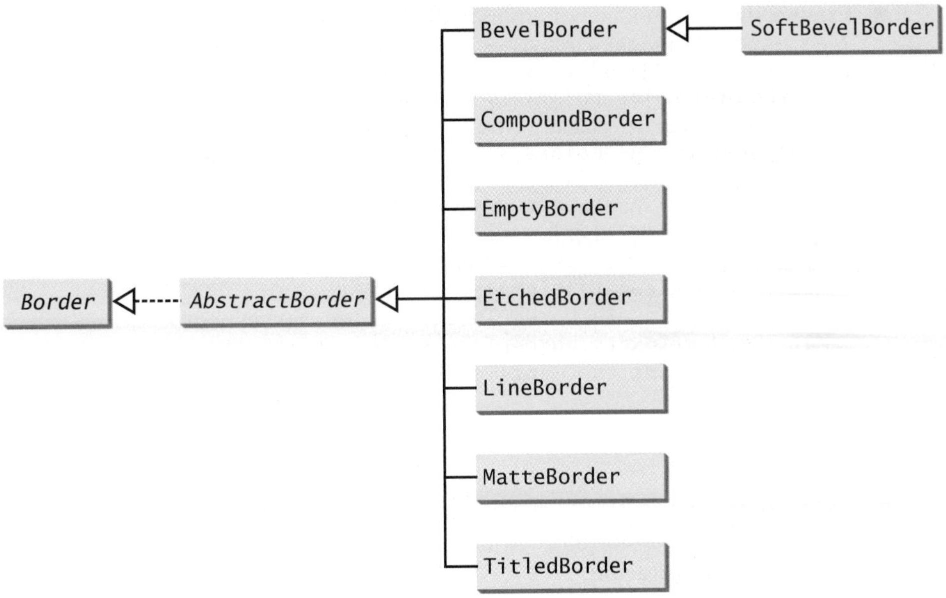
Border
AbstractBorder
BevelBorder
SoftBevelBorder
CompoundBorder
EmptyBorder
EtchedBorder
LineBorder
MatteBorder
TitledBorder

FIGURE 33.18 The Border interface defines Swing borders.

- **BevelBorder** is a 3D-look border that can be lowered or raised. BevelBorder has the following constructors, which create a BevelBorder with the specified bevelType (BevelBorder.LOWERED or BevelBorder.RAISED) and colors:

```
BevelBorder(int bevelType)
BevelBorder(int bevelType, Color highlight, Color shadow)
BevelBorder(int bevelType, Color highlightOuterColor,
            Color highlightInnerColor, Color shadowOuterColor,
            Color shadowInnerColor)
```

- **SoftBevelBorder** is a raised or lowered bevel with softened corners. SoftBevelBorder has the following constructors:

```
SoftBevelBorder(int bevelType)
SoftBevelBorder(int bevelType, Color highlight, Color shadow)
SoftBevelBorder(int bevelType, Color highlightOuterColor,
                Color highlightInnerColor,
                Color shadowOuterColor,
                Color shadowInnerColor)
```

- **EmptyBorder** is a border with border space but no drawings. EmptyBorder has the following constructors:

```
EmptyBorder(Insets borderInsets)
EmptyBorder(int top, int left, int bottom, int right)
```

- **EtchedBorder** is an etched border that can be etched-in or etched-out. EtchedBorder has the property etchType with the value LOWERED or RAISED. EtchedBorder has the following constructors:

```
EtchedBorder() // Default constructor with a lowered border
EtchedBorder(Color highlight, Color shadow)
EtchedBorder(int etchType)
EtchedBorder(int etchType, Color highlight, Color shadow)
```

- **LineBorder** draws a line of arbitrary thickness and a single color around the border. LineBorder has the following constructors:

```
LineBorder(Color color) // Thickness 1
LineBorder(Color color, int thickness)
LineBorder(Color color, int thickness, boolean roundedCorners)
```

- **MatteBorder** is a mattelike border padded with the icon images. MatteBorder has the following constructors:

```
MatteBorder(Icon tileIcon)
MatteBorder(Insets borderInsets, Color matteColor)
MatteBorder(Insets borderInsets, Icon tileIcon)
MatteBorder(int top, int left, int bottom, int right, Color
  matteColor)
MatteBorder(int top, int left, int bottom, int right, Icon
  tileIcon)
```

- **CompoundBorder** is used to compose two Border objects into a single border by nesting an inside Border object within the insets of an outside Border object using the following constructor:

```
CompoundBorder(Border outsideBorder, Border insideBorder)
```

- **TitledBorder** is a border with a string title in a specified position. TitledBorder can be composed with other borders. TitledBorder has the following constructors:

```
TitledBorder(String title)
TitledBorder(Border border) // Empty title on another border
TitledBorder(Border border, String title)
TitledBorder(Border border, String title,
             int titleJustification, int titlePosition)
TitledBorder(Border border, String title,
             int titleJustification, int titlePosition,
             Font titleFont)
TitledBorder(Border border, String title,
             int titleJustification,
             int titlePosition, Font titleFont, Color
               titleColor)
```

For convenience, Java also provides the `javax.swing.BorderFactory` class, which contains the static methods for creating borders shown in Figure 33.19.

For example, to create an etched border, use the following statement:

```
Border border = BorderFactory.createEtchedBorder();
```

Note

All the border classes and interfaces are grouped in the package `javax.swing.border` except `javax.swing.BorderFactory`.

Note

Borders and icons can be shared. Thus you can create a border or icon and use it to set the `border` or `icon` property for any GUI component. For example, the following statements set a border `b` for two panels `p1` and `p2`:

```
p1.setBorder(b);
p2.setBorder(b);
```

javax.swing.BorderFactory
+createBevelBorder(type: int): Border
+createBevelBorder(type: int, highlight: Color, shadow: Color): Border
+createBevelBorder(type: int, highlightOuter: Color, highlightInner: Color, shadowOuter: Color, shadowInner: Color): Border
+createCompoundBorder(): CompoundBorder
+createCompoundBorder(outsideBorder: Border, insideBorder: Border): CompoundBorder
+createEmptyBorder(): Border
+createEmptyBorder(top: int, left: int, bottom: int, right: int): Border
+createEtchedBorder(): Border
+createEtchedBorder(highlight: Color, shadow: Color): Border
+createEtchedBorder(type: int): Border
+createEtchedBorder(type: int, highlight: Color, shadow: Color): Border
+createLineBorder(color: Color): Border
+createLineBorder(color: Color, thickness: int): Border
+createLoweredBevelBorder(): Border
+createMatteBorder(top: int, left: int, bottom: int, right: int, color: Color): MatteBorder
+createMatteBorder(top: int, left: int, bottom: int, right: int, tileIcon: Icon): MatteBorder
+createRaisedBevelBorder(): Border
+createTitledBorder(border: Border): TitledBorder
+createTitledBorder(border: Border, title: String): TitledBorder
+createTitledBorder(border: Border, title: String, titleJustification: int, titlePosition: int): TitledBorder
+createTitledBorder(border: Border, title: String, titleJustification: int, titlePosition: int, titleFont: Font): TitledBorder
+createTitledBorder(border: Border, title: String, titleJustification: int, titlePosition: int, titleFont: Font, titleColor: Color): TitledBorder
+createTitledBorder(title: String): TitledBorder

FIGURE 33.19 `BorderFactory` contains the static methods for creating various types of borders.

Listing 33.9 gives an example that creates and displays various types of borders. You can select a border with or without a title. For a border without a title, you can choose a border style from Lowered Bevel, Raised Bevel, Etched, Line, Matte, or Empty. For a border with a title, you can specify the title position and justification. You can also embed another border into a titled border. Figure 33.20 displays a sample run of the program.

Here are the major steps in the program:

1. Create the user interface.

   a. Create a `JLabel` object and place it in the center of the frame.

   b. Create a panel named `jpPositon` to group the radio buttons for selecting the border title position. Set the border of this panel in the titled border with the title "Position".

   c. Create a panel named `jpJustification` to group the radio buttons for selecting the border title justification. Set the border of this panel in the titled border with the title "Justification".

   d. Create a panel named `jpTitleOptions` to hold the `jpPosition` panel and the `jpJustification` panel.

   e. Create a panel named `jpTitle` to hold a check box named "Titled" and the `jpTitleOptions` panel.

f. Create a panel named `jpBorderStyle` to group the radio buttons for selecting border styles.

g. Create a panel named `jpAllChoices` to hold the panels `jpTitle` and `jpBorderStyle`. Place `jpAllChoices` in the south of the frame.

2. Process the event.

Create and register listeners to implement the `actionPerformed` handler to set the border for the label according to the events from the check box, and from all the radio buttons.

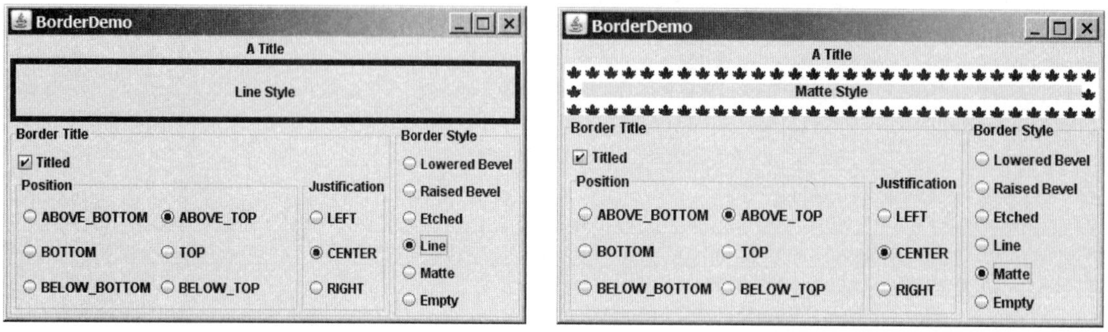
BorderDemo
A Title
Line Style
Border Title
Titled
Position
ABOVE_BOTTOM
ABOVE_TOP
BOTTOM
TOP
BELOW_BOTTOM
BELOW_TOP
Justification
LEFT
CENTER
RIGHT
Border Style
Lowered Bevel
Raised Bevel
Etched
Line
Matte
Empty
BorderDemo
A Title
Matte Style
Border Title
Titled
Position
ABOVE_BOTTOM
ABOVE_TOP
BOTTOM
TOP
BELOW_BOTTOM
BELOW_TOP
Justification
LEFT
CENTER
RIGHT
Border Style
Lowered Bevel
Raised Bevel
Etched
Line
Matte
Empty

(a) (b)

FIGURE 33.20 The program demonstrates various types of borders.

LISTING 33.9 BorderDemo.java

```
import java.awt.*;
import java.awt.event.ActionListener;
import java.awt.event.ActionEvent;
import javax.swing.*;
import javax.swing.border.*;

public class BorderDemo extends JApplet {
  // Declare a label for displaying message
  private JLabel jLabel1 = new JLabel("Display the border type",
    JLabel.CENTER);

  // A check box for selecting a border with or without a title
  private JCheckBox jchkTitled;

  // Radio buttons for border styles
  private JRadioButton jrbLoweredBevel, jrbRaisedBevel,
    jrbEtched, jrbLine, jrbMatte, jrbEmpty;

  // Radio buttons for titled border options
  private JRadioButton jrbAboveBottom, jrbBottom,
    jrbBelowBottom, jrbAboveTop, jrbTop, jrbBelowTop,
    jrbLeft, jrbCenter, jrbRight;

  // TitledBorder for the label
  private TitledBorder jLabel1Border;

  /** Constructor */
  public BorderDemo() {
    // Create a JLabel instance and set colors
    jLabel1.setBackground(Color.yellow);
```

create UI

```
    jLabel1.setBorder(jLabel1Border);

    // Place title position radio buttons
    JPanel jpPosition = new JPanel();
    jpPosition.setLayout(new GridLayout(3, 2));
    jpPosition.add(
      jrbAboveBottom = new JRadioButton("ABOVE_BOTTOM"));
    jpPosition.add(jrbAboveTop = new JRadioButton("ABOVE_TOP"));
    jpPosition.add(jrbBottom = new JRadioButton("BOTTOM"));
    jpPosition.add(jrbTop = new JRadioButton("TOP"));
    jpPosition.add(
      jrbBelowBottom = new JRadioButton("BELOW_BOTTOM"));
    jpPosition.add(jrbBelowTop = new JRadioButton("BELOW_TOP"));
    jpPosition.setBorder(new TitledBorder("Position"));

    // Place title justification radio buttons
    JPanel jpJustification = new JPanel();
    jpJustification.setLayout(new GridLayout(3,1));
    jpJustification.add(jrbLeft = new JRadioButton("LEFT"));
    jpJustification.add(jrbCenter = new JRadioButton("CENTER"));
    jpJustification.add(jrbRight = new JRadioButton("RIGHT"));
    jpJustification.setBorder(new TitledBorder("Justification"));

    // Create panel jpTitleOptions to hold jpPosition and
    // jpJustification
    JPanel jpTitleOptions = new JPanel();
    jpTitleOptions.setLayout(new BorderLayout());
    jpTitleOptions.add(jpPosition, BorderLayout.CENTER);
    jpTitleOptions.add(jpJustification, BorderLayout.EAST);

    // Create Panel jpTitle to hold a check box and title position
    // radio buttons, and title justification radio buttons
    JPanel jpTitle = new JPanel();
    jpTitle.setBorder(new TitledBorder("Border Title"));
    jpTitle.setLayout(new BorderLayout());
    jpTitle.add(jchkTitled = new JCheckBox("Titled"),
      BorderLayout.NORTH);
    jpTitle.add(jpTitleOptions, BorderLayout.CENTER);

    // Group radio buttons for title position
    ButtonGroup btgTitlePosition = new ButtonGroup();
    btgTitlePosition.add(jrbAboveBottom);
    btgTitlePosition.add(jrbBottom);
    btgTitlePosition.add(jrbBelowBottom);
    btgTitlePosition.add(jrbAboveTop);
    btgTitlePosition.add(jrbTop);
    btgTitlePosition.add(jrbBelowTop);

    // Group radio buttons for title justification
    ButtonGroup btgTitleJustification = new ButtonGroup();
    btgTitleJustification.add(jrbLeft);
    btgTitleJustification.add(jrbCenter);
    btgTitleJustification.add(jrbRight);

    // Create Panel jpBorderStyle to hold border style radio buttons
    JPanel jpBorderStyle = new JPanel();
    jpBorderStyle.setBorder(new TitledBorder("Border Style"));
    jpBorderStyle.setLayout(new GridLayout(6, 1));
    jpBorderStyle.add(jrbLoweredBevel =
      new JRadioButton("Lowered Bevel"));
```

```
    jpBorderStyle.add(jrbRaisedBevel =
      new JRadioButton("Raised Bevel"));
    jpBorderStyle.add(jrbEtched = new JRadioButton("Etched"));
    jpBorderStyle.add(jrbLine = new JRadioButton("Line"));
    jpBorderStyle.add(jrbMatte = new JRadioButton("Matte"));
    jpBorderStyle.add(jrbEmpty = new JRadioButton("Empty"));

    // Group radio buttons for border styles
    ButtonGroup btgBorderStyle = new ButtonGroup();
    btgBorderStyle.add(jrbLoweredBevel);
    btgBorderStyle.add(jrbRaisedBevel);
    btgBorderStyle.add(jrbEtched);
    btgBorderStyle.add(jrbLine);
    btgBorderStyle.add(jrbMatte);
    btgBorderStyle.add(jrbEmpty);

    // Create Panel jpAllChoices to place jpTitle and jpBorderStyle
    JPanel jpAllChoices = new JPanel();
    jpAllChoices.setLayout(new BorderLayout());
    jpAllChoices.add(jpTitle, BorderLayout.CENTER);
    jpAllChoices.add(jpBorderStyle, BorderLayout.EAST);

    // Place panels in the frame
    setLayout(new BorderLayout());
    add(jLabel1, BorderLayout.CENTER);
    add(jpAllChoices, BorderLayout.SOUTH);

    // Register listeners
    ActionListener listener = new EventListener();
    jchkTitled.addActionListener(listener);
    jrbAboveBottom.addActionListener(listener);
    jrbBottom.addActionListener(listener);
    jrbBelowBottom.addActionListener(listener);
    jrbAboveTop.addActionListener(listener);
    jrbTop.addActionListener(listener);
    jrbBelowTop.addActionListener(listener);
    jrbLeft.addActionListener(listener);
    jrbCenter.addActionListener(listener);
    jrbRight.addActionListener(listener);
    jrbLoweredBevel.addActionListener(listener);
    jrbRaisedBevel.addActionListener(listener);
    jrbLine.addActionListener(listener);
    jrbEtched.addActionListener(listener);
    jrbMatte.addActionListener(listener);
    jrbEmpty.addActionListener(listener);
  }

  private class EventListener implements ActionListener {
    /** Handle ActionEvents on check box and radio buttons */
    public void actionPerformed(ActionEvent e) {
      // Get border style
```

empty border

```
      Border border = new EmptyBorder(2, 2, 2, 2);

      if (jrbLoweredBevel.isSelected()) {
```

bevel border

```
        border = new BevelBorder(BevelBorder.LOWERED);
        jLabel1.setText("Lowered Bevel Style");
      }
      else if (jrbRaisedBevel.isSelected()) {
```

bevel border

```
        border = new BevelBorder(BevelBorder.RAISED);
        jLabel1.setText("Raised Bevel Style");
```

```java
      }
      else if (jrbEtched.isSelected()) {
        border = new EtchedBorder();
        jLabel1.setText("Etched Style");
      }
      else if (jrbLine.isSelected()) {
        border = new LineBorder(Color.black, 5);
        jLabel1.setText("Line Style");
      }
      else if (jrbMatte.isSelected()) {
        border = new MatteBorder(15, 15, 15, 15,
          new ImageIcon(getClass().getResource
            ("image/caIcon.gif")));
        jLabel1.setText("Matte Style");
      }
      else if (jrbEmpty.isSelected()) {
        border = new EmptyBorder(2, 2, 2, 2);
        jLabel1.setText("Empty Style");
      }

      if (jchkTitled.isSelected()) {
        // Get the title position and justification
        int titlePosition = TitledBorder.DEFAULT_POSITION;
        int titleJustification = TitledBorder.DEFAULT_JUSTIFICATION;

        if (jrbAboveBottom.isSelected())
          titlePosition = TitledBorder.ABOVE_BOTTOM;
        else if (jrbBottom.isSelected())
          titlePosition = TitledBorder.BOTTOM;
        else if (jrbBelowBottom.isSelected())
          titlePosition = TitledBorder.BELOW_BOTTOM;
        else if (jrbAboveTop.isSelected())
          titlePosition = TitledBorder.ABOVE_TOP;
        else if (jrbTop.isSelected())
          titlePosition = TitledBorder.TOP;
        else if (jrbBelowTop.isSelected())
          titlePosition = TitledBorder.BELOW_TOP;

        if (jrbLeft.isSelected())
          titleJustification = TitledBorder.LEFT;
        else if (jrbCenter.isSelected())
          titleJustification = TitledBorder.CENTER;
        else if (jrbRight.isSelected())
          titleJustification = TitledBorder.RIGHT;

        jLabel1Border = new TitledBorder("A Title");
        jLabel1Border.setBorder(border);
        jLabel1Border.setTitlePosition(titlePosition);
        jLabel1Border.setTitleJustification(titleJustification);
        jLabel1.setBorder(jLabel1Border);
      }
      else {
        jLabel1.setBorder(border);
      }
    }
  }
}
```

etched border

line border

matte border

empty border

border on border

main method omitted

This example uses many panels to group UI components to achieve the desired look. Figure 33.20 illustrates the relationship of the panels. The Border Title panel groups all the options for setting title properties. The position options are grouped in the Position panel. The justification options are grouped in the Justification panel. The Border Style panel groups the radio buttons for choosing Lowered Bevel, Raised Bevel, Etched, Line, Matte, and Empty borders.

The label displays the selected border with or without a title, depending on the selection of the title check box. The label also displays a text indicating which type of border is being used, depending on the selection of the radio button in the Border Style panel.

The `TitledBorder` can be mixed with other borders. To do so, simply create an instance of `TitledBorder`, and use the `setBorder` method to embed a new border in `TitledBorder`.

The `MatteBorder` can be used to display icons on the border, as shown in Figure 33.20(b).

Chapter Summary

1. `javax.swing.JRootPane` is a lightweight container used behind the scenes by Swing's top-level containers, such as `JFrame`, `JApplet`, and `JDialog`. `javax.swing.JLayeredPane` is a container that manages the optional menu bar and the content pane. The content pane is an instance of `Container`. By default, it is a `JPanel` with `BorderLayout`. This is the container where the user interface components are added. To obtain the content pane in a `JFrame` or in a `JApplet`, use the `getContentPane()` method. You can set any instance of `Container` to be a new content pane using the `setContentPane` method.

2. Every container has a layout manager that is responsible for arranging its components. The container's `setLayout` method can be used to set a layout manager. Certain types of containers have default layout managers.

3. The layout manager places the components in accordance with its own rules and property settings, and with the constraints associated with each component. Every layout manager has its own specific set of rules. Some layout managers have properties that can affect the sizing and location of the components in the container.

4. Java also supports absolute layout, which enables you to place components at fixed locations. In this case, the component must be placed using the component's instance method `setBounds()` (defined in `java.awt.Component`). Absolute positions and sizes are fine if the application is developed and deployed on the same platform, but what looks fine on a development system may not look right on a deployment system on a different platform. To solve this problem, Java provides a set of layout managers that place components in containers in a way that is independent of fonts, screen resolutions, and operating systems.

5. In addition to the layout managers provided in Java, you can create custom layout managers by implementing the `LayoutManager` interface.

6. Java provides specialized containers `Box`, `JScrollPane`, `JTabbedPane`, and `JSplitPane` with fixed layout managers.

7. A Swing border is defined in the `Border` interface. Every instance of `JComponent` can set a border through the `border` property defined in `JComponent`. If a border is present, it replaces the inset. There are eight concrete border classes: `BevelBorder`, `SoftBevelBorder`, `CompoundBorder`, `EmptyBorder`, `EtchedBorder`,

LineBorder, MatteBorder, and TitledBorder. You can use the constructors of these classes or the static methods in javax.swing.BorderFactory to create borders.

Review Questions

Section 33.2

33.1 Since JButton is a subclass of Container, can you add a button inside a button?

33.2 How do you set an image icon in a JFrame's title bar? Can you set an image icon in a JApplet's title bar?

33.3 Which of the following are the properties in JFrame, JApplet, and JPanel?

```
contentPane, iconImage, jMenuBar, resizable, title
```

Section 33.3

33.4 How does the layout in Java differ from those in Visual Basic?

33.5 Discuss the factors that determine the size of the components in a container.

33.6 Discuss the properties preferredSize, minimumSize, and maximumSize.

33.7 Discuss the properties alignmentX and alignmentY.

33.8 What is a CardLayout manager? How do you create a CardLayout manager?

33.9 Can you use absolute positioning in Java? How do you use absolute positioning? Why should you avoid using it?

33.10 What is BoxLayout? How do you use BoxLayout? How do you use fillers to separate the components?

Sections 33.4–33.7

33.11 How do you create a custom layout manager?

33.12 What is JScrollPane? How do you use JScrollPane?

33.13 What is JTabbedPane? How do you use JTabbedPane?

33.14 What is JSplitPane? How do you use JSplitPane?

33.15 Can you specify a layout manager in Box, JScrollPane, JTabbedPane, and JSplitPane?

Section 33.8

33.16 How do you create a titled border, a line border, a bevel border, and an etched border?

33.17 Can you set a border for every Swing GUI component? Can a border object be shared by different GUI components?

33.18 What package contains Border, BevelBorder, CompoundBorder, EmptyBorder, EtchedBorder, LineBorder, MatteBorder, TitledBorder, and BorderFactory?

Programming Exercises

Section 33.3

33.1* (*Demonstrating FlowLayout properties*) Create a program that enables the user to set the properties of a FlowLayout manager dynamically, as shown in Figure 33.21. The FlowLayout manager is used to place 15 components in a panel. You can set the alignment, hgap, and vgap properties of the FlowLayout dynamically.

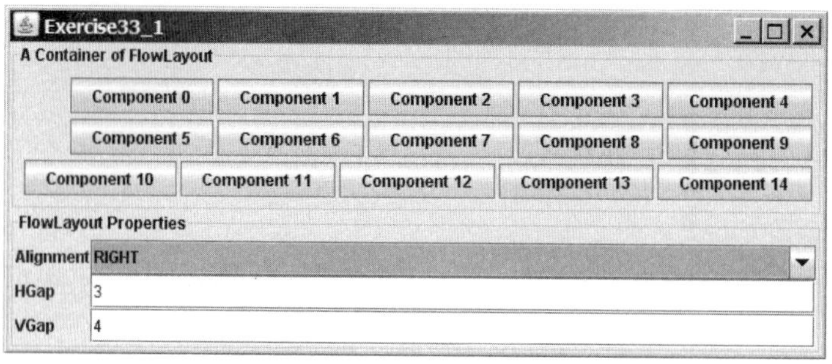
Exercise33_1
A Container of FlowLayout
Component 0
Component 1
Component 2
Component 3
Component 4
Component 5
Component 6
Component 7
Component 8
Component 9
Component 10
Component 11
Component 12
Component 13
Component 14
FlowLayout Properties
Alignment
RIGHT
HGap
3
VGap
4

FIGURE 33.21 The program enables you to set the properties of a `FlowLayout` manager dynamically.

33.2* (*Demonstrating* `GridLayout` *properties*) Create a program that enables the user to set the properties of a `GridLayout` manager dynamically, as shown in Figure 33.22(a). The `GridLayout` manager is used to place 15 components in a panel. You can set the `rows`, `columns`, `hgap`, and `vgap` properties of the `GridLayout` dynamically.

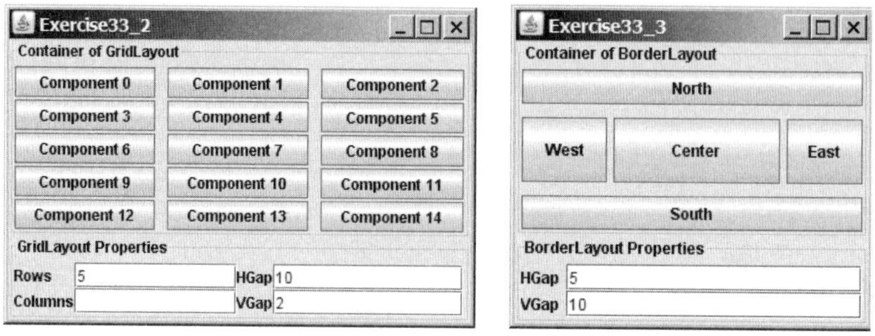
Exercise33_2
Container of GridLayout
Component 0
Component 1
Component 2
Component 3
Component 4
Component 5
Component 6
Component 7
Component 8
Component 9
Component 10
Component 11
Component 12
Component 13
Component 14
GridLayout Properties
Rows
5
Columns
HGap
10
VGap
2
Exercise33_3
Container of BorderLayout
North
West
Center
East
South
BorderLayout Properties
HGap
5
VGap
10

(a) (b)

FIGURE 33.22 (a) The program enables you to set the properties of a `GridLayout` manager dynamically. (b) The program enables you to set the properties of a `BorderLayout` manager dynamically.

33.3* (*Demonstrating* `BorderLayout` *properties*) Create a program that enables the user to set the properties of a `BorderLayout` manager dynamically, as shown in Figure 33.22(b). The `BorderLayout` manager is used to place five components in a panel. You can set the `hgap` and `vgap` properties of the `BorderLayout` dynamically.

33.4* (*Using* `CardLayout`) Write an applet that does arithmetic on integers and rationals. The program uses two panels in a `CardLayout` manager, one for integer arithmetic and the other for rational arithmetic. The program provides a combo box with two items Integer and Rational. When the user chooses the Integer item, the integer panel is activated. When the user chooses the Rational item, the rational panel is activated (see Figure 33.23).

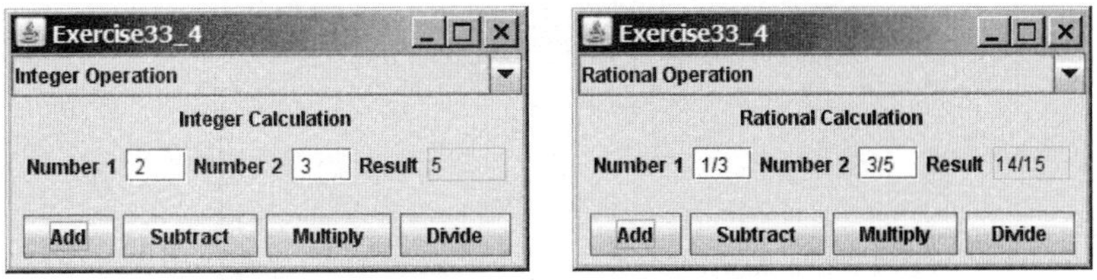
Exercise33_4
Integer Operation
Integer Calculation
Number 1 2 Number 2 3 Result 5
Add Subtract Multiply Divide
Exercise33_4
Rational Operation
Rational Calculation
Number 1 1/3 Number 2 3/5 Result 14/15
Add Subtract Multiply Divide

FIGURE 33.23 `CardLayout` is used to select panels that perform integer operations and rational number operations.

33.5* (*Using null layout*) Use a null layout to lay out a calculator, as shown in Figure 18.18(a).

Sections 33.4–33.8

33.6* (*Using tabbed panes*) Modify Listing 33.7, DisplayFigure.java, to add a panel of radio buttons for specifying the tab placement of the tabbed pane, as shown in Figure 33.24.

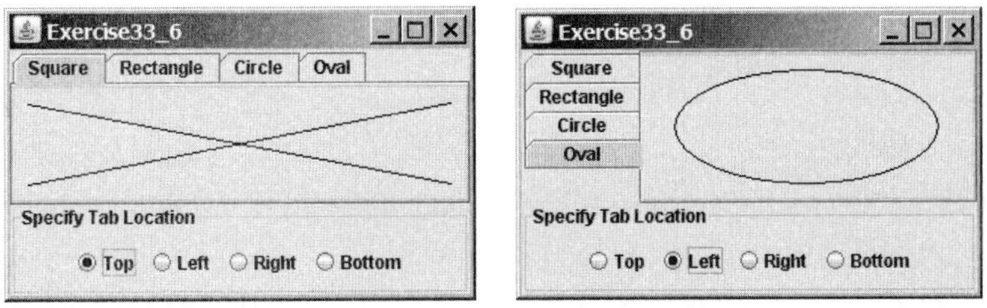
Exercise33_6
Square Rectangle Circle Oval
Specify Tab Location
Top Left Right Bottom
Exercise33_6
Square
Rectangle
Circle
Oval
Specify Tab Location
Top Left Right Bottom

FIGURE 33.24 The radio buttons let you choose the tab placement of the tabbed pane.

33.7* (*Using tabbed pane*) Rewrite Exercise 33.4 using tabbed panes instead of `CardLayout` (see Figure 33.25).

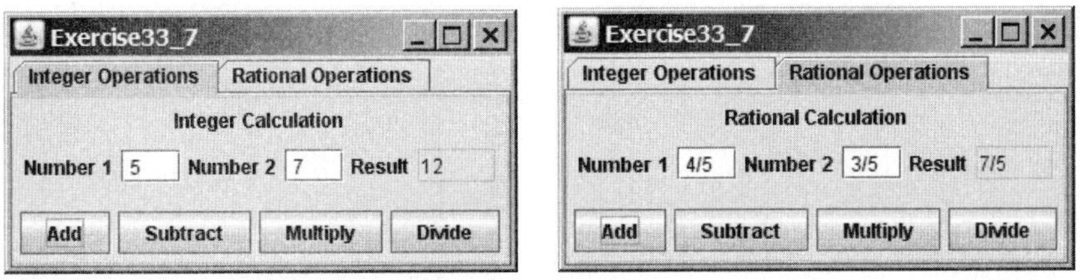
Exercise33_7
Integer Operations Rational Operations
Integer Calculation
Number 1 5 Number 2 7 Result 12
Add Subtract Multiply Divide
Exercise33_7
Integer Operations Rational Operations
Rational Calculation
Number 1 4/5 Number 2 3/5 Result 7/5
Add Subtract Multiply Divide

FIGURE 33.25 A tabbed pane is used to select panels that perform integer operations and rational number operations.

33.8* (*Using `JSplitPane`*) Create a program that displays four figures in split panes, as shown in Figure 33.26. Use the `FigurePanel` class defined in Listing 15.3, FigurePanel.java.

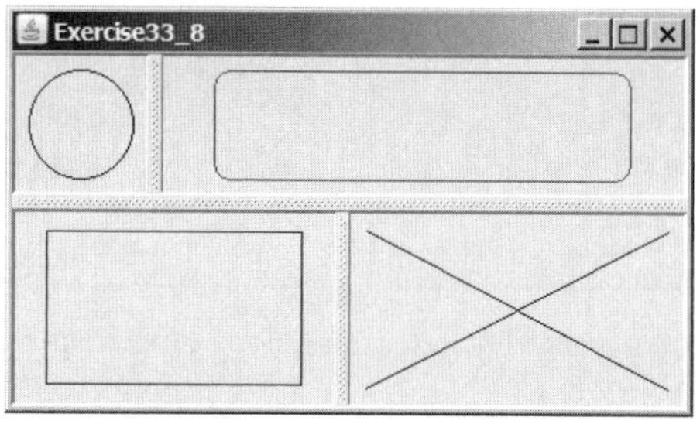
Exercise33_8

FIGURE 33.26 Four figures are displayed in split panes.

33.9* (*Demonstrating* `JSplitPane` *properties*) Create a program that enables the user to set the properties of a split pane dynamically, as shown in Figure 33.27.

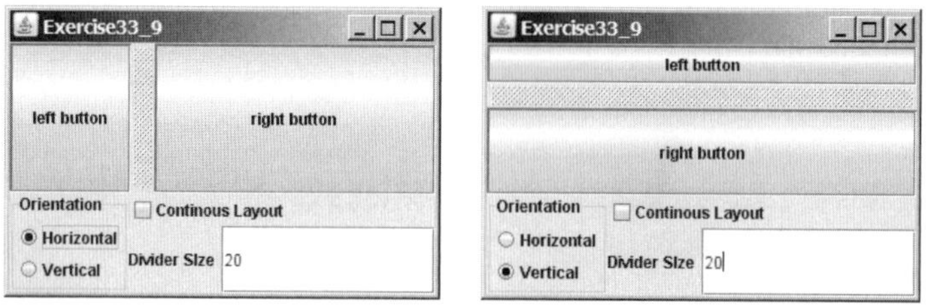
Exercise33_9
left button
right button
Orientation
Continous Layout
Horizontal
Vertical
Divider Size
20
Exercise33_9
left button
right button
Orientation
Continous Layout
Horizontal
Vertical
Divider Size
20

FIGURE 33.27 The program enables you to set the properties of a split pane dynamically.

33.10* (*Demonstrating* `DiagonalLayout` *properties*) Rewrite Listing 33.5 `ShowDiagonalLayout.java` to add a panel that shows the properties of a `DiagonalLayout`. The panel disappears when the `DiagonalLayout` radio button is unchecked, and reappears when the `DiagonalLayout` radio button is checked, as shown in Figure 33.28.

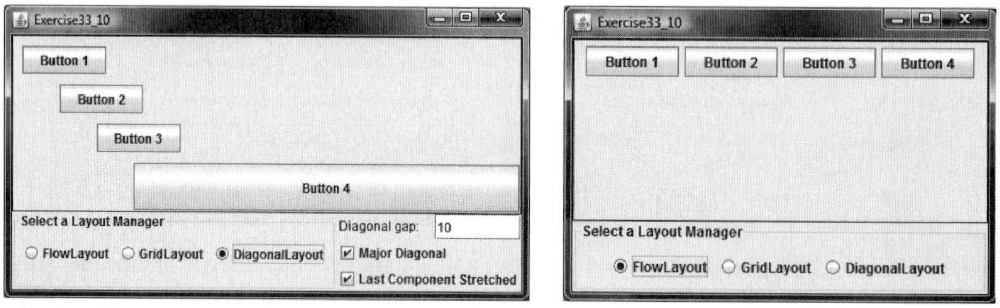
Exercise33_10
Button 1
Button 2
Button 3
Button 4
Select a Layout Manager
FlowLayout
GridLayout
DiagonalLayout
Diagonal gap:
10
Major Diagonal
Last Component Stretched
Exercise33_10
Button 1
Button 2
Button 3
Button 4
Select a Layout Manager
FlowLayout
GridLayout
DiagonalLayout

FIGURE 33.28 The program enables you to set the properties of the `DiagonalLayout` dynamically.

CHAPTER 34

MENUS, TOOLBARS, AND DIALOGS

Objectives

- To create menus using components `JMenuBar`, `JMenu`, `JMenuItem`, `JCheckBoxMenuItem`, and `JRadioButtonMenuItem` (§34.2).
- To create popup menus using components `JPopupMenu`, `JMenuItem`, `JCheckBoxMenuItem`, and `JRadioButtonMenuItem` (§34.3).
- To use `JToolBar` to create toolbars (§34.4).
- To use `Action` objects to generalize the code for processing actions (§34.5).
- To create standard dialogs using the `JOptionPane` class (§34.6).
- To extend the `JDialog` class to create custom dialogs (§34.7).
- To select colors using `JColorChooser` (§34.8).
- To use `JFileChooser` to display Open and Save File dialogs (§34.9).

34.1 Introduction

Java provides a comprehensive solution for building graphical user interfaces. This chapter introduces menus, popup menus, toolbars, and dialogs. You will also learn how to use `Action` objects to generalize the code for processing actions.

34.2 Menus

menu

Menus make selection easier and are widely used in window applications. Java provides five classes that implement menus: `JMenuBar`, `JMenu`, `JMenuItem`, `JCheckBoxMenuItem`, and `JRadioButtonMenuItem`.

menu item

`JMenuBar` is a top-level menu component used to hold the menus. A menu consists of *menu items* that the user can select (or toggle on or off). A menu item can be an instance of `JMenuItem`, `JCheckBoxMenuItem`, or `JRadioButtonMenuItem`. Menu items can be associated with icons, keyboard mnemonics, and keyboard accelerators. Menu items can be separated using separators.

34.2.1 Creating Menus

The sequence of implementing menus in Java is as follows:

1. Create a menu bar and associate it with a frame or an applet by using the `setJMenuBar` method. For example, the following code creates a frame and a menu bar, and sets the menu bar in the frame:

```
JFrame frame = new JFrame();
frame.setSize(300, 200);
frame.setVisible(true);
JMenuBar jmb = new JMenuBar();
frame.setJMenuBar(jmb); // Attach a menu bar to a frame
```

2. Create menus and associate them with the menu bar. You can use the following constructor to create a menu:

```
public JMenu(String label)
```

Here is an example of creating menus:

```
JMenu fileMenu = new JMenu("File");
JMenu helpMenu = new JMenu("Help");
```

This creates two menus labeled `File` and `Help`, as shown in Figure 34.1(a). The menus will not be seen until they are added to an instance of `JMenuBar`, as follows:

```
jmb.add(fileMenu);
jmb.add(helpMenu);
```

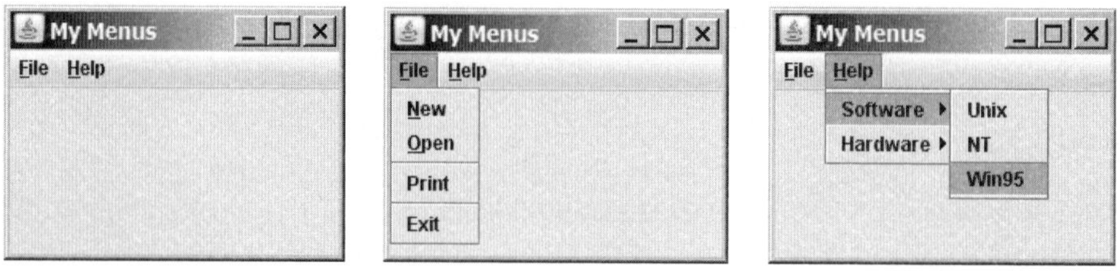
My Menus
File Help
My Menus
File Help
New
Open
Print
Exit
My Menus
File Help
Software
Hardware
Unix
NT
Win95

(a) (b) (c)

FIGURE 34.1 (a) The menu bar appears below the title bar on the frame. (b) Clicking a menu on the menu bar reveals the items under the menu. (c) Clicking a menu item reveals the submenu items under the menu item.

3. Create menu items and add them to the menus.

```
fileMenu.add(new JMenuItem("New"));
fileMenu.add(new JMenuItem("Open"));
fileMenu.addSeparator();
fileMenu.add(new JMenuItem("Print"));
fileMenu.addSeparator();
fileMenu.add(new JMenuItem("Exit"));
```

This code adds the menu items New, Open, a separator bar, Print, another separator bar, and Exit, in this order, to the File menu, as shown in Figure 34.1(b). The **addSeparator()** method adds a separator bar in the menu.

3.1 Creating submenu items. You can also embed menus inside menus so that the embedded menus become submenus. Here is an example:

```
JMenu softwareHelpSubMenu = new JMenu("Software");
JMenu hardwareHelpSubMenu = new JMenu("Hardware");
helpMenu.add(softwareHelpSubMenu);
helpMenu.add(hardwareHelpSubMenu);
softwareHelpSubMenu.add(new JMenuItem("Unix"));
softwareHelpSubMenu.add(new JMenuItem("NT"));
softwareHelpSubMenu.add(new JMenuItem("Win95"));
```

This code adds two submenus, **softwareHelpSubMenu** and **hardwareHelpSubMenu**, in **helpMenu**. The menu items **Unix**, **NT**, and **Win95** are added to **softwareHelpSubMenu** (see Figure 34.1(c)).

3.2 Creating check-box menu items.You can also add a **JCheckBoxMenuItem** to a **JMenu**. **JCheckBoxMenuItem** is a subclass of **JMenuItem** that adds a Boolean state to the **JMenuItem**, and displays a check when its state is true. You can click a menu item to turn it on or off. For example, the following statement adds the check-box menu item **Check it** (see Figure 34.2(a)).

```
helpMenu.add(new JCheckBoxMenuItem("Check it"));
```

3.3 Creating radio-button menu items. You can also add radio buttons to a menu, using the **JRadioButtonMenuItem** class. This is often useful when you have a group of mutually exclusive choices in the menu. For example, the following statements add a submenu named Color and a set of radio buttons for choosing a color (see Figure 34.2(b)):

```
JMenu colorHelpSubMenu = new JMenu("Color");
helpMenu.add(colorHelpSubMenu);

JRadioButtonMenuItem jrbmiBlue, jrbmiYellow, jrbmiRed;
colorHelpSubMenu.add(jrbmiBlue =
  new JRadioButtonMenuItem("Blue"));
colorHelpSubMenu.add(jrbmiYellow =
  new JRadioButtonMenuItem("Yellow"));
colorHelpSubMenu.add(jrbmiRed =
  new JRadioButtonMenuItem("Red"));

ButtonGroup btg = new ButtonGroup();
btg.add(jrbmiBlue);
btg.add(jrbmiYellow);
btg.add(jrbmiRed);
```

4. The menu items generate **ActionEvent**. Your listener class must implement the **ActionListener** and the **actionPerformed** handler to respond to the menu selection.

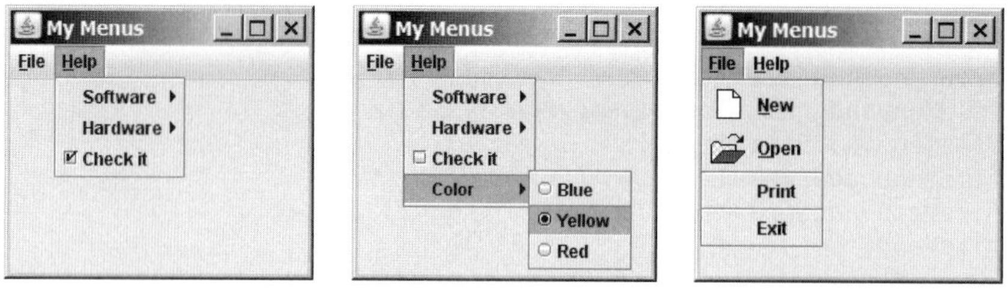
My Menus
File Help
Software
Hardware
Check it
My Menus
File Help
Software
Hardware
Check it
Color
Blue
Yellow
Red
My Menus
File Help
New
Open
Print
Exit

(a) (b) (c)

FIGURE 34.2 (a) A check box menu item lets you check or uncheck a menu item just like a check box. (b) You can use `JRadioButtonMenuItem` to choose among mutually exclusive menu choices. (c) You can set image icons, keyboard mnemonics, and keyboard accelerators in menus.

34.2.2 Image Icons, Keyboard Mnemonics, and Keyboard Accelerators

The menu components `JMenu`, `JMenuItem`, `JCheckBoxMenuItem`, and `JRadioButtonMenuItem` have the `icon` and `mnemonic` properties. For example, using the following code, you can set icons for the New and Open menu items, and set keyboard mnemonics for File, Help, New, and Open:

```
JMenuItem jmiNew, jmiOpen;
fileMenu.add(jmiNew = new JMenuItem("New"));
fileMenu.add(jmiOpen = new JMenuItem("Open"));
jmiNew.setIcon(new ImageIcon("image/new.gif"));
jmiOpen.setIcon(new ImageIcon("image/open.gif"));
helpMenu.setMnemonic('H');
fileMenu.setMnemonic('F');
jmiNew.setMnemonic('N');
jmiOpen.setMnemonic('O');
```

The new icons and mnemonics are shown in Figure 34.2(c). You can also use `JMenuItem` constructors like the ones that follow to construct and set an icon or mnemonic in one statement.

```
public JMenuItem(String label, Icon icon);
public JMenuItem(String label, int mnemonic);
```

By default, the text is at the right of the icon. Use `setHorizontalTextPosition(SwingConstants.LEFT)` to set the text to the left of the icon.

To select a menu, press the ALT key and the mnemonic key. For example, press ALT+F to select the File menu, and then press ALT+O to select the Open menu item. Keyboard mnemonics are useful, but they only let you select menu items from the currently open menu.

accelerator

Key accelerators, however, let you select a menu item directly by pressing the CTRL and accelerator keys. For example, by using the following code, you can attach the accelerator key CTRL+O to the Open menu item:

```
jmiOpen.setAccelerator(KeyStroke.getKeyStroke
  (KeyEvent.VK_O, ActionEvent.CTRL_MASK));
```

The `setAccelerator` method takes a `KeyStroke` object. The static method `getKeyStroke` in the `KeyStroke` class creates an instance of the keystroke. `VK_O` is a constant representing the `O` key, and `CTRL_MASK` is a constant indicating that the `CTRL` key is associated with the keystroke.

Note

As shown in Figure 17.1, **AbstractButton** is the superclass for **JButton** and **JMenuItem**, and **JMenuItem** is a superclass for **JCheckBoxMenuItem**, **JMenu**, and **JRadioButtonMenuItem**. The menu components are very similar to buttons.

34.2.3 Example: Using Menus

This section gives an example that creates a user interface to perform arithmetic. The interface contains labels and text fields for Number 1, Number 2, and Result. The Result text field displays the result of the arithmetic operation between Number 1 and Number 2. Figure 34.3 contains a sample run of the program.

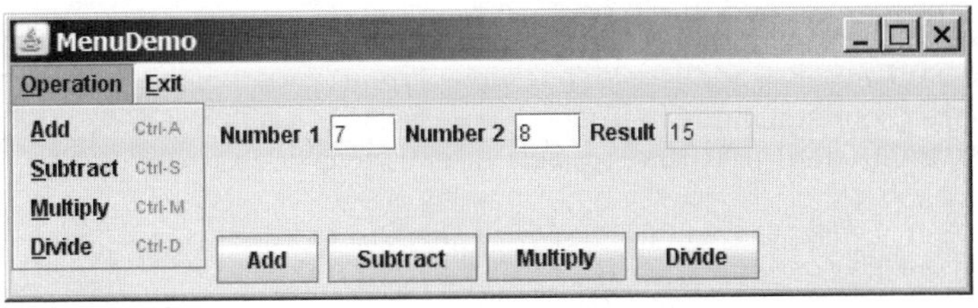
MenuDemo
Operation
Exit
Add
Ctrl-A
Subtract
Ctrl-S
Multiply
Ctrl-M
Divide
Ctrl-D
Number 1
7
Number 2
8
Result
15
Add
Subtract
Multiply
Divide

FIGURE 34.3 Arithmetic operations can be performed by clicking buttons or by choosing menu items from the Operation menu.

Here are the major steps in the program (Listing 34.1):

1. Create a menu bar and set it in the applet. Create the menus Operation and Exit, and add them to the menu bar. Add the menu items Add, Subtract, Multiply, and Divide under the Operation menu, and add the menu item Close under the Exit menu.
2. Create a panel to hold labels and text fields, and place the panel in the center of the applet.
3. Create a panel to hold the four buttons labeled Add, Subtract, Multiply, and Divide. Place the panel in the south of the applet.
4. Implement the **actionPerformed** handler to process the events from the menu items and the buttons.

LISTING 34.1 MenuDemo.java

```
import java.awt.*;
import java.awt.event.*;
import javax.swing.*;

public class MenuDemo extends JApplet {
  // Text fields for Number 1, Number 2, and Result
  private JTextField jtfNum1, jtfNum2, jtfResult;

  // Buttons "Add", "Subtract", "Multiply" and "Divide"
  private JButton jbtAdd, jbtSub, jbtMul, jbtDiv;

  // Menu items "Add", "Subtract", "Multiply","Divide" and "Close"
  private JMenuItem jmiAdd, jmiSub, jmiMul, jmiDiv, jmiClose;

  public MenuDemo() {
    // Create menu bar
    JMenuBar jmb = new JMenuBar();

```

menu bar

set menu bar
exit menus
add menu items
accelerator
buttons
register listener
register listener

```
    // Set menu bar to the applet
    setJMenuBar(jmb);

    // Add menu "Operation" to menu bar
    JMenu operationMenu = new JMenu("Operation");
    operationMenu.setMnemonic('O');
    jmb.add(operationMenu);

    // Add menu "Exit" to menu bar
    JMenu exitMenu = new JMenu("Exit");
    exitMenu.setMnemonic('E');
    jmb.add(exitMenu);

    // Add menu items with mnemonics to menu "Operation"
    operationMenu.add(jmiAdd= new JMenuItem("Add", 'A'));
    operationMenu.add(jmiSub = new JMenuItem("Subtract", 'S'));
    operationMenu.add(jmiMul = new JMenuItem("Multiply", 'M'));
    operationMenu.add(jmiDiv = new JMenuItem("Divide", 'D'));
    exitMenu.add(jmiClose = new JMenuItem("Close", 'C'));

    // Set keyboard accelerators
    jmiAdd.setAccelerator(
      KeyStroke.getKeyStroke(KeyEvent.VK_A, ActionEvent.CTRL_MASK));
    jmiSub.setAccelerator(
      KeyStroke.getKeyStroke(KeyEvent.VK_S, ActionEvent.CTRL_MASK));
    jmiMul.setAccelerator(
      KeyStroke.getKeyStroke(KeyEvent.VK_M, ActionEvent.CTRL_MASK));
    jmiDiv.setAccelerator(
      KeyStroke.getKeyStroke(KeyEvent.VK_D, ActionEvent.CTRL_MASK));

    // Panel p1 to hold text fields and labels
    JPanel p1 = new JPanel(new FlowLayout());
    p1.add(new JLabel("Number 1"));
    p1.add(jtfNum1 = new JTextField(3));
    p1.add(new JLabel("Number 2"));
    p1.add(jtfNum2 = new JTextField(3));
    p1.add(new JLabel("Result"));
    p1.add(jtfResult = new JTextField(4));
    jtfResult.setEditable(false);

    // Panel p2 to hold buttons
    JPanel p2 = new JPanel(new FlowLayout());
    p2.add(jbtAdd = new JButton("Add"));
    p2.add(jbtSub = new JButton("Subtract"));
    p2.add(jbtMul = new JButton("Multiply"));
    p2.add(jbtDiv = new JButton("Divide"));

    // Add panels to the frame
    setLayout(new BorderLayout());
    add(p1, BorderLayout.CENTER);
    add(p2, BorderLayout.SOUTH);

    // Register listeners
    jbtAdd.addActionListener(new ActionListener() {
      public void actionPerformed(ActionEvent e) {
        calculate('+');
      }
    });
    jbtSub.addActionListener(new ActionListener() {
```

```
      public void actionPerformed(ActionEvent e) {
        calculate('-');
      }
    });
    jbtMul.addActionListener(new ActionListener() {
      public void actionPerformed(ActionEvent e) {
        calculate('*');
      }
    });
    jbtDiv.addActionListener(new ActionListener() {
      public void actionPerformed(ActionEvent e) {
        calculate('/');
      }
    });
    jmiAdd.addActionListener(new ActionListener() {
      public void actionPerformed(ActionEvent e) {
        calculate('+');
      }
    });
    jmiSub.addActionListener(new ActionListener() {
      public void actionPerformed(ActionEvent e) {
        calculate('-');
      }
    });
    jmiMul.addActionListener(new ActionListener() {
      public void actionPerformed(ActionEvent e) {
        calculate('*');
      }
    });
    jmiDiv.addActionListener(new ActionListener() {
      public void actionPerformed(ActionEvent e) {
        calculate('/');
      }
    });
    jmiClose.addActionListener(new ActionListener() {
      public void actionPerformed(ActionEvent e) {
        System.exit(0);
      }
    });
  }

  /** Calculate and show the result in jtfResult */
  private void calculate(char operator) {
    // Obtain Number 1 and Number 2
    int num1 = (Integer.parseInt(jtfNum1.getText().trim()));
    int num2 = (Integer.parseInt(jtfNum2.getText().trim()));
    int result = 0;

    // Perform selected operation
    switch (operator) {
      case '+': result = num1 + num2;
                break;
      case '-': result = num1 - num2;
                break;
      case '*': result = num1 * num2;
                break;
      case '/': result = num1 / num2;
    }

```

register listener

register listener

register listener

register listener

register listener

register listener

register listener

calculator

```
137      // Set result in jtfResult
138      jtfResult.setText(String.valueOf(result));
139    }
140 }
```

main method omitted

The program creates a menu bar, `jmb`, which holds two menus: `operationMenu` and `exitMenu` (lines 17–30). The `operationMenu` contains four menu items for doing arithmetic: Add, Subtract, Multiply, and Divide. The `exitMenu` contains the menu item Close for exiting the program. The menu items in the Operation menu are created with keyboard mnemonics and accelerators.

The user enters two numbers in the number fields. When an operation is chosen from the menu, its result, involving two numbers, is displayed in the Result field. The user can also click the buttons to perform the same operation.

The private method `calculate(char operator)` (lines 120–139) retrieves operands from the text fields in Number 1 and Number 2, applies the binary operator on the operands, and sets the result in the Result text field.

Note

placing menus

The menu bar is usually attached to the window using the `setJMenuBar` method. However, like any other component, it can be placed in a container. For instance, you can place a menu bar in the south of the container with `BorderLayout`.

34.3 Popup Menus

popup menu

A popup menu, also known as *a context menu*, is like a regular menu, but does not have a menu bar and can float anywhere on the screen. Creating a popup menu is similar to creating a regular menu. First, you create an instance of `JPopupMenu`, then you can add `JMenuItem`, `JCheckBoxMenuItem`, `JRadioButtonMenuItem`, and separators to the popup menu. For example, the following code creates a `JPopupMenu` and adds `JMenuItems` into it:

```
JPopupMenu jPopupMenu = new JPopupMenu();
jPopupMenu.add(new JMenuItem("New"));
jPopupMenu.add(new JMenuItem("Open"));
```

A regular menu is always attached to a menu bar using the `setJMenuBar` method, but a popup menu is associated with a parent component and is displayed using the `show` method in the `JPopupMenu` class. You specify the parent component and the location of the popup menu, using the coordinate system of the parent like this:

```
jPopupMenu.show(component, x, y);
```

popup trigger

Customarily, you display a popup menu by pointing to a GUI component and clicking a certain mouse button, the so-called *popup trigger*. Popup triggers are system dependent. In Windows, the popup menu is displayed when the right mouse button is released. In Motif, the popup menu is displayed when the third mouse button is pressed and held down.

Listing 34.2 gives an example that creates a text area in a scroll pane. When the mouse points to the text area, clicking a mouse button displays a popup menu, as shown in Figure 34.4.

Here are the major steps in the program (Listing 34.2):

1. Create a popup menu using `JPopupMenu`. Create menu items for New, Open, Print, and Exit using `JMenuItem`. For the menu items with both labels and icons, it is convenient to use the `JMenuItem(label, icon)` constructor.

2. Add the menu items into the popup menu.

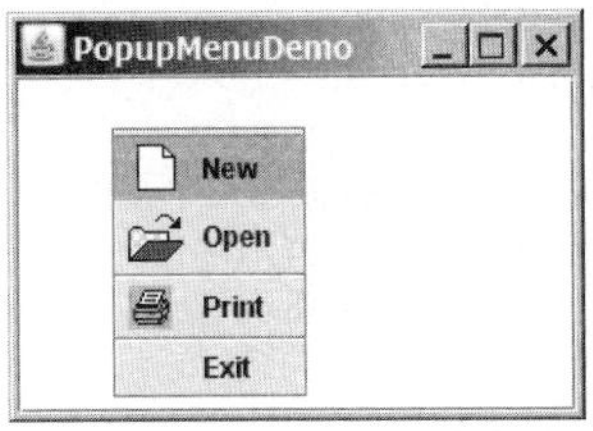
PopupMenuDemo
New
Open
Print
Exit

FIGURE 34.4 A popup menu is displayed when the popup trigger is issued on the text area.

3. Create a scroll pane and add a text area into it. Place the scroll pane in the center of the applet.
4. Implement the `actionPerformed` handler to process the events from the menu items.
5. Implement the `mousePressed` and `mouseReleased` methods to process the events for handling popup triggers.

LISTING 34.2 PopupMenuDemo.java

```
import javax.swing.*;
import java.awt.*;
import java.awt.event.*;

public class PopupMenuDemo extends JApplet {
  private JPopupMenu jPopupMenu1 = new JPopupMenu();
  private JMenuItem jmiNew = new JMenuItem("New",
    new ImageIcon(getClass().getResource("image/new.gif")));
  private JMenuItem jmiOpen = new JMenuItem("Open",
    new ImageIcon(getClass().getResource("image/open.gif")));
  private JMenuItem jmiPrint = new JMenuItem("Print",
    new ImageIcon(getClass().getResource("image/print.gif")));
  private JMenuItem jmiExit = new JMenuItem("Exit");
  private JTextArea jTextArea1 = new JTextArea();

  public PopupMenuDemo() {
    jPopupMenu1.add(jmiNew);
    jPopupMenu1.add(jmiOpen);
    jPopupMenu1.addSeparator();
    jPopupMenu1.add(jmiPrint);
    jPopupMenu1.addSeparator();
    jPopupMenu1.add(jmiExit);
    jPopupMenu1.add(jmiExit);

    add(new JScrollPane(jTextArea1), BorderLayout.CENTER);

    jmiNew.addActionListener(new ActionListener() {
      public void actionPerformed(ActionEvent e) {
        System.out.println("Process New");
      }
    });
    jmiOpen.addActionListener(new ActionListener() {
      public void actionPerformed(ActionEvent e) {
        System.out.println("Process Open");
      }
    });
    jmiPrint.addActionListener(new ActionListener() {
      public void actionPerformed(ActionEvent e) {
```

popup menu

add menu items

register listener

register listener

register listener

register listener

register listener

show popup menu

show popup menu

main method omitted

```
39          System.out.println("Process Print");
40        }
41      });
42      jmiExit.addActionListener(new ActionListener() {
43        public void actionPerformed(ActionEvent e) {
44          System.exit(0);
45        }
46      });
47      jTextArea1.addMouseListener(new MouseAdapter() {
48        public void mousePressed(MouseEvent e) { // For Motif
49          showPopup(e);
50        }
51
52        public void mouseReleased(MouseEvent e) { // For Windows
53          showPopup(e);
54        }
55      });
56    }
57
58    /** Display popup menu when triggered */
59    private void showPopup(java.awt.event.MouseEvent evt) {
60      if (evt.isPopupTrigger())
61        jPopupMenu1.show(evt.getComponent(), evt.getX(), evt.getY());
62    }
63  }
```

The process of creating popup menus is similar to the process for creating regular menus. To create a popup menu, create a `JPopupMenu` as the basis (line 6) and add `JMenuItem`s to it (lines 17–23).

To show a popup menu, use the `show` method by specifying the parent component and the location for the popup menu (line 61). The `show` method is invoked when the popup menu is triggered by a particular mouse click on the text area. Popup triggers are system dependent. The listener implements the `mouseReleased` handler for displaying the popup menu in Windows (lines 52–54) and the `mousePressed` handler for displaying the popup menu in Motif (lines 48–50).

simplify popup menu

Tip

Java provides a new `setComponentPopupMenu(JPopupMenu)` method in the `JComponent` class, which can be used to add a popup menu on a component. This method automatically handles mouse listener registration and popup display. Using this method, you may delete the `showPopup` method in lines 59–62 and replace the code in lines 47–55 with the following statement:

```
jTextArea1.setComponentPopupMenu(jPopupMenu1);
```

34.4 JToolBar

toolbar

In user interfaces, a *toolbar* is often used to hold commands that also appear in the menus. Frequently used commands are placed in a toolbar for quick access. Clicking a command in the toolbar is faster than choosing it from the menu.

Swing provides the `JToolBar` class as the container to hold toolbar components. `JToolBar` uses `BoxLayout` to manage components by default. You can set a different layout manager if desired. The components usually appear as icons. Since icons are not components, they cannot be placed into a toolbar directly. Instead you place buttons into the toolbar and set the icons on the buttons. An instance of JToolBar is like a regular container. Often it is placed in the north, west, or east of a container of BorderLayout.

The following properties in the JToolBar class are often useful:

- **orientation** specifies whether the items in the toolbar appear horizontally or vertically. The possible values are JToolBar.HORIZONTAL and JToolBar.VERTICAL. The default value is JToolBar.HORIZONTAL.
- **floatable** is a boolean value that specifies whether the toolbar can be floated. By default, a toolbar is floatable.

Listing 34.3 gives an example that creates a JToolBar to hold three buttons with the icons representing the commands New, Open, and Print, as shown in Figure 34.5.

ToolBarDemo

FIGURE 34.5 The toolbar contains the icons representing the commands New, Open, and Print.

LISTING 34.3 ToolBarDemo.java

```
import javax.swing.*;
import java.awt.*;

public class ToolBarDemo extends JApplet {
  private JButton jbtNew = new JButton(
    new ImageIcon(getClass().getResource("image/new.gif")));
  private JButton jbtOpen = new JButton(
    new ImageIcon(getClass().getResource("image/open.gif")));
  private JButton jbPrint = new JButton(
    new ImageIcon(getClass().getResource("image/print.gif")));

  public ToolBarDemo() {
    JToolBar jToolBar1 = new JToolBar("My Toolbar");
    jToolBar1.setFloatable(true);
    jToolBar1.add(jbtNew);
    jToolBar1.add(jbtOpen);
    jToolBar1.add(jbPrint);

    jbtNew.setToolTipText("New");
    jbtOpen.setToolTipText("Open");
    jbPrint.setToolTipText("Print");

    jbtNew.setBorderPainted(false);
    jbtOpen.setBorderPainted(false);
    jbPrint.setBorderPainted(false);

    add(jToolBar1, BorderLayout.NORTH);
  }
}
```

buttons

toolbar

add toolbar

main method omitted

A `JToolBar` is created in line 13. The toolbar is a container with `BoxLayout` by default. Using the `orientation` property, you can specify whether components in the toolbar are organized horizontally or vertically. By default, it is horizontal.

By default, the toolbar is floatable, and a floatable controller is displayed in front of its components. You can drag the floatable controller to move the toolbar to different locations of the window or can show the toolbar in a separate window, as shown in Figure 34.6.

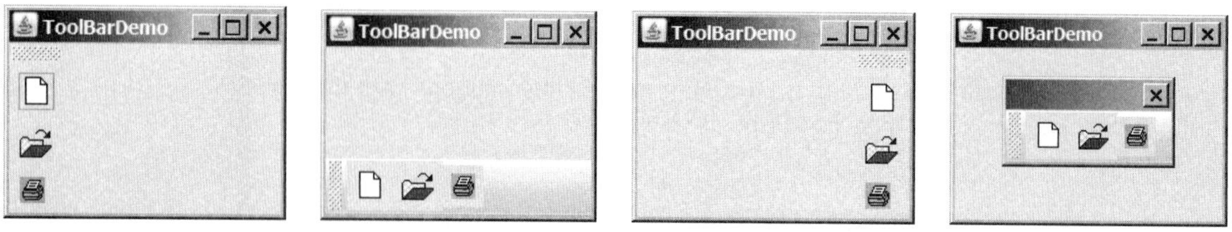
ToolBarDemo
ToolBarDemo
ToolBarDemo
ToolBarDemo

FIGURE 34.6 The toolbar buttons are floatable.

You can also set a title for the floatable toolbar, as shown in Figure 34.7(a). To do so, create a toolbar using the `JToolBar(String title)` constructor. If you set `floatable` false, the floatable controller is not displayed, as shown in Figure 34.7(b). If you set a border (e.g., a line border), as shown in Figure 34.7(c), the line border is displayed and the floatable controller is not displayed.

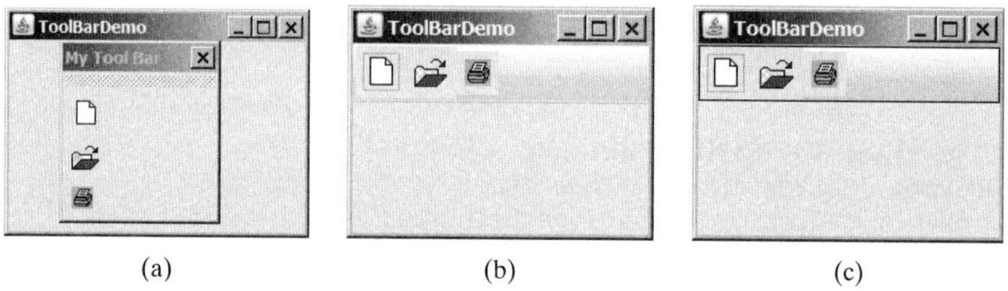
ToolBarDemo
My Tool Bar
ToolBarDemo
ToolBarDemo
(a)
(b)
(c)

FIGURE 34.7 The toolbar buttons can be customized in many forms.

Tip

For the floatable feature to work properly, do the following: (1) place a toolbar to one side of the container of `BorderLayout` and add no components to the other sides; (2) don't set border on a toolbar. Setting a border would make it non-floatable.

34.5 Processing Actions Using the `Action` Interface

Often menus and toolbars contain some common actions. For example, you can save a file by choosing *File*, *Save*, or by clicking the save button in the toolbar. Swing provides the `Action` interface, which can be used to create action objects for processing actions. Using `Action` objects, common action processing can be centralized and separated from the other application code.

The `Action` interface is a subinterface of `ActionListener`, as shown in Figure 34.8. Additionally, it defines several methods for checking whether the action is enabled, for enabling

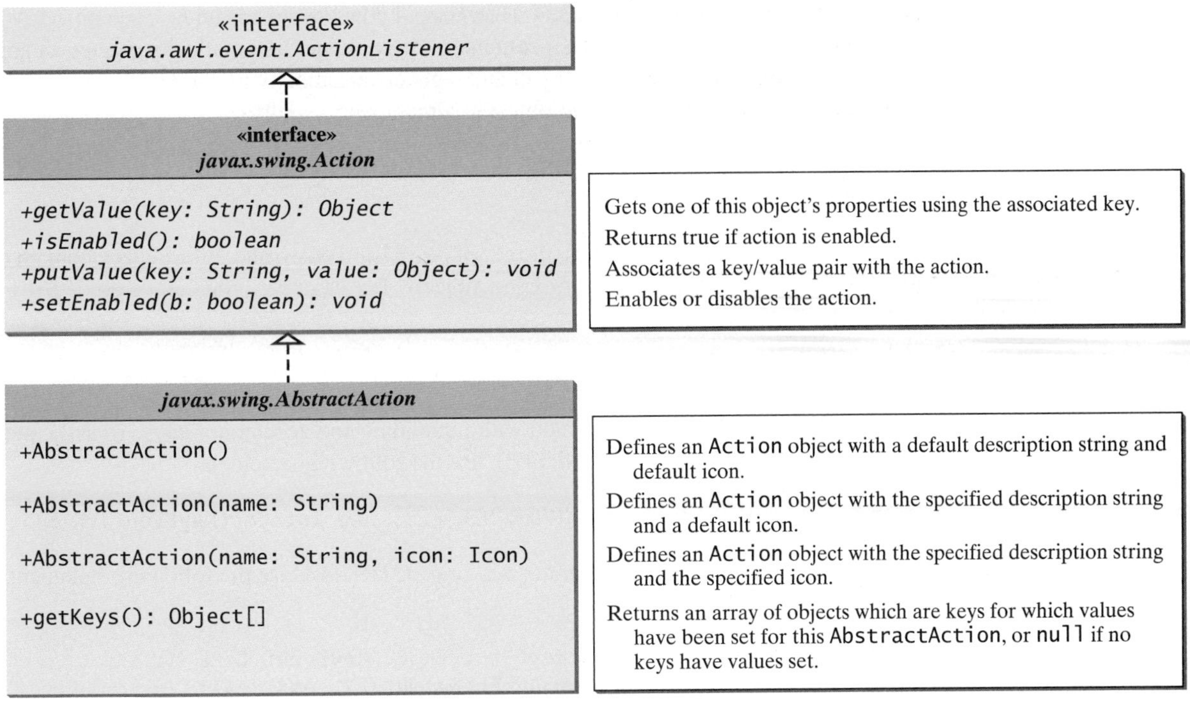
«interface»
java.awt.event.ActionListener
«interface»
javax.swing.Action
+getValue(key: String): Object
+isEnabled(): boolean
+putValue(key: String, value: Object): void
+setEnabled(b: boolean): void
Gets one of this object's properties using the associated key.
Returns true if action is enabled.
Associates a key/value pair with the action.
Enables or disables the action.
javax.swing.AbstractAction
+AbstractAction()
+AbstractAction(name: String)
+AbstractAction(name: String, icon: Icon)
+getKeys(): Object[]
Defines an Action object with a default description string and default icon.
Defines an Action object with the specified description string and a default icon.
Defines an Action object with the specified description string and the specified icon.
Returns an array of objects which are keys for which values have been set for this AbstractAction, or null if no keys have values set.

FIGURE 34.8 The `Action` interface provides a useful extension to the `ActionListener` interface in cases where the same functionality may be accessed by several controls. The `AbstractAction` class provides a default implementation for `Action`.

and disabling the action, and for retrieving and setting the associated action value using a key. The key can be any string, but four keys have predefined meanings:

Key	Description
`Action.NAME`	A name for the action
`Action.SMALL_ICON`	A small icon for the action
`Action.SHORT_DESCRIPTION`	A tool tip for the action
`Action.LONG_DESCRIPTION`	A description for online help

`AbstractAction` is a default implementation of the `Action` interface, as shown in Figure 34.8. It implements all the methods in the `Action` interface except the `actionPerformed` method. Additionally, it defines the `getKeys()` method.

Since `AbstractAction` is an abstract class, you cannot create an instance using its constructor. However, you can create a concrete subclass of `AbstractAction` and implement the `actionPerformed` method. This subclass can be conveniently defined as an anonymous inner class. For example, the following code creates an `Action` object for terminating a program.

```
Action exitAction = new AbstractAction("Exit") {
  public void actionPerformed(ActionEvent e) {
    System.exit(0);
  }
};
```

Certain containers, such as `JMenu` and `JToolBar`, know how to add an `Action` object. When an `Action` object is added to such a container, the container automatically creates an appropriate component for the `Action` object and registers a listener with the `Action` object. Here is an example of adding an `Action` object to a menu and a toolbar:

```
jMenu.add(exitAction);
jToolBar.add(exitAction);
```

Several Swing components, such as `JButton`, `JRadioButton`, and `JCheckBox`, contain constructors to create instances from `Action` objects. For example, you can create a `JButton` from an `Action` object, as follows:

```
JButton jbt = new JButton(exitAction);
```

`Action` objects can also be associated with mnemonic and accelerator keys. To associate actions with a mnemonic key (e.g., ALT+E), use the following statement:

```
exitAction.putValue(Action.MNEMONIC_KEY, new Integer(KeyEvent.VK_E));
```

To associate actions with an accelerator key (e.g., CTRL+E), use the following statement:

```
KeyStroke exitKey =
  KeyStroke.getKeyStroke(KeyEvent.VK_E, KeyEvent.CTRL_MASK);
exitAction.putValue(Action.ACCELERATOR_KEY, exitKey);
```

Listing 34.4 gives an example that creates three menu items, Left, Center, and Right, three toolbar buttons, Left, Center, and Right, and three regular buttons, Left, Center, and Right, in a panel, as shown in Figure 34.9. The panel that holds the buttons uses the `FlowLayout`. The actions of the left, center, and right buttons set the alignment of the `FlowLayout` to left, right, and center, respectively. The actions of the menu items, the toolbar buttons, and the buttons in the panel can be processed through common action handlers using the `Action` interface.

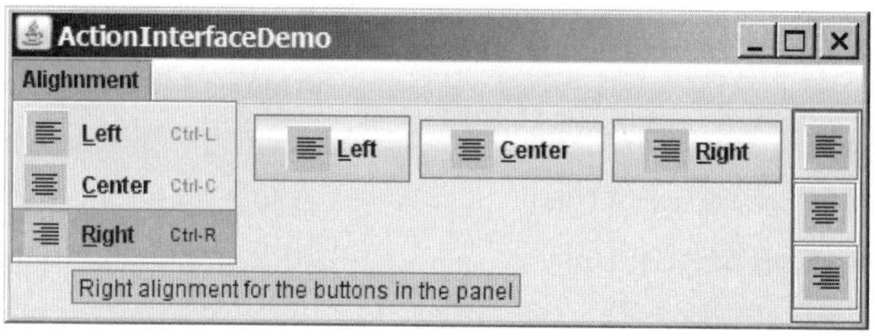
ActionInterfaceDemo
Alignment
Left Ctrl-L
Center Ctrl-C
Right Ctrl-R
Left
Center
Right
Right alignment for the buttons in the panel

FIGURE 34.9 Left, Center, and Right appear in the menu, in the toolbar, and in regular buttons.

LISTING 34.4 ActionInterfaceDemo.java

```
import java.awt.*;
import java.awt.event.*;
import javax.swing.*;

public class ActionInterfaceDemo extends JApplet {
  private JPanel buttonPanel = new JPanel();
  private FlowLayout flowLayout = new FlowLayout();

  public ActionInterfaceDemo() {
    // Create image icons
    ImageIcon leftImageIcon = new ImageIcon(getClass().getResource(
```

image icon

```java
      "image/leftAlignment.png"));
    ImageIcon centerImageIcon = new ImageIcon(getClass().getResource(
      "image/centerAlignment.png"));
    ImageIcon rightImageIcon = new ImageIcon(getClass().getResource(
      "image/rightAlignment.png"));

    // Create actions
    Action leftAction = new MyAction("Left", leftImageIcon,
      "Left alignment for the buttons in the panel",
      new Integer(KeyEvent.VK_L),
      KeyStroke.getKeyStroke(KeyEvent.VK_L, ActionEvent.CTRL_MASK));
    Action centerAction = new MyAction("Center", centerImageIcon,
      "Center alignment for the buttons in the panel",
      new Integer(KeyEvent.VK_C),
      KeyStroke.getKeyStroke(KeyEvent.VK_C, ActionEvent.CTRL_MASK));
    Action rightAction = new MyAction("Right", rightImageIcon,
      "Right alignment for the buttons in the panel",
      new Integer(KeyEvent.VK_R),
      KeyStroke.getKeyStroke(KeyEvent.VK_R, ActionEvent.CTRL_MASK));

    // Create menus
    JMenuBar jMenuBar1 = new JMenuBar();
    JMenu jmenuAlignment = new JMenu("Alighnment");
    setJMenuBar(jMenuBar1);
    jMenuBar1.add(jmenuAlignment);

    // Add actions to the menu
    jmenuAlignment.add(leftAction);
    jmenuAlignment.add(centerAction);
    jmenuAlignment.add(rightAction);

    // Add actions to the toolbar
    JToolBar jToolBar1 = new JToolBar(JToolBar.VERTICAL);
    jToolBar1.setBorder(BorderFactory.createLineBorder(Color.red));
    jToolBar1.add(leftAction);
    jToolBar1.add(centerAction);
    jToolBar1.add(rightAction);

    // Add buttons to the button panel
    buttonPanel.setLayout(flowLayout);
    JButton jbtLeft = new JButton(leftAction);
    JButton jbtCenter = new JButton(centerAction);
    JButton jbtRight = new JButton(rightAction);
    buttonPanel.add(jbtLeft);
    buttonPanel.add(jbtCenter);
    buttonPanel.add(jbtRight);

    // Add toolbar to the east and panel to the center
    add(jToolBar1, BorderLayout.EAST);
    add(buttonPanel, BorderLayout.CENTER);
  }

  private class MyAction extends AbstractAction {
    String name;

    MyAction(String name, Icon icon) {
      super(name, icon);
      this.name = name;
    }

```

create action

menu

toolbar

button

custom action

constructor

constructor

handler

main method omitted

```
72      MyAction(String name, Icon icon, String desc, Integer mnemonic,
73          KeyStroke accelerator) {
74        super(name, icon);
75        putValue(Action.SHORT_DESCRIPTION, desc);
76        putValue(Action.MNEMONIC_KEY, mnemonic);
77        putValue(Action.ACCELERATOR_KEY, accelerator);
78        this.name = name;
79      }
80
81      public void actionPerformed(ActionEvent e) {
82        if (name.equals("Left"))
83          flowLayout.setAlignment(FlowLayout.LEFT);
84        else if (name.equals("Center"))
85          flowLayout.setAlignment(FlowLayout.CENTER);
86        else if (name.equals("Right"))
87          flowLayout.setAlignment(FlowLayout.RIGHT);
88
89        buttonPanel.revalidate();
90      }
91    }
92 }
```

The inner class `MyAction` extends `AbstractAction` with a constructor to construct an action with a name and an icon (lines 67–70) and another constructor to construct an action with a name, icon, description, mnemonic, and accelerator (lines 72–79). The constructors invoke the `putValue` method to associate the name, icon, description, mnemonic, and accelerator. It implements the `actionPerformed` method to set a new alignment in the panel of the `FlowLayout` (line 81–90). The `revalidate()` method validates the new alignment (line 89).

Three actions, `leftAction`, `centerAction`, and `rightAction`, were created from the `MyAction` class (lines 19–30). Each action has a name, icon, description, mnemonic, and accelerator. The actions are for the menu items and the buttons in the toolbar and in the panel. The menu and toolbar know how to add these objects automatically (lines 39–41, 46–48). Three regular buttons are created with the properties taken from the actions (lines 51–54).

34.6 JOptionPane Dialogs

You have used `JOptionPane` to create input and output dialog boxes. This section provides a comprehensive introduction to `JOptionPane` and other dialog boxes. A *dialog box* is normally used as a temporary window to receive additional information from the user or to provide notification that some event has occurred. Java provides the `JOptionPane` class, which can be used to create standard dialogs. You can also build custom dialogs by extending the `JDialog` class.

The `JOptionPane` class can be used to create four kinds of standard dialogs:

- **Message dialog** shows a message and waits for the user to click OK.
- **Confirmation dialog** shows a question and asks for confirmation, such as OK or Cancel.
- **Input dialog** shows a question and gets the user's input from a text field, combo box, or list.
- **Option dialog** shows a question and gets the user's answer from a set of options.

These dialogs are created using the static methods `showXxxDialog` and generally appear as shown in Figure 34.10(a).

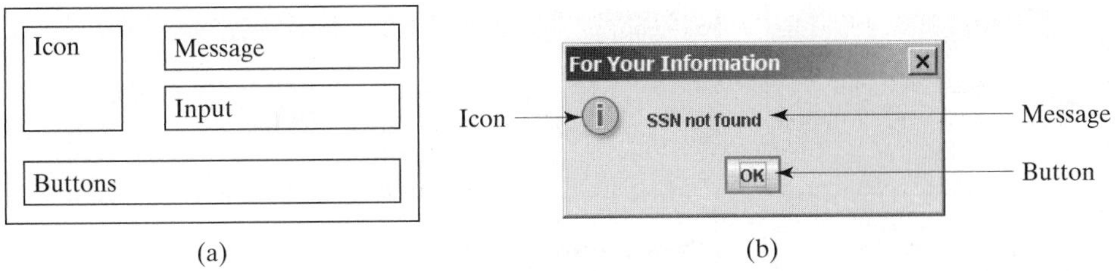
Icon
Message
Input
Buttons
(a)
For Your Information
Icon
SSN not found
Message
OK
Button
(b)

FIGURE 34.10 (a) A JOptionPane dialog can display an icon, a message, an input, and option buttons. (b) The message dialog displays a message and waits for the user to click OK.

For example, you can use the following method to create a message dialog box, as shown in Figure 34.10(b):

```
JOptionPane.showMessageDialog(null, "SSN not found",
  "For Your Information", JOptionPane.INFORMATION_MESSAGE);
```

34.6.1 Message Dialogs

A *message dialog* box displays a message that alerts the user and waits for the user to click the *OK* button to close the dialog. The methods for creating message dialogs are:

```
public static void showMessageDialog(Component parentComponent,
                                     Object message)
public static void showMessageDialog(Component parentComponent,
                                     Object message,
                                     String title,
                                     int messageType)
public static void showMessageDialog(Component parentComponent,
                                     Object message,
                                     String title,
                                     int messageType,
                                     Icon icon)
```

The parentComponent can be any component or null. The message is an object, but often a string is used. These two parameters must always be specified. The title is a string displayed in the title bar of the dialog with the default value "Message".

The messageType is one of the following constants:

```
JOptionPane.ERROR_MESSAGE
JOptionPane.INFORMATION_MESSAGE
JOptionPane.PLAIN_MESSAGE
JOptionPane.WARNING_MESSAGE
JOptionPane.QUESTION_MESSAGE
```

By default, messageType is JOptionPane.INFORMATION_MESSAGE. Each type has an associated icon except the PLAIN_MESSAGE type, as shown in Figure 34.11. You can also supply your own icon in the icon parameter.

The message parameter is an object. If it is a GUI component, the component is displayed. If it is a non-GUI component, the string representation of the object is displayed. For example, the following statement displays a clock in a message dialog, as shown in Figure 34.12. StillClock was defined in Listing 15.10.

```
JOptionPane.showMessageDialog(null, new StillClock(),
  "Current Time", JOptionPane.PLAIN_MESSAGE);
```

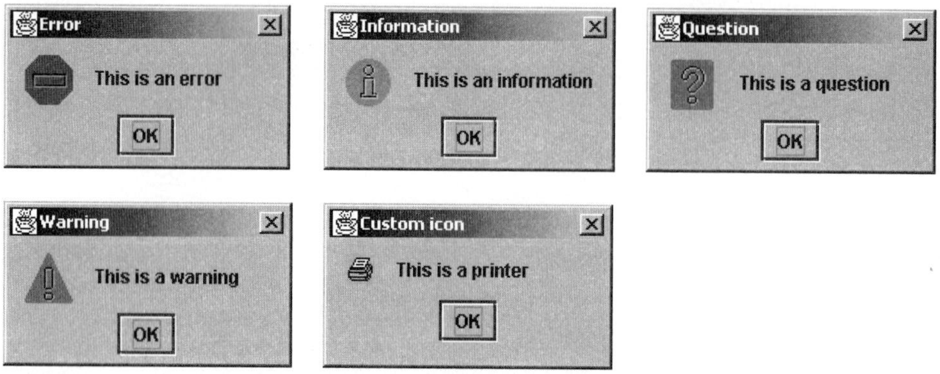
Error
This is an error
OK
Information
This is an information
OK
Question
This is a question
OK
Warning
This is a warning
OK
Custom icon
This is a printer
OK

FIGURE 34.11 There are five types of message dialog boxes.

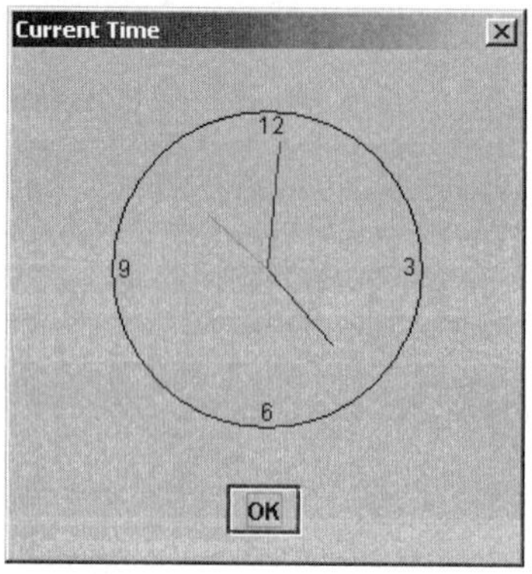
Current Time
12
9
3
6
OK

FIGURE 34.12 A clock is displayed in a message dialog.

34.6.2 Confirmation Dialogs

A message dialog box displays a message and waits for the user to click the *OK* button to dismiss the dialog. The message dialog does not return any value. A *confirmation dialog* asks a question and requires the user to respond with an appropriate button. The confirmation dialog returns a value that corresponds to a selected button.

The methods for creating confirmation dialogs are:

```
public static int showConfirmDialog(Component parentComponent,
                                    Object message)
public static int showConfirmDialog(Component parentComponent,
                                    Object message,
                                    String title,
                                    int optionType)
public static int showConfirmDialog(Component parentComponent,
                                    Object message,
                                    String title,
                                    int optionType,
                                    int messageType)
public static int showConfirmDialog(Component parentComponent,
                                    Object message,
                                    String title,
                                    int optionType,
                                    int messageType,
                                    Icon icon)
```

The parameters parentComponent, message, title, icon, and messageType are the same as in the showMessageDialog method. The default value for title is "Select an Option" and for messageType is QUESTION_MESSAGE. The optionType determines which buttons are displayed in the dialog. The possible values are:

```
JOptionPane.YES_NO_OPTION
JOptionPane.YES_NO_CANCEL_OPTION
JOptionPane.OK_CANCEL_OPTION
```

Figure 34.13 shows the confirmation dialogs with these options.

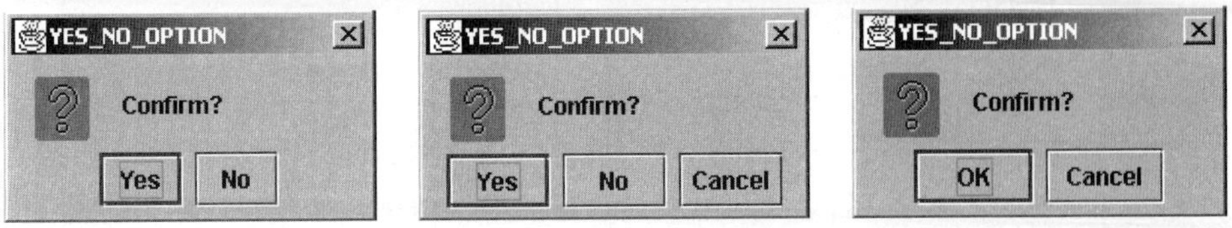
YES_NO_OPTION
Confirm?
Yes
No
YES_NO_OPTION
Confirm?
Yes
No
Cancel
YES_NO_OPTION
Confirm?
OK
Cancel

FIGURE 34.13 The confirmation dialog displays a question and three types of option buttons, and requires responses from the user.

The showConfirmDialog method returns one of the following int values corresponding to the selected option:

```
JOptionPane.YES_OPTION
JOptionPane.NO_OPTION
JOptionPane.CANCEL_OPTION
JOptionPane.OK_OPTION
JOptionPane.CLOSED_OPTION
```

These options correspond to the button that was activated, except for the CLOSED_OPTION, which implies that the dialog box is closed without buttons activated.

34.6.3 Input Dialogs

An *input dialog* box is used to receive input from the user. The input can be entered from a text field or selected from a combo box or a list. Selectable values can be specified in an array, and one of them can be designated as the initial selected value. If no selectable value is specified when an input dialog is created, a text field is used for entering input. If fewer than twenty selection values are specified, a combo box is displayed in the input dialog. If twenty or more selection values are specified, a list is used in the input dialog.

The methods for creating input dialogs are shown below:

```
public static String showInputDialog(Object message)
public static String showInputDialog(Component parentComponent,
                                     Object message)
public static String showInputDialog(Component parentComponent,
                                     Object message,
                                     String title,
                                     int messageType)
public static Object showInputDialog(Component parentComponent,
                                     Object message,
                                     int messageType,
                                     Icon icon,
                                     Object[] selectionValues,
                                     Object initialSelectionValue)
```

The first three methods listed above use a text field for input, as shown in Figure 34.14(a). The last method listed above specifies an array of `Object` type as selection values in addition to an object specified as an initial selection. The first three methods return a `String` that is entered from the text field in the input dialog. The last method returns an `Object` selected from a combo box or a list. The input dialog displays a combo box if there are fewer than twenty selection values, as shown in Figure 34.14(b); it displays a list if there are twenty or more selection values, as shown in Figure 34.14(c).

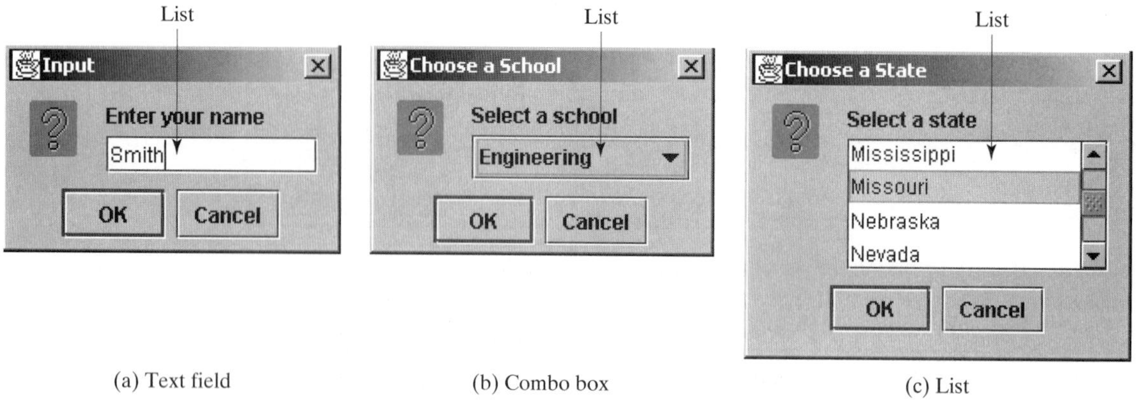
List
Input
Enter your name
Smith
OK
Cancel
(a) Text field
List
Choose a School
Select a school
Engineering
OK
Cancel
(b) Combo box
List
Choose a State
Select a state
Mississippi
Missouri
Nebraska
Nevada
OK
Cancel
(c) List

FIGURE 34.14 (a) When creating an input dialog without specifying selection values, the input dialog displays a text field for data entry. (b) When creating an input dialog with selection values, the input dialog displays a combo box if there are fewer than twenty selection values. (c) When creating an input dialog with selection values, the input dialog displays a list if there are twenty or more selection values.

Note

The `showInputDialog` method does not have the `optionType` parameter. The buttons for input dialog are not configurable. The *OK* and *Cancel* buttons are always used.

34.6.4 Option Dialogs

An *option dialog* allows you to create custom buttons. You can create an option dialog using the following method:

```
public static int showOptionDialog(Component parentComponent,
                                   Object message,
                                   String title,
                                   int optionType,
                                   int messageType,
                                   Icon icon,
                                   Object[] options,
                                   Object initialValue)
```

The buttons are specified using the `options` parameter. The `initialValue` parameter allows you to specify a button to receive initial focus. The `showOptionDialog` method returns an `int` value indicating the button that was activated. For example, here is the code that creates an option dialog, as shown in Figure 34.15:

```
int value =
  JOptionPane.showOptionDialog(null, "Select a button",
    "Option Dialog", JOptionPane.DEFAULT_OPTION,
    JOptionPane.PLAIN_MESSAGE, null,
     new Object[]{"Button 0", "Button 1", "Button 2"}, "Button 1");
```

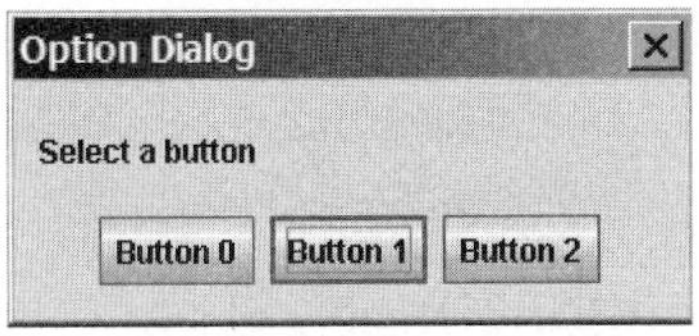
Option Dialog
Select a button
Button 0
Button 1
Button 2

FIGURE 34.15 The option dialog displays the custom buttons.

34.6.5 Example: Creating `JOptionPane` Dialogs

This section gives an example that demonstrates the use of `JOptionPane` dialogs. The program prompts the user to select the annual interest rate from a list in an input dialog, the number of years from a combo box in an input dialog, and the loan amount from an input dialog, and it displays the loan payment schedule in a text area inside a `JScrollPane` in a message dialog, as shown in Figure 34.16.

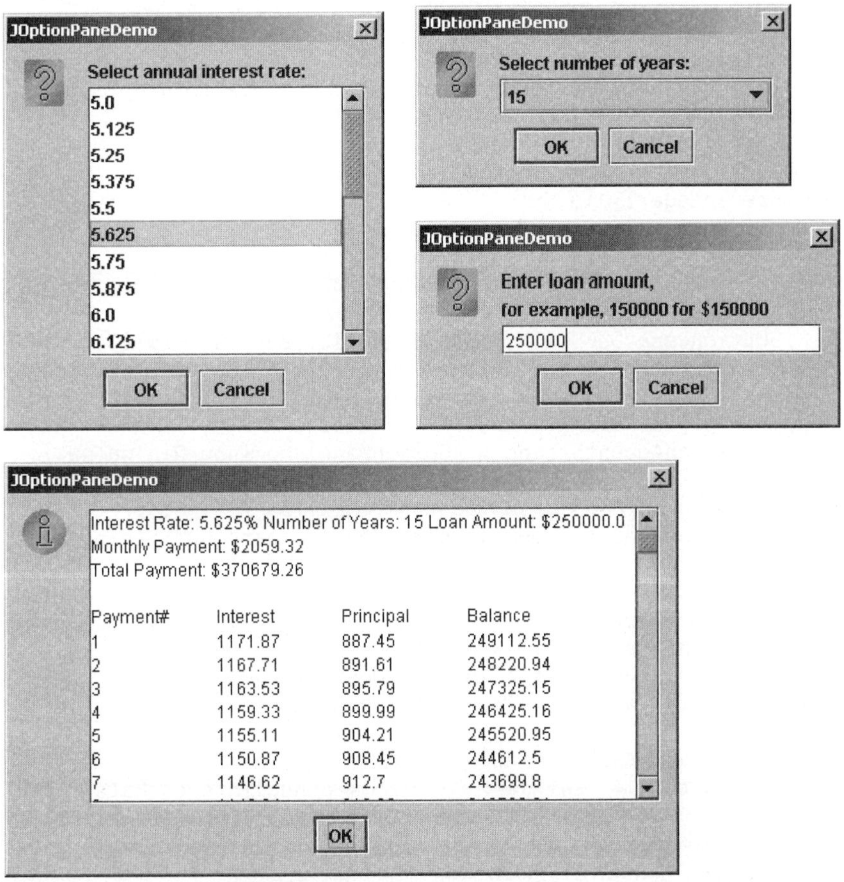
JOptionPaneDemo
Select annual interest rate:
5.0
5.125
5.25
5.375
5.5
5.625
5.75
5.875
6.0
6.125
OK
Cancel
JOptionPaneDemo
Select number of years:
15
OK
Cancel
JOptionPaneDemo
Enter loan amount,
for example, 150000 for $150000
250000
OK
Cancel
JOptionPaneDemo
Interest Rate: 5.625% Number of Years: 15 Loan Amount: $250000.0
Monthly Payment: $2059.32
Total Payment: $370679.26
Payment# Interest Principal Balance
1 1171.87 887.45 249112.55
2 1167.71 891.61 248220.94
3 1163.53 895.79 247325.15
4 1159.33 899.99 246425.16
5 1155.11 904.21 245520.95
6 1150.87 908.45 244612.5
7 1146.62 912.7 243699.8
OK

FIGURE 34.16 The input dialogs can contain a list or a combo box for selecting input, and the message dialogs can contain GUI objects like `JScrollPane`.

Here are the major steps in the program (Listing 34.5):

1. Display an input dialog box to let the user select an annual interest rate from a list.
2. Display an input dialog box to let the user select the number of years from a combo box.

3. Display an input dialog box to let the user enter the loan amount.
4. Compute the monthly payment, total payment, and loan payment schedule, and display the result in a text area in a message dialog box.

LISTING 34.5 JOptionPaneDemo.java

input dialog

input dialog

input dialog

```
import javax.swing.*;

public class JOptionPaneDemo {
  public static void main(String args[]) {
    // Create an array for annual interest rates
    Object[] rateList = new Object[25];
    int i = 0;
    for (double rate = 5; rate <= 8; rate += 1.0 / 8)
      rateList[i++] = new Double(rate);

    // Prompt the user to select an annual interest rate
    Object annualInterstRateObject = JOptionPane.showInputDialog(
      null, "Select annual interest rate:", "JOptionPaneDemo",
      JOptionPane.QUESTION_MESSAGE, null, rateList, null);
    double annualInterestRate =
      ((Double)annualInterstRateObject).doubleValue();

    // Create an array for number of years
    Object[] yearList = {new Integer(7), new Integer(15),
      new Integer(30)};

    // Prompt the user to enter number of years
    Object numberOfYearsObject = JOptionPane.showInputDialog(null,
      "Select number of years:", "JOptionPaneDemo",
      JOptionPane.QUESTION_MESSAGE, null, yearList, null);
    int numberOfYears = ((Integer)numberOfYearsObject).intValue();

    // Prompt the user to enter loan amount
    String loanAmountString = JOptionPane.showInputDialog(null,
      "Enter loan amount,\nfor example, 150000 for $150000",
      "JOptionPaneDemo", JOptionPane.QUESTION_MESSAGE);
    double loanAmount = Double.parseDouble(loanAmountString);

    // Obtain monthly payment and total payment
    Loan loan = new Loan(
      annualInterestRate, numberOfYears, loanAmount);
    double monthlyPayment = loan.getMonthlyPayment();
    double totalPayment = loan.getTotalPayment();

    // Prepare output string
    String output = "Interest Rate: " + annualInterestRate + "%" +
      " Number of Years: " + numberOfYears + " Loan Amount: $"
      + loanAmount;
    output += "\nMonthly Payment: " + "$" +
      (int)(monthlyPayment * 100) / 100.0;
    output += "\nTotal Payment: $" +
      (int)(monthlyPayment * 12 * numberOfYears * 100) / 100.0 + "\n";

    // Obtain monthly interest rate
    double monthlyInterestRate = annualInterestRate / 1200;

```

```
52     double balance = loanAmount;
53     double interest;
54     double principal;
55
56     // Display the header
57     output += "\nPayment#\tInterest\tPrincipal\tBalance\n";
58
59     for (i = 1; i <= numberOfYears * 12; i++) {
60       interest = (int)(monthlyInterestRate * balance * 100) / 100.0;
61       principal = (int)((monthlyPayment - interest) * 100) / 100.0;
62       balance = (int)((balance - principal) * 100) / 100.0;
63       output += i + "\t" + interest + "\t" + principal + "\t" +
64         balance + "\n";
65     }
66
67     // Display monthly payment and total payment
68     JScrollPane jsp = new JScrollPane(new JTextArea(output));
69     jsp.setPreferredSize(new java.awt.Dimension(400, 200));
70     JOptionPane.showMessageDialog(null, jsp,
71       "JOptionPaneDemo", JOptionPane.INFORMATION_MESSAGE, null);
72   }
73 }
```

message dialog

The `JOptionPane` dialog boxes are *modal*, which means that no other window can be accessed until a dialog box is dismissed.

You have used the input dialog box to enter input from a text field. This example shows that input dialog boxes can also contain a list (lines 12–14) or a combo box (lines 23–25) to list input options. The elements of the list are objects. The return value from these input dialog boxes is of the `Object` type. To obtain a `double` value or an `int` value, you have to cast the return object into `Double` or `Integer`, then use the `doubleValue` or `intValue` method to get the `double` or `int` value (lines 15–16 and 26).

You have already used the message dialog box to display a string. This example shows that the message dialog box can also contain GUI objects. The output string is contained in a text area, the text area is inside a scroll pane, and the scroll pane is placed in the message dialog box (lines 68–71).

34.7 Creating Custom Dialogs

Standard `JOptionPane` dialogs are sufficient in most cases. Occasionally, you need to create custom dialogs. In Swing, the `JDialog` class can be extended to create custom dialogs.

As with `JFrame`, components are added to the `contentPane` of `JDialog`. Creating a custom dialog usually involves laying out user interface components in the dialog, adding buttons for dismissing the dialog, and installing listeners that respond to button actions.

The standard dialog is *modal*, which means that no other window can be accessed before the dialog is dismissed. However, the custom dialogs derived from `JDialog` are not modal by default. To make a dialog modal, set its `modal` property to `true`. To display an instance of `JDialog`, set its `visible` property to `true`.

Let us create a custom dialog box for choosing colors, as shown in Figure 34.17(a). Use this dialog to choose the color for the foreground of the button, as shown in Figure 34.17(b). When the user clicks the *Change Button Text Color* button, the Choose Color dialog box is displayed.

Create a custom dialog component named `ColorDialog` by extending `JDialog`. Use three sliders to specify red, green, and blue components of a color. The program is given in Listing 34.6.

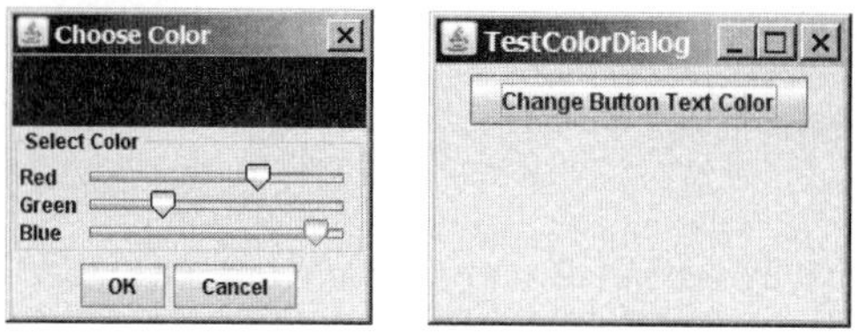
Choose Color
Select Color
Red
Green
Blue
OK
Cancel
TestColorDialog
Change Button Text Color

(a) (b)

FIGURE 34.17 The custom dialog allows you to choose a color for the label's foreground.

LISTING 34.6 ColorDialog.java

color value
sliders
buttons
constructor
constructor
create UI

```
import java.awt.*;
import java.awt.event.*;
import javax.swing.*;
import javax.swing.event.*;

public class ColorDialog extends JDialog {
  // Declare color component values and selected color
  private int redValue, greenValue, blueValue;
  private Color color = null;

  // Create sliders
  private JSlider jslRed = new JSlider(0, 128);
  private JSlider jslGreen = new JSlider(0, 128);
  private JSlider jslBlue = new JSlider(0, 128);

  // Create two buttons
  private JButton jbtOK = new JButton("OK");
  private JButton jbtCancel = new JButton("Cancel");

  // Create a panel to display the selected color
  private JPanel jpSelectedColor = new JPanel();

  public ColorDialog() {
    this(null, true);
  }

  public ColorDialog(java.awt.Frame parent, boolean modal) {
    super(parent, modal);
    setTitle("Choose Color");

    // Group two buttons OK and Cancel
    JPanel jpButtons = new JPanel();
    jpButtons.add(jbtOK);
    jpButtons.add(jbtCancel);

    // Group labels
    JPanel jpLabels = new JPanel();
    jpLabels.setLayout(new GridLayout(3, 0));
    jpLabels.add(new JLabel("Red"));
    jpLabels.add(new JLabel("Green"));
    jpLabels.add(new JLabel("Blue"));

    // Group sliders for selecting red, green, and blue colors
    JPanel jpSliders = new JPanel();
    jpSliders.setLayout(new GridLayout(3, 0));
    jpSliders.add(jslRed);
```

```
    jpSliders.add(jslGreen);
    jpSliders.add(jslBlue);

    // Group jpLabels and jpSliders
    JPanel jpSelectColor = new JPanel();
    jpSelectColor.setLayout(new BorderLayout());
    jpSelectColor.setBorder(
      BorderFactory.createTitledBorder("Select Color"));
    jpSelectColor.add(jpLabels, BorderLayout.WEST);
    jpSelectColor.add(jpSliders, BorderLayout.CENTER);

    // Group jpSelectColor and jpSelectedColor
    JPanel jpColor = new JPanel();
    jpColor.setLayout(new BorderLayout());
    jpColor.add(jpSelectColor, BorderLayout.SOUTH);
    jpColor.add(jpSelectedColor, BorderLayout.CENTER);

    // Place jpButtons and jpColor into the dialog box
    add(jpButtons, BorderLayout.SOUTH);
    add(jpColor, BorderLayout.CENTER);
    pack();

    jbtOK.addActionListener(new ActionListener() {
      public void actionPerformed(ActionEvent e) {
        setVisible(false);
      }
    });

    jbtCancel.addActionListener(new ActionListener() {
      public void actionPerformed(ActionEvent e) {
        color = null;
        setVisible(false);
      }
    });

    jslRed.addChangeListener(new ChangeListener() {
      public void stateChanged(ChangeEvent e) {
        redValue = jslRed.getValue();
        color = new Color(redValue, greenValue, blueValue);
        jpSelectedColor.setBackground(color);
      }
    });

    jslGreen.addChangeListener(new ChangeListener() {
      public void stateChanged(ChangeEvent e) {
        greenValue = jslGreen.getValue();
        color = new Color(redValue, greenValue, blueValue);
        jpSelectedColor.setBackground(color);
      }
    });

    jslBlue.addChangeListener(new ChangeListener() {
      public void stateChanged(ChangeEvent e) {
        blueValue = jslBlue.getValue();
        color = new Color(redValue, greenValue, blueValue);
        jpSelectedColor.setBackground(color);
      }
    });
  }

```

listeners

```
107   public Dimension getPreferredSize() {
108     return new java.awt.Dimension(200, 200);
109   }
110
111   /** Return color */
112   public Color getColor() {
113     return color;
114   }
115 }
```

Create a test class to use the color dialog to select the color for the foreground color of the button in Listing 34.7.

LISTING 34.7 TestColorDialog.java

listener

main method omitted

```
import javax.swing.*;
import java.awt.*;
import java.awt.event.*;

public class TestColorDialog extends JApplet {
  private ColorDialog colorDialog1 = new ColorDialog();
  private JButton jbtChangeColor = new JButton("Choose color");

  public TestColorDialog() {
    setLayout(new java.awt.FlowLayout());
    jbtChangeColor.setText("Change Button Text Color");
    jbtChangeColor.addActionListener(new ActionListener() {
      public void actionPerformed(ActionEvent e) {
        colorDialog1.setVisible(true);

        if (colorDialog1.getColor() != null)
          jbtChangeColor.setForeground(colorDialog1.getColor());
      }
    });
    add(jbtChangeColor);
  }
}
```

The custom dialog box allows the user to use the sliders to select colors. The selected color is stored in the `color` variable. When the user clicks the *Cancel* button, color becomes `null`, which implies that no selection has been made.

The dialog box is displayed when the user clicks the *Change Button Text Color* button and is closed when the *OK* button or the *Cancel* button is clicked.

Tip

Not setting the dialog modal when needed is a common mistake. In this example, the dialog is set modal in line 24 in ColorDialog.java (Listing 34.6). If the dialog is not modal, all the statements in the *Change Button Text Color* button handler are executed before the color is selected from the dialog box.

34.8 JColorChooser

You created a color dialog in the preceding example as a subclass of `JDialog`, which is a subclass of `java.awt.Dialog` (a top-level heavy-weight component). Therefore, it cannot be added to a container as a component. Color dialogs are commonly used in GUI programming. Swing provides a convenient and versatile color dialog named `javax.swing.JColorChooser`. `JColorChooser` is a lightweight component inherited from `JComponent`. It can be added to any container. For example, the following code places a `JColorChooser` in an applet, as shown in Figure 34.18.

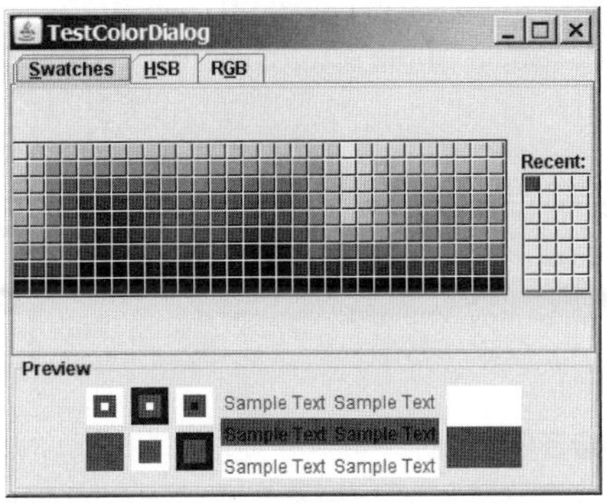
TestColorDialog
Swatches
HSB
RGB
Recent:
Preview
Sample Text Sample Text
Sample Text Sample Text
Sample Text Sample Text

FIGURE 34.18 An instance of `JColorChooser` is displayed in an applet.

create `JColorChooser`

```
public class JColorChooserDemo extends javax.swing.JApplet {
  public JColorChooserDemo() {
    this.add(new javax.swing.JColorChooser());
  }
}
```

Often an instance of `JColorChooser` is displayed in a dialog box using `JColorChooser`'s static `showDialog` method:

```
public static Color showDialog(Component parentComponent,
                               String title,
                               Color initialColor)
```

For example, the following code displays a `JColorChooser`, as shown in Figure 34.19.

```
Color color = JColorChooser.showDialog(this, "Choose a color",
  Color.YELLOW);
```

The `showDialog` method creates an instance of `JDialog` with three buttons, *OK*, *Cancel*, and *Reset*, to hold a `JColorChooser` object, as shown in Figure 34.19(a). The method displays a

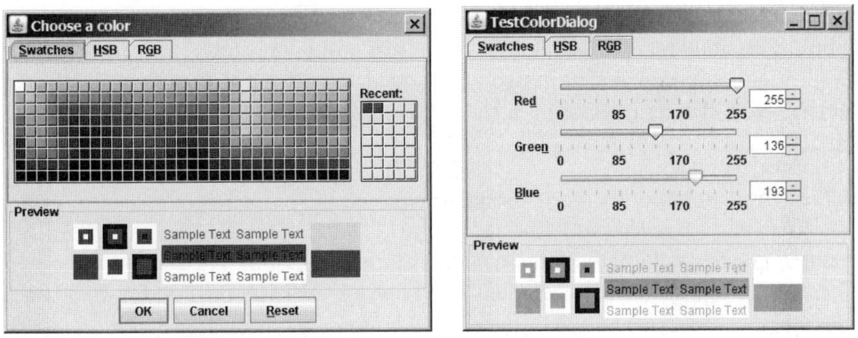
Choose a color
Swatches
HSB
RGB
Recent:
Preview
Sample Text Sample Text
Sample Text Sample Text
Sample Text Sample Text
OK
Cancel
Reset
TestColorDialog
Swatches
HSB
RGB
Red
Green
Blue
0
85
170
255
255
136
193
Preview
Sample Text Sample Text
Sample Text Sample Text
Sample Text Sample Text

(a) (b)

FIGURE 34.19 An instance of `JColorChooser` is displayed in a dialog box with the *OK*, *Cancel*, and *Reset* buttons.

modal dialog. If the user clicks the *OK* button, the method dismisses the dialog and returns the selected color. If the user clicks the *Cancel* button or closes the dialog, the method dismisses the dialog and returns `null`.

`JColorChooser` consists of a tabbed pane and a color preview panel. The tabbed pane has three tabs for choosing colors using Swatches, HSB, and RGB, as shown in Figure 34.19(b). The preview panel shows the effect of the selected color.

Note

`JColorChooser` is very flexible. It allows you to replace the tabbed pane or the color preview panel with custom components. The default tabbed pane and the color preview panel are sufficient. You rarely need to use custom components.

34.9 JFileChooser

The `javax.swing.JFileChooser` class displays a dialog box from which the user can navigate through the file system and select files for loading or saving, as shown in Figure 34.20.

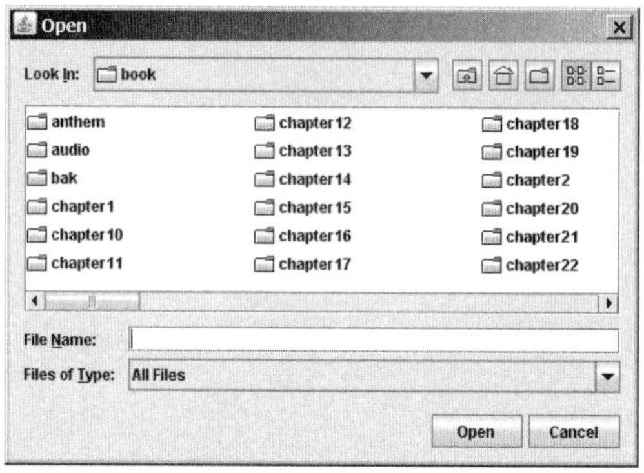
Open
Look In:
book
anthem
audio
bak
chapter1
chapter10
chapter11
chapter12
chapter13
chapter14
chapter15
chapter16
chapter17
chapter18
chapter19
chapter2
chapter20
chapter21
chapter22
File Name:
Files of Type:
All Files
Open
Cancel

FIGURE 34.20 The Swing `JFileChooser` shows files and directories, and enables the user to navigate through the file system visually.

Like `JColorChooser`, `JFileChooser` is a lightweight component inherited from `JComponent`. It can be added to any container if desired, but often you create an instance of `JFileChooser` and display it standalone.

`JFileChooser` is a subclass of `JComponent`. There are several ways to construct a file dialog box. The simplest is to use `JFileChooser`'s no-arg constructor.

The file dialog box can appear in two types: open and save. The *open type* is for opening a file, and the *save type* is for storing a file. To create an open file dialog, use the following method:

```
public int showOpenDialog(Component parent)
```

This method creates a dialog box that contains an instance of `JFileChooser` for opening a file. The method returns an `int` value, either `APPROVE_OPTION` or `CANCEL_OPTION`, which indicates whether the *Open* button or the *Cancel* button was clicked.

Similarly, you can use the following method to create a dialog for saving files:

```
public int showSaveDialog(Component parent)
```

The file dialog box created with `showOpenDialog` or `showSaveDialog` is modal. The `JFileChooser` class has the properties inherited from `JComponent`. It also has the following useful properties:

- **`dialogType`** specifies the type of this dialog. Use `OPEN_DIALOG` when you want to bring up a file chooser that the user can use to open a file. Likewise, use `SAVE_DIALOG` to let the user choose a file for saving.
- **`dialogTitle`** is the string that is displayed in the title bar of the dialog box.
- **`currentDirectory`** is the current directory of the file. The type of this property is `java.io.File`. If you want the current directory to be used, use `setCurrentDirectory(new File("."))`.
- **`selectedFile`** is the file you have selected. You can use `getSelectedFile()` to return the selected file from the dialog box. The type of this property is `java.io.File`. If you have a default file name that you expect to use, use `setSelectedFile(new File(filename))`.
- **`multiSelectionEnabled`** is a `boolean` value indicating whether multiple files can be selected. By default, it is `false`.
- **`selectedFiles`** is a list of the files selected if the file chooser is set to allow multi-selection. The type of this property is `File[]`.

Let us create an example of a simple text editor that uses Swing menus, toolbar, file chooser, and color chooser, as shown in Figure 34.21, which allows the user to open and save text files, clear text, and change the color and font of the text. Listing 34.8 shows the program.

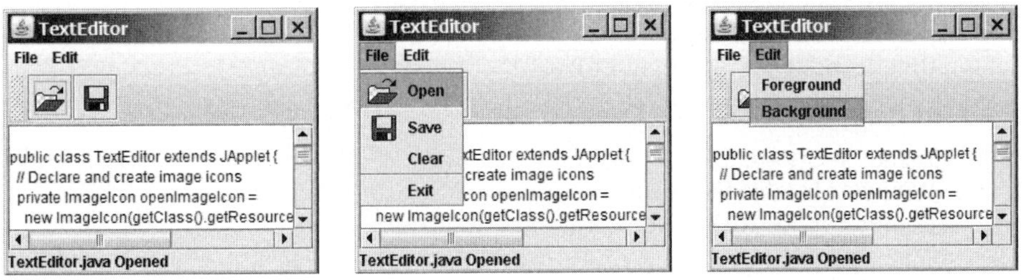
TextEditor
File
Edit
Open
Save
Clear
Exit
Foreground
Background
public class TextEditor extends JApplet {
// Declare and create image icons
private ImageIcon openImageIcon =
new ImageIcon(getClass().getResource
TextEditor.java Opened

FIGURE 34.21 The editor enables you to open and save text files from the File menu or from the toolbar, and to change the color and font of the text from the Edit menu.

LISTING 34.8 TextEditor.java

```
import java.io.*;
import java.awt.*;
import java.awt.event.*;
import javax.swing.*;

public class TextEditor extends JApplet {
  // Declare and create image icons
  private ImageIcon openImageIcon =
    new ImageIcon(getClass().getResource("image/open.gif"));
  private ImageIcon saveImageIcon =
    new ImageIcon(getClass().getResource("image/save.gif"));

```

create UI

```
  // Create menu items
  private JMenuItem jmiOpen = new JMenuItem("Open", openImageIcon);
  private JMenuItem jmiSave = new JMenuItem("Save", saveImageIcon);
  private JMenuItem jmiClear = new JMenuItem("Clear");
  private JMenuItem jmiExit = new JMenuItem("Exit");
  private JMenuItem jmiForeground = new JMenuItem("Foreground");
  private JMenuItem jmiBackground = new JMenuItem("Background");

  // Create buttons to be placed in a toolbar
  private JButton jbtOpen = new JButton(openImageIcon);
  private JButton jbtSave = new JButton(saveImageIcon);
  private JLabel jlblStatus = new JLabel();

  // Create a JFileChooser with the current directory
  private JFileChooser jFileChooser1
    = new JFileChooser(new File("."));

  // Create a text area
  private JTextArea jta = new JTextArea();

  public TextEditor() {
    // Add menu items to the menu
    JMenu jMenu1 = new JMenu("File");
    jMenu1.add(jmiOpen);
    jMenu1.add(jmiSave);
    jMenu1.add(jmiClear);
    jMenu1.addSeparator();
    jMenu1.add(jmiExit);

    // Add menu items to the menu
    JMenu jMenu2 = new JMenu("Edit");
    jMenu2.add(jmiForeground);
    jMenu2.add(jmiBackground);

    // Add menus to the menu bar
    JMenuBar jMenuBar1 = new JMenuBar();
    jMenuBar1.add(jMenu1);
    jMenuBar1.add(jMenu2);

    // Set the menu bar
    setJMenuBar(jMenuBar1);

    // Create toolbar
    JToolBar jToolBar1 = new JToolBar();
    jToolBar1.add(jbtOpen);
    jToolBar1.add(jbtSave);

    jmiOpen.addActionListener(new ActionListener() {
      public void actionPerformed(ActionEvent e) {
        open();
      }
    });

    jmiSave.addActionListener(new ActionListener() {
      public void actionPerformed(ActionEvent evt) {
        save();
      }
    });

    jmiClear.addActionListener(new ActionListener() {
```

```
      public void actionPerformed(ActionEvent evt) {
        jta.setText(null);
      }
    });

    jmiExit.addActionListener(new ActionListener() {
      public void actionPerformed(ActionEvent evt) {
        System.exit(0);
      }
    });

    jmiForeground.addActionListener(new ActionListener() {
      public void actionPerformed(ActionEvent evt) {
        Color selectedColor =
          JColorChooser.showDialog(null, "Choose Foreground Color",
            jta.getForeground());

        if (selectedColor != null)
          jta.setForeground(selectedColor);
      }
    });

    jmiBackground.addActionListener(new ActionListener() {
      public void actionPerformed(ActionEvent evt) {
        Color selectedColor =
          JColorChooser.showDialog(null, "Choose Background Color",
            jta.getForeground());

        if (selectedColor != null)
          jta.setBackground(selectedColor);
      }
    });

    jbtOpen.addActionListener(new ActionListener() {
      public void actionPerformed(ActionEvent evt) {
        open();
      }
    });

    jbtSave.addActionListener(new ActionListener() {
      public void actionPerformed(ActionEvent evt) {
        save();
      }
    });

    add(jToolBar1, BorderLayout.NORTH);
    add(jlblStatus, BorderLayout.SOUTH);
    add(new JScrollPane(jta), BorderLayout.CENTER);
  }

  /** Open file */
  private void open() {
    if (jFileChooser1.showOpenDialog(this) ==
      JFileChooser.APPROVE_OPTION)
      open(jFileChooser1.getSelectedFile());
  }

  /** Open file with the specified File instance */
  private void open(File file) {
    try {
```

color chooser

color chooser

file chooser

```
133       // Read from the specified file and store it in jta
134       BufferedInputStream in = new BufferedInputStream(
135         new FileInputStream(file));
136       byte[] b = new byte[in.available()];
137       in.read(b, 0, b.length);
138       jta.append(new String(b, 0, b.length));
139       in.close();
140 
141       // Display the status of the Open file operation in jlblStatus
142       jlblStatus.setText(file.getName() + " Opened");
143     }
144     catch (IOException ex) {
145       jlblStatus.setText("Error opening " + file.getName());
146     }
147   }
148 
149   /** Save file */
150   private void save() {
151     if (jFileChooser1.showSaveDialog(this) ==
152       JFileChooser.APPROVE_OPTION) {
153         save(jFileChooser1.getSelectedFile());
154     }
155   }
156 
157   /** Save file with specified File instance */
158   private void save(File file) {
159     try {
160       // Write the text in jta to the specified file
161       BufferedOutputStream out = new BufferedOutputStream(
162         new FileOutputStream(file));
163       byte[] b = (jta.getText()).getBytes();
164       out.write(b, 0, b.length);
165       out.close();
166 
167       // Display the status of the save file operation in jlblStatus
168       jlblStatus.setText(file.getName()  + " Saved ");
169     }
170     catch (IOException ex) {
171       jlblStatus.setText("Error saving " + file.getName());
172     }
173   }
174 }
```

main method omitted

The program creates the File and Edit menus (lines 34–45). The File menu contains the menu commands Open for loading a file, Save for saving a file, Clear for clearing the text editor, and Exit for terminating the program. The Edit menu contains the menu commands Foreground Color and Background Color for setting foreground color and background color in the text. The Open and Save menu commands can also be accessed from the toolbar, which is created in lines 56–58. The status of executing Open and Save is displayed in the status label, which is created in line 24.

`jFileChooser1`, an instance of `JFileChooser`, is created for displaying the file dialog box to open and save files (lines 27–28). `new File(".")` is used to set the current directory to the directory where the class is stored.

The `open` method is invoked when the user clicks the Open menu command or the Open toolbar button (lines 62, 108). The `showOpenDialog` method (line 125) displays an Open dialog box, as shown in Figure 34.20. Upon receiving the selected file, the method `open(file)` (line 127) is invoked to load the file to the text area using a `BufferedInputStream` wrapped on a `FileInputStream`.

The save method is invoked when the user clicks the Save menu command or the Save toolbar button (lines 68, 114). The showSaveDialog method (line 151) displays a Save dialog box. Upon receiving the selected file, the method save(file) (line 153) is invoked to save the contents from the text area to the file, using a BufferedOutputStream wrapped on a FileOutputStream.

The color dialog is displayed using the static method showDialog (lines 87, 98) of JColorChooser. Thus you don't need to create an instance of JFileChooser. The showDialog method returns the selected color if the *OK* button is clicked after a color is selected.

Chapter Summary

1. *Menus* make selection easier and are widely used in window applications. Java provides five classes that implement menus: JMenuBar, JMenu, JMenuItem, JCheckBoxMenuItem, and JRadioButtonMenuItem. These classes are subclasses of AbstractButton. They are very similar to buttons.

2. JMenuBar is a top-level menu component used to hold menus. A menu consists of *menu items* that the user can select (or toggle on or off). A menu item can be an instance of JMenuItem, JCheckBoxMenuItem, or JRadioButtonMenuItem. Menu items can be associated with icons, keyboard mnemonics, and keyboard accelerators. Menu items can be separated using separators.

3. *A popup menu*, also known as a *context menu*, is like a regular menu, but does not have a menu bar and can float anywhere on the screen. Creating a popup menu is similar to creating a regular menu. First, you create an instance of JPopupMenu, then you can add JMenuItem, JCheckBoxMenuItem, JRadioButtonMenuItem, and separators to the popup menu.

4. Customarily, you display a popup menu by pointing to a GUI component and clicking a certain mouse button, the so-called *popup trigger*. Popup triggers are system dependent. In Windows, the popup menu is displayed when the right mouse button is released. In Motif, the popup menu is displayed when the third mouse button is pressed and held down.

5. Swing provides the JToolBar class as the container to hold toolbar components. JToolBar uses BoxLayout to manage components. The components usually appear as icons. Since icons are not components, they cannot be placed into a toolbar directly. Instead you place buttons into the toolbar and set the icons on the buttons. An instance of JToolBar is like a regular container. Often it is placed in the north, west, or east of a container of BorderLayout.

6. Swing provides the Action interface, which can be used to create action objects for processing actions. Using Action objects, common action processing for menu items and toolbar buttons can be centralized and separated from the other application code.

7. The JOptionPane class contains the static methods for creating message dialogs, confirmation dialogs, input dialogs, and option dialogs. You can also create custom dialogs by extending the JDialog class.

8. Swing provides a convenient and versatile color dialog named `javax.swing.JColorChooser`. Like `JOptionPane`, `JColorChooser` is a lightweight component inherited from `JComponent`. It can be added to any container.

9. Swing provides the `javax.swing.JFileChooser` class that displays a dialog box from which the user can navigate through the file system and select files for loading or saving.

Review Questions

Section 34.2

34.1 How do you create a menu bar?

34.2 How do you create a submenu? How do you create a check-box menu item? How do you create a radio-button menu item?

34.3 How do you add a separator in a menu?

34.4 How do you set an icon and a text in a menu item? How do you associate keyboard mnemonics and accelerators in a menu item?

Section 34.3

34.5 How do you create a popup menu? How do you show a popup menu?

34.6 Describe a popup trigger.

Section 34.4

34.7 What is the layout manager used in `JToolBar`? Can you change the layout manager?

34.8 How do you add buttons into a `JToolBar`? How do you add a `JToolBar` into a frame or an applet?

Section 34.5

34.9 What is the `Action` interface for?

34.10 How do you add an `Action` object to a `JToolBar`, `JMenu`, `JButton`, `JRadioButton`, and `JCheckBox`?

Section 34.6

34.11 Describe the standard dialog boxes created using the `JOptionPane` class.

34.12 How do you create a message dialog? What are the message types? What is the button in the message dialog?

34.13 How do you create a confirmation dialog? What are the button option types?

34.14 How do you create an input dialog with a text field for entering input? How do you create a combo box dialog for selecting values as input? How do you create a list dialog for selecting values as input?

Sections 34.7–34.10

34.15 How do you show an instance of `JDialog`? Is a standard dialog box created using the static methods in `JOptionPane` modal? Is an instance of `JDialog` modal?

34.16 How do you display an instance of `JColorChooser`? Is an instance of `JColorChooser` modal? How do you obtain the selected color?

34.17 How do you display an instance of `JFileChooser`? Is an instance of `JFileChooser` modal? How do you obtain the selected file? What is the return type for `getSelectedFile()` and `getSelectedDirectory()`? How do you set the current directory as the default directory for a `JFileChooser` dialog?

Programming Exercises

Sections 34.2–34.3

34.1* (*Creating an investment value calculator*) Write a program that calculates the future value of an investment at a given interest rate for a specified number of years. The formula for the calculation is as follows:

```
futureValue = investmentAmount × (1 + monthlyInterestRate)^(years×12)
```

Use text fields for interest rate, investment amount, and years. Display the future amount in a text field when the user clicks the *Calculate* button or chooses Calculate from the Operation menu (see Figure 34.22). Show a message dialog box when the user clicks the **About** menu item from the Help menu.

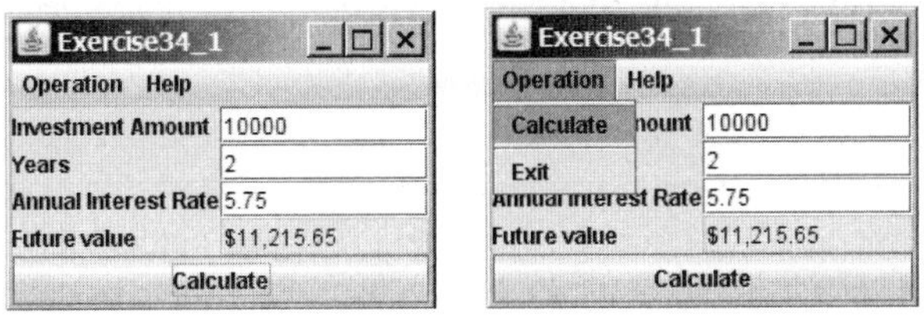
Exercise34_1
Operation
Help
Investment Amount
10000
Years
2
Annual Interest Rate
5.75
Future value
$11,215.65
Calculate
Exercise34_1
Operation
Help
Calculate
Exit
2
5.75
Future value
$11,215.65
Calculate

FIGURE 34.22 The user enters the investment amount, years, and interest rate to compute future value.

34.2* (*Using popup menus*) Modify Listing 34.1, MenuDemo.java, to create a popup menu that contains the menus Operations and Exit, as shown in Figure 34.23. The popup is displayed when you click the right mouse button on the panel that contains the labels and the text fields.

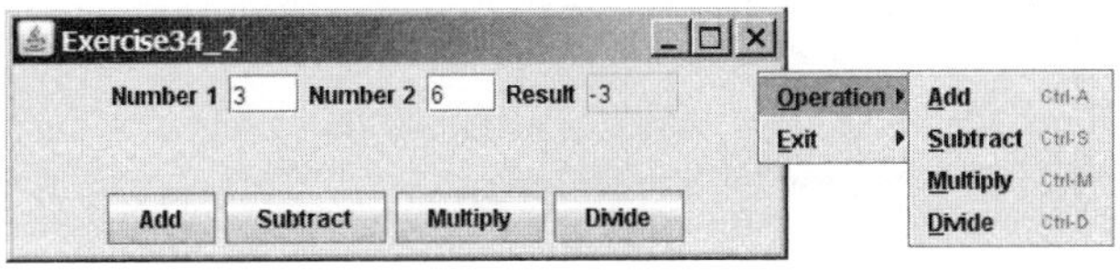
Exercise34_2
Number 1
3
Number 2
6
Result
-3
Add
Subtract
Multiply
Divide
Operation
Exit
Add
Ctrl-A
Subtract
Ctrl-S
Multiply
Ctrl-M
Divide
Ctrl-D

FIGURE 34.23 The popup menu contains the commands to perform arithmetic operations.

Sections 34.4–34.5

34.3** (*A paint utility*) Write a program that emulates a paint utility. Your program should enable the user to choose options and draw shapes or get characters from the keyboard based on the selected options (see Figure 34.24). The options are

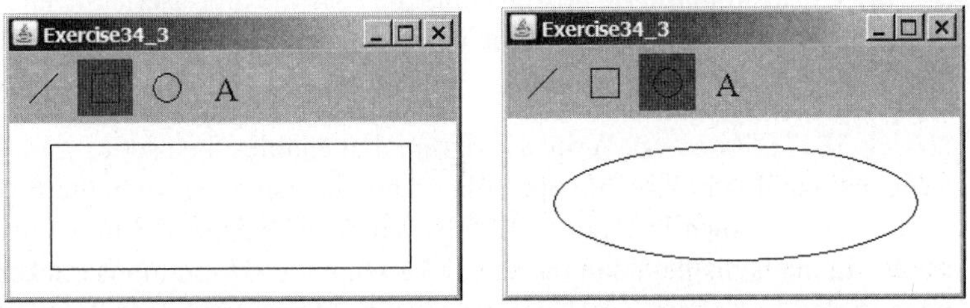
Exercise34_3
A
Exercise34_3
A

FIGURE 34.24 This exercise produces a prototype drawing utility that enables you to draw lines, rectangles, ovals, and characters.

displayed in a toolbar. To draw a line, the user first clicks the line icon in the toolbar and then uses the mouse to draw a line in the same way you would draw using Microsoft Paint.

34.4* (*Using actions*) Write a program that contains the menu items and toolbar buttons that can be used to select flags to be displayed in an `ImageViewer`, as shown in Figure 34.25. Use the `Action` interface to centralize the processing for the actions.

Exercise34_4
Flags
CA
US
Select the US flag to display

FIGURE 34.25 The menu items and tool buttons are used to display selected images in the `ImageViewer`.

Sections 34.6–34.10

34.5* (*Demonstrating `JOptionPane`*) Write a program that creates option panes of all types, as shown in Figure 34.26. Each menu item invokes a static `showXxxDialog` method to display a dialog box.

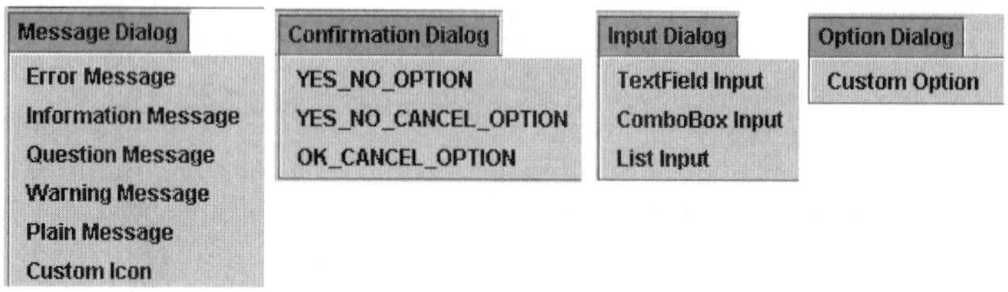
Message Dialog
Error Message
Information Message
Question Message
Warning Message
Plain Message
Custom Icon
Confirmation Dialog
YES_NO_OPTION
YES_NO_CANCEL_OPTION
OK_CANCEL_OPTION
Input Dialog
TextField Input
ComboBox Input
List Input
Option Dialog
Custom Option

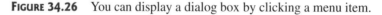

FIGURE 34.26 You can display a dialog box by clicking a menu item.

34.6* (*Creating custom dialog*) Write a program that creates a custom dialog box to gather user information, as shown in Figure 34.27(a).

Login
Username peter
Password •••
OK
Cancel
Exercise34_7
Professor Y. Daniel Liang, PhD
Department of Computer Science
Armstrong Atlantic State University
11935 Abercorn Street
Savannah, Georgia 31419-1997
* telephone: (912) 921-5440
* fax: (912) 921-5606
* liang@armstrong.edu
* http://www.cs.armstrong.edu/liang
Filename signature.txt
Browse

(a) (b)

FIGURE 34.27 (a) The custom dialog box prompts the user to enter username and password. (b) The program enables the user to view a file by selecting it from a file open dialog box.

34.7* (*Using `JFileChooser`*) Write a program that enables the user to select a file from a file open dialog box. A file open dialog box is displayed when the *Browse* button is clicked, as shown in Figure 34.27(b). The file is displayed in the text area, and the file name is displayed in the text field when the *OK* button is clicked in the file open dialog box. You can also enter the file name in the text field and press the *Enter* key to display the file in the text area.

34.8* (*Selecting an audio file*) Write a program that selects an audio file using the file dialog box, and use three buttons, *Play*, *Loop*, and *Stop*, to control the audio, as shown in Figure 34.28. If you click the *Play* button, the audio file is played once. If you click the *Loop* button, the audio file keeps playing repeatedly. If you click the *Stop* button, the playing stops. The selected audio files are stored in the folder named **anthems** under the exercise directory. The exercise directory contains the class file for this exercise.

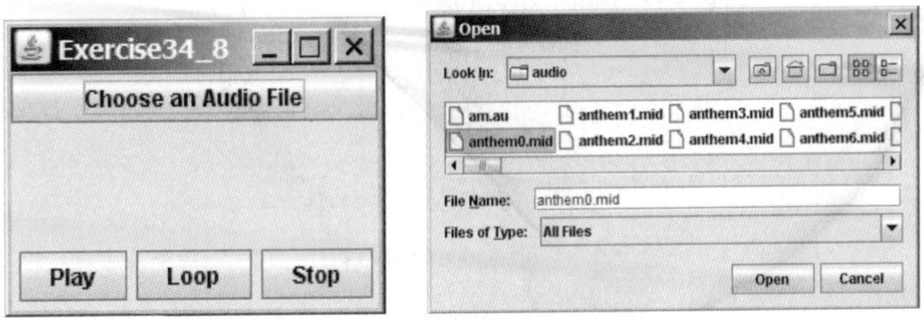
Exercise34_8
Choose an Audio File
Play
Loop
Stop
Open
Look In:
audio
am.au
anthem0.mid
anthem1.mid
anthem2.mid
anthem3.mid
anthem4.mid
anthem5.mid
anthem6.mid
File Name:
anthem0.mid
Files of Type:
All Files
Open
Cancel

FIGURE 34.28 The program allows you to choose an audio file from a dialog box and use the buttons to play, repeatedly play, or stop the audio.

34.9** (*Playing TicTacToe with a computer*) The game in §18.9, "Case Study: TicTacToe," facilitates two players. Write a new game that enables a player to play against the computer. Add a File menu with two items, New Game and Exit, as shown in Figure 34.29. When you click New Game, it displays a dialog box. From this dialog box, you can decide whether to let the computer go first.

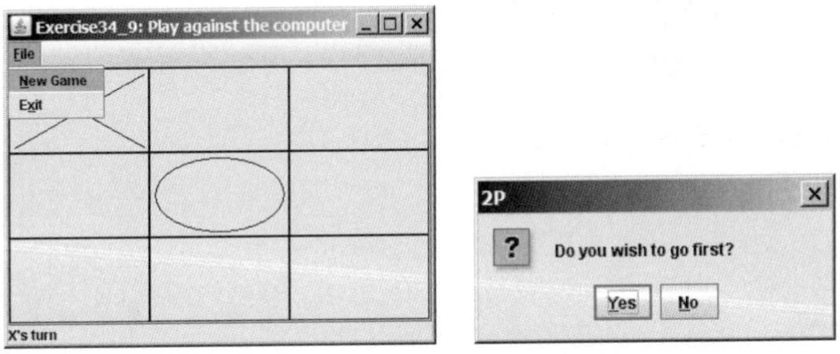
Exercise34_9: Play against the computer
File
New Game
Exit
X's turn
2P
Do you wish to go first?
Yes
No

FIGURE 34.29 The new TicTacToe game enables you to play against the computer.

CHAPTER 35

MVC AND SWING MODELS

Objectives

- To use the model-view-controller approach to separate data and logic from the presentation of data (§35.2).
- To implement the model-view-controller components using the JavaBeans event model (§35.2).
- To explain the Swing model-view-controller architecture (§35.4).
- To use `JSpinner` to scroll the next and previous values (§35.5).
- To create custom spinner models and editors (§35.6).
- To use `JList` to select single or multiple items in a list (§35.7).
- To add and remove items using `ListModel` and `DefaultListModel` (§35.8).
- To render list cells using a default or custom cell renderer (§35.9).
- To create custom combo box models and renderers (§35.10).

35.1 Introduction

The Swing user interface components are implemented using variations of the MVC architecture. You have used simple Swing components without concern for their supporting models, but in order to use advanced Swing components, you have to use their models to store, access, and modify data. This chapter introduces the MVC architecture and Swing models. Specifically, you will learn how to use the models in `JSpinner`, `JList`, and `JComboBox`. The next chapter will introduce `JTable` and `JTree`.

35.2 MVC

The model-view-controller (MVC) approach is a way of developing components by separating data storage and handling from the visual representation of the data. The component for storing and handling data, known as a *model*, contains the actual contents of the component. The component for presenting the data, known as a *view*, handles all essential component behaviors. It is the view that comes to mind when you think of the component. It does all the displaying of the components. The *controller* is a component that is usually responsible for obtaining data, as shown in Figure 35.1.

model

view

controller

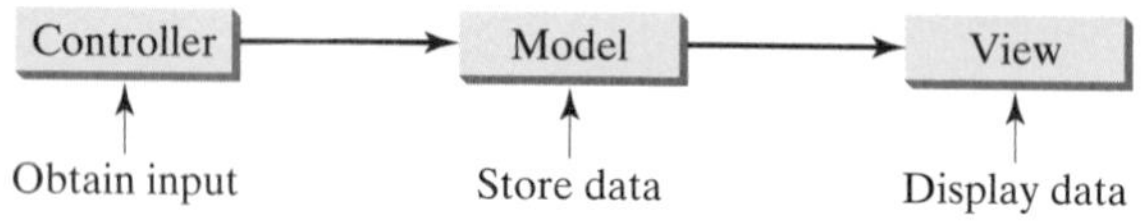
Controller
Model
View
Obtain input
Store data
Display data

FIGURE 35.1 The controller obtains data and stores it in a model. The view displays the data stored in the model.

MVC benefits

Separating a component into a model and a view has two major benefits:

- It makes multiple views possible so that data can be shared through the same model. For example, a model storing student names can be displayed simultaneously in a combo box and a list box.
- It simplifies the task of writing complex applications and makes the components scalable and easy to maintain. Changes can be made to the view without affecting the model, and vice versa.

A model contains data, whereas a view makes the data visible. Once a view is associated with a model, it is synchronized with the model. This ensures that all of the model's views display the same data consistently. To achieve consistency and synchronization with its dependent views, the model should notify the views when there is a change in any of its properties that are used in the view. In response to a change notification, the view is responsible for redisplaying the viewing area affected by the property change.

The Java event delegation model provides a superior architecture for supporting MVC component development. The model can be implemented as a source with appropriate event and event listener registration methods. The view can be implemented as a listener. Thus, if data are changed in the model, the view will be notified. To enable the selection of the model from the view, simply add the model as a property in the view with a set method.

Let us use an example to demonstrate the development of components using the MVC approach. The example creates a model named `CircleModel`, a view named `CircleView`, and a controller named `CircleControl`. `CircleModel` stores the properties (`radius`, `filled`, and `color`) that describe a circle. `filled` is a boolean value that indicates whether a circle is filled.

`CircleView` draws a circle according to the properties of the circle. `CircleControl` enables the user to enter circle properties from a graphical user interface. Create an applet with two buttons named *Show Controller* and *Show View*, as shown in Figure 35.2(a). When you click the *Show Controller* button, the controller is displayed in a frame, as shown in Figure 35.2(b). When you click the *Show View* button, the view is displayed in a separate frame, as shown in Figure 35.2(c).

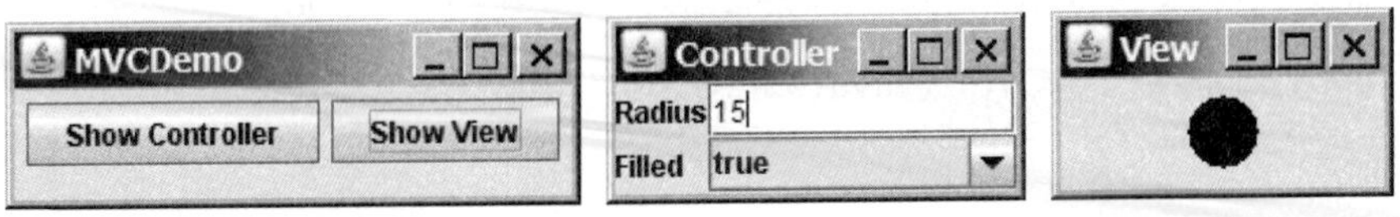
MVCDemo
Show Controller
Show View
Controller
Radius 15
Filled true
View

(a) (b) (c)

FIGURE 35.2 The controller obtains circle properties and stores them in a circle model. The view displays the circle specified by the circle model.

The circle model contains the properties `radius`, `filled`, and `color`, as well as the registration/deregistration methods for action event, as shown in Figure 35.3.

date model

When a property value is changed, the listeners are notified. The complete source code for `CircleModel` is given in Listing 35.1.

LISTING 35.1 CircleModel.java

properties

fire event

```
import java.awt.event.*;
import java.util.*;

public class CircleModel {
  /** Property radius. */
  private double radius = 20;

  /** Property filled. */
  private boolean filled;

  /** Property color. */
  private java.awt.Color color;

  /** Utility field used by event firing mechanism. */
  private ArrayList<ActionListener> actionListenerList;

  public double getRadius() {
    return radius;
  }

  public void setRadius(double radius) {
    this.radius = radius;

    // Notify the listener for the change on radius
    processEvent(
      new ActionEvent(this, ActionEvent.ACTION_PERFORMED, "radius"));
  }

  public boolean isFilled() {
    return filled;
  }

  public void setFilled(boolean filled) {
    this.filled = filled;

    // Notify the listener for the change on filled
```

fire event

```
    processEvent(
      new ActionEvent(this, ActionEvent.ACTION_PERFORMED, "filled"));
  }

  public java.awt.Color getColor() {
    return color;
  }

  public void setColor(java.awt.Color color) {
    this.color = color;

    // Notify the listener for the change on color
```

fire event

```
    processEvent(
      new ActionEvent(this, ActionEvent.ACTION_PERFORMED, "color"));
  }

  /** Register an action event listener */
```

standard code

```
  public synchronized void addActionListener(ActionListener l) {
    if (actionListenerList == null)
      actionListenerList = new ArrayList<ActionListener>();

    actionListenerList.add(l);
  }

  /** Remove an action event listener */
```

standard code

```
  public synchronized void removeActionListener(ActionListener l) {
    if (actionListenerList != null && actionListenerList.contains(l))
      actionListenerList.remove(l);
  }

  /** Fire ActionEvent */
```

standard code

```
  private void processEvent(ActionEvent e) {
    ArrayList list;

    synchronized (this) {
      if (actionListenerList == null) return;
      list = (ArrayList)actionListenerList.clone();
    }

    for (int i = 0; i < list.size(); i++) {
      ActionListener listener = (ActionListener)list.get(i);
      listener.actionPerformed(e);
    }
  }
}
```

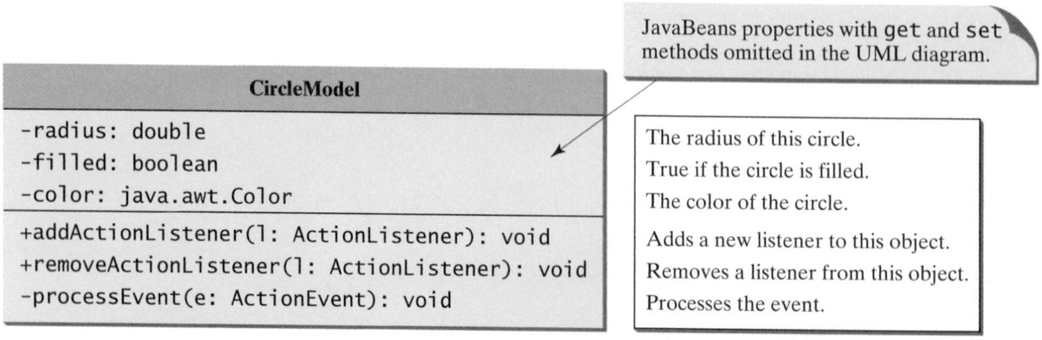
JavaBeans properties with get and set methods omitted in the UML diagram.
CircleModel
-radius: double
-filled: boolean
-color: java.awt.Color
+addActionListener(l: ActionListener): void
+removeActionListener(l: ActionListener): void
-processEvent(e: ActionEvent): void
The radius of this circle.
True if the circle is filled.
The color of the circle.
Adds a new listener to this object.
Removes a listener from this object.
Processes the event.

FIGURE 35.3 The circle model stores the data and notifies the listeners if the data change.

Note

The registration/deregistration/processEvent methods (lines 54–80) are the same as in lines 49–82 in Listing 32.2, CourseWithActionEvent.java. If you use a GUI builder tool such as NetBeans and Eclipse, the code can be generated automatically.

view

The view implements **ActionListener** to listen for notifications from the model. It contains the model as its property. When a model is set in the view, the view is registered with the model. The view extends **JPanel** and overrides the **paintComponent** method to draw the circle according to the property values specified in the model. The UML diagram for **CircleView** is shown in Figure 35.4 and its source code is given in Listing 35.2.

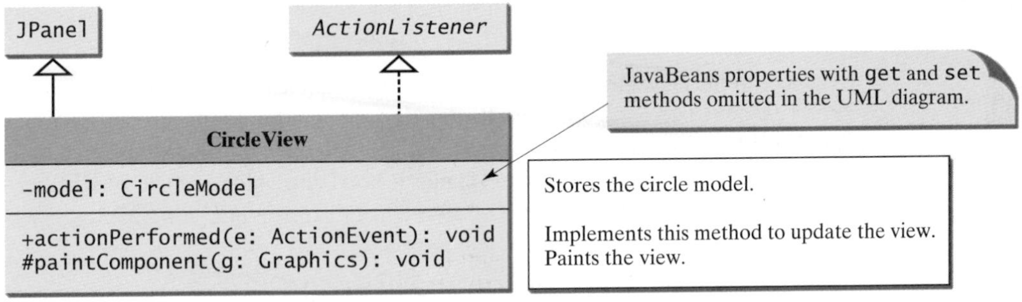
JPanel
ActionListener
CircleView
-model: CircleModel
+actionPerformed(e: ActionEvent): void
#paintComponent(g: Graphics): void
JavaBeans properties with get and set methods omitted in the UML diagram.
Stores the circle model.
Implements this method to update the view.
Paints the view.

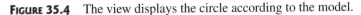

FIGURE 35.4 The view displays the circle according to the model.

LISTING 35.2 CircleView.java

model | set model | paint view

```
import java.awt.*;
import java.awt.event.*;

public class CircleView extends javax.swing.JPanel
    implements ActionListener {
  private CircleModel model;

  public void actionPerformed(ActionEvent actionEvent) {
    repaint();
  }

  /** Set a model */
  public void setModel(CircleModel newModel) {
    model = newModel;

    if (model != null)
      // Register the view as listener for the model
      model.addActionListener(this);

    repaint();
  }

  public CircleModel getModel() {
    return model;
  }

  public void paintComponent(Graphics g) {
    super.paintComponent(g);

    if (model == null) return;

    g.setColor(model.getColor());

```

```
    int xCenter = getWidth() / 2;
    int yCenter = getHeight() / 2;
    int radius = (int)model.getRadius();

    if (model.isFilled()) {
      g.fillOval(xCenter - radius, yCenter - radius,
        2 * radius, 2 * radius);
    }
    else {
      g.drawOval(xCenter - radius, yCenter - radius,
        2 * radius, 2 * radius);
    }
  }
}
```

The controller presents a GUI interface that enables the user to enter circle properties **radius**, **filled**, and **color**. It contains the model as its property. You can use the **setModel** method to associate a circle model with the controller. It uses a text field to obtain a new radius and a combo box to obtain a **boolean** value to specify whether the circle is filled. The source code for **CircleController** is given in Listing 35.3.

LISTING 35.3 CircleController.java

model

create UI

```
import java.awt.event.*;
import java.awt.*;
import javax.swing.*;

public class CircleController extends JPanel {
  private CircleModel model;
  private JTextField jtfRadius = new JTextField();
  private JComboBox jcboFilled = new JComboBox(new Boolean[]{
    new Boolean(false), new Boolean(true)});

  /** Creates new form CircleController */
  public CircleController() {
    // Panel to group labels
    JPanel panel1 = new JPanel();
    panel1.setLayout(new GridLayout(2, 1));
    panel1.add(new JLabel("Radius"));
    panel1.add(new JLabel("Filled"));

    // Panel to group text field, combo box, and another panel
    JPanel panel2 = new JPanel();
    panel2.setLayout(new GridLayout(2, 1));
    panel2.add(jtfRadius);
    panel2.add(jcboFilled);

    setLayout(new BorderLayout());
    add(panel1, BorderLayout.WEST);
    add(panel2, BorderLayout.CENTER);

    // Register listeners
    jtfRadius.addActionListener(new ActionListener() {
      public void actionPerformed(ActionEvent e) {
        if (model == null) return; // No model associated yet.
        model.setRadius(new
          Double(jtfRadius.getText()).doubleValue());
      }
    });
```

```
    jcboFilled.addActionListener(new ActionListener() {
      public void actionPerformed(ActionEvent e) {
        if (model == null) return;
        model.setFilled(
          ((Boolean)jcboFilled.getSelectedItem()).booleanValue());
      }
    });
  }

  public void setModel(CircleModel newModel) {
    model = newModel;
  }

  public CircleModel getModel() {
    return model;
  }
}
```

set model

Finally, let us create an applet named `MVCDemo` with two buttons, *Show Controller* and *Show View*. The *Show Controller* button displays a controller in a frame, and the *Show View* button displays a view in a separate frame. The program is shown in Listing 35.4.

LISTING 35.4 MVCDemo.java

```
import java.awt.*;
import java.awt.event.*;
import javax.swing.*;

public class MVCDemo extends JApplet  {
  private JButton jbtController = new JButton("Show Controller");
  private JButton jbtView = new JButton("Show View");
  private CircleModel model = new CircleModel();

  public MVCDemo() {
    setLayout(new FlowLayout());
    add(jbtController);
    add(jbtView);

    jbtController.addActionListener(new ActionListener() {
      public void actionPerformed(ActionEvent e) {
        JFrame frame = new JFrame("Controller");
        CircleController controller = new CircleController();
        controller.setModel(model);
        frame.add(controller);
        frame.setSize(200, 200);
        frame.setLocation(200, 200);
        frame.setVisible(true);
      }
    });

    jbtView.addActionListener(new ActionListener() {
      public void actionPerformed(ActionEvent e) {
        JFrame frame = new JFrame("View");
        CircleView view = new CircleView();
        view.setModel(model);
        frame.add(view);
        frame.setSize(500, 200);
        frame.setLocation(200, 200);
        frame.setVisible(true);
```

create model

create UI

set model

set model

```
36        }
37      });
38    }
39 }
```

main method omitted

The model stores and handles data, and the views are responsible for presenting data. The fundamental issue in the model-view approach is to ensure consistency between the views and the model. Any change in the model should be notified to the dependent views, and all the views should display the same data consistently. The data in the model is changed through the controller.

The methods `setRadius`, `setFilled`, and `setColor` (lines 21, 33, 45) in `CircleModel` invoke the `processEvent` method to notify the listeners of any change in the properties.

The `setModel` method in `CircleView` sets a new model and registers the view with the model by invoking the model's `addActionListener` method (line 18). When the data in the model are changed, the view's `actionPerformed` method is invoked to repaint the circle (line 9).

The controller `CircleController` presents a GUI. You can enter the radius from the radius text field. You can specify whether the circle is filled from the combo box that contains two `Boolean` objects, `new Boolean(false)` and `new Boolean(true)` (lines 8–9).

In `MVCDemo`, every time you click the *Show Controller* button, a new controller is created (line 18). Every time you click the *Show View* button, a new view is created (line 30). The controller and view share the same model.

35.3 MVC Variations

A variation of the model-view-controller architecture combines the controller with the view. In this case, a view not only presents the data, but is also used as an interface to interact with the user and accept user input, as shown in Figure 35.5.

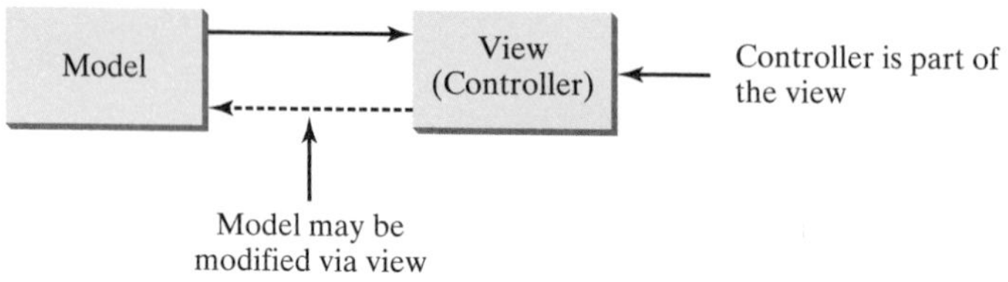
Model
View
(Controller)
Controller is part of the view
Model may be modified via view

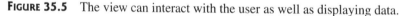

FIGURE 35.5 The view can interact with the user as well as displaying data.

For example, you can modify the view in the preceding example to enable the user to change the circle's radius using the mouse. When the left mouse button is clicked, the radius is increased by `5` pixels. When the right mouse button is clicked, the radius is decreased by `5` pixels. The new view, named `ViewController`, can be implemented by extending `CircleView`, as follows:

mouse listener

right button?

```
public class ViewController extends CircleView {
  public ViewController() {
    // Register mouse listener
    addMouseListener(new java.awt.event.MouseAdapter() {
      public void mousePressed(java.awt.event.MouseEvent e) {
        CircleModel model = getModel(); // Get model

        if (model == null) return;

        if (e.isMetaDown())
          model.setRadius(model.getRadius() - 5); // Right button
```

```
        else
          model.setRadius(model.getRadius() + 5); // Left button
      }
    });
  }
}
```

Another variation of the model-view-controller architecture adds some of the data from the model to the view so that frequently used data can be accessed directly from the view. Swing components are designed using the MVC architecture. Each Swing GUI component is a view that uses a model to store data. A Swing GUI component contains some data in the model, so that it can be accessed directly from the component.

35.4 Swing Model-View-Controller Architecture

Every Swing user interface component (except some containers and dialog boxes, such as `JPanel`, `JSplitPane`, `JFileChooser`, and `JColorChooser`) has a property named *`model`* that refers to its data model. The data model is defined in an interface whose name ends with `Model`. For example, the model for button component is `ButtonModel`. Most model interfaces have a default implementation class, commonly named `DefaultX`, where `X` is its model interface name. For example, the default implementation class for `ButtonModel` is `DefaultButtonModel`. The relationship of a Swing component, its model interface, and its default model implementation class is illustrated in Figure 35.6.

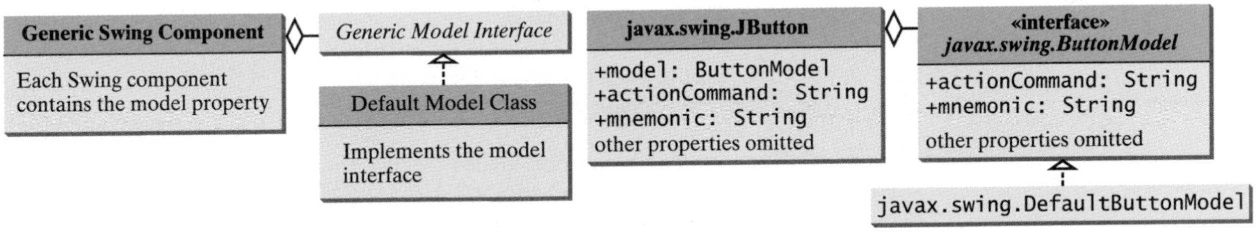
Generic Swing Component
Each Swing component contains the model property
Generic Model Interface
Default Model Class
Implements the model interface
javax.swing.JButton
+model: ButtonModel
+actionCommand: String
+mnemonic: String
other properties omitted
«interface»
javax.swing.ButtonModel
+actionCommand: String
+mnemonic: String
other properties omitted
javax.swing.DefaultButtonModel

(a) Generic Swing model-view architecture (b) `JButton` model-view implementation

FIGURE 35.6 Swing components are implemented using the MVC architecture.

For convenience, most Swing components contain some properties of their models, and these properties can be accessed and modified directly from the component without the existence of the model being known. For example, the properties `actionCommand` and `mnemonic` are defined in both `ButtonModel` and `JButton`. Actually, these properties are in the `AbstractButton` class. Since `JButton` is a subclass of `AbstractButton`, it inherits all the properties from `AbstractButton`.

When you create a Swing component without specifying a model, a default data model is assigned to the `model` property. For example, lines 9–10 in the following code set the `actionCommand` and `mnemonic` properties of a button through its model.

```
1 public class TestSwingModel1 {
2   public static void main(String[] args) {
3     javax.swing.JButton jbt = new javax.swing.JButton();
4
5     // Obtain the default model from the component
6     javax.swing.ButtonModel model = jbt.getModel();
7
8     // Set properties in the model
9     model.setActionCommand("OK");
10    model.setMnemonic('O');
11
```

get model

set model properties

```
    // Display the property values from the component
    System.out.println("actionCommand is " + jbt.getActionCommand());
    System.out.println("mnemonic is " + (char)(jbt.getMnemonic()));
  }
}
```

```
actionCommand is OK
mnemonic is O
```

You can also create a new model and assign it to a Swing component. For example, the following code creates an instance of **ButtonModel** (line 7) and assigns it to an instance of **JButton** (line 14).

create model

set model properties

set a new model

```
1 public class TestSwingModel2 {
2   public static void main(String[] args) {
3     javax.swing.JButton jbt = new javax.swing.JButton();
4
5     // Create a new button model
6     javax.swing.ButtonModel model =
7       new javax.swing.DefaultButtonModel();
8
9     // Set properties in the model
10    model.setActionCommand("Cancel");
11    model.setMnemonic('C');
12
13    // Assign the model to the button
14    jbt.setModel(model);
15
16    // Display the property values from the component
17    System.out.println("actionCommand is " + jbt.getActionCommand());
18    System.out.println("mnemonic is " + (char)jbt.getMnemonic());
19  }
20 }
```

```
actionCommand is Cancel
mnemonic is C
```

It is unnecessary to use the models for simple Swing components, such as **JButton**, **JToggleButton**, **JCheckBox**, **JRadioButton**, **JTextField**, and **JTextArea**, because the frequently used properties in the models of these Swing components are also the properties in these components. You can access and modify these properties directly through the components. For advanced components, such as **JSpinner**, **JList**, **JComboBox**, **JTable**, and **JTree**, you have to work with their models to store, access, and modify data.

35.5 JSpinner

A spinner is a text field with a pair of tiny arrow buttons on its right side that enable the user to select numbers, dates, or values from an ordered sequence, as shown in Figure 35.7. The keyboard up/down arrow keys also cycle through the elements. The user may also be allowed to type a (legal) value directly into the spinner. A spinner is similar to a combo box but is sometimes preferred because it doesn't require a drop-down list that can obscure important data.

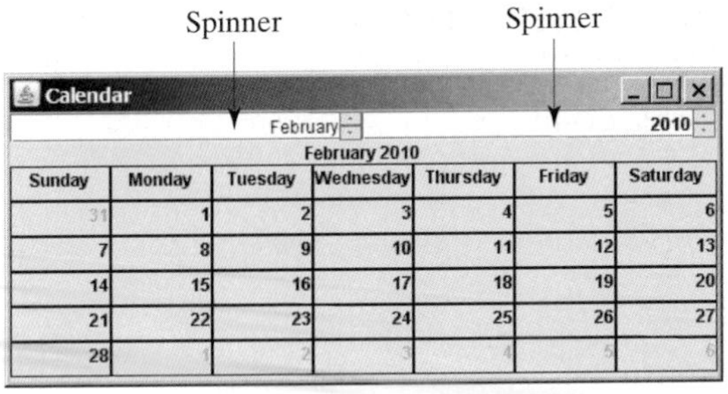
Spinner
Spinner
Calendar
February
2010
February 2010
Sunday
Monday
Tuesday
Wednesday
Thursday
Friday
Saturday

FIGURE 35.7 Two `JSpinner` components enable the user to select a month and a year for the calendar.

Figure 35.8 shows the constructors and commonly used methods in `JSpinner`. A `JSpinner`'s sequence value is defined by the `SpinnerModel` interface, which manages a potentially unbounded sequence of elements. The model doesn't support indexed random access to sequence elements. Only three sequence elements are accessible at a time—current, next, and previous—using the methods `getValue()`, `getNextValue()`, and `getPreviousValue()`, respectively. The current sequence element can be modified using the `setValue` method. When the current value in a spinner is changed, the model invokes the `stateChanged(javax.swing.event.ChangeEvent e)` method of the registered listeners. The listeners must implement `javax.swing.event.ChangeListener`. All these methods in `SpinnerModel` are also defined in `JSpinner` for convenience, so you can access the data in the model from `JSpinner` directly.

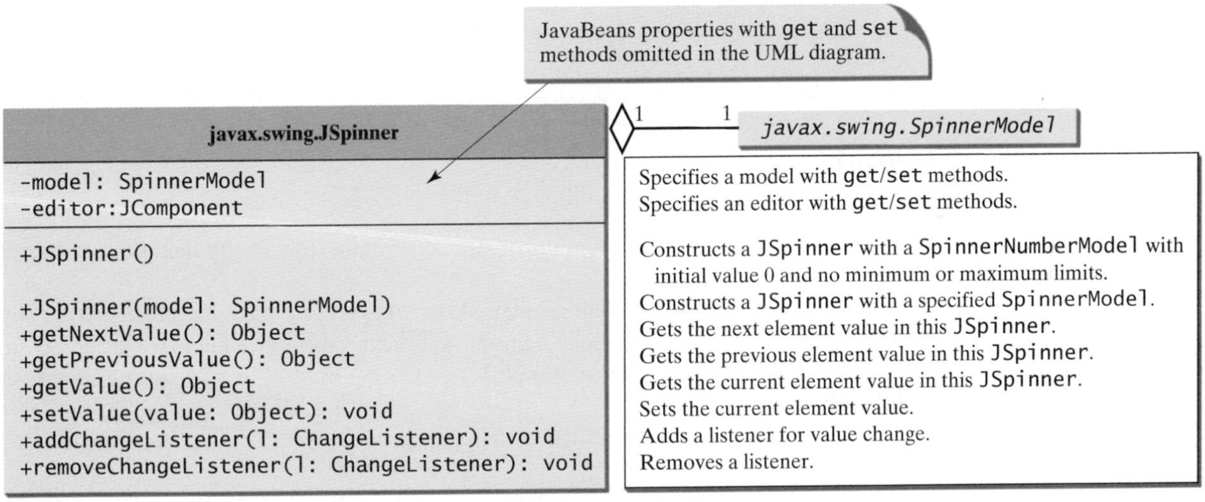
JavaBeans properties with get and set methods omitted in the UML diagram.
javax.swing.JSpinner
-model: SpinnerModel
-editor:JComponent
+JSpinner()
+JSpinner(model: SpinnerModel)
+getNextValue(): Object
+getPreviousValue(): Object
+getValue(): Object
+setValue(value: Object): void
+addChangeListener(l: ChangeListener): void
+removeChangeListener(l: ChangeListener): void
1
1
javax.swing.SpinnerModel
Specifies a model with get/set methods.
Specifies an editor with get/set methods.
Constructs a JSpinner with a SpinnerNumberModel with initial value 0 and no minimum or maximum limits.
Constructs a JSpinner with a specified SpinnerModel.
Gets the next element value in this JSpinner.
Gets the previous element value in this JSpinner.
Gets the current element value in this JSpinner.
Sets the current element value.
Adds a listener for value change.
Removes a listener.

FIGURE 35.8 `JSpinner` uses a spinner model to store data.

Note

If you create a `JSpinner` object without specifying a model, the spinner displays a sequence of integers.

Listing 35.5 gives an example that creates a `JSpinner` object for a sequence of numbers and displays the previous, current, and next numbers from the spinner on a label, as shown in Figure 35.9.

LISTING 35.5 SimpleSpinner.java

spinner

spinner listener

main method omitted

```
1 import javax.swing.*;
2 import javax.swing.event.*;
3 import java.awt.BorderLayout;
4
5 public class SimpleSpinner extends JApplet {
6   // Create a JSpinner
7   private JSpinner spinner = new JSpinner();
8
9   // Create a JLabel
10  private JLabel label = new JLabel("", JLabel.CENTER);
11
12  public SimpleSpinner() {
13    // Add spinner and label to the UI
14    add(spinner, BorderLayout.NORTH);
15    add(label, BorderLayout.CENTER);
16
17    // Register and create a listener
18    spinner.addChangeListener(new ChangeListener() {
19      public void stateChanged(javax.swing.event.ChangeEvent e) {
20        label.setText("Previous value: " + spinner.getPreviousValue()
21          + " Current value: " + spinner.getValue()
22          + " Next value: " + spinner.getNextValue());
23      }
24    });
25  }
26 }
```

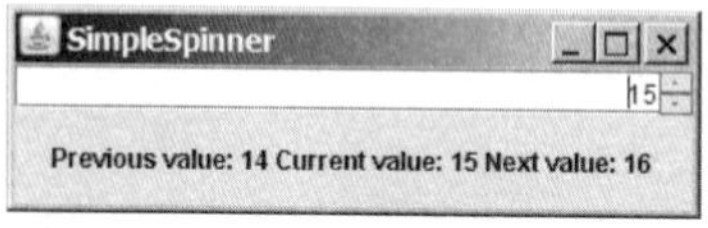
SimpleSpinner
15
Previous value: 14 Current value: 15 Next value: 16

FIGURE 35.9 The previous, current, and next values in the spinner are displayed on the label.

A `JSpinner` object is created using its no-arg constructor (line 7). By default, a spinner displays a sequence of integers.

An anonymous inner class event adapter is created to process the value change event on the spinner (lines 18–24). The previous, current, and next values in a spinner can be obtained using the `JSpinner`'s instance methods `getPreviousValue()`, `getValue()`, and `getNextValue()`.

To display a sequence of values other than integers, you have to use spinner models.

35.6 Spinner Models and Editors

`SpinnerModel` is an interface for all spinner models. `AbstractSpinnerModel` is a convenient abstract class that implements `SpinnerModel` and provides the implementation for its registration/deregistration methods. `SpinnerListModel`, `SpinnerNumberModel`, and `SpinnerDateModel` are concrete implementations of `SpinnerModel`. The relationship among them is illustrated in Figure 35.10. Besides these models, you can create a custom spinner model that extends `AbstractSpinnerModel` or directly implements `SpinnerModel`.

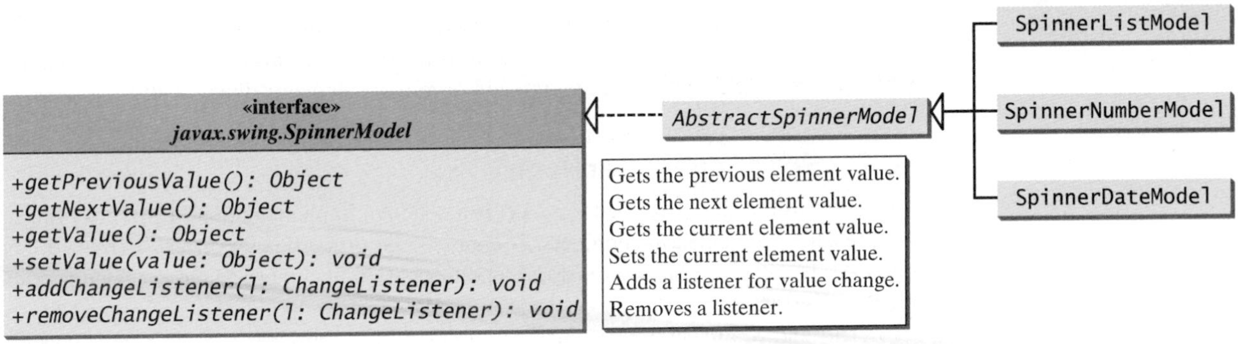
«interface»
javax.swing.SpinnerModel
+getPreviousValue(): Object
+getNextValue(): Object
+getValue(): Object
+setValue(value: Object): void
+addChangeListener(l: ChangeListener): void
+removeChangeListener(l: ChangeListener): void
Gets the previous element value.
Gets the next element value.
Gets the current element value.
Sets the current element value.
Adds a listener for value change.
Removes a listener.
AbstractSpinnerModel
SpinnerListModel
SpinnerNumberModel
SpinnerDateModel

FIGURE 35.10 `SpinnerListModel`, `SpinnerNumberModel`, and `SpinnerDateModel` are concrete implementations for `SpinnerModel`.

35.6.1 `SpinnerListModel`

`SpinnerListModel` (see Figure 35.11) is a simple implementation of `SpinnerModel` whose values are stored in a `java.util.List`.

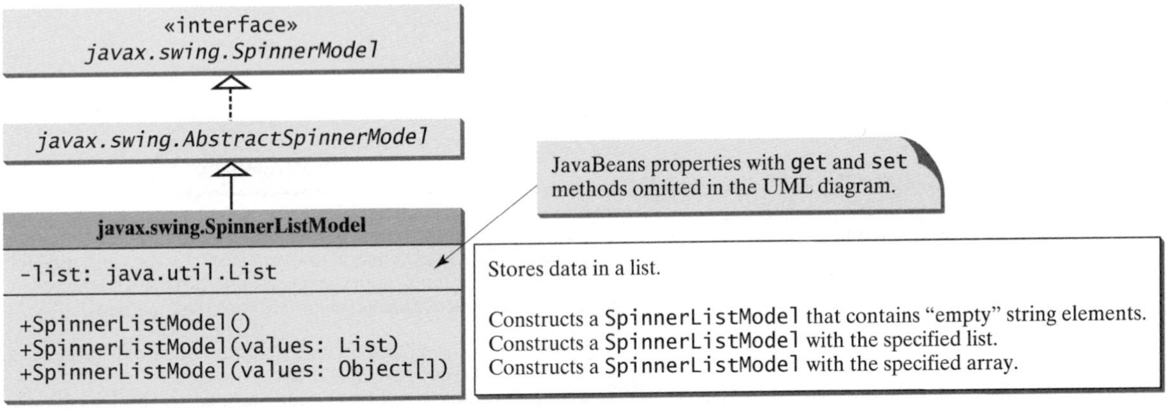
«interface»
javax.swing.SpinnerModel
javax.swing.AbstractSpinnerModel
javax.swing.SpinnerListModel
-list: java.util.List
+SpinnerListModel()
+SpinnerListModel(values: List)
+SpinnerListModel(values: Object[])
JavaBeans properties with get and set methods omitted in the UML diagram.
Stores data in a list.
Constructs a SpinnerListModel that contains "empty" string elements.
Constructs a SpinnerListModel with the specified list.
Constructs a SpinnerListModel with the specified array.

FIGURE 35.11 `SpinnerListModel` uses a `java.util.List` to store a sequence of data in the model.

You can create a `SpinnerListModel` using an array or a list. For example, the following code creates a model that consists of values Freshman, Sophomore, Junior, Senior, and Graduate in an array.

```
// Create an array
String[] grades = {"Freshman", "Sophomore", "Junior",
  "Senior", "Graduate"};

// Create a model from an array
model = new SpinnerListModel(grades);
```

Alternatively, the following code creates a model using a list:

```
// Create an array
String[] grades = {"Freshman", "Sophomore", "Junior",
  "Senior", "Graduate"};

// Create an ArrayList from the array
list = new ArrayList(Arrays.asList(grades));

// Create a model from the list
model = new SpinnerListModel(list);
```

The alternative code seems unnecessary. However, it is useful if you need to add or remove elements from the model. The size of the array is fixed once the array is created. The list is a flexible data structure that enables you to add or remove elements dynamically.

35.6.2 SpinnerNumberModel

SpinnerNumberModel (see Figure 35.12) is a concrete implementation of SpinnerModel that represents a sequence of numbers. It contains the properties maximum, minimum, and stepSize. The maximum and minimum properties specify the upper and lower bounds of the sequence. The stepSize specifies the size of the increase or decrease computed by the nextValue and previousValue methods defined in SpinnerModel. The minimum and maximum properties can be null to indicate that the sequence has no lower or upper limit. All of the properties in this class are defined as Number or Comparable, so that all Java numeric types may be accommodated.

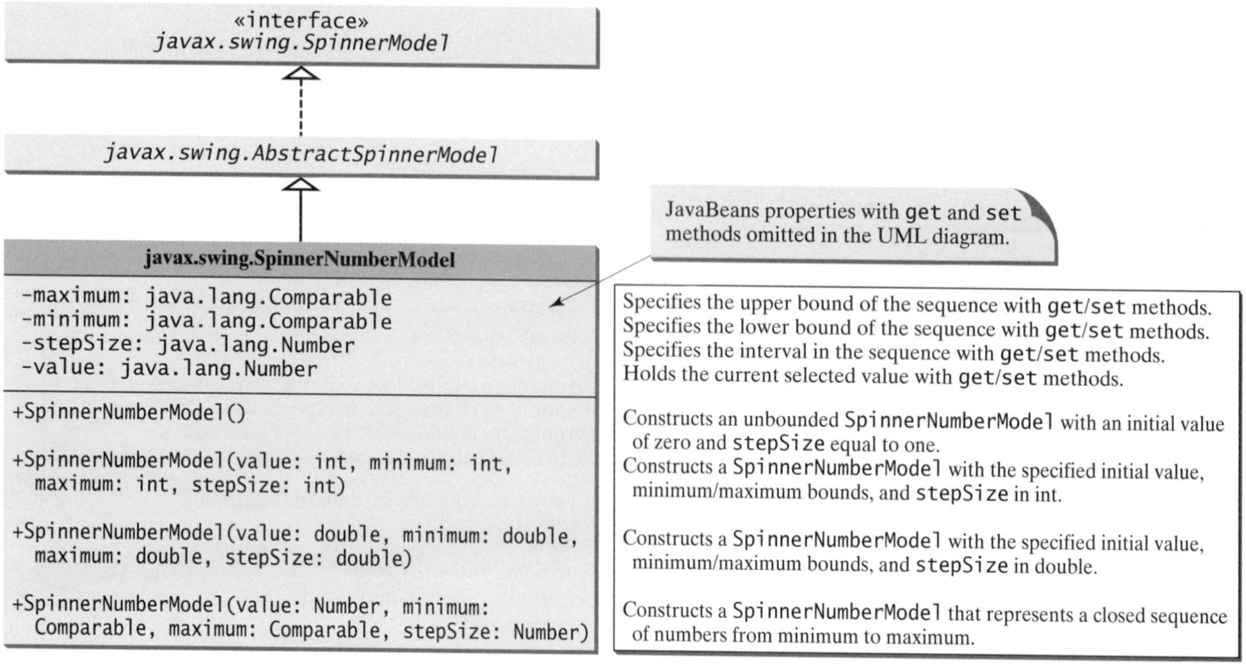
«interface»
javax.swing.SpinnerModel
javax.swing.AbstractSpinnerModel
JavaBeans properties with get and set methods omitted in the UML diagram.
javax.swing.SpinnerNumberModel
-maximum: java.lang.Comparable
-minimum: java.lang.Comparable
-stepSize: java.lang.Number
-value: java.lang.Number
+SpinnerNumberModel()
+SpinnerNumberModel(value: int, minimum: int, maximum: int, stepSize: int)
+SpinnerNumberModel(value: double, minimum: double, maximum: double, stepSize: double)
+SpinnerNumberModel(value: Number, minimum: Comparable, maximum: Comparable, stepSize: Number)
Specifies the upper bound of the sequence with get/set methods.
Specifies the lower bound of the sequence with get/set methods.
Specifies the interval in the sequence with get/set methods.
Holds the current selected value with get/set methods.
Constructs an unbounded SpinnerNumberModel with an initial value of zero and stepSize equal to one.
Constructs a SpinnerNumberModel with the specified initial value, minimum/maximum bounds, and stepSize in int.
Constructs a SpinnerNumberModel with the specified initial value, minimum/maximum bounds, and stepSize in double.
Constructs a SpinnerNumberModel that represents a closed sequence of numbers from minimum to maximum.

FIGURE 35.12 SpinnerNumberModel represents a sequence of numbers.

You can create a SpinnerNumberModel with integers or double. For example, the following code creates a model that represents a sequence of numbers from 0 to 3000 with initial value 2004 and interval 1.

```
// Create a spinner number model
SpinnerNumberModel model = new SpinnerNumberModel(2004, 0, 3000, 1);
```

The following code creates a model that represents a sequence of numbers from 0 to 120 with initial value 50 and interval 0.1.

```
// Create a spinner number model
SpinnerNumberModel model = new SpinnerNumberModel(50, 0, 120, 0.1);
```

35.6.3 SpinnerDateModel

`SpinnerDateModel` (see Figure 35.13) is a concrete implementation of `SpinnerModel` that represents a sequence of dates. The upper and lower bounds of the sequence are defined by properties called `start` and `end`, and the size of the increase or decrease computed by the `nextValue` and `previousValue` methods is defined by a property called `calendarField`. The `start` and `end` properties can be `null` to indicate that the sequence has no lower or upper limit. The value of the `calendarField` property must be one of the `java.util.Calendar` constants that specify a field within a `Calendar`. The `getNextValue` and `getPreviousValue` methods change the date forward or backward by this amount. For example, if `calendarField` is `Calendar.DAY_OF_WEEK`, then `nextValue` produces a date that is 24 hours after the current value, and `previousValue` produces a date that is 24 hours earlier.

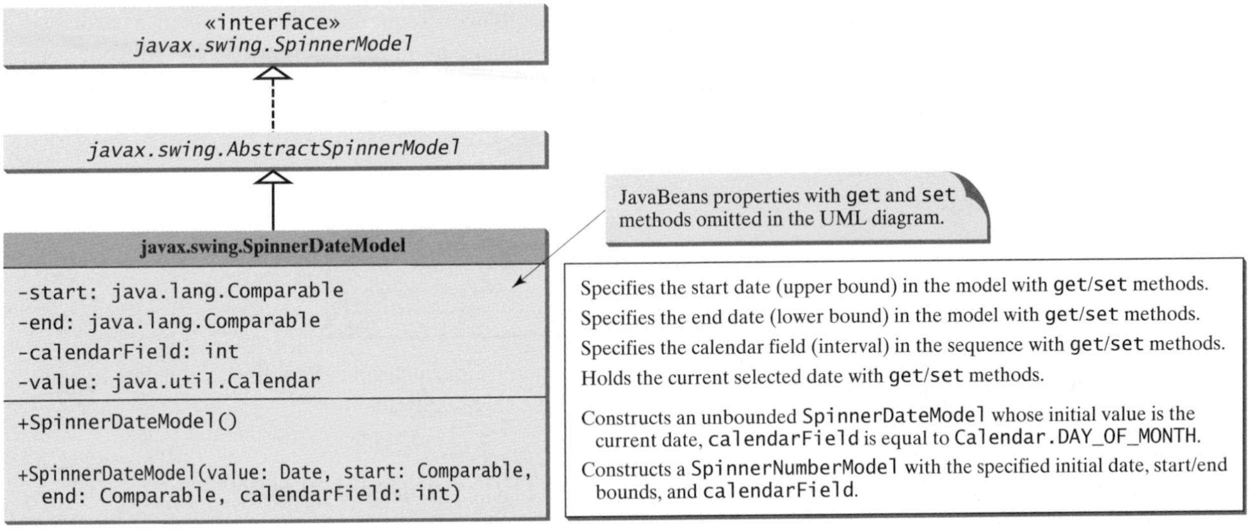
«interface»
javax.swing.SpinnerModel
javax.swing.AbstractSpinnerModel
JavaBeans properties with get and set methods omitted in the UML diagram.
javax.swing.SpinnerDateModel
-start: java.lang.Comparable
-end: java.lang.Comparable
-calendarField: int
-value: java.util.Calendar
+SpinnerDateModel()
+SpinnerDateModel(value: Date, start: Comparable, end: Comparable, calendarField: int)
Specifies the start date (upper bound) in the model with get/set methods.
Specifies the end date (lower bound) in the model with get/set methods.
Specifies the calendar field (interval) in the sequence with get/set methods.
Holds the current selected date with get/set methods.
Constructs an unbounded SpinnerDateModel whose initial value is the current date, calendarField is equal to Calendar.DAY_OF_MONTH.
Constructs a SpinnerNumberModel with the specified initial date, start/end bounds, and calendarField.

FIGURE 35.13 `SpinnerDateModel` represents a sequence of dates.

For example, the following code creates a spinner model that represents a sequence of dates, starting from the current date without a lower/upper limit and with calendar field on month.

```
SpinnerDateModel model = new SpinnerDateModel(new Date(), null, null,
  Calendar.MONTH);
```

35.6.4 Spinner Editors

A `JSpinner` has a single child component, called the *editor*, which is responsible for displaying the current element or value of the model. Four editors are defined as static inner classes inside `JSpinner`.

- **`JSpinner.DefaultEditor`** is a simple base class for all other specialized editors to display a read-only view of the model's current value with a `JFormattedTextField`. `JFormattedTextField` extends `JTextField`, adding support for formatting arbitrary values, as well as retrieving a particular object once the user has edited the text.
- **`JSpinner.NumberEditor`** is a specialized editor for a `JSpinner` whose model is a `SpinnerNumberModel`. The value of the editor is displayed with a `JFormattedTextField` whose format is defined by a `NumberFormatter` instance.
- **`JSpinner.DateEditor`** is a specialized editor for a `JSpinner` whose model is a `SpinnerDateModel`. The value of the editor is displayed with a `JFormattedTextField` whose format is defined by a `DateFormatter` instance.

- **JSpinner.ListEditor** is a specialized editor for a JSpinner whose model is a SpinnerListModel. The value of the editor is displayed with a JFormattedTextField.

The JSpinner's constructor creates a NumberEditor for SpinnerNumberModel, a DateEditor for SpinnerDateModel, a ListEditor for SpinnerListModel, and a DefaultEditor for all other models. The editor can also be changed using the setEditor method. The JSpinner's editor stays in sync with the model by listening for ChangeEvents. The commitEdit() method should be used to commit the currently edited value to the model.

35.6.5 Example: Using Spinner Models and Editors

This example uses a JSpinner component to display the date and three other JSpinner components to display the day in a sequence of numbers, the month in a sequence of strings, and the year in a sequence of numbers, as shown in Figure 35.14. All four components are synchronized. For example, if you change the year in the spinner for year, the date value in the date spinner is updated accordingly. The source code of the example is given in Listing 35.6.

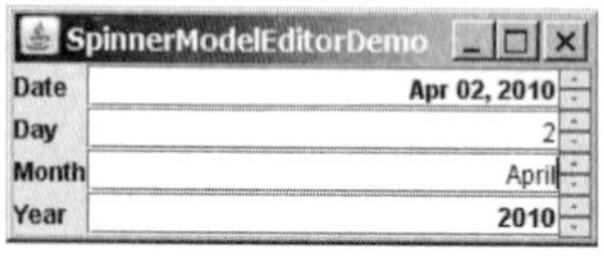
SpinnerModelEditorDemo
Date
Apr 02, 2010
Day
2
Month
April
Year
2010

FIGURE 35.14 The four spinner components are synchronized to display the date in one field and the day, month, and year in three separate fields.

LISTING 35.6 SpinnerModelEditorDemo.java

spinners

create UI

```java
import javax.swing.*;
import javax.swing.event.*;
import java.util.*;
import java.text.*;
import java.awt.*;

public class SpinnerModelEditorDemo extends JApplet {
  // Create four spinners for date, day, month, and year
  private JSpinner jspDate =
    new JSpinner(new SpinnerDateModel());
  private JSpinner jspDay =
    new JSpinner(new SpinnerNumberModel(1, 1, 31, 1));
  private String[] monthNames = new DateFormatSymbols().getMonths();
  private JSpinner jspMonth = new JSpinner
    (new SpinnerListModel(Arrays.asList(monthNames).subList(0, 12)));
  private JSpinner spinnerYear =
    new JSpinner(new SpinnerNumberModel(2004, 1, 3000, 1));

  public SpinnerModelEditorDemo() {
    // Group labels
    JPanel panel1 = new JPanel();
    panel1.setLayout(new GridLayout(4, 1));
    panel1.add(new JLabel("Date"));
    panel1.add(new JLabel("Day"));
    panel1.add(new JLabel("Month"));
    panel1.add(new JLabel("Year"));

```

```
    // Group spinners
    JPanel panel2 = new JPanel();
    panel2.setLayout(new GridLayout(4, 1));
    panel2.add(jspDate);
    panel2.add(jspDay);
    panel2.add(jspMonth);
    panel2.add(spinnerYear);

    // Add spinner and label to the UI
    add(panel1, BorderLayout.WEST);
    add(panel2, BorderLayout.CENTER);

    // Set editor for date
    JSpinner.DateEditor dateEditor =
      new JSpinner.DateEditor(jspDate, "MMM dd, yyyy");
    jspDate.setEditor(dateEditor);

    // Set editor for year
    JSpinner.NumberEditor yearEditor =
      new JSpinner.NumberEditor(spinnerYear, "####");
    spinnerYear.setEditor(yearEditor);

    // Update date to synchronize with the day, month, and year
    updateDate();

    // Register and create a listener for jspDay
    jspDay.addChangeListener(new ChangeListener() {
      public void stateChanged(javax.swing.event.ChangeEvent e) {
        updateDate();
      }
    });

    // Register and create a listener for jspMonth
    jspMonth.addChangeListener(new ChangeListener() {
      public void stateChanged(javax.swing.event.ChangeEvent e) {
        updateDate();
      }
    });

    // Register and create a listener for spinnerYear
    spinnerYear.addChangeListener(new ChangeListener() {
      public void stateChanged(javax.swing.event.ChangeEvent e) {
        updateDate();
      }
    });
  }

  /** Update date spinner to synchronize with the other spinners */
  private void updateDate() {
    // Get current month and year in int
    int month = ((SpinnerListModel)jspMonth.getModel()).
        getList().indexOf(jspMonth.getValue());
    int year = ((Integer)spinnerYear.getValue()).intValue();

    // Set a new maximum number of days for the new month and year
    SpinnerNumberModel numberModel =
      (SpinnerNumberModel)jspDay.getModel();
    numberModel.setMaximum(new Integer(maxDaysInMonth(year, month)));

```

date editor

number editor

spinner listener

spinner listener

spinner listener

```
87      // Set a new current day if it exceeds the maximum
88      if (((Integer)(numberModel.getValue())).intValue() >
89          maxDaysInMonth(year, month))
90        numberModel.setValue(new Integer(maxDaysInMonth(year, month)));
91
92      // Get the current day
93      int day = ((Integer)jspDay.getValue()).intValue();
94
95      // Set a new date in the date spinner
96      jspDate.setValue(
97        new GregorianCalendar(year, month, day).getTime());
98    }
99
100   /** Return the maximum number of days in a month. For example,
101     Feb 2004 has 29 days. */
102   private int maxDaysInMonth(int year, int month) {
103     Calendar calendar = new GregorianCalendar(year, month, 1);
104     return calendar.getActualMaximum(Calendar.DAY_OF_MONTH);
105   }
106 }
```

main method omitted

A `JSpinner` object for dates, `jspDate`, is created with a default `SpinnerDateModel` (lines 9–10). The format of the date displayed in the spinner is MMM dd, yyyy (e.g., Feb 01, 2006). This format is created using the `JSpinner`'s inner class constructor `DateEditor` (lines 41–42) and is set as `jspDate`'s editor (line 43).

A `JSpinner` object for days, `jspDay`, is created with a `SpinnerNumberModel` with a sequence of integers between `1` and `31` in which the initial value is `1` and the interval is `1` (lines 11–12). The maximum number is reset in the `updateDate()` method based on the current month and year (lines 88–90). For example, February 2004 has 29 days, so the maximum in `jspDay` is set to 29 for February 2004.

A `JSpinner` object for months, `jspMonth`, is created with a `SpinnerListModel` with a list of month names (lines 14–15). Month names are locale specific and can be obtained using the `new DateFormatSymbols().getMonths()` (line 13). Some calendars can have 13 months. `Arrays.asList(monthNames)` creates a list from an array of strings, and `subList(0, 12)` returns the first 12 elements in the list.

A `JSpinner` object for years, `spinnerYear`, is created with a `SpinnerNumberModel` with a sequence of integers between `1` and `3000` in which the initial value is 2004 and the interval is 1 (lines 16–17). By default, locale-specific number separators are used. For example, 2004 would be displayed as 2,004 in the spinner. To display the number without separators, the number pattern #### is specified to construct a new `NumberEditor` for `spinnerYear` (lines 46–47). The editor is set as `spinnerYear`'s editor (line 48).

The `updateDate()` method synchronizes the date spinner with the day, month, and year spinners. Whenever a new value is selected in the day, month, or year spinner, a new date is set in the date spinner. The `maxDaysInMonth` method (lines 102–105) returns the maximum number of days in a month. For example, February 2004 has 29 days.

A `JSpinner` object can fire `javax.swing.event.ChangeEvent` to notify the listeners of the state change in the spinner. The anonymous event adapters are created to process spinner state changes for the day, month, and year spinners (lines 54–73). Whenever a new value is selected in one of these three spinners, the date spinner value is updated accordingly. In Exercise 35.3, you will improve the example to synchronize the day, month, and year spinners with the date spinner. Then, when a new value is selected in the date spinner, the values in the day, month, and year spinners will be updated accordingly.

This example uses `SpinnerNumberModel`, `SpinnerDateModel`, and `SpinnerListModel`. They are predefined concrete spinner models in the API. You can also create custom spinner models (see Exercise 35.4).

35.7 JList and Its Models

The basic features of JList were introduced in §17.9, "Lists," without using list models. You learned how to create a list and how to respond to list selections. However, you cannot add or remove elements from a list without using list models. This section introduces list models and gives a detailed discussion on how to use JList.

JList has two supporting models: a list model and a list-selection model. The *list model* is for storing and processing data. The *list-selection model* is for selecting items. By default, items are rendered as strings or icons. You can also define a custom renderer that implements the ListCellRenderer interface. The relationship of these interfaces and classes is shown in Figure 35.15.

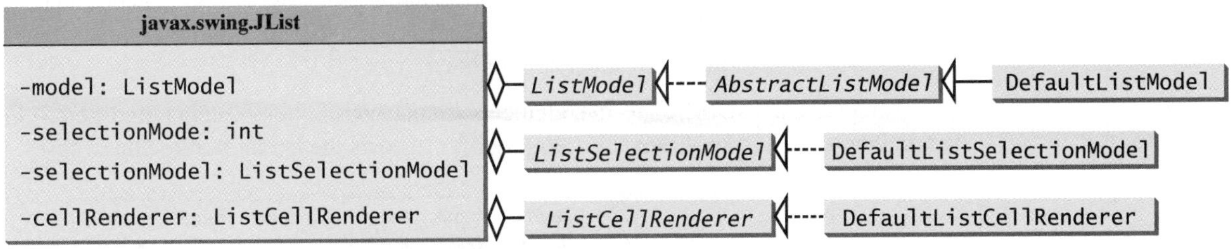
javax.swing.JList
-model: ListModel
-selectionMode: int
-selectionModel: ListSelectionModel
-cellRenderer: ListCellRenderer
ListModel
AbstractListModel
DefaultListModel
ListSelectionModel
DefaultListSelectionModel
ListCellRenderer
DefaultListCellRenderer

FIGURE 35.15 JList contains several supporting interfaces and classes.

35.7.1 JList Constructors, Properties, and Methods

Figure 35.16 shows the properties and constructors of JList. You can create a list from a list model, an array of objects, or a vector.

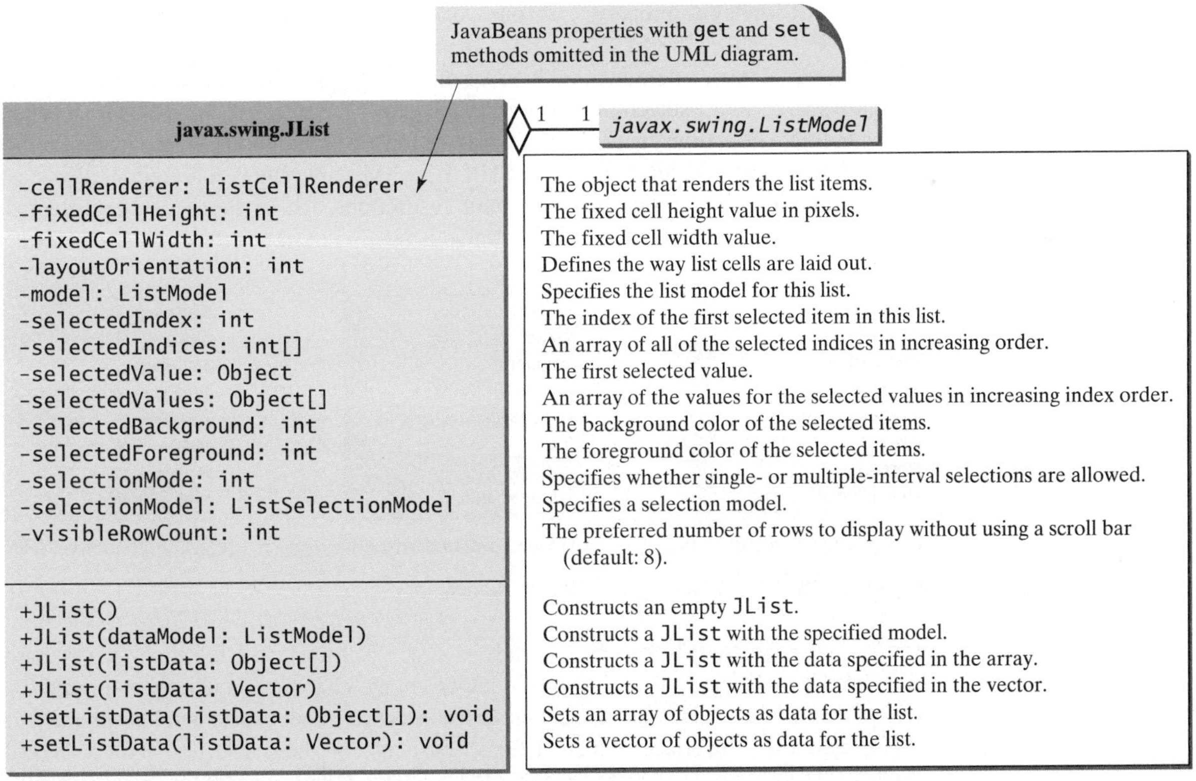
JavaBeans properties with get and set methods omitted in the UML diagram.
javax.swing.JList
1
1
javax.swing.ListModel
-cellRenderer: ListCellRenderer
-fixedCellHeight: int
-fixedCellWidth: int
-layoutOrientation: int
-model: ListModel
-selectedIndex: int
-selectedIndices: int[]
-selectedValue: Object
-selectedValues: Object[]
-selectedBackground: int
-selectedForeground: int
-selectionMode: int
-selectionModel: ListSelectionModel
-visibleRowCount: int
+JList()
+JList(dataModel: ListModel)
+JList(listData: Object[])
+JList(listData: Vector)
+setListData(listData: Object[]): void
+setListData(listData: Vector): void
The object that renders the list items.
The fixed cell height value in pixels.
The fixed cell width value.
Defines the way list cells are laid out.
Specifies the list model for this list.
The index of the first selected item in this list.
An array of all of the selected indices in increasing order.
The first selected value.
An array of the values for the selected values in increasing index order.
The background color of the selected items.
The foreground color of the selected items.
Specifies whether single- or multiple-interval selections are allowed.
Specifies a selection model.
The preferred number of rows to display without using a scroll bar (default: 8).
Constructs an empty JList.
Constructs a JList with the specified model.
Constructs a JList with the data specified in the array.
Constructs a JList with the data specified in the vector.
Sets an array of objects as data for the list.
Sets a vector of objects as data for the list.

FIGURE 35.16 JList displays elements in a list.

35.7.2 List Layout Orientations

The `layoutOrientation` property specifies the layout of the items using one of the following three values:

- `JList.VERTICAL` specifies that the cells should be laid out vertically in one column. This is the default value.
- `JList.HORIZONTAL_WRAP` specifies that the cells should be laid out horizontally, wrapping to a new row as necessary. The number of rows to use is determined by the `visibleRowCount` property if its value is greater than `0`; otherwise the number of rows is determined by the width of the `JList`.
- `JList.VERTICAL_WRAP` specifies that the cells should be laid out vertically, wrapping to a new column as necessary. The number of rows to use is determined by the `visibleRowCount` property if its value is greater than `0`; otherwise the number of rows is determined by the height of the `JList`.

For example, suppose there are five elements (item1, item2, item3, item4, and item5) in the list and the `visibleRowCount` is 2. Figure 35.17 shows the layout in these three cases.

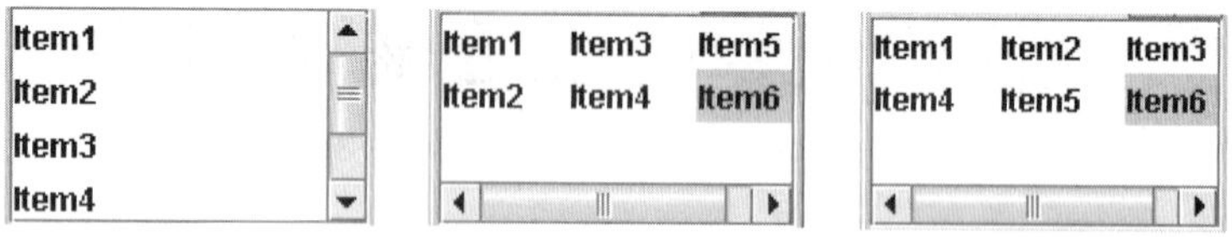
Item1
Item2
Item3
Item4
Item1 Item3 Item5
Item2 Item4 Item6
Item1 Item2 Item3
Item4 Item5 Item6

(a) Vertical (b) Vertical wrap (c) Horizontal wrap

FIGURE 35.17 Layout orientation specifies how elements are laid out in a list.

35.7.3 List-Selection Modes and List-Selection Models

The **`selectionMode`** property is one of the three values (`SINGLE_SELECTION`, `SINGLE_INTERVAL_SELECTION`, `MULTIPLE_INTERVAL_SELECTION`) that indicate whether a single item, single-interval item, or multiple-interval item can be selected, as shown in Figure 35.18. Single selection allows only one item to be selected. Single-interval selection allows multiple selections, but the selected items must be contiguous. These items can be selected all together by holding down the SHIFT key. Multiple-interval selection allows selections of multiple contiguous items without restrictions. These items can be selected by holding down the CTRL key. The default value is `MULTIPLE_INTERVAL_SELECTION`.

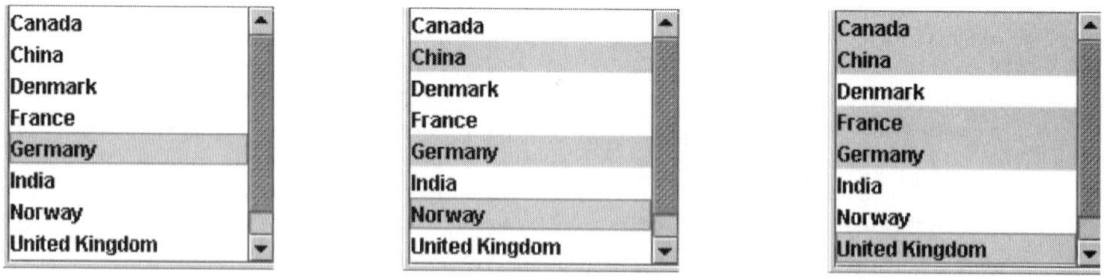
Canada
China
Denmark
France
Germany
India
Norway
United Kingdom

(a) Single selection (b) Single-interval selection (c) Multiple-interval selection

FIGURE 35.18 A list has three selection modes.

The **`selectionModel`** property specifies an object that tracks list selection. `JList` has two models: a list model and a list-selection model. *List models* handle data management, and *list-selection models* deal with data selection. A list-selection model must implement the `ListSelectionModel` interface, which defines constants for three selection modes (`SINGLE_SELECTION`, `SINGLE_INTERVAL_SELECTION`, and `MULTIPLE_INTERVAL_SELECTION`), and registration methods for `ListSectionListener`. It also defines the methods for adding and removing selection intervals, and the access methods for the properties, such as `selectionMode`, `anchorSelectionIndex`, `leadSelectionIndex`, and `valueIsAdjusting`.

By default, an instance of `JList` uses `DefaultListSelectionModel`, which is a concrete implementation of `ListSelectionModel`. Usually, you do not need to provide a custom list-selection model, because the `DefaultListSelectionModel` class is sufficient in most cases. List-selection models are rarely used explicitly, because you can set the selection mode directly in `JList`.

35.7.4 Example: List Properties Demo

This example creates a list of a fixed number of items displayed as strings. The example enables you to dynamically set `visibleRowCount` from a spinner, `layoutOrientation` from a combo box, and `selectionMode` from a combo box, as shown in Figure 35.19. When you select one or more items, their values are displayed in a status label below the list. The source code of the example is given in Listing 35.7.

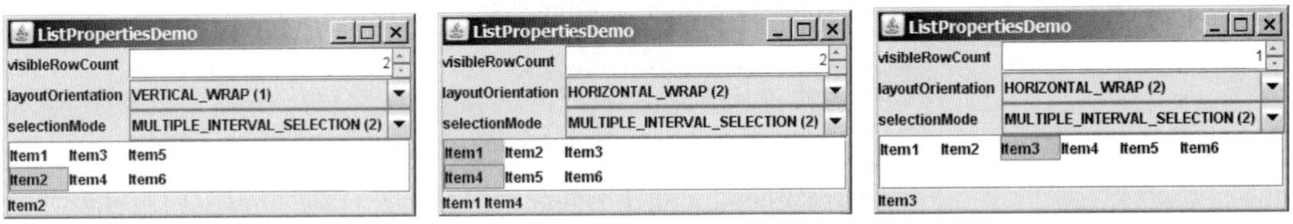

ListPropertiesDemo
visibleRowCount
layoutOrientation
selectionMode
VERTICAL_WRAP (1)
HORIZONTAL_WRAP (2)
MULTIPLE_INTERVAL_SELECTION (2)
Item1 Item2 Item3 Item4 Item5 Item6
Item2
Item1 Item4
Item3

FIGURE 35.19 You can dynamically set the properties for `visibleRowCount`, `layoutOrientation`, and `selectionMode` in a list.

LISTING 35.7 ListPropertiesDemo.java

```
import java.awt.*;
import java.awt.event.*;
import javax.swing.*;
import javax.swing.event.*;

public class ListPropertiesDemo extends JApplet {
  private JList jlst = new JList(new String[] {"Item1",
    "Item2", "Item3", "Item4", "Item5", "Item6"});
  private JSpinner jspVisibleRowCount =
    new JSpinner(new SpinnerNumberModel(8, -1, 20, 1));
  private JComboBox jcboLayoutOrientation =
    new JComboBox(new String[]{"VERTICAL (0)",
      "VERTICAL_WRAP (1)", "HORIZONTAL_WRAP (2)"});
  private JComboBox jcboSelectionMode =
    new JComboBox(new String[]{"SINGLE_SELECTION (0)",
      "SINGLE_INTERVAL_SELECTION (1)",
      "MULTIPLE_INTERVAL_SELECTION (2)"});
  private JLabel jlblStatus = new JLabel();

  /** Construct the applet */
  public ListPropertiesDemo() {
    // Place labels in a panel
    JPanel panel1 = new JPanel();
    panel1.setLayout(new GridLayout(3, 1));
    panel1.add(new JLabel("visibleRowCount"));
    panel1.add(new JLabel("layoutOrientation"));
    panel1.add(new JLabel("selectionMode"));

```

list
spinner
combo box
combo box
create UI

```
    // Place text fields in a panel
    JPanel panel2 = new JPanel();
    panel2.setLayout(new GridLayout(3, 1));
    panel2.add(jspVisibleRowCount);
    panel2.add(jcboLayoutOrientation);
    panel2.add(jcboSelectionMode);

    // Place panel1 and panel2
    JPanel panel3 = new JPanel();
    panel3.setLayout(new BorderLayout(5, 5));
    panel3.add(panel1, BorderLayout.WEST);
    panel3.add(panel2, BorderLayout.CENTER);

    // Place elements in the applet
    add(panel3, BorderLayout.NORTH);
    add(new JScrollPane(jlst), BorderLayout.CENTER);
    add(jlblStatus, BorderLayout.SOUTH);

    // Set initial property values
    jlst.setFixedCellWidth(50);
    jlst.setFixedCellHeight(20);
    jlst.setSelectionMode(ListSelectionModel.SINGLE_SELECTION);

    // Register listeners
```

spinner listener

```
    jspVisibleRowCount.addChangeListener(new ChangeListener() {
      public void stateChanged(ChangeEvent e) {
        jlst.setVisibleRowCount(
          ((Integer)jspVisibleRowCount.getValue()).intValue());
      }
    });

```

combo box listener

```
    jcboLayoutOrientation.addActionListener(new ActionListener() {
      public void actionPerformed(ActionEvent e) {
        jlst.setLayoutOrientation(
          jcboLayoutOrientation.getSelectedIndex());
      }
    });

```

combo box listener

```
    jcboSelectionMode.addActionListener(new ActionListener() {
      public void actionPerformed(ActionEvent e) {
        jlst.setSelectionMode(
          jcboSelectionMode.getSelectedIndex());
      }
    });

```

list listener

```
    jlst.addListSelectionListener(new ListSelectionListener() {
      public void valueChanged(ListSelectionEvent e) {
        Object[] values = jlst.getSelectedValues();
        String display = "";

        for (int i = 0; i < values.length; i++) {
          display += (String)values[i] + " ";
        }

        jlblStatus.setText(display);
      }
    });
  }
}
```

main method omitted

A `JList` is created with six string values (lines 7–8). A `JSpinner` is created using a `SpinnerNumberModel` with initial value `8`, minimum value `-1`, maximum value `20`, and step `1` (lines 9–10). A `JComboBox` is created with string values `VERTICAL (0)`, `VERTICAL_WRAP (1)`, and `HORIZONTAL_WRAP (2)` for choosing layout orientation (lines 11–13). A `JComboBox` is created with string values `SINGLE_SELECTION (0)`, `INTERVAL_SELECTION (1)`, and `MULTIPLE_INTERVAL_SELECTION (2)` for choosing a selection mode (lines 14–17). A `JLabel` is created to display the selected elements in the list (lines 18).

A `JList` does not support scrolling. To create a scrollable list, create a `JScrollPane` and add an instance of `JList` to it (line 44).

The fixed list cell width and height are specified in lines 48–49. The default selection mode is multiple-interval selection. Line 50 sets the selection mode to single selection.

When a new visible row count is selected from the spinner, the `setVisibleRowCount` method is used to set the count (lines 53–58). When a new layout orientation is selected from the `jcboLayoutOrientation` combo box, the `setLayoutOrientation` method is used to set the layout orientation (lines 60–65). Note that the constant values for `VERTICAL`, `VERTICAL_WRAP`, and `HORIZONTAL_WRAP` are `0`, `1`, and `2`, which correspond to the index values of these items in the combo box. When a new selection mode is selected from the `jcboSelectionMode` combo box, the `setSelectionMode` method is used to set the selection mode (lines 67–72). Note that the constant values for `SINGLE_SELECTION`, `SINGLE_INTERVAL_SELECTION`, and `MULTIPLE_INTERVAL_SELECTION` are `0`, `1`, and `2`, which correspond to the index value of these items in the combo box.

`JList` fires `javax.swing.event.ListSelectionEvent` to notify the listeners of the selections. The listener must implement the `valueChanged` handler to process the event. When the user selects an item in the list, the `valueChanged` handler is executed, which gets the selected items and displays all the items in the label (lines 74–85).

35.8 List Models

The preceding example constructs a list with a fixed set of strings. If you want to add new items to the list or delete existing items, you have to use a list model. This section introduces list models.

The `JList` class delegates the responsibilities of storing and maintaining data to its data model. The `JList` class itself does not have methods for adding or removing items from the list. These methods are supported in `ListModel`, as shown in Figure 35.20.

All list models implement the `ListModel` interface, which defines the registration methods for `ListDataEvent`. The instances of `ListDataListener` are notified when the items in the list are modified. `ListModel` also defines the methods `getSize` and `getElementAt`. The `getSize` method returns the length of the list, and the `getElementAt` method returns the element at the specified index.

`AbstractListModel` implements the `ListModel` and `Serializable` interfaces. `AbstractListModel` implements the registration methods in the `ListModel`, but does not implement the `getSize` and `getElementAt` methods.

`DefaultListModel` extends `AbstractListModel` and implements the two methods `getSize` and `getElementAt`, which are not implemented by `AbstractListModel`.

The methods in `DefaultListModel` are similar to those in the `java.util.Vector` class. You use the `add` method to insert an element to the list, the `remove` method to remove an element from the list, the `clear` method to clear the list, the `getSize` method to return the number of elements in the list, and the `getElementAt` method to retrieve an element. In fact, the `DefaultListModel` stores data in an instance of `Vector`, which is essentially a resizable array. Swing components were developed before the Java Collections Framework. In future implementations, `Vector` may be replaced by `java.util.ArrayList`.

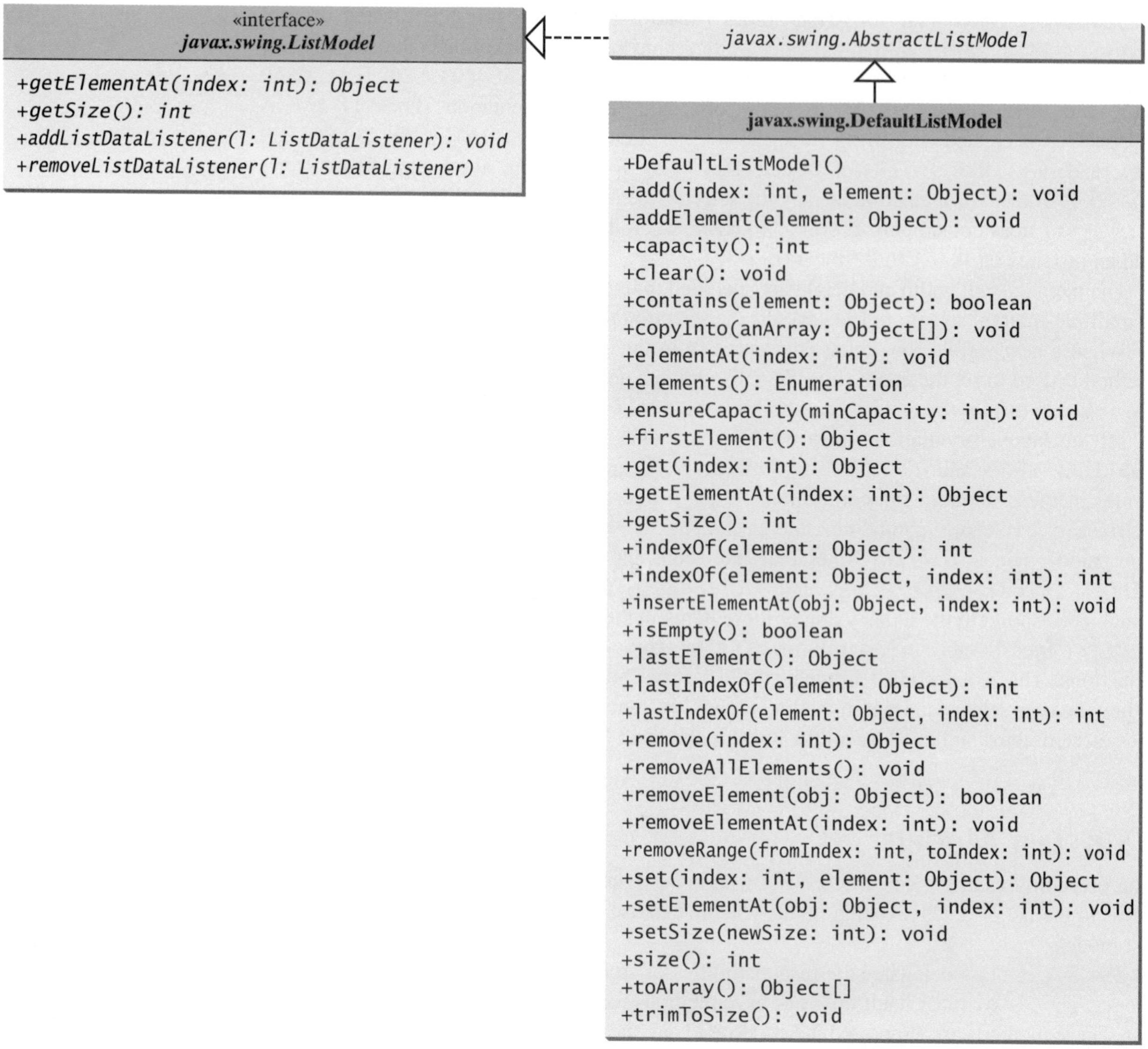
«interface»
javax.swing.ListModel
+getElementAt(index: int): Object
+getSize(): int
+addListDataListener(l: ListDataListener): void
+removeListDataListener(l: ListDataListener)
javax.swing.AbstractListModel
javax.swing.DefaultListModel
+DefaultListModel()
+add(index: int, element: Object): void
+addElement(element: Object): void
+capacity(): int
+clear(): void
+contains(element: Object): boolean
+copyInto(anArray: Object[]): void
+elementAt(index: int): void
+elements(): Enumeration
+ensureCapacity(minCapacity: int): void
+firstElement(): Object
+get(index: int): Object
+getElementAt(index: int): Object
+getSize(): int
+indexOf(element: Object): int
+indexOf(element: Object, index: int): int
+insertElementAt(obj: Object, index: int): void
+isEmpty(): boolean
+lastElement(): Object
+lastIndexOf(element: Object): int
+lastIndexOf(element: Object, index: int): int
+remove(index: int): Object
+removeAllElements(): void
+removeElement(obj: Object): boolean
+removeElementAt(index: int): void
+removeRange(fromIndex: int, toIndex: int): void
+set(index: int, element: Object): Object
+setElementAt(obj: Object, index: int): void
+setSize(newSize: int): void
+size(): int
+toArray(): Object[]
+trimToSize(): void

FIGURE 35.20 `ListModel` stores and manages data in a list.

default list model

Note

In most cases, if you create a Swing GUI object without specifying a model, an instance of the default model class is created. But this is not true for **`JList`**. By default, the **`model`** property in **`JList`** is not an instance of **`DefaultListModel`**. To use a list model, you should explicitly create one using **`DefaultListModel`**.

Listing 35.8 gives an example that creates a list using a list model and allows the user to add and delete items in the list, as shown in Figure 35.21. When the user clicks the *Add new item* button, an input dialog box is displayed to receive a new item.

LISTING 35.8 ListModelDemo.java

```
import java.awt.*;
import java.awt.event.*;
import javax.swing.*;

```

```
 5 public class ListModelDemo extends JApplet {
 6   private DefaultListModel listModel = new DefaultListModel();
 7   private JList jlst = new JList(listModel);
 8   private JButton jbtAdd = new JButton("Add new item");
 9   private JButton jbtRemove = new JButton("Remove selected item");
10
11   /** Construct the applet */
12   public ListModelDemo() {
13     // Add items to the list model
14     listModel.addElement("Item1");
15     listModel.addElement("Item2");
16     listModel.addElement("Item3");
17     listModel.addElement("Item4");
18     listModel.addElement("Item5");
19     listModel.addElement("Item6");
20
21     JPanel panel = new JPanel();
22     panel.add(jbtAdd);
23     panel.add(jbtRemove);
24
25     add(panel, BorderLayout.NORTH);
26     add(new JScrollPane(jlst), BorderLayout.CENTER);
27
28     // Register listeners
29     jbtAdd.addActionListener(new ActionListener() {
30       public void actionPerformed(ActionEvent e) {
31         String newItem =
32           JOptionPane.showInputDialog("Enter a new item");
33
34         if (newItem != null)
35           if (jlst.getSelectedIndex() == -1)
36             listModel.addElement(newItem);
37           else
38             listModel.add(jlst.getSelectedIndex(), newItem);
39       }
40     });
41
42     jbtRemove.addActionListener(new ActionListener() {
43       public void actionPerformed(ActionEvent e) {
44         listModel.remove(jlst.getSelectedIndex());
45       }
46     });
47   }
48 }
```

list model

list

add items

button listener

button listener

main method omitted

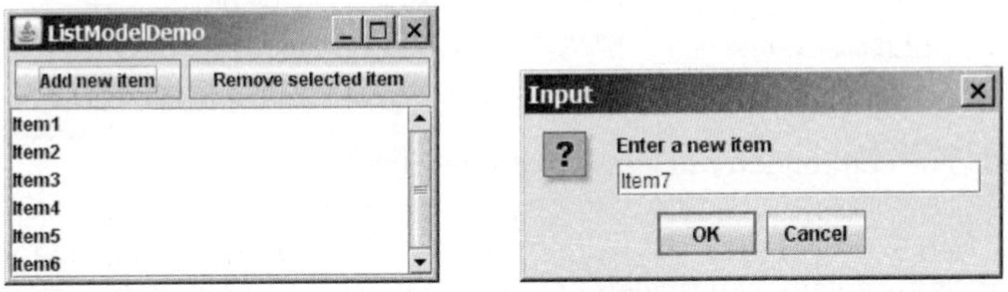
ListModelDemo
Add new item
Remove selected item
Item1
Item2
Item3
Item4
Item5
Item6
Input
Enter a new item
Item7
OK
Cancel

FIGURE 35.21 You can add elements and remove elements in a list using list models.

The program creates `listModel` (line 6), which is an instance of `DefaultListModel`, and uses it to manipulate data in the list. The model enables you to add and remove items in the list.

A list is created from the list model (line 7). The initial elements are added into the model using the `addElement` method (lines 13–19).

To add an element, the user clicks the *Add new item* button to display an input dialog box. Type a new item in the dialog box. The new item is inserted before the currently selected element in the list (line 38). If no element is selected, the new element is appended to the list (line 36).

To remove an element, the user has to select the element and then click the *Remove selected item* button. Note that only the first selected item is removed. You can modify the program to remove all the selected items (see Exercise 35.6).

What would happen if you clicked the *Remove selected item* button but no items were currently selected? This would cause an error. To fix it, see Exercise 35.6.

35.9 List Cell Renderer

The preceding example displays items as strings in a list. JList is very flexible and versatile, and it can be used to display images and GUI components in addition to simple text. This section introduces list cell renderers for displaying graphics.

In addition to delegating data storage and processing to list models, JList delegates the rendering of list cells to list cell renderers. All list cell renderers implement the ListCellRenderer interface, which defines a single method, getListCellRendererComponent, as follows:

```
public Component getListCellRendererComponent
  (JList list, Object value, int index, boolean isSelected,
   boolean cellHasFocus)
```

This method is passed with a list, the value associated with the cell, the index of the value, and information regarding whether the value is selected and whether the cell has the focus. The component returned from the method is painted on the cell in the list. By default, JList uses DefaultListCellRenderer to render its cells. The DefaultListCellRenderer class implements ListCellRenderer, extends JLabel, and can display either a string or an icon, but not both in the same cell.

For example, you can use JList's default cell renderer to display strings, as shown in Figure 35.22(a), using the following code:

```
JList list = new JList(new String[]{"Denmark", "Germany",
  "China", "India", "Norway", "UK", "US"});
```

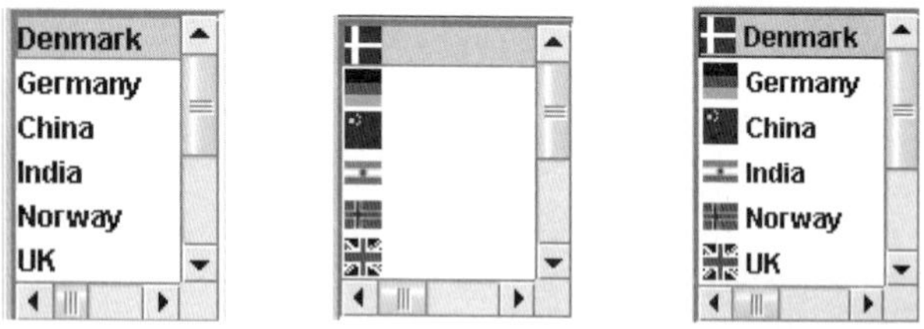
Denmark
Germany
China
India
Norway
UK
Denmark
Germany
China
India
Norway
UK

(a) Strings (b) Icons (c) Icons and strings

FIGURE 35.22 The cell renderer displays list items in a list.

You can use JList's default cell renderer to display icons, as shown in Figure 35.22(b), using the following code:

```
ImageIcon denmarkIcon = new ImageIcon(getClass().getResource(
  "image/denmarkIcon.gif"));
...
JList list = new JList(new ImageIcon[]{denmarkIcon, germanyIcon,
  chinaIcon, indiaIcon, norwayIcon, ukIcon, usIcon});
```

How do you display a string along with an icon in one cell, as shown in Figure 35.22(c)? You need to create a custom renderer by implementing `ListCellRenderer`, as shown in Figure 35.23.

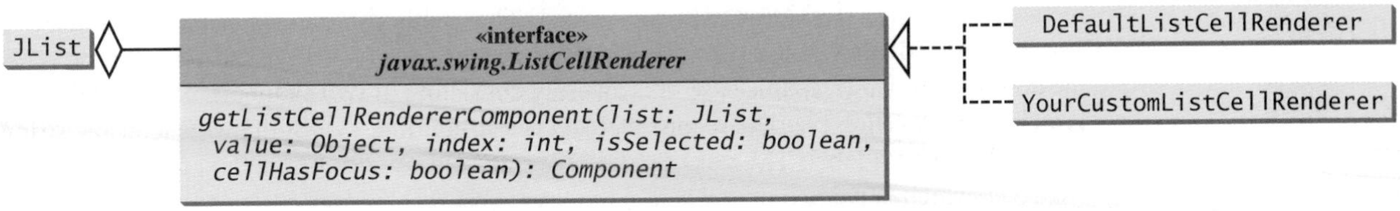
JList
«interface»
javax.swing.ListCellRenderer
getListCellRendererComponent(list: JList, value: Object, index: int, isSelected: boolean, cellHasFocus: boolean): Component
DefaultListCellRenderer
YourCustomListCellRenderer

FIGURE 35.23 `ListCellRenderer` defines how cells are rendered in a list.

Suppose a list is created as follows:

```
JList list = new JList(new Object[][]{{denmarkIcon, "Denmark"},
  {germanyIcon, "Germany"}, {chinaIcon, "China"},
  {indiaIcon, "India"}, {norwayIcon, "Norway"}, {ukIcon, "UK"},
  {usIcon, "US"}});
```

Each item in the list is an array that consists of an icon and a string. You can create a custom cell renderer that retrieves an icon and a string from the list data model and display them in a label. The custom cell renderer class is given in Listing 35.9.

LISTING 35.9 MyListCellRenderer.java

```
import java.awt.*;
import javax.swing.*;
import javax.swing.border.*;

public class MyListCellRenderer implements ListCellRenderer {
  private JLabel jlblCell = new JLabel(" ", JLabel.LEFT);
  private Border lineBorder =
    BorderFactory.createLineBorder(Color.black, 1);
  private Border emptyBorder =
    BorderFactory.createEmptyBorder(2, 2, 2, 2);

  /** Implement this method in ListCellRenderer */
  public Component getListCellRendererComponent
      (JList list, Object value, int index, boolean isSelected,
       boolean cellHasFocus) {
    Object[] pair = (Object[])value; // Cast value into an array
    jlblCell.setOpaque(true);
    jlblCell.setIcon((ImageIcon)pair[0]);
    jlblCell.setText(pair[1].toString());

    if (isSelected) {
      jlblCell.setForeground(list.getSelectionForeground());
      jlblCell.setBackground(list.getSelectionBackground());
    }
    else {
      jlblCell.setForeground(list.getForeground());
      jlblCell.setBackground(list.getBackground());
    }

    jlblCell.setBorder(cellHasFocus ? lineBorder : emptyBorder);

```

cell component

set icon

set text

cell selected

return rendering cell

```
32       return jlblCell;
33     }
34 }
```

The `MyListCellRenderer` class implements the `getListCellRendererComponent` method in the `ListCellRenderer` interface. This method is passed with the parameters `list`, `value`, `index`, `isSelected`, and `isFocused` (lines 13–15). The `value` represents the current item value. In this case, it is an array consisting of two elements. The first element is an image icon (line 18). The second element is a string (line 19). Both image icon and string are displayed on a label. The `getListCellRendererComponent` method returns the label (line 32), which is painted on the cell in the list.

If the cell is selected, the background and foreground of the cell are set to the list's selection background and foreground (lines 22–23). If the cell is focused, the cell's border is set to the line border (line 30); otherwise, it is set to the empty border (line 30). The empty border serves as a divider between the cells.

any GUI renderer

Note

The example in Listing 35.9 uses a `JLabel` as a renderer. You may use any GUI component as a renderer, returned from the `getListCellRendererComponent` method.

Let us develop an example (Listing 35.10) that creates a list of countries and displays the flag image and name for each country as one item in the list, as shown in Figure 35.24. When a country is selected in the list, its flag is displayed in a label next to the list.

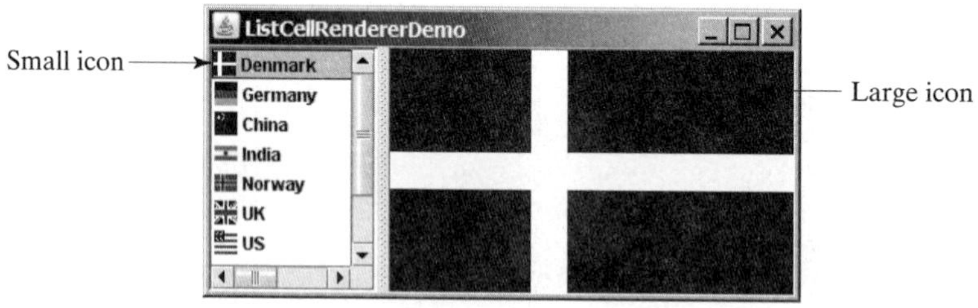
Small icon
ListCellRendererDemo
Denmark
Germany
China
India
Norway
UK
US
Large icon

FIGURE 35.24 The image and the text are displayed in the list cell.

LISTING 35.10 ListCellRendererDemo.java

nation strings

small icons

big icons

list model

```
import javax.swing.*;
import javax.swing.event.*;
import java.awt.*;

public class ListCellRendererDemo extends JApplet {
  private final static int NUMBER_OF_NATIONS = 7;
  private String[] nations = new String[]
    {"Denmark", "Germany", "China", "India", "Norway", "UK", "US"};
  private ImageIcon[] icons = new ImageIcon[NUMBER_OF_NATIONS];
  private ImageIcon[] bigIcons = new ImageIcon[NUMBER_OF_NATIONS];

  // Create a list model
  private DefaultListModel listModel = new DefaultListModel();
```

```
14
15   // Create a list using the list model
16   private JList jlstNations = new JList(listModel);
17
18   // Create a list cell renderer
19   private ListCellRenderer renderer = new MyListCellRenderer();
20
21   // Create a split pane
22   private JSplitPane jSplitPane1 = new JSplitPane();
23
24   // Create a label for displaying image
25   private JLabel jlblImage = new JLabel("", JLabel.CENTER);
26
27   /** Construct ListCellRenderer */
28   public ListCellRendererDemo() {
29     // Load small and large image icons
30     for (int i = 0; i < NUMBER_OF_NATIONS; i++) {
31       icons[i] = new ImageIcon(getClass().getResource(
32         "image/flagIcon" + i + ".gif"));
33       listModel.addElement(new Object[]{icons[i], nations[i]});
34
35       bigIcons[i] = new ImageIcon(getClass().getResource(
36         "image/flag" + i + ".gif"));
37     }
38
39     // Set list cell renderer
40     jlstNations.setCellRenderer(renderer);
41     jlstNations.setPreferredSize(new Dimension(200, 200));
42     jSplitPane1.setLeftComponent(new JScrollPane(jlstNations));
43     jSplitPane1.setRightComponent(jlblImage);
44     jlstNations.setSelectedIndex(0);
45     jlblImage.setIcon(bigIcons[0]);
46     add(jSplitPane1, BorderLayout.CENTER);
47
48     // Register listener
49     jlstNations.addListSelectionListener(new ListSelectionListener() {
50       public void valueChanged(ListSelectionEvent e) {
51         jlblImage.setIcon(bigIcons[jlstNations.getSelectedIndex()]);
52       }
53     });
54   }
55 }
```

list

list cell renderer

split pane

image label

load image icons

add elements

load image icons

set renderer

list listener

main method omitted

Two types of icons are used in this program. The small icons are created from files `flagIcon0.gif`, ..., `flagIcon6.gif` (lines 31–32). These image files are the flags for Denmark, Germany, China, India, Norway, UK, and US. The small icons are rendered inside the list. The large icons for the same countries are created from files `flag0.gif`, ..., `flag6.gif` (lines 35–36). The large icons are displayed on a label on the right side of the split pane.

The `ListCellRendererDemo` class creates a list model (line 13) and adds the items to the model (line 33). Each item is an array of two elements (image icon and string). The list is created using the list model (line 16). The list cell renderer is created (line 19) and associated with the list (line 40).

The `ListCellRendererDemo` class creates a split pane (line 22) and places the list on the left (line 42) and a label on the right (line 43).

When you choose a country in the list, the list-selection event handler is invoked (lines 49–53) to set a new image to the label in the right side of the split pane (line 51).

35.10 JComboBox and Its Models

The basic features of JComboBox were introduced in §17.8, "Combo Boxes," without using combo box models. This section introduces combo models and discusses the use of JComboBox in some detail.

A combo box is similar to a list. Combo boxes and lists are both used for selecting items from a list. A combo box allows the user to select one item at a time, whereas a list permits multiple selections. When a combo box is selected, it displays a drop-down list contained in a popup menu. The selected item can be edited in the cell as if it were a text field. Figure 35.25 shows the properties and constructors of JComboBox. The data for a combo box are stored in ComboBoxModel. You can create a combo box from a combo box model, an array of objects, or a vector.

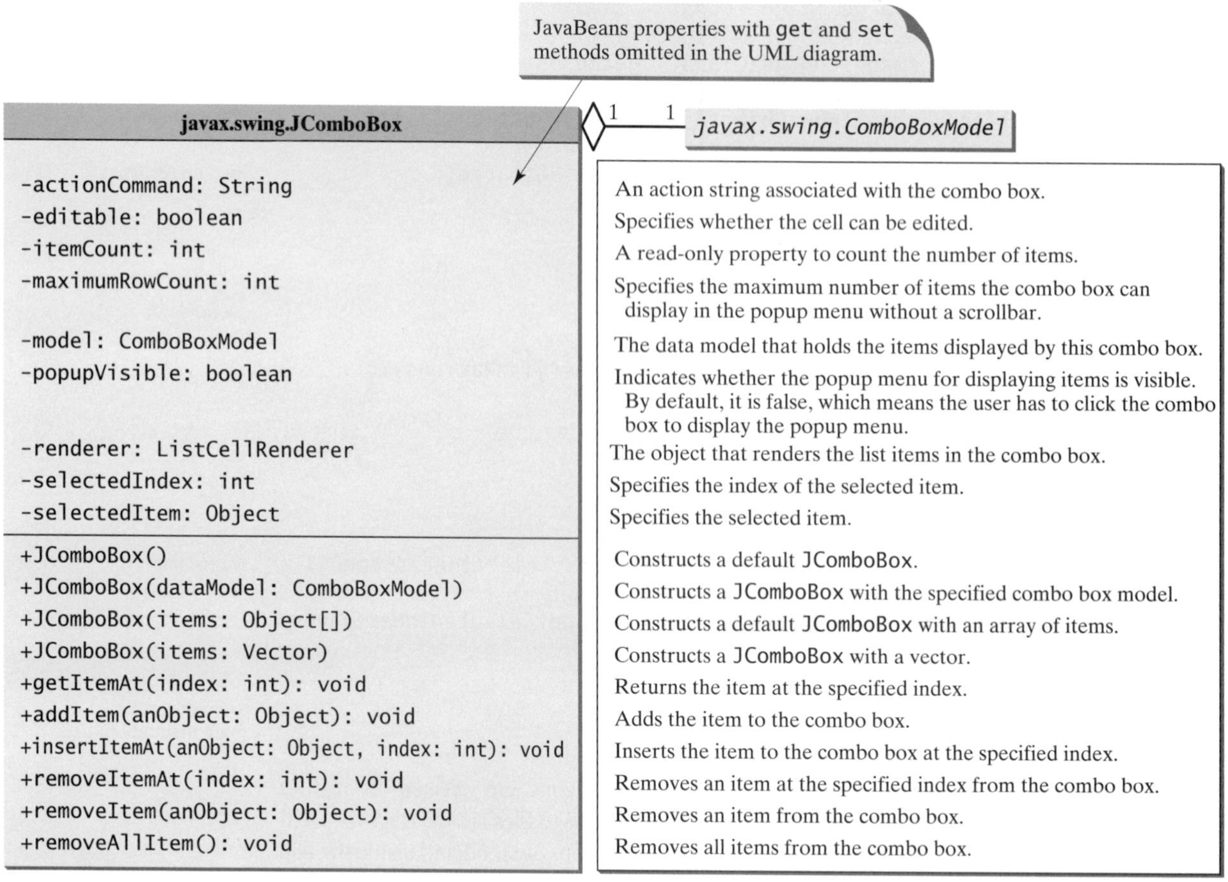
JavaBeans properties with get and set methods omitted in the UML diagram.
javax.swing.JComboBox
1
1
javax.swing.ComboBoxModel
-actionCommand: String
-editable: boolean
-itemCount: int
-maximumRowCount: int
-model: ComboBoxModel
-popupVisible: boolean
-renderer: ListCellRenderer
-selectedIndex: int
-selectedItem: Object
+JComboBox()
+JComboBox(dataModel: ComboBoxModel)
+JComboBox(items: Object[])
+JComboBox(items: Vector)
+getItemAt(index: int): void
+addItem(anObject: Object): void
+insertItemAt(anObject: Object, index: int): void
+removeItemAt(index: int): void
+removeItem(anObject: Object): void
+removeAllItem(): void
An action string associated with the combo box.
Specifies whether the cell can be edited.
A read-only property to count the number of items.
Specifies the maximum number of items the combo box can display in the popup menu without a scrollbar.
The data model that holds the items displayed by this combo box.
Indicates whether the popup menu for displaying items is visible. By default, it is false, which means the user has to click the combo box to display the popup menu.
The object that renders the list items in the combo box.
Specifies the index of the selected item.
Specifies the selected item.
Constructs a default JComboBox.
Constructs a JComboBox with the specified combo box model.
Constructs a default JComboBox with an array of items.
Constructs a JComboBox with a vector.
Returns the item at the specified index.
Adds the item to the combo box.
Inserts the item to the combo box at the specified index.
Removes an item at the specified index from the combo box.
Removes an item from the combo box.
Removes all items from the combo box.

FIGURE 35.25 JComboBox displays elements in a list.

JComboBox delegates the responsibilities of storing and maintaining data to its data model. All combo box models implement the ComboBoxModel interface, which extends the ListModel interface and defines the getSelectedItem and setSelectedItem methods for retrieving and setting a selected item. The methods for adding and removing items are defined in the MutableComboBoxModel interface, which extends ComboBoxModel. When an instance of JComboBox is created without explicitly specifying a model, an instance of DefaultComboBoxModel is used. The DefaultComboBoxModel class extends AbstractListModel and implements MutableComboBoxModel, as shown in Figure 35.26.

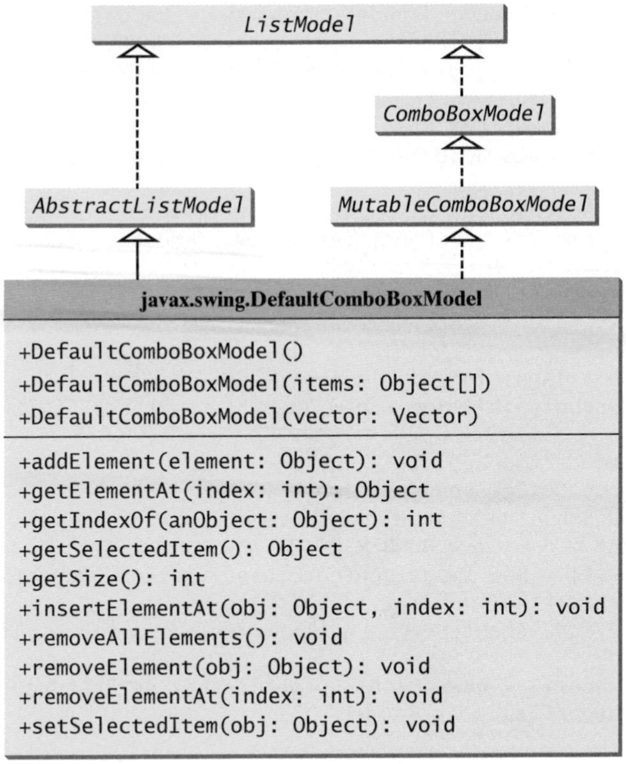
ListModel
ComboBoxModel
AbstractListModel
MutableComboBoxModel
javax.swing.DefaultComboBoxModel
+DefaultComboBoxModel()
+DefaultComboBoxModel(items: Object[])
+DefaultComboBoxModel(vector: Vector)
+addElement(element: Object): void
+getElementAt(index: int): Object
+getIndexOf(anObject: Object): int
+getSelectedItem(): Object
+getSize(): int
+insertElementAt(obj: Object, index: int): void
+removeAllElements(): void
+removeElement(obj: Object): void
+removeElementAt(index: int): void
+setSelectedItem(obj: Object): void

FIGURE 35.26 `ComboBoxModel` stores and manages data in a combo box.

Usually you don't need to use combo box models explicitly, because `JComboBox` contains the methods for retrieving (`getItemAt`, `getSelectedItem`, and `getSelectedIndex`), adding (`addItem` and `insertItemAt`), and removing (`removeItem`, `removeItemAt`, and `removeAllItems`) items from the list.

`JComboBox` can fire `ActionEvent` and `ItemEvent`, among many other events. Whenever a new item is selected, `JComboBox` fires `ItemEvent` twice, once for deselecting the previously selected item, and the other for selecting the currently selected item. `JComboBox` fires an `ActionEvent` after firing an `ItemEvent`.

Combo boxes render cells exactly like lists, because the combo box items are displayed in a list contained in a popup menu. Therefore, a combo box cell renderer can be created exactly like a list cell renderer by implementing the `ListCellRenderer` interface. Like `JList`, `JComboBox` has a default cell renderer that displays a string or an icon, but not both at the same time. To display a combination of a string and an icon, you need to create a custom renderer. The custom list cell renderer `MyListCellRenderer` in Listing 35.9 can be used as a combo box cell renderer without any modification.

Listing 35.11 gives an example that creates a combo box to display the flag image and name for each country as one item in the list, as shown in Figure 35.27. When a country is selected in the list, its flag is displayed in a panel below the combo box.

LISTING 35.11 ComboBoxCellRendererDemo.java

```java
import java.awt.*;
import java.awt.event.*;
import javax.swing.*;

public class ComboBoxCellRendererDemo extends JApplet {
  private final static int NUMBER_OF_NATIONS = 7;
  private String[] nations = new String[] {"Denmark",
```

nation strings

small icons / big icons / combo box model / combo box / list cell renderer / image label / load image icons / add elements / load image icons / set renderer / action listener / main method omitted

```
 8       "Germany", "China", "India", "Norway", "UK", "US"};
 9     private ImageIcon[] icons = new ImageIcon[NUMBER_OF_NATIONS];
10     private ImageIcon[] bigIcons = new ImageIcon[NUMBER_OF_NATIONS];
11
12     // Create a combo box model
13     private DefaultComboBoxModel model = new DefaultComboBoxModel();
14
15     // Create a combo box with the specified model
16     private JComboBox jcboCountries = new JComboBox(model);
17
18     // Create a list cell renderer
19     private MyListCellRenderer renderer = new MyListCellRenderer();
20
21     // Create a label for displaying image
22     private JLabel jlblImage = new JLabel("", JLabel.CENTER);
23
24     /** Construct the applet */
25     public ComboBoxCellRendererDemo() {
26       // Load small and large image icons
27       for (int i = 0; i < NUMBER_OF_NATIONS; i++) {
28         icons[i] = new ImageIcon(getClass().getResource(
29           "image/flagIcon" + i + ".gif"));
30         model.addElement(new Object[]{icons[i], nations[i]});
31
32         bigIcons[i] = new ImageIcon(getClass().getResource(
33           "image/flag" + i + ".gif"));
34       }
35
36       // Set list cell renderer for the combo box
37       jcboCountries.setRenderer(renderer);
38       jlblImage.setIcon(bigIcons[0]);
39       add(jcboCountries, java.awt.BorderLayout.NORTH);
40       add(jlblImage, java.awt.BorderLayout.CENTER);
41
42       // Register listener
43       jcboCountries.addActionListener(new ActionListener() {
44         public void actionPerformed(java.awt.event.ActionEvent e) {
45           jlblImage.setIcon
45             (bigIcons[jcboCountries.getSelectedIndex()]);
46         }
47       });
48     }
49   }
```

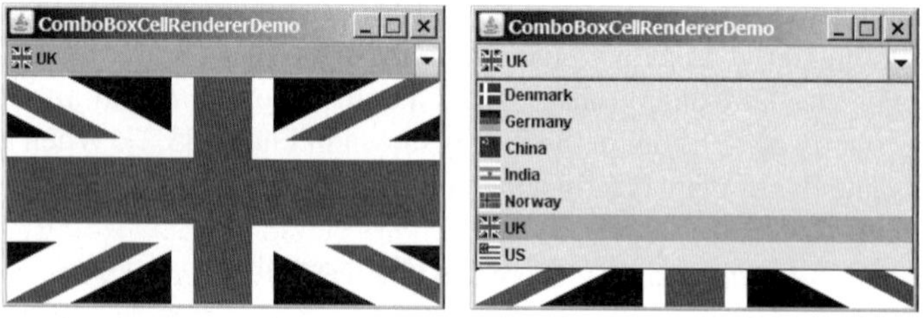
ComboBoxCellRendererDemo
UK
ComboBoxCellRendererDemo
UK
Denmark
Germany
China
India
Norway
UK
US

FIGURE 35.27 The image and the text are displayed in the list cell of a combo box.

The program is very similar to the preceding example in Listing 35.10. Two types of image icons are loaded for each country and stored in the arrays `icons` and `bigIcons` (lines 27–34). Each item in the combo box is an array that consists of an icon and a string (line 30).

MyListCellRenderer, defined in Listing 35.9, is used to create a cell renderer in line 19. The cell renderer is plugged into the combo box in line 37.

When you choose a country from the combo box, the action event handler is invoked (lines 44–46). This handler sets a new image on the label (line 45).

Key Terms

Chapter Summary

1. The fundamental issue in the model-view approach is to ensure consistency between the views and the model. Any change in the model should be notified to the dependent views, and all the views should display the same data consistently. The model can be implemented as a source with appropriate event and event listener registration methods. The view can be implemented as a listener. Thus, if data are changed in the model, the view will be notified.

2. Every Swing user interface component (e.g., JButton, JTextField, JList, and JComboBox) has a property named *model* that refers to its data model. The data model is defined in an interface whose name ends with Model (e.g., SpinnerModel, ListModel, ListSelectionModel, and ComboBoxModel).

3. Most simple Swing components (e.g., JButton, JTextField, JTextArea) contain some properties of their models, and these properties can be accessed and modified directly from the component without the existence of the model being known.

4. A JSpinner is displayed as a text field with a pair of tiny arrow buttons on its right side that enable the user to select numbers, dates, or values from an ordered sequence. A JSpinner's sequence value is defined by the SpinnerModel interface. AbstractSpinnerModel is a convenient abstract class that implements SpinnerModel and provides the implementation for its registration/deregistration methods. SpinnerListModel, SpinnerNumberModel, and SpinnerDateModel are concrete implementations of SpinnerModel. SpinnerNumberModel represents a sequence of numbers with properties maximum, minimum, and stepSize. SpinnerDateModel represents a sequence of dates. SpinnerListModel can store a list of any object values.

5. A JSpinner has a single child component, called the *editor*, which is responsible for displaying the current element or value of the model. Four editors are defined as static inner classes inside JSpinner: JSpinner.DefaultEditor, JSpinner.NumberEditor, JSpinner.DateEditor, and JSpinner.ListEditor.

6. JList has two supporting models: a list model and a list-selection model. The *list model* is for storing and processing data. The *list-selection model* is for selecting items. By default, items are rendered as strings or icons. You can also create a custom renderer implementing the ListCellRenderer interface.

7. JComboBox delegates the responsibilities of storing and maintaining data to its data model. All combo box models implement the ComboBoxModel interface, which extends the ListModel interface and defines the getSelectedItem and setSelectedItem methods for retrieving and setting a selected item. The methods

for adding and removing items are defined in the MutableComboBoxModel interface, which extends ComboBoxModel. When an instance of JComboBox is created without explicitly specifying a model, an instance of DefaultComboBoxModel is used. The DefaultComboBoxModel class extends AbstractListModel and implements MutableComboBoxModel.

8. Combo boxes render cells exactly like lists, because the combo box items are displayed in a list contained in a popup menu. Therefore, a combo box cell renderer can be created exactly like a list cell renderer by implementing the ListCellRenderer interface.

Review Questions

Sections 35.2–35.3

35.1 What is model-view-controller architecture?

35.2 How do you do implement models, views, and controllers?

35.3 What are the variations of MVC architecture?

Section 35.4

35.4 Does each Swing GUI component (except containers such as JPanel) have a property named model? Is the type of model the same for all the components?

35.5 Does each model interface have a default implementation class? If so, does a Swing component use the default model class if no model is specified?

Sections 35.5–35.6

35.6 If you create a JSpinner without specifying a data model, what is the default model?

35.7 What is the internal data structure for storing data in SpinnerListModel? How do you convert an array to a list?

Sections 35.7–35.9

35.8 Does JList have a method, such as addItem, for adding an item to a list? How do you add items to a list? Can JList display icons and custom GUI objects in a list? Can a list item be edited? How do you initialize data in a list? How do you specify the maximum number of visible rows in a list without scrolling? How do you specify the height of a list cell? How do you specify the horizontal margin of list cells?

35.9 How do you create a list model? How do you add items to a list model? How do you remove items from a list model?

35.10 What are the three list-selection modes? Can you set the selection modes directly in an instance of JList? How do you obtain the selected item(s)?

35.11 How do you define a custom list cell renderer?

35.12 What is the handler for handling the ListSelectionEvent?

Section 35.10

35.13 Can multiple items be selected from a combo box? Can a combo box item be edited? How do you specify the maximum number of visible rows in a combo box without scrolling? Can you specify the height of a combo box cell using a method in JComboBox? How do you obtain the selected item in a combo box?

35.14 How do you add or remove items from a combo box?

35.15 Why is the cell renderer for a combo box the same as the renderer for a list?

Programming Exercises

Section 35.2

35.1*** (*Creating MVC components*) Create a model, named `ChartModel`, which holds data in an array of double elements named `data`, and the names for the data in an array of strings named `dataName`. For example, the enrollment data {200, 40, 50, 100, 40} stored in the array `data` are for {"CS", "Math", "Chem", "Biol", "Phys"} in the array `dataName`. These two properties have their respective get methods, but not individual set methods. Both properties are set together in the `setChartData(String[] newDataName, double[] newData)` method so that they can be displayed properly. Create a view named `PieChart` to present the data in a pie chart, and create a view named `BarChart` to present the data in a bar chart, as shown in Figure 35.28(a).

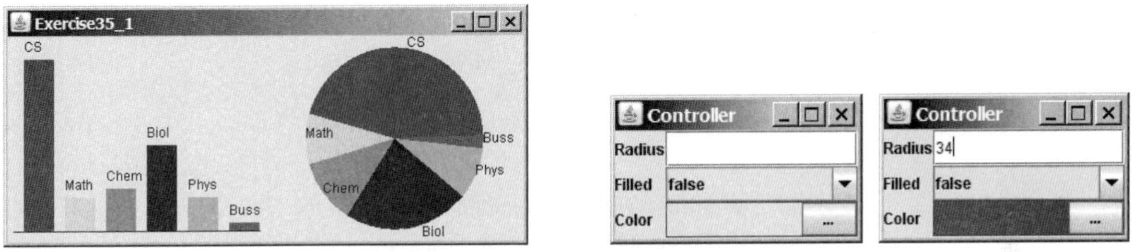
Exercise35_1
CS
Biol
Math
Chem
Phys
Buss
CS
Math
Buss
Phys
Chem
Biol
Controller
Radius
Filled
false
Color
Controller
Radius
34
Filled
false
Color

(a) (b)

FIGURE 35.28 (a) The two views, `PieChart` and `BarChart`, receive data from the `ChartModel`; (b) Clicking the eclipse button displays the color chooser dialog box for specifying a color.

(*Hint*: Each pie represents a percentage of the total data. Color the pie using the colors from an array named colors, which is {`Color.red`, `Color.yellow`, `Color.green`, `Color.blue`, `Color.cyan`, `Color.magenta`, `Color.orange`, `Color.pink`, `Color.darkGray`}. Use `colors[i % colors.length]` for the *i*th pie. Use black color to display the data names.)

35.2* (*Revising Listing 35.3 CircleController.java*) `CircleController` uses a text field to obtain a new radius and a combo box to obtain a Boolean value to specify whether the circle is filled. Add a new row in `CircleController` to let the user choose color using the `JColorChooser` component, as shown in Figure 35.28(b). The new row consists of a label with text Color, a label to display color, and an eclipse button. The user can click the eclipse button to display a `JColorChooser` dialog box. Once the user selects a color, the color is displayed as the background for the label on the left of the eclipse button.

Sections 35.5–35.6

35.3** (*Synchronizing spinners*) The date spinner is synchronized with the day, month, and year spinners in Listing 35.6, SpinnerModelEditorDemo.java. Improve it to synchronize the day, month, and year spinners with the date spinner. In other words, when a new value is selected in the date spinner, the values in the day, month, and year spinners are updated accordingly.

35.4* (*Custom spinner model*) Develop a custom spinner model that represents a sequence of numbers of power 2—that is, 1, 2, 4, 8, 16, 32, and so on. Your model should implement `AbstractSpinnerModel`. The registration/deregistration methods for `ChangeListener` have already been implemented in `AbstractSpinnerModel`. You need to implement `getNextValue()`, `getPreviousValue()`, `getValue()`, and `setValue(Object)` methods.

35.5* (*Reversing the numbers displayed in a spinner*) The numbers displayed in a spinner increase when the up-arrow button is clicked and decrease when the down-arrow button is clicked. You can reverse the sequence by creating a new model that extends `SpinnerNumberModel` and overrides the `getNextValue` and `getPreviousValue` methods. Write a test program that uses the new model, as shown in Figure 35.29.

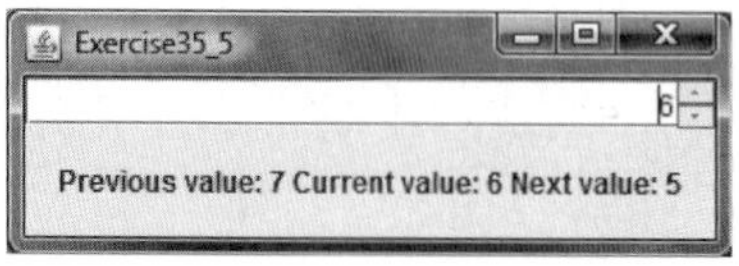
Exercise35_5
6
Previous value: 7 Current value: 6 Next value: 5

FIGURE 35.29 The numbers in the spinner are in decreasing order.

Sections 35.7–35.9

35.6* (*Removing selected items in a list*) Modify Listing 35.8, ListModelDemo.java, to meet the following requirements:

- Remove all the selected items from the list when the *Remove selected item* button is clicked.
- Enable the items to be deleted using the DELETE key.

35.7* (*Custom list cell renderer*) Listing 35.10, ListCellRendererDemo.java, has two types of images for each country. The small images are used for display in the list, and the large ones are used for display outside the list. Assume that only the large images are available. Rewrite the custom cell renderer to use a `JPanel` instead of a `JLabel` for rendering a cell. Each cell consists of an image and a string. Display the image in an `ImageViewer` and the string in a label. The `ImageViewer` component was introduced in Listing 15.13, ImageViewer.java. The image can be stretched in an `ImageViewer`. Set the dimension of an image viewer to 32 by 32, as shown in Figure 35.30. Revise Listing 35.10 to test the new custom cell renderer.

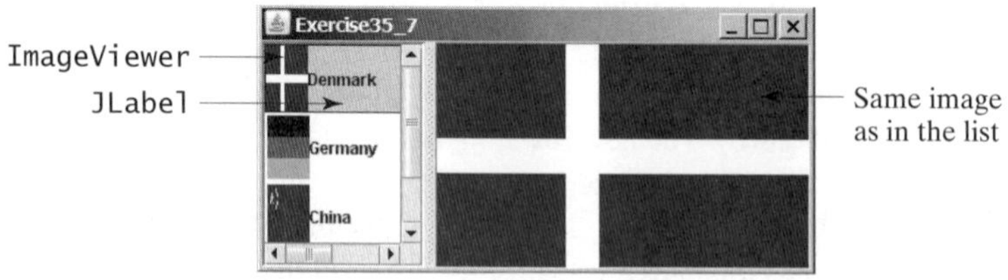
ImageViewer
JLabel
Exercise35_7
Denmark
Germany
China
Same image as in the list

FIGURE 35.30 `ImageViewer` is used to render the image in the list.

35.8* (*Deleting selected items in a list using the DELETE key*) Modify Listing 35.10, ListCellRendererDemo.java, to delete selected items from the list using the DELETE key. After some items are deleted from the list, the index of a selected item in the list does not match the index of the item in the `bigIcons` array. As a result, you cannot use the image icon in the `bigIcons` array to display the image to the right side of the split pane. Revise the program to retrieve the icon from the selected item in the list and display it, as shown in Figure 35.31.

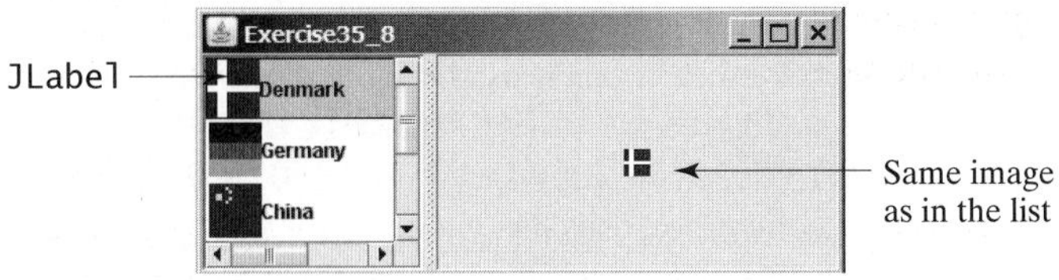
JLabel
Exercise35_8
Denmark
Germany
China
Same image
as in the list

FIGURE 35.31 Images in the list are also used for display in the label placed in the right side of a split pane.

35.9** (*Rendering figures*) Create a program that shows a list of geometrical shapes along with a label in an instance of `JList`, as shown in Figure 35.32(a). Display the selected figure in a panel when selecting a figure from the list. The figures can be drawn using the `FigurePanel` class in Listing 15.3, FigurePanel.java.

35.10** (*List of clocks*) Write a program that displays a list of cities and their local times in a clock, as shown in Figure 35.32(b). When a city is selected in the list, its clock is displayed in a large picture on the right.

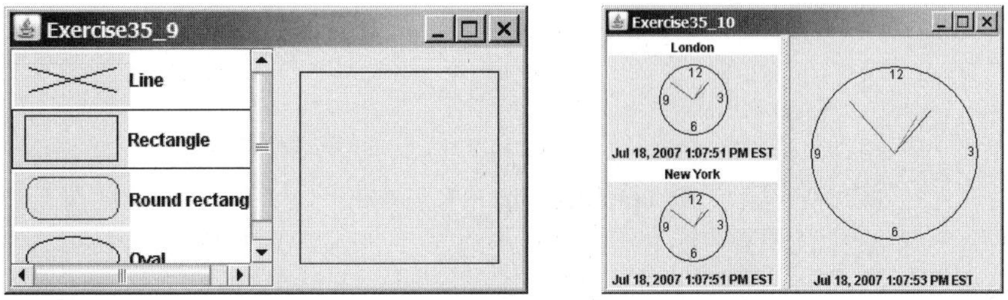
Exercise35_9
Line
Rectangle
Round rectang
Oval
Exercise35_10
London
Jul 18, 2007 1:07:51 PM EST
New York
Jul 18, 2007 1:07:51 PM EST
Jul 18, 2007 1:07:53 PM EST

(a) (b)

FIGURE 35.32 (a) The list displays geometrical shapes and their names; (b) The list displays cities and clocks.

Section 35.10

35.11** (*Creating custom cell renderer in a combo box*) Create a program that shows a list of geometrical shapes along with a label in a combo box, as shown in Figure 35.33(a). This exercise may share the list cell renderer with Exercise 35.9.

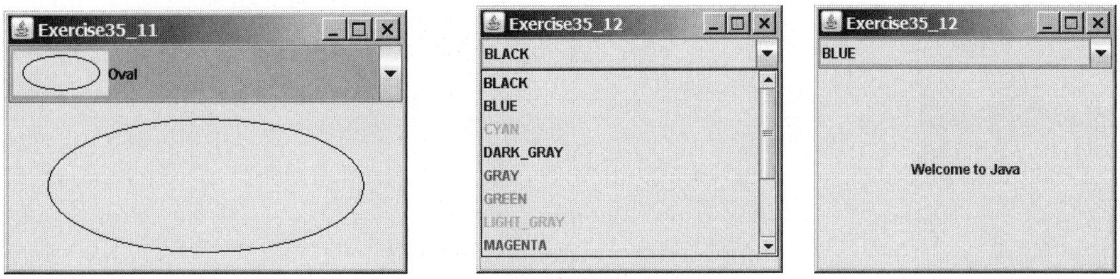
Exercise35_11
Oval
Exercise35_12
BLACK
BLACK
BLUE
CYAN
DARK_GRAY
GRAY
GREEN
LIGHT_GRAY
MAGENTA
Exercise35_12
BLUE
Welcome to Java

(a) (b)

FIGURE 35.33 (a) The combo box contains a list of geometrical shapes and the shape names. (b) The combo box contains a list of color names, each using its own color for its foreground.

35.12** (*Rendering colored text*) Write a program that enables the user to choose the foreground colors for a label, as shown in Figure 35.33(b). The combo box contains 13 standard colors (BLACK, BLUE, CYAN, DARK_GRAY, GRAY, GREEN, LIGHT_GRAY, MAGENTA, ORANGE, PINK, RED, WHITE, YELLOW). Each color name in the combo box uses its own color for its foreground.

35.13* (*Deleting a selected item in a combo box using the DELETE key*) Modify Listing 35.11, ComboBoxCellRendererDemo.java, to delete the selected item from the combo box using the DELETE key.

Comprehensive

35.14* (*Calendar*) Write a program that controls a calendar using a spinner, as shown in Figure 35.7. Use the `CalendarPanel` class (see Listing 31.4) to display the calendar.

CHAPTER 36

JTABLE AND JTREE

Objectives

- To display tables using `JTable` (§36.2).
- To process rows and columns using `TableModel`, `DefaultTableModel`, `TableColumnModel`, `DefaultTableColumnModel`, and `ListSelectionModel` (§§36.3–36.5).
- To enable auto sort and filtering on table model (§36.4).
- To add rows and columns, delete rows and columns in a table (§36.5).
- To render and edit table cells using the default renderers and editors (§36.6).
- To render and edit table cells using the custom renderers and editors (§36.7).
- To handle table model events (§36.8).
- To display data in a tree hierarchy using `JTree` (§36.9).
- To model the structure of a tree using using `TreeModel` and `DefaultTreeModel` (§36.10).
- To add, remove, and process tree nodes using `TreeNode`, `MutableTreeNode`, and `DefaultMutableTreeNode` (§36.11).
- To select tree nodes and paths using `TreeSelectionModel` and `DefaultTreeSelectionModel` (§36.12).
- To render and edit tree nodes using the default and custom renderers and editors (§36.14).

36.1 Introduction

The preceding chapter introduced the model-view architecture, Swing MVC, and the models in `JSpinner`, `JList`, and `JComboBox`. This chapter introduces `JTable` and `JTree`, and how to use the models to process data in `JTable` and `JTree`.

36.2 `JTable`

`JTable` is a Swing component that displays data in rows and columns in a two-dimensional grid, as shown in Figure 36.1.

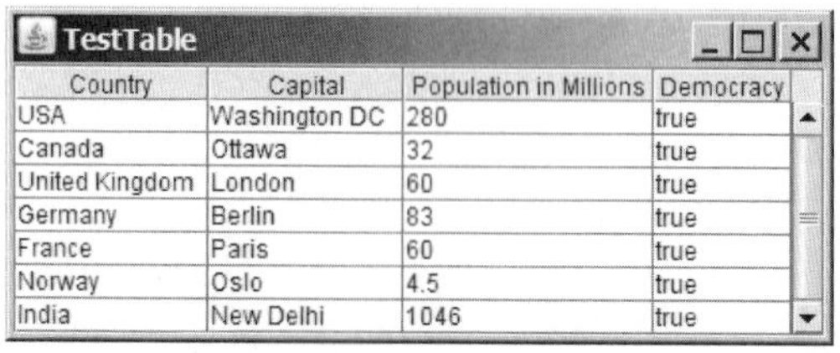
TestTable
Country | Capital | Population in Millions | Democracy
USA | Washington DC | 280 | true
Canada | Ottawa | 32 | true
United Kingdom | London | 60 | true
Germany | Berlin | 83 | true
France | Paris | 60 | true
Norway | Oslo | 4.5 | true
India | New Delhi | 1046 | true

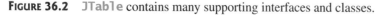

FIGURE 36.1 `JTable` displays data in a table.

`JTable` doesn't directly support scrolling. To create a scrollable table, you need to create a `JScrollPane` and add an instance of `JTable` to the scroll pane. If a table is not placed in a scroll pane, its column header will not be visible, because the column header is placed in the header of the view port of a scroll pane.

`JTable` has three supporting models: a table model, a column model, and a list-selection model. The *table model* is for storing and processing data. The *column model* represents all the columns in the table. The *list-selection model* is the same as the one used by `JList` for selecting rows, columns, and cells in a table. `JTable` also has two useful supporting classes, `TableColumn` and `JTableHeader`. `TableColumn` contains the information on a particular column. `JTableHeader` can be used to display the header of a `JTable`. Each column has a default editor and renderer. You can also create a custom editor by implementing the `TableCellEditor` interface, and create a custom renderer by implementing the `TableCellRenderer` interface. The relationship of these interfaces and classes is shown in Figure 36.2.

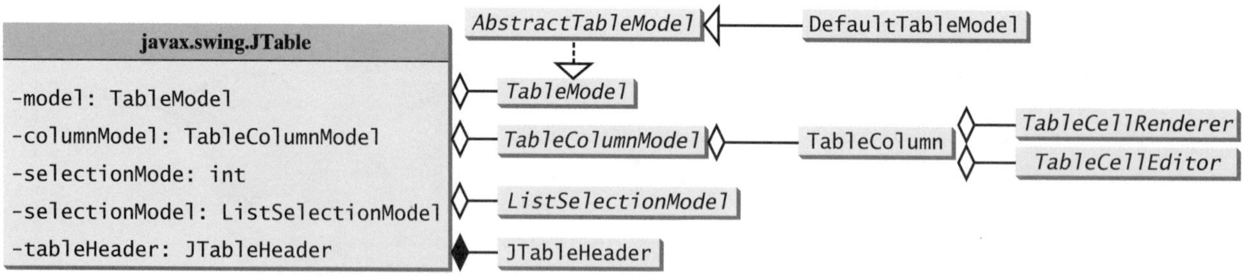
javax.swing.JTable
-model: TableModel
-columnModel: TableColumnModel
-selectionMode: int
-selectionModel: ListSelectionModel
-tableHeader: JTableHeader
AbstractTableModel
DefaultTableModel
TableModel
TableColumnModel
TableColumn
TableCellRenderer
TableCellEditor
ListSelectionModel
JTableHeader

FIGURE 36.2 `JTable` contains many supporting interfaces and classes.

Note

All the supporting interfaces and classes for `JTable` are grouped in the `javax.swing.table` package.

Figure 36.3 shows the constructors, properties, and methods of `JTable`.

JavaBeans properties with get and set methods omitted in the UML diagram.

javax.swing.JTable	
-autoCreateColumnsFromModel: boolean	Indicates whether the columns are created in the table (default: true).
-autoResizeMode: int	Specifies how columns are resized (default: SUBSEQUENT_COLUMNS).
-cellEditor: TableCellEditor	Specifies a cell editor.
-columnModel: TableColumnModel	Maintains the table column data.
-columnSelectionAllowed: boolean	Specifies whether the column can be selected (default: false).
-editingColumn: int	Specifies the column of the cell that is currently being edited.
-editingRow: int	Specifies the row of the cell that is currently being edited.
-gridColor: java.awt.Color	The color used to draw grid lines (default: GRAY).
-intercellSpacing: Dimension	Specifies horizontal and vertical margins between cells (default: 1, 1).
-model: TableModel	Maintains the table model.
-rowCount: int	Read-only property that counts the number of rows in the table.
-rowHeight: int	Specifies the row height of the table (default: 16 pixels).
-rowMargin: int	Specifies the vertical margin between rows (default: 1 pixel).
-rowSelectionAllowed: boolean	Specifies whether the rows can be selected (default: true).
-selectionBackground: java.awt.Color	The background color of selected cells.
-selectionForeground: java.awt.Color	The foreground color of selected cells.
-showGrid: boolean	Specify whether the grid lines are displayed (write-only, default: true).
-selectionMode: int	Specifies a selection mode (write-only).
-selectionModel: ListSelectionModel	Specifies a selection model.
-showHorizontalLines: boolean	Specifies whether the horizontal grid lines are displayed (default: true).
-showVerticalLines: boolean	Specifies whether the vertical grid lines are displayed (default: true).
-tableHeader: JTableHeader	Specifies a table header.
+JTable()	Creates a default JTable with all the default models.
+JTable(numRows: int, numColumns: int)	Creates a JTable with the specified number of empty rows and columns.
+JTable(rowData: Object[][], columnData: Object[])	Creates a JTable with the specified row data and column header names.
+JTable(dm: TableModel)	Creates a JTable with the specified table model.
+JTable(dm: TableModel, cm: TableColumnModel)	Creates a JTable with the specified table model and table column model.
+JTable(dm: TableModel, cm: TableColumnModel, sm: ListSelectionModel)	Creates a JTable with the specified table model, table column model, and selection model.
+JTable(rowData: Vector, columnNames: Vector)	Creates a JTable with the specified row data and column data in vectors.
+addColumn(aColumn: TableColumn): void	Adds a new column to the table.
+clearSelection(): void	Deselects all selected columns and rows.
+editCellAt(row: int, column: int): void	Edits the cell if it is editable.
+getDefaultEditor(column: Class): TableCellEditor	Returns the default editor for the column.
+getDefaultRenderer(col: Class): TableCellRenderer	Returns the default renderer for the column.
+setDefaultEditor(column: Class, editor: TableCellEditor): void	Sets the default editor for the column.
+setDefaultRenderer(column: Class, editor: TableCellRenderer): void	Sets the default renderer for the column.

FIGURE 36.3 The JTable class is for creating, customizing, and manipulating tables.

The JTable class contains seven constructors for creating tables. You can create a table using its no-arg constructor, its models, row data in a two-dimensional array, and column header names in an array, or row data and column header names in vectors. Listing 36.1 creates a table with the row data and column names (line 20) and places it in a scroll pane (line 23). The table is displayed in Figure 36.1.

LISTING 36.1 TestTable.java

column names
row data
create table
scroll pane
main method omitted

```
 1 import javax.swing.*;
 2
 3 public class TestTable extends JApplet {
 4   // Create table column names
 5   private String[] columnNames =
 6     {"Country", "Capital", "Population in Millions", "Democracy"};
 7
 8   // Create table data
 9   private Object[][] data = {
10     {"USA", "Washington DC", 280, true},
11     {"Canada", "Ottawa", 32, true},
12     {"United Kingdom", "London", 60, true},
13     {"Germany", "Berlin", 83, true},
14     {"France", "Paris", 60, true},
15     {"Norway", "Oslo", 4.5, true},
16     {"India", "New Delhi", 1046, true}
17   };
18
19   // Create a table
20   private JTable jTable1 = new JTable(data, columnNames);
21
22   public TestTable() {
23     add(new JScrollPane(jTable1));
24   }
25 }
```

autoboxing

Note

Primitive type values such as `280` and `true` in line 10 are autoboxed into `new Integer(280)` and `new Boolean(true)`.

`JTable` is a powerful control with a variety of properties that provide many ways to customize tables. All the frequently used properties are documented in Figure 36.3. The `autoResizeMode` property specifies how columns are resized (you can resize table columns but not rows). Possible values are:

```
JTable.AUTO_RESIZE_OFF
JTable.AUTO_RESIZE_LAST_COLUMN
JTable.AUTO_RESIZE_SUBSEQUENT_COLUMNS
JTable.AUTO_RESIZE_NEXT_COLUMN
JTable.AUTO_RESIZE_ALL_COLUMNS
```

The default mode is `JTable.AUTO_RESIZE_SUBSEQUENT_COLUMNS`. Initially, each column in the table occupies the same width (75 pixels). With `AUTO_RESIZE_OFF`, resizing a column does not affect the widths of the other columns. With `AUTO_RESIZE_LAST_COLUMN`, resizing a column affects the width of the last column. With `AUTO_RESIZE_SUBSEQUENT_COLUMNS`, resizing a column affects the widths of all the subsequent columns. With `AUTO_RESIZE_NEXT_COLUMN`, resizing a column affects the widths of the next columns. With `AUTO_RESIZE_ALL_COLUMNS`, resizing a column affects the widths of all the columns.

Listing 36.2 gives an example that demonstrates the use of several `JTable` properties. The example creates a table and allows the user to choose an Auto Resize Mode, specify the row height and margin, and indicate whether the grid is shown. A sample run of the program is shown in Figure 36.4.

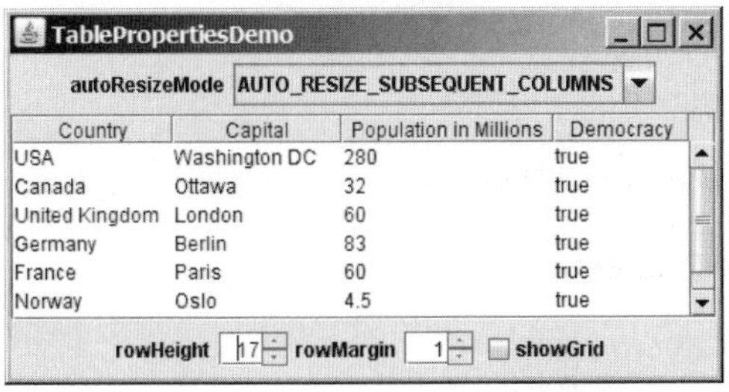
TablePropertiesDemo
autoResizeMode AUTO_RESIZE_SUBSEQUENT_COLUMNS
Country Capital Population in Millions Democracy
USA Washington DC 280 true
Canada Ottawa 32 true
United Kingdom London 60 true
Germany Berlin 83 true
France Paris 60 true
Norway Oslo 4.5 true
rowHeight 17 rowMargin 1 showGrid

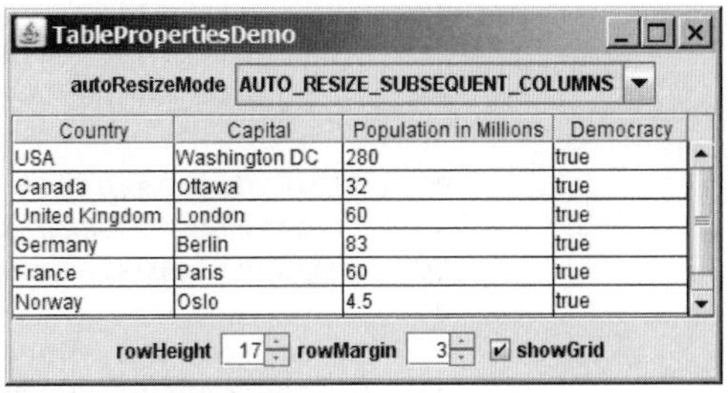
TablePropertiesDemo
autoResizeMode AUTO_RESIZE_SUBSEQUENT_COLUMNS
Country Capital Population in Millions Democracy
USA Washington DC 280 true
Canada Ottawa 32 true
United Kingdom London 60 true
Germany Berlin 83 true
France Paris 60 true
Norway Oslo 4.5 true
rowHeight 17 rowMargin 3 showGrid

FIGURE 36.4 You can specify an autoresizing mode, the table's row height and row margin, and whether to show the grid in the table.

LISTING 36.2 TablePropertiesDemo.java

```java
import java.awt.*;
import java.awt.event.*;
import javax.swing.*;
import javax.swing.event.*;

public class TablePropertiesDemo extends JApplet {
  // Create table column names
  private String[] columnNames =
    {"Country", "Capital", "Population in Millions", "Democracy"};

  // Create table data
  private Object[][] rowData = {
    {"USA", "Washington DC", 280, true},
    {"Canada", "Ottawa", 32, true},
    {"United Kingdom", "London", 60, true},
    {"Germany", "Berlin", 83, true},
    {"France", "Paris", 60, true},
    {"Norway", "Oslo", 4.5, true},
    {"India", "New Delhi", 1046, true}
  };

  // Create a table
  private JTable jTable1 = new JTable(rowData, columnNames);

  // Create two spinners
  private JSpinner jspiRowHeight =
    new JSpinner(new SpinnerNumberModel(16, 1, 50, 1));
  private JSpinner jspiRowMargin =
    new JSpinner(new SpinnerNumberModel(1, 1, 50, 1));

  // Create a check box
  private JCheckBox jchkShowGrid = new JCheckBox("showGrid", true);

  // Create a combo box
  private JComboBox jcboAutoResizeMode = new JComboBox(new String[]{
    "AUTO_RESIZE_OFF", "AUTO_RESIZE_LAST_COLUMN",
    "AUTO_RESIZE_SUBSEQUENT_COLUMNS", "AUTO_RESIZE_NEXT_COLUMN",
    "AUTO_RESIZE_ALL_COLUMNS"});

  public TablePropertiesDemo() {
    JPanel panel1 = new JPanel();
    panel1.add(new JLabel("rowHeight"));
    panel1.add(jspiRowHeight);
```

column names

table data

table

spinners

combo box

create UI

```java
    panel1.add(new JLabel("rowMargin"));
    panel1.add(jspiRowMargin);
    panel1.add(jchkShowGrid);

    JPanel panel2 = new JPanel();
    panel2.add(new JLabel("autoResizeMode"));
    panel2.add(jcboAutoResizeMode);

    add(panel1, BorderLayout.SOUTH);
    add(panel2, BorderLayout.NORTH);
    add(new JScrollPane(jTable1));

    // Initialize jTable1
```

table properties

```java
    jTable1.setAutoResizeMode(JTable.AUTO_RESIZE_OFF);
    jTable1.setGridColor(Color.BLUE);
    jTable1.setSelectionMode(ListSelectionModel.SINGLE_SELECTION);
    jTable1.setSelectionBackground(Color.RED);
    jTable1.setSelectionForeground(Color.WHITE);

    // Register and create a listener for jspiRowHeight
```

spinner listener

```java
    jspiRowHeight.addChangeListener(new ChangeListener() {
      public void stateChanged(ChangeEvent e) {
        jTable1.setRowHeight(
          ((Integer)(jspiRowHeight.getValue())).intValue());
      }
    });

    // Register and create a listener for jspiRowMargin
```

spinner listener

```java
    jspiRowMargin.addChangeListener(new ChangeListener() {
      public void stateChanged(ChangeEvent e) {
        jTable1.setRowMargin(
          ((Integer)(jspiRowMargin.getValue())).intValue());
      }
    });

    // Register and create a listener for jchkShowGrid
```

check-box listener

```java
    jchkShowGrid.addActionListener(new ActionListener() {
      public void actionPerformed(ActionEvent e) {
        jTable1.setShowGrid(jchkShowGrid.isSelected());
      }
    });

    // Register and create a listener for jcboAutoResizeMode
```

combo box listener

```java
    jcboAutoResizeMode.addActionListener(new ActionListener() {
      public void actionPerformed(ActionEvent e) {
        String selectedItem =
          (String)jcboAutoResizeMode.getSelectedItem();

        if (selectedItem.equals("AUTO_RESIZE_OFF"))
          jTable1.setAutoResizeMode(JTable.AUTO_RESIZE_OFF);
        else if (selectedItem.equals("AUTO_RESIZE_LAST_COLUMN"))
          jTable1.setAutoResizeMode(JTable.AUTO_RESIZE_LAST_COLUMN);
        else if (selectedItem.equals
               ("AUTO_RESIZE_SUBSEQUENT_COLUMNS"))
          jTable1.setAutoResizeMode(
            JTable.AUTO_RESIZE_SUBSEQUENT_COLUMNS);
        else if (selectedItem.equals("AUTO_RESIZE_NEXT_COLUMN"))
          jTable1.setAutoResizeMode(JTable.AUTO_RESIZE_NEXT_COLUMN);
        else if (selectedItem.equals("AUTO_RESIZE_ALL_COLUMNS"))
          jTable1.setAutoResizeMode(JTable.AUTO_RESIZE_ALL_COLUMNS);
```

```
104       }
105     });
106   }
107 }
```

main method omitted

If you know the row data in advance, creating a table using the constructor `JTable(Object[][] rowData, Object[] columnNames)` is convenient. As shown in line 23, a `JTable` is created using this constructor.

Two `JSpinner` objects (`jspiRowHeight`, `jspiRowMargin`) for selecting row height and row margin are created in lines 26–29. The initial value for `jspiRowHeight` is set to `16`, which is the default property value for `rowHeight`. The initial value for `jspiRowMargin` is set to `1`, which is the default property value for `rowMargin`. A check box (`jchkShowGrid`) is created with label `showGrid` and initially selected in line 32. A combo box for selecting `autoResizeMode` is created in lines 35–38.

The values of the `JTable` properties (`autoResizeMode`, `gridColor`, `selectionMode`, `selectionBackground`, and `selectionForeground`) are set in lines 57–61.

The code for processing spinners, check boxes, and combo boxes is given in lines 64–106.

36.3 Table Models and Table Column Models

`JTable` delegates data storing and processing to its table data model. A table data model must implement the `TableModel` interface, which defines the methods for registering table model listeners, manipulating cells, and obtaining row count, column count, column class, and column name.

TableModel

The `AbstractTableModel` class provides partial implementations for most of the methods in `TableModel`. It takes care of the management of listeners and provides some conveniences for generating `TableModelEvents` and dispatching them to the listeners. To create a concrete `TableModel`, you simply extend `AbstractTableModel` and implement at least the following three methods:

AbstractTableModel

- `public int getRowCount()`
- `public int getColumnCount()`
- `public Object getValueAt(int row, int column)`

The `DefaultTableModel` class extends `AbstractTableModel` and implements these three methods. Additionally, `DefaultTableModel` provides concrete storage for data. The data are stored in a vector. The elements in the vector are arrays of objects, each of which represents an individual cell value. The methods in `DefaultTableModel` for accessing and modifying data are shown in Figure 36.5.

DefaultTableModel

Listing 36.3 gives an example that demonstrates table models. The example creates a table model (line 16), plugs the model to the table (line 20), appends a row to the table (line 25), inserts a row before the first row (line 26), removes a row with index 1 (line 28), adds a new column (line 29), and sets new values at specified cells (lines 30–32). Figure 36.6 shows the output of the program.

LISTING 36.3 TestTableModel.java

```
 1 import javax.swing.*;
 2 import javax.swing.table.*;
 3
 4 public class TestTableModel extends JApplet {
 5   // Create table column names
 6   private String[] columnNames =
 7     {"Country", "Capital", "Population in Millions", "Democracy"};
 8
 9   // Create table data
10   private Object[][] data = {
```

column names

row data

create table model
create table
scroll pane
add row
insert row
remove row
add column
set value
main method omitted

```
    {"USA", "Washington DC", 280, true},
    {"Canada", "Ottawa", 32, true}
  };

  // Create a model
  private DefaultTableModel tableModel =
    new DefaultTableModel(data, columnNames);

  // Create a table
  private JTable jTable1 = new JTable(tableModel);

  public TestTableModel() {
    add(new JScrollPane(jTable1));

    tableModel.addRow(new Object[]{"France", "Paris", 60, true});
    tableModel.insertRow(0, new Object[]
      {"India", "New Delhi", 1046, true});
    tableModel.removeRow(1);
    tableModel.addColumn("Area");
    tableModel.setValueAt(10, 0, 4);
    tableModel.setValueAt(20, 1, 4);
    tableModel.setValueAt(30, 2, 4);
  }
}
```

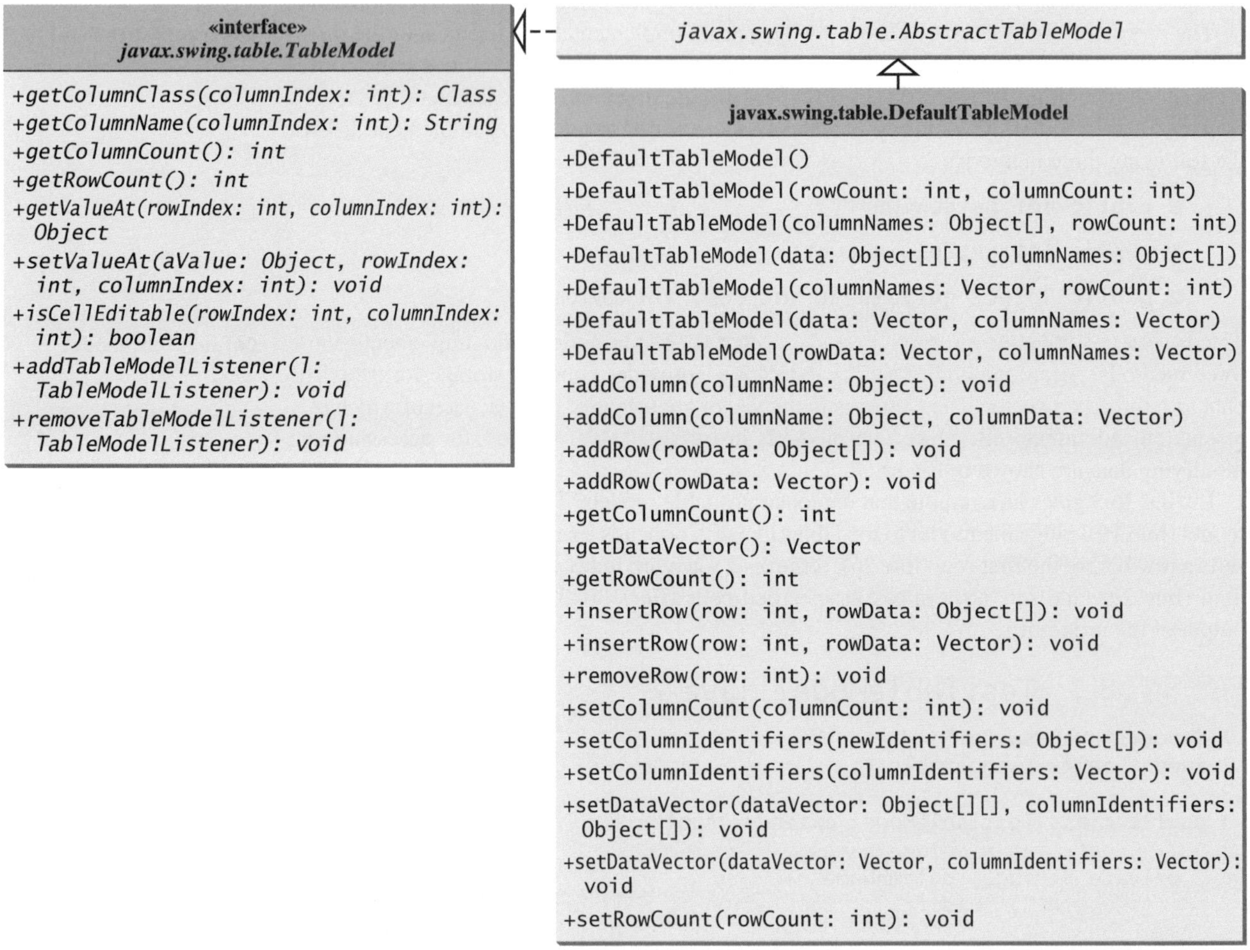
«interface»
javax.swing.table.TableModel
+getColumnClass(columnIndex: int): Class
+getColumnName(columnIndex: int): String
+getColumnCount(): int
+getRowCount(): int
+getValueAt(rowIndex: int, columnIndex: int): Object
+setValueAt(aValue: Object, rowIndex: int, columnIndex: int): void
+isCellEditable(rowIndex: int, columnIndex: int): boolean
+addTableModelListener(l: TableModelListener): void
+removeTableModelListener(l: TableModelListener): void
javax.swing.table.AbstractTableModel
javax.swing.table.DefaultTableModel
+DefaultTableModel()
+DefaultTableModel(rowCount: int, columnCount: int)
+DefaultTableModel(columnNames: Object[], rowCount: int)
+DefaultTableModel(data: Object[][], columnNames: Object[])
+DefaultTableModel(columnNames: Vector, rowCount: int)
+DefaultTableModel(data: Vector, columnNames: Vector)
+DefaultTableModel(rowData: Vector, columnNames: Vector)
+addColumn(columnName: Object): void
+addColumn(columnName: Object, columnData: Vector)
+addRow(rowData: Object[]): void
+addRow(rowData: Vector): void
+getColumnCount(): int
+getDataVector(): Vector
+getRowCount(): int
+insertRow(row: int, rowData: Object[]): void
+insertRow(row: int, rowData: Vector): void
+removeRow(row: int): void
+setColumnCount(columnCount: int): void
+setColumnIdentifiers(newIdentifiers: Object[]): void
+setColumnIdentifiers(columnIdentifiers: Vector): void
+setDataVector(dataVector: Object[][], columnIdentifiers: Object[]): void
+setDataVector(dataVector: Vector, columnIdentifiers: Vector): void
+setRowCount(rowCount: int): void

FIGURE 36.5 `TableModel` stores and manages data in a table and `DefaultTableModel` provides a default implementation for `TableModel`.

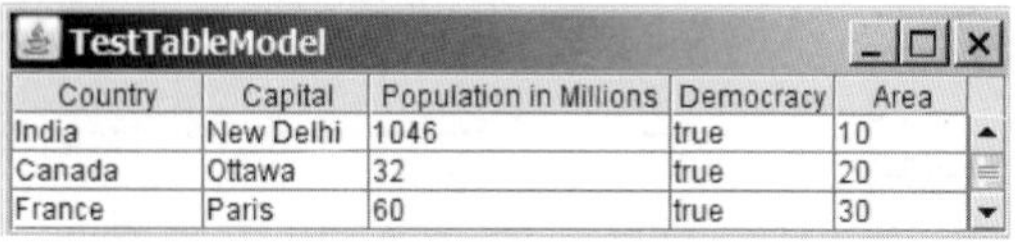
TestTableModel
Country | Capital | Population in Millions | Democracy | Area
India | New Delhi | 1046 | true | 10
Canada | Ottawa | 32 | true | 20
France | Paris | 60 | true | 30

FIGURE 36.6 `TableModel` and `DefaultTableModel` contain the methods for adding, updating, and removing table data.

`TableModel` manages table data. You can add and remove rows through a `TableModel`. You can also add a column through a `TableModel`. However, you cannot remove a column through a `TableModel`. To remove a column from a `JTable`, you have to use a table column model.

Table column models manage columns in a table. They can be used to select, add, move, and remove table columns. A table column model must implement the `TableColumnModel` interface, which defines the methods for registering table column model listeners, and for accessing and manipulating columns, as shown in Figure 36.7.

TableColumnModel

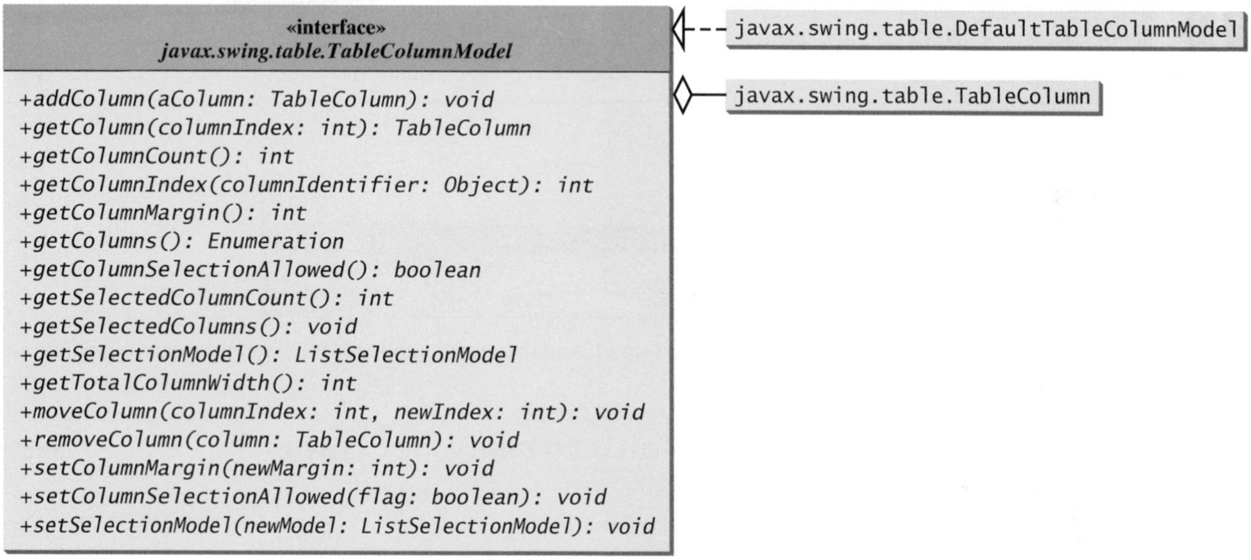
«interface»
javax.swing.table.TableColumnModel
+addColumn(aColumn: TableColumn): void
+getColumn(columnIndex: int): TableColumn
+getColumnCount(): int
+getColumnIndex(columnIdentifier: Object): int
+getColumnMargin(): int
+getColumns(): Enumeration
+getColumnSelectionAllowed(): boolean
+getSelectedColumnCount(): int
+getSelectedColumns(): void
+getSelectionModel(): ListSelectionModel
+getTotalColumnWidth(): int
+moveColumn(columnIndex: int, newIndex: int): void
+removeColumn(column: TableColumn): void
+setColumnMargin(newMargin: int): void
+setColumnSelectionAllowed(flag: boolean): void
+setSelectionModel(newModel: ListSelectionModel): void
javax.swing.table.DefaultTableColumnModel
javax.swing.table.TableColumn

FIGURE 36.7 `TableColumnModel` manages columns in a table and `DefaultTableColumnModel` is a concrete implementation of it.

`DefaultTableColumnModel` is a concrete class that implements `TableColumnModel` and `PropertyChangeListener`. The `DefaultTableColumnModel` class stores its columns in a vector and contains an instance of `ListSelectionModel` for selecting columns.

DefaultTableColumnModel

The column model deals with all the columns in a table. The `TableColumn` class is used to model an individual column in the table. An instance of `TableColumn` for a specified column can be obtained using the `getColumn(index)` method in `TableColumnModel` or the `getColumn(columnIdentifier)` method in `JTable`.

TableColumn

Figure 36.8 shows the properties, constructors, and methods in `TableColumn` for manipulating column width and specifying the cell renderer, cell editor, and header renderer.

Listing 36.4 gives an example that demonstrates table column models. The example obtains the table column model from the table (line 21), moves the first column to the second (line 22), and removes the last column (lines 23). Figure 36.9 shows the output of the program.

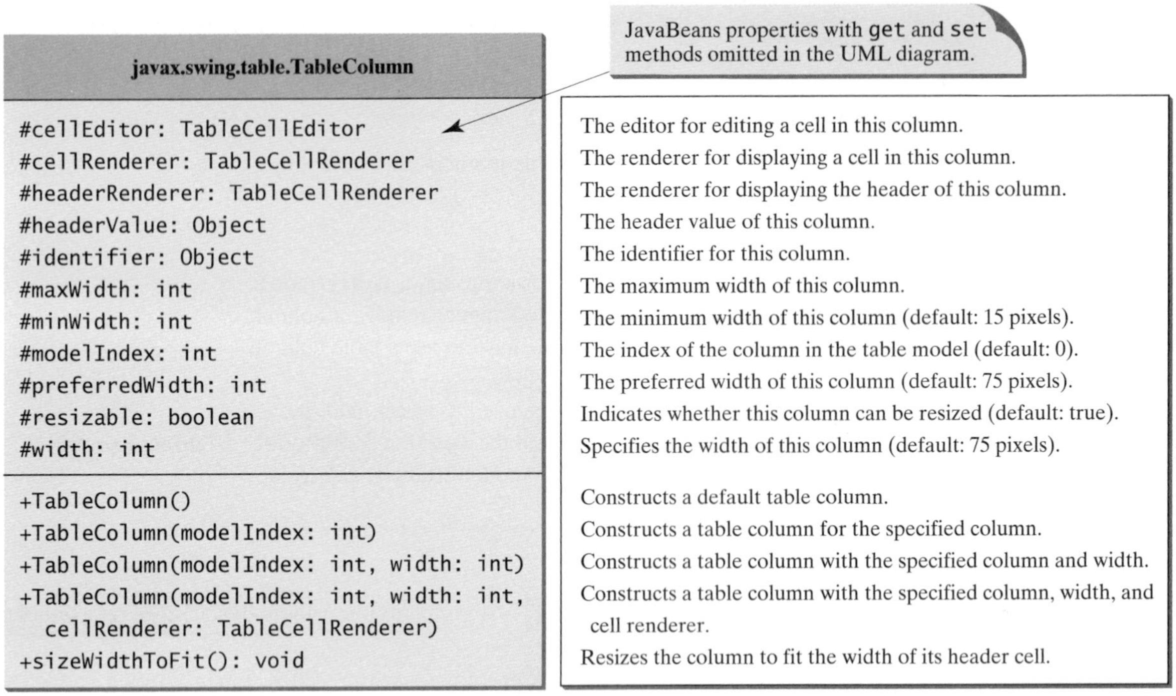
JavaBeans properties with get and set methods omitted in the UML diagram.
javax.swing.table.TableColumn
#cellEditor: TableCellEditor
#cellRenderer: TableCellRenderer
#headerRenderer: TableCellRenderer
#headerValue: Object
#identifier: Object
#maxWidth: int
#minWidth: int
#modelIndex: int
#preferredWidth: int
#resizable: boolean
#width: int
+TableColumn()
+TableColumn(modelIndex: int)
+TableColumn(modelIndex: int, width: int)
+TableColumn(modelIndex: int, width: int, cellRenderer: TableCellRenderer)
+sizeWidthToFit(): void
The editor for editing a cell in this column.
The renderer for displaying a cell in this column.
The renderer for displaying the header of this column.
The header value of this column.
The identifier for this column.
The maximum width of this column.
The minimum width of this column (default: 15 pixels).
The index of the column in the table model (default: 0).
The preferred width of this column (default: 75 pixels).
Indicates whether this column can be resized (default: true).
Specifies the width of this column (default: 75 pixels).
Constructs a default table column.
Constructs a table column for the specified column.
Constructs a table column with the specified column and width.
Constructs a table column with the specified column, width, and cell renderer.
Resizes the column to fit the width of its header cell.

FIGURE 36.8 The `TableColumn` class models a single column.

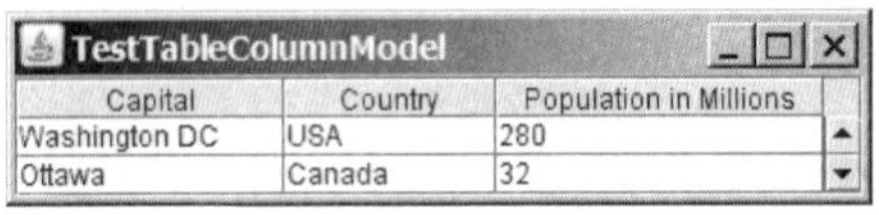
TestTableColumnModel
Capital
Country
Population in Millions
Washington DC
USA
280
Ottawa
Canada
32

FIGURE 36.9 `TableColumnModel` contains the methods for moving and removing columns.

LISTING 36.4 TestTableColumnModel.java

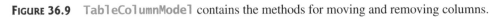

```
import javax.swing.*;
import javax.swing.table.*;

public class TestTableColumnModel extends JApplet {
  // Create table column names
  private String[] columnNames =
    {"Country", "Capital", "Population in Millions", "Democracy"};

  // Create table data
  private Object[][] data = {
    {"USA", "Washington DC", 280, true},
    {"Canada", "Ottawa", 32, true}
  };

  // Create a table
  private JTable jTable1 = new JTable(data, columnNames);

  public TestTableColumnModel() {
    add(new JScrollPane(jTable1));

    TableColumnModel columnModel = jTable1.getColumnModel();
    columnModel.moveColumn(0, 1);
```

```
    columnModel.removeColumn(columnModel.getColumn(3));
  }
}
```

remove a column

main method omitted

Note

Some of the methods defined in the table model and the table column model are also defined in the `JTable` class for convenience. For instance, the `getColumnCount()` method is defined in `JTable`, `TableModel`, and `TableColumnModel`, the `addColumn` method defined in the column model is also defined in the table model, and the `getColumn()` method defined in the column model is also defined in the `JTable` class.

TableHeader

`JTableHeader` is a GUI component that displays the header of the `JTable` (see Figure 36.10). When you create a `JTable`, an instance of `JTableHeader` is automatically created and stored in the `tableHeader` property. By default, you can reorder the columns by dragging the header of the column. To disable it, set the `reorderingAllowed` property to `false`.

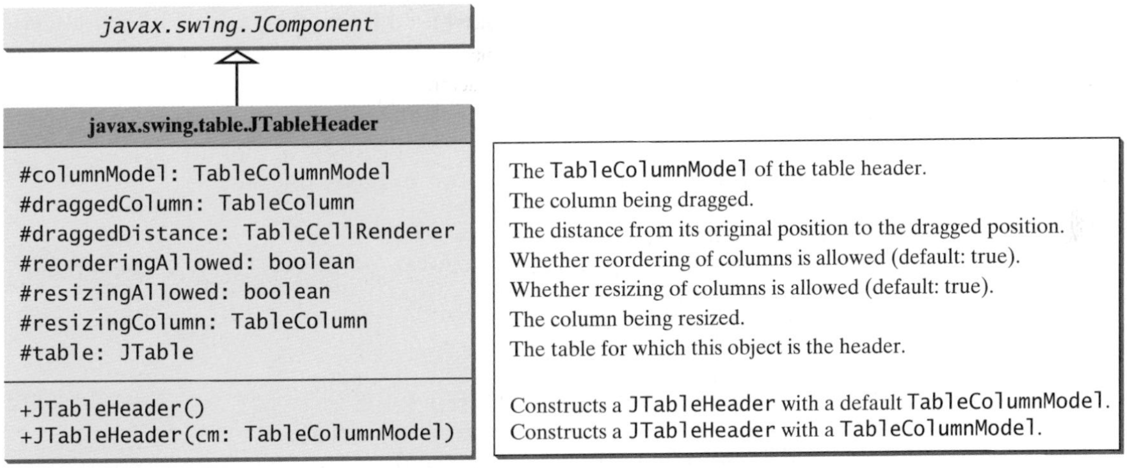
javax.swing.JComponent
javax.swing.table.JTableHeader
#columnModel: TableColumnModel
#draggedColumn: TableColumn
#draggedDistance: TableCellRenderer
#reorderingAllowed: boolean
#resizingAllowed: boolean
#resizingColumn: TableColumn
#table: JTable
+JTableHeader()
+JTableHeader(cm: TableColumnModel)
The TableColumnModel of the table header.
The column being dragged.
The distance from its original position to the dragged position.
Whether reordering of columns is allowed (default: true).
Whether resizing of columns is allowed (default: true).
The column being resized.
The table for which this object is the header.
Constructs a JTableHeader with a default TableColumnModel.
Constructs a JTableHeader with a TableColumnModel.

FIGURE 36.10 The `JTableHeader` class displays the header of the `JTable`.

36.4 Auto Sort and Filtering

Auto sort and filtering are two useful features. To enable auto sort on any column in a `JTable`, create an instance of `TableRowSorter` with a table model and set `JTable`'s `rowSorter` as follows:

create a **TableRowSorter**

setRowSorter

```
TableRowSorter<TableModel> sorter =
  new TableRowSorter<TableModel>(tableModel);
jTable.setRowSorter(sorter);
```

When the table is displayed, you can sort the table by clicking a column head, as shown in Figure 36.11.

You can specify a filter to select rows in the table. The filter can be applied on one column or all columns. The `javax.swing.RowFilter` class contains several static methods for creating filters. You can use the `regexFilter` method to create a `RowFilter` with the specified regular expression. For example, the following statement creates a filter for the rows whose first column or second column begin with letter `U`.

create a filter

```
RowFilter rowFilter = RowFilter.regexFilter("U.*", int[]{0, 1});
```

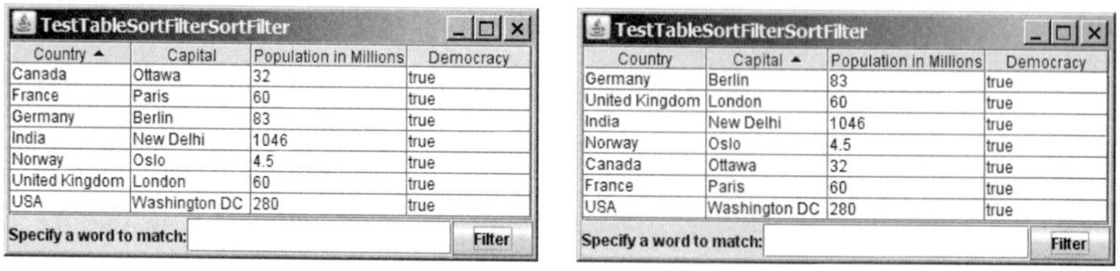
TestTableSortFilterSortFilter
Country ▲ | Capital | Population in Millions | Democracy
Canada | Ottawa | 32 | true
France | Paris | 60 | true
Germany | Berlin | 83 | true
India | New Delhi | 1046 | true
Norway | Oslo | 4.5 | true
United Kingdom | London | 60 | true
USA | Washington DC | 280 | true
Specify a word to match:
Filter
TestTableSortFilterSortFilter
Country | Capital ▲ | Population in Millions | Democracy
Germany | Berlin | 83 | true
United Kingdom | London | 60 | true
India | New Delhi | 1046 | true
Norway | Oslo | 4.5 | true
Canada | Ottawa | 32 | true
France | Paris | 60 | true
USA | Washington DC | 280 | true
Specify a word to match:
Filter

(a) (b)

FIGURE 36.11 (a) The table is sorted on Country. (b) The table is sorted on Capital.

The second argument in the `regexFilter` method specifies a set of column indices. If no indices are specified, all columns are searched in the filter.

To enable filtering, you have to associate a filter with a `TableRowSorter`, which is set to the `JTable`'s `rowSorter` property.

set filter in **JTable**

Listing 36.5 gives an example that demonstrates auto sort and filtering in `JTable`.

LISTING 36.5 TestTableSortFilter.java

column names

row data

create table

create **TableRowSorter**

set sorter

```
import javax.swing.*;
import javax.swing.table.*;
import java.awt.BorderLayout;

public class TestTableSortFilter extends JApplet {
  // Create table column names
  private String[] columnNames =
    {"Country", "Capital", "Population in Millions", "Democracy"};

  // Create table data
  private Object[][] data = {
    {"USA", "Washington DC", 280, true},
    {"Canada", "Ottawa", 32, true},
    {"United Kingdom", "London", 60, true},
    {"Germany", "Berlin", 83, true},
    {"France", "Paris", 60, true},
    {"Norway", "Oslo", 4.5, true},
    {"India", "New Delhi", 1046, true}
  };

  // Create a table
  private JTable jTable1 = new JTable(data, columnNames);

  // Create a TableRowSorter
  private TableRowSorter<TableModel> sorter =
      new TableRowSorter<TableModel>(jTable1.getModel());

  private JTextField jtfFilter = new JTextField();
  private JButton btFilter = new JButton("Filter");

  public TestTableSortFilter() {
    // Enable auto sorter
    jTable1.setRowSorter(sorter);

    JPanel panel = new JPanel(new java.awt.BorderLayout());
    panel.add(new JLabel("Specify a word to match:"),
      BorderLayout.WEST);
    panel.add(jtfFilter, BorderLayout.CENTER);
    panel.add(btFilter, BorderLayout.EAST);
```

```
40
41      add(panel, BorderLayout.SOUTH);
42      add(new JScrollPane(jTable1), BorderLayout.CENTER);
43
44      btFilter.addActionListener(new java.awt.event.ActionListener() {
45        public void actionPerformed(java.awt.event.ActionEvent e) {
46          String text = jtfFilter.getText();
47          if (text.trim().length() == 0)
48            sorter.setRowFilter(null);
49          else
50            sorter.setRowFilter(RowFilter.regexFilter(text));
51        }
52      });
53    }
54  }
```

remove filter

set a filter

main method omitted

The example creates a `TableRowSorter` (line 25) and sets the sorter in `jTable1` (line 33). The program lets the user enter a filter pattern from a text field, as shown in Figure 36.12. If nothing is entered, no filter is set (line 48). If a regex is entered, clicking the *Filter* button sets the filter to `jTable1` (line 50).

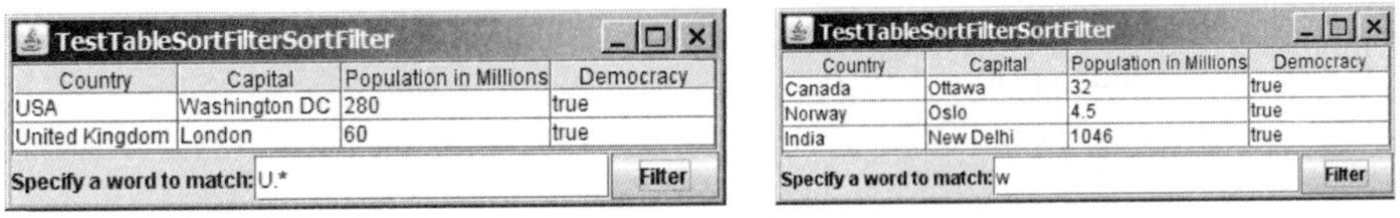
TestTableSortFilterSortFilter
Country
Capital
Population in Millions
Democracy
USA
Washington DC
280
true
United Kingdom
London
60
true
Specify a word to match:
U.*
Filter
(a)
TestTableSortFilterSortFilter
Canada
Ottawa
32
Norway
Oslo
4.5
India
New Delhi
1046
w
(b)

FIGURE 36.12 (a) Filter the table with regex `U.*`. (b) Filter the table with regex `w`.

36.5 Case Study: Modifying Rows and Columns

This case study demonstrates the use of table models, table column models, list-selection models, and the `TableColumn` class. The program allows the user to choose selection mode and selection type, add or remove rows and columns, and save, clear, or restore the table, as shown in Figure 36.13(a).

The *Add New Row* button adds a new empty row before the currently selected row, as shown in Figure 36.13(b). If no row is currently selected, a new empty row is appended to the end of the table.

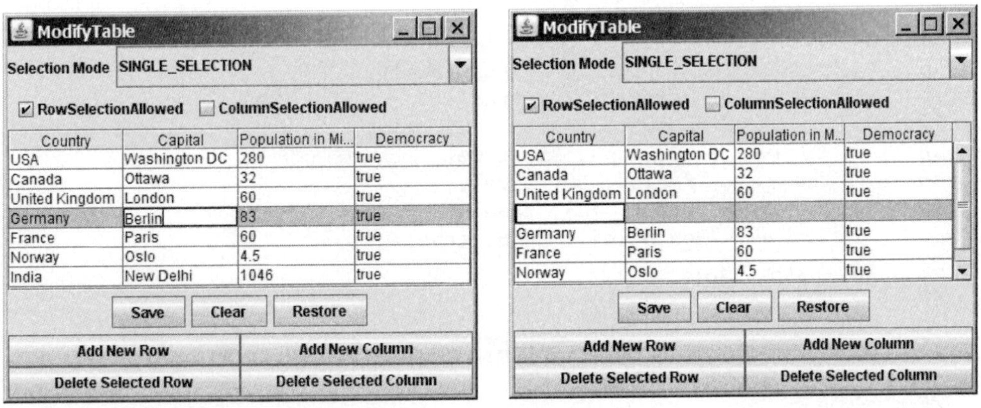
ModifyTable
Selection Mode
SINGLE_SELECTION
RowSelectionAllowed
ColumnSelectionAllowed
Country
Capital
Population in Mi...
Democracy
USA
Washington DC
280
Canada
Ottawa
32
United Kingdom
London
60
Germany
Berlin
83
France
Paris
60
Norway
Oslo
4.5
India
New Delhi
1046
true
Save
Clear
Restore
Add New Row
Add New Column
Delete Selected Row
Delete Selected Column
(a)
(b)

FIGURE 36.13 You can add, remove, and modify rows and columns in a table interactively.

When you click the *Add New Column* button, an input dialog box is displayed to receive the title of the column, as shown in Figure 36.14(a). The new column is appended in the table, as shown in Figure 36.14(b).

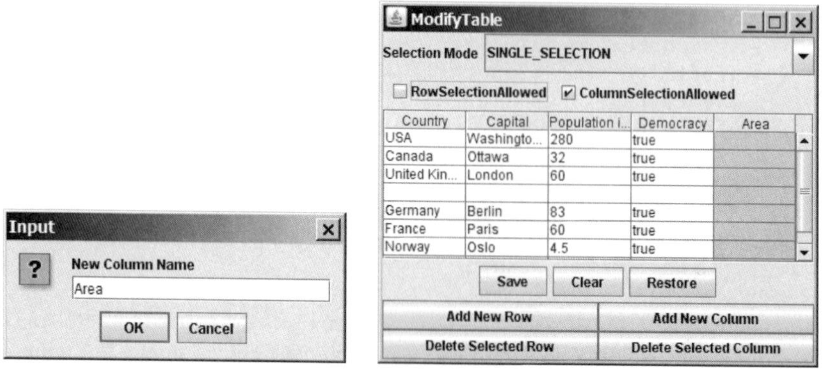
Input
New Column Name
Area
OK
Cancel
ModifyTable
Selection Mode
SINGLE_SELECTION
RowSelectionAllowed
ColumnSelectionAllowed
Country
Capital
Population i...
Democracy
Area
USA
Washingto...
280
true
Canada
Ottawa
32
true
United Kin...
London
60
true
Germany
Berlin
83
true
France
Paris
60
true
Norway
Oslo
4.5
true
Save
Clear
Restore
Add New Row
Add New Column
Delete Selected Row
Delete Selected Column

(a) (b)

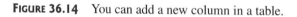

FIGURE 36.14 You can add a new column in a table.

The *Delete Selected Row* button deletes the first selected row. The *Delete Selected Column* button deletes the first selected column.

The *Save* button saves the current table data and column names. The *Clear* button clears the row data in the table. The *Restore* button restores the saved table.

Listing 36.6 gives the program.

LISTING 36.6 ModifyTable.java

column names

table data

table model

table

```
import java.awt.*;
import java.awt.event.*;
import javax.swing.*;
import javax.swing.table.*;
import java.io.*;
import java.util.Vector;

public class ModifyTable extends JApplet {
  // Create table column names
  private String[] columnNames =
    {"Country", "Capital", "Population in Millions", "Democracy"};

  // Create table data
  private Object[][] rowData = {
    {"USA", "Washington DC", 280, true},
    {"Canada", "Ottawa", 32, true},
    {"United Kingdom", "London", 60, true},
    {"Germany", "Berlin", 83, true},
    {"France", "Paris", 60, true},
    {"Norway", "Oslo", 4.5, true},
    {"India", "New Delhi", 1046, true}
  };

  // Create a table model
  private DefaultTableModel tableModel = new DefaultTableModel(
    rowData, columnNames);

  // Create a table
  private JTable jTable1 = new JTable(tableModel);
```

```java

  // Create buttons
  private JButton jbtAddRow = new JButton("Add New Row");
  private JButton jbtAddColumn = new JButton("Add New Column");
  private JButton jbtDeleteRow = new JButton("Delete Selected Row");
  private JButton jbtDeleteColumn = new JButton(
    "Delete Selected Column");
  private JButton jbtSave = new JButton("Save");
  private JButton jbtClear = new JButton("Clear");
  private JButton jbtRestore = new JButton("Restore");

  // Create a combo box for selection modes
  private JComboBox jcboSelectionMode =
    new JComboBox(new String[] {"SINGLE_SELECTION",
      "SINGLE_INTERVAL_SELECTION", "MULTIPLE_INTERVAL_SELECTION"});

  // Create check boxes
  private JCheckBox jchkRowSelectionAllowed =
    new JCheckBox("RowSelectionAllowed", true);
  private JCheckBox jchkColumnSelectionAllowed =
    new JCheckBox("ColumnSelectionAllowed", false);

  public ModifyTable() {
    JPanel panel1 = new JPanel();
    panel1.setLayout(new GridLayout(2, 2));
    panel1.add(jbtAddRow);
    panel1.add(jbtAddColumn);
    panel1.add(jbtDeleteRow);
    panel1.add(jbtDeleteColumn);

    JPanel panel2 = new JPanel();
    panel2.add(jbtSave);
    panel2.add(jbtClear);
    panel2.add(jbtRestore);

    JPanel panel3 = new JPanel();
    panel3.setLayout(new BorderLayout(5, 0));
    panel3.add(new JLabel("Selection Mode"), BorderLayout.WEST);
    panel3.add(jcboSelectionMode, BorderLayout.CENTER);

    JPanel panel4 = new JPanel();
    panel4.setLayout(new FlowLayout(FlowLayout.LEFT));
    panel4.add(jchkRowSelectionAllowed);
    panel4.add(jchkColumnSelectionAllowed);

    JPanel panel5 = new JPanel();
    panel5.setLayout(new GridLayout(2, 1));
    panel5.add(panel3);
    panel5.add(panel4);

    JPanel panel6 = new JPanel();
    panel6.setLayout(new BorderLayout());
    panel6.add(panel1, BorderLayout.SOUTH);
    panel6.add(panel2, BorderLayout.CENTER);

    add(panel5, BorderLayout.NORTH);
    add(new JScrollPane(jTable1),
      BorderLayout.CENTER);
    add(panel6, BorderLayout.SOUTH);

```

buttons

combo box

check boxes

create UI

```
    // Initialize table selection mode
    jTable1.setSelectionMode(ListSelectionModel.SINGLE_SELECTION);

```

add row

```
    jbtAddRow.addActionListener(new ActionListener() {
      public void actionPerformed(ActionEvent e) {
        if (jTable1.getSelectedRow() >= 0)
          tableModel.insertRow(jTable1.getSelectedRow(),
            new java.util.Vector());
        else
          tableModel.addRow(new java.util.Vector());
      }
    });

```

add column

```
    jbtAddColumn.addActionListener(new ActionListener() {
      public void actionPerformed(ActionEvent e) {
        String name = JOptionPane.showInputDialog("New Column Name");
        tableModel.addColumn(name, new java.util.Vector());
      }
    });

```

delete row

```
    jbtDeleteRow.addActionListener(new ActionListener() {
      public void actionPerformed(ActionEvent e) {
        if (jTable1.getSelectedRow() >= 0)
          tableModel.removeRow(jTable1.getSelectedRow());
      }
    });

```

delete column

```
    jbtDeleteColumn.addActionListener(new ActionListener() {
      public void actionPerformed(ActionEvent e) {
        if (jTable1.getSelectedColumn() >= 0) {
          TableColumnModel columnModel = jTable1.getColumnModel();
          TableColumn tableColumn =
              columnModel.getColumn(jTable1.getSelectedColumn());
          columnModel.removeColumn(tableColumn);
        }
      }
    });

```

save table

```
    jbtSave.addActionListener(new ActionListener() {
      public void actionPerformed(ActionEvent e) {
        try {
          ObjectOutputStream out = new ObjectOutputStream(
            new FileOutputStream("tablemodel.dat"));
          out.writeObject(tableModel.getDataVector());
          out.writeObject(getColumnNames());
          out.close();
        }
        catch (Exception ex) {
          ex.printStackTrace();
        }
      }
    });

```

clear table

```
    jbtClear.addActionListener(new ActionListener() {
      public void actionPerformed(ActionEvent e) {
        tableModel.setRowCount(0);
      }
    });

```

restore table

```
    jbtRestore.addActionListener(new ActionListener() {
```

```
150       public void actionPerformed(ActionEvent e) {
151         try {
152           ObjectInputStream in = new ObjectInputStream(
153             new FileInputStream("tablemodel.dat"));
154           Vector rowData = (Vector)in.readObject();
155           Vector columnNames = (Vector)in.readObject();
156           tableModel.setDataVector(rowData, columnNames);
157           in.close();
158         }
159         catch (Exception ex) {
160           ex.printStackTrace();
161         }
162       }
163     });
164 
```

row selection allowed

```
165     jchkRowSelectionAllowed.addActionListener(new ActionListener() {
166       public void actionPerformed(ActionEvent e) {
167         jTable1.setRowSelectionAllowed(
168           jchkRowSelectionAllowed.isSelected());
169       }
170     });
171 
```

column selection allowed

```
172     jchkColumnSelectionAllowed.addActionListener(
173       new ActionListener() {
174       public void actionPerformed(ActionEvent e) {
175         jTable1.setColumnSelectionAllowed(
176           jchkColumnSelectionAllowed.isSelected());
177       }
178     });
179 
```

choose selection mode

```
180     jcboSelectionMode.addActionListener(new ActionListener() {
181       public void actionPerformed(ActionEvent e) {
182         String selectedItem =
183           (String) jcboSelectionMode.getSelectedItem();
184 
185         if (selectedItem.equals("SINGLE_SELECTION"))
186           jTable1.setSelectionMode(
187             ListSelectionModel.SINGLE_SELECTION);
188         else if (selectedItem.equals("SINGLE_INTERVAL_SELECTION"))
189           jTable1.setSelectionMode(
190             ListSelectionModel.SINGLE_INTERVAL_SELECTION);
191         else if (selectedItem.equals("MULTIPLE_INTERVAL_SELECTION"))
192           jTable1.setSelectionMode(
193             ListSelectionModel.MULTIPLE_INTERVAL_SELECTION);
194       }
195     });
196   }
197 
```

get column names

```
198   private Vector getColumnNames() {
199     Vector<String> columnNames = new Vector<String>();
200 
201     for (int i = 0; i < jTable1.getColumnCount(); i++)
202       columnNames.add(jTable1.getColumnName(i));
203 
204     return columnNames;
205   }
206 }
```

main method omitted

A table model is created using `DefaultTableModel` with row data and column names (lines 25–26). This model is used to create a `JTable` (line 29).

The GUI objects (buttons, combo box, check boxes) are created in lines 32–50 and are placed in the UI in lines 53–88.

The table-selection mode is the same as the list-selection mode. By default, the selection mode is `MULTIPLE_INTERVAL_SELECTION`. To match the initial value in the selection combo box (`jcboSelectionMode`), the table's selection mode is set to `SINGLE_SELECTION`.

The *Add New Row* button action is processed in lines 93–101. The `insertRow` method inserts a new row before the selected row (lines 96–97). If no row is currently selected, the `addRow` method appends a new row into the table model (line 99).

The *Add New Column* button action is processed in lines 103–108. The `addColumn` method appends a new column into the table model (line 106).

The *Delete Selected Row* button action is processed in lines 110–115. The `removeRow(rowIndex)` method removes the selected row from the table model (line 113).

The *Delete Selected Column* button action is processed in lines 117–126. To remove a column, you have to use the `removeColumn` method in `TableColumnModel` (line 123).

The *Save* button action is processed in lines 128–141. It writes row data and column names to an output file using object stream (lines 133–134). The column names are obtained using the `getColumnNames()` method (lines 198–205). You may attempt to save `tableModel`, because `tableModel` is an instance of `DefaultTableModel` (lines 25–26) and `DefaultTableModel` is serializable. However, `tableModel` may contain nonserializable listeners for `TableModel` event.

The *Clear* button action is processed in lines 143–147. It clears the table by setting the row count to `0` (line 145).

The *Restore* button action is processed in lines 149–163. It reads row data and column names from the file using object stream (lines 154–155) and sets the new data and column names to the table model (line 156).

36.6 Table Renderers and Editors

Table cells are painted by cell renderers. By default, a cell object's string representation (`toString()`) is displayed and the string can be edited as it was in a text field. `JTable` maintains a set of predefined renderers and editors, listed in Table 36.1, which can be specified to replace default string renderers and editors.

TABLE 36.1 Predefined renderers and editors for tables

Class	*Renderer*	*Editor*
`Object`	`JLabel` (left aligned)	`JTextField`
`Date`	`JLabel` (right aligned)	`JTextField`
`Number`	`JLabel` (right aligned)	`JTextField`
`ImageIcon`	`JLabel` (center aligned)	
`Boolean`	`JCheckBox` (center aligned)	`JCheckBox` (center aligned)

The predefined renderers and editors are automatically located and loaded to match the class returned from the `getColumnClass()` method in the table model. To use a predefined renderer or editor for a class other than `String`, you need to create your own table model by extending a subclass of `TableModel`. In your table model class, you need to override the `getColumnClass()` method to return the class of the column, as follows:

```
public Class getColumnClass(int column) {
  return getValueAt(0, column).getClass();
}
```

By default, all cells are editable. To prohibit a cell from being edited, override the `isCellEditable(int rowIndex, int columnIndx)` method in `TableModel` to return `false`. By default, this method returns `true` in `AbstractTableModel`.

To demonstrate predefined table renderers and editors, let us write a program that displays a table for books. The table consists of three rows with the column names Title, Copies Needed, Publisher, Date Published, In-Stock, and Book Photo, as shown in Figure 36.15. Assume that dates and icons are not editable; prohibit users from editing these two columns.

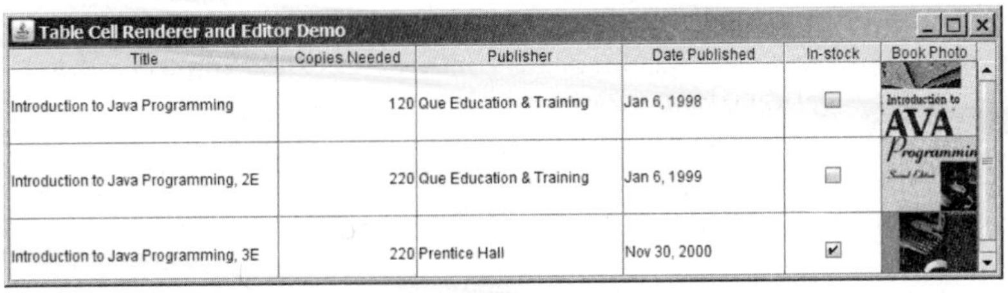
Table Cell Renderer and Editor Demo
Title
Copies Needed
Publisher
Date Published
In-stock
Book Photo
Introduction to Java Programming
120
Que Education & Training
Jan 6, 1998
Introduction to Java Programming, 2E
220
Que Education & Training
Jan 6, 1999
Introduction to Java Programming, 3E
220
Prentice Hall
Nov 30, 2000

FIGURE 36.15 You need to use a custom table model to enable predefined renderers for Boolean and image cells.

Listing 36.7 gives a custom table model named `MyTableModel` that overrides the `getColumnClass` method (lines 15–17) to enable predefined renderers for Boolean and image cells. `MyTableModel` also overrides the `isCellEditable()` method (lines 20–24). By default, `isCellEditable()` returns `true`. The example does not allow the user to edit image icons and dates, so this method is overridden to return `false` to disable editing of date and image columns. For a cell to be editable, `isCellEditable()` in the table model must be `true`.

LISTING 36.7 MyTableModel.java

```
1 import javax.swing.*;
2 import javax.swing.table.*;
3 import java.util.*;
4
5 public class MyTableModel extends DefaultTableModel {
6   public MyTableModel() {
7   }
8
9   /** Construct a table model with specified data and columnNames */
10  public MyTableModel(Object[][] data, Object[] columnNames) {
11    super(data, columnNames);
12  }
13
14  /** Override this method to return a class for the column */
15  public class getColumnClass(int column) {
16    return getValueAt(0, column).getClass();
17  }
18
19  /** Override this method to return true if cell is editable */
20  public boolean isCellEditable(int row, int column) {
21    Class columnClass = getColumnClass(column);
22    return columnClass != ImageIcon.class &&
23      columnClass != Date.class;
24  }
25 }
```

column class

cell editable?

If you create a `JTable` using a table model created from `MyTableModel`, the default renderers and editors for numbers, Boolean values, dates, and icons are used to display and edit these columns. Listing 36.8 gives a test program. The program creates a table model using `MyTableModel` (line 36). `JTable` assigns a predefined cell renderer and a predefined editor to the cell, whose class is specified in the `getColumnClass()` method in `MyTableModel`.

LISTING 36.8 TableCellRendererEditorDemo.java

```
1 import java.awt.*;
2 import javax.swing.*;
3 import java.util.*;
4
5 public class TableCellRendererEditorDemo extends JApplet {
6   // Create table column names
7   private String[] columnNames =
8     {"Title", "Copies Needed", "Publisher", "Date Published",
9      "In-stock", "Book Photo"};
10
11   // Create image icons
12   private ImageIcon intro1eImageIcon = new ImageIcon(
13     getClass().getResource("image/intro1e.gif"));
14   private ImageIcon intro2eImageIcon = new ImageIcon(
15     getClass().getResource("image/intro2e.gif"));
16   private ImageIcon intro3eImageIcon = new ImageIcon(
17     getClass().getResource("image/intro3e.jpg"));
18
19   // Create table data
20   private Object[][] rowData = {
21     {"Introduction to Java Programming", 120,
22      "Que Education & Training",
23       new GregorianCalendar(1998, 1-1, 6).getTime(),
24       false, intro1eImageIcon},
25     {"Introduction to Java Programming, 2E", 220,
26      "Que Education & Training",
27       new GregorianCalendar(1999, 1-1, 6).getTime(),
28       false, intro2eImageIcon},
29     {"Introduction to Java Programming, 3E", 220,
30       "Prentice Hall",
31       new GregorianCalendar(2000, 12-1, 0).getTime(),
32       true, intro3eImageIcon},
33   };
34
35   // Create a table model
36   private MyTableModel tableModel = new MyTableModel(
37     rowData, columnNames);
38
39   // Create a table
40   private JTable jTable1 = new JTable(tableModel);
41
42   public TableCellRendererEditorDemo() {
43     jTable1.setRowHeight(60);
44     add(new JScrollPane(jTable1),
45       BorderLayout.CENTER);
46   }
47 }
```

column names (line 7)
image icons (line 12)
row data (line 20)
table model (line 36)
table (line 40)
main method omitted (line 47)

The example defines two classes: `MyTableModel` and `TableCellRendererEditorDemo`. `MyTableModel` is an extension of `DefaultTableModel`. The purpose of `MyTableModel` is to override the default implementation of the `getColumnClass()` method to return the class of the column, so that an appropriate predefined `JTable` can be used for the column. By default, `getColumnClass()` returns `Object.class`.

36.7 Custom Table Renderers and Editors

Predefined renderers and editors are convenient and easy to use, but their functions are limited. The predefined image icon renderer displays the image icon in a label. The image icon cannot be scaled. If you want the whole image to fit in a cell, you need to create a custom renderer.

A custom renderer can be created by extending the `DefaultTableCellRenderer`, which is a default implementation for the `TableCellRenderer` interface. The custom renderer must override the `getTableCellRendererComponent` method to return a component for rendering the table cell. The `getTableCellRendererComponent` method is defined as follows:

```
public Component getTableCellRendererComponent
  (JTable table, Object value, boolean isSelected,
   boolean isFocused, int row, int column)
```

This method signature is very similar to the `getListCellRendererComponent` method used to create custom list cell renderers.

This method is passed with a `JTable`, the value associated with the cell, information regarding whether the value is selected and whether the cell has the focus, and the row and column indices of the value. The component returned from the method is painted on the cell in the table. The class in Listing 36.9, `MyImageCellRenderer`, defines a renderer for displaying image icons in a panel.

LISTING 36.9 `MyImageCellRenderer.java`

```
import javax.swing.*;
import javax.swing.table.*;
import java.awt.*;

public class MyImageCellRenderer extends DefaultTableCellRenderer {
  /** Override this method in DefaultTableCellRenderer */
  public Component getTableCellRendererComponent
      (JTable table, Object value, boolean isSelected,
       boolean isFocused, int row, int column) {
    Image image = ((ImageIcon)value).getImage();
    ImageViewer imageViewer = new ImageViewer(image);

    return imageViewer;
  }
}
```

override method

`getImage()`
create image viewer

return image viewer

You can also create a custom editor. `JTable` provides the `DefaultCellEditor` class, which can be used to edit a cell in a text field, a check box, or a combo box. To use it, simply create a text field, a check box, or a combo box, and pass it to `DefaultCellEditor`'s constructor to create an editor.

Using a custom renderer and editor, the preceding example can be revised to display scaled images and to use a custom combo editor to edit the cells in the Publisher column, as shown in Figure 36.16. The program is given in Listing 36.10.

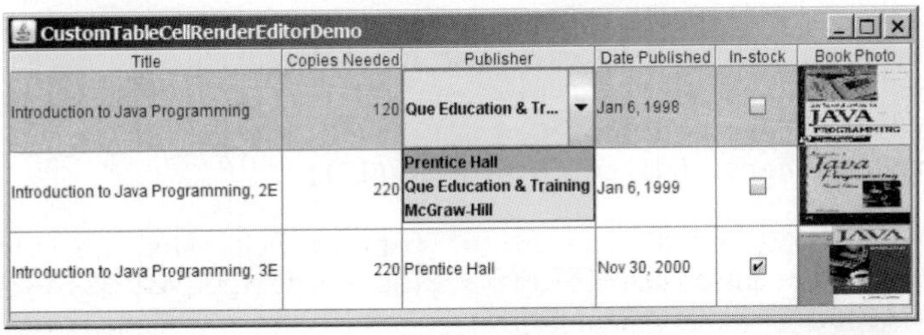
CustomTableCellRenderEditorDemo
Title
Copies Needed
Publisher
Date Published
In-stock
Book Photo
Introduction to Java Programming
120
Que Education & Tr...
Jan 6, 1998
Introduction to Java Programming, 2E
220
Prentice Hall
Que Education & Training
McGraw-Hill
Jan 6, 1999
Introduction to Java Programming, 3E
220
Prentice Hall
Nov 30, 2000

FIGURE 36.16 A custom renderer displays a scaled image, and a custom editor edits the Publisher column using a combo box.

LISTING 36.10 CustomTableCellRendererEditorDemo.java

column names
image icons
row data
table model
table
set renderer
combo box
set editor

```
import java.awt.*;
import javax.swing.*;
import javax.swing.table.*;
import java.util.*;

public class CustomTableCellRendererEditorDemo extends JApplet {
  // Create table column names
  private String[] columnNames =
    {"Title", "Copies Needed", "Publisher", "Date Published",
     "In-stock", "Book Photo"};

  // Create image icons
  private ImageIcon intro1eImageIcon =
    new ImageIcon(getClass().getResource("image/intro1e.gif"));
  private ImageIcon intro2eImageIcon =
    new ImageIcon(getClass().getResource("image/intro2e.gif"));
  private ImageIcon intro3eImageIcon =
    new ImageIcon(getClass().getResource("image/intro3e.jpg"));

  // Create table data
  private Object[][] rowData = {
    {"Introduction to Java Programming", 120,
     "Que Education & Training",
      new GregorianCalendar(1998, 1-1, 6).getTime(),
      false, intro1eImageIcon},
    {"Introduction to Java Programming, 2E", 220,
     "Que Education & Training",
      new GregorianCalendar(1999, 1-1, 6).getTime(),
      false, intro2eImageIcon},
    {"Introduction to Java Programming, 3E", 220,
      "Prentice Hall",
      new GregorianCalendar(2000, 12-1, 0).getTime(),
      true, intro3eImageIcon},
  };

  // Create a table model
  private MyTableModel tableModel = new MyTableModel(
    rowData, columnNames);

  // Create a table
  private JTable jTable1 = new JTable(tableModel);

  public CustomTableCellRendererEditorDemo() {
    // Set custom renderer for displaying images
    TableColumn bookCover = jTable1.getColumn("Book Photo");
    bookCover.setCellRenderer(new MyImageCellRenderer());

    // Create a combo box for publishers
    JComboBox jcboPublishers = new JComboBox();
    jcboPublishers.addItem("Prentice Hall");
    jcboPublishers.addItem("Que Education & Training");
    jcboPublishers.addItem("McGraw-Hill");

    // Set combo box as the editor for the publisher column
    TableColumn publisherColumn = jTable1.getColumn("Publisher");
    publisherColumn.setCellEditor(
      new DefaultCellEditor(jcboPublishers));

```

```
59      jTable1.setRowHeight(60);
60      add(new JScrollPane(jTable1),
61        BorderLayout.CENTER);
62    }
63 }
```

main method omitted

This example uses the same table model (MyTableModel) that was created in the preceding example (lines 37–38). By default, image icons are displayed using the predefined image icon renderer. To use MyImageCellRenderer to display the image, you have to explicitly specify the MyImageCellRenderer renderer for the Book Photo column (line 46). Likewise, you have to explicitly specify the combo box editor for the Publisher column (lines 56–57); otherwise the default editor would be used.

When you edit a cell in the Publisher column, a combo box of three items is displayed. When you select an item from the box, it is displayed in the cell. You did not write the code for handling selections. The selections are handled by the DefaultCellEditor class.

When you resize the Book Photo column, the image is resized to fit into the whole cell. With the predefined image renderer, you can see only part of the image if the cell is smaller than the image.

36.8 Table Model Events

JTable does not fire table events. It fires events like MouseEvent, KeyEvent, and ComponentEvent that are inherited from its superclass, JComponent. Table events are fired by table models, table column models, and table-selection models whenever changes are made to these models. Table models fire TableModelEvent when table data are changed. Table column models fire TableColumnModelEvent when columns are added, removed, or moved, or when a column is selected. Table-selection models fire ListSelectionEvent when a selection is made.

To listen for these events, a listener must be registered with an appropriate model and implement the correct listener interface. Listing 36.11 gives an example that demonstrates how to use these events. The program displays messages on a text area when a row or a column is selected, when a cell is edited, or when a column is removed. Figure 36.17 is a sample run of the program.

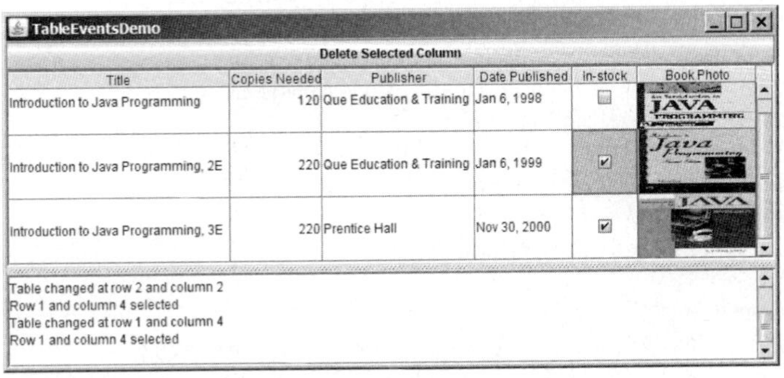
TableEventsDemo
Delete Selected Column
Title
Copies Needed
Publisher
Date Published
in-stock
Book Photo
Introduction to Java Programming
120
Que Education & Training
Jan 6, 1998
Introduction to Java Programming, 2E
220
Que Education & Training
Jan 6, 1999
Introduction to Java Programming, 3E
220
Prentice Hall
Nov 30, 2000
Table changed at row 2 and column 2
Row 1 and column 4 selected
Table changed at row 1 and column 4
Row 1 and column 4 selected

FIGURE 36.17 Table event handlers display table events on a text area.

LISTING 36.11 TableEventsDemo.java

```
import java.awt.*;
import java.awt.event.*;
import javax.swing.*;
import javax.swing.event.*;
import javax.swing.table.*;
```

```
import java.util.*;

public class TableEventsDemo extends JApplet {
  // Create table column names
```
column names
```
  private String[] columnNames =
    {"Title", "Copies Needed", "Publisher", "Date Published",
     "In-stock", "Book Photo"};

  // Create image icons
```
image icons
```
  private ImageIcon intro1eImageIcon =
    new ImageIcon(getClass().getResource("image/intro1e.gif"));
  private ImageIcon intro2eImageIcon =
    new ImageIcon(getClass().getResource("image/intro2e.gif"));
  private ImageIcon intro3eImageIcon =
    new ImageIcon(getClass().getResource("image/intro3e.jpg"));

  // Create table data
```
table data
```
  private Object[][] rowData = {
    {"Introduction to Java Programming", 120,
     "Que Education & Training",
      new GregorianCalendar(1998, 1-1, 6).getTime(),
      false, intro1eImageIcon},
    {"Introduction to Java Programming, 2E", 220,
     "Que Education & Training",
      new GregorianCalendar(1999, 1-1, 6).getTime(),
      false, intro2eImageIcon},
    {"Introduction to Java Programming, 3E", 220,
      "Prentice Hall",
      new GregorianCalendar(2000, 12-1, 0).getTime(),
      true, intro3eImageIcon},
  };

  // Create a table model
```
table model
```
  private MyTableModel tableModel = new MyTableModel(
    rowData, columnNames);

  // Create a table
```
table
```
  private JTable jTable1 = new JTable(tableModel);

  // Get table column model
```
column model
```
  private TableColumnModel tableColumnModel =
    jTable1.getColumnModel();

  // Get table selection model
```
selection model
```
  private ListSelectionModel selectionModel =
    jTable1.getSelectionModel();

  // Create a text area
  private JTextArea jtaMessage = new JTextArea();

  // Create a button
  private JButton jbtDeleteColumn =
    new JButton("Delete Selected Column");

  public TableEventsDemo() {
    // Set custom renderer for displaying images
    TableColumn bookCover = jTable1.getColumn("Book Photo");
    bookCover.setCellRenderer(new MyImageCellRenderer());

```

```
    // Create a combo box for publishers
    JComboBox jcboPublishers = new JComboBox();
    jcboPublishers.addItem("Prentice Hall");
    jcboPublishers.addItem("Que Education & Training");
    jcboPublishers.addItem("McGraw-Hill");

    // Set combo box as the editor for the publisher column
    TableColumn publisherColumn = jTable1.getColumn("Publisher");
    publisherColumn.setCellEditor(
      new DefaultCellEditor(jcboPublishers));

    jTable1.setRowHeight(60);
    jTable1.setColumnSelectionAllowed(true);

    JSplitPane jSplitPane1 = new JSplitPane(
      JSplitPane.VERTICAL_SPLIT);
    jSplitPane1.add(new JScrollPane(jTable1), JSplitPane.LEFT);
    jSplitPane1.add(new JScrollPane(jtaMessage), JSplitPane.RIGHT);
    add(jbtDeleteColumn, BorderLayout.NORTH);
    add(jSplitPane1, BorderLayout.CENTER);

    tableModel.addTableModelListener(new TableModelListener() {
      public void tableChanged(TableModelEvent e) {
        jtaMessage.append("Table changed at row " +
          e.getFirstRow() + " and column " + e.getColumn() + "\n");
      }
    });

    tableColumnModel.addColumnModelListener(
      new TableColumnModelListener() {
      public void columnRemoved(TableColumnModelEvent e) {
        jtaMessage.append("Column indexed at " + e.getFromIndex() +
          " is deleted \n");
      }
      public void columnAdded(TableColumnModelEvent e) {
      }
      public void columnMoved(TableColumnModelEvent e) {
      }
      public void columnMarginChanged(ChangeEvent e) {
      }
      public void columnSelectionChanged(ListSelectionEvent e) {
      }
    });

    jbtDeleteColumn.addActionListener(new ActionListener() {
      public void actionPerformed(ActionEvent e) {
        if (jTable1.getSelectedColumn() >= 0) {
          TableColumnModel columnModel = jTable1.getColumnModel();
          TableColumn tableColumn =
              columnModel.getColumn(jTable1.getSelectedColumn());
          columnModel.removeColumn(tableColumn);
        }
      }
    });

    selectionModel.addListSelectionListener(
      new ListSelectionListener() {
      public void valueChanged(ListSelectionEvent e) {
        jtaMessage.append("Row " + jTable1.getSelectedRow() +
```

table model listener

column model listener

selection model listener

```
124                  " and column " + jTable1.getSelectedColumn() +
125                  " selected\n");
126          }
127        });
128     }
129 }
```

main method omitted

To respond to the row and column selection events, you need to implement the valueChanged method in ListSelectionListener. To respond to the cell-editing event, you need to implement the tableChanged method in TableModelListener. To respond to the column-deletion event, you need to implement the columnRemoved method in TableColumnModelListener. Let's use the same table from the preceding example, but with a button added for deleting the selected column and a text area for displaying the messages.

A table model is created using MyTableModel (lines 39–40), which was given in Listing 36.7. When a table is created (line 43), its default column model and selection model are also created. Therefore, you can obtain the table column model and selection model from the table (lines 46–51).

When a row or a column is selected, a ListSelectionEvent is fired by selectionModel, which invokes the handler to display the selected row and column in the text area (lines 120–127). When the content or structure of the table is changed, a TableModelEvent is fired by tableModel, which invokes the handler to display the last row and last column of the changed data in the text area (lines 86–91). When a column is deleted by clicking the *Delete Selected Column* button, a ColumnModelEvent is fired by tableColumnModel, which invokes the handler to display the index of the deleted column (lines 93–107).

36.9 JTree

JTree is a Swing component that displays data in a treelike hierarchy, as shown in Figure 36.18.

A Sample Tree
JTree
colors
blue
violet
red
yellow
sports
basketball
soccer
football
hockey
food

FIGURE 36.18 JTree displays data in a treelike hierarchy.

All the nodes displayed in the tree are in the form of a hierarchical indexed list. The tree can be used to navigate structured data with hierarchical relationships. A node can have child nodes. A node is called a *leaf* if it has no children; a node with no parent is called the *root* of its tree. A tree may consist of many subtrees, each node acting as the root for its own subtree.

A nonleaf node can be expanded or collapsed by double-clicking on the node or on the node's handle in front of the node. The handle usually has a visible sign to indicate whether the node is expanded or collapsed. For example, on Windows, the + symbol indicates that the node can be expanded, and the – symbol, that it can be collapsed.

Like JTable, JTree is a very complex component with many supporting interfaces and classes. JTree is in the javax.swing package, but its supporting interfaces and classes are all included in the javax.swing.tree package. The supporting interfaces are TreeModel, TreeSelectionModel, TreeNode, and MutableTreeNode, and the supporting classes are DefaultTreeModel, DefaultMutableTreeNode, DefaultTreeCellEditor, DefaultTreeCellRenderer, and TreePath.

While JTree displays the tree, the data representation of the tree is handled by TreeModel, TreeNode, and TreePath. TreeModel represents the entire tree, TreeNode represents a node, and TreePath represents a path to a node. Unlike the ListModel or TableModel, TreeModel does not directly store or manage tree data. Tree data are stored and managed in TreeNode and TreePath. DefaultTreeModel is a concrete implementation of TreeModel. MutableTreeNode is a subinterface of TreeNode, which represents a tree node that can be mutated by adding or removing child nodes, or by changing the contents of a user object stored in the node.

The TreeSelectionModel interface handles tree node selection. The DefaultTreeCellRenderer class provides a default tree node renderer that can display a label and/or an icon in a node. The DefaultTreeCellEditor can be used to edit the cells in a text field.

A TreePath is an array of Objects that are vended from a TreeModel. The elements of the array are ordered such that the root is always the first element (index 0) of the array. Figure 36.19 shows how these interfaces and classes are interrelated.

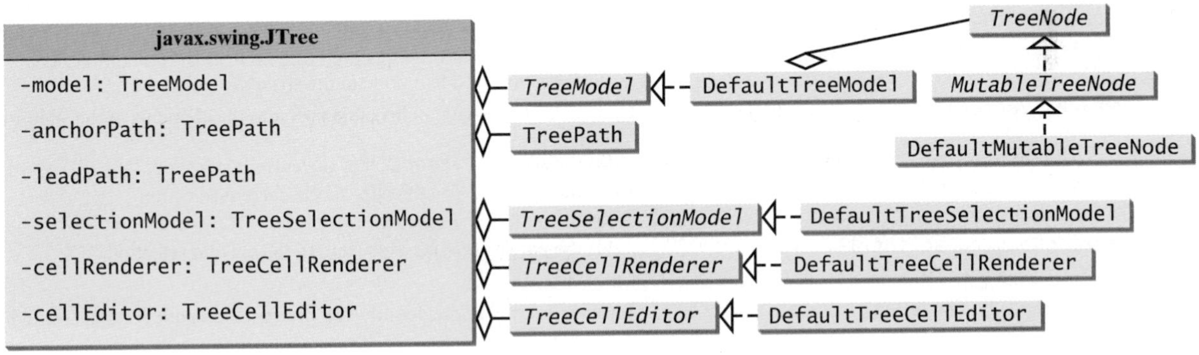
javax.swing.JTree
-model: TreeModel
-anchorPath: TreePath
-leadPath: TreePath
-selectionModel: TreeSelectionModel
-cellRenderer: TreeCellRenderer
-cellEditor: TreeCellEditor
TreeModel
DefaultTreeModel
TreeNode
MutableTreeNode
DefaultMutableTreeNode
TreePath
TreeSelectionModel
DefaultTreeSelectionModel
TreeCellRenderer
DefaultTreeCellRenderer
TreeCellEditor
DefaultTreeCellEditor

FIGURE 36.19 JTree contains many supporting interfaces and classes.

Figure 36.20 shows the constructors, frequently used properties, and methods of JTree.

The JTree class contains seven constructors for creating trees. You can create a tree using its no-arg constructor, a tree model, a tree node, a Hashtable, an array, or a vector. Using the no-arg constructor, a sample tree is created as shown in Figure 36.18. Using a Hashtable, an array, or a vector, a root is created but not displayed. All the keys in a Hashtable, all the objects in an array, and all the elements in a vector are added into the tree as children of the root. If you wish the root to be displayed, set the rootVisible property to true.

All the methods related to path selection are also defined in the TreeSelectionModel interface, which will be covered in §36.12, "TreePath and TreeSelectionModel."

Listing 36.12 gives an example that creates four trees: a default tree using the no-arg constructor, a tree created from an array of objects, a tree created from a vector, and a tree created from a hash table, as shown in Figure 36.21. Enable the user to dynamically set the properties for rootVisible, rowHeight, and showsRootHandles.

JavaBeans properties with `get` and `set` methods omitted in the UML diagram.

javax.swing.JTree	
`#cellEditor: TreeCellEditor`	Specifies a cell editor used to edit entries in the tree.
`#cellRenderer: TreeCellRenderer`	Specifies a cell renderer.
`#editable: boolean`	Specifies whether the cells are editable (default: false).
`#model: TreeModel`	Maintains the tree model.
`#rootVisible: boolean`	Specifies whether the root is displayed (depending on the constructor).
`#rowHeight: int`	Specifies the height of the row for the node displayed in the tree (default: 16 pixels).
`#scrollsOnExpand: boolean`	If true, when a node is expanded, as many of the descendants as possible are scrolled to be visible (default: 16 pixels).
`#selectionModel: TreeSelectionModel`	Models the set of selected nodes in this tree.
`#showsRootHandles: boolean`	Specifies whether the root handles are displayed (default: true).
`#toggleClickCount: int`	Number of mouse clicks before a node is expanded (default: 2).
`-anchorSelectionPath: TreePath`	The path identified as the anchor.
`-expandsSelectedPaths: boolean`	True if paths in the selection should be expanded (default: true).
`-leadSelectionPaths: TreePath`	The path identified as the lead.
`+JTree()`	Creates a `JTree` with a sample tree model, as shown in Figure 36.18.
`+JTree(value: java.util.Hashtable)`	Creates a `JTree` with an invisible root and the keys in the `Hashtable` key/value pairs as its children.
`+JTree(value: Object[])`	Creates a `JTree` with an invisible root and the elements in the array as its children.
`+JTree(newModel: TreeModel)`	Creates a `JTree` with the specified tree model.
`+JTree(root: TreeNode)`	Creates a `JTree` with the specified tree node as its root.
`+JTree(root: TreeNode, asksAllowsChildren: boolean)`	Creates a `JTree` with the specified tree node as its root and decides whether a node is a leaf node in the specified manner.
`+JTree(value: Vector)`	Creates a `JTree` with an invisible root and the elements in the vector as its children.
`+addSelectionPath(path: TreePath): void`	Adds the specified `TreePath` to the current selection.
`+addSelectionPaths(paths: TreePath[]): void`	Adds the specified `TreePaths` to the current selection.
`+addSelectionRow(row: int): void`	Adds the path at the specified row to the current selection.
`+addSelectionRows(rows: int[]): void`	Adds the path at the specified rows to the current selection.
`+clearSelection(): void`	Clears the selection.
`+collapsePath(path: TreePath): void`	Ensures that the node identified by the specified path is collapsed and viewable.
`+getSelectionPath(): TreePath`	Returns the path from the root to the first selected node.
`+getSelectionPaths(): TreePath[]`	Returns the paths from the root to all the selected nodes.
`+getLastSelectedPathComponent()`	Returns the last node in the first selected `TreePath`.
`+getRowCount(): int`	Returns the number of rows currently being displayed.
`+removeSelectionPath(path: TreePath): void`	Removes the node in the specified path.
`+removeSelectionPaths(paths: TreePath[]): void`	Removes the node in the specified paths.

FIGURE 36.20 The `JTree` class is for creating, customizing, and manipulating trees.

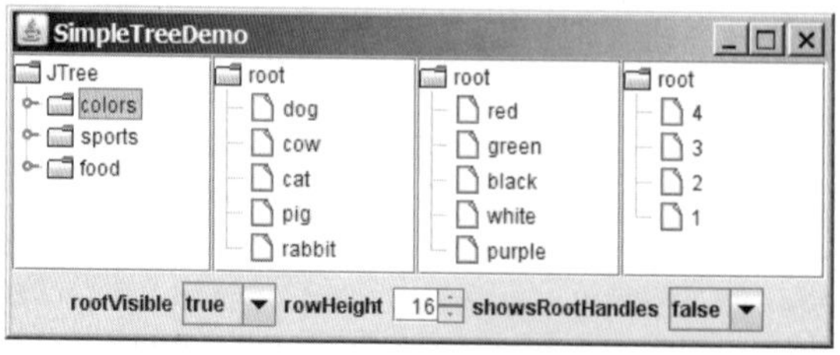
SimpleTreeDemo
JTree
colors
sports
food
root
dog
cow
cat
pig
rabbit
root
red
green
black
white
purple
root
4
3
2
1
rootVisible
true
rowHeight
16
showsRootHandles
false

FIGURE 36.21 You can dynamically set the properties for `rootVisible`, `rowHeight`, and `showRootHandles` in a tree.

LISTING 36.12 SimpleTreeDemo.java

```
import java.awt.*;
import java.awt.event.*;
import javax.swing.*;
import javax.swing.event.*;
import java.util.*;

public class SimpleTreeDemo extends JApplet {
  // Create a default tree
  private JTree jTree1 = new JTree();

  // Create a tree with an array of Objects.
  private JTree jTree2 = new JTree(new String[]
    {"dog", "cow", "cat", "pig", "rabbit"});

  // Create a tree with a vector
  private Vector vector = new Vector(Arrays.asList(
    new Object[]{"red", "green", "black", "white", "purple"}));
  private JTree jTree3 = new JTree(vector);

  private Hashtable<Integer, String> hashtable =
    new Hashtable<Integer, String>();
  private JTree jTree4;

  // Create a combo box for selecting rootVisible
  private JComboBox jcboRootVisible = new JComboBox(
    new String[]{"false", "true"});

  // Create a combo box for selecting showRootHandles
  private JComboBox jcboShowsRootHandles = new JComboBox(
    new String[] {"false", "true"});

  // Create a spinner for selecting row height
  private JSpinner jSpinnerRowHeight = new JSpinner(
      new SpinnerNumberModel(16, 1, 50, 1));

  public SimpleTreeDemo() {
    jTree1.setRootVisible(false);

    hashtable.put(1, "red");
    hashtable.put(2, "green");
    hashtable.put(3, "blue");
    hashtable.put(4, "yellow");
    jTree4 = new JTree(hashtable);

    JPanel panel1 = new JPanel(new GridLayout(1, 4));
    panel1.add(new JScrollPane(jTree1));
    panel1.add(new JScrollPane(jTree2));
    panel1.add(new JScrollPane(jTree3));
    panel1.add(new JScrollPane(jTree4));

    JPanel panel2 = new JPanel();
    panel2.add(new JLabel("rootVisible"));
    panel2.add(jcboRootVisible);
    panel2.add(new JLabel("rowHeight"));
    panel2.add(jSpinnerRowHeight);
    panel2.add(new JLabel("showsRootHandles"));
    panel2.add(jcboShowsRootHandles);

```

tree 1

tree 2

tree 3

tree 4

tree

combo box listener

spinner listener

main method omitted

```
59     add(panel1, BorderLayout.CENTER);
60     add(panel2, BorderLayout.SOUTH);
61 
62     // Register listeners
63     jcboRootVisible.addActionListener(new ActionListener() {
64       public void actionPerformed(ActionEvent e) {
65         boolean rootVisible =
66           jcboRootVisible.getSelectedItem().equals("true");
67         jTree1.setRootVisible(rootVisible);
68         jTree2.setRootVisible(rootVisible);
69         jTree3.setRootVisible(rootVisible);
70         jTree4.setRootVisible(rootVisible);
71       }
72     });
73 
74     jcboShowsRootHandles.addActionListener(new ActionListener() {
75       public void actionPerformed(ActionEvent e) {
76         boolean showsRootHandles =
77           jcboShowsRootHandles.getSelectedItem().equals("true");
78         jTree1.setShowsRootHandles(showsRootHandles);
79         jTree2.setShowsRootHandles(showsRootHandles);
80         jTree3.setShowsRootHandles(showsRootHandles);
81         jTree4.setShowsRootHandles(showsRootHandles);
82       }
83     });
84 
85     jSpinnerRowHeight.addChangeListener(new ChangeListener() {
86       public void stateChanged(ChangeEvent e) {
87         int height =
88           ((Integer)(jSpinnerRowHeight.getValue())).intValue();
89         jTree1.setRowHeight(height);
90         jTree2.setRowHeight(height);
91         jTree3.setRowHeight(height);
92         jTree4.setRowHeight(height);
93       }
94     });
95   }
96 }
```

Four trees are created in this example. The first is created using the no-arg constructor (line 9) with a default sample tree. The second is created using an array of objects (lines 12–13). All the objects in the array become the children of the root. The third is created using a vector (lines 16–18). All the elements in the vector become the children of the root. The fourth is created using a hash table (lines 39–43). A `Hashtable` is like a `Map`. `Hashtable` was introduced earlier than Java 2 and has since been replaced by `Map`. It is used in the Java API (e.g., `JTree`), which was developed before Java 2. The keys of the hash table become the children of the root.

`JTree` doesn't directly support scrolling. To create a scrollable tree, create a `JScrollPane` and add an instance of `JTree` to the scroll pane (lines 46–49).

The example enables you to specify whether the root is visible and whether the root handles are visible from two combo boxes (lines 63–83). It also lets you specify the row height of the node in a spinner (lines 85–94).

36.10 TreeModel and DefaultTreeModel

The `TreeModel` interface represents the entire tree. Unlike `ListModel` or `TableModel`, `TreeModel` does not directly store or manage tree data. `TreeModel` contains the structural information about the tree, and tree data are stored and managed by `TreeNode`.

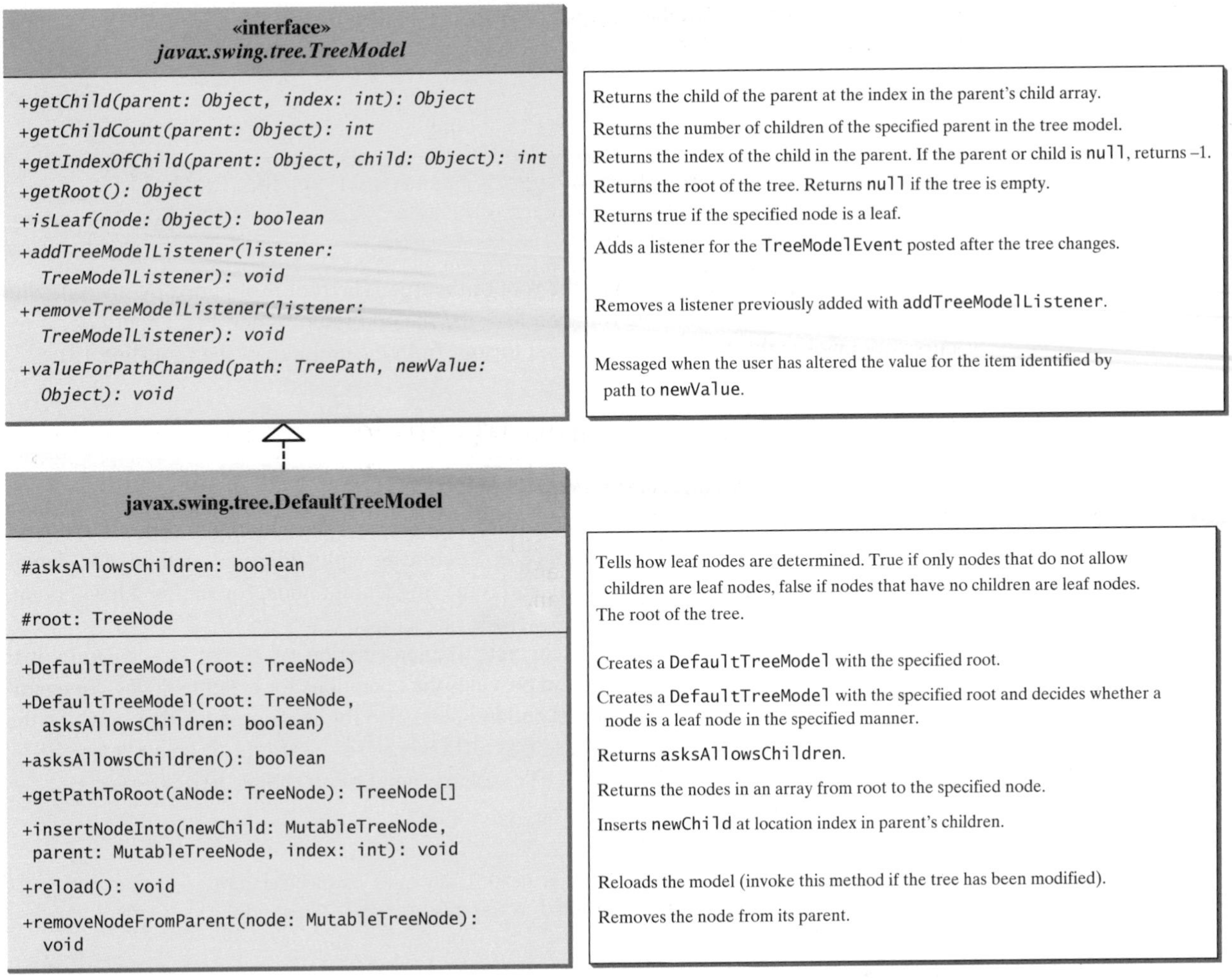
«interface»
javax.swing.tree.TreeModel
+getChild(parent: Object, index: int): Object
+getChildCount(parent: Object): int
+getIndexOfChild(parent: Object, child: Object): int
+getRoot(): Object
+isLeaf(node: Object): boolean
+addTreeModelListener(listener: TreeModelListener): void
+removeTreeModelListener(listener: TreeModelListener): void
+valueForPathChanged(path: TreePath, newValue: Object): void
Returns the child of the parent at the index in the parent's child array.
Returns the number of children of the specified parent in the tree model.
Returns the index of the child in the parent. If the parent or child is null, returns –1.
Returns the root of the tree. Returns null if the tree is empty.
Returns true if the specified node is a leaf.
Adds a listener for the TreeModelEvent posted after the tree changes.
Removes a listener previously added with addTreeModelListener.
Messaged when the user has altered the value for the item identified by path to newValue.
javax.swing.tree.DefaultTreeModel
#asksAllowsChildren: boolean
#root: TreeNode
+DefaultTreeModel(root: TreeNode)
+DefaultTreeModel(root: TreeNode, asksAllowsChildren: boolean)
+asksAllowsChildren(): boolean
+getPathToRoot(aNode: TreeNode): TreeNode[]
+insertNodeInto(newChild: MutableTreeNode, parent: MutableTreeNode, index: int): void
+reload(): void
+removeNodeFromParent(node: MutableTreeNode): void
Tells how leaf nodes are determined. True if only nodes that do not allow children are leaf nodes, false if nodes that have no children are leaf nodes.
The root of the tree.
Creates a DefaultTreeModel with the specified root.
Creates a DefaultTreeModel with the specified root and decides whether a node is a leaf node in the specified manner.
Returns asksAllowsChildren.
Returns the nodes in an array from root to the specified node.
Inserts newChild at location index in parent's children.
Reloads the model (invoke this method if the tree has been modified).
Removes the node from its parent.

FIGURE 36.22 TreeModel represents an entire tree and DefaultTreeModel is a concrete implementation of it.

DefaultTreeModel is a concrete implementation for TreeModel that uses TreeNodes. Figure 36.22 shows TreeModel and DefaultTreeModel.

Once a tree is created, you can obtain its tree model using the getModel method. Listing 36.13 gives an example that traverses all the nodes in a tree using the tree model. Line 1 creates a tree using JTree's no-arg constructor with the default sample nodes, as shown in Figure 36.18. The tree model for the tree is obtained in line 4. Line 5 invokes the traversal method to traverse the nodes in the tree.

LISTING 36.13 TestTreeModel.java

```
 1 public class TestTreeModel {
 2   public static void main(String[] args) {
 3     javax.swing.JTree jTree1 = new javax.swing.JTree();
 4     javax.swing.tree.TreeModel model = jTree1.getModel();
 5     traversal(model, model.getRoot());
 6   }
 7
 8   private static void traversal
 9       (javax.swing.tree.TreeModel model, Object root) {
10     System.out.print(root + " ");
11     if (model.isLeaf(root)) return;
12     for (int i = 0; i < model.getChildCount(root); i++) {
```

default tree (line 3)
tree model (line 4)
getRoot (line 5)
is leaf? (line 11)
getChildCount (line 12)

getChild

```
13       traversal(model, model.getChild(root, i));
14     }
15   }
16 }
```

```
JTree colors blue violet red sports basketball soccer football
food hot dogs pizza ravioli
```

The `traversal` method starts from the root of the tree. The root is obtained by invoking the `getRoot` method (line 5). If the root is a leaf, the method returns (line 11). Otherwise, it recursively invokes the `traversal` method to start from the children of the root (line 13).

36.11 TreeNode, MutableTreeNode, and DefaultMutableTreeNode

While `TreeModel` represents the entire tree, `TreeNode` stores a single node of the tree. `MutableTreeNode` defines a subinterface of `TreeNode` with additional methods for changing the content of the node, for inserting and removing a child node, for setting a new parent, and for removing the node itself.

`DefaultMutableTreeNode` is a concrete implementation of `MutableTreeNode` that maintains a list of children in a vector and provides the operations for creating nodes, for examining and modifying a node's parent and children, and also for examining the tree to which the node belongs. Normally, you should use `DefaultMutableTreeNode` to create a tree node. Figure 36.23 shows `TreeNode`, `MutableTreeNode`, and `DefaultMutableTreeNode`.

depth-first traversal

Note

In graph theory, depth-first traversal is defined the same as preorder traversal, but in the `depthFirstEnumeration()` method in `DefaultMutableTreeNode`, it is the same as postorder traversal.

creating trees

Note

You can create a `JTree` from a root using `new JTree(TreeNode)` or from a model using `new JTree(TreeModel)`. To create a tree model, you first create an instance of `TreeNode` to represent the root of the tree, and then create an instance of `DefaultTreeModel` fitted with the root.

Listing 36.14 gives an example that creates two trees to display world, continents, countries, and states. The two trees share the same nodes and thus display identical contents. The program also displays the properties of the tree in a text area, as shown in Figure 36.24.

LISTING 36.14 TreeNodeDemo.java

tree nodes

add children

```
import java.awt.*;
import javax.swing.*;
import javax.swing.tree.*;
import java.util.*;

public class TreeNodeDemo extends JApplet {
  public TreeNodeDemo() {
    // Create the first tree
    DefaultMutableTreeNode root, europe, northAmerica, us;

    europe = new DefaultMutableTreeNode("Europe");
    europe.add(new DefaultMutableTreeNode("UK"));
```

```
13      europe.add(new DefaultMutableTreeNode("Germany"));
14      europe.add(new DefaultMutableTreeNode("France"));
15      europe.add(new DefaultMutableTreeNode("Norway"));
16
17      northAmerica = new DefaultMutableTreeNode("North America");
18      us = new DefaultMutableTreeNode("US");
19      us.add(new DefaultMutableTreeNode("California"));
20      us.add(new DefaultMutableTreeNode("Texas"));
21      us.add(new DefaultMutableTreeNode("New York"));
22      us.add(new DefaultMutableTreeNode("Florida"));
23      us.add(new DefaultMutableTreeNode("Illinois"));
24      northAmerica.add(us);
25      northAmerica.add(new DefaultMutableTreeNode("Canada"));
26
27      root = new DefaultMutableTreeNode("World");
28      root.add(europe);
29      root.add(northAmerica);
30
31      JPanel panel = new JPanel();
32      panel.setLayout(new GridLayout(1, 2));
33      panel.add(new JScrollPane(new JTree(root)));
34      panel.add(new JScrollPane(new JTree(new DefaultTreeModel(root))));
35
36      JTextArea jtaMessage = new JTextArea();
37      jtaMessage.setWrapStyleWord(true);
38      jtaMessage.setLineWrap(true);
39      add(new JSplitPane(JSplitPane.VERTICAL_SPLIT,
40        panel, new JScrollPane(jtaMessage)), BorderLayout.CENTER);
41
42      // Get tree information
43      jtaMessage.append("Depth of the node US is " + us.getDepth());
44      jtaMessage.append("\nLevel of the node US is " + us.getLevel());
45      jtaMessage.append("\nFirst child of the root is " +
46        root.getFirstChild());
47      jtaMessage.append("\nFirst leaf of the root is " +
48        root.getFirstLeaf());
49      jtaMessage.append("\nNumber of the children of the root is " +
50        root.getChildCount());
51      jtaMessage.append("\nNumber of leaves in the tree is " +
52        root.getLeafCount());
53      String breadthFirstSearchResult = "";
54
55      // Breadth-first traversal
56      Enumeration bf = root.breadthFirstEnumeration();
57      while (bf.hasMoreElements())
58        breadthFirstSearchResult += bf.nextElement().toString() + " ";
59      jtaMessage.append("\nBreath-first traversal from the root is "
60        + breadthFirstSearchResult);
61    }
62  }
```

add children

main method omitted

You can create a `JTree` using a `TreeNode` root (line 33) or a `TreeModel` (line 34), whichever is convenient. A `TreeModel` is actually created using a `TreeNode` root (line 34). The two trees have the same contents because the root is the same. However, it is important to note that the two `JTree` objects are different, and so are their `TreeModel` objects, although both trees have the same root.

A tree is created by adding the nodes to the tree (lines 9–29). Each node is created using the `DefaultMutableTreeNode` class. This class provides many methods to manipulate the tree (e.g., adding a child, removing a child) and obtaining information about the tree

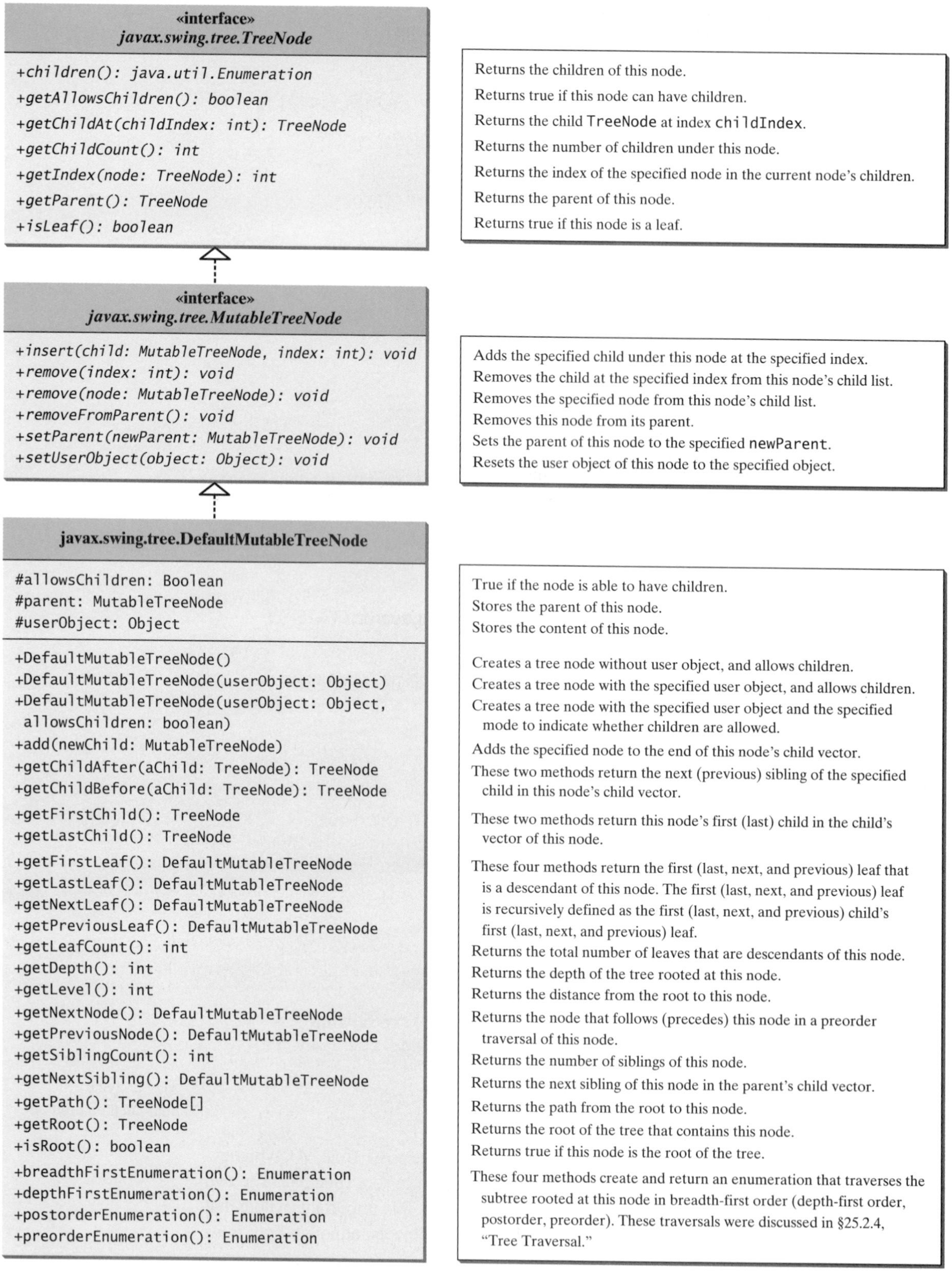
«interface»
javax.swing.tree.TreeNode
+children(): java.util.Enumeration
+getAllowsChildren(): boolean
+getChildAt(childIndex: int): TreeNode
+getChildCount(): int
+getIndex(node: TreeNode): int
+getParent(): TreeNode
+isLeaf(): boolean
Returns the children of this node.
Returns true if this node can have children.
Returns the child TreeNode at index childIndex.
Returns the number of children under this node.
Returns the index of the specified node in the current node's children.
Returns the parent of this node.
Returns true if this node is a leaf.
«interface»
javax.swing.tree.MutableTreeNode
+insert(child: MutableTreeNode, index: int): void
+remove(index: int): void
+remove(node: MutableTreeNode): void
+removeFromParent(): void
+setParent(newParent: MutableTreeNode): void
+setUserObject(object: Object): void
Adds the specified child under this node at the specified index.
Removes the child at the specified index from this node's child list.
Removes the specified node from this node's child list.
Removes this node from its parent.
Sets the parent of this node to the specified newParent.
Resets the user object of this node to the specified object.
javax.swing.tree.DefaultMutableTreeNode
#allowsChildren: Boolean
#parent: MutableTreeNode
#userObject: Object
+DefaultMutableTreeNode()
+DefaultMutableTreeNode(userObject: Object)
+DefaultMutableTreeNode(userObject: Object, allowsChildren: boolean)
+add(newChild: MutableTreeNode)
+getChildAfter(aChild: TreeNode): TreeNode
+getChildBefore(aChild: TreeNode): TreeNode
+getFirstChild(): TreeNode
+getLastChild(): TreeNode
+getFirstLeaf(): DefaultMutableTreeNode
+getLastLeaf(): DefaultMutableTreeNode
+getNextLeaf(): DefaultMutableTreeNode
+getPreviousLeaf(): DefaultMutableTreeNode
+getLeafCount(): int
+getDepth(): int
+getLevel(): int
+getNextNode(): DefaultMutableTreeNode
+getPreviousNode(): DefaultMutableTreeNode
+getSiblingCount(): int
+getNextSibling(): DefaultMutableTreeNode
+getPath(): TreeNode[]
+getRoot(): TreeNode
+isRoot(): boolean
+breadthFirstEnumeration(): Enumeration
+depthFirstEnumeration(): Enumeration
+postorderEnumeration(): Enumeration
+preorderEnumeration(): Enumeration
True if the node is able to have children.
Stores the parent of this node.
Stores the content of this node.
Creates a tree node without user object, and allows children.
Creates a tree node with the specified user object, and allows children.
Creates a tree node with the specified user object and the specified mode to indicate whether children are allowed.
Adds the specified node to the end of this node's child vector.
These two methods return the next (previous) sibling of the specified child in this node's child vector.
These two methods return this node's first (last) child in the child's vector of this node.
These four methods return the first (last, next, and previous) leaf that is a descendant of this node. The first (last, next, and previous) leaf is recursively defined as the first (last, next, and previous) child's first (last, next, and previous) leaf.
Returns the total number of leaves that are descendants of this node.
Returns the depth of the tree rooted at this node.
Returns the distance from the root to this node.
Returns the node that follows (precedes) this node in a preorder traversal of this node.
Returns the number of siblings of this node.
Returns the next sibling of this node in the parent's child vector.
Returns the path from the root to this node.
Returns the root of the tree that contains this node.
Returns true if this node is the root of the tree.
These four methods create and return an enumeration that traverses the subtree rooted at this node in breadth-first order (depth-first order, postorder, preorder). These traversals were discussed in §25.2.4, "Tree Traversal."

FIGURE 36.23 TreeNode represents a node.

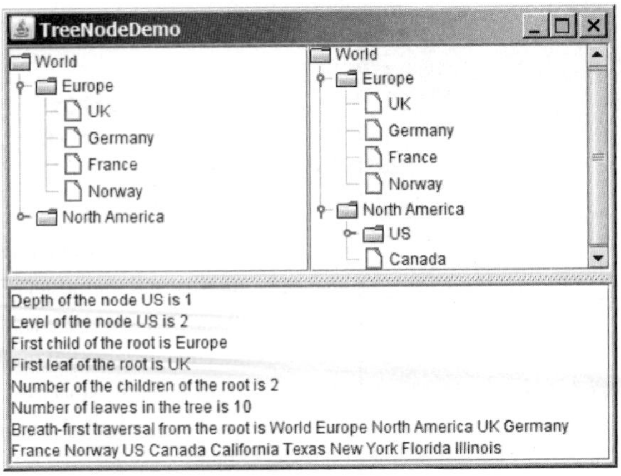
TreeNodeDemo
World
Europe
UK
Germany
France
Norway
North America
World
Europe
UK
Germany
France
Norway
North America
US
Canada
Depth of the node US is 1
Level of the node US is 2
First child of the root is Europe
First leaf of the root is UK
Number of the children of the root is 2
Number of leaves in the tree is 10
Breath-first traversal from the root is World Europe North America UK Germany
France Norway US Canada California Texas New York Florida Illinois

FIGURE 36.24 The two trees have the same data because their roots are the same.

(e.g., level, depth, number of children, number of leaves, traversals). Some examples of using these methods are given in lines 43–60.

As shown in this example, often you don't have to directly use `TreeModel`. Using `DefaultMutableTreeNode` is sufficient, since the tree data are stored in `DefaultMutableTreeNode`, and `DefaultMutableTreeNode` contains all the methods for modifying the tree and obtaining tree information.

36.12 TreePath and TreeSelectionModel

The `JTree` class contains the methods for selecting tree paths. The `TreePath` class represents a path from an ancestor to a descendant in a tree. Figure 36.25 shows `TreePath`.

javax.swing.tree.TreePath	
+TreePath(singlePath: Object)	Constructs a TreePath containing only a single element.
+TreePath(path: Object[])	Constructs a path from an array of objects.
+getLastPathComponent(): Object	Returns the last component of this path.
+getParentPath(): TreePath	Returns a path containing all but the last path component.
+getPath(): Object[]	Returns an ordered array of objects containing the components of this TreePath.
+getPathComponent(element: int): Object	Returns the path component at the specified index.
+getPathCount(): int	Returns the number of elements in the path.
+isDescendant(aTreePath: TreePath): boolean	Returns true if aTreePath contains all the components in this TreePath.
+pathByAddingChild(child: Object): TreePath	Returns a new path containing all the elements of this TreePath plus child.

FIGURE 36.25 `TreePath` represents a path from an ancestor to a descendant in a tree.

You can construct a `TreePath` from a single object or an array of objects, but often instances of `TreePath` are returned from the methods in `JTree` and `TreeSelectionModel`. (obtain tree paths) For instance, the `getLeadSelectionPath()` method in `JTree` returns the path from the root to the selected node. There are many ways to extract the nodes from a tree path. Often you use the `getLastPathComponent()` method to obtain the last node in the path, and then the `getParent()` method to get all the nodes in the path upward through the link.

The selection of tree nodes is defined in the `TreeSelectionModel` interface, as shown in Figure 36.26. The `DefaultTreeSelectionModel` class is a concrete implementation of the `TreeSelectionModel` that maintains an array of `TreePath` objects representing the current selection. The last `TreePath` selected, called the *lead path*, can be obtained using the `getLeadSelectionPath()` method. To obtain all the selection paths, use the `getSelectionPaths()` method, which returns an array of tree paths.

«interface»
javax.swing.tree.TreeSelectionModel

`+addSelectionPath(path: TreePath): void`	Adds the specified `TreePath` to the current selection.
`+addSelectionPaths(paths: TreePath[]): void`	Adds the specified `TreePaths` to the current selection.
`+clearSelection(): void`	Clears the selection.
`+getLeadSelectionPath(): TreePath`	Returns the last path in the selection.
`+getSelectionCount(): int`	Returns the number of paths in the selection.
`+getSelectionPath(): TreePath`	Returns the first path in the selection.
`+getSelectionPaths(): TreePath[]`	Returns all the paths in the selection.
`+getSelectionMode(): int`	Returns the current selection mode.
`+removeSelectionPath(path: TreePath): void`	Removes path from the selection.
`+removeSelectionPaths(paths: TreePath[]): void`	Removes paths from the selection.
`+setSelectionMode(mode: int): void`	Sets the selection mode.
`+setSelectionPath(path: TreePath): void`	Sets the selection to path.
`+setSelectionPaths(paths: TreePath[]): void`	Sets the selection to paths.
`+addTreeSelectionListener(x: TreeSelectionListener): void`	Registers a `TreeSelectionListener`.
`+removeTreeSelectionListener(x: TreeSelectionListener): void`	Removes a `TreeSelectionListener`.

`javax.swing.tree.DefaultTreeSelectionModel`

FIGURE 36.26 The `TreeSelectionModel` handles selection in a tree and `DefaultTreeSelectionModel` is a concrete implementation of it.

tree selection modes

`TreeSelectionModel` supports three selection modes: contiguous selection, discontiguous selection, and single selection. *Single selection* allows only one item to be selected. *Contiguous selection* allows multiple selections, but the selected items must be contiguous. *Discontiguous selection* is the most flexible; it allows any item to be selected at a given time. The default tree selection mode is discontiguous. To set a selection mode, use the `setSelectionMode(int mode)` method in `TreeSelectionModel`. The constants for the three modes are:

- `CONTIGUOUS_TREE_SELECTION`
- `DISCONTIGUOUS_TREE_SELECTION`
- `SINGLE_TREE_SELECTION`

bypass `TreeSelectionModel`

Note

When you create a `JTree`, a `DefaultTreeSelectionModel` is automatically created, and thus you rarely need to create an instance of `TreeSelectionModel` explicitly. Since most of the methods in `TreeSelectionModel` are also in `JTree`, you can get selection paths and process the selection without directly dealing with `TreeSelectionModel`.

Listing 36.15 gives an example that displays a selected path or selected paths in a tree. The user may select a node or multiple nodes and click the *Show Path* button to display the properties of the first selected path or the *Show Paths* button to display all the selected paths in a text area, as shown in Figure 36.27. The *Show Path* button displays a path from the last node up to the root.

LISTING 36.15 TestTreePath.java

```
import java.awt.*;
import java.awt.event.*;
import javax.swing.*;
import javax.swing.tree.*;
```

```
public class TestTreePath extends JApplet {
  private JTree jTree = new JTree();
  private JTextArea jtaOutput = new JTextArea();
  private JButton jbtShowPath = new JButton("Show Path");
  private JButton jbtShowPaths = new JButton("Show Paths");

  public TestTreePath() {
    JSplitPane splitPane = new JSplitPane(JSplitPane.HORIZONTAL_SPLIT,
      new JScrollPane(jTree), new JScrollPane(jtaOutput));

    JPanel panel = new JPanel();
    panel.add(jbtShowPath);
    panel.add(jbtShowPaths);

    add(splitPane, BorderLayout.CENTER);
    add(panel, BorderLayout.NORTH);

    jbtShowPath.addActionListener(new ActionListener() {
      public void actionPerformed(ActionEvent e) {
        TreePath path = jTree.getSelectionPath();
        jtaOutput.append("\nProcessing a single path\n");
        jtaOutput.append("# of elements: " + path.getPathCount());
        jtaOutput.append("\nlast element: "
          + path.getLastPathComponent());
        jtaOutput.append("\nfrom last node in the path to the root: ");
        TreeNode node = (TreeNode)path.getLastPathComponent();
        while (node != null) {
          jtaOutput.append(node.toString() + " ");
          node = node.getParent();
        }
      }});

    jbtShowPaths.addActionListener(new ActionListener() {
      public void actionPerformed(ActionEvent e) {
        jtaOutput.append("\nProcessing multiple paths\n");
        javax.swing.tree.TreePath[] paths = jTree.getSelectionPaths();
        for (int i = 0; i < paths.length; i++)
          jtaOutput.append(paths[i].toString() + "\n");
      }});
  }
}
```

default tree
text area
Show Path button
Show Paths button
split pane
Show Path button
selected path
path count
last node
get parent
Show Paths button
selected paths
display a path
main method omitted

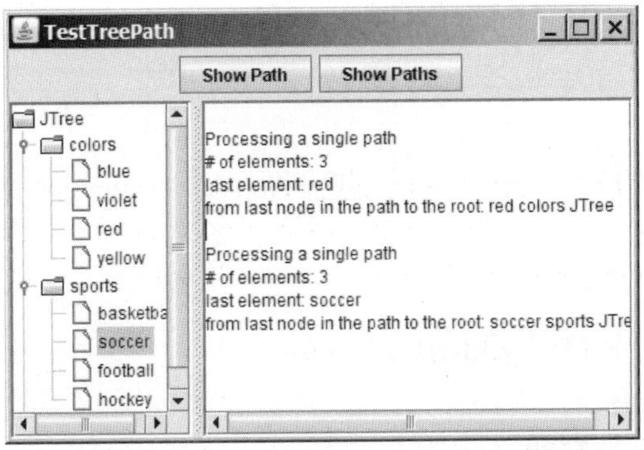
TestTreePath
Show Path
Show Paths
JTree
colors
blue
violet
red
yellow
sports
basketba
soccer
football
hockey
Processing a single path
# of elements: 3
last element: red
from last node in the path to the root: red colors JTree
Processing a single path
# of elements: 3
last element: soccer
from last node in the path to the root: soccer sports JTre

FIGURE 36.27 The selected path(s) are processed.

The `getSelectionPath()` method invoked from a `JTree` returns a `TreePath` in line 25. The first node in the path is always the root of the tree. The `getPathCount()` invoked from a `TreePath` returns the number of the nodes in the path (line 27). The `getLastPathComponent()` invoked from a `TreePath` returns the last node in the path (line 29). The return node type is `Object`. You need to cast it to a `TreeNode` (line 31) in order to invoke the `getParent()` method from a `TreeNode` (line 34).

While the `getSelectionPath()` method (line 25) returns the first selected path, the `getSelectionPaths()` method (line 41) returns all the selected paths in an array of paths.

36.13 Case Study: Modifying Trees

Write a program to create two trees that display the same contents: world, continents, countries, and states, as shown in Figure 36.28. For the tree on the left, enable the user to choose a selection mode, specify whether it can be edited, add a new child under the first selected node, and remove all the selected nodes.

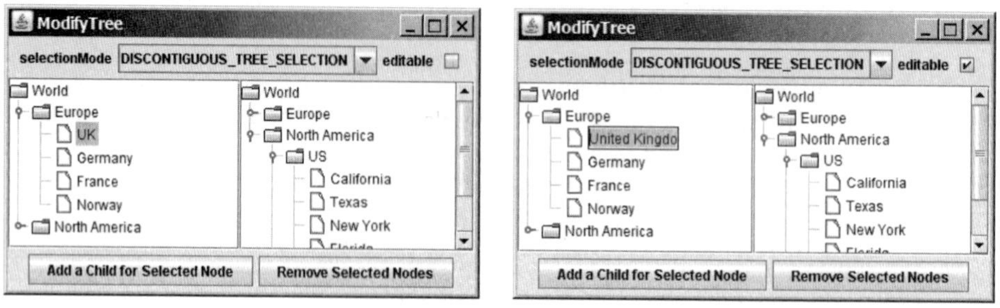
ModifyTree
selectionMode
DISCONTIGUOUS_TREE_SELECTION
editable
World
Europe
UK
Germany
France
Norway
North America
US
California
Texas
New York
Add a Child for Selected Node
Remove Selected Nodes
United Kingdo

(a) (b)

FIGURE 36.28 You can rename a node, add a child, and remove nodes in a tree dynamically.

You can choose a selection mode from the selectionMode combo box. You can specify whether the left tree nodes can be edited from the editable check box.

When you click a button, if no nodes are currently selected in the left tree, a message dialog box is displayed, as shown in Figure 36.29(a). When you click the *Add a Child for Selected Node* button, an input dialog box is displayed to prompt the user to enter a child name for the selected node, as shown in Figure 36.29(b). The new node becomes a child of the first selected node. When you click the *Remove Selected Nodes* button, all the selected nodes in the left tree are removed.

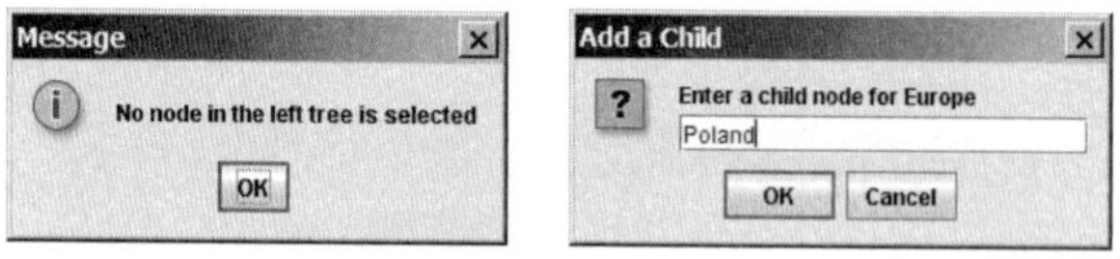
Message
No node in the left tree is selected
OK
Add a Child
Enter a child node for Europe
Poland
OK
Cancel

(a) (b)

FIGURE 36.29 You can add a new node to the tree.

Listing 36.16 gives the program.

LISTING 36.16 `ModifyTree.java`

```
import java.awt.*;
import java.awt.event.*;
import javax.swing.*;
import javax.swing.tree.*;
```

```java

public class ModifyTree extends JApplet {
  // Create a combo box for choosing selection modes
  private JComboBox jcboSelectionMode = new JComboBox(new String[]{
    "CONTIGUOUS_TREE_SELECTION", "DISCONTIGUOUS_TREE_SELECTION",
    "SINGLE_TREE_SELECTION"});

  // Create a check box for specifying editable
  private JCheckBox jchkEditable = new JCheckBox();

  // Create two buttons
  private JButton jbtAdd =
    new JButton("Add a Child for Selected Node");
  private JButton jbtRemove = new JButton("Remove Selected Nodes");

  // Declare two trees
  private JTree jTree1, jTree2;

  public ModifyTree() {
    // Create the first tree
    DefaultMutableTreeNode root, europe, northAmerica, us;

    europe = new DefaultMutableTreeNode("Europe");
    europe.add(new DefaultMutableTreeNode("UK"));
    europe.add(new DefaultMutableTreeNode("Germany"));
    europe.add(new DefaultMutableTreeNode("France"));
    europe.add(new DefaultMutableTreeNode("Norway"));

    northAmerica = new DefaultMutableTreeNode("North America");
    us = new DefaultMutableTreeNode("US");
    us.add(new DefaultMutableTreeNode("California"));
    us.add(new DefaultMutableTreeNode("Texas"));
    us.add(new DefaultMutableTreeNode("New York"));
    us.add(new DefaultMutableTreeNode("Florida"));
    us.add(new DefaultMutableTreeNode("Illinois"));
    northAmerica.add(us);
    northAmerica.add(new DefaultMutableTreeNode("Canada"));

    root = new DefaultMutableTreeNode("World");
    root.add(europe);
    root.add(northAmerica);

    jcboSelectionMode.setSelectedIndex(1);

    JPanel p1 = new JPanel();
    p1.add(new JLabel("selectionMode"));
    p1.add(jcboSelectionMode);
    p1.add(new JLabel("editable"));
    p1.add(jchkEditable);

    JPanel p2 = new JPanel(new GridLayout(1, 2));
    p2.add(new JScrollPane(jTree1 = new JTree(root)));
    p2.add(new JScrollPane(jTree2 =
      new JTree(new DefaultTreeModel(root)))); // Same root as jTree1

    JPanel p3 = new JPanel();
    p3.add(jbtAdd);
    p3.add(jbtRemove);

    add(p1, BorderLayout.NORTH);
```

combo box

check box

buttons

trees

tree nodes

fill nodes

create **jTree1**

create **jTree2**

choose selection mode
set selection mode
choose editable
set editable
add child
get selected node
add new node
reload tree model
remove node
get selected paths

```
    add(p2, BorderLayout.CENTER);
    add(p3, BorderLayout.SOUTH);

    // Register listeners
    jcboSelectionMode.addActionListener(new ActionListener() {
      public void actionPerformed(ActionEvent e) {
        if (jcboSelectionMode.getSelectedItem().
            equals("CONTIGUOUS_TREE_SELECTION"))
          jTree1.getSelectionModel().setSelectionMode(
            TreeSelectionModel.CONTIGUOUS_TREE_SELECTION);
        else if (jcboSelectionMode.getSelectedItem().
            equals("DISCONTIGUOUS_TREE_SELECTION"))
          jTree1.getSelectionModel().setSelectionMode(
            TreeSelectionModel.DISCONTIGUOUS_TREE_SELECTION);
        else
          jTree1.getSelectionModel().setSelectionMode(
            TreeSelectionModel.SINGLE_TREE_SELECTION);
      }
    });

    jchkEditable.addActionListener(new ActionListener() {
      public void actionPerformed(ActionEvent e) {
        jTree1.setEditable(jchkEditable.isSelected());
      }
    });

    jbtAdd.addActionListener(new ActionListener() {
      public void actionPerformed(ActionEvent e) {
        DefaultMutableTreeNode parent = (DefaultMutableTreeNode)
          jTree1.getLastSelectedPathComponent();

        if (parent == null) {
          JOptionPane.showMessageDialog(null,
            "No node in the left tree is selected");
          return;
        }

        // Enter a new node
        String nodeName = JOptionPane.showInputDialog(
          null, "Enter a child node for "+ parent, "Add a Child",
          JOptionPane.QUESTION_MESSAGE);

        // Insert the new node as a child of treeNode
        parent.add(new DefaultMutableTreeNode(nodeName));

        // Reload the model since a new tree node is added
        ((DefaultTreeModel)(jTree1.getModel())).reload();
        ((DefaultTreeModel)(jTree2.getModel())).reload();
      }
    });

    jbtRemove.addActionListener(new ActionListener() {
      public void actionPerformed(ActionEvent e) {
        // Get all selected paths
        TreePath[] paths = jTree1.getSelectionPaths();

        if (paths == null) {
          JOptionPane.showMessageDialog(null,
            "No node in the left tree is selected");
          return;
        }
```

```
126
127         // Remove all selected nodes
128         for (int i = 0; i < paths.length; i++) {
129           DefaultMutableTreeNode node = (DefaultMutableTreeNode)
130               (paths[i].getLastPathComponent());
131
132           if (node.isRoot()) {
133             JOptionPane.showMessageDialog(null,
134               "Cannot remove the root");
135           }
136           else
137             node.removeFromParent();
138         }
139
140         // Reload the model since a new tree node is added
141         ((DefaultTreeModel)(jTree1.getModel())).reload();
142         ((DefaultTreeModel)(jTree2.getModel())).reload();
143       }
144     });
145   }
146 }
```

remove node

reload tree model

main method omitted

Two JTree objects (jTree1 and jTree2) are created with the same root (lines 56–58), but each has its own TreeSelectionModel. When you choose a selection mode in the combo box, the new selection mode is set in jTree1's selection model (line 69–83). The selection mode for jTree2 is not affected.

When the editable check box is checked or unchecked, the editable property in jTree1 is set accordingly. If editable is true, you can edit a node in the left tree.

When you click the *Add a Child for Selected Node* button, the first selected node is returned as parent (lines 93–94). Suppose you selected Europe, UK, and US in this order; parent is Europe. If parent is null, no node is selected in the left tree (lines 96–100). Otherwise, prompt the user to enter a new node from an input dialog box (lines 103–105) and add this node as a child of parent (line 108). Since the tree has been modified, you need to invoke the reload() method to notify that the models for both trees have been changed (lines 111–112). Otherwise, the new node may not be displayed in jTree1 and jTree2.

When you click the *Remove Selected Nodes* button, all the tree paths for each selected node are obtained in paths (line 119). Suppose you selected Europe, UK, and US in this order; three tree paths are obtained. Each path starts from the root to a selected node. If no node is selected, paths is null. To delete a selected node is to delete the last node in each selected tree path (128–138). The last node in a path is obtained using getLastPathComponent(). If the node is the root, it cannot be removed (lines 132–135). The removeFromParent() method removes a node (line 137).

36.14 Tree Node Rendering and Editing

JTree delegates node rendering to a renderer. All renderers are instances of the TreeCellRenderer interface, which defines a single method, getTreeCellRendererComponent, as follows:

```
public Component getTreeCellRendererComponent
  (JTree tree, Object value, boolean selected, boolean expanded,
   boolean leaf, int row, boolean hasFocus);
```

You can create a custom tree cell renderer by implementing the TreeCellRenderer interface, or use the DefaultTreeCellRenderer class, which provides a default implementation for TreeCellRenderer. When a new JTree is created, an instance of DefaultTreeCellRenderer is assigned to the tree renderer. The DefaultTreeCellRenderer class maintains three icon properties named `leafIcon`, `openIcon`, and `closedIcon` for leaf nodes, expanded nodes, and collapsed nodes. It also provides colors for text and background. The following code sets new leaf, open and closed icons, and new background selection color in the tree:

```
DefaultTreeCellRenderer renderer =
  (DefaultTreeCellRenderer)jTree1.getCellRenderer();
renderer.setLeafIcon(yourCustomLeafImageIcon);
renderer.setOpenIcon(yourCustomOpenImageIcon);
renderer.setClosedIcon(yourCustomClosedImageIcon);
renderer.setBackgroundSelectionColor(Color.red);
```

Note

The default leaf, open icon, and closed icon are dependent on the look-and-feel. For instance, on Windows look-and-feel, the open icon is − and the closed icon is +.

`JTree` comes with a default cell editor. If `JTree`'s `editable` property is `true`, the default editor activates a text field for editing when the node is clicked three times. By default, this property is set to `false`. To create a custom editor, you need to extend the `DefaultCellEditor` class, which is the same class you used in table cell editing. You can use a text field, a check box, or a combo box, and pass it to `DefaultCellEditor`'s constructor to create an editor. The following code uses a combo box for editing colors. The combo box editor is shown in Figure 36.30(a).

```
// Customize editor
JComboBox jcboColor = new JComboBox();
jcboColor.addItem("red");
jcboColor.addItem("green");
jcboColor.addItem("blue");
jcboColor.addItem("yellow");
jcboColor.addItem("orange");

jTree1.setCellEditor(new javax.swing.DefaultCellEditor(jcboColor));
jTree1.setEditable(true);
```

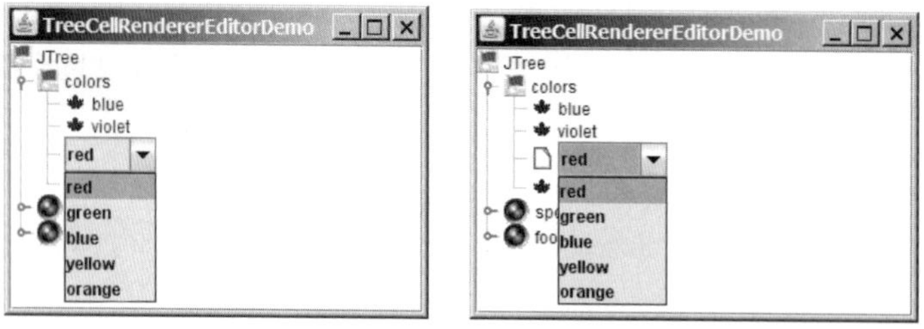
TreeCellRendererEditorDemo
JTree
colors
blue
violet
red
red
green
blue
yellow
orange
TreeCellRendererEditorDemo
JTree
colors
blue
violet
red
red
green
blue
yellow
orange

(a) (b)

FIGURE 36.30 You can supply a custom editor for editing tree nodes.

There are two annoying problems with the editor created in the preceding code. First, it is activated with just one mouse click. Second, it overlaps the node's icon, as shown in Figure 36.30(a). These two problems can be fixed by using the `DefaultTreeCellEditor`, as shown in the following code:

```
jTree1.setCellEditor
  (new javax.swing.tree.DefaultTreeCellEditor(jTree1,
   new javax.swing.tree.DefaultTreeCellRenderer(),
   new javax.swing.DefaultCellEditor(jcboColor)));
```

The new editor is shown in Figure 36.30(b). Editing using DefaultTreeCellEditor starts on a triple mouse click. The combo box does not overlap the node's icon.

36.15 Tree Events

JTree can fire TreeSelectionEvent and TreeExpansionEvent, among many other events. Whenever a new node is selected, JTree fires a TreeSelectionEvent. Whenever a node is expanded or collapsed, JTree fires a TreeExpansionEvent. To handle the tree-selection event, a listener must implement the TreeSelectionListener interface, which contains a single handler named valueChanged method. TreeExpansionListener contains two handlers named treeCollapsed and treeExpanded for handling node expansion or node closing.

The following code displays a selected node in a listener class for TreeSelectionEvent:

```
public void valueChanged(TreeSelectionEvent e) {
  TreePath path = e.getNewLeadSelectionPath();
  TreeNode treeNode = (TreeNode)path.getLastPathComponent();
  System.out.println("The selected node is " + treeNode.toString());
}
```

Chapter Summary

1. JTable has three supporting models: a table model, a column model, and a list-selection model. The *table model* is for storing and processing data. The *column model* represents all the columns in the table. The *list-selection model* is the same as the one used by JList for selecting rows, columns, and cells in a table. JTable also has two useful supporting classes, TableColumn and JTableHeader. TableColumn contains the information on a particular column. JTableHeader contains the information on the header of a JTable. Each column has a default editor and renderer. You can also create a custom editor by implementing the TableCellEditor interface, and you can create a custom renderer by implementing the TableCellRenderer interface.

2. Like JTable, JTree is a very complex component with many supporting interfaces and classes. While JTree displays the tree, the data representation of the tree is handled by TreeModel, TreeNode, and TreePath. TreeModel represents the entire tree, TreeNode represents a node, and TreePath represents a path to a node. Unlike the ListModel or TableModel, the tree model does not directly store or manage tree data. Tree data are stored and managed in TreeNode and TreePath. A TreePath is an array of Objects that are vended from a TreeModel. The elements of the array are ordered such that the root is always the first element (index 0) of the array. The TreeSelectionModel interface handles tree node selection. The DefaultTreeCellRenderer class provides a default tree node renderer that can display a label and/or an icon in a node. The DefaultTreeCellEditor can be used to edit the cells in a text field. The TreePath class is a support class that represents a set of nodes in a path.

3. JTable and JTree are in the javax.swing package, but their supporting interfaces and classes are all included in the javax.swing.table and javax.swing.tree packages, respectively.

REVIEW QUESTIONS

Sections 36.2–36.7

36.1 How do you initialize a table? Can you specify the maximum number of visible rows in a table without scrolling? How do you specify the height of a table cell? How do you specify the horizontal margin of table cells?

36.2 How do you modify table contents? How do you add or remove a row? How do you add or remove a column?

36.3 What is autoresizing of a table column? How many types of autoresizing are available?

36.4 What are the properties that show grids, horizontal grids, and vertical grids? What are the properties that specify the table row height, vertical margin, and horizontal margin?

36.5 What are the default table renderers and editors? How do you create a custom table cell renderer and editor?

36.6 What are the default tree renderers and editors? How do you create a custom tree cell renderer and editor?

36.7 How do you disable table cell editing?

Sections 36.8–36.14

36.8 How do you create a tree? How do you specify the row height of a tree node? How do you obtain the default tree model and tree-selection model from an instance of `JTree`?

36.9 How do you initialize data in a tree using `TreeModel`? How do you add a child to an instance of `DefaultMutableTreeNode`?

36.10 How do you enable tree node editing?

36.11 How do you add or remove a node from a tree?

36.12 How do you obtain a selected tree node?

PROGRAMMING EXERCISES

Sections 36.2–36.7

36.1* (*Creating a table for a loan schedule*) Exercise 31.5 displays an amortization schedule in a text area. Write a program that enables the user to enter or choose the loan amount, number of years, and interest rate from spinners and displays the schedule in a table, as shown in Figure 36.31. The step for loan amount is $500, for number of years is 1, and for annual interest rate is 0.125%.

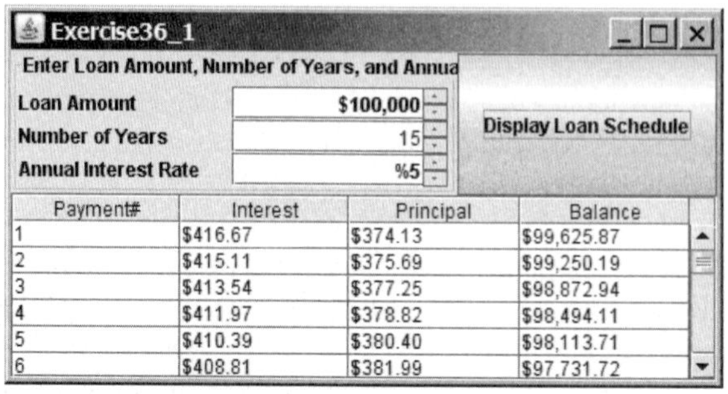
Exercise36_1
Enter Loan Amount, Number of Years, and Annua
Loan Amount
$100,000
Number of Years
15
Annual Interest Rate
%5
Display Loan Schedule
Payment#
Interest
Principal
Balance
1 $416.67 $374.13 $99,625.87
2 $415.11 $375.69 $99,250.19
3 $413.54 $377.25 $98,872.94
4 $411.97 $378.82 $98,494.11
5 $410.39 $380.40 $98,113.71
6 $408.81 $381.99 $97,731.72

FIGURE 36.31 The table shows the loan schedule.

36.2* (*Deleting rows and columns*) Listing 36.6, ModifyTable.java, allows you to delete only the first selected row or column. Enable the program to delete all the selected rows or columns. Also enable the program to delete a row or a column by pressing the DELETE key.

36.3** (*Creating a student table*) Create a table for student records. Each record consists of name, birthday, class status, in-state, and a photo, as shown in Figure 36.32(a). The name is of the `String` type; birthday is of the `Date` type; class status is one of the following five values: Freshman, Sophomore, Junior, Senior, or Graduate; in-state is a `boolean` value indicating whether the student is a resident of the state; and photo is an image icon. Use the default editors for name, birthday, and in-state. Supply a combo box as custom editor for class status.

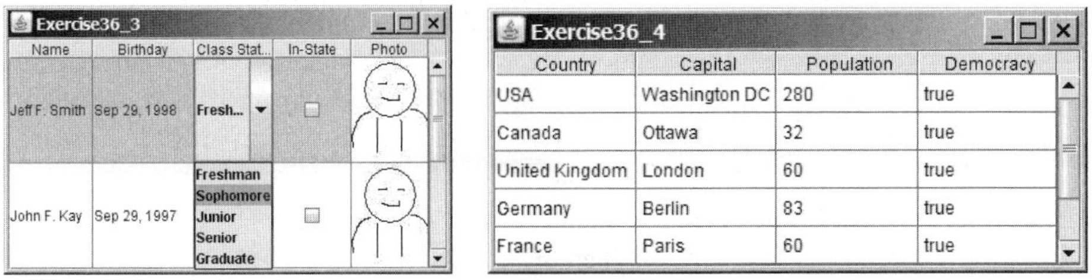
Exercise36_3
Name
Birthday
Class Stat...
In-State
Photo
Jeff F. Smith
Sep 29, 1998
Fresh...
Freshman
Sophomore
Junior
Senior
Graduate
John F. Kay
Sep 29, 1997
Exercise36_4
Country
Capital
Population
Democracy
USA
Washington DC
280
true
Canada
Ottawa
32
true
United Kingdom
London
60
true
Germany
Berlin
83
true
France
Paris
60
true

(a) (b)

FIGURE 36.32 (a) The table displays student records. (b) The data in the file are displayed in a `JTable`.

36.4* (*Displaying a table for data from a text file*) Suppose that a table named Exercise36_4Table.txt is stored in a text file. The first line in the file is the header, and the remaining lines correspond to rows in the table. The elements are separated by commas. Write a program to display the table using the `JTable` component. For example, the following text file is displayed in a table, as shown in Figure 36.32(b).

```
Country, Capital, Population, Democracy
USA, Washington DC, 280, true
Canada, Ottawa, 32, true
United Kingdom, London, 60, true
Germany, Berlin, 83, true
France, Paris, 60, true
Norway, Oslo, 4.5, true
India, New Delhi, 1046, true
```

36.5*** (*Creating a controller using `JTable`*) In Exercise 35.1, you created a chart model (`ChartModel`) and two views (`PieChart` and `BarChart`). Create a controller that enables the user to modify the data, as shown in Figure 36.33.

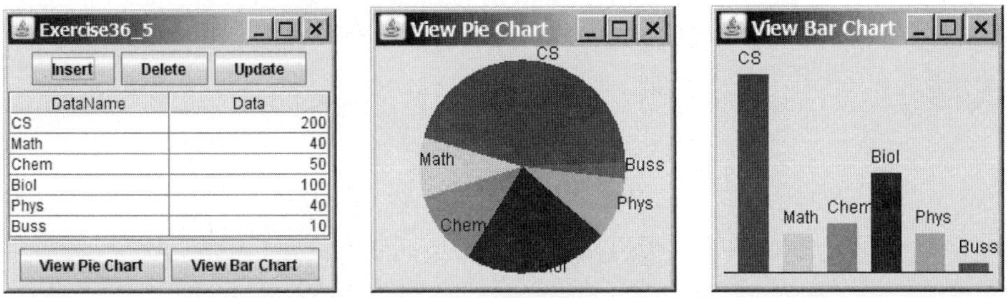
Exercise36_5
Insert
Delete
Update
DataName
Data
CS
200
Math
40
Chem
50
Biol
100
Phys
40
Buss
10
View Pie Chart
View Bar Chart
View Pie Chart
CS
Math
Buss
Phys
Chem
View Bar Chart
CS
Biol
Math
Chem
Phys
Buss

FIGURE 36.33 You can modify the data in the controller. The views are synchronized with the controller.

You will see the changes take effect in the pie-chart view and the bar-chart view. Your exercise consists of the following classes:

- The controller named `ChartController`. This class uses a table to display data. You can modify the data in the table. Click the *Insert* button to insert a new row above the selected row in the table, click the *Delete* button to delete the selected row in the table, and click the *Update* button to update the changes you made in the table.
- The class `MyTableModel`. This class extends `DefaultTableModel` to override the `getColumnClass` method so that you can use the `JTable`'s default editor for numerical values. This class is the same as in Listing 36.7.
- The classes `ChartModel`, `PieChart`, and `BarChart` from Exercise 35.1.
- The main class `Exercise36_5`. This class creates a user interface with a controller and two buttons, *View Pie Chart* and *View Bar Chart*. Click the *View Pie Chart* button to pop up a frame to display a pie chart, and click the *View Bar Chart* button to pop up a frame to display a bar chart.

Sections 36.8–36.14

36.6* (*Creating a tree for book chapters*) Create a tree to display the table of contents for a book. When a node is selected in the tree, display a paragraph to describe the selected node, as shown in Figure 36.34(a).

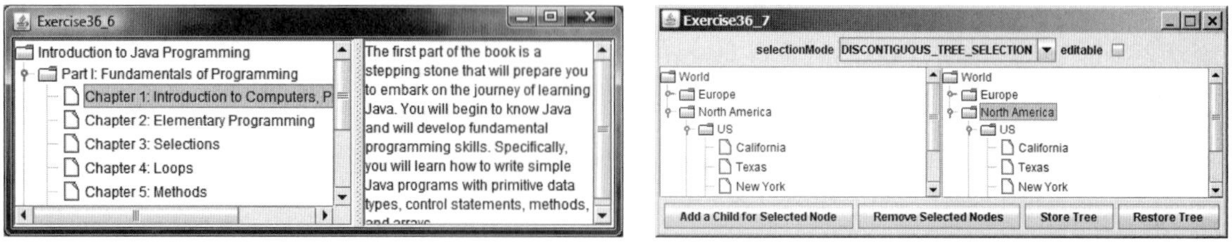
Exercise36_6
Introduction to Java Programming
Part I: Fundamentals of Programming
Chapter 1: Introduction to Computers, P
Chapter 2: Elementary Programming
Chapter 3: Selections
Chapter 4: Loops
Chapter 5: Methods
The first part of the book is a stepping stone that will prepare you to embark on the journey of learning Java. You will begin to know Java and will develop fundamental programming skills. Specifically, you will learn how to write simple Java programs with primitive data types, control statements, methods,
Exercise36_7
selectionMode
DISCONTIGUOUS_TREE_SELECTION
editable
World
Europe
North America
US
California
Texas
New York
World
Europe
North America
US
California
Texas
New York
Add a Child for Selected Node
Remove Selected Nodes
Store Tree
Restore Tree

(a) (b)

FIGURE 36.34 (a) The content of the node is displayed in a text area when the node is clicked. (b) You can store tree data to a file and restore them later.

36.7* (*Storing and restoring trees*) Modify Listing 36.16, ModifyTree.java, to add two buttons, as shown in Figure 36.34(b) to store and restore trees. Use the object I/O to store the tree model.

36.8* (*Traversing trees*) Create a tree using the default `JTree` constructor and traverse the nodes in breadth-first, depth-first, preorder, and postorder.

36.9*** (*File explorer*) Use `JTree` to develop a file explorer. The program lets the user enter a directory and displays all files under the directory, as shown in Figure 36.35.

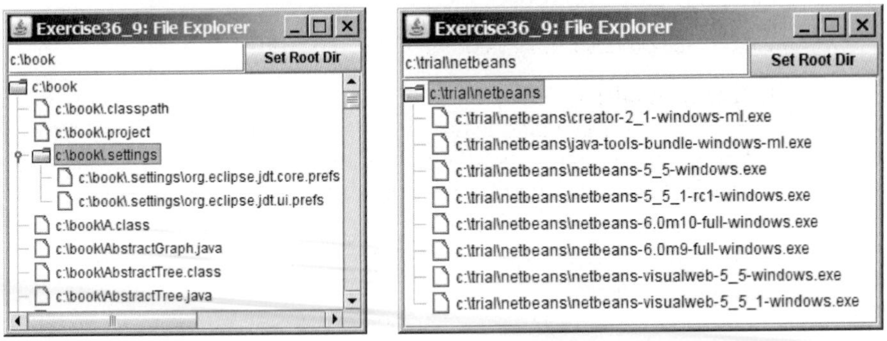
Exercise36_9: File Explorer
c:\book
Set Root Dir
c:\book
c:\book\.classpath
c:\book\.project
c:\book\.settings
c:\book\.settings\org.eclipse.jdt.core.prefs
c:\book\.settings\org.eclipse.jdt.ui.prefs
c:\book\A.class
c:\book\AbstractGraph.java
c:\book\AbstractTree.class
c:\book\AbstractTree.java
Exercise36_9: File Explorer
c:\trial\netbeans
Set Root Dir
c:\trial\netbeans
c:\trial\netbeans\creator-2_1-windows-ml.exe
c:\trial\netbeans\java-tools-bundle-windows-ml.exe
c:\trial\netbeans\netbeans-5_5-windows.exe
c:\trial\netbeans\netbeans-5_5_1-rc1-windows.exe
c:\trial\netbeans\netbeans-6.0m10-full-windows.exe
c:\trial\netbeans\netbeans-6.0m9-full-windows.exe
c:\trial\netbeans\netbeans-visualweb-5_5-windows.exe
c:\trial\netbeans\netbeans-visualweb-5_5_1-windows.exe

FIGURE 36.35 The file explorer explores the files in a directory.

36.10** (*Adding and deleting tree nodes using the INSERT and DELETE keys*) Modify Listing 36.16, ModifyTree.java, to add a new child node by pressing the INSERT key, and delete a node by pressing the DELETE key.

CHAPTER 37

JAVA DATABASE PROGRAMMING

Objectives

- To understand the concept of database and database management systems (§37.2).
- To understand the relational data model: relational data structures, constraints, and languages (§37.2).
- To use SQL to create and drop tables and to retrieve and modify data (§37.3).
- To learn how to load a driver, connect to a database, execute statements, and process result sets using JDBC (§37.4).
- To use prepared statements to execute precompiled SQL statements (§37.5).
- To use callable statements to execute stored SQL procedures and functions (§37.6).
- To explore database metadata using the `DatabaseMetaData` and `ResultSetMetaData` interfaces (§37.7).

37.1 Introduction

You may have heard a lot about database systems. Database systems are everywhere. Your social security information is stored in a database by the government. If you shop online, your purchase information is stored in a database by the company. If you attend a university, your academic information is stored in a database by the university. Database systems not only store data, they also provide means of accessing, updating, manipulating, and analyzing data. Your social security information is updated periodically, and you can register in courses online. Database systems play an important role in society and in commerce.

This chapter introduces database systems, SQL, and how to develop database applications using Java. If you already know SQL, you may skip §§37.2–37.3.

37.2 Relational Database Systems

database system

A *database system* consists of a database, the software that stores and manages data in the database, and the application programs that present data and enable the user to interact with the database system, as shown in Figure 37.1.

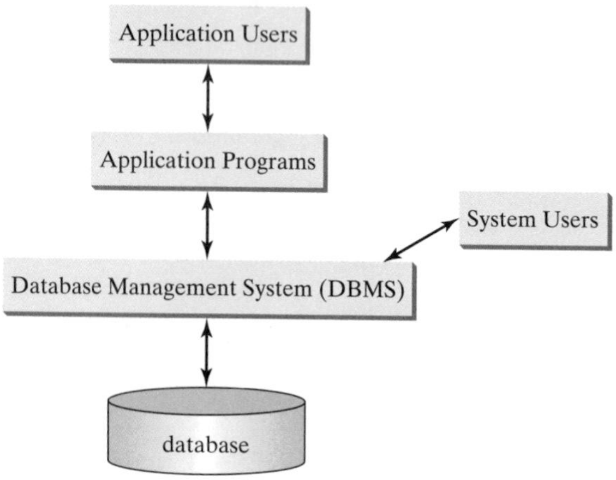
Application Users
Application Programs
System Users
Database Management System (DBMS)
database

FIGURE 37.1 A database system consists of data, database management software, and application programs.

DBMS

A database is a repository of data that form information. When you purchase a database system, such as MySQL, Oracle, IBM, Microsoft, or Sybase, from a software vendor, you actually purchase the software comprising a *database management system* (DBMS). Database management systems are designed for use by professional programmers and are not suitable for ordinary customers. Application programs are built on top of the DBMS for customers to access and update the database. Thus application programs can be viewed as the interfaces between the database system and its users. Application programs may be standalone GUI applications or Web applications, and may access several different database systems in the network, as shown in Figure 37.2.

Most of today's database systems are *relational database systems.* They are based on the relational data model, which has three key components: structure, integrity, and language. *Structure* defines the representation of the data. *Integrity* imposes constraints on the data. *Language* provides the means for accessing and manipulating data.

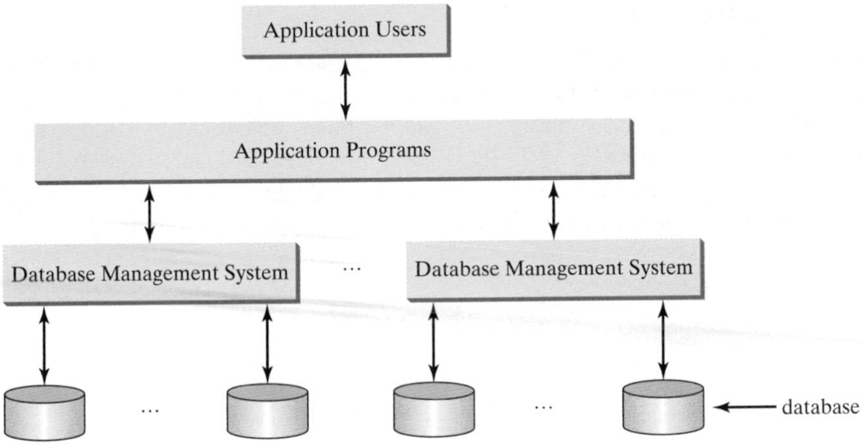
Application Users
Application Programs
Database Management System
...
Database Management System
...
...
database

FIGURE 37.2 An application program may access multiple database systems.

37.2.1 Relational Structures

relational model

The relational model is built around a simple and natural structure. A relation is actually a table that consists of nonduplicate rows. Tables are easy to understand and easy to use. The relational model provides a simple yet powerful way to represent data.

tuple

attribute

A row of a table represents a record, and a column of a table represents the value of a single attribute of the record. In relational database theory, a row is called a *tuple* and a column is called an *attribute*. Figure 37.3 shows a sample table that stores information about the courses offered by a university. The table has eight tuples, and each tuple has five attributes.

Relation/Table Name

Columns/Attributes

Course Table

Tuples/ Rows

courseId	subjectId	courseNumber	title	numOfCredits
11111	CSCI	1301	Introduction to Java I	4
11112	CSCI	1302	Introduction to Java II	3
11113	CSCI	3720	Database Systems	3
11114	CSCI	4750	Rapid Java Application	3
11115	MATH	2750	Calculus I	5
11116	MATH	3750	Calculus II	5
11117	EDUC	1111	Reading	3
11118	ITEC	1344	Database Administration	3

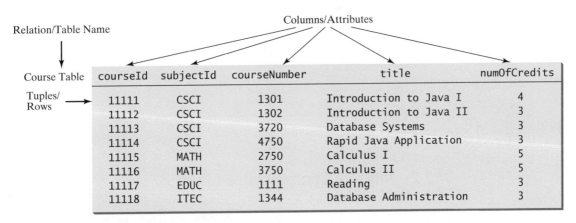

FIGURE 37.3 A table has a table name, column names, and rows.

Tables describe the relationship among data. Each row in a table represents a record of related data. For example, "11111", "CSCI", "1301", "Introduction to Java I", and "4" are related to form a record (the first row in Figure 37.3) in the `Course` table. Just as data in the same row are related, so too data in different tables may be related through common attributes. Suppose the database has two other tables, `Student` and `Enrollment`, as shown in Figures 37.4 and 37.5. The `Course` table and the `Enrollment` table are related through their common attribute `courseId`, and the `Enrollment` table and the `Student` table are related through `ssn`.

Student Table								
ssn	firstName	mi	lastName	phone	birthDate	street	zipCode	deptID
444111110	Jacob	R	Smith	9129219434	1985-04-09	99 Kingston Street	31435	BIOL
444111111	John	K	Stevenson	9129219434	null	100 Main Street	31411	BIOL
444111112	George	K	Smith	9129213454	1974-10-10	1200 Abercorn St.	31419	CS
444111113	Frank	E	Jones	9125919434	1970-09-09	100 Main Street	31411	BIOL
444111114	Jean	K	Smith	9129219434	1970-02-09	100 Main Street	31411	CHEM
444111115	Josh	R	Woo	7075989434	1970-02-09	555 Franklin St.	31411	CHEM
444111116	Josh	R	Smith	9129219434	1973-02-09	100 Main Street	31411	BIOL
444111117	Joy	P	Kennedy	9129229434	1974-03-19	103 Bay Street	31412	CS
444111118	Toni	R	Peterson	9129229434	1964-04-29	103 Bay Street	31412	MATH
444111119	Patrick	R	Stoneman	9129229434	1969-04-29	101 Washington St.	31435	MATH
444111120	Rick	R	Carter	9125919434	1986-04-09	19 West Ford St.	31411	BIOL

FIGURE 37.4 A `Student` table stores student information.

Enrollment Table			
ssn	courseId	dateRegistered	grade
444111110	11111	2004-03-19	A
444111110	11112	2004-03-19	B
444111110	11113	2004-03-19	C
444111111	11111	2004-03-19	D
444111111	11112	2004-03-19	F
444111111	11113	2004-03-19	A
444111112	11114	2004-03-19	B
444111112	11115	2004-03-19	C
444111112	11116	2004-03-19	D
444111113	11111	2004-03-19	A
444111113	11113	2004-03-19	A
444111114	11115	2004-03-19	B
444111115	11115	2004-03-19	F
444111115	11116	2004-03-19	F
444111116	11111	2004-03-19	D
444111117	11111	2004-03-19	D
444111118	11111	2004-03-19	A
444111118	11112	2004-03-19	D
444111118	11113	2004-03-19	B

FIGURE 37.5 An `Enrollment` table stores student enrollment information.

37.2.2 Integrity Constraints

integrity constraint

An *integrity constraint* imposes a condition that all the legal values in a table must satisfy. Figure 37.6 shows an example of some integrity constraints in the `Subject` and `Course` tables.

In general, there are three types of constraints: domain constraints, primary key constraints, and foreign key constraints. *Domain constraints* and *primary key constraints* are known as *intrarelational constraints*, meaning that a constraint involves only one relation. The *foreign key constraint* is *interrelational*, meaning that a constraint involves more than one relation.

Domain Constraints

domain constraint

Domain constraints specify the permissible values for an attribute. Domains can be specified using standard data types, such as integers, floating-point numbers, fixed-length strings, and variant-length strings. The standard data type specifies a broad range of values. Additional constraints can be specified to narrow the ranges. For example, you can specify that the `numOfCredits` attribute (in the `Course` table) must be greater than 0 and less than 5. You can

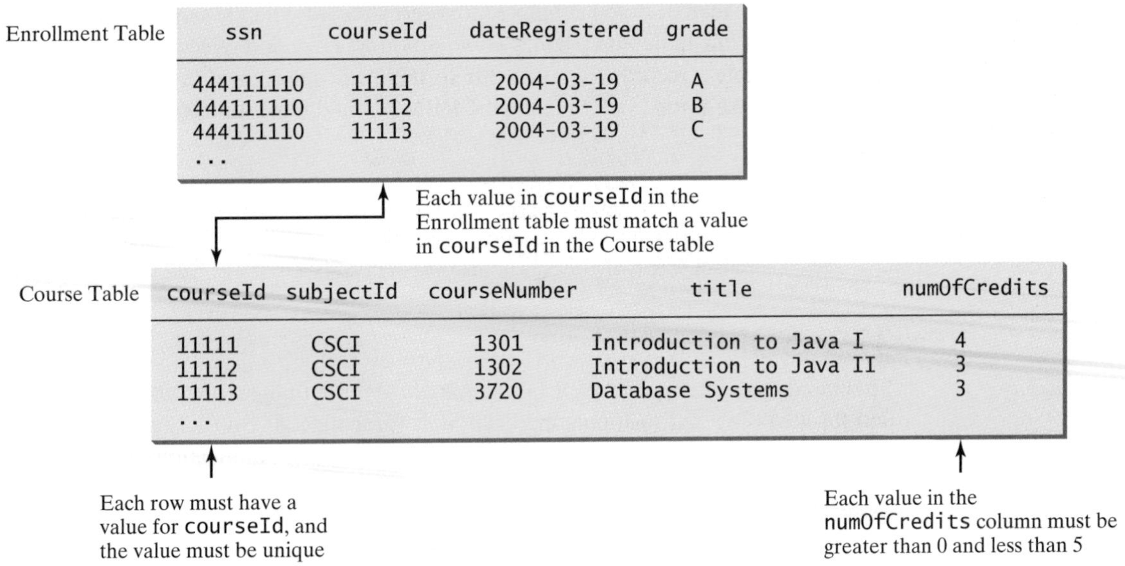
Enrollment Table
ssn courseId dateRegistered grade
444111110 11111 2004-03-19 A
444111110 11112 2004-03-19 B
444111110 11113 2004-03-19 C
...
Each value in courseId in the Enrollment table must match a value in courseId in the Course table
Course Table
courseId subjectId courseNumber title numOfCredits
11111 CSCI 1301 Introduction to Java I 4
11112 CSCI 1302 Introduction to Java II 3
11113 CSCI 3720 Database Systems 3
...
Each row must have a value for courseId, and the value must be unique
Each value in the numOfCredits column must be greater than 0 and less than 5

FIGURE 37.6 The `Enrollment` table and the `Course` table have integrity constraints.

also specify whether an attribute can be `null`, which is a special value in a database meaning unknown or not applicable. As shown in the `Student` table, `birthDate` may be `null`.

Primary Key Constraints

primary key

superkey

To understand primary keys, it is helpful to know superkeys, keys, and candidate keys. A *superkey* is an attribute or a set of attributes that uniquely identifies the relation. That is, no two tuples have the same values on a superkey. By definition, a relation consists of a set of distinct tuples. The set of all attributes in the relation forms a superkey.

A *key* `K` is a minimal superkey, meaning that any proper subset of `K` is not a superkey. A relation can have several keys. In this case, each of the keys is called a *candidate key*. The *primary* key is one of the candidate keys designated by the database designer. The primary key is often used to identify tuples in a relation. As shown in Figure 37.6, `courseId` is the primary key in the `Course` table.

Foreign Key Constraints

foreign key

In a relational database, data are related. Tuples in a relation are related, and tuples in different relations are related through their common attributes. Informally speaking, the common attributes are foreign keys. The *foreign key constraints* define the relationships among relations.

Formally, a set of attributes *FK* is a *foreign key* in a relation *R* that references relation *T* if it satisfies the following two rules:

- The attributes in *FK* have the same domain as the primary key in *T*.
- A nonnull value on *FK* in *R* must match a primary key value in *T*.

As shown in Figure 37.6, `courseId` is the foreign key in `Enrollment` that references the primary key `courseId` in `Course`. Every `courseId` value must match a `courseId` value in `Course`.

Enforcing Integrity Constraints

auto enforcement

The database management system enforces integrity constraints and rejects operations that would violate them. For example, if you attempted to insert a new record ('11115', 'CSCI', '2490', 'C++ Programming', 0) into the `Course` table, it would fail because the credit hours must be greater than 0; if you attempted to insert a record with the same primary key as an existing record in the table, the DBMS would report an error and reject the operation; if you attempted to delete a record from the Course table whose primary key value is referenced by the records in the Enrollment table, the DBMS would reject this operation.

Note

All relational database systems support primary key constraints and foreign key constraints. Not all database systems support domain constraints. On the Microsoft Access database, for example, you cannot specify the constraint that numOfCredits is greater than 0 and less than 5.

37.3 SQL

database language

Structured Query Language (SQL) is the *language* for defining tables and integrity constraints and for accessing and manipulating data. SQL (pronounced "S-Q-L" or "sequel") is the universal language for accessing relational database systems. Application programs may allow users to access a database without directly using SQL, but these applications themselves must use SQL to access the database. This section introduces some basic SQL commands.

standard SQL

Note

There are many relational database management systems. They share the common SQL language but do not all support every feature of SQL. Some systems have their own extensions to SQL. This section introduces standard SQL supported by all systems.

SQL can be used on MySQL, Oracle, Sybase, IBM DB2, IBM Informix, Borland Interbase, MS Access, or any other relational database system. This chapter uses MySQL to demonstrate SQL and uses MySQL, Access, and Oracle to demonstrate JDBC programming. The book's Web site contains the following supplements on how to install and use three popular databases: MySQL, Oracle, and Access:

MySQL Tutorial
- Supplement IV.B: Tutorial for MySQL

Oracle Tutorial
- Supplement IV.C: Tutorial for Oracle

Access Tutorial
- Supplement IV.D: Tutorial for Microsoft Access

37.3.1 Creating a User Account on MySQL

Assume that you have installed MySQL 5 with the default configuration. To match all the examples in this book, you should create a user named *scott* with password *tiger*. You can perform the administrative tasks using the MySQL GUI Administrator tool or using the command line. Here are the steps to create a user from the command line:

1. From the DOS command prompt, type

   mysql –uroot -p

   You will be prompted to enter the root password, as shown in Figure 37.7.

2. At the mysql prompt, enter

   use mysql;

3. To create user **scott** with password **tiger**, enter

   create user 'scott'@'localhost' identified by 'tiger';

   grant select, insert, update, delete, create, drop,
   execute, references on *.* to 'scott'@'localhost';

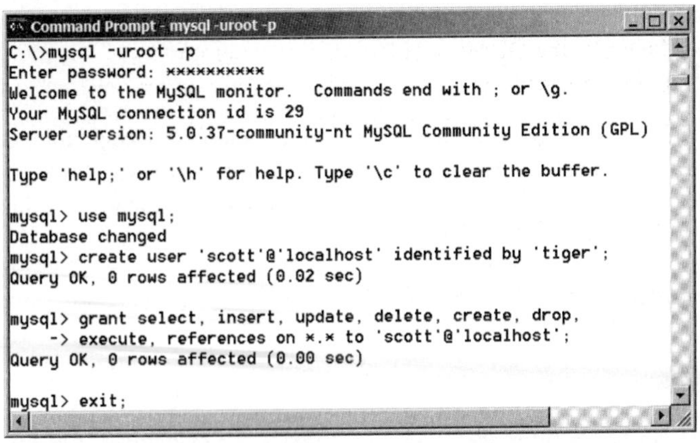
Command Prompt - mysql -uroot -p
C:\>mysql -uroot -p
Enter password: **********
Welcome to the MySQL monitor. Commands end with ; or \g.
Your MySQL connection id is 29
Server version: 5.0.37-community-nt MySQL Community Edition (GPL)
Type 'help;' or '\h' for help. Type '\c' to clear the buffer.
mysql> use mysql;
Database changed
mysql> create user 'scott'@'localhost' identified by 'tiger';
Query OK, 0 rows affected (0.02 sec)
mysql> grant select, insert, update, delete, create, drop,
    -> execute, references on *.* to 'scott'@'localhost';
Query OK, 0 rows affected (0.00 sec)
mysql> exit;

FIGURE 37.7 You can access a MySQL database server from the command window.

4. Enter

   exit;

   to exit the MySQL console.

Note

On Windows, your MySQL database server starts every time your computer starts. You can stop it by typing the command `net stop mysql` and restart it by typing the command `net start mysql`.

start mysql
stop mysql

By default, the server contains two databases named **mysql** and **test**. The **mysql** database contains the tables that store information about the server and its users. This database is intended for the server administrator to use. For example, the administrator can use it to create users and grant or revoke user privileges. Since you are the owner of the server installed on your system, you have full access to the mysql database. However, you should not create user tables in the mysql database. You can use the test database to store data or create new databases. You can also create a new database using the command `create database` ***`databasename`*** or drop an existing database using the command `drop database` ***`databasename`***.

37.3.2 Creating a Database

To match the examples in the book, you should create a database named **javabook**. Here are the steps to create it:

1. From the DOS command prompt, type

   mysql –uscott -ptiger

   to login to mysql, as shown in Figure 37.8.

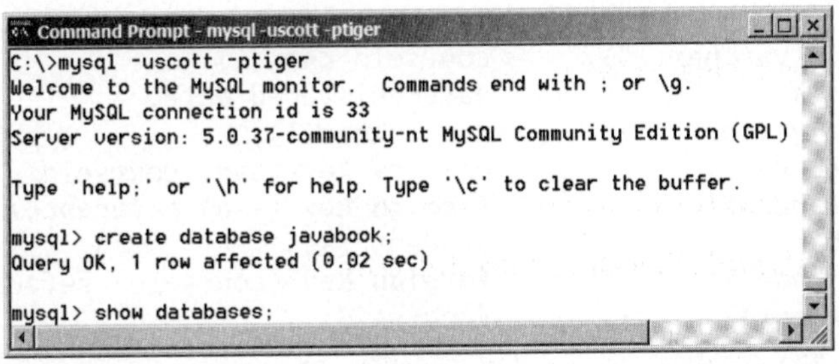
Command Prompt - mysql -uscott -ptiger
C:\>mysql -uscott -ptiger
Welcome to the MySQL monitor. Commands end with ; or \g.
Your MySQL connection id is 33
Server version: 5.0.37-community-nt MySQL Community Edition (GPL)
Type 'help;' or '\h' for help. Type '\c' to clear the buffer.
mysql> create database javabook;
Query OK, 1 row affected (0.02 sec)
mysql> show databases;

FIGURE 37.8 You can create databases in MySQL.

2. At the mysql prompt, enter

create database javabook;

For your convenience, the SQL statements for creating and initializing tables used in the book is provided in Supplement IV.A. You can download the script for MySQL and save it to script.sql. To execute the script, first switch to the **javabook** database using the following command: **use javabook;** and then type

run script file

source script.sql;

as shown in Figure 37.9.

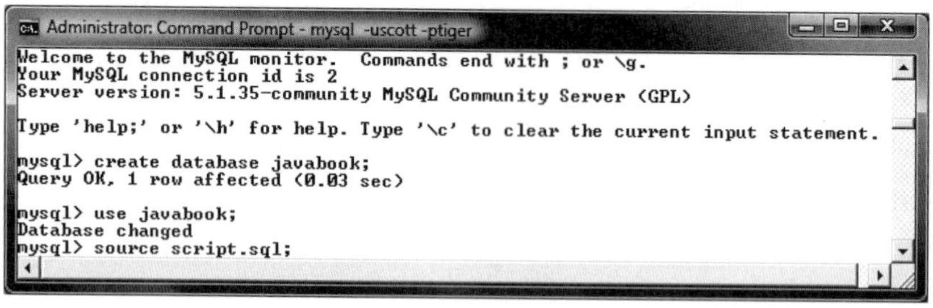
Administrator: Command Prompt - mysql -uscott -ptiger
Welcome to the MySQL monitor. Commands end with ; or \g.
Your MySQL connection id is 2
Server version: 5.1.35-community MySQL Community Server (GPL)
Type 'help;' or '\h' for help. Type '\c' to clear the current input statement.
mysql> create database javabook;
Query OK, 1 row affected (0.03 sec)
mysql> use javabook;
Database changed
mysql> source script.sql;

FIGURE 37.9 You can run SQL commands in a script file.

37.3.3 Creating and Dropping Tables

Tables are the essential objects in a database. To create a table, use the `create table` statement to specify a table name, attributes, and types, as in the following example:

create table

```
create table Course (
  courseId char(5),
  subjectId char(4) not null,
  courseNumber integer,
  title varchar(50) not null,
  numOfCredits integer,
  primary key (courseId)
);
```

This statement creates the `Course` table with attributes `courseId`, `subjectId`, `courseNumber`, `title`, and `numOfCredits`. Each attribute has a data type that specifies the type of data stored in the attribute. `char(5)` specifies that `courseId` consists of five characters. `varchar(50)` specifies that `title` is a variant-length string with a maximum of 50 characters. `integer` specifies that `courseNumber` is an integer. The primary key is `courseId`.

The tables `Student` and `Enrollment` can be created as follows:

```
create table Student (
  ssn char(9),
  firstName varchar(25),
  mi char(1),
  lastName varchar(25),
  birthDate date,
  street varchar(25),
  phone char(11),
  zipCode char(5),
  deptId char(4),
  primary key (ssn)
);
```

```
create table Enrollment (
  ssn char(9),
  courseId char(5),
  dateRegistered date,
  grade char(1),
  primary key (ssn, courseId),
  foreign key (ssn) references
  Student (ssn),
  foreign key (courseId) references
  (courseId)
);
```

> **Note**
>
> SQL keywords are not case sensitive. This book adopts the following naming conventions: Tables are named in the same way as Java classes, and attributes are named in the same way as Java variables. SQL keywords are named in the same way as Java keywords.

naming convention

If a table is no longer needed, it can be dropped permanently using the `drop table` command. For example, the following statement drops the `Course` table:

create table

```
drop table Course;
```

If a table to be dropped is referenced by other tables, you have to drop the other tables first. For example, if you have created the tables `Course`, `Student`, and `Enrollment` and want to drop `Course`, you have to first drop `Enrollment`, because `Course` is referenced by `Enrollment`.

Figure 37.10 shows how to enter the create table statement from the mysql console.

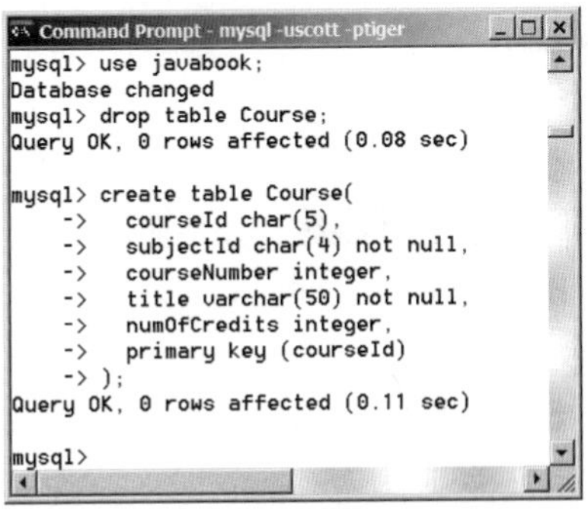
Command Prompt - mysql -uscott -ptiger
mysql> use javabook;
Database changed
mysql> drop table Course;
Query OK, 0 rows affected (0.08 sec)
mysql> create table Course(
-> courseId char(5),
-> subjectId char(4) not null,
-> courseNumber integer,
-> title varchar(50) not null,
-> numOfCredits integer,
-> primary key (courseId)
->);
Query OK, 0 rows affected (0.11 sec)
mysql>

FIGURE 37.10 The execution result of the SQL statements is displayed in the MySQL console.

If you make typing errors, you have to retype the whole command. To avoid retyping, you can save the command in a file, and then run the command from the file. To do so, create a text file to contain commands, named, for example, test.sql. You can create the text file using any text editor, such as NotePad, as shown in Figure 37.11(a). To comment a line, precede it with two dashes. You can now run the script file by typing `source test.sql` from the SQL command prompt, as shown in Figure 37.11(b).

Test - Notepad
File Edit Format Help
create table Course (
courseId char(5),
subjectId char(4) not null,
courseNumber integer,
title varchar(50) not null,
numOfCredits integer,
primary key (courseId)
);
Command Prompt - mysql
mysql> drop table Course;
Query OK, 0 rows affected (0.00 sec)
mysql> source c:\book\Test.sql
Query OK, 0 rows affected (0.00 sec)
mysql>

(a) (b)

FIGURE 37.11 (a) You can use Notepad to create a text file for SQL commands. (b) You can run the SQL commands in a script file from MySQL.

37.3.4 Simple Insert, Update, and Delete

Once a table is created, you can insert data into it. You can also update and delete records. This section introduces simple insert, update, and delete statements.

The general syntax to insert a record into a table is:

```
insert into tableName [(column1, column2, ..., column)]
values (value1, value2, ..., valuen);
```

For example, the following statement inserts a record into the Course table. The new record has the courseId '11113', subjectId 'CSCI', courseNumber 3720, title 'Database Systems', and creditHours 3.

```
insert into Course (courseId, subjectId, courseNumber, title, numOfCredits)
values ('11113', 'CSCI', '3720', 'Database Systems', 3);
```

The column names are optional. If they are omitted, all the column values for the record must be entered, even though the columns have default values. String values are case sensitive and enclosed inside single quotation marks in SQL.

The general syntax to update a table is:

```
update tableName
set column1 = newValue1 [, column2 = newValue2, ...]
[where condition];
```

For example, the following statement changes the numOfCredits for the course whose title is Database Systems to 4.

```
update Course
set numOfCredits = 4
where title = 'Database Systems';
```

The general syntax to delete records from a table is:

```
delete [from] tableName
[where condition];
```

For example, the following statement deletes the Database Systems course from the Course table:

```
delete Course
where title = 'Database System';
```

The following statement deletes all the records from the Course table:

```
delete Course;
```

37.3.5 Simple Queries

To retrieve information from tables, use a select statement with the following syntax:

```
select column-list
from table-list
[where condition];
```

The select clause lists the columns to be selected. The from clause refers to the tables involved in the query. The optional where clause specifies the conditions for the selected rows.

Query 1: Select all the students in the CS department, as shown in Figure 37.12.

```
select firstName, mi, lastName
from Student
where deptId = 'CS';
```

37.3.6 Comparison and Boolean Operators

SQL has six comparison operators, as shown in Table 37.1, and three Boolean operators, as shown in Table 37.2.

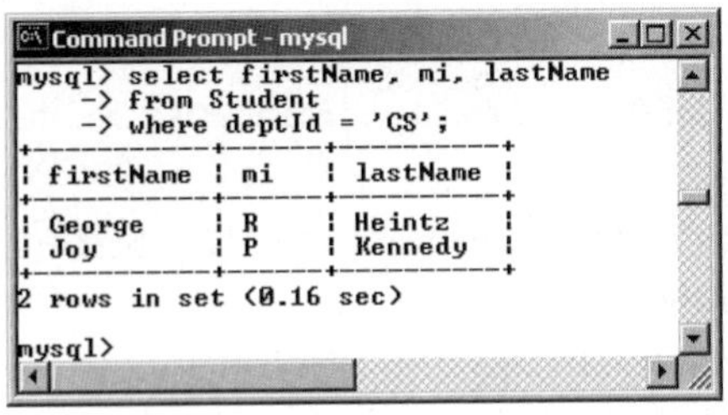
Command Prompt - mysql
mysql> select firstName, mi, lastName
-> from Student
-> where deptId = 'CS';
firstName | mi | lastName
George | R | Heintz
Joy | P | Kennedy
2 rows in set (0.16 sec)
mysql>

FIGURE 37.12 The result of the select statement is displayed in a window.

TABLE 37.1 Comparison Operators

Operator	*Description*
=	Equal to
<> or !=	Not equal to
<	Less than
<=	Less or equal to
>	Greater than
>=	Greater than or equal to

TABLE 37.2 Boolean Operators

Operator	*Description*
`not`	logical negation
`and`	logical conjunction
`or`	logical disjunction

Note

The comparison and Boolean operators in SQL have the same meaning as in Java. In SQL the `equal to` operator is =, but in Java it is ==. In SQL the `not equal to` operator is <> or !=, but in Java it is !=. The `not`, `and`, and `or` operators are !, && (&), and || (|) in Java.

Query 2: Get the names of the students who are in the CS dept and live in the zip code 31411.

```
select firstName, mi, lastName
from Student
where deptId = 'CS' and zipCode = '31411';
```

Note

To select all the attributes from a table, you don't have to list all the attribute names in the select clause. Instead you can just use an *asterisk* (*), which stands for all the attributes. For example, the following query displays all the attributes of the students who are in the CS dept and live in zip code 31411:

```
select *
from Student
where deptId = 'CS' and zipCode = '31411';
```

37.3.7 The `like`, `between-and`, and `is null` Operators

SQL has a `like` operator that can be used for pattern matching. The syntax to check whether a string `s` has a pattern `p` is

`s like p` or `s not like p`

You can use the wild-card characters `%` (percent symbol) and `_` (underline symbol) in the pattern `p`. `%` matches zero or more characters, and `_` matches any single character in `s`. For example, `lastName like '_mi%'` matches any string whose second and third letters are `m` and `i`. `lastName not like '_mi%'` excludes any string whose second and third letters are `m` and `i`.

Note

On the earlier version of MS Access, the wild-card character is *, and the character ? matches any single character.

The `between-and` operator checks whether a value `v` is between two other values, `v1` and `v2`, using the following syntax:

> `v between v1 and v2` or `v not between v1 and v2`
>
> `v between v1 and v2` is equivalent to `v >= v1 and v <= v2`, and `v not between v1 and v2` is equivalent to `v < v1 or v > v2`.

The `is null` operator checks whether a value `v` is `null` using the following syntax:

> `v is null` or `v is not null`

Query 3: Get the social security numbers of the students whose grades are between 'C' and 'A'.

```
select ssn
from Enrollment
where grade between 'C' and 'A';
```

37.3.8 Column Alias

When a query result is displayed, SQL uses the column names as column headings. Usually the user gives abbreviated names for the columns, and the columns cannot have spaces when the table is created. Sometimes it is desirable to give more descriptive names in the result heading. You can use the column aliases with the following syntax:

```
select columnName [as] alias
```

Query 4: Get the last name and zip code of the students in the CS department. Display the column headings as Last Name for lastName and Zip Code for zipCode. The query result is shown in Figure 37.13.

```
select lastName as "Last Name", zipCode as "Zip Code"
from Student
where deptId = 'CS';
```

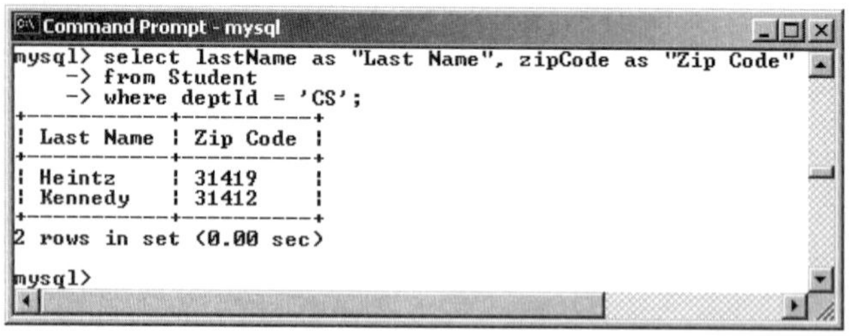
Command Prompt - mysql
mysql> select lastName as "Last Name", zipCode as "Zip Code"
-> from Student
-> where deptId = 'CS';
Last Name	Zip Code
Heintz	31419
Kennedy	31412
2 rows in set (0.00 sec)
mysql>

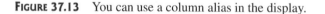

FIGURE 37.13 You can use a column alias in the display.

Note

The `as` keyword is optional in MySQL and Oracle but is required in MS Access.

37.3.9 The Arithmetic Operators

You can use the arithmetic operators * (multiplication), / (division), + (addition), and – (subtraction) in SQL.

Query 5: Assume that a credit hour is 50 minutes of lectures; get the total minutes for each course with the subject CSCI. The query result is shown in Figure 37.14.

```
select title, 50 * numOfCredits as "Lecture Minutes Per Week"
from Course
where subjectId = 'CSCI';
```

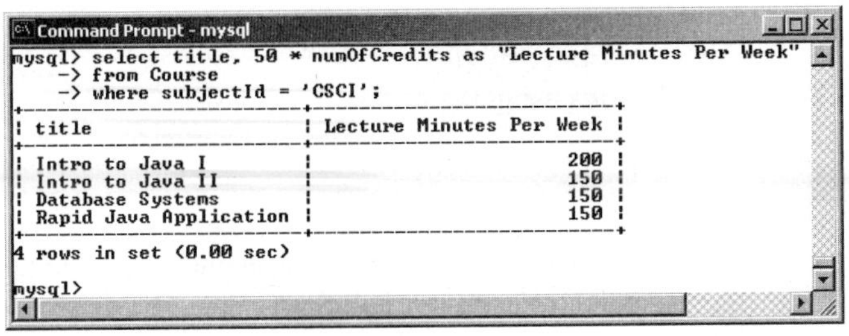
Command Prompt - mysql
mysql> select title, 50 * numOfCredits as "Lecture Minutes Per Week"
-> from Course
-> where subjectId = 'CSCI';
title
Lecture Minutes Per Week
Intro to Java I
Intro to Java II
Database Systems
Rapid Java Application
200
150
150
150
4 rows in set (0.00 sec)
mysql>

FIGURE 37.14 You can use arithmetic operators in SQL.

37.3.10 Displaying Distinct Tuples

SQL provides the `distinct` keyword, which can be used to suppress duplicate tuples in the output. For example, the following statement displays all the subject IDs used by the courses:

```
select subjectId as "Subject ID"
from Course;
```

This statement displays all the subject IDs. To display distinct tuples, add the `distinct` keyword in the `select` clause, as follows:

```
select distinct subjectId as "Subject ID"
from Course;
```

When there is more than one item in the `select` clause, the `distinct` keyword applies to all the items that find distinct tuples.

37.3.11 Displaying Sorted Tuples

SQL provides the `order by` clause to sort the output using the following general syntax:

```
select column-list
from table-list
[where condition]
[order by columns-to-be-sorted];
```

In the syntax, `columns-to-be-sorted` specifies a column or a list of columns to be sorted. By default, the order is ascending. To sort in descending order, append the `desc` keyword after `columns-to-be-sorted`. You could also append the `asc` keyword, but it is not necessary. When multiple columns are specified, the rows are sorted based on the first column, then the rows with the same values on the first column are sorted based on the second column, and so on.

Query 6: List the full names of the students in the CS department, ordered primarily on their last names in descending order and secondarily on their first names in ascending order. The query result is shown in Figure 37.15.

```
select lastName, firstName, deptId
from Student
where deptId = 'CS'
order by lastName desc, firstName asc;
```

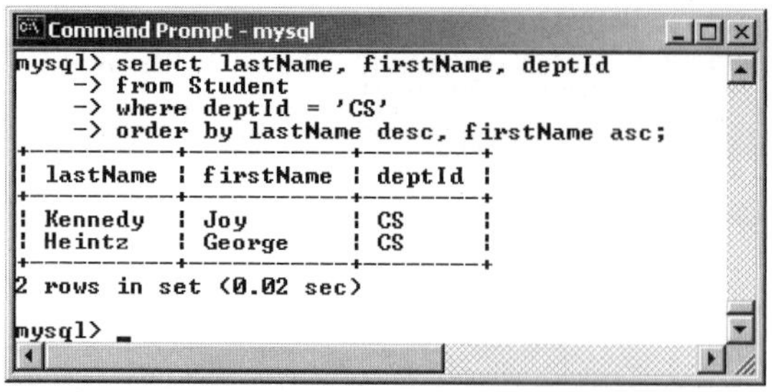
Command Prompt - mysql
mysql> select lastName, firstName, deptId
-> from Student
-> where deptId = 'CS'
-> order by lastName desc, firstName asc;
lastName	firstName	deptId
Kennedy	Joy	CS
Heintz	George	CS
2 rows in set (0.02 sec)
mysql> _

FIGURE 37.15 You can sort results using the `order by` clause.

37.3.12 Joining Tables

Often you need to get information from multiple tables, as demonstrated in the next query.

Query 7: List the courses taken by student Jacob Smith. To solve this query, you need to join tables `Student` and `Enrollment`, as shown in Figure 37.16.

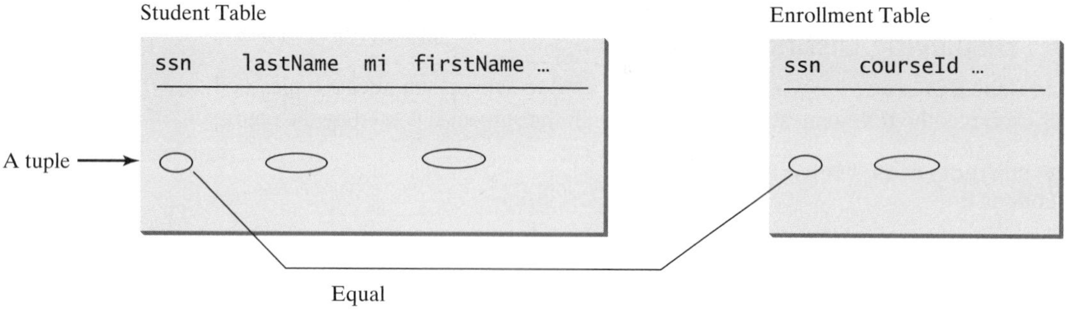
Student Table
ssn lastName mi firstName ...
A tuple
Enrollment Table
ssn courseId ...
Equal

FIGURE 37.16 `Student` and `Enrollment` are joined on `ssn`.

You can write the query in SQL:

```
select distinct lastName, firstName, courseId
from Student, Enrollment
where Student.ssn = Enrollment.ssn and
  lastName = 'Smith' and firstName = 'Jacob';
```

The tables `Student` and `Enrollment` are listed in the `from` clause. The query examines every pair of rows, each made of one item from `Student` and another from `Enrollment`, and selects the pairs that satisfy the condition in the `where` clause. The rows in `Student` have the last name, Smith, and the first name, Jacob, and both rows from `Student` and `Enrollment` have the same `ssn` values. For each pair selected, `lastName` and `firstName` from `Student` and `courseId` from `Enrollment` are used to produce the result, as shown in Figure 37.17. `Student` and `Enrollment` have the same attribute `ssn`. To distinguish them in a query, use `Student.ssn` and `Enrollment.ssn`.

For more features of SQL, see Supplement IV.H and Supplement IV.I.

37.4 JDBC

The Java API for developing Java database applications is called *JDBC*. JDBC is the trademarked name of a Java API that supports Java programs that access relational databases. JDBC is not an acronym, but it is often thought to stand for Java Database Connectivity.

JDBC provides Java programmers with a uniform interface for accessing and manipulating a wide range of relational databases. Using the JDBC API, applications written in the

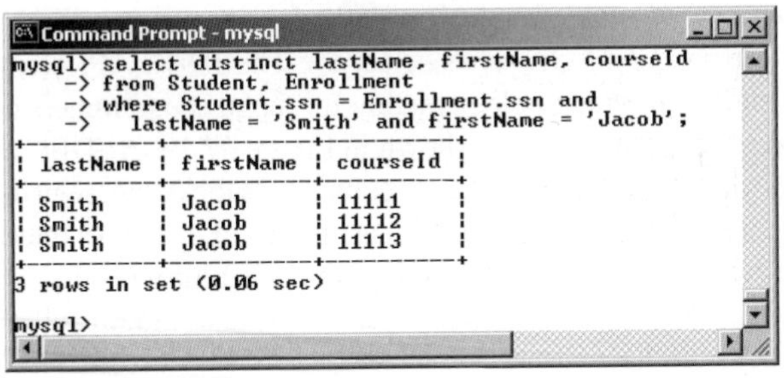
Command Prompt - mysql
mysql> select distinct lastName, firstName, courseId
-> from Student, Enrollment
-> where Student.ssn = Enrollment.ssn and
-> lastName = 'Smith' and firstName = 'Jacob';
lastName	firstName	courseId
Smith	Jacob	11111
Smith	Jacob	11112
Smith	Jacob	11113
3 rows in set (0.06 sec)
mysql>

FIGURE 37.17 Query 7 demonstrates queries involving multiple tables.

Java programming language can execute SQL statements, retrieve results, present data in a user-friendly interface, and propagate changes back to the database. The JDBC API can also be used to interact with multiple data sources in a distributed, heterogeneous environment.

The relationships between Java programs, JDBC API, JDBC drivers, and relational databases are shown in Figure 37.18. The JDBC API is a set of Java interfaces and classes used to write Java programs for accessing and manipulating relational databases. Since a JDBC driver serves as the interface to facilitate communications between JDBC and a proprietary database, JDBC drivers are database specific and are normally provided by the database vendors. You need MySQL JDBC drivers to access the MySQL database, and Oracle JDBC drivers to access the Oracle database. For the Access database, use the JDBC-ODBC bridge driver included in JDK. ODBC is a technology developed by Microsoft for accessing databases on the Windows platform. An ODBC driver is preinstalled on Windows. The JDBC-ODBC bridge driver allows a Java program to access any ODBC data source.

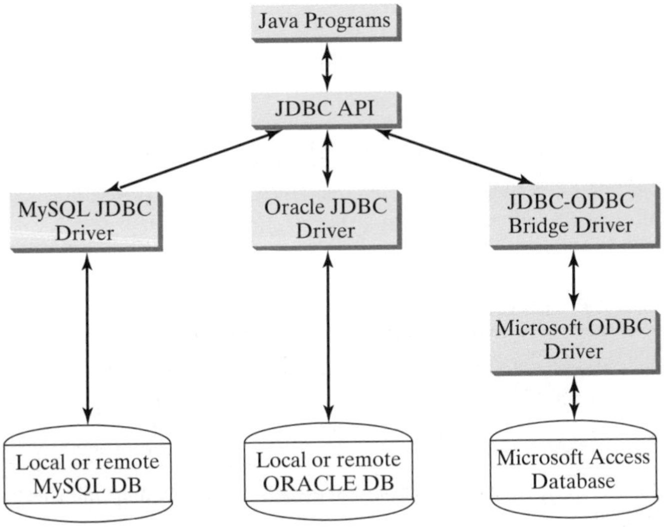
Java Programs
JDBC API
MySQL JDBC Driver
Oracle JDBC Driver
JDBC-ODBC Bridge Driver
Microsoft ODBC Driver
Local or remote MySQL DB
Local or remote ORACLE DB
Microsoft Access Database

FIGURE 37.18 Java programs access and manipulate databases through JDBC drivers.

37.4.1 Developing Database Applications Using JDBC

The JDBC API is a Java application program interface to generic SQL databases that enables Java developers to develop DBMS-independent Java applications using a uniform interface.

The JDBC API consists of classes and interfaces for establishing connections with databases, sending SQL statements to databases, processing the results of the SQL statements, and obtaining database metadata. Four key interfaces are needed to develop any database application using Java: Driver, Connection, Statement, and ResultSet. These interfaces define a framework for generic SQL database access. The JDBC API defines these interfaces. The JDBC driver vendors provide implementation for them. Programmers use the interfaces.

The relationship of these interfaces is shown in Figure 37.19. A JDBC application loads an appropriate driver using the Driver interface, connects to the database using the Connection interface, creates and executes SQL statements using the Statement interface, and processes the result using the ResultSet interface if the statements return results. Note that some statements, such as SQL data definition statements and SQL data modification statements, do not return results.

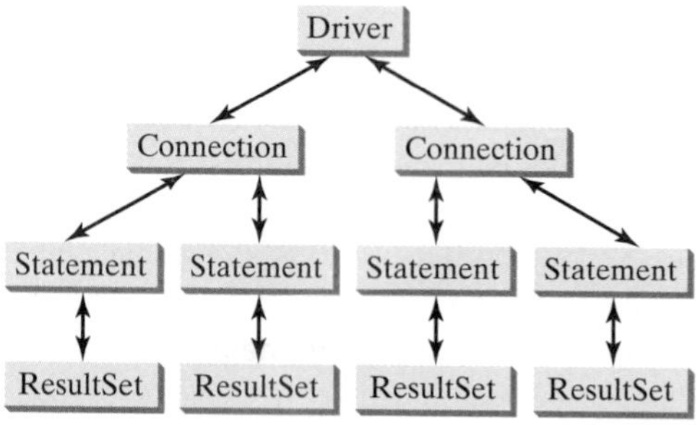
Driver
Connection
Connection
Statement
Statement
Statement
Statement
ResultSet
ResultSet
ResultSet
ResultSet

FIGURE 37.19 JDBC classes enable Java programs to connect to the database, send SQL statements, and process results.

The JDBC interfaces and classes are the building blocks in the development of Java database programs. A typical Java program takes the steps outlined below to access the database.

1. Loading drivers.

An appropriate driver must be loaded using the statement shown below before connecting to a database.

```
Class.forName("JDBCDriverClass");
```

A driver is a concrete class that implements the java.sql.Driver interface. The drivers for Access, MySQL, and Oracle are listed in Table 37.3.

TABLE 37.3 JDBC Drivers

Database	*Driver Class*	*Source*
Access	sun.jdbc.odbc.JdbcOdbcDriver	Already in JDK
MySQL	com.mysql.jdbc.Driver	Companion Web site
Oracle	oracle.jdbc.driver.OracleDriver	Companion Web site

mysqljdbc.jar
ojdbc6.jar

The JDBC-ODBC driver for Access is bundled in JDK. The MySQL JDBC driver is contained in mysqljdbc.jar (downloadable from www.cs.armstrong.edu/liang/intro8e/book/lib/mysqljdbc.jar). The Oracle JDBC driver is contained in ojdbc6.jar (downloadable from www.cs.armstrong.edu/liang/intro8e/book/lib/ojdbc6.jar). To use the MySQL and Oracle drivers, you have to add mysqljdbc.jar and ojdbc6.jar in the classpath using the following DOS command on Windows:

```
set classpath=%classpath%;c:\book\mysqljdbc.jar;c:\book\ojdbc6.jar
```

If your program accesses several different databases, all their respective drivers must be loaded.

> **Note**
>
> why load a driver?
>
> `com.mysql.jdbc.Driver` is a class in `mysqljdbc.jar`, and `oracle.jdbc.driver.OracleDriver` is a class in `ojdbc6.jar`. `mysqljdbc.jar` and `ojdbc6.jar` contain many classes to support the driver. These classes are used by JDBC, but not directly by JDBC programmers. When you use a class explicitly in the program, it is automatically loaded by the JVM. The driver classes, however, are not used explicitly in the program, so you have to write the code to tell the JVM to load them.

> **Note**
>
> automatic driver discovery
>
> Java 6 supports automatic driver discovery, so you don't have to load the driver explicitly. At the time of this writing, however, this feature is not supported for all drivers. To be safe, load the driver explicitly.

2. Establishing connections.

To connect to a database, use the static method `getConnection(databaseURL)` in the `DriverManager` class, as follows:

```
Connection connection = DriverManager.getConnection(databaseURL);
```

where `databaseURL` is the unique identifier of the database on the Internet. Table 37.4 lists the URLs for the MySQL, Oracle, and Access databases.

TABLE 37.4 JDBC URLs

Database	*URL Pattern*
Access	`jdbc:odbc:dataSource`
MySQL	`jdbc:mysql://hostname/dbname`
Oracle	`jdbc:oracle:thin:@hostname:port#:oracleDBSID`

For an ODBC data source, the `databaseURL` is `jdbc:odbc:dataSource`. An ODBC data source can be created using the ODBC Data Source Administrator on Windows. See Supplement IV.D, "Tutorial for Microsoft Access," on how to create an ODBC data source for an Access database.

Suppose a data source named ExampleMDBDataSource has been created for an Access database. The following statement creates a `Connection` object:

connect Access DB

```
Connection connection = DriverManager.getConnection
  ("jdbc:odbc:ExampleMDBDataSource");
```

The `databaseURL` for a MySQL database specifies the host name and database name to locate a database. For example, the following statement creates a `Connection` object for the local MySQL database `javabook` with username *scott* and password *tiger*:

connect MySQL DB

```
Connection connection = DriverManager.getConnection
  ("jdbc:mysql://localhost/javabook", "scott", "tiger");
```

Recall that by default MySQL contains two databases named *mysql* and *test*. §37.3.2, "Creating a Database," created a custom database named `javabook`. We will use `javabook` in the examples.

The `databaseURL` for an Oracle database specifies the *hostname*, the *port#* where the database listens for incoming connection requests, and the *oracleDBSID* database name to locate a database. For example, the following statement creates a **Connection** object for the Oracle database on liang.armstrong.edu with username *scott* and password *tiger*:

connect Oracle DB

```
Connection connection = DriverManager.getConnection
  ("jdbc:oracle:thin:@liang.armstrong.edu:1521:orcl",
   "scott", "tiger");
```

3. Creating statements.

If a **Connection** object can be envisioned as a cable linking your program to a database, an object of **Statement** can be viewed as a cart that delivers SQL statements for execution by the database and brings the result back to the program. Once a **Connection** object is created, you can create statements for executing SQL statements as follows:

```
Statement statement = connection.createStatement();
```

4. Executing statements.

An SQL DDL or update statement can be executed using **executeUpdate(String sql)**, and an SQL query statement can be executed using **executeQuery(String sql)**. The result of the query is returned in **ResultSet**. For example, the following code executes the SQL statement ***create table Temp (col1 char(5), col2 char(5))***:

```
statement.executeUpdate
  ("create table Temp (col1 char(5), col2 char(5))");
```

The next code executes the SQL query **select firstName, mi, lastName from Student where lastName = 'Smith'**:

```
// Select the columns from the Student table
ResultSet resultSet = statement.executeQuery
  ("select firstName, mi, lastName from Student where lastName "
    + " = 'Smith'");
```

5. Processing **ResultSet**.

The **ResultSet** maintains a table whose current row can be retrieved. The initial row position is **null**. You can use the **next** method to move to the next row and the various **get** methods to retrieve values from a current row. For example, the code given below displays all the results from the preceding SQL query.

```
// Iterate through the result and print the student names
while (resultSet.next())
  System.out.println(resultSet.getString(1) + " " +
    resultSet.getString(2) + ". " + resultSet.getString(3));
```

The **getString(1)**, **getString(2)**, and **getString(3)** methods retrieve the column values for **firstName**, **mi**, and **lastName**, respectively. Alternatively, you can use **getString("firstName")**, **getString("mi")**, and **getString("lastName")** to retrieve the same three column values. The first execution of the **next()** method sets the current row to the first row in the result set, and subsequent invocations of the **next()** method set the current row to the second row, third row, and so on, to the last row.

Listing 37.1 is a complete example that demonstrates connecting to a database, executing a simple query, and processing the query result with JDBC. The program connects to a local MySQL database and displays the students whose last name is Smith.

LISTING 37.1 SimpleJDBC.java

```
1 import java.sql.*;
2
3 public class SimpleJdbc {
4   public static void main(String[] args)
5       throws SQLException, ClassNotFoundException {
6     // Load the JDBC driver
7     Class.forName("com.mysql.jdbc.Driver");
8     System.out.println("Driver loaded");
9
10    // Establish a connection
11    Connection connection = DriverManager.getConnection
12      ("jdbc:mysql://localhost/javabook" , "scott", "tiger");
13    System.out.println("Database connected");
14
15    // Create a statement
16    Statement statement = connection.createStatement();
17
18    // Execute a statement
19    ResultSet resultSet = statement.executeQuery
20      ("select firstName, mi, lastName from Student where lastName "
21        + " = 'Smith'");
22
23    // Iterate through the result and print the student names
24    while (resultSet.next())
25      System.out.println(resultSet.getString(1) + "\t" +
26        resultSet.getString(2) + "\t" + resultSet.getString(3));
27
28    // Close the connection
29    connection.close();
30  }
31 }
```

load driver

connect database

create statement

execute statement

get result

close connection

The statement in line 7 loads a JDBC driver for MySQL, and the statement in lines 11–13 connects to a local MySQL database. You may change them to connect to an Access or Oracle database. The last statement (line 29) closes the connection and releases resource related to the connection.

Note

run from DOS prompt

If you run this program from the DOS prompt, specify the appropriate driver in the classpath, as shown in Figure 37.20.

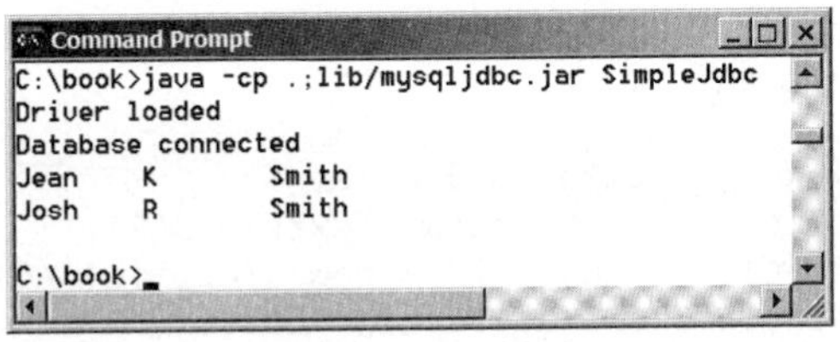
Command Prompt
C:\book>java -cp .;lib/mysqljdbc.jar SimpleJdbc
Driver loaded
Database connected
Jean K Smith
Josh R Smith
C:\book>_

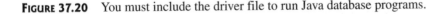

FIGURE 37.20 You must include the driver file to run Java database programs.

The classpath directory and jar files are separated by commas. The period (.) represents the current directory. For convenience, the driver files are placed under the **lib** directory.

Caution

the semicolon issue

Do not use a semicolon (;) to end the Oracle SQL command in a Java program. The semicolon may not work with the Oracle JDBC drivers. It does work, however, with the other drivers used in the book.

auto commit

Note

The `Connection` interface handles transactions and specifies how they are processed. By default, a new connection is in autocommit mode, and all its SQL statements are executed and committed as individual transactions. The commit occurs when the statement completes or the next execute occurs, whichever comes first. In the case of statements returning a result set, the statement completes when the last row of the result set has been retrieved or the result set has been closed. If a single statement returns multiple results, the commit occurs when all the results have been retrieved. You can use the `setAutoCommit(false)` method to disable autocommit, so that all SQL statements are grouped into one transaction that is terminated by a call to either the `commit()` or the `rollback()` method. The `rollback()` method undoes all the changes made by the transaction.

37.4.2 Accessing a Database from a Java Applet

Using the JDBC-ODBC bridge driver, your program cannot run as an applet from a Web browser because the ODBC driver contains non-Java native code. The JDBC drivers for MySQL and Oracle are written in Java and can run from the JVM in a Web browser. This section gives an example that demonstrates connecting to a database from a Java applet. The applet lets the user enter the SSN and the course ID to find a student's grade, as shown in Figure 37.21. The code in Listing 37.2 uses the MySQL database on the localhost.

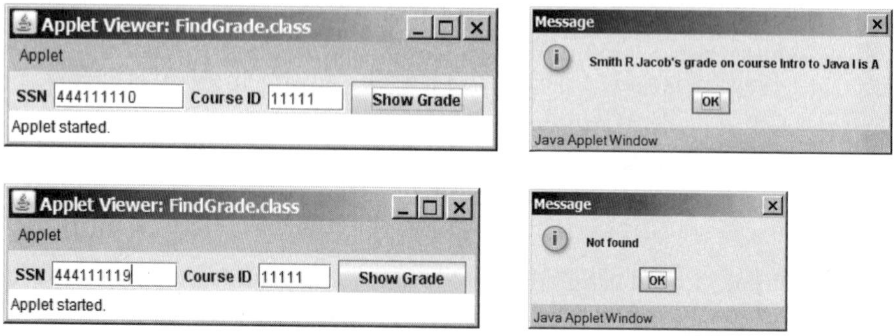
Applet Viewer: FindGrade.class
Applet
SSN 444111110
Course ID 11111
Show Grade
Applet started.
Message
Smith R Jacob's grade on course Intro to Java I is A
OK
Java Applet Window
Applet Viewer: FindGrade.class
Applet
SSN 444111119
Course ID 11111
Show Grade
Applet started.
Message
Not found
OK
Java Applet Window

FIGURE 37.21 A Java applet can access the database on the server.

LISTING 37.2 FindGrade.java

```
import javax.swing.*;
import java.sql.*;
import java.awt.*;
import java.awt.event.*;

public class FindGrade extends JApplet {
  private JTextField jtfSSN = new JTextField(9);
  private JTextField jtfCourseId = new JTextField(5);
  private JButton jbtShowGrade = new JButton("Show Grade");

  // Statement for executing queries
  private Statement stmt;

  /** Initialize the applet */
  public void init() {
    // Initialize database connection and create a Statement object
    initializeDB();

```

```
    jbtShowGrade.addActionListener(
      new java.awt.event.ActionListener() {
      public void actionPerformed(ActionEvent e) {
        jbtShowGrade_actionPerformed(e);
      }
    });

    JPanel jPanel1 = new JPanel();
    jPanel1.add(new JLabel("SSN"));
    jPanel1.add(jtfSSN);
    jPanel1.add(new JLabel("Course ID"));
    jPanel1.add(jtfCourseId);
    jPanel1.add(jbtShowGrade);

    add(jPanel1, BorderLayout.NORTH);
  }

  private void initializeDB() {
    try {
      // Load the JDBC driver
      Class.forName("com.mysql.jdbc.Driver");
//      Class.forName("oracle.jdbc.driver.OracleDriver");
      System.out.println("Driver loaded");

      // Establish a connection
      Connection connection = DriverManager.getConnection
        ("jdbc:mysql://localhost/javabook", "scott", "tiger");
//    ("jdbc:oracle:thin:@liang.armstrong.edu:1521:orcl",
//     "scott", "tiger");
      System.out.println("Database connected");

      // Create a statement
      stmt = connection.createStatement();
    }
    catch (Exception ex) {
      ex.printStackTrace();
    }
  }

  private void jbtShowGrade_actionPerformed(ActionEvent e) {
    String ssn = jtfSSN.getText();
    String courseId = jtfCourseId.getText();
    try {
      String queryString = "select firstName, mi, " +
        "lastName, title, grade from Student, Enrollment, Course " +
        "where Student.ssn = '" + ssn + "' and Enrollment.courseId "
        + "= '" + courseId +
        "' and Enrollment.courseId = Course.courseId " +
        " and Enrollment.ssn = Student.ssn";

      ResultSet rset = stmt.executeQuery(queryString);

      if (rset.next()) {
        String lastName = rset.getString(1);
        String mi = rset.getString(2);
        String firstName = rset.getString(3);
        String title = rset.getString(4);
        String grade = rset.getString(5);

```

button listener

load driver

Oracle driver commented

connect to MySQL database

connect to Oracle commented

create statement

execute statement

show result

```
78         // Display result in a dialog box
79         JOptionPane.showMessageDialog(null, firstName + " " + mi +
80           " " + lastName + "'s grade on course " + title + " is " +
81           grade);
82       } else {
83         // Display result in a dialog box
84         JOptionPane.showMessageDialog(null, "Not found");
85       }
86     }
87     catch (SQLException ex) {
88       ex.printStackTrace();
89     }
90   }
91 }
```

main method omitted

The `initializeDB()` method (lines 36–56) loads the MySQL driver (line 39), connects to the MySQL database on host liang.armstrong.edu (lines 44–45), and creates a statement (line 51).

You can run the applet standalone from the `main` method (note that the listing for the `main` method is omitted for all the applets in the book for brevity) or test the applet using the appletviewer utility, as shown in Figure 37.21. If this applet is deployed on the server where the database is located, any client on the Internet can run it from a Web browser. Since the client may not have a MySQL driver, you should specify the driver in the archive attribute in the applet tag, as follows:

```
<applet
  code = "FindGrade"
  archive = "FindGrade.jar, lib/mysqljdbc.jar"
  width = 380
  height = 80
>
</applet>
```

create archive file

Note

For information on how to *create an archive file*, see Supplement III.Q, "Packaging and Deploying Java Projects." The FindGrade.jar file can be created using the following command:

```
c:\book>jar -cf FindGrade.jar FindGrade.class FindGrade$1.class
```

applet security restriction

Note

To access the database from an applet, *security restrictions* make it necessary for the applet to be downloaded from the server where the database is located. Therefore, you have to deploy the applet on the server.

security hole

Note

There is a *security hole* in this program. If you enter `1' or true or '1` in the SSN field, you will get the first student's score, because the query string now becomes

```
select firstName, mi, lastName, title, grade
from Student, Enrollment, Course
where Student.ssn = '1' or true or '1' and
      Enrollment.courseId = ' ' and
      Enrollment.courseId = Course.courseId and
      Enrollment.ssn = Student.ssn;
```

You can avoid this problem by using the `PreparedStatement`.

37.5 PreparedStatement

Once a connection to a particular database is established, it can be used to send SQL statements from your program to the database. The **Statement** interface is used to execute static SQL statements that contain no parameters. The **PreparedStatement** interface, extending **Statement**, is used to execute a precompiled SQL statement with or without parameters. Since the SQL statements are precompiled, they are efficient for repeated executions.

A **PreparedStatement** object is created using the **preparedStatement** method in the **Connection** interface. For example, the following code creates a **PreparedStatement preparedStatement** on a particular **Connection connection** for an SQL **insert** statement:

```
Statement preparedStatement = connection.prepareStatement
  ("insert into Student (firstName, mi, lastName) " +
   "values (?, ?, ?)");
```

This **insert** statement has three question marks as placeholders for parameters representing values for **firstName**, **mi**, and **lastName** in a record of the **Student** table.

As a subinterface of **Statement**, the **PreparedStatement** interface inherits all the methods defined in **Statement**. It also provides the methods for setting parameters in the object of **PreparedStatement**. These methods are used to set the values for the parameters before executing statements or procedures. In general, the set methods have the following name and signature:

```
setX(int parameterIndex, X value);
```

where *X* is the type of the parameter, and **parameterIndex** is the index of the parameter in the statement. The index starts from **1**. For example, the method **setString(int paramterIndex, String value)** sets a **String** value to the specified parameter.

The following statements pass the parameters "Jack", "A", and "Ryan" to the placeholders for firstName, mi, and lastName in **PreparedStatement preparedStatement**:

```
preparedStatement.setString(1, "Jack");
preparedStatement.setString(2, "A");
preparedStatement.setString(3, "Ryan");
```

After setting the parameters, you can execute the prepared statement by invoking **executeQuery()** for a SELECT statement and **executeUpdate()** for a DDL or update statement.

The **executeQuery()** and **executeUpdate()** methods are similar to the ones defined in the **Statement** interface except that they have no parameters, because the SQL statements are already specified in the **preparedStatement** method when the object of **PreparedStatement** is created.

Using a prepared SQL statement, Listing 37.2 can be improved as in Listing 37.3.

LISTING 37.3 FindGradeUsingPreparedStatement.java

```
import javax.swing.*;
import java.sql.*;
import java.awt.*;
import java.awt.event.*;

public class FindGradeUsingPreparedStatement extends JApplet {
  private JTextField jtfSSN = new JTextField(9);
  private JTextField jtfCourseId = new JTextField(5);
  private JButton jbtShowGrade = new JButton("Show Grade");

```

load driver

connect database

placeholder

prepare statement

execute statement

```
  // PreparedStatement for executing queries
  private PreparedStatement preparedStatement;

  /** Initialize the applet */
  public void init() {
    // Initialize database connection and create a Statement object
    initializeDB();

    jbtShowGrade.addActionListener(
      new java.awt.event.ActionListener() {
      public void actionPerformed(ActionEvent e) {
        jbtShowGrade_actionPerformed(e);
      }
    });

    JPanel jPanel1 = new JPanel();
    jPanel1.add(new JLabel("SSN"));
    jPanel1.add(jtfSSN);
    jPanel1.add(new JLabel("Course ID"));
    jPanel1.add(jtfCourseId);
    jPanel1.add(jbtShowGrade);

    add(jPanel1, BorderLayout.NORTH);
  }

  private void initializeDB() {
    try {
      // Load the JDBC driver
      Class.forName("com.mysql.jdbc.Driver");
//      Class.forName("oracle.jdbc.driver.OracleDriver");
      System.out.println("Driver loaded");

      // Establish a connection
      Connection connection = DriverManager.getConnection
        ("jdbc:mysql://localhost/javabook", "scott", "tiger");
//      ("jdbc:oracle:thin:@liang.armstrong.edu:1521:orcl",
//       "scott", "tiger");
      System.out.println("Database connected");

      String queryString = "select firstName, mi, " +
        "lastName, title, grade from Student, Enrollment, Course " +
        "where Student.ssn = ? and Enrollment.courseId = ? " +
        "and Enrollment.courseId = Course.courseId";

      // Create a statement
      preparedStatement = connection.prepareStatement(queryString);
    }
    catch (Exception ex) {
      ex.printStackTrace();
    }
  }

  private void jbtShowGrade_actionPerformed(ActionEvent e) {
    String ssn = jtfSSN.getText();
    String courseId = jtfCourseId.getText();
    try {
      preparedStatement.setString(1, ssn);
      preparedStatement.setString(2, courseId);
      ResultSet rset = preparedStatement.executeQuery();

```

show result

```
71        if (rset.next()) {
72          String lastName = rset.getString(1);
73          String mi = rset.getString(2);
74          String firstName = rset.getString(3);
75          String title = rset.getString(4);
76          String grade = rset.getString(5);
77
78          // Display result in a dialog box
79          JOptionPane.showMessageDialog(null, firstName + " " + mi +
80            " " + lastName + "'s grade on course " + title + " is " +
81            grade);
82        }
83        else {
84          // Display result in a dialog box
85          JOptionPane.showMessageDialog(null, "Not found");
86        }
87      }
88      catch (SQLException ex) {
89        ex.printStackTrace();
90      }
91    }
92  }
```

main method omitted

This example does exactly the same thing as Listing 37.2 except that it uses the prepared statement to dynamically set the parameters. The code in this example is almost the same as in the preceding example. The new code is highlighted.

A prepared query string is defined in lines 50–53 with **ssn** and **courseId** as parameters. An SQL prepared statement is obtained in line 56. Before executing the query, the actual values of **ssn** and **courseId** are set to the parameters in lines 67–68. Line 69 executes the prepared statement.

37.6 CallableStatement

The **CallableStatement** interface is designed to execute SQL-stored procedures. The procedures may have **IN**, **OUT** or **IN OUT** parameters. An **IN** parameter receives a value passed to the procedure when it is called. An **OUT** parameter returns a value after the procedure is completed, but it contains no value when the procedure is called. An **IN OUT** parameter contains a value passed to the procedure when it is called, and returns a value after it is completed. For example, the following procedure in Oracle PL/SQL has **IN** parameter **p1**, **OUT** parameter **p2**, and **IN OUT** parameter **p3**.

IN parameter
OUT parameter
IN OUT parameter

```
create or replace procedure sampleProcedure
  (p1 in varchar, p2 out number, p3 in out integer) is
begin
  -- do something
end sampleProcedure;
/
```

Note

The syntax of stored procedures is vendor specific. Oracle PL/SQL is used for demonstrations of stored procedures in this book. PL/SQL is a procedural language extension of SQL. It is a fully functional programming language whose syntax is very similar to Ada's.

A **CallableStatement** object can be created using the **prepareCall(String call)** method in the **Connection** interface. For example, the following code creates a **CallableStatement cstmt** on **Connection connection** for procedure **sampleProcedure**.

```
CallableStatement callableStatement = connection.prepareCall(
  "{call sampleProcedure(?, ?, ?)}");
```

`{call sampleProcedure(?, ?, ...)}` is referred to as the *SQL escape syntax*, which signals the driver that the code within it should be handled differently. The driver parses the escape syntax and translates it into code that the database understands. For this case, `sampleProcedure` is an Oracle PL/SQL procedure. The call is translated to a string `"begin sampleProcedure(?, ?, ?); end"` and passed to an Oracle database for execution.

You can call procedures as well as functions. The syntax to create a SQL callable statement for a function is:

```
{? = call functionName(?, ?, ...)}
```

`CallableStatement` inherits `PreparedStatement`. Additionally, the `CallableStatement` interface provides methods for registering `OUT` parameters and for getting values from `OUT` parameters.

Before calling a SQL procedure, you need to use appropriate set methods to pass values to `IN` and `IN OUT` parameters, and use `registerOutParameter` to register `OUT` and `IN OUT` parameters. For example, before calling procedure `sampleProcedure`, the following statements pass values to parameters `p1` (`IN`) and `p3` (`IN OUT`) and register parameters `p2` (`OUT`) and `p3` (`IN OUT`):

```
callableStatement.setString(1, "Dallas"); // Set Dallas to p1
callableStatement.setLong(3, 1); // Set 1 to p3
// Register OUT parameters
callableStatement.registerOutParameter(2, java.sql.Types.DOUBLE);
callableStatement.registerOutParameter(3, java.sql.Types.INTEGER);
```

You may use `execute()` or `executeUpdate()` to execute the procedure depending on the type of SQL statement, then use get methods to retrieve values from the OUT parameters. For example, the next statements retrieve the values from parameters `p2` and `p3`.

```
double d = callableStatement.getDouble(2);
int i = callableStatement.getInt(3);
```

Let us define an Oracle function that returns the number of the records in the table that match the specified `firstName` and `lastName` in the `Student` table.

```
create or replace function studentFound
  (first varchar2, last varchar2)
  -- Do not name firstName and lastName. 6/4/00 YDL
  return number is
  numberOfSelectedRows number := 0;
begin
  select count(*) into numberOfSelectedRows
  from Student
  where Student.firstName = first and
    Student.lastName = last;

  return numberOfSelectedRows;
end studentFound;
/
```

Suppose the function `studentFound` is already created in the database. Listing 37.4 gives an example that tests this function using callable statements.

LISTING 37.4 TestCallableStatement.java

```
1 import java.sql.*;
2
3 public class TestCallableStatement {
4   /** Creates new form TestTableEditor */
5   public static void main(String[] args) throws Exception {
6     Class.forName("oracle.jdbc.driver.OracleDriver");
7     Connection connection = DriverManager.getConnection(
8       "jdbc:oracle:thin:@liang.armstrong.edu:1521:orcl",
9       "scott", "tiger");
10
11     // Create a callable statement
12     CallableStatement callableStatement = connection.prepareCall(
13       "{? = call studentFound(?, ?)}");
14
15     java.util.Scanner input = new java.util.Scanner(System.in);
16     System.out.print("Enter student's first name: ");
17     String firstName = input.nextLine();
18     System.out.print("Enter student's last name: ");
19     String lastName = input.nextLine();
20
21     callableStatement.setString(2, firstName);
22     callableStatement.setString(3, lastName);
23     callableStatement.registerOutParameter(1, Types.INTEGER);
24     callableStatement.execute();
25
26     if (callableStatement.getInt(1) >= 1)
27       System.out.println(firstName + " " + lastName +
28         " is in the database");
29     else
30       System.out.println(firstName + " " + lastName +
31         " is not in the database");
32   }
33 }
```

load driver (line 6)
connect database (line 7)
create callable statement (line 12)
enter **firstName** (line 17)
enter **lastName** (line 19)
set IN parameter (line 21)
set IN parameter (line 22)
register OUT parameter (line 23)
execute statement (line 24)
get OUT parameter (line 26)

```
Enter student's first name: Jacob [Enter]
Enter student's last name: Smith [Enter]
Jacob Smith is in the database
```

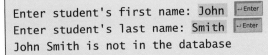

```
Enter student's first name: John [Enter]
Enter student's last name: Smith [Enter]
John Smith is not in the database
```

The program loads an Oracle driver (line 6), connects to an Oracle database (lines 7–9), and creates a callable statement for executing the function **studentFound** (lines 12–13).

The function's first parameter is the return value; its second and third parameters correspond to the first and last names. Before executing the callable statement, the program sets the first name and last name (lines 21–22) and registers the **OUT** parameter (line 23). The statement is executed in line 26).

The function's return value is obtained in line 26. If the value is greater or equal to 1, the student with the specified first and last name is found in the table.

You can define procedures and functions in MySQL 5. The equivalent function for studentFound in MySQL can be defined as follows:

MySQL function

```
drop function if exists studentFound;

delimiter //

create function studentFound(first varchar(20), last varchar(20))
  returns int
begin
  declare result int;

  select count(*) into result
  from Student
  where Student.firstName = first and
    Student.lastName = last;

  return result;
end;
//

delimiter ;
```

37.7 Retrieving Metadata

database metadata

JDBC provides the DatabaseMetaData interface for obtaining databasewide information and the ResultSetMetaData interface for obtaining information on the specific ResultSet, such as column count and column names.

37.7.1 Database Metadata

The Connection interface establishes a connection to a database. It is within the context of a connection that SQL statements are executed and results are returned. A connection also provides access to database metadata information that describes the capabilities of the database, supported SQL grammar, stored procedures, and so on. To obtain an instance of DatabaseMetaData for a database, use the getMetaData method on a connection object like this:

```
DatabaseMetaData dbMetaData = connection.getMetaData();
```

If your program connects to a local MySQL database, Listing 37.5 displays the database information, as shown in Figure 37.22.

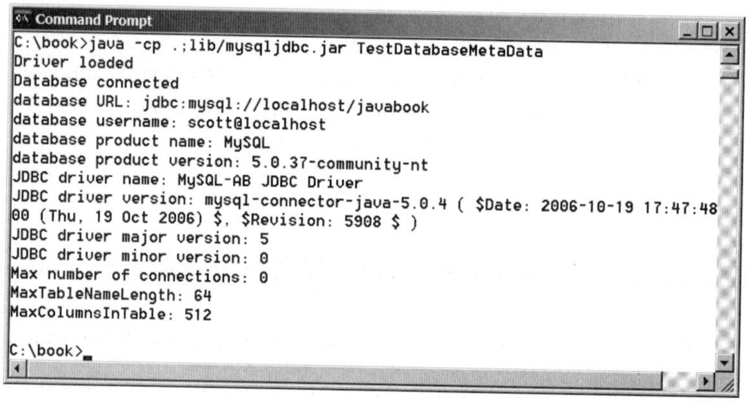
Command Prompt
C:\book>java -cp .;lib/mysqljdbc.jar TestDatabaseMetaData
Driver loaded
Database connected
database URL: jdbc:mysql://localhost/javabook
database username: scott@localhost
database product name: MySQL
database product version: 5.0.37-community-nt
JDBC driver name: MySQL-AB JDBC Driver
JDBC driver version: mysql-connector-java-5.0.4 ($Date: 2006-10-19 17:47:48
00 (Thu, 19 Oct 2006) $, $Revision: 5908 $)
JDBC driver major version: 5
JDBC driver minor version: 0
Max number of connections: 0
MaxTableNameLength: 64
MaxColumnsInTable: 512
C:\book>

FIGURE 37.22 The DatabaseMetaData interface enables you to obtain database information.

LISTING 37.5 TestDatabaseMetaData.java

```
import java.sql.*;

public class TestDatabaseMetaData {
  public static void main(String[] args)
      throws SQLException, ClassNotFoundException {
    // Load the JDBC driver
    Class.forName("com.mysql.jdbc.Driver");
    System.out.println("Driver loaded");

    // Establish a connection
    Connection connection = DriverManager.getConnection
      ("jdbc:mysql://localhost/javabook", "scott", "tiger");
    System.out.println("Database connected");

    DatabaseMetaData dbMetaData = connection.getMetaData();
    System.out.println("database URL: " + dbMetaData.getURL() );
    System.out.println("database username: " +
      dbMetaData.getUserName());
    System.out.println("database product name: " +
      dbMetaData.getDatabaseProductName());
    System.out.println("database product version: " +
      dbMetaData.getDatabaseProductVersion());
    System.out.println("JDBC driver name: " +
      dbMetaData.getDriverName());
    System.out.println("JDBC driver version: " +
      dbMetaData.getDriverVersion());
    System.out.println("JDBC driver major version: " +
      dbMetaData.getDriverMajorVersion());
    System.out.println("JDBC driver minor version: " +
      dbMetaData.getDriverMinorVersion());
    System.out.println("Max number of connections: " +
      dbMetaData.getMaxConnections());
    System.out.println("MaxTableNameLength: " +
      dbMetaData.getMaxTableNameLength());
    System.out.println("MaxColumnsInTable: " +
      dbMetaData.getMaxColumnsInTable());

    // Close the connection
    connection.close();
  }
}
```

load driver

connect database

database metadata

get metadata

37.7.2 Obtaining Database Tables

You can find out the tables in the database through database metadata using the `getTables` method. Listing 37.6 displays all the user tables in the test database on a local MySQL. Figure 37.23 shows a sample output of the program.

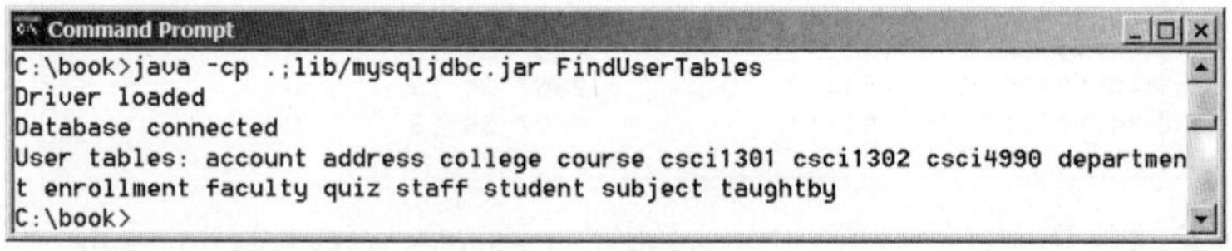
Command Prompt
C:\book>java -cp .;lib/mysqljdbc.jar FindUserTables
Driver loaded
Database connected
User tables: account address college course csci1301 csci1302 csci4990 departmen
t enrollment faculty quiz staff student subject taughtby
C:\book>

FIGURE 37.23 You can find all the tables in the database.

LISTING 37.6 FindUserTables.java

load driver

connect database

database metadata

obtain tables

get table names

```
1 import java.sql.*;
2
3 public class FindUserTables {
4   public static void main(String[] args)
5       throws SQLException, ClassNotFoundException {
6     // Load the JDBC driver
7     Class.forName("com.mysql.jdbc.Driver");
8     System.out.println("Driver loaded");
9
10    // Establish a connection
11    Connection connection = DriverManager.getConnection
12      ("jdbc:mysql://localhost/javabook", "scott", "tiger");
13    System.out.println("Database connected");
14
15    DatabaseMetaData dbMetaData = connection.getMetaData();
16
17    ResultSet rsTables = dbMetaData.getTables(null, null, null,
18      new String[] {"TABLE"});
19    System.out.print("User tables: ");
20    while (rsTables.next())
21      System.out.print(rsTables.getString("TABLE_NAME") + " ");
22
23    // Close the connection
24    connection.close();
25  }
26 }
```

Line 17 obtains table information in a result set using the `getTables` method. One of the columns in the result set is TABLE_NAME. Line 21 retrieves the table name from this result set column.

37.7.3 Result Set Metadata

The `ResultSetMetaData` interface describes information pertaining to the result set. A `ResultSetMetaData` object can be used to find the types and properties of the columns in a `ResultSet`. To obtain an instance of `ResultSetMetaData`, use the `getMetaData` method on a result set like this:

```
ResultSetMetaData rsMetaData = resultSet.getMetaData();
```

You can use the `getColumnCount()` method to find the number of columns in the result and the `getColumnName(int)` method to get the column names. For example, Listing 37.7 displays all the column names and contents resulting from the SQL SELECT statement *`select * from Enrollment`*. The output is shown in Figure 37.24.

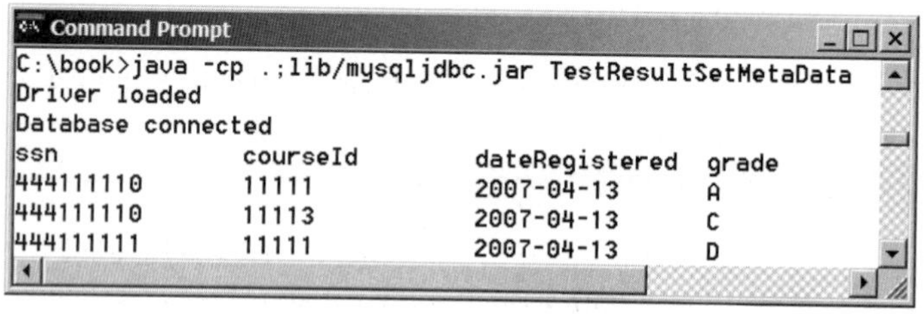
Command Prompt
C:\book>java -cp .;lib/mysqljdbc.jar TestResultSetMetaData
Driver loaded
Database connected
ssn courseId dateRegistered grade
444111110 11111 2007-04-13 A
444111110 11113 2007-04-13 C
444111111 11111 2007-04-13 D

FIGURE 37.24 The `ResultSetMetaData` interface enables you to obtain resultset information.

LISTING 37.7 TestResultSetMetaData.java

```
import java.sql.*;

public class TestResultSetMetaData {
  public static void main(String[] args)
      throws SQLException, ClassNotFoundException {
    // Load the JDBC driver
    Class.forName("com.mysql.jdbc.Driver");
    System.out.println("Driver loaded");

    // Establish a connection
    Connection connection = DriverManager.getConnection
      ("jdbc:mysql://localhost/javabook", "scott", "tiger");
    System.out.println("Database connected");

    // Create a statement
    Statement statement = connection.createStatement();

    // Execute a statement
    ResultSet resultSet = statement.executeQuery
      ("select * from Enrollment");

    ResultSetMetaData rsMetaData = resultSet.getMetaData();
    for (int i = 1; i <= rsMetaData.getColumnCount(); i++)
      System.out.printf("%-12s\t", rsMetaData.getColumnName(i));
    System.out.println();

    // Iterate through the result and print the student names
    while (resultSet.next()) {
      for (int i = 1; i <= rsMetaData.getColumnCount(); i++)
        System.out.printf("%-12s\t", resultSet.getObject(i));
      System.out.println();
    }

    // Close the connection
    connection.close();
  }
}
```

load driver

connect database

create statement

create resultset

resultset metadata

column count

column name

KEY TERMS

database system 1274
domain constraint 1276
foreign key constraint 1277
integrity constraint 1276
primary key constraint 1277
relational database 1274
Structured Query Language (SQL) 1278

CHAPTER SUMMARY

1. This chapter introduced the concepts of database systems, relational databases, relational data models, data integrity, and SQL. You learned how to develop database applications using Java.

2. The Java API for developing Java database applications is called *JDBC*. JDBC provides Java programmers with a uniform interface for accessing and manipulating a wide range of relational databases.

3. The JDBC API consists of classes and interfaces for establishing connections with databases, sending SQL statements to databases, processing the results of SQL statements, and obtaining database metadata.

4. Since a JDBC driver serves as the interface to facilitate communications between JDBC and a proprietary database, JDBC drivers are database specific. A JDBC-ODBC bridge driver is included in JDK to support Java programs that access databases through ODBC drivers. If you use a driver other than the JDBC-ODBC bridge driver, make sure it is on the classpath before running the program.

5. Four key interfaces are needed to develop any database application using Java: `Driver`, `Connection`, `Statement`, and `ResultSet`. These interfaces define a framework for generic SQL database access. The JDBC driver vendors provide implementation for them.

6. A JDBC application loads an appropriate driver using the `Driver` interface, connects to the database using the `Connection` interface, creates and executes SQL statements using the `Statement` interface, and processes the result using the `ResultSet` interface if the statements return results.

7. The `PreparedStatement` interface is designed to execute dynamic SQL statements with parameters. These SQL statements are precompiled for efficient use when repeatedly executed.

8. Database *metadata* is information that describes the database itself. JDBC provides the `DatabaseMetaData` interface for obtaining databasewide information and the `ResultSetMetaData` interface for obtaining information on the specific `ResultSet`.

Review Questions

Section 37.2

37.1 What are superkeys, candidate keys, and primary keys? How do you create a table with a primary key?

37.2 What is a foreign key? How do you create a table with a foreign key?

37.3 Can a relation have more than one primary key or foreign key?

37.4 Does a foreign key need to be a primary key in the same relation?

37.5 Does a foreign key need to have the same name as its referenced primary key?

37.6 Can a foreign key value be null?

Section 37.3

37.7 Create the tables `Course`, `Student`, and `Enrollment` using the `create table` statements in Section 37.3.1, "Creating and Dropping Tables." Insert rows into `Course`, `Student`, and `Enrollment` using the data in Figures 37.3, 37.4, and 37.5.

37.8 List all CSCI courses with at least four credit hours.

37.9 List all students whose last names contain the letter *e* two times.

37.10 List all students whose birthdays are null.

37.11 List all students who take Math courses.

37.12 List the number of courses in each subject.

37.13 Assume that each credit hour is 50 minutes of lectures. Get the total minutes for the courses that each student takes.

Section 37.4

37.14 What are the advantages of developing database applications using Java?

37.15 Describe the following JDBC interfaces: `Driver`, `Connection`, `Statement`, and `ResultSet`.

37.16 How do you load a JDBC driver? What are the driver classes for MySQL, Access, and Oracle?

37.17 How do you create a database connection? What are the URLs for MySQL, Access, and Oracle?

37.18 How do you create a `Statement` and execute an SQL statement?

37.19 How do you retrieve values in a `ResultSet`?

37.20 Does JDBC automatically commit a transaction? How do you set autocommit to false?

Section 37.5

37.21 Describe prepared statements. How do you create instances of `PreparedStatement`? How do you execute a `PreparedStatement`? How do you set parameter values in a `PreparedStatement`?

37.22 What are the benefits of using prepared statements?

Section 37.6

37.23 Describe callable statements. How do you create instances of `CallableStatement`? How do you execute a `CallableStatement`? How do you register `OUT` parameters in a `CallableStatement`?

Section 37.7

37.24 What is `DatabaseMetaData` for? Describe the methods in `DatabaseMetaData`. How do you get an instance of `DatabaseMetaData`?

37.25 What is `ResultSetMetaData` for? Describe the methods in `ResultSetMetaData`. How do you get an instance of `ResultSetMetaData`?

37.26 How do you find the number of columns in a result set? How do you find the column names in a result set?

Programming Exercises

37.1* (*Accessing and updating a `Staff` table*) Write a Java applet that views, inserts, and updates staff information stored in a database, as shown in Figure 37.25(a). The *View* button displays a record with a specified ID. The `Staff` table is created as follows:

```
create table Staff (
  id char(9) not null,
  lastName varchar(15),
  firstName varchar(15),
  mi char(1),
  address varchar(20),
  city varchar(20),
  state char(2),
```

```
  telephone char(10),
  email varchar(40),
  primary key (id)
);
```

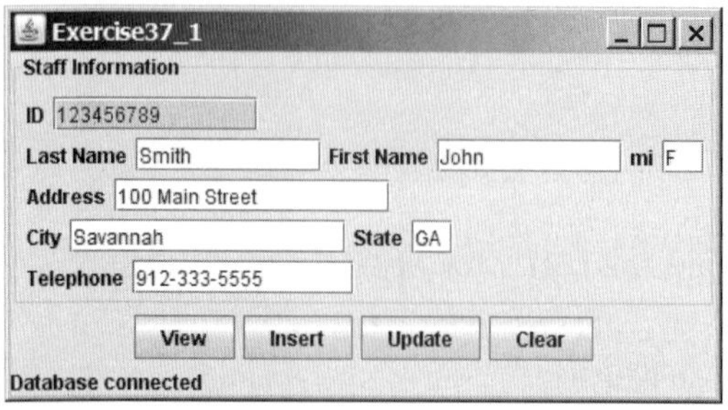
Exercise37_1
Staff Information
ID 123456789
Last Name Smith
First Name John
mi F
Address 100 Main Street
City Savannah
State GA
Telephone 912-333-5555
View
Insert
Update
Clear
Database connected

(a)

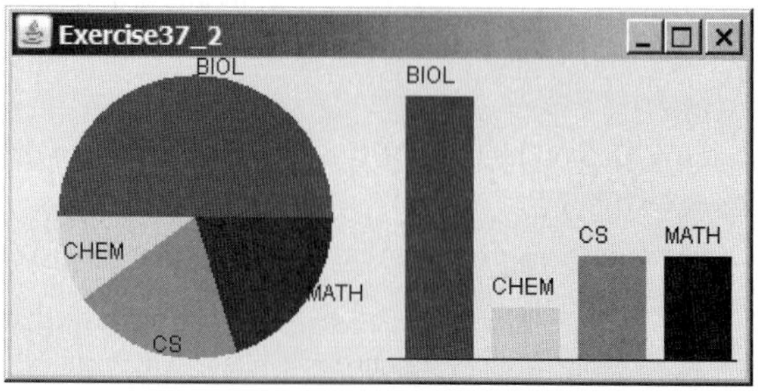
Exercise37_2
BIOL
CHEM
CS
MATH
BIOL
CHEM
CS
MATH

(b)

FIGURE 37.25 (a) The applet lets you view, insert, and update staff information. (b) The PieChart and BarChart components display the query data obtained from the data module.

37.2** (*Displaying data*) Write a program that displays the number of students in each department in a pie chart and a bar chart, as shown in Figure 37.25(b). The number of students for each department can be obtained from the Student table (see Figure 37.4) using the following SQL statement:

```
select deptId, count(*)
from Student
where deptId is not null
group by deptId;
```

Use the PieChart component and the BarChart component created in Exercise 35.1 to display the data.

37.3* (*Connection dialog*) Develop a JavaBeans component named DBConnectionPanel that enables the user to select or enter a JDBC driver and a URL and to enter a username and password, as shown in Figure 37.26. When the *OK* button is clicked, a Connection object for the database is stored in the connection property. You can then use the getConnection() method to return the connection.

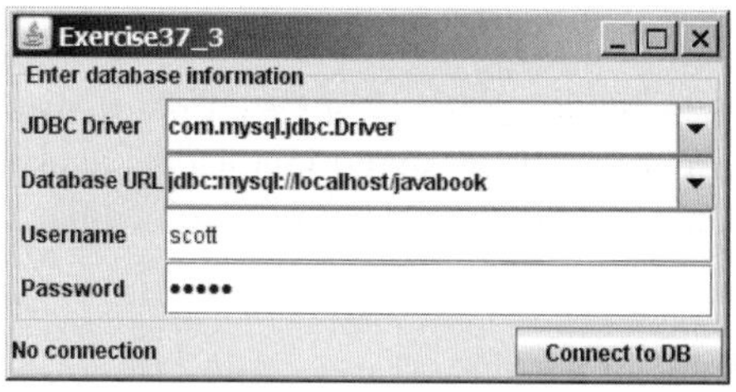
Exercise37_3
Enter database information
JDBC Driver com.mysql.jdbc.Driver
Database URL jdbc:mysql://localhost/javabook
Username scott
Password •••••
No connection
Connect to DB

FIGURE 37.26 The DBConnectionPanel component enables the user to enter database information.

37.4* (*Finding grades*) Listing 37.2, FindGrade.java, presented an applet that finds a student's grade for a specified course. Rewrite the program to find all the grades for a specified student, as shown in Figure 37.27.

Exercise37_4
SSN 444111111
Show Grade
Stevenson K John's grade on course Intro to Java I is D
Stevenson K John's grade on course Intro to Java II is F
Stevenson K John's grade on course Database Systems is A
3 courses found
Exercise37_4
SSN 444111119
Show Grade
no courses found for this SSN

FIGURE 37.27 The applet displays the grades for the courses for a specified student.

37.5* (*Displaying table contents*) Write a program that displays the content for a given table. As shown in Figure 37.28(a), you enter a table and click the *Show Contents* button to display the table contents in the text area.

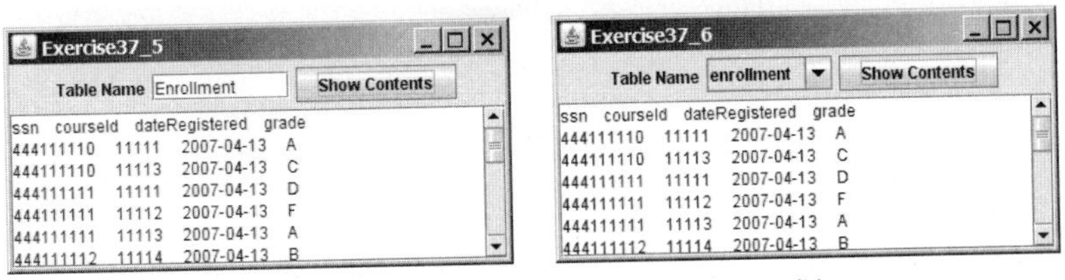
Exercise37_5
Table Name Enrollment
Show Contents
ssn courseId dateRegistered grade
444111110 11111 2007-04-13 A
444111110 11113 2007-04-13 C
444111111 11111 2007-04-13 D
444111111 11112 2007-04-13 F
444111111 11113 2007-04-13 A
444111112 11114 2007-04-13 B
Exercise37_6
Table Name enrollment
Show Contents
ssn courseId dateRegistered grade
444111110 11111 2007-04-13 A
444111110 11113 2007-04-13 C
444111111 11111 2007-04-13 D
444111111 11112 2007-04-13 F
444111111 11113 2007-04-13 A
444111112 11114 2007-04-13 B

(a) (b)

FIGURE 37.28 (a) Enter a table name to display the table contents. (b) Select a table name from the combo box to display its contents.

37.6* (*Finding tables and showing their contents*) Write a program that fills in table names in a combo box, as shown in Figure 37.28(b). You can select a table from the combo box to display its contents in the text area.

37.7**(*Populating database*) Create a table named `Quiz` as follows:

```
create table Quiz(
  questionId int,
  question varchar(4000),
  choicea varchar(1000),
  choiceb varchar(1000),
  choicec varchar(1000),
  choiced varchar(1000),
  answer varchar(5));
```

The `Quiz` table stores multiple-choice questions. Suppose the multiple-choice questions are stored in a text file named Exercise37_7.txt in the following format:

```
1. question1
a. choice a
b. choice b
c. choice c
d. choice d
Answer:cd
```

```
2. question2
a. choice a
b. choice b
c. choice c
d. choice d
Answer:a
...
```

Write a program that reads the data from the file and stores it in the `Quiz` table. (Exercise37_7.txt is contained in **c:\book**).

APPENDIXES

APPENDIX A

Java Keywords

The following fifty keywords are reserved for use by the Java language:

`abstract`	`double`	`int`	`super`
`assert`	`else`	`interface`	`switch`
`boolean`	`enum`	`long`	`synchronized`
`break`	`extends`	`native`	`this`
`byte`	`for`	`new`	`throw`
`case`	`final`	`package`	`throws`
`catch`	`finally`	`private`	`transient`
`char`	`float`	`protected`	`try`
`class`	`goto`	`public`	`void`
`const`	`if`	`return`	`volatile`
`continue`	`implements`	`short`	`while`
`default`	`import`	`static`	
`do`	`instanceof`	`strictfp`*	

The keywords **goto** and **const** are C++ keywords reserved, but not currently used, in Java. This enables Java compilers to identify them and to produce better error messages if they appear in Java programs.

The literal values `true`, `false`, and `null` are not keywords, just like literal value `100`. However, you cannot use them as identifiers, just as you cannot use `100` as an identifier.

assert is a keyword added in JDK 1.4 and **enum** is a keyword added in JDK 1.5.

*The **strictfp** keyword is a modifier for method or class to use strict floating-point calculations. Floating-point arithmetic can be executed in one of two modes: *strict* or *nonstrict*. The strict mode guarantees that the evaluation result is the same on all Java Virtual Machine implementations. The nonstrict mode allows intermediate results from calculations to be stored in an extended format different from the standard IEEE floating-point number format. The extended format is machine-dependent and enables code to be executed faster. However, when you execute the code using the nonstrict mode on different JVMs, you may not always get precisely the same results. By default, the nonstrict mode is used for floating-point calculations. To use the strict mode in a method or a class, add the **strictfp** keyword in the method or the class declaration. Strict floating-point may give you slightly better precision than nonstrict floating-point, but the distinction will only affect some applications. Strictness is not inherited; that is, the presence of **strictfp** on a class or interface declaration does not cause extended classes or interfaces to be strict.

APPENDIX B

The ASCII Character Set

Tables B.1 and B.2 show ASCII characters and their respective decimal and hexadecimal codes. The decimal or hexadecimal code of a character is a combination of its row index and column index. For example, in Table B.1, the letter A is at row 6 and column 5, so its decimal equivalent is 65; in Table B.2, letter A is at row 4 and column 1, so its hexadecimal equivalent is 41.

TABLE B.1 ASCII Character Set in the Decimal Index

	0	*1*	*2*	*3*	*4*	*5*	*6*	*7*	*8*	*9*
0	nul	soh	stx	etx	eot	enq	ack	bel	bs	ht
1	nl	vt	ff	cr	so	si	dle	dcl	dc2	dc3
2	dc4	nak	syn	etb	can	em	sub	esc	fs	gs
3	rs	us	sp	!	”	#	$	%	&	’
4	(	)	*	+	,	–	.	/	0	1
5	2	3	4	5	6	7	8	9	:	;
6	<	=	>	?	@	A	B	C	D	E
7	F	G	H	I	J	K	L	M	N	O
8	P	Q	R	S	T	U	V	W	X	Y
9	Z	[	\	]	∧	–	‘	a	b	c
10	d	e	f	g	h	i	j	k	l	m
11	n	o	p	q	r	s	t	u	v	w
12	x	y	z	{	|	}	~	del		

TABLE B.2 ASCII Character Set in the Hexadecimal Index

	0	*1*	*2*	*3*	*4*	*5*	*6*	*7*	*8*	*9*	*A*	*B*	*C*	*D*	*E*	*F*
0	nul	soh	stx	etx	eot	enq	ack	bel	bs	ht	nl	vt	ff	cr	so	si
1	dle	dcl	dc2	dc3	dc4	nak	syn	etb	can	em	sub	esc	fs	gs	rs	us
2	sp	!	”	#	$	%	&	’	(	)	*	+	,	–	.	/
3	0	1	2	3	4	5	6	7	8	9	:	;	<	=	>	?
4	@	A	B	C	D	E	F	G	H	I	J	K	L	M	N	O
5	P	Q	R	S	T	U	V	W	X	Y	Z	[	\	]	∧	–
6	‘	a	b	c	d	e	f	g	h	i	j	k	l	m	n	o
7	p	q	r	s	t	u	v	w	x	y	z	{	|	}	~	del

APPENDIX C

Operator Precedence Chart

The operators are shown in decreasing order of precedence from top to bottom. Operators in the same group have the same precedence, and their associativity is shown in the table.

Operator	*Name*	*Associativity*
()	Parentheses	Left to right
()	Function call	Left to right
[]	Array subscript	Left to right
.	Object member access	Left to right
++	Postincrement	Right to left
--	Postdecrement	Right to left
++	Preincrement	Right to left
--	Predecrement	Right to left
+	Unary plus	Right to left
-	Unary minus	Right to left
!	Unary logical negation	Right to left
(type)	Unary casting	Right to left
new	Creating object	Right to left
*	Multiplication	Left to right
/	Division	Left to right
%	Remainder	Left to right
+	Addition	Left to right
-	Subtraction	Left to right
<<	Left shift	Left to right
>>	Right shift with sign extension	Left to right
>>>	Right shift with zero extension	Left to right
<	Less than	Left to right
<=	Less than or equal to	Left to right
>	Greater than	Left to right
>=	Greater than or equal to	Left to right
instanceof	Checking object type	Left to right

Operator	*Name*	*Associativity*
==	Equal comparison	Left to right
!=	Not equal	Left to right
&	(Unconditional AND)	Left to right
^	(Exclusive OR)	Left to right
|	(Unconditional OR)	Left to right
&&	Conditional AND	Left to right
||	Conditional OR	Left to right
?:	Ternary condition	Right to left
=	Assignment	Right to left
+=	Addition assignment	Right to left
-=	Subtraction assignment	Right to left
*=	Multiplication assignment	Right to left
/=	Division assignment	Right to left
%=	Remainder assignment	Right to left

APPENDIX D

Java Modifiers

Modifiers are used on classes and class members (constructors, methods, data, and class-level blocks), but the final modifier can also be used on local variables in a method. A modifier that can be applied to a class is called a *class modifier*. A modifier that can be applied to a method is called a *method modifier*. A modifier that can be applied to a data field is called a *data modifier*. A modifier that can be applied to a class-level block is called a block modifier. The following table gives a summary of the Java modifiers.

Modifier	*class*	*constructor*	*method*	*data*	*block*	*Explanation*
(default)*	√	√	√	√	√	A class, constructor, method, or data field is visible in this package.
public	√	√	√	√		A class, constructor, method, or data field is visible to all the programs in any package.
private		√	√	√		A constructor, method or data field is only visible in this class.
protected		√	√	√		A constructor, method or data field is visible in this package and in subclasses of this class in any package.
static			√	√	√	Define a class method, or a class data field or a static initialization block.
final	√		√	√		A final class cannot be extended. A final method cannot be modified in a subclass. A final data field is a constant.
abstract	√		√			An abstract class must be extended. An abstract method must be implemented in a concrete subclass.
native			√			A native method indicates that the method is implemented using a language other than Java.

*Default access has no modifier associated with it. For example: **class Test {}**

Modifier	*class*	*constructor*	*method*	*data*	*block*	*Explanation*
`synchronized`			√		√	Only one thread at a time can execute this method.
`strictfp`	√		√			Use strict floating-point calculations to guarantee that the evaluation result is the same on all JVMs.
`transient`				√		Mark a nonserializable instance data field.

APPENDIX E

Special Floating-Point Values

Dividing an integer by zero is invalid and throws `ArithmeticException`, but dividing a floating-point value by zero does not cause an exception. Floating-point arithmetic can overflow to infinity if the result of the operation is too large for a `double` or a `float`, or underflow to zero if the result is too small for a double or a `float`. Java provides the special floating-point values `POSITIVE_INFINITY`, `NEGATIVE_INFINITY`, and `NaN` (Not a Number) to denote these results. These values are defined as special constants in the `Float` class and the Double class.

If a positive floating-point number is divided by zero, the result is `POSITIVE_INFINITY`. If a negative floating-point number is divided by zero, the result is `NEGATIVE_INFINITY`. If a floating-point zero is divided by zero, the result is NaN, which means that the result is undefined mathematically. The string representation of these three values are Infinity, -Infinity, and NaN. For example,

```
System.out.print(1.0 / 0); // Print Infinity
System.out.print(-1.0 / 0); // Print -Infinity
System.out.print(0.0 / 0); // Print NaN
```

These special values can also be used as operands in computations. For example, a number divided by `POSITIVE_INFINITY` yields a positive zero. Table E.1 summarizes various combinations of the `/`, `*`, `%`, `+`, and `-` operators.

TABLE E.1 Special Floating-Point Values

x	*y*	*x/y*	*x*y*	*x%y*	*x + y*	*x − y*
Finite	± 0.0	± ∞	± 0.0	NaN	Finite	Finite
Finite	± ∞	± 0.0	± 0.0	x	± ∞	∞
± 0.0	± 0.0	NaN	± 0.0	NaN	± 0.0	± 0.0
± ∞	Finite	± ∞	± 0.0	NaN	± ∞	± ∞
± ∞	± ∞	NaN	± 0.0	NaN	± ∞	∞
± 0.0	± ∞	± 0.0	NaN	± 0.0	± ∞	± 0.0
NaN	Any	NaN	NaN	NaN	NaN	NaN
Any	NaN	NaN	NaN	NaN	NaN	NaN

Note

If one of the operands is NaN, the result is NaN.

APPENDIX F

Number Systems

1 Introduction

binary numbers

Computers use binary numbers internally, because computers are made naturally to store and process 0s and 1s. The binary number system has two digits, 0 and 1. A number or character is stored as a sequence of 0s and 1s. Each 0 or 1 is called a *bit* (binary digit).

decimal numbers

In our daily life we use decimal numbers. When we write a number such as 20 in a program, it is assumed to be a decimal number. Internally, computer software is used to convert decimal numbers into binary numbers, and vice versa.

hexadecimal number

We write computer programs using decimal numbers. However, to deal with an operating system, we need to reach down to the "machine level" by using binary numbers. Binary numbers tend to be very long and cumbersome. Often hexadecimal numbers are used to abbreviate them, with each hexadecimal digit representing four binary digits. The hexadecimal number system has 16 digits: 0–9, A–F. The letters A, B, C, D, E, and F correspond to the decimal numbers 10, 11, 12, 13, 14, and 15.

The digits in the decimal number system are 0, 1, 2, 3, 4, 5, 6, 7, 8, and 9. A decimal number is represented by a sequence of one or more of these digits. The value that each digit represents depends on its position, which denotes an integral power of 10. For example, the digits 7, 4, 2, and 3 in decimal number 7423 represent 7000, 400, 20, and 3, respectively, as shown below:

$$\boxed{7 \mid 4 \mid 2 \mid 3} = 7 \times 10^3 + 4 \times 10^2 + 2 \times 10^1 + 3 \times 10^0$$

$$10^3\ 10^2\ 10^1\ 10^0 = 7000 + 400 + 20 + 3 = 7423$$

base

radix

The decimal number system has ten digits, and the position values are integral powers of 10. We say that 10 is the *base* or *radix* of the decimal number system. Similarly, since the binary number system has two digits, its base is 2, and since the hex number system has 16 digits, its base is 16.

If 1101 is a binary number, the digits 1, 1, 0, and 1 represent 1×2^3, 1×2^2, 0×2^1, and 1×2^0, respectively:

$$\boxed{1 \mid 1 \mid 0 \mid 1} = 1 \times 2^3 + 1 \times 2^2 + 0 \times 2^1 + 1 \times 2^0$$

$$2^3\ 2^2\ 2^1\ 2^0 = 8 + 4 + 0 + 1 = 13$$

If 7423 is a hex number, the digits 7, 4, 2, and 3 represent 7×16^3, 4×16^2, 2×16^1, and 3×16^0, respectively:

$$\boxed{7 \mid 4 \mid 2 \mid 3} = 7 \times 16^3 + 4 \times 16^2 + 2 \times 16^1 + 3 \times 16^0$$

$$16^3\ 16^2\ 16^1\ 16^0 = 28672 + 1024 + 32 + 3 = 29731$$

2 Conversions Between Binary and Decimal Numbers

binary to decimal

Given a binary number $b_n b_{n-1} b_{n-2} \ldots b_2 b_1 b_0$, the equivalent decimal value is

$$b_n \times 2^n + b_{n-1} \times 2^{n-1} + b_{n-2} \times 2^{n-2} + \ \ldots \ + b_2 \times 2^2 + b_1 \times 2^1 + b_0 \times 2^0$$

Here are some examples of converting binary numbers to decimals:

Binary	**Conversion Formula**	**Decimal**
10	$1 \times 2^1 + 0 \times 2^0$	2
1000	$1 \times 2^3 + 0 \times 2^2 + 0 \times 2^1 + 0 \times 2^0$	8
10101011	$1 \times 2^7 + 0 \times 2^6 + 1 \times 2^5 + 0 \times 2^4 + 1 \times 2^3 + 0 \times 2^2 +$ $1 \times 2^1 + 1 \times 2^0$	171

decimal to binary

To convert a decimal number d to a binary number is to find the bits $b_n, b_{n-1}, b_{n-2}, \ldots, b_2, b_1$, and b_0 such that

$$d = b_n \times 2^n + b_{n-1} \times 2^{n-1} + b_{n-2} \times 2^{n-2} + \ \ldots \ + b_2 \times 2^2 + b_1 \times 2^1 + b_0 \times 2^0$$

These bits can be found by successively dividing d by 2 until the quotient is 0. The remainders are $b_0, b_1, b_2, \ldots, b_{n-2}, b_{n-1}$, and b_n.

For example, the decimal number 123 is 1111011 in binary. The conversion is done as follows:

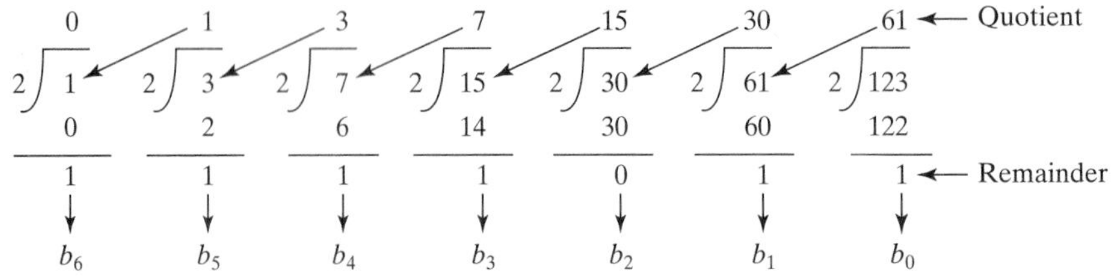
Quotient
Remainder

Tip

The Windows Calculator, as shown in Figure F.1, is a useful tool for performing number conversions. To run it, choose *Programs*, *Accessories*, and *Calculator* from the *Start* button, then under *View* select *Scientific*.

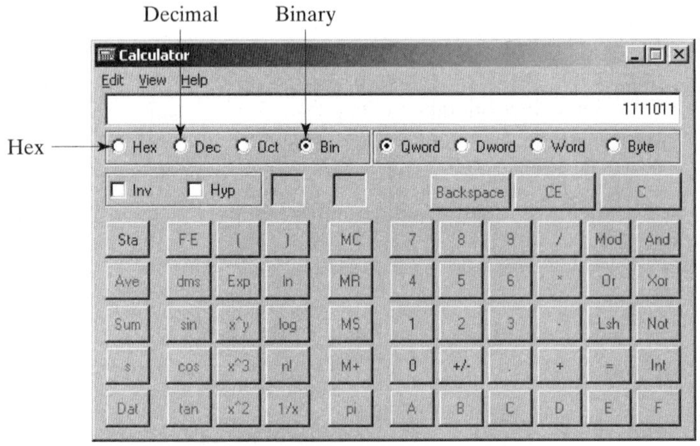
Decimal
Binary
Hex
Calculator
1111011
Hex
Dec
Oct
Bin
Qword
Dword
Word
Byte

FIGURE F.1 You can perform number conversions using the Windows Calculator.

3 Conversions Between Hexadecimal and Decimal Numbers

hex to decimal

Given a hexadecimal number $h_n h_{n-1} h_{n-2} \ldots h_2 h_1 h_0$, the equivalent decimal value is

$$h_n \times 16^n + h_{n-1} \times 16^{n-1} + h_{n-2} \times 16^{n-2} + \ldots + h_2 \times 16^2 + h_1 \times 16^1 + h_0 \times 16^0$$

Here are some examples of converting hexadecimal numbers to decimals:

Hexadecimal	**Conversion Formula**	**Decimal**
7F	$7 \times 16^1 + 15 \times 16^0$	127
FFFF	$15 \times 16^3 + 15 \times 16^2 + 15 \times 16^1 + 15 \times 16^0$	65535
431	$4 \times 16^2 + 3 \times 16^1 + 1 \times 16^0$	1073

decimal to hex

To convert a decimal number d to a hexadecimal number is to find the hexadecimal digits $h_n, h_{n-1}, h_{n-2}, \ldots, h_2, h_1$, and h_0 such that

$$d = h_n \times 16^n + h_{n-1} \times 16^{n-1} + h_{n-2} \times 16^{n-2} + \ldots + h_2 \times 16^2 + h_1 \times 16^1 + h_0 \times 16^0$$

These numbers can be found by successively dividing d by 16 until the quotient is 0. The remainders are $h_0, h_1, h_2, \ldots, h_{n-2}, h_{n-1}$, and h_n.

For example, the decimal number 123 is 7B in hexadecimal. The conversion is done as follows:

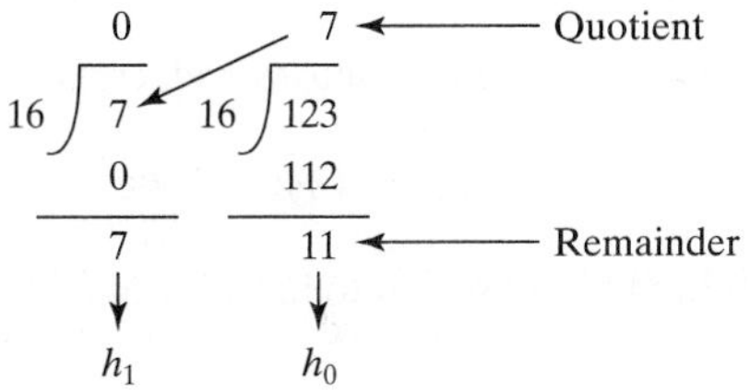
0
7
Quotient
16
7
16
123
0
112
7
11
Remainder
h_1
h_0

4 Conversions Between Binary and Hexadecimal Numbers

hex to binary

To convert a hexadecimal to a binary number, simply convert each digit in the hexadecimal number into a four-digit binary number, using Table F.1.

For example, the hexadecimal number 7B is 1111011, where 7 is 111 in binary, and B is 1011 in binary.

binary to hex

To convert a binary number to a hexadecimal, convert every four binary digits from right to left in the binary number into a hexadecimal number.

For example, the binary number 1110001101 is 38D, since 1101 is D, 1000 is 8, and 11 is 3, as shown below.

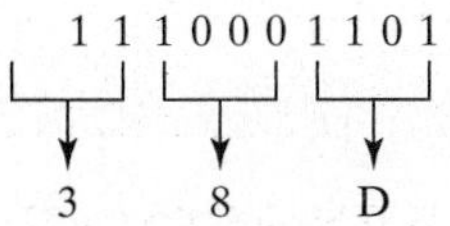
1 1 1 0 0 0 1 1 0 1
3
8
D

TABLE F.1 Converting Hexadecimal to Binary

Hexadecimal	*Binary*	*Decimal*
0	0000	0
1	0001	1
2	0010	2
3	0011	3
4	0100	4
5	0101	5
6	0110	6
7	0111	7
8	1000	8
9	1001	9
A	1010	10
B	1011	11
C	1100	12
D	1101	13
E	1110	14
F	1111	15

(*Note*: Octal numbers are also useful. The octal number system has eight digits, 0 to 7. A decimal number 8 is represented in the octal system as 10.)

REVIEW QUESTIONS

1. Convert the following decimal numbers into hexadecimal and binary numbers.

```
100; 4340; 2000
```

2. Convert the following binary numbers into hexadecimal and decimal numbers.

```
1000011001; 100000000; 100111
```

3. Convert the following hexadecimal numbers into binary and decimal numbers.

```
FEFA9; 93; 2000
```

INDEX

J

K

L

M

N

O

P

Q

R

S

T

U